History of Washington County, Ohio, with illustrations and biographical sketches.

Anonymous

History of Washington County, Ohio, with illustrations and biographical sketches.
Anonymous
British Library, Historical Print Editions
British Library
1881
739 p. ; 4°.
10408.k.3.

The BiblioLife Network

This project was made possible in part by the BiblioLife Network (BLN), a project aimed at addressing some of the huge challenges facing book preservationists around the world. The BLN includes libraries, library networks, archives, subject matter experts, online communities and library service providers. We believe every book ever published should be available as a high-quality print reproduction; printed on- demand anywhere in the world. This insures the ongoing accessibility of the content and helps generate sustainable revenue for the libraries and organizations that work to preserve these important materials.

The following book is in the "public domain" and represents an authentic reproduction of the text as printed by the original publisher. While we have attempted to accurately maintain the integrity of the original work, there are sometimes problems with the original book or micro-film from which the books were digitized. This can result in minor errors in reproduction. Possible imperfections include missing and blurred pages, poor pictures, markings and other reproduction issues beyond our control. Because this work is culturally important, we have made it available as part of our commitment to protecting, preserving, and promoting the world's literature.

GUIDE TO FOLD-OUTS, MAPS and OVERSIZED IMAGES

In an online database, page images do not need to conform to the size restrictions found in a printed book. When converting these images back into a printed bound book, the page sizes are standardized in ways that maintain the detail of the original. For large images, such as fold-out maps, the original page image is split into two or more pages.

Guidelines used to determine the split of oversize pages:

• Some images are split vertically; large images require vertical and horizontal splits.
• For horizontal splits, the content is split left to right.
• For vertical splits, the content is split from top to bottom.
• For both vertical and horizontal splits, the image is processed from top left to bottom right.

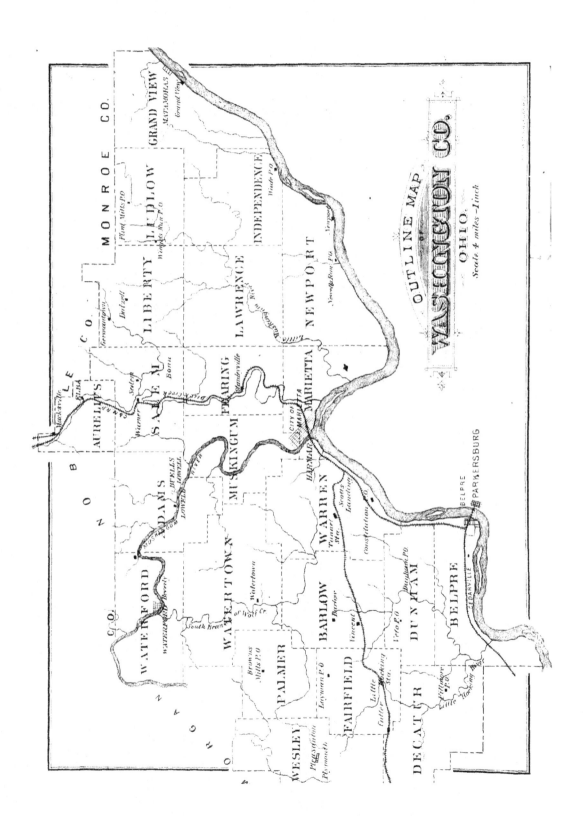

OUTLINE MAP

WASHINGTON CO.

OHIO.

Scale 4 miles =1inch

1788.

HISTORY

OF

WASHINGTON COUNTY,

OHIO,

WITH

ILLUSTRATIONS AND BIOGRAPHICAL SKETCHES.

H. Z. WILLIAMS & BRO.

PUBLISHERS.

1881.

FROM PRINTING HOUSE OF W. W. WILLIAMS. CLEVELAND, OHIO.

PREFATORY NOTE.

In placing this History of Washington County before their patrons, the publishers feel that they have faithfully fulfilled all pledges made at the outset, and that their work will stand the tests of candid criticism.

That a volume containing, as does this, upwards of seven hundred royal quarto pages of printed matter—considerably more than three-quarters of a million words presenting at least ten thousand facts and twice ten thousand names—should be absolutely free from error, no thinking person will expect; and while we do not claim unerring accuracy, we are confident, such has been the conscientious care of our corps of writers and gatherers of facts, that the work we now place before the public does not contain any serious errors of statement, and that the sins of omission are not numerous or great. No pains have been spared to make the history at once comprehensive and correct. The task which confronted the writers when they began the preparation of the History of Washington County was one of arduous responsibility, but having entered upon it we believe that they have labored zealously and judiciously, and the publishers have no hesitancy in resting the result of their labors with the public.

The general history of Washington county, and the history of Marietta were principally prepared by Mr. Alfred Mathews. The history of the origin and doings of the Ohio Land company, and the events which were of chief importance to those who effected the initial settlement at Marietta are vividly narrated by Mr. Mathews. It far surpasses any other narrative extant of the same facts, both as to detail and interesting manner of statement.

Chief among the assistants were Mr. Benjamin S. Grosscup and Clarence G. Reynolds, among whose productions we may mention respectively the chapters devoted to Waterford and Belpre. The Military History, as is elsewhere indicated, is the work of S. J. Hathaway, esq., of Marietta. The History of the Washington County Bar was written by R. E. Harte, esq. An interesting chapter appears accredited to Anselm T. Nye, and a large portion of another, of especial value, is from the pen of William P. Cutler. Miss Mary Cone contributed the biography of General Rufus Putnam. The history of Marietta college was furnished by President Andrews. Other residents of the city of Marietta and Washington county have contributed to various departments and credit is given them, individually, in connection with their work.

The fact that the writers in our employ have availed themselves of every opportunity for research in the original authorities and sources of information, will be patent to every reader. The many valuable manuscripts which have been preserved and gathered into the college library, and others in private possession were generously proffered for their use, and have been advantageously consulted. A large amount of historical lore has been gathered, little by little, through personal interviews with the few living repositories of old-time memories. With a solitary exception, the people of Marietta and of Washington county have been courteous and cordial in extending to our corps of writers whatever aid was in their power. Of this class, and among those whose position has enabled them to be of especial service, we may mention the Hon. William P. Cutler, Anselm T. Nye, esq., Miss Mary C. Nye, Miss Julia Cutler, Mrs. Sarah Cutler Dawes, Mrs. Dr. Z. D. Walter, President I. W. Andrews, R. M. Stimson, esq., William F. Curtis, Captain C. M. Cole, Hon. Harlow Chapin, Miss Mary Monette, George T. Hovey and Beman Gates, of Marietta; Colonel John Stone and Captain George Dana, of Belpre; Dr. Joseph M. McElhinney, of Newport; E. S. McIntosh, General H. F. Devol and Stephen Powers, of Waterford. To these, to the members of the press, the pastors of the several churches and the obliging county officials, and to hundreds of others, in behalf of the writers engaged on this volume we return most cordial thanks.

CONTENTS.

HISTORICAL.

CONTENTS.

ILLUSTRATIONS.

3

HISTORY

OF

WASHINGTON COUNTY, OHIO.

CHAPTER I.

ABORIGINAL OCCUPATION OF OHIO.

DURING a long period—one which, perhaps, had its beginning soon after the forced exodus of the semi-civilized, pre-historic people, and which extended down to the era of the white man's actual knowledge—the upper Ohio valley was probably devoid of any permanent population. The river teemed with fish, and the dense luxuriant wood abounded in game, but no Indian wigwams dotted the shores of the great stream, no camp-fires gleamed along its banks, and no maize-fields covered the fertile bottom lands or lent variety to the wild vernal green. An oppressive stillness hung over the land, marked and intensified rather than broken, and only made more weird by the tossing of the water upon the shores and the soft mysterious sounds echoed from the distance through the dim aisles of the forest. Nature was lovely then as now, but with all her pristine beauty the valley was awful in the vastness and solemnity of its solitude. No where was human habitation or indication of human life.

This was the condition of the country when explored by the early French navigators, and when a century later it became the field for British and American adventurers. There was a reason for this desertion of a region rich in all that was dear to the red man. The river was the warway down which silently and swiftly floated the canoe fleets of a fierce, relentless, and invincible enemy. That the dreaded devastaters of the country when it was occupied by the ancient race had made their invasions from the northward by way of the great stream is suggested by the numerous lookout or signal mounds which crown the hills on either side of the valley, occupying the most advantageous points of observation. The Indians who dwelt in the territory included in the boundaries of Ohio had, when the white men first went among them, traditions of oft repeated and sanguinary incursions made from the same direction, and dating back to their earliest occupation of the country. History corroborates their legends, or at least those relating to less ancient times. The Iroquois or Six Nations were the foes whose frequent forays, made suddenly, swiftly, and with overwhelming strength, had carried dismay into all the Ohio country and caused the weaker tribes to abandon the valley, penetrated the interior and located themselves on the upper waters of the Muskingum, the Scioto, the Miamis, and the tributaries of the lake, where they could live with less fear of molestation. The Six Nations had the rude elements of a confederated republic, and were the only power in this part of North America who deserved the name of government.* They pretentiously claimed to be the conquerors of the whole country from sea to sea, and there is good evidence that they had by 1680 gained a powerful sway in the country between the great lakes, the Ohio and the Mississippi, and were feared by all the tribes within these limits. The upper Ohio was called by the early French the river of the Iroquois, and was for a long time unexplored through fear of their hostility.

But little is definitely known of the Indian occupation of the Ohio country prior to 1750, and scarcely anything anterior to 1650. As far back in American history as the middle of the seventeenth century it is probable that the powerful but doom-destined Eries were in possession of the vast wilderness which is now the thickly settled, well improved State of Ohio, dotted with villages and cities and covered with the meshes of a vast net-work of railroads. Most of the villages of this Indian nation, it is supposed, were situated along the shore of the lake which has been given their name. The Andastes are said by the best authorities to have occupied the valleys of the Alleghany and upper Ohio, and the Hurons or Wyandots held sway in the northern peninsula between the lakes. All were genuinely Iroquois, and the western tribes were stronger than the eastern. The Iroquois proper (the Five Nations increased afterward to Six by the alliance of the Tuscarawas) formed their confederacy in the beginning of the seventeenth century, and through

---

* James R. Albach's Annals of the West.

consolidation of strength overwhelmed singly and successively the Hurons, the Eries, and the Andastes. The time of the massacre of the Erie nation—for the war upon them culminated in a wholesale murder—is usually set down by antiquarians and historians as 1655, and the victory over the Andastes is, on good evidence, placed in the year 1672. About the same time a tribe, supposed to have been the Shwanees, were driven from the Ohio valley and far towards the Gulf of Mexico. And so the territory now Ohio became a land without habitation and served the victorious Iroquois as a vast hunting ground. Whether the Iroquois conquered the Miamis and their allies, the Illinois, is a question upon which leading students of Indian history have been equally divided. The Miamis had no traditions of ever having suffered defeat at the hands of the great confederacy, and their country, the eastern boundary of which was the Miami river, may have been the western limit of the Six Nations' triumph. That they were often at war with the Iroquois is not disputed, however, by any writers of whom we have knowledge.

Although the Six Nations were the nominal owners of the greater part of the territory now constituting the State of Ohio, they did not, after the war with the Canadian colonists broke out in 1663 (and probably for some years previously), exercise such domination over the country as to exclude other tribes. Such being the case, the long deserted and desolate wild was again the abode of the red man, and the wigwams of the race again appeared by the waters of the Muskingum, the Scioto, and the Miamis; by the Tuscarawas, the Cuyahoga, and the Maumee.

Concerning what, so far as our knowledge extends, may be called the second Indian occupation of Ohio, we have authentic information. In 1764 the most trustworthy and valuable reports up to that time secured, were made by Colonel Boquet as the result of his observations while making a military expedition west of the Ohio. Previous to the time when Colonel Boquet was among the Indians, and as early as 1750, traders sought out the denizens of the forest, and some knowledge of the strength of tribes and the location of villages was afforded by them. The authentic history of the Ohio Indians may be said to have had its beginning some time during the period extending from 1750 to 1764.

About the middle of the last century the principal tribes in what is now Ohio were the Delawares, the Shawnees, the Wyandots (called the Hurons by the French), the Mingoes, an offshoot of the Iroquois, the Chippewas, and the Tawas, more commonly called the Ottawas. The Delawares occupied the valleys of the Muskingum and Tuscarawas; the Shawnees, the Scioto valley; and the Miamis, the valleys of the two rivers upon which they left their name; the Wyandots occupied the country about the Sandusky river; the Ottawas had their headquarters in the valleys of the Maumee and Sandusky; the Chippewas were confined principally to the south shore of Lake Erie; and the Mingoes were in greatest strength upon the Ohio, below the site of Steubenville. All of the tribes, however, frequented, more or less, lands outside of their ascribed divisions of territory, and at different periods from the time when the first definite knowledge concerning them was obtained down to the era of white settlement, they occupied different locations. Thus the Delawares, whom Boquet found in 1764 in greatest number in the valley of the Tuscarawas had, thirty years later, the majority of their population in the region of the county which now bears their name, and the Shawnees, who were originally strongest upon the Scioto, by the time of St. Clair and Wayne's wars had concentrated upon the Little Miami. But the Shawnees had also as early as 1748 a village, known as Logstown, on the Ohio, seventeen miles from the site of Pittsburgh.* The several tribes commingled to some extent as their animosities toward each other were supplanted by the common fear of the enemy of their race. They gradually grew stronger in sympathy and more compact in union as the settlements of the whites encroached upon their loved domain. Hence the divisions, which had in 1750 been quite plainly marked, became, by the time the Ohio was fringed with the cabins and villages of the pale face, in a large measure, obliterated. In eastern Ohio, where the Delawares had held almost undisputed sway, there were now to be found also Wyandots,† Shawnees, Mingoes, and even Miamis from the western border—from the Wabash, Miami, and Mad rivers. Practically, however, the boundaries of the lands of different tribes were as here given.

The Delawares, as has been indicated, had their densest population upon the upper Muskingum and Tuscarawas, and they really were in possession of what is now the eastern half of the State from the Ohio to Lake Erie. This tribe, which claimed to be the elder branch of the Lenni-Lenape, has by tradition and in history and fiction been accorded a high rank among the savages of North America. Schoolcraft, Loskiel, Albert Gallatin, Drake, Zeisberger, Heckewelder, and many other writers have borne testimony to the superiority of the Delawares, and James Fennimore Cooper in his attractive romances has added lustre to the fame of the tribe. According to the tradition preserved by them the Delawares, many centuries before they knew the white man lived in the western part of the continent, and separating themselves from the rest of the Lenni-Lenape migrated slowly eastward. Reaching the Alleghany river they, with the Iroquois, waged war successfully against a race of giants, the Allegewi, and still continuing their migration settled on the Delaware river, and spread their population eventually to the Hudson, the Susquehannah, and the Potomac. Here they lived, menaced and often attacked by the Iroquois,

---

* This village and Shawneetown, at the mouth of the Scioto, were the only exceptions to the abandonment of the upper Ohio valley noted at the opening of this chapter.

† Gist, however, found, in 1750, the town on Whitewoman creek, called Muskingum, "inhabited by Wyandots" and containing about one hundred families. This was undoubtedly an isolated government.

As late as 1791, the Indian war being in progress, the different tribes were massed in what is now the northwestern part of the State, and their old abiding places, their favorite regions, were of course deserted. Delawares, Shawnees, Miamis, Mingoes, Senecas, Chippewas, and others were upon the Maumee, and its tributaries.

and finally, as some writers claim, they were subjugated by the Iroquois through stratagem. The Atlantic coast became settled by Europeans and the Delawares also being embittered against the Iroquois, whom they accused of treachery, they turned westward and concentrated upon the Alleghany. Disturbed here again by the white settlers a portion of the tribe obtained permission from the Wyandots (whom they called their uncles, thus confessing their superiority and reputation of greater antiquity) to occupy the lands along the Muskingum. The forerunners of the nation entered this region in all probability as early as 1745, and in less than a score of years their entire population had become resident in this country. They became here a more flourishing and powerful tribe than they had ever been before. Their warriors numbered not less than six hundred in 1764. The Delawares were divided into three tribes, the Unamis, Unalachtgo, and the Minsi, also called the Monseys or Muncies. The English equivalents of these appellations are the Turtle, the Turkey, and the Wolf. The tribe bearing the latter name exhibited a spirit that was quite in keeping with it, but the Delawares as a rule were less warlike than other nations, and they more readily accepted Christianity.

The principal chiefs among the Delawares were White Eyes and Captain Pipe. The former was the leader of the peace element of the nation and the latter of the tribes who were inclined to war. There was great rivalry between them and constant intrigue. White Eyes died about the year 1780. and Captain Pipe gained the ascendancy among his people. It was principally through his influence that the Delawares were drawn into a condition of hostility towards the whites, and he encouraged the commission of enormities by every artifice in his power. He was shrewd, treacherous, and full of malignity, according to Heckewelder, Drake and other writers on the Indians of the northwest, though brave, and famous as a leader in battle. White Eyes though not less noted as a warrior seemed actuated by really humane motives to fight only when forbearance was impossible. He encouraged the establishment of the Moravian Indian missions and was the firm friend of their founders, though he never accepted Christianity. His greatest influence was exerted over the Delawares after the death, in 1776, of Netawatmees, a celebrated chief, who, during his lifetime, had combatted the reforms which White Eyes advocated. Buckougahelas was another of the Delaware chiefs, and was celebrated principally for his action in what is now the western part of the State. Others were King Newcomer (after whom the present Newcomerstown was named) and Half King. There dwelt among the Delawares of the Upper Muskingum at one time a white woman who had great influence among them and after whom a creek was named—Whitewoman's creek.

Most of the Delaware towns were at the vicinity of the forks of the Muskingum, or the confluence of the Tuscarawas and Muskingum, and that region is rich in the old Indian names. The Delawares had no village on the lower Muskingum, and so far as is known none in what is now Washington county, this region, like almost the whole of the Ohio valley, being devoid of inhabitants and regarded as a hunting ground.

The Muskingum river derives its name from the Delawares, and was originally Mooskingom. The literal meaning of this term is Elk's Eye, and it was probably so called because of its clearness. The Tuscarawas undoubtedly took its name from an Indian town which was situated where Bolivar now is. The name according to Heckewelder meant "old town" and the village bearing it was the oldest in the valleys.

The Shawnees were the only Indians of the northwest who had a tradition of a foreign origin, and for some time after the whites became acquainted with them they held annual festivals to celebrate the safe arrival in this country of their remote ancestors. Concerning the history of the Shawnees there is considerable conflicting testimony, but it is generally conceded that at an early date they separated from the other Lenape tribes and established themselves in the south, roaming from Kentucky to Florida. Afterward the main body of the tribe is supposed to have pushed northward, encouraged by their friends the Miamis, and to have occupied the beautiful and rich valley of the Scioto until driven from it in 1672 by the Iroquois. Their nation was shattered and dispersed. A few may have remained upon the upper Scioto and others taken refuge with the Miamis, but by far the most considerable portion again journeyed southward and, according to the leading historians, made a forcible settlement on the head waters of the Carolina. Driven away from that locality they found refuge among the Creeks. A fragment of the Shawnees was taken to Pennsylvania and reduced to a humiliating condition by their conquerors. They still retained their pride and considerable innate independence, and about 1740 encouraged by the Wyandots and the French, carried into effect their long cherished purpose of returning to the Scioto. Those who had settled among the Creeks joined them and the nation was again reunited. It is probable that they first occupied the southern portion of their beloved valley, and that after a few years had elapsed the Delawares peacefully surrendered to them a large tract of country further north.[*] It is conjectured by some students that the branch of the Shawnees who lived for a term of years in the south were once upon the Suanee river and that the well known name was a corruption of the name of the nation of Tecumseh. This chief, whose fame added lustre to the annals of the tribe, is said to have been the son of a Creek woman whom his father took as a wife during the southern migration. The Shawnees were divided into four tribes[†]—the Piqua,[‡] Kiskapocke, Mequachuke, and Chillicothe.

---

[*] Some of the Delaware chiefs who visited Philadelphia during the Revolution spoke figuratively of having "placed the Shawnees in their laps."

[†] This information is derived from a communication in the Archæological American, written in 1819 by Colonel John Johnston, then Indian agent, and located at Piqua, Ohio.

[‡] It was from the fact of these that the Indian village and the present town of Piqua, Miami county, derived their names. The name Pickaway, which has been given to one of the older counties of Ohio, but which was originally applied to the "plains" within its limits is a corruption of Piqua.

Those who deny to the American Indians any love for the beautiful and any exercise of imagination might be influenced to concede them the possession of such faculties and in a high degree, by the abundance of their fanciful traditions, of which their account of the origin of the Piqua is a good example. According to their practical legend the tribe began in a perfect man who burst into being from fire and ashes. The Shawnees said to the first whites who mingled with them, that once upon a time when the wise men and chiefs of the nation were sitting around the smouldering embers of what had been the council fire, they were startled by a great puffing of fire and smoke, and suddenly, from the midst of the ashes and dying coals, there arose before them a man of splendid form and mien, and that he was named Piqua, to signify the manner of his coming into the world—that he was born of fire and ashes. This legend of the origin of the tribe, beautiful in its simplicity, has been made the subject of comment by several writers as showing in a marked manner the romatic susceptibility of the Indian character. The name Megoachuke signifies a fat man filled—a man made perfect, so that nothing is wanting. This tribe had the priesthood. The Kiskapocke tribe inclined to war, and had at least one great war chief—Tecumseh. Chillicothe is not known to have been interpreted as a tribal designation. It was from this tribe that the several Indian villages on the Scioto and Miami were given the names they bore, and which was perpetuated by application to one of the early white settlements. The Shawnees have been styled "the Bedouins of the American wilderness" and "the Spartans of the race." To the former title they seem justly entitled by their extensive and almost constant wanderings, and the latter is not an inappropriate appellation, considering their well known bravery and the stoicism with which they bore the consequences of defeat. From the time of their reestablishment upon the Scioto until after the treaty of Greenville, a period of from forty to fifty years, they were constantly engaged in warfare against the whites. They were among the most active allies of the French, and after the conquest of Canada continued, in concert with the Delawares, hostilities which were only terminated by the marching of Colonel Boquet's forces into the country of the latter. They made numerous incursions into Pennsylvania, the Virginia frontier, harassed the Kentucky stations, and either alone or in conjunction with the Indians of other tribes, actually attacked or threatening to do so, terrorized the first settlers in Ohio from Marietta to the Miamis. They took an active part against the Americans in the war for Independence and in the Indian war which followed, and a part of them, under the leadership of Tecumseh, joined the British in the War of 1812.

The Wyandots or Hurons had their principal seat opposite Detroit, and smaller settlements (the only ones within the limits of Ohio, probably, except the village on White woman creek,) on the Maumee and Sandusky. They claimed greater antiquity than any of the other tribes, and their assumption was even allowed by the Delawares. Their right to the country between the Ohio and Lake Erie from the Alleghany to the Great Miami, derived from ancient sovereignty or from the incorporation of the three extinct tribes (the Eries, Andastes, and Neutrals) was never disputed, save by the Six Nations. The Jesuit missionaries who were among them as early as 1639, and who had ample advantages for obtaining accurate information concerning the tribe, placed their number at ten thousand. They were both more civilized and more warlike than the other tribes of the northwest. Their population being, comparatively speaking, large and at the same time concentrated, they naturally gave more attention than did other tribes to agriculture. Extensive fields of maize adjoined their villages. The Wyandots on the score of bravery have been given a higher rank than any of the other Ohio tribes.* With them flight from an enemy in battle, whatever might be the odds of strength or advantage of ground, was a disgrace. They fought to the death and would not be taken prisoners. Of thirteen chiefs of the tribe engaged in the battle of Fallen Timbers, Wayne's victory, only one was taken alive, and he badly wounded.

The Ottawas existed in the terriory constituting Ohio only in small numbers and have no particular claims for attention. They seem to have been inferior in almost all respects to the Delawares, Wyandots, and Shawnees, though as the tribe to which the great Pontiac belonged they have been rendered quite conspicuous in history.

The Miami Indians were, so far as actual knowledge extends, the original denizens of the valleys bearing their name, and claimed that they were created in it. The name in the Ottawa tongue signifies mother. The ancient name of the Miamis was Twigtwees. The Mingoes or Cayugas, a fragment of the Iroquois, had only a few small villages, one at Mingo Bottom, three miles below Steubenville, and others upon the Scioto. Logan came into Ohio in 1772 and dwelt for a time at the latter town, but two years later was on the Scioto.

---

* William Henry Harrison and other eminent authorities pay the highest tribute to the valor of the Wyandot warriors, and give abundant proofs of their assertions.

CHAPTER II.

OWNERSHIP OF THE NORTHWEST.

The Claims of France, Founded on Discovery and Occupation.—England's Claim Based Upon Discovery and Settlement of the Atlantic Coast and Treaties of Purchase.—Treaty of Paris in 1763.—Ohio as a Part of France and Canada.—The "Quebec Bill."—Title Vested in the Confederated States by Treaty in 1783.—Conflicting Claims of States.—Virginia's Exercise of Civil Authority.—The Northwest Territory Erected as Botetourt County.—Illinois County.—New York Withdraws Claim.—Virginia's Deed of Cession.—Massachusetts Cedes Her Claim Without Reservation.—"The Tardy and Reluctant Sacrifice of State Pretensions to the Public Good," Made by Connecticut.—A Serious Evil Averted.—The States Urged to their Action by New Jersey, Delaware and Maryland.—Extinguishment of the Indiana Title.—Difficulty of Making Satisfactory Provisions.—A Harsh and Unjust Policy.—Washington's Influence Causes More Humane Treatment of the Indians.—Treaty of Fort Stanwix.—Treaty of Fort McIntosh.—George Rogers Clark, General Butler and S. H. Parsons Confer with Several Tribes at the Mouth of the Miami.—Measures of the Treaty Ineffectual to Preserve Peace.—Great Improvement in the Attitude of the Government.—Indian Tribes Recognized as Rightful Owners.—Appropriations made to Purchase Title from Them.

FRANCE, resting her claim upon the discovery and explorations of Robert Cavalier de la Salle and Marquette, upon the occupation of the country, and later, upon the provisions of several European treaties (those of Utrecht, Ryswick, Aix-la-chapelle), was the first nation to formally lay claim to the soil of the territory now included within the boundaries of the State of Ohio as an integral portion of the valley of the Mississippi and of the northwest. Ohio was thus a part of New France. After the treaty of Utrecht, in 1713, it was a part of the French province of Louisiana, which extended from the gulf to the northern lakes. The English claims were based on the priority of their occupation of the Atlantic coast, in latitude corresponding to the territory claimed; upon an opposite construction of the same treaties above named; and last but not least, upon the alleged cession of the rights of the Indians. England's charters to all of the original colonies expressly extended their grants from sea to sea. The principal ground of claim by the English was by the treaties of purchase from the Six Nations, who, claiming to be conquerors of the whole country and therefore its possessors, asserted their right to dispose of it. A portion of the land was obtained through grants from the Six Nations and by actual purchase made at Lancaster, Pennsylvania, in 1744. France successfully resisted the claims of England, and maintained control of the territory between the Ohio and the lakes by force of arms until the Treaty of Paris was consummated in 1763. By the provisions of this treaty Great Britian came into possession of the disputed lands, and retained it until ownership was vested in the United States by the treaty of peace made just twenty years later. We have seen that Ohio was once a part of France and of the French province of Louisiana, and as a curiosity it may be of interest to refer to an act of the British Parliament, which made it an integral part of Canada. This was what has been known in history as the "Quebec Bill" passed in 1774. By the provisions of this bill the Ohio river was made the southwestern, and the Mississippi river the western boundary of Canada, thus placing the territory now constituting the States of Ohio, Indiana, Illinois, Michigan, and Wisconsin under the local jurisdiction of the Province of Quebec.

Virginia had asserted her claims to the whole of the territory northwest of the Ohio, and New York had claimed titles to portions of the same. These claims had been for the most part held in abeyance during the period when the general ownership was vested in Great Britian, but were afterwards the cause of much embarrassment to the United States. Virginia, however, had not only claimed ownership of the soil, but attempted the exercise of civil authority in the disputed territory as early as 1769. In that year the colonial house of burgesses passed an act establishing the county of Botetourt, including a large part of what is now West Virginia and the whole territory northwest of the Ohio, and having, of course, as its western boundary the Mississippi river. This was a county of vast proportions—a fact of which the august authorities who ordered its establishment seem to have been fully aware, for they inserted the following among other provisions of the act, viz:

WHEREAS, The people situated upon the Mississippi in the said county of Botetourt will be very remote from the court house, and must necessarily become a separate county as soon as their numbers are sufficient, which will probably happen in a short time, be it therefore enacted by the authority aforesaid that the inhabitants of that part of the said county of Botetourt, which lies on the said waters, shall be exempted from the payment of any levies to be laid by the said county for the purpose of building a court house and prison for said county.

It was more in name than in fact, however, that Virginia had jurisdiction over this great county of Botetourt through the act of 1769. In 1778, after the splendid achievements of General George Rogers Clarke—his subjugation of the British posts in the far west, and conquest of the whole country from the Ohio to the Mississippi—this territory was organized by the Virginia legislature as the county of Illinois. Then, and not until then, did government have more than a nominal existence in this far extending but undeveloped country, containing a few towns and scattered population. The act, which was passed in October, contained the following provisions:

All the citizens of the commonwealth of Virginia who are already settled, or shall hereafter settle on the western side of the Ohio, shall be included in a distinct county which shall be called Illinois; and the governor of this commonwealth, with the advice of the council, may appoint a county lieutenant or commandant-in-chief, during pleasure, who shall appoint and commission so many deputy commandants, militia officers and commissaries, as he shall think proper, in the different districts, during pleasure, all of whom, before they enter into office, shall take the oath of fidelity to this commonwealth, and the oath of office, according to the form of their own religion. And all officers to whom the inhabitants have been accustomed, necessary to the preservation of peace and the administration of justice, shall be chosen by a majority of citizens, in their respective districts, to be convened for that purpose by the county lieutenant or commandant, or his deputy, and shall be commissioned by the said county lieutenant, or commandant-in-chief.

John Todd was appointed as county lieutenant and civil commandant of Illinois county, and served until his death (he was killed in the battle of Blue Licks, August 18, 1782), being succeeded by Timothy de Montbrun.

New York was the first of the several States claiming right and title in western lands to withdraw the same in favor of the United States. Her charter, obtained March 2, 1664, from Charles II, embraced territory which had formerly been granted to Massachusetts and Connecticut. The cession of claim was made by James Duane, William Floyd, and Alexander McDougall, on behalf of the State, March 1, 1781.

Virginia, with a far more valid claim than New York, was the next State to follow New York's example. Her claim was founded upon certain charters granted to the colony by James I, and bearing date respectively, April 10, 1606; May 23, 1609; and March 12, 1611; upon the conquest of the country by General George Rogers Clarke; and upon the fact that she had also exercised civil authority over the territory. The general assembly of Virginia, at its session beginning October 20, 1783, passed an act authorizing its delegates in Congress to convey to the United States in Congress assembled all the right of that commonwealth to the territory northwest of the Ohio river. The act was consummated on March 17, 1784. By one of the provisory clauses of this act was reserved the Virginia Military district, lying between the waters of the Scioto and Little Miami rivers.

Massachusetts ceded her claims, without reservation, the same year that Virginia did hers (1784), though the action was not formally consummated until the eighteenth of April, 1785. The right of her title had been rested upon her charter, granted less than a quarter of a century from the arrival of the Mayflower, and embracing territory extending from the Atlantic to the Pacific.

Connecticut made what has been characterized as "the last tardy and reluctant sacrifice of State pretensions to the common good"* on the fourteenth of September, 1786. She ceded to Congress all her "right, title, interest, jurisdiction, and claim to the lands northwest of the Ohio, excepting the Connecticut Western Reserve," and of this tract jurisdictional claim was not ceded to the United States until May 30, 1801.

The happy, and, considering all complications, speedy adjustment of the conflicting claims of States and consolidation of all rights of title in the United States was productive of the best results both at home and abroad. The young nation, born in the terrible throes of the Revolution, went through a trying ordeal, and one of which the full peril was not realized until it had been safely passed. Serious troubles threatened to arise from the disputed ownership of the western lands, and there were many who had grave fears that the well-being of the country would be impaired or at least its progress impeded. The infant Republic was at that time closely and jealously watched by all of the governments of Europe, and nearly all of them would have rejoiced to have witnessed the failure of the American experiment, and they were not destined to be gratified at the expense of the United States. As it was, the most palpable harm, caused by delay, was the retarding of settlement. The movement towards the complete cession of State claims was accelerated as much as possible by Congress. The national legislature strenuously urged the several States in

1784 to cede their lands to the confederacy to aid the payment of the debts incurred during the Revolution and to promote the harmony of the Union.*

The States of New Jersey, Delaware, and Maryland had taken the initiative action and been largely instrumental in bringing about the cession of State claims. The fact that they had no foundation for pretensions of ownership save that they had equally in proportion to their ability with the other States assisted in wresting these lands from Great Britian, led them to protest against an unfair division of the territory—New Jersey had memorialized Congress in 1778, and Delaware followed in the same spirit in January, 1779. Later in the same year Maryland virtually reiterated the principles advanced by New Jersey and Maryland, though more positively. Her representatives in Congress emphatically and eloquently expressed their views and those of their constituents in the form of instructions upon the matter of confirming the articles of confederation.

The extinguishment of the Indian claims to the soil of the northwest was another delicate and difficult duty which devolved upon the Government. In the treaty of peace, ratified by Congress in 1784, no provision was made by Great Britian in behalf of the Indians—even their most faithful allies, the Six Nations. Their lands were included in the boundaries secured to the United States. They had suffered greatly during the war and the Mohawks had been dispossessed of the whole of their beautiful valley. The only remuneration they received was a tract of country in Canada, and all of the sovereignty which Great Britian had exercised over them was transferred to the United States. The relation of the new government to these Indians was peculiar. In 1782 the British principle, in brief, that "might makes right" —that discovery was equivalent to conquest, and that therefore the nations retained only a possessory claim to their lands, and could only abdicate it to the government claiming sovereignty—was introduced into the general policy of the United States. The legislature of New York was determined to expel the Six Nations entirely, in retaliation for their hostility during the war. Through the just and humane counsels of Washington and Schuyler, however, a change was wrought in the Indian policy, and the Continental Congress sought henceforward in its action to condone the hostilities of the past and gradually to dispossess the Indians of their lands by purchase, as the growth of the settlements might render it necessary to do so. It was in pursuance of this policy that the treaty of Fort Stanwix was made, October 22, 1784. By this treaty were extinguished the vague claims which the confederated tribes, the Mohawks, Onondagas, Senecas, Cayugas, Tuscarawas, and Oneidas, had for more than a century maintained to the Ohio valley. The commissioners of Congress in this transaction were Oliver Wolcott, Richard Butler, and Arthur Lee. The Six Nations were represented by two of their ablest chiefs, Cornplanter and Red Jacket, the former for peace and the latter for war. La Fayette was present at this treaty and importuned the Indians to preserve peace with the Americans.

By the treaty of Fort McIntosh, negotiated on the twenty-first of January, 1785, by George Rogers Clark, Richard Butler, and Arthur Lee, was secured the relinquishment of all claims to the Ohio valley held by the Delawares, Ottawas, Wyandots, and Chippewas. The provisions of this treaty were as follows:

ARTICLE 1st—Three chiefs, one from the Wyandot and two from the Delaware nations, shall be delivered up to the commissioners of the United States, to be by them retained till all the prisoners taken by the said nations or any of them shall be restored.

ARTICLE 2nd—The said Indian nations and all of their tribes do acknowledge themselves to be under the protection of the United States and of no other sovereign whatever.

ARTICLE 3rd—The boundary line between the United States and the Wyandot and Delaware nations shall begin at the mouth of the river Cuyahoga, and run thence up the said river to the portage between that and the Tuscarawas branch of the Muskingum; then down the said branch to the forks at the crossing-place above Fort Laurens; then westwardly to the portage of the Big Miami, which runs into the Ohio, at the mouth of which branch the fort stood which was taken by the French in the year one thousand seven hundred and fifty-two; then along the said portage to the Great Miami or Owl river, and down the southeast side of the same to its mouth; thence down the south shore of Lake Erie to the mouth of the Cuyahoga where it began.

ARTICLE 4th—The United States allot all the lands contained within the said lines to the Wyandot and Delaware nations, to live and to hunt on, and to such of the Ottawa nation as now live thereon; saving and reserving for the establishment of trading posts six miles square at the mouth of the Miami or Owl river and the same at the portage of that branch of the Miami which runs into the Ohio, and the same on the cape of Sandusky, where the fort formerly stood, and also two miles square on the lower rapids of Sandusky river; which posts and the land annexed to them, shall be for the use and under the government of the United States.

ARTICLE 5th—If any citizen of the United States, or other person not being an Indian, shall attempt to settle on any of the lands allotted to the Wyandot and Delaware nations in this treaty, except on the lands reserved to the United States in the preceding article, such person shall forfeit the protection of the United States, and the Indians may punish him as they please.

ARTICLE 6th—The Indians who sign this treaty, as well in behalf of all their tribes as of themselves, do acknowledge the lands east, south, and west of the lands described in the third article, so far as the said Indians claimed the same, to belong to the United States, and none of their tribes shall presume to settle upon the same or any part of it.

ARTICLE 7th—The post of Detroit, with a district beginning at the mouth of the river Rosine on the west side of Lake Erie and running west six miles up the southern bank of the said river; thence northerly, and always six miles west of the strait, till it strikes Lake St. Clair, shall also be reserved to the sole use of the United States.

ARTICLE 8th—In the same manner the post of Michilimackinack with its dependencies, and twelve miles square about the same, shall be reserved to the use of the United States.

ARTICLE 9th—If any Indian or Indians shall commit a robbery or murder on any citizen of the United States, the tribe to which such offenders may belong shall be bound to deliver them up at the nearest post, to be punished according to the ordinance of the United States.

ARTICLE 10th—The Commissioners of the United States, in pursuance of the humane and liberal views of Congress, upon the treaty's being signed, will direct goods to be distributed among the different tribes for their use and comfort.

The treaty of Fort Finney, at the mouth of the Great Miami, January 31, 1786, secured the cession of whatever claim to the Ohio valley was held by the Shawnees. George Rogers Clark, Richard Butler, and Samuel H. Parsons* were the Commissioners of the United States. James Monroe, then a member of Congress from Virginia and afterwards President of the United States, accompanied General Butler, in the month of October preceding the treaty, as far as Limestone† (now Maysville, Kentucky). The party, it is related, stopped at the mouth of the Muskingum and (in the words of General Butler's journal) "left fixed in a locust tree" a letter recommending the building of a fort on the Ohio side. By the terms of this treaty the Shawnees were confined to the lands west of the Great Miami. Hostages were demanded from the Indians, to remain in the possession of the United States until all prisoners should be returned, and the Shawnees were compelled to acknowledge the United States as the sole and absolute sovereign of all the territory ceded to them, in the treaty of peace, by Great Britain. The clause embodying the latter condition excited the jealousy of the Shawnees. They went away dissatisfied with the treaty, though assenting to it. This fact, and the difficulty that was experienced even while the treaty was making of preventing depredations by white borderers, argued unfavorably for the future. The treaty was productive of no good results whatever. Hostilities were resumed in the spring of 1786, and serious and widespread war was threatened. Congress had been acting upon the policy that the treaty of peace with Great Britian had invested the United States with the fee simple of all the Indian lands, but urged now by the stress of circumstance the Government radically changed its policy, fully recognizing the Indians as the rightful proprietors of the soil, and on the second of July, 1787, appropriated the sum of twenty-six thousand dollars for

*† General Samuel H. Parsons, an eminent Revolutionary character, was one of the first band of Marietta pioneers, and was appointed first as associate and then as chief judge of the Northwest Territory. He was drowned in the Big Beaver river, November 17, 1789, while returning to his home in Marietta from the north, where he had been making the treaty which secured the aboriginal title to the soil of the Connecticut Western Reserve.

†† General Butler's Journal in Craig's "Olden Time," October, 1847

the purpose of extinguishing Indian claims to lands already ceded to the United States and for extending a purchase beyond the limits heretofore fixed by treaty.

Under this policy other relinquishments of Ohio territory were effected through the treaties of Fort Harmar, held by General St. Clair, January 9, 1789, the treaty of Greenville, negotiated by Anthony Wayne, August 3, 1795, and various other treaties made at divers times from 1796 to 1818.* But of these it is beyond our province to speak in this chapter.

CHAPTER III.

ADVENT OF THE WHITE MAN.

La Salle Upon the Ohio Two Hundred Years Ago.—Possibility of his Having Explored the Muskingum.—The "Griffin" on Lake Erie.—French Trading Stations.—Routes Through the Wilderness.—The English Supersede the French.—Interest in the West Exhibited by Governor Spotswood, of Virginia, in 1710.—The Transmontane Order Founded.—Licenses Issued for Trading with the Indians, by the Governor of Pennsylvania, in 1740.—Systematic Exploration of the Ohio Valley by Celeron de Bienville.—At the Mouth of the Muskingum in 1749.—Leaden Plate Buried.—Discovered in 1798.—Pickawillamy, the First Building Erected by the English in Ohio.—Organization of the Colonial Ohio Land Company, in Virginia, in 1748.—Preparation Made to Establish a Colony.—French Resistance.—War of Britain Against the French and Indians.—Its Results.—Franklin's Plans for Western Settlements.—George Washington upon the Ohio. His Favorable Impressions of the Country.—Immense Schemes for Western Colonization.—Indian Hostility and Imperfection of Land Title the Probable Cause of their Failure.—The First English Military Expedition upon Ohio Soil.—Colonel Boquet Wins a Bloodless Victory on the Upper Muskingum.—Thomas Hutchins.—Hostility of the Shawnees.—Logan.—Lord Dunmore's War.—The Battle of Point Pleasant.—The Breaking Out of the Revolutionary War.—An Event of Immeasurable Importance in the West.—General George Rogers Clark's Conquest of the Northwest.—Value of His Foresight and Decisive Action.—His Services Unappreciated.—Miscellaneous Military Invasions.—The Establishment of the Moravian Missions on the Muskingum—The Massacre.

THE adventurous La Salle, there is every reason to believe, was the first white man who trod the soil of the destined State of Ohio, and the first whose eyes beheld the Beautiful river. With a few followers and led by Indian guides he penetrated the vast country of the powerful Iroquois until, as Parkman says, he reached "at a point six or seven leagues from Lake Erie, a branch of the Ohio, which he descended to the main stream," and so went onward as far as the "falls," or the site of Louisville. His men abandoning him there, he retraced his way alone. This, according to the best authorities, was in the winter of 1669-70, over two hundred years ago. And it is not improbable that one hundred and eighteen years before Marietta was settled this intrepid French explorer had encamped at the mouth of the Muskingum. Indeed, there is some reason to believe that he made his way from Lake Erie to the Ohio by the Cuyahoga, the Tuscarawas, and Muskingum, though the preponderance

*It is a fact worthy of note, and one of which we may well be proud, that the title to every foot of Ohio soil was honorably acquired from the Indians.

of evidence points to the Alleghany as the route followed. Ten years later La Salle unfurled the first sail ever set to the breeze upon Lake Erie, and upon the Griffin, a schooner of forty-five tons burden, made the voyage to Lake Huron. In 1682 he reached the Mississippi, descended to its mouth, and there solemnly proclaimed possession of the vast valley in the name of his king.

The French had a trading station on the Maumee near the site of Toledo, as early as 1680, and according to Bancroft they had a route through the western wilderness from Canada to the Mississippi; by the way of the Maumee, Wabash, and Ohio rivers in 1716; and another only a little later from Presque Isle (Erie) by the Alleghany and Ohio. About 1740, however, the French traders were superseded by the English.

Governor Alexander Spotswood of Virginia became interested in the western country early in the eighteenth century; engaged in exploring the Alleghanies in 1710; discovered a passage through them in 1714, and entered with great ardor upon the scheme of taking practical possession of the Ohio valley. He founded the Transmontane order, whose knights were decorated with a golden horseshoe bearing the legend "*Sic jurat transcendere montes,*" and urged upon the British sovereign the importance of gaining a foothold in the west before the French had gained too powerful an ascendancy. His suggestions were not regarded, and many years later the British government had cause to remember with regret the wise policy they had neglected to act upon. Although no systematic plan of exploration or settlement was followed, individuals from time to time passed the great barrier and visited the valley of the *la belle riviere.* There have been handed down certain vague traditions that the English had trading posts on the Ohio as early as 1730, and it is known positively that they had soon after that time. In 1744 the governor of Pennsylvania issued licenses for trading with the Indians as far west as the Father of Waters. John Howard had descended the Ohio in 1742 and been captured on the Mississippi by the French; and six years later Conrad Weiser, acting in behalf of the English, visited the Shawnees at Logstown (below the site of Pittsburgh) bearing gifts with which to win their favor. About the same time George Crogan and Andrew Montour, the half breed of a Seneca chief bore liberal presents to the Miamis, in return for which the Indians allowed the whites to establish a trading post and build a stockade at the mouth of Loramies creek on the Great Miami (within the present county of Shelby). The fort, built in 1751, which was called Pickawillamy, has been cited by some writers as the first English settlement in Ohio. The building, which was undoubtedly the first erected by the British on the soil of the State, was destroyed in June, 1752, by a force of French and Indians.

Prior to the middle of the century the French strenuously reasserted their ownership of the northwest, and did actually take possession of what is now the northern part of Ohio, building a fort and establishing a trading station at Sandusky. Celeron de Bienville made a systematic exploration of the Ohio valley and formally declared by process verbal the ownership of the soil. On the sixteenth of August, 1749, he was at the mouth of the Muskingum. This fact was revealed in 1798 by the discovery of a leaden plate which had been buried by him and which set forth that the explorer sent out by the Marquis de la Gallissoniere, captain general of New France, agreeably to the wishes of His Majesty, Louis XV, had deposited the plate as a monument of the renewal of possession of *la riviere Oyo*, otherwise *la belle riviere*, and all those which empty into it, and of all the lands of both sides even to the sources of the said rivers, and which had been obtained by force of arms and by treaties, especially those of Ryswick, Utrecht, and Aix-la-chappelle. The plate was found protruding from the bank after a freshet, by some boys, who, ignorant of its antiquarian value, cut away a considerable portion of it to melt into bullets, lead there being very scarce. The plate was finally secured by Paul Fearing, one of the Marietta pioneers, and the inscription was translated by William Woodbridge (afterwards governor of Michigan) but then a young man, who had been studying French at Gallipolis. Considerable difficulty was experienced in making the translation as a portion of the inscription had been cut away by the finders of the plate, but the larger part remaining enabled the student to supply the missing words. The plate was nearly twelve inches from top to bottom and about seven and a half in breadth.[*] A similar plate was found in 1846 at the mouth of the Kanawha. They were doubtless deposited at the mouths of all the principal tributaries of the Ohio.

The French had a very just claim to the Ohio valley, but it was destined that they should not hold it and already events were shaping which eventually led to the overthrow of their authority and the vesture of title and possession in the English crown.

The Colonial Ohio Land company was organized in Virginia in 1748 by twelve associates, among whom were Thomas Lee, and Lawrence and Augustine, brothers of George Washington. Under their auspices Christopher Gist explored the Ohio as far as the falls, travelling a portion of the time with Croghan and Montour. The company secured a royal grant of half a million acres of land in the Ohio valley. In 1753 preparations were made to establish a colony. The French exhibited an intention of resistance, and the royal governor of Virginia sent George Washington, then a young man, to the commander of the French forces to demand their reason for invasion of British territory. Washington received an answer that was both haughty and defiant. Returning to Virginia he made known the failure of his mission. The project of making a settlement was abandoned, and preparations were immediately made for the maintenance of the British claim to the western valley by force of arms. The result was the union of the colonies, the ultimate involvement of England in the war that ensued, the defeat of the French, and the vesture in the British

crown of the right and title to Canada and of all the territory east of the Mississippi and south to the Spanish possessions, excepting New Orleans and a small body of land surrounding it. Benjamin Franklin had previously tried to effect a union of the colonies and had been unsuccessful. He had proposed a plan of settlement in 1754, and suggested that two colonies should be located in the west—one upon the Cuyahoga and the other upon the Scioto, "on which," he said, "for forty miles each side of it and quite up to its head is a body of all rich land, the finest spot of its bigness in all North America, and has the peculiar advantage of sea coal in plenty (even above ground in two places) for fuel when the wood shall have been destroyed."

But little advantage was taken by the English of the ascendancy they had gained. About the only men who visited the country northwest of the Ohio were traders. The frontiers of Pennsylvania and Virginia were settled in due time, but as the title to the soil on the other side of the Ohio was not perfected no attempt was made for several years to occupy the country. Kentucky had even been penetrated by the pioneers, of whom Daniel Boone was a type, and many setttlements founded before attention was again seriously given to the country north of the Ohio.

George Washington made a journey down the Ohio in 1770. He was accompanied by Dr. Craik, Captain (afterwards Colonel) William Crawford (who was burned to death at the stake within the present limits of Wyandot county in 1782), and several other white men, also by a party of Indians. The little company embarked on the Ohio from Fort Pitt, October 20th, and on the night of the twenty fifth camped out "about half way down the Long Reach" (Grand view). Washington's journal continues:

October 26th. . . . At the lower end of the Long Reach, and for some distance up it, on the east side, is a large bottom, but low and covered with beech near the river shore, which is no indication of good land.

The Long Reach is a straight course of the river for about eighteen to twenty miles, which appears more extraordinary as the Ohio in general is remarkably crooked. There are several islands in this Reach, some containing a hundred or more acres of land, but all I apprehend liable to be overflowed.

On the night of October 26th Washington encamped "at a creek about twelve miles below the Three Islands," which was "pretty large at the mouth and just above an island." This was the Little Muskingum.

Under date of October 27th occurs the following entry:

Left our encampment a quarter before seven, and after passing the creek near which we lay and another of much the same size, and on the same side [this was Duck creek], also one island about two miles in length, but not wide, we came to the mouth of the Muskingum, distant from our encampment about four miles. This river is about a hundred and fifty yards wide at the mouth; it runs out in a gentle current and clear stream, and is navigable a great way into the country for canoes. From Muskingum to Little Kanawha is about thirteen miles. This is about as wide as the mouth of the Muskingum, but the water much deeper. It runs up towards the inhabitants of Monongahela. . . . About six or seven miles below the mouth of the Little Kanawha we came to a small creek on the west side which the Indians call Little Hockhocking, but before we did this we passed another small creek on the same side near the mouth of that river, and a cluster of islands afterward. The lands for two or three miles below the Little Kanawha appear broken, and indifferent, but opposite to the Little Hockhocking there is a bottom of good land.*

Largely through Washington was the interest in the west revived. Immense schemes for settlement and land speculation were projected. A huge company was organized which included the Old Ohio company and the Walpole scheme as well as recognizing the bounties of the Virginia volunteers in the French war. Doubtless some of these plans for the devlopement of the west would have succeeded had it not been for Indian hostilities upon the border settlements already established, and the probability of a long continuance of the perturbed condition of affairs generally. Colonel Henry Boquet had made the first English military expedition into the Ohio country in 1764, his purpose being to punish and awe the Indians and recover from them the captives they had taken during the previous years on the Pennsylvania and Virginia borders. He was successful in the accomplishment of each one of his objects. The expedition was directed against the Delawares upon the Muskingum and Tuscarawas. No blood was shed, the Indians assenting to the terms of a treaty prepared by Colonel Boquet, and delivering to him over two hundred prisoners. Upon the twenty-eighth of November the army of about fifteen hundred men returned to Fort Pitt, which point they had left on October 3d. This expedition for a time tranquilized the Indians of the Ohio country, and the next ten years passed peacefully and without the occurrence of any important event. With Colonel Boquet was Thomas Hutchins (of whom we shall have frequent occasion to speak). He served in the capacity of military engineer and was geographer to the king of Great Britain. Hutchins published a large book upon the western country with which he became very familiar from long continued services as explorer. In later years as geographer of the United States he superintended the survey of the "seven ranges," and it was largely through his influence that the Ohio company was led to locate their purchase upon the Muskingum.

But returning to the period from which we retrograded to speak of the Boquet expedition, we find in 1774 that the Shawnees have become bitterly hostile, principally on account of the prospect of losing their land and because of the murder of the kindred of Logan, the famous Mingo, who was now dwelling with them at the Old Chillicothe town on the Scioto (where is now the village of Westfall, Pickaway county). Logan had "fully glutted his vengeance" upon the white settlements of the Monongahela country, and numerous atrocities had been committed all along the border. To quell the turbulence that prevailed Lord Dunmore, the then royal governor of Virginia, organized an army of invasion of the Indian country. He had a desire for military renown and decided to assume personal command of the larger division, while he entrusted the other, consisting of about eleven hundred men raised west of the Blue Ridge, to

General Andrew Lewis. The forces of the latter were attacked by the Indians on the tenth of October south of the Ohio, and the ensuing combat, known as the battle of Point Pleasant, was one of the most desperate and bloody in the annals of the west. The contending forces were very nearly equal, it is claimed by most writers, but there is strong probability that the Indians were much weaker in numbers than the army which they assailed. The whites lost half of their officers and fifty-two men killed, while the Indian loss was estimated at two hundred and thirty-three. Lord Dunmore's division passed through a bloodless campaign. They descended the Ohio to the mouth of the Hocking river, and there built Fort Gower. The governor was here at the time of the battle of Point Pleasant, and had sent messengers to Lewis ordering him to march toward the Scioto towns. Dunmore marched through the territory included in Athens county and onward to the Pickaway (originally Piqua) plains, below the site of Circleville. There he was met by Lewis' decimated division, whom he could hardly keep from falling upon the Indians to avenge the death of their comrades at Point Pleasant. A treaty was held at Camp Charlotte, which was attended and acquiesced in by all of the leading chiefs of the villages except Logan. Lord Dunmore dispatched John Gibson to confer with the haughty Mingo, and his visit elicited the famous speech, which Jefferson pronounced equal in eloquence to any ever made by the great orators of civilized nations.

Already the premonitory signs of that discontent which developed into the Revolution of American independence were exhibiting themselves, and soon the conflict was begun which riveted the attention of the world upon the colonies. The Revolutionary period was almost barren of event in the west. There was one event, however, of immeasurable importance. The time had come when the destiny of the Great West—of the Northwestern Territory—was to be decided. The man who was to shape its destiny was, in 1774, an officer in Lord Dunmore's army, and in 1776 a pioneer settler in Kentucky—George Rogers Clark. He was a realization of the ideal soldier—cool, coruageous, and sagacious, and at once the most powerful man and the most picturesque character in the whole west. It was his foresight and prompt, efficient action which at the close of the war made the Northwest Territory a portion of the United States instead of leaving it in the possession of the British.* He foresaw that even if the colonies should be victorious in their war for independence they would be confined to the eastern side of the Alleghanies, unless the west was a special field of conquest. After failing to interest the house of Burgesses he made an appeal to Patrick Henry, the governor of Virginia, and from him he succeded in obtaining the authority which he needed, viz.: commissions that empowered him to raise seven companies of soldiers, and to seize the British posts in the northwest.

---

*The journey extended to the Big Kanawha. On his way back Washington, accompanied by Crawford, walked across the big bend, now in Meigs county, and again taking his boat proceeded up the river, arriving at Fort Pitt November 21.

"The cession of that great territory, under the treaty of 1873, was due mainly to the foresight, the courage and endurance of one man, who never received from his country an adequate recognition of his great service."—Hon. James A. Garfield: Address, 1873.

In January, 1778, he was at Pittsburgh securing provisions and ammunition; in June he was marching through the unbroken forest at the head of a small but valiant army, principally composed of his fellow pioneers from Kentucky. His march was directed towards the Illinois country. His able generalship and courage soon placed the garrisons of Cahokia, Kaskaskia, and St. Vincent in his possession, and his equally great tact enabled him to win over the French inhabitants to the American cause and make of them warm allies.

Two other expeditions were made by General Clark—both against the Indians upon the Miamis—one in 1780 and the other in 1782. Other expeditions into or through Ohio territory were made as follows: by Colonel Bradstreet (simultaneously with Boquet's expedition—1764) along Lake Erie to Detroit, accompanied by Major Israel Putnam (the major general of the Revolution); by Colonel Angus McDonald (just prior to Dunmore's invasion); by General Lachlin McIntosh in 1778 (to the Tuscarawas, where he built the first English fort, with a parapet and stockade, intended as a permanent work, in Ohio); by Colonel John Bowman in 1779; by General Daniel Broadhead in 1781; by Colonel Archibald Lochry in the same year; by Colonel Williamson in 1782; by the fated William Crawford in the summer of the year last mentioned; by Colonel Benjamin Logan in 1786; and still others of less importance by Daniel Boone, Simon Kenton, Colonel Edwards, and Colonel Todd, at various times during the decade preceding the settlement of the territory. In drawing a rapid outline of the history of this western land it is sufficient merely to mention these various military incursions of the Indians' domain, and we have spoken more at length of General Clark's expedition because its results have a wide, general interest, and of Dunmore's invasion, because nearer the legitimate field of our work. Enough has been said to bring to mind the fact that prior to the arrival of the New England pioneers the Ohio country was the scene of many actions and events, and though a wilderness inhabited only by the roving savage had already a history.

One other topic remains to be touched upon briefly in the conclusion of this chapter, and it is one of painful and peculiar interest. We have in mind the Moravian missions on the Muskingum, and use the word painful, as the horrible massacre perpetrated there—the blackest stain on Ohio history—comes to mind. We say also a peculiar interest, and that phrase is suggested by the fact that the Moravians had better claims to be considered as settlers than any other dwellers north of the Ohio, prior to the arrival of the New England colony, and however inadequate such claims may appear it must at least be admitted that these "monks of Protestantism"* presented to the western world a phase of civilization and religion which was both picturesque and inspiring, and, also, that one of them at least, the Rev. John Heckewelder, was in after years prominently identified with affairs of State and in close association with the Marietta settlers.

*Madame de Stael.

As early as 1761 the Delaware Indians on the Tuscarawas branch of the Muskingum were visited by a Moravian missionary, the Rev. Christian Frederick Post. In March of the following year John Heckewelder became his companion and assistant. Only a few months, however, were spent in missionary labor, for in the fall the Indians who had first welcomed them, became suspicious that their sojourn there was only a ruse through which a foothold was to be gained leading to settlement, and Post and Heckewelder were obliged to leave the country to save their lives. Not until ten years had passed by was another attempt made by the zealous religionists to plant a mission among the savages. In 1772 Rev. David Zeisberger founded Schoenbrunn (Beautiful Spring) on the west side of the river and near the site of New Philadelphia, Tuscarawas county, and twenty-eight persons located there. Gnadenhutten (Tents of Grace) was established the same year seven miles below Schoenbrunn. The Rev. George Jungman, Rev. John Roth and Rev. John Etwin came out as missionaries from Pennsylvania the same year; and with the last named, immigrated to Zeisberger's station a large company of converted Indians, bringing with them the implements of industry. Good log huts were built in the regularly laid out village, a large chapel reared in which to hold religious services, the ground tilled, and every measure taken that was considered needful in the formation of a permanent settlement. The simple, quiet life went on very pleasantly, and all was peace and prosperity. Much did the Delaware chiefs and the few traders who visited Schoenbrunn marvel to see so many Indians living together after the manner of the whites, and devoting themselves to agriculture rather than the chase. They had abjured war and all savage customs. New converts were made almost daily, and the pious missionaries felt well rewarded for their patient toil and gave praise to Him whom they regarded as the prime author of their success. So many accessions were made by the Moravians that in 1776 Zeisberger formed another colony, village or station, near the present town of Coshocton, and gave it the name Lichtenan. In 1780 Salem was founded five miles below Gnadenhutten, and the Rev. John Heckewelder became its regular preacher. All went well with the people at the mission stations until the British, fearing or pretending to fear, that they were performing various services for the Americans, forcibly removed them in September, 1781, to Sandusky. There they were sorely distressed by lack of provisions, and in the latter part of the following winter obtained permission to return to their old stations and gather the corn which they had planted the summer before, and to secure if possible any of the valuables they had been obliged to leave behind them when they were hurried away. They came down from Sandusky in February, and the first of March found them busily engaged in plucking the corn which had been left standing during the winter, and packing it for transportation to their famishing brethren. "The weather during the greater part of February," says Doddridge, "had been uncommonly fine, so that the war parties from Sandusky visited the settlements and began depredations earlier than usual. One of the parties fell upon a family named Wallace and murdered all of its members, exhibiting even greater brutality than usually characterized their atrocities. The early period at which the fatal visitation was made led to the conclusion that the murderers were either Moravians or that the warriors had their winter quarters at their towns on the Muskingum. In either case the Moravians being at fault, the safety of the pioneer settlements required the destruction of their establishments at that place.*" A force of eighty or ninety men was immediately organized, and led by Colonel David Williamson set out for the Muskingum. On their arrival at Gnadehutten they found the Indians in the fields gathering their corn and with their arms by them as was the common custom, for the purpose of shooting game, and also to guard against attack. The unsuspecting Indians hearing the whites' protestations of peace and good will, and being informed that they had come to remove them to Fort Pitt and place them under the protection of the Americans, gave up their arms and began with all speed to prepare food for the white men and themselves for the proposed journey. A party of men sent out for the purpose soon brought in the Indians from Salem, and with the Gnadenhutten Indians they were placed in block-houses and confined under an armed guard. Colonel Williamson then cooly put the question to his men, should the prisoners be taken to Pittsburgh or dispatched. Sixteen or eighteen men only out of the eighty or ninety men leaned towards the side of mercy. The majority were for murdering them and were impatient to begin their hellish work. The Moravians had foreseen their fate as soon as they had been placed in confinement, and in the hour of extremity exhibited the steadfastness of their simple faith by singing the hymns and breathing the prayers that Heckewelder and Zeisberger had taught them. Some of them appealed for mercy when the murderers came among them to begin their work, but the greater number, sustained by their acquired religious faith or natural stoicism, met death with majestic composure. The executioners, with tomahawks, war-clubs, and knives, entering the crowded slaughter-pens struck down the defenseless and innocent captives until their arms grew tired, and then their places were taken by others of those white savages who thirsted for blood; and the dreadful carnage went on until ninety-six lives had been taken. Of these sixty-two were grown persons, of whom one-third were women, and the remaing thirty-four were children of various ages, from those just entering manhood or womanhood down to babes on their mothers' breasts. Neither the grey hairs of old age nor the mute, appealing innocence of childhood were protection from the fury and the brutality of these fiends in the form of men. Of all the Indians gathered in the block-houses only two escaped. Those at Schoenbrunn fled before the approach of Williamson's men and none of them were taken. This massacre occured on the seventh of March, 1782, just six years and one month

before the landing of the pioneers at the mouth of the Muskingum.

The wanton butchery of these inoffensive Moravians, more than any other event in western history, had the effect of making the Indians hostile to the Americans, and therefore, naturally, inclining them to amity with the British. This was an end which the latter people constantly sought to effect by every method of intrigue. There is some reason, too, for the belief that Williamson's men were led to the Moravian towns and incited to the commission of the stupendous massacre through the shrewd wiles of the British. It seems to be authoritatively established that the murderers of the Wallace family retreated by way of Gnadenhutten, and that one of them bartered with an unsuspecting young woman there for food, and in payment gave her a garment which he had stripped from Mrs. Wallace or one of the other victims, and that this garment was seen and recognized by some of the pursuing party as one which had been familiar to them at their homes. This fact may partly explain, but cannot in the slightest measure justify, the murder of ninety-six persons. It is sufficient, at any rate, to suggest the suspicion that to a dark stratagem of the English emissaries in the west, was attributed the foulest deed in the history of the border. The Indians, wrought into frenzied passion, began that malignant, remorseless, and unceasing raiding of the borders which terrorized the frontiers from Fort Pitt to the falls of the Ohio. Their evil deeds were more numerous than ever before and their treatment of prisoners more inhuman. One of the first acts of retaliation upon the Americans, strangely enough, was visited upon Colonel William Crawford, an intimate friend and companion at arms of Colonel Williamson. But the diabolical cruelty that was practiced upon him was only one of the many horrible deeds which were the outgrowth of the white man's crime.

CHAPTER IV.

AFFAIRS IN THE WEST FROM 1785 TO 1788.

First Ordinance for the Government of the Northwest Territory—It Proves Practically Inoperative—Ordinance of May 20, 1785, for Survey of Western Lands—The Plan Prescribed—Surveyors Appointed by Congress—One from Each State—"Squatter" Settlers on Ohio Soil—Illegality of Their Position—A Proclamation of Warning Addressed to Them—General Richard Butler Disperses Them in 1785, While on His Way to the Miami—Extracts from His Journal—Butler Chooses Location for a Fort at the Mouth of the Muskingum—Hon. James Monroe, of Virginia, descends the Ohio with Baxter—Major Doughty Builds Fort Harmar—Description of the Work—The Gardens—Memento for Doughty in the Name of a Peach—Joseph Buell's Experience in the West—Daily Life at Fort Harmar—Depredations by Roving Bands of Indians—Scarcity of Provisions—Company Ordered out to Protect the Surveyors—The "Seven Ranges"—General Benjamin Tupper—Journal of John Mathews—Indians Harass the Men Engaged at Surveying—Narrow Escape from Destruction—Seeking Safety at Wheeling—Mathews Meets General Putnam at Sumrill's Ferry.

IN 1784 a committee, of which Thomas Jefferson was chairman, reported to Congress an ordinance providing

---

* Notes on the Early Settlement and Indian Wars in Western Virginia and Pennsylvania by Joseph Doddridge.

for the establishment and maintenance of government in the Northwest Territory. It contained an article prohibiting slavery after the year 1800. This clause, was stricken out, however, before the ordinance came to its passage upon the twenty-third of April. This measure of 1784, although it remained nominally in force until repealed by the Ordinance of 1787, was really inoperative—a dead letter. Repeated though unsuccessful efforts were made to so improve the bill as to render possible the development of the west under it. Something, however, was accomplished by the Ordinance of 1784. It paved the way, however imperfectly, for a subsequent act of national legislation. This, the first step tending directly toward the sale and settlement of the lands northwest of the Ohio was taken by Congress in 1785. On the twentieth of May the ordinance for ascertaining the mode of disposal of these lands was passed and as soon as possible thereafter put into practical action. By this ordinance it was provided that a surveyor should be appointed from each State, who should take an oath before the geographer of the United States for the faithful discharge of his duty. The surveyors were to be under the general direction of the geographer, and as soon as qualified were to proceed with their work of dividing the territory "into townships of six miles square by lines running due north and south and others crossing these at right angles as near as may be, unless where the boundaries of the late Indian purchases may render the same impracticable." Each surveyor was to be allowed pay for his services at the rate of two dollars for every mile in length he should run, including wages of chain carriers, markers, and all expenses. It was prescribed that the first line running north and south as aforesaid should begin on the river Ohio at a point due north from the western termination of a line which had been run at the southern boundary of Pennsylvania, and that the first line running east should begin at the same point and extend throughout the whole territory. The ordinance instructed the geographer to designate the townships or fractional parts of townships by numbers, progressivley from south to north; beginning each range with number 1; and to designate the ranges by progressive numbers to the westward, the first rangs extending from the Ohio to Lake Erie being marked number 1. The geographer was personally to attend to the running of the first east and west line and the latitudes of the extremes of the first north and south line and of the mouths of the principal rivers. The surveyors were also charged with the duty of carefully noting on the plats to be made of the lands, all mines, salt licks or springs, mill seats, mountains, water courses, and the nature of the soil. The plats of townships were to be marked in subdivisions of a mile square by lines running in the same direction as the external lines. It was further provided that as soon as several of the townships had been surveyed the geographer should transmit plats of the same to the board of treasury, who should record the same with the report in well bound books, to which the Secretary of War should have access. This official was to take by lot a number of townships and

fractional parts of townships, both of those to be sold entire and those to be sold in lots, such as would be equal to one-seventh part of the whole seven ranges, for the use of the Continental army. The board of treasury, it was provided, should from time to time cause the remaining number to be drawn for in the name of the thirteen States. The board of treasury was to sell (for not less than one dollar per acre) at public vendue, after proper notification, the lands not distributed to the several States, the plan prescribed being that township 1 should be sold entire, and township number 2 in the same range in lots; and thus in alternate order through the whole of the first range, and in the second range the same alternation should be observed, though beginning the reverse of the first range. The United States reserved out of every township the four lots 8, 11, 26, and 29, for future sale. Lot number 16 in every township was to be reserved for the maintenance of public schools in the township, and one-third of all gold, silver, lead, or copper mines to be sold as Congress should in the future direct. Further than the provisions stated the ordinance reserved the towns of Gnadenhutten, Schoenbrunn, and Salem, on the Muskingum, and lands surrounding them, for the use of the Christian Indians formerly settled there.

Congress elected six days after the passage of the ordinance the surveyors whose duty it should be to run the first line with glass and chain, northwest of the Ohio. Nathaniel Adams was chosen for New Hampshire; Rufus Putnam for Massachusetts; Caleb Harris for Rhode Island; William Morris for New York; Adam Hoops for Pennsylvania; James Sampson for Maryland; Alexander Parker for Virginia; Absalom Tatum for North Carolina; William Tate for South Carolina; and, nearly two months later, Isaac Sherman for Connecticut. At the time these appointments were made General Putnam was engaged in surveying for Massachusetts certain lands which she possessed in Maine, and therefore General Benjamin Tupper was appointed to serve in his place. Caleb Harris and Nathaniel Harris resigned and Colonel Ebenezer Sproat and Winthrop Sargent were respectively chosen to fill their places.[*]

Even as early as the Revolution a few hunters, trappers, and traders had located along the west bank of the Ohio, and it was apprehended that after the treaty of Fort McIntosh squatter settlers and speculators would throng those portions of the territory adjacent to Pennsylvania and Virginia and that evil results would follow this intrusion and exercise of "squatter sovereignty." A few irresponsible men had already made temporary homes along the river, and there was every reason to believe that the number who would do so, unless prevented by immediate and strong measures, would be sufficiently large to be productive of serious evil. Congress foreseeing this movement and its possible results, on the fifteenth of June, 1785, authorized the Indian commissioners to publish the following proclamation and circulate it in the territory:

*General Benjamin Tupper, Colonel Ebenezer Sproat, and Winthrop Sargent, as will appear in subsequent chapters, were among the early settlers at Marietta and prominent citizens of the State of Ohio.

Whereas, it has been represented to the United States, in Congress assembled, that several disorderly persons have crossed the Ohio and settled upon their unappropriated lands; and whereas it is their intention, as soon as it shall be surveyed, to open offices for the sale of a considerable part thereof, in such proportions and under such other regulations as may suit the convenience of all the citizens of the United States, and others who may wish to become purchasers of the same—and as such conduct tends to defeat the object they have in view, is in direct opposition to the ordinances and resolutions of Congress, and highly disrespectful to the Federal authority, they have, therefore, thought fit, and do hereby issue this their proclamation, forbidding all such unwarrantable intrusions, and enjoining all those who have settled thereon to depart with their families and effects without loss of time, as they shall answer the same at their peril.

In the autumn of 1785 General Richard Butler passed down the Ohio on his way to attend the treaty with the Indians at the mouth of the Little Miami. He has left, in the form of a diary or journal, an account of his journey which throws much light on the then condition of the country. He makes several entries relating to the squatter inhabitants on the Ohio shore:

* Friday October 1, 1785. Passed Yellow Creek, and found improvements on both sides of the river. Put in at one Jesse Penniman on the north side five miles below Yellow creek. Warned him off; called on one Pry who I warned off also; this appears to be a shrewd, sensible man.

. . . . I told him as well as the others, that Congress was determined to put all of the people off of the lands, and that none would be allowed to settle but the purchasers, and that these and these only would be protected; that troops would be down next week, who have orders to destroy every house and improvement on the north side of the river, and that garrisons will be placed at Muskingum and elsewhere, and that if any person or persons attempted to oppose Government, they may depend on being treated with the greatest rigor. He seems not well pleased, though he promised submission. . . . .
Passed on to the Mingoe towns, where we found a number of people, among whom one Ross seemed to be the principal man of the settlers on the north side of that place. I conversed with him, and warned him and the others away.
Sunday, October 2nd. . . . . Called at the settlement of Charles Morris, whose house has been pulled down and he has rebuilt it. At this place found one Walter Kean, who seemed but a middling character and rather of the dissentious cast; warned all of these off, and requested they would inform their neighbors, which they promised to do. Colonel Monroe spoke to them also, which had weight, as I informed them of his character.† Called at the settlement of Captain Hoglan, who we also warned off, his house had also been thrown down and rebuilt. We informed him of the impropriety of his conduct, which he acknowledged, and seemed very submissive, and promised to remove and to warn his neighbors off also.
Tuesday, October 4th. I directed one corporal and three soldiers to stay at Zanes till Captain O'Hara would send a good boat from Fort McIntosh. . . . I wrote to Colonel Harmar for three other men to join these as an escort to the Miami, and to give Major Dougherty (Doughty) orders to pull down every house on his way to Muskingum, that is on the north side of the Ohio. . . .
Wednesday, October 5th. . . . Met . . . some of the inhabitants from Fishing creek, one of whom had made a settlement on the north side of the Ohio, warned him off and gave him two of the proclamations of Congress. . . . .

Three days later General Butler notes in his journal that "there is good improvement on the north side" nearly opposite the Little Kanawha. He also found settlements on the head of the first island below the Little Hockhocking, and also on the Ohio shore further down the river. To the people on the island who "seemed to be very reasonable people," and where the writer of the journal saw several women who appeared clean and decently dressed," he sent some proclamations, but sterner

measures were resorted to in the case of the settlers below, as appears from the entry under date of Monday, October 10th.

General Butler's journal also gives information in regard to many other matters of interest, among them the location of Fort Harmar. In Virginia and Kentucky measures had been taken for what would have been really, an irresponsible invasion of the Indian country. This action, which threatened to precipitate a disastrous war hastened in all probability the action of the confederation in taking measures for the effectual strengthening of the frontier. It was determined to establish several posts northwest of the Ohio. Fort Laurens had been built in 1778 upon the Tuscarawas, near the old Indian town of Tuscarawas and one mile south of the site of the present village of Bolivar. It was injudiciously located, and was abandoned one year after its erection. General Butler while on his journey in 1785 chose the site for Fort Harmar. Before leaving Fort McIntosh he had prepared and left with Colonel Harmar, the commandant of the post, a paper in which he expressed the opinion that "the mouth of the Muskingum would be a proper place for a post to cover the frontier inhabitants, prevent intruding settlers on the land of the United States, and secure the surveyors." In his journal under date of Saturday, October 8th, he writes:

"Sent Lieutenant Doyle and some men to burn the houses of the settlers on the north side and put up proclamations.
Went on very well to the mouth of the Muskingum and found it low. I went on shore to examine the ground most proper to establish a post on, find it too low, but the most eligible is in the point on the Ohio side. Wrote to Major Doughty and recommended this place with my opinion of the kind of work most proper. Left the letter, which contained other remarks on the fort, fixed to a locust tree.

A few days later the general instructed a man whom he met ascending the Ohio to take the letter from the mouth of the Muskingum to Major Doughty.

A short time later Major Doughty, with a detachment of United States troops under his command, arrived at the mouth of the Muskingum, and began the erection of a post which was not fully completed until the spring of 1786.

The fort stood very near the point on the western side of the Muskingum, and upon the second terrace above ordinary flood water. It was a regular pentagon in shape, with bastions on each side, and its walls enclosed but little more than three quarters of an acre. The main walls of defence, technically called "curtains," were each one hundred and twenty feet long and about twelve or fourteen feet high. They were constructed of logs laid horizontally. The bastions were of the same height as the other walls, but unlike them were formed of palings or timbers set upright in the ground. Large two-story log buildings were built in the bastions for the accommodation of the officers and their families, and the barracks for the troops were erected along the curtains, the roofs sloping toward the centre of the enclosure. They were divided into four rooms of thirty feet each, supplied with fireplaces, and were sufficient for the accommodation of a regiment of men,* a larger number, by the way, than

---

*General Butler's Journal in Craig's "Olden Time"—October and November, 1847.

†This was Colonel James Monroe, member of Congress from Virginia.

* American Pioneer, volume one, 1842, contribution by Dr. S. P. Hildreth.

was ever quartered in the fort. From the roof of the barracks building towards the Ohio river there arose a watch tower, surmounted by the flag of the United States. This tower was also used as a guard-house. There were other buildings within the enclosure—an arsenal, a store-house, and several smaller structures. The main gate was toward the river with a sally-port on the side fronting on the hills. A well was dug near the centre of the enclosure to supply the garrison with water in case of siege, but, happily, it was never needed, and we are told that ordinary water was brought from the river. The timber used in the construction of the fort was that of the heavy forest which covered its site and several acres of land round about. The area cleared was nearly all utilized for gardening purposes under the direction of Major Doughty, who seems to have had a remarkable fondness for tilling the soil and considerable taste and knowledge as a horticulturist.* Fort Harmar was named after General (then Colonel) Harmar, who was the commander of the regiment to which Major Doughty was attached, and for some time commandant of the fort at the mouth of the Muskingum.

Joseph Buell (afterward one of the prominent early settlers at Marietta) was on the frontier for nearly a period of three years, dating from the latter part of December, 1785, and he spent a considerable portion of his time at Fort Harmar. His journal† affords some interesting glimpses of life in the garrison and affairs in the western country during the years immediately preceding its settlement. Much is said in the beginning of the hardships of army life, the depravity of the troops, and the severity of the punishments inflicted for various offences. Drunkenness and desertion were prevalent evils. The punishment for the former and other venal misdemeanors was not infrequently flogging to the extent of one hundred or even two hundred lashes, and the death penalty, without the process of court-martial, was inflicted upon deserters. Buell relates that three men, the finest soldiers in the company, deserted at Fort McIntosh, and being captured were shot by order of Major Wyllis, who commanded the fort—an act which the chronicler characterizes as the most inhuman that he ever saw. The pay of the soldiers at that time guarding the frontier was only three dollars per month.

March 12, 1786, Buell (still at Fort McIntosh) notes that "Generals Parsons and Butler," the latter the author of the journal from which we have made extracts in this chapter, "arrived here from the treaty at Miami."

It is shown by a later entry that the prevention of settlement northwest of the Ohio was still engaging the troops:

April 3rd. Major Wyllis and Captain Hamtramck, with his company, went down the river on command to disperse the frontier people settling on the Indian shore, or the right bank of the Ohio.

On the 4th of May, 1786, Captain Zeigler's and Strong's companies, embarked for Muskingum; and from this date forward the entries in the journal relate to occurrences at Fort Harmar.

May 8th. We arrived at Muskingum, where we encamped in the edge of the woods, a little distance from the fort.

10th. Captain Zeigler's company embarked for the Miami, and our company moved into the garrison, where we were engaged several days in making ourselves comfortable.

12th. Began to make our gardens, and had a very disagreeable spell of weather, which continued for twenty-two days raining in succession.

June 9th. Two boats arrived from Miami, and report that the Indians had murdered several inhabitants this spring. We are getting short of meat for the troops.

10th. Five frontiersmen came here to hunt for the garrison, and brought with them a quantity of venison.

19th. News arrived here that the Indians had killed four or five women and children at Fish creek, about thirty miles northeast from this garrison.

July 4th. The great day of American independence was commemorated by the discharge of thirteen guns, after which the troops were served with extra rations of liquor, and allowed to get as drunk as they pleased.

8th. We are brought down to half-rations, and have sent out a party of men to hunt. They returned without much success, although game is plenty in the woods.

9th. We discovered some Indians crossing the Ohio in a canoe, below the garrison, and sent a party after them, but could not overtake them.

10th. Ensign Kingsbury, with a party of nine, embarked for Wheeling in quest of provisions.

12th. Captain Strong arrived from Fort Pike.

16th. We were visited by a party of Indians, who encamped at a little distance from the garrison, and appeared to be very friendly. They were treated kindly by the officers, who gave them some wine, and the best the garrison afforded.

17th. Our men took up a stray canoe on the river. It contained a pair of shoes, two axes and some corn. We suppose the owners were killed by the Indians. Same day Lieutenant Kingsbury returned with only a supply of food for six or seven days.

18th. Captain Strong's company began to build their range of barracks, to make ourselves comfortable for the winter.

19th. This day buried the fifer to Captain Hart's company. Our funerals are conducted in the following manner. The men are all paraded without arms, and march by files in the rear of the corpse. The guard, with arms, march in front, with their pieces reversed; and the music in the rear of the guard, just in front of the coffin, playing some mournful tune. After the dead is buried they return in the same order, playing some lively march.

21st. A boat arrived from Fort Pitt with intelligence of a drove of cattle at Wheeling for this garrison.

22nd. Lieutenant Pratt, with a party of men, went up by land to bring down the cattle.

23d. Colonel Harmar arrived at the garrison. The troops paraded to receive him, and fired a salute of nine guns.

26th. Captain Hart went with a party of men to guard the Indians of the Muskingum.

27th. Lieutenant Pratt arrived with ten head of cattle, which revived our spirits, as we had been without provisions for several days.

29th. Three hunters came into the fort and informed us that they had seen a party of Indians lying in the woods. We sent out some men, but discovered nothing.

August 2d. Our garrison was alarmed. Captain Hart was walking on the bank of the river, and said he saw Indians on the other side of the Ohio, and saw them shoot one of our men who was out hunting, and beheld him fall. Colonel Harmar immediately sent the captain with a party of men after them. They crossed the river and found one man asleep on the ground, and another had been shooting at a mark. They had seen no Indians.

11th. Captain Hart's company were ordered to encamp in the open ground outside of the fort, as the men are very sickly in the barracks.

23d. Captain Hart and his company embarked for Wheeling with orders to escort and protect the surveyors in the seven ranges.

September 1st. Captain Tunis, the Indian, came to the fort and reported the Indians designed to attack our garrison, and that they were bent on mischief. We were all hands employed in making preparations

---

*A portion of the cleared ground was planted with peaches, and the second or third year after, fine fruit was obtained from this orchard, probably the first in Ohio. One variety has been quite largely cultivated in Marietta and its vicinity, and named after its originator "the Doughty peach."

†The journal of Joseph Buell has been in part published in "Pioneer History of Ohio," by S. P. Hildreth. We make some extracts from it, both in this and subsequent chapters. Buell had the position of orderly in Captain Strong's company of Colonel Harmar's regiment.

to receive them, lining the bastions, clearing away all the weeds and brush within a hundred yards of the fort. We likewise cut up all our corn and broke down the bean poles, to prevent their having any shelter within rifle shot distance.

6th. Captain Tunis left the garrison to return to his nation and bring us further information.

7th. The troops received orders to parade at the alarm post at daybreak, and continue under arms until after sunrise.

12th. Still busy making preparations for the Indians, and expect them every day.

21st. Ensign Kingsbury was ordered to take a party of men into the commandant's house, and put it in the best order for defence, and to remain there during the night.

26th. The troops are again brought to half rations. I went with a party of men after a raft of timber to construct our barracks.

27th. Lieutenant Smith embarked in quest of provisions. We are on short allowance, and expect the Indians every day to attack us. Our men are very uneasy, laying various plans to desert, but are so closely watched that it is very difficult for them to escape.

October 2nd. Lieutenant Smith returned with provisions sufficient only for a short time. We are busily occupied in erecting the barracks.

10th. Major Doughty and Captain Strong left here for New England.

11th. The Indians made us a visit, and stole one of our horses as it was feeding in the woods.

16th. Captain Tunis called again at the fort and says the Indians had repented of their design to attack the garrison.

November 3rd. Captain Tunis and a number of Indians with two squads, came into the garrison. At night they got very drunk and threatened the guard with their tomahawks and knives.

5th. Uling, a trader on the river, arrived with provisions.

9th. The hunters brought in about thirty deer and a great number of turkeys.

25th. Captain Hart's and McCurdy's companies came in from the survey of the seven ranges. They had a cold, wearisome time; their clothes and shoes wore out, and some of their feet badly frozen.

December 3rd. Uling arrived with twenty kegs of flour and ten kegs of whiskey and some dry goods.

Our rations now consist of a little venison, without any bread; as a substitute we have some corn and potatoes. The weather is very cold and the river full of ice.

13th. Lieutenant Pratt embarked in a boat for Flinn's Station (now Belleville) distant thirty miles below the garrison, for a load of corn and potatoes. The troops are in great distress for provisions. About twelve miles below they landed on account of the storm and their boat was carried off by the ice with a considerable amount of goods in it.

19th. Weather more moderate. Ensign Kingsbury embarked for Flinn's Station to make another trial for provisions.

22d. Ensign Kingsbury returned with about sixty bushels of corn and twenty of potatoes.

24th. We drew for our station about a peck of frozen potatoes. As Christmas is so near we are making all the preparations in our power to celebrate it.

25th. This being Christmas day, the sergeant celebrated it by a dinner to which was added a plentiful supply of wine.

January 31, 1787. Hamilton Kerr, our hunter, began to build a house on the island a little above the mouth of the Muskingum, and some of our men were ordered out as a fatigue party to assist him, under the command of Lieutenant Pratt.

February 11th. The weather has been very fine, and there is prospect of an early spring.

15th. Sergeant Judd went with a party of men to assist some inhabitants to move their families and settle near the garrison.

16th. Hamilton Kerr moved his family onto the island.

18th. Several families are settling on the Virginia shore opposite the fort.

24th. Isaac Williams arrived with his family to settle on the opposite shore of the river. Several others have joined him, which makes our situation in the wilderness much more agreeable.

27th. Major Hamtramck arrived from Fort Steuben in order to muster the troops. The same day some of the hunters brought in a buffalo, which was eighteen hands high and weighed one thousand pounds.

April 1st. The Indians came within twelve miles of the garrison, and killed an old man and took a boy prisoner.

5th. Lieutenant Smith went out with a party of men on a scout and discovered Indians on a hill within half a mile of the garrison.

9th. Ensign Kingsbury went on command with a party to bring in one of the hunters, fifty miles up the Muskingum, for fear of the Indians, who, we hear, are bent on mischief.

25th. One of our men discovered two Indians attempting to steal our horses a little distance from the fort.

May 1st. This is St. Tammany's day, and was kept with the festivities usual to the frontiers. All the sergeants in the garrison crossed the Ohio to Mr. Williams and partook of an excellent dinner.

7th. Twenty-one boats passed on their way to the lower country, Kentucky. They had on board five hundred and nine souls, with many wagons, goods, etc.

14th. John Stockley, a fifer in Captain Strong's company, deserted. He was pursued and overtaken twelve miles from the garrison, brought back, and ordered to run the gauntlet eleven times, through the troops of the garrison, stripped of his Continental clothing, and drummed out of the fort, with a halter around his neck, all of which was punctually executed.

21st. This evening I sent a young man, who cooked for me on Kerr's island, about half a mile above the fort after some milk; he was seen to jump into the river near the shore, when about a third of a mile from the garrison. We supposed some of the people were playing in the water. He did not return that evening, which led me to fear he had lost his course. In the morning a party was sent after him. They discovered fresh signs of Indians, and found his hat. They followed the trail, but did not find them. We afterwards heard that they had killed and scalped him. The Indians were a party of Ottawas.

The writer of the journal on the twentieth of May started down the Ohio with Captain Strong's company, and did not return to Fort Harmar until the twenty-first of November, having spent the interim at the Miami garrison, Fort Finney, Port Vincent, and other frontier localities in the lower Ohio country. During the period after his return, and prior to the landing of the Ohio company's colony, the journal contains no important entries, and we here leave it, to resume a survey of its pages in subsequent chapters.

While the various incidents of frontier army life above narrated or referred to were occurring at Fort Harmar, the eastern part of what is now Washington county, and the country north of it, was the theatre of a different kind of action. The surveyors mentioned in the first part of this chapter were traversing the country which was to be divided into "the seven ranges."

General Butler records the fact that he met the surveyors and the United States geographer at the west line of Pennsylvania, on the thirtieth of September, and dined with them. There was some discord among the members of the party, and Captain Hutchins was apprehensive of the safety of his company, unless the Indian chiefs should personally assure him of their good-will. A beginning had been made in the survey, but it was very soon abandoned.

General Benjamin Tupper, soon after the passage of the ordinance of May 20, 1785, providing for the survey and sale of the western lands, had gone as far as Pittsburgh with the idea of beginning the work which had been assigned to him. The Indians, however, who were dissatisfied with the terms of the treaty of Fort McIntosh, and alleged that they had been imposed upon, assumed a very hostile attitude, and threatened with death any persons who should engage in surveying the lands northwest of the Ohio. The risk was so great that common prudence dictated delay until further conference with the disaffected tribes and an amicable adjustment of their relations with the United States should be effected. General Tupper returned to New England.* The treaty of Fort Finney was negotiated in January, 1786, and temporary peace, at least, being promised the surveyors (General Tupper among them), made their way west in the following June, and began their labors.

These men (in one sense the pioneers—the advance guard of the great army of occupation which was to cross the Ohio)—led a career of adventure and danger, and accomplished the work to which they had been appointed only by overcoming many difficulties. Some idea of the sufferings they experienced has already been suggested by extracts from Joseph Buell's journal describing the condition of the soldiers who had been sent to guard them on their return to Fort Harmar. A more definite and a very interesting account of the progress of the survey is given in the journal of John Mathews.† He arrived at Pittsburgh July 29, 1786, and finding that the surveyors had gone down the Ohio to Little Beaver creek, followed and overtook them. After the troops who were to guard them had arrived from Fort Steuben, the work of the surveyors was begun, and Mathews went out with Captain Adam Hoops, the surveyor from Pennsylvania, to run the lines in the second range of townships. They remained out from the middle of August to the first of September, and then returned to the camp at Little Beaver, which they found deserted except by General Tupper, Captain Morris, and an assistant. Mr. Mathews made arrangements to go out with General Tupper on the survey of the seventh range, and started on the seventh of September. On the evening of the 9th they camped at the end of the fourth range. The next entry in the journal we quote:

Sunday, 10th. Camped near the end of the fifth range. Major Sargent, who surveys the fifth range, came to our camp and informed us that one of his hands had left him, which much embarrassed the progress of his work. General Tupper not being ready to begin work, as the geographer had not yet completed the sixth range, I went with Major Sargent to assist him for a few days, and General Tupper proposed to send his son Anselem,‡ who had gone to the geographer's camp, also, the next day to assist us. * * * *

Monday, 11th. Anselem Tupper came to our camp about ten o'clock, and he and myself carried the chain.

14th. Mr. Anselem Tupper and myself, with a hunter, left Major Sargent's camp in order to fall in with General Tupper on the geogra-

pher's line, whom we found encamped near the end of the sixth range. *

*   *   *   *   *

15th. Decamped and moved to the westward six miles, where we joined the geographer's camp on Sandy creek, a large branch of the Tuscarawas.

Sunday, 17th. This morning I went to a camp of Indians who were returning from Fort McIntosh to their town. It was eighty rods above us on the creek. They were about eight in number, men and women. They had rum with them, and had a drunken frolic the night before, but appeared decent and friendly.

18th. General Tupper began his range, and our camp moved to the west about three miles to a large branch of the Tuscarawas, called Nine Shilling. After running on the line about three-fourths of a mile an express arrived from Major Hamtramck's camp at Little Beaver, with word that the Indians were assembling at the Shawnees towns and intended making a general attack upon the surveyors. Captain Hutchins and General Tupper thought it unsafe to proceed any further. Notice was immediately sent to Captain Morris, who had gone about one mile and a half on the west boundary of the seventh range, and we all returned to the ground we left this morning and passed the night.

19th. At nine A. M. decamped and marched for Little Beaver. Our party consisted of about fifty men, thirty-six of whom were troops under the command of Lieutenant Percy. Encamped at night near the first mile post of the sixth range.

The party continued their march, being met on the third day by Major Hamtramck and the whole of his command, and on the twenty-third of September reached Hamtramck's station, on the Ohio, five miles below Little Beaver. By the fourth of October, the feeling of alarm having partially subsided, the surveyors determined to go on with their work; and, on the eleventh, having made the necessary preparations, they again started into the wilderness. Mr. Mathews went with Major Sargent, who was to survey the fifth range. They proceeded westward on "Crawford's old trail" until they reached the place where they were to begin work. After carrying on the survey for about two weeks their pack horses were stolen by the Indians, who they discovered had been lying near their camp (within eighty rods of it the journal says), and had probably been watching them for several days. The journal relates that

"When the commander of the escort, Captain Hart, was informed of the loss of our horses, he immediately commenced building a blockhouse on the most advantageous ground in the vicinity of our camp."

"31st. We this morning dispatched a man for Major Hamtramck's camp, on Wheeling rivulet, informing him of our situation and requesting more horses, so that we might proceed on our range. Although we were apprehensive of danger, we finished the west boundary of the seventh township this day. On our return to camp we found the blockhouses in such a state as to afford a good shelter in case of an attack from the Indians."

Soon after the company returned to Wheeling, General Tupper started for Massachusetts on the twenty-second of November, and early in the following month Colonel Ebenezer Sproat and some others of the surveyors left for their homes. Captain Hutchins, the United States geographer, departed for New York on the twenty-seventh of January, 1787. The survey was suspended for the season. Mathews who went to Fort Steuben to take charge of the commissary department for the winter, notes that the surveyors again took up their work in the woods during April. With ranging degrees of success it was carried slowly and tediously on, during the spring and early summer, without the occurrence of any important incidents. Some of the surveyors who had recommenced work early in the season, came into Wheeling on the fifth of May, considerably alarmed, as they had

---

*We pause here briefly to note, the fact elsewhere to be enlarged upon, that it was during this first visit to the west that General Tupper became favorably and even enthusiastically possessed of the idea of making a New England settlement in the Ohio country; and it was during his visit to Massachusetts in the winter of 1785-86 that the first direct movement was made toward the formation of a company for the purpose of colonization. General Tupper visited General Putnam; they spent nearly a whole night in talking over the scheme of immigration, and the result of their earnest conference was seen in the public prints of the State on the twenty-fifth of January, 1786, in the form of an advertisement headed "Information," signed by the generals, and designed to test the spirit of the people in regard to the formation of The Ohio company.

†John Mathews, of New Braintree, Massachusetts, was a nephew of General Rufus Putnam. He came to the western country before he had arrived at his majority, with the view of obtaining employment in the survey of the seven ranges, and to gain knowledge concerning the country. He was afterwards one of the Ohio company's surveyors, and settled in 1796 in Muskingum county.

‡Major Anselem Tupper was among the early settlers at Marietta, and was a surveyor in the employment of the Ohio company. He died at Marietta in 1808.

4

heard through one of the Zanes of the murder of a family on Fishing creek, by the Indians. Early in June the surveyors had all arrived at the mouth of Indian Wheeling creek on the Ohio, and being met there by the troops sent from Fort Harmar to act as escort, went out into the wilderness to their respective ranges. It was the policy of Congress to continue the surveys if it was possible to do so. There were indications that the summer would be a troublous time. The surveyors were several times obliged to leave their work and seek safety at Wheeling or other points along the river. One party of Indians, supposed to be Chippewas, who hovered about the locality mentioned, were followed and attacked by the whites who killed one of them, and wounded two more. Several other skirmishes took place.

The author of the journal from which we have given extracts, had but little to do with the survey after the spring of 1787, but was in the country all of the time acting in various capacities, and travelling about from Fort Steuben, Pittsburgh and Wheeling to Fort Harmar and other points. In the later entries of his journal (from November, 1787, to April 7, 1788,) is found mention of several characters who were among the pioneers of the Ohio company. In November, 1787, he met Colonel Return J. Meigs at Pittsburgh, and at Washington (Pennsylvania) he met Anselem Tupper (in January, 1788), with whom he remained some time, completing plats of surveys. On the second of February he came across Major Hoffield White "with twenty-two men from New England," and on the seventeenth at Sumrill's ferry, he makes the following entry in the journal:

I had the pleasure of seeing my honored uncle, General Putnam, by whom I received a number of letters from my friends.

CHAPTER V.

INCEPTION OF THE EMIGRATION IDEA AND ORGANIZATION OF THE OHIO COMPANY.

Review of the History of the West—Early Time Spirit of Emigration in New England.—"The Military Company of Adventurers" Propose Settlement in Mississippi.—Rufus Putnam goes thither with his Uncle Israel.—Feature of the Scheme of Colonization.—Effect on the New England Mind.—The Revolutionary War.—By the Camp-Fires in the Watch of the Night.—Washington Directs the Attention of the Soldiers to the West During the Darkest Days of the Conflict. —Impoverishment of the Revolutionary Officers at the Close of the War.—Condition of the Country.—Officers Petition Government for a Grant of Land.—Their Plan of Western Settlement.—General Putnam's Letter to Washington.—Its Wise Suggestions.—Some of Them Adopted with Beneficial Results.—Washington's Influence Unavailing to Secure Action of Congress.—Impatience of the Officers for the Realization of their Plans.—Something of their Character and Condition After the War.—"Financial Settlement Certificates."—Their Depreciated Value.—Speculators Purchase them to their own Advantage.—Loyalty to the Government.—Shay's Rebellion.—Virginia's Action in Regard to Lands for her Soldiers.—Destiny.—New England to Effect First Settlement in the West rather than the "Old Dominion."—Opportunity and Advantages of the Latter State. —General Putnam Again Addresses Washington.—Reply to his Letter.—"Justice and Gratitude to the Army" Demand the Granting of the Officers' Petition.—Despair of Succeeding in the Old Scheme.— A New One Boldly Entered on.—General Tupper's Visit to the West. —His All Night Conference with General Putnam.—They Publish a Call for the Organization of the Ohio Company.—Delegates Elected.— Meet at "Bunch of Grapes" Tavern in Boston.—Certificates of Agreement Adopted.—Progress of the Company's Affairs.—A Purchase in the Ohio Company Decided upon.—Dr. Manasseh Cutler Employed as Agent of the Company.—Canvass for the Location on the Muskingum.

In the preceding pages has been given something of the history of the west while it was still a wilderness, the ownership of which was successively vested in France, in the British crown, in Virginia, and in the Confederated Colonies of America. Something of the history of the Indian tribes of the northwest has been shown; of the advent of the white man as an adventurer among them; of the invasion of the country by armed forces who came to conquer; and of its peaceful penetration by the zealous missionaries who came to propagate a faith. Some idea has been given of the operations of explorers and political economists; of the feeling that prevailed in Virginia in respect to the country; and the unsuccessful projects for its colonization. In the last few years of the period prior to the red letter year, 1788, we have witnessed just over the boundary, in the easternmost edge of the vast territory, unlawful settlers driven from their homes; we have seen the frontier surveyors at their work, harassed by Indians; and we have seen a fort arise in the forest at the mouth of the Muskingum. At the far western boundary, upon the Mississippi, are a few French settlers and possibly there are a score or so of transient residents upon the Maumee—mere traders. But the northwest is still practically an unknown land, explorers to the contrary notwithstanding, a desolate though beautiful wild inhabited by savage tribes, its vast latent wealth awaiting, as it had for ages, the talismanic touch of civilization.

Far away upon the Atlantic sea board forces were at work a score of years anterior to 1788 which were not only to form the first settlement but to plant New England morals, law, and institutions upon this vast inland domain of the nation. Ideas were in inception, which as the prime impetus in a long chain of causes and effects were to swell the tremendous result and effect the destiny not alone of the west but of the Republic from sea to sea.

It is a pleasant thought that in the British war against the French, General Putnam (at the time of his enlistment in 1757, nineteen years of age) and many others assisted in wresting from the enemy and in securing to their sovereign the very territory which was to become their home, and it is a diagreeable fact that they had finally so dearly to purchase a small portion of the domain which they had twice bought by bravery of arms. The very men who fought to win for England the territory which the French disputed, in 1755–1760, were foremost to win it from her twenty years later, and thus twice exhibited the hardihood and heroism of their natures.

Something of the spirit of emigration manifested itself in New England after the conclusion of the French and Indian war, and was in fact an outgrowth of that struggle. An organization of ex-soldiers of the colonies was formed, called "The Military Company of Adventurers," whose purpose it was to establish a colony in West Florida (now Mississippi). Although the project had been entered upon soon after the establishment of peace, it was not until the year 1772 that anything was accomplished. General Lyman, after several years' endeavor, succeeded in procuring a grant of a tract of land. It was decided to explore the tract, and a company of surveyors, of which the celebrated Israel Putnam was the leader, went out in January, 1773, for that purpose. Rufus Putnam was a member of the party. The examination was satisfactory, and several hundred families embarked from Massachusetts and Connecticut to make a settlement. They found to their chagrin that the King's grant had been revoked, and the settlement was therefore abandoned. Those who did not fall sick and die returned to their homes. Such was the disastrous end of this project of settlement, which, had it succeeded, might possibly have changed the whole political history of the United States. It seems at least to be within the realm of probability that had a settlement been planted in Mississippi, Massachusetts would not have made the initial settlement in the Ohio country and extended her influence over the territory from which five great States have been created. The enterprise of founding a colony in the far south, thwarted as it was, undoubtedly had its effect upon the New England mind, and was one of the elements which prepared the way for the inauguration of a new scheme of emigration in later years. The dream which had been fondly indulged in for a long term of years, was not to be forgotten even when the opportunity for its realization had passed away.

Soon, however, there arose a subject for thought which overshadowed all others. What men of shrewd foresight had long expected had come to pass. The colonies were arrayed against the mother country in a battle for independence. We shall not here attempt to follow Generals Putnam, Parsons, Varnum, and Tupper, Major Winthrop Sargent, Colonel Ebenezer Sproat, and the many other brave soldiers who became Ohio company emigrants, through the perils of those seven dark years of the Revolution. But is it not natural to suppose that some of them who had been interested in the old colonization project talked of it around their camp fires? Is it not probable that the review of the past suggested the possibility of forming in the future another military colony, in which they should realize the bright hopes that had once been blasted? It seems natural that in the long lulls between the periods of fierce activity this topic should have come up frequently in conversation, or at least that it should have appeared as a vague but alluring element in many pictures of the future painted by hopeful imaginations. It is evident from perusal of General Putnam's autobiography that he had indulged the hope of emigration to "some remote land rich in possibilities "for many years before he led the little New England colony to the Muskingum. He had very likely cherished the hope unceasingly from the time when the military company of adventurers was organized, and doubtless the journey to that far away strange and beautiful Mississippi had served as a stimulus to quicken his desire for the realization of a project which would employ so much of his energy and enterprise, and afford so fine an opportunity for the achievement of a life success. We know that Washington, during the darkest days of the Revolution, directed the attention of his companions at arms to the west, as a land in which they might take refuge should they be worsted in the struggle, but happily it was not to be that contingency which should cause the movement of emigration toward the Ohio. If during the war the western country was the subject of an occasional estray, light thought, the time was to come when it should be uppermost in the minds of many of the soldiers and practically considered, not as a land in which they must seek to take refuge from a victorious foe, but as one in which they might retrieve the losses they had sustained in repelling the enemy. It must be borne in mind that the independence of the American colonies was dearly bought as indeed has been all the great good attained in the history of the world. The very men by whose long continued, self-sacrificing devotion and bravery, the struggle against the tyrannical mother country had been won, found themselves at the close of the war reduced to the most straitened circumstances, and the young nation ushered into being by their heroism was unable to alleviate their condition. These were the times which tried men's souls. Nowhere was the strain any more severe than in Massachusetts and Connecticut. The joy which peace brought after seven years of war was in most localities too deep to be voiced by noisy demonstration, and it was not unmingled with forebodings of the future. "The rejoicings," says a local historian,[*] "were mostly expressed in religious solemnities." There were still difficult problems to be solved—and there was the memory of husbands, fathers, sons, brothers, and lovers who would not return with the victorious patriots, and it may in many cases have been difficult "to discern the noise of the shout of joy from the noise of the weeping of the people."

---

[*] Ellen D. Larned, in the History of Windham County, Connecticut.

For the purpose of more adequately representing the feeling which prevailed in New England during the years following the war, we shall revert to the time when the great struggle was drawing to a close. Then the subject of western colonization was strongly agitated and the movement which culminated in the Ohio company's purchase and settlement had its inception. As the object which they had been fighting to achieve had been attained, the soldiers saw that their occupation was gone and looked about them for a new means of subsistence. Congress had in 1776 made an appropriation of lands by the laws of which it was provided that a colonel who should serve through the war should receive five hundred acres, a lieutenant colonel four hundred and fifty, and so on down to a private soldier who should be entitled to one hundred acres. The act was extended to the general officers in 1780, and it was arranged that a major general should receive one thousand one hundred acres and a brigadier eight hundred and fifty acres. In the summer of 1783 seeing that the final reduction must soon take place the officers to the number of two hundred and eighty-eight, anxious for definite action, petitioned Congress that the lands they were entitled to might be located in the country bounded on the north by Lake Erie, on the east by Pennsylvania, southeast and south by the river Ohio and west by a line beginning on the Ohio twenty-four miles west of the mouth of the Scioto, thence running north to the Miami of the lakes (Maumee) and down that stream to its mouth. "This tract," they said, "would be sufficient in extent, and the land of such quality and situation as may induce Congress to assign and mark it out as a tract or territory suitable to form a distinct government in time to be admitted as one of the Confederate States of America." This tract, it was claimed, "was not the property of or within the jurisdiction of any particular State"—which, by the way, was an erroneous assumption, as Virginia at that time laid claim to the whole northwest.

General Rufus Putnam was interested in the project. Like most of the other officers he was impoverished by the war, and had been so long engaged in the profession of arms that he necessarily knew little of any other. How earnestly he had entered into the scheme with his brother officers, and how thoroughly he had pondered the subject of western settlement is shown by a letter which he wrote to George Washington to enlist his great influence in favor of the petitioners. The letter shows that many of the wisest measures afterward adopted by the National Government in its plan for the disposal of the public domain, had their origin in the mind of the writer. It therefore has a broad and deep value as a matter of history, and as it is scarcely less interesting as exhibiting the spirit of the patriots in Massachusetts and Connecticut at the time it was written, we have thought it well to print it entire:

NEW WINDSOR, June 16, 1783.

SIR.—As it is very uncertain how long it may be before the honorable Congress may take the petition of the officers of the army for lands between the Ohio river and Lake Erie into consideration, or be in a situation to decide thereon, the going to Philadelphia to negotiate the business with any of its members or committee to whom the petition may be referred, is a measure none of the petitioners will think of undertaking. The part I have taken in promoting the petition is well known, and therefore needs no apology when I inform you that the signers expect that I will pursue measures to have it laid before Congress. Under these circumstances I beg leave to put the petition in your excellency's hands, and ask with the greatest assurance your patronage of it. That Congress may not be wholly unacquainted with the motives of the petitioners, I beg your indulgence while I make a few observations on the policy and propriety of granting the prayer of it, and making such arrangements of garrisons in the western quarter as shall give effectual protection to the settlers and encourage immigration to the new government; which, if they meet your approbation and the favor be not too great, I must request your excellency will give them your support and cause them to be forwarded, with the petition, to the president of Congress, in order that when the petition is taken up, Congress or their committee may be informed on what principles the petition is grounded. I am, sir, among those who consider the cession of so great a tract of territory to the United States, in the western world, as a very happy circumstance and of great consequence to the American empire; nor have I the least doubt but Congress will pay an early attention to securing the allegiance of the motives as well as provide for the defence of the country in case of a war with Great Britain or Spain. One great means of securing the allegiance of the natives, I take to be the furnishing them with such necessaries as they stand in need of, and in exchange receiving their furs and skins. They have become so accustomed to the use of firearms that I doubt if they could gain a subsistence without them, at least they will be very sorry to be reduced to the disagreeable necessity of using the bow and arrows as the only means of killing their game; and so habituated are they to the woollen blankets, etc., etc., that absolute necessity alone will prevent their making use of them.

This consideration alone, is I think, sufficient to prove the necessity of establishing such factories as may furnish an ample supply to these wretched creatures; for unless they are furnished by the subjects of the United States, they will undoubtedly seek elsewhere, and like all other people, form their attachments where they have their commerce; and then in case of war will always be certain to aid our enemies. Therefore, if there were no other advantages in view than that of attaching them to our interests, I think good policy will dictate the measure of carrying on a commerce with these people; but when we add to this the consideration of the profit arising from the Indian trade in general, there cannot, I presume, be a doubt that it is the interest of the United States to make as early provision for the encouragement and protection of it as possible. For these and many other obvious reasons, Congress will no doubt find it necessary to establish garrisons in Oswego, Niagara, Michilimackinac, Illinois, and many other places in the western world.

The Illinois and all the ports that shall be established on the Mississippi, may undoubtedly be furnished by way of the Ohio, with provisions, at all times, and with goods whenever a war shall interrupt the trade with New Orleans. But in case of a war with Great Britain, unless a communication is open between the river Ohio and Lake Erie, Niagara, Detroit, and all the ports seated on the great lakes will inevitably be lost without such communication; for a naval superiority on lake Ontario and the seizing of Niagara, will subject the whole country bordering on the lakes to the will of the enemy. Such a misfortune will put it out of the power of the United States to furnish the natives, and necessity will again oblige them to take an active part against us.

Where and how this communication is to be opened shall be next considered. If Captain Hutchins, and a number of other map makers, are not out in their calculations, provisions may be sent from the settlements on the south side of the Ohio by the Muskingum or Scioto to Detroit, or even to Niagara, at a less expense than from Albany, by the Mohawk, to those places. To secure such communication (by the Scioto, all circumstances considered, will be the best) let a chain of forts be established; these forts should be built upon the banks of the river, if the ground will admit, and about twenty miles distant from each other, and on this plan the Scioto communication will require ten or eleven stockaded forts, flanked by block-houses, and one company of men will be a sufficient garrison for each, except the one at the portage, which will require more attention in the construction and a larger number of men to garrison it. But besides supplying the garrisons on the great lakes with provisions, etc., we ought to take into consideration the protection that such an arrangement will give to the frontiers of Virginia, Pennsylvania, and New York. I say New York, as we shall undoubtedly extend our settlements and garrisons from the Hudson to Oswego. This done and a garrison posted at Niagara, whoever will inspect the map must be convinced that all the Indians on the

waters of the Mohawk, Oswego, Susquehanna, and Allegheny rivers and in all the country south of the lakes Ontario and Erie, will be encircled in such a manner as will effectually secure their allegiance and keep them quiet, or oblige them to quit the country.

Nor will such an arrangement of forts from the Ohio to Lake Erie be any additional expense, for unless this gap is shut, notwithstanding the garrisons on the lakes and from Oswego to the Hudson, yet the frontier settlers on the Ohio, by Fort Pitt to the Susquehanna, and all the country south of the Mohawk, will be exposed to savage insult, unless protected by a chain of garrisons which will be far more expensive than the arrangement proposed, and, at the same time, the protection given to these States will be much less complete; besides, we should not confine our protection to the present settlements, but carry the idea of extending them at least as far as the lakes Ontario and Erie.

These lakes form such a natural barrier that when connected with the Hudson and Ohio, by the garrisons proposed, settlements in every part of New York and Pennsylvania may be made with the utmost safety; so that these States must be deeply interested in the measures, as well as Virginia, who will by the same arrangement have a great part of its frontier secured and the rest much strengthened, nor is there a State in the Union but will be greatly benefitted by the measure, considered in any other point of view, for, without any expense, except a small allowance of purchase money to the natives, the United States will have within their protection seventeen million, five hundred thousand acres of very fine land, to dispose of as they think proper.

But I hasten to mention some of the expectations which the petitioners have respecting the conditions on which they hope to obtain the lands. This was not proper to mention in the body of the petition, especially as we pay for grants to all members of the army who wish to take up lands in that quarter.

The whole tract is supposed to contain about seventeen million four hundred and eighteen thousand two hundred acres, and will admit of seven hundred and fifty-six townships of six miles square, allowing to each township three thousand and forty acres for the ministry, schools, waste lands, ponds and highways; then each township will contain of settlers' lands twenty thousand acres, and in the whole fifteen million, one hundred and twenty thousand acres. The land to which the army is entitled by resolve of Congress, referred to in the petition, according to my estimate, will amount to two million one hundred and six thousand eight hundred and fifty acres, which is about the eighth part of the whole. For the survey of this the army expect to be at no expense, nor do they expect to be under any obligation to settle these lands or do any duty to secure their title to them; but in order to induce the army to become actual settlers in the new government, the petitioners hope Congress will make a further grant of lands on condition of settlement, and have no doubt but that honorable body will be as liberal to all those who are not provided for by their own States, as New York has been to the officers and soldiers who belong to that State; which, if they do, it will require about eight million acres to complete the army, and about seven million acres will remain for sale. The petitioners, at least some of them, are much opposed to the monopoly of the lands, and wish to guard against large patents being granted to individuals, as, in their opinion, such a mode is very injurious to a country, and greatly retards its settlement, and whenever such patents are tenanted it throws too much power into the hands of a few. For these and many other obvious reasons, the petitioners hope that no grant will be made but by townships of six miles square, or six by twelve, or six by eighteen miles, to be subdivided by the proprietors to six miles square, that being the standard by which they wish all calculations to be made, and that officers and soldiers, as well as those who petition for charters on purchase may form their associations on one uniform principle, as to number of persons or rights to be contained in a township, with the exception only that when the grant is made for services already done, or on condition of settlement, if the officers petition with the soldiers for a particular township, the soldier shall have one right only to a captain's three, and so in proportion with commissioned officers of every grade.

These, sir, are the principles which give rise to the petition under consideration; the petitioners, at least some of them, think that sound policy dictates the measure, and that Congress ought to lose no time in establishing some such chain of posts as have been hinted at, and in procuring the tract of land petitioned for, of the natives; for, the moment this is done, and agreeable terms offered to the settlers, many of the petitioners are determined not only to become adventurers, but actually to remove themselves to this country; and there is not the least doubt but other valuable citizens will follow their example, and the probability is that the country between Lake Erie and the Ohio will be

filled with inhabitants, and the faithful subjects of the United States so established on the waters of the Ohio and the lakes as to banish forever the idea of our western territory falling under the dominion of any European power. The frontiers of the old States will be effectively secured from savage alarms, and the new will have little to fear from their insults.

I have the honor to be, sir, with every sentiment, your excellency's most obedient and very humble servant,

RUFUS PUTNAM.

General Washington.

It will be observed that in the foregoing letter the admirable township system of New England is suggested as an element in the plan for settling and developing the western country. That measure was adopted very nearly as General Rufus Putnam originally advocated it, and it has been in the opinion of very many students of political economy[*] one of the most important factors in building up the civilization of the northern States and advancing them beyond the southern, in which the township system has only a nominal existence.

But to return to the matter directly in hand. Washington used his utmost influence to advance the object sought by the petitioners, and urged by General Putnam, but without avail. He wrote a communication to Congress, which he forwarded with the long letter he had received, but no legislation affecting the interests of the petitioners was enacted. The General Government had not yet a perfect title to the territory northwest of the Ohio, and even, if it had, Congress would undoubtedly have been tediously slow in taking the initiative in disposing of the domain which, in after years, was to be squandered with the most prodigal hand.

As time progressed, the New England Revolutionary officers and soldiers interested in western immigration became more and more impatient to realize their hopes. They were poorer than their neighbors who had not been in the field; and if they had more of pride, that was only natural from the lives they had led, and surely they had a right to feel proud of the services they had rendered. One who was among them, and a close observer, says that they had a better and more dignified bearing than before the war, dressed more handsomely, and were improved in manners and conversation.[†] Many of them were members of the Masonic order and of the Cincinnati, an order which was established to maintain the

---

[*] De Tocqueville, in his "Democracy in America," was perhaps the first writer who brought this subject prominently into consideration, and Judge Tourgee, author of the reconstruction novels "A Fool's Errand" and "Bricks without Straw" may be mentioned as the best known late writer who has dwelt upon the township plan as accounting in large measure, for the difference between the conditions of the north and south. In 1830, in the senate of the United States, Daniel Webster, in discussing the modes for the disposal of land—the northern and the southern—after speaking of the latter as the one which had shingled over the country in which it had been applied with conflicting titles and claims, causing the two great evils in a new country, of speculation and litigation, said. "From the system actually established these evils are banished. Now, sir, in effecting this great system, the first important measure on the whole subject, New England acted with vigor and effect, and the latest posterity of those who settled northwest of the Ohio, will have reason to remember with gratitude her patriotism and her wisdom. New England gave the system to the West, and while it remains, there will be spread over all the west one monument of her intelligence in matters of government and her practical good sense."

[†] Reminiscences of Colonel Ichabod Nye. (Mss.)

friendships of the war between the colonial officers and their French associates, and to aid the widows and the orphans of those who had fallen. It was by no means strange that, the war being ended and these men returned to their homes among people with whom they could not be wholly in sympathy, and from whom they had been separated seven long years, they should seek to perpetuate the newer ties that had been closely knit in common trials and dangers. These men, it must be remembered, did not receive money in *pay* for their fatigue, exposure and suffering, but final certificates in *settlement.* They were almost valueless, for the country had not the money to make them good. In 1784 they were worth only about three shillings and sixpence or four shillings to the pound, face value, and as late as 1788 they brought not more than five or six shillings. Even at these ruinous rates many holders had to part with them, and there were speculators who realized some profit from the transactions. Some lost property which would have been the support of their old age, because unable to raise comparatively trifling sums with which to save it. Thus illy were these men who had gained the Nation's independence requited. They rebelled at the idea of living in destitution and deficiency among people of relatively easy circumstances, and the thought of toiling at menial manual labor they could not entertain. Still, they were willing to work to gain a livelihood, but preferred to do that in a new country where they would all be in a condition of equality. They looked upon the western country, which should have been their free inheritance, as a land in which they could begin anew the toilsome grind of life. Still, in their perplexed, humiliated condition, they never wavered in loyalty; and, when the lower populace in Massachussetts, beginning to feel the distress caused by the long, costly war, broke forth in the first organized rebellion in the United States (Shay's insurrection), these soldiers were found, like General Benjamin Tupper, actively engaged upon the side of law and order.

There was an action, too, at this time, far away in Virginia, which could not be without its effect upon the waiting New Englanders. In 1783 the legislature of the Old Dominion authorized a deed ceding her claim to the territory northwest of the Ohio, with a very important reservation. A rich body of lands lying between the Scioto and the Little Miami, now known as the Virginia Military district, was reserved to be given to Virginia's Revolutionary soldiers of the continental line, or, in other words, to pay their bounty awards.

But in spite of this advantage possessed by Virginia in the privilege retained for her troops, and in spite of her contiguity to the territory, it was to be first settled by New Englanders, and leavened by New England law. And the events which were to lead to that consummation were closely following each other in Massachusetts and Connecticut.

Impelled anew, in all probability by the action of Congress, March 1, 1784, in accepting Virginia's cession, General Putnam again addressed George Washington in the interests of the New England officers. His letter was as follows:

RUTLAND, April 5, 1784.

DEAR SIR: Being unavoidably prevented from attending the general meeting of the Cincinnati at Philadelphia, as I had intended, where I once more expected the opportunity in person of paying my respects to your excellency, I cannot deny myself of addressing you by letter, to acknowledge with gratitude the ten thousand obligations I feel myself under to your goodness, and most sincerely to congratulate you on your return to domestic happiness; to enquire after your health, and wish the best of Heaven's blessings may attend you and your lady.

The settlement of the Ohio country, sir, engrosses many of my thoughts, and much of my time since I left the camp has been employed in informing myself and others in respect to the nature, situation, and circumstances of that country, and the practicability of removing ourselves there; and if I am to form an opinion on what I have seen and heard on the subject, there are thousands in this quarter who will emigrate to that country as soon as the honorable Congress makes provisions for granting lands there, and locations and settlements can be made with safety, unless such provision is too long delayed; I mean until necessity turn their views another way, which is the case with some already, and must soon be the case with many more. You are sensible of the necessity as well as the possibility of both officers and soldiers fixing themselves in business somewhere, as soon as possible, as many of them are unable to lie longer on their oars waiting the decision of Congress, on our petition, and, therefore, must unavoidably settle themselves in some other quarter, which, when done, the idea of removing to the Ohio country will probably be at an end, with respect to most of them. Besides, the commonwealth of Massachusetts have come to a resolution to sell their eastern country for public securities, and should their plan be formed, and propositions be made public before we hear anything from Congress respecting our petition and the terms on which the lands petitioned for are to be obtained, it will undoubtedly be much against us, by greatly lessening the number of Ohio associates.

Another reason why we wish to know, as soon as possible what the intentions of Congress are respecting our petition, is the effect such knowledge will probably have on the credit of the certificates we have received on settlement of accounts. Those securities are now selling at no more than three shillings and six pence, or four shillings on the pound, which in all probability might double, if not more, the moment it was known that the Government would receive them for lands in the Ohio country. From these circumstances, and many others which might be mentioned, we are growing quite impatient, and the general inquiry now is, When are we going to the Ohio? Among others, Brigadier General Tupper, Lieutenant Colonel Oliver and Mayor Ashley have agreed to accompany me to that country the moment the way is open for such an undertaking. I should have hinted these things to some member of Congress, but the delegates from Massachusetts, although exceedingly worthy men, and in general would wish to promote the Ohio scheme, yet, if it should militate against the particular interests of that State, by draining her of inhabitants, especially when she is forming the plan of selling the eastern country, I thought they would not be very warm advocates in our favor, and I dare not trust myself with any of the New York delegates, with whom I was acquainted, because that government is wisely inviting the eastern people to settle in that State; and as to the delegates of other States, I have no acquaintance with any of them.

These circumstances must apologize for my troubling you on this subject, and requesting the favor of a line, to inform us in this quarter what the prospects are with respect to our petition and what measures have been or are likely to be taken with respect to settling the Ohio country.

I shall take it as a very particular favor sir, if you will be kind enough to recommend me to some character in Congress acquainted with, and attached to, the Ohio cause, with whom I may presume to open a correspondence.

I am, sir, with the highest respect, your humble servant,

RUFUS PUTNAM.

General Washington.

General Putnam, in reply, received the following letter* from Washington, but, as will be observed, after a considerable delay.

MOUNT VERNON, June 2, 1784.

DEAR SIR: I could not answer your favor of the fifth of April from Philadelphia, because General Knox, having mislaid it, only presented

---

* The original is in the library of Marietta college with many other papers of rare value, presented by by Hon. William R. Putnam.

the letter to me in the moment of my departure from that place. The sentiments of esteem and friendship which breathe in it, are exceedingly pleasing and flattering to me, and you may rest assured they are reciprocal.

I wish it was in my power to give you a more favorable account of the officers' petition for lands on the Ohio, and its waters, than I am about to do. After this matter and information respecting the establishment for peace were my inquiries, as I went through Annapolis, solely directed, but I could not learn that anything decisive had been done in either.

On the latter, I hear Congress are differing about their powers, but as they have accepted of the cession from Virginia and have resolved to lay off ten new States, bounded by latitudes and longitudes, it should be supposed that they would determine something respecting the former before they adjourn, and yet I very much question it, as the latter is to happen on the 3rd—that is, to-morrow. As the Congress who are to meet in November next, by the adjournment, will be composed of an entire new choice of delegates, in each State, it is not in my power, *at this time*, to direct you to a proper correspondent in that body. I wish I could, for persuaded I am, that to some such cause as you have assigned, may be ascribed the delay the petition has encountered, for *surely, if justice and gratitude* to the army and general policy of the Union were to govern in this case, there would not be the smallest interruption in gratifying its request. I really feel for these gentlemen, who, by the unaccountable delays (by any other means than those you have suggested) are held in such an awkward and disagreeable state of suspense, and wish my endeavors could remove the obstacles. At Princetown, before Congress left that place, I exerted every power I was master of, and dwelt upon the argument you have used, to show the propriety of a speedy decision. Every member with whom I conversed acquiesced in the reasonableness of the petition All yielded, or seemed to yield, to the policy of it but plead the want of cession of the land to act upon; this is made and accepted, and yet matters as far as they have come to my knowledge, remain in *statu quo.*

I am, dear sir, with my sincere esteem and regard,

Your most obedient servant,

GEORGE WASHINGTON.

All of the efforts of General Putnam assisted by the strongest influence of the Father of his Country were unavailing to secure those simple measures of justice which would have relieved those Revolutionary officers of New England from their embarrassed and desperate situation. As time went slowly by they gave up even the little hope that had sustained them while waiting Congressional measures. Despairing of the success of the old scheme they finally adopted a new one, resolving to purchase outright what the Nation refused to bestow as the hard earned remuneration of their services. Early in 1786 the idea of Ohio immigration began to form into that shape in which it became effective.

It has been shown in a former chapter that General Benjamin Tupper, in the early autumn of 1785, had gone to the Ohio country to engage in surveying under the ordinance passed by Congress May 20th of that year, and it will be remembered that owing to the hostility of the Indians and consequent hazard of entering upon the work, he returned to New England. General Tupper was one of the men who had been most intently engaged in planning western settlements, and was undoubtedly a coworker with his intimate old friend, General Putnam, he advocating and agitating the scheme which had proved unsuccessful. He returned from the west filled with admiration of that portion of the country which he had seen, and made enthusiastic through the descriptions given by traders of the region farther down *la belle riviere* than he had journeyed. Doubtless he pondered upon the idea of removing to the west, during the

whole time spent there, and was chiefly occupied with the subject while making the tedious return to his home. Early in January he visited, at his house in Rutland, Worcester county, Massachusetts, General Putnam, and there these two men, who may be properly called the founders of the Ohio company, earnestly talked of their experiences and their hopes in front of the great fire, while the night hours fast passed away. In the language of one whom it is fair to suppose had preserved the truthful tradition of that meeting: "A night of friendly offices and conference between them gave, at the dawn, a development — how important in its results! — to the cherished hope and purpose of the visit of General Tupper." * As the result of that long conversation by a New England fireside, appeared the first mention in the public prints of the Ohio company. The two men had thought so deeply and carefully upon the absorbing theme of colonization, were so thoroughly impressed with the feasibility of their plans as they had unfolded them, so impatient to put them to that test, that they felt impelled to take an immediate and definite step. They could no longer rest inactive. They joined in a brief address, setting forth their views and feeling the opinion of the people. It appeared in the newspapers on the twenty-fifth of January, and read as follows:

INFORMATION

The subscribers take this method to inform all officers and soldiers who have served in the late war, and who are by a late ordinance of the honorable Congress to receive certain tracts of land in the Ohio country, and also all other good citizens who wish to become adventurers in that delightful region, that from personal inspection, together with other incontestible evidences, they are fully satisfied that the lands in that quarter are of a much better quality than any other known to the New England people, that the climate, seasons, products, etc., are in fact equal to the most flattering accounts that have ever been published of them; that being determined to become purchasers and to prosecute a settlement in that country, and desirous of forming a general association with those who entertain the same ideas, they beg leave to propose the following plan, viz.: That an association by the name of The Ohio Company be formed of all such as wish to become purchasers, etc., in that country, who reside in the commonwealth of Massachusetts only, or to extend to the inhabitants of other States as shall be agreed on.

That in order to bring such a company into existence the subscribers propose that all persons who wish to promote the scheme, should meet within their respective counties (except in two instances hereinafter mentioned) at 10 o'clock A. M. on Wednesday, the fifteenth day of February next, and that each county or meeting there assembled choose a delegate or delegates to meet at the Bunch of Grapes Tavern, in Boston, on Wednesday, the first day of March next, at 10 o'clock A M., then and there to consider and determine upon a general plan of association for said company, which plan, covenant, or agreement, being published, any person (under condition therein to be provided) may, by subscribing his name, become a member of the company.

Then follow the places of meeting:

At Captain Webb's, in Salem, Middlesex; at Bradish's, in Cambridge, Hampshire; at Pomeroy's in North Hampton, Plymouth; at Bartlett's, in Plymouth, Barnstable, Dukes and Nantucket counties; at Howland's, in Barnstable, Bristol; at Crocker's, in Taunton, York; at Woodbridge's, in York, Worcester; at Patch's, in Worcester, Cumberland and Lincoln; at Shotluck's, in Falmouth, Berkshire, at Dibble's, in Lenox.

RUFUS PUTNAM,

BENJAMIN TUPPER.

RUTLAND, January 10, 1786.

The plan suggested by General Putnam and Tupper was carried out, and upon the first day of March, the

* Arius Nye, in Transactions of the Ohio Historical and Philosophical society.

delegates from the several counties assembled at the Bunch of Grapes tavern, the designated place in Boston, (which was then a considerably smaller city than is now the capital of Ohio), and there discussed in conventional form the proposed organization of the Ohio company. The delegates present at that historical meeting were: Manasseh Cutler, of Essex; Winthrop Sargent and John Mills, of Suffolk; John Brooks and Thomas Cushing, of Middlesex; Benjamin Tupper, of Hampshire; Crocker Sampson, of Plymouth; Rufus Putnam, of Worcester; Jelaliel Woodbridge and John Patterson, of Berkshire; Abraham Williams, of Barnstable.

General Putnam was made chairman of the convention, and Major Winthrop Sargent, secretary. Before adjournment a committee of five was appointed to draft a plan of an association, as "from the very pleasing description of the western country, given by Generals Putnam and Tupper and others, it appeared expedient to form a settlement there." That committee consisted of General Putnam, Dr. Manasseh Cutler, Colonel Brooks, Major Sargent, and Captain Cushing.

On Friday, March 3d, the convention reassembled and the committee reported the following

Articles of agreement entered into by the subscribers for constituting an association by the name of the Ohio company.

PREAMBLE.

The design of this association is to raise a fund in Continental certificates, for the sole purpose and to be appropriated to the entire use of purchasing lands in the western territory belonging to the United States, for the benefit of the company and to promote a settlement in that country.

ARTICLE 1ST.—That the fund shall not exceed one million of dollars in Continental specie certificates, exclusive of one year's interest due thereon (except as hereafter provided), and that each share or subscription shall consist of one thousand dollars as aforesaid, and also ten dollars in gold or silver, to be paid into the hands of such agents as the subscribers may elect.

ARTICLE 2ND.—That the whole fund of certificates raised by this association, except one year's interest due thereon, mentioned under the first article, shall be applied to the purchase of lands in some one of the proposed States northwesterly of the river Ohio, as soon as those lands are surveyed and exposed for sale by the commissioners of Congress according to the ordinance of that honorable body, passed the twentieth of May, 1785, or on any other plan that may be adopted by Congress, not less advantageous to the company. The one year's interest shall be applied to the purpose of making a settlement in the country and assisting those who may be otherwise unable to remove themselves thither. The gold and silver is for defraying the expenses of those persons employed as agents in purchasing the lands and other contingent charges that may arise in the prosecution of the business. The surplus, if any, to be appropriated as one year's interest on the certificates.

ARTICLE 3RD.—That there shall be five directors, a treasurer and secretary, appointed in manner and for the purposes hereafter provided.

ARTICLE 4TH.—That the prosecution of the company's designs may be the least expensive and at the same time the subscribers and agents as secure as possible, the proprietors of twenty shares shall constitute one grand division of the company; appoint the agent, and in case of vacancy by death, resignation or otherwise, shall fill it up as immediately as can be.

ARTICLE 5TH.—That the agent shall make himself accountable to each subscriber for certificates and invoices received, by duplicate receipts, one of which shall be lodged with the secretary; that the whole shall be appropriated according to articles of association, and that the subscriber shall receive his just dividend according to quality and quantity of lands purchased, as near as possibly may be, by lot drawn in person or through proxy, and that deeds of conveyance shall be executed to individual subscribers, by the agent, similar to those he shall receive from the directors.

ARTICLE 6TH.—That no person shall be permitted to hold more than

five shares in the company's funds and no subscription for less than a full share will be admitted; but this is not meant to prevent those who cannot or choose not to adventure a full share, from associating among themselves, and by one of their number subscribing the sum required.

ARTICLE 7TH.—That the directors shall have the sole disposal of the company's fund for the purposes before mentioned; that they shall by themselves, or such person or persons as they may think proper to entrust with the business, purchase lands for the benefit of the company, where and in such way, either at public or private sale, as they shall judge will be the most advantageous to the company. They shall also direct the application of the one year's interest, and gold and silver, mentioned in the first article, to the purposes mentioned under the second article in such way and manner as they shall think proper. For these purposes the directors shall draw on the treasurer from time to time, making themselves accountable for the application of the moneys agreeably to this association.

ARTICLE 8TH.—That the agents being accountable to the subscribers for their respective divisions, shall appoint the directors, treasurer and secretary, and fill up all the vacancies which may happen in these offices respectively.

ARTICLE 9TH.—That the agents shall pay all the certificates and moneys received from subscribers into the hands of the treasurer, who shall give bonds to the agents, jointly and severally, for the faithful discharge of his trust; and also on his receiving certificates or moneys from any particular agent shall make himself accountable therefor, according to the condition of his bonds.

ARTICLE 10TH.—That the directors shall give bonds, jointly and severally, to each of the agents, conditioned that the certificates and moneys they shall draw out of the treasury shall be applied to the purposes stipulated in these articles; and that the lands purchased by the company shall be divided among them within three months from the completion of the purchase, by lot, in such manner as the agents or a majority of them shall agree, and that on such division being made, the directors shall execute deeds to the agents, respectively, for the proportions which fall to their divisions, correspondent to those the directors may receive from the commissioners of Congress.

ARTICLE 11TH.—Provided, that whereas a sufficient number of subscribers may not appear to raise the fund to the sums proposed in the first article, and thereby the number of divisions may not be completed, it is therefore agreed that the agents of divisions of twenty shares each shall, after the seventeenth day of October next, proceed in the same manner as if the whole fund had been raised.

ARTICLE 12TH.—Provided, also, that whereas it will be for the common interest of the company to obtain an ordinance of incorporation from the honorable Congress, or an act of incorporation from some one of the States in the Union (for which the directors shall make application), it is therefore agreed that in case such incorporation is obtained, the fund of the company (and consequently, the shares and divisions thereof) may be extended to any sum, for which provision shall be made in said ordinance or act of incorporation, anything in this association to the contrary notwithstanding.

ARTICLE 13TH.—That all notes under this association may be given in person or by proxy, and in numbers justly proportionate to the stockholder or interest represented.

These articles of agreement were unanimously adopted and subscription books were immediately opened. A committee was appointed, consisting of three members, to transact necessary business, and some other measures taken to advance the project of the association; but in spite of all the exertions made there was but little progress in the affairs of the Ohio company. When the next meeting was held, a little more than a year from the time of the first, that is, upon March 8, 1787, it was found that the total number of shares subscribed for was only two hundred and fifty. And yet, all untoward circumstances considered, that was probably a fair exhibit, and more than was expected. One active friend of the movement, General Tupper, was the greater part of the year in the west. The influence of the others was very largely counteracted by events of an alarming nature— the dissatisfaction which finally culminated in Shay's re

HISTORY OF WASHINGTON COUNTY, OHIO.

bellion. That civil commotion growing out of the imposition of heavy taxes upon the already impoverished people threatened for a time exceedingly dire results, but fortunately, it was speedily quelled. It served as a startling illustration, however, of the general depression in New England, and of the desperation to which men can be driven by ill condition. Possibly the outbreak gave a slight impetus to the progress of the Ohio company's project, by way of increasing the disposition of some citizens to seek in the west a new home. General Tupper, whose immediate neighborhood was "deeply infected with the sedition," returned from his second visit to the Ohio country in time to take a prominent part in subduing the revolt. The dawn of 1787 witnessed the pacification of the troubled country, but no marked increase in prosperity.

It was reported at the meeting held on the eighth of March at Brackett's tavern in Boston, that "many in the commonwealth of Massachusetts, also at Connecticut, Rhode Island and New Hampshire are inclined to become adventurers, who are restrained only by the uncertainty of obtaining a sufficient tract of country, collectively, for a good settlement."

It was now decided to make direct and immediate application to Congress for the purchase of lands, and General Putnam, Dr. Manasseh Cutler and General Samuel H. Parsons were appointed directors and especially charged with this business. General Parsons had previously been employed to negotiate for a private purchase, had petitioned Congress, and a committee of that body had been appointed to confer with him. "To that committee," says Dr. Cutler, "he proposed a purchase on the Scioto river," but as the proprietors in Massachusetts "were generally dissatisfied with the situation and lands on the Scioto and much preferred the Muskingum," the negotiation was suspended. The directors now employed Dr. Cutler to make a purchase upon the Muskingum. It was considered desirable that the negotiations be commenced and the purchase consummated as soon as possible, as other companies were forming, the spirit of private speculation rapidly increasing, and there was a fear that the lands which the Ohio company wished to possess would be bought by some other organization, or perhaps some part of them by individuals.

Just here the query arises: why were the New Englanders so anxious to purchase lands upon the Muskingum, rather than upon the Scioto, or elsewhere in the territory? To this question there are various answers. In the first place the greater part of the Federal territory was unfitted for settlement by the fact that it was occupied by the Indian tribes. None of these, however, had their residence in the lower Muskingum region, and it was only occasionally resorted to by them, when upon their hunting excursions. Then, too, the people who proposed making a settlement beyond the Ohio were very naturally influenced by the proximity of well established stations upon the east and south of the river; they doubtless preferred the Virginians rather than the Kentuckians, as neighbors. The lower Scioto offered no more alluring an aspect than the lower Muskingum. The best bodies of lands on each river are fifty miles from their mouth. To penetrate so far into the interior, however, as the site of either Chillicothe or Zanesvile would have been, at the time the Marietta settlement was made, was unsafe. The location of Fort Harmar, which we have seen was built in 1785—86, doubtless had its influence upon the Ohio company. Thomas Hutchins, the United States geographer, who had formerly been geographer to the king of Great Britain, and had travelled extensively in the west, had said and written much in favor of the Muskingum country, and as we shall see in the following chapter strongly advised Dr. Cutler to locate his purchase in this region. Other explorers and travellers had substantiated what Hutchins had said. General Butler and General Parsons, who had descended the Ohio to the Miamis, were deeply impressed with the desirableness of the tract of country now designated as southeastern Ohio, and the latter, writing on the twentieth of December, 1785, from Fort Finney (mouth of the Little Miami), to Captain Jonathan Hart, at Fort Harmar, said: "I have seen no place since I left you that pleases me so well for settlement as Muskingum." General Benjamin Tupper doubtless added important testimony supporting that of Hutchins, Parsons, Butler, and others. General Parsons, it has been asserted, became most strongly possessed of the belief that the Muskingum region was the best part of the territory, because one of the Zanes who had been many years in the west told him that the Scioto or Miami regions offered superior attractions, and he suspected that the old frontiersman artfully designed to divert attention from the Muskingum that he might have the first choice of purchase himself when the lands were put on sale. It is probable, too, that the prospect of establishing a system of communication and commerce between the Ohio and Lake Erie, by way of the Muskingum and Tuscarawas and Cuyahoga, and between the Ohio and the seaboard, by way of the Great Kanawha and the Potomac, (a plan which Washington had thought feasible before the Revolutionary war), had its weight. It is not probable that the New Englanders, interested in immigration, were ignorant of the existence of minerals in the Muskingum region, and they may have been far-seeing enough to have appreciatively estimated the value of their presence.

CHAPTER VI.

*THE ORDINANCE OF 1787 AND THE OHIO COMPANY'S PURCHASE.

THE Ohio company could have employed as their agent before the Congress of the old confederation, no better man than the Rev. Manasseh Cutler. He possessed an education of unusual solidity, and with it a versatile genius. These qualities of strength were rendered readily effective by his possession of a keen insight of human character, and of courtly grace in conversation. Dr. Cutler was at this time forty-five years of age, ripe and yet vigorous. Twenty-two years before he had graduated at Yale, and the intervening years had studied and taken degrees in the three learned professions—law, divinity and medicine. At the time he undertook the Ohio company's important mission he was the pastor of a congregational church at Ipswich (afterward Hamilton), Massachusetts, but he was best known as a scientist, and it has been said of him that in that capacity "he was, perhaps, second to no living American except Franklin." He had written upon meteorology, astronomy and botany, and was well known in the literary and social circles of New York and Boston.

It is probable that in the dignified divine, the student and book-worm which Dr. Cutler was, the people with

whom he associated in New York did not suppose there existed a thorough and shrewd knowledge of the world, and they were doubtless thrown off their guard by his bland manners, genial social qualities and good humor, and swayed more powerfully by his diplomacy because he seemed almost entirely devoid of it, added to his varied qualifications for the work assigned him. Dr. Cutler had the great advantage of being wholly in earnest. He was an enthusiast upon the subject which engaged him. He lived in the midst of the men interested in the scheme of western immigration, knew nearly all of them personally, and was fully in sympathy with them. He had in fact seen, and shared in, their hardships during the war, having served as a chaplain in the army through two campaigns. He was present at the time of the organization of the Ohio company, and one of the committee who drew up its articles of association, and was afterward made a director with General Putnam and General Parsons. From that time on until the Ohio company as an organization had concluded its work, he was almost constantly engaged in its service, and it was through his activity and acumen that the great measures of the association were accomplished in Congress, not only in 1787 but in 1792. Dr. Cutler and General Putnam were from first to last the leading spirits of the Ohio company, the office of the former being principally the management of the difficult and delicate negotiations with the General Government, and that of the latter the superintendency of the internal affairs of the organization.

The relations of the two men were intimate and cordial. Each seems to have entertained the most thorough respect for the other. Yet they were as dissimilar as two men well could be. One was thoroughly educated, cultured, accomplished; the other a strong, rugged man, almost entirely lacking in knowledge, save by the kind acquired little by little in the experience of life, but full of wisdom, possessing the genius of uncommon common sense, great strength of purpose and vast executive ability.* Either of these men would undoubtedly have made a failure in the position of the other. But in the places which they did occupy no men could have been more efficient.

A journal† which Dr. Cutler kept during his stay in New York affords very interesting reading, and

---

*The ordinance of 1787 and the Ohio purchase were parts of one and the same transaction. The purchase would not have been made without the ordinance, and the ordinance could not have been enacted except as an essential condition of the purchase. William F. Poole, in *North American Review* for April, 1876.

---

*Very complete biographies of Dr. Cutler and General Putnam will be found among the sketches of men prominent in the history of Washington county and the Ohio company.

† Dr. Cutler's journal was written at the request of one of his daughters, who brought him two blank books just as he was about to start upon his journey, and charged him, among other things, to write full descriptions of the toilets and dresses of the ladies whom he met. Hence we find many entries upon comparatively trivial subjects, interspersed with the grave descriptions of great men and the chronicling of important actions; but even the former, at this age, have a peculiar attractiveness, and give to the journal not only a graceful lightness but a vividness which it would lack undoubtedly had it been written under other circumstances. Only small portions of this invaluable diary have been published, and the part which is best known is probably that which has been given to the public in James Parton's "*Life and Times of Benjamin Franklin,*" and which consists of a beautiful, personal description of the great philosopher. There are three manuscript copies of the journal, and it is from one of them, in the possession of Mrs. Sarah Cutler Dawes, of Marietta, a granddaughter of Dr. Cutler's, that we make the extracts given in this chapter.

is of great value, because the *only* account of the negotiation of that important purchase made by the Ohio company. It also contributes to the illumination of the somewhat mysterious history of the famous Ordinance of 1787. The journal reveals the breadth and depth of character, and the consummate shrewdness of its writer, and it also suggests to the reader something of the grace of person and address which Dr. Cutler possessed, and which have formed a prominent theme for many writers to dwell upon. The extracts we present, full as they are, form only a small part of the journal, for from a mass of matter on various topics, we quote little which has not a direct bearing upon our two allied subjects—the Ordinance of 1787 and the Ohio company's purchase.

Dr. Cutler left his home in Ipswich, afterwards called Hamilton, in the latter part of June for New York, where the Continental Congress was then in session. Public conveyances were not in common use, and he used his own, a one-horse shay or sulky. On Sunday, June 24th, he was in Lynn and preached there in Mr. Parsons' pulpit. He went on to Cambridge the same day and remained there over night, lodging with Dr. Williams, although he had intended "going to President Willard's, of Harvard college."

Of the next day we give his own account:

Monday, June 25th. Waited on Dr. Willard this morning, who favored me with a number of introductory letters to gentlemen at the southward ** Received several from Dr Williams and went with him to Boston. Received letters of introduction from Governor Bowdoin, Mr. Winthrop, Dr. Warren, Dr. Dexter, Mr. Guild, Mr. Belknap, etc.; conversed with General Putnam, received letters; settled the principles on which I am to contract with Congress for lands on account of the Ohio company.

Dr. Cutler arrived at Middletown, Connecticut, on Saturday, the thirtieth of June, and preached there Sunday. This town was the home of General Parsons, who, as we have seen, was well acquainted with the western country. The doctor had a long talk with him concerning his business in Congress, and secured an addition to his bundle of letters to prominent public men. But to resume the journal:

Thursday, July 5th. About three o'clock I arrived at New York by the road that enters the Bowery. Put up my horse at the sign of the Plow and the Harrow, in the Bowery barns. After dressing myself I took a walk into the city. When I came to examine my letters of introduction I found them so accumulated that I hardly knew which to deliver first. As this is rather a curiosity to me I am determined to procure a catalogue, although only a part are to be delivered in New York. . . .

. [Here occurred a list of over fifty names, among them being Rev. Dr. Rogers, Sir John Temple, Lady Temple, General Knox and Hon. Richard Henry Lee, M. C., Melancthon Smith, M. C., Colonel Carrington, M. C.,* Hon. R. Sherman, M. C., General St. Clair, president of Congress, and others of New York, and among those at Philadelphia, Dr. Franklin, Dr. Rush, Dr. Shippen, Hon. Timothy Pickering, David Rittenhouse, etc.]

Friday, July 6th. This morning delivered most of my introductory letters to members of Congress. Prepared my papers for making my application to Congress for the purchase of lands in the western country for the Ohio company. At eleven o'clock I was introduced to a number of members on the floor of Congress chamber, in the city hall, by Colonel Carrington, member from Virginia. Delivered my petition for purchasing lands for the Ohio company and proposed terms and conditions of purchase. A committee was appointed to agree on terms of negotiation and report to Congress. Dined with Mr. Dane.

Saturday, July 7th. Paid my respects this morning to Dr Holton and other gentlemen. Was introduced by Mr Ewing and Mr. Rittenhouse to Mr. Hutchins, the United States geographer. Consulted him where to make our location. Dined with General Knox.

Monday, July 9th. Waited this morning very early on Mr. Hutchins. He gave me the fullest information of the country from Pennsylvania to the Illinois, and advised me, by all means, to make our location on the Muskingum, which was decidedly, in his opinion, the best part of the whole western country. Attended the committee before Congress opened and then spent the remainder of the forenoon with Mr. Hutchins.

Attended the committee at Congress chamber; debated on terms, but were so wide apart that there appears but little prospect of closing a contract.

Called again on Mr. Hutchins, consulted him further about the place of location. Spent the evening with Dr Holton and several other members of Congress in Hanover square.

Tuesday, July 10th. This morning another conference with the committee. As Congress was now engaged in settling the form of government for the Federal Territory, for which a bill has been prepared, and a copy sent to me (with leave to make remarks and propose amendments) which I had taken the liberty to remark upon and prepare several amendments, I thought this the most favorable time to go on to Philadelphia. * Accordingly, after I had returned the bill with my observations, I set out at 7 o'clock.

Dr. Cutler returned from Philadelphia upon the seventeenth of July. We resume our quotation from his journal:

July 18th. Paid my respects this morning to the president of Congress, General St. Clair. Called on a number of friends. Attended at the City Hall on members of Congress and their committee. We renewed our negotiations.

July 19th. Called on members of Congress very early in the morning, and was furnished with the ordinance establishing a government in the western Federal Territory. It is in a degree new modelled. The amendments I proposed have all been made except one, and that is better qualified. It was that we should not be subject to Continental taxation, unless we were entitled to a full representation in Congress. This could not be fully obtained, for it was considered in Congress as offering a premium to emigrants. They have granted us representation with the right of debating, but not voting, upon our being first subject to taxation.

The ordinance of 1787 † passed upon the thirteenth of

---

* This is the first of several allusions which show the doctor's shrewd policy. He sedulously cultivated the acquaintance of the southern members, and evidently from the first relied upon their assistance in carrying his measures.

* Colonel Carrington, Richard Henry Lee and Melancthon Smith were three of the five members of Congress who reported the Ordinance of Freedom.

* Dr. Cutler's visit to Philadelphia was for the purpose of seeing Franklin and other scientific men, with whom he had corresponded.

†Following is the full text of the instrument:

An ordinance for the government of the territory of the United States northwest of the river Ohio:

Be it ordained by the United States in Congress assembled, That the said territory, for the purpose of temporary government be one district, subject, however, to be divided into two districts, as future circumstances may, in the opinion of Congress, make it expedient.

Be it ordained by the authority aforesaid, That the estates both of resident and nonresident proprietors in the said territory dying intestate, shall descend to and be distributed among the children, and the descendants of a deceased child, inequal parts—the descendants of a deceased child, or grandchild, to take the share of the deceased parent in equal parts among them; and when there shall be no children or descendants, then in equal parts to the next of kin in equal degree; and among collaterals, the children of a deceased brother or sister of the intestate shall have, in equal parts among them, the deceased parent's share, and there shall, in no case, be a distinction between kindred of the whole

July, and from its most important provision often termed "the Ordinance of Freedom," was the "last gift of the Congress of the old confederation to the country, and it was a fit consummation of their glorious labors." It was the product of what we may call inspired statesmanship, the foundation upon which five great commonwealths were to be built up, the fundamental law, the constitution of the Northwest Territory, and a sacred compact between the old colonies and the yet uncreated States to come into being under its benign influence. It forever proscribed slavery upon the soil of the great territory that it organized, and it is undoubtedly true that to this ordinance the people of this great Nation owe thanks for the final complete suppression of slavery within its borders. Had the institution of slavery been established between the Ohio and Mississippi, its strength as a system would have resisted all reforming measures and crushing forces and the United States to-day have been a slave-holding power. And so the Congress of 1787 "builded wiser than they knew," and more grandly. But when we pass the broader significance and vaster value of the ordinance, and look upon it simply as the act of legislation providing for the opening, development, and government of the territory, we find it alike admirable and effective. It provided for successive forms of territorial government, and upon it were based all of the territorial enactments and much of the subsequent State legislation. It was so constructed as to give the utmost encouragement to immigration, and it offered the greatest protection to those who became settlers, for "when they came into the wilderness," says Chief Justice Chase, "they found the law already there. It was impressed upon the soil, while as yet it bore up nothing but the forest." Mr. Chase further says: "Never, probably, in the history of the world, did a measure of legislation so accurately fulfil, and yet so mightily exceed the anticipation of the legislators," and again "the ordinance has well been described as having been a pillar of cloud by day and of fire by night, in the settlement and government of the northwest States." In

1837, Judge Timothy Walker in an address delivered at Cincinnati, pronounced the ordinance as approaching "as nearly to absolute perfection as anything to be found in the legislation of mankind," and said "upon the surpassing excellence of this ordinance, no language of panegyric would be extravagant." Daniel Webster expressed his profound admiration of the instrument in his famous reply to Hayne, "We are accustomed," said he, "to praise the lawgivers of antiquity; we help to perpetuate the fame of Solon and Lycurgus; but I doubt whether one single law, of any lawgiver, ancient or modern, has produced effects of more distinct, marked and lasting character than the Ordinance of 1787. We see its consequences at this moment, and we shall never cease to see them, perhaps, while the Ohio shall flow."

This ordinance, New England in its character and prohibiting slavery, was impressed upon the northwest by southern votes. It was an act of legislation in close relation to the Ohio company's purchase, and the evidence that the man who negotiated that purchase was the author of its most important measures seems indisputable.

The authorship of the ordinance of 1787 has been variously ascribed to Nathan Dane, Congressman from Massachusetts, Rufus King of the same State, and Thomas Jefferson, and arguments more or less weighty have from time to time been advanced to support their claims or those of their friends. Thomas Jefferson went to France as Minister three years before the passage of the Ordinance of 1787 and did not return until eighteen months after. He was, however, identified with the inoperative ordinance of 1784, introduced the clause prohibiting slavery after the year 1800, which did not pass, and was probably the father of the idea of making the ordinance a compact, which was retained in the formation of the later ordinance. The country escaped the introduction of slavery under the specious plea that it was to exist only until 1800, and the northwest escaped the establishment of the geographical divisions with such names as Chersonesus, Assenisipia, Polypotamia, Pelesipia, Sylvania,

---

and half blood, saving in all cases to the widow of the intestate her third part of the real estate for life and one third part of the personal estate; and this law relative to descents and dower shall remain in full force until altered by the legislature of the district; and until the governor and judges shall adopt laws, as hereinafter mentioned, estates in the said territory may be divided or bequeathed by wills, in writing, signed and sealed by him or her, in whom the estate may be (being of full age) and attested by three witnesses, and real estate may be conveyed by lease or release, or bargain and sale, signed, sealed and delivered by the person, being of full age, in whom the estate may be and attested by two witnesses, provided such wills be duly proved and such conveyance be acknowledged, or the execution thereof duly proved, and be recorded within one year after proper magistrates, court and registers shall be appointed for that purpose, and personal property may be transferred by delivery, saving, however, to the French and Canadian inhabitants and other settlers of the Kaskaskias, St. Vincent and the neighboring villages, who have heretofore professed themselves citizens of Virginia, their laws and customs now in force among them, relative to the descent and conveyance of property.

Be it ordained by the authority aforesaid, That there shall be appointed, from time to time, by Congress, a governor, whose commission shall continue in force for the term of three years, unless sooner revoked by Congress. He shall reside in the district and have a freehold estate therein in one thousand acres of land while in the exercise of his office. There shall be appointed, from time to time, by Congress a secretary, whose commission shall continue in force for four

years, unless sooner revoked; he shall reside in the district and have a freehold estate therein in five hundred acres of land while in the exercise of his office; it shall be his duty to keep and preserve the acts and laws passed by the legislature, and the public records of the district, and the proceedings of the governor in his executive department; and transmit authentic copies of such acts and proceedings every six months to the secretary of Congress. There shall also be appointed a court to consist of three judges, any two of whom to form a court, who shall have a common law jurisdiction, and reside in the district and have each therein a freehold estate in five hundred acres of land while in the exercise of their offices; and their commissions shall continue in force during good behavior.

The governor and judges, or a majority of them, shall adopt and publish in the district such laws of the original States, criminal and civil, as may be necessary and best suited to the circumstances, and report them to Congress, from time to time; which laws shall be in force in the district until the organization of the general assembly therein, unless disapproved of by Congress; but afterwards the legislature shall have authority to alter them as they shall think fit.

The governor, for the time being, shall be commander-in-chief of the militia, appoint and commission all officers in the same below the rank of general officers; all general officers shall be appointed and commissioned by Congress.

Previous to the organization of the general assembly, the governor shall appoint such magistrates and other civil officers, in each county or township, as he shall find necessary for the preservation of the peace

Michigania, Saratoga, Illinoia, Metropotamia, and Washington—although as regards number merely the creation of ten rather than five States might have been very largely to the political advantage of the people of the territory. Mr Jefferson's claim of authorship appears to end with the history of this ordinance. Mr. King was undoubtedly the author of the anti-slavery clause in an ordinance which secured some attention in 1785, but he was not even a member of the Congress of 1787. Mr. Dane's claim is combatted chiefly on the ground that it was never made while any of the other men, who, from their position, were supposed to know about the formation of the ordinance, were alive; on the ground that he had none of those graces of composition which are exhibited in the ordinance; and upon the ground that he was very young (thirty-four years) and did not enter upon the fullest understanding either of the work that had been done to prepare Congress for the action, or the importance of the measures under consideration. In addition to these facts there is the consideration that Massachusetts did not warmly favor the idea of the western emigration. Mr. King had been accused of introducing measures which were calculated to prevent immigration and in one or two entries in Dr. Cutler's journal, which we shall give in their proper place, it is shown that the writer did not have much confidence in Dane's friendliness to the Ohio company's purchase. If unfriendly to that measure or representing a constituency of which the majority were opposed to the plan, would he not also be unfriendly to the enactment of an ordinance, which must, from its nature, encourage emigration? And yet "Mr. Dane," says a student of the subject,* "doubtless wrote the draft and performed the clerical duties of the committee" who

*William F. Poole in the *North American Review* for April, 1876. He has examined the whole subject of the authorship of the Ordinance in an elaborate but remarkably clear and concise article. We briefly summarize some of his evidence.

and good order in the same. After the general assembly shall be organized, the power and duties of magistrates and other civil officers, shall be regulated and defined by the said assembly; but all magistrates and other civil officers, not herein otherwise directed, shall, during the continuance of this temporary government, be appointed by the governor.

For the prevention of crimes and injuries the laws to be adopted or made shall have force in all parts of the district, and for the execution of process, criminal and civil, the governor shall make proper divisions thereof; and he shall proceed, from time to time, as circumstances may require, to lay out the parts of the district, in which the Indian titles shall have been extinguished, into counties and townships, subject, however, to such alterations as may thereafter be made by the legislature.

So soon as there shall be five thousand free male inhabitants of full age in the district, upon giving proof thereof to the governor, they shall receive authority, with time and place, to elect representatives from their counties or townships to represent them in the general assembly: provided that for every five hundred free male inhabitants, there shall be one representative, and so on, progressively, with the number of free male inhabitants shall the right of representation increase until the number of representatives shall amount to twenty-five; after which the number and proportion of representatives shall be regulated by the legislature: provided that no person be eligible or qualified to act as a representative unless he shall have been a citizen of one of the United States three years, and be a resident in the district, or unless he shall have resided in the district three years; and in either case, shall likewise hold in his own right, in fee simple, two hundred acres of land within the same: provided also that a freehold in fifty acres of land in the district, having been a citizen of one of the States and being resident in the district, or the like freehold and two years'

reported the ordinance. He took the liberty of withholding the anti-slavery clause until the second reading under the belief that it could not pass, but afterward, discovering the sentiment of Congress, added it. It was strange that Mr. Dane should have been in ignorance of the feeling that existed in Congress, for that feeling had been newly created. Very naturally he supposed that an anti-slavery clause could not be passed for every ordinance containing one had been voted down. The last ordinance had contained no restriction of slavery, no provision for education, and no articles of compact. Still it had come down to the ninth of July, 1787, only four days before the ordinance of freedom was passed, and was doubtless regarded as the future law of the Northwest Territory, only needing final action as it had passed its first and second readings.

But suddenly there came a change. The forces were put in operation which were to clothe the northwest with a beneficent law and forever to withhold slavery from five great States. The first outward intimation of the change was the appointment, on the ninth of July, of a new committee, authorized to prepare and submit to Congress a plan of government for the Federal Territory. It consisted of Colonel Carrington, of Virginia, Nathan Dane, of Massachusetts, Richard Henry Lee, of Virginia, Mr. Kean, of South Carolina, and Mr. Smith, of New York. The three new members were all southerners. Carrington was chairman. These southern Congressmen were the friends of Dr. Cutler. He had been introduced to most of the members, as his journal shows, by Colonel Carrington.

Dr. Cutler had come before Congress to purchase, for a company composed chiefly of Massachusetts men, a large body of public lands. The purchase would have been almost entirely valueless in the opinion of most of those Ohio company associates if they could not

residence in the district, shall be necessary to qualify a man as an elector of a representative.

The representative thus elected shall serve for the term of two years; and in case of the death of a representative, or removal from office, the governor shall issue a writ to the county or township for which he was a member to elect another in his stead, to serve for the residue of the term.

The general assembly or legislature shall consist of the governor, legislative council, and a house of representatives. The legislative council shall consist of five members to continue in office five years, unless sooner removed by Congress, any three of whom may be a quorum; and the members of the council shall be nominated and appointed in the following manner, to wit: As soon as representatives shall be elected, the governor shall appoint a time and place for them to meet together, and when met, they shall nominate ten persons, residents in the district, and each possessed of a freehold in five hundred acres of land, and return their names to Congress, five of whom Congress shall appoint and commission to serve as aforesaid; and whenever a vacancy shall happen in the council by death or removal from office, the house of representatives shall nominate two persons, qualified as aforesaid, for each vacancy, and return their names to Congress, one of whom Congress shall appoint and commission for the residue of the term. And every five years, four months at least before the expiration of the time of service of the members of the council, the said house shall nominate ten persons, qualified as aforesaid, and return their names to Congress, five of whom Congress shall appoint and commission to serve as members of the council five years, unless sooner removed. And the governor, legislative council, and house of representatives shall have authority to make laws, in all cases, for the good government of the district, not repugnant to the principles and articles in this ordi-

have the land to which they proposed to emigrate, covered with the law to which they had been accustomed. They were fully in accord with the spirit which seven years before had prohibited slavery in Massachusetts. The ordinance of freedom was, as an act of legislation, the natural predecessor of the sale to the Ohio company. It was considered by Congress, after the plan had been fully examined, very desirable that the public domain should be advantageously disposed of, and that a colony should be established in the Federal Territory. Such a colony would form a barrier against the British and Indians, it was argued, and this initiative step would be followed speedily by other purchases in which additional settlements would be founded. The south had a greater interest in the west than had New England, and Virginia especially, from her past protection, future prospect and geographical location, was interested in, and eager for, the development of the country beyond the Ohio. There was a strong feeling of disaffection in Kentucky and imminent danger that that territory would embrace the first favorable opportunity to join her fortunes with Spain. "The desire of the people," says Albach in his Annals of the West, "for a separation from the district of Virginia had familiarized their minds to the idea of a separation from the confederacy." Virginia, and the south in general, may have justly regarded the planting in the west of a colony of men whose patriotism was well known, a measure calculated to bind together the old and new parts of the Nation, and promote union. It is presumable that much was said by Dr. Cutler upon these advantages and that it was their importance in the eyes of southern members which led them to permit the creation and enactment of such an ordinance as the Ohio company desired. Another inducement for the southern members of Congress to pass an anti-slavery ordinance rather than to relinquish the possibility of deriving a revenue from the sale of lands, and the benefits attending the colonization of the west, was undoubtedly a shrewd provision in the

anti-slavery clause itself. Article sixth of the ordinance, after prohibiting slavery in the territory northwest of the Ohio river contained the following words: "Provided always, that any person escaping into the same, from whom labor or service is lawfully claimed in any one of the original States, such fugitive may be lawfully reclaimed and conveyed to the person claiming his or her service." This allowance to the south of the right to reclaim fugitive slaves was made as a concession that the passage of the ordinance with the prohibitory measure might not be imperilled. This was an idea that had not before been broached in Congress, and the same or similar prohibitory measures in former ordinances (those advocated by Jefferson and Rufus King) without the concession, had resulted in their speedy rejection by the votes of the very States by which the Ordinance of 1787 was passed. The provision was a splendid stroke of diplomacy.

The committee having the ordinance in charge, as we have seen, conferred with Dr. Cutler, and were evidently anxious to please him, for, as his journal states, they sent him a copy of the ordinance "with leave to make remarks and propose amendments." He did make amendments, went to Philadelphia, returned, found that the ordinance had been passed and, to use his own language, "the amendments   .   .   .   all made except one" which "was better qualified." This was the one relating to taxation. The ordinance was adopted on the thirteenth of July, there being only one dissenting vote, that of Mr. Yates, of New York, which was neutralized, as there were two other delegates from the same State who voted to adopt. Eight States were represented (of which only three were northern)—Delaware, Virginia, North Carolina, South Carolina, Georgia, New York, New Jersey and Massachusetts. The ordinance was therefore carried by the southern States. What Dr. Cutler inserted was, according to good evidence, the clauses relating to religion, morality, education and slavery.

In his subsequent labors for the Ohio company his

---

nance established and declared. And all bills having passed by a majority in the house, and by a majority in the council, shall be referred to the governor for his assent; but no bill or legislative act whatever, shall be of any force without his assent. The governor shall have power to convene, prorogue and dissolve the general assembly when, in his opinion, it shall be expedient.

The governor, judges, legislative council, secretary, and such other officers as Congress shall appoint in the district shall take an oath or affirmation of fidelity, and of office; the governor before the president of Congress, and all other officers before the governor. As soon as a legislature shall be formed in the district, the council and house assembled in one room, shall have authority, by joint ballot, to elect a delegate to Congress, who shall have a seat in Congress, with a right of debating, but not of voting, during this temporary government.

And for extending the fundamental principles of civil and religious liberty, which form the basis whereon these republics, their laws, and constitutions, are erected; to fix and establish those principles as the basis of all laws, constitutions, and governments, which forever hereafter shall be formed in the said territory; to provide, also, for the establishment of States, and permanent government therein, and for their admission to a share in the Federal councils on an equal footing with the original States, at as early periods as may be consistent with general interest.

It is hereby ordained and declared by the authority aforesaid, that the following articles shall be considered as articles of compact between the original States and the people and States in the said territory, and forever remain unalterable unless by common consent, to-wit:

"ARTICLE 1. No person demeaning himself in a peaceable and orderly manner shall ever be molested on account of his mode of worship or religious sentiments in the said territory.

"ARTICLE 2. The inhabitants of said territory shall always be entitled to the benefits of the writ of *habeas corpus* and of trial by jury; of a proportionate representation of the people in the legislature, and of judicial proceedings according to the course of the common law. All persons shall be bailable except for capital offences, where the proof shall be evident or the presumption great. All fines shall be moderate, and no unsual or cruel punishment shall be inflicted. No man shall be deprived of his liberty or property but by the judgment of his peers, or the law of the land; and should the public exigencies make it necessary, for the common preservation, to take away any person's property, or to demand his particular service, full compensation shall be made for the same; and in the just preservation of rights and property it is understood and declared that no law ought ever to be made, or have force in the said territory, that shall in any manner whatever interfere with or effect private contracts or engagements, bona fide, and without fraud, previously formed.

"ARTICLE 3. Religion, morality, and knowledge, being necessary to good government and the happiness of mankind, schools and the means of education shall forever be encouraged. The utmost good faith shall always be observed towards the Indians; their lands and property shall never be taken from them without consent; and in their property, rights, and liberty, they shall never be invaded or disturbed, unless in just and lawful wars, authorized by Congress; but laws founded in justice and humanity shall, from time to time, be made for preventing

course was precisely such as might have been expected of the man who would write, "Religion, morality and knowledge being necessary to good government and the happiness of mankind, schools and the means of education shall forever be encouraged."

And now for the direct evidence that Dr. Cutler was the author of the clauses claimed—the two ideas which made the northwest what it is in civilization and morality.

In 1847 Dr. Joseph Torrey, of Salem, Massachusetts son-in-law of Dr. Cutler, writing to Judge Ephraim Cutler, of Washington county, about some papers he had examined at Temple Cutler's in Hamilton, says:

Saw among these documents the Ordinance of 1787 on a printed sheet. On its margin was written that Mr Dane requested Dr. Cutler to suggest such provisions as he deemed advisable, and that at Dr. Cutler's instance was inserted what relates to religion, education and slavery. These facts have long been known to me as household words.

In 1849 Temple Cutler wrote to his brother, Judge Ephraim Cutler, of the ordinance, that "Hon. Daniel Webster is now convinced that the man whose foresight, suggested some of its articles, was our father."

In the same year as the above, and upon the twenty-fourth of November, Judge Cutler answered an inquiry as follows:

I visited my father at Washington during the last session he attended Congress (1804). . . . We were in conversation relative to the political concerns of Ohio, the ruling parties, and the effects of the constitution (of Ohio) in the promotion of the general interest; when he observed that he was informed that I had prepared that portion of the Ohio constitution which contained the part of the ordinance of July, 1787, which prohibited slavery. He wished to know if it was a fact. On my assuming that it was, he observed that he thought it a singular coincidence, as he himself had prepared that part of the ordinance while he was in New York negotiating the purchase of the lands for the

---

wrong being done to them and for preserving peace and friendship with them.

"ARTICLE 4TH.—The said territory, and the States which may be formed therein, shall forever remain a part of this confederacy of the United States of America, subject to the articles of confederation, and to such alterations therein as shall be constitutionally made, and to all the acts and ordinances of the United States in Congress assembled, conformable thereto. The inhabitants and settlers in the said territory shall be subject to pay a part of the Federal debts, contracted or to be contracted, and a proportional part of the expenses of government, to be apportioned on them by Congress, according to the same common rule and measure by which the apportionments thereof shall be made on the other States; and the taxes for paying their proportion shall be laid and levied by the authority and direction of the legislatures of the district or districts, on new States as in the original States, within the time agreed upon by the United States in Congress assembled The legislatures of those districts or new States shall never interfere with the primary disposal of the soil by the United States in Congress assembled, nor with any regulation Congress may find necessary for securing the title to such soil to the bona fide purchasers. No tax shall be imposed on lands the property, of the United States; and in no case shall non-resident proprietors be taxed higher than residents. The navigable waters leading into the Mississippi and St. Lawrence and the carrying places between the same, shall be common highways, and forever free, as well to the inhabitants of the said territory as to the citizens of the United States, and those of any other States that may be admitted into the confederacy, without any tax, import, or duty therefor.

ARTICLE 5TH.—There shall be formed in the said territory not less than three nor more than five States; and the boundaries of the States as soon as Virginia shall alter her act of cession and consent to the same, shall become fixed and established as follows, to wit: The western State in the said territory shall be bounded by the Mississippi, the Ohio and Wabash rivers; a direct line drawn from the Wabash and Port Vincents due north to the territorial line between the United States

---

Ohio company. I had then not seen the journal he kept while he was in New York at that time.*   .   .   .

We now resume our extracts from Dr. Cutler's journal, taking it up where it was left and following its entries respecting the purchase through to the close. That portion of the entry under date of July 19th, not already given, is as follows:

As there are a number in Congress opposed to my terms of negotiation and some to any contract, I wish now to ascertain the number for and against, and who they are, and must then, if possible, bring the opponents over. This I have mentioned to Colonel Duer, who has promised to assist me. Grayson, R. H. Lee, and Carrington, are certainly my warm advocates. Holton, I think, may be trusted. Dane must be carefully watched, notwithstanding his professions. Clark, Bingham, Yates, Kearney, and Ford, are troublesome fellows. They must be attacked by my friends at their lodgings If they can be brought over I shall succeed; if not, my business is at an end. Attended the committee this morning. They are determined to make a report to-day, and try the spirit of Congress. Dined with General Knox and about forty-two gentlemen, officers of the late Continental army, and among them Baron Steuben. General Knox gave us an entertainment in the style of a prince. I had the honor to be seated next the baron, who is a hearty, sociable old fellow. He was dressed in his military uniform, and with the ensigns of nobility, the shoe and garter. Every gentleman at the table was of the Cincinnati except myself, and wore his appropriate badges. Spent the evening at Dr. Holton's with Colonel Duer and several members of Congress, who informed me that an ordinance was passed in consequence of my petition, but, by their account of it, it will answer no purpose.

July 20th.—This morning the secretary of Congress furnished me with the ordinance of yesterday which states the conditions of a contract, but on terms to which I shall by no means accede. I informed the committee of Congress that I could not contract on the conditions proposed, that I should prefer purchasing lands from some one of the States, who would give incomparably better terms; and therefore proposed to leave the city immediately. They appeared to be sorry no better terms were effected, and insisted on my not thinking of leaving Congress until another attempt was made. I told them I saw no prospect of contracting, and wished to spend no more time and money in a business so unpromising. They assured me that I had many friends in Congress who would make every exertion in my favor; that it was an object of great magnitude, and that I must not expect to accomplish it in less than two or three months. If I desired it they would take the

---

and Canada; and by the said territorial line to the Lake of the Woods and Mississippi. The middle State shall be bounded by the direct line, the Wabash from Port Vincents to the Ohio, by the Ohio, by a direct line drawn due north from the mouth of the Great Miami to the said territorial line, and by the said territorial line. The eastern State shall be bounded by the last mentioned direct line, the Ohio, Pennsylvania, and the said territorial line; provided, however, and it is further understood and declared, that the boundaries of these three States shall be subject so far to be altered that, if Congress should hereafter find it expedient, they shall have authority to form one or two States in that part of the territory which lies north of an east and west line, drawn through the southerly bend or extreme of Lake Michigan. And whenever any of the said States shall have sixty thousand free inhabitants therein, such State shall be admitted, by its delegates into the Congress of the United States, on an equal footing with the original States, in all respects whatever, and shall be at liberty to form a permanent constitution and State government; provided the constitution and government so to be formed shall be republican, and in conformity to the principles contained in these articles; and so far as it can be consistent with the general interest of the confederacy, such admission shall be allowed at an earlier period and when there may be a less number of free inhabitants in the State than sixty thousand.

ARTICLE 6TH.—There shall be neither slavery nor involuntary servitude in the said territory otherwise than in the punishment of crimes, whereof the party shall have been duly convicted; provided, always, that any person escaping into the same from whom labor or service is lawfully claimed in any one of the original States, such fugitive may be lawfully reclaimed, and conveyed to the person claiming his or her labor or services as aforesaid.

matter up that day on different grounds and did not doubt they should obtain terms agreeable to my wishes. Colonel Duer came to me with proposals from a number of the principal characters of the city, to extend our contract and take in another company, but that it should be kept a profound secret. He explained the plan they had concocted and offered me generous conditions if I would accomplish the business for them. The plan struck me agreeably, Sargent insisted on my undertaking it, and both urged me not to think of giving the matter up so soon. I was convinced it was best for me to hold up the idea of giving up a contract with Congress, and making a contract with some of the States, which I did in the strongest terms, and represented to the committee and to Duer and Sargent the difficulties I saw in the way, and the improbability of closing a bargain when we were so far apart; and told them I conceived it not worth while to say anything further to Congress on the subject. This appeared to have the effect I wished The committee were mortified and did not seem to know what to say; but still urged another attempt. I left them in this state but afterward explained my views to Duer and Sargent who fully approved my plan. Promised Duer to consider his proposal. We had agreed last evening to make a party to Brooklyn, on Long Island, which is a small village opposite New York, divided from it by East river; Duer, Webb, Hammond, Sargent, with others were of the party. * * I spent the evening closeted with Colonel Duer and agreed to purchase more land, if terms can be obtained, which will probably forward the negotiation.

July 21st.—Several members of Congress called on me early this morning. They discovered much anxiety about a contract, and assured me that Congress, on finding that I was determined not to accept their terms, and had proposed leaving the city, had discovered a much more favorable disposition, and believed, if I renewed my request, I might obtain conditions as reasonable as I desired. I was very indifferent, and talked much of the advantages of a contract with one of the States. This I found had the desired effect. At length I told them that if Congress would accede to the terms of my proposal, I would extend the purchase from the tenth township from the Ohio and to the Scioto inclusively; by which Congress would pay more than four millions of the public debt; that our intention was to secure, a large and immediate settlement of the most robust and industrious people in America; and that it would be made systematically, which must instantly enhance the value of Federal lands, and prove an important acquisition to Congress. On these terms I would renew the negotiation, if Congress was disposed to take the matter up again. Dined with General Webb at the Mess house in Broadway, opposite the Play house. Spent the evening with Mr. Dane and Mr Millikin. They informed me that Congress had taken up my business again.

July 23rd.—My friends had made every exertion in private conversation to bring over my opponents in Congress. In order to get at some of them so as to work powerfully on their minds, we were obliged to engage three or four persons before we could get at them. In some instances we engaged one person who engaged a second, and he a third, and so on to the fourth, before we could effect our purpose. In these manœuvres I am much beholden by the assistance of Colonel Duer and Major Sargent. The matter was taken up this morning in Congress and warmly debated until three o'clock, when another ordinance was obtained. This was not to the minds of any of my friends, who were considerably increased in Congress, but they conceived it to be better than the former, and they had obtained an additional clause empowering the board of treasury to take order upon this ordinance and complete the contract upon the general principles contained in it, which still left room for negotiation. Spent the evening with Colonel Grayson and members of Congress from the southward, who were in favor of a contract. Having found it impossible to support General Parsons as a candidate for governor, after the interest that General St. Clair had secured, and suspecting that this might be some impediment in the way (for my endeavors to make interest for him were well known), and the arrangements for civil officers being on the carpet, I embraced the opportunity frankly to declare that for my own part and ventured to engage for Major Sargent—if General Parsons could have the appointment of first judge and Sargent, secretary, we would be satisfied; and I heartily wished that his excellency, General St. Clair, might be governor, and that I would solicit the eastern members to favor such an arrangement This I found rather pleasing to the southern members, and they were so complacent as to ask repeatedly what office would be agreeable to me in the western country. I assured them I wished for no appointment to the civil line. Colonel Grayson proposed the office of one of the judges, which was seconded by all the gentlemen present. The obtaining an appointment, I observed, had never come into my

mind, nor was there any civil office I should at present be willing to accept. This declaration seemed to be rather surprising, especially to men who were so much used to solicit or be solicited for appointments of honor or profit. They seemed to be the more urgent on this head. I observed to them, although I wished for nothing for myself, yet I thought the Ohio company entitled to some attention; that one of our judges besides General Parsons should be of that body, and that General Putnam was the man best qualified and would be most agreeable to that company, and gave them his character. We spent the evening very agreeably until a late hour.

July 24th.—I received this morning a letter from the board of treasury, inclosing the resolutions of Congress, which passed yesterday, and requesting to know whether I was ready to close a contract on those terms. As the contract had now become of much greater magnitude than when I had only the Ohio company in view, I felt a diffidence in acting alone and wished Major Sargent to be joined with me, although he had not been formally empowered to act, for the commission from the directors was solely to me. It would likewise take off some part of the responsibility from me if the contract should not be agreeable. After consulting Duer I proposed it to Sargent, who readily accepted. We answered the letters from the board as jointly commissioned in making the contract. We informed the board that the terms in the resolve of Congress were such as we could not accede to, without some variation We therefore begged leave to state to the board the terms on which we were ready to close the contract, and that those terms were our *ultimatum*. This letter* was sent to the board, but the packet having just arrived from England, and another to sail next morning, it was not in their power to attend any further to our business for the day. Dined with Mr. Hilleyas, treasurer of the United States. I spent the evening with Mr. Osgood, president of the board of treasury, who appeared to be very solicitous to be informed fully of our plan. No gentleman has a higher character for planning and calculating than Mr. Osgood. I was therefore much pleased with having an opportunity of fully explaining it to him. We were unfortunately interrupted with company. We, however, went over the outlines, and he appeared well disposed.

July 25th. This morning the board of treasury sent our letter to the secretary of Congress, requesting him to lay it before Congress for approbation or rejection. But the dispatches from Europe received yesterday by the British packet, occupied the attention of Congress for that day. Mr. Osgood desired me to dine with him, assuring me that he had purposely omitted inviting any other company, that we might not be interrupted in going over our plan. I had been repeatedly assured that Mr. Osgood was my friend, and that he had censured Congress for not assenting to the terms I had offered; but such is the intrigue and artifice often practiced by men in power, I felt very suspicious, and was as cautious as possible. Our plan, however, I had no scruple to communicate, and went over it in all its parts. Mr. Osgood made many valuable observations. The extent of his information astonished me. His views of the continent of Europe were so enlarged that he appeared to be a perfect master of every subject of this kind. He highly approved of our plan, and told me he thought it the best formed in America. He dwelt much on the advantages of system in a new settlement; said system had never before been attempted; that we might depend upon accomplishing our purposes in Europe, and that it was a most important part of our plan. If we were able to establish a settlement as we proposed, however small in the beginning, we should then have surmounted our greatest difficulty; that every other object would be within our reach, and if the matter was pursued with spirit

---

* The letter, which was signed by Manasseh Cutler and Winthrop Sargent, addressed to this board of treasury, proposed the following conditions:

The subordinate surveys to be completed as mentioned in the act, unless the frequency of Indian interruption should prevent; the mode of payment to be half a million of dollars when the contract should be executed, another half million when the tract should be surveyed by the proper officers of the United States, and the remainder in six equal payments; the lands assigned for the establishment of a university to be as nearly as possible in the centre of the first million and a half acres paid for, for to fix it in the centre of the proposed purchase, might too long defer the establishment. (That is, the lands are to be located in the Ohio company's purchase proper, and not beyond these bounds, in the lands bought merely in the name of the company, and for which they had the refusal.) The letter further suggested that the purchasers, when the second payment should be made, should receive a deed for as great a quantity of lands as a million would pay for at the price agreed upon; that as most of the associates had embarked their private fortunes in the support of the purchase, no security should be required of them but the lands; and that they, the purchasers, should be entitled to no right of entry, or occupancy, except on the lands actually paid for, and to receive no deeds until their payments amounted to one million of dollars, and then only in proportion to such payment.

M Cutler

he believed it would prove one of the greatest undertakings ever yet attempted in America. He thought Congress would do an especial service to the United States, even if they gave us the land, rather than that our plan should be defeated; and promised to make every exertion in his power in my favor. We spent the afternoon and evening alone, and very agreeably.

July 26th. This morning I accompanied General St. Clair and General Knox on a tour of morning visits, particularly to the foreign ministers: Sieur Otto, French charge; Don Diego Guarduqoi, Spanish; Van Berckle, Dutch, a frank open Dutchman, who speaks bad English, but is very talkative. He is fond of conversing about the western country, and seems to interest himself much in the settlement of the western lands.

Being now eleven o'clock, General St. Clair was obliged to attend Congress. After we came into the street General St. Clair assured us he would make every possible exertion to prevail with Congress to accept the terms contained in our letter. He appeared much interested and very friendly, but said we must expect opposition. I was fully convinced it was good policy to give up Parsons and openly to appear solicitous, that St. Clair might be appointed governor. Several gentlemen have told me that our matters went on much better since St. Clair and his friends had been informed that we had given up Parsons and that I should have solicited the eastern members in favor of St. Clair's appointment. I immediately went to Sargent and Duer. We now went into the true spirit of negotiation with great bodies. Every machine in the city it was possible to set to work we now put in motion. Few, Bingham and Kearney are our principal opposers. Of Few and Bingham there is hope, but to bring over that stubborn mule of a Kearney is beyond our power. The board of treasury, I think, will do us much service, if Dr. Lee is not against us, though Duer assures me that I have got the length of his foot, and that he calls me a frank, open, honest New England man, which he considers as an uncommon animal; yet from his zealous, cautious make, I feel suspicious of him, especially as Mr. Osgood tells me he has made every attempt to learn his sentiments, but is unable to do so. His brother, Richard Henry Lee, is certainly our fast friend, and we have hopes he will engage him in our interests. Dined with Sir John Temple in company with several gentlemen. Immediately after dinner I took my leave of them and called on Dr. Holton. He told me Congress had been warmly engaged in our business the whole day; that the opposition was lessened, but our friends did not think it prudent to come to a vote, lest there should be a majority in favor. I left much discouraged, and told Dr. Holton I thought it in vain to wait any longer, and should certainly leave the next day. He cried out on my impatience, said if I obtained my purposes in a month from that time I should be far more expeditious than was common in getting much smaller matters through Congress; that it was of great magnitude, for it far exceeded any private contract ever made before in the United States; that if I should fail now I ought still to pursue the matter, for I should most certainly finally obtain the object I wished. To comfort me, he assured me it was impossible for him to conceive by what kind of an address I had so soon and so warmly engaged the attention of Congress; for since he had been a member of that body he assured me, on his honor, that he never knew so much attention paid to any one person who made application to them on any kind of business, nor did he ever know them more pressing to bring it to a close. He could not have supposed that any three men from New England, even of the first characters, could have accomplished so much, in so short a time. This I believe was mere flattery, though it was delivered with a very serious air; but it gave some consolation. I now learned very nearly who were for and against the terms. Bingham has come over, but Few and Kearney are stubborn. Unfortunately there are only eight States represented, and unless seven of them are in favor no ordinance can pass.* Every moment of this evening until two o'clock was busily employed. A warm siege was laid on Few and Kearney from different quarters, and if the point is not effectually carried, the attack is to be renewed in the morning. Duer, Sargent and myself have agreed that if we fail, Sargent shall go on to Maryland, which is not at present represented, and prevail on the members of that State to come on and interest themselves, if possible, in our plan. I am to go on to Connecticut and Rhode Island to solicit the members from those States to go on to New York, and to lay an anchor to windward with them. As soon as those States are represented Sargent is to renew the application, and I have prom-

*The vote of seven out of the thirteen States was necessary to carry any measure. No State could vote unless two of its delegates were present, and in that case both must vote the same way or their ballots would be neutralized. If three delegates were present the vote of two would carry the State.

ised Duer that if it is necessary I will then return to New York again.

The contingency for which this careful provision was made did not arise. We come now to the entry in the journal which describes the last day's action and the success of Dr. Cutler's labors:

Friday, July 27th.—I rose very early this morning, and after adjusting my baggage (for I was determined to leave New York this day) I set out on a general morning visit and paid my respects to all the members of Congress in the city, and informed them of my intention to leave the city that day. My expectations of forming a contract, I told them, were nearly at an end. I should, however, wait the decision of Congress, and if the terms which we had stated, and which I considered to be very advantageous to Congress, considering the state of the country, were not accepted, we must turn our attention to some other part of the country. New York, Connecticut, and Massachusetts, would sell us lands at half a dollar an acre, and give us exclusive privileges beyond what we had asked of Congress. The speculating plan concerted between the British of Canada, and the New Yorkers, was now well known. The uneasiness of the Kentucky people with respect to the Mississippi was notorious. A revolt of that country from the Union, if a war with Spain took place, was universally acknowledged to be highly probable; and most certainly a systematic settlement in that country, conducted by men strongly attached to the Federal Government, and composed of young, robust, hardy, and active laborers, who had no idea of any other than the Federal Government, I conceived to be an object worthy of some attention. Besides, if Congress rejected the terms now offered, there could be no prospect of any application from any other quarter. If a fair and honorable purchase could now be obtained, I presumed, contracts with the natives, similar to that made with the Six Nations, must be the consequence, especially as it might be much more easily carried into effect. These, and such like, were the arguments I urged. They seemed to be fully acceded to, but whether they will avail is very uncertain. Mr. R. H. Lee assured me he was prepared for one hour's speech, and he hoped for success. All urged me not to leave the city so soon, but I assumed an air of perfect indifference, and persisted in my determination, which had, apparently, the effect I wished. Passing the city hall as the members were going into Congress, Colonel Carrington told me he believed Few was secured, that little Kearney was left alone, and that he was determined to make one trial of what he could do in Congress. Called on Sir John Temple for letters to Boston; bade my friends good-bye, and as it was my last day, Mr. Henderson insisted on my dining with him and a number of his friends whom he had invited.

At half-past three I was informed that an ordinance had passed Congress on the terms stated in our letter, without the least variation, and that the board of treasury was directed to take order and close the contract. This was agreeable but unexpected intelligence. Sargent and I went immediately to the board, who had received the ordinance, but were then rising. They urged me to tarry the next day, and they would put by all other business to complete the contract, but I found it inconvenient, and after making a general verbal adjustment, left it with Sargent to finish what was to be done at present.

Dr. Lee congratulated me and declared he would do all in his power to adjust the terms of the contract, so far as was left to them, as much in our favor as possible. I proposed three months for collecting the first half million of dollars, and for executing the instruments of Congress, which was acceded to. By this ordinance we obtained the grant of near five millions of acres of lands, amounting to three and a half millions of dollars. One million and a half acres for the Ohio company, and the remainder for a private speculation, in which many of the principal characters in America are concerned. Without connecting this speculation similar terms and advantages could not have been obtained for the Ohio company. On my return through Broadway I received the congratulations of my friends in Congress and others with whom I happened to meet. At half-past six I took my leave of Mr. Henderson and family, where I had been most kindly and generously entertained. Left the city by way of the Bowery. . . .

On his way home Dr. Cutler again stopped at Middleton, Connecticut, and called on General Parsons. Under date of July 30th he enters the following in his journal:

When I had informed the general of my negotiations with Congress, I had the pleasure to find it not only met his approbation, but he expressed his astonishment that I had obtained terms so advantageous, which, he said, were beyond his expectation. He assured me he preferred the appointment of first judge to that of governor, especially if General St. Clair was governor. He proposed writing to General St. Clair and his friends in Congress that they would procure an appointment for me on the same bench; but I absolutely declined, assuring him I had no wish to go in the civil line.

The reader who has followed the extracts given from Dr. Cutler's journal has seen that the diplomatic lobbyist accomplished far more than he first set out to achieve. Instead of a million and a half acres of land, he made arrangements to purchase five and a half millions of acres.

A collossal scheme of land speculation and immigration was concocted, which looked for fulfilment not simply to New England but to the countries of the old world, especially Holland and France. There was reason to believe that the vast plan could be successfully carried out; and, had it been, results would have been exhibited in the west which we cannot imagine. Unfortunately, however, the sanguine men who joined in securing the services of Dr. Cutler to negotiate a purchase for them, in connection with his bargain for the Ohio company, were doomed to disappointment. One of the illy developed results of that stupendous scheme was the settlement of the French at Gallipolis, in 1790, under the auspices of the Scioto company. They were defrauded, suffered innumerable hardships incident to pioneer life, for which they were poorly fitted; and, finally, failing to secure the lands for which they bargained, the larger part of them left Gallipolis, and, with much painful privation, found homes elsewhere, though a few remained at the scene of their early suffering, where some of their descendants still dwell. Much of the history of the Scioto company is shrouded in oblivion. It is certain, however, that Dr. Cutler and the Ohio company were in no degree responsible for the sad failure of that plan of immigration which brought the poor Frenchmen to America. Dr. Cutler acted only as the agent for the parties interested in the purchase, who could not by their own efforts secure the attention or favor of Congress. It is undoubtedly true that he obtained better terms for the Ohio company by including the other and making a huge purchase. To go further, it is improbable that Barlow and Duer had any wrong intent in their management of the Scioto company's business, but that really culpable parties were their sub-agents upon the other side of the Atlantic. But this is a topic, the consideration of which would take us far outside our province in writing a history of Washington county.

The amount of land for which Dr. Cutler secured the refusal for the Ohio company was one million five hundred thousand acres, but for reasons which will be hereafter shown, they finally became possessed of only nine hundred and sixty-four thousand two hundred and eighty-five acres.

At a meeting of the directors and agents of the Ohio company held at the Bunch of Grapes tavern, in Boston, August 29, 1787, Dr. Cutler made the following report of his action at New York:

That in consequence of resolves of Congress of the twenty-third and twenty-seventh of July last, he agreed on the conditions of a contract with the board of treasury of the United States, for a particular tract of land containing in the whole as much as the company's funds will pay for. Should the subscriptions amount to one million of dollars, agreeably to the articles of association, at one dollar per acre—from which price is to be deducted one-third of a dollar for bad lands and defraying the expenses of surveying, etc., etc.

That the land be bounded on the east by the western boundary of the seventh range of townships; south by the Ohio; west by a meridian line to be drawn through the western cape of the Great Kanawha river, and extending so far north that a due east and west line from the seventh range of townships to the said meridian line, shall include the whole.

This tract to be extended so far northerly as to comprehend within its limits, exclusively of the above purchase, one lot of six hundred and forty acres in each township for the purposes of religion; an equal quantity for the support of schools, and two townships of twenty-three thousand and forty acres each for an university, to be as near the centre of the whole tract as may be; which lots and townships are given by Congress and appropriated for the above uses forever; also three lots of six hundred and forty acres each in every township, reserved for the future disposition of Congress; and the bounty lands of the military associators to be comprised in the whole tract; provided they do not exceed one-seventh part thereof.

That five hundred thousand dollars be paid to the board of treasury upon closing the contract.

In consideration of which, a right of entry and occupancy for a quantity of land equal to this sum, at the price stipulated be given, and that as soon as the geographer or some proper officer of the United States shall have surveyed and ascertained the quantity of the whole, the sum of five hundred thousand dollars more be paid, amounting in the whole to one million dollars, for which the company are to be put in possession of the whole moiety of the lands above described, and receive a deed of the whole from the said board of treasury.[*]

It was resolved "that the above report and the proceedings of Dr. Cutler be fully approved, ratified and confirmed," and on the first of September it was ordered that the contract be closed. The same day the record shows that directors' and treasurer's bonds were entered into "in the sum of twenty thousand dollars each, at six shillings the Mexican dollar."

On the twenty-seventh of October, 1787, the contract was closed at New York, and signed by Samuel Osgood and Arthur Lee of the board of treasury of the United States, and Manasseh Cutler and Winthrop Sargent, for the Ohio company.[*] It was formed in all respects as foreshadowed by Dr. Cutler's report (which we have presented above), even to the provisions in regard to college, townships, and ministerial lands.

In this connection a letter from Manasseh Cutler to his son, Judge Ephraim Cutler, written as late as 1818, is very interesting. He says:

The fact is, the people of Ohio are wholly indebted to me for procuring the grant of those townships (for the university) and the minister's lands in the Ohio company's purchase; and, indeed, for similar grants in Judge Symmes' purchase. When I applied to Congress for the purchase, no person, to my knowledge, had an idea of asking for such grants. When I mentioned it to Mr. Sargent and others friendly to the measure, they were rather opposed, fearing it would occasion an increased price for the lands. I had previously contemplated the vast benefit that must be derived from it in a future time, and I made every exertion to obtain it. Mr. Sargent, indeed, cordially united with me in endeavoring to surmount the difficulties which appeared in the way, till the object was obtained. It is well known to all concerned with me in transacting the business of the Ohio company, that the establishment of a university was a first object and lay with great weight on my mind.[†]

---

* From the Ohio company's journal.
* The original contract is in the library of Marietta college.
†From William F. Poole's article in *North American Review*.

CHAPTER VII.

FROM NEW ENGLAND TO OHIO.

Preparations for Planting a Colony at the Mouth of the Muskingum.—Activity of Leaders in the Ohio Company.—Personal Persuasion.—Dissemination of Information Concerning the West.—A Pamphlet on the Ohio Country Published by Dr. Cutler in 1787.—Prediction that in Fifty Years the Northwestern Territory would Contain More People than all New England.—Prophecy that Western Rivers would be Navigated by Steamboats, Made Twenty Years before Fulton's Success on the Hudson.—Causes which Operated to Prevent Immigration.—Opposition Brought into Existence, and Taking the Form of Ridicule.—"Putnam's Paradise" and "Cutler's Indian Heaven."—Quotations from Cotemporaneous Correspondence of Hazard and Belknap.—Cutler and Sargent as Enthusiasts.—Various Inquiries in Regard to the West—Anxiety Regarding the Attitude of the Indians.—Letter from Washington to Lafayette.—Preparations of the Ohio Company as an Organization.—Plan Agreed upon for a City at the Confluence of the Muskingum and Ohio.—Scheme for the Division of the Lands.—Surveyors Employed.—Boat Builders and Mechanics.—General Rufus Putnam Appointed Superintendent of the Colony.—Meeting of the Company at Providence, Rhode Island.—Measures Taken for Securing Education and Religious Instruction in the New Settlement.—Boat Builders and Mechanics Leave Danvers, Massachusetts, December, 1787, for the Youghiogeny.—The Second Party Rendezvous at Hartford, Connecticut, January 1, 1788.—Putnam Detained by Business at New York.—He Overtakes the Party.—Crossing the Alleghanies in Winter.—Slow Progress and Privations of the Pioneers.—Arrival at the "Yoh."—Boats Built and Provisions Bought.—The "Mayflower."—The Company Leaves Sumrill's Ferry April 1st.—Extracts from the Journal of Joseph Buell.—Stopping by the Way.—Beauty of the Ohio.—Advancement of Vegetation.—Arrival at the Muskingum.—An Apochryphal Account of the Origin of the Term "Buckeye State."—Names of the Forty-seven Pioneers.

THE year 1787 was one full of doing and rich in result. The constitution of the United States was adopted, the Ordinance of Freedom enacted, and the Ohio company's purchase negotiated—the first of a series of transactions by which a revenue was obtained from the public domains to lessen the National debt and restore prosperity.

The year was a busy one with the leading men of the Ohio company. Both before and after the passage of the ordinance and the negotiation of the purchase, they were actively engaged in securing subscriptions and in finding men to go out to the Ohio country. General Putnam, General Tupper, General Parsons, Winthrop Sargent, and Dr. Cutler were using all of their influence to promote the affairs of the company, and to induce emigration. The latter was a difficult work. Personal persuasion was resorted to, and the public prints were used to disseminate knowledge concerning the west and the scheme for its settlement. Dr. Cutler published at Salem a pamphlet (though anonymously), which had a large circulation. It gave the fullest information attainable in regard to the lands beyond the Ohio, especially the Muskingum region, and contained some prophecies which were probably regarded as the wildest kind of improbabilities born of an imaginative brain, and yet nearly all that was said in the sanguine prophecies of Dr. Cutler, came to pass. He asserted that in fifty years the Northwestern Territory would contain more people than all New England, and that many people then living would see the western rivers navigated by steam. We find the following passage, copied from the original pamphlet:

The current down the Ohio and Mississippi, for heavy articles that suit the Florida and West India markets, such as Indian corn, flour, beef, lumber, etc., will be more loaded than any streams on earth. The distance from the Muskingum to the Mississippi is one thousand miles, from thence to the sea is nine hundred miles. The whole course is run in eighteen days, and the passage up these rivers is not so difficult as has been represented. It is found by late experiments that sails are used to great advantage against the current of the Ohio, and it is worthy of observation, that in all probability, steamboats will be found to do infinite service in all our river navigation.

This was written twenty years before Fulton's successful application of steam to navigation. But Miller, in Scotland, the same year that Dr. Cutler wrote, had demonstrated the practicability of the employment of steam for propelling boats. Dr. Cutler was a scientific man, in every way abreast of the age in which he lived—in many ways ahead of it. He doubtless knew of Miller's encouraging experiments, and his prediction regarding steamboats on the western rivers may have been principally based upon the achievement of that genius toiling on the other side of the Atlantic. But the people generally in that time, more than now, regarded the success of almost all novel and wonderful undertakings as impossible. There were doubtless many good New Englanders who regarded as an impracticable visionary the man who predicted steam navigation on the Ohio, and he was doubtless derided for this prophecy (if the authorship of the pamphlet was discovered) as he was for his zeal in advocating immigration.

After the purchase had been made preparations for removal to the Muskingum were carried on more actively than before, and as the time for an actual emigration approached, adverse criticism became more outspoken than it had been before.

There were various incentives to combat the movement that was steadily gaining ground. Families were divided as to opinions upon western settlement, and arguments arose between friends upon personal grounds as well as differences between factions. It must often have been the case that a father opposed his sons in their desire to seek their fortune in a new land, that wives opposed their husbands, and sweethearts their lovers. People who could not or would not emigrate, themselves very naturally disliked the idea of having their relatives and friends venture into the far west to find permanent homes. Opposition often took the form of ridicule. The enthusiasm with which the chief characters of the Ohio company labored to develop their plans, and the roseate-hued accounts that were given of the country to which a colony was to be sent, provoked some merriment and some sneering. The Ohio valley was dubbed "Putnam's Paradise" and "Cutler's Indian Heaven," and these and other names came into quite common use even among the men who were friendly to the movement these phrases were intended to ridicule. From the prominence in negotiating the purchase and his subsequent devotion to the Ohio company's interest, Dr. Cutler's name seemed to have been oftener mentioned in connection with the colonization movement than any other. Ebenezer Hazard,* writing to the

---

*Hon. Ebenezer Hazard was at this time Postmaster General and Treasurer of Congress. The Rev. Jeremy Belknap was in 1787 pastor of a church in Boston. Both were quite eminent historians. Their correspondence has been published.

Rev. Jeremy Belknap in 1787, says: "Cutler and Sargent are enthusiasts in the cause; and really, some degree of enthusiasm is necessary in all great undertakings." As the time drew nigh when the Ohio company was to send out the pioneers the people became more and more familiar with the subject of emigration, which was then a new one in Massachusetts and her sister states, and people began to make intelligent inquiries in regard to the country toward which the movement was directed, and the prospects of peace or war with the Indians. In a letter from Belknap to Hazard the writer after speaking of the lawlessness and vindictiveness of the Kentuckians, propounds the queries:

Whether the neighborhood of such a set of rascals will not be injurious to the Muskingum? Will the Indians make a distinction if the New England people should behave themselves differently towards them? Have they a good title from the Indians to the land? Or, if they have from some, will not others put in a claim?

Similar questions to these were doubtless asked by hundreds. Mr. Hazard writes that he "should not be fond of going there (to Muskingum) before the settlers had enjoyed one year's profound peace." There were many who were of this way of thinking. But notwithstanding danger, there were a few who had decided to be of the first company of adventurers, many more who had determined to go later, after a beginning had been effected, and it appears that in September, 1787, at least two families were on their journey to the Ohio company's purchase, though they must have fallen by the way as they did not reach their destination. On the twenty-ninth of the month Mr. Hazard wrote to Mr. Belknap:

Two families from Cutler's parish, Sawyer and Porter, by name, passed through here yesterday on their way to this Indian Heaven, with two or three wagons, built in the western styles. Some people pitied them as sheep going to the slaughter; others wished themselves in company, so different are the opinions of men, and I might add, women on the subject.

Mr. Hazard himself thought favorably of the Ohio company. He wrote:

I have thoughts of hiring a farm and retiring into the woods, where I may at least enjoy liberty, and that not without some hopes of independence, and Cutler's Indian Heaven (where I own a seat) has been more than half seriously in contemplation.

What Washington thought of the emigration scheme of some of his old officers and brother patriots is shown by a letter he wrote February 7, 1787, to Lafayette:

A spirit of emigration to the western country is very predominant Congress has sold in the year past a pretty large quantity of lands on the Ohio for public securities, and thereby diminished the public debt considerably. Many of your military acquaintances, such as Generals Parsons, Varnum and Putnam, Colonels Tupper, Sproat and Sherman, with many more, propose settling there. From such beginnings much may be expected.[*]

While individual efforts were being made to induce emigration, and with the result of producing a very general interest in the subject, the Ohio company as an organization was engaged in measures of practical preparation for the great work that lay before its members. On the thirtieth of August, 1787 (the day after Dr. Cutler had made his verbal report of the action of Congress in granting him the refusal of the lands), the company roughly mapped out upon paper the city near the conflu-

ence of the Muskingum and Ohio, which was to be Marietta. Five thousand seven hundred and sixty acres were to be reserved for the city and common. It was resolved that "within the said tract and in the most eligible situation there be appropriated sixty squares, in an oblong form of ten squares in front and six deep, with streets one hundred feet in width; that four of the said squares be reserved for public use, and the remaining fifty-six divided into house lots, each to contain twelve of sixty feet front and one hundred feet depth, and six of fifty-three feet front by one hundred and fifty feet depth, amounting in the total to one thousand and eight lots." This plan was to be followed as nearly as the situation of the ground would permit. (It was afterwards changed considerably.) It was also decided that the lots should be drawn for, and that each one should become a part of each proprietary share. It was further resolved that one hundred houses should be built, thirty-six by sixteen feet in dimensions, on three sides of one of the oblong squares, and that for their protection they should be connected or surrounded by a stockade. (Here is the first suggestion of Campus Martius.) At this meeting General James M. Varnum was elected a director, and Richard Platt, of New York, treasurer. The meeting was continued to the first of September, and on November 21st (the contract having been closed October 27th), another meeting was held, at Cromwell's Head tavern, Boston, for the consideration of various important details in the arrangements. At this meeting the plan of the proposed city was altered by the insertion of a provision that the lots should be ninety feet front by one hundred and eighty in depth, and that the centre street should be one hundred and fifty feet in width. The following resolutions were adopted, a part of which never came into effect, because the lands to which they would have applied never came into the possession of the company:

Resolved—That the lands of the Ohio company may be allotted and divided in the following manner, anything to the contrary in former resolutions notwithstanding, viz: Four thousand acres near the confluence of the Muskingum and Ohio rivers for a city and commons and contiguous to this, one thousand lots of eight acres each, amounting to eight thousand acres.

Upon the Ohio in fractional townships, one thousand lots of one hundred and sixteen and forty-three one hundredths acres, amounting to one hundred and sixteen thousand four hundred and eighty acres.

In the townships on the navigable rivers, one thousand lots of three hundred and and twenty acres each, amounting to three hundred and twenty thousand acres.

And in the inland towns one thousand lots of nine hundred and ninety-two acres each, amounting to nine hundred and ninety-two thousand acres, to be divided and allotted as the agents shall hereafter direct.

Resolved, further, That there be the following reservations, viz: One township at the falls of the Great Hockhocking river; one township at the mouth of the Great and Little river of that name, and one township opposite the mouth of the Great Kanawha river; which reservations may be allotted and decided as the directors and agents shall see fit.

Resolved. That the army bounty rights be considered in part payment of the shares of military associates in the ratio of one dollar to every acre to which they are entitled; and that this rule be observed by the agents of the subscribers in rendering their returns, and by the agents appointed by the directors for the several payments to the board of treasury.

Resolved. That no further subscriptions be admitted after the first day of January next, and that all interest, arising on sums paid since the payment of the first half-million to the board of treasury, until the second payment be completed, shall accrue to the benefit of the com-

---

[*] Sparks' Life of Washington, volume 19, page 319.

pany's funds; and that the agents pay all the money they may have in their possession into the treasury of the company by the first day of March next.

Resolved. That the eight acre lots be surveyed and a plat or map thereof be made, with each lot numbered thereon, by the first Wednesday in March next, and that a copy thereof be immediately forwarded to the secretary and the original retained by the companys superintendent; that the agents meet on the first Wednesday in March next, at Rice's tavern, in Providence, State of Rhode Island, to draw for said lots in numbers, as the same shall be stated upon the plat; that a list of the drawings be transmitted by the secretary to the superintendent, and a copy thereof preserved in the secretary's office.

Resolved. That this meeting of the directors and agents of the Ohio company be and is hereby adjourned to the first Wednesday in March, 1788, to be then holden at Rice's tavern, in the town of Providence, and State of Rhode Island.

Although the company had adjourned to meet in March the directors and agents came together again only two days later, or upon the twenty-third of November, at Brackett's tavern, where the following decisions were agreed upon and placed on file in the company's records:

Ordered. That four surveyors be employed under the superintendent hereinafter named, that twenty-two men shall attend the surveyors; that there be added to this number twenty men, including six boat-builders, four house carpenters, one blacksmith, and nine common workmen.

That the boat-builders shall proceed on Monday next, and the surveyors shall rendezvous at Hartford the first day of January next, on their way to the Muskingum.

That the boat-builders and men, with the surveyors, be proprietors in the company; that their tools and one axe and one hoe to each man and thirty pounds weight of baggage shall be carried in the company's wagons, and the subsistence of the men on the journey be furnished by the company.

That upon their arrival at the places of destination, and entering on the business of their employment, the men shall be subsisted by the company and allowed wages at the rate of four dollars each per month until discharged.

That they be held in the company's service until the first day of July next, unless sooner discharged, and that if any of the persons employed shall leave the service, or wilfully injure the same, or disobey the orders of the superintendent, or others acting under him, the person so offending shall forfeit all claim to wages,

That their wages shall be paid the next autumn in cash, or lands, upon the same terms as the company purchased them. That each man furnish himself with a good small-arm bayonet, six flints, a powder-horn and pouch, priming wire and brush, half a pound of powder, one pound of balls, and one pound of buckshot. The men so engaged shall be subject to the orders of the superintendent and those he may appoint, as aforesaid, in any kind of business they shall be employed in, as well for boat building and surveying, as for building houses, erecting defences, clearing lands, and planting, or otherwise, for promoting the settlement; and as there is a probability of interruption from enemies, they shall also be subject to orders as aforesaid in military command during the time of their employment.

That Colonel Ebenezer Sproat, from Rhode Island; Mr. Anselem Tupper, and Mr. John Mathews, from Massachusetts, and Colonel R. J. Meigs, from Connecticut, be the surveyors.

That General Rufus Putnam be the superintendent of all the business aforesaid, and he is to be obeyed and respected accordingly; that he be allowed for his services forty dollars a month and his expenses, to commence from the time of his leaving home.*

On March 5th the directors and agents assembled pursuant to adjournment, at Rice's tavern, Providence, Rhode Island, General Parsons being chairman. On this occasion the lots of the city (on paper) at the mouth of the Muskingum, were drawn for in the names of the proprietors, each share being entitled to one. One thousand shares were represented, the agents and the number of proprietary shares they represented being as fol-

lows: Edward Harris, forty; John May, thirty-five; Eliphalet Day, eighteen; Manasseh Cutler, one hundred and fifty-one; William Dodge, seventeen; Ephraim Cutler, nineteen; Winthrop Sargeant, one hundred and sixty-six; Benjamin Tupper, thirty-seven; Henry Jackson, thirteen; William Corliss, one hundred and twelve; Nathaniel Freeman, twelve; Rufus Putnam, sixty-two; S. H. Parsons, ninety-nine; Joel Barlow, twenty-seven; Archibald Crary, one hundred and two; Ebenezer Sproat, forty-three; Benjamin Tallmadge, forty-seven—one thousand.

A number of the agents mentioned were represented, as were of course the proprietors, by proxies. While this business was being transacted the pioneer party were on their way to the Muskingum country.

By far the most important measure acted upon at this meeting was that looking toward the establishment of schools and churches. The action was of importance in itself, and doubly interesting as showing the spirit of the men who formed the New England Ohio company. It was in exact accordance with the desires exhibited by Dr. Cutler in the ordinance and conditions of purchase. A committee was appointed "to consider the expediency of employing some suitable person as a public teacher at the settlement now making by the Ohio company." Its members were Dr. Cutler, General Varnum, and Colonel John May. They made a report in the following language:

That the directors be requested to pay as early attention as possible to the education of youth and the promotion of public worship among the first settlers; and that, for these important services, they employ, if practicable, an instructor eminent for literary accomplishments and the virtue of his character, who shall also superintend the first scholastic institutions, and direct the manner of instruction; and to enable the directors to carry into execution the intentions expressed in this resolution, the proprietors, and others of benevolent and liberal minds are earnestly requested to contribute, by voluntary donation, to the formation of a fund to be solely appropriated thereto.*

Prior to the later transactions we have chronicled the Ohio company's party of pioneers were on their way to the Muskingum. The first party, consisting of twenty-two men, and including the boat-builders and mechanics, started from Danvers, Massachusetts, on the first of December, 1787.† They were under the command of Major Haffield White, who seems also to have been commissary, and were sent ahead to build boats on the Youghiogheny which, in western parlance, was commonly called the "Yoh." The advance company arrived at Sumrill's Ferry on this stream (about thirty miles above Pittsburgh), on the twenty-third of January, after a wearisome journey.

The other party, including the surveyors and their assistants and a number of the proprietors of the Ohio company, rendezvoused at Hartford, Connecticut, on the first of January, 1788. They were met here by General Putnam who was to have commanded the march, but as he was under the necessity of going to New York, the

---

† The Ohio company's journal.

* It was under the provisions of this resolution that the Rev. Daniel Story was employed and sent to the Ohio company's settlement, as the first ordained minister in the Northwest Territory. His character and services are spoken of at length in the chapter on the churches of Marietta.

† Autobiography of General Rufus Putnam (MS).

company went forward in command of Colonel Ebenezer Sproat. General Putnam dispatching his business at New York, pressed forward and overtook the company at Lincoln's inn on the Lanterdale creek, January 24th. In his autobiography General Putnam says that this creek "was hard frozen, but not sufficient to bear the wagon, and a whole day was spent in cutting a passage. So great a quanity of snow fell this day and night, as quite blocked up the road; it was with much difficulty we got the wagon so far as Coopers, at the foot of the Tuscarawas mountains (now Strawsburg), where we arrived the twenty-ninth." As serious an obstacle to the progress of the pioneers as the snow had been up to this time it was much worse in the mountains. General Putnam says that they "found nothing had crossed the mountains since the great snow and in the old snow, twelve inches deep, nothing but pack horses." But the march of these resolute, hardy men toward their destination was not to be stayed by storm or the almost impossible condition of the narrow winding mountain trails which were dangerous enough at any time. "Our only resource" reads the brief, and simple narrative, "was to build sleds, and harness tandem, and in this manner with four sleds, and men marching in front, we set forward and reached "Yoh" the fourteenth of February.

For two weeks the little company consisting of a few more than a score of men, but all active, strong and hopeful, were winding slowly around the mountain passes, breaking a way through the deep snow for their jaded horses to draw along the cumbersome sledges with their heavy loads of baggage and provisions. Only a few miles were gained each day and that with the utmost toil. At night the men slept around huge blazing fires, which they often had difficulty in kindling. They suffered much from the arduousness of their labor by day and their exposure at night. General Putnam writing to Dr. Cutler some time after the arrival of the pioneers at the Muskingum said: "It would give you pain and me no pleasure to detail our march over the mountains or our delays afterwards on account of bad weather or other misfortunes."

Arriving at the Youghiogheny in the middle of February, and expecting to find preparations so far advanced for the journey down the Ohio that they could soon start, General Putnam and his associates were again disappointed. It is stated in the same letter from which we have quoted above, that there were "no boats built, no boards or planks in readiness, or person capable of building a canoe, much less a boat, among the party— mill froze up and no boards to be had. He (Major White) had, however, three canoes such as they were, on the stocks; and five of his men were sick with the small-pox, which they took by inoculation."

The latter part of February and the whole of the month of March was consumed in building boats. The three canoes which Major White had on the stocks were completed, and lumber being brought from a considerable distance a galley was built, which had an estimated capacity of fifty tons, and a flatboat of about three tons burthen, designed to be used as a ferry boat by the set-

tlers at the station, and was named the Adelphia. The canoes were hewn from logs. The large boat, which was called the Adventure Galley, and which General Putnam speaks of as the Union Galley, was afterwards appropriately named the Mayflower, in commemoration of the ship which brought across the ocean the Plymouth colony. Her bows were raking or curved; she was decked over and strongly built throughout. She was designed to pass and repass between Marietta and Buffalo creek or Cross creek, to carry letters and merchandise, but proving too large and unwieldy she was used only for a few trips.

In the afternoon of the first day* of April, which was a Tuesday, the little flotilla left Sumrill's ferry, on the Youghiogheny, and, floating down that stream to the Monongahela, was borne onward to the Ohio. Several stoppages were made to take on provisions, which had been bought the few weeks previous and brought to the river. Among other stores were "three thousand weight of flour, two thousand of which was at nine shillings a hundred, and one thousand at ten shillings, or one dollar sixty-six cents," bought of one man, and seven thousand pounds of another at the price last mentioned, also several bushels of beans. Many of the purchases were made by John Mathews, a nephew of General Putnam, who had been in the west since the summer of 1786 as a surveyor. Numerous extracts from his journal have been given in a former chapter of this work, and we now present several more, which, however unimportant, are interesting as contemporary jottings in regard to the journey of the colony:

Thursday, April 3rd. . . General Putnam arrived with coals at the mouth af Harman's creek before sunrise, and not being acquainted, fell some below the landing. Esquire Foster and myself attended to getting the provisions to the river, and a very disagreeable time we had of it, on account of the rain. I am to take General Putnam's horse by land to Buffalo tomorrow.

Friday, 4th. I left Greathouse's in the morning. Found Colonel Sprout at McMahan's, and rode with him to Wells' mills, and hurried on the provisons to the landing. From thence we went to the mouth of Buffalo, where the boat had arrived. She will not be loaded to-day.

Saturday, 5th. . . . Our boats tarried all day in the mouth of the creek, and we have everything to put on board in the morning. They also took on here a quantity of poplar boards for the erection of temporary huts, until more substatial buildings could be built.

Sunday, 6th Cloudy and rainy all day. At half past eight o'clock A. M. everything on board, and we started for Muskingum. . . . At four o'clock P. M. came to at "Round Bottom" and proposed waiting until nine or ten o'clock in the evening, in order to arrive at Muskingum in the forenoon. At half-past nine got under way and run all night, without meeting with any accident.

One may imagine something of the feelings of those first adventurers to Ohio as they floated down *la belle riviere*. The season was well advanced and there was a noticeable difference between the condition of the vegetation in the country passed on the last half of the journey and that of the upper Ohio. The forest which clad the hills was etherialized by the first touch of kindly spring and the virgin soil of the many beautiful islands was

---

* In Hildreth' Pioneer History and Charles M. Walker's History of Athens County, it is stated that the journey from the Youghiogheny was begun upon the second of April. General Putnam's autobiography is authority for the statement that it was upon the first.

mantled with the vernal green of scores of luxuriant shrubs and grasses and vines, strange to the eyes which now beheld them. The shores were for the most part devoid of the indications of human life. Only upon the Virginia side did the voyagers see an occasional cabin, and they lost even the slight sense of companionship that these afforded as they drew nearer to their destination, so that they looked with even more of joy than they otherwise would upon the rough log buildings and bristling stockade of Fort Harmar, and the little cabins of Isaac Williams and his fellow pioneers on the Virginia bank. As their boats swept around the curves and new landscapes were revealed how eagerly must those pioneers have watched for the first appearance of the place that was to be their home, the lands that some of them were individually to own, till, live and die upon. We can imagine groups of questioners gathered about John Mathews and Anselem Tupper, the only men in the company who had any personal knowledge of the "lands at the confluence of the Muskingum and Ohio," on which it had been decided far away in Massachusetts that a city should be built.

The morning of the seventh of April (which was Monday) was cloudy and during the greater part of the day rain fell. As the afternoon passed away the pioneers knew that the place of their destination could not be far away, and watched closely for some sign which would indicate it. Just as they had floated by the foot of Kerr's Island Captain Devol said to General Putnam, "I think it is time to take an observation; we must be near the mouth of the Muskingum." The current bore the boats onward at a good speed, and although many eyes were watching anxiously for the Muskingum they did not see it until too late to round into the harbor it afforded. The rain and fog and the huge sycamores upon the banks leaning over the outlet obscured it, undoubtedly, until they were quite near it. Fort Harmar was also unseen. The strong current of the Muskingum swerved the boats from their course, shot them way out into the Ohio, and before the pioneers were fully conscious of their whereabouts they had swept so far down the stream that they were unable to regain the place where they had intended to disembark. A landing was affected not far below the fort, and the commandant, Major Doughty sending some soldiers to their aid General Putnam's little band towed the boats up the stream, and, crossing the Muskingum, landed upon the site of Marietta (at the point) about noon.*

* It is traditionally asserted that in an episode which speedily followed the landing at Marietta originated the application to the early settlers of the name "Buckeyes," which afterwards became a kind of genuine appellation for all the people of Ohio, and led in fact to the second christening of the first commonwealth of the Northwest Territory with the sobriquet of "the Buckeye State."

It has been frequently related that two of the pioneers on springing ashore at the point, selected trees to be felled to the earth, and began a good-natured rivalry in chopping to see which one should first lay low a monarch of the forest. Strict regard for probability compels one to doubt whether either tree could with propriety be called a "monarch." They were undoubtedly about the smallest trees discoverable which were still large enough to have passed the undignified age of saplings. But however this may have been does not effect the story. One man selected, according to the tradition, a hard wood tree—a gum tree—and

They were welcomed by a party of about seventy Wyandot and Delaware Indians, warriors, women, and children, of whom the famous Captain Pipe was the principal character. The pioneers undoubtedly looked upon this friendly greeting as an omen of peace and good-will and their vague fears were tranquillized. The work of landing a portion of their provisions and the boards brought from Buffalo creek for the erection of temporary places of shelter was begun immediately, and General Putnam's large tent, known as a marquee,* was soon riased.

The pioneers who arrived on the "Mayflower" at the site of Marietta, were forty-seven† in number, and their names are embraced in the following list:

* This marquee was a very large one, and was taken, with some other baggage, on board the store boats of Burgoyne's army, a few days before its surrender, by the intrepidity of Major Goodall, who was attached to General Putnam's regiment. It had probably belonged to some of the general officers of the enemy. In the division of the spoils it fell to General Putnam, and now, eleven years after that event, was doing service on the banks of the Ohio, in the far wilderness of the Northwest Territory. . . *New England Historical and Genealogical Register*, October, 1860 Note to journal of Rev. Manasseh Cutler (Journey to Marietta, 1788), by Dr S P. Hildreth.

† The number is commonly stated as forty-eight. Colonel Return Jonathan Meigs, however, who is usually included in the list and who was really with the pioneer party on the upper Ohio, is shown by Joseph Buell in his journal, and by other authorities, to have arrived on the twelfth of April.

the other, a buckeye, the wood of which is very soft. Very naturally the buckeye fell first to the ground, and from this circumstance its name is said to have been given to the settlers and to the State. The successful man is said to have been Captain Daniel Davis, of Killingly, Connecticut The chief champion of the story has been a New England clergyman of the Reformed Episcopal church, J P. Davis, by name, who had been engaged in compiling a genealogy of the Davis family, and who, when in Ohio in 1879, made several contributions to the newspapers upon this subject. He accounts for the fact that Ohio is called "the Buckeye State," and its people "Buckeyes" by the result of the chopping competition, and supports the authenticity of the story handed down from one generation to another by the statement that "during ninety years it has not been contradicted by any history or denied by any counter-statement "

In this the reverend writer was mistaken, not only has a counter-statement been made, but it was published many years ago, and by a most excellent authority, Dr S. P. Hildreth. In his biography of Colonel Ebenezer Sproat, he says that his "tall commanding person, . . . soon attracted their (the Indians) attention, and they gave him the name of *Hetuck*, or Big Buckeye. From this, no doubt, originated the name of buckeye, now applied to the natives of Ohio, as the phrase was familiar to all the early settlers at Marietta. The name was commonly used at as early a date as 1791. Thus it appeared that Dr. Hildreth, himself a resident of Marietta, early in the present century, writing many years ago—prior at least to 1852—when he had exceptionally good advantages for gleaning items of pioneer history, either knew nothing of the Davis story or regarded it so doubtful as not to be entitled to a place in either of his two volumes made up of the minutiæ of early local occurrences. Still the Davis story may be true.

Standing against its plausibility, however, is the common trend of evidence, afforded by a number of early pioneers who have left accounts of the application of the term Buckeye. Some of them seem to have had knowledge of the Davis tradition, but their explanations agree with, rather than contradict, Dr. Hildreth's statement. Briefly to summarize what has been given as the opinion of many of the pioneers and their descendants, we may say that the company of forty-seven, the first settlers of Marietta, arrived early in a well-advanced spring; that the flowers of the Buckeye were the first that met their sight, and from this circumstance they may have called the country in which they had taken up their residence Buckeye land or Buckeye settlement, or alluded to themselves as Buckeyes, from the fact that they appeared simultaneously with the blossoms of these trees. Again, it has been suggested by some that because of the tall, erect forms, and the soldierly bearing

General Rufus Putnam, superintendent of the colony.

Colonel Ebenezer Sproat, Major Anselem Tupper, and John Mathews, surveyors.

Major Haffield White, steward and quartermaster.

Captain Jonathan Devol.	Jervis Cutler.
" 　Josiah Munroe.	Samuel Cushing.
" 　Daniel Davis.	Daniel Bushnell.
" 　Peregrine Foster.	Ebenezer Corry.
" 　Jethro Putnam.	Oliver Dodge.
" 　William Gray.	Isaac Dodge.
" 　Ezekiel Cooper.	Jabez Barlow.
Phineas Coburn.	Allen Putnam.
David Wallace.	Joseph Wells.
Gilbert Devol, jr.	Israel Danton.
Jonas Davis.	Samuel Felshaw.
Hezekiah Flint.	Amos Porter, jr.
Josiah Whitridge.	John Gardner.
Benjamin Griswold.	Elizur Kirtland.
Theophilus Leonard.	Joseph Lincoln.
William Miller.	Earl Sproat.
Josiah White.	Allen Devol.
Henry Maxon.	William Mason.
William Moulton.	Simeon Martin.
Benjamin Shaw.	Peletiah White.

These men, on Monday, the seventh of April, 1788, made the first lawful, organized English settlement within the limits of the great Northwest Territory.

of many of those pioneers of 1788, the Indians may have called them Buckeyes, or given them the appellation in their language equivalent to that term, after that species of tree, which is notably tall and perfectly straight. Or, the name might have been given by the Indians on account of the time of their advent. Either of these motives for the bestowal of the name would have been in entire accordance with the poetical and descriptive system of Indian nomenclature. The name having once been applied in a general way, it followed naturally that Colonel Sproat, who "towered like a Saul, a full head above the height of other men," should have been dubbed by the Indians as Dr. Hildreth says, the Big Buckeye.

There is another possibility. Muskingum (originally Mooskingom) means Elks Eye river. May it not also have been called Bucks Eye or *Buckeye* river, and the name have been either adopted by the settlers at its mouth, or applied to them by the Indians?

It has been very generally believed that Jervis Cutler, son of Dr. Manasseh Cutler, was the first one of the forty-seven to jump ashore at the mouth of the Muskingum, but upon the *west or Fort Harmar side*. He there cut down a small tree with a small axe which he drew from his coat.

When the boat reached the east or Marietta side of the Muskingum, it is said Allen Putnam and Amos Porter had a race, and both made desperate leaps to see who should have the honor of first putting foot on the shore. Putnam won, springing on to the bank five seconds ahead of Porter, and so was the first pioneer who landed at Marietta.

CHAPTER VIII.

PROGRES OF SETTLEMENT AND IMPROVEMENT.

The Farmers Delighted with their New Home.—Bright Prospects.—General Putnam to Dr. Cutler.—Washington's Opinion of the Colony.—Hopes Disappointed.—Combination of Adverse Circumstances.—Opposition ·to Emigration in New England from various motives.—Fear of Indian Hostility.—Derision of the West by Wits and Wags.—Parodies upon Panegyrics.—Caricatures Published.—"I am going to Ohio" and "I have been to Ohio."—Employment of the Settlers During the first Season Clearing Land, Planting and Surveying.—The Great Cornfield.—Uneasiness Regarding the Attitude of the Indians.—The Building of Campus Martius.—Dwelling-Houses.—New Arrivals in the Colony.—The first Families.—General Arthur St. Clair Governor of the Territory.—His Formal Reception at the "Bowery."—Opening of the first Court.—Proceedings of the Ohio Company.—Troubles Respecting Section Twenty-nine.—The "City" and the Ancient Works Named.—Measures for the Encouragement of Settlement.—A Plan for Donating Lands Agreed Upon.—Lots of One Hundred Acres Each to be given Actual Settlers.—A Committee Appointed to Explore the Purchase and Select Locations for Settlements.—The first Offshoots of the Original Colony.—Belpre and Waterford.—Wolf Creek Mills.—Settlements at Big Bottom, Meigs' Creek, and the Forks of Duck Creek.—Measures for the Encouragement of Improvements.—Kindly and Protective Policy of the Ohio Company.—Loans Made to Needy Settlers.—General Putnam's Contract with the Scioto Company.—Houses Built at Gallipolis.—Arrival of Four Hundred French Emigrants.—Their Pitiable Condition.—Number of Men and Families in the Ohio Company's Territory.—Complete List of Arrivals During 1788, 1789, and 1790.

THE members of the little pioneer company who landed from the Mayflower April 7th, and the few who followed them to the Muskingum during the early months of the season, found much to delight them, and were happy in the midst of their strange surroundings. Doubtless there were some who felt at times the comparative isolation and loneliness of their condition, and whose minds fondly and sadly reverted to the friends they had left behind them, and the old familiar scenes—the happy homes—in little New England villages. But such feelings were transitory. There was food for other thought in the busy bustling life of the new colony—the activity impelled by varied human interests. The forest was to be cleared away, the ground was to be titled, seed planted, houses built, preparations made for the reception of loved ones who could not immigrate with their husbands and fathers, and who were looking eagerly forward for a reunion with them in the land of their adoption. And so these pioneers labored with a zest and earnestness of purpose which doubled their accomplishment. To them the country seemed all that was desirable. There was a suggestion of New England in the rugged hills which surrounded them, and a fertility in the soil of the valleys which they had never seen equalled. Their new life, or the new chapter in life, had opened auspiciously, and the future appeared bright with promise.

Gen. Putnam wrote to Dr. Cutler, about the middle of May: "The men are generally in good health, and I believe much pleased with the country; that I am so myself you may rest assured. I can only add, the situation of the city plat is the most delightful of any I ever saw." And another of the colonists said: "This country, for fertility of soil and pleasantness of situation, not only exceeds my expectations, but exceeds any part of Europe or America I ever was in."

The prospects of the colony were as fair as its best

CAMPUS MARTIUS 1791

friends could have wished. The aspect of its affairs appeared promising alike to those immediately interested and to those who were outsiders. George Washington wrote from Mt. Vernon on the nineteenth of June, 1788, to Richard Henderson, an inquirer in regard to western lands, the following eulogium of the Ohio company's settlement:

No colony in America was ever settled under such favorable auspices as that which has just commenced at the Muskingum. Information, property, strength, will be its characteristics. I know many of the settlers, personally, and there never were men better calculated to promote the welfare of such a community. If I was a young man, just preparing to begin the world, or if in advanced life and had a family to make a provision for, I know of no country where I should rather fix my habitation than in some part of the region for which the writer of the queries seems to have a predilection.*

But notwithstanding the qualifications of these men of whom Washington wrote in glowing terms; in spite of the fair prospect which opened before the Ohio company, no one of the characteristics mentioned in the letter except "information" was soon to be possessed by the settlement began April 7, 1788, at the Muskingum. "Property and strength" were attained very slowly and only through a long, hard struggle. With its splendid organization, systematic methods and capable men, the Ohio company, there was every reason to believe, would rapidly develop its purchase and present every aspect of thrift and prosperity in its settlements. But there was a great disparity between the actual results achieved and the sanguine expectations which the pioneers indulged The period of five years of Indian war, which closely followed the inauguration of the settlement, was the principal preventive of progress. Other causes conspired to retard the fulfilment of well grounded hopes. The failure of the Scioto company doubtless led some people to mistrust the ability of the Ohio company to carry out its plans, and the organization suffered in some degree from unwise elements in its own policy, from the failure of its treasurer and from the strong opposition to western settlement which was aroused in New England. When all of the unusual obstacles which lay in the way of the company are considered in addition to those which are common to pioneer life, the small advancement of the colony during the first ten or twenty years of its existence does not seem strange, but on the other hand there is cause for wonder that the New Englanders in Ohio were not completely and irretrievably overwhelmed.

Relegating to subsequent chapters the sad story of the Indian war, the cessation of improvement and the embarrassment of the Ohio company, which was caused by it, we shall endeavor to give an idea of the earlier impediments to progress and of what was accomplished anterior to 1791. And, that the reader may more thoroughly understand why the increase in population was so small, comparatively, during the earliest years of the settlement, before the Indian war had opened in earnest, let us turn again to glance at the condition of public feeling in Massachusetts. It is a question whether the worst results of the Indian war would not have been averted had not the undue fear of that war restrained emigration.

In other words, if the progress of settlement had not been stayed by the dread of Indian hostilities, would not the Ohio company's colony have become strong enough by 1791 to have passed in perfect safety through the period of five years succeeding. The exact effect upon emigration of the few Indian depredations and hostilities prior to 1791 cannot be known, but the exaggerated stories of border barbarities circulated in New England must have served to keep many a would-be pioneer at home.

But the uncertainty in regard to the attitude of the Indians, at first, and the terror created by the appalling colors in which at a later day pictures of their incursions were painted, were by no means the only agencies operating against emigration.

One of the most potent of the causes tending to defeat the full accomplishment of the Ohio company's plans was the ridicule of western emigration in New England. Timothy Flint, a Massachusetts man, personally acquainted with many of the Ohio company settlers, in his little book on the west,* has the following paragraph describing the feeling which had an existence in the region in which he dwelt:

The first travellers to explore Ohio availed themselves of the full extent of the traveller's privilege in regard to the wonders of this new land of promise and the unparalleled fertility of the soil. These extravagant representations of the grandeur of the vegetation and the fertility of the land at first excited a great desire to emigrate to this new and wonderful region But some returned with different accounts, in discouragement . A reaction took place in the public mind.

The wags of the day exercised their wit in circulating caricatured and exaggerated editions of the stories of the first adventurers, that there were springs of brandy, flax that bore little pieces of cloth on the stems, enormous pumpkins, and melons and the like. Accounts the most horrible were added of hoop snakes of such deadly malignity that a sting which they bore in their tails, when it punctured the bark of a green tree, instantly caused its leaves to become sear and the tree to die. Stories of Indian massacres and barbarities were related in all their horrors The country was admitted to be fertile, but was pronounced excessively sickly, and poorly balancing by that advantage all these counterpoises of sickness, Indians, copper-headed and hoop snakes, bears, wolves and panthers

Much of derision seems to have been directed against Dr. Cutler, no doubt because he was a leading man in the Ohio company and because he was an enthusiast. The author from whom we have already quoted, says:

Dr. Cutler, at the time of his being engaged in the speculation of the Ohio company's purchase, had a feud—it is not remembered whether literary, political or religious—with the late learned and eccentric Dr. Bently, of Salem, Massachusetts Dr. Bently was the chief contributor to a paper, which he afterward edited. The writer still remembers, and can repeat doggerel verses by Dr Bently upon the departure of Dr Cutler on his first trip to explore his purchase on the Ohio.

Very interesting reading indeed, would these verses make for the present generation of the men of the west.

One word said against the western country had doubtless more effect than ten said in its favor, and so the few people who returned from the settlement of the Muskingum may have done much to prevent others from journeying thither. One of them, Theophilus Knight, an adventurer to the west in the summer of 1788, said that himself and two companions returned because they did not think "it was so much better than any other country that it would pay a man for carrying a large family to such a

---

*Spark's Life of Washington, volume IX, page 385.

* Indian Wars of the West, page 144.

wilderness, inhabited by savages and wild beasts of the forest."

At a later period than that of which we have written the opposition to emigration was increased rather than diminished, and derision of the Government and its friends became more general, more outspoken and more broad. It assumed in fact the form of burlesque. One early resident* of Ohio has said:

The powerful engine of caricature was set in motion. I have a distinct recollection of a picture I saw in boyhood, prefixed to a penny anti-moving-to-Ohio pamphlet, in which a stout, ruddy, well-dressed man on a sleek, fat horse, with a label "I am going to Ohio," meets a pale and ghastly skeleton of a man, scarcely half dressed, on the wreck of what was once a horse, already bespoken by the more politic crows, with a label "I have been to Ohio."

The attention of the little band of pioneers, who landed at the Muskingum the seventh of April, 1788, was first directed to the building of small cabins or huts for shelter. These were in part constructed of the poplar boards brought from Buffalo creek, and they were of the smallest and rudest kind which would afford any protection from the weather; for a more important work than building comfortable or commodious houses lay before the company. They had to make preparations for those whom they expected soon to arrive, and also to sow and plant that they might have a harvest for their maintenance in the autumn.

The survey was commenced on the ninth of April that the lots might be ready to assign to the new immigrants as soon as they should arrive.

Colonel Ebenezer Sproat and John Mathews, with thirteen men, engaged in this work, but their progress was slow, as General Putnam wrote to a friend, "because of rainy weather and their being obliged to survey so much more land than was expected in order to obtain lands suitable to the purpose. They did not complete their work of laying off the necessary lots until the middle of May. At that time General Putnam wrote: "The city lots will be ready to draw by the first Wednesday of July, as proposed at the meeting in Providence, but the others will not."

While the surveyors were carrying on their work, the remainder of the men were engaged under the immediate supervision of General Putnam in clearing land and deadening timber. The first clearing was at the point, on the east side of the Muskingum, and it is there that the first houses were built. In six days as many acres were cleared, though of course roughly. The forest fell fast under the blows of a score of axes, and by the latter part of May the greater part of the land had been planted. Several small pieces of ground cleared by individual labor — by the several proprietors who were of the pioneer company, or who had arrived later in the spring—had been planted earlier. But the great cornfield, planted for the common good of the colony, cleared and made ready for a crop by the men in the employ of the Ohio company, was not seeded until the time designated. It included nearly or perhaps quite an hundred

and thirty acres, and the settlers were gratified at the richness of the soil which was exhibited by the rapid growth of this fine crop. One letter writer chronicled the fact that "the corn has grown nine inches in twenty-four hours, for two or three days past." It was of this cornfield of which Dr. Cutler, when visiting the colony in August, said: "It astonished me on account of its magnitude. I should be as soon lost in it on a cloudy day as in a cedar swamp." The field occupied a portion of the high plain back of the site of Campus Martius (which was not built until after the crop was planted) and extended southward towards the Ohio, so as to include in its limits the great mound. It must not be understood that all of this land was cleared. In a portion of it the trees were deadened by girdling, and the leaves remaining upon some of them so shaded the ground as to interfere with the growth of the crop. Only about one-third of the field was plowed or harrowed, the rest being broken up for planting with hoes. Very little besides corn was raised the first season.* The other crops planted were chiefly those of the garden, and were grown in small quantity. Beans and potatoes were the principal of these.

During all the time that the labor of surveying, clearing and planting land was going on, we may imagine that the pioneers found much beside to interest them, and to form subjects for conversation. The ancient works with their far extending walls, the great mound, the graded way leading down to the Muskingum, and the huge platforms of earth, or truncated pyramids caused universal wonder alike among the educated and the unlearned, and were carefully examined. There was much to admire in the verdure-clad hills and the beautiful valleys of which the fertility was asserted by the most luxuriant growth of herbage and every variety of plant life which had a home in this latitude. Many strange forms of vegetation greeted the eyes of the curious and admiring. Game was abundant in the woods, and during the first few months richly furnished the rude but substantial larders of the pioneers. Later in the year the Indians drove away or killed off the larger game, but during the summer and early fall of 1788 nearly all varieties of animals and fowl known to the western country abounded in the woods. Hunting was engaged in with zest not alone for the sport which it afforded but for the value of the products of the chase. One of the pioneers writing home to New England, says: "We have started twenty buffaloes in a drove. Deer are as plenty as sheep with you. Beaver and otter are abundant. I have known one man to catch twenty or thirty of them in two or three nights. Turkeys are innumerable."

A general feeling of content existed among the settlers. All were pleased with their surroundings, with the climate of the country, the prospect for the future, and the attainments of the first few months. They had reason to be thankful for the enjoyment of good health. As late as

---

*Judge Timothy Walker, in address delivered before the Ohio Historical and Philosophical society at Cincinnati in 1837, and published in the "Transactions."

* The first wheat sown in the Ohio company's purchase, and in the State of Ohio, was a small quantity sown near Campus Martius, late in the fall of 1788, by Captain Trueman Guthrie, who brought a small quantity of seed with him from Connecticut.

July no man in the colony had been sick. This in a new country was remarkable.

But one cause of uneasiness remained, though it was probably little thought of except by General Putnam and a few others who occupied stations of responsibility in the colony. Some precaution was deemed necessary to insure safety in case of the manifestations of Indian hostility. The fortification known as Campus Martius (military camp) arose as an expression of this fear, as an evidence of the isolation of the colony and a tangible reminder of its danger. Little did the builders of that defence apprehend the hardships, perils, and atrocities of which its picture reminds their descendants of to-day. General Putnam had suspended the survey about the middle of May, because of the uncertainty of the Indians remaining at peace, but it was resumed and carried on with little interruption—and that not because of hostilities—through the season and, in fact, through the year 1788. Preparations for a treaty had been made soon after the landing of the pioneers, but it was not finally negotiated until the beginning of 1789 (as will be shown in the following chapter). Several times during the summer Captain Pipe of the Delaware tribe and other chiefs and warriors visited Fort Harmar and the little settlement on the east side of the Muskingum. They had dined with General Putnam in his marquee and made great professions of friendship, but had expressed displeasure at the building of houses and planting of crops before the making of a treaty.

Taking into consideration the feeling that existed among the Indians, the Ohio company decided to carry out a plan which should give the settlers protection in case it was needed. The first measure taken toward this work was the cutting of a road through the woods from "the point" where most of the houses were built, to the site which was selected for the stockade, which was a mile away, up the Muskingum. The ground was well chosen. It was the margin of the plain which had once been the bank of the Muskingum. On either side there were small ravines; in the rear stretched the smooth and gently rising plain, and in the front there was a somewhat abrupt descent to the lowest river terrace which, about one hundred and fifty yards distant, was washed by the Muskingum. The location is best described to those not familiar with it by the statement that it is bounded by Washington and Second streets, respectively upon the south and east. Here in the form of a parallelogram, the sides of which measured one hundred and eighty feet each, was built the stockade which for five years was to be the dwelling place and refuge of a large portion of the Ohio company's colony. The sides were formed of continuous lines of dwelling houses two stories in height. They were constructed of timber four inches thick, sawed by hand, and fitted together at the corners in the same manner as those of a hewed log house. At the corners were block-houses, solidly made and of quite imposing appearance. They were a trifle higher than the houses which formed the sides of the fort, were covered with shapely four square roofs, three of which were surmounted at their apexes with towers intended to be used as sentry

boxes, large enough to accommodate four men each. On the fourth there was a tower very similar to the others, but capped with a cupola for the reception of a bell, "which," says a letter writer of the period, "we are told is coming on as a present from a gentleman in Boston."[*]

The block-houses projected six feet beyond the sides of the stockade. They were twenty feet square at the ground, and the second story of each projected two feet over the lower. Heavy gates were hung at the entrances in the south and west fronts, and over that in the latter (toward the Muskingum) was a house of logs or hewed timber, projecting like the second floors of the corner block-houses. This was intended for the protection of the gate in case of an attack. The watch-towers were found inconvenient of access after the Indian war broke out, and small, square bastions were built at each angle of the stockade for the accommodation of the sentries. In those at the southwest and northeast angles small cannon were placed. In addition to the two rows of windows along the sides of the fort, the walls were pierced with loop-holes for musketry. The houses were nearly all provided with good brick chimneys, the bricks being made upon the ground and burned by men experienced in that line of industry. Good shingle roofs afforded a protection from the weather. Shingle-making was then a difficult and slow work. They were split from blocks about two and a half feet long, and sloped with the axe, and at the end exposed to the weather were nearly or perhaps quite an inch thick. Several of the houses included in Campus Martius were built at private expense, and were finished in detail as the owner's fancy dictated, but all conformed in general design to the plan by the superintendent and considered most advantageous to the general good. There were seventy-two rooms of eighteen feet square and upwards, in this work of defence, and it was estimated that when necessity required nearly nine hundred people could be shielded from an enemy in the enclosure.

As a basis of this estimate it is supposed that twelve persons should occupy a room. Campus Martius, however, never contained half as many people as the number mentioned. In the centre of the enclosure, which measured one hundred and forty-four feet each way, a well eighty feet deep (which still remains in use), was dug to supply water in the event of a siege. Near the well was placed a large sundial[†] made by Major Anselm Tupper, which marked the flight of time—slow albeit—through all the Indian war, and was kept for many years as an interesting relic of the pioneers.

Although the greater part of the work of building Campus Martius was accomplished during the first year

* In the MS journal of the Ohio company appears the following entry:
Upon information from Colonel May that Mr. Joseph May, of Boston, had presented a bell to the Ohio company for the first public building to be erected in the territory of the company, and such building ordered by the agents,

Resolved, That the thanks of the company be presented to that gentleman, and the directors be requested to take measures for transferring it from Boston to the Muskingum.

†This sundial was owned for many years by A. T. Nye, esq., and was consumed in his hardware store on the occasion of the great fire in Marietta in 1857.

of the settlement, and in fact much of it by August, the
details of the defence were not completed until the Indian war broke out in earnest in 1791. The illustration
represents it at that time in its finished state. Rows of
palings were planted from corner to corner of the block-
houses, sloping outward at an angle of forty-five degrees,
and supported by posts and railing. At a distance of
twenty feet from these sharp raking pickets, and surrounding the entire work, was a line of heavy palings
eight or ten feet in height; and again outside of this there
was an *abatis* formed of the boughs of trees with the
smaller limbs pointed and projecting outwards. The
work thus perfected was almost absolutely impregnable.
It is probable that the obvious strength of the defence
discouraged attack, for during the whole period of Indian disturbance no attempt was made against it, and so
far as is known no plan ever formed for an assault.

Campus Martius, judging from the picture of it (which
is in all essential matters historically correct), must have
presented a striking appearance with its background of
fields and wooded hills, and really have merited the enthusiastic words of one of the pioneers, who, in writing
home, said it was "the handsomest pile of buildings on
this side of the Alleghany mountains."

Upon the shore of the Muskingum, directly in front
of the stockaded fort, was constructed a substantial timber wharf at which lay moored the Mayflower, the lesser
craft and canoes when not in use, plying back and forth between Campus Martius and Fort Harmar, or "the point."

Beside the dwellings in Campus Martius about twenty-
five, mostly at "the point," were built during the season.

We must now return to the narrative of some important history of the year 1788 over which we have passed
in chronicling the building of Campus Martius.

The first company of pioneers of the Ohio company's
settlement were followed to the shores of the Muskingum
during the summer of 1788 by many more, of whom
some were adventurers, but the majority people seeking
permanent homes.

In May came General Samuel Holden Parsons, a man
already familiar with the western country, who was now
under appointment as judge of the territory. Also in the
same month there arrived Captain William Dana, Ebenezer Battelle, Major Jonathan Haskell, Colonel Israel Putnam, Aaron Waldo Putnam, Major Robert
Bradford, Jonathan Stone, Major Winthrop Sargent, Colonel William Stacey, and Colonel John
May.* The latter came down the river from Pittsburgh with quite a party, not all of whom, however, were
settlers. He has made note of the fact that on board of
the boat forty-two feet long were "twenty-seven men, two
cows, two calves, seven hogs and nine dogs, besides eight
tons of baggage."

In the month of June there were many more arrivals,
among them Hon. James M. Varnum, judge of the territory, Major Dean Tyler, Griffin and Charles Greene,
Colonel Joseph Thompson, Dr. Jabez True and Paul
Fearing. The two last named are known to have arrived on the sixteenth. Judge Varnum, as is shown by
Colonel May's journal, came upon the fifth, "with about
forty souls in company."

Judge Varnum, one of the ablest and noblest men in
the Ohio company's colony, was an invalid when he came
to the Muskingum. His wife was unable to accompany
him. James Owen and wife were of his party, and Mrs.
Owen acted as his nurse until death claimed him, early
in 1789. She was the first woman who settled in the
Ohio company's colony. There were, however, several
at Fort Harmar, the wives of the officers, before the arrival of the forty-seven pioneers. They could not be
called with propriety settlers. They were merely temporary sojourners at a United States military post. The
Owen family did not remain in the country through the
Indian war, but returned soon after, and were known as
most estimable people. Some of their descendants now
reside in Washington county. Mrs. Owen performed
very valuable humane services during the prevalence of
small-pox in Marietta in 1790, and from this fact, and
also, perhaps, in consideration of her being the first
woman inhabitant of Marietta, the Ohio company gave
her one of the donation lots of one hundred acres in extent. The family emigrated from South Kingston, Rhode
Island. Mrs. Owen died in 1800* and her husband ten
years later.

No other families arrived in the settlement until August. †On the nineteenth of that month six families
landed. They were those of General Benjamin Tupper,
Colonel Ichabod Nye (son-in-law of the former) Major
Nathaniel Cushing, Major Nathan Goodale, Major Asa
Coburn, sr., and Andrew Webster, his son-in-law. The
first four mentioned reached Wellsburgh (Buffalo creek),
Virginia, in July, and waited there six weeks for Major
Coburn and Andrew Weber. Colonel Ichabod Nye left
them, and with two single men came down the river on
the Virginia side, bringing the horses. He arrived
August 9th. The ladies of the above families, within a
day or two after their arrival, were called upon by the
wives of the officers at the fort and soon invited them to
partake of the hospitality that the garrison afforded.
Other families came out later, but the dates of their
arrival, with one or two exceptions, have not been preserved. The family of Ebenezer Battelle undoubtedly
landed in December. He had come out in May, with
Colonel John May, but went to Baltimore to meet his

*Colonel John May, of Boston, kept a journal which has been pub-
lished and is very interesting reading for the antiquarian and student of
western history. We shall have frequent occasion to quote from it.
It appears from this journal that Colonel May arrived at "the delightful Muskingum" at three o'clock in the afternoon of Monday, May
26th. Colonel May was one of the agents of the Ohio company. He
cherished the hope of settling permanently in the colony, but did not
realize it. He died in Boston in 1812.

*A. T. Nye in Marietta *Register.*

†With the party who arrived on the nineteenth of August was one
man who had a keen and curious interest in seeing the territory
owned by the Ohio company. That man was the Rev. Manasseh
Cutler, who had negotiated the purchase with Congress—a leading
man in the counsels of the company from the first. He came not as a
settler, but as an observer of the colony he had been so largely influential in planting upon the Ohio. He remained at Marietta until the
ninth of September, and then went up the river with Colonel Vigo to
Pittsburgh, from whence he returned to Massachusetts.

COMMODORE ABRAHAM WHIPPLE.

family in October. Colonel Robert Oliver's family arrived November 18th, as is shown by a letter written that day by Rowena Tupper. She says: "What do I hear below? Colonel Oliver is now landing. I fly to meet them." Arrivals were, indeed, the cause of excitement and joy to a degree which can hardly be realized in this age of quick mail and telegraph facilities. Altogether, says General Putnam, fifteen families arrived during 1788. Hildreth says the same. But in a list made of settlers, General Putnam gives the names of *nineteen* families who were in Marietta before the close of the year. There were sixteen at least whose names have been preserved, as follows: General Benjamin Tupper, Andrew Webster, Colonel Ichabod Nye, James Owen, Nathaniel Cushing, Asa Coburn, sr., Major Nathan Goodale, Asa Coburn jr., Benjamin Converse, Griffin Greene, Charles Greene, Benoni Hurlburt, Nathaniel Moody, Israel Pierce, Robert Oliver, and Ebenezer Battelle. Commodore Abraham Whipple was a noted arrival of this year. Colonel Ichabod Nye says in his autobiography that "during the fall five or six other families arrived and other adventurers and workmen. Some had returned to New England for their families. The winter began with about a hundred or more in the settlement." Rufus Putnam states that in addition to the pioneer party eighty-four men came to the settlement during 1788, making in all one hundred and thirty-two.[*]

General Arthur St. Clair, governor of the Northwest Territory, arrived in Marietta on the ninth of July. He had been commissioned by Congress October 16. 1787, the commission to take effect on the first of February, 1788. At the time of his appoinment he was president of Congress, but prior to that had been a general in the Revolutionary war; had fought gallantly in the French and Indian war, and carried a standard at the storming of Quebec, in 1759. Like most of the Revolutionary officers, he was impoverished by the long struggle for independence.[†] He was undoubtedly in full sympathy with the worn-out veterans who were the leading men of the only English settlement in the territory he was to govern, and his appointment was certainly agreeable to their desires. His arrival was an event of importance to the little community. "This," says Colonel May, "is in a sense the birthday of this western world." Hitherto law had only a nominal existence. Now government was to be organized; the governor was to dwell in the new settlement. It had already been foreseen by some of the leading men of the Ohio company that when other settlements were founded the governor might make one of them his residence. This they wished to prevent. Colonel May who, when on his way to the Muskingum, met St. Clair at Pittsburgh, and felt obliged to tarry and make him a visit, says:

For one I confess I am moved to the visit by two motives; one the respect due to the governor of the Western Territory; the other, a little selfish, as we wish him to make the Muskingum the seat of government and place of his residence. And we have no doubt if proper at-

tention is paid to these little matters, as well as to those of greater magnitude, the object will be accomplished."[*]

The formal reception of the governor was postponed until the fifteenth, but "his landing was announced by the discharge of fourteen cannon, and all rejoiced at his coming."[†] He was domiciled at Fort Harmar.

In the afternoon of the day set for the official welcoming, the governor came over to the Marietta side of the Muskingum in the barge belonging to Fort Harmar, on the oars of which, we are told, the word "Congress" was painted in bright letters. He was escorted by the garrison officers and by Major Winthrop Sargent, secretary of the territory, and was received, says Hildreth, "by General Putnam, the judges of the territory, and the principal inhabitants of the new colony." The formal inauguration of government in the Northwest Territory took place in the "Bowery," which was not as might be supposed one of Nature's shady temples but a structure reared with hands.[‡] The secretary read the Ordinance of Freedom, the commission of the governor, those of the judges, and his own; a short address of welcome was made to his excellency and "three cheers closed the ceremonies of the day." The people generally were presented to Governor St. Clair and the utmost good feeling prevailed. One of the officers present wrote of the occasion "These people appear the most happy folks in the world, greatly satisfied with their new purchase, and they certainly are the best informed, most courteous and civil to strangers of any people I have yet met with."[§] Shortly after this occasion, and within the month of July, the first laws of the territory were framed and published, and Washington county was established—but of these subjects we shall speak elsewhere.

Another interesting ceremonial which occurred not long after the governor's arrival in the colony was the opening of the first court in the Northwest Territory. The demonstration was simple from necessity; there was not much of pomp or splendor in the ceremony, but it must have been suggestive to the denizens of this isolated pioneer settlement of an idea that was majestic. The formal establishment of the institution which is at once the people's palladium and the organized exemplar of civilization's most distinctive force and characteristic quality, could not have been other than an absorbingly interesting incident in the lives of those who witnessed it. On Tuesday, the second of September, 1788, the people and the officers from Fort Harmar formed in procession at "the point" and marched to Campus Martius, escorting the governor, territorial judges, and the judges of the court of common pleas. In front was the sheriff of the county of Washington, Colonel Ebenezer Sproat, tall, erect and of a fine military bearing, with his drawn sword and wand of office. The spectacle was a strange one to the few friendly Indians who were present, for it was the first

---

[*] The subject of settlement is briefly treated here, as a full and correct list of the settlers of 1788, 1789 and 1790 is presented at the conclusion of this chapter.

[†] See Biography.

[*] Colonel May's journal, page 53.

[†] Ibid, page 83.

[‡] "Our long bowery is built on the east bank of the Muskingum."— Colonel May's journal, page 78.

[‡] Major Denny's military journal.

ceremonial which they had seen the white men perform, and it doubtless had upon their minds an awing effect. Arrived at the garrison the procession filed into the northwest corner of the block-house, and the great hall was filled with people. The Rev. Manasseh Cutler opened the exercises of the day with solemn prayer. The commissions of the judges, the clerk, and the sheriff were then read, after which the court of common pleas of Washington county was opened for business by the proclamation of the sheriff, beginning in the old form with the monitory, "Oyez, oyez, oyez." "Although this scene was exhibited thus early in the settlement of the State, few ever equalled it in the dignity and exalted character of its principal participators."[*] As there were no cases to be tried, the court was immediately adjourned. The first judges were General Rufus Putnam, General Benjamin Tupper, and Colonel Archibald Crary, the sheriff, as has been stated, Colonel Sproat, and the clerk, Colonel R. J. Meigs. Paul Fearing, esq., was admitted an attorney, and was the first in the territory.

The Ohio company was actively engaged during the whole of the period that has been sketched. Consideration of the unforseen difficulties which arose occupied much of the time of the directors and agents. New plans had to be devised and put in operation, and in many cases measures which had been deemed adequate to the end in view had to be materially modified to meet existing circumstances. The progress of the company's affairs, although for the most part smooth enough, was not entirely without the halting and unevenness which indicated cross purposes on the part of some of the members. There was something in the way of internal strife, though it was not serious. Colonel May gives some intimation of this in an entry in his journal:

General Varnum and his party are making difficulties about the eight acre lots not being drawn contiguous to the city; also with respect to the Scioto purchase. . . . General Putnam did not strictly adhere to orders given at Brackett's tavern at Boston and Rice's at Providence.[†]

The same writer found considerable fault with the slow progress that had been made in the company's colony, late in May, the day after his arrival, jotting down the following language:

As to our surveying, buildings, etc., they are in a very backward way. Little appears to be done and a great deal of time and money misspent.[‡]

The first meeting of the Ohio company, west of the mountains, was held July 2nd, and continued by adjournment, until August 14th. There were present Samuel Holden Parsons, Rufus Putnam, and James M. Varnum, directors, and the following agents (each of whom represented the number of shares indicated): Colonel John May, 36; Major Winthrop Sargent, 166; Colonel Archibald Crary, 102; Major William Corliss, 112; Colonel Return Jonathan Meigs, 99; Captain Aaron Barlow, 25; Colonel Ebenezer Sproat, 43; Major Haffield White, 20; General Putnam, 66. Total shares represented, 669. At this meeting the city at the mouth of the Mus-

kingum was named Marietta. Among other business transacted the first day, was the action in regard to the three-acre lots. It was moved, as a measure looking toward the safety and well-being of the colony, "that the lots 21, 30, and fractional parts of 35 and 36, of township number 2, in range 8, and numbers 19, 25, and 20, and fractional parts of 31 in the third township of range 8, the same being in commons laid out adjoining the city, be laid out in one thousand and five three-acre lots."

The mile square section No. 29, reserved out of every township for the support of religion, happening to be that on which the city was laid out, the company made a strenuous effort to have an exception made in this case. It was proposed to Congress that other lands should be reserved instead of this section, but the arrangement could not be effected. Hence it was given up, greatly to the disappointment of the proprietors, and other lots were laid out at the mouth of the great Hockhocking. Portions of the section, however, were leased for a term of years. Section No. 16, set apart for the use of schools, which fell near the mouth of Duck creek, was also leased in lots. The common lands, "between the highway and Muskingum and in Market square," it was decided might be assigned to individuals for gardens for the term of ten years (from March 1, 1788), on condition that they should be cleared within two months, fenced by March 1, 1792, and that within three years trees should be set out.

The ancient works received attention at this meeting. It was resolved that the elevated square, No. 11, be called *Quadranaou;* No. 19, *Capitolium;* No. 61, *Cecelia;* and that "the great road through the covert way" be named *Sacra Via.* It was further resolved that the reserved public square in the city, including the buildings at the block-house, be called *Campus Martius.*

The company took action on many matters intended to advance the interests of the colonists, and among the other resolutions which appear in their record[*] is the following, under date of August 13, 1788:

WHEREAS, It is necessary that mills be erected as soon as possible, it is ordered that any persons who shall build a wind-mill on the banks of the Ohio, and near the mouth of the Muskingum, by the first of December next, shall have right to occupy a tract of land one hundred and fifty feet east and west and two hundred feet north and south for a term of twenty years.

This tempting offer was not accepted, and it was not until sometime later that the colonists had the benefit of a mill within the limits of their purchase.

"It soon became evident," says General Putnam,[†] "that some new plan must be adopted to divide lands or the settlement would come to naught, and to remedy this the proprietors were notified to meet at Marietta the first Wednesday of December, 1788, and devise a plan. This they failed to do, and the agents, under the circumstances, conceiving that they had the authority to act in the matter, on February 6, 1789, repealed the resolutions for the division of lands passed at Boston November 21, 1787, and adopted the following:

---

* Marietta *Intelligencer,* March 10, 1842.
† Colonel May's journal, page 63.
‡ Ibid, page 59.

* MS. Journal of the Ohio Company.
† Autobiography of General Rufus Putnam (MS).

Resolved, That there shall be granted to persons who shall settle in such places within the purchase as the agents may think most conducive to advance the general interest of the proprietors, and under such restrictions and limitations as they shall think proper, lands not exceeding one hundred acres, out of each share in the fund of the company, and that a committee be appointed to investigate the purchase so far as may, in their opinion, be necessary in order to point out and fix upon proper plans and places for settlements.

As early as July this matter had been under consideration. The inability of the directors to dispose of any lands within the purchase had prevented the growth of the settlement, for thousands of emigrants had passed down the Ohio, many of whom it was believed would have located in the Ohio company's purchase had they been able to buy lands. Most of them were on their way to Kentucky but were not the owners of any lands there. General Putnam, Samuel Parsons, and Colonel Archibald Crary, who were appointed a committee for the consideration of this matter, rehearsed the foregoing facts to the shareholders and made a report, in concluding which they said: "We are of the opinion that giving a part of the lands to industrious people, on performing certain duties in settling, clearing, etc., will be very much for the interest of the proprietors." It was in accordance with this spirit that the action was taken by the agents which we have above indicated.

A committee, consisting of General Rufus Putnam, John Dodge, Griffin Greene, Alexander Oliver, Jonathan Devol, Colonel Robert Oliver, R. J. Meigs, Captain Dana, and Major Nathan Goodale, was appointed to explore the purchase and select suitable locations for settlements. It was decided to grant lands in one hundred acre parcels as contemplated by the resolution, and it was further provided that "no settlement should consist of less than twenty men able to bear arms, they to be well provided with arms and ammunition, and to erect such works of defense as should be appointed by the committee. The company made the following further requirements, viz: Each settler to furnish lands for highways when needed; to build, within five years, a dwelling house to be at least eighteen by twenty-four feet in dimensions; to plant not less than fifty apple and twenty peach trees within three years; to clear and put in meadow or pasture fifteen acres and into tillage not less than five acres within five years; to be constantly provided with arms and be subject to military duty.

The time had now arrived when Marietta should put forth her first off-shoot. Among the locations favorably mentioned by the exploring committee was the tract of land extending along the Ohio, a short distance above and four or five miles below the Little Kanawha, terminating two miles above the Little Hocking, and the broad alluvial bottom below the latter stream. During the winter of 1788–89 lots were surveyed and platted in these localities, and a company of about forty associates (as they were called) was organized to make a settlement. In reality there were four settlements (the lower being usually called Newbury), and they included sixty-eight lots. The lots being drawn the settlers began moving onto them early in April, 1789. Here the same slow, hard processes were repeated, which had resulted in the

attainment of the improved condition of things at the mouth of the Muskingum. The settlers built little cabins along the river bank, clearing away the forest around them. The community was made up of men of sterling character—most of them schooled in the long struggle of the Revolutionary war for the future that was before them. They began hopefully and toiled on in privation, patiently enduring the many hardships of their lot, and endeavoring to see in the future a reward for their labors. They did not know how soon they should suffer other ills than those which they already encountered, but the time was fast approaching when the fortitude of every man should be put to the severest test. This group of settlements was called Belle Prairie, which term became contracted to Belleprie, and finally to the present form—Belpre.

What was called the "second association" was formed also in the winter of 1788–89, for the purpose of making a settlement about twenty miles up the Muskingum on an allotment of donation lands, and also upon Wolf creek. The association numbered thirty-nine members and being afterward increased by the addition of one new member, took forty lots of one hundred acres each. A village, now Beverly, was laid out on the "peninsula," on the west side of the Muskingum and in a bend of Wolf creek. The settlement was made on the twentieth of April, 1789, by nineteen men, who leaving Campus Martius rowed up the Muskingum in canoes to the place of their destination. By the middle of May cabins were built for each family and gardens made. By the middle of July corn was growing among the girdled trees and upon the fertile plain, which had probably been tilled by the Indians, as when the settlement was made it was covered only with bushes and small saplings. A blockhouse was also erected during the summer. As the Wolf creek settlement was made simultaneously with that on the Muskingum (and, in fact, depending upon it) Colonel Robert Oliver, Major Haffield White, and Captain John Dodge, with a company of laborers erected what was known as the Wolf Creek mills, the first mill in the State of Ohio. This name was applied not alone to the building but to the settlement—the little cluster of houses which were also erected at this point, one mile from the mouth of the creek, though the term Millersburgh was also often used. These two settlements (that upon the Muskingum and that upon Wolf creek) were covered by one name, Plainfield, which, however, remained in use but a short time, being superseded by Waterford. The mill was of great service to the settlers in the immediate vicinity and also to the people of Marietta, both before and during the war. We have now mentioned briefly the two principal offshoots of the Marietta colony.*

There were several other small settlements made prior to the war. In the fall of 1790 an association of thirty-six members founded the ill-fated settlement at Big Bottom, which is fully described in the following chapter.

*For a full account of the early affairs of Belpre and Waterford the reader should see the chapters devoted respectively to them, and for the occurrences during the Indian war, the two chapters which follow this.

The same season a block-house was built for twenty men at Meigs creek, and a few settlers took up hundred acre donation lots at the forks of Duck creek, and in the meantime a few cabins appeared along the Ohio from the Muskingum to Duck creek.

Lands had been granted Captain Enoch Shepherd early in 1789, for the erection of mills on Duck creek, but the project did not result successfully, and Shepherd and his partners, Colonel Ebenezer Sproat and Thomas Stanley, lost all of the time and money they had expended. This saw-mill was completed in September, 1789, but a flood so injured it and the dam that they could not easily be repaired, and as the Indian war soon afterwards came on, the enterprise was abandoned.

In the year 1790 one hundred and twenty acres of land was granted Dudley Woodbridge in section three, township number four, range eleven, on condition that he should build a good horse-mill, and at the same time Robert Potts, from New London, Connecticut, was given permission to build a mill, and land was granted him for that purpose on Mill creek, two miles north of Marietta. Neither of these projects was realized, because of the more frequent occurrence of Indian hostilities which indicated an increased hazard in following any occupation, which necessitated removal from the immediate vicinity of the garrisons. The Robert Potts mill building was nearly completed when the danger became so great as to cause the workmen to abandon the building, and it was soon after destroyed by the Indians.

It must be borne in mind that during the years 1789 and 1790 the settlers were almost constantly harassed by the savage neighbors, and several murders were committed, but we have reserved for full consideration in subsequent chapters the topics of Indian affairs and the period of war.

Another grist-mill was projected by some of the Belpre settlers, among whom were Griffin Greene and Robert Bradford. The mouth of the Little Hocking was chosen as the location and the Ohio company donated to the builders a tract of one hundred and sixty acres of land. Work was begun in 1790 under the supervision of two experienced millwrights from Redstone, Pennsylvania, and very gratifying progress made, but the opening of the Indian war in January, 1791, put a stop to operations, and no mill was erected at this locality until after the restoration of peace. The people returned to the laborious method of grinding their corn by hand or pounding it in mortars until the completion of the famous floating mill, at Belpre, built by Captain Jonathan Devol, an ingenious mechanic, at the suggestion of Griffin Greene, who had seen one in Holland a number of years before. This mill was built upon two boats, one a large canoe made from a sycamore tree trunk, and the other a flat boat forty-five feet in length and ten feet wide. The grinding stones were placed upon the largest boat and the water wheel between this and the smaller. A small frame house was erected over the machinery. When the mill was in readiness for use it was towed to a point not far from Farmers Castle, and abreast of the middle of Backus' (afterward Blannerhassett's) island, where it was an-

chored in a strong current. This mill was owned by seven persons, and the capital of the stock company which they formed was divided into twelve shares. The cost of construction was fifty-one pounds and eight shillings in Massachusetts currency. This was quite a large sum of money to be expended at that time, but it proved a good investment. The situation of the mill rendered it safe from destruction at the hands of the Indians, and it was of immense service during the whole period of the war, not alone to the people of Belpre, but to the residents of Marietta as well. It is said that from twenty-five to fifty bushels of grain could be ground per day at this mill, according to the swiftness of the current.

Turning backward chronologically to the year 1789, we see in Marietta a continuation of the work of improvement carried on so diligently in 1788. The settlement felt severely the loss of those men who had gone out to Belpre and Waterford, for although quite a large number of accessions were made to the population, not many of the late comers were men to be compared in character with those who had taken their departure.

The results accomplished showed plainly the loss, for although the best was done under the circumstances, no more corn was planted than during the first season, and comparatively little building or other improvement was carried on.

General Varnum died in January of this year, and his place as director of the Ohio company was filled by the election of Griffin Greene. The company in February passed a resolution ordering that "the seventh of April should forever be considered as a day of public festival in the territory of the company." The Rev. Daniel Story, of Massachusetts, employed by Dr. Cutler for the Ohio company as preacher and teacher, arrived in the spring and began his labors as chaplain of the new settlement. He preached not only at Campus Martius and the Point, but made pastoral visits to Belpre and Waterford, using on those occasions a log canoe. His visits were made quite regularly through the years 1789 and 1790, and only suspended when the danger from Indian attacks was considered too great.

The Ohio company continued in the exercise of its wise and kindly policy toward the people in its settlements. The surveys were continued when the attitude of the Indians would permit, and donation allotments were surveyed in several localities, amounting in all to fifty-seven thousand acres.

The condition of healthfulness among the settlers, which has been remarked upon as existing through the summer of 1788 did not prevail during the two years following, and a dearth of food became an additional and serious evil. Under these circumstances the Ohio company humanely came to the assistance of its people and made small loans without interest to those among them who were sick or destitute, supplying a total of about three thousand dollars. Much of this sum was lost, as when the Indian war came on many of the settlers were unable to carry on their avocations by which they otherwise would have obtained money with which to discharge their indebtedness.

In the summer of 1790 General Putnam, who had contracted with William Duer, of the Scioto company, to erect houses at Gallipolis for the expected French emigrants, employed, at his own expense, Captain William Burnham and forty men, to perform the work. General Putnam expended two thousand dollars, which was a total loss. The Scioto company had been premature in selling lands and inducing emigration before they had completed their purchase of Congress. The company failed, and Duer became a bankrupt. The poor duped Frenchmen arrived in this country in the summer, and on the sixteenth of October were at Marietta on their way to the village which Putnam's men had built for them. They came to Marietta in six Kentucky flatboats, and numbered four hundred souls. The odd dress, wooden shoes, and strange tongue of the emigrants made them the subject of much curious observation, and awakened a general interest among the settlers. There was no little pity for these unfortunate foreigners among those at Marietta who knew the probabilities in regard to their losing the lands which they expected to settle upon, and the almost penniless condition of the majority made their situation doubly deplorable. All that was possible was done to make their condition bearable, and a few of the French who remained permanently at Marietta were cared for until able to provide for their own wants. The greater proportion of the four hundred tarried briefly and went on to Gallipolis, and, owing to the troubles which soon after beset the Ohio company settlers, the woes of the French were less thought of than would otherwise have been the case. The Ohio company was obliged to exert every power to provide for its own emigrants. The total number of men in the company's territory was now upwards of three thousand. The total number arrived was about five hundred, but fully two-fifths had come as adventurers, or if emigrating with the intention of making a permanent settlement, had either returned to New England, or sought homes in Pennsylvania, Virginia, or Kentucky. During the first year the number of males who came to the colony was one hundred and thirty-three; during 1789 the number was one hundred and fifty-two, and during 1790, one hundred and sixty-five. Nearly one hundred families had come to the settlement during the three years.

In conclusion we present General Putnam's list* of the arrivals in the Ohio company's purchase during the first three years of settlement.

A LIST OF THE EMIGRANTS OF 1788, 1789 AND 1790.

SEVENTEEN HUNDRED AND EIGHTY-EIGHT.

[The list does not include the members of the pioneer party who arrived April 7th.]

Bryant, Bazaleel,	Backus, James,
Battelle, Ebenezer, family,	Brayman, James,
Cushing, Nathaniel, family,	Converse, Benjamin, family,
Converse, James,	Crary, Archibald,
Crary, Frederick,	Cheever, Joshua,
Cheever, Lot,	Chouchip, Jeffrey,
Coburn, Asa, family,	Coburn, jr., Asa, family,
Coburn, Nicholas,	Dana, William, family (1789),
Dana, Luther,	Dana, Edmund,
Denney, Samuel,	Dicks, Nathan,
Dunham, Daniel, family (1789),	Delano, Cornelius,
Dorrence, Samuel,	Elliott, Richard,
Eldridge, Sylvanus,	Fearing, Paul,
Fuller, Oliver,	Greene, Griffin, family,
Greene, Richard,	Greene, Philip,
Greene, Charles, family,	Gilbert, Jonathan,
Goodale, Major Nathan, family,	Goodale, Timothy,
Gridley, William, family (1789),	Hurlburt, Benoni, family,
Hart, Selah,	Hutchinson, Thomas,
Holland, ——,	Ingersoll, George,
Kimble, Ephraim,	Knowles, Charles,
Knight, Theophilus,	Kerr, Hamilton,
Lasa, John,	Lunt, Ezra,
Lunt, William P.,	Leach, James,
Lord, Thomas,	Laughton, Dick (half Indian),
Minot, James,	Miller, John (half Indian),
Mitchell, John,	Mitchell, Samuel,
Matthewson, Jeffrey,	Mathews, Abel,
McGuffey, Neil,	Moody, Nathaniel, family,
Owen, James, family,	Nye, Ichabod, family,
Pierce, Stephen, family (1789),	Parsons, Samuel H.,
Oliver, Robert, family,	Pierce, Israel, family,
Oliver, Launcelot,	Oliver, Alexander, family,
Putnam, Israel,	Oliver, William,
Rice, Oliver,	Putnam, Waldo A.,
Stratton, John,	Sargent, Winthrop,
Skinner, John,	Stratton, Samuel,
Stanley, Elias,	Stone, Jonathan, family (1789),
Stacey, Col. William, family (1789)	Stebbins, Samuel,
Tupper, General Benjamin, family,	Shipman, Joshua, family (1789),
Tyler, Dean,	True, Jabez,
Tupper, Edward W.,	Tupper, Judah (died in war),
Varnum, James (died Jan. 1789),	Tupper, jr., Benjamin,
Woodward, Levi,	Wright, Simeon,
Whittemore, Ebenezer,	Webster, Andrew, family,

[In all eighty-five men, making with the first party forty-eight, a total of one hundred and thirty-three arrivals of males during the year.]

SEVENTEEN HUNDRED AND EIGHTY-NINE.

Ayres, Ebenezer, family.	Brown, David, family,
Babcock, Abijah,	Baker, Thaddeus,
Bull, Howell,	Breck, William,
Buell, Joseph, family (1790),	Bradford, Robert, family,
Bullard, Asa,	Baldwin, Abel,
Bull, Aaron,	Bent, Silas, family,
Bent, Silas, jr.,	Beadle, Benjamin,
Barker, Joseph, family,	Baldwin, Davis, (Gallipolis)
Barker, Isaac, family,	Blake, David, family,
Blake, Simeon,	Burnham, William,
Baldwin, David,	Baker, Benjamin,
Bullard, Eleazer,	Bagley, Henry
Cummins, Joseph,	Cald, Arnold,
Casey, Wanton,	Cady, Squire,
Cushing, Elijah,	Cogswell, Daniel, family,
Clark, Arnold,	Clough, Aaron,
Cory, Thomas,	Clark, Joseph,
Dodge, John, family,	Devol, Gilbert, esquire, family,

* Among the papers of General Putnam there appears a list of the settlers in the Ohio company's purchase during the years 1788, 1789 and 1790, or to the opening of the Indian war. This list, which is undoubtedly reliable, forms the only complete record of the settlement of Washington county, and has never heretofore appeared in print. It includes all who came to the county during the years above mentioned, except those men who were hired by the Ohio company, most of whom had no intention of remaining permanently in the colony. Many of those whose names are given did not continue in the Ohio company's lands, but either removed to other settlements in Ohio, Virginia or Kentucky or returned to New England. Those who remained through the Indian war (or fell victims to it) are indicated by a star. The French settlers, and those who removed to Gallipolis (quite a large class) are designated by General Putnam, and as we have thought that part of the record might be of interest to many readers, it is copied with the original indications or notes opposite the names. The whole is a literal transcript of the original document by the painstaking and careful superintendent of the colony.

Devol, Wanton, family,
Devol, Jonathan,
Davis, William,
Davis, Samuel,
Foster, Paul,
Fairchild, Major,
Greene, John,
Gibson, Thomas,
Gilman, Benjamin, family (1790),
Hamilton, Nathaniel,
Kelley, James, family (killed 1791),
Kinney, Nathan,
Leaveus, Joseph, family,
Lucas, Isaac,
Lord, Elisha,
McClure, Andrew,
Mixer, Isaac,
Miller, Edward,
Munsell, Levi, family,
Mayo, Daniel,
Mitchell, John,
Miles, John,
Newton, Sylvanus, family,
Newell, William,
Patten, James,
Putnam, David,
Parson, Enoch,
Porter, Thomas, family,
Parker, William, family,
Phillips, Ezra,
Rouse, Michael,
Rowel, Daniel,
Sprague, Joshua, family,
Strong, Joseph,
Shepherd, Enoch, jr.,
Story, William,
Stacey, William, jr.,
Stacey, John,
Smith, John,
Sawyer, Nathaniel, family,
Stone, Israel, family (1790),
Stanley, Thomas, family,
Smith, Jonathan,
Smith, Stephen,
Platt, Smith,
Tias, Eliphalet,
———, Daniel,
Tuttle, Linus,
Woodbury, Nathan,
Webster, Luke,
Whiting, Elisha,
Winsor, Christopher, family,
Wilson, George, family,
Wilson, Jeremiah, family,
Whipple, John H.,
Dunham, jr., Daniel,
Patterson, James, family,
Story, Joseph,
Delano, Cornelius.

Devol, Gideon,
Drown, Solomon,
Dodge, John T.,
Flagg, Gersham, family,
Farley, Thomas,
Fearing, Noah,
Greene, Abraham,
Gilman, Joseph, family,
Griffin, Caleb,
Haskell, Jonathan,
Knight, Theophilus,
King, Zebulon (killed 1789),
Lathbe, John,
Leaveus, John,
May, John,
Mitchell, Robert,
Mills, William,
Meigs, R. J., jr., family (1791),
Miles, Benjamin, family,
Mervin, Picket
Mills, Charles,
Morse, Moses,
Newell, Samuel, family,
Oaks, Joel,
Putnam, Ezra, jr.,
Pierce, Phineas,
Porter, Ebenezer, family,
Prime, Joseph, family,
Plummer, Jonathan,
Russell, John,
Rouse, John, family,
Smith, James, family,
Story, Daniel,
Shepherd, Enoch, family,
Shiner, William,
Slocumb, Benjamin, family,
Stacey, Joseph, family,
Stacey, Philip,
Story, Andrew, family,
Sprague, William, family,
Sprague, Jonathan,
Springer, Peleg,
Stacey, Rufus,
Shaw, Thomas, family (1790),
Thompson, Joseph,
Tilas, Alexander,
Tuttle, Joel, family,
White, John,
Woodbridge, Dudley, family,
Walker, James,
Warren, Elijah,
Wells, David, family,
Wilson, William, family,
Whipple, Abraham, family,
Wells, Thomas,
Maxon, Richard, family,
Patterson, Nathaniel,
Smith, Benjamin,

Brown, Aaron (Gallipolis),
Batchelder, Gideon (Gallipolis),
Bebee, Frederick,   "
Call, David,
Cushman, Nathaniel,
Comas Lansnett (French),
Choate, Isaac,
Chopman, Joseph
Caldwell, James,
Comas, John,
Callin, French,
Christophe, French,
Dudley, Asa,
Dorsey, James,
Drown, John,
Dennit (French),
Devol, Christopher,
Demsey, Isaac (Gallipolis),
Ford, William, family,
Frothingham, Peter,
Fustlay (French),
Farewell, Jonathan,
Fleming, Andrew (Gallipolis),
Goldsmith, Zaccheus (Gallipolis),
Guthrie, Stephen,
Guthrie, Truman,
Greene, Casey,
Henderson, Edward,
Hackney, Joseph,
Hawkins, Christopher,
Harris, John,
Harte, John (Gallipolis),
James, John, jr.,
Jennings, Joshua,
Jordan & Son (French),
Lewis, Samuel (Gallipolis),
Loring, Israel,
Lake, Archibald, family,
Lake, William, family,
Little, Nathaniel, jr., family,
Lynot, William,
Lalorcey (French),
Lloyd, David,
Label (French),
Moor, John (Gallipolis),
McIntosh, Nathan,
Miller, Joseph,
Mark (French),
Meron (French),
Athone (French),
Nye, Ebenezer, family,
Mills, Benjamin,
Olney, Coggswell, family,
McCullock, William,
Putnam, Ezra, family,
Patterson, Benjamin, family,
Potts, Robert,
Petal, Joseph (French),
Piana (French),
Potter, William (Gallipolis),
Proctor, Jacob (Gallipolis),
Palmer, Frederick (Gallipolis),
Richardson, Phineas (Gallipolis),
Rogers, Joseph (killed 1792),
Rue, Henry,
Ransford, Joseph, family,
Shh, Thomas (Gallipolis),
Sheldon, Jonathan (Gallipolis),
Sholes, Richard (Gallipolis),
Smith, Joseph (Gallipolis),
Smith, William,
Stephens Jacob,
Sprague, Nehemiah,
Shepherd, John,
Shoemann, family, (French),
Tenner, George, family,
Farmer, Jacob,

Brow, Nathaniel,   "
Butler David,   "
Beau, Daniel,   "
Carson, David,
Chople, Antoine (French),
Choate, Francis,
Choate Joshua,
Carroll Michael (Gallipolis),
Camp, John (killed at Big Bottom),
Calter (French),
Chevelett (French),
Crage, William (French),
Davenport, Gould,
Day, John,
David (French),
Delatre (French),
Dodge, Abraham (Gallipolis),
Dunlay, William,   "
Ford, William, jr.,
Frye, Joseph,
Fulham, John,
Fleming, Aride (Gallipolis),
Gilbraith, Thomas (Gallipolis),
Griffin, Asahel,
Guthrie, Elias,
Guthrie, Joseph, family,
Goodenough, Daniel,
Hart, William,
Harris, Edward, family,
Hinckley, Nathaniel,
Hammon, Zoath, family,
James, John, family,
James, William,
Isham, Russell,
Jowrdom (French),
Loring, Daniel family,
Lake, Thomas, family,
Lake, Andrew,
Little, Nathaniel, family,
Lygnum, Joseph,
Luxumburgh (French),
Leggett, Alexander,
Labelle, Francis (French),
Maynard, Daniel (Gallipolis),
McElwee, John,
Merrill, Simeon,
McLeland, Samuel,
Meacham (French),
Lewis (French),
Nealy, Thomas,
Nisewonger, John, family,
McNemarre, John,
O'Brien, Ichabod,
Ovrey (French),
Porter, Samuel,
Potts, James,
Potter, Rouse,
Pamey, Jean (French),
Pierre, Jean (French),
Page, Nathan (Gallipolis),
Potter, Benjamin (Gallipolis),
Randall, Ebenezer (Gallipolis),
Rue, Reuben (Gallipolis),
Reed, Enoch, family,
Roder, ——— (French),
Robbins, Isaac,
Sergent, Roger (Gallipolis),
Safford, Robert (Gallipolis),
Snow, David (Gallipolis),
Seamans, Samuel,
Simonds, Joseph (wounded 1792),
Sparhawk, Noah,
Smith, John,
Simkins, Daniel,
Scott, Alexander,
Thomas, Samuel (Gallipolis),
Finley, John,

[The total number of men who arrived during 1789 was one hundred and fifty-two, and the number of families fifty one.]

SEVENTEEN HUNDRED AND NINETY.

Bliss, Amos, family,
Allison, Robert, family,
Arvin (French),
Anthony (French),
Backus, Elijah,
Bethel, Edward,
Buck, John,
Blackburn, Andrew,
Begnear (French),
Barber, Ezekiel, family,
Browning, William,
Burlingame, Christopher, family,
Bridge, Samuel,

Allen, Justus,
Andre (French),
Applegate, Joseph,
Andrews, John (Gallipolis),
Paker Timothy,
Bailey, Caleb,
Baldwin, Jonathan (Gallipolis),
Bureau, Peter (French),
Badwell, Elijah (Gallipolis),
Bent, Rufus,
Barnes, Samuel,
Bridge, William,
Brown, David, jr. (Gallipolis),

Thierry, ——, family (French),
Tryon, ——, family, (French),
Votier, ——,
Utter, Joseph, family,
Utter, Samuel,
Waterman, John,
Worth, John,
Waldow, Zachariah,
Wood, Joseph,
Waugh, Joseph,
Kerr, Matthew (killed in 1791),
Warth, Robert (killed in 1791),

Tantroff, Antoine (French),
Vanmetre, William,
Venard, Pierre (French)
Vellermine, ——,
Utter, Reuben,
Waterman,Sherman (killed in 1794),
Weight, Jonathan,
Wiser, Jacob,
Worth, George,
Wasson, William, (Gallipolis),
Troop, Zebulon (killed at Big Bottom),

[The total number of arrivals (men) in 1790, was two hundred; inclusive of French one hundred and sixty-five—number of families thirty-one. Of the whole number of French people, thirty-five men and two families remained some time at Marietta.]

CHAPTER IX.

THE INDIAN WAR.

NOTWITHSTANDING the fact that Campus Martius had been built and some other measures taken, such as common prudence would suggest, the New Englanders, in their western home, had no very serious apprehensions of a state of general Indian hostility. As has been shown they were welcomed to the banks of the Muskingum by a large party of Delawares, under Captain Pipe, who made many protestations of friendship; their settlement was made under the conditions of an ordinance which exhibited a great and humane consideration of the Indians' right; the General Government had en-

tered upon a policy which promised an amicable, advantageous and speedy arrangement of Indian affairs in the west, and the settlers themselves, with no past record of antagonism toward the red man of the forest, sought, by fair and honorable treatment, to merit and retain his good-will. They certainly were regarded much more favorably by the Indians than were the pioneers upon the other side of the Ohio. The frontiersmen of western Pennsylvania and Virginia, and the Kentucky borderers, had been engaged for a long term of years in a warfare that was both defensive and offensive against the northwestern tribes, and looked upon the Indian as a creature without any rights they were bound to respect; as something little better, if any, than a wild beast, and equally with the latter a pest to be exterminated, if possible, by rifle and tomahawk, and every savage means known to the frontier.

The Indians at once hated and feared the "Long Knives," as they had named the Virginians, and they doubtless formed their whole idea of the white race upon their knowledge of this class, which they had known the longest and most unfavorably. During the seven years previous to the war, which began on Ohio soil in 1791, it was estimated, says Colonel and Judge Barker,* that on the frontiers south and west of the Ohio river, the Indians killed and took prisoners fifteen hundred people, stole two thousand horses and other property to the value of fifty thousand dollars.

Let it be borne in mind by those who would seek for cause, and endeavor to locate right and wrong, that these denizens of the western world, savages as they were, had only to look a few years backward to be reminded of the perpetration of the most perfidious outrages against their race, by the whites. Savages as they were, they had never struck at the civilized people such cruel and treacherous blows as those by which the kindred of Logan fell at Yellow Creek, or those by which were massacred the peaceful Moravian Delawares, upon the Tuscarawas. No atrocities of the Indians equalled in enormity those of the whites. We only allude to these occurrences to suggest the feeling which doubtless lurked in the breasts of the western Indians when the first settlements were made northwest of the Ohio. There were other causes, more immediate and more potent, which combined, ultimately wrought the nations of the northwest into the heat of that hostility which terrorized the whites from 1790 to 1795. Many of the tribes had only imperfectly comprehended the treaties of Fort McIntosh, Fort Stanwix, and Fort Finney; some were illy satisfied with the provisions which they did understand, and reluctantly assented to, while others refused to attend the treaties, or were improperly represented in them, i. e., by their young men, who were unauthorized to act in council. Those who had entered into the compacts and ceded right in the soil, in good faith, regretted their assent when they saw the white man actually enter their old-time domain, and cabins arise in the clearings; for the great natural boundary once crossed, the Indians seem to have realized that the tide could not be long stayed, even at treaty bounda-

*Colonel Barker's Reminiscences.

ries, and were jealous of future encroachments. Their disquietude was augmented by the intrigues of the British, who still held their posts in the northwest, traded with the Indians, wishing to retain them as allies, and to prevent the settlement of this region by the Americans, desired them to hold possession of it. The temper of the Indians was influenced by the white men among them to the highest pitch, and eventually, by the artifices of British agents, the services of Brant, the famous half-breed, were secured, and he effected the powerful confederation by which St. Clair was defeated.

Having given the reader a general view of the causes which conspired to bring on the war, we shall revert to some occurrences of which it is our province to treat specifically. The war did not commence in the Ohio company's purchase until January, 1791, but for the sake of unity, and to give an adequate idea of the situation, we shall in this chapter give an account of a number of events which occurred in 1788 and 1789.

It was the policy of the General Government to allay, as far as possible by peace processes, the dissatisfaction among the Indians, and Governor St. Clair had been especially charged with this delicate and difficult duty. In anticipation of his arrival in the territory preparations were made for holding a treaty, which it was intended should be confirmatory of the previous treaties, and should also embody some additional pacificatory measures. In June, 1788, the locality soon after named Duncan's Falls, upon the Muskingum, about sixty miles from its mouth, was designated as a place of meeting, and in the latter part of the month Lieutenant McDowell, with a party of thirty men from Fort Harmar, was sent out to convey to this spot provisions and presents, and to build there a council-house and huts for the shelter of those who might attend the contemplated treaty. The locality had been agreed upon rather than Fort Harmar, as really a concession to the Indians, being one of their favorite gathering places, and near a region in which they had one of their most considerable populations. The men from the fort encamped and proceded with the work they had been instructed to perform, and in the meantime the Indians assembled in large numbers, among them being Delawares, Wyandots, members of the Six Nations, Ottawas, Chippewas, and others. On the night of July 12th an attack was made on the tent in which the goods were stored. The sentries were suddenly fired upon and a movement quickly made to follow up the surprise, but the Indian volley being promptly returned by the sentries, and the remainder of the guard being roused from their slumber, coming to the rescue, the party was repulsed before they could effect their purpose, which was doubtless to obtain plunder. The attacking party lost one member and had one wounded by the volley from the soldiers' muskets. In the morning it was found that the dead Indian was a Chippewa, and the Delawares coming into the camp and disclaiming any connection with the attack, to show their friendliness, brought to Lieutenant McDowell six of the Chippewas, whom they averred were of the assailing party. These Indians, whom the Delawares instructed the commandant to do with as he saw

fit in retaliation for the hostility of the night before, were taken to Fort Harmar and there held as prisoners until they made their escape.* All thought of making a treaty at this time and place was now given up, and the labor that had been expended in making preparations was a loss. The goods were sent back to Fort Harmar in the large boat belonging to the Ohio company, which, with another, had been sent up the Muskingum immediately after the arrival at Marietta by rumor of the Indians' perfidy. The boats made the trip to Duncan's Falls and back in seven days. Duncan's Falls† was so named from Major Duncan, a trader who was waiting for the assembling of the Indians to barter for their furs and skins. A mulatto servant who was with him was killed by the Indians the same night they attacked the soldiers.

During the summer and fall of 1788 the Indians remained in the vicinity of the infant settlement and evinced in many ways their hostility toward the whites. Their hatred seemed to constantly increase during this period, and some individuals and tribes who had formerly been considered friendly showed signs of disaffection. Some, however, maintained a respectful attitude throughout the season, and a few exhibited unmistakable sincerity and much warmth of regard for the pioneers. At council held by the several tribes, congregated at Duncan's Falls, the Chippewas and Ottawas announced themselves as against making any treaty, and in favor of war which should only be suspended when the white settlers were driven south and east of the Ohio. The Delawares, Wyandots, and Indians of the Six Nations would not join with them in this expression of enmity, and after a delay of some weeks the Chippewas and Ottawas affected to be reconciled, and asserted that they had no evil intentions. They were too weak of themselves to make war upon the whites, and being unable to draw the more powerful tribes, such as the Delawares and Wyandots, into an offensive alliance, they put on an appearance of friendliness and confined their animosities to the destruction of game in the vicinity of the settlements, and an occasional covert attack upon isolated and unprotected individuals. The Delawares were represented among the hostile bands who roamed the country by a few renegades who had deserted the tribe. The great body of this nation, however, maintained, until the war had commenced in earnest, an honorable peace. Captain Pipe, their leading chief, who, it will be remembered, welcomed the pioneers to the shores of the Muskingum April 7th, dined on several occasions with General Putnam and with the officers at Fort Harmar. He expressed warm friendship, but deprecated the building of houses in Marietta and raising of crops until the treaty had been made.

---

*July 28th.—(1788)—At five o'clock A. M., as I was cleaning my rifle . . . I heard a confused noise at the garrison of men and dogs, and two guns went off. This drew my attention more particularly. Presently I saw two Indians come tumbling over a fence into a field of corn. It proved to be two of the Indian prisoners who had made good their escape. The sentinels who lost them were tried by court-martial, and whipped one hundred lashes in the evening.—Colonel May's journal.

†Duncan's Falls, of the Muskingum, were where the town of Taylorsville, Muskingum county now is, but were obliterated by the slack-water improvement of the river.

The whites had constant knowledge of the presence of evil disposed savages in the country, as well as of those who were friendly. The woods about Marietta were full of carrion, and it was evident that some of the hostile parties were killing all of the game they could under the impression that the food supply of the settlers might be thus cut off. Stripping the slain animals of their skins, they left the carcasses to rot or be devoured by bears and wolves. Alarming rumors of impending danger from attack were occasionally received by the settlers.* The season passed, however, without the occurrence of any actual hostilities.

Impatience was felt on the part of the Ohio company's settlers and the officers at Fort Harmar to effect a treaty as soon as was possible.

Gyantwahia the Cornplanter, a leading chief of the Six Nations (Seneca tribe, the same to which Logan belonged) with about forty Indians arrived at Fort Harmar in September, escorted by a company of soldiers from Fort Pitt, under command of Captain Zeigler. He was a civilized savage, friendly to the United States, and he used his best endeavors to enhance the interests at once of the whites and his own race, by preserving peace. The Ohio company were not unmindful of his great influence or unthankful for his exercise of that influence.† In November a son of the famous Brant came with two hundred warriors to Duncan's Falls and sent an express to Governor St. Clair, asking that the treaty should be held at that place. The governor's refusal to meet in treaty at the spot where but a few months before the Indians had treacherously assailed the guard, incensed Brant, and it was suspected that he used his influence to deter the Shawnees and some other Indians from attending the treaty, when it was finally held at Fort Harmar.

Two hundred warriors arrived at Fort Harmar on the thirteenth of December. They came from the northward along the west shore of the Muskingum, quite a number of them mounted, but the greater proportion of them walking. The flag of the United States was borne aloft at the head of the column, and as they drew near the fort they fired three rifles in the air to indicate that they were friendly and had no use for loaded guns. "The salute," says Hildreth, "was returned by the cannon and musketry of the soldiers, for several minutes, sounding so much like a real engagement of hostile bands that the old officers at Campus Martius were quite animated with the sound." Troops, with music playing, escorted the visitors into the fort, and then began the formal preliminaries which led to the formation of the treaty, a slow work, which was not consummated until January 9, 1789. The negotiations were carried on in the council house, which stood near the bank of the Muskingum, a short distance north of the garrison. A council fire was kindled here, and around it gathered the Indian sachems and chiefs in their conference with Governor St. Clair, his staff of civilians and the officers from Fort Harmar. The venerable John Heckewelder, Moravian missionary, who had been for many years among the Delawares on the Tuscarawas, was present and exerted a benign influence during the progress of the treaty. General Richard Butler served as a commissioner at this treaty. Three interpreters, Nicholson, Williams and La Chappelle, acted as the principal agents between the Indians and whites when their services were needed, which was not continually, as some of the chiefs could speak the English tongue quite fluently. Governor St. Clair was subject to the gout, and during the treaty suffered from an acute attack. He was carried on a chair daily by the soldiers to the council house.

In reality two treaties were made on this occasion, each of which, so far as appearances indicated, was highly satisfactory to all parties concerned. The first treaty was with the Indians of the Six Nations, and was signed by twenty-four of their chiefs. It was merely confirmatory of the previous treaties, but for the renewal of their assent to the provisions which had been stipulated the Six Nations were given presents, in goods, to the value of three thousand dollars. Simultaneously with the progress of this treaty a council was carried on from day to day with the Wyandots, Delawares, Ottawas, Chippewas, Pottowtoamies and Sacs, which confirmed and extended the treaty of Fort McIntosh. In addition to the provisions of former treaties in regard to councils, some of the measures of the treaty of Fort Harmar were as follows: The Indians were to be allowed to hunt within the territory ceded to the United States so long as they should demean themselves peaceably. Trade was to be opened with the several nations. They were enjoined to afford protection to all regularly licensed traders in their midst, and the treaty stipulated that to the end that they might not be imposed upon in their traffic, no person should be allowed to reside at the towns or hunting camps who was

---

*Colonel May's journal under date of Monday, July 23, contained mention of one such rumor:

"Henry Williams alarmed us a little this evening when he returned from the Virginia shore; he brought information that our settlement was to be attacked this night by three strong parties of Chippewa Indians—so said the report—to relieve the prisoners. We have sent this information over to the garrison. It proved false, however, but it made some trouble for us. We may always expect trouble while travelling through this life, which is nothing more than a wilderness world. We ought to make the best use we can of these matters, small and great. At Boston we have frequent alarms of fire and inundations of the tides; here the Indians answer the same purpose."

†The agents of the Ohio company at a meeting held in January, 1789, passed the following:

"WHEREAS, the Gyantwahia, or the Cornplanter, a chief of the Seneca nation, has since the treaty of peace in 1784, between the United States and Indian nations, in many instances been of great service to the United States, and the friendship he has manifested to the proprietors of lands purchased by the Ohio company has been of particular service to them, therefore

Resolved, That one mile square of the donation lands be granted to the Gyantwahia and his heirs forever, in such place as the committee appointed to examine proper places of settlement shall assign, and that the duties and conditions required of other settlers shall in this case be dispensed with, and the committee are directed to give him a deed.—Ohio company's journal, page 54.

Subsequently the directors passed a resolution referring to the above, and authorizing the exploring committee to lay out a mile square of land on the river Muskingum.

Cornplanter died at Cornplanterstown, Pennsylvania, February 18, 1836, aged about one hundred years. A monument was erected to his memory by authority of the legislature of Pennsylvania, expressed by act of March, 1866, and upon the occasion of its completion and unveiling Hon. James Snowden, of Philadelphia, delivered an address.

not provided with a license bearing the seal of the governor of the territory northwest of the Ohio. Should any nation of Indians meditate a war against the United States, and knowledge of the same come to any of the tribes party to the treaty, they were to give immediate notice to the governor, and they were to attempt to prevent any hostile nation from marching through their country against the United States, or any one of them. In like manner the United States was to give notice to the Indian nations of any harm that might be meditated against them. Settlement by white men upon the lands of the Indians was forbidden, and stipulations were made that each party to the treaty should give up murderers.* A memorandum was annexed, to the effect that the Wyandots had laid claim to the lands that had been granted to the Shawnees at the treaty held at Fort Finney, and had declared that as the Shawnees had been so restless and made so much trouble, they now dispossess them unless they should now assent to peace. The treaties were concluded upon the ninth of January and ratified upon the twelfth.

So overjoyed were the Marietta settlers with the result of Governor St. Clair's conference with the Indians, that they provided a dinner at Campus Martius, to which the principal chiefs were invited,† and also the officers from Fort Harmar. The feast passed off pleasantly and harmoniously, the Indian chiefs behaving with "very great decorum." Wine was served, and Cornplanter and other chiefs made speeches breathing the spirit of warmest friendship. On the day following the Indians dispersed. Then the year 1789 opened auspiciously for the frontier settlements.

The people at Marietta felt a deep sense of gratitude toward Governor St. Clair for the peace he had secured, and at a public meeting held on the fourth of February, they appointed Colonel Archibald Crary, Colonel Robert Oliver, Mr. Backus, Major Haffield White and Major Sargent, to draw up an address which should express to

---

* American State Papers--Indian Affairs, vol. V.

† The following letter of invitation to the Indians was published in the *Massachusetts Spy* soon after the occurrence narrated, and reproduced in Hildreth's Pioneer History:

"*To Messrs. Nicholson, Williams, and LaChappelle, Indian interpreters at Fort Harmar:*

"You are requested to inform the Wyandots, Delawares, Chippewas, Ottawas, Miamis, Pottawatomies, and Sacs, with the Senecas and such of the Five Nations as are present, that we are desirous of celebrating the good work which the Great Spirit has permitted our father, the governor, with our brother, General Butler, and their sachems and chiefs so happily to accomplish, for which purpose we will prepare an entertainment on Monday next, at two o'clock, and our brothers, the sachems and chiefs, to whom we now send tokens, are requested to attend at that time; that we may in friendship and as true brothers, eat and drink together, and smoke the pipe of everlasting peace; and evince to the whole world how bright and strong is the chain which the thirteen United States hold fast at one end, and the Wyandots, etc., at the other. We are very sorry we cannot entertain all of our brethren together, with their wives and children; but as we have come into this country a very long way, some of us forty or fifty days' journey toward the rising sun, and could not bring much provision along with us, it is now out of our power. We trust the Great Spirit will permit us to plant and gather our corn, and increase our stores, and their children and children's children may be told how much we shall all rejoice to make glad their hearts when they come to see us."

him their appreciation of his services. They fulfilled the task, and subsequently the following was forwarded to him as voicing the sentiments of the people—and, by the way, a testimonial which must have given the old Federalist governor some pleasant thoughts to relieve the pain caused by the bitter aspersions generally made when his great reverse of fortune came upon him:

To His Excellency, Arthur St. Clair, esq., Governor and Commander-in-Chief of the Territory of the United States Northwest of the River Ohio:

We, the citizens of Marietta, assembled at Campus Martius, beg leave to address your excellency with the most cordial congratulations upon the happy issue of Indian affairs. For this event, so interesting to the United States at large, and to this settlement in particular, we hold ourselves indebted, under God, to your excellency's wisdom and unremitting exertions displayed during the long and tedious negotiation of the treaty. It was with pain and very affectionate sympathy that we beheld this business spun out by the Indian nations through so many tedious months and to a season of the year, which from its inclemency must have endangered and perhaps impaired the health and constitution of a character under whose auspices and wise administration of government we hope to be a good and happy people.

But the inhabitants were not long to rest in the lull of peace which they had secured and fondly fancied they should permanently enjoy. Some of the Indian tribes were not represented in the treaty at all. Some, as the Shawnees, by but few of their braves and others, as they afterward claimed, not by their chiefs, but by young men who were unauthorized to act.* The Chippewas asserted that they had had no share of the goods distributed at the treaty.† [Tahre, the Crane of the Wyandots, and Captain Pipe of the Delawares, were among the well known chiefs who acknowledged the treaty of Fort Harmar to be binding.] The truth seems to have been that many of the tribes not present at the treaty resented the right of those who were there to barter away their lands, basing their opinion upon the agreement which they averred had been made in their general council in 1788, that no bargain or sale would be considered valid unless generally assented to.

Hostilities were commenced in the spring following the making of the treaty, the Indians passing by the Ohio company's settlements to strike their old enemies, the "Long Knives." Over twenty Virginians were killed or taken prisoners. The Wabash Indians and the Shawnees harassed travellers going up or down the Ohio. Depredations were committed all along the border from Pittsburgh to Louisville.

Upon the first of May, 1789, the first blow was struck within the limits of the Ohio company's purchase. Captain Zebulon King was killed at Belpre. He had located at the middle settlement with the Belpre company of associates a short time before, had been allotted his land and was engaged in clearing it when he was shot down

---

* Le Gris, the great chief of the Miamis, in April, 1790, said to Gamelin that the Muskingum treaty was not made by chiefs or delegates, but by young men acting without authority.—Albach's Annals of the West, p. 525.

† Massass, a Chippewa, and one who had signed the treaty at Fort Harmar, said at Greenville in 1795, "at that treaty (Fort Harmar) we had not good interpreters, and we were left partly unacquainted with many particulars of it. . . . If our uncles, the Wyandots, and grandfathers, the Delawares, have received presents, they have kept them to themselves.—Ibid, p. 524.

by an enemy in concealment, who, as soon as he had fallen, sprung to his side, scalped him and fled. Two Indians were engaged in the murder. The settlers at Belpre were thrown in a state of terrible consternation by this sudden taking off of one of their number.

This act had proved, conclusively, that the Indians could not be trusted, and no one knew how soon they might claim another victim, or surprise and destroy the whole of the little band.

From this time on, not alone at Belpre, but at Marietta and the other settlements, there was great distress. Indian signs were frequently found in the woods, and it was well known that they were often lurking in ambush to take advantage of those who should expose themselves. Men went forth to their work of clearing with apprehensions which made them ill at ease, and the women remaining in the cabins were filled with a nameless dread of danger to themselves and their loved ones away. The dark forest, surrounding the little clearings where the white man's axe had made it possible for the warm sun to reach the virgin soil, was a *terra incognita*, which imagination peopled with hords of savages plotting the destruction of the pioneers' cabins. As a matter of fact there were but few Indians in the immediate vicinity of the Ohio company's settlements, even at the time the greater outrages were perpetrated, and they were roving bands who came down from what is now the interior of the State. But the terror of the pioneers was none the less deep and intense if it was very often vague and the product of excited fancy. Any sound, however common, echoing through the forest—the cry of a bird, the snapping of a dry twig, caused man or woman to start with fright, such was the tension of their nerves, and to listen with anxious and troubled looks for any further breaking of silence that might possibly indicate the proximity, or the approach of a stealthy enemy.

In the month of August the little Belpre settlement was again horrified by the commission of an Indian atrocity. Two boys were killed at Meig's station, a small stockade on the Little Kanawha, a mile from its mouth. They had gone out Saturday, towards night, from their home, a small log cabin, to the block-house, not more than forty rods away, and their parents were alarmed at their failure to return. The next day their bodies were found in the edge of the woods, near a cornfield, where they had gone to feed the cows. They had been tomahawked; no gun had been fired, and the boys had probably made no outcry. The same night a woman, sleeping near the port-hole in the block-house, was awakened by a glare of light by her bedside and a stifling sensation caused by smoke. A fire brand had been thrust through the port-hole and was blazing upon the floor. The woman's awakening had doubtless saved the occupants from death by fire, or if they had escaped that, butchery by the Indians. A party of men went out from Belpre, under arms, and assisted in the burial of the murdered boys.

Upon the seventh of August John Mathews, the surveyor, and his party of assistants and soldiers were attacked by a strong band of Indians in what is now Lawrence county. Several were killed in this attack, and Mathews narrowly escaped. In spite of the admonitions of his friends and a full personal knowledge of the danger to which he was exposed, Mr. Mathews had carried on the labor of surveying the ranges west of Marietta, all through the season. The Indians had an especial dislike for the surveyors, who were running lines through the forest, and had frequently exhibited their hostility toward the men who three years previously had surveyed the "seven ranges." Mr. Mathews had become accustomed to the dangers of the wilderness while assisting in the work to which allusion has been made, and hence was not seriously alarmed when he discovered evidences that the Indians were about. On the morning of the sixth he had seen the tracks of a man and a horse, and had discovered that one of his own horses was missing. At night one of his assistants, Patchen by name, reported that he had seen moccasin tracks in several places and followed them to where they joined the trail found in the morning. It was the almost universal belief among the men that the trail they had discovered was that of a party of Indians who had made a plundering expedition to some of the Virginia settlements and were now returning toward the Scioto, where doubtless their villages were situated. As a measure of proper precaution, however, the corporal of the guard was ordered to keep sentries out during the night, and just before dawn, when the darkness of night was turning to gray, (this being the favorite time among the Indians for making their attacks), the whole force was called to arms and a reconnoissance made. No signs of a foe were to be seen, and at broad day, all danger past, as it was supposed, the soldiers went into camp. They had not been long returned and were scattered about the camp, some sitting upon their blankets and some kindling fires, when they were startled by two rifle shots, occurring almost simultaneously. Mathews was sitting upon his blanket, only partly dressed, and Patchen was by his side. The latter threw up his hands and exclaimed: "My God, I am killed!" and fell backward, dead. Mathews, turning toward him, saw a wound in his breast from which the blood gushed forth. He had scarcely time to notice the fate of his companion and friend, for the first shots were quickly followed by a volley, the Indians rising from their concealment and taking aim with a deliberation which made their fire a deadly one. The soldiers had sprung to their feet at the first discharge, only to become better targets for the Indians' rifle balls, and they all fell, either mortally wounded or dead, with the exception of the corporal, between whom and the assailants there was a large tree which hid him from their view and saved his life. With a wild and horrible yell the Indians sprang forward into the camp, and as they rushed upon their dead and wounded victims with tomahawks and knives, Mathews and three other men fled in an opposite direction, followed by several of the enemy, who, however, soon gave up the chase. Mathews legs and feet were bare, and he suffered in his flight through the stiff underbrush and briers, exceedingly. His companion's coat was arranged to shield him, but his feet, still uncovered, became so blistered after he had run several miles and reached the Ohio, that he could not endure the pain; so the two men set about making a raft of logs which they fastened together with grape vines. Before they had completed this work a Kentucky boat came down the river, which they boarded and upon which they found the other two men, who had reached the river farther up stream. Four miles down the Ohio they came upon the Ohio company's boat, in charge of Colonel Return J. Meigs. Before night the corporal arrived and the survivors were reunited. He had fallen over a log in his flight, and had lain behind it and watched the Indians until they had plundered and abandoned the camp. They had scalped the killed, broken the muskets of the soldiers upon the trees and rocks, taken everything of value, including some of the dead men's clothing. The compass, with its delicately vibrating needle, they had contemplated with mingled wonder, admiration and amusement. On the same day that this bloody attack was made Colonel Meigs, lying on his boat in the river, had become alarmed at the discovery of fresh Indian signs, and dropped down stream to the point where is now situated the village of Burlington. Here his men had hastily built a block-house for defence in case of necessity. Meigs and Mathews now resorted to this little stronghold and remained there until the tenth of August, when another party of surveyors, who had been out under a Mr. Backus, arrived, and they then went up the river, resolving to give up the work of surveying for an indefinite time. Three days later, having stopped at a convenient point, a squad of well armed men accompanied Mathews to the scene of the attack. He discovered the ghastly remains of the murdered men, which had been torn and partly devoured by wolves. It was thought that the attacking party on this occasion were Shawnees, and the testimony of some friendly Wyandots and Delawares was to that effect.

Not many more incidents of Indian hostility were to be set down in the annals of 1789, and in spite of the several alarming events which occurred during the summer, the inhabitants of the several settlements carried on their usual avocations and were fairly prosperous. Some precautions were taken, but after a time individuals and communities ceased to exercise that constant care and watchfulness, which was their surest safeguard. They became accustomed to danger, and to a certain extent contemptuous of it. The settlers at Waterford (then called Plainfield), which was now the frontier post, received upon the third of May, a letter from General Putnam, which informed them of the murder of Captain King, at Belpre, upon the first. They assembled, organized a military company and made plans for the building of a block-house, which was finished early in July, under the direction of Colonel Robert Oliver. William Gray was chosen captain of the military; David Wilson, sargent; and Andrew Webster, corporal. The block-house and the military organization were happily not necessary during 1789 and 1790, but there came a time when their practical utility was beyond dispute.

The capture of John Gardner, at Waterford, in September, 1789, was a peculiar incident, illustrating the boldness and ingenuity of the Indians, and the thoughtlessness of the whites at this period. It is true that it was nominally a time of peace, and yet several evil acts had been committed by the savages within a few months, and it is difficult to see how a man who had been all of this time in the frontier country would allow himself to fall into such a trap as did Gardner. He was a young man from Marblehead, Massachusetts, had been bred a sailor, and had come to the west as did many others, in search of fortune and adventure. He had entered into a kind of a partnership with Jervis Cutler to clear up some land, and on the day he was taken prisoner was alone in the woods, Custer having gone to Marietta for the purpose of procuring provisions. Four Indians and a white man came within a few feet of him before they were perceived, and when he chanced to raise his eyes and did see them, they beckoned to him; he walked over to them and they coolly made him their prisoner. One relieved him of his gun, another threw a slip noose over his head, and two of them taking hold of his hands led him away. This was done so close to other men engaged at work that the Indians would scarcely have dared to fire their guns. As the captive was led away and the party passed along the ridge near Wolf Creek mills, then building, Gardner could catch an occasional glimpse through the hazel thicket which bordered the path of the men, his comrades and fellow pioneers, hewing timbers and placing them in position. He could easily have made himself heard by them, but had he called out a tomahawk sunk in his brain would have been the penalty. What thoughts passed through the mind of the young man can be better imagined than described. He was a captive of ten savages, marching away he knew not whither, to a fate which he dared not think upon, while down below him in the valley were friends, who, ignorant of his misfortune, were cheerily laboring at the mill. Gardner was not destined, however, to long remain a prisoner with the Shawnees (for to that tribe his captors belonged), and on the second night effected his escape, a proceeding which required much patience and nerve. He slept tightly bound with deerskin thongs, and lying across a bowed sapling, to which he was also made fast, and upon the boughs of which the Shawnee warriors had tied cow-bells, which, should the prisoner make an unusual movement, would produce a clangor sufficient to bring every Indian from slumber to his feet. A gentle rain fell that night and favored the plans of the captive, who had resolved even at the risk of his life to escape. The leathern thongs softened and made pliable by the moisture were by two or three hours of straining so stretched as to permit Gardner to slip his hands through them, and that being done he released with fearful slowness the bent sapling, fearing that on any instant some of his captors would awake, and that he would either be killed or retaken and subjected to torture. At last the tree had risen to its natural position, and not a bell had sounded however faintly. Stepping silently among the prostrate and oblivious Indians the young man secured his gun and went out into the darkness of the forest, proceeding slowly and cautiously at first least he should yet wake the sleepers at the camp, but as he got farther away from them, and the sound of the snapping of the dry twigs under his feet could not by any possibility reach their ears, running at full speed. He walked or ran all day, travelling eastward, and never stopping save to drink from the little streams that he crossed. He was without food and dared not fire his gun as he had but one load of ammunition, and knew not when he should need that for a sterner purpose than bringing down game. At night he feared to kindle a fire, least it should reveal to those whom he imagined pursued him his whereabouts. He slept in a hollow log, the ends of which he filled with brush to keep away wolves. The second day of his flight, towards evening, he came to the Wolf Creek mills, and there met Jervis Cutler, who was on his way back to Waterford from Marietta, and entirely ignorant of his friend's disappearance and his four days of thrilling experience.

This is the simple story of one of those few romantic and exciting Indian adventures of which southeastern Ohio was the theatre, which, although serving to illustrate the dangers to which the inhabitants were daily exposed, still presents no element of blood-curdling horror. Well had it been for the pioneer settlements of Washington county if the chronicling of this history made no page sadder than is this.

During the spring of 1790 many reports and rumors reached Marietta of outrages perpetrated by the Shawnees at the mouth of the Scioto, but the Ohio company's settlements were left undisturbed.

By fall, however, there were ominous indications of a general war. In June Major Doughty, with one hundred and fifty men from Fort Harmar, had gone down the Ohio and commenced building Fort Washington, within the present limits of Cincinnati. A little later, General Harmar arrived there with three hundred men, and his force being increased by the addition of nearly a thousand militia men from Kentucky, Virginia, and Pennsylvania, he marched into the Indian country, and destroyed several large villages upon the Miami of the Lakes (Maumee). General Harmar's force suffered two defeats, one upon the nineteenth and the other upon the twenty-second of October, and lost a large number of men. The failure of this expedition was doubtless largely due to the inefficiency of the militia, and dissensions among the officers. General Harmar was severely condemned, and his action was investigated by a court of inquiry, with the result, however, of entirely exonerating him from blame. The Indians did not regard seriously the destruction of their towns, and seemed to magnify their victory over the army, it being currently reported among them that five hundred of the Americans had been killed. They were exasperated by the slight losses they had sustained through the invasion of their country, and emboldened by the fact that they had defeated the forces sent out against them. They made open threats now that "before the leaves should again come forth, not a single cabin fire of the whites should burn north of the Ohio." It was rumored that they were marching in large

force against the settlements upon the Muskingum and the Miamis.

About the time that General Harmar set out to bring the Indians to terms, or to chastise them, the attitude of the British was fully revealed. Governor St. Clair sent a letter to the governor of Detroit, informing him of the expedition that was to be made, and that the United States had no intention of molesting any of the British posts, and also requesting that no aid be furnished the hostile Indians in the way of furnishing them arms or ammunition. The letter was delivered by Return J. Meigs, jr. (afterwards governor of Ohio), who, accompanied by John, a son of Commodore Abraham Whipple, made the perilous journey to Detroit through the great wilderness, inhabited only by savages, and trackless save for the narrow trails worn by moccasined feet. A horse which these men took with them to carry their provisions was stolen by the Indians, and they made the greater part of the journey on foot. The British governor received Meigs with very distant manner, but, after considerable delay, consented to return a formal answer, which was exceedingly noncommittal in its character. Meigs was informed that it would be extremely hazardous to return to Marietta as he had come, even with a flag of truce, and he made therefore a long journey by water to Presque Isle, from thence over to the Allegheny and down that stream to the Ohio, and thence to his home by boat. Soon after this the Americans had positive proof that agents of the British were furnishing with military stores the very tribes which were most hostile.

General Harmar returned to the fort bearing his name in November, which, according to a good authority,[*] had been, during a portion at least of his absence, in charge of one of the sergeants of militia, Colonel Joseph Barker. Captain Zeigler was, however, the officer in command most of the time during the Indian war.[†]

Before the expedition of Harmar was entered upon the Ohio company had taken some precautions intended to strengthen the settlements within the purchase against Indian attack. The disastrous outcome of the campaign caused these measures for protection to be redoubled. Campus Martius was put in a good state of repair, and by authority of the Secretary of War an additional corps of men was raised to serve as guards for the several settlements. In November Colonel Sproat, commandant of the militia, was authorized to enlist scouts or rangers, and this number was subsequently increased to ten. They were sent out daily to scout the woods for signs of the enemy.

Hostilities had been continued upon the Ohio during the summer, and Governor St. Clair, writing to the Secretary of War upon the nineteenth of September, 1790, mentioned the fact that Captain McCurdy's boat had been fired upon between Marietta and Fort Washington, and that five or six men had been killed.

No events of serious nature, however, occurred within the limits of the Ohio company's lands. Indians hov-

*Horace Nye in *Western Recorder,* 1847.

†Testimony of the Ohio company's journal; Dr. S. P. Hildreth in American Pioneer and Pioneer History; Thomas Wallcut's journal, etc.

ered around the settlements, and the indications of their presence were oftened discovered by the spies, but they committed no depredations other than stealing a few horses.

Indeed, so peaceful had been the lives of the pioneers during the season and so promising did the future appear, that the regular occupations of the inhabitants were not only carried on, but new enterprises engaged their attention, and new institutions were brought into being in the western world. For the convenience of the members the Belpre association had divided into three settlements, which were called the "upper," "lower," and "middle" stations. A new association, alluded to in the preceding chapter, had been formed, and in the fall of 1790 had made a settlement at Big Bottom, * upon the Muskingum, which had attracted attention from its great beauty and richness. The association was composed of thirty-six members, but only eighteen went originally to the station, and one of these, the leader of the little colony, Colonel William Stacey, it appears did not remain there. Isaac Meeks, a Virginian frontiersman, was employed as hunter in the settlement, and brought with him his wife and two children. A block-house of good size was erected on the left bank of the river, and upon the lower bottom. One cabin was erected a short distance from the block-house, and was occupied by Francis and Isaac Choate, while another which had been a part of the "tomahawk improvement" made several years before by some Virginia squatter, was fitted up and occupied by Asa and Eleazer Bullard, brothers. These cabins were each about twenty rods from the defence which the associates built, the first above and the latter below. The settlement was composed principally of young men, inexperienced, and poorly qualified to occupy the frontier part which they did.

"They had neglected," says Colonel Barker,* "to enclose their house with palisades, and ceasing to complete the work the general interest was lost in that of the convenience of each individual. Another error was the neglect of any regular system of defence, and the omission of setting sentries. Those most familiar with the Indians had little doubt of their hostility, and had strongly opposed the settlers going out that fall, and advised them to remain until spring, by which time the question of war or peace would probably be decided." They were impatient, however, and had gone out, to invite by their exposed situation an Indian attack. And so it came about that the war began in earnest in the Ohio company's purchase, at this settlement. The massacre which occurred here on the second of January, 1791, was the bloodiest event in the annals of the first settlement of Ohio, and it not only terrorized the inhabitants of Marietta, Waterford and Belpre, but sent a thrill of horror into all of the border settlements of Virginia and Pennsylvania which left their people, accustomed as they

had long been to Indian attrocities, filled with foreboding for many a day.

The early part of the winter of 1790–91 was of unusual severity, and this fact undoubtedly made not only the young men at Big Bottom, but the settlers at all of the other stations less careful in guarding against Indian attack than they would otherwise have been, for the winter was very generally regarded as a season when there was immunity from depredations by the savages, and especially was this true when it was one of great cold.* The Indians, therefore, in making this attack in the winter, made an exception to their common custom and exceeded their usual shrewdness. It is supposed that they had originally designed falling upon and massacreing the settlers at Waterford (whom they had doubtless learned were not as watchful as they had formerly been), but that coming first to the Big Bottom settlement and recognizing their opportunity there, they had after holding a hasty council, decided to attack it.

The Indians, as it was subsequently learned, crossed the river upon the ice a few rods above the upper cabin, and then the warriors were divided into two parties. A small number of the savages made their way to the cabin occupied by the Choates and another and much larger party simultaneously, by a short detour, arrived at the block-house. No eye had observed them, and their quick but cautious approach had not started the dogs to barking. The Choate brothers and two men, Thomas Shaw and James Patten, who were living with them, were eating their supper, and upon the entrance of the Indians it seems, supposed them to be friendly and invited them to partake. To avert suspicion until they could fully project their plan of action, the Indians did actually help themselves to food, but after a lapse of not more than two or three minutes, and after having disposed themselves about the apartment in such manner as to best meet any resistance that might be made, they indicated by signs that their hosts were prisoners and quickly bound them with some thongs which they discovered in the cabin. The four men, taken by surprise and confronted by more than their own number, offered no opposition, and made no remonstrance. Scarcely a word was spoken. While quiet capture was effected at the cabin a scene of carnage was being enacted at the block-house. The inmates had gathered around the large fireplace, some engaged in preparing the evening meal and others having come in from work warming themselves by the genial blaze, when the door was thrown suddenly open and a volley of musketry poured death into their midst. Several fell lifeless to the floor, and one, Zebulon

---

* Big Bottom was so named because the broadest portion of the valley between the mouth of the Muskingum and Duncan's Falls. Windsor township, of Morgan county (adjoining Washington upon the east and south), included this historic locality in its limits.

* Reminiscences of Colonel Joseph Barker—MSS.

*Joseph Doddridge in his valuable and very reliable Notes on the Settlement and Indian Wars of the Western parts of Virginia and Pennsylvania (p. 262) has the following upon this topic:

.   .   " During the long continued Indian wars sustained by the first settlers of the western country they enjoyed no peace excepting in the winter season, when owing to the severity of the weather the Indians were unable to make their excursions into the settlements. The onset of winter was therefore hailed as a jubilee by the early inhabitants of the country, who throughout the spring and the early part of the fall had been cooped up in their little uncomfortable forts.

.   .   .   To our forefathers the gloomy months of winter were more pleasant than the zephyrs of spring and the flowers of May."

Throop, who was bending over a frying pan in which he was cooking venison for supper, sank down upon the blazing logs. The shots were fired from without, while one of the Indians who had burst the door in held it open. No sooner had the guns been emptied than with a fiendish yell the savages leaped through the smoke to finish with their tomahawks the butchery began with powder and ball. So sudden and fierce was the onslaught that but little resistance could be made, and one after another the inmates of the block-house were dispatched. Only one Indian was wounded, and he by the wife of Isaac Meeks, the Virginia hunter. She had witnessed the brutal slaying of her two children, had seen their brains dashed out and their bodies cast upon the fire, and with the courage of madness she seized an axe and struck wildly at one of the murderers. The blow came very near proving fatal at the instant (and did inflict a wound from which it was afterward thought the Indian would die), but it was quickly avenged by a companion of the assaulted one, who, coming up behind her as the woman was again raising the heavy axe to strike, cleft her skull with his tomahawk. The air was filled with the wild yells of the Indians, the moans of the dying, the agonizing shrieks and the supplications of those on whom the cruel death blow had not yet descended. All were quickly dispatched except Phillip, a son of Colonel William Stacey, who, during the excitement of the massacre, had cowered down in a corner of the room and pulled some bed clothes over himself. He was discovered after the bloody work of killing and scalping the men had been completed, by an Indian who was assisting in gathering up the various articles of plunder to remove them. As soon as his hiding-place was revealed a tomahawk was raised to kill him, and the terrified boy who threw himself at the feet of his would-be murderer, would have been dispatched in spite of his piteous entreaties if another Indian had not interposed and saved him. His brother, John Stacey, was the last one of the party killed. He had managed, unperceived, to climb through a scuttle hole into the low upper story or loft of the house, and from there made his way onto the roof, when he was fired upon and killed by some of the party who had remained outside during the progress of the butchering. On seeing the Indians upon the ground and knowing that his last chance of escape was shut off, he had fallen down in despair and cried out: "I am the only one left, for God's sake spare my life," but the only answer was the ringing rifle shot and an exultant cry from the fierce warriors below him.

The Ballards—Asa and Eleazer—who had been drawn from their cabin by the noise of the muskets and the loud shouts of the savages—caught sight of young Stacey as he emerged upon the roof and heard his agonizing appeal to the merciless enemy, and quickly comprehending the situation sprang back into their cabin, secured their rifles and fled, keeping the building between them and the Indians. They closed the door as they hurriedly left the cabin, and had got only a few rods away when they heard it burst open and the still bloodthirsty savages uttering imprecations and exclamations of chagrin upon discover-

ing their escape. Of the nineteen persons imperilled in this sudden and unsuspected attack, these two men were the only ones who escaped. Four were taken prisoners at the Choate cabin, and one, the boy—Philip Stacey—at the block-house, while twelve were killed. Their names were Ezra Putnam, Zebulon Throop, John Stacey, John Camp, Jonathan Farewell, James Couch, John Clark, William James, Isaac Meek, his wife and two children. Colonel William Stacey, William Smith, and some of the other associates were not present at the time of the attack. Had the first named been at the block-house the massacre would very likely have been prevented, and even had his advice been acted upon the great calamity might have been averted. Only a few days before the massacre he had urged the young men to put their block-house in better order to resist an attack, should one be made, to discontinue work at sundown, have doors and windows securely closed, palisades erected around the building, and sentries posted at good points of observation to warn the little garrison of the approach of an enemy. Had these precautions been observed it would have been impossible for the Indians to have made a successful attack, or at least to commit a wholesale murder as they did. The men had good arms and a sufficient number of them, but they were standing in the corner of the block-house when the Indians, without any warning, entered, and overwhelmed the surprised and terror-stricken group gathered about the fire.[*]

The escape of the Ballards was very fortunate. Had the Indians succeeded in capturing or killing them they doubtless would have come down on the Waterford and Wolf Creek Mills settlements and repeated the horrors of the Big Bottom massacre, but as the two men had fled they surmised that they would carry warning to those stations, and the party returned, with the exception of a few forming a scouting band who, it was subsequently discovered, penetrated the forest to the southeast and hovered threateningly around Wolf Creek Mills.

The Ballards in their flight came upon a hunting camp about four miles from the scene of the massacre, and there found Captain Joseph Rodgers, an experienced woodsman (who was afterwards a ranger or spy for the Marietta settlement) and a friendly Mohican Indian. They were wrapped in their blankets and asleep by the fire. Awakened and told the probable fate of the Big Bottom settlers, they seized their guns and leaving everything else behind them that they might make greater haste, started out in the darkness for the settlement at the mills. On arriving there they found that many of the heads of families were in Marietta attending the court of quarter sessions, and the news that they brought caused the utmost agitation among the women and children. Captain Rodgers immediately assumed direction of the preparations for defence, and his presence did much toward allaying the feeling of consternation which

*The story of the massacre is taken principally from Hildreth's Pioneer History, as are many of the local incidents of the Indian war. Other authorities on the same subjects have been consulted, viz: The recollections of Colonel Barker (MSS), and a series of valuable papers by Horace Wye, published in the *Western Recorder* in 1847.

filled the minds of the people. The situation was a desperate one. There had been no block-house erected here as the Ohio company directors had suggested there should be, and the absence of a number of the men materially increased the danger to which the remainder would be subjected in case of an attack, which was momentarily expected. Captain Rodgers' word was law, and he hastily notified all of the inhabitants to assemble in Colonel Robert Oliver's cabin, which was the largest and strongest. Water was carried from the creek until all the tubs, casks, buckets, and other available articles were filled and others prepared to quench the flames should the Indians set fire to their cattle fort, and the windows and door strongly barricaded, the company passed the long night, fearing, hoping, praying, peering into the darkness through the loop holes which had been made between the logs, listening for any sound that should bring intelligence of the stealthy enemy, waiting with tense nerves for whatever might come, and resolved, should it be the worst, to defend themselves as best they could, and sell their lives as dearly as possible. There were about thirty persons, men, women and children, crowded in the little cabin, and of this number only seven were men. Outside under cover of some palings was posted a sentry. Just before dawn he saw some Indians approach, and it was feared that they would make an attack, but as they undoubtedly saw that the people were on their guard they retreated in a short time. Daylight brought a very blessed relief to the feelings of the women and children, and even the men, for they had had every reason to apprehend an attack.

The people of Waterford had been made acquainted with the news of the attack on the Big Bottom settlement in the night by Samuel Mitchell from the mills. The settlement extended nearly two miles along the river, but every cabin was visited, either by Mitchell or by James and Daniel Convers, whom he had aroused first to help him spread the alarm. As the news was carried from door to door, terrified people aroused from their sleep, came hurrying to the block-house, carrying little else than such arms as they could command. Seventy persons passed the night in a room about fifteen feet square. There were more men here in proportion to the total number of inhabitants than at the mills, and the block-house was considered a very good defence and while the situation was not as harrowing as at the last named settlement, the people nevertheless passed a night which was full of apprehension and suspense.

Two days after the massacre Captain Rodgers led a company of men to Big Bottom. They met a company from Marietta headed by Anselem Tupper and together they found that the Indians after taking the lives of the twelve persons and carrying a quantity of provisions out of the house had pulled up the flooring, piled it over the bodies of their victims and set fire to the whole. The block-house had not long been built, was constructed of beech logs, and had been only partly consumed. Most of the bodies, however, were so disfigured by the tomahawk and by fire as to be unrecognizable. William James' remains were identified by his great size; he had measured

six feet four inches in stature and was of massive build otherwise. The ground being frozen very hard a grave was dug within the walls of the big cabin, where it had been prevented from freezing by the fire, and there these victims of a savage war were buried, side by side as they had fallen and the charred charnel-house, remained in the now solitary and soundless forest as a grim shelter from the rain, and snow, a desolate monument to the memory of the brave, unfortunate pioneers who slept beneath it, and a landmark which, to the hunter or scout passing it afar off, had a horrible suggestiveness of the fate which might be his. No attempt was made to again form a settlement here until after the Greenville treaty had been made in 1795. This beautiful locality in the valley of the Muskingum is now pointed out to the traveller as the scene of a terrible Indian massacre in early times but there remains no relic there of the bloody event, which made it classic ground in border annals. The landscape is one of gentle, pastoral loveliness, which seems to hold in sympathy as its appropriate settings human habitations —the abodes of simple but satisfying happiness—and the beholder may feel arise within him as he reflects upon the past and contemplates the present, the reverent phantasy that in recompense for the dark deed which once outraged Nature here, the Creator has breathed upon her bosom the benison of eternal peace.

Of the five men taken prisoners at Big Bottom, one, young Philip Stacey, died of sickness, the other four were ultimately returned to their friends.

The party of Indians, which numbered twenty-five to thirty, it was discovered were Delawares and Wyandots— tribes which had heretofore been at peace with the whites. But they had now been drawn into the alliance of hostile tribes, and a war club was found upon the ground of the massacre, left as a formal declaration of war.

We have already seen the immediate effect of the Big Bottom horror in the Wolf Creek Mills and Waterford settlements, and now let us turn our glance to contemporaneous affairs at Belpre and Marietta, the latter the centre of activity and government in the Ohio company's purchase. Let the reader imagine, if he can, the consternation which the report of the massacre caused at the settlements. The news was brought to Marietta in the forenoon of the day succeeding the disaster. The messengers who had been sent out by Captain Rodgers, at the same time as Samuel Mitchell was despatched to Waterford, had gone aside from the trail in the darkness of the night, and hence were delayed.

When they arrived the court of quarter sessions had just been opened, and the alarm caused its speedy adjournment. There were many in attendance in various capacities, from the settlements of Waterford and Belpre. Filled with the most terrible apprehensions of what might have befallen their families and friends in the weakened settlements, which had at the best inadequate defences, they lost no time in striking out through the woods for their homes, some going afoot and some upon horses, but all pushing ahead with the greatest rapidity possible to learn the worst, if it must be so, and hardly daring to hope that they should find their dear ones unmolested. Messengers had been sent to Belpre and the same scenes of agitated, impatient endeavor to strengthen their situation had occurred as at Waterford and Wolf creek. The best preparations possible to resist attack had been hurriedly made; but the little community, weakened by the absence of some of its best men, was not in condition to have resisted successfully if the Indians had made a determined onslaught. The people passed a night of terror, and were much relieved when the absent ones returned on the following day.

The residents of Marietta had not the same grounds for fear that existed at Belpre and the other outlying settlements. They had the strength of greater numbers. Among them there were several characters of great resoluteness and wide experience in warfare, and nearly all of them had led the lives of soldiers. They had, too, the protection of Fort Harmar and of Campus Martius, which was of a very superior order of defence.

But with all of these advantages the inhabitants were nevertheless filled with terror for the blow which had completely annihilated one settlement, struck as it was by Indians who had formerly been at peace, and coming just after the disastrous ending of General Harmar's campaign, seemed to them at first only the precursor of a series of atrocities which must inevitably overwhelm them. To add to the embarrassment of their situation the garrison at the fort had been reduced, and Governor St. Clair, who alone had authority to call on the adjoining States for troops was absent. The Ohio company was in this crisis thrown entirely upon its own resources, and it took prompt and efficient action.

The company was called together as soon as the news of the massacre was brought in (January 3rd) and the deliberations of the body were carried on, from day to day, until the tenth. Upon the fifth the following resolutions * were adopted:

Whereas, There is reason to believe that the campaign made against the Shawnees and other Indian nations the last year is so far from humbling the Indians and inducing them to sue for peace, that on the contrary a general war will ensue, which has already broke out against the people settled in the Ohio company's purchase by the surprise of the block-house and breaking up the settlement at Big Bottom on the evening of the second instant, in which disaster fourteen people were killed and three others are missing. The governor and secretary being out of the territory, the militia of Virginia and Pennsylvania cannot be called upon to our aid, no relief, in the nature of things, can be expected from the general Government in time to give us immediate relief and protection, and from the present state of Fort Harmar very little can be expected for defending our out-settlements.

Under these circumstances we conceive all our settlements to be in the utmost danger of being swallowed up, before any foreign aid can be obtained, unless prevented by immediately drawing in some of our settlements, erecting better defences at Marietta and those outposts that shall be agreed upon to remain, by having all our military strength drawn to certain points and a particular system of defence established; therefore,

Resolved, That the inhabitants of all the out-settlements be and they are hereby advised to remove all their women and children to the town of Marietta as soon as possible, where houses must be provided for their reception, and as far as reasonable the expenses paid by the directors out of the company's funds.

Resolved, That such additional works as are necessary for the defence

* From the Journal of the Ohio company.

of the town of Marietta and the fort at Wolf Creek Mills, and one at Belpre, ought to be made as soon as possible, and the directors are requested to take measures accordingly.

Resolved, That application be made to the commanding officer at Fort Harmar, requesting him to give us such protection as the state of his command will permit, and also that he will please to represent our defenceless condition to the Minister at War, and use such measures as he can with propriety, to procure us the defence necessary for protecting our settlements.

Resolved, That the directors wait on Captain Zeigler, the commanding officer at Fort Harmar, with this resolve.

Resolved, That Lieutenant Colonel Commandant Sproat be and he is hereby requested to detach three subaltern officers, or one captain and two subaltern (at his discretion), three sergeants, three corporals, one drummer, and sixty privates, for the purpose of garrisoning the town of Marietta, Belpre and Wolf Creek settlements, to serve until sufficient aid is granted for our protection in some other way, unless discharged, and in order to encourage a sufficient number to engage voluntarily in such detachment and submit themselves to military discipline and such labor in erecting defences as Continental troops are liable to.

Resolved, That their pay shall be as follows, viz: The commissioned officers, the same as in the Federal troops; the sergeants ten, the corporals nine, the drummer nine, and the privates eight dollars per month; and the subsistence of the officers and men shall be the same as allowed to the troops in the pay of the United States; and the directors are requested to make arrangements accordingly; and it being found by experience that the greatest art of Indian war consists in surprising their enemy, to prevent which, as far as lies in our power.

Resolved, That six of the best woodsmen be employed as scouts or spies about the settlements, to be engaged at such price as Lieutenant Colonel Commandant Sproat shall be able to procure them.

And, whereas, we place the highest confidence in the General Government of the United States, that upon a proper representation of the present situation of these settlements, they will reimburse the necessary expense we shall be at in defending ourselves against the common enemy.

These resolutions were transmitted to the judges of the court of quarter sessions with a stirring appeal to them to use their influence with the General Government to secure its aid. One clause of the communication contained the following:

"We cannot now be silent when we find ourselves after an ineffectual campaign exposed, unprotected to the fury of an irritated enemy. It is with pain we have heard the cruel insinuation of those who have been disaffected to the settlement of this country. It is not possible that those men who have pursued into these woods that path to an humble competence, which was pointed out to us by the commander-in-chief of the American armies, should be doomed the victims of a jealous policy to see the mangled bodies exposed, a spectacle to prevent emigration.

"We are fully assured of the parental tenderness of the Government of the United States. It is this assurance which has induced us through your honors' interposition to ask their speedy assistance.

We will remark here that the Ohio company during the war expended over eleven thousand dollars for the protection of its settlers, and that no part of that sum was ever refunded by the General Government. An account was kept of all moneys paid out to soldiers and scouts or for military stores, or the erection of works of defence, under the supposition that it would be repaid by Congress. The loss was a considerable one to the otherwise impoverished people.

On the eighth of January General Rufus Putnam wrote to General Knox, Secretary of War, and to George Washington, President of the United States. The communication to the latter contains a good and, so far as the writer is aware, the best contemporary account of the situation.

On the evening of the second of January, 1791, the Indians surprised a new settlement of our people at a place on the Muskingum called the Big Bottom, nearly forty miles up the river, in which disaster eleven men, one woman, and two children were killed; three men are missing and four others made their escape. Thus, sir, the war which was partial before the campaign of last year is, in all probability, become general. I think there is no reason to suppose that we are the only people on whom the savages will wreak their vengeance, or that the number of hostile Indians has not increased since the late expedition.

Our situation is truly critical; the governor and secretary both being absent, no assistance from Virginia or Pennsylvania can be had. The garrison at Fort Harmar, consisting at this time of little more than twenty men, can afford no protection to our settlements, and the whole number of men in our settlement capable of bearing arms, including all civil and military officers, do not exceed two hundred and eighty-seven, many of them badly armed.

We are in the utmost danger of being swallowed up, should the enemy push the war with rigor during the winter; this, I believe will fully appear by taking a short view of our several settlements, and I hope justify the extraordinary measures we have adopted for want of legal authority to apply for aid in the business. The situation of our people is nearly as follows:

At Marietta are about eighty houses in the distance of one mile, with scattering houses about three miles up the Ohio. A set of mills at Duck creek, four miles distant, and another mill two miles up the Muskingum. Twenty-two miles up this river is a settlement, consisting of about twenty families (this alludes to Waterford); about two miles from them on Wolf creek are five families and a set of mills.

Down the Ohio, and opposite the Little Kanawha, commences the settlement called Belle Prairie, which extends down the river with little interruption about twelve miles and contains between thirty and forty houses. Before the late disaster we had several other settlements, which are already broken up. I have taken the liberty to enclose the proceedings of the Ohio company and justices of the sessions on this occasion, and beg leave, with the greatest deference, to observe that unless Government speedily sends a body of troops for our protection, we are a ruined people.

The removal of the women and children, etc., will reduce many of the poorer sort to the greatest straits; but if we add to this the destruction of their corn, forage, and cattle by the enemy, which is very probable to ensue, I know of no way they can be supported; but if this should not happen, where these people are to raise bread for another year is not easy to conjecture, and most of them have nothing left to buy with.

But my fears do not stop here; we are a people so far detached from all others in point of situation that we can hope for no timely relief in case of an emergency from any of our neighbors; and among the number that compose our military strength, almost one-half are young men, hired into the country, intending to settle by and by; these, under present circumstances, will probably leave us soon, unless prospects should brighten; and as to new settlers, we can expect none in our present situation; so that instead of increasing in strength, we are likely to diminish daily; and if we do not fall a pray to savages, we shall be so reduced and discouraged as to give up the settlement, unless Government shall give us timely protection. It has been a mystery with some why the troops have been withdrawn from this quarter and collected at the Miami; that settlement is, I believe, within three or four days' march of a very populous part of Kentucky, from whence, in a few days, they might be reinforced with several thousand men, whereas we are not within two hundred miles of any settlement that can probably more than protect themselves.[*]

At Marietta during the months following the outbreak of the war, all was activity. Improvements were made at Campus Martius, and a company of men were busily employed under the direction of Colonel William Stacey in building defences at the "Point." About twenty houses and cabins, on an area of four acres of ground, were surrounded with palisades. Four block-houses were built, two of which stood respectively on the Ohio and Muskingum fronts, at the terminations of the lines of palings; the third on the innermost or northern corner of the enclosure, and the fourth on the eastern line, about midway between the one last mentioned and the Ohio river bank. Colonel Ebenezer Sproat was placed in command. As the war progressed small cannon were

placed in two of the block-houses, loaded with pieces of iron and leaden balls about the size of cannister shot. Sentries were kept at night upon the box turrets of the block-houses, and a watch was on duty also during the day. The cannon were used a few times to warn the garrison of danger and to call in those who might be in the fields at work, when the rangers reported Indians in the vicinity.

At Belpre Colonel Battelle and Colonel Cushing had already built at the middle settlement two block-houses for their families, and it was decided to construct additional defences at this locality, which was very nearly opposite the centre of Backus' island. Eleven more houses were built, making thirteen in all. They were arranged in two rows parallel with the river front, and the first row immediately upon it. A wide space was left between the two lines of houses, and palisades were erected around the whole group. Like the block-houses built elsewhere in the Ohio company's purchase and in common use upon the frontier, these were two stories in height and the upper floor projected over the lower, and was pierced with loop-holes through which, should the Indians attempt to effect an entrance at the lower doors or windows they could be fired upon. The houses were about twenty-two feet square, laid up with round logs, about a foot in diameter, and were provided with bullet-proof doors and window shutters, made of oak puncheons or planks. Small gateways opened upon the river, from which the water for the garrison was brought, and there were larger ones at the ends and rear, through which teams of oxen could be driven to haul wood or supplies, and which were also to be used for the admission of the cattle in case Indians appeared in the vicinity. Upon the corner block-house, farthest from the river, watch-towers were built, and in these sentries were kept at night during the greater part of the period of Indian war. A flag-staff was raised which bore aloft the flag of the United States, and near it was placed a small cannon or blunderbus, which turned upon a swivel and could be so pointed as to discharge a fire into any part of the garrison, should it be invaded. It was fired regularly every morning during the seasons of spring and summer when Indians were supposed to be in the neighborhood of the settlement, and its loud report answered by the reverberations from the hills may have had the effect of producing a wholesome awe among them when they heard it. In every house a large hogshead was placed and kept filled with water to be used in case the Indians should fire the buildings, or a conflagration be caused through accident. It was one of the duties of the officer of the day to see that these casks were kept constantly filled, and that the defences were in the best of order. Major Nathan Goodale was the officer in command during the earliest part of the war, and retained the place until he removed from the garrison in 1793, when he was superseded by Colonel Cushing. As soon as the fortification was ready for occupancy the families of the upper and lower settlements moved in, and the garrison was appropriately named Farmer's Castle. The strength of the garrison was about seventy able-bodied men, and altogether the inmates of

---

[*]American State Papers, Volume V; also Albach's Annals of the West.

the castle numbered about two hundred and twenty persons. The Ohio company paid for the building of several of the block-houses at Farmers' Castle, and employed rangers for that settlement as they did for the Marietta garrison.

At Waterford the settlers, who, after the massacre of the Big Bottom pioneers, had considered themselves in imminent peril, made preparations with great haste to render their condition safe. They were joined in a council by the men from the mills, the day after the deadly attack which had terrorized the whole group of Ohio company settlements, and after a brief conference it was decided to concentrate their strength. Wolf Creek Mills, being the smaller station of the two, was abandoned. The families moved over to Waterford, and Fort Frye was built in a bend on the east side of the Muskingum, about half a mile below the site of Beverly. Palisades were set in the ground, enclosing an area of about three-quarters of an acre of ground, in the form of an irregular triangle. At each corner were block-houses, twenty feet square, with projecting upper stories, and the two longer sides were occupied by dwelling-houses. A well was dug in the centre of the enclosure to afford water in case of an Indian siege; and a blacksmith shop was also erected, that the inmates would not be obliged to make the dangerous journey to Marietta to obtain repairs on their arms or agricultural implements. The fort was finished in about six weeks, the settlers working with the utmost diligence and being afforded assistance by the Ohio company, which sent to them a dozen good laborers. The gates were hung early in March, and the fort was then in excellent condition to resist any onslaught which the Indians were liable to make, though a determined attack by a very superior force could have overwhelmed it at any time. The garrison contained about forty men capable of bearing arms, and was under the command of Captain William Gray. Dr. Thomas Farley practiced medicine; Dr. Nathan McIntosh was surgeon's mate; Neal McGuffey, Andrew McClure, William McCullock, and William Neal were the rangers.

The inhabitants of the Ohio company's lands were now under pressure of the sternest necessity assembled at three points—Marietta, Belpre, and Waterford. The small, outlying settlements had been abandoned, and for the present all thought of returning to them was futile. The settlers saw before them a prospect of great inconvenience, arising from their confinement and crowded condition in the garrisons, and they were apprehensive that they would come to absolute want, if unable to visit the lands on which they had begun farming, and make a subsistence from the soil. They were able to congratulate themselves, however, that their lives were thus far spared, and that their present mode of living, at least, assured them of comparative safety.

CHAPTER X.
THE INDIAN WAR—CONTINUED.

WHILE preparations had been making locally to resist the Indians, Governor St. Clair and the General Government were maturing measures for securing a settled peace. The plan proposed was threefold: to send a messenger to the western Indians with offers of a peaceable adjustment of difficulties, at the same time to prepare expedition parties which should make expeditions into the enemy's country if the peace proposition was not entertained, and to organize an overwhelming army to take possession, build forts in and hold the territory northwest of the Ohio.

Buckongahelas, the war chief of the Delawares; Blue Jacket, of the Shawnees, and Little Turtle, of the Miamis, were engaged in forming a confederacy of all the tribes northwest of the Ohio to drive the whites from the country. The people of western Virginia had been greatly alarmed by the recent outrages of the savages near their border, and had memorialized their governor upon the defenseless condition of the border, and in response to their solicitations authority had been given for raising troops to penetrate the Indian country. St. Clair was in Pittsburgh in April, receiving volunteers and detachments of the regular army, horses, provisions, arms and equipments. On the fifteenth of May he reached Fort Washington, and his army was gradually concentrated there. In the fall with an army twenty-three hundred strong, exclusive of militia, peace negotiations having proved futile, he marched northward toward the seat of the greatest Indian population (most of the tribes were then gathered upon the Maumee and the Wabash in the country adjacent) building forts at the sites of the present villages of Hamilton and Eaton, in the westernmost tier of Ohio counties, and Fort Jefferson in the present county of Darke. Continuing his march he met the allied tribes and suffered the most disastrous defeat (not even excepting Braddock's) in the history of American arms in the west. But of that later.

If the glance that has swiftly swept over the far away region on the historiographic map, which represents the theatre of St. Clair's invasion and battle, be returned to southeastern Ohio, it will be seen that although the main line of Indian operations was after the early summer of 1791 along what is now the western boundary of our State, there has still been through all of the season from snow to snow Indian alarm, Indian depredation, Indian murder, upon the Muskingum.

Early in March the Indians attacked Fort Frye, committed hostilities at Belpre and killed Captain Joseph Rodgers, the brave ranger at Marietta.

The notice given by the Ballards had saved the people of Waterford in January, but in February another war party composed of some of the Wyandots and Delawares in the Sandusky country was preparing to proceed against this settlement. Early in March the hostile band had reached Duncan's Falls, about forty miles above Waterford, and encamped there preparatory to striking the intended blow. It so happened that the agent through whom their plans for a repetition of the horrors of Big Bottom were to be defeated was with them, a friendly Indian of King Philip's tribe, named John Miller, who had been at Marietta and Waterford and knew nearly all of the Ohio company settlers. He had come from Rhode Island, where he had been among white men nearly all his life, within 1788 with General Varnum, and in the fall of 1790 had gone with George, the college educated son of Captain White Eyes (Koquethogechton) the Delaware chief, from the Muskingum to Sandusky, in the capacity of guide and hunter. Wishing to return he had joined the war party, although it seems permission to do so had been reluctantly obtained, the Indians being distrustful of him on account of his known association with the whites. Their suspicions had increased during the march toward the Muskingum, and some of the party had proposed killing him for fear he should prove treacherous. Arriving at Duncan's Falls, the pleasant memories he had of kind friends at Waterford, made him even more anxious than he had been before to save them from the terrible fate that seemed impending. If he could escape he would be able to carry them warning of their danger, but to effect an escape from a party of alert warriors, who were jealously watching his every movement, was not an easy matter. To avoid at least being compelled to join in the attack on his old associates he purposely wounded his foot with a hatchet while

cutting wood. When the Indians set out from the camp upon the ninth of March to take up quarters nearer the settlement they intended to strike, Miller was left behind, as he had hoped to be, for he had planned an escape, but some of the more suspicious of the band took a precaution which he had not looked for, and which for a time filled his mind with consternation. They had not thought his wound alone sufficient to keep him a prisoner at the camp, and so tied his hands tightly together. He lay perfectly still for a long time after the departure of the braves, fearing that they might have left some of their number to secretly observe his movements, but when he felt sure that if such was the case the watchers' patience would have become exhausted, he began the tedious task of freeing himself. For hours he painfully worked the thongs back and forth, and finally got them so stretched that he could slip them from his hands. Then he collected some logs and drift wood, and with his hatchet cut grape vines with which he bound several pieces together in the form of a rude raft, and he also fashioned a paddle. Supplying himself liberally from the stock of powder and balls, which the Indians had left at the camp, and throwing into the water all that he could not carry, he was ready for departure.

Just as daylight was fading away in the wild valley, he pushed his frail craft out into the stream. The river was high and the strong current carried him along with little effort on his part, at a good rate of speed. All night he floated silently down stream, sometimes fast and sometimes slowly, but never coming to a full stop, even to prepare a meal, for he had with him a small quantity of dried venison, with which he satisfied his hunger. The long night had passed and the sky was just beginning to show the light of dawn, when Miller found himself opposite the mouth of Bald Eagle creek, and knew that he was not many miles from the people whom he was endeavoring, at the risk of his own life, to give warning of the danger that was threatening them. Suddenly he caught sight of a blazing camp fire on the river bank, which he well knew to be that of the Delawares and Wyandots. It was too late for him to abandon his raft and make a detour through the woods, and his only hope was in the chance of passing down stream unnoticed by the keen visioned savages above him. He threw himself prostrate upon the little raft and remained perfectly motionless, hoping that if seen at all the craft would be mistaken for one of those clumps of floating debris which abound in streams when at flood tide. He heard rifle shots, and supposed that he had been discovered, but no rifle bullets whistled near him, and he surmised that the Indians had been shooting at turkeys in the tree tops or some other game. He was soon out of danger, borne onward by the kindly current, in the uncertain light of dawn, and with a thankful heart he plied his paddle and shot rapidly along, taking not a moment's rest until, sweeping around a bend in the river, he saw Fort Frye just ahead upon the left bank.

The structure was new to him, but he was aware from other objects and the familiar appearance of the landscape that he had arrived at the Waterford settlement.

He landed above the stockade, and making his way cautiously toward it lest he should be mistaken for a hostile Indian and shot, he called out to the sentry, giving his name, and stating that he wanted to come into the garrison. After a few minutes' delay, he was admitted. Captain Gray and a number of the older men in the garrison gathered about Miller and listened to what he had to say. There were many who suspected the faithful Indian who had done them this invaluable service, of being a spy sent in by the hostile savages to learn the strength of the garrison, the place of the defences, and daily routine of life. He had been some time away from the settlement, and although he possessed when with them a good character, they knew not how association with the people of his own race might have operated in estranging his friendship and reviving savage instincts. It was thought best, however, to proceed as if there was no doubt of the truth of the assertions which he made, and preparations were immediately begun to strengthen the condition of the garrison.

The outer works were not yet all completed, and the gates had not yet been hung. This was accomplished in two days' time. The watch was doubled. No attack had been made up to this time, and no signs of Indians discovered by the rangers who were now on the alert, and scouring the woods in every direction several miles from the fort. The suspicion that Miller had not acted in good faith, was now more strongly and generally entertained than before, and many regretted that he had been allowed to go from the fort. He had said that if he was captured he would be put to death with great torture, requested the loan of a canoe to go to Marietta, and had signified his intention of going from there directly to his old home in Rhode Island. He had been given a letter to the directors of the Ohio company at Marietta, and had left the garrison, and it was subsequently ascertained had, after receiving a reward for his unselfish act, indeed gone east. But this the settlers at Waterford did not know at the time, and opinions were expressed that he had returned to the Indians in the northwest, who it was suspected had sent him out to gain full knowledge of the condition of the settlements prior to fitting out a war party.

It transpired that the reason the band which Miller had outwitted did not immediately fall upon Waterford, was to be explained by the fact that they had changed their plan after leaving the camp at Duncan's Falls, and resolved to strike their first blow at the little settlement at the forks of Duck creek, which they were unaware had been abandoned after the Big Bottom massacre. Finding that they had no opportunity to murder upon Duck creek they returned to the Muskingum on the evening of the second day after the alarm had been given. On the following morning, March 11th, they made the attack. The inhabitants of Fort Frye had by this time laid aside their extreme cautiousness, and a number of them had gone out before daylight to feed their cattle and perform various duties. The Indians, anticipating this had ambushed themselves in various localities com-

manding the cabins where the cattle were sheltered, or the approaches to them.

Wilbur Sprague, a young man, had gone to the cabin formerly occupied by the Sprague family to milk a cow, and emerging, milk pail in had, was fired upon by several Indians in concealment. One of the balls struck his hip and almost disabled him. He ran eighty or a hundred rods to the fort, however, a number of the enemy being in close pursuit, and did not sink down until near the gate, when he took advantage of the protection afforded by a large stump, until his brothers ran out and carried him in. A volley was fired at the brave young men as they lifted their burden, and another as they halted to open the gate. The balls pierced the heavy oak puncheons by their side, but they escaped without the slightest injury. Two of the spies, McGuffey and McCullock, hurried out when they heard the shooting to learn the cause. McCullock was deceived by an Indian stratagem and came very near being lured to his death. Some of the Indians were dressed in match coats and hats similar to those of the soldiers in the garrison, and he went readily toward them until warned by Wanton Devol, who cried out at the top of his voice: "They are going to shoot you!" McCullock sprang back just in time to save his life, a shot fired at him killing his dog, which had followed him from the block-house. He ran in a zig-zag course toward the gate, and although made a target for several shots was untouched. Another narrow escape was that of Samuel and William Sprague, who were among those who had paid little regard to the report brought in by the Indian, John Miller, and thinking that there were no savages about, started down the river for Merietta in a canoe. They had gone about a quarter of a mile when they heard the firing at the garrison, and after considering for a moment the safest plan to pursue—for John's warning then instantly flashed into their minds—they rowed back to the fort, passing very close to one party of Indians, though out of sight, close to the bank of the river. They entered at the water gate and were safe. A constant fire was kept up from the garrison, and the attacking party, seeing that there was small chance of winning the battle, retreated out of range of the guns and confined their hostility to the killing of the cattle, destroying about twenty-five fine animals, and driving nearly a dozen away, among them being two yokes of oxen, which were afterwards identified by a prisoner at Sandusky.

The only Indian who received any harm in the brief skirmish was one who was shot a very long distance off by Judge Devol, who fired through one of the loop-holes of the fort with an old ducking gun of very great length of barrel. The Indian was one of a party who, supposing themselves beyond the reach of a musket ball, were making very offensive and tantalizing gestures. He was evidently wounded in the leg or hip, for he went away with a marked limp. After nightfall an eccentric old bachelor, Jabez Barlow, who had been living at his cabin a mile below the fort, in spite of the remonstrances of his associates, came into the garrison exhibiting every symptom of having undergone a severe ordeal. He had gone toward the fort when he heard the first guns fired in the morning, but turned back, having made up his mind that it was only some of the men firing at a mark, when he saw in the door of his cabin an Indian. Barlow dropped flat on the ground among the underbrush and leaves, and had remained there all day, scarcely daring to move a muscle for fear that he would be seen by some of the savages and killed. After this experience he was glad to remain an inmate of the garrison.

Although the Indians retreated after this ineffectual attempt to destroy the Waterford garrison, they did not return to Sandusky, but, dividing into small parties, went immediately into the vicinities of Belpre and Marietta, where they lay in wait for such persons as might venture outside of the stockades.

Upon the twelfth of March, the day after the attack at Fort Frye, Waldo Putnam, a grandson of the famous Revolutionary general, and son of Colonel Israel Putnam, with Nathaniel Little, were fired upon at Belpre, and narrowly escaped death. They had gone out from "Farmers Castle" to milk and feed the cows, half a mile below, and while young Putnam was milking, Little, who was on lookout, caught sight of an Indian a few rods away, with his gun levelled to fire. The gun rang out and the ball tore up the earth where Putnam had been sitting, he having sprung aside when his companion gave the alarm by calling out "Indians! Indians!" The men ran toward the garrison, three Indians who sprang from concealment in the edge of the woods pursuing and firing at them until they were driven off by a party of men who came out with arms, having heard the gun shot. Disappointed by their failure to take human life, the Indians sought to vent their ire by killing cattle, as they had done at Waterford. They killed several and wounded others, among them two large and very valuable oxen, which were afterwards brought into the fort. One of them was butchered, being so badly hurt that it could not live, and the other recovered. This was the first actual hostility at Belpre after the building of "Farmers Castle."

Two days after the hostilities at Waterford, and the day after the fortunate escape of Putnam and Little at Belpre —upon the thirteenth of March, which was Sunday— Captain Joseph Rodgers and Edward Henderson, the two rangers employed at Campus Martius, started out on a scout up the Muskingum. As Rodgers passed the guard at the gate he had remarked: "Well, boys, to-day we take a scalp or lose one." It seems that Rodgers had had an ominous dream in the night, and when morning came was in a very sombre frame of mind. Questioned about his dejection and refusal to partake of breakfast he had related his dream, and the officers of the day, impressed with his earnestness and foreboding spirit, urged him to remain in the garrison and let another ranger go out on the tour of observation. He said "No, I shall never shrink from duty because of a dream." These remarks and the manner of brave Captain Joseph Rodgers were brought vividly to mind when Henderson arrived breathless at Marietta, after night had fallen, and told of the fate of his comrade—how he had been shot down by In-

dians lurking in ambush. The ominous dream, but little thought of in the morning, was then the topic of awed conversation in little groups at Campus Martius, the garrison at the Point and Fort Harmar.

The two rangers had made their usual circuit, and, in the whole day's tramp through the woods, had discovered no Indians or signs of their having been in the vicinity. At night, when returning, and within a mile of home, two Indians rose up suddenly from behind a log directly ahead and fired upon them. Rodgers fell, shot through the breast, into Henderson's arms. "I am a dead man," said he, "you must save yourself." Henderson fled down the hill with the fleetness of a deer, and as he ran two more Indians rose from their hiding-place and fired their rifles at him. The silk handkerchief bound about his head, after the manner in which they were commonly worn by the scouts, was cut by one of the balls, which also grazed his scalp, and the other passed through the collar of his hunting shirt. After running a few rods directly away from Campus Martius he discovered that his pursuers had got ahead of him, and so he turned to the right, ran up a ravine and crossed over the hills to Duck creek, in his flight passing the Indian camp, where one of the party was so intently engaged in cooking supper that he did not notice him. Henderson had now eluded the two Indians who had followed him, and though aching to revenge the death of his comrade, did not dare to fire upon the Indian in camp, as the shot would have revealed his whereabouts. When Henderson arrived at the Point and hurriedly told his experience, the alarm gun was fired and answered from Fort Harmar and Campus Martius. The inhabitants were filled with alarm, and expecting an immediate attack, the ordinary dwelling-houses were quickly deserted by their occupants, who sought refuge in the block-houses.

In the morning the confusion subsided, and about ten o'clock a number of men went out from Campus Martius and the Point garrison to bring in the body of the murdered ranger. It was found stripped of clothing, but undisfigured except by the removal of the scalp. The men bore it into Marietta upon a litter made of poles and the burial took place upon the east side of Second street. Captain Rodgers' death was severely felt at Marietta and in the other settlements, as he had been much liked as a man, and the settlers had a great respect for his bravery and sagacity. It will be remembered that he assumed command at Wolf Creek Mills on the occasion of the Big Bottom massacre and exhibited great efficiency in making preparations for defence and in notifying the people of Waterford, Marietta and Belpre of the danger that threatened them. He had been a ranger from the fall of 1790, and one of the bravest who ever served in that capacity. He was a native of Pennsylvania, a man of large and powerful build and had served in the Revolutionary war. Hamilton Kerr was engaged to fill his place as spy. He was thoroughly familiar with the woods, having been for two years a hunter at Fort Harmar. Matthew Kerr, the father of Hamilton, was killed in the summer of this year. He had settled, as has been related in a former chapter upon Kerr's island, prior to the arrival of the Ohio company colony, and soldiers had been detailed from Fort Harmar to assist him in building his cabin. After the war had commenced in earnest Kerr had removed to the garrison at the forest but had left his cattle at the little island clearing, and made daily trips there in his canoe to feed them. One day he found a horse tied in an empty barn, which he took with him to the garrison conjecturing, and correctly, that it had been left there by Indians who had been on a plundering expedition in Virginia, and who were still lurking in the vicinity to commit further depredations. The next day June 17th, he went up again to attend to his stock though advised not to by his sons, who feared that the Indians who had lost the horse would be lying in wait to murder, if possible, the person, who had taken it. Kerr went, however, and just as he was about to land from the canoe, four Indians fired upon him. He fell back pierced by three rifle balls, and one of the assailants springing into the water, made his way to the canoe, scalped the old man and pushed the boat out into the stream. It was picked up, when it reached the mouth of the Muskingum, and a party was immediately sent out to pursue the murderers, but they were not to be found.

In July, William Smith, who was acting as one of the sentries for a party of men who were cutting timber on the ridge back of the garrison, was alarmed by a great commotion among the cattle, which came rushing by him showing every indication of fear of which the brute is capable. Smith thinking Indians were near fled to the spot where the men had been working, and as they had gone to the garrison, time for quitting work having arrived, he quickly followed them. He told his story, and it was more than corroborated when on examination an arrow was found still sticking in the flesh of one of the cows. It being thus made evident that Indians were again in the neighborhood of the garrison, and that they knew where the cattle ranged, it was thought best to make a demonstration which should intimidate the Indians and make them at least remain at a respectful distance from the garrison. A company of forty men was accordingly made up consisting about equally of soldiers from Fort Harmar and volunteers from the Point garrison and Campus Martius. One party led by a lieutenant went up the Muskingum valley and the other, which was the stronger, starting directly toward the abandoned mills that had been built by Shepherd and Sproat, on Duck creek, two miles above the Ohio. This division was led by Henderson and Hamilton Kerr, the former of whom was thirsting to avenge the death of his old comrade, Captain Rodgers, and the latter that of his father. Hitherto these men had been unable to come upon the Indians, but to-day they met with a small band. The two parties had reunited and fallen upon a trail which they followed to the crest of the hill looking down upon the mills. While they were anxiously surveying the valley beneath them for an appearance of the savages they saw six of them cross the stream at a riffle from the east and go toward a small deserted cabin, where the men formerly engaged at the mill had lived. Henderson led a small party in a detour by which he hoped to gain a position

comanding the other side of the house, which the Indians had now entered, while Kerr remained with the rest of the men at the spot from which they had first caught sight of their skulking enemy.

Before the moving party could make the intended circuit an Indian came out of the house and around upon the side toward Kerr. According to the plan agreed upon no shots were to be fired until Henderson and his companion had reached a proper station from which to open fire, but upon seeing this Indian, Kerr, unable to restrain himself as he thought of them under of his father, brought his rifle to his shoulder and fired. The Indian fell, not dead, but wounded, and Kerr, rushing forward, dispatched him, plunging his hunting knife again and again into his body. George Kerr shot at and wounded another Indian, but so slightly that he was able to escape with the rest. In the blanket of the dead Indian was found a halter, all in one piece, ingeniously cut from a buffalo skin, and several other articles. It is a fact of history illustrating the savagery of which some of the whites were capable, that the head of this Indian was cut off, impaled upon a pole and carried aloft at the front of the company of hunters as they returned to Campus Martius.* The next day the body was brought in for a Dr. McIntosh, who boiled it to get the bones for a skeleton, which, it appears, he was too ignorant to put together after the work of nature had been undone. The Indians who learned of the disposition that had been made of the dead body, were filled with disgust and superstitious horror.

Proofs of the presence of Indians were discovered almost every day, although weeks sometimes elapsed, and even months, when no serious depredations were committed. Indications of an attempt at the surprisal and murder of some of the men, were discovered one day in July, near what is now Mound cemetery. A large number of men had been working in a field of flax and oats, owned by General Putnam, and situated just east of the mound square, and had so nearly finished the task of harvesting that it was thought unnecessary for the whole force to go out the last day. A careful watch during the progress of the work had failed to discover any signs of Indians, and consequently sentries were disposed of, and General Putnam's sons, William, Rufus, and Edwin, his son-in-law, William Browning, and Augustus Stone, a boy ten or twelve years of age, were selected to finish the job. When the others were ready to start early in the morning they found that Browning had gone to the Point garrison on some errand, and unwilling to go to their work without him, waited until about ten o'clock, when he returned. They then went to the field, and before going to work deeming it advisable to reconnoitre the ground, Augustus Stone ascended the mound while the others tramped through the standing corn surrounding it. Very soon

* Hildreth does not mention this circumstance though he does that which we relate subsequently. This baharity, committed in the exultation of revenge, is vouched for by Horace Nye in the *Western Recorder* of April 8, 1847. He says, after relating the incident: "I remember going with my mother to our garden, when hearing the yell of some of the men we discovered the procession they had formed. Horrible sight."

they discovered numerous fresh tracks of moccasined feet around the margin of the field and in the vicinity of the mound, and hastily retreated to Campus Martius. The tracks had doubtless been made early that morning by Indians who intended to shoot down the workmen when they came into the field, but who had doubtless become impatient and left when the usual hour for beginning work had passed, the sun risen high in the heavens and no man appeared. The delay caused by Browning's absence from Campus Martius, in the morning, had saved all their lives. The necessity of working in the fields, planting, and harvesting, was important even during the most threatening periods of the war. A famine would soon have ensued if the crops had not been carefully cared for. The settlers to gain a mere subsistence were forced to expose themselves to attack. If they could have remained steadily in their garrisons there would be fewer deeds of violence to record in these pages, but they had two enemies to contend with, and in seeking to provide against starvation many fell victims to the savages.

Sometime during the summer of 1791—the exact date is not known—James Kelley was killed on the Virginia shore about twenty miles below Marietta, at the Belleville garrison. He had settled in Marietta in 1788 with his wife and three children, James, John, and Joseph. Their fourth child, Arthur St. Clair Kelley, was the first child born in Marietta. Kelley and his family removed from Marietta to Waterford, and from there to Belleville. The father and two sons were one day working in a small field of corn quite near the block-house, when they were surprised by a party of Indians. Mr. Kelley had no gun or other arms to defend himself with, and was instantly killed. John succeeded in reaching the block-house, Joseph, then about seven or eight years of age, was captured and carried away. The widowed mother fearing to remain at Belleville after the killing of her husband, made her way with her three children to Marietta, where she remained through the period of the war as an inmate of Campus Martius. She received no tidings from her little son Joseph, and mourned him as dead, but when the war was over, and Wayne held his great treaty at Greenville in 1795, the boy was brought in among many other captives and surrendered to the commissioners. Return Jonathan Meigs, sr., who was present, took charge of the little fellow and returned him to his mother.

It occasionally happened that the simple, but solemn Sunday services at the garrisons were rudely interrupted by Indian alarms. The troops were mustered every Sunday morning for inspection, agreeably to a militia law, and afterward "headed by Colonel Sproat with his drawn sword, the civil officers and the clergyman, with the fife and drum, marched to the hall for divine service." Almost all of the people were congregated on such occasions and most of them kept their arms by their sides or conveniently near. Once, as the Rev. Daniel Story was preaching in the northwest block-house of Campus Martius, and the people closely listening to his sermon, Peter Niswonger, one of the rangers, burst into the garrison with the startling information that Indians were in

the neighborhood. Instantly the preacher ceased his discourse, the congregation was thrown into confusion, and the alarming "long roll" of the drum resounded through the stockade as the signal for every man to hasten to his post. A party was soon made up, consisting of six rangers, ten or twelve citizen volunteers, and as many soldiers, to apprehend if possible the Indians whose presence had been discovered by Niswonger. They embarked in canoes and went up the Ohio to the mouth of Duck creek. Landing there the shrewd woodsmen were not long in discovering a fresh trail, which led them over to the waters of the Little Muskingum. In a hollow between the hills and about half a mile east of the stream, the smoke of a camp fire was seen curling up through the trees. Dividing the company into two parties the rangers attempted to flank the Indians, but before they could do so the Indians had become alarmed by some movement made by the incautious soldiers, and the fight was precipitated by their flight. The Indians ran up the small creek on which they had encamped, but two of the band leaving the rest ascended the spur of a hill. The spies who had pushed ahead to intercept the fugitives fired on these two, and one of them fell, wounded through the hips, just as he had gained the foot of a low rocky ledge, up which his companion had clambered. The second Indian could have made his escape, but bravely stood by to protect the wounded one. He fired at Peter Anderson who saved himself by jumping behind a tree, and in another moment the Indian fell dead, shot through by several balls from the guns of the rangers. They had completely surrounded him, so that the tree to which he had taken offered him no protection. The wounded Indian escaped while the attention of the whites was upon his protector. There had been seven Indians in the party.

The five who had escaped the rangers, finding themselves safe, made a detour through the woods and came up in the rear of the camp from which they had been driven, where the soldiers were now regaling themselves with the contents of the kettle which had been left boiling upon the fire. The first intimation of danger that the soldiers, satisfying their hunger, had, was the report of five rifles and the whistling of as many balls close to their heads. One man fell into the creek exclaiming "I am killed," and the others ran to the rangers for protection. When the whole party returned to the camp they found the soldier whom they had supposed to be killed or fatally wounded, still lying in the bed of the creek, but on pulling him out and making an examination only a mere surface scratch was found on his person. The Indians had again retreated after scaring the soldiers, and though the rangers went some distance in the direction they had taken, they saw nothing of them. A scalp was taken from the dead Indian and carried into the garrison. Had it not been for the indiscretion of the soldiers, green in Indian fighting, it was thought the whole party could have been destroyed, but as it was the rangers felt as if some good had been accomplished, for it was by such retaliations as this that the Indians were prevented from becoming even bolder in their depredations and murders than they had been, and to approach the settlements less frequently and with more caution. Ordinarily, after such a movement against them, they refrained for a considerable time from harassing the people.

During the same month—September—the little community at Belpre was again horrified by the murder of one of its members. Although there had been several hostile visits of the savages to this settlement the killing of Benoni Hurlburt upon the twenty-eighth of September was the first that had taken place since the actual beginning of the war. Hurlburt had been brought up in the frontier country, and had come to Marietta in 1788 from Pennsylvania. For some time he had been with the Belpre associates, and had followed the calling of a hunter and trapper, and with the assistance of his sons and Joshua Fleehart had kept the garrison pretty well supplied with meat. He had a natural instinct for the chase, and was never happier than when in the woods. He always dressed in deerskin and had adopted many of the customs of the Indians. Feeling very confident of his ability to elude the savages he had often ventured long distances down the river and back through the forest, either alone or with a trusty companion, and but little fear of his safety was felt at the garrison. On the day that he met his death he had gone down the Ohio to the mouth of the Little Hocking, a distance of about three miles, in company with Fleehart, another experienced woodman. Their object was to visit traps which they had set for fur-bearing animals, and to secure any game that they could as the garrison larder was very low. On the way down they heard a sound as of turkeys gobbling, on the north shore, but, as Fleehart, after listening closely for some time found that the noise proceeded from Indians hidden in the underbrush, who were endeavoring to lure them to the bank, they only paddled their canoe faster down stream.

They neither saw nor heard anything to further alarm them, and soon after they had reached the mouth of the Little Hocking, Hurlburt went ashore and travelled through the woods near the creek, while Fleehart paddled the canoe slowly up stream. Not many minutes elapsed before the report of a rifle reached the man in the canoe. His practiced ear telling him that it did not come from his companion's gun, he instantly thought of Indians, and supposing that if Hurlburt was shot they would run to the bank to see what had become of the canoe, he ran it aground on the opposite bank and concealed himself in a place from which he could fire upon them to the best advantage. Presently he heard the loud barking of two dogs which had followed Hurlburt, but after a few seconds the noise ceased, and listening intently he could faintly hear the groans of a man in great pain, and the peculiar guttural voices of Indians as they carried on in low tones a hurried conversation. They were probably discussing whether or no they should search for the companion of the man they had made their victim, but they did not approach the creek, and after the elapse of about an hour Fleehart entered his canoe and went up to the garrison. On the following morning a party of men went down to secure the body

of the murdered hunter. They found it without difficulty. By the side of the corpse lay the lifeless dog, whose barking as it faithfully tried to guard the body of its master had been heard by Fleehart until it was silenced by a tomahawk stroke. Hurlburt had been scalped, as all the victims of the Indians were, but was otherwise unmutilated.

The death of Hurlburt was a severe shock to the people at Farmer's Castle. Besides being the loss of a good man, and one whom all had liked, the killing was a fresh illustration of the dangers to which all were exposed, and of the boldness of the enemy. Other hostile demonstrations had been made, but as human life had not been taken the impression created had been less deep than that which was now experienced. Waldo Putnam and Nathaniel Little had been a second time surprised by the Indians at the exact spot at which they were fired upon, as hitherto related, and had with great difficulty made their retreat to the fort. The Indians had also killed or driven away many cattle, and the associates had organized a mutual insurance society, to make good from a common fund each others' losses in this line. Horses were not kept at all. They were regarded as certain to be stolen, and offered too strong a temptation to the Indians to visit the settlement.

In October the Marietta settlement suffered a loss which exceeded any previous ones. This time the hostile blow was struck by a party of Shawnees, led by the famous Tecumseh. He and his warriors had been on a marauding expedition on the Little Kanawha and Hughes rivers in Virginia, and in making a circuit to return, fell upon the trail of Nicholas Carpenter and five men in his employ, who were driving some cattle to Marietta from Clarksburgh. Carpenter had several times made ventures of a similar character to the one in which he was now engaged, and had brought many cattle over from the older and securer settlements, for the garrison at Fort Harmar and the people of Marietta. On this occasion he had reached a small stream falling into the Ohio six miles above Marietta, and encamped upon it for the night. As they had seen no signs of Indians while upon their return, and the men being all very tired, no sentries were set, and all fell into a sound sleep, after they had partaken of their evening meal, the cattle being allowed to roam at large and feed upon the wild pea vines. The horses were hobbled, the bells upon them unmuffled, and they, too, were turned loose to forage for themselves during the night. The little camp included Carpenter, a little son ten years of age, and five men: Jesse Hughes, —— Ellis, George Leggitt, —— Barnes, and John Paul. Early in the morning the men were astir, refreshed with their long, unbroken slumber, and Carpenter, as was his custom, prepared for devotional exercises. The men took seats around the fire and were silent, while Carpenter opened his hymn-book and began to read from it a song of worship. Just as the first reverent and impressive words were uttered by the good old man, the hushed camp was startled by the loud cracking of rifle shots and the terrible war whoop of six or seven Indians who arose from behind a large fallen tree. Ellis fell dead upon the ground, and John Paul was shot through the hand. All but poor Ellis sprang toward their guns, which were leaning against a large sycamore, but before they could all reach them the savages were in their midst.

Some fled, and some, unable to do so, made a strong fight, but resistance was useless. Burns was killed by the tomahawks and knives of the Indians, after what must have been a hotly contested encounter. When the place was visited afterwards, by a company of men from Marietta, his body was found, bearing many wounds, while in his cold and rigid hand his knife was still closely grasped, and the grass and weeds for several yards around were tramped down and the underbrush broken. Carpenter and his little boy were not immediately killed, but being taken prisoners, were dispatched not long after the attack, at a little distance from the camp in which they had gone to sleep the night before with the fullest sense of security. The body of Carpenter was found wrapped in a blanket, and his scalp had not been taken. This fact was thought to be traceable to the intercession of one of the captors, whose gun had been repaired without charge by Carpenter, who was a gunsmith by trade, at Marietta, the year before. Carpenter was left without arms with which to defend himself, as Hughes, when he had leaped to his feet after the first fire, had seized, in his excitement, both Carpenter's rifle and his own, and fled with them. He was a very strong and swift runner, but as he was only partly dressed at the time of the attack, was at a disadvantage. His leggings, being unlaced, fell down, and tripped him at almost every step, until he finally stopped and tore them completely off. As he did so his pursuers gained upon him, and one of them threw a tomahawk, which grazed his head, and would have cleft the skull had it struck fairly. Freed from his entanglement, Hughes easily distanced the Indians, and so made his escape. John Paul, the man wounded by the first fire, also saved his life by his fleetness of foot. Leggitt was chased nearly two miles, overtaken, and tomahawked, making the last of five, out of the seven persons, who were killed. Hughes and Paul arrived at the garrison at the Point, and gave the sad intelligence of the affair to the friends of Carpenter and the other men slain. More definite information, however, than they were able to give, was brought in by a negro boy, who arrived about sundown at Isaac Williams', on the Virginia side of the river, opposite the mouth of the Muskingum. He had been taken prisoner by Tecumseh and his little band of Shawnees, at Neil's station, near the mouth of the Little Kanawha, and had been with them several days. When the Indians had come upon the camp of the whites they had left him, with his hands bound, and tied to a tree, some distance in the rear. He had managed to escape, and, lying concealed in a hazel thicket, had witnessed several incidents of the massacre, for such it was. The Indians, after finishing their bloody work and finding the black boy gone, had probably come to the conclusion that he had got a considerable distance toward Marietta, and so immediately retreated down the Ohio, fearing pursuit as soon as the alarm had been given.

After the killing of Carpenter and his men, those who returned on expeditions beyond the immediate vicinity of the garrisons used the utmost caution. There were several alarms during the fall and once or twice Indians were seen in the vicinity of Belpre, Marietta and Waterford, but there were no further hostilities of serious nature during the season. At Waterford there had been no trouble since the profitless attack on the fort in March, except the capture of Daniel Converse, which occurred in the month following. Converse, a young man who has heretofore been alluded to, was at work with some companions in the woods a short distance from Fort Frye, when a party of nine Ottawa and Chippewa Indians rose up from behind a brush fence and fired upon them. His companions fled to the garrison and Converse, left alone was taken prisoner and carried away to Sandusky, and from there to Detroit. The period of his captivity was only about six weeks. He passed through varied experiences, was treated for the most part very kindly, and finally made his escape and worked his way slowly eastward from one British post to another until he reached the American settlements, and then journeyed through to his home at Killingly, Connecticut, where he remained until 1794, when he again ventured to the west and located at Marietta.

Upon the fifth of December of this year Major Denny stopped at Marrietta on his way from Fort Washington (Cincinnati) to Philadelphia, and brought the unexpected and alarming news of the terrible disaster that had overtaken St. Clair's army. The battle had been fought November 4th, at a point which can now be best located as in the northern part of Darke county, near the western boundary of the State, less than two hundred miles in a direct line from Marietta, and less than one hundred from Fort Washington, between which place and the upper Ohio, keel-boats and canoes were almost daily passing, and yet, in the year 1791 it took more than a month for the report of the most important event which had ever occurred in the west to reach Marietta.

St. Clair's army, which we left sometime ago marching into the Indiana country, twenty-three hundred strong, reduced by sickness and desertion to between fourteen and fifteen hundred, had been overwhelmed in a single engagement with the forces of the powerful Indian confederacy, and upwards of six hundred men were killed, including many officers, while two hundred more were wounded. Fifty-six women were also butchered of the hundred or more who had followed the army. The Indians fought with terrible fury and showed no quarters. The vast slaughter they had made did not glut their vengeance or satisfy the hatred of the savages, and the grossest indecencies and acts of extremest cruelty were perpetrated in hundreds of cases upon the dying. Wounded men were pinned to the earth with great stakes driven through their bodies, and as the Indians were incensed by the understanding that this was a war for land, they crammed the throats of those who had fallen—the disabled and the dead—with the sand and clay of the battlefield.

Great was the alarm at Marietta and the other settlements in the Ohio company's purchase, in common with those of the entire frontier of a thousand miles, extending from the Allegheny to the Mississippi, when the news of St. Clair's defeat was received. They had felt confident that the result of the campaign would be permanent peace, and now they feared that the Indians would be more daring and bold than ever before, and would come upon them wtih overpowering numbers. When the greatest fear existed at Pittsburgh, throughout western Pennsylvania and Virginia, and along the Kentucky border, the state of feeling among the Ohio company settlers, it may be easily imagined, did not fall far short of absolute panic. Indeed, many, fearing that the Indians would now carry out their threat of extinguishing every white man's fire north of the Ohio, were upon the point of fleeing from the country. The situation was truly a serious one, for there was every reason to believe that instead of being assailed by small predatory bands of Indians, who had not joined the confederacy, the settlements would now be attacked by large forces and that the garrisons would either be taken through the onslaught of superior numbers or beseiged and starved out. The alarm was at its height during the first few days after the reception of the news of St. Clair's defeat and then gradually subsided as those to whom the people looked as leaders evinced a determination to retain their land and began promptly to make preparations for strengthening their position. Several of the old defences were improved, and a new block-house was built upon the bank of the Muskingum, near Fort Harmar by Judge Joseph Gilman and his son, Benjamin Ives Gilman.

A company of soldiers were sent to Fort Harmar about the beginning of the year 1792, and the people felt much safer than they had during the last month of 1791. Confidence was slowly renewed by the enactment of wise measures by the Ohio company, and by the presence of an increased number of soldiers at the several garrisons, Fort Frye and Farmer's Castle, as well as at Marietta. Small detachments were sent out and changed at frequent intervals. Arms were received occasionally by individuals, but the Government did not fully supply the garrisons until the summer of 1792, when Colonel Sproat received a quantity of muskets, with bayonets affixed, fresh from the factory. The winter passed away without the occurrence of any hostilities, and the people generally followed the various iudustries which they chose and made considerable progress in the improvement of their homes and preparations for the spring planting.

As pleasant weather came on the settlers were again filled with apprehensions of attack, and it is probable that their worst fears would have been realized had it not been that the General Government was already making preparations for another campaign, which should be prosecuted with all possible vigor, and that the Indians, aware of the assembling of General Wayne's army at Pittsburgh, were holding councils and gathering strength for resistance. Thus their attention was in a measure diverted from the Ohio company's settlements, and from those in the Miami country, and along the Virginia and Kentucky border.

The first demonstration of Indian hostility in the spring of 1792 was at one of the Belpre group of settlements, six miles below "Farmers Castle," known as Newbury. Several families had located here at the time Belpre proper was settled and had, on the breaking out of the war, January 2, 1791, abandoned their cabins and moved to the central stockade. Early in the spring, or late in the winter of 1792, forced to gain a subsistence from the soil, they again repaired to the lands to till them. Two block-houses were built and surrounded with heavy palings. The original settlement had been made by fourteen associates. Thirteen men were now at the little stockade, and four of them had families with them. Upon the thirteenth of March a man named Brown, from the upper Ohio region, arrived at the settlement bringing his wife and four children and all his worldly goods. He had bought a small tract of land about half a mile above the block-houses, and on the day after his arrival went up to it, accompanied by one of his sons and a man to plant some young trees he had brought with him, carefully wrapped up, from his former home. It was his intention to set them out around the little cabin (built by one of the settlers in 1789); which he fondly hoped to see the happy. peaceful home of his family. Towards night Brown's wife went out to meet her hushand and walk back with him to the stockade and to see (if she had time to reach him before he stopped work) the results of the day's labor. She took with her a babe and her two little girls, and was also joined by Persis Dunham, aged about fourteen years, daughter of Widow Dunham, and a great favorite among the settlers. The latter led one of the children by the hand and followed a little behind Mrs. Brown. A Mr. Leaveus was at work near the stockade, and they stopped for a few minutes to converse with him and then passed on. Presently Leavens heard the woman scream, and looking up from his work saw two Indians rush toward her, and after two or three blows with their tomahawks retreat toward the high bank, waving a bleeding scalp in their hand. The outcry made by Mrs. Brown and Persis Dunham had also been heard by a number of men near the stockade, and they rushed toward the spot from which the sound came. Brown, too, had heard the dying shrieks of his wife, and came running toward her, directly in the path of the retreating Indians. They pursued him away from the stockade, and as he had no arms it was supposed by those who witnessed his flight that he was soon overtaken and killed. The men from the fort found the bodies of Mrs. Brown, one of her children and Persis Dunham and carried them to the block-house, from whence they were taken to the grave upon the following day. One child, they thought, had escaped the tomahawk by lagging a considerable distance in the rear after the party had left Leaveus. The babe at Mrs. Brown's breast had a great gash across its forehead, from which the blood had flowed over the murdered mother's bosom. Very singularly and unexpectedly, after removal to the block-house, the babe exhibited signs of life, and by careful treatment was fully revived and eventually restored to health. The little girl who was supposed to be uninjured was discovered, upon undressing, to bear a knife wound, which she had been too much excited to feel, and she died shortly afterward from its effects. The Indians had not been pursued, as the men, from the boldness of the attack, judged that they must be present in large force to attack the fort, and had, consequently, hastened to take possession of and defend it.

Late in the evening the guards were accosted by a voice which came outside of the palings and which they recognized as that of Mr. Brown. He and his son and man companion had managed to conceal themselves under the bank of the river and had lain there keeping perfectly quiet until they felt reasonably sure the Indians had left, when they had ventured out under cover of the darkness, with some fear that they might still be captured or killed, and made their way to the fort. They were not admitted until the men in the garrison had become thoroughly convinced that their words were not forced from them under terrible threats by the Indians whom they supposed all along to have captured them, and now suspected were compelling them to lure their fellows to open the gate of the stockade that they might rush in and massacre its occupants. After close questioning in regard to the particulars of their escape they were made to walk several times around the enclosure to show that there were no Indians present and then allowed to enter, the whole garrison standing on guard as they did so. This precaution, which is reliably vouched for, may be thought excessive by some reader who does not take into account all of the circumstances under which it was exercised, but to those who will give the subject a little thought it will not seem unnatural. The inhabitants had before them the dead bodies of three fellows who had but a few hours before been murdered by the Indians; they were filled with awe at the sudden taking away of three bright, happy lives; they had every reason to suppose that a large band of savages were in their neighborhood, and they knew their enemy to be capable of just such shrewd stratagem as this which they feared was being attempted upon them. The incident serves well to illustrate the intensity of terror caused by an Indian attack, and the extreme to which the wariness of these early settlers was occasionally developed. The Newbury settlement was abandoned shortly after this demonstration of hostility, and the occupants of the stockade again took refuge at "Farmers' Castle," where they had the strength of greater numbers and systematic regulation of garrison life.

Late in the afternoon of a beautiful June day, in 1792, R. J. Meigs, jr. (afterwards governor of Ohio), was, with some others, attacked between Fort Harmar and Campus Martius. They had been down the Muskingum in a canoe, to work upon a lot which Mr. Meigs owned, and when returning to their boat, after the close of working hours, were suddenly confronted in a narrow pathway by two Indians. One of them fired at Meigs, who chanced to move aside just in time to dodge the shot, and it took effect in the shoulder of Joseph Symonds, who accompanied him. Symonds, although wounded quite severely, plunged into the Muskingum and soon

swam to a safe distance. A negro boy, who was the third person in the party, fled along the path toward the tree at the roots of which the canoe was tied, closely followed by the same Indian who had pursued Symonds. The boy made his way into the water, but, being unable to swim, was quickly overtaken. His captor tried to drag him ashore, evidently intending to make him a prisoner; but, as the terrified boy resisted, he struck him with his tomahawk, tore a scalp lock from his head and left him. With blood streaming from his head, the poor black boy sank down in the water, and, when reached a minute or two later, by Edward W. Tupper and the Frenchman, J. P. R. Bureau, was dead. Meigs, upon the flight of his companions, faced the remaining Indian, who was the one who had fired upon him, and endeavored to intimidate him by presenting his gun and threatening to fire. It happened that the gun had been discharged a few minutes before meeting the Indians, and they were doubtless aware of it, for the Indian who now confronted Meigs only laughed at the weapon which was intended to awe him, and advanced still closer toward it. Meigs recognized the savage as one who had, in 1790, accompanied him through the wilderness to Detroit, and exclaimed, with some astonishment, "Why! Charley, is that you?" but at the same instant, seeing that his foe was not to be mollified by the recollection of former friendship, clubbed his gun and rushed upon him, striking a powerful blow which the Indian caught upon his musket. As Meigs fled, his old time friendly guide dropped his gun and pursued him, tomahawk in hand. A short, swift race brought them to a small run which Meigs cleared at a single bound, while his pursuer, seeing that he was gaining no ground, and probably fearing that he might be taken by the soldiers who had now come out from the garrison, stopped and threw his hatchet at his intended victim. It missed its mark, and, with a loud yell, expressing his rage, the Indian retreated. The other Indian, who had killed the black boy, had been several times fired upon, but he, too, got away, and apparently uninjured. Mr. Bureau and Horace Nye, then a young boy, had passed up the same pathway that Meigs was ambushed on, only half an hour before. Mr. Nye, in after years, used to relate that Bureau had several times attempted to fire his gun at a pigeon, but that it had only "flashed in the pan," and thought that to this fact they were saved from attack and probably death, as he had no doubt the Indians were aware of his presence, and ready to fall upon them had the gun been discharged. Mrs. Nye, knowing that her son was absent from Campus Martius, was much alarmed when she heard the firing, and rushed out of the river gate just in time to meet him as he was returning.

The year 1792 was one of less disaster and alarm in the Ohio company's settlements than any other during the period of the Indian war. The events we have already narrated were the only serious exhibitions of hostility made during the year.

General Putnam was absent nearly all of the autumn, having been appointed by General Washington as commissioner to negotiate a treaty with the Indian tribes lving on the Wabash—the Pottawatomies, Eel River Indians, Kaskaskias, Onatainons, Pinkashaws, Kickapoos, Peorias, and others, accompanied by the Rev. John Heckewelder, Moravian missionary, who was at the general's request appointed as interpreter; he finally induced the tribes to assemble their chief men at Vincennes in September, and upon the twenty-seventh of that month concluded a treaty with them. General Putnam was taken sick soon after the completion of the treaty and did not reach home for several weeks. By the terms of the treaty he had made the Indians were to remain at peace with, and recognize the authority of, the United States, and they were also to send a number of their chiefs on to Philadelphia to have a talk with the Great Father. Fourteen of them, conducted by an officer of the army, arrived at Marietta on the seventeenth of November, on their way to the capital, and were served with a dinner and handsomely entertained, both at the Point garrison and Campus Martius. Colonel Barker says in his manuscript reminiscences that after receiving attention from the citizens at the Point, where they landed from their boats, "Colonel Oliver went down with some of the men from Campus Martius and led them back through the mud. On their entering, the drum struck a salute, the guards presented arms, the cannon was fired in the north east bastion whereat the Indians dodged and looked surprised. General Putnam and Dr. Stacey received them and they marched to the general's to dine." Colonel Ichabod Nye says "under all the circumstances the entertainment was very novel and the scene peculiarly striking. Shut up in garrison and at war with the other tribes of the forest, shaking hands with our red guests and the appellation of brother passing from one to the other, seemed to renew the scenes of the first year's settlement and make us all forget that war was on our borders." Anselem Tupper wrote some clever doggerel upon the dinner of the chiefs, in which he refers, among other pleasantries, to the fact that "old Hetuck" (Colonel Sproat) was not invited to the gathering, as the Campus Martius people had not been asked to meet the chiefs when they were entertained at the Point, and speaks of the appreciation of Mrs. Putnam's culinary productions which the wild men of the woods exhibited. The visit of the chiefs was altogether a very pleasant occasion and one which was ever remembered by those who were present.

At Belpre the immunity from attack during the season of 1792, after the murder of Mrs. Brown, her children, and Persis Dunham, had been the cause of great thanksgiving, and the settlers had become more hopeful than at any other time since the breaking out of the war. The feeling of comparative safety, the overcrowded condition of Farmers' Castle, and the desire of the settlers to be nearer the lands which they owned, and must look to for their subsistence, led them to construct additional blockhouses at the upper and lower settlements, which they had abandoned after the Big Bottom massacre. The reinvestment of the settlements took place in the winter of 1792–93. One garrison was built three miles above, nearly opposite the mouth of the Little Kanawha, on Captain Stone's land, and the other a mile and a half below, on Major Nathan Goodale's farm. They were called respectively Stone's and Goodale's garrisons.

The buildings for the accommodation and protection of the families were ready for occupation in February, 1793, and most of the associates had moved into them by the close of the month. At Goodale's garrison the inmates had scarcely become settled in their new quarters when their leader, the man upon whom they principally relied through the war, was taken from them. Upon the first day of March, one week after moving to the new garrison, Major Goodale had gone out to work upon his land, not more than forty rods from the little stockade, and within plain view of it.

There was but little apprehension of an Indian attack at this time, for the river was full bank, and that condition of the water was generally regarded as in the nature of a protection, the Indians at such times not being apt to stem the tide in their canoes, and usually avoided expeditions over land because of the difficulty of crossing the swollen streams. Then, too, General Wayne's army, which had been assembling at Pittsburgh, was now moving toward Cincinnati, and boats full of armed men were daily to be seen going down the Ohio—a sight which was suggestive of security.

Somebody at the garrison after Major Goodale had been at work for some time, noticed that his oxen were standing still, and that neither their owner nor his assistant, an Irishman, named John Magee, were near them. An hour passed and the same eye which had noticed this again fell upon the oxen, which had not changed their location in the field. Then for the first time there was an apprehension of something wrong. Two or three men went out to discover whether there was any ground for their fears or not. They felt relieved upon finding Magee unconcernedly at work. Surely he would be aware of it had any violence been committed. But as the men saw nothing yet of Major Goodale, they went on to the place where his oxen had been standing idle, and as they still found no sign of the owner's presence, they began a search for him. Their fears were not very strong; they would not have been surprised to have heard Goodale's voice at any moment, or to have seen him emerge from the woods. But suddenly the searchers came upon marks which told the whole story—fresh moccasin tracks in the snow which still remained on the ground in the shade of the forest which surrounded the clearing. The truth dawned upon them then that Major Goodale had been taken prisoner. There were no blood marks upon the ground, no indications of a struggle, and the capture had certainly been conducted without noise or otherwise Magee's attention would have been attracted and he would have given the alarm. Immediately a small party of men set out upon the trail the Indians had left, but they soon lost it, and on the following day a number of skilled woodsmen and rangers were alike unsuccessful in the pursuit and gave it up. Major Goodale had been taken as a captive instead of suffering death, but he was one of those prisoners who never returned. His family was most deeply distressed by the news of his capture and the whole garrison, indeed, all of the Belpre settlements, were filled with gloom. This was the most serious loss that had been experienced by the people of the beautiful prairie. Hopes were entertained by the grief-stricken family and by his old associates that Major Goodale would some day return, but these hopes were given over as month after month passed away, the remaining years of the war dragged their slow length along and no tidings came to cheer them. Even after peace was established in 1795 by the treaty of Greenville, many captives returned to their friends, and news received of others, there was still no word to dispel the uncertainty with which this case was clothed. Not until 1799 was anything heard which threw light on the fate of this good, brave man. The story of the capture of a man on the Ohio was then related by some Indians at Detroit, and the particulars were such as to leave little doubt that the prisoner they spoke of was Major Goodale. According to their narrative he was taken by eight Indians who were concealed behind the trees on the bank awaiting an opportunity to fall upon some unwary white man, and they were quite positive that the captive had become a prey to disease and died somewhere on the Maumee or Sandusky rivers. There were some people who gave but little credence to this story, and believe the unfortunate pioneer to have been killed near the Hocking river, where Joshua Fleehart some years later found a skeleton, which, from the absence of a tooth, they thought to be that of Goodale.

The people of the Belpre settlements, robbed of the man whose mere presence had in a measure always inspired them with a feeling of safety, became more keenly sensitive to their exposed condition. The war had become harder upon them than upon the settlers of either Marietta or Waterford.

Two weeks after the event which we have related they drew up and forwarded a petition to General Washington, whom many of them well knew, setting forth their exposed condition and losses by the Indians. It stated that six of their number had been killed, beside the recent loss of Major Goodale; that one-third of their cattle and produce had been destroyed, and that they were fearful of a total breaking up of the settlement unless the Government should afford them the protection of a larger number of men. It was represented that there were two hundred and one persons in the three settlements, fifty-two of whom were men, and that their usual guard consisted only of a corporal and four soldiers sent out from the post at Marietta.*

During the remainder of the year, however, the settlement, contrary to the apprehension of its people, was left in peace, and although the memory of former events cast a gloom over the inmates of Farmer's Castle and of Stone's and Goodale's garrisons they had no additional horrors to disturb them, and gave their attention to the raising of crops more fully than they had been able to do during the two years previous. A good yield rewarded them, and they were able, as were also the Waterford

*Biography of Mathew Goodale, by Dr. S. P. Hildreth

settlers, to sell considerable quantities of corn and some other provisions to the contractors who were engaged in supplying Wayne's army, which was concentrating at Cincinnati and preparing to enter the Indian country. The preparations under Mad Anthony Wayne had also diverted the Indians to such a measure that their plundering expeditions were made much less frequently than before. Their condition improved by the money they had secured from the army contractors, and which they sorely needed—free, comparatively, from depredations by the Indians, and looking forward to a speedy establishment of peace, the settlers at the several little forts in the Ohio company's purchase were less heavy-hearted than they had been since the beginning of the war. They were eager for the arrival of that time which they believed to be not far off, when, relieved from the fear of a wily, relentless and cruel foe, they could practice the arts of peace and devote themselves to the building up of their fortunes and the securing of happy homes. The day when they could do this was not so near as they fondly imagined. Although enjoying a lull in hostilities there was still before them a dreary period of Indian war, nearly two years in extent, in which these frontier colonies were destined to receive many a sudden and savage blow, to the bereavement of families and communities.

Bird Lockhart, a celebrated hunter living in the little garrison which Isaac Williams had established on the Virginia side of the Ohio, had an exciting adventure with Indians early in the winter of 1793-1794. He had gone to the headwaters of a small run now known as Worthington's run, to shoot some deer for Mr. Williams who was convalescing from a severe sickness, and felt a strong desire for venison. Lockhart's rifle soon brought down two fine deer which, after dressing, he threw across his old horse, and started for home, which, he judged, was eight miles distant. As he was making his way, by the side of his horse, slowly along an old trial or trace, he came suddenly upon two Indians. Lockhart sprang behind a tree, and the Indians followed his example. One of them, however, chose so small a tree in his haste that he was only partially protected, and Lockhart instantly noticing the circumstance, fired upon him. He fell, wounded through the hips, and entirely helpless. As soon as his rifle rang out upon the still air, the other Indian came forward, thinking that he could shoot the white hunter down, but Lockhart had apprehended this, and reloaded with such expedition that as his adversary came forward, he was almost ready to use his gun again. The Indian seeing that he could not take him at a disadvantage, quickly sought shelter behind another tree without firing. In this situation the two remained for several hours, each listening to detect any cautious movement, and furtively endeavoring to catch sight of the other. As night approached, Lockart began to feel uneasy, fearing that the Indian under cover of darkness would make his escape, and consequently he availed himself of his knowledge of a stratagem to draw the enemy's fire. It was one so old and well known that it must be practiced very adroitly in order to deceive. Placing his large slouch hat upon the ramrod of his gun, he slowly pushed it into view of the Indian in such a manner as to make him believe that the hat was in its proper place, and the wearer cautiously attempting to gain a view of the enemy. If he pushed it forward an inch too far, or allowed it to swing upon the end of the ramrod, the trick would be exposed. Lockhart hardly dared to hope for success, but at length he heard a rifle shot, and his hand detected a slight jarring of the ramrod as the ball pierced the hat, and sped onward on the harmless journey. He allowed the hat to fall to the ground, and so completely was the marksman deceived that he soon came forward, no doubt expecting to take the scalp of the white man whom he supposed he had killed. Lockhart allowed him to come very close, and then stepping from behind the tree with gun ready cocked, shot him through the heart. The next day a party of men went out, led by Lockhart expecting to find the bodies of two Indians, but could discover only the last one shot. The wounded Indian who, before Lockhart's departure, had crawled away a considerable distance, had not ventured to approach as he still had a loaded gun in his hands. It was supposed that he had caught Lockhart's old horse, and rode him until he had fallen in with some other Indians. The animal was found on Carpenter's creek, about six miles above Marietta, a distance to which he would not have strayed alone.

The hunters and rangers took great risks during the Indian war, but their coolness and courage usually saved them, and when their peculiar occupation was gone, most of them were still residents of southeastern Ohio, having become settlers in the land they had been chiefly instrumental in protecting from the ravages of the Indians. Of the same class as Bird Lockhart was the Belpre ranger, Joshua Fleehart. He, it is said traditionally, was in fact a leader among these brave men employed to roam the forest to discover indications of the approach of the Indians. No man among the rangers, either at Farmer's Castle, Marietta, or Waterford, was more skilful in following a hidden trail, or more daring in meeting the enemy. He was thoroughly conversant with the habits, not alone of the Indians, but of the wild beasts of the forest, and his shrewdness seemed never to fail him. He was admirably endowed by nature for the wild life which he led, being not only very active, but of the most powerful build, tough and sinewy, and over six feet in height. Before the war he lived upon the island afterwards famous as Blannerhassett's, and when Farmer's Castle was built, after the alarm of the settlers, he was employed as hunter and ranger for the garrison. An incursion made by this man into the heart of the Indian country well illustrates his hardihood and that of his class.

In the winter of 1793-94 he penetrated the forest alone within fifteen or twenty miles of the large Shawnees village of Chillicothe (which was on the north fork of Paint creek, a few miles west of the site of the present city of the same name, settled over two years later), and there took up his residence, and remained for nearly three months. It being winter, there was little need of his services at Farmer's Castle, and he yearned for more activity and excitement than garrison life afforded. He spent the season trapping beaver and hunting bears, the former along the small tributaries of the Scioto, and the latter among the hills, and led a happy, free life, at the same time accumulating a goodly store of valuable furs. He had built a little bark hut not far from the bank of the Scioto, and in some willows, several miles below, he secreted the canoe in which he had made his journey. When warm weather came, which that year was in the latter part of February, he began preparations for his return to Belpre, tying up his furs in bundles and storing them in his canoe. He was aware that, as the snow had almost disappeared danger from Indian attack was largely increased, and he had one day been admonished of the peril of his situation by hearing a rifle shot, though far away in the direction of the Indian town. On the day he had set for his departure he ate his last meal in the little hut which had given him shelter all the winter, and had started to walk down the river to his canoe, when his eye fell upon a solitary Indian slowly approaching with eyes intent upon the ground, examining, as he surmised, the tracts which he had made the day before as he came to his lodging place. Fleehart secreted himself behind a tree, and when the Indian had come near enough, took deliberate aim and sent a heavy rifle ball upon a sure death errand. He rushed immediately upon the fallen redskin to secure his scalp, but being diverted by a number of glistening brooches and other ornaments upon the dead warrior's breast and arms, began to tear them off and place them in the bosom of his hunting shirt. As he was thus engaged a rifle ball passed through his clothing, and looking in the direction whence the report had come he saw three Indians rapidly approaching. He took to flight and the Indians followed him as closely as they could, firing as they ran. Several times he stopped behind trees hoping to get a shot at his foes, but as they, on each occasion, immediately tried to flank him he was obliged again and again to run. The chase continued several miles on the level bottom, and finally, Fleehart, resolving to end the chase, shaped his course toward the high, steep hill which walled the valley. The Indians were encouraged now, for they believed they could at least come near enough, as the runner toiled up the ascent, to bring him to earth with their rifles, but they were chagrined after pressing ahead with all of the rapidity they could to see Fleehart spring up the rugged side of the hill with speed scarcely abated, and before they could fire upon him he had gained such a height that their shots were harmless, though one of them cut the handle of his hunting knife. The pursuers now gave up the chase, and Fleehart, making a long circuit among the hills, reached the place where his canoe was hidden just as darkness came on. He pushed out into the middle of the Scioto, paddled his canoe with vigor for several hours and went rapidly down stream. Being very tired he lay down toward the middle of the night, and quietly sleeping, the current swept him onward until he awoke at dawn and found himself floating out upon the broad bosom of the Ohio. From the mouth of the Scioto he pushed his canoe up stream, keeping close to the south shore, and in a few days reached Belpre. On numerous other occasions Fleehart was absent on long excursions into the forest, alone or with companions and he was usually the first to sally from the garrison when Indians were seen in the vicinity.

The winter of 1793-94 passed quietly and peacefully at the several settlements. The spring, which in time of peace, the husbandman everywhere hails with joy, brought gloomy feelings to the settlers. Predatory incursions were again made by the Indians when the snow had disappeared, and again was Belpre the scene of horrible murder.

John Armstrong, an emigrant from Pennsylvania, had arrived in the fall of 1793, and during the succeeding winter resided at the upper settlement, occupying with his wife and large family of children, a portion of Isaac Barker's block-house, which formed a part of the defence known as Stone's garrison. In the spring, Armstrong and Peter Mixner, who together owned a floating mill moored in the rapid current near the Virginia shore, moved to that side of the river in order to more conveniently manage their useful property and avoid the trouble of frequently crossing the stream. There were already two cabins there, of which Armstrong took the lower and his friend the upper, but after residing in his for a few weeks, Mixner built another, a few rods farther up stream, and beyond the limit of the little clearing. As soon as it was ready for occupation the family was transferred to it. Mrs. Armstrong had taken up her residence on the Virginia shore very unwillingly. Her parents had both been killed by Indians only a short time before in Mifflin county, Pennsylvania, and the remembrance of that event with all of its sickening details was constantly in her mind. Perhaps too she had a presentiment that the same fate was to overtake her and her children. Her husband relying upon the close proximity of the garrison and the block-house upon the island, was not apprehensive of danger, neither did Mixner and his wife seem to be troubled at all by fears of attack. The fate of which Mrs. Armstrong had a horrible foreboding came upon her in the night of the twenty-fourth of April. Her husband was awakened in the night by the loud barking of his watch-dog, and grabbing his rifle he went out without dressing himself, elated with the idea of getting a shot at a bear, for one had been in the vicinity of his hog-pen the night before, and he supposed that a second visit was the cause of the present disturbance. He had gone but a few steps from his cabin when he saw indistinctly through the darkness several forms which he knew to be Indians. Hastily firing his gun at them and hallowing for help, he retreated into the cabin, barred the door and ascended to the loft, where three of his children were sleeping. Mrs. Armstrong was aroused, and just as the Indians broke down the door, was endeavoring, with an infant in her arms, to climb out of the chimney, which was unfinished and quite low. She was instantly tomahawked, as were also two young children, and all three were quickly scalped. The murderers then turned their attention to the loft, from which they heard sounds, and two or three of them going up the ladder, found Elizabeth Armstrong, a girl fourteen years of age, and two

boys younger, whom they brought down and compelled to gaze upon their lifeless mother and infant brother and sister lying upon the blood-drenched puncheon floor. Armstrong had forced an opening through the roof and made his escape to the mill, where his two oldest sons were. Mixner and his wife were aroused by the shot which Armstrong had fired and the crashing in of the cabin door, listened for any further sounds that might indicate the cause of the disturbance, and overheard the Indians talking. Mrs. Mixner had been a prisoner among the Wyandots and she recognized the language as that of this nation. She could not catch every word, but enough was understood to indicate that the Indians were speculating upon the whereabouts of the people who had lived in the upper cabin which was now empty. Mixner hurriedly got his family into his canoe and paddled out into the river. When opposite the Armstrong cabin they could distinctly hear the sobs of the girl and crying of the boys, who, taken prisoners, were perhaps apprehending the fate to come momentarily upon them which had already overtaken three of the family. Mixner arrived at the garrison about the same time that Armstrong did, and the story which they told created much alarm. No attack was made, however, and at day dawn a party of men from Stone's, joined by others from the island block-house, went over to the Armstrong cabin and found the frightful scene which they had been led to expect awaited them. The bodies of Mrs. Armstrong and her children were brought to the Ohio side and buried. Armstrong and Mixner had supposed that all of the inmates of the cabin had been slaughtered, and the truth was not known until the visit was made in the morning. The Wyandots were pursued that day by a strong party headed by the rangers. Their trail was easily followed for some distance up the Ohio to a place where the Indians had raised their sunken canoes, and later in the day was again discovered some distance up the Hocking river where the boats had been abandoned. The footprints of the children were distinctly preserved in the soft earth of the bank. Fearing that the little captives would be tomahawked should the party be overtaken and engaged in a fight, the pursuit was given up and the men returned to the garrison. They learned that there had been about twenty Wyandots in the band and that when they attacked the Armstrong cabin they were returning from the vicinity of Clarksburgh, where they had also committed some murders. The three children were all ultimately restored to freedom, though not until after the close of the war. Jeremiah, aged eight years at the time of the capture, was adopted by the celebrated chief Tahre (the Crane), and a portion of the period of his captivity was passed at Wyandot town, on the site of Columbus, in which city he afterwards lived for many years.

At Waterford there had been no hostilities for so long a period that the settlers, whose number had been increased by the arrival of several families and single men, resolved this spring—1794—to send out a colony. A block-house was accordingly erected at the confluence of Olive Green creek and the Muskingum, four miles above Waterford; several ordinary cabins were clustered around it, and all were enclosed within a stockade. The settlers here were Able Sherman and wife, their son Ezra and his wife, and two unmarried sons of the former, but grown men; Ezekiel Hoit, wife and children; Aaron Delong, wife, son and two daughters; Mathew Gallant, wife, and children, and George Ewing, wife and children. [The last named became the pioneer settler of Ames township, Athens county. Among his children at Olive Green was one in his fifth year destined to be eminent in the counsels of the Nation—Thomas Ewing.] Altogether the station contained about thirty persons. This little settlement, as will be seen presently, was not exempt from Indian atrocities. One of its leading men, the head of a family, fell a victim to the savages a few weeks after removal to his new home. But for the present we leave the people of the infant settlement of Olive Green, pursuing the usual avocations of the pioneer, and looking forward hopefully to the time when they would be entirely free from danger and from the restraint of life within a stockade.

On the tenth of May Robert Warth was killed almost within a stone throw of Fort Harmar. He was at work for, and only a few rods from, Benjamin Ives Gilman, when two Indians who had hidden behind a brush pile rose up and fired upon him. Had they seen Gilman he would doubtless have been shot also, but after they had both emptied their rifles they were unable to cut off his retreat to the fort. John Warth, one of the rangers, ran out when he heard the report of the guns, and catching sight of the Indians running up the steep hillside, one of them waving the bloody scalp of his brother, fired upon them, and probably with effect, as their exultant yells were instantly hushed and the one with the scalp was noticed to start as if wounded and with difficulty scaled the hill. Several years later the bones of an Indian were found walled up in a little cave near the path by which the murderers of Robert Warth retreated. So it is possible that this, the last hostility of Marietta, was avenged.

Early in June another atrocity was perpetrated within the limits of the Ohio company's purchase. Abel Sherman, of Olive Green, taking his rifle, went out to search for the cows which had been missing for several days, and which his fellow inmates of the new garrison feared had been detained by the Indians to draw them out Thinking that possibly they might have joined the cattle belonging at Fort Frye, or that the rangers there might have seen them in the woods, he directed his steps down the Muskingum to that garrison. He did not arrive there until towards sundown, and some of the more prudent settlers tried to persuade him to remain with them until morning. suggesting that the absence of the cows was a sure indication that Indians were in the vicinity; but the old man, regardless of danger, started upon his return. An hour later the inmates of the Olive Green block-house heard the report of two guns, and Ezra Sherman, sure that one of them was his father's, and that he had been attacked by the dreaded enemy, took down his rifle from the wall and ran as fast as possible in the direction from which

the sound of the firing had come. He soon reached the spot—only a quarter of a mile away—upon which the encounter had taken place, and found his father dead and scalped. The body lay in a little patch of May apples or mandrakes, and it was evident that the kind and thoughtful old man had been surprised while gathering some of them to take to the children at the garrison which he was nearing, for the bosom of his hunting shirt was filled with them. The next morning a party of men went up from Fort Frye and buried him near the mouth of the run by which he had fallen, and which to this day is known as "Dead Man's run." The utmost consternation and grief were caused at Olive Green when young Sherman came in with the news of his father's death. The settlers had all seen much of the horrors of Indian warfare, but this sudden taking off of one of their own small circle, produced a deeper impression than any prior event, and made them more keenly alive to the danger. During the few subsequent months they lived in constant fear of attack or the waylaying of some of their members.

There is a sequel to the story of the murder of Abel Sherman. In the summer of 1798, when the prosperity of peace was beginning to bless the country, and industrial pursuits had replaced the savage employment of hunting men and beasts, a company of salt makers at work on Salt creek, in Muskingum county, was visited by an Indian known as Silverheels, who lived in the vicinity and was generally regarded as a well-disposed, good-natured child of the forest, and half-pitied as a lingering, lone, and melancholy individual of the vanquished race. He had been drinking when he came to the salt-makers' camp, and was there given more of the crazing firewater, under the influence of which, emerging from his habitual sombre taciturnity, he became loquacious and boastful. His tongue ran on fast and excitedly in narration of achievements in the chase, and presently of deeds of prowess and adventure in the war with the whites. The men for the most part listened with idle interest to what they considered the vaporings of vanity, but there was one among them who was strangely thrilled by the narration of an encounter which took place on the Muskingum in the summer of 1794. The narrative fitted in nearly all of its details the killing of Abel Sherman, and the man who was so deeply moved was his son, Josiah. As one circumstance after another was mentioned, which the young man knew to be true of the murder of his father, his fury arose almost to the pitch of frenzy. He could with difficulty restrain himself from springing upon the drunken Indian, exultingly dwelling upon his father's death, and slaying him upon the spot, but he reflected that possibly the savage had only known of the circumstance he so graphically detailed from hearing them told by others, and he controlled his passion, not even making the slightest remark upon the story which had aroused it. But he was filled with a determination to satisfy his doubts in the matter. He did not relax his stern intention to be executioner should he become sure of Silverheel's guilt, but he resolved first to investigate. The Indian, with tongue loosed by liquor, had told how the old man had been shot down while gathering May apples, that his hunting shirt bosom was filled with them; remarked upon the peculiar formation of his head (a kind of a double crown), which had enabled his slayer to secure a very large scalp, which he said he had divided in two, and obtained fifty dollars for at the British post at Detroit, and in conclusion said that the gun of the murdered man had been placed in a hollow log near the scene of the tragedy. Young Sherman anxious to gain the corroborating testimony which the firing of the gun would afford, soon after went to the spot where his father had fallen. There, sure enough, in a hollow log where the murderer had placed it four years previously, was the large, peculiar musket his father had owned. The iron barrel and the lock which still contained the carefully prepared flint, were thickly encrusted with red rust, and the stock was so rotten that it broke as it was lifted from its hiding-place. The finding of the gun had a strong effect upon Josiah Sherman. He regarded it as proof positive of the truth of the drunken Indian's words, and no longer doubted that the savage had indeed committed the act of which he boasted. Not many days later two hunters traversing the woods came upon the dead body of Silverheels, bearing the mark of a rifle ball over the heart.

The narrative of the incident forms a digression from the account of the war, but we give it in this connection as it was a direct outgrowth of an event of 1794. Another digression is now in order. Turning from the recital of local occurrences we see that while they have been the exciting topics of the settlers' conversation in Washington county, General Wayne had been carrying terror into the Indian country along the Miamis, the Whitewater, the Wabash, the Auglaize and Maumee.

In the autumn of 1793 and the following winter and spring, peace negotiations having proved unavailing, he had built Fort Recovery, near the field on which St. Clair's army had been defeated in November, 1791; Fort Wayne, where the Indiana town of that name now stands, and Fort Defiance, at the confluence of the Auglaize and Maumee; and now preparatory to striking a blow which should compel peace, he was awaiting an answer to his last amicable offer, "actuated by the purest principles of humanity and urged by pity for the errors in which bad and designing men" had led the confederated tribes. But the Indians were for war. Little Turtle (Michikinaqua), of the Miamis, alone in the council, was for peace. "We have beaten the enemy," said he, "twice, under separate commanders. We cannot expect the same good fortune always to attend us. The Americans are now led by a chief who never sleeps. The night and the day are alike to him; and during all the time that he has been marching upon our villages, notwithstanding the watchfulness of our young men, we have never been able to surprise him. Think well of it. There is something whispers to me, it would be prudent to listen to his offers of peace."

The decisive "battle of Fallen Timbers," or as it is sometimes called the battle of the rapids of the Miami (Maumee), occurred upon the twentieth of August, 1794.

It was followed by a vigorous campaign, which secured the results already gained by Wayne's great victory, and practically terminated the Indian war, and tranquilized the whole border country. Still some Indian depredations were committed until nearly a year later, or August 3, 1795, when peace was formally declared, and the old treaties of purchase ratified by the treaty of Greenville.

An attempt was made to keep up strict discipline in the Ohio company's garrisons during the period intervening between Wayne's victory and his treaty, but the settlers generally felt so secure after the former event that they could not be restrained and often took great risks. Belpre, which all through the war seemed a fated post, had yet to suffer one more loss. Jonas Davis, a young man, resident at Stone's garrison (the upper settlement), one day in February, 1795, while on his way back from Marietta, where he had gone on some errand, discovered an old skiff among some driftwood by the Ohio river, and on the following morning went up a distance of three miles to break it up and get the nails out of it. Nails were very scarce and hard to get at that time, and Davis had especial need for some as he was preparing a little cabin which he intended to occupy with his bride expectant, a daughter of Isaac Barker, as soon as their marriage should take place, and the time set for that ceremony was so near that both of the young people had provided themselves with their wedding garments. The young man on reaching the boat had begun to pull it to pieces, and it was supposed was so intently engaged that he did not hear the approach of an enemy, and was shot down without a moment's warning. He was missed from the garrison at evening and his betrothed was thrown into great distress as the night passed away and he did not return. In the morning a party of men who went out to look for him, led by the rangers, discovered his body lying by the wrecked boat, a small axe which he had been using, still in the tight grip of his dead hand. He had been scalped and stripped of his clothing. The death of Davis made a deep impression upon the Belpre settlers, and four young men from Stone's garrison, who had been among his warmest friends, determined to avenge him if possible. As soon as they heard the particulars of the murder they started in pursuit of the Indians, led by John James, one of the bravest and most alert of the men at their settlement. At Gallipolis they were joined by four volunteers and from that point they scouted up Raccoon creek. One of their men was taken sick the first day out, and as another was obliged to return with him, but six were left in the party. They pushed on, however, and on the following day reached the headwaters of Symmes' creek, where the Gallipolis rangers had said a party of Indians were engaged in hunting. A beaver skin cap was found which had been left by an Indian to mark the place where he had set a trap. This discovery corroborating the rangers' assertion, the men knew they were in the immediate vicinity of an Indian camp and supposed it to be that of a band to which the murderers of Davis belonged. They accordingly concealed themselves and holding a whispered council decided to fall upon the Indians under cover of night. Fortunately they were baffled in their design. An Indian returning from a hunt found their trail and was following it toward their hiding-place, when he was seen by Joseph Miller, one of the party, who quickly raised his rifle and fired at him. The Indian fell, evidently badly hurt, and John James rushed toward him tomahawk in hand, intending to dispatch him. As he did so the wounded Indian partly raised himself from the ground and uttered a ringing war-whoop, which was quickly answered from the camp only two or three hundred yards away, and by so many voices that the party of whites were much alarmed. They had supposed the camp to contain not more than their own strength, but fully a score of voices had been raised in response to the call of the wounded Indian, and almost immediately as many Indians came into view, rushing through the tangled undergrowth of the forest. James and his party seeing that the odds were so largely against them took to flight, and, assisted by the friendly darkness which had settled about them, soon put a considerable distance between them and their pursuers. The Indians, unable to follow their trail set their dogs on the retreating party, and followed on, guided by the sound of their barking. Two or three of the animals were silenced either with musket balls or tomahawk, and thus deprived of their lead the Indians lost ground rapidly. Arriving at the east fork of Symmes' creek, a difficulty arose which threatened to so long delay the fugitives as to allow their foes to overtake them.

There had been heavy rains, and the stream, ordinarily small, was now swollen so that it covered the entire bottom in the little valley. A raft was quickly made (a common expedient among the borderers and Indians, but when they attempted to cross upon it it became entangled in the submerged bushes and no effort that could be made would dislodge it. Abandoning the raft the six men, now so wet and cold that they were seriously hampered in their movements, made their way along the bank until they came to a place where it was possible to ford the stream. Taking their position upon a high bank which commanded this fording-place, they halted for rest and a chance to take advantage of their pursuers. They expected the Indians soon to make their appearance and intended to fire down upon them while they were in the water. After waiting an hour or more and hearing nothing of the Indians they pushed on to Raccoon creek, which they crossed upon a raft, and travelling rapidly all day reached Gallipolis just at evening, having been on foot twenty-four hours with the exception of two or three very brief intervals of rest, and travelled about fifty miles. The Gallipolis rangers the next day discovered that the Indians had followed the young men until they were within two or three miles of the settlement. The young men returned more leisurely to Belpre. Their expedition had taken them one hundred miles from home into the midst of the forest. During their absence they were the subject of a great deal of solicitude at the garrison, and all felt much relieved when they returned.

The closing tragedy of the war in Washington county took place in the summer of this year—1795—and the scene of its enactment was the vicinity of Waterford which since the futile attack upon the garrison in 1791 had not only suffered less annoyance from petty depredations than the Marietta and Belpre settlements, but by some kind fate or dispensation of Providence, had—although several of its people were taken captives—lost not a single man by death. [Abel Sherman, it must be remembered, was when killed a resident at Olive Green.] Indians had frequently been in the vicinity of Fort Frye during the continuance of the war, but they did not seem to cherish any such malice against the settlers as they did against the Virginians, "the Long Knives," and they were known several times to have peacefully passed by the Waterford people only to fall on the settlements south of the Ohio with relentless fury. They had been longer at war with the Virginians and hating them most thoroughly, never letting an opportunity go by for inflicting injury upon them, and often made long expeditions for the express purpose of assailing their little stations. While they had a bitter and long continued feud with the latter and many old hostilities to avenge, they were actuated in the war upon the Ohio settlers by less intense hostility—a feeling which arose principally from their dislike of seeing what they considered an encroachment upon their lands. The frequency of murderous attacks at Belpre was probably owing very largely to the situation of the settlement, upon the Ohio directly in the way of war parties returning from Virginia, who often chagrined by lack of success there sought to satisfy their desire for murder or plunder at the newer settlement. It is probable that had there been during the latter part of the war period any general desire on the part of the Indians to destroy the Ohio company's settlements, Waterford would have been the first assailed, and by a large war party. As it was the few small depredations committed there were the work of bands numbering three or four or a half dozen Indians, and those probably renegades wandering through the forest, and in obedience to their savage instincts committing murder when they could but seeking principally for plunder, or prisoners from whom they could exact labor or money for ransom. Judge Gilbert Devol and his son, Wanton, had a narrow escape from a company of Indians encamped on the banks of the Muskingum one summer day in 1793; and it had most of the time during the war been taken for granted that there were Indians in the vicinity, and precautions accordingly adopted. Since Wayne's victory, however, the settlers had lived more carelessly, and the rangers been less vigilant than of old.

This was the condition of affairs in the summer of 1795, and still as the treaty had not yet been made the members of the colony retained in some degree their prudent method of conducting their affairs. A number of young men—William Ford, Jacob Proctor, William Hart, John and Sherman Waterman, who had drawn adjoining donation lots on the south branch of Wolf creek, about four miles distant from Fort Frye—agreed to assist each other in clearing the timber, and both because it was pleasant and also prudential adopted the plan of working together in rotation a day at a time upon the five lots. On the twenty-first of May they were engaged in clearing on John Waterman's land. A house, or cabin rather, had already been built here, and as the day was showery they remained near it that they might take refuge under its roof when driven from their work. An unusually hard rain having set in they resorted to the cabin, and Sherman Waterman, when the rain had partially abated, remembering that he needed some fresh hemlock boughs for his sleeping berth, went out to cut them. He had not been gone long when the four men remaining in the cabin were startled by the report of a rifle. Silence and sombre gravity replaced the merriment of a moment before, and each man seizing his rifle sprang to a loop-hole to be ready in case of an attack. Presently Waterman came running toward the door pursued by several Indians. It was evident from his gait that he had been hurt, but he came onward at a fast run until near the door when he sank down groaning with pain. Terrified with fear that the Indians would now come up on him with their tomahawks he cried out to those within for assistance. To rush out and bring him into the cabin was to run a fearful risk of death, but among the pioneers when an emergency arose requiring self-sacrificing courage or prompt action there was always some man who could be relied upon to furnish these essentials. In this case it was William Hart. He was quickly at Waterman's side, lifted him from the ground, and amid a shower of bullets sprang back into the cabin door unharmed, though some of the rifle balls had narrowly missed him. A vigorous fire was kept up from the loopholes and the Indians soon retreated. Waterman was in a dying condition. William Hart volunteered to carry the news of the attack down to Waterford garrison. A number of men, led by the ranger McDuffey, came back with him, and took the wounded man in a canoe to a block-house below, owned by Dean Tyler, and there, after great agony endured with really heroic fortitude, Sherman Waterman passed away that night—the last victim of Indian war in Washington county.

Wayne's treaty, otherwise known as the treaty of Greenville, was concluded at Greenville, Darke county, Ohio, upon the tenth of August, 1795, and a permanent peace was secured in the northwest. The basis of the treaty was the one made at Fort Harmar in January, 1789.

The whole number of white persons killed during the period of hostility in the Ohio company's lands, or on the Virginia shore opposite, was thirty-eight. Ten were taken captive, and of these, two died of sickness or were killed. Only four Indians were known to have been killed, though twice as many were supposed to have fallen victims to the white man's rifle.

During the period represented in the foregoing pages, there were other terrors than those of Indian stealth and Indian attack to be endured by the settlers, and they were terrors before which bravery and strength were impotent. Disease and famine, the attendant evils of war, made their dread appearance in the little garrisons. The winter of 1788–89 was one of want to many of the settlers, but scarcely a foretaste of what they were to experience. While bread was not to be had, there was still a sufficient quantity of corn to sustain life—and there was little besides in the way of food until the river opened in the spring, when those who had money could buy flour. There was no meat to be had except that which could be secured by the hunters, and they fared poorly, as the Indians had killed off all the larger game, the bears and deer, while waiting about Marietta to attend the treaty. The year 1790 brought a worse condition of things. The corn crop of the preceding fall had been so badly damaged by an early frost that it was unfit to be eaten, and produced sickness and vomiting similar to that caused by the "sick wheat" which appeared occasionally when the country was new. During the winter of 1789–90 corn fit for consumption rose to the enormous price, for those times, of one dollar per bushel, and by the last of spring following it brought two dollars. With the scarcity of game, the failure of the corn crop, and the fact that there were no domestic animals which the owners could afford to kill, the fish, with which the rivers abounded, became the principal article of food, and the one which saved many people from absolute starvation. It was only with the practice of the most rigid economy that the people were able to hold out this year until a new crop could be raised. There was little money in the possession of the settlers, and they could only make small purchases in the spring, when the boats began running. The Ohio company made small loans to those who were most needy, and the few individuals who had more than enough food for their own use were very liberal with those who were worse off, sharing with them, perhaps to their own early disadvantage. Many articles were made use of as edibles which were not generally considered of any economic value, as potatoe tops, nettles, the tender buds and shoots of various shrubs and trees, and numerous roots. Sassafras and spice bush bark were brought into common use as a substitute for tea. Their scarcity made all staple articles very dear. Salt brought eight dollars per bushel and in smaller quantities much higher prices, as, for instance, fifty cents per quart. The settlers could therefore illy afford to salt down their fish or meat. In the spring the sap of the maples was secured in as large quantities as possible, and boiled down into syrup or sugar, and those articles, now esteemed as luxuries, were served as substantial food.

So nearly famished were the inhabitants at Belpre and Marietta when the new crop began to grow, that they could not wait for them to attain maturity, but plucked small and green vegetables, such as beans, peas, corn, and summer squashes, and boiling them with sparse handfulls of coarse corn meal from the last of their hoarded store, made a kind of vegetable soup which to their half-starved lips was an hundred-fold more grateful than is the most luxurious dish to the epicure in the midst of plenty. During the terrible season of famine, Isaac Williams, the Virginia frontiersman who had settled opposite the mouth of the Muskingum, exhibited the nobleness of his nature in many acts of generosity.

He had raised a very large quantity of corn, which, planted much earlier than that of the Belpre and Marietta settlers, who had first to clear and fence their lands, was so matured when frost came as to be uninjured. He was beset by speculators, who wished to buy his entire crop at the large price of one dollar and a quarter per bushel, but uniformly refused to have anything to do with them, and sold his corn to those who needed it for food, at the usual price in years of plenty, fifty cents per bushel. Nor would he sell to any man more than was necessary for the subsistence of his family. It was his usual custom to inquire of an applicant the number of persons in his household, and sell him a proportionate number of bushels. To those who had not money to buy even at his moderate price, he readily gave credit, and in not a few cases made actual donations. The settlers very generally availed themselves of his benevolence, and the good old man, denying himself riches, had the nobler satisfaction of having relieved distress, and perhaps warding off absolute starvation.

Pestilence made its appearance before famine. The small-pox was introduced among the Point settlers at Marietta in January, 1790—and it must be borne in mind that Jenner's discovery of vaccination had not then been given as a boon to mankind, and the loathsome disease was much more dreaded than now. A sick man named Welch was put on shore by a Kentucky boat. He was taken to the house of James Owen and soon discovered to have the small-pox. Great consternation and excitement followed. A meeting of the inhabitants was called and it was decided to build a house for the sick man. This was accordingly done and he was taken to it and there died. Mrs. Owen contracted the disease but recovered. The pestilence spread fast and inoculation was resorted to as a preventive of the worst form of the disease. Houses were put up for the reception of the sick at a considerable distance from the other dwellings. Eight persons died; two of them the number who had been inoculated.

Again in August, 1793, the settlers at the Point were alarmed by the appearance in epidemic form of the scarlet fever. It broke out among Captain Haskell's soldiers, and was probably caused by the malaria from the low ground around, and the streets within the Point garrison, which had been overflowed in March by a flood of the Ohio. The court of quarter sessions had the infected persons removed to Devol's island, but the disease had already spread, and a number of deaths occurred. The small-pox broke out again, and so the people were assailed at once by two insidious foes within the defence they had raised to protect themselves from their enemies, the Indians.

Belpre had its share in the evils of pestilence as it did of the horrors of warfare. Scarlet fever broke out at Farmer's Castle in the summer of 1792, attended by putrid sore throat. The cause was unknown, though it was doubtless the unhealthful condition of life unavoidable in a crowded garrison. It was confined principally to the children, and about fifteen of them were its victims. After the scarlet fever had subsided, and during the summer and autumn bilious and intermittent fevers prevailed, though happily in mild forms.

That more dreaded scourge—small-pox—again made its appearance in the over-crowded garrison in September, 1793, being introduced by Benjamin Patterson, one of the rangers, who had been inoculated at Marietta. It was not strange that the people who were huddled together in close quarters, guarding themselves from the Indians, who had already surprised and killed several of their number;—who had suffered from famine, and who had just seen their loved little ones carried off by fever, should feel that they were doomed to destruction. They knew that the terrible pest must sweep through their cramped quarters, and so, after holding a council, resolved upon heroic measures, and sent for Dr. True, of Marietta, to inoculate them all in their own houses. Farmer's Castle was one great hospital. Under every roof there was some person suffering from the mild form which they had taken voluntarily to themselves from the more virulent. The fatality of the disease was confined by inoculation, so that of one hundred persons affected only five died. At Goodale's garrison there were two or three more deaths. But the terrible scourge had been prevented from doing its worst. Though sorely tried, the little settlement was destined neither to succumb to the Indian, to famine, to fever, nor to pestilence.

CHAPTER XI.

LATER HISTORY OF THE OHIO COMPANY.

A Review of Some Important Matters.—The Price of Public Lands Reduced.—An Injustice to the Ohio Company.—The Rise of Securities.—Forfeited Shares in the Ohio Company's Stock Sold to the Trustees of the Scioto Company.—Plans for a Final Settlement with Congress.—Trouble Caused by Speculative Stockholders.—They Desire that the Contract of Purchase be Forfeited.—The Directors at Philadelphia in 1792.—Their Petition to Congress.—Critical Condition of the Company's Affairs.—Effect of the Indian War.—Failure of and Loss by the Treasurer, Richard Platt.—The Scioto Company Fails to Meet Its Obligation.—Impossibility of Carrying Out the Original Contract—The Only Hope of the Company and Its Settlement, a Release.—Favorable Action of Congress.—Three Patents Issued to Rufus Putnam, Manasseh Cutler, Robert Oliver and Griffin Greene, as Trustees of the Ohio Company.—Boundaries of the Purchase—The Donation Tract.—Beneficent Policy of the Company.—Division of the Lands.—Eleven Hundred and Seventy-three to Each of Eight Hundred and Seventeen Shares.—Names of the Members of the Ohio Company.—Number of Shares Owned by Each Person.—A Pendant to the History of the Company, Reaching Down to Recent Years.

MUCH of the later history of the Ohio company which would have been chronologically in order in the preceding pages, has been intentionally reserved for consideration connectedly in a single chapter. The most interesting topic is that which includes the release of the Ohio company from its original contract and its final settlement with Congress in 1792; but, to convey an adequate idea of the necessities of this release, and the difficulties and the perils which the company passed through, it will be necessary to review some events of prior years.

In May, 1789, at a meeting of the company held at Marietta, General Putnam and Dr. Cutler (the latter then at his house in Massachusetts), were empowered to ascertain from the different agents the number of unpaid shares, which were represented by them, to declare them forfeited, sell them if possible, and effect a final settlement with the Government. The affairs of the company were in a very unsatisfactory condition They had paid to the Government on account of their purchase which required a million. They had no title to any part of their lands, although under their right of entry they had made a settlement and considerable improvement, and had set off to each shareholder one city lot, one three-acre lot and one one hundred and sixty-acre lot. Until the company was able to complete the division of the lands as contemplated in the articles of association, the shares were useless to the holders and almost worthless. The securities in which they were payable, had appreciated in value more than one hundred per cent. There appeared therefore, but a faint prospect of selling the forfeited shares, and unless they were sold, the final payment to the Government could not be made as provided in the original contract.

In January, 1790, the Secretary of the Treasury, Alexander Hamilton, in a report to Congress on methods of funding the public debt, recommended that the price of the public lands be fixed at twenty cents per acre, payable in coin or Government securities. With the intention of applying to Congress for a reduction in the price of the lands, General Putnam went to New York in January, 1790. He arrived upon the thirtieth, and was joined by Dr. Cutler late in February. Pending the action of Congress on the recommendation of Secretary Hamilton, they did not present their petition. Early in April it became evident that nothing could be done during that session to secure a reduction of the price of the Ohio company's lands. The friends of the company in Congress, however, were sanguine that at the next session they would be able to secure a reduction in price at least equivalent to the rise in the value of securities. William Duer, Royal Flint and Andrew Craigie, as trustees of the Scioto company, held an option from the board of treasury to purchase all the lands west of the Ohio company's territory to the Scioto river, and as far north as the tenth township. They desired to purchase of the Ohio company a tract of land near the mouth of the Big Kanawha, upon which they could locate a number of French emmigrants who had already sailed. General Putnam proposed to them that they should buy the forfeited shares of the Ohio company (the number of which was concluded, from the best attainable information, to be one hundred and forty-eight), take the three acre lots, the eight acre lots, the city lots and one hundred and sixty acre lots already set apart for those shares in the portion of the Ohio company's tract which had been surveyed, and locate the remainder, one hundred and ninety-six thousand five hundred and forty-four acres, in a compact body fronting on the Ohio river, below the Big Kanawha.

They accepted, and on the twenty-third of April, 1790, Putnam and Cutler, for the Ohio company, made a contract for sale to Duer, Flint and Craigie of the tract described. The consideration was one thousand four hundred and eighty-eight dollars in specie, to be paid in sixty and ninety days; eight thousand eight hundred and eighty dollars in indents of interest, to be paid in six months, and the remainder to be paid when the Ohio company made its final settlement with Congress, at the same price per acre which that company should secure, and in the same public securities which they should pay for lands.

Duer, Flint and Craigie surrendered also to the Ohio company their right of preemption or option of purchase of all the lands north of the Ohio company's purchase to the tenth township. They were to have the same right to enter upon and occupy the lands comprised in the forfeited shares as was given the Ohio company by their contract with Congress, but no deed of conveyance was to be executed or demanded until the payments were fully completed. This contract was rightly deemed of great value to the Ohio company.* In case they should ultimately obtain a reduction in the price of their lands to twenty or twenty-five cents per acre, the amount already paid to the United States would entitle them to a larger amount of better lands in the territory comprised in the right of preemption released to them. To obtain this reduction and its application to the Ohio company's contract, they had secured a powerful ally in Colonel William Duer, formerly secretary of the board of treasury, an intimate and confidential friend of Washington and Hamilton, a man of high social standing and of reputed great wealth. If their effort in obtaining a reduction of prices failed, the original contract was at least secure.

The Indian war which broke out in September, 1790—for that was the time at which General Harmar started upon his expedition—prevented the directors from going on to New York, as they had expected to do, to continue negotiations for a settlement. The failure of the Government to take prompt and adequate measures for the protection of the settlements stopped immigration. With great difficulty many who had already settled in various parts of the purchase were prevented from returning to the east, and some did return.

A portion of the shareholders who had bought shares for speculation and had no other interest than a pecuniary one in the success of the settlement, demanded that the securities in the hands of the treasurer of the company (about twenty-five thousand dollars), applicable to the final payment, be at once divided among the shareholders, and if necessary, the contract be forfeited. Nothing but the

---

*At a meeting of the Ohio company's agents, June 11, 1790, at which six hundred and fifty shares were represented, the following resolution was adopted, by 621 yeas to 29 nays:

Resolved, That the sale of certain tracts of lands made by the Honorable Rufus Putnam and Rev. M. Cutler to the trustees of the Scioto company be approbated, and it is hereby approbated, and that the thanks of the agents and proprietors be given to Rufus Putnam and Mr. Cutler for their attention to the business of a settlement with Congress.—The Ohio company's journal.

firmness and good sense of Rufus Putnam and Manasseh Cutler prevented the destruction of the colony.

In February, 1792, General Putnam, Dr. Cutler, and Colonel Robert Oliver—a majority of the directors—met in Philadelphia, where Congress was then in session. The special agents and proprietors were notified by a circular letter to assemble at Philadelphia at once, bringing with them all documents necessary to make a final settlement with the treasurer of the company, Colonel Richard Platt. The directors presented a petition asking Congress that the whole amount of lands included in the company's contract (one million, five hundred thousand acres) might be deeded to them for the payment of five hundred thousand dollars, already made, and that a grant of one hundred thousand acres additional be made to the company to compensate them for lands they had donated to actual settlers and to those performing military duty, and for the expenses they were incurring in maintaining troops which properly belonged to the Government. The petition, after setting forth the facts heretofore represented, and appealing to Congress "to retrieve this unfortunate company from inevitable ruin," concluded with an earnest and touching expression of the worst fears felt by the subscribers and by the people in the settlements:

A very considerable part of the military strength of the settlement depends upon the non-proprietors to whom lands have been promised on condition of performance of military duty to the end of the present war and should the closing of this present contract be postponed until future session of Congress the company cannot fulfil their engagements to them, and if not done the directors are confidently assured that these people will desert the settlement, the inevitable consequence of which must be that a great part if not the whole of the settlements will be abandoned. Nor does the hazard of a total desertion depend only on those people. The resident proprietors sensibly feel the great loss of men and property which they have sustained, as well as the extreme distress and suffering they endured the last year. There is every reason to believe that unless they are retrieved from that State of suspense and uncertainty respecting their title, with which their minds have been so long exercised, they will make no further exertions to defend a settlement from which they are at any time liable to be driven, that if the scalping-knife and the tomahawk do not prevent an escape they will immediately retreat to some place of greater security. We will only add that the most of your petitioners have with much anxiety left their families exposed every moment to an attack from the Indians to repair to this place for the purpose of closing their contract, and should they be obliged to return without effecting this object we fear the evils we have suggested and many more will unavoidably take place.

The situation was bad enough, but it was to be worse. The agents did not assemble in Philadelphia until the eleventh of April, and before a settlement could be effected with Colonel Platt, there occurred a panic in New York and Platt failed, owing the Ohio company nearly fifty thousand dollars. Duer also failed and was thrown into prison. Flint and Craigie were carried down by Duer's failure. No payments had been made by these men, as the directors of the Scioto company on account of their contract for purchase of the forfeited shares, and it was therefore surrendered and cancelled. The committee of Congress to whom were referred the directors' petition, reported favorably to its passage, but for some reason which does not clearly appear there was much opposition to it. The probable reason was the fact which had become widely known through meetings of the dissatisfied shareholders that the company had in its treasury a large amount of securities which could be paid on account of the balance due on the contract.

A critical juncture in the affairs of the Ohio company and the settlers had been reached. Besides the combination of adverse circumstances which threatened to overwhelm the company, "the second payment, five hundred thousand dollars was now due," says General Putnam,[*] according to the terms of the original contract, and "non-payment it was feared would forfeit lands which had already been paid for." It was impossible to make the payment, and the company's only hope was in securing a release from the obligations incurred and more liberal terms, as contemplated in the petition. "In this mount of difficulties," adds Putnam, "Divine Providence so overruled the minds of men that Congress passed an act authorizing the President" to take those measures which practically answered the prayers of the company, and retrieved it from ruin. The bill authorizing a settlement as it finally passed April 21, 1792, directed that a deed be made to the Ohio company for seven hundred and fifty thousand acres, by fixed boundaries, for the five hundred thousand dollars in securities which had already been paid into the treasury of the United States; another for two hundred thousand two hundred and eighty-five acres additional, or about one-seventh of the amount of the original contract, to be paid for in land warrants (a large amount of which had been turned over by Colonel Platt), and a third for one hundred thousand acres in trust to be given in tracts of one hundred acres each to actual settlers. The donation tract was saved only by the vote of Vice President Adams.

Colonel Benjamin Tallmadge was chosen treasurer of the Ohio company, vice Platt, and was directed to sell all the securities on hand, reserve ten thousand dollars to pay for further work on the survey, and to divide the remainder, pro rata, among the shareholders, through their respective agencies.

Upon the tenth of May the President, in pursuance of the act of April 21st, issued three patents[†] to Rufus Putnam, Manasseh Cutler, Robert Oliver, and Griffin Greene, in trust for the Ohio company of associates. The patents were signed by George Washington, President, and Thomas Jefferson, Secretary of State. With the exception of one to the State of Pennsylvania, March 3, 1792, these are the first land patents issued by the Government.[‡]

The lands which came into the possession of the company through these patents amounted to a total of nine hundred and sixty-four thousand two hundred and eighty-five acres, or including the donation tract, one million sixty-four thousand two hundred and eighty-five—instead of the amount originally contracted for—one million five hundred thousand acres. The bill for the relief of the company at first contained a clause providing that the company might secure a conveyance for the remainder

---

[*] In autobiography.

[†] The original patents and the contract of October 27, 1787, are in the library of Marietta college.

[‡] Centennial address by Israel Ward Andrews, LL. D., president of Marietta college.

of the one million five hundred thousand acres on the payment for the same within six years at the rate of twenty-five cents per acre, but this provision was lost in the senate.

The boundaries of the Ohio company's purchase as finally fixed by survey are as follows: Beginning on the Ohio river upon the western boundary line of the fifteenth range of townships (opposite the mouth Guyandotte); thence running northerly to a point about one mile north of the south line of township number seven; thence westerly to the western boundary of the sixteenth range; thence northerly to the north line of township number thirteen; thence easterly to a point about one mile east of the west boundary of range eleven; thence north four miles; thence east to the western boundary of the seventh range; thence south along that line to the Ohio; thence along the Ohio to the place of beginning. This tract includes the whole of the present counties of Athens and Meigs, and portions of Washington, Morgan, Gallia, Vinton, Jackson and Hocking.

The donation tract lies in the northeast part of the territory above described, and is about twenty-one miles long by eight in width. The boundaries are described as follows:* Beginning on the western boundary line on the seventh range of townships at the northeast corner of the seven hundred and fifty thousand acre tract; thence running north to Ludlow's line (surveyed by Israel Ludlow at the northern boundary of the original purchase of one million five hundred thousand acres); thence along that line westwardly to the tract containing two hundred and fourteen thousand two hundred and eighty-five acres; thence south to the boundary of the seven hundred and fifty thousand acre tract; thence along that boundary, easterly to the place of beginning.

The directors of the Ohio company were the trustees of the donation tract. They had the land surveyed and boundaries established in May, 1793, and prescribed rules for their own government in donating the lands. It was decided that the settlers then in the tract should be provided with lots first.

General Putnam was appointed as the surveyor of the lands and superintendent of the donation tract business. The deeds were nearly all made out by him.

By the middle of July, 1793, seventeen thousand acres had been divided into one hundred and seventy lots. These were included in nine allotments, located in the vicinity of the Muskingum and Wolf creek. The total number of lots drawn during the year was one hundred and eighty-six. The lots which had been donated as lying outside of the tract, were covered by a new division, known as the fifth division, by which one-hundred acre lots were drawn in the company's lands as a part of each share.

There remains not much to be said of the Ohio company. When the final settlement was made with Congress its mission was practically closed. The influence, however, of the organization under whose auspices the State of Ohio and the great Northwest was opened, re-

mained an active and potent force in the life and progress of the west.

Owing to the continuance of the Indian war, which was not ended until the treaty of Greenville, heretofore alluded to, in the summer of 1795, the surveys were not completed as soon as would otherwise have been the case. The college lands, two townships (Nos. 8 and 9 in the fourteenth range, now known as Ames and Alexander, in Athens county), were selected and surveyed in the winter of 1795-96, and so was carried out one of the wisest and most beneficent measures of the company, one which had engaged the attention of its leading men from the time the organization was effected, in 1787.

Another act of the company about this time exhibited the broad and kindly policy which had ever been one of its characteristics. The land on which the poor French settlers had located, at Gallipolis, sold to the Scioto company by the Ohio company, had reverted to the latter through the inability of the other party to pay for it. In November the lands were sold to the settlers at the low price of one dollar and twenty-five cents per acre.

The last meeting of the Ohio company west of the mountains, was called at Marietta November 23, 1795, and the directors and agents continued in session until January 29, 1796. The final partition or division of lands was made at this time, and on the first of February sworn to before Josiah Monroe, justice of the peace. By this division there were set off to each share in the stock of the company the following lands: First division, one eight-acre lot; second division, one three-acre lot; third division, one city lot; Fourth division, one one-hundred-and-sixty-acre lot; fifth division, one one-hundred-acre lot; sixth division, one six-hundred-and-forty-acre lot, and one two-hundred-and-sixty-two-acre lot; total, one thousand one hundred and seventy-three acres.

Following is a list of the members of the Ohio company, among whom the lands were divided. There were eight hundred and nineteen shares classified in sixteen agencies; this order has been followed in making the list, the names being alphabetically arranged under each agency. Where an individual owned more than one share the number is given. Where two or more names appear in the same line there was a partnership in the share or shares. The list includes the names of many eminent characters and a very large number which are familiar to residents of Washington county. There are others which will appear strange, even to those persons best acquainted with the settlement of the Ohio company's purchase. A large proportion of this class belong to individuals who bought shares from purely speculative motives, and never settled in the territory of which they owned a part.

JOEL BARLOW'S AGENCY—NINETEEN SHARES.

Joel Barlow and associates, 3 shares; Abijah Colton; Joseph Day and associates; Abiel Griswold; Sylvanus Griswold; Peleg Heath and associates; Ebenezer Hinckley and associates, Thomas Lord, assignee; Timothy Hosmer; Elizabeth Judd; Daniel Jones; Abel Mathews and associates; Thomas Stanley and associates; Nathaniel Terry; John Watson, 2 shares; Samuel Wyllis; Nathan Williams.

WILLIAM CORLISS' AGENCY—ONE HUNDRED AND EIGHT SHARES.

Samuel Aborn, 3 shares; Welcome Arnold, 4 shares; Nathan Angel, 3 shares; Moses Brown, jr., to Nicholas Brown, 3 shares; Nicholas

---

* Land Laws of Ohio.

Brown, 5 shares; John Brown, 5 shares; James Brown, 5 shares; Alice Brown, 2 shares, Sally Brown, 2 shares; Sarah Brown, 4 shares; Abigail Brown, alias Francis, 2 shares; Obediah Bowen; Shubael Burr, Samuel Burr; Jabez Bowen, 2 shares; William Bowen; William Bradford; William Barton; Nicholas Brown, jr.. Nicholas Brown, 3 shares; Asahel Carpenter, William Corliss, John Corliss; Benjamin Cumstock, John Carter; George Corliss, William Bowen; George Corliss, William Sessions; George Corliss, Joseph Nightengale; John Child; Thomas Carpenter; Charles De Wolf; Marquis De Chapedelaine, Thomas L. Halsey, 3 shares; Mary Demount, Rebecca Demount; Jedediah Ensworth; Josiah Green, Boon Vaughn; James Grammon, Christopher Winsor; Nathan Grosvenor; Thomas L., Halsey; Enos Hitchcock; William Humphrey; Amos Horton; William Holroyd; John Jenks, Joseph Jenks, 2 shares; John Mumford; James Munroe; David W. Marsh; James Manning, William Corliss, William Holroyd, Nightingale and Clark, 5 shares; Jeremiah Olney, 2 shares; Christopher Olney; Nicholas Power; Saunders Pitman; Joseph and William Russell, 2 shares; John Spurr; Cyprian Sterry; Archibald Stewart, 2 shares; Stephen Smith; Henry Smith; Thomas Sabin; Simeon Thayer, John Walker; Joseph Winsor, John Woldron; Samuel Wyatt; Nathan Waterman; Nathaniel Wheaton; Samuel Wardwell.

A. GRAY'S AGENCY—SEVENTY-ONE SHARES.

Stephen Arnold, Thomas Arnold; William Arnold, 8 shares; Israel Bowen; James Brown, son of Nathaniel, Joseph Briggs; John L. Boss; John Breeze, 2 shares; William S. Brown; Abijah Babcock; Peleg Clark; Archibald Crary, Samuel King; Archibald Crary, Simeon Martin; Wanton Casey, 2 shares; James Corydon; Isaac Senter; Ethan Clark; Jonathan Devol; Nicholas Easton, 2 shares; John Fulham, Major Fairchild; George Gibbs; William Greene, governor, 2 shares; Charles Greene; Elihu Greene & Co., Elihu and Christopher Greene; William Greene, son of Nathaniel, Griffin Greene; Catharine Greene; Griffin Greene; Caleb Gardner, 2 shares; Job Greene; William Hammond; Alexander Hamilton, Robert Stephens; Thomas Howland; Thomas Hughes; Henry Hunter; Zebulon King, his heirs; Daniel Lyman; David Olyphant, 2 shares; Anne Olyphant; Peter Phillips, Northrop Daniel; Abraham Redwood, 3d, Christopher Champlin; Thomas Rice; Henry Rice; Adam Richmond, Abraham R. Rivera; Jacob R. Rivera; Thomas Rumrill, Hannah Sheffield; Benjamin Slocum; Robert Stephens; Nicholas P. Tillinghast, 2 shares; Waterman Tibbets; Peter Turner, 3 shares; John Topham; Pardon Tillinghast (West Greenwich); Pardon Tillinghast (Exeter); William Tew; William Vernon; James M. Varnum, Samuel Fowler; Elizabeth Whitman.

M. CUTLER'S AND DODGE S AGENCY—EIGHTY-SIX SHARES.

John Atchinson, 3 shares; Samuel Adams; William Burnham; John Burnham, 3 shares; Joseph Barrel, 5 shares; Augustus Blanchard; Nathaniel Brown; William Bartlett; Manasseh Cutler, 5 shares; William Cleveland; Ephraim Cutler to Joseph Multon; Ehpraim Cutler; Lot Cheever; Ezekiel Cooper and Jethro Putnam; Richard Dodge, Nathan Woodbury; Isaac Dodge, Oliver Dodge; Jonathan Deane, 2 shares; John Dodge, of Beverly, 2 shares; Nathaniel Deane, jr.; Moses Everett; John Friend; Daniel Fuller; Ezekiel Goldthwait, Nathaniel and Stephen Porter; Jesse Gay; Hugh Henderson; Samuel Hildreth, 2 shares; Thomas Hartshorn; John J. Herd, 2 shares; Samuel Hitchburn, Daniel Story; Stephen Jewett, Benjamin I. Gilman; Porter Lummis; Peter Oliver; David Pearce, jr., 5 shares, Obediah Parsons; Allen Putnam, Amos Porter, David Pearce, 4 shares; William Pearce, 2 shares; Matthew Park, Elijah Thorp; John Safford; Winthrop Sargent, of Boston, 2 shares; Peter Shaw; Winthrop Sargent, of Glocester; William Story, Daniel Story; George Stephens; John Treadwell, 2 shares; Israel Thornike, 2 shares; Robert Williams, jr., 4 shares; Benjamin Wadsworth, 3 shares; Elisha Whitney, William Burleigh; Jonathan Williams, 2 shares; William Burnham, 2 shares; Joseph Willard.

EPHRAIM CUTLER'S AGENCY—THIRTEEN SHARES.

Ebenezer Atwood; Alpheus Converse, 2 shares; Benjamin Converse, his heirs; Aaron Clough; 'Squire Cady; John Douglass; Daniel Davis; Isaac Knight; Joseph Leaveus; Jonathan Russell; Jesse Whipple; George Wilson, George Wilson and heirs.

E. DOWNER'S AGENCY—EIGHTEEN SHARES.

Henry Bowers, jr., 2 shares; John Bowers; Eleazer Baker; Stephen Cook; Eliphalet Downer, 2 shares; Nathaniel H. Furnass; Charles Knowles; Baker & Lamb; John Lamb; William Marshall; Nathaniel Ruggles; William Rhodes; John Stratton; Elisha Whitney, 2 shares; John Waldo.

FREEMAN'S AGENCY—NINE SHARES.

Joseph Bates; Barakiah Bassett; Joseph Nye, of Norwich, 5 shares; Joseph Thomas; Abraham Williams.

E HARRIS' AGENCY--THIRTY-ONE SHARES.

Jacob Brown; John Bond, Samuel Webster, Jonathan Call, Jabez B. True; Jonathan Cass; Samuel Currier; Timothy Dexter, 5 shares; Samuel L. Dexter; Jeremiah Fogg; Benjamin Ives Gilman; Edward Harris, 3 shares; Ezra Lunt, 4 shares; William Moulton; Josiah Munroe, Haffield White, Thomas Odiorne, Dudley Odlin, Benjamin Ives Gilman; Stephen Swasey, Joseph Swasey, jr.; Jabez True; Samuel Tenney; Nathaniel Whitmore, 2 shares; Amos Whitmore.

JACKSON'S AGENCY —THIRTEEN SHARES.

John Hurd; George Ingersoll; John Coffin Jones, 5 shares; Henry Jackson and associates; John Lucas; Rufus Putnam, 2 shares; Job Sumner, Jesse Sumner, William Torrey.

MAY'S AGENCY—THIRTY-FIVE SHARES.

James Bowdoin, 5 shares; Thomas Blake; William Breck; Benjamin Cobb, 2 shares; William Dall; Ebenezer Dorr; Elbridge Gerry; William Hoskins; John Lucas; John May, jr.; Joseph May; Henry K. May; William R. May; Frederick May; John May, William Marshall; Samuel H. Perkins; James Patterson, 2 shares; Thomas Russell, 5 shares; John Sprague; Winthrop Sargent, John May and James Smith; Russell Sturgis; Elisha Ticknor; Robert Williams, jr.; Ebenezer Wales.

PARSONS' AGENCY—NINETY-ONE SHARES.

David Adams, 2 shares; Caleb Atwater; Samuel Broome, 5 shares; Jeremiah Butler; Isaac Burnham; Nathan Beers; David Bull; James Backus; John H. Buell; Moses Cleveland, 2 shares, Wheeler Coit; Levi Chapman; Levi Chapman, Samuel Shipman; Elnathan Camp; Eliphalet Dyer; Samuel Dorrance; Richard Douglass; James Davenport, John Deshon, Jonathan Deming, John Deshon, Andrew Fitch; Samuel Frothingham, Ebenezer Frothingham; Thomas Grosvenor; Peter Heyleger, 5 shares, Jedediah Huntington, Azariah Lathrop; Nehemiah Hubbard, 2 shares; Elijah Hubbard; Jonathan Heart, Abigail Heart; David Humphreys, Elisha Lord; Christopher Leffingwell; Humphrey Lyon, William Lord; Joshua Miles, 2 shares; John Morgan; John Meigs; John Newton, jr., Abner Lord, Samuel H. Parsons, William Parsons, etc., 5 shares; Jeremiah Platt, 5 shares; Samuel H. Parsons, 2 shares; Humphrey Pratt, Israel Putnam, 4 shares; William Parsons; Enoch Parsons; Jonas Prentiss; Joshua Parsons, Edward Miller; Mehetable Parsons, John Nisewonger; John Pierpont, David F. Sill, Elias Stillwell, Abraham Scranton; Abigail Savage; George Starr; Jonathan Trumbull; Daniel Tyler, jr.; Gad Tallcott; Benjamin Throop, Robert Walker, Joseph Walker, John R. Watrous, Daniel Watrous; Andrew Backus, John P. Jones, his heir, John Davenport, John P. Jones, his heir; Andrew Huntington, John P. Jones, his heir; Timothy Larrabel, John P. Jones, his heir; Elijah Lathrop, jr., John P. Jones, his heir.

PUTNAM'S AGENCY -FIFTY-NINE SHARES.

Samuel Brazier, Francis Choat; Timothy Bigelow, Silas Bent; Silas Bent; William Browning, jr., John Burnham; William Caldwell, Nathan Goodale, 2 shares; Caleb Clapp, 2 shares; Jonathan Choat, Benjamin Miles, Nathaniel Cushing and associates; Asa Coburn and associates, 3 shares; Joshua and Daniel Clapp; Daniel Clapp; Elijah Dix, 2 shares; Frederick Frye; Isaac Farewell; Peregrine Foster; Samuel Frost; Dwight Foster; Paul Fearing, Samuel Flagg; Nathan Goodale, 2 shares; Benjamin Haywood, Elias Hall and associates, 2 shares; Daniel Loring; John Lyon, John Mathews and associates; Joel Marble; Thomas Nixon; William R. Putnam; Edwin Putnam; Ezra Putnam; William Rice; Henry Reidle, 2 shares; John Reed, John Miles; Oliver Rice, 2 shares; John Stanton, of Boston; John Stanton, of Worcester; Joseph Stephens, Jonathan Stone, 2 shares; Caleb Strong; Daniel Strong, 2 shares, John Sprague, 2 shares; Benjamin Stone and associates; Winthrop Sargent, 2 shares; Isaiah Thomas, Nicholas Pike; Benjamin Tupper, his heirs.

SARGENT'S AGENCY—ONE HUNDRED AND FORTY-EIGHT SHARES.

Joseph Ashton; Ercurius Beatty, 3 shares; Daniel Britt; Philander Brazier; Elizabeth Bowdoin, 4 shares; Anne Brown; James Bradford, his heirs; Leonard V. Borland; Sebastian Beaumin; William Constable, 5 shares; Henrietta Colden, 5 shares; David Cobb; Edward Carrington, 4 shares; John H. Chevallie, 2 shares; Caleb Champney; Florence Crowley; Thomas H. Condy; Ebenezer Crosby; John Delafield; De Neufville, 2 shares; Ebenezer Denny; John Doughty, Hamilton Kerr; John Doughty; Israel Evans, 2 shares; William Edgar, 5 shares; Andrew Frauncis; John Green, William Gridley; Alexander Hamilton, 3 shares; Joseph Hardy; Michael Hillegas; Josiah Harmar, 2 shares; Ebenezer Hazzard, Abijah Hammond, 5 shares; Jonathan Haskell; Elnathan Haskell; John Jeffers; Henry Jackson; Henry

Kuhl, Charles Knowles, 2 shares, Henry Knox; John Lawrence, 3 shares; Walter Livingstone, 3 shares; Arthur Lee, 2 shares; Isaac Ledyard, 2 shares; Brockholst Livingstone, 5 shares; Christopher Marshall; John May, Winthrop Sargent; William M. Morris; William McComb, 5 shares, John Mercer; Alexander McComb, 5 shares; William McCurdy; Elizabeth McComb, John Murray; Joseph May; Joseph Nourse, James Nicholson, 3 shares, Rufus Putnam; John Pratt, 2 shares, John Rose; Platt Rogers; Thomas Seward, John Dyer, 2 shares; Paschal N. Smith, 5 shares; Caleb Swan; Melancthon Smith; Derrick Schuyler; David Strong, Annanias R. Sacket; Arthur St. Clair; Evart W. Swart, John M. Scott; Sarah Sears; Robert Underwood, 2 shares; William Wickham; Matthew Witzell; Joseph Williams, 2 shares, Jeremiah Williams; Frederick Wizenfeldt, James O'Hara; Thomas Wallcutt; David Zeigler, 2 shares; William M. Morris.

SPROAT'S AGENCY—FORTY-THREE SHARES.

Israel Angel, Israel Angel, Christopher Windsor; Israel Angel, Jeffrey Matthewson, Samuel Aborn; Thomas Coles; John L. Dexter, 4 shares; Solomon Drown; Caleb Fisk, 2 shares; Theodore Foster; Oliver Fuller; Peleg Fisk; Libbens Loomis, 2 shares; Christopher Lippet; John Mawney, Elisha Mowry, jr.; Matthew Manchester, 3 shares; Ebenezer Macomber; Cogshall Olney. 3 shares; William Peck; Ebenezer Sproat, 2 shares; Ebenezer Sproat (drawn in name of Joseph Coit in E. Cutler's agency); David Sayles; Earl Sproat; Thomas Smart; Daniel Tillinghast, 3 shares, Samuel Thewber, jr.; Edward Thewber; William Wheaton; Abraham Whipple, 2 shares; Joseph Wilkinson.

TUPPER'S AGENCY—THIRTY SHARES.

Moses Ashley, Asa Hill; John Alden; Samuel Buffington; Daniel Dunham (his heirs); Asa Graves, Joseph Spencer, Noah Goodman, Aaron Howe; Samuel Kenshaw; Aaron Howe, Elijah Hunt, Perez Morton; Huldah Tupper; Ichabod Nye; Robert Oliver and associates, 2 shares, Alexander Oliver and associates; Rufus Putnam; Andrew Peters and associate, 2 shares; Asahel Pomeroy; John Quigley and associates; William Stacey, 4 shares; Calvin Smith and associate; Enoch Shephard; Benjamin Tupper, 2 shares; Benjamin Tupper, jr.; Anselem Tupper; Edward W. Tupper.

TALLMADGE'S AGENCY—FORTY-THREE SHARES.

Seth Bird, Alexander Catlin; Reuben Fox; Joseph Guthrie, 2 shares; Abel Hine; Benjamin Hunting and associates; Benjamin Hunting, etc., James Post; Benjamin Hunting, etc., David Hedges; Benjamin Hunting, etc., David Pierson; Benjamin Hunting, Augustus F. Tallmadge; David Hedges and Thomas Wickham; David Hedges and David Gardiner, 2 shares; David Hedges and Fuah Davis; David Hedges and John Beardsley, David Judson, 2 shares; Ephraim Kirby; David Leavitt, jr., & Co.; James Morris, 3 shares; Samuel Southmayd; Timothy Skinner; Heman Swift, B. Tallmadge & Co.; Heman Swift, Ebenezer Nye, Josiah Starr, 2 shares; Reuben Smith, Nathaniel Taylor; Benjamin Tallmadge, 5 shares; Henry F. Tallmadge; Uriah Tracey; William S. Tallmadge; John Tallmadge for Benjamin Tallmadge & Co., Elijah Wadsworth.

There is an interesting pendant to the history of the Ohio company, which reaches down to recent years. In the treasury of the company there were a number of Revolutionary certificates of the State of Georgia, which, owing to an irregularity in their endorsement, had been refused by the treasurer of the United States. Being unnegotiable, these certificates were practically valueless, and hence were undivided by the company. When the final partition was made, and the lands of the company set off to the shareholders, the certificates formed the only remaining property of the company (if property they could be called), except a small amount of personalty. The only value left in the shares was that which was contingent upon the negotiability of the Georgia certificates. There were few members of the company who believed that they would be recognized by the Government, and hence it was altogether a natural thing that the owners should part with their shares for trivial considerations.

Nahum Ward, a New England man, (grandson of Major General Artemas Ward, the first major general of the army), came to Marietta in 1810, and began a career as land speculator, in which capacity he eventually became the owner of colossal interests and wielded most powerful influences. He saw in the Georgia certificates the possibility of a fortune, and in order to become their possessor began to buy up the shares of the Ohio company, securing most of them for merely nominal sums. During all of the time he was prosecuting his affairs as land dealer and absorbing the shares of the company, he was making a study of the history of the Georgia certificates, and as he progressed in his investigations he became each day and year more thoroughly convinced of his ability to realize not only their face value, but the amount of interest on them, compounded at six per cent., from the year of their issuance (1777) down to the time at which payment should be secured. At a meeting of the surviving shareholders of the Ohio company, held at Providence, Rhode Island, in 1836, Mr. Ward was elected treasurer. In this capacity, representing the company as well as himself, after a long and careful preparation, he brought suit, in 1857, before the United States circuit court by an eminent attorney—John A. Rockwell, of Connecticut—for the payment of the certificates in his possession. It was represented that Mr. Ward was the legal holder of forty-three loan office certificates for the sum of four hundred dollars each, issued by authority of Congress, granted on the twenty-third of February, 1777, and to be payable in 1781; that these certificates were countersigned "by order of J. A. Treutlen, governor of Georgia," by E. Davis, jr.; that said Davis was duly authorized and appointed to countersign the certificates on behalf of the State of Georgia, by the governor of the State; that the United States had in repeated instances recognized their liability to pay, and had actually paid other certificates of the same issue, and had paid four years' interest upon those in the possession of Mr. Ward; that no objection was made that the paper was invalid until many years after the endorsement of interests upon the certificates, and then not from any want of genuineness, but upon the technical ground that the countersigning (by E. Davis, jr.,) was irregular; that there was evidence amounting to demonstration that the United States received a valuable consideration for the certificates, and that they came regularly into the possession of the Ohio company and that of the petitioner.

The counsel for the United States argued that there was no proof that the claimant was the treasurer of the Ohio company; that the company was not an incorporation, and the joint effects of the individuals composing it, if any, would pass to the survivor and his executors; that the certificates in question were not legally issued, E. Davis, jr., not being properly authorized as a commissioner to countersign them; that Alexander Hamilton, Secretary of the Treasury, refused in 1790 and 1791, to fund the certificates; that the payment of interest on the certificates was no proof of their validity; and that there was no positive proof that the United States had received any consideration for the certificates.

The judgment of the court was for the claimant. It was stated as the opinion of the court that the United

States was indebted in the amount due on the forty-three certificates with interest upon them and a bill was reported (based upon an estimation of each certificate at two hundred and eighty-two dollars and forty-four cents) for the relief of Nahum Ward in the sum of sixty thousand eight hundred and seventy-six dollars and ninety-nine cents. The judgment upon being reported back to Congress was, however, reversed, and an appeal was then taken to the Supreme court.

Mr. Ward was thoroughly convinced of the perfect equity of his claim. The preparation for presenting it had cost him years of his life and large sums of money. The ablest counsel working with the incentive of large contingent fees had made exhaustive efforts to win the suit. The amount for which judgment was secured in the Court of Claims did not represent the full measure of the claimant's expectation, but was within the limit prescribed by Congress, governing the amount to be sued for. The claim, with compound interest constantly increasing, amounted before litigation was finally suspended, to several millions of dollars. Mr. Ward constantly pursued his object until his death in 1861, and he was so thoroughly satisfied of the justness of the claim and so determined that the labors of years should not be lost that in his will he enjoined his heirs to carry on the suit. In accordance with his desire in 1870, William S. Ward appeared as the plaintiff in the case before the Supreme court of the United States, his counsel being ex-Attorney General Stanbery, Thomas Ewing, jr., and Judge Charles R. Rhodes. A judgment was affirmed adverse to the claimants, from which, however, Justice Field dissented, saying that he was of opinion that the demand of the plaintiff was a just obligation of the United States, as binding as any part of the public debt of the country.

And so was closed probably forever, the long continued litigation of Ward vs. the United States, growing out of the old Georgia Revolutionary certificates, which had formed a portion of the moneys of the Ohio company.

CHAPTER XII.

THE ERA OF PEACE.

PEACE came to the pioneer settlements after the war as the springtime comes to nature after long weary winter. Peace was the sunshine under which the land blossomed with prosperity.

The close of the war brought joy almost unspeakable to the long imprisoned and sorely harassed settlers in the Ohio company's purchase, and to all the people of the far-reaching frontier—not alone to those in the territory northwest of the beautiful river, but to all along the border of Pennsylvania, of Virginia, and of Kentucky. One old time writer says: "Never since the golden age of the poets did the 'siren song of peace and farming' reach so many ears and gladden so many hearts as after Wayne's treaty in 1795."

The Marietta, Belpre, and Waterford settlers relieved from the restraint of garrison life—and relieved from the necessity of it—went fearlessly forth to pursue those avocations from which they had been in a great measure debarred ever since their arrival in the country. Each man took possession of his own land,* and if a cabin had not before been erected upon it, proceeded to build one. The work of clearing land and sowing seed was carried on as it had never been before. The virgin soil which had been for ages shaded by the heavy forest was bared to the sunlight, and plenteous yields of grain and corn appeared to attest its richness. Men labored cheerily

---

* A few individuals had seen fit to venture beyond the protecting walls of the garrison before the Indian war was at an end. The family of Levi Chapman, it is said, was the first that left any of the stockades to settle on a farm in Washington county. Chapman, with a family of eight boys and four girls, arrived in Marietta in 1794, and in the same year located on Duck creek, where the village of Whipple now stands, a detachment of soldiers going out with him as a guard, and assisting him to erect a block-house. Harvey Chapman, the youngest son of Levi is still living (at Kenton, Hardin county, Ohio), at the age of ninety-three years, and is the only one of the family left. He was about seven years of age when the family came to Marietta. Some of the descendants of Levi Chapman are now living upon Duck creek, some in Marietta, and others in Zanesville.

and with a will now that they were assured of the safety of their homes and families. Every endeavor possible was made to secure the advantages which had so long been denied these distressed and well-nigh helpless people. There seemed a general desire to make present industry atone for the enforced idleness of the past. As fast as was possible in the sparsely peopled district, roads were opened and bridges built, though for many years the rivers and the lesser streams were the highways and byways of communication and commerce. Mills were erected to accommodate the increased needs of the people, and new commodities—articles usually thought necessities, but which were luxuries to the pioneers who had long been without them—were brought into the country. Not many articles, however, were brought, for there was but little money in the settlements. So far as was possible the pioneer men and women confined themselves to the use of those materials for clothing and those food staples which they could produce by their own labor. The skins of animals were very commonly made into clothing. There were many men in the country who had complete outfits of deerskin, and a few families in which little else was used.

For several years buckskin was retained in use by those following agricultural occupations, and was almost universally employed for trousers for men and boys. The men wore what were commonly called hunting shirts—garments resembling coats, made to fit the form quite loosely, and worn belted or tied about the waist with a sash or deerskin thongs. These hunting shirts were ordinarily made of "linsey woolsey," woven by the women of the wearer's household. Hemp and flax were raised in abundance, and there were few women who were not adepts in weaving it into cloth. Spinning and weaving were with them almost constant occupations. In nearly every cabin there was a wheel and a loom. The patient toil of deft fingers kept the family clothed and saved the outlay of money from the scanty store, for finer, but not more serviceable cloth. Only a small proportion of the residents in the Ohio company's territory wore any other than homespun clothes, though there were, of course, some who maintained the old custom of dressing in finer fabrics, and in a style of stately elegance. Cotton was grown in small quantities for a few years, and upon the rich bottom lands a very fair yield was obtained, but it was soon demonstrated that the climate was not sufficiently warm for the profitable growing of this crop and its culture was given up. There were many, however, who wore cloth made from cotton grown by themselves along the Ohio and Muskingum. Captain Jonathan Devol constructed an ingenious machine by which the seed was separated from the fibre. Cotton was not the only product of the semi-tropical regions which the pioneers raised within the present limits of Washington county. Rice of a very good quality was grown at an early day. Neither of the southern staples, however, was found to be so practically successful as to warrant the continuance of their culture after money became so plentiful that they could be purchased when needed.

There was one article which, perhaps, more than any other, the early settlers felt the need of, and which was very scarce and very dear. It was salt. The price in cash for one bushel of coarse salt was eight dollars. Those who had money could illy afford to pay such a price, and there were many who could not if they would. Some persons experienced considerable inconvenience from being deprived of a sufficiency of this important food condiment. So great was the need that a company was formed for the operation of the salt springs in the upper Muskingum county. It was known to the settlers that the Indians had made salt somewhere in the vicinity of Salt creek (a small stream that flows into the Muskingum at Taylorsville, Muskingum county, which locality was known before the slack water improvements were made at Duncan's Falls). An attempt made to discover these springs, however, during the Indian war, was unsuccessful. In 1796, an exploring party sent out for the purpose, found the valued saline springs. When they returned with the good news a company was immediately organized by the inhabitants for prosecuting the manufacture of salt. Some idea of the dearth of money at this time may be suggested by the statement of the fact that the number of shares was set at fifty and the shares were worth one dollar and fifty cents each. A capital of seventy-five dollars, however, was sufficient for the accomplishment of the company's purposes. A party of men were sent to the locality of the springs. They sunk a well fifteen feet deep and three feet in diameter, near the edge of the creek. A section of a hollow sycamore tree was put down to exclude the fresh water and a common sweep and fall was rigged for drawing the precious salt water to the surface.

In the meantime men had been sent to Pittsburgh, and with a portion of the company's modest capital had bought twenty-four iron kettles. These were boated down the Ohio to the Muskingum, and up the latter stream to Duncan's Falls, from whence they were "packed" on horses seven miles to the well. A furnace was built in which the kettles were set, and a shelter being provided the work of making salt was begun. The fires were kept up night and day, the fifty associates of the company being divided into ten squads of five men each, who worked for two weeks at a time, and divided the watches to suit themselves. An enormous quantity of wood was burned, a yoke of oxen being kept constantly employed in hauling and a man in cutting it. At the best only about one hundred pounds of salt could be made each day and night, and it was of a poor quality, being dark colored and strongly tinctured with a bitter substance—probably muriate of lime. It was probably worth when manufactured about three dollars per bushel, but even had it cost as much as the salt brought over the mountains the manufacture would have been advantageous as the outlay was principally that of labor instead of money. The work of salt boiling was carried on for several years, the men often enduring great hardship, and on one occasion, at least, during the first winter, in intensely cold weather, narrowly escaping death, from being lost in the woods while attempting to make their way to Marietta for the purpose of securing provisions.

During the year 1796 great numbers of emigrants, many of whom had been anxiously awaiting the close of the Indian war, came down the Ohio. It is estimated that upwards of a thousand Kentucky boats or "broadhorns" floated down the river. Each boat had on board from one to two families or men. Kentucky, which before the settlement of Marietta had a population of more than thirty thousand, received large accessions from this emigration, and the group of settlements in the Symmes purchase were considerably increased in strength. A few of these pioneers, mostly from Virginia, were destined for Chillicothe, which was founded this year by Nathaniel Massie, and others located at Manchester on the Ohio (in the present limits of Adams county), which, under the name of Massie's station, had been established in the spring of 1791. Nearly all of the Virginia emigrants located in the military district reserved by the Old Dominion between the Scioto and Little Miami. The Symmes Purchase settlers were almost to a man from New Jersey. The settlement of the Ohio company's purchase depended now, as originally, almost entirely upon New England. The impression that the lands owned by this company were very sterile, had gained wide credence, and many who would doubtless have settled within the limits of the tract had they depended upon personal examination for their knowledge, being prejudiced, passed by. The increase in population was very slow, but most of the newcomers, like the original settlers, were men of far better character than the majority of those in other pioneer communities. If the progress of settlement and improvement in the Ohio company's territory was less in degree than in the richer regions farther west, it was better in kind. The undesirable elements of frontier society were in a very small minority. The majority of the emigrants were men of small fortune, liberal education, good morals, and indomitable energy. They were men who were satisfied to make the slow but sure advancement in condition which a capital of industry insures.

All of the emigrants who owned or desired to own lands in the Ohio company's purchase stopped at Marietta prior to making permanent locations. In the spring of 1797 a number of men, among whom were Alvan Bingham, Silas Bingham, Isaac Barker, William Harper, John Wilkins, Robert Linzee, Edmund, William and Barak Dorr, John Chandler and Jonathan Watkins,[*] urged by General Putnam, settled in the college townships, now known as Ames and Alexander, in Athens county. They loaded their effects in canoes, floated down the Ohio to the Hockhocking, and rowed up that stream to the place of their destination. Upon the bottoms along the river and upon the site of Athens was thus begun the settlement of the interior of the purchase.

One of the prominent pioneer interior settlements within the county of Washington was in Barlow township. It was the most remote from the settlements on the Ohio and Muskingum, being about the same distance from each. The nearest settlement upon the westward was on Federal creek, sixteen miles distant. The settlement

[*] Charles M. Walker's History of Athens County.

13

was made by James Lawton and Nathan Proctor with their families in 1800, and the spot was probably chosen chiefly for the reason that it was near the intersection of the trails or traces which led from Belpre to Waterford and from Marietta to Athens.

Other settlements were formed about the same time in various localities remote from the Ohio and Muskingum but the majority of the early residents were located along the principal streams, and in the vicinity of the old and, by this time, well established communities of Marietta, Belpre and Waterford, and there were several of the back townships which were without any inhabitants at the beginning of the present century; and were very thinly settled a score of years later. The lands adjoining the streams were the first to be improved, for two reasons. First, they were richer and offered a better return for the husbandman's labor in clearing and tilling; and secondly, their location upon the streams made them more readily accessible. The streams were the thoroughfares on which nearly all traffic and communication was carried on. The best road within the boundaries of Washington county was probably that from Marietta to Zanesville, opened in 1798, but even this was, during the greater part of the year, practically impassable for laden wagons. The interior of the county was a wilderness penetrable only with great difficulty, and the few settlers who had taken up lands remote from the streams were almost completely isolated from fellowship with men. In the eastern end of the county the same order of things prevailed as in the western. The lands first bought from the Government and earliest settled were along the Ohio. The only practical difference between the development of the territory included in the seven ranges and that in the Ohio company's purchase was that in the former the population was made up almost entirely of Virginians and Pennsylvanians, and that the settlement was later than in the Ohio company's lands. Through all of these lands the slow, laborious task of clearing away the forest and rearing homes went on continuously, and lives were wrought out in patient, honorable heroism, which has been in a measure lost sight of in the glare of more startling, but not more valuable achievement.

While that portion of Washington county west of the Muskingum and along its eastern shore was the especial field of the New England settlers, they also pushed their way into some of the lands farther eastward which were not included in the Ohio company's purchase. The country around Marietta was of course settled by them and at an early day. Later, but still in the closing years of the past century, many of the immigrants from Massachusetts and her neighboring States made themselves homes within the present boundaries of Newport township, also in Fearing and in the southwestern corner of Lawrence. At a later period the country north of Fearing was thinly settled by the same class.

By the year 1800 the aspect of the country was very materially changed. Many of the log cabins on the farms had by this time been replaced by more commodious and comfortable frame houses, and the little barns hastily erected for the shelter of a single yoke of oxen, perhaps, or the storage of a small crop had given way to larger ones which still were not two ample for the harvests of corn and grain from the broad, newly cleared acres. More thorough methods of tilling the soil were adopted, as the practice became possible and improved implements could be either manufactured or procured from the east. But even the best of these were very primitive and ill adapted to the purposes designed and had to be made up by the increase of energy in their use.

Notwithstanding the advancement that had been made, very large portions of the country at present embraced in the limits of Washington county were in almost as wild a state as they were prior to the original settlement. There were large tracts of unbroken forest in which the game was still so plentiful that the Indians regarded them as good hunting grounds. They came into the country in large bands annually until the last grand hunt in the winter of 1810–11, and until that time bear continued in considerable abundance. Deer were also very plenty until this hunt was held. It was evidently the purpose of the Indians to destroy or drive the game from the country, as they had done in 1788 and 1789. After the hunt the carcasses of many deer were found in the woods bordering the settlements in Washington and Athens counties, which appeared to have been wantonly killed by the savages.* The buffalo and the elk were not exterminated until 1800.

The smaller kinds of animals were to be found in vast numbers. The woods were alive with wolves, foxes, opossums, rabbits, raccoons, ground hogs, squirrels and birds, and they proved a serious pest to the farmers. The wolves and squirrels were especially troublesome, the former prowling in the vicinity of the sheep pens and often committing depredations, and the latter overrunning the cornfields and completely ruining the crops, unless a constant watch was kept over the fields. Immense flocks of pigeons darkened the air in the fall by their flight, and broke down the branches of the forest trees where they alighted in countless number. A good idea of the vastness of these flocks is given by an observant and perfectly credible tourist of 1803:

The vast flight of pigeons in this country seem incredible. But there is a large forest in Waterford, containing several hundred acres, which has been killed in consequence of their lighting upon it during the autumn of 1801. Such numbers lodged upon the trees that they broke off large limbs, and the ground below is covered, and in some places a foot thick, with their dung, which has not only killed all the undergrowth, but all the trees are as dead as if they had been girdled.†

A letter received in 1803 by the writer of the above, from a friend in Marietta, says:

I have visited two pigeon roosts and have heard of a third. Those I have seen are astonishing. One is supposed to cover a thousand acres, the other is still larger. The destruction of timber and brush on such large tracts of land by these small animals is almost incredible. How many millions of them must have assembled to effect it, especially as it was done in the course of a few weeks ‡

Orchards of thrifty trees gave a home-like appearance

*Reminiscences of Judge Ephraim Cutler in Charles M. Walker's History of Athens County.

† "Journal of a Tour into the Territory Northwest of the Alleghany Mountains," by Thaddeus Mason Harris.

‡ Letter from the Rev. Daniel Story to Thaddeus Mason Harris, dated Marietta, June 3, 1803.

to many of the farms, and early in the present century were so well advanced as to be of very great value. The earliest introduction of fruit was in the year 1794. Israel Putnam, the son of Colonel Israel and grandson of General Israel, the wolf-slayer, when he arrived at Belpre on the second of May, in the year mentioned, unloaded among his other effects a few apple scions, which were set in his brother's garden. In 1796 he sent from the east a larger lot of scions, which were distributed among the settlers by William Rufus Putnam, to whom they were consigned. They were carried across the mountains in saddle-bags, and being well packed in beeswax, arrived in good condition, and nearly all of them were successfully engrafted. The list, by which it appears there were twenty-three varieties, has been preserved, and we here give it a place. It included Putnam sweets, Seek-no-farthers, Early Chandlers, Late Chandlers, Gillyflowers, Pound Royals, Naturalings, Rhode Island Greenings, Yellow Greenings, Golden Pippins, Long Island Pippins, Tollman Sweetings, Streaked Sweetings, Honey Greenings, Kent Pippins, the Cooper apple, Streaked Gillyflowers, Black Gillyflowers, Beauties, Queenings, Englins Pearmain, Green Pippins, and Spitzenbergs. Thus early were the best varieties of apples known in New England introduced in the pioneer western settlement.

Over twenty years later, in 1818, the same Israel Putnam who had made this beginning in fruit culture, established a nursery at his home upon the Muskingum, in old Union township, from which came nearly all of the apple trees in Washington county until comparatively recent years. The scions from this nursery were also brought out from New England, and included almost exactly the same variety as that given in the foregoing list, showing that the selections made in 1796 were satisfactory ones. Among the several new varieties were the Calvert Sweetings, Newton Pippins, and one which was given the name of the Muskingum apple.

Fine cattle were brought into the country by Colonel Israel Putnam, father of the Israel Putnam to whom the people were indebted for the introduction of fruit. He brought oxen of a superior breed to Marietta. in 1788; and, in 1795, procured cows from which he raised some of the best stock in the settlements. It was largely through the good beginning made by him, and his practical, intelligent devotion to agriculture and stock raising, that Belpre became a famous farming locality at an early day, and especially noted for its dairy products. Large quantities of superior cheese were made and shipped down the river, and Belpre was as much noted for the quantity and quality of the cheese manufactured by her farmers as are now some of the grazing counties in the Western Reserve.

Sheep raising was also begun at an early day, and the Hon. Paul Fearing was one of the first who paid any attention to this department of husbandry. The earliest mention of Merino sheep, however, occurs in the journal of the younger Israel Putnam, under date of September, 1809. It describes his journey to Wakatomica, and his return with two full bred Merino rams and fifteen half bred rams, which he put with his ewes at his farm upon the Muskingum. It appears from the record that he continued improving his flock until the year 1812. Paul Fearing was similarly engaged at about the same period, and paid very close attention to the care of his flocks, raising several hundred choice sheep from a few which he purchased at enormous expense. Benjamin Ives Gilman, it appears, was associated with him for some time. Merinos had then only recently been imported by the leading farmers in the eastern States, and these men, in what was at that time the far west, showed a very remarkable progressiveness and enterprise in thus early availing themselves of the costly means of improvement. It appears from an old letter (February 14, 1811,) that Messrs. Fearing and Gilman bought of Colonel Humphrey, the noted importer, one full-blooded Merino ram, for which they gave sixteen hundred acres of land. Sheep raising was during the early years of the settlement, and as late as 1825, attended with some difficulties which the farmers of the present day do not experience. The chief danger to the flocks was from wolves, which were still numerous. Israel Putnam lost ninety-seven sheep in eight months, from wolves or dogs—chiefly the former. Benjamin Dana, who owned a large farm twenty miles up the Muskingum, and kept about a thousand head of Saxons, in order to preserve them from the wolves drove them into small yards every night. These yards or pens were surrounded with high fences, sloping inward. Wolves could readily get in but could not get out, and never harmed the sheep, it is said, after finding they were entrapped. They were frequently found among the sheep in the morning and killed.

It had been confidently expected that after the close of the Indian war the Ohio company's settlements would quickly receive large accessions of population, and yet such was not the case. The student of history who seeks the cause will find it in the opening of the Connecticut Western Reserve. The Ohio company's leading spirits, and the friends of the organization had not feared the result of Virginia's action in reserving in 1784 a large tract of land for her Revolutionary soldiers. It could have little effect upon the weal or woe of the Muskingum settlements. The Ohio company did not look to Virginia for settlers. A considerable amount of emigration was diverted from the pioneer colony of the northwest by the well advertised attractions of the Symmes' purchase, but had no other divergence in the stream occurred the company's lands would have been quite thickly settled, in all probability, by the close of the first decade of the present century. Connecticut, it will be remembered, did not make her deed of cession until 1786. Definite action tending toward the colonization of her immense reservation (three million three hundred and sixty-six thousand nine hundred and twenty-one acres by actual survey) was not taken until 1795. In that year the State sold her lands for one million two hundred thousand dollars to the Connecticut Land company composed of forty-eight shareholders. The survey of the Western Reserve quickly followed, and the draft, or division, followed that. Thus there was thrown upon the market a large body of fine

lands, to which the people of Connecticut who entertained ideas of emigrating westward naturally looked for their future homes. The prospective opening of the Reserve had deterred many from locating elsewhere, and the mother State had done all in her power to direct the minds of her people to the New Connecticut. Now that it was open and ready for settlement, a current of emigration immediately set toward it, flowing feebly and slowly at first, but with strength and volume constantly increasing until the waves of population had covered all northeastern Ohio. The pioneers of the Reserve were nearly all from Connecticut, a State in which the Ohio company's influence had been extensively exerted, and which was commonly supposed would prove as rich a source of emigration to the company's territory as Massachusets. As the Connecticut Reserve was less remote from the mother State by which its interests were sedulously fostered, it was not strange that it received nearly all of the emigrants who went westward from Connecticut and many from the contiguous commonwealths, and that the developement of the Ohio company's purchase was retarded proportionately.

Another cause of the slow increase in the population of the Ohio company's purchase and of Washington county was the almost universal belief that the hill lands were entirely valueless. The fact that the bottom lands were the first settled has been heretofore alluded to. A map of the county in 1810, indicating habitations and improvements would show very few settlers except along the streams. The country immediately surrounding some of the oldest settlements would appear unbroken by civilization. For many years those who sought lands on finding that the rich alluvions had been taken up, journeyed on to find what they desired farther westward in Ohio or in Indiana or Illinois. It was only when these more desirable lands farther westward had increased considerably in price that the hill land came into general demand. Another era of settlement and development then began in Washington county. The emigrants of this period—say from 1820 to 1835 or 1840—coming in from the middle as well as the New England States, and even from foreign shores, changed and improved in a marked degree the condition of the country. In 1805 Watertown was probably the only township in Washington county of which the whole territory had been dotted with improvements and which exhibited anything like evenness in the distribution of its inhabitants. It was the first township generally improved although its settlement did not begin until after that of several other localities, and did not progress so fast. The cause of its evenness of development probably lay in the fact that its surface was, as compared with other portions of the county, not roughly broken or hilly. What we may call the second period of settlement resulted in giving other townships something of the advantages already possessed by Watertown. The new settlers taking up lands which the original pioneers had refused had a hard task before them, and saw smaller prospective rewards for their labor; but they were generally men of smaller expectations and humbler hopes than their predecessors, and they were more easily satisfied. Most of them were men of small means, but sturdy ability to labor, and possessed those well grounded habits of industry and economy which are always productive of thrift, whatever may be the nature of the surrounding circumstances. To their energy and frugality the people of the county are indebted for a vast increase in the value of its lands. From the comparative sterile hills, which the New Englanders as a rule despised and avoided, they have wrung, by patient toil, a livelihood, and in very recent years their gains have been largely increased by scientific, sensible application of those fertilizing elements which the hill soil has lacked.

The elements making up the population of the second period of emigration are varied and several of them possess features of especial interest, which are much more fully treated elsewhere in this volume, than in the present chapter.* Beside the population derived from the eastern and middle States the county has a considerable number of Scotch, Quakers and Germans. Each of these elements has a strong showing in the neighborhood, and one of them—the German—is to be found in all parts of the county.

The pioneers of the Scotch nationality located in Barlow township. The first family of this people in the county was probably that of John Harvey who arrived in 1817, and the second, William Andrews. John Flemming came in about 1820, and the settlement was farther increased by the addition of the Breckenridge family. These pioneers from Scotland were followed by other settlers, and in a few years so many had arrived that their population spread into the adjourning townships of Dunham and Warren, and even in Belpre. The immigration began as has been stated in 1817, was encouraged in 1828, and for a considerable period later, by Nahum Ward, esq., of Marietta, a large landholder, who went to Scotland, and there published "A Brief Sketch of the State of Ohio, one of the United States of North America, with a map delineating the same into counties." Both through Mr. Ward's endeavors and independent of them, the Scotch immigration increased until the neighborhood, of which the Barlow settlement was the beginning, became thickly populated with the people of the canny race, who prospering themselves, enriched the country in which they had made their homes.

The Quaker element in Washington county is principally confined to the western part, though a few reside in the east end. Wesley was the township first settled by these people, and they came in from the north in 1840. A movement had been made toward the Ohio, from Jefferson and Belmont counties, and many Quakers had located in Morgan county, where the names of Penn and Pennsville have been left as indications of the nature of the population which filled that portion of the county. From the township of Penn a slow but steady stream of immigration flowed into the extreme western tier of townships in Washington county. Wesley in which the

first settlement was made, has now the largest number of this class, but Decatur, Fairfield and Palmer have a considerable element. The whole western end of the county has been materially benefited by the Quaker settlers. Wherever they have gone, land has increased in value, and the moral well being of the people has been enhanced.

By far the largest foreign element in the county is the German. The settlement by people of this nationality may be said to have commenced early in the thirties—1832-'33-'34—being the years when the pioneer families arrived. Fearing township was the locality in which the earliest settlers made their homes, and they soon spread into Marietta township, Adams, Salem, Liberty, Lawrence, and Newport, and now there is no township in the county which has not at least a liberal sprinkling of German population. The largest immigration was from 1840 to 1850 and was nearly equalled in the decade following. One feature in the German settlement was the establishment of the village of Bonn, in Salem township, by Nahum Ward, esq., who induced many Germans to come to this country, and endeavored to build up for them and by them a little manufacturing centre. Spinning and silk manufacturing were the principal industries entered upon. They did not, however, meet with remarkable success, and the village of Bonn, of which very sanguine hopes were one time entertained, amounted to little more than a convenient trading place for the German settlers in Salem and the north part of Fearing. While the Germans generally in Washington county and especially those of them who were early settlers, were of Protestant faith, a Catholic element of considerable strength has slowly gathered in Muskingum, Watertown, Adams, and Warren. The latter township has a large German population, amounting probably to a third of the entire number of inhabitants and in the country back from the river fifty per cent. while a large portion of the original German settlers west of the Muskingum and east of it but in its immediate vicinity were of foreign birth. The majority of those in the eastern end are native born.

There is a considerable element of Irish population in the territory included in the old township of Union (now divided between Muskingum, Watertown, and Adams). Probably fifty per cent. of the inhabitants of this part of the county are Irish born, or of Irish descent. The work on the Muskingum improvements brought many laborers into the county, a large proportion of whom were Irish. When the Government work was completed, many of these men found themselves in possession of sufficient amounts of money to make the first payments upon, or buy outright, small farms. They naturally located in as compact a body as possible, and took up all the purchasable farming lands in the territory described.

There remains one other class of population to be spoken of. In addition to their scattered population, the colored people have in Washington county several distinct settlements. The first colored man who owned land in the county was undoubtedly Richard Fisher, a mulatto, who prior to 1800 dwelt in Salem township, on the west fork of Duck creek. It does not appear that more

---

* In the several township histories many facts in regard to nationality and characteristics of population are given as well as statements in regard to dates of settlement and names of pioneers. Hence the whole subject is in this chapter merely treated in a general way.

HERMAN BLENNERHASSETT.

than a score of individuals of the colored race lived in the county at any one time until about 1835, when a little community came into being in Barlow township, which increased both numerically and in property until its people were able to have their own church and school, and live in almost every sense independent of outsiders. Many of these colored people have accumulated modest properties, and some own large farms and live surrounded by every comfort possessed by their white neighbors. There is another and much smaller colony of colored people in Warren township, and a third in the south part of Adams. This is made up of families from Virginia, who, during and after the war of the Rebellion, became residents of Belmont county, and in 1875 made themselves homes at their present location. Their advancement in condition has been equal in result to that of the Barlow colored settlers, and attained much more quickly. They have a church of their own, and are in a generally prosperous state.

Another movement remains to be mentioned. While Washington county was receiving a slow but steady flow of emigration, a stream had set forth to the ever receding great west. From the land first settled by the sterling men of Massachusetts and her sister States of the Atlantic seaboard, the sons of those pioneers were going out as pioneers to the regions beyond the Mississippi. This was not an emigration effected through any colonization scheme, but by individual choice and independent action. It was, therefore, slow and its result not conspicuous. It was a powerful agency, however, in modifying the relative proportions of the two great elements in the population. Nearly all of the newcomers—the settlers who belong to what we have called the second period of emigration—were of foreign birth, and almost to a man those who removed were native born Americans. This being the fact, it follows as a matter of course that the western part of the county suffered most by the emigration. Upon the other hand the eastern end gained quite largely through an emigration from Belmont and Monroe counties. These causes combined soon became of sufficient force to be of some importance as affecting the relative political strength of the east and west sides of the county.

In the west, too, there has been some effect, however small, resultant from Washington county emigration. Marietta has borne no slight share in the great duty of social transmission, and so when the centennial anniversary of the settlement of Ohio shall have come her citizens can claim some degree of proprietorship in the advancement which has been made in Kansas and Iowa, and Minnesota, and all the younger States in the newer west.

An eloquent and renowned orator on the occassion of the two hundredth anniversary of the settlement of a Massachusetts town, which has a namesake in Washington county, used these words: "While our thoughts today are carried back to the tombs of our fathers beyond the sea, there are millions of kindred Americans beyond the rivers and mountains whose hearts are fixed on the Atlantic coast, as the cradle of their political existence.

.   .   .   A mighty wilderness has been colonized almost within our day."[*]

And now a mightier wilderness has been added to the realm of civilization, and while our thoughts, as the first century of western life draws to a close, are carried back to the tombs of our fathers—not in old England, but in New England—there are others beyond farther rivers and more distant mountains, whose hearts are fixed upon the shores of the Ohio, the Muskingum, and Lake Erie, as the land of their nativity or of ancestral recollection.

CHAPTER XIII.

POLITICAL MEASURES AND EVENTS FROM 1788 TO 1803.

Washington County as the Northwest Territory—The First Grade of Territorial Government—Peculiarities of the Early Laws—Formed upon British Statutes—Severity of Punishments—The Whipping Post, Pillory and Stocks—Second Grade of Territorial Government Organized—A Petition for the Allowance of Slavery—Carrying out the Policy of the Marietta Colony—"Support, Religion and Learning"—Corporation Organized for Leasing the Ministerial and School Lands—Form of Lease—Party Feeling Increasing—Dissatisfaction with Governor St. Clair—A State Government Suggested—Opposition on the Part of Putnam and Cutler—The Feeling in Washington County—Reasons Advanced against the Organization of a State—Bitterness of Feeling—Congress Passes an "Enabling Act"—Constitutional Convention Called—The Question of Slavery—Determination to Introduce it in a Modified Form—Judge Ephraim Cutler's Stand Against it—The Poetry of History—The State of Ohio Recognized by Congress, and Government Organized—Some Later Measures Exhibiting the Influence of Washington County.

WE have intentionally omitted from the preceding chapters a detailed statement of the organization and enactments of the Territorial Government that the subject might be presented in connection with those subsequent measures the first constitutional convention and the establishment of the State government. In each of these measures Washington county had an important agency. In 1788 Marietta was practically coextensive with the Northwest Territory. In 1789 the Marietta and Cincinnati groups of settlements were the only English colonies in the territory. Marietta was at first the more influential, but her political prestige waned as the settlement of the territory, and then of the State, increased, and as Federalism was supplanted as a national power by the Jeffersonian Democracy.

The first act of Congress for the purpose of carrying into action the Ordinance of 1787 was the election of Governor St. Clair, which has been heretofore alluded to. He was chosen upon the fifth of October, 1787. Winthrop Sargent was elected secretary the same day, and upon the sixteenth of the same month Samuel Holden Parsons, James Mitchell Varnum, and John Armstrong judges of the territory. John Armstrong subsequently declined the appointment and Congress elected John Cleves Symmes to fill the vacancy. †

---

[*] Edward Everett, at Salem, Massachusetts, September 18, 1828.

†For the successors of these officers, and also for those who acted in other capacities, see the following chapter containing a complete roster.

Upon the ninth of July, 1788, Governor St. Clair arrived at Marietta (where Judges Varnum and Parsons, and Secretary Winthrop Sargent had preceded him) and upon the eighteenth the government of the Northwest Territory was formally organized, in the presence of all the citizens of Marietta—and in fact all of the English-speaking people of the territory. The Ordinance of 1787 was read, the commissions of the governor, the judges present, and of the secretary. Governor St. Clair made a dignified and elegant address, and was responded to by General Rufus Putnam.

The government thus established was the first territorial government ever organized by Federal authority. It was in many respects peculiar, but as a whole exceedingly admirable, and it is doubtful if the ingenuity of man could have formulated a wiser and more beneficial system of authority, the time and conditions being considered. The fundamental law was the Ordinance of 1787, on which were based the constitutions of the five great States carved from the territory. Of the formation of this compact—which affirmed the principles of political and religious liberty, and which forever perpetuated them in the northwest—much has been said in an earlier chapter of this work. The ordinance vested the executive power in the governor, the judicial in a general court, and the legislative power in the governor and the judges, acting as a legislative council. Provision was also made for the election of a secretary, who, in case of the governor's resignation or removal, should be clothed with all of the powers of the governor.

The peculiarity of the government was that the people had no voice in it. This peculiarity was in a measure necessary, and of course for a purpose which can be easily understood, but if it was for the most part advantageous, it was also liable to abuse. In the exercise of authority the officers were responsible only to the General Government—they received their appointments from Congress until after the adoption of the constitution in 1789, and then from the President—and where there was a disposition for arbitrary action there was every opportunity for it. Such a disposition did exist, and toward the close of the period of territorial government caused much bitterness and produced some effects which curiously enough are still existent in the State government.

The first law enacted was formed July 26, 1788, published in Philadelphia in 1792, and was entitled

"A LAW

for regulating and establishing the militia of the United States northwest of the river Ohio, published at the city of Marietta upon the twenty-fifth day of July, in the thirteenth year of the independence of the United States and of our Lord one thousand seven hundred and eighty-eight, by his excellency, Arthur St. Clair, esquire, governor and commander-in-chief, and the honorable and James Mitchell Varnum, esquire, judges."

The ordinance of 1787 authorized the governor and judges to adopt and publish in the territory from time to time such laws of the old States, civil and criminal, as they saw fit, and report them to Congress. This provision, however, was not strictly obeyed. The officers made new laws almost as frequently as they adopted old ones, being often compelled to this course by the needs of the time. During the first year of settlement the governor, Judge Varnum and Judge Parsons assembled at Marietta in their legislative capacity, enacted a number of laws which were submitted to Congress, but were not approved on the ground that the governor and judges were empowered only to adopt existing laws, from the codes of the original States,* but notwithstanding the fact that these laws failed to secure the ratification of Congress they continued in force for various lengths of time—some of them until the second grade of territorial government was established—though most of them were superseded in 1795 by a code adopted in compliance with the terms of the ordinance at a legislative session held at Cincinnati. These laws were known as the Maxwell code, from the name of the printer, William Maxwell. The pamphlet containing them was the first piece of job printing done in the Northwest Territory. The only other legislative session under the first code of territorial government was held in 1798, and then only a few additional laws were adopted.†

There was much that was peculiar in the old territorial laws. They were formed largely upon English statutes, and the punishments inflicted under them were often very severe. The pillory and stocks were made accessories of the court house. The first law for whipping was passed at Marietta September 6, 1788, under the title of "A law respecting crimes and punishments." Section 1 provided that when three or more persons, constituting a mob, should commit unlawful acts, and fail to disperse when told to do so, each offender, on conviction, "shall be fined in a sum not exceeding three hundred dollars, and be whipped not exceeding thirty-nine stripes, and find security for good behavior for a term not exceeding one year." For a second offence the whipping would be repeated, as well as the fine and security, and the offender committed to jail until the sentence be satisfied. For breaking into a house, store or shop in the night, for the purpose of stealing, the punishment was thirty-nine stripes, security for good behavior, or in default, imprisonment for a term of not more than three years. If in the perpetration of the crime the person should commit any violence, or be so armed as to indicate intention of violence, he should forfeit all estate, real or personal, to the territory, out of which the party injured should be compensated, and the criminal should be committed to jail for a period not exceeding forty years.

For perjury, or refusing to be sworn to a fact, the penalty prescribed was a fine of sixty dollars, or the laying on of not more than thirty-nine lashes, and the criminal moreover was to be set in the pillory for a space of time not exceeding two hours. For arson, or aiding in the commission of the crime, the punishment was whipping to the extent of thirty-nine lashes, two hours in the pillory, three years or less in jail, and the forfeiture of all property to the territory. It was further provided by this law respecting crimes and punishments that a child

* Jacob Burnet's Notes on the Northwestern Territory.
† Charles B. Flood, esq., in Ohio secretary of State's report, 1879.

or servant refusing to obey lawful commands of the parent or master, on complaint to a justice of the peace, could be sent to the jail or the house of correction; or for striking his parent or master be whipped not exceeding ten stripes. A person convicted of drunkenness it was provided should be fined five dimes for the first offence, and one dollar for every subsequent offence. Failure to pay the fine subjected the person convicted to the stocks for the space of one hour. The person who committed larceny was compelled to pay two-fold retribution for the first offence, or if the money or property taken be not recovered, be whipped not exceeding thirty-nine lashes. In case the offender had not property, it was decreed that the sheriff, by direction of the court, should bind such person to labor for a term not exceeding seven years. The law from which the foregoing provisions have been taken concluded with the following clauses, which serve to convey a further idea of the severity of opinion transplanted from Old England and New England to the primal settlement of the western wilderness:

SEC. 21. Whereas, idle, vain, and obscene conversation, profane cursing and swearing, and more especially the irreverently mentioning, calling upon, or invoking the Sacred and Supreme Being by any of the divine characters in which he hath graciously condescended to reveal his infinitely beneficent purposes to mankind, are repugnant to every moral sentiment, subversive of every civil obligation, inconsistent with the ornaments of polished life, and abhorrent to the principles of the most benevolent religion. It is expected, therefore, if crimes of this kind should exist, their will not find encouragement, countenance, or approbation in this territory. It is strictly enjoined upon all officers and ministers of justice, upon parents, and others, heads of families, and upon others of every description, that they abstain from practices so vile and irrational, and that by example and precept, to the utmost of their power, they prevent the necessity of adopting and publishing laws with penalties on this head; and it is hereby declared that government will consider as unworthy of its confidence all those who may obstinately violate these injunctions.

SEC. 22. Whereas, mankind, in every stage of informed society, have consecrated certain portions of time to the particular cultivation of the social virtues, and the public adoration and worship of the common Parent of the universe; and,

Whereas, a practice so rational in itself, and conformable to the divine precepts, is greatly conducive to civilization, as well as morality and piety; and,

Whereas, for the advancement of such important and interesting purpose most of the Christian world have set apart the first day of the week as a day of rest from common labor and pursuits, it is therefore enjoined that all service labor, works of necessity, and charity only excepted, be wholly abstained from on said day.*

The later laws adopted or enacted under the territorial government bore a close resemblance to those of which we have already spoken.

In 1792 provision was made for the establishment of a court house, county jail, pillory, whipping-post and stocks in every county of the territory (there were then but four counties in existence—Washington, Hamilton, St. Clair and Knox). In 1795 a law was adopted from the Pennsylvania statutes, entitled "A law limiting imprisonment for debt, and subjecting certain delinquents and debtors to servitude," providing that no person should be kept in prison for debt or fines longer than the second day of the session next of his commitment, unless the plantiff should make it appear that the person imprisoned had some estate that he would not disclose and

in such case the court should examine all persons suspected to be privy to the concealment of such estate, and if no sufficient estate was found the debtor should make satisfaction by personal and reasonable servitude according to the judgment of the court (but only if the plaintiff requires it), not exceeding seven years. If the plaintiff refused to receive the debtor as his slave for the term named (according to the age of the debtor and whether married or single), the debt was discharged. A law selling men into servitude for fines and costs, for maining and disfiguring a person was adopted from the Kentucky criminal code in 1798, but this law was afterwards held to be unconstitutional, as Kentucky was not in existence as a State when the ordinance of 1787 was passed.

The governor and judges of the territory adopted, among other Virginia laws, one entitled "A law declaring what laws shall be in force," which declared that the common law of England, and all statutes or acts in aid of it, made prior to the reign of King James I, should be in full force in the territory until repealed by legislative authority, or disapproved by Congress. This proceeding was questioned by some authorities at the time, but no change was made until the organization of the State government.

Altogether there were enacted or adopted, during the period of the first grade of territorial government, nearly one hundred laws (beside the one which included the British laws), and, although open to some criticism, it has been said of them by one of Ohio's greatest jurists, "that it may be doubted whether any colony, at so early a period after its first establishment, ever had so good a code of laws."*

The second grade of the territorial government was organized in 1799, in pursuance of a provision of the ordinance of 1787, giving authority for such a step when the territory shall contain "five thousand free male inhabitants of full age." The governor having discovered this qualification to exist, upon October 29, 1798, issued his proclamation directing the voters to hold elections for territorial representatives on the third Monday of December following. The result was the election of: Return Jonathan Meigs, Washington county; Paul Fearing, Washington county; William Goforth, Hamilton county; William McMillan, Hamilton county; John Smith, Hamilton county; John Ludlow, Hamilton county; Robert Benham, Hamilton county; Aaron Caldwell, Hamilton county; Isaac Martin, Hamilton county; Shadrack Bond, St. Clair county; John Small, Knox county; John Edgar, Randolph county; Solomon Sibley, Wayne county; Jacob Visgar, Wayne county; Charles F. Chabert de Joncaire, Wayne county; Joseph Darlinton, Adams county; Nathaniel Massie, Adams county; James Pritchard, Jefferson county; Thomas Worthington, Ross county; Elias Langham, Ross county; Samuel Findlay, Ross county; Edward Tiffin, Ross county.

The legislature assembled at Cincinnati, January 22, 1799, and nominated ten men from whom the National Government, chose the following five to constitute the legislative council of the territory and continue in office five years: Jacob Burnet, of Cincinnati, Hamilton county; Henry Vandenburg, of Vincennes, Knox county; Robert Oliver, of Marietta, Washington county; James Findlay, of Cincinnati, Hamilton county; David Vance, of Vanceville, Jefferson county.

The council and house of representatives met at Cincinnati on the sixteenth of September, 1798, and organized for the discharge of their duties. Of the council, Henry Vandenburg was elected president and William C. Schenck, secretary. Of the house, Edward Tiffin was chosen speaker and John Riley, clerk.

The territory now had a legislature of which one branch was elective, but Governor St. Clair, by his use of the unqualified veto power with which he was invested, practically annulled the will of the peoples' branch of the legislature. Of thirty bills passed, eleven were vetoed.

There was, however, much business of public importance transacted at this, the first session of the territorial legislature. William Henry Harrison was elected to Congress by a majority of one vote over the governor's son, Arthur St. Clair, jr. The earnest attention of the legislators was given to the subject of education and to the preparation of laws supplementary to or supplanting those formerly enacted. The legislature adopted a joint remonstrance addressed to Congress against the power given to the governor to veto all acts which he pleased and against his exclusive exercise of authority in erecting counties.

By far the most interesting and significant subject before the body at this session was that of introducing slavery into the territory. It came up in the form of a petition from a number of the Virginia officers praying for permission to move with their slaves into the Virginia military districts (the lands lying between the Scioto and Little Miami rivers). There were some members of the legislature who were friendly to the prayer of the Virginians, but their favor was of no consequence. The Ordinance of 1787 rose up now in its majesty as the safeguard of liberty and the legislature had really no more discretion in the case than had that of Virginia or Kentucky. There would have been but few votes though in favor of the petition had the matter rested with the legislature. It would doubtless have been opposed both as a matter of right and policy.*

The first session of the legislature was prorogued by the governor December 19, 1799, until the first Monday of November, 1800, at which time the body reassembled at Chillicothe, which place had been made the capital by act of Congress of May 7, 1800.

Congress having passed (on May 7, 1800) an act establishing the Indiana territory (including the present States of Indiana and Illinois) and William Henry Harrison having been appointed governor, it was necessary to elect a delegate to Congress to fill his place as well as to elect one for the succeeding term. William McMillen, of Cincinnati, was chosen to serve out the unexpired

term, and Paul Fearing, esq., of Marietta, to serve from 1801 to 1803. The second session of the territorial legislature was brief, closing December 9, 1800.

There was one act passed at this session of 1800 which was of especial importance to Washington county, and is interesting as an exhibition of the continuance of the wise and beneficent policy of the Ohio company, and of those measures which through the labor and influence of Dr. Manasseh Cutler had been inserted in the Ordinance of 1787. We allude to an "Act authorizing the leasing of the lands granted for the support of schools and religious purposes in the county of Washington,"—bearing date of November 27, 1800.*

This law created and established a corporation by the name of "The trustees for managing lands granted for religious purposes, and for the support of schools, in the county of Washington, within the Ohio company's purchase," which corporation consisted of seven persons, "capable of suing and being sued," etc., viz: Griffin Greene, Robert Oliver, Benjamin Ives Gilman, Isaac Pierce, Jonathan Stone, Ephraim Cutler, and William Rufus Putnam. It was provided that this corporation should meet annually on the first Monday of April, at which meeting the trustees should elect officers, and until the first meeting should be held the legislature appointed that Griffin Greene should serve as chairman, Benjamin Ives Gilman as clerk, and William Rufus Putnam as treasurer. The law was a very long one, explicit and exhaustive in its specifications. The trustees were originally empowered with the leasing of section twenty-nine, in the second township of the eighth range (that on which Marietta is built), but a few years later this business was relegated to another board of trustees appointed especially for the purpose. The corporation, however, attended to the leasing of all the other ministerial as well as school sections, in the Ohio company's purchase.

There is, perhaps, no better means of conveying to the reader an idea of the painstaking care with which the public lands were granted, and the original purpose for which they were granted, carried out, than the presentation in these pages of a copy of one of the leases. It will be noticed that the lease is specific in its character, compels the making of improvements upon the property, and speaks very plainly in almost every line of the New England spirit of good order, progress and thrift, which in many ways was made to flourish upon western soil. The corporation trustees impressed upon the original indentures their seal, bearing as its devise an altar with the old-time horns at either side, and surrounded by the legend, "Support Religion and Learning." Here flourished the fruit of the good seed sown in the ordinance of 1787.

The following is a literal copy of one of the corporation's leases for one of the school sections, located as will be noticed in the extreme western part of the Ohio company's purchase:

THIS INDENTURE made the first day of April in the year of our Lord one thousand eight hundred and one, between the "trustees for managing lands granted for religious purposes, and for the support of

---

schools in the county of Washington, within the Ohio company's purchase," of the one part: and Hugh Boyle, esq., of Ames in the county of Washington, Northwest Territory, of the other part, witnesseth, that the said trustees, in pursuance of the seventeenth section of a law of the territory aforesaid, passed the twenty-seventh day of November one thousand eight hundred, intitled, "An act authorizing the leasing of land granted for the support of Schools, and for religious purposes in the county of Washington," have granted, leased, and to farm let unto the said Hugh Boyle, his heirs and assigns, a certain tract or parcel of land situate in the township of Ames aforesaid, butted and bounded as follows, viz: Mile lot No. 16 in the Twelfth township in the Fifteenth range granted for the support of schools

.   .   .   .

for the term of seven years, commencing from and after the first day of April, instant, on conditon that the following improvements shall be made which the said Hugh Boyle covenants and agrees to make, do and perform-on penalty of one hundred dollars in which sum he binds himself, his heirs and assigns to pay to the trustees aforesaid if the following conditions are not complied with on his part, viz: not to make unnecessary waste of timber nor to injure sugar trees, and within seven years from the commencement of his term to clear twelve acres of all the trees, brush and wood, two acres of which shall be suitable orchard ground, and set out or planted with two hundred apple trees, thrifty and of a proper size to set in an orchard; which orchard shall be enclosed by itself with a good and lawful fence and kept in constant repair, and no animals of any kind suffered to feed or graze therein; the remainder of the aforesaid twelve acres to be of the most suitable land for meadow, and seeded in a proper manner with herdsgrass and clover seeds, and the said meadow shall be fenced and improved in a good husbandlike manner. Furthermore, the said Hugh Boyle covenants; that within the term of his lease he will clear six acres in a suitable manner for pasturing and seed the same with a proper quantity of clover and herdsgrass seed; and also, that he will clear in a proper manner and have under improvement and cultivation at the end of his term twenty acres of tillage land; and that at the end of his term, the several lots of land covenanted and agreed to be cleared as aforesaid shall be separately enclosed with a good and sufficient fence agreeably to the law of the territory, when the said Hugh Boyle is to yield peaceable and quiet possession.

IN WITNESS whereof the said trustees have caused William Rufus Putnam, their clerk, to subscribe his name and affix the seal of the corporation, and the said Hugh Boyle hath also interchangeably set his hand and seal the day and year first above written.

Signed, sealed and delivered }
    in presence of   }

BENJAMIN BEADLE.   HUGH BOYLE.
JAMES CAMERON.   WM. RUFUS PUTNAM.

Returning to our brief outline of territorial history we will note that the third session of the legislature was held at Chillicothe, beginning upon November 23, 1801, in accordance with the conditions of adjournment. There were several new members in the legislature and the following was the roll: Epraim Cutler, of Washington county; William Rufus Putnam, of Washington county; Moses Miller, of Hamilton county; Francis Dunlavy, of Hamilton county; Jeremiah Morrow, of Hamilton county; John Ludlow, of Hamilton county; John Smith, of Hamilton county; Jacob White, of Hamilton county; Daniel Reeder, of Hamilton county; Joseph Darlington, of Adams county; Nathaniel Massie, of Adams county; Zenas Kimberley, of Jefferson county; John Milligan, of Jefferson county; Thomas McCune, of Jefferson county; Edward Tiffin, of Ross county; Elias Langham, of Ross county; Thomas Worthington, of Ross county; Francois Joncaire Chabert, of Wayne county; George McDougal, of Wayne county; Jonathan Schieffelin, of Wayne county; Edward Paine, of Trumbull county.

Edward Tiffin was speaker. Robert Oliver, of Marietta, was chosen president of the legislative council. The session closed upon the twenty-third of January, 1802, to

meet in Cincinnati in November of the same year, but it was not destined to assemble again. The territorial government was very soon to be superseded by State government. The removal of the seat of government from Chillicothe, says Jacob Burnet, was in consequence of the assembling of a mob on two evenings to insult Governor St. Clair and several members of the legislature, a proceeding which passed unrebuked by the village authorities.[*]

Party feeling had not until about the time of this session of the legislature, ran high, but Jefferson was now President, and his adherents were increasing in force in the west. On the other hand the territorial governor (Federalist) was losing strength, partly because of his use of the veto power, and from various other reasons. There was a growing uneasiness on the part of many under the territorial government, and in this session of the legislature the question of the formation of a State government came up for consideration. Judge Ephraim Cutler and William Rufus Putnam, the members from Washington county, were the leaders of the small minority opposing the formation of the State government, and it was chiefly against them that the demonstration of the mob above spoken of was directed. William Rufus Putnam had made a speech at a supper, in which he expressed the sentiment: "The Scioto — may its waters lave the borders of two great States;" and his words were thought to have been the chief agency in inflaming the spirit of the more violent element of the Chillicothe people. They expected the State to be formed as it now exists, or at least that the Miami would be the western boundary, and hoped that Chillicothe would be the capital. The people of Washington county were opposed to the formation of a State government at that time, and, indeed, were commonly imbued with the desire that their representative had expressed. This idea was advocated later, in fact, by the legislative council, which body petitioned Congress to make the boundary of the eastern division of the territory the Scioto river—a measure which, had it been granted, would have postponed for a considerable time its admission as a State, because of the lack of the requisite population (sixty thousand) specified by the ordinance of 1787 as the number which entitles any division to admittance to the Union.

Messrs. Cutler and Putnam were in perfect accord in this matter of the formation of a State government, with their constituency. If we turn back to look at the history of Washington county at a period a few months anterior to the occurrences we have narrated we shall see that there was a great activity of public opinion upon the subject. Various township meetings were held at which the proposition to form a State government was fully discussed and strongly opposed. On the seventeenth of June, 1801, an anti-State meeting was held at Marietta, made up of delegates from the several townships as follows: For Marietta, the Hon. Paul Fearing and Elijah Backus; Belpre, Isaac Pierce and Silas Bent; Waterford, Robert Oliver and Gilbert Devol; Adams, Joseph Bar-

---

[*] Burnet's Notes on the Northwestern Territory.

ker; Newport, Philip Witten and Samuel Williamson; Middletown (later Athens, now Athens county), Alvin Bingham; Gallipolis, Robert Safford. The meeting was organized by the election of Gilbert Devol as chairman and Joseph Barker as secretary. A very able and strong address was delivered by Colonel Joseph Barker, summing up the objections to organizing a State goverment. The convention, after listening to the speech of Colonel Barker, and remarks of several other delegates, adopted the following resolution, which was afterwards sent to their representatives:

Resolved, That in our opinion it would be highly impolitic and very injurious to the inhabitants of this territory to enter into a State government at this time. Therefore we, in behalf of our constituents, do request that you would use your best endeavors to prevent and steadily oppose the adoption of any measures that may be taken for the purpose.*

The reasons advanced against entering into a State government, in Washington county, were many and cogent. It was argued that the benefits to be obtained over those already possessed would be insignificant; that the expenses of a State government would be very heavy, whereas the chief support of the territorial government was derived from the National exchequer, and that the large expense necessitated would fall chiefly, or, at least, in undue proportion, upon the settlers in the Ohio company's purchase, while the Congress lands, constantly improving in value, would be exempt from taxation. There was much force in this argument. It meant that the first settlers of the country—those who had borne the brunt of the struggle not only against the wilderness but against a savage foe—would be obliged to pay a heavy revenue from their well-nigh depleted pockets for what would do them no good, while the newer settlers coming into the country after peace was fully established, and many of whom could reap some advantage from the founding of a State government, would be comparatively small supporters of it. The Washington county people, too, were now upon the weaker side in politics, and their leading men could expect no offices under the State. This was undoubtedly an element which entered into the consideration of some men, but there was another reason of greater weight of which little or nothing was said. The hope existed that two States might sometime be carved from the territory now included in Ohio, and that of the easternmost one of these, bounded upon the west by the Scioto river, Marietta might be the capital.

Paul Fearing, then a member of Congress, opposed the State government movement with great strength, and made a speech against it in March, 1802, when the question as to whether Congress should or should not pass an act enabling the people of the eastern division of the territory to hold a constitutional convention and organize a State government, was before the House.

As the time for the decision of the question drew nigh, there was developed much bitterness among the partizans upon each side, and many hot words were said or written by public men. On the one side there were charges that the advocates of the change were actuated chiefly

by their desire to gain offices which a State organization must create, and by a desire to favor the National administration. On the other hand those who favored admission to the Union criticised, in violent terms, the policy of Governor St. Clair, and freely spoke of him as a tyrant, and his friends (by whom they meant all who clung to the old form of government), as "aristocrats and Tories."

The friends of the State government idea were nowhere else stronger than in Chillicothe. All of the men of influence in that place belonged to the State government party, and several of them lent their whole strength to the furtherance of the cause at Washington. Thomas Worthington (afterward governor of Ohio) went on to Washington at the suggestion of a committee, appeared before Congress, and strongly urged the passage of the "enabling act" at the season when that measure was taken up for consideration.

The act was passed April 30, 1802. It authorized the holding of a convention and the organization of a State government, and prescribed the limits of the State. Delegates were elected in the various counties upon the twelfth of October, 1802, in conformance to published notice, and the convention assembled at Chillicothe upon the first of November. The delegates were as follows:

From the county of Washington—Ephraim Cutler, Rufus Putnam, Benjamin Ives Gilman, and John McIntire.

From the county of Adams—Joseph Darlington, Thomas Kirker, and Israel Donalson.

From the county of Belmont—James Caldwell.

From the county of Hamilton—Francis Dunlady, John Paul, Jeremiah Morrow, John Wilson, Charles Willing Byrd, William Goforth, John Smith, and John Reily.

From the county of Jefferson—Rudolph Bair, John Milligan, and George Humphrey.

From the county of Ross—Edward Tiffin, Nathaniel Massie, Thomas Worthington, Michael Baldwin, and James Grubb.

From the county of Trumbull—Samuel Huntington.

The convention organized by the election of Edward Tiffin, of Chillicothe, as president, and Thomas Scott as secretary.

On the third day of the session the question was put "whether or no it was expedient at this time to form a constitution and a State government." The journal shows that Ephraim Cutler, of Washington county, cast the only vote in the negative.*

The other three members from Washington, like him, were opposed to the measure, but seeing that their re-

---

* Biography of Captain Joseph Barker, by S. P. Hildreth.

*Judge Cutler, in a conversation several years later, gave the following reminiscence: "I never gave a vote of which I was more proud. The settlements were remote from each other, and still laboring under the difficulties incident to pioneer communities. They were poor; the expense of a State government was much greater than that of the territorial; and, above all, I felt that by waiting a few years we might be admitted on much more favorable terms than at that time. It was desirable that the vote should be unanimous. There was no debate on the question. General Putnam and Mr. Gilman wished me to vote with them. I told them I could not. The old general told me I was as stubborn as a bull—to go my own way."

monstrance must prove ineffectual, voted with the majority. The convention adjourned upon November 19th, having completed its labors and formed a constitution which was from that time the law of the State of Ohio, although it was never submitted to the people, "which," says a writer, "was the more remarkable as the convention itself was called by Congress, without any request on the part of the legislature, and without the opinion of the inhabitants being taken."* There were but seven votes in favor of submitting the constitution for approval or disapproval, viz.: those of the four members from Washington county—Messrs. Putnam, Cutler, Gilman, McIntire, Bazaleel Wells and Nathan Updegraff, of Jefferson county; and John Reily, of Hamilton.

The constitution was a very admirable one, as broadly democratic as such an instrument could be and exhibiting an extreme in that respect which was perhaps attributable to the arbitrariness of the government of St. Clair, from which a majority of the members of the Constitutional convention had been impatient to escape.

Although the Washington county members of the convention of 1802 had been opposed to the forming of a constitution "at that time," they had a large influence in creating the instrument and some of its best measures were inserted by them.

There was one topic before the convention of absorbing interest. Few people of this day know how narrowly the State of Ohio escaped being made slave territory in the year 1802. The monster knocked for admittance at the door which had been closed to it by the Ordinance of 1787, and the door was even set ajar for the entrance of the colossal evil. But there were men to meet and thrust it back and close that door again and forever. Foremost among these was Ephraim Cutler of Washington county, son of Manasseh Cutler who had fifteen years before placed in that fundamental law of the northwest, the Ordinance of Freedom, the words "There shall be neither slavery nor involuntary servitude in the · · territory." Here was the poetry of history.

It was claimed by some members of the convention that the Ordinance of 1787 was not binding upon the State as it had not been assented to by the State, and hence there was an attempt to introduce slavery in a modified form in spite of the prohibition. · Had it so been introduced there is reason to believe that it could not have been crushed out, the ordinance to the contrary notwithstanding.

John W. Brown of Hamilton county, chairman of a committee appointed to prepare a bill of rights, reported a clause which provided that no person should be held in slavery if a male after he was thirty-five years of age; and if a female, after twenty-five years of age. Judge Cutler was a member of the committee. He moved to have the clause laid upon the table until the next meeting, when, he suggested, each member should present a clause expressive of his own views. The committee met the next morning, and Judge Cutler presented

the clause which was ultimately made a part of the constitution. After considerable discussion a vote was had in the committee, by which the Brown clause was rejected and the Cutler clause adopted, the vote standing five to four. The measure, however, had several perils to pass through. While it was before the committee of the whole another endeavor was made to change the clause in such manner as to sanction slavery. And now we quote Judge Cutler's graphic words from a recorded conversation:

"I well remember the excited feeling of General Putnam on the occasion. I had been for a day or two confined to my room by sickness He came to see me, accompanied by Benjamin Ives Gilman, his large white eyes almost starting from their sockets, his form more erect than usual. "Cutler" said he, in a voice of thunder, "get up, get well and be in your place to-morrow." Gilman too, was greatly agitated. He was rubbing his hands as he was wont, when anything troubled him, and exclaimed, "We must prevent this. I cannot, will not live in a community where such injustice is sanctioned by law." I went to General McIntire and prevailed on him to stay away and not vote; there would be a tie, unless we could bring over one more. Milligan, of Jefferson county, had often in the Territorial legislature spoken against slavery, but in the convention he had voted with the Virginia party. In the course of my speech I happened to catch his eye and the very language he had used in debating that question occurred to me. I put it home to him, and he seemed to shrink under it. When the vote was taken, Milligan sang out his aye but with so weak and trembling a sound that the whole house was convulsed with laughter. For my own part I never before felt so fearful a responsibility and never made so great an effort."

Elsewhere Judge Cutler says:

"Thus an overruling Providence by His wisdom makes use of the weak often to defeat the purposes of the great and wise, and to His name be the glory and praise."

The influence of Jefferson was undoubtedly exerted to plant slavery upon Ohio soil. He argued that the extension of slavery would weaken it. It was commonly thought that the exclusion of slavery would operate against immigration to Ohio from the slave States, and that such a clause as that which Mr. Brown sought to introduce would encourage such emigration. This consideration was the chief cause of the pertinacity with which some of those members of the convention, whose districts principally depended upon the south for population, labored for the pro-slavery clause. It may be added that Judge Cutler, the principal agent in the defeat of this measure for the introduction of the modified slavery wedge, was the author also of those measures in the constitution which related to religion and education. Herein was another coincidence. The Washington county man was supplementing again the action of the Massachusetts man—his father; was perpetuating in the constitution of Ohio what the latter had first expression and force in the ordinance for the Northwest.

The State of Ohio for the organization of which an enabling act was passed April 30, 1802, by Congress, was first recognized as a State by that body upon the nineteenth of February, 1803, which seems the proper date to ascribe as that of the birth of the State.* Quite a number of different dates are given as those which Ohio became a State among them November 29, 1802,

* President Israel Ward Andrews, of Marietta college, in Centennial Historical Address.

* When was Ohio admitted into the Union—by President Israel Ward Andrews, of Marietta college. In Secretary of States' Report for 1879.

the day on which the constitutional convention adjourned, and March 1st and 3d, 1803, respectively the dates of the meeting of the first legislature and of the formal organization of the government.

It is not our purpose to follow the history of Ohio, for the briefest outline would be beyond the province of this work, and there was not that close and intimate connection between Washington county and the affairs of the State which existed between the county and the territorial government, and which justified the bestowal of so much attention (for a merely local history), upon the latter.

Washington county has contributed to the civil service of the State men of eminence and worth—men who have been identified with the greatest measures enacted for the public good, and who have left their mark as legislators and as public servants in various capacities. Their names, with the dates of service, appear in the following chapter.

In conclusion, it is fitting that we should refer to two important measures of the period of early State government, both brought about by a Washington county man, and one of them having its principal effect in southeastern Ohio—Washington and other counties. The reform in method of taxation, and the establishment of a general school system were two topics which engaged Judge Ephraim Cutler at about the same time. Prior to 1825 the unimproved lands in the State were taxed by the acre without regard to valuation, "a system than which," said Samuel F. Vinton, "ingenuity could not devise one more unequal, unjust, and oppressive." Judge Cutler, while representative for the county in 1819-20, introduced a resolution proposing that all lands should be taxed at their real or relative values. The resolution passed the house, but it was not until 1825 that its author secured its passage by the senate, of which body he was then a member, having been elected in 1823. He then secured its adoption through the convincing argument that to firmly establish the State credit (as the friends of public improvements were then very anxious to do in order to build the Ohio canal) it was absolutely necessary to have a broad, equitable, judicious system of raising the revenue. The *ad valorem* plan of taxation which was brought into vogue, was not only a great boon to the long distressed and burdened people of Washington and other thinly-settled counties, but an invaluable aid to the State, as it materially assisted the canal commissioners to procure the loan which they needed, in New York.

In 1822 Judge Cutler was appointed one of the seven commissioners to report a system of education, to be uniform throughout the State, and well supported by general taxation and by judicious management of the school lands or the funds from them. The report of Mr. Kilbourn said that Judge Cutler was the father of this admirable system adopted in 1825, which remained in vogue for many years.

Judge Cutler was elected to the legislature and the senate upon the very issues which he fought through to the end, and won. And the people of Washington county, as his constituency, thus exhibited an adherence

to those principles planted in the colony by the pioneer fathers, which have ever been at work leavening the body politic and building up the fabric of the splendid edifice —the State of Ohio.

CHAPTER XIV.

CIVIL HISTORY OF WASHINGTON COUNTY.

The Proclamation of Governor St. Clair Establishing the County—Its Vast Boundaries—Other Counties Established—Division of Washington into Townships—The First Court House and Jail—Excitement in Regard to Location of the Present Court House—The Donors of the County Lots—Infirmary—The Children's Home—Roster of Washington County—The Territorial Officers—Representatives in Congress—Members of the General Assembly—Members of Constitutional Conventions—Judges of the Courts—The County Officers from 1788 to 1880.

WASHINGTON COUNTY, originally embracing about half the territory now included in the State of Ohio, was established by proclamation of Governor Arthur St. Clair on the twenty-sixth of July, 1788.* Following is the law, which contains a full description of boundaries:

"By his Excellency, Arthur St. Clair, esq., governor and commander-in-chief of the Territory of all the United States northwest of the river Ohio,

A PROCLAMATION

To all persons to whom these presents shall come, greeting:

WHEREAS, by the ordinance of Congress of the thirteenth of July, 1787, for the government of the territory of the United States northwest of the river Ohio, it is directed that for the due execution of process, civil and criminal, the governor shall make proper divisions of the said territory, and proceed from time to time, as circumstances may require, to lay out the part of the same where the Indian title has been extinguished, into counties and townships, subject to future alterations as therein specified. Now, know ye, that it appearing to me to be necessary, for the purposes above mentioned, that a county should be immediately laid out, I have ordained and ordered, and by these presents do ordain and order, that all and singular the lands lying and being within the following boundaries, viz: Beginning on the bank of the Ohio river where the western boundary line of Pennsylvania crosses it, and running with that line to Lake Erie, thence along the southern shore of said lake to the mouth of the Cuyahoga; thence up said river to the portage between that and the Tuscarawas branch of the Muskingum; thence down the branch to the forks, at the crossing place above Fort Laurens; thence with a line to be drawn westerly to the portage of that branch of the Big Miami on which the fort stood that was taken by the French in 1742, until it meets the road from the lower Shawneestown to the Sandusky; thence south to the Scioto river; thence with that river to its mouth, and thence up the Ohio to the place of beginning; shall be a county, and the same is hereby erected into a county named and to be called hereafter the county of Washington; and the said county of Washington shall have and enjoy all and singular the jurisdiction, rights, privileges and immunities whatever, to a county belonging and appertaining, and which any other county that may hereafter be erected and laid out, shall or ought to enjoy, conformably to the ordinance of Congress before mentioned. In witness whereof I have hereunto set my hand and caused the seal of the Territory to be affixed this twenty-sixth day of July, in the thirteenth year of Independence of the United States, and in the year of our Lord one thousand seven hundred and eighty-eight.

(Signed) A. ST. CLAIR."

---

* The date as given above was discovered by President Andrews, of Marietta college, in an examination of the State papers at Washington to be the correct one. It has usually been stated that the county was erected on the twenty-seventh; Atwater's History of Ohio says the twenty-sixth.

The next county proclaimed was Hamilton, January 2, 1790. Then followed the erection from 1790 to 1795 of the counties of St. Clair, Knox, Randolph, and Wayne, lying in the Northwest Territory, and outside of the present limits of Ohio. Adams was next erected July 10, 1797. Jefferson followed in order, being erected July 29, 1797, as the eighth in the Territory and fourth in the boundaries of Ohio. The establishment of the last named materially lessened the size of Washington, as did also the creation of Ross in 1798. Trumbull, the county of the Western Reserve, was not erected until 1800. Belmont was proclaimed in 1801. After the organization of the State government counties were created quite fast, and the old territorial counties were reduced in size correspondingly. Muskingum was formed in 1804; Gallia in 1803; Athens in 1805; Monroe in 1815; Morgan and Meigs in 1819.

The division of Washington county into townships was not effected until December, 1790, and was done by the court of quarter sessions. Marietta, Belpre, and Waterford, including respectively the three settlements, were established and contained immense tracts of country. Marietta extended from the seventh range to the western boundary of the ninth range (twelve miles), and extended south so as to include township No. 2 in the ninth range. Belpre and Waterford were of similar size. Gallipolis was bounded upon the north by a line drawn westward from the north line of township No. 3, in the eleventh range, upon the west by the Scioto and on the south by the Ohio river. In the northern end of the county extending to the lake were two townships—Warren, adjoining Pennsylvania, and Middletown, further west. These townships were taken off by the establishment of Jefferson county in 1797. In December, 1797, the townships of Adams and Salem were established, the latter extending from the donation tract to the north line of the county, and being five miles in width. A new Middletown, embracing nearly all of what is now Athens county, was established in December, 1798. Newtown, formed from the north part of Waterford, and extending to the north line· of the county, was formed the same year as the above, also Newport. There were nine townships in the county in 1800, of which six—Marietta, Belpre, Waterford, Salem, Adams, and Newport, were within its present limits, and three—Gallipolis, Middletown, and Newport, outside. To conclude: The dates of the establishment of the townships have been as follows: *

Marietta, Belpre and Waterford, 1790; Adams and Salem, 1792; Newport, 1798; Grandview, 1802; Watertown and Roxbury, 1806; Fearing, 1808; Wesley and Warren, 1810; Union, 1812; Lawrence, 1815; Aurelius and Barlow, 1818; Ludlow, 1819; Decatur, 1820; Liberty, 1832; Jolly and Independence, 1840; Fairfield and Palmer, 1851; Dunham, 1856; Muskingum, 1861. Of the foregoing twenty-five townships three have ceased to exist, viz: Roxbury, Jolly and Union.

The first court house in Washington county was built in

* For fuller particulars upon this subject the reader is referred to the township histories.

1798, and the following year, under the superintendence of Dudley Woodbridge, esq., and Griffin Greene—the latter being the architect—contracts were made with Joshua Wells to frame and raise the building; with Joshua Shipman to weatherboard ard shingle it; with James Lawton to do the mason work, and with Gilbert Devol, jr., to furnish the iron—grating, spikes, bolts, etc. —in all three thousand weight, for which he was to have sixteen cents per pound. The main building was forty-five feet in length and thirty-nine in breadth, two stories high. The walls were three feet thick and made of double tiers of yellow poplar logs, eighteen inches square, neatly hewed and dovetailed at the corners of the building. The logs were so laid as to break joints like masonry, and were held together by heavy iron bolts. The front room in the upper story was the court room. It was forty by thirty feet in dimensions, lighted by seven windows and heated by two large fireplaces. "Here," says Hildreth, "Paul Fearing, R. J. Meigs, and Jacob Burnet, the earliest attorneys northwest of the river Ohio, displayed their youthful powers and unfolded talents that few at this day can excel. Here Charles Hammond and Philemon Beecher for many years attended as barristers, specially the latter. Here also Thomas Ewing, esq. (the elder), first essayed his mighty powers and began that bright career of popular fame which elevated him to some of the first stations of the government. A host of others have also here commenced their careers in the labyrinths of the law."* The two lower rooms were occupied by the jailer and his family. A passage between them led to the jail in the rear part of the structure, which like the court house proper was very strongly built. No imprisoned malfactor ever broke from this jail. The jury rooms were in the rear of the court room, over the jail. The roof over the old courthouse corresponded with the rest of the building, being constructed of very heavy timbers, and covered with thick shingles, nearly or perhaps quite three feet in length. A cupola surmounted the roof in which was hung the same bell which is in the present court house. For many years this bell was rung regularly at nine o'clock morning and evening and at noon, and was tolled upon the occasion of the death of any inhabitant. It bears the inscription, "1802—Barazilia Davidson, Norwich, Connecticut"—the name being that of the man who cast it.

The oldest portion of the present court house was finished in 1823. As early as 1819 the need of a new building became apparent, and after the subject had been agitated for some time a committee was appointed by a citizens' meeting to report upon the matter. The committee consisted of Governor Return J. Meigs, Hon. Levi Barber, and D. H. Buell, esq. These gentlemen reported in favor of the present location upon the thirteenth of April, and on the following day the county commissioners endorsed their opinion. For two years little or no action was taken, but in 1821 the commissioners advertised for a plan, and employed Joseph Holden to collect the materials for building. It was decided that the building should contain four principal offices, each to be sixteen feet square and, that the dimensions of the whole structure should be forty-eight feet each way. Much opposition to the location arose, and there was considerable discussion as to the relative merits of various sites. The commissioners were annoyed with scores of petitions and personal appeals for location in a dozen different places. Some wished the building to be erected upon the elevated square on Washington street, some upon the lot, where Judge Ewart has latterly lived, then known as the Thierry property, and others on Fifth street, south of the cemetery. In the spring of 1822 it was decided to locate it on Fifth street, but a few weeks later a majority of the citizens assembled at a meeting, and voted in favor of the Thierry property as the location. The commissioners changed their plan in conformance to the general desire, but a few weeks later decided on the corner of Putnam and Second streets, and the work was begun so soon that opponents to that location had no time to effect another change. Governor Meigs' influence secured the building of the edifice at a little distance back from Putnam street. This was done that the view (then a very fine one) from the house of his friend, Dr. S. P. Hildreth, might not be obscured.

The addition upon the north which looks older than the front building, was erected in 1854. The main building was again improved in 1876. The lot occupied by the court house was donated by Colonel Ebenezer Sproat.

The jail was built in 1848. It occupies the site of the old court house and jail which we have described. This lot was given to the county by Judge Dudley Woodbridge. While the old jail and court house occupied the site of the present jail, the lot on which the court house now stands was in use as the place of punishment for criminals. The pillory, stocks and whipping post stood there, and curious throngs of people assembled around them when either one was in use. The lot was also a pound. It was selected in 1800 for the double purpose by Messrs. Robert Oliver, Griffin Greene and Robert Safford.

The poor were provided for by the township authorities until 1840. Although a law was passed as early as 1816, authorizing county poor houses, no movement was made under it in Washington county until 1835. In that year land was bought of Dr. Jonas Moore for one thousand two hundred dollars, and a contract was made with Messrs. Daniels, Westgate and Alcock to erect a building for the sum of two thousand and forty dollars. Samson Cole, Eben Gates and Wyllys Hall were appointed directors in 1835. In 1838 many petitions were received for changing the location of the poor house, and in conformance to them the present farm was bought—one hundred and ninety-eight acres of land—for two thousand five hundred and thirty-six dollars and fifty-eight cents. In 1850 the name "poor house" was changed by act of the legislature to county infirmary.

The Children's Home of Washington county is an institution which has a peculiar interest, both because of the nature of its beginning and growth, and because the first institution of the kind in the State. Miss C. A. Fay (now Mrs. Ewing) has the honor of being the founder of the Children's Home, and of having given the initial impetus to this branch of charity in the State. Various scenes of distress led Miss Fay to concern herself for the welfare of children, and in 1858, upon the first of April, her plans had been so far realized that she opened a small home or asylum for children upon Moss run, in Lawrence township, about twenty miles from Marietta, where, with her savings as a school-teacher, she had bought twelve acres of land and built a small house. Her plan was to care for orphan children, with some assistance from the county, (her allowance for each child per week never exceeding one dollar and twenty cents,) and from individuals benevolently disposed. She took nine children from the infirmary to begin with, and a few years later had at one time more than thirty, and in the ten years of her service in this charity which she had conceived, she had one hundred and one under her charge, for most of whom she secured homes. Miss Fay's labors were of the heroic kind, were arduous, perplexing, and involved the sacrifice of almost every enjoyment of life, save that of doing good. She was employed almost constantly, but found time while attending to her family of little ones, at the humble home she had provided for them, to exert an influence upon the public mind in favor of legislation for having Children's Homes established and supported by taxation. Finally a bill introduced in the State legislature by Hon. W. F. Curtis, of this county, and given the earnest support of Hon. S. S. Knowles, senator from this district, was passed, authorizing the establishment, support, and regulation of children's homes in the several counties of the State. This act passed in March, 1866, and as amended, April 7, 1867. Very shortly after the former date a purchase was made of the farm of one hundred acres, one mile above Marietta, on the east bank of the Muskingum, on which the fine buildings of the Home now stand. The price paid was eighteen thousand dollars. The property is now valued at upwards of thirty thousand dollars, the increase being largely in the value of the buildings erected. March 1, 1867, Mrs. A. G. Brown, having been appointed matron of the Home, entered upon the discharge of the duties of the office by assisting in preparing and arranging the several apartments of the institution for the reception and care of such children as were ready to be admitted; and on the first of April, 1867, the children from Mrs. Ewing's were brought in, and from that date the Home has been in full operation. Mrs. Brown continued to serve as matron until April 1, 1868, and was succeeded by Rev. Ira M. Preston and wife as superintendent and matron, who served one year, whose successors were Dr. Simeon D. Hart and wife, who have served as superintendent and matron since the first of April, 1869.

Since its organization upwards of five hundred children have been admitted to the institution. The institution, a direct outgrowth of Mrs. Ewing's Home, was the first organized in the State, under the law. It has received the benefit of careful attention from the friends of the poor in Washington county, has most of the time had about a hundred inmates, and has been productive of an immense amount of good.

CIVIL ROSTER.*
MEMBERS OF CONGRESS.

After the adoption of the second grade of territorial government, in 1799, the whole Northwest Territory was represented in Congress by a single delegate. William Henry Harrison, of Hamilton county, was the first, and was succeeded, in 1800, by William McMillen, of the same county. Paul Fearing, of Washington county, was elected in 1801 and served until 1803. State government was then organized, and Jeremiah Morrow, of Warren county, was the sole delegate until 1813. From that time until 1823 Washington county was an integral part of the Third Congressional district, of which the following gentlemen were the representatives for the terms indicated:

William Creighton, jr., of Ross, 1813-17; Levi Barber, of Washington, 1817-19; Henry Brush, of Ross, 1819-21; Levi Barber, of Washington, 1821-23.

Until 1833 Washington county was a portion of the Seventh district, and was represented:

Samuel T. Vinton, of Gallia, 1823-33.

From 1833 to 1843 the county was in the Sixth district, and represented as follows:

Samuel F. Vinton, of Gallia, 1833-37; Calvary Morris, of Athens, 1837-43.

From 1843 to 1853 the county was a portion of the Thirteenth district, which was represented as follows:

Perley B. Johnson, of Morgan, 1843-45; Isaac Parrish, of Morgan, 1845-47; Thomas Ritchie, of Perry, 1847-49; William A. Whittlesey, of Washington, 1849-51; James M. Gaylord, of Morgan, 1851-53.

From 1853 to 1863 the district was the Sixteenth:

Edward Ball, of Muskingum, 1853-57; Cydnor B. Tompkins, of Morgan, 1857-61; William P. Cutler, of Washington, 1861-63.

From 1863 to the present the district has been the Fifteenth, and represented as follows:

James R. Morris, of Monroe, 1863-65; Tobias A. Plants, of Meigs, 1865-69; Eliakim H. Moore, of Athens, 1869-71; William P. Sprague, of Morgan, 1871-75; Nelson H. Van Vorhes, of Athens, 1875-79; Adoniram J. Warner, of Washington, 1879-81; Rufus R. Dawes of Washington, 1881.

MEMBERS OF STATE CONSTITUTIONAL CONVENTIONS.

Ephraim Cutler, Benjamin Ives Gilman, John McIntire, Rufus Putnam, 1802; Thomas W. Ewart, William P. Cutler, 1850-51; Harlow Chapin, 1873-74.

MEMBERS OF TERRITORIAL LEGISLATURE.
(Senators.)

Robert Oliver (president), 1799-1803.

(Representatives.)

Paul Fearing, Return J. Meigs, 1799-1801; Ephraim Cutler, William R. Putnam, 1801-1803.

MEMBERS OF STATE LEGISLATURE.*
(Senators.)

Joseph Buell, 1803, First; Joseph Buell, Elijah Backus, 1803, Second; Joseph Buell, 1804, Third; Joseph Buell, Hallam Hempstead, 1805, Fourth; Hallam Hempstead, 1806, Fifth; John Sharp, 1807-1808, Sixth and Seventh; William Woodbridge, 1811-12-13, Tenth, Eleventh, and Twelfth; William R. Putnam, 1814, Thirteenth; John Sharp, 1815-16, Fourteenth and Fifteenth; Sardine Stone, e, 1817-22, Sixteenth to Twenty-first; Ephraim Cutler, 1823-24, Twenty-second and Twenty-third; William R. Putnam, 1827-28, Twenty-sixth and Twenty-seventh; Arius Nye, 1831-32, Thirtieth and Thirty-first; Isaac Humphrey, 1839-40, Thirty-eighth and Thirty-ninth; Rufus E. Harte, 1845-46, Forty-fourth and Forty-fifth; George W. Baker, 1849-50, Forty-eighth and Forty-ninth; Harley Lafflin, 1854, Fifty-first; Davis Green, 1858, Fifty-third; William F. Curtis, 1864, Fifty-sixth; Samuel S. Knowles, 1866, Fifty-seventh; Rodney M. Stimson, 1870-72, Fifty-ninth and Sixtieth; Perez B. Buell, 1874, Sixty-first; John Irvine, 1878,

(Representatives.)

William Jackson, 1803, First and Second assembly; Seth Carhart, 1804, Third; Levi Barber, 1806, Fifth; Joseph Palmer, 1807, Sixth; William Woodbridge, 1808, Seventh; William R. Putnam, 1809, Eighth; S. P. Hildreth, William R. Putnam, 1810, Ninth; S. P. Hildreth, 1811, Tenth; Sardine Stone, 1812-13, Eleventh and Twelfth; John Sharp, 1814, Thirteenth; Henry Jolly, 1815, Fourteenth; Sardine Stone, 1816, Fifteenth; Nathaniel Hamilton, 1817, Sixteenth; Joseph Barker, 1818, Seventeenth; Ephraim Cutler, 1819, Eighteenth; Timothy Buell, 1820-21, Nineteenth and Twentieth; Ephraim Cutler, 1822, Twenty-first; William Skinner, 1823, Twenty-second; John Cotton, 1824, Twenty-third; William R. Putnam, 1825-26, Twenty-fourth and Twenty-fifth; Arius Nye, 1827-28, Twenty-sixth and Twenty-seventh; Joseph Barker, jr., 1829-30, Twenty-eighth and Twenty-ninth; James M. Booth, 1831-32, Thirtieth and Thirty-first; Silas Cook, 1833, Thirty-second; Joseph Barker, jr., 1842, Thirty-third; Isaac Humphrey, 1835-36, Thirty-fourth and Thirty-fifth; Walter Curtis, 1837-38, Thirty-sixth and Thirty-seventh; William A. Whittlesey, 1839, Thirty-eighth; Arius Nye, 1840, Thirty-ninth; Truxton Lyon, 1841, Fortieth; George M. Woodbridge, 1842, Forty-first; William Glines, 1843, Forty-second; William P. Cutler, 1844-45-46 (Speaker in 1846), Forty-third, Forty-fourth and Forty-fifth; George W. Barker, 1847, Forty-sixth; Seth Woodford, 1848-49, Forty-seventh and Forty-eighth; Ebenezer Battelle, jr., 1850, Forty-ninth; Levi Bartlett, 1852, Fiftieth; Thomas Ross, 1854, Fifty-first; Samuel Hutchinson, James Lawton, 1856, Fifty-second; A. S. Bailey, O. Lewis Clark, 1858, Fifty-third; John Haddon, 1860, Fifty-fourth; O. Lewis Clark, 1862, Fifty-fifth; Mark Green, 1864, Fifty-sixth; A. L. Curtis, A. L. Haskin, James B. Green (to fill vacancy caused by death of Mr. Haskin), 1866, Fifty-seventh; Samuel M.

---

*From appendix to Centennial Historical address, by President Israel Ward Andrews—with additions to date.

*Washington county has at times been associated with others both in the election of senators and representatives. We give only the names of those who were residents of the county.

Richardson, Perez B. Buell, 1868, Fifty-eighth; John A. Brown, 1870, Fifty-ninth; William G. Way, 1872, Sixtieth; John Varley, 1874, Sixty-first; Henry Bohl, Gilbert Smith, 1876-78, Sixty-second and Sixty-third; Thomas W. Moore, 1880.

JUDGES OF THE GENERAL COURT.

Samuel H. Parsons, October 16, 1787, died November 17, 1789; James M. Varnum, October 16, 1787, died January 10, 1789; John C. Symmes, February 19, 1788, to 1803 (State formed); Greene Turner, September 12, 1789, resigned in 1798; Rufus Putnam, March 31, 1790, resigned December 22, 1796; Joseph Gilman, December 22, 1796 to 1803 (State formed); R. J. Meigs, jr., February 12, 1798 to 1803 (State formed).

JUDGES OF THE COURT OF COMMON PLEAS.

Rufus Putnam, Benjamin Tupper, Archibald Crary, Joseph Gilman, Dudley Woodbridge, Robert Oliver, Daniel Loring, John G. Petit, Isaac Pierce, Griffin Greene, Ephraim Cutler, Peregrine Foster.

JUDGES OF THE COURT OF QUARTER SESSIONS OF THE PEACE.

Joseph Gilman, Isaac Pierce, Robert Oliver, Dudley Woodbridge, Josiah Munroe, John G. Petit, Griffin Greene, William R. Putnam, Samuel Williamson, Joseph Barker, Ephraim Cutler, Henry Smith, Philip Whitten, Alvin Bingham, Thos. Stanley, Seth Cathcart, Robert Safford, William Harper, William Burnham, Joseph Buell.

JUDGES OF PROBATE COURT.

Rufus Putnam, October, 1788, resigned December, 1789; Joseph Gilman, December, 1789, resigned December, 1796; Paul Fearing, March, 1797, to March, 1803; T. W. Ewart, February, 1852, to October, 1852; Davis Green, October, 1852, to February, 1855; William Devol, February, 1855, to February, 1858; C. R. Rhodes, February, 1858, to February, 1866; C. F. Buell, February, 1861, to February, 1864; L. W. Chamberlain, February, 1864, to February, 1870; A. W. McCormick, February, 1870, to February, 1876; C. T. Frazyer, February, 1876, to February, 1882.

PRESIDENT JUDGES OF THE COURT OF COMMON PLEAS IN THE CIRCUIT INCLUDING WASHINGTON COUNTY.

(Under the State Constitution of 1802.)

Calvin Pease, 1803-08; William Wilson, 1808-19; Ezra Osborne, 1819-26; Thomas Irwin, 1826-40; John E. Hanna, 1840-47; Arius Nye, 1847-50; A. G. Brown, 1850-52.

ASSOCIATE JUDGES OF THE COURT OF COMMON PLEAS.

Griffin Greene, 1803-08; Joseph Buell, 1803-10; Joseph Wood, 1803-08; Esekiel Deming, 1808-24; William Hempstead, 1808-10; Paul Fearing, 1810-17; Thomas Lord, 1810-17; Henry Jolly, 1817-24; John Sharp, 1817-23; J. M. Chamberlain, 1823-24; Walter Curtis, 1824-37; Henry P. Wilcox, 1824-25; Alexander Warner, 1824-30; John Cotton, 1825-47; Joseph Barker, 1830-43; Oliver Loring, 1837-47; Isaac Humphreys, 1843-43; Ebezener Gates, 1843-44; Joseph Barker, jr., 1844-52; Bial Stedman, 1847-52; William R. Putnam, jr., 1847-52.

Judges of the Court of Common Pleas in the subdistrict composed of Washington, Athens, Meigs, and Gallia counties:

Simeon Nash, 1852-62; John Welch, 1862-65; E. A. Guthrie, 1865-74; William B. Loomis, 1868-73; T. A. Plants, 1873-75; L. B. Hibbard, January, 1875, to October, 1875; J. T. Cartwright, February, 1875, to October, 1875; J. P. Bradbury, October, 1875, to February, 1882; S. S. Knowles, October, 1875, to February, 1882.

PROSECUTING ATTORNEYS.

This officer was appointed by the courts under the territory. The State law of 1803 gave the appointment to the supreme court, and that of 1805 to the court of common pleas. From 1833 the people have elected. The term is two years.

Paul Fearing, September 9, 1788 to 1794; Return Jonathan Meigs, jr., 1794 to 1798; Matthew Backus, 1798 to 1808; William Woodbridge, 1808 to February 6, 1815; Caleb Emerson, February 6, 1815, to April 10, 1821; John P. Mayberry, April 10, 1821, to October 30, 1829; Arius Nye, October 30, 1829, to August 17, 1840; David Barber, October 26, 1840, to April 3, 1845; Arius Nye, April 3, 1845, to March 8, 1847; William D. Emerson, March 8, 1847 to March, 13, 1848; William S. Nye, March 13, 1848, to March, 1850; Davis Green, March, 1850, to April 5, 1852; Rufus E. Harte, April 5, 1852, to October 4, 1852; Samuel B. Robinson, October 4, 1852, to January, 1855; Charles R. Rhodes, January, 1855, to January, 1857; Samuel B. Robinson, January, 1857, to January, 1859; Charles R. Barclay, January, 1859, to January, 1861; Frank Buell, January, 1861, to April, 1861; Melvin Clarke, April, 1861, to October 11, 1861; William S. Nye, October 11, 1861, to January, 1862; David Alban, January, 1862, to January, 1868; Walter Brabham, January, 1868, to January, 1870; Reuben L. Nye, January, 1870, to January, 1872; Walter Brabham, January, 1872, to January, 1874; Samuel B. Bobinson, January, 1874, to January, 1876; Frank F. Oldham, January, 1876, to January, 1880; David Alban, January, 1880.

CLERKS OF THE COURT OF COMMON PLEAS.

Under the territory the title for clerk of the court of common pleas was prothonotary. This officer and the clerk of the court of quarter sessions were appointed by the governor. Under the State constitution of 1802 court appointed its own clerk for seven years. Under that of 1851 the people elect, for three years.

Return Jonathan Meigs, September 9, 1788-June 9, 1795; Benjamin Ives Gilman, June 9, 1795-July, 1803; Edward W. Tupper, July, 1803-October 31, 1808; Giles Hemstead, October 31, 1808-January 1, 1809; Levi Barber, January 1, 1809-March 1, 1817; George Dunlevy, March 1, 1817-October 31, 1836; Thomas W. Ewart, October 31, 1836-October 21, 1851; William C. Taylor, October 21, 1851-February, 1852; George S. Gilliland, February, 1852-July, 1852; William C. Taylor, July, 1852-February, 1854; O. Lewis Clarke, February, 1854-February, 1857; Jasper S. Sprague, February, 1857-February, 1863; Willis H. Johnson, February, 1863-February, 1866; Jewett Palmer, February, 1866-February, 1872; Daniel P. Torpy, February, 1872-February, 1878; Christian H. Etz, February, 1878-February, 1881.

SHERIFFS.

Under the territory the governor appointed. Under the State the people elect, for two years. Sheriffs are eligible only four years in six.

Ebenezer Sproat, September 2, 1788-1802; William Skinner, 1802-3; John Clark, 1803-10; William Skinner, 1810-12; Timothy Buell, 1812-14; Alexander Hill, 1814-16; Timothy Buell, 1816-October, 1820; Silas Cook, October, 1820-October, 1824; Jesse Loring, October, 1824-October, 1828; Robert R. Green, October, 1828-October, 1832; Jesse Loring, October, 1832-October, 1834; Benjamin M. Brown, October, 1834-October, 1838; John Test, October, 1838-October, 1842; George W. Barker, October, 1842-October, 1846; Junia Jennings, October, 1846-October, 1850; Jesse Hildebrand, October, 1850-January, 1853; Marcellus J. Morse, January, 1853-January, 1857; Mark Green, January, 1857-January, 1861; Augustus Winsor, January, 1861-January, 1865; Jackson A. Hicks, January, 1865-January, 1869; Samuel L. Grosvenor, January, 1869-January, 1873; George Davenport, January, 1873-January, 1877; William T. Stedman, January, 1877, January, 1879; Daniel B. Torpy, 1879.

COUNTY COMMISSIONERS.

Provision was made for three such officers by a law adopted from the Pennsylvania code by the governor and judges in 1795, and confirmed by the territorial legislature in 1799. They were to be appointed by the court of quarter sessions. The State law of 1804 provided for their election by the people, one each year, the term of office being three years.

The following were appointed under the law of the territory: William R. Putnam, Paul Fearing, Oliver Rice, Gilbert Devol, Jonathan Haskell, Simeon Deming, Isaac Pierce. Of these, Isaac Pierce served until 1804, W. R. Putnam until 1805, and Simeon Deming until 1806. The list of those elected in successive years is as follows:

Nathaniel Hamilton, 1804; John Sharp, 1805; Paul Fearing, 1806; Nathaniel Hamilton, 1807; Joseph Barker, 1808; Paul Fearing (resigned), 1809; John Sharp (for two years), 1809; Nathaniel Hamilton, 1810; Daniel Goodno, 1811; Henry Jolly, 1812; Nathaniel Hamilton, 1813; Daniel Goodno, 1814; William Skinner, 1815; Titan Kemble, 1816; John B. Regnier, 1817; Daniel Goodno, 1818; Titan Kemble (resigned), 1819; John B. Regnier (died), 1820; Samuel Beach (two years), 1821; Amzi Stanley (one year), 1821; Daniel Goodno, 1821; Joseph Barker, 1822; William R. Putnam, 1823; Daniel H. Buell (resigned), 1824; Joseph Barker, 1825; Thomas White (one year), 1825; William Pitt Putnam, 1826; Silas Cook (one year), 1826; Anselm T. Nye, 1827; Seth Baker (one year), 1828; Joel Tuttle, 1829; Jabish F. Palmer (two years), 1829; Anselm T. Nye, 1830; Jabish F. Palmer, 1831; Ebenezer Battelle, 1832; William Pitt Putnam, 1833; John D. Chamberlain, 1834; Robert K. Ewart, 1835; Daniel H. Buell, 1836; John D. Chamberlain, 1837; William Dana, 1838; Daniel H.

Buell, 1839; John D. Chamberlain, 1840; James Dutton, 1841; Douglas Putnam, 1842; Hiram Gard, 1843; William West, 1844; Douglas Putnam, 1845; Boylston Shaw, 1846; Lewis H. Greene, 1847; Douglas Putnam, 1848; John Breckenridge, 1849; George Stanley, 1850; Douglas Putnam, 1851; Walter Curtis, 1852; Benjamin Rightmire, 1853; William Mason, 1854; Walter Curtis, 1855; Charles Dana, 1856; William R. Putnam, 1857; Joseph Penrose, 1858; Zachariah Cochrane, 1859; James McWilliams, 1860; J. J. Hollister, 1861; William Thomas, 1862; Anthony Sheets (resigned), 1863; J. J. Hollister, 1864; George Benedict, 1865; James Little, (one year), 1865; James Little, 1866; Seymour Clough, 1867; George Benedict, 1868; Thomas Caywood, 1869; Mark Green (resigned), 1870; Joseph Penrose, 1871; Cyrenius Buchanan (two years), 1871; John Hall, 1872; Pemberton Palmer, 1873; John Pool, 1874; John Potter, 1875; Moses A. Malster, 1876; John Hoppel, 1877; Philip Mattern, 1878; Robert Mullenix, 1879; William Thompson, 1880.

COUNTY AUDITORS.

The office was created in 1820. The general assembly appointed the first auditor. In 1821 the auditor was required to be elected by the people each year. In 1824 the law made the term two years.

The successive auditors have been: Royal Prentiss, 1820-5; William A. Whittlesey, 1825-38; James M. Booth, 1838-40; Joseph P. Wightman, 1840-2; James M. Booth, 1842-6; Sala Bosworth, 1846-54; Horatio Booth, 1854-6; Frederick A. Wheeler, 1856-64; Zadok G. Bundy, 1864-8; John V. Ramsey, 1868-70; John T. Matthews, 1870-6; Benjamin J. McKinney, 1876-81.

COUNTY RECORDERS.

Under the territory the recorder—styled register till 1795—was appointed by the governor. By the law of 1803 the associate judges appointed, for seven years. By the law of 1829 the people elect, for three years.

Enoch Parsons, 1788-90; Dudley Woodbridge, April, 1790-June, 1807; Giles Hempstead, June, 1807-June, 1814; George Dunlevy, June, 1814-June, 1817; Daniel H. Buell, June, 1817-October, 1834; James M Booth, October 1834-November, 1837; Daniel P. Bosworth, November, 1837-October, 1843; Stephen Newton, October, 1843-November, 1855; William B. Mason, November, 1855-January, 1862; Manly Warren, January, 186–May, 1864; William Warren (appointed), May, 1864-January, 1865; George J. Bartmess, January, 1865-August, 1866; A. T. Ward (appointed), August, 1866-January, 1867; James Nixon, January, 1867-81.

COUNTY TREASURERS.

The governor appointed till the formation of the State. By the law of 1803, the associate judges appointed. By the law of 1804, the commissioners appointed annually. Since 1827 the people have elected, for two years. By the constitution of 1851 the treasurer is eligible only four years in six.

Jonathan Stone, 1792-1801; Jabez True, 1801-17; Joseph Holden, 1817-28; Weston Thomas, 1828-30; Royal Prentiss, 1830-2; Michael Deterly, 1832-6; Eben-

15

ezer Gates, 1836-8; Robert Crawford, 1838-50; Abner L. Guitteau, 1850-6; Stephen Newton, 1856-8; Ebenezer B. Leget, 1858-60; William B. Thomas, 1860-2; Rufus E. Harte, 1862-6; William B. Mason, 1866-8; Lewis Anderson, 1868-70; Ernest Lindner, 1870-74; William S. Waugh, 1874-8; William R. Goddard, 1878-80; John Molst, 1880.

COUNTY COLLECTORS.

For some years prior to 1804 there were township collectors, and they performed some service in 1805. The office of county collector was abolished in 1827.

Nathanael Cushing, 1804-6; William Burnham, 1806-7; Obadiah Lincoln, 1807-8; Timothy Buell, 1808-20; Jesse Loring, 1820-2; Timothy Buell, 1822-3; Jesse Loring, 1823-7.

CORONERS.

Provision was made in 1788 for a coroner in each county, to be appointed by the governor. The first State constitution also provided for one to be elected every two years by the people, and a law of 1854 continued the provision. The list appended is believed to be correct from 1812 to the present time; there is some uncertainty as to the previous periods.

Charles Green (territory); Joel Bowen, 1803; Joseph Holden, 1806; Alexander Hill, 1812; Silas Cook, 1814; Samson Cole, 1816; Silas Cook, 1818; John Merrill, 1820; Griffin Greene, 1824; Francis Devol, 1834; Warden Willis, 1836; Lawrence Chamberlain, 1838; John T. Clogston, 1844; Lawrence Chamberlain, 1846; Chauncey T. Judd, 1850; Finley Wilson, 1852; James H. Jones, 1853; Chauncey T. Judd, 1855; Benjamin F. Stone, 1857; Louis Soyez, 1859; Allen M. Creigbaum, 1860; Lemuel Grimes, 1864; Simeon D. Hart, 1866; Herman Michaelis, 1868; Philip Emrich, 1870; Marcellus J. Morse, 1872; T. C. Kiger, 1874; Conrad Krigbaum, 1876; J. Fullman, 1880.

COUNTY SURVEYORS.

From 1803 to 1831 the surveyor was appointed by the court of common pleas, and commissioned by the governor. Since 1831 the election has been by the people, for three years.

Levi Barber, November, 1805-July, 1816; William R. Putnam, July, 1816-October, 1826; William R. Browning, February, 1827-May, 1832; Benjamin F. Stone, May, 1832-November, 1841; Levi Bartlett, November, 1841-October, 1851; L. W. Chamberlain, October, 1851-December, 1861; R. W. St. John, December, 1861-December, 1864; Charles E Gard* (appointed) January, 1865-December, 1865; John A. Plumer, February, 1866-January, 1875; J. P. Hulbert, January, 1875-1881; D. F. Dufer, January, 1881.

INFIRMARY DIRECTORS.

These officers were appointed by the commissioners from 1836 until 1842, when they were required to be elected by the people, one each year, to serve three years.

Samson Cole, 1836-42; Eben Gates, 1836-42; Wyl-

*Samuel N. Hobson was elected October, 1864, but resigned.

lys Hall, 1836-42; James Dunn, 1842-9; Thomas F. Stanley, 1842-44; William R. Putnam, jr., 1842-5; Samuel Shipman, 1844-7; Brooks Blizzard, 1845-51; John Collins, 1847 59; James M. Booth, 1849-50; James Dunn, 1850-61; James Dutton, 1850-3; James S. Cady, 1853-6; Robert T. Miller, 1854-60; Levi L. Fay, 1856-62; Robert B. Cheatham, 1860-3; Junia Jennings, 1861-70; John Dowling, 1862-5; William West, 1863-6; James Dunn, 1865-8; F. A. Wheeler, 1866-75; Samuel E. Fay, 1868-71; H. W. Corner, 1870-3; Charles Athey, 1871-4; George W. Richards, 1873-6; William Caywood, 3d, 1874-80; John Dowling, 1875-8; Charles A. Cook, 1876-9; John Dowling, 1878-81; John Strocker, 1879-82; Charles Athey, 1880-3.

TRUSTEES OF THE CHILDREN'S HOME.

By the act of March 20, 1866, five trustees were to be appointed by the county commissioners, to serve one year each. By the act of April 10, 1867, the number of trustees was reduced to three, and the term of service extended to three years.

Douglas Putnam, June, 1866, to March, 1868; William R. Putnam, June, 1866, to March, 1877; Frederick A. Wheeler June, 1866, incumbent; William S. Ward, June, 1866, to May, 1871; Augustin Dyar, June, 1866, to March, 1868; Wylie H. Oldham, June, 1871, to June, 1875; W. Dudley Devol, September, 1875, incumbent; George Benedict, March, 1877, incumbent.

CHAPTER XV.

THE BENCH AND THE BAR OF WASHINGTON COUNTY.*

Early Courts of the Territory and of Washington County—Their Constitution and Jurisdiction—Judges Varnum and Parsons—Paul Fearing the First Attorney in the Northwest—Sketches of Other Attorneys—Joseph Gilman—Return Jonathan Meigs, Jr.—Elijah Backus—Lewis Cass—Benjamin Ruggles—M. Backus—William Woodbridge—Gustavus Swan—Caleb Emerson—John P. Mayberry—Arius Nye—William A. Whittlesey—Charles R. Rhodes—Thomas W. Ewart—S. S. Knowles—Other Lawyers who have practiced in Washington County early and late.

The ordinance for the government of the territory of the United States northwest of the river Ohio, passed by the last Congress of the Confederation, provided for successive forms of territorial government; and the first temporary form provided for, was organized by the appointment of a governor and three judges.

The judges constituted a supreme court of common law jurisdiction, styled the general court.

In addition to their purely judicial functions, the judges, conjointly with the governor, were vested with the legislative power of the temporary government.

The first settlement of the territory made at the mouth of the Muskingum, was in April, 1788, and the first municipal code of the pioneers consisted merely of re-

* By Hon. R. E. Harte.

gulations, drawn up by Colonel Meigs, and published by posting on a tree on the banks of the river.

In about three months after the landing of the pioneers, Governor St. Clair and the judges arrived in the territory, and on the eighteenth of July the governor was formally received by the inhabitants at Marietta, the Ordinance of 1787 and the commissions of the governor and judges were read, an inaugural address was made by the governor, and a response made thereto by General Putnam in the name of all the people, and the first form of government provided by the ordinance was formally established within the territory.

The county of Washington, including within its limits about one-half of the present State of Ohio, was established by proclamation of the governor July 26, 1788.

Laws were enacted by the governor and judges, fixing the terms of the general court, establishing county courts of common pleas, courts of general quarter sessions of the peace, courts of probate, and of single justices of the peace.

The county court of common pleas consisted of a number of judges, not less than three, nor more than seven appointed in each county and commissioned by the governor.

The general court of quarter sessions of the peace consisted of three or more justices of the peace of the county, appointed by the governor, had a limited criminal jurisdiction, and held four sessions a year. Single judges of the common pleas and single justices of the peace were also clothed with certain civil and criminal powers. The court of probate had the ordinary jurisdiction of probate court.

This judicial system continued during the eleven years of the government of the governor and judges, and the three years of the territorial legislature of the Northwest Territory.

Under the State constitution of 1802 the judiciary consisted of judges of the supreme court, president and associate judges of common pleas courts, appointed by joint ballot of both houses of the general assembly for the term of seven years, and justices of the peace elected by the electors of township for three years.

Under the constitution of 1851 the present system of supreme, district, common pleas, probate and justice courts was organized.

The first court of common pleas of the county was opened in the hall in the northwest block-house of Campus Martius, at Marietta, September 2, 1788—Gen. Rufus Putnam, Gen. Benjamin Tupper and Col. A. Crary, judges.

The first court of general sessions of the peace was held on the ninth of the same month in the southeast block-house; General Putnam and General Tupper justices of the quorum; Isaac Pearce, Thomas Lord, and R. J. Meigs, jr., assistant justices. The grand jurors were William Stacy, foreman, Nathaniel Cushing, Nathan Goodale, Charles Knowles, Anselem Tupper, Jonathan Stone, Oliver Rice, Ezra Lunt, John Matthews, George Ingersoll, Jonathan Devol, Samuel Stebbins, Jethro Putnam and Jabez True.

The following account relating to the opening of the first Washington county court is taken from Dr. Andrews' Centennial address:

The first court held in the Territory was that of the court of common pleas at Campus Martius, September 2, 1788. A procession was formed at the Point, where most of the settlers resided, in the following order The high sheriff with his drawn sword; the citizens; the officers of the garrison at Fort Harmar; the members of the bar; the supreme judges; the governor and clergymen; the newly-appointed judges of the court, Generals Rufus Putnam and Benjamin Tupper. Rev. Dr. Manasseh Cutler, one of the directors of the Ohio company, then here on a visit, opened the court with prayer; and Colonel Ebenezer Sproat, the sheriff, made official proclamation that "a court is opened for the administration of even-handed justice, to the poor and the rich, to the guilty and the innocent, without respect of persons" General Putnam, alluding to this first court, says: "Happily for the credit of the people, there was no suit, either civil or criminal, brought before the court."

PERSONAL SKETCHES.

MAJOR GENERAL SAMUEL HOLDEN PARSONS was born at Lyme, Connecticut, in 1737. He graduated at Harvard college in 1756; studied law in the office of his uncle, George Matthew Griswold, and was admitted to the bar in 1759, and settled at Lyme in the practice of his profession. In 1761 he married the daughter of Richard Mathew, of Lyme, and in 1762 was elected member of the general assembly of the colony of Connecticut, and by successive reelections held that position until 1774, when he removed from Lyme to New London.

In the stirring times preceding the Declaration of Independence by the colonies, Mr. Parsons was an ardent patriot, and to him has been attributed the first suggestion of a meeting of commissioners from the colonies to consult as to their general welfare. Mr. Parsons was one of the bold men of Connecticut, who, after the battle of Lexington, conceived the project, and by whose exertions in raising money and troops, the project was by Colonel Allen gallantly carried into effect, to-wit: The surprisal and seizure of Forts Ticonderoga and Crown Point, whereby command of Lake Champlain and the main route to Canada was obtained. This was the first offensive blow struck by the colonies in the war for independence.

In 1775 Mr. Parsons was commissioned by the colony of Connecticut as colonel of a regiment raised for defence of the colony, and was actively engaged in the battle of Long Island.

In 1776 he was appointed by Congress brigadier general and was with the army at the battle of White Plains. The most important operation of the campaign of 1777, to-wit, the capture of prisoners and the destruction of the enemy's ships and supplies at Sag Harbor, was designed by General Parsons and executed under his directions, and received from Congress a complimentary notice. During most of the years 1778 and 1779 he was stationed at West Point and the Highlands and rendered valuable service. In 1780 he was commissioned by Congress as major general. For his bold and successful enterprise for the relief and protection of the inhabitants between New York and Greenwich he received the thanks of Congress. At the close of the war he resumed the practice of law at Middletown, Connecticut.

In 1786 General Parsons, with General Butler, of Pittsburgh, and George Rogers Clark, by appointment of Congress, held an important treaty with the Indians at the mouth of the Great Miami.

In 1789 he was appointed by Congress one of the judges of the supreme court for the territory northwest of the river Ohio, and in May, 1788, removed to Marietta and entered upon the discharge of his duties.

In 1789 he was appointed by the State of Connecticut a commissioner to hold a treaty with the Wyandot Indians of the Western Reserve, and visited that country to make preparations for holding the treaty. In descending the rapids of the Big Beaver river on his return he was drowned, November 17, 1789, aged fifty-two years.

GENERAL JAMES MITCHELL VARNUM was a descendent of Samuel Varnum who emigrated from Wales to this country in 1649, and settled at Dracut, Massachusetts. He was born at Dracut in 1749, graduated at Providence college, now Brown university, in the first class in 1769, studied law in the office of Oliver Arnold, Providence, Rhode Island, was admitted to the bar in 1771, and settled at East Greenwich in the practice of his profession. He took an active part in the controversy between the colonies and Great Britain, had a taste for military life, and shortly after the battle of Lexington was appointed colonel of one of the three regiments raised by Rhode Island in 1775. During 1776 he served as colonel in the colonial army, and in 1777 was promoted by Congress to the rank of brigadier general. During 1777 and 1778 he was with the army and commanded at Red Bank and Mud Island. In 1780 he was elected a delegate to Congress from Rhode Island, and was an active and influential member of that body. After the war he resumed the practice of law at East Greenwich, and was engaged in most of the important cases in the State. As an advocate and orator he was considered the equal of Patrick Henry. In 1786 General Varnum was again elected representative to Congress and noted for his brilliant eloquence. In 1787, upon the organization of the Ohio Land company at Boston, he was elected a director of the company, and soon after the passage of the ordinance of that year establishing the Northwest Territory, he was elected by Congress one of the judges of the territory, and in the spring of 1788 he left his home in Rhode Island for Marietta and arrived there in June, and entered upon the discharge of the duties of his office. He was the orator of the day at the celebration of American ·Independence held at the Point in Marietta July 4, 1788, and his address was noted for its many beauties of sentiment and language. He was in poor health, when he arrived at Marietta but was able to attend the meetings of the directors of the Ohio company, and assisted the governor and the other judges in forming a code of laws for the government of the Northwest Territory. He died at Marietta January 10, 1789, at the early age of forty, and his funeral was attended with great ceremony.

RUFUS PUTNAM was appointed by the President, in 1790, one of the judges of the supreme court for the territory northwest of the Ohio river, and served until 1796. A full biographical sketch of General Putnam will be found in another part of this volume.

JOSEPH GILMAN was born in Exeter, New Hampshire, in 1736. In the struggles of the colonists for liberty and independence, he took a decided part for the Whigs, and had their entire confidence. He was chairman of the committee of safety for New Hampshire, and, as such, made large advances from his own personal resources for the purchase of supplies for the State troops. Upon the formation of the Ohio company he became an associate, and, with his wife, Rebecca Ives Gilman, and his son, Benjamin Ives Gilman, removed to Marietta in 1789.

By Governor St. Clair, he was appointed to and held the offices of probate judge, judge of the court of quarter sessions, and judge of the court of common pleas.

In 1796 he was appointed by the President of the United States one of the judges of the general court for the Northwest Territory, and attended the sittings of that court at Marietta, Cincinnati, Detroit and other places at which that court was held.

Judge Gilman was highly respected and esteemed for his learning and abilities as a jurist and scientist, and for his pleasing social qualities. He died in 1806, aged seventy years.

RETURN JONATHAN MEIGS, JR., served, by appointment of the President of the United States, as one of the judges of the supreme court of Northwest Territory from 1798 until 1803.

A sketch of the life of Governor Meigs is given in another part of this volume.

PAUL FEARING.—As more fully set forth in Dr. Hildreth's Biographical Memoirs, Mr. Fearing was born in Wareham, Plymouth county, Massachusetts, February 28, 1762, and was the son of Noah and Mary Fearing. Of his early childhood but little is known; but as the boy is said to be the father of the man, he was doubtless an upright, open-hearted youth. The minister of the parish prepared him for college, as was common in that day, and he was graduated at Harvard in 1785. Having decided on law for a profession, he studied in the office of Esquire Swift, of Windham, Connecticut, and was admitted as an attorney in the courts of law of that State in September, 1787. During this year the Ohio company was matured, for establishing a colony in the Northwest Territory, and was a general topic of conversation in New England. The glowing descriptions of the country and climate in the valley of the Ohio caught the fancy of many young men, as well as older persons, and he decided on visiting that distant region. On the first of May, 1788, he embarked at Boston for Baltimore, where he arrived on the sixteenth of that month. Here he put his trunk into a wagon, and commenced the journey across the mountains on foot. He reached Pittsburgh on the tenth of June, and embarked the same day in a boat for Marietta, where he arrived on the sixteenth. On the fourth of July he participated in the first proceedings had on the bank of the Muskingum in honor of the day, and on the twentieth listened to the first sermon ever preached in the English tongue northwest of the Ohio river. On the second of September, 1788, he attended the first county common pleas court held in the

RETURN J. MEIGS.

county, and was admitted an attorney at law of the courts of the Territory. On the ninth of this month the county court of quarter sessions of the peace sat for the first time, and he was appointed counsel in behalf of the United States for Washington county.

The last of January, 1789, he set out on a journey to New England, in company with several persons, among whom was General Parsons. They went up the Ohio in a boat, but when about half way to Wheeling the floating ice became so troublesome that they left the river and went up by land. The travel over the mountains was accomplished on horseback in twenty six days, from Wheeling to Middleborough, in Massachusetts. He returned in August, by way of Alexandria, and being a fine pedestrian, again crossed the mountains on foot. He reached Red Stone, a famous port for boats on the Monongahela, on the fourteenth of the month. While waiting here for a rise in the river, Commodore Whipple came on with his family and that of his son-in-law, Colonel Sproat. With them he embarked in a small boat on the twenty-sixth of November, and reached Marietta on the thirtieth.

The following year was passed in attending to his law business, which began to increase some, as the emigration this season was very great. In November, 1790, he was appointed a deputy contractor for supplying the troops at Fort Harmar with fresh meat at the low rate of thirteen dollars and thirty-three cents a month and rations. Labor of all kinds was at a depressed state, a common hand on a farm getting only four dollars, and a private soldier three dollars.

Mr. Fearing's first attempt as an advocate before the court of quarter sessions was rather discouraging; but the embarrassment he first experienced vanished in his next trial, and he was able to deliver himself fluently and with fine effect. His frank, manly civility and sound, discriminating mind made him a favorite with the people, as well as the courts, and he had at his command much of the law business of the country. The Hon. R. J. Meigs was his first competitor at the bar, and for the favor of the public. Mr. Meigs was the more prompt and witty, with a ready flow of language, and Mr. Fearing was the more industrious and patient in investigation, so that, in final results they were very well matched.

When the troops left Fort Harmar, Mr. Fearing's intimate friend, Major Doughty, made him a present of his dwelling house, a well finished log building, standing in the southwest angle of the fort. During the war Mr. Fearing and his father occupied this house, which afforded a safe retreat from the attacks of Indians.

In the month of November, 1795, Mr. Fearing was married to Miss Cynthia Rowe, at his own home at Fort Harmar.

In 1797 he was appointed judge of probate for Washington county.

After the close of the war the county filled up rapidly, and in 1799 the first legislature held its session in Cincinnati. In 1800 the second session was held, and in this he was a member. During this period he was chosen a delegate to represent the Territory in Congress, which

post he filled for 1801 and 1802, with credit to himself and to the entire satisfaction of the people.

After his return to private life he resumed the practice of law with increased reputation. On his farm a little below the mouth of the Muskingum he erected a neat dwelling-house, and planted an extensive orchard of the choicest fruits, of which he was an intelligent and successful cultivator. He was one of the first in Ohio who paid attention to the raising of merino sheep. His flocks embraced several hundreds of these valuable animals, propagated from a few individuals bought at enormous prices.

In 1810 he was appointed associate judge of the court of common pleas. In this office he served seven years with much credit as a sound, just, and impartial judge.

In 1814 he was appointed master commissioner in chancery.

From the first entering of the lands of the Ohio company for taxation by the State, he acted very extensively as an agent for the shareholders in the eastern States. In this way a large portion of his time was occupied.

In his disposition, Mr. Fearing was remarkably cheerful and pleasant, much attached to children, and never happier than when in their company. He had great sympathy for the poor and the oppressed, and was ever ready to stretch forth his hand and open his purse for their relief.

He died the twenty-first day of August, 1822, after a few days' illness, a victim to the fatal epidemic fever which ravished the country for two or three years, aged sixty years. His wife died the same day, a few hours after, in the forty-sixth year of her age.

ELIJAH BACKUS was born at Norwich, Connecticut; was a graduate of Yale college, and was admitted to the bar in Connecticut in the year 1800. Shortly thereafter he came to Marietta and engaged in the practice of law. Wyllis Silliman, of Zanesville, was associated with him as a partner.

Mr. Backus held the office of receiver of public moneys of the United States. In 1801 he established the *Gazette* newspaper, of which he was editor. In 1803 he was a member of the Ohio senate. He was owner of the island in the Ohio river, now called Blennerhasset island, and sold it to Mr. Blennerhasset.

In 1808 Mr. Backus removed to Ruskin, Illinois, and died there in 1812.

LEWIS CASS was born at Exeter, New Hampshire, October 9, 1782. In 1799 he was employed as teacher at Wilmington, Delaware, where his father, Major Jonathan Cass, of the army, was stationed. In 1800 he removed with his father's family to Marietta, studied law there, and in 1802 was admitted to the bar and removed to Zanesville and commenced practice.

In 1806 he married Elizabeth Spencer, of Wood county, Virginia, and the same year was elected a member of the Ohio legislature. From 1807 to 1813 he was State marshal. In the War of 1812 he was colonel of a regiment of Ohio volunteers, under General Hull, and soon promoted to the rank of brigadier general.

In 1813 he was appointed governor of the territory of Michigan, and held that office for eighteen years. In 1831 he was appointed by President Jackson, Secretary of War, and was at the head of the war department at the commencement of the Florida war. In 1836 he was appointed minister to France, and served in that capacity until 1842, when he resigned. In 1845 he was elected United States Senator from the State of Michigan. In 1848 he was the Democratic candidate for President of the United States, but failed of election on account of a division of his party in the State of New York. In 1849 he was reelected to the Senate for the remainder of his original term. As Senator he opposed the Wilmot Proviso, although instructed by the legislature of his State to vote for it. He did not vote for the fugitive slave bill. In 1851 he was again elected Senator from Michigan. In 1852 he was a candidate before the Democratic convention at Baltimore for the nomination for the Presidency, but was not successful. In 1857 he was appointed Secretary of State by President Buchanan. In December, 1860, disapproving of the action of the President in refusing to reinforce Major Anderson and provision Fort Sumter, he promptly resigned his office as member of the cabinet. Through the war of the Rebellion his sympathies were with the National cause.

General Cass died at Detroit June 17, 1866.

He was a man of integrity, of great ability as scholar, jurist, and statesman, and his public career of more than half a century was honorable to himself and the Nation.

BENJAMIN RUGGLES was born at Woodstock, Connecticut, February 21, 1783. He attended the Brooklyn academy, and graduated from that institution. He studied law with Judge Peters, at Hartford, and was there admitted to the bar.

In 1807 he moved to Marietta, Ohio, and there pursued with success the practice of his profession. His profound learning, skill and care as a counsellor won for him public commendation.

In 1810 he was elected by the legislature of the State to succeed Calvin Pease as president judge of the third circuit. Shortly after his election to the judgeship he moved from Marietta to St. Clairsville.

In 1815 he was elected by the legislature to the United States Senate, and resigned the office of judge after having ably filled it for five years.

In 1821, and again in 1827, he was reelected to the Senate of the United States, and during his career of eighteen years in Congress as Senator from Ohio, he rendered valuable services to his State and the Nation. For many years he was chairman of the Senate committee on claims.

He was president of the caucus, held at Washington in 1824, which nominated William H. Crawford, of Georgia, for the Presidency.

In 1833, at the expiration of his third term as senator, he retired from public life and gave his attention to Agricultural pursuits, especially the cultivation of fruits and the introduction of choice varieties.

In 1840 he was favorably spoken of, in various parts of the country, for the office of Vice-President of the United States.

He died at his residence in St. Clairsville, September 2, 1857. As a statesman Judge Ruggles had the confidence of the senate and of the people. As a jurist his great ability was not as conspicuous in open court as in chambers. Though lacking, in some measure, the gifts of an orator, as a consulting attorney he had few superiors. As a private citizen he was highly respected. He was generous in his impulses, liberal in his views, and exerted an excellent moral influence wherever he was known.

THOMAS BACKUS was born at Norwich, Connecticut, in 1785; graduated at Yale college; studied law in the office of his father Elijah Backus, at Marietta, and was there admitted to the bar in 1808. He was married to Temperance Lord in 1810, and in 1811 removed to Franklinton, Franklin county, Ohio, and engaged in the practice of law, and in 1820 was appointed prosecuting attorney.

In 1823 he removed to Union county, Ohio, and was there appointed prosecuting attorney, and during his term of office died October 25, 1825.

WILLIAM WOODBRIDGE was born in Norwich, Connecticut, August 30, 1780. He received his early education in his native State, studied law in Litchfield, Connecticut, and, with his father, emigrated to the Northwest Territory in 1791, settling in Marietta.

In 1806 he was admitted to the bar in Ohio, and in the following year was elected to the assembly of that State.

From 1808 until 1814 he was prosecuting attorney for his county, and also a member of the Ohio State Senate.

During the latter year, without solicitation, he received the appointment of secretary of the territory of Michigan, from President Madison, and removed to Detroit and entered upon the performance of the duties of his new office.

He was elected the first delegate to Congress from Michigan, in 1819, and forwarded the interests of his constituents in a manner to elicit the warmest approbation.

He was appointed judge of the supreme court of the territory in 1828, and performed the duties of that office four years.

He was one of the members of the convention which framed the State Constitution, in 1835, and was elected a State senator under it in 1837.

He was chosen to succeed Stevens T. Mason as governor of the State, in 1839, and served during one term. At the expiration of his term of office as governor, he was elected a United States Senator, and served in that capacity from 1841 until 1847.

While in the Senate, he took a leading part in much of the important legislation of that body, both as a member of a number of the principal committees and also as a debater upon the floor of the Senate.

His last days were spent in retirement in Detroit, where he died October 20, 1861.

Governor Woodbridge was an eminent jurist and constitutional lawyer, and at the time of his death was the oldest and most distinguished member of the Detroit bar. He was a man of true principle and honor, who had served the public for many years with fidelity and integrity, and who died leaving to his children an unblemished name.

DAVID PUTNAN, became a member of the Washington county bar about 1808. A sketch of his life will be found in this volume elsewhere.

GUSTAVUS SWAN was born at Peterborough, New Hampshire, in 1787. By his own exertions he obtained a good clerical and scientific education. He studied law at Concord, New Hampshire, and was admitted to the bar of that State. In 1810 he came to Marietta, and was admitted to the bar of Ohio. From Marietta he moved to Franklin county, and engaged in the practice of law. In 1812 and again in 1817 he was representative in the Ohio legislature. In 1823 he was elected judge of the common pleas court, and at the expiration of his term of office, resumed the practice of law in Columbus, and continued there until 1843.

Judge Swan was an eloquent and able advocate, and his practice in Franklin and neighboring counties was large. After 1843 he devoted himself more exclusively to his duties as president of the State bank of Ohio. He died at Columbus, February 6, 1860.

CALEB EMERSON was born August 21, 1779, at Ashby, Massachusetts. It appears from some fragmentary memoranda among the papers he left, written in the last years of his life, that he lost both his parents early; that his mother died when he was six weeks old; that his father lost his health in the Revolutionary war, and his property by Continental money; that he was brought up by persons who were not of his kin; and that he was a student at law and assistant editor for some time before he left New England for Ohio, in the fall of 1808.

There remain to his descendants very few of the letters he received previous to 1820. Of the documents connected with his New England life, the most important is a file of letters from James Elliott, esq., a lawyer of Brattleborough, Vermont. Mr. Elliott appears to have been his early friend and counsellor, and showed much interest in his future advancement. In the earliest of these letters, dated January 3, 1801, he speaks of the young man's correct and friendly letter (addressed to him from Mason, postmarked Amherst, New Hampshire) and says it bears the marks of an honest mind, and the promise of future excellence. He desires to know his age, profession and prospects, his place of residence, amusements of infancy and course of study, and wishes to correspond with him occasionally.

In a subsequent letter Mr. Elliott speaks approvingly of his purpose to go west, but advises him first to spend a year or two in a law office, as in a new country the farmer, merchant and lawyer might all be combined in one person. He recommends that he cultivate his literary tastes, and promises to aid him.

In February, 1806, then at Washington city, Mr. Elliott addresses him as a student at law at Amherst, New Hampshire, having ascertained his then residence from the publisher of the *Farmers' Cabinet* at that place, whom he was probably assisting in the editorship of that journal.

Mr. Elliott frequently posted him up in the proceedings of Congress for the subsequent two years, and was one of several well known persons in that part of New England to give him recommendations as to general good character and proficiency in law studies, when he left for Marietta, Ohio.

Governor Tiffin, of Ohio, had advised a friend of Mr. Emerson's, at Washington, that it was not necessary for an applicant for admission to the Ohio bar to appear before the judges in session, but he could apply to any judge separately, who, if satisfied of his competency, could give him his certificate, and then he would apply to another judge, and the several certificates he received would entitle him to admission.

One of his remaining letters is one of recommendation from Hon. Paul Fearing, then a judge, dated September 13, 1809 (to General Philemon Beecher, of Lancaster, Ohio) of Mr. Emerson, as a suitable candidate for admission to the Ohio bar, and doubtless he was admitted about that time. He opened a law office at Marietta, visiting some of the neighboring county courts.

He married, July 29, 1810, Miss Mary Dana, daughter of Captain William Dana, of Belpre, Ohio, one of the early emigrants from New England; by whom he had several children, all but the earliest now living.

In the same year began his connection with the *Western Spectator*, a weekly journal of Marietta, to which was annexed a small book-store. The first number seems to have been issued about the twenty-third of October, 1810. He gave it up July 31, 1813, but continued the practice of the law, and was appointed prosecuting attorney of Washington county in February, 1815, and was continued in that office till April, 1821. In October, 1820, while residing on Front, between Scammell and Worcester streets, the dwelling house he occupied was consumed by fire, and most of the furniture and clothing of the family, and nearly all his valuable papers were destroyed. He and his family experienced great kindness and hospitality from the citizens of Marietta. His law business was continued.

In 1822 a fever, supposed to result from the miasmatic influences of the Ohio shore, prevailed extensively in Marietta township and elsewhere. Mr. Emerson's family was down with it for a considerable time, usually leaving only one or two able to wait on the rest. He was afterwards prostrated with a sickness which brought him very near the gates of death. After his recovery he had an abiding conviction that close application to a law office was ruinous to his health; and though his connection with legal matters was more or less maintained to the last years of his life, his time was largely given to horticultural and other industrial pursuits, mingled with literary, political, and social activities, and efforts in behalf of religious, moral, and educational institutions in Marietta.

He and his wife joined the Marietta Baptist church, which then worshipped four miles above the village about the year 1822, and remained in its communion to the last.

Being one of the earliest trustees of Marietta college, and remaining such during his life, he displayed an abiding interest in its growth.

In the year 1836 he was editor of the *Marietta Gazette*, a firm advocate for the right of free discussion. Certain lecturers about that time, in behalf of negro emancipation, were in danger of being mobbed, but the energetic philanthropists of Washington county secured for them fair treatment. In December, 1837, the *Marietta Gazette* passed into the hands of Mr. Isaac Maxon.

Several years later an advantageous sale of Mr. Emerson's three acre lots near Marietta, gave him leisure for literary effort. He wrote much in favor of emancipation, for journals both at home and abroad.

During the last ten or twelve years of his life he took great interest in the early history of Ohio, and especially of Washington county, and made extensive collections of old newspapers and other documents calculated to preserve a knowledge of the past, and to some extent lectured on these subjects. His duties as master commissioner in chancery, and as administrator for several estates, gave him opportunities for travel, where he could gather up such material. Probably the most complete of his essays on these subjects was an article in the North American Review, which includes the details of Dr. Manasseh Cutler's mission to Congress in behalf of the Ohio company, for the purchase of the well known tract which bears its name.

In 1845 he took an active part in bringing the celebrated case of the captured Ohioans, which involved, in part, the question of boundary between Ohio and Virginia, to the notice of the State authorities. His sympathies were strongly enlisted for the oppressed and downtrodden.

He died March 14, 1853, at his homestead in Marietta, aged seventy-three and one half years.

JOHN PENNYBACKER MAYBERRY was born March 1, 1790, at Pine Forge near the village of New Market, Virginia. His home was located in the loveliest portion of the beautiful valley of the Shenandoah. This is now a historic location from the fact that during the late civil war this homestead was the scene of many of the severest struggles for the possession of the valley.

His father was an Irish gentleman, having emigrated to America in early life. His mother was descended from German ancestors. Her maiden name was Rebekah Pennybacker. She was one of the large family of Pennybackers so well known throughout Pennsylvania.

John P. Mayberry, while in the valley of the Shenandoah, studied law under the eminent Judge Allen, of New Market, Virginia. Before completing his studies, however, in the year 1810, his father determined to seek a new home in the rich lands beyond the mountains, and his son John accompanied him, purchasing plantations near Belleville, Wood county, Virginia. They there settled. After a brief sojourn upon the plantations he became deputy sheriff of Wood county. In 1812 he visited Richmond, and made application for admission to practice in the State courts, and was given a certificate.

After his return, however, wishing to pursue his studies and perfect himself in other branches of the law, he went to Ohio, attracted by the reputation of Judge Fearing, of Harmar, Ohio, who was the first lawyer admitted to the bar in that State, the attorney of the Ohio company and the leading legal mind in the Northwest Territory. Here he had the advantage of an extensive library, and finished his studies with Judge Fearing in 1815. On the fifteenth of August, 1816, he married the only daughter of his preceptor, Lucy Willis Fearing, with whom he lived over fifty years. In 1817 he removed with his family to Parkersburgh, Virginia, and soon after was elected as a representative of the Whig party to the house of delegates at Richmond and served during the term of 1817 and 1818. In 1818 he left Richmond to accept the position of receiver of public moneys tendered him by the United States Government. This necessitated his return to Marietta, Ohio, where he succeeded Colonel Levi Barber, who was elected to Congress. The business of this office was very extensive as the territory was fast filling up, and the Government lands selling rapidly. His experience while in office illustrates the purity and honesty of the pioneer settlers of the northwest. The law existing at that time required receiver to deposit all moneys received, in the United States repositories situated at Cincinnati and Chillicothe, and the payments were to be made in the same coin as was paid to the receiver. The gold and silver received during the quarter had to be transported from Marietta to the points above named. At that time the woods were unfrequented and obscure, and the country sparsely settled, making it a perilous journey to transport six or eight thousand dollars in gold and silver on horseback. Yet these trips were made at the expiration of each quarter by Mr. Mayberry, accompanied by his father, or Henry or Silas Fearing, and Colonel David Barker, and during his term of office of over ten years, neither he himself nor his messengers were disturbed in their journeys to and fro. Mr. Mayberry was receiver until the year 1829. During this period he was also elected prosecuting attorney of Washington county, faithfully performing his duties and giving entire satisfaction to the public.

Retiring from these two important offices, and after settling his affairs relative thereto, he left Ohio and returned to his old home at Parkersburgh, and engaged in mercantile business. As was the custom in those days he made frequent journeys over the mountains to Philadelphia on horseback for the purpose of purchasing his stock in trade. While still engaged in merchandising he was elected prosecuting attorney for the county of Wood. In 1832 he was again called from private life, being elected to the house of delegates. At the expiration of this term he was reelected by his well satisfied constituents, and although not seeking or having any desire of office, he was again returned in 1837 and 1838, to the house of delegates; his ripe experience and sound judgment making him a great power, giving him the foremost position among the legislators.

The first recognition of any material importance which Parkersburgh or Wood county received from the State legislature of old Virginia in the way of improvement and bringing them into public notice was the establishment of the Northwestern Virginia turnpike road leading from Winchester in the valley of Virginia over the Alleghanies to Parkersburgh, a distance of two hundred and fifty miles. This great work was completed while Mr. Mayberry was in the house of delegates, and to his exertion, no doubt is West Virginia indebted for this great benefit.

He acquired wealth by prudent investments in real estate, together with the inheritance which his wife received from her father's estate.

Mr. Mayberry, in his long public life at Marietta, Parkersburgh, and Richmond, made friends with all whom he came in contact, and such was his even temperament that even in sharp political contests his urbanity of manner and kindliness for all humanity left his career destitute of enemies. He was a ripe scholar and a trained thinker, commanding in stature, with a pleasing address. He was a perfect type of a Virginia gentleman, of Washington's time. His manner and mien occasioning many of his friends to believe his resemblance to Washington very marked. Had his ambition led him to continue his public career his political associates were confident he would have taken a ranking position in national affairs among the great statesmen of that day, but turning aside from the allurements of public life, he returned to the quiet old home he loved so well in Parkersburgh. His house and grounds soon became shaded with the fine old trees he had planted. His office door under the shade of the catalpa was a charmed spot to all who came under the restful influence of the peaceful atmosphere. Happiness and contentment followed him like a shadow. The old men loved to linger with him, and the young men came to listen to the fine talk of the grand old gentleman. He devoted much of his time in later years to the rearing of blooded horses and to the improvement of the plantations he owned in the State. In his stables were some of the finest imported stock in the south and west, many of the descendants of the stables being favorite horses of the present time. He died while his favorite horse Lath was running; expired sitting in his carriage November 15, 1866, closing a life of nearly seventy-seven years, leaving his wife and son as the only immediate relatives to deplore his loss, as he was himself the last member of his father's family. And when the news came that the pure and noble John P. Mayberry was no more, a multitude mourned over the loss of a great and good man.

ARIUS NYE was the son of Colonel Ichabod Nye, and grandson of General Benjamin Tupper, two of the pioneers who with their families, made, at the mouth of the Muskingum in 1788, the first settlement in the territory northwest of the river Ohio. He was born in Campus Martius—"the stockade"—at Marietta, December 27,

1792. During his boyhood educational facilities at the new settlement were quite limited, yet mainly by his own exertions, he obtained what is now called a good common school education. In 1807 he went to Springfield, afterwards to Putnam in Muskingum county, and engaged in merchandizing.

In 1815 he married Miss Rowena, daughter of Dr. Joseph Spencer, of Vienna, Virginia, and sister of Mrs. General Cass. He was a director in the Bank of Zanesville before he was twenty-one years of age. During 1817-18 he studied law, was admitted to the bar, and began to make his mark in Muskingum county. In the autumn of 1822, or spring of 1823, he moved to Gallipolis, at the beginning of the sickly season, when he was taken sick with the prevailing epidemic, or malarial fever. In 1824-5 he removed to Marietta and there acquired a large and lucrative law practice. For several years after removing to Marietta he was elected and served as cashier of the Bank of Marietta. In 1827 he was elected representative in the State legislature, and re-elected in 1828. In 1831 he was elected State senator and served two years. At the time of the great flood in 1832 he removed his office from Putnam street to the old Ohio company's office on Washington street, where he kept his office until he was elected judge. He early acquired a large law library, and by 1837 probably had accumulated the largest law library of any lawyer in southeast Ohio. In 1840 he was again elected representative in the State legislature.

His son, A. Spencer Nye, became associate with him in practice as A. Nye & Son, continuing as a firm until 1846. In 1847 he was elected president judge of the district composed of the counties of Washington, Morgan, Athens, Meigs, Gallia, and Lawrence. The district was large and difficult of access during portions of the year, there being no railroads, and especially during the spring and autumn, county seats were difficult to reach. His health broke down under his labors on the bench, and he resigned in 1850. After his health improved he associated with him Mr. David Alban, and practiced as Nye & Alban until the commencement of the war, when Mr. Alban enlisted in the army. Thereafter as lawyer, generally associated in business with some younger member of the bar, he gave his attention to cases which were brought under his notice. His last illness was protracted and painful, but borne with fortitude. He died at his home in Marietta, July 27, 1865, in the seventy-third year of his age.

Judge Nye was an original, self-reliant, self-made man—a man of feeling, thought, and conviction. He will long survive in the memory of his friends; in the impressions which he made on the community where he lived, and in the legislation of his native State. At the time of his death he had obtained a wider celebrity than any other Marietta man. This was due to his strong character, to his industry, to his devotion to every accepted trust, to his public spirit, and above all to his inflexible integrity of mind and heart. As a jurist he ranked among the first chancery and criminal lawyers of the west. He was deeply read in the learning of the profession, and thoroughly imbued with the lofty spirit of its great masters.

WILLIAM A. WHITTLESEY was born at Danbury, Connecticut, in 1796. In 1816 he was graduated at Yale college, and for some time thereafter, was employed as teacher. In 1818 he came to Canfield, Ohio, entered the office of his uncle, the Hon. Elisha Whittlesey, as student at law, being fellow-student there with J. M. Giddings, and in 1820 was admitted to the bar. In 1821 he came to Marietta, and entered upon the practice of his profession. In 1825 he was elected auditor of the county, and for two successive years held that office, and received the public commendation for the faithfulness, care and ability, with which he discharged its duties.

In 1839 he was the candidate of the Democratic party for representative in the Ohio legislature, and was elected.

In 1841 and for several years following, he was associated with Gen. Charles B. Goddener, of Zanesville, in the practice of law in Washington county. In 1848 he was elected member of Congress from ———— district comprising the counties of Washington, Morgan and Perry. He declined being a candidate for reelection.

In 1856 and again in 1860, and again in 1862 he was elected mayor of the city of Marietta, and for six years discharged the duties of that office in an approved and satisfactory manner.

For some time previous to his death Mr. Whittlesey suffered from painful disease, but bore his affliction with fortitude and resignation. He died November 6, 1866, at Brooklyn, New York, where he had gone for medical treatment, leaving one surviving child, a daughter, now the wife of ——— Mitchell, of St. Cloud, Minnesota. His remains were brought back to Marietta, and buried in the Mound cemetery by the side of his deceased son, the lamented Captain W. B. Whittlesey, a brave and noble officer, who was killed at the battle of Mission Ridge in November, 1863.

The following is an extract from the report of a committee, appointed by the bar of Washington county to give expression of the sentiments of the profession, in relation to Mr. Whittlesey's death:

With feelings of the deepest sorrow and regret we, the members of the Washington county bar, have heard of the death of our late associate, the Hon. William A. Whittlesey. During the whole period of our connection with the profession in this county, we have been witnesses of the estimable qualities of the deceased.

As a lawyer, his discriminating mind, his legal acquirements, the friendliness and honesty of his counsels, his urbanity in the court-room, and his uniform courtesy and kindness toward the junior members of the profession have elicited our esteem, and endeared him in our recollections.

As a citizen and neighbor, the kindliness of his disposition, his liberality, his cheerfulness and his remarkable freedom from all feelings of envy, resentment and ill-will won for him the respect and friendship of all who knew him.

DAVID BARBER, son of Hon. Levi Barber was born at Harmar, Washington county, Ohio, August 14, 1804. He was educated at Washington college, Pennsylvania, and graduated from that institute in 1825. He studied law with the Hon. John P. Mayberry, of Marietta; was admitted to the bar in 1829, and engaged in the practice of his profession at Harmar.

In 1840 he was elected prosecuting attorney of the county. In 1845 he was again elected prosecuting attorney.

About 1876 he moved to the State of Illinois, and is located near Quincy, extensively engaged in agricultural pursuits.

LEVI HART GODDARD, son of Hon. Calvin Goddard, was born at Norwich, Connecticut, in 1810. He studied law and was admitted to the bar in his native State. In 1835 he removed to Marietta, Ohio, and then engaged in the practice of his profession. After a short residence in Marietta he returned to Norwich and there resumed the practice of law and continued the same until the time of his death. He died of pneumonia, in 1862.

Mr. Goddard was a lawyer of learning and ability, as counsellor and consulting attorney, and his amiable and cheery social qualities made for him hosts of friends. He was married in 1835 to Miss Mary Woodbridge Perkins, of Norwich.

RUFUS E. HARTE, was born in Middlebury, now embraced in the corporation limits of Akron, Ohio. He attended the academy at Tallmadge and the preparatory department of the Western Reserve college at Hudson. In 1833 he was graduated at Yale college, Connecticut. He studied law with Hon. Gregory Powers, of Akron. In 1835, at the session of the supreme court at Medina, he was admitted to the bar. In 1837 he located at Marietta and engaged in the practice of his profession, associated with Mr. W. A. Whittlesey as Whittlesey & Harte.

In 1839 he was married to Julia Holden, daughter of Mr. Joseph Holden, of Marietta.

In 1845 he was elected senator in the Ohio legislature from the district composed of the counties of Washington, Morgan and Perry.

In 1851 he was elected prosecuting attorney for the county of Washington.

In 1852 he was elected, by the trustees of the benevolent institutions of Ohio, superintendent of the institution for the blind, and resided at Columbus four years, discharging the duties of that office.

In 1856 he returned to Marietta and resumed the practice of law, associated therein with Mr. Melvin Clarke.

In 1861 he was elected treasurer of Washington county, and held that office for a period of four years.

In 1880 he was elected mayor of the city of Marietta, and is now discharging the duties of that office.

CHARLES F. BUELL, son of Daniel H. Buell, of Marietta, was born in Washington county, Ohio, March 12, 1814. He was a student in Marietta college and Kenyon college; studied law with Hon. Samuel F. Vinton, of Gallipolis, and was admitted to the bar in 1837. He practiced law a short time at Gallipolis, and about a year at Georgetown, Brown county, Ohio. In 1839 he returned to Marietta and engaged in the practice of his profession.

In 1860 he was elected probate judge of Washington county. After serving three years in that office he resumed the practice of law at Marietta, where he now resides.

WILLIAM D. EMERSON, eldest son of Caleb and Mary (Dana) Emerson, was born at Marietta, July 9, 1813. He was prepared for college by Rev. Luther G. Bingham, then pastor of the Congregational church at Marietta. At the age of sixteen he entered the Ohio university at Athens, from which he graduated in 1833, with the highest honors of his class. He was one of the teachers in the high school which opened up in Library hall, on Front street, which afterwards unfolded into Marietta college. In 1836 he was assistant editor with his father on the Marietta *Gazette*. His health failing in this department, he went west and spent two years as a common school teacher. The scenery of the wide west seems to have inspired his poetic fancy, and some of his finest poems, which aftewards came into print, were produced at this time.

He returned to Marietta in 1839, studied law, was admitted to the bar in 1841, and for several years kept a law office with his father. In 1845 he prepared and published the first map of Washington county. He was prosecuting attorney of that county for one year, ending March, 1848, filling the unexpired term of Arius Nye, esq., who was appointed presiding judge. He was assistant clerk in the commercial court of Cincinnati from 1848 to 1852, and for four years after made up records in the clerk's office of the Cincinnati and Hamilton county courts. He kept a law office in Cincinnati till 1860. Since that time he has devoted himself mainly to literary pursuits. The bent of his mind was more for literature than jurisprudence. In 1851 he issued Occasional Thoughts in Verse, for private distribution. In 1874 he issued a second volume of verse, and is now preparing a second edition of an agricultural work.

ARIUS SPENCER NYE, son of Arius Nye was admitted to the bar about 1840, and in company with his father practiced law at Marietta as Nye & Son.

In 1846 he was elected cashier of the Ross County bank, branch of the State bank of Ohio and removed to Chillicothe, where he now resides.

DARWIN E. GARDNER, son of William and Sarah B. (Earl) Gardner, was born at Norwalk, Ohio, January 25, 1820.

Pursuant to his father's wishes, and to some extent under his supervision, he pursued a thorough course of preparatory studies and about 1839 was graduated at the Western Reserve college. He studied law with Judge Crowell of Warren, Ohio, and was admitted to the bar at Newark in 1841.

The same year he located at Marietta and commenced the practice of his profession and successfully prosecuted the same at that place until 1851, when he removed to Cleveland, and soon thereafter to Toledo, where, until the time of his death he was extensively and prosperously engaged in the purchase and sale of real estate. He died at Toledo August 5, 1867, at the age of forty-seven. Mr. Gardner was an able lawyer, and an enterprising and successful man of business, and in the several places of his residence had the confidence and esteem of his fellow citizens. He was married in 1842, to Miss Elizabeth P. Putnam, of Hudson, Ohio who died in 1846, and in 1859 he married Miss Sarah Williams of Norwalk.

WYLIE H. OLDHAM, son of Samuel and Rebecca Oldham, was born November 21, 1819, at the old homestead in Ohio county, Virginia, where his grandfather and father lived and died. When about one year old, he was taken to the State of New York, where his father was employed as a missionary, teaching the Seneca Indians, lived in Cornplanter's town, remembered well the wild scenes in which his early boyhood was spent. Leaving there at five and a half years of age, he acquired such an education as the primitive schools of Virginia then afforded. In 1832 he entered the private academy at West Alexander, Washington county, Pennsylvania, under the charge of Rev. John McCluskey, pastor of the Presbyterian church of that place and pursued his academic studies under his care until September, 1836, when he entered the junior class in Washington college. He was a member of the Washington Literary society, graduated in June, 1838, and took the first honor of his society and second of his class (the first honor of the class being by a rule of the faculty due that year to the Union society which alone prevented his obtaining the first honor of his class). In the fall of 1838 he went to Mount Vernon, Ohio, and spent one year in teaching. In the fall of 1839 he went to Lexington, Kentucky, and taught one year, near the home of Henry Clay, visiting him frequently in 1840. He studied law with Isaac Hoge at Moundsville, Virginia, and was admitted to the bar in 1842. Shortly after he was elected prosecuting attorney. He represented Marshall county in the Virginia legislature in 1846-7 and 8. He practiced law at Moundsville from the time he was admitted to the bar until May, 1865. May 23, 1844, he married Mary Curtis, daughter of R. C. Curtis of Moundsville.

In May, 1865 he moved to Marietta, Ohio, where he resided until the time of his death, engaged extensively and successfully in the practice of his profession. He died July 22, 1875. Mr. Oldham's memory will be cherished by his neighbors and acquaintances on account of his marked characteristics in social life. The cordiality of his greetings, the vivacity of his conversation, his wit-beaming repartee and entire freedom from censoriousness made him everybody's favorite and his company was eagerly sought and merrily enjoyed by his associates.

Mr. Oldham was an orator, and as statesman and lawyer his speeches and arguments were models of beauty and eloquence. He was a good citizen, a liberal contributor to benevolent enterprises, a man of principle honor and fidelity, whose death was deeply lamented by all who knew him.

JOHN T. GUITTEAU, son of Benjamin Guitteau, was born in Fearing township, Washington county, Ohio, in 1821.

He was educated at Marietta college; studied law with Hon. Arius Nye, of Marietta, and was admitted to the bar in 1842. He commenced practice at Urbana, Ohio, associated with Hon. Thomas Corwin, and about 1843 moved to Cincinnati. After a residence of three or four years at Cincinnati he removed to New York city, where he now resides, engaged in the practice of law.

CHARLES R. RHODES was born in Zanesville, November 5, 1819; the third child of Dr. Dudley Woodbridge Rhodes. He went to school in the preparatory department of Kenyon college in 1835, entered the freshman class in 1836, and graduated in course of 1840, taking the second honor of his class.

He entered his name as a student of law in the office of Messrs. Goddard & Converse, Zanesville, and was admitted to the bar at Newark, Ohio, in 1843. The same year he removed to St. Louis, Missouri, to establish himself as a lawyer, where he remained until the fall of 1836. The same year, having married Miss Mary E. Ward, the third child of Hon. Nahum Ward, of Marietta, he returned to Ohio, and made his residence in Marietta, where he still resides.

In January, 1855, he was elected prosecuting attorney, and continued in that office until January, 1857. In February, 1858, he was elected probate judge of Washington county, and continued in office until February, 1861.

During the War of the Rebellion the people living in the little township along the Ohio river, were kept in a constant state of alarm, apprehending incursions from the lawless bands of rebels roving through West Virginia. Mr. Rhodes organized a company of from forty to sixty men, which, through the friendly assistance of Colonel William Craig, quartermaster of the United States army stationed in Marietta, he was able to arm and equip, and which he, as captain, kept in thorough drill and discipline, prepared for the emergencies of the times.

He was appointed by the governor of the State (Hon. Rutherford B. Hayes) delegate to the National Commercial convention, which met at Cincinnati, and the following year he was again appointed by the governor delegate for southeastern Ohio to the same convention, which met at Baltimore.

Mr. Rhodes' whole life in Marietta has been closely identified with the manufacturing and commercial enterprises of the town, and especially with the history and prosperity of St. Luke's Protestant Episcopal church and Sunday-school, for more than thirty years a member and secretary of the vestry, many times their delegate to the diocesan convention, and for more than twenty years superintendent of the Sunday-school.

MELVIN CLARKE was born at Ashfield, Massachusetts, November 15, 1818, and was the oldest of a family of eight children. He was the son of Stephen and Roxy Alden Clarke, and of the seventh generation in a direct line from John Alden, of Mayflower fame. His early education was derived from the common schools of Whately, Franklin county, Massachusetts; a few terms spent in select school, and a few months at the academy at Conway, Massachusetts. He came west in the fall of 1838, and taught school in Kentucky, at Parkersburgh, in West Virginia, and in this county for a series of years. Meanwhile he was studying law, and was admitted to the bar in 1843, and settled in law practice at McConnels-

ville, Morgan county, Ohio, and continued in the practice there for ten years.

In 1853 he removed to Marietta, and continued to practice his profession until the beginning of the war. He became a leading member of the bar, and an influential citizen.

Of his mind the distinguishing features were clearness and strength of comprehension. He had the ability to analyze, arrange, and present, in a forcible manner, the evidence in a case, and conducted, with marked talent, the important causes committed to him.

Impelled by motives of patriotism, he, with others, was actively instrumental, at the breaking out of the war, in raising and organizing the Thirty-sixth regiment, Ohio volunteer infantry, and was appointed its lieutenant colonel, and served in that capacity as a brave and gallant officer until killed by a shot from a ten-pound shell at the battle of Antietam, September 17, 1862.

He was buried with military honors in Mound cemetery, at Marietta, and a monument erected to his memory by his army comrades and associates of the bar.

He married Miss Dorcas Dana, daughter of William Dana, of Newport, Ohio, for his first wife, who died about 1850, and left one son, Joseph D. Clarke, who was killed in the war at City Point, Maryland, in 1864. He married, as his second wife, Miss Sophia Browning, of Belpre, Ohio. He was, at the time of his death, a member of the Congregational church, of Marietta.

SAMUEL JAMES ANDREWS, fourth son of Rev. William Andrews, was born at Danbury, Connecticut, July 30, 1817. He graduated at Williams college in 1839, and came to Marietta in May, 1844. He remained a member of the Marietta bar not quite a year, when he left the practice of law and began the study of theology. He was settled over the Congregational church at East Windsor, Connecticut, for some years, since which he has resided at Hartford, engaged in literary pursuits, and in giving instruction in Trinity college. The degree of Doctor of Divinity has been conferred upon him by Union college, Schenectady, New York.

SAMUEL B. ROBINSON was born at Washington, Pennsylvania, February 15, 1814, and was educated at Washington, now Washington and Jefferson, college, of that State. In 1835 he was editor of the *Washington Reporter*. In 1836, with his widowed mother and her family, he moved to Lake Chute and shortly thereafter to Beverly, Ohio. In 1837, at Beverly, in partnership with John Dodge, he engaged in mercantile business and continued therein for seven years. He studied law, Hon. Isaac Paine being his preceptor, and was admitted to the bar in 1844, and entered upon the practice of his profession in Beverly.

In 1846 he married Colina N., youngest daughter of John Dodge, of Beverly.

In 1846 he was elected prosecuting attorney of the county. In 1873 he was again elected prosecuting attorney, and the duties of this office he ably and faithfully discharged. Mr. Robinson was never of robust frame, and during the latter period of his life was in very poor health. On the night of January 2, 1878, while travelling by steamer from Beverly to Marietta, he fell overboard and was drowned. His body was recovered and buried by the side of his deceased wife in the Beverly cemetery. During his career in life as editor, merchant, and lawyer, Mr. Robinson deserved and received the confidence and esteem of his fellow citizens.

DAVIS GREEN, son of Rev. Allen Green, was born in Tyler county, Virginia, February 11, 1822. In 1823 his parents came to Ohio and settled on a farm in Belmont county.

Davis attended, in the winter season, the schools of his neighborhood and at the age of twenty-one years completed his education at Madison college, Guernsey county. In 1842 and the two following years he was partially engaged in teaching, and in the meantime studied law in the office of Judge Evans of Cambridge. For nearly a year after the fall of 1845 he was editor and part owner of the *Guernsey Times*.

In 1846 he was admitted to the bar at Mount Vernon and in the fall of the same year located at Marietta and commenced the practice of law. By close application and diligence he soon became prominent in his profession.

In 1849 he was elected prosecuting attorney of the county, and for two years ably discharged the duties of that office.

In 1854 he was elected probate judge, and served his three years' term to the entire satisfaction of the public.

In 1856 he was elected one of the electors for Ohio of President and Vice-President of the United States, and voted for Fremont and Dayton.

In 1858 he was elected senator in the Ohio legislature from the district composed of Washington and Morgan counties, and was an eloquent, influential and highly esteemed member from that body.

In 1861 at the breaking out of the Rebellion he took a decided and prominent part in defence of the Government, and labored unremittingly to encourage and promote the cause of the Union.

Judge Green was a man of great energy, industry and determination, and bid fair to become a jurist and statesman of high rank. In the prime of his life and the midst of his influence he died at Marietta, August 22, 1862. He was married in 1851 to Miss Columbia Ferguson, who is now the wife of Dr. D. Walter, of Marietta.

WILLIAM SPENCER NYE, son of Arius Nye, was graduated at Marietta college, in 1843. He studied law with his father, and was admitted to the bar in 1845.

He commenced practice in Marietta, associated with his brother, Dudley S. Nye, as D. S. & W. S. Nye.

He was elected and served as prosecuting attorney of the county from March, 1848, to March, 1850. About 1854 he was appointed attorney for the Marietta & Cincinnati railroad company. In 1861 he was again prosecuting attorney of the county. Shortly thereafter he removed to Chillicothe, Ohio, where he died of typhoid fever in 1862.

Mr. Nye was an accomplished gentleman, and a lawyer of fine abilities and attainments. A rather sensitive and retiring disposition inclined him to shrink somewhat from the more rugged conflict of the court room practice, and to thus take a less conspicuous position as a trial lawyer than his legal learning and acumen entitled him to occupy. It was for his breadth, soundness and candor of view, as a counsellor, that he was best known in the profession.

His disposition was peculiarly amiable, and in his domestic and social life he was a most genial companion, and warmly attached to himself all who knew him intimately.

SELDEN S. COOKE, son of Rev. Parden Cooke, was admitted to the bar in November, 1843, at the session of the supreme court in Morgan county, and commenced practice at Marietta. In 1849 and 1850 he was elected and served as recorder of the city of Marietta.

In 1851 he removed to Chillicothe, Ohio, where he now resides, engaged in the practice of law.

DUDLEY SELDEN NYE, son of Arius Nye, was admitted to the bar at the November term, 1843, of the supreme court, sitting in Morgan county. In 1847 he and his brother, William S. Nye, associated themselves in the practice of law at Marietta, succeeding to the business of Arius Nye & Son, as D. S. & W. S. Nye, and continued to practice until the autumn of 1852.

In 1852 he removed to Tennessee, and in the spring of 1855 removed to Council Bluffs, Iowa, and in 1857 was elected county judge of Pottawatomie county, in that State. In November, 1862, he returned to Marietta, where he now resides, engaged in the practice of law.

HENRY A. TOWNE was born January 5, 1826, at Litchfield, Herkimer county, State of New York. Upon the death of his father, Rev. Abner Towne, pastor of the Presbyterian church at Litchfield, his mother returned with her son, then five months old, to her parents at Amherst, Massachusetts; and coming afterwards to Gallipolis, Ohio, the residence of her brother, Hon. S. F. Vinton, married May 28, 1831, Dr. Robert Safford, of Putnam, Ohio, now the ninth ward of Zanesville, at which time the subject of this sketch became a resident of Ohio. He entered Marietta college when fifteen years of age, and graduated in 1845; was admitted to the bar at Cincinnati, Ohio, in 1849, and practiced law at Marietta, Ohio, in partnership with Hon. William A. Whittlesey from 1849 to 1854, and afterwards with David Green, esq, now deceased, until his removal to Portsmouth, Ohio, December 1, 1855, where he entered upon the practice of the law. He married, December 18, 1856, Harriet Nye, daughter of Judge Arius Nye, now deceased.

In 1858 he was elected one of the judges of the court of common pleas of the seventh judicial district of Ohio, and held that position until July, 1870, when he resigned and resumed the practice of law at Portsmouth.

He has been connected with several of the furnaces of the Hanging Rock iron region, and is now a stockholder and director in the Globe Iron company, of Jackson,

Ohio; and is also a stockholder and director in the Scioto Star Fire-brick works at East Portsmouth, Ohio.

In April, 1879, he was elected mayor of the city of Portsmouth, and is now discharging the duties of that office. In 1880 he was appointed supervisor of census of the fourth district of Ohio, and superintended the taking of the census in the eleven counties comprising the district.

RODNEY M. STIMSON was born in Milford, New Hampshire, October 26, 1824. He attended Philips' Exter academy, New Hampshire, during three years preceding 1845, when he entered Marietta college and graduated from that institution in 1847. He studied law, and in 1849 was admitted to the bar at Marietta. Soon thereafter he removed to Ironton, Lawrence county, Ohio, and there established the *Register*, a newspaper which, as editor and proprietor, he successfully conducted for twelve years. In 1862 he removed to Marietta, and there edited and published the *Marietta Register* during the ten years following. In 1869 he was elected senator in the Ohio legislature and was reelected in 1871, serving four years. In 1877 he was appointed State librarian, and for two years acceptably discharged the duties of that office. His residence is at Marietta where he has a library of over two thousand carefully selected volumes, has charge of the Marietta College library, and is also treasurer of that institution. He devotes his time to literary pursuits. He has been twice married, first in 1851, and again in 1862.

SAMUEL S. KNOWLES son of Samuel and Clarissa Curtis) Knowles, was born in Athens, Ohio, August 25), 1825. In 1846 and the three years following he was a student in the academy and the Ohio university at Athens. After finishing his course of studies at the university he read law with Lot L. Smith and L. Jewett at Athens, and was admitted to the bar in 1851. During the same year he was elected prosecuting attorney of Athens county, was reelected in 1853, and held that office for four years. In 1861 he removed from Athens to Marietta, engaging in the latter place in the practice of his profession. In 1864 he was commissioned captain of a company in the One Hundred and Forty-eight regiment, Ohio national guard, and served with his company, stationed at Bermuda Hundred, until September of that year, when the regiment was mustered out of service. In 1864 he was elected mayor of the city of Marietta, and reelected in 1866, serving four years. In 1865 he was elected senator in the Ohio legislature from the counties of Washington, Morgan, and Noble, serving two years. In 1875 he was elected judge of the court of common pleas, of the Third subdivision, of the Seventh judicial district of Ohio, to fill a vacancy caused by the resignation of Judge Plants, and in 1878 he was reelected for the full term of five years, and is now engaged in the discharge of the duties of his office. He was married January 23, 1852, to Henrietta, youngest daughter of Captain Charles Devol, of Hockingport, Athens county.

THOMAS W. EWART, LL. D., was born February 27, 1816, at Grandview, Washington county, Ohio. His mother, Mary Cochran, was a native of West Virginia, of Scotch descent; and his father, Robert K. Ewart, a Pennsylvanian, of Irish parentage. Thomas received such early education as he could obtain in the common schools of that date, in which he was a diligent and ambitious student.

September 30, 1831, he left school and farm, and entered as an assistant in the office of clerk of the court of Washington county, where he improved his time not demanded in the office in studies under private instructors. He was appointed clerk of the court of this county in December, 1836, and continued in office until October, 1851. While still clerk of the court he was elected to represent Washington and Morgan counties in the Constitutional convention of 1850, which formed the present constitution of Ohio, and was one of its youngest members. On the expiration of his term as clerk of the court he was elected probate judge of Washington county, the first under the new constitution.

In the meantime, while in the prosecution of official duties as clerk of the court, he had pursued a rigid course of legal study under Judge Nye, and when attending the Constitutional convention at Cincinnati in 1851, was admitted to practice in the courts of Ohio.

He held the office of probate judge one year, and resigned to practice his profession, in which he has had a good degree of success, and attained a prominent position as a lawyer of recognized ability. He has recently opened an office and is practicing law at Columbus, Ohio.

In politics he was a Whig, serving as chairman of the central committee of the county for many years. At the organization of the Republican party he identified himself with that party and so continues.

As a citizen he has been active, enterprising, seeking the welfare of the community; especially so in connection with the temperance and Sunday-school movements.

A member of, and liberal contributor to, the Baptist church, he has been superintendent of the Marietta Baptist Sunday-school forty years, and deacon of that church thirty years.

In 1838 he married Grace Dana, of Newport, who died in 1854; and in 1855 he married his present wife, Jerusha Gear, daughter of Rev. H. Gear, late of Marietta, deceased.

WILLIAM P. RICHARDSON was born in Washington county, Pennsylvania, May 25, 1824. In 1841 he entered Washington college and pursued there a three-years' course of study. In 1846 he enlisted as a volunteer in the "Steubenville Greys," a company raised for the Mexican war, and assigned to the Third Ohio regiment. After his return from Mexico he was engaged for several years teaching in Brooke county, Virginia, and Harrison county, Ohio, and in the meantime studied law with Allen C. Turner, of Cadiz, and was there admitted to the bar in 1852. In 1853 he moved from Harrison county to Woodsfield, in Monroe county, Ohio, and after a year's employment as principal of the Monroe academy, commenced there the practice of law in partnership with L. C. Wise, and afterwards with Edward Nechbold.

In 1855 he was elected prosecuting attorney for Monroe county, and was reelected in 1857 and again in 1859. In 1861, soon after the attack on Fort Sumter, he raised two companies of volunteers, which were assigned to the Twenty-fifth Ohio infantry, three years' service, of which regiment he was appointed major, and soon after lieutenant colonel, and with that rank proceeded to the field. In 1862 he was promoted to the colonelcy of his regiment. In 1863, at the battle of Chancellorsville he was wounded in the right shoulder, and on account of the severity of the wound was an invalid for eight months. In January, 1864, he was detailed as president of a general court-martial at Camp Chase, near Columbus, Ohio, and in February following was placed in command of that post. In October, 1864, he was elected attorney general of the State of Ohio, and it was his intention to retire from the army, but upon the urgent solicitation of Governor Brough, he resigned the attorney generalship and remained in the service. The same year he was brevetted brigadier general. In 1865 he was ordered to Charleston, from thence to Columbia, and finally to Darlington, in command of the district of East South Carolina. In June, 1866, he resigned his position in the army. In July, 1866, he was appointed collector of internal revenue for the Fifteenth district of Ohio, and in November moved from Woodsfield to Marietta. In May, 1869, he resigned his office of collector, and since then has been engaged at Marietta in the successful practice of his profession as lawyer. As a commanding officer General Richardson possessed the confidence and esteem of his men. His services in detached positions have been frequently commended. He has been connected professionally with various enterprises, and was a director of the Marietta & Cleveland railroad. He was married in 1848 to Sarah E. Smith, of Brooke county, West Virginia, who died at Marietta, May 11, 1879.

HARVEY HOLLAND was born in Oswego county, New York, June 19, 1815.

In 1818 he came with his father to Woodsfield, Monroe county, Ohio.

In 1839 he moved from Woodsfield to Ludlow township, Washington county, Ohio. He was elected and served two terms as justice of the peace, and in the meantime studied law, and in 1853 was admitted to the bar. He continues to reside in Ludlow engaged in the practice of law in Washington and adjoining counties.

DAVID ALBAN studied law in the office of Hon. Samuel F. Vinton, of Gallipolis, Ohio.

In the spring of 1855 he was admitted to the bar by the district court sitting in Gallia county.

In the summer of 1855 he removed to Marietta and commenced practice in partnership with Hon. Arius Nye.

In 1862 he volunteered as a private soldier in the United States service, and served with his regiment, the Eighty-seventh Ohio volunteer infantry, until he was taken prisoner at Harper's Ferry, September 13, 1862, and parolled.

In 1861 he was elected prosecuting attorney of the

county, and was reelected in 1863 and in 1865, serving for six consecutive years.

For several years he has been associated with Hon. W. B. Loomis, in the law firm of Loomis & Alban, now engaged in the practice of law at Marietta.

In 1879 he was again elected prosecuting attorney of the county, and now holds that office.

RODNEY K. SHAW is a native of Copenhagen in the town of Denmark, county of Lewis, and State of New York, born December 13, 1829. His early opportunities for improvement were those of the district school, and as clerk in his father's store. At twenty he began an academic course at Union academy at Belleville, New York, which was continued at Lowville academy, Lowville, New York, until his admission to the bar. He pursued the study of the law in the offices of Hon. N. B. Sylvester, now of Saratoga, New York, and Hon. E. S. Merrell, of Lowville. He taught at intervals and during vacation, teaching one year each in Virginia and Mississippi. Previous to his admission to the bar he was awarded a life certificate by the department of public instruction of New York. He was admitted to the bar at the general term of the supreme court of New York at Utica, January 2, 1855, and practiced four years in his native county. In 1859 his father having become a helpless invalid, he came to West Virginia, and cared for him until his death.

In March, 1860, he entered the office of Thomas W. Ewart as a clerk, was admitted to the bar on motion, at the April term of the district court in 1860, and continued as clerk in Mr. Ewart's office until the summer of 1861, when he was given a lieutenant's commission to recruit for the Sixty-third Ohio volunteer infantry. At the organization of the regiment he was made captain of company G, one of the companies raised in Washington county, and served with that regiment in the Ohio brigade until the fall of 1862, when he was discharged on surgeon's certificate.

In the fall of 1863 he became a partner of Thomas W. Ewart, and continued in that relation until 1870, under the firm names of Ewart & Shaw, Ewart, Shaw & Sibley, and again as Ewart & Shaw, and since 1870 has been practicing alone. He is a member of the American Bar association.

CHARLES R. BARCLAY located at Beverly, Ohio, and commenced the practice of law about 1856. He was elected mayor of Beverly, and served one term. In 1858 he was elected prosecuting attorney of the county, and served two years. After a residence of a few years in Beverly, he removed to Missouri, and in that State is successfully engaged in the practice of his profession.

WILLIAM B. LOOMIS was born in New London, Connecticut, February 1, 1837. In the spring of 1840 he came with the family of his father, Christopher C. Loomis, to Marietta, Ohio, where his father engaged in the mercantile business. He attended the Marietta academy, and completed his early education at the Marietta high school, having in 1853 graduated with the first class of graduates from that school. After leaving school he was engaged for a few months as merchants' clerk, after which he was employed as deputy clerk of the court of common pleas and clerk of the probate court of Washington county, Ohio. During his clerkship in those courts he studied law with Messrs. Clarke & Ewart, and in April, 1857, was admitted to the bar by the district court in Washington county. He then engaged in the practice of his profession at Marietta, in partnership with Thomas W. Ewart, esq., which relation continued until the fall of 1859. In the spring of 1860 he became the law partner of Melvin Clarke, and so continued until Colonel Clarke was killed in the battle at Antietam in 1862. He was married October 1, 1860, to Harriet Frances Wheeler, daughter of F. J. Wheeler, esq., of Marietta. In 1862 he was elected city solicitor of the city of Marietta, which office he held for four years. From the spring of 1863 to May, 1865, he was associated with the late Judge Simeon Nash, of Gallipolis, as partner in the practice of law at Marietta, when he became the law partner of Samuel S. Knowles, and so remained until June, 1868, at which time he was elected judge of the court of common pleas of the third subdivision of the seventh judicial district of Ohio, and held that position for five years.

In March, 1879, his wife died, and in June, 1880, he was married to Mrs. N. C. Hodkinson, of Marietta.

After his retirement from the bench he resumed his position at the bar, and is now senior member of the law firm of Loomis & Alban, of Marietta, successfully engaged in the practice in the State and Federal courts.

WILLIAM M. RAMSEY was born in Washington county, Pennsylvania. In 1845 he came with the family of his father, Dr. Robert Ramsey, to Beverly, Washington county, Ohio, where his father commenced, and for two years acceptably and successfully continued, the practice of medicine.

In 1847, upon the decease of his father, he returned with the family from Beverly to Washington county, Pennsylvania, where his early education was obtained. He studied law with Hon. William Montgomery, of Washington, Pennsylvania.

In 1857 he was admitted to the bar; located in Marietta, Ohio, and commenced practice as an attorney at law. In 1858 he was a candidate for the office of prosecuting attorney, nominated by the Democratic party. In 1859 he removed from Marietta to Cincinnati, where he entered upon the practice of his profession, in which he has been eminently successful, and has attained a high position as a member of the Ohio bar. He was married in 1860 to Miss Mary Frances Hart, of Cincinnati.

HENRY MANASSEH DAWES was born at Malta, Morgan county, Ohio, March 11, 1832. He was the eldest son of the late Henry Dawes, a prominent and active citizen of that county, and a grandson of Manasseh Cutler, whose life is recorded in this volume. His boyhood was spent at Malta, from whence he came to Marietta about the year 1850, and pursued a regular course at Marietta college, graduating in 1855, after which he studied law in the office of the late Hon. Davis Green, and was admitted to the bar at the April term of the district court of Wash-

ington county, 1858. He at once became a partner of Judge Green, and continued in the practice at Marietta until his death, which occurred August 13, 1860.

Mr. Dawes was endowed with a mind of unusual strength, quick perception, and fine reasoning powers, and his talents and acquirements gave promise of great professional success and distinction.

Descended from a line of ancestors who participated in the stormy events of the Revolution, he seemed to have inherited the patriotic spirit of that period, and developed an early fondness for the study of the political history of the country, and for active participation in political discussion. When yet a student he delivered a course of lectures upon the life and times of Henry Clay, the "Great American Commoner," in which he gave evidence that he comprehended the spirit of our institutions. He was also a frequent contributor to the local press on these subjects.

A man of decision and firmness, unyielding where principle was involved, he was at the same time genial, generous, and courteous to all, and having a face full of tenderness and indicating a frank and kindly nature, he was one whom to know well was both to respect and love. His untimely death was the cause of general sorrow and regret, and deprived the bar of a member who would have honored the calling.

FRANK BUELL was born at Lowell, Washington county, Ohio, April 24, 1837. He studied law with Hon. W. A. Whittlesey, of Marietta, and in January, 1859, was admitted to the bar. In 1859 he was elected prosecuting attorney of the county. In 1861, at the breaking out of the war of the Rebellion, he resigned his office as prosecuting attorney and was commissioned as captain of company B, Eighteenth Ohio regiment, in the three months' service. Afterwards, in the fall of the same year, from recruits residing on the borders of Ohio and West Virginia, he raised an artillery company, the Pierpont battery, and by the governor of West Virginia was appointed and commissioned captain of the same. With his command he was in the campaigns in West Virginia, under Generals Fremont, Schenck, and Siegel, was engaged in several severe artillery duels, and in the battles of Cross Keys, Port Republic and Cedar Mountain.

On the twenty-second of August, 1862, at Freeman's Ford, in Fauquier county, Virginia, whilst engaged in an artillery skirmish, a shell from the enemy's battery struck the ground beneath his horse, and bursting, a piece passed through the horse and broke the captain's thigh. The horse fell dead across the captain's body, inflicting internal injuries from which he died in a few hours.

Captain Buell, during his short career as soldier, was the favorite with his command, and his services were highly commended by his superior officers. His speedy promotion to a colonelcy of artillery was contemplated by the Government.

WALTER BRABHAM was born in Loudoun county, Virginia, September 29, 1812. He obtained his early education at the common schools of that county, and commenced the study of law with William Benton, esq.

In 1835 he moved from Virginia to Ohio, and in Morgan county, and afterwards in Washington county, was engaged for several years in the business of teaching, merchandizing, and farming.

In 1859, having completed a course of law studies, under the preceptorship of Hon. Davis Green, of Marietta, he was admitted to the bar and commenced the practice of law.

In 1867 he was elected prosecuting attorney of Washington county, and was again elected to the same office in 1871, and acceptably discharged the duties thereof until 1873.

He continues to reside at Harmar, engaged in the practice of law.

M. D. FOLLETT was admitted to the bar in the fall of 1858. A sketch of Mr. Follett is given elsewhere in this work.

REUBEN L. NYE, son of Ichabod H. Nye and Miriam C. Linnel, of Granville, Ohio, was born at Marietta, October 28, 1836; attended Marietta high school and preparatory department, Marietta college; was for several years employed as a clerk in the hardware store of his uncle, A. T. Nye; studied with his uncle, Arius Nye, and was admitted to practice, 1860.

He volunteered as a private soldier, April 15, 1861, and served with his regiment, Seventeenth Ohio volunteers, in West Virginia, until July following, when he was commissioned second lieutenant Thirty-sixth Ohio volunteers; promoted to captain, April, 1862; served through the war and mustered out at Columbus, July 27, 1865. The last year of his service he was employed on staff and court-martial duty in departments of the Cumberland and West Virginia.

He commenced practice at Marietta, in the fall of 1865, with Colonel David Alban; afterwards associated with H. L. Sibley, as Sibley & Nye; and now with F. F. Oldham, as Nye & Oldham. Married Helen McLeod, of Topsfield, Massachusetts, May 21, 1867. He was elected prosecuting attorney of Washington county in 1869, and served as such from January, 1870, to January, 1872. He was elected solicitor of the city of Marietta in 1872 and 1874, and served as such for a period of four years. He held the office of register in bankruptcy under the act of 1867.

HIRAM L. GEAR, son of Rev. H. Gear, was born at Marietta, Ohio, December 1, 1842, prepared for college in the High school of Marietta, and entered Marietta college in 1858, and graduated therefrom in 1862.

After acting as tutor in Marietta college for one year, he read law with Thomas W. Ewart, and then removed to California, where he was admitted to practice by the supreme court of that State. He was an energetic young man, of a logical turn of mind, and entered heartily into the active business life of the community; and, while at Quincy, Plumas county, California, was elected prosecuting attorney. Subsequently he became editor of the Plumas County *Herald*, at Quincy, California, which position he held until his return to Marietta in the fall of 1870. Here he again engaged in the practice of the law,

as partner in the firm of Ewart, Gear & Ewart, and continued in that business until the fall of 1872, when, impelled by the impression that he ought to preach the gospel as his father had done, he left the law and became a minister, preaching at Newport, Ohio, Norwalk, Ohio, and finally he was called to the position of superintendent of State missions of the Baptist denomination, which position he now holds, residing at Granville, Ohio.

THOMAS R. SHEPPARD, son of Charles J. Sheppard, was born in Washington county, Ohio, and was educated in the public schools of Marietta city.

In 1864 he volunteered as a private soldier in the One Hundred and Forty-eighth regiment, Ohio volunteer infantry, National Guard, and served until he was mustered out with the regiment. He studied law in the office of Messrs. Knowles & Loomis, of Marietta, and in 1867 was admitted to the bar. Soon afterwards he removed to Mississippi, where he remained until 1871, engaged in the practice of law.

Since 1871 he has been located and practicing in Marietta, Ohio.

HIRAM L. SIBLEY was admitted to the bar of Marietta in April, 1865. A sketch of him is given elsewhere in this work.

JOSHUA T. CREW, son of Thomas and Ann (Andrews) Crew, was born at Chesterfield, Morgan county, Ohio, October 5, 1844. He studied law with M. D. Follett, of Marietta, was admitted to the bar in 1868, and commenced practice at Marietta, in partnership with Mr. Follett.

In 1869 he removed from Marietta to McConnellsville.

In 1876 he located at Zanesville, where he now resides, engaged in the practice of law.

JAMES W. COLLETT, was born in Wood county, West Virginia, April 23, 1828, and was educated at Parkersburgh, Virginia. He was engaged for some years in mercantile business at Newport, Washington county, Ohio. He studied law with Hon. Davis Green, at Marietta, and in 1868, was admitted to the bar. He resides at Newport and is engaged in the practice of his profession.

WILLIAM G. WAY was born at Marietta, Ohio, July 22, 1842. He studied law with Hon. W. H. Oldham, of Marietta, and was admitted to the bar at a term of the district court for Washington county, April 8, 1869, and commenced practice in Marietta.

In 1869 he was a candidate for prosecuting attorney, but was defeated. In 1871 he was elected representative in the Ohio legislature, served one term, and refused a renomination. In 1876 he was elected solicitor of the city of Marietta, and reelected in 1878 and 1880. He continues to reside at Marietta, engaged in the practice of his profession.

THOMAS EWART was born October 4, 1847, at Marietta, Ohio. He attended the public schools of Marietta and Marietta college until 1866, and then attended Dennison university, at Granville, Ohio, for three years, and graduated there in 1869. He read law with Ewart & Shaw, and was admitted to practice at the district court of Noble county, Ohio, in the fall of 1870. He then began the practice of law at Marietta, Ohio, with his father, Thomas W. Ewart, under the firm name of Ewart, Gear & Ewart, where he has continued in the practice to the present time, except a year and a half spent at Indianapolis in 1873 and 1874.

LUMAN W. CHAMBERLAIN, son of John D. and Thiora (Grow) Chamberlain, was born at Watertown, Ohio, December 1, 1828. He attended common schools and Western Liberal institute at Marietta, and taught school several terms.

In 1851 he was elected county surveyor, and by successive reelections held that office for ten years. In 1862 he was elected assistant sergeant-at-arms of the Ohio house of representatives, and served as such during the sessions of 1862 and 1863. In 1863 he was elected probate judge of Washington county, and reelected in 1866, serving six years.

In 1870, having completed a prepartory course of law studies with Hon. Thomas W. Ewart, he was admitted to the bar, and has since been engaged at Marietta in the practice of his profession, now associated with John A. Hamilton as Chamberlain & Hamilton.

MANLY W. MANN was admitted to the bar at Columbus, Ohio, about 1870. His residence is at Coal Run, Washington county, Ohio, where he is engaged in the practice of his profession.

SEYMOUR J. HATHAWAY, son of Luther, and Clarissa (Ripley) Hathaway was born in Macedon, Wayne county, New York, January 27, 1844. In 1853 he came with his father and family who then moved from Macedon to Marietta, Ohio.

In 1861, at the breaking out of the war, he was a student in the freshman class of the Marietta high school, when he enlisted in Captain William B. Mason's company, Third regiment Ohio militia, called into service by Governor Dennison, and served three months.

In 1864-5 he was engaged with the law firm of Ewart & Shaw, and afterwards with that of Knowles & Loomis in examining records and making abstracts of title to lands in the oil regions of southeastern Ohio.

In 1865, having pursued the required preparatory course of studies, he entered the freshman class of Marietta college and graduated at that institution in 1869. The same year he began the study of law with M. D. Follett, esq., of Marietta, and was admitted to the bar in 1871, and commenced practice at Marietta.

In 1874 he was elected city solicitor of Marietta city, and by direction of the council immediately began the revision of the city ordinances, which work was completed early in 1875.

He continues his residence at Marietta engaged in the practice of law.

He was married in 1876 to Miss Mary C. Means, daughter of William C. Means, of Marietta..

JOHN A. HAMILTON, son of Dr. David and Ruth (Allen) Hamilton, was born at Pittsburgh, Pennsylvania, August 2, 1847. In 1853 he came with his father's family to Marietta, Ohio, attended the public schools there

for his preliminary education, and completed it at the high school in that city.

In 1863 he entered the army as volunteer in the Second Ohio artillery. In 1864 he was detailed as private secretary to General Hugh Ewing, then commanding the Second division, district of Kentucky, and filled that position until 1865, when he was mustered out of the service.

He then returned to Marietta where for two or three years he was engaged in mercantile business.

In 1871, having completed a course of law studies with Colonel Alban, he was admitted to the bar. Since then he has been engaged in the practice of his profession at Marietta; a partner from 1871 to 1874 in the firm of Knowles, Alban & Hamilton; from 1874 to 1875 in the firm of Knowles & Hamilton, and since 1875 in the firm of Chamberlain & Hamilton.

He was married in 1872 to Mary M. Martin, of Pittsburgh, Pennsylvania.

CORNELIUS T. FRAZYER was born in New York city, June 15, 1836. He came to Washington county, Ohio, in the latter part of February, 1865; was deputy clerk of common pleas from June, 1872 to January, 1876; was admitted to the bar in this State in June, 1871; was elected probate judge in October, 1875, for three years from February 14, 1876, and reelected in the fall of 1878.

HARVEY HOLLAND, JR., son of Harvey Holland above mentioned, was born in Ludlow, Washington county, Ohio, July 6, 1845. In 1866 and for several years thereafter he was engaged in teaching, and in the meantime studied law and was admitted to the bar in 1872. In 1875 he located at Marietta and commenced the practice of law.

In 1878, on account of feeble and failing health he was obliged to abandon his law practice, and after travelling in the south seeking, unsuccessfully, restoration of strength he returned to Ludlow, where he now resides.

JOHN IRVINE, son of Dr. William Irvine, was born in Brownsville, Pennsylvania, October 17, 1835. He obtained his early education at the Brownsville academy.

In 1852 he removed with his widowed mother from Pennsylvania to Ohio, and settled in the western part of Washington county on a farm.

In 1866 he was appointed collector of tolls on the Muskingum improvement, and served in that capacity eleven years.

In 1872, having finished a course of law studies under the preceptorship of W. Brabham, esq., he was admitted to the bar and commenced practice in Harmar.

The same year he was elected mayor of Harmar, and was reelected in 1874.

In 1877 he was elected senator in Ohio legislature for the counties of Washington, Morgan and Noble, and served two years.

He continues to reside at Harmar engaged in the practice of law.

He was married in 1854 to Miss Fanny Irvine, of Decatur, Ohio.

FRANK F. OLDHAM, son of W. H. Oldham, above named was born at Moundsville, Virginia, March 3, 1849. He attended the Morgantown, West Virginia, academy during the four years preceding 1865, when he moved with his father to Marietta, Ohio, and in 1866 entered Marietta college, and graduated therefrom in 1870 with the highest honors of his class. He studied law with his father at Marietta, attended law lectures at Cincinnati, and was admitted to the bar in 1872. Immediately after his admission to the bar, he entered at Marietta, upon the practice of his profession, the first year in partnership with his father and W. G. Way, as Oldham, Way & Oldham; for the next four years with W. B. Loomis as Loomis & Oldham, and since 1876 in partnership with R. L. Nye, as Nye & Oldham.

In 1875 he was the nominee of the Democratic party for the office of prosecuting attorney of the county, and was elected, and reelected in 1877.

In January, 1876, he was married to Miss Betty W. Lovell, granddaughter of Mr. A. T. Nye, of Marietta.

JEWETT PALMER, son of Jewett Palmer who removed from New Hampshire to Washington county, Ohio, in 1818, was born at Fearing, Washington county, Ohio, May 7, 1840.

At the breaking out of the war he enlisted in Captain Frank Buell's company, B, Eighteenth regiment Ohio volunteer infantry, in the three months' service. At the close of this service he returned to Washington county, and with James Stanley, of Salem, recruited a company for the Thirty-sixth Ohio volunteer infantry, and was commissioned as captain of the same, and with that rank proceeded to the field and served with the regiment. In May, 1864, he was promoted to the rank of major. In November, 1864, after participating in the battle of Cedar Creek, the last battle in which his regiment was engaged, he resigned his commission and returned to Salem, Ohio.

In 1865 he was elected clerk of the court of Washington county, Ohio, and was reelected in 1868, and for the period of six years satisfactorily discharged the duties of that office.

In April, 1872, having pursued a course of legal studies with Everett, Green & Everett, of Marietta, he was admitted to the bar, opened an office at Marietta, and commenced practice as attorney and solicitor of patents.

In 1874 he was elected mayor of the city of Marietta, and was reelected in 1876.

In October, 1876, he resigned the mayoralty to accept the position of collector of internal revenue for the Fifteenth district of Ohio, tendered him by President Hayes, and since then has continued his residence at Marietta, engaged in the discharge of the duties of his office as collector.

In September, 1866, he was married to Miss Saida M. Scott, of Marietta.

ANDREW W. MCCORMICK was born in Greene county, Pennsylvania. He came to Marietta and published the Marietta *Republican* for some years preceding the fall of 1861, when he entered the military service, became captain in the Seventy-seventh Ohio volunteer infantry, was wounded, and twice taken prisoner during the war.

In 1867 he was admitted to the bar in Washington county. In 1869 he was elected probate judge of the county, and was reelected in 1872. He practiced law in Marietta from 1876 until 1878, when he removed to Cincinnati.

JASPER LISK was admitted to the bar about 1872. He resides at Matamoras, Washington county, Ohio, and is engaged in the practice of law.

FREDERICK J. CUTTER was born at Watertown, Washington county, Ohio, October 6, 1839. In 1859 he went to Cincinnati, and during the latter portion of his six years' residence in that city he attended Herron's seminary and Professor Clive's private school. In 1865 he entered the sophomore class of Marietta college and was graduated at that college in 1868. During the four years following he was engaged in teaching and in the care and management of his father's farm in Union township.

In 1872 he commenced reading law with Hon. T. W. Ewart, of Marietta, and in April, 1875, was admitted to the bar. In 1876 he opened an office in Marietta, where he is now engaged in the practice of his profession. He resides in Watertown township.

JAMES E. WAY, son of Joshua and Lucinda (Bishop) Way, was born in Union township, Washington county, Ohio, April 9, 1857. He received his early education at the common schools of Washington and Monroe counties, and attended the high schools at Woodsfield and Caldwell.

He studied law with Messrs. Oldham & Way, at Marietta, was admitted to the bar in 1875, and practiced for two years with Pearson & Doherty, of Woodsfield. In 1877 he returned to Marietta and formed a law partnership with his brother, William G. Way. In 1878 he removed to Beverly, Ohio, and engaged, and still continues, in the practice of his profession at that place.

In 1879 he was the nominee of the Democratic party for prosecuting attorney for Washington county, but was not elected.

In February, 1877, he was married to Miss Mary E. Hanson, of Stafford, Union county.

WILLIAM LOREY was born in Prussia about 1827. He emigrated to this country in 1849, came to Marietta in 1855, and established, and for about ten years, published the *Marietta Democrat*, the first German paper printed in the county.

In 1869 he was admitted to the bar in Washington county, and was engaged in the practice of law at Marietta until the time of his death in 1881.

CHARLES A. COOK, son of Silas Cook, esq., was born November 3, 1825. He studied law in the office of W. G. Way, of Marietta, and was admitted to the bar at a session of the district court for Washington county, April 3, 1877. He resides at Marietta, engaged in the practice of law.

DAVID R. ROOD, son of Richard H. and Mary A. (Williams) Rood, was born at McConnelsville, Ohio, February 23, 1847.

In 1849 he removed with his parents to Washington county, where he obtained his early education at the common schools.

In 1864 he entered the army as volunteer in company L, First Ohio volunteer cavalry, and served in the escort of Major General George H. Thomas until the close of the war.

In 1865 he was mustered out of service, and at Marietta entered upon a course of study preparatory to teaching. In 1868, and for several of the following years he was engaged in teaching, and in the meantime studied law with Hon. S. S. Knowles. In 1877 he was admitted to the bar at Athens, Ohio. In 1878 he opened a law office at Belpre, Ohio, where he is now engaged in the practice of his profession, associated with S. Ridgway, at Marietta, as Rood & Ridgway.

JOHN W. TRAUTMAN was born in Alleghany county, Pennsylvania, November 29, 1849, and obtained his early education in that county. In 1870 he came to Ohio and located in Harmar, Washington county. He studied law with Hon. John Irvin, and in 1877 was admitted to the bar, and commenced practice.

In 1878 he was elected by the house of representatives of Ohio, as first assistant sergeant-at-arms, and served in that capacity during two sessions of the legislature.

In 1879 he resumed the practice of law at Harmar, where he now resides.

JOHN W. McCORMICK was born at Brownsville, Monroe county, Ohio, December 25, 1850. In 1869 he came with his parents to Washington county, and at Marietta pursued a course of preparatory studies. In 1875 he was graduated at Marietta college.

He commenced the study of law with Messrs. Loomis & Alban, and completed the same with Mr. M. D. Follett, and in 1878 was admitted to the bar.

In the spring of 1879 he commenced the practice of law at Marietta, and is now engaged therein at that place.

JAMES ROSS, was born in Belmont county, Ohio, in 1839. In October, 1861, he volunteered as a private soldier, and afterwards reenlisted as a veteran in the Seventy-third regiment, Ohio volunteer infantry. He was engaged in many hard fought battles; marched with Sherman to the sea; was commissioned as first lieutenant, and having served through the entire war, was mustered out of service with his regiment in 1865.

In 1878 he was admitted to the bar, and is now located in Wesley township, Washington county, engaged in the practice of law.

M. WILBER REA was born at Rea's Run, Washington county, Ohio. He attended the Gallia academy at Gallipolis, Ohio, and the Normal School at Lebanon, Ohio. At the age of seventeen years he began teaching, and taught for a number of years. He was engaged for a time with his brother in store-keeping and tobacco-packing at Newport, Ohio. He studied law and graduated at Cincinnati Law school in 1878. In 1879 he commenced and is now engaged in the practice of law at Marietta.

F. R. McCORMICK, son of A. W. McCormick, was graduated at Marietta college in 1874. He studied law with his father, and in 1876 was admitted to the bar. In 1878 he removed to Cincinnati, where, associated with his father he is now engaged in the practice of law.

ALFRED DEWEY FOLLETT, son of Martin D. Follett and Harriet L. Shipman, was born in Marietta, Ohio, March 30, 1858. In September, 1872, he entered Marietta college and graduated therefrom in July, 1876, with the highest honors of his class. In September, 1877, he entered Cornell university and took a post graduate course in history, philosophy, political economy, constitutional law and literature. On his return to Marietta he commenced the study of law and in February, 1880, was admitted to the practice of law by the supreme court of Ohio. Since then he has been engaged in the practice of law with his father at Marietta.

SIDNEY RIDGWAY, son of Thomas Ridgway, was born in Washington county, Ohio, May 20, 1850. In 1868 and 1869 he attended the academy at Marietta; in 1874 was graduated at Marietta college; in 1875 he was elected justice of the peace for Union township, Washington county; in 1877 was the nominee of the Republican party for representative in the Ohio legistature, but was not elected; in 1877 was engaged as teacher in the public schools of Lowell, Washington county, and in 1879 having completed a course of law studies under the preceptorship of Ewart, Sibley & Ewart, at Marietta, he was admitted to the bar. He is now engaged in the practice of his profession at Marietta, associated with D. R. Rood, of Belpre, as Rood & Ridgway.

CHARLES W. RICHARDS, son of George H. Richards, was born at Marietta, Ohio, May 11, 1856. He attended the public schools of his native city; studied law two years with Messrs. Loomis & Alban, and was admitted to the bar in Washington county in April, 1879.

In April, 1880, he was elected justice of the peace of Marietta township. He resides at Marietta, engaged in the practice of his profession, and in the discharge of his duties as justice of the peace.

CHARLES RICHARDSON, son of W. P. Richardson, was born at Woodsfield, Ohio, March 28, 1857. He studied law with his father, and was admitted to the bar in 1879. He is associated with his father in the practice of law at Marietta, Ohio.

JOHN C. PRESTON, son of Frederic and Joanna (Chapin) Preston, was born at Ludlow village near Beverly, Ohio, October 3, 1831. A part of his early life was spent at Columbus, Ohio, where he attended school at the seminary. About 1852 he became a resident of Beverly, where he has held the office of justice of the peace for a period of six years, of postmaster sixteen years, and of mayor six years.

In 1878 he was admitted to the bar, and at Beverly commenced and still continues in the practice of his profession. In 1855 he married Harriet Anderson, who died in 1871. In 1876 he married his present wife, Mrs. Kate Shoop, of McConnellsville.

LOWELL W. ELLENWOOD was born in Washington

county, Ohio, August 7, 1855. He studied law with Messrs. Chamberlain & Hamilton, of Marietta, and in 1879 graduated at the law school in Cincinnati, and was admitted to the bar. In 1880 he located at Marietta, where he now resides, and engaged in the practice of his profession.

CHAPTER XVI.*

WAR OF 1812.

Cause of the War—Situation in Washington County—The Federalists—Reminiscences of John Stone, James Lawton, Joel Deming—Caleb Emerson's Statement as to why the Draft was Resorted to—Battle of Tippecanoe—Expedition of General Hull—Colonel Lewis Cass—Captain Sharp's Company—Surrender of Hull—Call for Troops—Expedition of General E. W. Tupper—General Harrison's Movements—Journal of Captain James Flagg—Companies of Captains Sharp, Flagg, Buell, Hill, Thorniley and Devol—Siege of Fort Erie—Perry's Victory—Proctor and Tecumseh Defeated by Harrison—Treaty of Peace—Battle of New Orleans—Rolls of Companies in War of 1812—Biographical Sketches of Officers, War of 1812—General E. W. Tupper—Captains Sharp, Flagg, Thorniley, Hill, Buell, Devol, Lieutenant Danielson and Major Horace Nye, Captain Jason R. Curtis, Captain Robert C. Barton.

OHIO had been settled twenty-four years when the war with Great Britain broke out. Some progress had been made in subduing the wilderness, numerous settlements had been formed, new counties organized, and the census of 1810 shows that, with an area of four thousand square miles, she had at that time but two hundred and thirty thousand seven hundred and sixty-nine inhabitants, and Washington county, by the same census, five thousand

---

*The military history of Washington county is from the pen of S. J. Hathaway, of Marietta.

*Among the many who were anxious to have the fine record of Washington county, in the War of the Rebellion, adequately represented in this history were Colonel William R. Putnam, E. S. McIntosh, M. P. Wells and Douglas Putnam; but Colonel Putnam, chairman of the military committee during the war, was the moving spirit in having the present military history prepared. He it was who invited the gentlemen named to support the undertaking.

I have attempted to develop Colonel Putnam's idea of what such a history should be in the following pages, which I began January 13, 1881, and completed in about four months. Meanwhile Colonel Putnam departed, and the hand that could have placed the seal of approval on the work was paralyzed in death. I have therefore submitted the Military History to President J. W. Andrews and General R. R. Dawes, who have endorsed the work.

I am under obligations to General B. D. Fearing, of the Ninety-second Regiment, General H. F. Devol, of the Thirty-sixth regiment, Colonels A. W. McCormick and W. B. Mason, of the Seventy-seventh regiment, Colonel Douglas Putnam, jr., of the Ninety-second regiment, Captain James G. Parker, of the Thirty-sixth regiment, Major Joseph B. Daniels, of the Ninth cavalry, Captain R. K. Shaw, and Captain R. S. Mason, of the Sixty-third regiment, Lieutenant J. S. McCowan, of the One Hundred and Seventy-fifth regiment, Alex. H. Birkey, of Buell's battery, John Caywood, of Seventh cavalry, Major George F. Rice, of the Thirty-ninth regiment, Lieutenant John Burke, of the Seventy-third regiment, Captain W. L. DeBeck, battery K, First artillery, Captain J. F. Huntington, battery H, First artillery, and others, for services in preparing the sketches of their respective organizations, and to A. T. Nye, sr., Rotheus Hayward, Hiram Hill and T. P. Flagg, of Clayton, Illinois, for information and documents relating to the War of 1812.

S. J. HATHAWAY.

---

nine hundred and ninety-one. A large part of the State was still in its natural condition, and part of it held by tribes of Indians. The settled portion was all southeast of a line drawn from Cleveland in a southwesterly direction. It was through this wild country that the soldiers of 1812 marched to the falls of the Ohio, at Louisville; and the gratitude of the country is due to them not so much for the amount of fighting done as for the hardships endured in traversing these pathless forests and holding important posts on the far frontier. In those days the facilities for travel were limited, horses and wagons were scarce, while clothing and all the equipments of an army were difficult to provide so far from the centres of supply, and much of it, when obtained, was not suitable for the kind of service demanded—that of fighting Indians, marching through dense forests, tangled thickets and extended swamps.

The people of the Northwest Territory had always been accustomed to the maintenance of a warlike attitude. The young State of Ohio had a well organized militia, and the service of a militia man in those days meant something. They had, from 1790 to 1795, a fierce war with a powerful combination of Indians, including the Miamis, Wyandots, Delawares, Pottawatomies, Shawnees, Chippewas, Ottawas and other tribes of the Territory, all under the great Miami chief, Michikiniqua, whose war-cry was "Drive the white man east of the Ohio." General Anthony Wayne, August 20, 1794, had totally defeated them on the Miami; and since the treaty with them at Greenville, August 3, 1795, the Indians had not molested the settlements until the beginning of the war we are now discussing.

From 1798 to 1800 the war with France occurred. From 1801 to 1805 the war with the pirates of Tripoli was waged. Thus had the new generation grown up, and the new settlements been formed almost under the shadow of the sword and scalping-knife; and the population, accustomed to rely on the fruits of the chase as well as agriculture and other pursuits, was largely made up of hardy hunters, good woodsmen, and men who had made a successful fight against the ruder forces of nature.

The War of 1812, as far as this country was concerned, was fully justified. The mother country had acknowledged our independence, but would not accord us the privileges of freedom. She had impressed our seamen, searched our ships on the high seas, and made almost innumerable aggressions on our commerce, and last, but not least, had incited the Indians on the frontier to renew their savage hostilities, and for these causes war was declared June 18, 1812. President Madison in his proclamation of war, dated June 19, 1812, urges all citizens of the Republic to sustain the administration in the impending struggle. One would suppose that such an appeal was superfluous, but it had a meaning at that time which we can the better understand by consulting the political history of the day. Thomas Jefferson had already founded the Democratic party by which Madison had been elected. It was the war party. The Federalists were opposed to the war, in this much at least, that they believed that the object sought could be accomplished by negotiation without a resort to arms. The war party, however, carried the day, and the verdict of history is that they were right. This feeling of opposition was well developed in Washington county. It was, however, more of a non-interest than opposition.

In the spring of 1878 A. T. Nye, sr., of Marietta, received several letters from old citizens of the county, written in response to inquiries made by Mr. Nye in regard to the War of 1812, which we give as the best statement readily obtainable of the situation in this county in those days, John Stone, esq., of Belpre, wrote as follows:

The patriotism of Belpre did not prompt her citizens to deeds of peril on the Canada lines. The people believed the Government could have made a treaty if it had taken the right course. The Berlin and Milan decrees of Napoleon were as obnoxious as the British orders in council, and to declare war against one government and not the other was to discriminate. If war was the remedy to maintain our rights, we were in every way unprepared for it.

The blundering management of the war in the northwest gave cause for the severest criticism, and perhaps gave rise to the idea of the necessity of a Silver Grey organization. Colonel Nathaniel Cushing had command of a company of Silver Greys, whose valor had been tried in their youth, who had seen Indians since, heard the war whoop and helped to bury the scalped dead, but the men who threw up their caps for the War of 1812 looked upon these old soldiers as Tories, and sometimes called them so. Perhaps I might mention some circumstances to show who they were, how well they bore the appellation, not accepted it, and how they stood when a Tory was an enemy to his country. There was some shipping away from the legal call of the militia officers, but enough were found to fill the drafts as they occurred. All who went into the service were given honorable discharges. There were a great many sick and ailing when an order for draft was announced, so much so that old Mr. Allen, who did the ferrying at the mouth of the Little Hocking, and who was commonly known as Old Charon, said: "Nearly all the drafted men profaned themselves sick."

Edmund B. Dana and Bial Stedman were captains in the regiment of Washington county militia as then organized. They were citizens of Belpre, and Belpre at that time contained double the territory it does now. The bounds of military companies were fixed by regimental boards of officers. Hence Captain Dana's company, though called a Belpre company, extended into Warren, while Captain Stedman's company was all in Belpre, and within the bounds of these two companies were formed the Silver Greys. I am not aware that either Captain E. B. Dana or Captain Bial Stedman performed any other service than to call out the requisition made on their companies and other duties connected with that service. I was a corporal in Captain Dana's company, and performed the duty of notifying the drafted men in the draft of 1813. It was the duty of commanders of companies when they received a requisition to draft the number of men called for and forward them to the place of rendezvous; they were not authorized to use compulsion. If the drafted man did not go or furnish a substitute he was subject to a fine. Officers were detailed in the order of the dates of their commissions, and took with them their non-commissioned officers, governed by a rule fixed by law. A suit grew out of the drafting of an apprentice who never returned to service, in which case the aggrieved master, a strong advocate of the war, sought his remedy in court against the captain, and paid the costs in Goodno vs. Bial Stedman, on appeal from William Browning's docket; whether he cursed the war I don't know, but have no doubt he cursed his luck and the captain, too.

Omitting all dates, Quartermaster or Contractor Craig purchased a large number of ox teams in Belpre and vicinity, and forwarded them to headquarters under his nephew W. P. Putnam, wagonmaster, Absalom Misner, Major Reed, and Cummings Porter, teamsters, which duties they performed in a satisfactory manner and were honorably discharged.

The drafted men who served were Elam Frost, Nehemiah Morse, Lemuel Cooper, Samuel Barkley. The men who hired substitutes were Jervis Burroughs, William Burroughs, and I think George Dana and Joseph Dilley. The substitutes were Joel Bennett, Curtis and Hinman. Pardon Cook served in the company commanded by Captain Charles Devol; Barkley and others from Belpre were in Captain John

Thornilley's company; Captain Dana's company extended into Warren and Cooper may have been a citizen of that township at the time.

To comfirm the statement that Belpre folks were called Tories a drafted man says, "When spoken to I was always called Tory except at roll call."

James Lawton, of Barlow, responded as follows:

In regard to the War of 1812, a large class of the then voters thought it unnecessary and impolitic. My father and most of his neighbors took that view of it. Of course, we rejoiced at our victories, but farther than that took but little interest in it. Doubtless the case was very different in some quarters, and many prominent citizens participated in it, but with comparatively few exceptions it was not the case here.

Joel Deming's letter was in substance as follows:

I can recollect many events of the War of 1812. There were a number of young men went from Waterford into the service, Elias Wolcott, Lorey Ford, Elisha Mallory, Norman Hart, Benedict Hutchins, Duty Green, David Deming, William Henry, Alexander Walker, Neal Walker, who all lived to return except Norman Hart.

In the summer or early fall of 1812 General Edward W. Tupper came to Marietta to recruit a force of volunteers for the war. A consultation was held between leading men as to the propriety of raising men in this manner, and it was decided to resort to the draft. Caleb Emerson, in the *Western Spectator*, of which he was the editor in 1812, says that it was feared that the volunteers would be from the ranks of the Democratic party, which was strongly in favor of the war, and thus the chances of success at the approaching October election would be endangered, whereas, if the draft was resorted to, men of both parties would be taken. The result was that the young men, and others without families, who could conveniently go, were not afforded a chance to volunteer, but men with families to support, and others who were not well suited for soldiers were forced into the service. General Tupper left without any recruits.

From the military papers of Captain Rotheus Hayward, late of Waterford township, furnished by Rotheus Hayward, it appears that on February 15, 1814, he was ordered to furnish men for the service. Thereupon Corporal John Craft was given a list of thirteen members of Captain Hayward's company, with orders "to begin at the first and proceed down the list until he found two men who were willing to serve, and warn them to appear at Anthony McCandish's in Waterford, on Wednesday, February 23, 1814, armed and equipped as the law directs, to march on a tour of duty, to rendezvous at Franklinton, in this State." The men who were willing to go were Edward Miller and William Prewit.

The attempt, however, to class the Federalists with the Tories was a failure, for many of them were Revolutionary soldiers, and the whole tenor of their lives amply disproved the charge. We are inclined to believe that it was merely a campaign epithet used to help James Madison to his second term in the White House. The War of 1812 really began the year previous, although no formal declaration was made; it was the same conflict, and many Indians that fought at Tippecanoe, in 1811, doubtless fought with Tecumseh and General Brock the year following.

An early intimation of the pending war was afforded the citizens of Washington county by the landing, at Marietta, of the old Fourth regiment, United States infantry, commanded by Colonel Boyd, during the summer of 1811. They were mostly from New Hampshire and Massachusetts, a fine looking and intelligent body of men, who were destined to see hard service. They passed on their way to join General William Henry Harrison at Vincennes, where they were met by several regiments of mounted volunteers from Kentucky. General Harrison, with this force, moved on up the line of the Wabash, and on November 7, 1811, at Tippecanoe creek, Indiana, met and defeated the Indians under the Prophet, brother of Tecumseh. The Indians lost one hundred and seventy killed and one hundred wounded; the Americans sixty-two killed and one hundred and twenty-six wounded. The Fourth United States infantry lost heavily in this battle. Captain Robert C. Barton, a Washington county man, commanded a company, and General Harrison, in his report of the battle, mentioned Captain Barton for his gallant conduct. The Fourth United States infantry were stationed at Fort Harrison and Vincennes during the winter, and in May, 1812, marched to Urbana, Ohio, and joined the northwestern army.

The certainty of war with Great Britain prompted the Government, in the winter of 1811-12, to call for three regiments from Ohio to serve in the northwest; the plan being to move this force early in the spring and occupy Detroit, which, in event of a war, would be an important strategic point in movements against Canada.

Brigadier General William Hull was at that time governor of the Territory of Michigan, and early in May he arrived with his staff from Washington city and assumed command of the northwestern army. General Hull had seen service in the Revolutionary War, and under General Anthony Wayne, at the storming of Stony Point, had distinguished himself, but he had lost his youthful vigor, and lacked the inspiring presence of "Mad Anthony" to urge him on to deeds of valor, as the sequel will show. The three regiments asked from Ohio were promptly furnished. They were the First, Second and Third regiments of Ohio volunteers, commanded respectively by Colonel Duncan McArthur, of Ross county; Colonel James Findlay, from the western part of the State, and Colonel Lewis Cass, from Muskingum county.

Colonel Cass gathered a few companies at Zanesville in May, 1812, and proceeded thence down the Muskingum, to Marietta, where he was joined by Captain John Sharp with the Washington county company. Colonel Cass arrived at Marietta May 25th, and was received amid the firing of cannon and other public demonstrations. On the next day he departed for Cincinnati, his men numbering two hundred and fifty in all, travelling in keel boats. On their arrival at Cincinnati they were joined by two hundred more men. From there they marched to Dayton.

After obtaining the consent of the Indian tribes through whose country the expedition was to march, General Hull moved forward through the pathless forests, the unbroken wilds of Ohio to the foot of the Maumee rapids, where he arrived June 30, 1812, and by July 4th the Fourth United States infantry took possession of Fort Detroit.

The other regiments coming up, encamped around the fort.

A sufficient number of bateaux (a boat somewhat larger than a skiff) having been procured the expedition by July 9th was ready to cross the Detroit river and invade Canada. They accordingly moved up the river on that day in the following order: first, the Fourth United States infantry Lieutenant Colonel James Milier; second, the First regiment Ohio volunteers, Colonel Duncan McArthur; third, the Second regiment Ohio volunteers, Colonel James Findlay; fourth, the Third regiment Ohio volunteers Colonel Lewis Cass. Thus the Third regiment became the right wing of the army. Arriving at the point selected for the crossing, they entered the bateaux at daylight, and launched out upon the broad river in perfect alignement, the right a little in advance. They reached the other shore in due time, formed on the bank, but were not attacked as they expected. Marching down to Sandwich opposite the fort, they encamped. A reconnoisance in force was soon made, in the direction of Malden, by Colonels McArthur and Cass capturing a battery over the Canada river, four miles above Malden. Several other reconnoisances were undertaken which developed the fact that the enemy were weak and disposed to avoid an engagement.

General Hull, from some reason best known to himself, on the seventh of August ordered the whole force to recross the river and occupy their old position which movement was effected without molestation and the invasion of Canada ended. The enemy now crossed opposite Malden and interrupted communications with Ohio. On the ninth of August a strong detachment was sent down to drive them back. Here was fought the battle of Brownston, in which the National army lost sixty-eight men. The enemy were defeated, driven back to Canada and communications with Ohio restored.

The officers commanding the troops under General Hull now discovered that something was wrong at headquarters; that the old general was either a coward or a traitor, and giving matters their most charitable construction, it was thought he ought to be deposed from command.

An effort to accomplish this change was started, all the officers signing a petition, their names being arranged in a circle so that no one came first. The design was to place one of the Ohio colonels in command, but nothing came of it.

On August 15th the British opened on Fort Detroit from a battery located on the opposite shore, which could not possibly have dislodged the garrison at Fort Detroit without a heavy supporting force which they did not have. This fort had been designed and laid out by army engineers, and was—what it was intended to be—a very formidable work; heavily armed, and surrounded by common stretching back for a mile or more to the forests, across which an enemy would have to approach without cover, a circumstance which, in event of attack, would have deprived general Brock of the aid of six hundred Indians under Tecumseh, who would never have approached the fort across the open plain in the face of the artillery on the bastions and curtain walls of this formidable fortress. The total effective force of General Hull was two thousand three hundred officers and men, well supplied with artillery, independent of the guns in advanced batteries.*

The force of Brock consisted of two hundred and thirty British regulars, four hundred Canadian militia, and the six hundred Indians above mentioned, to which was attached a battery of three six-pound and two three-pound guns. Besides this there were in Fort Detroit ammunition, arms and equipments in abundance.

General Brock, with his forces, crossed below Detroit on the morning of August 16, 1812, before dawn and marched up to within a mile of the fort and sent Tecumseh with his Indians by a detour around to the west side, keeping them concealed in the woods. Brock promptly sent in his demand for a surrender, which General Hull accepted, and the Northwestern army was no more.

This army was composed of brave men who were anxious for a fight, yet their reputation and opportunity for destruction were thus basely compromised and surrendered by General Hull without cause or justification.

General Hull was afterward tried by court martial and sentenced to be shot, but was spared on account of former services.

The Government, during General Hull's operations at Detroit, had called for additional troops from Ohio to support him. These were collected at Urbana by Governor Meigs, and among them was the Second brigade of Ohio militia, commanded by General Edward W. Tupper, with Horace Nye as brigade major, both citizens of Washington county. The brigade consisted of one regiment from the eastern part of the State, commanded by Colonel Charles Miller, of Coshocton; one regiment from Gallia and Athens, the county below, commanded by Colonel Robert Safford, of Gallia; and a battalion under command of Major James Galloway, of Xenia, with two companies of scouts of about twenty-five men each—one commanded by Captain Thomas Hinckson, the other by Captain Wood. The whole effective force was about one thousand, until subsequently reduced by sickness.*

At the rapids of the Maumee there had been planted some three hundred acres of corn, in clearings made at that point. About October 30, 1812, General Tupper, being informed of the above fact, through his scouts sent out from Fort McArthur, and having also learned through an Indian interpreter captured by the same scouts, that there was an expedition of some thirty British and five hundred Indians, on the way to secure this corn for the Indians to live on during the winter, he at once resolved to defeat them in their undertaking. A courier was sent to General Winchester, who was lying within forty miles of the cornfields with three thousand men, in order that

the general might be on the alert to either drive the enemy back or cut off his retreat. Meanwhile General Tupper determined to proceed at once to the rapids with what force he had—some six hundred effective combatants, with a six-pound gun drawn by six horses. The field-piece was, however, abandoned the second day out from camp, and the carriage broken up; this was about the eighth of November. General Winchester had been notified of the departure of the expedition, of its object, and the length of time the subsistence taken would enable them to stay away from the base of supplies.

When General Tupper arrived at the rapids he found the Maumee so swollen that it was impossible to cross. The scouts reported the enemy on the opposite side some distance from the rapids, and as yet unaware of the approach of Tupper and his command. After an unsuccessful attempt to cross his force he marched down the river until opposite the Indian camp, still undiscovered. Captain Hinckson, however, with nine of his scouts came on to three Indians, who had crossed to the cornfields. Shots were exchanged, killing one Indian and wounding another. The whole Indian encampment was aroused and agitated at once, like a hive of bees that had been disturbed. They dashed up the river for the ford, but upon arrival there found Tupper and his men ready for them. This was not what they expected, and they immediately resorted to their usual Indian strategy of picking off the stragglers. After several hours of desultory firing, the Indians were driven back at every approach, and many of them killed in the water while attempting to recross. They seemed to have quite a number of horses and used them to ferry the warriors over. These horses were afterwards ascertained to be the same captured from General Hull, at Detroit. The rations of the command being exhausted they fell back slowly to Fort Findlay, on the river Auglaize. The Indians did not attempt to follow.

Had General Winchester cooperated with General Tupper, there is no doubt but that the whole detachment of British and Indians would have been either captured or so punished that the subsequent disaster at the river Raisin would not have occurred.* The motive of General Winchester in not seconding this movement was a desire to thwart the plans of General Harrison; at least this is the construction given to his actions by cotemporary writers.

The winter of 1812–13 was a very severe one, and the troops on the frontier suffered greatly, especially from lack of sufficient clothing. The time of most of the brigade was out by the last of February, 1813, and General Tupper and his staff, with the men whose time had expired, were discharged and returned home.

During the War of 1812 Washington county furnished seven companies, some volunteers, some militia, some regulars, to-wit: Captain Sharp, already mentioned as

---

*The guns surrendered by Hull were as follows: Iron—seven twenty-four-pounders, in water battery; two twenty-four-pounders, on new field carriages; eight twelve-pounders, in and around fort; five nine-pounders, in and around fort; three six-pounders, in and around fort; four twelve-pounders, not mounted. Brass—three six-pounders, at fort; two four-pounders, at fort; one three-pounder, at fort; one eight-inch howitzer, at fort; one five and one-half inch howitzer, at fort; one mortar; total, thirty-eight pieces.

*From Reminiscences by Major Horace Nye.

*General Harrison's order to General Tupper is dated October 4, 1812, and the report of the expedition October 12th, showing that they were out some seven or eight days. The object was partly a reconnoisance in force and partly to surprise any force of the enemy that might have been in the vicinity of the rapids.

being in the Third regiment, Ohio volunteers, so basely surrendered by Hull at Detroit; Captain Timothy Buell, who went out in May and also in August, 1813. The latter were mounted volunteers. They went to Zanesville; from there to Franklinton, a post situated opposite what has since become Columbus. They went from there to Mansfield, when the emergency at Fort Meigs being over, they returned home.

Captain John Thorniley's company was made up by draft. They were in the infantry, and formed part of the First regiment of Ohio militia, and were called out in the fall of 1813, and their term of service expired March 13, 1814, which term included seven days for returning home, one hundred and forty miles. The company was stationed at Fort Stephenson most of the time of their term of service.

Captain Charles Devol's company of dragoons was called out October 20, 1812. They reported for duty, but not being needed were ordered to hold themselves in readiness to march on short notice, which they did until the emergency was over.

Captain James Flagg's company were drafted men called out the same day as Captain Devol's.

October 20, 1812, the following is the captain's journal:

A. D. 1812:

Journal of the First company of militia detached from the First regiment, First brigade and Third division of Ohio militia.

On Tuesday, the twentieth October, the company rendezvoused at Dolonel Davis', in Waterford.

On the twenty-first we took up our march at 3 o'clock P. M. and marched seven miles to Stevens.

22d. We marched to the salt works, twenty and one-half miles.

23d. Arrived at Zanesville, ten and one-half miles, where we found good accommodations.

Sunday, November 1st, we took up our march for Mansfield; went three miles and camped.

Monday, 2d, we marched nine and one-half miles.

Tuesday, 3d, to Newark, thirteen miles.

Wednesday, 4th, we camped on Mr. Davis' farm, fifteen miles from Newark—rainy night.

Thursday, 5th, we marched to Mt. Vernon, ten miles, and camped.

Friday, 6th, we marched eight miles and camped—rainy weather.

Saturday, 7th, we marched to Lewis' block-house, fourteen miles—twenty-eight hours steady rain.

Sunday, 8th, lay in camp—rainy day.

Monday, 9th, I went with five of our men to the Indian village called Greentown, where we fell in with the Pennsylvania troops. Very wet and rainy; we got very wet.

Tuesday, 10th, went to look for a lost man; he was not to be found.

Wednesday, 11th, sent a scout of fourteen men to look for the lost man; the man returned about twelve o'clock the third day from camp.

Thursday, 12th, we left Potato camp and marched six miles to Mr. Hill's and camped on the same ground the Pennsylvania troops did.

Friday, 13th, marched to Burns' mill, four miles, and camped within three miles of Mansfield.*

Here the journal ends. The outfit of the company receipts for October 20, 1812, was as follows:

Fifty arms and bayonets, fifty cartridge boxes, one wagon, four set of horse gears, four horses, two tents, two bags, six axes; and at Zanesville they received two more tents, eight pots, two kettles and powder and ball.

In this connection it is curious to note what one ration for a soldier was, to-wit: "One and one-fourth pounds beef, or four and three-fourth pounds salted pork, eighteen ounces of bread or flour, one gill of rum, whiskey or brandy, and at the rate of two quarts of salt, four

*From original furnished by T. P. Flagg, esq., Clayton, Illinois.

quarts vinegar, four pounds soap and one pound and a half of candles to every hundred rations;" also what the uniform of a soldier of 1812 was, to-wit: The regulation coat was a "swallow tail," made of dark blue cloth, faced and trimmed with buff, buttons of white metal, with "U. S. A." on them. The hat was a tall bell-crowned affair, with no brim except a small visor in front. To this costume was added the "stock" for the neck, of polished leather, wide enough to fit up snug under the chin.

Captain Alexander Hill's company was recruited principally in Washington county for the regular army in the summer of 1813, and was part of the Nineteenth United States infantry. Captain Hill was, in the fall of 1813, ordered by Colonel George Paul, commanding the regiment and having charge of the recruiting station of Zanesville, to report at that place. Captain Hill after his arrival at Zanesville was ordered to Detroit, arriving there after the battle of the Thames. The company was next ordered back to Zanesville by Colonel Paul, soon after arriving there. Captain Hill was placed in command of a battalion of the Ninth infantry and ordered to report at Fort Erie, in Canada, near the head of the Niagara river, where he arrived before the battle at that place in 1814.

On July 31st the British, under General Drummond, appeared before the fort with about four thousand five hundred men and laid siege. The garrison now began a vigorous use of spades, perfecting the works which were quadrangular in shape. They also constructed some advanced works, in which were placed guns with proper infantry supports. On August 2d the firing from the opposing batteries began which continued until August 15th. General Gaines, having arrived a few days before, was in command at the fort at this time, and on the fourteenth had discovered signs of a new movement in the enemy's camp. He accordingly put his forces in best shape possible for an attack and awaited developments. About two o'clock in the morning, August 14th, the enemy, under Lieutenant Colonel Fisher, thirteen hundred strong, attacked the left, when the Twenty-first regiment, under command of Major Wood, and Towson's battery repulsed them and fell back. The firing had scarcely subsided on the left when Lieutenant Colonel Drummond and Colonel Scott, with fifteen hundred picked men, moved up to the assault on the right. The night was exceedingly dark, but by the commands of the enemy's officers two columns were discovered approaching. Boughton and Hardings' volunteers and the Ninth United States infantry were manning the works on the right, but owing to the unfinished condition of an advanced bastion the enemy carried it and turned the guns on the defenders of the fort. The battle now raged furiously, but by renewed exertion the enemy was driven back and Colonel Scott and Lieutenant Colonel Drummond, the leaders of the assault, killed, but the British still held the captured bastion. The passage from this bastion to the body of the fort was in a great measure closed by the position of the block-house there located. This, though in a ruinous condition at the time, had been occupied the evening before by Lieutenant

Colonel Trimble with a detachment of the Ninteenth infantry, including Captain Oliver Hill's company, whose well-directed fire, at the same time that it galled the enemy severely in the bastion, had completely defeated every attempt he made to penetrate farther.

The column of Colonel Scott being now routed, the guns of the Douglass battery were so directed as to cut off all communication between the contested bastion and the enemy's reserve—and a party of desperate fellows were about to rush in and finish the work, when a spark being communicated by some means to an ammunition chest under the platform, the bastion with those who occupied it were blown into the air together."[*]

The enemy's loss and that of the National forces in this engagement were estimated at the time as follows: British, two hundred killed and wounded and two hundred prisoners; United States troops, three officers and eight to ten killed and fifteen to twenty wounded.

The British now waited reenforcements and soon received two full regiments, established a new battery, and recommenced the cannonade. This state of things continued until September 17th, when a counter assault was undertaken in two columns, commanded respectively by Generals Porter and Miller. This sortie was well conducted and successful in driving the enemy from his entrenchments. The victorious columns, satisfied with having beaten the enemy in his chosen position, returned within the works of Fort Erie, and four days afterward the British broke camp and retired rapidly down the river, thus ending a siege of fifty-one days.

The victory of Commodore Perry near Put-in-Bay Island, Lake Erie, September 10, 1813, relieved the whole Northwest Territory of the presence of hostile forces. The British and Indians retired to Canada, abandoned Detroit, and but for the urgent demands of Tecumseh would have abandoned the whole of Lower Canada. Tecumseh, however, insisted upon a vigorous resistance to the advance of General Harrison, who pressed close on the retiring enemy.

On October 5, 1813, with what forces the combined efforts of Tecumseh and General Proctor could muster, battle was offered at the Moravian town on the River Thames. General Harrison engaged the enemy with a fine body of Kentucky mounted riflemen who carried confusion and destruction into the ranks of the British, but met with a vigorous resistance from the Indians. The Kentuckians, however, attacked them vigorously, and after a desperate resistance defeated and routed them, killing their celebrated chief, Tecumseh. The theatre of war was from this time on transferred to Niagara frontier and the east, and continued with uniform success to the American arms both on land and sea. The sharpest fighting, however, of the War of 1812, was done on the ocean, and the people of the United States can always refer with pride to that series of brilliant victories won by American seamen, who seemed sent by an avenging Nemesis to redress the long standing grievances and punish Great Britain for her wrong and oppression.

[*] From Frost's Remarkable Events in the History of America (1848).

The battle of New Orleans was fought January 8, 1815, fifteen days after the treaty of peace was signed at Ghent, the news not arriving until after the battle, presenting one of the anomalies of history, a thing that could not happen at the present day with our great facilities for transmitting information. The Senate confirmed the treaty of Ghent February 17, 1815, and President Madison made proclamation of the fact the following day.

We have said nothing of many important conflicts of the War of 1812, as the scope of this sketch was to give only that part in which troups from Washington county figured; and considering the population of the county at that time, we may say that she did her part nobly and would have done much more had the occasion offered.

COMPANIES FROM WASHINGTON COUNTY.

(Rolls obtained from official files in Washington, D. C.)

Muster-roll of a company of volunteers under the command of John Sharp, captain of a company, under the act of Congress of the sixth of February, 1812, and afterwards under the command of Colonel Lewis Cass:

COMMISSIONED OFFICERS.

Captain John Sharp, Lieutenant William Sawyer, Ensign Jacob Trowbridge.

NON-COMMISSIONED OFFICERS.

First Sergeant John H. Simon, Second Sergeant Thomas Green, Third Sergeant Chester Wilcox, Fourth Sergeant Otis Record, First Corporal Peter F. Schenck, Second Corporal William Crane, Third Corporal David Miskimens, Fourth Corporal James Elwell, Musician Christian B. Smith.

PRIVATES.

Joseph Clark, Benjamin Beers, James Mall, Abraham Lyon, David Williams, William Goldsmith, William Lynch, Brazilla Browning, Samuel Null, John Shingler, John Skinner, Alvin Benedict, Samuel Nixon, James Gary, Joseph Rogers, Joseph Knox, John Black, Jacob Nechilow, William Duncan, Harris Ellis, Lewis Frazy, Benjamin Badgeley, Philip Langdon, William Anderson, James T. Downing, Joseph Fox, John Ward, Samuel Murphy, Ezra Kelly, Jabez Tuttle, John T. Robertson, Samuel McMullen.

CAPTAIN JAMES FLAGG'S COMPANY.

Muster-roll of a company of militia commanded by Captain James Flagg; ordered into the service of the United States on the twentieth day of October, 1812, by the authority of his excellency, R. J. Meigs, governor of the State of Ohio, and commanded by Samuel Connel, major commandant.

Commencement of service October 20, 1812, expiration of service January 11, 1813.

COMMISSIONED OFFICERS.

Captain James Flagg, Lieutenant Benedict Hutchison, Ensign Nathaniel Olney.

NON-COMMISSIONED OFFICERS.

First Sergeant Dora Ford, Second Sergeant John Greenman, Third Sergeant David Trobridge, Fourth Sergeant Peletiah White, First Corporal Jacob Larne, Second Corporal Charles Thomas, Third Corporal Joseph Whilton, Fourth Corporal John Haskel.

PRIVATES.

Daniel Alpha, George Abbot, James Adams, James Anderson, John Baker, John Barret, Nathan Briton, Seth D. Burbank, Jonah Burchet, Philip Cady, Simeon Chapman, George Castle, William Cline, Daniel Coleman, Henry Coverstone, George Daugherty, Thomas Dennis, Daniel Dunahue, Asa Emerson, James Ewings, Stanton Fordice, James Goodwin, John Gosset, George Harris, Curtis Hinman, James Hutchison, James Hutchins, John Imgles, John Kid, James Knight, Elisha Malery, Nehemiah Morris, Gilbert Otis, Daniel Penny, Richard D. Priest, Pardon Starkes, James B. Walker, James Whitton.

Total officers, eleven; privates, thirty-eight.

We do certify that the said company of infantry were regularly drafted from the militia of the State as a part of her quota, and mustered, and that they served the time specified, and that the muster-roll as it stands is accurate and just.

JAMES FLAGG, Captain.
BENEDICT HUTCHINS, Lieutenant.

I do certify on honor that the said company of infantry was regularly drafted from the militia of this State, that they were commanded by me, and served the full time specified, and that the muster-roll, as it stands, is accurate and just.

SAMUEL CONNELL,
Major Commandant.
FRANKLINGTON, September 19, 1813.

I certify that the company of militia mustered on the within muster-roll were in the service of the United States.

RETURN J. MEIGS,
Governor of Ohio.

A list of names, with rank, in Captain Alexander Hill's company, Nineteenth United States infantry, War of 1812.

COMMISSIONED OFFICERS.

Captain Alexander Hill, First Lieutenant Charles L. Cass, Second Lieutenant John Carrel, Third Lieutenant Alexander Patterson, Ensign Nathan Reeves.

NON-COMMISSIONED OFFICERS.

First Sergeant John Elliott, Second Sergeant Stephen Worthington, Third Sergeant Allen Lowry, Fourth Sergeant Elijah Adams, Fifth Sergeant Ambrose A. Ford, First Corporal Manna Root, Second Corporal John Franks, Third Corporal William Wallace, Fourth Corporal Daniel Moore, Fifth Corporal Cyrus Baily, Sixth Corporal John L. Gordon, Musician Christian B. Smith, Musician William Spurgon

PRIVATES.

James Armstrong, William Arnold, Abraham Badgly, Nichola Bumgarner, James Brooks, John Barker, Adam Bair, John Bowman, Ebenezer Buckly, Jacob Brosius, Thomas Clark, Nathan Cross, Israel Cross, John Cox, Lewis Clapper, Shirley Callogg, Samuel Cooper, Henry Crown, Joseph Dean, Jehu Dealy, Noah Demster, William Elliott, John Fishback, Samuel Fisher, Ira L. Foster, Joseph Fisher, Matthias Gates, John Gates, Jesse Graham, Thomas Grey, James Garner, Joseph Heaton, John Hill, Elisha Heitt, James Hillyard, Samuel Higley, Samuel Henning, John Johnston, David Johnston, W. M. Lockhart, William Lyons, John Lyons, John Loveland, Ephraim Lucas, Jacob Monteith, Samuel Morfoot, William Morgan, John McCombs, Nehemiah Morse, John McMullen, John Mowry, Andrew Millburn, Stephen Mowry, George Osborn, Benjamin Patrick, Hira Pettee, James Prichett, John Potts, Daniel Paine, John Ridingour, William Reynolds, Gabriel Root, John Swift, Oliver Stockings, John D. Smith, John W. Smith, John Stanley, John Silvers, Christian Standsburg, Philip Swagert, Benjamin Snyder, William Syder, William A Strong, Jesse Spalding, Nicholas Teel, John Taylor, Daniel Trumble. Total, ninety-three.

Pay roll of a company of Ohio militia, commanded by Captain John Thorniley, of the First regiment of Ohio militia, in the service of the United States, stationed at Fort Stephenson by order of General John S. Gano, commencing January 6, 1814, and expiring March 13, 1814, including seven days for returning home one hundred and forty miles, both days inclusive.

COMMISSIONED OFFICERS.

Captain John Thorniley, Lieutenant David Merideth, Ensign Elisha Chapman.

NON-COMMISSIONED OFFICERS.

First Sergeant St. Clair Kelly, Second Sergeant Thomas Addy, Third Sergeant Daniel McCleain, Fourth Sergeant Lemuel Cooper, First Corporal Solomon Tise, Second Corporal William Smith, Third Corporal William Henkins, Fourth Corporal Daniel Alpha, Drummer William Magee, Fifer David Cox.

PRIVATES.

John Archer, Jerid Andrew, Jonah Birchet, John Bell, Daniel Booth, Perry G. Banthan, William Bird, Henry Baner, Samuel Barkey, Jesse Brown, Joel Bennet, Robert Corbit, William Clark, George Cline, Samuel Crouch, Simon Chapman, John Creig, Hezekiah Chapman, John Connet, Abraham Connet, Jonathan Darling, Mathew Davidson, David Edwards, Luke Emerson, Jeremiah Fugate, Abner Furgusen, Ephraim Frost, John Gose, Norman Hart, Thomas Hill, Thomas Hartley, Keitis Henman, George Harris, Benjamin Hepsen, William Jolly, John Kisley, William Kidd, John Lynn, Benjamin Lamb, Thomas Marshall, Joseph T. Milford, Andrew McCleain, Thomas Newal, James Oglesbay, Presseley Petty, William Ramsey, John Ramsey, Thomas Ramsey, Nicholas Row, John Skinner, John Saltingstall, John Smith, Jonathan Sills, Francis Stanley, Zephaniah Tisen, Solomon Tipton, Jacob Vulgermot, Alexander Vaughan, Richard Willis, William Walker, James Riley.

Muster roll of a company of dragoons (of the State of Ohio) commanded by Captain James Devol, called into the service of the United States on the twentieth day of October, 1812, by the authority of his Excellency, Return J. Meigs, governor of the State of Ohio.

COMMISSIONED OFFICERS.

Captain Charles Devol, First Lieutenant Josiah Scott, Second Lieutenant Washington Olney.

NON-COMMISSIONED OFFICERS

First Sergeant James White, Fourth Sergeant William White, First Corporal John Clark, Second Corporal Pardon Cook, Third Corporal Samuel Reed.

PRIVATES.

Solomon Brown, Thomas Browning, Moses Finch, Gilbert Olney, Argalus Pixley, John Quigley, Joseph Shuttlesworth, Joshua Tucker, Samuel Whipple, Paulus E. Wood

"We do acknowledge to have received of Return J. Meigs, jr., esq., the sums annexed to our names respectively, in full for our pay for a tour of duty in Captain Timothy Buell's company of Ohio mounted militia, under the command of his excellency, the governor of Ohio, called into the service of the United States on the first of August, 1813, upon the requisition of Major General Harrison, commanding the Eighth Military district:"

COMMISSIONED OFFICERS.

Captain Timothy Buell, First Lieutenant Peletiah White, Second Lieutenant Sylvanus Olney.

NON-COMMISSIONED OFFICERS.

Ensign James Liggett, First Sergeant Nathaniel Hamilton, Second Sergeant George Nixon, Third Sergeant Jabez Palmer, Fourth Sergeant Salmon D Buell, First Corporal Samuel Nott, Second Corporal Edward Corner, Third Corporal John Darrough, Fourth Corporal Nicholas Chapman.

PRIVATES.

Timothy Blackmor, Daniel Coleman, John Corns, John C. Clark, Elisha Coleman, Z. Cuddington, Henry Delong, Thomas Dunbar, Richard Demont, Thomas Dennis, Benjamin Ellis, Timothy Gates, jr., Stephen Gates, William ——— (worn from original), Henry Havens, Zebulon Jennings, Titus Kimball, R. Lawrence, jr., Robert Liggett, John Longhery, William Longhery, Alexander McCoy, Jacob Miller, Robert Magee, John McConnell, Samuel Miller, Jacob Multon, Benjamin F. Palmer, John Perry, John R Porter, William Brevelt, Horace Quigley, Dennis Raur, James Ray, Clark Springer, John Scott, Nathaniel Smith, John Taylor, Jonathan Wilson, Jonathan Whitney, Police E. Wood.

Captain Buell was out in May, 1813, with a company, as has been mentioned, but the rolls of the company have not been preserved, and can not be found at Washington, as will be seen by the following letter from the Third Auditor:

TREASURY DEPARTMENT,
THIRD AUDITOR'S OFFICE,
WASHINGTON, March 31, 1881.

SIR: In reply to your letter of the twenty-eighth instant, herewith returned, I have to inform you that Captain Timothy Buell has no other service in the Ohio militia, War of 1812, than that which has already been furnished you.

Respectfully,
E. W. KNIGHTLY,
Auditor.

S. J. HATHAWAY, ESQ., Marietta, Ohio.

Pay roll of a detachment of Ohio militia, commanded by Lieutenant John Devault, of Colonel McDonald's regiment, late in the service of the United States, from the thirty-first of January, 1815, commencement of service, to the tenth of April, 1815, expiration of service, or of this settlement:

COMMISSIONED OFFICER.

Lieutenant John Devault.

NON-COMMISSIONED OFFICERS.

Sergeant Levi Bevington, Corporal James Playwell.

PRIVATES.

Henry Aye, George Chadd, Ephraim Doty, William Harrison, Philip Hobaugh, John Harter, Benjamin Long, Robert Mitchell, Samuel Moore, Benjamin Neely, George Rhodes, Richard Shacles, John Sanders, Ezra Travis, David Thompson, Caleb Wright, Morris Yates.

Pay roll of a company of Ohio militia, commanded by Lieutenant John Devault, of Colonel James Stuart's regiment, late in the service of the United States, from the twenty-sixth of July, 1813, commencement of service, to the sixteenth of August, 1813, on expiration of service or of this settlement:

COMMISSIONED OFFICER.

Lieutenant John Devault.

NON-COMMISSIONED OFFICERS.

Second Sergeant Isaac House, Third Sergeant Thomas Devault, Second Corporal Gilbert Hurley, Third Corporal Morris Baker.

PRIVATES.

William Hurley, Jacob Dunkle, John Collender, Benjamin Roebuck, William Dyer, William Kerr, Joseph Ohaner, David Hays, Daniel Sharrot, Oliver Kyle, Joseph Windle, George Roebuck.

BIOGRAPHICAL SKETCHES OF OFFICERS, WAR OF 1812.

GENERAL EDWARD W. TUPPER.

Edward W. Tupper, son of General Benjamin Tupper, an officer in the Revolutionary army, was born in Chesterfield, Hampshire county, Massachusetts, in 1771. His father was an officer of the Revolution, from the commencement of the war, in 1775, until its close, in 1788. The subject of this notice was, at the opening of this war, only four years old. His father, with several other families, came to Marietta in August, 1788. These were the first families who came to Marietta. Edward W. Tupper was then seventeen years of age. He was in Campus Martius during the Indian war, and began his business life at its close.

At the organization of the State government, in 1803, he was appointed clerk of the court of common pleas, and of the supreme court, for Washington county, which offices he continued to hold until he left Marietta. At an early period he opened a store for the sale of general merchandise, at the corner of Second and Putnam streets, Marietta. In 1802 he established a ship-yard at the foot of Putnam street, and built the brig Orlando.

This vessel went out under command of Captain Matthew Miner, with Anselem Tupper for second officer, in 1804. The Orlando was at New Orleans July 4, 1804, at the time of the first celebration of that day after Louisiana was ceded to the United States. She made her first voyage to the Mediterranean and Black sea, as far as Trieste on the latter.

In 1807 Edward Tupper built two gun-boats, under contract with the United States Government.

In 1803 he built the house well known as the residence of the late Nahum Ward, and, since that, of his son, William S. Ward. This property he held until after he left Marietta, and sold it to Mr. Ward. It was occupied, for some years, by General Joseph Wilcox and his family.

On the third of May, 1804, Mr. Tupper married Mrs. Bethia S. Putnam, widow of Dr. William Pitt Putnam—who was a brother of the

late David Putnam, of Harmar. The house built by him, in 1803, was their residence while they remained in Marietta. In 1809 or 1810, he removed to Gallipolis. He was one of the most prominent and useful men of the place, and he had few superiors in southeast Ohio. He represented Gallia county in the legislature for several terms. Some time, before leaving Marietta, he had been elected to the office of brigadier general of militia, of the counties of Washington, Athens, and Gallia.

Soon after the commencement of the War of 1812, Governor Meigs made a requisition for a brigade to be raised in this division, composed of counties along the southern and western portion of the State. This brigade was organized at Urbana in August, 1812, and the command of it was assigned to General Tupper—he being the oldest brigadier general in the division. The surrender of the army under Hull prevented this brigade from advancing beyond McArthur's block-house, where they went into camp, and where they remained for a considerable part of the following winter. In January, 1813, General Tupper learned that the British and Indians were collecting their forces at the foot of the rapids of the Maumee, to carry away a quantity of corn which had been left standing during the winter. He immediately made preparations for driving them away. Many of his men were unfit for duty, but he called for volunteers from among those fit for service to go on the expedition to the rapids. About six hundred responded, and a forced march of several days was made to the Maumee, through the Black swamp, then frozen over. On arriving at the rapids the river was found to be so high that it was not possible to get the troops over in condition to make an attack. Only about two companies passed over, and these found their ammunition so wet that they had to withdraw. It became necessary, therefore, for the troops to fall back a short distance, for the purpose of drying their clothes and their ammunition. Next morning, however, all were fit for active duty; meantime, the Indians, having learned of the approach of our troops, marched up towards the rapids, on horseback, for the purpose of making an attack. They attempted to cross the river with a large force, but were driven back by our troops with considerable loss. The British and Indians retreated, and abandoned the corn, which was afterwards used by General Harrison's army. Our troops lost no men, but some few stragglers from the ranks, who were killed by Indians. None of the troops of this brigade were from Washington county, except Horace Nye, brigade major. They returned to Camp McArthur after an absence of four days. In February, 1813, the brigade was advanced to Fort Meigs, where it was under command of General Harrison. About the first of March, 1813, their term expired, and they were mustered out of service. The following is a copy of the letter discharging General Tupper and his command:

"HEADQUARTERS CAMP MEIGS,
MIAMI RAPIDS, 21st Feb'y, 1813.

"Dear Sir:

"The term of service for which the greater part of your brigade was engaged having expired, and the remaining part not forming a command even for a field officer, you will be pleased to consider yourself and them discharged as soon as they arrive at Urbana. On your way to the latter place, and whilst there, you will be pleased to give such directions with regard to the troops and public property as you may deem proper. I cannot take my leave of you without expressing my sense of zeal and ability with which you have discharged your duty in every instance whilst acting under my orders, and my wishes for your health and happiness.

"With great respect, I am
"Your obedient servant,
"WILLIAM HENRY HARRISON.

"Brigadier General Edward W. Tupper."

In September, 1813, General Tupper, then senior brigadier general, organized a regiment of drafted men at Zanesville, which went out under command of Colonel Bay, of Guernsey county. One company of this regiment was from Washington county, and was commanded by Captain John Thorniley.

After the war General Tupper continued to reside at Gallipolis until his death in September, 1823. Mrs. Tupper died in 1858.

CAPTAIN JOHN SHARP.

The subject of this sketch was born in 1771, at a place in Pennsylvania, then known as the "Burnt Cabins." He came to Washington county about the year 1800, settled on the Little Muskingum, in Lawrence township, near where the townships of Marietta, Newport, and Lawrence, have their corner.

He was of large stature and inclined to corpulency, and was a man of force and influence in the affairs of Washington county, in his time.

When the call for volunteers came in the spring of 1812, Captain Sharp raised a company and joined Colonel Cass' regiment when he passed from Zanesville down the Muskingum and Ohio to Cincinnati. The troops lay over at Marietta one day, were received by the citizens with an artillery salute and other demonstrations of public approval. They took on board Captain Sharp's company, and on April 25, 1812, proceeded on to Cincinnati. They were transported in keel boats. This regiment was the Third Ohio volunteer infantry, army of Ohio.

After participating in the hardships and fatigues of the march to the rapids of the Maumee, Captain Sharp was there detailed, for what purpose is not known, probably to command the escort, to go on board a schooner laden with the sick, baggage of the officers and army stores of General Hull's army. The schooner was accompanied by a boat also loaded with army stores. This was to facilitate the march of the army, which was hastening forward to occupy Detroit. Dr. James Reynolds, surgeon's mate of the army of Ohio, was in charge of the schooner and boat, but took up his quarters on the boat. They sailed July 1, 1812, from the mouth of the Maumee for Detroit, but in passing Malden the schooner was captured by the British, with all on board, including Captain John Sharp, Lewis Dent, paymaster, a lieutenant of the Fourth United States infantry, and about fifty soldiers. The boat escaped. They were afterwards exchanged, and Captain Sharp arrived home soon after the surrender of Hull, and it may be said of this affair of the schooner that it saved the officers and men on board the disgrace of being surrendered by General Hull.

Captain Sharp was chosen senator from Washington county for 1808, representative for 1814, senator again for 1815 and 1816. He was for some years one of the judges of the county court. He died very suddenly in 1823.

CAPTAIN JAMES FLAGG.

James Flagg was born near Springfield, Massachusetts, May 17, 1779, and came to this county about 1790. December 4, 1803, he was married to Sarah Corner. They settled near Cornersville, in Washington county, where he followed his trade of blacksmithing, until the breaking out of the war with Great Britain, at which time he was captain of a company of militia.

Captain Flagg was designated to command a company for active service October 15, 1812, and started for the field October 20th of the same year, for a term of service of six months, but was honorably discharged January 13, 1813. He filled the office of magistrate in the county for many years. His children were: Edna P., wife of Silas Richardson; William C., who married Valeria Hays; Gersham Flagg, who married —— Cisler; Thomas P., who married Sarah Corner; Susan Flagg, wife of David Racer; Catharine Flagg, wife of James Rood; Sarah Flagg, wife of Marian Rood; Mary E., wife of John Corner. Captain Flagg's sister, Cynthia, was the wife of Joseph Kelley and mother of Mrs. Levi Barber, of Harmar, Ohio. Captain James Flagg died in 1854, at Cornersville, in this county, respected and honored by his acquaintances and friends.

CAPTAIN JOHN THORNILEY.

The subject of this sketch was born in England July 17, 1781, and came to this country April, 1795. The means of conveyance were at that early day limited, especially through the western wilds and over the Alleghanies. He, with his father and the family, walked to Pittsburgh, Pennsylvania, where they built boats, and came down the Ohio river to Marietta, after being six months on the way. They settled near the Little Muskingum in Marietta township of this county. When the war with Great Britain broke out in 1812, Captain Thorniley commanded a company of militia, and was assigned to the command of a company of drafted men called out in the fall of 1813. His company was in the second battalion of the First regiment of the First brigade, Third division Ohio, militia, and was stationed at Fort Stephenson, Captain Thorniley commandant, Lower Sandusky.

Captain Thorniley was married July 12, 1810, to Mary Compton. He died August, 1844. The names of his children are as follows: William, Mary, Ann, Thomas, John, James, George, Caleb, Elizabeth, Harriet, and Adaline Thorniley.

CAPTAIN ALEXANDER HILL.

He was of Scotch-Irish descent, and was born February 28, 1777, in the County of Antrim, Ireland, near Belfast, and landed at Philadelphia in 1784. His parents were strict Scotch Presbyterians, and Captain Hill doubtless owed much of his success in life to the wholesome training of his youth. Force of circumstances put him in the way of learning the cabinetmaker's trade, though his tastes strongly impelled him to a seafaring life.

Captain Hill started from Pittsburgh with an English emigrant named Alcock, in canoes lashed together, expecting to have gone to New Orleans and shipped as a sailor at that point, but on arriving at Marietta, in 1798, he found it inadvisable to proceed further without more money than he possessed. He, therefore, plied his trade at Marietta, and soon found that the demand for furniture to supply the new settlers was increasing, and offering opportunities for active and profitable business in that line. He established the first furniture factory in that county, and the cabinetmaker of those days was also the undertaker, and Captain Hill constructed the first coffin that was placed in Mound cemetery.

Captain Hill was married in 1801 to Sarah Foster, daughter of Ephraim Foster, a Revolutionary soldier.

Captain Hill now became prosperous, and the idea of going to sea was abandoned. He was accustomed to load a boat (one of the old time "broad horns") every year with furniture for the southern market, generally going to New Orleans, and either walking back or going around by sea to Philadelphia, and thence across the mountains in a wagon train. On one of these trips south the broad-horn had just reached New Madrid, Missouri, at the time of the great earthquake, which occurred in that country in 1811, and it was with much difficulty that the boat was rescued from destruction.

At the breaking out of the war with Great Britain Captain Hill was a major in the State militia. In the spring of 1813 he received a commission as captain in the Twenty-seventh United States infantry, and on April 22, 1813, he advertised for recruits in the counties of Washington, Athens, and Gallia. He was ordered with his men to Zanesville, and the Twenty-sixth and Twenty-seventh regiments were consolidated, and the Nineteenth United States infantry formed out of the two.

Captain Hill, in the fall of 1813, was ordered to Detroit, and is said to have been placed in command of Malden. He was ordered from there to Zanesville, and from there to Fort Erie. He took part in the battle and siege of that fort, his company being stationed on the right in a block-house, from which they maintained a destructive fire on the enemy, who had captured an outlying work, but could not hold it. The battalion of the Nineteenth infantry, in this battle, was commanded by Major Trimble, and the garrison and post by General Gaines.

Soon after his return from the war Captain Hill was summoned to New York to attend a court-martial. Meeting General Gaines there he asked the general what he thought of the conduct of his men, seeing that it was the first time many of them had been in battle. "Why, sir," said General Gaines, "I could not have expected better service from veterans."

Upon his return from the war, his term of enlistment being for one year, he opened a tavern in Marietta, under the "Sign of the Swan." Captain Hill was elected sheriff of Washington county as the successor of Captain Buell in 1815.

Captain Hill kept tavern until 1827, when, owing to the prevalence of the use of spirituous liquor and necessity almost of keeping a bar if he kept hotel, he decided rather than do it to quit, and accordingly, with his own hand, sawed down his sign-post and closed the tavern. His Scotch Presbyterian training was stronger than the greed for gain. The furniture business was not neglected during these years, but kept up, and when the market would justify it, a boat was loaded for the south, and the outcome was uniformly profitable until the fall of 1836, when he entered into a contract with the State to build the dam and one-half the canal at Lowell, the State being engaged at that time in providing slack water navigation for the Muskingum river; but Captain Hill died in February, 1841, before the work was completed, leaving his heirs to finish the contract, the consideration of which was eighty-five thousand dollars. This money enabled the heirs to settle the estate and pay the debts of Captain Hill, who had become somewhat embarrassed, financially.

Captain Hill was of temperate and exemplary habits, and considering the extent and character of his public services, had very few enemies. He had seven sons and two daughters; one son and daughter died in childhood. Ephraim Hill died of the prevailing fever in 1823, aged nineteen years. The remaining children all grew up to mature age. They were John, Hugh, Jessie, Hiram A., Daniel Y., and Eliza Hill.

Eliza Hill was married to Spencer T. Bukey, June, 1835. He was a son of Hezekiah Bukey, a pioneer who settled on and owned a tract of land in Virginia, nearly opposite to Marietta. The children of Spencer T. Bukey were Van H., Alexander H., John, Joseph T., and Sarah Bukey.

Wallace Hill, son of John Hill, was lieutenant of company B, Eighteenth Ohio volunteer militia, for the three months' service, April, 1861. Alexander H. Bukey, son of Spencer T. Bukey, was a private in the same company; also served as commandant of a gun in Buell's battery during the war. Subsequently Wallace Hill was lieutenant in company C, First West Virginia light artillery, familiarly known as Buell's Pierpoint battery, command by Captain Frank Buell, and after the death of Captain Frank Buell, at the battle of Freeman's Ford, August 22, 1862, Wallace Hill became captain of the battery, and so continued during the remainder of the war.

Frank Hill, son of Hiram A. Hill, born 1847, was appointed third sergeant of company A, One Hundred and Forty-eighth Ohio National guards, Samuel S. Knowles, captain, and on July 23, 1864, was appointed commissary sergeant of the regiment.

Ephraim A. Hill, son of Daniel Y. Hill, served three months in company A, Eighty-seventh Ohio volunteer infantry, and returning enlisted in battery K, Second Ohio heavy artillery, and served until April 15, 1865, when he died at Knoxville, Tennessee.

Alexander Hill, son of John Hill, served in the same company Van H. Bukey enlisted in—the Eleventh West Virginia infantry—October 16, 1861; was commissioned first lieutenant February, 1862; captain August, 1862; major March, 1863; lieutenant colonel August, 1863; colonel November, 1864; Brigadier general, by brevet, May, 1865.

John Bukey enlisted in company D, Eleventh West Virginia infantry, and was promoted from sergeant, orderly, second lieutenant, to first lieutenant in January, 1865.

Joseph T. Bukey enlisted as a musician in company D, Eleventh West Virginia infantry, and was afterwards drum major of the regiment. In 1865 he enlisted for three years in company A, First United States dragoons; served his term on the Pacific slope, and then re-enlisted in the Twenty-second United States infantry, and was accidentally drowned at Sitka, Alaska, May 12, 1872.

CAPTAIN TIMOTHY BUELL.

He was born October 18, 1768, at Killingworth, now Clinton, Connecticut, son of David Buell, of same place; came to Ohio June 15, 1789, and settled at Cincinnati, Ohio, where he is said to have built the first brick house in that city. Wishing to live near his friends and relatives, who had settled in Washington county, he returned to Marietta When the conspiracy of Aaron Burr began to attract public attention, in 1806, the President of the United States sent out a confidential agent to Marietta to ascertain the true situation and relations between Burr, Blennerhasset, and the expedition then being fitted out. This agent became convinced, from what he saw, that the enterprise of Burr and Blennerhasset, if not treasonable, was at least alarming He therefore went to Chillicothe, and laid the matter before the Ohio legislature, then in session; and on the second of December procured an act to be passed, "authorizing the governor to call out the militia on his warrant to any sheriff or militia officer, with power to arrest boats on the Ohio river, or men supposed to be engaged in this expedition, who might be held to bail in the sum of fifty thousand dollars, or imprisoned, and the boats confiscated." Under this act a company of militia was called out, with orders to capture and detain the boats (which were being built about six miles above Marietta, on the Muskingum), and the provisions, with all others descending the Ohio under suspicious circumstances. This force was placed under command of Captain Timothy Buell. One six-pound gun was placed in a battery on the river bank at Marietta, and pickets disposed at proper places along the shores to watch the river and give the alarm if any persons attempted to pass with the suspected boats. The dispositions of Captain Buell resulted in the capture of all but one of Mr. Blennerhasset's boats, which escaped during a very dark night.

After General Hull's surrender, the British and Indians began to move southward from Detroit and infest the territory opened up by their victory, and in the spring of 1813 they gathered in force and laid siege to Fort Meigs, situated at the rapids of the Maumee. General Harrison immediately made a requisition on Ohio for troops, and Governor Meigs called for mounted volunteers to hasten to the relief of the beleaguered garrison. Captain Buell immediately raised a company of mounted men, and on May 12, 1813, left Marietta for the rapids. Captain Robert C. Barton, who was highly spoken of in the battle of Tippecanoe, was lieutenant, and Manly Morse, ensign. After being some days on the march, they were met with instructions to return, as the enemy had retreated. Over four thousand mounted men, in Ohio, turned out under this call, and all but a few were sent back. Governor Meigs arrived at his home in Marietta (the same now owned by Hon. M. D. Follett) about the last of May, and Captain Buell, on arriving at Marietta, drew up his men in front of the governor's house and tendered

their services for any expedition he might direct. The governor responded in very complimentary terms as to their promptness and patriotism in going to the relief of Fort Meigs. He observed that he was the more gratified at their demonstration of zeal in their country's cause, as it was the first specimen of public military spirit which had been exhibited in the county of Washington since the commencement of the war. That henceforth he augured a revival of a redeeming spirit of military energy worthy of the county which bears the name of the illustrious Father of his Country. To those gentlemen who had aided the company in equipments he returned his sincerest thanks. Of those who had endeavored to discountenance the expedition, he observed that such merited, what they must eventually receive, the contempt of all honorable men. The company was then honorably discharged.

On August 1, 1813, to meet a similar emergency at Fort Meigs, the mounted volunteers were again called upon, and they responded with the same readiness. Captain Buell gathered another company and went to the front, but before they had arrived at the scene of action the British and Indians had fled, and an order from General Harrison gave them his thanks and an "honorable discharge." This was the last demonstration of the British and their allies in the northwest. The victory of Commodore Perry, in September, 1813, compelled them to retire to Canada.

Captain Timothy Buell and Alexander McConnell were elected to represent the district composed of Morgan and Washington counties in the nineteenth general assembly, 1820, and Captain Buell and William M. Dawes to represent the same district in the twentieth general assembly. Captain Buell was sheriff of the county for several years, being succeeded in that office by Captain Alexander Hill, in 1815. He was also a magistrate for many years. Died February 6, 1837.

Captain Buell was the brother of General Joseph Buell, and grandfather, on the maternal side, of Major General Don Carlos Buell. His children were. Eliza Buell, born at Marietta August 22, 1798, died August 3, 1823; Joseph H. Buell, born October 20, 1812; William Plummer Buell, born June 18, 1815; Milo M. Buell, born September 18, 1817; Hiram B. Buell, born in 1824; George D. Buell, born in 1826; and Columbia Buell, born in 1828. Of these, Eliza married Hon. Salmon D. Buell, April 9, 1816, who was son of Hon. Salmon Buell, of Ithica, New York. Their children were: General Don Carlos Buell, born near Marietta, March 23, 1818; Sally M. Buell, born near Marietta, February 26, 1820; and Aurelia A. Buell, born near Marietta, February 27, 1822, wife of Hon. William F. Curtis, of Marietta.

LIEUTENANT TIMOTHY E. DANIELSON.

There is a degree of sadness connected with the life of this young officer who came to Marietta about the year 1804, from Brimfield, Connecticut. His father was General Timothy Danielson, of Union, Connecticut, who died in 1791. The widow (his mother), Eliza Danielson, married Hon. William Eaton, of Brimfield, Connecticut, August 21, 1872.

Mr. Eaton had been for many years connected with the diplomatic service of the United States, and stationed in the Barbary States.

Upon his return to this country in 1803, he had promised young Timothy a position in his suite when he should return. Mr. Eaton however changed his mind, and took out a younger brother, Mr. E. E. Danielson.[*]

This was a great disappointment to Timothy E. Danielson, and he left home for the west, arriving at Marietta shortly after the departure of his stepfather in 1804.

Great care and attention had been given to the education of the children of Mrs. Danielson, both by General Danielson and Mr. Eaton, and young Danielson turned his training to account by teaching school in Marietta for several years.

At the opening of the War of 1812, Danielson was commissioned as lieutenant in the regular army, and July 29, 1812, he advertised for recruits—headquarters at Marietta. The recruits were taken for either three or five years. With what men he could raise he left for the front, and entered the Seventeenth United States infantry. He was taken with malarial fever, and died December 21, 1812, at Fort Winchester.

We have the following notice of his death: Died at Fort Winchester December 21, 1812, after a long illness which he bore like a soldier, Lieutenant Timothy E. Danielson, of the Seventeenth United States regiment.[†]

Caleb Emerson was appointed his administrator, and among his effects was a large assortment of law books, medical works and a general assortment of other works.

---

* He was afterwards, upon his return to this country, killed in a duel with a naval officer.

† Western Spectator, January 23, 1813.

MAJOR HORACE NYE.

Horace Nye came to Ohio when a child, August, 1788, with his father, Colonel Ichabod Nye. From that time until his death Ohio was his home, and until 1813 his residence was Marietta.

He was the grandson of General Benjamin Tupper, a soldier, and the son of Colonel Nye, also a soldier, and was surrounded by men who put themselves under strict military discipline during the Indian war, while living in Campus Martius. Thus he became a soldier himself, and was all through life noted for his military bearing and soldierly qualities.

Though but a child, he shared in the privations and hardships and dangers of the garrison, and at an early age began to share in the toils, and to form habits of endurance and energy.

His life was coeval with the first settlement of the State, and the history and experience of its tragic scenes and patient toils and heroic sufferings were as familiar to him as household words.

He furnished many facts from memory to the historian, and published some valuable sketches of early times. In the summer of 1812 he was called into the service of his country as brigade major, in General E. W. Tupper's brigade of Ohio militia. This brigade was composed of troops mostly from southern Ohio, and was called into service shortly before the surrender of General Hull at Detroit. The men were ordered to the frontier—Ohio then being a frontier State—and spent most of the winter near Urbana and McArthur's block-house. They suffered much from bad quarters, bad food, poor clothing and the severity of the winter. Later they were advanced to Fort Meigs, where they remained until their return of service expired. The service rendered was important and severe. Major Nye returned home in the spring of 1813, and during the following summer engaged successfully in business in Putnam, Ohio.

Few men ever lived who have established a better character for uprightness of purpose and unbending integrity. He scorned the idea of bending his principles to expediency or of smothering his honest convictions. He was a reader, a thinker and a keen observer of men. For thirty years he was a member of the Presbyterian church, and to know the right was with him to do it. Always the friend of the slave he was an advocate of immediate emancipation.

In 1835 his life and property were threatened by a Zanesville mob. There was a little band of Abolitionists in Putnam, of which he was one, and when the mob threatened to burn the town, he saw no reason to change his views, but armed himself under the authority of the mayor, and purposed to fire at the word of command. He would have braved the dungeon or the stake in defence of the inalienable rights of man.

He was born at Chesterfield, Massachusetts, June 8, 1786, and died at Putnam, Ohio, February 15, 1859.

CAPTAIN JASON R. CURTIS.

Jason R. Curtis was born in 1785 at Warren, Litchfield county, Connecticut, removed to Marietta in 1792, and married Mary Clark, daughter of Major John Clark. Captain Curtis served during the War of 1812, as aid-de-camp of Governor R. J. Meigs, with the rank of captain. Jason R. Curtis, father of Hon. William F. Curtis, died in Marietta September 12, 1834.

CAPTAIN ROBERT C. BARTON.

Robert C. Barton came to Marietta during the War of 1812. We have not been able to obtain any facts as to him, except that he commanded a company under General Harrison at the battle of Tippecanoe, and was mentioned by General Harrison in his report of that battle for gallant conduct. He was afterwards, during the same war, first lieutenant under Captain Timothy Buell in a company of mounted volunteers, and was also on duty with Governor Meigs, probably as aid-de-camp.

CHAPTER XVII.

WAR OF THE REBELLION

Causes of the War—Leaders North and South, Political Campaign of 1860—Position of the People of Washington County as to the War—Public Meeting January 8, 1861—Progress of Public Sentiment—View of the Country April, 1861—War Begun at Sumter—Call of the President for Troops—The "Union Blues"—Ceremonies on Departure of First Company—The Beverly Company—Militia System of Ohio—Preparing for Invasion—Appeal to the Governor for Aid—Arrival of Colonel Barnett's Artillery—Camp Putnam Established—The Military Situation—Governor Dennison's Plan of a Campaign Successful—McClellan's Communications—Battle of Bull Run—Romance no more, but Dead Reality—New Policy Inaugurated—Call for Five Hundred Thousand Men for Three Years—Hon. William P. Cutler's Offer—Thirty-sixth Regiment—First Three Years Company—Groesbeck's (Thirty-ninth) Regiment—Company L, First Ohio Volunteer Corps—Buell's, De Beck's and Huntington's Batteries—Seventy-seventh Regiment—Sixty-third Regiment—Camp Tupper Established—Military Committee Appointed—Close of the Year 1861—Beginning of Governor Tod's Administration—First Volunteer Killed in Battle—"Shiloh"—Washington City Threatened—The "Putnam Guards"—Organization of the Ninety-second Regiment—Parkersburgh in Danger—The Draft—Camp Marietta Established—Battles of South Mountain and Antietam—Death of Colonel Melvin Clarke—Battle of Corinth—Organization of Company H (the "Newton Guards")—Seventh Cavalry Alarm along the Border—Military Strength of Marietta—Close of 1862.

THE WAR OF THE REBELLION—INTRODUCTORY.

Reader, let us stand together on a crest of the Alleghanies, commanding a splendid prospect to the westward. It is a bright clear day in September, the year 1788. Here lies the course of the wagons of the mountains up from the east and down to the west, the grand thoroughfare of emigration, now scarcely begun westward. We see spread out before us a grand expanse of forest and stream. In the far distance from north to south is the Mississippi river. On the hither side, like a silver thread from northeast to southwest, winds the Ohio river. On the north, like burnished shields, lie the great lakes Erie, Huron, Michigan and Superior, and spread out between these bounds, like an open scroll, lies the Northwest Territory. The pleasing fancy cherished so long in Connecticut and Virginia that those old commonwealths owned strips of country from the Atlantic westward to the South sea, or more familiarly the Pacific, have been exploded and abandoned, and the claims of those States in the Northwest Territory formally released.

Look at the vast expanse of forest in the foreground, undulating like the green waves of the ocean and traversed by silvery streams flowing to the Ohio or to the lakes. Westward in the far distance the country breaks away from the forests and spreads out into broad savannahs, studded with groves, and beyond the eye detects the sheen of the Father of Waters.

This vast domain possesses the finest climate of the continent. In a similar climate the human race attains its highest development. Neither too hot or too cold, but finely tempered as a Damascus blade. Mother of energy, endurance, enterprise and civilization, this beautiful land lying before us will certainly be fruitful and productive. Vast in extent, encumbered by the finest timber, the growth of centuries, it is now a wilderness. The primeval forest clothes it like a garment. The great valley of the Ohio falls away to the southwest with nothing to disturb its placid stillness but here and there an Indian guiding his rude canoe.

Excepting a few settlements on the hither side of the Ohio river, the whole is one vast solitude—but hold, there at the junction of the Ohio and Muskingum, the blue smoke curls up, and a clearing appears. The white man has come to take possession, and he has come to stay; now through the aisles of the stately forest is heard the woodman's axe. The Indian pauses on the trail while hunting the bear, the deer, or the wild turkey, to listen; and he creeps through the thicket to obtain a view of the newcomers, who are soon to dispossess him and bring a nobler race to take possession. But, reader, think not these fertile acres, fraught with such great possibilities, have been overlooked and forgotten.

This settlement is but the result of a cause that went before. That cause was as subtle in its results as the falling dew or gentle rain, and came as silently. Every inch of land, from the great lakes on the north to the Ohio on the south, is held as firmly as though caught by hooks of steel, and every man, woman and child destined to be born in and to occupy and cultivate this land can not, if they would, escape its influence. The Ordinance of 1787, the second great charter of American progress and liberty, has silently gone into possession. Law, enthroned in a temple built without hands, has assumed sovereignty over a vast domain, having as yet but few occupiers, but waiting for the teeming millions of the future. "Law it is," as the Hindoo says, "which is without name or color, or hands or feet, which is the smallest of the least and the largest of the large; all, and knowing all things; which hears without ears, sees without eyes, moves without feet, and seizes without hands."

Let us now turn to the southward, there lie Virginia and Kentucky soon to be settled from eastern Virginia and the Carolinas by a brave and hardy race, but wedded to the institution of human slavery. There is but the narrow Ohio between the north land and the south, yet even at this early date the forerunners of the race to come are separated very widely in sentiment by the institution referred to. And their children shall grow up with the cherished sentiments of their parents, instilled into ther minds at their mothers' knee, to be intensified by each political contest, and confirmed as time advances in their various opinions. Time will show to what dread extent two great contending ideas will carry the sections. Oh! pine on the crest of storm swept Alleghany sigh, and ye mothers in the far off clearings weep for the evil days to come, and that so fair a patrimony should be destined to witness so fierce a struggle between such noble men, children of a common brotherhood,

When this soft turf, that rivulets sands,
    Were trampled by a hurrying crowd,
And fiery hearts and armed hands
    Encountered in the battle-cloud.

Ah! never shall the land forget
    How gushed the life-blood of her brave —
Gushed, warm with hope and courage yet,
    Upon the soil they fought to save.

It is necessary in writing the military history of the first county and oldest settlement in the Northwest Territory to bring prominently to the front that great ordinance which has so largely shaped the destinies of the populous commonwealths of Ohio, Illinois, Michigan, and Wisconsin, especially as that ordinance contained the germinal cause that made the States named to go with the Government, when the crisis of revolution came. Let us therefore examine very briefly that part of the ordinance which pertains to the subject in hand—the cause of the War of the Rebellion. That it was no sudden growth all will readily admit. The men, south of the Ohio and north of the same, were generally of a common origin, Amerians all. It will not do to say that these States would have gone with the North in 1861, had there never been such an ordinance as the one referred to. Indiana, Illinois, and Ohio, at least, could have been slave States as easily and consistently as Virginia and Kentucky, having substantially the same climate, the same products and therefore the same demand for slave labor; but the fundamental law governing the territory, out of which all these States were erected, prohibited slavery, and thus each State constitution contained a clause of similar prohibition.

The article of the ordinance referred to is as follows:

ARTICLE 6. There shall be neither slavery nor involuntary servitude in the said Terrritory otherwise than in punishment of crimes, whereof the party shall have been duly convicted: provided always that any person escaping into the same from whom labor or service is lawfully claimed in any one of the original States, such fugitive may be lawfully reclaimed and conveyed to the person claiming his or her labor or service, as aforesaid.

The Jeffersonian ordinance of 1784 providing for the government of Kentucky and the Southwest, contained nothing in regard to slavery; an amendment had been offered, putting an end to the peculiar institution after the year 1800, but failed of passage by one vote, the delegate of one State, New Jersey being temporarily absent. On what a slender thread often hang the destines of millions! The Resolutions of 1798 as passed by the Kentucky legislature were preeminently a State Rights document. They were a natural outgrowth of the doctrine of slavery; and as that institution increased so did the States Rights heresy.

We quote the first resolution which is a sample of all the others:

RESOLVED, That the several States composing the United States of America are not united on the principle of unlimited submission to their General Government, but that by a compact under the style and title of a Constitution of the United States, and of amendments thereto, they constituted a General Government for special purposes—delegated to that Government certain definite powers, reserving, each State to itself, the residuary mass of right to their own self-government; and that whensoever the General Government assumes undelegated powers, its acts are unauthoritative, void, and of no force; that to this compact each State acceded as a State, and as an integral party, its co-States forming, as to itself, the other party; that the Government, created by this compact, was not made the exclusive or final judge of the extent of the powers delegated to itself; since that would have made its discretion, and not the constitution, the measure of its power; but that as in all other cases of compact among powers having no common judge, each party has an equal right to judge for itself, as well of infractions, as of the mode and measure of redress.

Similar resolutions were passed by the legislature of Virginia the year following. They were afterwards re-

MAJ. GEN. DON CARLOS BUELL

peated, but not until they had largely sown the seed of rebellion and revolution.

In the earlier days of the Republic the great question of slavery, and especially of States Rights, had already been formulated and stated in terms that were not materially altered during all the great political contests that followed.

Patrick Henry, June 4, 1788, in the Virginia convention called to ratify the new constitution of the United States, said:

"That this is a consolidated government is demonstrably clear; and the danger of such a government is, to my mind, very striking. I have the highest veneration for those gentlemen (the framers of the constitution); but, sir, give me leave to demand, What right had they to say *We, the people?* My political curiosity, exclusive of my anxious solicitude for the public welfare, leads me to ask who authorized them to say, *We, the people, instead of we the States?* States are the characteristics and the soul of a confederation. If the States be not the agents of this compact, it must be one great, consolidated National government of the people of all the States. . . . . . I need not take much pains to show that the principles of this system are extremely pernicious, impolitic and dangerous."

Washington, in his Farewell Address, said:

"Citizens by birth or choice of a common country, that country has a right to concentrate your affections. The name of American, which belongs to you in your National capacity, must always exalt the just pride of patriotism more than any appellation derived from local discriminations."

Alexander Hamilton, June 18, 1787, in the debate on the new constitution, said:

"The general power, whatever be its form, if it preserves itself, must swallow up the State governments, otherwise it would be swallowed up by them. It is against all the principles of good government to rest the requisite powers in such a body as Congress. Two sovereignties cannot exist within the same limits."

The people of the States formed out of the Northwest Territory were by education and tradition, and more especially by virtue of the moulding power of a great fundamental law, opposed to slavery and to the doctrine of States Rights. They naturally went with the North; and we believe we are justified in saying that the North could not have succeeded in the war for the Union if the States named had refused to cooperate.

Previous to the war, through much discussion and many political campaigns, the people of the States named, as well as the balance of the great North, had settled, as far as they were concerned, the momentous question forced upon them by the slave power. The venerable John Quincy Adams, ex-President, in his gallant fight for the right of petition in Congress, was one of the first to take up the gage and begin the battle, and he was successful. Then followed that noble galaxy of leaders, Joshua R. Giddings, William Lloyd Garrison, John Greenleaf Whittier, Henry Ward Beecher, William Cullen Bryant, Wendell Phillips, Charles Sumner, Gerrett Smith, Cassius McClay, Owen Lovejoy, Benjamin Lundy and a host of others, who appealed to the North in the name of liberty and humanity, and eventually carried the great majority to victory in the Presidential campaign of 1860.

The people of the South also were led by men of ability, who fought long and hard for what they considered truth and justice, and they have left their mark upon their generation. Some of them, indeed, in certain localities, are deemed martyrs to a noble cause, lost and hopeless though it be, forever. Beginning with John C.

Calhoun, the great advocate and expounder of the States Rights doctrine, there were Jefferson Davis, Judah P. Benjamin, Henry A. Wise, R. Barnwell Rhett, Alexander H. Stephens, James M. Mason, John Slidell, John B. Floyd, William L. Yancy, Robert Toombs, Isham G. Harris, and many others, under whose teaching and leadership the great States of the South were induced to try the arbitrament of the sword to decide their grievances.

Thus the two sections of the country with the leaders named and entertaining the principles they did, glowing with the white heat of a great political campaign, gradually drifted asunder. In the south free speech was denied to northern men. Northerners at the south on business were violently treated and hundreds returned, bringing the story of their treatment home. John B. Floyd, Buchanan's Secretary of War, had quietly removed cannon and other munitions of war to southern arsenals, and these and many other events which occurred in swift succession, enhanced the excitement. Early in January, 1861, news of an alarming character began to be received, and the "War News" headings of the newspapers had come to be so common as to be regularly looked for by the readers.

Mr. Dennison, governor of Ohio, while reviewing the situation in his message to the legislature, January 7, 1861, says:

The patriotism of the country is justly alarmed. The unity of the Government is denied. Doctrines subversive of its existence are boldly advocated and made the basis of State action, under the pretended right of a State to secede from the Confederacy at its pleasure, in peace or war, constitutional liberty is imperilled, revolution is meditated, and treason is justified.

On the occasion of my inauguration I felt it to be my duty to warn my countrymen against those hostile designs against the Federal Union. But then they were in speculation only. Now they are in act. Shall they be consummated? Shall the National Government be degraded into a mere league between independent States, existing only by their appearance, subordinate to them and subject to be destroyed at the pleasure of any State of the Confederacy? Or shall it continue to be maintained, as it has always been maintained, as a government proper — sovereign within its prescribed sphere—as the States are sovereign within their prescribed spheres—founded on the adoption of the people as were the States, and creating direct relations between itself and the individual citizens, which no State authority has power to impair or disturb, and which nothing can dissolve but revolution.

The people of Washington county fully endorsed these sentiments. They had stood arrayed against each other in the two great political parties, but when the Union was threatened, irrespective of party they gave their allegiance to the Government of the fathers. On the evening of January 8, 1861, pursuant to a call for a union meeting, the people of Marietta and vicinity, including a number of citizens from the adjoining county of Wood, Virginia, assembled at the court house, in Marietta, and the mayor, Hon. William A. Whittlesey, was chosen chairman; Hon. T. W. Ewart and C. F. Buell, secretaries. Thereupon a committee consisting of Melvin Clarke, Arius Nye, Rufus E. Harte, Andrew W. McCormick, Davis Green, Douglas Putnam, William West, David C. Skinner and Charles F. Buell, were appointed to draw up resolutions expressive of the sentiment of the people on the condition of the country. The meeting then adjourned to 2 P. M., January 12th. On the day named

19

a large number of citizens of Washington county and of Wood county, Virginia, without distinction of party, assembled at the court house, and the committee, through Melvin Clarke, reported resolutions at length, condemning the secession movement and affirming their devotion to the cause of the Union.

The following are the second and seventh resolutions passed:

II. The doctrine of the secession of a State has no warrant in the constitution, but, on the contrary, is in its effects fatal to the Union, and subversive of all the ends of its creation, and in our judgment secession is revolution; and while we fully admit the right of revolution for the causes set forth in the Declaration of Independence, or for others of equal force, and while we are grieved to say that the Government and citizens of several of the States, both north and south, have been guilty of acts of great injustice toward others, yet facts do not exist which warrant a resort to that last and final remedy, revolution, and we have still an abiding faith in the capacity and adaptation of the General Government to redress all grievances suffered by its citizens, whatever their origin.

VII. Notwithstanding former differences of opinion on this subject, for the purpose of making a final adjustment of the unfortunate controversy now raging in our country, we are willing to accept as the basis of a compromise, the reenactment of the eighth section of the Missouri Compromise act; or we are willing to adopt the principle, that the whole subject of slavery in the territories, shall be left to be determined by the will of the *bona fide* residents of such territory, provided they also be left free to elect their own officers, executive and judicial, as well as legislative.

The history of the progress of public sentiment in this county is but a repetition of that of many others in the State. The people of Ohio would have compromised with the south gladly; but it is an old story, often told, how the southern leaders disregarded all overtures. They were bent on having a new government, founded upon the institution of human slavery and awaited their opportunity. In the fullness of time that oppportunity came.

But, reader, come again with me to the crest of high Alleghany and let us look once more westward. It is noontide of a beautiful day in April, 1861. Seventy-three years have elapsed since the first settlement of the Northwest Territory. To the southwest are the broad valleys of the Ohio. In the far west, by the shore of the Mississippi is Illinois On the north, like burnished shields, lie the great lakes. The forests have melted away. No more does the Indian lurk in the thicket or guide his rude canoe on the broad Ohio; but the great Anglo Saxon has built his domicile beside every stream, and his cattle graze upon the hills and in all the valleys. On the Ohio, the great steamer, bearing the commerce of populous States, pursues her way. Instead of a few hamlets, we see the populous valleys of Virginia. In place of the lone wagon trail over the mountain, is the wonderful railroad, connecting Ohio and the east. . Instead of the small settlement at the mouth of the Muskingum, we see a thriving city, and the county of Washington with thirty-six thousand five hundred inhabitants. The wilderness has been subdued, and out of it has grown Ohio with two million three hundred and forty thousand, Indiana with one million three hundred and fifty-five thousand, Illinois with one million seven hundred and fifty thousand, Michigan with seven hundred and fifty thousand, and Wisconsin with seven hundred and eighty thousand inhabitants. Cultivated fields interspersed with woodland extend as far as the eye can reach and the thrifty son of toil has made the land "to blossom like the rose." Peace and prosperity have wrought their perfect work. Great cities have sprung up. Thousands of manufactories, giving employment to a million of workmen, dot the land. Institutions of learning are scattered here and there over the whole land. Unexampled prosperity! Amazing transformation! Surely this Northwest Territory has more than fulfilled its early promise. Sad, that the wheels of industry should be stopped, the plough left standing in the furrow, the college deserted, and that the red hand of war should paralyze a State in the full tide of prosperity, sending mourning to so many hearts and disaster to so many homes; but such is war.

At the hour of 4:30 on the morning of April 12, 1861, the boom of a mortar on Sullivan's Island, in Charleston harbor, gave notice to the country and to Major Anderson, pent within the walls of Fort Sumter, that the war was begun. The news was not wholly unlooked for, yet the dread reality was difficult to comprehend. Soon, however, the patriotic impulse of the people obtained control and carried everything before it. Washington county was thoroughly aroused. The news of the beginning of hostilities reached Marietta on Saturday morning, April 13th, and on Monday morning the call of the President for seventy-five thousand men was received. Captain Frank Buell, of the Union Blues, a Marietta company, called his men together the same evening, and the company promptly tendered their services, were at once accepted by the governor, and ordered to march on the following Monday morning. The company was soon filled more than to the maximum, officers elected and preparations made for departure at the date named.

As this was the first company from this county to offer its services to the Government, and as this was an event of great moment at the time, we give the names of this company and a short sketch of the events attending their departure.

COMMISSIONED OFFICERS.

Captain Frank Buell, First Lieutenant Dennis O'Leary, Second Lieutenant William H. Bisbee, elected major of Eighteenth Ohio volunteer infantry, May 29, 1861; Second Lieutenant Wallace Hill.

NON-COMMISSIONED OFFICERS.

First Sergeant John Theis, Second Sergeant Daniel Y. Hill, Third Sergeant Owen O'Neal, Fourth Sergent Theodore G. Field, First Corporal Wallace W. Withrow, Second Corporal John D. Holden, Third Corporal Samuel C. Skinner, Fourth Corporal George B. Haskins, Musician Louis Fourgeres, Musician Manly Warren, Musician Ebenezer Corry.

PRIVATES.

Amos Mordecai, Eli P. Boring, Frank H. Bosworth, R. H. Bull, William Bryan, Robinson Blain, Jacob Bower, Benjamin Bragg, Absalom Boring, George R. Burris, Alexander H. Dukey, John F. Booth, Guy Barrows, Henry Claus, John Clark, Peter L. Coniffe, Stephen H. Collins, Charles Clogston, George Coon, Joseph Corey, E. Corey, Daniel Close, John Chase, John Calvert, David Craig, Thomas Dyar, David Dow, George W. Devin, Juthro Davis, Thomas Driscoll, Thomas C. Daily, Hannibal Dibble, D. T. Deming, Henry Eastman, William N. Foulke, Thomas Fisher, Jeremiah Fairhurst, Daniel Goodman, Allen Green, William Gay, L. R. Green, Milton Gillingham, Henry Henning, John Henning, George B. Haskins, Albert Hamilton, Thomas Hatfield, William Holden, Henry Kellner, August Kropp, Herman Ketchner, Lafayette La Grange, Philip Loufman, Levi F. Lamotte, Frederick Living, J. H. Lapham, Milton H. Laughlin, Augustus Morris, John Mahnkin, Wesley Miner, John N. Miner, George

Moore, Wilbur F. Morse, Leonidas R. Merber, Lewis Munroe, Thomas McNamara, John McCullough, George McCadden, John Neigham, Reuben L. Nye, Thomas North, James S. Parker, Anthony Padden, Wallace W. Pixley, William Parker, George Pixley, Michael Padden, James Phelps, Jewett Palmer, jr., Thomas Phelps, Daniel Quimby, Philetus S. Ripley, George W. Ridgeway, John Ranger, William Robinson, Walter Reppert, Milton Regnier William Ranger, James H. Sniffen, William Stewart, Daniel Soler, John L. Shaw, Elijah G. Smith, Peter Sherrer, Jacob Shaw, William Spence, Ordam Snier, Horatio Stark, John W. Smith, Robert Shiers, Henry B. Stanton, James Stanley, William N. Scott, William H. Snodgrass, Charles W. Sprengle, Tartus L. Stewart, Hugh Shoop, David Shockley, James Turner, Thomas R. Thorniley, Samuel Tracey, Abner Tucker, T. W. Terry, Oscar Underwood, George Vickers, James Voschel, Gordon B. West, Charles B. Wetson, Jacob Wood.

Quite a number whose names appear in the above list were not accepted, being under age, over age, or physically unfit for service. On Sunday evening before the departure of the company a meeting was held at the Congregational church in Marietta, all the other churches meeting at the same place.

The church was crowded with an earnest and attentive throng, seats being reserved at the front for the volunteers. They marched in. The choir sang the National hymn "My country, 'tis of thee." After which Rev. Dr. Wicks preached from the text—Isaiah xi: 4—a sermon full of patriotic zeal and devotion to country. The concluding part of his sermon was more directly to the volunteers, and was in part as follows:

Never did I think to perform such a task as this; never imagined that I could stand in the midst of such an assembly, to give the parting word from this sacred desk to a company of volunteer soldiers enlisted in their country's defence. Yet let me say, that strange and painful as the service is, it is no unwilling part that I perform. I have never been an advocate for war. I have preached the gospel of peace and good tidings. I would that there were no such necessity laid upon you and upon me; yet my heart is with you, my countrymen, and I bid you God speed in this work, though it may be a mission of death to many.

.   .   .   .   .   .

In the name, therefore, of God, and from this house of God, where prayer shall continually ascend for you, we bid you go forward, we give you our blessing, and shall not cease to implore the blessing of heaven upon you. Your cause is ours. Dear as you are to us, and bound in the tenderest ties of earthly kindred, yet for our country's service and the maintenance of all that is most precious in human society, we give you up, sons, brothers, husbands though you be, to stand in the deadly breach. We know well the danger. Some of you may not return to us again. Your ranks may be fearfully thinned, though it is not certain but that we who remain here behind at home may be called to fall first at our own firesides. It is not certain yet where the blow will first be struck. The danger is widespread and threatening, and we cannot escape it. God be thanked that we are all aroused as one man to meet it, and that he has given us one heart to take the sword of justice to avenge that accursed treason, which, considering all the circumstances of the case, is without a parallel in the history of the world, and which demands the most signal, summary punishment that violated law can inflict.

In the name then of our loved country, in the name of fathers and mothers, and sisters and wives, whom you love; in the name of the ministers of our holy region; in the name of God—that God who loveth truth and justice, and is terrible to the evil doer, we bid you go and God go with you. May He make your arm strong, and your hearts courageous to do valiant service, while you are ever cheered in the darkest hour, when the missiles of death load the air, and there are many here who will not cease to pray for you and commend you in humble supplication to heaven.

Dr. Wicks was followed by Dr. L. G. Leonard, of the Baptist church, who with Rev. Mr. Wakefield, of Harmar, and Rev. Mr. Mumford, of the Unitarian church, occupied the pulpit. D. P. Bosworth, president of the Washington County Bible society, then addressed the volunteers and presented each with a neat pocket edition of the New Testament. At the close of the ceremony Reuben L. Nye, one of the volunteers, ascended the pulpit stairs, "and responded in behalf of the company in an exceedingly appropriate and eloquent speech."

Dr. Leonard then closed the exercises with the benediction.

This was in the oldest church in Ohio, and these ceremonies are said to have been the most impressive and effecting ever witnessed within its walls.

Before the volunteers left for Columbus on Monday morning, the ladies of the city of Marietta presented them with a splendid silk flag. This was in the presence of an immense crowd on the commons, Melton Clarke making the presentation speech and Captain Frank Buell responding.

Thus cheered and encouraged, and with the benediction of the entire community upon them, the first company of volunteers from Washington county left for the war. Their progress up the Muskingum was like a triumphal march. People flocked to the landings to greet them as the steamer approached. At Lowell the entire population turned out, and cheer upon cheer was given. Speeches were made, and a purse of over sixty dollars was raised for them. After the boat was gone, Albert Chandler and Warner Green started a subscription paper to raise money for the equipment of a company, and for the support of the families of those who should volunteer. In one hour's time, thirteen hundred dollars were subscribed, one man, James S. Stowe, pledging five hundred dollars. At Beverly, the citizens had already formed a company of home guards of over a hundred strong, and as the steamer approached they fired a salute. The Beverly brass band then played a patriotic air, and were followed by the Beverly vocal band, who sung the stirring song, "My Native Land." Speeches were made—George P. Buell responding on behalf of the company. It is said, on good authority, that Colonel E. S. McIntosh, an old citizen, probably upon a timely suggestion, bought up all the underwear in town and presented it to the volunteers. The company went into quarters at Camp Jackson, Columbus, and were assigned to the Eighteenth regiment as company B, of that regiment.

A company of volunteers of about one hundred strong was organized at Beverly, April 23, 1861, called the Washington guards. The following were the commissioned officers: John Henderson, captain; Thomas Ross, first lieutenant; Oliver H. P. Scott, second lieutenant. They were assigned to the Eighteenth regiment, and became company K, of that organization.

The militia system of Ohio, under the fostering care of Governor Chase, had, at the beginning of the war, grown to be an institution of some consequence, and in nearly every county of the State could be found one or more companies, with more or less proficiency in drill, and the tactics, according to the length of time such companies had been organized and the efficiency of their officers.

When the war broke out these military organizations were of great utility in furnishing men somewhat familiar with the military art, to take the lead in forming companies and regiments out of the mass of raw volunteers offered the State.

Ohio was, at the time, divided into military divisions. The Seventh division comprised the counties of Fairfield, Hocking, Perry, Scioto, Lawrence, Jackson, Pike, Newton, Washington, Athens, Meigs, and Gallia. The whole of this large district was under the command of Major General Jesse Hildebrand—headquarters at Marietta. This division was subdivided as follows: Fairfield, Hocking, and Perry counties, under command of Brigadier General N. Schleich—headquarters at Lancaster; Scioto, Lawrence, Pike, Jackson, and Vinton counties, under command of Brigadier General Peter Kinney—headquarters at Portsmouth; Washington, Athens, Meigs, and Gallia counties, under command of Brigadier General Robert A. Constable—headquarters at Athens.

General Hildebrand's staff was as follows: Colonel A. W. McCormick, assistant adjutant general and division inspector; Colonel John Marshall, assistant quartermaster general; Colonel Melvin Clarke, assistant judge advocate general; Colonel A. L. Haskins, assistant engineer-in-chief; Major J. B. Hovey, Major I. R. Waters, and Major W. B. Whittlesey, aids.

On April 22, 1861, in pursuance of orders received from Columbus, General Hildebrand issued his general order No. 1, calling on the people of the Seventh division for ten thousand men. Whenever eighty men should be secured they were authorized to form an infantry company, and if forty men be secured, a light artillery company, and to elect one captain, one first lieutenant, one second lieutenant, four sergeants, four corporals, and two musicians. This was promptly responded to, more men being offered than could be used, under the President's call, the quota of the State being thirteen regiments.

The language of the general order as to the disposition of the men was as follows:

All companies which may be organized in counties near the Ohio river to remain where organized, to defend the frontier, while all other companies will hold themselves in readiness to march when and wherever the President of the United States, through the Governor of Ohio, may direct.

General Hildebrand and his staff soon afterwards tendered their services to the Government; but the general and the most of the members of his staff were destined to other duties, and to act important parts on widely separated fields, and in commands tried by the storm of battle, where the glory of a military uniform was little thought of. The general himself died in the service, at Alton, Illinois. He was a man of good presence, brave, and did good service as commandant of a brigade at Shiloh. His career will be more fully noticed further on. Colonel McCormick was severely wounded at the battle of Shiloh, in a charge by Forest's Texan cavalry. Colonel Clarke, while in command of the Thirty-sixth Ohio, was killed by a cannon shot at Antietam. Colonel Haskins died of injuries received while colonel of the Sixty-third Ohio, and Captain Whittlesey was killed at the battle of Mission Ridge, while leading his company in that memorable charge.

During the first two years of the war there was great fear along the border and in Washington county, of raids by the rebels. News came to Marietta on Sunday, April 21, 1861, that a large body of rebels was about to descend on Parkersburgh, and great alarm was felt as to the threatening attitude of affairs, and the following dispatch was sent to the capital:

MARIETTA, OHIO, April 21—5 P. M.

To Governor Dennison:

It is rumored that rebel troops are on their way to Parkersburgh, Virginia. We do not know what credit to give this report. It is, however, reasonable to suppose that Parkersburgh, being the terminus of one branch of the Baltimore & Ohio railroad, will be made in any event a base of operations by the rebel military, and that we are in danger of being overrun by foraging parties and perhaps worse events. We therefore feel that an absolute necessity exists of being at least prepared with a full supply of arms and ammunition, of which we are wholly destitute. We may also need more troops than can be raised on the border, and experienced drill officers. We shall at once organize a home guard, which we believe it to be of the utmost importance to arm. We want especially cannon, and as many as we can have. We think there can be no possible doubt of the existence of an overwhelming necessity for the occupancy of this point and Belpre, opposite Parkersburgh, at once. A messenger will leave for Columbus to-night.

A. T. NYE,
President of City Council.
M. CLARKE,
Of Major General Hildebrand's staff.

The messenger sent was Beman Gates, esq., who went to Columbus and laid the matter before the governor, with what success will be seen further on.

On the next day, pursuant to a resolution passed by the city council of Marietta, on Saturday, April 20th, a large number of citizens of the county assembled at the court house to arrange for home defence. Two committees were appointed to carry out the objects of the meeting, one to raise money for the benefit of the families of volunteers, consisting of Hon. William R. Putnam, J. S. Sprague, and Henry Fearing; the other a committee of safety, consisting of Colonel John Mills, William P. Cutler, William R. Putnam, Davis Green, Anselem T. Nye, Harlow Chapin, Rufus E. Harte, David C. Skinner, and the mayor, Hon. William A. Whittlesey.

Measures for the defence of the county, and especially of Marietta city, were adopted. Arms and ammunition were needed, and very few, if any, arms were to be had. Meanwhile, in order to utilize the means of defence at hand, two iron cannon, in the city, were put in readiness for active service, and an order was given to the foundry of A. T. Nye, jr., to cast solid shot for fixed ammunition. In response to the dispatch and to the personal application of Mr. Gates, the governor ordered the First regiment, light artillery, Third brigade, Fourth division of Ohio volunteer militia, from Cleveland and vicinity, to report at Marietta for the defence of that point.* The regiment was made up of six companies,

---

*Mr. Reid, in Ohio in the War, says: "Governor Dennison, as early as April 19th, four days before the call for volunteers, determined to protect the exposed points. Marietta, Parkersburgh, and Gallipolis were the points, and Marietta was considered the place of greatest danger. Colonel Barnett, of Cleveland, had already tendered the services of himself and command, and he was ordered to report at Columbus. Meantime, on Sunday, April 21st, the Columbus machine shops were opened at the request of the governor, and before night two hundred solid shot were cast. The next day, the twenty-second, the battery arrived, and went by way of Loveland to Marietta." And in a foot note he says: "As the battery entered Columbus, a committee of

citizens from Marietta arrived to represent their danger to the governor and to ask for succor. They found that his foresight had already secured them, and some of the committee, turning immediately back, reached Marietta again on the same train which bore the battery they had gone to ask."

of twenty men each, and six guns, under command of Colonel James Barnett.

On Tuesday night, April 23rd, the regiment arrived and went into camp at the fair grounds. This was the first camp established, and was named Camp Putnam, in honor of General Rufus Putnam, of the Revolutionary war. These were the first troops to arrive in Washington county. The next was the Fourteenth regiment Ohio volunteer militia, raised in the Tenth congressional district, and commanded by Colonel James B. Steedman. Then came the Eighteenth regiment, on its way to Virginia. The latter regiment was made up as follows:

Company A, Lawrence County guards, Captain Roders; company B, Marietta Blues, Captain Buell, company C, Lawrence County guards, Captain Bolles; company D, Vinton County guards, Captain Caldwell; company E, Lawrence County guards, Captain Merrill; company F, Meigs County guards, Captain Curtis, company G, Galia County guards, Captain Aleshire; company H, Meigs County guards, Captain Waller; company K, Washington County guards, Captain Henderson; company L, Jackson County guards, Captain Hoffman. Regimental officers, elected at Parkersburgh, Virginia: colonel, J. R. Stanley, of McArthur; lieutenant colonel, William Bolles, of Ironton; major, William H. Bisby, of Marietta; quartermaster, Beman Gates. Mr. Gates afterwards resigned, and John C. Paxton was appointed.

At this point it will be well to understand the situation. The rebels had penetrated western Virginia and pushed their forces along both branches of the Baltimore & Ohio railroad, from Grafton westward, towards Parkersburgh, and along the northern branch toward Wheeling, burning bridges and trestle works as they went. This spread general alarm throughout western Virginia, to Wheeling, Parkersburgh, and along the border in Ohio. Governor Dennison resolved that the line of battle should not be on the border of Ohio, but along the natural line made by the Alleghanies. And this was against the advice of General McClellan, who counselled delay, but the governor was positive, and his plan prevailed. Accordingly, on the twenty-sixth of May, the following movement was ordered: The Fourteenth regiment, Colonel Steedman, stationed at Zanesville, and the Eighteenth, Colonel Stanley, stationed at Camp Jackson, were ordered to Marietta to support Barnett's battery. The Seventeenth regiment, Colonel Connell, stationed at Lancaster, was ordered to Zanesville. The Fifteenth regiment, Colonel Andrews, stationed at Zanesville, was ordered to Bellaire, to await orders. The Sixteenth regiment, Colonel Irvine, stationed at Columbus, was ordered to Zanesville to support Colonel Andrews. The Nineteenth regiment, Colonel Beatty, and the Twenty-first, Colonel Norton, stationed at Cleveland, were ordered to Columbus, there to await orders. Colonel Steedman, with the Fourteenth and a part of Barnett's artillery, crossed to Virginia on the morning of May 27th, arriving at Parkersburgh at eleven o'clock, being the first troops to enter southern territory, Ellsworth, with the New York Zouaves, entering Virginia from Washington at 2 P. M. After putting a quietus on the secession element in Parkersburgh, they moved out on the Baltimore

& Ohio railroad, rebuilding bridges and trestle works as they advanced. Colonel Irvine, with his regiment at Bellaire, crossed the day following, and was joined by a regiment of loyal Virginians, under Colonel Kelley, and they pushed on out the northern branch of the Baltimore & Ohio, repairing and rebuilding bridges and trestles. The two columns met and formed a junction at Grafton, Virginia. After them the gallant sons of Ohio and Indiana went pouring into Virginia, driving the rebels before them. Fifteen miles beyond Grafton, at Philippi, they fought the first battle of the war, and gained a victory.

Thus, by the foresight and energy of Governor Dennison, was West Virginia saved to the Union, important railway communications recovered and held, and Ohio and the border protected from invasion and predatory warfare.

On the twenty-third of June, pursuant to an order of the adjutant general of the State, the following militia companies arrived and were distributed along the railroad between the city of Marietta and Athens to guard the Marietta & Cincinnati railroad, known as the "old line." General McClellan feared that his communications would be interrupted and that his supplies might be cut off by the destruction of the bridges and trestle works on this railroad, which was an important matter at that time. These companies were: company F, First regiment, Captain Miller, thirty men; company B, Second regiment, Captain King, thirty men; company F, Second regiment, Captain Garrett, thirty men; company D, Second regiment, Captain Menken, fifteen men; company E, Third regiment, Captain Buckner, forty men; company G, Third regiment, Captain J. H. Carter, sixty men. The whole under command of Lieutenant Colonel A. E. Jones. Afterwards four of these companies were relieved by four Washington county companies, one of which was the Union Blue company recruited up after the three months men had gone, commanded by Captain William B. Mason; the Fireman Zouaves, Captain S. F. Shaw—both companies from Marietta—one company from Harmar, Captain Joseph B. Daniels, and one—the Belpre guards—commanded by Captain F. H. Loring, from Belpre. They were distributed along the railroad in squads, and were armed, clothed and subsisted the same as other volunteers. This service although not especially dangerous, was important, and as these companies are not elsewhere recorded we give them below as far as possible to ascertain their names:

COMMISSIONED OFFICERS.

Captain F. H. Loring; Lieutenant James King.

NON-COMMISSIONED OFFICERS.

Orderly Sergeant A. P. Sherman, Sergeant J. L. O'Neal, John Mitchell, C. W. Stone, John Drain.

CORPORALS.

A. H. Browning, P. W. Simpson, E. M. O'Neal, A. D. Stone.

PRIVATES.

H. G. Allen, D. C. Allen, James R. Barrows, George Ballard, Daniel Breckenride, William Baker, W. W. Botkin, William Berry, Samuel Barkley, Jacob Clark, A. F. Downer, Moses Dugan, George Dunlevy, J. G. Ellenwood, Council Flowers, George Flowers, L. R. Forbes, George Gage, Alexander Galbraith, George Hutchinson, John Haddow, George A. Howe, John Hutchinson, D. B Horton, C. B. Kirkpatrick, Fremont Kirkpatrick, Henry Kirkpatrick, Corwin H. Loring, George Lysle, George M. Conaughey, Joseph Marsh, Joseph Miller, James Mendenhall, James McGaffey, F. F. Newport, J. R. Newport, M. Noland, Joseph Noland, F. Odenshan, E. K. O'Neal, William Powell, James Powell, Josiah Rutherford, Jacob Rutherford, B. B. Stone, Frank Stone, George G. Stone, William F. Shee, Joseph Sterlin, William F. Sayre, Henry Schram, Harrison Smith, John A. Shipe, S. C. H. Smith, Milton Stone, F. B. Simpson, Martin Tharp, John Thompson, William White, Noah Welch.

Roll of Captain William B. Mason's company D, in the First regiment, Third brigade, Seventh division of Ohio volunteer militia, enrolled on the twenty-seventh day of July, 1861, and mustered into the service of the State of Ohio the twenty-seventh day of July, 1861.

COMMISSIONED OFFICERS.

Captain William B. Mason, First Lieutenant James McCaddon, Second Lieutenant James Lewis.

NON-COMMISSIONED OFFICERS.

First Sergeant W. L. Theis, Sergeants George W. Kennedy, Robert H McKittrick, Louis Schmidt; Corporals Jacob Unger, John Mahuken, John Plug, William L. Porterfield; Bugler Louis Schlicker.

PRIVATES.

George Baldwin, Frank Braddock, Peter Beck, George Booth, John Burke, Frederick Becker, John Dow, John Danker, Henry Estman, John W. Eaton, David M. Grimes, William Hose, Seymour J. Hathaway, Andrew Holden, Luther M. Ingraham, David F. Jones, Frank E. Jett, Arius Nye Kennedy, Joel Kennedy, David H. Lewis, Dennis Mulhane, John J. Medlicott, Patrick C. Meers, Frank McCaddon, Theodore McCaddon, Frederick Mahuken, Michael Manly, George W. Reynolds, John Ratgen, Nicholas Roeder, William Robinson, Frank Shafer, William W. Skinner, William H. Storrs, Richard Siebers, William Salzman, Samuel Tracy, Frank Towsley, Jacob Wood, J. Henry Wellbrook, Julius Wenland.

Muster roll of Captain Joseph B. Daniels' company, First regiment, Third brigade, Seventh division, of Ohio volunteer militia, commanded by Major O. Bennett.

COMMISSIONED OFFICER.

Captain Joseph B. Daniels (both lieutenants refused to respond to the call).

NON-COMMISSIONED OFFICERS.

First Sergeant Arthur B. Chapin, Sergeants William S. Judd, Diton Fearing, George Maxon; Corporals George Reppert, George Marsh, Abram Daniels, Otis J. Chambers, Drummer John Knox.

PRIVATES.

Daniel Bingham, William Bingham, Joseph Boyd, John Chambers, Salmon Chambers, Charles Dugan, James Doughitt, William Dugan, John Edelston, Dennis A. Finch, Charles L. Gates, John Huff, Isaac Lucas, Solon Mathews, Horatio W. Mason, Thomas McNamara, Henry E. Nugent, Samuel H. Niece, Madison J Naylor, James S. Parker, William Parker, Samuel H. Putnam, Simon Readin, Byron P. Reppert, William W. Rice, Darwin A. Scott, William Snodgrass, William Tunnicliff, James Wright, Luther Wright, John L. Young.

We have now passed the opening chapter of the war as far as it relates to Washington county. This was the romantic period of the contest, if such a thing can be said of so grim a subject. The hardships, dangers and privations of active service had not been fully realized. The theory at first entertained that armed resistance could be put down in a three months' campaign was soon dismissed, and the enormous strength of the Rebellion began to be understood.

On July 21st the great battle of Bull Run was fought and lost, the flower of the Union army destroyed, or turned into a fleeing rabble, and a great mass of war material swallowed up in the vortex of war. It was hard to believe this news, but what seemed at that time a dire disaster proved, in reality, a loud note of warning, and

to that extent, at least, beneficial. It broadened the views of the administration as to war measures. Henceforward the war was to be carried on more aggressively, and on a gigantic scale. The President, on the day after the battle, issued a call for five hundred thousand three years' men. Another outburst of patriotic feeling ensued. This was the first great call to arms. The country was stirred to its centre, and the scenes of volunteering that followed were grand. It was from these five hundred regiments that the vital power to crush the Rebellion came. They furnished the great bulk of the officers who finally led our armies to victory.

The Representative of this district at that time was the Hon. William P. Cutler, who was attending a called session of Congress. Having received enquiries about raising a regiment in Washington county he telegraphed as follows:

WASHINGTON, D. C., July 23, 1861.

M. Clarke and J. Hildebrand:

Government will probably accept an infantry regiment if ready in fifteen days. Can you raise it? I will bear all incidental expenses of raising it. Answer.   WILLIAM P. CUTLER.

The response sent was that Washington county could and would do it.

This was the beginning of the Thirty-sixth regiment, companies for which began to rendezvous immediately at Marietta.

Colonel John Groesbeck, of Cincinnati, had offered to raise and equip a regiment at his own expense, and the liberality of this offer attracted general attention and commendation. The companies for that regiment were about this time gathering at Camp Colerain, near Cincinnati. There was a company in Marietta at this time known as the "Washington County Rifle Guards." They resolved to join Groesbeck's regiment. Lieutenant W. II. Edgerton came from Newport with a battalion of men and joined the guards, the election of officers resulted as follows:

John C. Fell, captain; William H. Edgerton, first lieutenant; Henry W. Shepard, second lieutenant.

This was the first three years' company that left the county. They numbered one hundred and fifteen men. Upon leaving Marietta July 22, 1861, for the war, they were escorted by a Marietta company called the Fireman Zouaves, Captain S. F. Shaw, the German brass band, and a large concourse of citizens, relatives and friends. They marched through the streets, Ohio and Front, from their headquarters at the old woollen factory and across to the Harmar depot The Zouaves, finding that the guards had no colors, presented their beautiful flag, through Captain Shaw, who made the presentation speech, which was responded to by Captain Fell in appropriate words, and which act of courtesy was received with cheers by the departing volunteers. This company became company B, and Groesbeck's regiment the Thirty-ninth Ohio volunteer infantry.

The following is the complete roster:

COMPANY B, THIRTY-NINTH OHIO VOLUNTEER—FIRST THREE YEARS COMPANY.

COMMISSIONED OFFICERS.

Captain John C. Fell, First Lieutenant William H. Edgerton, Second Lieutenant Henry W. Shepard.

PRIVATES AND NON-COMMISSIONED OFFICERS.

Henry Adams, Furman Abbot, Jacob Abendshau, J. Abernachard, Samuel Ackerson, William C. Buck, John C. Buck, Henry Bast, C. Briggs, P. Bronson, Wilson Congdon, J. S. Carver, James Cahoon, John Cisler, B. Congdon, John Congdon, H. Coleman, T. J. Conner, M. L. Cook, G. W. Chapman, J. Carson, William Carpenter, David C. Day, E. J. Douglass, W. W. Dye, K. Davis, L. K. Dutton, J Fifer, G. Elbfritz, J. Ebinger, Lewis W. Linch, W. Fise, H. Farnsworth, William Grass, B. F. Gilpin, A. H. Gardz, J. W. Goodrich, J. Goddard, I. Green, D. D. Huntsman, William Hobby, C. Hallet, D. D. Hughes, J. Hutchinson, W. Hackathan, Lyman Hall, Luther Hathaway, L. Hyer, Jacob Johnson, A. Johns, William Kennedy, William J. Kemp, Frederick K. Lebzer, A. W. S. Landy, Joseph H. Lapham, T. Lang, E. J. Ludgen, Smith Ming, William S. Morse, James McCall, George Moore, M. McManus, Neil McLaughlin, A F. Moore, W. Miller, M. Miller, L. Mine, J. McCullough, A. A. Middleswart, G. W. Middleswart, Lewis Noe, David P. Pugh, Daniel Pfaff, Ebenezer Pearce, George Payne, C. Pfaff, F. B. Reckard, C. L. Russell, E. H. Richards, Nedor Roon, C. Riesch, C. W. Reynold, A. Rudig, William Rouse, F. W. Ranger, D. S. Reynolds, George T. Rice, Moses Smith, George Soler, John Stewart, Frederick Solzer, William St. Clair, C. J. Skidmore, N. H. Shaw, Matthew Stricker, William Stewart, S H. W. Smith, J. E Schmidt, Eli Steen, F. Snodgrass, W. J. Seevers, J. F. Snoetast, J. E. Smith, William Theis, John E. Thurman, R. Taylor, John Wood, Henry Wendelker, S. Wells, Lewis Zimmer, L. Zimmerman.

The second company was "Koenig's German Rifles," which was raised in one week. It was composed mainly of Germans, and included many of the best shots of that nationality in the county. They elected Jacob Koenig captain, and left for Camp Colerain July 31, 1861, deferring the election of the other officers until their arrival in camp. The company became company F, Thirty-ninth Ohio volunteer infantry.

About the first of August, 1861, the "Muskingum company" went into camp at Marietta, the first of the gallant Thirty-sixth regiment. They were composed of the young men of the valley of the Muskingum, immediately above Marietta. Twenty of them were from Rainbow and the neighborhood of Devol's dam, and comprised the best, and in fact, nearly all the young men in that locality. They were officered as follows: Captain Hiram F. Devol, First Lieutenant J. Gage Barker, Second Lieutenant J. C. Selby, First Sergeant Miles A. Stacy. The next company was the "Salem Light Guard,"* a splendid body of men, officered as follows: Captain Jewett Palmer, jr., First Lieutenant James Stanley, Second Lieutenant Ernst Lindner, First Sergeant John A. Palmer. Soon the Thirty-sixth regiment was full.

Captain T. W. Moore's company was raised in the vicinity of Tunnel Station, in Washington county, and were considered a fine body of men, and Captain Adney's

* Before the departure of the guards from Salem the ladies of that place presented the company with a fine flag, their spokesman addressing the departing volunteers in appropriate words. Their captain, Jewett Palmer, jr., responded as follows:

"Ladies of Salem: We thank you for this stand of colors; we know and fully appreciate the spirit which prompted you in procuring them for us, and knowing this we receive them promising as we do to defend them if necessary with our lives, and to return them to your hands. It may be tattered and torn, but not dishonored.

"In speaking of this noble ensign of freedom, it is not necessary to enumerate the causes which by degrees have brought about this very presentation. Suffice it to know that on the fourteenth day of April last, for the first time since this flag has had a national existence, it was struck, and that too, by fraternal hands raised in rebellion against it; therefore we consider it the duty of every loyal citizen to rally beneath its folds and march in solid phalanx to the defence of our country."

was from the west end of Washington and from Athens county. The governor appointed Melvin Clarke lieutenant colonel, Professor Ebenezer B. Andrews, major; Benjamin D. Fearing, adjutant, and John M. Woodbridge, quartermaster. Neither of these officers had any military education, and it was decided to secure a regularly educated army officer, if possible, as colonel of the regiment. Major E. B. Andrews, to carry out this idea, went to Columbus to lay the matter before Governor Dennison. At first it was supposed that Colonel Sill would be appointed; but Colonel Sill, a member of the governor's staff, was needed in organizing the thousands of raw recruits then flocking to the Ohio camp. Major Slemmer, however, of the regular army, inspector general on the staff of General Rosecrans, was designated as commanding officer, for the time being—the same Lieutenant A. J. Slemmer who was in command of Fort Pickens, at the entrance of Pensacola harbor, Florida, when the war began, and who, by his prompt refusal to surrender, and promptness in preparing for defence, saved that important fortification to the Union.

The Thirty-sixth was, on August 30th, ordered into Virginia, Major Slemmer joining the regiment at Parkersburgh; but soon after Colonel George Crook, of the Eighth United States infantry, was assigned to the command of the regiment, and began at once the task of drilling and disciplining both officers and men.

The advent of Colonel Crook was an event of great importance to the Thirty-sixth. He won the confidence and respect of the men, and imparted to the regiment a character for discipline and good behavior that they never lost during subsequent terms of service.

During the months of September and October of 1861, several important commands were in process of formation in Washington county. Colonel T. C. H. Smith, of Marietta, was commissioned as lieutenant colonel of the First Ohio cavalry; and soon after, on September 11th, Captain Thomas J. Patten, and Lieutenant John D. Barker went into Camp Putnam with sixty men for that regiment, which became company I, First Ohio volunteer cavalry. At the same time Pierpoint battery, De Beck's battery, Huntington's battery, the Sixty-third Ohio volunteer infantry, the Seventy-seventh Ohio volunteer infantry, were all enlisting men—the men that were shortly to do such gallant service for their country.

Captain Frank Buell who was always devoted to his men, had become dissatisfied at Ohio's treatment of the volunteers, and with the delay of the State authorities in paying off his men, recently returned from the three months' service, and he therefore resolved to raise a company of artillery for the new State of West Virginia. He had no difficulty in securing a sufficient number of men, many of the old company of three months' men joining him, the entire company being from Marietta and vicinity. They were accepted by Governor Pierpont, whose name they took, and were known as Buell's Pierpont battery and Battery C, First regiment West Virginia, light artillery. They left October 9th for Camp Carlisle on Wheeling Island, West Virginia. A large concourse of citizens and friends witnessed their departure. The Young

America brass band accompanied them to Wheeling, the leader and one of their number, William Jenvey, having joined the battery.

At this time Captain William Craig, of the regular army, had charge of the army stores and military depots at Bellaire, Marietta and Parkersburgh, with headquarters at Marietta. He desired to raise a regiment for the war, and was commissioned by Governor Dennison as colonel, for that purpose. He was a graduate of West Point, and was much esteemed as an officer and gentleman. The prospects for raising the regiment seemed good, and it was christened the Sixty-third Ohio volunteer infantry. Alexander L. Haskins, a civil engineer of Marietta, was appointed major, and the lieutenant colonelcy temporarily left vacant.

About the same time a vigorous movement was inaugurated to raise a regiment for Colonel Jesse Hildebrand, who stood high in the State militia service, and had strong hold upon the popular heart. He had, for a long time, been the favorite military man of the county, and many people wished to have him command a Washington county regiment. His friends had expected that he would command the Thirty-sixth, but a regular army officer was appointed. His cause was urged upon Governor Dennison, but to no purpose. The governor was hampered in some way, and could not act. He had learned by this time that there was a war department in this country, and governed his actions accordingly. Colonel Hildebrand finally tendered his service to Governor Pierpont who did not need any urging to take advantage of the situation, and at once issued a commission to Hildebrand as colonel, and ordered him to rendezvous his men at Parkersburgh. This led to an emphatic protest by the friends of the colonel.* About this time the War Department authorized Governor Dennison to commission all Ohio officers who were promised commissions by Governor Pierpont, and so the merits of Colonel Hildebrand were recognized, and he was immediately commissioned by the governor to raise a regiment of three years men in Washington county. W. De Hass

* Memorial numerously signed by citizens of the city of Marietta.

MARIETTA, OHIO, September 14, 1861.

We, the undersigned citizens of Marietta, Ohio, having felt a deep interest in the appointment of General J. Hildebrand to the command of a regiment, regret very much that the governor of Ohio refused to commission him to such command, and we regret still more that General Hildebrand is after many efforts of his numerous friends to procure for him the aforesaid command, compelled to either remain out of the service of our country or take command of a regiment in the State of Virginia, which command we understand he is about to take, and which patriotic course in him we do most sincerely and heartily endorse:

W. F. Curtis, A. N. Hill, W. A. Whittlesey, James B. Hovey, Isaac N. Goldsmith, H. B. Shipman, H. H. Drown, A. T. Nye, B. F. Hart, Arius Nye, David Allan, Davis Green, W. P. Cutler, John Mills, Douglas Putnam, E. W. Buell, James Holden, Jesse Vickers, H. Brenan, C. E. Glines, George S. Jones, William S. Ward, James M. Booth, J. S. Sprague, H. Purch, E. F. Hill, Jacob Cram, Thomas W. Ewart, J. A. Hicks, A. Finch, George W. Wilson, D. G. Mathews, Charles B. Hall, J. R. Waters, John Hall, A. L. Haskins, A. Tupper Nye, jr., Warner Green, John Scott, jr., Joseph Holden, jr., James McLeod, R. E. Harte, E. Winchester, D. B. Bosworth, S. P. Hildreth, W. H. Buell, John Marshall, John W. Thomas, A. W. McCormick, L. Sayes, Horatio Booth, C. E. Sherman, W. L. Ralston, Charles F. Buell, Hugh Donahoe, L. A. Jones, George Benedict, F. A. Lovell, J. M. Hook, E. C. Dawes, W. G. Bloomfield and others.

was appointed lieutenant colonel, and Benjamin D. Fearing at that time serving as adjutant of the Thirty-sixth, was appointed major.

Here then were two regiments authorized to be raised at the same time, in the county, and this naturally led to some friction between the parties interested in these different organizations. The fact of Colonel Craig being a West Pointer, acted against him as well as in his favor. The volunteer could never exactly understand the regular army officers' manner and style of doing things, and they often charged him with being haughty and tyrannical with the common soldier. No doubt great injustice was done Colonel Craig in this way, but he had able defenders, and they only intensified the opposition. The result was that the Seventy-seventh was soon full and ready for service, while the Sixty-third was slow in getting men. Finally the Sixty-third was ordered to Columbus to consolidate with the Fifty-second, but that proved an unfortunate combination, and the Sixty-third returned again to Marietta for the purpose of filling up its ranks. The Twenty-second regiment, a fragmentary organization at Camp Dennison, was ordered to Marietta to consolidate with the Sixty-third, and arrived January 30, 1862. Colonel William Craig having resigned the colonelcy, John W. Sprague, a captain in the Seventh regiment, was appointed colonel, and after remaining in Camp Putnam until February 18, 1862, they received marching orders and departed for Paducah, Kentucky.

Colonel Jesse Hildebrand, immediately after being commissioned by Governor Dennison, received orders to form a camp and recruit up a regiment, which was to become the gallant Seventy-seventh. Accordingly, he chose a public square in Marietta, the Quadranaon, and named it Camp Tupper, for General Anselem Tupper. On the south side, along the line of Third street, he built ten barracks, for as many companies, and on the elevated square in the camp, a field piece was placed for firing a morning and evening gun. The regiment was rapidly filled. Many of the recruiting lieutenants held meetings through the east side of the county, as did the Rev. William Pearce, who afterwards became the chaplain of the regiment. On January 9, 1862, the regiment received marching orders, and went to Camp Dennison.

Governor Dennison, in the fall of 1861, finding that the recruiting and handling of a large number of soldiers entailed an immense amount of labor upon the executive department, and especially on the adjutant general, resolved to systematize and divide the work so that each county would have its share, and at the same time have competent supervision and proper attention given to details incident to the service. He accordingly divided the State into military districts, which were the same as the congressional districts. Each district had over it a district military committee, appointed by the governor, and they appointed a committee of five for each county, and the county military committee appointed a committee of three in each township. These were the men to whom the governor appealed in emergencies, and they appealed directly to the people. Their duties were varied and often arduous, at times requiring their con-

stant attention to the exclusion of all other business. They served without pay, and considering the character and value of the service rendered, deserve to be gratefully remembered.

The military committee appointed in the fall of 1861 for Washington county were William R. Putnam, chairman, Samuel F. Cooke secretary, and John Newton, Mark Green, and George W. Baker.

The township committees appointed at the same time by the committees were as follows:

Adams—Dr. William F. Clark, Dennis Gibbs, Jonas Mason. Aurelius—Thomas Ellison, Samuel L. Berkley, Theodore Jevres. Barlow—J. W. Merrill, H. E. Vincent, William Breckenridge. Belpre—O. R. Loring, John Stone, Joseph Potter. Decatur—William P. Gamble, Jonah McGirr, W. C. Smith. Dunham—J. J. Hollister, William A. Chevalier, Edward McLarty. Fairfield—Dr. J. W. Marsha, John B. Farris, William Thompson. Fearing—Joseph W. Stanley, Orin Chapman, F. G. Guitteau. Grandview—Samuel F. Cooke, Moses Meeks, John Pool. Independence—John G. Thomas, Squire D. Riggs, Dr. Valentine. Lawrence—A. J. Dye, A. W. Dye, J. M. Caywood. Ludlow—George W. Harvey, Christopher Dickson, William Bell. Liberty—Jackson A. Hicks, John H. Jamison, John Roberts. Newport—Luther Edgerton, Aaron Edgell, Edgar O'Neal. Palmer—John Breckenridge, sr., J. M. Murdough, D. J. Richards. Salem—Josiah Morgan, Henry Schofield, Moses Blake. Marietta City—George Benedict, First ward; David C. Skinner, Second ward; Thomas W. Ewart, Third ward. Muskingum—Colonel William West, William F. Curtis, Johnson Bean. Harmar—David Putnam, Colonel D. Barber, Henry Fearing. Waterford—Enoch S. McIntosh, Samuel B. Robinson, Mathew Patterson. Warren—Moses Morris, Dean Briggs, August S. Bailey Wesley—S. C. Van Law, Robert Hodgin, J. P Bruce. Watertown—W. F. Lasure, Henry McGrew, H. L. Deming. Union—Wesley Coombs, J. B Dyar, Samuel Maxwell.

It was upon the county military committee, however, that the most of the labor and responsibility fell. They were charged with the entire business of recruiting in their counties; and could adopt such measures to hasten the work as they thought proper. All candidates for commissions had to have an endorsement by the county committee, and they were enjoined to be very careful whom they recommended. They were also charged with collecting clothing and supplies for the army. No further praise need to be bestowed upon the conduct of the military committee of Washington county than to say that through all the emergencies and trying ordeals of four years of the war the same men first appointed were retained to the end.

In closing the year 1861 there are many things that might be said in regard to the management of military affairs outside as well as in this county, about which there was great difference of opinion at the time, but it is not the province of this history to discuss such matters nor have we room for an extended examination, but one thing should be said, at least, a word in justification of Governor Dennison. The governor was not renominated, but was passed with a commendatory resolution and David Tod, a war Democrat, taken up in his stead, and elected. Governor Dennison sought no vindication nor asked any one to defend his course, but left it to the future and the sober judgment of the citizens of Ohio to vindicate him, and he has, indeed, been fully justified. He said "Ohio must lead in the war," and he nobly endeavored to make good the promise. The war found him a plain but versatile and talented civilian, with no knowledge of military affairs and with a staff totally un-

acquainted with the demands and emergencies about to overtake them. When hostilities began, and the thousands of citizen soldiers began to crowd into the capital city, it was utterly impossible to meet their demands with even the barest necessities of camp life, and so on, during the succeeding weeks as each new exigency arose, it was met manfully and all demands filled as soon as possible; but Governor Dennison fully realized the great burdens imposed upon him and laid his plans to meet them, and in a short time he had so fully mastered the situation that he was enabled to give his attention to other matters than the mere details of military organization. He planned the first campaign against the enemy in West Virginia which was a grand success, but enough offence had already unavoidably been given to the volunteers, fresh from the comforts of home, to raise a great clamor against him, which extended to every part of the State from which a three months' man had come. The legislature took up the cudgel also and asked for the resignation of certain members of his staff, but the governor, firm, yet dignified, declined to dismiss them, and knowing that he was doing all that could be done, continued to work out his task, and the sequel showed that he did his work well and that a greater part of the complaints were causeless and unjustified by the facts.

When Governor Tod took the reins of government in January, 1862, he found the State fully organized and ready for a vigorous war administration. Many of the men who were subsequently to distinguish themselves and reflect honor upon their native State had already been commissioned by Governor Dennison, and gone to the field.

Mr. Whitelaw Reid, in Ohio in the War, says of the opening of Governor Tod's administration:

With trained assistants, and organized system, and the work thus gradually coming upon him, Governor Tod speedily mastered his new duties. There was no opportunity for distinguishing his administration by the redemption of a State, or the appointment of officers who were soon to reach the topmost round of popular favor, or the adoption of independent war measures during a temporary isolation from the General Government. But what there was to do he did prudently, systematically, and with such judgment as to command the general approval of his constituents.

There was, however, room for all the zeal of patriotism to have full play. The war was constantly affording opportunities for men in authority to show what they were made of, and the year 1862 furnished its full share.

The first soldier from Washington county to be killed in action was Albert W. Leonard, private of company C, Second West Virginia cavalry. He was killed in an action on Jennie's creek, Kentucky, January 7, 1862. His command was in pursuit of Humphrey Marshall, and, on turning a curve in the road, was attacked by the enemy, young Leonard falling at the first volley. He was the son of J. D. Leonard, at that time living at Matamoras, but for many years previous a resident of Marietta. His captain, Thomas Neal, said of him: "Officers and men will attest to his bravery on the field, his exemplary conduct as a soldier, and his honest, upright course as a comrade."

On April 6, 1862, the great battle of Shiloh took place.

It was a momentous and memorable event, as being the first great engagement for our western troops, and one exciting especial interest in Washington county as being the first battle in which the Seventy-seventh regiment was engaged, having seven companies from this county. It was not until the ninth that the full news of the battle was received, and it revealed a tale of slaughter and suffering that startled and aroused the communtiy. On April 10th a public meeting was called at the court house in Marietta to provide means of assistance for the wounded. Beman Gates, William F. Curtis, George M. Woodbridge, Henry Fearing, Dr. Benjamin F. Hart, and George Benedict were sent at once to Cincinnati to make arrangements with the sanitary commission for the relief of the wounded from Washington county, and if necessary to go directly to the battle-ground. Meanwhile ladies assembled at the Episcopal church and made up four boxes of hospital stores, which, together with three hundred dollars in money, were sent along with the committee. A standing committee consisting of Davis Green, W. R. Putnam, W. F. Curtis, I. W. Andrews and Stephen Newton were appointed to raise subscriptions and render such aid to the wounded as occasion might thereafter require.

In this engagement the Seventy-seventh bore a gallant part, and on the third day, while in the advance in pursuit of the enemy, were charged upon by Forest's Texan cavalry and rode down and literally cut to pieces. Their conduct was worthy of regulars. The commanding general of the division neglected to have the Union cavalry within supporting distance, which exposed the infantry to a destructive charge. General Hildebrand, in his official report, says of the battle:

Early on the morning of Sunday, 6th inst., our pickets were fired upon, and shortly after seven o'clock the enemy appeared in force, presenting himself in columns of regiments, at least four deep. He opened immediately upon our camp a heavy fire, following up rapidly with shell. I ordered an advance. The Seventy-seventh and Fifty-seventh regiments were thrown forward to occupy a certain position, but encountered the enemy in force within three hundred yards of our camp. Unfortunately, we were not supported by artillery, and were compelled to retire under cover of our camp, the engagement becoming general along the entire front of the command. A battery having been brought to support our right, the Fifty-seventh and Seventy-seventh stood gallantly side by side for four hours, contending with a force of at least four to one. The battery having been forced from its position, and the infantry both on our right and left having fallen back, it finally became necessary that the regiments forming part of my command should fall back lest their retreat be effectually cut off.   .   .   .   The night I passed on the battlefield in company with Colonels Buckland, Cockerel, Rice and other officers.

That night was one of intense interest on both sides. Beauregard, impatient for the morning light, that he might complete the work so auspiciously begun; and Sherman and Grant hoping for Buell with his fresh divisions, to reinforce the Union army. Buel arrived and crossed, and one of his officers remarked to a gunboat officer, "We will show you some man-of-war fighting to-morrow," and they kept the promise well. Marching to the front they relieved the exhausted troops engaged the day before and drove the rebel army back, regaining the lost ground, and the victory was complete.

General Hildebrand says of Monday's battle:

On monday morning I marched near the field of battle, forming near

the rear, holding my force in readiness to enter into action at any moment, when called upon. We remained in this position, until the enemy had retreated and the victory achieved.

On the eighth instant, in compliance with your order, I marched my brigade, accompanied by a large cavalry force, also by Buckland's brigade, on the Corinth road, about four miles from camp. Halting in an open field, skirmishers were sent forward, who discovered rebel cavalry in considerable force, exhibiting a disposition to fight. The skirmishers immediately fired upon the enemy, when the Seventy-seventh regiment, under command of Lieutenant Colonel De Hass, was ordered up to support them. Soon after forming in line a large body of cavalry made a bold and dashing charge on the skirmishers and the whole regiment. So sudden and rapid was the charge, shooting our men with carbines and revolvers, that they had not time to reload, and fell back, hoping our cavalry would cover the retreat. Unhappily our own cavalry was not sufficiently near to render essential assistance. The rebel cavalry literally rode down our infantry, shooting, sabering, and trampling them under foot. We sustained a loss in killed, wounded, and missing of fifty-seven—nineteen killed on the spot, thirty wounded, and the balance missing. Of the latter, two captains and one second lieutenant are numbered. Captain A. W. McCormick and Captain A. Chandler were meritorious officers. This I may also say of Lieutenant Criswell.   .   .   .   .
With regard to the officers and men who participated in the battle of Pittsburgh, and the affair of Tuesday, I am happy to bear testimony to the fidelity, bravery, and devotion of all.   .   .   .
Major B. D. Fearing, who was immediately in command of the Seventy-seventh regiment, acquitted himself with as much skill, bravery and military bearing as an old officer of long experience, and was not excelled by any other field officer who came under my observation.

In a letter to his wife the general says:

To the credit of the Seventy-seventh and Fifty-seventh be it said, that they fought on their own ground for four hours, against at least four times their number, nor did they fall back in the least until completely overpowered with numbers, and to show how well they fought over two hundred rebels fell and lay dead on the battle-ground in front of our lines, besides double that number wounded, while there were not fifty in both of our regiments, killed, and about a hundred and fifty wounded. I was in the fight all day Sunday, but on Monday held my command as a reserve, ready to bring it into action at any minute needed. The shells and balls flew as thick as hailstones around me on Sunday, but still I came out untouched.   .   .   .   .
The Seventy-seventh has lost in killed, wounded and missing over two hundred, and, in short, I may say that the Seventy-seventh was in the hardest and most important part of the engagement. The rebels fought like devils, they were determined to whip us. They had the best of the battle on Sunday, but we returned the compliment on Monday! I cannot describe to you the awfulness of this most terrible battle, but if I ever live to get home I will try to give you some idea of what it was like.

The roll of killed, wounded and missing of the Seventy-seventh sufficiently attests the brave stand they made. The following is a recapitulation of the whole number:

Company A—4 killed, 13 wounded, 3 missing; total, 20. Company B—4 killed, 10 wounded, 6 missing; total, 20. Company C—3 killed, 10 wounded, 3 missing; total, 16. Company D—5 killed, 18 wounded, total, 23. Company E—6 killed, 13 wounded, 10 missing; total, 29. Company F—2 killed, 11 wounded, 1 missing, total, 14. Company G—9 killed, 10 wounded, 11 missing; total, 30. Company H—4 killed, 8 wounded, 19 missing; total, 31. Company I—11 wounded; total, 11. Company K—5 killed, 9 wounded, 16 missing, total, 30. Total—42 killed, 113 wounded, 69 missing—Total, 224.

Colonel Hildebrand himself exhibited fine, soldierly qualities in this action, and when the Union line was driven back on Sunday he was of great service in rallying the men, not only of his own brigade but of other brigades, and his portly figure and fearless demeanor inspired many a company with renewed confidence and turned them again to the front; and he was, no doubt, of great service in saving the army from complete route before overpowering numbers.

Colonel T. C. H. Smith, of the First Ohio volunteer

cavalry, in a letter to George M. Woodbridge, of Marietta, written from the field of battle, April 12, says:

"Hildebrand and Fearing showed distinguished courage. The first account I had of Hildebrand was from a major of the Fifteenth Illinois, who, unasked, gave me an account of their part in the fight, of their being surprised and their field officers killed, etc. While we were scattered there came along a Colonel Hildebrand rallying the men. I don't know what State he is from, or what his regiment is, but he showed grit. We rallied under him, and fought there until they sent Lieutenant Colonel —— to command us."

On the twenty-sixth of May the startling news was received that Washington city was about to be attacked, followed by a dispatch from the governor of the State calling for troops. The call designated three classes that would be received for the term of three years, for the term of three months, and for guard duty within the State, and saying: "Everything is valueless to us if our Government is overthrown."

This dispatch was accompanied by another, directed to the Washington county military committee, as follows:

"Astounding as the fact may be, Washington city is in imminent danger. You will please raise, without delay, one hundred men, and send them as fast as raised to Camp Chase, where they will be organized and equipped, and such as are not willing to proceed to Washington will perform guard duty in place of the regiment now at Camp Chase.

DAVID TOD, Governor."

A meeting of citizens was immediately called to take action. Upon assembling at the usual place of holding such meetings in Marietta, R. H. Harte was chosen chairman, and G. R. Rosseter, secretary. Judge Green then addressed the assembly, and was followed by William R. Putnam, who made a stirring appeal to men of all ages to respond promptly to the call of their country. Rev. D. H. Moore, a Methodist minister of Marietta, spoke, saying that he "had held back from enlisting by the advice of his friends long enough, and now he was bound to go at all hazards." The court house was filled to overflowing, and this declaration of the reverend gentleman had a stirring effect. Others followed in patriotic appeals, and enlistment rolls being circulated quite a number of names were secured. The students of Marietta college held a meeting and twenty-five young men offered themselves as volunteers.

The following is the closing part of an appeal sent out through the country as a hand-bill:

We call upon our fellow citizens at once to stand forth for their country in this emergency! Your country calls, and it is the duty of patriotic citizens to obey the call! Old Washington to the rescue! Volunteers along the banks of the Muskingum river should be in readiness to take the steamer for Zanesville on Wednesday. Volunteers from other parts of the county will report themselves immediately to the undersigned at Marietta.

WILLIAM R. PUTNAM,
Chairman military committee Washington county.
Marietta, May 26, 1862.

On the twenty-eighth the company embarked on the steamer Ema Graham for Zanesville, and a large concourse of citizens assembled on the commons at Marietta to see them embark. The company was named the Putnam guards, in honor of Judge William R. Putnam, chairman of the military committee. On arriving at Camp Chase they elected Rev. D. R. Moore captain, who was afterwards lieutenant colonel of the Eighty-

seventh when in the three years' service; E. S. Aleshire, first lieutenant, and J. R. Jenkins, second lieutenant, and became company A, Eighty-seventh regiment. This regiment was at Harper's Ferry, under Colonel Mills, when the surrender took place, and were paroled, their time being out.

On the second of July, 1862, the President called for three hundred thousand more volunteers for three years, and Ohio's quota was about forty thousand. Governor Tod issued an earnest appeal to the military committees and the citizens of the State, calling upon them to furnish the men. The military committee of the county resolved that old Washington should not be behind in any emergency, and invited a general meeting of the citizens of the county in Marietta, on July 19th. Meantime a meeting of the military committees of the counties comprising the third military district was held in Marietta, to promote concerted action, and to provide officers for the new regiment, which was to be the Ninety-second.

On the fifteenth of July they assembled, members present:

Athens: J. M. Dana, T. F. Wildes, W. R. Golden, and W. T. Brown.

Meigs: J. V. Smith, G. W. Cooper, J. J. White, D. A. Smith, and George Eiselstein.

Noble: E. G. Dudley, Jabez Belford, W. H. Frazier, and Dr. M. Martin.

Washington, William R. Putnam, G. W. Barker, John Newton, and S. F. Cooke.

Monroe: Not represented.

Colonel William R. Putnam, chairman; J. M. Dana, and J. Belford, secretaries.

A committee consisting of G. W. Cooper, of Meigs, E. G. Dudley, of Noble, W. R. Golden and G. W. Barker, of Washington, having been appointed to devise a plan of organization for the new regiment, reported that the several counties of the district should furnish the following number of companies: Washington, three; Noble, two; Monroe, two; Athens, one, and Meigs, one. Monroe county not being represented they adjourned until July 22d, and upon the adjourned meeting elected officers for the Ninety-second regiment, and passed the resolutions following:

Resolved, that we pledge ourselves one to another, to use all diligence in recruiting our respective portions of the Ninety-second regiment, and that we will exert ourselves to the extent of our ability to maintain harmony and good feeling in our proceedings, upon which we feel will depend, to a great degree, our success, as well in recruiting as in every other branch of the service in this military district.

Resolved, that we call upon every loyal man in this military district to aid us with his might and strength and means to recruit the men called for to fill up the Ninety-second regiment.

Resolved, that we go home and go to work.

Resolved, that we make everybody else go to work.

With this declaration of purpose to raise a regiment for the war these gentlemen went home, and we shall presently see with what success.

The mass convention of the citizens of the county, called to meet on the nineteenth of July, assembled at the court house in Marietta, at ten o'clock A. M. of that day, and Colonel David Barber, of Harmar, was chosen chairman, and S. B. Robinson, of Beverly, secretary.

The object of the meeting having been stated by the chairman of the military committee, the following gentlemen were appointed to report resolutions: R. E. Harte, Davis Green, C. R. Rhodes, E. S. McIntosh, and Douglas Putnam. After the resolutions had been prepared Mr. Harte reported them, and they were unanimously adopted; they declared the confidence of the citizens of the county in the Government and in the power of the country to sustain itself in the struggle for equal rights and in the integrity of the Union, and pledged anew the men and means of the county to carry out the war to a successful issue. After remarks by George Benedict and William F. Curtis, an effort was inaugurated to raise a fund to assist in recruiting three hundred men in the county for the new regiment. Two thousand one hundred dollars was raised in about five minutes. In the afternoon Hon. W. P. Cutler, having returned from a session of Congress, made an eloquent and forcible speech upon the situation of public affairs.. Further subscriptions raised the total to three thousand five hundred and fifteen dollars. This amount was further increased to four thousand and twenty-six dollars by the twenty-fourth of July, Henry Fearing, of Harmar, donating a house and lot in Beverly, worth nine hundred dollars. August 1st, the war fund amounted to five thousand and eighty-one dollars. William Pitt Putnam, of Belpre, obligated himself to pay eight dollars a month to two volunteers and a third volunteer fifteen dollars bounty.

On July 28th the following despatch was received at Marietta.

PARKERSBURGH, July 28, 1862—1:50 P. M.

To the mayor of Marietta:

Send us all the men and arms you can at once. We are about to be attacked by a force of rebels.

M. P. AMISS, mayor.

Soon one hundred men were raised, and Lieutenant George T. Rice, being home on recruiting service from the Thirty-ninth regiment, was placed in command, as captain, also Lieutenant Robert Booth, of the Sixty-third regiment, and Lieutenant C. B. Way, of the Eleventh Virginia were appointed lieutenants, and Manly Warren, orderly sergeant. They marched to the depot to take a train for the beleaguered city, but there received a second dispatch "we are not yet attacked and no reenforcements are needed now."

On August 4th the call for a draft of three hundred thousand nine months' men came, and this, in addition to the calls for three years' men, made the quota of Washington county under both at two thousand and thirty. The total number of enrolled militia at that date was six thousand and eighty-nine, making two calls equal to about thirty-three per cent. of the whole number of militia in the county.

The draft commissioner for this county was George Benedict; provost marshal, William F. Curtis, of Marietta; examining surgeon, Dr. James Little, of Beverly. After several postponements by Governor Tod the draft finally took place on October 1st as follows: Adams, eleven; Barber, nine; Fairfield, four; Fearing, fifteen; Grandview, six; Independence, two; Lawrence, nine; Liberty, six; Ludlow, ten; Palmer, three; Union, one;

Warren, seven; Watertown, seven; Wesley, sixteen—total, one hundred and seven, which was afterwards increased to one hundred and thirty-one. A great effort was made to save the county from the draft, and large sums of money were raised in all parts of the county to facilitate enlistments. Barlow was down for over two hundred dollars; Waterford, over twelve hundred dollars in addition to one thousand dollars subscribed to the county war fund previously. To this must be added large sums in every township, of which we can find no record, running up into the thousands. It should be said, however, in regard to drafted men from this county, that a greater portion of them volunteered for three years when they reached Camp Dennison, and some even before. Noble county had over three hundred men drafted, Monroe sixty-one, Morgan one hundred and sixty-seven, and Muskingum two hundred and ninety-three, Gallia two hundred and seventeen. Athens, Lawrence and Scioto escaped.

Judge William R. Putnam having been placed in command of the post at Marietta, with rank of colonel, was authorized to lease ground and erect additional barracks. Accordingly, in September, of 1862, he selected a site which, at that time, lay between the fair grounds and the Muskingum river, and constructed quarters to accommodate the new regiment. By the nineteenth of September the Ninety-second regiment was complete; it contained as good material as any regiment from this part of the State, the men being from among the best citizens of the district, and its subsequent history fully justified the expectation of its friends. The time in camp at Marietta was devoted to drill and disciplining the men for active service. On October 7th they received orders to march, and left Camp Putnam for Gallipolis. Many of those who marched out on that October day with such fine martial bearing were destined never to return. Again Washington county was sending forth her bravest and best, but the sacrifice was not considered too great for the issues at stake.

On October 12th the battle of South Mountain was fought, in which the Thirty-sixth was engaged. It was in this battle that the future brigade commander of the Thirty-sixth was severely wounded—Colonel Rutherford B. Hayes, the successor of Grant to the Presidency. On the seventeenth of July the Thirty-sixth was hotly engaged in the great battle of Antietam, in which its colonel, Melvin Clarke, was killed, and loosing heavily in non-commissioned officers and men.

The great battle of Corinth took place on October 4th, resulting in a crushing defeat to the armies of Price and Van Dorn, and not without great loss to the Union army. The Sixty-third regiment, containing two companies of Washington county men, stood the brunt of the charge at Fort Robinet, and lost very heavily in officers and men—fully forty-five per cent. Colonel J. W. Sprague, of that regiment, said of his regiment: "The loss of my regiment has been terrible, but I have the consolation of believing that no braver or truer set of men were ever taken into battle. Every officer distinguished himself for gallantry and daring."

In October, 1862, Captain Arthur D. Eells, recruited a company of cavalry for a new regiment authorized by the governor. Captain Eells' company was recruited very rapidly, as he was a popular man and had seen service as captain of company F, Second West Virginia cavalry, from which position he resigned in May, 1862, on account of ill-health, but by October of the same year was again engaged in the service of his country, as captain of company H, Seventh Ohio volunteer cavalry. At the date of leaving for the front the company had one hundred and one men, officered as follows: Captain, Arthur Eells, First Lieutenant, William L. Tripp, Second Lieutenant, John J. Smith.

The year 1862 was one of great military activity in Washington county. Over two thousand men were sent out, many to fill up old regiments, but the greater part to form new organizations, which were, in the main, recruited for three years' service. The danger of invasion from Virginia had thoroughly aroused the county, and the militia companies throughout the townships were called out for drill at regular intervals. The citizens of Marietta during the summer closed their places of business at four o'clock P. M., and all the ablebodied men, including the Silver Grays, turned out to drill.

On Tuesday, August 26th, Colonel William R. Putnam, commandant of Camp Marietta, received a dispatch from Governor Tod, saying, "You are in danger of invasion on the border; prepare for it." The citizens of Marietta then had the following companies: Silver Grays, Captain D. P. Bosworth, First Lieutenant C. J. Sheppard, Second Lieutenant R. E. Harte; Home Guards, Captain Charles R. Rhodes, First Lieutenant James Lewis, Second Lieutenant John B. Dutton; First ward company, Captain Robert Booth, First Lieutenant Dan Y. Booth, Second Lieutenant Philip Schramm; Second ward company, Captain R. E. Harte (promoted from Silver Grays), First Lieutenant Samuel C. Skinner, Second Lieutenant Lewis Theiss; Third ward company, Captain John S. Conley, First Lieutenant S. J. Dutton, Second Lieutenant Joseph S. Stephens; Bloomfield Guards, Captain Nathaniel F. Bishop, First Lieutenant Joseph E. Hall, jr., Second Lieutenant D. A. Belden; Putnam Light Artillery, Captain A. T. Nye, jr., Lieutenant Charles A. Hall, Gunner John Hall. On September 13th Ernst Lindner having resigned as adjutant of the Thirty-sixth regiment and residing for the time being in Marietta, was placed in command of the companies of Marietta and Harmar, by order of the commandant of the Washington county militia. The companies were placed as follows: A, Captain Charles R. Rhodes; B, Captain Rufus E. Harte; C, Captain Nathaniel F. Bishop; D, Captain Oscar Underwood; E, Captain Robert Booth; F, Captain I. W. Andrews; G, Captain D. P. Bosworth; H, Captain Casper Crouss; I, Captain John W. Conley; K, Captain W. B. Hollister. Smith J. Dutton was appointed adjutant, and D. P. Bosworth, jr., sergeant major; George Payne, sr., drum major. We give these details to show how pressing the emergency was considered and how the men of those days rallied to meet it. The city of Marietta was laid off for the purposes of guard duty into beats, and for many weeks the night patrol paced the streets expecting a border foray.

Many brave sons of Washington county fell in the year 1862, among them Captain Frank Buell, Captain Theodore Greenwood, Colonel Melvin Clarke, and Lieutenant J. J. Steenrod.

The closing event of the year was the arrival in the county of Major General J. D. Cox and staff on December 7th, who established at Marietta the headquarters of the department of West Virginia, which included the State of West Virginia and the bordering counties of Ohio from Wheeling to the Big Sandy. General Cox remained until April 8, 1863, when he went to Columbus, Ohio, having been assigned to a new command.

CHAPTER XVIII.

WAR OF THE REBELLION—CONTINUED.

Battle of Stone River - Emancipation—Secret Political Organizations—Battle of Chancellorsville - Lee's Army Invades the North—Battle of Gettysburgh—Capture of Vicksburgh—The Morgan Raid—Battles of Chickamauga and Mission Ridge—The Brough Campaign—The Veterans Reenlist—Death of Colonel Jesse Hildebrand—Beginning of Governor Brough's Administration New Militia Law—Conference of the War Governors—Call of Governor Brough for Thirty Thousand Ohio National Guards—Departure of the One Hundred and Forty-eighth Ohio National Guard—General Steele's Arkansas Expedition—Battle of Marks Mills and Capture of the Seventy-seventh Regiment—Raid of Hunter, Crook and Averill—The Great Flank Movements of Grant and Sherman—The Atlanta Campaign—Sherman's Movements to the Right—March to the Sea—March Through the Carolinas—Battles of Averysborough and Bentonville—General Sheridan in the Shenandoah Valley—Battles of Opequan, Fisher's Hill and Cedar Creek—Battle of Nashville—Army of the Potomac—Battles of the Wilderness—Petersburgh—Sheridan's Raid—Wilson's Great Raid—Grant's Movements to the Left - Evacuation of Richmond—Surrender of Lee at Appomattox—Great Rejoicing—Assassination of President Lincoln—The Soldier Becomes a Citizen Again.

THE year 1863—the great battle year of the war—was ushered in by two important events: the memorable battle of Stone River and the emancipation proclamation striking the shackles from three millions of slaves. Washington county had not been strongly for the abolition of slavery, but the fierce logic of war had convinced the most conservative that the time had come and they heartily approved the action of Abraham Lincoln when he issued the emancipation edict to take effect January 1, 1863, and the grand Union party of Ohio, which swept everything before it in the great political contest of the year, endorsed the conduct of the war by a hundred thousand majority for John Brough. The partisan feeling that characterized this campaign was something fearful to contemplate, the party of the Union could brook no resistance, and there was a strong tendency to brand as traitors all who were not in its ranks, when in fact many good and true men of the opposition were devoted to their country and to the preservation of the Union; but some of the opposition were not for the Union or the war, and were so outspoken and active in their course that they were arrested in their course as was their leader C. L. Vallandigham, but not like him arrested, tried, convicted and sent south.

On the thirty-first of March the citizens of Marietta, Harmar and vicinity formed what was known as the Union league, with the object of binding together all loyal men of all trades and professions, in a common union to maintain the power, glory and integrity of the Nation, to spare no endeavor to maintain unimpaired the National unity, both in principle and territorial boundary, and to vote for no man for office whose loyalty is questionable or who is not willing to support the principles set forth in the foregoing declaration. The officers elected were George M. Woodbridge, president; H. H. Brown, vice-president; S. S. Porter, secretary; W. F. Curtis, treasurer; M. H. Needham, J. H. Best, Daniel Y. Hill, John M. Hook, W. S. Ward, Thomas F. Jones, Beman Gates, Lewis Lenhart, B. F. Pixley, W. W. Hutchinson, George E. Stratton, and William H. Smith, executive committee. The formation of this society was doubtless prompted by the formation of lodges of Knights of the Golden Circle and Sons of Liberty in the county by the opposition.

On the first of May occurred the great battle of Chancellorsville in which Huntington's, De Beck's and Pierpont's batteries were engaged, and when J. F. Huntington's battery H, First Ohio light artillery, made a gallant stand against great odds holding the enemy in check until deserted by the supporting infantry. For his conduct in this battle Captain Huntington was promoted to chief of artillery of his division.

In the same action Colonel Rufus R. Dawes, an old Washington county boy, bore a conspicuous part, in carrying out Fighting Joe Hooker's plans for crossing the Rappahannock prior to the battle. A surgeon of the Sixth Wisconsin, which regiment Lieutenant Colonel Dawes then commanded, was an eye-witness to the achievement. He says:

The steep bank on the opposite side was lined with rifle pits from which our troops on this side tried in vain for several hours to dislodge the enemy. It was impossible to lay the pontoon bridges on which to cross the corps until the rifle pits were cleared, and to throw troops across in boats for this purpose was a necessary condition of success.

It was regarded by all as a most desperate and perilous undertaking, and none but troops of tried valor could be relied on.

The Sixth Wisconsin was one of the two regiments (Twenty-fourth Michigan was the other) which had the honor of being the "forlorn hope" selected to cross the river and carry the heights beyond. When the order was given to "fall in" not a man faltered or hesitated a moment, though fully conscious of the danger he was to meet. I shook hands with Lieutenant Colonel Dawes, as I honestly believed for the last time, and said "God bless and protect you." Our troops double-quicked down the slope on this side, sprang into the boats, and pushed out boldly across the river under a perfect storm of bullets. The river, which is about one hundred and fifty yards wide at this point, was soon passed, and our brave men sprang ashore, dashed up the hill, capturing the rebs in the rifle pits, and in less than twenty minutes from the time the order to march was given on this side, our regiment was formed in line of battle on the top of the opposite shores. Lieutenant Colonel Dawes stood up in the boats while crossing, and assisted in pushing his boat along, and seized the colors to rally the regiment as soon as a landing was effected. I rejoiced greatly when I saw the rebels on the opposite side "skedaddling" in fine disorder. It seemed a miracle no more were hurt.

Early in June the threatening movements of the enemy

under Lee alarmed the cabinet at Washington, and the President issued a call for one hundred thousand six months' men to be raised in the States of Maryland, Pennsylvania, Ohio, and West Virginia. Lee had divided his army into three grand divisions, cut loose from the base, and it was reported that one of these divisions was intended for the invasion of West Virginia and Ohio, another to strike the western part of Pennsylvania, and the third to invade Maryland. Under this call Ohio was to have furnished thirty thousand men, but the call for six months was soon found to be very injudicious, and two thousand was the total number from Ohio, of which none were from Washington county. Lee's movements were witnessed with great alarm, but it was soon evident that he was not expecting to divide his forces but bent on taking Philadelphia and New York, and carrying the war into the north.

The Rebel invasion culminated at Gettysburgh, where he was met by General Meade with the army of the Potomac, and the greatest battle of the war and the one most momentous in the results involved, was fought. Washington county was represented by Buell's Pierpoint battery, Huntington battery and DeBeck's battery under command of Captain J. F. Huntington. They fought nobly and stood to their guns as only veterans can. Who can describe the battle, who will ever adequately chronicle the deeds of heroism there enacted? It will never be done. Lines of battle five miles long, Round Top, Cemetery Hill, Culp's Hill, Wolf Hill, Power's Hill, Benner's Hill, all the scenes of charge and counter-charge, and all in one great battle. Let us take a bit out of this great master-piece, this crowd of heroic achievements and let it stand for all the rest: "Agate" then the *nom de plume* of Whitelaw Reid, correspondent of the Cincinnati *Gazette*, wrote:

Let me give one phase of the fight—fit type of many more. Some Massachusetts batteries—Bigelow's Captain Phillip's, and Captain McGilory, of Maine—were planted on the extreme left, advanced, now well down to the Emmitsburgh road, with infantry in their front—the first division, I think, of Sickles' corps. A little after five, a fierce rebel charge drove back the infantry and menaced the batteries. Orders are sent Bigelow on the extreme left, to hold his position at every hazard short of sheer annihilation, till a couple more batteries can be brought to his support. Reserving his fire a little, then with depressed guns opening with double charges of grape and canister, he smites and shatters, but cannot break the advancing line. His grape and canister are exhausted, and still, closing grandly up over their slain, on they come. He falls back on spherical case, and pours this in at the shortest range. On, still onward, comes the artillery defying line, and still he holds his position. They are within six paces of the guns—he fires again, once more, and he blows devoted soldiers from his very muzzles. And, still mindful of that solemn order, he holds his place, they spring upon his carriages, and shoot down his horses! And then, his Yankee artillerists still about him, he seizes the guns by hand, and from the very front of that line drags two of them off. The caissons are further back—five out of the six are saved. That single company, in that half hour's fight, lost thirty-three of its men, including every sergeant it had. The captain himself was wounded. Yet it was the first time it was ever under fire! I give it simply as a type. So they fought along that firey line!

The rebels now poured on Phillips' battery, and it, too, was forced to drag off the pieces by hand, when the horses were shot down. From a new position, it opened again; and at last the two reenforcing batteries came up on the gallop. An enfilading fire swept the rebel line: Sickles' gallant infantry charged, the rebel line swept back on a refluent tide—we regained the lost ground, and every gun just lost in this splendid fight.

Buell's battery was in the thickest of the fight and fired over twelve hundred rounds. De Beck's battery lost two pieces. Huntington's battery was forced to retire for fresh ammunition. Let Captain Huntington tell the story himself:—* "Started from Taneytown with my brigade, at 4 A. M., second inst., reached Gettysburgh at 2 P. M., and about four o'clock was ordered to relieve some of the First corps, who were in the battle the day before. Position of our army peculiar, the line forming a triangle with the apex towards the enemy, whose line was in front around ours, we having the advantage of being able to throw troops across, while the enemy had to go around. The salient part of our line was an elevated piece of ground just on the edge of town, on which was a beautiful cemetery, and here, at the centre, my batteries were posted—a position fine for artillery, yet quite exposed, being swept by rebel batteries in front and on our left flank. Shelling was going on vigorously, when we took position, and we replied with great vigor. Meanwhile the tremendous attack was made on our left. Had this been successful every battery on the hill must have been taken, as our only line of retreat was by the Baltimore pike, directly in our rear. At one time when our left was forced back by a tremendous charge of the enemy, I thought "the jig was up" with us, but fresh troops were just brought up, and the enemy fell suddenly back. Just before dark, another column attacked our batteries on the hill, which were supported by part of the Eleventh corps, who, as their custom is, gave way, and part of Captain Ricketts' battery of my brigade, in the extreme front, was actually taken. General Carroll, with his brigade, of old Shields' fire-eaters, came up just in the nick of time. Carroll sung out, 'Where is Huntington? 'Here I am, general,' I said. 'I am sent here' he continued, 'to support something or some one—where is the enemy?' I showed him their advancing line, and he commanded, 'Forward! double quick march!' And in they went, turned the advancing rebels, and saved the batteries. It was sharp while it lasted. Ricketts' battery lost seventeen killed and wounded and five prisoners in that charge." We quote further:

The night was spent in preparing for the struggle of the next day (July 3rd). At 4 A. M., Friday, the enemy attacked the right of our line. From that to eleven the musketry never slackened for a single moment. Such a sustained fire I never heard before, and to look at the place it was terrible. The rebels charged up a hill against log breast-works, lined with our splendid infantry. I was on the ground afterwards. It was a sickening sight. In one place I traced the line of an entire company, shot dead where they stood, with the captain at his post. Here General Ewell's adjutant general was killed, while trying to rally his men.

After this fight there was a lull, but about 2 P. M., while a knot of officers were lying down near my battery to avoid the sharpshooters, who were constantly firing at us, all at once there came a most terrible storm of iron. They had been quietly placing their batteries in position, and opened at a signal. The howling of the shells, the deadly hiss of the solid Wentworth, and the crash of the twelve-pound spherical case, was awful beyond description. Most of the fire came from the left, and my battery was then faced to the front; we had to change the position of the guns under that fire. For the first time the men of battery H hesitated to obey my orders; but they were almost exhausted by fatigue and intense heat, and it was only for a moment that they forgot their duty. We soon had our guns around, and opened one section

* Letter to Mrs. Huntington July 6th.

to the left, another to the front, and the third I could not work for the want of men able to stand on their feet. Captain Wallace Hill's battery (Pierpoint) behaved most nobly. I never saw guns served better than theirs, until they fired their last round. I ordered them to leave the field, and replaced them with Captain Edgell's (New Hampshire) battery. Meanwhile, my own was about exhausted, and, feeling the importance of maintaining the fire at this point, I started to the reserve headquarters, with Orderly Fred Regnir, to run the gauntlet of the enemy's batteries for a mile, every shot that came over our batteries striking in our track—no pleasure trip to be sure—but we got through Could obtain no relief, as every battery was already engaged. Starting back, I met my battery coming out, its ammunition exhausted, and one piece dismounted by solid shot Under cover of this fire the enemy made their last charge on our left, suffered awfully, and were utterly routed—their last effort

General Grant, after a series of battles and brilliant manœuvres around Vicksburgh, had penned up the rebel General Pemberton, and by July 4th had compelled him to surrender. The fourth of July, 1863, was a glad day for the National cause. "To whom shall we Grant the Meade of praise?" was telegraphed throughout the country; but Grant's star was in the ascendant. Meade's victory was grand, but his tactics were defensive, while Grant's were aggressive. These victories occasioned general rejoicing. The friends of the Union throughout the north now saw the beginning of the end. The gloom that had overshadowed the past year was dissipated, and the name of Grant was thenceforth to be the watchword to victory and the omen of success.

THE MORGAN RAID.

It was in July of 1863 that John Morgan made his raid through southern Ohio, passing through Washington county, an account of which follows.

John Morgan, with his bold troopers, had, up to July, 1863, made numerous raids and forays across the mountains of eastern Kentucky and Tennessee into the Blue Grass region of Kentucky. These forays were a source of alarm to the Unionist, and exultation to the secessionist. He generally captured all the good horses within his reach, provoked a vigorous pursuit, and although he uniformly had to get out much faster than he came in, he generally accomplished all that he set out to do.

Encouraged by his successes he planned a grand raid to the northward, which should give the northern people a taste of war as well as the sunny south. General Bragg, however, ordered Morgan not to go beyond the State of Kentucky. Bragg was then confronted by General Rosecrans, at Stone River, and the object sought to be accomplished was to strike the communications and rear of the Union army, and divert the flanking columns of Rosecrans from annoying Bragg, the supposition being that a strong force sent to the rear would engage the attention of a large part of the Union cavalry, and the sequel proved this to be true.

Collecting a body of cavalry, numbering about two thousand five hundred men, with two twenty-pound Parrot rifle cannon and four other guns of lighter metal, he was ready for the enterprise. Basil Duke, the "brains of John Morgan," was second in command, with Colonels Cluke, Dick Morgan, and others of lesser note commanding regiments.

He crossed the Cumberland at Burkesville, Kentucky,

July 3, 1863, and, marching rapidly north, drove or evaded all the Union forces that disputed his progress, and on the eighth arrived on the banks of the Ohio at Bradenburgh, Kentucky. He gave out as he went that he should attack Louisville. He captured two steamers, the J. J. McCoombs and Alice Dean, and disregarding his instructions, crossed the Ohio, burned the steamers, and disappeared among the hills of Indiana.

General Judah, commanding the Union cavalry in Kentucky, began at once a vigorous pursuit. Colonel Garrard, of the Seventh Ohio cavalry, in command of a brigade composed of the Seventh and Second Ohio cavalry, Forty-fifth Ohio mounted infantry, Law's howitzer battery, and the First Kentucky cavalry, started the same day Morgan crossed the Cumberland, where Garrard had been watching him, and was joined, at Bardstown, Kentucky, by General Hobson with Shackelford's brigade, consisting of the Third, Eighth, Ninth, and Twelfth Kentucky cavalry, and two pieces of artillery. Hobson assumed command, and the whole force hurried on after the raider.

Morgan, after getting safely across into Indiana, gave out, seemingly as in confidence, to prisoners, that he was moving on Indianapolis, but immediately afterwards bore off to the eastward, crossed the Ohio line, and was soon in the neighborhood of Cincinnati. Upon nearing that city he gave out that he expected to attack Hamilton, but instead passed by so close to the great city that part of his command, embarrassed by the darkness and the labyrinth of streets in the suburbs, came near losing their way. This was the night of July 13th.

General Burnside was in command in Cincinnati and General Judah was there also hurrying up with fresh cavalry.

Ohio was soon thoroughly aroused. Governor Tod, July 12th, issued a proclamation calling out the militia of all the southern and southwestern counties.

Morgan, no doubt, endeavored to enhance the prevailing alarm, hoping to make his escape more certain amid the general uproar before any definite or concerted action could be taken to intercept him. Onward he went eastward, his men plundering everybody without fear or favor, through the counties of Warren, Clermont, Brown, Adams, Pike, Jackson, and Meigs, while detachments from the main body made detours through other counties, and the whole body bringing up at Portland, near Buffington's Island, on the evening of the eighteenth, and would doubtless have crossed at once but for the threatening appearance of an earthwork then and there appearing.

Morgan had run the gauntlet of the militia through the State, with Hobson but a few hours in the rear, eager to bring the raider to bay after the long pursuit. Tired, jaded and harassed, and withal heavily loaded with booty, the rebels rested at the river, expecting in the morning to make a short job of the earthwork and cross to the Virginia shore.

Let us now turn to the scene of operations in Washington county, and see what was being done there to capture the bold raider.

Governor Tod, in his proclamation, had ordered "all the militia companies in Washington, Monroe, Noble, Meigs, Morgan, Perry, Hocking, and Athens, to report forthwith to Colonel William R. Putnam at Camp Marietta, who was to organize them into battalions or regiments and appoint temporary officers therefor." Immediately following the proclamation came a telegram from Governor Tod to Colonel Putnam, stating that three thousand militia had been ordered to Marietta. At this date there were one hundred and seventy-five six months' men in camp, including company A, One Hundred and Twenty-eighth Ohio volunteer infantry. Governor Tod telegraphed on the fourteenth that Morgan had crossed the Little Miami, and was probably making for some ford near Marietta. Colonel Putnam at once began to act—first, to prevent Morgan crossing the Ohio; second, to keep him west of the Muskingum; and, third, to shut his forces between the Ohio river and Marietta & Cincinnati railroad if possible. He therefore set about guarding the fords as the first part of the programme. On the fourteenth there were four hundred and fifty-seven men in camp, but no arms had arrived, although a thousand stand had been promised by the governor. At this time Captain D. L. Wood, of the Eighteenth United States infantry, was stationed at Marietta, and Lieutenant J. W. Conine, aide-de-camp to General Cox, was in immediate command of the six months' men at Camp Marietta. On July 10th the following order was issued:

HEADQUARTERS, CAMP MARIETTA, O., July 15, 1863.
Special Order No. 1.

The following companies now at camp are hereby detached under command of Captain D. L. Wood, Eighteenth United States infantry, and will put themselves in readiness to march.

Marietta artillery company, Lieutenant Nye commanding.

Volunteer mounted company, Captain Bloomfield commanding.

Company A, One Hundred and Twenty-eighth Ohio volunteer infantry, Captain Stedman commanding.

Captain J. P. Putnam's company, Captain Putnam commanding.

Post Quartermaster Croxton will provide transportation and forage for five (5) days for fifty (50) horses. Post Commissary R. B. Treat will turn over to Charles Jones (who will act as quartermaster of the detachment), twelve hundred and fifty (1250) rations.

Surgeon S. D. Hart will be acting surgeon.

By order of WM. R. PUTNAM,
Colonel Commanding.

Captain Woods instructions were as follows:

You are hereby ordered to assume command of the troops detached by special order No. 1 of this date, and proceed with them to the ford below Parkersburgh, where you will make such disposition as you deem fit and proper to prevent the rebel forces now in the State from crossing at that place.

WM. R. PUTNAM,
Colonel Commanding.

But now an unforseen difficulty arose. Lieutenant Cornine refused to allow the United States troops in Camp Marietta to be moved without orders from a higher source. Governor Tod was telegraphed, and all that day spent in waiting for an answer. The answer came finally ordering Lieutenant Cornine to obey all orders from Colonel Putnam, and Captain Wood started early on the morning of the sixteenth. The expedition numbered about three hundred men. The cannon were two iron pieces that had been used in Marietta and Harmar for firing salutes, and the arms for the infantry and cavalry were such as could be hastily gathered in the city and Camp

Marietta. Captain Wood reached Blennerhasset island the same day, and began entrenching, informing Colonel Putnam by telegraph of the fact. Captain Wood had stopped short of the point intended to be covered by the movement. At this time four thousand two hundred and fifty-nine men reported for duty, and Captain R. B. Wilson, of Meigs county, was ordered to proceed to Mason City, West Virginia, with his company and that of Captain George G. Woodward armed as infantry, to prevent Morgan crossing at that point. On the same day (seventeenth) the following order was sent to Captain Wood, at Blennerhasset island:

The shoal at the foot of Blennerhasset island is deemed impracticable on account of quicksand. The ford you were to guard is at the foot of Buffington's island. You will therefore take your forces to that point. Use the flats and steamer Logan in conjunction with Captain Wilson, in transporting your forces, sending baggage overland, if necessary. Delay Captain Wilson as little as possible.

Lieutenant Conine will report to you with reenforcements as soon as they can be armed.

By this arrangement Captain Wood and his little force reached Buffington at 7 P. M. of the seventeenth, and at once began to intrench, throwing out pickets and preparing for such defence as his limited means afforded. Captain Wilson proceeded to Mason City.

In the meantime Captain Henry Best, on July 13th, with his own company and those of Captains Stone, Dana, Pugh, and Rutherford, had been ordered to proceed on the steamer Buck to Blennerhasset island and open the channel so that the gunboats could pass, and on the way down remove all boats of every description to the Virginia shore, which order was faithfully carried out. Captain Wilson arrived at Mason City at 11 P. M. of the seventeenth, and hearing that the rebels had appeared about five miles back of Middleport, he crossed the river and advanced promptly but cautiously through the darkness and took up a position three miles to the rear of that place. Here Morgan's men, or a part of them, advanced, captured a scouting party of Captain Wilson's force, pushed on to within a quarter of a mile of Wilson, when they were fired on, and delayed until noon of the eighteenth, when the Twenty-third Ohio infantry came up, and an attack was immediately made by the two commands on the rebels, resulting in their retreat. On the nineteenth, Captain Wilson was ordered up to Bowman's run, seven miles up the Ohio from Middleport, where he made such dispositions of his men as to capture seventy-seven men and officers, and eighty horses. Captain Wilson took his prisoners to Pomeroy, when he was ordered six miles below to guard another ford, and arrived just in time to prevent a body of Morgan's men from crossing, and turned them back on their pursuers, who captured them.

By July seventeenth a thousand stand of arms arrived, and Colonel Putnam ordered Lieutenant J. W. Conine, with a detachment consisting of the companies of Captains Knowles, Moore, Jaynes, Brown, Seaman, Dyar, Jenkins, Comley, and Davenport, to proceed on board the steamer Eagle and reinforce Captain Wood, and report to that officer for orders. The Eagle got fast aground on a bar, and Conine disembarked, marched his men to the mouth of the Little Hocking, and bivouacked, deciding to act independent of Captain Wood. At this time there were reported for duty seven thousand and sixty-four men, with scarcely any arms in camp, but in order to utilize these men as far as practicable they were provided with spades, axes, and picks, and sent to the proper places to fell trees and obstruct the lines of retreat along the supposed route of Morgan.

Hon. William P. Cutler on the eighteenth was ordered to obstruct the roads between the line of the Marietta & Cincinnati railroad and the Ohio river. He had in his command the railroad employes, Captain Holmes' company, and that of Captain Grewell; and at Cutler's Station and Big run he was joined with three more companies under Captains Waugh, Maxwell, and Dee. With these forces, Mr. Cutler says, in his report: "We succeeded in accomplishing the object in a thorough manner from Big Hocking (including all roads leading into the ravines of that stream), as far east as the road leading from Vincent to the Ohio river by way of Daniel Shaw's, in Dunham township."

On the seventeenth General Burnside telegraphed Colonel Putnam that if Morgan was driven from the ford at Buffington, he would probably strike for Marietta, the roads therefore were to be well obstructed, the flooring of the bridge across the Muskingum torn up, and rifle pits so constructed as to command the crossing. General Cox who was with General Burnside at Cincinnati, telegraphed that if the roads were so obstructed as to prevent Morgan dodging north between Athens and Marietta, there was force enough following to crush or capture him. Three companies under John Newton were sent up the Muskingum to remove all boats to the east side of the stream, and three more under command of Captain Levi Barber were sent to blockade the roads between Coolville and Little Hoking. Meantime, mounted scouts were sent out from Mr. Cutler's camp, and from all points practicable, and the best information possible obtained as to the enemy's movements. Several companies were stationed at the Marietta bridge, and such arrangements made that the drawbridge could be turned at a moment's notice. In addition to the rifle pits a barricade of bales of hay was made commanding the bridge and the ford below. On the night of July 17th Colonel B. P. Runkle's forces arrived at Scott's landing three miles below Marietta.

Let us now return to Morgan's command whom we left on the evening of the eighteenth, near Buffington's Island.

Basil Duke, in his "History of Morgan's Cavalry," says:

July 18th, at 3 A. M., we moved on. By this time the militia had turned their attention seriously to felling trees, and impeding our progress in every conceivable way. Advanced guard was forced to carry axes to cut away frequent blockade. In passing on the eighteenth near Pomeroy, there was one continual fight, but not wholly with militia, for some regular troops now appeared. We had to run a terrible gauntlet for nearly five miles, through a ravine, on the gallop.

We reached Portland (Buffington) about 8 P. M., and the night was one of solid darkness. General Morgan consulted one or two of his officers upon the propriety of at once attacking an earthwork, thrown up to guard the ford. From all the information he could gather, this work was manned with about three hundred infantry—regular troops, and two heavy guns were mounted in it. Our arrival at this place after dark had involved us in a dilemma. If we did not cross the river that night, there was every chance of our being attacked on the next day by heavy odds—by infantry sent after us from Kentucky, and by gunboats at the ford, which we could not drive off, as we had not more than three cartridges apiece for our artillery. General Morgan fully appreciated these reasons for getting across the river that night, as did those with whom he advised, but there were also very strong reasons against attacking the work at night; and without the capture of the work which commanded the ford, it would be impossible to cross. Attacks in the dark are always hazardous experiments, in this case doubly so as we knew nothing of the ground and could not procure guides. Our choice of the direction in which to move to the attack would have been purely guesswork. The defenders of the work had only to lie still and fire with artillery and musketry directly to their front, but the assailants would have had a line to preserve, and to exercise great care lest they should fall foul of each other, in the obscurity. . . He determined, therefore, to take the work at early dawn, and hoped to effect a crossing rapidly before the enemy arrived.

Captain D. L. Wood in his report to Colonel Putnam says: "On the morning of the eighteenth I made a line of entrenchments covering the approach to the ford, sent out cavalry scouts and ascertained that the enemy were advancing on me in force. I had all my stores removed to the boat (steamer Starlight) and ordered it to be ready to move. At half past seven o'clock the enemy appeared in force in front of my works, at which time my forces were in line to receive them as best I could. At twelve o'clock, having received an order from General Scammon to retire, I did so. Being hardly pressed by the enemy, I was obliged to abandon my artillery."

. . .

Lieutenant C. B. Lewis, of the One Hundred and Twenty-eighth Ohio volunteer infantry, was officer of the day; posted pickets at different points around the ford to watch for the approach of the rebels, and while out on the picket line was taken prisoner by the rebels the night before the battle.

BATTLE OF BUFFINGTON'S ISLAND.

The valley in which Morgan encamped on the night of July 18th was about eight hundred yards wide at the lower end and gradually narrowed above until the hills approached near to the river at the upper end. The river road coming from Pomeroy was upon the bank of the river. About midway of the valley a road winds into the valley to the river. The rebels had encamped on the night of the eighteenth (Saturday night) in the corn fields at the end of a private lane running parallel to the road on which General Judah was approaching from the direction of Pomeroy. A dense fog covered all the bottom lands. General Hobson had with his command followed Morgan for two weeks, and on the night of the eighteenth went into camp to rest both horses and men. Colonel Garrard, of the Seventh Ohio cavalry, remonstrated with Hobson for delaying the march at the critical point of the pursuit, but Hobson decided to halt. Colonel Garrard then asked permission to continue the pursuit that night, and in reply was informed that he might take his regiment and "go to hell."[*] So Garrard kept on in pursuit. General Judah pressing forward during the night with his command was, with his staff

including Major Daniel McCook, early in the morning of the nineteenth, in the advance, and when within a short distance of the ford, there being a dense fog, came unexpectedly upon the rebel cavalry, who received them with a volley and pursued, killing Major McCook, wounding several and taking some prisoners together with one piece of artillery. General Judah, now hurried his forces forward, and the fog suddenly lifting disclosed the enemy in the valley before them. While Judah was bringing his forces into action, Lieutenant O'Neil, of the Fifth Indiana cavalry, appeared on another road with but fifty men and charged two different regiments so desperately that they were broke and left the captured gun, also their prisoners. Meanwhile Colonel Garrard with the Second and Seventh Ohio cavalry came in by the road about the middle of the valley and charged them in flank and rear. Captain Fitch with the gunboat Moose now attacked from the river, playing on them with his twenty-four pound Dahlgreen guns. With Judah up, Hobson up and the gunboats up, the situation of Morgan became not only interesting but desperate.

Judah and Hobson, from different points, soon opened on the rebel ranks with shell, and, according to Basil Duke's account, the air was fairly filled with pieces of shell, compelling the enemy to retreat. Duke was in command of the line designed to cover the retreat, with instructions to make the best fight he could, and but for being attacked in the flank, would have given General Judah a more stubborn resistance than they did. General Duke attempted to retreat in good order, but soon a regular stampede took place, many made a rush for the ford, others ran from point to point over this field, taking a new direction at the chance explosion of a shell near by. The most of the rebels, however, still clung to the booty stolen on the march.

The victors now closed in on them and captured between seven and eight hundred, including Basil Duke, Colonel Dick Morgan, Colonels Smith, Ward and Hoffman. All their artillery, wagons, etc., were captured. About twelve hundred men, under Morgan, escaped, and, pressing on up the river, tried to cross at Belleville, but were headed off by the gunboat Moose. A few got across, and some were killed in the river. The bulk of the raiders, however, turned away from the river and disappeared among the hills. It is a remarkable fact that two out of the six or seven guns captured were twenty-pound parrots, which Morgan had dragged over his extended line of march, and had he not run out of ammunition, would doubtless have given the gunboats as well as his other pursuers a more desperate battle than he did. The Union loss was five killed and twenty-five wounded. Rebel loss, twenty killed, wounded not known.

In regard to the conduct of Captain Wood, the Rebellion Record has the following:[*]

Captain Wood, of the Eighteenth regulars, while stationed at Marietta as mustering officer, was induced to take command of two companies of volunteers, and proceeded to Buffington bar on Saturday. He found the steamer Starlight aground, with only two men aboard, and loaded with three thousand barrels of flour. He immediately un-

---

* From one of the Seventh cavalry.

* Frank Moore's Rebellion Record, Volume VII, page 267.

loaded the vessel, raised steam and manned the boat, from the captain to the deck-hand, with his men, and run her out of the range of Morgan's guns, which, before he could get away, had arrived on the bank. Before leaving with his little band of true gallants, he rolled his two heavy pieces of artillery over into a ravine, so that the enemy could neither take nor use them. After the fight, Captain Wood reported to General Judah for duty with the boat, and was highly complimented by the general and placed in charge of several hundred of the prisoners to bring to Cincinnati. Had the boat not been seized by Captain Wood when it was, Morgan would have had it and crossed the river with it, for the gunboats did not arrive till Sunday morning, while Morgan was there the night before. So let Marietta be proud of her gentlemen soldiers who were not too proud to carry coal or do any work which would hinder the enemies of the Union and help her defenders.

Captain Wood and his command returned to Camp Marietta from Cincinnati, July 25th.

When Major McCook was shot, the country lost a noble patriot, who had sent his distinguished sons to the war and only remained at home himself on account of the infirmities of age. The horse he rode remained in the hands of the enemy. There is an interesting incident related in regard to the horse, "Old Joe," as he was called, which we give as we heard it:

When Captain Arthur D. Eells, H Seventh Ohio volunteer cavalry, on the failure of his health, left the army at Somerset, Kentucky, he sold his horse "Joe" to Major John Dalman, at that time paymaster, who took the horse to Cincinnati. Very soon after this John Morgan made his raid through Indiana and Ohio.

When Morgan and his troops were passing near Cincinnati, a force of volunteers gathered to pursue him. Old Major McCook went to Dalman's stable and took the horse Joe, and, with the others, followed Morgan, overtaking him, as we have seen, at Buffington. As soon as Major McCook fell, the horse galloped over the field at will. Soon the Seventh Ohio cavalry attacked the rebels on the flank and rear, and the horse, doubtless recognizing familiar voices in the direction of the gallant Seventh, galloped through the tumult and confusion of the battle to the position of the Seventh cavalry and took his wonted place in the line, much to the edification of the boys, who shouted, "Look! there comes Captain Eells' horse, Old Joe."

So ended the battle of Buffington's Island, in which there were more men killed than some of the famous battles in Mexico.

About three hundred and fifty rebels succeeded in getting across at the different fords, and between one and two hundred were taken prisoners after becoming detached from the main body. Morgan himself was half way across at the upper Buffington ford, when he saw that a large part of his command were so hard pressed that they would not be able to escape, and he turned back and continued his flight north, but doubled on his track and again attempted to cross near Blennerhasset's island, but was foiled in this and compelled to make a detour to get out of the trap set for him by Colonel Putnam. In order to do this he marched outside the lines of Mr. Cutler and Lieutenant Conine and the other forces sent out to obstruct and hold the roads leading to the river. He was, however, followed by Shackelford, and also by a force of militia sent forward by Colonel Runkle, under command of Colonel Hill. These moved by boat up the Muskingum, and landed at McConnelsville, July 23d, just as Morgan crossed at Eaglesport seven miles above. Colonel Hill took an unfrequented road over the hills and succeeded in flanking Morgan, and getting his artillery into position, opened on the rebels and threw them into confusion. They dropped their guns, booty,

and everything that would impede progress and fled, followed by Hill as long as his artillery could get positions from which to shell them, keeping up the pursuit until about four P. M., when General Shackelford's cavalry came up and relieved the militia, now very much exhausted, whom Colonel Hill ordered back to the Muskingum.

Thus harassed the remnant of the raiders pursued their toilsome march. General Brooks, who had taken up his headquarters at Wellsville, Ohio, finding that there was a strong probability of Morgan crossing the Cleveland & Pittsburgh railroad at Salineville, sent Colonel Gallagher, with a regiment of six months' men, to a point about two miles from that place, and had them posted advantageously near the supposed place of crossing. Major Way, with the Ninth Michigan cavalry, was also moving up to the same point. In a short time the expected rebels made their appearance, coming around a bend in the road. On catching sight of the infantry they halted and turned their horses' heads in another direction. Before they could get out of the trap Major Way, with two hundred men of the Ninth Michigan cavalry, dashed among them and commenced cutting right and left. The rebels made but a brief resistance, when they broke in utter confusion. The scene that followed was almost ludicrous, and could only be matched by the previous stampede at Buffington's Island. Men dismounted, threw down their arms and begged for quarter, whilst others galloped around wildly in search of a place of escape and were "brought to time" by a pistol shot or saber stroke.

Morgan himself was riding in a carriage drawn by two white horses. Major Way saw him, and galloping up, reached for him. Morgan jumped out at the other side of the carriage, leaped over a fence, seized a horse, and galloped off as fast as horse flesh, spurred by frightened heels, could carry him. About two hundred succeeded in escaping with him. In the buggy thus hastily evacuated by Morgan were found his rations, consisting of a loaf of bread, some hard-boiled eggs, and a bottle of whiskey.*

The number of rebels killed in this engagement was five or six; number wounded not stated; prisoners, about two hundred, together with horses and arms. A few Union cavalry men were wounded.

About two o'clock P. M. of the same day the forces in pursuit of Morgan closed in around him in the vicinity of West Point, between New Lisbon and Wellsville. The rebels were finally compelled to take refuge on a bluff, and finding escape impossible, they surrendered to Colonel Shackelford and the militia, who now started on a general hunt for straggling rebels, brought in numbers of them, found concealed in the woods, all of whom were sent to Columbus.

A rebel account states that Morgan on this raid captured six thousand prisoners, all of whom were paroled, destroyed thirty-four important bridges, and the railroad tracks in sixty places, that they lost twenty-eight commissioned officers killed, thirty-four wounded, and two hun-

* Correspondence Cleveland *Herald* July 27, 1863.

dred and fifty men killed, wounded and captured; that by Federal accounts, they killed more than two hundred, wounded at least three hundred and fifty, and captured as above mentioned, six thousand; that the damage to railroads, steamboats and bridges, added to the destruction of public stores and depots, cannot fall short of ten million dollars; that they captured three pieces of artillery, and one twenty-four pounder at Lebanon, which they destroyed, one Parrot three-inch gun at Brandenburgh, and a twelve-pounder at Portland; that the Copperheads and Butternuts were always in the front opposing them; that occasionally they would meet a pure "Southron," generally a person banished from the border states.

The above mentioned account was written by one of the raiders who escaped at Buffington, and as far as it relates to the Union loss, is not trustworthy, being an over-estimate, but as far as relates to the destruction of property is doubtless not up to the mark.

Morgan and his officers were confined in the penitentiary, from which prison Morgan and six others made their escape November 27, 1863, by cutting through the stone floors of three cells with knives carried off from the prison table, till they reached the air chamber below and tunneling thence under the prison walls into the outer yard, and climbing the surrounding prison wall by the aid of ropes made from their bed clothes. An investigation into the cause of the escape showed that the usual routine of sweeping the cells was omitted in the case of those occupied by the rebels, and they were thus enabled to cover up and conceal their work. The omission to sweep was at the suggestion of one of the directors of the penitentiary.

Morgan reached his hiding-place beyond the mountains of Kentucky and Tennessee in safety, and afterwards led several bands of raiders into the Blue Grass, in one of which he was killed in a skirmish, while endeavoring to escape from a house in a little village in East Tennessee.

THE MILITIA.

Under order to organize the force assembled at Camp Marietta during the Morgan raid, Colonel Putnam appointed on his own staff:

Josiah H. Jenkins, assistant adjutant general; P. B. Putnam, quartermaster; George O. Hildreth, post hospital surgeon; James Little, post hospital surgeon; F. D. Howell, post hospital surgeon; B. F. Culver, post hospital assistant surgeon; John W. White post hospital assistant surgeon; Michael Edwards, post hospital assistant surgeon; Joseph M C. Moorhead, examining surgeon; William Beebe, examining surgeon; William Ackley, examining surgeon; besides a corps of clerks and assistants.

ATHENS COUNTY MILITIA.

A. D. Jaynes, colonel; E. L. DeWitt, colonel; Jared Moris, adjutant. Names of Company commandants—Charles Mathenry, E. D. Harper, reported July 14th; Charles Goodspeed, Elias Grewell, Edward Wheeler, C. Cooper, F. L. Junrod, C. Winget, I. C. Shotts, A. D. Jaynes, H. Nauna, and Daniel Fulton, reported July 16th; Charles Stout and James M. Holmes, reported July 17th; S. H. Smith, E. Stalder and E. P. Pickett, reported July 18th.

Highest number men from Athens county, one thousand eighty-two; total number companies, seventeen.

MEIGS COUNTY MILITIA.

Nathaniel M. McLaughlin, colonel; William B. Skrevner, major. Names of Company Commandants—I. H. Rutherford, L. E. Campbell, John Barrot, G. G. Woodward and R. B. Wilson, reported July 16th; John F. Martin, Minor Reed and S. Riggs, reported July 17th. Total nmber companies, nine; highest number men reported, seven hundred and six.

MONROE COUNTY MILITIA.

Joseph Kelley, colonel. Company Commandants—R. T. Beiber, S. C. Kelley, Henry Scott, J. M Evans, reported July 17th; J. L. Watson, S. F. Ellsworth, G. W. Bennett, C. M. Stewart, J. M. Jones. J. A. Fleischmann, C. B. Way, H. R. Mason, Joshua Way, J. Daugherty, Max Albert, A. C. McElroy and Elias Hoppmann, reported July 18th; Peter Dover, George Ring and J. Roemer, reported July 20th; John Mallory, J. J. Hurd, James Adams, J. F. Culverhouse and J. Rupp, reported July 21st; W. Truax, July 22d; and M. Thoenen, John Bellman and John Monroe, July 24th.

Total number companies, twenty-nine; highest number men reported one thousand three hundred and sixty-seven.

NOBLE COUNTY MILITIA.

William P. Sprague, colonel; William H. Frazier, adjutant.

Company Commandants—Pearson Mordeck, James A. Morrison, B. B. Taylor, Asa Barton, and John Hesson, reported July 15th; D. L. Weems, July 16th; J. R. Rickley, Louis Headly, Lorenzo Powell, Israel Harris, July 17th; Dudley Evans, Enoch Wilkinson, William Fowler, J. M. Walters, James Gibson, William L. Parks, William Ogle, C. Clymer, David McGary, Robert Bary, and Robert Hayne, July 18th. J. F. Briggs, George E. Geddes, July 19th.

Number of companies, twenty-three; highest of men reported on any one day, two thousand one hundred and twelve.

PERRY COUNTY MILITIA.

W. Cook, colonel; S. F. Muzzy, colonel; A. W. Poundston, adjutant.

Company Commandants—D. W. Marsh, John S. Nixon, Obediah Larimer, J. Mackin, and W. H. Spencer, reported July 17th; John Dike, A. T. Sharp, J. Clark, James C. Ritchey, James R. Fulton, and W. L. Harbough, July 18th.

Number of companies, eleven; highest number of men reported, eight hundred and fifty-six.

HOCKING COUNTY MILITIA.

David Little, colonel.

Company Commandants—Samuel Creighton, Abraham McLain, John O. Kennedy, D. Little, and John Oaks, reported July 18th.

Number of companies, five; highest number of men reported, three hundred and forty-four.

MORGAN COUNTY MILITIA.

John C. Ellston, jr., colonel; William B. Loomis, adjutant; Frederick W. Wood, colonel; Bearly Davis, adjutant.

Company Commandants—J. H. Roland, reported July 14th; A. J. Harte, J. McVay, H. R. Seaman, Sidney Newton and Thomas Hammond, reported July 15; J D. Lashley, George Hedges and William Balding reported July 16th, J. L. Pierrot, S. S. Jenkins, William Miller, James B. Tannehill, John Henderson, H. R. Hughes, E. G. Caulson, H. B. White, Charles McCarthy, John Preston, reported July 17th; H. C. Harvey, P. D. Danford, John Rollison, William McIntire, G. B. Fowler, F. G. Phillips and Thomas Vicroy, reported July 18th; D. D Scott and John Fouraker, reported July 19th.

Total number companies, twenty-eight; highest number of men reported, two thousand three hundred and sixty-two.

WASHINGTON COUNTY MILITIA.

J. Mills, Kendrick, colonel commanding; Thomas W. Moore,* colonel First regiment; Joseph B. Kinkead,* colonel First regiment; Thomas Day, colonel First regiment; Edwin Cood, colonel Second regiment; Joseph Dyar, colonel Third regiment; O. P. Scott, colonel Fourth regiment.

Company Commandants—Augustus Dyer, and A. T. Nye, jr., reported July 14th; S. S. Knowles, J. W. Tripp, John Holst, jr., K. Krauss, Elijah Locker, John W. Conley, Henry Kelley, David P. Pugh, P. L. Cole, J. H. Brown, W. L. Baldwin, and J. L. W. Newton, reported July 15th; D. Y. Hill, E. M. Howland, Loring E. Stone, J. P. Sanford, Charles A. Cook, George Davenport, John Magee, Charles H. Cook, R. P. Delley, B. Racer, H. M. Brown, M. Ryan, J. W. Brabham, J. M. Warren, E. D. Smith, and Thomas W. Moore, reported July 16th; Oscar Liackey, J. A. Brown, Jacob Hagar, G. R. Goddard, Washington Wilson, G. B. Turner, July 17th; J. P. Kinkead, Charles Luckens, C. H. Goddard, John E. Smallwood, John Dretchell,

---

* Relieved to command men on detached duty.

J. F. Deshler, and S. P. Willis, July 18th; William Smith, J. D. Gates. July 19th, J. C. Campbell, and Israel N. Dye, July 20th.

Total number of companies, forty-seven; highest number of men reported, two thousand and thirty-nine.

Besides these, there were volunteers under command of S. Mason, Major Bloomfield, J. W. Brabham, D. Y. Hill, one hundred and ninety-eight men, and six months' men in camp at this time numbering two hundred and fifty. In addition to the companies already enumerated, six others from counties outside the first military district came in with six hundred and thirty-four men. The daily aggregate of forces reported at Camp Marietta during the Morgan raid was as follows: On July 13th, the day after the Governor's proclamation, there were in camp one hundred and seventy-five men—the militia had not yet started; July 14th, 457; fifteenth, 1,732; sixteenth, 4,259; seventeenth, 7,064; eighteenth, 11,782; nineteenth, 12,082; twentieth (owing to an order from the governor to send the militia home), 6,434; twenty-first, 5,826; twenty-second, 3,939; twenty-third, 2,721; twenty-fourth, 3,372; twenty-fifth, 2,466; twenty-sixth, 2,389; twenty-seventh, 2,384; twenty-eighth, 449; twenty-ninth, 284; all the militia disappearing again.

AGGREGATE FROM COUNTIES.

On July 19th there were reported at Camp Putnam, either as on duty or in camp, militia and other soldiers, as follows:

NAMES OF COLONELS COMMANDING.		NUMBER OF MEN
Colonel E. L. DeWitt, Athens county; militia		1,036
" D. Little, Hocking county, "		337
" N. M. McLaughlin, Meigs county, "		708
" Joseph Kelley, Monroe county, "		1,355
" J. C. Elston, jr., Morgan county, "		2,364
" W. P. Sprague, Noble county, "		2,117
" L. F. Muzzy, Perry county, "		827
" J. M. Kendrick, Washington county,"		3,039
All others		252
Total		12,082

The results of the operations planned at Camp Marietta were to compel Morgan to make an extended detour to the northward, thereby saving a large tract of country from devastation. Another and more important result was the preventing of his escape across the river, at Buffington. There is no doubt but that the timely arrival of Captain Wood at Buffington, and the construction of the earthwork mentioned, prevented Morgan from crossing with his entire command the night before the battle. The statement of General Basil Duke heretofore referred to fully corroborates this fact. Captain Wood left the fortification under orders from General Scammon, of the Kanawha department, a superior officer, and he left none too soon. Six hours later and the rebels would have attacked him, overpowered his small force, captured the steamer and ferried their troops across before either Judah or Hobson, or the gunboats, could have prevented it.

There are few men that could have handled so large a body of men so well, under such circumstances, as Colonel Putnam did these who came so suddenly upon his hands. They came by the thousands, wholly unarmed, unequipped and unorganized. His action in this situation was admirable, preserving his usual fine equanimity

through it all; and superintending the details of the whole camp, he still had time enough to plan for the capture and detention of Morgan. Down the Ohio, out on the line of the Marietta & Cincinnati railroad as far as the Big Hocking, up the Muskingum, up Duck creek, up Little Muskingum as far as Woodsfield, and up the Ohio, everywhere his regiments and companies were prepared to repel and delay the invaders. While we say this of the commandant of Camp Marietta, we must not forget that grand array of militia, twelve thousand strong, who sprang to the defence of their invaded State, many of them leaving their crops unharvested in the fields, and often compelled to march by their own fields that needed their attention, and doing it without a word of complaint; many leaving their stores, their shops, and employments that required hourly attention, to engage in an uncertain enterprise, the danger of which at the time seemed threatening and hazardous.

It was fully demonstrated by Morgan's raid that no freebooting foray, no matter how well planned or how well carried out, could succeed on Northern soil, and this raid was the last of the kind ever attempted.

On September 19th and 20th occurred the battle of Chickamauga, in which the following regiments having Washington county men in them were engaged: The Ninety-second, Thirty-sixth, and Eighteenth infantry, and First Ohio cavalry. They fought nobly to save the day in this most desperate battle, losing heavily—the Ninety-second seven killed, seventy-eight wounded, including Colonel D. B. Fearing, and twenty missing; the Thirty-sixth twelve killed, including Colonel Jones, sixty-five wounded, and eighteen missing.

The First Ohio cavalry, in this battle, were ordered to charge, through some mistake, and had started toward the enemy's line, some three hundred in number, with sabers drawn; it would have been a second Balaklava, where the famous "six hundred" composing the Light brigade, made such a hopeless charge, but for a timely countermand of the order.

The famous charge at Chickamauga, made by Turchin's brigade, in which were the Thirty-sixth and Ninety-second regiments, should not be passed without adequate mention. A correspondent of the Cincinnati *Commercial* says:

After resisting several heavy charges the brigade changed direction by filing to the left, into the woods skirting the road on that side, and were halted and brought to a front, leaving the brigade in columns by companies, forming two lines of battle, the Eleventh Ohio and Eighteenth Kentucky in front, and the Ninety-second and Thirty-sixth in the rear. Hardly had this been completed when a rebel battery opened a perfect storm of shell and grape-shot into our ranks. This was entirely unexpected to us. It seems a whole division of the enemy had passed entirely around our left, and, coming up in our rear, expected to capture the entire left wing of our army.

Just at the moment the rebels opened General Thomas rode up:

"Whose brigade is this?"

"General Turchin's," was promptly answered.

"General, can your brigade break through those lines?"

"Yes, I guess so, if any brigade can."

"Very well, do it at once."

General Turchin had been commanding our brigade but a short time, but long enough to gain the confidence of his men. Rising in his stirrups he gave the command —"About face—forward, double-quick—charge bayonets—mar-c-h!" With a yell, the volume of which was decreased not a whit by the fact that the men fully realized that everything depended on the success of this movement, they did charge.

The enemy were drawn up in three lines in an open field, and as we emerged from the woods delivered a volley that tore thrugh our ranks, but failed to check the onward course of our men, who returned the fire, charged bayonets, and dashed into them before they could reload

The rebels broke in the wildest confusion, while cheer upon cheer from our brave boys added swiftness to their flight. A running fight now ensued which baffles description. The smoke arising from the discharge of so many guns, and the thick clouds of dust completely obscured both rebel and federal, while the hoarse commands of the officers, endeavoring to keep their men in line, the lurid flash of artillery, and the bursting of shell and rattling of grapeshot, which the rebels continued to pour into our ranks, at short range, from three points, made up a picture as nearly resembling Pandemonium as any one need wish to see.

On this charge our brigade captured about six hundred prisoners and four pieces of cannon, but were so closely pushed that we had to abandon the cannon, and half of our prisoners escaped in the confusion, but three hundred were marched along and sent safely through to Chattanooga that night.

Officers of the reserve, who had a fair view of the whole charge, describe it as the grandest spectacle imaginable.

Lieutenant Colonel Douglas Putnam, jr., who took command of the Ninety-second after Colonel Benjamin D. Fearing was wounded, says in his report of the battle:

The smallness of the loss was due to the very skilful management of Colonel Fearing, and his coolness and bravery while under fire and in command.

Major Golden assisted me in every possible manner, and did himself credit. Captains Grosvenor and Whittlesey are especially deserving of notice for bravery and coolness, and for the manner in which their companies were managed. After Colonel Fearing was wounded Captain Grosvenor took command of the left wing, Major Golden going to the right. I feel under obligations to Adjutant George B. Turner, whose assistance was invaluable to me, and whose coolness and forethought were manifested on every occasion. He is deserving of especial notice and commendation. Surgeon J. D Cotton was with us whenever it was possible for him to reach us, and left nothing undone for the comfort of the wounded Quartermaster Priestly showed himself to be a brave man, and was on the field attending to the wants of the men.

The next great battle in which Washington county figured was Mission Ridge. Rosecrans had planned to carry the enemy's position on the ridge and on Lookout Mountain, and when Grant relieved him everything was ready to his hand. Bragg, with his rebel legions forty thousand strong, held high Lookout and Mission Ridge fully fortified and bristling with cannon; but Sherman, with the army of the Mississippi, had reenforced Grant, and now everything, by November 23rd, was ready. Sherman, by a detour, had quietly taken position to the northeast unknown to the enemy, and was now ready to cross the Tennessee river and attack the northern fortifications on the ridge. Hooker had crossed the Tennessee by a pontoon bridge at Bridgeport, southwest of Chattanooga, and was ready to storm Lookout Mountain. Meanwhile "Pap" Thomas, with the army that had fought its way from Stone River to the Chattanooga, moved out from the centre. Let an eye witness relate the story:*

The day was bright and beautiful; the rays of the sun, reflected from ten thousand bayonets, dazzled the beholder's eyes; the men were dressed as if for holiday; proud steeds, bearing gallant riders, galloped along the lines; every eminence about the city was crowded with spectators; and for the first time in my experience I saw soldiers of the Union march to battle to the beat of the spirit-drum. This was indeed the "pomp and circumstance" of war; and it is no wonder that the rebels

whom we afterward captured declared they did not think we were going to make an attack upon them, but had our troops out for a review or dress parade. .   .   .   On the eventful day of which I write, I saw an exaultant and lofty pride, a high and patriotic hope, a firm and deep resolve expressed in the countenance of each soldier as I had never seen them expressed before, and no one could doubt, as he looked upon them, that they would go that day wherever they were bidden, even should they be compelled to pass through surges of vindictive fire.

Thomas' men moved out swiftly, drove in the enemy's pickets, and captured his first line, known as Orchard Ridge, where they intrenched. The next day, the twenty-fourth, Hooker attacked Lookout, and fought his celebrated "battle among the clouds," driving the rebels from their position; and Sherman, having constructed a pontoon bridge across the Tennessee, above, had attacked and carried the north end of Mission Ridge. Accordingly, on November 25th, everything was ready for the final grand assault on the stronghold of the enemy on Mission Ridge. The rebel General Bragg, trusting to the natural strength of his position, had sent off part of his command, under Longstreet, to capture Burnside at Knoxville, and from his eyrie on the ridge surveyed with complacency the preparations of his foe for the attack. At last Grant was ready, and at the preconcerted signal of six guns, fired at intervals of two seconds, the assault began all along the line, up the steep side of the mountain. Soon the grand roll of musketry, and a line of smoke encircling the mountain, told that they had started the enemy from his lair. A long line of blue, broken into triangles, with their points toward the crest of the mountain (fifteen of them), and at each apex a stand of colors marks the centre of the regiment. Upward they rush. Anon, a standard goes down, which means that the entire color guard have been shot.

Mr. Furay continues:

And still the Union troops pressed on, scaling nnwaveringly the sides of Mission Ridge; the blood of their comrades renders their footsteps slippery; the toil of the ascent almost takes away their breath; the rebel musketry and artillery mow down their thinned ranks—but still they press on! Not once do they even seem to waver. The color-bearers press ahead, and plant their flags far in advance of the troops; and at last—O, moment of supreme triumph!—they reach the crest and rush like an avalanche upon the astonished foe. Whole regiments throw down their arms and surrender; the rebel artillerists are bayonetted by their guns, and the cannon which had a moment before been thundering on the Union ranks, are now turned about, pouring death into the midst of the mass of miserable fugitives who are rushing down the eastern slope of the ridge *

Lieutenant Colonel H. F. Devol, commanding the Thirty-sixth regiment in this battle, in his official report, says:

My regiment was assigned to the centre of the first line, the Eleventh Ohio volunteer infantry on my right, and the Ninety-second Ohio volunteer infantry on the left. Two companies, B and H, were thrown forward as skirmishers. Remaining there until three o'clock, we moved forward a short distance, halted, deployed, and immediately again moved in line of battle through a skirt of woods. As soon as we reached the open ground the enemy opened on us with artillery from the top of Missionary Ridge. We were then ordered to double-quick, which we did, passing the second line of the enemy's breast-works, which were occupied by General Beatty's brigade; reached the base of the ridge, where also were some troops under cover. We rushed up the ridge as fast as possible, under a terrible enfilading fire from both right, left, and front. Near the top, and about six rods from the enemy's breastworks, we passed over (I think) the Ninth Kentucky volunteer infantry. Reaching the breast-works, where the enemy lay, a terrible, almost hand-to-hand fight ensued. Stubbornly did the enemy

---

*W. S. Furay, correspondent Cincinnati *Gazette*.

contest the works. There we took a number of prisoners, which I passed to the rear without a guard. Those of the enemy who escaped made a second stand on the crest, from four to six rods beyond; but they were at once killed, captured, or routed. On our left was a heavy force of the enemy's infantry, and two pieces of artillery. The infantry kept up a constant fire. The artillery fired two rounds, when we made a charge on it and captured the two pieces, but not until they had succeeded in getting them some distance down the eastern slope of the ridge to the rear. They were unlimbered and immediately hauled back to the top of the ridge by the men, and placed in position. The taking of the artillery was done, mainly, under the superintendence of Sergeant Adney, of company B, and Sergeant Holliday, of company H. Some men from the Eleventh and Ninety-second Ohio volunteer infantry assisted in hauling the guns back.

Captain J. C. Selby, company K, was wounded in the right arm (which has since been amputated) near a log cabin, to the left of where we went up the ridge. First Lieutenant O. J. Wood, company B, when in command of the company, was seriously wounded, the ball passing through from left to right side and through the right lung. Second Lieutenant J. W. Hanlin, company H, was slightly wounded in the leg.

It would be in vain for me to try to express how nobly and with what daring both officers and men conducted themselves, in this their fifth great battle. Never as yet have they fallen back under fire in the face of the enemy. In this all seemed eager to fight, and under the leadership of their general, felt confident of success. I would particularize, did I not have to mention the whole.

The Thirty-sixth lost nine killed, sixty-five wounded and five missing, and the Ninety-second, twelve killed and forty-two wounded. Among the former killed were Captain W. Beale Whittlesey and Adjutant George B. Turner, both promising young officers, from Marietta, a fuller account of whose lives will be found further on. Lieutenant Colonel Douglas Putnam, jr., received a severe wound in the ankle. Mission Ridge was the most peculiar battle of the war. No other presented such natural obstacles to be overcome at such high altitudes. Bragg had forty thousand men, and Grant, seventy-five thousand, but the advantages of position in Bragg's favor fully made up for the disparity of numbers. Grant went to Chattanooga on crutches to relieve Rosecrans, but now his fame travelled on the wings of the wind. To Vicksburgh, through a fortunate turn of affairs, he had added Mission Ridge, and the country went wild with enthusiasm for Grant. He was made lieutenant general, and Sherman taking command of the army at Chattanooga, soon began his march on Atlanta.

The year 1863 closed without any further great battles, and the Union armies generally went into winter quarters. Nearly all of the three years' men reenlisted as veterans, showing their devotion to country and the flag, and their great interest in carrying the conflict to a successful close.

The regiments having companies from Washington county, who reenlisted, furnished veterans as follows: Eighteenth regiment, sixty-two; Thirty-sixth regiment, three hundred and sixty-four; Thirty-ninth regiment, five hundred and thirty-four; Sixty-third regiment, four hundred and fifty-five; Seventy-seventh regiment, three hundred and four; First cavalry, two hundred and eighty-five; Second West Virginia cavalry, three hundred and thirty-three; First light artillery, five hundred and fifteen, and also Pierpont battery, eighty. The Thirty-ninth Ohio furnished more veterans than any other regiment from Ohio, and Washington county more veterans than any other county in the State, except Hamilton.

Upon the return of the veterans from the front on thirty days' furlough, they were met with a continuous ovation. The citizens of Washington county greeted them with gratitude and respect.

The roll of dead officers and soldiers for the year 1863 includes many good names, none, however, more lamented than Colonel Jesse Hildebrand, a fuller notice of whom will be found in another part of this work.

CHAPTER XIX.

WAR OF THE REBELLION CONTINUED—1864-65.

Beginning of Governor Brough's Administration—New Militia Law—Ohio National Guard—Conference of the Governors—Call of Governor Brough for Thirty Thousand Ohio National Guards—Response.

GOVERNOR BROUGH entered upon his term with a more emphatic endorsement than any former governor ever had in the State, receiving over one hundred thousand majority, of which Washington county contributed as follows: Home majority, eight hundred and sixty-five; soldier's majority, eight hundred and four; total majority, one thousand six hundred and sixty-nine. This was a very decided endorsement of the war policy and was an emphatic pledge to devote the resources of the county to the prosecution of the war, not only by furnishing additional soldiers, but money through taxes and voluntary contributions to support the families of the soldiers left behind as the wards of the Nation, and the history of 1863, 1864 and 1865 shows how fully the county came up to the work. The whole amount of money thus furnished can never be known. The value of the service rendered could not be measured by money because it involved the expenditure of the best energies, finest talent and noblest courage, involving loss of life and of all that men hold most dear, but the feeling was benevolent and deep seated in the hearts of the people that no sacrifice was too costly to serve the Union, for without union all the rest was worthless. Now the fine theories of other days, the high periods and eloquence of the statesmen and patriots of the illustrious past were being forged into the life and experience of the Nation. Men were living what before they had only dreamed. The great battle year of 1863 had developed heroes and leaders. The Nation had grappled with and worsted the foe, and it was now only a question of time as to how long the rebellion would hold out.

In the spring of 1864 the legislature passed a new militia law repealing the one enacted the previous year requiring military encampments. The new body of State soldiery thus summoned into existence was the Ohio National guards that was soon to become so famous in the annals of the State.

From the time Governor Brough was inaugurated a new impetus was given to all the military affairs of the State, which in no way reflected on the able administration of his illustrious predecessor, David Tod. Governor

Brough was a man of strong feelings and convictions, and he greatly desired to see the war end in an honorable peace. He was anxious to help the President and vigilant in watching for opportunities to help on the good work. The invasion of the State during the last year had induced the governor and legislature to favor a thorough militia organization, and Governor Brough, fearing incursions by the enemy along the southern border of the State, sent Ex-Governor Dennison to Washington to urge upon the Secretary of War the necessity of putting State regiments into the service along the border and on the northern line at proper posts, to discourage any invasion from Canada which was feared, but the Secretary denied the necessity. Failing in this, and the circumstances of the situation showing that soon all must either be gained or lost by striking heavy blows, thick and fast, Governor Brough adopted the theory that the next best way to prevent invasion was to keep the enemy busy at home. He, therefore, argued that all veterans and volunteers should be in the field in the immediate presence of the enemy, ready to push him to the wall, and that all soldiers on guard duty should be relieved and sent to the front. The National guards offered a partial solution of the problem, and seeking the cooperation and counsel of the governors of other States, he arranged for a meeting of the governors of Indiana, Illinois, Iowa, and Wisconsin, to be held at Washington, where it was decided to offer the President the services of the militia of the States named for one hundred days. The offer was couched in the following terms:

WAR DEPARTMENT,
WASHINGTON CITY, April 21, 1864.

To the President of the United States:

I. The governors of Ohio, Indiana, Illinois, Iowa, and Wisconsin, offer to the President infantry troops for the approaching campaign, as follows. Ohio, thirty thousand; Indiana, twenty thousand; Illinois, twenty thousand, Iowa, ten thousand; Wisconsin, five thousand.

II. The term of service to be one hundred days, reckoning from the date of muster into the service of the United States, unless sooner discharged.

III. The troops to be mustered into the service of the United States by regiments, when the regiments are filled up, according to regulations of the War Department; the whole number to be furnished within twenty days from date of notice of the acceptance of this proposition.

IV. The troops to be clothed, armed, equipped, subsisted, transported, and paid as other United States infantry volunteers, and to serve in fortifications, or wherever their services may be required, within or without their respective States.

V. No bounty to be paid the troops, nor the services charged or credited on any draft.

VI. The draft for three years' service to go on in any State or district where the quota is not filled up, but if any officer or soldier in this special service should be drafted, he shall be credited for the service rendered.

JOHN BROUGH, Governor of Ohio.
O. P. MORTON, Governor of Indiana.
RICHARD YATES, Governor of Illinois.
W. M. STONE, Governor of Iowa.

The President accepted the offer two days after, and on the same day the adjutant general of Ohio received a dispatch from Governor Brough to call out thirty thousand of the Ohio National guard for one hundred days' service. They were to rendezvous at the nearest practicable point in their respective counties. A week was given

for the muster, and by sundown of May 2, 1864, over thirty thousand of Ohio's substantial citizens reported for duty, and demanded to be sent on to the post of duty. Such an uprising had not been seen since the first alarm of Sumter. Governor Brough at one stroke, like that of a magician's wand, had summoned an army into existence. Over forty regiments, containing thirty-four thousand men, responded to the call and were accepted, thus relieving thirty thousand veterans to go to the front.

The situation in Washington county as to the draft at this time was very encouraging. Under all the calls of 1863, and the calls of March 14, 1864, for two hundred thousand more, there was an excess of one hundred and ninety-two to the credit of different townships, but as the credit of one township would not help the deficiency of another, it so happened that fifty-four men were drafted as follows: Belpre, ten; Decatur, twenty-one; Dunham, one; Lawrence, four; Liberty, fifteen; Ludlow, three.

The draft, therefore, had nothing to do with the great uprising of the National guard, although the guards were, by a subsequent arrangement, credited to Ohio on her quota.

The Washington county regiment of the National guard, organized under the militia law of 1863, remained substantially the same under the new law creating the Ohio National guard. It was the Forty-sixth regiment but the number was changed to One Hundred and Forty-eighth. The regiment was commanded by Colonel Thomas W. Moore, of Warren township, and all but two companies were from Washington county. Three companies having come from Vinton county they were consolidated with the eight from Washington county, and on May 22, 1864, they left Marietta for Harper's Ferry. A fuller account of the services of the regiment will be found further on in this work.

General Banks, supported by Commodore Porter, with a fleet of gunboats, during the month of March, 1864, started up the Red river, and General Steele with the army under his command from Little Rock, Arkansas, to effect a junction with Banks, but the rebels having driven Banks back, turned their whole force upon Steele. On April 25, the brigade, consisting of the Thirty-sixth Iowa, Forty-third Indiana, and Seventy-seventh Ohio regiments, under command of Lieutenant Colonel Drake, of the Thirty-sixth Iowa, was sent from General Steele's army to guard an empty train of two hundred and seventy wagons returning to Pine Bluffs. The whole force numbered about fifteen hundred, with a battery of four guns. When the train reached Marks Mills it was attacked by Shelby's cavalry, estimated at seven thousand, and the Thirty-sixth and Forty-third, after a gallant fight were driven back; the Seventy-seventh guarding the rear hurried up on the double quick to the help of the Forty-third and Thirty-sixth, running over five miles. They charged the enemy with a yell, and killed them by the score, but found an overpowering force of rebels closing in on them from every side. "They fought desperately hand-to-hand and foot to foot," says an eye witness, but all in vain; they were all taken prisoners except one lieutenant and forty men, who cut their way out and

ercaped to the Union lines after travelling over one hundred miles, smimming many streams and eating nothing for forty-eight hours. Captain McCormick and Lieutenant Smithson were taken prisoners with the rest, and marched from the battle-field to the prison pen at Tyler, Texas, marching fifty-two miles in twenty-four hours. The negro servants of the officers were shot at once after the surrender.

This was the second term in rebel prisons for Captain McCormick, he having been rode down, shot and captured at Shiloh, by the Texan cavalry.

One of the men of company C, Seventy-seventh, tore the colors from the staff and wrapped it around him, when the rebels were within twenty yards of it, cut his way through the rebel lines and brought the colors into camp, in triumph. The flag has nineteen holes in it.*

The Union loss in killed and wounded was about two hundred and fifty, the rebel loss was much larger, estimated at the time by Union officers at one thousand. The Seventy-seventh lost as follows: Killed, seven; mortally wounded, one; severely wounded, fourteen; slightly wounded, seventeen; wounded prisoners, six; prisoners, three hundred; paroled, seven; missing, eighteen; total, three hundred and seventy.

A rebel officer in a letter to General Fagan, of Dick Taylor's army, gives the following account of the battle of Marks Mills:

After driving Steele into Camden, General Fagan started with three thousand five hundred cavalry for Little Rock, but fell in with the enemy at Marks Mills, where we had a terrible fight. Our arms were finally victorious, and we succeeded in capturing about fifteen hundred prisoners, two hundred and fifty wagons, and five pieces of artillery. It was a complete rout and few of the enemy escaped.

In June the great raid of Generals Hunter, Crook, and Averill, took place. They destroyed the military institute at Lexington, Virginia, and did great damage to the enemy. The Second Virginia cavalry and Thirty-sixth regiment took a gallant part in this expedition.

July 24th the Thirty-sixth regiment was in the battle of Winchester, and lost heavily, and all along the line the soldiers from Washington county were getting in their work.

The war had now resolved itself into two great movements—Grant on Richmond and Sherman on Atlanta. Sherman had gathered within his grasp the armies of the departments of the Ohio, the Cumberland, the Tennessee, and the Arkansas, and after a thorough understanding with Grant, he began his famous campaign against Atlanta. Washington county had companies in five regiments which took part in this campaign, the First and Ninth cavalries, the Thirty-ninth, Sixty-third and Ninety-second regiments, besides men in the Seventy-third, thirty-third, and other regiments.

Sherman, by a series of brilliant flank movements to the right compelled the enemy to abandon every position from Dalton to Atlanta, and fought the battles of Rocky Face Ridge, Resaca, Pumpkin Vine Creek, Kenesaw Mountain, Nicojack Creek, Peachtree Creek, the battles around Atlanta and Jonesborough. In all these battles,

making about one hundred and twenty days of nearly constant fighting, he lost but one—that of Kenesaw Mountain, which was immediately retrieved by another movement on the right flank, compelling the enemy to evacuate Kenesaw. The rebel authorities being dissatisfied with the Fabian policy of Johnson, removed him and placed Hood in command at Atlanta, where, by July 22, 1864, Sherman had extended his lines in the form of a semi-circle, partially enclosing the city and the enemy's works. Hood, on the day named, wishing to begin a strong and aggressive policy, quietly stole out and got on the flank and rear of the gallant McPherson before the movement was fully known to the Union generals. Here occurred one of the most desperate and hard fought battles of the war, the rebels hoping to surprise and beat McPherson, and then each of the other divisions in turn made charge after charge on our lines. The Thirty-ninth regiment was in the thickest of this engagement, and suffered severely, losing one-third of the entire number in killed and wounded. Our line was beaten back and several batteries captured, and more than all, McPherson killed. Sherman hurried Schofield up to the scene and after a hard struggle, lasting until night, drove the enemy back with a loss of eight thousand, the Union loss being three thousand seven hundred and twenty-two. General John W. Sprague says:

Before Atlanta, on the twenty-second of July, the Twenty-seventh and Thirty-ninth rendered their greatest service of the war. A great opportunity was here made the most of. Upon the valor of the Sixteenth corps rested the safety of all our trains, and perhaps that of a part of the Army of the Tennessee. It is safe to say that no regiments of the corps had more responsibility in the great battle than did these two. None, certainly, proved truer to their trust. Twice they charged the enemy who essayed to take possession of the open field where they were fighting, and twice they drove him back ingloriously to the woods.*

Sherman finally, by another movement to the right and rear of Atalanta, cut the enemy's communications, destroyed all railroads leading into the city when it was abandoned, and on September 1st Sherman's triumphant legions marched in and took possession. Reorganizing his army and sending part of it with Thomas to Nashville, Sherman retained and consolidated the remaining forces into four corps, the Fourteenth, Fifteenth, Seventeenth, and twentieth, which, together with Kilpatrick's cavalry, numbered about sixty-five thousand men.

After perfecting his arrangements, Sherman by November 11th was ready to begin his famous "march to the sea." The army marched in two columns, the right with the Fifteenth and Seventeenth corps, commanded by General O. O. Howard, and the left, with the Fourteenth and Twentieth corps, led by General H. W. Slocum. Each wing had a pontoon train, and kept their line of march about twenty miles apart. Kilpatrick, with the cavalry hovered around the front demonstrating first on one flank and then on the other to deceive the enemy as to the real intentions of Sherman. By thus widening his lines he enabled the foraging parties to cover forty miles of territory from which to obtain subsistence for the troops, and they lived well. On December 10th, after marching two hundred and fifty-five miles, being six

---

*Letter of Lieutenant Gordon B. West to his sister Miss Lottie West.

22

*Address at reunion of the Ohio brigade, October 3, 1878.

weeks on the way, they arrived at Savannah. Soon Fort McAllister fell, and the grand march was successfully ended. It is an extra honor to have been with Sherman on this "march to the sea" for history presents few parallels to it, and though little fighting was done it was a grand achievement, and far-reaching in its results.

After resting and refitting his army, Sherman, on February 1, 1865, started northward through the Carolinas, devastating the country and teaching the South Carolinians a few lessons in the hardships of war as he went. General Johnston having been restored to the command of the decimated divisions of his old army, hurried up from the southwest on the trail of Sherman, to intercept him, but by skilful handling of the cavalry, General Sherman deceived Johnston into believing that he was going to Charlotte, North Carolina, and as soon as the rebel force had concentrated there turned to the eastward and started direct to Goldsborough, where he expected to be joined by the divisions of General Schofield. Johnston, however, by rapid marches intercepted four divisions of the left wing on March 15th, at Averysborough, on a narrow swampy neck of land, between Cape Fear and South rivers, North Carolina. The rebels under General Hardee, estimated at twenty thousand, attacked the Union lines with great spirit, hoping to beat them before reenforcements could be brought up. By a rapid movement to the left the enemy's flank was turned, and being pressed in front by other divisions, they were repulsed.

A gallant officer from Washington county, General B. D. Fearing, commanding the old "McCook brigade," was on the left of the line, and General Davis ordered him "to check the enemy and hold them if it cost his whole brigade."

The charge of General Fearing was made with spirit and accompanied with hard fighting. The general had his horse shot under him, and was himself wounded, a minnie-ball passing through his right hand from the wrist forward, carrying away the thumb, fore-finger and left portion of the hand. Being permanently disabled by this wound, General Fearing, now at the age of twenty-seven years, was mustered out of the service, having, as a private, taken part in the first, and as commander of a brigade, in the last important battle of the war *

At Bentonville, on March 18th, the enemy made their last attack, Johnston hoping by a swift and heavy assault to break the left wing before the other could be brought to reinforce it. Johnston accordingly made several desperate charges on our left wing. In the first, two brigades of Carlin's division were driven back, losing three guns.* Slocum thereupon stood on the defensive, placing four divisions in line to the front and making such slight defensive works as they could, while Kilpatrick attacked the enemy on the left. The left received six fierce assaults from Johnston's army. They came on after the old style, line upon line, closing up the gaps made by our fire, but were met by equal discipline and coolness, and by superior numbers. Our artillery did terrible execution on the foe, inflicting heavy loss on his devoted ranks. The rebels had hoped to crush Slocum, but they were disappointed. Night came, and nothing had been gained; and during the night Slocum brought up and

* From General Fearing's Biographical Sketch, Ohio in the War.

disposed three more divisions, rendering his position safe, and Johnston fortified, but made no more attacks. Sherman and his entire army came up next day, and movements were immediately begun to cut off the wiley Johnston, but he decamped that night, and Sherman, with the entire army, moved on to Goldsborough. After paying a hasty visit to Grant at City Point, Sherman again began operations against the enemy, which speedily ended in the surrender of Johnston and the collapse of the confederacy.

While these memorable events were transpiring, and Sherman was establishing for himself a name and fame equal to that of any military chieftain of modern times, equally brilliant successes were attending the Union arms in other fields, in which Washington county figured.

In August, 1864, Grant desiring to have a trusty lieutenant on the Potomac and Shenandoah, sent General Phil Sheridan to take command of those armies. Sheridan's instructions were comprised principally in two words—"Go in!"—and he went in.

On September 13th he confronted the rebel General Early on Opequan creek, near Berryville, in the Shenandoah valley, a few miles south of Harper's Ferry, and on the nineteenth, at 2 A. M., began dispositions for battle. General Crook, with the Eighth corps (the army of West Virginia), including the Second Virginia cavalry and the Thirty-sixth Ohio volunteer infantry, was sent out on the right to turn the enemy's left flank, while the Sixth and Nineteenth corps assaulted the enemy in front, but were met with a vigorous resistance, and Grove's and Rickett's divisions were repulsed with great loss.

From Greeley's Great American Conflict the following account of that battle is taken:

The One Hundred and Fifty-sixth New York had barely forty men grouped around its colors. Captain Rigby, Twenty-fourth Iowa, was seen retreating firmly, deliberately followed by a sergeant and twelve men, who, reaching the assigned rallying point, halted, faced to the front, and gave three hearty cheers. Five minutes later that platoon had been swelled by other such to a battalion; while Captain Bradbury, First Maine battery, had, by Grover's order, posted two guns in a gap and opened on the exultant rebels, who, charging to seize them, received a volley in the rear from the One Hundred and Thirty-first New York, which General Emory had rallied and posted in a projection of wood, with orders not to fire until the enemy should have passed them. As they staggered under this unexpected salute, a volley from the newly-formed line in their front sent them pell mell back across the fields to their original cover.

And now a shout from the far right, shut out from view by woods and hills, announced that the turning movement was effected—that our cavalry under Torbert and Crook, with his Eighth corps, have struck the enemy's left flank, and are charging it under a terrible fire. Instantly redoubled fire breaks out along our central front, in spite of the general scarcity of cartridges; and these being soon exhausted, Colonel Thomas, Eighth Vermont, ordered his men to charge at double-quick with the bayonet. In vain general officers shouted "Halt!" "Lie Down!" "Wait for supports!" etc.; for while some were still confused and vacillating, a staff officer from the right galloped in front, and pointed with his sabre to the woods which sheltered the enemy. At once all dissent was silenced, all hesitation at an end. The whole centre, as one man, swept forward cheering, and plunged into the woods, meeting there Crook's corps, charging from the flanks. All the rebels who could still travel were by this time going or gone.

A height in the rear, still held by the enemy, was soon stormed by Crook and carried, and Early retreated to his second position, Fisher's Hill, south of Winchester, but was attacked by Sheridan's victorious columns, beaten, and compelled to retreat ignominiously, followed by Sheridan's cavalry, destroying everything as they went, and what they missed going up they destroyed on their way back, "so that nothing should be left to invite the enemy to return."

On October 9th, General Sheridan, in compliance with an order from Washington, went to that city, and by the eighteenth had returned as far as Winchester. Meanwhile, Early, chafing under his recent defeats, had demanded and received reinforcements. Planning to take advantage of Sheridan's absence and effect a surprise, he stole out of his lair at dusk on the evening of the eighteenth, and to insure silence his men were divested of canteens and other equipments that would be likely to make a noise in marching. The Union army, six miles distant, lay encamped at Cedar creek, with Crook's army of West Virginia in front, the Nineteenth corps half a mile behind, and the Sixth corps to the right and rear of the Nineteenth, Kitching's division behind Crook's left, and the cavalry, under Torbert, on the right of the Sixth. This army was perfectly unsuspicious of an attack, as they were in a measure justified in being. Early had divided his forces in two columns to take our army on both flanks. An hour before sunrise the rebels were in position, and had not been discovered by our pickets, and our army slumbered in peace, with the deep slumber of the early morning upon them, when all at once there came a crash of musketry on the morning air, and the rebels rush over the trenches and upon the gallant veterans of so many well-fought fields. They seize their arms, the hurried command is given to form, but the rebel line presses them out of their camp, and by their rapid pursuit prevent any formation. The enemy, perfectly familiar with every foot of ground, rushed on, and the army of West Virginia took its way as best it could towards Winchester. The Sixth corps attempted to stay the rebel advance, and the Nineteenth, to the right, offered a stubborn resistance to the rebel onslaught, but gradually fell back.

The Sixth fell back in good order, and the whole army after losing twenty-four guns and twelve hundred prisoners was in full retreat. The rebels stopped to plunder our camps. Meantime Sheridan riding out of Winchester found the first stragglers of the retreat and at once took in the situation. Putting spurs to his horse he rode with all speed to the scene of action, turning back the soldiers and cheering them with such remarks as, "Face the other way, boys! we are going back to our camps—we are going to lick them out of their boots!" Hastily reforming the broken divisions he arranged anew a line of battle and in two charges sent the rebels flying up the valley, capturing twenty-three guns and fifteen hundred men and recovering the guns lost in the morning, and camping at the old camp so hastily abandoned in the early part of the day. This was the last of the Shenandoah campaign. Early's army was destroyed, and Sheridan had no enemy worth his attention to molest him in the valley.

T. Buchanan Read has given to posterity the following lines in relation to this famous battle:

Up from the South at break of day,
Bringing to Winchester fresh dismay,
The affrighted air with a shudder bore,
Like a herald in haste to the chieftain's door,
The terrible grumble and rumble and roar,
Telling the battle was on once more,
And Sheridan twenty miles away.

But there is a road from Winchester town,
A good, broad highway leading down;
And there, through the flash of morning light,
A steed, as black as the steeds of night,
Was seen to rush as with eagle flight.
As if he knew the terrible need
He stretched away with his utmost speed;
Hill rose and fell—but his heart was gay,
With Sheridan fifteen miles away.

The first that the general saw were the groups
Of stragglers, and then the retreating troops;
What was done—what to do—a glance told him both.
Then striking his spurs, with a terrible oath
He dashed down the line 'mid a storm of huzzas,
And the wave of retreat checked its course there, because
The sight of the master compelled it to pause.
With foam and with dust the black charger was gray;
By the flash of his eye, and his red nostril's play,
He seemed to the whole great army to say:
"I have brought you Sheridan all the way
From Winchester down to save the day!"

Hurrah! hurrah for Sheridan!
Hurrah! hurrah for horse and man!
And when their statues are placed on high,
Under the dome of the Union sky—
The American soldiers' Temple of Fame—
There with the glorious general's name
Be it said, in letters both bold and bright,
"Here is the steed that saved the day,
By carrying Sheridan into the fight
From Winchester- twenty miles away."

Washington county was represented at the battle of Nashville by one company in the First and one in the Seventh Ohio volunteer cavalry, one company in the Eighteenth Ohio volunteer infantry, besides a large number distributed through other Ohio regiments. This battle, fought December 15th and 16th, 1864, was the crowning triumph of General George H. Thomas, a perfect Waterloo to General Hood and the rebel army in the west. Thus ended the eventful year 1864. From the beginning of the year to the end it was a series of Union victories, and Washington county's sons were on every field. All during the great battle year she had kept a steady stream of recruits going to the front, where they stepped into the places made vacant by the loss in battle or in hospital. She had sent out nearly a thousand of her best citizens for the hundred days' service. She had furnished more veterans for reenlistment than any other county in the State excepting Hamilton, the number being four hundred and forty, Stark being next with four hundred. The counties of the Fifteenth district stood as follows: Meigs, 245; Athens, 246; Washington, 440; Morgan, 251; Monroe, 238—total number of veterans, 1420. During this year the grand army of the Potomac, under General Grant, had engaged the flower of the rebel army in Virginia, who fought stubbornly for every inch of ground. It was on May 11th that Grant telegraphed the Secretary of War:

We have now ended the sixth day of very heavy fighting. The result to this time is much in our favor.

Our losses have been heavy, as well as those of the enemy. I think the loss of the enemy must be greater.

We have taken over five thousand prisoners, whilst he has taken from us but few except stragglers.

I propose to fight it out on this line if it takes all summer

                         U. S. GRANT,

                  Lt. Gen Commanding.

It was this tenacious spirit and steady hammering that gradually overcame the rebel armies.

By the battles of the Wilderness and the other great engagements fought during the year 1864 between Grant and Lee the rebel forces were terribly reduced in number, so also were ours, but the great North stood ready to fill the ranks and to furnish the treasure to carry on the war indefinitely, while the South, already exhausted, could scarcely hope to supply fresh regiments or more money. Thus although Grant did not succeed in giving Lee a crushing defeat, he so weakened him that when he set down before Petersburgh and began his series of movements towards Richmond, he left Washington and the rear in a measure secure from molestation, that city being fully fortified and the fortifications being manned by the artillerists of the reserve—the heroes of many battles—who were not needed at Petersburgh. Among them were our Washington county Pierpont battery, also Huntington's battery.

The war had lasted nearly four years. Long and dreary they were, but filled with intensely exciting episodes. The people of the north were heartily tired of war and longed for peace. They had sent their bravest and best to the support of the Union and were ready for further sacrifices.

The following poem, by J. J. Piatt, was first printed August 6, 1864, in *Harper's Weekly*:

THE MOWER IN OHIO.

The bees in the clover are making honey, and I am making hay;
The air is fresh, I seem to draw a young man's breath to-day.

The bees and I are alone in the grass; the air is so very still
I hear the dam, so loud, that shines beyond the sullen mill.

Yes, the air is so still that I hear almost the sounds I cannot hear,
That, when no other sound is plain, ring in my empty ear;

The chime of striking scythes, the fall of the heavy swaths they sweep—
They ring about me, resting, when I waver half asleep;

So still, I am not sure if a cloud, low down, unseen there be,
Or if something brings a rumor home of the cannon so far from me.

Far away in Virginia where Joseph and Grant, I know,
Will tell them what I meant when first I had my mowers go.

Joseph he is my eldest—how his scythe was striking ahead!
William was better at shorter beats, but Joe in the long run led.

William he was my youngest; John between them, some how I see,
When my eyes are shut, with a little board at his head in Tennessee.

But William came home one morning early, from Gettysburgh last July
(The mowing was over already, although the only mower was I);

William, my captain, came home for good to his mother; an' I'll be bound
We were proud and cried to see the flag that wrapt his coffin round;

For a company from the town came up ten miles with music and gun—
It seemed his country claimed him then—as well as his mother her son.

But Joseph is yonder with Grant to-day, a thousand miles or near,
And only the bees are abroad at work with me in the clover here.

Was it a murmur of thunder I heard hummed again in the air?
Yet, may be, the cannon are sounding now their "Onward to Richmond"
     there.

For I saw my boys, across the field, by the flashes as they went,
Tramping a steady tramp as of old with the strength in their arms unspent;

Tramping a steady tramp they moved like soldiers that march to the beat
Of music that seems, a part of themselves, to rise and fall with their feet.

Tramping a steady tramp, they came with flashes of silver that shone,
Every step, from their scythes that rang as if they needed the stone—

(The field is wide and heavy with grass)—and, coming toward me they beamed
With a shine of light in their faces at once, and surely I must have dreamed!

For I sat alone in the cloverfield, the bees were working ahead;
There were three in my vision—remember old man; and—what if Joseph were dead!

But I hope that he and Grant (the flag above them both to boot)
Will go into Richmond together, no matter which is ahead or afoot!

Meantime alone at the mowing here—an old man somewhat gray—
I must stay at home as long as I can, making myself the hay.

And so another round—the quail in the orchard whistles blithe—
But first I'll drink at the spring below, and whet again my scythe.

The newspapers of the year 1864 were filled with discussions of the terms of peace and propositions for settlement of the existing war, but nothing could be accomplished. It remained for Grant, Sherman, Thomas, and Sheridan to show the way to an honorable peace. At the beginning of the year 1865 Sherman had virtually completed his part in the great drama. Thomas had defeated and utterly routed and destroyed the rebel army under Hood, at Nashville, leaving nothing to fear in the west. Sheridan, by his crushing defeat of Early, in the Shenandoah valley, had made a good beginning on his part, and with Crooks, Custer, and the others commanding that splendid body of cavalry, started on their great raid toward Richmond, broke down all opposition like a whirlwind, swept through Virginia at will, destroying railroads, canals, and everything in their track, and joined Grant at Petersburgh on March 27th. The final surrender of Lee and his remnant of an army was only a question of time, but Grant had his plans fully matured, and he now considered the time most opportune to close in on the rebel stronghold. He accordingly continued the flank movements to the left, placing Sheridan with his trusty cavalry on the extreme left, with orders to proceed southwestward and develop the enemy's position and strength. Washington county was represented in Sheridan's cavalry by company F, Second Virginia cavalry, as well as in other regiments. Heavy masses of infantry were sent out to support Sheridan, and then began the most skilful and brilliant handling of large bodies of cavalry of any part of the war. The enemy were compelled to throw out a heavy force to meet this new movement, and thereby weakened the garrison at Petersburgh and Richmond. A series of engagements took place, in which the Union troops were successful, taking many prisoners, and gaining many new and important positions, so that by April 2nd, Lee, realizing that his extended works around the two beleaguered cities had become untenable, sent the following dispatch from Petersburgh to Jefferson Davis, at Richmond: "My lines are broken in three places. Richmond must be evacuated this evening." It was Sunday, and Davis was at church. He at once went out, and by 10 P. M. the rebel government was well on its way towards Lynchburgh, securing their own safety, and leaving the army stores that Lee depended on for support during the retreat at Richmond. Lee, therefore, had to forage for subsistence, which greatly impeded his retreat. It was indeed a losing game from the first, to contend with hunger and greatly superior forces at the same time. Four trains of provisions had been sent from Lynchburgh to Appomattox station, and the rebels were pushing on with all haste to gain that point, but their horses were worn out, and they had no cavalry of any consequence. A man will stand hunger and fatigue and outlast several horses, in an emergency. So with Lee's grand army of northern Virginia, now reduced to barely thirty thousand men, the veterans of so many battles, they could still offer a stubborn resistance; but the dumb brutes, that pulled their wagons and cannon, were totally exhausted. Sheridan, taking in the situation, dispatched Crook and Custer to capture the four trains, intended for the rebel army. This they did by a rapid march, riding up to the astonished train men before they were aware of their danger; and when Lee's advance guards came up they found no provisions, but saw an impenetrable wall of blue-coats, blocking their further advance. Lee, coming up, ordered a charge, supposing there was nothing but cavalry to oppose him. Accordingly, on came the charging column, when, at the proper time, Sheridan rapidly drew off his cavalry, and revealed a heavy force of Union infantry, outnumbering the rebels two to one. The rebel line wavered, and seeing the cavalry on the right getting ready to charge their flank, they immediately sent in a white flag, which led to the famous interview between Grant and Lee and the surrender at Appomattox—the final collapse of the confederacy—the consummation so devoutly wished.

The glorious news caused the greatest rejoicing throughout the north. Governor Brough issued a proclamation announcing the great victories, and recommended April 14th, the anniversary of the fall of Sumter, as a fitting day on which to celebrate the fall of the Rebellion.

The people of Washington county needed no proclamation to urge them to celebrate. The news was no sooner received at Marietta, than the streets were filled with a joyful throng made up from all classes, old and young, grave and gay—every one that could make any kind of a gleeful noise was resolved to do it. The tinners did a good business in tin horns that day. Platoons of the best citizens went arm in arm down the street like drunken men, and the whole community was given up to rejoicing.

The programme for the fourteenth was as follows: National salute and ringing of bells at sunrise; 10 A. M., grand procession—Captain A. W. McCormick and Major Jewett Palmer, jr., just returned from the war, and Captain Levi Barber, commanding; 2 P. M., assembly of the people to listen to speeches, songs, etc., at corner of Greene and Front streets, Marietta; in the evening, general illumination, procession, fireworks, music, etc.

Hon. W. E. Stevenson, of Wood county, West Vir-

ginia; President J. W. Andrews, of Marietta college, and Hon. George W. Woodbridge, of Marietta, were the orators of the day. Just as the procession was forming a steamer landed, with the left wing of the Eighth United States colored infantry on board, six hundred men, under command of Major Long. They marched up to the common in front of the Congregational church for dress parade, in the presence of the assembled multitude. This occurrence, just at the time, was an eloquent commentary on the results of the great contest for human rights, now so successfully ended.

While these glad citizens were rejoicing and the illumination and fireworks were progressing so happily, there was being enacted in the far off capital of the Nation a tragedy that on the morrow would send a thrill of horror throughout the country. Abraham Lincoln, that evening, was assassinated. Alas! that so sad a morn should succeed so joyful a day. The flags that were displayed so proudly and exultantly Friday, on Saturday were draped in mourning for the great and good man, the martyred President. In compliance with the request of the Secretary of War, the day of the funeral, Wednesday, April 19th, was appropriately observed. The mayor of Marietta issued a proclamation asking all citizens of the city to desist from their ordinary occupation on that day, and attend religious services at the Centenary Methodist, and Congregational churches. This request was generally complied with, and the day was very generally observed. The speakers at the churches were Revs. W. M. Mullenix and C. D. Battelle, at the Centenary, and President J. W. Andrews and Rev. Thomas Wicks, at the Congregational. After the services an immense throng was formed in procession at the foot of Putnam street, under Colonel William R. Putnam as chief marshal, assisted by Major Jewett Palmer, jr., and Captain Levi Barber. They marched in the following order: Music, pall-bearers, colors, pall-bearers, clergy, mayor and council of Marietta, mayor and council of Harmar, citizens. The procession moved up Putnam to Second, up Second to Scammel, and down Scammel to Front, where a hollow square was formed, and the benediction pronounced by Rev. C. D. Battelle.

Thus ended the great Rebellion. Washington county had done her part fully, and with distinguished honor, and it was the delight of her citizens during the next few months to welcome back to their homes and to the ranks of peace, the veterans, the citizen soldiery she had sent forth, where they took their places, started again the wheels of industry and resumed the occupations they had left, and in a few months the blue-coats were lost to sight, but the wearers were destined never to be forgotten.

CHAPTER XX.

WAR OF THE REBELLION—CONTINUED.

Women's Work in the War.—The Marietta Military Hospital.—Short Sketches of the Military Organizations from the County.—Buell's Pierpoint Battery.—Huntington's Battery.—De Beck's Battery.—K, Second Ohio Heavy Artillery.—General Thomas' Body Guard (L, First Ohio Volunteer Cavalry)—Company H, Seventh Cavalry.—Company B, Ninth Cavalry.—Company F, Second West Virginia Cavalry.—Eighteenth Ohio Volunteer Infantry.—Thirty-sixth Ohio Volunteer Infantry.—Thirty-ninth Ohio Volunteer Infantry.—Sixty-third Ohio Volunteer Infantry.—Seventy-third Ohio Volunteer Infantry.—Seventy-seventh Ohio Volunteer Infantry.—Ninety-second Ohio Volunteer Infantry.—One Hundred and Forty-eighth Ohio National Guards.—The Silver Grays.—The Pony Section.—The War Editors.—Biographical Sketches of Officers from Washington County.—Major General Don Carlos Buell.—General B. D. Fearing.—General H. F. Devol.—General R. R. Dawes.—Colonel Jesse Hildebrand.—Colonel Melvin Clarke.—Colonel Ebenezer B. Andrew.—Colonel John C. Paxton.—Lieutenant Colonel Alexander L. Haskins.—Lieutenant Colonel Ephraim C. Dawes.—Major Jewett Palmer.—Major George T. Rice.—Captains Jacob Koenig, James C. Selby.—William B. Whittlesey.—Madison Hoon.—Frank Buell.—Augustus T. Ward.—Arthur D. Eells.—Theodore E. Greenwood.—John J. Jumper.—George B. Bartlett.—Lieutenants Levi J. Fouraker.—George B. Turner.—Timothy L. Condit.—Charles B. Gates.—Richard D. Mason.—Edgar P. Pearce.—Richard B. Cheatham.—Assistant Surgeon Pardon Cook, jr.—Luther Hathaway.—William L. Porterfield.—Roll of Honor.—History of the Washington County Soldiers Monument Association—Roll of the Dead

WOMEN'S WORK IN THE WAR.

WHILE recounting the deeds of Washington county soldiers, let us not forget the noble part taken by the women of the county during that struggle, in ministering to the wants of the Union soldiers and in alleviating that world of suffering in the hospital and camp, and on the field of battle.

Their work was done quietly and without ostentation, and they modestly hoped that by helping the sick and wounded of the grand armies, to bear their burdens of pain and disease, they should be counted as having done something for the Union.

They had husbands, sons, brothers, fathers and other very dear friends with Grant, Sherman or Sheridan, at the front. Not a day passed but that their hearts were troubled for the welfare of the loved ones. How anxiously did they look for the letters. If only a few lines were received, those few lines told the story that he was still among the living and battling for his country. How they tried the patience of the postmasters, especially after a great battle. "Are you sure there is no letter? Please look again," and then, perhaps, the mother, in her anxiety, before another mail, would send around the little boy to ask still again. Then there came too often, not the longed-for missive, but the telegram or hurried line from a comrade, stating that he was dead. Dead for his country, for liberty and union, in so much a great consolation, but how could even that console her who bent under the stroke. All the courage and fortitude was not displayed on the battle line. By thousands of hearthstones, here and there through the land, came occasions for great courage and great fortitude, especially when it was the bread-winner stricken down in his prime, leaving a young family, with none to provide.

Who can tell to what extent the loyal homes at the

north influenced men in the field. The brave words sent, the noble sentiments penned by fair hands, all glowing with patriotism and love at country. All honor to the noble women of the great north.

On Monday, October 28, 1861, seventy-five ladies of Marietta and Harmar met at the vestry of the Episcopal church, pursuant to a call of the United States sanitary commission, and organized by electing Mrs. Mumford, president; Mrs. Stephen Newton, vice-president; and Mrs. W. L. Rolston, secretary; Mrs. James Dunn, Mrs. Pardon Cooke, Mrs. T. P. Harshberger, Miss M. Woodbridge, Mrs. William S. Ward, Mrs. M. P. Wells, Mrs. C. B. Hall. Miss Phebe Fuller, Mrs. C. Regnier, Mrs. O'Leary, Mrs. Paul Bradbeck, Mrs. McLeod and Mrs. S. R. Turner, receiving committee; Mrs. James Ball, Mrs. Judge Green, Mrs. William Pearce, Mrs. L. Hathaway, Mrs. Bonner, Mrs. Beman Gates, Mrs. I. W. Andrews, Mrs. D. R. Sniffen, Mrs. H. Hill, Mrs. Levi Barber, Mrs. Oscar Chapin, Mrs. E. R. Cadwallader, committee for preparatory work.

The society was called the Union Soldiers' Relief association. Each member paid a small initiation fee with liberty to contribute as much more as possible. Application was made at once for material to make up into quilts, socks, slippers, comforts, etc. Donations of canton-flannel, fruits, half-worn calico, etc., were also received, which were speedily made up, boxed and ready to ship. Gallipolis hospital was the first place supplied, there being many men from Washington county lying there sick and destitute. Two boxes were sent within a few days, one filled with clothing and bedding from Marietta; the other with wine, jellies and fruit from Harmar.

The society met at the lecture room of the Episcopal church during all the war, varying the frequency of its meetings with the demand made upon them—usually meeting once a week.

Mrs. Rolston, in the first report, dated April 28, 1862, a semi-annual one, says:

We have had thirty-one regular meetings, and three extra ones. The attendance has ranged from seventy to eighty, and the average about twenty-five, and at no time has the interest flagged, for when few were here they worked the faster.

.   .   .   We have met from week to week, and this gathering has been a source of pleasure as well as profit, and will long be remembered a bright day amid the dark horrors of this war. The merry peals of laughter have lightened many a heart that came here sad.

.   .   .   When we learn through reports from the different hospitals of the west; how much the sufferings of our wounded soldiers have been alleviated by the sanitary commission we are amply repaid, and must feel like continuing our labors unwearied.

The German ladies of Marietta also formed a society, as did the ladies of Waterford, Barlow and Salem townships, and others of which we have no record.

In April, 1863, the Beverly *Advertiser* contained the following: "No accurate record of the contributions of the Waterford Township Soldiers' Aid society for three fourths of its existence can be procured, but recently its records show items, viz: one hundred and seventy-five dollars cash, one hundred and forty-three shirts, one hundred and seventy-four pairs socks, sixty-eight blankets, fifty-three handkerchiefs with canned fruits, lint, bandages, etc., in abundance.

The heart of old Waterford is wholly pledged to the glorious cause, and she has still enough sturdy sons of patriot sires, lovers of freedom and union to make the air of this part of the Muskingum valley exceedingly unwholesome to traitors.

In this connection it should be said that the first woman to subscribe to the Soldiers' Relief fund in the county was Mrs. William R. Putnam. On December 15 and 16, 1863, a special effort was made by the society at Marietta to raise funds by a sanitary fair. Contributions were sent in from all the townships in the vicinity, in money, apples, quinces, potatoes, turnips, onions, cabbages, pumpkins, butter, cheese, eggs, chickens, honey, dried and canned fruits, flour, buckets, ornamental and fruit trees, blankets, socks, furniture, and many other things—"almost everything that could be turned into money, or sent to the soldiers." From Union and Muskingum townships, large lots of fruits, vegetables, and trees were received. From Rainbow, fifty dollars in cash—Lowell, eighty-six dollars in cash and a large contribution in socks and canned fruits. Belpre, Warren, Barlow, Fearing, Salem, and Newport, all gave large contributions. A dinner was donated by the citizens of Marietta which added largely to receipts, the net amount cleared being one thousand nine hundred and ninety-one dollars and seventy-five cents.

The following are the items:

Cash contributions		$ 427 00
Receipts from door		234 70
"	from dinner	108.00
"	from supper	245 25
"	from fancy tables	243 10
"	from cake table	163.36
"	from grab box	39 30
"	from toys and confectionary	49 57
"	from pictures	43 00
"	from pipe of peace	33 50
"	from ring cakes	30 00
"	from guess cake	32 45
"	from auction	82.00
Sums from various sources		73 49
Receipts from Harmar table		339 30
Total		2166 52
Expenses		174 77
Net		$1991 75

Part of the above amount was paid over to the Harmar association, how much we cannot ascertain.

In Belpre the Ladies' Union circle on February 22, 1864, held a festival "for the aid of soldiers in the field," and cleared three hundred and seventy dollars, and so in all parts of the county the generous hearted women devoted themselves to the work.

At Bonn, in Salem township, they formed a branch No. 420 of what was called the "Union League of Loyal Women of America," an organization which originated in Illinois, having the same purpose as similar societies. This was begun in the fall of 1864 and continued during the balance of the war. It had between sixty and seventy members, and notwithstanding the lateness of the start they forwarded a number of invoices of sanitary supplies to the Cincinnati branch of the United States sanitary commission, amounting in all to about one hundred dollars. The fund remaining at the close of the war, amounted, August 2, 1865, to seventeen dollars and twenty cents which was donated to Washington County Soldiers' Monument association.

Among the many women of Washington county deserving of special mention, we can only notice one whose talents and industry gave her special prominence—Mrs. Francis Dana Gage, "Aunt Fanny Gage." She acquired a national reputation by her devotion to the cause of the freedmen and her untiring energy in working for the sanitary commission: "Through all the inclement winter weather (1863–4), through Pennsylvania, New York, Ohio, Illinois, and Missouri, she pursued her labors of love, never omitting an evening, when she could get an audience to address, speaking for soldiers' aid societies, and giving proceeds to those who worked only for the soldiers,—then for freedmen's associations. She worked without fee or reward, asking only of those who were willing, to give enough to defray her expenses—for herself—thankful if she received, cheerful if she did not."* Mrs. Gage was the daughter of Joseph Barker, late of this county, and Elizabeth Dana, a descendent of Mary Bancroft, thus being allied on maternal side to the well-known Massachusetts families of Dana and Bancroft. She has also acquired a reputation in literature from the beauty and pathos of her numerous poems.

On December 2, 1865, Mrs. Rolston made her final report, showing the work of the Marietta Soldiers' Relief association from October, 1861, to June, 1865, when the meetings ceased, as follows:

During the three and a half years over two thousand garments were made. Articles made—one thousand and forty shirts, three hundred and seventy-five pairs of drawers, sixty comforters, one hundred and sixteen sheets, two hundred and sixteen pillow-cases, fifty-nine pillows, two hundred and three towels, thirty-one pairs slippers, two hundred and seventy-one pairs socks, thirty-four pairs mittens, twelve pairs suspenders, three hundred and thirty-four pocket-handkerchiefs, twenty-one dressing-gowns; in all, two thousand eight hundred and thirty, besides many other articles for hospital use.

The association has been well supplied with material, which was made into bandages, compresses, towels, pocket-handkerchiefs, lint, etc.

There have been bought four thousand three hundred and thirty yards of cotton and flannel, besides much donated. Goods were sent once a month, or oftener, where most needed, generally to the Cincinnati branch of the United States Sanitary commission, but the hospital here (at Marietta), and those at Parkersburgh, Charleston, and Cairo, and sometimes regiments in the field, have been supplied.

Boxes sent: sixty-five—containing shirts, sheets, drawers, socks, mittens, blankets, towels, etc., to the number of three thousand five hundred and forty-three, besides slings, wound-supporters, eye-shades, pincushions, compresses, bandages, lint, etc., too numerous to mention.

In February, 1863, the hospital at Marietta having been abandoned, the military committee gave all the goods remaining there to the association.

More than six hundred cans and jars of fruit, at least forty gallons of pickles, several barrels of sauerkraut, more than twenty bushels of dried fruit, with various articles of hospital aid have been sent.

The association has never asked in vain for anything that could be of service to the soldier, nor have the citizens ever failed to respond to the call for money. The association has not been for one day out of funds. Voluntary contributions of ninety-three dollars and fifty cents have been received from different sources. The military committee gave, at different times, forty-five dollars; four public entertainments realized one thousand six hundred and seventy-six dollars and sixty-seven cents; a fee of five cents per month from members raised fifty-two dollars and ninety cents; with one hundred and fifteen dollars and fifty-eight cents interest on the money deposited, gives the total receipts one thousand nine hundred and eighty-three dollars and sixty-five cents.

The expenditures have been chiefly for materials for work, with inci-

---

* Women's Work in the Civil War.

dentals, such as fuel, boxes, although most of these have been donated. About fifty dollars have been given in small sums to soldiers and their families.

Receipts..................... ....$1,983 65
Expenditures........... .... 1,274 15

Balance in treasury.................................... 709 50
  This balance, by vote of the association, was given as follows: two hundred dollars to the Washington County Soldiers' Monument association; and five hundred and nine dollars and fifty cents to the Marietta Charitable association.
  After a vote of thanks to the vestry of St. Luke's church for the use of the lecture room for over three years, the association dissolved.
                                    S. C. ROLSTON,
                                         Secretary and treasurer.

The officers of the Marietta and Harmar society were as follows: 1861—Mrs. T. F. Mumford, president; Mrs. Stephen Newton, vice-president; Mrs. W. L. Rolston, secretary and treasurer. Work committee: Mrs. James Booth, Mrs. Beman Gates, Mrs. Davis Green, Mrs. Luther Hathaway, Mr. I. W. Andrews, Mrs. Bonner, Mrs. D. R. Sniffen, Mrs. Levi Barber, Mrs. Oscar Chapin, Mrs. E. R. Cadwallader.

The Harmar ladies formed a separate association in 1862.

1862—Mrs. Nahum Ward, president; Mrs. Melvin Clarke, vice-president; Mrs. W. L. Rolston, secretary and treasurer.

1863—Mrs. Nahum Ward, president; Mrs. William A. Whittlesey, vice-president; Mrs. R. P. James, second vice-president; Mrs. W. L. Rolston, secretary and treasurer. Work committee: Miss McFarland, Miss Hobby, Mrs. R. E. Harte, Mrs. Joseph Lovell.

1864 and 1865—Mrs. William A. Whittlesey, president; Mrs. B. W. Lovell, vice-president; Mrs. W. L. Rolston, secretary and treasurer. Work committee: Miss McFarland, Miss Hobby, and Mrs. R. E. Harte.

After the first year the Harmar ladies had their own association, an account of which, by Mrs. John Pool, is given herewith.

The foregoing is a brief record of the part taken by the women of Washington county during the great war for the preservation of the Union. It does not fully record their work. No historian will attempt to do it; for who could ever hope to adequately describe the burden of heart, the burden of work, and the burden of patriotism borne by the devoted women of the north during that eventful struggle. Let us honor them, and let posterity hold them in grateful remembrance.

SOLDIERS' AID SOCIETY OF HARMAR, OHIO.

Immediately following the departure of our volunteers from Marietta, Harmar and the adjoining towns, in response to President Lincoln's call for troops in 1861, to suppress the great Rebellion,—the loyal women, all aglow with the patriotism which had inspired the hearts of those who had so recently left—anxiously inquired in what way they, too, could serve their country.

The weeks preceding had been eventful and stirring times in the history of our quiet town, for the call for troops had met with a hearty and ready response. Students from the college, mechanics from factories and workshops, clerks from offices and stores, and young men from country homes had volunteered their services —companies had been formed and drilled in military tactics,—while over dwellings and stores the stars and stripes waved, and the streets resounded with the notes of warlike preparation.

At length marching orders were received, and the volunteers had left, and then to the mothers, wives and children of these—some of whom were sick and destitute, the attention and sympathy of the patriotic women was directed. Subscriptions had already been received from many of the citizens, to meet the present necessities of such as needed help, and as far as possible, generous assistance had been proffered.

Then, followed letters from our volunteers in camp, or on the march, some of whom unaccustomed to exposure, were sick, and requiring home comforts or articles of clothing. These supplies were immediately sent from private sources until, as the wants became greater, committees were appointed, who went from house to house soliciting donations.

Meanwhile, our troops had moved southward, rumors of anticipated battles were reported, and as the necessity of hospital supplies became apparent, meetings were held for consultation to meet the approaching emergency.

The various benevolent and church organizations were merged into soldiers' aid societies, and articles for the comfort of the sick and wounded were in constant preparation. The following ladies were prominently connected with the Harmar Aid society, and until the close of the war, closely identified with its interests: Mrs. Levi Barber, president; Mrs. Harlow Chapin, Mrs. Douglas Putnam, Mrs. David Putnam, Mrs. Henry Fearing, Mrs. Oscar Chapin, Mrs. Dr. Frank Hart, Mrs. L. Wheeler, Mrs. Dr. L. Hart, Mrs. S. Stratton, Mrs. W. Crawford, Mrs. Barber, Mrs. Rev. Wakefield, Mrs. Newton, Mrs. Fuller, and Mrs. L. Reppert.

To this committee a corps of young ladies was added, as follows: Miss Julia Barber, Miss V. Reppert, Miss Martha Putnam, Miss J. Wheeler, Miss E. Stratton, Miss E. Barber, Miss M. F. Newton, Miss Mary Hart, Miss A. Reppert. Through the newspapers, from the pulpit, and in every available way, urgent appeals were made for assistance, and from individuals and churches liberal donations were sent. From country societies and from sources unknown to us, supplies of delicacies, jellies, canned and dried fruits were added, which to the stores of clothing in readiness were carefully packed and consigned to surgeons in various regimental hospitals, who by letter had specified previously the articles most needed. From month to month this work went on, varied only by sad tidings of battles fought and the intelligence of many of our brave soldiers wounded or sick in hospitals, requiring special supplies, when boxes of bandages, lint, and the various appliances for hospital use were hastily prepared and dispatched. No official record has been preserved of shipments made to Western Virginia, Louisville, Pittsburgh Landing, Murfreesborough and other points, which were forwarded in request of surgeons and officers in Ohio regiments, with whom our society was in direct communication.

While sending supplies to distant hospitals, the ladies of the Aid society and others were not unmindful of the present wants and needs of the Union soldiers at our doors, to whom a helping hand could be extended. There were regiments encamped temporarily within the precincts of our own town—some awaiting transportation to the front or for regimental supplies, which had been detained or interrupted on the route thither, in consequence of which the soldiers were exhausted from want of proper food. The presence of these troops would stimulate anew the patriotism of the citizens, whose generosity was unbounded; and everything which could be provided for their comfort was most freely bestowed.

In these kindly offices of hospitality, of which also no record has been preserved, the capacity of the dwellings and the resources of the larder were often tested to their utmost limit; our doors were thrown wide open, and all who could be accommodated were most cordially invited to enter and served with impromptu meals, calling forth, as our guests departed, their warmest thanks, and leaving us with the cheering thought that we had "done what we could."

There were also unwritten kindnesses which could be rendered our Union soldiers on these occasions—sometimes in writing letters at their dictation, to wives, mothers, and sisters, far distant, bearing messages of comfort and cheer; to others some forgotten or lost article could be supplied, or some needed repair of clothing made, while to all words of encouragement and kindness could be spoken which were always gratefully appreciated. To those regiments, also, who were in transit to distant points, and who for long, weary hours were detained in railroad cars near the town, awaiting orders to move on to these we could render service. On many a cold and chilly morning the intelligence would come that these soldiers, too, were within reach of sympathy and help; and as speedily as possible messengers would be dispatched with plentiful supplies of hot coffee and sandwiches, distributed amid the cheers of the soldiers, to whom this unexpected repast was a welcome surprise.

Each day brought special demands upon the time and attention of our Aid society, either in supplying the wants of our troops passing through the town, or in preparing boxes of sanitary stores for points already designated.

There were also the families of our volunteers, who needed assistance. Liberal subscriptions had been repeatedly made for this purpose, by the citizens, and also for the purchase of hospital supplies. Numerous collections had been taken in the churches for the same object; and as larger cities and towns had raised sums of money by means of sanitary fairs and entertainments, it was proposed that a fair be held in Marietta, in which the ladies of Harmar be invited to unite. This plan met with hearty approval, and a committee was appointed, consisting of Mrs. Levi Barber and Mrs. John Poole, to make necessary arrangements. Subsequently other committees were added, to obtain articles of beauty and utility to be placed on sale, and for refreshments, etc., who canvassed the town thoroughly. After weeks of

preparation the fair was opened, with an admiring throng of visitors in attendance, and its success was assured. The receipts were unexpectedly large, many pleasant acquaintances formed, harmonious feelings prevailed, and results were in every respect satisfactory. The receipts, of which the ladies of Harmar received a fair proportion, were expended for the relief of soldiers' families, and paid in weekly instalments, after a careful investigation of the circumstances of each family had been made. The fund, amounting to several hundred dollars, was judiciously and systematically disbursed, bringing much comfort to the recipients and gratification to all those who by personal effort or influence had secured these results.

In all these beneficent efforts, extending through the war, and never ceasing until the conflict was over, the aid society was indebted to many of the citizens of Harmar for invaluable assistance, rendered in the prosecution of their work, at home and abroad, for which services, we record in behalf of the society, our appreciation and thanks.

The foregoing pages comprise but a fragmentary and imperfect report of the work accomplished by the Soldiers' Aid society of Harmar; but are submitted in the hope that they may be of some interest to the home workers, who were thus privileged to minister to some of the Union soldiers, without expectation of either mention or reward—but grateful then and now, for the opportunity of expressing, in the slightest degree, their gratitude to those brave men who were willing to sacrifice their lives in the service of our country.

THE MARIETTA HOSPITAL.

About May 26, 1861, a hospital was opened for the soldiers then in Camp Putnam. It was located on the upper or eastern side of Second street, a short distance from the camp, and was conducted and supported by the ladies of Marietta and Washington county, assisted by the officers in command at the camp. Drs. Frank Hart, Samuel Hart, and George O. Hildreth were in attendance when their services were needed, and always without pay. No records of this hospital have been preserved, but it was used more or less all through the war.

BATTERY C, FIRST WEST VIRGINIA LIGHT ARTILLERY.

COMMISSIONED OFFICERS.

Captain Frank Buell, mustered March 30, 1862, died from effects of wounds at battle of Freeman's Ford, August 23, 1862; Captain Wallace Hill, mustered August 1, 1862, promoted to captain August 1, 1862; First Lieutenant Dennis O'Leary, mustered March 30, 1862; First Lieutenant John G Theis, mustered August 1, 1862, promoted to junior first lieutenant; Second Lieutenant Theodore G. Field, mustered December 23, 1863, promoted to first sergeant August 1, 1862, to second lieutenant December 23, 1863, vice Langley, resigned; Second Lieutenant John W. Jacobs, mustered December 29, 1863, promoted from corporal, vice Miner, resigned, December 29, 1863.

NON-COMMISSIONED OFFICERS.

First Sergeant William H. Goldsmith, mustered March 31, 1864, veteran, Quartermaster Sergeant Thomas Phelps, mustered March 31, 1864, veteran; Sergeant Owen O'Neil, mustered March 31, 1864, veteran; Sergeant Alexander H. Bukey, mustered March 31, 1864, veteran, Sergeant L. R. Miraben, mustered March 31, 1864, veteran; Sergeant David Dow, mustered March 31, 1864, veteran; Sergeant Adam B. Rook, mustered February 24, 1864, veteran; Corporal Turrell Cusack; mustered March 31, 1864, veteran. Corporal John Meighan, mustered March 31, 1864, veteran; Corporal William F. Minster, mustered March 31, 1864, veteran; Corporal Charles Clogson, mustered March 31, 1864, veteran, promoted January 1, 1864; Corporal William H. Ranger, mustered March 31, 1864, veteran, Corporal Milton H. Laughlin, mustered March 31, 1864, veteran; Corporal John Lehnhard, mustered September 2, 1862, promoted to corporal September 1, 1862, Corporal George W. Stanley, mustered March 31, 1864, veteran; Corporal Jeremiah H. Dooley, mustered March 31, 1864, veteran; Corporal John H. Miner, mustered March 31, 1864, veteran; Corporal James Wright, mustered March 31, 1864, veteran, wounded at Bull Run, August 30, 1862; Corporal Frank R. Benan, mustered March 31, 1864, veteran; Corporal William Jenvey, mustered March 30, 1862.

BATTERY C, FIRST WEST VIRGINIA LIGHT ARTILLERY.

When President Lincoln made his first call for troops to serve three months, a company of infantry, under command of Captain Frank Buell, left Marietta in April, 1861, and as heretofore noticed became company B, Eighteenth Ohio volunteer militia. The other officers were Dennis O'Leary, first lieutenant; William Bisbee, second lieutenant, who was afterward elected major of the regiment, and Wallace Hill elected to fill the vacancy.

The company served in West Virginia under General Hill, and was most of the time guarding railroads. There was no engagement with the enemy and it was mustered out in August, 1861. This company reenlisted almost entire, as a battery of light artillery, the reenlistment dating from September 1, 1861. Owing to a misunderstanding among those in authority in Ohio, the service of the battery was offered to Governor Pierpont, of West Virginia, and accepted, and was named by the captain in the governor's honor.

The battery left Marietta for Wheeling, West Virginia, in October, 1861. The officers: Frank Buell, senior captain; Dennis O'Leary, junior first lieutenant; Wallace Hill, senior first lieutenant; John P. Theis, junior second lieutenant; William W. Witherow, second lieutenant.

The battery remained in Wheeling until ordered to Point Pleasant, West Virginia, for recruiting purposes, and from there to Charleston, West Virginia, where it remained till early in the spring of 1862, when it was ordered back to Wheeling and was mustered into the service of the United States, March 30, 1862. Here the injustice was done the battery of not dating the muster back to the date of enlistment, it having been in the service seven months.

These seven months had not been idly spent. Although not fully mounted, the battery had thorough and continued drill and practice in firing, with study of the tactics, so that when at this time they were fully equipped, they were by no means raw recruits.

The battery was supplied with six ten-pounder Parrott guns. After the effective work done with those guns at Cross Keys, Bull Run, Gettysburgh, and elsewhere, it would be hard to convince any member of this battery that it was not the most accurate shooting gun in the service.

General Fremont having taken command of the mountain department, the battery served under him during his campaign in West Virginia in the summer of 1862.

Leaving Wheeling in May for New Creek, West Virginia, we immediately proceeded to reinforce Milroy and Schenck, who were hard pressed by Stonewall Jackson

on the upper south branch of the Potomac. Here they were assigned to Stahl's brigade, of Blencker's division. Arriving at Franklin, in Pendleton county, they found Generals Schenck and Milroy had fought Jackson at Bull Pasture Mountain, but had been compelled to fall back to Franklin.

In the meantime Jackson, instead of remaining in front, as it was supposed he would, had gone over the mountains into the Shenandoah valley, and had driven General Banks out. In order to intercept Jackson, Fremont fell back from Franklin to Moorefield and crossed the mountains into the Shenandoah valley and struck Jackson's army on his retreat at Strasburgh. Jackson sent out a force and held Fremont in check near Strasburgh, where he had quite a skirmish, while his army passed up the valley. The next day Fremont started in pursuit, and the battery was assigned to the cavalry advance, and the Eighth West Virginia infantry and the Sixtieth Ohio infantry under Colonel Cluseret—the infantry was called the Cluseret light brigade. This colonel, afterward General Cluseret, was subsequently in the war of the French commune.

BATTLE OF TOM BROOK.

At Tom Brook, some few miles above Strasburgh, the battery came up with the enemy's rear and forced him to form. Here, for the first time, the battery met the foe, June 2, 1862. Unfortunately two of the guns were temporarily disabled by loosing the wheels while galloping into action, caused by the linch-pins bouncing out. This defect was afterward remedied throughout the army by using a pin with a clamp. The right and left sections, however, went into position under fire, which proved to be inaccurate, and when the centre section came up the chief of artillery, Colonel Pilsen, moved it to a position to the right and front some three hundred yards. The ground being very uneven, the progress was slow, which was trying to new troops going into their first engagement under fire, but every man stood to his post like a veteran, and all of them were complimented by the chief of artillery for coolness and accuracy of firing, which, all things considered, was admirable. The enemy was compelled to retreat.

The next day, at Woodstock, they met the enemy, and the next at Mt. Jackson, where "Stonewall Jackson," to delay the Union pursuit, burned the bridge over the Shenandoah. The river was very high and swift, which rendered fording impossible, and the current was too strong to admit of laying pontoons. They were compelled to wait till the water receded. The next morning was rather hazy. They were aroused very early by the "long roll" and the cavalry and artillery buglers calling to "boots and saddle." Orders were given to hitch up as quickly as possible, as the enemy had flanked us on the left. The river, some distance below the bridge, makes an abrupt turn, and the sentries had discovered, through the fog, as they thought, a six gun battery, which would enfilade their position and would open on them as soon as the fog lifted. During the bustle and confusion of a change of front the fog cleared away and disclosed six beautiful piles of rails, at about the usual interval of a battery of field guns in position. After great delay in laying the pontoon bridge, which was a clumsy affair, the battery again started in pursuit, this time bringing the enemy to bay a short distance above Harrisonburgh, where he had left the main turn-pike and started on a cross-road to the left, where he was vigorously attacked by the light brigade and the Pennsylvania Buck Tails. The deadly aim of the latter punished the rebels severely. Among their slain was the notorious General Ashby, Jackson's chief of cavalry. General Fremont, not wishing to bring on a general engagement, the enemy were not pushed, but were allowed to retire unmolested

CROSS KEYS.

The following morning the army of General Fremont moved out and found the enemy in position at Cross Keys, eight miles from Harrisonburgh, and about nine from Port Republic. Stahl's brigade, including the battery, held the left, Milroy the right, and Cluseret the centre. The battle had continued about four hours when Jackson massed on the left and swept Stahl's infantry from the field, driving all of the line to the left of the battery back to the rear, and leaving the battery in a very exposed position. Captain Buell hesitated to leave the field, and did not attempt to retire until the general in person ordered him to do so, as they were about to be surrounded and cut off. Finally the order was given to "limber to the rear." In doing so they were compelled to pass to the left and rear through a wood, on the other side of which were the victorious "Johnnies," coming up to capture a lone, unsupported battery, as they doubtless imagined, but they were badly mistaken, for there was the Buck Tail battalion, who deployed among the trees between the battery and the rebels, who, as soon as they saw the deer tails on their caps, fell back and allowed the battery to retire unmolested. Captain Buell, not wishing to desert his friends who had so bravely defended him, unlimbered the left section in the woods, determined to stand by the Buck Tails. Although in a military sense this movement would have been considered highly imprudent, yet it showed the indomitable courage of the man. On coming out of these woods the balance of the brigade, mistaking our battery for the enemy, opened fire doing perhaps better firing than they ever did before, killing one of the battery horses. It was by force that a demoralized infantry color bearer was induced to advance with his colors, when the firing was stopped. This ended the battle. Stahl's brigade lost about five hundred, while the troops to the right suffered but little loss and held their position.

At the request of Jackson an armistice was granted to bury the dead, and in the night he folded his tents, and, Arab-like, stole away.

The next morning the army was to move to the attack at 5 A. M., the battery in columns of sections, the infantry in columns of divisions, with a strong skirmish line in front ready to deploy instantly into line of battle. The signal to move was to be two cannon shots in succession. For some reason this signal was not given

until 9 A. M., or later, when we could distinctly hear fighting at Port Republic, where Carroll, with his brigade, was holding the bridge against Jackson's whole army. We moved on to port Republic, arriving in time to see the rear of the rebel army passing over the Blue Ridge mountains miles away.

The battery then fell back to Harrisonburgh, thence to Moorefield, thence crossed over the Blue Ridge, at Thornton's Gap, and joined Pope's army at Sperryville.

BATTLE OF FREEMAN'S FORD. *

One evening at dark an orderly dashed up with orders to fall back to Culpeper without delay; then came one of the most trying campaigns we ever experienced. We marched eleven days and nights, and never took the harness off our backs, and the only time we could get to cook would be when our advance would encounter the enemy, causing a check, or when we were guarding some ford while the infantry were passing. It was a terrible experience. At length the enemy were discovered strongly posted at Freeman's Ford.

Johnson's, De Beck's, Dickman's, and a portion of Weidrick's batteries had tried in vain to dislodge them, when we were ordered up with our long range Parrots. This was August 22, 1866. I shall never forget the last order Captain Buell ever gave me. I was then his color-bearer As soon as he received orders to go into position he turned with sparkling eye to me and exclaimed:

"Show your colors, Wil."

I unfurled my colors and rode by his side up the hill. The rebels having engaged so many of our batteries on that hill had the exact range, and every shell came thundering in our midst, cutting up the ground terribly. The rebels picked out every conspicuous mark; my brigade flag (a present from the Marietta ladies) soon drew their fire, when Lieutenant Hill ordered me to draw off to the left, as it formed too good a target. The battle waged warmer and warmer, our boys having got the range were soon enabled to send as good as we received; this was perceptible from the increasing wildness in the rebel fire.

Captain Buell, mounted on "Billy," a light dun horse, formed a fair and easy mark, passing continually along the line directing here, encouraging and applauding there; he appeared omnipresent. His daring recklessness soon drew the attention of officers on him General Milroy, renowned for gallantry, turning to his staff, remarked: "Gentlemen, if you desire to see a brave man look there." But all anticipations of our gallant captain's future were soon to be cut off. A shell, as fatally aimed as the bullet which laid our martyred President on a bloody bier, and set a Nation in mourning, struck his horse in the shoulder, and, passing through, broke his left leg. So suddenly did the horse fall that the captain, unable to extricate himself, was thrown violently forward as the horse fell backward, injuring the captain internally. As he fell four boys sprang to his side and carried him from the field. I was watching him as he fell. It appeared as if the grave had suddenly yawned wide and taken father, mother, brothers, sisters, friends, all, so blank did life appear to us, and I have heard many of our bravest and truest say that they were not ashamed to confess that they cried like children But our misfortune never for a moment interfered with the battle; if anything, all appeared to enter still more heartily into it, influenced, as they were, by a desire for revenge. Gun after gun was discharged with fearful rapidity. The men worked with a will that promised soon to turn victory's uncertain scale in our favor. Each and all appeared oblivious to all else than seeking a terrible retribution. Nor were our endeavors futile. Soon we beheld a wavering and wildness in their fire; soon one by one their guns ceased, until all became silent, and we saw them drawing from the field. Corporal A. H. Bukey, fortunately having his gun loaded, took deliberate aim as the last gun was leaving and fired. I saw horses rear, cannoneers scattered in a manner not laid down in artillery tactics, so I should judge the piece was dismounted. The battle was over.

Captain Buell died of his injuries, loved and lamented by his men, and respected and admired by all who knew him.

Orders came August 23, 1862, for the battery to leave its position at Freeman's Ford and take up the line of

---

*From account by William Jenvey.

march with their corps. They had not gone far when they encountered the enemy at Sulphur Springs, where they gained an easy victory, after an hour's vigorous shelling, driving them from their position, and enabling the corps to resume its march in peace.

The next day, the twenty-fourth, they met the enemy at Waterloo bridge, and held the bridge until the army had all passed, when they witnessed its destruction by the Union troops, and again sped on. The march now became a race between the Union forces and the rebels, on parallel lines, the objective point being Bull Run. During the still marches of midnight they could distinctly hear the rumbling of Jackson's artillery, and by day they would occasionally catch the gleam of lines of bright muskets in the sunlight.

SECOND BATTLE OF BULL RUN.

The following is from an account by William Jenvey:

Bull Run was at length reached on the evening of the twenty-eighth of August, 1862. Milroy's brigade deploying, encountered their skirmishers, drove them, and pushed back a portion of their lines, and enabled our whole line to take position that night. All slept on their arms and tried to snatch a few moments' sleep to enable them to do well their parts on the coming morrow.

The next day's sun found us all bustle and activity. Aids-de-camp on jaded horses, were dashing and tearing here and there, receiving and delivering orders. Brigade commanders were busy arranging and disarranging their lines. Division commanders, older and wiser, were coolly witnessing the preparatory manœuvres, and concentrating all their energies for the desired time.

Suddenly Milroy, advancing, sought the foe, and full soon did he find them, for with his characteristic recklessness he advanced too far and encountered a full rebel division. Not a whit intimidated, he deployed his lines and opened with a murderous fire, but numbers soon told on him. Rapidly his lines thinned, and he stood in imminent danger of being cut off; but, collecting all his energies, he charged, extricated himself, and rejoined our line.

By this time the battle had become general. Our battery, being in position near the Washington pike, was keeping clear all before it. Manœuvres and counter-manœuvres took place, yet neither side gained any advantage. After noon, Hooker and Kearney coming up and taking position with us, we gained visible successes; gradually we gained ground, though every step was hotly contested. Night closed on the combatants, leaving the Union forces in possession of fully a mile of conquered ground.

The "sun of Austerlitz" scarcely dawned with prospects of a more sanguinary conflict than did the sun of the thirtieth. McDowell had abandoned Thoroughfare Gap, Lee had largely reinforced Jackson, and we had been reinforced by several divisions of McClellan's Peninsular army.

Our battery was scattered on three parts of the field. The right, under Lieutenant Witherow, was ordered to report to General McLean, of Schenck's division. The centre section, disabled by the heavy and incessant firing of the previous day, was nevertheless kept close at hand ready for any emergency, while the left, under Lieutenant Hill, together with three brass guns placed under his command, advanced up the Washington pike, and poking their noses fair in the midst of the Johnnies, soon created havoc and dismay in the rebel ranks. The first day's fight taxed our energies greatly, but the exertions of the second were two-fold greater. The rebels outnumbered us greatly and punished us terribly. The part of the field on which our right section was in position, was a scene of terrible carnage, the rebels opening with artillery strove in vain to dislodge us, the infantry was then called into requisition. Advancing in perfect order they attempted to take the place by assault, a terrible discharge of canister met them and forced them back. Several times did they rally and advance, but as often were they repulsed. At last, largely reinforced, they took advantage of a piece of woods to our left and flanked us from that direction. Turning our guns on them we poured storms of canister into their faces, cutting swaths through their massive ranks. Piercing their column appeared like piercing a rubber ball, the hole was scarcely made before it closed. Notwithstanding the dreadful havoc, on they came, and still on until

they nearly grasped our guns. Our canister had all been expended. Bukey, intent on fighting to the last, inserted a shell minus either fuse or cap in his gun and sent it as a solid shot right through their ranks. McLean's brigade, not unlike the British Home Guards at Waterloo, sprang from their cover, and as we limbered to the rear to fall back they closed in on our rear and opened such a storm of musketry that mortal men could not withstand it. The rebel charge was thus checked, and we were allowed to draw off in peace. Lieutenant Witherow, on mounting his horse was badly wounded, eventually causing his discharge. Thomas Driscoll in the hurry forgot his sponge bucket, and on going back after it got several holes through his blouse, but fortunately none hit the brave fellow. Several horses were shot.

In the meantime Lieutenant Hill and the left section had been hard pressed. Being in position in the centre of the pike, he presented a fair target to the whole of the rebel artillery, and well did they improve their opportunity, for shot and shell and the more deadly shrapnel fell on all sides with one continuous roar and hiss, and added to this the whistling of the musket balls and the discharge of our own guns, it created confusion enough to try the bravest of hearts. During the whole engagement Siegel remained in our midst, his uniform and splendid staff drawing the fire of the rebel sharp-shooters on us quite briskly. After a while Hooker established himself with us, and also for a while Reno and Kearney. These generals centering in us caused the tide of war to roll all around us. Assaults would be made in front, then the task would be comparatively easy, but when the flanking charges came then came danger. Sergeant Wes Miner, having possessed himself of a musket, had busied himself during the whole engagement picking off sharp-shooters. One in particular we saw roll in the dust from his unerring aim.

To the right and left of us the day was going badly. Fitz John Porter, lying within hearing of our guns and knowing of the fearful slaughter, refused to support us. Our overtasked and outnumbered boys were gradually obliged to give way, still we in the centre held our own until the rebels concentrating their infantry and a portion of their artillery, opened on us most terribly; for a while it seemed as if nothing could stay there and live. At last a shell, surcharged with destruction, came hurtling along, and striking Sergeant Goldsmith's gun on the right side, glancing, struck the elevating screw and bursting severely wounded Corporal James Wright and John Eaton; the former in seven places, the most of them severe, the latter in four places and mortally. For a time all appeared confounded, so close did the shell come to all, and so severe was the concussion. The shell passed over Sumner Ellis' shoulder, for a time stunning him. Soon the confusion died away, and they found the extent of the injuries. To stay longer was madness, for certain death awaited them; so limbering up and carefully supporting their wounded comrades they coolly and slowly made way for the rear.

All had now become lost; "rout, ruin, panic scattered all." The baggage wagons, having been foolishly brought up to the very front, commenced a base and confused retreat, but one road led to the rear, and to this road all fled. Artillery, baggage wagons, ambulances and vehicles of almost every sort were locked in utter and inextricable confusion, unable to move themselves, and preventing egress to those who were retreating in good order. In vain did officers ride to the rear and entreat, and curse, and shoot, and cut, and do all that mortal man could do to stop the rout. No; fear had seized all, and all sought to save themselves. Our battery, by strange though lucky fortune, from their different parts of the field, found each other, and, although three pieces were disabled, we drew ourselves across the road, and drawing sabres and revolvers, refused to let a man pass. Staff and field officers perceiving our design, galloped to our aid and assisted in rallying. As soon as a battalion could be formed, an officer would put himself at their head and march them back. Thus our line was restored, and we were enabled to hold the enemy in check. Many a man did I see who, having escaped death in the two days' engagement, would be either shot or cut down for refusing to halt. It was hard, but it was necessary. The cause of the Union demanded that they should be checked, and even though it should cause the loss of the best half of the army, still it had to be done. The field of Bull Run was a terrible one; full eight thousand had fallen, but the Capital was saved and the rebel designs foiled. They marched into Maryland, and at Antietam they were most signally defeated.

The battery was not actively engaged at the battle of Fredericksburgh, but was in all the marches of that disastrous campaign, and was waiting within easy reach of the field during the battle, the men listening to the uproar of the engagement, and expecting momentarily to be ordered to the front. Finally the troops were all back across the Rappahanock, and the retreat was commenced.

Mr. Jenvey, wishing to get a view of the battle field before they left, says:

I succeeded in gaining an admirable spot where I could overlook the whole field. First, the Rappahanock rolled under my feet. So smoothly did it flow that one would not imagine that but the day before it was witness to such a dreadful encounter. Next, a vast plain, fully two miles in width, stretched itself under the low range of hills on which the rebel host was encamped. It looked to me impossible that men could charge as far as they did. The rebel entrenchments were on successive hills, each commanding the other, and all commanding the plain. Our artillery was unable to manage them, on account of the infantry intervening, thus throwing the brunt of the battle on the infantry and a portion of the cavalry. Still, the day would have gone well had General Franklin performed his duty. Oh! it appeared mockery to the gallant dead to allow such a man as him to walk the earth.

The following is from an account by William Jenvey:

BATTLE OF CHANCELLORSVILLE, MAY 2, 1863.

Captain Hill and I rode to the scene of conflict and such a scene! The rebels under Jackson, numbering from thirty to forty thousand, had attacked our right and rear, and had driven brigade after brigade in inextricable confusion, until all organization was lost. Colonels and brigade commanders were slain; division generals were riding about, their staffs either killed or scattered, striving to restore the line, wounded men were pouring back; detachments began to give way, then all gave way, and from a retreat it became one confused rout; men refused to obey orders and were shot down; color bearers in vain stopped on every elevation, striving to effect a rally; they rallied but to fall, for bullets from the throats of thirty thousand guns were carrying all before them. I retired with the retreating army until reaching my own battery, found the boys already loaded with cannister, and ready to fight to the last.

The rout at length reached our guns. We drew our sabres, handspikes, sponge staves, armed ourselves with stones, anything to keep the cowardly mob from our front. They crowded us so that we were unable to fire. At length all had got back, and we were left almost alone to check the onset of the victorious foe. As well might a child strive to dam up Niagara, but still we refused to give way, until General Schurz riding up, gave us peremptory orders to fall back. Nothing daunted, some one proposed "three cheers for the general," they were given, and then three times three. The general raised his hat in acknowledgement as gracefully as if on parade. After the battle we were complimented in a general order.

Captain Hill commanded "limber to the rear," and the order was executed without any confusion. The road was found completely blocked up, so we took to the woods. All went well until Sergeant Bukey's piece ran foul of a sapling; an axe was produced, the sapling cut, but by that time the rebels were close upon us. About eight of us were there. Out of the eight—Corporal Ranger while lifting at the gun, was hit badly in the side; Smith Miner and Henry Hutchinson slightly wounded, and Wiley Reeves captured, and five horses out of six fell. Can any one wonder that we were obliged to leave the gun. By this time the rebels had brought a piece of artillery captured from us to bear on us. They were but a short distance off, and we saw they would soon have a clean sweep of the road; so, remembering that "discretion was the better part of valor," we dashed off and rejoined the battery.

Just as Lieutenant Miner, disdaining to fall back any farther, had placed the boys in position with the artillery of the Twelfth corps, soon the rebels announced their intention to charge by the usual yell peculiar to them, so we were ready for them. As soon as they made their appearance we fired on them such a storm of shot and shell as would stop a whirlwind, were it composed of animal matter; nothing could withstand it, however brave or desperate; back they went, and cheer on cheer and the most derisive yells arose from our lines. While they were reforming we improved the opportunity, and commenced throwing up intrenchments. Night was coming on, but a good moon furnished enough light to fight by. The rebels, having reformed, advanced with deafening yells to encounter our iron hail. Trees were cut down on their heads, shell and shrapnell were exploded in their midst. At times it appeared as if the whole woodw as lighted up, so contin-

uous was our fire. Our line could be easily seen, 'as' could the rebel line, by the long glare of discharging muskets. Both lines stood close to each other, each seeking to destroy the other, but no human power of endurance could withstand the fire we hurled at them. The second time they broke and ran. Again while they were reforming did we further intrench ourselves. And thus did it continue, fight and intrench, fight and intrench, until tired nature could stand it no longer.

Morning at length dawned and brought with it prospects of a more sanguinary conflict than had been fought on the day and night previous.

We were encouraged as if ten thousand men had been captured by the report of "Stonewall" Jackson's death, as his name alone was sufficient to carry fear into the northern ranks.

I said the morning of the third gave prospects of a terrible engagement, nor were they unverified, for with the early dawn began the battle in front of the Third corps, and such musketry I never heard before or since. I was actually glad when our guns began their continuous roar so as to deafen me and prevent me from hearing the noise. I am safe in saying that at times 'from one hundred to one hundred and twenty-five thousand muskets would be going off at once, fairly making the ground shake with each discharge, and the battle in the woods made the noise doubly great. Little by little the rebels gained ground, until at last the Chancellor house was reached. The brave Hooker refused to relinquish his headquarters, although surrounded by danger. At length it had to be abandoned. Inch by inch we fell back, and every inch was hotly contested. At last night set in, and as if by mutual consent both armies wearied and worn rested from the contest.

On the morning of the fourth the Rappahanock was discovered to be rapidly rising and our provisions were nearly exhausted, with all of our trains on the other side. Hooker, fearful that the pontoons would be swept away, ordered the army to recross. We retired very reluctantly; to many of us it was the most reluctant thing we ever did, for we all went over confident of success.

Our boys behaved nobly throughout the whole engagement. Captain Hill, usually brave, surpassed himself. Lieutenant Miner acted in such a way as to receive the commendation of all, but were I to mention all who distinguished themselves, I should have to begin at the top of the battery roll and enumerate every one. Our casualties were as follows: Will Regnier, Smith Miner, Louis Fougeres, Henry Hutchinson, wounded, and Wiley Reeves captured, twenty horses lost, three caissons and one gun captured, the latter, however, was recaptured the ensuing fall. By the evening of the fourth the whole army had recrossed and were ordered to Brook's station.

About the last of May, 1863, the battery was transferred from the Eleventh corps to the artillery reserve, under General R. O. Tyler, and they remained in that splendid organization ever afterward.

The following is an account by William Jenvey:

BATTLE OF GETTYSBURGH.

We at length reached Taneytown, Pennsylvania, just one day's march from Gettysburgh. All of June 30, 1863, we remained here to allow the artillery to concentrate. All July 1st we heard heavy and incessant cannonading, but could gain no tidings, until toward evening reports came in announcing the disaster to the First and Eleventh Corps, and the death of General Reynolds. All this dampened our enthusiasm considerably, for we all perceived that our duties would be doubly severe to recover the lost ground, and restore confidence. The morning of the second we broke camp early and started briskly toward the contested ground, which we reached early, halted long enough to make coffee, when we were ordered into position on Cemetery hill. Those who are familiar with the history of that memorable day, will remember that Cemetery hill, situated as it was in the centre, and being the most advanced position of the line, was, as a consequence, all but the most hotly contested part of the field. Directly in our rear lay the Baltimore pike, a most tempting bait, leading as it did to Baltimore.

On a gallop under a heavy fire we dashed up the hill, unlimbered and prepared for action. Soon the conflict raged with redoubled fury, reinforcements were coming up and rapidly taking position, and by noon both lines were completed.

Stretching off to our left in a valley intervening between the two lines, lay a long dark line of blue coated men with gleaming bayonets. By their battle flags we recognized the Third corps, always on hand and always bearing their banners where death flies thick and fast. Their line was fully a quarter of a mile in advance of the Second corps, on their right, thus leaving an interval between the two flanks. General Meade was explaining to General Sickles the danger of his position, when the enemy made a furious assault upon his lines. The moment the rebel host appeared they discharged such a volley as to make the earth quake, their whole line blazed with a sulphurous light, their guns hurled death and destruction into the surprised ranks of our men. Gallantly the brave Third corps held its position. Sickles, dashing into the thickest of the fight, sought to retrieve the fortunes of the day, but was soon brought off bleeding and mangled, almost lifeless, a ball having broken his leg.[*]

Mortal men could not stand such a fire. They wavered, then rallied, then wavered again, then broke, and with terrific and appalling yells the rebel infantry pursued. Back fell our men, and still back until they were directly in our rear, until we thought our line was broken and all was lost, when lo! a long bright line of bayonets appear, quickly the men are deployed in the field, their knapsacks are unslung, their line formed and all are in readiness for the fray. By their battle flags we discern that the Fifth corps has opportunely come up, by the exultant and confident cheers they charged. A long bright flash burst from their ranks and havoc and dismay were sent into the enemy's ranks. Their line staggered. Another volley from our boys and they fell back. Just then a battery of twenty-pound Parrots secreted on Sugar Loaf hill, opened on them and cut swaths in their retreating ranks, and the orderly retreat was turned to a mob, all organization was lost, and with it all hope.

Many a southern hearthstone was minus a member, and many a sorrowing family can tell how their joy and pride was cut down in that fatal charge. Our lines were firmly reestablished.

All this time we had been actively engaged with the rebel artillery in our front. They were strong in force, and had been tasking us pretty severely. The sharpshooters, too, secreted behind a stone wall but a short distance away in our front, and had been annoying us terribly, but as yet no casualty had taken place. All were congratulating themselves when a shell too surely aimed, came crashing through the air. Louis Fourgeres saw and avoided it, but poor Stephen Braddock more unfortunate, was struck fair in the head, the shell taking as it went, a portion off the top part of his head. If his body had been made of stone, he could not have fallen more rigidly. He threw out his arms, and with a gentle oh! returned his soul to Him who gave it. His death for a time threw a gloom over all, for no one knew but he would be the next. I am convinced from the suddenness of the blow that he never knew the cause of his death.

So hotly were we engaged that no one had a leisure moment to remove him; there he lay grim and ghastly. Although I was commanding the gun next to the one on which Braddock was killed, and was but a few feet from him, still I was ignorant of the fact until quite a time afterward, when Lieutenant Thics informed me. So you may imagine how actively we were engaged. A lull soon occurred in the firing when Braddock's remains were carried off, and laid in their last resting place. Truly a soldier's burial was his, the noise of war was resounding on all sides when we laid him in his grave. He was wrapped in his blanket, a good deep grave dug, and a head board with his name carved on by a comrade, placed at the head. We left his body, but carried away a just appreciation of his worth as a man and a soldier.

Soon, however, under the renewed energy of the battle all else was forgotten, and little by little accidents happened, two of my horses had their fore legs cut off by one shell, and so close did it strike to Charley Boyce, their driver, that it knocked the dust over him, and stunned for a time. Supposing him killed, I ran to his assistance, but found him safe and cool as if nothing had happened. I ordered to unharness his crippled horses, take them to the rear, and have them shot, and am not positive that I did not see a glistening in the poor fellow's eyes, very much like a tear, when he received the order.

John Leinhard and Martin Wendelkin, both cannoneers on my gun, were standing side by side, taking ammunition out of the chest, when a shell came thundering between them, tearing off half the axle, and burying itself in the ground. Each looked at the other, and grasped their legs, thinking one at least was gone, so close did the shell pass, but finding themselves intact, they laughed and went on with their work. Another of my boys, whilst leaning against a wheel, heard a dull thud; on looking around, he found a musket ball, half buried in the wheel close by his head. Sergeant Dow seeing a shell coming too friendly a course, leaped aside, and escaped death. Captain Hill, while

walking up and down the line, encouraging all, nearly lost both his legs by a shell.

Seeing a shell coming bent on mischief, I called out "Look out." L. R. Moore on my right hearing me, fell to the ground, and the shell passed so close to him across his back, that he thought he was wounded, and placed his hands on his back like one in intense agony; he looked towards me, and seeing me laughing, found himself uninjured. He laughed also, and went on with his duty. It was now getting dark, and the fire of the artillery was beginning to die away, but still the sharpshooters kept up an incessant fire. I was standing by my gun when I felt a sharp stinging sensation in my throat. I clapped my hand to the spot, imagining myself badly wounded. I felt a second time, but found no blood, and came to the conclusion that it was nothing. The next morning, on mentioning the fact, I was told that there was a red streak across my throat.

About 10 o'clock P. M., the firing ceased, and every man laid down by his gun, and slept.

The next morning, July 3d, we awoke refreshed and ready for the attack, nor had we long to wait, for with the break of day began the engagement, and we kept up a brisk fire until about noon, when a deadly calm fell on the whole field.

Early in the morning a general officer rode up to Captain Hill and told him that they had learned that the rebels designed concentrating all their artillery on our front, to be supported by ten thousand picked men under Rhodes. The artillery was to destroy our lines, when the infantry was to charge and occupy them. He further said that General Meade could not afford us any support, and that we must defend ourselves to keep clear our front, and asked the captain if he could do it. Captain Hill answered, "If any men can, mine can," or words to that effect. The general replied that our position must be held at all hazards, or the day was lost. Knowing as we did the immense responsibility resting upon us, we shut our teeth and vowed we would hold our position.

The intense calm over the whole field we knew portended the anticipated attack, nor were we long in anticipation, for at a signal from a gun on the rebel right, the whole field was as convulsed as if an earthquake had occurred. The whole of the rebel artillery, estimated at from two hundred and twenty-five to two hundred and fifty guns, by General Meade in his official report, had opened on us at once. Mortal pen cannot describe the horrors of that unparalleled cannonade. Nearly five hundred guns were going all at once. The air was alive with shrieking and bursting shells, guns discharging, men shouting, and many crying out in pain, horses rearing and neighing as they were being horribly mangled, caissons bursting, carrying death and dismay to their possessors, until it appeared as if it was impossible for man to survive the destructive missiles. For four long hours did this continue. Men by scores and hundreds had been killed. In the first battery to our left forty men had been killed and wounded, and nearly all their horses. Four pieces had been disabled, and at one time we saw three of their limber chests blown up. I rode over their position the next morning, and the sight fairly sickened me. Their guns had to be hauled off in baggage wagons. Still, although our position was higher and more exposed, it appeared as though some guardian angel was watching over us, for our losses were but few. Charles Lacey, a driver on Sergeant O'Neil's gun, while keeping his horses still, was struck by half of a light twelve pounder shell above the right eye, killing him the same way as Braddock, but there he had to lay until after the battle, when we gave him a decent burial. James Loufman was struck in the breast with a piece of shell, but its force had been spent, causing no injury.

The battle still raged hotter and hotter. Our ammunition having given out, we fired back a few of the rebel shells, hot as they were, literally paying them back in their own coin. Our ammunition being exhausted, we were compelled to withdraw.

Our journey down the Chambersburgh pike was, if anything, hotter than the field itself, for it is proverbial that the rear is the most dangerous place, for on it is concentrated all the shot and shell that have passed over the front. We had no sooner got out of harm's way than the firing ceased. The artillery having failed to break our line, the rebel infantry was drawn up in line to attempt it. Right nobly they came, but it was to their death, for our whole line opened on them with full force, and sent such a deadly storm of canister into their ranks that it appeared as if the whole line was doomed. Fully one-third fell, as many more threw down their arms and surrendered, and the rest, demoralized and scattered, sought the shelter of the woods. Thus ended this memorable engagement. Skirmishing, it is true, was still kept up, but the heavy fighting was over. Some of the boys, on going over the field to our front and left, said that fully three acres could be traversed without touching the ground, so thickly were the bodies strewn. I was

---

[*] This wound necessitated amputation, and we find it recorded in another place by one who saw him borne from the field, that after his leg had been taken off and the wound dressed, this impetuous leader was borne from the field on a stretcher, lying with his hat drawn down over his eyes, his arms folded tightly on his breast and a cigar in his mouth.

content to take a view from our position. It was too horrible to take a nearer look at. We remained in position until noon of the fifth, when it was fully known that the rebels were retreating.

The battle being over and the rebels in full retreat, we started after them, nor were we loth to leave the place. For four days and nights had we been there almost without food, water, or sleep. Is it any wonder that the place had no fascination?

Men blame Meade for not following Lee more closely, and preventing his escape across the Potomac, but had they been there they could readily have seen the reason.

THE LAST BATTLE.

Lee having got fairly away, we started by easy and pleasant marches towards our old haunts. We camped at Warrentown, then at Culpeper, and when in the fall Lee slipped by us and again made demonstrations on Washington, we again took part in that "masterly fall-back." Although the rebels had the start, and the inside track, still, Meade hoped that by strategem he might defeat them. He placed the army in three columns, and marched them by three different roads, keeping each column in sight of the other nearly constantly, and the race became so close that when the head of our column reached and occupied Centreville Heights, the head of the rebel Hill's column could be seen crossing the old Bull Run bridge. Lee manœuvred around a good deal, hoping to find an assailable point, but not finding any, he again fell back. We in this campaign fought our last battle. The Second corps had been warmly engaged, their artillery had run out of ammunition, and it became necessary to relieve them. We were sent up to their relief, and hardly had we reached the front when a rebel battery of four guns opened on us from Mitchell's ford. We asked no better fun than to engage them. Dashing into position we soon exchanged cards, and opened an intimate acquaintance. A short time was sufficient. They tired of our acquaintance and very unceremoniously withdrew, leaving us exulting over our easy, and on our part bloodless victory. We followed Lee to the Rappahannock, where a part of our troops made such a gallant assault on his works, at Rappahannock Station. Here the gun captured from us at Chancellorsville was, to our great joy, recaptured.

Our battery reenlisted and came home on a veteran furlough, and returned expecting to take part in the anticipated engagements under Grant, but that general, having more artillery than he needed, sent us, in connection with a number of other batteries, to man the defences of Washington, where we remained until peace was declared and we were allowed to return to our homes, proud that we should never have cause to blush at our record.

BATTLE RECORD OF THE BATTERY.

Strasburg, Virginia, June 2, 1862; Tom Brook, Virginia, June 3, 1862; Mt. Jackson, Virginia, June 4, 1862, Cross Keys, Virginia, June 8, 1862; Port Republic, Virginia, June 9, 1862; Luray, Virginia, July 11, 1862; Cedar Mountain, Virginia, August 9, 1862; Freeman's Ford, Virginia, August 22, 1862; Sulphur Springs, Virginia, August 23, 1862; Waterloo Bridge, Virginia, August 24, 1862; Bull Run, Virginia, August 29, 1862; Bull Run, Virginia, August 30, 1862; Leesburgh, Virginia, September 17, 1862, Catlett's Station, Virginia, September 25, 1862; Chancellorsville, May 2, 1863; Gettysburgh, Pennsylvania, July 2 and 3, 1863; Mitchell's Ford, October 15, 1863.

HUNTINGTON'S BATTERY H, FIRST OHIO VOLUNTEER LIGHT ARTILLERY.

COMMISSIONED OFFICERS.

Captain James F. Huntington, mustered November 7, 1861, resigned on surgeon's certificate of disability October 26, 1863; Captain George W. Norton, mustered October 26, 1863, resigned March 21, 1864; Captain Stephen W. Dorsey, mustered April 13, 1864, mustered out with battery; First Lieutenant George W. Norton, mustered November 7, 1861, promoted to captain; First Lieutenant George Davenport, mustered November 7, 1861, resigned January 7, 1863; First Lieutenant Charles G. Mason, mustered March 12, 1862, resigned April 26, 1862; First Lieutenant William A. Ewing, mustered June 4, 1863, mustered out October 24, 1864; First Lieutenant Albert G. Merrill, mustered March 3, 1864, resigned October 12, 1864; First Lieutenant James Harris, mustered February 8, 1865, mustered out with battery; First Lieutenant William H. Perrigo, mustered February 8, 1865, mustered out with battery; Second Lieutenant Thomas M. Bartlett, mustered November 7, 1862, promoted; Second Lieutenant Martin B. Ewing, mustered November 7, 1862, promoted; Second Lieutenant Albert G. Merrill, mustered September 15, 1862, promoted; Second Lieutenant Frank B. Reckard, mustered January 7, 1863, promoted; Second Lieu-

tenant Albert Reagler, mustered May 9, 1864, mustered out with battery; Second Lieutenant Lewis B. Maxwell, mustered May 2, 1865, mustered out with battery; Second Lieutenant Silas H. Judson, mustered May 2, 1865, mustered out with battery; Second Lieutenant Wallace W. Pixley, mustered October 20, 1864, mustered out July 1, 1865; Second Lieutenant William E. Parmalee, mustered February 8, 1865, mustered out July 1, 1865.

In October, 1861, about sixty men were raised for the field artillery service, in Washington and Monroe counties. An arrangement was made to complete a battery by uniting them with about the same number of recruits from the vicinity of Toledo.

On November 6th the organization was perfected at Camp Dennison, and battery H, of the First light artillery, came into existence. The following was the roster of commissioned officers at that date: I. F. Huntington, of Marietta, captain; G. W. Norton, of Toledo, senior first lieutenant; George Davenport, of Salem, junior first lieutenant; M. B. Ewing, of Cincinnati, senior second lieutenant; T. M. Bartlett, of Cleveland, junior second lieutenant.

The junior subaltern never reported for duty with the battery, and was afterwards transferred. Private W. A. Ewing was promoted to the vacancy. Of the men thus brought together from opposite frontiers of the State, it is but justice to say, that in character and intelligence they were above the average.

The battery was armed with six James' guns—the old bronze six-pounder rifled to throw a thirteen-pound conical shot. It was admirably horsed—better than at any subsequent period.

In January, the battery being reported as ready for the field, it was sent to join General Lander's, afterwards Shield's division, near Cumberland, Maryland. It was first engaged at the battle of Winchester, March 22, 1862: losing one man, Private Jacob Tager, and one horse killed by the same shot. General Shields was wounded while sitting on his horse near the pieces watching the fire. The battery took part in the various operations in Shenandoah valley for the next two months. In May the division was ordered to march for Fredericksburgh and join McDowell's corps, then about to unite with the right wing of McDowell's army in an attack on Richmond.

When Shields' division was fairly out of the way, Stonewall Jackson returned and drove General Banks' small command out of the valley. The advance on Richmond was postponed, and Shields' division, followed by the bulk of McDowell's corps, was started post haste towards the valley. In combination with Fremont, who was to come in from Franklin, they were to "bag Jackson."

As usual, the string slipped—McDowell gave it up at Front Royal, and left Shields to follow Jackson on his own hook. The bridges of the Shenandoah had been burnt, and the stream was unfordable. Shields sent two brigades and three battalions, "H" among them, up the north bank to the village of Port Republic, where a bridge was standing.

Jackson proposed to cross at this point. He found these two brigades under General Tyler, of Ohio, likely to interfere with him. Fremont pressed him south of the river. On Sunday, June 8th, he checked that General at Cross Keys, and, crossing at Port Republic early the next morning, attacked Tyler's small command, expecting to wipe him out in season to return and join with Fremont. In this action battery H was severely handled. Posted on the left flank, without infantry support, a thick wood sheltered the enemy within pistol-shot of the guns. It was charged in front and flanked by the "Louisiana Tigers," and forced to retire, leaving two pieces on the field, having several men killed and wounded, with a large number of horses. Tyler's command made a gallant fight, and the enemy made no serious attempt to follow their retreat. Shields' division retired to Front Royal; the general resigned his command, and the division was broken up.

In July battery H arrived at Alexandria much reduced in strength by the casualties of service. Before the losses in men and material could be repaired, the battery was ordered to Marietta to join General Pike's army. At this place it was inspected and ordered back to Alexandria. Recruiting officers were sent to Toledo and Marietta who soon raised men to fill the attenuated ranks. The James guns were turned in and replaced by six ordnance guns, three inch wrought iron rifles. By this time General Pope was falling back on the defences of Washington. The battery joined him in time for the battle of Chantilly. After various marches and countermarches the battery permanently assigned to General Whipple's division, proceeded by rail from Washington to join McClellan in Maryland. Thenceforward it belonged to the army of the Potomac. The battery next came in contact with the enemy during a reconnoissance in Manassas gap with Piatt's brigade early in November, 1862.

After General Burnside succeeded to the command, the battery marched to Fredericksburgh. She was detailed with others to cover the laying of the center pontoon preparatory to the bloody and disastrous battle of Fredericksburgh. It took part in shelling the city, but did not cross the river. In Burnside's next attempt, known as the "mud march," battery H was one of those assigned to cover the crossing at Bank's ford. It reached the designated position and got back to the old camp by one of the hardest marches in its history.

During the winter of 1862-63, spent at Falmouth, Lieutenant Davenport resigned on a surgeon's certificate. Sergeant F. B. Richard was promoted to the junior lieutenantcy.

Battery H marched to Chancellorsville with Whipple's division of Sickle's corps. When the division went out to join the attack on Jackson's column as it crossed the front of Hooker's position, its batteries H, First Ohio, First and Thirteenth New York Independent, were left in a field near the turnpike. Here it became their duty to meet and repel a strong attack from Jackson's advance after the rout of the Eleventh corps. This was done so as to elicit the warmest commendation from General Sickles when he reached the field.

Early the next morning battery H was left in the same field with two regiments of infantry to make a show of resistance till the new line of defence was completed. The front attack of the enemy was repelled, but being outflanked, the infantry support having retreated in confusion, the battery was forced to retire as best it could through boggy ground and across a creek. It sustained a heavy loss in men and material—two pieces had to be left across the stream, the horses being killed or disabled.

After the return of the army to Falmouth, the artillery was reorganized and a strong reserve formed under General R. O. Tyler, United States Army. It was soon afterwards sent to Banks' Ford, on temporary duty, with the regular division of the Fifth corps. It marched with that division as far as Manassas Junction, *en route* for Gettysburgh, then rejoined the reserve. Just before this, First Lieutenant M. B. Ewing resigned to accept promotion into the First regiment, heavy artillery. Sergeant Albert Merrill became junior subaltern. At Fairfax Court House a new brigade was formed in the reserve, made up of company H, First Ohio, company C, First Virginia, and company L, First Pennsylvania. Captain Huntington, First New Hampshire independent battery, was assigned to the command; so the immediate charge of the battery devolved on Lieutenant Norton.

At Gettysburgh the battery, posted on Cemetery hill, was exposed to a heavy fire of artillery, as well as from sharpshooters near the edge of the town. Some of the best men in the battery fell in that hard-fought battle.

After the return of the army to Virginia, battery H, with Huntington's brigade, did out-post duty on the Rappahannock and Rapidan rivers. In November, 1863, the battery was at Warrentown, Virginia.

Captain Huntington, in consequence of an injury, resigned on a surgeon's certificate, to accept an appointment in the veteran reserve corps. Lieutenant Norton became captain. The battery took part in the Mine Run campaign, and passed the remainder of the winter of 1863-64 at Brandy Station.

In March Captain Norton resigned. Up to this time promotions had been made by seniority, a selection in the battery where the vacancy occurred. A new rule had been introduced about this time, under which Lieutenant S. W. Dorsey, as senior subaltern of the regiment, became captain of battery H.

Soon after the opening of the spring campaign, the battery was transferred to the Sixth corps, and with it fought at Spottsylvania. At the sanguinary action of Cold Harbor the battery was the first to take position, and was heavily engaged. In the advance on Petersburgh the battery held a very exposed position for three days and nights, trying to prevent the enemy from crossing the railroad bridges. In July the battery had a little vacation from siege duties.

In consequence of Early's raid on Washington, it was sent to that city, but after a very brief stay was ordered to return to the front of Petersburgh. For over two months the battery held the earthwork officially called Fort Sedgewick, but better known as Fort Hell, the hottest place on the line. Constantly under fire, no amount of active field service is so harassing and trying to soldiers.

The battery was among the first sent home after the surrender. The muster-out took place at Camp Taylor, near Cleveland, June 15, 1865. The roster of officers then stood as follows:

S. W. Dorsey, captain; James Harris and W. H. Pervigo, first lieutenants; W. W. Pixley and W. E. Parmelee, second lieutenants.

Battery H thus completed a record of arduous and honorable service. No man who ever fought at its guns need blush to tell his children, "I belonged to old Battery H." In the matter of losses in action the battery was remarkably fortunate. Few, if any, that saw so much service were equally so. The following is a resume of its career:

Whole number borne on the rolls during service, two hundred and sixty-two; killed in action, twenty-eight; died in hospital, fifteen; discharged on surgeon's certificates, forty; discharged expiration of enlistment, thirty-six; discharged for promotion, etc., eighteen; mustered out at Camp Taylor, one hundred and twenty-five.

About six of the original horses went through with the battery. Promotions from the enlisted men were as follows:

To commissions in the battery, seven; commissions in other batteries, three; commissions in heavy artillery, two; commissions in infantry, two; commission in United States navy, one; total, fifteen.

Battery H was present at the following battles and skirmishes:

Battles—Winchester, Port Republic, Chantilly, Fredericksburgh, Chancellorsville, Gettysburgh, Wine Run, Wilderness, Spottsylvania, Cold Harbor, Chickahominy, Petersburgh.

Skirmishes—Edenburgh, Strasburgh, Rudis Hill, New Market, Mount Jackson, Manassas Gap, Mitchell's Station, Bank's Ford, Weldron Railroad.

DE BECK'S BATTERY—K, FIRST OHIO VOLUNTEER LIGHT ARTILLERY.

ROSTER OF OFFICERS.

Captain William L. De Beck, mustered October 10, 1861, resigned May 11, 1863; Captain Louis Heckman, May 11, 1863, mustered out with battery; First Lieutenant George B. Haskins, October 10, 1861, resigned October 20, 1862; First Lieutenant John D. Holden, February 19, 1862, resigned March 27, 1862, First Lieutenant Henry F. Camp, March 27, 1862, died September 15, 1862; First Lieutenant Thomas M. Bartlett, September 15, 1862, resigned October 30, 1863, First Lieutenant Louis Heckman, October 20, 1862, promoted; First Lieutenant Charles M. Schilley, May 11, 1863, mustered out with battery; First Lieutenant Columbus Rodamour, October 15, 1863, mustered out with battery; First Lieutenant Andrew Berwick, October 30, 1863, mustered out with battery; Second Lieutenant John D. Holden, October 10, 1861, promoted; Second Lieutenant Louis Heckman, February 20, 1862, promoted; Second Lieutenant Henry F. Camp, January 7, 1862, promoted; Second Lieutenant Hiram B. Iams, March 27, 1862, resigned May 11, 1863; Second Lieutenant Charles M. Schilley, October 20, 1862, promoted; Second Lieutenant Columbus Rodamour, May 11, 1863, promoted, Second Lieutenant John H. Reis, May 11, 1862, promoted; Second Lieutenant Joseph Maloney, May, 9, 1864, mustered out with battery; Second Lieutenant Otto Marolotze, May 2, 1865, resigned June 10, 1865.

DE BECK'S BATTERY, "K," FIRST OHIO VOLUNTEER LIGHT ARTILLERY.

Washington county has just cause to be proud of the three batteries she furnished for the Union during the

civil war, viz: De Beck's "L" and Huntington's "H," of the First Ohio and Buell's Virginia First.

"De Beck's Battery," so called in honor of its organizer and first commander, Captain William L. De Beck, of Cincinnati, was first started, in June, 1861, under authority from the State of Virginia with headquarters at Williamstown, West Virginia, opposite Marietta, but recruiting in "Dixie" proving slow, October 10th, of the same year, the command was offered to Ohio, which was accepted, and the company went to Camp Dennison, near Cincinnati, where it was designated as "K" Company, First regiment Ohio volunteer light artillery. During the fall and winter of 1861 and 1862, the drilling and disciplining were incessant, and so proficient did the men become, that the governor of Ohio, as a special recognition, furnished the company six of the famous Wierd steel guns. March 1, 1862, the command went to Parkersburgh, West Virginia, and was incorporated into the army of West Virginia, then under General Rosecranz. Two weeks later, it went forward to Cumberland, Maryland, and reported to General Robert C. Schenck. A few days afterwards it was sent on a forced march, reaching the Wire Suspension bridge over the South Potomac, near Romney, and by its timely arrival, prevented a raid upon the Baltimore & Ohio railroad by a division of Stonewall Jackson's cavalry. For the promptness here displayed, the battery was publicly thanked by General Rosecrans, and Captain De Beck promoted to chief of artillery, on the staff of General Schenck. Early in April, 1862, "K" was engaged in engagements at Grassy Lick, Lost River, Moorefield and Crab Bottom Church, again receiving the thanks of the general.

May 8th of the same same year, after a forced night and day march, of more than one hundred miles, Schenck's army reached the overwhelmed forces of General Milroy, the combined army numbering seven thousand, at once engaging Jackson's army of twenty-three thousand in the fierce battle of Bull Pasture Mountain, which lasted till late in the night, and by mutual consent ending as a "drawn game." The Union army under Schenck, being largely outnumbered, withdrew that night, closely followed by Jackson in its retreat, fighting at Mountain Summit, Ighs' Church, Handy's Gap, Washington's Meadow, and Franklin; in all of which Jackson's attempt to cut the army off from its base of retreat was frustrated. During the five days and nights of this terrible retrograde movement, De Beck's battery was assigned the first place of honor, in covering the retreats and driving back the fierce onslaughts of Jackson, in which it was again so successful that General Fremont who had succeeded Rosecrans, in the presence of his staff and other commanding officers, thanked Captain De Beck for splendid work he had done, General Schenck adding that battery K had saved the army.

Fremont now started on his memorable march, to intercept Jackson in the Shenandoah valley, during which were fought the battles of Strasburgh, Middletown, Cedar Creek, New Market, Edinburgh, Woodstock, Mt. Jackson, Harrisonburgh, Rockingham Fields (where the rebel cavalry general, Ashby, was killed), and Cross

Keys, and in the latter the terrible firing of De Beck's battery, and work it did, exciting the greatest admiration of all officers and men from the highest to the lowest. Fremont was now succeeded by General Siegel, and Captain De Beck was chief of artillery of the army. While under Siegel, the battery took part in the great battles of Cedar Mountain, Freeman's Ferry, Kelly's Ford, Warrenton, Warrenton Junction, Bristow Station, New Baltimore (second), Chantilly and the second Bull Run, all under Pope.

After this K was assigned to the army of the Potomac, closing the year 1862 by taking part in Burnside's great and fatal battle of Fredericksburgh. General Joe Hooker was now made commander, and K battery was sent to the Eleventh corps under General O. O. Howard.

May 1st, 2d and 3d. battery K was in the terrible field at Chancellorsville, its discipline and drill never proving of greater value than when the Eleventh corps so unexpectedly became demoralized, and began its disastrous retreat. K battery was remained like a solid wall, with cannister and shrapnel again and again driving back the fierce charges of Jackson, remaining in position until our forces had either reformed their lines, or new troops came to the rescue. The next day, while temporarily serving in the Fifth corps under General Meade, the battery again distinguished itself, by driving back with cannister Longstreet's veterans. Captain De Beck being now called to another command, Lewis Heckman, senior first lieutenant, was commissioned captain, and took charge of the battery.

July 1, 2 and 3, 1863, was fought the greatest battle of the war, Gettysburgh, in which battery K was prominently engaged, its terrific fire on Cemetery Hill, eliciting the highest enconiums.

In October the battery went to the west with the Eleventh and Twelfth corps under Hooker, and at Chattanooga was incorporated into the army of the Cumberland, and while there, was participant in all of Grant's battles at Lookout Mountain, Missionary Ridge, etc., and during the rest of the war, remained at Stevenson and Bridgeport, Alabama, finally returning to Camp Dennison, where it was mustered out of service, delivering its guns over to the Ordnance Department of the United States, and having had the rare good fortune of never having surrendered a single gun to the enemy.

Gallant, noble Frank Buell died in battle, lamented and beloved by all the officers and men of the three batteries, while De Beck and Huntington had the good fortune to live through the contest, to see the country restored and reunited, and peace reigning throughout the land.

BATTERY K, SECOND OHIO HEAVY ARTILLERY.
COMMISSIONED OFFICERS.

Captain Daniel W. Hoffman, mustered August 22, 1863, promoted to major September 30, 1863; Captain Walter S. Bradford, June 16, 1865, mustered out with regiment. Captain Stowell S. Hazen, September 30, 1863, resigned June 24, 1865, First Lieutenant Richard Burns, August 25, 1863, promoted to captain of battery L; First Lieutenant Stowell S. Hazen, August 27, 1863, promoted to captain of battery K; First Lieutenant Thomas M. Sechler, September 30, 1863, resigned June 3, 1865; First Lieutenant Charles A. McManus, October 18, 1864, resigned June 24, 1865; First Lieutenant Francis Reichman, June 16,

1865, mustered out with regiment; Second Lieutenant Thomas M. Sechler, August 25, 1863, promoted to first lieutenant; Second Lieutenant Charles H. Newton, August 25, 1863, promoted to first lieutenant of battery D, and resigned January 19, 1865; Second Lieutenant George W. Bell, September 30, 1863, promoted to first lieutenant of battery B, on General Carter's staff at muster out of regiment; Second Lieutenant Thomas Underwood, September 15, 1864, mustered out with regiment; Second Lieutenant Henry A. Frary, mustered out with regiment.

This was a Washington county organization. By the middle of the year 1863 the National armies had made important captures of forts and other strongholds of the enemy. It became necessary to recruit a class of troops whose duty it should be to fortify, garrison and hold these captures. The Second regiment of heavy artillery was therefore authorized, and rank and file consisted of twenty-four hundred men.

K battery was mustered into the service September 7, 1863, at Covington barracks, Kentucky, and on October 11th, was removed to Mumfordsville. On May 26, 1864, it was transferred to Charleston, Tennessee, where, on the eighteenth of August, it was engaged with the enemy's cavalry, under Wheeler, and participated in the subsequent movements of General Ammen, moving to Fort Saunders and Knoxville, and on November 18, 1864, marched to open communication with the Union forces, then in a critical position at Strawberry plains. On November 20th, returned to Knoxville, and on December 7th, marched with General Ammen's command to Bean's Station, Tennessee. It occupied fortifications at Clinch Gap, Tennessee, until December 31, 1864, when it returned to Fort Lee, at Knoxville. Shortly thereafter the battery was ordered to Greenville, Tennessee, and thence to Nashville, where, on the twenty-third of August, 1865, it was mustered out of the service. On August 29, 1865, it was finally paid and discharged at Camp Chase.

COMPANY I, FIRST OHIO VOLUNTEER CAVALRY.
(General G. W. Thomas' Body Guard.)
REGIMENTAL OFFICERS.

Colonel Owen P. Ransom, mustered August 17, 1861, resigned; Colonel Minor Millikin, January 11, 1862, killed at Stone River December 31, 1862; Colonel Thomas C. H Smith, December 31, 1862, revoked; Colonel Beroth B. Eggleston, April 1, 1863, mustered out with regiment; Lieutenant Colonel Thomas C. H. Smith, August 23, 1861, promoted to colonel December 13, 1862, appointed brigadier general by President November 29, 1862, Lieutenant Colonel James Laughlin, December 31, 1862, resigned April 1, 1863; Lieutenant Colonel Valentine Cupp, April 1, 1863, died September 20, 1863; Lieutenant Colonel Thomas J. Pattin, September 20, 1863, mustered out with regiment; Lieutenant Colonel Stephen C. Writer, December 9, 1864, mustered out with regiment; Major John D. Moxley, February 25, 1865, A. A. A. G. at Camp Webster, Nashville, Tennessee; Major William McBurney, February 28, 1865, mustered out with regiment; Major Minor Millikin, August 24, 1861, promoted to colonel; Major Michael W. Smith, October 31, 1861, resigned June 10, 1862; Major E. B. Dennison, November 27, 1861, resigned June 10, 1862; Major James Laughlin, June 10, 1862, promoted to lieutenant colonel; Major Beroth B. Eggleston, June 20, 1862, promoted to colonel, Major J. W. Robinson, June 1, 1862, died; Major David A. B. Moore, September 7, 1862, killed at Stone River December 31, 1862; Major Valentine Cupp, December 31, 1862, promoted to lieutenant colonel; Major Thomas J. Pattin, December 31, 1862, promoted to lieutenant colonel; Major Stephen C. Writer, April 1, 1863, promoted to lieutenant colonel; Major James N. Scott, April 1, 1863, mustered out with regiment; Major John C. Frankenberger, September 20, 1863, mustered out; Surgeon Rudolph Wirth, September 7, 1861, resigned May 23, 1862; Surgeon John Cannan, February 1, 1862; Wilson V. Cowen, December 16, 1863, resigned October 4, 1864; Assistant Surgeon John Cannan, October 10, 1864, promoted to

surgeon; Assistant Surgeon John B. McDill, August 21, 1864, mustered
out; Chaplain J. M. Drake, December 13, 1864, resigned May 23, 1862.

COMPANY OFFICERS.

Captain Thomas J. Pattin, mustered September 17, 1864, promoted
to major; Captain John D. Barker, December 31, 1863, resigned January 21, 1864; Captain Henry C. Reppert, December 14, 1864, mustered
out with regiment; First Lieutenant John D. Barker, September 18,
1861, promoted to captain; First Lieutenant Samuel H. Putnam, September 7, 1862, resigned October 26, 1863; First Lieutenant Henry C.
Reppert, March 31, 1864, promoted to captain, First Lieutenant Robert B. Rhodes, January 6, 1865, mustered out May 5, 1863, as second
lieutenant; First Lieutenant Daniel W. Dye, July 24, 1865, mustered
out with regiment, Second Lieutenant Oscar H. Underwood, September 18, 1861, resigned May 29, 1862; Second Lieutenant Timothy L.
Condit, May 29, 1862, killed at Stone River December, 31, 1862; Second Lieutenant Samuel H. Putnam, November 20, 1862, promoted to
first lieutenant; Second Lieutenant Henry C. Reppert, December 31,
1862, promoted to first lieutenant; Second Lieutenant Robert B.
Rhodes, December 9, 1863, promoted to first lieutenant.

NON-COMMISSIONED OFFICERS.

First, second and third sergeants at date of muster out.

First Sergeant Edward P. Burlingame, March 31, 1864, mustered
out with regiment; Quartermaster Sergeant John Huff, March 31, 1864,
mustered out with regiment, Commissary Sergeant Henry Duden,
March 31, 1864, mustered out with regiment.

The following sketch of company L, First Ohio volunteer cavalry, was compiled from brief notes taken by
Sergeant E. P. Burlingame from a journal kept by him
during the war. Many soldiers kept journals, but few were
as fortunate as Mr. Burlingame in getting through all the
marches and battles and not losing them:

September 5, 1861, Governor Dennison authorized a
regiment of cavalry to be raised for the three years' service. Through the efforts of the military committee of
Washington county, and especially two members, John
Newton, esq., and Colonel William R. Putnam, together
with Thomas J. Pattin and John D. Barker, a company
was raised in this county, and by September 14, 1861,
ninety-three names were enrolled. Thomas J. Pattin
was elected captain, John D. Barker first lieutenant, and
Oscar H. Underwood second lieutenant.

On the seventeenth of the same month the company
reported at Camp Chase, and was assigned to the First
Ohio volunteer cavalry, as company L. They were mustered in on the eighteenth, received uniforms the twenty-first, horses the twenty-eighth, horse equipments October
22d, sabres and belts November 25th, and revolvers December 3d. Meanwhile they were exercised at mounted
and dismounted drill, until they became very efficient in
the manual of arms and cavalry evolutions.

December 11th, the regiment arrived at Louisville,
Kentucky, and on the twentieth were reviewed by General Don Carlos Buell, commanding the department.

January 30, 1862, the company made a short tour in
search of the rebel chief, John Morgan, but failed to
come up with him.

The regiment proceeded southward through Nashville
and on March 24th, encamped at Spring Hill, Tennessee, where a detail from company L was made as an
escort for General George H. Thomas, under command
of Lieutenant John D. Barker.

April 6, 1862, while on the March with General Buell's
army in the direction of Pittsburgh Landing, the cannonading at the battle of Shiloh was distinctly heard.

The regiment arrived at Pittsburgh Landing April 8th,
too late to take part in the battle, and were actively employed up to May 30th, having several skirmishes with
the enemy, and lost one man, William M. Robinson—
missing.

On June 4, 1862, they fought their first battle. Company L with part of company D were on picket duty
three miles from Booneville, at Carolina church, when
the rebels, four companies strong, attacked them. Forming hastily they checked the enemy's advance, and then
fell back in good order, to entice the enemy into the
open ground. The rebels, supposing they were retreating, charged with a yell, but our men wheeled by fours
and faced the enemy, opening on them with their Sharps'
carbines, Captain Pattin riding up and down the line,
urging the boys to "give it to them." The rebels having
a larger force now endeavored to flank them. They consequently were compelled to fall back still farther, turning
on the rebels several times, and finally reached their
supports at Booneville, when the enemy retired. The
company escaped without loss; two of company D, however, were wounded.

In July, 1862, the company was engaged in the siege
of Corinth, and on the twenty-fourth of that month
joined the regiment at Tuscumbia, Alabama. During
August they were engaged in scouting along the line of
the Nashville & Chattanooga railroad. September 30th
found the regiment at Louisville again under the command of General Buell, where they were clothed and
equipped and received four months' pay.

On October 2d company L was thrown out from Louisville to make a flank movement on the rebels who had
taken possession of Mt. Washington. Captain Pattin
advanced part of the company, dismounted, who were
supported by other troops; they were soon briskly engaged, when the enemy opened on them with grape and
cannister; they thereupon retired to give room to our
artillery; moving now to the other flank the company got
into the town, and the rebels rapidly retreated. Loss,
Henry Duden, wounded.

October 4, 1862, a detachment under Major Laughlin
having been sent out to the front, they left the direct road
to Bardstown, and proceeding *via* Fairfield, came into
it again at Bardstown fair-grounds. After some skirmishing we gained the road. Company L was formed parallel to the road, close up to the fence, and was on the left
of the line, disconnected. We had commenced letting
down the fence to enable us to get on to the road, but a
rush of cavalry from the direction of Louisville caused
us to make other disposition of our time. We were between a brigade of Texan rangers and Bardstown, and
they were charging down upon us in columns of platoons,
evidently intent upon cutting through. We fired a few
rounds at a right oblique, and the right having broken,
we had to fall back. The rebels were between us and
our reserves. We must run the gauntlet or jump a rail
fence and take a wide circuit around. Captain Pattin's
bridle rein caught on a gate latch, and he barely escaped
capture. Corporal Daniel W. Dye having dropped his
carbine, dismounted and picked it up, and with the reb-

els demanding his surrender, he put spurs to his horse and escaped. Jonathan H. Smith was mortally wounded after he had been compelled to surrender. Corporal Jacob Gano and privates Edward P. Bigelow, Calvin C. Broughton, Peter Cline, David M. Grimes, John Hoskinson and William Rice were captured and paroled. John Duden and William Reese were captured and dismounted, but watching their opportunity, they escaped.

On October 8th the detachment took part in the battle of Perryville, and bivouacked that night on the field.

By order of General Buell, Major Laughlin's detachment on October 10th started for Bardstown, with a large number of rebel prisoners, and on the fourteenth joined the regiment at Danville, Kentucky.

After another fruitless chase after Morgan, the company was for some time engaged in carrying dispatches from Gallatin to General Rosseau at Tyree Springs, Tennessee.

The regiment was about this time (November, 1862) brigaded with the Third Ohio cavalry, and the Second and Fifth Kentucky cavalry under Colonel Zahn of the Third Ohio. The Fourth Ohio cavalry was afterwards substituted for the Fifth Kentucky.

On December 30, 1862, Captain Pattin was ordered to take his platoon and with a section of artillery, to drive some rebel troops out of Lavergne, Tennessee. Upon coming in sight of the town the artillery was brought into position, and a few shots were fired as "feelers." One of these passing through a house took of the arm of Mr. Tidd of Harmar, Ohio, who was employed by the government, in putting up telegraph lines. The rebels retreated. Pattin pursued and captured a number of mules. The Second platoon, under Lieutenant Timothy L. Condit, accompanied the train, and both platoons met at Wilkes' crossroads, and went into camp there at 10 P. M.

THE BATTLE OF STONE RIVER.

December 31st we were preparing to break camp, when, from the right over the fields, came excited soldiers, with tales of disaster. General Willich's command had been surprised, and the plain was covered with his fleeing troops. The wounded, as they passed, inquired where they might find a hospital, and all seemed more or less panic-stricken. Hastily forming we proceeded to join the regiment, and hardly had we done so when the rebels opened on us with artillery; one of the first shots killing our major, David A. B. Moore. Acting under orders, we fell back to a new position. The enemy, mistaking the movement for a retreat, set up a cheer and charged. Upon our again facing them, however, they came to a sudden halt, and we engaged them with our carbines. Colonel Miliken was cool and brave. "Give it to them, boys," said he, "and if they get too close take your sabres to them." The disaster to General McCook's corps made it necessary for us to fall back again, that the line of battle might not be disconnected. We were closely followed by the rebels, who used the artillery at every opportunity. He had no artillery, and in this the enemy had the advantage. As we were compelled to go through fences we lost our formation

and became mixed up. This kept getting worse; we were like a drove, and still harder pressed, the foe riding down on us, and with their revolvers firing upon us as they came. We were nearing the pike; our line of communication to the rear, and the sight of the long line of wagons must have given the rebels encouragement. At this juncture Colonel Miliken ordered "Charge!" repeating the command. Seventy-five or a hundred men wheeled and dashed toward the enemy, but they took to flight. We pursued and had nearly overtaken them when a strong force was hurled against our right flank, and made retreat a necessity. This was a matter of difficulty, and in trying to make it seccessful Colonel Miliken and Lieutenant Timothy L. Condit, our best officers, were killed; Adjutant Scott was severely wounded, Sergeant George Warren and Bugler John Dulty were taken prisoners, and James S. Parker was captured, disarmed and shot in two places. He managed to escape with his horse. The rebels now had undisputed possession of the train. Our cavalry was scattered, discouraged and fleeing. It was late in the day ere we were again in order. Captain Pattin brought up the first battalion and took command of the company. The rebels were driven from the road by the Fourth regulars, and the fighting for the day, as far as we were concerned, was over. Our colonel died nobly. His loss was deeply lamented, for his place could never be filled. The death of Lieutenant Condit was a grief to all the company. He had no enemies; every one was a friend, and each felt an individual sorrow.

January 1, 1863. Fulton Guitteau was killed by a cannon ball. He belonged to the escort of Major General Thomas, and was on the field when killed. His comrades bear testimony to his excellent qualities as a soldier and his uniform courtesy and gentlemanly bearing.

We were not actively engaged to-day. The rebels advanced but once, and being met with grape and canister from a masked battery, they precipitately retired.

January 2d. The company was in order of battle all day. There was considerable skirmishing, but no general engagement by the Second brigade.*

January 3d. We held our position; raining all day.

The next day it was discovered the rebels had left Murfreesborough, and pursuit was begun, company L taking part, and on the fifth entered the town.

The company, soon after this battle, was assigned to duty carrying dispatches, until April 21, 1863, when the company was permanently detailed as escort of General George H. Thomas.

Captain T. J. Pattin having been promoted to major, Lieutenant Barker was now promoted captain of the company.

The duties of escort to a general in the field are aptly illustrated by the following incident on July 15, 1863:

During the operations against Tullahoma, Tennessee, we were engaged as orderlies and couriers, and in time of expected battle, as General Thomas' personal escort on the field. We are now at Winnefred's Ford, at Elk river, six miles north of Dercherd, Tennessee. To-day

*Second brigade, Second division of cavalry, commanded by Colonel Zahn, and afterward by Colonel Eli Long, Fourth cavalry.

General Thomas, accompanied by General Reynolds, went to General Rosecrans' headquarters at Estell Springs. When returning, as he was crossing Elk river, his horse stumbled over a stone and he was thrown into the water. Corporal John W. Price had charge of the detail then with the general, and was close behind him. The current was very rapid, and the general was being carried down stream unable to reach the shore. Corporal Price, without a moment's hesitation, sprang from his horse into the water, and, being over six feet high, by a few rapid strides, reached the general and caught hold of his coat tail. Setting himself against the current he tried to check their progress down the stream, but to no purpose; at each surge the general went under. Finally they reached the shore, the general much exhausted.

THE BATTLE OF CHICKAMAUGA.

September 18, 1863. At dusk General Thomas received a dispatch from General Rosecrans, through the signal corps, which caused orders to be issued immediately for breaking camp. We marched to Crawfish Springs, where General Thomas stopped to have an interview with General Rosecrans. The company, at 10 o'clock P. M., built fires and unsaddled, but remained ready for marching at a few minutes' notice. Troops and trains are passing rapidly towards Chattanooga. The fences on each side of the road are on fire, and diffuse light and warmth.

September 19th, at 2 o'clock A. M. we left Crawfish Springs and proceeded toward Chattanooga. A short time after daylight the general took a detail from the company, and with his staff took a road to the right, leaving the company to escort the headquarters train to Rossville. The road taken by General Thomas ran almost parallel to the line of battle which he proceeded to form as the troops came up. To secure certain advantages an advance was ordered early in the day, and the rebels were driven to the creek, but soon after they advanced and drove our men, capturing some artillery. There was evidently a slight panic, and the movement to the rear was being made in confusion and haste. Officers and men were mixed indiscriminately, and they rushed by the general, paying no heed to the injunction "look behind you." Had they done so they would have stopped, for the rebels had ceased to advance, and of those of our men who had remained to oppose them quite a good line was formed. The detail under Sergeant Daniel W. Dye made efforts to stop those who were fleeing, but it was some time ere they could be convinced that they were out of danger. Fortunately this was confined to but one brigade, and in the remainder of the battle it proved faithful and courageous. Another detail joined the general in the afternoon and performed whatever service was required. At night we stood around the field headquarters, ready at a call. The general sat on a log in the woods near a dim fire, dictating dispatches to his aid. At twelve o'clock he went to see General Rosecrans, a part of the company going as escort.

September 20th those of the company who were with the train yesterday came to the field, and those who were relieved to get rations and forage. These returned again in the afternoon. When the centre was forced to give way the escort was used to supply additional aids with orderlies, and a number of the company performed very satisfactorily the duties of staff officers. Captain John D. Barker, when returning from a distant point, whither he had gone with a message, not knowing that the centre was so far driven back, came unawares upon the rebels, who fired upon him, shooting his horse through the neck. Taking a more roundabout course he came in rear of the left and was again fired upon. At this same place General James A. Garfield, a few minutes later, had his horse shot from under him. Captain Barker reached the General and reported, and was sent with Captain Killogg, aid de camp, to conduct the loads of ammunition to General Reynolds. Here the services of the company were required. The rebels were in the rear of General Reynolds' position, and the ammunition was in some danger of being captured. A number of the company were deployed as skirmishers, and with raised pistols we advanced through a piece of woods on the left supposed to be occupied by the extreme right flank of the rebel army. This was not the case, however, until half an hour later, when General Turchin, with the Thirty-sixth and Ninety-second charged upon them and routed them completely. The ammunition was delivered to the proper officer and we returned to the general. During the afternoon a cloud of dust was seen to the rear at a distance, and as it came nearer troops were discovered. General Thomas had been watching them, and calling Corporal Franklin W. Prunty he instructed him to go and ascertain whether they were rebel or Union troops, cautioning him to be sure to return with a correct report. Rapidly galloping toward the approaching column, Corporal Prunty discovered that they carried the flag of the Reserve corps, and getting sufficiently near to remove all doubt of their being friends he turned back and reported the approach of General Steedman's division of the Reserve corps. The general himself, a few minutes later, came up and was assigned to duty on the right of the line held by General Thomas. At sunset the divisions on the left began to retire, and the general, after seeing everything in order, started late in the evening for Rossville, where the troops were concentrating. We lay down around the fire and being warm and weary fell asleep.

During the entire engagement the officers and men of the company performed valuable services. Captain Barker was on the field all the time, and rendered efficient service as an aide-de-camp. Lieutenants Putnam and Reppert were alternately on the field, and in command of the train guard. There was no manifestation of cowardice on the part of any member of the company. Those who witnessed the coolness of Quartermaster Sergeant John Huff, when danger was most imminent, will not forget it, and the quiet, determined manner in which private Benjamin S. Turner performed his duties was admirable. He realized that there was danger, but never let it keep him from his post of duty. Others are deserving of as great praise as these, but all did not become equally prominent.

After the battle of Chickamauga company L was with General Thomas during all the movements and engagements from Chattanooga and Mission Ridge to Atlanta. On November 19, 1863, the subject of reenlisting veterans came up and Corporal William H. Snodgrass reenlisted at once, one of the first in the army to pledge his services to the country for another term of three years. Afterwards many others of the company took the same step. On December 5, 1863, Captain J. D. Barker having been assigned to duty at headquarters of the department of the Cumberland as acting assistant inspector general, Lieutenant Henry C. Reppert assumed command, and retained that position to the end, receiving his commission as captain June 30, 1865.

On April 27, 1864, the company was joined by thirty-five recruits, and by May 4th they found themselves well equipped, rested, healthy, and ready for the arduous campaign before them. Then began General Sherman's brilliant movements, flanking the enemy to the right and compelling him each time to abandon one stronghold after another until he finally drew up before Atlanta, and then by another flank movement compelling him to abandon that also. During all these movements and battles General George H. Thomas was an important figure as well as a powerful factor in every important move. Sherman, no doubt, owed much of his success on this memorable campaign to his able lieutenants, his corps commanders. General Thomas was himself constantly in the field and his body guard were constantly subjected to dangerous and fatiguing service.

Mr. Burlingame relates the following incident which we give in full:

August 28, 1864. We reached Red Oak post office this evening During the day the larger part of the company was thrown out as flankers for the protection of the headquarters train. Soon after we arrived at Red Oak (on the Atlanta & West Point railroad) we received information that private Harrison Naylor had been captured by a squad of rebel cavalry about a mile to the rear. A detachment of the company under Sergeant Daniel W. Dye immediately went in pursuit of them and succeeded in falling upon them and capturing four prisoners with their horses, arms and equipments. Naylor was rescued and with him several others who had been captured earlier in the day. Corporal Henry Duden has the credit of capturing the prisoners, having with a few men followed them as they fled until he overtook them. These rebels were scouting here under special orders from General Hood to get information of our movements. Had they escaped that night they would the next day have been in Atalanta. They affirmed that but for having captured that cavalryman they would have successfully accomplished their object General Thomas expressed his satisfaction with the performance of the company on this occasion. Naylor had stopped in a sweet-potato patch a short distance from the road, and was engaged in digging potatoes when a voice called "Come here," in such a tone as to cause him to look around. From behind a fence there appeared a "Johnny" who, presenting a revolver, repeated his command, "Come here." Naylor was unable to resist the persuasive summons and yielded to the demand. Behind the fence concealed in the bushes and weeds were the rest of the party.

On September 2d, about two o'clock in the morning, heavy explosions were heard in the direction of Atlanta, and they broke camp early and moved towards the city and on the eighth moved up to Atlanta and went into camp, Hood and his army having retreated.

On November 6th, arrived at Chatanooga and began at once to build winter quarters. On January 6th, 1865, arrived at Nashville.

The company continued in service after the fall of Richmond and the final collapse of the Confederacy, scouring the country in the neighborhood of Nashville, Gallatin, Hartsville and Lebanon, Tennessee, looking after Government property and protecting loyal citizens until September 26, 1865, when the company was paid and mustered out at Nashville. The company before disbanding did something that showed their high opinion and regard for General George H. Thomas, the "Pap" Thomas who was so brave, so able and so "popular with the boys." It was a tribute to his social and personal worth.

The company contributed fifty dollars for the purchase of a full length colored photograph of General George H. Thomas, which was taken in charge by a committee, to be placed in the hands of the military committee of Washington county, for exhibition in the soldiers' gallery in connection with the company. And so we part, some to take the evening train for *home*. Others remain to spend a few days in Nashville as citizens.

Of the ninety-one enlisted men in the company, there were forty-one farmers, twenty-eight carpenters, smiths, machinists, moulders, masons, coopers, etc., ten clerks and students, and twelve of various occupations. Six were commissioned, thirty discharged at expiration of term of service, eighteen discharged for disability, one on writ of *habeas corpus*, twenty-seven reenlisted, one deserted, one missing in action, and eight dead.

SEVENTH OHIO VOLUNTEER CAVALRY.

REGIMENTAL OFFICERS.

Colonel Israel Gerrard, mustered September 18, 1862, refused promotion, mustered out with the regiment; Lieutenant Colonel George G. Miner, September 18, 1862, on detached duty; Major William Reany, September 20, 1862, mustered out July 4, 1865; Major Augustus Norton, December 28, 1862, resigned January 30, 1864; Major James McIntyre, July 1, 1863, resigned March 26 1864; Major William T. Simpson, March 28, 1864, resigned August 26, 1864; Major John Leaper, July 13, 1864; Major Solomon L. Green, October 12, 1864, mustered out with regiment; Surgeon Isaac Train, October 9, 1862, mustered out with regiment; Assistant Surgeon R. H. Tullis, November 6, 1862, died at Marietta, Georgia; Assistant Surgeon P. G. Barrett, June 9, 1863, honorably discharged October 26, 1864; Assistant Surgeon John Kraps, January 4, 1865, mustered out with regiment.

OFFICERS OF COMPANY H.

Captain Arthur D. Eells, August 27, 1862, resigned June 28, 1863; Captain Theodore F. Allen, April, 2, 1864, mustered out July 4, 1865; Captain Andrew Hall, brevet major, lieutenant colonel and colonel United States volunteers, April 2, 1864, mustered out with regiment; First Lieutenant William L. Tripp, September 2, 1862, resigned December 25, 1863; First Lieutenant John J. Smith, April 2, 1864, resigned as second lieutenant October 30, 1863; First Lieutenant Andrew J. Hardy, May 25, 1864, mustered out with regiment; Second Lieutenant John J. Smith, September 2, 1862, promoted to first lieutenant; Second Lieutenant Andrew J. Hardy, April 19, 1864, promoted to first lieutenant; Second Lieutenant Samuel C. Tappan, March 16, 1865, mustered out with regiment as first sergeant.

SEVENTH OHIO VOLUNTEER CAVALRY.

Company H, named at the time "Newton Guards," in honor of John Newton, esq., of the military committee of Washington county, was organized at Marietta, Ohio, September 8, 1862. It had been speedily enlisted by that popular officer, Captain Arthur D. Eells, who became the first captain of the company. On October 25, 1862, they were mustered in at Camp Marietta, and on the twenty-ninth were ordered to Ripley, Ohio, where they became company H, Seventh Ohio volunteer cavalry, the famous "river regiment." Over sixteen hundred men were offered for this regiment, so popular was this branch of the service at the time.

They left Ripley on January 2d and arrived at Lexington, Kentucky, January 8, 1863. On February 3d they were sent on a scouting expedition to Mt. Vernon, Kentucky, and on March 21st were again on a scout, this time meeting the rebel raider Basil Duke, near Mt. Sterling, Kentucky, on the twenty-second and driving him from the State.

With the other forces under General Gilmore they engaged in the pursuit of the rebel general Pegram's command, which had invaded Kentucky, and at Dutton's hill, near Somerset, where the enemy made a stand in a strongly entrenched position, a sharp battle took place. "Companies G, I, K, L and M made a gallant sabre charge, which decided the day, and the enemy fled in the greatest confusion," leaving in the hand of the companies that charged up the hill one hundred and thirty prisoners and forty-nine dead and wounded on the field. The rebels, however, had sent some veteran cavalry around to the rear and the Nationals had scarcely taken possession of the hill when from their rear was heard the rebel yell, and two regiments of rebels charged at full speed down the valley. They were met at once by a counter charge, led by Captain Saunders, of General Gilmore's staff (afterward General Saunders killed at Knoxville), who charged with companies E, F and H of the river regiment, routed and scattered the rebel charging columns, capturing from them nearly two hundred prisoners and two battle flags. Then followed a vigorous pursuit of the enemy for five miles or more up hill and down, through woods, shooting, shouting, taking prisoners, and strewing the woods with wounded, slain and all the debris of battle. At one place they came unexpectedly onto a company of women from Somerset, who had taken refuge in the woods; these began screaming and were expecting doubtless to be killed in a very short space of time, but the gallant troopers halted in their mad career and allowed the women to pass and then resumed the pursuit, which continued until darkness intervened.

The next work in hand was to drive Pegram beyond the Cumberland mountains, in May, 1863, which they did. Pegram, however, refused to stay whipped, and information being received that he had collected a force near Monticello, the Seventh, with four other cavalry regiments, all under Colonel A. V. Kautz, attacked the enemy June 9, 1863, and drove him from that place. On the return march the river regiment was in the rear of the column, with companies D and H thrown out as rear guard. Presently a huge cloud of dust to the rear announced the approach of the enemy. The two companies nerved themselves to check the rebel advance, and selected a position behind a stone wall. The enemy, coming up, received the well directed fire of the guard, which emptied several saddles; but the rebels, charging gallantly, drove the guard from its chosen position. Gal-

loping along the road, closely pursued by the enemy, the guard loaded their carbines, wheeled into line, and delivered a fire which checked the rebel advance for a moment. The rear guard was soon reinforced by the entire regiment, and afterwards by other regiments and a battery, when a close and desperate fight ensued, lasting till after dark, when both parties withdrew. This engagement was known as that of Rocky Gap. General Burnside complimented the regiment, in orders, for their service in this action, which he announced as "the spirited cavalry engagement at Rock Gap, Kentucky."

The regiment next engaged in cutting the Knoxville & Chattanooga railroad, at Lenoir station, marching from there to a point so close to Knoxville that they threw a few shells into the town. They then drew back and proceeded to Strawberry Plains, and burned a fine railroad bridge over the Holston, the depot, and large quantities of army supplies.

They next joined in the pursuit of the famous raider, John Morgan, who on July 3, 1863, had succeeded in crossing his command over the Cumberland, estimated at three thousand five hundred men. On the tenth Morgan crossed the Ohio at Brandenburgh, Kentucky, with Shackelford and his cavalry in hot pursuit, the route taken being through southern Indiana eastward through Ohio, Morgan having the advantage of twenty-four hours' start and all the fresh horses on the line of march. Morgan, becoming anxious for the safety of his command, had resolved to make a desperate effort to cross the Ohio at Buffington's island. His pursuers, however, were too close upon him. At daylight on the morning of July 19th the advance guard of the pursuing column drove in the rebel pickets, and the enemy was found in line of battle near Buffington's island. The river regiment, being in the advance, was the first to attack, and being reinforced by other troops, a sharp engagement ensued, which resulted in the defeat of the enemy, who fled from the field in the greatest disorder, leaving their artillery and dead and wounded on the field. The pursuit was continued until dark, up to which time eight hundred prisoners had been brought in, and the rest of the raiders scattered or hiding in the woods. After the pursuit ceased, a flag of truce was sent to Colonel Garrard, of the Seventh, the bearer announcing that Colonels Basil Duke and Howard Smith, of Morgan's command, with staff officers, had been cut off and were anxious to surrender. Two officers were sent to receive the surrender, and, upon arriving at the designated place, found that two colonels and several other officers and about fifty men had surrendered to *one soldier*, Sergeant Drake, of the Eighth Michigan cavalry.

The river regiment took part in the movement against Cumberland Gap, the gateway to East Tennessee, which stronghold was invested, and on September 9, 1863, the garrison of two thousand six hundred men, with fifteen pieces of artillery, surrendered, and the Seventh was detailed to receive the surrender.

On August 31st company H was acting as advance guard of the force moving on the Gap, and that night, being well in advance of the main column, they went into camp at a convenient place, and in the morning found they had gone into camp with a party of rebels. The enemy thinking there was a large force present "folded their tents and stole away" during the night, and stole some of the company's horses also. Camping with the enemy was an experiment they did not repeat.

On September 10th the Seventh cavalry took part in the night fight at Carter's station, in upper East Tennessee, driving the enemy away. They then repaired to Bull's gap, in Bey's mountain, forty miles east of Knoxville, and held that position until October 10th, when, in the battle of Blue Springs, it took part in the final charge, near nightfall, routing the rebels, who beat a hasty retreat.

On November 6th occurred the disastrous defeat at Rogersville, Tennessee, where the gallant Seventh, the Second Tennessee mounted infantry, and battery M, Second Illinois light artillery, in all about one thousand combatants, under command of Colonel Garrard of the Seventh, made a desperate stand against greatly superior numbers, losing one hundred and twelve men and some of its best officers. The orderly—Bugler Justus Schminke, a company H man from Marietta, was shot at his post by the side of Colonel Garrard. The enemy were said to number three thousand five hundred men.

From the thirteenth to the seventeenth of December, after the enemy retreated from Knoxville, the Seventh regiment was constantly fighting and skirmishing, subsisting during that time almost entirely on parched corn.

December 23, 1863, they engaged the rebels at New Market, and drove them out of that town Christmas day they crossed Bey's mountain and joined battle with a largely superior force of the enemy, and, after hard fighting all day, being surrounded at two different times, they were compelled to cut their way out.

The ten days following New Year's day, 1864, were the most dreary days in the history of the regiment; they and their comrades of the other regiments and army lay on the hills about Mossy creek, half starved. A bushel of corn meal was issued to a brigade of men for a day's rations. Horses died by the hundreds from starvation. It stormed fearfully, and the men were without shelter. There was but one blanket for every two men, and they were but scantily clothed for such severe weather.

On January 27, 1864, the regiment joined the force under General Sturgis, and gave battle to Morgan's and Armstrong's divisions of Wheeler's cavalry, at Fair Garden, Tennessee, defeating them and driving them across the French Broad river.

On June 11, 1864, the Seventh, with the force under General Burbridge, began the pursuit of Morgan's force, which had invaded Kentucky, and at daylight of June 12th, at Cynthiana, Kentucky, attacked, driving the rebels in confusion from the field. The left wing, led by company H, and commanded by Colonel Garrard, charged the enemy's right, broke through and reached the rear of the rebel line before it gave way on the centre or left, captured the bridge over the Licking river, on the rebel line of retreat, taking position on the opposite bank, with the rallying cry of "Rogersville," killed, wounded and captured a large number of the same

enemy who had defeated them at Rogersville, Tennessee, November 6, 1863. The regiment followed Morgan into the mountains of eastern Kentucky, until forage and supplies failed, when they returned. They had marched two hundred and seventy-two miles in six days and nights.

The regiment was ordered to join General Sherman's army then moving on Atalanta, and by July 26th arrived at that fated city, participated in all the movements around Atalanta, scouting and doing picket duty, until November 6th, when they were ordered to Nashville, where they arrived November 17, 1864.

On November 28, 1864, the Seventh was ordered to join the National forces, then retreating in the direction of Nashville, and at Duck river the regiment was surrounded by the enemy, and were compelled to cut their way out. At the battle of Franklin, Tennessee, the Seventh held the left of the line. In December, 1864, the regiment was assigned to the First brigade, Sixth division cavalry corps, commanded by General Wilson.

On December 15th the regiment participated in the great battle of Nashville, and, charging by squadrons, drove the enemy in its front a mile and a half, and captured four pieces of artillery, with men and horses. On the second day of the battle the regiment was actively engaged; and in the pursuit of Hood's army, on December 17th, marching by a detour to cut off the rebel rear guard, they struck the rebel centre at Franklin, and, charging into the town, found it swarming with rebels, who were fleeing and endeavoring to hide from their pursuers. The rebel officers were unable to bring their men into line, and hundreds of them were taken prisoners, including seven hundred officers and men, two thousand seven hundred rebel wounded, and a large number of National wounded in hospital at Franklin.

On Christmas day, 1864, the regiment engaged the rebel rear guard at Pulaski, drove them from that place in disorder, and captured three pieces of artillery, an ammunition train, etc. The pursuit ended on December 27th, when the rear guard of the defeated army of Hood crossed the Tennessee.

The Seventh then went into winter quarters at Gravelly Springs, Alabama, where they remained until March 22, 1865. At that date the cavalry corps commanded by General Wilson, started on the last great raid of the war. This force numbered about eighteen thousand men, the finest and best equipped body of cavalry of the war. They moved southward with irresistible momentum, driving the few scattered fragments of the rebel army like chaff before the wind. The object of the expedition was to cut off communication between the rebel armies of the east and west. The line of march of the Seventh regiment lay through Jasper, Georgia, Plantersville, Alabama, where three hundred prisoners were taken, Selma, Alabama, where a large number of prisoners were taken; at which place, on April 3d, the regiment had three thousand rebel prisoners in their possession. On April 12th they passed through Montgomery, the capital of Alabama; April 15th, through Tuskegee, Alabama. April 16th the regiment attacked Columbus, Georgia, at night, and captured the same, and on the eighteenth moved down the railroad toward the Andersonville prison pen ; and on the twentieth, while skirmishing with the enemy, a rebel officer appeared with a white flag, announcing the surrender of Lee at Appomatox, and end of the war. The pursuit was at once stopped, and the forces which a short time before had been engaged in deadly conflict joined hands and bivouacked on the same field.

The regiment went into camp at Macon, Georgia, on April 25th, and remained there until May 5th, when they were ordered to Atlanta, where they arrived May 9th.

On May 13th eighteen men from company H were detailed to guard Jefferson Davis, the president of the defunct confederacy, who had been captured in women's attire, endeavoring to effect his escape. He was taken to Augusta, Georgia.

On May 22d the regiment was ordered to Nashville, where they arrived June 6th, completing a ride of fifteen hundred miles on horseback.

June 30th the "River regiment" was mustered out of the United States service, and company H arrived at Marietta July 6, 1865.

The total number, including recruits, in the regiment during its service, was fourteen hundred; when mustered out it numbered eight hundred and forty, showing a loss of five hundred and sixty men by the casualties of war.

NINTH OHIO VOLUNTEER CAVALRY.

REGIMENTAL OFFICERS.

Colonel William D. Hamilton, mustered December 2, 1863, brevet brigadier general April 18, 1865; Lieutenant Colonel William D. Hamilton, October 30, 1863, promoted to colonel, Lieutenant Colonel Thomas P. Cook, December 2, 1863, discharged September 9, 1864; Lieutenant Colonel William Stough, October 1, 1864, mustered out with regiment; Major William D. Hamilton, December 6, 1862, promoted to lieutenant colonel; Major Thomas P. Cook, October 30, 1863, promoted to lieutenant colonel; Major William Sims, October 30, 1863, resigned June 21, 1864; Major John Williamson, December 2, 1863, resigned July 28, 1864; Major Henry Plessner, December 7, 1863, discharged January 13, 1865; Major Elijah Hoague, July 13, 1864, resigned March 9, 1865; Major William Stough, September 8, 1864, promoted to lieutenant colonel; Major L. H. Bowlus, October 1, 1864, mustered out with regiment; Major John W. Macumber, February 10, 1865, mustered out with regiment; Major James Irvine, May 31, 1865, mustered out with regiment; Major Joseph B. Daniels, February, 1864, mustered out with regiment; Surgeon C. M. Finch, October 5, 1863, mustered out with regiment; Assistant Surgeon William McMillen, March 26, 1863, mustered out with regiment; Assistant Surgeon James C. Thorpe, October 5, 1863, discharged April 18, 1864; Assistant Surgeon Charles H. Pinney, April 22, 1864, mustered out with regiment; Chaplain Ezekiel S. Hoagland, January 18, 1863, resigned August 20, 1864.

OFFICERS OF COMPANY B.

Captain John Williamson, mustered November 16, 1862, promoted to major; Captain Joseph B. Daniels, December 2, 1863, promoted to major; First Lieutenant Joseph B. Daniels, November 6, 1862, promoted to captain; First Lieutenant Richard B. Mason, December 22, 1863, deceased June 25, 1864; First Lieutenant James Stonehawker, July 30, 1864, mustered out with regiment; First Lieutenant Allen J. Alexander, February 10, 1865, honorably discharged March 25, 1865; Second Lieutenant Richard B. Mason, February 2, 1863, promoted to first lieutenant; Second Lieutenant James Stonehawker, October 10, 1863, promoted to first lieutenant; Second Lieutenant Allen J. Alexander, December 22, 1863, promoted to first lieutenant; Second Lieutenant Edward Ashley, May 31, 1865, mustered out with regiment; Second Lieutenant Bishop Martin, May 31, 1865, mustered out with regiment.

NINTH OHIO VOLUNTEER CAVALRY.

Company B, of this regiment, was from Washington county. They were raised in the fall of 1862, under the authority of Governor Tod, to make three new regiments of cavalry, the Eighth, Ninth and Tenth. Captain William D. Hamilton, of the Thirty-second Ohio volunteer infantry, then stationed at Winchester, Virginia, had been sent to Ohio to recruit another company for that regiment. He had secured fifty men, when his regiment, with others, was captured by "Stonewall" Jackson, on the fifteenth of September, 1862. Governor Tod then ordered Captain Hamilton to proceed at once to organize a cavalry regiment, to be called the Ninth Ohio volunteer cavalry.

The fifty recruits above referred to formed a nucleus for the new organization, which rendezvoused at Zanesville, and on December 1, 1862, seven companies were ready for muster. Three companies, however, were transferred to the Tenth cavalry, then organizing at Cleveland, to complete that regiment. The four remaining companies were ordered to Camp Dennison. They were designtaed as the First battalion of the Ninth cavalry, were equipped and drilled until April 23, 1863, when they were ordered to Lexington, Kentucky. The battalion under command of Captain Hamilton, numbering three hundred men, were soon actively engaged driving out raiders and marauders who were so frequently coming down from the Kentucky and Tennessee mountains into the Blue Grass region.

On June 15, 1863, they joined an expedition designed to penetrate into East Tennessee and find out the situation of the loyal inhabitants of that region. The whole force consisted of about two thousand mounted men, of which two hundred were from the battalion, including company B. Crossing the Cumberland river on the night of June 16th, they were soon at Pine Mountain gap, a rebel stronghold. Here the garrison was surprised and captured without firing a shot, and they passed on to Big Creek gap, the Ninth cavalry battalion in the advance. The rebel force at this gap evacuated and fled.

The objects of the raid were accomplished without further opposition, and they returned to London, Kentucky. The battalion on July 5th was ordered to move out after John Morgan, but Morgan having passed by, the battalion was ordered to watch and embarrass the progress of the rebel General Scott, who was reported moving to the support of Morgan. The battalion joined a hastily gathered force at Camp Dick Robinson, and went in pursuit of Scott, who had passed with his command to the right. They then had a running fight for ten days; the battalion marching at the rate of fifty-seven miles in twenty four hours, the men living chiefly on blackberries gathered at the roadside while the horses were resting.

On August 1st the battalion went from Stanford to Glasgow, Kentucky, and were there assigned to a cavalry brigade for General Burnside's advance into East Tennessee. The capture of Knoxville was effected without much opposition, and Major Hamilton was appointed provost marshal of the city, and the first battalion assigned to patrol and guard duty on the approaches of the city.

The Second battalion was organized November 6th, and the Third battalion December 16, 1863, thus completing the regiment. The two battalions were filled to their maximum, and together with one hundred recruits for the old battalion, were rendezvoused at Camp Dennison and furnished with horses, equipped with sabres and Smith carbines, and carefully drilled until February 6, 1864, when they were ordered by water to Nashville, Tennessee. Arriving at Louisville they were disembarked to follow some guerillas, who were reported to be making trouble in Kentucky. They marched through the country to Nashville without opposition. The regiment was then attached to the left wing of the Sixteenth army corps, and ordered to Athens, Alabama, for field duty along the Tennessee river.

Colonel Hamilton at this time went to Knoxville with orders from the First battalion to join the regiment. The severe campaign through which the First battalion had passed, ending at Knoxville, rendered an entire new equipment necessary. For this purpose they were ordered to Nashville, and after considerable delay waiting for horses, they were again ready for active service. Captain Joseph B. Daniels was now placed in command of the First battalion and so remained until the end—towards the last being in command of the entire regiment. The battalion now moved to Pulaski, Tennessee, and occupied that place about six weeks, Captain Daniels being in command of the post. Several movements were undertaken against the rebel cavalry under Wheeler and Forrest, for which the whole regiment combined, but were not permanently united until all of the battalions reached Athens, in April, 1864.

On the night of April 13, 1864, a company of the Ninth, which with others had been sent out to look for stock, was surrounded in a barn where they were sleeping. The attack was made by an Alabama regiment, and after a short struggle, two officers and thirty-nine men were captured. The remaining three companies soon came to the rescue, but not in time to rescue their comrades.

The non-commissioned officers and men thus taken were sent to Andersonville prison. Eight months after, a report from Orderly Sergeant Kennedy showed that twenty-five of their number had died from brutal treatment.

The two officers taken were Captain Joseph N. Hetzler and Lieutenant Frank H. Knapp, who were sent to Columbia, South Carolina. Lieutenant Knapp, after two efforts to escape, in which he was retaken by the aid of bloodhounds, finally succeeded in reaching Knoxville, Tennessee, after travelling three weeks, principally at night, securing food and assistance from the negroes. At one time he heard the hounds on his trail, and again would have been captured but for the generous assistance of a negro, who, after giving him something to eat, said: "Now, bress de Lord, massa Yank, you jist trust to me and we'll fool dem dogs. You trot along fust, den I'll come too, steppin' in your tracks. Go 'bout half a mile,

den you come to some watah; you take right through dat, den I'll keep on t'other way. See dem dogs is used to huntin' niggers, dey knows de smell, and likes to follow de black man's foot." "But," said the lieutenant, surprised at this singular offer, "the dogs will catch you and probably tear you to pieces." "Oh, massa," said he, "let dis nigger alone for dat, I'se fooled dem dogs afore for de Yanks, and, bress de Lord, I'll try it again. Now trot along, massa, for I hear dem dogs a comin'." Shortly after crossing the pond the lieutenant heard the hounds howling in the direction taken by the negro, and he was no longer disturbed by them. He afterwards joined the regiment at Savannah, Georgia, in January, 1865. Captain Hetzler remained a prisoner until near the close of the war, when he was exchanged.

Another battalion of the Ninth was sent out in the vicinity of Florence, to guard the river, thus, for a distance of fifty miles, the Tennessee was patrolled by the two battalions of the regiment, having frequent skirmishes with the enemy.

On May 5, 1864, the regiment arrived at Decatur, Alabama, and on the eighth the place was attacked by the enemy. The Ninth moved out beyond the works a mile and a half, to develop the enemy's strength. The country was about equally divided between timber and level, open land. The rebels formed on the open ground, and, as the Ninth swung around the timber, a battle ensued, in which the rebels were driven back in confusion. The regiment lost one man killed and three severely wounded. From this time until June 1st, cavalry skirmishes were of daily occurrence.

The Seventh Illinois infantry having been driven from Florence to Pulaski, the Ninth went to reinforce that regiment. After driving the enemy beyond Florence, they returned to Decatur.

The Ninth was engaged on various expeditions in the region about Atlanta up to the fall of that city, immediately before the evacuation being attached to the cavalry division under Colonel Garrard, on the extreme right of General Sherman's army. The First battalion was engaged in the battle of Jonesborough.

Four hundred men of the Ninth were now ordered to Nashville to procure horses. On the night of September 2, 1864, while the train containing the men was passing Big Shanty, Georgia, it was thrown from the track and six cars demolished. The enemy, concealed beside the track, opened fire on the wreck; the fire was returned, and the cowards fled. One man was killed and three wounded by the accident, and two killed and five wounded by the enemy's fire. Failing to procure horses at Nashville, the regiment proceeded to Louisville, and having received fresh horses returned to Nashville en route to the front.

This battalion arriving at Nashville found the rebel General Wheeler within twelve miles of the city, and they were sent out with other forces to meet and drive him back. They encountered him at various places during the next ten days until he was finally compelled to retire beyond the Tennessee. They soon received orders to report at once to Marietta, Georgia, to join the regiment which was to form a part of one of Sherman's new cavalry divisions in the "March to the Sea." The battalion found Marietta burned, and pressing on rapidly arrived at Atlanta November 17th, and found it evacuated, having marched eighty miles in thirty-six hours. They proceeded on to McDowell, seventeen miles southward, where they joined the balance of the regiment. They now numbered seven hundred effective men. From this time on they were busily engaged covering the march of the infantry, making false marches to deceive the enemy, and fighting almost daily, until December 4th, at Waynesborough, when a general engagement occurred, in which the Ninth made the second charge that broke the rebel lines.

Arriving at Savannah they were sent on an expedition during the progress of the siege, to destroy railroad communication with the city. Captain Joseph B. Daniels, with the First battalion, was ordered to approach and burn the bridge, and engaging the enemy with their Spencer carbines drove them to cover and burnt the bridge.

The army remained at Savannah after its evacuation until the latter part of January, 1865, at which time one hundred and fifty men of the Ninth, that had been left with the army of General Thomas, and who participated in the battle of Franklin and Nashville, joined the regiment.

On the night of February 3, 1865, the cavalry division crossed the Savannah river at Sisters' Ferry, forty miles above the city, and entered upon the march through the Carolinas. On the sixth the Ninth having the advance, engaged the enemy at a swamp near Barnwell. The men were dismounted and wading the swamp under cover of the timber, drove the enemy from their position. As they progressed through the Carolinas, the forage and grain grew scarce and together with wearing service in the swamps, rendered a great many horses unfit for service, and as a consequence many of cavalrymen were dismounted. These were organized into a "dismounted command." On the night of the ninth of March General Kilpatrick went into camp with the Third brigade and the dismounted men, about three miles in advance of the remainder of his command. On the tenth the rebels under General Hampton dashed in upon the camp, and captured the wagons, artillery and many of the officers and men before they had time to dress themselves. The dismounted men, however, opened a close and heavy fire upon the rebels, who were pillaging the camp. A sharp fight ensued, during which the artillerymen recovered their cannon, and opened on the enemy. The Second brigade soon arrived, and the rebels were forced to retire. The loss of the Nationals was twenty-five, and the rebels, seventy-five killed in this short but desperate contest.

In the battle of Averysborough, on March 15th, the Ninth supported the right flank of the Twentieth corps, and was in the thickest of the contest, and at the battle of Bentonville, North Carolina, March 18th to 21st, the final contest of the grand army under General Sherman, General Kilpatrick's entire command occupied the left

flank. The enemy being defeated, they occupied Goldsborough, and remained there until April 10th. They entered Raleigh after a slight skirmish April 14th. On the morning of the eighteenth, part of the rebel army occupied the village of Chapel Hill. General Wheeler's rebel cavalry covered the approach to the town, occupying a swamp through which the road passed. At daylight the regiment was ordered to effect a crossing if possible. Arriving at the swamp, the second battalion was ordered forward, dismounted, through the water. They advanced under cover of the cypress timber until the enemy came within range of their Spencer carbines. A spirited engagement ensued, in which the enemy were driven from their position, leaving a captain and staff-officer of General Wheeler, and three men dead on the field.

Orders in the meantime arrived from General Sherman suspending hostilities.

After the surrender the command was ordered to Concord, North Carolinia, where it remained until the last of July.

On August 2, 1865, the regimental colors and property were turned over at Columbus, Ohio, and the regiment was mustered out of the service.

SECOND VIRGINIA VOLUNTEER CAVALRY.

REGIMENTAL OFFICERS.

Colonel William M. Bolles, mustered September 16, 1861, resigned June 25, 1862; Colonel John C. Paxton, July 18, 1862, honorably discharged; Colonel William H. Powell, May 18, 1863, promoted to brigadier general; Lieutenant Colonel John C. Paxton, September 16, 1861; promoted to colonel; Lieutenant Colonel Rollin L. Curtis, August 19, 1862, resigned October 25, 1862; Lieutenant Colonel William H. Powell, December 5, 1862, promoted to colonel; Lieutenant Colonel David Done, May 18, 1863, resigned July 5, 1864; Lieutenant Colonel John J. Hoffman, July 14, 1864, mustered out; Lieutenant Colonel James Allen, November 26, 1864; Major Rollin L. Curtis, October 2, 1861, promoted to lieutenant colonel; Major John J. Hoffman, October 2, 1861, promoted to lieutenant colonel; Major Henry Stembach, February 5, 1862, mustered out; Major William H. Powell, August 19, 1862, promoted to lieutenant colonel; Major John McMahon, January 2, 1863; Major James Allen, April 29, 1864, promoted to lieutenant colonel; Major Charles E. Hambleton, July 14, 1864, mustered out; Major Edwin S. Morgan, November 26, 1864; Adjutant John P. Merrill, October 25, 1861, resigned June 5, 1862; Adjutant Elijah F. Gillon, November 5, 1862, resigned September 7, 1864; Adjutant Earl A. Cranston, November 12, 1861, resigned June 2, 1862; Adjutant George E. Downing, October 25, 1861, resigned May 1, 1862; Quartermaster Sayres G. Payton, October 2, 1861, mustered out; Quartermaster William Holden, October 23, 1861, resigned March 13, 1862; Commissary George S. South, January 2, 1863, mustered out at expiration of term; Surgeon Thomas S. Neal, October 25, 1861, resigned February 9, 1862; Surgeon Matthew McEwen, January 17, 1863; Assistant Surgeon Lucien L. Comstock, November 6, 1863, promoted to surgeon of Eighth West Virginia infantry; Assistant Surgeon Ozias Neltis, March 6, 1863, mustered out at expiration of term; Assistant Surgeon Edward L. Gillian, May 18, 1863; Chaplain Charles M. Bethauser, October 2, 1861, resigned October 12, 1862.

OFFICERS OF COMPANY F.

Captain Arthur D. Eells, November 22, 1861, resigned May 6, 1862; Captain Oliver H. P. Scott, June 26, 1862, resigned December 23, 1862; Captain George Millard, April 1, 1863, mustered out at expiration of term; Captain Henry F. Swentzel, November 26, 1864, promoted from Seventy-ninth Pennsylvania infantry to company E, and from company E to company F; Captain George W. Gilmore; Captain Ed. A. Rosser, promoted from company B; Captain E. S. Fisher; Captain Oliver C. Ong; First Lieutenant Oliver H. P. Scott, November 22, 1861, promoted to captain; First Lieutenant William M. Fortescue, June 26, 1862, promoted to captain of company I; First Lieutenant George Millard, November 5, 1862, promoted to captain; First Lieutenant

Lloyd B. Stephens, April 1, 1862, resigned July 13, 1864; First Lieutenant Charles C. Clise, November 26, 1864; Second Lieutenant William M. Fortescue, November 22, 1861, promoted to first lieutenant; Second Lieutenant George Millard, June 26, 1862, promoted to first lieutenant, Second Lieutenant Lloyd B. Stephens, November 5, 1862, promoted to first lieutenant; Second Lieutenant Oliver C. Ong, April 1, 1863, mustered out; Second Lieutenant Elisha T. Fisher, November 26, 1864.

The Second Virginia cavalry was recruited entirely from the border counties of Ohio. Commencing at Monroe all the counties were represented by one or more companies, ending with Lawrence county. Company F was the Washington county organization. Recruiting for it began in August, 1861, under the management of Captain Arthur D. Eells, and by September the company was in camp at Parkersburgh, West Virginia, where the regiment was mustered into service November 8th. The fall and early winter of 1861 were spent in drill on foot and sword exercise at Parkersburgh, West Virginia. In January the regiment was moved to Guandotte, West Virginia, where they received their horses and completed their drill mounted. The first engagement of the regiment was with General Humphrey Marshall January 6, 1862, on Point Creek, Kentucky. The Union forces were under the command of General (afterward President) Garfield. The first loss of Washington county in battle in the war was Albert W. Leonard, shot in the forehead while in a charge on James' Creek January 7, 1862. His body lies in Mound cemetery at Marietta. On the twenty-eighth of April company F left Guyandotte with the half of the regiment under Colonel William M. Bolles, and marched up the Big Kanawha, and over the Sewell mountains and joined the forces of Colonel Elliott of the Forty-seventh Ohio infantry at Meadow Bluff, Virginia. The summer of 1862 was spent in raiding and scouting the counties of Raleigh, Wyoming, Fayette, Greenbrier, Union and Nicholas. These trips brought on many skirmishes and some battles, that of Lewisburgh, May 23d, being quite severe. Company F was with Colonel Paxton, who left Camp Piatt November 24, 1862, and surprised the rebel General Jenkins at Sinking Creek, Virginia, capturing one hundred and seventeen prisoners, one hundred and ten horses, and two hundred and fifty stand of arms. This was one of the most severe marches made during the war, both as regards cold and hard riding. The troops were in the saddle for seventy consecutive hours on the latter part of their trip; and on their arrival at Summerville, West Virginia, numbers had to be lifted out of their saddle, they were so badly frozen. The winter of 1862–63 was spent at Camp Piatt on the Big Kanawha. With the spring of 1863 scouting began early. July 18th the company was in the severe fight at Wytheville, where both colonels were lost. Colonel Toland, of the Thirtyfourth Ohio volunteer infantry, in command of the expedition, was shot dead, and Colonel W. H. Powell, of the Second Virginia cavalry, wounded so badly as to be left and taken prisoner. In this battle one hundred and twenty-five prisoners were taken and seventy-five rebels were killed; Union loss, seventy-eight killed, wounded and missing, the houses in Wytheville having been used

as places of concealment from which to pick off the Union soldiers, even the women of the town taking part in the fight. The town was totally destroyed.

The regiment was also in engagements at Lewisburgh May 3d, November 7th, and December 12, 1863.

The winter of 1863–64 was spent at Charleston, West Virginia, and it was at this place that the regiment was brought up to its high standard of drill. The regiment started March 16, 1864, on a scout through Hurricane Bridge, Gyandotte, Trouts Hill and Wayne Court House. The weather was very cold on this trip.

May 1st the regiment was attached to General Averill's division, and with him was in the raid to Wytheville on the Virginia & Tennessee railroad. The route lay through Brownstown, Logan Court House, Wyoming, Tug Fork of Sandy and Jeffersonville. The rebels were met at Cove Gap, a few miles this side of Wytheville, under General John Morgan, and a very severe battle was fought. General Averill complimented the regiment in general orders, saying: "The general commanding desires to express his high appreciation of the steady and skilful evolutions of the Second Virginia cavalry under Colonel Powell upon the field of battle. It was a dress parade that continued without disorder under a heavy fire for over four hours." Company F was with the regiment and participated in all of the engagements on the Hunter road to Lynchburgh, Virginia; was also with it in the Shenandoah valley, being in the fight at Bunker Hill, Stevenson's depot, Winchester, Newton, Kearnstown, Fisher Hill, Mt. Jackson, Cross Keys, Port Republic, Brown's Gap, Luray, Harrisonville, Weirs Cave, Opequan, Martinsburgh, Williamsport, Hagerstown, Chambersburgh, Pennsylvania; St. Thomas, Pennsylvania; Moorfield, Virginia, and many other places. The winter of 1864–65 was spent in the Shenandoah valley, but when in 1865 General Sheridan went up the valley to Waynesborough and on over to the White House, Virginia, company F was along doing fine service. This company held the key to the hill at Dinwiddie Court House, Virginia; was in the charge at Five Forks, Ford's Station, Deep Creek, Namozin Church, Jettersville, and in the first charge at Sailors' Creek; also in the desperate engagement at Appomattox Court House, and on the morning of the ninth of April took part in the final charge on the flank of Lee's army, which would have resulted in the surrender of General Lee to General Custer but for the arrival of General Grant on the ground. After the surrender the company marched to Petersburgh where it remained with the regiment until the 23d of April, when it moved to intercept Johnson's army in North Carolina, but was ordered back at Halifax Court House. From there the company marched to Richmond, Virginia, thence to Washington City. In the grand review company F led the cavalry column in review. On the seventeenth of June the regiment was ordered to Texas via Louisville, Kentucky, but was stopped at Wheeling and mustered out, June 20, 1865.

Company F lost the first and last man killed in battle from Washington county.

The neighborhoods that furnished the most men to

John C. Partin

this company were, first, Coal Run; second, Plymouth; third, Moss Run; fourth, Marietta.

COMPANY F, EIGHTEENTH OHIO VOLUNTEER INFANTRY.

REGIMENTAL OFFICERS.

[Three years' service].

Colonel Timothy R. Stanley, mustered August 6, 1861, mustered out November 9, 1864; Colonel Charles H. Grosvenor, April 8, 1865, provost marshal; Lieutenant Colonel Josiah Given August 17, 1861, appointed Colonel Seventy-fourth regiment; Lieutenant Colonel Charles H. Grosvenor, March 16, 1863, promoted to colonel; Lieutenant Colonel John M. Benedict, April 8, 1865, mustered out with regiment; Major Charles H. Grosvenor, July 30, 1861, promoted to lieutenant colonel; Major J. M. Welch, March 16, 1863, mustered out November 9, 1864; Major John M. Benedict, February 1, 1865, promoted to lieutenant colonel; Major Robert B. Chappell, April 8, 1865, mustered out with regiment; Surgeon William P. Johnson, September 24, 1861, mustered out November 9, 1864; Surgeon Horace P. Kay, February 20, 1865, mustered out with regiment; Assistant Surgeon William W. Mills, September 24, 1861, resigned February 28, 1864; Assistant Surgeon Charles H. French, January 1, 1863, mustered out November 9, 1864; Assistant Surgeon Arthur C. Newell, May 2, 1865, mustered out October 9, 1865; Assistant Surgeon S. A. Baxter, May 29, 1865, mustered out October 9, 1865; Chaplain John Dillon, September 16, 1861, mustered out November 9, 1864

OFFICERS OF COMPANY F.

Captain John J. Jumper, mustered September 8, 1861, resigned October 4, 1863; First Lieutenant Robert R. Danford, September 8, 1861, resigned January 17, 1862; First Lieutenant William B. Williams, February 3, 1862, resigned February 8, 1863; First Lieutenant Charles M. Grubb, April 14, 1863, mustered out November 9, 1864; First Lieutenant David J. Searight, July 12, 1864, mustered out November 9, 1864; First Lieutenant John G. G. Carter, March 29, 1865, transferred to adjutant Eighteenth Ohio volunteer infantry, September 1, 1865; Second Lieutenant William B. Williams, September 8, 1861, promoted to first lieutenant; Second Lieutenant Charles M. Grubb, March 15, 1862, promoted to first lieutenant; Second Lieutenant David J. Searight, April 14, 1863, promoted to first lieutenant; Second Lieutenant John G. G. Carter, December 21, 1864, promoted to first lieutenant; Second Lieutenant James W. Slater, May 31, 1865, mustered out with regiment.

This company was made up of men from Beverly and Newport, Washington county, and Windsor and Ringgold, Morgan county, and was organized early in September, 1861, at Camp Putnam, Marietta, Ohio. John J. Jumper was elected captain.

About the middle of the month company F joined the regiment at Camp Wood, Athens, Ohio, and the regimental organization was completed at Camp Dennison, November 4, 1861.

From Camp Dennison the regiment went to Louisville, Kentucky, arriving November 7th and remaining there about a month, and marching from there to Bacon Creek, where they remained about two months and drilled. Arrived at Green river February 7, 1862, and on the next day started for Bowling Green, which place was occupied on the tenth. Remained there until the twenty-third. After the fall of Fort Donelson they proceeded to Nashville, Tennessee, a distance of sixty-two miles, in three days. At Nashville the regiment encamped until March 18th, suffering many privations and hardships, when they started for Huntsville, Alabama, arriving April 11th. Thence they went to Tuscumbia, Alabama, thence to Athens, Alabama, and deployed along the railroad.

May 1st they were attacked by Scott's rebel cavalry and driven back towards Huntsville, company F going as far as Madison station, where, falling in with a part of the Thirty-third Ohio, they halted and remained.

On May 3d company F and a detail from the Thirty-third Ohio and Twenty-second Kentucky acted as guard to a train that was gathering up cotton that had been used in fortifying at places between Huntsville and Athens, returning to the station at night, where they remained until the ninth, when they moved to Athens.

On the twenty-first company F, with four other companies, guarded a supply train to Huntsville, returning the next day, and remaining at Athens until the thirtieth, when they started for Fayetteville, arriving next day, and where they remained until June 23d, when they marched to Huntsville. All these movements were made under the command of General O. M. Mitchell, who had been sent southward by General Don Carlos Buell, commanding the army of the Ohio, to annoy the enemy and keep him busy while other and more important movements were being consummated.

The regiment at this time was brigaded with the Nineteenth and Twenty-fourth Illinois and the Thirty-seventh Indiana, under the command of Colonel Turchin. At one place during these movements, Tuscumbia, Colonel Turchin, with but a small force, including the Eighteenth regiment, held the town, which was surrounded by a greatly superior force of rebels. In order to keep up the appearance of a large force, however, he had the names of officers from a dozen regiments entered upon the hotel register of the town, whose regiments were supposed to be in camp, but in reality he had not more than six hundred men, all told. No citizens were allowed to leave the town. Soon General Buell ordered all the territory west of Decatur evacuated, and the regiment went to Athens, Alabama.

At Battle Creek they found the enemy in force across the stream, and shelled them, but received no response. July 1st, company F, with C and B, was on detached duty, but soon rejoined the regiment. July 13th the regiment started for Tullahoma, and camped at the foot of the mountain near that place, in the evening. On the fourteenth they passed up and over the mountain. Just at sunset they reached the summit, and began the descent by a very difficult route, reaching the valley about 8 P. M., without serious accident.

July 15th they marched from Decherd for Caledonia, where the regiment remained until July 24th, when they started for Tullahoma, arriving there the day following, when company F was thrown out as a picket guard around the town. August 8th they left Tullahoma for Duck river, and from there went to Manchester. September 3rd the regiment arrived at Murfreesborough, and September 8th arrived at Nashville, and remained there until December 10th, when the regiment went down the Franklin pike about four miles, and encamped until the twenty-sixth, when a general advance was ordered, which was continued until December 30th, when they went into the great battle of Stone River, which continued for three days with terrible carnage, in which the gallant Eighteenth did noble service.

In June, 1863, the regiment was with the force that crossed Lookout mountain into McLamore cove, and confronted Bragg at Dug Gap, September 11th, and the eighteenth, with the balance of the brigade, held the enemy in check.

At Chickamauga the regiment did not participate in the first day's battle, but on Sunday, September 20th, was in the thickest of the engagement, making several brilliant charges.

From this time until the expiration of their term of service the regiment was on engineering duty, and on October 20, 1864, was ordered to Camp Chase, to be mustered out, and on November 9th it was mustered out. Nearly one hundred men reenlisted as veterans, and with those whose time had not expired numbered two hundred and twenty-five men.

Upon reenlisting, the First, Second, Eighteenth, Twenty-fourth, and Thirty-fifth Ohio regiments were consolidated under the name of the Eighteenth Ohio, commanded by Lieutenant Colonel C. H. Grosvenor. The regiment took part in the battle of Nashville, December 6, 1864, losing four officers out of seven, and seventy-five men in killed and wounded out of less than two hundred.

The regiment was engaged from this time to the end of the war in garrison duty. In July, 1865, the regiment was stationed at Augusta, Georgia, and Colonel (now general) Grosvenor was assigned to duty as provost marshal general of the department, where they remained until October 9th, when they were ordered to Columbus, Ohio, to be mustered out, and were there honorably discharged October 22, 1865.

COMPANIES A, F, AND G, THIRTY-SIXTH OHIO VOLUNTEERS.

REGIMENTAL OFFICERS

Colonel George Crook, mustered September 12, 1861, appointed brigadier general September 7, 1862; Colonel Melvin Clarke, September 7, 1862, killed at Antietam September 17, 1862; Colonel Ebenezer B. Andrews, September 17, 1862, resigned April 9, 1863; Colonel William G. Jones, April 13, 1863, killed September 19, 1863, at Chickamauga; Colonel Hiram F. Devol, September 19, 1863, appointed brevet brigadier general July 20, 1865; Lieutenant Colonel Melvin Clarke, July 30, 1861, promoted to colonel September 16, 1862; Lieutenant Colonel E. B. Andrews, September 7, 1862, promoted to colonel September 17, 1862; Lieutenant Colonel Hiram F. Devol, September 17, 1862, promoted to colonel; Lieutenant Colonel William H. G. Adney, May 9, 1864, mustered out; Lieutenant Colonel William S. Wilson, March 8, 1865, mustered out with regiment; Major E. B. Andrews, July 28, 1861, promoted to lieutenant colonel September 16, 1862; Major Hiram F. Devol, September 7, 1862, promoted to lieutenant colonel; Major William H. G. Adney, September 17, 1862, promoted to lieutenant colonel; Major Jewett Palmer, jr., May 9, 1864, resigned November 30, 1864; Major William S. Wilson, December 30, 1864, mustered out; Major Benjamin J. Ricker, jr., February 3, 1865, transferred from Thirth-fourth Ohio volunteer infantry; Surgeon Robert N. Barr, August 22, 1861, resigned February 25, 1862, Surgeon J. H. Whitford, March 8, 1862, mustered out with regiment; Assistant Surgeon J. H. Whitford, August 23, 1861, promoted to surgeon; Assistant Surgeon Colin Mackenzie, March 8, 1862, resigned May 19, 1863; Assistant Surgeon John Dickerson, July 4, 1862, promoted to surgeon of new regiment; Assistant Surgeon James P. Welch, July 24, 1862, resigned September 18, 1864; Assistant Surgeon B. F. Holcomb, March 14, 1865, mustered out with regiment; Assistant Surgeon A. M. Beers, June 26, 1865, did not accept; Chaplain George V. Fry, August, 1861, resigned January 31, 1862; Chaplain J. G. Blair, July 25, 1864, mustered out; Chaplain G. W. Collier, August 30, 1861, mustered out; Chaplain William S. Taylor, February 1, 1862, resigned April 30, 1862; Quartermaster First Lieutenant Levi Barber, August 31, 1861, resigned November 29, 1862; Quartermaster Captain Thomas M. Turner, December 30, 1864, declined promotion, promoted to captain December 1, 1862, from first lieutenant, mustered out with regiment as regimental

quartermaster; Quartermaster First Lieutenant John M. Woodbridge, July 31, 1861, resigned; Chief Musician Ebenezer Cory, August, 1861, mustered out at expiration of three years; Chief Musician John Tenney, September, 1864, mustered out with regiment.

COMPANY OFFICERS.

Captain H. F. Devol, mustered August 1, 1861, promoted to major September 7, 1862; Captain Thomas W. Moore, August 24, 1861, resigned March 5, 1862; Captain Jewett Palmer, jr., August 24, 1861, promoted to major; Captain Reuben L. Nye, March 3, 1862, mustered out with regiment; Captain Joseph Kelly, March 5, 1862, mustered out with regiment; Captain James Stanley, June 6, 1862, honorably discharged November 25, 1864; Captain Augustus T. Ward, December 30, 1864, mustered out with regiment; Captain James Gage Barker, September 7, 1862, mustered out November 4, 1864; Captain James C. Selby, October 3, 1862, died of wounds September 14, 1864; Captain Wallace S. Stanley, December 30, 1864, mustered out with regiment; Captain James Haddow, December 30, 1864, mustered out with regiment; Captain Miles A. Stacy, December 30, 1864, resigned as first lieutenant December 1, 1864, Captain Jesse Morrow, December 30, 1864, mustered out with regiment; First Lieutenant James Gage Barker, August 13, 1861, promoted to captain; First Lieutenant Joseph Kelly, August 24, 1861, promoted to captain; First Lieutenant James Stanley, August 24, 1861, promoted to captain; First Lieutenant James C. Selby, March 5, 1862, promoted to captain; First Lieutenant A. F. Tiffany, September 17, 1862, resigned November 18, 1863; First Lieutenant O. J. Wood, November 29, 1862, resigned August 27, 1863; First Lieutenant Jesse Morrow, February 22, 1863, promoted to captain; First Lieutenant Miles A. Stacy, January 17, 1863, promoted to captain; First Lieutenant Augustus T. Ward, April 21, 1864, promoted to captain; First Lieutenant James Haddow, May 9, 1864, promoted to captain; First Lieutenant Samuel S. Grosvenor, December 30, 1864, honorably discharged as second lieutenant; First Lieutenant George W. Putnam, December 30, 1864, honorably discharged as second lieutenant; First Lieutenant S. W. Harvey, December 30, 1864, mustered out with regiment; First Lieutenant John A. Palmer, September 1, 1862, resigned June 18, 1863; Second Lieutenant James C. Selby, August 13, 1861, promoted to first lieutenant; Second Lieutenant A. F. Tiffany, August 24, 1861, promoted to first lieutenant; Second Lieutenant Ernst Lindner, August 24, 1861, resigned June 28, 1862; Second Lieutenant Reuben L. Nye, July 30, 1861, promoted to captain March 3, 1862; Second Lieutenant John A. Palmer, March 5, 1862, promoted to first lieutenant; Second Lieutenant O. J. Wood, February 5, 1862, promoted to first lieutenant; Second Lieutenant Miles A. Stacy, June 28, 1862, promoted to first lieutenant; Second Lieutenant Wallace S. Stanley, June 28, 1862, promoted to first lieutenant; Second Lieutenant Augustus T. Ward, September 17, 1862, promoted to first lieutenant; Second Lieutenant Jesse Morrow, July 28, 1862, promoted to first lieutenant; Second Lieutenant James Haddow, September 17, 1862, promoted to first lieutenant; Second Lieutenant Samuel L. Grosvenor, October 24, 1863, promoted to first lieutenant; Second Lieutenant George W. Putnam, October 24, 1862, promoted to first lieutenant; Second Lieutenant Ransom C. Wyatt, March 8, 1865, mustered out at expiration of service; Second Lieutenant Benajmin Bragg, March 8, 1865; mustered out with regiment; Second Lieutenant Samuel W. Harvey, April 21, 1864, promoted to first lieutenant.

Under the call of President Lincoln, July 22, 1861, for five hundred thousand men, Lieutenant Colonel Melvin Clarke was authorized to organize a regiment at Camp Putnam, Marietta, Ohio. He at once set about it, and hearing that a company was being formed at Lowell for the Thirty-ninth Ohio—Colonel Groesbeck— he met that company on its organization, August 1st, and made known his purpose, asking that the company report at Camp Putnam to form a nucleus for his regiment. He solicited the forming of companies in this and other counties, and the following reported and were mustered in: August 13th, company A; August 14th company B; August 14th, company C; August 22d, company D; August 22d, company E; August 24th, company F; August 24th, company G; August 24th, company H; August 24th, company I, August 31st, company K.

Nearly the maximum number being mustered in, the regiment was armed with the old United States muskets, and uniformed. Not having a colonel, the line officers had a well grounded notion that only a regular army officer could drill and make a standard regiment equal to the ambition of its members. This wish being favorably regarded by the field officers and governor, efforts were made to secure one through the Secretary of War.

In this condition the regiment was ordered, August 30, 1861, to the field, taking transports at Marietta for Parkersburgh. Six companies, A, B, F, G, H and I, under command of Major E. B. Andrews, were there met by Major A. J. Slemmer—at that time of General Rosecrans staff—under the charge of Major Slemmer were transported by cars to Walker station—a few miles out. From that point marched over the mountains. Company A had one man killed that day by the accidental discharge of a musket—Private Steward, from Pinchville.

Arrived at Elizabeth after dark, foot-sore and weary. The object of this forced march was to clear the country of bands of guerillas.

The next morning the advance was fired on by a squad of these fellows from a hill fronting the turn of the road. One of the men was wounded in the shoulder. A company was thrown forward as skirmishers and soon dislodged them. Camped at Reedy that night. The next day marched for Spencer, the county east of Roane county. The place was surrounded by guerillas and three of its loyal citizens had been killed by them. On the approach of the regiment they fled. The people were found in a truly pitiable condition—nothing but corn-meal to subsist on. Rations having given out the men were in much the same plight for two days. Scouts brought in a little beef, but salt there was none. This kind of diet was new, and on the whole it seemed as if the regiment was being roughly initiated. The supply train that three days later followed was surrounded at Reedy. A night march of two companies relieved and brought it forward. Guerillas seemed to be upon all the hills and frequently their signals could be heard. Like the foxes, they knew the woods and were never seen at their houses during the day, so it seemed impossible to catch them. This was a new kind of warfare for the regular major, and when the regiment moved away—being relieved by another command—he ordered flanking parties as skirmishers in advance of the column.

The day before leaving Spencer it was thought best to unload the muskets. A target at fifty yards was placed and the men in turn tried their skill. The small men at every discharge would be either upset or faced about. The recoil of those old muskets with their heavy charge of powder, ball and three buckshot was about as fatal at the rear as in front. The target was not hit. Loud was the cursing of the men. They saw their guns were useless, which accounted for their never bringing down a single bushwhacker, despite their many chances. The march lay through Arnoldsburgh, Bulltown, Sutton to Summerville, Nicholas county. Lieutenant Colonel Clarke, with the other four companies, C, D, E and K, soon joined the regiment, and in a few days Colonel George Crook, who had been appointed to command it, arrived to the great joy of the men.

At this period was laid the solid foundation which gave to the regiment confidence in the future and secured for it a place second to none in the service. Colonel Crook instituted a perfect system of drill and a school in which officers were drilled, and recitations regularly held; and the officers drilled the men. A large drill house was erected that all could use at the same time. Leather stocks—called by the men "dog collars," were worn under the chin to set the men up. The old muskets were exchanged for new Enfield rifles. The entire regiment was quartered in the houses of people who left at the approach of the Union army. This crowding in houses, change of diet—this seasoning process—caused sickness, typhoid fever, pneumonia and measles. This was a sad era. Fifty deaths was the fearful record. Expeditions were frequently sent out to hunt guerillas and to forage mainly for cattle—all quite successful. There was some lively skirmishing with the bushwhackers; but two men were seriously wounded. Early in the winter one company (A) was sent to Cross Lanes, eight miles distant, to hold that post and guard a ford over the Gauley river.

There was but little intercourse with the people; only a few were loyal to the flag; but we respected both person and property where they showed no open acts of disloyalty. Thus the winter passed. Our numbers were kept full by recruits. May 12, 1862, the regiment—a thousand strong—with cheerful hearts, took up its line of march in the direction of real business. Company B alone remained in charge of the train to come by another route. Forded Gauley river and marched much of the way by bridal paths. The march was a forced one, and the first two days were intensely hot, so that many gave out. The way led via Cold Knob and Frankfort, the object being to get in the rear of a Confederate force under General Heath, at Lewisburgh. At the same time a force under Colonel Gilbert approached from Gauley Bridge. General Heath was too wary and eluded the trap. The Union forces united at Lewisburgh, and consisted of the Thirty-sixth and Forty-fourth regiments and a battalion of the Second Virginia cavalry, all under command of Colonel Crook - about twelve hundred strong. From Lewisburgh, Colonel Crook, with this small force, marched through the mountains to White Sulpher Springs and Covington, to Jackson River depot, and destroyed the bridge at that point. The movement was so bold and rapid, and the enemy so surprised they dare not leave their mountain fastnesses to essay an attack.

A few days after the return of the expedition to Lewisburgh, May 23d, early in the morning, General Heath, with from two thousand five hundred to three thousand men, drove in the pickets and took a strong position on a hill on the opposite side of the town from where the Union forces were encamped, and commenced shelling the camp. The Thirty-sixth, under Colonel Clarke, and the Forty-fourth, under Colonel Gilbert, were ordered to charge the enemy in their position. Disappearing for a few moments in the streets of the town, the National forces suddenly emerged upon the rising ground in front of the rebels—the Thirty-sixth on the left and the Forty-fourth on the right of the line of battle. The rebel infantry was posted behind a rail fence, and between the lines was an open, clear field. Over this ground the Thirty-sixth charged with a yell, receiving a volley from the enemy.

Reserving fire until at close range, and giving the rebels scarcely time to reload, the men were upon them, and they broke in complete route. They escaped down the mountain, and firing the bridge over Greenbrier river rendered further pursuit impossible. In this the maiden battle of the Thirty-sixth regiment, it was pitted against the Twenty-second Virginia, which was recruited in the rich country of Greenbrier county and the Kanawha valley, and was armed with Mississippi rifles. The result of this victory was a loss to the Thirty-sixth of seven killed, forty-four wounded, and five captured on picket. The Forty-fourth lost much less. Rebel loss, sixty killed and left on the field, one hundred and seventy-five prisoners, four pieces of artillery, and three hundred stand of small arms. They carried off many of their slightly wounded.

This being a fair stand up fight, on ground of the rebels' own choosing, the plan of attack also their own, it increased the men's confidence in the future. It being a rebel town, the wounded who were straggling back were ill-treated; one was shot dead by a citizen. The Union dead were buried in a beautiful grove, and their graves surrounded by a picket fence by their comrades.

This battle occurring near the homes of many of the Confederate soldiers, their friends came in to care for both dead and wounded. The scenes there witnessed were very affecting. Mothers with their dead or wounded sons, sisters with their brothers, wives with husbands. It was truly a sad picture of the realities of war. Added to this was the mortification of defeat in their own country. The Union wounded were sent to Charleston in ambulances. Some were met there by relatives and taken home. Dyar B. McClure, of Warren, Washington county, badly wounded, died soon after reaching home.

After clearing up the wreck of battle and parolling the rebel wounded, May 29th, the regiment took up the line of march to Meadow Bluffs to be more accessible to supplies. They were joined here by the Forty-seventh Ohio, and on June 22d the entire force, under command of Colonel Crook, started to return General Heath's early call on them at Lewisburgh, by a visit to his camps at Union, Monroe county. Marched *via* Salt Sulphur springs, forded Greenbrier river the second day, and reached Union in the afternoon. The general, not caring for further acquaintance, had left for the mountains. The command then leisurely retraced its steps, and as it was a very fine country foraged its way back by another route. At Meadow Bluffs, drilling occupied most of the time until August 14th, when the regiment started for Camp Piatt, on the Kanawha river. Here, with most of the force under General Cox, they embarked on transports for Parkersburgh, *en route* to Washington and the army of the Potomac.

At Parkersburgh recruits were added to the regiment,

increasing its numbers to one thousand and twenty men. A happy day was spent here, the regiment mingling with their friends, who came to meet them, and to many it was the last meeting on earth. Left Parkersburgh on stock and freight cars, and went through without change. Through Washington, over the long bridge, through Alexandria, arriving at Warrenton junction August 25th, in advance of the rest of the Kanawha division, and were assigned by General Pope to duty at his headquarters. General Stonewall Jackson having broken in upon General Pope's rear, prevented any more of the division coming forward.

August 27th, in charge of headquarters, train fell back with the rest of the army, and encamped that night near the battle ground of Bristow Station. Marched through Manassa to Centreville, overlooking the second Bull Run battle. Company F was sent back to Bristow on special duty, joining the regiment next day.

In the succeeding battle of Bull Run the Thirty-sixth was held in reserve by General Pope, and on the evening of that defeat, performed signal service in arresting stragglers and fugitives from the battle, thus preventing thousands from hurrying back to Washington and creating a panic of dismay similar to that after the first battle of Bull Run.

September 2d the regiment fell back to Arlington heights, remaining there a few days. September 7th, marched through Washington; were reviewed by Secretary Chase and others from the balcony of the treasury department. The men were proud of their regiment, as compared with any they had seen in the eastern army, not merely because of their numbers (for they were often hailed with "What brigade is that?"), but in their marching and drill they knew they were second to none. Colonel Strother, better known as "Porte Crayon," said of the regiment, after witnessing one of its dress parades, that it executed the most perfect manual of arms he had ever seen in his army experience.

September 7th, after being joined by the rest of the Kanawha division, left Washington, the object being to repel Lee's invasion of Maryland. The Kanawha division had the advance of the entire Federal force, now commanded again by General McClellan; met the advance of Lee's army (General Stewart's cavalry) on the 2d, at Frederick, Maryland. They occupied the town. The Thirty-sixth marched to the attack in line of battle on the left of the pike, the Twenty-eighth Ohio on the right. Colonel Moore, of the Twenty-eighth commanding brigade, kept the pike leading directly into the town with a section of artillery. The moment he reached the town a rush by the enemy's cavalry captured the brave colonel and a few others; then fell back without fighting. The command of the brigade devolved on Colonel Crook, and that of the regiment on Lieutenant Colonel Clarke. The regiment never afterward had its old colonel as its commander. Reached Middletown the thirteenth; here opened the battle of South Mountain.

Early on the morning of the fourteenth, General J. D. Cox, commanding the division, was ordered to storm the mountain. The Thirty-sixth had position in the centre,

The Colors and Battle-flag of the Sixty-third Ohio Volunteer Infantry, crossed on the drum of Drum Major Robert Sturts, and resting the sword of Surgeon Arthur B. Monahan, suspended from drum stick in centre.

Note.—Only a few space at the upper corner and the fringe of the Battle flag remain. The names of the battles borne on the flags and staves are inscribed at the close of the history of the regiment.

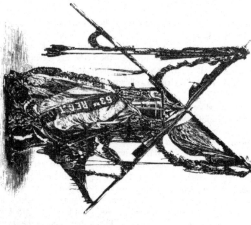

THE OHIO BRIGADE STARTING FOR ISLAND No. 10. THE 39TH OHIO EMBARKING ON THE UPPER TRANSPORT FOR THE UPPER FORT. Taken from "Ohio in the War," 2 vols., octavo, by permission of the Publisher, Wilstach, Baldwin & Co., Cincinnati.

and its march lay through the only open ground, without cover of any kind. The enemy, first with shell, and, as the line advanced, with canister and grape, poured into them a destructive fire. The musketry followed. The line never wavered although subjected to an enfilading fire from artillery, and musketry in front, posted behind a stone wall on the crest of the mountain. The regiment held its fire, the rebels cursing and yelling "You can't come over here." With loaded guns and fixed bayonets they reached the wall, then over it rattled the brave lads with a yell. Then followed a hand-to-hand fight with those who would not surrender or run away. Among the former was a confederate surgeon, who kept firing with his revolver until pierced with a bayonet. The regiment pursued the enemy into the woods beyond, killing and capturing a number, until ordered back in line with the right of our forces, who had not been quite so fortunate. The rest of the day was spent in repelling the efforts of the enemy to retake that line.

The Thirty-sixth lost a number in killed and wounded. Corporal Courtland Shepherd from Washington county, one of the colored guard, was killed. That night the regiment bivouacked among the rebel dead on their chosen ground. A detail rudely buried the Union dead at the rear near where they fell. In this, the second battle of the regiment, not a man was known to have failed in his duty. That night the enemy left the mountain, falling back and across Antietam creek. Early in the morning the Union army was in pursuit. That day (the fifteenth) and the sixteenth little else was done, but as the army came on to take up position, driving in the rebel skirmishers, the rebels from the heights about Sharpsburgh commenced throwing with their cannon pieces of iron rails and sledge hammers as far as our line. General Burnside, the corps commander, gave his command to understand that it was to have an easy victory as the enemy was out of ammunition. Alas, how fatal the delusion! About 10 A. M. on the seventeenth the Kanawha division was ordered to assault the stone bridge and carry it at all hazard. It could not be done till Colonel Crook by a skilful manœuvre with a battery cleared the heights of the enemy at the opposite end. When a crossing was effected the division was rapidly deployed in line of battle and a charge at once ordered. The ground being clear, excepting fences, and the regiment about the centre of the line, it drew a terrible fire from the enemy's artillery. In this charge Colonel Clarke fell, shot through the body by a large shell. The regiment drove the rebel infantry from their first line and was then halted. This part of the field being vital to the enemy they massed a heavy force on the left of the Union line and doubled it back. Colonel Crook drew his brigade with the rest of the division a short distance back under cover of rolling ground. In this movement the regiment did not forget its beloved commander, Colonel Clarke, but carried his remains with them in a blanket. It is but just to say here that Colonel Clarke, by unexampled bearing, even temper and gentlemanly deportment, had steadily won for himself the confidence and a warm place in the hearts of the entire regiment.

His remains were forwarded to his home at Marietta, where they now rest in the beautiful cemetery, and his grave is marked by a monument erected by his fellow officers.

The command of the regiment now devolved upon Major Andrews. That night the groans and cries of the helpless wounded of both armies between the two lines could be heard, but no help could safely reach them. The eighteenth passed with an occasional shot, but a vigilant watch was kept over the enemy. The following night Lee with his entire army escaped, fording the Potomac. After the battle the regiment was moved down near the mouth of Antietam creek, where it remained until October 6th, when the Kanawha division was ordered back to West Virginia. The march lay via Hagerstown to Hancock, then over the Baltimore and Ohio railroad to Clarksburgh. The regiment and brigade left this town the last of October for Charleston. The march lay through Summerville, the old familiar quarters of the regiment. Reached Charleston about the middle of November. After the active work of the summer and fall fall it was supposed that here on the lower bank of the Elk river the regiment would winter. Accordingly all actively set about making quarters out of such material as was at hand. Some were completed and all nearly so when, January 25th, transports came up the Kanawha river to convey General Crook with his command to the army of the Cumberland at Nashville, Tennessee. The men regretted to leave their newly constructed quarters, but such are the uncertainties of army life. Crowded on steamers the trip was exceedingly uncomfortable. Remained near Nashville till February 22d, when the Thirty-sixth, Eleventh, Eighty-ninth and Ninety-second Ohio, and Eighteenth Kentucky regiments, and Twenty-first Indiana battery, under command of General Crook reembarked for Carthage, Tennessee. At this place a good deal of important scouting occupied the time till early in June, when General Crook with his command marched to Murfreesborough. In the meantime Colonel Andrews resigned and William G. Jones was commissioned colonel of the regiment. General Crook's brigade was assigned to Major-General Reynolds's division, Fourteenth army corps, commanded by Major General George H. Thomas. June 24th, General Crook with his (Third) brigade, in advance of the corps, took up the line of march on the Manchester pike southward. Late in the day the Thirty-sixth had a few men wounded at Hoover's Gap. Next day moved to the left, to flank the enemy's position at Tullahoma. Found him gone in the direction of Bridgeport, the railroad crossing over the Tennessee river.

The pursuit was necessarily and aggravatingly slow, owing to the wretched condition of the roads, it having rained incessantly since the command left Murfreesborough. At Big Springs, a day's march further on, General Crook was relieved of the command of the brigade and given a division of cavalry, General J. B. Turchin taking his place.

In July moved up to University Place, a beautiful

26

place on a mountain, remained there some two weeks, with little else to do but fight jiggers (a little insect thick on the bushes) and look out for rattlesnakes. In August moved down the southeastern slope into Sweeden's cove; stopped a few days at Blue Springs, on Battle creek; marched on through Sequatchie valley to Jasper, Tennessee. This land abounded in very delicious peaches, of which many a heaping hatful was appropriated by the soldiers. September 2d crossed the river at Shell Mound in flats. From this point the march lay over Sand mountain into Lookout valley; moved on in the direction of Trenton, Georgia. Further up the regiment and command performed the task of pulling both artillery and baggage train to the top of Lookout mountain, crossing immediately down the other side into McLemore's cove. Here, on the seventeenth, the enemy made some demonstrations from Catlett's gap. Some manœuvring was done to mystify the enemy, and on the night of the eighteenth, after issuing a few rations, the entire command moved.

General Crittenden was being pressed in the direction of Rossville, northeast. This compelled a wearisome all-night march. At daylight, on the nineteenth, the regiment was at Crawfish Springs, and a little further on went into its place in line of battle. Soon the work of death commenced—the terrible battle of Chickamauga. Fierce cannonading for miles up and down the valley— a short lull—then the murderous work of the infantry began. The battlefield being largely in the woods seemed to impart a sentiment of awe to the work that was going on. The Thirty-sixth in position seemed a little to the left centre. Suddenly on the right the firing grew nearer and nearer. Many wounded were passing to the rear, the front holding its ground. General Reynolds, division commander, ordered the brigade to change front to the right. Barely was this manœuvre accomplished when through the ranks rushed some National troops closely pursued by the enemy. The solid front presented checked them, and their broken masses took cover behind trees and logs, giving them great advantage. Not a man of the regiment was known to have turned back unless wounded. The slaughter was fearful, especially on the right of the regiment. The brave Captain James Stanley's men, company D, were falling right and left. Something must be done. General Turchin was not there. Colonel Jones was mortally wounded; Major Adney was wounded. At this critical moment Lieutenant Colonel Devol ordered a charge. With an inspiring yell the men rushed forward and drove the enemy back and beyond their artillery. They had driven them several hundred yards when an aid was dispatched ordering the brigade back. Had the enemy closed that gap in the rear, the subsequent history of the Thirty-sixth and Eleventh Ohio and Eighteenth Kentucky regiments would have had a different reading. There was but little fighting on that part of the line the rest of the day. Exhausted the regiment lay on its arms keeping a skirmish line in front. Early the next morning, the twentieth, General Rosecrans caused word to be passed along the line that as it was the Sabbath fighting should not be provoked.

General Bragg being reinforced by Longstreet's corps was confident, and early opened the battle. The regiment was moved to the left and front. The enemy made repeated charges and as often were repulsed. Major General Thomas, in his official report of these charges, says: "The enemy attacked Johnson, Palmer, and Reynolds with fierceness which was continued at least two hours, making assault after assault with fresh troops, which was met by our troops with a most determined coolness and deliberation. Having exhausted his utmost energies to dislodge us, he apparently fell back entirely from our front, and we were not disturbed again till towards night." About four o'clock the enemy made a desperate effort and succeeded in forcing the lines back on the right and left of Reynolds' division, where, from the front and both flanks, the enemy poured their missiles of death. General Reynolds and other officers thought the entire division would have to surrender, and as evidence of their fears took off their shoulderstraps to conceal their rank. At this moment General Thomas, the "Rock of Chickamauga," ran the gauntlet and ordered a "change of front to the left on the enemy's flank, and get out, if possible." Like a statue he coolly sat on his horse, witnessed the execution of his order and then galloped back. The charge was a success. Many prisoners and a battery of artillery were captured. The latter could not be brought off. General Thomas further reports:

At 5.30 P. M. I started to see General Reynolds, and in passing through an open woods bordering the State road, I was cautioned by a couple of soldiers, who had been to hunt water, that there was a large rebel force in these woods, drawn up in line, and advancing toward me. Just at this time I called to General Reynolds and directed him to change the head of his column to the left and form a line perpendicular to the State road, his right resting on the road and to charge the enemy who were then in his immediate front. This movement was made with the utmost promptitude. Turchin threw his brigade upon the rebel force, routing and driving them in utter confusion. In this splendid advance more than two hundred prisoners were captured and sent to the rear. Turchin's brigade after driving the enemy a mile and a half was reassembled, and took its position on the ridge road with Robinson and Willich.

The day closed with seventy dead officers and men of the Thirty-sixth regiment lying in those woods. The night was spent in withdrawing to Rossville, next day (twenty-first) held the gap through the ridge covering Chattanooga. The twenty-second of September fell back into Chattanooga, and with the rest of the army vigorously set about fortifying. From this time to the first of November the army was in a state of siege on half rations. Early during the siege lost a dozen men on a reconnoissance. October 26th, Turchin's and Hayen's brigades were elected to take Brown's Ferry below Lookout mountain and thus cooperate with General Hooker in relieving the beleaguered army. This was successfully accomplished by selecting experienced boatmen from the Thirty-sixth and Ninety-second regiments. Quietly in the darkness of night they floated down in pontoons past the rebel pickets, landing and storming the heights at the ferry. Hooker's arrival brought the first sound crackers and meat the regiment had had for a month. Parched corn had been the only good diet that could be had. The regiment returned to Chattanooga in a few days. Hooker holding the ferry and starting from it on his famous charge up Lookout mountain.

November 25th, on the extreme left of the Fourteenth corps and army, the Thirty-sixth and Ninety-second, side by side, with the battle cry of "Chickamauga," charged Mission Ridge. The miles in length of the charging line of the blue, dotted here and there with the soldier's pride—his country's flag—was an inspiring sight, though the belching line of cannon and musketry from the enemy on the crest told fearfully on that column. The crest was reached, the breastworks taken—in many instances by a hand-to-hand fight. The regiment captured two pieces of artillery and many prisoners. Generals Grant and Thomas having followed closely, were cheered by the men as they passed by. The regiment lost in this charge eighty-three of its brave members. The following day pursued the enemy to Ringgold, Georgia, after which it returned to its tents in Chattanooga. Thus ended what commenced in the forests of Chickamauga and might be termed a continuation of the same battle.

As soon as possible the regiment made coffins and went out to Chickamauga (eight miles) to bring in its dead; only thirty-seven could be recognized, however—they having been covered with a shovelfull of earth when they fell. The rest had been gathered promiscuously with others and buried in rows, with only earth enough to partially cover them; near the widow Glen's house were long rows of the dead of both armies.

How the Nation's destroyers gloated over their temporary success at Chickamauga, while like vultures they looked down from Mission ridge and Lookout mountain, on its defenders! The men of the Thirty-sixth killed in these battles now rest in a lot selected by their comrades in the beautiful National cemetery at Chattanooga.

In February, 1864, the regiment reenlisted, and March 10th started for home on veteran furlough. At Cincinnati they separated for thirty days. At the expiration of that time were ordered to General Crook at Charlestown, West Virginia—he having been sent there to take command of the Third division, department of West Virginia. On reaching Charlestown the regiment was assigned to the First brigade, commanded by Colonel R. B. Hayes.

May 1st General Crook with his division started on a raid to the Virginia & Tennessee railroad. Several attempts on it had been made, but had failed. The march lay via Falls of Kanawha, Raleigh and Princeton. Had a slight skirmish at Princeton, and a few miles further on found the enemy in strong position at Cloyd's farm. Their position was at once charged and a severe engagement ensued, which resulted in driving the enemy from their works, capturing two pieces of artillery and mortally wounding and capturing the notorious rebel General Jenkins. Being reenforced, they made a stand a mile to the rear of their first position, but were easily routed. They retreated through Dublin depot and across New river. At the depot a large amount of wagons and other quartermaster and commissary stores were captured. Destroyed all that were not available, and burned the railroad bridge. This severed the railroad connection of Richmond with the Tennessee rebel forces.

Being so far from the base of his supplies General Crook was obliged to return—over Salt Pond mountain, through Union to Meadow Bluffs. Near Union Lyman Perrin, from Rainbow, Washington county, was shot dead in the road by a bushwhacker.

On reaching Meadow Bluffs orders were received to join General Hunter in the Shenandoah valley. As soon as the bare and foot-sore men could be cared for, and the expedition otherwise fitted up, the march began. It lay over old familiar ground in part—through Lewisburgh, White and Warm sulphur springs, and Goshen. At the latter place, a bridge spanning Calf Pasture river was burned and the railroad track destroyed nearly to Cravesville, where the mountain was crossed and a junction effected with General Hunter at Staunton. The march had been opposed by "Mudwall" Jackson, with a small force, which caused but little delay. June 10th the National forces left Staunton for Lynchburgh, skirmishing most of the way. "Mudwall" Jackson retreating across the North river into Lexington. After firing the bridge he took courage and with the help of the students at the military institute delivered himself of a brisk little fight. He soon gave way.

On entering Lexington, by order of General Hunter, the military institute and ex-Governor Letcher's house were burned. The loss of the Thirty-sixth was three killed and five wounded. From Lexington the army moved by way of Buchanan, thence across the Blue Ridge, between the Peaks of Otter, to Liberty. From this place bridges were burned and the railroad destroyed to within a short distance of Lynchburgh. At the old stone church, on the Liberty pike, the rebels were encountered and driven inside their fortifications. Night coming on, operations were suspended. By morning, June 18th, affairs had assumed a different aspect. The rebel General Early had arrived from Richmond with a heavy force, and at daylight opened with his artillery. It was evident that a greater than "Mudwall" was at hand. Heavy skirmishing was kept up by the infantry till about noon, when the Union force was most furiously assailed, but stood its ground, and in turn drove the enemy back within their works. General Hunter decided to withdraw, but affected to keep up appearances till after dark. The Thirty-sixth was deployed in front of the enemy, and an occasional shot delivered, giving time for the troops to get well under way; then quietly withdrawing, briskly marched until the rear of the column was reached. Then commenced one of the hardest marches of the war. Supplies were nearly exhausted, and foraging had to be resorted to, with an active enemy hanging on the rear. The retreat was continued *via* Liberty, Buford's Gap, Salem, Newcastle, Sweet and White Sulphur Springs, Lewisburgh, and Meadow Bluffs, to Charleston, on the Kanawha. Chapters might be written of the sufferings of the soldiers, marching from within hearing of the guns at Richmond across all the mountain ranges to the Ohio river. Many men, exhausted, fell out, and never were heard of again. Night and day without sleep or rest, it was march, march—that or starvation. During the last nine days the average was twenty miles per day. From June 27th to July 10th the starving, worn-out army rested—ate, slept, and was reclothed. They then embarked for Parkersburgh, *en route* east, General Crook having been ordered with his command east, to repel General Early in his invasion of Maryland. They reached Martinsburgh, by railroad, July 15th; thence marched to Halltown, near Harper's Ferry. General Crook was at Snicker's Gap, having followed and driven General Early across to the west side of the Shenandoah. Colonel Hayes' brigade (the Twenty-third and Thirty-sixth regiments) was ordered to form a junction with General Crook. They found the enemy in full force, and no possibility of communicating. After heavy skirmishing the little command found itself entirely surrounded by two divisions of the enemy's cavalry, and fought its way out towards Harper's Ferry. The Thirty-sixth lost three men killed and four wounded. July 22nd they joined General Crook at Winchester.

Two days later a battle was fought at Kernstown, three miles above Winchester, in which the Union troops were forced to retire, the enemy getting in on the flank in overwhelming numbers. The fighting continued till nine o'clock at night. The regiment lost in killed and wounded one hundred and twenty-seven men and officers. The army moved next day towards Martinsburgh, the enemy pursuing closely. At Martinsburgh the rebel cavalry charged into town, when General Crook turned on them and drove them back, capturing a few prisoners. The Thirty-sixth had two men wounded. Under cover of this feint General Crook moved on quietly that night to a ford over the Potomac, at Williamsport, and marched down to Harper's Ferry. The enemy's cavalry having passed through Maryland into Pennsylvania, General Crook's division was ordered to intercept them, and moved up through Middletown. That day, July 28th, the regiment suffered terribly with the heat. Many, including its colonel, were stricken with sunstroke. Hearing that the enemy had burned Chambersburgh and gone back, General Crook turned back to Harper's Ferry.

August 7th General Sheridan took command of the army, having added to it the Sixth corps, and· followed the Confederate forces up to Cedar creek, but at once fell back to Halltown, followed by General Early, reenforced from Lee's army. August 23d the enemy attacked early in the morning but did not follow it up. Colonel Hayes' brigade (Twenty-third and Thirty-sixth Ohio and Fifth West Virginia), sallied out, and drove in the enemy's skirmishers, capturing a number. August 26th another sortie was made; in this they were successful in capturing a number of officers and men, all from Kershaw's division.

Nothing more of interest occurred until September 3d. General Crook with his troops reached Berryville, halted, and were in the act of making coffee when rapid firing was heard in the direction of a regiment that had been sent forward on picket. At once the regiment started on the double-quick, but did not reach them till they were being driven back on the run, closely followed by the enemy. Taking advantage of a little embankment the regiment lay down, concealed until our pickets passed through. The enemy came on until within a few rods, when the men, with fixed bayonets, rose up and rushed forward to meet them, firing as they ran. The enemy was driven back on his main force and behind his artillery. Taking cover behind rocks and trees, firing was kept up till late in the night. General Sheridan not wishing to bring on a general engagement here the brigade was withdrawn. Captured a number of prisoners. The regiment's loss was twenty-five men. Captain J. C. Selby, a brave and true soldier, was mortally wounded.

Much marching and counter-marching was gone through with up to September 19th. The Nineteenth corps having come up, General Sheridan attacked General Early in his fortified position in front of Winchester, across the Opequan creek. The Sixth and Nineteenth corps were ordered to attack the enemy in front. General Crook's forces were held in reserve, but were soon ordered to the right of the line and to fall upon the enemy's left flank. On reaching that point Colonel Hayes' brigade was formed in the first line and moved to the attack. The enemy discovering this movement turned their artillery upon it with vigor. The brigade hurried forward and soon came upon an impassable swamp, and were moved by the right flank a short distance where fording was possible. The enemy's skirmishers were driven in. A short delay ensued until all the forces could come up, when a rush was made—the enemy was doubled up and back and completely routed. General Crook's little command of about four thousand now became the front, and pursued the fleeing rebels. Passing many pieces of artillery, seven battle-flags were captured, the blue coats and the "gray backs" mingling together. A large number of prisoners were left to the rear. The pursuit continued through and beyond Winchester, till dark. The regiment's loss was thirty-five in killed and wounded. In this battle the division commander was wounded and Colonel R. B. Hayes assumed command; Colonel H. F. Devol of the brigade; Lieutenant Colonel Adney of the regiment. Following the enemy up the valley they found him, September 22d, in position at Fisher's Hill, his right resting against Massanutten mountain, his left at the foot of North mountain—a very strong position. As at Opequan, the Sixth and Nineteenth corps confronted the enemy.

General Crook with his command wended his way, through gulch and brush, by the flank, to the foot and up the side of North mountain, unperceived by the enemy. When well on their flank, overlooking them, he halted, his orders were to "quietly move down on the enemy till within range, then raise the yell and go for them."

At the command, "Forward!" the men broke in utter disorder, and like an avalanche, and yelling like demons, fell upon the enemy. Piece after piece of their artillery was abandoned. The Union forces not being able to overtake them, they fled on up the valley. Four men of the regiment were wounded. The regiment followed the fugitive army to Harrisonburgh. Soon after, the army fell back to Cedar creek. The creek crosses at right angles to the valley from the foot of Massanutten mountain to North mountain. On the lower bank of this creek the army took up its position. The Nineteenth corps on the right, the Sixth corps in the centre, army of western Virginia (General Crook's command), on the left—Major General Wright, the ranking officer, in command of the entire force. After this disposition General Sheridan left for Washington. General Early, reenforced, came down and confronted the National forces, and from Massanutten mountain could overlook the entire line, and from that point planned his attack. Early in the morning of the eighteenth, the entire rebel infantry was moved down the stream to a ford, which, by neglect of General Wright, was not properly guarded, and captured the picket without alarm. After crossing their forces, under cover of darkness and a dense fog, about 4 o'clock on the morning of the nineteenth they attacked Colonel Thoburn (First division, which was to the left and front), with a heavy force, completely surprising him, capturing a battery, and putting to flight the entire division. The main force of the enemy, at the same time, in double column, moved partly to the rear of Hayes' (Second) division. At the first firing at the front, tents were struck, all packed, and lines were formed as the First division men came back. It was now light enough to see the enemy in large force. The Second division command firing and falling back held the enemy in check till General Crook's headquarters train was out of the way. Captain Beir, General Crook's adjutant general, and Colonel Thoburn were killed at this point. We were still forced back by weight of numbers and overlapping.

A little further back in some woods the First brigade turned and charged the enemy, who had extended his line, driving that part of the line back which had the effect to check the pursuit and gave time for the reforming of the entire line at a new position about one and a half miles from the camps. Skirmishers were thrown forward. The enemy was contented with throwing an occasional shell and plundering the deserted camps. The men of the regiment were furiously angry, and eager to wipe out the stain of the morning.

In this new line the Second division was on the left and near the Winchester pike. About ten o'clock General Sheridan came galloping up the pike, having heard the firing. He stopped in rear of the Thirty-sixth regiment, dismounted, and heard from General Crook the story of the morning. Remounting, he rode along the line to the right and was cheered, all feeling that now there was an efficient head over all. Coming back he again dismounted and lay down among the weeds in consultation with General Crook—sent aides directing the formation of the Nineteenth corps which had not been engaged in the morning. They reported all in position, then he sent orders to be in readiness to move forward. General Custer, commanding cavalry, was posted on the right of the infantry. About half-past 2 P. M. the entire line advanced and drove the enemy at every point. As the rebels could not cross their forces rapidly over the ford many were captured, and the cavalry swinging round in

their rear took many more. These, with forty-nine pieces of artillery and most of the enemy's train, were the trophies of the last battle in which the Thirty-sixth regiment participated, and the finale of General Jubal Early's army. The regiment's loss in this battle was thirty. The dead of the morning were stripped of their clothing. The regiment remained in the valley at and above Winchester. Marched to Martinsburgh, in a cold rain, and January 1, 1865, embarked on railroad trains for Cumberland. In that ride, lasting most of two days and nights, the men suffered greatly from cold. While at Cumberland was consolidated with the Thirty-fourth Ohio, retaining its number, Thirty-sixth. In April was sent back to Winchester and thence to Staunton, the object being to head off any of the rebel forces which might flee that way out of Richmond. At Winchester, April 15th, the news of the assassination of President Lincoln was received, and this was perhaps the saddest day in the experience of the regiment. Then soldier looked at soldier in silent wonder. It was truly the hush of death. The colors were draped, which emblem of respect never was removed. The regiment was at Staunton when General Lee surrendered and the Confederacy collapsed. In June was ordered back to Cumberland and thence to Wheeling. Perceiving there was no more need for soldiers in the field they made application at once to be mustered out. This took place at Wheeling, West Virginia, July 27th; went to Columbus, Ohio, were paid off and disbanded August 1, 1865.

To the above account of the Thirty-sixth regiment by General H. F. Devol, which is briefly and modestly put considering the value of the service rendered, we take pleasure in adding two farewell addresses:

HEADQUARTERS SECOND BRIGADE, FIRST DIVISION, }
DEPARTMENT WEST VIRGINIA, }
NEW CREEK, WEST VIRGINIA, April 6, 1865. }

To the officers and men of the First brigade, First division, Department West Virginia·

It is with very great regret that I have been compelled to part with the officers and men of the First brigade. With many of you I have been associated in the service almost four years, with three of the regiments of the brigade more than two years, and with all the regiments during the memorable campaign of 1864, the battle of Cloyd Mountain, the burning of New River bridge, and the night march over Salt Pond mountain under General Crook in May, the days and nights of marching, fighting and starving on the Lynchburgh raid in June, the defeat at Winchester and the retreat on the twenty-fourth and twenty-fifth of July, the skirmishing, marching and counter-marching in the Shenandoah valley in August, the bloody and brilliant victories in September, the night battle of Berryville, the turning of the enemy's left at Sheridan's battle of Winchester, the avalanche that swept down North mountain upon the rebel stronghold at Fisher's Hill, the final conflict in October, the surprise and defeat of the morning and the victory of the evening at Cedar Creek. These and a thousand other events and scenes in the campaign form part of our common recollections which we are not likely ever to forget. As long as they are remembered we shall be reminded of each other, and of the friendly and agreeable relations which so long existed between us. It is very gratifying to me that I was allowed to serve with you until we received together the tidings of the great victory which ends the Rebellion. Whatever may be your future, I shall not cease to feel a lively interest in everything which concerns your welfare and your reputation. Under the able and gallant officer who succeeds me—under whom we have served together with so much satisfaction—I am confident that your future will be worthy of your past. As an organization and as individuals, you have my most fervent wishes for your happiness and success.

R. B. HAYES,
Brigadier General.

The above address was accompanied by the following:

NEW CREEK, VIRGINIA, fifteenth April, 1865.

DEAR COLONEL:—I hope to see the Thirty-sixth again before I quit the service, but I have thought proper to send you a good-bye which you will oblige me by having read to your regiment on dress parade when convenient.   Sincerely,

R. B. HAYES.

Colonel H. F. Devol, Thirty-sixth Ohio veteran volunteers.

HEADQUARTERS THIRTY-SIXTH OHIO
VETERANS VOLUNTEER INFANTRY,
COLUMBUS, OHIO, July 30, 1865.

Officers and Soldiers of the Thirty-sixth:

The time has come when we will have to part; some of us never to meet again. I cannot sever the connection that has bound us together for four long and bloody years without expressing to you my high appreciation of your valor and patriotism, manifested on many a hard contested field; and I assure you that the feeling I entertain for you is more than common friendship. I love you for your patriotism, your manly devotion to principle, and the stern resolution you have ever exhibited through victory and defeat, and especially for the heroic conduct that characterized you during the memorable campaign of Lynchburgh, and many similar scenes. Your country owes you a debt of gratitude which it never can repay, and but few can appreciate. And when, by your determination to sustain the integrity of your distracted country, you reenlisted as veterans, you did that which challenged the admiration of the world, and won the crowning glory of you life.

I would have you feel a just pride for the hard-earned but glorious reputation which you now enjoy; and I would conjure you, by all that is held dear, never to do aught that would sully your fair fame. And when our connection as comrades in arms is severed, as it soon will be, I would have you often think of that dear old flag, under which, and for which, we all have fought, and entertain towards each other that friendly feeling which has ever characterized our past relations.

Many of our comrades, who started with us four years ago, to-day fill heros' graves! And while we mourn their loss, it is a happy thought to know that they did not die in vain, but that our country lives! Let their valorous deeds and heroic example ever be fresh in our memory. I am assured that the soldiers who acted nobly their part in the death struggles at Antietam, South Mountain, Mission Ridge, Cloyd Mountain, and through the arduous campaign in the Shenandoah Valley, and who learned to do and dare under such generals as McClellan, Rosecrans, Grant, Crook, and Sheridan, will be men wherever they are placed, and will clearly demonstrate the fact that fighting soldiers make peaceful citizens.

To convince you has been the highest aim of my life, and in parting with you I have the highest regard for all. I shall never cease to take an interest in your future welfare, and you may rest assured that the bond of brotherhood that has existed between us for so long a time may not easily be forgotten.

Comrades, you can go to your homes with the happy consciousness that you have done your duty to your country and yourselves, and when you again assume the privileges and responsibilities of citizenship, be as unflinching in defending the sacred Temple of Liberty with the ballot as you have with the bullet, and all will be well

May God bless and protect you,

H. F. DEVOL,
Col. and Brev. Brig. Gen'l, U. S. V.

The regiment, during its entire term of service, had a most excellent drum corps. The first half of the time in charge of Chief Musician Ebenezer Corey, the remainder in charge of Chief Musician John Tenney.

If space would permit, an individual mention of every officer would be but justice; each one having an honorable record of patriotic deeds, which were wrought out with great personal sacrifice, not one having the slightest stain. They cherished toward each other throughout only the kindest feelings; no jealousy, no rivalry, or anything that ever marred the fellowship of the true and noble brotherhood.

COMPANIES B AND F, THIRTY-NINTH OHIO VOLUNTEERS.

REGIMENTAL OFFICERS.

Colonel John Groesbeck, mustered August 24, 1861, resigned July 8, 1862; Colonel A. W. Gilbert, July 8, 1862, resigned October 1, 1862;

Colonel Edward F. Noyes, October 1, 1862, honorably discharged April 22, 1865; Colonel Daniel Webber, May 18, 1865, mustered out with regiment; Lieutenant Colonel A. W. Gilbert, July 27, 1861, promoted to colonel July 8, 1862; Lieutenant Colonel Edward F. Noyes, July 8, 1862, promoted to colonel October 1, 1862; Lieutenant Colonel Henry T. McDowell, October 1, 1862, mustered out; Lieutenant Colonel Daniel Webber, February 10, 1865, promoted to colonel; Lieutenant Colonel William C. Buck, May 18, 1865, mustered out as captain May 18, 1865; Lieutenant Colonel Henry A. Babbitt, June 6, 1865, mustered out with regiment; Major Edward F. Noyes, July 27, 1861, promoted to lieutenant colonel; Major Henry T. McDowell, July 8, 1862, promoted to lieutenant colonel; Major William H. Lathrop, October 1, 1862, colonel Third Alabama colored regiment April 20, 1864; Major John S. Jenkins, April 25, 1864, mustered; Major Daniel Webber, January 11, 1865, promoted to lieutenant colonel; Major Henry A Babbitt, May 18, 1865, promoted to lieutenant colonel; Major George T. Rice, June 6, 1865, mustered out with regiment; Surgeon Oliver W. Nixon, August 20, 1861, resigned May 31, 1862; Surgeon Thomas W. McArthur, May 31, 1862, resigned September 3, 1862; Surgeon John A. Follett, September 3, 1862, mustered out with regiment; Assistant Surgeon Thomas W. McArthur, August 20, 1861, promoted to surgeon; Assistant Surgeon Christian Forrester, May 31, 1862, promoted to surgeon September 3, 1862; Assistant Surgeon Pierre S. Starr, December 13, 1862, mustered out with regiment; Assistant Surgeon Lionel J. Smith, September 5, 1862; Assistant Surgeon William J. Andrews, May 18, 1865, mustered out with regiment; Chaplain Benjamin W. Childaw, August 20, 1861, resigned April 9, 1862.

COMPANY OFFICERS FROM WASHINGTON COUNTY.

Captain John C. Fell, mustered July 31, 1861, resigned April 12 1862; Captain Jacob Koenig, July 31, 1861, died; Captain William H. Pittinger, May 18, 1862, mustered out with regiment; Captain Ethan O. Hurd, July 3, 1862, resigned March 3, 1864; Captain William C. Buck, May 9, 1864, promoted to lieutenant colonel; Captain George T. Rice, January 11, 1862, promoted to major; Captain William H. Mintun, January 11, 1862, mustered out with regiment; Captain William Benze, January 11, 1862, mustered out; First Lieutenant William Edgerton, July 31, 1861, resigned June 25, 1862; First Lieutenant Ethan O. Hurd, July 31, 1861, promoted to captain; First Lieutenant Henry W. Sheppard, February 8, 1862, resigned June 10, 1862; First Lieutenant William C. Buck, June 25, 1862, promoted to captain; First Lieutenant August Kropp, July 3, 1862, resigned April 1, 1864; First Lieutenant George T. Rice, May 9, 1864, promoted to captain; First Lieutenant Ely Steen, January 11, 1865, mustered out with regiment; First Lieutenant Alexander McTaggert, February 10, 1865, resigned June 20, 1865; First Lieutenant William Snodgrass, May 18, 1865, discharged July 1, 1865; First Lieutenant Frank Fortman, July 20, 1862, resigned September 15, 1862; First Lieutenant William Benze, May 25, 1862, promoted to captain; First Lieutenant William H. Pittinger, January 11, 1865, promoted to captain; First Lieutenant Barney Shults, February 10, 1865, mustered out with regiment; Second Lieutenant Henry W. Sheppard, July 31, 1861, promoted to first lieutenant; Second Lieutenant William C. Buck, March 19, 1862, promoted to first lieutenant; Second Lieutenant George T. Rice, June 25, 1862, promoted to first lieutenant; Second Lieutenant Alexander McTaggart, July 11, 1865, promoted to first lieutenant; Second Lieutenant William Snodgrass, February 14, 1865, promoted to first lieutenant; Second Lieutenant Daniel Otterbein, May 18, 1865, mustered out with regiment; Second Lieutenant Buell Congdon, May 18, 1865; Second Lieutenant Charles Miller, July 31, 1861, resigned June 16, 1862; Second Lieutenant Frank Fortman, July 18, 1862, promoted to first lieutenant; Second Lieutenant William Benze, June 20, 1863, promoted to first lieutenant; Second Lieutenant Barney Shultz, July 11, 1865, promoted to first lieutenant.

The regimental organization was perfected August 16, 1861, at Camp Dennison, Ohio; ordered to St. Louis, Missouri, where they arrived August 19th; moved up the North Missouri railroad September 7th. September 12th, the regiment was divided, companies A, B, E, I and K, going toward St. Joseph. This detachment remained in northern Missouri until February, 1862. Companies A and I marched from St. Joseph to Liberty in pursuit of the enemy and back to St. Joseph, in September, then moved by rail to Chillicothe, when they rejoined B, E and K. These five companies marched from Chillicothe to Macon City, thence to St. Joseph and Chillicothe and back to Macon City and St. Joseph, at which latter place they arrived December 4, 1861. On the fifth of December they marched under Brigadier General Prentiss toward the Missouri river, reaching it at Lexington; proceeded to Carrolton and returned to Utica December 8, 1861. December 20th, moved to Palmyra, Missouri, and remained there until the middle of February, 1862, when the detachment moved by rail to St. Louis. Companies C, D, F, G and H, moved from Utica, Missouri, as part of the command of Brigadier General Sturgess to the relief of Lexington, which place was then besieged by the enemy under General Price. Arrived in sight of Lexington September 19th, but finding it impossible to cross the river, and having no artillery, the relieving force diverged and marched to Liberty, when they embarked on steamers for Kansas City, Missouri, October 15th, still under General Sturgess, took up line of march for Springfield, Missouri, by way of Osceola, Bolivar and Greenfield. Arrived at Springfield November 1st, having marched on that day thirty-nine miles, to reenforce General Fremont's grand army, which was reported to be in the presence of the enemy. On the ninth of November marched towards the Missouri river, reaching Sedalia by way of Warsaw November 16th, and by December 18th, reached Syracuse. February 2, 1862, took up line of march for St. Louis, by way of Boonville, Columbia, Fulton and St. Charles, and arrived at St. Louis February 19, 1862, when the entire regiment was reunited.

The regiment embarked on steamer February 22d, and arrived at Commerce, Missouri, on the twenty-fourth, and at New Madrid March 3d, when the regiment formed a part of Groesbeck's brigade, Stanley's division of General Pope's army of the Mississippi. During the next ten days made several reconnoissances and took part in the siege of New Madrid, March 13th and 14th. Assisted in the capture of the place March 14th, crossed the Mississippi April 7th, and on the 8th, in conjunction with other troops, captured five thousand and five hundred prisoners at Tiptonville, being the rebel force from Island No. 10. On same day marched to Island No. 10, and on the ninth returned to New Madrid. April 13th embarked on steamer to go down the river, arrived near Fort Pillow on the fifteenth, started for Pittsburgh Landing on the seventeenth, where the command arrived on the twenty-third, and disembarked. During the siege of Corinth from April 23d to May 29th, the regiment made many reconnoissances and was frequently engaged in skirmishes with the enemy. On the thirtieth they advanced upon the rebel works, found them deserted, and the Thirty-ninth was the first regiment to enter the entrenchments. For several days they pursued the rebels, and on the twelfth of June returned to Clear creek, four miles south of Corinth, and went into camp, where the regiment was armed with the Whitney rifle with sabre bayonet. August 20th, marched to Iuka under General Rosecrans and returned on September 12th. On September 14th the movement against General Price, who had occupied Iuka, began, and on the nineteenth they were engaged in the battle of Iuka, which was a bloody contest, resulting in a defeat to the enemy. They pursued the rebel forces several days and then turned back and reached Corinth October 3rd. The Thirty-ninth, in the dispositions for the great battle impending at that point, was stationed near Fort Robinet. After dark the Ohio brigade, which consisted of the Twenty-seventh, Thirty-ninth, Forty-third and Sixty-third Ohio regiments, marched to relieve one of the brigades of General Davie's division, which had been resisting the enemy's advance in front. The Ohio brigade was ordered to occupy the high ground near battery Robinet. Near the crest was formed the line of battle. Directly on the right of the earthwork covering the battery and streching across the Chewalla road, stood the men of the Sixty-third, next came the Twenty-seventh and farther still to the right was the Thirty-ninth regiment. On the left of the battery facing to the left and nearly at right angles with the main line, rested the Forty-third.*

The locality above mentioned was the scene of the desperate charge of October 4th, in which the Twenty-seventh, and especially the Sixty-third regiment, lost heavily, the Thirty-ninth escaping with slight loss, and the enemy were terribly punished and routed. The Thirty-ninth followed in pursuit of Van Dorn and Price for four days, and on October 12th returned to Corinth, where they remained until November 2d, and marched southward to a point five miles south of Oxford, Mississippi. On December 18th they moved by rail to Jackson, Tennessee, to reenforce General Sullivan, who was hard pressed by General Forrest's command. They then, on December 20th, moved toward the Tennessee river, and took part in the battle of Parker's Cross Roads, defeating Forrest there on December 31st. General Fuller says of this engagement, which was so overshadowed by the great battle of Stone River, in progress at the same time, that it never received adequate notice:

Colonel Dunham, of Indiana, was sent ahead with a brigade to intercept Forrest's march at Parker's Cross Roads, and the Ohio brigade was to follow the next morning. At four o'clock we started, and marched until daylight, when a halt was made for breakfast. That over, we moved on, and soon the sound of cannon in our front advised us that Forrest was attacking Dunham's brigade, and then began a struggle in which legs told. Within an hour and a half they marched seven miles without a halt, with ranks well closed; and when a hill was reached whence Forrest's men and guns were seen, the Ohio brigade formed in line of battle on the double-quick, and went down for them with such good will that every rebel gun unlimbered and in action was ours in five minutes, and Forrest's forces were galloping away—not all, however, for many had dismounted in the fight, and their horses left in the rear were captured and their riders surrendered. Six guns, four hundred horses, and three hundred and sixty officers and men were captured. This was quite an achievement, for Forrest was not beaten every day.

January 8, 1863, the regiment returned to Corinth, having marched over two hundred miles in three weeks, without Government rations, transportation, or ambulances. The regiment remained at Corinth until April

*From address of General John W. Fuller at the reunion of the Ohio brigade at Columbus, Ohio, October 3, 1878, further extracts from which will be found in the history of the Sixty-third regiment.

20th, when it moved with the expedition under General Dodge to the Tuscumbia valley, for the purpose of keeping the rebels busy in that direction while another expedition cut the railroads in the rear of General Bragg's army. General Dodge was confronted by the rebel forces under Forrest and Roddy, and on the twenty-eighth the regiment was engaged in the battle near Tuscumbia, defeating the rebels. They then marched sixteen miles beyond Tuscumbia, returned to Corinth May 2nd, and marched to Memphis, Tennessee, on May 10th. Here the regiment was allowed to rest and recuperate. General Fuller says:

When Grant directed everything at Memphis to come to him at Vicksburgh, the Ohio brigade was ordered to march and garrison the former city. This was your single "soft spot" of the war. Excepting this, your lot was always at the front; but here for some months you lounged in camp, guarded the gardens, flirted with the ladies, and seldom missed a "good square meal."

The regiment up to this time had lost, in killed and wounded and discharged, since its organization, about three hundred men, and had recruited about two hundred, and had an aggregate of eight hundred and thirty ready for duty.

The regiment remained in Memphis until October 18th, when they went to Prospect, Tennessee, marching a distance of two hundred and fifty miles, and arriving there November 13th. Here they lay encamped until the twenty-seventh of December, when the regiment reenlisted as veterans, and returned home on furlough for thirty days. "The measured tread of an army, keeping step, is heard; and that wondrous scene unfolds, which the whole world beholds—the marshalling of the veteran hosts! The soldiers of the ranks stand forth!   .   . 'Muster us again! for all the war muster us in!' From that patriotic hour was the doom of the Rebellion sealed."*

The Thirty-ninth regiment furnished more veterans than any other Ohio regiment. The Ohio brigade stood as follows: Thirty-ninth, five hundred and thirty-four men; Sixty-third, four hundred and fifty-five; Forty-third, four hundred and thirty-six; and the Twenty-seventh, four hundred and thirty-seven men.

At the expiration of the furlough the regiment returned to its former camp at Prospect, Tennessee, and from thence they moved on Decatur, Alabama. The town was captured by a night movement. The brigade was embarked above in seventy boats, which, with muffled oars, silently stole down until opposite, when, by the left flank, they were soon on shore, up the bank, and in line. The rebels, after exchanging a few shots, retired, completely surprised and defeated.

On May 1, 1864, the regiment marched to join General Sherman's grand army at Chattanooga. Here the great Atlanta campaign was commenced. Meeting the enemy at Resaca, the Thirty-ninth was, on May 13th, 14th, and 15th, in the front line of battle driving the rebels to their trenches with a loss of two men.

At Dallas, Georgia, on the twenty-seventh, they again met the enemy, driving him from his position, in which engagement the loss by the regiment was severe. The rebel army was next encountered at the base of Kennesaw mountain. Heavy skirmishing began on the thirteenth of June, in which the Thirty-ninth was constantly engaged during the several days' fighting, losing severely in killed and wounded. The rebels were finally compelled to leave their stronghold.

On July 4th the enemy was again encountered at Ruff's Mills, when the Thirty-ninth, together with the Twenty-seventh, made a gallant charge on the enemy's works, driving them out in confusion, and not giving them time to remove their dead and wounded, and capturing quite a number of prisoners. This engagement is known also by the name of Nicojack Creek. The colonel of the regiment, E. F. Noyes, lost a foot in this action and never joined the regiment afterwards.* Company B lost four severely wounded.

The rebels retreated, and the National army pursued until they were finally driven into their devoted city, Atlanta, around which scenes of terrible slaughter were soon to be enacted.

On July 22, 1864, the regiment together with the Twenty-seventh Ohio was ordered to a responsible position in the line of battle of that memorable day, and they held it.

"The men were directed to unsling knapsacks, fix bayonets, and lie down on the crest of the ridge, where the line was formed, for protection from the fire of the enemy which came from the wood in front. The Second division had formed a line conforming in the main to that of the Twenty-seventh and Thirty-ninth, on a parallel ridge to the left of the Thirty-ninth, but separated from that regiment by a deep transverse ravine. The enemy charged the Second division within a few minutes and were repulsed.

"Immediately afterward his line of battle came out of the timber in front of the Thirty-ninth and Twenty-seventh regiments, advancing in plain view and within easy range, when individual men of both regiments raised to their feet and taking deliberate aim discharged their pieces. No order could keep them down with such an opportunity to use their muskets effectually. In less time than it takes to relate it, both regiments were on their feet discharging their pieces with rapidity and telling effect on the foe; yet on he came until the Thirty-ninth and Twenty-seventh charged him in turn, driving him from the field into the wood. Meanwhile another body of the enemy in line of battle came out of the wood to the right of the Twenty-seventh, bearing down on its flank and rear. General Fuller directed that the three right companies of the regiment be retired to face this second assault. This was done, but it soon became evident that a change of front to the rear of the entire line was necessary. This change was make under a hot fire. In executing this movement, necessarily made with celerity and under trying conditions, in the face of a defiant and rapidly advancing foe, the Twenty-seventh became somewhat disordered; and my thanks are due to General

---

*General Fuller's address before the Ohio brigade.

* He is, at this writing, Minister to France.

Fuller for his timely assistance in forming the new line. He grasped the colors of the Twenty-seventh and with them designated the ground he wished the new line to occupy. The line was promptly formed there; several volleys fired by the Twenty-seventh and Thirty-ninth Ohio regiments, Eighteenth Missouri and Sixty-fourth Illinois (the latter two regiments until then in reserve), followed by a charge again drove the enemy from the field. The line now laid down facing the wood which was on its right flank in the beginning of the battle, under a raking fire from the timber for an hour or more, when the enemy retreated and the greatest battle of the campaign was over. This was a stand up open field fight, with only such protection as the muskets and bayonets afforded."*

This stubborn resistance in this part of the field saved the left wing of Sherman's army from defeat; the old Thirty-ninth and Twenty-seventh stood as an impenetrable wall in front of the enemy, not giving an inch of ground and repelling several distinct charges by the rebels. Our artillery, supported by the Ohio brigade, poured into the rebel columns closed *en masse*, their deadly fire, musketry, grape, and canister, causing them to melt away like dew before the morning sun, leaving the National forces the victors of the field. The Thirty-ninth lost one hundred and forty-four killed and wounded.

The regiment then moved to the west side of Atlanta, forming the right wing, where on the twenty-eighth of July another severe battle was fought in which the Thirty-ninth participated, repulsing the enemy with great loss. Thus almost every day the regiment was engaged in skirmishing until the final evacuation of the city, which occurred on the second of September, 1864, and in the meantime they marched to Jonesborough fifteen miles south of Atlanta, destroying ten miles of the Montgomery railroad while on the way. At the latter place we again met the enemy in force and repulsed him with great loss, driving him so far south as Lovejoy's Station. In all these movements the Thirty-ninth performed a conspicuous part. They then returned to Atlanta, where they enjoyed a rest of about thirty days. In the meantime Hood, with his army, had got in our rear, destroying our communications with Chattanooga and investing our stronghold at Allatoona Pass. General Corse commanded at that point and had one thousand nine hundred and forty-four men, the rebel general, French, many times that number. The rebels came on in full force and charged the devoted garrison, but were driven back with the loss of hundreds, still assault after assault was delivered with same result, while the Twenty-third corps, under General J. D. Cox, were hastening to the rescue, and flags conveying from peak to peak, the message from General Sherman to General Corse to "hold the fort," and "that he was coming with reenforcements." Sherman on learning that Corse was there, exclaimed, "He will hold out! I know the man!" and he did hold out, though seven hundred and seven (more than a third) of his men had fallen, when the enemy desisted, leaving two hundred and thirty-one dead and four hundred and

*Address of General M. Churchill, late Colonel of the Twenty-seventh regiment, at the reunion of the Ohio brigade.

eleven prisoners and eight hundred muskets on the field.

The Thirty-ninth was in the front during the pursuit of Hood, being the first regiment in the Ohio brigade commanded by General J. W. Fuller.

The rebels were driven across the Tennessee to be left to the tender mercies of General George H. Thomas, while Sherman made all haste to get ready for his "march to the sea." The regiment now no longer in the Ohio brigade, but in the First division of the Seventeenth Army corps, on the fifteenth of November, took up its line of march with that corps, down to the sea, with Sherman. They destroyed the railroads as they went, meeting with but little opposition until they arrived in front of Savannah on the ninth of December, making a distance of three hundred and fifty miles from Atlanta. Here they found the rebels strongly fortified, with Hardee in his last ditch. After opening communication with the sea by way of the St. Catharine sound, taking Fort McAllister on the way, and having several days' hard fighting around the city of Savannah, in all of which the Thirty-ninth participated, the rebels evacuated the city on the twenty-first of December, and it was immediately occupied by the National army.

About the middle of January, 1865, the Thirty-ninth embarked with other troops on transports, and went to Beaufort, South Carolina, and assisted in driving the rebels from their stronghold at Pocotaligo Station twenty-five miles northwest from Beaufort.

On the first of February the Thirty-ninth, with the other forces of the grand army, took up its line of march through the Carolinas, wading swamps and fighting the enemy from place to place. On the fourth of February they engaged the enemy at Revers bridge, repulsing him with severe loss, the Thirty-ninth losing two killed and three wounded.

Continuing the march they struck the Augusta & Charleston railroad at Midway station, moving on that road to Columbia, thence north to Waynesborough, thence east to Cheraw, driving the enemy before them and capturing at that point a large amount of ammunition and artillery, thence marched to Fayetteville, North Carolina, thence to Bentonville, where a severe battle was fought March 21st, in which the First division, Seventeenth army corps, was hotly engaged, the Thirty-ninth being in the centre of the brigade on the right of the line of battle. They firmly held their ground, while those on the right and left gave way, leaving both flanks exposed to a raking fire. The brigade finally formed in the shape of a horse shoe and succeeded in repulsing the enemy. The brigade then moved to a stronger position, lay on their arms all night and in the morning were ready to resume the fight, but the enemy was gone. The next day they moved to Goldsborough. Our loss in this engagement was twenty-three killed and wounded.

Here they rested until April 10th, when they resumed the line of march toward Raleigh, and arrived there on the fifteenth and went into camp two miles west of the city, enjoying a few days of rest. We then joined in the pursuit of the rebel forces under General Johnston. After marching fifteen miles a proposal was received by

General Sherman to surrender the rebel forces, which was finally consummated, and we again returned to Raleigh. We then marched to Richmond, the late rebel capital, a distance of one hundred and eighty miles, in seven days, and from there to Washington city.

After participating in the grand review of all the armies by President Lincoln, the heads of departments, diplomatic corps, and a large number of distinguished officers of the army and navy, and an immense throng of rejoicing citizens, the Thirty-ninth moved to Louisville, Kentucky, where it was mustered out of the United States service on July 9, 1865, the war being over.

Engagements in which the Thirty-ninth regiment participated:

New Madrid, Missouri, March 7, 10, and 13, 1862; Island No. 10, April 8, 1862; Farmington, Mississippi, May 8 and 9, 1862; Corinth, Mississippi, May 28 and 29, 1862; Iuka, Mississippi, September 19, 1862; Parkers Cross Roads, Tennessee, December 31, 1864, Resaca, Georgia, May 13 and 14, 1864; Dallas, Georgia, May 31, 1864; Kennesaw Mountain, Georgia, June 18, 23, 26, and 27, 1864; Ruffs Mills, Georgia, July 4, 1864; Atlanta, Georgia, July 22, 29 and 30, 1864; Savannah, Georgia, December 10, 1864; Rivers Bridge, South Carolina, February 4, 1865; Bentonville, North Carolina, March 21, 1865.

The Thirty-ninth regiment marched three thousand five hundred and twenty-one miles, by rail two thousand six hundred and eighty miles, by steamboat two thousand four hundred and five miles, total, eight thousand six hundred and six miles.

SIXTY-THIRD OHIO VOLUNTEER INFANTRY.

REGIMENTAL OFFICERS.

Colonel John W. Sprague, mustered January 23, 1862, promoted to brigadier general volunteers, Colonel Charles E. Brown, June 6, 1865, on detached duty at muster out of regiment, Lieutenant Colonel William E. Gilmore, October 17, 1861, resigned July 17, 1862; Lieutenant Colonel Alexander L. Haskin, July 17, 1862; Lieutenant Colonel J. Hunter Odlin, March 20, 1863; Lieutenant Colonel Charles E. Brown, March 20, 1863, promoted to colonel, Lieutenant Colonel Oscar L. Jackson, June 6, 1865, mustered out with regiment as major, Major Alexander L. Haskins, October 1, 1861, promoted, and honorably discharged March 20, 1863; Major J Hunter Odlin, October 1, 1862, resigned January 3, 1863; Major John W. Fouts, January 1, 1863, mustered out; Major Oscar L. Jackson, January 28, 1865, promoted to lieutenant colonel, Surgeon Isaac L. Crane, October 7, 1861, resigned January 28, 1863; Surgeon Arthur D. Monahan, January 28, 1863, mustered out July 21, 1865, Assistant Surgeon Arthur D. Monahan, November 7, 1861, promoted to surgeon; Assistant Surgeon J. O. Marsh, August 21, 1862, resigned October 2, 1862; Assistant Surgeon John B. McDeil, March 11, 1863, resigned May 31, 1865; Chaplain B. S. Fry, February 13, 1862, mustered out September 27, 1864, at expiration of term.

COMPANY OFFICERS.

Captain John W. Fouts, October 23, 1861, promoted to major; Captain Christopher E. Smith, October 26, 1861, resigned December 22, 1862; Captain Rodner K. Shaw, December 20, 1861, resigned August 30, 1862; Captain Charles J. Titus, December 20, 1861, resigned June 18, 1862; Captain O. W. Pollock, June 18, 1862, mustered out with regiment; Captain George Wightman, August 11, 1862, discharged October 19, 1864, Captain Winslow L. Bay, January 1, 1863, mustered out with regiment; Captain A. C Fenner, October 4, 1864, mustered out with regiment, Captain George B. Bartlett, November 12, 1864, mustered out with regiment; Captain M. A. Stewart, November 12, 1864, declined promotion, Captain Madison Hoon, June 28, 1865, mustered out with regiment, First Lieutenant Wesley J. Tucker, October 28, 1861, resigned June 18, 1862, First Lieutenant Henry S.

Burt, December 20, 1861, detailed on staff duty; First Lieutenant O. W. Pollock, December 26, 1861, promoted to captain; First Lieutenant Louis Schmidt, February 13, 1862, resigned August 24, 1864; First Lieutenant Richard B. Cheatham, June 18, 1862, died July 18, 1863; First Lieutenant A. C. Tenner, August 11, 1862, promoted to captain; First Lieutenant George B. Bartlett, July 18, 1863, promoted to captain; First Lieutenant A. J. Howard, August 11, 1864, declined promotion, First Lieutenant M. A. Stewart, September 26, 1864, returned commission, mustered out; First Lieutenant Angus McDonald, September 26, 1864, promoted to captain; First Lieutenant Wallace S. Roach, September 26, 1864, returned commission; First Lieutenant Madison Hoon, October 4, 1864, promoted to captain; First Lieutenant Alexander H. Brill, January 20, 1865, mustered out with regiment; First Lieutenant Wallace C. Bay, January 20, 1865, resigned May 23; 1865; Second Lieutenant Robert Booth, October 1, 1861, resigned June 28, 1862; Second Lieutenant Benjamin Knight, November 12, 1861, resigned September 3, 1862; Second Lieutenant Lewis L. Grubb, February 13, 1862, resigned May 26, 1862; Second Lieutenant George B. Bartlett, May 26, 1862, promoted to first lieutenant; Second Lieutenant Winslow L. Bay, January 30, 1862, promoted to captain; Second Lieutenant A. J. Howard, January 1, 1863, honorably discharged November 9, 1864; Second Lieutenant M. A. Stewart, January 1, 1863, mustered out; Second Lieutenant Angus McDonald, July 18, 1863, promoted to first lieutenant; Second Lieutenant Wallace S. Roach, June 30, 1863, mustered out; Second Lieutenant Alexander H. Brill, November 12, 1864, promoted to first lieutenant.

THE SIXTY-THIRD OHIO VOLUNTEER INFANTRY.

The Sixty-third Ohio volunteer infantry was formed by the consolidation of a battalion of six companies raised at Camp Worthington, Chillicothe, with a battalion of four companies raised at Camp Putnam, Marietta.* It was originally intended for two regiments—the Twenty-second, to be raised under the direction of, and to be commanded by, Colonel William E. Gilmore, and the Sixty-third, to be raised under the direction of, and to be commanded by, Colonel William Craig, then quartermaster in charge at Marietta. In December, 1861, the call for troops to be sent to the front became so pressing that the order for consolidation came, and the two battalions were united; the Twenty-second furnishing companies A, B, E, H, I, and K; and the Sixty-third furnishing four companies raised in Washington county —company C, commanded by Captain Christopher E. Smith; company B, commanded by Captain John W. Fouts; company F, commanded by Captain Charles J. Titus; and company G, commanded by Captain Rodney K. Shaw. The command of the regiment was given to Colonel Craig; William E. Gilmore was made lieutenant colonel, and Alexander L. Haskins major.

On the twenty-first of December, 1861, the regiment removed to Camp Dennison; and on the twenty-seventh of the same month it returned to Marietta, and encamped at Camp Tupper.

On the twenty-third day of January, 1862, Colonel Craig resigned, and the command of the regiment was given to Colonel John W. Sprague, formerly a captain in the Seventh Ohio. Colonel Sprague immediately took command, and proceeded to fit his regiment to enter the field by perfecting its drill and discipline.

On the eighteenth day of February, 1862, Colonel Sprague with his regiment was ordered to the field, and to report at Paducah, Kentucky. The regiment left

---

*By this consolidation it became practicable to transfer, and by order of the war department, the Thirteenth Missouri regiment, composed mostly of Ohio men and officers, was transferred to the credit of Ohio, and became the Twenty-second Ohio volunteer infantry.

Marietta late in the evening of the eighteenth; six companies under the command of Colonel Sprague, on the steamer Bostona, No. 2, and four companies under command of Major Haskins, on the steamer T. J. Rattin. Marietta gave one of the best proofs of her sympathy and interest for the success of the Union cause by turning out *en masse* at the landing to witness their departure. On Saturday the twenty-second of February, the command reached Paducah and reported for orders. Having been armed and drilled in Camp Marietta, it was ordered to proceed to Commerce, Missouri, and report to General Pope, then organizing the army of the Mississippi at that point. The regiment reached Commerce on Sunday morning, the twenty-third of February, being the second regiment to arrive at the rendezvous. It immediately debarked, and encamped and occupied the cemetery on the high ground in the rear of the town. Later in the day it was joined by the Twenty-seventh, Thirty-ninth, and Forty-third Ohio volunteer infantry, its companions in the organization known as the Ohio brigade. These four regiments were brigaded together, and were made the First brigade in the First division of the army of the Mississippi. General Schuyler Hamilton commanded the division one day; the command was then given to General David S. Stanley, one of Ohio's brigadier generals.

From the twenty-third to the twenty-seventh of February the army was actually employed in the collection of stores, and the organization of the divisions. On the morning of the twenty-eighth the line of march was taken up for New Madrid, the Ohio brigade taking the advance. The army arrived in sight of New Madrid on the third day of March, and at two o'clock in the afternoon of that day the Sixth-third was first brought into action. It moved forward in line of battle with the same steadiness and precision that it would in review. Its first experience gave it the *morale* of veterans. For three hours it remained in its trying position, exposed to the artillery fire of the two forts and a fleet of six gunboats, without the opportunity of using their arms. Late in the afternoon the army retired out of range, and went into camp. The day had been a cold raw March day, and in the afternoon it began to snow. En route the army had been restrained from using fences, or in any manner foraging. The cold and exposure brought from headquarters the order to take the top rail, for campfires. In a short time the boys were comfortable around the blazing campfires, and in the morning it was found the army "was not fenced in."

The Sixty-third shared in all the fights in and around New Madrid previous to its capture. In the reconnoisance on the seventh of March it took an exposed position, and for a short time the upper fort had its range, and made its situation uncomfortable, fortunately without casualty.

On the thirteenth of March the Ohio brigade was made the infantry support of the siege batteries. The Sixty-third on the right, the Thirty-ninth on the left, well up to the batteries, and the Twenty-seventh and Forty-third in reserve. The troops were exposed to a constant artillery fire from the dawn until sunset, when the cannonading ceased. The troops remained in the trenches at night, exposed to a most terrific thunderstorm, without shelter or fires, the ground flooded with water. The dawn revealed the fact that the enemy had abandoned the forts, and retreated during the darkness.

The Ohio brigade was complimented in general orders for its gallantry, and was awarded the privilege to first enter and plant their banners on the captured forts. On the evening of the eighteenth day of March the Sixty-third was detailed to haul one of the heavy siege guns from the forts at New Madrid to Point Pleasant, fourteen miles below, and opposite Tiptonville in Tennessee. This arduous labor was performed between dark and daylight, the regiment dragging its heavy load over roads impassable for teams. The next morning the rebel fleet were surprised to find a battery opposite Tiptonville, their only line of communication with their garrison at Island Ten.* This severe labor and its attendant exposure permanently disabled many men.† The regiment returned to camp, and with the army awaited the action of the engineers in removing the obstructions from the bayou, for the passage of the gunboat fleet, and the transports.

On the morning of the seventh of April, 1862, the regiment with Stanley's and Paine's divisions of the army of the Mississippi, embarked on the transports to cross the Mississippi river, and were transported to the Tennessee shore, opposite the lower port.‡ The expedition took up its line of march down the Mississippi for Tiptonville, to intercept the enemy, if they should attempt to retreat. The route lay through muddy corn and wheat fields, with occasionally a strip of woods, having no semblance of roads. The marching was tedious, frequent halts were necessary, as the feet would gather more of Tennessee mud than a man was able to carry. Night came upon them in the fields, and they were compelled to bivouac in the field, and without campfires. The march was resumed at daybreak, and it reached Tiptonville in time to witness the surrender of the army that had garrisoned Island Ten, which had abandoned the forts, and attempted to escape by Tiptonville and the river. The expedition had been successful in intercepting and capturing them. The sixty-third proceeded immediately to Island Ten and occupied the enemy's abandoned quarters for the night. The next morning the regiment returned on the transports to New Madrid and occupied its old quarters. It had borne a conspicuous part in all of the work of the army of the Mississippi, resulting in the

---

*The first casualty in the Sixty-third occurred March 24th, the carelessness of a companion wounding Elisha Roberts mortally and George W. Essex seriously.

†James W. Nye served during the New Madrid campaign with the Sixty-third as acting quartermaster, and was present on the field during all the battles at that point, although never having been mustered; his name does not appear on the rolls.

‡The embarkation of the Ohio brigade on the expedition is illustrated in the second volume of Ohio in the War, page 253. The Sixty-third is upon the transport crossing the river. The Thirty-ninth are in the act of embarking at the upper fort, the last of the battalion ready to move on the transport when the picture was taken and the gunboat with steam up ready for action, abreast the upper fort.

capture of all of the forts on the Mississippi above Fort Pillow.*

On the thirteenth day of April, 1862, the regiment embarked on the transport Silver Wave, and moved with the army of the Mississippi to Osceola, Askansas, and thence to Fort Pillow, and was present during the bombardment of that fort. On the seventeenth day of April, 1862, the army of the Mississippi, having received orders to reenforce the army of Tennessee, under Halleck, in front of Corinth, proceeded up the Mississippi and Tennessee rivers on the transports. On the twenty-third of April the Sixty-third landed at Hamburgh, Tennessee, four miles above the battle-ground of Shiloh. Stanley's division was posted on the left flank of the army, moving to the capture of Corinth, and during all the movement for its capture, the Sixty-third held its position, as the flanking regiment. It actively participated in all the reconnoissances and engagements in front of Corinth, including those at Monterey and Farmington. When the enemy moved out of Corinth on the thirtieth day of May, the Sixty-third moved out of the trenches in immediate pursuit of the retreating army. The Thirty-ninth Ohio, of our brigade, being the first to enter the rebel works, and Wallace Bruce, of Washington county, being the first to mount the works. The Sixty-third was kept in pursuit of Price's wing of the retreating army, six companies under Major Haskins proceeding to the Tuscumbia river on the Jacinto road, when it found the bridges burned, and was then recalled, and proceeded with the main body of the army in pursuit of Beauregard's army, to Boonville, the Ohio brigade having the advance of the infantry in this movement. † From Boonville, where the pursuit was abandoned, the regiment proceeded to Camp Clear Creek, near Corinth, and remained in camp at Clear Creek, Bear Creek, Iuka, and Burnsville.

On the seventeenth day of September, with Stanley's division, it participated in the battle of Iuka. After a tedious and forced march it came upon the enemy at the beginning of dusk, immediately formed in line of battle, advanced, and opened "that steady fire that always distinguished it in action." It was just getting well into its work when darkness put an end to the fighting, and the two armies bivouacked upon the field. The pickets of the two armies were posted so near as to be able to communicate by ordinary conversation; and pickets of the Ohio brigade were so far advanced as to cover the captured guns of Niel's Eleventh Ohio battery, which the rebels had been unable to remove. The morning's dawn revealed an abandoned rebel camp, and Niel's battery was restored to its gallant owners. An active pursuit was taken up, and from that time until the third of October, 1862, when it entered Corinth, the

Sixty-third was with Rosecrans' army, beating the bush to find and engage the enemy.

The regiment took a most active and honorable part in the battle of Corinth on the third and fourth of October, 1862, and it there proved itself worthy of a place in the history of a county named after the father of our country, to know that she was well and ably represented by an organization performing its whole duty in every great contest during the war, that upon the group of colors of her regiments and batteries are found the names of every great battle of the war. In the battle of Corinth the Sixty-third did great service, and won for itself a place beside the Eighteenth, Thirty-sixth, Thirty-ninth, Seventy-seventh, and Ninety-second, Buell's and Huntington's batteries, and the First, Seventh and Ninth cavalry. The Ohio brigade took so important a part in the battle of Corinth, which would probably have been lost but for their terrific fight, that it deserves to be described at length. We here copy the admirable description of General John W. Fuller, read at the brigade reunion on the sixteenth anniversary of the battle:

On the morning of October 3d, just sixteen years ago to-day, the enemy attacked the division of General Davies at the outer line of works, the line constructed by the rebels when Sidney Johnson and Beauregard held possession of the town. Davies had been ordered there to retard the enemy's advance, until Rosy should be ready to let Van Dorn come in. Van Dorn's superior strength enabled him to drive Davies from this line, but Davies' men fought stubbornly, and fell back over that two or three miles so slowly, that it was near night when they approached the outskirts of the town, and when reenforcements enabled Davies to stop the enemy's advance. After dark the Ohio brigade marched to relieve one of the brigades of Davies' division, and was ordered to occupy the high ground near battery Robinet. Near the crest was formed the line of battle. Directly on the right of the earthwork covering the battery, and stretching across the Chewalla road, stood the men of the Sixty-third; next came the Twenty-seventh, and farther still to the right was the Thirty-ninth regiment. On the left of the battery, facing to the left, and nearly at right angles with the main line, rested the Forty-third.

Let us go back through the intervening years, and in fancy place ourselves on the spot then occupied, and look again over that field which has since been famous. Before you, for three hundred yards, lie in confusion the few trees which have been felled to form a partial abattis. Beyond this stands the forest, and through both, leads, without obstruction, the road to Chewalla. To the right of the Thirty-ninth the line of battle is broken for three hundred yards, by an impassable swamp, beyond which we see the rising ground occupied by several brigades of our infantry, and on the extreme right, perhaps a mile away, the earthwork called Fort Richardson. Turning to look over your right shoulder, you may see what transpires in the streets of Corinth. Without changing your position you may, by looking over the other shoulder, see a part of the division of General McKean, and the redoubt called Battery Phillips, which form the left of Rosecrans' line of battle. If you come to a right about, you see directly in rear the cut through the hill where lies the Memphis railroad, and just over this, on still higher ground, stands Fort Williams, with a twenty pounder Parrot looking out of each embrazure. Your own batteries, company F. of Second United States, and company C, of First Michigan artillery, are ready for action on the high ground abreast of Fort Williams; all apparently so near, that but for their elevated position you might look down the cannons' throats. Here you waited during the long hours of the night of October 3d, and here you fought on the morning of the fourth.

The removal of Davies' skirmish line, which by some mistake was not made known to us, permitted the enemy to advance so closely that, although hidden by the darkness, you could hear him planting his guns in the edge of the forest, not more than three hundred yards in our front; and during the night the commander of that battery (I think from New Orleans) reconnoitering the ground between his guns and your line, was quietly captured, mounted though he was, by Captain (since General) Brown, of the Sixty-third Ohio.

---

*The first slave ever manumitted under the order of President Lincoln, to manumit slaves escaping from the rebel armies to the Union lines, was a body servant of General Jeff Thompson, who came to the lines of the Sixty-third at New Madrid and was manumitted by order of General David S. Stanley. The manumitted contraband was afterward taken to Ohio by General Sprague.

†During the time of the Sixty-third's service before Corinth the Eighth Wisconsin regiment was attached to Stanley's division, and the eagle, Old Abe, was a companion in arms of the boys of the Ohio brigade.

It was a night of suspense and anxiety to all. We knew that General Hackleman had been killed, and we had seen General Oglesby carried to the rear, with a wound we supposed was mortal. Hundreds more, wounded during the day's fight, had been borne to the hospitals, and the men of Davies' division, who had fought against great odds all day had been slowly driven back, seemed well nigh disheartened. You knew you had to meet an enemy not only strong and resolute, but who was also flushed with what he thought a victory. Hence you listened with anxiety to those sounds of preparation, so plainly heard from the hill, where, lying down without sleep, you waited for the assault. It seems strange, in view of the rapid and thorough mode of entrenching afterward acquired, that no attempt was made to fortify, especially since we now know how much superior the enemy was in numbers. But we had not then learned the use of spades.

With the earliest dawn of day, the rebel battery in front opens its fire. What a magnificent display! Nothing you had ever seen looked like the flashes of those guns! No rockets ever scattered fire like the bursting of those shells! Not long, however, for as soon as there is light enough to aim, the twenty-pounder Parrots in Fort Williams suddenly belch forth and make the place occupied by the rebel battery so hot that it is hurriedly withdrawn. Yet not all, for one gun has been abandoned, and some venturesome boys of the Sixty-third Ohio, with others of the First United States infantry, run forward, and pull it into our lines by hand.[*] Then came fierce fighting between the skirmishers. The enemy had the cover of the woods, while our men crept from log to log, in the endeavor to gain the better cover of the forest. Reenforcements to our skirmishers enabled them, after two hours' fighting to drive the rebels back, and gave the shelter sought, but not far off, the conformation of the ground was peculiarly fortunate for the enemy. He could lie on the crest of a series of ridges and sweep everything in his front, scarcely exposing a man to view. Behind these ridges he was massing his men for the assault.

About ten or eleven o'clock, our attention is diverted from the fierce skirmish in our immediate front by the advance of General Price's divisions, which are moving out of the woods to our right front, and marching upon the troops and fort which form the right of Rosecrans' line of battle. A splendid sight is that, as one rebel brigade after another moves in fine style over the ground which our position overlooks so plainly. The attack is fierce, and we soon are shocked to see our line give way and retire into the very town. We notice, too, some of our batteries drawn out of position and rapidly pulled to the rear. The guns of Fort Williams, and of our own batteries directly in our rear, are all turned to the right, and an enfilading fire sweeps through the rebel hosts with an effect very plainly visible; but, though disordered somewhat, they move on; fresh troops pour out of the woods, and we see the rebels rushing over the works on our right, and pouring into Corinth itself. A rolling fire is heard in the streets, and soon after the rebels begin to retire. They stand awhile at the works they had captured, but our boys are coming to the front again from the town. At this juncture, some regiments of Hamilton's division, not previously engaged, are thrown forward on the extreme right, where, as finely aligned as if on parade, they are pouring a stream of lead into the rebel ranks. A little later, we say to each other, most joyously, "Our boys are driving them back again."

But a fiercer fire than ever opens on our own skirmish line, and a constant hum of bullets tells us that our turn is coming now; and it proves to be the rebel centre moving for the main attack upon the place we occupy. Looking through the trees before us, we plainly see the rebel banners and their attacking columns advancing. The Forty-third changes front forward on its right company, and the Eleventh Missouri is rapidly brought forward and held in reserve, just behind the Sixty-third Ohio. Our skirmishers are driven back pell mell upon the line of battle; the artillery with us in Robinet, and the guns which play over our heads from the rear are firing rapidly, and some of your officers are running along the line ordering you to "Get down, and lie low, until they are close upon us." In another minute the head of a rebel column, coming along the Chewalla road, is seen near by, heading straight for the Sixty-third and Battery Robinet. Now you rise to your feet, and pour into the enemy that steady fire which fills the road with his dead, and *seems* to cause a halt; for, though the rear of his column moves steadily on, the head of it comes no nearer, but appears to melt away. But the enemy is firing too. Along the whole length of the Sixty-third, and portions of the Twenty-seventh and Forty-third, officers and men are falling fast.

Some scenes here witnessed, though almost as brief as if revealed by

a flash of lightning, are stamped indelibly upon our memories. Just where the Sixty-third adjoins the Twenty-seventh, three men go down together. One, in the front rank, is lifting his arms high in the air and slowly sinking down. The man behind, and covering the first, drops as if a thunderbolt had struck him, while another turns around, and with a look of agony upon his face, and trying to walk to the rear, moves but a step and falls. Captain McFadden, of the Sixty-third, shouts out his first command in battle and is dead! Lieutenant Webb, of the Twenty-seventh, endeavors to repeat the order to "fire low," and while his mouth is opened wide, a bullet enters. He throws up his hands, and falling on his face is still forever! But the men not hit, heed nothing; they fire incessantly, and their faces black with powder, make noticeable their flashing eyes and set teeth, so that they look like demons.

A minute later the column in the Chewalla road has disappeared, but a strong force a little farther to the west, is approaching the left of Robinet, and is making sad havoc in the ranks of the Forty-third This regiment has hardly finished its manœuvre of changing front, obstructed as is the field with logs and brush, and exposed moreover to a flank fire from the Chewalla road. A glance in their direction reveals a startling picture! Colonel Kirby Smith, commander of the regiment, is down, rider and horse together. Some men now raise him up; his face falls over towards us, and we see his cheek is red with blood. Lieutenant Heyl, the adjutant, trying to keep his saddle, clutches his horse's mane, but gradually looses grip, and before a comrade with outstretched arms can reach him, he is on the ground. A dozen more along the line drop in that instant, and the enemy's fire, from front and flank, is so severe that for a moment a rout is feared; but only for a moment, for Swayne here takes command of the regiment and is steadying the line, and General Stanley, who rode over to the right when he thought that all the fighting was to be done there, gallops back in the nick of time to help. His coming at that critical moment seemed like the arrival of reenforcements. And now this regiment takes sudden vengeance for its colonel's fall; for they drive back with great slaughter, the force which approaches to the left of Robinet, and shoot every rebel who shows his head above the parapet or tries to climb through the embrasures of the battery, when the final effort is made very soon thereafter, to carry the work by storm.

While the Forty-third is thus engaged, Colonel Rogers, commanding the Texan brigade, rides out from the woods, and with his troops moves along the Chewalla road heading for the battery and the Sixty-third. Another moment, his horse is shot and he is coming along the road on foot. His leading color-sergeant falls, when Rogers, picking up the colors, continues to advance with flag in hand. A cloud of rebel skirmishers on either side of the road are firing heavily on the Sixty-third and left wing of the Twenty-seventh, until forty-eight per cent. of the men of the former regiment are killed or wounded, and the line is so much thinned that Colonel Sprague and I, standing behind, can look right through it, and distinctly see the advancing rebels, now close at hand.

I shall always recollect how well Sprague looked at that eventful moment. Tall, and commanding in appearance, with sword in one hand and pistol in the other, he stood as a painter likes to portray an officer in battle. I shall remember, too, looking at the face of the rebel Colonel Rogers, when not distant more than thirty yards, and noting the peculiar expression it bore. He looked neither to the right nor left, neither at his own men nor at mine, but with eyes partly closed, like one in a hail-storm, was marching slowly and steadily upon us; and there flashed through my mind this question, "Is he stupid with drink, or is he simply resolved to calmly meet a fate which he foresees?" Before there was time to answer to myself the question, the rebel column in the road seemed to gain some tremendous impetus from the rear, for it suddenly rushed on like a great wave, threatening to sweep into the gap which had been shot through the Sixty-third, and to carry the redoubt by storm. The supreme moment had now come; and I turned to give the signal to the Eleventh Missouri, in reserve, and close behind. The leader of this regiment, perhaps ten minutes earlier, had received his orders; they had been sung out over the heads of his men, so that every soldier in the ranks knew what was wanted, and there was no need to repeat them now. "Forward!" shouted the major, as the regiment sprang up, and I had to run to the right to let them pass. With a short quick step, and alignment perfect, they filled up the gap which the enemy's fire had made, charging the rebel column on the head. The Twenty-seventh, under Spaulding, which had lost heavily, yet still was full of fight, joined by the plucky remnant of the Sixty-third, rushed forward at the same moment, charging the column obliquely on its left flank, when in an instant the whole scene changed. Rogers, with many of his men, lay dead before us, and those who were

---

[*] Company's B and G.

not prisoners, were flying back to the woods.* One moment, the rebels seemed to be swarming over us in thousands, our own lines looked thin and weak, we seemed threatened with destruction; the next, most of the living of the foremost rebels were our prisoners, a few hundreds, apparently, were running to the forest, while our boys seemed to have swelled into many thousands.

In the melee this banner of the enemy [pointing to a captured flag displayed in rear of the speaker], was captured by a private of the Twenty-seventh Ohio, Orrin B Gould, of company G, who I am glad to see is here to-night. But there was one red flag, I think the banner briefly borne by Rogers, which escaped us as by a miracle. Some bold Texan had picked it up almost from beneath our feet, and throwing the staff across his shoulders, ran in a zig-zag manner for the woods. He dodged behind a log a moment here, then behind a stump there; he was fired at by twenty men or more, 'and once, 'whether hit or not, tumbled headlong when striding a fallen tree. Yet he escaped with the banner after all; and as he passed over the ridge out of our sight, some of our boys who had missed him, gave him the cheer that was due a hero.

An incident may here be mentioned of the Forty-third. When the rebels made their final effort to break through our lines, Lieutenant Robinet, of the battery, severely wounded in the head, fell senseless under one of his guns. At this, most of his men ran to the rear. A moment later, some of the men of company A, of the Forty-third, entered the battery, and aided the few brave fellows who had stood their ground, to man the guns. The enemy was now retreating, and, in the excitement, a little drummer passed directly before the battery and jumped upon a log to see the rebels run. A piece had just been sighted and "ready, fire," followed before the little fellow was discovered. When the smoke cleared up, we saw that both his legs were torn away. Somehow there seemed a sting in the recollection that men of his own regiment had fired this shot And now came Colonel Noyes, of the Thirty-ninth, who was so far to the right that his men could only get an oblique fire, asking permission to bring his regiment to the Chewalla road, where they could take a hand when the next assault should come Two minutes later, the regiment was across the road, but the battle was over

That thrill of ecstasy which victory brings, was here intensified by an act of the commanding general. Rosecrans had lost his temper when the troops attacked by Price had temporarily given way, and had hardly time to become appeased by their subsequent good conduct. Still nursing his wrath, and having seen Van Dorn had met with a different reception at the hands of this brigade, he was disposed to extol the men who fought near Robinet, at the expense of those who had fallen back. So riding to the crest we occupied and pointing to the right, he said: "I have just come from a part of the field where some of our troops retreated like old women, but now I know, not only from what I heard and what I saw from a distance, but also from these piles, of dead along your front, that I am in the presence of brave men! So brave that I take my hat off in your presence, and thank you, in our country's name, for your great valor!" No soldier who heard these words will be likely to forget them, nor the appearance of Rosecrans as he addressed us, hat in hand.

The Sixty-third entered the fight with two hundred and seventy-five men. It held its line stubbornly during the whole fight, and lost six officers and one hundred and thirty-four men, killed and wounded. After the battle, the surviving half of the regiment joined in the pursuit of Van Dorn to Ripley, where the pursuit was abandoned and the regiment returned to Corinth. It remained in camp until the second of November, when it proceeded to join Grant's army. On the route it was reenforced by a battalion of the One Hundred and Twelfth Ohio, which had been consolidated with it, and its depleted ranks filled up. On the eleventh of December it went into camp at Oxford, Mississipi. Late in the evening of the sixteenth of December, the Ohio brigade received orders

to proceed to the rear and protect the lines of communication of the army, from the attacks of Van Dorn, and Forrest's cavalry. On the seventeenth of December it moved by rail to Jackson, Tennessee. Ten days were spent in marching and counter-marching, to intercept the enemy. On the twenty-seventh the regiment joined the command of General Sullivan. On the thirtieth of December Colonel Dunham with his brigade was sent to intercept Forrest at Parker's Cross Roads, and the Ohio brigade had orders to follow in the morning.

On December 31, 1862, at 4 o'clock A. M., the Ohio brigade moved out of its camp and marched until daylight, when it made a short halt for breakfast. Soon it is again on the move, in hunt of the raiders. Then the sound of cannon revealed to them that Forrest and Dunham are engaged, and that they were needed in the fight. In a moment the orders were given, "Unsling knapsacks!" and the road for a mile, occupied by the brigade, was strewn with knapsacks. "Brigade forward, double quick, march!" Then began a march that was worthy of the name. The old brigade went to the front to the music of the battle, on its muscle. It went for the purpose of getting there before the battle was over—and it made its legs tell.

Within an hour and a half it marched seven miles without a halt, with the ranks well closed and at a sight of the enemy deployed in line of battle on the double-quick, and within five minutes it had put Forrest's force to flight, captured six guns, four hundred horses, and three hundred and fifty men.

This record presents one of the best contests made by an infantry against a cavalry force during the war, and fitly rounded up the service of the Ohio brigade for the year 1862. The regiment pursued Forrest's retreating force to the Tennessee river, and then marched back to Corinth over rough, frozen roads, without supplies, but subsisting upon forage gathered on the route. It arrived at Corinth on the ninth of January, and went into winter quarters. Their knapsacks had been gathered and brought into camp by train, and the scene when the soldiers reclaimed their effects was ludicrous beyond description.

When General Grant moved to Vicksburgh the Sixty-third was ordered with the brigade to garrison Memphis, and proceeded there May 16, 1863, and remained there until the eighteenth of October, 1863. This was the only garrison duty done by the Ohio brigade during the war. At the latter date, it left Memphis to join the forces moving to the relief of the army of the Cumberland. On the thirteenth of November it arrived at Prospect, Tennessee. At that place, on January 2, 1864, the regiment reenlisted as veterans, and returned to their homes in Ohio on furlough. The regiment reassembled at Columbus, Ohio, February 18th, and from that point returned to Prospect, Tennessee. Early in the spring the Ohio brigade crossed the Tennessee river, and dispersed the rebel force at Decatur, Alabama. At that point it remained until it moved to join in the Atlanta campaign.

In the Atlanta campaign the Sixty-third participated in

---

* At the time the Eleventh Missouri came up, a clean gap had been shot away between the two wings of the Sixty-third, and eighteen men joined in the charge at the left of the Eleventh Missouri, and one hundred and twenty-seven between the Eleventh Missouri and the Twenty-seventh Ohio, and at the close of the charge the Sixty-third was the most advanced of the line and was requested to fall back and align with the Eleventh Missouri and the Twenty-seventh Ohio.

the battle of Resaca, companies A, C, and H, deployed as skirmishers, were among the first troops to reach the river at that place. On the sixteenth of May, 1864, it crossed Oostenaula, and participated in the actions at Adairsville and in and about Dallas. It sustained an important part in all the movements to dislodge the enemy from Kennesaw mountain. After the evacuation of Marietta, Georgia, the Sixty-third, with Sprague's brigade, was the extreme left of the army; on the twentieth of July moved to Decatur, Georgia, and had charge of the baggage train of the army of the Tennessee, and the twenty-first it rested quietly in Decatur, without incident to disturb it. At noon on July 22d, when the battle of that date was at its height,[*] Wheeler's cavalry with several batteries of artillery made a furious attack on Sprague's brigade, intending to capture it and the train. In this fight that slender brigade had a hand-to-hand contest for three hours with a superior force of rebel cavalry, and succeeded in holding its ground and safely removing the train. The regiment lost heavily in officers and men. For his gallantry and the faithful work of his men in this fight, Colonel Sprague was made brigadier general, and Lieutenant Colonel Charles F. Brown and Captain, afterwards Lieutenant Colonel, Oscar L. Jackson were brevetted brigadier generals for gallantry in battle, and the regiment was complimented by special order for its gallantry. In this battle General Brown lost his leg while at the head of the regiment, and his adjutant, Fower, was killed. After the fall of Atlanta the regiment was in the battle of Jonesborough. At the close of the Atlanta campaign, the Sixty-third joined in Sherman's marched to the sea, sharing in all the dangers and privations of that campaign. It was engaged in the action at Oliver station, and participated in all the movements resulting in the capture of Savannah. It was at the front, and on the tenth of December, 1864, it charged across the Ogechee canal, under a heavy infantry and artillery fire, and obtained a lodgment on the Savannah side. The ground having been secured, the men stacked arms by running bayonets in the ground, removed their clothing and wrung it, and moved on to the fight; the enemy keeping up their artillery fire in the meantime. The Sixty-third entered the city of Savannah on the Twenty-first of December, and remained in and around Savannah until the first of February, 1865. At that date it moved northward, on the line of the Salkahatchee river, and on the third of February it was ordered to and made a gallant assault upon the fort at Rivers Bridges, which it was unable to reach by reason of the intervening river and swamps. At this point it remained in line of battle twenty-four hours, in water and ice from knee to waist deep, holding the enemy engaged in the fort until another force made a detour, crossed the river and turned the fort, when it was abandoned. It then proceeded northward and entered Columbia, South Carolina, on the seventeenth day of February. It continued its march with the army in a northeasterly direction, through the Carolinas; and it participated in the battle

of Bentonville, the last battle of the war, and sustained its well earned reputation. On the thirty-first day of March the regiment had a lively skirmish with the enemy. The Sixty-third had shared, and born a conspicuous part in all the great campaigns of the west, in Sherman's march to the sea, and in his campaign through the Carolinas. After the surrender of Johnston it proceeded northward from Raleigh by Petersburgh, Richmond and Fredericksburgh to Alexandria. Thus after sharing all the campaigns of the west, it had the privilege as a victor of marching over the battle-grounds of the east, where all the great campaigns of the army of the Potomac were fought—and in its marches it had tramped the whole battle-ground of the war. It had fought in the lines with the infantry, and hand-to-hand successfully with the Forrest and Wheeler cavalry.

At Washington it took part in the great review, the grandest spectacle that the world ever witnessed—a veteran army in triumph, passing their country's capital, bearing their torn and battle-scarred banners, the emblems of a free and united country, eager to lay down their arms, to follow the advice and example of Washington, and pursue the avocations of peace. From Washington the regiment proceeded by railroad to Parkersburgh, West Virginia, and thence by boat to Louisville, Kentucky, where it was mustered out on the eighth day of July, A. D. 1865. It was commanded successively by Colonel John W. Sprague, Charles E. Brown, Major John W. Fouts and Captain (afterwards Lieutenant-Colonel) O. L. Jackson. Its colonel was made major-general by brevet, and Colonels Brown and Jackson brigadier generals by brevet for gallantry in action. Of the colonels of the Ohio brigade, J. L. Kirby Smith was killed, and Noyes, Swayne and Brown each lost a leg. Of its officers that became colonels of other regiments one officer deserves special mention. Surgeon Arthur B. Monahan was always conspicuous for his humane, gallant and soldierly bearing. Whenever his regiment was in action, Surgeon Monahan was at the front, and the unfortunate wounded received immediate care and attention. Thus was many a life saved by his untiring devotion.

The Sixty-third is proud that it was one of the regiments of a brigade that tramped the farthest of any in the army—a brigade that never turned its back to the enemy. It is proud of its battle flag[*] and colors, and their staves bearing the names of New Madrid, Island Ten, Farrington, Corinth, Iuka, Hatchie, Parker's Cross Roads, Decatur, Alabama, Resaca, Dallas, Kennesaw Mountain, Marietta, Decatur, Georgia, Siege of Atlanta, Jonesborough, Savannah, Rivers Bridges, and Bentonville,[†] Raleigh.

---

*It was in this battle that McPherson fell, near the Thirty-ninth Ohio, in the lines of the Ohio brigade.

*Of the battle flag of the Sixty-third that was once composed of the beautiful blue silk, with a silk embroidered eagle with spread wings, there remains but the fringe that adorned it when new, and about one foot square of the flag, near the spear point of the staff. The colors, torn and rent, still bear the names of their first battles (the latter ones being enscribed on the staff), and are stained with the blood of one of the color bearers.

†The Sixty-third in the Atlanta, Savannah and Carolina campaigns belonged to the first division of the Seventeenth army corps, army of the Tennessee. Its corps badge is an arrow legend "swift and certain."

COMPANY F, SEVENTY-THIRD OHIO VOLUNTEERS.
REGIMENTAL OFFICERS

Colonel Orland Smith, mustered October 3, 1861, resigned February 17, 1864; Colonel Richard Long, February 17, 1864, resigned June 27, 1864; Colonel Samuel H Hurst, July 13, 1864, not mustered, appointed colonel by brevet March 13, 1865; Lieutenant colonel Jacob Hyer, October 3, 1861, resigned June 21, 1862, brigadier general by brevet March 13, 1865; Lieutenant Colonel Richard Long, June 21, 1862, promoted to colonel; Lieutenant Colonel Samuel H. Hurst, February 17, 1864, promoted to colonel; Lieutenant Colonel Thomas W. Higgins, July 13, 1864, mustered out as major; Major Richard Long, December 20, 1861, promoted to lieutenant colonel; Major Samuel H. Hurst, June 21, 1862, promoted to lieutenant colonel; Major Thomas W. Higgins, November 5, 1862, promoted to lieutenant colonel, Major Thomas Lucas, July 13, 1864, resigned as captain September 11, 1864; Major Abishai Downing, July 17, 1865, mustered out as captain, Surgeon Jonas P. Safford, October 26, 1861, dismissed February 18, 1863; Surgeon Isaac N. Hines, December 31, 1862, mustered out at expiration of term; Surgeon John C. Preston, February 1, 1865, mustered out with regiment; Assistant Surgeon Isaac N. Hines, October 26, 1861, promoted to surgeon February 1, 1863; Assistant Surgeon James Segafoor, August 15, 1862, resigned October 24, 1862; Assistant Surgeon William Richardson, March 18, 1863, resigned June 27, 1864; Assistant Surgeon John C. Preston, March 19, 1863, promoted to surgeon; Assistant Surgeon Smith D. Steer, February 1, 1865, mustered out with regiment; Chaplain Joseph Hill, March 13, 1862, resigned December 17, 1862, Chaplain James R. Stilwell, June 20, 1865; Adjutant Frederick C. Smith, December 26, 1861, died April 25, 1862; Adjutant John Spence, March 1, 1863, resigned May 16, 1864; Adjutant John B. Smith, June 1, 1865, mustered out with regiment; Quartermaster William D. Wesson, October 22, 1861, commissary of subsistence July 17, 1862; Quartermaster Robert M. Rodgers, November 20, 1862, resigned November 5, 1863; Quartermaster William H. Eckman, May 11, 1864, resigned March 30, 1865; Quartermaster James Earl, March 27, 1865, served full term.

OFFICERS OF COMPANY F.

Captain Thomas Lucas, November 20, 1861, promoted to major; Captain George M. Doherty, January 1, 1863, died July 13, 1863; First Lieutenant Charles W. Stone, July 1, 1863, resigned July 5, 1864; First Lieutenant George M. Doherty, November 20, 1861, promoted to captain; First Lieutenant John Burke, March 28, 1865, served full term; First Lieutenant James Ross, May 1, 1865, served full term; Second Lieutenant John Mitchell, November 20, 1861, resigned December 23, 1862; Second Lieutenant Charles W. Stone, December 23, 1862, promoted to first lieutenant.

In September, 1861, Captain Orland Smith of the "Chillicothe Greys" was invited to take the colonelcy of a new regiment proposed to be organized, and Jacob Hyer was tendered the lieutenant colonelcy; both accepted, and the new organization became the gallant Seventy-third Ohio volunteer infantry. Company F of this regiment was raised mainly in old Washington county by Captain Thomas Lucas, and lacking sufficient men to raise it to the maximum number, he took the company to Chillicothe, where they were joined by a fragmentary company under George M. Doherty, who became first lieutenant, and John Mitchell, second lieutenant.

The other companies came from Ross, Highland, Pickaway, Jackson, Pike, and Athens counties. It is needless in the space allotted us to go into separate history of company F. Its history is so closely identified with that of the glorious old Seventy-third—that what we shall say of the regiment will include the company.

Few regiments had the fortune to paticipate in so many and so desperate engagements as this regiment. Starting as they did so early in the war and drifting almost at once into the great army of the Potomac, they soon became familiar with great armies, great battles and great commanders Company F, was organized Novem-

ber 20, 1861, at Camp Logan near Chillicothe, and January 24, 1862, the regiment was ordered to West Virginia. Arriving at Fetterman, they there met the Fifty-fifth, Seventy-fifth, and Eighty-second Ohio regiments, also just entering active service. On the third of February, the Seventy-third and Fifty-fifth Ohio moved to New Creek, where they found three regiments of Virginia infantry, a battery and a detachment of cavalry. They engaged the enemy at Moorfield for the first time, February 13th and 14th, driving him out, and were then ordered to Clarksburgh, where they remained a month, when they went to Weston, where they remained three weeks, and then were ordered to cross the mountains and join Milroy, who took up a position at McDowell, near Bull Pasture river, where, on May 8th, was fought the battle of McDowell, in which the Union forces were outnumbered and compelled to retreat.

General Fremont soon took command of the "Army of the Mountains," and the Seventy-third joined its fortunes to that army at Franklin. On May 25th, General Fremont's army left for the Shenandoah valley to engage "Stonewall" Jackson, who was driving General Banks' army down the valley. Then followed the battle of Cross Keys, the retreat of the enemy and the return of Fremont to Strasburgh and finally to Middletown, where the regiment had a chance to rest and recuperate. While here Fremont was superseded by Siegel, and the "Army of the Mountains" became the First corps army of Virginia. General Schenck was placed in command of the division, and Colonel N. C. McLean of the Seventy-fifth Ohio became commander of the brigade to which the Seventy-third was assigned, including the Fifty-fifth, Seventy-third, and Twenty-fifth Ohio regiments. On the seventh of July, they were in motion, and crossed the Blue Ridge, encamping on the eastern side at Sperryville. At the battle of Cedar Mountain, July 9th, the Seventy-third came up in the night, went into position in line of battle and awaited the dawn of day, to join in the engagement, but the enemy did not wait for them. August 24th, at the battle of Freeman's Ford, the Seventy-third supported the principal battery engaged in that famous artillery duel. At the second battle of Bull Run, August 28th and 29th the Seventy-third took a prominent part, going into the engagement with three hundred and twelve men and losing one hundred and forty-four killed and wounded, besides twenty prisoners, leaving one hundred and forty-eight for duty.

At the battle of Fredericksburgh, the regiment was held in reserve and did not participate. In January, 1863, they were again on the war path, this time with "Burnside stuck in the mud" in his memorable "mud march" on Fredericksburgh and masterly retreat.

General O. O. Howard now took command of the First corps, superseding General Siegel at his own request, and the corps name was changed to Eleventh corps army of the Potomac. General Barlow succeeded Colonel Smith in the command of the brigade. General Hooker now effected a thorough reorganization of the entire army, and armed and equipped them thoroughly. The work occupied the months of February, March and April, and the

Jewett Palmer

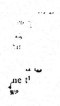

army of the Potomac, one hundred thousand strong at that time seemed capable of sweeping everything before it.

Then came the battle of Chancellorsville, May 2d, and the disheartening "fall back" across the Rappahannock. Then the race between Lee and Hooker for the north, Lee seeking to out-march and distance Hooker, and the latter bent on heading him off. Meanwhile Mead superseded Hooker, and on July 2d the two great armies confronted each other at Gettysburgh, in which three days of tremendous engagements the Seventy-third lost half its number, among the rest Lieutenant G. M. Doherty, of company F. The regiment, with the rest of the victorious army now returned to Virginia.

September 24th the Eleventh and Twelfth corps were ordered to Bridgeport, Alabama, to reenforce the army of the Tennessee, and the whole force of twenty thousand men was transferred by rail in five days, arriving September 30th. They then marched up the Tennessee and joined General Thomas near Brown's Ferry. On October 27th, at about midnight the enemy made an attack on General Geary and the Twelfth corps at Wauhatchie, Tennessee, and the Seventy-third with the division was ordered to their support. The Seventy-third and Thirty-third Massachusetts regiments being in advance, and coming onto the rebels charged up a steep and difficult hill, and upon arriving at the top were received with a deadly fire; but nothing daunted, they fixed bayonets and charged, driving the enemy in confusion from their entrenched position, breaking the rebel line, and compelling the entire attacking force to retire from Geary's position. Indeed, as soon as the Seventy-third Ohio and Thirty-third Massachusetts opened their fire the rebel fire on Geary's line fell off. The conduct of the Seventy-third on this occasion was characterized in the official dispatches of General Grant as "one of the most daring feats of arms of the war."

In the battle of Mission Ridge the Seventy-third formed a part of General O. O. Howard's corps that was pushed out on the left to make a junction with Sherman, and took position on the banks of the Chickamauga, on Sherman's extreme left. Meanwhile Thomas and Hooker had made their famous charge and captured the ridge. On January 4th the regiment went home on veteran furlough.

Upon its return the Seventy-third regiment was assigned to the Third brigade (Wood's), Third division (Butterfield's), and Twentieth corps (Hooper's) army of the Cumberland. The Seventy-third took part in the great Atalanta campaign, and in the battle of Resaca so acquitted itself as to be complimented by the division commander for brilliant conduct.

In the battle of New Hope Church, they occupied the extreme left, and, though in an exposed position and suffering severely, held their position until nightfall, losing three officers and seventy-two men in killed and wounded.

Around Kennesaw Mountain the Seventy-third was in several severe engagements, losing heavily; in front of Marietta, Georgia, sixteen, and in another engagement nineteen men in killed and wounded. On June 20th, they engaged in the battle of Peach Tree Creek, losing

eighteen men. The rebels were now hotly besieged in Atlanta, and the Seventy-third was constantly under fire and in the front line of works. Upon the evacuation, two companies of the Seventy-third, forming part of a reconnoissance, were the first troops to enter the city. In this campaign of one hundred and twenty days, the regiment had been under fire one hundred and three days, and lost two hundred and ten men and eight officers out of less than three hundred and fifty.

On November 15th, they started with Sherman on his memorable "March to the Sea," being in the Twentieth corps, under General Williams, and, in the left wing, commanded by General Slocum. The regiment reached Savannah without firing a shot.

January 2, 1865, the regiment crossed the Savannah into South Carolina, and entered upon its last campaign. At the battle of Averysborough the Seventy-third engaged the enemy, losing fifteen wounded.

On Sunday, March 19th, they took part in the battle of Bentonville, the last engagement of the war, loosing five men killed, and four officers and twenty-one men wounded.

After the march to Washington and the grand review, the Seventy-third was sent to Louisville, and on July 20th was mustered out, and returning to Camp Dennison, Ohio, was there finally paid off and discharged July 24th, after a service of three years and eight months.

It was always in actual service, never at posts or guarding communications. It marched several thousand miles, participated in twenty battles, not to speak of numerous skirmishes. On three occasions, in connection with its brigade, its behavior in battle decided the fortunes of the day. Its discipline and drill were uniformly the subject of remark in its brigade and division. As proof of its gallantry and services, out of a little more than twelve hundred members, including recruits, two hundred and eighty-five sleep beneath the sod, and five hundred and sixty-eight are now bearing about the scars of honorable combat, many of them crippled for life.[1]

CASUALTIES.

Killed in battle, 95; died of wounds, 61; died of disease, etc., 129; dead of the regiment, 285; wounded, not fatally, 568.

SEVENTY-SEVENTH OHIO VOLUNTEER INFANTRY.

REGIMENTAL OFFICERS.

Colonel Jesse Hildebrand, mustered October 5, 1861, died April 18, 1863; Colonel William B. Mason, April 18, 1863, mustered out December 31, 1864; Colonel William E. Stevens*, March 7, 1866, mustered out as lieutenant colonel, Lieutenant Colonel Wills De Hass‖, October 5, 1861, dismissed February 16, 1863; Lieutenant Colonel William E. Stevens, March 19, 1864, promoted to colonel; Lieutenant Colonel Charles H. Morris*, March 7, 1866, mustered out as captain; Major Benjamin D. Fearing, December 17, 1861, appointed lieutenant colonel Ninety-second Ohio volunteer infantry, August 26, 1862; Major William B. Mason, August 26, 1862, promoted to colonel; Major Louis E. Sisson‖, March 19, 1864, mustered out December 10, 1864; Major Charles H. Morris, November 14, 1865, promoted to lieutenant colonel; Major Robert E. Smithson, March 7, 1866, mustered out as captain; Surgeon James W. Warfield,† February 3, 1862, honorably discharged May 15, 1864; Surgeon Andrew Wall,§ August 11, 1864, mustered out with regiment; Assistant Surgeon Pardon Cook, October 29, 1861, died August 31, 1863; Assistant Surgeon Andrew Wall, September 8, 1862, promoted to surgeon; Assistant Surgeon Yearsley H. Jones, September 17, 1864, mustered out December 31, 1864; Chaplain William Pearce, January 4, 1862, resigned August 31, 1862; Chaplain James T. Holliday, July 13, 1864, mustered out December 31, 1864.

---

1 Ohio in the War.

28

COMPANY OFFICERS.

Captain William E. Stevens, company A, November 23, 1861, promoted to major; Captain William B. Mason, B, December 2, 1861, promoted to major; Captain Louis E. Sisson, C, December 10, 1861, promoted to major; Captain Enoch W. Blasdell, D, December 12, 1861, resigned February 25, 1863; Captain Andrew Smith, † E, December 12, 1861, resigned February 5, 1863; Captain James H. Lutgen, ‡ F, December 31, 1861, resigned March 16, 1864, Captain Andrew W. McCormick, G, December 31, 1861, brevet lieutenant colonel mustered out March 12, 1865; Captain Richard Fouraker, H, December 31, 1861, resigned September 2, 1862; Captain William P. Robinson, I, December 31, 1861, mustered out December 27, 1864, Captain Albert Chandler, K, January 4, 1862, mustered out January 3, 1865; Captain Isaac B. Kinkead, K, April 8, 1862, mustered out April 18, 1863; Captain Robert H. McKitrick, B, August 26, 1862, mustered out August 27, 1865; Captain Thomas Ross, H, September 2, 1862, dismissed March 29, 1864, Captain Thomas Garrett, † E, February 6, 1863, mustered out December 12, 1864, Captain Samuel S. McNaughton, D, February 25, 1863, mustered out January 16, 1865; Captain Charles H. Morris, A, April 18, 1863, promoted to major; Captain Thomas Mitchell, II, March 19, 1864, resigned December 9, 1864; Captain William H. Fisher, K, March 29, 1865, mustered out as first lieutenant March 5, 1865; Captain William W. Scott, C, March 29, 1865, resigned December 1, 1865; Captain Robert E. Smithson, E, March 29, 1865, promoted to major; Captain Samuel Fulton,* F, March 29, 1865, mustered out with regiment, Captain Robert H. Flemming, D, March 29, 1865, mustered out with regiment, Captain Henry L. Pugh, B, September 29, 1865, mustered out with regiment; Captain John L. McIntyre, E, November 14, 1865, mustered out with regiment as first lieutenant, Captain Leonard A. Marlow, C, December 30, 1865, mustered out with regiment; Captain Gordon B. West, E, March 7, 1866, mustered out as first lieutenant and regimental quartermaster; First Lieutenant Harvey Anderson,* A, November 23, 1861, resigned February 13, 1863; First Lieutenant Robert H. McKitrick, B, December 2, 1861, promoted to captain; First Lieutenant Thomast Mitchell, C, December 2, 1861, promoted to captain; First Lieutenant John Henricle, D, December 2, 1861, resigned September 20, 1862; First Lieutenant Thomas Garrett, E, December 2, 1861, promoted to captain, First Lieutenant Hershel B. White, ‡ F, December 2, 1861, discharged October 21, 1862; First Lieutenant Samuel S. McNaughton, G, December 2, 1861, promoted to captain; First Lieutenant William W. Scott, H, December 2, 1861, discharged August 31, 1862; First Lieutenant Horatio W. Mason, H, January 4, 1862, resigned March 6, 1862, First Lieutenant William West, regimental quartermaster, October 15, 1861, resigned June 5, 1862; First Lieutenant Thomas J. Cochran, adjutant, November 25, 1861, resigned October 6, 1862, First Lieutenant William H. Fisher, F March 6, 1862, promoted to captain; First Lieutenant Thomas Ross H, March 27, 1862, promoted to captain; First Lieutenant Edgar B Pearce, regimental quartermaster, June 5, 1862, mustered out December 31, 1864, First Lieutenant David F. Jones, B, August 26, 1862, mustered out December 10, 1864; First Lieutenant William P. Richner,* D, September 20, 1862, mustered out December 11, 1864; First Lieutenant Marion N. Burris, adjutant, October 6, 1862, resigned July 15, 1863; First Lieutenant Edward R. Moore, D, August 31, 1862, discharged August 1, 1863; First Lieutenant Hanson Criswell, † E, August 2, 1862, resigned June 26, 1863; First Lieutenant David A. Henery, F, October 31, 1862, resigned December 9, 1864; First Lieutenant William W. Scott, I, February 5, 1863, promoted to captain, First Lieutenant Charles A. Morris, A, February 13, 1863, promoted to captain; First Lieutenant Robert E. Smithson, G, February 25, 1863, promoted to captain; First Lieutenant Samuel Fulton, A, April 18, 1863, promoted to captain; First Lieutenant Charles J. Eagles, B, March 19, 1864, resigned December 9, 1864; First Lieutenant Henry L. Pugh, F, March 19, 1864, promoted to captain; First Lieutenant Robert H. Flemming, D, August 1, 1863, promoted to captain, First Lieutenant Nathan B. Smith, K, March 19, 1864, resigned as second lieutenant July 7, 1865, not mustered as first lieutenant; First Lieutenant John L. McIntyre, E, March 29, 1865, promoted to captain. First Lieutenant Leonard A. Marlow, C, March 29, 1865, promoted to captain; First Lieutenant Gordon B. West, G, March 29, 1865, promoted to captain; First Lieutenant Robert C. Berry, H, March 29, 1865, mustered out June 28, 1865; First Lieutenant Augustus McCarty, F, March 29, 1865, never mustered as lieutenant; First Lieutenant William W. Burns, C, March 29, 1865, mustered out with regiment; First Lieutenant Joseph M. Mitchell, A, March 29, 1865, mustered out with regiment; First Lieutenant William M. Atkinson, B, March 29, 1865, mustered out with regiment; First Lieutenant Benjamin T. Hill,* September 29,

1865, mustered out with regiment as first lieutenant and adjutant; First Lieutenant Henry H. Dye, November 14, 1865, resigned October 10, 1865, as second lieutenant; First Lieutenant William A. Day, E, November 16, 1865, mustered out with regiment as second lieutenant; First Lieutenant John Smith, ‡ K, December 30, 1865, mustered out with regiment as second lieutenant; First Lieutenant Thomas Wiseman, C, December 30, 1865, mustered out with regiment; First Lieutenant James P. Daugherty, March 7, 1866, mustered out with regiment as second lieutenant; Second Lieutenant Joseph J. Steenrod,* A, November 23, 1861, killed April 8, 1862, Second Lieutenant David F. Jones, B, December 2, 1861, promoted to first lieutenant, Second Lieutenant Marion N. Burris, C, December 10, 1861, promoted to first lieutenant; Second Lieutenant Edward R. Moore, D, December 12, 1861, promoted to first lieutenant; Second Lieutenant Hanson Criswell, † E, December 12, 1861, promoted to first lieutenant; Second Lieutenant Oliphant S Thomas, * G, December 10, 1861, died May 31, 1862; Second Lieutenant David A. Henery, ‡ F, December 21, 1861, promoted to first lieutenant, Second Lieutenant Levi J Fouraker, H, December 31, 1861, discharged October 21, 1863; Second Lieutenant Henry Hobletzell, ‖ I, December 31, 1861, dismissed January 8, 1863; Second Lieutenant William H Fisher, ‡ K, November 5, 1861, promoted to first lieutenant; Second Lieutenant Robert B. Griggs, K, March 6, 1862, discharged August 5, 1862, Second Lieutenant Charles H. Morris, A, April 8, 1862, promoted to first lieutenant; Second Lieutenant Thomas R. Campbell, B, August 26, 1862, died September 25, 1862; Second Lieutenant Robert E. Smithson, G, May 31, 1862, promoted to first lieutenant; Second Lieutenant Charles J. Eagler, B, August 26, 1862, promoted to first lieutenant; Second Lieutenant Jesse Hildebrand, jr., H, October 21, 1862, resigned January 23, 1864; Second Lieutenant Henry L Pugh, F, August 26, 1862, promoted to first lieutenant; Second Lieutenant Nathan B. Smith, ‡ K, October 21, 1862, promoted to first lieutenant; Second Lieutenant Gordon B. West, G, February 11, 1863, promoted to first lieutenant; Second Lieutenant John L. McIntyre, † G, January 1, 1863, promoted to first lieutenant; Second Lieutenant Jesse S. Province, I, May 1, 1862, mustered out December 27, 1864; Second Lieutenant Isaac B. Kinkead, K, November 1, 1862, promoted to first lieutenant, Second Lieutenant Samuel Fulton, A, February 13, 1863, promoted to first lieutenant; Second Lieutenant Robert H. Flemming, D, February 25, 1863, promoted to first lieutenant; Second Lieutenant Leonard A. Marlow, C, January 1, 1863, promoted to first lieutenant; Second Lieutenant Robert C. Berry, A, April 18, 1863, promoted to first lieutenant, Second Lieutenant William E. Smithson, B, November 1, 1863, mustered out December 11, 1864; Second Lieutenant Benjamin T. Hill, adjutant, March 29, 1865, promoted to first lieutenant; Second Lieutenant Henry H. Dye, H, March 29, 1865, resigned October 10, 1865; Second Lieutenant William A. Day, E, March 29, 1865, promoted to first lieutenant; Second Lieutenant John Smith, March 29, 1865, promoted to first lieutenant; Second Lieutenant Thomas Wiseman, C, May 31, 1865, promoted to first lieutenant; Second Lieutenant Joseph M. Mitchell, A, March 29, 1865, promoted to first lieutenant, Second Lieutenant William W. Burris, A, June 29, 1865, promoted to first lieutenant; Second Lieutenant Henry H. Clindenst, September 29, 1865, never mustered; Second Lieutenant Gamaliel J. Lund, B, November 14, 1865, mustered out with regiment as sergeant, Second Lieutenant Jeremiah Fish, † November 14, 1865, mustered out with regiment as sergeant; Second Lieutenant James P. Daugherty, November 14, 1865, promoted to first lieutenant; Second Lieutenant William H. Hose, November 14, 1862, mustered out with regiment, Second Lieutenant William H. Hanson, G, November 16, 1865, mustered out with regiment as sergeant; Second Lieutenant Christopher Black,* December 30, 1865, mustered out with regiment as sergeant; Second Lieutenant William H. Bingman, ‡ March 7, 1866, mustered out with regiment as sergeant.

Early in September, 1861, the quota of Ohio being full at the time, Governor F. Pierpont, of Virginia, commissioned Jesse Hildebrand, of Marrietta, Ohio, colonel, and Wills DeHass, of Wheeling, lieutenant colonel, to raise a regiment along the Ohio river for the United States service. It was soon manifest that the men composing the regiment would be nearly all recruited in Ohio, and as the Government would now accept them, Governor Dennison proposed to Colonel

Officers not from Washington county are marked: * Monroe, † Belmont, ‡ Morgan, ‖ West Virginia, § Cambridge, Ohio.

Hildebrand to enter the Ohio service, which proposition was accepted, and the organization was made the Seventy-seventh regiment of Ohio infantry. Recruiting officers were appointed October 10th, and the place of rendezvous was Camp Tupper, Marietta. With the exception of company A from Monroe county, company E from Belmont county, and company F from Morgan county, all the companies of the regiment were almost entirely composed of Washington county men—there being some recruits from Monroe and Noble counties in several of them.

By the last of December the regiment was full and many men recruited for it were transferred to the Sixty-third Ohio infantry. On the ninth of January, 1862, the Seventy-seventh left Marietta for camp Dennison, where the regiment was engaged in drilling until the seventeenth of February, when it was ordered to Cincinnati, and at once embarked on transports for Paducah, Kentucky, for service on the Tennessee. Landing at Paducah on the twentieth, it was assigned to General W. T. Sherman's division. After drilling and doing guard duty without arms till the ninth of March, it was armed and brigaded with the Fifty-third and Fifty-seventh Ohio and Fifth cavalry regiments, and embarked on transports for Pittsburgh Landing and other points on the Tennessee. Colonel Hildebrand being in command of the brigade, and Lieutenant Colonel DeHass absent, the regiment was under command of Major Benjamin D. Fearing. The regiment joined in the expedition to cut the enemy's communications by destroying the Memphis & Charleston railroad, and landed at the mouth of Yellow creek March 14th; but the heavy rains and the position of the enemy rendering this impracticable, the expedition returned next day and disembarked at Pittsburgh Landing on the sixteenth. On the seventeenth it marched under General Sherman to near Monterey, in the direction of Corinth, where the enemy was in heavy force, and returning went into camp at Shiloh Church on the eighteenth. Still other reconnoissances towards Purdy and Corinth were made, and on the first of April the regiment moved with the division, by transports, to Eastport, Mississippi, driving the enemy from Eastport towards Iuka. After its return to Shiloh, the Third brigade, of which this regiment was a part, was encamped on the left of the Corinth road, the right of the brigade resting on the Church.

The Seventy-seventh camped on the left of the Corinth road, its right resting on Shiloh church, which was used for regimental headquarters. On Friday evening, April 4th, Captain Mason's company, B, was on picket near the Lee house, in front of Shiloh church, and plainly heard beating of drums a short distance south. They wondered whether our troops were moving towards Corinth. When daylight came they discovered that the birds, rabbits, and squirrels were coming towards them and passing through the guard line, being too much frightened to notice the pickets, thus showing that a large body was near on the south. Captain Mason at once established a few new vidette posts at favorable points of observation, and before noon a squad of gray-coated

cavalry passed along the ridge, about seventy-five yards distant, several of them firing at the vidette. About two o'clock large bodies of cavalry were seen approaching the Union line, and filing off to the right, keeping under cover as much as possible. Soon after, column after column of infantry arrived at the same point, filing off to the right and left, taking up their position in line of battle. Several pieces of artillery also went into position on the ridge, just at the edge of the open field. Captain Mason, believing this display of the enemy worthy of reporting, sent Sergeant C. J. Eagler, now of Macksburgh, to inform Colonel Hildebrand just what had transpired, and then report back to the picket line. The sergeant promptly obeyed the order, and Colonel Hildebrand, brigade commander, says he at once went to division headquarters and repeated the report the captain had sent him, word for word. General Sherman ridiculed the idea of such a force being seen, and ordered the messenger arrested. In obedience to this order the colonel sent Captain Stevens, with a portion of his command, to arrest Eagler for bringing false and scary news from the front. On learning the object of his arrival, Captain Mason said to Captain Stevens: "You have not men enough to take Eagler; he has simply obeyed my orders, which he swore to do when he enlisted. Go back to headquarters and have the order changed to my arrest, for I am responsible, and have sent in the facts, as all on duty here know."

Captain Stevens returned, reporting the facts as related. Soon after, Colonel Hildebrand, with part of his staff, came out to the picket line, and, after saluting, said: "Captain Mason, what does all this mean?" He replied: "General, it means the enemy are directly in our front. Do you wish to see them? If so, ride to that little opening to the right, and about two rods in advance." He and his staff did so, accompanied by the captain, who pointed out the enemy, whom the colonel could see without the aid of a field-glass, when Colonel Hildebrand exclaimed: "My God! General Sherman has been deceived, for he told us to-day there was no enemy this side of Corinth, except some reconnoitring parties." He returned to camp, and took the precaution of doubling his picket line by detailing companies C and G, Captains Sisson and McCormick, to relieve company B, at dusk, Saturday evening. He also reported to General Sherman that he had been to the picket line, and it was true that the enemy were in our front in force, with the appearance of a determination to attack.

Notwithstanding these facts, orders were received near midnight, by company commanders of the Seventy-seventh, "Form your companies on the color-line at daybreak in the morning, move to the old drill-ground, and drill one hour before breakfast." Captain Mason, receiving this order with the rest, and knowing that Colonel Hildebrand knew the facts above related, went to him, and after talking a few minutes, casually asked who originated the order for regimental drill in the morning. Colonel Hildebrand picked up a paper from his desk and observed: "This is the order of General Sherman, but we know it will be a different ·drill on the morrow than any of us has ever seen." That order has always been a mystery to the Seventy-seventh.

Before daylight a battalion under Major Powell passed through our picket lines, reconnoitring, and at once became engaged with the enemy's advance. An orderly was sent by Captain McCormick to brigade headquarters with a report of this fact, and the officers in command of the pickets received orders to hold their ground as long as possible, and if hard pressed to fall back slowly, which orders were strictly obeyed, the pickets becoming engaged at daybreak. This was probably the first time Ohio troops were engaged with the enemy at Shiloh, it being in fact the opening day of that bloody contest.

At daylight the regiment was on its way to the drill-ground, but after having gone a few hundred yards, was overtaken by an orderly and ordered back, to breakfast and fall into line immediately. It returned, but before breakfast was over the orders were: "Seventy-seventh, fall into line, quick! Company B will move to the front, deploy as skirmishers, and move forward to the Lee house." The regiment formed, and the skirmishers advanced rapidly across the bridge, about fifty yards in front, and were ordered by the captain to deploy to the right. In a few minutes they were directly under fire of the enemy, and many were shot down—among the first killed being that noble soldier, George A. Booth, of Marietta.

On the night of April 5th, companies C and G, under Captains Sisson and McCormick, relieved company B, Captain Mason, on the picket line. When the pickets were changed that evening, the enemy was so near that his outposts could easily be seen by our men. General Sherman had, the night before, ordered that on the morning of the sixth of April the Seventy-seventh regiment should be posted covering the open field to the right of the Lee house, near the advance picket line. In the morning it was found impossible to reach that position, as the enemy had forced the pickets to fall back, so that the skirmish line of the regiment met them between the Lee house and the creek which ran in front of the camp. The pickets were reenforced by the skirmishers, and the brigade formed in line of battle between the church and the creek, covering the road to Corinth. Here the battle opened sooon after sunrise by a heavy fire of musketry on both sides, assisted on the Union side by Taylor's Chicago battery. The enemy had also artillery engaged at this point. The line of the enemy as they came down the western slope could be distinctly marked in the woods by the glitter of their polished muskets in the sunlight, and the fire was most deadly from the ponderous French rifled muskets with which the Seventy-seventh was armed. This position was held, with one slight change, for about two hours, and the valley was strewn thickly with the enemy's dead, while our losses were also heavy. After a bloody conflict of some hours, the left of the brigade was turned, and the Seventy-seventh changed position so that its left rested on the old church.

Writers of history give it the credit, in connection with the Fifty-seventh and a part of the Fifty-third, of holding the enemy so long in check at this point as to enable Sherman to save the fortunes of the day.

It was here that Colonel E. C. Dawes, a Washington county soldier, then adjutant of the Fifty-third (in connection with Captain, afterwards Colonel W. S. Jones), distinguished himself by rallying a part of his regiment and fighting bravely. The overwhelming numbers of the enemy sweeping around the left rendered it necessary, as the day advanced, after many hours of gallant fighting, for the brigade to again change to the ridge further north, contesting the ground with the foe, step by step, and losing brave men by the score. Each chosen position was, in its turn, assaulted and carried by the enemy till about the middle of the afternoon, when the line was formed and held till the conflict of the day closed with the dusk of evening.

On the morning of the seventh the regiment was promptly in line, waiting orders to move to the attack, but as General Buell's army had arrived and joined General Grant's forces, these fresh troops led the advance; and before noon the enemy were in full retreat without the Seventy-seventh being actively engaged that day—though being in supporting distance of the advance line the regiment was only a part of the time under fire. By the middle of the afternoon it occupied its old camp at the church.

*On Tuesday morning, April 8th, General Sherman's division moved out the Corinth road in pursuit of the retreating enemy. General Breckenridge's division of Hardee's corps, with Forrest's brigade of Confederate cavalry, covered the enemy's retreat. A battalion of cavalry having reported to General Sherman that "the woods was full of rebs," he asked Colonel Hildebrand to halt his brigade and send a regiment forward and "clean out the woods." Colonel Hildebrand selected his own regiment whose position was in the rear of the brigade. The regiment moved promptly forward, and in a few minutes its skirmishers were engaged with the enemy. Coming forward into line and to a halt, a sharp fire was opened upon the cavalry brigade in its front, which proved to be Wirt Adams' Mississippians, Forrest's Kentucky cavalry, and the Texas rangers. In a few moments it was seen that the cavalry were about to charge, and bayonets were fixed to receive them. On they came with dashing impetuosity, discharging their double-barreled shotguns as they came, thus killing and wounding enough to thin out our short line of battle. When within a rod or two of our line they halted and emptied their revolvers on our gallant men, while still out of reach of their bayonets. Then a dash was made to make prisoners of the survivors, which was partly successful, as Captain McCormick (having his right arm broken by a gunshot), Captain Chandler, Lieutenant Criswell, and about thirty-five men were captured—several others of them being badly

---

*On the night of the seventh a large part of the regiment did picket duty all night in the rain, Lieutenant Jeseph J. Steenrod being in command of the pickets. There were three alarms during the night so the men got no rest. Captain Stevens having been wounded, was unable to go on the expedition on the morning of the eighth, so Lieutenant Steenrod was in command of company A and was killed in battle. He was a noble officer.

wounded. But for the timely order of Colonel Hildebrand bringing the Fifty-third and Fifty-seventh Ohio
regiments to the rescue, the most of the regiment, and
with it General Sherman, would have been made prisoners. The general had so much faith in the regiment,
and appeared to doubt the report of his cavalry so much,
that he felt sure of the success of the movement, and was
almost abreast of the regiment when this powerful brigade
of the enemy's best cavalry charged down upon its
thinned ranks.

Among those killed in the battle on Sunday were non-
commissioned officers George A. Booth, Lorain Burris,
Jacob R. Batten, George A. Cavanaugh, John Cline,
John P. Calvert, James Flemming, Benjamin M. Kimberly and John Sanford. Lieutenant O. S. Thomas was
mortally wounded, and died May 31, 1862; and Sergeant
Major G. B. West was wounded.

So great had been our loss in the first day's fight in killed
and wounded, and by disease in camp, that the regiment
took but about two hundred and ten men into this battle
at Fallen Timbers," as it is sometimes called, about sixty-
five of whom it there lost. Among those killed here were
Lieutenant Joseph Steenrod, Andrew J. Duvall, William L.
Porterfield, John H. Kepburn, James M. Baker, Percival
Nott, Daniel Sipple, Lyman Wyss, and Royal A. Wright,
non-commissioned officers, with eighteen privates. Lieutenants Fisher, Fouraker, Garrett, White and Thomas
Mitchell, were wounded.

The regiment lost in the battles of Shiloh, including
the fight of Tuesday, one officer and fifty men killed,
seven officers and one hundred and ten men mounted,
besides several reported missing in action - now almost
certainly known to sleep on this bloody field in unmarked
graves. Its loss was, with two or three exceptions, the
largest of any regiment in the army. Three officers and
fifty-three men were captured, the privates being paroled
in a few days and the officers held till October, when
they were paroled and soon exchanged.

Colonel Jesse Hildebrand, himself a gallant officer, in
his report as brigade commander, says: "With regard
to the officers and men who participated in the affair at
Fallen Timbers, and at Shiloh, I am happy to bear testimony to the fidelity, bravery and devotion of all. Major
B. D. Fearing, who was in immediate command of the
Seventy-seventh Ohio volunteer infantry, was cool and
brave, and acquitted himself with as much skill as an old
officer of larger experience, and was not excelled by any
other field officer who came under my observation."
He also spoke of Captains Chandler and McCormick as
meritorious officers—the latter being since brevetted
major for "meritorious services in the battle of Shiloh."
Captain Mason, also, was distinguished for the part he
took in these three days' fight.

General Sherman, in published orders, speaks in high
terms of praise regarding the firmness in which the
Seventy-seventh held the position at Shiloh church
against such fearful odds, and credited with saving from
capture the Chicago artillery. He has since said much
more in commendation of these gallant heroes, which it
is hoped he will put into form for preservation in history.

After the battle and up to the capture of Corinth, May
30th, the Seventy-seventh took a prominent part in the
siege, being often under fire, and all the time engaged in
building works and otherwise aiding to capture the place
by regular approaches. It advanced in pursuit of the
retreating enemy as far as Chewalla, and during June
and until July 21st, it was on expeditions to Holly
Springs, Mississippi, Moscow, Macon, Lagrange, Tennessee, and other places. July 21st, it reached Memphis,
where the men did guard duty till August 27th, when
the regiment was ordered to Alton, Illinois, to guard
prisoners of war and recruit its thinned ranks—relieving
General Sherman's old regiment, the Thirteenth United
States infantry.

Being recruited up to a minimum the regiment was
ordered to join General F. Steele's expedition for the
capture of Little Rock and other places in Arkansas, leaving on the thirty-first of July, 1863, for Helena, where it
landed August 5th. It was here brigaded with the
Forty-third Indiana and Thirty-sixth Iowa, as the Third
brigade of the Third division of the Arkansas expedition,
and marched on the eleventh for the State capital. The
men were in fine condition, and endured the arduous
march with commendable spirit. They exhibited the
true spirit of tried soldiers in the various brushes with
the enemy on the way. Halting a brief period at Clar-
endon and Duval's Bluffs, the army marched, on the
first of September, across Grand Prairie without water,
through a broiling hot sun in which many of the men
were sun-struck, inflicting incurable if not fatal injuries,
reaching Brownsville in the evening. On the fourth of
September, the regiment made a feint on the enemy's
position at Bayou Meteor, accompanied by a few pieces
of artillery, shelling them from their position and returning to Brownsville. On this march the commanding
officer of the regiment, Colonel William B. Mason, met
with a serious accident; his horse becoming entangled in
fallen telegraph wires, was unmanageable, and the
colonel being thrown off with great force, received injuries which would ordinarily prove fatal, but a good
constitution and the skill and care of Surgeon Wall enabled him to live through them.

On the tenth of September the army drove the enemy
from Little Rock and entered the capital, where the
whole army encamped till December. The forces of
Generals Fagan, Marmaduke, Shelby, and others, were
hovering in the vicinity and awaiting an opportunity to
make an assault, and if possible retake the place. General Steele had the railroad repaired from Duval's Bluffs
to Little Rock, and officers and men of the Seventy-
seventh were detailed to run it, as well as to guard saw-
mills in the vicinity while lumber was cut to build winter
quarters. In this way, and in scouting the country,
guarding supply trains to Pine Bluffs, and conducting
court martial business, the officers and men were employed till December 20th, when almost all the men fit
for military duty reenlisted as veteran volunteers—a
movement towards reenlisting having begun in the regiment as early as October. On the 23d of December,
the regiment started to Columbus, Ohio, where it arrived

January 10, 1864, and on the twenty-second of January, the men were mustered as veterans and furloughed for thirty days. Colonel Mason, Captain McCormick, Captain Morris and Lieutenant Fisher, were appointed recruiting officers, and when the regiment reached Camp Dennison, the rendezvous, to start for the field, it had about two hundred recruits in its ranks.

Reaching its rendezvous February 26th, the regiment left, March 1st, for Little Rock, where it arrived on the seventeenth. It was ordered to march with General Steele's expedition, and left on the twenty-third for Shreveport, Louisiana, to cooperate with Banks' Red River expedition. At Spoonville, April 2d, a skirmish took place, but the regiment lost no men. At Okalona, on the third, it was again under fire, having a prominent position and bearing itself creditably while aiding Colonel Goetz to drive a battery from its position. At Elkin's Ford, on the sixth, it next met and assisted in driving the foe, as it did again at Prairie de Ann on the thirteenth. The army was attacked at Moscow on the thirteenth, but there was not much fighting. Arriving at Camden on the sixteenth, and driving out the enemy, it was learned from telegrams captured that General Banks' Red River expedition had been defeated. Our troops had started from Little Rock with only half rations of hard bread and quarter rations of pork, and had been long out of meat, subsisting partly on the country. General Clayton had started a supply train from Pine Bluffs to meet Steele's forces at Camden, but it did not arrive on time, and there was much suffering for food. After its arrival, General Steele ordered the thoroughly effective men of the brigade, except the guards at headquarters and at two mills that were grinding corn and the pickets of the division (which consisted of portions of the Seventy-seventh Ohio, Forty-third Indiana, and Thirty-sixth Iowa), to escort the empty wagon train back to Pine Bluffs, and on the twenty-third it crossed the Washita river on pontoon bridges and left Camden. Colonel Drake, of the Thirty-sixth Iowa, commanded the brigade, and Captain McCormick was elected by Colonel W. B. Mason as the senior officer present to command that portion of the Seventy-seventh that was detailed. About two hundred of the First Indiana and Seventh Missouri cavalry and a section of the Second Missouri battery accompanied the train. On the twenty-fifth of April this little force, guarding about two hundred and fifty wagons, found in battle array over six thousand mounted rebels at Marks' Mills, forty-five miles from Camden and about the same distance from Pine Bluffs. The enemy had taken another route from Camden and struck on our flank at this junction. The train was passing from Bayou Moro through woodlands over a narrow road, so it was stretched out some five miles long. In this condition it was not difficult for the enemy to divide the regiments at the cross-roads and attack them in detail. This was done, and their heavy force surrounded and captured the two other regiments, after a sharp fight. Hearing the battle open several miles ahead, while they were guarding the rear of the train, the commander of the detailed portion of the Seventy-seventh moved his command forward

on the double-quick, passing wagons and pieces of artillery mired in the swampy Moro bottoms. Moving as rapidly as possible the entire distance, and coming up almost breathless to Marks' Mills, the detachment of the Seventy-seventh arrived only in time to find that their comrades had been captured, and that they must fight the battle alone. The entire force of the enemy, except a few hundreds left guarding the prisoners, now confronted the gallant Ohio boys. Quickly throwing out skirmishers to protect the flanks, Captain McCormick at once formed his command in line of battle, in a good position, and endeavored to protect the remaining half of the train. For more than an hour longer was the enemy held at bay by this little band of about three hundred men, amidst a hotly contested conflict of arms. Twice was General Cabell's brigade in front of our noble boys driven back, causing the brigade commander to ask them if they were "going to let that little handful whip them." Meantime, Adjutant Flemming and Quartermaster Fisher, who had been sent out to the cross-roads to see if there was any danger of being flanked, reported that there was a heavy body of troops on the right, and another to the left and rear, threatening to surround the little Union band. These proved to be the brigades of General Dockery and General Shelby. Notwithstanding these fearful odds, the Seventy-seventh boys and their commander were unwilling to give up the conflict, but continued to pour well directed shots into the heavy lines of the enemy, defying the leaden hail which stormed around them. After keeping up this unequal contest for about two hours, the brave boys found their ammunition exhausted and themselves entirely surrounded and prisoners of war. The Union losses in this battle were two hundred and fifty killed and wounded, and about one thousand prisoners, the wagons also falling into the hands of the enemy. The enemy's losses in killed and wounded were much heavier, owing to the fact that the battle was in a piece of woodland, where they were unable to see how small a force they were fighting. Believing General Steele had reenforced the train guard, they were unwilling to make a dash to surround them at once, lest they should meet with a decided repulse; and advancing slowly in heavy lines, they formed a good target for the Ohio boys, who caused them to remark (when they found how few of our men they had been fighting), that they were "a dear lot of prisoners."

The enemy's loss was estimated at a thousand, killed and wounded. Three hundred and eighteen members of the Seventy-seventh, including eleven officers, became prisoners of war. They were marched, without stopping to eat or sleep, and almost without drink, sixty miles to the Washita river, before they were allowed an hour's rest. The commander of the guard apologized for this, and showed one of our officers the order of General Fagan, requiring him to cross the Washita before resting, lest General Steele should rescue the prisoners.

Captain McCormick was given the rank of brevet lieutenant colonel "for gallantry in the battle of Marks, Mills," and their commander says Captain McKitrick and Lieutenants Fulton, Scott, Marlow, Flemming, Mc-

Intire, David A. Henry, R. E. Smithson, Province, and N. B. Smith, also deserve well of this country for their part in the battle. They were all captured, as well as Lieutenants Atkinson, J. M. Mitchell, John Smith, Dye, Lund, Day and Black, afterwards commissioned, all of whom fought bravely.

General Steele, finding that the Banks expedition had met with disastrous defeat, was compelled to abandon Camden. Leaving the place in the night, by a pontoon bridge and a new road he had made, the enemy (which now far outnumbered his force) did not learn of his movements so as to overtake him till he reached the Saline river, at Jenkins' Ferry. Here, on the thirtieth of April, those of the Seventy-seventh who had not been at Marks' Mills (having been left at Camden because they were on picket and other guard duty), or not thoroughly equipped, or not fit for duty), were, with the rest of Steele's forces, engaged in a bloody battle. Fortunately the enemy was repulsed, and with heavy loss. In this encounter the Seventy-seventh lost, in killed and wounded, about half the number engaged, and a few were made prisoners. Part of the time they fought in water knee deep, the river being out of its banks. Those captured by the enemy at Marks' Mills, and at Jenkins' Ferry, were soon after marched about two hundred miles south, and confined for ten months in a military prison at Camp Ford, near Tyler, Texas, where thirty-eight of them died from starvation, exposure, and disease, and one, John Calvert, was shot dead, in a brutal manner, by a rebel guard, for getting too close "the dead line" when going for water.

Captain McCormick and Lieutenants Flemming, Scott, and Smithson, of the Seventy-seventh, and three men not of the regiment, escaped from the military prison one dark evening about the last of August, and started north, travelling by night with only the stars for a guide. Scott and Smithson travelled about a hundred miles and were retaken near Red river. The others marched about sixty miles towards the Union lines, but unfortunately the watch-dogs on a plantation got scent of them, and next morning two packs of blood-hounds, with squads of rebel cavalry, were on there track. After a tiresome chase through the tangled woods they were run down by the blood-hounds, and brought to bay. As orders were posted at the prison before they left that all prisoners who might escape should be shot if overtaken, the situation was considered one of peril. However, the enemy evidently took care to count the cost of such a course, as assurances were given by the cavalry that no harm should be done them if they would surrender. Being taken to Gilmore, a squad of fierce rebels, who probably never saw an army Union soldier, plied them with numerous insulting questions, which were answered in plain language without much care for the feelings of the doughty questioners. So they charged Captain McCormick with "treason to the State of Texas," and threatened to hang him for his pointed replies. The real soldiers of the guard seemed to relish the answers made to those who would insult an unarmed and defenceless prisoner, and they were restrained and advised to cease

questioning if they could not endure the responses. The prisoners were returned to Camp Ford a few days after, where they awaited another opportunity to escape, finally made unnecessary by the arrival of the paroling officers so long and anxiously looked for in vain. On being paroled the survivors marched to Shreveport, Louisiana, about one hundred miles, where they were placed on transports and conveyed to the mouth of Red river, and there delivered into the Union lines February 25, 1865, except Lieutenants Flemming, Fulton, and Atkinson, who were held in Texas till the end of the war for attempting to escape.

After being clothed and paid, and given a thirty days' furlough, these exchanged prisoners returned to the regiment in April.

On the expiration of the term of service, of the few original member who did not become veterans, and of those enlisted in 1862, and therefore could not reenlist, they were mustered out in 1864.

This left the command too small to maintain its organization as a regiment, and it was consolidated into a battalion of six companies, commanded by Colonel Stevens.

On the fifth of February, 1865, the battalion left Little Rock with General Steele for the Gulf department, and was at Fort Morgan, Alabama, when the paroled prisoners were released, and were near Mobile when they joined it. It was engaged in operations around Mobile, Fort Spanish, Blakely, McIntosh Bluffs, and other points in Alabama, in which Colonel Stevens and the boys won golden opinions, until June 1, 1865, when it took transports across the Gulf of Mexico for the Rio Grande, and remained on duty at Brazos and Clarksville, and then, from August 1, 1865, till March 8, 1866, at Brownsville, Texas, where it was mustered out and started for Columbus, Ohio, where the men were finally paid off and disbanded, March 26, 1866.

Only one of all Ohio's regiments remained longer in the service, and none served the country more faithfully, or suffered more for the cause of the Union.

NINETY-SECOND OHIO VOLUNTEER INFANTRY.

REGIMENTAL OFFICERS.

Colonel Nelson H. Van Vorhes, mustered August 15, 1862, resigned March 22, 1863; Colonel Benjamin D. Fearing, March 22, 1863, mustered out May 19, 1863, on account of wounds; Lieutenant Colonel Benjamin D. Fearing, August 15, 1862, promoted to colonel; Lieutenant Colonel Douglas Putnam, jr., March 22, 1863, honorably discharged April 11, 1864; Lieutenant Colonel John C. Morrow, April 28, 1864, mustered out with regiment; Major Dioclesian A. Smith, August 10, 1862, resigned February 1, 1863; Major Douglas Putnam, jr., February 1, 1863, promoted to lieutenant colonel, Major Elmer Golden, March 22, 1863, resigned December 8, 1863; Major John C. Morrow, December 8, 1863, promoted to lieutenant colonel, Surgeon Josiah D. Cotton, August 19, 1862, mustered out with regiment; Assistant Surgeon N. B. Sisson, August 16, 1862, resigned August 15, 1864; Assistant Surgeon J. D. Howell, August 20, 1862, resigned April 29, 1863; Assistant Surgeon A. M. Beers, August 26, 1864, mustered out with regiment; Chaplain Washington M. Grimes, December 1, 1862, resigned September 9, 1863.

COMPANY OFFICERS FROM WASHINGTON COUNTY.

Captain William Thorniley, mustered July 29, 1862, resigned April 9, 1863; Captain Francis H. Loring, July 30, 1862, mustered out with regiment; Captain Alexander Higgins, July 30, 1862, resigned May 9, 1863, Captain William Beale Whittlesey, June 1, 1863, killed at Mission

Ridge November 25, 1863; Captain Hamilton Middleswart, July 20, 1863, mustered out with regiment; Captain James W. Merrill, October 2, 1863, honorably discharged May 24, 1864; Captain Joseph Stephenson, November 25, 1863, mustered out with regiment; Captain Bradley B. Stone, November 18, 1864, mustered out with regiment; First Lieutenant Hamilton Middleswart, July 23, 1862, promoted to captain; First Lieutenant Douglas Putnam, jr., July 25, 1862, promoted to major; First Lieutenant James W. Merrill, July 28, 1862, promoted to captain; First Lieutenant Joseph Stephenson, July 28, 1862, promoted to captain; First Lieutenant David E. Putnam, February 1, 1863, honorably discharged November 24, 1863; First Lieutenant George B. Turner, June 1, 1862, died of wounds December 1, 1863; First Lieutenant Bradley B. Stone, July 20, 1863, promoted to captain; First Lieutenant Reason A. Bull, October 29, 1863, mustered out with regiment, First Lieutenant Charles A. Brown, June 14, 1864, mustered out with regiment; Second Lieutenant William Beale Whittlesey, July 23, 1862, promoted to first lieutenant; Second Lieutenant Thomas Day, July 26, 1862, resigned February 17, 1863; Second Lieutenant Bradley B. Stone, February 17, 1863, promoted to first lieutenant, Second Lieutenant George B. Turner, May 9, 1863, promoted to first lieutenant.

The Ninety-second Ohio was organized at Marietta, Ohio, during the months of August and September, 1862. It rendezvoused at Camp Marietta, then in command of Colonel William R. Putnam. Nelson H. Van Vorhes, the colonel, reported and assumed command on the first of October, 1862. As an officer of volunteers he had been on active duty at the front since April, 1861, and while the regiment was organizing he was still on duty with General Mitchell in Alabama. Benjamin D. Fearing, the lieutenant colonel, had seen service; was at Manassas as a private, had served on the staff of Generals Slemmer and Crook in Virginia, while serving as adjutant in the Thirty-sixth Ohio volunteer infantry, and evinced soldiership at Shiloh in command of one of the regiments of General Sherman's division. All the officers were gentlemen of experience and courage.

The men were the pick of the district—young, active, quick to learn, eager to do their best at all times, and proud of the good name and character of their regiment. The first service performed was before the colonel, lieutenant colonel or major had reported or the regiment had been mustered. Adjutant Putnam, with companies A, B and D, was ordered to move to Gallipolis, Ohio, and garrison that post at the time the rebels were driving Lightburn out of the Kanawha valley. While there they made two expeditions into Virginia. These companies soon after rejoined, when the regiment, numbering nine hundred and forty-nine, rank and file, was mustered into the United States service, uniformed, and armed with Austrian rifled muskets.

On October 7, 1862, the regiment was ordered to Point Pleasant, West Virginia, and made a part of the brigade of Colonel Gilbert. It took part in the expeditions up the Kanawha under General Cox, before whom the rebels retreated and were finally, after some skirmishing, driven beyond the mountains.

At Gauley Bridge it was transferred to brigade commanded by General Hugh Ewing and went into winter quarters, building log huts at Loupe creek, a few miles below Kanawha Falls. They were permitted to enjoy these comforts but a short time, when they were ordered to join the brigade of General George Crook and were stationed at Tompkins' farm on New river, which was at that time the outpost of the army of the Kanawha valley.

After the dark days of December, 1862, when the country struggled under the discouragements of Fredericksburgh and the seemingly indecisive battle of Murfreesborough, General Crook's brigade was hurriedly taken by transports to Nashville, Tennessee. The trip occupied over fourteen days and was attended with many hardships on account of the crowded condition of the boats. Remaining at Nashville about three weeks the regiment was ordered to proceed to Carthage, Tennessee. The trip occupied a week, and in no way was it more comfortable than our journey to Nashville. Many of the men were compelled to sleep in the hold, full of foul air, and became impregnated with disease which soon developed itself.

Those two months spent at Carthage will never be forgotten. Daily, for weeks, one or more burial parties fired the last salute over the grave of a comrade as he was committed to mother earth, in a town where no one sympathized with them, and where each grave was counted as taking away one more of their enemies. In less than two months over ninety men were buried.

The colonel, N. H. Van Vorhes was here compelled to resign on account of sickness, and Lieutenant Colonel Fearing was promoted to colonel. Major Smith having resigned, adjutant Putnam, by request of the officers, was made major, and after promotion of Colonel Fearing, was made lieutenant colonel.

Health once restored, the regiment was ordered south of the Cumberland and joined with the brigade the army of the Cumberland at Murfreesborough. The brigade, which was still under the command of General Crooks, was assigned to General Reynolds' division, Fourteenth army corps.

The regiment moved from Murfreesborough on the twenty-fourth of June, 1863, supporting Wilder's mounted infantry—one of the brigades of Reynold's division at Hoover's gap. The enemy were met and driven back, as they were pressing Wilder and attempting to recover the ground he had taken.

The march over the table lands of Tennessee, through a continuous rain—rains twenty-one days in succession—bivouacking nightly in mud so deep and soft as to make it necessary to cut boughs to lie on. Mouldy crackers and musty coffee, wet sugar and some bacon, are pleasant themes for the survivors to dwell upon now.

On Elk river the news of Gettysburgh and Vicksburgh was announced in the evening of July 4th and was hailed by a salute from the combined artillery of the army. Despondent hearts took courage; and with better weather and better supplies and full of hope, the regiment camped at Big Springs, Tennessee, resting and enjoying the change as only tired soldiers can.

While here General John B. Turchin, the old Hungarian soldier, assumed command. His vigorous efforts to secure green corn, blackberries, and fresh vegetables, speedily eradicated all traces of scurvy and disease contracted at Carthage, and put the regiment in good condition, mentally and physically, for active work. They bivouacked by the springs at University Place and foraged in the valleys, moving over the mountains and through

Sweden Cowen, stopping long enough to gather the green corn and ripe peaches.

On the second of September the regiment crossed the Tennessee river, at Shell Mound, in flatboats. On the third it led the advance over Sand Mountain, and on the next day moved to Trenton, Georgia. From here the brigade crossed the Lookout ranges, overcoming the seemingly impossible obstacles in so doing, and descending the Coopers gap into McLemoes cove, passed up the valley into Catlett's gap.

While here quite a sharp skirmish occurred, and the regiment held the head of the gap. Skirmishing continued here for parts of two days, and the Ninety-second was busily engaged.

On September 18th a night march was made (one that will never be forgotten by those participating in it) to Chickamauga. The regiment engaged the enemy on that bloody field, under Turchin, on the nineteenth and twentieth, and formed a part of the rear guard that saved the army. On the nineteenth, early in the day, Colonel Fearing was wounded and carried from the field, the command devolving upon Lieutenant Colonel Putnam. Lieutenant Merrill was wounded severely, captured and sent to our lines under a flag of truce.

On Sunday afternoon Turchin's brigade made the charge necessary to open connection with Granger, coming to reenforce General Thomas, who gave the command in person to the Ninety-second to lead the charge, which was made left in front. This charge is described by Van Horn, in his "Army of the Cumberland:"

The charge was made with great vigor, and the enemy was completely routed. Turchin's brigade drove this daring force entirely beyond Baird's left, capturing more than two hundred prisoners. This brigade . . . . . was posted by General Thomas, on the road leading through the ridge to the Dry Valley roads, to hold the ground, while the troops from the right and left passed by.

In this battle Lieutenant David E. Putnam, adjutant, was wounded and discharged on account of wounds, and George B. Turner, orderly sergeant of company F, was promoted to first lieutenant and made adjutant. Captain John Brown was mortally wounded, and soon after the battle died; also, Lieutenant G. T. Okey received a dangerous shell wound. W. B. Whittlesey, second lieutenant of company F, was promoted to first lieutenant, and on resignation of Captain Thorniley, of the same company, was promoted to captain in June, 1863; hence was in command of his company in this battle.

The regiment returned to Chattanooga, living in dog tents, with cold, wet weather, insufficient rations, etc., yet bore all with patience and fortitude. They made several reconnoissances and were ready for duty on a moment's notice. They formed a part, with Hazen's brigade, of the forlorn hope sent to open connection with General Hooker's arming corps, who were coming to the relief of the beleaguered and nearly starved army. As General Turchins described it: "Chattanooga was surrounded by two lines of fortifications, one built by brave men and one composed of dead mules, starved to death for their country's cause."

A part of the regiment floated past Lookout Mountain in scow boats, and the rest marched across Moccasin

29

Point, and were ferried over as the boats came down. The movement was so carefully planned, and executed with so much skill, that the enemy was taken completely by surprise, and perfect success crowned the effort. The army was revictualled and reenforced.

About November 20th the preliminary movement for the capture of Mission Ridge commenced. The Ninety-second, with Turchins' brigade, had been for some time expecting orders to assault, being in position for several days. On the afternoon of November 25th, the final assault was made. Captain Middlesworth, of company F, in connection with the skirmishers of the Thirty-sixth and Eleventh Ohio, cleared the rifle pits at the foot of the ridge. The brigade was ordered forward at double quick, and swept every obstacle before it. This charge has often been described. General John C. Breckenridge, who commanded the enemy's lines in front of this brigade, told the writer that the audacity of the attack—the sight of the steadily moving lines, silent but terrible in its advance—so demoralized his men that they became unmanageable, and, at last, gave way, not until there was almost a hand-to-hand encounter near the summit.

About half way up the hill the commanding officer, Lieutenant Colonel Putnam, fell wounded. Soon thereafter Captain Whittlesey was shot through the heart, but said to his men "Go on, I'm killed," and breathed his last. The men went on, sweeping over the top, in company with the Thirty-sixth, while the enemy retreated down the side.

The summit once gained, no rest was found by the breathless and worn column, as a force of the enemy came hastily from the left to reenforce their fleeing comrades. Here, while rallying the men for this assault, Adjutant Turner received his death-wound, being struck in the head by a large minnie ball. He lived for some days, however, but sank away.

By the death of these two young men, Washington county offered up her choicest material, and their funerals (on the same day) will ever be remembered. Both were brave and faithful officers. Lieutenant Townsend, of Athens county, was also killed, who was an excellent officer. The loss of the regiment was, in this assault, thirty-three per cent. of the officers and ten per cent. of the men. They took many prisoners and two guns.

The next day the regiment, under command of Captain Wheeler, started in pursuit of the enemy and returned soon to Chattanooga. Remaining here until February, 1864, when, under command of Captain I. C. Morrow, Major Golden having resigned, Fearing and Putnam both absent from wounds, they started south towards Dallas. They were engaged at Rocky Face Gap, losing heavily, some of the wounded being buried in the woods. From here they moved to Ringgold Gap, doing out-post duty. Here Captain Morrow was promoted to lieutenant colonel vice Putnam mustered out on account of wounds. Colonel Fearing returned in March, and Lieutenant B. B. Stone of company G, who was promoted from orderly sergeant, was made adjutant. The regiment took an active part in that campaign through Dallas. On the twenty-seventh of July, they were in line of Atlanta.

During August and September the regiment was in the neighborhood of Atlanta, taking parts in the charge at Jonesborough, Georgia. On the fourth of October, they broke camp and joined in pursuit of Hood, crossing the Chattahoochie.

At Kingston preparations were made for the march to the sea under Sherman, the sick provided for in hospitals, baggage sent to rear or destroyed, etc. On the sixteenth, they started. This march has been fully described, and no attempt to do so is needed here. They met the enemy at Bentonville, North Carolina, March 21st. Here Colonel Fearing, who was in command of a brigade, having been brevetted brigade general, was severely wounded in the hand, necessitating the amputation of a portion of it. Passing through Goldborough, Durham Station, and Raleigh, North Carolina, they moved onward through Virginia, reaching Washington on May 19th and taking part in the ever memorable grand review of the Twenty-fourth. Having orders to be mustered out of service, it was transported to Columbus, Ohio, and on the nineteenth of June, 1865, the Ninety-second Ohio volunteer infantry ceased to exist.

Their first colors were literally worn and shot into shreds, the second set now in the flag room at Columbus are mute witnesses of their regiment's history as they bear on their folds in letters of gold these names: Hoovers Gap, Chickamauga, Mission Ridge, Rocky Face Atlanta, The March to the Sea, Savannah, and the Carolinas.

THE SILVER GRAYS.

Among the many military organizations of Washington county for home defence, none was more self-sacrificing and patriotic than the one we have now to consider. The Silver Grays were among the very first to step forward and form in martial array at the beginning, and their moral influence in the community was great. Their appearance on parade, marching and going through the manual of arms was inspiring, and if a man had any of the martial spirit in him, the sight of these venerable men keeping step to the music of the Union was sure to arouse it.

Two of the members, William Warren and Junia Jennings, prepared the following account of the company in 1866, and we give it substantially as we find it:

Monday forenoon, April 22, 1861, was the time of the departure of the first company of volunteers from Marietta to aid in putting down the Rebellion, the Union Blues,—over one hundred men—under command of Captain Frank Buell. It was an effecting occasion, such as was never before known in Washington county, and may never be again. Strong men's nerves gave way, and the patriotic tear and firm resolve were seen upon every face. There was a brief speech by George P. Buell, esq., and amid cheers, the firing of cannon, and the waving of flags, the volunteers embarked upon the Muskingum packet from the common in front of the Congregational church, thousands of people being assembled.

The citizens then repaired to the court house and organized a meeting to take into consideration the state of public affairs. Hon. William A. Whittlesey, the mayor of Marietta, being called to the chair, secretaries and committees were appointed. Colonel William West, then in his sixty-sixth year, arose and said:

"Mr. chairman, I hold in my hand a resolution which I wish to offer for the consideration of this meeting. Such is the excitement of the occasion that I am not in the situation to either do justice to myself or the subject I wish to present, therefore, without comment, with the indulgence of the house, I will submit the resolution."

Silence reigned throughout the crowded house, and the colonel, with a voice tremulous with the deep feeling that pervaded all present, read:

"*Resolved,* That we, the citizens of Washington county, whose ages are sixty years and upwards, for the protection of our homes, our firesides, and our country's liberties, form ourselves into a military organization, to be called and known as the Silver Grays, of Washington county."

A hundred earnest voices seconded the motion for its adoption, and it was carried with a unanimous shout, and cheers for the Silver Grays.

A rush was made to be the first to enroll their names. James Dutton, being a little lame, had started first and had his name first down, followed by William Warren, second; Colonel West, third; Thomas Porter, fourth; Junia Jennings, fifth; and so on. Subsequently, men of forty-five years and upwards were enrolled.

It was resolved that each member of the company should supply himself with ammunition. The commissioned officers had red sashes, the rank and file, blue. A uniform was agreed upon, but circumstances did not favor its procurement. They were armed at once. George W. Barker, William Warren, and F. Wheeler were appointed a committee to ask the county commissioners to procure a flag to be raised on the court house.

Through the exciting days of 1862, especially when the rebels pressed upon the border everywhere throughout the whole line, in August and September, the Silver Grays were out in full force and vigor. In the spring of 1863 their guns were taken by authority for use by a company of younger men, and that ended the Silver Grays, who, it is justice to say, did all the duties they were called upon to perform, and did them well. That they would have done excellent duty in repelling invasion, had it ever occurred, there is no doubt. Several of the members were deaf, and these were compelled to watch their comrades' motions to know what order the captain gave. Several used canes.

Their motto as set forth in the first article of their constitution was: "The Union, the Constitution, and the Flag of our Country, for the sustaining of which we pledge our lives, our fortunes, and our sacred honor."

ARTICLE 4. The company shall meet for exercise or other duty at such time and place as shall be determined on by the company on Saturday of each week at 2 P. M., provided that the captain or any other commissioned officer of our company is hereby empowered and required in cases of danger or emergency to cause a fire bell to be rung, which shall be a signal for the company to assemble at the court house at a minute's warning.

Colonel William West was first elected captain, but declined; Major George W. Barker was then elected, but his time of service was short. For a time they met every evening, at five o'clock, for drill.

May 11, 1861, three weeks after the first organization, officers were elected by ballot, who continued to the end, as follows:

COMMISSIONED OFFICERS.

Captain Daniel P. Bosworth, First Lieutenant Charles J. Sheppard, Second Lieutenant Rufus E. Harte.

NON-COMMISSIONED OFFICERS.

First Sergeant Junia Jennings, Second Sergeant Thomas Porter, Third Sergeant Frederick Buck, Fourth Sergeant Hugh Brenan.

PRIVATES.

James Dutton, William Warren, Colonel William West, Isaac C. Fuller Daniel Protsman, E. W. T. Clark, Lemuel Grimes, Montgomery Sayre, John Skipton, Jacob Middleswart, Joel Deming, William A. Whittlesey, James Brown, John M. Slocomb, Theodore Scott, G. W. Barker, Isaac Maxon, John Goodman, Levi Bartlett, Joseph E. Hall, Robert T. Miller, J. W. L. Brown, L. J. P. Putnam, Henry Armstrong, W. C. McCarty, John Mills, Joseph Jones, J. L. Reckard, T. P. Harshberger, D. R. Sniffen, T. J. Westgate, Isaac Kidd, John Test, James McLeod, D. Stevens, F. A. Wheeler, H. H. Wheatley, John Miles, Lewis Leonhart, John Eaton, James H. Dye, George Payne, L. M. Parker, Merritt Judd, John Armstrong, J. J. Parker, Hugh Hill, Austin Edgerton, John Marshall, Hugh Clancey, Matthew Wylie, J. J. Preston, Barker Devol, James Dunn, George Greenwood, J. H. Nye, Owen Franks, Philo Doan, A. M. Shanklin, Calvin Hildreth, William Scott, R. D. Hollister, Elisha Allen, Graydon Medicott, Robert Johnson, George Stanley, James B. Matthews, Stephen Alcock, John Richards, J. J. Hollister, A. L. Guitteau, B. F. Stone, D. Atkinson, David Wright, John R. Tucker, J. M. Eels, Lucius Brigham, S. P. Hildreth, J. B. Dyar, James Ferguson, William P. Skinner, Rosswill Turney, Charles Sullivan, A. Woodruff, Warren Wilcox, John

Stricker, John Lehnhart, Joseph H. Steward, Wyllys Hall, Shadrach Wood, Silas Slocomb, Jacob Snyder, E. Eveleigh, J. Pfeiffer, William Wylie, Colonel Augustus Stone, Nathaniel Holden, Jacob Lauder, David Cline, Austin Berkley, Amos Dye.—Total, one hundred and seven.

THE "PONY SECTION."

During the war Marietta was prolific in fifers and drummers. The first to enter the service were those who joined the Eighteenth Ohio volunteer militia, in the three months' service.

Ebenezer Corey and Louis Fourgeres were the musicians of company B, the old Union Blues. After the Eighteenth entered Virginia they were distributed along the Baltimore & Ohio railroad as guards. Ebenezer Corey was appointed drum major of the Eighteenth June 6, 1861, and soon went to Marietta to recruit a martial band.

This resulted in the enlistment of nine young men, most of whom knew nothing of the use of fife or drum, but who became quick learners. On June 17, 1861, they started for Virginia, learning the notes on the way. They were—Charles Holden, George K. Jenvey, William Jenvey, John Tenney, Henry Langley, Frank R. Brenan, Fred Regnier, James Judd, and Henry Corey, and others, among whom were Manly Warren, Louis Fourgeres, and Stephen Mass, from Washington county; they made the "Pony Section," so called from their size and age.

At Bridgeport they drilled and practiced—result a few tunes and sunburnt ears. They then went to Clarksburgh, still training for the war, when they, with the whole regiment, were transferred to Oakland, and made a fruitless march over the mountains under General Hill, after General Garnett's rebel forces. As the time of the regiment had expired, one hot July day they came back to Marietta and awaited patiently their discharge, with hardly a taste of hard service.

Their martial strains awoke many responsive chords in the hearts of the patriotic people, and the band was invited to take a trip up the Muskingum to Zanesville. Every courtesy was shown them along the route, and they awakened the valley by their ringing music. At Zanesville and Beverly they were treated with especial favor.

On their discharge five enlisted in Buell's battery; three with the major in the Thirty-sixth Ohio volunteer infantry, in a fine band, which timed the steps of many brave ones in their march to duty and victory; one went into Huntington's battery, and one in the Second West Virginia cavalry. All did brave duty through the war. One of whom died in the service—Charles A. Holden. Such was the "Pony Section."

ONE HUNDRED AND FORTY-EIGHTH OHIO NATIONAL GUARDS.

REGIMENTAL OFFICERS.

Colonel Thomas W. Moore, mustered May 18, 1864, Washington county; Lieutenant Colonel Isaac B. Kinkead, May 18, 1864, Washington county; Major William L. Edmiston, May 18, 1864, Vinton county; Adjutant Thomas Day, May 18, 1864, Washington county; Quartermaster Allen R. Darrow, May 18, 1864 Washington county; Surgeon William Beebe, May 18, 1864, Washington county; Assistant Surgeon Benjamin F. Culver, May 18, 1864, Washington County; Drum Major Darius Towsley, May 18, 1864; Washington county.

COMPANY OFFICERS.

Captain Samuel S. Knowles, company A, mustered May 17, 1864, Washington county, Captain John P. Sanford, B, May 17, 1864, Washington county, Captain Joseph J McDowell, C, May 17, 1864, Vinton county; Captain William F. Dawson, D, May 17, 1864, Washington county; Captain Isaiah H. McCormick, E, May 17, 1864, Vinton county; Captain George B. Turner, F, May 18, 1864, Washington county; Captain Joseph M McElhinney, G, May 18, 1864, Washington county; Captain John Mitchell, H, May 17, 1864, Washington county, Captain David J. Richards, I, May 17, 1864, Washington county; First Lieutenant Wallace Wolcott, K, May 17, 1864, Washington county; First Lieutenant Charles B. Gates, A, May 17, 1864 died May 31, 1864, at Harper's Ferry, Maryland, First Lieutenant William W. West, B, May 17, 1864, Washington county; First Lieutenant Harson P. Ambrose, C, May 17, 1864, Vinton county; First Lieutenant John Randolph, D, May 17, 1864, Washington county, First Lieutenant Nathaniel Murphy, E, May 17, 1864, Vinton county, First Lieutenant Leonidas P. Pond, F, May 17, 1864, Washington county; First Lieutenant Augustus Leonard, G, May 18, 1864, Washington county; First Lieutenant Austin L. Curtis, H, May 18, 1864, Washington county; First Lieutenant W. L. Woodford, I, May 17, 1864. Washington county; First Lieutenant A. S. Bailey, K, May 17, 1864, Washington county; Second Lieutenant Smith J. Dutton, A, May 17, 1864, Washington county; Second Lieutenant William H. Jennings, B, May 17, 1864, Washington county; Second Lieutenant Robert S. Barnhill, C, May 17, 1864, Vinton county, Second Lieutenant Benjamin Arnold, D, May 17, 1864, Washington county, Second Lieutenant Samuel G. Scott, E, May 17, 1864, Vinton county, died at Bermuda Hundred, Second Lieutenant Benjamin F. Robinson, F, May 17, 1864, Washington county, Second Lieutenant John C. Wood, G, May 18, 1864, Washington county; Second Lieutenant Alexander H. Browning, H, May 17, 1864, Washington county; Second Lieutenant Robert Alexander, K, May 17, 1864, Washington county.

ONE HUNDRED AND FORTY-EIGHTH OHIO VOLUNTEER INFANTRY, OHIO NATIONAL GUARDS.

In response to the call of Governor Brough the Forty-sixth regiment, Ohio National guards, numbering six hundred and fifty-four men of Washington county, reported for duty at Marietta on the second day of May, 1864. Subsequently the Ninety-sixth battalion, of Vinton county, was consolidated with the Forty-sixth regiment, forming the One Hundred and Forty-eighth regiment, Ohio volunteer infantry. The regiment was mustered into the service on the seventeenth and eighteenth of May. The officers were all Washington county men, except Major Edmiston and Captains McDowell and McCormick. The colonel had been a captain in the Thirty-sixth Ohio; the lieutenant colonel had been a lieutenant in the Seventy-seventh Ohio; and the major had been a captain in the Eighteenth Ohio. Several of the line officers, also, had been in the service, and nearly the whole regiment had been tried, briefly but laboriously, during the Morgan raid of the previous year. Company A, in particular, had been called out repeatedly, and on two or three occasions had been sent to Virginia, when the border was threatened. An unusual proportion of the men in this company were students of Marietta college and merchants, and it is worthy of remark that during one hundred and thirty-six days' service it was the only company in the regiment that did not lose a man by sickness.

On the twenty-third of May the regiment left Marietta for the field. Scarcely had the train passed out of sight of the town when an accident occurred to it, on the Union branch of the Marietta & Cincinnati railroad, by which Jeremiah Stuckey, of company A, was killed. John H. McKimm, of Athens county, and Alexander S.

Nugent, of Franklin, Pennsylvania, students in the preparatory department of Marietta college, who were accompanying their friends in the regiment to Parkersburgh, were killed. William Hildebrand, William Flemming, and First Lieutenant Gates were seriously injured. Lieutenant Gates went forward with the regiment, but he had received such internal injuries that, coupled with pneumonia, it resulted in his death on the thirty-first, six days after the regiment had arrived at Harper's Ferry. This accident, together with the subsequent death of Lieutenant Gates, cast a gloom over the regiment and throughout the community from which its members had been gathered. Although the youngest officer, and one of the youngest men in the regiment, no one was more generally known and more universally beloved than Charles Beman Gates. The various testimonials of affection and regret from the college societies with which he was connected, and from the officers of his regiment, are evidences of the high esteem in which this youthful, Christian patriot was held by his associates.

After remaining about two days at Harper's Ferry, the regiment moved to Washington, and on the ninth of June left that city for White House, on the Pamunkey. On the eleventh it left White House, arrived at Bermuda Hundred on the twelfth, and on the thirteenth went into General Butler's intrenchments at the front. On the sixteenth seven companies, under command of Lieutenant Colonel Kinkead, left Bermuda Hundred for City Point. On the ninth of August, by the explosion of an ordnance boat at City Point, three men of the regiment were killed—S. E. Graham, of company H, Joseph H. Smith, of company D, and Joseph D. Clarke, of company A. Young Clarke was only about seventeen years old, was a member of the preparatory department in Marietta college, and was the oldest son of Colonel Melvin Clarke, of the Thirty-sixth Ohio, who was instantly killed while gallantly leading his regiment at the battle of Antietam, September, 1862. Sire and son, both instantly killed in their country's service, are buried side by side in the Marietta Mound cemetery. The total loss of the regiment by death was forty. On the twenty-ninth of August the One Hundred and Forty-eighth Ohio left City Point, and arrived at Marietta on the fifth of September. On the thirteenth a public dinner was given to the regiment by the citizens of the county, and on the fourteenth it was mustered out of the service.*

THE WAR EDITORS.

Any account of the eventful period of the war for the Union would be incomplete without some notice of the war editors of Washington county, the men who stood by the administration of Abraham Lincoln and encouraged the people at home and the soldiers in the field with brave words and patriotic sentiments.

T. L. Andrews was editor of the Marietta *Intelligencer* during the first year, and did much towards sustaining a healthy public policy. A. W. McCormick was the editor of the Marietta *Republican* at the beginning and so continued up to late in the fall of 1861, when he raised a

_____
*From Ohio in the War.

company and went into the Seventy-seventh regiment. E. Winchester edited the *Home News*, and his local column was always a mine of interest both to soldiers and citizens. In June, 1862, R. M. Stimson purchased and combined the *Home News* and *Intelligence* and christened the new paper the Marietta *Register*.

All these editors did good work for the cause of the Union. Although Mr. McCormick differed in politics from the administration, yet he stood by the Union, and soon threw down the pen and took up the sword for his country. To Mr. Stimson, however, we are indebted for steady, unflinching support, and for work that told in the county. His proprietorship of the Marietta *Register* spanned the halcyon days of the Republican party in Washington county, which service the people have shown their appreciation of by twice sending him to the State senate.

_____

BIOGRAPHIES OF OFFICERS OF THE WAR OF THE REBELLION.

DON CARLOS BUELL,

major general and commander of one of the principal Union armies in the War of the Rebellion, son of Salmon D. and Eliza Buell, was born March 23, 1818, on a farm owned by his grandfather, Judge Salmon Buell, which has since become the site of the town of Lowell, on the Muskingum river twelve miles above Marietta. He was named after an uncle, Don Carlos Buell, a young lawyer of Ithica, New York, who entered the volunteer service as a captain of artillery, and died in the Canada frontier, in the War of 1812. The lines of his progenitors on both sides come together again in the sixth preceding generation in the person of Samuel Buell born at Windsor, Connecticut, September 2, 1641. Judge Salmon Buell, on the grandfather's side, a lawyer by profession, was born in New York in 1764, served at the age of sixteen in the Revolutionary war, and became a senator and judge of the court of appeals of New York. He moved to Marietta about the year 1816, and in 1824 to Hamilton county, where he died in 1828. Captain Timothy Buell, the grandfather on the mother's side, was born in Connecticut in 1768, moved to Marietta in 1789, and died on his farm three miles above that place in 1837. He served in the War of 1812, represented Washington county in the legislature, and was sheriff of the county several years.

Soon after the death of his father, which occurred in August, 1823, the subject of this sketch was taken under the care of his uncle, George P. Buell, esq., of Lawrenceburgh, Indiana; and with an intermission of about five years passed in Marietta under the roof of his stepfather, George W. Dunley, esq., he remained with his relations at Lawrenceburgh until 1837, when he was appointed to a cadetship at West Point. He was graduated and commissioned in the army in 1841, and served in the Florida war and in the west until the Mexican war. He served through that war from the beginning to the end; participating in the battles of Ralo Alto, Resacca de la Ralma, Monterey, the siege of Vera Cruz, and the battles of Contreras and Cherubusco, and received the brevet of captain and major. He was severely wounded in the battle of Cherubusco. The following record of his grades up to 1850 is taken from Gardner's Military Dictionary, published in that year:

Don Carlos Buell, cadet in 1837; second lieutenant Third infantry first of July, 1841; first lieutenant June, 1846, brevet captain for gallant and meritorious conduct in the several conflicts at Monterey, Mexico, twenty-third of September, 1846, distinguished in battle of Cerro Gordo; brevet major for gallant and meritorious conduct in the battles of Contreras and Cherubusco, twentieth August, 1847, and severely wounded in the latter; assistant adjutant general, January, 1848.

He was on duty in Washington in 1848, and subsequently, up to the war of the Rebellion, served as assistant adjutant general at various department headquarters, in the east, west, south, and on the Pacific, and in the war department at Washington. In December, 1860, he was sent by Mr. Floyd, Secretary of War, to Charleston, South Carolina, with verbal instructions for Major Robert Anderson, who was in command of the Government troops in the harbor, under the critical circumstances which the movement of secession had already created. After inspecting the forts, and making some suggestions with reference to their preparation for defence, he communicated verbally to Major Anderson the instructions he had received, and then a written memorandum of them, foreseeing the responsibility which coming events were likely to throw upon that officer. This memorandum, which is published in the Robinson record, has a historical interest, since it contains the authority upon which Major Anderson took the decisive step of abandoning Fort Moultrie, and concentrating his command in Fort Sumter.

Memorandum of verbal instructions to Major Anderson, First artillery, commanding Fort Moultrie, South Carolina:

FORT MOULTRIE, SOUTH CAROLINA, }
December 11, 1860. }

You are aware of the great anxiety of the Secretary of War that a collision of the troops with the people of this State shall be avoided, and of his studied determination to pursue a course with reference to the military force and forts in this harbor which shall guard against such a collision. He has, therefore, carefully abstained from increasing the force at this point, or taking any measures which might add to the present excited state of the public mind, or which would throw any doubt on the confidence he feels that South Carolina will not attempt, by violence, to obtain possession of the public works, or interfere with their occupancy.

But as the counsel and acts of rash and impulsive persons may possibly disappoint these expectations of the Government, he deems it proper that you should be prepared with instructions to meet so unhappy a contingency. He has, therefore, directed me, verbally, to give you such instructions.

You are carefully to avoid every act which would needlessly tend to provoke aggression; and for that reason you are not, without evident and imminent necessity, to take up any position which could be construed into the assumption of a hostile attitude. But you are to hold possession of the forts in this harbor, and if attacked you are to defend yourself to the last extremity.

The smallness of your force will not permit you, perhaps, to occupy more than one of the three forts, but an attack on, or attempt to take possession of, any one of them, will be regarded as an act of hostility, and you may then put you command into either of them which you may deem most proper to increase its power of resistance.

You are also authorized to take similar steps whenever you have tangible evidence of a design to proceed to a hostile act

D. C. BUELL,
Assistant Adjutant General.

The commencement of the civil war found General Buell a lieutenant colonel, and a little later colonel, and the third officer in rank in the adjutant general's department of the regular army. He was under orders for duty on the Pacific coast in April, 1861, and sailed for San Francisco a few days after the firing on Fort Sumter. He was commissioned a brigadier general and recalled to Washington in August. In September and October he organized and disciplined a division in the army of the Potomac, and, on the twelfth of November was assigned to the command of the "Department of the Ohio, composed of the States of Ohio, Michigan, Indiana, that portion of Kentucky east of the Cumberland river, and the State of Tennessee, with headquarters at Louisville, Kentucky." Next to the department of the Potomac this was regarded the most important command in the contest which was then opening. The condition of affairs in Kentucky was thought to be extremely critical. One-third of the State was in the possession of the rebel forces, under whose protection a provisional government was inaugurated at Russellville; while further invasion was threatened from East Tennessee by Zollicoffer through Cumberland Gap, and by Humphrey Marshall from Virginia through Pound Gap. It was affirmed that the Union element was confined in a great part to the old men, and that the mass of the young men were on the eve of joining the rebel ranks; and many persons believed that a strong and prudent hand was required to preserve the State from a condition of practical, if not avowed revolt. The Government had in the State a new and imperfectly organized force of about twenty-five thousand men, while General Sherman, who had recently relieved General Anderson in the command, reported to the war department that the occasion demanded two hundred thousand men. Under these circumstances General Buell assumed command at Louisville on the fifteenth of November, relieving General Sherman, and entered upon the task before him. That task was to gather in the raw regiments that were forming in the different States of his department; organize, equip, and discipline an army; maintain the supremacy of the Union; control the secession element, and give confidence to the loyal citizens of Kentucky; expel from its borders the armed forces of the Confederacy, and carry the arms and authority of the Government into the States in rebellion. Those who fail to keep in mind the general state of confusion and excitement which pervaded the country at that time, the passion and energy of the insurrection, the magnitude of the physical obstacles to be overcome, the total lack of military training and experience among the people, and the scarcity of available officers for the various staff functions, will not appreciate the difficulty of the work to be performed, or do justice to the services of that early period of the war, in comparison with those of a later date, when the military arm of the Government had by practice grown strong and skilful, and the power and confidence of the confederacy had received its first fatal shock. The army which General Buell then formed and put into the field, called the army of the Ohio, afterwards the army of the Cumberland, was the largest of the original army organizations except the army of the Potomac, and it assumed from the first an efficiency and *esprit de corps* which gave it a marked prominence in the subsequent events of the war.

While the work of organization was going on, the aggressive attitude of the enemy had to be counteracted, and, as is usual under such circumstances, the temper of the southern people and the enthusiasm of revolution gave to their troops a sort of efficiency which had to be offset by the steadier methods of discipline in the northern armies. The main Confederate line at Bowling Green under Albert Sidney Johnson, menaced Louisville, and its partisan cavalry, rendered exceptionally efficient for such service by the personal qualities of the material, and operating in a hot, unfriendly population, produced results which were altogether out of proportion to its numerical strength. To repel an invasion in northeastern Kentucky under General Humphrey Marshall, a brigade was organized and placed under the command of General Garfield, then colonel of the Forty-second Ohio infantry, who defeated Marshall in several engagements, and drove him out of the State.

The following are the instructions under which General Garfield acted, and the general orders commending his success:

HEADQUARTERS DEPARTMENT OF THE OHIO, }
LOUISVILLE, December 17, 1862. }

Colonel James A. Garfield, Forty-second Ohio Regiment, Commanding Brigade,

SIR: The brigade organized under your command is intended to operate against the rebel force threatening, and indeed actually committing, depredations in Kentucky, through the valley of the Big Sandy.

The actual force of the enemy, from the best information I can gather, does not probably exceed two thousand or two thousand and five hundred, though rumor places it as high as seven thousand. You can better ascertain the true state of the case when you get on the ground.

You are apprised of the position of the troops placed under your command. Go first to Lexington and Paris, and place the Fortieth Ohio regiment in such position as will best give a moral support to the people in the counties on the route to Prestonburgh and Piketon, and oppose any further advance of the enemy on that route. Then proceed with the least possible delay to the mouth of the Big Sandy and move with the force in that vicinity up that river and drive the enemy back, or cut him off. Having done that, Piketon will probably be the best position for you to occupy to guard against further incursions. Artillery will be of but little if any service to you in that country. If the enemy have any it will encumber and weaken them rather than strengthen them.

Your supplies must mainly be taken up the river; and it ought to be done as soon as possible, while the navigation is open. Purchase what you can in the country through which you operate. Send your requisitions to these headquarters for funds and ordnance stores, and to the quartermaster and commissary at Cincinnati for other supplies.

The conversations I have had with you will suggest more details than can be given here. Report frequently and fully upon all matters concerning your command.

Very respectfully your obedient servant,

D. C. BUELL,
Brigadier General Commanding.

HEADQUARTERS DEPARTMENT OF THE OHIO, }
LOUISVILLE, KENTUCKY, January 20, 1862. }

General Orders No. 40.]

The general commanding takes occasion to thank Colonel Garfield

and his troops for their successful campaign against the rebel force under General Marshall on the Big Sandy, and their gallant conduct in battle. They have overcome formidable difficulties in the character of the country, the condition of the roads, and the inclemency of the season; and, without artillery, have in several engagements, terminating with the battle on Middle Creek on the eleventh inst , driven the enemy from his entrenched positions, and forced him back into the mountains with the loss of a large amount of baggage and stores, and many of his men killed or captured.

These services have called into action the highest qualities of a soldier—fortitude, perseverance, courage.

By command of GENERAL BUELL.

JAMES B. FRY, A. A. G., Chief of Staff.

In December, the confederate general, George B. Crittenden, recently assigned to the command of General Zollicoffer's column, crossed the Cumberland river nearly opposite Somerset, fortified himself at Mill Spring, and threatened central Kentucky. On the thirty-first of December General George H. Thomas was sent with his division, to attack him. The battle of Mill Spring, with a signal victory to the Union arms, was the result of this expedition. Various other expeditions and operations of minor importance, were also executed.

The following are the principal instructions and orders relating to this expedition:

HEADQUARTERS DEPARTMENT OF THE OHIO, }
LOUISVILLE, KENTUCKY, December 29, 1861. }

General:

I send you a sketch of the country about Somerset, which shows more of the roads than your maps. We conversed about the advance on Zollicoffer through Columbia, and if you remember my idea it is hardly necessary to add anything on the subject. It is for you to move against his left and endeavor to cut him off from his bridge, while Schoepf, with whom of course you will communicate, attacks in front. The maps will indicate the proper moves for that object. The result should be at least a severe blow to him, or a hasty flight across the river. But to expect the former, the movement should be made rapidly and secretly, and the blow should be vigorous and decided. There should be no delay after your arrival. It would be better not to have undertaken it if it should result in confining an additional force merely to watching the enemy.

Take such portion of the cavalry from Columbia as you think necessary. Draw all the supplies you can from the country, and move as light as possible.

Having accomplished the object, be ready to move promptly in any direction, but wait until you hear from me, unless circumstances should require you to move without delay, as I may want you to proceed from there to the other matter about which we have conversed.

Very respectfully, your obedient servant,

D. C. BUELL.

GEORGE H. THOMAS,
Brigadier general commanding First division, Lebanon.

HEADQUARTERS FIRST DIVISION DEPARTMENT OF THE OHIO, }
CAMP NEAR WEBB'S CROSS ROADS, KENTUCKY, }
January 13, 1862. }

Brigadier General D. C. Buell, commanding department of the Ohio, Louisville, Kentucky.

GENERAL: After two days of the hardest work I have reached this place, sixteen miles from Columbia, with the advance brigade of my division. The provision and ammunition train with a portion of one brigade is still in the rear, and will probably not reach here to-night. The road which has been represented as good, is the worst I ever saw, and the recent rains have made it one continuous quagmire from Columbia to this place. We are still seventeen miles from the position of the enemy by the shortest road, viz: that across the headwaters of Wolf creek, leaving Harrison to the left. This road is represented by my scouts as much worse than the roads the command has already passed over. It is next to impossible to procure either forage or subsistence in the country, and entirely impracticable to haul over this road at this season of the year. It is therefore necessary to do one of two things, either to go to Jamestown and eventually down the river to Burkesville, thereby cutting off all communication between Mill Spring and Nashville by the river, or work our way by this road to Somerset and join General Shoepf. We can never get supplies in any other way. Should my division proceed on to Somerset, it would be impossible to get down the river by the road on this side during the winter, and as Shoepf's force is sufficient to keep the enemy in check, I would respectfully suggest that the troops now with me proceed at once to Jamestown and eventually to Burkesville, from which point their services can be made available in any operations in the direction of Bowling Green.

Very respectfully, your obedient servant,

GEORGE H. THOMAS,

Brigadier General U. S. V., commanding.

HEADQUARTERS DEPARTMENT OF THE OHIO, }
LOUISVILLE, January 17, 1862. }

Brigadier General G. H. Thomas, commanding First Division.

GENERAL: I have received your letter of the thirteenth, from Webb's Cross Roads. You will, before this time, have received my letter of the same date, sent with your messenger. I hope that letter will have determined your action. It is not sufficient to hold Zollicoffer in check. He must be captured or dispersed. I think the situation offers the opportunity of affecting the former. If you consider your force insufficient, telegraph me from Somerset. The lines have been extended to that place. It will not be desirable to march your command to Somerset, but rather take a position in front of the enemy, so as to draw your supplies from Somerset, and be in convenient position to move down upon him. I am assured that you can get an abundance of forage from the country in the direction of Liberty. If you can buy meal, don't haul flour. It is not necessary to subsist your command, but it is not necessary that the established rations shall be exactly followed.

I am aware that the roads are in a horrible condition. They must be improved. The only way to do that effectually, when trains are to pass over them several times, is to corduroy or puncheon them, sixteen feet wide. I have given orders for this to be done on the Danville and Somerset roads. General Schoepf sends a regiment on that duty from Somerset, and General Wood, with three regiments, is to do the same from Danville. See that it is pushed forward energetically from Somerset. It ought to be completed in a few days.

Take some means of informing yourself constantly of the movements of the enemy, and apprise me daily by telegraph.

You could not march to Burkesville, and it is not desirable that you should be there.

Very respectfully,

Your obedient servant,

D. C. BUELL,

Brigadier General Commanding.

HEADQUARTERS DEPARTMENT OF OHIO, }
LOUISVILLE, KENTUCKY, January 23, 1862 }

General Orders No. 46.

The general commanding has the gratification of announcing the achievement of an important victory, on the nineteenth inst , at Mill Spring, by the troops under General Thomas, over the rebel forces, some twelve thousand strong, under General George B. Crittenden and General Zollicoffer.

The defeat of the enemy was thorough and complete, and his loss in killed and wounded was great. Night alone, under cover of which his troops crossed the river from their intrenched camp and dispersed, prevented the capture of his entire force. Fourteen or more pieces of artillery, some fifteen hundred horses and mules, his entire camp equipage, together with wagons, arms, ammunition, and other stores to a large amount, fell into our hands.

The general has been charged by the general in chief to convey his thanks to General Thomas and his troops for their brilliant victory. No task could be more grateful to him, seconded as it is by his own cordial approbation of their conduct.

By command of BRIGADIER GENERAL BUELL.

JAMES B. FRY, A. A. G., Chief of Staff.

The subject of a general plan of campaign to be executed as soon as the necessary force was prepared, received the early attention of the new commander, and in a letter, written twelve days after his arrival in Louisville, he submitted to the general-in-chief, General McClellan, his views on that subject. The same plan was, a little later, proposed to General Halleck, who commanded the adjoining department—Missouri. The main confederate force in the west, under the command of General Albert Sidney Johnston, with headquarters at Bowling

Green, Kentucky, occupied Bowling Green, fortified behind Barren river. Fort Donelson, on the Cumberland; Fort Henry, on the Tennessee, and Columbus, on the Mississippi. General Buell's plans proposed that Halleck, with a land and naval force, should attack the centre of this line on the Cumberland and Tennessee, while we attacked or turned Bowling Green and moved directly on Nashville. This plan, substantially, was at length executed, though without the concert which, would perhaps, have given better results. General Halleck was not prepared to coöperate when invited, and finally moved without concert, having no idea of further progress than the capture of Fort Henry. But the prompt reenforcements, amounting first and last to twenty-four regiments, with artillery, sent by Buell to the river expedition, and his movement upon Bowling Green and Nashville, brought about a more complete and extended success than Halleck contemplated.

The authorship of the general plan of these operations has been the subject of considerable discussion, though it is difficult to see how there should be any doubt about the matter. It has been claimed by General Grant for himself, and General Sherman claimed it for General Halleck; the letter on which Grant's claim is based was dated the twenty-ninth of January, and only proposed to capture Forts Henry and Donelson, and the official records show that the subject was not broached by Halleck before the twentieth of January. The following are the letters in which the plan was proposed to Generals McClellan and Halleck, by General Buell, on the twenty-seventh of November and third of January respectively:

LOUISVILLE, KENTUCKY, November 27, 1861

MY DEAR GENERAL.—I have not written you very frequently because I could not write definitely, and because such, perhaps exaggerated, importance do I attach to secrecy in these matters, that I have hesitated to put my own thoughts to paper, and I now ask you to keep them to yourself. It is certainly possible that in the end you may have to observe how far the consummation will have fallen short of my plans.

I hope you have not supposed that the introduction of the reenforcements through this point has had any reference to a defence of Louisville. That has not entered my mind at all. I assume that to be safe in any event. I do not place high estimate on Buckner's force at Bowling Green, and I have no such thought as that he will attempt to advance. His position is purely defensive, and he will be quite content if he can maintain that. I have, therefore, thought of no such thing as fortifying Louisville. Sherman threw up a little work at the mouth of Salt river. It may have been judicious when he did it. I have not seen the necessity of it since, though it does no harm.

If you will look carefully at the map you will see that Louisville affords the best base that can be taken for land operations from the north upon any part of Tennessee. The railroad to Lebanon curves around to the northeast behind Salt river, giving, besides the Nashville railroad, three good pike roads, which converge to a point of easy communication for three columns about Glasgow—one by the mouth of Salt river, coming into the railroad at Elizabethtown, one by Bardstown and New Haven, and coming into the direct pike road to Gallatin and Nashville, and one by Lebanon, Shepherdsville, and Greensburgh into the same road, while Lebanon junction, New Haven, and Lebanon form convenient points for the departure of as many columns. Lebanon also affords a point of departure for a column on East Tennessee as short as any route; for wagon transportation as short as the route from Cincinnati by Lexington, and shorter and less attended with delay by railroad. Nothing could be more convenient. This point has the further advantage of bringing everything under my eye. I could know nothing of what would be done from a base at Cincinnati. These advantages will not fail to impress themselves upon you without going more into detail.

And now for a plan of campaign. Up to the organization of columns behind Salt river, all the plans I have in view at present concur. Beyond that they diverge, and may be stated briefly thus: First, to establish a sufficient force before Bowling Green to hold Buckner there, while a column moves into East Tennessee by Somerset, and the route we had in view; second, to hold him in check while a column moves rapidly past him on Nashville by the turnpike via Gallatin, and third, holding him in check at Bowling Green and throwing in columns on both the Somerset and Nashville routes. The choice of these must depend on circumstances, which may vary in the meantime, or which may not now be clearly perceived. In conjunction with either of these should be the movement of the flotilla columns up the Tennessee and Cumberland, so as at least to land and winter near the State line, and cut off communication between Bowling Green and Columbus, and, perhaps run directly into Nashville. A strong demonstration should, at the same time, be made on Columbus by the Mississippi. The details of all this, such as the destruction of railroads, so as to cut off communication, and a thousand other details, I do not go into, nor is it necessary. You can imagine them all.

All this, I hope, you will at least say looks plausible; more than that, I hope it is reasonable, and believe it is practicable though I would not like you to forget that circumstances not fully foreseen may mar it in part. For the water movements, means are necessary which I have not the control of; that is, gunboats and transports. The troops which you promise from Missouri could be used for the purpose, and ought to move at my signal. I should take the troops from Paducah for one of them, and replace them by those which probably would not be as well disciplined and equipped.

Thus far I have studiously avoided any movements which to the enemy would have the appearance of activity or method. The points occupied are pretty much the same as when I arrived, except that a regiment has now and then been moved into position, and Thomas has gradually been closing in upon Lebanon. I shall in a couple of days, at most, complete the matter of organizing brigades and divisions as the troops come in, and begin to get them into position. We are now "lying around somewhat loose," and I shall not care much if some of our fragments have to look sharply after themselves. We are at the mouth of Salt river, Elizabethtown, Nolin, Columbia, Campbellsville, at the points on the Lebanon railroad, Somerset, London, Crab Orchard, and Dick Robinson, and on the lower Green river. The latter force is composed mostly of Kentucky regiments, half organized. I shall probably keep them to make a demonstration on Russellville and Hopkinsville at the proper time. We have occasional stampedes at the outposts, but I do not allow myself to be much troubled about them. Such an one we have now on the lower Green river, where Breckenridge is said to be advancing with eight thousand men. He may have two thousand five hundred or three thousand. Another at Somerset, where Zollicoffer is said to be crossing with ten thousand. He may have four or five thousand, and he may cross a regiment or two.

As the troops come they go into camp five miles from the city, under Mitchell, who is attentive and subordinate, and where they replenish their worn out clothes and outfit and go to drilling. Nelson has been in camp a day, and, I am informed, has already got into a difficulty with Mitchell; and, if I am rightly informed, has behaved very absurdly. As he is a veteran, some allowance must be made for him.

There are at Indianapolis seven regiments ready for service, but demoralized by the proximity of friends and the want of discipline and instruction. I propose to form them into a reserve and camp of instruction at Bardstown, which is a convenient place in many respects. I can make no use of them in an advance. The Kentucky regiments are only partially organized, and can be but little used at present.

If I were to go into my affairs, I should have the appearance of complaining over difficulties. I am greatly in need of general and staff officers. My own staff force is entirely insufficient, but I have no means of augmenting it with advantage. As for myself I should pay a very high compliment, if I hoped to come up to the expectations which you first formed. I am afraid I shall have to ask a little patience.

Very truly, yours,
D. C. BUELL.

MAJOR GENERAL GEORGE B. McCLELLAN,
Commanding United States army.

LOUISVILLE, KENTUCKY, December 10, 1861.

MY DEAR GENERAL:—As I informed you by telegraph, I received your letters on the third and fifth. I have by no means been unmindful of your wishes in regard to East Tennessee, and I think I can both appreciate and write in your sympathy for a people who have shown so much constancy. That constancy will still sustain them until the hour of deliverance. I have no fear of their being crushed. The allegiance of such people to hated rulers, even if it could be enforced for the moment,

will only make them the more determined and ready to resist when the hour of rescue comes.

The organization of the division at Lebanon has been with special reference to the object which you have so much at heart, though, fortunately, it is one which suits any contingencies that can arise. I shall hasten its preparation with all the energy and industry I can bring to bear. The plans which I have in view embrace that fully; but the details and the final determination—while there is yet time to watch the progress of circumstances which might affect our plans vitally—I think I should lack that ordinary discretion by which I hope to retain your confidence, if I did not reserve. When the preparation of that division is complete, which I hope will be very soon, if I then see reasons why it should be merged into the general line of operations, I will give you the reasons and you shall be the judge of them; and, if you do not see force in them, I assure you I will pursue your views with as much zeal and hopefulness, and, perhaps, more energy than if I entirely concurred in them. You do not know me well yet if you think I cannot do this. And now for the other side of the field. I feel more anxiety about it than any other, because I have less control over the means that ought to bear on it, and have less knowledge of their details if I had the control. I do not know well—scarcely at all—the description and capacity of the gunboats and transports that are to be used, and I do not know anything about the quality of the troops and officers. I have not seen Smith for seven years, and am afraid to judge him. I have never rated him as highly as some men. The expedition requires nothing more, as matters now stand, than ordinary nerve and good judgment, and ability to command men. The troops ought, of course, to be the best we can command. The object is not to fight great battles and storm impregnable fortifications, but, by demonstrations and manœuvring, to prevent the enemy from concentrating his scattered forces. In doing this, it must be expected there will be some fighting; it may be pretty good fighting. I suppose that ten thousand men, with two batteries, would not be too great an estimate for each of the rivers, if the enemy should do all that he probably can do. The precise manner of conducting expeditions depends so much on local knowledge that I can hardly venture on its details; but, at least, the expeditions should go as rapidly as possible to the nearest point where the road crosses the peninsula: that is, to Dover and Fort Henry. And the first thing then to be done is to destroy the bridges and ferries; then act momentarily on the defensive, unless the weakness of the enemy or a trepidation in his force should give a good opportunity to attack. I think the first serious opposition will be found at Fort Henry, and at an island battery four or five miles below Dover; but my information is not very complete as to the strength of these works. It would be probably necessary to stop there. Fort Henry is said by civilians to be strong. I cannot learn yet the number of guns. There have been some seven thousand troops there. We will probably find that number there. It is about six miles below the railroad bridge. I should not expect to meet any considerable force at Dover, but, perhaps, seven or eight thousand at Clarksville, where they are fortifying. If they succeed in getting out of Bowling Green, which, I believe, they will try to do as soon as they see us advancing, unless their force and armament are increased, of course the number at Clarksville may be expected to be greater.

The demonstration on Columbus and the Mississippi should, at least, be on such a scale that it can be converted into a real attack if they detach anything; better still, if it can attack in any event.

You must be patient if you find my letter vague and unsatisfactory. I have had to satisfy a deputation acting under a joint resolution of the legislature, that it was hardly necessary or expedient at this time to appoint a certain person "provost marshal, with all proper power, and giving to him such military force as he may deem essential for a prompt and proper enforcement and execution of the laws, and a suppression of all lawless and marauding excursions into northeastern Kentucky." I believe I succeeded pretty well, and perhaps after that I ought not to have attempted a coherent letter. Your own judgment will satisfy its deficiencies. Please have Rosecrans take care of his revolted subjects along the Big Sandy. We are established at Mumfordsville. Truly yours,
D. C. BUELL.

MAJOR GENERAL GEORGE B. McCLELLAN,
Commanding United States army.

HEADQUARTERS DEPARTMENT OF THE OHIO, }
LOUISVILLE, January 3, 1862. }

GENERAL: I received your dispatch, and, with more delay than I meant, proceed to the subject of it in compliance with your request, and, I may add, also at the wish of the President.

I do not underrate the difficulties in Missouri, and I think it is not extravagant to say that the great power of the rebellion in the west is arrayed on a front the planks of which are Columbus and Bowling Green, and the centre about where the railroad between these points crosses the Tennessee and Cumberland rivers. Including Nashville and the fortified points below, it is, I have no doubt, within bounds to estimate their force on that line at eighty thousand men; including a column about Somerset, Kentucky, in rear of their right flank, it is more.

Of this force, forty thousand may be set down as at Bowling Green; twenty thousand at Columbus, though you doubtless have more information on that point than I have; and twenty thousand at the centre Considering the railroad facilities which enable the enemy to concentrate in a few hours on any single point of this front, you will at once see the importance of a combined attack on its centre and flanks, or at least of demonstrations which may be converted into real attacks, and fully occupy the enemy on the whole front. It is probable that you may have given the subject, as far as Columbus and the Centre are concerned, more attention than I have. With reference to the former, at least, I can make no more than the general suggestion already expressed, that it should be fully occupied.

The attack upon the centre should be made by two gunboat expeditions, with, I should say, twenty thousand men on the two rivers. They should, of course, be organized with reference to the depth of the water in the rivers; and whether they should be of equal or unequal strength, would depend upon that and other considerations, and can hardly be determined until the moment of departure. The mode of attack must depend upon the strength of the enemy at the several points and the features of the localities. It will be of the first importance to break the railroad communication, and, if possible, that should be done by columns moving rapidly to the bridges over the Cumberland and the Tennessee. The former, probably, would not be reached as first, being some thirty-one miles above the first principal battery that I know of at Dover. The other is eighteen miles above Fort Henry—the first I know of on the Tennessee. If the expedition should not be strong enough to do the work alone, they should establish themselves firmly at the nearest possible point, and remain at least until they ascertained that reenforcements from my column or some other source would not reach them. By uniting they could establish themselves permanently under the protection of the gunboats.

I say this much rather to lay the subject before you, than to propose any definite plan for your side. Whatever is done should be done speedily, within a few days. The work will become more difficult every day. Please let me hear from you at once.

Very truly, yours,
D. C. BUELL,
Brigadier General Commanding.

GENERAL H. W. HALLECK,
Commanding Department of the Missouri.

The events happened in this order: The gunboats under Commodore Foot, supported by a land force under General Grant, captured Fort Henry, February 6th; Grant and the navy, with the reenforcements which Buell had sent, appeared before Fort Donelson February 12th and 14th; Buell's force appeared before Bowling Green, commenced crossing and demonstrating towards Nashville, February 14th, Johnston having, on his approach, burnt the bridges and retired to Nashville. Fort Donelson surrendered to Grant, February 16th, and on the approach of Buell, Johnston burnt the bridges over the Cumberland, and retired south from Nashville, which Buell occupied February 25.

The following order, issued on this occasion, is not so interesting for the announcement of the mere fact of occupation, as for the policy which it avowed in the prosecution of the war:

HEADQUARTERS DEPARTMENT OF THE OHIO, }
NASHVILLE, TENNESSEE, February 26, 1862. }

General Order No. 13a]

The General Commanding congratulates his troops that it has been their privilege to restore the national banner to the capital of Tennessee. He believes that thousands of hearts in every part of the State will swell with joy to see that honored flag reinstated in a position from which it was removed in the excitement and folly of an evil hour; that

the voice of her own people will soon proclaim its welcome, and that their manhood and patriotism will protect and perpetuate it.

The general does not deem it necessary, though the occasion is a fit one, to remind his troops of the rule of conduct they have hitherto observed and are still to pursue. We are in arms, not for the purpose of invading the rights of our fellow countrymen anywhere, but to maintain the integrity of the Union, and protect the constitution under which its people have been prosperous and happy. We cannot, therefore, look with indifference on any conduct which is designed to give aid and comfort to those who are endeavoring to defeat these objects, but the action to be taken in such cases rests with certain authorized persons, and is not to be assumed by individual officers or soldiers. Peaceable citizens are not to be molested in their persons or property. Any wrongs to either are to be promptly corrected and the offenders brought to punishment. To this end all persons are desired to make complaint to the immediate commander of officers or soldiers so offending, and if justice be not done promptly, then to the next commander, and so on until the wrong is redressed. If the necessities of the public service should require the use of private property for public purposes, fair compensation is to be allowed. No such appropriation of private property is to be made except by the authority of the highest commander present, and any other officer or soldier who shall presume to exercise such privilege shall be brought to trial. Soldiers are forbidden to enter the residences or grounds of citizens on any plea without authority.

No arrests are to be made without the authority of the commanding general, except in case of actual offence against the authority of the Government; and in all such cases the fact and circumstances will immediately be reported in writing to headquarters through the intermediate commanders.

The general reminds his officers that the most frequent depredations are those which are committed by worthless characters who straggle from the ranks on the plea of being unable to march; and where the inability really exists, it will be found in most instances that the soldier has overloaded himself with useless and unauthorized articles. The orders already published on this subject must be enforced.

The condition and behavior of a corps are sure indications of the efficiency and fitness of its officers. If any regiment shall be found to disregard that propriety of conduct which belongs to soldiers as well as citizens, they must not expect to occupy the posts of honor, but may rest assured that they will be placed in positions where they cannot bring shame on their comrades and the cause they are engaged in. The Government supplies with liberality all the wants of the soldier. The occasional deprivations and hardships incident to rapid marches must be borne with patience and fortitude. Any officer who neglects to provide properly for his troops, or separates himself from them to seek his own comfort, will be held to a rigid accountability.

By command of General Buell.

JAMES B. FRY, A. A. G., Chief of Staff.

The confederate forces concentrated south of the Tennessee river, under the command of Albert Sidney Johnston, after the evacuation of Nashville, and Buell's command, for military operations, was, on the twelfth of March, merged into that of Halleck. After sending a division under General O. M. Mitchel to occupy north Alabama, organizing a division under General G. W. Morgan to operate from Kentucky against Cumberland Gap, and leaving a suitable force at Nashville and other places on his lines of communication, Buell marched in the latter part of March with five divisions, about thirty-seven thousand men, to form a junction with the forces of Halleck on the Tennessee river. He arrived at Savannah, the place appointed for the junction, with his leading division the evening before the battle of Shiloh, or Pittsburgh Landing. When the battle opened the following morning, he ordered forward the division (Nelson's) already arrived, sent instructions to the rear divisions to press on by forced march, and in person went to the river on a steamer to the field of battle. The head of his column, under Nelson, arrived in time to repel an attack which the confederates made immediately at the landing, to which the troops of Grant had been driven back at the close of the first day. Three of his divisions came up that night, a fourth the following day, and at daylight on the seventh the enemy was attacked, and by four o'clock in the evening, driven from the field. General Lew Wallace's fresh division, and such other fragments of Grant's army as retained any organization from the disaster of the previous day, took part in the battle of the seventh. The confederates fell back to Corinth, which they fortified, and from which they were forced to retire May 30th, by the combined armies under Halleck. The army of the Ohio, under Buell, occupied the centre in this advance.

After the retreat of the confederates from Corinth, Buell with his army was again detailed to operate against East Tennessee. He moved into north Alabama with four divisions (twenty-five thousand men), making (June 31st) his headquarters temporarily at Huntsville, while repairing the railroads to his base of supplies at Louisville, three hundred miles distant. His remaining division, under General Thomas, arrived July 31st. The movement from the first was delayed by the orders of Halleck, requiring him to repair and guard the Memphis & Charleston railroad east of Corinth.

In the meantime the confederate forces in East Tennessee were reenforced by General Bragg, with the bulk of the Corinth army, making an aggregate force of not less than sixty thousand men, which by the twenty-eighth of July was available for prompt concentration at Chattanooga or elsewhere in East Tennessee. Its superior cavalry force operated with great effect upon the long lines of the Union army, breaking up the railroads and cutting off its supplies.

The effort to defeat these partisan operations by combining light infantry with the totally insufficient Union cavalry, and by local guards, was unsuccessful, and on the tenth of August the confederate cavalry under Forrest and Morgan, effectually severed the line of supplies of the Union army by an extensive destruction of the railroad north of Nashville.

About the same time the whole confederate force in East Tennessee assumed the offensive. General Kirby Smith, starting from Knoxville, passed the mountains to the left of Cumberland Gap, which the division under General G. W. Morgan had occupied and fortified in time.

Upon hearing of Smith's movement Buell dispatched General Nelson with a few experienced officers and two batteries of artillery to organize such troops as could be got together in Kentucky to repel Smith's invasion. Smith encountered Nelson's force, composed of raw troops, at Richmond, defeated it (August 30th) and advanced into central Kentucky, threatening Louisville and Cincinnati.

Simultaneously with Smith's advance Bragg crossed the Tennessee river at and near Chattanooga with the bulk of his army, threatening middle Tennessee and Nashville. The Union army, which occupied various points for repairing the roads and with a view to the forward movement for which it had been preparing, was immediately put in readiness for concentration.

McCook, with his own and Crittenden's divisions, was ordered from the mouth of Battle creek up the Sequatchy valley to watch and oppose the enemy's advance, and when pressed, to fall back for concentration on the road to McMinnville. He advanced a short distance and returned, supposing that the enemy had already anticipated him on the McMinnville road. This supposition proved to be incorrect, and it threw the army out of position for efficient observation, gave an erroneous impression of the rate of the enemy's progress, and kept the army a week about McMinnville awaiting his approach, of which at the end of that time there was yet no intelligence. The army was now reduced to ten days' supplies, and assuming Nashville to be the enemy's first objective point, it was necessary to put the army in a position which would enable it best to oppose that design and at the same time reopen its communication with Louisville. Orders were therefore given on the thirtieth of August for concentrating at Murfreesborough on the fifth of September. Pending this movement the head of Bragg's column crossed the mountain and appeared at Sparta on the second of September, and instead of turning towards Nashville, moved towards the Cumberland river, which it crossed at Carthage and Gainsborough. This change in the anticipated route of the enemy caused the movement of the Union army upon Nashville, and the sending of a division for the protection of Bowling Green, where some supplies had been gathered; and on learning that the bulk of the confederate army was marching in the same direction, Buell started with the army of the Ohio in pursuit, after leaving a suitable force to hold Nashville, which he had previously commenced to fortify. The enemy halted involuntarily at Glasgow, but continued his march to Mumfordsville, where a Federal force of about four thousand men, with artillery, strongly fortified, but heedlessly exposed to such a danger by the authority at Louisville, not then under Buell's command, surrendered to Bragg on the seventeenth without resistance. There was skirmishing between the two armies and preparations for battle at Mumfordsville, but on the twenty-first the confederate army, followed closely by the Union army, moved towards Louisville until near Elizabethtown, when it turned off toward Bardstown. That deflection indicated a speedy junction of Bragg and Kirby Smith, and perhaps an attack on Louisville, where a force of raw troops was gathering. Instead, therefore, of turning off to continue the pursuit, Buell marched directly on to Louisville, where his rear division arrived on the night of the twenty-ninth.

The new regiments were immediately incorporated into the old organizations, and on the first of October the army moved against the enemy, who then occupied Bardstown and Frankfort. The news of this advance brought to a hurried conclusion the ceremonies of inaugurating a State governor at Frankfort, in which Bragg was at the moment engaged. Sharp skirmishing occurred in both lines, the confederates retiring for concentration until the Bardstown column reached Perryville, where, October 8th, a severe but indecisive battle, lasting until night, was fought between portions of the two armies. The Union army moved forward at six o'clock next morning to renew the battle, but the confederates had withdrawn. There was further concentration on both sides and manœuvring for battle, but on the twelfth Bragg commenced to retreat on Cumberland Gap. He was followed, and his rear guard engaged at various points as far as London, when seeing no prospect of further advantage, Buell, October 17th, discontinued the pursuit, and directed his army by way of Glasgow and Bowling Green upon Murfreesborough, in anticipation of Bragg's movement against middle Tennessee and Nashville. Pending this movement, October 30th, the army being then in the vicinity of Glasgow and Bowling Green, he turned over the command to General Rosecrans, in obedience to news from Washington. Previously, September 29th, while at Louisville, he had been ordered to relinquish the command to General Thomas, but the order was countermanded at the request of Thomas and others.

In reporting, October 16th, the movement he had determined upon, he added:

While I shall proceed with these dispositions, deeming them to be proper for the public interest, it is meet that I should say that the present time is, perhaps, as convenient as any for making any change that may be thought desirable in the command of this army.

He was thanked by the department for the service rendered, but there immediately arose some disagreement between him and the department as to the plan of further operations. He, however, adhered to his views, and continued the movement which he had announced, and, as stated, surrendered his command pending its execution.

In November a court of inquiry was ordered to investigate his operations during the summer and fall. The court was in session more than five months, and much oral and documentary evidence was taken; but the proceedings were never published, and when called for some years afterwards by Congress, the voluminous record was found to have disappeared from the archives of the War department. Twice after the inquiry General Buell was offered commands under his juniors, Sherman and Camby, but declined. He was then mustered out of the volunteer service May 23, 1864, and on the first of June resigned his commission in the regular army. In 1865 he took part in coal and iron interest in Kentucky, where he now (1881) resides.

In this sketch nothing has been attempted but a brief outline of the more prominent facts, omitting many important details, and all discussion of the actual or relative value of General Buell's services as a commander during the Rebellion. The fact is not to be ignored that perhaps no high officer in the war was the subject of so much party criticism as he during the last six months of his command. Though in his own mind repelling the injustice of this criticism, he has not seen proper to make much public protest against it, and it does not come within the scope of this sketch to analyze facts for the purpose of pointing out how much of the harsh judgment was bestowed without discernment or justice, how much was due to a state of the public mind, which, it must be confessed, was often disposed to regard passionate, or at least practical partizanship, as an element of patriotic duty, and how much to the machinations of hostile ambitions and personal resentment. It does not appear that the War department shared fully in the disapprobation to which a portion of the public press gave loud expression, but it yielded to a popular clamor, or rather to the dictation of political and personal influences which first shaped the popular prejudice, and then derived strength and reward from its support. It may, however, be proper to say in the direction of impartial criticism, that in reviewing the operations of the army under General Buell in the summer and fall of 1862, and comparing them with similar operations of other dates and other commanders on the same and other fields, it is impossible not to be impressed by the contrast in the popular feeling with reference to the different periods. These contrasts indicate, perhaps, a more politic conformity of the later commanders to the popular idea of the war, and fortunately, also to a more patient appreciation by the popular judgment of the obstacles to be overcome.

The following is the order with which General Buell relinquished the command of the army:

HEADQUARTERS ARMY OF THE OHIO, }
LOUISVILLE, KY., October 30, 1862. }
General Orders, No. 150.]

In obedience to orders from the headquarters of the army, Major-General Buell relinquishes the command of the district and Army of the Ohio to Major-General W. S. Rosecrans.

It is impossible for the general without feelings of regard and a warm interest in their future success, to part with troops whom he has been the instrument of converting for the most part from raw levies into a powerful army, honored by common consent for its discipline and efficient organization, for its *esprit de corps*, and for victories unqualified by a single reverse, and whose fortunes he has followed for a twelve month over a field of operations embracing considerable portions of our States, through difficulties and dangers which its fortitude and courage have mastered without accident or failure. It has recently, by a rapid march of some five hundred miles with limited subsistence, often with an inadequate supply of water, returned to Kentucky and driven from her borders a powerful army; and having reestablished its communications is now well on its way to meet the enemy at other points. The occasion is not convenient for recounting its services during the past twelve months, but the army may safely recur to them with pride. If anything has not been accomplished which was practicable within the sphere of its duty, the general cheerfully holds himself responsible for the failure.

The general reflects with pride that the army under his command has for the most part been free from petty jealousies and intrigues—that it has neither indulged in vain boasting, nor tarnished its high character by bickerings and low criminations. It will enhance his gratification if it shall carry to its new commander—who already has earned its confidence and respect by distinguished service—the same noble qualities which have characterized it since its organization. He will pray that it may be the instrument of speedily restoring the Union to its integrity; and there is no individual in its rank in whose honor and welfare he will not feel a special interest.

By command of Major-General Buell.

JAMES B. FRY, colonel and chief of staff.

GENERAL H. F. DEVOL.

Among the regiments in the late Rebellion to which Washington county contributed her "bravest and best," the gallant Thirty-sixth stands prominent. The history of this regiment is sketched at another place in this volume, but an outline of the life of its worthy colonel will be of interest, both to his military friends and the public.

H. F. Devol, the youngest son of Stephen Devol, jr., was born in Waterford township August 6, 1831. His boyhood was spent in the country school and on his father's farm. At the age of sixteen, a courageous spirit, and a desire for more extended educational advantages led him to seek independence from parental dictation. He then attended Beverly academy for a short time, and two years later made his first trip south in the produce trade. From this time till the opening of the Rebellion Mr. Devol devoted his summers to farming and his winters to flatboating and trade.

He married, May 15, 1856, Adelaide A. Dyer, of Muskingum township, by whom he had two children— Hattie A., and Carroll, who is a graduate of Pennsylvania Military institute, and was, in 1879, appointed by President Hayes lieutenant in the regular army. Mrs. Devol died July 10, 1860.

In the winter of 1860 Mr. Devol witnessed the first overt acts of the important drama in which he became an actor. Being south with a cargo of produce he experienced some of the inconveniences of that disturbed period. The spirit of secession was aroused, and northern merchants became objects of hatred. Their boats were not permitted to land at many places, while at others obstructions were thrown in the way of sales and collections. Mr. Devol, however, did not suffer serious financial loss, but his experience aroused him to action on returning home. He had been a witness of secession. It was in store for him to take a part in the bloodiest acts of the tragedy then opening, and eventually to stand in the line of triumphant soldiery with a full share of military glory.

When the first call for volunteers for the three years' service was made, Mr. Devol set to work to enlisting a company, from Waterford, Adams and Muskingum townships. It was the intention to enroll this company in the Thirtieth Ohio volunteer infantry, then being formed at Cincinnati. Mr. Devol had acted without a commission and without direction, and borne all the expenses out of his own pocket. When the company met at Lowell for organization, Colonel Melvin Clarke appeared with a commission to organize a new regiment, and informed Captain Devol that Colonel Groesbeck's regiment (Thirtieth Ohio volunteer infantry) was full. Captain Devol enlisted his men in the new regiment, and when the quota was full they were properly enrolled as "company A."

The company was reported August 1, 1861, and Mr. Devol was commissioned captain August 13th. From the time of being mustered in until peace illuminated their blood-stained bayonets, the Thirty-sixth was in active, efficient, and dangerous service, and during all that period Mr. Devol was with his men—with them both in camp and battlefield. He was promoted to the rank of major, September 7, 1862; to lieutenant colonel September 16, 1862, and to the colonelcy, for valuable and valiant conduct on the field of Chickamauga, October 13, 1862. In this battle Colonel Devol took a conspicuous and important part. When the battle opened Colonel

Jones was in command of the regiment and General Turchin of the brigade. In the afternoon the brigade was thrown in front of the enemy's centre. At a critical moment the advance line was driven back and Turchin's brigade, consisting of the Thirty-sixth and Ninety-second Ohio and Fourteenth Kentucky, was brought in face of a hot fire. To retreat would be disastrous. Brave boys were falling fast, and Lieutenant Colonel Devol, impatient for an order, grasped the situation, assumed command, and ordered a charge. A moment later positions were changed. The rebel ranks were broken and the brave brigade, encouraged by the bold movement of their temporary commander, followed close in pursuit for a distance of more than three hundred yards, when a retreat was ordered. They passed back through the gap in the enemy's line which this bold charge had brought to a halt, and given the Union troops time to reorganize on that day. Colonel Devol proved his soldierly instincts. Colonel Jones had been mortally wounded, and the brigade commander was not at his post. It was left for a lieutenant colonel to give the command which materially effected the fortunes of that celebrated battle. General Thomas and General Reynolds heartily complimented his soldierly conduct.

At Berryville an incident occurred which exemplifies his bravery. The brigade was ordered by General Hayes, then in command, to lie down to escape a destructive fire of the enemy. But in disobedience to the protestations of their soldiers, General Hayes and Colonel Devol remained standing at their posts where they could watch changing movements.

Colonel Devol was always found with his regiment and, indeed, was in one more engagement than his regiment. His rank during the greater period of the war was that of colonel, but on several occasions he was thrown in command of a brigade. This was the case at Cedar Creek, when General Hayes' brigade was under his command. At this battle the army of West Virginia, under command of General Crook, to which this brigade belonged, was held as a flanking column. But General Devol, in the excitement of progressing battle, lost his place, and was not a little surprised to find himself urging on with characteristic energy a strange command, engaged in the thickest of the fight. This is an episode of the war which General Hayes delights to tell. Few officers can claim the honor of having been in as many fights as their command, but Cedar Creek places the colonel of the Thirty-sixth one ahead of his regiment. Colonel Devol was brevetted brigadier general July 20, 1865.

During the war he had the singular good fortune to escape with only two slight wounds, and his robust body suffered but little from disease. He enjoyed the friendship and cordial respect of his associates in office and his men. He was always jealous of the fame of his regiment and always ready to protect its standing.

When the time for which the Thirty-sixth enlisted had expired General Devol was found ready to reengage in the service of the Union, and the regiment cheerfully went with him.

At the conclusion of hostilities in 1865 the rank and file

of our volunteer soldiery felt that they had accomplished that for which they suffered the pains and dangers of war, and were anxious to return to their families and farms. High salaried officers were accused of selfishly detaining the troops; but General Devol was entirely free from any accusation in this regard. Through his management and influence the regiment with which he went into the service and in which he had a warm interest was one of the first Ohio regiments mustered out of the service.

The war over, he returned to Waterford, and in 1866 he purchased the mercantile establishment of Charles Bowen, where he has since devoted himself closely to business. He has never had an ambition for political preferment, but is by no means indifferent to the duties of citizenship. His political creed was enunciated in his farewell address to the Thirty-sixth, when he said:

Comrades, you can go to your homes with the happy consciousness that you have done your duty to your country and yourselves; and when you again resume the privileges and responsibilities of citizenship, be as unflinching in defending the sacred Temple of Liberty with the ballot as you have been with the bullet, and all will be well.

He was appointed by General Hayes, while governor of Ohio, one of the trustees of Athens asylum for the insane. The relations between the President and himself have been the most cordial since their acquaintance in the Rebellion.

General Devol is a leading member of the Beverly Presbyterian church, is superintendent of the Sunday-school, and a valuable supporter of religious and moral movements in the community. He has acquired a handsome competence, and uses it liberally both in public improvements and in answering the prayers of multiplied charities. General Devol married, April 3, 1867, Harriet E. Bowen, by whom he had four children, George H., Mary B., Florence W., and Ermine B.

GENERAL RUFUS R. DAWES.

The year 1861 found Rufus R. Dawes in Jeneau county, Wisconsin. He had graduated with the class of 1860 at Marietta college, and like many young men who strike out from home at that period, had gone to the west which offered newer and broader fields of advancement. Born July 4, 1838, he was then in his twenty-third year. Upon the beginning of hostilities, he at once raised a company. This was in April, 1861. He was chosen captain and commissioned May 3, 1861. The company was composed principally of lumbermen and farmers, and was known as "The Lemonwier Minute Men." The company became "K," of the Sixth Wisconsin volunteer infantry.

They were mustered into the United States service at Madison, Wisconsin, July 16, 1861, for three years, and went at once to Washington, D. C. They were kept in camp of instructions during the winter of 1861-2. In the spring of 1862 they were with General McDowell, attached to the "pendulum division oscillating between Fredericksburgh and Catlett's Station, while General McClellan was enacting the tragedy of the Peninsula campaign. On July 1, 1862, Captain Dawes was promoted to major of the regiment.

On the morning of August 21, 1865, commenced the battle of the Rappahannock. Major Dawes' regiment was engaged three days supporting artillery and skirmishing at the fords. Captain Frank Buell was killed a short distance to their right at Freeman's Ford.

The battle of Gainsville was fought on the evening of August 28th. His brigade and a New York and Pennsylvania regiment engaged, at short musket range, Ewell's division of Stonewall Jackson's army. These six regiments suffered a loss of twelve hundred killed and wounded in forty-five minutes firing. Our troops held their ground. This was conceded to have been one of the most desperate struggles against large odds that occurred during the war.

In the second battle of Bull Run his regiment was hotly engaged, and suffered a severe loss. They left the field in perfect line before the enemy and the regiment formed the basis of two new alignements of the corps to check the advancing enemy. They left the field at 10 o'clock, P. M., covering the retreat of the entire army.

At the battle of South Mountain, Major Dawes commanded the left wing of his regiment which formed part of the assaulting column. They lost ninety killed and wounded out of four hundred engaged. General McClellan pronounced the brigade, for their admirable conduct on this occasion, equal to the best troops of any army in the world.

In the battle of Antietam he commanded the regiment during most of the battle, and took two hundred and eighty-six officers and men into action, of whom one hundred and fifty-two were killed or wounded. The flag staff of the regiment was struck while in Major Dawes, hands—all of the color guards having been disabled, it became necessary for him to carry the colors to maintain his organization.

At the battle of Fredericksburgh his regiment was engaged on the left of the line of General Franklin's grand division. Loss not severe. In Burnside's mud march his regiment took part, suffering severely from cold, rain, mud and hunger. Major Dawes was promoted to lieutenant colonel, March 24, 1863.

At the battle of Fitzhugh's Crossing, April 29, 1863, the Sixth Wisconsin and Twenty-fourth Michigan, under command of Lieutenant Colonel Dawes, were selected by General John F. Reynolds to force a crossing of the Rappahannock below Fredericksburgh. They rowed across the river in pontoon boats under musketry fire from the enemy's rifle pits; charged up a precipitous bank, captured the rifle pits and two hundred prisoners. General Reynolds pronounced it the most gallant dash he ever witnessed. Lieutenant Colonel Dawes was slightly wounded in the hand in this action.

In the battle of Chancellorsville his regiment participated, but was not heavily engaged, and covered the retreat of the army, crossing the last at the United States ford.

At the battle of Gettysburgh, Lieutenant Colonel Dawes commanded the regiment, and was engaged on the first of July. He charged upon and captured officers, men and battle flag of the Second Mississippi rebel regiment. In this charge he lost two hundred men killed and wounded, of four hundred and fifty in the line. General Doubleday, commanding the corps, in his official report, uses the following language as to the engagement:

The moment was a critical one, involving the defeat, perhaps the utter route of our forces. I immediately sent for one of Meredith's regiments, the Sixth Wisconsin, a gallant body of men, whom I knew could be relied upon. Forming them rapidly perpendicular to the line of battle, on the enemy's flank, I directed them to attack immediately. Lieutenant Colonel Dawes, their commander, ordered a charge, which was gallantly executed. The enemy made a hurried attempt to change front to meet the attack, and flung his troops into a railroad cut for safety.   .   .   .   The cut was carried at the point of the bayonet, and two regiments of Davis' (rebel) brigade taken prisoners.

Of the retreat through Gettysburgh the general says:

The Sixth Wisconsin marched through the streets in a body, stopping from time to time to return the fire of the enemy, and giving hearty cheers for the good old cause and the Sixth Wisconsin volunteers.

He says further:

The commander of the regiment, Lieutenant Colonel R. R. Dawes, proved himself one of the ablest officers on the field.

Brigadier General Solomon Meredith wrote to the governor of Wisconsin:

The Sixth Wisconsin was temporarily detached from my command, and although they met a superior force, yet they captured an entire regiment of the enemy. I can pay these gallant men no higher tribute than to testify, as I here do, that on this, as upon all other occasions, Lieutenant Colonel Dawes, his officers and men, fully sustained the honor of your State.

Second day.—Lieutenant Colonel Dawes, when arriving at Culp's Hill, began at once the construction of rifle pits, without orders. This example, promptly followed on the right, undoubtedly saved a defeat there. The enemy carried the rifle pits on Culp's Hill, on the right of the Sixth Wisconsin, about 8 P. M. Lieutenant Colonel Dawes charged upon and dislodged the Tenth Virginia (rebel) regiment, and repossessed the works in his own front. The line of pits was on the slope of the hill. They charged from the summit with an irresistible momentum, rolling the enemy down the hill before them.

Third day.—The Sixth Wisconsin was not heavily engaged, but from its position on Culp's Hill, overlooked the whole field of battle.

Battle of Mine Run.—Took part in the engagement, but were not heavily engaged.

In the battles of the Wilderness—first day—his regiment was desperately engaged on the morning of May 5th. They advanced upon the enemy through woods, brush, and swamps, driving them along their own front; but the assaulting column had exposed their flank, and not being properly supported, the enemy suddenly attacked them in flank and rear, and the corps (Fifth) was thrown into confusion and forced back. The fighting in the swamps and brush was entirely with muskets and bayonets, and owing to the intermingling of hostile lines in thick underbrush, it was terribly fierce and bloody.

On the second day the Sixth Wisconsin was moved to the right, to the relief of the Second corps, and was ordered to attack the enemy early in the morning of the sixth. Accordingly, at daylight they moved out to the

assault. Then ensued one of the most deadly musketry struggles of the war. Hill's corps was forced back two miles, when suddenly Longstreet's corps came into action, and at 10 o'clock A. M. the National line was forced back as far as Spottsylvania Court House road. May 6, 1864, Lieutenant Colonel Dawes assumed permanent command of the regiment.

After the terrible fighting of the two days above mentioned, they skirmished all day of the seventh, and marched all that night toward Spottsylvania Court House.

Battle of Laurel Hill or Tod's Tavern.—About 10 o'clock A. M. of the eighth they encountered General Hood's division of Longstreet's corps, and immediately gave battle, attacking them and driving them back to the summit of a low range of hills with slopes covered with thick underbrush. At this point the Union advance was checked and forced back with some loss. Colonel Dawes formed his regiment as a basis of a new alignement of the division, upon which they immediately entrenched. The enemy advanced about 12 o'clock M., and were easily repulsed. The two lines now confronted each other for several days, skirmishing heavily, at short range. On the tenth the Sixth Wisconsin, with other troops, made an unsuccessful charge on the enemy, who was now strongly entrenched. All day of the eleventh was taken up in heavy skirmishing.

In the battle of May 12th Colonel Dawes' regiment was, with other troops, engaged in two desperate and unsuccessful assaults on the enemy's position, in columns five lines deep, the slaughter being simply horrible. The leaves took fire from burning wads, and the wounded between the lines were burned to death under the eyes of their comrades, who were powerless to aid them. The impracticability of carrying this strongly entrenched position by assault, with a column broken by scrambling through thick laurel brush, was so clearly demonstrated on the ninth that some of the bravest soldiers fell on their faces, crying: "That's played out; you can't shove us into that slaughter pen again."

Battle of Spottsylvania Court House.—Immediately after this they marched on the double-quick five miles to the left, where General Hancock had carried the enemy's line. A bitter struggle had been raging all day between the enemy and troops of the Sixth army corps for the possession of a salient called by newspaper correspondents "The Angle of Death." The Sixth Wisconsin, with four other regiments, was selected by General Russell (afterwards killed at Fisher's Hill) as a forlorn hope to assault this salient. Fortunately, General Hancock countermanded the order. The ground in front of this work was wet and boggy, and the tramp of forty thousand feet had rendered it a mortar-bed of mud. In this mud were hundreds of dead soldiers. Here they formed their line with orders to pour a continued fire into the enemy's works, and here, throughout the whole night of May 12th, they worked at loading and firing. Morning disclosed the enemy falling back before troops who came to the relief of the Sixth Wisconsin and the four other regiments above mentioned. The men, utterly exhausted with fighting and marching so long sustained, sank down in the mud, many using the dead bodies of their comrades for pillows, and caught their first sleep for thirty-six hours. Words cannot be readily found to fitly describe the extreme hardship of this service. All night of the thirteenth they marched, wading creeks waist deep, flanking the works they had failed to take by assault. They went into position directly before Spottsylvania Court House, the morning of the fourteenth, the troops being so much scattered by the hard night's march that General Grant's order to assault could not be obeyed.

Battle of Jericho Ford.—In the pursuit of General Lee, the Fifth corps, having the advance, pushed across the North Anna river at Jericho Ford, and was immediately attacked by General A. P. Hill's rebel corps. Half of the Fifth corps had not crossed, and those that were over, including Colonel Dawes' regiment, were not in position. But it was the first open field fight since crossing the Rapidan, and the boys gloried in the chance of getting twice their number of the enemy on an open field. They, accordingly, within fifteen minutes, drove them into their works. This brilliant affair was highly complimented by General Grant in general orders.

On the twenty-ninth Colonel Dawes' regiment was engaged in a heavy skirmish, demonstrating against the enemy's entrenched position near Hanover Junction.

Battle of Bethesda Church.—The advance division of the Fifth corps was attacked near this church, thirteen miles from Richmond, and after a short and spirited action the enemy was completely beaten. Colonel Dawes commanded during this engagement the Sixth Wisconsin, Seventh Wisconsin, and Nineteenth Indiana regiments.

Battle of Cold Harbor.—The Union army had now pushed on in pursuit of the enemy to within nine miles of Richmond, where they were found strongly entrenched. Three days of heavy skirmishing ensued but no direct assault was made along Colonel Dawes' front, but the regiment nevertheless lost severely.

In the battle of Petersburgh June 18th, Colonel Dawes' regiment was engaged in an unsuccessful assault on the entrenchments, losing severely, and holding their line nearer the enemy's works than any other corps of the army. For two weeks they lived in holes in the ground, from which to raise a head in daylight was almost certain death.

Mine Explosion.—After the explosion of the mine, Colonel Dawes' regiment was sent forward to drive the enemy's skirmishers in front of the Sixth corps and suffered some loss.

Colonel Dawes was commissioned colonel July 5, 1864. He was mustered out August 10, 1864, by reason of expiration of term of service; having served three years and something over three months. Colonel Dawes was the only man of his regiment who passed through all of the above engagements without serious injury. He never was a day in hospital, and never was absent from his regiment when in battle or skirmish.

Colonel Dawes was commissioned brigadier general by brevet March 13, 1865, for meritorious services during the war.

He was married January 18, 1864, to Miss Mary B. Gates, daughter of Beman Gates, of Marietta.

In this brief sketch we have endeavored to give the military services of one of Washington county's most distinguished soldiers. Of the civil career of General Dawes we have not space to speak, further than to say that he was the popular candidate of the Republican party for representative in Congress from this (fifteenth) district at the October election in 1880, and was elected by a handsome majority.

COLONEL JESSE HILDEBRAND.

Jesse Hildebrand was of German extraction, his ancestry coming to this country sometime between the years 1700 and 1730. He was born in Pennsylvania, near the New York State line, on the twenty-second day of May, 1800, and was the first white child born in that portion of the State, the so-called "Corn" or "Planter" Indians then occupying the soil. His mother being an invalid, the child was placed in the care of an Indian woman, who tenderly cared for him, and became so attached to her charge that she was loth to give him up when the mother's health again permitted her to take charge of him. When he was about two years of age his parents sold the farm and removed to near Pittsburgh, but only remained there a short time when they pushed on farther west, finally arriving at Marietta, Ohio, where they found their future home. His parents both lived to an advanced age.

Our subject early in life developed a strong predilection for a military life, and would have entered the regular army had it not been for his love for, and care of, his mother. He was noted as a "drummer boy," and when about eighteen became drum major of the regiment at Marietta. He was a personal friend of President Jackson, who commissioned him an officer of militia. He was for many years a brigadier general of militia, and subsequently became major general. General Hildebrand always had a fine staff completely uniformed and equipped during this period of his military career.

Colonel Hildebrand, although a Democrat, believed thoroughly in the supremacy of the National to State authority, and in the hour of the Nation's peril did not hesitate as to his duty. In October, 1861, he began to raise the Seventy-seventh regiment for the active service of his country. He was appointed and commissioned its colonel, and in January, 1862, he left Marietta in command of a full regiment, and was soon at the front. The brigade of which he was in command, met the first outset of the enemy at Shiloh, and in that action distinguished himself for gallantry and courage, and for his persevering efforts in rallying his men in the face of disaster. General Sherman, who witnessed Colonel Hildebrand's conduct on this occasion, enthusiastically declared him to be the bravest man he ever knew. He afterwards endured a severe march through Tennessee and north Mississippi, finally arriving at Memphis. His regiment had become sadly reduced by battle and disease, and in August, 1862, was detailed for service at the military prison, Alton, Illinois, Colonel Hildebrand becoming commandant of the post, where he remained until his death. The unusual hardship and exposure to which he had been subject while in the field finally resulted in pneumonia, and at 2:30 o'clock P. M., Saturday, April, 1863, the brave soldier passed away.

The news of his death caused universal sorrow here in Marietta where he was so well and favorably known. A committee of arrangements for his funeral was appointed, consisting of Mayor Whittlesey, George M. Woodbridge, John Marshall, Henry Fearing, L. W. Reppert, I. R. Waters, J. B. Hovey, and Major William B. Mason, Seventy-seventh Ohio volunteer infantry, and appropriate resolutions to the memory of the deceased were adopted. The funeral services were held at the Putnam Street church, and the remains were followed to Mound cemetery, under military escort, by his family, the clergymen, members of his staff when general, members of the Seventy-seventh regiment present and a large concourse of citizens.

When the news of Colonel Hildebrand's death reached General Sherman, he sent his widow the following letter of condolence, which contains the highest testimonial to Colonel Hildebrand's worth as a soldier and a man:

HEADQUARTERS FIFTEENTH ARMY CORPS, NEAR VICKSBURGH,
May 2, 1863.

Mrs. Colonel Hildebrand, Marietta, Ohio,

DEAR MADAM: You must feel that the kindly relations which existed between Colonel Hildebrand and myself will warrant my tender of deep and heartfelt sympathy with the family he has left to mourn his absence. Colonel Hildebrand served under my immediate command during the eventful campaign from the time we left Paducah until we reached the Mississippi at Memphis. That was one of the most successful epochs in the war, and you and your children will have cause to treasure the memory of the part your husband took in it. At Memphis the Seventy-seventh was detached from me, but it was understood that it was to return, and I have several letters from the colonel of his hope soon to take the field, but his Maker has called him away, and we are left to mourn his absence. I could recall many little scenes of our camp life to illustrate the honest, fearless character of Colonel Hildebrand, the interest he took in his men, always with them doing his duty like a brave soldier, as he was, never complaining, never talking of turning back. He was not the man to dream of peace until it should be won fairly and honestly. But I will, if I live, at some future time see his family and children, and tell them of their father, and of things that will make them proud of his name, and stimulate them to equal him in his pure and excellent character.

Accept the assurance of my heartfelt sympathy in your deep affliction, and believe me

Your friend,
W. T. SHERMAN,
Major General.

In civil life Colonel Hildebrand was widely known. For a number of years he was a mail contractor and owned the stage line between Marietta and Zanesville. In October, 1850, he was elected sheriff of Washington county and served two years.

Colonel Hildebrand was married in 1826 to Mrs. S. Perkins Fowler, and was the father of seven children. Eliza, the eldest, now Mrs. Henry E. Marks, resides in Washington, D. C. Her husband entered the service in the late war as lieutenant from that district. Arius Gilead, the second, died in Washington in 1876, and is buried in the Congressional cemetery in that city; Elodiannas, the third, died in infancy; W. W., the fourth, entered the service as a private, but while on his way to the front was injured by a railroad accident and brought home to Marietta injured for life; Francis Isabel, the fifth, resides at the old home; Anna Maria, the sixth, died in childhood; Cynthia E., the youngest, now Mrs. Henry J. Bradford, is in the Government employ at Dalton, Massachusetts. Her husband was a naval officer and served all through the war. He died in the service September 16, 1873, at the age of thirty-five. In one of the naval expeditions up the Savannah river Mr. Bradford was the officer on shipboard who volunteered to go into the interior with a flag of truce and in some engagement saw all of his brother officers disappear before the enemy's fire, leaving no trace of their presence on shipboard but their own blood.

COLONEL MELVIN CLARKE.

Melvin Clarke was born at Ashfield, Massachusetts, November 15, 1818. His father was a farmer near Northampton. His mother was a descendant of one of the Mayflower emigrants, and a sister of Gilbert Alden, who died a few years since in Salem, township of this (Washington) county, where he settled about twenty-five years ago.

Of the early years of Colonel Clarke's history little has been learned for the purposes of this sketch, except that his advantages for education were limited to those afforded by a New England common school, with perhaps a few months training at an academy. His subsequent attainments show that these were well improved. He came to Marietta in the fall of 1838, when about twenty years of age, and was engaged, for the two succeeding winters in teaching at Newport in this county, and for the next two years he assisted Rev. Mr. Hawks in a select school at Parkersburgh, Virginia. He also taught for a short time in Kentucky. During the period of his employment as a teacher he was also engaged in the study of the law, under the instruction of the late Arius Nye, of Marietta.

Colonel Clarke was admitted to the bar in 1843 and began the practice of his profession at McConnelsville. On the twenty-first of May, 1844, he married Dorcas Dana (daughter of William Dana, of Newport), who died at McConnelsville in the spring of 1852, leaving one son, Joseph Dana Clarke, who, like his father, entered the service of his country in the late war, and was killed by the explosion of ammunition at City Point, August 9, 1864, in the nineteenth year of his age. He was a young man of good promise, the recollection of whose life and character is a pleasure and satisfaction to his friends.

In the fall of 1852 Colonel Clarke removed to Marietta and began what afterwards proved to be a large practice at the bar of Washington county with the Hon. Thomas W. Ewart, under the firm name of Clarke & Ewart. He continued the practice of his profession here until his entrance into the army in 1861.

On the twenty-sixth of August, 1854, Colonel Clarke was married to Sophia Browning, who survives him, and with their three children resides at Belpre in this county.

When, in April, 1861, this terrible war broke upon the country, the flood of patriotism which swept into the army seventy-five thousand young men, did not carry Colonel Clarke into the ranks. He was not a soldier by nature, and nothing but an imperative sense of duty could take him away from more congenial pursuits, and from those most dear to him. But when it became apparent that the struggle upon which the Nation had entered, was not one of a day, and when, sometime after the second call for troops, it seemed that Washington county was not coming quite up to the rank in the supply of men, Colonel Clarke, finding it necessary to urge others to imperil their lives in the cause, could no longer withhold his own, and said that "he believed it to be his imperative duty to enter the army."

Having, with others, written to the Hon. William P. Cutler, then member of Congress from this district, the following telegram was received:

WASHINGTON, D. C., July 23, 1861.

M. Clarke and J. Hildebrand:

Government will probably accept an infantry regiment if ready in fifteen days. Can you raise it? I will bear all incidental expenses of raising it. Answer.

WILLIAM P. CUTLER.

This telegram was the beginning of the Thirty-sixth regiment, Ohio volunteers. Colonel Clarke's commission as lieutenant colonel bears date the thirtieth day of July, 1861. He was mustered into the United States service with the regiment at Marietta.

When the main body of the regiment, under Major Slemmer, marched into Virginia, Colonel Clarke was placed in command of the post at Parkersburgh, which was held by him with a detachment of the Thirty-sixth, consisting of companies C, D, E, and K, and a small number from each of the other companies, with one or two squadrons of the Second Virginia cavalry. He was relieved from this command about the first of October, moved with the detachment of his regiment to Camp Piatt, on the Kanawha, and marched thence to join the other part of the regiment under Colonel Crook at Summerville—his detachment serving as guard to a large train with supplies for the post, and the Enfield rifles which were to rearm the regiment.

During the remainder of the fall Colonel Clarke rendered efficient service in superintending the erection of the drill house in which, through the succeeding winter, the regiment received under Colonel Crook, its first and most effective drill and discipline. He also commanded some of the detachments which were sent out from the post against the guerillas who infested its vicinity.

In April, 1862, he received a short leave of absence, from which he returned just in time to take part in the maiden battle of the regiment at Lewisburgh, May 23d. In August following the regiment, with the greater part of the forces serving in the Kanawha valley, was transferred to General Pope's immediate command in eastern Virginia, and participated (though not in action) in the latter part of the disastrous campaign closing with the

31

battle of Bull Run. It was observed by Colonel Clarke's associates that he shared very largely in the feeling of despondency and gloom which pervaded the army at that time.

Lee's first invasion of Maryland followed, and the army under McClellan was moved back to Washington in pursuit.

At Frederick City, on the twelfth of September, the Kanawha division being in the advance, and the Thirty-sixth regiment upon the skirmish line, Colonel Moore, of the Twenty-eighth Ohio, commanding the First brigade, riding forward into the town with a small body of cavalry and one piece of artillery, was taken prisoner by the evacuating enemy. This advanced Colonel Crook to the command of the brigade, and Colonel Clarke to that of the regiment. The battle of South Mountain followed on the fourteenth, the regiment taking part in the gallant charge made by the Kanawha division early in the day, which drove the rebels from their stronghold at the top of the mountain, a position the importance of which was shown by their desperate but vain assaults to regain it. In the afternoon of that day Colonel Clarke said to a friend that "he believed God had appointed to each his time to die, and that if a man was in the discharge of his duty he would die no sooner in the army than at home." On the evening of the sixteenth he wrote of the bravery of the regiment, and that he was safe and unhurt in the midst of such carnage.

The terrible battle of Antietam followed on the seventeenth. Colonel Clarke fell about 5 o'clock in the afternoon, when our line on the left had nearly reached its most advanced position towards Sharpsburgh, from which we were soon afterwards compelled to retire to the bridge for want of sufficient force.

The casualties in the regiment at Antietam were few owing to the fact that it was not sent down to the bridge (where the greatest part of the loss on the left occurred) until a well directed fire of grape had forced the enemy from his position on the opposite bank of the creek. The Thirty-sixth was not exposed to infantry fire until the advance at 4 o'clock P. M. Other regiments of our brigade, particularly the Eleventh Ohio, lost heavily at the bridge.

It is a remarkable fact that the loss of the Thirty-sixth in officers was light during the war, and that the only officers killed outright on the battle-field were Colonels Clarke and Jones, the former at Antietam and the latter at Chickamauga, though others died from wounds received in action.

The promotion of Colonel Crook to the rank of brigadier general made vacant the colonelcy of the regiment, which was filled by the promotion of Colonel Clarke. Of this, however, he was never informed. His commission was issued and bears date the seventh of September, 1862.

Colonel Clarke's remains were brought to Marietta and buried with military honors in the Mound cemetery, where a monument, erected by the officers of his regiment and brother members of the bar, stands over his grave.

Colonel Clarke was a man of vigorous mind, of very general intelligence, a good thinker, not easy in the expression of his thoughts, but logical in style and forcible in manner, successful, and of high standing as a lawyer. He was a man of very decided opinions, and frank in the expression of them, yet respectful to those who differed from him. There was nothing like deceit in his character. Colonel Clarke was energetic, and, to strangers, had the appearance of austerity in his manner, but, nevertheless, he was kind hearted and generous. He was a valuable citizen, and a brave, Christian soldier. The period of his service in the army was not long, but the record is honorable. Of his gallantry, none, I am sure, of those who saw him fall at Antietam, will doubt. His death was a public sacrifice.

COLONEL EBENEZER B. ANDREWS.

Ebenezer Baldwin Andrews was born at Danbury, Connecticut, April 29, 1821. He was the youngest of six sons of Rev. William Andrews, for many years the pastor of the Congregational church in Danbury. After spending a year at William's college, he entered the sophomore class in Marietta college, and graduated in 1842. Among his fellow students he was a leading man, noted for geniality and humor, and universally popular. After a short time spent in teaching, he pursued a course of theological study at Princeton. In 1846 he became pastor of the Congregational church at Housatonic, Massachusetts, and afterward he was settled over a church in New Britain, Connecticut.

In 1851, coming to Marietta to deliver the address before the alumni at commencement, he made such an impression as an orator and a man of culture, that he was elected to the chair of natural science in Marietta college. Professor Beach, one of his pupils, writes thus:

In his college work, Professor Andrews early became specially interested in geological investigations, and during his stay here the study of geology was made very prominent. His teaching in this department was suggestive and stimulating. His students were sure to think geology a great and living science. During a series of years he conducted his senior classes on exploring expeditions which will not be forgotten by any who participated in them. The writer remembers with much interest the explorations made by the class of 1859, through the wildest parts of Washington county, and which occupied five days. The enthusiasm of the professor, as well as his unfailing good humor and his rich resources of wit and anecdote made it a memorable journey to the young men who followed him.

When in 1861, we were plunged into civil war, Prof. Andrews was appointed major of the Thirty-first Ohio regiment. He secured a release from his college duties, and engaged in the service of his country. He served with his regiment in West Virginia and on the Potomac, and, after Antietam, was made its colonel. His military life is best set forth in the following extracts from communications from those who served with him, and were familiar with his career as an army officer.

General B. D. Fearing, who was the first adjutant of the Thirty-sixth Ohio, says:

Few are familiar with the embarrassements that surrounded those entrusted with the recruiting and organizing of infantry during the late civil war. Briefly, they may be summed up thus: The public had

to be stimulated to the point of encouraging enlistment. Constant thought and labor were required to foster the effort made to popularize enlistments. Extended correspondence had to be carried on with the military committees of the different counties in the district, with the officers recruiting for the regiment, and with many of the families of the men enlisted. As the companies arrived at the camp of instruction, all their wants, and there were not a few, had to be provided for without any delay. As the companies arrived at the camp in detachments under the recruiting officers,—and not infrequently they reached the camp during the night time—it was a very exhausting work to care for them and see that they did not suffer. This Major Andrews did, in the care of the Thirty-sixth regiment, as those friendly to the soldiers, and the military committees of Washington county are prompt to testify. In accordance with the custom in those early war days, the recruiting officers were instructed to have the enlisted men bring nothing to camp with them except what they were willing to abandon, when furnished with the Government outfit. I remember well how much perplexed and embarrassed Colonel William R. Putnam, commandant of the camp of instruction at Marietta, was, when it was reported to him by officers of the companies after the first night in camp, that the men were actually suffering from the chill of the night.

Major Andrews immediately suggested that Colonel Clarke himself should secure from the patriotic citizens of Marietta blankets and comforts to meet the needs of the regiment. This suffering was more particularly in those companies recruited at a distance, and whose friends could not easily reach them. It was fortunate for the regiment that Major Andrews was so situated that he could give his undivided thought and time to the care of the soldiers

Colonel Clarke was a veteran practitioner at the bar. He had upon his hands the ordinary business of the lawyer as well as the care of several estates, and his time was necessarily occupied day and night in putting his affairs in order for the long absence of the war. While his advice was always at the command of his fellow officers, yet the vexations and great responsibilities following the sudden gathering of a thousand men just from the farm into the confinement of a camp, had to be met directly by Major Andrews. Every soldier had a thousand and one questions that must be answered each hour of the day, in those early times, before they felt the discipline of camp life, and before the regimental commander was relieved by the company officers, who had themselves to assume their position between the soldier and the commander of the regiment. Major Anderson was preeminently qualified to do all this work.

The following incident, from the same communication, shows the self-sacrificing and patriotic spirit of the subject of our sketch:

Information had reached Major Andrews that the regiment would soon be called into active service in West Virginia, by General Rosecrans, for the relief of the town of Spenser, which was in his rear, and for whose relief he had no troops at command. This stimulated Major Andrews to use extraordinary efforts to prepare the regiment as speedily as possible for service It was determined by the friends of the regiment that, if possible, the services of a regular army officer should be secured to command this splendid body of volunteers. There seemed to be no one at that time that could accomplish this but Major Andrews. His extended reputation as a scientific man, and his acquaintance with the leading men of the State, gave him excellent allies in Washington. Although his services were in great demand in the camp, yet it was decided that he should go to Washington. Availing himself of his personal acquaintance with Secretary Chase to reach President Lincoln, he succeeded in presenting himself, accompanied by Lincoln and Chase, before Secretary Cameron, and, in face of the order that had just been issued, that no more details should be made from the regular army to the volunteers, he secured the assent of Cameron to the detailing of a West Point man to the command of the regiment, if a suitable one could be found. To this zealous work of Major Andrews, at Washington, may without doubt be attributed all the valuable results that followed the appointment of Colonel Crook to the command of the Thirty-sixth regiment.

I am now convinced that this extraordinary effort on the part of Major Andrews was not absolutely essential, since Colonel Clarke had large experience as a teacher, had held official positions in civil life, and was a man of great courage, and of undoubted qualifications for the command of a regiment. The history of the regiment proves also that many of the subordinate officers were possessed of the same qualifications. It would be hard to find two men so unselfish and truly patriotic as Colonel Clarke and Major Andrews showed themselves to be, in thus giving up their own promotion, and in seeking so zealously to discover a man to hold the honorable position, that by right belonged to them."

The following extract is from a letter from General J. D. Cox, who commanded the department of West Virginia during Col. Andrews' service in that State.

"When Colonel Andrews joined my command in 1861, as major of the Thirty-sixth Ohio, I at once saw that he was a cool, brave and conscientious officer, arrogating nothing to himself from his previous standing as an intellectual and scientific man, but determined to learn his new duties with thoroughness and with modesty. As one immediately charged with the enforcement of the ideas of discipline of Colonel Crook, the major's task at the beginning was a hard one. The regiment was, as all volunteer regiments necessarily are, slow in seeing the immense importance of the discipline and drill, which a commandant, taken from the regular army, knew to be the indispensable condition of success, and, in the end, of the well-being of the regiment itself. Much of the ordinary unpopularity of the earlier stages of this instruction and discipline fell on Major Andrews. He did not shrink from it or avoid it. He sought no shelter under apologies; did not shoulder off the burden upon his superiors, but loyally obeyed the injunctions he received, as a faithful subordinate without complaint or criticism. He had faith that in the end, the honesty of his purpose, the usefulness of the discipline, and the good will to the regiment, which dictated it, would all be recognized."

.   .   .   Major Andrews took an honorable part in both the battles last named (South Mountain and Antietam.—Ed.) and by his modest but business-like and steadfast courage and coolness proved that he had in no small degree the characteristics of the true soldier.

The following is from General Crook:

Of Colonel Andrews' army life, so far as I was acquainted with it, I can only speak in terms of highest praise. The readiness with which he adapted himself to the duties of his new position has always been a matter of surprise to me. The value of his services at Summerville, where he was in charge of the construction of the camp, the hygiene of the men, the management of the hospital and the preparation of the food of the soldiers was inestimable, as it relieved me from a responsibility which is one of the most onerous of all the duties devolving upon the commander of an inexperienced regiment. No matter how distasteful or how much at variance with his former experience, every duty committed to him was zealously and skilfully performed to my entire satisfaction. It only remains that I should testify to his courage and gallantry in action. The Thirty-sixth Ohio did heroically and won for me my star, and I need only add that Colonel Andrews always aided by his word and example the reputation for bravery and general good conduct which the regiment so nobly maintained to the end. To his personal efforts was very largely due the organization of the Thirty-sixth, and I feel that I owe him a personal debt of gratitude, as I have understood that it was mainly through Colonel Andrews' efforts that I obtained the command of the regiment of which he was the first major.

At the close of his army life, in 1863, Professor Andrews resumed his position at Marietta college. He had already become known as an eminent geologist, and especially as an authority in the geology of eastern Ohio and West Virginia. In 1869 he resigned his chair in Marietta, to accept the position of assistant geologist in the geological survey of Ohio. To this work he gave several years of assiduous and successful labor, removing from Marietta to the more central position of Lancaster, Ohio. His work upon the coal fields of southeastern Ohio was universally recognized as admirable and thorough, and it widely extended his reputation as a geologist. After the close of the geological survey Professor Andrews continued his residence in Lancaster, giving his attention to the preparation of a text-book on geology, which has proved very acceptable. He also found large employment as a consulting geologist, whose opinions as to the nature and value of the mineral resources of southern Ohio and West Virginia were highly valued.

He died at Lancaster, Ohio, August 14, 1880.

COLONEL JOHN C. PAXTON.

John C. Paxton was born in Gettysburgh, Pennsylvania, February 22, 1824. At the age of ten years he began life for himself, and from that day his generous hand lent assistance to his parents, and a more dutiful and loving son never lived than he. At an early age he came to Ohio and engaged in the mercantile business at Sharon, Noble county, until 1853. In 1845 he was united in marriage to Agnes Greenlee, who was to the end of her life a faithful partner and sympathetic wife.

He removed with his family to Marietta in 1853, and engaged in business pursuits. In 1854, while in the south, he had the misfortune to contract the small-pox, and returning home, the whole family were stricken with the disease which bereft the household of the cherished wife and mother. In 1857 he married for his second wife, Sophia L. Reed, of Lancaster, Pennsylvania, who still survives.

Mr. Paxton's temperament made him restless and imperative. He travelled into every State and territory, and he acquired a knowledge of the resources and society of the entire country. Several years of his mature life were spent in Salt Lake City, where an intimate acquaintance with the practices of Mormonism taught him to hate, with all the bitterness of his intense nature, the execrable doctrines of that peculiar people.

Writers of all periods have united in extolling the valiant deeds of military heroes. The man who enlists his body and soul in the cause of his country is deserving of the highest honor, no matter what his military rank may be. War has not inappropriately been likened to a drama, in which the officers play the leading *roles*, but the success of the whole depends upon the acting of each character. Another point of likeness is that each *role* requires its own peculiar actor. The bold and dashing colonel who carries assault to victory is no less deserving of honor than the general in command who has planned the preliminary movements.

It will be necessary to understand the character of Colonel Paxton, and to know the field in which he was ordered to operate, before proceeding to a consideration of his merits as a military man.

He was a man of strong talent, but nervous, impulsive and often erratic. He had a pointed insight into affairs, and his opinions and resolutions, though quickly formed, were usually correct. His wit was pungent and keen; incisive sarcasm gave him peculiar power in controversy. In the social circle he was at his best, vivacious and witty and enjoying a story or a joke exceedingly. His friendship was devoted and true, his hatred intense. A large heart made him generous to a fault, and he was always ready to contribute to the necessities of the unfortunate.

During the crisis of secession in 1860 he was in Louisiana, and was present at the convention when the State was voted out of the Union. He was present when the vote was carried to tear down the old flag then floating over the capitol. His loyal eyes saw the raising of the first rebel flag in Louisiana. When he had seen the banner which he always worshipped torn into shreds and trampled under foot in the streets of Louisiana, he could restrain his impetuous spirit no longer. He hastened north with the determination that nothing which he could do should be left undone in the great contest then at hand.

Colonel Paxton began his military career in the three months' service as quartermaster for the Eighteenth Ohio volunteer infantry. At the expiration of his term of service he returned to Marietta, and in August, 1861, recruited a regiment of cavalry. The history of the movements and services in this regiment will be found at the proper place in this volume. But it will be in place here to notice the difficulties under which Colonel Paxton labored. With an ardent leader and ambitious followers, the Second Virginia cavalry was stationed in the narrow valleys of West Virginia to rout bushwackers and break up camps of the enemy. No section of country within the whole range of the Rebellion imposes as great physical obstructions to military movements as West Virginia. Considering the conformation of the country, the condition of the roads, and the character of the service, Colonel Paxton is entitled to the highest praise for his persevering, brave and dashing leadership. "He was accused," says General Fearing, "of being rash, but such rashness in a cavalry officer is oftentimes a virtue. The same rashness evinced by an infantry officer would be unpardonable and lead to a court-martial. It was the custom during the early stages of the war for cavalry officers to pre-estimate results and magnify the strength of the enemy. Imagined insurmountable obstacles in the front often caused them to turn back from an assault or an expedition which might easily have been accomplished with small loss. This fact led General Hooker, as late as the battle of Chancellorsville, to make the assertion while enraged at an unsuccessful expedition of cavalry, that the man could not be found who had ever seen a dead cavalryman.

Although Colonel Paxton may not have been a cool, calculating director of movements, he was never found wanting when an opportunity was presented for a bold charge. And when a court or commission was appointed to examine into the qualifications of officers then serving in the valley, Colonel Paxton was the first man ordered before the committee of which Colonel Hayes (since President Hayes) was chairman. Colonel Hayes put the question: "Colonel, suppose you were marching along a flat top mountain with a train, how would you dispose of your troops to protect it?" "Well, answered Colonel Paxton, "I would throw out a squad of men on each side to protect the train in case of an attack." "Well, colonel," said Colonel Hayes, "suppose an attack were made on you when in that position, what command would you give?" Colonel Paxton scratched his head a moment, then said, "I don't know colonel, what command you would give, but I would say, 'Go for them, boys, and give them h—l." That ended the examination.

Colonel Paxton's bravery or patriotism was never questioned. General Powell, in a recent letter to Mrs. Downing, his daughter, says:

Permit me to say that, having been intimately acquainted with the

decased from the organization of our regiment, in August, 1861, to the time of his leaving the service, in 1863, he was the idol of his regiment; kind and generous to his command; attentive to their wants, and jealous of their good name as soldiers. No truer or more earnest man ever drew a sword in defence of our National Government than Colonel John C. Paxton.

General Fearing, from whom we have already quoted, says further:

Colonel Paxton had the essential qualifications of a successful officer in his branch of the service. Under different circumstances and surroundings he would have taken rank with Custer, Merritt, Grierson, Hatch, Wilson, Kilpatrick, Torbert, Averill, and a host of other cavalry officers who won renown in the Rebellion. . . . The military friends of Colonel Paxton cannot but regret the circumstance whereby he was not placed in association with trained soldiers, who would have given scope and direction to his splendid fighting qualities.

General J. D. Cox, whose good opinion it is a distinguished honor to have, pays this tribute to him as a man and soldier:

When I think of him he always appears as I knew him in the prime of his early manhood in West Virginia, handsome, dashing, fearless, a bold rider and a daring scout. His patriotic determination to see service in the war for the Union made him enter a West Virginia regiment when Ohio's quota was full, and he gave his whole heart to his work. He was disposed to be impatient of restraint, but for a commander whom he trusted and respected he was ready at any moment to imperil his life. His impetuosity sometimes led him into collision with others, especially if he doubted their earnestness or their enterprise. These were, however, the faults of an excess of zeal, and will appear merits when contrasted with their opposites. He had most of the qualities of a first class cavalry officer, and was never happier than when detailed for some dangerous adventure requiring both intelligence and daring.

Colonel Paxton in going into the war had followed the impulse of his convictions, and as long as he remained in the service was not only the brave soldier who fought for glory but also the devoted patriot who had a heart in the cause. In a letter written to his family, dated "Camp Piatt, Virginia, February 22, 1863," he shows his feeling in regard to the war. This was at a time when the army in the field had reason to be discouraged by the indifference of some of their constituency at home. We quote one paragraph of the letter.

My position is one of great care and responsibility, and I can honestly say I wish it was done. I have seen enough of war in the last twenty months to satisfy both my curiosity and my ambition, but I have not seen enough of this war until I see it closed in favor of our glorious flag and the Union; and I know I but reflect the sentiments of my regiment when I say so. We are all tired and wish to be at home with our families, but not until all is quiet at the front. Then, if traitors (tories is a better word) at home wish our services you may rest assured they shall have the benefit of them.

Colonel Paxton left the service in 1863. When the war had closed he was as heartily in favor of "burying the past" as in 1860 he had been impatient to crush out the Rebellion. He believed that the sooner the north and the south could unite in a fraternal Fourth of July shout of patriotism the better it would be for the whole country. He says in a published letter in 1874:

I never was in sympathy with the organization, the Grand Army of the Republic as organized at the close of the war, nor of its child, "Decoration Day." I believe, from the history of such affairs in other countries, that the sooner the marks of our civil war are obliterated, the better it would be for what we fought for "one whole country." Soldiers' reunions there is no objection to, but my understanding as to the object of Decoration Day was to afford an opportunity for civilians women and children, aided by the clergy and politicians, to pay a formal respect to dead soldiers; living soldiers could stand and look on and feel proud of the respect paid to their dead comrades. It was an innocent proceeding, well adapted for the persons it was intended for, but never was in my opinion that which would create or fire a patriotic people or fighting soldiery. Let the past be gone. I believe the boys in their "little beds" are quite as well off as their living comrades. They are free of the tax, in pains and aches, their comrades in their rear are paying, every step they take, to the present "slow music of the Union."

Colonel Paxton possessed a sound judgment, a strong mind, and remarkable versatility of talent. Had he enjoyed the advantages in early life of a judicious mental training he would undoubtedly have achieved distinction as a writer. He was not a politician in the common acceptation of the term. But he was a man of public spirit favoring every kind of public improvement intended for the development of the country. From what has been written some idea may be formed of the principles and character of our subject. He was one of those peculiar men whom it is impossible to accurately portray with pen. He died at his residence in Marietta, February 28, 1881, of paralysis, after two years of intense suffering.

LIEUTENANT COLONEL ALEXANDER L. HASKINS.

The subject of this sketch was born in Shushan, Washington county, New York, March 18, 1822. He received a liberal school education and was engaged in St. Louis, Missouri, several years before going to Marietta, as teacher, and adopted the profession of civil engineer. He was married on October 6, 1853, to Miss Addie G. Gerken, of Marietta.

When the Marietta & Cincinnati railroad was being constructed, Colonel Haskins was employed as assistant engineer in locating the line, and as engineer in charge of various parts of the work, especially that part laid out between Marietta and Bellaire.

At the beginning of the war he was civil engineer of the city of Marietta, and when the Sixty-third Ohio volunteer infantry was raised he was commissioned major of that regiment. When the regiment went to the field the attainments of Colonel Haskins as an engineer were called into requisition, and he was constantly employed in locating military works, roads, etc.

On July 17, 1862, he was promoted to lieutenant colonel of his regiment. The arduous duties of the camp and field proved more than his health would stand, and he was honorably discharged March 20, 1863, on account of impaired health.

Colonel Haskins followed his profession of civil engineer up to the fall of 1865, when he was elected to the fifty-seventh general assembly as representative from Washington county.

Colonel Haskins was civil engineer of the city of Marietta during the years 1855, 1858, 1859, 1860, and 1861. In January, 1866, while at Logansport, Indiana, on some business connected with a railroad on which he had been engaged as engineer, he was taken suddenly ill and died, January 13, 1866. His widow still resides in Marietta. One son and one daughter are living.

The house of representatives upon the reception of the news of his death passed resolutions regarding the deceased, part of which we give in closing this brief notice of a noble life. The introduction of the resolutions elicited remarks from various members.

Hon. A. L. Curtis, his colleague from this county, and Hon. T. M. Davey, of Lawrence, spoke in terms of high commendation of Colonel Haskins, not only as a soldier but as a man of pure mind, Christian character, and social, genial disposition.

After the preamble, the House passed the following resolutions:

Resolved, That this House bear testimony of the high character and integrity of Hon. A. L. Haskins, who won the esteem of his fellow members by his urbane manners and frank courteous bearing.

Resolved, That in the untimely death of A. L. Haskins this house has lost an able and highly esteemed member, and the community a good citizen, whose worth will live in the memory of all who knew him.

Resolved, That in further testimony of respect for the memory of our late colleague and brother, this house do now adjourn.

The house accordingly adjourned.

LIEUTENANT COLONEL EPHRAIM C. DAWES.

Ephraim Cutler Dawes, born May 27, 1840; graduated at Marietta college, June 26, 1861; mustered into service as first lieutenant and adjutant of the Fifty-third Ohio volunteer infantry, September 26, 1861; promoted major January 26, 1863; served under Sherman in his Mississippi campaign, in his march from Big Black to Chattanooga, and in the pursuit of Longstreet across the mountains of East Tennessee in November and December, 1863, without baggage or tents, and subsisting on less than half rations. He participated in Sherman's Georgia campaign; and at Dallas, Georgia, May 28, 1864, he received two wounds, one in the head, and a second, very severe, in the face, a minnie ball carrying away most of the lower jaw. He was brevetted lieutenant colonel and honorably discharged from service on account of his wound, October 31, 1864. He was engaged in the following battles: Pittsburgh Landing (Shiloh), Tennessee, April 6 and 7, 1862; Fallen Timbers, Tennessee, April 8, 1862; Siege of Corinth, Tennessee and Mississippi, May, 1862; Siege of Vicksburgh, Mississippi, June, 1862; Jackson, Mississippi, July 10–16, 1863; Mission Ridge, Tennessee, November 25, 1863; Resaca, Georgia, August 13, 14, 15, 1864; Dallas, Georgia, May 27, 28, 1864.

MAJOR GEORGE T. RICE.

George T. Rice was born December 16, 1823, in Macedon, Wayne county, New York, son of Nathan and Docas Rice. He married Miss Minerva Jane Ripley, daughter of John and Betsey Ripley, of the same place, and in 1852 removed to Marietta, Ohio.

He enlisted as a private in company B, Thirty-ninth regiment, July 22, 1861, was appointed second sergeant and served as such until July 11, 1862, when he was commissioned second lieutenant; he served as such until May 9, 1864, when he was commissioned as first lieutenant company E, January 11, 1865; was commissioned as captain and transferred to command of company C, June 6, 1865; was commissioned as major of the regiment and served as such until the regiment was discharged, July 9, 1865.

Major Rice, at the close of the war, removed from Marietta to Macedon, New York, and afterwards located permanently at Rollin, Michigan, where he now resides, and is engaged in the mercantile business.

CAPTAIN JACOB KOENIG.

Jacob Koenig was born in 1816, in the town of Desloch, dukedom of Hessia, Germany. At the age of twenty-one he joined the army, and was a faithful soldier for six years in company I, infantry, of the dukedom of Hessia, receiving an honorable discharge on April 1, 1842. After being discharged he remained at home about two weeks, when he sailed for the United States, landing in New York city in May, 1842. He was married in New York on May 7, 1843, to Julia A. Maas, born in Mannheim, Bavaria, who had landed in New York about two weeks before him.

While residing in New York city he served in the New York State militia for fourteen years, the first seven as a private, and the last as lieutenant. He came to Marietta in July, 1856. In July, 1861, he organized company F, Thirty-ninth Ohio volunteer infantry, and was elected captain of the same.

The newspapers of 1861 published in Marietta, speak of Captain Koenig's company as the "German Rifles." The company was a militia company for a short time prior to enlistment for three years, and after the first vote to go into the service, it was recruited up to the maximum, one hundred men, and left for Camp Colerain, near Cincinnati, all inside of one week. Captain Koenig was a brave soldier, and exceedingly kind to the men in his command. During his term of service he also served as assistant inspector general of the Fifth division, Sixteenth army corps. He died at Memphis, Tennessee, on the twenty-first day of August, 1863, leaving a wife and five children, viz: Jacob, Julia, Caroline, Philip, and William, all of whom are still living.

CAPTAIN JAMES C. SELBY.

Captain James C. Selby was born in Washington county, Ohio, on the third day of December, 1838. His father was Jeremiah J. Selby, a native of New York. The maiden name of his mother was Rosana D. Stone. At the age of four years he lost his father. His mother was his only guardian till after he was fourteen years of age. Having received a good common school education, he followed the occupation of farming, and also that of carpenter.

At the outbreak of the Rebellion he enlisted in the Union army on July 29, 1861, at Lowell, Washington county, Ohio. On August 24, 1861, (at Marietta, Ohio) he was mustered in as second lieutenant of company A, Thirty-sixth Ohio volunteer infantry. A few days after

he left with his company and regiment for the field. He was promoted to first lieutenant and assigned to company F, Thirty-sixth Ohio volunteer infantry, March 5, 1862.

At the battle of Antietam, Maryland, while making a charge, a piece of a shell went through his haversack, tearing it to pieces and scattering his hardtack over the ground.

He was promoted to captain and assigned to company K, Thirty-sixth Ohio volunteer infantry, October 30, 1863. (Commissioned October 13, 1863.)

At the battle of Mission Ridge, Tennessee, November 25, 1863, he lost his right arm and was sent to the hospital, where he remained till January, when he went home. In about six weeks he joined his regiment again, and took command of his company even before he was able for duty. He had his sword changed to carry on his right side, and learned to write with his left hand in a few days.

At the battle of Berryville, Virginia, September 3, 1864, he received a gun shot wound in his right thigh, severing the vein and shattering the bone. He remained in the field hospital at Berryville two or three days, and was then removed to the general hospital at Annapolis, Maryland, where he died in ten days after he was wounded. When informed that he must die, he received it with perfect calmness, sent for the chaplain and made the necessary disposition of his property, and asked his nurse to write his lieutenant to make out his monthly returns for him.

In the regiment he was respected as a soldier and gentleman—brave to desperation, generous to a fault, possessed of an iron will, a good moral character, and a kind heart. He was loved and desired to be loved by all his comrades.

CAPTAIN WILLIAM BEALE WHITTLESEY.

William Beale Whittlesey, son of Hon. William A. Whittlesey and Jane H. Whittlesey, of Marietta, Ohio, was born at Marietta, October 2, 1841. Even in boyhood he showed a taste and ambition for military life, and when a young man under age he was made an aid de camp of General Hildebrand in the State militia.

In September, 1857, at the age of seventeen, he entered the freshman class and was graduated in the summer of 1861.

In the fall of 1862 he aided in raising a company, and was commissioned second lieutenant of company F, Ninety-second Ohio volunteer infantry. The regiment remained in Kanawha valley until the first of 1863, when it was ordered to Nashville, and attached to the army of the Cumberland. It afterwards joined the Fourteenth army corps, under that noblest of noble generals, George H. Thomas, and formed one of the many regiments which met Bragg at Chickamauga, September 17 and 18, 1863. As it became evident that a battle was imminent, Whittlesey talked freely of it— wondering how he would stand fire—how he would act, and asked the writer if he fell *doing his duty* to so state it to his father. He went into that battle and, in his earnestness, unnecessarily exposed himself—taking position in *front* of his company and directing their fire. He escaped without injury—was commended in the official report of the battle, and afterwards a vacancy occurring was made captain.

The regiment remained in Chattanooga during that fall, and formed part of the forlorn hope under command of General Baldy Smith, by which communication was opened with General Hooker, coming to our relief from Bridgeport. A part went by small flat-boats in the night, passed the enemy's pickets at Lookout mountain, while the remainder marched across the neck and joined them at Brown's Ferry, where a crossing was made, the boats being used to form a pontoon bridge. The army provisioned and reenforced, preparations soon began for the assault of General Bragg, securely posted on Mission Ridge and Lookout Mountain. From the summit of the latter, shells were frequently thrown into our camp from a battery stationed there. It was not many days before the ominous order was issued to prepare three days' cooked rations, and one hundred rounds of ammunition. All soldiers knew its meaning, and were also well aware that no boy's play was before them. Whittlesey made the requisite preparations and then awaited the command to move—making first his will, in which he remembered the Psi Gamma society, of which he was an enthusiastic member when in college. He expressed a wish that if struck by a ball, it might be through the heart. He led his company up that hill—so steep that it was no easy task to climb it when no enemy was on the top; and when near the top, a minnie ball went crashing through his heart. Telling his men to go on, that he was killed, he breathed his last amid the smoke and carnage of that long to be remembered evening.

The cord that bound son to father seemed to possess the qualities of the electric wire; the shock that took the life of the son signalled the father, a thousand miles away. On the next Thanksgiving day, 1863, taking his usual morning walk, Mr. Whittlesey said to a friend: "I feel that there has been a great battle, and Beale is killed." He was advised to dismiss it as a fond father's fancy, and went home. Soon after, seeing another friend coming towards his house, he said: "There comes Mr. P. to tell me of Beale's death"—which was too true—the telegram from Dr. Cotton, the regimental surgeon, sent that morning from Chattanooga, conveyed the sad news—news that made that Thanksgiving day one memorable in more than one family, and among the friends and acquaintances of Whittlesey and Turner. The funerals of both were held the same day some weeks afterwards. The bodies lay in state in Psi Gamma hall for a season. Mr. Whittlesey never seemed to recover from the shock of Beale's death, and soon followed him.

CAPTAIN MADISON HOON.

Captain Hoon, Sixty-third Ohio volunteer infantry, was reared on a farm in Waterford township; volunteered with J. W. Fouts and was mustered into service at the organization of the company at Camp Putnam, in Marietta, Ohio, October 9, 1861, and was appointed corporal; was promoted to sergeant of his company, then to sergeant major of the regiment, then to first lieutenant, and lastly to captain. Captain Hoon served through the war; was mustered out with the regiment at Louisville, Kentucky, July 8, 1865; went to his home, and died of disease the same fall. Captain Hoon gained his promotions by true merit, both in business and as a commander. Sagacious in battle, considerate in camp, he won the confidence of his men and the respect of all who knew him.

CAPTAIN FRANK BUELL.

Frank Buell was born in Adams township, Washington county, Ohio, April 24, 1837, and was killed at the battle of Freeman's Ford, Virginia, August 22, 1862. He was the youngest son of P. B. Buell, a native of New York, and grandson of Judge Salmon Buell. His mother was a native of eastern Virginia, and belonged to one of the oldest and best families of that region. His childhood and boyhood were spent at the farm home. At the age of eighteen he went to Washington, District of Columbia, where he spent a year assisting his brother, George P. Buell, esq., of the *National Democratic Review*. On his return to Washington he continued the study of the law, which he had commenced while in Washington. He was admitted to practice at the age of twenty, and opened a law office at Marietta, Ohio. He was elected city solicitor of the city of Marietta, and within the first two years of his practice was elected prosecuting attorney of Washington county, which position he resigned to go into the army, at the commencement of the late civil war.

His was one of the first companies in Ohio to offer its services to the governor; was mustered into the Eighteenth regiment Ohio volunteer militia, in the three months' service, at the close of which he recruited a company for the artillery service, known as "Buell's Pierpont Battery," made up largely of Ohio men, but went out as a West Virginia battery, and distinguished itself as one of the best drilled, hardest fighting batteries in the army. It would have gone out as an Ohio battery had Captain Buell received the recognition from his own State to which he felt that he was entitled. But he was not the man to be trifled with, nor to be turned aside in the pursuit of the great object of his patriotism and ambition by those whom accidental authority had placed in his way.

From the time when Captain Buell's battery was ordered to the front, it seems to have been given posts of danger, and was often placed where desperate action was necessary. At the time of his death he was acting lieutenant colonel, and was in command of the reserve artillery under General Siegel, in General Pope's command. Promotion awaited him, had he survived this (to him) fatal engagement. This unfortunate, but not inglorious campaign of General Pope's resulted in great sacrifice of life. The artillery immediately under command of Captain Buell was covering the retreat of General Pope's arm, and held position on the east bank of the Rapphannock river. It was in this position that he fell. He was on horseback. A shell passed through his horse, killing his horse instantly, and causing his own death a few hours later. Shells had passed under and above him, showing that he—on his light colored horse was a conspicuous mark, in full view of, and at which the enemy was taking deliberate aim. He refused, however, to dismount, or to change his position on the field. This was almost exclusively an artillery fight, was at short range, the river only separating the Federal and Confederate batteries, and is spoken of as one of the most terrible artillery battles of the late war, and in which the Federal batteries triumphed having driven the enemy from position.

If there is such a thing as resignation to death, it must come to the hero who falls in the hour of victory.

It is a remarkable fact that Captain Buell was killed in his mother's native county—Fauquier county, Virginia. Only a few miles from where he fell she was born and spent her early life, leaving there at the age of twenty to find a home in (the then far west) Ohio,— never to return. Fifty years later her youngest son (the subject of this sketch) found his way to that region—not to visit her childhood's home, as a sacred spot, nor to brighten her declining years by his return, but to fall in terrible conflict, and then to rest (for a while) in a soldier's grave.

His remains were reinterred in the family cemetery at the Buell homestead, when the members of his battery who had followed him with the same inspiration with which he had led them, erected to his memory a monument, on which they inscribed the admiration they entertained for him as an officer, and their regard for him as a man.

The impress of genius—a term too often tamely used —is sure in the short but marked life of Frank Buell. The noble man into which he developed was apparent in him as a boy. Almost without the aid of schools he became a scholar, and without the life-long drill he became the thorough and accomplished soldier.

CAPTAIN AUGUSTUS T. WARD.

Augustus T. Ward was born October 11, 1840, in Fearing township, Washington county, Ohio. He was the second son and fourth child of Robert and Lucy M. Ward; the former an English emigrant, the latter a native of the township.

He was brought up on a farm, attending the district school in summer terms until the age of nine, and winter schools until he was sixteen, after which he taught common schools during the winter until 1861.

When the Rebellion broke out in 1861 he was filled with indignation at the insults the flag received from the traitors of the south, but did not enter the army on the first call of President Lincoln, because of his parents strong desire that he should remain at home. After the expiration of the term of the three months troops, and

when the second call was made for three hundred thousand men, he felt that his country needed his services, and that he owed her his first duty. Captain Jewett Palmer, jr., (afterward major) was at that time enlisting a company for the Thirty-sixth Ohio infantry, at Lower Salem, of this county, and Ward hastened to enroll his name with the young patriots there assembled. This was on the twelfth day of August, 1861. Captain Palmer marched his company to Camp Putnam, at Marietta, the same evening and reported to Lieutenant Colonel M. Clarke, commanding regiment.

Ward was appointed drummer of his company next day, a position of which he was extremely proud.

He served in that capacity until the first of February, 1862, when he was placed in the ranks of his company by his colonel.

He was immediately appointed second sergeant of his company (G) by Captain Palmer, and served as such until the sixth of April following, when a vacancy occurring in the first sergeantcy, he was appointed to fill that position. The two last appointments were made while the regiment was in bararcks at Summerville, West Virginia.

Having served faithfully as first sergeant through Pope's and McClellan's campaigns in the east in August and September, 1862, and for gallantry in the battles of South Mountain and Antietam, he was promoted to second lieutenant (commission dating from the latter engagement), and assigned to duty in company A of the Thirty-sixth regiment, of which J. Gage Barker, of Muskingum, was then captain, and John L. Palmer, of Salem, first lieutenant. He served as second lieutenant through the campaign of Rosecrans to Chattanooga, and under Thomas during the winter of 1863 and 1864, in camp at that place. Remained with the regiment on its reenlistment as veterans, in February, 1864, visiting home then for the first time since his entry into service.

On the expiration of the veteran furlough the regiment was ordered to Charlestown, West Virginia, where he received a commission as first lieutenant, dated April 21, 1864, and assigned to duty in the same company, in which he remained until the thirteenth of January, 1865, when he received his appointment to a captaincy, commission dated December 31, 1864.

While first lieutenant he passed through the raids to the Virginia & Tennessee railroad and to Lynchburgh, under General Hunter, and the memorable campaign of General Sheridan in the Shenandoah valley, fighting his last battle at Cedar Creek, on the nineteenth day of October, 1864.

As captain he was assigned to the command of company F of his regiment, of which company he retained command until the muster out and discharge of the regiment, which took place at Columbus, Ohio, July 31, 1865.

Having served nearly four years honestly and faithfully, and seen the honor of the American flag completely established and the rebellion crushed, he received his discharge with a degree of satisfaction that only an old soldier can feel, and retired from the army with the entire good will of his company.

The following is a list of engagements in which he bore a gallant and honorable part:

Lewisburgh, West Virginia, May 23, 1862; South Mountain, Maryland, September 14, 1862; Antietam, Maryland, September 17, 1862; Hoover's Gap, Tennessee, June 24, 1863; Chickamauga, Georgia, September 19 and 20, 1863; Mission Ridge, Tennessee, November 25, 1863; Cloyd Mountain, Virginia, May 9, 1864; New River Bridge, Virginia, May 10, 1864; Kernstown, Virginia, July 23, 1864; Berryville, Virginia, September 3, 1864; Opequan, September 19, 1864; Fisher's Hill, September 22, 1864; Cedar Creek, October 19, 1864. Besides these he was engaged in eight or ten skirmishes, more or less dangerous and bloody.

After his discharge he returned at once to his farm in his native township.

[In the summer of 1865 the Military committee of Washington county caused a letter to be written to each of the officers in the army from this county, requesting them to give a short account of their life in the service, and the foregoing was written by Captain Ward in response to such letter.]

In the year following the close of the war Mr. Bartmess, the county recorder, having died, Captain Ward was appointed to fill the vacancy. He afterwards engaged in business in Marietta, in which he was very successful.

In 1869 he was married to Kate L. Wakefield, daughter of B. A. Wakefield, of Lawrence county. The following are their children: Charles Augustus, born July 27, 1870; Willia Wakefield, born March 25, 1872.

Captain Ward was compelled to give up business on account of failing health. The disease, doubtless the result of exposure in the service, now made rapid strides, and Captain Ward seeking relief by change of air and medical treatment, went to Green Springs, Ohio, where he died on the thirteenth day of August, 1874.

CAPTAIN ARTHUR D. EELLS.

Arthur D. Eells was born at Unadella, Otsego county, New York, February 6, 1838. He was the son of John Eells, formerly of New Canaan, Connecticut, and a grandson of General John Mead, who served his country through the Revolutionary war. Captain Eells came to Marietta in February, 1859. Soon after the rebellion broke out he commenced recruiting men for the Union army and in August, 1861, took a squad of twenty odd men to Parkersburgh, West Virginia, and continued to recruit men for the Union army until about the twenty-sixth of October, 1861, when the Second Virginia cavalry regiment was organized and he was commissioned captain of company F, the regiment being mostly composed of Ohio men. Soon after the regiment was organized it was sent to Guyandotte, on the Ohio river, and remained there through the winter of 1861-62. In May, 1862, the regiment in part joined General Crook's brigade, at Lewisburgh, West Virginia, and went on the raid through the mountains to White Sulpher Springs, Covington, and Jackson Depot, tearing up the railroad

track and doing much damage to the enemy. The march was so rapid that the enemy was entirely taken by surprise and could not gather force sufficient to attack them. General Crook with his little army returned to Lewisburgh. The day previous to the battle of Lewisburgh Captain Eells with a small detail of men was sent out by General Crook on a reconnoitring expedition. On this expedition he came very near being captured, having gone very nearly within the lines of the enemy's pickets. He and his men escaped by strategy, as he personally learned from prisoners captured in the Lewisburgh fight the next day. While at a farmer's house he learned facts that were of sufficient moment to put him on the alert, and in a very careless way gave orders to his men to fall back to the main force, indicating that there was quite a force close at hand. One of the men at the farm house was a rebel soldier in citizen's dress, who at once reported these facts to the enemy, as one of the prisoners told Captain Eells the next day that they thought by letting him go that they would likely capture the main body of men, not supposing that he would venture to come so near their lines with such a small squad of men. Captain Eells and his men after having got a reasonable distance from the enemy made good time in getting back to headquarters with his men, and reached camp at about nine o'clock in the evening of the twenty-second of May and made his report to General Crook giving him valuable information. In the early morning of May 23d General Crook was attacked; the enemy drove in his pickets and the fight commenced. The enemy numbered from twenty-five hundred to three thousand men, and were defeated, losing six men killed, one hundred and seventy-five prisoners and many wounded, four pieces of artillery and a large number of small arms. This was a grand victory for General Crook and his brave little army. In one of Captain Eells' scouting expeditions he came suddenly on a rebel picket armed with a double-barrelled shotgun. The picket fired one barrel of his gun at Eells, who returned the fire with his revolver. The picket dropped his gun and ran into the woods, evidently wounded. Captain Eells captured the gun and brought it home with him. The hardships of army life and the mountain campaigns were more than his health could bear. Some time in June, 1862, he resigned his commission and came back to Marietta. With quiet and rest came better health and renewed strength. In the following August the Government called for a regiment of cavalry for border service, to be known as the River regiment. Captain Eells at once commenced recruiting men for this regiment. In a very few days he reported to the military committee of Washington county that he had a company of one hundred men ready for the service. He went to Columbus and was commissioned as captain of company H, Seventh Ohio volunteer cavalry, August 25, 1862. He was very soon ordered to report with his company at Ripley on the Ohio river above Cincinnati, notwithstanding the regiment was raised for border service. Early in December of the same year the regiment was ordered to the front. They crossed the Ohio river below Maysville into

32

Kentucky, reaching Lexington about the first of January, 1863. While in camp at Lexington Captain Eells was taken sick with typhoid fever and was unable to do any military duty until some time in April following. He joined his regiment at Stanford, Kentucky, and was on duty until the twenty-third of June, 1863. While stationed at Somerset, Kentucky, it became evident to him that he could not stand the hardships of an active army life. It was often remarked by his brother officers that there was not another man in the regiment who would think he was able to do military duty even when he was in his best health. He was full of hope, always cheerful and ready for duty, a good soldier, and every man in the regiment his friend. He greatly desired to live to see the war ended. He never for a moment doubted the final result. On the twenty-eighth of June, 1863, he sent in his resignation and severed his connection with his company and regiment as a comrade and an officer. He came back to Marietta with the hope that rest and good care would again bring him better health and more strength. But not so; the exposures and hardships of an army life had done the work for him—the destroyer's hand was on him—his health gradually failed him. His ambition and cheerful disposition kept him up even to the last, and when death came he was ready for the call and died with the courage of a Christian soldier the thirteenth of September, 1864, and was buried in Mound cemetery at Marietta, Ohio.

CAPTAIN THEODORE E. GREENWOOD.

Captain Theodore Edgerton Greenwood, only son of George Greenwood, esq., and Elizabeth Edgerton Greenwood, was born at Newport, Washington county, Ohio, February 7, 1838. He entered the preparatory department of the Marietta college at the age of sixteen, and entered the freshman class in September, 1855. During his college course he united with the Congregational church at Marietta, and always remained a consistent member. He graduated in the summer of 1859, at the head of his class. At the death of Tutor Washburne he was made tutor and filled that position acceptably for the remainder of the year. He spent part of the following year in the study of the law, but subsequently decided to choose a business career. But the breaking out of the Rebellion spoiled his plans, as it spoiled those of so many ardent young men in 1861. As early as the autumn of 1860, he began to study Scott's Tactics, and in a confidential talk with a college friend, said: "Any observant man can see that we are on the eve of a terrible war between the North and the South, and the man of military knowledge will be the man of power, who can help his country in her hour of need." At the beginning of hostilities young Greenwood did not see his way clear for leaving his parents for the field. He however accepted the position of post quartermaster at Marietta, and in the autumn of the same year was called to a more important position of the same kind at Wheeling, West Virginia.

But he was not satisfied with this kind of service; he believed that he was needed in the field. Accordingly, having at length satisfied the claims of filial duty which had before detained him, he resigned his position, and, in June, 1862, having enlisted in the military service, was appointed on the staff of General Rosecrans, who had become acquainted with him in West Virginia, but was now in command of a portion of the army of the Tennessee. Greenwood started immediately for the field, full of ardor, gratified to be at length where he would have an opportunity to do his part in the great struggle. His letters of that date are full of the spirit of his station. But his service was short; a single summer in the climate of Mississippi cut him down. Weakened by disease, he concealed his condition as much as possible from his general, and in the battle of Iuka, September 19th, he was placed in a position of much danger and responsibility. The line was broken, and Greenwood, by his courage and skill, succeeded in stopping a detachment that was flying before the enemy, and restored order to that part of the line. General Rosecrans testifies that "Captain Greenwood's conduct was admirable." But the exertion and excitement were too great for his strength. On the second day after the battle he was completely prostrated, and was taken in an ambulance to Jacinto, Mississippi, where he rapidly sank, and a week later, on the twenty-seventh of September, 1862, passed away.

CAPTAN JOHN J. JUMPER.

John J. Jumper was born in Manchester township, Morgan county, Ohio, September 6, 1830, son of George and Elizabeth Jumper, who afterwards removed to Washington county. John was married on September 13, 1851, at Reinersville, Morgan county, Ohio, and his widow, Mrs. M. E. Jumper, still lives at Beverly, Ohio. In August, 1861, Captain Jumper raised a company for the three years' service, and after remaining at Camp Putnam, Marietta, until his company was full, he joined the Eighteenth Ohio volunteer infantry at Camp Wool, Athens, Ohio, and his company became F, of that regiment.

While in the army he did good service, and would have continued until the close but for a severe attack of chronic diarrhœa, compelling him to resign, and of which disease he died September 13, 1864, at Beverly, Ohio.

CAPTAIN G. B. BARTLETT.

Captain G. B. Bartlett enlisted with J. W. Fouts at Beverly, and was mustered in and made a corporal at the organization of the company, D, at Marietta, October 9, 1861; was promoted to sergeant, January 1, 1862, and to second lieutenant May 26, 1862, and on the tenth of June started to Ohio on recruiting service, with headquarters at Chillicothe and at Marietta. While returning to his regiment, which was at Corinth, Mississippi, he was detached as acting assistant quartermaster, and acting assistant commissary sergeant of the engineers' department of the army of the Mississippi, and went with Grant on his expedition against Vicksburgh, becoming personally responsible for all the tools and materials used in the construction of the famous canal at that place, served in that capacity three months; then at the earnest request of his colonel, J. W. Sprague, returned to his regiment, and was promoted to first lieutenant July 1, 1863, and to captain November 12, 1864, and transferred to the command of company A, where he served to the close of the war.

LIEUTENANT LEVI J. FOURAKER.

Levi J. Fouraker was born in Morgan county, Ohio, September 8, 1838, where he lived until August, 1852, when he came to Washington county with his parents, and remained with them until April, 1861. He enlisted a few days after the breaking out of the war, in Captain John Henderson's company, K, Eighteenth Ohio three months' regiment, and at the expiration of his term of service volunteered in company H, Seventy-seventh Ohio, Colonel Hildebrand commanding. Upon organizing the company he was elected second lieutenant, and Richard Fouraker, his father, captain of the company. After the regiment landed at Pittsburgh Landing, Tennessee, Lieutenant Fouraker served faithfully on scouting and other duty, until the Seventy-seventh was ordered into camp at Shiloh Church, when Lieutenant Fouraker was placed in command of the first picket guard sent out from that point, which guard was stationed near the place afterwards known as the battle-field of Fallen Timbers.

Lieutenant Fouraker fought with his command through the battle of Shiloh, April 6th and 7th, and was taken prisoner with many others, on the eighth, at the battle of Fallen Timbers, and when a prisoner of war was basely shot by the rebel cavalry and subsequently brought into camp, nearly dead. He stayed in the field hospital a few days, when he was sent to the Cincinnati hospital, and from there to his father's house, where he died of his wounds March 5, 1875, aged thirty-six years.

Lieutenant Fouraker was always jovial, agreeable, and a good companion. He was brave to a fault, and had no enemies. His comrades had learned to love and respect him as a true soldier, when he fell at his post of duty.

ADJUTANT GEORGE B. TURNER.

George Butler Turner was a son of Samuel R. Turner, esq., and Hannah B. Turner, of Marietta, Ohio, and was born at New London, Connecticut, November 13, 1840.

From the age of eight years his home was at Marietta. He graduated at the high school, then finished his preparation for college under a private tutor, entered the freshman class in the fall of 1858, and passed through his course with the highest credit, graduating with the class of 1862. His parents were at the time in the east, and he informed them by letter that he felt it his duty to engage in the great struggle to save the Union, and

soon thereafter was enrolled in company F, Ninety-second Ohio volunteer infantry, in which W. Beale Whittlesey was a lieutenant. He was made orderly sergeant of the company, and filled the position very satisfactorily.

Although of seemingly frail constitution and one likely to succumb to the hardships and trials of a soldier's life, yet he seemed to stand it well, so far as I can now remember, being usually in good health, always bright and cheerful. An earnest Christian, he was at all times consistent, yet by no means obtrusive in asserting his faith. His everyday life commended his belief to all those associating with him. In battle he was cool and self-possessed. At Chickamauga, at a critical time, Colonel Fearing and his adjutant were both wounded, and word was brought to the writer, on the right wing, to assume command; Turner, then acting as sergeant major, notified me of it, kindly urging me to keep cool, and all would be well. At this battle the adjutant, D. E. Putnam, was so badly wounded as to render his discharge a necessity, and Turner, who had been promoted, was made adjutant of the regiment as soon as it could be done; in which capacity he acted after the date of that battle, September 18, 1863.

On the afternoon of November 25, 1863, the Ninety-second regiment, with less than four hundred fighting men, formed a part of the column that assaulted and captured Mission Ridge. Turner lived to reach the summit unharmed. The commanding officer of the regiment had been wounded, Whittlesey and other officers killed, and others wounded in the assault, which was a very difficult one, the hill being steep and rough. The summit once reached and the enemy driven over, he assumed command of the shattered line, now three times decimated, in about a half hour and with drawn sword rallied the men about him and led them to aid in repelling a brigade of the enemy who were coming to the assistance of their comrades in our front. He here received his mortal wound, a large minnie ball striking him just behind the ear; no doubt he was facing the men urging them forward at the time.

Everything was done that could be, but his wound was mortal. He was evidently expecting death, and while he talked but little, seemed to draw comfort from his pocket testament, opened at the fourteenth and fifteenth chapters of St. John. General Turchin, who commanded the brigade, called, and in speaking of Turner's bravery and ability, offered him a position on his staff, asking him if he would like it. The reply came at once—"I am willing to go and do that in which I can be the most useful." He gradually sank, became delirious, and when it was thought best to remove him to the officers' hospital, gave the writer his hand, saying, "Good bye, colonel, good bye; we will both go home together." He went home that night, living but a few hours afterwards. He died December 1, 1863. Just before going into this last battle he wrote a letter home, to be mailed in case he should be killed, which closed with these words—"If I return not with the victors, think not the sacrifice too great for the interests at stake."

LIEUTENANT TIMOTHY L. CONDIT.

Killed in the battle of Murfreesborough, December 31, 1862.

Timothy L. Condit was born at Cleveland, Ohio, in December, 1837. In 1852 he entered the office of the Marietta *Intelligencer* as an apprentice. He devoted three years to the mastery of his trade as a printer. During this time spare moments were occupied in diligent preparation for college. He so far succeeded in fitting himself, that, after one year more spent partly in the preparatory department, and partly in working at his trade, he entered college the most thoroughly prepared of any member of his class. This leadership he maintained throughout the course, graduating in 1860, as the valedictorian of that year. Principally by his own labor as a printer, he secured the money to pay his way through college. The perseverance and force to achieve such marked success against such obstacles, of themselves stamp Condit as a young man of devoted purpose, great industry, and no ordinary ability.

In 1856 he united with the Congregational church at Marietta, and felt called to prepare for the ministry, but before the fall term of the theological seminary began he felt a stronger call to enter the service of his country, and decided to volunteer. In pursuance of this decision, he entered company L, of the First Ohio cavalry, as a private soldier, for three years' service. An educated gentleman, with influential friends in places of authority, he could have had a commission for the asking. Deeming himself unprepared for the responsibility of command, he refused to ask one. Through the camps and campaigns of his regiment, a gallant body of soldiers, Condit faithfully performed his arduous duties, adorning his humble position by maintaining amid all trials, temptations, and sufferings, his Christian profession and gentlemanly bearing. On the twenty-ninth of May, 1862, he was promoted to be second lieutenant in his company.

On the thirty-first of December, 1862, on the battlefield of Murfreesborough, in the thickest of the fight, and at the head of his squadron, Condit was shot dead.

Two companies of his regiment, on duty guarding a wagon train, were suddenly overwhelmed in the fierce onset of the attack by the Confederate army. Said a private soldier who rode with Condit on that day, "When the lieutenant was killed they were all around us; we could not see any way out. The lieutenant said the only way was to charge and then retreat. He rode forward to lead and was killed." To make way for his men to get out Condit died. Arnold Winkelried, when he gathered to his breast the spears of the Austrian phalanx died not a more heroic death.

His body was recovered from the battlefield, and now lies buried in the Mound cemetery at Marietta. As a token of appreciation of the character and service of this noble Christian patriot and martyr, the society of the alumni, and his fellow-soldiers of the First Ohio cavalry, placed a monument over his resting place.

LIEUTENANT CHARLES BEMAN GATES. *

Looking back to the dark years when so many homes were made desolate that the whole country seemed to sit in one common bereavement, there yet stand in the memory spots where the shadows rested with unwonted heaviness; where the time and manner in which death came, and the relations of the dead to the living, gave elements of peculiar and overwhelming sadness to the sorrowful stroke.

Lieutenant Gates was the only son of Beman Gates, esquire, and Betsy Shipman Gates, of Marietta. He was born October 30, 1844, and entered Marietta college in 1861.

Already in these early days of the war, his heart and soul were enlisted in his country's cause, and he entered college rather than the army, only because of his extreme youth. In the recruiting camp which was established at Marietta, the officers were drilled regularly by an army officer, and at his request his father obtained permission for him to join in the drill. He joined the force which was organized in Marietta for defence and guard duty, and was present at Buffington, when John Morgan attempted to cross the Ohio at that point. In this kind of duty he became proficient in the manual of arms, and satisfied in part his desire to help his country in her need, while at the same time he continued his studies.

Meantime the war raged on. Victories and defeats alike added to the Nation's dead, and the voice of mourning filled the land. Regiments which went away with full ranks, had come back piecemeal, on crutches, on cots, and in coffins. The day when man enlisted under the inspiration of fife and drum had passed away. The dark days of the spring of 1864 had come, and the Government was laboring desperately to recruit the armies which were melted away in the terrible battles of the wilderness campaign.

Young Gates felt that the time had come when he must give himself wholly to his country's service. Friends tried to dissuade him, feeling that to break away in the midst of his education was a sacrifice that was not called for. But he remained firm in his conviction that it was his duty to go, and his parents yielded their consent, feeling that to withhold it would be to crush all manliness in him. He enlisted in the One Hundred and Forty-eighth regiment, which was formed in response to the call of Governor Brough, was chosen first lieutenant of his company, and was duly commissioned.

On the twenty-third day of May, at 2 o'clock P. M., he left with his regiment for the front by rail, via Parkersburgh to Harper's Ferry. When about five miles below Marietta the train was thrown from the track down an embankment; two of his fellow students were killed, and he received severe internal injuries. Unwilling to turn back, he proceeded with his regiment; but his injuries, aggravated by exposure to rain, marching and camping without tents, resulted in his death at Harper's Ferry, May 31, 1864.

Thus he was cut down at the very threshold of the

---

*By Professor D. E. Beach.

service which he had longed for. He had followed Greenwood and Condit and Whittlesey and Turner to their last resting place, and he entered this service with a full realization of the dangers involved, expressing his readiness to give up his life for his country. The sacrifice was required of him, while the experiences which are dear to the soldier were denied him.

In his college course he developed business rather than professional qualities. He was especially devoted to the more practical branches of study. He was greatly attached to his literary society, and took an active part in the frequent debates upon the questions which were then absorbing the public mind. He read more for information than amusement, and his essays which were often upon some political subject showed quick perception, penetration and sound judgment. With his fellow students he was universally popular. He was thoroughly unselfish, generous, often to his own detriment, as he frequently permitted his own record to suffer, through a desire to serve others. Through all his intercourse with his fellows, there ran a thoughtful regard for the feelings of others, and a fine, delicate sense of honor which won for him the warm affection and esteem of a large circle of friends, both in his own and the other college classes.

There were few residents of Marietta, old or young, to whom his bright intelligent face was not familliar; and his pleasant, respectful ways and frank, hearty friendliness had endeared him to all. He was devoid of all affectation, and slow to manifest the deeper feelings of his heart, yet no one who was intimate with him could fail to see that a deep reverence and affection for his parents was the strongest sentiment of his nature; so strong that it held him firmly from the temptations to which his sociable, funloving disposition rendered him peculiarly liable, and became a constant incentive to honorable effort.

He was maturing rapidly and gave every promise that he was passing to a successful and honorable manhood.

His death came with a weight of swift sorrow which words cannot measure or express. A telegram brought to his parents the tidings of his critical condition, and they hastened to Harper's Ferry by the first train, but reached there only to find that he was already dead, and they returned, bringing with them the lifeless form of him who had left them a short week before in the strength and beauty of his early manhood.

In all the sad experiences of the war, perhaps nothing shows more strongly the fearful cost at which the country was saved, than cases like this, when an only and tenderly loved son was taken, leaving a sharp sense of bereavement and irreparable loss which the passing years do not lessen, and which even religion can only soften, but can not take away.

LIEUTENANT RICHARD D. MASON.

Lieutenant Richard D. Mason, the subject of this sketch, was born in Adams township, Washington county, son of Adolphus and Betsey B. Mason. He received a common school education.

He was elected second lieutenant of company B, Ninth Ohio cavalry, which rendezvoused at Camp Marietta, and was mustered in at Zanesville January 17, 1863. From Zanesville the company moved to Camp Dennison, where they were armed and equipped. They then proceeded to Kentucky. Lieutenant Mason was with his company during its term of service up to the time of his death, acquitting himself with credit. After the siege of Knoxville, Lieutenant Mason was promoted to first lieutenant, and soon after obtained leave of absence to return home. While at home he was married to Miss Elizabeth Shepard. Returning to his company at Pulaski, Tennessee, he was taken with chronic diarrhea on June 24, 1864. "Thus perished as gallant a young patriot as ever drew sword in defence of his country."

LIEUTENANT RICHARD B. CHEATHAM.

R. B. Cheatham, Sixty-third Ohio volunteer infantry, volunteered with J. W. Fouts, and was mustered in at the organization of the company, October 9, 1861, as first sergeant of the company, served in that capacity with his company up to the twenty-sixth day of May, 1862, when he was promoted to first lieutenant of his company (D), served in that capacity up to the time of his death, in 1864. He died in camp at Memphis, after a two days' illness. Lieutenant Cheatham was a good soldier and an efficient officer, always ready for duty and seldom absent from his company, who deeply regretted his loss.

LIEUTENANT EDGAR P. PEARCE.

Edgar P. Pearce was born in London, England, November 27, 1840. Two years later his father removed with his family to this country, taking up his residence at Cleveland, Ohio; afterwards, in 1848, at Marietta. Here the subject of this sketch grew to manhood, passing through the public schools of the city. Having learned the printers' trade, he worked several years in the office of the Marietta *Intelligencer*. He then filled a clerical office at the bank of Marietta for some years. In his twenty-first year he enlisted as a private in the Seventy-seventh regiment, and soon after was appointed quartermaster's sergeant of the regiment.

After the battle of Shiloh he was promoted to first lieutenant and assistant quartermaster. He was next detached from the regiment and made brigade quartermaster; and when General Steele was organizing his expedition to join General Banks, Lieutenant Pearce was appointed chief quartermaster of the expedition, which position he filled with distinguished ability. He was always a favorite with his commanding officers, owing to his genial disposition and peculiar talents and ability in the quartermasters' department. When the Seventy-seventh regiment was reduced to battalion, on account of its thinned ranks, a reduction of regimental officers took place, and lieutenant Pearce was honorably discharged, together with others.

He was married on January 26, 1865, to Miss Mary

D. Ewart, eldest daughter of Hon. T. W. Ewart, of Marietta. As a partner in the firm of Pearce & Triem, he pursued the business of druggist for some years, in Marietta. He was the popular cashier of the Caldwell National bank, at Caldwell, Ohio, for several years. In the fall of 1872 he returned to Marietta in failing health, and died of consumption July 7, 1873, aged thirty-two years and seven months, much loved and lamented by a large circle of friends.

SURGEON PARDON COOKE.

Pardon Cooke, jr., was born January 10, 1823, at Parkersburgh, West Virginia, son of Rev. Pardon and Mary Cooke. The family removed to Ohio in September, 1832. In March, 1852, he graduated at the Starling Medical college, Columbus, Ohio.

He was married in November, 1852, to Mary Ellen, eldest daughter of Hon. William Forrest Hunter, of Woodsfield, Ohio, soon after which he settled in Marietta and began the practice of his profession.

He was commissioned as assistant surgeon of Ohio volunteers October 29, 1861, and assigned to duty in General Cox's division, in the Kanawha Valley. In February, 1862, he was assigned to duty as assistant surgeon of the Seventy-seventh regiment, and remained at his post until the time of his death, which occurred October 31, 1863, on a steamer, on the White river, near Duvall's Bluff, Arkansas.

LUTHER HATHAWAY.

In looking over the chapter of a life, especially after it is closed, we can readily see the leading characteristics, ambitions and desires that prompted the course of that life; and in the study of biography the chief benefit is derived from these salient points. We can gather from the field of every life, many flowers, many examples that may stimulate others to noble endeavor. Let us gather only these. Thus far will the general reader be interested and no farther. More than that is for local consumption of friends and relatives. The life before us presents many such points, of which we mention but a few.

First—Devotion to the cause of the country. For a year before the war Mr. Hathaway was in Kentucky, where every business interest would have prompted him either to oppose the Union or remain indifferent, but his letters of that period show that he stood by the Union as it was without equivocation; and upon his return in 1861 he at once enlisted as a private in the United States service. He placed his life in the scale. No higher duty can be discharged, or greater sacrifice made by a citizen than that.

Second—We would mention a pure life. Having been converted in early life he united with the Baptist church, and ever after remained a consistent member thereof.

Third—That which is included in the above—fidelity to domestic relations.

Fourth—A high appreciation of education as a means of developement and as the right road to advancement. In one of his last letters to his wife, he tells her that no sacrifices they might make in educating their children would be too great for the end to be attained. His constant effort and solicitude was to bring up and educate his children properly.

Mr. Hathaway learned the trade of carpenter and joiner when a young man, but as he grew older it became his strong desire to own and cultivate land, as he was reared on a farm and such pursuits were more congenial to him. His tastes in this direction led him to take an agricultural journal for many years. He believed the life of a farmer to be the most independent and satisfactory of all; but the strong swirl of American life and the necessities of the hour led him in a different path. The better desire and the better purpose had to give way to the more pressing duties of daily life.

Luther Hathaway was born at Savoy, Berkshire county, Massachusetts, December 31, 1817. He was the youngest son of Nathaniel Gilbert and Vashti (Seymour) Hathaway, and counted among his ancestors on the paternal side, Governor William Bradford and Sir Humphrey Gilbert, the navigator and discoverer.*

His father and mother were both born at Taunton, Bristol county, Massachusetts, from which town they removed to Savoy.

From Berkshire his father removed to Macedon, Wayne county, New York, where Luther and his brothers and sisters received such education as was customary in New England families of those days. He was married August 29, 1842, to Clarissa Louise, daughter of John and Betsey (Elliot) Ripley, at Macedon, New York. The children of this marriage were Seymour Judson, born at Macedon January 27, 1844; and John Gilbert, born at the same place November 24, 1850.

Mr. Hathaway with his family removed to Marietta in the spring of 1853, where he resided until the breaking out of the war, when, upon his return from Danville, Kentucky, he enlisted in company B, Thirty-ninth Ohio volunteer infantry, July 22, 1861. Upon arriving at Camp Colerain, near Cincinnati, he was appointed hospital steward of the regiment. Soon afterwards the Thir-

* To those interested in genealogical matters the following will be of interest. The progenitor of the name came from Devonshire, England, in the year 1635, landing at Barnstable, Bristol county, Massachusetts. In Freetown, Taunton, and Fall River, in the same county, the early families remained for many years. All of the Hathaway name trace their ancestry to the same county, whether spelled Hadaway, Hatheway, or Hathaway. In the published life of Major General Samuel Gilbert Hatheway is the following: "Nathaniel Gilbert, a descendent of Sir Humphrey Gilbert, married Welthia, granddaughter of Governor William Bradford. Their daughter, Welthia Gilbert, married Ebenezer Hathaway, and these were the grandparents of Samuel Gilbert Hathaway. Ezra Chase, a descendant of John Alden, married a Gilbert, and their daughter, Hannah, married Shadrach Hathaway. These were the parents of Samuel Gilbert Hathaway." Colonel Ebenezer Hathaway, above mentioned, was the grandfather of Lemuel Hathaway, whose son was Nathaniel Gilbert Hathaway. During the Revolutionary war many of the Gilberts, and a few of the Hathaways went with the king and were banished, going to New Brunswick; those remaining were true to their country, and their names are found on the rolls of the Revolutionary army, some of the name attaining to positions of honor and trust, both in civil and military life.

Luther Hathaway

ty-ninth left for Missouri, and he accompanied the regiment on all its hard and extended line of march over that State during the winter of 1861–62; having for a messmate and friend the Rev. B. W. Chidlaw, chaplain of the regiment.

After the fall of Island No. 10, a general hospital was organized at New Madrid, Missouri, and Mr. Hathaway was designated to take charge of the same, being detached from the regiment. He so remained detached up to the time of his death.

During the winter of 1862–3 preparations were made for an advance on Vicksburgh, the next rebel stronghold below Island No. 10, and he assisted and superintended the fitting up, at Columbus, Kentucky, of the large Mississippi steamer Nashville for a floating hospital. When completed he was placed in charge. General Grant soon began to concentrate his forces for an advance on Vicksburgh, and when the army and flotilla arrived in front of that city, the Nashville was anchored in the river ready to receive the sick and wounded soldiers.

Before leaving Columbus, Kentucky, Mr. Hathaway's health was in such condition as would have warranted a release from duty, but he stood to his post. While at New Madrid he had been detailed as physician and surgeon to accompany various cavalry expeditions into the enemy's country. This was a position he had an ambition to fill, and he was fast becoming competent to fill it successfully by the study of medicine during his spare hours, and by his varied experience in camp and field. In these expeditions the active life on horseback preserved his usual health and vigor, but when he started south on the Nashville, the confinement and care of the hospital, and the heat and malaria of the southern rivers began to tell upon his health. Upon arriving at Vicksburgh he was in reality unfit for duty, but he still remained at his post. He died April 1st. His remains were embalmed and sent to Marietta. He was buried with Masonic honors in Mound cemetery, April 14, 1863.

The family then removed to Macedon, New York, where Clarissa L. Hathaway, his wife, died December 27, 1863.

His son, S. J. Hathaway, having begun preparation for college at Marietta in the winter of 1863, remained and graduated at Marietta college in 1869.

His son, J. G. Hathaway, after attending the Macedon Centre academy, in Macedon, New York, for several years, returned to Marietta in the spring of 1869, and engaged on the engineer corps then surveying the Cleveland & Marietta railroad until its completion, when he learned the photographer's business with J. D. Cadwallader, esq., at Marietta. He was married, in 1875, to Miss Annetta Morse, and removed to Portsmouth, Ohio, the same year.

Rev. B. W. Chidlaw writes in regard to Mr. Hathaway:

Of Luther Hathaway I have many pleasant memories, and shall ever hold him in high esteem. I first met him at Camp Dennison, near Cincinnati, where the Thirty-ninth Ohio volunteer infantry was organized in July, 1861. He was appointed hospital steward, and I as chaplain was brought into intimate relations with him. He was every way well fitted for the position; humane, kind, skilful, and industrious, like a ministering angel he faithfully served his country in caring for the sick and wounded soldiers. As a Christian I found him a helper in my labors, ever anxious to render my services acceptable and useful to the suffering soldiers in the hospital. He always prepared the way for my ministrations in the gospel and encouraged me in my work and labor of love. As a man I always found him faithful and self-sacrificing in duty, an unflinching friend of his Government and country, ready for service in defence of the Union and the suppression of the Rebellion.

He was a true friend, a sincere Christian, and a man of noble purposes. His death at the post of duty all of his officers and comrades greatly deplored and sincerely mourned.

B. W. CHIDLAW,
Chaplain Thirty-ninth Ohio Volunteer Infantry.

WILLIAM L. PORTERFIELD.

William L. Porterfield was born in Butler county, Pennsylvania, February 8, 1839. At the age of fifteen his family came to Marietta, Ohio. Here he attended school and was graduated from the high school in 1859. He engaged in teaching until the breaking out of the Rebellion. In November, 1861, he enlisted in company B, Seventy-seventh Ohio volunteer infantry, then encamped in Marietta, and was appointed second sergeant of his company. In January, 1862, the regiment was ordered to Cincinnati, and soon after was sent up the Tennessee to Pittsburgh Landing, there to take part in the great battle of Shiloh. Porterfield survived the first two days' heavy fighting, taking a gallant part therein, to be slain on the third day, April 8th, in the memorable charge of the Texan cavalry. He was almost instantly killed by a shot in the neck. His remains were brought to Marietta and interred in Mound cemetery. Thus perished, in his first battle, this young soldier, at the age of twenty-three.

CAPTAIN JACOB CRAM.

Jacob Cram was born at Marietta in August, 1820. He was the son of Jonathan and Sally Dodge Cram. His father was one of the early merchants of Marietta, coming to this county in 1816.

He had two wives: Miss Lethe Devol, and upon her death Miss Caroline V. Blocksom, of Zanesville, Ohio.

At the time of the call for troops to repel the Morgan raid, Mr. Cram raised a company of cavalry and took command of the same July 16, 1863. They were called the Putnam Guards, in honor of Colonel William R. Putnam, and were, with Captain Wood's command, ordered to the fords at Buffingtons island, where Captain Cram's company did good service as scouts. On the night of the eighteenth Captain Cram with others, was taken prisoner, and the same night General Scammon, of the Kanawha division, ordered Wood to abandon his position, which he did, taking his force on board the steamer Starlight, and repairing to Ravenswood. Where Captain Cram was during the battle of the next morning is not known. He was wearing, when the Morgan raid took place, a suit of butternut brown, and wore it at

Buffington. After the battle Captain Cram was employed as an aid-de-camp to a Union officer, and his duties in this capacity led him to pass frequently between two Union camps about three quarters of a mile apart. On the morning of July 20th, while thus engaged, he was halted by some Union soldiers, who, from his butternut clothing, mistook him for a rebel, and as he rode on without stopping, they shot him, robbed him, and he was buried where he fell.

Thus fell Captain Cram, who in his anxiety to serve his country, had found death where he had a right to least expect it. He had been in poor health when the raid began, but the invasion of his native State roused him to action, and he resolved to go and help repel the invaders at any cost.

His remains were afterwards removed and reinterred in the Mound cemetery at Marietta. He left a widow and three children.

JOHN ALEXANDER PALMER.

John Alexander Palmer, fourth child of Jewett and Rachel (Campbell) Palmer, was born in Washington county, Ohio, October 19, 1829.

He married Margaret McAfee April 6, 1856, by whom he had two children. His life was passed upon his farm, and his winters usually spent in teaching until the breaking out of the war of the Rebellion. In August, 1861, he enlisted in the company then being recruited in Salem, by his brother Jewett, for the Thirty-sixth Ohio infantry. On the organization of the company he was appointed first sergeant. He entered the field with his regiment, and bore his full share of its hard campaigning and battles. He was promoted to second lieutenant March 20, 1862, and to first lieutenant on the first of September following. Owing to the failure of his health, he resigned his commission on January 18, 1863, and returned home. He died on the twenty-third of the following March, from the effects of exposure in the service. His high character as a Christian and patriot is well known. As a citizen and neighbor he was full of kindly impulses and quiet, good deeds. The organization and prosperous growth of the First Universalist church of Salem, this county, and of Palmer Lodge, of Odd Fellows, of the same place, are very largely due to his influence and earnest, energetic labors.

"His life was gentle; and the elements
So mix'd in him, that nature might stand up,
And say to all the word.—*This is a man!*"

ROLL OF HONOR—WAR OF 1861 TO 1865.

The following is a list of volunteers in the service of the United States during the war of the Rebellion, compiled from papers of the military committee, Washington county, newspaper lists, assessor's lists 1863 and 1864, lists of deceased soldiers, adjutant general's report, West Vir-

ginia, 1864 and 1865, company rolls, so far as they could be obtained, and from personal inquiry. Two persons have spent over six weeks in preparing and correcting the same.*

The roll is as full and accurate as it can be made without great expense and trouble.

It will prove a source of just pride to the people of the county, generally, as well as to the descendants and friends of those whose names are here recorded, and will be a standing challenge to the patriotism of the future to emulate the example of the volunteers of 1861–5.

ADAMS TOWNSHIP.

Allison, James, age 37, volunteer, 1865, Thirty-sixth regiment, company C.

Allison, Stephen, age 25, volunteer, July 20, 1861, three years, Twenty-seventh regiment, company D, corporal, attained rank of captain served four years, mustered out July 20, 1865; reenlisted as a veteran.

Allison, C. M., age 28, volunteer, three years, Ninth cavalry, company B, corporal, died in May, 1865, at Decatur, Alabama, of diarrhœa.

Allison, Lucien, age 33, 1865, Thirty-sixth regiment, company C.

Allison, Levi, Second regiment, company B.

Allison, Robert, age 24, volunteer, October 17, 1862, three years, Ninth cavalry, company B, private, served two and a half years, mustered out July 20, 1865.

Armstrong, Isaac, age 20, volunteer, July 20, 1861, three years, Thirty-sixth regiment, company A, private, served five months, died in service December 9, 1861, at Somerville, Virginia.

Armstrong, William, age 18, volunteer, October 17, 1862, three years, Ninth cavalry, company B; private, served two years and nine months, mustered out July 20, 1865.

Asbeenshheet Daniel, age 20, volunteer, October 14, 1862, three years, Ninth cavalry, company B, private, two years and nine months, mustered out July 20, 1865.

Atherton, Wiliam H., age 40, substitute, Seventy-eighth regiment, company D; mustered out July 11, 1865.

Augustine, John, age 23, Seventy-eighth regiment, company D, regular.

Augustine, Matt, volunteer, 1865, One Hundred and Seventy-eighth regiment, company D.

Badgeley, Isaac, age 27, Seventy-seventh regiment, company D.

Balch, John, volunteer, October 22, 1863, three years, Thirty-sixth regiment, company A, private.

Bowman, Ed, age 41, three years, Seventy-seventh regiment, company K, private, served three years, honorably discharged, reenlisted as a veteran.

Bowman, William, age 19, three years, Seventy-seventh regiment, company K, served three years, reenlisted as a veteran.

Brooker, Deemore, Seventy-seventh regiment, company H.

Brooker, Darius, age 16, volunteer, February, 1, 1864, three years, Ninth cavalry, company B, private, served eighteen months, mustered out July 20, 1865.

Brooker, Brainard, age 23, volunteer, October 24, 1862, three years, Ninth cavalry, company B, private, served three years, mustered out July 20, 1865, marched with Sherman to the sea, permanently detailed with division and ambulance train.

Brown, George W., age 21, volunteer, Seventy-seventh regiment, company K, died December 25, 1864, reenlisted as a veteran, died at Little Rock, Arkansas.

Brown, Charles, age 32, Thirty-ninth regiment, company D.

Brown, William, age 26, August 8, 1864, Seventy-seventh regiment, company K, served one year and seven months, mustered out March 8, 1866,

Brown, Gartrail, age 52, volunteer, three years, Seventy-seventh regiment, company K, reenlisted as a veteran.

Burtis, John, Seventy-seventh regiment, company H.

Butts, George, Seventy-seventh regiment, company H.

Campton, Peter, Seventy-seventh regiment, company H.

Campton, William, age 23, volunteer, February 1, 1864, three years, Ninth cavalry, company B, private, mustered out July 20, 1865.

Campton, John, age 20, volunteer, February 1, 1864, three years,

*Miss Addie Irish and Mrs. Mary M. Hathaway.

Ninth cavalry, company B, private, served one year and five months, mustered out July 20, 1865.

Cutherwood, William, age 30, volunteer, October 17, 1862, three years, Ninth cavalry, company B, attained rank of quartermaster sergeant, discharged for disability May, 1864, reduced to ranks after eighteen months of service.

Chandler, Albert, age 39, volunteer, September, 1861, three years, Seventy-seventh regiment, company K, captain, served three years, mustered out January 4, 1865, taken prisoner April 8, 1862.

Chapman, Rector, age 23, volunteer, October 17, 1862, three years, Ninth cavalry, company B, teamster, served two years and nine months, mustered out July 20, 1865.

Cheesman, William E., volunteer, Seventy-seventh regiment, companies K and A; reenlisted as a veteran.

Clay, Timothy, age 40, volunteer, October 15, 1862, three years, Ninth cavalry, company B, private, served two years and nine months, mustered out July 20, 1865, teamster.

Clay, Orange, age 44, volunteer, three years, Seventy-seventh regiment, company K, reenlisted as a veteran.

Coffee, Adoniram, age 18, volunteer, October 21, 1862, three years, Ninth cavalry, company B, private.

Coffeen, H. T. C., age 24, Sixty-sixth regiment, discharged July 15, 1865.

Cobb, Joseph, age 20, 1863, Sixty-third regiment, company F, mustered out July 8, 1865.

Cobb, Isaiah, age 31, 1865, Sixty-third regiment, company F, private.

Coles, Isaac, age 21, volunteer, Sixty-third regiment, company F.

Cowee, F. P., age 27, volunteer, February 15, 1864, three years, Thirty-sixth regiment, company F, private, served one year and four months, honorably discharged June 5, 1865, on account of wound.

Cowen, Reuben.

Crane, William G., age 21, volunteer, October 28, 1862, three years, Ninth cavalry, company B, sergeant, served two years and nine months, mustered out July 20, 1865.

Crane, Charles C., age 44, United States navy, mustered out, gunboat.

Davis, Paul W., Seventy-seventh regiment, company K, reenlisted as a veteran.

Davis, William S., age 23, volunteer, July 20, 1861, three years, Twenty-seventh regiment, company D, private, attained rank of corporal, served four years, mustered out July 20, 1865, transferred to gunboat service September, 1864, reenlisted as a veteran.

Davis, George S., age 20, volunteer, October 25, 1865, three years, Ninth cavalry, company B, private, honorably discharged, 1865, for physical disability.

Davis, Frederick, age 22, volunteer, October 17, 1862, three years, Sixty-ninth regiment, company B, private, served three years, mustered out July 20, 1865, discharged for physical disability, recovered and reentered service.

Davis, Edmond, age 25, volunteer, July 29, 1861, three years, Thirty-sixth regiment, company A, private, deserted, sentenced to lose wages, imprisoned, but subsequent bravery reinstated him in honorable standing.

Davis, Hugh A., age 32, volunteer, Seventy-seventh regiment, company K., reenlisted as a veteran.

Davis, Squire D., Seventy-seventh regiment, company K., deserter.

Davis, Dudley, age 35, volunteer, three years, Ninth cavalry, company B, corporal, attained rank of sergeant, discharged at close of war, transferred to navy.

Davis, Andrew J., age 21, volunteer, October 18, 1862, three years, Ninth cavalry, company B, private, served two years and nine months, mustered out July 20, 1865.

Davis, Brown A., age 37, volunteer, Seventy-seventh regiment, company K, died April 8, 1862, killed at Fallen Timber.

Davis, Daniel W., age 41, volunteer, three years, Seventy-seventh regiment, company K.

Devol, Luther, age 17, volunteer, January, 1863, three years, Ninth cavalry, company B, private, served one year and six months, mustered out July 20, 1865, reenlisted as a veteran.

Denwell, Martin, volunteer, 1865, Thirty-sixth regiment, company H.

Devol, J. Hervy, age 33, volunteer, February 1, 1862, three years, One Hundred and Ninety-third regiment, company E, corporal, served three years, mustered out August 4, 1865.

Dobbin, John, age 36, volunteer, three years, Seventy-seventh regiment, company K, died April 19, 1862, mortally wounded at Fallen Timber, near Shiloh, Tennessee, April 8, 1862.

Dobbin, William, age 22, volunteer, three years, Seventy-seventh regiment, company K, reenlisted as a veteran.

Dobbin, Isaac, age 45, volunteer, October, 1862, for three years, Ninth regiment, cavalry, company B, farrier, served two years and nine months, mustered out July 20, 1865, company blacksmith.

Dobbins, Henry, fall of 1864, One Hundred and Eighty-fourth regiment, company D, private, mustered out September 20, 1865.

Dobbins, William.

Driscoll, Stukely, age 42, volunteer, three years, Seventy-seventh regiment, company K, private, served three years, reenlisted as a veteran.

Driscoll, George B., volunteer, 1865, One Hundred and Seventy-fourth regiment, company D, mustered out June 28, 1865.

Driscoll, Merritt, volunteer, 1865, One Hundred and Seventy-fourth regiment, company D, mustered out June 28, 1865.

Drum, Lewis, 1861, served three months.

Drum, Jacob, age 47, volunteer, November 22, 1861, for three years; First artillery, company K, private, served three years, mustered out January 16, 1865.

Flagg, William, Seventy-seventh regiment, company K.

Farmer, Thomas, age 46, three years, Seventy-seventh regiment, company K, served three years, honorably discharged.

Farmer, John, Seventy-seventh regiment, company K, served two years, honorably discharged for disability.

Grant, Daniel L., age 34, volunteer, Seventy-seventh regiment, company K, died July, 1862, of fever.

Grant, Jefferson, age 24, volunteer, 1865, Thirty-sixth regiment, company H.

Grimes, Peter, age 22, Ninth regiment, cavalry, company B.

Griggs, Wallace, age 24, volunteer, August, 1863, three years, Ninety-second regiment, company F, corporal, died at Carthage, Tennessee, April 29, 1864, of typhoid fever.

Griggs, Robert, age 20, volunteer, three months, Seventy-seventh regiment, company B, October 17, 1862, three years, Ninth regiment, cavalry, company B, private.

Griggs, Charles A., age 17, volunteer, July 29, 1861, three years, Thirty-sixth regiment, company A, private, reenlisted as a veteran.

Hall, Josiah W., age 44, discharged, then entered invalid corps, finally missing.

Hall, George W., age 19, Seventy-seventh regiment, company H.

Hall, John, Ninety-second regiment, company F.

Hall, Elijah, age 17, Seventy-seventh regiment, company H.

Hall, Dudley, age 53, Seventy-seventh regiment, company H, honorably discharged for physical disability.

Hanson, Finley, age 43, drafted, Ninth regiment, cavalry, company B, discharged before leaving camp, homesick.

Haynes, John, age 38, volunteer, 1865, One Hundred and Eighty-sixth regiment, company E.

Henager, Herman, volunteer, Sixty-third regiment, company G, mustered out July 8, 1865.

Henager, William H., volunteer, October 28, 1862, three years, Ninth cavalry, company B, private, honorably discharged.

Henager, Charles, volunteer, 1865, One Hundred and Seventy-fourth regiment, company H, discharged in 1865 as no longer wanted, detailed as dispatch carrier, died of wounds received in battle, September 1, 1873.

Hiltabiddle, William, Sixty-third regiment, company F.

Hoover, W. H., volunteer, 1865, Seventy-seventh regiment, company H.

Hoover, D. T., substitute volunteer, 1865, Eighteenth regiment, company C.

Hoover, Andrew, Seventy-seventh regiment, company K, died October 4, 1863.

Hoover, Aaron, age 51, Seventy-seventh regiment, company H, reenlisted as a veteran.

Hughey, James L., age 24, Seventy-seventh regiment, company G.

Hughey, Andrew, volunteer, three years, Thirtieth regiment, blacksmith, served three years, mustered out, reenlisted as a veteran.

Humiston, Jason, age 24, drafted, Seventy-seventh regiment, died in service at Alton.

Hutcheson, John, age 21, volunteer, January 17, 1862, three years, Ninth cavalry, company B, corporal.

Hutcheson, Edward, age 23, volunteer, three years, Seventy-seventh regiment, company K, died in hospital in Alton, Illinois.

Huzzy, D. J.

Jenne, Stephen, age 18, volunteer, August 12, 1862, three years, Ninety-second regiment, company H, corporal.

Judd, Chauncey, age 21, volunteer, Ninety-second regiment, company F, mustered out June 10, 1865.

Judd, Lewis, Thirty-sixth regiment, company H, mustered out July 27, 1865.

Keith, Peter B., age 26, volunteer, three years, Seventy-seventh regiment, company K, died November, 1862, captured at Fallen Timber, paroled, died in hospital at Washington, D. C., of hardships while a prisoner.

Kirkpatrick, Ralph, age 39, volunteer, One Hundred and Eighty-second regiment, company C, private, died July 13, 1865, Camp Chase, Ohio.

Kimberly, Benjamin, age 46, volunteer, Seventy-seventh regiment, company H, died April 6, 1862, killed at Shiloh.

Kile, Samuel C., age 19, October 17, 1862, three years, Ninth cavalry, company B, private, corporal, served three years, mustered out July 20, 1865.

Kile, Oliver W., age 21, volunteer, October 17, 1862, three years, Ninth cavalry, company B, corporal, attained the rank of fourth sergeant, served two years and nine months, mustered out July 20, 1865.

Landsittle, Jacob, Thirty-ninth regiment, company F, musician.

Langly, Marion A., Seventeenth regiment, company H.

Lewis, Otis, age 20, Sixty-third regiment, died.

Lewis, Stephen B., age 43, volunteer, December 8, 1861, three years, First light artillery, company K, artificer, served three years, mustered out January 16, 1865.

Living, John, age 19, volunteer, July 29, 1861, three years, Thirty-sixth regiment, company A, private, served three years, died January 18, 1864, killed at battle of Cedar creek.

Long, George, age 21, volunteer, July 29, 1861, three years, Thirty-sixth regiment, company A, private, captured at Winchester in 1864, reenlisted as a veteran.

Long, James, age 18, volunteer, Seventy-seventh regiment, company K.

Lucas, George W., age 27, volunteer, October 18, 1862, three years, Ninth cavalry, company B, corporal, served two years and nine months, mustered out July 20, 1865, teamster.

Lucas, Isaac, age 25, Sixty-third regiment, company G, died April, 1862, mortally wounded.

Longley, Marion A, age 17, volunteer, February 10, 1864, Seventeenth regiment, company H, captain.

Mason, William B., age 37, volunteer, June 15, 1861, three years, Seventy-first regiment, company D, captain, served four months, resigned October 12, 1861.

Mason, William W., age 20, volunteer, three years, Sixty-third regiment, company D, died May 30, 1862, died at Corinth, Mississippi.

Mason, R. D, age 27, volunteer, October 9, 1862, three years, Sixty-ninth regiment, company B, second lieutenant, attained the rank of first lieutenant, served one year and nine months, died June 24, 1864, at Pulaski, Tennessee.

Mason, Horatio, volunteer, three years, Thirty-sixth regiment, company A.

Mason, Elijah J., age 18, volunteer, First artillery, company C, mustered out.

Mason, Jacob, aged 34, Sixty-third regiment, company F, mustered out July 8, 1865, discharged for physical disability, entered again February 11, 1865.

Mason, Oscar, age 24, volunteer, three years, Sixty-third regiment, company D, served one year, honorably discharged on account of physical disability.

Mason, Reuben S., age 27, volunteer, three years, Sixty-third regiment, companies D and F, lieutenant, transferred to Fifty-fifth colored infantry.

McAtee, Samuel M., agee 17, volunteer, three years, Sixty-third regiment, company F, mustered out July 8, 1865, reenlisted as a veteran.

McAtee, Francis, volunteer, July 29, 1861, three years, Thirty-sixth regiment, company A, private, served four years, mustered out July 27, 1865, reenlisted as a veteran.

McCarty, Christopher, volunteer, 1865, One Hundred and Seventy-fourth regiment, company B.

McCarty, Lucien, three years, Ninety-second regiment, company E, private, mustered out June 10, 1865.

McCurdy, Joshua, age 43, volunteer, Ninety-second regiment, company E, private, died April 23, 1863, at Carthage, Tennessee.

McHugh, John, age 26, 1865, One Hundred and Eighty-fourth regiment, company D.

McKenny, James, jr., age 35, volunteer, Seventy-seventh regiment, company H.

Merriam, William S., age 18, volunteer, October 22, 1862, three

years, Ninth cavalry, company B, corporal, attained captain, served two years and nine months, mustered out, July 20, 1865, in general hospital at Springfield, Illinois, part of time for sore eyes.

Miller, Charles, Thirty-ninth regiment.

Miller, Thomas, Seventy-seventh regiment, company K.

Moore, Aaron, age 53, Seventy-seventh regiment, company K.

Moore, Zedick J., age 24, volunteer, One Hundred and Seventy-eighth regiment, company F, private, died March 7, 1865, at Arlington Heights.

Moore, P. R., age 35, volunteer, Thirty-sixth regiment, company C.

Morris, William, age 27, volunteer, Seventy-seventh regiment, company H, died 1863, of small-pox.

Morris, John, age 17, Ninth cavalry, company B, transferred to the Tenth in January, 1862.

Morris, Allen, age 18, volunteer, July 29, 1861, three years, Thirty-sixth regiment, company A, private, reenlisted as a veteran.

Nott, Percival, age 48, volunteer, three years, Seventy-seventh regiment, company H, private, died April 8, 1862, mortally wounded at Pittsburgh Landing, April 8, 1862.

Nott, William, age 16, Seventy-eighth regiment, company H

Nott, Benjamin, age 46, volunteer, July 29, 1861, three years, Thirty-sixth regiment, company A, private, served three years, mustered out in 1864.

Olney, Orin, Seventy-seventh regiment, company K.

Otis, Harrison G., age 26, volunteer, reenlisted June, 1864, Twelfth and Twenty-third regiments, company H, lieutenant, attained captain, mustered out July 26, 1865, wounded in Winchester, July, 1864.

Owen, Alexander D, age 18, volunteer, First cavalry, company M.

Owen Daniel, age 36, volunteer, September 28, 1861, three years, Thirty-sixth regiment, company A, private, served three years, mustered out 1864, lost his speech by severe cold in his third year of service.

Owen, James D., age 22, volunteer, First Light artillery, company K, served ten months, honorably discharged on account of physical disability.

Owen, Oscar F., age 19, volunteer, July 29, 1861, three years, Thirty-sixth regiment, company A, private, served three years, mustered out in 1864.

Owen, Vincent B., age 20, volunteer, July 20, 1861, three years, Twenty-seventh regiment, company B, private, served three years, mustered out July, 1864, wounded seventeen days before time expired.

Owen, Sylvester D., volunteer, First regiment, company C.

Owen, W. D., aged 28, volunteer, Ninth cavalry, private, died April, 1864, at Pulaski, Tennessee, of diarrhea.

Palmer, Henry, age 17, volunteer, Thirty-sixth regiment, company C.

Palmer, William, age 17, volunteer, October 15, 1862, three years, Ninth cavalry, company B, private, served two years and eight months, mustered out July 20, 1865, sick during first year, afterwards performed duty.

Penwell, Martin, Thirty-sixth regiment, company H.

Perkins, Albert, volunteer, Sixty-third regiment, company F, honorably discharged on account of disability, arm broken below elbow.

Perkins, John, age 33, Sixty-third regiment.

Plummer, Robert L., age 38, volunteer, November 15, 1861, three years, First artillery, company K, sergeant, served three years and two months, mustered out January 16, 1865.

Porter, Hardy, age 30, volunteer, winter of 1864–65, Thirty-sixth regiment, company H.

Pratt, Davis, age 17, volunteer, January 9, 1863, three years, Ninth cavalry, company B, private, served two years and a half, mustered out July 20, 1865.

Ripley, Hiram, age 18, volunteer, July 29, 1861, three years, Thirty-sixth regiment, company A, private, served two years and four months, died November 28, 1862, wounded at Mission Ridge, died four days later.

Roach, W. S., age 18, volunteer, October 14, 1861, three years, Sixty-third regiment, company F, sergeant, attained second lieutenant, served three years and four months, mustered out July 8, 1865, slight wound at Coal Run.

Roach, William W., age 20, One Hundred and Eighty-sixth regiment, company E.

Roach, Lyman, age 18, First artillery, company K, captured near Savannah, October 12, 1864, confined at Florence, South Carolina, starved till nearly insane, paroled in three months, and mustered out in June, 1865.

Rollin, Edward, age 39, 1865, Thirty-sixth regiment, company C.

Rose, James, Eighteenth regiment, company D.

Rose, Thompson, age 19, Sixty-third regiment, company F, died July 22, 1864, reenlisted as a veteran, killed at Decatur, answered first call.

Rose, Isaiah, age 20, volunteer, Sixty-third regiment, company F.

Ross, Nathaniel, age 20, volunteer, April 28, 1861, three years, First artillery, company K, private, attained corporal, served three years, mustered out in 1864, captured the first time at Decatur, Georgia, July 22, 1864, and twice afterwards wounded while returning to Union line, answered first call.

Ross, William, age 19, volunteer, July 29, 1861, three years, Thirty-sixth regiment, company A, private, served three years, mustered out July 27, 1864, reenlisted as a veteran.

Ross, Russell D., age 17, volunteer, September 28, 1861, three years, Thirty-sixth regiment, company A, private, served three months, died December, 1861, at Somersville, West Virginia, of typhoid fever, a good soldier.

Ross, Daniel N., age 21, Second Virginia cavalry, company E.

Ross, Sampson? Sixty-third.

Rummer, Perley, age 19, volunteer, Sixty-third regiment, company F, mustered out July 8, 1865.

Rummer, W. J., age 36, volunteer, 1865, Thirty-sixth regiment, company A, private, mustered out July 27, 1865.

Sayles, Burgess A., Seventy-seventh regiment, company K, died October 2, 1862, of fever, buried at National cemetery, Little Rock, Arkansas.

Severance, Church B., age 22, volunteer, July 29, 1861, three years, Thirty-sixth regiment, company A, private, served nine months, honorably discharged July 25, 1862, on account of physical disability.

Severance, Arthur, age 34, volunteer, 1865, Thirty-sixth regiment, company C.

Shattuch, Benjamin, volunteer, 1865, Thirty-sixth regiment, company E.

Shinn, Alexander.

Shaw, Charles, age 19, died.

Shinn, Alfred C., age seventeen, volunteer, Seventy-seventh regiment, company K, died January 5, 1862, typhoid fever, Corinth, Mississippi.

Shinn, Samuel D., age 18, volunteer, Seventy-seventh regiment, company K, died June 1, 1862, wounded and taken at Fallen Timber, died at Huntsville, Alabama, prisoner for two months.

Shivers, George, age 23, volunteer, three years and three months, Seventy-seventh regiment, company H, reenlisted as a veteran, injured by a shell and afterwards made insane by heavy cannonading.

Shockley, Henry, age 19, volunteer, July 29, 1861, three years, Thirty-sixth regiment, company A, private, reenlisted as a veteran.

Shockley, N. D., age 48, volunteer, three years, Seventy-seventh regiment, company K, private, died August 9, 1862, captured at Fallen Timber April 8, 1862, died a prisoner.

Shockley, William, age 17, three years, Ninety-second regiment, company F, private, died February 4, 1863, taken sick in service, was brought home and died.

Simons, Orrin, age 40, volunteer, 1865, Thirty-sixth regiment, company C.

Simons, O. H., age 18, First artillery, company C.

Skinard, Ed. age 25, Thirty-sixth regiment, company C.

Smith, Charles, age 42, volunteer, Ninety-second regiment, company H, slightly wounded in hand.

Spear, James T., age 22, volunteer, July 29, 1861, three years, Thirty-sixth regiment, company A, private, detailed for an Indiana battery, wounded once.

Spear, Gideon, age 20, volunteer, three years, Thirty-sixth regiment, company D, mustered out July 27, 1865, reenlisted as a veteran.

Spears, Ivan, Thirty-sixth regiment, company D, killed at Chickamauga.

Spooner, Daniel, age 22, Ninth cavalry, company B, sergeant, mustered out at expiration of service, July 20, 1865.

Spooner, Isaac, age 24, volunteer, three years, Ninety-second regiment, hospital steward, served three years, discharged.

Sprague, Daniel F., age 21, volunteer, First artillery, company H, mustered out.

Sprague, H. O., age 20, August 8, 1862, three years, Ninety-second regiment, company H, sergeant, served one year, died April 16, 1863, at Carthage, Tennessee, in service, of great service in disciplining troops.

Stackhouse, Franklin, volunteer, Ninety-second regiment, company D, wounded at Buzzard's Roost, in hospital one year, died at Chattanooga from chills and fever.

Stackhouse, John, age 48, volunteer, 1862, three years, Ninety-second regiment, company H, private, served two years, died.

Stackhouse, W. W., volunteer, fall 1864, One Hundred and Eighty-fourth regiment, company D, private, mustered out September 20, 1865.

Steed, Abraham, age 20, volunteer, January, 1864, three years, Ninth cavalry, company B, private, served eighteen months, mustered out July 20, 1865

Steed, John, age 22, volunteer, July 29, 1861, three years, Thirty-sixth regiment, company A, private, reenlisted as a veteran.

Stewart, John V., volunteer, 1865, Thirty-sixth regiment, company A, answered first call for seventy-five thousand, and was captured at Harper's Ferry.

Striker, John, age 19, volunteer, Ninth cavalry, company B, mustered out July 20, 1865, served full term, well throughout service.

Thayer, James E., volunteer, 1864, Seventy-seventh regiment, company H.

Thayer, Ephraim, Seventy-seventh regiment, company B.

Votial, James, age 30, volunteer, 1865, One Hundred and Eighty-sixth regiment, company L.

Waller, Thomas, volunteer, Seventy-seventh regiment, company K, died April 8, 1862, mortally wound at Fallen Timber.

Ward, Isaac, Seventy-seventh regiment, company B, deserted before leaving Camp Tupper, influenced by disloyal friends.

Ward, Morris, age 17, Seventy-seventh regiment, company K.

Ward, W. G., age 35, Seventy-seventh regiment, company B.

Weatherby, William, age 26, January 1, 1862, three years, First artillery, company K, private, served three years, mustered out 1865.

Williamson, John, age 35, volunteer, November 6, 1862, three years, Ninth cavalry, company B, captain, attained rank of major, served one year and nine months, resigned July 28, 1864, an account of physical disability, at Chattanooga

Williams, Jesse, age 28, volunteer, 1864, One Hundred and Seventy-sixth regiment, company I.

Williams, J. W., volunteer, Twelfth cavalry, company D, reenlisted as a veteran.

Wilson, Benjamin, age 19, Seventy-seventh regiment, company K.

Wilson, William, age 37, volunteer, three years, Seventy-seventh regiment, company K, reenlisted as a veteran.

Wilson, George W., age 34, volunteer, January 16, 1864, three years, First artillery, company K, private, served one year and six months, mustered out July 31, 1865.

Wilson, John, age 16, Seventy-seventh regiment, company K.

Wilford, Charles, Seventh cavalry

Wright, Josiah, age 23, volunteer, September 12, 1862, three years, Seventeenth cavalry, company H, served three years, mustered out July 4, 1865.

Wright, Amos, age 23, volunteer, November 19, 1861, three years, Second Virginia cavalry, company I, corporal, served three years and seven months, mustered out June 30, 1865, reenlisted as a veteran.

Zollars, Zephaniah, volunteer, Eighteenth regiment, honorably discharged on account of disability.

Zollars, James, age 23, volunteer, three years, Thirty-sixth regiment, company A, private, reenlisted as a veteran.

Rose, Sanfron, Sixty-third regiment.

RECAPITULATION.

De Beck's battery	8
First artillery	2
Huntington's battery	1
Ninth Ohio cavalry	38
Seventh Ohio cavalry	2
Second Virginia cavalry	2
One each in First and Twelfth Ohio cavalry	2
Seventy-seventh Ohio	59
Thirty-sixth Ohio	39
Sixty-third Ohio	20
Ninety-second Ohio	12
One Hundred and Seventy-fourth Ohio	5
Eighteenth Ohio (three years)	3
Eighteenth Ohio (three months)	2
Twenty-seventh Ohio	3
Thirty-ninth Ohio	3
One Hundred and Eighty-fourth Ohio	3
One Hundred and Eighty-sixth Ohio	3
Seventeenth and Seventy-eighth Ohio, two each	4
One each in First, Twelfth, Twenty-third, Second, Thirtieth, Sev-	

enty-first, Sixty-sixth, One Hundred and Seventy-sixth, One Hundred and Seventy-eighth, One Hundred and eighty-second, and One Hundred and Ninety-third, United States navy, not designated, eight, in all...... 20

Total number soldiers......... 227
Died.. 31

AURELIUS TOWNSHIP.

Allen, Alexander J., volunteered October 9, 1862, Ninth cavalry, company B, private, attained rank of first lieutenant, served two years and nine months, mustered out July 20, 1865.

Allen, James, age 20, volunteer, three years, Thirty-sixth regiment, company G, private, served three years, mustered out, captured at Chickamauga, and in rebel prison seventeen months.

Alban, William, age 18, volunteer, February 10, 1864, three years, Seventy-seventh regiment, company G, private, served two months, died April, 1864, of chronic diarrhœa.

Atkinson, William Monroe, aged twenty, volunteer, 1861, three years, Seventy-seventh regiment, company B, corporal, attained rank of sergeant, served two years six months, mustered out; second enlistment, age 22, volunteer, 1864, three years, Seventy-seventh regiment, company R, sergeant, attained rank of first lieutenant, served two years, mustered out March 8, 1866, captured in Marks' Mills, and in rebel prison fourteen months.

Archer, Cornelius, three years, Seventy-seventh regiment, company B.

Barker, William K., age 17, volunteer, 1861, three years, Thirty-sixth regiment, company B, private, veteran enlistment, age 19, volunteer, 1864, Thirty-sixth regiment, company E, private, mustered out July, 1865.

Barker, Levi Tuttle, age 16, volunteer, February, 1864, three years, Seventy-seventh regiment, company B, private, captured at Marks' Mills, and ten months in rebel prison.

Barnes, William E., age 37, volunteer, 1862, three years, Ninety-second regiment, company H, bugler, served three years, mustered out June 10, 1865.

Barnes, Owen, volunteer, 1861, three years, Seventy-seventh regiment, company B, veteran enlistment, volunteer, 1864, three years, Seventy-seventh regiment, company B.

Barnes, William L., volunteer, 1861, three years, Seventy-seventh regiment, company B.

Barnes, William Wilson, volunteer, 1864, one year, One Hundred and Seventy-sixth regiment.

Betz, Charles, First cavalry, company L.

Brown, William James, age 22, volunteer, 1861, three years, Thirty-sixth regiment, companies E and D, private, served three years, mustered out 1864.

Carmical, James, age 32, volunteer, 1862, three years, Ninety-second regiment, company H, private, attained rank of sergeant; second enlistment, volunteer, three years, One Hundred and Ninth United States colored infantry, second lieutenant.

Burton, William, age 30, volunteer, 1861, three years, Thirty-sixth regiment, companies A and H, private, attained rank of fifer, served three years, mustered out in 1864.

Copeland, John, age 35, volunteer, three years, Ninety-second regiment, company D, sergeant, died 1863, from wounds received at Chickamauga.

Davidson, John, age 19, volunteer, December, 1861, three years, Seventy-seventh regiment, company G, private; veteran enlistment, volunteer, February, 1861, three years, Seventy-seventh regiment, companies G and E, private.

Davidson, William, age 20, volunteer, August, 1864, Seventy-seventh regiment, companies G and E, private, served eight months, died March 23, 1865.

Davis, Brown, age 20, Seventy-seventh regiment, company H.

Dearth, Nehemiah H., age 21, volunteer, 1862, three years, Seventy-seventh regiment, company B, private, served two years; veteran enlistment, 1864, three years, Seventy-seventh regiment, company B, private, served one year six months, died July 19, 1865, of chronic diarrhœa, at Clarksville.

Delong, Jones, Seventy-seventh regiment, company B.

Dilley, James L., age 20, volunteer, October 17, 1861, three years, Sixty-third regiment, company G, drummer, served two years, mustered out July 15, 1865; veteran enlistment, age 22, volunteer, December, 1863, three years, Sixty-third regiment, company G, drummer, served two years, six months, lost right leg above the knee at battle of Rice's Station, April 6, 1865.

Dilley, Clinton, age 22, volunteer, December, 1861, three years, Seventy-seventh regiment, company B, private, died 1862, from the effects of a wound in the head and shoulders.

Dilley, Richard H., age 17, volunteer, 1861, three years, Sixty-third regiment, company G, drummer, served two years; veteran enlistment, age 19, volunteer, December, 1863, three years, Sixty-third regiment, company G, drummer, served two years six months, mustered out in 1865, was drum major during part of this service.

Dilley, Joseph, one year, One Hundred and Seventy-fourth regiment, company D.

Gerrez, Didier, age 17, volunteer, August, 1861, three years, Thirty-sixth regiment, company A, private.

Gerrez, Lafayette, age 19, volunteer, December, 1862, three years, Thirty-sixth regiment, company A, private.

Gilmore, John T., six months, One Hundred and Twenty-ninth regiment, company F.

Grant, John H., age 21, volunteer, Forty-second regiment, company D, private, died September, 1863, of typhoid fever.

Grass, Adam, Thirty-sixth regiment, company G.

Groselas, Jacob, Thirty-sixth regiment, company F.

Grubb, James D., age 20, volunteer, July, 1861, three years, Thirty-sixth regiment, company A, private, attained rank of corporal.

Hall, Justus W., age 18, substitute, May 15, 1864, one hundred days, One Hundred and Forty-eighth regiment, company F, private, served three ond one-half months, died August 29, 1864, of chronic diarrhœa, interred at home.

Hanson, William, age 21, volunteer, 1861, three years, Seventy-seventh regiment, company G, sergeant; veteran enlistment, February, 1864, three years, Seventy-seventh regiment, company G, sergeant.

Harper, William, Seventy-seventh regiment, company B.

Hess, Christian, Seventy-seventh regiment, company K.

Hess, Jacob, Thirty-ninth regiment, company F.

Hess, Justin, Fourth cavalry, company K.

Harvey, William, age 37, volunteer, 1862, three years, Ninety-second regiment, company H, private, served three years, mustered out June 10, 1865.

Hilton, James W., age 18, volunteer, December, 1864, three years, Seventy-seventh regiment, company B, private, died in 1864, in prison, at Tyler, Texas.

Holland, John Thomas, age 17, volunteer, 1862, three years, Ninety-second regiment, company H, private, served three years, mustered out June 10, 1865.

Holland, William Nelson, age 18, volunteer, 1862, three years, Ninety-second regiment, company H, private, served three years, mustered out June 10, 1865.

Jackson, Thomas Putnam, age 40, volunteer, July, 1861, three years, Thirty-sixth regiment, company A, private, served two years and six months, honorably discharged January 10, 1864.

Jackson, Andrew, Thirty-sixth regiment, company G.

Jackson James N., Seventh cavalry, company H.

James, John W., One Hundred and Sixteenth regiment, company H.

Johnson, William A., Twenty-fifth regiment.

Linten, George, age 40, volunteer, August, 1861, three years, Thirty-sixth regiment, company G.

Longfellow, Samuel, age 33, volunteer, February, 1864, three years, Seventy-seventh regiment, companies H and E, private, served one year, died February, 1865.

Lund, Gamiel J., age 16, volunteer, November 15, 1861, three years, Seventy-seventh regiment, company B, private, attained rank of lieutenant, served four years and four months, mustered out March 29, 1866, wounded in shoulder at Marks' Mills.

Masters, Zephaniah, three years, Seventy-seventh regiment, company B, private, died February 1, 1863, of chronic diarrhœa.

Littlefield, William, Tenth regiment, company B, died.

Mathews, Samuel B., age 20, volunteer, October 1, 1862, three years, One Hundred Sixteenth regiment, company H, private, attained rank of sergeant, served three years, mustered out in 1865, captured at Winchester and in prison one month, then in hospital five months, transferred to Sixty-second Ohio volunteer infantry.

Matthews, Henry C., age 18, volunteer, August 22, 1862, three years, One Hundred and Sixteenth regiment, company H, private, served three years, mustered out in 1865, lost one foot in a charge at Petersburgh, April 2, 1865.

Matthews, James Garnet, age 16, volunteer, August, 1863, six months, Fourth cavalry, company C, private, served seven months, mustered out in 1864; second enlistment, age 17, August, 1864, one year, One Hundred and Seventy-fourth regiment, company D, corporal, mustered out in 1865.

McKee, Samuel, Thirty-sixth regiment, company D.

McMahan, G. W., Seventy-seventh regiment, company G, honorably discharged.

Meredith, John, age 30, Seventy-seventh regiment, company G, private.

Meredith, New, volunteer, Ninety-second regiment, company H, private, died April 4, 1865, of scurvy at Nashville, Tennessee.

Miller, John, age 27, volunteer, 1864, three years, Seventy-seventh regiment, company B, private, died October 26, 1864, in Tyler prison, Texas.

Miller, Henry, volunteer, 1864, one year, One Hundred and Sixty-fourth regiment, company D.

Monroe, George Alburn, age 20, volunteer, 1863, six months, Fourth cavalry, company C, private, served seven months, mustered out 1864, second enlistment, age 31, substitute, 1864, one hundred days, One Hundred and Forty-eighth regiment, company F, private, served five months, mustered out 1864.

Morris, James, age 19, volunteer, February, 1864, three years, Seventy-seventh regiment, company B, private, died July 2, 1864, at Tyler, Texas.

Nesselrode, Perley J., volunteer, July 29, 1861, three years, Thirty-sixth regiment, company A, private, served two years and four months died November 25, 1863, at Mission Ridge.

Nesselrode, R. H., July 29, 1861, three years, Thirty-sixth regiment, company A, private, served two years and four months, honorably discharged December 10, 1863, for disability.

Parker, Isaac, Seventy-seventh regiment, company B.

Ogle, Willard, Ninety-second regiment, company H.

Peaker, Joseph, Seventh cavalry, company H.

Peaker, Peter, Seventh cavalry, company H.

Peaker, John, Seventh cavalry, company H.

Peaker, Charles, Sixty-third regiment, company G.

Pierce, J., Sixty-third regiment, company G, killed September 20, 1863.

Perkins, Charles, age 19, July, 1861, three years, Thirty-sixth regiment, company A, private, served three years, mustered out 1864, believed to have been captured.

Perkins, William Burns, age 17, volunteer, 1861, three years, Seventy-seventh regiment, company B, private, killed April 8, 1862.

Reed, Erastus, age 35, volunteer, August, 1861, three years, Ninety-second regiment, company H, served three years, mustered out June 1, 1865.

Roads, William, volunteer, three years, Thirty-sixth regiment, company G.

Rodgers, I. H., Seventy-seventh regiment, company B.

Shafer, John, age 28, volunteer, July 29, 1861, three years, Thirty-sixth regiment, company A, private, served one year and six months, honorably discharged January 4, 1863, shot through both legs above knees at Lewisburgh, Virginia.

Shafer, James R., age 20, volunteer, 1862, three years, Thirty-sixth regiment, company A, private, served two years; veteran enlistment, age 22, volunteer, 1864, three years, Thirty-sixth regiment, company A, private, served one year and six months, mustered out July 27, 1865.

Smith, George W., Ninety-second regiment, company H.

Shafer, Albert D., age 18, July 29, 1861, three years, Thirty-sixth regiment, company A, private, served two and a half years; veteran enlistment, age 20, 1864, three years, private, served one and a half years, mustered out July 27, 1865.

Smith, James W., age 19, volunteer, January 21, 1864, three years, Ninety-second regiment, company H, private.

Smithson, Robert Emmet, age 30, volunteer, 1861, three years, Seventy-seventh regiment, company G, private, veteran enlistment, age 32, volunteer, 1864, three years, Seventy-seventh regiment, companies G and E, private, attained rank of captain, mustered out March 7, 1866.

Smithson, H. N., Seventy-seventh regiment, company B, died 1863.

Smithson, William, age 24, volunteer, 1861, three years, Seventy-seventh regiment, company B.

Smithson, Richard C., age 21, volunteer, August 2, 1862, three years, Ninety-second regiment, company H, sergeant, served three years, mustered out June 10, 1865.

Smith, Horatio Nelson, age 17, volunteer, November 14, 1861, three years, Seventy-seventh regiment, company B, private, served one year, died October 7, 1863.

Still, Chester T., age 24, volunteer, June 10, 1861, three years, Twenty-fifth regiment, company I, private, attained rank of blacksmith, served three years, mustered out in 1864.

Still, John F., age 23, three years, Thirtieth regiment, company K, private, served nine months; second enlistment, volunteer, August 1, 1861, three years, Thirtieth regiment, company K, blacksmith, served two years, mustered out in 1865.

Smith, Jonathan, Ninety-second regiment, company A.

Still, Martin Luther, age 20, volunteer, 1862, Thirty-sixth regiment, company G, private, attained rank of sergeant, served three years, mustered out in January, 1865.

Stone, David, Thirty-sixth regiment, company G.

Taylor, William, volunteer, 1862, three years, Ninety-second regiment, company H.

Tumberlake, Thomas, Twenty-fifth regiment, company I.

Tilton, Benjamin, One Hundred and Sixteenth regiment.

Unger, Andrew, age 23, volunteer, three years, Ninety-second regiment, company H, private, mustered out June 16, 1865.

Unger, Jeremiah, age 21, volunteer, July 29, 1861, three years, Thirty-sixth regiment, company A, private, served two and one-half years; veteran enlistment, age 23, volunteer, 1864 three years, Thirty-sixth regiment, company A, corporal, attained rank of sergeant, served one and a half years, mustered out July 27, 1865, never sick in service.

Vertican, F. W., First cavalry.

Vanfleet, Garrett, Seventy-seventh regiment, company F.

Vaughn, Ira, age 21, substitute, May 2, 1865, one hundred days, One Hundred and Forty-eighth regiment, company F, private, served three months, died August 4, 1864, and buried under another man's name.

Waller, Thomas J., volunteer, 1863, six months, One Hundred and Twenty-ninth regiment, company F, private

Walter, Isaac, Ninety-second regiment, company H.

Walter, Warren Norton, age 39, volunteer, 1861, for three years, Thirty-sixth regiment, company G, private, served three years, mustered out in 1864.

Walter, Jay Clark, age 30, volunteer, August 11, 1861, three years, Ninety-second regiment, company H, blacksmith, served three years, mustered out June 10, 1865.

Walter, Seth Eugene, age 23, volunteer, 1862, three years, Ninety-second regiment, company H, private, served two years, died November 13, 1864.

Ward, Thomas, Fourth cavalry, company C.

Ward, James, age 24, volunteer, 1862, three years, Ninety-second regiment, company H, private, died April 1, 1863.

Ward, Isaac, age 21, volunteer, 1862, three years, Ninety-second regiment, company H, private, attained rank of corporal, served three years, mustered June 10, 1865.

Ward, Stephen, age 21, volunteer, 1861, three years, Seventy-seventh regiment, company B, private, deserted before regiment left Marietta.

Weekly, Thomas, Thirty-sixth regiment, company G

West, William Milton, age 16, volunteer, August 4, 1863, six months, One Hundred and Twenty-ninth regiment, company F, private, mustered out in 1864; second enlistment, age 17, volunteer, September 14, 1864, one year, One Hundred and Seventy-sixth regiment, company G, private, served nine months, mustered out June 19, 1865.

Waters, Zephaniah, Seventy-seventy regiment, company B.

Walford, John, age 24, volunteer, 1861, three years, Seventy-seventh regiment, company B, private, died April 6, 1862, killed at Battle of Shiloh.

Wolford, Isaac, Seventy-seventh regiment, company B.

Woster, Jacob, volunteer, July, 1861, three years, Thirty-sixth regiment, company A, private; veteran enlistment, volunteer, 1864, three years, Thirty-sixth regiment, company A, private.

West, William N., One Hundred and Twenty-ninth regiment, company F.

Yoho, Job, Seventy-seventh regiment, company B.

Zollars, Nathan.

Zollars, Frederick, 1864, one hundred days, One Hundred and Forty-eighth regiment, company A.

RECAPITULATION.

Seventh Ohio cavalry	4
Fourth Ohio cavalry	3
First Ohio cavalry	2
And one each in Fourth Ohio independent battalion cavalry and Ninth Ohio cavalry	2
Seventy-seventh Ohio	37
Thirty-sixth Ohio	30
Ninety-second Ohio	20
One Hundred and Forty-eighth Ohio	4
One Hundred and Twenty-ninth Ohio	4

BARLOW TOWNSHIP.

Alexander, Henry, May, 1864, one hundred days, One Hundred and Forty-eighth regiment, company F, private, served four months, mustered out September 14, 1864.

Austin, Lemuel, age 20, volunteer, April, 1864, Twenty-seventh colored regiment, company I.

Austin, Salathiel, age 17, volunteer, Twenty-seventh colored regiment, company I.

Butler, Charles W., volunteer, Fifth colored regiment; company I, killed.

Butler, Henry, volunteer, Fifth colored regiment, company I.

Breckenridge, Hugh, volunteer, May, 1864, one hundred days, One Hundred and Forty-eighth regiment, company F, private, served four months, mustered out September 14, 1864.

Breckenridge, Andrew, volunteer, May, 1864, one hundred days, One Hundred and Forty-eighth regiment, company F, private, served four months, mustered out September 14, 1864.

Bartlett, James, volunteer, May, 1864, one hundred days, One Hundred and Forty-eighth regiment, company F, private, served four months, mustered out September 14, 1864.

Bartlett, John, age 17, volunteer, November 4, 1861, three years, Seventy-seventh regiment, company D, private, served four years, mustered out July 27, 1865, reenlisted as a veteran, wounded at Shiloh.

Beach, Alfred P., age 19, volunteer, August, 1861, three years, Thirty-sixth regiment, company F, private, attained the rank of corporal, served four years, mustered out July 27, 1865, reenlisted as a veteran, and was wounded at Shenandoah.

Beach, Cydnor T., age 20, volunteer, February 25, 1864, Thirty-sixth regiment, company F, private, served one year and five months, mustered out July 27, 1865.

Ball, James W., age 27, volunteer, May, 1864, one hundred days, One Hundred and Forty-eighth regiment, company F, private, served four months, mustered out September 14, 1864.

Calvert, John P., minister, age 28, volunteer, November 1, 1861, three years, Seventy-seventh regiment, company K, first sergeant, served five months, died April 7, 1862, mortally wounded at Shiloh April 6th.

Clark, John, volunteer, Ninety-second regiment, company G, private.

Chapman, Ezra A., age 32, volunteer, August 8, 1861, three years, Thirty-sixth regiment, company F, private, served three years, mustered out September 3, 1864, detailed for messenger service.

Chapman, Hiel, volunteer, May, 1864, one hundred days, One Hundred and Forty-eighth regiment, company F, corporal, served four months, mustered out September 14, 1864.

Clay, Nicholas, volunteer, Thirty-sixth regiment, company F, private, served two and one-half years, honorably discharged for disability.

Carlin, James P., age 18, volunteer, November 17, 1862, three years, One Hundred and Twenty-fifth regiment, company E, private, served two years, honorably discharged November 17, 1864, wounded at Mission Ridge November 25, 1863, finally discharged for disability.

Conly, Hugh, age 38, volunteer, 1861, three years, Thirty-sixth regiment, company F, private, served three years, mustered out 1864, wounded at Lewisburgh, Virginia.

Coop, Benjamin F., age 28, volunteer, November 4, 1861, three years, Seventy-seventh regiment, company D, private, served two years, died September 8, 1863, from wound received at Shiloh.

Cooksey, Townsend, company C, corporal.

Cunningham, Francis M., age 17, volunteer, September, 1861, three years, Thirty-sixth regiment, company F, private, served five months, died February 24, 1862.

Daniels, Charles W., age 18, volunteer, August 1, 1861, three years, Thirty-sixth regiment, company F, private, served three years, mustered out September, 1864.

Deming, Henry, May, 1864, one hundred days, One Hundred and Forty-eighth regiment, company F, private, served four months, mustered out September 14, 1864.

Dunbar, Warren K., age 20, volunteer, November 30, 1861, three years, Fifty-third regiment, company H, private, served one year, died October 11, 1862, died at Memphis.

Dustin, John, May, 1864, one hundred days, One Hundred and Forty-eighth regiment, company F, sergeant, served four months, mustered out September 14, 1864.

Dunsmoor, Harvey, volunteer, May, 1864, one hundred days, One Hundred and Forty-eighth regiment, company F, private, served four months, mustered out September 14, 1864.

Dunsmore, Perley, volunteer, May, 1864, one hundred days, One Hundred and Forty-eighth regiment, company F, corporal, served four months, mustered out September 14, 1864.

Danley, Joel M., age 24, volunteer, three years, Ninety-second regiment, company G, private, died May 20, 1863, of pneumonia, at Carthage, Tennessee.

Evans, Simeon, age 48, volunteer, August 26, 1861, three years, Thirty-sixth regiment, company F, private, served one year and four months, honorably discharged December 24, 1862, for disability in early service in West Virginia.

Evans, David E., age 25, volunteer, September 27, 1861, three years, Thirty-sixth regiment, company F, private, served two years, honorably discharged September, 1863, for disability, died three weeks after reaching home.

Evans, Charles E., volunteer, May, 1864, one hundred days, One Hundred and Forty-eighth regiment, company F, private, served four months, mustered out September 14, 1864.

Ferguson, H. C., Eighteenth regiment, company K.

Fleming, Robert H., age 18, volunteer, November, 1861, three years, Seventy-seventh regiment, company D, private, attained rank of captain, served four years and four months, mustered out March 8, 1866, wounded at Shiloh, captured at Marks' Mills, and in prison for thirteen months, detailed as clerk for colonel of regiment.

Fleming, James, age 21, volunteer, November, 1861, three years, Seventy-seventh regiment, company D, private, attained rank of orderly sergeant, served five months, died April 6, 1862, killed at Shiloh.

Gates, David, volunteer, May, 1864, one hundred days, One Hundred and Forty-eighth regiment, company F, private, served four months, mustered out September 14, 1864.

Gooding, George, volunteer, May, 1864, one hundred days, One Hundred and Forty-eighth regiment, company F, fifer, discharged, wounded at Harper's Ferry.

Gooding, Harvey, age 16, volunteer, May, 1864, one hundred days, One Hundred and Forty-eighth regiment, company F, private, served four months, mustered out September 14, 1864.

Gooding, Franklin, age 19, volunteer, July 3, 1861, three years, Thirty-ninth regiment, company B, private, served one year, honorably discharged in 1862 for disability.

Green, Dan P., May, 1864, one hundred days, One Hundred and Forty-eighth regiment, company I, private, served four months, mustered out September 14, 1864.

Green, Henry, age 20, volunteer, August, 1861, three years, Thirty-sixth regiment, company F, private, attained rank of corporal, served four years, mustered out July 27, 1865, reenlisted as a veteran.

Greenlees, Andrew, volunteer, May, 1864, one hundred days, One Hundred and Forty-eighth regiment, company F, private, served four months, mustered out September 14, 1864.

Graham, Robert, Ninety-second regiment, company G, private.

Gould, James, age 20, volunteer, November 5, 1861, for three years, Seventy-seventh regiment, company D, private, attained sergeant, reenlisted with the regiment.

Haddow, James, age 34, volunteer, August 1, 1861, for three years, Thirty-sixth regiment, company F, first sergeant, attained captain, served four years, mustered out July 27, 1865, in all active service of the regiment, wounded at Kerntown July 24, 1864, and reenlisted as a veteran.

Harvey, David, aged 22, volunteer, October 28, 1861, for three years, Seventy-seventh regiment, company D, first sergeant, served one year and two months, died January 28, 1863; discharged for disability, died at Barlow April 24, 1863.

Harvey, Robert, aged 19, volunteer, August 1, 1861, for three years, Thirty-sixth regiment, company F, private, attained first sergeant, served three years, died May 29, 1864, killed at Cloyd's Mountain, Virginia, and buried near the field by his comrades.

Harvey, Andrew, volunteer, May, 1864, for one hundred days, One Hundred and Forty-eighth regiment, company F, private, mustered out September 14, 1864.

Harvey, Samuel W., aged 21, volunteer, August, 1861, for three years, Thirty-sixth regiment, company F, private, attained rank of first lieutenant, served four years, mustered out July 27, 1865, reenlisted as a veteran, wounded at Lewisburgh in 1862, and at Opequan in 1864.

Harvey, William, aged 16, volunteer, September, 1861, for three years, Thirty-sixth regiment, company F, private, served three years, honorably discharged October 5, 1864; sick three months, wounded and taken at Chickamauga September 12, 1863, paroled after twelve days, exchanged May 23, 1864, in hospital nine months.

Harvey, S. Fletcher, volunteer, May, 1864, for one hundred days, One Hundred and Forty-eighth regiment, company F, private, discharged September 25, 1864, reenlisted as a veteran, detailed for picket and post duty.

Henry, Julius, May, 1864, for one hundred days, One Hundred and Forty-eighth regiment, company F.

Hill, George W., aged 23, volunteer, October, 1862, for nine months. Sixty-second regiment, company I, private, honorably discharged November, 1862; slightly wounded when charging a bayonet

Hoffman, Samuel H., aged 18, volunteer, September 27, 1861, for three years, Thirty-sixth regiment, company F, private, served three years, mustered out October 26, 1864, served as mounted orderly with General Turchin for nine months.

Hoffman, John W., aged 19, volunteer, April 22, 1861, for three months, Eighteenth regiment, company K, private, attained first sergeant, served two years, died April 27, 1863, reenlisted, was sick but joined before recovering, died at Nashville, Tennessee, of typhoid fever.

Hoffman, David S., aged 22, volunteer, August 6, 1861, for three years, Thirty-sixth regiment, company F, private, served three, mustered out September 7, 1864. He was detailed often as regimental carpenter, recruiting service, as commissary sergeant and as clerk of commissary of subsistence.

Hoffman, Richard A., aged 17, volunteer, August 1, 1861, for three years, Thirty-sixth regiment, company F, clerk, attained quartermaster sergeant, served three years and nine months, discharged May 8, 1865, while out on duty taken by enemy June, 1864, while being taken to Andersonville jumped from train, and reached our lines July 20th, afterward served as citizen's clerk in quartermaster department in Sherman's army

Hoffman, William W., volunteer, May, 1864, for one hundred days, One Hundred and Forty-eighth regiment, company F, sergeant, died August 16, 1864.

Hoffman, Francis A., volunteer, May, 1864, for one hundred days, One Hundred and Forty-eighth regiment, company F, private, mustered out September 14, 1864, served on detail duty as orderly, on mail boat from Fort Monroe to Bermuda, Kansas.

Hoisington, George, aged 30, volunteer, August 1, 1861, for three years, Thirty-sixth regiment, company F, private, served three years, discharged August 28, 1864, was in all the chief engagements of his regiment, wounded at Mission Ridge in ankle, six months in hospital.

Jones, John, jr., aged 39, volunteer, October 14, 1861, for three years, First light artillery, company H, served one year and five months, died May 29, 1863; was struck by three balls at Chancellorsville May 2, 1863, taken by rebels and exchanged, and died of amputation of leg.

Jones, Jacob, volunteer, May, 1864, for one hundred days One Hundred and Forty-eighth regiment, company F, private.

Kinkhead, George W., aged 18, volunteer, October 14, 1862, for three years, Seventy-seventh regiment, company K, private, three years, captured at Mark's Mills April 25, 1864, was held with regiment for ten months, after furlough of thirty days rejoined regiment

Kinkhead, Isaac B., aged 25, volunteer, October 8, 1861, for three years, Seventy-seventh regiment, company K, orderly sergeant, attained lieutenant colonel, mustered out May 14, 1862, at Shiloh was appointed captain in place of Captain Chandler, supposed to be dead, on his return he was mustered out and put on detached service till June 17, 1863.

Kinkhead, David N., aged 24, volunteer, February, 1864, Seventy-seventh regiment, company D, private, served nine months, died November, 1864, taken prisoner at Mark's Mills but escaped, reported killed on a foraging expedition in Arkansas.

Kinkhead, John P., aged 21, volunteer, July 7, 1863. Second heavy artillery, company K, artificer.

Lamb, William A., aged 47, volunteer, September, 1864, for one year, Sixth Virginia infantry, company D, private, served nine months; honorably discharged June 10, 1865; served on post duty among the guerillas in West Virginia.

Lamb, Leonidas G., aged 22, volunteered February 13, 1865, One Hundred and Eighty-sixth regiment, company G, served seven months, discharged September 25, 1865, on post duty at Bermuda Hundred, Virginia.

Lamb, William F., May, 1864, for one hundred days, One Hundred and Forty-eighth regiment, company F, died July 31, 1864.

Lawton, Ezra J., aged 21, volunteer, August 1, 1861, for three years, Thirty-sixth regiment, company F, private, attained first sergeant, served nine months, died April 19, 1862, was promised a commission as lieutenant, but attacked by pneumonia and died at Summersville.

Lawton, Richard G., volunteer, May, 1864, for one hundred days, One Hundred and Forty-eighth regiment, company F, wardmaster, served four months, mustered out September 14, 1864

Lawton, Arthur, aged 35, volunteer, August, 1861, for three years, Thirty-sixth regiment, company F, private, hospital nurse, served three years, honorably discharged September, 1864; discharged for disability incurred by camp disease.

Lawton, Isaiah B., aged 24, volunteer, August, 1862, for three years, Ninety-second regiment, company G, private, attained surgeon's clerk, served two years and six months, honorably discharged February 27, 1864; discharged at Chattanooga for disability.

Love, Charles W., age 20, volunteer, August 1, 1861, three years, Thirty-sixth regiment, company F, private, served three years, discharged September, 1864.

Lewis, William H., age 28, volunteer, August 8, 1864, Twenty-seventh regiment, United States colored infantry, company K, private, served one year, discharged September 7, 1865

Lockmiller, James, volunteer, October 14, 1861, three years, First light artillery, company H, died of camp fever

Lewis, Charles, age 26, volunteer, August 10, 1864, Twenty-seventh regiment, United States colored infantry, company D, private, served one year and four months, died December 13, 1865.

Lukins, Eli B., age 34, volunteer, January, 1864, Eighteenth regiment, colored infantry, company B, private, served four years and six months, discharged July 1, 1865.

Male, Aaron, age 25, volunteer, August 11, 1864, Fifth regiment, company F, private, died in 1865, at Columbus, Ohio.

McMain, James L., age 18, volunteer, February 27, 1864, Thirty-sixth regiment, company F, private, discharged March 17, 1865, in hospital most of the time, never in active service, discharged for disability.

McGathy, William H., volunteer, One Hundred and Twenty-fifth regiment, company E, private, wounded at Chattanooga.

Morris, Benajah, age 25, volunteer, August 13, 1862, three years, Ninety-second regiment, company G, private, served two years and nine months, discharged May 12, 1865

Miller, Stephen O., age 13, volunteer, three months, Thirteenth regiment, private, captured at Harper's Ferry and paroled.

Morrow, Joseph William, age 27, volunteer, February 4, 1862, Sixty-third regiment, company H, private, discharged October 4, 1863, as disabled.

Miller, William K., age 21, volunteer, July 21, 1861, three years, Thirty-ninth regiment, company B, private, attained the rank of corporal, served four years, discharged July 9, 1865.

Miller, Josiah, age 26, volunteer, March, 1864, Thirty-sixth regiment, company F, served one year, discharged July 28, 1865

Miller, Hiram H., age 15, volunteer, November, 1861, three years, First artillery, company H, private, attained the rank of fife major, reenlisted in 1862

Miller, Isaac, age 49, volunteer, November, 1861, three years, First artillery, company H, private, served nine months, died September 1, 1863

Morris, George M., volunteer, May, 1864, one hundred days, One Hundred and Forty-eighth regiment, company F, private, honorably discharged, was sick at Bermuda with brain fever and paralysis and brought home.

Morris, Joseph P., May, 1864, one hundred days, One Hundred and Forty-eighth regiment, company F, private.

Morris, John W., age 18, volunteer, October 23, 1861, three years, Seventy-seventh regiment, company D, private, served one year and five months, honorably discharged March 12, 1863, for disability, was wounded at Shiloh, April 6, 1862, died July 1, 1864, at Camden, Arkansas.

Moore, Frank A., volunteer, February 15, 1865, Thirty-sixth regiment, company F, private, served five months, mustered out July 27, 1865.

Morris, William H., age 23, volunteer, August 1, 1861, three years, Thirty-sixth regiment, company F, private, attained the rank of first sergeant, served four years, mustered out July 27, 1865, in active service throughout the period, reenlisted as a veteran

McClure, Thomas J., age 24, volunteer, 1861, three months, Second regiment, private, served three months, on guard duty.

McCarty, Thomas, age 29, volunteer, August, 1862, three years Ninety-second regiment, company G, private, served nine months, died June 1, 1863.

Merrill, James W., age 30, volunteer, July 28, 1862, three years, Ninety-second regiment, company G, first lieutenant, attained the rank of captain, served one year and ten months, honorably discharged May 24, 1864, on account of wounds received in the service, wounded and taken prisoner at Chickamauga, September 20, 1863, paroled and exchanged September 29th, and made captain.

Murchy, John, Ninety-second regiment, company G, died January, 1862, of pneumonia, at Nashville.

McKibben, William A., volunteer, May, 1864, one hundred days, One Hundred and Forty-eighth regiment, company B, orderly, discharged.

Norris, Adam, age 23, volunteer, August 20, 1864, one year, One Hundredth regiment, United States colored infantry, private, served one year, discharged September 15, 1865, first served on commissary and hospital duty, afterwards on the field.

Ormiston, Alexander, volunteer, October 12, 1861, three years, Sixty-third regiment, company G, corporal, served four years, discharged July, 1865

Ormiston, Isaac A., volunteer, May, 1864, one hundred days, One Hundred and Forty-eighth regiment, company F, private, served four months, mustered out September 14, 1864.

Ormiston, James F., volunteer, May, 1864, one hundred days, One Hundred and Forty-eighth regiment, company F, private, served four months, mustered out September 14, 1864.

Parsons, William, age 33, volunteer, August 1, 1864, three years, Twenty-seventh regiment, United States colored infantry, company B, corporal, served one year, discharged September 7, 1865

Payne, Darius, age 18, volunteer, April 23, 1861, three months, Eighteenth regiment, company K, sergeant, attained the rank of first sergeant, served four years, discharged October 18, 1865, reenlisted in September, 1862, in company C, One Hundred and Twenty-fifth regiment, Ohio volunteer infantry, as sergeant, was wounded twice.

Preston, Daniel L., age 21, volunteer, August 1, 1861, three years, Thirty-sixth regiment, company F, private, served three years, discharged September 5, 1864, wounded twice.

Palmer, I. F., volunteer, May, 1864, one hundred days, One Hundred and Forty-eighth regiment, company F, private, served four months, discharged September 14, 1864.

Phillips, Thomas G., age 29, volunteer, August 15, 1861, three years, Eighteenth regiment, company F, private, honorably discharged July 18, 1862, for physical disability, reenlisted August 19, 1864, one year, One Hundred and Eighty-second regiment, company C, corporal, attained the rank of sergeant, discharged July 7, 1865

Pond, L. P., volunteer, May, 1864, One hundred and forty-eighth regiment, company F, first lieutenant, served four months, mustered out September 14, 1864, sick, sent to Fort Dennison, then transferred to veteran corps.

Proctor, Joseph H., age 23, volunteer, August 15, 1862, three years, Ninety-second regiment, company G, private, served three years, discharged July, 1865.

Rigg, John C., Thirty-sixth regiment, company A, private.

Pugh, J. L., volunteer, May, 1864, one hundred days, One hundred and forty-eighth regiment, company F, served four months, discharged September 14, 1864.

Rogers, S. H., Thirty-sixth regiment, company F, private.

Richards, Henry S., age 20, volunteer, November 5, 1861, three years, Seventy-seventh regiment, company D, private, attained the rank of sergeant, reenlisted as a veteran.

Robinson, Joseph, Sixty-third regiment, company F, private, died July 20, 1863, chronic diarrhœa.

Richards, Luman D., age 19, volunteer, February 15, 1864, Seventy-seventh regiment, company D, private.

Robinson, Benjamin, volunteer, October, 1861, three years, Thirty-sixth regiment, company F, private, honorably discharged May 23, 1863, wounded and captured at Chickamauga, paroled and exchanged in May, 1864, wounded and captured at Winchester, July 24th, paroled and exchanged, discharged.

Saylor, Solomon, age 18, volunteer, September 13, 1861, three years, Thirty-sixth regiment, company F, private, served three years, discharged October 23, 1864.

Saylor, Edward, three years, Thirty-sixth regiment, company F, private, mustered out July 27, 1865, never wounded, but in all the engagements with his regiment.

Saylor, Jacob, age 16, volunteer, November 30, 1861, three years,

Fifty-third regiment, company H, private, served four years, mustered out August 16, 1865.

Smith, David, volunteer, 1861, three years, Seventh cavalry, company H, private, served three years, died July 8, 1864, captured at Chickamauga, September 20, 1863, and taken to Andersonville prison, where he died.

Scott, Henry, volunteer, Fifth cavalry, company I, corporal, died April 7, 1865, died in hospital in North Carolina.

Tiffany, Alfonzo, volunteer, August, 1861, three years, Thirty-sixth regiment, company F, second lieutenant, attained the rank of first lieutenant, served two years, resigned 1863.

Turner, George B., volunteer, May, 1864, one hundred days, One Hundred and Forty-eighth regiment, company F, captain, served four months, discharged September 14, 1864, discharged at close of term, reenlisted in company F, Thirty-sixth Ohio volunteer infantry, and served till mustered out with regiment.

Turner, Duncan, volunteer, May, 1864, one hundred days, One Hundred and Forty-eighth regiment, company F, private, served four months, mustered out September 14, 1864

Turner, David, volunteer, 1863, nine months, First Virginia cavalry, private, served nine months, discharged 1864.

Tompkins, A. W., volunteer, May, 1864, one hundred days, One Hundred and Forty-eighth regiment, company F, private, served four months, mustered out September 14, 1864.

Vincent, Cyrus E., age 18, volunteer, June 15, 1863, One Hundred and Twenty-ninth regiment, company A, private, died October 29, 1863, died of lung fever at Cumberland Gap, Maryland.

Tuttle, James, volunteer, May, 1864, one hundred days, One Hundred and Forty-eighth regiment, company F, private, served four months, mustered out September 14, 1864

Vanvaley, John W., age 18, volunteer, March 18, 1865, Eighteenth regiment, company I, private, detailed on post duty.

Vincent, Anselem, age 30, volunteer, August, 1861, three years, Thirty-sixth regiment, company F, private, discharged January 14, 1863, discharged on account of disability, enlisted again in 1864 and served till discharged with regiment.

Vincent, John C., age 20, volunteer, May, 1864, one hundred days, One Hundred and Forty-eighth regiment, company F, first sergeant, served four months, discharged September 14, 1864.

Vanvaley, Joseph S., volunteer, May, 1864, one hundred days, One Hundred and Forty-eighth regiment, company F, corporal, served four months, discharged September 14, 1864.

Vincent, O. B., volunteer, May, 1864, one hundred days, One Hundred and Forty-eighth regiment, company F, private, served four months, discharged September 14, 1864, detailed for telegraph service.

Young, John R., age 25, volunteer, October 11, 1862, three years, Seventy-seventh regiment, company H, sergeant, served three years, discharged October 14, 1865, wounded and captured at Marks' Mills, April 25, 1864, paroled, exchanged, and after six months' disablement resumed duty.

Young, George, volunteer, Seventy-seventh regiment, company H.

Wilson, Alexander, Sixty-third regiment, company G.

Wilson, Martin, Sixty-third regiment, company G.

RECAPITULATION.

Huntington's battery	5
Battery K, Second Huntington artillery	1
One each in Fourth Virginia cavalry, Seventh Ohio, and Thirteenth Ohio	3
One Hundred and Forty-eighth Ohio National Guard	38
Thirty-sixth Ohio	33
Seventy-seventh Ohio	15
Ninety-second Ohio	9
Sixty-third Ohio	5
Fifth colored infantry	5
Eighteenth Ohio (three years)	3
Eighteenth Ohio (three months)	3
Twenty-seventh United States colored infantry	5
Thirty-ninth Ohio	2
One Hundred and Twenty-fifth Ohio	2
Fifty-third Ohio	2
One each in Second Ohio infantry, Twelfth Ohio, Sixth Virginia infantry, Sixty-second Ohio, One Hundredth United States colored infantry, One Hundred and Twenty-ninth Ohio, One Hundred and Eighty-second Ohio, One Hundred and Eighty-sixth Ohio, in all	8
Total number soldiers	137
Died	21

BELPRE TOWNSHIP.

Allen, Davis C., volunteer, 1862, three years, Ninety-second regiment, company G, sergeant, in battles of Chattanooga, Mission Ridge, and Lookout Mountain.

Allen, Harvey G., volunteer, May, 1864, one hundred days, One Hundred and Forty-eighth regiment, company H, private, served four months, discharged, September 14, 1864.

Allen, Loring P.

Barkley, Samuel W., age 18, volunteer, January, 1862, Seventy-third regiment, company F, corporal, served two years, died May 22, 1864, fought at Chancellorsville, Gettysburgh, Lookout Valley, and Resaca, where he was mortally wounded May 15th.

Barrows, James K., volunteer, discharged.

Armstrong, Alexander H., age 22, volunteer, September 26, 1861, One Hundred and Eighty-third regiment, company D, second lieutenant, died May 8, 1865, from exposure while in camp.

Batten, Lewis M., volunteer, May, 1864, one hundred days, One Hundred and Forty-eighth regiment, company H, private, served four months, discharged September 14, 1864.

Barcus, James M., volunteer, May, 1864, one hundred days, One Hundred and Forty-eighth regiment, company H, private, served four months, discharged September 14, 1864.

Berry, William, First light artillery, company H.

Bellows, Benjamin T., volunteer, private, honorably discharged May 31, 1865.

Bellows, Orrin M., age 22, volunteer, August, 1862, three years, Ninety-second regiment, company G, private, served six months, died February 26, 1863, of brain fever.

Bellows, Abram M., age 16, volunteer, February 22, 1865, Ninety-first regiment, company B, private.

Bodkin, William Wallace, age 17, volunteer, October 30, 1861, Seventy-third regiment, company F, private, discharged May 30, 1864, wounded at Gettysburgh very severely, and reenlisted as a veteran in 1865.

Bodkins, Charles, age 43, volunteer, August 15, 1862, Seventh cavalry regiment, company I, private, served one year and eight months, died April 7, 1864, captured at Rogersville, Tennessee, taken to Belle Isle, removed sick to hospital at Richmond where he died.

Breckenridge, D. M., volunteer, May 18, 1864, one hundred days, One hundred and Forty-eighth regiment, company H, private, attained rank of adjutant's clerk, served four months, discharged September 14, 1864.

Breckenridge, Charles D., volunteer, May 18, 1864, one hundred days, One Hundred and Forty-eighth regiment, company H, private, served four months, discharged September 14, 1864, disabled and not on duty, but reenlisted with One Hundred and Seventy-ninth regiment, company H, September 28, 1864, and was discharged with regiment.

Blow, John H., volunteer, Ninety-second regiment, private, attained rank of corporal, discharged January 28, 1865.

Blough, Rufus, volunteer, one hundred days, One Hundred and Forty-eighth regiment, company H, private, died July 7, 1864, of camp disease and measles.

Berry, James B., age 38, volunteer, 1864, one hundred days, One Hundred and Forty-eighth regiment, company H, private, discharged September 14, 1864.

Bellows, Avery S., age 24, volunteer, August 9, 1862, three years, Ninety-second regiment, company G, private, served one year and four months, discharged December 19, 1863, sick for ten months, discharged for disability.

Brown, John A., age 29, volunteer, May, 1864, one hundred days, One Hundred and Forty-eighth regiment, company H, orderly sergeant, served four months, discharged September 14, 1864.

Cox, Jefferson, Seventh cavalry, company I.

Campbell, Charles H., age 40, volunteer, May 16, 1864, one hundred days, One Hundred and Forty-eighth regiment, company H, corporal, served four months, discharged September 14, 1864.

Campbell, Theodore W., age 20, volunteer, May 18, 1864, one hundred days, One Hundred and Forty-eighth regiment, company H, private, four months, discharged September 14, 1864.

Clark, John, age 23, volunteer, three years, Seventy-third regiment, company F, private, died August, 1862, from a gunshot wound received at the battle of Bull Run.

Campbell, Currun, volunteer, August 4, 1862, private, injured by accident June 9, 1863, remained in hospital till August 14th.

Chick, John C., One Hundred and Sixteenth regiment, company I.

Clark, John J., age 31, volunteer, August, 1862, three years, Ninety-second regiment, company G, private, three years, discharged June 29,

1865, in March, 1864, was transferred to company H, veteran reserve corps, wounded at Fort Stephens, District Columbia, July 12, 1864.

Clark, Jacob, Seventy-third regiment, company F, killed in action at Cross Keys.

Cole, William R., age 19, volunteer, July 27, 1861, three years, Thirty-ninth regiment, company K, private, served one year, discharged October 14, 1862, for disability.

Coleman, Alfred, Thirty-ninth regiment, company K.

Curtis, Henry C., volunteer, May 18, 1864, one hundred days, One Hundred and Forty-eighth regiment, company H, private.

Curtis, Columbus B., age 30, volunteer, May 18, 1864, one hundred days, One Hundred and Forty-eighth regiment, company H, sergeant, four months, discharged September 14, 1864.

Curtis, A. S., age 34, volunteer, May 18, 1864, one hundred days, One Hundred and Forty-eighth regiment, company H, first lieutenant, four months, discharged September 18, 1864.

Dalzell, James, age 24, August 4, 1862, three years, Ninety-second regiment, company G, private, served three years, captured at Carthage, Tennessee, March 8, 1863, taken to Libby prison, parolled and exchanged in June, and discharged with regiment June, 1865.

Davis, J. T., age 18, volunteer, May 18, 1864, for one hundred days, One Hundred and Forty-eighth regiment, company H, private, served four months, discharged September 14, 1864, sick most of the time and out, returned and was discharged with his company.

Davidson, Eh, age 34, volunteer, May 18, 1864, served one hundred days, One Hundred and Forty-eighth regiment, company H, corporal, died 1865, taken sick at City Point, remained in hospital till two weeks after the regiment's discharge, and returned home.

Deeble, Charles H., age 17, volunteer, March 4, 1864, Seventy-third regiment, company F, musician, attained the rank of orderly, served one year and four months, discharged July 20, 1865, was in all the battles of his regiment after his enlistment, and discharged with it.

Deeble, Joseph, age 42, volunteer, May 18, 1862, one hundred days, One Hundred and Forty-eighth regiment, company H, wagon-master, served four months, discharged September 14, 1864, died October 8, 1864.

Dexter, John L., age 27, volunteer, August 2, 1861, Thirty-ninth regiment, company K, private, served three years and two months, discharged July, 1865, neither sick, wounded or captured during service.

Dexter, Francis, age 25, volunteer, May 18, 1862, One Hundred and Forty-eighth regiment, company H, private, discharged August, 1864, sick but not wounded or captured during service.

Dustin, Charles E., age 49, volunteer, 1862, Seventy-third regiment, company D, private, served three weeks, died 1862, killed at Bull Run three weeks after enlistment, had previously served in the Florida war.

Eskey, Samuel S., age 31, volunteer, May 18, 1864, one hundred days, One Hundred and Forty-eighth regiment, company H, private, served four months, died September, 1864

Fletcher, Amasa S., age 19, volunteer, August, 1862, Ninety-second regiment, company G, private, served two years and nine months, discharged May 19, 1865, wounded at Atlanta, Georgia, and disabled for several months.

Flowers, Counree O., age 24, volunteer, August 25, 1862, three years, Seventh cavalry, company I, attained the rank of orderly, served three years, mustered out July 4, 1865

Fish, David, Seventy-third regiment, company F, died 1862.

Flowers, George, age 25, volunteer, March 7, 1865, One Hundred and Ninety-sixth regiment, company F, private, discharged March 13, 1865, sick and discharged from hospital.

Fletcher, John V., age 19, volunteer, August, 1861, Thirty-ninth regiment, company B, private, honorably discharged, discharged at close of term and reenlisted in the Thirty-ninth Ohio volunteer infantry.

Forbes, Leander, Seventh cavalry, company H, died March 5, 1863.

Fletcher, Henry H., age 15, volunteer, September, 1861, Ninth Virginia regiment, company D, adjutant, attained the rank of orderly, honorably discharged, discharged at close of term and reenlisted in the Fourth Ohio volunteer infantry.

Frost, Charles, Ninth Virginia regiment, company K.

Foster, William, age 24, volunteer, 1862, three years, Seventy-fifth regiment, company D, private, discharged December, 1864.

Frazer, Amos, Seventy-fifth regiment, company D.

Gilchrist, Daniel N., age 19, volunteer, May, 1864, one hundred days, One Hundred and Forty-eighth regiment, company H, private, served four months, discharged September, 1864.

Gilchrist, James H., age 20, volunteer, August 2, 1862, One Hundred and Sixteenth regiment, company I, private.

Galbraith, John, age 18, volunteer, November 7, 1862, Seventy-third

34

regiment, company D, private, served two years and eight months, discharged July 26, 1865.

Galbraith, Archibald, age 21, volunteer, November, 1861, Eleventh Virginia regiment, company D, private, served seven months, discharged June, 1862, after his discharge reenlisted in company K, Second Ohio heavy artillery.

Galbraith, James, age 20, volunteer, August, 1862, Ninety-second regiment, company G, private, served three years, discharged 1865, captured at Chickamauga September 20, 1863, imprisoned in Belle Isle, Libby, Andersonville, Danville, Charleston and Florence prisons, exchanged March 4, 1865, sick for seven weeks, then sent home and discharged.

Green, James M., age 23, volunteer, August, 1861, Thirty-ninth regiment, company K, corporal, attained the rank of sergeant, discharged, sick first with typhoid fever and camp disease, and then in active service, discharged and reenlisted as a veteran September 28, 1864, in company H, One Hundred and Seventy-ninth regiment, and discharged with company June 17, 1865.

Green, Andrew J.

Hall, John D., age 29, volunteer, May, 1864, one hundred days, One Hundred and Forty-eighth regiment, company H, private, died 1864, taken with measles and died a few weeks after enlistment.

Hall, James, age 20, volunteer, May, 1864, one hundred days, One Hundred and Forty-eighth regiment, company H, private, died 1864, died in hospital at Bermuda Hundred.

Hall, Jeremiah, age 22, volunteer, May, 1864, one hundred days, One Hundred and Forty-eighth regiment, company H, private, died 1864, died of measles in hospital at Point of Rocks.

Haze, Truman, volunteer, May, 1864, one hundred days, One Hundred and Forty-eighth regiment, company H, private, died 1864, taken sick at City Point and died in hospital at Washington after discharge of regiment.

Hitchcock, Myson K., volunteer, 1862, One Hundred and Sixteenth regiment, company B, corporal, attained the rank of chief of orderly, died May 22, 1865, mortally wounded at Petersburgh.

Hutchinson, John, Ninety-second regiment, company G.

Hunter, George, age 41, volunteer, May, 1864, one hundred days, One Hundred and Forty-eighth regiment, company H, private, died July 1, 1864, taken sick and left in hospital partially recovering, rejoined his regiment, again taken sick and died.

Horton, D. B., Third Iowa cavalry, company I.

Henderson, Warren, age 59, volunteer, May, 1864, one hundred days, One Hundred and Forty-eighth regiment, company H, private, died August 27, 1864, taken sick at City Point and died in hospital at Fortress Monroe.

Johnston, Valentine E., age 46, volunteer, November 7, 1862, three years, Seventy-third regiment, company F, private, discharged May 18, 1865, became disabled by rheumatism and blindness in October, 1864, discharged for disability.

Johnston, Joseph W., age 20, volunteer, November 11, 1861, Seventy-third regiment, company F, private, attained the rank of color corporal, mustered out July 20, 1865, wounded twice.

Johnston, James P., age 23, volunteer, August 8, 1862, three years, Seventy-third regiment, company F, private, served three years, mustered out January 20, 1865.

Kirkpatrick, Henry, age 19, volunteer, three years, Seventy-third regiment, company F, private, attained the rank of corporal, died August 27, 1863.

Kirkpatrick, T. M., age 20, volunteer, three years, Seventy-third regiment, company F, private, died September 5, 1862, of wounds at Alexandria, Virginia.

Kirkpatrick, C. B., volunteer, three years, Seventy-third regiment, company F, sergeant, discharged in 1862 for disability.

Lockwood, Hugh, age 22, volunteer, February, 1865, Fifth Kentucky cavalry, private, honorably discharged May, 1865, for disability.

Loring, Franklin, volunteer, July, 1862, three years, Ninety-second regiment, company G, captain, served three years, mustered out July 10, 1865.

Loring, Corwin, age 21, volunteer, May, 1864, one hundred days, One Hundred and Forty-eighth regiment, company H, private, served four months, mustered out September 14, 1864.

Loring, Corwin H., Forty-seventh Iowa regiment, private, died in 1863 at Helena, Arkansas.

Lyle, George, volunteer, Seventy-third regiment, company F, private.

McCullough, H., Thirty-ninth regiment, company K.

McFarland, S. R. W., age 22, volunteer, August 29, 1862, three years, Seventh cavalry, company H, private, attained the rank of cor-

poral, served three years, mustered out July, 1865, wounded near Pulaski, Tennessee.

Menzie, Rufus C., age 43, volunteer, August, 1862, three years, Ninety-second regiment, company G, private, served two years and ten months, mustered out June 10, 1865.

Mitstead, Isaac, Second Virginia regiment, company K.

Mitchell, John, Seventy-third regiment, company F.

Mosel, James, Ninety-second regiment, company G.

Moore, Amstead, Seventy-fifth regiment, company I.

Newport, J. Ross, volunteer, September 1, 1862, three years, Seventh cavalry, company H, sergeant, served one year and three months, died December 11, 1863, mortally wounded at Morristown, December 10th.

Noland, George W., age 29, volunteer, May, 1864, One Hundred and Twenty-second regiment, company B, private, served ten months, mustered out July 30, 1865.

O'Neil, Ezra H., age 21, volunteer, November 18, 1861, three years, Seventy-third regiment, company F, private, attained the rank of orderly sergeant, served two years and three months, honorably discharged February, 1864, severely wounded at Gettysburgh.

Powell, Jesse, age 20, volunteer, August, 1864, had been a slave, enlisted in a colored regiment in Columbus.

Plumley, William, age 33, drafted, died in 1863 before he got in a regiment.

Plumley, J.

Reid, James, volunteer, January, 1864, Seventy-third regiment, company F, private, served one year and five months, honorably discharged June, 1865, for disability.

Rutherford, Jacob, age 28, volunteer, navy, ensign, resigned June 20, 1865.

Rutherford, Josiah S., age 23, volunteer, September 25 1862, three years, Seventh cavalry, company H, private, served two years and ten months, mustered out July, 1865.

Robinson, William, age 20, volunteer, May, 1864, one hundred days, One Hundred and Forty-eighth regiment, company H, private, served four months, mustered out September 14, 1864, reenlistment, February, 1865, Thirty-sixth regiment, company H, private, served six months, mustered out July 27, 1865.

Shipe, Isaac N., volunteer, December 31, 1861, three years, Seventy-third regiment, company F, private, served three years, mustered out in 1864, reenlistment, volunteer, 1864, three years, Seventy-third regiment, company F, private, served seven months, mustered out July 20, 1865, wounded at Cross Keys, December 9, 1864, captured and in prison for three months at Florence, South Carolina, paroled March, 1865.

Shipe, John A., volunteer, three years, Seventy-third regiment, company F, private, wounded at Bull Run, fell back, and never since seen or heard from.

Stone, George G., age 20, volunteer, three years, Seventy-third regiment, company F, died July 25, 1863, of softening of the brain.

Stone, Edward D., age 22, volunteer, August 10, 1861, three years, Thirty-ninth regiment, company K, private, attained rank of orderly sergeant, served four years, mustered out July 9, 1865.

Stone, Charles W., age 22, volunteer, three years, Seventy-third regiment, company F, attained rank of second lieutenant, resigned July 5, 1864.

Stone, John M., age 22, volunteer, June, 1861, three years, Thirty-ninth regiment, company K, corporal, attained rank of quartermaster clerk, served three years, mustered out in 1864.

Stone, Bradley P., age 21, volunteer, August, 1862, three years, Ninety-second regiment, company G, sergeant, attained rank of captain, served three years, mustered out June 10, 1865.

Stone, Bolivar S., age 38, volunteer, May, 1864, one hundred days, One Hundred and Forty-eighth regiment, company H, private, died July 17, 1864.

Stone, Augustus D., age 28, volunteer, May, 1864, one hundred days, One Hundred and Forty-eighth regiment, company H, private, mustered out September 14, 1864.

Stone, Franklin, age 26, volunteer, May, 1864, one hundred days, One Hundred and Forty-eighth regiment, company H, private.

Stoneman, Philip, age 19, volunteer, August 2, 1861, three years, Thirty-ninth regiment, company K, private, served three years, died July 22, 1864, killed at Atlanta.

Stoneman, William.

Shram, Henry, age 21, volunteer, 1861, three years, artillery, died July 4, 1863.

Stage, Andrew, Seventh cavalry, company H.

Starling, Marion, age 16, volunteer, March, 1864, One Hundred and Sixteenth regiment, company I, private.

Shaw, Jacob H., age 20, volunteer, August, 1862, three years, Ninety-second regiment, company G, corporal, attained rank of orderly sergeant, served three years, mustered out June 10, 1865, and wounded at Mission Ridge November 25, 1864.

Sweezy, Francis M., age 17, volunteer, November 7, 1862, three years, Seventy-third regiment, company H, private, attained rank of corporal, served two and two-thirds years, mustered out July, 1865, captured at Gettysburgh August 21, 1863, taken to Belle Isle, and parolled.

Sweezy, John L., age 17, volunteer, May, 1864, one hundred days, One Hundred and Forty-eighth regiment, company H, private, four months, mustered out September 14, 1864, second enlistment, February 9, 1865, Sixth Virginia regiment, private, mustered out June 10, 1865.

Shire, William, Seventy-fifth regiment, company I.

Swan, Samuel B., age 19, volunteer, August 4, 1862, Ninety-second regiment, company G, private, attained corporal, served three years, discharged June 19, 1865.

Swan, David R., age 19, volunteer, February, 1865, One Hundred and Ninety-first regiment, company B, private.

Sloter, Michael F., age 30, volunteer, August 11, 1862, three years, Ninety-second regiment, company G, private, served three years, discharged June 10, 1865, was sick and detailed as nurse in hospital, never in action.

Schoonover, Augustus D, volunteer, September 12, 1862, three years, Seventh cavalry, company I, private, served three years, mustered out July 4, 1865.

Schoonover, Walter H., age 23, volunteer, September 12, 1862, three years, Seventh cavalry, company I, corporal, served three years, mustered out July 4, 1865.

Schoonover, Jacob F., age 20, volunteer, February 22, 1865, One Hundred and Ninety-first regiment, company B, private, attained sergeant.

Shotwell, Isaac, volunteer, May, 1864, one hundred days, One Hundred and Forty-eighth regiment, company H, private, served four months, discharged September, 1864, sick in hospital at return of regiment.

Shotwell, Ezra M., age 19, volunteer, May, 1864, one hundred days, One Hundred and Forty-first regiment, company A, private, served four months, discharged September, 1864.

Smith, Arnold, volunteer, Eleventh Virginia regiment, company A, drum major, attained color-bearer.

Smith, S. C. H., Seventh cavalry, company H.

Starr, George W., age 22, volunteer, September 14, 1862, three years, Third Virginia cavalry, company E, private, attained first lieutenant, served three years, mustered out June 30, 1865, detached on various duties.

Stoneman, William, age 16, volunteer, August 2, 1861, three years, Thirty-ninth regiment, comyany K, private, killed at Stricker's Gap,

Teeters, George W., Ninety-second regiment, company G.

Travis, Ezra, age 18, volunteer, August 15, 1861, three years, Seventy-third regiment, company F, private, captured at Atlanta, imprisoned in Andersonville, and at Jackson, Florida, and released April, 1865.

Travis, Lewis, age 19, volunteer, May, 1864, one hundred days, One Hundred and Forty-eighth regiment, company H, private, served four months, discharged September, 1864.

Travis, Jacob, age 23, volunteer, August 11, 1862, three years, Ninety-second regiment, company F, private, served three years, discharged January 19, 1865, captured at Chickamauga, but escaped.

Travis, William, aged 29, volunteer, August 11, 1862, three years, Ninety-second regiment, company F, private, discharged June 19, 1865.

Templar, Austin, volunteer, August 7, 1862, three years, Ninety-second regiment, company G, private, served three years, discharged June 19, 1865, wounded at Chickamauga and at Savannah.

Templar, Amos, volunteer.

Thorpe, Martin R., age 18, volunteer, December, 1861, Seventy-fifth regiment, private, attained adjutant, wounded at Chancellorsville, reenlisted as a veteran.

Van Gilden, George H., age 19, volunteer, February, 1864, Thirty-ninth regiment, company K, private, discharged July, 1865.

Watson, John K., age 24, volunteer, May, 1864, one hundred days, One Hundred and Forty-eighth regiment, company H, private, served four months, discharged September 14, 1864.

Watson, Daily, age 20, volunteer, May, 1864, one hundred days, One Hundred and Forty-eighth regiment, company H, private, served four months, discharged September, 1864, was in hospital at Point of Rocks with measles and camp disease.

Watson, Jacob, age 18, volunteer, August 11, 1862, three years, Ninety-second regiment, company F, private, served three years, discharged June 20, 1865, never off duty during enlistment.

Weaver, Hanson, volunteer, January 23, 1862, three years, Sixty-third regiment, company F, private.

Winans, Francis, age 21, volunteer, January 23, 1862, three years, Sixty-third regiment, company F, private, died September, 1862, of diphtheria.

Weaver, William, Twenty-seventh Illinois, company D.

Winans, Benjamin, age 23, volunteer, January 23, 1862, three years, Sixty-third regiment, company F, captured near Atlanta, Georgia, in 1864, and imprisoned, exchanged and reached home in July, 1865, in reduced condition.

Walker, Henry M., volunteer, May, 1864, one hundred days, One Hundred and Forty-eighth regiment, company H, private, served four months, discharged September, 1864.

White, Leander I, Seventy-fifth regiment, company D.

White, Henry L., age 23, volunteer, June 20, 1861, Thirty-ninth regiment, company K, private, served four years, discharged July, 1865, reenlisted in 1863, and was detailed for clerk duty.

White, Arastus H., age 19, volunteer, August 14, 1862, three years, One Hundred and Sixteenth regiment, company B, private, served three years, discharged June 24, 1865, wounded at Hatcher's Run.

White, Sydney P., age 19, volunteer, March 4, 1864, One Hundred and Sixteenth regiment, company B, private, attained orderly, was in thirteen different actions, and was transferred to company B, Sixty-second regiment.

White, William W., age 21, volunteer, November 13, 1861, Seventy-fifth regiment, company D, private, died in hospital May 17, 1864, of intermittent fever, captured at Gettysburgh and exchanged.

Williams, David, age 22, volunteer, May, 1864, One Hundred and Forty-eighth regiment, company H, private, served four months, discharged September 14, 1864.

Williams, George W., volunteer, May, 1864, One Hundred and Forty-eighth regiment, company H, private, served four months, discharged September 14 1864.

William, George W., age 37, drafted September, 1864, one year, Seventeenth regiment, company K, private, discharged 1865.

RECAPITULATION.

DECATUR TOWNSHIP.

Aglen, John S., age 16, volunteer, November 13, 1863, One Hundred and Twenty-fifth regiment, company K, private.

Batchelor, Daniel, substitute, May, 1864, one hundred days, One Hundred and Forty-first regiment, company A, private.

Ballard, Philip A., age 18, volunteer, September 15, 1863, six months, Fourth Virginia cavalry, private, served six months, discharged March 1864, wounded once, captured in 1863 at Winchester and imprisoned at Belle Isle twenty-three days, died December 26, 1864, chronic diarrhœa reenlistment, volunteer, May 1864, one hundred days, One Hundred and Forty-eighth regiment, company D, private, served four months, discharged September, 1864.

Barrows, Bradley P., age 42, volunteer, August 22, 1862, three years, One Hundred and Sixteenth regiment, company I, private, served three years, discharged June 14. 1865.

Broadhead, Francis M., age 27, volunteer, November, 1861, three years. First Virginia cavalry, company E, private, attained rank of quartermaster sergeant, served two years and seven months, died July 1, 1863, killed while scouting just after the battle of Gettysburgh.

Basim, John, Eleventh Indiana light artillery, died October 4, 1864, of pneumonia.

Burk, Henry, age 36, volunteer, May, 1864, one hundred days, One Hundred and Forty-eighth regiment, company D, private, served four months, discharged September, 1864.

Burk, James, age 19, volunteer, August 2, 1861, three years, Thirty-ninth regiment, company K, served four years, discharged June, 1865, injured while tearing up railroad track at Goldsborough, North Carolina, and discharged for disability.

Burk, Samuel, age 22, volunteer, December 30, 1861, three years, Seventy-third regiment, company F, private, served three years and seven months, discharged July 24, 1865.

Burg, George W., age 30, volunteer, 1862, three years, Seventy-third regiment, company F, private, served three years, discharged July 16, 1865, captured at McDowell, Virginia, sent to Staunton, Libby, Salisbury and Belle Isle, paroled and exchanged September, 1862, and rejoined his regiment October 3, 1862, wounded, first at Gettysburgh, second, Lookout Mountain, captured at Goldsborough, March, 1865, taken to southern prisons and paroled May 25th, discharged with regiment.

Brandeberry, William C., age 26, volunteer, December 30, 1861, three years, Seventy-third regiment, company F, private, served three years and seven months, discharged July 24, 1865.

Brandeberry, John H , age 17, volunteer, November 15, 1863, One Hundred and Twenty-fifth regiment, company K, private, served one year and seven months, discharged June 7, 1865, wounded at Resaca, discharged for disability.

Brooker, Marcellus, age 16, volunteer, December 30, 1861, three years, Seventy-third regiment, company F, private, served three years discharged January 1, 1864, reenlisted, volunteer, January 1, 1864, Seventy-third regiment, company F, private, served six months, discharged July 24, 1865, captured twice.

Brooks, James, age 46, volunteer, August 11, 1862, three years, Ninety-second regiment, company G, private, served one year, discharged 1863, taken with camp disease and fever, and brought home by his wife.

Beebe, Theodore, age 27, volunteer, August 15, 1862, three years Seventy-third regiment, company F, corporal, served three years, discharged July 26, 1865, never sick, wounded or prisoner.

Beebe, Guy, age 22, volunteer, October 11, 1861, three years, Seventy-third regiment, company F, private, attained rank of sergeant, served four years, discharged July 26, 1865, never lost a day's duty.

Beebe, James, age 15, volunteer, June 21, 1861, three years, Thirty-ninth regiment, company K, private, served four years discharged July 19, 1865, wounded at Atlanta, and home sick three months.

Beebe, Festus, age 16, volunteer, February 16, 1864, Seventy-third regiment, company F, private, served one year and five months, discharged July 26, 1865.

Beebe, Charles, age 18, volunteer, June 12, 1861, three years, Thirty-ninth regiment, company K, private, served four years, discharged July 19, 1865, wounded at Corinth, May 28, 1862.

Blair, Alexander, age 22, volunteer, August, 1861, three years, Thirty-sixth, company F, private, served three years, honorably discharged in September, 1864.

Blair, Thomas, age 21, volunteer, October, 1861, three years, Thirty-sixth regiment, company F, private, served three months, died January 29, 1862.

Blair, Alvin, age 17, volunteer, August 2, 1861, three years, Thirty-ninth regiment, company K, private, died in 1862 of measles, at Mowsa.

Bennett, Isaac, age 35, volunteer, August 9, 1862, three years, Ninety-second regiment, company G, private, discharged June 21, 1865.

Bennett, William, age 22, volunteer, October 19, 1861, three years, Thirty-sixth regiment, company F, private, died in February, 1862, at Summerville, West Virginia, of measles.

Bennett, Gordon, volunteer, August 1, 1861, three years, Thirty-sixth regiment, company F, private, served three years, honorably discharged in 1864, slightly wounded at Lewisburgh, Virginia.

Carlin, D. B., Eighteenth regiment, company C, lieutenant.

Chambers, William, age 39, volunteer, February 27, 1865, One Hundred and Eighty-ninth regiment, company F, private.

Chambers, James, age 18, volunteer, July 20, 1861, three years, Thirty-ninth regiment, company K, private, honorably discharged in 1863; reenlisted December 23, 1863, private, attained rank of hospital steward, served four years, discharged July 9, 1865.

Chambers, Martin V., age 21, volunteer, June 18, 1861, three years, Thirty-ninth regiment, company K, private, died July 5, 1864, mortally wounded at Kennesaw Mountain, July 4, 1864.

Campbell, James, age 22, volunteer, August 2, 1861, three years, Thirty-ninth regiment, company K, private, reenlisted in 1863, hospital nurse, served four years, discharged in June, 1865.

Campbell, Luther T., age 17, volunteer, September 12, 1861, three years, Fifty-third regiment, company B, private, served three years, discharged August 11, 1865.

Campbell, Elijah, age 17, volunteer, June 29, 1863, Second heavy artillery, company K, private.

Campbell, William, age 15, volunteer, March, 1864, Fifty-third regiment, company B, private.

Croy, Robert, Ninety-second regiment, company G, sick several times.

Conant, Sanford, age 29, volunteer, August 12, 1862, three years, Ninety-second regiment, company G, private, served three years, discharged June, 1865, transferred to veteran reserve corps.

Cutlip, Henry, age 41, volunteer, three years, One Hundred and Seventy-sixth regiment, company I, private, died June 12, 1863, at Chickamauga, Tennessee.

Deasy, Luke, age 21, volunteer, October, 1861, three years, Seventy-third regiment, company F, private, served three years, discharged December 31, 1864, wounded at Lookout Mountain.

Ellis, Alexander M., age 21, volunteer, November 16, 1861, three years, Seventy-third regiment, company F, private, served eleven months, discharged October 3, 1862, for disability.

Ellis, Albert, age 24, volunteer, September 7, 1861, three years, First cavalry, company N, private, discharged 1865, transferred to veteran reserve corps.

Ellis, Reuben H., volunteer, May, 1864, one hundred days, One Hundred and Forty-first regiment, company G, private, served four months, discharged September, 1864.

Ellis, Ethan G., age 29, volunteer, June 27, 1863, Second heavy artillery, company H, private.

Ellis, John W., age 25, volunteer, August, 1862, three years, Ninety-second regiment, company G, private, died March 8, 1863, at Camp Gallatin, cause unknown.

Ellis, James I., volunteer, three years, Ninety-second regiment, company I, private, died July, 1863, at Camp Gallatin, after three months' sickness.

Ellis, Charles C., age 15, volunteer, December 18, 1863, three years, Eighteenth regiment, company A, corporal, wounded at Nashville.

Evans, David, volunteer, Fourth colored infantry, company D, private, died 1864, at Fortress Monroe.

Fairbanks, Cornelius, substitute, May, 1864, one hundred days, One Hundred and forty-eighth regiment, company H, private, served four months, mustered out September, 1864.

France, John W., age 19, volunteer, 1861, three years, Seventy-third regiment, company F, private, served three years, died May 25, 1864, mortally wounded at Dallas, Georgia, May 25, 1864.

France, George W., age 32, volunteer, August 5, 1862, three years, Ninety-second regiment, company G, private, served one year and five months, honorably discharged January 6, 1864.

France, William H., age 25, volunteer, December 18, 1863, One Hundred and Twenty-fifth regiment, company K, private, served one year and four months, discharged April 17, 1865, for disability, wounded near Dallas, Georgia, June 2, 1864.

Frye, James C., age 26, volunteer, September 29, 1864, Seventy-first regiment, company B, private, served nine months, discharged June 12, 1865, sick with camp disease in Tennessee.

Frye, George N., age 21, August, 1861, three years, Eighteenth regiment, company C, private, served six months, died February 3, 1862, in hospital at Louisville.

Fish, S. H., volunteer, December 30, 1861, three years, Seventy-third regiment, company F, private, two years and seven months, discharged July 24, 1865.

Gaughan, Anthony, 1861, three years, Thirty-ninth regiment, company K, private, served three years, discharged, reenlisted, while waiting discharge as a veteran went into Louisville, on a pass and supposed to have died by foul means.

Grimes, Owen, volunteer, December 30, 1861, three years, Seventy-third regiment, company H, private, honorably discharged 1864 for disability.

Giddings, Charles, age 37, volunteer, February 23, 1865, one hundred days, One Hundred and Eighty-ninth regiment, company F, private, discharged May 15, 1865, for disability.

Haynes, Andrew A., age 18, volunteer, May, 1864, one hundred days, One Hundred and Forty-eighth regiment, company D, private, served four months, mustered out September 14, 1864.

Haynes, Austin I., age 18, volunteer, December 30, 1861, three years, Seventy-third regiment, company F, private, died May 14, 1862, of measles.

Henderson, Isaac, Fourth regiment, company B.

Howell, Josephus, volunteer, August, 1862, three years, Ninety-second regiment, company G, private, three years, discharged June 19, 1865, transferred to veteran reserve corps.

Hicks, Thomas F., age 23, volunteer, December 30, 1861, three years, Seventy-third regiment, company F, private, served four years, discharged July, 1863; reenlisted as a veteran.

Johnson, William A., age 17, volunteer, August 1, 1863, six months, Fourth Virginia cavalry, company E, private, served six months, discharged February 6, 1864, from cavalry service; reenlisted May, 1864, one hundred days, One Hundred and Forty-eighth regiment, company D, private, served four months, discharged September, 1864.

Johnson, Worthy A., age 16, volunteer, May, 1864, one hundred days, One Hundred and Forty-eighth regiment, company A, private, served four months, discharged September 14, 1864.

Johnson, Samuel, drafted, One Hundred and Seventy-sixth regiment, company I, and Sixty-fifth regiment, company G, private, died in 1865, captured and supposed to have died in the hands of the rebels.

Johnson, Marion N., volunteer, October 16, 1863, six months, Fourth Virginia cavalry, company E, private, served five months, mustered out March 6, 1864; reenlisted May, 1864, one hundred days, One Hundred and Forty-eighth regiment, company D, private, served four months, discharged September, 1864; reenlisted the third time in company B, One Hundred and Ninety-second regiment.

Johnson, Corwin, volunteer, October 16, 1863, six months, Fourth Virginia cavalry, company E, private, served five months, mustered out May 6, 1864; reenlisted May, 1864, one hundred days, One Hundred and Forty-eighth regiment, company D, private, served four months, discharged September, 1864.

Johnson, William H., age 21, volunteer, 1861, three years, Seventy-third regiment, company F, private, served three years and three months, honorably discharged August 31, 1864, wounded at Lookout Mountain in 1863, reenlisted as a veteran.

Jarvis, George P., age 17, volunteer, August 7, 1862, three years, Ninety-second regiment, company B, private, served three years, discharged June 19, 1865, sick in Georgia, captured near close of war in Georgia, and taken to Andersonville, was parolled a month after and soon discharged.

King, Wilton, age 19, volunteer, August 26, 1861, three years, Thirty-ninth regiment, company K, private, attained rank of orderly sergeant, served four years, discharged August 1, 1865, wounded July 4, 1864, reenlisted as a veteran.

King, John, age 24, volunteer, August, 1861, three years, Thirty-sixth regiment, company F, private, three years, honorably discharged August, 1864, at expiration of his time.

King, Abel D., volunteer Fourth Virginia cavalry, company E, sergeant, discharged March 6, 1864; reenlisted February 23, 1865, Thirty-sixth regiment, company F, served five months, discharged July 27, 1865.

King, William, age 17, volunteer, February 27, 1865, one hundred days, One Hundred and Ninety-fourth regiment, company I, private.

King, Nathan P., age 17, volunteer, June 10, 1864, three years, Thirty-ninth regiment, company K, private, died June 19, 1864, from wound received at battle of Kennesaw Mountain, June 18, 1864.

Kelly, Samuel, age 21, volunteer, June 22, 1861, three years, Thirty-ninth regiment, company K, private, served three years, honorably discharged August, 1864.

Lee, Jonathan R., substitute, May, 1864, one hundred days, One Hundred and Forty-first regiment, company A, private.

Lucas, J. C., Eighteenth Virginia cavalry, company C.

Loraine, Louis J., volunteer, October 16, 1863, six months, Fourth regiment, company E, private, served five months, mustered out March 6, 1864; reenlisted in One Hundred and Ninety-first regiment Ohio National guards, also in One Hundred and Ninety-second regiment, company G, Ohio volunteer infantry.

Lucas, Oliver, Eighteenth regiment, company C.

Meek, Jacob, age 31, volunteer, October, 1861, three years, Eighteenth regiment, company A, private, died in 1863 at Chickamauga.

Meek, Samuel, age 19, volunteer, October, 1861, three years, Eighteenth regiment, private, company A, served three years, honorably discharged, November, 1864, sick with yellow fever and rheumatism, wounded and captured at Stone River, in Atlanta, Montgomery, and Libby prisons, wounded at Chickamauga.

Myers, William, volunteer, One Hundred and Twenty-eighth regiment, served ten months, transferred to One Hundred and Twenty-ninth artillery.

Montgomery, A. H., age 20, volunteer, February 26, 1864, Eighteenth regiment, company A, private.

Marshall, William, age 23, volunteer, October 21, 1861, three years, Seventy-third regiment, company F, private, served four years, discharged July 20, 1865, reenlisted as a veteran.

Mellow, Samuel, age 20, volunteer, September 19, 1862, three years, Seventy-third regiment, company B, private, served three years, discharged July 24, 1865, detailed as teamster, wounded.

Moore, William M., age 20, volunteer, May, 1864, one hundred days, One Hundred and Forty-eighth regiment, company D, private, served four months, discharged September 14, 1864.

Miller, Manuel, age 38, drafted, October, 1864, Seventy-first regiment, company B, private, served eight months, mustered out June, 1865.

Moran, Anthony, age 35, volunteer, December 30, 1861, three years, Seventy-third regiment, company F, private, served four years, mustered out July 20, 1865, wounded at second Bull Run, reenlisted as a veteran.

McDaniel, Frederick P., age 25, volunteer, December 13, 1861, three years, First Virginia cavalry, company E, private, served seven months, died July 18, 1862, of fever.

McGirr, William P., age 31, volunteer, August 26, 1861, three years, Thirty-sixth regiment, company F, private, served three years, honorably discharged September 3, 1864

Mead, Charles K., volunteer, August 2, 1861, three years, Thirty-ninth regiment, company K, private, served five months, died January 6, 1862, of camp disease.

Newel, Erastus R., age 36, volunteer, 1862, three years, Fifty-third regiment, company E, private, died June 6, 1863.

Nolan, Zachary, age 17, volunteer, October 19, 1864, Seventy-eighth regiment, company F, private, served nine months, discharged July 11, 1865.

Nolan, Allan, age 19, volunteer, 1862, one year, Eighteenth regiment, company C, private, served one year, honorably discharged in 1863

Nolan, Enoch, age 25, volunteer, February 14, 1865, One Hundred and Seventy-sixth or One Hundred and Eighty-sixth regiments, company I, private, died April, 1865, of measles.

Nolan, Ryley, age 18, volunteer, October, 1863, six months, Fourth Virginia cavalry, private, served nine months, honorably discharged July, 1864, reenlisted in One Hundred and Eighty-sixth regiment, company I.

Newman, John, December 30, 1861, three years, Seventy-third regiment, company F, served three years, honorably discharged in 1864.

Norman, Azariah, volunteer, Fifth colored infantry, company G, died.

Norman, Amos, volunteer, Fifth colored infantry, company G, honorably discharged.

O'Neal, William J., age 18, volunteer, August 2, 1861, three years, Thirty-ninth regiment, company K, corporal, served four years, discharged July, 1865; reenlisted as a veteran.

Parsons, W., age 23, volunteer, 1862, three years, Seventy-third regiment, company F, private, served three years, discharged July 24, 1865.

Parsons, Josiah W., age 18, volunteer, 1862, Seventy-third regiment, company F., private, died near Dallas, Georgia.

Parsons, Robert K.

Plan, Trueman E., age 18, volunteer, 1861, Eighteenth regiment, company C, private, served one year, discharged 1862, drafted 1864, Eighteenth regiment, company F, private, discharged July, 1865, both times for disability.

Ritenour, Joseph S., age 25, volunteer, February 16, 1864, Seventy-third regiment, company D, private, one year, wounded at Atlanta, and died of fever, April 23, 1865.

Ridenour, J. R., age 26, volunteer, Seventy-second regiment, company F, Private, died May 1, 1865, of chronic disease.

Romine, Peter, age 27, volunteer, November 4, 1862, three years, Fifty-third regiment company E, private, wounded at Kennesaw Mountain.

Rowland, John W., age 28, volunteer, November 3, 1861, three years, Fifty-third regiment, company E, private, mustered out.

Rowland, James E, age 20, volunteer, February 3, 1864, Seventy-third regiment, company F, private, served one year and five months, discharged July 24, 1865.

Ross, James, Seventy-third regiment, company F.

Russel, Emanuel, age 24, volunteer, August 22, 1862, One Hundred and Sixteenth regiment, company I, private, wounded and captured at Staunton, Virginia, imprisoned at Andersonville, discharged June 14, 1865.

Russel, Washington, age 16, volunteer, August 6, 1862, three years, Ninety-second regiment, company A, private, attained rank of first sergeant, served three years, discharged June 10, 1865.

Snider, Thomas H., age 22, volunteer, August 31, 1862, three years, Seventy-third regiment, company D, private, two years and eight months, discharged for disability April 18, 1865.

Snider, John W., age 19, volunteer, August 31, 1862, three years, Seventy-third regiment, company F, private, transferred to Infantry corps.

Sampson, Thomas E, volunteer, August 22, 1864, Fifth regiment colored infantry, company F, private, wounded at Deep Bottom, near Richmond.

Shrader, William, age 27, volunteer, November 1, 1862, three years, Seventy-third regiment, company F, private, captured near Monterey, Virginia, held four months in Libby, Salisbury, and Belle Isle prisons, parolled, honorably discharged,

Smith, William C., age 39, volunteer, February 22, 1864, three years, Thirty-ninth regiment, company K, private, served one year and five months, wounded before Atlanta, discharged July 9, 1865.

Smith, Alexander F., age 34, volunteer, May, 1864, one hundred days, One Hundred and Forty-eighth regiment, company D, private, served four months, discharged September 14, 1864.

Smith, James F., age 29, volunteer, May, 1864, one hundred days, One Hundred and Forty-eighth regiment, company D, private, killed in an explosion at City Point.

Smith, Joseph A, age 24, volunteer, February 22, 1864, Thirty-ninth regiment, company K, private, served one year and four months, discharged July 9, 1865

Starling, George, Ninety- second regiment, company G, died.

Storts, Joseph B., age 18, volunteer, February 9, 1864, Seventy-third regiment, company F, private, one year and five months, discharged July 26, 1865.

Storts, H. Andrew, age 20, substitute, May, 1864, one hundred days, One Hundred and Forty-eighth regiment, company H, private, mustered out September, 1864.

Storts, Philander, age 31, volunteer, March 22, 1864, Eighteenth regiment, company F, private, served one year, discharged July 15, 1865.

Tate, John, volunteer, died in hospital June 15, 1865.

Taylor, John W., volunteer, Eighteenth regiment, company B.

Taylor, Benjamin G, age 27, volunteer, August, 1862, three years, Ninety-second regiment, company G, private, three years, mustered out June, 1865.

Taylor, William M., volunteer, Eighteenth regiment, company B.

Turrel, William P, age 25, volunteer, August 4, 1862, three years, Ninety-second regiment, company F, private, served ten months, discharged June 12, 1863, for disability.

Weakly, Thomas, May, 1864, one hundred days, One Hundred and Forty-eighth regiment, company D, private, served four months, discharged September, 1861, reenlisted May, 1865, Thirty-sixth regiment, private, died in 1865.

RECAPITULATION.

One each in Eleventh Ohio, Independent battery, batteries H and
K, Ohio heavy artillery, in all.. 3
Fourth Virginia cavalry... 7
First Virginia cavalry... 2
First Ohio cavalry.. 1
Seventy-third Ohio.. 28
Thirty-ninth Ohio... 15
Ninety-second Ohio... 13
One Hundred and Forty-eighth Ohio.................................... 14
Eighteenth Ohio (three years)... 13
Thirty-sixth Ohio... 8
Fifty-third Ohio.. 5

One Hundred and Twenty-fifth Ohio.................................... 3
One Hundred and Forty-first Ohio..................................... 3
One Hundred and Sixteenth Ohio....................................... 2
Seventy-first Ohio.. 2
One Hundred and Eighty-sixth Ohio.................................... 2
Fifth colored regiment.. 3
One Hundred and Eighty-ninth Ohio.................................... 2
One Hundred and Seventy-sixth Ohio................................... 3
One Each in Fourth Ohio, Fourth colored regiment, Seventy-second Ohio, Sixty-fifth Ohio, Seventy-eighth Ohio, One Hundred and Twenty-eighth Ohio, One Hundred and Ninety-fourth Ohio one not designated, in all.................................... 7

Total number of soldiers...................... 136
Died... 26

DUNHAM TOWNSHIP.

Andrew, Thomas A., First Virginia light artillery, company H.

Berry, William E., age 31, volunteer, October 29, 1861, three years, battery H, private, served three years, discharged October 28, 1864, captured and imprisoned at Lynchburgh and Belle Isle.

Beach, Hiram, age 22, volunteer, three years, Thirty-sixth regiment, company F, private, died July, 1862, of typhoid fever.

Basim, David, age 28, volunteer, May, 1864, one hundred days, One Hundred and Forty-eighth regiment, company G, private, discharged September, 1864.

Baker, Manuel, age 30, volunteer, three years, Thirty-sixth regiment, company F, private, died March, 1864, in Andersonville prison pen, of starvation.

Calder, Philip C., age 31, volunteer, September 10, 1862, three years, Eighty-eighth regiment, company B, private, served three years, discharged July 3, 1865.

Cammel, M. M., volunteer, three years, Ninety-second regiment, company F, private, attained the rank of sergeant, died July 16th, of typhoid fever.

Drain, John, age 22, volunteer, 1864, one hundred days, One Hundred and Forty-eighth regiment, company H, private, served four months, discharged September, 1864.

Ellenwood, Dudley H, age 21, volunteer, October 23, 1861, Seventy-seventh regiment, company D, private, discharged June 18, 1862, for disability.

Farley, George, Seventy-third regiment, company F.

Fish, David, age 18, volunteer, December 30, 1861, Seventy-third regiment, company F, private, served nine months, died October, 1862, of measles.

Farley, George, jr., Seventy-third regiment, company F.

Frazer, Evan, age 35, volunteer, August, 1862, three years, Ninety-second regiment, company G, private, discharged June 10, 1865.

Gorham, Samuel Earl, age 39, volunteer, May, 1864, one hundred days, One Hundred and Forty-eighth regiment, company H, corporal, killed by explosion at City Point August 9, 1864.

Gorham, Daniel H., age 32, volunteer, December 1, 1861, three years, battery H, corporal, served three years and six months, discharged June 13, 1865, reenlisted as a veteran.

Green, James, Thirty-ninth regiment, company K.

Hollister, A. D., age 20, volunteer, June 18, 1861, three years, Thirty-ninth regiment, company K, private, served four years, discharged July 9, 1865, wounded at Atlanta, reenlisted as a veteran.

Hall, John, age 24, volunteer, three years, Seventy-third regiment, company F, private, died August 9, 1864, at Fortress Monroe, of measles.

Hall, James, age 18, volunteer; three years, Seventy-third regiment, company F, private, died June, 1864, at Point of Rocks, of measles.

Hollister, Austin A., age 17, volunteer, May, 1864, one hundred days, One Hundred and Forty-eighth regiment, company G, private, served four months, discharged September, 1864.

Irwin, William, volunteer, First Virginia light artillery, company H.

Mankin, Rufus M., age 29, volunteer, August 15, 1862, three years, Eighty-eighth regiment, company B, private, served three years, discharged July 3, 1865.

Mankin, Daniel E., age 22, volunteer, May, 1864, one hundred days, One Hundred and Forty-eighth regiment, company K, sergeant, served four months, discharged September, 1864.

Mankin, Francis F., age 42, volunteer, May, 1864, one hundred days, One Hundred and Forty-eighth regiment, company H, private, served four months, honorably discharged September, 1864.

Mankin, Ezra, age 23, volunteer, May, 1864, one hundred days, One

Hundred and Forty-eighth regiment, company K, private, served four months, discharged September, 1864.

McClure, Dyer G., age 18, volunteer, 1861, Thirty-sixth regiment, company A, private, died June 19, 1862, mortally wounded at Lewisburgh, Virginia.

McClure, Alonzo, age 18, volunteer, May, 1864, one hundred days, One Hundred and Forty-eighth regiment, company K, private, served four months, discharged September, 1864.

McClure, Henry O., age 23, volunteer, 1861, three years, Thirty-sixth regiment, company A, private, attained the rank of sergeant, discharged in 1864, at expiration of term.

McGill, John M., age 26, volunteer, 1861, battery H, private, killed at Port Republic, June 9, 1862.

McGill, Hugh, age 25, volunteer, February, 1864, three years, Thirty-sixth regiment, company F, private, attained the rank of corporal, served one year and four months, discharged June 27, 1865.

McGill, William B., age 20, May, 1864, one hundred days, One Hundred and Forty-eighth regiment, company H, private, discharged September, 1864, sick and returned home by general order of war department.

McKinney, Robert D., age 19, volunteer, August 17, 1864, one hundred days, One Hundred and Seventy-fourth regiment, company E, private, discharged from hospital.

McTaggart, Alexander, age 20, volunteer, August, 1861, three years, Thirty-ninth regiment, company H, private, attained the rank of lieutenant, wounded at Atlanta, resigned just before the regiment was discharged, reenlisted in 1864, three years, Thirty-ninth regiment.

McTaggart, Neil, age 18, volunteer, January 2, 1862, three years, Seventy-seventh regiment, company D, private, reenlisted for three years in the same regiment and company, captured at battle of Mark's Mills, imprisoned ten months at Camp Ford.

Mitchell, George B., age 21, volunteer, August 15, 1862, three years, Eighty-eighth regiment, company B, private, discharged July 3, 1865

Mitchell, Thomas, age 21, volunteer, 1865, private, served four months, mustered out.

Mitchell, David, volunteer, First artillery, company H, private, mustered out.

Mitchell, John, Seventy-third regiment.

Noland, Sylvester, age 25, volunteer, August 8, 1862, three years, Seventy-third regiment, company F, private, discharged May, 1865, for disability, wounded at battle of Gettysburgh.

Noland, James A., age 18, volunteer, October 23, 1863, three years, Thirty-ninth regiment, company K, private, served thirteen months, discharged on account of some flaw in his enlistment papers, reenlisted February 9, 1864, Thirty-second regiment, company B, mustered out July, 1865.

Noland, John, age 18, volunteer, February 15, 1865, Thirty-sixth regiment, company H, private, died July 20, 1865.

Noland, Augustus, age 32, volunteer, February, 1865, One Hundred and Ninety-sixth regiment, company F, private.

Noland, Loring, age 20, volunteer, November, 1861, three years, Seventy-third regiment, company F, private, discharged November 1862, from hospital, reenlistment, February 15, 1865, Thirty-sixth regiment, company H, mustered out in 1865.

Noland, Joseph M., age 18, volunteer, October 31, 1864, three years First artillery, company H, private, discharged June 15, 1865, captured at Chancellorsville, and prisoner thirty days.

Norton, Charles R., age 19, volunteer, May, 1864, one hundred days, One Hundred and Forty-eighth regiment, private, served four months, mustered out September, 1864.

Pauley, Benjamin T., age 15, volunteer, December 5, 1862, three years, Sixty-third regiment, company D, private, discharged July 17, 1865.

Rodgers, Sanderson H., age 19, volunteer, August, 1861, three years, Thirty-sixth regiment, company F, discharged October 24, 1864, wounded at Chickamauga, and afterwards on detached duty in provost marshal's office.

Rodgers, Charles J., age 18, volunteer, February 14, 1865, one year, One Hundred and Eighty-sixth regiment, company I, private, died April 9, 1865, at Cleveland, Tennessee.

Rardin, Alonzo, age 27, volunteer, August 1, 1861, three years, Thirty-sixth regiment, company F, private, served two and one-fourth years, died November 25, 1863, killed in battle of Mission Ridge.

Rodgers, Edward P., age 16, volunteer, February 14, 1865, one year, One Hundred and Eighty-sixth regiment, company I, private, discharged on surgeon's certificate.

Reynolds, Emanuel, age 28, volunteer, February, 1864, Seventy-

seventh regiment, company G, private, was discharged June 30, 1865

Sayres, James M., age 24, volunteer, June, 1862, three months, Eighty-fifth regiment, company F, discharged by surgeon's certificate; reenlistment, volunteer, September 24, 1862, three years, Eighty-eighth regiment, company B, private, died August 5, 1865, of hemorrhage of lungs.

Sayres, Isaac T., age 20, volunteer, September 24, 1862, three years, Eighty-eighth regiment, company B, private, discharged October 26, 1863, by surgeon's certificate.

Sayres, William, age 24, volunteer, June, 1862, three months, Eighty-fifth regiment, teamster, reenlistment, volunteer, Eleventh Virginia regiment, company A, private, discharged July 3, 1865.

Sayres, Richard C., age 20, volunteer, June, 1862, three months, Eighty-fifth regiment, reenlistment, volunteer, September, 1863, Eleventh Virginia regiment, company A, private, mustered out in 1865.

Sayres, I. T., age 18, volunteer, September, 1863, three years, Eleventh Virginia regiment, company A, private.

Sayres, George, age 17, volunteer, September, 1863, three years, Eleventh Virginia regiment, company A, private, discharged July 24, 1865, wounded in front of Richmond.

Shaw, James, age 18, volunteer, May, 1864, one hundred days, One Hundred and Forty-eighth regiment, comyany H, private, served four months, mustered out September, 1864.

Shipton, William, age 27, volunteer, August 9, 1862, three years, Ninety-second regiment, company F, private, served two and five-twelfths years, discharged March 31, 1865, from hospital, wounded in front of Atlanta.

Stanton, Smith, volunteer, 1864, Seventy-third regiment, company F, private, mustered out July 20, 1865.

Tilton, Douglas, age 19, volunteer, August 1, 1861, three years, Thirty-sixth regiment, company F, private, served two months, died October 20, 1861, at Sumnerville, Virginia.

Todd, Alfred, age 54, volunteer, September 29, 1861, three years, Second Virginia cavalry, company B, private, served three years, mustered out November 29, 1864.

Todd, George (adopted), age 18, volunteer, November 8, 1861, three years, Second Virginia cavalry, company B, private, served three years and five months, mustered out June 30, 1865.

Wilson, Benjamin F., age 28, volunteer, August, 1862, three years, Ninety-second regiment, company F, private, mustered out June 10, 1865.

Wayson, Henry, Seventy-third regiment, company F, died.

Wayson, Alexander, Seventy-third regiment, company F.

RECAPITULATION.

Huntington's battery	5
Battery H, First Virginia light artillery	2
Second Virginia cavalry	2
One Hundred and Forty-eighth Ohio national guard	11
Seventy-third Ohio	11
Thirty-sixth Ohio	10
Eighty-eighth Ohio	5
Ninety-second Ohio	4
Thirty-ninth Ohio	4
Eleventh Virginia	4
Eighty-fifth Ohio	3
Seventy-seventh Ohio	3
One Hundred and Eighty-sixth Ohio	2
And one each in Thirty-second Ohio, Sixty-third Ohio, One Hundred and Seventy-fourth Ohio, One Hundred and Ninety-sixth Ohio, not designated one.	5
Total number of soldiers	66
Died	9

FAIRFIELD TOWNSHIP.

Addis, Benjamin F., aged 23, volunteer, October, 1861, for three years, Fifty-third regiment, company I, private, attained corporal, served three years, discharged November 1, 1864.

Addis, Thomas M., aged 24, volunteer, for three months, Eighteenth regiment, guard served three months, captured at Shiloh Aril 8, 1862, in prison for a year, on being released, sick and in hospital, reenlisted as a veteran, volunteer, 1861, for three years, Seventh regiment, company K, sergeant, served four years, discharged June 18, 1865, again captured at Mark's Mills, held for ten months, discharged for disability.

Barr, Elias, aged 44, volunteer, May, 1864, for one hundred days, One Hundred and Forty-eighth regiment, company F, private, served one hundred days, discharged August, 1864.

Bracken, Reed P., aged 20, volunteer, August 12, 1862, for three years, Ninety-second regiment, company G, private, attained corporal, served three years, discharged June 20, 1865.

Blair Alexander, Thirty-sixth regiment, company F.

Bracken, Craig, volunteer, for three months, Eighty-seventh regiment, private, served three months, discharged, reenlisted, volunteer, January 7, 1864, First cavalry, company H, private, served one year and four months, died June 25, 1865, captured during first enlistment at Harper's Ferry, but parolled, died of consumption at Atlanta

Bowman, Christian, aged 23, volunteer, 1861, Seventy-seventh regiment, company D, private, discharged September, 1862, wounded while sick and in hospital, discharged for disability.

Buck, J. A., Thirty-ninth regiment, company K.

Barnes, William, volunteer, 1861, Seventy-third regiment, company F, private, discharged for disability.

Burritt, J C, Eighteenth regiment, company C.

Campbell, Charles W., aged 19, volunteer, August 19, 1861, Seventy-seventh regiment, company D, private, served one year and three months, discharged November 12, 1862, discharged for disability.

Campbell, Thomas H., aged 22, volunteer, October 19, 1861, Seventy-seventh regiment, company D, private, attained corporal.

Callahan, George E., Ninety-second regiment, company G, died March 6, 1863, at Carthage, Tennessee.

Cary, Cornelius, aged 24, volunteer, October 17, 1861, three years, First artillery, company H, private, served three years, discharged 1864, as a veteran.

Cottle, Lewis, aged 28, volunteer, November, 1861, Seventy-seventh regiment, company D, private.

Cottle, Thornton F., aged 19, volunteer, November, 1861, Seventy-seventh regiment, company D, private, died April 6, 1862, killed at Shiloh.

Croy, Robert, aged 30, veteran, August 5, 1862, for three years, Ninety-second regiment, company G, private, served three years, mustered out June, 1865, took part in all the regiment actions.

Croy, Greer, aged 23, volunteer, October 12, 1861, for three years, Thirty-sixth regiment, company F, private, attained color corporal, served three years and four months, discharged February, 1865, wounded first at Antietam, second at Chichamauga, third Cedar Creek, discharged as a disabled veteran.

Croy, Duncan, aged 16, volunteer, August 4, 1862, for three years, Ninety-second regiment, company G, private, served three years, mustered out June, 1865, sick during first year

Croy, Calvin, aged 16, volunteer, May, 1864, for one hundred days, One Hundred and Forty-eighth regiment, company F, private, served one hundred days, mustered out August, 1864, reenlistment, volunteer, February 17, 1865, Ninety-second regiment, company G, private, served four months, mustered out June, 1865.

Croy, William, age 26, volunteer, August 9, 1862, three years, Ninety-second regiment, company G, private, served three years, mustered out 1865, detailed as wagonmaster for one year.

Croy, David, age 21, volunteer, August 6, 1862, three years, Ninety-second regiment, company G, private, served three years, mustered out June 10, 1865.

Croy, Nathan, age 21, volunteer, May, 1864, one hundred days, One Hundred and Forty-eighth regiment, company G, private, served one hundred days, mustered out August, 1864.

Dawson, William F, volunteer, One Hundred and First Pennsylvania infantry, first lieutenant, attained captain, discharged May 1, 1863, on account of disability.

Dewees, Caleb, volunteer, 1861, three years, Seventy-third regiment, company F, private, attained corporal, served two years, killed at Gettysburgh

Double, Edward, age 27, volunteer, August 12, 1861, three years, Thirty-sixth regiment, company G, private, attained orderly sergeant, served four years and seven months, discharged March 27, 1865, captured at Cumberland Gap but escaped.

Dunbar, David, age 27, volunteer, August 15, 1862, three years, Ninety-second regiment, company G, private, served three years, discharged June 29, 1865, wounded at Chickamauga and transferred to veteran reserved corps.

Dunsmoore, Lucius J., age 18, volunteer, May, 1864, one hundred days, One Hundred and Forty-eighth regiment, company D, private, served one hundred days, mustered out in September, 1864, died July 21, 1865, of injuries received at City Point.

Ellis, David F., age 22, October 14, 1862, three years, Sixty-third regiment, company G, private, served two years and two months, mustered out December 26, 1864

Ellis, Lewis H., age 20, volunteer, May, 1862, one hundred days, One Hundred and Forty-eighth regiment, company D, private, served one hundred days, mustered out in September, 1864.

Faires, Cyreneus B., age 17, volunteer, September 5, 1861, three years, Second Virginia cavalry, company H, private, served one year and seven months, died in April, 1863, of typhoid fever.

Faires, Edward G., age 15, volunteer, May, 1864, one hundred days, One Hundred and Forty-eighth regiment, company G, private, served one hundred days, mustered out in September, 1864.

Fitzgerald, Garret, age 33, volunteer, 1861, three years, Seventy-third regiment, company B, private, served two years, discharged in 1863 on account of disability.

Goddard, Peter F., age 17, volunteer, October 9, 1861, Second regiment Virginia cavalry, company H, private, died October 1, 1862, died of typhoid fever.

Goddard, Harvey H., age 20, volunteer, August 6, 1862, three years, Ninety-second regiment, company G, private, died March 6, 1863, in hospital.

Goddard, George R., age 17, volunteer, May, 1864, one hundred days, One Hundred and Forty-eighth regiment, company G, private, mustered out September, 1864.

Gallaher, Patrick, Seventy-seventh regiment, company H.

Gallagher, James, age 15, volunteer, 1861, three years, Seventy-seventh regiment, company D, private, reenlisted in 1863, Seventy-seventh regiment, company D, captured at Mark's Mills, in Tyler prison ten months.

Hart Lucien, age 20, volunteer, October 10, 1864, Ninth regiment cavalry, private, served nine months, mustered out July, 1865.

Hart, William R., age 22, volunteer, September 26, 1861, Seventieth regiment, company F, private, attained the rank of orderly sergeant.

Hart, Wilson S., age 20, volunteer, June, 1862, three months, Eighty-seventh regiment, company A, private, served three months, mustered out September, 1862, captured at Harper's Ferry and parolled.

Haynes, John T., age 26, volunteer, May, 1864, one hundred days, One Hundred and Forty-eighth regiment, company D, corporal, served three months, mustered out September, 1864.

Haynes, Isaac P., age 24, volunteer, May, 1864, one hundred days, One Hundred and Forty-eighth regiment, company D, private, served three months, mustered out September, 1864.

Hill Isaac, age 26, volunteer, 1861, First regiment artillery, company H, private, served four years, mustered out July 31, 1865, reenlisted as a veteran.

Hull Daniel, age 34, volunteer, May, 1864, one hundred days, One Hundred and Forty-eighth regiment, company G, private, served one hundred days, died October 26, 1864, of measles.

Hull, Samuel, age 28, volunteer, August, 1862, Ninety-second regiment, company G, private, attained the rank of sergeant, died March 12, 1863, of measles at Nashville.

Hull, Reuben E., age 21, volunteer, October, 1861, three years, Second regiment Virginia cavalry, company II, private, attained the rank of first sergeant, served three years, mustered out October, 1864, reenlisted October, 1864, Second regiment Virginia cavalry, company H, first sergeant, mustered out February, 1865.

Hunter, Charles, age 21, volunteer, 1861, Seventy-third regiment, company F, private, died May 19, 1865, of consumption.

Johnson, John D., Thirty-sixth regiment, company F.

Jones, William D., volunteer, January, 1864, three years, First regiment cavalry, company L, private.

Johnson, Zeno C., Thirty-sixth regiment, company F, private, died.

Kidwell, Alexander D., age 19, volunteer, December 31, 1861, Seventy-seventh regiment, company D, private.

Johnson, E. M., Seventy-seventh regiment, company D.

Lucas, Thomas, volunteer, 1861, three years, Seventy-third regiment, company F, captain, mustered out 1864, discharged by surgeon's certificate.

Meek, William J., Ninety-second regiment, company G.

Marple, James W., age 21, volunteer, May, 1864, one hundred days, One Hundred and Forty-eighth regiment, company D, private, served one hundred days, mustered out September, 1864.

Moore, George, aged 21, volunteer, February 15, 1864, Thirty-ninth regiment, company K, private, mustered out July 9, 1865.

Meer, Patrick C., volunteer, 1861, Seventy-third regiment, company F, private, discharged, cause unknown.

Mocer, David, Thirteenth regiment, company H.

Miller, Elbridge, aged 19, volunteer, September 6, 1861, three years, Second Virginia cavalry, company F, private, served three years, mustered out November, 1864, captured at Somerville, West Virginia, May

12, 1863, in Libby prison eleven months, parolled and exchanged in 1864.

Morrow, William, Sixty-fifth regiment, company H.

Morrow, Andrew D., aged 24, volunteer, February 25, 1861, two years, Sixty-third regiment, company H, private, served two years, reenlisted, volunteered January 1, 1863, Sixty-third regiment, company H, saddler, served two years and six months, mustered out July, 1865.

M'Namery, William, aged 20, volunteer, February, 1864, Seventy-third regiment, company F, private, mustered out May, 1865, wounded at Goldsborough, North Carolina.

Marple, Wesley, Sixty-third regiment, company G, private, died June 20, 1862, at Corinth, Mississippi, of typhoid fever.

Murphy, William, volunteer, 1861, Sixth Kentucky cavalry, private, died, 1863, shot through the head.

Nichol, Thomas, aged 22, volunteer, October, 1861, Seventy-seventh regiment, company D, private, attained rank of corporal, served on detached service, and reenlisted as a veteran.

O'Donnel, John, volunteer, November, 1861, three years, Seventy-third regiment, company F, private, three years, mustered out 1864, wounded at second Bull Run fight, captured and parolled on the field.

Pennock, Jacob, aged 20, volunteer, March 9, 1865, One Hundred and Ninety-sixth regiment, company F, private, died April 27, 1865, of typhoid fever.

Reid, Hugh, aged 21, volunteer, December 31, 1861, two years, Seventy-seventh regiment, company D, private, served two years, captured at Mark's Mills, and imprisoned at Camp Ford, Texas, for ten months, reenlisted, volunteered, December 19, 1863, Seventy-seventh regiment, company D, private.

Sayler, Edward J, age 21, volunteer, August 1, 1861, three years, Thirty-sixth regiment, company K, private, served three years, reenlisted as a veteran, was wounded at Winchester, September, 1863.

Stephens, Thomas, age 16, volunteer, October 2, 1862, Ninth cavalry, company B, private.

Thompson, William, age 36, volunteer, May, 1864, one hundred days, One Hundred and Forty-eighth regiment, company F, corporal, served one hundred days, mustered out in September, 1864.

Tait, Michael, age 45, volunteer, 1861, Seventy-third regiment, company F, private, died in 1863 in hospital.

Tait, Edward, age 14, volunteer, 1861, Seventy-third regiment company F, private.

Walker, James, age 44, volunteer, February, 1862, three years, Seventy-seventh regiment, company D, private, died April 21, 1862, in consequence of wound received at Shiloh.

Walborn, Elias, age 18, volunteer, February 17, 1864, Thirty-sixth regiment, company F, private, served two months, mustered out April 27, 1865.

Wible, Levi, age 28, volunteer, October 26, 1861, Sixty-third regiment, company G, private, attained rank of sergeant, reenlisted as a veteran, severely wounded and captured at Atlanta, in prison at Andersonville eight months, parolled, and was on board the Sultana when she exploded on the Mississippi river, died.

Wible, Joseph, age 22, volunteer, August 28, 1861, two years, One Hundredth Pennsylvania infantry, company D, private, served two years, reenlisted, captured at James Island, South Carolina, June 3, 1862, in prison at Columbia four months and parolled, captured second time at Petersburgh, March 25, 1865, in Libby prison five days and parolled, discharged with his company.

RECAPITULATION.

Huntington battery	3
Second Virginia cavalry	4
First Ohio cavalry	2
Ninth Ohio cavalry	2
Sixth Kentucky cavalry	1
Seventy-seventh Ohio	13
One Hundred and Forty-eighth Ohio National guard	12
Ninety-second Ohio	11
Seventy-third Ohio	10
Thirty-sixth Ohio	7
Sixty-third Ohio	5
Thirty-ninth Ohio	3
Eighty-seventh Ohio (three months)	2
One each in Fifty-third Ohio, Eighteenth Ohio (three months), Eighteenth Ohio (three years), One Hundredth Pennsylvania, One Hundred and First Pennsylvania, Sixty-fifth Ohio, Seventieth Ohio, One Hundred and Ninety-sixth Ohio, in all	8
Total number of soldiers	78
Died	16

FEARING TOWNSHIP.

Abbott, William James, age 21, volunteer, August 6, 1861, three years, Thirty-sixth regiment, company G, drummer, attained to the rank of principal musician, served two years and six months, honorably discharged, reenlistment, age 23, volunteer, three years, Thirty-sixth regiment, company G, quartermaster, attained rank of orderly, served one year and six months, mustered out

Athey, Hezekiah, age 42, drafted, 1862, nine months, Seventy-seventh regiment, company B, private, served nine months, mustered out.

Athey, Charles Wesley, age 18, volunteer, October, 1861, three years

Athey, James L., age 17, volunteer, February 26, 1863, three years, Seventy-seventh regiment, company B, private.

Athey, John Wesley, age 17, volunteer, October 18, 1861, three years, Seventy-seventh regiment, company B, private, reenlistment.

Bartmess, George J., volunteer, August 12, 1861, three years, Thirty-sixth regiment, company G, private, honorably discharged September 12, 1862, for disability.

Bartlett, Frederick, volunteer, August 19, 1862, three years, Seventh cavalry, company H

Bell, John Thomas, age 18, volunteer, August 30, 1862, three years, Seventh cavalry, company H, private, served two years and ten months, mustered out June 29, 1865.

Brown, Leroy S, volunteer, August 3, 1862, three years, Seventh cavalry, company H, private, discharged from service on account of disability.

Boye, Charles, age 16, volunteer, 1861, three years, First Virginia light artillery, company C, private, mustered out July 1, 1865, reenlisted as a veteran.

Britton, Thomas, age 34, volunteer, August 12, 1862, three years, Thirty-sixth regiment, company D, private, served three years, mustered out July 9, 1865

Brown, John Howell, volunteer, May 28, 1862, three months, Eighty-seventh regiment, company A, sergeant, one battle, served four months, mustered out October 1, 1862.

Brown, William, age 23, volunteer, September, 1861, three years, First cavalry, company L, private.

Brown, Daniel

Brown, James Pedre, age 18, volunteer, May 28, 1862, three months, Eighty-seventh regiment, company A, private, one battle, served four months, mustered out September, 1862

Carver, T S, Second Virginia regiment, company H.

Carver, Sampson James, age 16, volunteer, First cavalry, company G.

Chapman, Seldon, age 22, volunteer, 1863, three years, Second heavy artillery, company K, private, attained to rank of corporal

Chapman, Levi O, volunteer, Seventh cavalry, company H.

Chapman, Hiram H, age 21, volunteer, August 13, 1862, three years, Ninety-second regiment, company H, private, served two years and ten months, mustered out June 10, 1865.

Doan, Richard, age 27, volunteer, July 25, 1863, three years, Second heavy artillery, company K, private, mustered out August 23, 1865.

Dowling, James R., age 25, volunteer, August 12, 1862, three years, Thirty-sixth regiment, company D, private, served three years, mustered out July 4, 1864, wounded at Chickamauga and transferred to veteran reserve corps

Dowling, John W, age 24, volunteer, October, 1862, three years, Seventh cavalry, company H, private, served two years and nine months, mustered out June 29, 1865

Dowling, Lewis W., age 21, volunteer, May 28, 1862, three months, Eighty-seventh regiment, company H, private, one battle, served four months, mustered out October 1, 1862.

Drum, Jacob, volunteer, August 3, 1862, three years, Sixty-third regiment, company C, private.

Flanders, John, age 24, drafted, 1862, nine months, Seventy-seventh regiment, company B, private, served ten months.

Flanders, Augustus, age 23, volunteer, September 3, 1862, three years, Seventh cavalry, company H, private, served three years.

Flanders, Henry, age 22, volunteer, August, 1861, three years, Thirty-sixth regiment, company I, private, served seven months, died March 17, 1862, at Summersville, Virginia, of typhus fever.

Flanders, Jasper C., age 21, substitute, 1864, one hundred days, One Hundred and Forty-eighth regiment, private.

Flanders, Joseph, age 19, March 14, 1864, three years, Sixty-second regiment, company I, private, served one year and five months, mustered out August, 1865.

Flanders, Enos, age 23, substitute, 1864, one hundred days, One Hundred and Forty-eighth regiment, company A, private.

Guitteau, Benjamin Fulton, age 21, volunteer, 1861, three years, First cavalry, company L, private, killed January 2, 1863, at battle at Stone River.

Hall, James, age 20, volunteer, August 13, 1861, three years, Thirty-sixth regiment, company G, private, served three years, mustered out.

Hallet, Charles, Second Huntington artillery, company K.

Henning, John Henry, age 29, volunteer, April 17, 1861, three months, Eighteenth regiment, company B, private served four months, mustered out August 28, 1861, reenlistment, age 29, volunteer, September, 1861, three years, First Virginia cavalry, company C, private, mustered out, veteran enlistment, age 31, volunteer, March 31, 1864, three years, First Virginia light artillery, company C, private.

Henning, Charles Henry, age 22, volunteer, April 17, 1861, three months, Eighteenth regiment, company B, private, served four months, mustered out August 28, 1861, reenlistment, age 22, volunteer, 1861, three years, First Virginia light artillery, company C, private, served two years, died October 31, 1863

Hill, Ira, age 27, volunteer, September 2, 1862, three years, Seventh cavalry, company H, private, served three years, mustered out 1865.

Hill, Isaac, age 18, volunteer, August, 1862, three years, Thirty-sixth regiment, company I, private, served three years, mustered out July 3, 1865.

Himebaugh, John H., age 21, volunteer, February 1, 1864, three years, Seventh cavalry, company H, private, served one year and six months, mustered out June 29, 1865.

Hobby, William Alexander, age 32, volunteer, July 22, 1861, three years, Thirty-ninth regiment, company B, served three years, mustered out 1864, sick, and transferred to Fifteenth regiment, company D, Invalid corps.

Howland, Jesse, second heavy artillery, company K.

Horne, George Winfield, age 16, volunteer, August 1, 1863, three years, Second heavy artillery, company K, private, served two years, mustered out August 23, 1865

Ifler, Jacob, First Virginia light artillery, company C.

Kaneff, George Washington, volunteer, August 27, 1862, three years, Seventh cavalry, company L, private, attained rank of sergeant, served three years, mustered out.

Kaneff, Charles Wesley, age 21, volunteer, February 3, 1864, three years, Seventh cavalry, company L, private.

Kidd, Nathaniel Evans, age 30, volunteer, May, 1864, one hundred days, One Hundred and Forty-eighth regiment, company B, private.

Kidd, Jesse M., age 25, volunteer, September 8, 1862, three years, Seventh cavalry, company H, private

Kidd, Joseph, Seventy-seventh regiment, company B.

Kimmick, George, age 17, volunteer, October 5, 1864, one year, Seventh Virginia regiment, company C, private, served nine months, mustered out June 26, 1865.

Kimmick, William, volunteer, December 12, 1863, Thirty-sixth regiment, company B.

Kimmick, William Henry, age 16, volunteer, December, 1863, one year, United States gunboat, cabin boy, attained rank of steward, mustered out.

Kurbs, Leonard.

Lane, Thomas, age 36, substitute, May 2, 1864, one hundred days, One Hundred and Forty-eighth regiment, company A, private, served five months, mustered out September 30, 1864.

Lankford, H. H., age 20, volunteer, August, 1861, three years, Thirty-sixth regiment, company G, private, attained rank of corporal, served three years, mustered out 1864, reenlistment, age 23, substitute, April 3, 1865, one year, Eighteenth regiment, company I.

McCall, James, age 35, volunteer, December 27, 1861, three years, Seventy-seventh regiment, company H, private, served one year, died January 1, 1862, at Alton, Illinois, of small pox.

Morris, Thomas, age 28, volunteer, September 8, 1862, three years, Seventh cavalry, company H, private, served seven months, honorably discharged April 3, 1863, pulmonary tuberculosis.

Newberg, William, age 17, volunteer, January 16, 1864, three years, First cavalry, company L, private.

Nicol, Robert Elder, age 35, substitute, May, 1864, one hundred days, One Hundred and Forty-eighth regiment, company B, private, mustered out September 24, 1864, died October 3, 1864.

Noe, Lewis, volunteer, July 14, 1862, three years, Thirty-sixth regiment, company G.

Page, May, 1864, one hundred days, One Hundred and Forty-eighth regiment.

Page, May, 1864, one hundred days, One Hundred and Forty-eighth regiment.

Palmer, Miles L., age 22, volunteer, August 29, 1862, three years, Seventh cavalry, company H, private.

Pfaff, Lewis, age 26, substitute, May, 1864, one hundred days, One Hundred and Forty-eighth regiment, company A, private.

Pfaff, Daniel, age 21, volunteer, July 22, 1861, three years, Thirty-ninth regiment, company B, private, served three years and one month, mustered out August, 1864.

Pfaff, Conrad, aged 18, volunteer, December 27, 1861, three years, First Virginia light artillery, company C, private, served two years and six months, honorably discharged 1864, veteran enlistment, age 20, volunteer, March 31, 1864, three years, First Virginia light artillery, company C, served one year and three months, mustered out June 28, 1865.

Prewett, Brazil, age 21, volunteer, Seventh cavalry, company L, private.

Price, John W., volunteer, 1861, three years, First cavalry, company L, private, reenlisted as a veteran.

Price, Logan, age 19, volunteer, September 1, 1861, three years, First Virginia light artillery, company A, private, served two years and six months, honorably discharged, veteran enlistment, age 21, volunteer, March 31, 1861, three years, First Virginia light artillery, company C, mustered out June 28, 1865.

Robinson, W Lynch, volunteer, July, 1862, three years, Ninety-second regiment, company F, private, served three years, mustered out June 10, 1865.

Robinson, Joseph, age 48, volunteer, three years, Sixty-third regiment, company H, private, died July 20, 1863, at Covington, Kentucky, of chronic diarrhœa

Robinson, Charles H., age 35, volunteer, August 9, 1862, three years, Ninety-second regiment, company F, private, served three years, mustered out June 10, 1865, last two years in invalid corps in Frederick City.

Rodgers, Mason C., volunteer, March 30, 1862, three years, First Virginia light artillery, company C, private, died March 17, 1863.

Rodgers, Frederick, volunteer, March 30, 1862, three years, First Virginia light artillery, company C, private, died December 24, 1862, mortally wounded at the battle of Cross Keys.

Schultice, Adam, age 21, volunteer, August 13, 1862, three years, Sixty-third regiment, company G, private, veteran reenlistment, age 22, volunteer, three years, Sixty-third regiment, company G.

Shelden, Charles, One Hundred and Sixteenth regiment, company G.

Scevers, Benjamin, volunteer, August 20, 1862, three years, Thirty-sixth regiment, company D, private.

Simmons, John, age 29, volunteer, one year, One Hundred and Seventy-ninth regiment, company F, private.

Sinclair, William, Thirty-ninth regiment, company B, private, died August 10, 1862, of fever, at Corinth, Mississippi.

Stanley, William, January 25, 1861, three years, Twelfth regiment, company D, private, served one year, honorably discharged December 25, 1862.

Stanley, W. T., volunteer, three years, Thirty-sixth regiment, company K, second lieutenant, attained rank of captain, honorably discharged November 25, 1864.

Stanley, George, volunteer, First Virginia light artillery, company C, private, attained rank of corporal, mustered out 1865.

Taylor, Reuben, age 17, volunteer, three years, Seventy-seventh regiment, company B, private, died June 25, 1864, in rebel prison at Tyler, Texas

Theis, Jacob, age 20, October 13, 1864, one year, Seventy-eighth regiment, company D, private, served nine months, mustered out July 11, 1865.

Thornton, William, age 18, volunteer, August 12, 1861, three years, Thirty-sixth regiment, company G, private, attained rank of orderly, served two and one-half years, honorably discharged, veteran enlistment, age 20, volunteer, February 24, 1864, three years, Thirty-sixth regiment, company G, private, attained rank of orderly, served six months, mustered out July 27, 1865.

Troudner, George Adam, age 18, volunteer, March, 1862, three years, First Virginia light artillery, company C, private, served two years, honorably discharged, veteran enlistment, age 20, volunteer, October 31, 1864, three years, First Virginia light artillery, company C, private, mustered out June 28, 1865.

Tucker, John R., age 56, volunteer, April, 1861, three months, Nineteenth regiment, company G, private, served three months, mustered out August, 1861.

Tucker, Abner, age 22, volunteer, April 17, 1861, three months, Eighteenth regiment, company B, private, mustered out August 28,

1861, reenlisted, volunteer, Thirty-sixth regiment, private, reenlisted, volunteer, First light artillery, company C, private, reenlisted, age 26, volunteer, Eighteenth regiment, company C, private, honorably discharged.

Ward, Augustus, volunteer, 1861, three years, Thirty-sixth regiment, company A, drummer, served two and one-half years, reenlisted, three years, Thirty-sixth regiment, company A, lieutenant, attained rank of captain, served one and one-half years, mustered out July 9, 1865.

Ward, Everett R., age 18, volunteer, August 8, 1864, one year, First Virginia light artillery, company H, private, served ten months, honorably discharged May 24, 1865.

Warren, Robert L., volunteer, October, 1861, three years, First Virginia cavalry, company E, private, honorably discharged, reenlisted as a veteran.

Warren, Charles, Seventh Virginia regiment, company E.

Waxler, Archibald V., age 23, volunteer, August 19, 1862, three years, Thirty-sixth regiment, company G, private, attained rank of corporal, died November 18, 1864, killed West.

Whitney, Simon H., age 27, volunteer, October 5, 1862, three years, Seventh cavalry, company H, private, served seven months, died May, 10, 1863, of typhoid fever.

Young, John R., age 23, volunteer, August 12, 1861, three years, Thirty-sixth regiment, company G, private, attained rank of corporal, served two years and six months, honorably discharged, veteran enlistment, age 25, volunteer, February 1, 1864, three years, Thirty-sixth regiment, company G, corporal, attained rank of sergeant, served one year and six months, mustered out July, 1865.

Young, Thomas Andrews, age 17, volunteer, March, 1865, one year, One Hundred and Eighty-ninth regiment, company H, private.

Young, Douglass H., age 22, volunteer, September, 1861, three years, First Virginia light artillery, company C, private, served one month, honorably discharged, second enlistment, age 23, volunteer, August 12, 1861, three years, Thirty-sixth regiment, company D, private, served three years, mustered out June 22, 1865.

Young, Lewis, volunteer, October 1, 1861, Fifty-eighth regiment, company K.

Zimmer, Lewis, age 20, volunteer, September 26, 1861, three years, Sixty-third regiment, company G, private, served one year, died October 3, 1862, shot in battle at Corinth.

RECAPITULATION.

Buell's Pierpont battery.. 12
Battery K, Second heavy artillery.. 4
Battery H, First Virginia light artillery.. 1
Seventh Ohio cavalry.. 15
First Ohio cavalry.. 6
First Virginia cavalry.. 1
Sixty-third Ohio.. 4
Thirty-sixth Ohio.. 18
Seventy-seventh Ohio 8
One Hundred and Forty-eighth Ohio National Guard.. 8
Three each in Thirty-ninth Ohio, Ninety-third Ohio, Eighty-Seventh Ohio (three months) Eighteenth (three months) in all.. .. 12
Seventh Virginia infantry.. 2
Eighteenth Ohio (three years).. 2
And one each in Second Virginia infantry, Sixty-second Ohio, Fifty-eighth Ohio, Twelfth Ohio, Nineteenth Ohio, Seventy-eighth Ohio, One Hundred and Sixteenth Ohio, One Hundred and Seventy-ninth Ohio, One Hundred and Eighty-ninth Ohio, and two not designated, in all.. 11

Total number soldiers.. 109
Died 11

GRANDVIEW TOWNSHIP.

Adams, Thomas Dunn, age 23, volunteer, August, 1861, Seventh Virginia infantry, company C, private, served three years, mustered out in November, 1864.

Adams, William A. S., age 17, volunteer, September 12, 1864, one year, Sixth Virginia infantry, company C, private, served nine months, mustered out June 10, 1865.

Armstrong, Robert, One Hundred and Sixteenth regiment, company D, killed in service.

Austin, George Greenwood, age 21, volunteer, 1861, three years, Second Virginia cavalry, company C, bugler, veteran reenlistment, 1864, three years.

Arthur, William D., age 18, volunteer, October 5, 1861, three years,

Seventy-seventh regiment, company C, private, served one year, honorably discharged October 12, 1862

Arthur, J. Armstrong, age 16, volunteer, October 5, 1861, three years, Seventy-seventh regiment, company C, private; veteran enlistment, February 1864, three years.

Aten, George, age 32, drafted, September 27, 1864, one year, Fifty-first regiment, company D, private, served nine months, mustered out June 20, 1865.

Ballentine, John, age 24, volunteer, November, 1861, three years, Seventy-seventh regiment, company C, private, served one year, honorably discharged.

Ballentine, Robert, age 16, volunteer, October 5, 1861, Seventy-seventh regiment, company C, private, veteran enlistment, February, 1864, three years, private, attained the rank of corporal.

Ballentine, Hugh, age 14, volunteer, February, 1864, three years, Twenty-fifth regiment, company C, private.

Barber, J. Daubigne, age 24, volunteer, October 8, 1861, three years, Second Virginia cavalry, company C, first sergeant, attained rank of first lieutenant, served two years, killed in action near Winchester, July 27, 1864.

Barentz, Dwight, age 24, volunteer, January 25, 1865, one year, One Hundred and Eighty-fourth regiment, company A, private, served seven months, mustered out in September, 1865.

Barentz, Martin, age 18, volunteer, March, 1865, one year, One Hundred and Eighty-seventh regiment, company G, private.

Barnes, Vachel Hall, age 22, volunteer, August, 1862, three years, Ninety-second regiment, company H, corporal, died.

Barnes, Francis Adams, age 18, volunteer, September, 1861, three years, Second Virginia cavalry, company C, private, served one year, honorably discharged in 1862, second enlistment, age 20, volunteer, August, 1863, six months, Fourth Virginia cavalry, company G, first lieutenant; third enlistment, age 21, volunteer, September, 1864, one year, One Hundred and Eightieth regiment, company F, first lieutenant, served ten months, mustered out July, 1865.

Barnhart, Leonard, age 29, volunteer, October 5, 1861, three years, Seventy-seventh regiment, company C, private, served three and one-half years, mustered out in March, 1865.

Barnhart, William, age 22, volunteer, February, 1864, three years, Seventy-seventh regiment, company C, private.

Barnhart, George M, age 39, volunteer, February 15, 1865, one year, One Hundred and Eighty-seventh regiment, company G, private.

Barnhart, Chester, age 33, volunteer, March 8, 1864, Seventh Virginia, private, killed June 3, 1864, in action at Cold Harbor, Virginia.

Barnhart, James William, volunteer, Seventh Virginia, killed.

Barrett, John C., age 18, volunteer, February 20, 1865, one year, One Hundred and Eighty-seventh regiment, company G, private.

Beaver, Perry, age 23, volunteer, 1861, three years, Seventy-seventh regiment, company C, private, served three years, mustered out December 12, 1864

Beaver, James, age 19, volunteer, August, 1861, three years, Seventy-seventh regiment, company C, private, served seven months, died in May, 1862, at Covington, Kentucky.

Beaver, George W., age 31, drafted and volunteer, 1862, three years, Seventy-seventh regiment, company C, private.

Beaver, Calvin, age 19, volunteer, November 1861, three years, Seventy-seventh regiment, company C, private, served three years, mustered out December 12, 1864.

Beaver, Michael, age 23, volunteer, November, 1861, three years, Seventy-seventh regiment, company C, private, served two months, discharged.

Beegle, Daniel M., age 17, substitute and volunteer, 1862, three years, Seventy-seventh regiment, company C, private.

Biddle, Perry, age 43, volunteer, December 16, 1861, three years, Seventy-seventh regiment, company I, private, served two years, died December 14, 1863.

Biddle, Loyd Adelbert, age 17, volunteer, October 22, 1861, three years, Seventy-seventh regiment, company I, private; veteran enlistment, February, 1864, company C.

Biddle, John Quincy, age 15, volunteer, October 22, 1861, three years, Seventy-seventh regiment, company C, private, served five months, honorably discharged March 15, 1862; reenlistment, age 18, volunteer, February, 1864, three years, Seventy-seventh regiment, company C, private.

Bradfield, Charles, age 18, volunteer, February, 1864, three years, Seventy-seventh regiment, company C, private.

Broadright, Henry, age 22, volunteer, October, 1861, three years, Second Virginia cavalry, company I, private, attained corporal, died.

Brooks, John, age 35, drafted, September 27, 1864, one year, Fifty-first regiment, company D, private, served nine months, mustered out June 20, 1865.

Bruce, Samuel, age 42, volunteer, August 6, 1861, three years, Seventy-seventh regiment, company C, private, served nine months, died April 23, 1862.

Burnet, John L. Jones, age 16, volunteer, May 18, 1863, three years, Seventy-seventh regiment, company C, private.

Burris, Marion, age 23, volunteer, October 5, 1861, three years, Seventy-seventh regiment, company C, private, attained the rank of second lieutenant, resigned; reenlistment, age 27, substitute, February, 1865, one year, Twentieth regiment, company B, private.

Burris, William W., age 18, volunteer, December 12, 1861, three years, Seventy-seventh regiment, company C, private; veteran enlistment, age 20, volunteer, February, 1864, three years, Seventy-seventh regiment, company C, private, attained the rank of first lieutenant.

Burris, John Martin, age 18, volunteer, February 8, 1864, three years, Sixty-second Pennsylvania regiment, company I, private, served seventeen months, mustered out July 3, 1865.

Burris, William, age 22, volunteer, 1861, three years, Second Virginia cavalry, company C, private, mustered out in 1864.

Burns, Stimson, age 16, volunteer, February, 1865, one year, One Hundred and Eighty-Seventh regiment, company G, private.

Byers, Jacob, age 35, volunteer, August 15, 1862, three years, One Hundred and Sixteenth regiment, company E, private, served three years, mustered out June 14, 1865

Callagan, John, age 47, volunteer, 1861, three years, Seventy-seventh regiment, company C, private, killed January 8, 1862.

Calvert, Alexander, age 25, volunteer, August 29, 1862, three years, Fourteenth Virginia regiment, company E, corporal.

Calvert, Washington, age 25, volunteer, October 8, 1861, three years, Sixty-third regiment, company F, private, attained the rank of corporal, served ten months, honorably discharged August 23, 1862.

Calvert, Ezekiel, First artillery, company K.

Campbell, Joseph, age 23, volunteer, August 23, 1861, three years, Seventy-seventh regiment, company C, private, served nine months, honorably discharged May 26, 1862.

Cameron, John B., volunteer, Seventy-seventh regiment, company G.

Cameron, John R., Seventy-seventh regiment, company G.

Cameron, Andrew.

Carrol, George, age 38, volunteer, October 28, 1861, three years, Seventy-seventh regiment, company C, private, one year, died October 4, 1862.

Carrol, Thomas, Seventy-seventh regiment, company I.

Cline, Martin Van, age 34, volunteer, August 1, 1861, three years, Seventh Virginia regiment, company D, private, served one year, honorably discharged October 6, 1862, for disability.

Cline, Theodore, volunteer, One Hundred and Eighty-seventh regiment, company G.

Cluter, M. V., volunteer, Seventy-seventh regiment, company C.

Cooper, James, Ninety-second regiment, company H.

Cooper, John, volunteer, Ninety-second regiment, company H, private, killed in service.

Cooper, Robert, Sixty-third regiment, company F; reenlistment, volunteer, 1865, one year, One Hundred and Eighty-seventh regiment, company G, private.

Cunningham, William Henry, One Hundred and Eighty-seventh regiment, company G.

Cunningham, James, age 24, drafted, September 27, 1864, one year, Fifty-first regiment, companies I and D, private, served eight months, honorably discharged June 1, 1865.

Cunningham, Robert H., age 19, volunteer, February 14, 1865, one year, Fifty-first regiment, company G, private.

Custer, David, age 48, volunteer, January 5, 1862, three years, Seventy-seventh regiment, company C, private, served two years, honorably discharged February, 1864.

Dailey, Hamilton, age 18, volunteer, February 28, 1864, three years, Fifteenth regiment, company C, private.

Dailey, William, One Hundred and Twenty-fifth regiment, company H.

Davis, John, age 36, volunteer, August, 1862, three years, Ninety-second regiment, company H, private, served three years, mustered out June 10, 1865.

Davis, Peter, Second cavalry, company C, died.

Dayly, Wesley, age 18, volunteer, October 19, 1861, three years, Seventy-seventh regiment, company C, private, served five months, died March 30, 1862, at Paducah, Kentucky.

Dickey, Samuel M., age 41, volunteer, 1861, three years, Seventy-seventh regiment, company C, private, honorably discharged, reenlistment, age 45, substitute, October, 1864, three years, Seventy-seventh regiment, company C, private, mustered out in 1865.

Dodds, Joseph, age 19, volunteer, September 13, 1861, three years, Second Virginia cavalry, company C, private, attained corporal, served two years and a half, reenlistment, volunteer, 1864, three years, Second Virginia cavalry, company C, corporal, served one year and four months, mustered out in 1865.

Dorff, Charles, age 17, volunteer, October 20, 1861, three years, Second Virginia cavalry, company C, private, reenlistment, age 19, volunteer, 1864, three years, Second Virginia cavalry, company C, private, mustered out in 1865.

Dorff, Reuben, age 16, volunteer, 1864, three years, Second Virginia cavalry, private, mustered out in 1865.

Dorff, William, age 18, volunteer, September, 1861, three years First light artillery, company K, corporal, attained sergeant, reenlistment, age 21, volunteer, 1864, three years, First light artillery, company K, sergeant, mustered out in 1865.

Deegan, William C., age 20, volunteer, October, 1861, three years, Sixty-third regiment, company F, corporal, attained sergeant.

Dye, James, One Hundred and Ninety-fourth regiment, company I, private, died.

Eaton, William, Seventy-seventh regiment, company C.

Easthorn, James P., age 30, volunteer, September 12, 1861, three years, Seventy-seventh regiment, company C, private, reenlisted as a veteran, volunteer, February, 1864, three years, Seventy-seventh regiment, company C, private, attained corporal.

Easthorn, John J., aged 19, volunteer, May, 1861, three years, Twenty-fifth regiment, company B, private, served one year, died, mortally wounded at the battle of Cross Keys, Virginia.

Easton, Daniel, Twenty-fifth regiment.

Eddy, Going, age 40, volunteer, August 27, 1861, three years, Seventh Virginia infantry, company D, private, served ten months, honorable discharged in June, 1862.

Eddy, David, age 24, volunteer, October 18, 1861, three years, Seventy-seventh regiment, company I, private, reenlisted as a veteran, age 26, volunteer, February, 1864, three years, Seventy-seventh regiment, company I, private.

Eddy, Alpheus, age 18, volunteer, August, 1861, three years, First light artillery, company K, private, served two years and a half, enlisted as a veteran, age 20, volunteer, 1864, three years, First light artillery, company K, private, died in 1864.

Eddy, Going, jr., age 17, volunteer, July 25, 1863, six months, Fourth Virginia cavalry, company G, private, served seven months, mustered out in March, 1864, reenlistment, age 18, volunteer, 1864, three years, First light artillery, company K, private, mustered out in 1865.

Eddy, William, age 15, volunteer, July, 1863, six months, Fourth Virginia cavalry, company G, private, served seven months, mustered out in 1864, reenlistment, age 16, volunteer, 1864, three years, First light artillery, company K, private, mustered out in 1865.

Edgill, John, age 15, volunteer, August, 1861, three years, Seventy-seventh regiment, company C, private, enlisted as a veteran, age 18, volunteer, 1864, three years, Seventy-seventh regiment, company C, private.

Edmonds, Robert, age 19, volunteer, October 28, 1861, three years, Seventy-seventh regiment, company C, private, enlisted as a veteran, age 21, volunteer, 1864, three years, Seventy-seventh regiment, company C, private.

Edmonds, William, aged 17, volunteer, July, 1861, three years, Fourth Virginia, company C, private, honorably discharged in March, 1865.

Edmonds, John, age 16, volunteer, February, 1864, three years, Seventy-seventh regiment, company C, private.

Elrod, James, age 25, volunteer, three years, Seventy-seventh regiment, company C, private.

Eoffie, Hiram, age 17, volunteer, June 4, 1861, three years, Fourth Virginia, company C, served two years, honorably discharged in September, 1863, enlisted as a veteran, age 20, volunteer, February, 1864, three years, Seventy-seventh regiment, company C, private.

Eoffie, Sardine, age 17, volunteer, October 10, 1861, three years, Seventy-seventh regiment, company C, private, enlisted as a veteran, age 19, volunteer, February, 1864, three years, Seventy-seventh regiment, company C, private.

Eoffie, Lander, age 19, volunteer, 1864, three years, One Hundred and Sixteenth regiment, company C, private, died in September, 1864, shot in hospital at Cumberland, Maryland.

Eoffle, Marion, volunteer, February 14, 1865, one year, Seventy-seventh regiment, company C, private.

Evans, John F., volunteer, Seventh Virginia, company C, Second lieutenant, attained first lieutenant, mustered out August 19, 1863, on account of wound received at Chancellorsville.

Ferguson, James S., volunteer, October 20, 1861, three years, Seventy-seventh regiment, company C, private, served six months, died April 20, 1862.

Ferguson, Thomas, age 32, volunteer, 1861, three years, Seventy-seventh regiment, company C, private, died in 1862.

Ferguson, John, Seventy-seventh regiment, company C, private.

Filley, Buell, age 18, volunteer, September 3, 1861, three years, Seventy-seventh regiment, company D, private, served two and a half years, reenlisted as a veteran, February, 1864, three years, Seventy-seventh regiment, company D, private, served one year, died April 23, 1865, of diarrhœa, at Natchez, Mississippi.

Fisher, Henry, drafted, Seventy-seventh regiment, company B.

Forance, George, Seventeenth regiment, company B

Frazier, George R., age 16, volunteer, August 1, 1861, three years, Seventh Virginia, company D, private, mustered out July 1, 1863.

Fouracre, Charles W., Fifteenth regiment, company D.

Frey, William Henry, age 22, volunteer, August, 1862, three years, Ninety-second regiment, company C, private, served three years, mustered out June 10, 1865.

Fry, William Everett, age 36, volunteer, August 13, 1862, three years, Ninety-second regiment, company H, private, served three years, mustered out June 10, 1865.

Gibson, Robert, age 25, volunteer, September 23, 1864, one year, One Hundred and Eightieth regiment, company F, private, mustered out June 10, 1865.

Gatten, Robert, Second Virginia cavalry, company A.

Gooseman, Israel, age 18, volunteer, October 10, 1861, three years, Second Virginia cavalry, company C, private, served three years, mustered out October 1, 1864, wounded in action near Raleigh.

Gray, Walter, age 19, volunteer, August, 1861, three years, Thirty-sixth regiment, company E, private, reenlisted as a veteran, 1864, three years, Thirty-sixth regiment, company E, private, mustered out July, 1865.

Gray, Philip, age 16, volunteer, February 25, 1864, three years, Seventy-seventh regiment, company C, private.

Gray, William, age 15, volunteer, February 25, 1864, three years, Seventy-seventh regiment, company C, private, served three months, died June 6, 1864, at Little Rock, Arkansas.

Griggs, John C., age 15, volunteer, October 1, 1861, three years, Seventy-seventh regiment, company I, private, reenlisted as a veteran February, 1864, three years, Seventy-seventh regiment, company I, private.

Guirt, William, First light artillery, company K, private.

Gully, Cyrus, Ninth cavalry, company B.

Hackethorn, William, age 31, volunteer, September, 1861, three years, First light artillery, company K, private, served three years, mustered out, 1864.

Harvey, Lucien Levant, age 28, volunteer, December, 1861, three years, First light artillery, company H, private, served three years, mustered out, 1864.

Harvey, Franklin C., volunteer, 1863, six months, Fourth Virginia cavalry, company G, private, served seven months, mustered out March, 1864, reenlisted as a substitute in 1864, one year, Fifth regiment, company D, private, served nine months, mustered out June 22, 1865.

Harvey, Theodore I, age 17, volunteer, February, 1864, three years, Seventy-seventh regiment, company C, private.

Hays, John, age 30, volunteer, August 25, 1861, three years, Seventy-seventh regiment, company C, private, attained the rank of corporal, served two and a half years, reenlisted as a veteran February, 1864, three years, Seventy-seventh regiment, company C, private, served one year and three months, honorably discharged June, 1865.

Heddleston, Finley, age 38, volunteer, March 23, 1864, three years, First light artillery, company K, private.

Hessam, Samuel T., substitute, September, 1864, one year, Fifth regiment, company D, private, served nine months.

Hill, Daniel, Seventy-eighth regiment, company G, died.

Hill, Porter, age 27, volunteer, August 1, 1861, three years, Seventh Virginia, company D, private, served three years, mustered out August 27, 1864.

Holland, Alexander, age 19, volunteer, May, 1861, three years, Twenty-fifth regiment, company C, private, served three years, mus-

tered out, 1864, reenlisted March, 1865, one year, One Hundred and Ninety-fourth regiment, company C, attained the rank of captain.

Holland, William, age 18, volunteer, February 15, 1864, three years, Seventy-seventh regiment, company C, private.

Holland, Harvey, age 16, volunteer, February 15, 1864, three years, Seventy-seventh regiment, company C, private.

Hood, D., Fifty-first regiment, company D.

Howell, John H., age 19, volunteer, November 16, 1861, three years, Sixty-second regiment, company K, private, reenlisted as a veteran, 1864, three years, Sixty-second regiment, company K, private, attained the rank of corporal, honorably discharged September, 1865.

Howell, George, age 18, substitute, March, 1865, one year, Thirty-ninth regiment, company C, private, served four months, mustered out July, 1865.

Howell, James, drafted, discharged

Howell, Andrew, First light artillery, company K.

Hines, John, volunteer, 1861, three years, Seventy-seventh regiment, company C.

Honnel, David, volunteer, Twenty-third regiment, company G.

Hines, John, jr., volunteer, three years, Seventy-seventh regiment, company C.

Jarvis, John E., age 21, volunteer, 1863, three years, Fifty-ninth regiment, company A, private, killed.

Jarvis, Ashbury, age 19, volunteer, 1861, three years, Seventy-seventh regiment, company I, served three years, mustered out in 1864.

Jewell, James, volunteer, February 24, 1864, three years, Seventy-seventh regiment, company C, private.

Justice, John W., age 22, volunteer, January 18, 1864, First light artillery, company K, corporal, mustered out.

Jewell, Samuel, volunteer, three years, Seventy-seventh regiment, company C, private

Justice, Josiah, First light artillery, company K.

Johnson, James, age 35, volunteer, March 25, 1865, one year, One Hundred and Ninety-fourth regiment, company I, private, served three months, honorably discharged May, 1865.

Johnson, John D., Twenty-seventh regiment, company I.

Jones, Calvin D., age 20, volunteer, 1861, three years, First light artillery, company K, veteran reenlistment, age 22, volunteer, 1864, three years, First light artillery, company K, mustered out 1865.

Jones, Johiel, age 16, volunteer, December 25, 1861, three years, Seventy-seventh regiment, company C, private, served two years, veteran reenlistment, age 18, volunteer, February, 1864, three years, Seventy-seventh regiment, company C, private, served four months, shot himself, and died June 20, 1864.

Keigley, Jacob, age 22, volunteer, November 10, 1861, three years, Seventy-seventh regiment, company C, private, served one year, died December 14, 1862, at Alton, Illinois.

Kendle, Elias, Sixty-seventh regiment, company K, private.

Kette, Ferdinand, age 16, volunteer, 1863, six months, Fourth Virginia cavalry, company G, private, reenlistment, age 17, volunteer, March 1, 1865, one year, Nineteenth regiment, company I, corporal, served eight months, mustered out in 1865

Kilmer, John, drafted September, 1864, one year, Thirty-second regiment, company C, private.

Kirkbride, Martin, age 18, volunteer, March 24, 1864, three years, First light artillery, company K, private, served sixteen months, mustered out July, 1865.

Knapp, Wilson L., age 30, drafted September 27, 1864, one year, Fifty-first regiment, company D, private, served nine months, mustered out June 20, 1865.

Landy, Alvy William, age 22, volunteer, July 22, 1861, three years, Thirty-ninth regiment, company B, private, served two years and six months, reenlistment, age 24, volunteer, January 1, 1864, three years, Thirty-ninth regiment, company B, private, served one year and five months, died June 17, 1865.

Larcombe, Charles, age 22, volunteer, November 8, 1861, three years, Second Virginia cavalry, company C, private, attained rank of quartermaster sergeant, served three years and seven months, mustered out July, 1865.

Ledger, Frederick, age 29, drafted 1864, one year, Thirty-second regiment, company C, mustered out 1865.

Ledger, Daniel, age 23, volunteer, September 4, 1861, three years, First light artillery, company K, private, served two years and six months, veteran enlistment, age 25, volunteer, 1864, three years, First light artillery, company K, corporal, attained rank of sergeant, served one year and six months, mustered out July 18, 1865.

Leonard, Albert W., age 19, volunteer, November 8, 1861, three years, Second Virginia cavalry, company C, private, served two months, killed at Jennie's Creek, Kentucky, January 7, 1862

Linn, Hiram, age 22, volunteer, August, 1862, three years, Ninety-second regiment, company K, private.

Linn, William, age 20, volunteer, August, 1862, three years, Ninety-second regiment, company K, private, served one month, honorably discharged, second enlistment, volunteer, 1863, six months, Fourth Virginia cavalry, company G, teamster, served seven months, mustered out March, 1864.

Lipincott, Samuel, age 26, volunteer, August 27, 1861, three years, Seventy-seventh regiment, company B, private, served two years and six months, veteran enlistment, volunteer, 1864, three years, Seventy-seventh regiment, company B, private

Lisk, James, age 22, volunteer, September 27, 1861, three years, First light artillery, company K, private, served five months, died of measles at Camp Dennison, March 4, 1862.

Lisk, Nicholas, age 18, volunteer, February, 1864, three years, Seventy-seventh regiment, company C, private, served one year and two months, honorably discharged June, 1865.

Little, Leander, age 18, volunteer, March 24, 1864, three years, First light artillery, company K, private, served one year and three months, mustered out July 18, 1865.

Little, Thomas, age 19, substitute, February 27, 1865, one year, Forty-third regiment, company H, private, served four months, honorably discharged July 14, 1865.

Little, John, volunteer, one year, One Hundred and Eighty-seventh regiment, company G, private, served one year, died in service.

Little, Daniel, age 17, volunteer, 1863, six months, Fourth Virginia cavalry, company G, private, served seven months.

Lowery, Daniel, age 22, volunteer, November 23, 1861, three years, Seventy-seventh regiment, company C, private, served four months, killed at Chattanooga, April 8, 1862.

Lowman, William Henry, age 18, volunteer, November 30, 1861, three years, Seventy-seventh regiment, company C, private, served five months, died May 1, 1862

Lowther, William W., Twenty-fifth regiment, company C.

Marks, D. R., volunteer, January 1, 1862, three years, Seventy-seventh regiment, company C, served one year, honorably discharged January 16, 1863.

Marlow, Leonard A., age 22, volunteer, August, 1861, three years, Seventy-seventh regiment, company C, sergeant, attained rank of second lieutenant.

Masters, Thomas A., age 23, volunteer, April 29, 1861, three years, Twenty-fifth regiment, company B, private, served three years, mustered out July 20, 1864

Mathers, Francis M., age 18, substitute, April, 1865, one year, Eighteenth regiment, company E, private, served six months, honorably discharged October 9, 1864.

Meeks, Gideon, age 24, volunteer, August, 1862, three years, Ninety-second regiment, company H, private, one year, died November, 1863

McBee, Jesse, age 21, volunteer, September 10, 1861, three years, First light artillery, company K, private, served three and a half years, mustered out January 16, 1865.

McCall, James, age 18, volunteer, October 18, 1861, three years, Sixty-second regiment, company K, private, reenlisted as a veteran, age 20, volunteer, 1864, three years, Sixty-second regiment, company K, private, attained rank of corporal.

McCall, Benjamin, age 16, volunteer, November 1, 1862, three years, Seventy-seventh regiment, company C, private.

McCullough, John, age 19, volunteer, September, 1861, three years, First light artillery, company K, private, served two and a half years, reenlisted as a veteran, 1864, volunteer, 1864, three years, First light artillery, company K, corporal, served one and a half years, mustered out July 18, 1865.

McCullom, Isaac, age 18, volunteer, August 1, 1861, three years, Seventh Virginia, company D, private, mustered out July 1, 1865

McCullom, John, Seventy-seventh regiment, company I

McKnight, William Seman, age 32, drafted, September, 1864, one year, Seventy-first regiment, company I, private.

McMahan, William, volunteer, One Hundred and Sixteenth regiment, company D.

Miller, John, March 3, 1864, three years, Seventh Virginia, company D, honorably discharged for disability.

Miller, James, One Hundred and Eighty-seventh company G.

Miller, Frederick, age 27, drafted, October, 1864, one year, Thirty-second regiment, company C, private, served eleven months, mustered out August 27, 1865

Minder, Jacob, age 16, volunteer, August 22, 1864, one year, One Hundred and Eightieth regiment, company F, private, served eleven months, mustered out July 12, 1865.

Mitchell, Joseph M., age 20, volunteer, August, 1861, three years, Seventy-seventh regiment, companies C and A, sergeant, attained rank of orderly sergeant, reenlisted as a veteran, 1864, three years, Seventy-seventh regiment, company C, orderly sergeant, attained rank of first lieutenant.

Mitchell, Israel, age 17, volunteer, February 20, 1865, one year, Eighteenth regiment, company F, private, served seven months, mustered out July 22, 1865.

Moore, John, age 33, volunteer, August, 1861, three years, Seventh Virginia, company D, private, served nine months, honorably discharged for disability May 6, 1862.

Moore, Shadrick, age 17, volunteer, February 24, 1862, three years, Seventy-seventh regiment, company C, private, served one and a half years, honorably discharged July 22, 1865, reenlisted, age 18, July 22, 1865, five years, First United States light artillery, company D, private.

Moore, William, age 27, volunteer, 1861, three years, Seventh Virginia, company D, private, attained to rank of corporal, enlisted as a veteran 1864, three years, wounded at the battle of the Wilderness, July 1, 1865, mustered out.

Moore, Sheldon M., age 22, volunteer, 1861, three years, Seventh Virginia, company D, private, one year, honorably discharged October, 1863.

Myers, William Larwell, age 19, volunteer, March 31, 1864, three years, Seventh Virginia, company D, private, attained rank of corporal, served one year and three months, mustered out July 1, 1865, enlisted as a veteran.

Myers, John, age 24, volunteer, October 20, 1861, three years, Second Virginia cavalry, company C, private, served two years, honorably discharged November 19, 1865, enlisted as a veteran November 20, 1863, three years, served one and a half years, mustered out June 30, 1865.

Myers, Henry, one year, Fifty-first regiment, company D, private.

McWilliams, Lewis H., age 20, volunteer, One Hundred and Eightieth regiment, company C, private, died of fever at Columbus, Ohio, October 1, 1864.

Nenn, Jonas, age 44, volunteer, 1865, one year, One Hundred and Ninety-fourth regiment, company I, private, served seven months, mustered out October, 1865.

Nenn, George, age 17, volunteer, 1863, served six months, Fourth Virginia cavalry, company G, private, served seven months, mustered out March, 1864, reenlisted September, 1864, one year, Eighteenth regiment, company F, served nine months, mustered out July, 1865.

Nenn, John, age 16, substitute, 1865, one year, Twentieth regiment, company D, private, served three months, mustered out July 15, 1865.

Newman, Henry, age 17, volunteer, February 21, 1865, one year, One Hundred and Eighty-ninth regiment, company F, private, seven months, mustered out September 28, 1865.

Oliver, Hillery, age 33, volunteer, September 26, 1864, one year, One Hundred and Eightieth regiment, company F, private, served nine months, mustered out July, 1865.

Oliver, John Weston, age 26, volunteer, February, 1865, one year, One Hundred and Eighty-seventh regiment, company G, private.

Parker, Isaac, age 39, volunteer, 1861, three years, First light artillery, company H, private, served three years, mustered out 1864.

Pan, James H., Thirty-sixth regiment, company G

Petty, Daniel, Twenty-seventh regiment, company D.

Pitcher, William, volunteer, 1865, one year, One Hundred and Ninety-fourth regiment, company I.

Poole, James Jackson, age 27, volunteer, August, 1861, three years, Seventh Virginia, company D, private, served one year, killed at Antietam in 1862.

Poole, Charles, age 33, volunteer, March 3, 1865, one year, One Hundred and Ninety-fourth regiment, company I, private, three months, honorably discharged June, 1865.

Poole, Richard, age 36, volunteer, August 22, 1864, one year, Eighteenth regiment, company F, private, served eleven months, mustered out July 12, 1865.

Porter, Daniel, Eighteenth regiment, company B.

Potts, Richard, age 34, volunteer, October 18, 1861, three years, Sixty-second regiment, company K, private, served seven months, honorably discharged May 9, 1862.

Powell, George W., volunteer, Seventh Virginia, company D, private, attained rank of second lieutenant, mustered out July 1, 1865.

Racy, William, volunteer, Third Virginia cavalry, company C.

Ramsay, Joseph, Forty-fifth regiment, company C, died in prison

Riggs, Daniel B., age 18, volunteer, August 1, 1861, three years, Thirty-sixth regiment, company C, private, hung himself October 15, 1861.

Rienict, Gearhard C., age 33, volunteer, March 7, 1865, one year, Thirty-sixth regiment, company G, private, served five months, mustered out July 27, 1865

Rindle, Charles, Sixty-first regiment, company C, private.

Ritter, Henry, Seventy-seventh regiment, company C.

Robinson, David, One Hundred and Eighty-seventh regiment, company G.

Sandford, John, age 40, volunteer, August 26, 1861, three years, Seventy-seventh regiment, company C, died.

Scott, Isaac, One Hundred and Eightieth regiment, company F.

Scott, John, age 16, volunteer, November, 1861, three years, Seventy-seventh regiment, company C, private, second enlistment, substitute, May, 1864, one hundred days, One Hundred and Forty-eighth regiment, company G, private, served four months, mustered out 1864, third enlistment, volunteer, October 1, 1864, one year, Fifteenth light artillery, private, served eight months, mustered out June 8, 1865.

Robinson, David, One Hundred and Eighty-seventh regiment, company G.

Sandford, Clark.

Springer, John, volunteer, 1861, three years, First regiment, company H, private, served eight months, honorably discharged

Shaner, William, Twenty-fifth regiment, company B.

Springer, Henry J., age 21, volunteer, February, 1865, one year, One Hundred and Eighty-seventh regiment, company G, private.

Salisbury, Henry, Twenty-seventh regiment, company B.

Springer, George, age 19, volunteer, February, 1865, one year, One Hundred and Eighty-seventh regiment, company G, private, mustered out.

Sandford, Nathan, Twenty-fifth regiment, company K.

Springer, John, age 17, volunteer, March, 1865, one year, One Hundred and Ninety-fourth regiment, company I, private, mustered out.

Springer, Samuel, Seventy-seventh regiment, company I.

Stephens, Stacy H., age 22, volunteer, September, 1864, one year, One Hundred and Eightieth regiment, company F, private, served ten months, mustered out July 25, 1865

Snodgrass, John S., Sixty-third regiment, company F.

Stephenson, Joseph, volunteer, 1862, three years, Ninety-second regiment, company H, captain.

Sandford, M., Twenty-fifth regiment, company K.

Stephenson, Joseph Albert, age 16, volunteer, September, 1864, one year, One Hundred and Eightieth regiment, company F, private, served ten months, mustered out July 25, 1865.

Shaner, Leander, Eighty-sixth regiment, company A.

Stewart, Hiram C., age 15, volunteer, August, 1861, three years, Seventh Virginia, company D, private, honorably discharged, veteran enlistment, age 17, volunteer, three years, Seventh Virginia, company D, private, died.

Still, Leonard, volunteer, September, 1864, one year, Seventh Virginia, company D, private, mustered out July 1, 1865.

Shaner, George L., One Hundred and Twenty-ninth regiment, company F.

Still, Thomas, age 18, volunteer, September, 1864, one year, Seventh Virginia, company D, private, served six months, died February 23, 1865.

Swatswood, Levi K., First light artillery.

Swatswood, William, Seventy-seventh regiment, company I.

Talbot, William Bruce, age 18, volunteer, April, 1861, three months, Eighteenth regiment, company E, private, served four months, mustered out August, 1861, second enlistment, age 18, volunteer, 1861, three years, Second Virginia cavalry, companies K and E, private, attained rank of sergeant, served two years, veteran enlistment, age 20, volunteer, 1863, three years, Second Virginia cavalry, company E, sergeant, served one year and six months, mustered out July 1, 1865.

Thorp, Isaiah, age 24, volunteer, August 20, 1862, three years, Ninety-second regiment, company H, private, served one year, killed at Chattanooga September 19, 1863.

Thorp, Isaac, age 28, volunteer, August 20, 1861, three years, Seventy-seventh regiment, company C, private, attained rank of corporal, veteran enlistment, age 20, volunteer, February, 1864, three years, Seventy-seventh regiment, company C, private.

Thorp, William, age 19, volunteer, 1863, six months, Fourth Virginia cavalry, company G, private, served seven months, mustered out March

1864, reenlistment, age 20, volunteer, 1864, one year, Seventy-seventh regiment, company C, private, died September 23, 1865, in prison, Brownsville, Texas.

Thorp, John Henry, age 16, volunteer, February, 1864, three years Seventy-seventh regiment, company C, private.

Thompson, Orvill, age 18, volunteer, November 8, 1861, three years, Second Virginia cavalry, company C, private, served two years, discharged November 25, 1863, for disability, died.

Thompson, James, age 42, volunteer, October, 1861, three years, Sixty-second regiment, company K, private, served seven months, honorably discharged, June 1862.

Thompson, Sampson, age 16, volunteer, October 18, 1861, three years, Sixty-second regiment, company K, private, served seven months, honorably discharged, June, 1862, reenlistment, age 17, volunteer, October 23, 1862, three years, Seventy-seventh regiment, company C, private

Thompson, William S., age 28, substitute and volunteer, 1862, three years, Ninth cavalry, company B, sergeant, honorably discharged, June 8, 1865

Thompson, Edgar, age 26, volunteer, August 9, 1862, three years, Ninety-second regiment, company H, private, served four months, honorably discharged, December, 1862

Thompson, Benjamin, Sixty-second regiment, company K.

Tice, John J., age 43, volunteer, October 27, 1861, three years, Seventy-seventh regiment, company G, sergeant, veteran enlistment age 45, volunteer, February, 1864, three years, Seventy-seventh regiment, company L, teamster

Tice, Harvey, age 15, volunteer, October 27, 1861, three years, Seventy-seventh regiment, company G, private, veteran enlistment, age 17, volunteer, February, 1864, three years, Seventy-seventh regiment, company E, private.

Tice, Henry William, volunteer, Seventy-seventh regiment, company I, private.

Trimble, Francis, age 40, volunteer, October, 1861, three years, First light Artillery, company K, private, veteran enlistment, age 42, volunteer, February, 1864, three years, First light artillery, company K, private, died May 22, 1864.

Ullom, Sylvanus, age 19, volunteer, May, 1861, three years, Twenty-fifth regiment, company B, private, veteran enlistment, age 21, volunteer, three years, Twenty-fifth regiment, company C, private, died.

Unger, Jonas, age 36, volunteer, September 27, 1864, one year, One Hundred and Eightieth regiment, company F, private, served ten months, mustered out July 25, 1865

Vickers, Albert, age 19, volunteer, November 11, 1861, three years, Seventy-seventh regiment, company C, private.

Waters, John, One Hundred and Sixteenth regiment, company A.

Watson, Jacob, Seventy-seventh regiment, company D.

Watson, William, age 32, volunteer, August 1, 1861, three years, Seventh Virginia regiment, company D, corporal, died April 1, 1862, at home

Wells, Clinton, age 18, substitute, 1865, one year, Sixty-third regiment, private, served six weeks, mustered out May, 1865.

Williams, Lewis, One Hundred and Eightieth regiment, company F.

West, Michael, Eighteenth regiment, company F.

Williamson, Nelson, age 24, volunteer, November, 1861, three years, Seventy-seventh regiment, company G, private, served five months, died March 20, 1862, at Pittsburgh Landing.

Willis, James, age 48, substitute, October 8, 1864, one year, Forty-third regiment, company D, private, served nine months, mustered out July 12, 1865.

Wilson, Andrew V., age 19, volunteer, August 29, 1861, three years, Seventy-seventh regiment, company C, private, attained rank of sergeant, served three years, mustered out 1864

Wilson, John, age 21, volunteer, September, 1864, one year, One Hundred and Eightieth regiment, company F, private, honorably discharged 1865.

Winton, Clark, age 28, volunteer, September 7, 1861, three years, Second Virginia cavalry, company C, private, served three and one-fourth years, mustered out December 3, 1864, reenlistment, age 31, volunteer, March 1, 1865, one year, One Hundred and Ninety-fourth regiment, company I, sergeant, served eight months, mustered out October 28, 1865

Woodburn, John Thomas, age 31, drafted, September, 1864, one year, Fifty-first regiment, company D, private, served eight months, mustered out June 10, 1865.

Wilson, James, volunteer, Thirty-third regiment, company D.

RECAPITULATION.

De Beck's battery	20
Huntington's battery	3
And one each in First Ohio light artillery, First United States light artillery	2
Second Virginia cavalry	16
Fourth Virginia cavalry	9
Ninth Ohio cavalry	2
And one each in Second Ohio cavalry, Third Virginia cavalry	2
Seventy-seventh Ohio	85
Seventh Virginia infantry	20
Ninety-second Ohio	12
One Hundred and Eightieth Ohio	11
One Hundred and Ninety-fourth Ohio	8
Fifty-first Ohio	8
One Hundred and Eighty-seventh Ohio	14
Eighteenth Ohio (three years)	6
Eighteenth Ohio (three months)	1
Twenty-fifth Ohio	10
Sixty-second Ohio	6
Sixty-third Ohio	5
One Hundred and Sixteenth Ohio	5
Thirty-sixth Ohio	4
Fifteenth Ohio	3
Twenty-seventh Ohio	3
Thirty-second Ohio	3
Thirty-ninth Ohio	2
Twentieth Ohio	2
Fourth Virginia infantry	2
Fifth Ohio	2
Forty-third Ohio	2
And one each in Sixth Virginia infantry, Thirty-third Ohio, Nineteenth Ohio, Seventeenth Ohio, Twenty-third Ohio, Fourteenth Virginia, Forty-fifth Ohio, Fifty-ninth Ohio, Sixty-second Pennsylvania, Sixty-first Ohio, Sixty-seventh Ohio, Seventy-first Ohio, Seventy-eighth Ohio, Eighty-sixth Ohio, One Hundred and Twenty-fifth Ohio, One Hundred and Twenty-ninth Ohio, One Hundred and Forty-eighth Ohio National guards, One Hundred and Eighty-fourth Ohio, One Hundred and Eighty-ninth Ohio, not designated, 2; in all	21
Total number soldiers	272
Died	45

INDEPENDENCE TOWNSHIP.

Baldwin, Perry, age 43, volunteer, October, 1861, three years, First regiment, company F, private.

Barr, Lewis, volunteer, 1862, three years, One Hundred and Sixteenth regiment, company F, private, served three years, mustered out June 14, 1865.

Blewer, James, Seventy-seventh regiment, company G.

Barnhart, James W., three years, Ninety-second regiment, company D

Blewer, Hiram, Seventy-seventh regiment, company G

Beabout, James, age 18, March 4, 1865, one year, Forty-third regiment, company G, private, served four months, mustered out July 13, 1865.

Boyle, Thomas M., Seventy-seventh regiment, company C.

Beaver, Francis M., age 21, volunteer, August 20, 1861, six months, Fourth Virginia cavalry, company G, private, mustered out.

Beaver, Abraham, age 17, volunteer, 1861, three years, Seventy-seventh regiment, company C, private, second enlistment, age 21, drafted, March 23, 1865, one year, Thirty-ninth regiment, company C, private.

Beck, Preston, age 17, volunteer, three years, Ninety-second regiment, company F, private.

Beabour, James.

Beagal, Milton, age 22, volunteer, three years, Seventy-seventh regiment, company C, private.

Begal, Jeremiah, age 18, volunteer, 1861, three years, First cavalry, company L, private, served three years, mustered out in 1864.

Belville, George, Fourteenth regiment, company F.

Bennett, Simeon, age 25, drafted, March 23, 1865, one year, Thirty-ninth regiment, company G, private, served three months, mustered out July, 1865

Belville, James, Fifth regiment, company H

Bowie, Eli, age 18, volunteer, February 27, 1864, three years, Thirty-sixth regiment, company F, private, served seventeen months, mustered out July, 1865.

Bowie, Harvey, age 18, volunteer, August, 1864, one year, Thirty-sixth regiment, company F, private.

Blower, D., Seventy-seventh regiment, company G.

Broom, James, age 37, volunteer, February, 1865, one year, One Hundred and Ninety-sixth regiment, company F, private.

Brown, George, age 40, drafted, March 23, 1865, one year, Sixty-third regiment, company I, private, served seven weeks, mustered out May 15, 1865.

Brown, James, One Hundred and Ninety-sixth regiment, company H, private.

Carson, James, age 27, volunteer, August, 1862, three years, One Hundred and Sixteenth regiment, company F, private, served two years, died October 28, 1864, in Andersonville prison.

Carson, Thomas, age 22, volunteer, October 28, 1861, three years, Seventy-seventh regiment, company G, private, served one year, died October 4, 1862, of measles.

Carson, Andrew, age 20, volunteer, October 22, 1861, three years, Seventy-seventh regiment, company G, private, served four months, died February 8, 1865, of measles at Camp Dennison.

Chapman, George, age 21, volunteer, July 22, 1861, three years, Thirty-ninth regiment, company B, private, served fourteen months, honorably discharged September 8, 1863, second enlistment, age 24, volunteer, May, 1864, one hundred days, One Hundred and Forty-eighth regiment, company G, private, served four months, mustered out in 1864

Chapman, Vivian, age 20, volunteer, 1862, three years, Ninety-second regiment, company F, private, served three years, mustered out June, 1865.

Chapman, James, volunteer, 1861, three years, Seventy-fifth regiment, company B.

Chapman, William, age 36, volunteer, June 19, 1863, six months, One Hundred and Twenty-ninth regiment, company F, private, served nine months, mustered out March 5, 1864.

Chapman, John, Ninety-second regiment, company H.

Chapman, Joseph, age 38, volunteer, February, 1865, one year, One Hundred and Ninety-sixth regiment, company F, private, mustered out 1865

Climan, John, age 17, substitute, March, 1865, one year, Sixty-third regiment, served seven weeks, mustered out May, 1865.

Cline, Jacob.

Cline, Isaiah, age 32, volunteer, 1861, three years, Seventy-seventh regiment, company C, private, died September 15, 1862.

Cline, Joel, age 33, drafted, September, 1864, one year, Fifty-first regiment, company G, private, mustered out in 1865.

Cline, Marion, age 21, drafted, March, 1865, one year.

Cline, Luther, age 18, volunteer, 1861, three years, Seventy-seventh regiment, company G, private.

Cowen, Robert, age 46, drafted, September 26, 1864, one year, Forty-third regiment, company A, private, mustered out in 1865.

Davis, Bradford, age 17, volunteer, October 28, 1861, three years, Seventy-seventh regiment, company C, private, served fourteen months, December, 1862, veteran enlistment, age 20, volunteer, December 20, 1863, three years, Seventy-seventh regiment, company C, private, served one year and eight months, honoraby discharged August 12, 1865.

David, James B., aged 40, drafted, September 28, 1864, one year, Fifty-first regiment, company G, private mustered out May 22, 1865.

Davis, Joel P., aged 20, volunteer, April 2, 1865, one year, One Hundred and Ninety-seventh regiment, company I, private, served four months, mustered out August, 1865

Decker, Samuel.

Dilley, Jonathan, volunteer, May, 1864, one hundred days, One Hundred and Forty-eighth regiment, company G, private, served three months, mustered out September, 1864.

Donley, Francis M., aged 18, volunteer, December, 1863, three years, Fifth cavalry, company K.

Eddy, Alfred, aged 36, drafted, March 23, 1865, one year, honorably discharged June 6, 1865.

Edwards, John, aged 19, volunteer, August 27, 1861, three years, Seventy-seventh regiment, company C, private, served one year, died September 28, 1864.

Edwards, Richard, aged 19, volunteer, 1863, six months, Fourth Virginia cavalry, company G, private, served eight months, mustered out 1864, reenlisted, age 20, volunteer, August 24, 1864, one year, One Hundred and Seventy-fifth regiment, company K, private, mustered out June 20, 1865.

Ellifritz, James P., aged 28, volunteer, August 8, 1862, three years,

Ninety-second regiment, company F, private, served one year and four months, died November 25, 1863.

Ellifritz, George W., aged 21, volunteer, August 8, 1862, three years, Ninety-second regiment, company F, private, served three years, mustered out June 10, 1865.

Ellis, John J., Sixth regiment, company G, private.

Farnsworth, John C., aged 18, volunteer, July, 1861, three years, Thirty-ninth regiment, company B, private, served two years and six months, reenlisted as veteran, aged 20, volunteered three years, Thirty-ninth, company B, private, served one year and six months, mustered out July 9, 1865.

Farnsworth, Samuel S., aged 25, volunteer, September 19, 1864, three years, Thirty-sixth regiment, company C, private, honorably discharged.

Farnsworth, Henry, aged 23, volunteer, August, 1861, three years, First Virginia cavalry, company F, private, mustered out

Farnsworth, Thomas D., aged 18, volunteer, August, 1861, three years, First Virginia cavalry, company F, private, reenlisted as veteran, aged 20, volunteer, 1864, three years, First Virginia cavalry, company F, private.

Farnsworth, Joseph, aged 34, volunteer, May, 1864, one hundred days, One Hundred and Forty-eighth regiment, company G, private, served four months, mustered out September, 1864.

Fleming, Leander, aged 20, volunteer, May, 1864, one hundred days, One Hundred and Forty-eighth regiment, company G, private, served four months, mustered out September, 1864

Fryman, Alexander, aged 18, substitute, February 28, 1865, one year, Forty-third regiment, company G, private, served four and one half months, mustered out July 13, 1865.

Francis, B., Fourth Virginia cavalry, company G.

Goddard, Joseph, aged 19, volunteer, August, 1861, three years, Seventh Virginia cavalry, company B, private.

Gilbert, Isaac, Seventy-seventh regiment, company E.

Goodman, John Henry, aged 21, drafted, March 23, 1865, one year, Thirty-ninth regiment, company C, private, served three months, mustered out July 9, 1865.

Goodrich, John, aged 27, volunteer, 1861, three years, First light artillery, company K, private, mustered out 1865.

Gouer, John, Seventy-seventh regiment, company G.

Grandon, George W., aged 22, volunteer, March 7, 1865, one year, One Hundred and Ninety-sixth regiment, company F, private, served six months, mustered out September 11, 1865.

Green, Isaac N., Ninety-second regiment, company H.

Greenback, William, aged 27, drafted, September 27, 1864, one year, Fifty-first regiment, company D, private, served nine months, mustered out June 20, 1865.

Haught, Bennett, aged 29, substitute, October, 1864, one year, Fifty-first regiment, company G, private, served nine months, mustered out June 20, 1865.

Haynes, Crawford, aged 16, volunteer, March, 1864, three years, Thirty-sixth regiment, companies F and K, private.

Heinselm, Christian, aged 23, volunteer, October 23, 1861, three years, Seventy-fifth regiment, company B, private, attained corporal, served three years, mustered out December 22, 1864.

Heinselm, Martin, aged 21, volunteer, October 23, 1861, three years, Seventy-fifth regiment, company B, private, served three years, mustered out 1864.

Heinselm, Jacob, aged 23, drafted March 23, 1865, one year, Thirty-ninth regiment, company D, private, served three months, mustered out July, 1865.

Hicks, Ambrose.

Hicks, John, volunteer, 1861, three years, Second Virginia cavalry, company G, private, served seven months, honorably discharged, reenlistment, volunteer, May, 1864, one hundred days, One hundred and Forty-eighth regiment, company G, private, served four months, mustered out September, 1864, third enlistment, drafted, September, 1864, one year, Eighty-eighth regiment, company G, served six months, died April, 1865.

Hill, Thomas G., age 30, volunteer, three years, Seventy-seventh regiment, company G, private, died April 8, 1862, killed at Pittsburgh Landing.

Hoffman, Conrad G., age 36, volunteer, May, 1864, one hundred days, One Hundred and Forty-eighth regiment, company G, mustered out, September, 1864.

Homan, John L., Seventy-seventh regiment, company B.

Hornet, David.

Hutchinson, James, age 23, volunteer, July, 1861, three years, Thirty-

ninth regiment, company B, private, served six months, died January 23, 1862

Jobes, George, Ninety-second regiment, company F, died.

Jones, John R., age 23, volunteer, November 20, 1861, three years, Seventy-seventh regiment, company G, private, served two years, 1863, veteran enlistment, age 25, volunteer, February, 1864, three years, Seventy-seventh regiment, company G, private, attained rank of corporal.

Justice, Phineas J., age 36, volunteer, September 10, 1861, three years, First light artillery, company K, private, served three years, mustered out November 5, 1864.

Justice, John William, age 22, volunteer, November 15, 1861, three years, First light artillery, company K, private, veteran enlistment, age 24, volunteer, 1864, three years, First light artillery, company K, private, served three years and eight months, mustered out July 31, 1865.

Justice, Reuben J., age 20, volunteer, February, 1864, three years, Seventy-seventh regiment, company C, private.

Kemp, Nathan, age 51, volunteer, October 23, 1861, three years Seventy-fifth regiment, company B, private, served ten months, honorably discharged September 4, 1862.

Kemp, William J., age 17, volunteer, July 22, 1861, three years, Thirty-ninth regiment, company B, private, died July, 1862.

Kerns, Andrew J., age 33, volunteer, drafted, March 23, 1865, one year, Thirty-ninth regiment, company C.

Kidder, Rufus, age 29, One Hundred and Forty-eighth regiment, company G, private

Kidder, Erastus, age 21, volunteer, May, 1864, one hundred days, One Hundred and Forty-eighth regiment, company G, private, reenlistment, age 22, volunteer, February, 1865, one year, One Hundred and Ninety-fifth regiment, company I, private.

Kidder, Carolus, age 20, volunteer, February, 1865, one year, One Hundred and Ninety-fifth regiment, company I, private.

Kiggins, Joseph, age 18, October, 1861, three years, Seventy-seventh regiment, company C, private, reenlistment, age 20, volunteer, 1864, three years, Seventy-seventh regiment, company C.

Kiggins, Samuel, age 17, volunteer, 1864, three years, Seventy-seventh regiment, company C, private

Kiggins, Elijah W., age 19, volunteer, May, 1864, one hundred days, One Hundred and Forty-eighth regiment, company G, private, served four months, mustered out September, 1864, reenlistment, age 20, volunteer, March 9, 1865, one year, One Hundred and Ninety-sixth regiment, company F, private, served six months, mustered out September 11, 1865.

Landy, Calvin, age 19, substitute, March, 1865, one year, Eighteenth regiment, company E, private, served five months, died August 26, 1865.

Lee, Peter, age 20, volunteer, August 22, 1862, three years, One Hundred and Sixteenth regiment, company F, private, served three years, mustered out August 8, 1865.

Lee, William, age 33, drafted, March 23, 1865, one year, Thirty-ninth regiment, company C, private.

Lever, James, Seventy-seventh regiment, company G.

Luddington, Henry, age 40, drafted, September 27, 1864, one year, Fifty-first regiment, company G, private, served ten months, mustered out June 20, 1865.

Martin, John, age 19, Ninety-second regiment, company F, died April 15, 1863, of typhoid fever, in Tennessee.

McFarland, Amos M., age 30, drafted, September 27, 1864, one year, Fifty-first regiment, company G, private, served ten months, mustered out June 20, 1865

McKean, Samuel, age 18, volunteer, March, 1865, one year, One Hundred and Ninety-fifth regiment, company K, private.

McFarland, William F., age 21, substitute, May, 1864, one hundred days, One Hundred and Thirty-second regiment, company B, private, served three months, died August 17, 1864.

McFarland, Amos M., age 19, substitute, October, 1864, one year, Sixty-second regiment, company I, private, served seven months, died May 17, 1865.

Merical, John, Seventy-seventh regiment, company G.

Miles, William, age 41, volunteer, August 1, 1861, three years, Seventh Virginia, company D, private, served three years, mustered out August 27, 1864.

Mellen, Franklin S., Seventy-seventh regiment, company G.

Miller, John, age 25, drafted, March 23, 1865, one year.

Murphy, William, age 21, volunteer, September 3, 1861, three years, Seventy-seventh regiment, company C, private, served three years, mustered out 1864.

Moore, Grandville, age 18, volunteer, November, 1861, three years, Seventy-seventh regiment, company G, private.

Noffsinger, Matthias, age 18, volunteer, November, 1861, three years, Seventy-seventh regiment, company G, private, served five months, died April 8, 1862, killed.

Osten, James.

Parr, James, age 26, drafted, September 27, 1864, one year, Fifty-first regiment, company G, private, served ten months, mustered out June 20, 1865.

Powell, Reuben, volunteer, 1863, six months, Fourth Virginia cavalry, company G, private, served six months, mustered out with regiment.

Parr, Lorenzo D., age 19, volunteer, February, 1865, one year, Nineteenth regiment company I.

Powell, James, Fifty-third regiment, company B.

Patterson, Henry, age 51, volunteer, February, 1864, three years, Thirty-sixth regiment, company G, private, served ten months, discharged January 5, 1865.

Paynter, Daniel, aged 26, volunteer, October 28, 1861, three years, First Virginia regiment, company F, private, served three years, mustered out November 26, 1864.

Pickle, Matthias, One Hundred and Ninety-fifth regiment, company I.

Peterson, Thomas, age 35, volunteer, August 22, 1862, three years, One Hundred and Sixteenth regiment, company F, private, served three years, mustered out 1865.

Powell, Jesse, Thirty-sixth regiment, company K.

Pittman, Jacob, age 19, substitute, March 28, 1865, one year, Eighteenth regiment, company E, private, served four months, mustered out August 9, 1865.

Powell, George, Seventy-seventh regiment, company G.

Pool, Alexander, age 25, volunteer, 1861, three years, Seventy-fifth regiment, company B, private, served two years, died November, 1863.

Rea, Thompson N., age 23, volunteer, August, 1863, six months, Fourth Virginia cavalry, company G, private, served five months, died January, 1864.

Rea, Samuel Kemper, age 20, volunteer, September, 1862, three years, Seventh cavalry, company H, private, served one year, died August, 1863.

Ray, John, Seventy-seventh regiment, company K.

Rea, James Richard, age 20, volunteer, August 11, 1862, three years, Ninety-second regiment, company F, corporal, served three years, mustered out June 10, 1865.

Rea, Philip Greene, age 18, volunteer, 1863, six months, Fourth Virginia cavalry, company G, private, mustered out, reenlistment, age 19, volunteer, 1864, one hundred days, One Hundred and Forty-eighth regiment, company G, private, mustered out.

Rea, William Henry, age 20, volunteer, 1863, six months, Fourth Virginia cavalry, company G, private, attained rank of quartermaster sergeant, mustered out, reenlistment, age 21, volunteer, May, 1864, one hundred days, One Hundred and Forty-eighth regiment, company G, private, mustered out September 15, 1865.

Riggs, David, volunteer, May, 1864, one hundred days, One Hundred and Forth-eighth regiment, company G, corporal, mustered out

Riggs, Asbury, age 20, volunteer, August 20, 1863, six months, Fourth Virginia cavalry, company G, private, served seven months, mustered out March 8, 1864, reenlistment, age 21, volunteer, March 31, 1864, three years, First light artillery, company K, private, served one year and three months, mustered out July 19, 1865.

Roth, Nicholas, age 22, volunteer, 1861, three years, Seventy-seventh regiment, company G, private, died April, 1862, killed at Pittsburgh Landing.

Roth, Jacob, age 18, volunteer, September 20, 1864, one year, Seventy-seventh regiment, company E, private, served ten months, mustered out July 31, 1865.

Scott, William, Seventy-seventh regiment, company K, private, died October 3, 1863, at Little Rock, Arkansas.

Sheppard, James, age 21, volunteer, 1862, three years, Ninety-second regiment, company G, private, mustered out June, 1865, died March 23, 1862.

Shockley, Squire, age 29, volunteer, December 10, 1861, three years, Seventy-fifth regiment, company B, private, served three years, died March 23, 1862.

Sipple, Daniel, age 21, volunteer, November, 1861, three years, Seventy-seventh regiment, company G, private, served five months, died April 8, 1862.

Sipple, William, age 22, volunteer, February 14, 1865, one year,

One Hundred and Eighty-sixth regiment, company I, private, served seven months, mustered out September 25, 1865.

Skinner, James, age 19, volunteer, three years, Seventy-seventh regiment, company G, private, died January 24, 1862, of measles, at Camp Dennison.

Skinner, George, age 25, drafted, March 23, 1865, one year, Thirty-ninth regiment, company G, private, served three months.

Stump, John, Seventh Virginia, company B, died.

Thomas, John L., age 22, volunteer, December, 1861, three years, Seventy-seventh regiment, company E, sergeant, served three years and three months, mustered out March, 1865.

Tice, Solomon, three years, Seventy-seventh regiment, company G, private.

Tice, William P., age 21, volunteer, November, 1861, three years, Seventy-seventh regiment, company G, private, served one year, died April 29, 1862, mortally wounded at Louisville.

Tice, Jacob, drafted, March 13, 1865, one year, Thirty-ninth regiment, company C, private.

Tice, William Harrison, drafted, September 27, 1864, one year, Twentieth regiment, company E, private, honorably discharged.

Tice, George W., age 38, drafted, March 25, 1865, one year, Thirty-ninth regiment, company C, private, served three months, mustered out July 9, 1865.

Tice, Lewis, age 33, drafted, September, 1864, one year, Twentieth regiment, company E, private, served eight months, mustered out May 30, 1865.

Tool, Alexander, Seventy-seventh regiment, company B, died.

Tice, Noah, age 17, volunteer, November 4, 1861, three years, Seventy-seventh regiment, company G, private, honorably discharged in 1863, reenlisted September 17, 1864, one year, One Hundred and Eighty-second regiment, company C, private, served ten months, mustered out July 17, 1865.

Tice, Henry, age 14, volunteer, November, 1861, three years, Seventy-seventh regiment, company G, private.

Todd, James, age 35, volunteer, three years, Ninety-second regiment, company G, private, died April 22, 1865, at Nashville, Tennessee.

Voshel, John, age 26, volunteer, three years, Seventy-seventh regiment, company G, private, died November 5, 1863, at Alton, Illinois.

Ward, John, Ninety-second regiment, company F.

Ward, Jacob, age 18, volunteer, August, 1862, three years, Ninety-second regiment, company C, private, served nine months, died May 14, 1863.

Wells, Christopher, drafted, March 25, 1865, one year, Thirty-ninth regiment, company C, private, served three months, mustered out July 9, 1865.

Wells, Samuel, drafted, March, 1865, one year, Thirty-ninth regiment, company C, private, served three months, mustered out July 9, 1865.

Wells, Sheffield B., age 19, volunteer, July, 1861, three years, Thirty-ninth regiment, company B, private, served nine months, died in April, 1862.

Wells, Nelson F., age 17, volunteer, October 31, 1861, three years, Eighteenth Kentucky regiment, company F, private, served two years, veteran enlistment, age 19, volunteer, 1864, three years, Eighteenth Kentucky regiment, company F, private, served one and a half years, mustered out July 18, 1865.

Wells, Lewis Henry, age 16, volunteer, 1863, six months, One Hundred and Twenty-ninth regiment, company F, private, served seven months, mustered out in March, 1864, second enlistment, substitute, 1864, one hundred days, One Hundred and Forty-eighth regiment, company G, private, served four months, mustered out September, 1864, third enlistment, age 17, substitute, 1865, one year, Eighteenth regiment, company C, private.

Widger, Ananias, age 23, substitute, April, 1865, one year, Thirty-ninth regiment, company C, private, served three months.

Williams, John, age 19, August 29, 1863, three years, Fourth Virginia cavalry, company G, private, died.

Williamson, Stephen, Seventy-fifth regiment, company B.

Wilson, Richard, age 45, volunteer, 1862, three years, One Hundred and Sixteenth regiment, company F, private, served one year, honorably discharged.

Wiseman, Thomas, age 23, volunteer, October, 1861, three years, Seventy-seventh regiment, company C, corporal, attained the rank of sergeant, veteran enlistment, 1864, three years, Seventy-seventh regiment, company C, sergeant, attained rank of lieutenant.

Yonally, Jesse, age 40, drafted, September, 1864, one year, Fifty-first regiment, company G, private, served nine months, mustered out June, 1865.

Yonally, Asa, age 33, volunteer, February, 1865, one year, Thirty-sixth regiment, company C, private, served five months, mustered out July, 1865.

Yonally, Solomon, age 27, volunteer, 1861, three years, Seventy-seventh regiment, company G, private, served seven months, honorably discharged June, 1862.

RECAPITULATION.

DeBeck's battery	4
Fourth Virginia cavalry	9
First Virginia cavalry	2
And one each in Second and Seventh Virginia cavalry, First, Fifth, and Seventh Ohio cavalry, in all	5
Seventy-seventh Ohio	41
Ninety-second Ohio	14
Thirty-ninth Ohio	16
Seventy-fifth Ohio	8
Fifty-first Ohio	8
Thirty-sixth Ohio	7
One Hundred and Forty-eighth Ohio National guard	13
One Hundred and Sixteenth Ohio	5
One Hundred and Ninety-sixth Ohio	5
One Hundred and Ninety-fifth Ohio	4
Eighteenth Ohio (three years)	3
Seventh Virginia	2
One Hundred and Twenty-ninth Ohio	2
Forty-third Ohio	3
Sixty-third Ohio	2
Twentieth Ohio	2
One each in the First, Fourteenth, Fifth, Sixth, Nineteenth, Fifty-third, Sixty-second, Eighty-eighth, One Hundred and Ninety-seventh, One Hundred and Seventy-fifth, One Hundred and Eighty-second, One Hundred and Eighty-sixth, One Hundred and Thirty-second, First Virginia, Eighteenth Kentucky, not designated 7, in all	22
Total number of soldiers	168
Died	31

LAWRENCE TOWNSHIP.

Alexander, Samuel, age 38, volunteer, September 1, 1864, one year, One Hundred and Seventy-ninth regiment, company F, private, served ten months, mustered out June, 1865.

Alexander, A., age 28, volunteer, September 1, 1864, one year, One Hundred and Seventy-ninth regiment, company F, private, served ten months, mustered out June, 1865.

Atkinson, James, Thirty-sixth regiment, company F.

Atkinson, William Templeton, age 22, volunteer, May, 1864, one hundred days, One Hundred and Forty-eighth regiment, company G, private, died July 23, 1864.

Atkinson, Charles, age 20, volunteer, August 23, 1864, one year, Thirty-sixth regiment, company F, private, served eleven months, mustered out July, 1865.

Atkinson, George Templeton, age 18, volunteer, February 23, 1864, three years, Thirty-sixth regiment, company F, private, served one year and six months, mustered out July, 1865.

Bartmess, Washington, age 25, volunteer, 1862, three years, One Hundred and Sixteenth regiment, company F, private.

Bartmess, Jacob S., age 21, volunteer, March 28, 1863, three years, Thirty-eighth regiment, company D, private, served two years and three months, mustered out July, 1865.

Bartmess, Samuel, age 20, volunteer, October 16, 1863, six months, Fourth regiment Virginia cavalry, company M, private, served six months, mustered out with regiment.

Bender, Frederick, age 36, drafted, March 23, 1865, one year, Eighteenth regiment, company F, private.

Baumes, Jacob, Seventy-seventh regiment, died.

Bony, Simon, age 36, drafted, September 27, 1864, one year, Sixty-sixth regiment, company B, private, served two months and two weeks, died December 14, 1864, at Nashville, Tennessee, of consumption.

Boswell, James R., age 29, volunteer, August 8, 1862, three years, Ninety-second regiment, company F, private, served one year, honorably discharged August 23, 1863, reenlisted, age 32, drafted, September 28, 1864, one year, Sixty-sixth regiment, company E, private, served eight months, mustered out June 2, 1865.

Bowie, James R., Seventy-seventh regiment, company D, died at Alton, Illinois.

Boye, Eli, Thirty-sixth regiment, company G.

Britton, Luther Dale, age 33, drafted, September 28, 1864, one year,

Seventy-first regiment, company F, private, served five months, died February, 1865, at Louisville, of smallpox.

Britton, William Henry, age 19, volunteer, August 30, 1863, six months, Fourth regiment Virginia cavalry, company G, private, mustered out, reenlisted, age 20, volunteer, August 12, 1864, one year, One Hundred and Seventy-fifth regiment, company K, private, served ten months, mustered out June 27, 1865.

Brooks, David, age 23, volunteer, March 21, 1864, three years, First regiment light artillery, company K, private, served one year and three months, mustered out July, 1865.

Bull, Reason H., age 36, volunteer, August, 1862, three years, Ninety-second regiment, company F, sergeant, attained rank of second lieutenant, served two years and ten months, mustered out 1865.

Bull, William R., Ninety-second regiment, company F.

Calvert, Alfred, age 47, substitute, September, 1864, one year, Seventy-first regiment, company C, private.

Cantwell, Joseph M., age 25, volunteer, 1861, three years, Seventy-seventh regiment, company D, private, died July, 1862.

Carpenter, Samuel, age 40, volunteer, December, 1861, three years, Seventy-seventh regiment, company H, private, served five months, died May 19, 1862.

Carpenter, Alexander, age 25, volunteer, December, 1861, three years, Seventy-seventh regiment, company D, private, served two years, honorably discharged February, 1864, reenlisted as a veteran, age 27, volunteer, February, 1864, three years, Seventy-seventh regiment, company D, private.

Casady, Amzi, age 21, volunteer, 1862, three years, Ninety-second regiment, company F, private, served three months, died of smallpox January 23, 1865.

Clasey, Wine Rood, age 42, drafted, March 23, 1865, one year, Thirty-ninth regiment, company B, private, mustered out July 27, 1865.

Cline Peter, age 23, volunteer, 1861, three years, First regiment cavalry, company D, private.

Covey, Morgan, One Hundred and Seventy-fifth regiment, died May 22, 1865, at Columbia, Tennessee.

Cline John, drafted, September, 1864, one year, Fifty-fifth regiment, company D, private, mustered out.

Cameron, Andrew, volunteer, 1864, one year, One Hundred and Seventy-fifth regiment, company K, private, served one year, mustered out with regiment.

Close, Daniel, August 14, 1862, three years, First regiment Virginia light artillery, company A, private.

Clute, John, Thirty-sixth regiment, company E.

Cockings, James, age 26, drafted, March, 1865, one year, Thirty-ninth regiment, company B, private, served three months, mustered out July 9, 1865.

Conner John, Eighteenth regiment, company C.

Covey, Marion, Ninety-second regiment, company F.

Covey, William Mason, age 18, volunteer, February 29, 1864, three years, Thirty-sixth regiment, companies F and K, private, served seventeen months, mustered out July, 1865.

Cunningham Wilson, age 34, volunteer, 1861, three years, Seventy-seventh regiment, company H, private, honorably discharged May, 1862.

Callahan, Oliver, volunteer, 1864, one year, One Hundred and Seventy-fifth regiment, company K, private, served one year, mustered out with regiment.

Cuthbert, Ralph, volunteer, August 9, 1862, three years, Ninety-second regiment, company F, private, served two years and six months, mustered out June 6, 1865.

Cuthbert, Ralph W., age 18, volunteer, September, 1863, six months, Fourth Virginia cavalry, company G, private, served eight months, mustered out May, 1864, reenlistment, age 19, volunteer, August 6, 1864, one year, One Hundred and Seventy-fifth regiment, company K, private, attained rank of corporal, served nine months, died May 11, 1865, effects of exposure at the battle of Nashville.

Cuthbert, Ralph D., age 25, volunteer, September, 1863, six months, Fourth Virginia cavalry, company G, private, served eight months, mustered out May, 1864.

Dye, Morgan, Ninety-second regiment, company F.

Davis, Frank, age 29, Ninety-second regiment, company H, died May, 1864, at Atlanta, Georgia, gun-shot.

Dye, Amos, Seventy-seventh regiment, company H.

Dickes Charles, age 34, drafted, September 28, 1864, one year, Thirty-third regiment, company I, private, served nine months, mustered out July 5, 1865.

Dye, John Ely, Ninety-second regiment, company F.

Draher, John, age 23, drafted, March 23, 1865, one year, Thirty-ninth regiment, company B, private.

Dye, Daniel W., volunteer, September, 1861, three years, First cavalry, company I., corporal, attained rank of first lieutenant, served four years, mustered out September 28, 1865.

Draper, Adam, age 16, substitute, 1862, three years, Seventy-seventh regiment, company B, private.

Dye, Ross N., First cavalry, company H.

Dunlap, William, age 20, volunteer, 1862, three years, Ninety-second regiment, company F, private, died in March, 1864, at Nashville, Tennessee.

Drew, Jesse P., Thirty-sixth regiment, company H.

Dye, Thomas, First cavalry, company L.

Dye, Minor M., volunteer, 1864, one year, One Hundred and Seventy-fifth regiment, company K, corporal, served one year, mustered out with regiment.

Dye, S. P., Ninety-second regiment, company F.

Dye, Dudley, Seventy-seventh regiment, company H.

Davis, Isaiah, volunteer, 1863, six months, Fourth Virginia cavalry, company K, private, mustered out with regiment.

Early, William, age 24, substitute, 1862, Seventy-seventh regiment, company G, private, died 1863, Alton, Illinois, of lung fever.

Early, James, volunteer, 1862, three years, One Hundred and Sixteenth regiment, company F, private.

Early, Thomas, volunteer, 1861, three years, Seventy-Seventh regiment, company D, private, reenlistment, volunteer, 1864, three years, Seventy-seventh regiment, company D, private.

Early, George Washington, volunteer, 1861, three years, Seventy-seventh regiment, company G, private, veteran enlistment, volunteer, 1864, three years, Seventy-seventh regiment, company G, private.

Early, John Morris, volunteer, 1861, three years Seventy-seventh regiment, company G, private, veteran enlistment, volunteer, 1864, three years, Seventy-seventh regiment, company G, private.

Early, John Alexander, drafted, March 23, 1865, one year, Thirty-ninth regiment, private, served five months, mustered out August 26, 1865.

Early, William Thomas, drafted, March 23, 1865, one year, Thirty-ninth regiment, company G, private, served three and one-half months, mustered out July 18, 1865.

Efaw, Lugenius, volunteer, August 17, 1862, three years, One Hundred and Sixteenth regiment, company F, private.

Eifler, Charles.

Eifler, Jacob.

Evilsiser, Samuel Hunt, age 29, volunteer, August 5, 1862, three years, Ninety-second regiment, company F, private, served three years, mustered out June 10, 1865.

Evilsiser, Jonathan, age 20, volunteer, July, 1862, three years, Ninety-second regiment, company F, private, died September, 1863, mortally wounded at Chickamauga.

Evilsiser, Josiah, age 19, volunteer, February, 1864, three years, Thirty-sixth regiment, company K, private, served one and one-half years, mustered out July, 1865.

Foster, George, Thirty-sixth regiment, company G.

Forest, Andrew, age 20, volunteer, July 31, 1861, three years, Thirty-ninth regiment, company B, private, served three years, mustered out 1864.

Foster, John, Thirty-sixth regiment.

Foster, Archibald, age 28, volunteer, September, 1861, three years, Thirty-sixth regiment, company G, private, served three months, died December 25, 1861, of typhoid fever, at Summersville.

Foster, James, age 26, volunteer, February, 1864, three years, Thirty-sixth regiment, company G, private, served one year, honorably discharged 1865.

Foster, Josephus, age 22, volunteer, 1861, three years, Thirty-sixth regiment, company G, private.

Foster, Albert, age 20, volunteer, 1861, three years, Thirty-sixth regiment, company G, private, served three years, mustered out 1864.

Frazer, Adam, Seventy-seventh regiment, company B.

Gilsher, Jacob, age 20, volunteer, 1861, three years, Thirty-ninth regiment, company B, private, veteran enlistment.

Gist, William, age 45, volunteer, September 5, 1864, one year, One Hundred and Seventy-ninth regiment, company F, private.

Gitchell, John Wesly, age 27, volunteer, May, 1864, one hundred days, One Hundred and Forty-eighth regiment, company G, corporal, attained rank of sergeant, reenlistment, age 28, drafted, March, 1865, one year, Sixty-third regiment, private.

Gitchell, Joseph Harmen, age 21, volunteer, May, 1864, one hundred days, One Hundred and Forty-eighth regiment, company G, private.

Greathouse, McDonald, age 23, drafted, March, 1865, one year, Thirty-ninth regiment, company G, private, served three and a half months, mustered out July 18, 1865.

Greathouse, Peter, age 26, volunteer, August 6, 1862, three years, Ninety-second regiment, company F, private, served one and two-thirds years, honorably discharged in 1864.

Green, Isaac Newton, age 24, volunteer, August 12, 1862, three years, Ninety-second regiment, company H, private, served two and ten-twelfths years, mustered out June, 1865.

Groves, James, volunteer, 1864, one year, One Hundred and Seventy-fifth regiment, company K, private, attained the rank of corporal, served one year, mustered out with regiment.

Guist, James, age 19, volunteer, 1862, three years, Ninety-second regiment, company F, private, died May 10, 1864, of typhoid fever, at Carthage, Tennessee.

Guyton, Jacob, age 32, drafted September 28, 1864, one year, Twenty-third regiment, company A, private, honorably discharged May 8, 1865.

Harris, Isaac, age 19, Ninety-second regiment, company F, died at Camden, Tennessee.

Harris, William, age 20, volunteer, 1863, three years, Ninety-second regiment, company F, private, served five months, died March 31, 1864.

Harshy, William Wesley, age26, volunteer, August, 1862, three years, Ninety-second regiment, company F, private, served two years and six months, mustered out June 10, 1865.

Haught, Levi, age 37, volunteer, 1861, three years, Seventy-seventh regiment, company F, private.

Haught, Joshua, age 19, volunteer, August 24, 1864, one year, Thirty-sixth regiment, company F, private, served ten months, mustered out June 27, 1865.

Henning, William, aged 33, volunteer, August 7, 1862, three years, Ninety-second regiment, company F, private, served two and ten-twelfths years, mustered out June 10, 1865.

Hill, McIntosh, volunteer, August 12, 1862, three years, Thirty-sixth regiment, company I, private.

Hoff, Washington George, age 31, volunteer, August 4, 1862, three years, Ninety-second regiment, company F, private, served ten months, died June 12, 1865, of chronic diarrhœa.

Hoff, Kingsbury, age 24, volunteer, August 8, 1862, three years, Ninety-second regiment, company F, private, served two and ten-twelfths years, mustered out June, 1865.

Hoff, Ford Plum, age 16, volunteer, October 3, 1864, one year, First Virginia cavalry, company L, private, served eight months, honorably discharged June, 1865.

Immel, George, age 18, volunteer, August 11, 1862, three years, Ninety-second regiment, company F, private, served two and ten-twelfths years, mustered out June 10, 1865.

Jameson, James, age 23, volunteer, August 11, 1862, three years, Ninety-second regiment, company F, private, served two and ten-twelfths years, mustered out June 10, 1865.

John, Anthony, Seventy-Seventh regiment, company D, died.

Johnson, William, age 31, volunteer, August 3, 1861, three years, Eighteenth United States regiment, company C, private, three years, mustered out August 3, 1864, detailed and served as teamster.

Kelly, Benjamin, Twenty-Seventh regiment, company D.

Kemp, Nathan, age 22, volunteer, November 5, 1861, three years, First Virginia light artillery, company C, private, served two and one-third years, honorably discharged March, 1863, veteran enlistment, age 24, volunteer, March 31, 1864, three years, First Virginia light artillery, company C, served one and one-fourth years, mustered out.

Kemp, Abram, age 21, volunteer, August 6, 1861, three years, Thirty-sixth regiment, company G, private, served three years, mustered out in 1864.

Kemp, Charles Wesley, age 18, volunteer, February 29, 1864, three years, Thirty-sixth regiment, company G, private, served one and a half years, mustered out July, 1865.

Kemp, John D, age 17, volunteer, February 29, 1864, three years, Thirty-sixth regiment, company G, private, served one and a half years, mustered out July, 1865.

Kennedy, Jacob, Ninety-second regiment, company F.

La Grange, Lafayette, age 33, substitute, 1864, three years, Ninth cavalry, company B, private, mustered out in 1865.

Martin, Wilson, 1862, three years, One Hundred and Sixteenth regiment, private.

Masters, Joseph.

Matchett, George.

Mathers, William, age 21, volunteer, September, 1861, three years, Twenty-Seventh regiment, company D, private.

Macbeth, John, First cavalry, company L.

Mathers, Henry, age 20, volunteer, 1863, six months, reenlistment, volunteer, September, 1864, one year, First cavalry, company L, private.

Maxon, George, age 30, volunteer, discharged

Maxon, Henry, age 18, volunteer, August 12, 1863, six months, Fourth Virginia cavalry, company G, private, served seven months, mustered out March 11, 1864, reenlistment, age 19, volunteer, August, 1864, one year, First cavalry, company F, private, served nine months, mustered out May 20, 1865.

Mayer, George, One Hundred and Sixteenth regiment, company F, died.

Maxon, Edwin, age 17, substitute, May, 1864, one hundred days, One Hundred and Forty-eight regiment, company F, private, reenlistment, age 17, volunteer, September, 1864, one year, first cavalry, company L, private.

McAffee, John, age 44, drafted, September 28, 1864, one year, Seventy-first regiment, company C, private, served eight and a half months, mustered out June 12, 1865.

McAllister, James A., age 24, volunteer, September 6, 1861, three years.

McAllister, Charles Alden, age 19, volunteer, September 16, 1861, three years, Eighteenth regiment, company F, private, served three and a half years.

McAllister, John M, age 18, volunteer, August 8, 1862, three years, Seventh cavalry, company H, private, died.

McAllister, William, age 17, volunteer, August, 1862, three years, Seventh cavalry, company H, private, reenlistment, age 18, volunteer August, 1863, six months, Fourth Virginia cavalry, company M, attained the rank of corporal, served eleven months, mustered out June 23, 1864, third enlistment, age 19, volunteer, September, 1864, one year, Fifteenth regiment, company F, attained the rank of corporal, served nine months, mustered out June 8, 1865.

McBeath, John, First cavalry, company G.

McCowen, Isaac S., age 19, volunteer, August 17, 1863, six months, Fourth Virginia cavalry, company G, corporal, served seven months, mustered out March 4, 1864, reenlistment, age 20, volunteer, October 8, 1864, one year, One Hundred and Seventy-fifth regiment, company K, first lieutenant, served nine months, mustered out June 27, 1865.

McCullough, D.

McElfresh, Nathan M., age 18, substitute, September 30, 1864, one year, Seventy-eight regiment, company H, private, served eight months, mustered out May 30, 1865.

McElfresh, Samuel Wilson, age 25, volunteer, October, 1863, three years, Ninety-second regiment, company F, private, served one year and eight months, mustered out 1865.

McElfresh, John W., age 19, volunteer, October, 1863, three years, Ninety-second regiment, company F, private, served one month, died November, 1863, of smallpox.

McGee, William, age 19, volunteer, April, 1861, three months, Eighteenth regiment, reenlistment, age 19, volunteer, August, 1861, three years, Thirty-sixth regiment, company G, veteran enlistment, age 21, volunteer, 1864, three years, Thirty-sixth regiment, company G.

McGee, George, age 17, volunteer, August 12, 1861, three years, Thirty-sixth regiment, company G, veteran enlistment, age 19, volunteer, 1864, three years, Thirty-sixth regiment, company G.

McGee, John Wesley, age 16, volunteer, October 25, 1862, three years, One hundred and sixteenth regiment, company F.

Mendenhall, William A., age 37, volunteer, October 7, 1862, three years, Ninety-second regiment, company F, private, served one year, honorably discharged 1863.

Mercal, Amos, Seventy-seventh regiment, company, D died February 17, 1863.

Miller, John, age 34, drafted, March 23, 1865, one year, Sixty-third regiment, private.

Myer, John, age 22, drafted September 28, 1864, one year, Seventy-first regiment, company H, private, served eight and a half years, mustered out June 12, 1865,

Martin, Robert, One Hundred and Sixteenth regiment, company F, died.

Myer, Henry, age 20, drafted, September 28, 1864, one year, Seventy-first regiment, company H, private, served eight and a half months, mustered out June 12, 1865.

Porter, William H , age 22, volunteer, December, 1861, one year, Seventy-seventh regiment, company H, private, served six months, died June 12, 1862, mortally wounded.

Pierce, Henry, Thirty-sixth regiment, company G.

Porter, Thomas J , age 15, volunteer, December 12, 1861, three years, Seventy-seventh regiment, company D, private, served ten months, honorably discharged October, 1862, reenlistment, age 29, drafted March 23, 1865, one year, Thirty-ninth regiment, company D, private, served three months.

Powell, Daniel, age 35, drafted March 25, 1865, one year, Thirty-ninth regiment, company G, private, served three and a half months, mustered out July 18, 1865.

Powell, Jesse, age 35, volunteer, February, 1864, three years, Thirty-sixth regiment company F, private.

Pratt, Phillip, age 45, drafted, March 23, 1865, one year, Thirty-ninth regiment, company B, private, served four months, mustered out July 22, 1865.

Pratt, James, age 22, drafted, March 23, 1865, one year, Thirty-ninth regiment, company B, private, served four months, mustered out July 22, 1865.

Quimby, Allen, age 53, volunteer, July 15, 1863, six months, One Hundred and Twenty-ninth regiment, company F, private, served eight months, mustered out March 5, 1864.

Quimby, Fulton G., age 18, volunteer, August 12, 1861, three years, Thirty-sixth regiment, company G, private, served two and a half years, honorably discharged, veteran enlistment, age 20, volunteer, February 22, 1864, three years, Thirty-sixth regiment, company G, private, honorably discharged.

Quimby, George Wesley, age 17, volunteer, 1862, three years, Ninety-second regiment, company G, private, died October 17, 1863.

Quimby, Charles Wesley, age 16, volunteer, July, 1864, six months, One Hundred and Twenty-ninth regiment, company F, private, served eight months, mustered out March, 1864, reenlisted, substitute, 1865, one year, Eighteenth regiment, company E, private.

Ray, James D, age 17, volunteer, August 7, 1862, three years, Ninety-second regiment, company F, private, two years and ten months, mustered out June 10, 1865.

Reynolds, John R., age 19, volunteer, September, 1861, three years, First Virginia light artillery, company C, private, honorably discharged.

Roke, William J

Rice, Thomas, age 20, volunteer, October, 1863, six months, Fourth Virginia cavalry, company M, private, served six months, mustered out, reenlisted 1864, one year, One Hundred and Seventy-fifth regiment, company K, private, attained rank of sergeant, served one year, mustered out June, 1865

Russell, John, volunteer, 1863, six months, Fourth Virginia cavalry, company M, private, served six months, mustered out with regiment.

Robinson, C. E , Thirty-sixth regiment, company G.

Schminke, John, age 22, volunteer, August, 1862, three years, Seventh cavalry, company H, private.

Schrader, John, age 19, volunteer, 1861, three years, Seventy-seventh regiment, company D, private, veteran enlistment, 1864, three years.

Scott, James, One Hundred and Twenty-fifth regiment, company E.

Smith, Joseph, volunteer, February, 1864, three years, Thirty-sixth regiment, company F, private.

Smith, G. W , One Hundred and Sixteenth regiment, company F.

Snodgrass, B. F., volunteer, Thirty-ninth regiment, company B, private, died May 28, 1862, of chronic diarrhœa at Farmington, Mississippi.

Snodgrass, William A., age 20, volunteer, July 22, 1861, three years, Thirty-ninth regiment, company B, private, attained rank of sergeant, veteran enlistment February, 1864, three years, sergeant, attained rank of first lieutenant, mustered out July 9, 1865.

Snodgrass, George W., age 31, volunteer, August 5, 1862, three years, Ninety-second regiment, company F, private

Snodgrass, Hiram, age 19, volunteer, August, 1863, six months, Fourth Virginia cavalry, company G, private, served seven and a half months, mustered out March 8, 1864, reenlisted September, 1864, one year, One Hundred and Seventy-fifth regiment, company K, private, attained the rank of corporal, mustered out June 27, 1865.

Stackhouse, William, age 21, volunteer, August 12, 1861, three years, Thirty-sixth regiment, company G, private, served three years, mustered out September 3, 1864.

Statts, Alfred, age 19, volunteer, August, 1861, three years, First cavalry, company L, private, served two and a half years, honorably discharged, veteran enlistment 1864, three years, served one and a half years, mustered out September 26, 1865.

Steen, James, age 21, volunteer, August, 1802, three years, One Hundred and Sixteenth regiment, company F, private, served seven months, honorably discharged April 1, 1863.

Steen, Joseph, age 19, volunteer, 1863, six months, One Hundred and Twenty-ninth regiment, private, mustered out 1864, reenlisted August 5, 1864, one year, Thirty-sixth regiment, company F, private.

Steen, Hamilton, age 19, volunteer, August 5, 1864, one year, Thirty-sixth regiment, company F, private

Stephens, A. W., Seventy-seventh regiment, company D.

Strickley, A., Ninety-second regiment, company F.

Sultan, Samuel, Thirty-sixth regiment, company F

Taylor, Richard P., age 40, volunteer, September 15, 1864, one year, One Hundred and Seventy-fifth regiment, company K, private, served eight months, died May 29, 1865.

Templeton, George W., age 18, volunteer, February 22, 1864, three years, Seventy-seventh regiment, company D, private, served six months, died August 21, 1864.

Fletcher, Daniel, age 34, volunteer, 1861, three years, Seventy-seventh regiment, company D, private, veteran enlistment 1864, three years.

Tippens, Edward, age 25, volunteer, November, 1861, three years, Seventy-seventh regiment, company D, private, honorably discharged.

Tippens, Napoleon, age 20, drafted, September, 1864, one year, Forty-third regiment, company K, private, mustered out June 22, 1865.

Waggoner, Peter, Seventy-seventh regiment, company H

Walker, Martin, age 30, August, 1861, three years, Thirty-sixth regiment, company G, private, served six months, honorably discharged, reenlistment, May 28, 1862, three months, Eighty-fifth regiment, Ohio State guards, private.

Walker, Aaron, age 25, volunteer, May 28, 1862, three months, Eighty-seventh regiment, company A, private.

Van Dyne, George, Thirty-sixth regiment, company F.

Walker, Ezra A., age 17, volunteer, October 3, 1861, three years, Thirty-sixth regiment, company G, private, honorably discharged, veteran enlistment, February, 1864, three years, private, served three and a half years, mustered out July 9, 1865.

Wright, John, age 25, volunteer, August 26, 1861, three years, Eighteenth regiment, companies H and C, private, veteran enlistment, three years, Eighteenth regiment, companies H and C, private.

Wright, Nathan, age 20, volunteer, August, 1862, three years, Ninety-second regiment, company F, private, honorably discharged.

Walker, Annanias, Thirty-sixth regiment, company G.

Yaho, Peter, One Hundred and Sixteenth regiment, company F.

Zimmerman, Lorenzo, age 21, volunteer, September 16, 1861, three years, First cavalry, company G, private, served one and a half years, honorably discharged November 6, 1862.

West, S. A.

RECAPITULATION.

Buell's Pierpont battery	2
One in battery A, First Pennsylvania light artillery, and one in De Beck's battery, in all	2
Fourth Virginia cavalry	11
First Ohio cavalry	10
First Virginia cavalry	2
Seventh Ohio cavalry	3
Ninth Ohio cavalry	1
Thirty-sixth Ohio	34
Ninety-second Ohio	34
Seventy-seventh Ohio	25
Thirty-ninth Ohio	14
Seventy-first Ohio	6
One Hundred and Forty-eighth Ohio	4
Sixty-third Ohio	2
Eighteenth Ohio (three years)	5
Eighteenth Ohio (three months)	1
One Hundred and Twenty-ninth Ohio	3
One Hundred and Seventy-fifth Ohio	11
One Hundred and Seventy-ninth Ohio	3
Twenty-seventh Ohio	2
One Hundred and Sixteenth Ohio	10
Sixty-sixth Ohio	2
One each in Fourth Virginia infantry, Twenty-fifth Ohio, Forty-third Ohio, Eighty-fifth and Eighty-seventh Ohio (three months) Fifteenth Ohio, Seventy-eighth Ohio, Twenty-third Ohio, Eighteenth United States, Thirty-third Ohio, Thirty-eighth Ohio, Fifty-second Ohio, and Fifty-fifth Ohio, in all	13
Not designated	7
Total number of soldiers	193

Died 20

LIBERTY TOWNSHIP.

Abbott, William, age 19, volunteer, December 25, 1861, three years, Fifty-eighth regiment, company A, private, served fourteen months, honorably discharged May 1, 1863, lost left arm in the attack upon Vicksburgh December 29, 1863.

Abbest, William Thomson, age 20, volunteer, October 20, 1861, three years, Seventy-seventh regiment, company D, private, served six months, killed at Shiloh, April 8, 1862.

Allison, Samuel, age 19, volunteer, September, 1864, three years, One Hundred and Seventy-fifth regiment, company K, private, served five months, died March 15, 1864, of measles, at Columbia.

Alexander, A. C., volunteer, One Hundred and Seventy-ninth regiment, company F, private.

Amos, James, age 35, drafted, March, 1865, one year, Sixty-third regiment, private, served five months, mustered out August 15, 1865.

Amos, Mordecai, age 25, volunteer.

Bahrenburg, John P., age 34, volunteer, September, 1864, one year, One Hundred and Seventy-ninth regiment, company F, sergeant, served ten months, mustered out June 27, 1865.

Barnes, A. L., volunteer, One Hundred and Seventy-fifth regiment, company K.

Barnet, Albertis, age 22, volunteer, August, 1864, one year, One Hundred and Seventy-fifth regiment, company K, private, served six months, died February, 1865, of measles, at Columbia.

Barnhart, Joseph W., age 25, substitute, 1862, Ninth cavalry, company D, private.

Beardmore, William, age 32, volunteer, September 5, 1864, one year, One Hundred and Seventy-ninth regiment, company F, private, served ten months, mustered out June 27, 1865.

Boston, Michael, age 19, volunteer, February, 1864, three years, Seventy-seventh regiment, company G, private.

Boston, Leander, age 21, volunteer, May, 1861, three years, Twenty-fifth regiment, private, died 1862, in Virginia.

Boston, Jacob, age 40, drafted, September, 1864, one year, Fifty-first regiment, company G, private, died 1865, Nashville, Tennessee, of lung disease.

Bowers, Valentine, age 28, volunteer, September 5, 1864, one year, One Hundred and Seventy-fifth regiment, company K, private, served ten months, mustered out June 27, 1865.

Bowers, John Wesley, age 21, volunteer, November, 1861, three years, Seventy-seventh regiment, company D, private, veteran enlistment, volunteer, 1864, three years, Seventy-seventh regiment, company D, private.

Bowers, Jacob Asbury, age 18, volunteer, August 11, 1862, three years, Ninety-second regiment, company F, private, served two years and nine months, honorably discharged May 21, 1865, wounded in left thigh at Mission Ridge.

Brown, Alexander, age 34, volunteer, September 5, 1864, one year, One Hundred and Seventy-ninth regiment, company F, private, served nine and one-half months, mustered out June 17, 1865.

Brown, James, volunteer, 1861, three years, Thirty-sixth regiment, company G, private, served three years, mustered out 1864, transferred to invalid corps.

Brown, Samuel Smith, age 15, volunteer, September 29, 1861, three years, Thirty-sixth regiment, company E, private, veteran enlistment, age 17, volunteer, 1864, three years, Thirty-sixth regiment, company E, private, blacksmith.

Burford, John Alexander, age 17, volunteer, March, 1864, three years, Twentieth regiment, company I private, served eight months, died November 18, 1864, of measles, at Gallipolis.

Burnet, Simeon.

Bush, Josephus, age 36, volunteer, February, 1864, three years, One Hundred and Sixteenth regiment, company E, private, served six months, died September 17, 1864.

Bush, Abraham, age 31, volunteer, September 20, 1861, three years, Thirty-sixth regiment, company G, private, veteran enlistment, volunteer, February, 1864, three years, Thirty-sixth regiment, company G, private.

Bush, William, age 29, volunteer, August, 1862, three years, One Hundred and Sixteenth regiment, company C, private, served ten months, mustered out June, 1865.

Campbell, John M., Ninety-second regiment, company F, private.

Cline, John, age 36, volunteer, 1861, three years, Seventy-seventh regiment, company D, sergeant, killed at Shiloh, April 7, 1862.

Cline, Joshua, age 22, volunteer, 1862, three years, Ninety-second regiment, company F, private, served nine months, died April 9, 1862.

Congleton, Burris, age 33, drafted, March 23, 1865, one year, Thirty-ninth regiment, company D, private, served four months, mustered out July 27, 1865.

Congleton, Joseph, age 22, volunteer, August 15, 1862, three years, Ninety-second regiment, company H, private, attained the rank of corporal, served two years and ten months, mustered out in June, 1865.

Congleton, James, age 21, volunteer, February 20, 1864, three years, Thirty-sixth regiment, company K, private, served one year and five months, mustered out July 9, 1865.

Congleton, Thomas, age 33, volunteer, September 1, 1864, one year, One Hundred and Seventy-ninth regiment, company F, private, served ten months, mustered out July 27, 1865.

Congleton, William, age 34, volunteer, September, 1864, one year, One Hundred and Seventy-fifth regiment, company K, private, died in December, 1864.

Congleton, Lewis, age 26, substitute, May, 1864, one hundred days, One Hundred and Forty-eighth regiment, company D, private, served four months, mustered out September 14, 1864.

Congleton, James, age 21, volunteer, 1862, three years, Thirty-sixth regiment, company G, private, died in February, 1862, of fever at Summerville, West Virginia.

Congleton, John, age 19, volunteer, December, 1861, three years, Seventy-seventh regiment, company D, private, honorably discharged.

Congleton, Thomas, age 19, volunteer, February, 1864, three years, Seventy-seventh regiment, company D, private.

Coon, Peter, age 21, volunteer, November, 1861, three years, Seventy-seventh regiment, company D, private, served nine months, died July 11, 1862.

Coon, Sampson, age 38, volunteer, November, 1861, three years, Seventy-seventh regiment, company D, private, served six months, died April 9, 1862.

Coon, Simpson, age 37, volunteer, September 16, 1864, one year, One Hundred and Seventy-sixth regiment, company I, private, served eight months, died May 9, 1865.

Coon, Wilson, age 33, volunteer, January 1, 1862, three years, Seventy-seventh regiment, company D, private, served four months, honorably discharged May 5, 1862.

Coon, Samuel, age 27, volunteer, 1864, one year, Thirty-sixth regiment, company G, private, died April 27, 1865.

Coon, William, age 29, volunteer, September, 1864, one year, One Hundred and Seventy-ninth regiment, company F, private, served nine months and two weeks, mustered out in June, 1865.

Coon, Orlena, age 40, volunteer, September 12, 1864, One Hundred and Seventy-sixth regiment, company I, private, served nine months, mustered out in June, 1865.

Coon, Michael, age 22, volunteer, November 9, 1862, three years, Seventy-seventh regiment, company D, private, served two years and eleven months, died October 6, 1864, of fever, at Little Rock, Arkansas.

Coon, Orlena, age 18, substitute, August 8, 1864, one year, Seventieth regiment, company C, private, served ten months, mustered out in May, 1865.

Covey, Morgan, age 23, volunteer, September 2, 1864, one year, One Hundred and Seventy-fifth regiment, company K, private, served eighth months and two weeks, died May 21, 1865, at Columbia, Tennessee.

Cranston, William, age 28, volunteer, September 5, 1864, one year, One Hundred and Seventy-fifth regiment, company K, served ten months, mustered out in June, 1865.

Dolman, John W., age 18, volunteer, September 26, 1861, three years, Thirty-sixth regiment, company E, private, served two years and six months, honorably discharged in 1864, reenlisted as a veteran, volunteer, 1864, three years, Thirty-sixth regiment, company E, private, served one year and four months, mustered out July 9, 1865.

Dolman, Charles Morgan, aged 17, volunteer, February, 1864, three years, Seventy-seventh regiment, company D, private.

Donaldson, John B., age 33, volunteer, September, 1864, one year, One Hundred and Seventy-ninth regiment, company F, private, served nine months, mustered out in June, 1865.

Donthitt, William, drafted.

Dunlap, William, age 18, volunteer, 1862, three years, Ninety-second regiment, company F, private, served four months, died December 9, 1862.

Dunlap, Robert, age 17, volunteer, February, 1864, three years, Seventy-seventh regiment, company D, private,

Dunlap, Moses S., age 16, volunteer, March, 1865, one year, Thirty-

sixth regiment, company C, private, served two months, honorably discharged in May, 1865.

Eisnach, Philip, age 34, volunteer, December 4, 1861, three years, First light artillery, company H, private, served six months, died in June, 1862.

Ekey, Lewis Milton, age 17, volunteer, February, 1864, three years, Seventy-seventh regiment, company D, private, served one year and two months, died April 6, 1865.

Erb, John, age 17, volunteer, September 26, 1864, one year, First cavalry, company L, private, served one year, mustered out September 13, 1865.

Epler, William, age 43, three years, Seventy-seventh regiment, died March 7, 1863, of pleurisy, at Alton, Illinois.

Farley, Isaac, age 31, volunteer, December 8, 1861, three years, Seventy-seventh regiment, company D, private, served one month, died January 5, 1862.

Feltor, Isaac, age 22, volunteer, August 7, 1862, three years, Ninety-second regiment, company F, private, served two years and ten months, mustered out June 10, 1865.

Fulton, David, age 44, volunteer, three years, Seventh cavalry, company H, private, died April 14, 1863, of rheumatism, at Covington, Kentucky.

French, Ezra, age 45, drafted March 23, 1865, one year, Sixty-third regiment, private, served two months, mustered out May 20, 1865.

Gatchett, John Barnes, age 37, volunteer, September 5, 1864, one year, One Hundred and Seventy-ninth regiment, company F, private, served ten months, mustered out in June, 1865.

Gearheart, George Thomas, age 19, volunteer, September 21, 1863, six months, Fourth Virginia cavalry, company G, private, served six months, mustered out March 8, 1864, reenlistment, volunteer, August 30, 1864, one year, One Hundred and Seventy-fifth regiment, company K, private, served ten months, mustered out in June, 1865.

Gearheart, Joseph, age 16, volunteer, February, 1864, Seventy-seventh regiment, company D, private.

Gill, Henry Patterson, age 18, substitute, May, 1864, one hundred days, One Hundred and Forty-eighth regiment, company B, private, served four months, mustered out September 14, 1864.

Gleason, George Milton, age 31, volunteer, December 25, 1861, three years, Seventy-seventh regiment, company D, private, veteran enlistment, volunteer, 1864, three years, Seventy-seventh regiment, company D, private.

Glover, Samuel, age 39, volunteer, September, 1864, one year, One Hundred and Seventy-ninth regiment, company F, corporal, served ten months, mustered out in June, 1865.

Glover, Sylvester, age 20, volunteer, August, 1862, three years, Ninety-second regiment, company F, private, served two years and ten months, mustered out June 10, 1865.

Granville, H., Second Virginia cavalry, company C.

Gregory, John, age 20, volunteer, September 3, 1864, one year, One Hundred and Seventy-ninth regiment, company F, private, served ten months, mustered out June 10, 1865.

Gregory, George William, age 22, volunteer, September 3, 1864, one year, One Hundred and Seventy-ninth regiment, company F, private, served ten months, mustered out June 10, 1865.

Grey, Jesse, volunteer, three years, Seventy-seventh regiment, company D, private, honorably discharged in April, 1864.

Grey, Joshua, volunteer.

Gruther, G., volunteer, three years, Thirty-sixth regiment, company G, private, died in 1861, of typhoid fever at Summerville.

Groves, Henry, age 24, volunteer, 1861, three years, Thirty-sixth regiment, company F, private, served ten months, died June 3, 1862.

Gruther, John, age 21, three years, Thirty-sixth regiment, company G, private, died in 1861, of typhoid fever, at Summerville, West Virginia.

Groves, William Augustus, age 21, volunteer, 1861, three years, Sixty-third regiment, company D, private, served two years and six months, died in June, 1864, mortally wounded.

Gruther, ——, age 21, volunteer, three years, Thirty-sixth regiment, company G, private.

Groves, Charles Stewart, age 20, volunteer, August, 1864, one year, One Hundred and Seventy-fifth regiment, company K, private, served ten months, mustered out in June, 1865.

Hall, John, age 20, volunteer, February 17, 1865, one year, Thirty-sixth regiment, company G, private, served five and one-half months, mustered out July 9, 1865.

Hern, Jacob Winget, age 26, volunteer, three years, Seventy-seventh regiment, company G, private, died April 25, 1864, at battle of Mark's Mills, Arkansas.

Hall, James, age 29, volunteer, 1861, three years, Seventy-seventh regiment, company A, private, veteran enlistment, age 31, volunteer, 1864, three years, Seventy-seventh regiment, company A, private.

Hall, William, age 27, drafted May 19, 1864, three years, One Hundred and Twenty-second regiment, company H, private, served one year, mustered out in June, 1865.

Harris, Stephen, age 18, volunteer, August 13, 1863, three years, Second heavy artillery, company H, private, served one year and seven months, died March 28, 1865.

Hartwig, Peter, age 22, substitute, May, 1864, one hundred days, One Hundred and Forty-eighth regiment, company A, private, served four months, mustered out September 14, 1864.

Hartwig, John, age 18, volunteer, August 15, 1862, three years, Thirty-sixth regiment, company I, private, served two years and ten months, mustered out July 9, 1865.

Heslop, George, age 37, volunteer, September, 1864, one year, One Hundred and seventy-fifth regiment, company K, private, served ten months, mustered out June, 1865.

Hill, Elverton Newell, age 34, August 29, 1862, three years, Seventh cavalry, company H, private, served six months, honorably discharged February 20, 1863.

Hill, James Amos, age 16, volunteer, September 14, 1864, one year, One Hundred and seventy-sixth regiment, company I, private, served four months, died January 14, 1865.

Hughes, Benjamin F., age 21, volunteer, three years, Seventy-seventh regiment, company D, private, died April 8, 1862, at battle of Fallen Timber, Tennessee.

Hoit, John A., volunteer, Ninety-second regiment, company H, private.

Hughes, David S., age 19, volunteer, three years, Seventy-seventh regiment, company D.

Howell, David, age 36, volunteer, December 12, 1861, three years, Seventy-seventh regiment, company A, private, died 1863, at Little Rock, Arkansas.

Hughey, William, age 29, volunteer, November, 1861, three years, Seventy-seventh regiment, company G, private, served one year and five months, died April, 1863.

Johnson, Andrew C., age 26, volunteer, September 5, 1864, one year, One Hundred and Seventy-ninth regiment, company F, private, served nine months, mustered out June, 1865.

Jordon, John, age 42, volunteer, 1861, three years, Sixty-third regiment, company G, private, served two months, honorably discharged.

Jordon, William, age 17, volunteer, October 1, 1861, three years, Sixty-third regiment, company G, sergeant, served three years, mustered out 1864, veteran enlistment, age 20, substitute, February 28, 1865, one year, Forty-third regiment, company A, private, served four and a half months, mustered out July 13, 1865.

Kelly, William, aged 19, volunteer, May 2, 1861, three years, Twenty-fifth regiment, company F, private, served eight months, died December 29, 1861, of fever, at Cheat Mountain, West Virginia.

Kelley, Isaac Newton, aged 17, volunteer, October, 1861, three years, Seventy-seventh regiment, company D, private, served six months, died May 2, 1862, of fever, at Camp Dennison, Ohio.

King, Jesse, aged 26, volunteer, September, 1864, one year, One Hundred and Seventy-fifth regiment, company K, private, served nine and one half months, honorably discharged June, 1865.

King, John Merical, aged 20, volunteer, September 20, 1861, three years, Second Virginia cavalry, company F, private, honorably discharged, veteran enlistment, aged 22, volunteer, 1864, three years, Second Virginia cavalry, company F, private.

King, Nicholas, aged 19, volunteer, 1861, three years, Thirty-sixth regiment, company I, private, served three years, mustered out 1864.

King, William, aged 20, volunteer, September, 1864, one year, One Hundred and Seventy-fifth regiment, company K, private, served ten months, mustered out June 27, 1865.

Kirk, Mark, aged 34, drafted, March, 1865, one year, Thirty-ninth regiment, company D, private.

Kirkman, Samuel, aged 26, volunteer, One Hundred and Twenty-second regiment, company H, died 1864, of diarrhœa, at Annapolis, Maryland.

Lamington, Josiah B., aged 34, volunteer, February 12, 1864, three years, Ninety-second regiment, company K, private, served sixteen months, mustered out June, 1865.

Love, Thomas, aged 38, volunteer, August, 1862, three years, Ninety-second regiment, company F, private, served seven months, died March 6, 1863.

Love, Hugh, aged 32, volunteer, August 30, 1864, one year, One Hundred and Seventy-fifth regiment, company K, private, served ten months, mustered out 1865.

Love, Robert, aged 23, volunteer, August 15, 1862, three years, Ninety-second regiment, company K, private, served two years and ten months, mustered out June 10, 1865.

Love, William, aged 18, volunteer, August 9, 1862, three years, Ninety-second regiment, company F, private, served one year and six months, died February 25, 1864.

Love, Solomon, aged 16, volunteer, December 31, 1861, three years, Second Virginia cavalry, company F, private, honorably discharged 1864, veteran enlistment, aged 18, volunteered 1864, three years, Second Virginia cavalry, company F, private, mustered out 1864.

Masters, Benjamin, aged 48, volunteer, 1861, three years, Seventy-seventh regiment, company D, private, died April 6, 1862.

Masters, Joshua, aged 17, volunteer, 1861, three years, Seventy-seventh regiment, company D, private, honorably discharged August 5, 1862, reenlisted, aged 19, volunteer, February, 1864, three years, Seventy-seventh regiment, company D, private, died August 22, 1865, at Brownsville, Texas, of chronic diarrhœa.

Masters, Thomas H., aged 23, volunteer, March 1, 1865, one year, One Hundred and Seventy-ninth regiment, company D, private, mustered out June, 1865.

McAfflee, Thomas, aged 42, volunteer, March 1, 1865, one year, One Hundred and Seventy-ninth regiment, company F, private, served five months, mustered out July 26, 1865.

McAfflee, Joseph Francis, aged 16, volunteer, September, 1864, one year, One Hundred and Seventy-ninth regiment, company F, private, served ten months, mustered out June 27, 1865.

McLead, Elias, aged 38, volunteer, September 1, 1864, one year, One Hundred and Seventy-ninth regiment, company F, private, served nine months, honorably discharged June 8, 1865.

McLead, John, aged 18, volunteer, March 13, 1865, one year, One Hundred and Seventy-ninth regiment, company F, private, served two months, honorably discharged May 25, 1865.

McPeck, Lemuel, aged 26, drafted, March 3, 1865, one year, Thirty-ninth regiment, company D, private, served two months, died May 24, 1865, at Philadelphia, Pennsylvania, of fever.

Mirach, Garrison, aged 28, volunteer, August, 1862, three years, One Hundred and Sixteenth regiment, company F, private, served one year and ten months, died June 25, 1864.

Mirach, William, aged 24, volunteer, August 1, 1861, three years, Thirty-sixth regiment, company F, private, served three years, mustered out September 13, 1864.

Miracle, Jesse, age 22, volunteer, August 1, 1861, three years, Thirty-sixth regiment, company F, private, served two and a half years, honorably discharged, veteran enlistment, age 24, volunteer, February, 1864, three years, Thirty-sixth regiment, company F, private, served one year and five months, murdered at Cumberland, Maryland, January, 1865.

Miracle, John, age 19, volunteer, October, 1861, three years, Sixty-third regiment, company D, private, served two years, honorably discharged December, 1863, veteran enlistment, age 21, volunteer, December, 1863, three years, Sixty-third regiment, company D, private, served one year and a half, mustered out.

Miracle, Isaac, age 16, volunteer, August 10, 1864, one year, Ninety-second regiment, company F, private, served ten months, mustered out June 10, 1865.

Miracle, John Long, age 22, volunteer, 1861, three years, Thirty-sixth regiment, company F, private, served three years, mustered out September 3, 1864.

Miller, Robert, age 25, drafted, 1862, nine months, Seventy-seventh regiment, company D, private, served seven months, died April 11, 1863.

Moore, William, age 23, volunteer, October 15, 1861, three years, Sixty-third regiment, company D, private, died July 22, 1862, of small-pox, at Memphis, Tennessee.

Mossbury, William A., age 16, volunteer, August 11, 1864, one year, One Hundred and Seventy-ninth regiment, company F, private, served ten months, mustered out June 17, 1865.

Mossbury, William, drafted, March, 1865, one year, Twenty-seventh regiment, private.

Mull, George William, age 20, substitute, May, 1864, one hundred days, One Hundred and Forty-eighth regiment, company K, private.

Mullenix, Thomas, Thirty-sixth regiment, company G.

Mullenix, Owen, age 17, volunteer, November 21, 1861, three years, Seventy-eighth regiment, company G, private, veteran reenlistment, age 20, volunteer.

Murdock, James, age 27, volunteer, September 5, 1864, one year, One Hundred and Seventy-ninth regiment, company F, private, served ten months, mustered out June 27, 1865.

Myres, Jonathan, volunteer, 1862, three years, Seventh cavalry, company H, private, served one year and a half, died March 15, 1864.

Myres, James, age 21, volunteer, January, 1864, three years, First cavalry, company L, private, one year and eight months, mustered out September 26, 1865.

Myres, David, age 20, volunteer, August 15, 1864, one year, Thirty-sixth regiment, company G, private, served eight months and a half, honorably discharged May, 1865.

Myres, William, age 17, volunteer, June 20, 1863, six months, Fourth cavalry, company I, private, served nine months, mustered out March 12, 1864, reenlistment, age 18, volunteer, August 15, 1864, one year, Thirty-sixth regiment, company G, honorably discharged from service May, 1865.

Oliver, James, age 21, volunteer, August, 1861, three years, Thirty-sixth regiment, company G, private, attained the rank of corporal, died May, 1864.

Palmer, Harris James, age 23, volunteer, August 18, 1862, three years, Thirty-sixth regiment, company I, private, served eighteen months, killed September 19, 1863, at Chickamauga.

Parker, John, Thirty-sixth regiment.

Phelps, Jacob Eden, age 24, volunteer, August, 1862, three years, One Hundred and Sixteenth regiment, company F, private, attained the rank of corporal.

Phelps, Benjamin, age 17, volunteer, July 19, 1863, six months, One Hundred and Twenty-ninth regiment, company F, private, served eight months, mustered out March 11, 1864, reenlistment, age 18, substitute, February 23, 1865, one year, Forty-third regiment, company E, private, mustered out.

Porter, Thomas, age 40, volunteer, February 24, 1865, one year, One Hundred and Seventy-ninth regiment, company F, private, served six and a half months, mustered out September 6, 1865.

Rice, Joseph Allan, age 22, volunteer, November 8, 1861, three years, Seventy-seventh regiment, company D, corporal, honorably discharged in 1862.

Ray, Ezra Deming, age 21, volunteer, August 29, 1864, one year, One Hundred and Seventy-fifth regiment, company K, private, served ten months, mustered out June 25, 1865.

Rees, Jonathan, age 29, volunteer, December 5, 1861, three years, Seventy-seventh regiment, company A, private, died June, 1865, at Galveston, Texas, of camp disease.

Roberts, William, age 20, volunteer, October 6, 1862, three years, Seventh cavalry, company H, served two years and eight months, honorably discharged June 19, 1865.

Schneider, Lewis, age 24, volunteer, December, 1861, three years, Sixty-fifth regiment, company E, died September, 1863

Schneider, Frederick, age 21, volunteer, November 9, 1861, three years, Fifty-eighth regiment, company A, private, served three years and two months, mustered out January 14, 1865.

Schneider, William, age 19, volunteer, November 9, 1861, three years, Fifty-eighth regiment, company A, private, served three years and two months, mustered out January 14, 1865.

Schram, Jacob, age 29, drafted March 23, 1865, three years, Thirty-ninth regiment, company D, private, served three and a half months, mustered out July 9, 1865.

Selken, Henry, volunteer, September 6, 1864, one year, One Hundred and Seventy-ninth regiment, company F, private, served five and a half months, died January 26, 1865.

Stegner, Jacob, age 22, three years, Ninety-second regiment, company K, private, died October, 1863, at Gallatin, Tennessee.

Selken, John, volunteer, 1861, three years, Thirty-sixth regiment, company G, private.

Selken, James, age 18, volunteer, February 29, 1864, three years, Thirty-sixth regiment, company G, private, served one year and five months, mustered out July, 1865.

Shaw, John M., age 21, volunteer, 1862, three years, Ninety-second regiment, company F, private; reenlistment, age 22, volunteer, February, 1865, one year, Thirty-sixth regiment, company C, private.

Slobohn, Henry, age 20, volunteer, August 11, 1862, three years, Ninety-second regiment, company F, served two years and ten months, mustered out June 10, 1865.

Slobohn, John H., age 18, volunteer, August 11, 1862, three years, Ninety-second regiment, company F, served two years and ten months, honorably discharged 1865.

Smith, Elias D., age 26, volunteer, September 3, 1864, one year,

One Hundred and Seventy-ninth regiment, company F, sergeant, served nine months and fifteen days, mustered out June 17, 1865.

Smith, George Alexander, age 22, volunteer, September, 1862, three years, Seventh cavalry, company H, honorably discharged June 8, 1865.

Smith, William P., age 18, substitute, May, 1864, one hundred days, One Hundred and Forty-eighth regiment, company G, private, mustered out September 14, 1864.

Stewart, John, age 34, volunteer, August 26, 1864, one year, One Hundred and Seventy-ninth regiment, company F, private, served nine months and fifteen days, mustered out June 17, 1865.

Stidd, John.

Scott, Abijah, Thirty-sixth regiment, company G.

Scranton, William, One Hundred and Seventy-fifth regiment, company K.

Stollar, John, age 27, volunteer, three years, One Hundred and Seventy-ninth regiment, company F, died at Nashville, Tennessee, February 18, 1865

Swaney, William, age 26, drafted, 1862, One Hundred and Fourteenth regiment, company C.

Telles, William, age 22, volunteer, Thirty-sixth regiment, died 1863.

Taylor, John, age 45, volunteer, Thirty-sixth regiment, company E, private, died December 25, 1863.

Taylor, Ezra, age 30, volunteer, August 29, 1862, three years, Seventh cavalry, company H, private, served three years, mustered out July 4, 1865.

Taylor, David, age 22, volunteer, September 3, 1864, one year, One Hundred and Seventy-ninth regiment, company F, private, served ten months, honorably discharged July 5, 1865.

Taylor, Theodore, age 20, volunteer, August, 1864, one year, One Hundred and Seventy-fifth regiment, company K, private, served ten months, discharged for disability and died at home.

Taylor, Isaac, age 18, volunteer, September 6, 1864, one year, Seventy-eighth regiment, company I, private, mustered out 1865

Vanway, Burris, age 29, volunteer, 1863, six months, One Hundred and Twenty-ninth regiment, company F, private, mustered out 1864, reenlistment, age 30, substitute, May, 1864, one hundred days, One Hundred and Forty-eighth regiment, company F, private, mustered out September, 1864.

Vanway, William Johnson, age 17, volunteer, 1863, six months, Fourth Virginia cavalry, company G, private, mustered out June.

Vanway, Joseph Osborn, age 44, drafted, March, 1865, one year, Thirty-ninth regiment, company D, private, served four months, mustered out July, 1865.

Vanway, Robert L., age 28, volunteer, December 8, 1861, three years, Seventy-seventh regiment, company D, private, veteran enlistment, age 30, volunteer, February, 1864, three years, Seventy-seventh regiment, company D, private.

Vanway, Isaac, age 22, volunteer, February, 1864, three years, Seventy-seventh regiment, company D, private, died of diarrhœa at Fort Morgan, Alabama, May 31, 1865

Walters, James P., age 17, volunteer, August 8, 1864, one year, One Hundred and Seventy-ninth regiment, company F, private served ten months, mustered out May, 1865

Walters, William T., age 18, volunteer, July 7, 1863, three years, Second heavy artillery, company K, private, served one year and ten months, honorably discharged May, 1865.

West, George Washington, volunteer, 1861, three years, Seventy-seventh regiment, company D, private, veteran enlistment, volunteer, February, 1864, three years, Seventy-seventh regiment, company D, private.

West, Jonathan, age 23, volunteer, August, 1862, three years, Ninety-second regiment, company H, private, served eight months, died March 24, 1863

West, Levi, age 22, volunteer, 1862, three years, One Hundred and Sixteenth regiment, company A, private.

West, Joshua, age 19, volunteer, August, 1864, one year, One Hundred and Seventy-sixth regiment, company G, private, served ten months, mustered out June 27, 1865.

Westbrook, William Thomas, age 23, volunteer, August 11, 1863, three years, Ninety-second regiment, company H, private.

Wiley, Daniel, age 24, volunteer, September, 1864, one year, One Hundred and Seventy-sixth regiment, company I, private, served nine months, mustered out June, 1865.

Williams, Henry, volunteer, December 11, 1861, three years, Seventy-seventh regiment, company D, private, served seven months, died August 23, 1862.

Wilson, Owen D., age 34, volunteer, September 5, 1864, one year, One Hundred and Seventy-ninth regiment, company F, private, served ten months, mustered out June, 1865.

Wright, Hiram, Seventy-seventh regiment, company G.

RECAPITULATION.

One each in batteries, H and K, Second Ohio heavy artillery, and Huntington's battery....	3
Seventh Ohio cavalry....	6
Fourth Virginia cavalry....	2
First Ohio cavalry....	2
Second Virginia cavalry....	3
One each in Fourth Ohio cavalry and Ninth Ohio cavalry....	2
Seventy-seventh Ohio....	34
Thirty-sixth Ohio....	30
One Hundred and Seventy-ninth Ohio....	28
One Hundred and Seventy-fifth Ohio....	14
One Hundred and Forty-eighth Ohio....	6
Sixty-third Ohio....	7
Thirty-ninth Ohio....	5
Ninety-second Ohio....	20
Seventy-eighth Ohio....	2
One Hundred and Twenty-ninth Ohio....	2
One Hundred and Sixteenth Ohio....	5
One Hundred and Seventy-sixth Ohio....	5
Fifty-eighth Ohio....	3
Twenty-fifth Ohio....	2
One Hundred and Twenty-second Ohio....	2
Forty-third Ohio....	2
One Each in Twentieth Ohio, Twenty-seventh Ohio, Sixty-fifth Ohio, Seventieth Ohio, Fifty-first Ohio, One Hundred and Fourteenth Ohio....	6
Total number of soldiers....	193
Died....	47

LUDLOW TOWNSHIP.

Adams, George Washington, age 28, volunteer, September 20, 1861, three ears, Thirty-sixth regiment, company B, private, honorably discharged, reenlisted.

Adams, James M., age 26, volunteer, February 28, 1865, one year, Thirty-sixth regiment, company G, private, served five months, mustered out July 27, 1865.

Adams, James, age 22, drafted September 27, 1864, one year, Sixty-second regiment, company A, private, served eleven months, mustered out August 8, 1865.

Adams, Lewis, age 18, volunteer, September, 1864, one year, One Hundred and Seventy-ninth regiment, company F, private, mustered out in June, 1865.

Adamson, Barnet, age 17, substitute, October 12, 1864, one year, Seventy-eighth regiment, company F, private, served nine months, mustered out July 11, 1865.

Baker, Henry, age 25, drafted, September, 1864, one year, Fifty-first regiment, company G, private, died February, 1865.

Baker, James William, age 20, volunteer, December 5, 1861, three years, Seventy-seventh regiment, company G, served four months, mortally wounded, a d died April 8, 1862.

Baker, Samuel, age 16, volunteer, December 5, 1861, three years, Seventy-seventh regiment, company G, private, served five months, died May 25, 1862.

Boston, Jacob, age 42, Fifty-second regiment, died in 1865, at Nashville, Tennessee, of lung disease.

Battin, John, age 35, drafted, September, 1864, one year, Fifty-first regiment, company G, private, served eight months, died May 27, 1865.

Battin, Samuel, Seventy-seventh regiment, company G, died.

Bell, William B., One Hundred and Sixteenth regiment, company F.

Bellville, Cornelius, age 20, volunteer, March 10, 1865, one year, One Hundred and Ninety-sixth regiment, company F, private, served six months, mustered out September 12, 1865.

Bellville, Isaiah, age 17, substitute, May, 1865, one year, One Hundred and Ninety-sixth regiment, company H, private, served four months, mustered out in 1865.

Boston, John L., Seventy-seventh regiment, company G.

Bowersock, Adam L., age 23, volunteer, October 25, 1861, three years, First light artillery, company K, private, served one year, honorably discharged October 6, 1862.

Cline, ———, volunteer, 1863, six months, Fourth Virginia cavalry, private, served six months, mustered out with regiment.

Cline, Jonathan, Thirty-sixth regiment, company E.

Cooper, Robert, Sixty-third regiment, company F.

Courim, John T., age 25, volunteer, 1862, three years, Ninety-second regiment, company H, private, mustered out.

Craig, Sylvester, age 21, volunteer, July 31, 1864, one year, Ninety-second regiment, company K, private.

Craig, John T., age 17, substitute, July 29, 1864, one year, Seventieth regiment, company H, private.

Cross, Jackson, Seventy-seventh regiment, company G.

Day, William Alfred, age 16, volunteer, November, 23, 1861, three years, Seventy-seventh regiment, company G, corporal, attained rank of sergeant, veteran enlistment, age 18, volunteer, February, 1864, three years, Seventy-seventh regiment, company E, attained rank of lieutenant.

Denbon, Elisha, age 28, volunteer, August 31, 1861, three years, Seventy-seventh regiment, company A, corporal, veteran enlistment, age 30, volunteer, February, 1864, three years, Seventy-seventh regiment, company A.

Denbon, Thomas, age 27, volunteer, 1861, three years, Seventy-seventh regiment, company I.

Dixon, Albert, age 23, volunteer, October 21, 1861, three years, Seventy-seventh regiment, company C, served seven months, died May 29, 1862.

Dixon, Jacob.

Duvall, Andrew J., age 34, volunteer, October, 1861, three years, Seventy-seventh regiment, company G, sergeant, served six months, killed at Shiloh April 8, 1862.

Dowell, Jesse, Seventy-seventh regiment, company I.

Earley, John, age 35, drafted September 26, 1864, one year, Fifty-first regiment, company G, private, served nine months, mustered out in June, 1865

Edwards, Samuel, Thirty-sixth regiment, company E.

Edwards, Benjamin R., age 37, volunteer, September, 1862, three years, One Hundred and Sixteenth regiment, company F, private, served eight months, honorably discharged May 20, 1863.

Enochs, John, age 23, drafted, September 27, 1864, one year, Sixty-sixth regiment, company I, private, mustered out in July, 1865.

Felton, Conrad, age 21, volunteer, 1861, three years, First light artillery, company K.

Flanagan, James H., age 35, volunteer, February 17, 1865, one year, Thirty-sixth regiment, company C, private, mustered out.

Flanagan, Thomas J., age 27, volunteer, September 20, 1861, three years, Thirty-sixth regiment, company J, private, served three years, mustered out in 1864.

Fleming, Porter, age 38, volunteer, March 8, 1865, one year, One Hundred and Ninety-sixth regiment, company F, private, served six months, mustered out September 11, 1865.

Flint, David D., age 22, volunteer, November 11, 1861, Seventy-seventh regiment, company C, private, served one year, died November 23, 1862.

Flint, James, age 22, substitute, Thirty-sixth regiment, company C, private.

Fox, James, age 44, substitute, October 12, 1864, one year, Fifty-first regiment, company D, private.

Fryman, Isaac, age 27, volunteer, 1862, three years, Seventy-seventh regiment, company G, private.

Fulmer, Jacob, age 40, volunteer, 1862, three years, Seventy-seventh regiment, company G, private, died April 27, 1863.

Ganet, Andrew C., Second Virginia cavalry, company C.

Gault, Andrew, age 44, volunteer, September 7, 1861, three years, Second Virginia cavalry, company C, private, served three years, mustered out November 8, 1864.

Gualt, Peter, age 18, substitute, November, 1864, one year, Sixty-sixth regiment, company K, private, mustered out in February.

Giffen, Robert, age 36, volunteer, February 24, 1865, one year, Thirty-sixth regiment, company E, private, served five months, mustered out July 27, 1865.

Girt, Henry, age 33, volunteer, September, 1861, three years, Thirty-sixth regiment, company G, private.

Griffin, Charles Allen, age 22, volunteer, March, 1864, three years, Seventy-seventh regiment, company D, private.

Groves, Porter Flint, age 19, volunteer, December 10, 1861, three years, Seventy-seventh regiment, company G, private, served four months, died in April, 1862, mortally wounded.

Hall, John, Thirty-sixth regiment, company C.

Hall, Thomas, age 33, drafted, March 23, 1865, one year, Thirty-ninth regiment, company E, private, served three months.

Handlon, Rufus, Seventy-seventh regiment, company I, private, died October 19, 1864, in Tyler, Texas, prisoner of war.

Haught, Elijah, age 42, volunteer, 1862, three years, Seventy-seventh regiment, companies G and E, private.

Haught, William, age 23, volunteer, December 7, 1861, three years, Seventy-seventh regiment, company G, private, served three years, mustered out December 23, 1864.

Haught, Leonard, age 21, volunteer, December 7, 1861, three years, Seventy-seventh regiment, company G, private, served three years, mustered out December 23, 1864.

Haught, Levi, Seventy-seventh regiment, company G.

Hearn, Granville, age 37, volunteer, October 22, 1861, three years, Second Virginia cavalry, private, veteran enlistment, age 39, volunteer, 1864, three years, Second Virginia cavalry, mustered out in 1865, served as teamster greater part of time.

Hearn, Jacob W., age 27, volunteer, February, 1864, three years, Seventy-seventh regiment, company G, private, one battle, served two months, died April 25, 1864, killed.

Hearn, Daniel D., age 21, volunteer, October 25, 1861, three years, First light artillery, company K, private, veteran enlistment, age 23, volunteer, 1864, three years, First light artillery, company K, private, mustered out.

Hearn, Harris, age 17, volunteer, September 13, 1861, three years, Thirty-Sixth regiment, company G, private, missing September, 1863, captured or killed, or both, at Chickamauga.

Hearn, Josiah, age 15, volunteer, December, 1861, three years, Seventy-seventh regiment, company I, private, served four months, died in April, 1862, mortally wounded.

Hendershott, Brown, age 21, volunteer, February 22, 1864, three years, Seventy-seventh regiment, company G, private, served ten months, honorably discharged May, 1865.

Hendershott, H., Sixth cavalry, company E.

Holland, Arius, age 17, volunteer, August 1, 1864, one year, Ninety-second regiment, company H, private, served ten months, mustered out June 10, 1865.

Hood, John Bendoah, age 26, volunteer, February 28, 1864, three years, Seventy-seventh regiment, company D, private, served fourteen months, honorably discharged May, 1865.

Hood, Thomas A., age 24, volunteer, February 28, 1864, three years, Seventy-seventh regiment, company D., private, served fourteen months, died April 29, 1865.

Host, John Moffat, Ninety-second regiment, company H.

Host, William H., Seventy-seventh regiment, company D.

Jay, George, age 27, volunteer, July 27, 1861, three years, Seventh Virginia regiment, company D, private, served two years and six months, honorably discharged in 1863, veteran enlistment, volunteer, January 1, 1864, three years, Seventh Virginia regiment, company D, private, served one year and six months, mustered out August 6, 1865

Joy, Matthew, age 26, volunteer, November 15, 1861, three years, First light artillery, private, attained corporal, served two years, honorably discharged 1864, veteran enlistment, age 28, volunteer, February 1, 1864, three years, First light artillery, company K, corporal, served one year and six months, mustered out 1865.

Joy, Eliel Long, age 26, volunteer, February, 1864, three years, Seventy-seventh regiment, company G, private, served four months, died June 21, 1864.

Joy, Bishop, Seventy-seventh regiment, company G.

Joy, Mordecai B., age 23, volunteer, October, 1862, three years, Seventy-seventh regiment, company G, private.

Joy, David, age 19, volunteer, July 16, 1861, three years, Twenty-seventh regiment, company D, private, second enlistment, age 20, volunteer, November 27, 1862, three years, Seventy-sixth regiment, company I, private.

Kinard, I., Seventy-seventh regiment, company C.

Kinney, John Thomas, age 35, volunteer, October 20, 1861, three years, First light artillery, company K, private, served two years and three months, honorably discharged, reenlisted as a veteran, volunteer, January 16, 1864, three years, First light artillery, company K, private, served one year and six months, mustered out in July, 1865.

McMullin, Ezra, age 33, volunteer, February 17, 1865, one year, Thirty-sixth regiment, company C, private, served three months, honorably discharged May 19, 1865.

McDowell, Lewis, First light artillery, company A.

McVay, Esau, age 31, volunteer, December 9, 1861, three years, Seventy-seventh regiment, company I, private, served nine months, honorably discharged September 8, 1862.

Mendenhall, William T., age 18, volunteer, August 2, 1862, three

years, Ninety-second regiment, company H, private, served three years, mustered out June 10, 1865.

Moor, Landon Norman, age 17, volunteer, February 27, 1864, three years, Seventy-seventh regiment, company D, private, served one year and three months, honorably discharged June 8, 1865.

McBeth, William, Fourth Virginia, died at Gettysburgh, Pennsylvania.

Morey, William H., Thirty-sixth regiment, company G.

Mulinex, David B., age 19, volunteer, August 11, 1862, three years, Ninety-second regiment, company H, private, served ten months, honorably discharged June 22, 1863.

Mulinex, John, age 24, volunteer, February, 1864, three years, Seventy-seventh regiment, company D.

Parker, John C., age 23, volunteer, August, 1861, three years, Thirty-sixth regiment, company G, private, reenlisted as a veteran, February, 1864, three years, Thirty-sixth regiment, company G, private.

Parker, Robert L., age 24, drafted, March 23, 1865, three years, Thirty-ninth regiment, company G, private, served three months, mustered out July 9, 1865.

Parker, Henry, Fifty-first regiment, company G, veteran.

Parker, John A., age 18, volunteer, October 31, 1861, three years, Seventy-seventh regiment, company C, private, reenlisted as a veteran, February, 1864, three years, Seventy-seventh regiment, company C.

Parr, Jacob, age 22, volunteer, October 4, 1862, three years, Seventy-seventh regiment, company G, private.

Parr, William Lafayette, age 18, volunteer, February 22, 1864, three years, Seventy-seventh regiment, company G, private.

Piatt, James, age 22, volunteer, 1861, three years, Thirty-sixth regiment, company C, died March 2, 1862, mortally wounded.

Prior, Howard, age 35, drafted, September 27, 1864, one year, Forty-third regiment.

Piatt, James G., Thirty-ninth regiment, company G.

Provance, Joseph, volunteer, December, 1861, one year, Seventy-seventh regiment, company I, nine months, honorably discharged in September, 1862.

Provance, David, volunteer, 1861, one year, Ninth Virginia, company A, mustered out in 1865, reenlisted as a veteran, volunteer, 1864, one year, Ninth Virginia, company A.

Provance, John William, age 42, volunteer, February 22, 1865, one year, One Hundred and Eighty-ninth regiment, company F, mustered out in 1865

Provance, David S., aged 25, volunteer, 1861, three years, Seventy-seventh regiment, company I, private, honorably discharged in October, 1862

Provance, James, age 17, volunteer, May, 1861, three years, Twenty-fifth regiment, company C, private, died in May, 1868, mortally wounded.

Provance, John, age 19, volunteer, 1861, three years, Seventy-seventh regiment, company I, private.

Rake, William Jasper, One Hundred and Sixteenth regiment, company F.

Rew, David, Thirty-sixth regiment, company G.

Read, Joseph, age 38, volunteer, December 4, 1861, three years, Seventy-seventh regiment, company G, private, reenlisted as a veteran, volunteer, February, 1864, three years.

Read, Jacob, age 16, volunteer, February 29, 1864, three years, Seventy-seventh regiment, company G, private.

Rees, Oliver, age 44, volunteer, 1865, one year, Thirty-sixth regiment, company G, private, mustered out in July, 1865.

Rees, David, age 26, volunteer, September 14, 1861, three years, Thirty-sixth regiment, company G, private, served two years and six months, reenlisted as a veteran, volunteer, February, 1864, three years, Thirty-sixth regiment, company G, private, served one year and six months, mustered out in July, 1865.

Rees, Thomas, age 21, volunteer, September 11, 1861, three years, Thirty-sixth regiment, company G, private, served two years and six months, reenlisted as a veteran, volunteer, February, 1864, three years, Thirty-sixth regiment, company G, private, served one year and six months, mustered out in July, 1865.

Rinard, Isaac, age 20, volunteer, October 25, 1861, three years, Seventy-seventh regiment, company C, private, reenlisted as a veteran, volunteer, February, 1864, three years, Seventy-seventh regiment, company C, private.

Russell, Levi, age 19, volunteer, 1861, three years, Seventy-seventh regiment, company C, private, reenlisted as a veteran, volunteer, February, 1864, three years, Seventy-seventh regiment, company C, died April 13, 1864.

Russell, Samuel, One Hundred and Seventy-fifth regiment, company K.

Sample, William, age 28, volunteer, September 19, 1861, three years, Thirty-sixth regiment, company G, private, served three years, mustered out September 27, 1864.

Sample, Samuel B., age 19, volunteer, September 14, 1861, three years, Thirty-sixth regiment, company G, private, drowned.

Scott, Abijah, Fifty-first regiment, company G.

Scott, Benjamin, age 18, volunteer, December 9, 1861, three years, Seventy-seventh regiment, company G, private, three years, served nine months, honorably discharged August 28, 1862.

Scott, Howard, age 16, volunteer, February 6, 1864, three years, Seventy-seventh regiment, company G, private, served seven months, died September 1, 1864.

Scott, Basil, age 21, volunteer, February 22, 1865, one year, Thirty-sixth regiment, company C, private, served five months, mustered out July 27, 1865.

Smith, Clark, age 24, volunteer, 1862, three years, Seventh cavalry, company H, private.

Smith, David, age 39, drafted, September 27, 1864, one year, Fifty-first regiment, company G, private, served nine months, honorably discharged July 4, 1865.

Snodgrass, Stacy S., age 29, volunteer, November 11, 1861, three years, Seventy-seventh regiment, company I, private, veteran enlistment, age 31, volunteer, February, 1864, three years, Seventy-seventh regiment, company I, private.

Snodgrass, George Washington, age 19, volunteer, August 15, 1862, three years, Ninety-second regiment, company H, private, served three years, mustered out, June 10, 1865.

Snodgrass, Samuel, age 20, substitute, 1865, one year, Sixty-third regiment, private, mustered out May, 1865.

Still, James Leroy, age 30, drafted, March, 1865, one year, Thirty-ninth regiment, company E, private, served three months, mustered out July 9, 1865.

Strahl, Charles, aged 22, volunteer, 1861, three years, Seventy-seventh regiment, private.

Strahl, Martin, volunteer, three years, Seventy-seventh regiment, private.

Strahl, Joseph, age 19, substitute, October, 1864, one year, Thirty-third regiment, company B, private, served nine months, mustered out July 20, 1865.

Swallow, George Washington, age 36, volunteer, May, 1861, three years, Twenty-fifth regiment, company H, private, honorably discharged, second enlistment, 1863, six months, Fourth Virginia cavalry, private, mustered out, third enlistment, May, 1864, one hundred days, One Hundred and Forty-eighth regiment, company A, private, mustered out, 1864.

Swallow, James M., age 20, volunteer, August, 1862, three years, Ninety-second regiment, company H, private, served eight months, died April 14, 1863.

Thomas, Alexander, age 16, volunteer, February 5, 1862, three years, Seventy-seventh regiment, company C, private, served three months, honorably discharged May 9, 1862.

Thomas, Samuel, age 19, volunteer, December 12, 1861, three years, Seventy-seventh regiment, company G, private, served eleven months, honorably discharged November 20, 1862.

Thomas, Ezer, age 26, volunteer, November, 1861, three years, Seventy-seventh regiment, company G, private, served six months, died May 7, 1862.

Thomas, Jacob, drafted September, 1864, one year, Thirty-ninth regiment, company E.

Thomas, Leander, drafted September, 1864, one year, Thirty-ninth regiment, company E.

Tice, Sherwood, age 23, volunteer, February, 1864, three years, Seventy-seventh regiment, company G, private.

Tice, Henry.

Turner, George W., age 44, drafted September, 1864, one year, Fifty-first regiment, company D, private, served eight months, honorably discharged June, 1865.

Weddle, William, age 37, volunteer, October 10, 1861, three years, First light artillery, company K, private, served sixteen months, honorably discharged October 20, 1863

Williams, Daniel, age 17, volunteer, March 22, 1865, one year, Thirty-sixth regiment, company E, private, honorably discharged May 15, 1865.

Wilson, Richard, One Hundred and Sixteenth Ohio, regiment, company F.

MARIETTA TOWNSHIP

Alcock, Thomas, age 44, volunteer, May, 1864, one hundred days, One Hundred and Forty-eighth regiment, company B, corporal, served five months, mustered out October, 1864.

Baldwin, Saint Clair, age 41, volunteer, May 1, 1861, three years, Tenth regiment, company I, private, attained rank of corporal, served three years, mustered out 1864, regular veteran enlistment, age 44, volunteer, 1864, First New York light artillery, company L, private, served eight months, mustered out July 17, 1865.

Beach, John Berwick, age 21, volunteer, October 15, 1861, three years, Seventy-seventh regiment, company B, sergeant, served two years and three months, honorably discharged February, 1864, veteran enlistment, age 23, volunteer, 1864, three years, Seventy-seventh regiment, company B, sergeant, died September 1, 1866, lost leg in army.

Beach, Asa Pardee, volunteer, February 10, 1864, three years, Seventy-seventh regiment, company B, private.

Bartmess, George J., Thirty-sixth regiment, company G, private, died.

Bean, James F., Seventh Virginia cavalry, company H.

Berry.

Blancet, William H., three years, Eighteenth regiment.

Bodman, Frederick, Thirty-ninth regiment, company F.

Boughton, Calvin C., age 20, volunteer, September, 1861, three years, First cavalry, company L, private, served three years, mustered out 1864

Buell, Timothy L., age 26, volunteer, September, 1862, three years, Seventh cavalry, company H, private, attained rank of sergeant, served three years, mustered out 1865.

Bush, William, One Hundred and Sixteenth regiment, company C.

Cain, James Gibson, age 26, volunteer, May, 1864, one hundred days, One Hundred and Forty-eighth regiment, company B, private, served five months, mustered out October, 1864.

Cain, Martin S., age 22, volunteer, May, 1864, one hundred days, One Hundred and Forty-eighth regiment, company B, private, served five months, mustered out October, 1864.

Campbell M. M., Ninety-second regiment, company F.

Campbell, S. Madison, age 18, volunteer, September, 1862, three years, Seventh cavalry, company H, private, attained rank of corporal, served two years and ten months, mustered out 1865.

Campbell, Thomas R., volunteer, Seventy-seventh regiment, company B, private, died September 25, 1862.

Campbell, William R., volunteer, three years, First Virginia light artillery, company C, private, mustered out June 28, 1865.

Carpenter, Jasper N., volunteer, May, 1864, one hundred days, One Hundred and Forty-eighth regiment, company B, private, served four months, mustered out September 14, 1864.

Chambers, William, age 23, volunteer, September, 1862, three years, Seventh cavalry, company H, private, served four months, honorably discharged January, 1863.

Chambers, Ellis T., age 21, volunteer, 1862, three years, Ninety-second regiment, company F, private.

Classpil, George.

Clogston, Charles, volunteer, three years, First Virginia light artillery, company C, private, attained rank of corporal, mustered out June 28, 1865.

Cole, William Henry H., age 21, volunteer, September, 1862, three years, Seventh cavalry, company H, private, served two years and ten months, mustered out 1865.

Cole, Hiram Howe, age 21, volunteer, May, 1864, one hundred days, One Hundred and Forty-eighth regiment, company B, private, served five months, mustered out October, 1864.

Cole, John W. B., age 18, volunteer, June, 1863, three years, First cavalry, company L, private, served eight months, died September 10, 1864, of typhoid fever, near Atlanta.

Coombs, William, age 18, volunteer, 1862, three years, Ninety-second regiment, company F, private, attained rank of corporal, mustered out June 10, 1865.

Conkle, Jacob, age 15, volunteer, July, 1863, six months, Fourth Virginia cavalry, company D, private, served nine months, mustered out March, 1864, reenlistment, age 16, volunteer, April, 1864, three years, Seventh Virginia cavalry, company D, private, served one year and two months, mustered out July, 1864.

Conkle, Abner, age 16, volunteer, 1865, one year, Thirty-sixth regiment, company F, private, served four months, mustered out July, 1865.

Cook, Charles Augustus, age 32, volunteer, August 12, 1861, three years, Thirty-sixth regiment, company G, private, served five and one-half months, honorably discharged January 31, 1862.

Corner, Whitney R., age 21, volunteer, February, 1864, three years, First cavalry, company L, private, served one year and six months, mustered out September 26, 1865.

Coraig, George, volunteer, 1862, three years, Ninety-second regiment, company F, private, attained rank of corporal, served three years, mustered out 1865.

Crickard, William C., age 20, volunteer, April, 1863, three years, First Virginia light artillery, company C, private, served two years and three months, mustered out June 28, 1865.

Curtis, William, age 17, volunteer, May, 1862, three months, Eighty-seventh regiment, company A, corporal, served four months, mustered out October 1, 1862.

Dailey, Isaac, First regiment light artillery, company K.

Davis, John, Thirty-sixth regiment, company I.

Davis, Albert, Seventy-seventh regiment, company B.

Davis, Willard, age 38, volunteer, 1861, three years, Seventy-seventh regiment, company B, private, honorably discharged 1862.

Dibble, Hannibal, age 21, volunteer, May 27, 1861, three months, Eighteenth regiment, company B, private, served three months, mustered out August 28, 1861, second enlistment, age 21, volunteer, September, 1861, three years, First Virginia light artillery, company C, private, served two years and six months, 1864, third enlistment, age 24, volunteer, March 31, 1864, three years, First Virginia light artillery, company C, private, served one year and three months, honorably discharged 1865.

Dotson, Michael, age 28, volunteer, May, 1864, one hundred days, One Hundred and Forty-eighth regiment, company B, private, served five months, mustered out September 14, 1864.

Dotson, Joseph, Third regiment, company B.

Dotson, Samuel, volunteer, September 16, 1861, three years, First cavalry, company L, corporal.

Douglas, Edward J., age 24, volunteer, July 22, 1861, three years, Thirty-ninth regiment, company B, private, served three years, mustered out August 2, 1864, transferred to company D, veteran reserve corps.

Dye, David L., Seventh cavalry, company H.

Fuller, Ira, age 19, volunteer, May, 1864, one hundred days, One Hundred and Forty-eighth regiment, company B, private, served five months, mustered out September 14, 1864.

Dye, Sanford, volunteer, May, 1864, one hundred days, One Hundred and Forty-eighth regiment, company B, private, four months, mustered out September 14, 1864.

Guise, Abram F., First cavalry, company C.

Gurley, John, Thirty-sixth regiment, company C.

Harris, Henry M., volunteer, September 16, 1861, three years, First cavalry, company L, private.

Harsha, William, age 19, volunteer, September 16, 1861, three years, First cavalry, company L, private, served two years and six months, honorably discharged 1864, veteran enlistment, age 21, volunteer, 1864, three years, First cavalry, company L, corporal, served one year and six months, mustered out September 26, 1865.

Harsha, Robert, age 19, volunteer, First cavalry, company L, private.

Hart, Jeremiah, Seventh cavalry, company H.

Hays, John, age 17, volunteer, 1861, three years, Ninth Virginia regiment, company C, private, served two years and six months, honorably discharged 1864, veteran enlistment, age 19, volunteer, 1864, three years, Ninth Virginia regiment, company C, private, attained rank of sergeant, served one year and six months, mustered out 1865.

Hemmeger, William, age 27, volunteer, November 17, 1863, three years, Ninety-second regiment, company F, private, served one year and eight months, mustered out July 20, 1865, transferred to Thirty-first when the Ninety-second was discharged.

Henneger, Alfred, age 18, volunteer, October, 1861, three years, Seventy-seventh regiment, company B, private, served two years and three months, honorably discharged 1864, veteran enlistment, age 20, volunteer, February, 1864, three years, Seventy-seventh regiment, company B, private, served two years.

Henrehan, James, age 17, volunteer, 1861, three years, First Virginia light artillery, company C, private, served two years, honorably discharged 1864, veteran enlistment, age 19, volunteer, March, 1864, three years, First Virginia light artillery, company C, private, served one year and three months, mustered out 1865.

Hill, Daniel Y., volunteer, April, 1861, three months, Eighteenth regiment, company B, private, served three months, August, 1861.

Hill, John, volunteer, May, 1864, one hundred days, One Hundred and Forty-eighth regiment, company B, private, served four months, mustered out September, 1864.

Hill, Edward Thomas, age 26, volunteer, February 13, 1864, three years, Seventy-seventh regiment, companies H and D, private.

Hill, Wallace, age 18, volunteer, three years, Seventy-seventh regiment, company B, private, died May 6, 1863, at Alton, Illinois, of measles.

Hill, Ephraim A., age 17, volunteer, May, 1862, three months, Eighty-seventh regiment, company A, private, served four months, mustered out October 1, 1862, reenlistment, age 18, volunteer, August 9, 1863, three years, Second heavy artillery company K, private, died April 3, 1865, of intermittent fever.

Hoffman, John Henry, age 17, volunteer, May 28, 1862, three months, Eighty-fifth regiment, company F, private, mustered out, reenlistment, age 19, volunteer, February 2, 1864, three years, First cavalry, company L, private, one year and eight months, mustered out September 26, 1865.

Hoit, Jeremiah, age 31, volunteer, September, 1862, three years, Seventh cavalry, company H, private, served two years and eight months, mustered out July 4, 1865.

House, Amos, age 37, volunteer, May, 1864, one hundred days, One Hundred and Forty-eighth regiment, company B, private, served four months, mustered out September 14, 1864.

House, John, age 30, volunteer, May, 1864, one hundred days, One Hundred and Forty-eighth regiment, company B, private, served four months, mustered out September 14, 1864.

Hutchenson, H. Underhill, age 33, volunteer, October 22, 1861, three years, Seventy-seventh regiment, company B, private, attained to rank of corporal, served three years, mustered out October 20, 1864.

Kerr, John, age 22, volunteer, September, 1861, three years, Thirty-sixth regiment, company G, private, served three years, mustered out.

Magee, George, age 19, volunteer, September 16, 1861, three years, First cavalry, company L, private, served three years, mustered out in 1864.

Magee, Hiram, age 18, volunteer, November, 1861, three years, Seventy-seventh regiment, company B, private, served two and one-fourth years, honorably discharged February, 1864, veteran enlistment, age 20, volunteer, February, 1864, three years, Seventy-seventh regiment, company B, private, served two years.

Magee, Ansel Ward, volunteer, January 4, 1864, three years, First cavalry, company L, private, served one and two-thirds years, mustered out September 26, 1865.

Maxon, Russell W., age 18, volunteer, January, 1864, three years, First cavalry, company L, private, served eight months, died September 20, 1864.

McGrath, Thomas, age 24, volunteer, September 1, 1861, three years, First Virginia light artillery, company C, private, served two and a half years, honorably discharged March, 1864, veteran enlistment, age 26, volunteer, March 31, 1864, three years, First Virginia light artillery, battery C., private, served one year and three months, mustered out June, 1865.

McGregory, B., Seventy-seventh regiment, company B.

Miller, John William, age 24, volunteer, May, 1864, one hundred days, One Hundred and Forty-eighth regiment, company B, corporal, mustered out September, 1864.

Miller, Robert Taylor, age 23, volunteer, May, 1864, one hundred days, One Hundred and Forty-eighth regiment, company D, private, mustered out September, 1864.

Miller, Charles Augustus, age 20, volunteer, September 2, 1862, three years, Seventh cavalry, company H, private, attained the rank of corporal, mustered out July 4, 1865.

Miller, James.

Mitchell, Edward S., age 19, volunteer, August 8, 1862, three years, Seventh cavalry, company H, private, served one year, died in 1863, of chronic diarrhœa.

Nelson, Philip O., age 16, volunteer, January, 1864, three years, First cavalry, company L, private, served one and a half years, mustered out September 26, 1865.

Nixon, Zebulon J, age 20, volunteer, 1861, three years, Thirty-sixth regiment, company A, veteran enlistment, age 22, volunteer, 1864, three years, Thirty-sixth regiment, company A.

Nixon, Edward William, age 19, volunteer, 1864, one hundred days, One Hundred and Forty-eighth regiment, company B, private, mustered out September 14, 1864.

Northrop, J. Thurston, age 17, volunteer, September 2, 1862, three years, Seventh cavalry, company H, private.

Northrup, Henry A., substitute, May, 1864, one hundred days, One Hundred and Forty-eighth regiment, company F, private, mustered out September, 1864, second enlistment, volunteer, February 15, 1865, one year, Thirty-sixth regiment, company C, private, served five and a half months, mustered out August, 1865.

Oliver, David, age 26, volunteer, 1862, three years, Ninety-second regiment, company F, private, mustered out June 10, 1865.

Oliver, Albert, age 18, volunteer, July 19, 1861, three years, Thirty-ninth regiment, company B, private, served two years and six months, honorably discharged in 1863, veteran enlistment, age 20, volunteer, 1864, three years, Thirty-ninth regiment, company B, private, served one year and six months, mustered out July 9, 1865.

Oliver, Thomas, age 16, volunteer, Seventy-seventh regiment, company I, private.

Oliver, Henry, age 17, volunteer, 1863, six months, Fourth cavalry, company C, private, reenlistment, age 17, volunteer, February, 1864, three years, Thirty-sixth regiment, company G, private, died August, 1864, killed at Fredericktown, Maryland.

Otis, H. L., Twenty-third regiment, company H.

Posey, Dudley, age 18, volunteer, July 28, 1862, three years, Ninety-second regiment, company F, fifer, served eight and a half months, honorably discharged March 15, 1863.

Posey, Henry Clay, age 17, volunteer, March 31, 1864, three years, Thirty-sixth regiment, company F, private, served one and a half years, mustered out July 27, 1865.

Priest, William Henry, age 23, volunteer, 1862, three years, Ninety-second regiment, company F, private, honorably discharged 1865.

Priest, John Sumner, age 19, volunteer, March 6, 1864, three years, Thirty-sixth regiment, company F, private, served one month, died April 6, 1864.

Rake, Abraham, Seventh cavalry, company H, died.

Rake Elias, Seventh cavalry, company H, died at Marietta, Ohio.

Rake, John, jr., Seventh cavalry, company H, killed at Rocky Gap, Kentucky.

Reckard, Wesley J., age 24, volunteer, September, 1861, three years, First cavalry, company L, private, served seven and a half months, honorably discharged June 2, 1862

Reeves, Abram, volunteer, August 9, 1862, three years, Ninety-second regiment, company F, private, served two years and eight months, mustered out June 10, 1865

Reeves, Isaac, volunteer, Ninety-second regiment, company F, died February 23, 1864, gunshot.

Reeves, Isaac, jr., age 18, volunteer, July 29, 1862, three years, Ninety-second regiment, company F, private, served one year and six months, honorably discharged May 29, 1865.

Richardson, Edward L., age 18, volunteer, February 15, 1864, three years, Seventy-seventh regiment, company B, private, served six months, died February 25, 1864, Tyler, Texas, prisoner of war.

Riley, John Newton, age 18, volunteer, September 2, 1862, three years, Seventh cavalry, company H, private, served two years and nine months, died August, 1864.

Riley, Judson, age 17, volunteer, February, 1864, three years, First cavalry, company L, private, served one year and six months, mustered out August, 1865.

Riley, John, age 21, volunteer, September 16, 1861, three years, First cavalry, company L, private, served fifteen months, honorably

discharged, reenlistment, age 24, volunteer, May, 1864, one hundred days, One Hundred and Forty-eighth regiment, company B, corporal, mustered out September, 1864.

Riley, Warren, age 19, volunteer, September, 1861, three years, First cavalry, company L, private, served nine months, honorably discharged June 22, 1862, reenlistment, age 22, volunteer, February 10, 1864, three years, First cavalry, company L, private, attained rank of corporal, served one year and six months, mustered out September 26, 1865.

Robinson, Lucius L., age 20, volunteer, March, 1865, one year, One Hundred and Eightieth regiment, company F, private.

Robinson, Charles Eli, age 16, volunteer, January, 1864, three years, Thirty-sixth regiment, company G, private, served one year and six months, mustered out July, 1865.

Rood, D. R., volunteer, three years, First cavalry, company L, private.

Rumbles, Charles, Thirty-sixth regiment, company H.

Sanford, George Philip, age 20, volunteer, August, 1861, three years, Second Virginia cavalry, company F, corporal, served two years and six months, veteran enlistment, age 22, volunteer, 1864, three years, Second Virginia cavalry, company F, corporal, attained rank of sergeant.

Sanford, Thomas Spencer, volunteer, May, 1864, one hundred days, One Hundred and Forty-eighth regiment, company B, private.

Sanford, John P., volunteer, May, 1864, one hundred days, One Hundred and Forty-eighth regiment, company B, captain, served four months, mustered out September 14, 1864.

Sanford, Charles Henry, age 24, volunteer, August, 1861, three years, First cavalry, company L, private, served two years and six months, honorably discharged, veteran enlistment, age 26, volunteer, 1864, three years, First cavalry, company L, private, served one year and six months, mustered out August, 1865.

Sawers, George W., volunteer, May, 1864, one hundred days, One Hundred and Forty-eighth regiment, company B, private, served four months, mustered out September, 1864.

Scott, Jacob Hanson, age 19, volunteer, May, 1864, one hundred days, One Hundred and Forty-eighth regiment, company G, drummer, served four months, mustered out September 14, 1864.

Sheldon, Hiram, age 21, volunteer, three years, One Hundred and Sixteenth regiment, company D.

Sheldon, Charles, volunteer, May, 1864, one hundred days, One Hundred and Forty-eighth regiment, company A, private.

Sheppard, Thomas R., age 19, volunteer, May, 1864, one hundred days, One Hundred and Forty-eighth regiment, company A, private, served four months, mustered out September, 1864.

Smith, Moses, age 48, volunteer, 1861, three years, Thirty-ninth regiment, company B, corporal, served ten months, honorably discharged for disability May 23, 1862.

Smith, Joshua Pitt, age 26, volunteer, May, 1864, one hundred days, One Hundred and Forty-eighth regiment, company B, private, served four months, mustered out September, 1864.

Smith, David Chesmy, age 24, volunteer, May, 1864, one hundred days, One Hundred and Forty-eighth regiment, company B, private, four months, mustered out September, 1864.

Snyder, Joseph B., age 21, volunteer, August, 1862, three years, Ninety-second regiment, company F, sergeant, one year, died October 13, 1863.

Stanhope, John William, age 13, volunteer, 1861, three years, Seventy-seventh regiment, companies C and E, drummer, honorably discharged, veteran enlistment, age 15, volunteer, 1864, three years, Seventy-seventh regiment, companies C and E, drum major.

Strickler, Isaac, Ninety-second regiment, company F.

Stuckey, Jeremiah, age 35, substitute, May, 1864, one hundred days, One Hundred and Forty-eighth regiment, company A, private, died May, 1864.

Thornley, William, volunteer, July, 1862, three years, Ninety-second regiment, company F, captain, served nine months, resigned April 9, 1863.

Thornley, Willis Hall, volunteer, November, 5, 1861, three years, Seventy-seventh regiment, company B, private, attained rank of corporal, served three years, mustered out December 10, 1864.

Thornley, Warren, age 17, volunteer, May, 1864, one hundred days, One Hundred and Seventy-eighth regiment, company B, private, served four months, mustered out September, 1864.

Thornley, James, volunteer, July 9, 1862, three years, Ninety-second regiment, company F, private, served three years, mustered out 1865, transferred to invalid corps in 1863.

Thorniley, Nathan De Witt, age 20, volunteer, August 9, 1862, three years, Ninety-second regiment, company F, private, served one year, died September 4, 1863, of consumption, at Nashville.

Thorniley, Rinaldo R., age 23, volunteer, August 9, 1862, three years, Ninety-second regiment, company F, private, served one year and four months, honorably discharged December 7, 1863.

Wells, John C., three years, Ninety-second regiment, company F, private.

Wendland, Julius, Seventy-seventh regiment, company B, private.

Wendland, Robert, Twenty-eighth regiment, company K, private.

West, James Compton, age 39, volunteer, May, 1864, one hundred days, One Hundred and Forty-eighth regiment, company B, orderly sergeant, mustered out September, 1864.

West, William Wilson, age 34, volunteer, May, 1864, one hundred days, One Hundred and Forty-eighth regiment, company B, first lieutenant, mustered out September, 1864.

West, Thomas Jefferson, age 21, volunteer, May, 1864, one hundred days, One Hundred and Forty-eighth regiment, company B, corporal, mustered out September, 1864.

West, Henry Clay, age 18, volunteer, August 30, 1861, three years, Thirty-sixth regiment, company G, private, attained the rank of sergeant, served three years, mustered out in 1864.

West, Leslie Coombs, age 16, volunteer, May, 1864, one hundred days, One Hundred and Forty-eighth regiment, company B, drummer, mustered out September, 1864.

Wilson, Matthew W., age 30, volunteer, May, 1864, one hundred days, One Hundred and Forty-eighth regiment, company B, sergeant, mustered out September, 1864.

Wilson, Milo, age 29, volunteer, May, 1864, one hundred days, One Hundred and Forty-eighth regiment, company B, private, mustered out September, 1864.

Woodward, Orlando, age 18, volunteer, January 19, 1864, three years, Thirty-ninth regiment, company B, fifer, served one year and a half, mustered out July 9, 1865.

Yeardley, Frank B., volunteer, three years, Thirty-ninth regiment, company B, private, died.

Yeardley, John, volunteer, Seventy-seventh regiment, company B.

Wright, William, Seventy-seventh regiment, company C.

RECAPITULATION.

Buell's Pierpont battery	8
And one each in First New York light artillery, De Beck's battery, battery K, Second Ohio heavy artillery, in all	3
First Ohio cavalry	20
Seventh Ohio cavalry	15
One each in Fourth Virginia cavalry, Ninth Virginia cavalry, Fourth Ohio cavalry, Second Virginia cavalry, in all	4
One Hundred and Forty-eighth Ohio National guard	32
Seventy-seventh Ohio	19
Ninety-second Ohio	18
Thirty-sixth Ohio	14
Thirty-ninth Ohio	6
Eighteenth Ohio (three months)	2
One Hundred and Sixteenth Ohio	2
Eighty-seventh Ohio	2
And one each in Tenth Ohio, Eighteenth Ohio, Seventh Virginia, Third Ohio, Eighty-fifth Ohio, Twenty-third Ohio, Twenty-eighth Ohio, and One Hundred and Eightieth Ohio, and one not designated, in all	9

Total number soldiers	134
Died	14

HARMAR TOWNSHIP.

Adams, Horatio N., age 25, volunteer, three years, Ninety-second regiment, company F, private, died January 27, 1863, at Gallipolis, of dropsy.

Alexander, Robert, volunteer, May, 1864, one hundred days, One Hundred and Forty-eighth regiment, private.

Berry, Zenas Asa, age 18, volunteer, February 4, 1865, one year, fifth cavalry, company D, private, served nine months, mustered out October 30, 1865.

Briant, Permenus, age 40, volunteer, September 21, 1864, one year, First light artillery, company H, private, served nine months, mustered out June 15, 1865, detailed as artificer.

Bartlett, Sylvester, volunteer, August, 1864, gunboat, private, honorably discharged.

Bartlett, H., age 18, volunteer, November 1, 1861, Sixty-third regi-

ment, company D, private, attained the rank of corporal, served three years and eight months, mustered out July 8, 1865, reenlisted as a veteran.

Bruch, James, Eleventh regiment.

Babcock, William Winslow, age 44, May, 1864, One hundred days, One Hundred and Forty-eighth regiment, company A, private, served four months, mustered out September, 1864.

Babcock, James Whitney, jr., age 20, substitute, May, 1864, one hundred days, One Hundred and Forty-eighth regiment, company K, private, served four months, mustered out September, 1864

Boring, Absolom, age 43, January 5, 1864, First cavalry, company L, private, served one year and eight months, mustered out September 26, 1865.

Bauer, Jacob, First cavalry, company L.

Barker, Jesse H, age 19, volunteer, July 29, 1861, three years, Thirty-sixth regiment, company A, corporal, attained the rank of commissary sergeant, served two years and five months, mustered out January 1, 1864.

Bisbee, William H., volunteer, May, 1861, three months, Eighteenth regiment, attained the rank of major, served four months, mustered out September, 1864.

Boeshar, Christian, volunteer, Thirty-ninth regiment, company F.

Bishop, William, volunteer, First cavalry, company L, private.

Briant, Andrew J., age 22, volunteer, 1862, three years, Ninety-second regiment, company F, private, served three years, mustered out June 12, 1865, sick and after one year detailed in the commissary department.

Beckwith, B., age 33, volunteer, August 18, 1864, one year, First cavalry, company H, private, served ten months, mustered out June 20, 1865.

Boyd, Joseph, age 36, volunteer, August, 1862, three years, Ninety-second regiment, company G, private, served three years, mustered out June 12, 1865.

Barber, Henry, age 20, August 1, 1861, three years, Thirty-sixth regiment, company F, drummer, served two years, honorably discharged August 21, 1863, for disability.

Brown, John William, age 18, substitute, March 19, 1865, one year, Eighteenth regiment, company H, private, served seven months, mustered out October 9, 1865.

Barber, Levi, volunteer, August, 1861, three years, Thirty-sixth regiment, captain, one year and three months, resigned November 29, 1862.

Brickwady, Jacob, volunteer, Thirty-ninth regiment.

Chambers, Salmon M., age 20, volunteer, October, 1861, three years, First cavalry, company L, private, served four years, mustered out September 13, 1865, enlisted as a veteran.

Chambers, Otis J., volunteer, three years, First cavalry, company L, private.

Carpenter, Theodore, age 17, volunteer, 1865, one year, Thirty-sixth regiment, company B, private, mustered out July 27, 1865.

Caywood, William, age 50, substitute, May, 1864, one hundred days, One Hundred and Forty-eighth regiment, company A, private, served four months, mustered out September, 1864.

Caywood, John William, age 24, volunteer, September 1, 1862, three years, Seventh cavalry, company H, corporal, attained the rank of sergeant, served three years, mustered out July 4, 1865.

Chapin, Arthur B, age 19, volunteer, September 16, 1861, three cavalry, company L, sergeant, served three years, mustered out 1861.

Childers, Otis L., age 20, volunteer, February 16, 1862, three years, First cavalry, company L, private, served three years, mustered out September 13, 1865.

Childers, Joseph H, age 22, volunteer, August 5, 1863, three years, First light artillery, company H, private, served two years, mustered out July 31, 1865.

Childers, Simon, volunteer, Twenty-first Illinois, company D, died August 1, 1862.

Congdon, Buell, age 27, volunteer, July 22, 1861, three years, Thirty-ninth regiment, companies B and F, private, attained rank of orderly sergeant, served four years, mustered out July 9, 1865, reenlisted as a veteran.

Congdon, John G., age 59, volunteer, October 17, 1861, three years, Seventy-seventh regiment, company K, private, honorably discharged for disability.

Chamberlain, William.

Corey, David, Thirty-sixth regiment, company A.

Dailey, Thomas Cook, age 24, volunteer, May 27, 1861, three months, Eighteenth regiment, company B, private, served three months, mustered out August 28, 1861, reenlistment, volunteer, August 6, 1862, three years, First light artillery, company H, private, attained rank of sergeant, served two years and ten months, honorably discharged June 14, 1865

Dailey, William H , age 21, volunteer, September, 1861, three years, First cavalry, company L, private, mustered out September 26, 1865, reenlisted as a veteran, was discharged once for disability.

Daniels, James B., Thirty-ninth regiment, company B.

Daniels, Joseph B., age 34, volunteer, November, 1862, three years, Ninth cavalry, company B, first lieutenant, attained rank of captain, served three years, mustered out August 2, 1865.

Davis, Albert A., volunteer, three years, Seventy-seventh regiment, company K, private, died April 6, 1862, killed at Shiloh.

Devol, Simeon, M., age 19, volunteer, August, 1861, Thirty-sixth regiment, company A, private, served eight months, honorably discharged 1862, second elistment, volunteer, six months, Fourth Virginia cavalry, company D, private, served six months, mustered out, third enlistment, substitute, May, 1864, one hundred days, One Hundred and Forty-eighth regiment, company A private, served four months, mustered out September, 1864, fourth enlistment, substitute, April, 1865, one year Eighteenth regiment, company I, private, served six months, mustered out, 1865.

Dilley, James, jr, age 30, volunteer, June 3, 1861, three years, tenth regiment, company G, private, served three years, mustered out 1864, captured, in prison three weeks.

Douthitt, James, volunteer, Ninety-second regiment, company F.

Duden, John, age 21, volunteer, September 16, 1861, three years First cavalry, company L, private, served three years, mustered out September 17, 1864.

Duden, Henry, age 20, volunteer, February 1, 1862, three years, First cavalry, company L, private, attained rank of commissary sergeant, served three years and seven months, mustered out September 26, 1865, reenlisted as a veteran.

Duden, Charles, age 19, volunteer, October, 1861, three years, Seventy-seventh regiment, company D, private, attained rank of sergeant, served seven months, died May, 1862, at Camp Dennison, of typhoid fever.

Dye, Sanford, May, 1864, one hundred days, One Hundred and Forty-eighth regiment, company B, private.

Dye, Sereno, volunteer, Thirty-sixth regiment, company F, private

Dye, Daniel H., volunteer, Ninety-second regiment, company F.

Eddleston, Hugh B , age 18, volunteer, September 16, 1861, three years, First cavalry, company L, private, served three years, mustered out September 17, 1864.

Eddleston, John C., age 16, volunteer, September 1, 1861, First Virginia light artillery, company C, private, served three years, died October 26, 1864, of intermittent fever, at Alexandria, Virginia.

Farley, George, Thirty-ninth regiment, company K.

Farley, John W., First cavalry, company L.

Fearing, Francis D., age 21, volunteer, August, 1862, three years, First light artillery, company H, private, served five months, died January 3, 1863, of typhoid fever.

Fearing, Benjamin D., volunteer, 1861, three years, Seventy-seventh regiment, major, attained rank of brevet brigadier general, mustered out May, 1865, transferred to the Ninety-second.

Finch, Darius, First cavalry, company L.

Gillingham, Milton, age 32, volunteer, 1861, three months, Eighteenth regiment, company B, private, served four months, mustered out September, 1861, reenlistment, September 16, 1861, three years, First cavalry, company L, private, four years, mustered out September 13, 1865.

Green, George L, age 18, volunteer, January 15, 1864, First cavalry, company L, private, served one year, honorably discharged for disability February 27, 1865.

Gates, Charles L., age 37, volunteer, January, 1864, First cavalry, company L, private, served eight months, mustered out September 26, 1865, in hospital three months.

Goodin, Stephen, May, 1864, one hundred days, One Hundred and Forty-eighth regiment, company K.

Gossett, Ephraim, age 35, substitute, May, 1864, one hundred days, One Hundred and Forty-eighth regiment, company I, private, four months, mustered out September, 1864.

Hall, Lyman W., volunteer, First cavalry, company L, private.

Hale, Alexander S , age 28, August 1, 1861, three years, Thirty-sixth regiment, company F, private, served four years, mustered out July 27, 1865, reenlisted as a veteran.

Hale, William Owen, age 17, volunteer, July 24, 1863, six months, Fourth Virginia cavalry, company D, private, served eight months,

mustered out March, 1864, second enlistment May, 1864, one hundred days, One Hundred and Forty-eighth regiment, company K, private, served four months, mustered out September 14, 1864, third enlistment February 18, 1865, one year, Thirty-sixth regiment, company C, private, served five months, mustered out July 27, 1865.

Hale, Simeon, age 28, volunteer, Sixty-third regiment, company II, private.

Hill, William, Thirty-sixth regiment, company A.

Harlow, Thomas C., volunteer, First cavalry, company C, private.

Hart, Percival P., age 26, volunteer, 1862, steamer Pattin, served eight months, honorably discharged for disability 1863, died June 12, 1863.

Hart, David W., age 23, volunteer, 1861, three years, First cavalry, company C, first sergeant, attained rank of first lieutenant, served four years, mustered out September 13, 1865.

Hart, Samuel, age 31, volunteer, January 11, 1862, three years, Seventy-fifth regiment, surgeon, brevetted lieutenant colonel, served three years and seven months, honorably discharged August 5, 1865, on duty with Sixteenth United States regiment at battle of Chattanooga, afterwards in charge of United States general hospital at Chattanooga, Tullahoma, Murfreesborough, and Nashville.

Henrich, John, Seventy-seventh regiment, company D.

Hill, Samuel G., volunteer, August 11, 1862, three years, Ninety-second regiment, company F, sergeant, served three years, mustered out June 10, 1865.

Hill, William.

Hollister, Arthur, volunteer, Second Ohio heavy artillery company K, private.

Hoff, James, age 17, volunteer, July 6, 1863, Fourth Ohio volunteer cavalry, company C, served eight months, honorably discharged March, 1864, reenlisted March, 1864, Thirteenth Ohio volunteer cavalry, company A, second sergeant, served four months, died July 30, 1864.

Henry, Jacob, age 16, volunteer, 1861, three years, Thirty-ninth regiment, company F, corporal, three years, mustered out 1864.

Huntsman, Cyrus S., volunteer, Seventh cavalry, company II, died in service.

Huntsman, D. D., volunteer, Thirty-ninth regiment, company B.

Ingraham, Ralph, volunteer, three years, Seventy-seventh regiment, company D, private, died April 2, 1862, at Paducah, Kentucky.

Jewell, Albert, volunteer, First Michigan.

Johnson, Charles, volunteer, Tenth regiment.

Jack, David L., Ninety-second regiment, company E, private.

Judd, Charles Hildreth, age 34, volunteer, August 22, 1862, three years, Nineteenth regiment, company A, corporal, detailed clerk, served two years, honorably discharged for disability September 25, 1864.

Maxon, George W., First light artillery, company H.

Matthews, Stephen, age 35, volunteer, October 16, 1861, three years, Seventy-seventh regiment, company K, private, served one year, honorably discharged August 8, 1862, captured at Shiloh, in prison one month and paroled.

Matthews, Solon, age 30, volunteer, August 7, 1862, three years, First light artillery, company H, private, served three years, mustered out June 14, 1865.

Lancaster, Frank, three months, Eighty-seventh regiment, company A, private, second enlistment July 6, 1863, Fourth Virginia cavalry, company C, private, attained rank of corporal, third enlistment March, 1864, Thirteenth cavalry, company A, sergeant, honorably discharged July 18, 1865.

Marsh, Brigham, age 31, volunteer, January 5, 1864, three years, First cavalry, company L, private, served one year and eight months, mustered out September 26, 1865.

Matthews, Stephen D., volunteer, Seventy-seventh regiment, company E, honorably discharged.

Matthews, John, volunteer, First cavalry.

Matthews, Solon, volunteer, First light artillery, company H.

McCulloch, Anthony W., volunteer, March 5, 1864, three years, First cavalry, company L, private.

Maxon, George W., First light artillery, honorably discharged.

McGinty, Michael, age 33, volunteer, February 3, 1864, three years, Seventy-third regiment, company F, private, died at Columbus of brain fever in 1855.

McGinty, Neil, age 24, volunteer, February 3, 1864, three years, Seventy-third regiment, company F, private, served one year and five months, mustered out July 20, 1865.

Merwin, Lewis P., First cavalry, company L, private.

Mervin, George W., volunteer, Eighteenth United States, company I, private.

Milligan, John, age 25, substitute, October 1, 1864, Fifteenth Tennessee, company K, private, served nine months, honorably discharged for disability July, 1865.

Milligan, William, age 21, volunteer, 1861, three years, First cavalry, company L, private, served four years, transferred to infantry August, 1865.

Milligan, George, age 23, volunteer, 1863, Sixty-third regiment, company H, private, served one year, died 1864.

Morton, Jackson, volunteer, First cavalry, company L.

Muncy, Isaac, age 17, volunteer, August 13, 1864, one year, First cavalry, company H, private, served one year, honorably discharged, 1865.

Muncey, John D., age 25, volunteer, January 5, 1864, First cavalry, company L, private, transferred to Ninth United States colored artillery, company E, March, 1865.

Muncey, Montgomery, age 20, volunteer, January 11, 1864, First cavalry, company L, private, transferred to Ninth United States colored artillery, company E, March, 1865.

Naylor, Harrison, age 19, volunteer, June, 1861, First cavalry, company L, private, mustered out and reenlisted as a veteran.

Naylor, James M., age 17, volunteer, September 1, 1861, three years, First Virginia light artillery, company C, private, mustered out 1865.

Nugent, Henry E., age 21, volunteer, July 2, 1863, three years, Second heavy artillery, company K, private, honorably discharged June 23, 1865.

Pattin, Thomas J., volunteer, 1864, First cavalry, company L, captain, attained rank of lieutenant colonel, mustered out.

Plant, Daniel A., volunteer, Thirty-ninth regiment, company B.

Parker, James, age 24, volunteer, April 19, 1861, three months, Eighteenth regiment, company B, private, served four months, mustered out August 28, 1861, reenlistment, volunteer, February 16, 1861, three years, First cavalry, company L, private, wounded December 31, 1862, and honorably discharged for disability June 15, 1863.

Parks, Miles, volunteer, First Virginia cavalry, company L, private.

Price, William, age 36, volunteer, May, 1864, one hundred days, One Hundred and Forty-eighth regiment, private.

Pryor, Nathan, volunteer, First cavalry, company L, private.

Putnam, Samuel H., age 26, volunteer, September 16, 1861, three years, First cavalry, company L, sergeant, attained rank of first lieutenant, resigned October 26, 1863.

Putnam, Douglas, jr., volunteer, July, 1862, three years, Ninety-second regiment, first lieutenant, attained rank of lieutenant colonel, honorably discharged April 11, 1864.

Pugh, Thomas, age 41, substitute, November 9, 1864, Sixty-seventh regiment, company B, private, served five months, wounded at Fort Gregory, and discharged for disability May 31, 1865.

Quimby, George, volunteer, May, 1864, one hundred days, One Hundred and Forty-eighth regiment, company L.

Quimby, Daniel.

Rardin, Thomas, volunteer, Thirty-ninth regiment, company B, private.

Regnier, Frederick A., volunteer, First light artillery, company H.

Rainey, Milton, volunteer, First cavalry, company L.

Rice, William, age 23, volunteer, 1861, three years, First cavalry, company L, private, served three years, mustered out in 1864.

Reppert, H. Clay, volunteer, three years, First cavalry, company L, second lieutenant, attained rank of captain, mustered out September 28, 1865.

Reppert, Walter, volunteer, February 1, 1863, three years, First cavalry, company L, corporal.

Regnier, Charles F., age 17, volunteer, August 13, 1862, three years, First light artillery, company H, private, served three months, honorably discharged December 13, 1862, for disability.

Rash, Charles, volunteer, Thirty-ninth regiment, company B, private.

Reese, Samuel, age 31, volunteer, August 3, 1862, three years, Ninety-second regiment, company F, private, served three years, honorably discharged June 10, 1865, detailed as teamster.

Russell, Charles, volunteer, three years, Thirty-ninth regiment, company B, private.

Roush, James, age 28, volunteer, September 30, 1864, one year, First cavalry, company H, private, served nine months, mustered out June 17, 1865.

Roberts, William, volunteer, October 6, 1862, three years, private, honorably discharged June 19, 1865.

Sears, Uz Hoy, age 23, volunteer, May 9, 1861, three years, Ninth Pennsylvania, company D, private, served three years, mustered out in 1864.

Shears, Isaac, volunteer, January 4, 1864, three years, First cavalry, company L, private.

Scott, John, age 50, volunteer, three years, 1861, Seventy-seventh regiment, company K, orderly sergeant, died May 4, 1862, of congestion of the brain.

Scott, Darwin, age 18, volunteer, 1861, three years, First cavalry, company L, private, served four years, mustered out September 13, 1865, reenlisted as a veteran.

Scott, William, age 23, Seventy-seventh regiment, company I.

Schilling, Joseph, age 17½, volunteer, May, 1864, one hundred days, One Hundred and Forty-eighth regiment, company A, private, served four months, mustered out in September, 1864.

Shepard, Henry, age 35, volunteer, July, 1861, three years, Thirty-ninth regiment, company B, second lieutenant, attained rank of first lieutenant, served one year, resigned June 10, 1862.

Skinner, Adolphus M., age 19, volunteer, March 23, 1864, three years, First Virginia cavalry, company C, private, served one year and four months, honorably discharged July 11, 1865, wounded July 24, 1864, afterward served as hospital nurse.

Shepard, Courtland, jr., volunteer, three years, Thirty-sixth regiment, company A, private, killed at Antietam September 17, 1862.

Smith, Jonathan, First cavalry, company L.

Smith, William H., age 24, volunteer, 1863, United States navy, master's mate.

Smith, John W., age 19, volunteer, April, 1861, Eighteenth regiment, company B, private, served three months, mustered out in 1861, reenlistment, 1861, three years, First cavalry, company L, private, honorably discharged in 1862 for disability.

Smith, Elijah G., age 57, volunteer, October 21, 1861, First light artillery, company H, private, honorably discharged April 17, 1863, for physical disability, reenlistment, volunteer, July 8, 1863, Second heavy artillery, private, honorably discharged on account of physical disability.

Smith, Jeremiah, volunteer, October, 1862, three years, Ninety-second regiment, company F, private, served three years, mustered out June 10, 1865.

Smith, Henry M., age 18, volunteer, February, 1862, three years, Sixty-third regiment, private, served two years and three months, killed at Kennesaw Mountain, June 26, 1864.

Snodgrass, William H., First cavalry, company L.

Steward, George, age 35, substitute, May, 1864, one hundred days, One Hundred and Forty-eighth regiment, company K, private, served four months, mustered out September, 1864.

Stewart, Jonathan C., First cavalry, company L.

Stevens, Hugh, Seventy-seventh regiment, company K.

Stremple, Charles, age 20, volunteer, 1861, three months, Eighteenth regiment, company B, private, mustered out August 28, 1861, reenlisted in company B, Eighteenth Ohio battery, and died April, 1862, in Kentucky.

Stremple, Henry, volunteer, First cavalry, company L, private.

Stiles, Benjamin F., First cavalry, company L.

Sugden, Edmonds J., age 19, volunteer, July 22, 1861, three years, Thirty-ninth regiment, company B, private, served three years, mustered out August, 1864, detailed for hospital service.

Sugden, Thomas Henry, age 19, volunteer, December, 1863, Sixty-third regiment, company F, drummer, mustered out July 8, 1865.

Struhl, Joseph S., volunteer, 1862, six months, Eighty-seventh regiment, company A, discharged March 12, 1863, reenlistment, volunteer, March 14, 1864, three years, orderly sergeant, attained the rank of captain, mustered out August 18, 1865.

Thurman, John H., volunteer, Thirty-ninth regiment, company B, died in service.

Tunecliff, William, January 16, 1864, three years, First cavalry company L, private.

Turner, Thomas M., volunteer, December, 1862, three years, Thirty-sixth regiment, first lieutenant, attained the rank of captain, quartermaster.

Thorniley, Thomas, volunteer, First cavalry, company L, died August 22, 1864, at Nashville, Tennessee.

Tise, Jacob, Thirty-sixth regiment, company C.

Tise, Philip B., Thirty-sixth regiment, company C.

Underwood, Oscar H., age 61, volunteer, February, 1861, three years, First cavalry, company C, second lieutenant, served nine months, resigned October, 1861.

Walters, William E., Ninety-second regiment, company F, private, honorably discharged.

Wells, John W., volunteer, August 6, 1862, three years, First light

38

artillery, company H, private, served three years, mustered out June 14, 1865.

Walton, Josiah, age 42, volunteer, October, 1862, three years, Ninety-second regiment, company F, private.

Wilson, Rector R., age 26, volunteer, January 4, 1864, First cavalry, company L, blacksmith, served one year and eight months, mustered out September 13, 1865.

Wilson, William, age 18, substitute, May, 1864, one hundred days, One Hundred and Forty-eighth regiment, company K, private, mustered out September, 1864, detailed as telegraph operator.

Whiting, Theodore, age 17, volunteer, August 31, 1862, three years, Eleventh Virginia regiment, company D, private, died June 6, 1863, of consumption.

Young, Daniel S., age 52, volunteer, three years, Seventy-seventh regiment, company K, private, died September 7, 1863, never in active service.

Young, John Lewis, age 41, volunteer, October 9, 1861, three years, First Ohio light artillery, company H, orderly sergeant, served one year, honorably discharged October 15, 1862, for disability.

Young, John Lewis, jr , age 14, volunteer, November 16, 1861, three years, First Ohio light artillery, company H, private, served three years, honorably discharged November 16, 1864

Ward, James Edwin, age 17, volunteer, Seventy-seventh regiment, company D, private, served eleven months, reenlistment, volunteer, July 6, 1863, six months, independent battalion of cavalry, company C, private, served eight months, discharged March 12, 1864, reenlistment, volunteer, March 14, 1864, Thirteenth cavalry, company A, corporal, in fifteen battles, served one year and four months, mustered out July 18, 1865.

RECAPITULATION.

Huntington's battery.. 12
Buell's Pierpont battery.. 2
Battery K, Second heavy artillery.............................. 3
First Ohio light artillery...................................... 1
Eighteenth Ohio Independent battery........................... 1
First Ohio cavalry.. 54
Seventh Ohio cavalry... 2
Fourth Virginia cavalry.. 2
Fourth independent battalion of Ohio volunteer cavalry........ 5
Thirteenth Ohio cavalry.. 4
And one each in Fifth cavalry, and Ninth cavalry.............. 2
United States navy... 1
Gunboat service.. 2
Thirty-sixth Ohio.. 16
Thirty-ninth Ohio.. 15
Ninety-second Ohio... 12
One Hundred and Forty-eighth Ohio National guard.............. 14
Sixty-third Ohio... 5
Eighteenth Ohio (three months)................................ 5
Eighteenth Ohio (three years)................................. 2
Seventy-seventh Ohio... 12
Eighty-seventh Ohio (three months)............................ 2
Seventy-third Ohio... 2
And one each in Eleventh Ohio, Twenty-first Illinois, Tenth Ohio, Seventy-fifth Ohio, First Michigan, Nineteenth Ohio, Eleventh Virginia, Ninth Virginia, Eighteenth United States, Fifteenth Tennessee, Sixty-seventh Ohio, and one not designated........ 12
                                                             ——
        Total number of soldiers.......................... 173
Died........ 17

MARIETTA CITY—FIRST WARD.

Abbott, William, age 26, volunteer, August 2, 1862, three years, Ninety-second regiment, company H, private, served two years, honorably discharged October 28, 1864, reenlisted, aged 29, substitute, April 1, 1865, Eighteenth regiment, company H, private, served five months, honorably discharged October, 1865.

Abbott, Farnum, volunteer, 1861, three years, Thirty-ninth regiment, company B, private.

Abbott, Charles, volunteer, United States navy.

Ackerson, Ephraim, age 26, volunteer, August 14, 1862, three years, Thirty-ninth regiment, company B, private, served three years, mustered out, veteran enlistment, age 29, volunteer, December, 1864, Thirty-ninth regiment, company B, private, served seven months, mustered out July 9, 1865

Ackerson, Abraham, age 19, volunteer, August 14, 1862, three years, Thirty-ninth regiment, company B, private, mustered out, veteran enlistment, age 22, volunteer, December, 1864, Thirty-ninth regiment,

company B, private, served seven months, mustered out July 9, 1865.

Ackerson, George Washington, age 16, volunteer, December, 1864, Thirty-ninth regiment, company B, private, served seven months, mustered out July 9, 1865.

Adams, Joseph John, age 29, volunteer, September 16, 1861, three years, First cavalry, company L, private, served three years, mustered out September, 1864.

Alcock, Charles T., age 20, volunteer, September 1, 1862, three years, Seventh cavalry, company H, bugler, attained rank of chief bugler, served two years and ten months, mustered out July 4, 1865.

Anderson, Joseph Hall, age 27, volunteer, November 10, 1863, three years, Ninety-second regiment, company F, private, attained orderly sergeant, served one year and nine months, mustered out July, 1865.

Aplin, Joseph, age 22, volunteer, November 8, 1861, three years, First Ohio light artillery, company H, private, served three years and eight months, mustered out July 31, 1865, reenlisted as a veteran.

Atkinson, Jonathan, volunteer, three years, Thirty-ninth regiment, company B, private.

Audebert, C., age 57, volunteer, Seventy-seventh regiment, company H, private.

Bacher, Henry, age 24, volunteer, Sixty-first regiment, three years, Thirty-ninth regiment, company F, musician.

Baldwin, George Edward, age 22, volunteer, August 3, 1862, three years, First Ohio light artillery, company H, private, discharged February 8, 1864, for disability.

Barker, John, volunteer, Seventy-fifth regiment, company F.

Barrows, Charles Cole, age 27, volunteer, August 9, 1862, three years, Thirty-ninth regiment, company B, private, served three years, mustered out July 9, 1865, reenlisted as a veteran.

Bell, Mathias, age 34, volunteer, gunboat engineer, served one month.

Bickert, Ambrose, age 26, volunteer, 1861, three years, Thirty-ninth regiment, company F, private, three years, honorably discharged 1864.

Bordman, Frederick, Thirty-ninth regiment, company F.

Booth, Robert, age 44, volunteer, October 1, 1861, three years, Sixty-third regiment, company G, second lieutenant, served seven months, resigned May 26, 1862.

Booth, John Thomas, age 20, volunteer, May 27, 1861, three months, Eighteenth regiment, company B, private, mustered out August 8, 1861, wounded in right wrist at Chickamauga, second enlistment, volunteer, August 12, 1861, three years, Thirty-sixth regiment, company G, first corporal, attained second sergeant, served three years, mustered out August 17, 1864.

Booth, George, age 16, volunteer, August 14, 1861, Thirty-sixth regiment, company E, drummer, honorably discharged April 1, 1862.

Booth, Joseph Robinson, age 14, volunteer, October, 1861, Sixty-third regiment, company G, musician, served six months, honorably discharged April, 1862.

Booth, Frank, age 17, volunteer, 1816, First Ohio light artillery, company K, private, honorably discharged 1862, captured at Harper's Ferry September 3, 1862, and paroled, reenlistment, volunteer, May 28, 1862, three months, Eighty-seventh regiment, company A, private, served four months, mustered out October 1, 1862.

Brenan, William Augustine, age 18, volunteer, September 1, 1861, three years, First Virginia light artillery, company C, private, mustered out, reenlisted as a veteran.

Brenan, Frank R., age 17, volunteer, September, 1861, three years, First Virginia light artillery, company C, private, mustered out, served in the three months' service of company G, Eighteenth regiment, reenlisted as a veteran.

Brenan, John Victor, aged 16, volunteer, September, 1861, three years, First Virginia light artillery, company C, private, mustered out, reenlisted as a veteran.

Broadhurst, William J., age 35, volunteer, March 27, 1862, three years, First Virginia light artillery, company C, private, served eleven months, honorably discharged February 15, 1863, for disability.

Brookover, Charles, age 18, volunteer, January, 1865, one year, One Hundred and Eighty-ninth regiment, company E, private, served seven months, mustered out October, 1865.

Bruce, Robert, age 23, volunteer, June 28, 1861, Fifteenth Massachusetts regiment, company B, private, one year, mustered out 1862, wounded at Ball's Bluff.

Bruce, Napoleon, volunteer, October, 1861, Fifteenth Massachusetts regiment, company B, private.

Bruce, Wallace, age 18, volunteer, July 22, 1861, Thirty-ninth regiment, company B, private, served four years, mustered out July 9, 1865, on detailed service as private orderly, reenlisted as a veteran.

Bukey, John S., age 15, volunteer, May 12, 1862, three years, Eleventh Virginia cavalry, company D, sergeant, attained rank of first lieutenant, resigned May 18, 1865.

Bukey, Alexander H., age 22, volunteer, May 29, 1861, three months, Eighteenth regiment, company B, private, served three months, mustered out August 8, 1861, reenlistment, volunteer, September 1, 1861, First Virginia light artillery, company G, corporal, attained rank of seargeant, mustered out.

Bukey, Joseph T., volunteer, January, 1862, three years, Eleventh Virginia cavalry, drum major, served three years, mustered out 1865.

Bukey, Van H., age 25, volunteer, October 28, 1861, three years, Eleventh Virginia cavalry, company D, private, attained rank of colonel, served three years and two months, mustered out December 26, 1864.

Buck, Silas, Twelfth Virginia cavalry, assistant surgeon.

Buck, George, paymaster.

Burk, John, volunteer, Seventy-third regiment, company F, private.

Burns, Israel, age 35, volunteer, February, 1864, Thirty-ninth regiment, company B, private, served one year and five months, mustered out July 9, 1865.

Carpenter, William, age 17, volunteer, July, 1861, three years, Thirty-ninth regiment, company B, private, served three years, mustered out July 9, 1864, veteran enlistment, age 21, volunteer, January, 1865, navy, private, discharged September, 1865.

Carpenter, Samuel, Seventy-seventh regiment, company H, private.

Caywood, John W., volunteer, three years, Seventh cavalry, company H, private, attained rank of sergeant, mustered out with regiment.

Chase, John Wallace, age 19, volunteer, September, 1862, three years, Thirty-ninth regiment, company B, private, served two years and ten months, discharged July 9, 1865.

Cherry, Henry, age 19, volunteer, May 28, 1862, six months, Eighty-seventh regiment, company A, private, captured twice and in prison in Texas ten months, reenlistment, February, 1864, three years, Seventy-seventh regiment, company B, private.

Cherry, Albert, age 17, volunteer, August 21, 1863, three years, Second Ohio heavy artillery, company K, private, served two years, mustered out August 23, 1865.

Clarke, George, age 16, volunteer, August 10, 1864, one year, One Hundred and Eighty-second regiment, company C, private, served one year, mustered out.

Clogston, Luther E., age 34, volunteer, September 16, 1861, three years, First Ohio volunteer cavalry, company L, private, served three years, mustered out September 16, 1864.

Clogston, Ansel, age 22, volunteer, May, 1864, one hundred days, One Hundred and Forty-eighth regiment, company A, private, mustered out September, 1864.

Clogston, Charles, age 18, volunteer, April 17, 1861, three months, Eighteenth regiment, company B, private, served three months, mustered out August 8, 1861, reenlistment, volunteer, Eighteenth regiment, company B, private, attained rank of corporal, mustered out, reenlisted as a veteran.

Cooley, William W., Thirty-sixth regiment, company K.

Cusic, L., volunteer, First light artillery, company H, private.

Davis, Jethro, age 34, volunteer, November, 1863, three years, Thirty-ninth regiment, company B, private, served one year and eight months, mustered out July 9, 1865.

Davenport, George, volunteer, 1861, three years, First light artillery, company H, first lieutenant, resigned January 7, 1863.

Daggett, William S., Twentieth Illinois regiment.

DeBeck, William L., volunteer, August, 1861, three years, First light artillery, company K, captain, served one year and nine months, resigned May 11, 1863.

Davis, Solomon, Seventy-seventh regiment, company B.

Dooley, Jeremiah, age 18, volunteer, three years, First Virginia light artillery, company C, corporal, mustered out 1865, reenlisted as a veteran.

Dotson, Joseph, age 19, volunteer, June, 1861, three years, Twenty-fourth regiment, company D, private, served three years and four months, mustered out October, 1864.

Douthitt, James, age 34, volunteer, August 10, 1862, three years, Ninety-second regiment, company F, private, attained rank of sergeant, served three years, mustered out June 10, 1865.

Douthitt, Augustus, age 18, volunteer, April, 1865, one year, Ninety-second regiment, company F, private, mustered out of service June 10, 1865.

Dow, David, age 19, volunteer, May, 1861, three months, Eighteenth regiment, company B, private, mustered out August 8, 1861, reenlist-

ment, volunteer, October 21, 1861, First Virginia light artillery, company C, private, attained rank of sergeant, mustered out.

Dow, John, age 18, volunteer, January 1, 1862, three years, First Virginia light artillery, company C, private, mustered out, reenlisted as a veteran.

Dye, George, age 21, volunteer, September 16, 1861, three years, First Ohio volunteer cavalry, company L, private, attained rank of commissary sergeant, served three years, honorably discharged September 17, 1864.

Dye, William, age 20, volunteer, August, 1864, gunboat, private, served eleven months, mustered out July, 1865.

Dyer, Thomas, age 25, volunteer, April, 1861, three months, Eighteenth regiment, company B, private, served three months, mustered out with regiment, reenlistment, age 25, volunteer, July, 1861, three years, Thirty-ninth regiment, company B, private, 1865, mustered out with regiment.

Dulty, John, age 40, volunteer, September 14, 1861, three years, First cavalry, company L, bugler, served three years, mustered out 1864, captured at Stone River.

Eaton, John W., age 19, volunteer, September 1, 1861, three years, First Virginia light artillery, company C, private, served one year, died September 3, 1862, mortally wounded at Bull Run, second battle.

Elleford, William, age 27, volunteer, September 1, 1861, three years, First Virginia light artillery, company C, private, served two years and seven months, honorably discharged April 12, 1864, disability.

Evans, L. G., age 17, volunteer, 1862, three years, Forty-ninth regiment, company B, private, served thee years, honorably discharged 1865.

Everly, Frederick, age 17, volunteer, July 20, 1861, three years, Thirty-ninth regiment, company F, private, served three years, mustered out July, 1864, wounded July 22, 1864, in front of Atlanta.

Field, Joseph, age 16, volunteer, February 2, 1864, Seventy-seventh regiment, drummer, served one month, died March 5, 1864, of typhoid fever, at Little Rock.

Frisby, Charles L., age 26, volunteer, Fifty-third regiment, private, died May 26, 1863.

Flesher, Adam, age 21, volunteer, Seventh cavalry, company H, saddler, mustered out July 4, 1865.

Frisby, Richard, volunteer, One Hundred and Seventy-seventh regiment, company H, private.

Fougeres, Louis, age 18, volunteer, May, 1861, three months, Eighteenth regiment, company B, musician, served three months, mustered out August 8, 1861, reenlisted, volunteer, September 1, 1861, First Virginia light artillery, company C, fifer, mustered out.

Getth, Michael, age 21, volunteer, May 28, 1862, three months, Eighty-seventh regiment, company A, private, mustered out September, 1862, reenlisted, volunteer, August 23, 1864, one year, gunboat, private, mustered out.

Getth, Henry, age 18, volunteer, August 23, 1864, one year, gunboat, private, mustered out.

Geer, Peter, age 16, volunteer, July 22, 1861, three years, Thirty-ninth regiment, company B, private, attained rank of corporal, served three years, mustered out July 9, 1865, reenlisted as a veteran.

Goldsmith, William, age 21, volunteer, September 1, 1861, three years, First Virginia light artillery, company C, private, mustered out, reenlisted as a veteran, captured at Harper's Ferry, and again at Mark's Mills, April 25, 1864, and in prison ten months.

Goldsmith, John, age 20, volunteer, 1862, three months, Eighty-seventh regiment, company A, private, reenlisted, volunteer, February, 1864, Seventy-seventh regiment, company B, private.

Goodman, John, age 23, volunteer, May, 1862, six months, Eighty-seventh regiment, company A, private, captured and parolled with the regiment at Harper's Ferry.

Goodman, Daniel, age 20, volunteer, April 17, 1861, three months, Eighteenth regiment, company B, private, mustered out August 28, 1861.

Goodman, Nathaniel, age 18, volunteer, three years, Thirty-sixth regiment, company G, private.

Green, Abraham, age 35, volunteer, December 19, 1861, three years, Seventy-seventh regiment, company H, sergeant, served two years, died October 23, 1863.

Gwin, Abraham, age 18, volunteer, January 22, 1864, First Ohio volunteer cavalry, company L, private, served one year and seven months, honorably discharged August 30, 1865, for disability.

Hall, George Buster, age 19, volunteer, May, 1862, six months, Eighty-seventh regiment, company A, fifth sergeant, reenlistment, volunteer, 1863, gunboat, master's mate, served two years, honorably discharged October, 1865.

Harte, W. James, age 19, volunteer, 1862, three months, Eighty-seventh regiment, company A, reenlistment, December, 1862, gunboat, midshipman, served nine months, came home a parolled prisoner, also in one hundred days' service.

Haskins, Colonel Alex. L., volunteer, October 1, 1861, three years, Sixty-third regiment, lieutenant colonel, served one year and five months, honorably discharged March 20, 1863.

Hathaway, Luther, age 44, volunteer, July 21, 1861, three years, Thirty-ninth regiment, company B, private, detailed hospital steward, served one year and seven months, died April 1, 1863.

Haskins, George B., volunteer, October 10, 1861, three years, First light artillery, company K, first lieutenant, served one year, resigned October 20, 1862.

Harris, James, volunteer, July 22, 1864, one year, Twentieth colored regiment, company H, corporal, served one year, mustered out August 12, 1865.

Henton, James, age 20, volunteer, 1861, Fourteenth regulars, company C, sergeant, attained rank of adjutant.

Henton, Albert, age 21, volunteer, August, 1862, three years, Thirty-sixth regiment, company A, corporal, served two years, died September 3, 1864, shot at the battle of Barryville.

Henson, Tapley, volunteer, Seventh regiment, company C, private.

Highland, Patrick, age 30, volunteer, 1861, three years, Seventy-third regiment, company F, private, served one year, discharged August, 1862, for disability.

Highland, John, age 25, volunteer, December, 1863, Seventy-third regiment, company F, private, honorably discharged July, 1865.

Highland, Patrick, age 24, volunteer, 1861, Seventy-third regiment, company F, private, mustered out July, 1865, wounded at Cross Keys and the battle of Lookout Mountain.

Hodkinson, Jonathan, volunteer, Thirteenth Pennsylvania regiment, company I, private.

Hodkinson, Thomas, volunteer, Twelfth Pennsylvania regiment, company I, private.

Hildebrand, Jesse, age 62, volunteer, August, 1861, three years, Seventy-seventh regiment, colonel, one and two-thirds years, died April 18, 1863, at Alton, Illinois.

Hill, John, age 26, volunteer, August 13, 1862, three years, First Virginia light artillery, company C, private, mustered out in 1865.

Hill, Alexander, volunteer, three years, Second heavy artillery, company K, private.

Hill, Wallace, volunteer, January 25, 1861, three years, First Virginia artillery, company C, first lieutenant, attained the rank of captain, mustered out with battery.

Holden, Charles Asa, age 20, volunteer, May, 1861, three months, Eighteenth regiment, company B, fifer, served three months, mustered out August 8, 1861, reenlistment, volunteer, September, 1861, First Virginia light artillery, company C, private, served one year, died December 7, 1862.

Holden, Shipman B., age 22, volunteer, May, 1862, Eighty-seventh regiment, company A, private, served five months, mustered out October 1, 1862, captured and parolled.

Holden, Amos Price, age 21, December, 1861, three years, First Virginia light artillery, company C, private, mustered out, reenlisted as a veteran.

Huff, Amon P., volunteer, three years, First Virginia light artillery, company C, private, mustered out in 1865, reenlisted as a veteran.

Judd, Merit, age 58, volunteer, December 2, 1861, Seventy-seventh regiment, company K, private, mustered out August 9, 1862.

Jams, Hiram, volunteer, three years, First Ohio light artillery, company K, first lieutenant.

Judd, James Grover, age 17, volunteer, June, 1861, Eighteenth regiment, company C., drummer, mustered out, reenlistment, volunteer, July, 1863, Thirty-sixth regiment, company I, drummer, served two years, mustered out July 27, 1865.

Judd, Frank L., age 16, Seventy-seventh regiment, company A, fifer, honorably discharged, August 1862, second enlistment, volunteer, May, 1864, one hundred days, One Hundred and Forty-eighth regiment, company A, private, served four months, mustered out September 1864, third enlistment, substitute, March, 1865, Eighteenth regiment, company I, private, served seven months, mustered out October 9, 1865.

Jones, Anthony, volunteer, Seventy-seventh regiment, company H, private, taken with heart disease, served nine months as dispatch carrier for telegraph office, then furloughed and discharged.

Kennedy, George Washington, age 39, volunteer, September 1, 1861, three years, Seventh cavalry, company H, private, honorably discharged May 27, 1865.

Kennedy, Arius H., age 21, volunteer, January 22, 1863, three years,

Third Virginia cavalry, company H, private, served two years, mustered out June 30, 1865.

Kennedy, William, age 16, volunteer, three years, Thirty-ninth regiment, company B, private, served one year, honorably discharged for disability, reenlistment, volunteer, July, 1863, three years, Seventy-seventh regiment, company B, private, served three months, discharged September, 1863.

Kennedy, Elisha, age 17, volunteer, February, 1864, three years, Thirty-ninth regiment, company B, private, served one and five-twelfths years, mustered out July 9, 1865.

Kennedy, Joel, Thirty-ninth regiment, company B.

Koenig, Jacob, age 45, volunteer, July, 1861, three years, Thirty-ninth regiment, company F, captain, served two years, died August 23, 1863, of flux and fever.

Koenig, Jacob James, age 18, volunteer, August 26, 1861, three years, Thirty-ninth regiment, company F, drummer, three years, mustered out in 1864.

Koon, Weedon, age 41, volunteer, December, 1861, Seventy-seventh regiment, companies I and E, private, reenlisted as a veteran, captured and in prison for ten months.

Koon, George, age 19, volunteer, July, 1861, three years, Thirty-ninth regiment, company B, private, served four years, mustered out July 9, 1865.

Lammott, Levi F., age 18, volunteer, May, 1862, Eighty-seventh regiment, company A, private, captured and parolled at Harper's Ferry, in Seventy-seventh regiment, served on detached duty as clerk, second enlistment, volunteer, December, 1863, Seventy-seventh regiment, company H, private.

Lammott, Eugene R. A., age 14, 1861, Seventy-seventh regiment, company H, drum major.

Lasure, Nathan, age 19, volunteer, September 1, 1861, First Virginia light artillery, company C, private, served three and nine-twelfths years, mustered out June 28, 1865.

Lemgo, Henry, age 28, volunteer, 1861, three years, Thirty-ninth regiment, company F, private, three years, mustered out August, 1864.

Langley, David, volunteer, Thirty-ninth regiment, company B.

Langley, George W., volunteer, Thirty-ninth regiment, company B, private.

Langley, Lewis D., age 19, volunteer, March 30, 1862, three years, First Virginia light artillery, company C, private, served two years, honorably discharged April 28, 1864, for disability.

Laughlin, Milton H., three years, First Virginia light artillery, company C, private, attained rank of corporal, mustered out, reenlisted as a veteran.

Langley, Henry M., volunteer, First Virginia light artillery, company C, second lieutenant, resigned April 22, 1863.

Loffman, Leon, Sixty-third regiment, company F.

Loffman, Philip, volunteer, three years, First Virginia light artillery, company C, private, mustered out in 1865, reenlisted as a veteran.

Loffman James, age 28, volunteer, three years, First Virginia light artillery, company C, private, mustered out in 1865, reenlisted as a veteran.

Lord, Henry, age 20, volunteer, May 28, 1862, three years, Eighty-seventh regiment, company A, third sergeant, served four months, mustered out September 20, 1862, captured and parolled at Harper's Ferry, reenlisted November 16, 1863, One Hundred and Twenty-fifth regiment, company K, quartermaster sergeant, served one year and five months, mustered out June 8, 1865.

Marvin, James, age 15, volunteer, October, 1861, Eleventh Virginia, company D, private, served seven months, second enlistment May, 1862, three months, Eighty-fifth regiment, company B, private, mustered out June, 1862, third enlistment August 18, 1864, one year, United States navy, private, served eleven months, mustered out July 21, 1865.

Marwin, John, age 15, volunteer, October 12, 1864, one year, Seventy-seventh regiment, company G, private.

McCallister, John S., age 18, volunteer, September 1, 1861, three years, First Virginia light artillery, company C, private, served three years and nine months, mustered out June 28, 1865, reenlisted as a veteran.

McCormick, Captain A. W., volunteer, December, 1861, three years, Seventy-seventh regiment, company G, captain, honorably discharged.

McFarland, B. Powell, age 36, volunteer, August, 1862, Thirty-ninth regiment, company B, corporal, served two years, killed at Kennesaw Mountain June 26, 1864.

McKibben, Edwin, age 16, volunteer, March 31, 1864, Thirty-sixth regiment, company F, private, in six battles, served one year and three months, mustered out July 27, 1865.

McKittrick, Robert H., volunteer, 1861, three years, Seventy-seventh regiment, first lieutenant, attained rank of captain, served three years, mustered out 1864.

McLaughlin, Neil, age 33, volunteer, July 28, 1861, three years, Thirty-ninth regiment, company B, private, served four years, mustered out July 9, 1865, reenlisted as a veteran.

McManns, Michael, age 35, volunteer, 1861, Thirty-ninth regiment, company B, private, served four years, mustered out July 9, 1865.

McNaughton, Samuel S., volunteer, 1861, three years, Seventy-seventh regiment, first lieutenant, attained rank of captain, mustered out.

Miller, Frederick, age 18, volunteer, September 1, 1861, three years, First light artillery, company K, bugler, attained rank of second lieutenant, served four years, mustered out July 22, 1865, did good service at Chancellorsville.

Miner, Robert W., age 33, volunteer, September 1, 1861, three years, First Virginia light artillery, company C, private, attained rank of second lieutenant, served one year and nine months, mustered out June, 1863.

. Miner, Smith, volunteer, September 1, 1861, First Virginia light artillery, company C, private, served four years, mustered out June 28, 1865, enlisted as a veteran, detailed as commissary sergeant for nine months.

Miner, John N., volunteer, April, 1861, three months, Eighteenth regiment, company B, private, served three months, mustered out August 8, 1861, reenlisted September 1, 1861, three years, First Virginia light artillery, company C, private, attained rank of corporal, served three years and nine months, mustered out June 28, 1865

Miraben, Leonidas R., age 24, volunteer, May, 1861, three months Eighteenth regiment, company B, private, served three months, mustered out August 8, 1861, reenlisted February 28, 1862, three years, First Virginia light artillery, company C, sergeant, served three years and four months, mustered out June 28, 1865.

Moore, Lewis Roe, age 17, volunteer, February 28, 1862, three years, First Virginia light artillery, company C, private, served three years and four months, mustered out June 28, 1865.

Moore, A. F., Thirty-ninth regiment, company B.

McGirr, William P., Thirty-sixth regiment, company F.

Morgaridge, Daniel J., age 19, volunteer, November 19, 1861, three years, Second Virginia cavalry, company F, bugler, mustered out with regiment, reenlisted as veteran.

Morgaridge William, age 23, volunteer, August 1, 1861, three years, Eighteenth regiment, company B, private, in five battles, served three and a half years, honorably discharged, February, 1865, captured at Chickamauga, and in prison fifteen months.

Morgaridge, R. Arthur, age 25, volunteer, July, 1862, three years, Thirty-ninth regiment, company B, private, served three years, mustered out July 9, 1865.

Mahnken, John, volunteer, three years, First Virginia light artillery, company C., private, mustered out June 28, 1865, reenlisted as a veteran.

Mulhane, Dennis, age 35, volunteer, March, 1864, First Virginia light artillery, company C, private, served one year, mustered out June 28, 1865.

O'Neil, James H., United States navy.

Otis, Timothy, age 22, volunteer, May, 1862, three months, Eighty-seventh regiment, company A, private, served four months, mustered out October 1, 1862, captured April 25, 1864, and in prison ten months, reenlistment, volunteer, December, 1863, Seventy-seventh regiment, company B, private.

Otterbein, Daniel, age 23, volunteer, July 28, 1861, three years, Thirty-ninth regiment, company B, private, attained rank of second lieutenant, served four years, mustered out July 9, 1865, reenlisted as a veteran.

, O Leary, Dennis, age 32, volunteer, March 30, 1862, three years, First Virginia artillery, company C, first lieutenant, served three years and four months, mustered out June 28, 1865.

Painter, Thomas, age 22, volunteer, July 22, 1861, Thirty-ninth regiment, company B, private, attained rank of blacksmith, served four years, mustered out July 9, 1865, reenlisted as a veteran.

O'Neal, Thompson, First Virginia light artillery.

Parker, Adoniram, age 34, volunteer, August, 1862, Thirty-ninth regiment, company B, private, served two years, died of wounds October 1, 1864.

Patton, George D. W., age 23, substitute, October 14, 1862, three years, Seventy-seventh regiment, company B, private, served three years, captured at Marks' Mills and in prison for ten months, mustered out October 16, 1865.

Payne, A. D., Sixty-fourth regiment, drum major, resigned.

Phillips, Lyman, age 28, volunteer, September, 1861, three years, First veteran Ohio cavalry, company L, private, served three years, mustered out 1864.

Phillips, Robert E., Third brigade, quartermaster, honorably discharged for disability.

Quigley, James, age 36, volunteer, September 1, 1861, three years, First light artillery, company K, private, served three years, mustered out 1864.

Quigley, Patrick J., age 15, volunteer, October, 1861, three years, First Virginia light artillery, company C, private, served three years, mustered out 1864.

Ranger, William Henry, age 20, volunteer, May, 1861, three months, Eighteenth regiment, company B, private, served three months, mustered out August 8, 1864, reenlistment, volunteer, September, 1861, three years, First Virginia light artillery, company C, private, served four years, wounded at Chancellorsville May 2, 1863, mustered out June 28, 1865.

Ranger, Francis Wesley, age 18, volunteer, July 22, 1861, three years, Thirty-ninth regiment, company B, private, served four years, mustered out July 9, 1865.

Reckard, Frank R., volunteer, First light artillery, company H, first lieutenant.

Reckard, James L, age 19, volunteer, September 1, 1862, three years, Seventh Ohio cavalry, company H, private, attained the rank of corporal, served three years, mustered out July 4, 1865.

Reinhart, Andrew J., age 18, volunteer, August 10, 1863, three years, Eleventh Virginia, company D, private, served one year and ten months, mustered out June 17, 1865

Rice, George T., age 38, volunteer, July 22, 1861, three years, Thirty-ninth regiment, company B, private, attained the rank of major, served four years, mustered out July 9, 1865, reenlisted as a veteran.

Richards, Timothy, age 40, volunteer, February, 1864, three years, First Virginia light artillery, company C, private, honorably discharged October, 1864, became blind and sent to hospital till discharged.

Riley, Ulysses, Seventy-seventh regiment, company D.

Richards, Thomas, age 37, volunteer, September, 1862, three years, First Virginia light artillery, company C, private, served two years, died September 2, 1864.

Richards, John, age 35, volunteer, October 27, 1864, one year, First Virginia light artillery, company C, private, served nine months, mustered out June 28, 1865.

Richards, Edward H, volunteer, July 22, 1861, three years, Thirty-ninth regiment, company B, private, served three years, mustered out in 1864.

Ripley, Henry E., age 38, volunteer, September 1, 1861, three years, First Virginia light artillery, company C, private, served four years, mustered out June 28, 1865, reenlisted as a veteran.

Ripley, Philetus S., volunteer, September 1, 1861, three years, First Virginia light artillery, company C, private, served four years, mustered out June 28, 1865, reenlisted as a veteran.

Rodgers, George Washington, age 22, volunteer, August 30, 1861, three years, Second Virginia cavalry, company F, private, attained the rank of corporal, served four years, mustered out June 30, 1865, reenlisted as a veteran.

Rodgers, Robert, age 16, volunteer, December, 1861, Seventy-seventh regiment, company B, private, served four years, mustered out March 8, 1866, reenlisted as a veteran, captured at Mark's Mills and in prison ten months.

Rewell, Martin V., First cavalry

Schmidt, Louis, age 39, volunteer, October 4, 1861, three years, Sixty-third regiment, company F, second lieutenant, attained the rank of first lieutenant, served three years, honorably discharged August 24, 1864, for disability.

Schmidt, Edwin William, age 19, volunteer, July 6, 1861, three years, Forty-seventh regiment, company G, private.

Shires, Robert, age 19, volunteer, April 17, 1861, three months, Eighteenth regiment, company B, private, served four months, mustered out August 28th, reenlistment, volunteer, October, 1861, Sixty-third regiment, company D, drummer.

Shires, George, volunteer, October, 1862, Sixty-third regiment, company B, private, served three years, mustered out July 7, 1865.

Sherer, Peter, age 25, volunteer, April 17, 1861, three months, Eighteenth regiment, company B, private, mustered out August 28, 1861, reenlisted, volunteer, December, 1861, First Virginia light artillery, company C, private, served three and a half years, mustered out June 28, 1865.

Slattery, Patrick William, age 18, volunteer, May, 1861, three months, Twenty-second regiment, company G, private, served three months, reenlistment, volunteer, September 1, 1861, First Virginia light artillery, company C, private, served three years and nine months, mustered out June 28, 1865.

Smith, William L., age 14, volunteer, June, 1861, three months, Twenty-second regiment, company B, drummer, served three months, mustered out, reenlisted, volunteer, August, 1861, three years, Twenty-second regiment, company B, drummer, served three years and three months, mustered out in 1864.

Smith, John Charles, age 18, volunteer, January 1, 1862, three years, First Virginia light artillery, company C, private, attained the rank of corporal, mustered out June 28, 1865.

Slump, John, volunteer.

Snider, Peter Bratton, age 48, volunteer, September 12, 1862, three years, Thirty-ninth regiment, company B, private, served three years, mustered out July 9, 1865.

Smith, Moses, volunteer, July 1, 1861, three years, Thirty-ninth regiment, company B, private, honorably discharged in 1863.

Snider, Jacob Bratton, age 19, volunteer, September 12, 1862, three years, Thirty-ninth regiment, company B, private, served three years, mustered out June, 1865, served three months in an independent company called Cadwallader Grays, on detailed service as clerk.

Steed, Z.

Snider, William T., age 21, volunteer, 1862, three months, Eighty-seventh regiment, company A, private, served three months, mustered out September 20, 1862, captured at Harper's Ferry, reenlistment, age 23, volunteer, August 18, 1864, one year, navy, private, served eleven months, mustered out July, 1865.

Snider, John, age 20, volunteer, August 18, 1864, one year, navy, private, served eleven months, mustered out July, 1865.

Snodgrass, William H., volunteer, September 18, 1861, three years, First cavalry, company L, private, reenlisted as a veteran.

Stephens, Joseph R., age 19, volunteer, September 1, 1861, three years, Second Virginia cavalry, company E, private, served three years in 1864, captured and in prison five months.

Swift, John, age 19, volunteer, May, 1864, one hundred days, One Hundred and Forty-eighth regiment, company A, private, mustered out September, 1864.

Stone, Thompson, volunteer, Thirty-ninth regiment, company F, private.

Stilt, Jacob, age 19, volunteer, 1861, three years, First Virginia light artillery, company C, private.

Stuffledom, Calvin, volunteer, Sixty-third regiment, company G, private.

Toothaker, Frank B., age 18, volunteer, 1862, three years, Seventh Ohio cavalry, company H, private, detailed for clerk service.

Stump, L., Thirty-ninth regiment, company F, private.

Towsley, Darius, age 48, volunteer, 1862, three months, Eighty-seventh regiment, drum major, taken prisoner at Harper's Ferry.

Towsley, Frank, age 18, volunteer, March 10, 1862, three years, First Ohio light artillery, company K, private, served three years, mustered out in 1865.

Tracy, Wesley, age 23, volunteer, May 1, 1862, three years, First Virginia light artillery, company C, private, served nine months, honorably discharged February 16, 1863, for disability.

Towsley, John, age 16, volunteer, May, 1862, three months, Eighty-seventh regiment, company A, drummer, served four months, mustered out September 20, 1862, reenlistment, age 18, volunteer, May, 1864, one hundred days, One Hundred and Forty-eighth regiment, company A, drummer, served four months, mustered out, 1864.

Towsley, George, age 11, volunteer, June, 1862, three months, Eighty-seventh regiment, company G, drummer, served four months, mustered out September 20, 1862, reenlistment, volunteer, May, 1864, one hundred days, One Hundred and Forty-eighth regiment, company F, drummer, served four months, mustered out September, 1864.

Tracy, Samuel S., age 22, volunteer, December, 1863, three years, Seventy-seventh regiment, company B, private.

Warren, Manly, age 30, volunteer, April 27, 1861, three months, Eighteenth regiment, company B, fifer, served four months, mustered out August 28, 1861.

Way, Charles Bosworth, age 27, volunteer, October 1, 1861, three years, Eleventh Virginia, company D, private, attained the rank of second lieutenant, resigned April, 1863.

Wells, Charles Elijah, age 16, volunteer, 1861, three years, Thirty-sixth regiment, company D, private, served one year, died January 14, 1862, typhoid fever, at Summersville, West Virginia.

Wheatley, Isaac, age 22, volunteer, May, 1862, three months, Eighty-seventh regiment, company A, private, mustered out September 20, 1862, reenlistment, volunteer, January 11, 1864, three years, First Ohio cavalry, company L, private, served one year and seven months, mustered out September 13, 1865.

Wheeler, Julius Frank, age 18, volunteer, August 13, 1863, three years, First heavy artillery, company L, private, served two years, mustered out August 25, 1865.

Tripp, William L., volunteer, 1862, Seventh cavalry, company H, first lieutenant, resigned December 25, 1863.

Turder, George Butler, age 23, volunteer, August 22, 1862, three years, Ninety-second regiment, company F, private, attained rank of adjutant, served one year and four months, died December 1, 1863, mortally wounded at Mission Ridge, November 25.

Turner, Frederick V., age 21, volunteer, June, 1852, three months, Eighty-seventh regiment, company A, private, served three months, mustered out September 20, 1862, captured at Harper's Ferry and paroled.

Wilson, William, age 20, volunteer, April 18, 1861, three months, Eighteenth regiment, company K, private, served three months, mustered out August, 1861, second enlistment, volunteer, 1861, three years, Second Virginia cavalry, company F, corporal, attained rank of sergeant, mustered out 1865.

Winchester, Albert, age 17, volunteer, August 27, 1861, three years, Thirty-sixth regiment, company D, private, served five months, discharged January 23, 1862, for physical disability (too young) much on detailed service, reenlistment, volunteer, August 16, 1862, three years, Thirty-ninth regiment, company B, private, served three years, honorably discharged June 21, 1865.

Withrow, William Wallace, age 21, volunteer, April, 1861, three months, Eighteenth regiment, company B, first corporal, mustered out August 28, 1861, reenlistment, volunteer, January 25, 1862, three years, First Virginia light artillery, company C, second lieutenant, resigned December 28, 1862, wounded at second Bull Run battle, August 30, 1862.

Withrow, James, age 21, volunteer, May, 1852, three months, Eighty-seventh regiment, company A, private, served two months, honorably discharged July 30, 1862.

Williams, Charles B., age 29, volunteer, October 18, 1861, three years, Sixty-third regiment, company G, private, attained rank of corporal, served three years and ten months, mustered out July 8, 1865, reenlisted as a veteran.

Wood, John, age 35, volunteer, August, 1861, three years, First light artillery, company K, private, served four years, mustered out July 31, 1865, reenlisted as a veteran.

Wood, Alfred Spencer, age 18, volunteer, January 2, 1864, three years, First Ohio cavalry, company L, private, one year and eight months, mustered out September 26, 1865.

Wright, James M., age 26, volunteer, September 1, 1861, three years, First Virginia light artillery, company C, private, attained rank of corporal, served four years, mustered out June 28, 1865, wounded at second Bull Run battle.

Zoller, George, age 20, volunteer, July 22, 1861, three years, Thirty-ninth regiment, company B, private, served eight months, died March, 1862.

Wallace, Thomas, volunteer, Seventy-Seventh regiment, private.

Wells, Henry, volunteer, Eighty-sixth regiment, company F, private.

RECAPITULATION.

Thirty-ninth Ohio	42
Buell's Pierpont battery	46
Seventy-seventh Ohio	25
Eighteenth Ohio (three months)	17
Eighteenth Ohio (three years)	4
Eighty-Seventh Ohio (three months)	19
First Ohio cavalry	9
Seventh Ohio cavalry	6
Second Virginia cavalry	3
Huntington battery	5
Sixty-third Ohio	9
Thirty-sixth Ohio	11
De Beck's battery	7
Eleventh Virginia	6
Seventy-third Ohio	4
One Hundred and Forty-eighth Ohio	5
Fifteenth Massachusetts	2
Ninety-second Ohio	5
United States navy	6
Gunboat service	6

Battery K, Second Ohio heavy artillery........................ 2
Twenty-second Ohio (three months)........................... 2
And one each in the Seventy-fifth Ohio, Eighty-fifth Ohio (three months), One Hundred and Eighty-ninth Ohio, Twelfth Virginia, One Hundred and Eighty-second Ohio, Twentieth Illinois, Twenty-fourth Ohio, Forty-ninth Ohio, One Hundred and Seventy-seventh Ohio, Fifty-third Ohio, Twentieth colored United States infantry, Fourteenth United States infantry, Seventh Ohio, Thirteenth Pennsylvania infantry, Twelfth Pennsylvania, Third Virginia cavalry, One Hundred and Twenty-fifth Ohio, Sixty-fourth Ohio, Forty-seventh Ohio, Twenty-third Ohio (three years, First Ohio heavy artillery, Eighty-sixth Ohio, making in all.................. 21
Not designated.................................. 2
　　　　Total number of soldiers.......................... 235

Died.. 14

MARIETTA CITY—SECOND WARD.

Abendshau, Jacob, age 20, volunteer, July 22, 1861, three years, Thirty-ninth regiment, company B, private, mustered out in 1865, wounded twice, reenlisted as a veteran.

Anderson, Edward A., age 18, volunteer, May, 1862, three months, Eighty-seventh regiment, company A, private, served six months, mustered out September, 1862, captured and paroled.

Bailey, Benjamin P., first enlistment, age 17, volunteer, November, 1861, three years, Nineteenth Massachusetts regiment, company H, private, honorably discharged June, 18, 1862, reenlistment, age 20, substitute, May, 1864, one hundred days, One Hundred and Forty-eight regiment, company A, private, served three months, mustered out September, 1864.

Baker, Alpheus, volunteer, Ninety-second regiment, company F, crippled in service.

Buck, William C., volunteer, July, 1861, three years, Thirty-ninth regiment, company B, sergeant, attained to rank of lieutenant colonel, served three years and ten months, mustered out May 15, 1865.

Buell, Frank, age 25, volunteer, April, 1861, three months, Eighteenth regiment, company D, captain, served three months, mustered out, reenlisted October, 1861, three years, First Virginia light artillery company C, captain, died August 30, 1862, killed at Freeman's Ford, Virginia.

Bosworth, Daniel Perkins, age 21, volunteer, April 13, 1863, United States navy, master's mate, attained to rank of acting ensign, honorably discharged October, 1865.

Braddock, Stephen A., age 24, volunteer, July, 1862, First Virginia light artillery, company C, private, served one year, died July 2, 1863, killed at Gettysburgh.

Bruce, Wallace, volunteer, Thirty-ninth regiment, company B, private.

Chambers, Samuel L., volunteer, January 18, 1864, three years, Thirty-ninth regiment, company B, private, mustered out July 9, 1865.

Burlingame, E. P., First cavalry, company L.

Cook, Pardon, jr., age 40, volunteer, 1861, Seventy-seventh regiment, assistant surgeon, served two years, died, August 21, 1863, of chills, sick one week.

Coleman, Henry, age 29, volunteer, July 22, 1861, three years, Thirty-ninth regiment, company B, private, served three years, mustered out in 1864.

Contner, William, age 18, volunteer, November, 1861, three years, Sixty-third regiment, company F, private, mustered out July 18, 1865, reenlisted as a veteran.

Contner, Charles, substitute, one year, Sixty-third regiment, private, discharged.

Corey, Ebenezer, age 53, volunteer, April, 1861, three months, Eighteenth regiment, company B, fifer, attained to rank of drum major, served four months, honorably discharged August 8, 1861, reenlistment, volunteer, Thirty-sixth regiment, drum major, served three years, mustered out August 1, 1865.

Corey, Jonathan H., age 18, volunteer, June, 1861, three months, Eighteenth regiment, company C, drummer, served two months, discharged August 8, 1861, reenlistment, Thirty-sixth regiment, companies C and G, drummer, mustered out August 1, 1865.

Corey, Joseph, age 18, volunteer, April 17, 1861, three months, Eighteenth regiment, company B, private, served four months, mustered out August 8, 1861, reenlistment, volunteer, January, 1862, three years, Seventy-seventh and Sixty-third regiment, company G, sergeant, attained to rank orderly sergeant, served six months, died, July 18, 1862, of typhoid fever.

Corey, Decatur, age 18, volunteer, April 14, 1864, Thirty-sixth regi-

ment, company A, private, died July 24, 1864, killed at the battle of Winchester.

Creal, George, Fifth United States colored infantry, company I.

Davis, Charles, age 27, volunteer, August 9, 1862, three years, Thirty-sixth regiment, company A, private, served two years and four months, discharged December 17, 1864, discharged for disability, wounded severely in the jaw at Dallas, Georgia, May 28, 1864, and discharged.

Dawes, Ephraim C., age 21, volunteer, July, 1861, three years, Fifty-third regiment, adjutant, attained to rank of major, served three years and six months, honorably discharged in 1865 on account of wound.

Eells, Arthur D., volunteer, November, 1861, three years, Second Virginia cavalry, company F, captain, served six months, resigned May 6, 1862, reenlistment, August 25, 1862, three years, Seventh cavalry, captain, resigned June 28, 1863.

Fell, John C., volunteer, July, 1861, three years, Thirty-ninth regiment, company B, captain, resigned April 12, 1862

Field, Joseph, age 19, volunteer, 1861, three years, Seventy-seventh regiment, company G, private, detailed as drummer, died March 5, 1864, at Little Rock, Arkansas.

Ferguson, Noah Wilson, age 15, volunteer, May 1862, three years, Eighty-seventh and One hundred and Twenty-fifth regiments, companies A and K, fifer, served three years and four months, mustered out September 25, 1865, served much on detailed service.

Franks, Lafayette, age 16, volunteer, September, 1861, three years, First Virginia light artillery, company C, private, attained to rank of corporal, served three years and eight months, mustered out June 28, 1865, had previously served three months as railroad guard.

Garnett, Thomas, age 28, volunteer, August 15, 1862, three years, Thirty-sixth regiment, company F, private, served two years and ten months, mustered out June 27, 1865.

Garen, Irenius A., age 17, volunteer, October 25, 1861, three years, First Virginia light artillery, company H, private, attained rank of corporal served three years and eight months, mustered out June 28, 1865.

Garen, Dudley D., age 16, volunteer, October 25, 1861, First Virginia light artillery, company H, private, served three years and eight months, mustered out June 28, 1865.

Giles, Edward, age 30, volunteer, August 10, 1864, one year, Fifth colored infantry, company G, private, served one year, mustered out August 22, 1865, a slave until the capture of New Madrid, Missouri.

Green, Richard L., volunteer, June, 1861, Twenty-fifth regiment, company H, captain, died September 5, 1862.

Grimes, David, age 29, volunteer, September, 1861, three years, First cavalry, company L, private, detailed as teamster, served three years, mustered out in 1864.

Grimes, Peter, Ninth cavalry.

Groves, Henry J., age 25, substitute, 1865, one year, Forty-third regiment, private, served seven months.

Groves, Edward, age 20, volunteer, August 15, 1862, three years, First Virginia light artillery, company C, private, served three years, mustered out June 28, 1865

Guyton, John, age 31, volunteer, September, 1861, three years, First cavalry, company L, bugler, served three years, mustered out in 1864.

Huberling, Jacob, age 21, substitute, May, 1864, one hundred days, One Hundred and Forty-eighth regiment, company A.

Hall, James Eli, age 29, volunteer, August 6, 1862, One Hundred and Fourth regiment, company G, corporal, attained rank of sergeant, served two years and ten months, honorably discharged June 17, 1865.

Harris, Samuel, age 25, volunteer, September 27, 1861, three years, Second Virginia cavalry, company F, sergeant, served three years and nine months, mustered out June 25, 1865, captured at Front Royal, Virginia, and sent to Libby Prison for three months.

Hayes, Lewis, age 19, volunteer, July 31, 1861, three years, Thirty-ninth regiment, company B, private, served three years, honorably discharged August 26, 1864.

Henneman, George, age 22, volunteer, 1861, three years, Thirty-ninth regiment, company B, private, attained rank of sergeant, served three years, honorably discharged 1864.

Holden, William, age 21, volunteer, May, 1861, three months, Eighteenth regiment, company B, captain, mustered out with regiment, reenlisted for three years and appointed assistant quartermaster.

Holden, John B., age 19, volunteer, October, 1861, three years, Eighteenth regiment, company B, and First light artillery, company K, second lieutenant, attained rank of first lieutenant, resigned March 27, 1862.

Jones, David F., age 27, volunteer, October 14, 1861, three years,

Seventy-seventh regiment, company B, private, attained to rank of first lieutenant, served three years, resigned December 10, 1864.

Jones, Alexander, age 19, volunteer, October 14, 1861, Seventy-seventh regiment, company B, private, served one year, died September 12, 1862, of yellow fever, at Alton, Illinois.

Jones, Joseph, age 23, volunteer, September 7, 1862, Seventy-second Indiana regiment, company E, private, died March 31, 1863, typhoid fever.

Knowles, Samuel S., volunteer, May, 1864, one hundred days, One Hundred and Forty-eighth regiment, company A, captain, served four months, mustered out September 14, 1864.

Kropp, August, age 29, volunteer, April 14, 1861, three years, Thirty-ninth regiment, company B, private, attained to rank of first lieutenant, served three years, resigned April, 1864, was first in three months' service of company B, Eighteenth regiment.

Kelly, Joseph, volunteer, August, 1861, three years, Thirty-sixth regiment, company F, first lieutenant, attained to rank of captain, mustered out July 27, 1865.

Lapham, Joseph H., age 17, volunteer, July 22, 1861, three years, Thirty-ninth regiment, company B, corporal, attained to rank of sergeant, served four years, mustered out July 9, 1865, reenlisted as a veteran.

Lapham, Owen Theodore, age 17, volunteer, May, 1864, one hundred days, One Hundred and Forty-eighth regiment, company A, private, served four months, mustered out September, 1864, was offered seven hundred dollars to go as a substitute, but preferred to serve as a volunteer, reenlisted, volunteer, February 4, 1865, one year, Thirty-sixth regiment, company G, private, served five months, mustered out July 27, 1865.

Lapham, Luther T., age 16, volunteer, May, 1864, one hundred days, One Hundred and Forty-eighth regiment, company A, private, served four months, mustered out September, 1864, reenlisted, volunteer, February 4, 1865, one year, Thirty-sixth regiment, company G, private, served five months, mustered out July 27, 1865.

Lewis, David H., age 20, volunteer, Thirty-ninth regiment, company B.

Lewis, Samuel M., age 19, substitute, May, 1864, one hundred days, One Hundred and Forty-eighth regiment, company A, private, mustered out September, 1864, reenlistment, substitute, March, 1865, one year, Eighteenth regiment, company C, private, served five months, mustered out October, 1865.

McGin, Alexander C., age 38, volunteer, May, 1864, one hundred days, One Hundred and Forty-eighth regiment, company A, second sergeant, served four months, mustered out September, 1864.

McElroy, E. R., volunteer, Thirty-sixth regiment, company E.

McGirr, William P., age 22, volunteer, September, 1861, three years, Thirty-sixth regiment, company A, private, served three years, mustered out 1864.

McElroy, H. P., volunteer, Thirty-sixth regiment, company E.

Meister, Christian, age 21, volunteer, July 27, 1861, three years, Thirty-ninth regiment, company F, private, served three years, mustered out July 27, 1864.

McGuire, Patrick, volunteer, 1864, one year, One Hundred and Eighty-first regiment, company F, private, served ten months, mustered out 1865, second enlistment, One Hundred and Twenty-ninth regiment, company A, third enlistment, One Hundred and Forty-eighth regiment, company A.

McIntosh, Silas, volunteer, Twenty-seventh regiment.

Medlicott, John, volunteer, May, 1863, three years, Second Virginia cavalry, company G, lieutenant, discharged September 27, 1864.

Moore, George, age 18, volunteer, July 22, 1861, three years, Thirty-ninth regiment, company B, private, served three years, died July 22, 1864, killed.

Moore, William, age 16, volunteer, September 7, 1862, three years, Second heavy artillery, company K, private, served one year and four months, honorably discharged January 7, 1864, reenlistment, volunteer, February 1, 1865, one year, Thirty-sixth regiment, company C, private, served six months, mustered out July 27, 1865.

Morse, William, S., age 18, volunteer, July 22, 1861, Thirty-ninth regiment, company B, private, mustered July 9, 1865, reenlisted as a veteran.

Morse, John P. D., age 18, volunteer, August 13, 1862, three years, First Virginia light artillery, company C, private, five battles, served two years and ten months, mustered out June 28, 1865.

Nye, Reuben L., age 25, volunteer, April 17, 1861, three months, Seventeenth and Eighteenth regiments, company B, private, served four months, mustered out August, 1861, wounded near Harper's Ferry, reenlistment, August, 1861, three years, Thirty-sixth regiment, company G, second lieutenant, attained the rank of captain, served four years, mustered out July 27, 1865, brevetted lieutenant colonel of volunteers, March 13, 1865.

Nye, Edward C., volunteer, June, 1862, three months, Eighty-seventh regiment, served four months, mustered out September, 1862, reenlistment, December 23, 1863, naval service, acting master's mate ensign, honorably discharged November 4, 1865

Nott, Perley J., volunteer, Thirty-sixth regiment, company A, private.

Ohle, William Henry, age 15, volunteer, November, 1861, three years, Seventy-seventh regiment, companies E and G, drummer, reenlisted as a veteran.

Ohle, Charles, age 15, volunteer, December, 1863, three years, Thirty-ninth regiment, company B, private, served one year and seven months, mustered out July 9, 1865.

Parker, George, age 18, volunteer, August 30, 1862, three years, Seventh cavalry, company H, private, served three years, mustered out July 4, 1865, detailed for two and a half years as orderly.

Parker, Isaac D., age 28, volunteer, November 14, 1861, three years, Seventy-seventh regiment, company B, private, served three years, mustered out December 10, 1864.

Paxton, John C., volunteer, September 16, 1861, three years, Second Virginia cavalry, lieutenant colonel, attained rank of colonel, served one year and eight months, discharged May 7, 1863.

Paxton, S. G., age 30, volunteer, September 12, 1861, three years, Second Virginia cavalry, lieutenant, attained rank of regimental quartermaster, served three years, mustered out November 28, 1864.

Payne, George, volunteer, Seventy-seventh regiment, company B, honorably discharged.

Pfiefer, John, age 27, volunteer, January 20, 1864, three years, Thirty-ninth regiment, company B, private, served one year and six months, mustered out July 9, 1865.

Pfiefer, William, age 21, volunteer, Thirty-seventh regiment, company A, private, second enlistment, volunteer, Thirty-ninth regiment, company B, private, third enlistment, volunteer One Hundred and Thirty-fifth colored infantry, company K, private.

Pixley, Frank, age 17, substitute, May, 1864, one hundred days, One Hundred and Forty-eighth regiment, company A, private, served four months, mustered out September, 1864, reenlistment, volunteer, February 8, 1865, one year, Thirty-sixth regiment, company H, private, served five months, mustered out July, 1865.

Porterfield, William L., age 21, volunteer, October 14, 1861, Seventy-seventh regiment, company B, sergeant, attained rank of lieutenant, served six months, died April 8, 1862, at Shiloh.

Rucker, William P., on General Crook's staff.

Ranger, John, age 31, volunteer, April, 1861, three months, Eighteenth regiment, company B, private, served five months, mustered out September, 1864, reenlistment, volunteer, October 21, 1861, three years, First Virginia light artillery, company H, private, served three years, honorably discharged October 20, 1864.

Richards, Timothy, age 40, volunteer, January 19, 1864, three years, First Virginia light artillery, company C, private, discharged October 24, 1864, for blindness.

Rees, Samuel, volunteer, three years, Ninety-second regiment, company F, private, mustered out June 28, 1865.

Sayre, Simeon S., age 27, volunteer, August 13, 1862, three years, First Virginia light artillery, company C, private, served three years, mustered out June 28, 1865.

Shiefley, Gottlieb, volunteer, One Hundred and Sixteenth regiment, company K, second lieutenant, resigned September 17, 1864.

Schlicher, Lewis, age 23, volunteer, 1862, three years, Seventy-seventh regiment, company B, bugler, reenlisted as a veteran.

Schlicher, Frederick, age 20, volunteer, 1862, three years, Seventy-seventh regiment, company D, private, attained rank of sergeant, reenlisted as a veteran.

Schlicher, Daniel, age 17, volunteer, 1861, three years, First light artillery, company L, private, served four years, mustered out July 31, 1865, reenlisted as a veteran.

Schmidt, Lewis, volunteer, February, 1862, Sixty-third regiment, first lieutenant, resigned August 24, 1864.

Schmidt, Emanuel, age 28, volunteer August, 1861, three years, Thirty-ninth regiment, company F, private, attained rank of corporal, served three years, honorably discharged, 1864.

Shafer, Frank, age 35, volunteer, February 28, 1862, three years, Thirty-ninth regiment, company F, private, served one year and two months, honorably discharged April 28, 1863, for disability.

Smith, T. C. H., age 42, volunteer, August 23, 1861, three years,

First cavalry, lieutenant colonel, attained rank of brigadier general, served four years, mustered out 1865, is paymaster in the United States army.

Sheldon, Hiram H., One Hundred and Sixteenth regiment, company G.

Smith, Edwin, volunteer, 1861, three years, Forty-seventh regiment, company G, private, killed at Vicksburgh May 30, 1863.

Steed, James, age 22, volunteer Sixty-third regiment, company D.

Steed, William, volunteer, Sixty-third regiment, company D.

Stricker, Matthew, age 22, volunteer, July 22, 1861, three years, Thirty-ninth regiment, company B, private, served four years, mustered out July 9, 1865.

Stricker, Morris, volunteer, Thirty-ninth regiment, company B.

Stricker, William, age 22, volunteer, May, 1862, Eighty-seventh regiment, company A, corporal, served four months, mustered out September, 1862.

Talbott, Jake T., age 20, volunteer, May, 1864, one hundred days, One Hundred and Forty-eighth regiment, company A, served four months, mustered out September, 1864.

Tappan, Samuel C., volunteer, Seventh cavalry, company H, private, attained rank of second lieutenant, mustered out March 18, 1865.

Tenney, George Champion, age 20, volunteer, May, 1862, three months, Eighty-seventh regiment, company A, private, served four months, mustered out September, 1862, reenlistment, volunteer, May, 1864, one hundred days, One Hundred and Forty-eighth regiment, company A, corporal, served four months, mustered out 1864, also member of the independent company in Marietta.

Tenney, John, age 16, volunteer, June, 1861, three months, Eighteenth regiment, company C, fifer, served three months, mustered out September, 1862, reenlisted as a veteran, October 4, 1861, three years, Thirty-sixth regiment, company E, musician, served four years, mustered out July 27, 1865.

Tenney, Edward P., age 12, volunteer, May, 1864, one hundred days, One Hundred and Forty-eighth regiment, company A, fifer, served four months, mustered out September, 1864, failed to pass muster on account of age and size, and so received no pay for service.

Theis, Louis, age 26, volunteer, August, 1863, six months, Fourth Virginia cavalry, company D, first lieutenant, served six months, mustered out in 1864.

Theis, John G., age 22, volunteer, April 17, 1861, three months, Eighteenth regiment, company B, orderly sergeant, served five months, mustered out September, 1864, reenlistment, volunteer, 1861, three years, First Virginia light artillery, second lieutenant, attained rank of first lieutenant, served four years, mustered out July 28, 1865.

Theis, Christian, age 18, substitute, May, 1864, one hundred days, One Hundred and Forty-eighth regiment, company A, private, served four months, mustered out September, 1864.

Theis, William, volunteer, Thirty-ninth regiment, company F.

Tidd, Charles Theodore, age 17, volunteer, 1861, three years, Fourth Virginia cavalry, company F, drummer, served three years, mustered out in 1864.

Tucker, William, Ninety-second regiment, company F.

Wehers, George, age 21, volunteer, August, 1861, three years, Thirty-ninth regiment, company F, private, served four years, mustered out July 9, 1865, reenlisted as a veteran.

Welk, William, First cavalry, company L, discharged.

Wendlekin, Henry, age 24, volunteer, May, 1864, one hundred days, One Hundred and Forty-eighth regiment, company A, private, served four months, mustered out September, 1864.

Wendlekin, Martin, age 19, volunteer, August 13, 1862, three years, First Virginia cavalry, company L, private, served one year, honorably discharged April 12, 1864, for disability.

Wendlekin, John, Fifth cavalry.

Whillesey, William Beale, age 21, volunteer, July, 1862, three years, Ninety-second regiment, company F, second lieutenant, attained rank of captain, served one year and three months, killed at Mission Ridge, November 25, 1863.

Wood, Jacob S., age 45, volunteer, December 10, 1861, three years, First light artillery, company K, private, served three years and six months, mustered out July 31, 1865.

Williamson, I., Second Virginia cavalry, company F.

Wood, J. L., volunteer, First light artillery, company H.

Tappen, S. C., Seventh cavalry, company H.

Wright, Amos, age 21, volunteer, November 19, 1861, three years, Second Virginia cavalry, company F, private, attained the rank of corporal, served three years and seven months, mustered out June 30, 1865, reenlisted as a veteran.

39

RECAPITULATION.

Buell's Pierpont battery	2
First Virginia artillery	2
Huntington's battery	2
One each in battery L, First Ohio light artillery and DeBeck's battery	2
First Ohio cavalry	5
Second Virginia cavalry	7
Seventh Ohio cavalry	4
Fourth Virginia cavalry	2
And one each in Ninth and Fifth Ohio cavalry	2
United States navy	2
Thirty-ninth Ohio	22
One Hundred and Forty-eighth Ohio National guard	13
Seventy-seventh Ohio	11
Thirty-sixth Ohio	17
Eighteenth Ohio (three months)	9
Eighteenth Ohio (three years)	2
Sixty-third Ohio	6
Eighty-seventh Ohio (three months)	5
Ninety-second Ohio	4
Fifth United States colored infantry	2
One Hundred and Sixteenth Ohio	2
One each in the Seventeenth, Fifty-third, One Hundred and Twenty-fifth, Tweny-fifth, Forty-third, One Hundred and Fourth, Eighty-first, Twenty-ninth, Twenty-seventh, Thirty-seventh, One Hundred and Thirty-fifth, and Forty-seventh Ohio, Forty-second Indiana, and Nineteenth Massachusetts, making in all	14
Total number of soldiers	124
Died	12

MARIETTA CITY—THIRD WARD.

Andrews, Ebenezer B., age 40, volunteer, July, 1861, three years, Thirty-sixth regiment, major, attained colonel, served one year and eight months, resigned April 9, 1863.

Armstrong, Charles, age 28, volunteer, February, 1864, three years, Thirty-ninth regiment, company B, private, served one year and six months, mustered out July 9, 1865.

Armstrong, John, age 16, volunteer, May, 1864, one hundred days, One Hundred and Forty-eighth regiment, company H, private, served four months, mustered out in September, 1864.

Atkinson, John, age 18, volunteer, July 22, 1861, three years, Thirty-ninth regiment, company B, private, served four years, mustered out July 9, 1865.

Atkinson, Frederick, age 16, volunteer, November, 1861, three years, Seventy-seventh regiment, company A, private, reenlisted as a veteran, captured at Mark's Mills, and in prison ten months.

Bast, Henry, age 39, volunteer, July 20, 1861, three years, Thirty-ninth regiment, company B, corporal, served nine months, honorably discharged April 5, 1862, for disability.

Bast, Frederick, age 15, volunteer, September, 1864, one year, Fifth regiment, private, ran away from home.

Batchelor, William, age 45, volunteer, September 1, 1862, three years, Seventh cavalry, company H, commissary sergeant, honorably discharged May 17, 1865, for disability.

Block, John, age 36, substitute, 1862, Seventy-seventh regiment, private, served nine months, reenlisted in 1863, Second light artillery, company K, private, served two years, mustered out in 1865.

Boomer, Charles D., age 30, volunteer, November, 1861, three years, Seventy-seventh regiment, company B, private, served one year and five months, died April 30, 1863, suicide.

Booth, George Albert, age 19, volunteer, October 20, 1861, three years, Seventy-seventh regiment, company B, private, served six months, died in April, 1862, mortally wounded at Shiloh.

Booth, Frederick E., age 17, volunteer, October 20, 1861, three years, Seventy-seventh regiment, company B, private, mustered out in July, 1865.

Clarke, Melvin, volunteer, 1861, three years, Thirty-sixth regiment, lieutenant colonel, attained colonel, killed at Antietam September 17, 1862.

Cline, Samuel, Ninety-second regiment, company H.

Clarke, Joseph D., volunteer, May, 1864, one hundred days, One Hundred and Forty-eighth regiment, company A, private, killed by an explosion at City Point August 9, 1864.

Congdon, James W., age 36, volunteer, July 22, 1861, three years, Thirty-ninth regiment, company B, second sergeant, served one year and four months, honorably discharged November 11, 1862, for disability, reenlisted, volunteer, January, 1864, Thirty-ninth regiment, company B, private, served six months, honorably discharged June 13, 1864.

Condit, Timothy, age 24, volunteer, 1861, three years, First cavalry, company L, private, attained second lieutenant, killed at Murfreesborough December 31, 1862.

Conner, John, age 43, volunteer, November 12, 1861, three years, Seventy-seventh regiment, company C, private, served eight months, honorably discharged July 14, 1862, for disability.

Conner, John, jr., age 21, volunteer, November, 1861, Sixty-third regiment, company F, private, served two months, died of measles in January, 1861.

Coomer, Henry, age 18, substitute, May, 1864, one hundred days, One Hundred and Forty-eighth regiment, company A, private, served four months, mustered out in September, 1864, reenlisted, volunteer, February, 1865, one year, Thirty-sixth regiment, company H, private, served five months, mustered out July 27, 1865.

Cotton, J. D., volunteer, 1862, three years, Ninety-second regiment, sergeon, mustered out June 10, 1865.

Darrow, Allen R., age 38, volunteer, May, 1864, one hundred days, One Hundred and Forty-eighth regiment, first lieutenant and regimental quartermaster, served four months, mustered out in September, 1864, one of the original members of the National guards, organized in Marietta in 1863.

Dutton, Leander, age 27, volunteer, July 22, 1864, Thirty-ninth regiment, company B, sergeant, served one year, honorably discharged in 1862, for disability.

Dutton, Smith, age 26, volunteer, May, 1864, one hundred days, One Hundred and Forty-eighth regiment, company A, second lieutenant, served four months, mustered out in September, 1864, was a member of the National guards.

Dye, Henry, Seventy-seventh regiment, company H.

Dye, Elijah, age 19, volunteer, July 22, 1861, Thirty-ninth regiment, company B, private, served four months, detailed as butcher, and died of measles November 7, 1861.

Dye, Jacob, age 16, substitute, May, 1864, one hundred days, One Hundred and Forty-eighth regiment, company A, private, served four months, mustered out in September, 1864.

Ellis, Sumner, age 17, volunteer, November, 1861, three years, First Virginia light artillery, company C, private, served three years and seven months, mustered out in 1865.

Essman, Henry, age 25, volunteer, March 30, 1862, three years, First Virginia light artillery, company C, private, mustered out in 1865.

Field, Theodore G., age 29, volunteer, 1861, three years, First Virginia light artillery, company C, first corporal, attained lieutenant, mustered out with the battery.

Gaddle, Jacob, 1863, six months, Fourth Virginia cavalry, company C, private, served six months, mustered out.

Gates, Charles Bemans, age 19, volunteer, May, 1864, one hundred days, One Hundred and Forty-eighth regiment, company A, First regiment, first lieutenant, served four months, died May 31, 1864, of pneumonia at Harper's Ferry, was one of the company of National guards.

Gear, George R., age 22, volunteer, August 15, 1862, three years, Thirty-ninth regiment, company B, private, attained the rank of sergeant, served three years, mustered out July 9, 1865.

Given, Abraham, First Virginia artillery.

Guckert, Henry, volunteer, July, 1861, three years, Thirty-ninth regiment, company F, private, served four years, mustered out July 9, 1865.

Grass, William, age 19, volunteer, July 22, 1861, Thirty-ninth regiment, company B, private, served four years, mustered out July 9, 1865, reenlisted as a veteran, wounded at Atlanta.

Grass, Henry, age 11, volunteer, November, 1862, three years, One Hundred and Fourteenth regiment, company E, drummer, served three years, honorably discharged.

Haynes, Charles, Thirty-sixth regiment.

Henning, Henry, volunteer, March, 1862, three years, First Virginia light artillery, company C, private, died August 13, 1863, at Washington, D. C.

Huntington, J. F., volunteer, November, 1861, three years, First Ohio, company H, captain, served two years, resigned October 26, 1863.

Jenvy, William, age 19, volunteer, March, 1862, three years, First Virginia light artillery, company C, bugler, mustered out 1863.

Jeynes, James, Eleventh regiment, company E, died October 12, 1864.

Jenvey, George K., age 18, volunteer, November 19, 1861, three years, Second Virginia cavalry, company F, served three years and seven months, mustered out June 30, 1865, reenlisted as a veteran.

Jones, Charles.

Jett, George, age 17, volunteer, February 17, 1865, one year, Thirty-sixth regiment, company H, private, served six months, mustered out July 28, 1865.

Jenkins, Josiah H., age 26, volunteer, May, 1862, three months, Eighty-seventh regiment, company A, second lieutenant, mustered out September 20, 1862.

Kasper, Krus, Thirty-ninth regiment, company F.

Kendricks, John Mills, age 26, volunteer, August, 1861, Thirty-third regiment, first lieutenant, attained the rank of adjutant, served one year and one month, resigned September, 1862.

King, George W., volunteer, three years, Thirty-ninth regiment, company B, private, died.

Kuntz, John, age 18, volunteer, July 31, 1861, three years, Thirty-ninth regiment, company F, private, served three years, mustered out 1864

Lacey, Charles, age 21, volunteer, March, 1862, three years, First Virginia light artillery, company C, private, died July 3, 1863, killed at Gettysburgh.

Lehnhardt, John Jacob, age 19, volunteer, August 13, 1862, three years, First Virginia light artillery, company C, four battles, served two years and ten months, mustered out June 28, 1865.

Long, Lewis, age 16, volunteer, November 4, 1861, three years, First Virginia light artillery, company G, private, served three years and nine months, mustered out July 8, 1865, reenlisted as a veteran.

Mahnken, John, age 24, volunteer, September 1, 1861, three years, First Virginia light artillery, company E, private, served three years and nine months, mustered out June 28, 1865, reenlisted as a veteran.

Maloy, Barney, age 24, volunteer, December, 1861, three years, First Virginia light artillery, company C, private, served three and a half years, mustered out June 28, 1865, reenlisted as a veteran.

Maloy, Alexander E., age 21, volunteer, December, 1861, three years, First Virginia light artillery, company C, private, mustered out June 28, 1865, reenlisted as a veteran.

Maloy, James Henry, age 21, volunteer, 1862, three years, First Virginia light artillery, company C, private, mustered out June 28, 1865.

Merabin, L. R., volunteer, three years, First Virginia light artillery, company C, private, captured at Rodgersville, Tennessee, and imprisoned, nothing further heard of him.

Misenhelder, William, age 35, volunteer, September, 1862, three years, Seventh cavalry, company H, private, died.

Miller, Henry J., age 38, volunteer, September 20, 1862, three years, Seventh cavalry, company H, private, served two years and nine months, mustered out June 29, 1865.

Morris, Augustus, age 22, volunteer, April, 1861, three months, Eighteenth regiment, company B, served four months, mustered out September, 1861, reenlisted as a veteran, volunteer, September, 1861, three years, First Virginia light artillery, company C, private, served three years and nine months, mustered out June 28, 1865.

Morris, William H., age 21, volunteer, January 18, 1862, three years, gunboat, private, served two and one-half years, honorably discharged 1864, by reason of yellow fever appearing on board the gunboat.

Newton, Charles H., age 21, volunteer, July, 1863, three years, Second Ohio heavy artillery, company K, second lieutenant, attained rank of first lieutenant, served one year and seven months, honorably discharged February, 1865.

Payne, George, age 56, volunteer, November 15, 1861, Seventy-seventh regiment, company B, drum major, served five months, honorably discharged April 17, 1862.

Payne, Abram Darrow, age 27, volunteer, October 14, 1861, Sixty-fourth regiment, company B, musician, honorably discharged May 7, 1863.

Payne, George L., age 23, volunteer, July 22, 1861, Thirty-ninth regiment, company B, principal musician, honorably discharged January, 1863, for disability.

Pearce, William, age 58, volunteer, January, 1862, three years, Seventy-seventh regiment, chaplain, resigned 1862.

Pearce, Charles, age 25, volunteer, August 13, 1862, three years, Seventy-seventh regiment, company D, private, attained orderly, served three years, mustered out July 25, 1865.

Pearce, Edgar P., June, 1862, three years, Seventy-seventh regiment, company D, first lieutenant, mustered out March 8, 1866, brigade quartermaster in General Steele's army.

Pearce, Ebenezer, age 27, volunteer, 1861, three years, Thirty-ninth regiment, company B, private, served three years, mustered out 1864.

Petre, Frederick, age 34, volunteer, 1861, three years, First light artillery, company H, private, honorably discharged March, 1862, for disability.

Petre, Charles, age 21, volunteer, December 8, 1861, three years, First Virginia light artillery, company C, private, served three years and six months, mustered out June 28, 1865, reenlisted as a veteran.

Pfaff, Lewis, age 20, volunteer, July 31, 1861, three years, Thirty-ninth regiment, company F, private, served three years, mustered out 1864, detailed for duty in a battery two years of the time.

Pixley, William W., volunteer, First light artillery, company H, private.

Reiter, Nicholas, age 36, volunteer, August 12, 1861, three years, First Virginia light artillery, company H, private, served one year and six months, died 1863, of lung fever.

Rudig, Adam, age 44, volunteer, February, 1864, one year, Thirty-ninth regiment, company F, private, served thirteen months, died March, 1865, of diarrhœa.

Rudig, Jacob, age 19, volunteer, February, 1864, one year, Thirty-ninth regiment, company F, private, served one year and four months, mustered out July 9, 1865.

Schminke, Augustus, age 32, volunteer, October, 1862, three years, Seventh cavalry, company H, bugler, served one year, died November 6, 1863, killed at Rogersville, Tennessee.

Schneider, Philip, aged 30, volunteer, October, 1861, three years, Thirty-ninth regiment, company F, private, served one year, honorably discharged December, 1862, his team ran away and injured him

Scisson, Lewis E., volunteer, 1861, three years, Seventy-seventh regiment, company C, captain, attained major, mustered out.

Shaw, Sidney F., age 37, volunteer, October 23, 1862, three years, Fifteenth Virginia regiment, company G, captain, acting chief engineer of West Virginia.

Shaw, Rodney K., age 31, volunteer, August, 1861, three years, Sixty-third regiment, company B, second lieutenant, attained captain, served one year, resigned September 18, 1862, for disability.

Shaw, Nathaniel H., age 41, volunteer, July 8, 1861, three years, Thirty-ninth regiment, company B, private, served three months, honorably discharged October 4, 1861, for disability.

Snider, John B., Thirty-ninth regiment, company B.

Shockley, David, age 23, volunteer, 1861, three years, First light artillery, company H, private, served four years, mustered out July 31, 1865, reenlisted as a veteran.

Simmons, Orrin, First Light artillery, company K.

Sinclair, Jesse B., age 16, volunteer, 1861, three years, Seventy-seventh regiment, company B, drummer, attained corporal, served four years, mustered out July 15, 1865, reenlisted as a veteran, was captered at Mark's Mills, and in Tyler prison, Texas, for ten months.

Stoful, John, Fifth regiment, company A.

Smith, Samuel H. W., aged 23, volunteer, July, 1861, three years, Seventy-seventh regiment, company B, private, three years, honorably discharged, October 8, 1864, detailed as printer and served as such for eighteen months, reenlistment, substitute, 1865, one year, Thirty-ninth regiment, company B, private.

Smith, J. J.

Snider, Peter, Thirty-ninth regiment, company B.

Sniffen, James, Seventh cavalry, company H.

Stewart, T. R., Thirty-sixth regiment, company G, died October 20, 1861, of of typhoid pneumonia.

Sniffen, J. Wesley, Seventh cavalry, company H.

Solar, George, volunteer, three years, Thirty-ninth regiment, company B, private, died.

Stump, Lawrence, age 27, volunteer, February, 1864, three years, Thirty-ninth regiment, company B, private, served one year, died April 4, 1865, of wound in the lungs.

Thomas, James L., volunteer, Seventy-seventh regiment, company E, private.

Styner, First light artillery, company H.

Thomas, Samuel R., volunteer, Seventy-seventh regiment, company E, honorably discharged.

Vandine, Samuel, age 29, volunteer, May, 1862, three months, Eighty-eighth regiment, private, served four months, mustered out September, 1862, reenlistment, volunteer, May, 1864, one hundred days, One Hundred and Forty-eighth regiment, private, served four months, mustered out in September, 1864.

Wellbrook, Henry, age 35, volunteer, February, 1862, three years, Sixty-third regiment, company F, private, served one month, died March 31, 1864, of diarrhœa, at St. Louis.

Wilson, John, volunteer, honorably discharged.

Warren, George, age 36, volunteer, September, 1861, three years, First cavalry, company L, sergeant, served three years, honorably discharged in 1864, reenlistment volunteer, October 12, 1864, one year, Twenty-first Kentucky, company I, private, honorably discharged October 24, 1865.

Wildt, Joseph B., jr., volunteer, First light artillery, company H, private, honorably discharged, July, 1862.

Wildt, Joseph, volunteer, Fifty-eighth regiment, captain.

Walters, Thomas B., volunteer, March 21, 1863, Sixth regiment, served one year, company D.

Shaw, Sidney F., age 28, volunteer, Sixty-third regiment, lieutenant, reenlistment, volunteer, September, 1862, Fifteenth Virginia, company G, captain, attained rank of chief engineer, which position he held from October 16, 1864, to July 1, 1865, when he was made major.

Wells, William.

RECAPITULATION.

Buell's Pierpont battery (First Virginia artillery)	12
First Virginia light artillery	3
Huntington's battery	7
Battery K, Second heavy artillery	2
De Beck's battery	1
Seventh Ohio cavalry	6
First Ohio cavalry	2
One each in Fourth Virginia cavalry and Second Virginia cavalry	2
Thirty-ninth Ohio	26
Seventy-seventh Ohio	16
One Hundred and Forty-eighth Ohio National guards	8
Thirty-sixth Ohio	6
Ninety-second Ohio	2
Sixty-third Ohio	4
And one each in Fifth Ohio, One Hundred and Fourteenth Ohio, Eleventh Ohio, Eighty-seventh Ohio (three months), Thirty-third Ohio, Eighteenth Ohio (three months), Sixty-fourth Ohio, Sixty-seventh Ohio, Fifteenth Virginia infantry, Eighty-eighth Ohio, Fifty-eighth Ohio, Sixth Ohio, Fifteenth Virginia infantry, Twenty-first Kentucky infantry, and one in gunboat service, making in all	15
Total number soldiers	108

MUSKINGUM TOWNSHIP.

Andrews, Christian, age 26, volunteer, September 1, 1862, three years, First Virginia light artillery, company C, private, served two years and nine months, mustered out June 30, 1865, reenlisted as a veteran.

Andrews, Daniel, Sixty-third regiment, company F.

Arend, Daniel, age 19, volunteer, October, 1861, three years, Sixty-third regiment, company F, private, served ten months, honorably discharged on account of rheumatism.

Baker, Alpheus, age 41, August 5, 1862, three years, Ninety-second regiment, company F, private, served fourteen and one-half months, honorably discharged November 26, 1862

Barker, John D., age 29, volunteer, September, 1861, three years, First cavalry, company L, first lieutenant, attained rank of captain, served three years and four months, resigned January 21, 1864

Barker, J. Gage, age 26, volunteer, July 29, 1861, three years, Thirty-sixth regiment, company A, first lieutenant, attained rank of captain, served three years and two months, resigned October, 1864, wounded at battle of Berryville, September 3, 1864, and severely at Winchester.

Barker, Arthur W., age 24, volunteer, July 29, 1861, three years, Thirty-sixth regiment, company A, private, honorably discharged April 24, 1863, transferred December 10, 1861, to accept an appointment, wounded severely at Antietam, September 17, 1862, second enlistment, volunteer, three years, Thirty-sixth regiment, company A.

Barker, Jesse H., volunteer, July 29, 1861, three years, Thirty-sixth regiment, company A, private, attained rank of commissary sergeant, served three years, honorably discharged in 1864, for disability.

Barker, Luther D., volunteer, May, 1864, one hundred days, One Hundred and Forty-eighth regiment, company A, private, served one hundred days, mustered out September, 1864.

Barnhart, William, volunteer, July 29, 1861, three years, Thirty-sixth regiment, company A, private, served three years, mustered out 1864.

Barnhart, William, age 19, volunteer, July 5, 1863, six months, Fourth independent batallion cavalry, private, served nine months, mustered out March 12, 1864, reenlistment, age 20, volunteer, September 5, 1864, one year, One Hundred and Seventy-fourth regiment, company D, private, served ten months, mustered out June 28, 1865.

Barnhart, Jasper, age 19, volunteer, July 5, 1863, six months, Fourth independent batallion cavalry, private, served nine months, mustered out March 12, 1864, reenlistment, age 20, volunteer, September 5, 1864, one year, One Hundred and Seventy-fourth regiment, company D, private, served ten months, mustered out June 28, 1865.

Bartlett, Henry, age 19, volunteer, three years, Sixty-third regiment, company D, private, mustered out July 8, 1865, reenlisted as a veteran.

Baumgardner, John G., age 18, volunteer, March 31, 1865, one year, Thirty-sixth regiment, company G, private, served four months, mustered out July 27, 1865.

Bell, Wilson, aged 27, volunteer, 1861, three years, Thirty-ninth regiment, company B, private, mustered out July 9, 1865, reenlisted as a veteran.

Bell, George Washington, age 25, volunteer, December 3, 1863, three years, Thirty-sixth regiment, company K, private, served one year and six months, mustered out June, 1864.

Bell, William, age 17, volunteer, July 5, 1863, six months, Fourth independent batallion cavalry, private, served nine months, mustered out March 12, 1864, reenlistment, age 18, volunteer, September 15, 1864, one year, One Hundred and Seventy-fourth regiment, company D, sergeant, attained rank of orderly sergeant, served ten months, mustered out June 28, 1865.

Bey, Frederick, age 21, volunteer, October 12, 1862, three years, Seventh cavalry, company H, blacksmith.

Bingham, William H., age 34, volunteer, August, 1862, three years, First light artillery, company H, private, discharged.

Bishop, Lycurgus, age 29, volunteer, 1862, three years, First light artillery, company H, died June 14, 1863.

Burlingame, E. P., volunteer, September 14, 1861, three years, First cavalry, company L, private, attained rank of first sergeant, served four years, mustered out September 26, 1865, veteran, reenlisted.

Bragg, Benjamin, age 21, volunteer, April 17, 1861, three months, Eighteenth regiment, company B, private, served four months, mustered out August 23, 1861, reenlistment, age 21, volunteer, July 29, 1861, three years, Thirty-sixth regiment, company A, corporal, attained rank of second lieutenant, served two years and six months, mustered out July 27, 1865, veteran enlistment, age 23, volunteer, February, 1864, three years, Thirty-sixth regiment, company A, sergeant, attained rank of second lieutenant, served one year and six months, mustered out July 27, 1865.

Brown, Asa, One Hundred and Forty-eighth regiment.

Briggs, Felix, age 28, volunteer, Twenty-third Kentucky regiment, company I, private, died January 24, 1864.

Briggs, T. L.

Briggs, Sabinus, age 24, volunteer, One Hundred and Thirty-ninth Pennsylvania, company H, reenlistment.

Creal, George, age 26, volunteer, July 29, 1863, three years, Fifth colored infantry, company I, private, served two years, honorably discharged September 22, 1865.

Cook, Jacob, age 16, volunteer, October, 1861, three years, Sixty-third regiment, company F, private, served six months, died May 1, 1862.

Dabold, Jacob,[*] volunteer, May, 1864, one hundred days, One Hundred and Forty-eighth regiment, company A, private.

Danner, William, age 42, volunteer, February 14, 1865, one year, Thirty-sixth regiment, company C, private, served five and one-half months, mustered out July 27, 1865.

Davis, Freeman L., volunteer, three years, First cavalry, company L.

Davis, Herman, volunteer, three years, Thirty-sixth regiment, company A, private, served three years, mustered out.

Deeker, John, Thirty-ninth regiment, company F.

Devol, Stephen, volunteer, July 29, 1861, three years, Thirty-sixth regiment, company A, private, served two and a half years, mustered out in February, 1864, veteran enlistment, volunteer, February, 1864, three years, Thirty-sixth regiment company A, private, served one year and a half, mustered out July 27, 1865.

Devol, Charles H., age 20, volunteer, July 29, 1862, three years, Thirty-sixth regiment, company A, private, attained rank of corporal, served three years, mustered out July 27, 1865.

Devol, William, age 19, volunteer, August 12, 1862, three years, Thirty-sixth regiment, company A, private, mustered out July 27, 1865.

Devol, Benjamin, substitute, May, 1864, one hundred days, One Hundred and Forty-eighth regiment, company A, private, served four months, mustered out September, 1864, reenlisted, one year, Eighteenth regiment, company I, private, mustered out.

Devol, Harris, age 18, volunteer, July 29, 1861, three years, Thirty-sixth regiment, company A, private, served three years, mustered out in 1864.

Dyar, Joseph, age 25, volunteer, July 29, 1861, three years, Thirty-sixth regiment, company A, corporal, honorably discharged.

Tile, Henry, Sixteenth regiment, company A.

Gilpin, Daniel, age 23, substitute, October 6, 1864, one year, Seventy-eighth regiment, company E, private, served nine months, mustered out June 26, 1865.

Gilpin, Jackson, age 17, volunteer, October 6, 1864, one year, First cavalry, company L, private, served nine months, mustered out June 26, 1865.

Hamilton, Albert G., age 24, volunteer, August 2, 1863, three years, Second heavy artillery, company K, private, served two years, mustered out August 23, 1865.

Hamilton, John A., age 16, volunteer, August 27, 1863, three years, Second heavy artillery, company K, private, served one year and nine months, honorably discharged May 12, 1865.

Haney, James, age 23, volunteer, 1861, three years, Sixty-third regiment, company G, private, served one year, honorably discharged in 1862, reenlistment, age 26, volunteer, 1864, three years, Seventy-seventh regiment, company D, private, served one year, mustered out in 1865

Heckler, John, Thirty-sixth regiment, company A.

Heckler, Joseph, Thirty-sixth regiment, company A.

Heckler, Godfrey, Thirty-sixth regiment, company A.

Hill, Prescott, age 29, volunteer, January 5, 1864, three years, Seventy-seventh regiment, companies H and D, private.

Hill, William, volunteer, three years, Thirty-sixth regiment, company A, private.

Kidwell, George Washington, age 16, volunteer, Seventy-seventh regiment, company D, died.

Ladd, William, age 32, volunteer, August 12, 1862, three years, Thirty-sixth regiment, company A, private, died.

Ladd, Salathiel, age 28, volunteer, 1861, three years, Thirty-sixth regiment, company A, private, served three years, mustered out in 1864.

Ladd, John Asher, age 22, volunteer, three years, Thirty-sixth regiment, company A, private, died.

Lancaster, J. Leroy, age 27, volunteer, August 9, 1862, three years, Thirty-sixth regiment, company A, private, served two years and eleven months, mustered out July 27, 1865.

Lancaster, William, age 21, volunteer, July 29, 1861, three years, Thirty-sixth regiment, company A, private, served four years, mustered out July 27, 1865, reenlisted as a veteran.

Lancaster, Francis, age 19, volunteer, May 28, 1862, three months, Eighty-seventh regiment, company A, private, served four months, mustered out October 1, 1862, reenlisted twice.

Lancaster, F. T., Thirteenth cavalry, company A.

Lancaster, Mordecai, age 17, volunteer, May 28, 1862, three months, Eighty-seventh regiment, company A, private, served four months, reenlisted as a veteran, killed by explosion at Petersburgh.

Marshall, William, age 21, volunteer, 1861, three years, Thirty-sixth regiment, company A, private, attained rank of corporal, served two years, died in 1863, mortally wounded June 29, 1863.

Maxwell, S. Newton, age 23, volunteer, May 28, 1862, three months, Eighty-seventh regiment, company A, served four months, mustered out October 1, 1862.

Mellor, Walter H., age 37, volunteer, May, 1864, three months, One Hundred and Forty-eighth regiment, company K, orderly sergeant.

Monett, A. Lake, age 22, volunteer, May 28, 1862, three months, Eighty-seventh regiment, company A, private, served four months, mustered out, October 1, 1862.

Monett, Moses M., age 18, volunteer, July 29, 1861, three years, Thirty-sixth regiment, company A, private, served six months, honorably discharged January 31, 1862.

More, Alfred, Thirty-ninth regiment, company B.

Nye, Charles N., volunteer, May 28, 1862, three months, Eighty-fifth regiment, company B, private, mustered out October 1, 1862, reenlisted May, 1864, one hundred days, One Hundred and Forty-eighth regiment, company A, orderly sergeant, four months, mustered out September, 1864.

Otten, John, volunteer, reenlisted as a veteran.

Palmer, David P., age 18, volunteer, July, 1861, three years, Thirty-sixth regiment, company G, private, served three years, mustered out September, 1864, wounded at Mission Ridge.

Perrin, Lyman, volunteer, July 29, 1861, three years, Thirty-sixth regiment, company A, private, served two years and nine months, reenlisted as a veteran, killed by a bushwhacker May, 1864.

Pixley, George, age 21, volunteer, April 17, 1861, three months, Eighteenth regiment, company B, private, served four and a half months, mustered out August 28, 1861.

Putnam, Israel Pitt, age 29, volunteer, November 15, 1861, three years, First Virginia light artillery, company C, corporal, served two years and two months, honorably discharged February 16, 1863.

Putnam, George W., age 21, volunteer, July 29, 1861, three years, Thirty-sixth regiment, company A, sergeant, attained rank of first lieutenant, served three and a half years, resigned January 13, 1865.

Putnam, William Rufus, volunteer, commanding Camp Putnam, Ohio, colonel.

Ridgeway, George, volunteer, Eighteenth regiment, company B, died.

Ridgeway, Joseph, Thirty-sixth Iowa.

Rhodes, Joseph, age 33, volunteer, September 14, 1861, three years, First cavalry, company L, private, mustered out 1864.

Robinson, William, First cavalry, company L, died.

Ross, William, Ninth cavalry, company B.

Ross, Griffin, Ninth cavalry, company B.

Saner, Henry, age 24, volunteer, October 6, 1862, three years, Seventh cavalry, company H, private, served two years and eleven months, honorably discharged September 3, 1864.

Saner, Conrad, age 23, volunteer, October 6, 1862, three years, Seventh cavalry, company H, private, served two years and eight months, honorably discharged May 24, 1865.

Selby, James Cahoun, age 22, volunteer, 1861, three years, Thirty-sixth regiment, company A, second lieutenant, attained rank of captain, served three years, mortally wounded at Berryville, Virginia, September 3, 1864, died September 14, 1864.

Shaw, John L., age 35, volunteer, April 17, 1861, three months, Eighteenth regiment, company B, private, served four and a half months, mustered out August 28, 1861.

Schwartz, Martin, Thirty-sixth regiment, company A.

Smith, George P., volunteer, August, 1862, three years, Thirty-sixth regiment, company A, private, attained rank of sergeant, served three years, mustered out August 28, 1865.

Smith, Christopher C., volunteer, August 11, 1862, three years, Thirty-sixth regiment, company A, private, served one and a half years, honorably discharged February 29, 1864.

Smith, John, age 24, volunteer, August 24, 1861, three years, Thirty-sixth regiment, company A, private.

Snider, Henry, May, 1864, one hundred days, One Hundred and Forty-eighth regiment.

Spears, James, Thirty-sixth regiment, company A.

Stackhouse, Wallace, age 48, volunteer, three years, Ninety-second regiment, company H.

Stacy, Miles A, volunteer, July, 1861, three years, Thirty-sixth regiment, company A, orderly sergeant, attained rank of captain, served four years, mustered out July 27, 1865.

Stacy, James.

Stacy, Joel Elliot, age 21, volunteer, July 29, 1861, three years, Thirty-sixth regiment, company A, private, served two and a half years, mustered out February, 1864, veteran enlistment February, 1864, three years, Thirty-sixth regiment, company A.

Stacy, Arius F, age 18, volunteer, August 24, 1861, three years, company A, private, served three years, mustered out 1864.

Steed, James, volunteer, 1861, three years, Sixty-third regiment, company D, private.

Steer, Edward, age 18, volunteer, July 29, 1862, three years, Ninety-second regiment, company F, private, served three years, mustered out June 10, 1865.

Stewart, Frank, volunteer, July 29, 1861, three years, Thirty-sixth regiment, company A, private, killed.

Stow, Seldon S., age 19, volunteer, July 29, 1861, three years, Thirty-sixth regiment, company A, private, served four years, mustered out July 27, 1865, reenlisted as a veteran.

Stow, Charles R., age 17, volunteer, 1862, three years, Thirty-sixth regiment, company A, private.

Strohl, William, age 29, volunteer, November 11, 1862, three years, One Hundred and Twenty-fifth regiment, company E, private, attained rank of corporal, served two years and ten months, mustered out September 25, 1865.

Strohl, Joseph, volunteer, May 28, 1862, three months, Eighty-seventh

regiment, company A, private, served four months, mustered out October 1, 1862, reenlistment, volunteer, June 28, 1863, six months, Fourth independent battalion cavalry, company C, sergeant, served eight months, mustered out March 12, 1864, third enlistment volunteer, March 14, 1864, three years, Thirteenth cavalry, companies A, K, and E, orderly sergeant, attained rank of captain, served one year and four months, mustered out August 10, 1865.

Swartz, Martin, age 19, volunteer, August, 1861, three years, Thirty-sixth regiment, company G, private, served two years and six months, mustered out February, 1864, veteran enlistment, volunteer, February, 1864, three years, Thirty-sixth regiment, company G.

Wagoner, Theobald, company A.

Wagoner, Michael, age 19, volunteer, August 2, 1863, three years, Second heavy artillery, company K, private, served two years, mustered out August 23, 1865.

Ward, J. Edwin, age 17, volunteer, 1861, three years, Seventy-seventh regiment, company D, private, served eleven months, honorably discharged 1862, reenlistment, age 19, volunteer, July 6, 1863, six months, Fourth independent battalion cavalry, company C, private, served eight months, mustered out March 12, 1864, third enlistment, age 20, volunteer, March 14, 1864, three years, Thirteenth cavalry, company A, corporal, served one year and four months, mustered out July, 1865.

Wellspring, John, volunteer, October 20, 1861, three years, First light artillery, company H, private, served two years, honorably discharged September 22, 1863.

Wendleken, Henry W., age 18, substitute, April 1, 1865, one year, Eighteenth regiment, company E, private, served six and one-half months, mustered out October 19, 1865.

West, Gordon B, age 20, volunteer, April 17, 1861, three months, Eighteenth regiment, company B, private, served four and one-half months, mustered out August 28, 1861, reenlistment, 1863, three years Seventy-seventh regiment, company E, lieutenant, attained rank of captain, mustered out March 8, 1866, reenlisted as a veteran.

Welking, Philip, Thirty-ninth regiment, company B.

Wood, Osmer J., volunteer, July 29, 1861, three years, Thirty-sixth regiment, companies A and K, sergeant, attained rank of first lieutenant, served two years, resigned August 27, 1863

Wood, Gustavus Adolphus, volunteer, July 29, 1861, three years, Thirty-sixth regiment, company A, corporal, served two years and five months, honorably discharged December 7, 1862, wounded at Antietam, September 17, 1862, and at Chickamauga, September 19, 1863.

RECAPITULATION.

Huntington's battery................................	3
Buell's Pierpont battery.............................	2
Battery K, Second Ohio heavy artillery..............	3
First Ohio cavalry.................................	6
Fourth Ohio independent battalion cavalry...........	5
Seventh Ohio cavalry...............................	3
Thirteenth Ohio cavalry............................	3
Ninth Ohio cavalry.................................	2
Thirty-sixth Ohio..................................	46
Sixty-third Ohio...................................	6
One Hundred and Forty-eighth Ohio..................	7
Thirty-ninth Ohio..................................	5
Seventy-seventh Ohio...............................	5
Eighteenth Ohio (three months).....................	5
Eighty-seventh Ohio................................	5
Eighteenth Ohio (three years)......................	2
Ninety-second Ohio.................................	3
One Hundred and Seventy-fourth Ohio................	3
One each in Twenty-third Kentucky, Thirty-sixth Iowa, One Hundred and Thirty-ninth Pennsylvania, Fifth colored infantry, Sixteenth Ohio, Seventy-eighth Ohio, Eighty-fifth Ohio (three months), One Hundred and Twenty-fifth Ohio, not designated two....................................	10
Total number of soldiers........	111
Died...	13

NEWPORT TOWNSHIP.

Adams, Moses, age 46, volunteer, May, 1864, one hundred days, One Hundred and Forty-eighth regiment, company G, private, served four months, mustered out September, 1864.

Adams, Alcynus, age 17, volunteer, May, 1864, one hundred days, One Hundred and Forty-eighth regiment, company G, private, served four months, mustered out September, 1864.

Adkins.

Bobb, Reese Smith, age 31, volunteer, May, 1864, one hundred days, One Hundred and Forty-eighth regiment, company G, corporal, served four months, mustered out September, 1864.

Ballentine, William Henry, age 30, volunteer, May, 1864, one hundred days, One Hundred and Forty-eighth regiment, company G, corporal, served four months, mustered out September, 1864.

Ballentine, George Kimberly, age 20, volunteer, August, 1861, three years, Sixth Virginia regiment, company G, private, attained the rank of sergeant, three years, mustered out October, 1864.

Ballentine, John T., age 18, volunteer, August, 1861, three years, Sixth Virginia regiment, company G, private, three years, mustered out October, 1864.

Ballentine, William Edward, age 17, volunteer, August, 1861, three years, Sixth Virginia regiment, company G, private, served three years, mustered out October, 1864.

Baldwin, Sinclair, volunteer, company A.

Baldwin, Silas, age 22, volunteer, September 1, 1861, three years, First Virginia light artillery, company C, private, served two years and six months, mustered out in 1864, reenlistment, age 24, volunteer, 1864, three years, First Virginia light artillery, company C, private, served one year, mustered out June 28, 1865.

Barker, Joseph, age 28, volunteer, May, 1864, one hundred days, One Hundred and Forty-eighth regiment, company B, corporal, served four months, mustered out September, 1864.

Batelle, Charles D., age 16, volunteer, May, 1864, one hundred days, One Hundred and Forty-eighth regiment, company G, fifer, served four months, mustered out September, 1867.

Bell, Austin, age 18, volunteer, 1861, three years, Thirty-sixth regiment, company G, private.

Bell, William Henry, age 42, volunteer, August 22, 1862, three years, One Hundred and Sixteenth regiment, company F, drummer, attained the rank of private, three years, mustered out June, 1865.

Blakely, Lewis, Second Arkansas light artillery, died.

Blakely, William Hervy, age 21, volunteer, September 9, 1861, three years, Eighteenth regiment, company F, private, served three years and three months, mustered out December 15, 1864.

Blakely, Andrew S., age 17, volunteer, September 9, 1861, three years, Eighteenth regiment, company F, private, served four years, mustered out October 9, 1865, reenlisted as a veteran.

Bosworth, Sumner, May, 1864, one hundred days, One Hundred and Forty-eighth regiment, company G, private, served four months mustered out September, 1864.

Burge, C., volunteer, First Virginia regiment, company I, died.

Britton, Charles-Russel, age 16, volunteer, August, 1863, six months, One Hundred and Twenty-ninth regiment, company F, private, served eight months, mustered out March 11, 1864, reenlistment, May, 1864, one hundred days, One Hundred and Forty-eighth regiment, company G, private, served four months, mustered out September, 1864.

Bush, John L., age 48, volunteer, 1864, one hundred days, One Hundred and Forty-eighth regiment, company G.

Bush, William Casner, volunteer, Thirty-sixth regiment, company G.

Bush, Josephus, age 18, volunteer, July 13, 1863, six months, One Hundred and Twenty-ninth regiment, company F, private.

Carpenter, David, age 31, volunteer, May, 1864, one hundred days, One Hundred and Forty-eighth regiment, company G, private, mustered out September, 1864, reenlistment, age 32, drafted March, 1865, one year, honorably discharged.

Carpenter, Jasper, age 31, volunteer, May, 1864, one hundred days, One Hundred and Forty-eighth regiment, company B, private, mustered out September, 1864.

Carver, Isaac P., age 18, volunteer, January 1, 1862, three years, First Virginia light artillery, company C, private, served two years, honorably discharged in 1864, veteran enlistment, age 20, volunteer, 1864, three years, First Virginia light artillery, company C, private, served one year and six months, mustered out June 28, 1865.

Conner, Joseph Long, age 32, drafted March 23, 1865, one year, Forty-third regiment, served two months, honorably discharged May 24, 1865, by reason of instructions from the War Department.

Chapeell, Conrad.

Conner, Thomas Jason, age 19, volunteer, July 22, 1861, three years, Thirty-ninth regiment, company B, corporal, attained rank of sergeant, three years, mustered out in 1864.

Cooke, Milton Gilbert, age 47, volunteer, September 6, 1861, three years, First cavalry, company L, blacksmith, served one year and six months, honorably discharged.

Cree, John R., age 21, volunteer, May 28, 1862, three months, Eighty-fifth regiment, company F, private, mustered out.

Cooke, James Monroe, age 16, August 13, 1861, three years, Thirty-ninth regiment, company B, private, served four years, mustered out July 9, 1865, reenlisted as a veteran.

Crandall.

Crocker, Joseph, age 42, volunteer, May, 1864, one hundred days, One Hundred and Forty-eighth regiment, company G, corporal.

Crumbley, E. A., age 38, volunteer, May, 1864, one hundred days, One Hundred and Forty-eighth regiment, company G, private, mustered out in September, 1864.

Cunningham, Michael, age 40, volunteer, August 6, 1862, three years, Ninety-second regiment, company F, private, honorably discharged.

Cutshaw, William, age 18, volunteer, 1864, three years, One Hundred and Seventy-fifth regiment, company K, private, died.

Cutshaw, Sheppard, age 16, volunteer, 1864, Eighth Virginia cavalry, company C.

Cutshaw, Shannon, age 15, volunteer, 1864, one year, One Hundred and Seventy-fifth regiment, company K, private, died at Nashville, Tennessee.

Dana, Frederick F., age 18, volunteer, September 1, 1862, three years, Seventh cavalry, company H, served three years, mustered out July 4, 1865.

Dale, Edward R., Seventy-seventh regiment.

Dana, Charles L.

Davis, Hamilton F., age 16, volunteer, October 8, 1861, three years, Seventy-seventh regiment, company B, private, served two years and four months, honorably discharged, veteran enlistment, age 19, volunteer, 1864, three years, Seventy-seventh regiment, company B, private, served five months, died July 1, 1864, died in prison in Tyler, Texas.

Davis, John Wilson, age 19, drafted March 23, 1865, one year, Thirty-ninth regiment, company B, private, served four months, mustered out July 9, 1865.

Davis, K. B., age 23, volunteer, July, 1863, six months, One Hundred and Twenty-ninth regiment, company F, private, served nine months, mustered out March 11, 1864, reenlistment, substitute, May, 1864, one hundred days, One Hundred and Forty-eighth regiment, company G, private, served four months, mustered out in September, 1864.

Davis, James W., age 22, volunteer, April, 1861, three months, Eighteenth regiment, company C, private, four and one-half months, mustered out in August, 1861, reenlistment, substitute, May, 1864, one hundred days, One Hundred and Forty-eighth regiment, company K, private, served four months, mustered out September, 1861.

Davis, Henry Edward, age 20, volunteer, September 1, 1862, three years, Seventh cavalry, company H, private, served one year and seven months, died April 4, 1864, a prisoner at Andersonville, captured November 15, 1863, in Kentucky.

Davis, Sandford, age 33, volunteer, May, 1864, one hundred days, One Hundred and Forty-eighth regiment, company G, private, served four months, mustered out September, 1864.

Dick, J., age 16, volunteer, 1861, three years, Eighteenth regiment, company F, private, served three years, mustered out in 1864.

Dolson, Emanuel, volunteer, May, 1861, three years, Twenty-fifth regiment, private, served eleven months, honorably discharged March, 1862, for disability, a prisoner, captured at Rogersville, November 6, 1863, reenlistment, volunteer, 1862, three years, Seventh cavalry, company H, private, served one year and ten months, died July 20, 1864.

Dotson, George, age 17, volunteer, August, 1864, one year, Second heavy artillery, company K, private, served ten months, honorably discharged May 25, 1865, from hospital after three months sickness.

Dowens, George, age 57, volunteer, October 19, 1861, three years, Sixty-third regiment, company F, fife major, honorably discharged for disability.

Edgell, Benjamin Ellis, age 23, volunteer, July, 1863, six months, One Hundred and Twenty-ninth regiment, company F, orderly sergeant, mustered out.

Edgerton, Luther, volunteer, First cavalry, company L, died May 13, 1862, of fever, at Louisville, Kentucky.

Edgerton, William H., volunteer, July, 1861, three years, Thirty-ninth regiment, company B, first lieutenant, resigned June 25, 1862.

Edwards, Benjamin, May, 1864, one hundred days, One Hundred and Forty-eighth regiment, company G, private, served four months, mustered out September, 1864.

Edwards, Dennis, age 25, volunteer, 1862, three years, Ninety-second regiment, company F, private.

Elson, Lewis, age 33, volunteer, August, 1862, three years, Eleventh Virginia regiment, company D, private, served two years and nine months, mustered out June, 1865.

Farley, Pearson, age 45, volunteer, one hundred May, 1864, days, One Hundred and Forty-eighth regiment, company G, private, served four months, mustered out September, 1864.

Farley, John, age 18, volunteer, May, 1864, one hundred days, One Hundred and Forty-eighth regiment, company G, private, served four months, mustered out September, 1864.

Francis, A. J., age 29, volunteer, August, 1862, three years Ninety-second regiment, company F, private, served one year, died, November 1, 1863, of chronic diarrhœa in Chattanooga.

Francis, Stephen, age 27, volunteer, August 8, 1862, three years, Ninety-second regiment, company F, private, served two years and ten months, mustered out June, 1865.

Friedel, Andrew, May, 1864, one hundred days, One Hundred and Forty-eighth regiment, company G, private, served four months, mustered out September, 1864.

Gano, Jacob, age 21, volunteer, September, 1861, three years, First cavalry, company L, corporal, attained rank of sergeant, served three years, mustered out 1864.

Garrison, Rodney S., age 20, volunteer, July 22, 1861, three years, Thirty-ninth regiment, company B, private, served one year, honorably discharged 1862, reenlistment, age 23, volunteer, May, 1864, one hundred days, One Hundred and Forty-eighth regiment, company G, private.

Gates, Jewett, age 23, volunteer, 1862, three years, Ninety-second regiment, company G, private, served three months, died 1864.

Goddard, George, age 35, drafted, March 23, 1865, one year, Thirty-ninth regiment, company G, private, served four months, mustered out July 9, 1865.

Greene, Christopher, age 55, volunteer, May, 1864, one hundred days, One Hundred and Forty-eighth regiment, company G, sergeant, served four months, mustered out September, 1864.

Greene, James Brown, age 31, volunteer, May, 1864, one hundred days, One Hundred and Forty-eighth regiment, company G, private, attained rank of sergeant.

Gregg, Levi.

Greenwood, Frank, age 16, volunteer, May, 1864, one hundred days, One Hundred and Forty-eighth regiment, company G

Guilinger, Michael, age 16, volunteer, January 22, 1864, three years, Ninety-second regiment, company F, private, served one and one-half years, honorably discharged 1865.

Guilinger, Thomas, age 44, volunteer, May, 1864, one hundred days, One Hundred and Forty-eighth regiment, company B, private.

Guilinger, Jacob H., age 37, volunteer, May, 1864, one hundred days, One Hundred and Forty-eighth regiment, company G, private, attained rank of corporal.

Haight, Charles C., age 21, volunteer, August 26, 1861, three years, Sixth Virginia regiment, company G, sergeant, served three years, mustered out.

Haight, George Washington, age 19, volunteer, May, 1862, thirteen months, One Hundred and Eighty-fifth regiment, company F, private, mustered out 1862, at Bermuda Hundred.

Hall, Eli Worthington, age 17, substitute, May, 1864, one hundred days, One Hundred and Forty-eighth regiment, company G, private, served six weeks, died July 6, 1864, at Bermuda Hundred.

Hall, Oscar, age 14, volunteer, September 1, 1862, three years, Ninety-seventh regiment, company A, private, served five months, died January, 1863, in hospital, Tennessee.

Haynes, Alfred, age 16, substitute, May, 1864, one hundred days, One Hundred and Forty-eighth regiment, company G, private, served four months, mustered out September, 1864.

Hays, Preston G., age 19, volunteer, May, 1864, one hundred days, One Hundred and Forty-eighth, regiment, company G, private, served four months, mustered out September, 1864.

Hazel, Frederick, age 18, volunteer, January 18, 1864, three years, First cavalry, company L, private, served one year and four months, honorably discharged May 31, 1865.

Higgins, Thomas Neely, age 33, May, 1864, one hundred days, One Hundred and Forty-eighth regiment, company G, private, served four months, mustered out, September 1864.

Hill, Addison, age 18, volunteer, November, 1861, three years, Seventy-seventh regiment, company B, private, served two years, mustered out December, 1863, reenlistment, volunteer, 1864, three years, Seventy-seventh regiment, company B, private.

Hill, Cornelius, age 41, volunteer, one hundred days, One Hundred and Forty-eighth regiment, company B, private, died July 19, 1864, of chronic diarrhœa, at Bermuda Hundred.

Hill, William Wallace, age 18, volunteer, October, 1861, three years,

Seventy-seventh regiment, company B, private, one battle, served one and one-half years, died May 3, 1863, of measles, at Alton, Illinois.

Hill, Henry McKibben, age 23, volunteer, October 22, 1862, three years, Seventy-seventh regiment, company B, private.

Hutchinson, Charles, volunteer, Thirty-sixth regiment, company E, private.

Hughes, David D., age 16, volunteer, July 18, 1861, three years, Thirty-ninth regiment, company B, private, served four years, mustered out July 9, 1865, reenlisted as a veteran.

Jobes, John, volunteer, May, 1864, one hundred days, One Hundred and Forty-eighth regiment, company B, private, died.

Jobes, Carby, age 37, drafted March 23, 1865, one year, Thirty-ninth regiment, company B, private, served four months, mustered out July 9, 1865.

Johnson, E. A., First Virginia regiment.

Johnson, A. F., Fourteenth Virginia regiment.

Lang, Ebenezer, age 17, volunteer, May, 1864, one hundred days, One Hundred and Forty-eighth regiment, company G, private, served four months, mustered out September, 1864.

Lang, William, age 20, volunteer, August 24, 1861, three years, Sixth Virginia regiment, company G, private, served three years, mustered out 1864.

Larkins, Elias, First cavalry, company L.

Leonard, Augustus, age 34, volunteer, May, 1864, one hundred days, One Hundred and Forty-eighth regiment, company G, first lieutenant, served four months, mustered out September, 1864.

Little, Arthur B., volunteer, October 25, 1862, three years, Seventh cavalry, company H, corporal, attained the rank of sergeant, served three years, mustered out July 4, 1865.

Little, Thomas O., age 22, volunteer, 1861, three years, First cavalry, company L, private, served three years, honorably discharged, reenlistment, volunteer, 1864, three years, First cavalry, company L, private.

Matheny, John, Seventh cavalry, company H.

Manley, Bryan, First Virginia artillery, company C.

Mathers, John, age 38, volunteer, 1861, three years, Sixty-third regiment, company G, private, served nine months, honorably discharged in 1862, reenlistment, substitute, private.

Mathers, Alexander, age 21, volunteer, September, 1861, three years, Seventy-fifth regiment, company D, private, served two years, honorably discharged September, 1863, for disability.

Mathers, Matthew, age 21, volunteer, January, 1865, one year, First cavalry, company L, private.

Mathers, Joseph, age 17, volunteer, January, 1865, one year, First cavalry, company L, private.

Matthews, David, volunteer, Seventy-seventh regiment, company D, private.

Matthews, Edward, Seventy-seventh regiment, company G, private, died April 27, 1862, near Cincinnati.

McDaniels, J.

McCoy, Thomas A., age 26, volunteer, May, 1864, one hundred days, One Hundred and Forty-eighth regiment, company B, private, served four months, mustered out September, 1864.

McCallister, Charles, Eighteenth regiment.

McElfresh.

McElhinney, Joseph M., volunteer, May, 1864, One Hundred and Forty-eighth regiment, company G, captain, served four months, mustered out September, 1864.

McIntire, Fidellus, age 32, volunteer, August 11, 1862, three years, Ninety-second regiment, company F, private, served three years, mustered out June 15, 1865.

McLain.

McPeak, Jasper, volunteer, 1862, three years, Ninety-second regiment, company F, private, served one year and eight months, died April 19, 1863, at Carthage, Tennessee, of fever.

McVey, Thomas Jett, age 18, volunteer, November 14, 1861, three years, Seventy-seventh regiment, company B, private, taken prisoner at Shiloh and not heard from since

Middleswartz, H. F., volunteer, July, 1862, three years, Ninety-second regiment, company F, first lieutenant, attained the rank of captain, served three years, mustered out June 19, 1865

Middleswartz, George W., age 23, volunteer, July 22, 1861, three years, Thirty-ninth regiment, company B, private, served four years, mustered out July 9, 1865, reenlisted as a veteran.

Middleswartz, H. F., age 22, volunteer, July 22, 1861, three years, Thirty-ninth regiment, company B, private, served four years, mustered out July 9, 1865, reenlisted as a veteran.

Middleswartz, N., age 22, volunteer, May, 1864, one hundred days, One Hundred and Forty-eighth regiment, company B, private, served four months, mustered out September, 1864.

Miller, Greenbury, drafted, spring of 1865.

Moor, Abijah, age 22, volunteer, October 23, 1861, three years, Seventy-fifth regiment, company B, private, served three years and two months, mustered out December, 1864.

Newlen, Henry, age 30, volunteer, November 26, 1861, three years, Seventy-seventh regiment, company G, private, served three years, mustered out December 23, 1864.

Newlen, David, age 27, 1864, one hundred days, One Hundred and Forty-eighth regiment, company G, private.

Newlen, Martin, age 24, volunteer, November 26, 1861, three years, Seventy-seventh regiment, company G, private.

Nine, George, Fourth Virginia cavalry, company G.

Newlen, Ira, age 17, volunteer, November 26, 1861, three years, Seventy-seventh regiment, company G, private, mustered out December, 1863, reenlistment, volunteer, December, 1863, three years, Seventy-seventh regiment, company G, private.

Noland, Stephen, age 33, volunteer, May, 1864, one hundred days, One Hundred and Forty-eighth regiment, company G.

Nine, Jacob.

Noland, Augustus, age 27, volunteer, May, 1864, one hundred days, One Hundred and Forty-eighth regiment, company G.

Nine, Lewis, volunteer, Thirty-ninth regiment, company B, private, killed at New Madrid.

Noland, Johnston, age 24, volunteer, May, 1864, one hundred days, One Hundred and Forty-eighth regiment, company G.

Noland, Justus, age 21, volunteer, 1862, three years, Seventh cavalry, company H, private, served one year and eight months, died March, 1864, at Camp Nelson, of small-pox.

Nolan, Philip.

Osborn, Joseph, Eighteenth regiment, company F.

O'Blenas, Henry, age 19, volunteer, May 28, 1862, three months, Eighty-fifth regiment, company F, corporal, mustered out, reenlistment, volunteer, May, 1864, one hundred days, One Hundred and Forty-eighth regiment, company G, sergeant, served four months, mustered out September 1864

O'Blenas, Abram Guyton, age 18, volunteer, May 28, 1862, three months, Eighty-fifth regiment, company F, private, mustered out, second enlistment, age 19, volunteer, 1863, six months, One Hundred and Twenty-ninth regiment, company F, private, mustered out March 11, 1864, third enlistment, age 20, volunteer, 1864, one hundred days, One Hundred and Forty-eighth regiment, company G, private, served four months, mustered out September, 1864.

O'Neil, Gilbert, age 25, volunteer, September, 1861, three years, First cavalry, company L, private, served two years, honorably discharged in 1863 by reason of deafness, reenlistment, age 29, volunteer, May, 1864, one hundred days, One Hundred and Forty-eighth regiment, company G, private, four months, mustered out September, 1864.

O'Shurn, Ezra J., age 18, volunteer, September 16, 1861, three years, Eighteenth regiment, company F, private, served three years and two months, honorably discharged November 9, 1864, veteran enlistment, November, 1864, three years, Eighteenth regiment, companies F and B, private, served five months, honorably discharged April, 1865.

Paxton, Martin, Thirty-sixth regiment, private.

Paxton John L., First Virginia light artillery, private.

Peckens, Austin W., age 23, volunteer, August, 1861, three years, Eighteenth regiment, company F, private, served one year and eight months, honorably discharged April, 1863, on account of wound in right breast, received at Stone River.

Peckens, H. Sheppard, age 20, volunteer, August, 1861, three years, Eighteenth regiment, company F, private, served three years and three months, mustered out November 9, 1864, reenlistment, substitute, one year, Eighteenth regiment, company F, private, attained rank of corporal, mustered out October 9, 1865.

Peckens, George Conner, age 18, volunteer, 1861, three years, Eighteenth regiment, company F, private, served nine months, honorably discharged in 1862 for disability.

Pegg, Henry, age 20, volunteer, November 18, 1861, three years, Seventy-seventh regiment, company G, private.

Petty, Henry Wesley, age 26, May, 1864, one hundred days, One Hundred and Forty-eighth regiment, company B, private.

Pryor, Nathan, age 21, volunteer, September, 1861, three years, First cavalry, company L, private, served two years and four months, mustered out January, 1864, reenlistment, volunteer, January, 1864, three years, First cavalry, company L, private.

Reese, William, age 21, volunteer, September, 1861, three years, First cavalry, company L, private, served three years, mustered out in 1864.

Reynolds, Daniel S., age 42, volunteer, 1861, three years, Thirty-ninth regiment, company B, private, mustered out, reenlisted as a veteran.

Reynolds, Charles Wesley, age 16, volunteer, July, 1861, three years, Thirty-ninth regiment, company B, private, reenlisted as a veteran.

Reynolds, Theodore M., age 15, volunteer, February 18, 1862, three years, Sixty-third regiment, company G, drummer, honorably discharged, second enlistment, age 17, substitute, 1864, one hundred days, One Hundred and Forty-eighth regiment, company G, private, served four months, mustered out September, 1864, third enlistment, age 18, volunteer, March 10, 1865, one year, One Hundred and Ninety-sixth regiment, company F, served three months, honorably discharged June 14, 1865.

Ritchie, Isaac, age 27, drafted, March 23, 1865, one year, Thirty-ninth regiment, company I, private, served four months, honorably discharged July, 1865.

Ritchie, St. Clair, age 17, volunteer, September 1, 1861, three years, First Virginia light artillery, company C, private, served three years and nine months, mustered out June 28, 1865 reenlisted as a veteran.

Ritchie, William, age 18, volunteer, January 21, 1864, three years, First Virginia light artillery, company C, private, served eighteen months, mustered out June 28, 1864.

Ross, Welland, Thirty-third regiment, company F.

Rowland, Rufus Henry, age 20, volunteer, August 10, 1862, three years, Ninety-second regiment, company F, drummer, served three years, mustered out June 10, 1865.

Rowland, Robert S., age 20, volunteer, August 28, 1862, three years, Seventh cavalry, company H, private, served three years, mustered out June 10, 1865.

Scott, Maxwell, age 49, volunteer, October, 1861, three years, Sixty-third regiment, company F, private, served eight months, honorably discharged July 5, 1862, for disability.

Seacord, D.

Seevers, Daniel D, age 44, volunteer, May, 1864, one hundred days, One Hundred and Forty-eighth regiment, company G, private.

Seevers, Richard D., age 40, volunteer, July 22, 1861, three years, Thirty-ninth regiment, company B, private, served thirteen months, honorably discharged August, 1862, for disability, reenlistment, volunteer, January 11, 1864, three years, Thirty-sixth regiment, company K, private, served ten months, died November 15, 1864, of wound received at Winchester, July 24, 1864.

Seevers, Abram, age 42, volunteer, May, 1864, one hundred days, One Hundred and Forty-eighth regiment, company G, private, served one and a half years.

Seevers, James, age 16, volunteer, March, 1862, three years, Third Virginia cavalry, company H, private, mustered out.

Seevers, William James, age 22, volunteer, February 9, 1864, three years, Thirty-ninth regiment, company B, private, served eighteen months, mustered out July 9, 1865.

Sexton, Linsey, Second Virginia cavalry, company D.

Shreves, Thomas, age 36, volunteer, March, 1864, three years, Thirty-sixth regiment, company K.

Shreves, James Wesley, age 19, volunteer March, 1864, three years, Thirty-sixth regiment, company F.

Smith, J. Higgins, age 22, volunteer, 1861, three years, First cavalry, company L, private.

Smith, James Keith, age 43, volunteer, May, 1864, one hundred days, One Hundred and Forty-eighth regiment, company G.

Smith, George W., age 37, volunteer, May, 1864, one hundred days, One Hundred and Forty-eighth regiment, company G.

Smith, Samuel Thomas, age 34, volunteer, May, 1864, one hundred days, One Hundred and Forty-eighth regiment, company G.

Smith, S. R., Ninth cavalry.

Smith, George, age 30, drafted, March 23, 1865, one year.

Smith, Henry, age 21, volunteer, 1864, three years, First cavalry, company L, private, served one year and four months, honorably discharged July 4, 1865.

Smith Jonathan, Seventy-seventh regiment, died.

Stewart, John, Thirty-sixth regiment, company B.

Stewart, J. H., age 32, volunteer, September, 1861, three years, First cavalry, company L, private, served three years, mustered out 1864.

Stewart, Ira, age 19, volunteer, September, 1861, three years, First cavalry, company L, private, served four months, died January, 1862, of typhoid fever.

Thomas, George W., age 16, volunteer, August 12, 1863, six months, One Hundred and Twenty-ninth regiment, company D, private, served eight months, mustered out April, 1864, reenlistment age 17, volunteer, August 12, 1864, one year, One Hundred and Seventy-ninth regiment, company I, private, served nine months, mustered out June 18, 1865.

Thompson, Edgar, Ninety-second regiment, company K, private, died.

Thompson, S., age 21, volunteer, 1862, three years, Ninety-second regiment, company F, private, served three years, mustered out 1864, served last two years in invalid corps.

Tidd, George Washington, age 18, volunteer, August 7, 1862, three years, Ninety-second regiment, company F, private, served two years and nine months, mustered out June 10, 1865.

Tidd, Charles Wesley, age 17, volunteer, August 18, 1863, six months, Fourth Virginia cavalry, company G, private, served four months, died December 17, 1863, at Clarksburgh, Virginia, of typhoid fever.

Turner, Benjamin Stokely age 18, First cavalry, company L.

Turner, William Parker, age 16, volunteer, September 26, 1874, one year, First cavalry, company H, private, served eight months, honorably discharged 1865.

Tuttle, One Hundred and Forty-eighth regiment.

Unger, Jacob, Ninety-second regiment, company F.

Vanway, Moses, age 24, volunteer, September, 1863, three years, First Virginia light artillery, died.

Vanway, James, age 37, volunteer, November 9, 1861, three years, Seventy-seventh regiment, company G, private, served three years, mustered out, 1864.

Vanway, William, age 36, drafted, March 23, 1865, one year, Thirty-ninth regiment, company B, private, served four months, honorably discharged July 9, 1865.

Vanway, Isaac, age 23, Ninety-second regiment, company F, private, died April, 1863.

Vanway, Thomas Mills, age 21, volunteer, 1861, three years Seventy-seventh regiment, company G, private.

Ward, Martin, volunteer, Seventy-seventh regiment, company E, private, in prison at Tyler, Texas, died July 8, 1864.

West, Stephen A., age 22, volunteer, November 29, 1861, three years, Seventy-seventh regiment, company D, private, served three years, mustered out December 11, 1864, reenlistment, age 25, substitute, March 28, 1865, one year, Eighteenth regiment, company C, private.

Wetzel, James, One Hundred and Twenty-fifth regiment, died.

Whitsel, James, One Hundred and Twenty-fifth regiment, died.

Wetzel, Joseph.

Wheeler, Jesse, age 46, volunteer, May, 1864, one hundred days, One Hundred and Forty-eighth regiment.

Wheeler, John, age 21, volunteer, September 1, 1861, three years, First light artillery, company K, private, served two years and six months, honorably discharged, enlisted as a veteran, volunteer, 1864, three years, First light artillery, company K, private.

Wheeler, Lewis, age 20, volunteer, September, 1861, three years, First light artillery, company K, private, reenlisted as a veteran, volunteer, 1864, three years, First light artillery, company K, private.

Whiston, Silas Adkins, age 24, volunteer, 1862, three years, Seventh cavalry, company H, private, served three years, mustered out July 4, 1865.

White, Walter Cole, age 23, volunteer, May, 1864, one hundred days, One Hundred and Forty-eighth regiment, company G, orderly sergeant.

Williams, Sylvester, age 16, volunteer, March, 1863, three years, Seventh Virginia, company D, died.

Williamson, James, age 24, volunteer, October 23, 1861, three years, Seventy-fifth regiment, company B, private, served three years and three months, mustered out December 12, 1864.

Wilson, William, age 29, volunteer, May, 1864, one hundred days, One Hundred and Forty-eighth regiment, company G, private.

Wood, Soranus Shaw, age 25, volunteer, September 1, 1862, three years, Seventh cavalry, company H, corporal, attained sergeant, served two years and nine months, mustered out June 12, 1865.

Wood, Joseph E., volunteer, May, 1864, one hundred days, One Hundred and Forty-eighth regiment, company G, corporal, mustered out in September, 1864.

Wood, John C., age 21, volunteer, May, 1862, three years, Eighty-fifth regiment, company F, private, reenlistment, volunteer, May, 1864, one hundred days, One Hundred and Forty-eighth regiment, company G, second lieutenant, served three months, mustered out in September, 1864.

Wood, William Ware, age 17, volunteer, 1861, three years, First cavalry, company L, private, died of chronic diarrhoea in 1864.

Woodward, John, age 36, volunteer, May, 1864, one hundred days, One Hundred and Forty-eighth regiment, company B, private.

Wright, Luther.

Zanilley, B. F., Thirty-ninth regiment, company B, died.

Zanilley, John, Thirty-ninth regiment, company B.

RECAPITULATION.

Buell's battery	5
Huntington's battery	4
Second Arkansas light artillery	1
Battery K, Second Ohio heavy artillery	1
First Ohio cavalry	18
Fourth Virginia cavalry	2
First Virginia light artillery	2
De Beck's battery	3
Seventh Ohio	10
Second Virginia cavalry	1
Third Virginia cavalry	1
Ninth Ohio cavalry	1
One Hundred and Forty-eighth Ohio National guard	58
Seventy-seventh Ohio	16
Thirty-ninth Ohio	19
Ninety-second Ohio	15
Sixth Virginia infantry	5
Eighteenth Ohio (three years)	10
One Hundred and Seventy-fifth Ohio	2
One Hundred and Twenty-ninth Ohio	6
Thirty-sixth Ohio	8
Sixty-third Ohio	4
Seventy-fifth Ohio	3
Eighty-fifth Ohio	4
One Hundred and Twenty-fifth Ohio	2

And one each in the Twenty-fifth Ohio, One Hundred and Sixteenth Ohio, One Hundred and Eighty-fifth Ohio, One Hundred and Seventy-ninth Ohio, One Hundred and Ninety-sixth Ohio, Forty-third Ohio, Ninety-Seventh Ohio, Thirty-third Ohio, First Virginia, Seventh Virginia, Eleventh Virginia, Fourteenth Virginia, and nine not designated, in all......................... 21

Total number of soldiers 211

Died. 32

PALMER TOWNSHIP.

Agin, William, volunteer, May, 1864, one hundred days, One Hundred and Forty-eighth regiment, company F, served four months, mustered out September, 1864.

Berfield, Humphrey, age 19, volunteer, October 19, 1861, three years, Seventy-seventh regiment, company D, private, attained rank of orderly sergeant, mustered out December 11, 1864, on detached service part of time.

Beswick, George, volunteer, three years, Sixty-third regiment, company H, private.

Biggins, Brazil B., age 27, volunteer, November, 1862, three years, Sixty-third regiment, company H, private, wounded at Corinth, reenlisted.

Biggins, James H., age 15, volunteer, August, 1862, three years, Ninety-second regiment, company G, private, died of measles March 14, 1863.

Biggins, Thomas W., age 42, volunteer, November, 1862, three years, Sixty-third regiment, company H, private, died of fever December, 1864.

Brown, Andrews, age 36, volunteer, Seventy-seventh regiment, company B, private, killed in battle of Shiloh April 6, 1862.

Brown, Silas A., age 23, volunteer, May, 1864, one hundred days, One Hundred and Forty-eighth regiment, company I, private, mustered out September, 1864, sick most of time.

Brown, Charles A., age 27, volunteer, August 7, 1862, three years, Ninety-second regiment, company G, third sergeant, attained rank of first lieutenant, mustered out June 10, 1865, wounded at Chickamauga, captured and parolled.

Brown, John A., age 18, volunteer, September 5, 1864, three years, Eighteenth regiment, company F, private, attained rank of corporal, served one year, mustered out October 9, 1865, sick most of time.

Camp, David H., age 22, volunteer, November 16, 1861, three years, Sixty-third regiment, company F, private, attained rank of orderly sergeant, mustered out July 8, 1865, reenlisted as a veteran.

Camp, George L., age 27, volunteer, August 15, 1862, three years,

Ninety-second regiment, company G, private, served three years, mustered out June 8, 1865.

Carter, John G., Eighteenth regiment, company F

Campbell, Harvey, age 33, volunteer, May, 1864, one hundred days, One Hundred and Forty-eighth regiment, company F, corporal, served four months, mustered out September, 1864, detailed for clerk service, also orderly and commissary.

Cooper, Armine R., age 21, volunteer, August 5, 1861, three years, Thirty-sixth regiment, company F, private, served four years, mustered out July 27, 1865, reenlisted as a veteran.

Danley, Joseph, age 39, volunteer, May, 1864, one hundred days, One Hunderd and Forty-eighth regiment, company I, private, died of measles June, 1864.

Danley, William E., volunteer, May, 1864, one hundred days, One Hundred and Forty-eighth regiment, company I, private, served four months, mustered out September, 1864.

Danley, Harvey, age 22, volunteer, May, 1864, one hundred days, One Hundred and Forty-eighth regiment, company I, private, served four months, mustered out September, 1864.

Danley, James, volunteer, May, 1864, one hundred days, One Hundred and Forty-eighth regiment, company I, private.

Danley, Joel N., age 25, volunteer, August 15, 1862, three years, Ninety-second regiment, company D, corporal, served seven months, died at Carthage, of measles, March 20, 1863.

Danley, John W., age 32, volunteer, January 1, 1864, three years, First cavalry, company L, private, mustered out September, 1865.

Dunsmore, Carmi S., volunteer, Ninety-second regiment, company G.

Ferguson, Daniel, age 27, volunteer, October, 1861, three years, Seventy-seventh regiment, company D, private, reenlisted as a veteran.

Ferguson, Andrew, age 19, volunteer, May, 1864, one hundred days, One Hundred and Forty-eighth regiment, company F, private, served four months, mustered out September, 1865.

Fowler, L. R., volunteer, Fourth Virginia, company D, private.

Gard, James H., age 35, volunteer, August 1, 1863, six months, Fourth Virginia cavalry, company D, private, served seven months, mustered out March 7, 1864

Guy, Hezekiah F., age 19, volunteer, October 28, 1863, One Hundred and Twenty-second regiment, company C, corporal, served one year and eight months, mustered out June 26, 1865, sick with smallpox and wounded at Winchester.

Hildebrand, Jesse, age 39, volunteer, October, 1862, three years, Seventy-seventh regiment, company A, second lieutenant, served one year and three months, resigned January 23, 1864.

Hemphill, Orson, age 21, volunteer, May, 1864, one hundred days, One Hundred and Forty-eighth regiment, company I, corporal, served four months, mustered out September, 1864.

Huston, John P., volunteer, May, 1864, one hundred days, One Hundred and Forty-eighth regiment, company F, private.

Hoon, James P., age 34, volunteer, May, 1864, one hundred days, One Hundred and Forty-eighth regiment, company I, private, served four months, mustered out September, 1864.

Jenkins, Samuel, volunteer, Second Virginia cavalry, company F.

Lake, George, age 18, volunteer, June, 1862, three months, Eightyseventh regiment, private, served three months, mustered out September 20, 1862, reenlistment, 1863, three years, Second heavy artillery, private.

Lazure, E. E., age 21, volunteer, October 23, 1861, three years, Second Virginia cavalry, company F, private, served three years and nine months, mustered out July 4, 1865, reenlisted as a veteran.

Morris, Thomas C., age 17, volunteer, February 7, 1865, Thirtysixth regiment, company H, private, honorably discharged July 27, 1865, sick most of the time with camp disease.

Morris, Jonathan G., age 15, volunteer, October 29, 1861, three years, Sixty-third regiment, company G, private, served three months, died of measles January 23, 1862.

Morris, John, volunteer, Seventy-seventh regiment, company B, private.

Morris, Benajah K., volunteer, Ninety-second regiment company G, private.

Morris, William, age 34, volunteer, May, 1864, one hundred days, One Hundred and Forty-eighth regiment, company I, private, served four months, mustered out September, 1864.

Morris, R. S., age 22, substitute, August 13, 1862, three years, Ninety-second regiment, company G, private, served three years, mustered out July 1, 1865, transferred to veteran reserve corps.

Murdough, J. G., age 30, volunteer, May, 1864, one hundred days,

One Hundred and Forty-eighth regiment, company F, private, served four months, mustered out September, 1864.

Murdough, Charles J., age 22, volunteer, August, 1862, three years, Ninety-second regiment, company G, private, served one year and eight months, died April 29, 1864.

Nulton, Henry, age 26, volunteer, 1861, three years, Seventy-seventh regiment, company B, private.

Palmer, James D., age 18, volunteer, February 11, 1864, three years, Sixty-third regiment, company F, private, died March 18, 1864, of measles.

Perry, Armstrong H., age 23, volunteer, August 12, 1861, three years, Second Virginia cavalry, company F, private, served one year and five months, honorably discharged January, 1863, for disability.

Payne, Joseph D., age 25, volunteer, May, 1864, one hundred days, One Hundred and Forty-eighth regiment, company I, private, served four months, mustered out September, 1864

Payne, Francis M., age 21, volunteer, May, 1864, one hundred days, One Hundred and Forty-eighth regiment, company I, private, served four months, mustered out September, 1864.

Pugh, John A., age 17, volunteer, February 9, 1865, Thirty-Sixth regiment, company H, private, served five months, mustered out July 27, 1865.

Pugh, Henry L., volunteer, 1861, three years, Seventy-seventh regiment, companies F and D, fifer, attained rank of captain, mustered out March 8, 1865

Pugh, Austin, age 34, volunteer, May, 1864, one hundred days, One Hundred and Forty-eighth regiment, company F, private, served four months, mustered out September, 1864.

Reed, Joseph, age 19, volunteer, August, 1862, three years, Ninetysecond regiment, company F, private, served three years, mustered out June, 1865, wounded at Chickamauga, and afterwards on various detached service.

Skipton, William, age 33, May, 1864, one hundred days, One Hundred and Forty-eighth regiment, company I, corporal, served four months, mustered out September, 1864.

Sheets, Hiram, died.

Smith, Henry, volunteer, May, 1864, one hundred days, One Hundred and Forty-eighth regiment, company I.

Trotter, James, volunteer, May, 1864, one hundred days, One Hundred and Forty-eighth regiment, company F, private.

Trotter, Richard, volunteer, May, 1864, one hundred days, One Hundred and Forty-eighth regiment, company F, private.

RECAPITULATION.

Second heavy artillery	1
Second Virginia cavalry	3
Fourth Virginia cavalry	1
First Ohio cavalry	1
One Hundred and Forty-eighth Ohio National guard	20
Ninety-second Ohio	9
Seventy-seventh Ohio	7
Sixty-third Ohio	6
Thirty-sixth Ohio	3
Eighteenth Ohio (three years)	2
One each in Eighty-seventh Ohio, One Hundred and Twenty-second Ohio, Fourth Virginia, not designated one, in all	4
Total number of soldiers	55
Died	9

SALEM TOWNSHIP.

Alden, Jonathan, age 39, volunteer, 1862, three years, Ninety-second regiment, company H, private, served three years, mustered out June 10, 1865.

Alden, Benjamin G., volunteer, 1862, three years, Ninety-second regiment, company H, private, attained the rank of second lieutenant, resigned October 14, 1863.

Alden, Philetus, volunteer, 1862, three years, Ninety-second regiment, company H, private, served three years, mustered out June 10, 1865.

Baesshar, Christian, Thirty-ninth regiment, company F.

Bartell, Frederick, age 23, volunteer, 1862, three years, Seventh cavalry, company H.

Bay, Jacob F., age 21, volunteer, October 12, 1862, three years, Seventh cavalry, company H, blacksmith, served two years and nine months, mustered out July 4, 1865.

Best, John, age 20, volunteer, April 13, 1864, three years, Thirtysixth regiment, company A, private, in six battles, served one year and three months, mustered out July 27, 1865.

Boye, Theodore, volunteer, May 28, 1862, three months, Eighty-seventh regiment, company A, corporal, in one battle, served four months, mustered out October 1, 1862.

Boye, August, volunteer, May 28, 1862, three months, Eighty-fifth regiment, private, served four months, mustered out October 1, 1862.

Brown, Jacob, age 20, volunteer, August 15, 1864, one year, One Hundred and Seventy-fourth regiment, company D, private, served ten months, mustered out June 28, 1865.

Chandler, Isaac, age 17, volunteer, August 24, 1864, one year, One Hundred and Seventy-fourth regiment, company D, private, served ten months, died June 30, 1865, of intermittent fever, at Charlotte, North Carolina.

Chapman, Sidney D., age 22, volunteer, 1862, three years, Ninety-second regiment, company H, private, attained the rank of corporal, served one year, died November 19, 1863, mortally wounded at Chickamauga September 19, 1863.

Close, Allen, age 22, volunteer, August 12, 1861, three years, Thirty-sixth regiment, company G, private, served three years, mustered out in 1864.

Clay, Benjamin F., volunteer, July 29, 1861, three years, Thirty-sixth regiment, company A, private.

Clay, Daniel, volunteer, 1863, six months, Fourth cavalry, company C, private.

Crawford, William, volunteer, 1862, three years, Seventh cavalry, company H, private, served three years, mustered out with regiment.

Crawford, John, volunteer, August, 1861, three years, Thirty-sixth regiment, company G, private, served three years, reenlistment, December, 1863, three years, Thirty-sixth regiment, company G, private, served one year, mustered out with regiment.

Dauber, Frederick, age 22, volunteer, 1862, three years, Seventh cavalry, company H, attained the rank of corporal, served three years, mustered out July 4, 1865.

Deitz, Frederick, age 21, volunteer, 1863, six months, Fourth cavalry, company C, sergeant, mustered out, reenlistment, age 22, volunteer, 1864, three years, Thirteenth cavalry, company C, second lieutenant, mustered out August 10, 1865.

Delong, Charles, age 30, volunteer, August 12, 1861, three years, Thirty-sixth regiment, company G, private, served four years, mustered out July 27, 1865, reenlisted as a veteran.

Delong, Charles R., Thirty-sixth regiment, company G.

Dice, John.

Dillon, William Henry, age 17, volunteer, October 31, 1861, three years, Seventy-seventh regiment, companies A and G, private, served five months, died May 8, 1862, at Shiloh, of homesickness.

Doan, Richard, age 37, volunteer, August, 1863, three years, Second heavy artillery, company K, private, mustered out in 1865, transferred to invalid corps.

Doan, Josiah M., age 25, volunteer, 1861, three years, Thirty-sixth regiment, company G, private, served four years, mustered out July 27, 1865, reenlisted as a veteran.

Doan, Archibald S., age 23, volunteer, 1861, three years, Twelfth regiment, company D, private, attained the rank of sergeant, served three years, mustered out in 1864.

Doan, David C., volunteer, 1862, three years, Ninety-second regiment, company H, private, served three years, mustered out in 1865.

Doan, Edwin T., age 20, volunteer, May 28, 1862, three months, Eighty-seventh regiment, company A, private, in one battle, served four months, mustered out October 1, 1862, reenlistment, age 21, volunteer, August, 1863, three years, Second heavy artillery, company K, sergeant, attained the rank of orderly sergeant, served two years, mustered out August 23, 1865.

Doud, Conner, volunteer, 1862, three years, Thirty-sixth regiment, company G, private, served three years, mustered out July 27, 1865.

Ewing.

Fantz, Frederick, 1862, three years, Ninth cavalry, company B, private, served three years, mustered out July 20, 1865.

Feldner, Henry, age 20, volunteer, 1861, three years, Sixty-third regiment, company G, private, served four years, mustered out July 8, 1865.

Dressler, Michael.

Feldnor, Samuel, age 17, volunteer, September 9, 1862, three years, Sixty-third regiment, company G, private, served three years, mustered out July 8, 1865.

Fenn, Benjamin, volunteer, three years, Thirty-sixth regiment, company G.

Fisher, Thomas, age 21, volunteer, April 17, 1861, three months, Eighteenth regiment, company B, private, served four months, mus-

tered out August 28, 1861, badly wounded at South Mountain, second enlistment, 1861, three years, Thirty-sixth regiment, company G, private, honorably discharged 1862, third enlistment, 1863, three years, Second heavy artillery, company K, sergeant, attained rank of second lieutenant, served two years, mustered out in 1865.

Flanders, Alden, age 23, volunteer, August, 1863, six months, Seventh cavalry, company C, fifer, served eight months, mustered out in March, 1864.

Fulton, Robert, age 20, volunteer, August, 1862, three years, Seventh cavalry, company H, private, attained rank of corporal, served three years, mustered out July 3, 1865.

Gibson, Henry J., volunteer, Thirty-sixth regiment, company G, private, died September 12, 1862, of wounds received at battle of South Mountain.

Goodwill, Jeremiah A., volunteer, Ninety-second regiment, company F, died.

Gould, Luther W., age 17, volunteer, July, 1861, three years, Thirty-sixth regiment, company G, private, served six months, died January 21, 1862, of measles and pneumonia.

Gould, Daniel W., age 24, 1862, three years, Ninth cavalry, company B, three years, honorably discharged in 1865.

Gray, James C., age 21, volunteer, May 27, 1862, three months, Eighty-seventh regiment, company A, private, in one battle, served four months, mustered out 1862, reenlistment, 1863, six months, Fourth independent battalion cavalry, company C, corporal, served eight months, mustered out in March, 1864.

Gray, John, volunteer, Seventy-seventh regiment, company A, died.

Gray, Thomas, volunteer, January, 1864, three years, Twelfth regiment, company D, private, died in Andersonville prison.

Guitteau, Hamilton H., age 25, volunteer, 1862, three years, Ninety-second regiment, company H, private, attained rank of sergeant, three years, mustered out June 10, 1865.

Hayt, Theodore, age 31, volunteer, July 29, 1861, three years, Thirty-sixth regiment, company A, sergeant, served two years, honorably discharged November, 1863.

Hallet, Howard, Twenty-fifth regiment, company I.

Hallet, Asa Davis, age 18, volunteer, 1861, three years, Forty-second regiment, company D, private, attained rank of corporal, mustered out at expiration of service.

Hardy, Andrew J., volunteer, 1862, three years, Seventh cavalry, company H, sergeant, attained rank of lieutenant, served three years, mustered out July 4, 1865.

Hardy, James M., volunteer, 1862, Seventh cavalry, company H, private, served three years, mustered out July 4, 1865.

Harris, Daniel, age 26, volunteer, 1862, three years, Seventh cavalry, company H, private, served three years, mustered out July 4, 1865.

Harth, Daniel, age 24, volunteer, 1861, three months, Sixteenth regiment, private, mustered out, second enlistment, volunteer, 1861, three years, Thirty-first regiment company K, private, served two years and six months, mustered out December 26, 1863, veteran enlistment, age 26, volunteer, 1863, three years, Thirty-first regiment, company K, private, served one year and six months, mustered out July 9, 1865.

Hazen, Charles D., age 24, volunteer, 1862, three years, Ninety-second regiment, company H, corporal, attained rank of sergeant, served three years, mustered out June 10, 1865.

Hazen, Stowell S., volunteer, 1861, three years, Twelfth regiment, company D, private, served one year, honorably discharged in 1862, disabled by wound received at Antietam, reenlistment, volunteer, 1863, three years, Second heavy artillery, company K, second lieutenant, attained rank of captain, resigned in 1865.

Hockingberry, Peter, volunteer, 1861, three years, Thirty-sixth regiment, company G, private.

Hockingberry, Oakley, volunteer, 1861, Thirty-sixth regiment, company G, private.

Hill, Irwin, volunteer, three years, Fourth cavalry, company C.

Hess, Jacob, volunteer, Sixty-third regiment, company I, honorably discharged.

Hoit, John A., age 27, volunteer, August, 1862, three years, Ninety-second regiment, company H, private, served three years, mustered out June 10, 1865.

Hoit, Nicholas G., age 18, volunteer, October 29, 1863, three years, Thirty-sixth regiment, company G, private, served one year and six months, died in April, 1865.

Howlan, Jesse, volunteer, Thirty-sixth regiment, company G, private, reenlisted, volunteer, Second Ohio heavy artillery, company K, private, mustered out with regiment.

Hunter, David C., age 24, volunteer, 1861, three years, Thirty-sixth regiment, company G, private, attained rank of sergeant, served four years, mustered out July 27, 1865, reenlisted as a veteran.

Happ, Zachariah, Second heavy artillery, company H, honorably discharged.

Hutchinson, W. H., volunteer, Seventy-seventh regiment, company K, honorably discharged.

Johnson, Henry W., volunteer, Ninety-second regiment, company H.

Kelly, Calvin V., age 18, September 3, 1864, one year, One Hundred and Seventy-ninth regiment, company F, private, served ten months, mustered out June 16, 1865.

Kyles, Frederick, three years, Thirty-sixth regiment, company G, private.

Lauer, John, volunteer, three years, Thirty-ninth regiment, company F, private.

Lenhardt, Henry, age 22, volunteer, Thirty-ninth regiment, company F, private, died December 1, 1862, of chronic diarrhœa, at Louisville, Missouri.

Lindamood, James, age 35, volunteer, August 8, 1862, three years, Ninety-second regiment, company K, private, served three years, mustered out June 10, 1865.

Lingo, Archelaus R., volunteer, three years, Twenty-fifth regiment, company I, sergeant, served four years, 1865, reenlisted as a veteran.

Lindner, Earnest, volunteer, August, 1861, three years, Thirty-sixth regiment, company G, lieutenant, attained rank of adjutant, served ten months, resigned June 28, 1862.

Lindner, Carl W., volunteer, May 28, 1862, three months, Eighty-fifth regiment, company F, private, served four months, mustered out October, 1862, reenlistment, volunteer, November, 1863, three years, Thirty-sixth regiment, company G, private, attained rank of corporal, served one year and eight months, mustered out July 27, 1865.

Magruder, John N., age 21, volunteer, three years, Thirty-six regiment, company G, private.

Magruder, Nahum W., age 18, volunteer.

Magruder, Asahel.

Marsh, William, age 18, volunteer, 1861, three years, Forty-second regiment, company D, private, served three years, mustered out, 1864.

Marsh, John, age 15, volunteer, August, 1863, six months, Fourth independent batallion cavalry, company C, private, served eight months, mustered out, March, 1864, reenlistment, 1864, one year, Twenty-third regiment, company G, private, mustered out 1865.

Matthews, John T., volunteer, June, 1861, three years, Third regiment, company C, private, attained rank of corporal, mustered out, wounded at Perryville, Kentucky, reenlistment, volunteer, 1864, three years, One Hundred and Ninety-third regiment, lieutenant, adjutant of regiment.

McCoy, Joshua, aged 20, volunteer, October 19, 1861, three years, Sixty-third regiment, company G, private, served two years, died August, 1863, of chronic diarrhœa at Memphis, Tennessee, transferred to gunboat service.

McKinsey—Thirty-six regiment, company H.

Moore, William H., age 37, volunteer, August 14, 1862, three years, Ninety-second regiment, company H, private, three years, mustered out June 10, 1865.

Moor, E. R., volunteer, 1861, three years, Seventy-seventh regiment, company D, second lieutenant, attained rank of first lieutenant, honorably discharged August 1, 1863.

Morgan, James Wheeler, age 24, volunteer, August, 1861, three years, Thirty-sixth regiment, company G, private, died November 5, 1861, of measles at Gallipolis.

Morgan, George Henry, age 22, volunteer, August, 1862, three years, Ninety-second regiment, company H, private, served three years, mustered out June 10, 1865.

Morse, Madison, age 51, volunteer, 1861, three years, Thirty-sixth regiment, company G, fifer, three years, mustered out 1864.

Morse, William Wallace, age 24, volunteer, 1861, three years, Twelfth regiment, company D, private, three years, died June 26, 1864, killed at the battle of Lynchburgh.

Morse, Wilbur Fisk, age 22, volunteer, April 17, 1861, three months, Eighteenth regiment, company D, private, served four months, mustered out August 28, 1861, reenlistment, volunteer, August, 1861, three years, Thirty-sixth regiment, company G, private, served three years, mustered out 1864.

Morse, Wilkinson M., age 20, volunteer, 1863, three years, Fifth Virginia cavalry, company G, private, served two years, mustered out in 1865.

Morse, Wayne, age 16, volunteer, March, 1865, one year, Thirty-sixth regiment, company G, private, honorably discharged in 1865.

Morse, Winslow W., age 18, May, 1864, one hundred days, One Hundred and Forty-eighth regiment, company A, private, served four months, mustered out September, 1864.

Munnel, George, age 20, volunteer, August, 1862, three years, Thirty-sixth regiment, company G, private, served one year, died September 20, 1863, of chronic diarrhœa, at Chattanooga.

Murdock, Churchill, age 20, volunteer, August, 1861, three years, Thirty-sixth regiment, company G, private, served three years, mustered out July 27, 1865.

Murdock, Andrew, Twenty-sixth regiment, company F.

Murdock, Lewis, age 18, volunteer, August, 1861, three years, Thirty-sixth regiment, company G, private, attained to rank of corporal, served four years, mustered out July 27, 1865.

Palmer, John A., volunteer, 1861, three years, Thirty-sixth regiment, company G, first sergeant, attained to rank of first lieutenant, resigned January 18, 1863.

Palmer, Jewett, jr., volunteer, August, 1861, three years, Thirty-sixth regiment, company G, captain, attained to rank of major, served three years and three months, resigned, November 29, 1864, reenlisted as veteran.

Payne, Orrin, volunteer, 1862, three months, Eighty-seventh regiment, company A, private, mustered out with regiment.

Perkins, Miles O., volunteer, 1864, three years, Thirty-sixth regiment, company G, private, mustered out July 27, 1865.

Pfaff, Christopher J., age 19, volunteer, September 1, 1862, three years, Seventh cavalry, company H, served three years, mustered out July 4, 1865.

Poland, Zimri, age 17, volunteer, February, 1864, three years, Thirty-sixth regiment, company G, private, served one year and six months, mustered out July 27, 1865.

Porter, Daniel, volunteer, August, 1862, three years, Ninety-second regiment, company H, private, served three years, mustered out with regiment.

Reese, Thomas, volunteer, three years, Thirty-sixth regiment, company G.

Roth, Henry, volunteer, Third regiment, company K.

Roth, Christian, Seventy-seventh regiment, company K.

Sankford, Franklin, age 16, volunteer, December 7, 1861, three years, Seventy-seventh regiment, company K, private, served eight months, honorably discharged, August 11, 1862, for disability.

Schofield, William, volunteer, January, 1864, three years, Twelfth regiment, company D, private, served one year, mustered out at end of war.

Schofield, Joseph C., age 18, volunteer, August, 1861, three years, Thirty-sixth regiment, company G, private, served four years, mustered out July 27, 1865.

Schofield, William A., age 18, volunteer, January, 1864, three years, Twelfth regiment, company D, private, served one year, mustered out at end of war.

Schofield, Charles M., age 20, volunteer, June, 1861, three years, Twelfth regiment, company D, private, attained to rank of sergeant, served three years, was in Andersonville prison eight months, reenlistment, volunteer, December, 1863, three years, Twelfth regiment, company D, first sergeant, served one year, mustered out with regiment.

Sherlick, Frederick, age 35, volunteer, August, 1862, three years, Ninety-second regiment, company H, private, served nine months, died April 7, 1863.

Smith, John, volunteer, Thirty-sixth regiment, company A.

Smith, Phillip, volunteer, Twenty-eighth regiment, company A.

Smith, Frederick, volunteer, One Hundred and Fifty-fifth regiment, company E.

Spears, John, age 18, volunteer, August, 1862, three years, Ninety-second regiment, company H, private, served one year, died October 14, 1863, of chronic diarrhœa.

Stanley, James, volunteer, August, 1861, three years, Thirty-sixth regiment, company G, first lieutenant, attained to rank of captain, served three years and three months, honorably discharged November 25, 1864, was in company B, Eighteenth Ohio volunteer infantry, three months

Stanley, Thomas, volunteer, August, 1861, three years, Thirty-sixth regiment, company G, private, attained to rank of sergeant, died, May 9, 1864, killed at Cloyd Mountain, West Virginia.

Stewart, Thomas R., volunteer, August, 1861, three years, Thirty-sixth regiment, company G, private, died October 21, 1862, of typhoid pneumonia.

Shaffer, Albert, Thirty-sixth regiment, company A.

Stickrod, Lewis, age 18, volunteer, August, 1861, three years, Thirty-sixth regiment, company G, private, served four years, mustered out July 27, 1865, reenlisted as a veteran, badly wounded.

Shaffer, James, Thirty-sixth regiment, company A.

Stickrod, Paul, age 16, volunteer, August, 1863, six months, Fourth cavalry, company C, private, served eight months, mustered out March 8, 1864, second enlistment, May, 1864, one hundred days, One Hundred and Forty-eighth regiment, served four months, mustered out September, 1864, third enlistment, 1865, one year, Eighteenth regiment, company E, private.

Smith, August, volunteer, One Hundred and Seventy-fourth regiment, company D.

Thomas, Rees, age 23, volunteer, 1861, three years, Third regiment, company C, private, served three years, mustered out in 1864.

Thomas, David, age 21, volunteer, May 28, 1862, three months, Eighty-seventh regiment, company A, private, served four months, mustered out October 1, 1862, second enlistment, age 22, volunteer, August, 1863, six months, Fourth independent battalion cavalry, company C, second lieutenant, served eight months, mustered out March, 1864, third enlistment, age 23, volunteer, March, 1864, three years, Thirteenth cavalry, company A, second lieutenant, attained the rank of captain, served one year and three months, mustered out August 10, 1865.

True, Melvin C., age 22, volunteer, August 12, 1861, three years, Thirty-sixth regiment, company G, private, attained the rank of orderly sergeant, served three years, mustered out in 1864.

True, Wilbur F., age 20, volunteer, August, 1862, three years, Ninety-second regiment, company H, private, served one year and six months, honorably discharged in 1864; while guarding a sutler's goods, a keg of tobacco fell on him and crippled him for life.

True, Joseph O., age 22, volunteer, August 12, 1861, three years, Thirty-sixth regiment, company G, private, served three years, mustered out in 1864.

True, Hanson W., age 20, volunteer, three years, Twenty-fifth regiment, company I, private, served three years, mustered out in 1864.

True, Hurd A., age 18, volunteer, 1862, three years, Thirty-sixth regiment, company G, private, three years, mustered out July 27, 1865.

True, Russel H., age 19, volunteer, May 28, 1862, three months, Eighty-seventh regiment, company A, private, served four months, mustered out October 1, 1862, second enlistment, age 20, volunteer, August, 1863, six months, Fourth independent battalion cavalry, company C, sergeant, served eight months, mustered out March 12, 1864, third enlistment, age 21, volunteer, March, 1864, three years, Thirteenth cavalry, company A, sergeant, attained the rank of lieutenant, served one year and three months, mustered out August 10, 1865

True, John A., age 20, volunteer, August, 1861, three years, Thirty-sixth regiment, company G, private, attained the rank of corporal, served four years, mustered out Ju'y 27, 1865, reenlisted as a veteran

Twiggs, Benjamin, age 23, volunteer, September, 1862, three years, Seventh cavalry, company H, private, served three years, mustered out July, 1865.

Waldeck, Simon, volunteer, three years, First cavalry, company L, private, served three years, court-martialed once.

Watkins, Hamilton, age 17, volunteer, August 16, 1864, one year, fifer, attained the rank of private, served ten months, mustered out, June 22, 1865.

Wharff, Charles W., Seventy-seventh regiment, company H, honorably discharged.

Wharff, George, age 17, volunteer, August 22, 1862, three years, One Hundred and Sixteenth regiment, company H, private, nineteen battles, served three years, mustered out June 14, 1865, had not a day's sickness.

Wharff, Oliver K., age 44, volunteer, 1861, three years, Eighteenth regiment, company H, private, served one year, honorably discharged in 1862, reenlistment, age 45, volunteer, August 22, 1862, three years, One Hundred and Sixteenth regiment, company H, private, served two years, honorably discharged in 1864.

Wheatstone, Joseph, age 17, volunteer, August, 1863, six months, Fourth independent battalion cavalry, company C, private, served eight months, mustered out March 12, 1864, reenlistment, age 18, volunteer, one year, One Hundred and Twenty-sixth regiment, company A, private, four battles, mustered out June 25, 1865.

Wheatstone, Isaac, age 17, volunteer, May 3, 1864, nine months, Ninety-second regiment, company H, private, served one year, mustered out June 10, 1865.

Wiess, W.

Wilson, Freeland C., volunteer, August, 1861, three years, Thirty-sixth regiment, company G, private, discharged in 1861.

Williams, Reese, age 17, volunteer, September 18, 1862, three years, One Hundred and Sixteenth regiment, company H, corporal, attained the rank of first lieutenant, served three years, mustered out June 14, 1865, badly wounded at Piedmont, Virginia, in 1864.

Williams, William, volunteer, Twenty-seventh regiment, company D.

Wilson, Riley, artillery, company A, died.

Wilson, William W., age 23, volunteer, 1861, three years, Third regiment, company C, corporal, attained the rank of sergeant, served three years, mustered out in 1864, wounded and captured at Rome, Georgia, on the straight raid, parolled.

Wilson, John, age 34, volunteer, January 1, 1862, three years, Thirty-sixth regiment, company A, private, served two years and nine months, died September 24, 1864.

Wilson, Eli, age 23, volunteer, August 1, 1864, one year, Thirty-sixth regiment, company A, private, served one year, mustered out July 27, 1865

Wilson, Amos, age 19, volunteer, July 29, 1861, three years, Thirty-sixth regiment, company A, private, served four years, mustered out July 27, 1865, reenlisted as a veteran.

Young, William, age 21, volunteer, 1862, three years, Ninety-second regiment, company H, private, died at Carthage, Tennessee, of chronic diarrhœa.

RECAPITULATION.

Battery K, Second Ohio heavy artillery	5
Battery H, Second Ohio heavy artillery	1
Seventh Ohio cavalry	10
Fourth independent battalion of Ohio volunteer cavalry	5
Fourth Ohio cavalry	5
Thirteenth Ohio cavalry	3
Ninth Ohio cavalry	2
First Ohio and Fifth Virginia cavalry, one each	2
Thirty-sixth Ohio	51
Ninety-second Ohio	20
Seventy-seventh Ohio	7
Eighty-Seventh Ohio	6
Twelfth Ohio	7
Sixty-third Ohio	4
Third Ohio	4
Three each in Thirty-ninth Ohio, Twenty-fifth Ohio, One Hundred Sixteenth Ohio and One Hundred and Seventy-fourth Ohio	12
Two each in Eighteenth Ohio (three years), Eighteenth Ohio (three months), Forty-second Ohio, Eighty-fifth Ohio, One Hundred and Forty-eighth Ohio National guard	10
One each in Sixteenth Ohio, Twenty-third Ohio, Twenty-seventh Ohio, Twenty-eighth Ohio, Thirty-first Ohio, One Hundred and Twenty-sixth Ohio, One Hundred and Fifty-fifth Ohio, One Hundred and Seventy-ninth Ohio, One Hundred and Ninety-third Ohio, and six not designated, in all	16
Total number of soldiers	151
Died	16

UNION TOWNSHIP.

Adams, Isaac N., age 16, volunteer, August, 1862, three years, Thirty-ninth regiment, company B, private, served nine months, died at Memphis, Tennessee, May 15, 1863, of bloody flux.

Atkinson, Samuel, Thirty-sixth regiment, company F, private, reenlisted as a veteran

Apple, Samuel, three years, Thirty-ninth regiment, company F, private, served three years, mustered out July 27, 1895

Bodman, Frederick, volunteer, Thirty-ninth regiment, company F.

Baker, John, age 23, drafted, 1865, one year.

Beebe, Jerry, May, 1864, one hundred days, One Hundred and Forty-eighth regiment, company I, served four months, mustered out September, 1864.

Beebe, Joseph, May, 1864, one hundred days, One Hundred and Forty-eighth regiment, company I, served four months, mustered out September, 1864.

Biedle, Jacob, Seventy-seventh regiment, company B, private, died in service.

Bostner, William, Seventy-seventh regiment, company C.

Callahan, Emery, volunteer, three years, Sixty-third regiment, company F, died in service.

Clark, John, volunteer, Thirty-ninth regiment, company B.

Craig, Stewart, volunteer, First cavalry.

Cutter, Lewis L., Seventy-seventh regiment, company B.

Cutter, William H., volunteer, Seventy-seventh regiment, company B, killed at the battle of Mark's Mills, April 30, 1864.

Cobb, William, Seventy-seventh regiment, company H.

Dice, John, age 21, drafted, 1865, one year.

Davis, Douglas, Seventy-seventh regiment, company H.

Emge, Adam, volunteer, three years, Sixty-third regiment, company G, reenlisted as a veteran.

Fouracker, Richard, age 52, volunteer, 1861, three years, Seventy-seventh regiment, company H, lieutenant, attained rank of captain, served one year, honorably discharged September 2, 1862, for physical disability.

Fouracker, Louis McK, age 25, volunteer, three years, Seventy-seventh regiment company H, sergeant, served three years, reenlisted as a veteran.

Fouracker, Levi James, age 23, volunteer, 1861, three years, Seventy-seventh regiment, company H, second lieutenant, honorably discharged October 21, 1862, died March 5, 1875, of wounds received at Shiloh.

Fouracker, Douglass W., age 20, volunteer, 1861, Seventy-seventh regiment, company H, orderly sergeant, died August 11, 1862, buried at Memphis, Tennessee.

Farmer, James, Seventy-seventh regiment, company H, honorably discharged for disability.

Harden, Enos, volunteer, Seventy-seventh regiment, company H, served six months, honorably discharged for disability.

Harden, James, age 20, Seventy-seventh regiment, company H, killed at Shiloh April 6, 1862.

Haines, Jacob, volunteer, Sixty-third regiment, company G, died.

Henry, Owen, May, 1864, one hundred days, One Hundred and Forty-eighth regiment, company K, private, served four months, mustered out September, 1864.

Kramer, Henry, Sixty-third regiment, company G, mustered out.

Liner, John, volunteer, Eighth regiment, company B, three years.

McAffie, Henry, age 22, substitute.

McKinney, James, Seventy-seventh regiment, company H, died January 2, 1862, in Union township.

Myres, William, volunteer, May, 1864, one hundred days, One Hundred and Forty-eighth regiment, company I, private, served four months, mustered out September, 1864.

Myres, Jacob, three years, Seventy-seventh regiment, company H, private, served three years.

O'Hern, James.

Power, David, volunteer, three years, Seventy-seventh regiment, company H, private, reenlisted as a veteran.

Power, James, substitute, Seventy-seventh regiment, company H.

Power, Robert, drafted 1865, died in 1865 of a swelling in the knee.

Pinkerton, Calvert, drafted 1865.

Rehmle, John, First cavalry, company L, died October 1, 1862, of diarrhœa.

Schlauback, Conrad, volunteer, three years, Thirty-ninth regiment, company B, private, mustered out July 9, 1865, reenlisted as a veteran.

Schilling, John, volunteer, three years, Thirty-ninth regiment, company F, served three years.

Sheppard, Thomas, May, 1864, one hundred days, One Hundred and Forty-eighth regiment, company I, served four months, mustered out September, 1864.

Shuster, William, May, 1864, one hundred days, One Hundred and Forty-eighth regiment, company I, served four months, mustered out September, 1864

Tilton, Leroy D., May, 1864, one hundred days, One Hundred and Forty-eighth regiment, company I.

Power, Tyrannus, May, 1864, one hundred days, One Hundred and Forty-eighth regiment, company I, served four months, mustered out September, 1864.

Roesh, John, drafted, 1865, one year, sent a substitute.

Weaver, Nicholas, age 44, drafted, 1865, one year, exempt from physical disability.

Witham, J. M., May, 1864, one hundred days, One Hundred and Forty-eighth regiment, company I, served four months, mustered out September, 1864.

Ladd, Richard, Sixty-third regiment, company G.

Ladd, Salathiel, Thirty-sixth regiment, company A, served his term.

Ladd, John, Thirty-sixth regiment, company A, died.

Miller, Austin, 1864.

Linn, Daniel O., Ninety-second regiment, company F.

RECAPITULATION.

WARREN TOWNSHIP.

Anderson, William, age 22, volunteer, February 24, 1864, three years, Thirty-sixth regiment, company K, private, served one year and five months, mustered out July 27, 1865.

Anderson, James, age 20, volunteer, March 5, 1864, three years, First Virginia light artillery, company C, private, served one year and three months, mustered out June 28, 1865.

Anderson, Edward, age 26, volunteer, May, 1864, one hundred days, One Hundred and Forty-eighth regiment, company K, private, served four months, mustered out September, 1864.

Asbury, Dudley E., age 25, volunteer, October 4, 1864, one year, One Hundred and First United States colored regiment, sergeant-major, served one year, mustered out October 1, 1865.

Appel, Valentine, age 21, volunteer, July 31, 1861, three years, Thirty-sixth regiment, company F, private, served three years, mustered out August 12, 1864.

Appel, Simeon, volunteer, three years, Thirty-ninth regiment, company F, private.

Baker, Manuel T., age 27, volunteer, August 1, 1861, three years, Thirty-sixth regiment, company F, private, served three and a half years, died February 10, 1865, captured at Winchester, July 24, 1864, imprisoned at Danville, where he died.

Baker, Francis, age 16, volunteer, spring of 1864, three years, Thirty-sixth regiment, company F, private, died March 16, 1864, of measles, at Chattanooga.

Baker, John L. A., age 39, volunteer, September 1, 1862, three years, Seventh cavalry, company H, private, served two years and ten months, mustered out July 4, 1865.

Bailey, Peter, age 31, volunteer, March 4, 1864, three years, One Hundred and Twenty-second regiment, company I, private, died May 7, 1864, wounded in the battle of the Wilderness, May 7, 1864, taken to Danville prison, and supposed to be dead.

Bailey, Daniel, age 25, volunteer, August 1, 1861, three years, Thirty-sixth regiment, company F, private, served four years, mustered out July 27, 1865, reenlisted as a veteran.

Bailey, Seth, age 19, volunteer, May, 1864, one hundred days, One Hundred and Forty-eighth regiment, company K, private, served four months, mustered out September, 1864.

Beckford, Otis, age 17, volunteer, August 9, 1861, three years, Thirty-sixth regiment, company F, private, served four years, mustered out July 27, 1865, reenlisted as a veteran.

Boothby, David, age 20, volunteer, May, 1864, one hundred days, One Hundred and Forty-eighth regiment, company K, private, served four months, mustered out September, 1864.

Boothby, Cornelus E., age 25, volunteer, May, 1864, one hundred days, One Hundred and Forty-eighth regiment, company K, private, served four months, mustered out September, 1864.

Boothby, Joseph N., age 24, volunteer, May, 1864, one hundred days, One Hundred and Forty-eighth regiment, company K, private, served four months, mustered out September, 1864.

Benedict, George, Second cavalry.

Brabham, Wellington, age 20, volunteer, October 1, 1864, First cavalry, companies H and L, private, served eight months, honorably discharged June 28, 1865, for disability.

Call, John, age 29, volunteer, March, 1864, Thirty-sixth regiment, company C, private, served five months, died in August, 1864, of measles.

Call, David, age 24, volunteer, October, 1862, three years, Ninety-second regiment, companies C and F, private, served five months, died March 18, 1863, of erysipelas, at Nashville, Tennessee.

Carpenter, Ezra J, age 19, volunteer, September 30, 1861, three years, Thirty-sixth regiment, company F, private, served two years and ten months, mustered out July 27, 1865, reenlisted as a veteran and detailed as a veteran.

Carpenter, Alfred, age 22, volunteer, August, 1861, three years, Thirty-sixth regiment, company F, private, served three years, died October 29, 1863, reenlisted as a veteran, killed at Winchester.

Carpenter, Spencer, age 18, volunteer, spring of 1862, three years, Seventy-seventh regiment, company G, private, served four years, mustered out March 8, 1865, reenlisted as a veteran.

Cecil, John T., age 27, volunteer, May, 1864, one hundred days, One Hundred and Forty-eighth regiment, company K, private, served four months, mustered out September, 1864.

Cecil, Edward S., age 24, volunteer, May, 1864, one hundred days, One Hundred and Forty-eighth regiment, company F, private, served four months mustered out September, 1864.

Cecil, George K., age 20, volunteer, May, 1864, one hundred days, One Hundred and Forty-eighth regiment, company K, private, served four months, mustered out in September, 1864.

Chalfant, Bazil, Seventy-seventh regiment, company D.

Chute, Albert, age 27, volunteer, December, 1861, three years, Sixty-third regiment, company I, private, served six months, honorably discharged June 16, 1862, for disability.

Cole, Hiram Harvey, age 25, volunteer, August, 1861, three years, Thirty-sixth regiment, company F, corporal, served two years, killed September 18, 1863, at Chickamauga.

Cole, Dudley, age 22, volunteer, October, 1862, three years, Ninety-second regiment, private, mustered out June 30, 1865.

Christopher, William H., age 18, volunteer, December 20, 1863, three years, Seventy-seventh regiment, company D, private, two years and three months, mustered out in March, 1866.

Christopher, Clark L., age 26, volunteer, May, 1864, one hundred days, One Hundred and Forty-eighth regiment, company K, private, served four months, mustered out in September, 1864.

Coffman, Charles, age 26, volunteer, May, 1864, one hundred days, One Hundred and Forty-eighth regiment, company K, private, served four months, mustered out in September, 1864.

Cochran, Charles, age 22, volunteer, October 16, 1862, three years, Seventy-seventh regiment, companies D and H, private, served three years and five months, mustered out March 8, 1866.

Crael, Charles, age 21, volunteer, September, 1861, three years, Thirty-sixth regiment, company F, corporal, served two years and ten months, mustered out July 27, 1865.

Daugherty, William, age 31, volunteer, August, 1861, three years, Thirty-sixth regiment, company F, sergeant, served three years, mustered out in 1864.

Devore, James, age 17, volunteer, winter of 1861, three years, Thirty-sixth regiment, company F, private, died June 19, 1864, wounded at Chickamauga.

Faris, Samuel, age 18, volunteer, August, 1862, three years, Thirty-sixth regiment, company F, private, served two years and nine months, honorably discharged June 14, 1865.

Ferril, Charles.

Finch, Lewis J., age 20, volunteer, August, 1861, three years, Thirty-ninth regiment, company B, private, served four years, mustered out July 9, 1865, reenlisted as a veteran.

Finch, William W., volunteer, Ninety-second regiment, company G.

Finch, Henry, age 17, volunteer, July, 1862, three years, Second heavy artillery, private, three years, mustered out August 23, 1865.

Froochel, Walter, volunteer, three years, Thirty-ninth regiment, company B, private.

Fish, Timothy, age 26, volunteer, 1863, three years, Second heavy artillery, private, missing and supposed to be dead.

Fish, James, age 25, December 25, 1863, three years, First cavalry, company L, served two years and nine months, private, mustered out September 28, 1865, in hospital several months with small-pox.

Fish, William, age 21, volunteer, three years, December, 1863. First cavalry, company L, private, died of measles in January, 1864

Farley, William, age 18, volunteer, Seventy-third regiment, company F, private, died at Chattanooga, Tennessee, July 10, 1864.

Farley, Kins, age 19, volunteer, Tenth cavalry, company L, private, died at Kingston, Georgia, June 17, 1864.

French, Columbus, age 31, volunteer, May, 1865, one hundred days, One Hundred and Forty-eighth regiment, company K, private, served four months, mustered out in September, 1864.

Gilpin, William R., age 23, volunteer, January, 1862, three years, Sixty-third regiment, company G, private, served three years and six months, mustered out July 8, 1865, reenlisted as a veteran.

Gilpin, Felix, age 16, volunteer, January 1, 1862, three years, Sixty-third regiment, company G, private, served three years and six months, died of small-pox March 26, 1864, wounded at Corinth, transferred to gunboat service January 3, 1863.

Gray, Frank S., volunteer, Thirty-sixth regiment, company F.

Greenwood, Theodore, age 21, volunteer, June, 1862, three years, captain, died September 27, 1862, quartermaster on General Rosecrans' staff

Hale, Selkirk, Thirty-sixth regiment, company F.

Hall, E. K., Twenty-second regiment.

Hall, W. II. G.

Hall, Alexander, Thirty-sixth regiment, company F.

Hanna, James, age 26, volunteer, August, 1861, three years, Thirty-sixth regiment, company F, corporal, served two years, honorably discharged in 1863, for disability.

Hanna, William W., age 21, volunteer, August, 1861, three years, Thirty-sixth regiment, company F, private, attained sergeant, served four years, mustered out July 27, 1865, reenlisted as a veteran.

Hart, Samuel M., age 35, May, 1864, one hundred days, One Hundred and Forty-eighth regiment, company K, private, served four months, mustered out in September, 1864

Harris, Joseph, Seventy-third regiment, company F.

Harris, Lewis, Seventy-third regiment, company F.

Harte, Miller H., age 19, volunteer, May, 1864, one hundred days, One Hundred and Forty-eighth regiment, company K, private, served four months, mustered out September, 1864

Hawkins, Thomas, age 25, volunteer, May, 1864, one hundred days, One Hundred and Forty-eighth regiment, company K, private, served four months, mustered out September, 1864

Hawkins, Granville, age 22, volunteer, August 16, 1861, three years, Thirty-ninth regiment, company B, private, served three years, mustered out August, 1864.

Hawkins, James, age 37, volunteer, spring of 1862, three years, Seventy-seventh regiment, company H, private, died January 14, 1864, of small-pox, at Alton, Illinois.

Henderson, James, age 36, volunteer, May, 1864, one hundred days, One Hundred and Forty-eighth regiment, company K, private, served four months, mustered out September, 1864, off duty with sickness most of the term.

Henderson, John S., age 21, volunteer, August, 1861, three years, Thirty-sixth regiment, company D, private, served four years, mustered out July 27, 1865, slightly wounded at Chattanooga.

Hohn, John, age 34, volunteer, August, 1862, three years, Ninety-second regiment, company G, private, served one year and two months, died October, 1863, wounded in the heel at Chickamauga, September 20, 1863, and died of lockjaw.

Holden, Andrew, age 35, volunteer, October 11, 1861, three years, Seventy-third regiment, company F, private, served three years and ten months, mustered out July 20, 1865.

Hollister, G. R., age 18, volunteer, May, 1864, one hundred days, One Hundred and Forty-eighth regiment, company K, private, served four months, mustered out September, 1864.

Hollister, John L., age 23, volunteer, August, 1862, three years, Thirty-sixth regiment, company F, private, served three years, mustered out July 27, 1865.

Hollister, Charles S., age 20, volunteer, August, 1863, three years, Second heavy artillery, private, served two years, mustered out August 23, 1865.

Hudson, John, Sixty-third regiment, company F.

Hutchinson, Joseph T., age 28, volunteer, September, 1861, three years, First Virginia light artillery, private, served two years, died September 12, 1863, of camp disease, in Virginia.

Hudson, Samuel, Sixty-third regiment, company F.

Hutchinson, Henry W., age 31, volunteer, September 1, 1861, three years, First Virginia light artillery, company C, private, honorably discharged 1863, for disability.

Hufferd, John W., age 16, August 1, 1861, three years, Thirty-sixth regiment, company F, private, served four years, mustered out 1865, reenlisted as a veteran

Hufferd, William H, age 16, volunteer, August, 1863, six months, One Hundred and Twenty-ninth regiment, company F, private, served seven months, honorably discharged March, 1864, reenlistment, age 17, volunteer, May, 1864, one hundred days, One Hundred and Forty-eighth regiment, private, served four months, mustered out September, 1864, reenlistment, volunteer, winter 1864-5, Thirty-sixth regiment, company F, private, mustered out July 27, 1865.

Ingram, Thomas M., age 15, volunteer, August, 1863, six months, One Hundred and Twenty-ninth regiment, company F, private, served seven months, mustered out March, 1864, reenlistment, May, 1864, one hundred days, One Hundred and Forty-eighth regiment, company F, private, served four months, mustered out September, 1864, reenlistment, volunteer, Thirty-second regiment, company B, private, mustered out May, 1865.

Johnson, Jacob, volunteer, February, 1864, three years, Thirty-sixth regiment, company F, private, mustered out July 27, 1864, sick for six months.

Johnson, Bloomfield, age 31, volunteer, May, 1864, one hundred days, One hundred and Forty-eighth regiment, company K, private, served four months, mustered out September, 1864.

Jones, Andrew, age 34, volunteer, December 4, 1863, three years, Seventy-sixth regiment, company D, corporal, mustered out July 15, 1865.

Lacy, Elisha, Thirty-sixth regiment, company K.

Leavers, W. J.

Lightfoot, John, age 20, volunteer, 1864, First cavalry, private, mustered, out September 28, 1865.

Lightfoot, James, age 21, volunteer, December, 1863, three years, Seventy-seventh regiment, company D, private, served two years and three months, mustered out March 8, 1864, captured in 1864, and in prison at Camp Ford ten months.

Lightfritz, Samuel, age 37, volunteer, May, 1864, one hundred days, One Hundred and Forty-eighth regiment, company F, private, served four months, mustered out September, 1864.

Lynch, Thomas, age 29, volunteer, May, 1864, one hundred days, One Hundred and Forty-eighth regiment, company K, private, served four months, mustered out September, 1864.

Malcolm, Andrew, age 15, volunteer, August 10, 1862, Thirty-sixth regiment, company F, private, served three years, mustered out July 27, 1865.

Moore, Thomas W., volunteer, August, 1861, three years, Thirty-sixth regiment, company F, captain, served seven months, resigned March 5, 1862, reenlistment, May, 1864, one hundred days, One Hundred and Forty-eighth regiment, colonel, served four months, mustered out September, 1864.

Malcolm, James M., age 24, volunteer, September, 1861, three years, Thirty-sixth regiment, company F, corporal, attained rank of sergeant, served three years and six months, mustered out, March, 1865.

Malcolm, John W., age 19, volunteer, September, 1861, three years, Thirty-sixth regiment, company F, private, served two years and ten months, died July 24, 1864, killed at Winchester.

Malcolm, Horace H., age 16, volunteer, May, 1864, one hundred days, One Hundred and Forty-eighth regiment, company K, private, served four months, mustered out September, 1864.

McClure, Andrew J., age 25, volunteer, April, 1864, three months, First Iowa artillery, private, mustered out for disability, reenlistment, volunteer, 1861, three years, First Iowa artillery, private, honorably discharged March, 1863.

McClure, Theodore D., age 21, volunteer, August, 1861, three years, Fortieth Illinois regiment, company G, colored sergeant, served three years, mustered out August, 1864.

McGovern, Peter, age 19, volunteer, 1861, two years, Second Virginia light artillery, company K, private, served two years, mustered out 1863, reenlistment, volunteer, 1863, Second cavalry, private

McGovern, Michael, age 17, volunteer, August, 1861, three years, Thirty-sixth regiment, company F, private, served three years, died September 29, 1865, wounded twice and died of lockjaw from second wound.

McGovern, Edward, age 16, volunteer, February, 1864, Thirty-sixth regiment, company F, private, served one year and four months, mustered out July 27, 1865.

Miller, Edward, Second cavalry, company L.

Moore, Henry, Twenty-fifth regiment, company B.

Morgan, Vincent, age 29, volunteer, September 26, 1864, Sixty-fifth regiment, company I, private, served nine months, mustered out June 16, 1865.

Morris, John R., age 30, volunteer, August 1, 1861, three years, Thirty-sixth regiment, company F, private, served one year and six months, honorably discharged February, 1863, for disability.

Morris, Joseph, age 20, volunteer, August 1, 1861, three years, Thirty-sixth regiment, company F, private, served four years, mustered out July 27, 1865, wounded at Winchester July 20, 1864, captured and in Danville seven months, furloughed home and rejoined regiment in April, 1865.

Morris, Daniel, age 20, volunteer, April, 1865, Eighteenth regiment, company I, private, mustered out

Patten, Thomas, age 37, volunteer, September 16, 1861, three years, First cavalry, company L, private, served three years, mustered out September, 1864.

Perdew, Henry, age 31, volunteer, April, 1862, three years, Seventy-seventh regiment, company H, private, died January 14, 1863, of smallpox at Alton

Prettyman, Eli, Seventy-seventh regiment, company H.

Pearce, Thomas R., age 42, volunteer, August, 1861, three years,

Thirty-sixth regiment, company F, private, served four years, mustered out, July 27, 1865, reenlisted as a veteran.

Pearce, Israel J., age 19, volunteer, September 1, 1862, three years, Seventh cavalry, company H, private, served two years and ten months, mustered out July, 1865.

Pryor, William, age 26, volunteer, July, 1862, three years, Ninety-second regiment, company F, private, served one year, honorably discharged June 17, 1863, for disability, lost his hearing.

Prettyman, John, Seventy-seventh regiment, company H.

Pryor, Francis, age 24, volunteer, July, 1862, three years, Ninety-second regiment, company F, private, served three years, honorably discharged July 17, 1865, wounded February 25, 1864, captured at Calhoun, Georgia, August 14, 1865, in various prisons seven months, and paroled, captured while detailed as train guard, sick four months, detailed as orderly, reenlisted as a veteran.

Pryor, Matthew, age 21, volunteer, September 11, 1861, three years, First cavalry, company L, private, served four years, mustered out September 28, 1865.

Pryor, Jasper, age 17, volunteer, August 13, 1863, three years, Second heavy artillery, company K, private, served four months, died December 12, 1863, of typhoid pneumonia.

Rannelly, Joseph, Second cavalry, company C.

Rannelly, William, Second cavalry, company C.

Reason, Oliver.

Reading, Simon J., age 22, volunteer, February 24, 1864, Thirty-sixth regiment, company K, private, served one year, and five months, mustered out July 27, 1865.

Reppert, Byron D., age 22, volunteer, September 1, 1861, three years, First Virginia light artillery, company C, private, served three years and six months, mustered out March 30, 1865.

Ritchey, Joseph, Seventy-seventh regiment, company H.

Roberts, Ezekiel, age 19, volunteer, July, 1861, three years, Thirty-sixth regiment, company A, private, served three years and eight months, mustered out March 10, 1865, wounded at Lewisburgh and at Winchester, captured at Martinsburgh and in prison one month.

Roberts, John, age 32, volunteer, April 6, 1863, Eighty-eighth regiment, company B, private, served two years and three weeks, mustered out July 3, 1865.

Rood, Vincent, age 19, volunteer, First light artillery.

Rumerfield, Aaron E., age 17, volunteer February 27, 1865, Thirty-sixth regiment, company F, private, served five months, mustered out July 27, 1865.

Roush, Absalom, age 17, volunteer, September 30, 1864, First cavalry, company H, private, served nine months, mustered out June 17, 1865.

Roush, William, age 25, volunteer, September 30, 1864, First cavalry, company H, private, served one year, mustered out September, 1865, was in the hundred days' service.

Rumbold, Charles H., age 24, volunteer, March 12, 1864, Thirty-sixth regiment, company B, private, served one year and four months, mustered out July 27, 1865, sick and in the hospital seven months.

Rumbold, Benjamin F., age 19, April 5, 1865, Thirty-sixth regiment, company B, private, served three months, mustered out July 27, 1865, was in the hundred days' service.

Rumbold, Joseph I., age 20, volunteer, October 4, 1864, First cavalry, company L, private, served four months, died February 13, 1865, of camp disease and pneumonia.

Shafer, Martin, age 24, volunteer, three years, Thirty-sixth regiment, company F, private, died June, 1864, by a shell, Lynchburgh, Virginia.

Sheid, John T., age 17, volunteer, February 2, 1864, Seventy-seventh regiment, company F, private, served two years, mustered out March 8, 1866.

Skipton, Hiram, age 25, volunteer, August, 1861, three years, Thirty-sixth regiment, company F, private, attained rank of corporal, served three years and nine months, mustered out May 27, 1865, wounded at Lexington, June 11, 1864.

Skipton, William.

Skipton, Samuel, age 38, volunteer, August, 1861, three years, Thirty-sixth regiment, company F, private, attained rank of corporal, served three years, mustered out August, 1864.

Scott, William W., volunteer, 1861, three years, Seventy-seventh regiment, first lieutenant, honorably discharged August 31, 1862.

Scott, Joseph C., age 19, volunteer, August, 1862, three years, Huntingdon battery, private, served two years and ten months, mustered out June, 1865.

Smith, Gilead, age 20, volunteer, December 10, 1861, Sixty-third regiment, company F, private, served one year, died January 17,

1863, wounded at Corinth, October 4, 1862, intermittent fever ensued, and caused his death.

Smith, George W., age 19, volunteer, May, 1864, one hundred days, One Hundred and Forty-eighth regiment, company F, private, served four months, mustered out September, 1864.

Smith, John, Seventy-seventh regiment, company H.

Stage, William J., age 40, volunteer, October 3, 1864, three years, First cavalry, company H, private, served one year, mustered out September, 1865.

Stage, Thomas, age 37, volunteer, May, 1864, one hundred days, One Hundred and Forty-eighth regiment, company F, private, served four months, mustered out September, 1864.

Strain, James M., age 43, volunteer, August 1, 1861, three years, Thirty-sixth regiment, company F, private, served three years and three months, honorably discharged October 27, 1864, wounded at Lexington, Virginia, in June, 1864.

Stump, John, age 33, volunteer, September 1, 1862, three years, Seventh cavalry, company H, private, served six months, died April 22, 1863, at Nicholasville, Kentucky, sick with inflammatory rheumatism three months.

Trachel, Walter, age 24, volunteer, July 22, 1861, three years, Thirty-ninth regiment, company B, private, served three years, mustered out July 30, 1864.

Tyrrel, William, volunteer, three years, Ninety-second regiment, private.

Turril, Henry L., age 20, volunteer, August, 1861, three years, Thirty-sixth regiment, company F, private, served three years, mustered out August, 1864, served also in Sixth Virginia infantry, wounded at battle of Winchester and in hands of the rebels ten days.

Turril, Charles, age 28, volunteer, August, 1861, three years, Thirty-sixth regiment, company F, private, in three battles, served one year, honorably discharged August, 1862, for disability.

Tunnecliff, William, age 28, volunteer, November, 1861, three years, First cavalry, company K, private, served three years and ten months, mustered out September 13, 1865, detached as clerk in quartermaster's department, reenlisted as a veteran.

Tunnecliff, Joseph, age 23, volunteer, May, 1861, three years, Fifth regiment, company C, private, served three years, mustered out June 20, 1864, captured in 1862, confined in Libby prison three months, and parolled.

Welch, Edward, October, 1861, three years, Seventy-third regiment, company F, private, served three years, died 1864, wounded three times at Winchester, died probably in January.

Wheeler, Lewis.

Wynn, A. D., age 30, volunteer, May, 1864, one hundred days, One Hundred and Forty-eighth regiment, company K, private, served four months, mustered out September, 1864.

Wynn, Joseph D., age 34, volunteer, August, 1861, three years, Thirty-sixth regiment, company F, sergeant, served three years, mustered out September, 1864, wounded twice.

Wynn, Amos D., age 28, volunteer, May, 1864, one hundred days, One Hundred and Forty-eighth regiment, company K, private, four months, mustered out September, 1864.

Wright, Benjamin, age 24, volunteer, August 1, 1861, three years, Thirty-sixth regiment, company F, corporal, attained rank of sergeant, served two years and nine months, died May 20, 1864, at Gallipolis.

Wright, David, age 22, volunteer, September, 1862, three years, Ninety-second regiment, company G, private, served one year and ten months, died July 17, 1864, died from wound received at the battle of Kennesaw Mountain, June 23, 1864.

Wright, William, age 18, volunteer, 1862, three years, Seventh cavalry, company H, private, died 1864, captured at Rogersville, Tennessee, and in various prisons, dying in Andersonville, from deprivation and hardship.

Vaughn, James, volunteer, August, 1861, three years, Thirty-sixth regiment, company F, private, served two years and seven months, died May 9, 1864, killed at Cloyd Mountain.

Zearing, Joseph, age 24, volunteer, August, 1861, three years, Thirty-sixth regiment, company F, fifer, served two years, died November 12, 1863, at Gallatin.

Zearing, William H., age 21, volunteer, August, 1861, three years, Thirty-sixth regiment, company F, private, served three years, mustered out September 9, 1864, was also in the three months' service.

Zearing, James E., age 19, volunteer, August, 1861, three years, Thirty-sixth regiment, company D, fifer, served three years, mustered out September 9, 1864.

Zearing, John L., age 17, volunteer, August, 1861, Thirty-sixth regiment, company F, private, served three years, mustered out September 9, 1864.

RECAPITULATION.

Buell's Pierpont battery	3
Huntington battery	1
Battery K, Second Ohio heavy artillery	1
Second heavy artillery	3
One each in First Ohio light artillery, First Virginia light artillery, First Iowa light artillery	3
First Ohio cavalry	11
Seventh Ohio cavalry	2
Second Ohio cavalry	2
Second Louisana cavalry	1
Thirty-sixth Ohio	52
One Hundred and Forty-eighth Ohio National guard	27
Seventy-seventh Ohio	13
Ninety-second Ohio	15
Sixty-third Ohio	5
Thirty-ninth Ohio	3
Seventy-third Ohio	4
One Hundred and Twenty-ninth Ohio	5
Second Ohio	2
And one each in Fifth Ohio, Twenty-second Ohio, Twenty-fifth Ohio, Eighteenth Ohio (three years) Thirty-second Ohio, Seventy-sixth Ohio, Sixty-fifth Ohio, Eighty-eighth Ohio, One Hundred and Twenty-second Ohio, First Iowa, Second Virginia, Fortieth Illinois, One Hundred and First United States colored infantry, not designated five, making in all	18
Total number of soldiers	167
Died	28

WATERFORD TOWNSHIP.

Allen, Leonidas, age 21, volunteer, August 14, 1861, three years, Eighteenth regiment, company F, private, died of typhoid fever at Louisville, Kentucky, June 30, 1863.

Alberry, Richard, age 25, volunteer, December 31, 1863, Second Virginia cavalry, company E, private, served one year and six months, mustered out July 1, 1865.

Alberry, John, age 21, volunteer, December 31, 1863, Second Virginia cavalry, company E, private, served one year and six months, mustered out July 1, 1865, reenlisted as a veteran.

Alberry, Antony, age 18, volunteer, December 31, 1863, Second Virginia cavalry, company E, private, served one year and six months, mustered out July 1, 1865.

Alberry, Joseph, age 15, volunteer, December 31, 1863, Second Virginia cavalry, company E, private, served one year and six months, mustered out July 1, 1865.

Anderson, William R., volunteer, Ninth cavalry, company B, private, died of fever.

Beach, Thomas H. B., age 28, volunteer, 1863, three years, Ninth cavalry, company B, mustered out July 30, 1865.

Becket, Humphry, age 22, volunteer, three years, Sixty-third regiment, company D, private, mustered out July 8, 1865, reenlisted as a veteran.

Becket, Jesse M., volunteer, September 15, 1861, three years, Second Virginia cavalry, company E, corporal, served three years, mustered out 1864.

Bishop, William, volunteer, three years, Thirty-sixth regiment, company A, private, mustered out July 27, 1865, reenlisted as a veteran.

Bishop, Henry, volunteer, three years, Thirty-sixth regiment, company A, private, mustered out July 27, 1865, reenlisted as a veteran, wounded at Berryville, West Virginia, September, 1864.

Bolun, Daniel, age 25, volunteer, September 15, 1861, three years, Second Virginia cavalry, company E, corporal, mustered out, reenlisted as a veteran.

Busman, James, volunteer, three years, Thirty-sixth regiment, company A, private.

Belman, James, Thirty-sixth regiment, company A.

Brown, Charles W., age 21, volunteer, October 6, 1861, three years, Sixty-third regiment, companies D and G, sergeant, attained rank of orderly sergeant, died of typhoid fever, 1862.

Brown, Samuel W., age 17, volunteer, December 17, 1861, three years, Sixty-third regiment, company B, musician, served one year and one month, discharged for disability January, 1863, wounded at Corinth, reenlistment, February, 1864, Sixty-third regiment, company B, served one year and five months, mustered out July 8, 1865.

Brown, William C., age 17, volunteer, August 14, 1862, three years,

ment, company F, private, served three years, mustered out September 9, 1864.

Thirty-sixth regiment, company A, private, served three years, mustered out July 27, 1865, severely wounded July 24, 1864.

Brown, John, age 18, volunteer, 1862, three years, Ninety-second regiment, company H, private, served three years, mustered out June 10, 1865.

Brown, William P., age 20, volunteer, three years, Eighteenth regiment, company F, private, mustered out October, 1865, reenlisted as a veteran.

Bucy, William T., volunteer, 1861, three years, Second Virginia cavalry, company F, private, served four years, mustered out 1865, reenlisted as a veteran.

Brown, John W., volunteer, August, 1864, One Hundred and Eighty-second regiment, private, served eleven months, mustered out July 7, 1865.

Brown, John, age 28, volunteer, Ninety-second regiment, company H, private, honorably discharged for disability.

Burris, Lorain, volunteer, three years, Seventy-seventh regiment, company H, private, killed April 6, 1862, at Shiloh.

Bartlett, George B., volunteer, October 9, 1861, three years, Sixty-third regiment, companies A and D, corporal, attained rank of captain, acting assistant quartermaster engineers' department, Mississippi, mustered out with regiment.

Burris, Franklin.

Burris, James, age 35, volunteer, September 1, 1861, Second Virginia cavalry, company E, private, mustered out 1865, reenlisted as a veteran.

Burris, Royal, Ninety-second regiment.

Burrows, James, volunteer, Second Virginia cavalry, private, mustered out July 30, 1865, reenlisted as a veteran.

Callahan, Cyrus, age 25, volunteer, three years, Second Virginia cavalry, company E, private, mustered out July 30, 1865.

Clark, Henry, age 29, volunteer, 1864, three years, One Hundred and Eighty-second regiment, company C, private, mustered out July 7, 1865.

Cheatham, Richard B., age 40, volunteer, 1861, three years, Sixty-third regiment, company D, sergeant, attained lieutenant, served two years, died in Memphis, Tennessee, July 18, 1863.

Craig, Samuel S., age 20, volunteer, Sixty-third regiment, company D, died, transferred to company C, First marine.

Crawford, A. W., volunteer, Ninety-second regiment, company H.

Crooks, Ralph, volunteer, 1861, three years, Thirty-sixth regiment, company A, private, served three years, mustered out in 1864.

Crawford, James, volunteer, three years, Sixty-third regiment, company F, private, reenlisted as a veteran.

Cross, John W., age 22, volunteer, 1864, One Hundred and Eighty-second regiment, private, died at Nashville, Tennessee.

Culver, B. F., age 22, volunteer, 1864, one hundred days, One Hundred and Forty-eighth regiment, assistant surgeon, served four months, mustered out with regiment.

Daoff, L., Seventy-seventh regiment, company H.

Dean, Charles, age 30, volunteer, 1862, three years, Ninety-second regiment, company H, private, served three years, mustered out June 10, 1865.

Dean, John, age 35, volunteer, December 23, 1863, three years, Eighteenth regiment, company F, hospital nurse.

Devol, Silas A., age 18, volunteer, August, 1861, three years, Thirty-sixth regiment, company A, private, served three years, mustered out in 1864.

Devol, Henry F., age 30, volunteer, August, 1861, three years, Thirty-sixth regiment, company A, captain, attained brigadier general, served four years, mustered out July 31, 1865.

Devol, Hiram.

Devol, Alexander C., age 17, volunteer, 1861, three years, Thirty-sixth regiment, company A, private, served three years, honorably discharged in 1864.

Devol, Isaac L., age 19, volunteer, March 14, 1865, Eighteenth regiment, company H, private, served seven months, mustered out October 9, 1865.

Devol, Gilbert, age 16, volunteer, March 14, 1865, Eighteenth regiment, company H, private, seven months, mustered out October 9, 1865.

Devol, Samuel, age 19, volunteer, January 1, 1863, three years, Second Virginia cavalry, company F, private, served two years and five months, mustered out June 30, 1865.

Dixon, Nicklow, age 19, volunteer, 1861, three years, Eighteenth regiment, company F, private, served three years, mustered out in 1864.

Dixon, Wilson, volunteer, 1861, three years, Eighteenth regiment, company F, private, served three years, mustered out in 1864.

Dickson, Isaac, age 19, volunteer, 1865, Eighteenth regiment, company H, private, mustered out October 9, 1865.

Dixon, William, age 19, volunteer, May, 1864, Fourth Virginia cavalry, private, served six months, mustered out in November, 1864.

Dobbins, James, age 30, volunteer, Ninety-second regiment, company H, private, honorable discharged for disability.

Dobbins, Anthony, volunteer, Thirty-sixth regiment, company A, private.

Dolen, Lewis C., age 16, volunteer, March, 1865, One Hundred and Ninety-sixth regiment, private, served sixth months, mustered out September 11, 1865.

Dyer, Charles, volunteer, 1861, three years, Second Virginia cavalry, company F, private, served four years, mustered out June 30, 1865, reenlisted as a veteran.

Dyer, John, age 21, volunteer, September 17, 1861, three years, Second Virginia cavalry, company F, private, reenlisted as a veteran, lost left arm near Winchester September 5, 1864.

Dyer, Samuel, age 18, volunteer, February, 1864, First cavalry, company L, private, served one year and seven months, mustered out September 13, 1865.

Eakins, James, age 24, volunteer, July 14, 1861, three years, Thirteenth regiment, musician, served eleven months, mustered out June 3, 1862.

Fisher, Joshua G., volunteer, January, 1864, Second Virginia cavalry, company F, sergeant, honorably discharged, wounded in Texas, and discharged for disability.

Flag, Luthur, volunteer, Twenty-fifth regiment, company H, private, died of fever.

Fletcher, Wesley T., age 25, volunteer, Fourteenth United States colored heavy artillery, private.

Fleming, David, volunteer, Seventy-seventh regiment, company F, private, died.

Fleming, Aaron.

Fouts, John W., volunteer, October, 1861, three years, Sixty-third regiment, company D, captain, attained the rank of major, served four years, mustered out July 8, 1865.

Gittings, Harry C., volunteer, Ninth cavalry, company B.

Gittings, Metamoras, age 22, volunteer, May 15, 1861, three years, Twenty-fourth regiment, company B, private, served eight months, died January, 1862, mortally wounded at Murfreesborough.

Gliddons, James L., volunteer, 1861, three years, Thirty-sixth regiment, company A, private, died May, 1862, mortally wounded at Lewisburgh.

Gooden, Henry, age 37, volunteer, August, 1862, three years, Ninety-second regiment, company H, private, served two years and ten months, mustered out June 10, 1865, wounded at Chickamauga.

Grubb, Charles M., volunteer, 1861, three years, Eighteenth regiment, company F, first lieutenant, served three years, mustered out November 9, 1864.

Gooden, Solomon M., age 26, volunteer, August, 1862, three years, Ninety-second regiment, company H, private, served one year and five months, died January 6, 1864, of diarrhœa.

Green, Obed, One Hundred and Eighty-second regiment.

Gooden, John, age 18, volunteer, Eighteenth regiment, company H, private.

Grubb, John, Thirty-third regiment, company F, private.

Gooden, Moses, age 32, September 1, 1862, One Hundred and Twenty-second regiment, company C, private, captured in battle of the Wilderness, fate unknown.

Grubb, Archibald, age 25, volunteer, three years, Second Virginia cavalry, company E, private, served three years, mustered out, wounded near close of his time.

Griever, Henry C., volunteer, Second heavy artillery, private, mustered out August, 1865.

Grubb, Goodsill, age 21, volunteer, 1861, three years, Thirty-sixth regiment, company A, private, reenlisted as a veteran.

Grubb, Lewis, age 26, volunteer, 1861, three years, Sixty-third regiment, company D, private, attained the rank of second lieutenant, served nine months, resigned May 26, 1862.

Hagerman, John B., volunteer, 1861, Sixty-third regiment, company D, lieutenant, resigned in 1861, reenlisted, volunteer, 1864, One Hundred and Eighty-second regiment, died.

Hagerman, John H., age 18, volunteer, Fourth Virginia cavalry, company D, lieutenant, died.

Hall, Theodore, age 21, volunteer, August, 1862, three years, Ninety-second regiment, company H, private, served three years, mustered out June 12, 1865.

Hall, John, age 23, 1861, three years, Second Virginia cavalry, company F, private, served three years, mustered out in 1864.

Hall, Alfred, volunteer, three years, Ninety-second regiment, company H, private.

Hall, Frederick, age 29, volunteer, August, 1862, three years, Ninety-second regiment, company H, private, served three years, mustered out June 10, 1865.

Haley, Edward, volunteer, August, 1861, three years, Thirty-sixth regiment, company A, private.

Harwood, William W., age 26, volunteer, 1861, three years, Thirty-sixth regiment, company A, private, attained the rank of commissary sergeant, served four years, mustered out July 27, 1865, reenlisted as a veteran.

Hastings, Adam, age 22.

Henderson, Samuel, volunteer, Seventy-seventh regiment, company K, private, died.

Henderson, Charles, volunteer, three years, Sixty-third regiment, company D, private, reenlisted as a veteran, killed on skirmish line at Big Shanty, Georgia, June 17, 1864.

Henderson, John, volunteer, May 7, 1861, three months, Eighteenth regiment, company K, captain, served three months, mustered out, August 28, 1861

Henderson, Thompson H., volunteer, 1862, three years, Ninety-second regiment, company H, private, served three years, mustered out June 10, 1865.

Higgins, Alexander H., volunteer, July 30, 1862, three years, Ninety-second regiment, company H, captain, served ten months, resigned May 9, 1863.

Hill, John, Eighteenth regiment, company F, private.

Hill, Samuel, age 20, volunteer, three years, Sixty-third regiment, company D, private, honorably discharged for disability, reenlistment, volunteer, Second Virginia cavalry, private, mustered out June 30, 1865.

Hill, Isaac V., age 21, volunteer, February 15, 1865, One Hundred and Eighty-sixth regiment, company I, private, served seven months, mustered out September 18, 1865.

Hill, Obadiah P., age 19, volunteer, October 10, 1861, three years, Sixty-third regiment, company D, private, attained the rank of captain, mustered out July 8, 1865.

Hoon, Samuel, age 20, volunteer, October 8, 1861, three years, Sixty-third regiment, company D, private, served two years and nine months, mustered out July 8, 1865, lost right leg at Decatur, Georgia, July 22, 1864.

Hoon, Madison, age 20, volunteer, October 1, 1861, three years, Sixty-third regiment, company D, corporal, attained rank of captain, served two years and nine months, mustered out July 8, 1865.

Hoon, John, aged 23, volunteer, May, 1861, three months, Eighteenth regiment, company K, private, served three months, mustered out August 28, 1861.

Hutchinson, Calvin A., volunteer, August 27, 1863, six months, Fourth Virginia cavalry, company D, captain, served ten months, mustered out June 23, 1864.

Humphrey, Samuel H., age 21, volunteer, August, 1862, three years, Ninety-second regiment, company H, private, served three years, mustered out June 10, 1865, transferred to invalid corps.

Hurlbut, Benoni W. H., age 18, volunteer, One Hundred and Eighty-second regiment, company C, private, served six months in the Fourth Virginia cavalry.

Jackson, Samuel L., age 18, volunteer, March, 1865, One Hundred and Ninety-sixth regiment, company F, private, served seven months, mustered out September 11, 1865, served six months in Fourth Virginia cavalry.

Jackson, John T., age 23, volunteer, October, 1861, three years, Sixty-third regiment, company D, private, served three years, mustered out 1864.

Jackson, A. M., Eighteenth regiment, company H, private.

Jackson, Frank, volunteer, 1865, One Hundred and Eighty-sixth regiment, private, mustered out September, 1865.

Jackson, B. F., age 21, volunteer, Eleventh Iowa regiment, company D, reenlisted February 14, 1865, One Hundred and Eighty-sixth regiment, company I, first lieutenant, served four months, resigned June 4, 1865.

James, Marion, age 19, volunteer, three years, Ninety-second regiment, company H, private, died September, 1863, of wounds received at Chickamauga.

Johnson, Robert, Ninety-second regiment, company H, private.

Johnson, Newton, age 20, volunteer, August 15, 1861, three years, Eighteenth regiment, company F, private.

Johnson, William, age 25, volunteer, 1861, three years, Sixty-third regiment, company D, private, mustered out July 8, 1863, reenlisted as a veteran.

Johnson, James, age 22, volunteer, 1861, three years, Sixty-third regiment, company D, private, mustered out July 8, 1865, reenlisted as a veteran.

Johnson, Benjamin, volunteer, three years, Sixty-third regiment, company D, private, honorably discharged for loss of speech.

Jordan, John, age 21, volunteer, six months, Fourth Virginia cavalry, company D, private.

Jordan, Mitchell, age 18, volunteer, six months, Fourth Virginia cavalry, company D, private, reenlisted, volunteer, May, 1864, one hundred days, One Hundred and Forty-eighth regiment, private, served four months, mustered out September, 1864.

Justice, George, age 15, volunteer, June 3, 1862, Eighteenth regulars, company F, corporal, wounded at Chickamauga and twice at Jonesborough.

Justice, William, age 15, volunteer, March, 1861, one year, Eighteenth regiment, company H, private, served one year, mustered out 1862, reenlisted, volunteer, six months, Fourth Virginia cavalry, private, served six months, mustered out.

Justice, Henry, age 15, volunteer, September, 1864, Thirty-eighth regiment, company I, private, served ten months, mustered out July, 1865.

Jumper, John, age 27, volunteer, August 15, 1861, three years, Eighteenth regiment, company F, captain, served two years and two months, resigned October 4, 1863, died September 13, 1864, of chronic diarrhœa.

King, Martin S., age 20, volunteer, three years, Second Virginia cavalry, company E, private, mustered out June 30, 1865, reenlisted as a veteran.

Kendal, John, age 23, volunteer, May, 1861, three months, Eighteenth regiment, company F, private, served three months, mustered out August 28, 1864, reenlistment, volunteer, 1861, three years, Eighteenth regiment, company F, private, served three years, mustered out 1864.

Kendall, Hiram, age 17, volunteer, 1861, three years, Eighteenth regiment, company F, private, served four years, mustered out October 9, 1865, reenlisted as a veteran.

Kirby, John, age 22, volunteer, 1862, three years, Ninety-second regiment, company H, private, three years, mustered out June 10, 1865.

Lady, Hiram, age 24, volunteer, three years, Sixty-third regiment, company D, private, mustered out July 8, 1865, reenlisted as a veteran.

Keghoe, J., volunteer, three years, Sixty-third regiment, company D, captain, reenlisted as a veteran.

Lang, James, age 19, volunteer, 1861, three years, Sixty-third regiment, company F, private, served three years, mustered out 1864, captured July 22, 1864, and held nine months.

Langhery, Thornton, volunteer, September, 1861, three years, Second Virginia cavalry, company F, private, served four years, mustered out June 30, 1865, reenlisted as a veteran.

Langley, Benjamin H., age 17, volunteer, three years, Second Virginia cavalry, company I', private, mustered out June 30, 1865.

Latamore, John W., age 18, volunteer, three years, Sixty-third regiment, company D, private, mustered out July 8, 1865, reenlisted as a veteran.

Long, Morris D., age 40, volunteer, 1862, three years, Ninety-second regiment, company H, orderly sergeant, served eighteen months, died of typhoid fever at Nashville.

Mason, H. W., Second Virginia cavalry, company F.

Mason, Franklin, age 16, volunteer, January 27, 1864, Sixty-third regiment, company F, private, served five months, mustered out July 8, 1865.

Mason, Winchester.

Mass, A. J., age 50, volunteer, April, 1861, served three months, Eighteenth regiment, company K, drummer, served four months, mustered out August 28, 1865.

Mankins, A. S., age 30, volunteer, 1862, Ninety-second regiment, company H, private.

McAttee, William H., age 20, volunteer, September, 1861, three years, Second Virginia cavalry, company F, private, served three years and nine months, mustered out June 30, 1865, reenlisted as a veteran, captured near Murfreesborough in 1862 and taken to Libby prison.

McCall, William R., age 17, volunteer, September, 1861, three years, Seventeenth regiment, company H, private, died.

McDonald, John, volunteer, three years, Ninety-second regiment, company H, private.

McDonald, James, age 38, volunteer, September 15, 1861,* three years, Eighteenth regiment, company F, private.

McDeed, John, volunteer. September 1, 1861, three years, Second Virginia cavalry, company F, private, mustered out June 30, 1865, reenlisted as a veteran.

McGuigan, Thomas D., age 28, volunteer, three years, Ninety-second regiment, company H, second sergeant, served one year, honorably discharged for disability.

McGuigan, John G., age 35, volunteer, August 15, 1862, three years, Fourteenth regiment, company D, second sergeant, died in 1863 of fever.

McGuigan, William E., age 30, volunteer, September 15, 1861, Second Virginia cavalry, company E, second sergeant, served thirteen months, discharged for disability in 1862.

McGuigan, Eli M., age 23, 1861, three months, Eighteenth regiment, company K, corporal, served three months, mustered out 1861, reenlistment December 24, 1863, First heavy artillery, company I, served one year and six months, mustered out July 25, 1865.

McKendry, Albert, age 25, volunteer, 1862, Ninety-second regiment, company H, private, honorably discharged for disability in 1863, wounded at Chickamauga.

McKendry, Elijah, age 20, volunteer, Thirty-sixth regiment, company A, private, reenlisted as veteran, missing.

McKelvey, William, age 18, volunteer, March, 1865, Eighteenth regiment, company H, private.

McMann, Orlof, age 17, volunteer, one hundred days, private, died at Winchester.

Morris, Philip, age 38, volunteer, December 31, 1863, Second Virginia cavalry, company E, private, served one year and six months, mustered out July 1, 1865.

Newton, Nathan, volunteer, three years, Second Virginia cavalry, company F, private, reenlisted as a veteran, wounded at Fisher's Hill and died at Winchester.

Newton, William A., age 23, volunteer, February 17, 1862, three years, Sixty-third regiment, company C., musician, served three years, mustered out July 8, 1865, reenlisted as a veteran, last eighteen months clerk in adjutant general's office.

Nickerson, Allen, age 21, volunteer, August 7, 1862, three years, Ninety-second regiment, company H, mustered out July 12, 1865, transferred to Fifteenth regiment, company G, veteran reserve corps.

Nickel, James, age 22, volunteer, three years, Second Virginia cavalry, company F, private, attained rank of sergeant, mustered out June 30, 1865, in three months' service, reenlisted as a veteran, offered a lieutenancy.

Nickel, William, age 24, volunteer, 1861, three months, Eighteenth regiment, company K, corporal, attained rank of sergeant, served three months, mustered out, reenlisted.

Nixon, James M., age 22, volunteer, October 1, 1861, three years, Eighteenth Iowa, company F, private, discharged for disability April 22, 1863, wounded at Murfreesborough, losing a leg.

Nixon, B. F., age 16, volunteer, October, 1863, three years, Eleventh Virginia regiment, company A, private, served one year and eight months, mustered out June 17, 1865, died August 1, 1865, from wound in leg.

Nixon, George E., age 21, volunteer, March 8, 1865, Eighteenth regiment, company F, private, served seven months, mustered out October 9, 1865.

Nixon, William M., age 29, volunteer, December 31, 1863, three years, Second Virginia cavalry, company E, private, served one year and six months, mustered out June 30, 1865.

Nixon, William, age 34, volunteer, 1862, three years, Ninety-second regiment, company H, private, mustered out June 10, 1865.

Norman, A. W., volunteer, October 1, 1861, three years, Eighteenth regiment, company H, private, served four years, mustered out October 9, 1865, reenlisted as a veteran.

Norman, Joseph G., volunteer, October 1, 1861, three years, Thirty-sixth regiment, company K, private, served four years, mustered out July 27, 1865, reenlisted as a veteran, was captured while sick at Winchester, and paroled.

Norman William, volunteer, 1865, One Hundred and Eighty-sixth regiment, company I, private, mustered out September 26, 1865.

Norman, Milton, age 32, volunteer, February 10, 1864, Twenty-seventh regiment, company D, private, mustered out July 11, 1865.

Null, Samuel, volunteer, Sixty-third regiment, company D, private, mustered out July 4, 1865, reenlisted as a veteran.

Norris, Peter, regulars.

Palmer, Isaac L., age 16, volunteer, July 24, 1861, three years Thirty-sixth regiment, company A, division teamster, served four years, mustered out July 27, 1865, reenlisted as a veteran, injured in July, 1864, and in hospital till December, 1864.

Palmer, John D., volunteer, April 22, 1861, three months, Third regiment, company G, private, served three months, second enlistment, June 25, 1861, Third regiment, company C, private, served three years, mustered out June 23, 1864, captured May 3, 1863, paroled May 15th, third enlistment, volunteer, August, 1864, One Hundred and Eighty-second regiment, company C, color sergeant, attained rank of orderly sergeant, served eleven months, mustered out July 7, 1865.

Palmer, George B., age 22, volunteer, January 1, 1863, three years, Second Virginia cavalry, company E, private, served two years and five months, mustered out June 30, 1865, after one year transferred to ambulance corps.

Palmer, Andrew B., age 18, volunteer, February 4, 1865, One Hundred and Twenty-sixth regiment, company I, private, served three months, died May 21, 1865, of measles.

Parcel, Theodore, age 13, volunteer, August, 1863, six months, Fourth Virginia cavalry, company D, private, served ten months, mustered out June 23, 1864.

Parsons, Hardeson, age 21, volunteer, August, 1861, three years, Thirty-sixth regiment, company A, private, served two years and six months, honorably discharged February, 1865, for disabilty, reenlisted as a veteran, wounded.

Parsons, Silas D., age 17, substitute, August, 1864, one year, One Hundred and Eighty-second regiment, company C, private, served eleven months, mustered out July 7, 1865.

Patterson, John, age 22, volunteer, three months, Fourth Virginia cavalry, company F, private, served three months, mustered out.

Perry, Richard, volunteer, Ninety-second regiment, company H, private, died January 6, 1864, of diarrhœa.

Pettibone, John W., age 30, volunteer, December 31, 1863, First cavalry, company L, supposed to be dead.

Philips, C. S., Thirty-sixth regiment, company A.

Pixley, Joseph, volunteer, 1864, Thirty-sixth regiment, company A, one year, mustered out July 27, 1865.

Pratt, Charles C., One Hundred and Eighty-second regiment, company C.

Preston, Benjamin, age 28, volunteer, 1862, Ninety-second regiment, color bearer, wounded October, 1863, and honorably discharged.

Pyle, George D., Second Virginia cavalry, company F, killed at Spencer Court House.

Quimby, Ezra, Seventy-seventh regiment, company H, private, reenlisted as a veteran.

Ramsey, Philip.

Reed, George, age 27, volunteer, June 4, 1861, three years, Twenty-fifth regiment, company H, private, served three years, mustered out in 1864.

Ramsey, James, age 16, volunteer, 1861, three years, Sixty-seventh regiment, private.

Reynolds, Charles, age 21, volunteer, July 14, 1861, three years, Thirteenth regiment, musician, served eleven months, mustered out June 3, 1862, served six months in Fourth Virginia cavalry.

Reyhoe, James F., age 26, volunteer, October, 1861, three years, Sixty-third regiment, company D, private, reenlisted as a veteran, afterwards raised a company of colored troops.

Richards, D. J., volunteer, May, 1864, one hundred days, One Hundred and Forty-eighth regiment, captain, served four months, mustered out September, 1864.

Roach, Rufus W., age 17, volunteer, November 6, 1863, three years, Sixty-third regiment, company F, private, attained the rank of corporal, served one year and eight months, mustered out July 8, 1865.

Roach, Marcellus S., age 17, volunteer, fall of 1861, three years, Sixty-third regiment, company F, corporal, served three years, mustered out in 1864, captured July 22, 1864, and in prison for nine months.

Roach, Wallace S., volunteer, fall of 1861, three years, Sixty-third regiment, company F, private, attained the rank of second lieutenant, mustered out July 8, 1865, reenlisted as a veteran.

Roberts, Elisha, age 20, volunteer, 1861, three years, Sixty-third regiment, company D, private, died March 24, 1862, killed by an accident near New Madrid.

Ross, Daniel, volunteer, 1861, three years, Second Virginia cavalry, company F, private, mustered out June 30, 1865, veteran, captured at Front Royal in the fall of 1864 and paroled, also in first three months' service.

Ross, James, age 21, volunteer, September 19, 1861, three years, Thirty-sixth regiment, company A, private, served three years and ten months, mustered out July 24, 1865, in first three months' service, re-enlisted as a veteran.

Ross, Franklin, age 18, volunteer, 1861, three years, Sixty-third regiment, company D, private, died June 17, 1864, veteran, killed on skirmish line at Big Shanty, Georgia.

Shockley, John, age 31, volunteer, three years, First Virginia light artillery, company C, private, mustered out in 1865.

Scott, Andrew E., volunteer, November 22, 1861, three years, Second Virginia cavalry, company E, captain, served two months, resigned January 12, 1862.

Scott, William H., volunteer, Seventy-seventh regiment, company D, private.

Scott, O. P. H., Second Virginia cavalry, company F, lieutenant, attained to rank of captain, resigned December 23, 1862.

Scott, Freeman, age 18, volunteer, August 28, 1863, three years, Second Virginia cavalry, company F, private, died.

Scroggan, John, One Hundred and Eighty-second regiment, company C.

Skillington, William O., age 22, volunteer, August 10, 1864, One Hundred and Eighty-second regiment, company C, private, mustered out July 14, 1865, served in the first months.

Skillington, Thomas, age 13, volunteer, August, 1863, Fourth Virginia cavalry, company D, private, died in August, 1863, a prisoner.

Slaters, James W. F., age 18, volunteer, fall of 1861, three years, Eighteenth regiment, company F, private, attained to rank of second lieutenant, served four years, mustered out October 9, 1865.

Slater, D. S., age 22, volunteer, fall of 1864, Eighteenth regiment, company F, private, one year, mustered out October 9, 1865.

Sleigh, George W., age 27, volunteer, 1862, three years, Ninety-second regiment, company A, private, attained to rank of sergeant, served three years, mustered out June 10, 1865.

Shipman, Joseph S., volunteer, 1862, three years, Ninety-second regiment, company H.

Smith, Charles, age 30, volunteer, Ninety-second regiment, company H, private.

Spayerman, John, Ninth cavalry, company B, private.

Spencer, George W.

Spooner, Cyrus, age 31, volunteer, January 1, 1863, Second Virginia cavalry, company F, private, served one and a half years, mustered out June 30, 1865.

Stewart, Tartus L., volunteer, three years, Ninety-second regiment, company H, private, died November 25, 1863, killed at Mission Ridge.

Stewart, John V.

Swift, jr., Lyman W., age 24, volunteer, December 4, 1861, three years, Seventy-seventh regiment, company F, private, served four years and four months, mustered out March 8, 1866, captured at Mark's Mills, and in prison nine months.

Swift, John, age 22, volunteer, Seventy-seventh regiment, company F, private, died August 10, 1862.

Taylor, Thomas C., volunteer, 1861, three years, One Hundred and Eighty-second regiment, company C, private.

Taylor, John, age 19, volunteer, June 8, 1861, three years, Twenty-sixth regiment, company D, private, served four years, mustered out August 1, 1865, wounded in 1864, and served in hospital till muster out.

Taylor, Theodore, age 19, volunteer, September, 1864, One Hundred and Eighty-second regiment, company C, private, served seven months, died March 23, 1865, of measles.

Thomas, —— Twenty-sixth regiment, company F.

Thurlow, Silas, Sixty-third regiment, company F.

Thornbury, William H., volunteer, August, 1861, three years, Thirty-sixth regiment, company A, private, served ten months, died June, 1864, killed at Lynchburgh.

Townsend, William C., age 22, volunteer, 1861, three years, Sixty-third regiment, company D, private, attained the rank of corporal, mustered out July 4, 1865, reenlisted as a veteran.

Truesdale, John W., age 16, three years, Eighteenth regiment, company F, private, served three years, mustered out.

Truesdale, Joseph F., age 16, volunteer, three years, Sixty-third regiment, company D, private, mustered out July 4, 1865.

Tyson, Ira, three years, Ninety-second regiment, company H, private.

Tyson, Charles, Eighteenth regiment, company H, private.

Vincent, W. J., age 31, January 1, 1864, Second Virginia cavalry, company F, private, served one year and six months, mustered out July, 1865.

Tucker, Wesley, age 25, volunteer, September, 1861, three years, Sixty-third regiment, first lieutenant, served nine months, resigned June 18, 1862, sergeant in first three months' service.

Tucker, James, age 22, volunteer, September, 1861, three years, Sixty-third regiment, company D, second sergeant, served seven months, honorably discharged in 1861, in first three months' service, discharged for disability.

Vincent, H., age 20, volunteer, three years, Sixty-third regiment, company D, private, mustered out July 4, 1865.

Vincent, C. W., age 17, volunteer, August 11, 1864, One Hundred and Eighty-second regiment, company C, corporal, served one year, mustered out July 7, 1865, served six months in Fourth Virginia cavalry.

Vincent, Marion, age 18, volunteer, July 24, 1861, three years, Thirty-sixth regiment, company A, private, served three years, honorably discharged in 1864, by reason of wounds.

Voschel, Ebenezer, volunteer, Sixty-third regiment, company H, private, died.

Walters, Ralph, age 31, volunteer, January 1, 1862, three years, Sixty-third regiment, company F, private, served three years and six months, honorably discharged, mustered out July 4, 1865, veteran.

Ward, Isaac, volunteer, three years, Seventy-seventh regiment, company H, private, mustered out March 8, 1866, veteran.

Whissen, Amos A., volunteer, April, 1861, three months, Seventeenth regiment, company H, first lieutenant, served three months, mustered out, reenlistment, volunteer, November 4, 1861, three years, Seventeenth regiment, company H, captain, served two years, resigned October 27, 1863, reenlistment, volunteer, October 1, 1864, One Hundred and Eighty-second regiment, company C, captain, attained rank of major, served nine months, mustered out July 7, 1865.

Whitney, James, age 25, volunteer, six months, Fourth Virginia cavalry, private, served six months, mustered out.

White, Hiram, age 28, volunteer, April 23, 1861, three months, Eighteenth regiment, company K, corporal, served four months, mustered out August 28, 1861.

Wilson, Daniel, age 25, volunteer, three years, Sixty-third regiment, company D, private, mustered out July 4, 1865, veteran, detached as ferryman in 1863.

Wilson, William, age 20, volunteer, September, 1864, three years, One Hundred and Seventeenth regiment, company F, private, served eleven months, mustered out August 1, 1865.

Wilson, James.

Winstanley, Peter, age 23, volunteer, August, 1862, three years, Ninety-second regiment, company H, private, served ten months, mustered out June 10, 1865.

Winstanley, James, age 32, volunteer, August 11, 1864, one year, One Hundred and Eighty-second regiment, company C, corporal, served eleven months, mustered out July 7, 1865.

Wood, Newton, age 20, volunteer, October 14, 1863, Eleventh Virginia regiment, company A, private, honorably discharged April 17, 1865, for disability.

Wood, William, age 17, volunteer, September 15, 1863, Eleventh Virginia regiment, company A, private, honorably discharged in 1865, wounded at battle of Petersburgh March 31, 1865, discharged on account of wound.

Worstall, George, age 35, volunteer, August, 1862, Ninety-second regiment, company H, private, served two years and ten months, mustered out June 10, 1865.

Wright, Horace, volunteer, Seventy-seventh regiment, company H, private, discharged.

Wright, Royal, volunteer, Seventy-seventh regiment, company H, private, died

Wright, Russell, Seventy-seventh regiment, company H.

RECAPITULATION.

WATERTOWN TOWNSHIP.

Adams, Demas, age 18, volunteer, September 13, 1861, three years, Eighteenth regiment, company, F, orderly sergeant, served three years, mustered out September, 1864, captured near Lookout Mountain, reenlistment, 1864, One Hundred and Eighty-sixth regiment, company I, attained the rank of second lieutenant, mustered out September 25, 1865, held in Libby prison and Belle Isle, six months.

Adams, Augustine, age 16, volunteer, October, 1861, three years, First light artillery, company H, private, served three years, mustered out October 23, 1864.

Adams, Hamlin M., age 25, volunteer, may, 1864, one hundred days, One Hundred and Forty-eighth regiment, company A, private.

Andrews, Samuel, volunteer, May, 1864, one hundred days, One Hundred and Forty-eighth regiment, company I, private, served four months, mustered out September, 1864.

Arnold, Joseph A, age 18, volunteer, May, 1864, one hundred days, One Hundred and Forty-eighth regiment, company I, private, served four months, mustered out September, 1864.

Bartlett, George, volunteer, three years, Sixty-third regiment, company D, private.

Beebe, Lyman, age 27, volunteer, May, 1864, one hundred days, One Hundred and Forty-eighth regiment, company I, private, served four months, mustered out September, 1864, detailed as hospital nurse.

Beebe, John W., age 20, volunteer, May, 1864, one hundred days, One hundred and Forty-eighth regiment, company I, private, mustered out September, 1864, sick.

Bohl, Conrad, age 35, volunteer, October 22, 1861, three years, Seventy-seventh regiment, company C, sergeant, honorably discharged for disability.

Brabham, John W., age 23, volunteer, August 27, 1861, three years, Seventy-seventh regiment, company H, private, served one year, honorably discharged September, 1862, wounded at Shiloh, reenlistment, May, 1864, one hundred days, One Hundred and Forty-eighth regiment, company K, private, served four months, mustered out September, 1864, third enlistment, October, 1864, one year, First cavalry, company L, private, served eight months, mustered out June, 1865.

Brabham, Rickard B., age 16, volunteer, 1861, three years, Seventy-seventh regiment, company H, private, discharged March 20, 1863, for disability.

Brabham, Stanton L., age 34, volunteer, August, 1861, three years, Seventy-seventh regiment, company H, wagonmaster, reenlisted as a veteran.

Bidel, Jacob, volunteer, Seventy-seventh regiment, company B, private, died.

Brabham, Thomas J., volunteer, August, 1861, three years, Seventy-seventh regiment, company H, private, served three years and three months, mustered out December, 1864.

Brabham, George W., age 26, volunteer, October 19, 1862, three years, Ninth cavalry, company B, private, died August 10, 1864, captured at Knoxville January 25, 1864, confined in Belle Isle and in Andersonville, where he died.

Brabham, Henry H., age 24, volunteer, October 19, 1862, Ninth regiment, company B, private, served three years, mustered out December, 1864.

Buchanan, George W., age 28, volunteer, August 11, 1862, three years, Eighty-seventh Indiana, company A, private, served three years, mustered out June, 1865, captured and parolled, wounded at Chickamauga.

Buchanan, Charles, age 23, volunteer, May, 1864, one hundred days, One Hundred and Forty-eighth regiment, company I, private, served four months, mustered out September, 1865.

Burchett, William T., age 25, volunteer, February 9, 1865, three years, Thirty-sixth regiment, company H, private, served five months, mustered out July 27, 1865.

Breckenridge, James F, one hundred days, One Hundred and Forty-eighth regiment, company D, private, died September 10, 1864, at Baltimore, Maryland.

Burris, Bernard, age 29, volunteer, October, 1861, three years, Seventy-seventh regiment, company H, private, reenlisted as a veteran.

Burris, Rufus, age 25, volunteer, October, 1861, three years, Seventy-seventh regiment, company H, private, honorably discharged for disability, reenlistment, October 6, 1864, one year, Seventy-first regiment, company F, private, captured and imprisoned four months.

Burris, Reuben, age 18, volunteer, October, 1861, three years, Seventy-seventh regiment, company H, private, honorably discharged for disability, reenlistment, Seventy-seventh regiment, company H, private, honorably discharged for disability.

Burris, John J., age 26, October, 1861, three years, Seventy-seventh regiment, company H, private, honorably discharged.

Burris, Francis M., age 18, volunteer, October, 1861, three years, Seventy-seventh regiment, company H, private, died April 6, 1862, killed at Shiloh.

Burris, Albert, age 18, volunteer, October, 1861, three years, Seventy-seventh regiment, company H, private, reenlisted as a veteran, captured near Camden and imprisoned at Camp Ford ten months.

Burris, Harvey, age 16, volunteer, October, 1861, three years, Seventy-seventh regiment, company H, private, honorably discharged for disability, reenlisted as a veteran.

Chamberlain, John D., jr, age 21, volunteer, May, 1864, one hundred days, One Hundred and Forty-eighth regiment, company I, private, served four months, mustered out September, 1865.

Colwell, William W., age 17, volunteer, 1861, three years, Seventy-seventh regiment, company C, honorably discharged for disability.

Colman, William H., age 18, volunteer, February, 1865, Thirty-sixth regiment, company H, private, mustered out July 27, 1865.

Colvin, Charles, Seventh cavalry.

Cooksey, T. H., age 29, volunteer, October 9, 1862, three years, ninth cavalry, company B, private, attained the rank of ordnance sergeant, honorably discharged June 12, 1865, for disability.

Cozzens, Samuel, age 24, volunteer, May, 1864, one hundred days, One Hundred and Forty-eighth regiment, company I, private, served four months, mustered out September, 1864.

Criswell, Isaac, age 34, volunteer, January 5, 1864, First cavalry, company C, private, served one year and eight months, mustered out September 13, 1865.

Creeser, Adam, age 17, volunteer, July 29, 1861, three years, Thirty-ninth regiment, company F, corporal, attained to rank of sergeant, served four years, mustered out July 9, 1865, reenlisted as a veteran.

Danielson, Leroy H., age 38, volunteer, May, 1864, one hundred days, One Hundred and Forty-eighth regiment, company I, private, served four months, mustered out September, 1864.

Day, Thomas, age 25, volunteer, August, 1862, three years, Ninety-second regiment, company F, second lieutenant, served five months, resigned January, 1863, reenlistment, volunteer, March, 1863, one hundred days, One Hundred and Forty-eighth regiment, adjutant, served four months, mustered out September, 1864.

Dauley, Hiel, One Hundred and Twenty-fifth regiment, company I.

Day, Alvin, age 18, volunteer, February, 1864, three years, Thirty-sixth regiment, company F, private.

Deming, Henry M., age 25, volunteer, August, 1861, three years, Thirty-sixth regiment, company F, private, served one year, honorably discharged July, 1862, first discharge for disability, second discharge sick at Washington and sent home, reenlistment, volunteer, May, 1864, one hundred days, One Hundred and Forty-eighth regiment, company I, private, served four months, mustered out in 1864.

Deming, Edward N., age 18, volunteer, October, 1861, three years, Seventy-seventh regiment, company B, private, captured at Shiloh, taken to Mobile, and supposed to be dead.

Deming, Lester C., age 19, volunteer, May, 1864, one hundred days, One Hundred and Forty-eighth regiment, company I, private, served four months, honorably discharged in 1864.

Devore, David A., age 20, volunteer, January, 1862, three years, Sixty-third regiment, company D, private, served seven months, honorably discharged August 13, 1862, died August 20th of diarrhœa.

Dickerson, Greensbury F., age 45, volunteer, September, 1862, three years, Seventy-seventh regiment, company H, private, served one year, honorably discharged September, 1863, for disability.

Dickerson, Milton H., age 16, volunteer, September, 1862, three years, Seventy-seventh regiment, company H, private, served nine months, died June 17, 1863, taken sick just after the battle of Shiloh.

Dickerson, Cassius M. C., age 15, volunteer, March 16, 1865, Eighteenth regiment, company K, private.

Ewing, Marquis, volunteer, three years, Seventy-seventh regiment, company H, private.

Fish, James, age 24, volunteer, 1864, First cavalry, private.

Fohl, John, age 21, volunteer, July 29, 1861, three years, Thirty-ninth regiment, company F, private, first sergeant, served four years, mustered out July 9, 1865, reenlisted as a veteran.

Ford, Daniel, age 44, volunteer, June 11, 1864, One Hundred and Twenty-second regiment, company G, private, four battles, served one year, mustered out June 26, 1865.

Gilpin, Manley, age 17, volunteer, October 14, 1861, three years, Sixty-second regiment, company I, private, served three years, mustered out October, 1864.

Gilpin, Joseph, age 20, volunteer, November, 1861, three years, Sixty-second regiment, company I, private, honorably discharged for disability, died in 1865.

Gilpin, James, age 15, volunteer, October, 1861, three years, Sixty-second regiment, company I, private, served ten months, honorably discharged August, 1862, for disability.

Gilpin, Jonas, volunteer, three years, Sixty-third regiment, company D, private, died.

Gilpin, Jonas, jr., age 20, volunteer, September, 1861, three years, Sixty-third regiment, company D, private, served ten months, died in 1862.

Gilpin, Matthew, December, 1863, Sixty-third regiment, company D, private, captured and supposed to have died in Andersonville prison

Gilpin, Sullivan, age 18, volunteer, April, 1861, three months, Eighteenth regiment, private, served four months, mustered out August 28, 1861, reenlisted as a veteran, September, 1861, three years, Sixty-third regiment, company D, served four years, mustered out July 8, 1865, wounded in the battle of the Wilderness, May, 1864.

Gilpin, Rufus, age 18, volunteer, October, 1863, three years, One Hundred and Twenty-second regiment, company C, private, served one year and nine months, mustered out July, 1865.

Gillmor, William W., age 24, volunteer, August 1, 1861, three years, Thirty-sixth regiment, company F, private, attained to rank of corporal, served four years, mustered out July 27, 1865, reenlisted as a veteran, captured at Lewisburgh, May, 23, 1862, in prison for four months, and wounded at Mission Ridge.

Gillmoor, Cromwell, age 31, volunteer, May, 1864, one hundred days, One Hundred and Forty-eighth regiment, company I, private, honorably discharged September, 1864, sick two months, and died three weeks after his return home.

Gossett, Warden, age 20, volunteer, 1861, three years, Seventy-seventh regiment, company H, private, honorably discharged November, 1862, sick most of the time and discharged for disability.

Gossett, Miles, age 16, volunteer, July, 1861, six months, Fourth Virginia cavalry, company D, private, served six months, mustered out February, 1862.

Gossett, Lindsay, age 28, volunteer, 1863, six months, Fourth Virginia cavalry, company B, private, served six months, mustered out.

Greene, Harvey, age 20, volunteer, August, 1861, three years, Thirty-sixth regiment, company F, private, served nine months, died May 1, 1862, of pneumonia, in West Virginia.

Greene, James P., age 25, volunteer, November, 1861, three years, Seventy-seventh regiment, company B, second sergeant, served seven months, died June, 1862, captured at Shiloh, April, 1862, imprisoned and died in prison hospital in Georgia.

Hagerman, George W., age 37, volunteer, May, 1864, one hundred days, One Hundred and Forty-eighth regiment, company I, private, served four months, mustered out September, 1864, detailed as provost guard, at Bermuda Hundred.

Hall, William, age 18, volunteer, November 26, 1861, three years, Sixty-third regiment, company F, private, honorably discharged for disability, reenlisted as a veteran.

Harry, John W., volunteer, six months, Fourth Virginia cavalry, private, served six months, mustered out.

Henry, George, age 27, volunteer, May, 1864, one hundred days, One Hundred and Forty-eighth regiment, company I, private, mustered out September, 1864, sick the whole time at Bermuda Hundred.

Henry, B. F., age 38, volunteer, May, 1864, one hundred days, One Hundred and Forty-eighth regiment, company I, private, served four months, mustered out September, 1864, detailed as provost guard at Bermuda Hundred.

Henry, John, age 18, volunteer, August 9, 1864, one year, gunboat, private, served one year, mustered out June 12, 1865.

Henry, Arius, N., age 23, volunteer, August, 1861, three years, Thirty-sixth regiment, company F, private, served ten months, honorably discharged June 1, 1862, for disability.

Henry, George, age 34, volunteer, May, 1864, one hundred days, One Hundred and Forty-eighth regiment, company I, private, served four months, mustered out September, 1864.

Henry, David, age 29, volunteer, October 28, 1861, three years, Sixty-third regiment, company F, private, served three years and nine months, mustered out July 8, 1865, reenlisted as a veteran.

Henry, Joseph, age 25, volunteer, October, 1862, Sixty-third regiment, company F, private, served two years, died September 26, 1864.

Hinton, Samuel, age 28, volunteer, October, 1861, three years, Seventy-seventh regiment, company F, private, served four years, mustered out March 8, 1866, captured at Sabine River, and in Camp Ford prison ten months.

Hinton, William B., age 30, volunteer, October, 1861, three years, Seventy-seventh regiment, company F, private, mustered out March 8, 1866, captured at Sabine River, and in Camp Ford prison ten months.

Hootsel, Joseph, volunteer, three years, Seventy-seventh regiment, company B, private.

Hootsel, Peter, volunteer, October, 1861, Seventy-seventh regiment, company B, private, died in Camp Ford prison.

Hootsel, John, age 19, volunteer, June, 1862, three months, eighty-seventh regiment, company A, private, mustered out September 20, 1862, reenlistment, February, 1865, Thirty-sixth regiment, company H, mustered out July 27, 1865.

Hootsel, Frank, volunteer, 1862, three years, Ninety-second regiment, company F, died.

Hootsel, George, volunteer, 1862, three years, Ninety-second regiment, company F.

Hootsel, William, volunteer, March, 1865, Eighteenth regiment, company K.

Humiston, Charles, age 30, volunteer, May, 1864, one hundred days, One Hundred and Forty-eighth regiment, company I, private, died, 1864, of measles

Humphrey, Orton E., age 19, volunteer, May, 1864, one hundred days, One Hundred and Forty-eighth regiment, company I, private, honorably discharged September, 1864.

Klinger, Joseph, age 19, volunteer, July 11, 1863, three years, Second heavy artillery, private, mustered out August 23, 1865.

Librand, Frederick, age 20, volunteer, June, 1861, three years, Thirty-ninth regiment, company F, private, served two years, honorably discharged 1863, for disability, reenlistment, May, 1864, one hundred days, One Hundred and Forty-eighth regiment, company I, private, served four months, mustered out September, 1864.

McGrew, Jesse, age 18, volunteer, May, 1864, one hundred days, One Hundred and Forty-eighth regiment, company I, private, served four months, mustered out September, 1864.

Martin, Henry W., age 20, volunteer, May, 1864, one hundred days, One Hundred and Forty-eighth regiment, company I, private, served four months, mustered out September, 1864, in hospital two months.

McFarland, W. P., age 36, volunteer, October, 1861, three years, Seventy-seventh regiment, company E, private, captured near Pine Bluffs and imprisoned in Camp Ford prison ten months.

Mellor, Thomas, age 29, volunteer, 1861, three years, Sixty-third regiment company D, private, served four months, died July 8, 1862.

Micham, William M., volunteer, Ninety-second regiment, company G, died.

Miser, Adam, age 21, volunteer, 1861, three years, Thirty-sixth regiment, company F, private.

Morris, John, age 29, volunteer, November, 1861, three years, Seventy-seventh regiment, company B, private, mustered out 1866, captured at Pine Bluffs, imprisoned at Camp Ford ten months, reenlisted as a veteran.

Morris, Elza, age 21, volunteer, November, 1861, three years, Seventy-seventh regiment, company D, private, died September 16, 1862, of fever.

Morris, Elwood, age 21, volunteer, November, 1861, three years, Seventy-seventh regiment, company D, private, honorably discharged for disability, died one month after his brother, October, 1862.

Morris, Harvey, age 22, volunteer, May, 1864, one hundred days, One Hundred and Forty-eighth regiment, company I, private, honorably discharged September, 1864.

McNeal, Cromwell, age 29, volunteer, October 16, 1861, Forty-first Illinois, assistant surgeon, died June 11, 1862, was attacked with measles, before full recovery was overdone by excessive labor at his post, and died.

McNeal, Franklin, age 25, volunteer, May, 1864, one hundred days, One Hundred and Forty-eighth regiment, company I, private, served four months, mustered out September, 1864.

Moliney, Reuben, volunteer, three years, Seventy-seventh regiment, company B.

Muncton, Enoch, age 30, volunteer, February 27, 1864, Thirty-sixth regiment, company K, private, mustered out May, 1865.

Newbanks, Alfred D., age 24, volunteer, October, 1861, three years, Seventy-seventh regiment, company B, private, died January 19, 1862, at Camp Putnam, of measles and pneumonia.

Neason, John, age 21, volunteer, August, 1861, three years, Thirty-sixth regiment, company F, private, died 1865, at Andersonville, of wound.

Palmer, Gabriel Y., age 20, volunteer, April, 1861, three months, Eighteenth regiment, private, served four months, mustered out August 28, 1861, reenlistment, July 6, 1861, three years, Thirty-sixth regiment, company F, served three years, mustered out August, 1864, wounded at Chattanooga, September 24, 1863, transferred to invalid corps, reenlistment, February 22, 1865, Forty-third regiment, company A, private, mustered out July 13, 1865.

Peter, Philip, age 42, volunteer, October, 1861, three years, Seventy-seventh regiment, company B, sergeant, served three years and three months, died January 8, 1865, captured April 25, 1864, imprisoned at Camp Ford, died in prison hospital.

Proctor, Alfred, age 20, volunteer, February 27, 1864, Thirty-sixth regiment, company F, private, died March 21, 1864, of measles.

Proctor, Edward, age 18, volunteer, March 27, 1864, three years, Thirty-sixth regiment, company F, private, served one year and four months, mustered out July 27, 1865.

Reed, George W., age 17, volunteer, 1863, six months, Fourth regiment, private, served eight months, mustered out, reenlistment, May, 1864, one hundred days, One Hundred and Forty-eighth regiment, company I, private, served four months, mustered out September, 1864

Radecker, William, age 22, volunteer, May, 1864, one hundred days, One Hundred and Forty-eighth regiment, company I, private, served four months, mustered out September, 1864.

Rice, William, Second cavalry.

Rigg, John C., age 21, volunteer, July 29, 1861, three years, Thirty-sixth regiment, company A, private, discharged March, 1865, captured at Chickamauga, imprisoned nine months, paroled, could not be discharged on account of parole till March 18, 1865.

Riley, George W., first enlistment, volunteer, three months, Eighty-fifth regiment, company F, private, served three months, mustered out, second enlistment, volunteer, August, 1863, six months, Fourth Virginia cavalry, company D, private, served six months, mustered out February, 1864, third enlistment, volunteer, May, 1864, one hundred days, One Hundred and Forty-eighth regiment, company I, private, served four months, mustered out September, 1864, fourth enlistment, age 25, volunteer, February 10, 1865, one year, Thirty-sixth regiment, company H, private, served five months, mustered out July 27, 1865.

Ross, Thomas, Seventy-seventh regiment, company H.

Riley, Albert, volunteer, 1863, six months Fourth Virginia cavalry, company D, private, served six months, mustered out March 15, 1864, reenlistment, May, 1864, one hundred days, One Hundred and Forty-eighth regiment, company I, private, served four months, mustered out September, 1864, reenlistment, February 10, 1865, one year, Thirty-sixth regiment, company H, private served five months, mustered out July 27, 1865.

Ryan, Thomas, age 25, volunteer, June, 1862, three months, Eighty-seventh regiment, company A, private, mustered out September 20, 1864.

Rutter, William C., age 41, volunteer, October, 1861, Seventy-seventh regiment, company B, private, served one year, died September 24, 1862, captured at Shiloh and died in prison at Macon, Georgia, of disease caused by privation and bad usage.

Remeley, John L., age 25, volunteer, October, 1861, three years, First cavalry, company L, private, died October 1, 1862, buried near Fort Blair, Kentucky

Schwartzeup, Adam, age 21, volunteer, 1861, Twenty-eighth regiment, private, died 1862 in hospital at Bull Run, Virginia.

Scott, Watson, Seventy-seventh regiment, company A.

Smith, Henry, age 21, volunteer, May, 1864, one hundred days, One Hundred and Forty-eighth regiment, company I, private, served four months, mustered out September, 1864.

Snow, C. P., age 44, volunteer, May, 1864, one hundred days, One Hundred and Forty-eighth regiment, company I, private, served four months, mustered out September, 1864.

Starling, Stephen, age 31, volunteer, May, 1864, one hundred days, One Hundred and Forty-eighth regiment, company I, private, honorably discharged September 20, 1864, left in hospital at Washington with measles, and not able to rejoin regiment.

Steber, Adam, volunteer, Thirty-sixth regiment, company B, private, died July 4, 1863, of erysipelas.

Steeber, Jacob, age 26, volunteer, October 8, 1861, First Virginia light artillery, company C, private, served three years and eight months, mustered out June 28, 1865, reenlisted as a veteran.

Webster, John L., age 31, volunteer, October, 1861, three years, Seventy-seventh regiment, company H, private, served six months, honorably discharged April, 1862, for disability, reenlistment, volunteer, May, 1864, one hundred days, One Hundred and Forty-eighth regiment, company I, private, served four months, mustered out 1864.

Webster, Andrew, age 19, volunteer, May, 1864, one hundred days, One Hundred and Forty-eighth regiment, company I, private, served four months, mustered out in September, 1864.

Wells, Adams, age 18, volunteer, 1861, Seventy-seventh regiment, company B, three years, private, died in January, 1863.

Wells, Ira, volunteer, Seventy-seventh regiment, company B, three years, private, died.

Wigner, W. D., age 21, volunteer, December, 1862, pilot on gunboat, mustered out in 1865, pressed as pilot into rebel service, ran his boat aground and escaped to Union lines, when the Diana was captured, and escaped by swimming, served as first-class pilot through the war.

Wilson, Daniel, age 25, volunteer, September, 1861, three years, Sixty-third regiment, company D, private, served four years, mustered out July 8, 1865, reenlisted as a veteran.

Waterman, Ralph O., age 36, volunteer, three years, Sixty-third regiment, company F, private, died at Jackson, Tennessee.

Waterman, Charles L., age 22, volunteer, July, 1863, six months, Fourth Virginia cavalry, company D, first corporal, attained first sergeant, served six months, mustered out in February, 1864, reenlisted, volunteer, May, 1864, one hundred days, One Hundred and Forty-eighth regiment, company I, served two months, July 23, 1864, died of camp fever, taken sick at Bermuda Hundred.

Winsor, Heary H., age 16, volunteer, September 1, 1863, six months, Fourth Virginia cavalry, private, served six months, mustered out in February, 1864, reenlisted, volunteer, May, 1864, one hundred days, One Hundred and Forty-eighth regiment, company I, served four months, mustered out in September, 1864.

Wolcott, Lewis, age 24, volunteer, August, 1861, three years, Thirty-sixth regiment, company F, private, died in hospital at Summerville, December 1, 1861.

Wolcott, Rollin, age 16, volunteer, July, 1863, six months Fourth Virginia cavalry, company D, private, served six months mustered out March 12, 1864, reenlisted, volunteer, March 20, 1864, Third United States cavalry, company D, private, served through the war.

Wolcott, Roscoe, age 22, volunteer, May, 1864, one hundred days, One Hundred and Forty-eighth regiment, company I, orderly, served four months, mustered out in September, 1864.

Wolcott, C. F., age 15, volunteer, October 24, 1861, three years, First light artillery, company H, private, corporal gunner, served three years, mustered out October 23, 1864.

Woodruff, Mark, age 18, volunteer, June, 1861, three years, Seventh Missouri cavalry, private, served two years and three months, honorably discharged September 1, 1863, reenlisted in March, 1864, Seventy-seventh regiment, company G, corporal, wounded twice, captured at Mark's Mills, taken sick and died on the journey.

Woodruff, Mansley, age 20, volunteer, August 1, 1862, one year, Sixtieth regiment, company K, private, mustered out October 10, 1862, reenlisted in February, 1865, One Hundred and Ninety-fourth regiment, company C, private, attained corporal, mustered out October 24, 1865, captured at Harper's Ferry, paroled and exchanged.

Woodruff, Anson, age 17, volunteer, March, 1864, Thirty-sixth regiment, company F, drummer, served one year and four months, mustered out July 27, 1865.

Woodruff, George N., age 18, volunteer, 1861, three years, Forty ninth regiment, private, served four years, mustered out in September, 1865, reenlisted as a veteran.

Woodruff, O. Jerome, age 41, May, 1864, volunteer, one hundred days, One Hundred and Forty-eighth regiment, company I, private, served four months, mustered out in September, 1864.

Waterman, Daniel, volunteer, three years, Seventy-seventh regiment, company B, private.

Vincent, Thomas, age 19, volunteer, November 25, 1861, three years, Seventy-seventh regiment, company B, private, served one year, honorably discharged November 26, 1862, for disability.

Quimby, Sol, volunteer, three years, Seventy-seventh regiment, company H.

Quimby, Hanford, volunteer.

RECAPITULATION.

Huntington's battery	2
Buell's battery	1
Second heavy artillery	1
Fourth Virginia cavalry	9
Ninth Ohio cavalry	3
Second Ohio cavalry	1
Seventh Ohio cavalry	1
Third United States cavalry	1
Seventh Missouri cavalry	1
First Ohio cavalry	4
Seventy-seventh Ohio	42
One Hundred and Forty-eighth Ohio	38
Thirty-sixth Ohio	20
Sixty-third Ohio	12
Ninety-second Ohio	4
Thirty-ninth Ohio	3
Eighteenth Ohio (three years)	3
Sixty-second Ohio	3
Eighteenth Ohio (three months)	2
Seventh Ohio	2
One Hundred and Twenty-second Ohio	2
Gunboat service	2
One each in Sixtieth Ohio, Forty-third Ohio, Forty-first Illinois, Forty-ninth Illinois, Twenty-eighth Pennsylvania, Eighty-seventh Indiana, Eighty-fifth Ohio, One Hundred and Twenty-fifth Ohio, One Hundred and Eighty-sixth Ohio, One Hundred and Ninety-fourth Ohio	10
Total number soldiers	146
Died	26

WESLEY TOWNSHIP

Baker, George H., age 16, volunteer, June, 1861, three years, Fourth Virginia cavalry, company D, private, served three years, mustered out June 23, 1864.

Baker, Francis, age 18, 1864, Thirty-sixth regiment, company F

Bachelor, Alexander, age 20, volunteer, August 14, 1862, three years. Ninety-second regiment, company G, private, died December 19, 1864, wounded at Chattanooga and also at Franklin, Tennessee, captured and died in hospital.

Barnes, Lewis H., age 19, volunteer, 1864, Thirty-sixth regiment, company B, private, died October 26, 1864, at Annapolis, Maryland.

Beebe, Guy, Seventy-third regiment, company F.

Brill, Benjamin F., age 19, volunteer, August 1, 1861, three years, Thirty-sixth regiment, company F, private, attained rank of sergeant, wounded and had typhoid fever, transferred to the invalid corps, reenlisted in the veteran reserve corps.

Brill, Alexander H., age 26, volunteer, October 27, 1861, three years, Sixty-third regiment, company G, private, attained rank of first lieutenant, mustered out July 8, 1865, sick with typhoid, billious, and intermittent fevers, detailed for recruiting service, reenlisted as a veteran.

Brill, John R., age 17, volunteer, May 17, 1864, one hundred days, One Hundred and Forty-eighth regiment, company D, private, served four months, mustered out September, 1864, reenlistment, February 15, 1865, Nineteenth regiment, company D, private, served eight months, mustered out October 21, 1865.

Brill, William H., age 25, volunteer, May, 1864, one hundred days, One Hundred and Forty-eighth regiment, company D, corporal, served four months, mustered out September, 1864.

Caldwell, William B., age 19, Seventy-seventh regiment, company B.

Callahan, George E., age 26, volunteer, August 12, 1862, three years, Ninety-second regiment, company G, private, died March 6, 1863, at Carthage, Tennessee.

Callahan, Ezekiel, age 35, Ninety-second regiment, company G, died.

Campbell Alexander A., age 40, volunteer, October 15, 1861, three years, Seventy-third regiment, company F, sergeant, served three years, honorably discharged in 1864, after the reenlistment acted as sergeant in pioneer company till put in charge of the ambulance train.

Carpenter, George W., age 33, volunteer, January 26, 1864, Thirty-sixth regiment, company A, private, served one year and six months, mustered out July 27, 1865.

Carr, R. C., Fifth regiment, company G.

Carwee, Seneca, Second cavalry, company F.

Clarke, Leander, age 19, Thirty-sixth regiment, company F.

Clayton, David E., age 25, volunteer, August, 1862, three years, Ninety-second regiment, company G, private, attained rank of sergeant, served two years and ten months, mustered out June 10, 1865.

Clayton, James A., age 24, volunteer, May, 1864, one hundred days, One Hundred and Forty-eighth regiment, company D, corporal, served four months, mustered out September, 1864

Clayton, Isaac C., age 21, volunteer, May, 1864, one hundred days, One Hundred and Forty-eighth regiment, company B, private, served four months, mustered out September, 1864

Coler, Charles H., volunteer, July 18, 1861, three years, Thirty-ninth regiment, company C, private, served four years, mustered out July 9, 1865, reenlisted as a veteran.

Coler, George M., age 20, volunteer, May, 1864, one hundred days, One Hundred and Forty-eighth regiment, company D, private, died August 20, 1864, of camp disease at City Point.

Coler, Patrick Perley, Seventy-seventh regiment, company F.

Coler, John E, age 22, volunteer, May, 1864, one hundred days, One Hundred and Forty-eighth regiment, company D, private, served four months, mustered out September, 1864, sick for two months.

Coler, Felix W., age 28, volunteer, May, 1864, one hundred days, One Hundred and Forty-eighth regiment, company D, private, died August 28, 1864, of congestion of the lungs.

Colwell, W. W., age 18, Seventy-seventh regiment, company B.

Cowee, Sardine, age 23, volunteer, February 27, 1864, One Hundred and Twenty-second regiment, company C, private, served one year and four months, mustered out June 26, 1865.

Cowee, John T, age 19, volunteer, February 20, 1864, One Hundred and Twenty-second regiment, company C, private, served one year and four months, mustered out June 26, 1865

Duer, George A, age 42, Thirty-sixth regiment, company F.

Cowee, Seneca A, age 21, volunteer, August 12, 1861, three years, Second Virginia cavalry, company F, private, served four years, mustered out June 30, 1865, much on detached duty in hospital.

Denny, Charles W., age 18, volunteer, Sixty-third regiment, company I, died December 30, 1864.

Ellis, Pierson, age 18, volunteer, October 9, 1861, three years, Second Virginia cavalry, company H, private, served three years and ten months, mustered out June 30, 1865, on detailed service as messenger and orderly, reenlisted as a veteran.

Ellis, Alonzo, age 35, Seventy-seventh regiment, company F, died.

Ellis, Asbury F., age 32, volunteer, October 14, 1861, three years, Sixty-third regiment, company G, private, served four months, honorably discharged February 17, 1862, for disability, reenlistment, volunteer, May, 1864, one hundred days, One Hundred and Forty-eighth regiment, company D, private, served four months, mustered out September, 1864.

Ellis, Lindley F., age 22, volunteer, Second Virginia cavalry, company H.

Ellis, Richard, Sixty-third regiment, company G.

Engle, Richard, age 32, Sixty-third regiment, company G.

English, Gideon, age 24, volunteer, March, 1864, Thirty-sixth regiment, company F, private, honorably discharged in 1865, sick and never in active service.

Fowler, Lester R., Seventy-fifth regiment, company B.

Faries, George, age 30, Fifth regiment, company C.

Gates, Leander S., age 22, volunteer, three years, Seventy-seventh regiment, company F, private.

Graham, James M, age 16, volunteer, October 20, 1861, three years, Fifty-third regiment, company B, private, served three years and ten months, mustered out August 12, 1865.

Graham, Finley B., age 17, volunteer, January 18, 1865, One Hundred and Ninety-third regiment, company E, private, served seven months, mustered out August 6, 1865.

Graham, Finley P., age 19, volunteer, August 18, 1862, Thirty-sixth regiment, company F, mustered out July 27, 1865, captured at Winchester, July 24, 1864, and in prison seven months, and then paroled.

Grosvenor, Samuel L., age 35, volunteer, three years, Thirty-sixth regiment, company B, private, attained to rank of first lieutenant, mustered out February 17, 1865.

Grosvenor, David, age 22, volunteer, August, 1862, three years, Thirty-sixth regiment, company F, private, served one year and four

42

months, died December 29, 1863, wounded at Mission Ridge, died from effects of wound.

Grosvenor, Ebenezer, age 34, Eighteenth regiment, company H.

Hacker, William, age 27, Thirty-sixth regiment, company F.

Haines, Josiah L., age 22, volunteer, November 8, 1864, Seventy-third regiment, company F, private, served eight months, mustered out July 20, 1865.

Haines, Charles L., age 20, volunteer, February, 8, 1864, Seventy-third regiment, company F, private, died in March, 1864, of measles, at Chattanooga.

Haines, Nathaniel A., age 18, volunteer, May, 1864, one hundred days, One Hundred and Forty-eighth regiment, company D, private, died May 21, 1864, drowned, seized with cramp while bathing.

Hampton, Amos, age 22, volunteer, August, 1862, three years Ninety-second regiment, company A, sergeant, died in 1863, from wound received at Chattanooga.

Hampton, Thomas, age 31, volunteer, February, 1864, Sixty-third regiment, company I, private, honorably discharged in 1865, captured at Winchester, July 24, 1864, and in Libby prison five months.

Hartman, John, age 19, Seventy-seventh regiment, company B.

Heald, William S., age 53, volunteer, December 11, 1861, three years, Seventy-third regiment, company F, private, served one year and five months, honorably discharged May, 1863, detailed as hospital nurse, discharged for disability.

Heald, Caleb M., age 27, volunteer, December 11, 1861, three years, Seventy-third regiment, company F, private, attained the rank of sergeant, served three years and seven months, mustered out July 11, 1865, transferred to Twelfth Ohio battery and reenlisted as a veteran.

Heald, Nathan, age 17, volunteer, November 11, 1861, three years, Seventy-third regiment, company F, private, died July 4, 1863, wounded in the battle of Gettysburgh, July 2.

Heald, Edmund, age 15, volunteer, December 11, 1861, three years, Seventy-third regiment, company F, private, attained the rank of corporal, served three years and seven months, mustered out July 20, 1865, reenlisted as a veteran.

Hecker, William, age 28, volunteer, March 30, 1864, Thirty-sixth regiment, company F, private, served one year and three months, honorably discharged in June, 1865, captured at Winchester, July 24, 1864, in prison seven months and in hospital seventeen weeks.

Hill, Spencer K., age 18, volunteer, August 22, 1861, three years, Thirtieth regiment, company K, private, attained the rank of corporal, in eighteen battles, served four years, mustered out August 13, 1865, reenlisted as a veteran.

Hill, George F., age 23, Thirty-ninth regiment, company C.

Hill, I. S., age 26, Seventy-fifth regiment, company G.

Hobson, Thomas C., age 19, volunteer, August 15, 1862, Ninety-second regiment, company G, private, died February 22, 1863, while aiding Lieutenant Merril, was captured, paroled for nine days, but stayed to assist the wounded, and died in Danville prison.

Hobson, Samuel M., age 32, volunteer, May, 1864, one hundred days, One Hundred and Forty-eighth regiment, company D, orderly sergeant, served four months, mustered out September, 1864.

Howland E. M., age 25, July, 1863, Twenty-fourth regiment, assistant surgeon, served three years, mustered out June 24, 1864, captured and in Libby prison three months, and exchanged.

Jones, Allen, age 28, Fifteenth regiment, company F.

Johnson, Jonathan, age 25, 1864, Seventy-seventh regiment, company F.

Julier, D. Alonzo, age 20, volunteer, fall of 1861, three years, Eighteenth regiment, company F, private, died March 29, 1862, at Nashville, Tennessee, of typhoid fever.

Kass, James, Seventy-third regiment, company F.

Kester, Aaron M., age 25, volunteer, September 4, 1861, three years, Thirty-sixth regiment, company F, private, died December 7, 1863, at home on sick furlough.

Kinkhead, Benton, age 16, volunteer, October 26, 1861, three years, Seventy-seventh regiment, company D, private, served three years and two months, honorably discharged December 11, 1864, wounded and captured April 25, 1864, in the battle of Mark's Mills, exchanged after two months' imprisonment.

Kinkhead, Julius, age 19, volunteer, December 12, 1861, three years, Seventy-seventh regiment, company D, private, served three years, mustered out December 11, 1864.

Lambert, Elwood, age 36, volunteer, May, 1864, one hundred days, One Hundred and Forty-eighth regiment, company D, private, served four months, mustered out September 14, 1864.

Lee, Edwin, age 28, volunteer, June 18, 1861, three years, Thirty-

ninth regiment, company K, private, served four years, mustered out July 9, 1865, reenlisted as a veteran.

Lee, Samuel, age 35, volunteer, May, 1864, one hundred days, One Hundred and Forty-eighth regiment, company D, corporal, served four months, mustered out September 14, 1864.

Lee, Wesley, age 26, volunteer, February, 1864, Fifty-third regiment, company B, private, mustered out August 11, 1865.

Lindy, H. H. I., age 19, volunteer, six months, Eighty-seventh regiment, company D, private.

Louthan, James, age 23, volunteer, November 11, 1861, three years, Seventy-third regiment, company F, private, mustered out July 20, 1865, home one year for disability on irregular discharge, ordered to report and remained with the regiment.

Louthan, John, age 27, volunteer, Thirty-sixth regiment, company F.

Lytle, Samuel, age 44, volunteer, September 16, 1861, three years, Eighteenth regiment, company F, private, served seven months, honorably discharged April 15, 1862.

Magers, William, age 17, volunteer, May, 1864, one hundred days, One Hundred and Forty-eighth regiment, company D, private, served four months, mustered out September, 1864.

Mains, Abram, age 31, volunteer, March 31, 1864, Thirty-sixth regiment, company F, private, served one year and three months, honorably discharged June 9, 1865, wounded October 19, 1864, at Cedar Creek, Virginia, and in hospital all winter.

Mains, Elijah, age 25, volunteer, February, 1862, three years, Second Virginia cavalry, company F, private, served three years and four months, mustered out June 30, 1865.

Mains, Simon H., age 20, volunteer, September 24, 1861, three years, Second Virginia cavalry, company F, private, served three years and nine months, mustered out June 30, 1865, reenlisted as a veteran.

Mains, Richard G., age 17, volunteer, September 25, 1861, three years, Seventeenth regiment, company H, private, honorably discharged in the winter of 1864, wounded and captured September 20, 1862, and in various prisons for fifteen months.

Marshall, Jesse B., age 29, volunteer, May, 1864, one hundred days, One Hundred and Forty-eighth regiment, company B, private, served four months, mustered out September, 1864.

Marsher, Samuel F., age 21, Eighteenth regiment, company F.

Marsher, Daniel P., age 20, Eighteenth regiment, company F.

Martin, Nathan, age 24, volunteer, January 6, 1862, Seventy-seventh regiment, company D, private.

Martin, Benjamin, age 21, volunteer, December 3, 1861, three years, Seventy-seventh regiment, company D, private, died May 2, 1862, from the effects of wounds received at Shiloh, March 6, 1862.

McKain, John B., Thirtieth regiment, company K.

McKain, Franklin, One Hundred and Ninety-third regiment, company E.

Miller, Nathan, age 19, volunteer, February 16, 1864, Thirty-sixth regiment, company K, private, served one year and five months, mustered out July 27, 1865

Miller, Thomas, age 18, Seventy-seventh regiment, company B.

Miller, Peter, age 19, volunteer, August 15, 1862, Ninety-second regiment, company G, private, served three years, mustered out June 10, 1865, wounded at Chickamauga, detailed for team service.

Miller, Oliver, age 18, volunteer, February 18, 1864, Seventy-third regiment, company F, private, served one year and four months, mustered out June, 1865, severely wounded at Atlanta, afterwards detailed as hospital nurse.

Mills, Christopher, age 18, volunteer, February, 1864, Sixtieth regiment, company E, private, honorably discharged August, 1865, off duty a good deal by sickness.

Mills, Thomas W., age 15, volunteer, October 26, 1861, three years, Seventy-seventh regiment, company D, private, served four years and five months, mustered out March, 1866, captured at Mark's Mills, April 25, 1864, and in Tyler prison for ten months, sick with fever two months.

Monroe, Abner S., age 17, volunteer, October 20, 1861, three years, Fifty-third regiment, company B, private, served four years, mustered out August 11, 1865, reenlisted as a veteran.

Morlan, Samuel, age 20, volunteer, August 15, 1862, three years, Ninety-second regiment, company G, second sergeant, attained the rank of orderly sergeant, died May 4, 1863, at Carthage, Tennessee.

Morlan, Barzillei, age 36, Third Virginia, company B.

Moshier, Daniel, age 18, volunteer, October 8, 1861, three years, Eighteenth regiment, company F, private, served three years, transferred to the invalid corps, honorably discharged September 26, 1864, for disability.

Moshier, Samuel T., age 20, volunteer, October 8, 1861, three years, Eighteenth regiment, company F, private, served three years, mustered out October, 1864, in hospital a good deal.

Morris, Nathan, age 18, volunteer, December 25, 1861, three years, Seventy-third regiment, company F, private, served six months, killed at the battle of Cross Keys June 8, 1862.

Morris, Elwood, age 21, volunteer, December 25, 1861, three years, Seventy-third regiment, company F, private, mostly on detached service and transferred to First veteran reserve corps.

Morris, Mordecai, age 20, volunteer, January 16, 1865, One Hundred and Ninety-third regiment, company E, private, served six months, mustered out August 4, 1865.

Morris, Silas S., age 19, volunteer, January 16, 1865, One Hundred and Ninety-third regiment, company E, private, served six months, mustered out August 4, 1865.

Morrow, James, Sixty-third regiment, company G, died.

Norris, William, age 28, Third colored regiment, company C, private, died June 15, 1865, at Goldsborough, North Carolina, of chronic diarrhœa.

Painter, John, age 23, Twenty-fifth regiment, company H.

Painter, William, age 19, Thirty-sixth regiment, company H.

Palmer, J. Amos, Fifth regiment, company G.

Penrose, Albert, age 20, volunteer, August 1, 1861, three years, Thirty-sixth regiment, company F, private, missing, probably killed at Winchester July 24, 1864.

Penrose, William, age 17, volunteer, February 22, 1865, one year, One Hundred and Eighty-ninth regiment, company F, private, mustered out September 26, 1865.

Pewthers, Charles J., age 32, volunteer, November 19, 1861, three years, Second Virginia cavalry, company F, corporal, died June 22, 1864, by explosion of ammunition wagon.

Pickering, Elwood E., age 16, volunteer, May, 1864, one hundred days, One Hundred and Forty-eighth regiment, company E, private, served four months, mustered out September, 1864, reenlistment, February 20, 1865, Fifty-third regiment, company B, private, mustered out August 11, 1865.

Pickering, Jasper C., age 18, volunteer, February 13, 1864, Fifty-third regiment, company B, mustered out August 11, 1865, wounded May 14, 1864, at Resaca.

Pickering, B. C., Seventy-third regiment.

Price, Jacob L., age 30, volunteer, February 5, 1864, three years, One Hundred and Twenty-second regiment, company C, private, served eight months, died October 19, 1864, mortally wounded September 19, 1864.

Rardin, Andrew, age 32, volunteer, May, 1864, one hundred days, One Hundred and Forty-eighth regiment, company D, private, served four months, mustered out September, 1864.

Rardin, Eli, age 33, volunteer, February, 1864, three years, Thirty-sixth regiment, company F, private, mustered out July 27, 1865, wounded July, 1864.

Rardin, Leroy L., volunteer, three years, First light artillery, company K, private, cannoneer, died May, 1862, of fever, in Franklin hospital.

Rardin, Levi H., volunteer, three years, First light artillery, company K, cannoneer, in fourteen battles, mustered out February, 1865.

Rardin, John C., age 17, volunteer, February, 1865, One Hundred and Eighty-eighth regiment, company E, private, mustered out September 21, 1865.

Rardin, Jacob C., age 26, volunteer, September, 1861, three years, Second Virginia cavalry, company F, private, honorably discharged March, 1863, for disability.

Rardin, William H. H., age 22, volunteer, September, 1861, three years, Second Virginia cavalry, company F, private, mustered out June 30, 1865, wounded at Guyandotte.

Randolph, Isaiah N., age 27, volunteer, August 13, 1862, three years, Thirty-sixth regiment, company F, private, mustered out July 27, 1865, wounded in battles of Winchester and Perrysville.

Reed, John W., age 17, volunteer, July 4, 1863, three years, First heavy artillery, company I, private, served two years, mustered out July 25, 1865.

Read, Stephen W., age 18, volunteer, September, 1861, First cavalry, company L, died of typhoid fever at Louisville, January, 1862.

Rester, Aaron, age 27, Thirty-sixth regiment, company F.

Rowland, John, age 17, volunteer, November, 1861, three years, Seventy-seventh regiment, company F, private, mustered out March 8, 1866, wounded at Shiloh, captured in the Red River expedition, held ten months.

Roman, Isaac, age 20, volunteer, October 8, 1861, three years, Sixty-third regiment, private, served one year, honorably discharged November, 1862, for disability, wounded at battle of Corinth, reenlistment May, 1864, one hundred days, One Hundred and Forty-eighth regiment, company D, sergeant, served four months, mustered out September, 1864.

Ross, James, age 26, volunteer, November 25, 1861, three years, Seventy-third regiment, company F, private, attained rank of first lieutenant, served one year and eight months, mustered out July 20, 1865, wounded at Resaca May, 1864.

Sharpe, Joel, age 19, volunteer, May, 1864, one hundred days, One Hundred and Forty-eighth regiment, company D, private, served four months, mustered out September, 1864, reenlistment February 22, 1865, One Hundred and Eighty-ninth regiment, company F, private, served seven months, mustered out September 28, 1865.

Shaner, Emmor, age 24, volunteer, August 8, 1862, three years, Thirty-sixth regiment, company F, private, served three months, honorably discharged November 24, 1862, for disability.

Sheets, Henry C, age 32, volunteer, September 24, 1861, three years, Eighteenth regiment, company I, private, served three years, mustered out November 9, 1864.

Sheets, Harrison, age 22, volunteer, October 8, 1861, three years, Eighteenth regiment, company F, private, served two years and three months, killed January 2, 1863, at Stone River.

Sheets, John W., age 21, volunteer, One Hundred and Twenty-ninth regiment, company A, private, died January 14, 1864, at Cumberland Gap.

Simpson, William, Fifth regiment, company G.

Shinn, James H., age 19, volunteer, One Hundred and Twenty-second regiment, company C, private, died 1864, at the battle of the Wilderness.

Sherman, Jasper, Sixty-third regiment, company F.

Sivill, Samuel N., age 44, volunteer, August 13, 1862, three years, Thirty-sixth regiment, company F, private, honorably discharged February 2, 1863, for disability.

Sivill, Tobias, age 16, volunteer, October 14, 1861, three years, Sixty-third regiment, company G, private, served three years and ten months, mustered out July 8, 1865.

Sivill, Nathan, age 18, volunteer, September 22, 1861, three years, Thirty-sixth regiment, company F, private, died February 8, 1862, o measels and typhoid fever.

Slotterback, Joseph, age 18, volunteer, March 2, 1864, Seventy-seventh regiment, company F, private, captured at Mark's Mills April 25, 1864, and died in Tyler prison June 29, 1864, of typhoid fever.

Slotterback, Henry, age 24, volunteer, February 23, 1864, Seventy-seventh regiment, company F, private, died July 6, 1864, of typhoid fever.

Smith, Thomas, age 34, volunteer, October, 1862, three years, Ninth cavalry, company B, corporal.

Smith, Josiah, age 18, volunteer, October 10, 1861, Second Virginia cavalry, company H, private, captured, and supposed to have died in prison

Smith, Wilton, age 22, Thirty-ninth regiment, company C.

Spear, Henry L., age 23, volunteer, February 29, 1864, Seventy-seventh regiment, company C, private, served two years, mustered out March 8, 1866, captured in Tyler prison for ten months.

Starman, Jonathan, Seventy-seventh regiment, company F.

Stoneman, John, age 23, volunteer, 1861, three years, Seventy-seventh regiment, company F, private, killed at Pittsburgh Landing, 1862.

Stoneman, Jasper, age 20, volunteer, 1861, three years, Sixty-third regiment, company G, sergeant, served seven months, died of typhoid fever at Nashville, June, 1862.

Tate, John, Fifth regiment, company G

Taylor, David, age 55, volunteer, October 11, 1861, three years, Seventy-third regiment, company F, private, served four months, honorably discharged February 11, 1862, discharged for disability and died at home, April 11, 1862, of lung disease

Taylor, William W., age 31, volunteer, August 18, 1861, three years, Eighteenth regiment, company C, private, served four months, mustered out October 9, 1865, reenlisted as a veteran, captured September, 1863, in Libby, Danville, Andersonville and Florence prisons.

Taylor, Brintnal, age 27, volunteer, three years, August 18, 1861, Eighteenth regiment, company C, private, honorably discharged February, 1865.

Taylor, Finley W., age 18, volunteer, August 18, 1861, three years, Eighteenth regiment, company C, private, served three years, mustered out November, 1864.

Taylor, John Wesley, age 15, volunteer, August 18, 1861, three years, Eighteenth regiment, company C, private, served three years, mustered out November 10, 1864, captured at battle of Stone River, held six weeks and parolled.

Taylor, Wilson P., age 14, volunteer, May, 1864, one hundred days, One Hundred and Forty-eighth regiment, company D, private, served four months, mustered out September, 1864, reenlistment, February 15, 1865, six months, One Hundred and Eighty-ninth regiment, company F, private, served seven months, mustered out September 25, 1865.

Underwood, William H , age 22, volunteer, September 22, 1861, three years, Nineteenth regiment, company D, private, attained rank of orderly sergeant, served four years, mustered out October 21, 1865.

Vanfleet, John, age 23, volunteer, October, 1861, three years, Seventy-seventh regiment, company F, private, missing, reenlisted as a veteran.

Way, Milton, age 18, volunteer, January 20, 1862, three years, Twentieth regiment, company I, private, served three years and five months, mustered out July 15, 1865.

Way, Samuel, age 24, volunteer, August, 1862, three years, Ninety-second regiment, company A, private, served seven months, died March 20, 1863, at Carthage.

Way, William, Twenty-eighth regiment, company I.

Wilson, Washington, age 24, volunteer, November 5, 1861, three years, Sixty-third regiment, company G, private, served nine months, honorably discharged August 27, 1862, for disability.

Wilson, James M., age 20, volunteer, November 3, 1861, three years, Sixty-third regiment, company G, corporal, died September, 1864, of camp disease at Atlanta, Georgia.

Wilson, Nathan, age 34, volunteer, May, 1864, one hundred days, One Hundred and Forty-eighth regiment, company D, private, served four months, mustered out September, 1864.

Wilson, James C., age 37, August 8, 1862, three years, Thirty-sixth regiment, company I, private, served two months, honorably discharged October 30, 1862, for disability, wounded at Antietam.

Wilson, Finley V., age 21, volunteer. August 1, 1861, three years, Thirty-sixth regiment, company F, private, mustered out October 6, 1864, wounded at South Mountain, Mission Ridge, and Winchester.

Wilson, Jacob B., age 19, volunteer, September, 1861, Seventeenth regiment, company H, private, died 1863, supposed to have been killed at Chickamauga.

Wilson, Andrew F., age 29, volunteer, May, 1864, one hundred days, One Hundred and Forty-eighth regiment, company D, corporal, served four months, mustered out September, 1864.

Wilson, Jacob P., age 21, volunteer, August, 1861, three years, Thirty-sixth regiment, company F, private, served three years, mustered out August 1, 1864.

Wilson, Harmon T., age 20, volunteer, August 8, 1862, three years, Thirty-sixth regiment, company F, private, killed September, 1864, at Berryville.

Wilson, Abram P., age 27, volunteer, September, 1861, three years, Thirty-sixth regiment, company F, private, served three years, mustered out August, 1864.

Wilson, William F., age 34, volunteer, May, 1864, one hundred days, One Hundred and Forty-eighth regiment, company D, private, served four months, mustered out September, 1864.

Witham, Nathan R., age 39, volunteer, May, 1864, one hundred days, One Hundred and Forty-eighth regiment, company D, private, served four months, mustered out September, 1864.

Witham, Wesley K., age 20, volunteer, February 15, 1865, six months, One Hundred and Eighty-ninth regiment, company F, private, served seven months, mustered out September 28, 1865.

Wood, Matthews, age 31, volunteer, October 6, 1862, three years, Ninth cavalry, company C, private, attained rank of corporal, honorably discharged June 13, 1865, for disability.

Yocum, John, age 18, Ninety-second regiment, company G.

RECAPITULATION.

De Beck's battery	2
First Ohio heavy artillery	1
Second Virginia cavalry	9
Ninth Ohio cavalry	2
One each in First Ohio cavalry and Second Ohio cavalry	2
Fourth Virginia cavalry	3
One Hundred and Twenty-second Ohio	4
Thirty-sixth Ohio	29
One Hundred and forty-eighth Ohio	23
Seventy-seventh Ohio	20
Seventy-third Ohio	17

Thirteen each in Sixty-third Ohio and Eighteenth Ohio (three years)	26
Ninety-second Ohio	9
Five each in the Fifth Ohio and and Fifty-third Ohio	10
Four each in Thirty-ninth Ohio, One Hundred and Eighty-ninth Ohio, One Hundred and Ninety-third Ohio	12
Two each in Seventeenth Ohio, Thirtieth Ohio, Seventy-fifth Ohio, Nineteenth Ohio	8
One each in Third Ohio, Fifteenth Ohio, Twenty-fourth Ohio, Twenty-fifth Ohio, Sixtieth Ohio, Twentieth Ohio, Twenty-eighth Ohio, Eighty-seventh Ohio, One Hundred and Twenty-ninth Ohio, One Hundred and Eighty-eighth Ohio, Third Virginia infantry	11
	—
Total number of soldiers	180
Died	33

RECAPITULATION OF SOLDIERS OF WASHINGTON COUNTY.

ARTILLERY.

First Virginia light artillery (Buell's battery)	109
First Ohio (DeBeck's battery)	56
First Ohio (Huntington's battery)	55
First Ohio light artillery (scattering)	10
Second Ohio heavy artillery (battery K)	25
Second Ohio heavy artillery (scattering)	10
One each in the Eleventh and Eighteenth Ohio independent batteries, First United States artillery, First New York artillery, Second Arkansas light artillery, First Iowa light artillery, and Fourteenth United States colored heavy artillery	7

CAVALRY (VOLUNTEERS).

First Ohio cavalry	163
Second Ohio cavalry	5
Fourth Virginia cavalry	12
Fifth Ohio cavalry	3
Seventh Ohio cavalry	105
Ninth Ohio cavalry	61
Thirteenth Ohio cavalry	11
First Virginia cavalry	7
Second Virginia cavalry	91
Third Virginia cavalry	4
Fourth Virginia cavalry	68
Fourth Ohio independent battalion	16
One each in the Sixth and Twelfth Ohio, Fifth, Seventh, and Ninth Virginia, Fifth and Sixth Kentucky, Third Iowa, Second Louisiana, Third United States, Seventh Missouri	11

INFANTRY (VOLUNTEERS).

First Ohio	2
Second Ohio	4
Third Ohio	8
Fifth Ohio	10
Tenth Ohio	3
Eleventh Ohio	2
Twelfth Ohio	10
Thirteenth Ohio	2
Fourteenth Ohio	2
Fifteenth Ohio	5
Sixteenth Ohio	2
Seventeenth Ohio	7
Eighteenth Ohio (three years)	104
Eighteenth Ohio (three months)	61
Nineteenth Ohio	5
Twentieth Ohio	6
Twenty-second Ohio	3
Twenty-third Ohio	6
Twenty-fourth Ohio	3
Twenty-fifth Ohio	26
Twenty-sixth Ohio	3
Twenty-seventh Ohio	13
Twenty-eighth Ohio	3
Thirtieth Ohio	4
Thirty-second Ohio	5
Thirty-third Ohio	6
Thirty-sixth Ohio	553
Thirty-eighth Ohio	2
Thirty-ninth Ohio	242
Forty-second Ohio	3
Forty-third Ohio	12

SOLDIERS MONUMENT, MARIETTA, O.

Forty-seventh Ohio.. 2
Fifty-first Ohio.. 25
Fifty-third Ohio... 16
Fifty-eighth Ohio... 4
Sixtieth Ohio.. 2
Sixty-second Ohio.. 13
Sixty-third Ohio.. 181
Sixty-fourth Ohio... 2
Sixty-fifth Ohio... 4
Sixty-sixth Ohio.. 5
Sixty-seventh Ohio... 4
Seventieth Ohio... 3
Seventy-first Ohio.. 11
Seventy-third Ohio... 101
Seventy-fifth Ohio.. 22
Seventy-seventh Ohio....................................... 593
Seventy-eighth Ohio.. 10
Eighty-fifth Ohio... 14
Eighty-sixth Ohio.. 2
Eighty-seventh Ohio.. 50
Eighty-eighth Ohio... 7
Ninety-second Ohio... 329
One Hundred and Fourteenth Ohio......................... 2
One Hundred and Sixteenth Ohio.......................... 50
One Hundred and Twenty-second Ohio..................... 12
One Hundred and Twenty-fifth Ohio....................... 13
One Hundred and Twenty-sixth Ohio....................... 2
One Hundred and Twenty-ninth Ohio...................... 25
One Hundred and Forty-first Ohio......................... 4
One Hundred and Forty-eighth Ohio....................... 411
One Hundred and Seventy-fourth Ohio..................... 14
One Hundred and Seventy-fifth Ohio...................... 38
One Hundred and Seventy-sixth Ohio...................... 8
One Hundred and Seventy-ninth Ohio..................... 35
One Hundred and Eightieth Ohio.......................... 12
One Hundred and Eighty-second Ohio..................... 21
One Hundred and Eighty-fourth Ohio..................... 4
One Hundred and Eighty-sixth Ohio....................... 14
One Hundred and Eighty-seventh Ohio.................... 14
One Hundred and Eighty-ninth Ohio...................... 9
One Hundred and Ninety-first Ohio....................... 2
One Hundred and Ninety-third Ohio....................... 6
One Hundred and Ninety-fourth Ohio..................... 10
One Hundred and Ninety-fifth Ohio....................... 4
One Hundred and Ninety-sixth Ohio....................... 15
First Virginia.. 2
Second Virginia.. 3
Fourth Virginia.. 4
Sixth Virginia.. 7
Seventh Virginia... 27
Ninth Virginia... 4
Eleventh Virginia.. 17
Fourteenth Virginia.. 2
Fifteenth Massachusetts.................................... 2
Eighteenth United States regulars......................... 3
Fifth United States colored regiment...................... 11
Twenty-seventh United States colored regiment............ 5
One each in the Fourth, Sixth, Seventh, Twenty-ninth, Thirty-first,
    Thirty-seventh, Forty-fifth, Forty-ninth, Fifty-second, Fifty-
    ninth, Sixty-first, Seventy-second, Seventy-sixth, Eighty-first,
    Eighty-ninth, Ninety-first, Ninety-seventh, One Hundred and
    Fourth, One Hundred and Seventeenth, One Hundred and Twen-
    ty-eighth, One Hundred and Thirty-second, One Hundred and
    Thirty-fifth, One Hundred and Fifty-fifth, One Hundred and
    Seventy-seventh Ohio, One Hundred and Seventy-eighth, One
    Hundred and Eighty-third, One Hundred and Eighty-fifth,
    One Hundred and Eighty-eighth, and One Hundred and Ninety-
    seventh Ohio, Third and Twelfth Virginia, Twentieth, Twenty-
    first, Twenty-seventh, Fortieth, Forty-first, and Forty-ninth Illi-
    nois, Twelfth, Thirteenth, Twenty-eighth, Sixty-second, One
    Hundredth, One Hundred and First, and One Hundred and
    Thirty-ninth Pennsylvania, Eighteenth, Twenty-first, and
    Twenty-third Kentucky, First, Thirty-sixth, Eleventh, and Forty-
    seventh Iowa, Forty-second and Eighty-seventh Indiana, First
    Michigan, Fifteenth Tennessee, Nineteenth Massachusetts, Four-
    teenth United States, One Hundred and Ninth, Fourth, One
    Hundred and First, One Hundredth, and Twentieth United

States colored, Tenth California.... 63
United States navy... 10
Gunboat service 10
Number with service not designated....................... 81
                                                        ————
    Total number soldiers and marines from Washington county..4052

THE SOLDIERS' MONUMENT.

The losses of the war fell heavily upon Washington county, and the number who lost their lives in the service seems large when compared with the total number who went out, and one of the first acts of the public-spirited citizens of the county after the war was over was to secure the erection of a suitable monument to commemorate the great sacrifice of life in the glorious cause of the Union. Accordingly, as early as June 7, 1865, a meeting was held in the interests of the enterprise.

On Wednesday forenoon, June 7th, immediately after the adjournment of the session of the county commissioners, the gentlemen constituting the board, to-wit: J. J. Hollister, W. Thomas, and Anthony Sheets, together with several other citizens, held a meeting at the office of the county auditor, to consider the propriety and feasibility of erecting a monument to the memory of the soldiers from Washington county, who have fallen in this war against the Rebellion. A. R. Darrow was appointed chairman, R. M. Stimson, secretary. J. J. Hollister made some feeling remarks as to the exceeding propriety of the noble object, and gave some facts and figures from the tax duplicate touching the increased wealth and prosperity of the county—showing that a tax of one mill on a dollar would raise thirteen thousand dollars.

Mr. Darrow, Captain McCormick, Hon. W. F. Curtis, Mr. Sheets, W. S. Ward, R. M. Stimson, R. E. Harte, and others, made brief remarks, and all agreed that the object ought and could be carried into effect, by taxation, or by subscriptions, or by both methods in conjunction—erecting a monument that should be an honor to the county, and to the noble dead whose names should be thereon engraved.

J. J. Hollister, A. R. Darrow, and R. E. Harte, were appointed a committee to devise a plan for the erection of the monument, to report at a future meeting.

It was resolved to call a meeting of the citizens of Washington county, to be held at the court house in Marietta, on Friday, July 14, 1865, at two o'clock, P. M., the day on which the county commissioners hold an adjourned session, to organize for the erection of the monument.

The hope was expressed that public-spirited citizens from every township in the county would be present. A. R. Darrow was chairman of this meeting and R. M. Stimson secretary. Accordingly, at the time and place named, the friends of the movement assembled and effected a temporary organization by electing F. A. Wheeler chairman, and Theodore G. Fields secretary. R. E. Harte chairman of the committee on permanent organization then reported a scheme of organization, including a preamble and nine articles, which was unanimously adopted and signed by forty-one citizens,* and the association adjourned to meet on the day named in the constitution for the regular annual meeting, the second Tuesday in August (8th), 1865, at two P. M.

One of the central ideas of the association was to construct a monument in such form that the names of the soldiers could be engraved on the monumental stone, an idea which was abandoned in the practical working out of the plan as will be seen further on in this sketch.

The association was duly incorporated under the laws of Ohio, and on August 8, 1865, the following named officers and trustees were elected: President, Rufus E. Harte, ex officio a trustee; clerk, Theodore G. Field; trustees for one year, John C. Paxton, J. W. Andrews and William F. Curtis; trustees for two years, Rufus R. Dawes, Enoch S. McIntosh and Henry H. Drown; trustees for three years, Samuel C. Skinner, T. W. Moore and A. W. McCormick.

The trustees began their work at once. They procured a handsomely lithographed certificate of membership graded at different prices, so that all, even the children, of a family could become members and thus help on the great undertaking. Agents were appointed in the different townships to solicit subscriptions, and to circulate the certificates of membership. On August 14, 1866, General R. R. Dawes, president of the trustees, reported the following assets:

Fees of membership..................................$1,426.00
Donation Soldiers' Aid Society, Marietta..................... 200.00
Ladies' League No. 420 Bonn................................. 17.20
Other sources... 16.00

　　Total...$1,659.20

Gen. Dawes pushed the sales of certificates of membership so that by August 13, 1867, he was enabled to turn over to Hon. W. F. Curtis, treasurer of the trustees, two thousand seven hundred and thirty-five dollars and nine cents. Up to that date the finances of the association were mainly under the direction of General R. R. Dawes. On August 19, 1868, Mr. Curtis reported two thousand eight hundred and ninety dollars and three cents. We find no further signs of the treasurer for five years.

When, on August 12, 1873, Mr. Curtis reported the fund at three thousand eight hundred and sixty-one dollars and thirteen cents, and in connection therewith he said: "The premium on the five twenty bond and the interest due on the Salem bond will increase the above amount to something over four thousand dollars," General Dawes moved the thanks of the association be tendered Mr. Curtis for his efficient efforts in increasing the funds in something over one thousand and two

* The following were the persons present at the first meeting: J. J. Hollister, J. W. Andrews, E. Corey, W. P. Skinner, L. W. Chamberlain, S. C. Skinner, R. M. Stimson, David Alban, J. C. Paxton, William B. Loomis, R. R. Dawes, T. G. Field, R. K. Shaw, S. B. Robinson, C. F. Buell, J. S. Sprague, S. S. Knowles, Eli Johnson, C. R. Rhodes, A. W. McCormick, William F. Curtis, R. E. Harte, T. W. Moore, A. R. Darrow, I. N. Carman, B. F. Hart, H. H. Drown, J. D. Cotton, F. A. Wheeler, W. B. Hollister, Owen Franks, Z. G. Bundy, John Jones, A. T. Nye, Thomas Henton, L. S. Protsman, S. Maxwell, D. P. Bosworth, W. S. Ward, B. F. Pixley, S. Newton.

hundred dollars, which motion was carried unanimously. The trustees now felt justified in receiving bids for the construction of the monument, and the following resolution was adopted:

Resolved, That a committee of three trustees be appointed to correspond with such persons as they may select, and receive proposals for a monument, and report at the next annual meeting of the association, the designs to be reported with the bids, and fully exemplified, provided that the cost of the monument shall not exceed six thousand dollars.
　　　　　　　　　　R. E. HARTE,
　　　　　　　　　　R. R. DAWES,
　　　　　　　　　　R. L. NYE,
　　　　　　　　　　　　　　Committee.

At the next annual meeting the committee reported having received a limited number of bids which upon examination proved unsatisfactory. The committee were then directed to procure other bids, and "that the designs should be for a shaft surmounted by a figure of a soldier in uniform, the material granite and the cost not to exceed five thousand dollars," and to report by September 20th the same year (1874), at which date it was voted to contract with T. O'Hare, of Cincinnati, Ohio, for a monument at the sum of four thousand five hundred and fifty dollars, which they did, the work to be delivered in six months. The contract was afterwards modified so that the material should be Quincy granite instead of "light granite," at an additional cost of one hundred and fifty dollars, making the total four thousand seven hundred dollars. The site for the monument was chosen after due consideration of all other points, it being a point on the common fifty feet from Front street and the same distance from the line of Putnam street, in the city of Marietta.*

The monument was completed in due time and was highly spoken of as a work of art. The art critic of a leading Cincinnati journal spoke in high terms of the work of Thomas O'Hare, more especially of the statue intended for the top. He said:

The sculptor has wisely refrained from an attempt to create in marble any ideal type of soldierly manhood; he has only striven to represent the young farmer-soldier, sun-browned and vigorous from healthy labor in the field, imbued with the natural heroism inherited by the descendants of a race of hunters, and sternly calm in the firm consciousness of duty. The young soldier figure is altogether characterized less by grace than by strength—not the trained strength of a well muscled athlete, but with ponderous physical force of a western laborer, with tendons hardened by field work, and such a frame work of bone as only those who live upon a phosphatic country diet possess.

We have no fancy warrior in this memorial statue, but only the image of a fair-haired country youth of rugged face and form, like hundreds who left their homes to die for the Union. Men and women, husbands and mothers, brothers and sisters of the soldier-dead of Ohio will recognize in the pathetic truthfulness of the marble features some memory of loved ones lost. And this is what the public demand in such works, and what even the most unpatriotic mind may admire.

It is rather a pity that the statue itself, which is but six feet high, is to stand upon a pedestal, twenty-six feet in height. At such an altitude the finer beauties of the statue cannot be advantageously seen. Considering the size of the pedestal, the statue should have been colossal.

INSCRIPTIONS.

The pedestal will, however, be very handsome—a quadrilateral shaft of Quincy granite, with belts of the same material bearing in raised letters the names: Gettysburgh, Mission Ridge, Shiloh, Corinth, Antietam.

* The other sites voted on were Camp Tupper, (Quadranaon) Capitolium Square, and a point on the common near the Congregational church.

Above the first belt will be the figure of an eagle with, outspread wings, perching on a shield in Carrara marble—the same material used in the statue.

On the east side of the die is a polished tablet, with this inscription:

Erected in memory of the soldiers of Washington county, Ohio, who lost their lives in the United States service in the war for the suppression of the rebellion of 1861.

Washington county was represented in the following and many other organizations: Thirty-sixth, Thirty-ninth, Sixty-third, Seventy-third, Eighty-seventh, Ninety-second, and One Hundred and Forty-eighth Ohio infantry, First, Seventh, and Ninth Ohio and Second West Virginia cavalry, and First Ohio and First West Virginia light artillery.

Names of the fallen may be seen at the recorder's office.

The base of the monument was completed May 31, 1875. In an excavation in the centre stone was placed a tin box hermetically sealed, in which were placed lists of county and city officers, etc.*

The monument having been completed, preparations were made without delay for the dedication. On May 14, 1875, the trustees had appointed R. E. Harte, R. R. Dawes, and the secretary, R. L. Nye, a committee on dedication, with instructions that the secretary correspond with General Rutherford B. Hayes, inviting him to deliver the dedicatory oration, but owing to other engagements he declined.

General W. T. Sherman, General John Pope, General George Crook, General Edward F. Noyes, and other distinguished military men, were invited to be present. General T. C. H. Smith, of Marietta, was finally chosen to deliver the oration, and September 17, 1875, fixed as the day for the ceremonies.

On the appointed day, at 10 A. M., a large concourse of people from different parts of the county, estimated at three thousand, assembled to witness the dedication. On the speakers' stand, near the monument, was General John Pope, of the regular army, General Manning F. Force, of Cincinnati, and others. General Smith's oration was an eloquent tribute to the noble dead of the county, of which we are able to give only the closing paragraphs: †

We should have done injustice to the manhood of these dead if we had neglected to recall this day their deeds as soldiers. We shall do more than injustice—we shall desecrate their memory as citizens who gave their lives for the common weal—if we fail on this occasion to ap-

preciate the animating spirit on our side, as distinguished from the passions and purposes which actuated and inflamed those on that side against which we strove, and over which, under God, we prevailed.

Do not think I talk party politics. The men who fought this war for us, to whatever party they may now belong, are above criticism as to their motives in public affairs, and their opinions are entitled to respect. I speak only of that on which, then, we all agreed, and ask that by the memory of these dead we may never give it up. Let us, to whatever party we belong, never give up the sentiment and the duty that united us in the war. The Rebellion was a crime against free government. If that conviction is given up by those who held it, the days of our Government are numbered. And so long as any considerable portion of our people refuse to accept that conviction, so long is our Government in danger.

Let us remember, then, we who were on the stage of action in the great contest, and you our inheritors remember, for what these dead fought—for what they died. And to all, and to future generations, let the appeal rise from the graves of those to whom we now dedicate this monument: "We, to tell of whom this stone was raised, ask of those who come after us that they see to it that we did not die in vain."

In the evening, at the city hall, a reunion of veterans was held, President Israel W. Andrews, of Marietta college, delivering the address of welcome. He referred in complimentary terms to the distinguished guests present; he welcomed the soldiers from far and near who were gathered together on the occasion to renew their acquaintance and friendship; he paid a tribute to the heroic dead whose memories it was sought to perpetuate by the monument dedicated, though a feeble expression of the gratitude of our people; he referred to the distinguished general of the army and the distinguished jurist, who had laid aside his duties as a private citizen to join the army when our country was in danger. His remarks were received with hearty applause.

General John Pope spoke in a feeling manner of the "ties of friendship between comrades who fought side by side on so many bloody fields." He referred to the subject then so much discussed of conciliating the South. In closing he said:

Let us remember the solemn legacy these dead men have bequeathed us, consecrated by their lives to maintain among ourselves, and to transmit to their and our descendants the results they laid down their lives to achieve.

Judge Force said:

But why are these dead so honored? Why is tribute given to them that is not given to wealth, or to power, or to learning? Is it because they were brave? Because they were patient? Because they were victorious? Because they were slain? No; it is none of these. It is because they died for us, because they gave themselves a cheerful sacrifice that our country might remain one, our free institutions stand perpetual. It is because of the work they did, but still more for the spirit in which they did it.

The monument erected to-day is a tribute of the people to public virtue. Let it stand as long as this Nation shall last. It will be honored so long as our institutions shall be upheld by a worthy people. Let it stand in our park, facing the setting sun, no mere ornament, but a lesson and a stimulus. As years roll by and generation succeeds generation, let old and young find in its sculptured face both history and admonition. As the sunlight plays about the inscription like the wind breathing upon Æolian strings, the letters will seem vocal, and chant, in earnest tones. The dead died to save their country, let the living so live as to keep it worthy."

After Judge Force had spoken, Hon. Oliver P. Morton, Senator of Indiana, being in the city, came upon the stage, and was called upon to speak. He thereupon referred, in eloquent terms, to the occasion and the commemorative object of the meeting, but confined his remarks to the National as against the States Rights idea.

---

* The following is a list of the articles in the box: Holy Bible, presented by the Washington County Bible society, Constitution of the United States, with manuel of same, by I. W. Andrews, presented by J. M. Fuller; Constitution of Ohio, with volume of Ohio laws, 1873; brief history of Washington County Soldiers' Monument association and a list of its officers from organization to date; constitution or articles of association of the Washington County Soldiers' Monument association; roll of the officers of Washington county; roll of officers of the city of Marietta; copies of the Marietta *Register*, *Times*, *College Olio*, and *Zeitung*; revised ordinances of the city of Marietta, presented by S. J. Hathaway; directory of the churches of Marietta and Harmar; Masonic calendar of American Union lodge and chapter and Harmar lodge. The constitution and by-laws and list of officers of the following benevolent societies: Elk Eye encampment and Marietta and Guttenburgh lodge of Odd Fellows, Manhattan and Muskingum tribes of red men, Reynold lodge Knights of Pythias, Marietta and Harmar lodges of Good Templars; also a roll of Pierpont battery; a copy of the Boston *Post*, one hundred years old; a premium list and list of officers of the Washington County Agricultural and Mechanical association, and various other articles presented by citizens.

† General Smith's address was published by Robert Clarke & Co., Cincinnati, Ohio, in 1875.

Speeches were also made by General A. J. Warner and Rev. John Tenney, of Marietta; also by John Beach, a one-armed soldier.

The main object of the association was now accomplished,* but the roll of the dead, referred to on the monument as recorded at the recorder's office remained unprepared until the spring of 1880. Mr. S. J. Hathaway having been elected secretary of the association in 1878, prepared a bill to enable soldiers' monument associations to record names of fallen soldiers, war of 1861 to 1865 inclusive.

The Hon. Henry Bohl, then representing Washington county in the State legislature, procured the passage of the bill May 27, 1879, so that the assessors in the spring of 1880 were required to take an enumeration of all deceased soldiers who enlisted from this county. A blank was prepared giving the facts. The assessors did their work as well as it could be done after so many years had elapsed since the war. This was supplemented by facts and data, procured at much labor and trouble, from other sources, until a sufficient degree of fullness and accuracy was obtained to justify the record to be made.

> How sleep the brave, who sink to rest,
> By all their country's wishes blest!
> When spring, with dewy fingers cold,
> Returns to deck their hallowed mould,
> She there shall dress a sweeter sod
> Than Fancy's feet have ever trod.
>
> By fairy hands their knell is sung;
> By forms unseen their dirge is sung;
> There Honor comes, a pilgrim gray,
> To bless the turf that wraps their clay;
> And Freedom shall awhile repair
> To dwell a weeping hermit there!

---

* Through the efforts of one of Marietta's public-spirited citizens—M. P. Wells, esq.—a neat iron fence was, in the spring of 1877, placed around the monument, part of the money to pay for which was donated by the Philomathean society, composed of young ladies of the Marietta high school. The same gentleman then followed up the work so well begun by moving for a donation of four cannon from the United States arsenal, at Washington, to place at the four corners of the monument. The Hon. A. J. Warner, our Representative in Congress from this district (thirteenth), procured the passage of a bill, approved June 8, 1880, donating to the association four twenty-pound Parrot guns. These were received in the summer of 1880, were let into four stone blocks and placed at the corners of the monument, as they now stand.

CAPTAIN CHARLES DEVOL.*

The subject of this sketch was born at Tiverton, Rhode Island, at a place known as Howland's Ferry, June 30, 1782. His father, Captain Jonathan Devol, was born in the same vicinity, where he had numerous connections.

In the fall of the year 1788 the family moved to Marietta, then in the Northwest Territory, he being then but six years of age. The journey took six weeks of incessant toil. When the family arrived at Marietta they found a wilderness to be conquered, requiring years of patient toil and entailing, at times, great privations. In the spring of 1789, his father and family, in company with a number of others, removed to Belpre and began that

---

* This biography was received too late for insertion in the proper place.

---

settlement. They had cleared a few acres, amid much suffering from scarcity of food, when the Indian war broke out, and for four years thereafter they were confined within the protecting walls of "Farmer's Castle," a strong palisade and log fortification built by the settlers for their safety. Near the close of the war, when only thirteen years old, he served as a soldier in Fort Harmar, performing the routine of duty and standing guard in the sentry-box during the darkest nights with the firmness of a man of thirty. He was, when a youth, noted for his courage and daring feats. At the close of the war he removed to a farm five miles above Marietta, on the Muskingum, where he erected a large mill, carried on shipbuilding with other various mechanical pursuits, in all of which his son Charles bore a part until he was twenty-one years of age.

During the War of 1812 Captain Charles Devol commanded a company of cavalry on the frontiers under General Harrison.

Just before the war he was married to Sallie Hoyt, daughter of Benajah Hoyt. At the close of the war he settled on a farm at the mouth of the Big Hocking river.

He served as a magistrate several years with credit to himself and the community in which he lived. Owing to the scarcity of physicians in those days men of tact and experience often had to act in the place of the doctors. Captain Devol filled this position in the community in which he lived, acting as doctor or dentist as occasion required. In religion he was a Congregationalist, and remained a consistent member of that church up to the time of his death. Captain Devol was endowed with a cheerful disposition, fine conversational powers, and a superior personal appearance. His affable manners won for him the lasting regard of all who knew him. He died from the effects of paralysis, August 28, 1845, at Chauncy, Athens county, Ohio, while on a business visit to Hon. Samuel F. Vinton.

The children of Captain Devol were: Sarah, who married Winchester Dana, the owner of the well known "Dana farm" just below Beverly; Henrietta, who married Samuel S. Knowles, prominent in Washington county as State senator and judge of the court of common pleas; Frank Devol, who removed to Mount Pleasant, Iowa, and there engaged in the hardware business; and Captain Prescott Devol.

Of Captain Prescott Devol we should make more than a passing notice did our space permit. Nature seldom endows a man so richly as she did the brave, adventurous, and generous "Pres" Devol. He was named after his father's intimate friend, Dr. Samuel Prescott Hildreth, of Marietta, and was born in March, 1822. When about twelve years of age he went to school at Marietta, and afterwards studied at the Ohio university at Athens. In addition to physical strength he possessed unusual vocal powers.

In the fall of 1840 he took a boat load of cord wood to Cincinnati. The Harrison campaign being then in full blast young Devol's vocal powers were in demand, being pressed into the service of the Whig party at Cincinnati, as he had no equals in singing campaign songs.

He was borne through the streets in a triumphal car, singing to the great amusement and edification of the throng that flocked to hear him. During the campaign he visited St. Louis and New Orleans, creating great excitement by his stirring political songs. He was afterwards clerk and then captain of one of the fast Clipper steamboats, then plying between Pittsburgh and Cincinnati, and such was his popularity that passengers would wait over to go with Captain "Pres" Devol. He went to Mexico during the Mexican war on a war vessel in the service of the United States. Upon his return, in the fall of 1846, he was married to Sarah, daughter of Gilbert Devol. He afterwards went to California upon the breaking out of the gold excitement, and from there to the Sandwitch Islands. He seems to have sailed in a whaling ship, and finally brought up in Chinese waters. When he left the Sandwitch Islands, such was his popularity with the officers of the ships of different nationalities gathered there that they fired salutes in his honor as he sailed out. When he arrived at China the impression prevailed there that he must be a superior personage of high rank. At least he soon found a position as captain of a Peruvian man-of-war sent for the protection of the Peruvian merchant ships in those waters. He was next in the service of China as captain of a large steamship. He was soon after commissioned as captain of a man-of-war by the king of Siam to cruise for pirates. In one of these cruises he encountered two pirate ships, engaged them, totally disabling one with cannon shot, and upon closing in to board her Captain Devol headed the boarding party in person. They surrendered, however, without further resistance. The other piratical craft also surrendered, and with these he returned to port. We next find Captain Devol organizing a gold mining expedition to the interior of Siam. While on this journey among the jungles and mountains of Siam he died from the effects of miasma, in his thirty-fifth year. He left a wife and one child.

CHAPTER XXI.
HISTORY OF PUBLIC IMPROVEMENTS IN WASHINGTON COUNTY.

Importance of the Rivers as Means of Communication in Early Days.—Dr. Manasseh Cutler on these Facilities for Commercial Intercourse in 1787.—The Need of a Through East and West Road Recognized by the Pioneers.—Proceedings in the Territorial Legislature in 1802.—The First Sum of Money Ever Appropriated for Internal Improvements Northwest of the Ohio.—Five Hundred and Forty-four Dollars and Forty-one Cents as the Beginning of Incalculable Millions.—Planning for Communication from the Atlantic Seaboard to the Ohio at the Beginning of the Century.—Measures of 1831.—The Muskingum Improvement and Baltimore & Ohio Railroad.—Washington County and the Marietta & Cincinnati Railroad.—Early and Late History.—The Cleveland & Marietta Railroad.

WASHINGTON county has a border on the Ohio river of over fifty miles. The convenient access thus afforded to nearly all her population to the best navigable water of the western country has been a source of wealth in the transportation to distant markets of her products. It has given an exceptionally high value to all the valley lands bordering the river.

Notwithstanding the provision by nature for the wants of her people in the line of commercial intercourse, the subject of more enlarged and varied kinds of transportation facilities has been regarded from the very foundation of its settlement as one of great importance.

At the time the contract was made with Congress for the Ohio company's lands, the only means of commercial intercourse that was deemed reliable was by water. Hence we find that Dr. Cutler, in a pamphlet issued by himself at the time he negotiated with Congress for the lands, in recommending the new country, calls attention to the various water routes as follows:

The communications between this country and the sea will be principally by the four following directions:

First.—The route through the Scioto and Muskingum to Lake Erie, and so to the Hudson river.

Second.—The passage up the Ohio and Monongahela to the portage, which leads to the waters of the Potumak. This portage is thirty miles, and will probably be rendered much less by the execution of plans now on foot for opening the navigation of those waters.

Third.—The Great Kanawha, which falls into the Ohio from the Virginia shore between the Hocking and the Scioto, opens an extensive navigation from the southeast, and leaves but eighteen miles portage from the navigable waters of James river, Virginia. This communication for the country between Muskingum and Scioto will probably be more used than any other for the exportation of manufactures and other light and valuable articles, and especially for the importation of foreign commodities, which may be brought from the Chesapeake to the Ohio much cheaper than they are now carried from Philadelphia to Carlisle and other thickly settled back counties of Pennsylvania.

Fourth—But the current down the Ohio and Mississippi, for heavy articles that suit the Florida and West India markets—such as corn, flour, beef, lumber, etc.,—will be more loaded than any streams on earth. The distance from the Scioto to the Mississippi is eight hundred miles; from there to the sea is nine hundred. This whole course is easily run in eighteen days, and the passage up these rivers is not so difficult as has usually been represented It is found by late experiments that sails are used to great advantage against the current of the Ohio; and it is worthy of observation that in all probability steamboats will be found to do infinite service in all our extensive river navigation.

The design of Congress and of the company is that the settlements shall proceed regularly down the Ohio river and northward to Lake Erie; and it is probable that the whole country above Miami will be brought to that degree of cultivation which will exhibit its latent beauties and justify those descriptions of travellers which have so often made it the garden of the world, the seat of wealth, and the centre of a great empire.

It must be borne in mind that at that time water lines alone were used for transportation of merchandise from the seaboard to the interior, and for the return, mainly, of furs to the seaboard. These water lines were navigated by light canoes pushed up the streams to the extreme limit that the water in the stream would allow, then carried over the distance required to meet the waters of a descending stream in the proposed route. Thus commerce with the Indians had been kept up for more than a century between the waters of the Hudson and the lakes, while the same system was applied to more western lines as the wants of population required. This explains the importance attached to the acquisition of an Ohio river frontage extending from above the Muskingum to the Scioto, thus giving control not only of the Ohio, but of the mouths of the Muskingum, Hocking, and Scioto on the Ohio side, and of the Great Kanawha on the Virginia side, the head waters of all these streams offering lines of portage either with the Chesapeake bay or the lakes. Probably the word steamboat first found its way into print, as applied to western waters, in the pamphlet above referred to.

But the attention of the pioneer fathers was not limited to these natural facilities for commercial intercourse. At that time Alexandria, on the Potomac, was regarded as the seaport of this region. It was at that port the early French emigrants landed and were met by Mr. Duer's agents, who conducted them by way of Simmrell's Ferry, on the head waters of the Youghiogheny, and thence by boats to Marietta, in 1790.

It became an object of great importance in the estimation of the early settlers to secure a direct route by land in the direction of Alexandria on the east and of Cincinnati on the west through Marietta. The following extracts from the proceedings of the territorial legislature show the interest then felt and the steps taken to open up this direct line from east to west through Marietta:

Friday, 15th January, 1802.

Mr. Ludlow, from the committee to whom was referred, the reports of the survey of a road made by Paul Fearing, Thomas Worthington, and John Reiley from Marietta in the county of Washington, through Chillicothe in the county of Ross, thence to Cincinnati in the county of Hamilton, made a report, which was read and ordered to be committed to the committee of the whole house on Saturday next.

Saturday, 16th January, 1802.

The house, according to the order of the day, resolved itself into committee of the whole on the reports of a survey of a road from Marietta to Cincinnati The committee of the whole reported several resolutions thereon which were agreed to by the house as followeth to wit :

Whereas, from the present state of the funds of the Territory, it would be inexpedient to appropriate any further sum or sums of money for establishing the road laid out by Paul Fearing, Thomas Worthington, and John Reiley, from Marietta through Chillicothe to Cincinnati than what has already been expended in surveying and laying out the same; and whereas by an act passed at the present session of the General assembly entitled "An act levying a tax on land for the year 1802 and for other purposes," the counties of Washington and Ross will, in a great measure, be enabled to open a road through said counties sufficient for present purposes, therefore,

Resolved, By the the legislative council and house of representatives, that so much of the reports and survey of said road as were made by Paul Fearing and Thomas Worthington, be delivered to one of the representatives from each of said counties of Washington and Ross, to be by them laid before the court of general quarter sessions of the peace of their respective counties for their information. Resolved also, that to defray the expenses already incurred in surveying and laying out said road there shall be allowed to the said Paul Fearing, Thomas Worthington, and John Reiley, the sum of four hundred and ninety-seven dollars and forty-one cents to wit: to Paul Fearing, eighty-seven dollars, to Thomas Worthington, two hundred and thirty-seven dollars and forty-one cents and to John Reiley, one hundred and seventy-three dollars; and also that there be allowed to Ephraim Cutler, esq , for his services and expenses in completing the exploring of that part of said road allotted to Paul Fearing, the sum of forty-seven dollars.

This sum of five hundred and forty-four dollars and forty-one cents was undoubtedly the first legislative appropriation of money for "internal improvements" northwest of the Ohio river, made by either State or Territorial authority. That was the first "highway" marked out in the "wilderness" by the pioneers of a Christian civilization.* Eastwardly it was designed at

* By the Indian treaty of June 21, 1752, it was agreed with the Miami Indians that a road should be laid out, beginning at Mills

that time to secure a road through Clarksburgh, Romney, and Winchester to the seaboard at Alexandria. Baltimore in time took the place of Alexandria as the sea-port, but a friendly and cooperative correspondence and effort was kept up for many years, between Marietta and these points, all looking to the establishment of what they expected and hoped would become a National thoroughfare from the seaboard to the west.

By the act of Congress April 30, 1802, providing for the admission of Ohio as a State into the Union, it was enacted that one twentieth part of the net proceeds of the lands lying within the said State, sold by Congress, from and after the nineteenth day of June next, after deducting all expenses, incident to the same shall be applied to the laying out and making public roads, leading from the navigable waters emptying into the Atlantic, to the Ohio State and through the same—such roads to be laid out under the authority of Congress, with the consent of the several States through which the road shall pass.

By an act of Congress passed March 3, 1803, it was provided that three per cent. of the land sales should be applied to the laying out, opening and making roads within said State, and to no other purpose whatever.

This act still left two per cent. of the land sales to be applied as originally designed—to roads leading from the seaboard to the Ohio river.

The following circular dated October 19, 1804, represents the views then held upon this important subject:

MARIETTA, October 19, 1804.

SIR. As it is expected that Congress at their next session will act upon the subject of appropriating two per cent. of the moneys arising from the sales of public lands in the State of Ohio, to the opening, making and repairing a road leading from the navigable waters of the Atlantic to the Ohio river, we take the liberty of suggesting for your consideration the following reasons in favor of appropriating the money on a road leading from the city of Washington to Marietta, or to some point on the river Ohio in its vicinity.

First—That no convenient road can be had from the city of Washington or its vicinity to the Ohio much below Marietta, and that a road leading to Marietta or its vicinity will be found to be nearly or quite as straight, and to pass over better ground, than a road leading to Charleston, Wheeling or Grave Creek, or to any other place on the river above Marietta.

Second—That a road striking the river at or near Marietta, would furnish a more direct and convenient communication from the seat of the General Government to Chillicothe, the seat of the Ohio State Government (between which place and Marietta an excellent State road will soon be completed, a competent sum being appropriated for that purpose); as likewise by the navigable water of the Muskingum and Hockhocking rivers, and by short and practicable land routes, to the rich and habitable lands in the State of Ohio.

Third—That the most convenient road from Washington city to Kentucky, Tennessee, the Indiana Territory and Louisiana will be found by adopting the above proposed route.

Fourth—That one principal object to be attained in making a road from the Atlantic waters to the river Ohio is to facilitate the transportation of goods and families from the Atlantic States to the lower parts of the State of Ohio, Kentucky, Tennessee, and the various territories of the United States in the western world; and this object would be attained in a much greater degree, by a road striking the Ohio as far down as Marietta, than by one leading to any place above; the Ohio

creek, near Fort Cumberland, to the mouth of Yough, thence to Pittsburgh, thence via Beaver, thence via head waters of Yellow Creek and Big Sandy to Tuscarawas line, thence via heads of Hocking, Scioto, Little Miami to Great Miami at the mouth of Loramie Creek and to the English Fort of Pickawillamy, thence westerly to the Wabash, also a branch to Harrisburgh, and a wagon road to Philadelphia.

at almost all times furnishing a good and safe navigation from Marietta downwards, and particularly at seasons when it is rendered dangerous above by shoals, rocks, sunken trees, ice, and other obstructions by which boats are often late in autumn, detained and injured to the loss of lives and property. It will be further remembered that the Muskingum river running nearly through the centre of the State of Ohio, empties itself into the Ohio river at Marietta, and that its navigable heads interlock with those of the Cuyahoga of Lake Erie; and transportation may, and (as the progress of population extends) will be effected, from Marietta to Lake Erie, by means of these rivers and the connecting carrying place between them. Signed,

R. J. MEIGS, JR.,
JOSEPH BUELL,
RUFUS PUTNAM,
MATTHEW BACKUS,
DAVID PUTNAM,
BENJAMIN IVES GILMAN,
PAUL FEARING,
DUDLEY WOODBRIDGE,
Committee of Town of Marietta.

This policy of the General Government in applying two per cent. of western land sales to building roads from the Atlantic waters to the Ohio river, resulted in the construction of the Cumberland and Ohio road, which was authorized by an act of Congress dated March 29, 1806. Its location was made through Wheeling, Zanesville, and Columbus.

The efforts, however, to secure a direct thoroughfare through Marietta were not abandoned. In 1831 the survey and location of a turnpike road were authorized by the legislature of Ohio, from Chillicothe, through Athens to Marietta. Ephraim Cutler, James Worthington and Charles Harper were appointed commissioners.

Mr. Andrew Young was detailed from the corps of canal engineers—then employed by the State—to make an instrumental survey of the route from Chillicothe through McArthur and Athens to Marietta. He reported a distance of one hundred and nine miles, and a cost for grading, culverts and bridges of one hundred and forty-seven thousand seven hundred and fifty-six dollars.

The Marietta and Newport turnpike company was organized, and the road built as far as Newport, connecting at that point with the Virginia northwestern turnpike.

MUSKINGUM SLACKWATER IMPROVEMENT AND BALTIMORE AND OHIO RAILROAD.

Stimulated by the success of the Ohio canal, and a prevailing desire to improve the natural advantages of their position, the people along the Muskingum valley began the agitation of plans to secure State aid, either in the way of a railroad or slackwater improvement of that river. Their interest in that subject was much increased by the hope that they might induce the Baltimore & Ohio Railroad company to look for a terminus of their road upon the Ohio river at the mouth of the Muskingum.

*"A public meeting was held at the court house, January 3, 1835, to consider the question of the improvement of the Muskingum river, and a memorial was prepared and laid before the legislature. A bill was introduced the following winter by Isaac Humphreys, representative from Washington county, ordering the work, and appropriating four hundred thousand dollars

* From the Centennial Address on Washington county by President Israel Ward Andrews, of Marietta college.

for the purpose. The bill passed the house February 5th, and the senate March 4th."

In compliance with the act of the legislature, under the direction of William Wall as acting commissioner, and David Bates as chief engineer, the work for the improvement of the Muskingum river was advertised to be let in the fall of 1836. The successful bidders were G. W. Manypenny, who secured the contract for building the dam at Zanesville; Josiah Spaulding, the lock at the same place; Hosmer, Chapin & Sharp, the dam at Taylorsville; Lyon, Buck & Wolf, the lock at the same place; Arthur Taggert, the lock and dam at Bald Eagle; Hosmer, Chapin & Sharp, the lock and dam at McConnelsville; Arthur Taggert, the lock and dam at Windsor; Lyon, Buck & Wolf, the lock and dam at Luke Chute; John McCune, the dam and canal at Beverly; Arthur Taggert, the lock at the same place; Lyon, Buck & Wolf, the lock at Lowell; Arthur Taggert, the lock and dam at Devols; Hosmer, Chapin & Sharp, the lock and dam at Marietta. The work was commenced in the spring of 1837 and completed in the fall of 1841. The size of the locks was changed from the original plan—which provided that they should be only one hundred and twenty feet long by twenty feet in width—to one hundred and eighty-five feet in length and thirty-six feet in width. Even this size admits only the smaller class of boats that navigate the Ohio. The supervisor and chief engineer, at the commencement and during the first two years progress of the work, was Samuel R. Curtis, a graduate of West Point—a most excellent man, but said to be in a measure deficient in practical knowledge and experience. The members of the several firms were distributed as follows: Mr. Taggert supervised all four of his contracts, Mr. Wolf at Taylorsville lock, Mr. John Buck at Luke Chute, Truton Lyon the lock at Lowell, Colonel Sharp at Taylorsville dam, Stephen R. Hosmer the lock and dam at McConnelsville, Harlow Chapin the Marietta lock and dam. It was considered at the time of the assigning of the different contracts that the dam and lock at Marietta was the most difficult to construct—and justly too—on account of the liability of back water from the Ohio river, and the other members of the firm insisted that Chapin, in consideration of having had the most experience, should perform the work, which was accordingly done.

The total cost of the Marietta or Harmar improvement was one hundred and twenty thousand dollars. The contractors all made money; there were no failures.

The commissioner adopted several rules to govern him in disposing of the contracts. One was that he would give no more contracts or jobs than there were members in a firm; another was when a person was the owner of the lands on which a dam and lock was proposed to be built, he (the owner) could, if he so elected, have the contract at the lowest responsible bid. Following this rule the firm of Hosmer, Chapin & Sharp, could have only three contracts, while the firm was the lowest on every contract except the one for building the dam at Zanesville. But the firm had the choice of contracts, and made the choice of Taylorsville dam, McConnelsville dam and lock, and Marietta lock and dam. A Mr. Proctor was the owner of the land where it was proposed to locate the Lowell dam, and he elected to take the contract at the lowest responsible bid, but did not desire to do the work, but to dispose of or sell his claim out. Mr. Alexander Hill was wanting work, but, unacquainted with such work, hesitated to pay Mr. Proctor his price—five hundred dollars—until he had consulted one of the firm of Hosmer, Chapin & Sharp, and was advised to lose no time in taking Mr. Proctor at his offer, and he did so, thereby securing the contract for the Lowell dam, which must have yielded him not less than twenty thousand dollars profit.

Great expectations were indulged in by the citizens of the Muskingum valley, before and after the beginning of the slack water improvement. Elaborate calculations were made, and spread broadcast along the valley, of the quantity of water power the construction of the dams would furnish, the number of mill stones that the flow of water in the river would furnish motive power to run, the number of barrels of flour that could and would be manufactured and exported. Untold numbers of manufacturing establishments would at once spring into existence, propelled by the abundance of water power; the finances of the State would at no distant day be placed on a firm and reliable basis, from the basis of this vast amount of water power. Added to this the tolls for freight and passengers would yield a revenue sufficient not only to pay the interest on the investment, but to wipe out the entire debt for its construction. These views were entertained by shrewd, conservative business men, while those more enthusiastic could see prosperity untold, with numerous cities, with a teeming population. Such opinions led to unnecessary increase in the expense of construction, and caused serious drawbacks to navigation as for instance, the unnecessary canals at Taylorsville, McConnelsville, Beverly, and Lowell.

Entertaining these extravagant views led to the formation of several companies to profit by the prospects presented for making a fortune. One composed of David Bates the chief engineer, Colonel Augustus Stone, Colonel John Mills, and Mr. Hatch, purchased a large tract of vacant ground in Harmar and laid it out in lots of small dimensions, forced the lock on the Harmar side of the river, where it should not have been, to favor the speculation; but the speculation was a failure. One other company was formed and purchased the land between the canal and river at a place they named Lowell, with the full expectation and anticipation that it would, in a brief space of time, throw old Lowell, its namesake, entirely in the shade; but the scheme was a failure; and the same may be said of Taylorsville and McConnelsville.

The Muskingum improvement was already in a fair way of being accomplished and was actually commenced before the railroad project really promised to be a success.

In the decision of the first the people had whatever influence could be brought to bear in shaping the legislature of the state of Ohio upon that subject; but upon the other they could exert no positive influence beyond the inducements that might flow from their position at the confluence of the two rivers.

In 1837 a committee appointed at a county meeting commissioned Judge Cutler to go to Baltimore to confer with Mr. Louis McLane, the president of the Baltimore & Ohio company, with regard to the route of that road which had been built about eighty miles.[*]

Judge Cutler was again requested by a meeting of citizens held November 30, 1839, to repair immediately to Baltimore and obtain interviews with the board of directors, and seek to impress on the minds of its members the great importance of terminating the road in this section of the Ohio valley.

The two absorbing subjects at that time were the Muskingum improvements on the one hand and the terminus of the Baltimore & Ohio railroad on the other hand.

The efforts of the citizens of Marietta and Washington counties, however, in calling the attention of Baltimore railroad managers to the advantages of a location of their great work upon a line most direct to Cincinnati and St. Louis as well as most accessible to the fertile interior of Ohio was so far successful that earnest efforts were made to secure legislation from the State of Virginia in accordance with that policy. The opening for public use of the Cumberland turnpike road to Wheeling had directed the attention of Baltimore merchants to that point on the Ohio river as the only one that would meet their views and interests. The city of Wheeling availed herself of this preference and exerted such an influence with the Virginia legislature that years of controversy were spent in an effort on the part of the more intelligent and far-seeing friends of the Baltimore road to reach the Ohio upon a direct route that would have given to Marietta the full advantage of her position.

Middle Island was the preferred route of those who had listened to representations urged by the agents from Marietta. Then as a next choice was Fishing creek and at one time Fish creek was accepted by the Baltimore managers as a compromise. But Wheeling influence prevailed and the Baltimore & Ohio company were obliged to accept Grave creek, twelve miles below Wheeling, as their point of entrance to the Ohio valley or continue a struggle that promised indefinite delay.

WASHINGTON COUNTY AND THE MARIETTA AND CINCIN-
NATI RAILROAD.

At this period the active efforts of Washington county in the way of actually building a railroad may be said to commence.

A special charter had been granted to the Belper & Cincinnati railroad company in 1845 to build a road to Cincinnati, with terminus on the Ohio river, either at Belpre or Harmar.

The company was organized at Chillicothe, and Washington county interests were represented in the board of directors by N. L. Wilson and William P. Cutler.

As the terminus of the Baltimore & Ohio was then undecided, they obtained from the legislature—with the consent and approbation of the Belpre & Cincinnati

*Centennial Address on Washington county, by President Israel Ward Andrews, of Marietta College.

directors the right to extend from Harmar up the Ohio valley to any point so as to connect with any railroad or other improvement that should be built to the Ohio river on the easterly side thereof.

This legislative grant of a right to extend from Harmar up the Ohio valley was procured in accordance with advice received from the manager of the Baltimore & Ohio company, and with their known wishes on that subject.

The following extract from a letter to Hon. W. P. Cutler from Louis McLane, then president of the company, sufficiently indicates their views and fully justifies the efforts made to bring the road to Harmar.

BALTIMORE, January 14, 1848.

Unless it should be indispensably necessary to prescribe some limit to the extension of your road, it would appear to me most advisable that the right should be obtained to extend it to any point on the Ohio at which the company should determine to connect with our road, or if a limitation be unavoidable, to obtain the right to extend it to any point on the Ohio river not higher up than the mouth of Fish creek. That would enable you certainly to connect with the projected improvement either from that point or Fishing creek, and I have very little doubt that before we finish our road to Wheeling our intersecting road will be authorized from the mouth of Fishing creek.

As the location and construction of the Marietta & Cincinnati railroad through the western part of the county, upon what is known as the "old line" has been a subject of much adverse criticism, and is now the occasion of a serious controversy, it is due to all the parties who were in any way responsible for that action, that the facts should be put upon record as they existed at the time when the necessary decisions had to be made. In the first place, it was a very serious undertaking, a very heavy job, to build two hundred miles of railroad across southern Ohio, where the water courses afforded no valleys of any great extent running in the proper direction, but all requiring a railroad line to be carried across and nearly at right angles to their courses. Second, it required the active and cordial cooperation of all the localities along the route. Third, the only points of any strength that could be brought into harmony with each other and the general object of the enterprise were Marietta, Athens, and Chillicothe, and the respective counties of which they were the county-seats. Greenfield, Hillsborough, and several smaller towns west of Chillicothe could contribute private, but not municipal aid.

The Belpre and Cincinnati charter, with Harmar as an available terminus, and with subsequent right of extension up the Ohio valley, so as to meet the views expressed in President McLane's letter as above quoted, made a cooperation of all the above named interests possible.

The first effort to build was by placing twenty-four miles between Chillicothe and Greenfield, and eleven miles east of Chillicothe under contract. This was soon followed by a second contract, extending to Byres station on the east and Blanchester on the west. At the date of these contracts the control of the company was in the hands of directors from Athens, Ross, and Highland counties. Washington county had but two representatives on the board, Messrs. Wilson and Cutler. The contract entered into would require at least three million dollars to complete them. The means applicable were

three hundred and fifty thousand dollars in municipal subscription to stock from Ross county and Chillicothe, and two hundred thousand dollars in private subscriptions between Chillicothe and Blanchester.

The road had really taken a leap in the dark when they ventured upon such large obligations with so slender support. But the more difficult problem to be solved was the extension from Byers station, a distance of seventy-five miles, to the Ohio river, over the most rough and expensive portion of the whole route, and for which they had at that time only a pledge of one hundred thousand dollars, voted by Athens county.

It was at this crisis and under these circumstances that municipal subscriptions were offered from Washington county, Marietta and Harmar, amounting to three hundred and fifty thousand dollars, and from individuals amounting to fifty thousand dollars, provided the company would locate and build their road through the western part of the county.

In addition to this offer of four hundred thousand dollars, the promise was held out by the citizens of Washington county that they would undertake to enlist a Philadelphia interest to take the place of the expected connection up the Ohio valley with the Baltimore & Ohio road, as that company had been forced, by the influence of Wheeling, to confine its terminus on the Ohio to that point.

This promise was subsequently fulfilled by subscriptions of seven hundred and fifty thousand dollars by the Pennsylvania railroad company and two hundred and fifty thousand dollars by the city of Wheeling to the common stock of the company.

It was found that the credit of mortgage bonds would be greatly enhanced by a through connection over the Pennsylvania road to Philadelphia and New York. The progress of surveys and locations on the Baltimore & Ohio line had developed grades of one hundred and sixteen feet to the mile, or long plains with shortest practicable curves.

The commerce of Baltimore at that time was not such as to impart any confidence that western products would seek that seaport over a line of road that was regarded as well nigh impracticable.

It was also ascertained that a practicable route could be obtained from Marietta eastward to Baltimore, by bridging the Ohio river in that vicinity to Williamstown, in Virginia, thence by way of Cow creek to Grafton, on the main stem of the Baltimore & Ohio road. A charter was secured to cover this route, and careful surveys made by the Independence railroad company proved that the through line from the seaboard to the great west could be built through Marietta and along the route of the old line several miles shorter than through Belpre and along the Hocking valley.

As the case then stood, when the question of a choice as between Belpre and Harmar came up for decision, the controlling facts on one side were, first, an offer of four hundred thousand dollars from Washington county, conditioned upon the road being built through Boston township; second, one million dollars from the Pennsylvania railroad company and city of Wheeling, on same condition; third, a route *via* Williamstown and Harmar, as between Baltimore and Cincinnati, shorter and cheaper than the one through Belpre and along the Hocking valley; fourth, the additional advantage of a seaboard route directly to Philadelphia and New York over grades of fifty-two feet per mile as compared with those on the Baltimore & Ohio line; fifth, a credit thus imparted to the mortgage securities of the road by the virtual indorsement of the scheme in large subscription to its stock by the Pennsylvania, then standing at the head of American railroads. In the opposite scale was laid one hundred thousand dollars voted by Athens county with assurance of as much more, all applicable to either route.

Appeals had been made both to Parkersburgh and the president of the Baltimore & Ohio company for aid in case the Belpre terminus should be adopted, but no encouragement whatever was given that any money could be expected from those sources. The conclusion reached at that time was quite unanimous by the board of directors of the Belpre & Cincinnati company—although the sympathies of all the members except the two from Washington county were strongly enlisted in favor of a direct connection through Belpre with Baltimore alone. But they all felt that even to have continued the work already under contract would have been little less than a swindle upon their own people, unless additional means equivalent to that which Washington county offered could be secured. The only alternative in the mind of any sane man at the time was to accept the proffered aid or abandon the enterprise at once.

That abandonment would undoubtedly have taken place if the aid thus offered had been rejected.

Upon the actual acceptance of the Washington county subscription—based upon a contract between the municipal authorities and the railroad company to locate and construct their road through Barlow township—Messrs. John Mills and Douglass Putnam were elected directors. Messrs. Beman Gates and W. S. Nye became members soon after, thus giving to Washington county six out of the nineteen members of the board. The name of the company was also changed to that of Marietta & Cincinnati railroad company.

The burden of the enterprise rested upon their shoulders from that time forward. The western members very soon secured the object of their most earnest efforts by having the line from Blanchester to the western limits of the Vinton county coal fields brought within the limits of certainty by the progress of grading and a favorable purchase of rails. They were, therefore, quite willing that the Washington county men should assume the active execution of a policy which they had devised and urged upon the board's acceptance. While, therefore, the cooperation of the western members, including those from Athens, was most cordial and at all times valuable, the active labors of planning and urging forward the work devolved mainly upon the Washington county members.

As a result of these labors and the adoption by the board of a comprehensive policy, embracing not only a direct route to Baltimore, but a still more valuable one to Philadelphia, the credit of the mortgage as well as municipal bonds did acquire a high value. Most favorable contracts were effected in England for rails, and the extra line from Blanchester to Wheeling was soon under contract in the hands of contractors of the highest standing in ability and experience.

A force of six thousand men and teams was soon at work with every prospect of consummating the high hopes that had become universally inspired, as to the complete success of the whole scheme.

But in 1854, after four years of most unremitting toil, and just as success seemed to be a question of only a short interval of time, a storm burst upon the managers from a quarter least expected, from which no human foresight could have protected them, and from a source entirely foreign to the enterprise.

News came from Europe that England and France had resolved upon war with Russia.

The financial agents of the company in New York soon gave warning that sales of bonds were diminishing. Monthly payments for work in progress had reached the large sum of one hundred and fifty thousand dollars per month. Advances were earnestly sought so as to keep contractors at work, but very soon all sales ceased and there was no alternative but to discharge every man and team from the line.

Thus, as it were in a day, the labors of years were thrown upon the hands of directors—a wreck.

This disaster could not in any way be charged upon the enterprise itself, or upon the policy that had given it so promising a start. As the court proved, that policy was the basis of recuperation and reconstruction.

Mr. Wilson undertook to negotiate sale of mortgage bonds in Europe and succeeded in organizing a syndicate to take a large amount based upon and connected with a purchase of seven thousand acres of mineral lands in Vinton county. It was a condition of the bond purchase that the shops should be located at Zaleski. The bond purchasers laid out that town on a large scale and named it after a Polish nobleman who had taken a large amount of the bonds.

In the meantime other members of the board succeeded in making a home market for a large amount of domestic bonds along the line to contractors and others interested in the completion of the road.

A large purchase of machinery was also made from eastern manufacturers on long time and favorable terms.

Messrs. Gates and Nye devoted their personal oversight and attention to the reorganization of the abandoned work and its prosecution between Byres and the Ohio river. The labor was performed—much of it in the winter—amidst all the difficulties and discouragements resulting from so serious a downfall—and was made doubly important from the fact that many subscriptions to domestic bonds had been made payable upon condition that the track should reach certain points at fixed times.

As a result of all these efforts the track was urged through to Harmar and opened for use in June 1857.

The labors and struggles of that period if fully presented would form and interesting chapter of personal devotion, untiring effort and skilful management on the part of the eastern members, and of cordial support by those who had sooner realized in part the expectations of the people, by having secured some running road.

But another storm had gathered its force and was ready to burst upon the heads of the directors, almost as soon as they had reached a temporary resting place upon the banks of the Ohio river.

In the fall of 1857 the failure of the Ohio Life and Trust company involved nearly every newly or partly finished railroad in the west in such financial embarrassment that bankruptcy was a general result.

In urging the work forward the directors had incurred personal liabilities amounting to over two hundred thousand dollars. This load of indebtedness was distributed among the thirteen members of the road, and when the crash came they found that all the securities that had a cash value had been absorbed, leaving only some third mortgage bonds and scraps of real estate—none of which could be readily converted into money. The advance of money or personal credits on the part of the directors was absolutely necessary to get the track through to Marietta. Without it that object could not have been attained.

This second disaster, however, did discourage or prevent further effort. Foreign holders of securities forced the road into the hands of a receiver—but steps were at once taken to reorganize the company by exchanging all indebtedness for stock, so that in 1860 a complete reorganization had been effected. During this interval a line was built from Scott's Landing to Belpre so as to make an "all rail" route over the Baltimore & Ohio road, and thus displace a water link which had proved almost fatal to through traffic.

From the time of the reorganization up to 1868 the management of the Marietta & Cincinnati railroad was almost exclusively in the hands of Washington county men. During that time money was raised to complete a large portion of the unfinished work on the eastern division, and an independent line was built from Loveland into Cincinnati through Madisonville, thus securing close connections with all western roads and the right of common use with the Indianapolis, Cincinnati & Louisville road of the passenger depot on Plum street.

At no time, however, has it been found practicable to resume the work between Harmar and Wheeling. The result has been that the Baltimore & Ohio company had a complete control over all through traffic and the policy was to patronize a barge line on the Ohio river from Parkersburgh, while their "all rail" business was done over the Central Ohio through Bellair. Local business alone was not sufficient to maintain the road and pay interest on the bonds that had been issued to build into Cincinnati and complete other portions of the road. Aid was sought from the Baltimore & Ohio managers in 1868. This was extended only upon condition of absolute control over the Marietta & Cincinnati road.

From that time all influential connection on the part of Washington county men has ceased and the entire responsibility of management of the property has devolved on Baltimore managers.

During the twelve years that the Marietta & Cincinnati railroad has been under an exclusively Baltimore control, the policy has been to devote its tracks and equipments mainly to an inter-State traffic between western grain fields and the elevator in Baltimore. It is only by succeeding in this effort that Baltimore can ever expect to retain her foreign shipping, and become a large commercial centre upon the Atlantic railroad.

This effort has forced the railroad managers to propose this through traffic at very low rates, in order to compete successfully with water routes and competing railroad lines.

In order to make up for lack of profit on the inter-State business, the highest rates have been charged upon local. The effect of this has been to discourage business enterprise along the route of the Marietta & Cincinnati road, and has forced the people of Marietta, Athens, Chillicothe, Greenfield, Jackson—all the strong points along the line—to build roads that would give them respectively outlets to other and competing railroads.

As a result of this entire policy, which has been on trial during the twelve years past, a complete wreck has been made of all the securities of the Marietta and Cincinnati road, as will be seen by the following statement, showing earnings, deficits and interest paid for borrowed money, copied from annual reports on file in office of railroad commissioners in Columbus.

This statement is made up by the difference between operating expenses, taxes, rentals, interest on floating debts, and other strictly general payments, and gross earnings for each year:

Year ending June 30.	Net Earnings.	Deficits.	Amounts Paid Bondholders for their Annual Interest.
1869	$33.751		$441,420
1870		$166,956	427,752
1871		106,581	522,752
1872		87,471	642,047
1873	221,191		682,371
1874	17,508		843,068
1875		14,263	837,282
1876		385,613	845,242
1877		356,919	724,156
1878		130,735	124,860
1879		141,421	None paid.
1880 (14 mo.)		210,399	None paid.
Total for 12 years, $272,450		$1,600,360	$6,090,951
Deduct net earnings from deficits,	272,450		

Shows a net deficit in 12 years of $1,327,910.

The increase in bonded and floating debt in twelve years has been $15,885,990.

The road has been in the hands of a receiver for about three years. His report made October 31, 1880, states that there are past due coupons on mortgage bonds, amounting to three million four hundred and twenty-seven thousand five hundred dollars, and says: "It cannot be expected that those arrearages can ever be paid, or that the company will ever be able to pay the excessive rates of interest accruing on its present funded debt, and the fixed rentals, and other charges now existing."

In order to save ten miles in distance, the Baltimore managers built thirty miles of new road along Hocking valley to Belpre, and have abandoned the use of that portion of their road that was built through the western portion of Washington county, upon the route fixed by contract between the municipal authorities of the county and the company, in 1862, now known as the "old line." The rental annually paid on the new road—the Baltimore short line—is about one hundred and fifty thousand dollars. During over six years that it has been used, it has absorbed nearly one million dollars of the earnings, while the bondholders are shown annual deficits. Such have been the results to the owners of the property from devoting the road to through traffic for the benefit of Baltimore city, while Washington county is wantonly deprived of that which cost the people in subscriptions, advances and taxes about one million four hundred thousand dollars. The people have appealed to the Legislature for relief and court aid to compel the railroad company to perform its duties to the public.

THE CLEVELAND AND MARIETTA RAILROAD.

The history of the enterprise which resulted in the building of this road is one of numerous failures. The company as originally organized was known as the Marietta & Pittsburgh railroad company, and it was brought into being for the purpose of constructing a road from Marietta to Dennison, Tuscarawas county, passing through the counties of Washington, Noble, Guernsey, Harrison, and Tuscarawas. The certificate of organization was filed September 29, 1868, and the first meeting of the stockholders, pursuant to a call of the corporators, was held December 8, 1868, at the First National bank of Marietta. The original corporators were William H. Frazier of Caldwell, William Glidden of Noble county, William C. Okey, W. P. Cutler, and R. R. Dawes. The stockholders elected the following gentlemen as the first directors of the company, viz ; W. P. Cutler, A. J. Warner, and R. R. Dawes, of Washington county, William Frazier, of Noble, Isaac Morton, Thomas Greene and William Lawrence of Guernsey. At a meeting of the directors held upon the same day William P. Cutler was chosen president, and R. R. Dawes, secretary. At the second meeting, held February 18, 1869, A. J. Warner resigned his place as director of the company and became, with James McArthur, party to a contract to construct the road from Marietta to Caldwell, a distance of thirty-three miles, the original purpose being to purchase the nearest good coal fields. They agreed to build the road for about seventeen thousand dollars per mile, taking their pay in the stock subscriptions and bonds of the road. The contract was made and submitted February 18, 1869, and the directors were ordered to place a mortgage upon the road and issue bonds to the amount of fifteen thousand dollars per mile. Construction was commenced in the summer of 1869. On June 30th the company was authorized to issue a mortgage of one million five hundred thousand dollars, it having been arranged to extend the construction from Caldwell to Dennison or some other point to connect with the "Pan Handle" or

Pittsburgh, Cincinnati & St. Louis railway. Of these bonds five hundred thousand dollars were to be used in payment for building that part of the road between Marietta and Caldwell already under contract. This action by the board of directors was ratified by the stockholders July 1, 1870. At the annual meeting of the stockholders December 14, 1870. It appears from the president's report that six miles of track had been laid. The grading was completed to Caldwell, and cross ties furnished for nearly the whole of the line. It was shown that the sum of one hundred and fifteen thousand eight hundred and seventy-nine dollars had been expended by the company, which by this time was largely in debt to the contractors.

At this meeting a new board of directors was elected, viz: William P. Cutler, R. R. Dawes, Samuel Shipman, James Dutton, of Washington county, William H. Frazier and David McKee of Noble. This board organized by the election of Mr. Cutler as president, Mr. Frazier as vice-president, Samuel Shipman as treasurer, and J. A. Kingsbury as secretary.

Up to this time no effort had been made to carry out the company's plan of extending the line north of Caldwell. At a meeting of the directors, May 1, 1871, the following resolution was adopted:

Resolved, That we deem it advisable to take the necessary steps at once toward extending our line northward from Caldwell, and that W. Richardson and Samuel Shipman be a committee to take all preliminary and necessary steps to attain that effect.

At the same meeting Mr. Warner submitted a proposition on behalf of the firm of Warner & McArthur, proposing to build the extension contemplated, and a resolution was passed authorizing the company to enter into a contract with them, the company agreeing to furnish the right of way. An agreement was executed on the twelfth of June following. The contractors immediately began the work of locating the line through to Newcomerstown, which point had finally been selected as the place of junction. At a meeting held November 30, 1871, the northern terminus of the road had been changed from Newcomerstown to Canal Dover, Tuscarawas county, and the contractors were given authority to take subscriptions in the name of the county, and to enter into contract, for rights of way. By this time the road was completed and rolling stock was moving over it between Marietta and Caldwell. Conductor P. M. Snyder, at present in the employ of the company, had the honor of running the first train over the road—from Marietta to Whipple, fourteen miles—on the first day of April, 1871.

On the first day of January, 1872, the fourth annual meeting of the company was held, and the following directors were chosen, viz: A. J. Warner, Samuel Shipman, W. Richardson, W. H. Frazier, Isaac Morton, A. Wilhelmi, and William P. Cutler.

A. J. Warner was chosen president, and from this time on almost the entire responsibility of the affairs of the company rested upon him. The company had become largely in arrears to the contractors, being unable to collect subscriptions fast enough to pay for the construction.

Arrangements were made with the several counties to provide subscriptions of stock to a given amount and to furnish right of way as conditioned prior to entering upon the construction of the road in them. As soon as the line was definitely located between Caldwell and Canal Dover a branch was projected to run from Liberty, Guernsey county, via Coshocton, to Mansfield, to be known as the Northwest Extension, which it was intended should become the main line. A considerable amount of money was subscribed, and county and township aid was voted to this line, but before work could be begun the panic of 1873 overtook the company and put an end to operations. Prior to this, however, Mr. Warner had negotiated the first mortgage bonds through parties in New York city and Amsterdam, which enabled the company to prosecute their work vigorously through the season of 1872.

February 11, 1873, the annual meeting for that year was held. The old board of directors was continued in office, with the exception of Mr. Richardson, whose place was filled by T. W. Ewart. During this year the name of the company was changed to that of the Marietta, Pittsburgh & Cleveland railway company; the "Marietta city branch" was built, affording connection with the Marietta & Cincinnati railroad at Front street; and a consolidated mortgage was authorized to be issued for the purpose of providing additional funds, and taking up the mortgage previously issued.

It may be remarked, that during the summer of 1873 the work of construction was pushed ahead with all of the rapidity possible. Most of the grading was done, ties provided, and the line was got in readiness for the laying of iron, except in the construction of the tunnels, of which four were proposed between Caldwell and Canal Dover. One of these it was necessary to complete before cars could be run on the road. On this tunnel, south of Newcomerstown, work was carried on night and day for several months. In order to hasten the track laying and get the road into running order the three other summits were crossed by steep grades and zig-zags. Progress, however, was considerably delayed, and the company and contractors were embarrassed by the tardiness of subscribers in paying the money they had promised, and the difficulty in selling bonds. But by employing every energy at their command and using their own funds the contractors pushed the road forward until the panic came on. The track was then laid nearly to Cambridge, from the south, and most of the way from Canal Dover to Newcomerstown, upon the north, but none of the road had been ballasted and the cuts and embankments were new and required constant attention. At this juncture it became a serious question whether it was possible to complete the line or whether it must be abandoned. Bonds could not be negotiated, and it was almost impossible to make any further collections on stock subscriptions. The floating debt was large and pressing.

Up to this time Mr. Warner was not personally involved beyond the direct obligations he had assumed as contractor in building the road. The construction of the road came to a halt. Mr. Warner, knowing that

if the work was long delayed the iron on hand must be sold and the enterprise fail completely, and the subscribers along the line not only lose all of the money they had paid in, but also lose the road, determined to carry the project through, even if he did so at the expense of heavily involving himself, personally. In February, 1874, he went to Europe, and after some time spent there succeeded in effecting a negotiation whereby the first bonds were substituted by the new consolidated bonds and additional funds provided for carrying on the work. The business of the road, however, which was largely dependent upon the development of the coal and iron field, came to a standstill, furnaces "blowing out" and rolling mills "shutting down." The road was left by these causes without sufficient earnings to pay the interest on the bonds. This complication of troubles, being supplemented and aggravated by an unparaleled flood in Duck creek, which did great damage along the southern part of the line, made it necessary to apply for a receiver. On August 5, 1875, A. J. Warner was appointed to this position by Judge Marsh of the Guernsey county court of common pleas. The road was operated by the receiver from this time until June 13, 1877, when it was sold under order of the court, Cyrus W. Field, John Paton, and Isaac Morton becoming the purchasers as trustees for the bondholders. The trustees conducted the business of the road until May 1, 1880, when, in accordance with an agreement made by the bondholders, the road was transferred to the new organization, the Cleveland & Marietta railroad company, a corporation duly formed under the State law, and having for directors Isaac Morton, of Cambridge; Douglass Putnam, of Marietta; Stanley Mathews, Larz Anderson, F. H. Short, and Charles W. West, of Cincinnatti; Cyrus W. Field, Charles Lanier, and John Paton of New York city; C. D. Willard, of Washington, District of Columbia; and S. C. Baldwin, of Cleveland. These directors elected Isaac Morton, president and treasurer, and S. C. Baldwin, vice-president and secretary.

The road was incomplete when it came into the hands of the trustees and they spent large amounts in building trestles, repairing bridges and tunnels, etc., their expenses charged to this account being in excess of the earnings of the road. It may be remarked that the same is in a large measure true of the operation of the road under its present management.

The reign of prosperity which has succeeded the long period of universal depression, the consequent development of the rich resources of the country through which the Cleveland & Marietta railroad passes, and the continuance of good management in the same line of policy as that which has obtained during the past three years, there can be no doubt, will make the line in the not far distant future, what it never yet has been, a paying property. Already the business has been very largely increased, and a contemplated connection with Cleveland by the new valley road, which, unlike the lines by which that outlet is now obtained, has no interests conflicting with the Cleveland and Marietta railroad, seems to be all that is necessary to make the business of this line all that may

44

be desired. The shipments of coal, iron ore, and petroleum must in the future be very large. For the year ending June 30, 1880, they are largely in excess of those for 1877. In the latter year seventy thousand tons of coal were carried, to only seventeen thousand tons of the former year, and a smaller proportionate increase is shown in the amount of oil carried. In 1877 it was only twenty-nine thousand tons; in the year ending in June, 1880, it was fifty-one thousand tons. Twenty-one thousand tons of iron ore were carried in the last fiscal year, and none in 1877. As the production of these staples increases, as it is now doing and seems destined to, increase in freightage must correspond. Agriculturally, too, the country is growing richer, more abundant crops being secured through the enrichment of the hill coal lands with phosphates. The chief inducement to build the road was the mineral deposits extending almost the whole length of the line. The road was carefully located with reference to the best and most easily available ores and coal, and its development of the mineral resources was all that was ever claimed for it by its projectors and builders. The line crosses the entire outcrop of the great Appalachian coal-field. No other road in Ohio or elsewhere passes through larger or better deposits of coal or iron.

The road, too, has opened a district before without railroad communication and has given an outlet to a number of interior towns formerly isolated. It also gave to Cambridge and Newcomerstown the full benefit of competition. One especial advantage which the road secured to Marietta, and one which saved its people many thousands of dollars every year, was the opening of communication between the city by the river and the valuable coal fields, which has operated to materially reduce the price of coal.

There has been a noteworthy freedom from accident upon this road, even from the first, but during the time when the road was operated by the trustees, from June, 1877, up to June of 1880, no passenger has been killed upon the line, and accidents of all kinds were reduced to the minimum. The total length of the main line is about one hundred miles. A large part of this is ballasted with stone and quite a number of miles with coal slack. It is kept in excellent condition through constant watchfulness. The road is under the direct management of S. C. Baldwin, vice-president and secretary, and J. C. Kingsbury, who has been connected with the road from its establishment, is the master of transportation.

CHAPTER XXII.

COUNTY SOCIETIES.

Organization of the Marietta Historical Society in 1842—The Present Washington County Pioneer Association, Organized in 1870—Brief Notes of Some of its Meetings—Its Officers—List of Members—The Agricultural and Manufacturing Society of Washington and Wood Counties, Organized in 1819—The First Fair Held in 1826—Premiums Offered for Wolf Scalps—The Present Washington County Agricultural and Mechanical Association, Organized in 1846—List of its Officers.

HISTORICAL AND PIONEER ASSOCIATIONS.

The first historical society which had an existence in Washington county, was organized in Marietta in 1842, as appears by the following circular, which was printed in the *American Pioneer* of that year, and which is believed to be the only record of the society in existence:

MARIETTA HISTORICAL ASSOCIATION.

Ephriam Cutler, president; Arius Nye, vice-president; Caleb Emerson, corresponding secretary; Arius S. Nye, recording secretary; William R. Putnam, John Mills, A. T. Nye, curators.

It is not a little singular that the known and acknowledged importance of history has heretofore induced so little effort for its accuracy. The classification of history as a branch of fictitious literature would, alas! for it, be not altogether false. We have recent indications of better things to come. The formation of historical societies, local as well as general, is very encouraging. The Marietta Historical association aims to establish a library, cabinet, and repository worthy of the oldest settlement in Ohio. The members hope their zeal may prove not incommensurate with their views. But the efficiency of the institution must depend much on the aid of others.

That aid is invoked in the furnishing of books, pamphlets, newspapers, memoirs and manuscripts illustrative of western history, particularly of Ohio, and especially of the earlier settlements. The donation of books is asked as a contribution for public utility. Any book, publication, record, or manuscript, will be acceptable. The association hopes to do its share in the preparation of western history, and respectfully suggests the formation everywhere of like associations, holding friendly correspondence and rendering mutual aid.

　　　　　EPHRAIM CUTLER, President.

　　　CALEB EMERSON, Corresponding Secretary.

MARIETTA, November 24, 1842.

A. T. Nye, esq., is authority for the statement that this society never held a meeting after the first, at which the organization was effected. Caleb Emerson, as its secretary, collected some valuable papers.

THE PIONEER ASSOCIATION OF WASHINGTON COUNTY.

After 1842 no other historical or pioneer society had an existence in Marietta or Washington county until the present one came into being in 1870. The first mention of this organization was the following call:

　　　　　　MARIETTA, November 19, 1869.

Dear Sir: Of the company of forty-eight men that landed at this place on the seventh of April, 1788, or the members of those families that landed here on the nineteenth of August following, none are now living. A few that came out at a later period still survive. In Cincinnati, and other places, "Pioneer Associations" have been formed, to keep alive the recollection of early events in the history of the State. It seems to us proper that in the oldest town in the State such an association should be formed. It has been deemed best to invite some of the sons of the pioneers to meet at the library room of the Marietta library on Tuesday, February 22, 1870, at 10 o'clock A. M., to take into consideration the propriety of forming such an association for this county, and if deemed best to enter into such an organization. You are respectfully invited to attend this meeting.

　　　　　Respectfully yours,

　　　　　　WILLIAM PITT PUTNAM.

　　　　　　A. T. NYE.

　　　　　　WILLIAM R. PUTNAM.

In pursuance of the above call a meeting was held, of

which Enoch S. McIntosh, of Beverly, was appointed chairman, and A. T. Nye, secretary. On motion of A. T. Nye it was resolved that it was expedient to organize a pioneer association in Washington county. On motion of John Mills, A. T. Nye was appointed to prepare and report to the meeting a constitution for the government of the proposed society. Mr. Nye reported the following, which was adopted:

CONSTITUTION.

PREAMBLE.

In view of the fact that all the company of pioneers that landed at Marietta on the seventh day of April, 1788, and the several members of the first families that landed there on the nineteenth of August, of the same year, have passed away, and that time is also making inroads upon the children of our pioneer fathers, it seems important that some organization should exist, having in view the perpetuation of the memory of those pioneer fathers and mothers, and the collection of papers which may give valuable information in regard to the early history of this county and State, we deem it expedient to form a Pioneer Association for Washington county, and adopt the following constitution:

ARTICLE 1. The society shall be known as the Pioneer Association of Washington county, Ohio.

ARTICLE 2. The object of the association shall be to cultivate social intercourse with each other, to gather and preserve personal narratives of persons and events connected with the early history of Washington county and the State, and generally any other information which may be valuable as a part of the history of the county and State.

ARTICLE 3. Any person may become a member of this association by signing the constitution and paying annually the sum of one dollar to the proper officers of the association, provided such person lived in the State prior to the year 1830. The wives of any members may become members, although they may not have resided in the State as early as that year. The association may, by a majority vote of members present at any meeting elect corresponding members

ARTICLE 4 The officers of the association shall be a president, vice-president, corresponding secretary, a recording secretary, treasurer, and an executive committee of five, who shall be elected by ballot annually, and who shall perform the duties usually assigned to such officers, and hold their offices until their successors are chosen.

ARTICLE 5. The annual meeting, at which the election of officers shall take place, shall be held on the seventh day of April, except when that day falls on Sunday, when the meeting shall be held on the Monday following.

ARTICLE 6 Other meetings may be called by the president or the executive committee at such times and places as they may appoint.

ARTICLE 7. The annual meeting of the society shall be held at Marietta.

ARTICLE 8. All moneys of the association shall be paid to the recording secretary, who shall make a record of the same and pay it over to the treasurer, taking his receipt for the amount.

ARTICLE 9. Expenditures of money shall be made on the order of the executive committee unless otherwise provided for.

ARTICLE 10. No alteration or amendment shall be made to this constitution except at an annual meeting and with the consent of not less than two-thirds of the members present.

After the adoption of the constitution the society adjourned, to meet in the afternoon at the same place. On coming to order at 2 o'clock P. M., the election of officers was taken up, with the following result: William R. Putnam, president; E. S. McIntosh, vice-president; Samuel Shipman, treasurer; John M. Woodbridge, recording secretary; A. T. Nye, corresponding secretary. Executive committee: Augustus Stone, Sumner Oakes, George W. Barker, Henry Fearing, William Pitt Putnam.

After resolving to celebrate the anniversary of the settlement of Marietta on the seventh of April next (1870), the society adjourned.

On this occasion the association assembled at the Congregational church in Marietta, and conducted a very interesting programme of services, opened with prayer by Rev. T. H. Hawks. The address, which was one of very interesting character, and highly appropriate to the occasion, was delivered by Dr. G. S. B. Hempstead, of Hanging Rock, Ohio, formerly of Marietta. This was followed by a narrative of Dr. John Cotton, prepared by Dr. S. P. Hildreth before his death, and read by Dr. J. Dexter Cotton. A. S. Curtis read a narrative of the Newberry settlement, made up of incidents which occurred soon after the location of that colony. The members of the association were photographed in a body. A collation was served in the new college building, after which the members enjoyed themselves socially, reviewing their reccollections of early years. In the evening historical exercises were again taken up, and a number of very interesting and valuable papers read.

Meetings similar to this have been held on the seventh of April each year.

Following are the present officers of the association: William R. Putnam;* president; E. S. McIntosh, vice-president; A. T. Nye, corresponding secretary; W. F. Curtis, recording secretary; Beman Gates, treasurer. Executive committee: Henry Fearing, L. J. P. Putnam, I. W. Andrews, William P. Curtis, B. F. Hart.

The following are the names of the persons who have been or are now members of the association: Augustus Stone, Benjamin F. Stone, Weston Thomas, E. L. McIntosh, John Mills, James Lawton, A. T. Nye, Henry Fearing, George W. Barker, Joel Deming, Sumner Oaks, John Test, Douglas Putnam, Ichabod H. Nye, Samuel Shipman, J. W. L. Brown, Edwin Guthrie, William R. Putnam, Henry W. Corner, Thomas W. Ewart, John M. Woodbridge, J. P. Sanford, Joseph E. Hall, Silas Slocumb, Henry Hay, Merritt Judd, Stephen Devol, Louis Anderson, William Warren, Mrs. H. D. Knowles, Samuel S. Knowles, Walter Curtis, Mrs. Phebe W. Putnam, Dennis Gibbs, J. D. Cotton, J. L. Record, James Dutton, Jesse Beach, John C. McCoy, Junia Jennings, C. M. Wood, James Dunn, James Furgason, John M. Hook, I. W. Putnam, M. Morse, O. R. Loring, John Newton, Stephen Newton, David Putnam, Levi Barber, William Knox, William F. Curtis, David Barber, Boylston Shaw, Cyrus Ames, A. Pixley, E. R. Robinson, Joseph Thompson, Samuel Dye, Courtland Sheppard, Rotheus Hayward, Joseph Hutchison, Samson Cole, Luther Edgarton, William Corner, Thomas Coffman, B. F. Harte, Sally H. Alcock, Dennis Adams, Pardon Cook, Truman Guthrie, Charles D. Cook, Benoni Hurlbert, J.S. Stow, A. T. Blake, Sardis Cole, Ephraim Gould, Mrs. Hannah M. Putnam, Sophia M. Byington, Melzer Nye, Isaac Muncton, John B. Stone, Walter C. Hood, Chas. DeLong, J. J. Preston, Jonas Mason, Sarah Therilly, L. J. P. Putnam, A. S. Bailey, John L. Corp, William B. Hollister, C. L. Guthrie, Aurelia R. Hollister, Jonathan Sprague, Elijah Sprague, Colonel J. C. Paxton, George Payne, James Armstrong, Abigail W. Brough, Charlotte P. Stone, John Stone, Mary Gates, C. C. Smith, B. F. Guthrie, W. C. Olney, William L. Ralston, James Holden, John W. Stanley, John D. Chamber-

*Colonel William R. Putnam, president of the association from its first organization, died May 1, 1881.

lain, Robert Leggett, Charles Bowen, George Bowen, S. F. Seely, H. A. Staley, John M. Truesdell, Mrs. C. J. McIntosh, Alpha Devol, William McIntosh, Eliza M. McIntosh, Betsy Fearing, Philip Biddeson, William S. Ward, T. J. Westgate, Horace Curtis, Thomas Ridgway, William Pitt Putnam, Josiah Henderson, Gilbert Devol, T. G. Guitteau, M. J. Morse, Mrs. Sarah C. Dawes, Harlow Chapin, Mrs. William Pitt Putnam, W. P. Cutler, Beman Gates, I. W. Andrews, Charles R. Rhodes, R. M. Stimson.

Honorary members: Hon. Winthrop S. Gilman, of New York; Dr. G. L. B. Hempstead, of Hanging Rock, Ohio.

THE FIRST AGRICULTURAL SOCIETY.

At a meeting of a number of citizens of Washington county—and of Wood county, Virginia—held February 22, 1819, at McFarland's hotel in Marietta, was taken the first action looking toward the organization of the first agricultural society which had an existence in this immediate region. Captain Jonathan Devol was chosen chairman and A. T. Nye clerk. A committee was chosen to form a constitution for a society and prepare an address to the people. Its members were Ephraim Cutler, Joseph Barker, and Alexander Henderson. They drew up the following constitution, which contains the rules on which the society was organized:

CONSTITUTION

Of the Agricultural and Manufacturing Society of Washington and Wood counties:

Favored with public patronage and encouragement agriculture and manufacture have ever been wont to flourish, especially whenever such favor has been bestowed in premiums on those who have excelled in the various productions of those great and important arts and a suitable spirit of emulation and enterprise thereby excited.

Under these impressions the subscribers have formed themselves into a society for the promotion and encouragement of improvements in agriculture and domestic manufactures in the counties of Washington (Ohio) and Wood (Virginia), and do hereby adopt the following articles as a constitution of government:

ARTICLE 1. This society shall be known by the name of the Agricultural and Manufacturing society of Washington and Wood counties.

ARTICLE 2. The officers of the society shall consist of a president, two vicepresidents, one recording and one corresponding secretary, and a treasurer, also a board of managers to consist of no more than twelve nor less than seven, provided always that the president and vicepresidents shall, *ex officio*, be members of the board.

ARTICLE 3. The society shall meet annually on the second Wednesday in November, unless otherwise provided by by-laws, at which meeting the officers of the society shall be elected (by ballot) by the members present, to hold their offices for one year or until others are elected in their stead.

ARTICLE 4. The board of managers shall have power to grant premiums as rewards of merit, exertion, discovery or improvement in the various branches of agriculture, economy in husbandry and useful domestic manufactures and the same to award, from time to time from the funds of the society; to make and establish such rules and by-laws as to them shall seem proper for the regulation and government of the society; and to do and transact all things necessary to carry into effect the intentions of this association.

ARTICLE 5. For the purpose of creating a fund to be used in promoting the object of this association, each member of this society on subscribing the constitution shall pay the sum of three dollars, and shall thereafter yearly and every year on or before the first day of February pay to the treasurer the like sum of three dollars, and in case of the non-payment thereof the person so neglecting shall be considered as voluntarily surrendering the privileges of his membership and no longer entitled to act in the society, but any member who may lose his membership by neglecting to make his annual payments, may be restored, on

motion, at an annual meeting by paying up his arrearages, provided always that all payments made before the first day of January next shall be considered as made for the year eighteen hundred and twenty.

ARTICLE 6. The funds of the society may be augmented from time to time by the patronage of the public; and in all cases where an individual shall bestow any money, or other article on the society for the purpose of encouraging any particular object within the institutions of the association, such donation shall be faithfully applied agreeably to the wishes of the donor.

ARTICLE 7. The first meeting of the society shall be at the court house in Marietta on the second Wednesday of November next, at ten o'clock A. M.

The same committee who drew up the foregoing constitution through the medium of the *American Friend*, published the following:

ADDRESS.

To the citizens of Washington and Wood counties:

FELLOW CITIZENS: In a country like ours, extremely favorable to the production of all the necessaries and some of the luxuries of life, agriculture is and must be the grand source of public and individual prosperity. Its interests are inseparably interwoven with those of commerce and manufactures. To promote these interests, in the improvements of our agricultural products and domestic fabrics, is the object of this society.

That the most happy and beneficial effects have resulted in all countries from the establishment of such societies is beyond all question. In our own, particularly, have they been eminently useful in correcting erroneous habits of culture and giving stimulus and facility to industry, by granting premiums to those who have excelled in practical husbandry, in domestic manufactures, in improving the different breeds of domestic animals and the various implements of husbandry.

To effect these desirable objects requires the exertions of experience and associated patriotism. Man is the child of habit. He is cold to precept and falters at experiment, but add the fame of example and you call into action the energies of his body and mind to the accomplishment of every object within the reach of perseverance and industry. Among the first objects contemplated by the society for the improvement of our agricultural and manufacturing interests, are the collection of such interesting facts as are the results of practical information, and encouragement and reward of experiments and improvements requiring time, care, situation and expense, not within the reach of every individual, and thus promote the interest of all by the encouragement of industry and enterprise and the improvement of productive labor. For the attainment of these objects we solicit the patronage of a liberal and enlightened public.

> EPHRAIM CUTLER,
> JOSEPH BARKER,
> ALEXANDER HENDERSON,
> Committee.

A meeting was held in pursuance of the call (in the seventh article of the constitution) at the court house and adjourned to the seventeenth of November, 1819. Upon that date there was a good attendance. Paul Fearing, esq., was chosen chairman and Dr. S. P. Hildreth clerk of the meeting. The business of organizing the society was then taken up and the choice of officers resulted as follows: President, Benjamin Ives Gilman; first vice-president, Christian Schultz; second vice-president, William R. Putnam; recording secretary, S. P. Hildreth; corresponding secretary, Nahum Ward; treasurer, David Putnam; board of managers, the president and vice-presidents, *ex officio*, with Ebenezer Battelle, John Griffith, J. B. Regnier, A. W. Putnam, A. Henderson, George Neale, Ephraim Cutler, Benjamin Dana, Paul Fearing.

After adopting resolutions looking towards the raising of funds and increase of membership the society adjourned.

It does not appear that any fair was held until 1826.

But in that year, upon October 18th, the agricultural and mechanical association had an exhibition at Marietta. The committee of arrangements consisted of Nahum Ward, S. P. Hildreth and John Mills. The president of the society at that time was Joseph Barker; the secretary, William A. Whittlesey; the marshal of the day, Captain F. Devol. A procession was formed in front of the court house, and escorted by a band of music, marched to the front of the congregational church, where president Barker delivered an address.

A dinner was served at three o'clock and the awards announced after the members of the society had regaled themselves. Henry Fearing took the first premium for the greatest crop of corn—nearly one hundred and five bushels per acre—a ten dollar Winan's plow. Colonel John Stone of Belpre got a similar premium for the largest yield of wheat, which was a little over thirty-two bushels per acre. He also received a ten dollar premium for the best corn and a similar one for the second best merino sheep. William P. Putnam had the second best crop of corn—ninety-eight and three-fourths bushels per acre. Stephen Dana, of Newport, had a premium for the best yield of potatoes—one hundred and seventy-six bushels from half an acre of ground. Mrs. William P. Putnam took a premium for a specimen of linen, and O. R. Loring and Wm. P. Putnam for domestic cheese.

The second fair was held in Marietta October 18, 1827. William Pitt Putnam, of Belpre was at that time president of the society.

In the spring prior to the first exhibition (March, 1826) it was resolved at a meeting of the society, that among the premiums should be given one of ten dollars to the person who should destroy the greatest number of wolves within the county between January 1, 1826, and October 1st, of the same year, and that another of five dollars should be given to the person killing the next largest number. Two whelps under the age of six months were to be considered equal to one old wolf.

THE PRESENT ASSOCIATION.

At a meeting held at the old court house in Marietta, June 24, 1846, with the Hon. Joseph Barker in the chair, and Darwin E. Gardner acting as secretary, this association was organized under an act of the legislature entitled "an act for the encouragement of agriculture," passed February 27, 1846, as the Washington County Agricultural society. At this meeting a constitution and by-laws were adopted, which continued in force as amended from time to time, until the adoption of its present constitution and by-laws. The present constitution was adopted by the board of directors August 5, 1875, and by the association at its annual meeting held September 9, 1875. The present by-laws were adopted by the board August 5, 1875.

At a meeting of the board held August 7, 1858, the name was changed to the Washington County Agricultural and Mechanical institute. At a meeting of the board, held June 29, 1867, the name was changed to the Washington County Agricultural and Mechanical association, its present name.

FAIRS OF THE ASSOCIATION.

First, October 15, 1846; second, October 20, 1847; third, September 28, 1848; fourth October, 18, 1849; fifth, October 10, 11, 1850; sixth, October 30, 31, 1851; seventh, October 14, 15, 1852; eighth, October 13, 14, 1863; ninth, October 12, 1854; tenth, October 10, 11, 12, 1855; eleventh, October 8, 9, 10, 1856; twelfth, October 7, 8, 9, 1857; thirteenth, October 6, 7, 8, 1858; fourteenth, October 5, 6, 7, 1859; fifteenth, October 3, 4, 5, 1860; sixteenth, September 18, 19, 1867; seventeenth, October 7, 8, 1868; eighteenth, October 12, 13, 14, 1869; nineteenth, October 4, 5, 6, 1870; twentieth, September 20, 21, 22, 1871; twenty-first, September 24, 25, 26, 1872; twenty-second, September 17, 18, 19, 1873; twenty-third, September 23, 24, 25, 1874; twenty-fourth, September 8, 9, 10, 1875; twenty-fifth, September 27, 28, 29, 1876; twenty-sixth, October 24, 25, 26, 1877; twenty-seventh, September 4, 5, 6, 1878; twenty-eighth, September 3, 4, 1879; twenty-ninth, September 29, 30, October 1, 1880; thirtieth, September 13, 14, 15, 16, 1881.

From the year 1861 to 1867 inclusive, on account of the war, no fairs were held.

The officers of the society consisted of a president, vice-president, secretary, treasurer, and seven managers, elected annually by the society, until January 11, 1871, when the constitution was amended by increasing the number of managers to eight, dividing them into two classes, and providing for the election annually of four to serve two years, and also by vesting in the board instead of the society, the election of the secretary and treasurer.

PRESIDENTS.

Joseph Barker, 1846; George Dana, 1847; Joseph Barker, 1848; William R. Putnam, jr., 1849; George W. Barker, 1850; William Devol, 1851; Seth Woodford, 1852; George W. Barker, 1853–4; A. B. Batelle, 1855–7 inclusive; L. J. P. Putnam, 1858–9; George W. Barker, 1860; George Dana, 1861–7 inclusive; John Newton, 1868; Augustine Dyar, 1869; John D. Barker, 1870; W. F. Curtis, 1871; John Newton, 1872–3; William R. Putnam, 1874; T. W. Moore, 1875–6; P. B. Buell, 1877; Pemberton Palmer, 1878–9; John Newton, 1880; F. J. Cutter, 1880–1.

VICE-PRESIDENTS.

Julius Deming, 1846; William R. Putnam, jr., 1847–8; William P. Cutler, 1849; Henry Coomes, 1850; E. T. Hayward, 1851; William Devol, 1852; Owen Franks, 1853; Beman Gates, 1854; Henry Fearing, 1855; Milton Clark, 1856; Levi Barber, 1857; John Breckenridge, 1858; Joseph Holden, 1859; William McIntosh, 1860; John Newton, 1861–7; John W. Conly, 1868–9; P. B. Buell, 1870; D. T. Brown, 1871; T. W. Moore, 1872–3; William B. Thomas, 1874; Pemberton Palmer, 1875–6; D. T. Brown, 1877; William Thompson, 1878; William Johnson, 1879; James W. Nye, 1880; Thomas Fleming, 1880–1.

SECRETARIES.

William R. Putnam, 1846; D. E. Gardner, 1847–8; Beman Gates, 1849–50; William S. Ward, 1851–2;

George M. Woodbridge, 1853; William S. Ward, 1854; L. D. Dana, 1855; W. W. Rathbone, 1855-9 inclusive; William S. Ward, 1860; Samuel C. Skinner, 1861-7; William B. Thomas, 1867-8-9-70; Jewett Palmer, 1871-2-3; William N. Ward, 1874; Henry Hay, 1874; C. T. Frazyer, 1875-81 inclusive.

TREASURERS.

Robert Crawford, 1846; Levi Barber, 1847; A. L. Guitteau, 1848-50; William B. Thomas, 1851-60; C. K. Leonard, 1861-74; W. H. Johnson, 1874-8; C. H. Newton (chosen August 7, 1878, to fill the vacancy occasioned by the removal out of the county of W. H. Johnson), 1878-81.

DIRECTORS.

J. W. Dana, B. C. Bailey, William Devol, J. D. Chamberlain, John Algeo, 1846; E. Battelle, jr., B. C. Bailey, J. W. Dana, Julius Deming, C. Tallman, 1847; J. W. Dana, John Breckenridge, Cyrus Ames, John Collins, William P. Cutler, 1848; Henry Fearing, J. W. Dana, J. Collins, William Devol, L. J. P. Putnam, 1849; John Breckenridge, A. T. Nye, William Devol, Isaac Atkins, William R. Putnam, jr., 1850; S. Woodford, D. C. Skinner, I. W. Putnam, E. W. T. Clarke, Beman Gates, William R. Putnam, jr., E. Gould, 1851; Beman Gates, George H. Richards, Louis Soyez, W. W. Rathbone, L. J. P. Putnam, John Palmer, Ezra O'Neal, 1852; A. B. Battelle, I. W. Putnam, William Devol, Henry Fearing, W. W. Rathbone, E. W. T. Clarke, J. D. Leonard, 1853; John Breckenridge, A. B. Battelle, E. W. T. Clarke, E. B. Andrews, I. W. Putnam, Henry Fearing, William Devol, 1854; George W. Barker, John Palmer, E. W. T. Clarke, Charles Dickey, John M. Slocomb, 1855; L. J. P. Putnam, I. W. Putnam, George W. Barker, E. B. Andrews, Henry Fearing, John Palmer, John M. Slocomb, 1856; L. J. P. Putnam, Henry Fearing, George W. Barker, I. W. Putnam, John Palmer, B. C. Bailey, William McIntosh, 1857; George W. Barker, Joseph Holden, jr., John Newton, George M. Woodbridge, George Dana, jr., William B. Shaw, E. Gould, 1858; William McIntosh, J. T. Hart, William S. Ward, George Dana, jr., A. B. Battelle, E. Gould, John Palmer, 1859; George Dana, jr., William R. Putnam, William L. McMahan, Darius Towsley, Joseph Leonard, William Scott, O. S. Chapman, 1860; W. R. Putnam, W. L. Rolston, George W. Barker, O. S. Chapman, Darius Towsley, S. F. Seeley, Robert Pugh, 1861-7.

[Owing to the war no fairs were held during the years 1861-6, and the managers elected at the annual meeting in 1860, held over until the annual meeting of 1867, except that June 15, 1867, Augustine Dyar was elected to fill the vacancy caused by the resignation of W. L. Rolston.]

O. S. Chapman, W. B. Shaw, Levi Barber, William R. Putnam, George W. Barker, Augustine Dyar, Joseph Penrose, 1868; A. L. Curtis, J. D. Barker, S. B. Smith, John Hall, G. R. Goddard, G. S. Hovey, F. Semon, 1869; I. W. Putnam, A. Dyar, Louis Lehnhard, Pemberton Palmer, J. W. Conly, Israel Devol, John Hall, 1870; W. W. Northrup, George Davenport, Israel Devol,

Moses Blake, T. K. Wells, William Thompson, John A. West, 1871 [January 11th, 1871, the number of directors was changed from seven to eight, and M. H. Needham was chosen as director. The directors were also at that time divided into two classes, and since then four are elected each year to serve for two years.]; George Davenport, Moses Blake, T. K. Wells, W. W. Northrup, William Thompson, James W. Nye, W. M. Buchanan, John A. West, 1872; William Thompson, James W. Nye, W. M. Buchanan, John A. West, W. W. Northrup, John Varley, Pemberton Palmer, T. K. Wells, 1873; W. W. Northrup, John Varley, Pemberton Palmer, T. K. Wells, William Thompson, James W. Nye, F. J. Cutter, Rufus Leget, 1874; William Thompson, F. J. Cutter, James W. Nye, Rufus Leget, A. A. Little, Theodore Devol, James Stevens, George R. Goddard, 1875; A. B. Little, Theodore Devol, James Stevens, George R. Goddard, William Thompson, James W. Nye, Rufus Leget, Robert Breckenridge, 1876; William Thompson, James W. Nye, Rufus Leget, Robert Breckenridge, A. B. Little, John C. Drake, F. J. Cutter, George R. Goddard, 1877; A. B. Little, George R. Goddard, F. J. Cutter, John C. Drake, Robert Breckenridge, Joseph Wood, W. L. Bay, C. W. Knox, 1878; Robert Breckenridge, Joseph Wood, W. L. Bay, C. W. Knox, George R. Goddard, A. B. Little, F. J. Cutter, John C. Drake, 1879; George R. Goddard, A. B. Little, F. J. Cutter, John C. Drake, George W. Coffman,* I. B. Lawton,† W. D. Devol, Jesse Sharp, John Blake, 1880; W. D. Devol, Jesse S. Sharp, John Blake, Robert Breckenridge, George Davenport, John Mills, jr., John Strecker, 1881.

Following is the constitution:

ARTICLE I.

SECTION 1.—Name.—This society shall be known as the Washington County Agricultural and Mechanical Association.

SECTION 2.—Object.—The object of this association shall be to promote the best interests of agriculture and mechanic arts, by disseminating useful information on those subjects, securing funds and distributing premiums, in accordance with the provisions of "An act for the encouragement of agriculture," passed February 27, 1846.

ARTICLE II.

SECTION 1.—Officers.—The officers of this association shall consist of a president, vice-president, secretary, treasurer, and eight managers, who shall constitute a board of directors for the general management of the affairs of the association.

SECTION 2.—Election of Officers.—The association shall annually, at the annual meeting, elect a president, vice-president, and four managers; and the board of directors shall, at the first regular meeting in each year, elect a secretary and treasurer for the current fair year.

SECTION 3.—Terms of Office.—The elective officers of the association, except when elected to fill an unexpired term, shall hold their respective offices for the terms following, to wit: The president, vice-president, secretary and treasurer, one year, the managers, two years, and until their respective successors are elected.

SECTION 4.—Commencement of Terms.—The terms of office of the president, vice-president, secretary and treasurer shall commence on the third Thursday of December in each and every year; and the term of office of the managers shall commence on the third Thursday of December next succeeding their election.

SECTION 5.—Vacancies.—The board of directors may fill any vacancy occurring in the elective offices, but only for the unexpired term; provided, however, that when a vacancy occurs, by resignation or otherwise

---

* Elected president to fill the vacancy caused by the resignation of F. J. Cutter elected by board vice John Newton, declined.

† Declined at the end of his first year and Robert Breckenridge elected to fill the vacancy.

of a manager elected for two years, and previous to the annual meeting next succeeding such manager's election, then the board shall fill such vacancy only for the unexpired term of the first year of such manager's term, and the association at its annual meeting next thereafter, shall elect a manager for the second year of such unexpired term.

SECTION 6.—Mode of Elections.—The elections hereinbefore provided for, shall be by ballot.

ARTICLE IV.

SECTION 1.—Membership.—Any resident in Washington county, Ohio, of the age of twenty-one years, upon the payment of one dollar to the treasurer, may become a member of the association; and thereupon shall receive a membership ticket, entitling him to admission to the fair grounds during the annual fair held in the year for which such ticket is given; and the term of such membership shall commence on the day previous to the first day of the annual fair held next thereafter.

ARTICLE V.

SECTION 1.—Annual Meeting.—The annual meeting of the association shall be held at such time and place as may be designated by the board of directors, due notice of which shall be published.

SECTION 2.—Meeting of Board of Directors.—The board of directors shall meet on the third Thursday of December in each year, which meeting shall be the first regular meeting of the board for the ensuing year, and said board shall meet thereafter at such times as they may from time to time designate.

Premiums offered and awarded by the association at its annual fairs since its organization:

No.	Year of Fair.	Premiums Off'd.	Premiums Award.	REMARKS.
1	1846	$104 00	$65 75	The society gave a free dinner at the "Exchange" in Harmar.
2	1847	110 00	90 75	No report on crops.
3	1848	227 75	124 50	Certificates were issued to persons awarded third premiums.
4	1849	245 42	105 75	Certificates were issued to persons awarded third premiums.
5	1850	271 00	93 00	Certificates were issued to persons awarded third premiums, and no reports were made on cattle, sheep, plowing and farming implements.
6	1851	328 25	218 64	No certificates issued this year.
7	1852	274 23	152 15	In addition to the money premiums the society gave seventeen copies of Ohio Cultivator and thirty-one books on farming, etc.
8	1853	567 25	332 75	A few books and papers were given in addition on awards.
9	1854	765 50	353 50	
10	1855	788 25	357 75	Diplomas issued to persons awarded third premiums.
11	1856	815 00	560 75	Diplomas issued to persons awarded third premiums, and also premiums awarded to S. Maxwell and E. Gould for greatest improvement in farms during last four years.
12	1857	1078 00	583 15	Trials of speed for a small purse.
13	1858	1626 75	772 85	Trials of speed for a small purse.
14	1859	1626 75	698 00	The board adopted a resolution that the track should not be used in future for trotting matches, and that fast horses must trot against time.
15	1860	1261 80	602 65	
16	1867	1306 75	465 50	A citizens' purse of $260 for trials of speed offered and awarded in addition.
17	1868	1057 80	376 00	$650 in addition for trials of speed, a base ball tournament, and a $50 silver cup to the best club.
18	1869	2045 00	470 50	In addition, trials of speed $340, velocipede race, $15.
19	1870	1681 00	946 50	In addition, trials of speed.
20	1871	2076 75	1281 25	In addition, trials of speed, $340.
21	1872	1354 75	1330 50	In addition, trials of speed, $721, and to Weston $125.
22	1873	2041 00	1215 00	In addition, trials of speed, $730.
23	1874	2058 00	1139 75	In addition, trials of speed, $800.
24	1875	2059 50	1177 50	In addition, trials of speed, $650, but only $240 paid.
25	1876	1822 00	1115 00	In addition, trials of speed, $500, and for tournament $50. Only fifty per cent. of premiums paid.
26	1877	1741 50	824 00	In addition, trials of speed, $535, baby show, $118 by society, and special premium by citizens.
27	1878	1862 75	899 50	In addition, trial of speed, $700. No premiums paid.
28	1879	1781 25	663 25	No trial of speed. Fifty per cent. only of premiums paid.
29	1880	1875 25	997 25	In addition, trials of speed, $735.
Total.		35783 32	18033 44	Not including premiums offered and awarded for trials of speed and other amusements.

CHAPTER XXIII.

PHYSICAL FEATURES OF WASHINGTON COUNTY.[*]

Boundaries—Some Peculiarities of the Ohio—The Surface Drainage of the County—Interesting Facts—The Causes of the Conformation of the Surface Cannot be Assigned—Soil—Extent of the Valley Lands—Benefit Derived from the Soluble Limestone—General Geological Features—Coal—"Seneca Oil" or Petroleum—Iron Ore.

WASHINGTON county is bounded upon the north by the counties of Monroe, Noble and Morgan, and on the west by Morgan and Athens. It is bounded upon the south and east by the Ohio river and has a shore line of nearly fifty-four miles. In this distance the stream falls thirty-two feet, giving an average fall of about seven inches a mile. This is not, however, uniform, for the river consists of a series of alternating pools and shallows. According to the government surveys there are in the aggregate about twenty-four miles of pools in which the water is seven feet deep or more, and the remaining thirty miles are made up of comparative shallows and ripples. The elevation of the Ohio above tide-water at the upper end of the county and one and one-fourth miles above Matamoras is five hundred and eighty-eight and three-tenths feet, and the elevation where the river leaves the county at the lowest point of Belpre township is five hundred and fifty-six and three-tenths feet. At a point nearly three miles above the mouth of the Little Kanawha, at Parkersburgh the elevation is precisely the same as that of Lake Erie—five hundred and sixty-five feet.

The surface drainage of Washington county is very complete. The county is divided into two proximately equal parts by the Muskingum river, which, entering the county at the northwest corner, flows to the Ohio with many meanderings, in a generally southeast direction. The principal affluents of the Ohio within the county, beside the Muskingum, are the Little Muskingum river, Duck creek, and the Little Hocking river. Wolf creek, which drains a considerable area in the northwest portion of the county, empties into the Muskingum a little above Beverly. The drainage system of the county presents some very interesting facts, says the late Professor Andrews. The Ohio, Muskingum, and Duck creek all converge toward a common centre—the last three uniting with the Ohio in Marietta township. The Ohio, which flows in a channel very nearly parallel with the Little Muskingum, is deflected northwesterly by the West Virginia hills, and meets the other streams mentioned. The slopes of nearly half a circle find their lowest point at a common centre in Marietta township. The Little Muskingum drains the southwestern part of Monroe county, and entering Washington county near the northeast corner, flows through Ludlow, Independence, Lawrence, Newport, and Marietta townships to the Ohio. Its branches also drain portions of Jolly and Grandview townships. All of Liberty township, except the northwest corner, is drained by Fifteen Mile creek, a branch coming

---

[*] This chapter is principally compiled from The Geological Survey of Ohio—1874 (in which the contribution on Washington county is by the late Professor E. B. Andrews), and from Delafield's Topographical Description.

in from the north. Duck creek flows nearly south through Washington county and drains a comparatively limited area, lying in Aurelius, Salem, Fearing, and Marietta townships. The Pawpaw branch extends into the northwest corner of Liberty, and Whipple's run rises in Fearing. There is within the county no western tributary of Duck creek of any considerable size, the watershed or dividing ridge between Duck creek and the Muskingum being very near the former stream. The northern tributaries of the Muskingum in the county are all small. Bear creek, Cats creek, and Big run are the chief, and drain Adams and the western part of Salem townships. On the western and southern side of the Muskingum its principal tributaries are two, Rainbow creek and Wolf creek, the former flowing eastward and entering the Muskingum in the township by the same name, and the latter with its several branches flowing northward and draining Watertown, Palmer, Wesley, and the northern parts of Fairfield, Barlow, and Warren, and small portions of some adjacent townships. The slope drained by the waters of Wolf creek in Washington county is proximately a northwestern one, and directly opposite the general slope of southern Ohio. It is a curious fact that some of the branches of this stream (in Warren township) have their rise within two miles of the confluence of the Muskingum and Ohio. Instead of flowing into the waters of the Ohio, these small streams go by a devious course to the north limit of the county and then find their way back by the channel of the Muskingum to join the Ohio, very near its source. In the southwestern part of the county is the Little Hocking river, the east branch of which rises in the southern part of Warren, just back of the Ohio river hills, and flows southwesterly through Dunham and Belpre to unite with the west branch in the extreme western part of the latter township. The west branch drains the southern part of Fairfield and Decatur, flowing in a generally southeasterly direction toward the Ohio. Thus it will be seen that the county presents a great variety of surface slopes. In the eastern half of the county the slope is southwestern and southern, while in the western it is chiefly northern and southeastern. The causes which determined the flow of the streams in these different directions cannot be assigned.

SOIL.

The immediate valleys of the Ohio and Muskingum are very rich and productive, and equal in fertility to any lands in the State. There are in the county about fifty-four miles in length along the Ohio river, and about thirty-two miles along the Muskingum. The county has therefore a large aggregate area of the finest alluvial soil. In these valleys are found the sandy drift terraces, which are generally at a level of from seventy to eighty feet above the streams. While the soil of the terraces is not so rich as that of the lower alluvial ground, it is nevertheless generally fertile, and being a warm and early soil, and easily cultivated, it is the favorite one for many crops. In the gravel and among the pebbles of these terraces there is a considerable quantity of limestone, which adds greatly to the fertility. The valleys of Duck

creek and the Little Muskingum are generally much narrower, and show no drift terraces. The alluvial soil in these valleys is composed of sedimentary materials, derived from the carboniferous strata of this county, and Noble and Monroe. From the nature of the strata, we should not expect, as a rule, a soil as rich as in the larger valleys of the Ohio and Muskingum, where there is a larger variety of soil-producing materials in the strata traversed, and especially more of limestone.

The soil on the hills and hillsides is determined in quality by the nature of the strata composing the hills. It is richest where there is an abundance of limestone, and poorest when derived from disintegrated sandstone. In some cases are found strata of highly soluble limestone of great fertilizing value, situated halfway up the hillsides, while above are sand rocks and sandy shales. Yet, the more sterile sandstone soil is often cultivated, and the rich limestone soil neglected. It has been estimated that the alluvial valley of the Muskingum is three-fourths of a mile wide. If so, there would be fifteen thousand, three hundred and sixty acres of land in the immediate valley. If we estimate the average width in both bottom and terrace land of the north bank of the Ohio, at one-half mile, we have seventeen thousand two hundred and eighty acres, and a total in the two valleys within the limits of Washington county of thirty-two thousand six hundred and forty. The largest deposits of limestone strata are perhaps those found along Wolf creek, but they are so low in the valley, indeed, often in the bed of the stream, that they produce little fertilizing effect. In Adams, Salem, and Liberty townships there are valuable deposits of highly soluble limestone, which are of the utmost importance agriculturally, and give to many farms a rich and almost self perpetuating soil. Such limestones are not altogether wanting in several other townships, but are most abundant in the townships named. The smoothest lands in the county, and those most attractive to the eye, excepting the more immediate river valleys, are found on the slope drained by the branches of Wolf creek in the townships of Barlow, Watertown, Palmer, etc. They are not, perhaps, the richest, for there is a deficiency in limestone, but they lie beautifully, and in their gentle undulations and gradual slopes are in marked contrast with the abrupt hills so common in other parts of the county. Taken as a whole, the soil of Washington county is in quality above the average of that of the counties of southern Ohio. Even its most rough and forbidding hills have, by the frugal and industrious German population, been rendered productive and attractive.

GENERAL GEOLOGICAL FEATURES.

The county lies wholly within the coal measures and in the upper portion of the series. There are no other geological formations represented in the county, if we except the surface materials, which constitute the drift terraces of the Muskingum and Ohio valleys, which are of quaternary age. There is in Barlow, on the northern slope of the Wolf creek waters, the evidence of a probable lake bed, which is also, doubtless, of quaternary age. The drift terraces constitute a uniform series of ancient gravel banks and sand-bars, formed at a time when the Ohio and Muskingum were at a far higher stage than now. The materials of these terraces were brought from the north, from areas once covered by large deposits of sand, gravel, bowlders, etc. Duck creek and Little Muskingum are not sufficiently far north to reach these drift areas, and, consequently, no true drift terraces are found on them. On the Little Muskingum and Duck creek there are some terraced banks, but they show more of the extra-limital materials found in the drift terraces, and were made by the deposit of the proper river sands, where the current of these streams met the back water of the Ohio, at the time when the waters of the latter were probably eighty or one hundred feet higher than now. In the drift gravel in the Ohio and Muskingum terraces we find a great scarcity of pebbles and small bowlders, very interesting in their lithological and palentological characters. In addition to granites, quartzites, and greenstones, and all forms of the harder rocks found north of the lakes, occur fossils of all the fossiliferous strata lying to the north. They are best preserved when embedded in cherty limestone.

The stratified rocks of the county all belong to the coal measure formation. It is common to divide the Ohio coal measures into two divisions—upper and lower—the dividing line being that of the Pittsburgh seam of coal. But the Pittsburgh and Wheeling seams are the same and the Pomeroy seam is identical with the Wheeling. If therefore the Pomeroy seam be taken as the base of the upper coal measures nearly all of Washington county lies in the upper series. The Pomeroy seam is found in fine development, west of the Washington county line on Federal creek and its branches in Rome, Berne and Ames townships and in Marion and Homer townships in Morgan county. But the seam dips to the eastward and is not seen anywhere in the west half of Washington county. In the undulations and uplifts in the eastern part of the county, however, it appears on Duck creek and Little Muskingum in the Newells Run uplift in Newport township. The most extensive seam of coal in the county is the one found eighty-five to one hundred feet above the Pomeroy seam, which has a wide range in Adams, Aurelius, Salem, Liberty, Fearing, Lawrence, Newport and other townships. This is the upper Salem coal or the sandstone seam, so called from the fact that in Salem it generally lies under a heavy sand rock. It is generally of sufficient thickness for profitable mining and is of good quality. There is a seam of coal about one hundred feet higher in the series found in many parts of the county, which is generally thin, but serves the purpose of local use. It is seldom sufficiently thick to warrant extensive mining. There is in Washington county an adequate supply of coal, only needing proper facilities for distribution. Unfortunately all the seams of coal in the hills bordering on the Ohio river are thin. The Pomeroy and the one about ninety feet above it are brought up in the Newells Run uplift but are too thin near the Ohio river for profitable mining. Upon the Muskingum the coal run seam, which is the one above the Pomeroy seam, is fairly developed. When mined with discrimination the better coal of the seam is of a very fair quality and suitable for all general uses. This coal meets a want on the river which could not otherwise be well supplied.*

Salt, in the form of rich brines, may be found in many parts of the county by sufficiently deep boring. Many oil wells have struck ample supplies of brine.

Petroleum† is found in considerable quantities in several townships east of the Muskingum. Speaking (1832) of this product of mother earth, Delafield, who calls it "spring oil," or "Seneca oil," says that "it has been known to the hunters and early inhabitants of the county since its first settlement. It is generally supposed to be the product of coal, at a great distance below the surface of the earth. It is, as is well known, an oleaginous substance, possessing a strong, disagreeable odor. This oil, by filtering it through charcoal, is almost deprived of its empyreumatic smell and can be used in lamps, as it affords a brilliant light. It is very useful, and therefore much employed in curing the diseases of, and the injuries done to, horses. It is a preventive against the attacks of the blowing-fly, and is perhaps the best substance known for the prevention of friction in machinery." At the time when Delafield wrote, the importance of petroleum as an article of commerce was not anticipated, and he makes no suggestion regarding the possibility of its being discovered in large quantity. He speaks, however, of the gas arising from salt wells, "which, when a light is applied, inflames and burns for days until extinguished by rain or a sudden gust of wind," and he also mentions "some pools of water through which gasses arise, and which consequently have acquired the name of 'burning springs.'"

Iron ores have been found in Washington county only in limited quantities, and seldom occur in such manner or of such worth as to warrant mining. It is usually of the variety popularly known as "bog iron ore." This is most commonly found along the streams, and especially on the hills of the Little Muskingum and Duck creek.

---

*See also statements in regard to coal formation in the several chapters of township history in this volume.

† Petroleum production is elsewhere fully considered.

45

Townships and Villages

of

Washington County.

MARIETTA.

CHAPTER XXIV.

MARIETTA—EARLY EVENTS—MORAL CONDITION OF THE COMMUNITY.

A Chapter of Initial Events—Various Names Proposed for the Settlement—First Fourth of July Celebration—First Deaths—General Varnum's Death and Burial- First Marriage—Seventh of April Celebrated—First Births—First Religious Meetings—First Mail Route—First Postmaster at Marietta—First Town Meeting—Thomas Wallcut, of Boston—Condition of the Settlement—Mixer, the Tavern-keeper—A Slave Sold in Marietta—Indignation Expressed—Grievances Presented to the Court—Debating Society—Earliest Social Amenities—The Governor's Daughter—Intemperance—Irreligion—Scarcity of Money—Names of Residents at Campus Martius, "the Point," and Fort Harmar—Marietta in 1803

> HERE, where but late a dreary forest spread,
> Putnam, a little band of settlers led,
> And now beholds, with patriot joy elate,
> The infant settlement become a STATE;
> Sees fruitful orchards and rich fields of grain,
> And towns and cities rising on the plain,
> While fair Ohio bears with conscious pride
> New, laden, vessels to the ocean's tide.
>
> —HARRIS TOUR, 1803

MARIETTA was the first crystalization of that idea which may be said to have had its inception in the midnight conference between two earnest men—General Benjamin Tupper and General Rufus Putnam—at the home of the latter in Rutland, Massachusetts, in January, 1786. Marietta was the first flower put forth in the west by a great plant firmly rooted and nurtured in New England soil.

So far as the history of Marietta is contained in that of the Ohio company it has already been given. The organization of that body, under whose auspices the settlement was made; the plans that were formed in New England for the laying out of the city at the mouth of the Muskingum; the purchase of the land; the journey and arrival of the pioneer band of forty-seven, and the progress of immigration and of improvement, have been very fully set forth in preceding pages. We have followed the pioneers—

> "Through a long warfare, rude,"

in which,

> "With patient hardihood,
> By toil, and strife, and blood,
> The soil was won."

The local events of that Indian war have been considered in their chronological order, with those at Belpre and Waterford, and in their relation to the broader aspect of the subject. It now remains our task to treat of those topics which, while not less important or interesting, belong more strictly to Marietta as a community.

In this chapter we present a number of the initial items of Marietta history, endeavor to give an idea of the char-

acter of its pioneers, and to show the condition of the settlement, morally as well as materially. The two succeeding chapters contain accounts of the beginnings and progress of mercantile business and manufacturing, and of navigation upon the Ohio and Muskingum. They are followed by the history of the religious and educational institutions and the professions, while subsequent chapters give the corporate and municipal history of the city and a wide range of miscellaneous matter, including such topics as the visits of distinguished individuals, reminiscences of slavery times, the sickly seasons, the great floods, temperance history early and late, burial places, the ancient works, etc.

NAME.

The city at the confluence of the Muskingum and Ohio was not originally known. It was for a short time quite commonly referred to by the residents and people at the east who expected to emigrate to the west, simply as Muskingum. It is interesting to learn that the choice of a name for the primal settlement in the Ohio company's purchase occupied much attention. Several appellations were suggested, some of which were ingenious and very appropriate; while others perhaps no less curiously formed or singularly adapted were certainly neither appropriate nor beautiful. Some of the names discussed are mentioned in the correspondence of two New England historians[*] of the time, from whom we have quoted in this volume. One of them writes September 25, 1878, "Yesterday I dined with Major Sargent who told me . . . . that the old Indian fortifications near the mouth of the Muskingum was to be the site of the new city which they talk of calling Castrapolis (a name invented by Mr. St. John) in memory of the Indian fortified camp."

The same letter writer, under date of May 17th, 1788 says:

> In my opinion, he (Cutler) cannot give the new city a more proper name than Protepolis. Urania seems to be quite out of the way Tempe would, I think, do much better. But I wanted something original. In this view Genesis would do. There are Montgomerys already.

The escape from Castrapolis and Protepolis is something for which the successive generations of Marietta people had they possessed any knowledge of it, would doubtless have been very thankful. Urania also would, indeed, have been quite out of the way. Tempe would have done much better. The name was suggested in all probability by the classical vale of Tempe.

---

[*] Correspondence of the Hon. Ebenezer Hazard and the Rev. Jeremy Belknap.

Dr. Manasseh Cutler was an advocate for the adoption of the name "Adelphia." He wrote to General Rufus Putnam, from Ipswich, Massachusetts, under date of December 3, 1787:

Saying so much about conveying letters reminds me of the necessity of a name for the place where you will reside. I doubt not you will early acquire the meaning of Muskingum, or you may meet with some other name that will be agreeable. At present, I must confess, I feel a partiality for the name proposed at Boston, and think it preferable to any that has yet been mentioned. I think that Adelphia will, upon the whole, be the most eligible. It strictly means brethren, and I wish it may ever be characteristic of the Ohio company.

By this name, Adelphia, suggested by Dr. Cutler, the settlement was called until July 2, 1788, when, at the first meeting of the Ohio company west of the mountains it was changed by the following resolution:

Resolved, That the city near the confluence of the Ohio and Muskingum be called Marietta, that the directors write to his excellency, the Count Moustiers (who was the French minister) informing him of their motive in naming the city, and request his opinion whether it will be advisable to present to her majesty of France, a public square.

The name was compounded, and very prettily, from that of the unfortunate young queen, Marie Antoinette. One of the squares in the city plat was named after her. The proffered compliment was never formally acknowledged, the queen soon after being plunged into the midst of the troubles which finally bore her down.

It was very natural that the pioneers should have chosen the name they did. They had a great respect and love for France. Many of them were personally acquainted with, and warmly attached to, Lafayette and his brother officers who had lent their valuable aid to the colonies in the Revolution. Marie Antoinette had ever been the friend of the infant nation and these New England patriots assembled upon the banks of the Ohio appreciated her constant and uniform kindliness as they did the brave self-sacrifice of the sons of France. One writer says that Marie Antoinette "was intended to be the 'nursing mother' of the infant settlement."*

THE FIRST AND SECOND FOURTH OF JULY CELEBRATIONS.

The observance of the Fourth of July, 1788,†—the twelfth anniversary of American independence—was the first public celebration in Marietta or the Northwest Territory. The day, Friday, was ushered in with the firing of a federal salute by the cannons at Fort Harmar, over which the flag of the United states floated and the bastions and curtains of which were decorated with standards. The celebration was upon the Marietta side of the Muskingum in the long bowery built by the side of the stream. At one o'clock General Josiah Harmar, all of the officers not on duty at the fort and several ladies joined the Marietta settlers and listened to the first oration of a political nature ever delivered in the State of

*Thaddeus Mason Harris.

†Fifty years later—in 1838—the Fourth of July was celebrated in Marietta under the auspices of the Mechanics' Lyceum, the oration being delivered by Charles Hendric. Dinner was served at the Mansion house, Colonel Joseph Barker presiding, assisted by A. Pixley. Toasts were responded to by Robert Smith, Isaac Moss, Colonel Barker, Thomas J. Clogston, James M Booth, John Grenier, William West, L. Dewey, Matthias Moot, J. G Glidden, E. Gates, and others. A procession marched through the streets, of which Isaac Maxon was chief marshal and John Lest the assistant marshal

Ohio, a most eloquent and appropriate address by the honorably James Mitchell Varnum, one of the judges of the territory, a man, by the way, of the loftiest and purest mind in whom tenderness and strength seem to have been equally developed, but whose influence was, alas, not long to be felt in the little settlement. He was even then when he spoke hopeful and cheering words for the future of the country and of the pioneer community, in a consumptive decline which closed his bright, beautiful life six months later.

A repast, consisting of all the substantials and delicacies which the woods and the streams and the gardens and the housewives' skill afforded, was served at the bowery. There was venison, barbecued, Buffalo steaks, bear meat, wild fowls, fish, and a little *pork* as the choicest luxury of all. One fish, a great pike weighing one hundred pounds and over six feet long—the largest ever taken by white men, it is said, in the waters of the Muskingum—was speared by Judge Gilbert Devol and his son Gilbert.

The day was not all sunshine. "At three o'clock," says Colonel John May, "just as dinner was on the table came on a heavy shower which lasted half an hour. However the chief of our provisions were rescued from the deluge, but injured materially. When the rain ceased the table was laid again; but before we had finished it came on to rain a second time. On the whole though we had a handsome dinner."

The following was the order of the toasts drank after dinner had been served:

1. The United States.
2. The Congress.
3. His most Christian Majesty.
4. The United Netherlands.
5. The friendly powers throughout the world.
6. The new Federal Constitution.
7. His Excellency General Washington and the Society of the Cincinnati.
8. His Excellency Governor St. Clair and the Northwestern Territory.
9. The memory of those who have nobly fallen in defence of American freedom.
10. Patriots and heroes.
11. Captain Pipe, chief of the Delawares, and a happy treaty with the natives.
12. Agriculture and commerce, arts and sciences.
13. The amiable partners of our delicate pleasures.
14. The glorious Fourth of July.

There were several Indians present. Colonel May says: "While I headed one end of the table there came to me a Delaware Indian, one of three petty chiefs. He said to me 'how do you do, brother Yankee.' I answered him politely and then seated him on my left. He ate with a healthy appetite, but when we began drinking the toasts he labored with all of his might to speak them, but made rather a ridiculous piece of work of it. When the cannon was fired at the toasts in honor of Generals Washington and St. Clair and the western territory, it made him start. The roar of a cannon is as disagreeable to an Indian as a rope is to a thief or broad daylight to one of your made up beauties."*

The writer of the above adds: "Pleased with the en-

*Journal of Colonel John May.

tertainment, we kept it up till after 12 o'clock at night, then went home and slept soundly until daylight." The celebration closed with a beautiful illumination of Fort Harmar. The recollection of one of the participants in this celebration, when he had become a gray headed grandsire has been handed down in Marietta by tradition, and, if not reproduced with literal exactness, there can at least be no doubt that the words express the opinion he held of the first Fourth of July jollification in the Northwest Territory:

Never had such a dinner since. We were one great family, loving God and each other, proud of our new home, and resolved on success. And we won it.*

The second celebration of the Fourth of July in Marietta, 1789, was an interesting occasion, but lacked the impressive significance of the first. At this time Return Jonathan Meigs, jr., then an attorney at law, afterwards governor of Ohio, was the speaker of the day. His oration was in verse—the first poem produced in the country northwest of the Ohio, a region which has since, considering that it has scarcely as yet emerged from the formative condition of its existence, given so much of poetry and other literature to the world. Meigs' muse sang in a lofty and prophetic strain. A portion of his roseate dream was never realized in the growth of Marietta. The sanguine seer might better perhaps have voiced his hopes at Cincinnati. Albach has indeed put his words into the mouth of John Cleves Symmes,† whom he imagines standing before and contemplating the site of the present metropolis of Ohio. We give an extract from the poem:

Enough of tributary praise is paid
To virtue living or to merit dead;
To happier themes the rural muse invites,
To calmest pleasures and serene delights;
To us, glad fancy brightest prospect shows;
Rejoicing nature all around us glows;
Here late the savage, hid in ambush, lay,
Or roamed the uncultur'd valleys for his prey;
Here frowned the forest with terrific shade;
No cultured fields exposed the opening glade.
How changed the scene ! See, nature, clothed in smiles,
With joy repays the laborer for his toils;
Her hardy gifts rough industry extends,
The groves bow down, the lofty forest bends;
On every side the cleaving axes sound,
The oak and tall beach thunder to the ground.
And see the spires of Marietta rise,
And domes and temples swell into the skies;
Here justice reign, and foul dissension cease;
Her walks be pleasant and her paths be peace.
Here swift Muskingum rolls his rapid waves;
There fruitful valleys fair Ohio laves;
On its smooth surface gentle zephyrs play,
The sunbeams tremble with a placid ray.
What future harvests on his bosom glide,
And loads of commerce swell the downward tide.
Where Mississippi joins in length'ning sweep
And rolls majestic to the Atlantic deep.
Along our banks see distant villas spread;
Here waves the corn, and there extends the mead;
Here sound the murmurs of the gurgling rills;
There bleat the flocks upon a thousand hills.
Fair opes the lawn, the fertile fields extend,
The kindly showers from smiling heaven descend;
The skies drop fatness upon the blooming vale;

From spicy shrubs ambrosial sweets exhale;
Fresh fragrance rises from the flow'rets bloom,
And ripening vineyards breathe a glad perfume;
Gay swells the music of the warbling grove,
And all around is melody and love.
Here may religion fix her blest abode,
Bright emanation of creative God.
Here charity extend her liberal hand,
And mild benevolence o'erspread the land;
In harmony the social virtues blend;
Joy without measure, rapture without end !*

THE FIRST RELIGIOUS MEETINGS.

The first sermon preached in Marietta and the first in a Protestant style in the State of Ohio to other than an Indian audience, was delivered on Sunday, July 20, 1788, by the Rev. William Breck, a New England man and a member of the Ohio company. [The French upon the Maumee may have held Roman Catholic services, and we know that Heckewelder and the other Moravian missionaries had preached years before to the Indians at the Muskingum stations.] The text chosen by the Rev. Mr. Breck was the sixth and seventh verses of the nineteenth chapter of Exodus:

Now, therefore, if you will obey my voice and keep my covenants; then ye shall be a peculiar treasure unto me above all people of earth; for all the earth is mine; and ye shall be unto me a kingdom of priests, and an holy nation.

The service was held upon the bank of the Muskingum, "before a numerous, well-informed and attentive assembly." The governor was present, and it has been recorded, "afterward expressed much satisfaction." He particularly remarked that "the singing far exceeded anything he had ever heard." "It was enchanting," continues the writer, from whom we have above quoted. "The grave, the tender, the solemn, and the pathetic were so happily blended, as to produce a most perfect harmony." Very impressive indeed must have been this first religious meeting upon the people who at home had been accustomed to regularly attend upon Sunday the preaching in the little New England village churches, and who had now been so long without such solace. †

The second sermon was delivered on August 24, 1788, by the Rev. Manasseh Cutler, who had arrived upon the nineteenth. He simply notes in his journal the following:

Sunday, August 24 —Cloudy this morning—very muddy. Attended worship in the public hall at Campus Martius. The hall was very full. I had but one exercise. People from the Virginia shore and garrison attended.

THE FIRST DEATH.

Death invaded the settlement for the first time August 25, 1788, the person taken being Nabby, a thirteen-year old child of Major Nathaniel Cushing, whose family, with several others, had arrived upon the nineteenth. Dr. Cutler says in his journal:

About three o'clock in the night I was called up to visit a child of Major Cushing's, supposed to be dying. Just before I got into the house it expired—the first person that died in the city of Marietta. The

---

*Mrs. F. D. Gage in Little Corporal.
†Albach's Annals of the West, page 482.

*Harris' Tour, 1803, (appendix).
†Journal of Colonel John May.   .   .   .   .   .   .
"A large number of people were assembled from the garrison, Virginia and our own settlement, in all about three hundred; some women and children, which was a pleasing sight, though something unusual to see. Mr. Breck made out very well; the singing excellent. We had ' Billings' to perfection."   .   .   .   .

child was very low when Major Cushing left New England. The disease was an *atrophia infantilus*—greatly emaciated; expected it would have expired in the boat on the way down. Dr. Scott, of the garrison, attended after its arrival here.

The first coming of the fell destroyer to the compact little colony in which all of the chords of life were more closely knit together, and sympathies more quick than in the larger, older, busier and more bustling communities of the far away, outside world, must have caused a depth of solemn feeling, such as can be but poorly imagined. Two days later the family of Major Cushing followed its youngest member to the grave with nearly all the people of the settlement, to which they had come only eight days before, as sympathizers. Dr. Cutler says, under date of August 27th: "At two o'clock attended the funeral of Major Cushing's child. A considerable number of people collected. The coffin was made of cherry tree wood. I proposed it should not be colored, as an example for the future."

DEATH AND BURIAL OF GENERAL VARNUM.

If the death of this infant caused sadness in the community and a feeling of solemnity because the first reminder of the mortality of all, that of General (or Judge) James Mitchell Varnum, which occurred on the tenth of January, plunged the people into the deepest grief. He was in the very prime of life, aged forty years. He had led, although so young a man, a distinguished career, and was one of the most active and influential men in the Ohio company and in the settlement; a judge of the territory; a man of fine and varied ability, and possessed of almost every admirable trait of character. He was respected in his public capacity, admired as a man and loved by all. Almost all of the leading men at Marietta had known him before his removal from New England, some of them as an officer in the Revolutionary army. His was the second death in Marietta. It was caused by consumption and occurred in less than eight months from the time of his arrival. The funeral took place upon the thirteenth of January, and was attended by all the people of the settlement, many from the garrison and the Virginia shore, and by a large number of Indian chiefs who had been present at the treaty of Fort Harmar, concluded upon the ninth. Dr. Solomon Drown delivered the funeral oration. All of the respect and honor possible was shown for the illustrious dead. The order of the procession which followed the body to the grave was as follows:

THE MILITARY UNDER CAPTAIN ZEIGLER.

MARSHALS.

Mr. Wheaton bearing the sword and military commission of the deceased on a mourning cushion.

Mr. Lord bearing the civil commission on a mourning cushion.

Mr. Mayo, with the diploma and order of Cincinnati on a mourning cushion.

Mr. Fearing, bearing the insignia of masonry on a mourning cushion.

PALL HOLDERS.

Griffin Greene, esq.
Judge Tuffer.
The secretary.

Judge Crary.
Judge Putnam.
Judge Parsons.

PRIVATE MOURNERS.

Charles Greene and Richard Greene, Frederick Crary and Philip Greene, Doctor Scott and Doctor Farley, Deacon Story and Doctor Drown, private citizens, two and two, Indian chiefs, two and two, the militia officers, the Cincinnati, the masons.

FIRST BIRTH.

The first child born in Marietta was a son of James Kelley, and Anna (Hart) Kelley, emigrants from Plainfield, Massachusetts, and was named after the governor, Arthur St. Clair Kelley. He was born December 30, 1788. The family afterward removed to Belleville, Virginia, and the father was killed there by the Indians on the seventh of April, 1791 (See chapter X, on the Indian War, page 76). The widow returned to Marietta and was given a home in Campus Martius. Arthur St. Clair Kelley passed his boyhood in Marietta, and died in Parkersburgh, Virginia, in 1823. The second child born was James Varnum Cushing, son of Nathaniel Cushing, the twenty-seventh of January 1789; the third Leicester G. Converse, son of Benjamin Converse, born on the seventh of February, 1789; the fourth Joseph Barker, son of Joseph Barker, born February 28, 1789. It will be noticed that only two months'intervened between the first and fourth births. (Other white children had been born in Ohio, but these were the first whose parents were pioneers and settlers. A child is said to have been born of a white woman in captivity, at Wakatomika, within the present limits of Muskingum county, in 1764; another upon the Scioto in 1770, the child of a white woman taken captive by the Shawnees and married by an Indian trader named Conner. John Lewis Roth, son of Rev. John Roth, the Moravian missionary, and wife, was born at Gnaddenhutten on the Tuscarawas July 4, 1773, and died at Bath, Pennsylvania, in 1841. Joanna Maria Heckewelder, daughter of the Rev. John Heckewelder, was born at Salem, one of the Moravian villages on the Tuscarawas, April 16, 1781. The last two of these births are well authenticated.

FIRST MARRIAGE.

On the sixth of February, 1789, the first marriage was solemnized between the Hon. Winthrop Sargent, secretary of the territory, and Rowena, daughter of General Benjamin Tupper. General Rufus Putnam, judge of the court of common pleas of Washington county, performed the ceremony. Mrs. Sargent died January 29, 1790, of child-birth, and was buried upon Sunday, January 31.*

THE SEVENTH OF APRIL CELEBRATED FOR THE FIRST TIME.†

The first anniversary of the settlement of Marietta was celebrated on the seventh of April, 1789. The Ohio

---

* Journal of Thomas Wallcut.

† The half-century celebration of the settlement of Marietta, April 7, 1838, was made an occasion of much interest. The exercises were held at the Congregational church. George M. Woodbridge, esq., delivered the oration. Colonel Joseph Barker was president, and Judge Ephraim Cutler and Joseph Barker, jr., vice-presidents. Beman Gates, esq., conducted the singing. Henry Fearing was chief marshal of the procession. A dinner was served at the Mansion house. Among the toasts was one to the memory of Judge Gilbert Devol, and his son Gilbert, who caught the great pike in the Muskingum on the fourth of July, 1788. Music was furnished during the day by the college band, which was led by Samuel Hall, a graduate of that year, in the first class which Marietta college sent out.

company, at a meeting held in February, had resolved that the anniversary of the landing of the forty-seven pioneers should forever be considered as a day of public festival in the territory of the Ohio company. At the same time the directors were authorized "to request some gentleman to prepare an address" for the approaching festival. They selected Dr. Solomon Drown, and he delivered a very suitable oration upon the occasion, in which he cordially congratulated the assembled people on the auspicious anniversary. The address, although for the most part rehearsing happy events was not without its element of sadness. The speaker alluded to General Varnum, who had passed away three months before:

. . . Of those worthies who have most exerted themselves in promoting this settlement, one, alas! is no more. One whose eloquence like the music of Orpheus, attractive of the listening crowd, seemed designed to reconcile mankind to the closest bonds of society. Ah! what avail his manly virtues now! Slow through yon winding path his corpse was borne, and on the sleepy hill interred with honors meet. What bosom refuses the tribute of a sigh on the recollection of that melancholy scene, when, unusual spectacle, the fathers of the land, the chiefs of the aboriginal nations, in solemn train attended; while the mournful dirge was rendered doubly mournful mid the gloomy, nodding grove. On that day even nature seemed to mourn. O Varnum! Varnum! thy name shall not be forgotten while gratitude and generosity continue to be the characteristics of those inhabiting the country once thy care. Thy fair fame is deeply rooted in our fostering memories, and,

" The force of boisterous winds and mouldering rain,
Year after year an everlasting train,
Shall ne'er destroy the glory of his name."

FIRST HOUSES.

The first frame house in Marietta was built in the summer of 1789, at the point, by Joseph Buell and Levi Munsell, and intended for a tavern. Captain Enoch Shepherd (brother of General Shepherd, who suppressed Shay's rebellion in Massachusetts) prepared the timber and lumber for this house, at McKeesport, Pennsylvania, and made it into a raft upon which he brought his family to Marietta. Colonel John May in the summer of 1788 built quite a pretentious house of hewed logs, which he said was "the first of the kind in the place." He describes his work as follows:

"This is an arduous undertaking and more than I intended. Am building from several motives. First, for the benefit of the settlement; second, from a prospect or hope of gain hereafter; third, for an asylum for myself and family should we ever want it; fourth, as a place where I can leave my stores and baggage in safety; and lastly, a foolish ambition, as I suppose it is. The house is thirty-six feet long, eighteen wide, and fifteen high; a good cellar under it and drain." . . .

MAIL ROUTE.—POST OFFICE.

Although a mail route had been established across the Alleghanys from Philadelphia to Pittsburgh as early as 1786, there was none to, or in, the Northwest Territory until 1795. The people at Marietta and Cincinnati had no communication with the east except by expresses or messengers, and these means of communication were slow, uncertain and insecure. In 1788 the Postmaster General required only that the mail to Pittsburgh be dispatched once in a fortnight.

*Journal of Colonel John May.

In the spring of 1794 a route was established from Pittsburgh by way of Washington, Pennsylvania, West Liberty, Virginia, and Wheeling to Limestone (now Maysville), Kentucky, and the military post, Fort Washington (Cincinnati). In May the Postmaster General, Timothy Pickering, wrote General Rufus Putnam:

. . . "Marietta will be a station for the boats to stop at as they pass, and doubtless it will be convenient to have a post office there. Herewith I send a packet to you to be put into the hands of the person you judge most suitable for postmaster."

General Putnam selected for the first postmaster of Marietta Return Jonathan Meigs, jr., who twenty years later became Postmaster General of the United States, which office he held for nine years.

The mail which was carried from Pittsburgh to Wheeling by land and from thence to Cincinnati by the river gave the inhabitants of Marietta an opportunity every two or three weeks to receive letters from, or send letters to, their friends in New England. The boats made the trip from Wheeling to Cincinnati in about six days and required twelve days or two weeks to ascend the river. The boats were manned by five or six persons, well armed to resist attack from the Indians. This occurred once, in November, 1794, at the mouth of the Scioto. One man was killed and the others narrowly escaped with their lives.

The first route established within the present limits of Ohio was from Marietta to Zanesville, in 1798. The schedule required that the post should leave Marietta every Thursday at 1 o'clock P. M., and arrive at Zanes town the following Monday at 8 o'clock A. M. Returning, the mail must leave Zanes town every Tuesday at 6 o'clock A. M., and arrive at Marietta on Wednesday, at 6 P. M. Daniel Converse was the first contractor. This route was discontinued in 1804, but afterward resumed. It was the only route within the present boundaries of the State in 1800. In 1802 a route was established from Marietta by way of Athens and Chillicothe to Cincinnati. Athens post office was not, however, established until 1804. James Dickey, of Athens county, was one of the post riders from Marietta to Chillicothe, a distance of about one hundred miles, between the years 1806 and 1814. Three riders each made one trip per week, and they suffered great hardships. By the year 1825 the mail was carried from Marietta to Zanesville once a week, to Chillicothe twice a week, and to Lancaster once in two weeks. Such were the mail facilities of southeastern Ohio less than sixty years ago.

With the exception of the Masonic lodge, organized in 1790, the post office is the oldest of Marietta institutions.*

*The following has been the succession of postmasters at Marietta from 1794 to the present: Return Jonathan Meigs, jr., May, 1794, to October, 1795; Josiah Munro, October, 1795, to 1801; David Putnam, 1801 to 1802; Griffin Greene, 1802 to 1804; Philip Greene, 1804 to 1806; Griffin Greene, jr., 1806 to 1815; Samuel Hoit, 1815 to 1818; Henry P. Wilcox, 1818 to 1825; David Morris, January, 1825, to August, 1825; Daniel H. Buell, 1825 to 1829; A. V. D. Joline, 1829 to 1841; A. L. Guitteau, 1841 to 1850; F. A. Wheeler, 1850 to 1853; Nathaniel Bishop, 1853 to 1857; A. W. McCormack, 1857 to 1861; Sala Bosworth, 1861 to 1870; W. B. Mason, 1870 to 1878; S. L. Grosvenor, 1878, present incumbent.

FIRST TOWN MEETING.

The first "town meeting" held in Marietta was upon February 4, 1789. Colonel Archibald Crary was chairman, and Colonel Ebenezer Battelle, clerk. There seems to have been need at this time for some additional laws bearing upon the community, and a police force to carry out the spirit of those already enacted. Colonel Crary, Colonel Robert Oliver, Mr. Backus, Major Sargent, and Major Haffield White were constituted a committee to devise a system of police and to draw up an address to the governor, who was then absent. The address, which was duly drawn up and forwarded, contained the following:

We must lament, with all the feelings of men anxious to live under the precepts of legal authority, the absence of your excellency and the judges of the territory, more particularly at this time, ere the system of laws has been completed. We feel most sensibly the want of them and the priviledge of establishing such city regulations as we are conscious should be derived alone from the sanction of your excellency's authority; and that nothing but the most absolute necessity can exculpate us in assuming even the private police of our settlement But the necessity and propriety of some system which may tend to health, the preservation of our fields and gardens, with other essential regulations, will, we flatter ourselves, apologize for our adopting it.   .   .   .

We see at this early day in the history of the settlement the earnest desire the people had for law and order. They had been accustomed to live under the exercise of authority and they desired to revive, so far as was possible here in the wilderness, in the little colony not yet a year old, that condition of society which they had left in the villages of New England.

A police system was reported upon March 17th, and a code of laws adopted which served comparatively well for the first few years. Rufus Putnam, Archibald Crary, Griffin Greene, Robert Oliver, and Nathaniel Goodale were appointed the first commissioners charged with the carrying out of the laws and the management of the police.

CONDITION OF THE SETTLEMENT.

Morally, Marietta was for a pioneer settlement far in advance of any other in the west. Cincinnati was considerably vitiated during the Indian campaigns by the presence of the army. Chillicothe, founded in 1796, was sadly demoralized by the settlement within its precincts of many of Wayne's soldiers. The Virginia and Kentucky pioneer settlements had as a general thing a large element of lawless people.

The people of Marietta, as a rule, were New Englanders and fully abreast of the New England sentiment of the time. What has already been said exhibits their lawloving nature. How deeply they abhored (as a majority) a laxity of morals has already been suggested on many pages of this volume.

The infant settlement, however, had some vicious citizens, such as are to be found in any community, and some crimes against society were perpetrated, which aroused great indignation in the bosoms of the better class of men.

A slave sold in Marietta! It reads strangely enough. Marietta, the initial settlement of the Ohio company— that beneficiently and wisely governed New England organization under whose very influence the ordinance of freedom was enacted!

A slave sold in Marietta! Such was the fact. It is well attested. Thomas Wallcut, of Boston, a member of the Ohio company, but not a settler, visited Marietta in 1789 and 1790, and took a deep interest in the affairs of the colony. It appears by his journal that Isaac Mixer, a tavern-keeper in the settlement, sold a little negro boy into slavery in Virginia, and allusion is made to other cases of negroes being sold. The editor of Mr. Wallcut's journal states that he was very decided in his opinions on the subject of slavery and offences against good morals, and he was always fearless in the expression of them. Early in 1790 he prepared an address to Governor St. Clair, in which the Mixer slave case is made the principal topic. The address also speaks of other evils, and the need of laws to check them. The extract we quote, shows that Mr. Wallcut was deeply indignant at the outrage of Mixer.

After some preliminary remarks complimentary to the governor, and speaking in general terms of "those natural, inherent and unalienable rights which we hold to be sacred, and which cannot be violated without endangering the public peace, liberty and safety," and setting forth that "infringement upon these rights ought not to go unpunished," the address continues:

We, therefore, beg leave to call to your Excellency's attention, and to earnestly recommend to your notice certain abuses and offences against the interests of society and good government which have taken place here, and against which it is said by some there is either no law, or that the laws are insufficient for remedying and punishing like offences in future.

The first thing we beg leave to mention is that a certain Isaac Mixer, an inhabitant and inn-keeper of this city and county, a man of notoriously vicious character, keeps a disorderly, riotous and ill-governed house, which is considered by the citizens in general as an intolerable nuisance to the place, and one that will not only bring an odium and prejudice against the inhabitants and their police, but is also in its tendency destructive of peace and good order and exemplary morals, upon which not only the well being but the very existence of society so much depends.

To remedy and prevent the like abuse in future we beg leave to suggest to your attention whether it is not immediately necessary that a law should be enacted for licensing and regulating taverns and other places of public resort with proper penalties.

We next beg leave to observe that we apprehend the said Isaac Mixer has committed a flagrant trespass upon the rights of humanity, the privileges of American subjects, and the peace and happiness of this jurisdiction, as well as the dignity of the United States, in selling a certain negro boy named Prince, about the age of seven years, out of this jurisdiction into the State of Virginia where slavery is tolerated by law. This atrocious crime, we presume, is against the divine and moral, as well as (according to Judge Blackstone) against the Jewish code, the common law of England, and the ordinance of Congress for the government of this territory, which we apprehend to be our constitution and therefore the supreme law of the land. And considering that this is the second instance that the said Mixer has shown his contempt and defiance of the aforesaid sacred rights of mankind, we cannot refrain from expressing to your excellency our apprehensions that if this evil is not speedily checked it may grow to the abominable and degrading traffic of buying and selling our fellow creatures in this place.[*]

The document of which this was a part was never presented to the governor, probably, for the reason that Mr. Wallcut had an opportunity to bring the subject before the court of quarter sessions. He says (under date of February 2, 1790)   .   .   .   "Mr. Woodbridge (Dudley), foreman, asked the jury if we had anything more to present, and nothing being offered, I proposed

---

*Journal of Thomas Walcutt, page 13.

for the consideration of the jury, four articles of complaint to be presented as grievances. I prefaced them with some observations on their necessity and propriety and the informality of the paper. With leave of the foreman I read them. The question was taken whether the jury would take them up and act upon them. Passed affirmatively." These grievances debated upon by the jury were as follows:

1st Grievance. No law against dueling, etc.

2nd Grievance. No incorporation of Marietta and therefore no way of providing for the poor and sick strangers.

3rd Grievance. No law licensing and regulating taverns.

4th Grievance. No law against the crime of buying and selling the human species.

It is significant of the state of public feeling in Marietta in the year 1790, that while for the correction of the first and third of these evils there were respectively only two and nine votes, there were eleven for the fourth. "The presentments of the jury," adds Mr. Wallcut, "concluded by referring the court to two former cases of two negroes being sold, and asking that they would concur in an application to the governor and judges for remedy of these complaints."

The writer from whom we have already quoted throws more interesting light upon the condition of the Marietta of 1790. His journal has numerous allusions to an institution which it is not surprising had an existence among the Muskingum pioneers—a literary and debating society, the first in Marietta. Paul Fearing, esq., was president of this society. At the first meeting of which there is any mention made, January 27th, the question for discussion was the following: "Is the civil government of the Northwest Territory, as it now stands by the ordinance of Congress, calculated to secure the peace, freedom and prosperity of the people, and what is wanting to obtain so desirable an object?"

The society were not unanimous, says Wallcut, in any opinion except that the ordinance or constitution would admit of amendments that might be very salutary, but that it is well framed for a temporary constitution; and taking futurity into consideration, some additions and amendments are necessary and proper. They, however, considered it as a compact that Congress cannot break or infringe without mutual consent.

One of the questions proposed for consideration at the next meeting was whether the police force of the city of Marietta was equal to the good government of the same, and what alteration, if any, was necessary. One proposed by Samuel Holden Parsons, however, and relating to the rights of navigation of the Mississippi, was chosen and debated upon the evening of February 11th. At a meeting held prior to this one, Enoch Parsons was elected president, Thomas Wallcut, secretary, and Joseph Prince, treasurer. Mention is only made of this debating society in one other place in the journal of Mr. Wallcut, and it is probable that, notwithstanding the number of educated men in the community who in ordinary times would have sustained it, it passed out of existence, owing to the excitement of the times, and the great activity with which all of the settlers were engaged in necessary pursuits. That it should even have been brought into existence at so early a period in the history of the settlement is a matter of wonder. It was an evi-

dence of the education and taste which pervaded this pioneer colony.

Social amenities began in Marietta when the first families arrived—the first ladies. This was upon the nineteenth of August, 1788. Upon the very next day an entertainment was given to the governor and officers of Fort Harmar, at the hall in Campus Martius. Dr. Cutler, who was present, having arrived the day before with the first families, notes that they "had a handsome dinner with punch and wine. The governor and the ladies from the garrison were very sociable. Mrs. Rowena Tupper and the two Mrs. Goodales dined, and fifty-five gentlemen."* . . . The writer says that Mrs. Harmar "is a fine woman," and speaks in a very complimentary manner of Captain McCurdy and lady.

Upon the twenty-sixth of the month Judge Symmes and company arrived, on their way to the Symmes purchase to become settlers. The visit must have been one of very lively interest to the people of Marietta and to those who were about to enter a life similar to that which they saw here. Judge Symmes was accompanied by his daughter, who is described as "a very accomplished young lady." She was called upon by several of the newly arrived ladies of Marietta, and with her father visited General Putnam and Dr. Cutler. They arrived in the evening and resumed their journey down the river upon the following day.

The governor's daughter, Louise St. Clair, came out with the rest of the family, except Mrs. St. Clair, from their home in the Ligonier valley, Pennsylvania, in 1790, and must have been a beautiful but strange figure in the little community. She was a boughsome beauty, brilliant and dashing, full of vivacity and action, wayward and unconventional in the extreme. Some of her hoydenish ways one can well imagine as calling forth the astonishment and displeasure of the dignified and rather severe majority. She compared to the more staid daughters of the pioneers as some brilliant tropical bird does to the brown thrush or the dove of the northern forest. Dashing through the woods in a scarlet riding habit, upon a fleet horse, alone, and even at such times as there was danger apprehended from the Indians, she was the picture of all that was high-lifed, careless and fearless. She was as active on foot as on horseback, could handle a rifle with wonderful dexterity, and in winter glided over the frozen Muskingum, equalling in her skating any of the young men and excelling most of them. Withal she was refined and highly cultivated intellectually. Several of the sons of the pioneers were madly in love with her. The verses which one of them wrote in her praise are still to be found in Marietta. Some time after the war she returned to the Ligonier valley, and it is said married a humble man in her father's employ.

Of the character of the men at Marietta much has already been said in the early chapters of this work. A large proportion of those who settled in the Ohio company's purchase prior to the close of the war were Revolutionary soldiers, and nearly all were from New Eng-

* Journal of Dr. Manasseh Cutler, in New England Historical and Genealogical Register.

land. There was probably more of learning, virtue, and dignity in this than in any other pioneer colony planted in America. For the most part they were men who held the religious views common in the land of their nativity. Deep piety was a characteristic of many, but there were a considerable number who were more or less imbued with infidel opinions. It was not the infidelity of Thomas Paine, but the light skepticism of France, received in a large degree from the French officers of the Revolutionary army.

Excess in the use of liquor was the greatest evil in the settlement. Hard drinking was not confined so closely as now to the vicious class, but indulged in by many of the best men in the community, and the use of liquor in moderation was almost universal. A number of the brightest minds in Marietta, at an early day, were ruined by intemperance. Men high in position and of otherwise exemplary character were among the victims.

A recent writer,* after making the statement that "at Marietta were several men of superior intellects who were infidels, and others who were intemperate," says: "And yet this pioneer town was probably one of the best examples of the society of pioneer times." He means evidently that it was one of the examples of the best society of pioneer times. It was far ahead, as we have heretofore remarked, of the other pioneer settlements of Ohio and the west generally.

During the period of the war (and the two years previous to it) money was very scarce in the settlement and provisions high. Many people were obliged to live in exceedingly straightened circumstances; others absolutely suffered. What little produce of the country could be spared was used in lieu of money, in exchange for commodities brought from the Eastern States or from Pittsburgh. Ginseng passed current. It was a local legal tender. Skins were also exchanged for goods with the traders and storekeepers. Whatever the settlers could produce by their own labors saved them an outlay from their small store of cash. "Sugar," says Colonel Barker, we make ourselves. Sugar (material for it) is plenty, but metal to boil it in is scarce. . . . When General Putnam was on and obtained the grant for the donation lands, Lady Washington sent out a keg of loaf made from maple sugar, to be distributed among the ladies of the officers of the Revolutionary army of the Ohio company's purchase.†

We have said that the prices upon all articles brought into the settlement were high. Calico commanded from a dollar to a dollar and seventy-five cents per yard, salt sold commonly from four to five dollars per bushel, and sometimes was as high as ten dollars. Tea was two dollars per pound, and other articles in proportion.

RESIDENTS DURING THE WAR.

Elsewhere in this work (chapter VII) has been given

General Putnam's list of arrivals at Marietta during the years 1788–89, and 1790. We now present a list* of those who were residents of Marietta—at Campus Martius, at "the Point," and in and near Fort Harmar—during the whole or a part of the period of the war.

To begin with, there were at Campus Martius the following:

General Rufus Putnam, wife, two sons and six daughters.

Governor Arthur St. Clair, son and three daughters.

General Benjamin Tupper, wife, three sons and a daughter.

Colonel Ichabod Nye, wife, and three sons.

Colonel Robert Oliver and wife, two sons, William and Robert, and two daughters, Nelly, married to Thomas Lord, the other to Captain William Burnham.

Thomas Lord and two apprentice boys—Benjamin Baker, and Amos R. Harvey.

Colonel R. J. Meigs, wife, and son, Timothy.

R. J. Meigs, jr., and wife. (He lived the larger part of the time at the Point.)

Colonel Enoch Shepherd, wife, and nine children: Enoch, Daniel, Luther, Calvin, Esther, Anna, Rhoda, Lorana, and Huldah.

Charles Greene, esq., wife, and three children: Sophia, Susan, and Charles; also Miss Sheffield, sister of Mrs. Greene, and afterwards wife of Captain Ziegler, of Fort Harmar.

Major Ezra Putnam, wife, and two daughters.

Major Haffield White and son, Peletiah.

Joshua Shipman, wife, and three children.

Wife and two sons and daughter of Captain Strong (who was attached to the army).

Captain Davis, wife, and five children.

James Smith, wife, and seven children.

John Russell, son-in-law of Smith.

Archibald Lake, wife, and three sons—Thomas, Andrew, and John.

Eleazer Olney, wife, and fourteen children.

Major Olney, wife, and two sons—Columbus and Discovery.

Ebenezer Corey and wife.

Richard Maxon, wife, and several children.

James Wells, wife and ten children. The sons were David, Joseph, Thomas, and Varnum. The daughters married as follows: Polly, to Richard Maxon; Nancy, to Thomas Carey; Susan, to Peletiah White; Betsy, to Jacob Proctor; and Sally, to Peleg Springer.

Major Coburn and wife, two daughters and three sons —Asa, Phinehas, and Nicholas.

Joseph Wood, wife, and one child.

Captain John Dodge, wife, and two sons—John and Sidney.

Robert Allison, wife, and children—three sons, young men, Charles, Andrew, and Hugh.

Elijah Warren, wife, and one child.

Gersham Flagg, wife, and children.

Widow of Joseph Kelley (who was killed in 1791) and mother of Arthur St. Clair Kelly, the first child born at Marietta.

---

* The late E. D. Mansfield, of Cincinnati, in "Personal Memories." His father, Jared Mansfield, was appointed by Jefferson, in 1803, as the successor of General Rufus Putnam, Surveyor General of the United States. The family lived for several years in Marietta. Mr. Mansfield was then a mere child. He wrote from common report upon the Marietta of earlier days.

†Colonel Joseph Barker's notes (Ms.)

* Derived for the most part from Hildreth's Pioneer History.

Single men—Major Anselem Tupper, Edward W. Tupper, Benjamin Tupper, jr., Rev. Daniel Story, Thomas Hutchinson, William Smith, Gilbert Devol, jr., Oliver Dodge, Alpheus Russell, Thomas Corey, and Azariah Pratt.

At or near Fort Harmar were the following families and single men:

Hon. Joseph Gilman and wife.

Benjamin Ives Gilman and wife. These families lived in a block-house above the fort.

Paul Fearing, a resident of Fort Harmar, Southwest block-house.

Colonel Thomas Gibson, an Indian trader, licensed for Washington county, occupied a block-house near the fort.

Hezekiah Flint and Gould Davenport, single men.

Mrs. Welch and several children lived at the fort. Her husband died of small-pox in 1790, and she married Thomas Hutchinson.

Preserved Seaman, wife and four sons—Samuel, Gilbert, Preserved, and Benajah. Samuel had a wife and several children and lived in the guard-house of the fort.

Benjamin Baker, wife and one child, lived in a small stone house just south of the fort.

George Warth, wife and five sons—John, George, Robert, Martin, and Alexander, and two daughters; lived in a log house between the fort and the river. Two of the sons were employed as rangers for the garrison during the war; Robert was killed by the Indians; George married Ruth, a sister of Joshua Fleehart, the Belpre ranger.

Joseph Fletcher married Catharine Warth.

Picket Meroin, married Polly Warth.

Francis Thierry and wife with two children were of the French emigrant party which arrived in 1790. Thierry was a baker. He lived afterwards for many years in Marietta. A daughter of Thierry's wife by a former marriage—Catharine La Lance, married Robert Warth, a short time before he was killed.

Monsieur Cookie was another of the French emigrants who remained at Fort Harmar.

Monsieur Le Blond, also French, carried on a distillery of cordials, and made wooden shoes.

Monsieur Shouman had been bred a gardener in France and followed that occupation near the fort. He had a wife and son, but his wife dying during the period of the war, he married the widow of Sherman Waterman, who was killed by the Indians.

Monsieur Gubbeau, another of the French emigrants, was a young man. He carried the mail in company with Pierre La Lance in 1795, from Marietta to Gallipolis.

At the Point garrison were the following families:

William Moulton, wife, one son, Edward, and two daughters. The father and son were members of the pioneer party of 1788. They were from Newburyport, Massachusetts, and the elder, who died in 1793, was a goldsmith by trade. Anna Moulton married Dr. Josiah Hart, and Lydia, Dr. Leonard.

Dr. Jabez True boarded with the Moulton family.

Captain Prince, a hatter by trade, from Boston, with wife and two children.

Moses Morse and wife. Morse owned a row of four log houses, which he rented to transient residents or people who were preparing cabins of their own.

Peter Nyghswonger, wife (Jane Kerr, sister of Hamilton Kerr, the spy), and several children occupied a cabin fronting on the Muskingum. Nyghswonger was himself a ranger and hunter. He moved westward after the war, following the game.

William Skinner dwelt at the point during the war and kept store, but afterwards removed to the Harmar side of the Muskingum.

J. McKinley was a partner with Skinner.

R. J. Meigs, jr., whom we have spoken of as a resident at Campus Martius, kept a store fronting on the Muskingum.

Charles Greene was in partnership with him.

Hon. Dudley Woodbridge, wife and children, lived in a block-house very near the Ohio. Between his house and the Ohio river he built a frame house in which he kept a store.

Captain Josiah Munroe, wife and two children lived near the centre of the enclosure or stockade.

Captain William Mills, wife, and one child, occupied a house near Munroe's.

Captain Jonathan Haskell, commander of a company of United States troops, also lived at this garrison.

Hamilton Kerr, the ranger, and his mother, lived in a small block-house.

Colonel Ebenezer Sproat, wife, and daughter, had a small house near the bank of the Ohio.

Commodore Abraham Whipple and family lived with Sproat, who was his son-in-law.

Joseph Buell, wife, and two children, and Levi Munsell and wife, lived in a large frame house heretofore spoken of—the first frame house built in Marietta—and kept tavern.

William Stacey (son of Colonel Stacey), wife and children.

Joseph Stacey (also a son of the colonel), wife and children.

James Patterson, wife and children.

Nathaniel Patterson, wife and children.

Captain Abel Mathews, wife and six children. (He was the father of John Mathews, of whom much is said in this volume).

Thomas Stanley, wife and four children.

Eleazer Curtiss, wife and children.

Simeon Tuttle, wife and family of children.

A number of the Ohio company's laborers occupied a row of cabins which stood upon the Ohio river bank but their names have not been preserved.

We have, in most cases, given nothing more than the names of these families—the first settlers of Marietta— as biographies of most of them are inserted at the close of the Marietta history, or elsewhere in this volume.

MARIETTA IN 1803.

The settlement, consisting of three small groups of dwellings—Campus-Martius, "The Point" garrison and

Fort Harmar—and containing during the war period, the people whose names we have given and a few others, had become by 1803, after eight years of peace, a flourishing little village. It is thus described by the Rev. Thaddeus Mason Harris, who arrived April 23, while making his "tour into the territory northwest of the Alleghany mountains:"

There are now within the town plat five hundred and fifty inhabitants, and ninety-one dwelling houses, sixty-five of which are frame or plank, eleven of brick, and three of stone. It contains also eight merchants' stores, nineteen buildings occupied by public officers and mechanics, three rope walks eight hundred and fifty feet long, a gaol and court house under the same roof, and an academy which is used at present as the place of worship.

Marietta is a place of much business, and is rapidly increasing in population. Ship building is already carried on to a considerable extent. A spirit of industry and enterprise prevails. Add to all the remarkable healthiness of the place, the benefit it receives from the growing settlements on the Muskingum, and the extensive navigation of that river, and it is easy to foresee that it will maintain a character as the most respectable and thriving town in the State.

The situation of this town is extremely well chosen, and is truly delightful. The appearance of the rivers, banks and distant hills is remarkably picturesque. Trees of different form and foliage give a vast variety to the beauty and coloring of the prospect, while the high hills that rise like a rampart all around, add magnificence and grandeur to the scene. Back of the town is a ridge finely clothed with trees.

According to the above statement, Marietta had a little more than one-third the present population of the village of Harmar, two hundred and eighty less than that of Beverly, eighty-one less than Matamoras, three hundred and fifty less than Belpre, and was almost exactly one-tenth the size of the Marietta of 1880—population five thousand four hundred and forty-four.

CHAPTER XXV.

MARIETTA—MERCANTILE BUSINESS AND MANUFACTURING.

The First Store in Marietta—Location of Business—Early Business Methods—Character of Mercantile Trade During the First Quarter Century—Monetary Terms—Prices During the Last Century—Prominent Business Men: Dudley Woodbridge, Charles Green, Edward W. Tupper, Joseph Lincoln, Abner Lord, Benjamin Ives Gilman, Augustus Stone, William Skinner, Abijah Brooks, Joseph Holden, Stephen B. Wilson, John Mills, Nathaniel Dodge, Robert Crawford, Jason R. Curtis, James Dunn, D. B. Anderson—Hat Making—Jewelry and Clock Making—Book Trade—Drug Trade—Dry Goods—Boots and Shoes - Hardware—Furniture—Taverns—Photography—Farming—Manufacture of Fabrics—Furniture Manufacture—Marietta Iron Works—Marietta Foundry—Gas Works—Book Binding—Brewing - Bucket Factories—Mills—Banking—Early Banking Laws—First Bank in the Northwest Territory—The Bank of Marietta—First National Bank—Marietta National Bank—Bank of Marietta—Bank of Exchange—Dime Savings Society—Oil—First Oil Wells—Seneca Oil—Oil Refining and Refineries.

MERCANTILE BUSINESS.*

The first store in Marietta—the first store in the Northwest Territory—was located on the corner of Muskingum

*No attempt is here made to give a detailed mercantile history of the city. If the general growth of business from the beginning to the present is outlined, and the name of the men who have taken a prominent part in trade, and in building up the city, shall be preserved, our purpose has been accomplished. It is not pretended that the dust has been so thoroughly brushed off the past that all the names, even of the more prominent and worthy of the merchants of a period of ninety-three years have been mentioned.

and Ohio streets, and was owned by Dudley Woodbridge. Business seems to have followed the river bank both ways from this point. As we shall proceed with this sketch, the location of stores first around the "point" and then up Muskingum street, will appear. At a later period Ohio street was the line of trade, and it was not until comparatively recent times that Front street was improved. Previous to 1830 Front street was almost a common, the grass and weeds scarcely ever being broken by a team or vehicle. It will be seen also that in the olden time Putnam street had a few stores. Business slowly advanced from the river westward, coming over flats and creeks, forming an unbroken line of stores on one side to Putnam, which in the unseen future may become the centre of trade. Green street and the cross streets connecting it with Ohio were avenues mainly to smaller shops and dwelling houses.

Harmar, with reference to the location of business was much like Marietta. The first stores faced the mouth of the Muskingum.

Mercantile business in some form or other had been carried on previous to the opening of the Woodbridge store already spoken of. An agent of Colonel John May, who at that time had a store at Wheeling, was doing business here for the Wheeling house in September, 1788. Colonel May in a letter which indicates that he was carrying on a general business in the western settlements, says: "Mr. Beck has been dispatched to Marietta—that was four days after I came here—with such goods as was supposed would sell. Hear from him about once a week. He is well and doing a moderate business. Our grand plan being broken all to pieces, we shall not make out a great summer's work, for there are many articles which cannot be sold at cost, unless by credit, and that, under existing circumstances, I can't think of doing. Of a great number who went to Kentucky in the trade of ling (ginseng) more than half will be bankrupt. In the way of exchange or barter I have taken other things, upwards of five hundred raccoon skins, some beaver, and one hundred and twenty deer skins and all the cash that would circulate into my hands.*" This exchange of furs for good was carried on by Pittsburgh and Wheeling merchants at a later day. But it is no where indicated that the business was transacted in a store in the proper sense of that term; supplies were received at stated intervals and distributed among the customers in exchange for whatever they had to dispose of.

Furs and salt were important articles of trade for a number of years. Salt, previous to its manufacture on the Muskingum, was brought to Marietta on pack-horses and sold by the quart or gallon at the rate of eight dollars per bushel. The enormous price and the indispensableness of the article made it important in the trade of the agents and early stores. From an account we learn the price of fur-skins in 1796: raccoon, two shillings; one and a quarter pound beaver, twelve shillings; muskrat, one shilling; wildcat, three shillings; fox, two to four shillings; otters, three dollars; bear skins were also in the market. Eleven raccoons and three foxes are at

* Journal of Colonel John May.

one place charged at two pounds, another entry runs: "two others valued at two dollars each." This strange mixing of money turns suggests the conservatism of business usages. Just now while the propriety of adopting the metric system of weights and measures is being much discussed, it will be interesting to note the hesitation with which the decimal system in monetary notation was adopted. The Continental Congress abolished the English system and made the dollar unit of notation in 1786. At the same time the coinage of the gold eagle and half eagle was ordered. A great variety of customs existed during the next fifteen or twenty years. There was not only a difference of usage among different business men, but, as the above quotation shows there was a mixing of the two systems on the same books. Six shillings were taken for a dollars unless otherwise specified. And here again there seems to have been another difficulty in the financial system of the latter part of the last century. A law was enacted in 1792, by Winthrop Sargent, then acting governor of the territory and the judges, regulating the fees of public officers, from which the following extract is taken, showing the inconveniences of having money variable in value and showing also that money must have a basis in intrinsic value. The act reads:

And whereas the dollar varies in its real value in the several counties in the territory, some provision in kind ought to be made, therefore: Be it enacted: that for every cent allowed by this act, one quart of Indian corn may be allowed and taken by the person to whom the fee is coming, as an equivalent for the cent, always at the election of the person receiving the same whether to receive his fee in Indian corn or in species at the sum affixed by the foregoing table of fees; one quart of Indian corn being always equal to one cent, and so on at that rate for a greater or less sum.

Imagine the difficulty of keeping accounts, first, with a mixed system of notation and second with a medium of exchange varying so much in the several counties as to require making an agricultural product the standard of value.

The decimal system was at first used as awkwardly as the metric system would be now by merchants in general. The usual way of keeping accounts was to have four colums headed D, d, c, m, or in some instances five columns headed E, D, d, c, m. Cents in old accounts are infrequently written as fractions of a dollar and the eagle was sometimes used as the unit of value.

A curious arrangement of names is found in the ledger kept by Judge Cutler at Waterford. A copy of the index to this ledger, in which the names are arranged in alphabetical order with reference to the Christian name, will be found in the chapter on Waterford.

The extensive produce and exchange business with New Orleans and other southern cities will be again referred to under the head of navigation and boat-building, as it had an important influence upon those industries. It also accelerated business development in general. This trade began as soon as the Muskingum valley and Ohio river bottoms were improved, and continued until the opening of the Rebellion.

The influence of the southern trade was not confined to multiplying stores and encouraging ship-building. It opened up the market which made the products of the farm more valuable, thus stimulating agriculture and hastening the developments of the county's resources.

In the early store everything marketable was bought and everything necessary to the comfort of enlightened people kept for sale, much after the fashion of the better class of country stores of the present time. In the progress of the growth of the city, business divided into its several natural departments.

Having hinted at the location and methods of business, we shall now attempt to outline its development, which began in earnest after the Indian war in 1795, after a paralytic period of more than four years.

Hon. Dudley Woodbridge, proprietor of the first store in the Northwest Territory, was born in Stonington, in 1747. He graduated at Yale college in 1766, married Lucy, daughter of Elijah and Lucy (Griswold) Backus, of Norwich, was bred to the bar, but on coming to Marietta in 1788,* engaged in mercantile business. He died at Marietta in 1823. The business at an early period was placed in charge of Dudley Woodbridge, jr., who came to Marietta in 1794 and was for more than fifty years a prominent merchant. His business during most of this period was located on Ohio street. Many of the men mentioned in this chapter were his partners and were benefitted by his friendship. He was the senior in the firm of Dudley Woodbridge, jr., & Co., of which Harman Blennerhassett was one of the partners. He was strong in his opinions and prejudices, but always sympathetic and charitable in the presence of want and distress. He was born November 10, 1778, and died in his seventy-fifth year. In his older years he was an enthusiastic worker in the Congregational church and Sunday-school. For a number of years he taught a large Bible class.

The second store in Marietta was opened by Charles Green, who came to Ohio the latter part of 1788, or early in 1789. During the Indian war he owned and lived in a house in Campus Martius. His place of business was on Ohio street, below Post, in a building erected for the purpose. About 1796 he erected a building further up the river. He also engaged in ship building early in the century, and was bankrupted by the embargo act.

General Edward Tupper came to Marietta with his father, General Benjamin Tupper, in 1788, being at that time seventeen years old. After the close of the Indian war he began merchandising on the corner of Putnam and Second streets. His wife was Berthia, daughter of William Pitt Putnam. Mr. Tupper was brigadier general of militia for the counties of Washington, Athens and Gallia. In 1807 he built the residence commonly known as the Ward property, on Putnam street. In 1809 or '10 he removed to Gallipolis.

One of the most successful of the early business men was Major Robert Lincoln, who was born in Massachusetts, in 1760. He was at Farmer's Castle during the Indian war, and at its close engaged in business in Marietta, on Ohio street. He at one time owned all the land on Ohio street between Post and Front, and several

* New England Historical and Genealogical Register.

lots on Front. In 1807 he erected, on the corner of
Front and Ohio streets, what was then the finest building in town. It was originally a large, square, brick
house, with ornamental mantels and stucco ceilings.
The building was arranged both for dwelling and business house; but Major Lincoln died about the time it
was finished. Colonel John Mills did business in this
house for many years. Frequent remodellings afterwards has left only the back walls of the building unchanged.

Colonel Abner Lord began business in Marietta about
1800. He emigrated from Lynn, Massachusetts, to Vienna, West Virginia, soon after the Indian war. Colonel
Lord's store was in a building which stood at the foot of
Front street, on the river bank. This house was afterwards occupied as a store by Joseph Holden. In the
spring freshet of 1827 or '8 a torch was applied and the
burning building sent floating down the river. Colonel
Lord removed to Franklin county in 1811, where he died
in 1821.

The name of Benjamin Ives Gilman is closely identified with the early business enterprises of the west side
of the Muskingum. He came with his father, Judge
Gilman, from Exeter, New Hampshire, in 1789. The
family was distinguished for social and intellectual culture. Benjamin Ives was married in 1790 to Hannah
Robbins, of New Hampshire, a lady of culture and education. Mr. Gilman opened a store in Harmar in 1792
and continued in business until about 1812. His
store, which was patronized by nearly all who lived
on that side of the river, was in a stone building, erected
for the purpose, located at the upper end of the square.
Mr. Gilman was also engaged in ship-building and banking. An extensive tract of land in Warren township,
known as the Gilman farm, was owned by him. In 1813
he engaged in business in Philadelphia, where he died in
1833.

Mr. Gilman was succeeded in Harmar by Colonel
Augustus Stone. Colonel Stone had been engaged as a
surveyor under General Mansfield in laying out Government lands. About 1809 he opened a store near the
foot of Oliver street. Four years later he moved to Harmar, where his store was largely patronized until reverses
overwhelmed him in 1842. He died at an advanced age
in 1879.

Colonel Levi Barber will be remembered as one of the
early merchants of the west side. His store fronted the
Muskingum. His residence was a double brick house,
which is still standing.

William Skinner, father of D. C. and William Skinner, prominent business men of a later date, was one of
the early merchants of Harmar, he was also one of the
directors of the bank. His son, Daniel C., carried on the
business in Harmar for some time, and afterwards, in
partnership with Weston Thomas, engaged in business
on Ohio street, Marietta.

James Whitney, whose name frequently appears in the
history of early Methodism in Marietta, was one of the
early merchants in Harmar. He was by trade a ship-
builder and worked for Benjamin Ives Gilman, in his

yard. After the embargo act had ruined the business,
Mr. Whitney opened a store below the square.

Abijah Brooks was, for a short time, a prominent merchant in Harmar. He began at Watertown, afterwards
removed to Waterford, and then to Harmar, where he
had a store on the corner of Ohio and Monroe streets.
He built the Exchange hotel about 1837, which proved
an unfortunate investment. His store was sometime
afterwards closed.

The extensive mercantile establishment now owned by
Colonel W. C. Moore was established by the Marietta
Iron company.

Joseph Holden was prominent among the early business men. He came to Marietta in 1803 and opened
a store in 1807. In 1837 he was succeeded by his sons,
William, Joseph and James, who carried on the business
under the firm name of W., J. & J. Holden, until January, 1843, when William retired. In 1852 James
became sole proprietor. He closed the business in 1857.
A sketch of Joseph Holden, sr., will be found in the
chapter of general biography.

Stephen B. Wilson had a store in the early part of the
century on the corner of Post and Muskingum streets in
a building erected by Earl Sproat. He was a native of
Virginia and married a daughter of Dr. Joseph Spencer
of Vienna. Noah L. Wilson, his son, was at a later
period one of the prominent merchants of the place.
He began as a clerk under Colonel Mills.

Opposite, on the corner of Montgomery and Muskingum, a store was kept by Mr. Avery, who began business
before the Indian war.

Colonel Ichabod Nye opened a store in 1810 in a
brick building erected for the purpose, on Putnam street,
just above Front. He continued for many years in mercantile business.

John Mills entered the list of Marietta business
men in 1815 in partnership with Dudley Woodbridge.
His connection with mercantile trade continued until
1865. From 1835 until 1847, he was in partnership with
Noah L. Wilson and W. F. Curtis; from 1847 to 1850
the firm was Mills, Iams & Dana; in 1850 the firm became, Iams, Dana & Co.; in 1865 Mr. Mills closed his
business with the firm of R. P. Iams & Co.

Nathaniel Dodge, of Hampton Falls, New Hampshire,
came to Ohio for permanent settlement in 1804. He
was a Revolutionary soldier and firm supporter of Washington. He purchased considerable property in Marietta
where he died in 1838. Two of his sons entered into
mercantile business in Marietta. Oliver Dodge was for
a time a partner of Augustus Stone, in Harmar. He
was afterwards captain and owner of a steamboat. He
died in Marietta in 1836. Nathaniel, second, began
business on Ohio street in partnership with Jonathan
Crane. When this partnership dissolved Mr. Dodge engaged in business in Parkersburgh where he died. Mr.
Crane removed the business to Muskingum street above
the Phœnix mills. He continued business here until
his death in 1821. Robert Crawford took charge of the
store and managed it for the family after his death.
Mr. Crane was a native of Hampton Falls, New Hamp-

shire. Three of the daughters of Nathaniel Dodge, first, married Marietta merchants; Sally married Jonathan Crain; Rebecca was first wife of Colonel Augustus Stone, and Hannah first wife of D. P. Bosworth.

Hat making was once a lucrative trade. Hat shops were as common and necessary in a town as shoe shops. The first hatter in Marietta of which we have any knowledge, was Seth Washburn, who had a shop on Ohio street. . From the accounts of James Dunn we learn that a Mr. Scott carried on the business in Harmar. Jason R. Curtis was the first manufacturer and tradesman in this line, whose business was of a permanent character. He began during the War of 1812. In 1818 he associated in partnership James Dunn who had a shop up the river, and visited the towns down along the river, selling his goods. At a later period he worked for Mr. Scott, of Harmar, and for Mr. Curtis. He continued in partnership with Mr. Curtis until 1825, when the business came under his control. In 1839 John Allison bought the shop or store as it had by this time become. Mr. Allison continued in business about five years, during which time his store was political headquarters. He was appointed register of the treasury by President Lincoln, and served in that important capacity for a period of twelve years. Three stores at present make a specialty of hats and furnishing goods: S. C. Wilhelm, established in 1877; W. A. Sniffin, 1877, and W. B. Mason, 1880.

During the pioneer years clock makers like hatters travelled about the country hunting purchasers for their manufacture, and doing repairing. A Mr. Harrison was one of this kind of tradesmen. D. B. Anderson was probably the first practical jeweler. He came from Utica, New York, and started a store on the corner of Front and Ohio streets, in 1817. He continued in business until 1854, when his son, D. B. Anderson, jr., came in charge, and has since been doing business on the corner of Front and Butler streets. J. W. Baldwin has been in this branch of business for some time. J. Whittling established a store in 1877.

S. and W. Slocumb, while in the shoe business, were agents for the American Bible society, and handled school and general books. The first book store, proper, was opened by Gurley & Cross, and McCoy & Stephens succeeded. From 1852 J. C. McCoy was proprietor until 1856, when C. E. Glines bought the stock, and has continued in the trade ever since. T. W. Morse opened a news depot in 1875. He also sells miscellaneous and school books.

In the early history of Marietta drugs were kept only by doctors whose offices were called apothecary shops. The first drug store was owned by Dr. Rignier, and was located on Ohio street, in "Flat-iron square." Dr. Regnier sold to Dr. John Cotton in 1818, who continued the business until his death in 1847. His son, J. D. Cotton, continued the business until 1850, when J. H. Hawes was associated in partnership, and the store was removed to near the corner of Front and Ohio streets. In 1851 the firm became Cotton & Buell, and in 1854 the store was removed to the Holden building on the opposite side of the street. Edward W. and William H. Buell

purchased the store in 1856, and in 1866 removed to the new building which they had erected a short distance above the old stand. E. W. Buell sold to W. H. Buell in 1869, and the firm changed to W. H. Buell & Co. in 1874. E. B. Perkins opened a drug store on the south side of Front street in 1848. This store was owned by Curier & Stimson, William Glines and others until 1864, when Hollister & Allen took charge. A. L. Curtis has owned the business since 1868. William Kayless opened a drug store on Front street, between the bridges, in 1856. He sold to Harte & Pearce, and they to Pearce & Treim. Theodore Treim now owns the business. A. J. Richards opened a store on the corner of Second and Green streets in 1875. Dr. J. C. Bartlett opened a store on Front street, near Putnam, in 1870. He sold to C. B. McCaskey in 1879.

Weston Thomas began business on Ohio street as early as 1820. He formed a partnership with D. C. Skinner and built a house on Ohio street, between Second and Front, where they had a store for a number of years. William B. Thomas succeeded.

Luther Edgerton began business with Dudley Woodbridge. He was for many years a successful merchant.

Abner L. Gitto opened a dry goods store in 1837 in the Clarke and Curtis building on Front street.

Samuel Shipman began business as a clerk under Colonel Mills in 1832. In 1837 he formed a partnership with his brother Charles and opened a dry goods store on Green street. In 1860 Samuel came into possession of the entire business and continued it until his death in 1880.

W. F. Curtis began a long and successful business career in 1841. He engaged more than any other merchant of his time in the southern trade spoken of in the introduction to this chapter. Mr. Curtis' name appears frequently in the sketch of banking.

The firm of William and Silas Slocumb were once prominent among Marietta business houses. Theirs was probably the first regular shoe store. They also carried on the manufacture of shoes on an extensive scale. Their cotemporaries in this branch of industry were W. L. Rolstan and Mr. Fisher, who remains in the business.

S. R. Turner began the dry goods business about 1850. In 1865 the firm became S. R. Turner & Son, and in 1881 S. R. Turner & Company. The store is situated on Front street, and is one of the largest and best stocked in the city.

Groceries have, until comparatively recent years, been kept in connection with other classes of goods. The principal individuals and firms now engaged in the grocery business are G. C. Best, established 1865; J. D. Otterbim, 1865; Jasper Sprague, 1862; Charles Weis, 1868; E. G. Brigham, 1871; F. R. Brenan, 1874; J. S. Stowe, jr., 1880; Lewis Hamlin, 1880, C. Schenkberg & Co., 1880.

The three-story building between Second and Third streets on Ohio, was erected by Wylis and Joseph E. Hall, about 1833. They occupied it as a boat store, having also a wharf boat. Their trade was largely with merchants in the surrounding country. Nearly all the goods for merchants on the Muskingum were received here.

Daniel P. Bosworth and George H. Wells began the hardware business in Marietta in 1840, on the north side of Front street. On the opposite side of the alley were two stores in the Holden building, one a dry goods store belonging to P. Fleming, the other a grocery, conducted by William Holden. In 1845 the firm became Bosworth, Wells & Co. The dry goods store just mentioned was purchased the same year, and the grocery two years later. In the spring of 1859 the firm began the erection of a block on the corner of Front and Monroe streets, now occupied by their stores. On the ninth of May of that year the old buildings burned, and the business was carried on, until the completion of the new block, on Ohio street.

A. T. Nye opened a hardware store on Front street in 1848, and continues in the business as senior partner, the firm name at present being Nye Hardware Company. Next to Bosworth, Wells & Company, this is the oldest hardware establishment in the city.

Stoves are handled by the hardware trade, but there are also special stove and tinware stores. Luthinger, Reck & Co. began business in 1874, Theis & Etz in 1879.

In 1867 the firm of Smith & Rodick opened a hardware store in the Booth building on Front street. The members of the firm were John Smith and Henry and Bernard Rodick. In May, 1871, Mr. Smith died, and in January, 1872, the firm name changed to Rodick Brothers. Their business increased rapidly, making it necessary for them to provide more commodious rooms. In the summer of 1878 the large, three-story brick building, a view of which is given on another page, was erected exclusively for their own use. Their store is one of the largest and best arranged in the State. They do both a wholesale and retail business.

The first furniture store in Marietta was started by Dana & Gray in 1855. Previous to that, furniture was made and sold in cabinet shops. Cabinet-makers of an early period were James M. Booth, Alexander Hill, Samuel Griggs, and a few others less known. The store started by Dana & Gray came into possession of J. W. Stanley in 1856. He continued the retail furniture business until 1881. Other stores are owned by Martin Schmidt, successor to Finley & Company, and Lewis Goebel.

TAVERNS.

Public houses of entertainment are either the strangers' paradise, or a place of persecution. This was as true in the eighteenth as it is in the nineteenth century, although the lapse of time has effected a transformation in their character. The good old familiar word tavern has given place to the more high-sounding term, hotel, and a stiff, mind-your-own-business air reigns where once was good cheer around hospitable fireplaces. The ideal landlord was, in the olden time, a jolly, good natured host, who looked after the comfort of his guests. The snob of self assumed importance who now too frequently stands behind the hotel counters in our smaller cities was then an unknown nuisance.

The first tavern was erected in Marietta by General Joseph Buell. It stood on the corner of Front and Green streets, and was the first frame house built north of the Ohio river. The timbers for its construction were cut and hewn on the Monongahela, and floated down the Ohio. It seems strange that building material should be brought to a country full of the best timber. But it must be remembered that here tools were scarce and laborers few.

This house was painted red, and received the name of "Red House." Red was the prevailing color for houses, as the paint was cheap and durable. The tavern was in charge of Levi Munsel, and for several years was the principal house of entertainment in the settlement.

A building framed at the same place, and occupied as a tavern by Stephen Shepard, stood where G. C. Best's store on Ohio street is now located. The building was removed in 1822, to make room for the present two-story brick block. The Shepard House was a gay place during the period of early settlement.

Further up the river was the McFarlan House, built as early as 1797. Moses McFarlan was a favorite among the flat-boatmen, and his house was a place of happy revelry. The bar in all those taverns was handy, and the whiskey cheap.

The Brophy House, a few doors farther up, will be remembered by many yet living. It was opened by Casper Smith, a German, whose wife had a cake shop in the same building. Smith died, leaving a good sized bag of gold, and his wife soon after married John Brophy, an Irishman, who carried on the business. The cake shop was made a bakery, and the small inn a jolly tavern. Mr. Brophy became quite wealthy. His house was Democratic headquarters.

Amos B. Harvey and Sampson Cole are also numbered among Marietta's landlords.

The hotel now known as the Brown House was built in the beginning of the century by Colonel Abner Lord for a residence. Caleb Emerson, Samuel Hoit, Rev. John Willard, and Dr. John Cotton resided in this house. After the death of Dr. Cotton in 1848, it was purchased by Charles Bizant and converted into a tavern.

The National House was built by A. W. Reckard.

The building now occupied by Mr. Gross, and known as the St. Cloud hotel, was built by Thomas Barker for a residence.

The Central House, on Second street, was built by Mrs. H. Reese, and opened as a hotel in 1880.

PHOTOGRAPHY.

W. P. Bennett opened a photographic gallery in 1862, and has been engaged in the art since that time. He has a valuable collection of pioneer photographs.

Cadwalleder & Tappan were at first located over the Bank of Marietta on Front street. In 1866 T. M. Tappan bought Mr. Cadwalleder's interest, and in 1868 Mr. Cadwalleder repurchased the instruments and has since been proprietor. In 1873 he removed to the Eell's building. A branch was opened at Parkersburgh in 1880.

Wm Mills

TANNERIES.

Marietta has had and still has peculiar advantages in the tanning industry. The material chiefly used in the process of leather-making is bark, and in quality and quantity of this material Washington county is peculiarly well favored. The first attempt at more than a rural business was made by Thomas Vinton, of Philadelphia, who constructed the necessary apparatus on the lot between Front and Second streets, near Sacra Via. Through inexperience in business and ignorance of the science of tanning, Mr. Vinton was unable to make the business a success.

In 1848 a firm, consisting of William L. Rolston, D. L. Skinner, Noah Wilson and William Nye, purchased the property from Mr. Vinton and began operations in 1845 after making many additions and repairs. This company, with a capital of fifty thousand dollars, soon found itself in possession of the largest business of the kind west of the Alleghany mountains. From 1860 to 1866 the firm of Skinner, Rolston & Co. had the reputation of having the model tannery of the west. About fifteen hundred cords of chestnut and oak bark were consumed annually, and the establishment had a capacity of five thousand skins per month. Agents of the firm were posted throughout the west for buying hides. St. Louis, Keokuk, Hamilton, Des Moines, and other Mississippi river towns being the principal points. Rough leathers were marketed in New York and Boston, fine leather in the west. Burning the tan was first successfully practiced in this establishment—a department of the business upon which advanced tanners had spent a great deal of money in experiments.

Another branch of industry carried on by this firm was the manufacture of quercitron. Black oak bark was easily obtained, and during the war the demand for this material was heavy. Tons of it were sent from Marietta to the eastern markets.

The death of William Nye made a reorganization of the firm necessary. In 1866 the buildings, grounds and machinery were sold at administrator's sale for eighteen thousand dollars; the stock invoiced twenty-five thousand dollars. This sale placed the establishment in the hands of A. Spencer Nye, of Chillicothe. The trade soon declined, and now the largest tanning establishment in Ohio is standing idle.

The first tannery in Marietta was established by Colonel Ichabod Nye in 1791. It was first located in the north part of the city. The business was afterwards permanently located on the corner of Sixth and Putnam streets, where it was continued till about 1820.

It is impossible even to name all who had previously engaged in this industry. Otis Wheeler was located on Green street, between Third and Fourth as early as 1826. James Furguson converted the Presbyterian church building on Third street below Green into a tannery after it had ceased to be used for the purpose for which it was built. The tannery on Second street near the Duck Creek railroad is an old stand. It was operated by J. H. Dye for twenty years and by him transferred to its present owner Mr. Meiser, and extensive business was estab-

47

lished in 1856, by John C. Fell, located near the Muskingum river. In the year 1862 the property was purchased by C. G. Fell, who continues to carry on the business. This tannery has one hundred vats and when operated to its full capacity, consumes five to eight hundred cords of bark annually. It has a capacity of fifteen hundred sides per annum.

G. Meister owns the largest tannery now operated in Marietta. It is located on Green street at the corporation line. Mr. Meister began in 1861, on a small scale, tanning about twenty-five hides per week. His establishment at present has a capacity of one hundred hides per week and consumes more than seven hundred cords of bark annually. Most of his hides are purchased in the city markets. The business is carried on to such an extent as to belong to the permanent industries of the town.

WOOLLEN MILLS.

For a long time the scheme was cherished by some of the most prudent and far sighted business men, of making Marietta a centre for the manufacture of wool. A trial, lacking nothing so far as investment of capital goes, was finally made by two wealthy companies. The bank accounts of each tell the result. The conditions seemed to promise success. Marietta, with abundant water, good transportation facilities, and located in the centre of an excellent wool producing territory, is apparently peculiarly adapted to this industry. Why, then, the failure? The reasons commonly assigned are, want of practical experience, prejudice throughout the west against home manufactured goods, and overpowering eastern competition.

The manufacture of woollen fabrics, during the period of early settlement, was a tedious and laborious process. The work was at first entirely done by hand. At a later period carding-machines were introduced while the washing, spinning and picking of the wool came under the list of domestic duties. The carding factories had connected with them machines for fulling and pressing the cloth. These factories were found very useful, and one or two were located at every centre of trade.

A factory for working cotton was built at Marietta in 1813, by a joint stock company, of which William Woodbridge, Joseph Holden, and S. P. Hildreth were directors. The building was located on Putnam street, between Fourth and Fifth, and was afterwards converted into the old academy. Dr. Nathan McIntosh and E. S. McIntosh, of Beverly, laid the brick. The property was afterwards purchased by Colonel Ichabod Nye, who carried on the business several years. About the same time Griffin Green built a factory on Fifth street. The machinery of both was run by horse-power.

Another horse power machine was started about 1840, on Third street, below Green, by Joshua Taylor, and at a later period Mr. Hoff engaged in the business on a small scale.

But the enterprise which attracted attention, and from which great results were expected, was undertaken in 1850, by a joint stock company, with a capital of thirty thousand dollars. The lot on the "Point" was purchased in January, and a large three-story brick building erected during the spring and summer. Six sets of the best machinery then in use was purchased, and business was commenced early in 1851, under the management of Robert Crawford and Mr. Fargo. The establishment was run to its full capacity for about two years. During the year 1853 the burden was found too heavy to carry, and operations were suspended. In 1857, Skinner, Rolston & Company purchased the building and machinery, at a cost of fifteen thousand dollars. Confident of being able to make the business a success, this firm put in repairs to the value of ten thousand dollars. The business was conducted for a few years on extensive, and, taking into account the income, on an expensive scale. The enterprise was finally abandoned, and the property, in 1866, sold to A. T. Nye & Son for other purposes.

MARIETTA CHAIR COMPANY.

The Marietta chair factory is the most successful and extensive business enterprise ever located at Marietta. The manufacture of furniture was first extensively engaged in by L. D. Dana and William J. Gray, in 1855, in a building erected for the purpose on the corner of Putnam and Seventh streets, on the site of the main building of the present company's works. The firm of Dana & Gray continued to manufacture furniture until January 18, 1866, when the present incorporated company was formed, with John Mills, president, and A. S. Cooper, secretary and treasurer. When this company took charge of the establishment, it had a capital stock of thirty thousand dollars, seventy-five workmen were employed, and the annual product was seventy-five thousand dollars. The policy of adding the net profits to the capital stock was adopted, and in January, 1874, the company was found to possess a capital of ninety thousand dollars.

On the tenth of February, 1874, a disastrous fire occurred. The entire factory, including machinery and a large quantity of stock, was destroyed; the warehouses alone were saved. The loss was estimated at forty-five thousand dollars, insured for fifteen thousand.

This unfortunate circumstance did not lose to Marietta her most important industry. The company soon began the erection of the large and commodious building now occupied. The plan was designed by John Mills, jr. This structure is excellently adapted to the purpose for which it was built. It is five stories high, and in size one hundred and seventy by fifty-four feet, and is as nearly fire-proof as practicable.

A peculiarity in the method of management is worthy of mention. The company furnishes all the machinery and power. The work is then contracted, the workmen being employed by the contractors. Each department is operated separately, the work passing from one to the other, after an examination by the superintendent.

This factory has built up an excellent reputation. Its products, a general variety of chairs, tables, etc., find a ready market all over the country. The factory proper occupies a floor space of fifty thousand feet; the warehouses, thirty thousand, two hundred and fifty workmen and one hundred caning girls are given regular employ-

ment. The value of the product for the year ending July, 1880, was about two hundred thousand dollars. The officers of the company are: President, John Mills; secretary and superintendent, A. S. Cooper; treasurer, John Mills, jr.; foreman, J. M. Eells; directors, John Mills, John Mills, jr., J. M. Eells, J. W. Stanley and M. D. Follett (for estate of S. Shipman).

MARIETTA IRON WORKS.

A company of which William H. Brown, John G. Stevens, John A. Williams, and B. S. Higley, were the leading members, was formed in 1866, for the purpose of building a rolling-mill. The officers chosen were William H. Brown, president; B. S. Higley, secretary and treasurer; John A. Williams, superintendent. Property was purchased and mills erected in Marietta township, about one mile below Marietta. Operations during the first two years were confined to the manufacture of bar and hoop iron. In 1868 the property was purchased by a new company, composed of William P. Cutler, R. R. Dawes, William H. Brown, B. S. Higley, and J. G. Stevens. Operations were at once enlarged by the addition of a mill for the manufacture of railroad iron, fishplate, and spikes, making the capacity of the entire mill thirty thousand tons per annum. The first officers of this firm were William H. Brown, president; B. S. Higley, secretary. In 1870 R. R. Dawes became president and T. D. Dale secretary and treasurer. From 1868 to 1873 the mills were operated to their full capacity, turning out nearly one million dollars worth of iron per annum, and employing two hundred and fifty men. It was the largest manufacturing industry during these years the county has ever had.

In 1873 a change of officers took place. The firm of Moore, Waters & Co., purchased the property, and in January, 1874, sold to J. A. Warner, who was at the head of a new company known as the Marietta Coke and Iron Company. James McArthur was vice-president and T. D. Dale secretary and treasurer. This company operated the works until 1876, when it succumbed to the general stagnation in the iron trade.

MARIETTA FOUNDRY.

The first movement toward establishing a foundry in Marietta was made by two men from Pittsburgh in 1829—one a Mr. Dobbin, a machinist, the other Larkin McElfresh. They contracted with Mr. Augustus Stone for a lot of ground on the west side of the Muskingum, at the foot of the Lancaster road. They were unable to pay for it, but by the assistance of Colonel Stone and James Whitney they succeeded in borrowing two thousand dollars from the bank of Marietta. With this money they built a foundry room and put up a stack. They commenced manufacturing in the latter part of 1829. But want of means interfered with their success. The property passed into the hands of Colonel Stone and James Whitney. A. T. Nye purchased it from them in 1830, and commenced what has proved to be a permanent business. The building afforded floor room for only five or six molders. The metal was reduced in what was known as a hot-air furnace, which remained in use until about

HISTORY OF WASHINGTON COUNTY, OHIO.

1840. Mr. McElfresh was retained as founder. Mr. Dobbins returned to Pittsburgh. Attention was first given to the manufacture of hollow-ware—dinner-pots, stew-kettles, spiders, dog-irons, grate bars, and cast plows, an article just introduced into the country. Previously the "Hog Nose" and "Bar Shear" were the only plows in use. Mr. Nye purchased of the Woods' Sons the right to manufacture the Jethro's wood cast-iron plow. At this time Marietta was the only place in northeastern Ohio where they were manufactured, and they came into general use in Washington, Athens, Gallia, Meigs, Lawrence, Scioto, and Jackson counties.

The salt makers on the Muskingum had experienced great difficulty in obtaining a clear article of salt. They had been using kettles manufactured at Dillon's furnace on Licking creek. Mr. Nye began the manufacture of salt kettles, using the Scioto county iron, which proved satisfactory, and this branch became a large part of the business. Fulton & Mizer, Clemens & Sherwood, Luther D. Barker, Alexander Simmons, and M. Hook, all extensively engaged in the manufacture of salt, purchased their kettles at the Marietta foundry.

The character of the work of this establishment varied with the wants of the country. In 1832-3 fanning-mill irons were in great demand. The manufacture of seven and nine plate heating stoves began about the same time, also several forms of cooking stoves, all for wood. The manufacture of coal stoves did not begin until about 1856. Castings for mills were also turned out. In 1854, A. T. Nye, jr., was associated in the business and the firm name became A. T. Nye & Son. In 1866 the old woollen mill property on the east side of the Muskingum, near the mouth, was purchased, a molding room was built on Post street, and the following year the business was removed. Stoves and hollow ware have been manufactured almost exclusively during the last five years. During 1880 about eight hundred tons of iron were consumed.

FRANKS' FOUNDRY.

Owen Franks built a foundry and machine shop on Second street in 1840, and engaged in the manufacture of engines, stoves, plows and general machinery. In 1845 boat-building became an important part of the industry. Between 1845 and 1870 about twenty large cotton steamers for the southern rivers were built by Mr. Franks, and supplied with machinery from his foundry. In 1850 the old buildings were removed, and the present commodious three-story shop erected. At present particular attention is given to the manufacture of engines and plows.

STRECKER'S BOILER WORKS.

George Strecker engaged in the manufacture of steam boilers in 1867. His shops located in Harmar, employ twelve men, and involve a capital of ten thousand dollars. Boilers of all kinds are manufactured, and repairing is an important branch of the business.

GAS WORKS.

An act was passed by the Ohio legislature March 6, 1857, incorporating the Marietta Gas company with a capital stock of fifty shares, one hundred dollars each. The incorporators named in the act are Z. Gingre, A. T. Nye, C. B. Hall, J. B. Hoval and A. T. Nye, jr. The first officers were: A. T. Nye, president; C. B. Hull, treasurer; A. T. Nye, jr., secretary. This company constructed the works, and continued to furnish gas at four dollars per thousand cubic feet until the beginning of 1867, when, on the ninth of January, the works passed into the hands of a new company, or rather a reorganization of the old company. The incorporators of the second company were: John Mills, D. C. Skinner, Beman Gates, Charles B. Hall, C. R. Leonard, Samuel Shipman, Thomas F. Jones, A. T. Nye, jr., and William Ward; capital stock, twenty-five thousand dollars. The officers elected were: Samuel Shipman, president; C. K. Leonard, treasurer, and Charles B. Hall, secretary. Colonel John Mills was elected president January 1, 1880. The present (1881) stockholders are: Charles B. Hall, Samuel Shipman, J. R. Waters, M. D. Follett, John Mills, D. C. Skinner, Mrs. C. K. Leonard, Mrs. Charles B. Hall and James K. Hall.

The works are now operated under a ten years lease by Emerson McMillan. Murray McMillan is superintendent. A controlling interest in the stock of the first company was owned by non-residents who dropped out upon the organization of the second company. The works are located on Green street, and mains extend through all the principal streets of the city.

BOOKBINDING.

Bookbinding was first carried on in Marietta by Silas Slocomb in 1835. Mr. Slocomb was at that time engaged in the manufacture and sale of shoes and made bookbinding merely a contingent business. The industry was afterwards for a time connected with the book trade by Crawford & Gurley, J. C. McCoy, and J. C. Glines.

In 1870 G. K. Jenvey was associated with Mr. Glines. The business was owned from 1874 till 1881 by E. R. Alderman and G. K. Jenvey, and conducted under the name of the Marietta bindery. G. K. Jenvey has been proprietor since January, 1881.

LOCK WORKS.

In 1871 a company was organized and buildings erected in Harmar for the purpose of engaging in the manufacture of locks. Of this company C. A. Falkner was president, and Dr. C. C. Warner, secretary and treasurer. The business was seemingly successful for nearly two years. Business was suspended in 1873 with great loss to the stockholders. The property was purchased in 1881 by the firm of W. T. Robinson & Co. at less than one-third the original cost.

BEER MAKING.

The first brewery in Marietta was located on the corner of Sixth and Montgomery streets. It had been occupied in the manufacture of common beer for several years, when, in 1860, B. E. Stoehr began to make lager beer. The brewery on Second, near Washington street, was built by a Mr. Heldt in 1865. It was owned and operated by G. N. Castle till 1869, from whom it passed into the hands of Rapp & Brother in 1869. George Schneider purchased the property in 1879, and has since been operating the establishment to its fullest capacity.

The old brewery on Montgomery street has been standing idle for some time.

BUCKET FACTORIES.

The shops in Harmar now owned by Putnam, Sons & Co., were established in 1850, by Darwin E. Gardner, who purchased land and erected buildings for general manufacturing purposes, in the upper part of the bottom. In 1852 the property was purchased by Putnam, Jewett & Co., and the works enlarged, and wooden-ware made a specialty. The shops came into possession of Pool & Co., in 1856, and during the same year were destroyed by fire, the loss being about thirty-five thousand dollars. The buildings were subsequently rebuilt, and the manufacture of engines became a large part of the business. Since 1864 the firm has been Putnam, Sons & Co. The manufacture of engines has been suspended. Capacity of bucket works, two thousand pieces per day.

MILLS.

Previous to 1811 there were no mills at the mouth of the Muskingum; Marietta and vicinity was dependent upon the mill at Devol's dam, which ground very slowly. Considerable flour was supplied in wet seasons by the mills on Wolf creek. The organization of a company and building of a steam mill at Harmar was, therefore, an important enterprise. This company consisted of David Putnam, William Skinner, Levi Barber, Paul Fearing, Oliver Dodge, and Benjamin J. Gilman. A substantial stone building was erected in 1811. This mill was successfully operated for some time, but after water power had come into effectual use, the ground of competition with water-mills was found unequal. The dividends of the company were small. The property, in 1847, was purchased by the Marietta Bucket company, which was organized that year.

In 1838 John O. Cram built a mill on the east bank of the Muskingum. This mill was successfully conducted by him until his death, 1860. The firm then became Cram & Conley, and in 1865 changed to Conley, Hall & Co. In 1871 Mr. Conley sold his interest to W. L. Rolston, and the firm name became Rolston, Hall & Co. The mill was in the meantime greatly enlarged and improved by the addition of modern machinery. The members of the firm at present are: W. L. Rolston, Joseph E. Hall, C. B. Hall, and James Wilson. The machinery is driven by water power transmitted by a turbine wheel fifty-two inches in diameter. During seasons of high water steam is applied. There are eight run of buhrs, capable of producing three hundred barrels of flour per day. It is chiefly a merchant mill, and employs in all departments twenty men.

The mill on the Muskingum near the foot of Washington street was built by John Wentelker about 1850. After several changes of ownership it passed into the possession of Strauss, Elston & Co., in 1878. This mill has a capacity of about one hundred barrels per day.

In 1853, the firm of Smith, Chapin & Buzzard converted the old saw-mill in Harmar into a grist-mill. This mill is located below the lock and is now owned by Dirk & Co.

There have been saw-mills in Marietta since the year of the first settlement. They were of the kind known as whip-saws, and were very simple in construction and correspondingly slow in operation. The more substantial of the early houses were made of logs sawed to an equal thickness and carefully joined at the corners. Some old buildings made in this way are still standing. Saw-mills, as population increased, became so numerous that it is impossible to mention more than those which became permanent industries.

The Marietta planing-mill, located on Third street below Green, was built in 1850 by a company consisting of J. E. Hall, O. Franks, J. O. Cram, George H. Richards, and R. P. Robinson. J. E. Hall, at different times, bought out the other partners, and now owns the mill. The business, which consists in handling all kinds of lumber and shingles, and manufacturing doors, sash, blinds, etc., was conducted by John and George B. Hall from 1867 till 1876, since by John Hall. About twenty men are employed.

George F. Elston & Co., built a saw-mill at the foot of Sacra Via in 1860. It was purchased by the Marietta Chair company in 1874, and is occupied in general custom work and sawing chair stock. The product for 1880 was thirty-four thousand dollars.

SMALLER MANUFACTURING.

William L. Bay is engaged in the manufacture of wagons, carriages, etc., on Second street. He has a complimentary local and general trade. Kelly & Brother also have a carriage factory on Second street. John Muisenhelder, Wilson & Morse, and Joseph A. Whitehead in Marietta, and W. B. Hollister, of Harmar, are engaged in the manufacture of tombstones and monuments.

BANKS AND BANKING.

Banking, in the early history of Ohio, was greatly disturbed by too much State interference. Banks were considered an important source of revenue, and the several laws regulating their establishment and management were framed with a view to making them profitable institutions to the State. The Bank of Marietta was subject to each of the several laws passed prior to 1845, and a sketch of those laws will give us a glimpse of the inside history of the corporation.

The earliest bank chartered was the Miami Exporting company, of Cincinnati, the bill for which was passed in April, 1803. Banking was with this company a secondary object, its main purpose being to facilitate trade, then much depressed; nor was it till 1808 that the first bank, strictly speaking, was chartered. During the same session the proposition of founding a State bank was considered and reported upon. It resulted in the establishment of the Bank of Chillicothe.

From that time charters were granted to similar institutions up to 1816, when the great banking law was passed, incorporating twelve new banks, extending the charters of old ones, and making the State a party in the

Douglas Putnam

profits and capital of the institutions thus renewed without any advance of means on her part. This was done in the following manner: Each new bank was at the outset to set apart one share in twenty-five for the benefit of the State, without payment, and each bank whose charter was renewed was to create for the State stock in the same proportion. Each bank, new and old, was yearly to set out of its profits a sum which would make, at the time the charter expired, a sum equal to one twenty-fifth of the whole stock, which was to belong to the State, and the dividends coming to the State were to be invested and reinvested until one-sixth of the stock was State property. The last provision was subject to change by·future legislatures.

This interest of the State in her banks continued until 1825, when the law was so amended as to change her stock into a tax of two per cent. upon all dividends made up to that time, and four per cent. on all made thereafter. But before the law of 1816, in February. 1815, Ohio had begun to raise a revenue from her banking institutions by levying upon their dividends a tax of four per cent. This law, however, was made null with the banks which accepted the terms of the law of 1816. After 1825 no change was made until March, 1831, when the tax was increased to five per cent.

Two important acts have since been passed by the legislature, to which we can only refer. In 1839 a law was passed appointing bank commissioners, who were to examine the various institutions and report upon their condition. This inquisition was resisted by some of the banks, and much controversy followed, both in and out of the general assembly.

In 1845 a new system of banking was adopted, embracing both the State bank and its branches and independent banks.

BANK OF MARIETTA.

The first corporation in the State which exercised banking powers exclusively, was chartered February 10, 1808, as the Bank of Marietta. The directors named in the charter were Rufus Putnam, president; Benjamin I. Gilman, William Skinner, Paul Fearing, Dudley Woodbridge, Earl Sproat, and David Putnam. This charter was for the term of ten years.

The bank began business with David Putnam cashier in the stone building on the west bank of the Muskingum river, a short distance above the dam and dock.

In 1813 the bank was moved to the Marietta side of the Muskingum, and occupied a one-story brick building located on the lot on Front street, above the Congregational church, where the residence of Charles R. Rhodes now is. About the time this change was made David Putnam resigned the cashiership, and was succeeded by David S. Chambers, who served in that capacity until 1815, when Alexander Henderson was elected to that position. While Mr. Henderson was cashier occurred the only attempt at bank burglary or robbery in Marietta. An attack was made upon George W. Henderson, a clerk, one dark, rainy night, while he was on his way to the bank to retire. The robber struck a heavy and unexpected blow, but the carrier of the keys was protected to such an extent by an umbrella that a severe stunning was the only result. Mr. Henderson raised the alarm and the robber made his escape.

In 1816 the charter, although not yet having expired, was extended, under the banking act of 1816, to January 1, 1843. Benjamin Putnam became cashier in 1822, and continued to hold the office until his death in 1825. William B. Barnes discharged the duties of the position until Arius Nye, esq., was elected in May, 1826. The bank purchased the lot and commenced the erection of a building on the north corner of Putnam and Front streets in 1831. This building was designed for a banking house and residence for the cashier or other officers. The first vault was constructed in this building, and when the place of business was removed April 1, 1833, from the old building, the first safe was thrown out as a valueless article. This safe, merely a heavy plank chest, barred with iron and secured by a padlock, is now in possession of the Bank of Marietta, and has been, for several years, exhibited as a relic at the Cincinnati expositions. A. T. Nye, who succeeded his brother Arius as cashier in 1838, occupied the residence part of the building from 1833 until it was sold to Joseph Holden. Business was suspended at the expiration of the charter on the first of January, 1843.

The successive presidents of this bank were Rufus Putnam, Benjamin I. Gilman, Dudly Woodbridge, Levi Barker, and John Mills. Of the last named gentleman an old citizen and banker has written: "The name of Colonel John Mills was long and favorably connected with this institution, he having served as president for many years, and in that capacity established the reputation of an honest, liberal and sagacious financier."

THE BANK OF MARIETTA,

a branch of the State Bank of Ohio, was organized and commenced business November 3, 1845, under the name of the Bank of Marietta, with John Mills president and Noah L. Wilson cashier. Business was conducted in the building occupied by the preceding bank for about two years, when the block on the east side of Front street, a few doors north of Green, was purchased and fitted up with a heavy vault and other modern furniture. On December 12, 1848, J. R. Crawford was appointed assistant cashier, and on December 12, 1849, I. R. Waters became clerk. February 4, 1831, I. R. Waters was appointed assistant cashier in place of J. R. Crawford, resigned. February 4, 1857, Noah L. Wilson resigned the cashiership and I. R. Waters was elected to the office. Colonel John Mills continued president until near the close of the charter, when the institution closed its business and gave place to the Marietta National bank, which began business March 14, 1865.

FIRST NATIONAL BANK OF MARIETTA.

Under the act of Congress "to provide a National currency secured by a pledge of United States stocks, and to provide for the circulation and redemption thereof," approved February 25, 1863, articles of association organizing a National bank in Marietta were entered into November 14, 1863.

The First National Bank of Marietta was fixed upon as the name of the association. Fifty thousand dollars was then subscribed as the capital stock of the bank, to be increased (subject to the limitations of the act) to two hundred thousand dollars. On the same day the stockholders (seven in number) proceeded to elect seven directors, as provided in the articles of association. The directors at once elected a president and cashier and appointed a committee to prepare by-laws, to be submitted to the directors at their next meeting.

On the twenty-fifth of the same month the committee reported by-laws, which were adopted. At the same meeting the stockholders were "required to pay fifty per cent of their subscriptions forthwith," which they did and more too, some paying the entire amount. A certificate to the amount paid, and that the necessary provisions of the law preparatory to commencing business had been complied with, was delivered to the comptroller of the currency on the third of December, and that officer, the next day, issued his certificate of authority for the association to commence banking.

The number of the bank on the official list is one hundred and forty-two. The room now (1881) occupied by Adams Express company, on Front street, was rented and fitted up for temporary use during the month of December, 1863, and on the fourth of January, 1864, the bank commenced business there.

The first circulating notes of the bank were received from the comptroller of the currency February 18, 1864. In November, 1864, the building at the corner of Front and Green streets, known as "Holden's corner," was purchased, a plan of alterations and improvements was adopted and committeee appointed to supervise the work of reconstruction and of building a vault for the safes and books of the association. During the summer of 1865 this work was carried on, and early in November of that year, the bank took possession of the new building.

CAPITAL STOCK.

As stated above, the bank commenced business with a capital of fifty thousand dollars. The next month, February, 1864, the directors voted that the capital stock might be increased fifty thousand dollars before the first of the succeeding May. This increase was promptly taken. In May, 1872, another increase of fifty thousand dollars was voted and taken by the then stockholders. The capital has not been changed since the payment of the second increase in July, 1872, but remains at one hundred and fifty thousand dollars. Semi-annual dividends have regularly been paid the stockholders—the one of November, 1880, having been the thirty-fourth since the bank was organized.

DIRECTORS AND OFFICERS.

During the first three years of the bank's existence the number of directors was seven. At the stockholders' meeting in January, 1867, the articles of association were so amended as to reduce the number, and since that time the board has consisted of but five members.

The list of directors (arranged in the order of their election) at this time, January, 1881, is as follows: Beman Gates, M. P. Wells, J. W. Andrews, C. B. Wells, and John Mills. Mr. Gates has been a director from the organization of the bank, also M. P. Wells, except during the year 1865. Mr. Andrews was first elected in 1867. C. B. Wells was elected in 1869, to succeed D. P. Bosworth, who had been a member (except for the year 1866), from the organization of the bank until his death in June, 1869. Colonel Mills was elected in September, 1877, to succeed Silas Slocomb who died the preceding July, after having served in the board ten and a half years. It thus appears that no changes have been made in the board of directors during a period of fourteen years, except to fill two vacancies caused by death.

Mr. Gates has been president from the date of the organization. The first vice-president was John Newton. He was elected in January, 1865, and held the office two years. He was succeeded by M. P. Wells, who still holds the office. William F. Curtis was the first cashier, and held the office through the years 1864 and 1865. Daniel P. Bosworth succeeded Mr. Curtis, and held the office three years—from January, 1866, to January, 1869. Edward R. Dale entered the service of the bank as teller in 1865, was elected assistant cashier in June, 1867, and was promoted to the cashiership as successor to Mr. Bosworth, in January, 1869. He is still cashier. Edward M. Booth was first employed in the bank in November, 1866, as teller. In 1870 he succeeded Mr. Dale as assistant cashier, and yet holds the office.

THE MARIETTA NATIONAL BANK

organized with Douglas Putnam president and I. R. Waters cashier, and began business in the rooms formerly occupied by the Bank of Marietta, on the fourteenth of March, 1865. January 8, 1867, F. E. Pearce was appointed cashier in place of I. R. Waters, resigned. I. R. Waters was elected president in place of Douglas Putnam, resigned, January 18, 1870. F. E. Pearce resigned the cashiership January 31, 1871, and D. G. Mathews was appointed to fill his place. Charles B. Hall became vice-president January 28, 1873, A. B. Waters became cashier August 31, 1875. Business was continued without any change until March 2, 1876. On that date the Marietta National bank, having closed up its business, the

BANK OF MARIETTA

was organized, as a private bank, with I. R. Waters president and A. B. Waters cashier. The business has been continued in the same building, purchased by the Bank of Marietta in 1847. A large fire and burglar proof Hall safe was purchased April 1, 1880. A striking contrast is presented when this heavy iron safe, with massive doors secured by combination and time locks, is compared with the wooden chest of which it is a successor.

BANK OF EXCHANGE.

The firm of Benedict Hall & Co., consisting of George Benedict, Charles B. and John Hall and G. G. Mathews, opened a banking house on Green street, in the Booth building, in 1854. This association closed up its business in March, 1859.

THE BANK OF MARIETTA.

John Newton and W. F. Curtis fitted up the building near the corner of Front and Ohio streets, and opened a bank known as the Bank of Marietta, June 1, 1868. John Newton was president and W. F. Curtis cashier. They continued the business until February 1, 1871, when they disposed of both building and business to a new association known as the

UNION BANK.

This bank, of which Douglas Putnam was president and F. E. Pearce cashier, was organized under the partnership laws of Ohio, in January, 1871. Business was discontinued at the end of the term of partnership—five years.

DIME SAVINGS SOCIETY.

The Dime Savings society was organized in January, 1872, through the efforts of Professor John L. Mills, who has acted as president ever since. The object of the incorporators was to establish an institution which would afford the industrious and frugal opportunities of safe investments of small sums. The general plan is to pay depositors a semiannual dividend on the money invested. W. H. Johnson was the first treasurer. Charles Newton next served in that capacity. He was succeeded by William Holden.

The society began business on the east side of Front street. In 1876 the room on the west side, formerly occupied by the Union bank, was then secured.

OIL BUSINESS.

Petroleum has been an important source of wealth in this county. The two sections where oil has been obtained are on Cow run, in Lawrence township, and at Macksburgh, in Aurelius. Reference is made to the chapters on those towns for a detailed sketch. Seneca oil was, for a number of years before, obtained in Pennsylvania and handled by the firm of Bosworth, Wells & Company, at Marietta. Their first purchase was in 1843, from Hughes' River, West Virginia. This firm handled about two hundred barrels per year, most of their sales being to manufacturers of liniments in larger cities. The "Mustang Liniment" firm was supplied from Marietta.

Since the first oil was produced in this county, in 1860, the total production has been nearly twelve times as much as all the other counties combined. The wells in the Cow Run region were most productive, but then, as at Macksburgh, the supply seems to be exhausted, and the pumps bring to the surface only limited quantities.

The first light crude oil sold in Marietta came from the Hoff farm, on Cow run. It was purchased by William Greenhill, in the summer of 1860. He sent it (ninety barrels) to Zanesville to have it refined.

The first oil refinery was built by M. Hodkinson, on the Muskingum river, just outside the corporation line, in 1861, and was run by Mr. Hodkinson and his sons, and Mr. Greenhill. In 1862, Madison McAllister and William Greenhill started a refinery about two miles above Marietta, on the Newport turnpike. A refinery was started on the corner of Second and Montgomery streets, in 1862, by R. P. Iams and George Hodkinson,

and was afterwards owned by R. P. Iams & Son. William Greenhill and Thomas Hodkinson built a refinery on Third street, between Ohio and Green, in 1863, but the concern was soon declared a nuisance, under the laws of Ohio, and was removed to near the mouth of Little Muskingum, and is the one now owned by O. M. Lovell & Son. William McCarty built a refinery on Green's road, near Fultonburgh, about 1863, which was afterwards removed to the present site, below Harmar, on the Ohio river. The Hodkinson refinery was burned in 1868, and was a severe loss to its owner. W. H. Buell became associated with Mr. Hodkinson in 1868, and their connection continued about four years, during which time the refinery was rebuilt and the business conducted successfully.

The refining business was quite profitable during the early years of the oil business, until about 1868. The panic of 1873 was disastrous to this industry. Failures were the rule rather than the exception. The Standard Oil company, one of the most gigantic monopolies in this country, was formed soon after, and made the blow doubly heavy. The leading railroads of the country were drawn into the Standard monopoly, and private arrangements were made for a rebate on freight rates. To such an extent was this carried that almost all the refiners of this part of the country were compelled to sell or combine with the Standard company, or were broken up.

The Ohio oil works, which is now the largest refinery in this section, having a capacity of twenty-five hundred barrels per week, was established in 1875, by Charles Leonard and George Rice. Mr. Rice purchased the property in 1877, and made extensive improvements. The Argand oil works, an extensive refinery situated one mile below Harmar, was built in 1878, and is owned by R. P. Iams and T. D. Dale. The business has been good for a few years, and refiners are making up for previous losses. The production of crude oil has been decreasing since 1870, and the low price discourages prospecting for new wells.

CHAPTER XXVI.

MARIETTA—NAVIGATION.

Ship-Building in 1800—Commodore Whipple and the St. Clair—List of Sea-going Vessels Built at Marietta Before the Passage of the Embargo Act—The Second Period of Ship-Building—The Barques Muskingum and Marietta—First Steamboat on the Ohio—General Remarks on the River Navigation—Its Advancement—Explosions in Early Years—List of Steamboats Built at Marietta and Harmar—River Improvement Along the Shore of Washington County—Navigation of the Muskingum—The Trip of the Rufus Putnam—First Boat to Marietta After the Slack Water Improvements Were Made.

SHIP-BUILDING.

Curiously enough the energies of the Marietta people in the line of navigation were first directed to the far away ocean. They built ships instead of river boats, and Marietta, two thousand miles from the sea, was made a port of clearance from which barques and brigs, full-rigged and laden with the produce of the country, sailed for foreign ports.

Ship-building was commenced in Marietta in the year 1800, and was a flourishing industry and very beneficial to the village until stopped in 1808 by Jefferson's unwelcome and unjust "embargo act." The first ship built was a small one—a brig—of one hundred and ten tons, named the St. Clair, in honor of the governor of the Northwest Territory. She was built for Charles Greene & Company by Stephen Devol. The St. Clair took a cargo of flour and pork, and in May, 1800, cleared for Havana, Cuba, under the command of Commodore Whipple, a gallant mariner of the Revolution, by whose hand had been fired the first gun at the British upon the ocean. The brig passed the falls of the Ohio in safety, and arrived at New Orleans early in July, where she lay for several days while taking in stores, anchored in the Mississippi, not tying up at the landing on account of the high price charged for that privilege by the Spanish. Before the close of July the St. Clair started for Havana, and Comodore Whipple was again upon the ocean wave with which he had been so familiar in his younger days. The occasion of the old commodore's return to the sea was made the subject of some verses by Captain Jonathan Devol, of Marietta. Neptune and the tritons are supposed to welcome the brave sailor:

"The triton crieth,
'Who cometh now from shore?'
Neptune replieth,
''Tis the old commodore.'
Long has it been since I saw him before.
In the year seventy-five from Columbia he came,
The pride of the Briton on ocean to tame;
And often, too, with his gallant crew
Hath he crossed the belt of ocean blue.
On the Gallic coast
I have seen him tost,
While his thundering cannon lulled my waves
And roused my nymphs from their coral caves,
When he fought for freedom with all his braves
    In the war of the Revolution.

But now he comes from the western woods,
Descending slow with gentle floods,
The pioneer of a might train,
Which commerce brings to my domain.
Up, sons of the wave,
Greet the noble and the brave—
Present your arms unto him.
His grey hair shows
Life's near its close;
Lets pay the honors due him.
Sea maids attend with lute and lyre,
And bring your conches my Triton sons;
A chorus blow to the aged sire
    A welcome to my dominions."

Commodore Whipple was the only man upon the St. Clair on this trip who understood navigation and had he met with accident, incapacitating him for service, the ship would have been at the mercy of the waves. The crew was made up mostly of landsmen. The first and second mates were good common sailors, but not competent to take an observation or ascertain latitude. The St. Clair sailed in safety to the Cuban capital where her

cargo was disposed of at advantageous terms. The money received for the flour and pork being invested in a cargo of sugar, the brig sailed in August for Philadelphia, Commodore Whipple in the meantime having met his son John, an accomplished navigator, whom he engaged as mate. Nearly all of the crew were taken sick with yellow fever before reaching Philadelphia and some of them before leaving the Cuban coast. Several died. The voyage was a remunerative one for the owners and encouraged the enterprising men of Marietta so that they continued building ships and sending them down the river to the sea. The St. Clair, which was the first rigged vessel built upon the Ohio, was sold in Philadelphia and her commander returned to Marietta by land.

The St. Clair was built near the foot of Monroe street, where Charles Greene & Co. established their shipyard. Several others were established about the same time. Benjamin Ives Gilman had one on the Harmar side of the river where the lock works are now located. Edward W. Tupper built ships at the foot of Putnam street on the Marietta side of the Muskingum. Colonel Abner Lord had a shipyard near where the Phœnix mills now stand. Colonel Joseph Barker built several ships and boats about six miles up the Muskingum, among the latter the flotilla engaged by Aaron Burr.

The following is a list of the ships built at Marietta at an early period, together with names of owners and commanders, furnished Colonel Ichabod Nye by James Whitney, Charles Greene & Company's master builder:

Brig St. Clair, 110 tons, Charles Greene & Co., built by Stephen Devol, in 1800, commanded by Commodore Whipple.

Ship Muskingum, built by J. Devol for B. I. Gilman, in 1801, 200 tons, Captain Crandon.

Brig Eliza Green, built by J. Devol for Charles Greene in 1801, 130 tons, Captain Hodgkiss.

Brig Marietta, by J. Whitney for Abner Lord, in 1802, Captain O. Williams, 150 tons.

Brig Dominie, by S. Crispin for D. Woodbridge, jr., 1802, Captain Lattimore, 140 tons.

Schooner Indiana, by J. Barker for E. W. Tupper, in 1802, Captain Merrill, 80 tons.

Brig Mary Avery, by D. Skilinger for G. Avery, 1802, Captain Prentiss, 150 tons.

Ship Temperance, 230 tons, built by James Whitney for A. Lord, in 1804, Captain Williams.

Brig Orlando, built by J. Barker for E. W. Tupper, in 1803, 160 tons, Captain Miner.

Schooner Whitney, built by J. Whitney for A. Lord.

Schooner McGrath, built by J. Whitney, for A. Lord, in 1803, Captains Williams and Wilson, 70 tons.

Brig Ohio, 170 tons, built by J. Devol, for McFarland & Co., in 1804, Captain Rose.

Brig Perseverance, 170 tons, by J. Whitney for B. I. Gilman, in 1805, Captain Wilson.

Ship Rufus King, 300 tons, by J. Whitney for Clark and B. I. Gilman, in 1806, Captain Clark.

Two gun-boats, by T. Vail for E. W. Tupper, in 1806.

Ship Tuscarawas, 320 tons, by W. McGrath,—Marshall S. Jones for A. Lord, 1806.

Ship I. Atkinson, by W. McGrath, for A. Lord, 320 tons, 1806.

Brig Hope, by A. Miller for Charles Greene, 120 tons, 1806.

Ship Francis, copper fastened, 350 tons, by J. Whitney for B. I. Gilman, Captain Wilson, 1807.

Ship Robert Hale, 300 tons, by J. Whitney for B. I. Gilman, Captain Holden, 1807.

Brig Golet, 120 tons, by W. McGrath for A. Lord, Captain Bennet, 1807.

Brig Rufus Putnam, 150 tons, by W. McGrath, Colonel Lord, Captain ——

Schooner Belle, 103 tons, by J. Whitney for Gilman and Woodbridge, Captain Boyle, 1808.

Schooner Maria, by J. Whitney for B. I. Gilman, 70 tons, 1814.

It will be noticed that all but one of the above mentioned boats were built prior to the passage of the embargo act. This was a severe blow to Marietta. Ship-building had become an important industry and employed a large number of men. Three rope-walks were in operation to supply the rigging and cordage for the ships. These, too, were of course suspended by the passage of the act. No other town in the whole country was injured so much in proportion to its size by this measure as Marietta.

Ship-building was not resumed until 1844. In the summer of this year the Marietta Ship company was organized, consisting of John Mills, William and S. Slocomb, Bosworth & Wells, William R. Wells, John O. Cram, and A. T. Nye, and subsequently Nye & Hayward. A shipyard was opened where the Phœnix mills now stand. The company employed Captain Ira Ellis, of Portland, Maine, as master builder, and Captain William R. Wells as superintendent of construction. The first ship built was the Muskingum, launched in January, 1845. She was rigged at Marietta, with the exception of her sails which were made in Boston and sent to New Orleans. She was placed in command of Captain William R. Wells, and on the first of March left Marietta, being towed to Cincinnati, where she took on a load of pork, lard, and oil-cake. From Cincinnati she was towed to New Orleans, and, securing her sails, departed for Liverpool. At the latter place she took a return cargo and sailing for Boston, reached that port in safety and was sold.

In the meantime, the Marietta, the exact counterpart of the Muskingum, had been built by the same company. Captain Wells took her from the mouth of the Mississippi to Boston with a cargo partly from Cincinnati and partly from New Orleans. Not finding a sale for her at Boston, as he had expected to, Captain Wells made two voyages to Cuba and one to Savannah. He then went to Montevideo with a cargo of salt. While there (on shore) he heard the name Muskingum spoken, and turning in the direction of the voice he saw a young man with a spy-glass watching a vessel coming into port. As she neared the harbor Captain Wells saw that it was indeed the Muskingum. She came to anchor by the side of the Marietta, and the sister barques, built at the same yard upon the same draft and measurements (they were each of about two hundred and fifty tons capacity) were thus united in a foreign port.

About the time the Marrietta was built the business of the company was placed in control of A. T. Nye, esq. The brig Waldhoning, of about two hundred and forty tons, was built by the Marietta Ship company in 1847, and left Marietta with Captain Jacob Cram as supercargo, and Captain Conway, of Portland Maine, as navigator. Taking on a load of pork at Madison, Indiana, she went down the Mississippi and to New York. Returning to New Orleans for an other cargo she got back to New York so late that she was quarantined and compelled to

remain outside so long that her cargo was considerably damaged. She was sold at New York.

The company built three schooners—the America and the Grace Darling, for a Mr. Kimball, of Salem, Massachusetts, each about one hundred and thirty tons capacity, and another of about the same size for a Mr. Cochrane of New Orleans.

A. B. and I. R. Waters built, in 1846, the barque John Farnum, their yard being at the point where A. T. Nye's foundry now stands. She was of two hundred and forty-nine tons burden. The John Farnum was launched in February, 1847, and towed to Portsmouth. She there took on a cargo of corn, went down the river and in May, 1847, during the great famine in Ireland, arrived at Cork. From there she returned to Philadelphia and was sold to the firm of Potter, McKeever & Co., of that city. Captain A. B. Waters had charge of the vessel and cargo, and Captain George Hatch was navigator. He was afterwards mayor of Cincinnati. The master builder of the John Farnum was Captain William Knox, of Harmar.

The last ship built in Washington county was one constructed at Little Hocking by a Captain Roberts, of California. She went out in 1866.

OHIO RIVER NAVIGATION.

In 1811 the Orleans, the first steamboat to descend the Ohio, passed Marietta. She was succeeded by the Comet, the Vesuvius, the Enterprise, the Ætna, the Dispatch, the Buffalo, the James Monroe, and in 1816 by the Washington. The Washington was the first boat whose success demonstrated the navigation of the western rivers to be practicable. This boat exploded her boilers near Harmar June 7, 1816. All the men on board except two or three were scalded, and six of them died. One man was blown overboard and drowned. Although several ladies were on board, they escaped without injury. The Washington was afterwards repaired and used in clearing out the Red river raft, and also was run on the river below Louisville. She was worn out in 1822. She was two hundred and twelve tons burthen.

The whole system of river navigation has undergone a vast and radical change since 1827. At that date towing was unknown. Everything was carried on the boat. Once in a while a boat would tow a disabled boat into port, but such things as barges were unheard of. The towing business began in the decade 1830–40. A few coal barges were first towed. Now the largest boats that pass Marietta take three hundred thousand bushels of coal in one tow. The average boat takes from one hundred and forty thousand to one hundred and sixty thousand bushels. This coal is towed from the Monongahela to Louisville for less than two cents a bushel.

An ordinary boat, from 1827 to 1831, was about one hundred feet long, eighteen feet beam, and about six feet hold, very strongly built. When light such a boat would draw from three and a half to four feet, and when loaded about six feet. She would carry from forty to eighty tons. Such a boat would have two boilers about twenty feet long and three feet in diameter.

An ordinary boat of the present date is from two hun-

48

dred to two hundred and thirty-five feet long, about thirty-six feet beam, six feet hold, draws only twenty inches light and about six feet loaded, carries from six hundred to eight hundred tons, and only has about twice the amount of boiler. The speed is very much greater than in the old days, with less steam in proportion to the size and load. The larger boats navigating the Ohio carry from fourteen hundred to eighteen hundred tons, and have less draft when light than the old boats had.

This wonderful increase in carrying capacity is owing to the vast improvements in boat-building, the boats being now made lighter and flat-bottomed. The increase in speed is owing to the great improvements in the machinery, better construction of furnaces, larger wheels, and a better proportioned power, and also to the burning of coal instead of wood. The improvement in the management of boats is also very great. The old habits of reckless intemperance among officers have, in a large measure, died out. Officers are carefully selected.,

The explosion of the Washington in 1816 has already been spoken of. There were quite a number of similar accidents during the early years of river navigation—far more than at present. The steamboat Kanawha exploded at Guyandotte June 24, 1829. This was one of the most serious casualties on the river. Four persons were instantly killed; four more died very shortly after, from injuries sustained, and quite a number of others were seriously hurt. Captain Hiram Burch, of Marietta, one of the pilots, but not at the time on duty, was thrown a considerable distance into the water and badly bruised. Captain Burch in his long experience upon the river met with several other accidents, but by a strange providence escaped death.

The steamboat Tri-color, Captain N. Drown, of Harmar, exploded at Wheeling, April 19, 1831. Captain Drown was killed and also Henry Cherry, Joseph Wortsell, and O. B. Nowland, of Marietta. Eight persons were killed and the same number severely injured.

Washington county was, as we have seen, identified at an early date in navigation and has always been largely interested in it. The boat yards of Harmar and Marietta have furnished a very large number of the boats engaged in the river navigation, as well as some ocean ships. Many a green country boy has started from Marietta for his first sea voyage. In the decade from 1820 to 1830 boat building began and has always been carried on quite extensively. Harmar has been the chief point for boat building in the county. Many boats have been built at Marietta, and a few small ones at other points. As complete a list as can be gotten of the boats built in Marietta and Harmar is here given.

STEAMBOATS BUILT AT HARMAR AND MARIETTA.

The steamer Mechanic, built near Marietta by Mr. Mitchell, owned by Captain Hall and others, 1823.

The steamer Rufus Putnam, built at Marietta for Captains Green and Dodge, 1823.

The steamer Red River, built at Harmar by James Whitney, for Captain Runbell, 1823

The steamer Marietta, built at Harmar by James Whitney, and owned by Whitney and Stone, 1823.

The steamer Muskingum, built at Marietta by ——— Hatch, for J. Rice and others, 1825.

The steamer Cherokee, built at Harmar by J. Whitney, for the contractors at Muscle Shoals, Tennessee, 1826.

The steamer Oregon, built by Captain J. Whitney and owned by himself and others, 1826.

The steamer Herald, built at Harmar by Captain J. Whitney, for Reating and Clark, 1826-27.

The steamer Isabella, built by Captain J. Whitney, owned by Captains Fearing, Green and others, 1826-27.

The steamer Atlantic, built at Harmar, by Captain J. Whitney, for Louisville contractors, 1831.

The steamer Chesapeake, built at Harmar by Captain Whitney, for Reating and Clark, 1831.

The steamer Java, built at Harmar, by Captain J. Whitney, for Captain Fearing and others, 1832.

The steamer Dispatch, built at Harmar by Hook & Knox, for Knox & McKee, 1833.

The steamer Philadelphia, built at Harmar by Hook & Knox, for Captain Dobbin, 1833.

The steamer Josephine, built at Harmar by Hook & Knox, for Captain Dobbin, 1833.

The steamer Tuscumbia, built at Harmar by Hook & Knox, for Captain Dobbin, 1834.

The steamer Hudson, built at Harmar by Hook & Knox, for Captain Dobbin, 1835.

The steamer Baltimore, built at Harmar by Captain William Knox, for Captain Weightman, 1836.

The steamer John Mills, built at Marietta by William Knox, for Captain Bosworth, 1836.

The steamer Stephen Girard, built at Harmar by Captain William Knox, for James Phillips, 1834.

The steamer Baltic, built at Harmar, 1836-37.

The steamer John Hancock, built at Harmar by Captain J. Whitney, for parties not now remembered, 1837.

The steamer Eclipse, built at Harmar by J. W. Whitney for Captain Knowles, 1837.

The steamer Orion, same place, same builder, 1837.

The steamer Isabella, same place, same builder, 1838.

The steamer Ann Calhoun, built at Harmar by Hook & Knox and owned by Columbus George, 1838.

The steamer Victoria, built at Harmar by William Knox and owned by G. Hook, of Mobile, Alabama, 1838.

The steamer Southerner, built at Harmar by William Knox for Charles Barney, of Mobile, Alabama, 1839.

The steamer Zanesville, built at Harmar by Whitney & Sharp, for Mr. Hutchinson and others of Zanesville, 1839.

The steamer Ganesville, same builders, owned by George Parker and others of Ganesville, 1839.

The steamer Elizabeth, built at Harmar by William Knox for Captain Miller, 1842.

The steamer Winfield Scott, built at Marietta by William Knox for Captain A. DeVinney, 1847.

The steamer Yallabusha, same place and same builder as above, owned by ———, 1847.

The steamer Empress, built at Harmar by William Knox for Captain Cox, 1848.

The steamer J. E. Thompson, built at Harmar by William Knox for the engineers on the Muskingum, 1849.

The steamer Little Thunder, same builder, same place, and same owners, 1849.

The steamer Tiber, built at Harmar by William Knox for Washington Kerr, 1850

The steamer Buckeye Belle, same place, same builder, owned by Captain H. Stull, 1850.

The steamer William Knox, built by William Knox, at Harmar, for Mr Chapin and others, 1850.

Ferry steamer for McConnelsville, built by William Knox, 1850.

The steamer Red River, built by William Knox, at Harmar, for Captain O. Franks, 1851.

The steamer Carrier, same place and same builder, owned by H. N. Booth, 1851.

The steamer Edward Manning, same place and builder, owned by Captain E. A. Davis, 1851.

The steamer Ohio No. 2, same place and builder, owned by Captain Blagg, 1855.

The steamer Creole, same place and builder, owned by Captain Hill.

The steamer Skipper, rebuilt by Knox for Captain J. Cram and others, 1857.

Tow boat West Columbia, built by Knox at Harmar, 1857.

The steamer Joseph Holden, built by Knox, at Harmar, for Captain O. Franks, 1858.

The steamer Ohio No. 3, same place and builder, owned by Captain Blagg and others, 1859.

The steamer Fanny McBurney, same place and builder, owned by Captain Drown and others, 1860.

The steamer Ohio Valley, 1862.

Wharf-boat, same place and builder, owned by Hall & Best, 1865.

The steamer J. H. Best, same place and builders, owned by J. H. Best, 1865.

The steamer Rose Franks and barge, same place and builder, owned by Captain Brinker, 1866.

The steamer Satawanee, same place and builder, same owner, 1877.

The steamer Ohio No. 4, same place and builder, owned by Captain Blagg and others, 1868.

The steamer Red Cloud, same place and builder, owned by Captain Brinker, 1868.

The steamer W. P. Thompson, same place and builder, owned by Captain Chancellor and others, 1868.

The steamer Boone, same place, William Knox & Son builders, Captain McClurg and others owners, 1877.

The steamer Oella, same builders as above, owned by Captain Berry, 1877.

The steamer Corner, same builders, owned by the Wheeling & Parkersburgh company, 1877.

The steamer W. F. Curtis, rebuilt by same builders, owned by Captain Brown, 1877.

The steamer Emma Graham, same builders, owned by Captain Williamson, 1877.

The steamer Kitty Nye, same builders, owned by Captain Berry, 1877-80.

Other steamers built during the past four years have been as follows: The Lizzie Cassell and the Mink for Captain Davis; the General H. F. Devol for Captain Martin; the Diurnal for Captain McClure; the J. H. McConnell for Captain S. Davis; the Scotio for Captain Stockdale, and La Belle for Captain Morris.

RIVER IMPROVEMENTS ALONG THE SHORE OF WASHINGTON COUNTY.

Until 1870 Marietta was a very bad landing place. Very few boats could make a landing at Marietta at all. The low water channel was on the Virginia side of the river, and the bar at the mouth of the Muskingum added still more to the difficulty.

A wharf boat was kept out in the river past the middle of the stream, and all the freight was carried to and from it, or else ferried across the Muskingum to and from Harmar.

The channel between the island and the Virginia shore above Marietta was always considered a bad one. The Duck Creek bar was at the head of the island, and the Muskingum bar at the foot. In 1866 the Government began to consider the matter of the improvement of the river in this part. Engineers were sent out, and reported in favor of a dam at the head of the island, shutting up the Ohio side of the river. This would, perhaps, have been best for general navigation, but it would have shut Marietta completely out from all the advantages of the river navigation. The people of Marietta opposed this plan strenuously, and sent a delegation to Washington to urge their interests. They succeeded in getting an order to the engineers to consult the interests of the town. In 1869 it was decided to shut up the Virginia side of the river at the head of the island, and in 1870 the contract for the dam was let to Captain Cole, of Harmar.

After the building of the dam, it was found that the water spread too soon below the island. To remedy this, a dike was built below the island, extending to a point opposite the mouth of the Muskingum. The work was entirely successful, and Marietta has now as good a landing as any place on the river. This work cost altogether forty-five thousand dollars.

There are various other dams and improvements along the shore of Washington county. These are at Blennerhassett's island, Muskingum island, Cole's island, Mill Creek island, Sheets Ripple, Collins Ripple and Petticoat Ripple. These have cost altogether something over one hundred and twenty-five thousand dollars. Nearly all of them have been made by Captain Cole, of Harmar, as have also the large majority of the completed works throughout the whole extent of the river.

NAVIGATION OF THE MUSKINGUM.

The Muskingum valley is very fertile and formerly produced more than it now does. Most of the produce was at an early day brought down the river to Marietta and thence to New Orleans or Cincinnati. Now railroads furnish nearer and easier markets, and very much less is taken down the river. This is the case, although navigation for steamers is now more regular and certain than it used to be.

Prior to 1836 steamers could only go up the river in high water, and had to run the risk of getting fast in the mud somewhere by a sudden fall in the river. Thus steam navigation was very uncertain. But in 1836 the State, at an immense expense, built dams and introduced the slack water system of navigation.[*] Since that time the navigation of the river has been certain and regular.

The Rufus Putnam, the first steamer that ascended the Muskingum river, was built at Marietta by Captain John Green, in 1822 or 1823, for the Ohio river trade. She was what we would now term a small side-wheel boat of sixty tons. At that time it was seldom that the Muskingum river was in such a condition as to admit of the ascent of a steamboat. In January, 1824, in passing up the Ohio, Captain Green found the Muskingum high enough by reason of a freshet to admit of his going up with his boat. He gave notice to the citizens of Marietta of his intention to make the trip, and in a short time his boat was crowded with passengers quite beyond her accommodations. She left Marietta on a Friday of the month of January, 1824. The current of the river was very strong and the progress of the boat very slow. She arrived at Waterford in the evening, between eight and nine o'clock, where several joined the Marietta party. At Luke's Chute the current was so strong that she was obliged to lay by for a considerable portion of the night, but she finally got through.

As no fuel had been provided, the captain had to depend on purchasing fuel on the route. The boat passed McConnelsville about the middle of the day on Saturday, and reached Zanesville about ten o'clock Saturday night. The banks of the river were lined with people,

_____
[*] See chapter on Public Improvements.

who having seen the lights of a steamboat at a distance, and not aware of any cause for the singular appearance, had assembled in uncertainty as to what to expect. The company on the boat were hospitably received, and many were entertained at private houses in Zanesville and Putnam. On Monday the boat made two excursion trips to Duncan's Falls and back, to gratify the desire of the people of Zanesville and Putnam to see her. Monday evening an entertainment was given the passengers and others by Judge Buckingham, of Putnam. Tuesday the boat started on her return trip. The current of the river was so strong that she descended to Marietta in about eight hours.*

The Rufus Putnam was sold by Captain Green into the lower Ohio trade, and was snagged near Port Chiert in 1826.

The first steamer which navigated the Muskingum after the slack-water improvement was made, was the Tuscarawas. She arrived in Marietta September 18, 1841, from Zanesville, and returned the same day.

Among the early boats on the Muskingum were the Zanesville, Dresden, Belle Zane, May Queen, Muskingum Valley, Dan Converse, and Julia Dean.

At a later date were the Emma Graham, Julia, Buckeye Belle, Malta, Viroqua, McIntyre, John Buck, Charlie Bowen, Charlie Potwin, Jonas Powell, J. H. Best, and Carrie Brooks.

The boats now running from Marietta are the Lizzie Cassell and General Devol for the through trade, and the Hubbell and a few smaller ones for the local trade.

CHAPTER XXVII.

MARIETTA—RELIGIOUS HISTORY—THE CHURCHES.

Ohio Company's Measures for the Support of Public Worship—Dr. Story Employed to go to Marietta—First Sermon in the Territory—Dr. Cutler's Preaching—Social Worship—Dr. Daniel Story's Arrival in 1789—Preaching During the Indian War—First Sunday-School—First Church Formed—The Congregational Church, Outline of its History—Pioneer Methodism—First Methodist Sermon in Marietta—The Yankee Circuit Formed—First Camp Meeting—Formation of a Church in Marietta—Its Growth and List of Ministers—First Presbyterian Church—Second Organization Known as First Presbyterian Church of Marietta—Fourth Street Church Organized—Universalist Society—The Early Baptist Church—Baptist Missionaries—Organization at Marietta—Little Muskingum Church—Episcopal Worship—St. Luke's Church—The German Societies—St. Paul's Evangelical—St. Lucas—Methodist—The Second Congregational Society, Marietta Township—St. Mary's Roman Catholic—Congregational Church, Harmar—The Unitarian Society—United Brethren Church—African Methodists—Religious Societies.

THE spirit of Puritan New England is manifested in the many healthy religious societies and handsome church edifices of Marietta. The members of the Ohio company considered religion the handmaid of education, and both essential to human progress. Through the in-

*This account of the trip of the Rufus Putnam up the Muskingum is taken from a statement given by A. T. Nye, esq., of Marietta, who was one of the passengers.

fluence of Rev. Dr. Cutler, who anticipated the difficulty of sustaining religious institutions in the new country, a reservation was incorporated in the land grant setting apart one section in each township for the support of religion, and it is to this reservation that some of the churches now flourishing in Marietta owe their existence.

At the last meeting of the agents of the Ohio company, held in Massachusetts, a resolution instructing the directors "to pay as early attention as possible to the education of youth and the promotion of public worship among the first settlers, and for these important purposes they employ, if practicable, an instructor, eminent for literary accomplishments and the virtue of his character   .   .   .   .   and to enable the directors to carry into execution the intentions expressed in this resolution, the proprietors and others of benevolent and liberal minds are earnestly requested to contribute by voluntary donation to the forming of a fund to be appropriated thereto."

Dr. Manassah Cutler was selected to carry out the instructions of this resolution, and he employed Rev. Daniel Story to go to Marietta as both minister and teacher.

The first sermon preached to white men in the territory now included in the State of Ohio, was delivered on the banks of the Muskingum by Rev. William Beck on the twentieth of July, 1788. His text was: "Now, therefore, if you will obey my voice indeed and keep my covenant, then ye shall be a peculiar treasure unto me above all people for all the earth is mine, and ye shall be unto me a kingdom of priests and an holy nation."

This sermon was preached in the hall of the northwest block-house. In the same hall, on the twenty-fourth of August, Dr. Cutler preached the second sermon ever delivered in the territory. He also preached on the thirty-first of August and seventh of September. Of his meeting on the seventh of September he says in his journal: "Had a very full meeting; many of the people from the Virginia side were present, and most of the gentlemen of the garrison."

Dr. Cutler attended the first funeral in the new settlement on the twenty-seventh of August. Soon after the arrival of the first families in August, General Benjamin Tupper organized social worship in the northwest block-house in Campus Martius, which was mainly conducted by him until the arrival of Rev. Daniel Story in the spring of 1789.

General Tupper was one of the organizers, and had been a deacon of the Congregational church of Chesterfield, Massachusetts.

When Rev. Daniel Story arrived early in 1789, it was determined to establish regular worship at Belpre and Waterford, and an arrangement was made by which the minister was to give about one-third of his time to these two charges. But the Indian war, which broke out in 1791, made it unsafe to leave the garrison, and services at Belpre and Waterford were necessarily suspended until the close of the war in 1795. During the progress of the war meetings were regularly held in the hall of the

northwest block-house, which had been fitted up with seats, and was capable of accommodating about one hundred and seventy-five people. Services were also occasionally held in the large room in the upper story of the frame house in the garrison at the Point. In 1791, soon after the settlers had been gathered within the garrison in consequence of the Indian war, the first Sunday-school north of the Ohio, and the second in America, was organized by Mrs. Mary Lake in the stockade.

Previous to December 6, 1796, there was no organized church in Marietta. The ministers, to whom reference has been made, were all members of the New England Congregational church, as were also most of the worshippers. There is evidence that the Episcopal service was read during the Indian war in one of the block-houses at the stockade, but the number of adherents to the Church of England at that time was very limited.

At a meeting held in Marietta December 4, 1796, to consider the propriety of forming a church, the matter was referred to a committee of three, consisting of Daniel Story, Benjamin Miles, and John Pratt. On the following day the committee reported a confession of faith and covenant, which was unanimously adopted. It was unanimously voted that "anyone who had been a member in regular standing of any regular Congregational church, or Presbyterian church, or of one of the dissenting Protestant churches of England whose sentiment in the fundamental principles of religion and discipline are agreeable to the gospel," should be permitted to sign the confession of faith and covenant.

*THE CONGREGATIONAL CHURCH

was regularly organized in Marietta on the sixth of December, 1796, by persons from Vienna, Virginia, Waterford, Belpre, and Marietta, nine of whom had been soldiers in the Revolutionary army; seventeen of the number were females and fifteen males.

Early in 1797 Rev. Mr. Story returned to Massachusetts. On the fourth of April it was resolved to call two ministers who should serve as pastors for the several churches of the surrounding settlements. At the same meeting Mr. Daniel Story was invited to become pastor. Mr. Story accepted the call on the ninth of April. He was ordained by an ecclesiastical council at Hamilton, Massachusetts, on the fifteenth of August. In this council Rev. Doctor Cutler represented the church at Marietta. Mr. Story took charge of the Marietta church a few months after his ordination and continued to serve as its pastor until the fifteenth of March, 1804, when he tendered his resignation. The financial support received by Mr. Story during his ministry was not sufficient to meet his current expenses, and at the time of his death the proceeds of his property, accumulated previous to leaving New England, proved insufficient to pay the debts incurred while laboring in the new settlement. He died in Marietta December 30, 1804, aged forty-nine years. He was buried in the northwest part of the Mound cemetery. Near the close of Dr. Story's ministry, a number of the

members of the First Religious society* signified their desire to withdraw, for the purpose of forming a Presbyterian church.

On the twenty-seventh of March, 1805, Samuel Prince Robbins, who had supplied the congregation for a short time after the resignation of Dr. Story, was elected to the pastorate of Marietta and neighboring churches. Mr. Robbins was solemnly ordained† in the house on Front street built by Governor Meigs, then in an unfinished condition. This house was used by the congregation for some time after this event. Mr. Robbins preached three Sundays at Marietta and one at Belpre, according to the terms of settlement.

From 1799 to the ordination of Mr. Robbins services were held in the Muskingum academy, which stood on the lot on Front street now occupied by the church.

Mr. Robbins' ministry, which was terminated by his death during the epidemic in 1823, is characterized by two notable events in the history of the church; one was the building of the present house of worship, in 1807, being at that time the finest church edifice in Ohio, and the other was the revival of 1820, which resulted in fifty-eight accessions to the church. The work of building was done under the superintendence of General Rufus Putnam, whose contribution toward its cost was very liberal. The total cost when dedicated, May 28, 1809, was about seven thousand three hundred dollars. The work was done in the best manner for that period. The interior has been repaired several times, but the general structure remains as when built and is apparently little affected by the lapse of seventy-three years.

The epidemic of 1823 greatly impaired the strength of the church. A number of the most substantial members, including the pastor, died, and public worship and the Sunday-school were suspended. From the death of Mr. Robbins till the election of Rev. Erastus Maltby to the pastorate December 9, 1824, the church was supplied by Rev. Mr. Krautz, a minister of the Old School Presbyterian church. Mr. Maltby did not accept the formal call, and how long he continued to supply the pulpit is not definitely known.

Rev. Luther G. Bingham was formally installed as pastor May 3, 1826, by the presbytery of Athens. The church was received under the care of the presbytery of Athens March 29, 1832. The plan of this union had been arranged by the general assembly and general association of Connecticut in 1801. This plan of union provided that congregations composed partly of Presbyterians and partly of Congregationalists might unite for the purpose of sustaining public worship, and the united church might have a voice in the presbytery. Mr. Bingham was ordained by the Presbyterian church and installed by the Presbytery of Athens, in which his church was represented until 1837, when the plan of union was annulled. The connection of the Presbytery of Athens

---

* The following sketch of this church is largely a condensation from a complete history of the church by A. T. Nye, the preparation of which cost him much time and patient labor.

* The name of the business corporation which has charge of the strictly temporal affairs of the church.

† Rev. Joseph Badger, the noted early evangelist of the northern part of the State, made his first and only visit to Washington county on this occasion.

and the Marietta church being terminated, the Congregational churches of Marietta, Harmar and Belpre met in convention and adopted a constitution and assumed the name of Marietta conference. The organization now embraces Marietta, Belpre, Harmar, Hockingport, Coolville, Cow Run, Stanleyville, Cedar Narrows, Cornersville, Lowell and Lawrence. There were large accessions to the church in 1829, 1833 and 1835. Mr. Bingham resigned in 1837. The connection of the church with Marietta college during his ministry will be fully noticed in the history of that institution. During the three years following the resignation of Mr. Bingham the church was supplied by Revs. O. P. Hoyt, F. M. Hopkins, J. H. Linsley, B. M. Palmer, and J. B. Walker. Rev. Thomas Wickes was installed as regular pastor July 28, 1840. He continued to serve the church until March 2, 1869, when he tendered his resignation. During the ministry of Mr. Wickes (in 1866) the church building was repaired at a cost of five thousand dollars. There were also twelve seasons of special religious interest and many additions to the membership.

A special church meeting was held May 2, 1869, at which Rev. Theron H. Hawkes was unanimously elected pastor. Dr. Hawkes was installed October 27, 1869. During the latter part of 1880 the church was repaired at a cost of about twelve hundred dollars.

Since its organization other religious societies have been organized from this church as follows: In 1804 a number were dismissed to the First Presbyterian church; in 1836, twenty-four, to constitute the Congregational church at Belpre; in 1840, twenty-five, for the Congregational church at Harmar; in 1841, nine, for the Old School Presbyterian church at Marietta; in 1843, twelve, for the Congregational church on Little Muskingum; in 1852, five, for Fearing Congregational church; and in 1865, forty-six to form the Fourth Street Presbyterian church. The deacons have been as follows: Dr. Josiah Hart, Dr. Joseph Spencer, Benjamin Mills, Nathan Proctor, Perley Howe, William R. Putnam, Jabez True, John Cotton, Douglass Putnam, William Slocomb, D. H. Buell, A. T. Nye, Dennis Adams, Samuel Shipman, Sala Bosworth, W. A. Fay, G. R. Rosscester, John M. Eells, William R. Putnam, E. B. Reed, T. D. Biscoe, and Asa B. Waters.

The whole number of members since organization is one thousand, five hundred and eighty-nine.

The first Bible society organized in the northwest was formed in this church in 1812, and was known as the Ohio Bible society. Several auxiliary societies were organized and depositories established. After the organization of the American Bible society, it was concluded to abandon the organization here.

As early as 1822 a young men's Bible society was organized mostly by members of the Congregational church. This association has since become the Washington County Bible society and has been the means of much good by distributing Bibles among the poor people of the county.

No Sabbath-school was organized under the auspices of the church until May, 1817, when Mr. Daniel Putnam, of Harmar, who had just returned from New York, determined to establish a Sunday-school in Marietta similar to those he had become acquainted with in the city. The school was opened in the academy, and was under the superintendence of Elisha Hutchinson, at that time principal of the academy. From that time to the present the church has regularly maintained a Sabbath-school. A greater part of the time a library has been kept up. At one time a number of schools in different parts of the town were in existence, but all have been merged into one.

The membership of this, the oldest religious organization, is distinguished for intelligence and refinement. No body of Christians can be found anywhere who worship God more understandingly than these descendants of the founders of the Northwestern Territory. This society is the parent of a sisterhood of churches in and around Marietta, and has always watched over and assisted each in a spirit of maternal affection and Christian charity. The church has faithfully obeyed the injunction of Dr. Manasseh Cutler, delivered to the first pastor on the occasion of his ordination: "To see the many new societies forming in your neighborhood supplied with faithful ministers, must ever be a cause near your heart. It is in every way highly important to them, for it intimately concerns their political and social, as well as their spiritual and eternal interests.

THE METHODIST EPISCOPAL CHURCH.

Methodism, in the early history of Marietta, met with strong and determined opposition. The loud and ardent sermons of the Wesleyan evangelists and missionaries who first travelled the circuits of Ohio were not well received by the more cold and intellectual New Englanders. The journals, autobiographies and letters of these missionaries show that they were not always treated with that kindness and cordiality which Christian charity would seem to demand, but their intolerant sermons, in which the settlers are characterized as deists and unbelievers, excuse in a measure such treatment. In spite of opposition and discouragement, the Methodist church pushed its missionary work with commendable zeal, and has been the means of accomplishing much good.

In 1799 Reese Woolfe, a circuit preacher in Virginia looked across the Ohio river and contemplated with regret a vast territory, with flourishing settlements, on which a Methodist preacher had never set foot. Rev. Robert Manley, who had been his assistant, was sent as a missionary, and on the twentieth of June, 1799, preached the first Methodist sermon in Marietta. He says he "found no place to rest the sole of his foot. There was no Laban to say to an itinerant preacher, 'Come in, thou blessed of the Lord.'" He was disinclined to tear down other denominations, and sought a field of labor in the country. In the towns were Congregational and Presbyterian churches, but the country was destitute of religious instruction. On Duck creek he found Solomon Goss, two members of whose family were Methodists. A number of small classes were founded, and a circuit organized. In 1800 Jesse Stoneman and James Quinn took charge of the circuit, and the church prospered in the country, but little progress was made in Marietta.

The pious and ardent George Atkins was sent to the "Yankee circuit," as it was called by the conference, in 1804. He resolved upon a bold adventure. A camp-meeting was appointed to be held near the stockade in Marietta. Members from the country erected a stand, fixed seats, and pitched their tents. The meeting materially strengthened the church in the country, "but the town people came, looked shy, and walked away." "There were no mighty works in town, by reason of unbelief."*

In 1805 Jacob Young and G. C. Light appointed a second camp-meeting. Jacob Young says:

There was great seriousness throughout the whole congregation and many, both of the country and the town, saw the importance of salvation.

The most prominent convert was Jonas Johnson, who in after years was one of the pillars of the church. He had been an infidel and was a charming singer. His singing made him a useful member during the revival seasons. "A lovely little class was organized in Marietta." For months and years this class met regularly, but suffered all kinds of persecution. The houses were stoned, the windows broken, and the chimneys closed up and the worshippers smoked out. This class was the first regular organization of the church in Marietta. The members were: Henry Fearing, of Harmar, Elijah Francis and wife, William Bell, Samuel Geren and wife, Jonas Johnson and wife, and Solomon Goss and wife. The first class leader was Jonas Johnson. The class or church, as it may now be called, was regularly supplied by the preacher of the Little Kanawha and Muskingum circuit. In 1806 the third camp-meeting was held, in Harmar, conducted by John Sale and Peter Cartwright. Among the converts at this meeting were Joseph Bartlett, John Drown, Christopher Carpenter, Robert McCabe and wife, Mrs. McClintick, Joseph Babcock and wife, James Whitney and wife, Andrew Lake and some of the Protsman family.

In 1809-10 there was a great revival and many were added to the church. But a dissension, which did much injury, seems to have grown out of this revival, some persons of doubtful virtue having been admitted into the membership, who brought reproach upon the whole organization. The enthusiastic little band, however, soon recovered its full powers. Up to about this time meetings had been held at private houses and in the academy. A brick school-house in Harmar was then used by the congregation until 1815, when the church on Second street was built. Meetings were held in Harmar in the old school-house until the present building, known as Crawford chapel, was completed in 1833.

In 1839 the church on Putnam street was built and appropriately named the "Centenary church" in commemoration of the centennial of Methodism.

In 1859 was organized the Whitney chapel congrega-

tion. Marietta and Harmar were made independent stations in 1848.*

In June, 1876, the Centenary and Whitney chapel congregations adopted articles of union and united.

Marietta, previous to 1808, was in the Little Kanawha and Muskingum circuits; from 1808 to 1820 the Marietta circuit; from 1820 to 1826, Marietta station; from 1826 to 1835, Marietta. circuit, which included Harmar till 1848.

About the year 1818 John Stewart, a colored man, was sent as a missionary to the Wyandot Indians. He returned to the conference, held in Marietta in 1822, with four of his Indian converts, John Hicks and Between-the-Logs, and two others. In 1826 the church was very much reduced, and it was doubtful whether an organization could be maintained. James Whitney wrote to the conference, "Send us Leroy Swomstedt or we are gone." Leroy Swomstedt was sent and during the following winter the church was blest with a glorious revival. One hundred and twenty-five members were added, and the congregation was again strong and vigorous. In 1842 the church experienced another great revival, conducted by J. C. Hunter and William Simmons, which resulted in one hundred and eighty seven additions to the membership. The fourth great revival was in 1856 while W. T. Hand was pastor. During that year two hundred and ten new members were received. There was also an extensive revival during the pastorate of A. C. Hurst.

The preachers have been: 1799, Robert Manley; 1803, George Askins; 1804, Jacob Young; 1805, Lowther Taylor, John Gage; 1806, Peter Cartwright; 1807, Solomon Langdon; 1809, John Holmes; 1810, David Young, V. Daniels; 1812; Isaac Quinn, Joseph S. Spahr; 1814, Marcus Lindsley; 1816, Cornelius Spinger; 1817, Thomas A. Morris; 1818, Samuel Hamilton; 1819, Jacob Hooper; 1820, Thurman Bishop; 1821, Abel Robinson; 1822, Cornelius Springer, D. Limerick; 1825, J. W. Kinney; 1826, Leroy Swomstedt; 1828, Samuel Hamilton; 1829, Jacob Young; 1830, J. W. Gilbert; 1831, Joseph Casper; 1832, Nathan Emory; 1833, Adam Poe; 1834, E. D. Roe; 1835, David Lewis; 1836, Azra Brown; 1838, W. P. Strickland; 1840, William Simmons; 1842, Frederick Merrick; 1843, J. S. Grover; 1844, J. W. White; 1845; E. V. Bing; 1846, Uriah Heath; 1847, William Young; 1848, E. M. Boring; 1849, Ansel Brooks; 1850, C. R. Lovel; 1852, J. W. Ross; 1853, J. W. Bush; 1854, T. D. Martindale; 1855, W. T. Hand; 1857, Andrew Carrol; 1858, A. G. Byers; 1859, T. J. N. Simmons; 1860, W. T. Harvey; 1862, H. K. Foster; 1863, C. D. Battelle; 1866, J. T. Miller; 1868, T. J. Ross; 1869, A. C. Hurst; 1872, C. B. Battelle; 1874, S. E. Frampton; 1876, T. H. Monroe; 1877; S. B. Mathews; 1880, G. W. Brown.

The following have been pastors at Harmar: 1848, W. H. Southerland; 1849, C. H. Lawton; 1850, A. M. Lorraine; 1851, C. W. Merrick; 1852, C. D. Mather, 1854, H. T. Magill; 1856, C. H. Frampton; 1857, E. H. Hall; 1859, E. V. Bing; 1861, I. T. King; 1863, T. S. Stivers; 1864, J. E. Sowers; 1866, W. S. Benner;

---

*Samuel Hamilton, in Methodist Magazine, 1830.

1868, T. S. Davis; 1869, R. H. Wallace; 1872, J. M. Weir; 1874, F. A. Spencer; 1876, C. F. Creighton; 1878, W. Abernathy; 1879, J. M. Jameson; 1880, A. T. Hieson,

The pastors of Whitney chapel were: 1859, J. B. Bradrick; 1861, D. H. Moore; 1862, E. M. Kirkham; 1865, M. M. Millenix; 1867, Earl Cranston, Levi Hall; 1868, F. W. Stanley; 1871, J. H. Acton; 1873, J. Van Law; 1875, James Kendall.

PRESBYTERIAN CHURCHES.

Just when the first Presbyterian church in Marietta was organized it is impossible to say. Rev. Stephen Lindley was employed as minister in January, 1804, and the second religious society was organized on the twentieth of that month. It is commonly supposed that the "Second Religious society" was formed of a colony from the "First Religious society," but such was not the case. On the twentieth of February, 1804, thirty-five persons withdrew from the Congregational church and probably joined the Presbyterian, but, as stated, a Presbyterian church had been organized and a pastor employed. January 25, 1813, the legislature incorporated the "First Presbyterian society of Marietta, called the Second Religious society." This must have been a large and vigorous organization. The causes which led to its decay are not known. Mr. Lindley became a chaplain in the War of 1812, and it is not probable that the church had any regular pastor after him. The last ministerial funds were drawn in 1818.

The Religious Meeting-House society, which was formed April 15, 1805, seems to have had some connection with this church. The object of the society was to build "a meeting-house in Marietta to be consecrated and devoted to the public worship of Almighty God." A building was commenced, but never finished. In this building (a large brick on Third street below Green,) Mr. Lindley preached for a time, and some of those most active in forming the society were among those who employed Mr. Lindley in 1804. This effort to establish Presbyterianism was probably felt to be premature, as an attempt was made in November, 1804, to compromise with the First Religious society on a basis which would secure a distinct communion for each congregation. Another attempt was made in 1805 "to unite with other Presbyterian congregations in the support of a pastor."

The second attempt to plant Presbyterianism in Marietta was made in 1841. On the fourth of December a church was organized, consisting of sixteen persons, eleven of whom were received into the communion by letter, and five on profession of faith. The church was organized by William Wallace, who was sent for that purpurpose by the presbytery of Lancaster. The members were Nancy Shepherdson, Angelina Amlin, Sarah Preston, Fanny Plumer, Cornelius Tinkham, Hattie Tinkham, Mercie B. Tinkham, Joshua and Elizabeth Taylor, William Sinclair, Mariam Sinclair, Phœbe Afflack, Eliza Mitchell, William and Martha Hill, and James Kennedy. William Hill and William Sinclair were elected first ruling elders. This church built the house on Third

street now owned by the African Methodist Episcopal church. It was known as the First Presbyterian church of Marietta, and maintained worship at intervals for about twenty years. Beach Grove church, in Newport township, was instituted as a branch of this society, and for a time worship was maintained at both places. The last recorded meeting in Marietta was August 16, 1862. The name was changed from First Presbyterian church of Marietta to Beech Grove Presbyterian church, in 1870.

The incipient action toward the formation of the Fourth Street Presbyterian church was taken at an apparently informal meeting held early in 1865, at which fourteen persons were present. For some time there had been a growing desire for a Presbyterian organization. Those accustomed to the Presbyterian form of government naturally felt somewhat strange in the other churches, and others felt that a Presbyterian church, in addition to being beneficial in a general way, would assist in building up Marietta college. The informal meeting just mentioned led to the appointment of a business meeting on the third of July, which was held at the house of Mrs. Sarah Dawes, and attended by thirteen persons. Of this meeting Silas Slocomb was chairman, and Dr. H. B. Shipman secretary. Action was taken with reference to providing for finances, obtaining a pastor, and procuring a place for worship. Prayer meetings were held regularly in private houses. The record of August 14, 1865, reads: "After the usual prayer meeting a call was made for the purpose of ascertaining the names of all who desired to become members of the new church."

The call was responded to by forty-three persons from the Congregational church and four from other churches, making in all forty-seven. Six new members were added at a subsequent meeting. The young congregation was not only strong in numbers, it was also well possessed of intelligence and pecuniary strength. All felt that there was a demand for the existence of the church, and all were determined that this demand should be supplied.

On Saturday, August 26, 1865, a confession of faith and covenant were adopted. On the following day the fifty-three members assented to the covenant and were then formed into a communion called the Fourth Street Presbyterian Church of Marietta. Rev. W. H. Ballantine presided, and Professor E. B. Andrews and Rev. C. D. Curtis assisted in the ordination ceremonies. This and subsequent meetings were held in the German church on the corner of Fourth and Scammel streets, afterwards the Baptist Mission chapel was used. At the time of the formal organization active preparations for building were in progress.

About the first of October, 1865, the present edifice on Fourth street was commenced, and the first meeting held in it was January 28, 1866, when the dedication services took place. The sermon was preached by the pastor, Rev. W. H. Ballantine. The total cost of the building and ground was about nine thousand dollars.

Mr. Ballantine resigned the pastorate on the last Sabbath in June, 1869. The present and second pastor was installed May 18, 1870. He had supplied the pulpit since October, 1869. The two first elders of the church were Silas Slocomb and Sula Bosworth. The first trustees were Dr. J. D. Cotton, S. Slocomb, S. Newton, R. R. Dawes, and G. H. Eels. Those who have since held the office are Dr. W. H. Brown, Dr. H. B. Shipman, A. B. Waters, S. Bosworth, C. H. Newton, and Henry Hay.

This church has from the first maintained a flourishing Sabbath-school. The average attendance was, the first year, about ninety. It is now nearly two hundred. This church has always taken a prominent part in benevolent work; always contributing liberally to all needy chaities. A Woman's Missionary society has been organized since 1872, and a Young People's Mission band is doing good work. The whole number of members since organization has been three hundred and forty-five; the whole number of dismissions, sixty; the whole number of deaths, eighteen.

THE UNIVERSALIST SOCIETY.

A Universalist society was organized in Marietta in 1817. On the second of February, 1832, the legislature passed an act to incorporate the "First Universalian Religious Library Association, of Marietta." It was the purpose of the society to build up a large collection of valuable miscellaneous books, and to this object the property which annually accrued to the society was appropriated. The more prominent members were Griffin Green, jr., James M. Booth, Stephen Hildreth, A. Pixley, Louis Mixer and Count de Bonny. It is not known just when the society began to hold religious services. The frame church, on Second street, was built in 1842. It was dedicated by J. T. Flanders, who was then regular pastor. One room of this building was fitted for the library, and used for that purpose until the books were destroyed during the flood in April, 1860. In March, 1850, the Western Liberal Institute was established and placed under the care of this church. A further notice of this institution will be found under the proper heading.

The ministers prior to the union with the Unitarian society were: J. T. Flanders, George S. Weaver, T. C. Eaton, Mr. Bartlet, Thomas Barron, Mr. Hicks, J. M. McMasters and J. W. Henley. The church, previous to the destruction of the library, in which the ministerial funds of thirty years had been invested, was in a very flourishing condition. The library contained about three thousand volumes, and many liberal Christians supported the society that they might receive in return the benefits of the library.

The conditions of the union with the Unitarian society, for the purpose of supporting public worship, is more fully treated in our history of that society. The church still exists as a legal body, and holds its property in trust.

A Universalist society was organized in Harmar in 1839, and continued in existence till 1849.

BAPTIST CHURCH.

The Baptist church dates its establishment in Washington county back to 1797. Elder Nehemiah Davis came with his family from Maine to Marietta in 1796. He was a regularly ordained Baptist minister, and preached in the several settlements of the county during the first and second years after his arrival. In 1797, a church was constituted in the Rainbow settlement on the Muskingum, twelve miles above Marietta, through his ministry. It was called the Rainbow church and had a membership scattered all over the territory some distance up and down the Muskingum and on Duck creek. Elder Davis bought land in Adams township and lived on it until 1805, when he moved to Athens county and there died.

Rainbow church prospered and rapidly grew in membership until 1804, when a dissension on the subject of open communion caused a division, most of the congregation embracing the doctrine of open communion. The names of those who held to the established faith were Elder Paul, who became pastor, Joseph Fuller, Mrs. Morris, Ebenezer Nye, Abraham Pugsley, Mr. and Mrs. Tresize and Otheniel Tuttle. This small band kept up its organization a few years but finally became extinct. Elder Davis connected himself with the seceding and larger branch. This branch continued the name of Rainbow Baptist church, and was in existence in 1820, though the name had probably been changed to the Adams church. This body was extinct before 1825, for the record of February 26, 1825, reads: Part of the Adams church, now dissolved, were received into the Marietta church. Several unsuccessful attempts had been made to bring this church back, as Ephraim Emerson expressed it, to the faith of the fathers. These attempts having failed, a few earnest Baptists of the close communion school feeling the necessity of an organization, took the incipient steps towards the establishment of a church at Marietta.

On Saturday, September 5, 1818, Ephraim Emerson, William Churchill, John Thorniley, Bain Posey, and Mary Case, met in the easterly part of Marietta and formed themselves into a church, and adopted articles of faith and covenant. All but one of them, says Professor Atkins, proved faithful to their covenant vows. They have years since passed from their earthly course, passed from the scene of their toil and trial and entered into rest. Let memory embalm their names.

The first communion service was conducted by Elder James McAboy, then pastor of the church of Parkersburgh, West Virginia, October 3d. Ephraim Emerson and William Churchill were chosen deacons, and at the next meeting, held October 17th, "the communion day was fixed on the third Sabbath of alternate months, at which time Rev. James McAboy was requested to attend as pastor." The church was now permanently organized.

For several years the members of this church were scattered over a considerable extent of territory, and services were held in various places both to accommodate members and to awaken an interest among those outside. By glancing through the records it will be seen that church was held "in the school-house at the mouth of Little Muskingum;" "in the school-house up the Little Muskingum;" "at Upper Newport;" "at Lower Newport;" "at Dye's settlement on Cat's creek;" and "candidates were received and baptized at Long Reach, West Virginia." The acts of these early Baptists interpret their zeal. The itinerant services of the early church were attended by all the communicants for miles around, and "some of them made it a point of duty to follow the ark and be present wherever the camp was pitched." No church was more genuinely missionary in spirit. It carried its preaching into every settlement and almost into every house, and laid an extensive foundation on which has since been built the religious home of many of Washington county's best people.

The organization was known as "Marietta church," and the town of Marietta was the natural centre, but meetings were held in the country for the first five years. After Caleb Emerson and wife became members, meetings were held in Marietta frequently at their house. There was no regularity of service, meetings being held wherever convenience or advantage seemed to dictate. Rev. James McAboy, by whom the church was formally constituted, was the first pastor. "For some three years," says the Western Religious Magazine, "Elder McAboy, then resident at Parkersburgh, preached and administered the ordinances of church once in two months. Deacons Emerson and Churchill and others held reading meetings on intervening Sabbaths. In 1821 the pastor began to devote one Sabbath in each month to this church. In 1823 he removed to Marietta and gave three-fourths of his time to the church. In 1821–2 an extensive revival resulted in many accessions to the church. In 1822 and 1823 meetings were interrupted by the devastating epidemics which pervaded the whole territory of the church."

The church, at the close of Elder McAboy's pastorate, November, 1825, had increased to ninety-one members. Most of these lived in the country, and many of them are remembered as founders of the branch organizations now flourishing in various parts of the county. The membership in Marietta was steadily increasing. Admission was obtained from the Parkersburgh association in 1825 to unite with the Meigs Creek association which had just been formed. Mr. McAboy was succeeded by Rev. Jeremiah Dale, who had been a valued laborer within the bounds of the church. It is said of Mr. Dale, "He was a man of fervent Christian spirit, devoted indefatigably to his work, animated with a passion to save souls, and his labors were greatly blessed beyond, as well as within, the territory of the Marietta church, for he set no limit to his field but his power of presence and endurance." The results of his labor at Cats creek and Newport were especially gratifying. Before the close of Mr. Dale's ministry five preaching stations had been organized. It has been truthfully said of this devoted pastor, "He had no home but the back of his horse." He travelled over four hundred miles a month to meet his appointments. Mr. Dale's pastorate, during which over three hundred members were added to the churches under his charge, was terminated by ill health in the summer of 1831. He died September 4, 1831, at Danvers, Massachusetts, his native home, where he had gone in the hope of recovering his strength.

During the next two years Rev. Alfred Dana served the church. Through his ministry the membership was increased and awakened. Rev. Allen Darrow was the next pastor. He resided in Marietta, but served the whole territory of the church except Lowell, which had become by this time an independent station. During the early years of his ministry meetings were held in Marietta in the old and new court houses, in the schoolhouse, in Library hall and in private dwellings. Measures were soon taken, however, for building a house of worship, and with the assistance of the Newport members the former house on Church street was ready for occupancy in April, 1836. That house was destroyed by fire in 1855. The present edifice on Putnam street is in process of erection at the time. Mr. Darrow resigned in 1837 to take charge of the Newport branch, which had been dismissed and made independent that year. By this time the branches had gained sufficient strength to cut loose from the parent stock and maintain an independent existence. Adams had been dismissed five years before. In 1837 Newport, Williamstown and Little Muskingum were constituted new churches. Long Reach church in West Virginia was constituted in 1838. "Six churches from the original one of five numbers."

Marietta church first enjoyed the entire service of a pastor in 1838, when Rev. Hiram Gear was chosen to that office. It was at first found necessary to ask assistance from the home missionary society, which was given or more properly loaned, for it has long since been repaid. The choice of Mr. Gear to the pastorate proved peculiarly fortunate. By his affable manner and strong sermons, he won the friendship and confidence of the citizens. He died February 20, 1843. The citizens testified their regard for him by erecting a monument to his memory.

Eber Crain ministered to the church until August, 1844, when he resigned on account of ill health.

Rev. Ira Corwin was called by the congregation October, 1844, and served until March, 1853. During his ministry the membership steadily increased and a good feeling existed. He resigned in December, 1852, but at the request of the congregation remained until the following March.

In September, 1853, Rev. J. P. Agenbrod accepted a call, and served as pastor two years.

Rev. L. G. Leonard became pastor in September, 1855, and during the following winter the church enjoyed the largest revival in its history. A new era of prosperity dawned which continues to the present time. Mr. Leonard served the church until July, 1863.

Rev. I. N. Carman was ordained pastor in July, 1864, having served the year previous as stated supply. During the winter of 1865 a revival resulted in forty accessions to the church, mostly from the Sunday-school. He added during his pastorate about ninety new members. He resigned in December, 1868.

Rev. J. D. Grieble became pastor in February, 1869. Rev. Mr. Grieble resigned March 10, 1869.

October 11, 1869, Marana Stone, D. D., was called to the pastorate, and served the church in that capacity until the fall of 1873, when he resigned to accept the call of the American Baptist Home Mission society, to hold institutes among the colored preachers of the south. He had been president of the Young Ladies' Baptist institute, at Grandview, and afterwards became president of Leland university, at New Orleans.

Dr. Stone was succeeded by James W. Riddle, who was ordained pastor February 26, 1874. Mr. Riddle resiged September 15, 1878.

George R. Gear, the present pastor, was ordained by a council March 26, 1879. These services were exceptionally interesting. The candidate had been baptized into the church at Marietta, and the ordination was conducted largely by former pastors: Allen Darrow, Cambridge, Ohio, moderator; L. B. Moore, Williamstown, West Virginia, reading of Scriptures; L. G. Leonard, Lebanon, ordination sermon; J. W. Carter, Parkersburgh, ordaining prayer; H. L. Gear, charge to candidate; C. H. Gunter, hand of fellowship.

Two liberal bequests are worthy of special mention in this connection. The following resolution was passed March 3, 1869:

That the following notice of the death of Deacon Thomas Heuton be entered on the record in connection with that portion of his will relating to the church:

"Departed this life, Monday, February 1, 1869, Deacon Thomas Heuton, aged fifty-five years, a man of disposition extremely retiring, loved by all who knew him, of rare beauty of character, and extremely attracted to the church of which he was a pillar and ornament."

The clause of the will relating to the church reads:

To the First Baptist church of Marietta of which I am a member, I give the sum of two thousand dollars, for the promotion of the Christian religion, as the said church or its trustees may deem proper, or the interests and wants of the church may require.

This liberal and unqualified gift was perfectly in harmony with the character of the noble man whose memory the church delights to honor.

September 27, 1871, T. W. Ewart deeded as a gift to the church, the lot on the corner of Fourth and Washington streets, on which was located what is now known as Mission chapel. He had for some time cherished the hope of seeing a second congregation organized, to which it was his purpose to donate this property. The hope was finally abandoned, and the property transferred to the first church.

The liberality of the Baptist congregation during the brightest period of its history, was highly commendable. During the year 1871 the treasurer received for all purposes, seven thousand three hundred and seventeen dollars and five cents, which was disbursed as follows: Church expenses, $4,775.76; Ohio Baptist Educational society, $204.40; association missions, $173.75; home and foreign missions, $528.87; Dennison university, $363; church debt, $1,497.90; the balance to new and weak congregations.

A new bell was purchased in December, 1874, which cost four hundred and seventy-five dollars. The money was raised by entertainments and subscriptions.

The church room was repaired and reseated in 1881.

LITTLE MUSKINGUM CHURCH.

The Little Muskingum Baptist church was dismissed from the Marietta church and organized with its present name in 1837, with twenty-nine members. Rev. A. Darrow served this church in connection with Newport until 1843. Rev. J. D. Riley ministered to this church from that date until August, 1874, with the exception of a year and a half, during which I. M. Winn officiated. J. C. Richardson succeeded Mr. Riley, and remained until 1876, when Mr. Riley again returned, and remained one year.

ST. LUKE'S CHURCH—EPISCOPAL.

Rev. Philander Chase, bishop of the diocese of Ohio, visited Marietta in August, 1820. He says he was well received and treated with kindness and hospitality, and that "a considerable number of persons in town and vicinity of great respectability and worth, expressed themselves sincerely attached to the church." He held two meetings in Marietta and one in Harmar on Wednesday, August 8th, and on the following morning administered the right of confession to seven persons. Incipient steps were taken at this time toward forming a parish by the name of St. Luke's church. The bishop says:

Nothing under the divine blessing seemed wanting to complete the fondest expectations of the promise of primitive Christianity at this place, but the labors of a pious, learned and active missionary for a few years.

In April, 1822, Philander Chase, jr., then a deacon, preached several times in Marietta. In 1825 Judge Arius Nye, a zealous member of the church returned to Marietta, and immediately undertook to effect an organization among the people whose sympathies were with the church. His efforts were rewarded with success, as the following article of association shows:

We, the inhabitants of Marietta and its vicinity, do hereby acknowledge and declare ourselves to be members and adherents of the religious society and parish of St. Luke's, of the Protestant Episcopal church, in the diocese of Ohio at Marietta, and agree to conform to such society and parish, to the constitution and cannons of that church in said diocese.

ARIUS NYE,	JAMES ENGLISH,
BILLY TODD,	A. V. D. JOLIM,
DANIEL H. BUELL,	EDWARD RECTOR.
JOHN K. JOLIM.	

MARIETTA, January 1, 1826.

Judge Arius Nye was appointed by Bishop Chase a lay reader. Mr. Nye kept up the services of the church for seven years until the parish had a rector. At the first meeting of the parish Arius Nye and Joseph Barker were elected wardens; Daniel H. Buell, Billy Todd, Alexander Henderson, Silas Hobby, and Joel Tuttle were appointed vestrymen; James English was first secretary of the parish.

Meetings were occasionally conducted by missionaries in the court house in Marietta, and in the old brick school-house in Harmar. In 1829 the parish had ten communicants. In 1832 Rev. John P. Robinson held services several times in the Congregational church. During that year a Sunday-school was organized and also St. Luke's circle, chiefly missionary in its objects.

Rev. John P. Robinson and J. Delafield were appointed a committee for the purpose of soliciting funds at the east with which to build a church, a parsonage, and to found a parish library.

Mr. Robinson declined the call to become rector, and

toward the latter part of the year Rev. John T. Wheat was elected. On the thirtieth of December the sacrament was administered to fourteen communicants. The success of the committee to solicit aid made it necessary that the church should be incorporated, which was done by act of the legislature on the ninth of January, 1833. Rev. John T. Wheat preached his inaugural sermon on the fourteenth of April, 1833. Active preparations were at once commenced for the building of a church, the corner-stone of which was laid August 20th. On the fifteenth of November the first services were held in the building, and on the seventeenth of October the building was consecrated by Bishop McIlvaine. During the rectorate of Mr. Wheat, which continued until the seventeenth of October, 1836, fifty-five were added to the membership, and when Rev. C. F. Haensel was installed he found fifty-five communicants. Since Mr. Haensel resigned the successive rectors have been: B. J. Bonner, to November, 1842; D. W. Tolfard, to November 19, 1843; Edward Winthrop, to May 24, 1847; D. W. Tolfard, to April 8, 1850; Rev. John Boyd, D. D., the present rector, was elected June 11, 1850. The first parsonage was built during the summer of 1850. Dr. Boyd's rectorship has been long and successful.

The old building soon became inadequate to the wants of the growing congregation, and a handsome new edifice was erected, which was consecrated on the twenty-fourth of September, 1857, by Bishop McIlvaine.

The parsonage was sold in 1862, and the convenient one now occupied by the rector built during that year. Dr. Boyd's continuous clerical service has been longer than any other clergyman in the county. Under his able ministrations the church has become one of the most influential in Marietta.

St. Luke's circle is an organization which deserves no unimportant place in the history of the parish. It was formed in 1832, by the ladies of the parish, for the purposes of promoting social union and replenishing the light treasury of the infant church. Considerable sums have frequently been contributed toward building and furnishing funds, and missionary work has received due attention.

St. Luke's sewing school is another institution of this church which deserves special attention. This society was instituted in 1873, by a number of ladies, for the purpose of teaching the children of poor or indifferent parents the art of sewing. Classes are held every Saturday when they engage in making garments out of material furnished by the society. The product of this work is donated to those in need.

ST. PAUL'S EVANGELICAL.

The first German religious society organized in Marietta and one of the first in Ohio was "St. Paul's Evangelical" connected with the Evangelical synod. About 1833, the German population began to increase quite rapidly.

Those inclined to attend public worship were kindly welcomed by the English churches. Many of them joined the Episcopal church, the service being translated for them. But there was a natural desire for worship in which all could freely participate and feel at home.

St. Paul's church was instituted in September, 1839, by John Lehnhard, Lewis Lehnhard, Jacob Theis and Messrs. Kallenbaugh, Heider and Hartwig. John Hebel joined the church soon afterward. This little congregation of men with their families met in private houses for a time and then procured the court room for regular services. C. Kobler was the first regular pastor. He was installed November 14, 1842. Previously services were conducted by stated supplies, the most prominent of whom were Reverend Mr. Runyer, Francisco Giolini, and A. Swartz. In the absence of a preacher one of the members read a sermon. Mr. Kobler filled the office of pastor about one year. During the next five years the church was very unfortunate in procuring ministers. Regularly ordained and pious clergymen of the denomination were scarce in the west and this unfortunate circumstance opened the way for imposters. Early in 1847, Dr. J. E. Freygang was installed as pastor. His ministery continued until August 24, 1848, when Jacob Mosbach was installed. The church had increased in numbers very rapidly and the members felt the need of a house of worship. Money for that purpose was raised by subscription and the work of building began in the summer of 1849. Just before the building was completed a change of pastors was deemed advisable, and Rev. Mr. Doener was elected to succeed. About the first of January, 1850, the new church was dedicated, the services being conducted by the pastor, assisted by Prof. George Rosscester, of Marietta college. The building cost about one thousand dollars and the lot about two hundred dollars.

The next pastor was Rev. Mr. Kress, who took charge early in 1853. A very sad circumstance is connected with Mr. Kress' life at Marietta. While he was coming from Zanesville on a boat, his daughter took sick and died. Her body was interred in Marietta cemetery. About a year after he had moved here, his son was accidentally drowned in the Muskingum. These two sad events, so closely connected, greatly affected Mr. Kress, and induced him to ask to be released from pastoral duties.

John H. Schienbeck was installed as pastor in November, 1857, and supplied the congregation till December, when D. Schultz succeeded, who was followed, in 1864, by one of the most eminent scholars in the church, Dr. Ruddolph. Dr. Ruddolph was a German by birth and education, and had for a number of years been chaplain of the Duke of Sax Weimar.

The remaining pastors have been: William F. Conner, from January, 1866, to August 15, 1868. G. Freidrigh, from September, 1868, to December, 1871. G. Geopken, from January 1, 1872, to January 1, 1879. Victor Broesel, from January 1, 1879, to the present.

The present membership is forty-five families. About one hundred families attend and assist in supporting this church. A Sunday-school was organized in 1848, and has been maintained since. The church is now in a very flourishing condition and the services of the sanctuary are well attended, there being usually about three hundred people present.

THOMAS W. EWART, LL. D.

Judge Thomas W. Ewart, the only son of Robert Kells Ewart and his wife, Mary Cochran, was born in Grand View township, Washington county, Ohio, on the twenty-seventh of February, A. D. 1816. On the paternal side he was of Scotch-Irish descent, his grandfather having come direct from the north of Ireland to western Pennsylvania, where he lived until the time of his death. After his death the family moved to Fishing Creek, near New Martinsville, West Virginia. R. K. Ewart was married to Mary Cochran in Tyler county, West Virginia, her home, about the year 1815, and the couple removed to Grand View township, Washington county, Ohio, in 1816, where the subject of this sketch was born on his father's farm. He was a delicate child, but attended school as regularly as his feeble constitution would permit, and proved to be a bright scholar, quick to learn and of retentive memory.

When about fifteen years of age an opportunity was afforded him of coming to Marietta and obtaining a business education. As his lack of physical strength seemed to unfit him for the arduous labor of farm life, and he had already about reached the limit of school advantages afforded by a country school of that day, his parents thought it best that he should improve the opportunity that was extended to him through the kindness of a friend in whom they had the utmost confidence. Accordingly at fifteen years of age he came to Marietta and entered the office of the county clerk, George Dunlevy, esq. Here he soon proved to be a very efficient deputy, winning high favor from the members of the bar, with whom he became very popular. When, a few years afterward, Mr. Dunlevy died, Mr. Ewart, who had then just attained the legal age, was appointed October 31, 1836, to the position of county clerk. His efficiency as an officer is sufficiently attested by the fact that he was continued by successive reappointments in the office for the next fifteen years.

Mr. Ewart early took an active interest in political affairs. He was identified with the Whig party, and for several years held the position of chairman of the county central committee in that party. After the rise of the Republican party he became identified with that organization, and continued to take an active part in politics, making frequent speeches in political campaigns. In 1850 he was elected a member of the Constitutional convention which formed our present State constitution, representing the senatorial district composed of Washington and Morgan counties. Hon. William P. Cutler was the other member from this county. Mr. Ewart was one of the youngest members of that body, and naturally did not take a very prominent part in its debates, although in all questions that came before it he took pains carefully to inform himself, that he might vote intelligently. The constitution provided for the organization of a new tribunal called the probate court. Before he reached home his party had nominated him for probate judge. He was elected to that office in February, 1852, but he resigned after holding the office about seven months, in order that he might enter upon the practice of law.

While in attendance upon the Constitutional convention at Cincinnati, he was admitted to the bar. He entered into a law partnership with Colonel Melvin Clarke, in October, 1852, and the new firm soon won a prominent position at the bar. Other partnerships at a later date were formed with Judge William B. Loomis, Captain R. K. Shaw, H. L. Gear, Captain H. L. Sibley, and his son, Thomas Ewart.

As a lawyer Mr. Ewart was distinguished for the thoroughness with which he prepared his cases, his ability in seizing the governing principles of his cases, and the energy and tenacity with which he advocated the cause of his client. His grasp of legal principles was comprehensive, and his presentation of facts skilful. He was honorable in his dealing with opponents, and firmly believed that the proper function of the lawyer was not "to make the worse appear the better reason," but fairly to represent the interests of his client.

He did not seek to encourage litigation; and was careful in entering upon causes to take those only in which there was, in his opinion, a real wrong to be righted, but when a case was once committed to his hands, he pushed it with all his energy.

For the last twenty five years he has usually represented one side or the other of almost every important civil cause, involving large amounts of money, or prominent business interests, tried in this county; and in such employment has uniformly acted with marked fidelity and ability. And during later years he has had considerable practice in neighboring counties in this State and West Virginia as well as in the Federal and Supreme courts of Ohio and Illinois.

The estimation in which his legal ability was held by others is made evident by the fact that in February, 1865, when a vacancy occurred in the office of judge of the court of common pleas in this district by the elevation of Judge John Welch to the supreme bench, the governor of Ohio tendered him the office thus made vacant. His business interests were such then as to forbid the acceptance of the appointment.

Mr. Ewart seriously felt the lack of a thorough collegiate education. While a young man in the office of county clerk, he entered upon a private course of study, devoting attention to mathematics, history, moral science and other branches. He was always a thoughtful reader and observer, and such a degree of intellectual culture did he reach by self-education, that in 1878 Denison University conferred upon him the title of Doctor of Laws. He was kind, social and affectionate in his family relations, and gave his children the fullest opportunities for thorough education.

In public business enterprises Mr. Ewart bore a prominent part. He was at various times identified with, as director and legal adviser, the old Marietta bank, the Marietta National bank, the Union Bank of Marietta, the Noble County bank, the Marietta Chair company, and the Marietta, Pittsburgh & Cleveland Railway company.

He was a public spirited man, and any enterprise which would result in the welfare of the community, was sure to have from him sympathy and support.

In religious life Mr. Ewart was very active. In early life, before he became of age, he became a Christian, and united with the Baptist church. At that time, there was no church of that denomination in the city, and he went to various points in the country, where meetings were held, walking several miles for the purpose. He was afterwards largely instrumental in the organization of a Baptist church in Marietta, and in the erection of a church building. He was always a very generous contributor to all benevolent enterprises. His sympathies were broad, taking in all worthy interests both at home and abroad. He was a staunch friend of Denison University at Granville, Ohio, and for upwards of twenty years one of its trustees. He took a great interest in Sabbath school work, frequently visiting different parts of the county, in the interest of Sabbath school extension. For thirty years he was superintendent of the Sabbath school of the First Baptist church of Marietta. Probably no man in Washington county has done more to promote Sabbath schools than Judge Ewart. In denominational interests he was active. For a period of about twenty years he was presiding officer of what is now known as the Marietta Baptist association, and he was ever on the alert to foster feeble churches in that association, and aid them in the erection of houses of worship. He acted one time as president of the State association of Baptists, and was for a time vice-president of the United States association of Baptists known as the Missionary union, presiding at one or two of their annual meetings.

In temperance work he bore a prominent part, being everywhere known as an uncompromising foe of the traffic in intoxicating liquors. His earnestness in this direction gained for him the bitter enmity of some whose interests were thus assailed, but this did not serve to deter him from advocating what he believed to be right.

Mr. Ewart took pleasure in speaking words of encouragement, and in giving practical assistance to worthy young men, whom he saw struggling with difficulty, and more than one remembers gratefully the help which he has thus received.

In 1838 he married Grace Dana, af Newport, by whom he had six children, four of whom still survive. She died in 1854. His second wife was Jerusha Gear, whom he married in 1855. By her he had six children, who are all living.

At one time Mr. Ewart was the possessor of a considerable amount of property, but the failure of men, for whom he had endorsed, and the general financial stringency of the past few years, swept away his posessions. Under an accumulation of troubles, his health failed and he has removed to Granville, Ohio, with his family, but leaving many warm friends in Washington county.

A very important crisis in the history of the church occurred in 1857. Z. E. Zobel, who had been pastor since 1854, was not giving satisfaction to the whole church. An effort to dismiss him led to a division and the organization of St. Lucas church, in the fall of 1857, with Mr. Zobel as pastor.

ST. LUCAS CHURCH.

The division in St. Paul's church, already spoken of, was the result partly of a difference of opinion on the question of church government, and partly of a local dissension among the members. A large portion of the membership was averse to synodical rule, and felt a desire for a society which should be congregational in its government and liberal in its doctrines. A dissension on a matter of church policy stimulated those who entertained this desire to organized action. Early in 1858, about forty persons held a meeting and organized St. Lucas Evangelical church. The exact date of this meeting is not known. The building on the corner of Fourth and Scammel streets, now used by this congregation, was purchased January 25, 1858, from the Protestant Episcopal church, at a cost of one thousand five hundred dollars. At a meeting held January 31, 1858, the following officers were elected: President, Jacob Grossclas; secretary, Daniel Hashler; treasurer, John Kuntz; trustees, John Pfaff, Henry Zisler, Peter Schlicher, John Peters, Jacob Hennerman and Jacob Lorenz. Of these first officers only three are now living—Peter Schlicher, Jacob Henman and Jacob Lorenz.

The church was inaugurated on the ninth of February by E. L. Zobel, the first pastor.

A neat parsonage was built in 1869 and an organ placed in the church in 1873. A Sunday-school was organized at the formal institution of the church and now numbers more than one hundred and fifty scholars and twenty teachers.

The ministers have been as follows: E. L. Zobel, Mr. Morsebach, Mr. Scipel, Mr. Fleicher, Mr. Gleischer, Mr. Arnold, Mr. Brickner, C. Moser, Jacob Bloss, Mr. Carmacher, Mr. Alech, M. Herberg, and Mr. Fritze.

The membership of this church is composed of enterprising and highly moral citizens. They are sincerely laboring for the advancement of Christian doctrine and Christian morality. The large band of faithful Sunday-school workers is an index of their zeal, while the character and every-day life of the members is an evidence of the good work being done.

GERMAN METHODIST CHURCH.

This church was formally organized in 1842, although meetings were held before that time. Paul Bodbeck was largely instrumental in instituting regular worship, and probably served as first pastor. The records of the early church are not complete, and therefore an accurate account of the organization cannot be obtained. The congregation purchased from the trustees of the Centenary church the house on Second street, until 1839 occupied by the Methodist congregation. This building was used until the new church on the corner of Fourth and Wooster was completed in 1877.

This congregation is now in a very flourishing condition. The membership numbers about one hundred and twenty-five. A Sunday-school has been maintained since soon after the organization of the church, and has a membership of about one hundred and fifty and a library of four hundred volumes.

SECOND CONGREGATIONAL CHURCH.

The Second Congregational church of Marietta township was organized March 3, 1859, by Rev. V. G. Fry. During the summer of 1858 Mr. Fry had been preaching at the Presbyterian church, Cedar Narrows Congregational church, Stanleyville and Lynch Methodist church. Upon invitation he included school district No. 8, Marietta township, in his appointments. In February, 1859, a protracted meeting was held in this church which resulted in the formation of the society with twenty-four members, twenty-one by profession and three by letter.

Mr. Fry acted as pastor until 1863, but having a wide field his visits were necessarily infrequent. Rev. John Noble was associated in the pastorate in 1873, and this church was supplied once each Sabbath. Mr. Noble was soon forced by ill health to resign the charge, and at the close of the year Mr. Fry accepted a call to Lexington, Ohio, and the society was left without a pastor. Up to this time there had been eleven additions to the membership. During 1864 and 1865 Rev. L. L. Fay and Professor J. L. Mills preached occasionally. During 1866 Professor Mills preached regularly. During 1867 there was no pastor and the society maintained a doubtful existence. In the winter of 1868 Rev. George Athey, of the United Brethren church, held an awakening revival in which the members of the Congregational church joined. A flourishing United Brethren class was organized, and both bodies worked together for nearly a year, when the United Brethren removed their services to Jenning's school-house, where they cultivated a much neglected field. Mr. J. H. Jenkins, then tutor in the college, preached for the second church once each Sabbath until 1872 when G. W. Wells became regular pastor in connection with the Little Muskingum church and served until 1876. He was succeeded by Rev. Eugene S. Reed, who remained until 1880, when Mr. Wells was recalled.

A comfortable frame church was built in 1869. A Sunday-school has been maintained during the summer months, since the date of its organization. The membership at the close of 1880 was seventy.

ST. MARY'S CATHOLIC CHURCH.

Prior to 1838 the Catholics in and around Marietta were attended by missionaries and priests from other places. In that year Rev. James McCaffrey was stationed in Marietta, and ministered to the communicants in all the neighboring towns. During the pastorate of Mr. McCaffrey the church was placed on a solid financial basis by the generous donation of a house and lot on Fourth street by Mrs. Mary Brophy. The house was a two-story brick, the first story of which was used as a church and the second story as the pastoral residence until 1850, when the new church, which had been in process of erection for about three years, was completed. The new church was built just above the old one on the same lot. The old building has since been removed. Rev. James McCaffrey remained in charge until June, 1849, when he was succeeded by Rev. Robert J. Lawrence, who in time was succeeded in April, 1850, by Rev. Peter Perry. During Mr. Perry's administration, which continued until October, 1855, it was found necessary to have more room to accommodate the increasing congregation, and the new church was commenced.

Rev. R. B. Hardey was the next pastor. He remained till May, 1857, when Rev. A. O. Walker took charge. Mr. Walker took upon himself the burden of freeing the church from the debt incurred by building. He visited many of the neighboring churches and solicited help. Not only enough money was procured to pay the debt but also enough to erect the main altar.

Rev. M. J Ryan succeeded to the partorate in May, 1862, and discharged the several duties of the office until his death, which occurred in July, 1869.

Rev. C. F. Schellamer, who was next appointed to the Marietta charge, had the church frescoed and stained glass put in the windows. In October, 1875, he was succeeded by Rev. Peter Thurheimer whose ministrations continued till September, 1878, when Rev. F. P. Campbell was appointed. In November, 1879, the present pastor, Rev. John B. Kuehn took charge of the congregation. He has arranged for the finishing of the tower and the purchase of a bell.

The church owns two city lots on Fourth street, below Green, on which the church edifice and parsonage stand, and a cemetery in the south part of the city. Until 1868 Marietta was in the diocese of Cincinnati; since that time it has been in the diocese of Columbus.

CONGREGATIONAL CHURCH—HARMAR.

On the first of January, 1840, thirty-seven persons met in the town hall in Harmar, and organized the Congregational church of Harmar. Twenty-five of the number were from the Congregational church of Marietta, nine from other churches and one was received on public profession. The meeting was conducted by Rev. J. H. Linsley, D. D., then president of Marietta college. He was assisted by Rev. D. Walker. A confession of faith and covenant, which are liberal and at the same time evangelical in doctrine, had been prepared by Dr. Linsley and were adopted at this meeting.

The ladies of the Congregational church of Marietta generously made a donation for the purchase of a communion set for the new church. During the first year there were nine accessions to the membership, five by letter and four on profession. Milo J. Hickok, a graduate of Middlebury college, Vermont, and Union Theological seminary, New York, was installed and ordained first pastor, on the fourth of May, 1842. The church had been supplied during the greater part of 1840 by Dr. Linsley and for a few months in 1841 by Rev. S. P. Robbins, son of the second pastor of the church in Marietta. The services attending the ordination of Mr.

Hickok were held in the Methodist church at Harmar, and were very interesting and impressive. The introductory prayer was made by Dr. Linsley, one of the founders of the church; the sermon by Rev. Henry Smith, D. D., of Marietta college; the ordaining prayer by Rev. Dyer Burgess; charge to the pastor by Dr. Linsley; right hand of fellowship by Rev. Thomas Wickes, of the Congregational church of Marietta; charge to the people by Dr. Kingsbury; concluding prayer by Rev. Hiram Gear, of the Baptist church.

Mr. Hickok was dismissed at his own request April 8, 1844. He afterwards became pastor of the church at Rochester, New York, where he received the degree of D. D., and later became a citizen of Marietta.

After the resignation of Mr. Hickok the pulpit was supplied for over a year by members of the college faculty.

Rev. Gideon Dana, after having served as stated supply for about two years was ordained second regular pastor October 20, 1847. The present church was built during the summer of 1847 on a lot donated by Mr. David Putnam, sr. It was dedicated November 27th, the services being conducted by the pastor and Rev. Dr. Wickes. The first Sabbath services were held in the church on the following day. During the winter of 1847–8 a series of concerts were given by a quartette of young men—Chandler Robbins, Horace Norton, G. H. Barbour and N. K. Beosley—and the proceeds given in the spring of 1848 for the purchase of a bell. Mr. Dana remained pastor until March 1, 1850, when he resigned.

Rev. David Gould supplied the pulpit till March 13, 1851, when a call was extended him, which he accepted. He was installed May 28, 1851, the installation sermon being preached by Rev. Thomas Wickes. Mr. Gould tendered his resignation May 11, 1854, on account of ill health, but his pastorate had been so entirely satisfactory to the congregation that his resignation was not accepted, but he was released from pastoral duties until January 1, 1855. The resignation was renewed in December, and accepted January 16th, with a resolution of regret.

Rev. William Wickefield was elected pastor January 22, 1855. Mr. Wickefield assumed the pastoral duties in April, and continued to serve the congregation with great acceptation until February 9, 1872, when he resigned. During his pastorate the church (in 1868) was repaired and refitted, and improved generally, at an expense of four thousand five hundred dollars, about half of which was paid by a single individual. The church is now one of the most comfortable in Washington county.

After the resignation of Mr. Wickefield, Professor J. L. Wells acted as supply until Rev. J. H. Jenkins became permanent supply in November, 1872. Mr. Jenkins was elected pastor January 8, 1873, and installed on the second of June. This church has been blessed with an abundant prosperity ever since its organization. The membership has steadily increased until there are at present about two hundred names on the roll. The whole number received since organization is four hundred and ninety. Since the present pastor took charge, one hundred and sixty-seven have been added to the membership.

To omit to mention the generous contributions of this church to the various causes of Christian beneficence, would be inexcusable. It is not possible to give anything like exact figures, for much has been given of which no record has been kept. Mr. Wickefield said in his sermon commemorative of the twentieth anniversary of the church: "Enough is known to make it safe to say that, including what has been expended in support of the Gospel at home, and the free will gifts for the causes of Christian benevolence and Christian education, the church has been enabled to devote to religious and benevolent purposes, during the twenty years, more than fifty thousand dollars." Enough is known to make it safe to say that that amount has been quadrupled during the second twenty years of the existence of the organization. One of the munificent acts of the man who has been deacon from the organization, and was clerk nearly thirty-five years, demands special mention. On New Year, 1869, as a free will offering, he annulled all outstanding bills, amounting to one thousand three hundred dollars. He had previously contributed toward improvements on the church about two thousand three hundred dollars, making in all a contribution of four thousand six hundred dollars for one year.

The deacons of the church since its organization have been Douglas Putnam, Daniel P. Bosworth, Seth Hart, Stephen Newton, Rotheus Hayward, Samuel Langbridge, George H. Ford, R. B. Hart, and C. M. Cole.

THE UNITARIAN SOCIETY.

If not among the first, at least among the early settlers of Marietta, there were some who held to the doctrine of Unitarianism. Peter Cartwright, the ardent Methodist evangelist, mentions with dismay the progress which "Universalism, Unitarianism and Liberalism" had made among the Yankee settlers as early as 1806.

On the twentieth of January, 1855, Nahum Ward, a wealthy and influential citizen, made a call through the *Marietta Intelligencer*, for a meeting of all who believed in the worship of God in unity, not in trinity, to meet at the court house February 3d, for the purpose of organizing a Unitarian, liberal, rational, religious society. In accordance with Mr. Ward's call a few friends met, and organized the First Unitarian society of Marietta. A basis of organization was adopted, of which the following is the cardinal principle:

Believing in the unity, and in the paternal character and merciful government of God; in man's natural capacity of virtue, and liability to sin; in the supernatural authority of Jesus Christ as a teacher sent from God; in his divine mission as a Redeemer; in his moral perfection as an example; in the remedial as well as retributive office and intention of divine punishments; in the soul's immediate ascension on release from the body to its account and reward; and that salvation rests not on superficial observance of rites, or on intellectual assent to creeds, or on any arbitrary decree, but under the grace of God on the rightness of the ruling affection, on humble faithfulness of life, and on integral goodness of character.

At this meeting Nahum Ward, William S. Ward and John C. McCoy were elected trustees. At a meeting

held January 9, 1858, R. D. Burr was elected first instructor of divine truth. The church edifice was erected entirely at the expense of Nahum Ward. The first corner-stone was laid July 2, 1855. The dedication services took place June 4, 1857. This church, situated at the corner of Third and Putnam streets, is one of the finest public buildings in Marietta.

In the spring of 1869 a successful movement was set on foot for uniting the First Unitarian society and the First Universalist church into one society to be known as the First Unitarian society, each of the separate churches, however, to preserve an independent existence. This union was permanently effected on the eighteenth of May, 1869. Since that date public worship has been supported by the united society. Each church yet preserves its identity, and each has its own organization as a church, the society being only a business organization, by which the union worship of the two churches is supported. The ministers supported by the First Unitarian society since its organization, have been: R. D. Burr, William L. Gage, E. C. Gild, T. J. Mumford, F. M. Holland and W. C. Finney before the union, and J. R. Johnson, T. S. Thatcher and J. T. Lusk since the union.

THE UNITED BRETHREN CHURCH.

This church was organized with a membership of about ninety, sometime during the winter of 1857. In the early part of that winter a series of protracted meetings were commenced by a preacher of the Wesleyan Methodist church in a mission meeting-house belonging to the Centenary church, in the part of town known as Texas. After these meetings had progressed some time under the direction of the Rev. Mr. Jones, the Wesleyan evangelist, a United Brethren preacher named Ciscel began to assist at the meetings. Under the efficient labor of these two brethren working in harmony, one of the greatest revivals ever known in Marietta, was started.

This revival did not conclude until more than one hundred had professed conversion, and expressed a desire to unite with the church. It was deemed advisable by the converts and others who had taken part in these meetings to organize a church of their own, and a vote was taken to decide with what denomination it should be connected. The vote showed a decided partiality for the United Brethren, and the conference at its next meeting formally received the new organization as the United Brethren church of Marietta. The Texas church was used for a house of worship until 1866, when the frame building on Fourth street, north of Green, was built. In 1879, the trustees of the church sold this building for a school-house and purchased Whitney chapel from the Methodists. The chapel was repaired and now affords the congregation a very comfortable place for services.

There are now about one hundred members. A Sunday-school was started soon after the organization of the church and now has a membership of more than one hundred and a well-selected library. The successive pastors have been Messrs. Dilly, Trover, Workman, Rinehart, Polton, Bower, Rock, and Booth.

AFRICAN METHODIST CHURCH.

It is not definitely known when this church was formally organized, but meetings were probably held as early as 1860, at first in private houses, and afterwards in the lecture room of the Baptist church. Rev. William H. Brown preached in the Odd Fellows' hall at Harmar, which the association had rented for the regular church services. During his ministry the members, although only five in number, determined to secure their own house of worship. The membership at this time consisted of Franklin Norman, Jane Norman, Susan Norman, Mrs. Fletcher, and Mrs. Strowders. In 1865 the society purchased the Old School Presbyterian church, on Third street. Since the Third street church was purchased the following ministers have served the congregation: Messrs. Brown, Ralph, Pettigrue, McTerry, Lee, Bell, Thomas, Cole, Whitman, Artis, and Davidson. The membership has steadily increased, and much good has been accomplished. The membership is now twenty-eight, and a wide-awake little Sunday-school has been maintained, which now numbers about forty, the average attendance being thirty-five. The Sunday-school has a small library.

RELIGIOUS SOCIETIES.

There were five religious societies organized from 1801 to 1806, all except one of which were extinct before 1820. None of these organizations had denominational designation, although perhaps all were in some way connected with denominational organizations.

The First Religious society was organized March 2, 1801, and continues to be the association which transacts the business of the Congregational church. When this society was organized it was strictly union in its character, Christians of all shades of opinion being included in its membership. Other religious societies which were organized soon after followed the example of the First church and society, of making the business organization independent of the church proper, which was of necessity in sympathy with some form of denominationalism. The First Religious society was directly connected with the Congregational church, the Second with the Presbyterian church, and the Religious Meeting-House society, which was organized April 15, 1805, probably was indirectly connected with the Presbyterian church. The Fourth Religious society was formed in 1805 by persons living east of Duck creek. This society drew its last ministerial dividend in 1812.

The Union Religious society, which was organized early in 1806, was formed almost wholly of residents of Harmar. It received dividends from the ministerial rents to 1818.

THE HALCYONS.

A new country is productive of new doctrines, particularly in matters of religion. Cutting loose from the scenes, the society, and the employments of childhood and life, breaks down natural reverence for old ideas and leads men into new systems of doctrine.

Abel Sargent, the founder of the Halcyon sect, visited Marietta first between 1801 and 1805. His doctrines were very similar to the faith of the modern Second Adventists, but great latitude on minor points were allowed. The doctrines commended themselves to many respectable people. Dr. McIntosh was perhaps the best known adherent. After the sect had declined as an organization he remained steadfast to the faith, and wrote a book, as will be seen by reference to his biography in another chapter. Sargent sought discussions with the clergy in different parts of the county and much personal controversy followed.

Peter Cartwright held a discussion with him in 1806 which led to an exposure. Sargeant announced his purpose to light a fire with light from heaven. A crowd was collected around a stump on which was placed some tinder. Bystanders were surprised and adherents delighted to see the prophecy fulfilled. Sargent praised God for sending fire from heaven, but the Methodist veteran reminded the witnesses that the smell of powder and brimstone indicated that the author of the fire lived in the lower regions.

The Halcyons declined after 1807 in point of numbers, a few, however, remained faithful. It no longer has an existence as a religious organization, but the doctrines in all essential respects are entertained by many people all over the country.

CHAPTER XXVIII.

MARIETTA—EDUCATIONAL MATTERS.

The Earliest School Teachers at Campus Martius, "The Point," and Fort Harmar—The Muskingum Academy—How Built—Subscription List—The Institute of Education—Hamar Academy—Western Liberal Institute—Public Schools of Marietta and Harmar—Their Reorganization in 1849—High School—History of Marietta College—Its Origin and Growth—Presidents—Early Instructors—Buildings — Library — Cabinets — Graduates—Societies—Donations —Directory and Faculty.

EARLY SCHOOLS AND TEACHERS.

Schools were opened in Marietta at as early a date after the founding of the settlement as was possible. The teachers were paid in part by the Ohio company, and in part by the parents of their pupils. The pioneer schools were located in each one of the three clusters of settlements, which have heretofore been described, and to which we have several times alluded—Campus Martius, "The Point," and Fort Harmar. The first at Campus Martius was held in the northwest corner block-house in the winter of 1788-89, and was taught by Major Anselem Tupper, an officer in the Revolutionary army, and son of General Benjamin Tupper. He was a young man of fine education and literary tastes. At a late period Benjamin Slocomb, of Rhode Island was a teacher at the stockade. He was a graduate of Brown university. He returned to his native State in 1805 or 1806. Major Tupper died in Marietta in 1808. At "The Point" the early teachers were Jonathan Baldwin, a man of talent and education from Massachussets; a Mr. Curtis, brother

of Eleazer Curtis, of the Newburgh settlement, and Dr. Jabez True. The former had his school most of the time in a cooper-shop, and the latter had the use of a room in one of the block-houses. Up to 1796 no school-house had been erected in Marietta and probably none in the State of Ohio. Mr. Baldwin became a settler at Waterford after the close of the war, and Mr. Curtis went to the Big Kanawha country. Dr. True died in Marietta in 1823.

As we have intimated, schools were opened upon the west side of the Muskingum about the same time that they were at Campus Martius and "the Point." But little is known, however, of the early teachers. One of the earliest of them, though at a period later than that to which the above mentioned belonged, was a Mr. Noble, a quaint old fellow, a bachelor, and, to quote the language of one of his first pupils, "a kindly old gentleman who loved his pupils and his snuff box." Another of those teachers was Benjamin F. Stone, who taught a school in a building which stood on the location now occupied by Mr. E. Luthringer as a tin-shop. Perhaps the most distinguished of those who taught in Harmar during early years was Mr. William Slocomb, whose reputation for thoroughness and culture attracted pupils from all parts of the settlement.

After the close of the Indian war the spirit of the New England pioneers, which had been expressed in the Ordinance of 1787, and in the resolutions of the Ohio company, asserted itself in the establishment of the first academy in the great Northwestern Territory.

THE MUSKINGUM ACADEMY.

The building of this school-house was proposed at a meeting of the inhabitants of Marietta, convened April 29, 1797, for the purpose of taking into consideration measures for promoting the education of the youths in the settlement. General Putnam was chairman of this meeting, and Return Jonathan Meigs, jr., clerk. It was resolved "that a committee of six be appointed to prepare a plan of a house suitable for the instruction of youth, and religious exercises, and to make an estimate of the expense and the most suitable means of raising the necessary moneys, and to fix upon a spot whereon to erect the house, and report on Saturday next at three o'clock, P. M." General Putnam, Paul Fearing, Griffin Greene, R. J. Meigs, jr., Charles Greene and Joshua Shipman were appointed the committee.

On the sixth of May the committee reported a plan for the building, estimating the cost of erecting and completing it at one thousand dollars; they also reported that their opinion was, that the best plan for raising the money was to assess the possessors of ministerial lands lying on the Ohio river between Hart's ditch and the north end of Front street, and between Front street and the Muskingum river, at the rate of one dollar for every one-third of an acre which they respectively possess; that the best place for the building was city lot 605; that a subscription be opened for raising the deficiency of money.

The report was accepted and a committee of five

appointed. The assessments and subscriptions were to be considered as loans to be repaid out of the taxes of the ministerial lands; in case these amounts were not hereafter repaid, the persons so assessed, subscribing and paying, were to become proprietors of the building, in proportion to the sums paid.

Joshua Shipman was authorized to contract for the necessary boards and planks. At the next meeting, Saturday, the thirteenth of May, it was decided to call the building the Muskingum academy. Shares were fixed at ten dollars, and the proprietors had votes according to the number of shares owned. A meeting of the proprietors could be called by the possessors of thirty shares.

The following is a copy of the subscription paper drawn up for the building of the academy:

MAY 13, 1797.

WHEREAS, It is in contemplation to build an academy at Marietta, to be called the Muskingum academy, by subscription, to be held in properties and moneys paid, the subscribers, desirous to carry so laudable an object into effect, do hereby, each for himself, undertake and promise to pay to Jabez True, treasurer, to the proprietors of the academy aforesaid, or his successors, in case any should be appointed by the proprietors, such sum or sums as they may, and do hereby severally affix to their names.

Rufus Putnam.	$300 00
Charles Greene.	40 00
Return J. Meigs, jr.	40 00
Jabez True.	30 00
Joseph Lincoln.	20 00
Ichabod Nye.	40 00
Joshua Shipman.	20 00
Ebenezer Sproat.	40 00
Paul Fearing.	20 00
Griffin Green.	20 00
John Collins.	10 00
Benjamin Tupper.	20 00
Earl Sproat.	20 00
Samuel Thorniley.	10 00
Joseph Buell.	20 00
Timothy Buell.	10 00
Francis Thierrey.	2 00
Azariah Pratt.	10 00
Ezra Putnam.	15 00
Ashbel Hale.	10 00
Gilbert Devol, in work.	20 00
Nathan McIntosh, in brick.	25 00
Luther Sheperd.	10 00
James White.	10 00
Perley Howe.	10 00
William Rufus Putnam.	30 00
William Bridge, in laying brick.	10 00
Josiah Munroe.	15 00
John Brough.	10 00
John Gilbert Petit.	10 00
Joel Bowen.	20 00
Levi Whipple.	10 00
William U. Parsons.	10 00
Thomas Lane.	10 00
Christopher Burlingame.	20 00
Joseph Gilman & Son.	40 00
Judson Guitteau.	10 00
Josiah Hart.	10 00
William Hart.	10 00
Jonathan Devol.	10 00
Stephen Pierce.	15 00
William Skinner.	30 00
John Mathews.	20 00
Dudley Woodbridge.	30 00
Daniel Story.	30 00
David Putnam.	20 00
Edwin Putnam.	20 00

On May 16th a committee, consisting of Paul Fearing, Charles Greene, and Joshua Shipman, was appointed with full power to erect and complete the academy in accordance with the plan submitted at a former meeting, with the addition of a cellar under the whole building; they were authorized to purchase city lot No. 605, and the adjoining one.

Funds still being wanting, it was decided to sell to the highest bidder seats numbered one to twenty-one; the purchaser to have exclusive right to such seats on all public occasions; seats eighteen to twenty-one were withdrawn.

On May 21, 1800, a subscription was opened for completing the building, and a committee was appointed to report on a system of education; the report of the committee was made and accepted May 26th.

The following are the articles relating to education:

ARTICLE 3. It shall be the duty of the preceptor to teach the pupils writing, reading, arithmetic, geography, English grammar, and the Latin and Greek languages; the different branches in which a pupil is to be taught to be signified to the preceptor by the parent or the guardian of the pupil.

ARTICLE 4. It shall be the duty of the preceptor to pay due attention to the language and manners, particularly, and to the deportment of the scholars generally, that they may be instructed to be civil and obliging to each other, and respectful everywhere, to all.

ARTICLE 5. It shall be the duty of the preceptor to cause some, or all of the pupils to learn select, entertaining, and instructive speeches and dialogues, adapted to their several capacities and ages, which they shall pronounce in the academy, before such audience as may attend on the quarter day, which shall be the last day of every quarter.

ARTICLE 6. It shall be the duty of the preceptor to see that the pupils do not injure the seats, doors, writing-tables, and windows of the academy, and to cause the pews and floors to be thoroughly swept by some of the pupils every Saturday noon, and the movable seats and tables to be placed in order for the reception of the congregation on the succeeding Sabbath.

ARTICLE 7. The hours of tuition shall commence at nine o'clock in the forenoon and end at twelve, and commence at two in the afternoon and end at five, except during the winter, when they shall begin at half-past one and end at half-past four, at which times the preceptor shall cause the bell to be rung.

ARTICLE 8. The prices of tuition to be paid to the preceptor for each quarter shall be, for reading and writing two dollars; for arithmetic, English grammar, the first rudiments of astronomy, and geography, two dollars and fifty cents; Latin, Greek, and mathematics, three dollars. There shall be paid for each pupil taught reading and writing, thirty cents; for those taught arithmetic, English grammar, and geography, forty cents; for Latin, Greek, and mathematics, fifty cents per quarter to the preceptor, who shall pay over the same to the academy, for its use to keep the academy in repair, and for such purposes as shall be directed by the proprietors.

On July 29, 1802 an improved plan of the building was presented. This included six new pews, which were sold that day at the following prices: Two for twenty-eight dollars, one for twenty-six dollars, and three for twenty-five dollars. The treasurer was then authorized to contract for building them. On the thirtieth of December this action was repealed, as its expediency was considered doubtful. At this meeting the following resolution was adopted:

WHEREAS. All professing Christians consider it as an essential branch of education to have their children, and those under their care, instructed in the principles of the Christian religion, and the public catechising has been always considered as a part of the duty incumbent on the minister or pastor of a religious society; therefore,

Resolved, That the minister or pastor of the first religious society in Marietta shall have the liberty, from time to time, to instruct the pupils of the several schools that may hereafter be kept in the Muskingum academy; provided it is not more than half a day in any one month, and that he give at least three days notice to the preceptor of the time preferred for the exercises aforesaid.

The house was forty feet in length by twenty-four feet in width, and was twelve feet high, with arched ceiling. There were two chimneys, and a cellar of the same size as the building in length and breadth. There was a lobby projection from the front; the roof was square. Opposite the door was a broad aisle, at the end of which was a pulpit against the wall. On the right and left of the pulpit was a row of slips. On each side of the door, against the wall, were two slips facing the pulpit, and at each end of the room, at each side of the chimney, one slip. These slips were stationary and were fitted with desks that could be let down, and there were also boxes in the seats for holding books and paper. In the centre of the room was an open space which could be filled with movable seats. The house was used for the double purpose of an academy and a place for public worship.

The academy was opened in 1800, and David Putnam, who was a graduate of Yale college, was the first teacher.

The teachers after 1800 were: 1801, David Putnam; 1801, Edwin Putnam; 1803, John Leavin; 1804, Benjamin F. Stone; 1807, David Gilmore; 1807, N. K. Clough; 1808, M. B. Belknap; 1808, Timothy E. Donalson; 1809, Caleb Emerson.

In January, 1816, the building was leased to the Marietta School association for sixty dollars per year. The interior was materially changed and a school of a higher grade than any in town was established, in charge of Elisha Huntingdon, a graduate of Dartmouth. He taught for two or three years. After leaving the school he studied medicine, and, returning to Massachusetts, was for many years a resident of Lowell, practising medicine there. He was also for some years mayor of Lowell, and, for one term, lieutenant governor of Massachusetts. He died in 1867 or 1868.

Doctor Huntington was succeeded in the academy by William Slocumb, who taught there several years. He afterwards went into business in Marietta, and finally removed to Rochester, New York, where he died in 1873.

The building and lot was sold at auction October 8, 1832, for four hundred and seventy-nine dollars and two cents, to D. C. Skinner, esq., who removed it to the lot south of the Rhodes block, on Second street, where it now stands. The building is now the property of Judge C. R. Rhodes, and is rented as a tenement house.

The original location of the Muskingum academy was between the old Governor Meigs house (now the property of M. D. Follett, esq.,) and the Congregational church.

OTHER EDUCATIONAL INSTITUTIONS.

From the time of the Muskingum academy, onward, the development of educational institutions was in two lines. Upon the one hand there was a succession of efforts to give the youths of the town, county, and surrounding region an advanced education through the medium of academys and institutes, and upon the other hand there was a development of the common schools.

The first of these lines of improvement reached its culmination in the establishment of Marietta college and the second developed the present public schools and the high school.

THE INSTITUTE OF EDUCATION.

The school which may be called the successor of the Muskingum academy was called The Institute of Education. It comprised an infant school, primary school, ladies' seminary, and high school, and was established by the Rev. L. G. Bingham, in 1830. With Mr. Bingham became associated, a year later, Mr. Mansfield French. Mr. M. Brown, a graduate of Williams' college, had charge of the high school the first two years of its existence and was superseded by Mr. Henry Smith, of Middlebury college, in 1832. The ladies seminary was started under the management of Miss Spaulding, of Ipswich, Massachusetts. In 1832, Miss D. T. Wells, now Mrs. D. P. Bosworth, became assistant in this department. It was the high school of this Institute of Education which was chartered in 1833, as the Marietta Collegiate institute. And it was this institution which two years later was chartered as Marietta college. Into the hands of the same corporation also came the ladies' seminary, but the schools were maintained as separate institutions. Miss Spaulding was succeeded by Miss Wells, and afterward Miss C. M. Webster, Miss S. Jaquith, and Mrs. L. Tenney were successively the principals. The trustees sold the property in 1843, but the school was continued for a number of years by Mrs. Tenney.

HARMAR ACADEMY.

In 1844 an academy was organized in Harmar, known as the Harmar academy. This was found to be a valuable adjunct to the schools already established. These schools, being of a lower grade, needed the stimulus which the academy supplied. From the first the academy received the hearty and liberal support of the citizens of Harmar. A suitable building was provided by the citizens, at an expense of about two thousand dollars, and many of those who were too poor to contribute money, contributed labor in the construction of the building. Distinguished teachers were invited to assume control of this school, and, from the catalogue of 1848, we find there were in attendance at the academy during 1847-8 one hundred and sixty-six different pupils. The reputation of this school may be understood when it is known that within two years after its organization, pupils were in attendance from all parts of the country. The catalogue of 1848 contains the names of pupils from all the more important settlements in the county, from McConnelsville, Xenia, Cincinnati, Wheeling, West Virginia; Governeur, New York; Wood county, West Virginia, and from many points in the contiguous counties. The male and female departments were separate. The Rev. Henry Bates, A. M., was principal of the male department, and Miss Sarah Jacquith principal of the female department. The principals were supported by twelve assistants.

The board of trustees of this date consisted of John Crawford, Douglas Putnam, Henry Fearing, Harlow Chapin and Silas T. Jewell. Upon the reorganization

of the public schools, in 1849, the academy became the high school department of these schools, and under the efficient administration of Mr. Bates, John Giles, George H. Howison and Robert S. Boreland, did valuable work.

THE WESTERN LIBERAL INSTITUTE

was a school of the higher class, organized by the Universalists of Marietta. The charter was obtained March 21, 1850. Felix Regnier, Joseph Holden, Owen Franks, George W. Barker, William Devol, William Pitt Putnam and L. J. P. Putnam and their associates were the corporators, and the first trustees were G. W. Barker, Owen Franks and James M. Booth. The first principal was Paul Kendall. Instruction was given to the youth of both sexes during the period the school remained in existence, which was about ten years. The trustees erected a building for the school upon Second street, south of Butler.

THE PUBLIC SCHOOLS.[*]

During the early years of the life of Marietta, while the several academies we have described were in existence, there were kept by divers persons at various times small select or private schools, and also the common district schools maintained under the law of 1821. There was little change or improvement prior to 1825. The small revenue then derived from the lease of school lands and the disfavor which the law of 1821 met with, here as elsewhere, in consequence of its charitable provisions for the poor, made the success of the schools dependent upon the liberality and wise encouragement they received from the citizens. This necessary support they received to an unusual degree.

Important school legislation being made from 1825 to 1829, the schools were placed on a more satisfactory footing.

REORGANIZATION OF THE SCHOOLS.

In May, 1849, the schools of Marietta were reorganized, and a graded system, embracing a union of all the schools, was adopted. For some years previous, the schools were five in number, in as many separate and independent districts. Female teachers were employed in these separate schools during the summer, and in winter their places were given to male teachers. The schools, under this plan, were conducted from six to eight months each year. At Akron, and a number of other places throughout the State, the graded or union system had been tried with excellent results, and it was determined to try the experiment in Marietta. The plan was first suggested in September, 1848, at the annual meeting of one of the five districts. It was agreed at this meeting to invite the other four districts to consider the matter at a joint meeting. As a result of this invitation, a joint meeting of all the directors was held, and a reorganization upon the union plan was recommended to the citizens. A public meeting being called, the change was endorsed, and as a result, in the following March, the first union board of education was elected. This board consisted of Dr. I. W. Andrews, T. W. Ewart, R. E. Harte, Lucius Brigham, E. H. Allen, and Robert Craw-

*By Professor John T. Duff.

ford. Under the direction of these gentlemen the union or graded system went into effect in May, 1849.

At first three grades were established, primary, secondary, and grammar. During the first year eight schools were established, to-wit: four primary, two secondary, and two grammar schools. These schools were taught in the buildings occupied by the district schools, two of which had been enlarged for the purpose. These schools were all taught by ladies except one grammar school for boys, which was taught by Mr. Theodore Scott.

HIGH SCHOOL.

There was no high school until 1850, when Mr. E. D. Kingsley was chosen superintendent of the schools, and organized that department. The first class graduated from the high school in 1853, and consisted of the following persons: Harriet L. Shipman, Sophia Browning, Mary C. Slocumb, Virginia N. Nye, Caroline E. Brigham, Maria R. Booth, Mary O. Tolford, Jane E. Butler, Elizabeth T. Soyez, Maria M. Morse, Vesta M. Westgate, Julia L. Holden, Rhoda M. Shipman, Mary P. Gilbert, John W. Morse, William B. Loomis, and Justus Morse, jr.

SUPERINTENDENTS AND PRINCIPALS.

Among the superintendents of the Marietta schools since the reorganization may be named E. D. Kingsley who remained in charge until 1855. Hon. M. D. Follett, of Marietta succeeded Mr. Kingsley. He remained two years, when he resigned to enter the practice of the law. E. A. Jones, at present superintendent of the Massillon, Ohio, schools, served as superintendent for two years. The present incumbent, C. K. Wells, was chosen as principal of the high school in the fall of 1879, since which time he has also performed the duties of superintendent in whole or in part.

Among the teachers of the High school at different periods may be named J. O. Gould; Prof. Geo. R. Rossiter, now professor of mathematics in Marietta college; Rev. George R. Gear, now pastor of the Baptist society of Marietta; Miss Lizzie Anderson and others. In addition to the present superintendent, the Marietta schools are ably managed by Prof. S. S. Porter, who for years has been the principal of the Washington Street schools; by Miss Lizie Anderson principal of the Greene Street schools, and by C. W. Hudson principal of the Third Street schools. The report of Superintendent Wells for April, 1881, shows that there are at present employed in the Marietta schools twenty-three teachers; the total enrollment of pupils, one thousand one hundred and thirty-two, and the average daily attendance one thousand and thirty-one. This includes the colored school which numbers thirty pupils, with a daily attendance of twenty-three.

REORGANIZATION OF HARMAR SCHOOLS.

Early in 1849, the attention of Douglas Putnam, Luther Temple and other citizens was called to the excellent results of the union or graded system which was then being introduced into many of the schools of the State, and through the interest of these gentlemen and others equally interested, the Harmar schools were re-

organized upon the union plan in the fall of 1849. The first union board of education consisted of Douglas Putnam, Luther Temple, John Crawford, Samuel Bussard E. G. Smith and S. T. Jewell. The Rev. Mr. Bates of the academy, was chosen teacher of the high school, and superintendent of the schools. Mrs. J. P. Stratton was chosen teacher of the grammar school, while Miss Mattie Fearing, now the wife of Captain T. M. Turner, of Cincinnati, and Miss Mary Crawford were selected as primary teachers.

Mr. Bates remained as superintendent of the schools until 1852 when he resigned, and John Giles, of McConnelsville, Ohio, was chosen to fill the vacancy. Mr. Giles remained in charge until 1858, when he was superseded by Mr. Boreland. Miss Stratton remained in the grammar department doing excellent work until 1852. After the withdrawal of Miss Fearing, Miss Lucy Abbott, afterwards the wife of Hon. Amos Layman, was appointed as teacher.

DISCONTINUANCE OF THE HIGH SCHOOL.

In 1863 the high department had become so reduced in numbers that it was deemed advisable by the board of education to discontinue it. It was provided, however, that all who should complete the grammar school course, should be transferred to the Marietta high school, the tuition to be paid from the tuition fund of the Harmar board of education. This plan remained in operation until the fall of 1876, when the board determined to reduce the course of study to eight years,—four primary and four grammar—thereby abolishing high school instruction. This arrangement has been continued to the present.

COLORED SCHOOLS.

At the reorganization of the Harmar schools, the board determined to establish no class schools, and colored pupils were assigned, without reference to their color, to whatever grade of school their attainments entitled them.

Martha E. Grey was the first colored pupil who passed a successful examintion for entrance into the High school. This was in 1873. In September of the same year she applied for admission into the Marietta High school, but her request was not granted. A separate school for colored youth is maintained in Marietta, but colored pupils are now received into the High school.

SUPERINTENDENTS AND TEACHERS IN HARMAR.

After the withdrawal of Mr. Boreland as superintendent in 1860, Mr. W. H. G. Adney, now professor of sciences in Meadville college, was chosen. He remained but one year, being succeeded by Mr. George H. Howison. At the expiration of the year Mr. Howison resigned, and Mr. Boreland was again placed at the head of the schools. He, in turn, was succeeded by Sarah L. Bosworth. The following year, the Rev. William Wakefield, a member of the board of education, was appointed to take a partial supervision of the schools, and for this service he was allowed a compensation of one hundred and fifty dollars. Mr. Martin R. Andrews, a graduate of Marietta college, was afterwards

chosen as superintendent. Mr. Andrews remained until 1870, when he resigned to accept the superintendency of the Steubenville, Ohio, schools. From 1871 to 1876, John T. Duff, a graduate of the Ohio university, was the superintendent, at which latter date he resigned to accept the superintendency of the Bellaire City schools. The present superintendent is Mr. John D. Phillips, who for many years was the principal of the Green Street grammar school of Marietta.

The superintendent of the Harmar schools is at present assisted by a corps of five teachers. The enrollment of pupils in the schools is about two hundred and eighty. Of the present corp of teachers, Miss Lydia N. Hart, and Miss Susan Daniels, have served continuously for fourteen and fifteen years respectively.

MARIETTA COLLEGE.*

Marietta college owes its existence and success to the character of the men who began upon the Muskingum the settlement of the northwest. There was a deep conviction on the part of many of the most intelligent men in southeastern Ohio that a literary institution of high order was essential to the educational and religious interests of a large region, of which Marietta was the centre. This conviction was confirmed by the opinions of men of high standing both west and east.

The enterprise was undertaken by men who understood that a long and arduous work was before them. They knew that an institution conducted with reference to genuine and thorough culture, with no resort to superficial methods or temporary expedients, must be of slow growth. They had but moderate means from which to draw, but their gifts were most generous. They gave expecting to give again and again, as they have done. They believed that such an institution as they proposed to establish was indispensable, and their faith in its success was strong from the beginning.

The college was the natural outgrowth of this settlement by the Ohio company. The descendants of the men of the Revolution and their associates in the Ohio company, whose ideas of civil society were embodied in the immortal ordinance of 1787, were the founders of Marietta college, and they have been its warmest and most steadfast friends and its most generous benefactors. To speak of no others, the families of the two Putnams—General Israel and General Rufus—of Dr. Manasseh Cutler and General Benjamin Tupper, have furnished eight trustees of the college, five of whom still hold to this relation.

The charter of Marietta college bears date February 14, 1835. The institution had, however, been in operation a short time under another name. An act of incorporation had been obtained December 17, 1832, for "The Marietta Collegiate Institute and Western Teachers' Seminary." This charter gave no power to confer

---

* In 1876 President Israel Ward Andrews prepared a historical sketch of Marietta college, at the request of the bureau of education, for the Centennial exhibition. It was published in the Ohio Centennial Volume upon Educational Institutions. The history as it here appears embodies the greater part of the sketch originally prepared, with much new matter from the same hand, and numerous corrections and additions, bringing it down to 1881.

degrees, and contained a section authorizing any future legislature to amend or repeal it. A new charter was obtained two years later, free from the repealing clause and giving the power to confer degrees.

The same gentlemen were named as corporators in both charters, viz: Luther C. Bingham, John Cotton, Caleb Emerson, John Mills, John Crawford, Arius Nye, Douglas Putnam, Jonas Moore, and Anselem T. Nye, though two of them, Messrs. Arius Nye and John Crawford, retired from the board about the time the college charter was obtained.

These gentlemen, and their succeesors, were constituted a body corporate and politic with perpetual succession, with all the powers and privileges incident to a corporation, to be known and distinguished by the name and style of "The Trustees of Marietta College."

There is no restriction or requirement as to residence, religious belief, or any other qualification. The State has no management or control of the institution, and no State official is a trustee *ex-officio*. It is not under the direction of any religious denomination, nor has any ecclesiastical body the power to appoint or nominate trustees. It was intended to be an institution where sound learning should be cultivated under the best religious influences; a Christian college, controlled by a board of trustees, with power to fill all vacancies in their body.

The charter has been modified but once. An amendment made December 21, 1844, authorized the board of trustees to increase the number of members at their discretion, provided it should not consist of more than twenty-five. The full number of members has never been reached; the present number of elected members (the president of the college is a member *ex-officio*, and has been unanimously elected to the presidency of the board of trustees) is twenty-one.

Of the seven trustees who continued to act under the charter of 1835, one left the board in 1845, on his removal to the east, three have deceased and three are still connected with the college.

Rev. Luther G. Bingham, a native of Cornwall, Vermont, and graduate of Middlebury college, was pastor of the Congregational church at Marietta, though a member of the presbytery of Athens when the college was founded. In connection with Mr. Mansfield French, he had established a high school at Marietta, and the building they had erected became the property of the college. Mr. Bingham left Marietta for Cincinnati in 1838, and a few years later removed to Brooklyn, New York. He was very active in the early history of the college, and his connection with it as trustee continued till 1845.

Hon. John Cotton, M. D., a lineal descendent of the distinguished clergyman of that name, who came to Boston in 1633, was born at Plymouth, Massachusetts, September 9, 1792, and was graduated at Harvard in 1810. He established himself as a physician at Marietta, and remained here till his death, April 2, 1847. Dr. Cotton filled many positions of usefulness, and was a most valuable member of the board of trustees. He was elected president of the board at its organization in

December, 1832, and continued president till the year 1838.

Caleb Emerson, esq., was born at Ashby, Massachusetts, August 21, 1779, and came to Ohio in 1808. He was a lawyer by profession and a man of philosophic mind, enriched by very wide reading. He married a daughter of Captain William Dana, one of the pioneers, whose descendants are numerous and of the highest respectability. Mr. Emerson was a trustee till his death, March 14, 1853.

Jonas Moore, M. D., another of the founders of the college, was also a native of Massachusetts, born March 9, 1781. His early manhood was spent at the south, but for many years he was a citizen of Marietta. He was a warm friend of the college, and gave generously to its funds. Dr. Moore died March 24, 1856.

The three surviving founders, John Mills, Douglas Putnam and Anselem T. Nye, are all natives of Marietta. They have all been prominent business men, and identified with the most important enterprises of the place. Colonel Mills was treasurer of the college from its founding till 1850, rendering this service gratuitously, the treasury being also almost always overdrawn, sometimes to the amount of several thousand dollars. Mr. Putnam has been the secretary of the board from the beginning. Both have been members of the executive committee from the first, and they are the two largest donors. Colonel Mills gave one thousand dollars when the college was founded; his last gift was ten thousand dollars. The sum of his donations is nearly twenty-three thousand dollars. Mr. Putnam's first gift was two hundred dollars, and his last twenty-five thousand dollars; the whole amounting to about fifty-thousand dollars.

Between 1835 and 1845, when the amendment in the charter authorized an increase of members, there was but one addition to the board—Rev. Addison Kingsbury, D. D., of Zanesville, who was elected in 1838, and who is still a member. Of those elected in 1845 and subsequently, the following gentlemen remained members till their decease: Henry Starr, esq., 1845-51; Rev. Charles M. Putnam, 1845-70; William Slocumb, esq., 1847-73; Noah L. Wilson, esq., 1849-67; Rev. Thomas Wickes, D. D., 1849-70; Hon. Simeon Nash, 1845-79; Hon. William R. Putnam, 1849-81; Samuel Shipman, 1859-80; Benjamin B. Gaylord, esq., 1864-80.

The Collegiate Institute went into operation in the autumn of 1833. Mr. Henry Smith, who was at the head of a high school in Marietta when the first charter was obtained, was elected professor of Latin and Greek in the winter of 1832-33. In May, 1833, Mr. Milo P. Jewett was made professor in the teachers' department, and in August Mr. D. Howe Allen was chosen professor of mathematics, and Mr. Samuel Maxwell, principal of the preparatory department. A freshman class was formed that fall, but becoming reduced in numbers, its members fell back into the next class, which was graduated in 1838.

The relations of these gentlemen to the institution remained unchanged under the charter of 1835, Professor Jewett having been transferred in the summer of 1834 to the chair of rhetoric and oratory. In the spring of 1835 Rev. Joel H. Linsley, of Boston, was elected president. Thus, when the Collegiate Institute became Marietta college, the faculty consisted of five members, a president, who was also professor of moral and intellectual philosophy, a professor of languages, a professor of rhetoric and oratory, a professor of mathematics, and a principal of the preparatory department.

President Linsley remained at the head of the institute till 1846, when he accepted the pastorate of a church in Greenwich, Connecticut. He devoted himself to the duties of his office with the utmost zeal and fidelity, rendering fruitful service, both as an instructor and in the general work of administration. All who knew him will recognize the truthfulness of the words penned by his successor concerning him:

To the deep-toned piety and spiritual fidelity of Dr. Linsley, the institution is largely indebted for the internal religious influence which prevailed, and the frequent and powerful revivals of religion which blessed it during the period of his presidency; and to his earnest conviction of the importance of the institution to the cause of Christ, and his stirring appeals from the pulpit, is to be ascribed much of the public confidence which it has secured, and the favor which it has met with from the friends of Christian education, both east and west.

Dr. Linsley was born at Cornwall, Vermont, July 16, 1790; was graduated at Middlebury college, 1818, was tutor from 1813 to 1815; practiced law at Middlebury, 1816-22; pastor of the South Congregational church, Hartford, Connecticut, 1824-32; pastor of Park Street church, Boston, Massachusetts, 1832-35; president of Marietta college, 1835-46; pastor of the Second Congregational church at Greenwich till his death, March 22, 1868. He received the degree of D.D. from Middlebury in 1837, and was a trustee of Yale college from 1855 till his death.

President Linsley was succeeded in the presidency by Professor Henry Smith, who had been Professor of Languages from the foundation of the college. The institution was fortunate in all the members of its first faculty. Four of them came directly from the Theological seminary at Andover, and their subsequent success attests the good judgment of the trustees in their appointment. Dr. Smith remained in the college longer than any of his associates, and his department of instruction furnished the opportunity to leave a decided impress upon the institution in its forming period. While those associated with him in laying the foundations of the college were men of fine ability and high attainments, some of them eminently so, it is not doing them injustice to say that the college is more indebted to him than to any other of its instructors for shaping its character, and making it a place of genuine and thorough culture. Few men have combined in a higher degree than Dr. Smith broad and exact scholarship, ability in instruction, and eminence in the pulpit. He resigned the presidency in the winter of 1854-5, and accepted an invitation to the chair of sacred rhetoric in Lane seminary, with which institution he was connected to the time of his death, with the exception of a few years at Buffalo, New York, as pastor of the North Presbyterian church. President Smith was graduated at Middlebury college in 1827, and was tutor there from

1828 to 1830. He received the honorary degree of D. D. at Middlebury in 1847, and that of LL. D. at Marietta in 1874. He died at Walnut Hills, January 14, 1879.

Dr. Smith's successor was the present president—Israel Ward Andrews, LL. D.

Professor Jewett (a graduate of Dartmouth in 1828), left the college in 1838. For many years he was at the head of a female seminary in Alabama, and then removed to Poughkeepsie, New York. It was during his residence there that Mr. Matthew Vassar decided to appropriate a portion of his property to the founding of a college for young ladies; and it was, doubtless, owing in part at least, to the influence of Professor Jewett, that this munificent gift, originally intended for another purpose, took an educational direction. He was appointed the first president of Vassar college, and visited Europe to examine institutions with reference to methods of instruction and courses of study. He is now living in Wisconsin. The degree of doctor of laws was conferred on Professor Jewett in 1861, by the university of Rochester, New York.

Professor D. Howe Allen (Dartmouth, 1829) was transferred from the chair of mathematics to that of rhetoric and oratory, at his own request, in 1838, on the resignation of Professor Jewett. His fitness for successful work as an instructor, and his personal influence over young men, were remarkable, and his loss was seriously felt when he accepted an invitation to Lane seminary in the early autumn of 1840. As professor of sacred rhetoric, and afterward of theology, he was eminently successful. Professor Allen was born at Lebanon, New Hampshire, July 8, 1808. The honorary degree of doctor of divinity was conferred upon him by Marietta college in 1848. His connection with Lane seminary remained till his death, though for some years he was laid aside from active duty. He died November 9, 1870.

Professor Samuel Maxwell (Amherst, 1829) was connected with the institution for more than twenty years, for the greater part of the time being in charge of the academy or preparatory department. He was a man of great personal excellence, and was most conscientious in the discharge of his duties. In 1855 he relinquished that work, and established a boarding school for lads. He was born at Lebanon, Connecticut, March 9, 1804, and died at Marietta, January 24, 1867.

Of the original faculty of five,* one only is now living—Doctor Milo P. Jewett. The following gentlemen have been professors for various periods, but are not now in active duty: Professor John Kendrick, a graduate of Dartmouth, 1826, and valedictorian of the class to which Chief Justice Chase belonged, succeeded Professor Allen in the chair of rhetoric, etc., in 1840, having for some years previously been a member of the faculty of Kenyon college. He was transferred to the department of ancient languages when Dr. Smith became president in 1846. In 1866 the department was divided, Dr. Kendrick retaining the Greek. He resigned in 1873,

having been in active service in the college for thirty-three years. Since that time he has been professor emeritus. *

Professor Hiram Bingham, a graduate of Middlebury, 1839, occupied the chair of geology and chemistry from 1846 to 1849, since which time he has been in the work of the ministry in northern Ohio.

Professor Ebenezer B. Andrews, an alumnus of the college, of the class of 1842, was elected to the department of geology, etc., in 1851. With the exception of two years in the army as colonel of the Thirty-sixth Ohio volunteer infantry, he continued to discharge the duties of this professorship till 1870, when he resigned to enter the service of the State in the geological survey.†

Professor Addison Ballard (Williams college, 1842) was professor of mathematics and natural philosophy from 1855 to 1857, having previously held the chair of rhetoric at Williams college. He is now professor at Lafayette college, Easton, Pennsylvania.‡

Dr. Ballard was succeeded by Professor Evan W. Evans (Yale, 1851), who occupied the mathematical chair till 1865. On the organization of Cornell university he was elected professor of higher mathematics in that institution. He died in 1874.

In 1860 Mr. Edward P. Walker (Marietta, 1856) was appointed professor of rhetoric and English literature. He had been tutor from 1856 to 1857. The hopes cherished by his friends and associates, that a long career of usefulness was before him, were cut off by his death, December 27, 1861.

After the resignation of Dr. E. B. Andrews, in 1870, the vacancy was filled by the appointment of Mr. William B. Graves (Amherst, 1862). Professor Graves had charge of the chemical and geological department till 1874, when he accepted an appointment in the Agricultural college at Amherst, Massachusetts.

Professor S. Stanhope Orris (College of New Jersey, 1862), succeeded Professor Kendrick in the Greek chair in 1873. He resigned in 1877 to accept the same chair at Princeton.

The gentlemen named above are all, besides the present faculty, who have held permanent professorships in the college, though a number have been acting professors for short periods, or have been lecturers. George O. Hildreth, M. D., lectured on chemistry and mineralogy from 1840 to 1843. Timothy S. Pinneo, M. D., was acting professor of mathematics in 1843-4. Professor Alonzo Gray gave instruction in 1844-5, and Professor W. W. Mather in the same department in 1845-6. Professor George R. Rosseter had charge of the Mathematical department in 1850-1, and Professor William Porter, now of Beloit college, gave instruction in the classical department from 1850 to 1852. Charles H. Raymond, M. D., lectured on chemistry in 1850-1, and Rev. Charles S. Le Duc gave instructions in mathe-

---

* It is worthy of note that three of these five were the valedictorians of their respective classes in college.

* Dartmouth college conferred upon him the degree of doctor of laws in 1870.

† The degree of doctor of laws was conferred on him by his *Alma Mater* in 1870. He died at Lancaster, Ohio, August 14, 1880.

‡ He received the degree of D. D. from Williams in 1867.

matics in 1852--3. Professor Erastus Adkins, formerly of Shurtleff college, gave instruction in Greek from 1857 to 1859, and in Greek and rhetoric from 1864 to 1866. Professor John N. Lyle, now of Westminster college, Missouri, had charge of the department of mathematics and natural philosophy from 1866 to 1868.

The present faculty numbers eight, including the principal of the academy and the tutor, four of them being graduates of the college.

Israel Ward Andrews, LL. D., succeeded Dr. Smith as president, being elected in January, 1855. He has filled this position continuously since, and served longer than any college president in the west, and, with perhaps one exception, longer than any in the United States. He entered the college as a tutor in the fall of 1838, having graduated from Williams college in the previous year, and taught an academy for a short time at Lee, Massachusetts.

In April, 1839, he was elected professor of mathematics, in which capacity he was employed until his presidency began. Dr. Andrews is the son of Rev. William and Sarah (Parkhill) Andrews, and was born at Danbury, Connecticut, January 3, 1815. He received the degree of D. D., from Williams' college in 1856, and that of LL. D. from Iowa in 1874, and from Wabash college in 1876.

Professor George R. Rosseter (Marietta, 1843,) was tutor from 1845 to 1847; acting professor of mathematics in 1850-1; principal of the academy from 1864 to 1868; and then was elected to the chair of mathematics, natural philosophy and astronomy.

Professor John L. Mills (Yale, 1835) was tutor at Yale from 1858 to 1861, professor of mathematics, etc., here from 1865 to 1866, and was then transferred to the chair of Latin.

Professor David E. Beach (Marietta, 1859) was principal of the academy for two years, from 1859 to 1861, and in 1869 was appointed professor of moral philosophy and rhetoric.

Professor Thomas D. Biscoe, a graduate of Amherst in 1863, tutor there one year, and Walker instructor in mathematics from 1866 to 1869, was appointed professor of chemistry and geology in 1874.

Professor Irving J. Manatt (B. A., Iowa college, 1869, and Ph. D., Yale, 1873) was tutor at Iowa college one year, acting professor at Dennison university two years, and was elected professor of Greek at Marietta in 1877.

Professor Martin R. Andrews (Marietta, 1869) has been principal of the academy since 1879, and the present tutor is Mr. William A. Batchelor, of the class of 1878.

It has been stated above that Professor Maxwell, the first principal of the academy, continued in charge of it till 1855. Since that time some graduate of the college has been principal, with the exception of two years, from 1862 to 1864, when it was under the care of Rev. Edward F. Fish, a graduate of Hamilton college.

Of the tutors, all have been alumni of the college except for the year 1838-9. The whole number of instructors--presidents, professors, principals of the academy,

and tutors—has been forty-seven, of whom thirty-one have been Marietta graduates. The institution has thus honored its own educational work by calling back its alumni, and committing to them the responsible work of instruction.

The experience of the college is decidedly favorable to the election of young men as professors. It has been seen that four of the five gentlemen composing the first faculty came directly from the theological seminary. Of the eighteen different professors, five only had been engaged in other professional work. These five had been pastors of churches, but, with one exception, that of President Linsley, their periods of clerical service had been short, ranging from two to six years. All but one entered upon their duties as professors at an early age. Twelve of the eighteen had been tutors, here or elsewhere, before becoming professors. Two of the three presidents were elected from the corps of professors; in both cases men who had come here in early manhood. The aggregate time spent by these two in the work of instruction in the college has amounted to sixty-five years.

One feature of the college was modified after a few years' experience. When the institution was opened, provision was made for daily labor, agricultural and mechanical, and each student was required to work three hours a day in summer, and two in winter. As early as 1838 the shops were directed to be rented, and manual labor became optional. The last mention of it in the annual catalogue is found in that for 1842-3.

PLAN OF EDUCATION AND COURSE OF STUDY.

In founding the institution, it was the purpose to establish a genuine college of the New England type. It has been seen that all the members of the original faculty had been educated in the eastern colleges, and the same is true of those trustees who had received a liberal education. Of the eighteen who have held permanent chairs in the college, three were graduates of Middlebury college, three of Dartmouth, two of Amherst, two of Williams, two of Yale, one of Princeton, one of Iowa, and four of Marietta. The institution was thus molded after the New England type, and its course of study and general plan continue to be substantially the same as in those colleges.

At first special arrangements were made for the instruction of teachers; but that department soon took the form of the scientific course, found in so many colleges, embracing all the languages pursued in the classical course except the ancient languages, with some additional work in mathematics and its applications. But while this course, though inferior to the classical, was good in itself, as is shown in the case of the few students who completed it, the difficulty was that the students did not remain to finish it. Whatever may have been the cause, this was the fact. While the regular course was completed by over sixty per cent. of those who entered it, this short course of three years was completed by only six per cent.

The experience of the college is decidedly adverse to

any alternative course of study not substantially equal in time and degree of culture to the full classical course. The philosophical course was established recently, the studies of which are the same as in the classical, except the Greek. For this the modern languages are substituted, both in the preparatory department, and in college.

With scarcely an exception, the professors have given no instruction in the preparatory department, nor have their energies been exhausted in attempting to carry on a number of parallel courses of study. Their strength has been concentrated upon the proper undergraduate course, and they believe that the result has shown the wisdom of this policy. The requisites for admission have been gradually increased, and such changes have been made from time to time in the studies of the course as experience and the progress of the times have made desirable. The optional system has not been regarded with favor. The first president, in his inaugural address, characterizes the theory that each should follow his own predilections, and pursue those studies only for which he has the most relish and the best capacity, as fallacious in theory and mischievous in practice. The same system was also discussed by the present president at his inauguration in 1855. He says: "This college has not wasted her energies, or jeoparded the interests of her young men by any rash experiments. She has pursued that course which the experience of the past and the wisdom of the most learned have pronounced to be the best adapted to secure the highest and most symmetrical development of the human intellect."

Whatever changes have taken place, the principles underlying and guiding have remained the same. Marietta has no hesitation in declaring a decided preference for the methods adopted at Yale and Williams over those at Charlottesville and Ithaca.

The custom, well nigh universal forty years ago, of attending morning prayers and recitation before breakfast, and at a very early hour, was changed at Marietta in 1840.

RELIGIOUS INFLUENCES.

The founders of the college were religious men, and their purpose was to establish a Christian institution. The design and aim have been to furnish the best facilities for instruction in all the branches of a liberal, non-professional education, and at the same time to bring the students under religious influences. A leading object was the training of young men for the work of the gospel ministry. One of the first donations was the sum of five thousand dollars, given by Deacon Samuel Train, of Medford, Massachusetts, toward a fund for aiding the students who were preparing for this work. But the institution is under no ecclesiastical control, and neither charter nor by-laws imposes any restriction in the election of trustees or professors. The first board of trustees, nine in number, had in it members of five different denominations. And the fund spoken of above is used to aid young men of promise belonging to any evangelical denomination.

The chapel services, held every morning, and attendance upon which is obligatory, consist usually of reading the Scriptures, singing and prayer. Until 1868 there was a chapel service every evening also. There is no chaplain, and on the Sabbath students attend those churches in town which their parents prefer, there being no preaching service in the chapel. All the classes have a Biblical exercise on Monday morning.

Thirty-seven per cent. of the alumni have studied for the ministry. It may also be stated that seventy-seven per cent. were professedly religious men at the time of their graduation, and that twenty-four per cent. were converted in college.

PREPARATORY DEPARTMENT.

From the first, a separate department has been in operation, with the object of preparing young men for college. Since 1840 it has been known as the Marietta academy. It has a permanent principal, who receives the same salary as a professor in the college. The course of study occupies three years, and the school, in its plan and appointments, is specially designed for those seeking a liberal education, though others are received. Of those admitted to the freshman class, about three-fourths on the average are prepared at this academy. The average annual attendance, as shown from all the catalogues, is seventy-six.

BUILDINGS.

The educational work of the college proper was carried on, till 1850, in a single building of very moderate dimensions. It is seventy-five feet by forty, four stories high, with a basement and an attic. The basement has long since ceased to be used for recitation rooms, as originally designed. The building is now used for students' rooms, except the Latin recitation room and the reading room. It was erected in 1832.

The second building is seventy-five feet by fifty-three, three stories high, with a tower. It was erected in 1850, according to the plans and under the supervision of Hon. R. E. Harte, of Marietta. On the first floor are the president's lecture room, the mathematical room, the chemical lecture room, and a working room for the chemical department. About half of the second story is occupied as a room for the college cabinet and apparatus. There are also the Greek room, the rhetorical room, and the Hildreth cabinet. In this last are deposited the specimens in natural history and geology presented to the college by the late S. P. Hildreth, LL. D. The two literary societies occupy the third floor.

This building, whose corner-stone was laid in 1845, with an address by Hon. Lewis Cass, who was a citizen of Marietta in his early manhood, was erected through the liberality of the people of Marietta. The room containing the cabinet and apparatus is named Slocomb hall, from William Slocomb, esq., one of the principal donors.

The third building of the group was finished in 1870, and was erected by the alumni and other students of the college. Its cost, including the fitting up of the two rooms of the libraries of the two literary societies, was about twenty-five thousand dollars. It is two stories high, and seventy-five by fifty feet on the ground. The lower story, which is sixteen and one-half feet high, is divided by a wide hall into two equal parts, one of which, intended for an alumni hall, is at present used as a chapel. The other half furnishes two fine rooms for the society libraries.

The whole of the second story, which is twenty feet high, is devoted to the college library. The room is surrounded with a gallery, and has twenty-five alcoves, each lighted with its own window.

On another part of the grounds is a building used for the preparatory department exclusively, thus keeping this department entirely distinct from the college. This building is of wood, while the others are of brick. The three forming the college group are on an elevated portion of the grounds, with a beautiful slope in front.

The outlay for buildings has been moderate. The trustees have acted on the principle that the real efficiency of an institution of learning is in men, with books and apparatus to work with, rather than buildings. There has been no ambition to erect fine edifices.

LIBRARIES, CABINETS, ETC.

As early as December, 1834, Professor Henry Smith obtained leave of absence, with continuance of salary, to go to Europe for the purpose of study. His departure was delayed, however, till the summer of 1836, and meanwhile efforts were made to raise funds for the purchase of books and apparatus. Most opportunely, though quite unexpectedly, the sum was increased by the gift of one thousand dollars from the estate of Samuel Stone, of Townsend, Massachusetts. A like amount was given to each of several colleges, for the purchase of books. The portion coming to Marietta was expended for philological works. Dr. Smith says: "These books were carefully selected and purchased, for the most part, by a personal attendance upon the great auction sales of Leipsic and Halle. In this way the institution came into possession of one of the most valuable collections of classical works in the west, and for a sum probably less than one-third the price it would have cost in this country."

In 1850 a special effort was made by a few friends to increase the library. Mr. Douglas Putnam gave two thousand five hundred dollars, Mr. N. L. Wilson one thousand five hundred dollars, Mr. William Sturges one thousand two hundred and fifty dollars, Colonel John Mills one thousand dollars, Mr. Winthrop B. Smith five hundred dollars, and others in smaller sums. President Smith expended most of this money abroad, thus increasing largely the number of works needed in the several departments of instruction. Subsequent purchases have been made from year to year, almost all with reference to the wants of the professors. The college library is thus largely professorial, the literary societies providing for the current literature.

In 1850 Dr. Samuel P. Hildreth, an eminent naturalist of Marietta, gave to the college his cabinet of minerals, etc., together with some five hundred volumes, chiefly scientific and historical. He continued to add to this collection till his death in 1863, since which time his son, George O. Hildreth, M. D., has made numerous additions.

Mrs. E. W. Lord, of Batavia, New York, in 1877, gave to the college about one thousand volumes and five hundred pamphlets, including the very valuable collection of educational works belonging to her husband, the late Asa D. Lord, M. D., at the time of his death superintendent of the State Institution for the Blind at Batavia, and for many years one of the most prominent and successful educators in Ohio.

President Henry Smith gave to the college, by will, his library of some twelve hundred volumes, and thirteen valuable oil paintings. A portion of the books are already on the shelves.

The college has also received many valuable works from Hon. William A. Whittlesey and Hon. William P. Cutler, both of Marietta. From various other sources the college has received books and pamphlets relating to this part of the west, and to the governmental history of the State and Nation, making it unusually rich in works of this character.

The number of volumes in the college library, including the Hildreth collection, is seventeen thousand six hundred, and the whole number in the various libraries is twenty-nine thousand.

Besides the collections in the Hildredth cabinet, which are in a room by themselves, the college has a valuable collection of fossils, minerals, shells, etc. The whole have recently been arranged, and the number of specimens is over thirty thousand.

The apparatus, though not extensive, includes some valuable instruments. Among them are a Holtz machine, induction coil, electric lamp, absorption spectroscope, binocular microscope, an air-pump of great power, a fine Atwood's machine, a theodolite, sextant, etc. There is also a quadrant belonging to and long used by General Rufus Putnam, who held the office of surveyor-general under President Washington. It was given to the college by his grandson, Hon. William Rufus Putnam.

COLLEGE SOCIETIES.

The two literary societies, the Alpha Kappa and the Psi Gamma, were formed in 1839, taking the place of the Phi Sigma, a society with two branches. They have large and handsome halls for their meetings, and commodious rooms for their libraries, which, together, contain over ten thousand volumes. There are four fraternities—three secret, and one anti-secret. Most of these have handsome halls. In 1860 a chapter of the Phi Beta Kappa society was established by Dr. John Kendrick (Dartmouth), General T. C. H. Smith (Harvard), and Professor E. W. Evans (Yale). A boating association is in successful operation. Their boat-house, in the city park, is a tasteful structure, and they make much use of the unsurpassed facilities furnished by the Muskingum.

GRADUATES.

The first class was graduated in 1838. From that time the series has been unbroken. The whole number of graduates is five hundred and seventeen, of whom five hundred and two are bachelor of arts, one bachelor of philosophy and fourteen of science.

The class (regular) of 1838 numbered four, that of 1875, numbered twenty-two. No class has been larger than that of 1875, and none smaller than that of 1838.

It has been stated before that over sixty per cent. of those entering the regular courses have completed the course. Taking all the catalogues published, extending from 1837-38 to 1880-81, the ratio of seniors to freshmen is as sixty-seven to one hundred. The ratio between the whole number of graduates and the whole number of freshmen is found to be the same—sixty-seven to one hundred. One-third of the alumni are from Washington county.

The graduates are distributed among the professions and occupations as follows: Clergymen, thirty-seven per cent.; business men, twenty-five per cent.; lawyers, seventeen per cent.; physicians, eight per cent.; teachers, eight per cent.; all others, five per cent.

Seventy-one of the alumni are the sons of clergymen—seventeen per cent. In an unusually large number of cases the college has had different students from the same families. Among her alumni may be found one hundred and fifty-one in groups of two, three and four in a family. Three families have sent four sons each; eleven have sent three each, and fifty-three have sent two each. Nineteen have graduated, whose fathers were students here before them. Forty of the graduates came from other colleges to finish their course here, and thirty-seven who have left Marietta, have received degrees elsewhere. It is believed that no student has been admitted here from another college, who did not bring the customary papers.

The following alumni have been missionaries: John F. Pogue, Sandwich Islands; Ira M. Preston, Africa; Nathaniel H. Pierce, American Indians; Jackson G. Coffing, Turkey; John H. Shedd, Persia; John P. Williamson, American Indians; Charles A. Stanley, China; William L. Whipple, Persia; John B. Cameron and William E. Fay are under appointment to go this year, one to Brazil and the other to Africa. Andrew J. McKim went to South America under the Seamen's Friends society.

The following have been professors in colleges: Erastus Adkins, Shurtleff college, and acting professor at Marietta; E. B. Andrews, Marietta college; George R. Rosseter, Marrietta college; R. A. Arthur, Ohio university; George H. Howison, St. Louis university, and Massachusetts institute of technology; Edward P. Walker, Marietta college; David E. Beach, Marietta college; John N. Lyle, acting professor at Marietta, and professor at Westminster college, Missouri; William G. Ballantine, Ripon college, Wisconsin, and Indiana university and Oberlin theological seminary.

Joseph F. Tuttle, D. D., has been president of Wabash college since 1862; General Willard Warner was United States Senator from Alabama; Hon. Joseph G. Wilson was one of the supreme judges of Oregon, and member of Congress; Hon. William Irwin is now governor of California; Hon. Alfred T. Goshorn is director general of the centennial international exposition.

The precise number of those who entered the army in the great war of 1861–65 can not now be given, but the relative number was large, both of graduates and under-graduates. Among those who lost their lives were the valedictorians of the classes of 1859, 1860 and 1862—Captain Theodore E. Greenwood, Lieutenant Timothy L. Condit, and Adjutant George B. Turner.

HONORARY DEGREES.

The honorary degree of doctor of laws has been conferred on twenty gentlemen; that of doctor of divinity on thirty-one; that of doctor of philosophy on one, and that of master of arts on forty-four.

The following persons have received the degree of LL. D.: Hon. Peter Hitchcock, 1845; Hon. Samuel F. Vinton, 1847; Hon. Gustavus Swan, 1855; Hon. Reuben Wood, 1851; Hon. Edward D. Mansfield, 1853; Samuel P. Hildreth, M. D., 1859; Hon. William Dennison, 1860; Hon. William V. Peck, 1860; Hon. Noah H. Swayne, 1863; Hon. Aaron F. Perry, 1865; Hon. Joseph G. Wilson, 1865; Hon. Chauncey N. Olds, 1869; Professor E. B. Andrews, 1870; Professor T. G. Wormley, 1870; Hon. Edward F. Noyes, 1872; Rev. Henry Smith, D. D., 1874; Hon. William Irwin, 1876; Hon. Emerson E. White, 1876; Hon. John F. Follett, 1879.

GRANTS AND ENDOWMENTS.

The college has been sustained entirely by private generosity. It has never received from the State or Nation an acre of land or a dollar of money. It was not founded in consequence of any large gift from an individual or family, nor did the town vote, or the people pledge, any sum for the sake of securing the institution at that point. The first effort to raise funds was after the charter had been obtained, and this was to pay for the property which the trustees had purchased, at a cost of eight thousand dollars. This sum was secured at Marietta, three donors giving one thousand dollars each.

This was the small beginning. But the founders and friends of the institution appreciated the importance of the enterprise, and their gifts have increased with their ability. Their example has had its influence upon others, and thus the college has retained its old friends and been gaining new ones. As illustrative of this continuance of interest, and the increase in successive donations from the same persons, a fact or two may be stated. Among the donors in the first effort, made in the spring of 1833, to raise eight thousand dollars, were seven men who gave in sums ranging from fifty dollars to one thousand dollars, making an aggregate of two thousand two hundred and fifty dollars. The total gifts to the college made by these seven gentlemen up to this time amount to ninety-eight thousand dollars, or over forty times the sum given at first. In 1847 a gentleman in southern Ohio gave fifty dollars. In 1857 he gave five hundred dollars. About ten years later he gave five thousand dollars. It is by such men that Marietta has been sustained.

The college has a number of scholarships on the basis of one thousand dollars each, nearly all of which are in the gift of the institution. The ability of the college to aid deserving young men has been greatly increased through the bequest of Hon. W. R. Putnam of thirty thousand dollars. Students who can do so may well pay some tuition, but others, if promising, need not abandon the purpose of securing a liberal education.

For some years prizes have been awarded to students in the three upper classes who have been distinguished for excellence in general scholarship during the previous year. Usually the sum of sixty dollars has been divided between the best two in each of these classes. Two small prizes for excellence in declamation have been given to two students in each of the sophomore and freshman classes. Recently rhetorical prizes have been awarded to the two or three in the junior class who have excelled in that department. These prizes are but partially endowed as yet, though they have been regularly paid. There is now also a prize in American history.

In 1843 an association was formed in the east under the name of the "Society for Promoting Collegiate and Theological Education at the West." Marietta was one of the institutions whose circumstances led to the formation of the society, and was one of the first five taken under its patronage. Aid was received through this source for about twenty years, and the cause of education owes great obligation to that society.

The college is beginning to receive aid in the form of legacies. Mrs. Mary Keyes and Mr. Daniel T. Woodbury, both of Columbus, made bequests of five thousand dollars each some years ago. President Henry Smith, who died in January, 1879, bequeathed his library and a collection of paintings, and made the college his residuary legatee, the bequest amounting to about thirty-four thousand dollars. Mrs. Smith has the use of the whole during her life. By the will of Hon. William Rufus Putnam, who died May 1, 1881, the college receives most of his property. It will probably be between thirty thousand and forty thousand dollars. About two years since Mr. and Mrs. Truman Hillyer, of Columbus, transferred to the college twenty-five thousand dollars, to which he has since added two thousand five hundred. This is subject to a life annuity.

It will be seen that bequests have already been made amounting to more than one hundred thousand dollars, and it is known that other persons have made testamentary provision, which will without doubt be secured to the college.

Allusion has already been made to the warm interest manifested in the college by the people of Marietta and its immediate vicinity. At its founding they gave generously, according to their ability, and each succeeding decade has witnessed a large increase in their benefactions. Their gifts to the present time have amounted to upwards of two hundred thousand dollars.

What has been said of the people where the institution is located may be as emphatically said of the trustees to whom the management of its affairs has been entrusted. The institution has been to them from the first a foster-child. They have regarded themselves appointed not merely to manage and control but to nourish and strengthen. They have encouraged benefactions in others by making them themselves. Their donations aggregate one hundred and seventy-five thousand dollars.

The alumni have manifested great liberality towards the college. Mention has already been made of the library building erected by them at a cost of twenty-five thousand dollars. Towards our alumni professorship more than sixteen thousand dollars has already been given. The various gifts from alumni and other former students amount to more than fifty thousand dollars. There is no more hopeful indication of the continued and increasing prosperity of an institution of learning than the enthusiasm and liberality of those who have been connected with it as students.

The following is a list of donors to the amount of one thousand dollars and upwards:

Douglas Putnam, $49,100; President Henry Smith, $35,000; William R. Putnam, jr., $30,700; Truman Hillyer, $27,500; John Mills, $21,800; Noah L. Wilson, $13,850; Charles W. Potwin, $10,000; Mrs. Valeria G. Stone, $10,000; Joseph Perkins, $6,800; Francis C. Sessions, $6,700; Benjamin B. Gaylord, $6,600; Mrs. Mary Keyes, $5,800; Samuel Train, $5,000; Preserved Smith, $5,000; Daniel T. Woodburry, $5,000; William P. Cutler, $5,000; A. J. Warner, $5,000; Samuel P. Hildreth, $4,100; John C. Calhoun, $3,800; Samuel Shipman, $3,775; President I. W. Andrews, $3,750; Thomas W. Williams, $3,600; Loyal Wilcox, $3,500; David C. Skinner, $2,925; William R. Putnam, sr., $2,800; Elizur Smith, $2,500; Rev. Dr. Joseph Eldridge and family, $2,400; Nahum Ward, $2,300; Cornelius B. Erwin, $2,200; John Newton, $2,100; L. G. Bingham, $2,000; Jonas Moore, $2,000; David Putnam, sr., $2,000; William Slocomb, $2,000; Anson G. Phelps, $2,000; Rev. William Van Vleck, $2,000; Samuel C. Morgan, $2,000; Mrs. Frances A. Morgan, $2,000; Dr. and Mrs. A. D. Lord, $2,000; Professor John Kendrich, $2,000; William Hyde, $2,000; Rufus R. Dawes, $1,800; William Shaw, $1,750; William H. Blymyer, $1,600; Professor John L. Mills, $1,575; Beman Gates, $1,525; John Bradley, $1,500; Anselem T. Nye, $1,500; Rev. George M. Maxwell, $1,500; William E. Dodge, $1,500; Samuel D. Warren, $1,500; William Sturges, $1,475; William A. Whittlesey, $1,400; J. Munro Brown, $1,300; Winthrop B. Smith, $1,300; E. C. Dawes, $1,300; Professor E. B. Andrews, $1,230; George Dana, sr., $1,100; Marcus Bosworth, $1,100; W. W. Wicks, $1,100; M. P. Wells, $1,100; Samuel Stone, $1,000; Samuel Williston, $1,000; Robert Hamilton, $1,000; Mrs. R. R. Hamilton, $1,000; William Johnson, $1,000; A. T. Goshorn, $1,000; A. H. Hinkle, $1,000; L. C. Hopkins, $1,000; John Field, $1,000; Cutler Laflin, $1,000; Legrand Lockwood, $1,000; William J. Breed, $1,000; R. M. White, $1,000; William Shaffer, $1,000; Henry Stanley, $1,000; Timothy W. Stanley, $1,000; Douglas Putnam, jr., $1,000; William E. London, $1,000; Mrs. John Mills, $1,000; Henry C. Brown, $1,000; Ezra Farnsworth, $1,000; John H. Hubbell, $1,000; E. R. Alderman, $1,000; Mrs. Ellenor Cook, $1,000; Professor George R. Rosseter, $1,000; G. H. Barbour, $1,000; George B. Collier, $1,000; John F. Follett, $1,000; George L. Laflin, $1,000.

Marlow Chapin

The names of the members of the corporation and faculty as now constituted (May, 1881), are as follows:

Israel W. Andrews, president.

John Mills, Anselem T. Nye, esq., Rev. Addison Kingsbury, D. D., Hon. William P. Cutler, General Rufus R. Dawes, Rev. Theron H. Hawks, D. D., Rev. William Addy, D. D., and M. P. Wells, esq., of Marietta; Douglas Putnam, of Harmar; Rev. E. P. Pratt, D. D., of Portsmouth; Rev. Henry M. Storrs, D. D., of Brooklyn, N. Y.; Francis C. Sessions, esq., Rev. William E. Moore, D. D., and Rev. Robert G. Hutchins, D. D., of Columbus; Rev. George M. Maxwell, D. D., Hon. Alfred T. Goshorn, William J. Breed, esq., and William H. Blymyer, esq., of Cincinnati; Hon. Charles W. Potwin, of Zanesville; Colonel Douglas Putnam, jr., and John Means, esq., Ashland, Kentucky.

FACULTY.

Israel W. Andrews, D. D., LL. D., president and Putnam professor of political philosophy.

John Kendrick, LL. D., Emeritus professor of the Greek language and literature.

George R. Rosseter, M. A., professor of mathematics and natural philosophy, and Lee lecturer on astronomy.

John L. Mills, M. A., professor of the Latin language and literature, and instructor in French.

David E. Beach, M. A., professor of moral and intellectual philosophy and rhetoric.

Thomas D. Biscoe, M. A., professor of the natural sciences.

Irving J. Manatt, Ph. D., professor of the Greek language and literature, and instructor in German.

Martin R. Andrews, M. A., principal of the preparatory department.

William A. Batchelor, B. A., tutor.

R. M. Stimson, M. A., librarian.

CHAPTER XXIX.

THE MEDICAL PROFESSION.

Character of Early Physicians—Biographical Sketches—Jabez True, Solomon Drown, Thomas Farley, William Pitt Putnam, Josiah Hart, William B. Leonard, John Baptiste Regnier, Nathan McIntosh, Robert Wallace, Samuel Prescott Hildreth, John Cotton, Jonas Moore, G. S. B. Hemstead, Morris German, Felix Regnier, Hugh Trevor, Shubel Fuller, Dr. Stearns, Wilson Stanley—Present Physicians—Seth Hart, George O. Hildreth, B. F. Hart, C. W. Eddy, J. D. Cotton, Simeon Hart, Samuel Hart, Z. D. Walter, James McClure, H. N. Curtis, Mrs. H. N. Curtis—Medical Societies.

PHYSICIANS.

Marietta has been favored with able and honest physicians since the year of the first settlement. It is frequently remarked that the professional classes of new settlements fill up with the failures of old and cultured communities. But the first settlement at Marietta was made under peculiar circumstances by some of the ablest and best men of New England, and among them were physicians of sterling qualities and genuine merit. It is the aim of this chapter to give sketches only of the more prominent practitioners from the first settlers to the present time.

Jabez True, son of Rev. Henry True, was born in Hampstead, New Hampshire, in 1760. It was the practice of the time for clergymen to instruct the youth and prepare young men for college. Mr. True had a class of this kind under his instruction. His son, Jabez, acquired sufficient knowledge of the languages to enable him to pursue a course of medicine with advantage. He read

medicine in his native town, and completed his course near the close of the Revolution. He volunteered his services as surgeon of a privateer and sailed for Europe. Soon after commencing the cruise the vessel was wrecked on the coast of Holland, and the mariners thrown on the mercy of the Hollanders. Dr. True remained in Europe until the cessation of hostilities, when he returned to America and began the practice of his profession in New Hampshire.

Dr. True became a member of the Ohio company in 1787, and came to Marietta in the spring of 1788. He built a small log office on Muskingum street. The new country did not afford a lucrative practice, but it was a fortunate circumstance that skilled physicians were present. He was employed at the opening of the Indian war as surgeon's mate for the troops and rangers, at a salary of twenty-two dollars per month. During this time he also taught a school a part of the time in one of the blockhouses of the garrison at the Point.

The small-pox and scarlet fever broke out in 1790 and made it necessary for the doctor to visit the settlements, which, during the Indian war, could only be done by water as none but trained rangers trusted themselves to enter the roadless forest; visits at that time even by water were extremely hazardous, but the sick required attention, and he frequently risked his life to respond to the calls of duty.

Dr. True was celebrated for his kindness and sympathy. So far as it was possible he patronized the prejudices of his patient and never resorted to radical remedies, except in cases of absolute necessity. "The result of his calm, deliberative judgment was generally correct, and his treatment of diseases remarkably successful, which was doubtless owing to its simplicity, for it is a lamentable fact that too many die from too many and improper remedies as well as from disease itself."[*]

After the close of the Indian war he improved a farm on the Ohio about a mile from Marietta, and took an interest in agricultural pursuits. His practice extended over a large area of territory, sometimes requiring him to ride twenty miles through forests and over bridgeless streams.

The practice of medicine at that time was by no means lucrative. The general poverty of the people necessitated low charges and in many cases no charges at all, neither for medicines or professional service.

Dr. True's devotion to the church cannot be omitted from any sketch of his life however brief. He joined the Congregational church at an early period of its organization and was for many years a deacon. His house was a home for itinerant preachers, and his purse always open to needy charities. He was the "Gains" of Marietta, although for a town of its population, it abounds in men zealous and liberal in promoting good works. Dr. True, for several of the last years of his life, served as county treasurer, a position which afforded him ease and a moderate income.

In 1806 Dr. True married Mrs. Mills, the widow of

---

[*] Dr. S. P. Hildreth.

Captain Charles Mills, an amiable and excellent woman. He had no children, but the children of his wife were treated with all the love and affection of a real father. He died during the epidemic of 1823.

Dr. Solomon Drown is known rather as a scholar and man of letters than as a physician. He came to Marietta in the summer of 1788, and attended on General Varnum as counsel during his sickness. He was selected to pronounce the eulogy at his funeral, which was published at the time in New England. He also delivered the address at the first Seventh of April celebration. About 1791 he was elected professor of botany and natural history in Brown university, of which he was a graduate. He filled the position for many years.

Dr. Thomas Farley came to Marietta in the summer of 1788 as the attending physician of General Varnum, who died of consumption in January, 1789. He was a son of General Farley, of Ipswich, Massachusetts, and studied medicine at Salem, under Dr. Holyoke, in 1782. Colonel Barker says of him: "He was a modest, amiable young man, always ready to obey the calls of humanity, and had the good will and confidence of all who knew him." He soon became discouraged with the new country and returned in the fall of 1790 to Massachusetts.

William Pitt, fourth son of Colonel William Putnam, and grandson of General Israel Putnam, was born in Brooklyn, Connecticut, in 1770. He attended the schools of the neighborhood in the winter and worked on a farm in the summer. He was placed under the tuition of Rev. Dr. Whitney at the age of sixteen, and pursued a course in Latin and other studies preliminary to reading medicine. At the age of eighteen he entered the office of Dr. Waldo, of Pomfret, the distinguished surgeon of the Revolution. He attended a course of lectures at Cambridge in 1791, and in 1792 came to Marietta. He spent a portion of his time at Belpre, where his brother lived, but the Indian war made general practice dangerous and unprofitable. In 1794 Dr. Putnam retured to Connecticut when he married Berthia G. Glysson, and in company with his father's family came to Marietta in 1795. In 1797 he purchased the lot on the corner of Fifth and Putnam streets, on which his brother David afterwards built the Mansion house, now occupied by Colonel Mills.

Dr. Putnam in 1799 having become discouraged, although he was highly esteemed and had a fair share of patronage, determined to give up practice and turn his attention to farming. He purchased two hundred acres on the Ohio river, eight miles above Marietta, and with characteristic energy plied his hand in the clearing. The fatigue and exposure of forest life brought on bilious fever of which he died, October 8, 1800, leaving no children to inherit his name or fortune. His widow subsequently married General Edward Tupper.

Josiah Hart.—A venerable physician, during the early period of Marietta's existence was Josiah Hart, who was born in Berlin, Connecticut, in 1738. He attended Yale college for the purpose of preparing for the ministry, but after graduating in 1762 changed his intention and entered on a course of medicine. His first wife died in 1777, leaving seven children, two of whom settled in Ohio. He married, for his second wife, Mrs. Abigail Harris, a blood relative of the celebrated Miles Standish, whom Longfellow has immortalized.

Dr. Hart came to Marietta in 1796, and was in active practice until 1811, when he removed to his farm where he died from spotted fever in 1812. His wife died a few hours after and both were buried the same day.

Doctor Hart was one of the first deacons of the Congregational church and was a consistent, pious Christian. He had a strong love for science and was a regular attendant at the meetings of a chemical society, composed of physicians and others. This society met two or three evenings in a week, where experiments were exhibited and lectures heard.

Doctor William B. Leonard, was born in England, in 1737, and was bred a surgeon. He was an associate of Apothecaries Hall, London, and in the prime of life served as surgeon in the British navy. In 1794 he determined to engage in woollen manufacture in America, and as machinery was at that time prohibited from being transported out of England, Doctor Leonard determined to clandestinely bring it on the vessel on which he had engaged passage, but was detected, and imprisoned. Having been discharged he came to America in 1797, and engaged in medical practice in Massachusetts until 1801, when he came to Marietta. Here he married Lydia Moulton, daughter of William Moulton, a highly respected pioneer.

Doctor Leonard was a skilful surgeon, but was rough in his manners and language. His fantastic dress excited a great deal of merriment, and caused him to be followed about the streets by a company of boys, on whom he frequently showered terrific profanity. His dress was patterned after the gaudy fashion of the times of Queen Elizabeth. In person he was thin and spare with very slender legs. He wore a blue broadcloth coat trimmed with gold lace and enormous gilt buttons, a waistcoat of crimson velvet with enormous pocket flaps. His pantaloons were tight and of the same material. Tight silk stockings dressed his slender legs and heavy silver buckles ornamented the knees and shoes. On his head he wore a full flowing periwig, of which he had half a dozen varieties, and crowned with a cocked beaver hat. Over this clownish dress he wore a large scarlet cloak. Like his dress, his books, instruments, and skeletons were of previous centuries. Doctor Hildreth preserved several of these articles as curious relics. One of the books is entitled "Secrets of Master Alexis," and is filled with such recipes as were in use then, centuries ago. The book was printed in 1562. Dr. Leonard died in 1806.

John Baptiste Regnier.—All the old citizens of the Duck Creek and Muskingum valleys and of Marietta remember John Baptiste Regnier, and most of them cherish his memory as a personal friend. Medicine exerts a greater personal influence over its patients than any other profession. The patient who recovers from a serious malady is likely to retain feelings of the profoundest gratitude toward the man who has rescued him from pain or death.

Mr. Regnier was the son of a Parisian native, and was born in Paris in 1769. His mother kept a small store for fancy goods, and is said to have been a very handsome and stylish woman.

The family was loyal to the Government and the king, and as a consequence were sufferers of the convulsions which revolutionized France. John had acquired a good education and special attainments in architecture and drawing, which he intended to follow as a profession. Like all the better class of French students, he had also attended scientific lectures, and had paid particular attention to the department of medicine. In 1790, when the young men were all called upon to enter the ranks of the revolutionists, the Regnier brothers who were loyalists decided upon leaving the country. John B., who was twenty years old, and Modeste, who was fourteen, joined the company of emigrants who had purchased lands from Joel Barlow, and came to the United States. They reached Marietta October 16, 1790. After a few days they embarked on boats, and proceeded to lands purchased from the Scioto Land company, and were among the founders of Gallipolis. Having lost their fortune and dreading the Indians, to whom they were unaccustomed, the two brothers left their forest home and went to New York. On their way up the Ohio the boat was upset and all the effects thrown out; among them was a curiously wrought octagonal cylinder, which was afterwards found in a sand-bar below, and exhibited in an eastern museum as a legacy of pre-historic art.

For the next eight or ten years Dr. Regnier suffered varying but cruel fortune. But those years of uncertainty and hardship threw him into the profession for which nature had intended him. In the year 1802 he entered the office of Dr. Lemoine, his French medical friend at Washington, Pennsylvania, and in 1803 came to Marietta for the purpose of entering the practice. Monsieur Thiery, a French baker, sold him a lot in Fearing township, on which he moved and made improvents. It soon became known that he was a "French doctor," and from that time on his practice grew and his purse was filled. There was an unusual amount of bilious fever, in the treatment of which he was remarkably successful. He also proved himself a skilled surgeon. One case particularly extended his reputation. A man had been caught in the branches of a falling tree and was bruised from head to foot. The pulsations of his heart had ceased and the body was already cold when the doctor arrived. He ordered the attendants to kill a sheep and bring him the warm pelt as quickly as possible. The steaming skin was wrapped around the bruised and naked, body, and a cure, which seemed almost miraculous, was accomplished.

In 1808 Dr. Regnier removed to Marietta where he had previously been frequently called as counsel, and attending physician. His practice was extended over a wider range of territory, and drew heavily on his physical powers. In Marietta he became a great social as well as professional favorite. He was a cheerful and interesting talker, was full of sympathy and always ready to give assistance.

He purchased a six acre lot and laid out the finest garden in the city. "It was a model from which divers individuals improved their own and ultimately implanted a permanent taste for this refining art to the citizens of Marietta."

He was one of the original members of the State Medical society organized in 1812. In 1818 he was elected county commissioner. In 1819 he sold his property in Marietta, to Dr. John Cotton, and purchased three hundred and twenty acres of land on Duck creek. He built a flouring- and saw-mill and a brick dwelling house. He also laid out roads, and built bridges. Up to that time the country was unimproved, but in a few years a prosperous settlement had grown up. He left Marietta with the intention of freeing himself of his laborious practice, but found it impossible. He was still called upon by his old patrons, in serious cases, and his strong humanity did not permit him to refuse. Broken down by overwork, he died of bilious remittent fever in August, 1821. Dr. Hildreth, his cotemporary and friend, has said of him:

Close discrimination and accurate observation of all phases and shades of diseases gave him wonderful tact in prognosis, the base of all successful practice, while his knowledge of the proper remedies rendered him very successful in their application. His colloquial powers were unrivaled, and at the bedside his cheerful conversation aided by the deep interest he actually felt in the sick, with his kind, delicate manner of imparting his instructions, always left his patients better than he found them, and formed a lasting attachment to his person in all who fell under his care. His death was lamented as a serious calamity, and no physician in this region of country has since fully filled the place he occupied in the public estimation.

Nathan McIntosh.—The subject of this sketch possessed the characteristic energy of his family. He was the son of Colonel William McIntosh, of Needham, Massachusetts, and born in 1762. His father was a man of considerable local note, having commaded a company in the Continental army, and subsequently served as colonel of militia. He was one of the delegates in the convention in Boston, in 1788, on the adoption of the constitution of the United States.

Nathan McIntosh, after receiving a suitable education, studied medicine in Boston, and was admitted to practice in 1786. In 1788 he decided on going west, and started for Marietta on horseback. When he reached Meadville, Pennsylvania, he was attacked with small-pox, and suffered severely from the loathsome disease. He practiced for a short time at Hagerstown, Pennsylvania, and Clarksburgh, Virginia, and then came to Marietta in 1790. He received the appointment of surgeon's mate at the Waterford garrison at the salary of twenty-two dollars a month. He married, in 1792, Rhoda Shepard, daughter of Colonel Enoch Shepard, of Marietta, and granddaughter of General Shepard, of Massachusetts.

In 1793 Dr. McIntosh decided to accept an invitation extended by leading citizens of Clarksburgh to locate at that place, and removed his family there in July, under escort of fifteen soldiers. He was soon in possession of a large practice, but being full of adventure suffered a serious financial misfortune. He contracted to build a bridge across the Monongahela river at Clarksburgh, and warranted it to stand a certain length of time. But soon after its completion the whole structure was swept away during a freshet.

Dr. McIntosh returned to Marietta in 1795 and resumed practice. His courteous and obliging manner and skill as a surgeon won him a large practice.

Jacob Young, the great itinerant Methodist, in his autobiography, commends the kindness of Dr. McIntosh in the most feeling terms. In 1805 the pioneer Methodist was stricken down with an attack of fever at a house where the surroundings were by no means pleasant. Dr. McIntosh took him to his house and not only doctored but nursed him during a long turn of sickness.

In religion Dr. McIntosh was a Halcyon, a sect embracing nearly the same doctrines propounded by the Second Adventists. He had previously been a Methodist. He wrote and lectured on religious and moral topics, being particularly severe on the secret societies. He published a volume on the subject of "Scripture Correspondences."

Dr. McIntosh, about 1806, turned his attention to the manufacture of bricks and building brick houses, working diligently in the brickyard and on walls. He died of fever September 5, 1823, during the prevailing epidemic. His family consisted of four sons and two daughters, a full biography of one of whom—Enoch S., will be found in the chapter on Waterford; the other children were Rhoda, wife of J. M. Chamberlain; William Whiting, Nathan Henry, Samuel Dooey, and Lucy Hulda, wife of Samuel Maxon, of Galia county.

Dr. Robert Wallace came from Pennsylvania to Marietta probably soon after the war. He was here in 1801. Dr. Regnier speaks of him as "a very intelligent druggist." A society of physicians and young men of scientific tastes, was formed in the early part of the century. Experiments were performed under Dr. Wallace's direction, and he also occasionally delivered scientific lectures. His oldest son, Mathew Wallace, was a Presbyterian clergyman. His second son, David, was a physician. The family removed to Cincinnati probably about 1809. Dr. David Wallace was one of the parties to the first and perhaps only only duel in the history of the county. In the spring of 1801, a difficulty arose which resulted in Dr. Wallace challenging John Woodbridge to a duel. The island opposite Marietta was the place selected and pistols were the weapons chosen. The parties accordingly met, but Wallace's courage failed and he was willing to ask pardon. Woodbridge was not thus easily satisfied. He cut a stick and gave Wallace a good dressing. They were both present at the Seventh of April celebration, which occurred soon after. The song composed for and sung upon that occasion closed with the stanza:

"Here population lifts her hand
And scatters round her jewels,
And must honor take its island,
Producing bloodless duels?"

No preface is necessary to an outline of the life of Dr. Samuel P. Hildreth. The reader already knows him, but an index to the labors of his busy and useful life, will be of interest and value.

He was born in Methuen, Essex county, Massachusetts, September 30, 1783. He was the son of Dr. Samuel Hildreth, and a descendent of Richard Hildreth, whose name is found amongst a company of twenty from the towns of Woburn and Concord, who, in 1652, petitioned the general court of Massachusetts bay, for a tract of land on the west side of Concord, or Musketaquid river, where they say "they do find a very comfortable place to accommodate a company of God's people upon." Samuel Prescott was of the sixth generation from Richard. Until he was fifteen years old he labored on a farm, there acquiring industrious habits and the power of physical endurance. A social library in the town afforded access to books, and a taste for reading was acquired at an early age, and until his death he was a devourer of books. After finishing the course of the common schools, he spent four seasons in Phillips academy in Andover, and at Franklin academy, which prepared him for entering college. In place, however, of completing a college course, he entered the office of Dr. Kittridge at Andover, and began the study of medicine. He received a diploma in 1805, from the Medical Society of Massachusetts, having attended lectures at Cambridge university.

Dr. Hildreth began practice at Hemstead, New Hampshire, the native home of Dr. Jabez True. He boarded in the family of John True, esq., through whom he learned of the professional success of Dr. True and the prospects for a young man at Marietta. From his boyhood he had entertained a desire to see the far west, and in September, 1806, left his New England home in the hope of realizing his ambition. The journey to Marietta was performed on horseback and consumed about one month. He says in his autobiography, "It was a land of strangers; but he was young and his heart buoyant with hope and expectation of good fortune. He soon obtained a share of the practice, the only physicians then being Dr. True and Dr. Hart. Dr. Leonard had recently died, and Dr. McIntosh had abandoned medicine. His rides sometimes extended over thirty miles through the wilderness, the settlements being few and far between."

Belpre was at that time without a physician, and at the solicitation of leading citizens, Dr. Hildreth decided to locate there. He arrived at Belpre on the evening of December 10th, just in time to see the deluded Blennerhassett leave his island paradise to embark in Aaron Burr's perilous expedition.

The summer of 1807 was a busy one for physicians. The epidemic which raged all along the Ohio was particularly severe in the neighborhood of Marietta. Few families at Belpre escaped. Dr. Hildreth was particularly fortunate in his treatment of these cases. Practice at Belpre was excessively laborious on account of the amount of riding necessary. Over exertion during the summer brought on an attack of inflammation of the hip which continued several months. In the spring of 1808 he returned to Marietta, where the practice required less riding. The epedemic of 1807 furnished him the subject for a paper which he printed in the tenth volume of

the New York Medical Repository. From this time he became known as an acute, discerning investigator and faithful writer on scientific and historical subjects. He, however, continued his large and laborious practice until a few months before his death, in 1863. He said his profession, during earlier years, kept him busily engaged and his scientific and historical labor could be pursued only by saving the "odds and ends of time."

Dr. Hildreth was a man of decided political opinions. In 1810 he was elected to represent Washington county in the legislature, and again reelected in 1811, when he defeated Judge Cutler, the Federalist candidate, by twenty votes. Hildreth was a supporter of Jefferson and Madison, whose political teachings at this time had displaced the doctrines of Washington and Hamilton. In the same campaign Hon. William Woodbridge defeated Hon. William R. Putnam for the State senate, Woodbridge being a Democrat and Putnam a Federalist. They were four able men, and after the administration of Monroe had broken party lines, all found a home in the political camp of the Whigs. Dr. Hildreth, however, was never again a candidate for office, but never neglected to vote. While in the legislature he drafted and succeeded in having passed the first law regulating the practice of medicine and establishing medical societies, which remained in force until 1819, when all laws on the subject were repealed.

He held the office of collector of non-resident taxes for the Third Ohio district from 1811 until the office was abolished in 1819.

He became clerk of the trustees of the ministerial lands in 1810, and discharged the duties of the office until his death in 1863.

He was a Republican from the formation of the party in 1854.

Dr. Hildreth carried his research into almost every department of science, but natural history was particularly fascinating. In 1812 he published a paper in the Medical Repository on the American colombo, with a drawing of the plant. It is proper to state in this connection that he had a remarkable genius in drawing. Insects and plants were represented with scrupulous accuracy, and engravings made from them have a permanent value. The illustrations in his geological and botanical reports were prepared by his own hand. They show artistic ability, as well as accurate observation and close discrimination.

In 1822 he published in the New York Medical Repository two articles, one on hydrophobia and one on a curious case of Siamese twins, found in his obstetric practice. A full history of the epidemic of 1822–23 was published in the Journal of Medical Science, Philadelphia, in 1824. The author was well qualified to write on this subject, as he had visited daily sixty to eighty patients, and in August, 1823, was himself attacked. He arrested the disease in a few days by taking Jesuit's bark, in quarter ounce doses. This was a trial of medicine to which few patients would submit. Sulphate of quinine had not yet come into use in Ohio, or by it many valuable lives might have been saved. An article was published in

1825 on the minor diseases, or sequela of the great epidemic, in the Western Journal of Medicine, Cincinnati. In 1819 he wrote a series of papers on the natural and civil history of Washington county, which appeared in Silliman's Journal in 1826. One of these articles gave a drawing and description of the spoonbill sturgeon found in the waters of the Ohio. In 1827, his articles contained descriptions and drawings of several freshwater shells found in the Muskingum, of which nothing had been known. His series of meteorological registers, published in that journal from 1828 till March, 1863, are useful for reference to writers on the climate of Ohio.

At the request of Professor Silliman, Dr. Hildreth undertook to explore the coal regions of the Ohio, the result of which was published in the Journal for January, 1836, under the title of "Observations on the bituminous coal deposits in the valley of Ohio, and the accompanying rock strata, with notices of the fossil organic remains, and the relic of vegetable and animal bodies, illustrated with a geological map, by numerous drawings of plants and shells, and by views of interesting scenery." The Journal says editorially that this was one of the most important of Dr. Hildredth's scientific labors, and by far the most valuable contribution which up to that time had appeared on the subject discussed. It filled an entire number (one hundred and fifty-five pages), of this Journal, and was profusely illustrated by figures of fossils, sections, and original drawings, embraced in thirty-six plates on wood. Articles on the history of the North American locust, saliferous rock formation, with a history of the manufacture, of salt from the first settlement of Ohio, Ten days in Ohio, a geological description of the country from Marietta to Chillicothe by way of Zanesville, and The Diary of a Naturalist, appeared in the same journal from 1830 to 1836.

In 1832 he wrote a history of the floods in the Ohio since the first settlement, which was published in the first volume of the transactions of the historical society of Ohio. In 1837 he was employed, in company with other geologists, to make a geological survey of the State. He delivered an address in 1839 before the medical society of Ohio, of which he was president, on the climate and diseases of southwestern Ohio, which was printed.

In 1830 Dr. Hildreth commenced the collection of a cabinet of natural history. While out on his daily professional rides he would stop to gather insects, shells, fishes, fossils, and minerals. He often employed boys in the country to do this service for him. When he returned from a drive he was in the habit of picking out the specimens he desired to keep, labelling them and placing them in cases. Duplicates were sent to eastern friends in exchange for books or specimens of that section. In the course of eight years his cabinet contained more than four thousand specimens, and his library a choice variety of works on natural history. Shortly before his death he donated his cabinet and library to Marietta college, where it is known as the Hildreth cabinet. "This donation made Dr. Hildreth one of four or five of the largest benefactors of the college."

52

In 1840 Dr. Hildreth turned his attention to writing a history of the first settlement of Ohio. He collected his material with great care from manuscripts and personal interviews, and wrote a book of five hundred and five pages, which will always be of interest and value. He was the means of preserving a variety of important history and interesting anecdote which would otherwise have been lost to posterity. His second volume of Lives of the Early Settlers of Ohio was published in 1852. These two books have a permanent place in history. Dr. Hildreth, besides, contributed many interesting historical papers to the Pioneer, and a history of the first settlement of Belleville was published in the Hesperian. A journal of diseases each month, with a bill of mortality, was kept from 1824 till his death. A large amount of manuscript of permanent value, though never published, besides many smaller articles were among the products of his busy pen.

R. M. Stimson in summing up the character of Dr. Hildreth says forcibly:

He looked on the bright side of things—loved beauty, although of an eminently practical turn of mind—was very fond of flowers, which he cultivated diligently. Industry and system in all that he did may be accounted among his marked points. Besides his laborious medical practice, he accomplished, very much as he himself expressed it, by "saving the odds and ends of time." Without having a brilliant mind he exemplified the fact that "industry is talent." He was exact in all his dealings, an honest man, a Christian. His was a complete life—be finished his work.

His life was gentle, and the elements so mixed in him that nature might stand up and say to all the world: This was a man.

Dr. Hildreth's able and productive pen gave him an extended acquaintance among the scientific men of his day. He was one of the first pioneers of science west of the Alleghany mountains and was regarded as one of the most acute observers of facts of his time. Professor Benjamin Silliman, his warm friend, has written a feeling tribute to his memory:

In his private life he illustrated every virtue of a Christian gentleman. Bright and cheerful by nature, he loved nature with the simple enthusiasm of a child. Industrious and systematic in a high degree, no moment of life was wasted. In his family we have seen a beautiful example of domestic happiness and warm-hearted hospitality. He lived with nature and nature's God—and among the patrons and coworkers in this journal, who have left its founder almost alone, no one has shed a purer and more mellow light in the horizon of his setting sun—no one has departed more loved and regretted by the senior editor.*

Dr. Hildreth died July 24, 1863, in his eightieth year. He had been in his usual good health, a well-preserved and happy old gentleman until a few weeks before his death. He sank away gradually, his mental faculties being preserved to the last. His funeral was on Sunday, July 26th, the services being in the Congregational church, of which he was a member. These last sad rites were conducted by Rev. Mr. Wickafield, of Harmar, and President Andrews, of Marietta college.

Dr. John Cotton was a physician well known and highly esteemed in his time, and is still remembered as a successful practitioner of physic and skilful surgeon. He was the son of Rev. Josiah Cotton, and was born in Plymouth, Massachusetts, in 1792. Rev. Josiah Cotton was

*Silliman's Journal, September, 1863.

a descendant of Rev. John Cotton, of Boston, and a graduate of Yale college. John entered Cambridge university at the age of fourteen and graduated in 1810 with honorable standing in his class. He received his medical degree at Cambridge in 1814, and began practicing in Andover, Massachusetts. In 1815 he married Susan Buckminster and came to Marietta, being attracted by the climate. In the latter part of the year he opened an office on the west side of the Muskingum, and soon acquired a comfortable practice, which grew with age and experience.

Dr. Cotton was an enthusiastic worker in the cause of religion. Immediately upon his arrival he set to work at organizing Sunday-schools, and in 1816 one had been opened on the west side and two on the east side. He continued an enthusiastic Sunday-school worker and teacher. He accumulated a large collection of theological books, and at the age of forty studied Hebrew that he might be able to understand more fully and explain more satisfactorily difficult passages in the Old Testament.

Dr. Cotton was ardent in his opinions. He soon became a local political leader, and in 1824 was chosen representative in the legislature. In 1825 he was chosen associate judge and filled the position till the time of his death. For a number of years he was chairman of the Whig Central committee, and proved himself an adroit politician. He took delight in scientific studies, and often lectured in the Marietta lyceum and the young ladies' seminary. Astronomy was his favorite theme. He delivered an address in Latin on the occasion of the installation of the first president of Marietta college. He was one of the original trustees of the college and for many years president of the board. He was also trustee of the medical college of Ohio. He died unexpectedly after a brief illness of three days, April 2, 1847.

Dr. Jonas Moore was a native of New Hampshire, and was in the senior year at Dartmouth when his father died, necessitating his return home. He never returned to graduate. His whole family was soon after carried off by scarlet fever, and he came to Marietta where he taught school and studied medicine with Dr. S. P. Hildreth. He next went to Louisiana where he practiced for a number of years. He afterwards became one of the leading physicians of Marietta, where he died in March, 1856. He was a trustee of the college and took deep interest in educational matters. He was of a scientific turn of mind and invented a number of mechanical devices for use in surgery. He was highly respected as a man.

Dr. G. M. P. Hempstead was a native of Connecticut, came to Ohio in 1802, and found good facilities for obtaining an education in Muskingum academy, where he was prepared for college. He was for a short time under the tutilage of Hon. Gustavus Swan, late of the supreme court, and Dr. Jonas Moore, of Marietta. He graduated from Ohio university in 1813, being the first literary graduate of that institution and consequently the first in Ohio. He received the degree of A. M. in 1822 and LL. D. in 1879. He began the study of medicine in

1813, and in 1816 went to Waterford where the spotted fever had become epidemic. He was there three or four months. He is now practicing in Portsmouth, Ohio.

Dr. Morris German was a native of Shenango county, New York. He attended lectures and received a diploma in New York city. He located in Harmar during the epidemic of 1823, and in a short time was in possession of a full practice, which was held until his death in 1835. Dr. German was a contemporary of Hildreth and Cotton, and held an honorable standing in the profession. He died at the age of thirty-nine.

Dr. Felix Regnier, the second son of Dr. J. B. Regnier, was born in Otsego county, New York, in 1801. When he was two years old his parents moved to Marietta, Ohio, where he received a liberal education and began the study of medicine under Dr. S. P. Hildreth. He received a diploma from the medical society of Ohio 1824, and that year began the practice of his profession at Gallipolis, Ohio. In 1831 he removed to Jacksonville, Illinois, where he remained two years and then came to Marietta. He had an office in Harmar and was regularly engaged in practice here until April, 1866. During the succeeding eleven years he travelled, in the hope of improving his wife's health. After her death in 1877 he removed to Carthage, Illinois, where he lives with his son, Austin B.

Dr. Hugh Trevor, a descendent of Sir Hugh Trevor, was born in County Down, Ireland, in 1806. He graduated at Trinity college, Dublin, and at the College of Surgeons, Dublin. He afterwards spent nine years in the hospitals of Paris. He came to Marietta in 1834, and began the practice of medicine. His medical knowledge was of a high order, and he had the confidence of a large class of people. While in Marietta he married Maria Holden, a daughter of Joseph Holden. In 1858 he removed to St. Joseph, Missouri, and in 1881 located in Quincy, Illinois, where he died in April, 1881.

Dr. Shubel Fuller was born in Canada in 1806. In 1818 his parents came to Marietta, and after passing through the schools of that period, began the study of medicine in the office of Dr. John Cotton. He attended lectures at the Ohio Medical college, Cincinnati, and opened an office in Marietta in 1835. Dr. Fuller was a successful physician, and conducted a large practice until the sickness which terminated in his death in February 17, 1857. Dr. Fuller was a descendant of the Plymouth Rock family of that name.

Dr. G. J. Stevens, an old practitioner, was located in Harmar for thirteen years. He was a native of Berkshire county, Massachusetts, where he was born in 1805. He attended lectures at Fairfield Medical college, and received a diploma in 1827. He practiced in New York, and in Portage and Summit counties, Ohio. He died at his home in Harmar in April, 1881.

Dr. Wilson Stanley was born and spent his early life in North Carolina, and graduated from the Homœopathic Hospital college, of Cleveland, Ohio. He practiced medicine for about ten years in Marietta, and moved to Memphis, Tennessee, in 1866, where he died within a year.

PRESENT PHYSICIANS.

Dr. Seth Hart began the practice of medicine in Harmar in 1827, and has been in active practice since that time, except during two brief periods. A full biography will be found in this volume.

Dr. George O. Hildreth, son of Dr. Samuel Prescott Hildreth, graduated at Ohio university in 1829, at the age of seventeen. He entered upon a course of medical study under the direction of his father, and attended lectures at Transylvania university, Kentucky, where he graduated in 1835. He was regularly associated with his father in practice until the death of the latter in 1863. Since then he has been alone, occupying the same house and office on Putnam street. His practice has continued over a period of forty-five years, with but a single intermission, during a period of four years—1849-53—which were spent in California. Dr. Hildreth has been pension examiner since 1863, and is highly esteemed as a physician and a man.

Benjamin Franklin Hart, M. D., was born in Watertown, Washington county, Ohio, January 3, 1823. He was a student of the Ohio Medical college, and received his degree from that institution in the spring of 1844. Subsequently, in 1864 he graduated from Bellevue college, New York. After completing his course at Cincinnati, he began practice in Marietta, and with the exception of a brief intermission, has continued until the present.

Dr. Hart took an active part in the War of the rebellion, visiting Pittsburgh Landing, Shiloh, and later, Gettysburg, Frederick city, Washington and Baltimore, to look after the needs of the Ohio soldiers He was one of the surgeons who engaged in the pursuit of John Morgan in his raid through Ohio. This work was performed gratuitously, and to the satisfaction of the sanitary commission. In 1864 he was appointed by Governor Brough military surgeon with the rank of major.

Dr. Hart is a member of the Ohio State Medical society, and of the American Medical association, and is one of the censors of the Columbus Medical college. He was a delegate to the International Medical congress at Philadelphia in 1876.

C. W. Eddy, M. D., is a resident of Marietta, having been born in this county. After receiving a liberal education at Beverly academy, he studied medicine in the office of Dr. C. S. Parker, and at Miami Medical college where he received his degree in 1877. He practiced first in Guernsey county. In April, 1879, he was appointed assistant physician for the Athens asylum, and was reorganized out in May, 1880, together with the whole staff. He has since been at Marietta.

Dr. Josiah Dexter Cotton, son of Dr. John Cotton, was born in Marietta May 19, 1822. He received his preliminary education at Marietta college, where he graduated in 1842. He began the study of medicine in his father's office, and in 1845 entered the medical college at Louisville, and was granted the degree of M. D. in 1847. He had previously been in practice in Lawrence county, about one year. In 1847 Dr. John Cotton died.

and Josiah D. succeeded to his business. He has been in constant practice in Marietta since, except three years, during the war, when he acted as surgeon for the Ninety-second Ohio, and brigade surgeon.

Dr. Simon D. Hart, at present superintendent and physician of the Washington County Children's home, engaged in the general practice of his profession from 1844 to 1869. He attended school at Marietta, and received his degree from Ohio Medical college, Cincinnati, in the spring of 1844, and opened an office in Coolville, Athens county, where he remained one year. During the next two years he practiced in Barlow, and in 1847 removed to Marietta. He received a fair share of public patronage until April, 1869, when his present position was tendered him. Dr. Hart married July, 1845, Lydia M. Lawrence, who has been matron of the home since its regular establishment.

Dr. Samuel Hart was born in Watertown township in 1830. He completed his studies at Marietta academy in 1849, and received a degree from the medical college of Ohio in 1852. He began practice in Marietta in 1853, and has continued till the present time, except during a period of four years of active surgical practice in the army in charge of a hospital, and two years spent in Bellevue hospital, New York. He also practiced in Massachusetts.

Dr. Z. D. Walter succeeded to the practice of Dr. W. Stanley in 1866. He was born of Quaker parentage, and spent his early life in Chester county, Pennsylvania. He received his education and afterward taught for two years at Westtown boarding school, a Quaker institution, and attended medical lectures at the Homœopathic Medical college of Pennsylvania, where he received his degree in 1866, since which time he has been in the practice at Marietta.

Dr. W. D. Putnam, of Harmar, studied medicine under Dr. Johnson Elliott, professor of surgery, of the university of Georgetown, Georgetown, D. C., and graduated from that institution in March, 1868. About a year afterward he came west and located at Lowell, this county. In November, 1872, he removed to Harmar, where he has since been engaged in the practice of his profession.

Dr. Putnam is the great-grandson of General Rufus Putnam, and grandson of Edwin. Putnam. His father was Franklin Putnam. He was born October 28, 1842, and was married February 5, 1867, to Emma J. Blane, of Hagarstown, Maryland. She died March 1, 1879.

Dr. J. B. Mellor, of Harmar, read with Dr. W. D. Putnam, and graduated at Miami college, Cincinnati, in the spring of 1878. Since then he has been in practice in Harmar.

Doctor James McClure has been practising in Marietta since 1871. He is a native of Salem, Meigs county, Ohio, and read medicine at Harrisonville, in the same county, under Dr. S. Day. He attended lectures at Starling Medical college in 1860 and 1861, and practised at Albany, Athens county, until the fall of 1863, when he entered the second course and graduated in 1864. He became surgeon for the Twenty-third Ohio volunteer

infantry, in May, 1864, and served in that capacity until the close of the war, when he returned to Albany and practiced there until coming to Marietta.

Dr. H. N. Curtis is a native of this county. He graduated at the New York Homœopathic Medical college in 1881, and began the practice of medicine in the spring of that year. Mrs. Curtis has the honor of being the first lady physician in Marietta. She graduated at the New York Medical College and Hospital for Women in 1881, and began practice with Doctors Walter and Curtis.

MEDICAL SOCIETIES.

The first medical society in the state was organized through the influence of Doctor S. P. Hildreth. It was a State society and followed by a district society. Before the war the first county society was organized, but was broken up after a few years by the opening of the Rebellion. "The Washington County Medical Society" was organized in July, 1873. The following physicians have served as presidents: J. D. Cotton, William Beebe, J. G. Stevens, G. O. Hildreth, B. F. Culver, and W. P. Beebe.

CHAPTER XXX.
MARIETTA—THE PRESS.

Earliest Newspapers in the West—The First Papers in Marietta, the Ohio Gazette and the Territorial and Virginia Herald—Messrs. Backus and Silliman—The Commentator—The Western Spectator—The American Friend—David Everett—Royal Prentiss—Marietta Gazette—The Marietta Intelligencer—Beman Gates—The Register—R. M. Stimson—E. R. Alderman—The Pilot the Pioneer in Democratic Journalism—The Jolines—The Western Republican—John Brough—The Democrat—Charles B. Flood—Marietta Republican—Amos Layman—Marietta Times—S. M. McMillen—The Leader—istory of the German Press.

THE beginning of the same century in which the west was settled witnessed the establishment of the first American newspaper. The Boston *News Letter* first saw the light April 24, 1704. The first paper west of the Alleghenies was the Pittsburgh *Gazette*, started in 1785. While preparations were making in New England, and in the Congress of the Old Confederation for the planting of the first colony northwest of the Ohio, the first newspaper in Kentucky was printed at Lexington by William Bradford. It was called the *Kentucke Gazette* and the first number bore date of August 17, 1787.

The pioneer of the press northwest of the Ohio was the *Centinel of the Northwest Territory*, issued at Cincinnati November 9, 1793. This is the paper from which the Cincinnati *Gazette* claims to be descended and from which it takes date and number, although its present name dates back only to 1815. The *Scioto Gazette* (Chillicothe) was established in the summer of 1800 and is still published under its original name. Its claim of being the oldest paper in Ohio is well based and indisputable. *The Ohio Gazette and the Territorial and Vir-*

B. F. Hart. M.D.

ginia Herald was first issued at Marietta December 7, 1801. Nine years later—in 1810—there were published in Ohio, according to Thomas' History of Printing, fourteen papers, four of which—the *Scioto Gazette, Supporter, Fredonian,* and *Independent Republican*—were at Chillicothe, and three—the *Whig, Liberty Hall,* and the *Advertiser*—at Cincinnati. The remaining seven were the *Ohio Gazette* and *Commentator,* at Marietta; the *Muskingum Messenger,* at Zanesville; the *Patriot,* at New Lisbon; *Western Herald,* at Steubenville; the *Impartial Expositor,* at St. Clairsville; and the *Western Star,* at Lebanon.

The first paper in Marietta, as we have said, was the *Ohio Gazette,* and *the Teritorial and Virginia Herald,* issued December 7, 1801. It was published by Wyllys Silliman and Elijah Backus, lawyers, who bought their material in Philadelphia. Their press was a wooden one with a stone bed, which is now in the office of the Marietta *Register.* The paper was printed upon Front street, near the Stockade, for the first few years, and afterward moved to "the Point." Elijah Backus performed most of the editorial duties upon the paper. In his salutatory, according to Caleb Emerson, who wrote a historical article upon the press in 1839, he apologized for adding "Virginia Herald" to the title of the paper. "He might," he says, "rest this apology upon the generous and extensive patronage he has received from the inhabitants of the western part of Virginia," but he desires to place it upon broader ground, and continues:

He is, indeed, proud in having this opportunity, at this time, and by this measure to give his fellow-citizens on both sides of the Ohio a pledge of his equal regard, and an example of that liberality of sentiment which is not only so decorous in private character, but which forms so important a pillar in the fabric of social and political happiness.

Breathing the same air—having the same wants—being capable of the same pleasures—talking the same language—living under the same National Government, what is there to limit or divide our affections? A river! A river whose kindred branches we inhabit—whose current, mild and unbroken, though composed of a thousand tributary streams, affords us an impressive lesson of unity and peace.

Surely this country ought to become one of the happiest under Heaven! Blessed with a friendly climate—a rich and diversified soil—a rapidly increasing population, and separated on all sides from the rest of the world by lakes and mountains, we form a world of our own which can be ruined only by our own follies. Shall we admit, that of all the most fatal, a spirit of discord?

At present we enjoy the protection of a Government recognizing an equality of rights and having liberty for its basis. May it be perpetual! But may we never forget that the best guarantors of our freedom will ultimately be found in the justness of our principles, and the harmony of our feelings.

The paper was Republican in politics and supported Jefferson. It was of course very small in size, but that fact did not interfere with the charging of a high subscription price—two dollars and fifty cents per annum. The paper was made up of national and foreign news—the latter about two months old, and advertisements, most of which were of a legal or official nature. There was little or nothing of the matter which now gives weekly newspapers their chief value, and which is usually termed "local."

Royal Prentiss, afterward an editor of the paper, and a well known citizen of Marietta, was a printer in the office of the *Ohio Gazette and Territorial and Virginia Herald* when it was first issued.

Mr. Backus was elected to the State senate in 1803, and afterwards removed to Pittsburg, where he died in 1807 or 1808.

Mr. Silliman was a member of the first State legislature, which assembled in March, 1803. He went to Zanesville as register of the land office under Jefferson's administration, and was for many years a well known lawyer there. He died in Zanesville some time in the forties.

Samuel Fairlamb became the proprietor of this paper in 1805, buying of Backus, who had two years before absorbed Silliman's interest. Fairlamb changed the name to *Ohio Gazette and Virginia Herald,* and continued to publish it, though with some irregularities, until the close of 1810. He was a Philadelphia printer. Removing to Zanesville he led a somewhat precarious existence, and died in the Muskingum County infirmary twenty years ago or more.

The Commentator and Marietta Recorder, a Federalist paper, started in opposition to the *Gazette,* was first issued September 16, 1807, by Dunham & Gardiner. Mr. James B. Gardiner was well known during early Whig days in Columbus and Xenia. The paper only remained in existence about two years, dying from lack of patronage.

The *Gazette* also lacked the support necessary to maintain its editor, and was sold out by the sheriff. In October, 1810, the *Western Spectator* was issued and took the place, in a certain sense, of the old *Gazette.* It was Federalist in politics and bore the motto "Be just and fear not." It was edited by one of the best known characters, and one of the ablest men, Marietta ever possessed—Caleb Emerson.[*] He was a vigorous writer, and made a very creditable paper. Joseph Israel was succeeded as printer or publisher in 1811 by Thomas G. Ransom. After a period of about two years and a half the paper was sold to the proprietor of the *American Friend,* which was first issued April 24, 1813. It was started as a Republican paper, and supported Madison's administration. The publisher was Thomas G. Ransom. David Everett, Timothy Buell, and D. H. Buell appear to have been associated in the ownership, and the first named was editor. He was the author of the lines, familiar to every school boy in the land, beginning:

> You'd scarce expect one of my age
> To speak in public on the stage,
> If I should chance to fall below
> Demosthenes or Cicero,
> Don't view me with a critic's eye,
> But pass my imperfections by.

He wrote these lines for a little pupil of his (Ephraim H. Farrer), while he was teaching school at New Ipswich, New Hampshire, his native State. He had read law at Amherst, New Hampshire, and attained considerable distinction as an editor in Boston; but his health having failed, he was obliged to seek a less vigorous climate, and so came to Marietta, arriving in March, 1813. He died of consumption December 21, 1813,

---

[*] See biography of Caleb Emerson in chapter upon the Bar of Washington County.

aged forty-four years, and was buried with Masonic honors. He was a man of splendid abilities.

The Buells retained possession of the *American Friend*, and D. H. Buell became editor upon the first of January, 1814. In April of the same year, Royal Prentiss took an interest in the publication of the paper, and continued in partnership with the Buells until 1816, when he bought them out, and thus became sole owner. Timothy and Daniel H. Buell were men of mark (the latter was the father of William H. Buell), and conducted the paper in a manner which commanded much respect. Mr. Prentiss maintained the character of the paper, and remained in control until 1833. During a portion of the time G. Prentiss was associated with him. The name was enlarged in 1823 to the *American Friend and Marietta Gazette*. Royal Prentiss was a man of true worth and great popularity, as is attested by the fact that he was township clerk, lieutenant colonel in the militia, auditor of Washington county, and the holder of several other offices of trust and honor. The paper was not remunerative to Mr. Prentiss, as is indicated by his valedictory, which appeared May 11, 1833. He says that during his nineteen years connection with the *Friend*, as proprietor, "the principal part of the mechanical labor has been performed by myself, without which, and close application to business, too, the paper could not have survived to the present." He gives as one of the reasons for selling, "that the profit of the business is not sufficient to remunerate me for the money and labor actually expended in carrying it on."

During a portion of the time that Mr. Prentiss owned the *Friend*, it was printed at his house on Fifth street, where Judge S. S. Knowles now lives. He was industrious and economical, but, with his revenue from the paper and from the several offices which he held, he managed to save only a small property.

The persons to whom Mr. Prentiss sold the paper in 1833 were John Delafield, jr., a young man of some literary pretensions, from New York, and Mr. Edward W. Nye (son of Colonel Ichabod Nye), now a resident of Williamstown, West Virginia. They dropped the first part of the name and left it simply the *Marietta Gazette*. During the next two years the paper was edited by Messrs. Delafield and Nye. Pazzi Lapham, a strolling printer, became interested in it in 1835, but remained only a short time. Messrs Delafield and Nye sold out in December, 1837. The former died at Memphis, in 1862. Isaac Moxon, the purchaser of the *Gazette*, was a strong Whig, but "thought a little slow by some of the younger men of the community." He has latterly lived in Illinois. During the period from 1837 to 1841 Caleb Emerson and his son, William D., the latter still living in Marietta, were engaged upon the *Gazette*, though with some irregularity.

Edmund B. Flagg came to Marietta in 1842 and took the position of editor and proprietor of the *Gazette*. He was a native of Maine and a graduate of Bowdoin college in 1835. In 1836 he was correspondent of the Louisville *Journal*, while travelling through Illinois and Missouri, and collected his correspondence and published it in two volumes bearing the title "The Far West." He was engaged in journalism in St. Louis and Louisville in 1837, 1838 and 1839, and in 1840 practiced law in Vicksburgh, with the distinguished Sargent S. Prentiss. While in Marietta he wrote two romances—"Carrero," and "Francis of Valois." He was consul to Venice in 1850, and published a book upon Venice afterward. In 1851 he became editor of a Democratic paper in New Orleans, and was in the employ of the Government during Buchanan's administration. Mr. Flagg was the last editor of the *Gazette*. It was merged, in 1842, with another paper—the *Intelligencer*—which had been started as a rival sheet three years before.

The Marietta *Intelligencer* appeared in the summer of 1839. This date marked the beginning of a new era in the history of the Marietta press. Beman Gates, the editor, was born in Montague, Franklin county, Massachusetts, January 5, 1818; moved with his father to Connecticut, in 1835, and in 1837, came west with a brother-in-law. It was his intention to go to Knoxville, Tennessee, and in fact he had an engagement there, but he was pleased with Marietta, and quite willing to seek no farther for a location. Still he would doubtless have gone on to Tennessee had he not been detained by his brother-in-law's illness. He decided to remain and was confident of finding something to do. He obtained a chance to do writing in the recorder's office, and soon began teaching vocal music in the college. Unexpectedly he received a proposition to become editor of a paper which had been projected, as a live Whig organ. The *Intelligencer* was started with young Gates (who had barely reached his twenty-first year) as editor, and George W. and Charles D. Tyler as the publishers. The Tyler boys, as they were called, were the members of the firm who had the practical knowledge. The elder, George W., was a perfect type setter and a fine pressman. He and his brother were both several years older than Mr. Gates, and each of them had a family. They had been printing for some time the Marietta and Washington county *Pilot*, edited by Charles B. Flood (a paper of which we shall have more to say in this chapter). The sum of six hundred dollars was raised by the Tylers though they were obliged to sell their houses to do it, and Mr. Gates added three hundred dollars borrowed money, to the capital. The firm immediately after deciding upon the issuance of a paper, bought a Washington hand-press, and a small quantity of large type, and the first *Intelligencer* was given to the light upon the twenty-ninth of August, 1839. Three hundred copies of the first issue were printed. The paper was larger than any previously issued in Marietta, and very handsomely printed. The subscription price was announced as two dollars per year. The following was the young editor's salutatory:

The general plan upon which this paper will be conducted has been set forth in the prospectus. The subscriber, in commencing his duties as editor, wishes it to be distinctly understood that he has no prejudices to foster, no partialities to indulge, and no invidious feelings to gratify. He is perfectly willing to be advised in regard to the manner of conducting it, but, after all, his own judgment must decide what course duty requires him to pursue. He will not suffer himself to be influenced by the opinions of others in any way incompatible with perfect freedom of thought and action. He speaks particularly on this point, because he has been charged with being under the control of influential men in this town.

In politics his motto will be, "Willing to praise, but not afraid to blame." He will be equally ready to bestow praise upon his political enemies, when merited, or censure upon his friends, when necessary It will therefore be conducted with impartial liberality, and no efforts shall be wanting on the part of the subscriber to render it distinguished by its practical utility.

Temperate and well written communications upon any subject that shall be deemed of general interest, will be thankfully received and inserted.

With this brief statement the first number or the *Intelligencer* is offered to the public, that by it they may judge of its merits and of the claims it has upon their patronage.

BEMAN GATES.

The *Intelligencer* received this notice in advance from the *Gazette:*

We understand the new paper, the *Marietta Intelligencer,* is to appear next week. This paper is to eclipse everything, exterminate Democracy, astonish the natives and swallow the *Gazette* with all its appendages. Now, to the latter performance we shall object. Although we labor under disadvantageous circumstances, not having asked or received from our business men, county or town officers, a pledge of their entire patronage, nor have we the assurance of aid by able writers to assist us in editing or writing, still we are not disposed to stop business just yet. It has been argued to some of our subscribers that they might as well discontinue the *Gazette* and subscribe for the *Intelligencer,* because the *Gazette* must stop at all events. Had not the gentlemen better stay their judgment for a time, and see if the community will that we shall be crushed in order to rear a favorite upon the ruin?

It was not until the Harrison campaign that the new Whig paper had three hundred paying subscribers, but the list more than doubled during the year 1840, and its success was assured. It drew heavily from the *Gazette.* Influential Whigs interested themselves in extending the circulation of the *Intelligencer,* for it was helping their cause.

In 1844 Charles D. Tyler sold out his interest in the paper to Mr. Gates, and in the following year George W. Tyler also sold out, but continued to print the paper until 1856. The first named moved to Ontonagon, Michigan, where he published a paper for several years, and then located in Missouri. From October, 1851, to January, 1861, the *Intelligencer,* was published both as a weekly and a tri-weekly. The circulation of the two editions was about eighteen hundred, and the weekly alone had more than twelve hundred, which was very large for the time.

In 1853 the New Orleans and Ohio telegraph line was established from Wheeling to the Gulf of Mexico, and in less than a month from the time the wires were put in use, Taylor was inaugurated President, and the *Intelligencer,* received his message by telegraph. Mr. Gates had regular paid correspondents at Pittsburgh and Cincinnati, and at Columbus during the sessions of the general assembly.

Caleb Emerson wrote a great deal for the paper. It is remembered that among other articles of a literary nature which he furnished, was a review, in 1840, of Carlyle's Sartor Resartus, which appeared at that time. At no other time has so much money been expended for journalistic labor in Marietta as during the sixteen years of Mr. Gates' connection with the *Intelligencer.* When the railroad brought in the Cincinnati papers, the field of the *Intelligencer* was narrowed and made more purely local, and competition with the dailies being impossible, the large outlay of money for telegraphic news was suspended.

Mr. Gates sold out in April, 1856, to Dr. T. L. Andrews. who was editor and proprietor until June, 1862, when he in turn sold out to Rodney M. Stimson, and a few years later removed to Iowa. Mr. Stimson, who took possession as editor and proprietor of the paper June 5th and changed its name to the *Marietta Register,* came well prepared for the task before him. He had been for twelve years, from 1850 to 1862, editor of an Ironton, Ohio, journal. He was born at Milford, New Hampshire, October 26, 1824; entered Phillips Exeter academy—the junior class—in 1845, and graduated at Marietta college in 1847. Mr. Stimson was a member of the State senate three years, being first elected in 1869 and reelected in 1871. He was State librarian from March, 1877, to March, 1879 (see longer biography in chapter on the Bar of Washington County). During the ten years in which he was editor of the *Register* Mr. Stimson not only made his paper an excellent one by the usual methods of good editorial work, but gave it an exceptional interest and value by the publication in its columns of a large amount of historical matter pertaining to Marietta and the region round about.

E. R. Alderman & Co. (the company was J. W. Dumble) took possession of the *Register* May 20, 1872. Mr. Dumble remained in the partnership until 1875, since which time Mr. Alderman has been the sole proprietor and editor. He was born in a log cabin near Athens August 29, 1839 (the day that the old *Intelligencer* was first issued). He was thrown on his own resources when a boy; went to school and taught school in the western part of Washington county; was in the mercantile business six years in Racine, Meigs county, and came to Marietta in 1867 and engaged in the general and life insurance business. The *Register* was enlarged by Mr. Alderman January 1, 1874, from an eight to a nine column paper.

We have now followed what may be called one succession of newspapers from the beginning down to the present. The *Register* it is claimed is the lineal descendent of the old *Ohio Gazette and the Virginia and Territorial Herald.*

There remains another succession to be spoken of— that which is represented by the *Marietta Times.* There were also several publications, for the most part short-lived, which belonged to neither of the lines of descent.

The first of this latter class (not heretofore alluded to) was the Marietta *Minerva,* first issued in October, 1823, by John K. and A. V. D. Joline, and suspended December 3, 1824.

The Marietta and Washington county *Pilot* was the first Democratic paper in the town, and the beginning of the succession to which the *Times* belongs. It appeared April 7, 1826, with the names of George Dunlevy and A. V. D. Joline as publishers. The latter had editorial control of the paper. The *Pilot* was at first neutral in politics, but in 1827 espoused the cause of Jackson. Party feeling ran very high in Marietta at this time. The *Friend* advocated the reelection of John Quincy Adams.

The campaign opened early, and was quite bitter locally. During the heated controversy between the local papers in 1828, an amusing incident occurred, and one which was rather embarrassing to the *Pilot*. In some manner, (probably through the agency of a printer of the *Friend* office) the letters at the head of the *Pilot* were transposed so as to read *Lipot*, and an edition of the paper was worked off and circulated before the mistake was discovered. The *Friend* in its next issue thus commented upon the change:

A SIGN.—Mr. Joline's editorial matter for once has a true heading. It came out last Saturday under the appropriate name of the *Lipot*. Whether he has blundered into the truth, or whether he has just begun to practice on his motto of "no concealment," we pretend not to determine. If he really means to fight no longer under false colors, he will do himself some little honor for candor, if not for truth.

Mr. Joline became postmaster at Marietta under Jackson in 1829 and remained in office until 1834. He subsequently went south and died in Memphis in 1845 or 1846. The last number of the *Pilot* was issued in May, 1830.

John Brough, afterwards auditor of State, and still later governor of Ohio, and his brother, Charles H., had learned the printer's trade under the Jolines, and buying the material of the defunct *Pilot*, they started the *Western Republican and Marietta Advertiser*, issuing the first number January 8, 1831. John Brough was at this time not twenty years of age. The *Friend* spoke of him as "Master" Brough. He showed, however, at this early age, considerable of the ability and force which were more fully developed in his later years. He made the *Republican* a strong paper, and supported Jackson's administration very energetically. His motto was, "Freedom of speech is man's inalienable birthright—the liberty of the press his impregnable safeguard." The paper was published in Marietta only about two years, then removed to Parkersburgh, and after a few months to Lancaster.

In the quarrel between Jackson and Calhoun the Broughs took the Calhoun side. The Nullifiers, as the Calhoun men were called, had only a very small representation in Washington county, and the paper lost its patronage; hence its removal.

Briefly, the career of this remarkable man, John Brough, was as follows: He was born in 1811 at his father's home, Cleona farm, at the mouth of Duck creek. His father died in the epidemic of 1823; his mother had been dead for several years, and the orphan boy at the age of twelve years entered the *Friend* office to learn the printer's trade under Royal Prentiss. He subsequently went to Athens, where he maintained himself while studying in one of the departments of the State university. From Athens he came to Marietta, and was the "Master Brough" and the "little lad" of the *Republican*. We have spoken of his removal to Lancaster. It was in that place that his talents received their first recognition. He was elected in 1838 as the representative of Fairfield and Hocking counties in the legislature. By this legislature he was chosen, when only twenty-eight years of age, State auditor, which office he filled with ability for six years. In 1845 he went to Cincinnati to study law. In 1841 he had bought the *Phenix* from Moses Dawson,

and started the *Enquirer* in company with his brother, Charles H. Brough. He was editor-in-chief of this paper in 1846-47, his brother having gone as a colonel into the Mexican war. In 1848 John Brough left the *Enquirer* and was elected president of the Madison & Indianapolis railroad. He remained in that position and exhibited great ability as a railroad manager until 1863, when he was elected governor of Ohio by one hundred and one thousand majority. He died while holding this position.

In 1834 a Democratic paper was started as the successor of the *Republican*, by John S. McCracken, who published it about eight weeks. Its support was insufficient; and one morning a note was found in the office, signed by McCracken, which ran thus: "I'm off, as the fly said when it lit on the mustard pot." The paper stopped.

The *Marietta Democrat* was started in August, 1835, by Charles B. Flood, who has since been, for several years, on the editorial staff of the daily Ohio *Statesman*, clerk of the Ohio senate and supervisor of public printing. He published the paper until 1838, when it was transferred to Jacob Baughey. It soon failed, and the material became the property of Daniel Radebaugh, jr., who issued in April, 1840, the first number of the *Washington County Democrat*, a paper which remained in existence for only a very short time. It was revived in 1844 by J. C. C. Carroll, and published until after the presidential election of that year, when it passed out of existence.

In 1849 the Democracy of the county had long been without an organ, when Amos Layman, who had but recently graduated from Marietta college and was reading law, was prevailed on to start a Democratic paper. He procured new material throughout, and gave the paper a new name—*The Marietta Republican*. Mr. Layman made the new Democratic organ a success, and it became a paying and prosperous paper. After conducting it for more than five years, he transferred it to Andrew W. McCormick, and accepted a position in the Indian service of the Government. Mr. Layman was afterward, for six years, the editor of the *Daily Ohio Statesman* of Columbus, succeeding George W. Manypenny. The duties of the position he performed creditably and acceptably during all the years of the civil war, and afterward, until he resigned it to take the office of clerk of the Ohio house of representatives. Mr. Layman held this position two terms, and has the reputation of having been the best clerk that body ever had. He afterward had the supervision of the publication of the debates and proceedings of the Constitutional convention of 1873-74; was executive clerk in the office of the Government during the administration of William Allen; and assisted the Codifying Commission of Ohio, from 1875 to 1880, in the work of revising and consolidating the statutes of the State. He was for a long series of years a member of the State Central and Executive committees of his party, and secretary thereof; was a delegate to the Democratic National convention of 1856, and one of its secretaries.

The Home News, a small quarto was first issued in

C. M. Cole

May, 1859, by E. Winchester, and in 1862 sold to R. M. Stimson, who merged it with the *Register*.

After the suspension of the *Republican*, in 1863, there was no Democratic paper in Marietta for nearly a year, but Walter C. Hood supplied the want by issuing, September 24, 1864, the *Marietta Times*. Hood sold out in 1871. He became State librarian while William Allen was governor, and died in February, 1875 while holding that office. He was a native of Somerset, Perry county, and previous to the time of his location in Marietta had established papers in Portsmouth and Ironton.

S. M. McMillen, the present editor of the *Times*, brought out the first issue that appeared under his management August 3, 1871, although he had been for a short period anterior to that time connected with the office. He has enlarged the *Times* to eight columns. Mr. McMillen is a native of Pennsylvania, and was born in Allegheny, August 19, 1840. He was connected with the Steubenville *Gazette* prior to coming to Marietta.

The newest candidate for public favor is the *Marietta Leader*, first issued by Frank A. Crippen and Will S. Knox, February 23, 1881. It is a handsome eight-column paper, of newsy character. Mr. Crippen was born March 1, 1845. He served some time on the Cincinnati papers; located in Marietta in 1878, and was local editor of the *Times* for two years previous to the establishment of the *Leader*. Mr. Knox is a son of M. G. Knox, and a grandson of Captain William Knox, of Harmar, and was born October 31, 1860.

There have been published several college magazines. The first was the Marietta *Collegiate Magazine* begun in June, 1854, and continued through three volumes of nine numbers each. The Marietta *Collegiate Quarterly* was first issued in November, 1865, by the senior class. Only one volume was issued. The Marietta *Olio* was started in November, 1872, and is still continued. After the first volume the name was changed to the *College Olio*. It is published by the two literary societies.

The German press history dates back to 1856. The first journal published in the German language in Marietta was issued August 3rd, of that year, by William Lorey, and bore the name *Der Marietta Demokrat*. This paper was published by Mr. Lorey until 1865, when it passed into the hands of Messrs. Mueller & Schultz, who shortly after abandoned its publication. It was then revived by its former publisher, Mr. Lorey, but he issued it only eighteen weeks and then suspended publication.

In 1861, Messrs. Joseph Wildt and Frederick Neuberger, under the firm name of Neuberger & Co., started a Republican German paper *Der Beolachter*. This paper was at first edited by Mr. Wildt and after he entered the Union army, by Doctor F. W. Neuberger. *Der Beolachter* only existed about nine months—German Republicans being too scarce in those days in Washington county, to give the paper a proper support. Mr. E. Schmidt, foreman of the office tried to revive the paper under another name but did not succeed. Mr. Wieldt died in 1875, in Cincinnati, and Doctor Neuberger died in 1867. E. Schmidt also died a few years ago, and Mr. Lorey a few months ago in Marietta.

In 1867 the Rev. Constantine Arnold, pastor of the German Protestant St. Luke's church, started an independent paper, *Der Patriot*, and published twenty-two numbers. He was granted the use of the material of the former *Beolachter*. This material had been bought by F. Neuberger & Company for five hundred dollars, and consisted of the type and presses of the once famous Cincinnati sheet, *Der Hochwachter*, an anti religious paper published by Frederick Hassaurek. Mr. Arnold was obliged to leave Marietta, and the paper ceased to be. In October, 1868, Mr. Winchester issued the first number of the *Marietta Zeitung*, published with the assistance of Mr. F. Neuberger, of the former *Beolachter*. Some twenty odd numbers were published by Mr. Winchester, and in April, 1869, he sold out to Jacob Mueller, who, assisted by his son, Louis Mueller, now conducts the paper. Mr. Mueller was born in Rheinish Bavaria, July 29, 1833, and came to America in 1849, after graduating from school and journeying through France. He located at Albany, New York, for a short time, and then became a resident of Cincinnati, where he resided for seventeen years. His wife having died, he removed to Marietta in 1866, and married as his second wife, in 1869, Lizzie, daughter of Colonel William C. Buck. He was engaged in commercial business prior to his purchase of *Der Zeitung*.

CHAPTER XXXI.

MARIETTA — SOCIETIES.

Masonry—American Union Lodge No. 1—The Oldest Institution in the State, and Antedating the American Government—Organization of the Lodge in Massachusetts in 1776—With the Revolutionary Army Through the War—Washington a Visitor—Seal of the Lodge —Rufus Putnam a Member—Reorganization of American Union Lodge, in Campus Martius, at Marietta, June 28, 1790, by Captain Jonathan Heart, of Fort Harmar—Recognized by the Grand Lodges of Massachusetts and Pennsylvania—Blennerhassett a Member—Lewis Cass—Rechartered by the Grand Lodge of Ohio in 1816—List of Masters—Centennial Celebration—American Union Chapter R. A. M. No. 1 Organized in 1792—Succession of High Priests—Harmar Lodge No. 390—Odd Fellowship—Marietta Lodge No. 67—Instituted by John Brough in 1846—Guttenburg Lodge (German)—Chartered in 1857—Harmar Lodge No. 115—Knights of Pythias—Miscellaneous Societies.

MASONRY.

AMERICAN UNION LODGE NO. 1, F. AND A. M.

This is the oldest institution in Marietta, and the oldest Masonic lodge in Ohio, or the five States originally the Northwest Territory. Its organization was effected prior to that of the American Government, and in the beginning of the Revolutionary struggle. In the winter of 1775-76 Boston was in the possession of the British, and the Patriot army was encamped before it. Among the soldiers of the Connecticut line there were a few Free Masons, who, anxious to enjoy the amenities of such intercourse as that to which they had been accustomed, resolved to organize a lodge in connection with the army, following a precedent which had long before been established in the British army. In the colony of Connecticut, from whence these officers and soldiers hailed, there was no organization which had authority to issue a warrant for a new lodge, and Boston being invested by the British the meetings of the Provincial grand lodge had been suspended. Of this organization John Rowe was grand master, and Richard Gridley deputy. The latter, who had power to act in the matter, was accessible, and to him application was made for authority to assemble and work as a regular lodge in connection with the Connecticut line of the army, then at Roxbury. In response was issued the following peculiar document, the warrant under which American Union Lodge was organized:

John Rowe, Grand Master; to Joel Clarke, esq., greeting.

By virtue of authority invested in us, I hereby, reposing special trust and confidence in your knowledge and skill of the ancient craft, do appoint and constitute you, the said Joel Clarke, esq., master of American Union Lodge, now erected in Roxbury, or wherever your body shall remove on the continent of America, provided it is where no grand master is appointed.

You are to promote in your lodge the utmost harmony and brotherly love and to keep up to the constitutions for the reputation of the craft. In your makings you are to be very cautious of the moral character of such persons, and also of visitors and such as desire to become members of your lodge (such as were not made before it). You are to transmit to the grand lodge a fair account of the choice of your officers, as well present as future. Any matters coming before your lodge that cannot be adjusted, you are to appeal to, and lay before the grand lodge for a decision. You are, as often as the grand lodge meets, to attend with your two wardens. Of the time and place the grand lodge meets you will have previous notice.

In order to support the grand lodge, your lodge is to pay into the hands of the grand secretary, each quarterly night, the sum of twelve shillings lawful money; all of which you will pay due regard to. This commission to remain in full force and virtue until recalled by me or my successor in office.

Given under my hand and the hands of the grand wardens (the seal of the grand lodge first affixed) this, the fifteenth day of February, Anno Mundi 5776, of salvation, 1776.

                                        RICHARD GRIDLLY, D. G. M.
                                        WILLIAM BURBECK, S. G W.
                              ————— , J. G. W.

The lodge which came into being in accordance with this communication was the first ever organized in America under American authority. Its first meeting was held and the lodge constituted at Waterman's tavern, Roxbury, Massachusetts, February 10, 1776. The original members as named on the minutes of the meeting were Colonel Joel Clark, Colonel John Park, Thomas Chase, esq., Ensign Jonathan Heart, Captain Joseph Hoiet, Colonel Samuel Holden Parsons, Captain Ezekiel Scott, ——— Whittlesey, and ——— Cotton, Fellow Crafts; and Colonel Samuel Wyllys Entered Apprentice. This military lodge throughout the whole period of the Revolution was with the army and held its meetings at such times as were thought proper and in whatever places the army chanced to be encamped. Shortly after the organization was effected a seal was made for the lodge. As the name American Union Lodge was supposed to have been suggested by Benjamin Franklin, so was the symbolism of the seal. Prominent in the device and surrounding the square and compasses appeared a chain of thirteen links, joined at the top by clasped hands. Above were the sun, moon and stars and below

three burning tapers. This seal was engraved by the celebrated patriot Paul Revere.

On August 13, 1776, the lodge held a meeting at New York. On the twenty-seventh of August a sanguinary battle took place on Long Island, in which the American army suffered serious loss. Among others who were taken prisoners were Right Worshipful Joel Clark, and upon the thirteenth of September two members, James Chapman and Micajah Gleason, were killed, and William Cleveland and John P. Wyllys taken prisoners. Colonel Clark died soon after in captivity, and, as many of the members were called away to other fields of action, the lodge was adjourned.

It was not again convened until February 15, 1779, when that portion of the army with which it was connected being in Connecticut, the secretary, Jonathan Heart, having issued a call, a meeting was held "at widow Sanford's, near Reading old meeting house." Jonathan Heart presided at this meeting. An election of officers took place, and Samuel Holden Parsons (afterwards prominent in the Ohio company, and one of the judges of the Northwest Territory) was elected master; Jonathan Heart, senior warden; and Elisha Marshall, junior warden. The master elect was not present, and seems not to have been at subsequent meetings for some time, as Jonathan Heart served in the capacity of master. Two days later the lodge met again at Mrs. Sanford's, when several additions were made to the membership. Other meetings were held upon the twenty-fourth, and upon the tenth, seventeenth, and twenty-fifth of March. On the twenty-fifth the members of the lodge dined together. On the seventh of May the lodge "closed without date," as the army was compelled to move.

On the twenty-fourth of June the lodge was at Nelson's Point, on the Hudson, Washington having established his headquarters at New Windsor. The twenty-fourth, being St. John's day, was duly celebrated. Being joined by a number of their Masonic brothers, the members of American Union lodge proceeded to the Robinson house, two miles down the river, where they were met by General Washington and his family, who dined with them. Here addresses were delivered by the Rev. Dr. Hitchcock and Major William Hull (the General Hull of War of '12 fame).

About this time another military lodge was organized, which consisted of soldiers of the Massachusetts line. It was named Washington lodge. Colonel Benjamin Tupper (afterwards a member of American Union lodge, one of the originators of the Ohio company and Marietta pioneer) was chosen senior warden. During the months of July, August and September, many prominent gentlemen of the army were initiated as members of American Union lodge, among whom were Colonel Rufus Putnam, Colonel Gamaliel Bradford, Dr. Elisha Skinner, Dr. Samuel Finley, Colonel John Brooks, afterwards governor of Massachusetts, Lieutenant James Baxter, Lieutenant Peleg Heath, Dr. Jonathan Graham, Captain Henry Ten Eyck, Asa Worthington, Captain Stephen Beats and Moses Cleaveland, after whom the city of Cleveland was named. The lodge passed a pleasant and profitable summer on the Hudson, but in December it was in session at Morristown, New Jersey, Captain Heart presiding. General Washington was again a visitor. In the midsummer of 1780 the lodge was again upon the Hudson. The movements of the army had prevented an election of officers at the proper time, and therefore one was held July 30th, with the result of choosing Captain Heart master. From this time onward, for a period of nearly two years, active military service prevented the possibility of holding lodge meetings, but in March, 1782, the lodge was again on the Hudson, and convened at the "Connecticut huts." Captain Heart was again elected master. The lodge held numerous meetings during the summer, and, in conjunction with Washington lodge, celebrated St. John's day at West Point. In October a meeting was held at Verplanck Point, and in March, 1783, we find it again at West Point. The great struggle for independence was now over, and the troops were awaiting discharge. The lodge, which for seven years had lived and moved with the American army, held its last meeting while connected with that army on April 23, 1783. It was upon that day adjourned to such a time as the master should choose to call it together.

The future was uncertain. It was destined, however, that American Union lodge should again be brought into active existence, and in a land which at the time of its adjournment had no inhabitants. Captain Heart who had been its master on the banks of the Hudson, was after a period of seven years to be its master upon the banks of the Ohio and the Muskingum.

The lodge was reorganized at Marietta June 28, 1790, —a little over two years from the time the first settlement was made. Judge James M. Varnum who died upon the tenth of January, 1789, had been buried with Masonic honors. This was the first Masonic work done in the State of Ohio. Very likely this solemn ceremony had suggested to the Masons in the little settlement the propriety of making more fast the ties of brotherhood which existed between them. They remembered that Captain Jonathan Heart, their old master, who was now the commandant of Fort Harmar just across the Muskingum, still had in his possession the warrant of their old army lodge, and they determined to revive it if possible. Upon the twenty-fifth of June, 1790, at Numsell & Buell's in Marietta, was gathered a company, consisting of the following members of the Masonic fraternity: Rufus Putnam, Benjamin Tupper, Griffin Greene, Robert Oliver, Ezra Lunt, William Stacey, William Burnham, Auselm Tupper, Thomas Stanley and Ebenezer Sproat. They framed a petition which set forth that "having considered the disadvantages that the brethren af the ancient and honorable society of Free and Accepted Masons, have labored under in this western hemisphere, relative to their further knowledge from the east, that W. Brother Jonathan Heart at Fort Harmar, would take them under his immediate patronage, and establish them on a permanent basis; and give them, and the other brethren of the fraternity in this quarter, an apportunity to meet him as soon as possibly consistent."

They received the following reply from Captain Heart:

Previous to the late Revolution all authority exercised in America with respect to masonry was derived from the grand lodge in Great Britain, delegated to deputies in and over certain districts, by virtue of which all lodges were then held The Federal territories not coming within the district of any grand lodge, holding under authority of the grand lodge of Great Britain and the United States, not as yet having formed a Federal head in masonry, it may be in doubt whether at this time there is any power in America having jurisdiction over the Federal territories From whence it follows the power is still in the grand lodge of Great Britain, unless there can be found some power which has been delegated other ways than through the present grand lodges and extending its jurisdiction to this country. Whether the warrant under which you wish to be convened affords protection is the next subject of enquiry.

This warrant was granted in the year 1776, previous to the Declaration of Independence, by Richard Gridley, esq , deputy grand master, whose authority extended to all parts of North America where no special grand masters were appointed, as may appear from the book of constitution, and as expressed in the same instrument. It will therefore follow that, there being no special grand master for this territory, a more ample authority for holding a lodge in this country could not be obtained, provided there was a competent number of the former members present But there are only two, viz. Brother Putnam and myself—who were actual enrolled members. To remove this objection, it is observable there are two others who are members and resident in this county, but at present at too great a distance to attend There are also two of the petitioners who were constant visitors of the lodge during the war, one of them a past master (Brother Bingham Tupper) who by custom is a member of all lodges. There are also others of the petitioners who have frequently visited the lodge at different times.

Wherefore, under every consideration with respect to your situation —the difficulty of obtaining authority—a doubt whether more ample authority can, at this time, be obtained, the right which is ever retained by the individuals of incorporating themselves where there is no existing power already lodged with particulars for that purpose.

Wherefore, being the present master of the lodge held under the authority of said warrant, as may appear by having recourse to the records deposited in Frederick's lodge, held at Farmington, State of Connecticut, and being the eldest Ancient Mason within said territory, I have thought proper with the advice of brother Putnam, member, and brother Benjamin Tupper, past master, to grant the request contained in your petition, and will meet you in Campus Martius, on Monday the twenty-eighth instant, at six o'clock P. M., for the purpose of forming you into a lodge.

I am, with every sentiment of respect, brethren,
Your most obedient and humble servant,
JONATHAN HEART,
M. A. U. lodge.

Under date of June 28, 1790, the minutes state that the brethren being convened by order of the worshipful Jonathan Heart, proceeded to open the lodge in due form. There were present Worshipful Brother Heart, master; Worshipful Brother Benjamin Tupper, past master Hampshire lodge, acting as senior warden; Brother Rufus Putnam, junior warden; and Brothers Thomas Stanley, William Burnham, Griffin Greene, William Mills, Robert Oliver, and William Stacey. The warrant of February 15, 1776, was read, and on motion of Rufus Putnam the seven brothers were proposed as members of the lodge, and being balloted for were admitted as members. Benjamin Tupper was chosen senior warden, and Rufus Putnam, junior warden. On the fifteenth of July another meeting was held, at which Anselem Tupper, who was elected secretary, delivered a very happy little speech. At the meeting of August 2d, the lodge was visited by Major John Doughty (who built Fort Harmar), then just returned from Cincinnati, where he had erected Fort Washington. On September 6th, the first petitioner prayed for admission to the lodge; this was Francis Choate, of Leicester, Massachusetts. On October 4th, Rev. Daniel Story, the minister and teacher employed for the settlements by the Ohio company, was admitted; also Josiah Munroe. In November the lodge secured a number of French visitors—the Marquis de Marnasia and others.— December 6th Jonathan Heart was reelected master. Nathaniel Cushing was a visitor. Colonel R. J. Meigs, sr., Colonel R. J. Meigs, jr., and Charles Greene were elected members. The master's degree was conferred upon the Rev. Daniel Story, December 8th. St. John's day was celebrated December 27th. A procession was formed and marched to the court house. Prayer was offered by Rev. Daniel Story, and an address made by Anselem Tupper. Regular meetings were held in 1791 (the worst year of the Indian war) as well as in 1790. Jonathan Heart was again elected master, and he held that position until compelled to go with the army into the Indian country. His resignation was tendered August 22d, and Rufus Putnam was chosen in his place, but requested to be excused. Robert Oliver was elected and served. Heart was killed at St. Clair's defeat, in the fall of the same year—November 4th.

The lodge was recognized early in 1791 by the Grand lodge of Massachusetts, and in 1792 by that of Pennsylvania. The former said to American Union lodge "your warrant is, beyond doubt, a perfect and good one, and must have its force and operation where you are until a a grand lodge is founded and established in your territory, when it will become your duty to surrender it and obtain in its place a warrant from the grand lodge that may have the government of masonry in your State." From Pennsylvania came a communication, of which the following is a portion:

It is with equal surprise and pleasure the Grand lodge of Pennsylvania received the intelligence of the formation of a lodge in the midst of the immense wilderness of the west; where but lately wild beasts and savage men were the only inhabitants, and where ignorance and ferocity contributed to deepen the gloom which has covered that part of the earth from creation. This day of light which has thus broke in upon the gloom and darkness of ages they consider as a happy presage that the time is fast approaching when the knowledge of masonry will completely encircle the globe and the most distant regions of the western hemisphere rival those of the eastern in masonic splendor.

The early years of the American Union lodge in Marietta were pleasant and prosperous ones, and as full of promise as the best friends of the organization could wish. Large accessions of membership were received, and the lodge numbered among its supporters the best men in the settlement and State.

In 1797—upon August 12th, the famous Harman Blennerhassett, being in the west for the purpose of preparing his island home for the arrival of his family, was a visitor to the lodge. He soon became identified with it, and in December was elected secretary.

In April 1800, news of the action of the Grand lodge of Pennsylvania upon the death of Washington was received, and American Union lodge made the following reply:

With you, we sincerely feel the loss we sustained in the death of Washington, our beloved brother. And though he never graced our meetings or processions with his presence, yet the happy effect of his Masonic and civil virtues, of his heroism, wisdom, patriotism and policy have reached the west. They have extended to every extremity of the United States, and like the sun at high meridian, have cheered, enlightened and animated, not only America, but the whole civilized world.

On the first intelligence of his demise, the lodge unanimously agreed to wear mourning for six months, as a great, respectful and affectionate tribute to his memory; and we cannot but receive sublime satisfaction in the intelligence, that our brethren in the east unite with us in respect, esteem and veneration for so distinguished and so amiable a character. He was indeed an illustrious brother, citizen and chief—in peace and war, in council and action, pre-eminent.

Among other eminent men who became members of American Union lodge during its early years was Lewis Cass. He was initiated in 1803, and was afterward master of the Zanesville lodge and grand master of the Masons in Ohio.

In January, 1808, a convention was held at Chillicothe, consisting of delegates from lodges then at work in the State, to form a Grand lodge. At this convention American Union Lodge No. 1, was represented by Robert Oliver, Ichabod Nye, and William Skinner. A Grand lodge was organized, and the venerable Rufus Putnam, though not present, was elected the first grand master of Masons in Ohio. He was not, however, installed, and the deputy, Thomas Henderson, of Cincinnati, performed the duties of the office during the year. At the session of the Grand lodge a year after, in January, 1809, a fraternal letter was received from General Putnam, declining to accept the office, because of his age and inability to perform its duties. His letter is a very touching one. He says: "My sun is far past the meridian; it is almost set; a few sands only remain in my glass; I am unable to undergo the necessary labors of that high and important office; unable to make you a visit at this time, without a sacrifice and hazard of health which prudence forbids."

For some cause not clearly known, American Union lodge, though continuing in activity, declined for some years to receive a charter from the Grand lodge of Ohio, and was not again represented in that body until the session at Chillicothe, in January, 1816. The new charter recognized the lodge by its present name—American Union Lodge No. 1—and was accepted by its members. It still lives, the oldest of over five hundred lodges in the State of Ohio.

The following list of the masters of American Union lodge will convey some idea of the characters who constituted this old organization: Joel Clark, 1776; Samuel H. Parsons, 1779; Jonathan Heart, 1779-91; Robert Oliver, 1791-3; Rufus Putnam, 1794; Daniel Story, 1794-6; Charles Greene, 1797; Rufus Putnam, 1798; Josiah Monroe, 1799; Griffin Greene, 1799; Rufus Putnam, 1800; Return Jonathan Meigs, 1801; Rufus Putnam, 1801; Daniel Story, 1802-3; Rufus Putnam, 1804-5; Ichabod Nye, 1806-8; Morris B. Belknap, 1809; Ichabod Nye, 1810-12; Levi Barber, 1813-15; Augustus Stone, 1816; Samuel Hoict, 1817; Anaxamander Warner, 1818-1819; Levi Barber, 1820; John Cotton, 1821; W. A. Whittlesey, 1825-6; James Dunn, 1827-8; James M. Booth, 1829-30; no meetings from 1830-43; James Dunn, 1843-5; Hugh Trevor, 1846-7; T. J. Westgate, 1848; Hugh Trevor, 1849; James Dunn, 1850; Hugh Trevor, 1851; M. J. Morse, 1852; Benjamin Soule, 1853; J. F. Cox, 1854; Benjamin Soule, 1855; T. J. Westgate, 1856; Pardon Cook, 1857; Thomas F. Jones, 1858-60; Charles

SAMPSON COLE.

The subject of this sketch is probably the oldest man now living in the county. He was born at Providence, Rhode Island, November 9, 1784. He was the oldest child of Nathan and Mary Jett Cole and a grandson of John Cole, one of the first settlers of Warren, as will be seen by reference to the chapter on that township.

Nathan Cole removed, with his family, in 1787, to Pittstown, Rensselaer county, New York. He afterwards removed to the Hoosac valley and remained there till 1803, when he came to this county and temporarily took shelter in a log house, nearly opposite the mouth of the Kanawha. He purchased land on the Ohio river bank, within the present limits of Dunham township, and, while a cabin was being built, Samson, then a boy of nineteen, and his younger brother, lodged in the covered wagons. The house was ready for occupancy in a week and the family moved into it.

Five years of toil in the forest and on the new farm greatly impaired the strong and vigorous constitution o young Cole. He had labored from early morn till late at night, cutting trees and rolling logs, and was now compelled to seek less straining employment. His father donated him a tract of land in Marietta township, or more properly gave it to him in remuneration for his services, for when the deed was being drawn up and the question was asked what consideration should be named, his father announced "twelve hundred dollars." His mother, who was present, feelingly added: "Yes, and every cent of it has been paid."

About 1809, Sampson Cole and his brother, Levi, built a boat and went into the salt business on the Kanawha. Sampson took charge of the transportation and Levi superintended the furnaces. In 1811 he married Mary Duncan, who was born in Fluvanna county, Virginia, March 8, 1792. He quit the river and moved on his farm. His wife died April 7, 1814, leaving one child, Ann Maria, who was born January 11, 1813. She died October 30, 1832.

Mr. Cole married for his second wife, November 30, 1815, Amy Chase, who was born in Otsego county, New York, November 23, 1792. He had served in various township offices, and was, at the time of his second marriage, deputy sheriff. He began housekeeping in the old court house. In 1816 his appointment was renewed by the sheriff, Captain Timothy Buell. In 1820 he built the house on Ohio street, which he occupied as a tavern for a number of years. This building is now occupied by his son-in-law, J. H. Stanley, as a residence. In 1829 he exchanged the farm on which he first settled in Marietta township, for two hundred acres about two miles from town, now known as the Cole farm. He removed to this place in 1849, and continued farming until 1862, when his son, William H. Cole, joined him, and took away the responsibilities which, in his old age, were becoming a burden. In 1871, Mr. Cole and his good wife, who had in every avocation been his co-worker, retired from the farm and sought rest among their old friends in town. In their house on Fourth street they resided in perfect contentment until July 12, 1878, when the association of more than sixty-two years of married life was broken by the death of Mrs. Cole.

Five children were the fruit of this second marriage: George, born July 25, 1817, died September 30, 1818; James Wallace, born July 23, 1819, died June 20, 1833; Charles, born July 3, 1822, died August 3, 1822; Sarah Elizabeth, wife of J. W. Stanley, born December 23, 1824; and William H., born April 12, 1835.

Mr. Cole, since the death of his wife, has been making his home with the two surviving children, Mrs. Stanley and William H. Cole. He is naturally of a happy temperament, and has been throughout his whole life, of nearly a century, highly respected by his neighbors and acquaintances. In his earlier life he spoke little of the past, but, in his ripe old age, he narrates in an interesting way, the experiences of his youth.

Up to about three years ago, he was a member of the Unitarian church, but has since experienced a change of faith and united with the Congregationalists.

E. Sherman, 1861-2; George T. Hovey, 1862; E. Locker, 1863; George T. Hovey, 1864-7; L. C. Davison, 1869; E. Winchester, 1870; George T. Hovey, 1871-6; James McClure, 1877-8; George T. Hovey, 1879-81.

It will be seen that George T. Hovey, the present master of American Union lodge, has held the position more years than any of his predecessors. He has opened the lodge four hundred and eight times; conferred apprentice degree one hundred and thirty-one times; fellowcraft's degree, one hundred and fifteen times; master mason's degree one hundred and ten times. In all he has conferred three hundred and fifty-six degrees on one hundred and forty-eight persons. He has presided during his terms of office at eighteen masonic trials and twenty-five funerals.

Since the first meeting of American Union lodge west of the mountains, at Campus Martius June 28, 1790, the lodge has had many places for assembling. Meetings were continued at the original hall until August 4, 1800, (although the greater part of the structure of Campus Martius was torn down soon after the close of the war) and the lodge then occupied rooms in Joel Bower's two story frame building, on the north side of Greene street between Front and Second streets. This building was consumed by fire March 24, 1801, and the lodge lost all of its property in the rooms, including the original charter from the Provincial Grand lodge of Massachusetts. The next meeting was held at Major Lincoln's inn, on the east corner of Post and Ohio streets, April 6, 1801. Meetings were continued in this location until December 5, 1803. At a meeting of this date it was resolved that the lodge accept the kind offer of Brother Rufus Putnam, tendering his office on the south side of Washington street (the building is still standing) for the accommodation of the lodge during the winter, free of charge. The lodge continued its meetings here until February 5, 1810, at which time it was decided in the future to hold its meetings in the third story of Ichabod Nye's brick store building, on the south side of Putnam street, near the court house, Mr. Nye agreeing to furnish the room and wood for fuel for twenty-five dollars a year. The lodge continued to assemble here until December 27, 1815. A meeting was held at the store room of Levi Barber, in Harmar, January 25, 1816, one at the court house February 13th, and one at Nye's store March 12th, of the same year. The lodge then rented a hall of Levi Barber, of Point Harmar, and occupied it from April 9, 1816, to December 27, 1822. This hall was in a stone building on the corner of Muskingum and Market streets. On leaving this locality rooms were rented of Henry P. Wilcox, over the post office on the southeast corner of Front and Putnam streets, at fifty dollars per year. Meetings were held here from February 18, 1823, to December 22, 1825. The next move of the lodge was into its own rooms in a building erected in partnership with the building committee of school district No. 1, near the east side of Front street and in the rear of Mr. William H. Buell's present drug store. In 1851 the rooms over N. Holden's store building, on the south side of Greene street were rented, and these were occupied until 1854, when the lodge leased the third story of John M. Woodbridge's building, on the east side of Front street, where meetings were held until July 22, 1873, when the lodge again moved into a hall of its own —the one at present in use on the north corner of Front and Butler streets.

The centennial celebration of American Union lodge at Marietta, upon St. John's Day (June 24th), 1876, was an interesting and grand occasion. Not less than three thousand strangers attended, coming into town from all parts of Ohio and adjoining States by railroad, by the Ohio and Muskingum boats, and from the surrounding country by carriages. Seats were arranged upon the college campus for three thousand persons, and a dinning hall in the park accommodated one thousand persons at a time. An immense procession with numerous bands of music paraded the streets, the buildings along which were beautifully decorated with flags and banners— the emblems of the Nation, and of Masonry—and with evergreens and flowers. At the college grounds a beautiful oration was delivered by P. G. M., Richard Vaux, of Philadelphia, and a historical address by C. Moore, of Cincinnati, editor of the Masonic *Review*. A centennial ode by Robert Morris was read, and the exercises closed with some brief, well-chosen remarks by M. D. Follett, esq. In the evening, at the city hall, a benefit entertainment was given for American Union lodge.

The lodge has now about one hundred and twenty members, and is in a prospering condition.

In closing this brief history of the oldest Masonic lodge in Ohio, we may appropriately allude to the late Colonel Augustus Stone who was its oldest member. He was born July 23, 1780; made a Mason in American Union lodge November 2, 1807, and served as secretary in 1808-9-10-11, and as master in 1816. He died at his home in Harmar, on the fourteenth of June, 1879, and was believed to have been at that time the oldest affiliated Mason, the oldest secretary, and the oldest Past Master in the United States.

AMERICAN UNION, CHAPTER R. A. M., NO. 1.

This chapter was organized in Marietta, June 6, 1792, under authority of American Union Lodge No 1, with Robert Oliver, Rufus Putnam, and Griffin Greene, as officers, and Daniel Story, Return Jonathan Meigs, and Joseph Woods, as additional members. The chapter was continued in existence until March 22, 1801, when the lodge hall, charter, and papers were burned, but was reorganized in January, 1804, on having the charter renewed by the grand lodge of Massachusetts. It was recognized by the grand chapter of Ohio upon its organization, and is probably the oldest chapter in the State. In the convention to organize the grand chapter, at Worthington, Ohio, October 21, 1816, American Union chapter was represented by companions Samuel Hoiet, Levi Barber, and Joseph Woods, the former of whom was chosen first grand high priest. The present charter of the chapter bears date of October 24, 1816, and is signed by Lincoln Goodall, grand secretary, *pro tem*. The charter members were Joseph T. Willard, H. P.; David

Trowbridge, K.; William Skinner, S.; Levi Barber, Augustus Stone, Sardine Stone, Anaxmander Warner, Oliver Dodge, Peter Howe, and Samuel Hoiet. The following were the high priests under the lodge charter: 1792, Robert Oliver; 1793 to 1796, Daniel Story; 1797 to 1799, Rufus Putnam; 1800 to 1803, Daniel Story; 1804 to 1808, Rufus Putnam; 1809 to 1814, Ichabod Nye.

The following is a list of the high priests who have presided over the chapter under its present charter, the are last nine of whom with the exception of James Dunn, living: 1816, Joseph T. Millard; 1817, Levi Barber; 1818, David Trowbridge; 1819, Anaxamander Warner; 1820, Levi Barber; 1821 to 1824, Dr. John Cotton; 1825, W. A. Whittlesey; 1826 to 1827, Dr. John Cotton; 1828 to 1845, (interregnum); 1846 to 1853, James Dunn; 1854, Dr. Hugh Trevor; 1855 to 1856, John Bigelow; 1857 to 1858, James Dunn; 1859 to 1861, W. B. Mason; 1862 to 1864, (no election); 1865 to 1867, T. F. Jones; 1868 to 1869, James B. Hovey; 1870 to 1874, C. P. Bartlett; 1875 to 1879, W. B. Mason; 1880, J. W. Holden; 1881, Z. D. Walter.

HARMAR LODGE NO. 390, F. AND A. M.

The gentlemen constituting this lodge held their first meeting on the eighth of June, 1867, and organized by electing A. S. Curtiss chairman, and William H. Smith secretary. They worked under a dispensation until October 16, 1867, when a charter was obtained from the Grand lodge of Ohio. The following were the charter members: J. M. Blair, A. S. Curtis, W. H. Bisbee, Elijah Locker, Augustus Stone, William H. Smith, O. J. Chambers, J. J. Vanderwarker, Thomas J. Pattin, William H. Boothby, S. H. Tidd, Emil Michelis, T. C. Fitch. George T. Hovey, of American Union Lodge, instituted this lodge under the charter and the following officers were elected: Elijah Locker, W. M.; A. S. Curtiss, S. W.; S. H. Tidd, J. W.; Thomas J. Pattin, treasurer; William H. Smith, secretary; Joel M. Blair, S. D.; William H. Boothby, J. D.; E. Michelis, tyler. The meetings of this lodge are now held in the hall on the north side of Church street, between Second and Third streets, where the lodge was instituted. The lodge has about sixty-five members.

INDEPENDENT ORDER OF ODD FELLOWS, MARIETTA LODGE NO. 67.

Marietta lodge No. 67, Independent Order of Odd Fellows was organized under a charter issued by the grand lodge of Ohio. The charter was granted Worley Adams, John P. Beach, D. H. Mortley, Oliver Porter and A. G. Westgate. All of the charter members except J. P. Beach were members of Valley Lodge No. 36, McConnelsville, Ohio. These members drew cards from Valley lodge for the purpose of applying to the grand lodge for a charter for Marietta lodge. And after Marietta lodge was instituted they again returned to membership in Valley lodge, McConnelsville.

John Brough, who was afterwards governor of Ohio, was appointed by the grand master of Ohio, special deputy to institute Marietta lodge. Governor Brough was a native of Marietta, and always took a great inter-est in every public measure that was for the advancement of the town. On the twenty-ninth day of August, 1846, Governor Brough came to Marietta, and on that day instituted Marietta Lodge No. 67. The exercises took place in the Masonic hall, in a brick school-house on the rear of the lot on Front street, now occupied by Horatio Booth's and W. H. Buell's brick store buildings. The first officers elected were John P. Beach, noble grand; M. N. Marsh, vice grand; W. F. Curtis, secretary; and Owen Franks, treasurer. Several petitions for membership were presented, and ten members were elected and initiated into the solemn rites of the order.

The lodge progressed very rapidly, as the order has all over the country. The membership has included since its organization over three hundred men by initiation and card.

The financial affairs of the lodge have kept up with the increase of membership, and a large amount has been expended in benefits to sick members. The trustees for the widow and orphan's fund have expended the means of the lodge in the relief of many widows and orphans. These expenditures, together with the amount paid for the burial of deceased brothers, and for charitable purposes, would foot up a very large sum. The lodge is now on a sound financial basis. The amount of bonds, notes and real estate at present held by the lodge is equal in value to seven or eight thousand dollars.

The officers elected January, 1881, are—Naham Bergen, noble grand; J. A. Whitehead, vice grand; F. S. Coleman, secretary; and George Benedict, treasurer.

The meeting night is Monday, and the place in the third story of the building on Green street owned by the heirs of the late Samuel Shipman.

GUTTENBERG LODGE, NO. 319.

Guttenberg lodge was instituted in the city of Marietta, Ohio, by Grand Master William Chidsey, on the twelfth day of June, 1857, and is consequently twenty-four years old. It always has worked, and does so at the present writing, exclusively in the German language. Jacob Grosscloss, Louis Leopold, Jacob Meagel, Joseph Wildt, John Theis, Charles F. Biszantz, and Henry Schmidt were the seven charter members of the same, all of whom are now deceased, except the last named, so that Henry Schmidt is the only surviving charter member at this time. The highest membership of the lodge since its existence was one hundred and twenty-two, and at the present time it has ninety-two members. Its membership has been very materially reduced by deaths and withdrawals of brethren for the purpose of instituting new lodges at Lowell and New Matamoras, in this county.

The lodge has always been regarded by the Grand lodge of Ohio as one of the best working lodges in the State. Since its existence it has paid many thousand dollars for relief to the sick, for funeral benefits for members and their wives, and support of widows and orphans, especially in the last past five years, when it had much sickness and many deaths, and it is hoped it may be able to continue to assist its worthy and distressed brethren, their widows and orphans, for many years to come.

Since its existence it has had forty-four past grands, a majority of whom are still living and members of the lodge.

The lodge pays five-dollar weekly sick benefits, and eighty-dollar funeral benefits at the death of a brother, and fifty dollars at the death of a brother's wife.

Since its existence it has furnished three representatives to the grand lodge of Ohio, for the Fifty-ninth district, as follows: Charles Tresch, in 1865 and 1866; Henry Bohl, in 1871 and 1872; Jacob Rech, in 1875 and 1876, and Henry Bohl again for 1881 and 1882.

Henry Bohl was appointed in 1878 by Grand Master Henry C. Hedges. of Mansfield, Ohio, as deputy grand master, but declined the honor in favor of Brother A. M. Creighbaum, of Marietta Lodge, No. 67. He was again appointed in 1880 by Grand Master H. P. Gravatt, of Columbus, Ohio, but again declined, this time in favor of Brother George Lauer, of Palmer Lodge, No. 351, Lower Salem, Ohio.

HARMAR LODGE, NO. 115.

This lodge was instituted August 5, 1848, by Edson B. Olds, grand master, with the following as charter members, viz.: Jonathan Soule, Willard Mansfield, William H. Widgen, William C. Olney, L. E. W. Warner, William L. McCowan and Joseph Rumbold. The first officers chosen were Jonathan Soule, N. G.; William C. Olney, V. G.; L. E. W. Warner, secretary; William H. Widgen, treasurer. The lodge has a membership of about thirty-five. A neatly furnished and attractive hall in the old brick building fronting on market square, and built by the Sons of Temperance, is the meeting place.

MISCELLANEOUS ORGANIZATIONS.

KNIGHTS OF PYTHIAS.

Raynald Lodge, No. 82, was organized in its present comfortable and well appointed lodgeroom, on Front street, May 27, 1875. The charter members were: A. P. Beach, Thomas Clark, M. Dye, W. C. Greenway, J. T. Mathews, M. McMillen, L. W. Phillips, W. T. Westgate, A. P. Brigham, L. D. Davis, J. M. Fuller, A. H. Hill, William B. Mason, R. D. McKinney, J. C. Smith, T. N. Woodruff, J. C. Folger and J. W. Sturgiss. The lodge has at present about thirty-five members.

INDEPENDENT ORDER OF RED MEN.

Manhattan tribe, No. 35, of this secret and benevolent order, was instituted January 27, 1868, and received its charter July 23d, of the same year. The first chiefs elected were as follows: Henry Bohl, sachem; Philip Schramm, senior sagamore; Fred Blume, junior sagamore; H. Michaelis, Ch. of R.; William Raeser, K. of W.; Charles Tresch, prophet. The lodge is in a flourishing condition, and has about half a hundred members.

DER MARIETTA TURN-VEREIN.

This society, which has for its object the physical and intellectual improvement of its members, and the fostering and promoting of the use of the German language and observance of German customs, was organized July 31, 1872. The original members were: A. Reinhart, first turnwart; A. Rech, vice-resident; William Raeser,

jr., treasurer; C. H. Etz, secretary; John Gerken, second turnwart; Fred Raeser, Charles Haberling, George Hennemann, John H. Lehnhard, F. Morganstern, George Bachmann, jr., William Becker, D. W. Strauss, Peter Kung, jr., Fred Meister, president; John F. Schmidt, John Wagner, and Louis Mueller. The society has at present but a small membership. During its best days the Turn-verin had, in the hall in Bosworth, Wells & Co.'s building, a very good apparatus for athletic exercises.

ST. JOSEPH'S CATHOLIC BENEVOLENT SOCIETY.

This society attached to the (Roman) Catholic church was organized June 6, 1869. The late Louis Schmidt was its first president; John A. Slattery was secretary, and L. Goeble treasurer. The society has about forty members, and the organization is thriving.

OHIO VALLEY COUNCIL NO. 543, ROYAL ARCANUM,

was instituted November 25, 1880, with the following charter members: E. P. Bartlett, George Caywood, R. B. Hoover, Murray McMillen, Zina Lapham, C. B. McCaskey, F. L. Coleman, J. C. McCarty, J. L. Reckard, William Wood, A. J. Richards, Louis McCollister, J. D. Cotton, L. B. Devol, and G. J. Lund. The officers are: J. D. Cotton, regent; R. B. Hoover, secretary. Meetings are held on the first and third Thursdays of every month.

CHAPTER XXXII.

MARIETTA—NATURAL PHENOMENA.

The Floods—Epidemics—Earthquakes—Flood of 1790—The Great Floods Prior to the Settlement of Marietta—High Water of 1832—Floods of 1847, 1852, and 1860—Earthquake Shocks of 1811 and 1812—Sickly Seasons of 1807, 1822, and 1823—Causes, Excessive Moisture and Drouth—Lists of Burials.

FLOODS.

To the people living along the banks of a mighty river the occasional rise of its waters is an occurrence which not only excites interest but causes deep concern. Especially is this the case in a village situated as is Marietta. The great floods in the Ohio have been the cause of very serious inconvenience to a portion of its people, and have done much damage to property. The town itself has been in some measure injured by these floods. The fact that a considerable portion of its plat is subject to inundation has operated against its improvement, and still greater harm has been caused undoubtedly by the reports (usually much exaggerated) that have gone abroad from time to time in regard to the damage caused by floods at this particular point. In view of these facts a brief history of the floods in the Ohio may not prove uninteresting.

The first flood which occurred in the Ohio river after the settlement was made at Marietta, was in 1790. Dr. Hildreth says, * that for a number of years after the

* In "Transactions of Ohio Historical and Philosophical Society." Volume I.

settlement there was no flood that did any damage. But one who was an eye witness * gives an account of this flood of 1790, which proves the contrary. He says, under date of February 19th: "We got up at sunrise this morning, the doctor calling and telling us the water rose so fast that it would soon be in the house, when we immediately got up. We soon had the tea kettle on and got our coffee boiled; and before we could get our breakfast done, the water came in so fast that the floor was afloat, and we stood in water to our buckles to drink the last dish. We had before got such articles upstairs as the water would injure. Everybody below the great bridge is obliged to move. Only three houses are out of the reach of the water, owing to their being placed so high." Messrs. Woodbridge (merchant), Rockwell, Wells (tailors), Mr. Bent, Prince, Webster, Moodey, Skinner, Mixer, Vietts, Lucas, Veal, Tuttle, Barber, Landon and Mathews are mentioned in the journal from which I have quoted, and the editor says that in the original a blank space is left as if the writer had intended to add the names of more sufferers. The "Point" was then lower than now, and the houses were not raised from the surface.

Previous to the settlement of Marietta there were three floods, of which we have some knowledge—in the years 1772, 1778 and 1784. The flood of 1872 occurred in June, and as noted by the pioneers at Wheeling, was five feet higher than that of 1832, backing up Wheeling creek to a level with the top of the falls. That of 1778 was seven feet less than the flood of 1772. In 1784—month of March—the waters of the Ohio rose to about the same height reached in 1832. †

The Indians who visited Marietta after peace had been declared, for the purpose of trading, seeing houses upon the low lands near the river, shook their heads ominously, and pointing to the spreading lower branches of the sycamores that lined the banks, said that they had seen the water reach them, and that some day the whites would see it equally high, also. The pioneers thought but little of these warnings, but the time came when some of them had occasion to remember the words of the Indians.

We have spoken of the flood of 1790 as the first which occurred after settlement. The second was in 1809. The water filled some of the lower streets, caused some annoyance, but did scarcely any damage. In 1813 occurred the third and in fact the first *big* flood after the making of the settlement. On the twenty-fifth of January the water commenced rising at Marietta, and in twenty-four hours the Ohio was "out of banks," and the flood still increasing at the rate of eight inches per hour. There had been much snow upon the ground, and upon the twenty-fourth a heavy rain had set in, which must have been general and prevailing over a large section of country. The water reached its greatest height at 6 o'clock on the morning of the twenty-eighth,

and began falling at midnight. The flood was about the same as that of 1860, the water being from seven to eight feet deep along Front street, between Putnam and the Point, and its height above low water mark being estimated at forty-five feet. The weather was very cold, and there was much suffering upon that account. The ice in the river was from twelve to eighteen inches thick, and was carried crashing against the buildings in the lower part of the town, adding greatly to the terror of the people. This was known as the ice flood. The heavy blocks of floating ice, and that which formed upon the backwater, did great damage as the flood subsided, in crushing down fruit trees and fences. The houses exposed to the flood were filled with mud and ice, and presented, with the surroundings of ruined trees, a most desolate appearance. Fortunately, the Muskingum was not high during this great rise of the Ohio. Had it been, the flood would have equalled, at Marietta, that of 1832, and possibly would have exceeded it.

Only two years and two months later—upon the first of April, 1815, occurred another flood, which, at Marietta, was a little higher than that of 1813. This time the Muskingum was greatly swollen in volume and so much higher than the Ohio that its turbid current rolled athwart the latter stream, carrying driftwood against the Virginia shore. This was the highest flood ever known in the Muskingum, and the settlers along the valley suffered very great losses, the bottom lands being completely stripped of small buildings and fences, stacks of hay, shocks of corn, and animals.

There were small floods in the year 1817 and 1818, but from 1815 until the great flood of 1832, there was no rise of the river sufficient to cause serious damage or inconvenience.

The long period during which the Ohio had scarcely passed the measure of "full bank" had caused people to well nigh forget that it was liable at any time to make a phenomenal rise and send its broad surging tide up around their houses and into their doors. In the winter of 1831-2, which was a very cold one, heavy ice had been formed in the Ohio, and snow covered the ground to the depth of a foot or more in the vicinity of Marietta, while at the headwaters of the river it was not less than three feet deep.

During the early part of the month of February there fell a great amount of rain. At Marietta the water commenced rising on the twelfth of February at noon. On the morning of the fourteenth it was over the banks. It continued rising until the seventeenth, regularly decreasing in rapidity until it began to fall. The height above low water mark reached by this flood was fifty feet. This was five feet and three inches more water than had ever been known by the residents. At Marietta there was great alarm at the time when the water reached its greatest height. A terrific thunder storm arose in the early hours of the seventeenth. The wind blew fiercely and great waves beat against the houses, threatening to bear them from their foundations and engulf them in the seemingly irresistable tide. Fortunately the wind abated after a short time, and the result was less disas-

---

* Thomas Wallcut's Journal, 1790.

† "A brief history of the floods in the Ohio river," S. P. Hildreth in "Transactions of the Ohio Historical and Philosophical Society." Volume I.

HON. THOMAS W. MOORE.

trous than had been apprehended. The damage, however, was very considerable along the entire length of the river. About twenty storehouses, barns and small dwellings were floated away from Marietta. The fire-engine house, a small frame building, with the engine and buckets, was floated away the night of the storm and seen six days later near Louisville. Most of the houses were never heard of, though some of them were discovered after the flood abated lodged upon the islands down the river, and a portion of their contents discovered. The water was above the second-story floors of many houses, was about nine feet deep along Front street, and in the house of A. T. Nye, on Putnam, about three feet in depth. The river was filled with the wrecks of flat-boats and floating buildings.

Many of the latter, from Pittsburgh, Wheeling and other places up the river, were found lodged upon the various islands, and men were employed for weeks after the flood in searching for flotsam and jetsam along the shores and bottom-lands. It was estimated that the damage along the Ohio was at least one thousand dollars per mile, upon the average, independent of the towns. The loss at Marietta was probably less than twenty thousand dollars. The most grossly exaggerated accounts went abroad of the condition of things at Marietta during the flood and of the damage done. Some statements placed the amount of loss at fifty thousand dollars. The *American Friend* defended the reputation of the town, and said that "one-half, or possibly one-third, of this amount would cover the loss," and that "the loss was small, as compared with that of other towns on the Ohio." As a specimen of the reports which went abroad, we quote a letter from Wheeling to the Philadelphia *Chronicle:*

The steamboat Columbus, which has just arrived, reports that not a vestige remains of many of the towns below. Marietta presents a most melancholy appearance. A large portion of the place has entirely disappeared, and in the higher parts of the town little more is to be seen than the tops of the chimneys. Nothing could be learned of the safety of the inhabitants, as the boat could not effect a safe landing.

Another paper had the following: "A gentleman recently from the West says that while running up the Ohio several hundred buildings were met floating down, and that at Marietta the steamboat in which he was passed through the streets and delivered its passengers at the third story windows of the houses." Steamboats did run up front street at the time of the flood. The reputation of Marietta, it is claimed by some, was helped, rather than hurt, by the flood of 1832. After the first reports had gone abroad and produced an unfavorable impression, it was shown conclusively that most of the other towns along the river had actually experienced greater damage. In March, of 1832, the *American Friend* contained the following paragraph upon the prospects of the town:

Our situation is salubrious and commanding. Many have decided to locate here, and a considerable influx of population is expected. Arrangements are making for the erection of more handsome and desirable buildings the coming season than have been put up in any one season before.

The flood of 1847 occurred in the month of December. This flood, which was generally very destructive, and at Cincinnati and some other points marked as high as that

of 1832, at Marietta lacked five and a half feet of the high water-mark of that year, and did very little damage.

In April, 1852, the water rose at Marietta to within four and a half feet of the flood of 1832. The Muskingum did not contribute materially to the condition of high water, otherwise the "great flood" would have been equalled.

The flood of 1860 was the largest since the flood of 1832, and only about three feet below it. The water was from seven to eight feet deep along Front street from Putnam to the "Point" April 13th, the water having commenced to rise in both rivers upon the tenth, and covering the "Point" by the night of that day. There was very little damage done. The people were put to considerable inconvenience, but the weather being very mild, this season of high water was rather regarded as a gala time. Boats were out upon the water evenings with singing parties, and there was more mirth than misery or discomfiture.

On January 22, 1862, the water covered Front street and was upon nearly all of the store floors.

The flood of February, 1881, was a little less in height than that of 1862, rising so as to cover Front street from the "Point" up to Putnam, on Saturday the twelfth, and remaining until Monday the fourteenth. On Bosworth & Wells' store floor it was about four inches deep; upon some others a foot or more. Quite a number of individual losses were sustained in Marietta and Harmar but none of them were very serious.

EARTHQUAKE SHOCKS.

Marietta felt slightly the earthquake shock of 1811 which extended throughout the Mississippi valley—using that term in its broadest sense—and which seemed to have its centre at New Madrid on the Mississippi. This occurred upon the sixteenth of December. At twenty-five minutes past two o'clock A. M., people were awakened by the shaking sensation, and many, springing from their beds, rushed forth into the streets. For a few seconds almost everybody was in doubt and wonder, but soon it was realized that the cause of their awakening was an earthquake. Many were excessively terrified; others cool and unfrightened, and some still in blissful ignorance of the commotion in mother earth. The second shock, however, aroused and brought to their senses those who had been unmoved by the first. The second rumbling of the earth and shaking of the buildings were felt at twenty minutes past three o'clock A. M. At half-past seven another period of violent trembling of the earth began, and continued for half an hour. Some people heard, or imagined that they heard, a dull sound as of a smothered explosion, or the falling of a heavy body. The effects of this earthquake were much more strongly felt at Zanesville than at Marietta. In the former place it is said that the cupola of the court house moved to and fro at eight o'clock in the morning, and that the iron rod surmounting it vibrated six or eight inches, while the oscillating motion of the sign posts and trees was generally observable. The shock lasted about four minutes.

Slight effects of the earthquakes of 1812—January 23d and February 4th—were also felt in Marietta, the first being much the strongest.

Marietta has suffered from three epidemics in 1807, 1822 and 1823. "Except in these three years" says Dr. Hildreth in a communication to a medical journal, "the town has been uniformly healthy and indeed remarkably so."

The sickness of 1807 was principally intermittent and remittent fevers. These diseases were prevalent up and down the Ohio river for hundreds of miles, and more malignant and fatal at various points in this region of country than at Marietta—notably so at Gallipolis. The spring of the year was very wet and all through the summer there were two or three rainy days for every fair one. The low grounds were covered in many places by stagnant water, and crops were, in some localities, entirely ruined by the excessive moisture. The elements of disease were all in existence and it would have been very surprising if general sickness had not prevailed. The fever made its appearance in July, and in the following month there was scarcely a family residing on the bottom lands which was not afflicted by it. The disease carried off a considerable number of the people of Marietta and Washington county, but the number of deaths after all was not large, compared to the number who were sick with the fever.

The epidemic of 1822 exceeded that of 1807, was similar in nature but proceeded from an exactly opposite condition of the weather. The summer of 1822, unlike that of 1807, was very dry and hot. There was not only little rain but what did come was not accompanied, as is usual in summer, by lightening, that great purifier of the atmosphere, and there was scarcely one strong, clearing wind from the north or northwest, during the season. Hot winds blew almost constantly from the south. The Ohio and Muskingum were reduced by the drouth, so that "they were mere brooks as compared with their usual size." The water was covered with a foul scum, and a green mould gathered upon the rank grass which grew along the shores and down into the beds of the streams. Dr. Hildreth's opinion was that "the fever had its origin from the sandbars and beaches of the Ohio river laid bare by the great drought." Some people thought that the disease was imported by the almost constantly blowing south wind. The fever varied from the mildest intermittent types, up to the genuine yellow fever. Ague, cholera morbus and dysentery were also prevalent. At one time, within a single square mile containing a population of about twelve hundred souls, four hundred were sick with some form of disease attributed to the drought and hot weather. Dr. Hildreth had about six hundred cases to care for between the first of July and the close of November. The fever was most widely disseminated in September. It first appeared upon the "plain" or higher ground in June, but in July most of the cases were in Harmar, and it did not become troublesome at the "Point" until August.

The proportion of deaths was about one to sixteen of the number of persons affected.

The people became much alarmed as the season advanced and the deaths became more numerous. On September 15th a public meeting was held at which committees were appointed to visit the sick, and supply them with whatever necessities they might be lacking. Upon the eighteenth another meeting was held, of which Dudley Woodbridge, jr., was chairman, and William A. Whittlesey, secretary. The reports of the committees appointed three days before showed that over three hundred persons were sick in Marietta—a number bearing about the same proportion to the population (two thousand) that twelve hundred would to the present. Resolutions were adopted setting forth that "the distressed situation of our fellow-citizens and friends calls for the utmost exertions and deepest humiliation;" that "we will exhort and encourage each other in visiting the sick," and that, "looking beyond the' sword of pestilence to Him who wields it, we humble ourselves before Almighty God, and recommend to our fellow citizens a day of public fasting, humiliation and prayer, imploring the pardon of our sins, individually, and as a people, the arrest of the pestilence which ravages our town, and grace to receive and do all things, as those who have hope in the Lord." Henry Dana Ward and William R. Putnam were appointed a committee to wait on the Rev. S. P. Robbins of the Congregational, and Rev. Cornelius Springer of the Methodist church, and "request them to agree upon a day of fasting, and if agreeable unite the congregations in its solemn service." The ministers gave public notice that Saturday, September 21st, would be observed, in accordance with the resolution of the citizens' meeting, as a day of fasting and prayer. The service was held at the Congregational church. It was noted a few days later by the *American Friend* that with the exception of fifteen or twenty who were quite low the people generally were recovering, and that very few new cases had occurred. It was not, however, until hard frosts came in November that the epidemic was stopped. No less than ninety-five persons died in Marietta township during June, July, August, September and October of 1822.

We are enabled to give a mortuary list for three months, nearly complete, and containing the names of some citizens of other parts of the county, who died during the prevalence of 1822:*

June 27, Charles F., son of Ephraim Ranger.
June 30, Frances, wife of Colonel George Turner.
July 10, Humphrey Hook (in Wood county) Virginia.
August 1, Mary, wife of Elder John Gates.
August 1, Abram Seevers (Fearng).
August 21, Hon. Paul Fearing (Harmar).
August 21, Cynthia, his wife (within six hours).
August 26, John Cornell.
August 26, Edmund Moulton.
August 27, wife of Captain Nathan Bowen.
August 30, Mrs. Catharine McClintick.
September 9, Joanna Lincoln.
September 9, Jauna R. Bowers.
September 9, Mrs. Merriam (in Adams).
September 10, Reuben Merriam (in Adams).

* From "Old Marietta Papers," No. XVII, in Marietta *Register*, by R. M. Stimson, esq.

September 14, Mrs. Nancy Bliss.
September 15, Aaron Smith.
September 16, Major Robert Bradford (Belpre).
September 16, Mrs. Persis Howe (Belpre).
September 19, Charlotte, wife of A. W. Putnam.
September 21, A. W. Putnam (in Belpre).
September 16, Mrs. Solniger (in Union).
September 19, Christian Ulmer.
September 20, John Miller.
September 20, Ann Eliza, wife of Levi Cole.
September 21, Justus Morse.
September 21, Silas Barter.
September 24, Jacob Schachtelien.
September 25, Elder John Gates.
September 25, Mrs. Mills.
September 25, John Drown (on the island).
September 26, Captain Obediah Lincoln.
September 26, John Clark.
September 26, Sarah, his wife.
September 27, Mrs. Deborah Erwin.
September 27, Hugh Dixon.
September 27, Tiffany Adams (in Warren).
September 28, Angelina Lincoln.
September 28, Harriet, wife of Wyllys Hall.
September 28, Caroline, wife of James Bliss.
September 28, Mary Ann, wife of Jasper Taylor.
September 28, Lucy, a woman of color.
September 30, Clarissa, wife of Captain Timothy Buell.
October 1, Jefferson Lincoln.
October 1, Wealthy A., wife of Richard Alcock.
October 1, infant son of John Kelley.
October 1, Mary, wife of S. D. W. Drown (on the island).
October 1, Solomon Jarvis (in Wood county, Virginia).
October 2, Titus Buck.
October 2, James Knight.
October 2, Manasseh, son of Ephraim Cutler (in Warren).
October 4, Colonel Jacob Ulmer.
October 5, Mark Anderson.
October 5, Mrs. Polly White (in Fearing).
October 6, Henry Winum.
October 7, Mrs. Mees.
October 8, Philip Cunningham.
October 8, William Judson.
October 9, Mrs. Lyon.
October 9, Eliza Anderson.
October 10, Abraham Sharp.
October 10, Mrs. Schachtelin.
October 10, Mrs. Lucretia Hempstead.
October 12, Jonas Livermore.
October 14, Charles Lincoln.
October 16, John Brough.
October 18, Dudley Dodge.
October 21, Henry Murphy.
November 4, Lydia, wife of William White (Fearing).
November 27, John Dye, sr.

Jonathan Guitteau and Joseph Babcock, of Marietta, died also during the epidemic, but the dates of their deaths are not known.

The sickness of 1823 seemed to be a new breaking out of that of 1822, but, unlike the epidemic of that year, this one was not confined to the water courses or their immediate vicinity. "The spring," says a newspaper writer[*] reviewing the subject, "was pleasant, with every prospect of a salubrious summer. But how sad the disappointment. The sickness broke out in June and pervaded nearly all parts of the west. · · ·

The country was deluged with rain in June and July, with very little thunder and lightening and no heavy winds. Every spot that could hold water was filled with it. Fields of wheat and corn were ruined and grass rotted. The low land exhaled noxious vapors, so that people in passing were obliged to put their hands to their

noses and hasten through some disgusting spots. In plowing in rich bottom lands, instead of the pleasant odors that usually arise from freshly plowed land a sickly smell would be sent forth. The rains ceased the last of August, but the systems of the people had become charged with miasma. · · · The disease was more malignant and fatal in the country than in town, especially in rich bottoms, where weeds grew in many places to the enormous height of fifteen or eighteen feet. In spite of the drawback on corn in the early part of the summer, the crop was heavy from its luxuriant growth and almost without cultivation, otherwise famine would have followed, for there were not well persons enough to take care of the sick, much less to cultivate their farms." Those who were attacked with the fever in 1822 usually escaped this year. July 17th was observed in Marietta as a day of fasting and prayer. Already the deaths had been quite numerous. From July 5th to the close of the month there were thirty-one deaths in Marietta and the immediate vicinity. The whole number of persons interred in Mound cemetery during July, August, September, and October was one hundred and forty-one. Of these seventy-two were residents of Marietta corporation; fifty-five were of the township outside of the corporation; and fourteen from other townships. The number of deaths in August was forty-six; in September forty-five: and in October nineteen. Upon the Harmar side of the Muskingum—Harmar was then included in Marietta corporation—there were eleven deaths.

The *American Friend* said: "The late sickness has made great, we had almost said irreparable, breaches in society, not only as it respects numbers, but the characters also of those taken away. In many cases children are left without any father or mother."

Following is a list of the deaths in Marietta or vicinity (those of persons buried in Mound cemetery) during the epidemic of 1823—from July to October inclusive.

July 5th, George Howe; 8th, Jacob Drake, 11th, son of S. Briggs; 13th, Mrs. Dempsey; 14th, Joseph Bartlett, T. J. H. Sandford, Mrs. Hill; 18th, Mrs. Mary A. Cunningham, William Taylor; 19th, Mrs. Bacon; 21st, John Locker; 22d, daughter of George Corner, Mrs. Livermore; 23d, Caleb Thornilly, Matthew Miner, son of Samuel Stone, child of Mr. Bacon; 24th, Harriet Hartshorn, Harriet Hearn, Mrs. Miner; 25th, Mrs. Miller, Mrs. Thornilly; 26th, Pamelia Rood, son of A. Daniels; 28th, Rachel Howe, Mrs. Hoff. Levi Benjamin; 29th, Leonard Foster, William Fulton, Anna Rogers; 30th, Jonathan Carms.

August 1st, Mr. Brown; 2d, Mr. Follett; 3d, son of Jacob Brown; 5th, Eliza Stanley, daughter of Broadhurst, James Lincoln; 6th, child of W. Holyoke, Mrs. Merrill, Mrs. Rood, D. Woodbridge, sr., child of D. Protsam; 8th, child of —— Pratt; 9th, Pearce Morse, William McAllister; 11th, child of A. Daniels; 12th, child of D. Murray; 13th, Joseph Harris, Harriet Goodwin; 14th Sally Druse, child of C. Thornilly, Mrs. Ezekiel Deming; 15th, Mrs. Dr. Jett, Mrs. Duncan; 16th, Mrs. Pratt; 17th, Mrs. Morse, child of T. Buell, child of R. McCabe; 18th, child of Mr. Wheeler, Mrs. Goodwin, Mrs. Keating; 19th, child of —— Cherry, Mr. Goodwin; 20th, John Phelps, 23d, child of J. Brown, child of J. Clark; 24th, child of William Talbot; 26th, Mrs. Guitteau; 27th, Ruth Johnson; 28th, Mrs. Browning, Mary Stone; 29th Eliza Palmer, son of J. Chase; 30th, Mrs. Stephen Hildreth, Emily Hoff, Andrew Webster, child of G. Gilbert.

September 1st, Judson Guitteau, Mrs. Spencer, Mr. Rood; 2d, son of J. Chase, Mrs. Pearce Morse; 3d, Rev. S. P. Robbins, Mrs. Garnet; 5th, Dr. N. McIntosh; 6th, Dr. Jabez True, Mary Stone, sr.; 11th, Mr. Needham; 12th, child of —— Mercer, John Gibson, Mr. Shoemaker, A. Shay, Mrs. Tucker; child of Mr. Brown; 14th, Luther

Edgarton sr.; 15th, Ephraim Foster, sr., 16th, child of Mrs. Harley; 17th, child of J. Graham; 18th, child of J. Chase; 19th, Elizabeth T. Willard, child of ———— Crandall; 20th, Ephraim Hill, child of J. Graham, child of J. J. Preston; 22d, Robert G. Duncan, woman (from Fearing), child of S. Lee, child of R. Mills; 24th, Rev. Joseph Willard, Caleb Barstow, Allen McNeil, child of William Alcock; 25th, Mrs. Deem; 26th, child of Mr. Locker; 27th, James Gilbert; 28th, Henry Gibson, child of Mr. Rich, child of J. Chase; 29th, Julia A. Geren, 30th, child of D. Gilbert, Mrs McCahe.

October 1st, Mrs. Evans, child of C. D. Bonney; 3d, Hopkins Green, Joshua Shipman, Mrs William M. Case; 6th, child of William Alcock; 12th, Lorenzo Protsam; 14th, child of E. Ryan; 15th, child of T. Buell; 17th, child of Wyllys Hall; 18th, Mrs. Crandall; 20th, child of J. Chase; 21st, Mrs. Bodwell, Mrs. Ryan; 22d, child of Mr. Bacon; 28th, Mrs. McCune, Mrs. Nat. Dodge; 29th, Edward Guitteau.

A long list of burials certainly to be made in a small village in four months. There were a few deaths that are not included in the above list: Ezra Crane, Lucretia Saltonstall, Amzi Stanley, Elizar Carver, Lydia Mc. Kawen, Anna Shepherd, Margaret Morse, and Sarah Wiseman.

CHAPTER XXXIII.

MARIETTA—REMINISCENCES OF SLAVERY DAYS.*

Remarks on the Growth of Anti-Slavery Sentiment by James Lawton—His Early Poem on Slavery--Something of His Character and Services for the Cause—Harry Bartlette's Freedom Paper—"Aunt" Lydia Pervis—James G. Birney's Anti-Slavery Newspaper in Cincinnati—Theodore Weld in Marietta—Rev. Bennet Roberts—Anti and Pro-Slavery Societies—The Prominent Pioneers of Abolition Sentiment—Mob Spirit Active—Fears of Violence—The Belpre Abduction Case—Peter H. Garner, Crayton J. Lorraine, and Mordecai Thomas Imprisoned at Parkersburgh and Refused Bail—The Question of Boundary Line.

THE manner in which the Northwestern Territory was secured to freedom has been already related in this work. The fact that most of the men who first came to Ohio were desirous of the extinction of slavery is undeniable, but in Washington county, as elsewhere, anti-slavery sentiment was a growth, and a general sketch of some of the causes of its growth may properly be given here.

In January, 1879, Mr. James Lawton, of Barlow, published an article in the Marietta *Register* from which the following extracts are taken. He says "That a systematic opposition to an institution which had grown with the growth of our country and strengthened with its strength, an institution acknowledged in our Constitution and secured by law, that such an institution should be assailed by citizens of the free States combined under a name which plainly indicated its annihilation, might well be deemed preposterous by many. On the other hand, the gross inconsistency of slavery with our National confession of faith, as expressed in our Declaration of Independence, together with the aggressive tendency of slavery, seemed to many minds to render combined opposition imperative. There was enough in the woes which slavery inflicted on its victims to arouse the indignation of every philanthropist; but the impetus given to

*By A. T. Nye, Esq., of Marietta.

anti-slavery views was perhaps less from the known sufferings of the enslaved than from the continually increasing demands of slavery for extension and domination. Reasonable persons who could make allowance for early training and habits formed where slavery ruled, were indignant at its threatened and actual infringements on the rights and privileges of those not connected with the institution,—such as its claim of jurisdiction over the Ohio river to low water-mark on this side, and the assumed dictation of what passengers on steam-boats should not discuss as topics of conversation—one known as an opponent of slavery being liable to mob law there. · · ·

In some of the slave states there were laws against incendiary speech or publications which might be so construed that anything said, written or exhibited against slavery there, would render any thus offending, liable to punishment. To illustrate the working of those laws I will state a fact. One of the oldest citizens of Belpre, in this county, made mention of something in reference to slavery, to a man engaged in making a flat-boat on the Virginia shore, which the workman seemed to doubt, but requested to see the paper which contained the article, which the Belpre man handed him the next day; and for that act he was threatened with and liable to imprisonment in the Parkersburgh jail for many years afterward, and other citizens of this county were not only threatened, but roughly handled while on necessary business on that side of the river, not for anything said or done there, but for their opinions. · · ·

Many thinking persons were brought to consider the subject of slavery more seriously, and to reflect on the consequences of such a despotic course, · · and felt constrained to throw their influence against slavery. · · But although most of the substantial portion of the community were in favor of free speech, and opposed to mob-violence, but few, comparatively, endorsed the abolition movement. · ·

I suppose no one doubts that the slave question tended to make slave property less secure in many parts, by causing discontent among the enslaved, but I doubt if more than a very small portion of abolitionists took any direct means to increase that discontent. Still the so-called "underground railroad" did exist, and many a dark subject found freedom through its labyrinths, but made his appearance as a fugitive before assistance was given."

Mr. Lawton was one of the early abolitionists of this county. As early as 1818 he wrote a short poem on the subject of slavery. It was first published in the *American Friend* with flattering comments, and about 1821 was printed, by Benjamin Lundy in a periodical published in Tennessee, called the "*Genius of Universal Emancipation*," with the remark "that as the writer was born in Marietta, he was young, and did not know that the line "Shall her fair banners o'er oppression wave," was literally true, that the United States flag did wave over the slave pens at Washington."

The lines as copied from the original in Mr. Lawton's hand writing, are as follows:

"SLAVERY—1819."

Shall man forever prove the scourge of man,
And thus subvert the great Creator's plan,
Who when he first bade nature spring from night
Clothed yon bright sun in robes of dazzling light,
Balanced the earth upon his firm decree,
Bade all be equal, all alike be free?
The darkest tenant of Angola's plains,
Feels the same current beating in his veins
As that which warms the fairest forms that shine.
Where beauty, wealth, and honor all combine,
The same affections warm his heart not less,
The same joys heighten, the same fears depress.
Then why despise the tincture of the skin,
Since all mankind are formed alike within?
One general life pervades each human frame,
All passions similar, all souls the same.
Yet cruel man, though impotent and vain,
Binds his own fellows in oppression's chain,
'Tis cruel sure, the limbs in chains to bind,
More cruel still to chain the human mind.
Ye Southern rulers, drop the afflicting rod,
No longer tempt the vengeance of a God.
For you, fair freedom loathes her sacred name,
For you Columbia mourns her tarnished fame,
Shall her fair banners o'er oppression wave?
Can freedom's pinions fan the toiling slave?
Confusion strange, to grasp in the same hand
The blood stained scourge, the peaceful olive wand.
Hail, Marietta! thou, my native town,
I'll sing thy praise, for freedom there is known.
No petty tyrants tread thy peaceful streets,
No mourning slave the passing stranger meets,
Blessed be thy name, while fair Ohio's waves
Shall part thy borders from the land of slaves.
May well fraught barges ever line thy shores,
And smiling plenty rest within thy doors.

Mr. Lawton was among the very first in Washington county to subscribe to anti-slavery papers, and he never repudiated the name Abolitionist, but he was not alone among our citizens in sympathy with the slave. He says: "The underground railroad did exist. One station on that line (in Decatur) was established in consequence of the suffering witnessed by one man in the separation of a slave family at Washington's Bottom, Virginia. Many things occurred to make men think, and to think, with some, meant to aid."

Before the late war there were but few colored families in Marietta. Among these was Harry Bartlette, who lived here many years, and was well known to all our citizens. He was a quiet and peaceful man, and, with his wife, a member of the Congregational church. He was born a slave, and the following paper gives some insight into his history:

COPY OF HARRY BARTLETTE'S FREEDOM PAPER.

To all to whom these presents may come:

Know Ye, that in October, 1817, I bought of George Neale, of Wood county, Virginia, a black man, named Harry Grey Bartlette, and that he lived with me in Belpre, Ohio, four years, for which he was to have his freedom, and he is now free, both by my consent and by the law of Ohio.

Given under my hand at Belpre, March 14, 1824.

EDMUND DANA.

Harry died in Marietta April 5, 1860. His wife, who was colored, claimed to have been born free and of French descent. She died in Marietta September 25, 1875.

Mr. Dana's object in buying Harry was that he might obtain his freedom. Some years later, owing to stringent laws, it became very difficult for any master to liberate his slaves, and equally difficult for anyone in Ohio to do for any slave what Mr. Dana did for Harry.

Another well known colored person who lived in Marietta was commonly called "Aunt Lydia." On her tombstone, in Mound cemetery, may be found the following:

Lydia Pervis, died January 1, —, aged seventy-five years. Though born in slavery, with a dark skin, Doctor Jonas Moore gave her temporal freedom, and Jesus gave her spiritual.

She was a member of the Methodist Episcopal church for many years, and at her death left property to the church worth eight hundred dollars.

Before 1830 doubtless many slaves were liberated by being purchased by humane persons on this side of the river.

The following paper, prepared by A. T. Nye, of Marietta, shows something of the excited state of feeling on the subject of slavery in Ohio in 1835.

The laws of Ohio in 1835 were very strict in relation to colored people coming from other States. Among other things it was required that they should give bonds never to become a township charge, and that a colored man could not be allowed to give testimony in a case where a white man was a party. These and similar provisions gave rise to many outrages against the colored people, especially in Cincinnati.

In 1833 or 1834 James G. Birney started an anti-slavery paper in Cincinnati, called the *Philanthropist.* About this time began the formation of anti-slavery societies in the west. A society was formed at Putnam, Ohio, in 1833. In the summer of 1835 Mr. Theodore Weld, a distinguished anti-slavery lecturer, came to Marietta for the purpose of lecturing on the subject of slavery. He brought a letter of introduction to A. T. Nye from his brother, Major Horace Nye, of Putnam, Ohio, a member of the anti-slavery society there. He was invited by A. T. Nye to make his home at his house. He particularly desired to lecture at the college. Because of the excited state of pro-slavery adherents here and throughout the State, it was not deemed safe or prudent by the faculty to allow such lectures to be delivered in the college buildings. Under an arrangement with the directors of the Marietta library the use of the library hall was granted him, on condition that he would hold meetings in the daytime only. Mr. Weld accordingly lectured in the afternoon for several weeks. He was an earnest and eloquent man. Many of the college students and citizens attended his lectures, which resulted in the formation of an anti-slavery society in Marietta. The pro-slavery mob feeling was held under restraint, though very restless and disposed to do mischief. No efforts were made, however, to disturb the meetings held by Mr. Weld.

Of the society formed at this time Rev. Bennet Roberts, of Watertown, was appointed president, and Samuel Hall, one of the oldest students in college, secretary. Other students became members. The society held meetings in different places. In the course of the season they had arranged to hold a meeting at the schoolhouse in Harmar, a building which fronted the commons.

While they were holding this meeting they were interrupted by a set of men who came with intent to break it up. Their threats and their conduct at the time drove the society out of the house. Several members escaped through the windows, and Mr. Hall and others who lived in Marietta were obliged to swim the river in order to get home in safety. The conduct of the mob was violent and offensive, and, though no one was injured, the effect of the disturbance was to strengthen the pro-slavery adherents, and the anti-slavery society met after that under an apprehension that the meetings might be disturbed. Until this time the mob spirit that had been so violent in other parts of the State had been kept in some measure of subjection here; but now it seemed that it might break out at any time. Threats of violence were frequently made, but no overt acts of riot were committed for some time.

In October, 1836, public notice was given that the first annual meeting of the anti-slavery society would be held at the Baptist church on Church street, and that Rev. Bennet Roberts would at that time deliver an address. It soon became evident that there was a mob spirit abroad in town, and a determination on the part of pro-slavery men to break up the meeting. The meeting of the society was advertised for Monday (about the middle of October). On the Saturday night previous the pro-slavery men held a meeting at the court house, the avowed object of which was to concert measures to prevent the holding of the anti-slavery meeting on Monday. The pro-slavery meeting was attended by a number of those who sympathized with the mob spirit. The meeting was rather boisterous, and a good deal of talk was indulged in as to what they would do. Ichabod Nye, William Slocomb, and Caleb Emerson, influential citizens, attended for the purpose of attempting to pacify the people assembled, and to prevent, if possible, any acts of violence. They were treated with rudeness, and insulting language was applied to them, but they did not leave. After a considerable amount of noise and talk, a resolution was passed to appoint a committee to visit the officers of the anti-slavery society for the purpose of inducing them to give up the meeting. Charles B. Flood was at the head of this committee, which was instructed to report to an adjourned meeting to be held on Monday morning. For some time previous to this, the mayor of the town, A. T. Nye, had received intimations, by letter and otherwise, that violence was meditated in case the anti-slavery meeting was held. Several leading citizens tendered him their services, the first to do so being George Dana, esq., of Belpre. The danger seemed to render it necessary that more than ordinary precautions should be taken to preserve peace. With the marshal, M. J. Morse, the mayor made what preparation seemed possible. The legal title of the ground on which the Baptist church was built was in the name of William Dana, of Newport. He became deeply interested in the condition of things and the measures being taken to prevent disturbance. He had given the society permission to occupy the church for the annual meeting. On Monday, the day set for the meeting, Mr. Dana left home early in the morning, and a short distance from home met Judge Joseph Barker going to Newport village on business. Mr. Dana stated the object of his trip to Marietta that day to Judge Barker, and the Judge turned about and came to Marietta with him. Mr. Dana said he would "rather see the church building torn to its foundations than that the right of free speech should be denied."

Monday morning the mayor and the marshal went to the church, and, by previous arrangement, a number of prominent citizens from town and county were there to aid them, if necessary, in preserving peace. Among these were: George Dana, of Belpre; George N. Burch, of Union; William Dana and Joseph Barker, of Newport; David Putnam, jr., James M. Amlin, George Burgess, Judson Hollister, Ichabod H. Nye, and others of Marietta and Harmar.

In the meantime the pro-slavery meeting assembled according to adjournment at the court house. The committee appointed at the previous meeting reported that it had handed a communication to Mr. Samuel Hall, secretary of the anti-slavery society, which he had received with the tongs and did not read. The meeting was highly indignant, and a great many hard speeches were made. It is said that Mr. A. V. D. Joline was much excited and said many things to excite others, at the same time repeatedly saying, "But I am not in favor of mobbing," or something to that purport. Colonel Ichabod Nye, Mr. Slocomb, and Mr. Emerson were again present, their reception by no means courteous, and it is said that Colonel Nye told Mr. Joline that he reminded him of a New England parson who, meeting some boys on their way to the salmon pond on Sunday, reproved them, saying, "You must not fish on Sunday, boys; but, boys, you know I like fish." This brought out a general laugh at Mr. Joline's expense. After a meeting of a boisterous nature, it was resolved that the "Abolitionists were beneath contempt," and the more considerate ones concluded it was best to go home. Another portion, however, were determined not to give the matter up, and they proceeded in a body to the Baptist church. When they arrived there the meeting was in progress and Mr. Roberts was speaking. Although their object had been to break up the meeting, the presence of so many men of character in the house seemed to deter them from the attempt, and their indignation now became directed toward Mr. Hall personally. Shortly after noon the meeting closed, and now began the most serious difficulty of the day. Those men who had come to disturb the meeting, by their conversation and threats seemed determined to inflict punishment on Mr. Hall. At the close of the meeting the mayor advised the friends of Mr. Hall to have him leave by the basement door at the rear of the building, rather than provoke disturbance by his presence on the street. This they attempted, but found the door locked, and therefore returned to the front part of the house. In the meantime the mob had discovered the movement and pushed toward the rear of the building for the purpose of intercepting Mr. Hall. This gave Mr. Hall a slight advantage.

He came out of the front door on Church street, James M. Amlin on one side of him and George Burgess on the other. They walked rapidly toward Fourth street, and were followed by the mob. The mayor warned the rioters of the consequences of any act of violence, and they, seeing the support that the mayor and marshal had at hand in the presence of prominent citizens, some of them carrying good stout canes, * seemed to lose courage, and the pursuit ended at Fourth street. Mr. Hall went on to the college in some haste, but uninjured.

The threats uttered during the day led the mayor to fear that some attempt might be made after nightfall to injure or destroy the college buildings. Accordingly he requested the students and some gentlemen from the country to remain at the college that night. The apprehensions of those at the college were kept alive by a drum which was kept in vigorous use in the lower part of town, supposed to be designed to call the pro-slavery partisans together. These manifestations were kept up until a late hour—probably to let down the courage of the mob, its spirit having been broken at the church. At all events it finally dispersed, and people generally except those at the college went home. Thus ended a memorable day in the history of the town. The excitement was intense, and the danger of an outbreak imminent, but the right of free speech was vindicated and the law sustained. The anti-slavery society lived for some years and there were always anti-slavery sentiments held by a considerable portion of our best citizens. It is not practicable here to mention in detail all the events which kept alive an interest in anti-slavery movements here, and some of the actors being yet alive are better fitted to give information than the writer of this article, but an affair which occurred ten years later became of national importance, and was briefly as follows, as published June, 1868, in the Marietta *Register:*

In 1845 six slaves of John H. Harward, of Washington's Bottom, Virginia, just below Blennerhassett's island, escaped into Ohio At the river bank a party of Ohio men, unarmed, met them to assist, but some Virginians having obtained knowledge of the purpose of the negroes were there in advance concealed in the bushes, and fully armed Al the baggage was being taken from the boat the Virginians rushed on them and secured five of the negroes and captured Peter M. Garner, Crayton J. Lorraine and Mordecai Thomas, white citizens of Ohio. The Virginians claimed that these men, who had never set foot on Virginia soil, were fellons and amenable to the laws of that State for an alleged offense not known to the laws of Ohio. They were forcibly carried over into Virginia on the night of July 9, 1845, and lodged in jail in Parkersburgh. No one in Virginia could be found to bail them, though Nahum Ward, A. T. Nye and William P. Cutler, offered to idemnify any Virginians who would become their bondsmen. Intercourse with their friends from Ohio was denied them, and Marietta lawyers employed to defend them were rejected. Subsequently the wives of the prisoners were permitted to visit them under guard.

August 16th a public meeting was held at the court house in Marietta "to take into consideration further measures for the liberation of Ohio citizens now in jail at Parkersburgh, and the vindication of the rights of Ohio." September 2d the prisoners, each collared by two men, were taken from jail to the court house in Parkersburgh and there pleaded "not guilty" to the charge of "enticing and assisting in the county of Wood, Virginia,", the six negroes to escape from slavery. Bail was again refused except by a Virginia freeholder, and the prisoners went back to jail. The jury found a special verdict of guilty turning on

*It is said that this was the only occasion on which Mr. George Dana, of Delpre, was ever known to carry a cane, and it was a strong one. Colonel Nye had a similar one in his hand at the court house.

"jurisdiction" in the case, to be tried by a higher court. The question of jurisdiction or boundary between the two States was argued before the court of appeals at Richmond, December 10-13th, and the court divided equally on the question whether the State line was at low water mark on the Ohio side of the river or above that. The men had been captured just above low water mark. At a special term of the court of appeals held in Parkersburgh, Garner, Lorraine and Thomas were admitted to bail in the sum of one hundred dollars each on their own recognizance, and were set at liberty January 10, 1846, having lain in jail six months Hon Samuel F. Vinton, of Gallipolis, argued the case for the prisoners before the superior court of Virginia. It was never decided. Peter M. Garner died at Columbus, Ohio, June 14, 1868, in his sixty-first year; Mordecai Thomas removed to Belmont county, and Crayton J Lorraine removed to Illinois This case was regarded with the deepest interest, and was of far more than local importance. Sixteen years later many of the actors in this affair were living to see the State of Virginia turned into a battle-ground in which the same principle was fought for, and to see a little later the overthrow of slavery accomplished.

CHAPTER XXXIV.

MARIETTA—SOME DISTINGUISHED VISITORS.

Louis Phillipe, King of France, and the French Baker, Thierry—General Lafayette's Visit in 1825 Accident to the Steamer Ben Franklin, of Marietta, on which he was a Passenger—Daniel Webster—Thomas Ewing as young Attorney and United States Senator—A Public Dinner in his Honor in 1837—John Quincy Adams at Marietta in 1843—His Address and Reception—An Impressive Occasion—Remarks on Caleb Emerson's Information and Conversational Powers.

So far as is known the first eminent character who visited Marietta was Louis Phillipe, King of France. While in exile he made an extensive tour of the United States, the itinerary for his western journeyings being prepared for him by Washington. He was in Marietta in 1798, probably late in January, as he arrived at New Orleans upon the seventeenth of the following month. It would be very interesting at this day to know what opinion the Bourbon king formed of this pioneer outpost of the young Republic, but his impressions of the place, or the thoughts inspired in him by his visit, if ever expressed, have not been chronicled for our perusal. He met at Marietta a humble countryman, Francis Thierry, the baker, and years after related the incident. It was introduced, with other anecdotes, by General Cass in his book on France* as indicating the remarkable retentiveness of Louis Phillipe's memory. He says:

At Marietta the party stopped and landed; and from a circumstance connected with the king's recollection of this town, it may not be out of place to allude to the faculty of memory which he possesses in a most extraordinary degree. . . . . The king once asked my informant if he was ever in Marietta. As it happened, this gentleman had spent some years of the early part of his life there, and was able to answer in the affirmative. "And did you know" said the king, "a French baker there, named Thierry?" This gentleman knew him verry well, and so answered the inquiry. "Well," said the king, "I once ran away with him"—and then proceeded to explain that in descending the Ohio he had stopped at Marietta, and had gone into the town in search of bread. He was referred to this same Mr. Thierry, and the baker not having a stock on hand, set himself to work to heat his oven to supply the applicant. While this process was going on the king walked over the town and visited the interesting ancient remains

* "France: Its King, Court and Government," by an American (General Lewis Cass).

which are to be found in the western part of it, near the banks of the Muskingum, and whose history and objects have given rise to such various and unsatisfactory speculations. The king took a sketch of some of these works, which are indeed among the most extensive of their class that are to be found in the vast basin of the Mississippi. On his return he found the ice in the Muskingum upon the point of breaking up, and Mr. Thierry so late in his operations that he had barely time to leap into the boat with the bread, before they were compelled to leave the shore, that they might precede the immense mass of ice which was entering the Ohio. Their French friend bore his misfortune like a philosopher, and though he mourned over the supposed grief of his faithful wife, he still urged the rowers to exert themselves, in order to place his young countryman beyond the chance of injury. They were finally successful, and after some time the good old man was taken ashore by a canoe that they hailed, well satisfied with his expedition. The travellers continued their voyage and met with but one sinister accident · · · and reached New orleans on the seventeenth of February, 1798.

In the year 1825 another illustrious Frenchman and one dear to the hearts of all Americans, made a very brief visit to Marietta. This was no other than General Lafayette. He had left Washington for a tour through the southwest upon the twenty-third of February, and in May was returning. He left Nashville on the sixth of that month, as a passenger on the steamboat Mechanic (the first steamboat built at Marietta), commanded by Captain Wyllys Hall, of Marietta, brother of Joseph Hall. On the night of Sunday, May 8th at 12 o'clock, when near the mouth of Deer creek, one hundred and twenty-five miles below Louisville the boat was wrecked by striking upon a snag, and it was only by a close chance that the passengers escaped. One account says that Lafayette was thrown into the water while endeavoring to reach the yawl; that he narrowly escaped drowning and that he lost eight thousand dollars. However this might be, it is a fact that Captain Hall, who devoted his entire attention to the passengers under his care, lost his secretary, containing thirteen hundred dollars. It was supposed to have fallen overboard during the lurching of the boat. No blame was attached to Captain Hall for the occurrence of the accident and his conduct afterward was highly praised, Lafayette gave him a little testimonial which read: "I eagerly seize this opportunity of doing justice to Captain Hall's conduct and acknowledging my personal obligations to him."

General Lafayette resumed his journey up the river upon the steamboat Herald, which "hove in sight" of Marietta about nine o'clock on the morning of Monday, May 23rd "and fired a gun which was supposed to be a signal that General Lafayette was on board." As she approached his name was seen across her bow in large letters, "and placed all doubts aside." The *American Friend and Marietta Gazette* of May 27th, 1825, had the following account of General Lafayette's visit:

· · · No preparations had been previously made for his reception, in consequence of its being generally believed that he would travel through the interior of the State. The general, however, landed and was escorted to the beautiful mansion of Nahum Ward, esq., (with whom he had become acquainted in Paris) where he continued for about an hour and received all those who chose to call upon him.

The news of his arrival was announced by the discharge of cannon, and the citizens began to flock around him, all eager to seize his hand and welcome him to the soil he so nobly defended—among them a few patriots of the Revolution paid him their respects, whose hands, when he once grasped them, he seemed unwilling to relinquish, and whose interviews were very feeling in themselves and rendered the scenes very interesting to the younger class. After being generally introduced to the citizens and the ladies who flocked to the place "to see and welcome the veteran," he informed them that he was sorry to part with them so soon and was again escorted by a large concourse of people to the beach from whence he embarked upon the Herald for Wheeling, amidst the acclamations and cheers of the people and the roaring of cannon.

Daniel Webster and Thomas Ewing were in Marietta the same year (1837) but not at the same time. The Marietta *Gazette* says that upon May 15, 1837, "Honorable Daniel Webster and lady arrived and landed at this place and after a short promenade passed on down the Ohio. There was no display in their appearance or conversation and Mr. Webster conversed in an easy and affable manner with those who accosted him."

Thomas Ewing was given a public dinner at Marietta September 2, 1837. He had been in Marietta often before, not as the distinguished statesman, but as the poor attorney. In 1816 he had won his first laurels as a lawyer in the old court house, which stood where the jail now is, and had received a small fee, of which he was more proud than of any of the large ones that he obtained in later years. On the occasion to which we have alluded he had just closed a term of seven years' brilliant service in the United States Senate, and was known and honored throughout the land. The dinner was served under the trees by the court house, within a few rods of the spot where the guest had twenty years before, as an obscure young man, won his first suit at law. A large concourse of people was now gathered to pay respect to the great orator and statesman. Judge Ephraim Cutler was president of the day, and the vice-presidents were Arius Nye, Joseph Barker, jr., General Dana, Dr. George Bowen, Judah M. Chamblerlain, William Mason, Thomas F. Stanley, and Major John Clark. The marshal was Captain Francis Devol. Mr. Ewing made an eloquent address, which was listened to by a large proportion of the citizens of Marietta. We will remark in this connection that Thomas Ewing, as a four-year-old lad came to Washington county with his father, George Ewing, from Virginia, in 1793, and lived for two years in the block-house at Waterford. His father was afterward the first settler in Ames township, Athens county.

Probably the most distinguished visitor ever entertained at Marietta was John Quincy Adams. His brief sojourn was fraught with the deepest interest, for aside from the eminence of the man whom the people assembled to honor, there was a suggestiveness in the occasion which was very impressive. It became known in the summer of 1843 that Mr. Adams had consented to lay the corner-stone of the Cincinnati observatory, and the citizens of Marietta tendered him an invitation to visit the place, as the first that was settled north of the Ohio. He accepted the invitation conditionally, agreeing to stop on his way up the river from Cincinnati if he should have no duties to perform which would conflict with his so doing. He was in Cincinnati upon the tenth of November. No definite time for his visit to Marietta could be fixed. It was understood throughout the town, however, that his coming would be announced in some unmistakable manner, as by the firing of cannon or the ringing of the Congregational church bell. At two o'clock in the

David Allen

afternoon of Wednesday, November 15th, the resounding boom of cannon announced the arrival of the steamer Ben Franklin, on which Mr. Adams was known to have left Cincinnati. The day was a little rainy, but that fact did not prevent the people from turning out *en masse* to greet the patriot whose influence had been potent in the affairs of the Nation from its beginning. A great crowd gathered at the Congregational church, and another at the steamboat landing. Some preparations had been made for the welcoming of the distinguished guest. Nahum Ward was chairman of the reception committee, and A. T. Nye and Noah L. Wilson marshals. Mr. Adams rode to the church in Mr. Ward's carriage, followed and escorted by a great concourse of people. The church was packed to its utmost capacity. The address of welcome was delivered by Deacon William R. Putnam, after which Mr. Adams spoke for half an hour or more extemporaneously upon the pioneers of the Ohio company. A graphic writer,* who was present, gives the following account of (and comment upon) the old statesman's remarks:

. . . He showed a minute acquaintance with the first movements which resulted in the settlement in Ohio. He spoke of the leading men in the enterprise, what part he had borne in the Revolutionary war, and what had been the leading influence he exerted in founding the colony and in raising it through the hardships of its first decade. He paid a noble tribute to the memory of this man, so dear to the Marietta people. He spoke also of bold Commodore Whipple, who "fired the first gun on the sea at the British," in the opening of the Revolutionary war," by heading the party which captured and burned the Gaspe in the waters of Rhode Island. He described Colonel Tupper, Return Jonathan Meigs, General Varnum, Colonel Parsons, the Devols, the Greens, the Putnams, Dr. Cutler and his son, the Fearings, and others. His knowledge of the families of the original settlers, where they came from, what they encountered on the journey, and after landing at the mouth of the Muskingum, their sufferings during the Indian wars, etc., surprised all present. What made it the more remarkable was, that there was then no published book from which he might have gleaned the facts, for Dr. Hildreth did not publish his Pioneers of Ohio until 1848, and his Lives of the Early Settlers of Ohio until 1852. I was afterwards informed that Mr. Adams accounted for his minute acquaintance with the early settlers of Ohio, by stating that he carefully read the accounts which were from time to time published in the newspapers of the day. Many of the pioneers were educated men, and wrote from the wilderness letters to their friends in New England, detailing carefully all the events transpiring in the colony. These were usually published in the Massachusetts newspapers and were read with as great avidity as a few years since people read the exciting letters from California. From this source Mr. Adams drew the materials of that admirable half hour's address, and the minuteness of his details, and the correctness of his names, dates, and other statements, proved the amazing accuracy and discipline of his memory.

After his remarks had been concluded an opportunity was afforded the people of meeting Mr. Adams personally. He descended from the pulpit, and one by one the congregation were presented to him. The writer from whom we have already quoted continues:

The first settlers were almost all gone, in fact I do not recall one who was present on this interesting occasion. However, there were many there who had come as children with the pioneers, or who had been born soon after the settlement was made. There were descendants of Israel Putnam, of Pomfret, through the line of his son, Colonel Israel Putnam. There were Deacon William Rufus Putnam and his son William Rufus, the son and grandson of General Rufus Putnam. There were the Nyes,

* "Lane" in the *Evangelist*. The real name of the writer is not known at this day. The Rev. Joseph F. Tuttle, president of Wabash college, wrote a number of years ago a similar article for the Cincinnati *Gazette*.

55

grandchildren and great-grandchildren of Colonel Benjamin Tupper. There were Judge Cutler and his son, the son and grandson of the Rev. Mannasseh Cutler, who negotiated with Congress the purchase of the land for the Ohio company. There were the descendents of Captain Joseph Barker, prominent among whom was Joseph Barker, esq., the first child born in Belpre township, which settlement was made soon after that at Marietta. Captain Barker himself had been dead only two months. The Danas, from Newport and Belpre, came also to welcome the sage of Quincy. One of these, Mr. George Dana, a plain farmer, of uncommon mental parts and acquirements, came up leading his little son, John Quincy Dana, and said to Mr. Adams, "Here is my youngest son, whom I have named to show my esteem for you." Mr. Adams immediately put his hand on the lad's head and said, "God bless you my son." Descendants of Jonathan Stone, Paul Fearing, Ebenezer Battelle, —— Devol, and other pioneers were introduced. It was a singularly impressive sight thus to have the children and grandchildren of the very men Mr. Adams had been speaking of, come up to shake his hand.

When this informal reception was brought to an end, Mr. Adams reentered Nahum Ward's carriage, and was driven to the great mound in the cemetery, the elevated squares and *Sacra Via* which he viewed with much interest. Before nightfall he had returned to the boat, and was on his way to Pittsburgh, accompanied by Caleb Emerson, Judge Ephraim Cutler and Judge Joseph Barker. Speaking of Mr. Adams and Mr. Emerson (the latter was called the "walking cyclopædia of Marietta"), the newspaper contributor from whom we have above quoted, says: "I am told that these remarkable men spent the greater part of the night in conversation," and, he adds, "a gentleman who was present told me that the conversation . . . was marvelous, and that the Sage of Quincy did not outshine his plain companion from Marietta, a statement I can easily credit, because few men had greater resources from which to draw than Mr. Emerson."

The Marietta *Intelligencer*, in its next issue after the occasion we have described, said that Mr. Adams' "visit to this place will be a day long remembered," and continued:

Old age will love to speak of it, and the family circle will repeat the story of his visit with feelings of gratitude and pleasure one to the other, and those now in the happy days of innocent childhood will tell to another generation that they have seen and shaken hands with the great defender of the rights of man.

CHAPTER XXXV.

MARIETTA—MUNICIPAL MATTERS.

Measures of the Ohio Company Relating to Marietta—The Ministerial Section—Petition For Incorporation—Marietta the First Town Incorporated in the Northwest—Changes in the Charter and System of Government—The Fire Department—City Hall—Roll of Marietta Officers From 1800 to 1881—Harmar Incorporated—List of Mayors.

THE early action of the Ohio company looking toward the laying out of the city at the confluence of the Ohio and the Muskingum, has already been related. The directors, at a meeting held in Boston, as shown by their manuscript journal, resolved "anything to the contrary in former resolutions notwithstanding," that four thousand acres of their land near the mouth of the Muskingum should be reserved for a city and commons and "that the city be so laid out into oblong squares as that each house lot shall consist of ninety feet in front and one hundred and eighty feet in depth, with an alley of ten feet in width through each square in its oblong direction, and that the centre street (which is Washington) crossing the city be one hundred and fifty feet wide." It will be easily seen by reference to the map that the "city" was laid out with reference to the Muskingum rather than the Ohio. The street nearest its bank was named Front and those parallel with it were numbered. The streets running at right angles were then named in honor of Revolutionary heroes.

Soon after the settlement was made it was

"Resolved (by the Ohio Company). That the common lands between the highway and the Muskingum and in Market Square may be assigned by the directors to persons, to occupy as gardens (reserving so much of the commons and in such places as the Directors judge necessary to pass from the Muskingum to the Ohio and to be by them ordered to be open), and the gardens so assigned shall be held the term of ten years from March 1st (1788), on condition that they shall be cleared within two months, and fenced by March 1, 1792, and that within three years trees be set out."

SECTION TWENTY-NINE.

It will be remembered that section twenty-nine in each township of the Ohio company's purchase was reserved for the support of religion. In Marietta township section twenty-nine happened to be included in the town plat and this fact caused the directors of the company a great amount of trouble. Upon November 26, 1795, the Ohio company passed the following resolutions relating to section twenty-nine, or as it is commonly called, the ministerial section:

WHEREAS, a part of lot No. 29, appropriated by Congress for the support of religion, was assumed by the agents of the Ohio company for the purpose of laying out the city of Marietta, under an apprehension that the same might be obtained from Congress, and

WHEREAS, many of the house-lots laid out as aforesaid, now fall within lot No. 29,

Resolved, unanimously, that provision shall be made in some part of the purchase to make good to the proprietors all such deficient lots; and in all cases where any lots have been intersected by the dividing lines of lot No. 29, of one said, and the proportion of one-fourth of said lot is recovered,

Resolved, That such lot shall be considered as retaining its former number, and belonging to the person in whose name it was drawn; and the superintendent of the survey is requested to ascertain the quantity of land so cut off from the city lots, which shall be provided for in some other place.

The ministerial section includes a large part of Marietta and of Harmar, and the boundary line may be described as follows: Beginning at the intersection of Sixth and Wayne streets in Marietta, on the Ohio river, the east line runs north, crossing Seventh street near the middle of square No. 71, Eighth and Hart streets at their intersection; thence to a point back of College Hill; thence due west, crossing Tupper at Seventh street, Sixth, Wooster, Fifth and Fourth streets to the northwest corner of Washington and Third streets; thence due south, crossing Second street, Front street near its intersection with Wooster, thence in same direction diagonally across the Muskingum river, entering Harmar at the intersection of Lancaster and Muskingum streets; thence midway between Second and Third streets and parallel with them to the Ohio river.

The territorial government, by act of November 27, 1800, authorized the leasing of the school and ministerial lands and established a corporation for managing the business. Griffin Greene, Robert Oliver, Benjamin Ives Gilman, Isaac Pierce, Jonathan Stone, Ephraim Cutler, and William Rufus Putnam were the trustees who originally composed the corporation.* Section 7 of the act set forth that as a portion of the town of Marietta was built on the fractional lot No. 29, and as it was reasonable that those persons who had built, or might build, valuable houses on the same should hold the land by a permanent lease, the trustees might lease any part of said land except such streets and commons as had been laid out. It was specified that the leases should be for ninety-nine years, renewable for ever, and that in no case was the annual rental to exceed ten dollars for one-third of an acre (except where more than one dwelling was built upon the same) and that in no case should the annual rental fall below one dollar for one-third of an acre.

In 1805 the leasing of the ministerial section was taken out of the hands of this corporation and a new one was established, and empowered with this especial duty. It was composed of William Rufus Putnam, Matthew Backus, Joseph Buell, Silas Bent, jr., Cornelius Hogland, Haffield White, Joseph Wood, William Skinner, and William Nixon. The act of 1805 was replaced by another in 1806, and in 1810—February 14th—one was passed reducing the number of trustees from nine to three. Thomas Stanley, John Sharp, and Cornelius Houghland were the commissioners appointed under the new act. In 1814 Timothy Buell was appointed trustee in the place of John Sharp, resigned.†

The owners of Marietta lots within the ministerial section can obtain a deed in fee simple from the governor of the State on payment of a sum sufficient to yield a yearly interest equivalent to the annual ministerial rent. Many of the property owners now hold these governor's deeds.

Upon December 14, 1795, the Ohio company took some action in regard to the lands on the west side of the Muskingum. The superintendent of surveys was directed to lay out city lots on the Harmar side of the river, "beginning where the north side of the two-acre tract appropriated to make good the fractional city lots shall end, after leaving a sufficient space for a street, thence going up the Muskingum as far as he may find land suitable for the purpose, leaving a sufficient street along the bank of the river, and also leaving convenient avenues or streets from the river back to the hill."‡ He was also instructed "to lay out as many house lots as the land might be suitable for, along both sides of the highway, leading from the river near Fort Harmar, west."

The same day the directors authorized the division of "Bake house square," and the laying off of the unappropriated land lying on the northeast bank of the Muskingum from the place where the university line intersects it up the river to the eight acre lots, into city or house lots. It was also resolved that "the superintend-

*Land Laws for Ohio.
†Land Laws for Ohio.
‡Journal of the Ohio company.

ent of surveys reserve out of such appropriation as great a width of land as the present reserve of ten squares for Campus Martius, and from thence to the river," which piece of land was reserved for a landing place or commons forever. Ten acres was reserved for a burying-ground, between city squares No. 33 and the three acre lots, in January, 1796; also, the elevated squares *Capitolium* and *Quadranaou*, and the land included in *Sacra Via*.

The lands lying in Campus Martius square and the garden lots attached—lots No. 1 to No. 18, inclusive—were held by the proprietors of the Ohio company without title, but the company, upon January 22, 1796, ordered them to be sold.

INCORPORATION.

The township of Marietta was established by the court of quarter sessions in 1790, but Marietta was not incorporated as a town until the year 1800. The town incorporation and the township of Marietta appear to have been coextensive under the first act, and to have so remained until 1825.

The first step taken toward securing the incorporation of the town was at a meeting of citizens held September 1, 1800. On this occasion Rufus Putnam, Return Jonathan Meigs, sr., Paul Fearing, Benjamin Ives Gilman, and William Rufus Putnam were appointed a committee to make application to the territorial legislature for the passage of an act authorizing the measure they wished to consummate. The following petition was shortly afterward forwarded to Chillicothe:

To his Excellency the Governor of the Territory Northwest of the Ohio, the Legislative Council and House of Representatives in General Assembly:

The petition of the subscribers, inhabitants of Marietta, respectfully showeth that your petitioners are desirous that the inhabitants of the township of Marietta may be incorporated into a body politic, and corporate, vested with power to regulate the internal police of said township, and provide for the incidental expenses arising within the same. Wherefore your petitioners pray you to take the subject into consideration, and enact a law granting them such privileges as are commonly enjoyed by incorporate towns in many of the States, composing the United States of America.

GRIFFIN GREENE,	JABEZ TRUE,
RUFUS PUTNAM,	CHARLES GREENE,
R. J. MEIGS, SR.,	EBENEZER SPROAT,
EARL SPROAT,	BENJAMIN TUPPER,
WILLIAM RUFUS PUTNAM,	GILBERT DEVOL, JR.,
WILLIAM SKINNER,	EDWIN PUTNAM,
JOSHUA SHIPMAN,	RICHARD GREENE,
JOHN BROUGH,	NATHAN MCINTOSH,
STEPHEN PIERCE,	MATTHEW BACKUS,
ICHABOD NYE,	JOHN H. WHITE,
DAVID PUTNAM,	GEORGE DYAR,

D. WOODBRIDGE.

On the back of the original manuscript of the above (which is in the handwriting of William Rufus Putnam) is the following note:

November 6, 1800. Referred to Meigs, Sibley, and Smith, who are appointed to examine the journal of last session, etc. Mr. Fearing added to said committee.

The act was passed soon after the above date, and approved by Governor St. Clair December 2, 1800.

Marietta was the first town incorporated in the Northwestern Territory. Athens was incorporated only four days later; Cincinnati, January 1, 1802, and Chillicothe, January 4, 1802.

The incorporation act was framed after those enacted in Massachusetts. It provided for the annual "town meeting," at which should be elected the chairman, a town clerk, treasurer, "three or five able and discreet persons of good moral character, to be styled the town council," assessors, overseers of the poor, supervisors of highways, fence viewer, and collector.

The act of 1800 was amended in 1812, and on January 8, 1825, which narrowed the town limits so as to include such parts of the old town as were contained in the plat as filed in the recorder's office. Three wards were established, the Second being that part of the town west of the Muskingum, and the First and Third including the territory now known as Marietta, upon the east side of the river. Under this act nine councilmen were elected on the first of March each year, and they chose the mayor, recorder and treasurer from their own number, and appointed the marshal, surveyor, clerk of the market, and all other town officers.

March 7, 1835, another act was passed. The boundaries of the town were left unchanged, but the system of election and government underwent a modification. The mayor, marshal, and nine trustees were elected annually. The mayor presided in the council, but had no vote. All of that part of Marietta lying east of the Muskingum was incorporated separately from that upon the west side March 15, 1837, and Harmar was incorporated March 23d. The act of 1837 divided Marietta into two wards. Otherwise it was similar in its provisions to that of 1835. In October, 1853, Marietta became a city of the second class in accordance with a State law of the previous year. In 1854 the corporation was divided into three wards, the First being the territory south of Butler street, and the Second and Third lying north of that street, separated by Fourth street.

FIRE DEPARTMENT.

Until quite recent years the fire department has not been regularly under municipal control, or patronage. The first fire in Marietta of which we have any knowledge was that which consumed "Bowen's Row" on the north side of Greene street, in 1804 or 1805. Very soon after this occurrence the citizens organized what was called a "fire brigade." Every householder kept a leather bucket, and when a fire broke out hastened to it, bucket in hand. Lines of men were then formed between the burning building and the nearest available water supply, and the buckets passed from one man to another, backward and forward. These buckets were made by Robert Johnson, a saddler. Some time prior to 1832 the little hand-engine, now managed by a company of boys, was brought to Marietta, and it was employed to excellent advantage several times during the years that elapsed before a larger one was procured.

The most disastrous fire that ever occurred in Marietta was in May, 1858. It originated in a barn back of the bank of Marietta, and, spreading rapidly, destroyed the large buildings in front, and made its way up Greene street nearly to Second.

Not long after this fire the Defiance Fire company (which is still in existence) was organized and a large hand-engine procured.

In 1871 the bonds of the city were issued to the amount of $12,000, and a Silsby steam fire engine was bought at an expense of $7,000. The amount originally provided by the council for the equipment of a fire company was found to be inadequate and further provision was made from time to time until the city had spent upwards of $16,000 for fire apparatus. The steamer was taken charge of by the Riverside Fire company, organized under the regulations of the council as expressed in an ordinance. Henry Best was the first chief. Since the completion of the city hall building the fire department quarters have been in that edifice.

In Harmar the same system prevailed at an early day to which we have alluded as existing upon the east side of the river. Almost every householder had a leather bucket. It is remembered by old residents that when emergencies demanded, the people were very prompt in rallying to suppress the flames, and that women as well as men served in the lines passing the buckets. "The Wave," a small hand-engine, was bought in Philadelphia in 1835. In 1875 the town council of Harmar, to keep abreast of the times in the matter of guarding against the destruction of property, bought of Burton & Sons, manufacturers at Waterford, New York, a fine steamer, for which they paid about three thousand five hundred dollars. The company organized to manage it has done excellent service when called upon.

CITY HALL.

The need of a city building appears to have been felt for several years before any definite measures were resorted to for supplying the deficiency. The city council decided in 1871 to erect a substantial brick building of a sufficient size to accommodate the city officers and the fire department, and afford a place of meeting for their body and their successors in office. The contract was awarded to W. W. McCoy, he being the lowest bidder, upon September 15th, and preparations were immediately begun for the work. It had been the intention of the council to build upon the commons, now commonly called the park, at the corner of Front and Putnam streets, but there was objection made to this location. An appeal to the court resulted in an injunction restraining the council from building on the common, and thereupon the present site of the city hall was purchased of M. P. Wells, esq. Work had been begun here when the city council, finding that there was much interest manifested in the matter, and a very general desire that the building should be much larger than had been contemplated, called a special election for the purpose of securing an accurate expression of public opinion. The ballots were prepared so as to read, "City Hall, yes," and "City Hall, no." The vote was very nearly unanimous for building a city hall, and, it being understood that the majority were in favor of a building which would answer all possible requirements and be an ornament to the town, the plans and specifications were changed, and a

new contract made with Mr. McCoy. The building committee consisted of Michael H. Needham, George S. Jones, and Dudley S. Nye. They examined several city halls in neighboring towns and reported plans which were adopted October 3, 1871. Work was immediately begun, and the building was finished and ready for occupancy by the first of February, 1873. The building cost about seventy thousand dollars, nearly all of which amount was expended in Marietta. The hall was formally opened February 4th, with a representation by amateurs (all Mariettians) of Bulwer's drama, "The Lady of Lyons." A congratulatory address to the people upon the completion of the building was delivered by General R. R. Dawes before the curtain was raised. Two other entertainments were given upon the evenings of February 6th and 7th. The proceeds of the three, which amounted to about one thousand dollars, was invested in scenery, which was presented to the city, and now ornaments the stage of the hall.

MARIETTA CIVIL LIST.[*]

Following is a list of the principal civil officers of the town from 1800 down to 1881:

OFFICERS.

1801.—Rufus Putnam, chairman town meeting; David Putnam, town clerk; Ichabod Nye, town treasurer; Rufus Putnam, Griffin Greene and Joseph Gilman, council.

1802.—Rufus Putnam, chairman town meeting; David Putnam, town clerk; Ichabod Nye, town treasurer; Rufus Putnam, Joseph Gilman and Dudley Woodbridge, council.

1803.—Rufus Putnam, chairman town meeting; David Putnam, town clerk; Ichabod Nye, town treasurer; Paul Fearing, Griffin Greene and John Brough, council.

1804.—Dudley Woodbridge, chairman town meeting; Nathaniel Gates, town clerk; Robert Wallace, town treasurer; Paul Fearing, Rufus Putnam and Dudley Woodbridge, council.

1805.—Dudley Woodbridge, chairman town meeting; Nathaniel Gates, town clerk; Robert Wallace, town treasurer; Dudley Woodbridge, William Skinner and Edward W. Tupper, council.

1806.—Dudley Woodbridge, chairman town meeting; Nathaniel Gates, town clerk; Robert Wallace, town treasurer; Levi Barber, Joseph Buell, William Taylor, Hallam Hempstead and Dudley Woodbridge, council.

1807.—Dudley Woodbridge, chairman town meeting; Nathaniel Gates, town clerk; Robert Wallace, town treasurer; Simeon Pool, Giles Hempstead and Edwin Putnam, council.

1808.—Edwin Putnam, chairman town meeting; Nathaniel Gates, town clerk; Seth Washburn, town treasurer; Edwin Putnam, Simeon Pool and Joseph Holden, council.

1809.—Paul Fearing, chairman town meeting; Benjamin Ruggles, town clerk; Seth Washburn, town treasurer; Jeremiah Dare, Hallam Hempstead and Edwin Putnam, council.

1810.—Seth Washburn, chairman town meeting; Samuel P. Hildreth, town clerk; Seth Washburn, town treasurer; William Woodbridge William Skinner and Jeremiah Dare, council.

1811.—Ichabod Nye, chairman town meeting; Samuel P. Hildreth, town clerk; Jabez True, town treasurer; William Woodbridge, Levi Barber and Joseph Holden, council.

1812.—Ichabod Nye, chairman town meeting; Samuel P. Hildreth, town clerk; Jabez True, town treasurer; William Woodbridge, Joseph Holden and James Sharp, council.

1813.—Ichabod Nye, chairman town meeting; Samuel P. Hildreth, town clerk; Jabez True, town treasurer; James Sharp, William Woodbridge and Robert Williamson, council.

1814.—Caleb Emerson, chairman town meeting; Samuel P. Hildreth, town clerk; Jabez True, town treasurer; William Woodbridge, James Sharp and Robert Williamson, council.

1815.—John Brough, chairman town meeting; Robert C. Barton,

---

* Prepared originally by S. J. Hathaway, esq., for appendix of "Revised Ordinances of Marietta," and now completed to date.

Henry Bohl

Hon. Henry Bohl, general insurance agent, was born July 4, 1844, in the kingdom of Bavaria, Germany. He came to this country with his father in May, 1855, and settled in Washington county, Ohio. He assisted him on the farm during the summer months, and attended school in the winter, until he was seventeen years old, when he left home and entered an engagement in the Marietta Chair factory, where he remained some four years. He next engaged in the clothing business as clerk for J. W. F. Brown, at Marietta, where he remained four years. In January, 1869, he engaged in local insurance in Marietta, and was very successful. His health, however, became very much impaired in 1871, and, by the advice of his physician, he concluded to dispose of his office and business, and engage in out door employment, which he did by accepting a special agency for the Home Insurance company, of Columbus, Ohio, but as his health did not improve, he removed in March, 1872, to Atlanta, Georgia, where he accepted a southern department of three states for the American Central Fire Insurance company, of St. Louis. In 1873 he was elected secretary of the Underwriters Association of the South, comprising eleven southern states, and being auxiliary to the National Board of Fire Underwriters, with headquarters at New York city.

Having nearly regained his health, and his family being anxious to return to their old home in Ohio, he removed again to Marietta in March, 1875, after an absence of two years, and took charge of a western department of three states for the American Central Insurance company, which he had managed in the South. He resigned this position in the autumn of 1875, and accepted the state agency for Ohio for the Milwaukee Mechanics Mutual Fire Insurance company, and also again embarked in the local insurance business at Marietta.

Mr. Bohl has always been a Democrat, casting his first vote in 1864 for George B. McClellan for President of the United States. From 1869 to 1871 he took an active interest in politics, and was for several years a member and secretary of the Democratic County Central committee. After his removal to the south, and during his residence there, he took no part in the movements of the day, but on his return home, his old political friends knowing him to be an effective worker, insisted on his again taking an active part in politics. In 1875 they urged him to accept the nomination for county treasurer, which, however, he declined emphatically, on the ground that he desired no political county office. He finally accepted the candidacy for representative to the Ohio legislature, and in October, 1879, he was elected by a majority of two hundred and fifty-one, running largely ahead of his ticket.

One of his first acts, after taking his seat in that body, was to introduce a resolution pledging the house of representatives of the people of Ohio to be in favor of a purely secular education, at the expense of the tax payers, without any division of the school fund, among any sect or sects, and to sustain and support the admirable provision of the Ohio constitution on that subject. This resolution received the unanimous vote of the house of representatives, and was introduced for the reason that the Republican party, in the political campaign of 1875, had charged their opponents with being in favor of a division of the public school funds. He also secured the passage of a bill by the house in 1877 making silver a legal tender in Ohio for all debts, public and private, silver at that time being demonetized by the National Government. On January 10, 1896, United States Senator Allen G. Thurman, of Ohio, addressed a letter to Mr. Bohl, defining his position on the financial question, which was forthwith published and read with great interest throughout the country, as the senator was then a prominent prospective candidate for President of the United States.

Mr. Bohl was reared in the communion of the German Reformed church, of which he and his family are now members.

He has taken a great interest in secret societies, being a member of the Masonic, Odd Fellows and Red Men societies. In 1871 he was elected representa-

tive to the grand lodge of Odd Fellows of Ohio, also great sachem of the State of Ohio of the Improved Order of Red Men. In 1892 he was elected representative to the United States grand lodge of the Improved Order of Red Men. In 1895 he was representative to the grand lodge of Odd Fellows of Georgia; and in 1896 again representative to the grand lodge of Odd Fellows of Ohio, being at this writing a member of the committee on legislation, one of a committee to receive and entertain the sovereign grand lodge of the world at Cincinnati next September, and one of the executive committee of the grand lodge of Ohio.

In May, 1876, he was elected by the Democratic State convention at Cincinnati as an alternate at-large to the National Democratic convention at St. Louis, and was afterward elected delegate-at-large from Ohio to said convention, filling the vacancy created by the absence of Hon. George H. Pendleton. He was also a member of the Democratic State Central committee in 1876. In 1877 he was renominated for representative and re-elected by five hundred and eighty-five majority. The sixty-third general assembly being Democratic, Mr. Bohl became at once one of the most influential members and leaders of the house of representatives, and took rank as one of its ablest debaters. He looked closely after the interests of his immediate constituents, securing a number of good appointments for his county, and the enactment of many local measures, protecting the real interests of said county, and presenting the removal of Beverly college to Pennsylvania, and many other important local measures. He was chairman of the committee on insurance of the house, also chairman of select committees asking Congress not to reduce the tariff on wood, steel and iron. He reported in favor of said resolutions as such chairman, and fought them through the house. He was also one of the house committee to prepare a bill to re-district the State for Congressional purposes, and wrote of a subcommittee, he wrote and reported to the Democratic caucus their report, which was unanimously adopted, and enacted into a law. He was also the author of all financial resolutions introduced and passed in the sixty-third general assembly, including one declaring "United States bonds payable, principal and interest, in silver, at the option of the Government," and instructing our Senators and Representatives in Congress to support the Bland silver bill without any amendments limiting free coinage, and censuring President Hayes and Secretary John Sherman for their opposition to the remonetization of the silver dollar. This resolution passed both houses, and was presented to the United States senate by Senator Thurman.

In 1878 Mr. Bohl was a prominent candidate for Congress in the thirteenth Ohio Congressional district, but, after more than eighty ballots, was defeated for the nomination by General A. J. Warner. In 1880 his name was prominently mentioned by the Democratic press of Ohio for secretary of state, but he declined to accept the nomination. He was delegate from the fifteenth district of Ohio to the Democratic National convention in 1880 at Cincinnati, being secretary of the Ohio delegation; and also chairman of the Democratic County Central committee of Washington county; was secretary of the Democratic State convention held at Cleveland in July, 1881.

Whilst a member of the Ohio legislature, he was opposed to all monopolies, and was the author of the resolution investigating the Standard Oil company in regard to railroad freight discriminations in Ohio.

His name, at this writing, is prominently used by the Democratic press and friends for the nomination for lieutenant governor of Ohio, and he has also been tendered the nomination for State senator by the Morgan county democracy, but he has declined to be a candidate for either position, on account of his large and pressing private business. Mr. Bohl is at this time serving as director in three Ohio insurance companies, and is vice-president of one.

town clerk; Joseph Holden, town treasurer; Robert Williamson, James Sharp and John Lawrence, council.

1816.—Caleb Emerson, chairman town meeting; Robert C. Barton resigned, and Royal Prentiss, town clerk; Joseph Holden, town treasurer; James Sharp, Giles Hempstead and Caleb Emerson, council.

1817.—James Sharp, chairman town meeting; Royal Prentiss, town clerk; Joseph Holden, town treasurer; James Sharp, Samuel Hoit and Robert Williamson, council.

1818.—James Sharp, chairman town meeting; Royal Prentiss, town clerk; Joseph Holden, town treasurer; James Sharp, Salmon Buell and Robert Williamson, council.

1819.—Caleb Emerson, chairman town meeting; Royal Prentiss, town clerk; Sampson Cole, town treasurer; Caleb Emerson, John Merrill and Amzi Stanley, council.

1820.—Ichabod Nye, chairman town meeting, Royal Prentiss, town clerk; Sampson Cole, town treasurer; Caleb Emerson, John Merrill and George Turner, council.

1821.—Ichabod Nye, chairman town meeting; Royal Prentiss, town clerk; John Mills, town treasurer; George Dunlevy, Daniel H. Buell and John Merrill, council.

1822.—John Clark, chairman town meeting; Royal Prentiss, town clerk; John Mills, town treasurer; George Dunlevy, Daniel H. Buell and John Merrill, council.

1823.—————, chairman town meeting; Royal Prentiss, town clerk; John Mills, town treasurer; George Dunlevy, Daniel H. Buell and John Cotton, council.

1824.—————, chairman town meeting; Royal Prentiss, town clerk; John Mills, town treasurer; Daniel H. Buell, John Cotton and George Dunlevy, council.

1825.—Daniel H. Buell resigned, and James M. Booth, mayor; Caleb Emerson, recorder; James Whitney, treasurer; William Slocomb, surveyor; Daniel H. Buell resigned, Joseph Holden, James M. Booth, Sampson Cole, James Whitney, Morris German, Notley Drown, John Cotton, Caleb Emerson and Ichabod Nye, council.

1826.—James M. Booth, mayor; John Crawford resigned, and John Mills, recorder; John Mills resigned, and James Whitney, treasurer; Daniel Protsman, marshal; David C. Skinner, surveyor; James M. Booth, James Dunn, Wyllys Hall, John P. Mayberry, James Whitney, John Crawford, John Mills, John Clark and Silas Cook, council.

1827.—James M. Booth, mayor; Royal Prentiss, recorder; James Whitney, treasurer; Enoch Hoff, marshal; David C. Skinner, surveyor; James M. Booth, Joseph Holden, Jude Hamilton, Morris German, Royal Prentiss, James Whitney, John Clark, Michael Deterly and Ichabod Nye, council.

1828.—James M. Booth, mayor; Royal Prentiss, recorder; James Whitney, treasurer; Genison Prentis, marshal; Douglas Putnam, surveyor; James B. Booth, Otis Wheeler, Charles Bosworth. James Whitney, Royal Prentiss, John P. Mayberry, John Clark, John Cotton and John Mills, council.

1829.—James M. Booth, mayor; Royal Prentiss, recorder; Amos Dunham, treasurer; Griffin Greene, marshal; Douglas Putnam, surveyor; James M. Booth, Otis Wheeler, John Cotton, Morris German, Amos Dunham, William R. Morton, John Mills, John Clark and Royal Prentiss, council.

1830.—James M. Booth, mayor; William P. Skinner, recorder, Robert Crawford, treasurer; Griffin Greene, marshal; William Slocomb, surveyor; James B. Booth, Otis Wheeler, David B. Anderson, Amos Dunham, William P. Skinner, William Knox, John Mills, Ichabod Nye and Robert Crawford, council.

1831.—James Dunn, mayor; William P. Skinner resigned, and Daniel P. Bosworth, recorder; Robert Crawford, treasurer; Griffin Greene, marshal; William Slocomb, surveyor; James M. Booth, James Dunn, David B. Anderson, William R. Morton, Joseph P. Wightman, Daniel P. Bosworth, William P. Skinner (resigned), Ichabod Nye, Robert Crawford and William Slocomb, council.

1832.—James Dunn, mayor; William Slocomb, recorder, Joseph P. Wightman, treasurer; Griffin Greene, marshal; Douglas Putnam, surveyor; James Dunn, Michael Deterly, Louis Soyez, William P. Morton, Joseph Thompson, Joseph P. Wightman, Ichabod Nye, Robert Crawford and William Slocomb, council.

1833.—Nahum Ward, mayor; Joseph P. Wightman, recorder; John Lewis, treasurer; Griffin Greene, marshal; Douglas Putnam, surveyor; John Lewis, Louis Soyez, Sampson Cole, Amos Dunham, Morris German, Joseph P. Wightman, Caleb Emerson, Nahum Ward and Anselm T. Nye, council.

1834.—Nahum Ward, mayor; Joseph P. Wightman, recorder; John Lewis, treasurer; Griffin Greene, marshal; Douglas Putnam, surveyor;

John Lewis, Nathaniel Bishop, Stephen Daniels, Joseph P. Wightman, Abijah Brooks, George Smith, Nahum Ward, Robert Crawford and Caleb Emerson, council.

1835.—Nahum Ward, mayor, M. Joseph Anders, recorder; James Withrow, treasurer, John Test, marshal, Douglas Putnam, surveyor; Stephen Daniels, James Withrow, Joseph E. Hall, M. Joseph Anders, William Knox, Lawrence Chamberlain, Nahum Ward, Anselm T. Nye and John Clark, council.

1836.—Anselm T. Nye, mayor; James M. Booth, recorder, Felix Regnier, treasurer. Marcellus J. Morse, marshal; ————, surveyor, Joseph E. Hall, James Withrow, Junia Jennings. Felix Regnier, M. Joseph Anders, Reuben Finch, Nahum Ward, Joseph Clark and Anselm T. Nye, council.

1837.—Anselm T. Nye, mayor; Thomas W. Ewart, recorder; Abner L. Guitteau, treasurer; Marcellus J. Morse, marshal; William R. Putnam, surveyor, James M. Booth, Junia Jennings, Stephen Daniels, John Mills, Thomas Vinton and Royal Prentiss council.

1838.—Anselm T. Nye, mayor; Thomas W. Ewart, recorder; Abner L. Guitteau, treasurer, James Marshall, marshal; William R. Putnam, surveyor; James M. Booth, Junia Jennings, Stephen Daniels, John Mills, Royal Prentiss and Samuel Geren, council.

1839.—Anselm T. Nye, mayor; Thomas W. Ewart, recorder; Daniel Protsman, treasurer; James Marshall, marshal; William R. Putnam, surveyor; James Booth, Junia Jennings, Thomas J. Westgate, William A. Whittlesey, John Mills and Samuel Geren, council.

1840.—Anselm T. Nye, mayor; Thomas W. Ewart, recorder; Daniel Protsman, treasurer; James Marshall, marshal; William R. Putnam, surveyor; Thomas J. Westgate, John T Clogston, Wyllys Hall, John Mills, Samuel Geren and Daniel P Bosworth, council.

1841.—Anselm T. Nye, mayor; Thomas W. Ewart, recorder; Daniel Protsman, treasurer; James Marshall, marshal, William R. Putnam, surveyor; Ethan H. Allen, Nathaniel Bishop, John T. Clogston, John Mills, Samuel Geren and Charles Hendrie, council.

1842.—Daniel H. Buell, mayor; Thomas W. Ewart, recorder; Daniel Protsman, treasurer; Thomas Porter, marshal; William R. Putnam, surveyor; Ethan H. Allen, Nathaniel Bishop, John T. Clogston, Thomas Vinton, Weston Thomas and Silas Slocomb, council.

1843.—Daniel H. Buell died, and Louis Soyez, mayor; John T. Clogston, recorder; Eli James, treasurer; Solomon Fuller resigned, and Thomas Porter, marshal; William R. Putnam, surveyor; Warren Wilcox, Hugh Hill, Charles Shipman, Silas Slocomb, Argalus Pixley, jr., and Robert Crawford, council.

1844.—Louis Soyez, mayor; John T. Clogston, recorder; Daniel P. Bosworth, treasurer; Thomas Porter, marshal; William R. Putnam, surveyor, Charles Shipman, Marcellus J. Morse, Nathaniel Bishop, Anselm T. Nye, Thomas W. Ewart and Silas Slocomb, council.

1845.—Louis Soyez, mayor; John T. Clogston, recorder; Daniel Protsman, treasurer, Junia Jennings, marshal; William R. Putnam, surveyor; Joseph L. Record, Horatio Booth, Lewis Mixer, William Holden, A Whittlesey and Thomas W. Ewart, council.

1846.—Louis Soyez, mayor; John S Clogston, recorder; Daniel Protsman, treasurer, Junia Jennings, marshal; William R. Putnam, surveyor; Marcellus J. Morse, Lewis Mixer, Charles Shipman, Theodore Scott, Thomas W Ewart and Anselm T. Nye, council.

1847.—Louis Soyez, mayor; Thomas W. Ewart, recorder; Benjamin Soule, treasurer; Frederick Buck, marshal; William R. Putnam, surveyor, Marcellus J. Morse, Lewis Mixer, John O. Cram, Theodore Scott, Anselm T. Nye and Joseph Jones, council.

1848.—Louis Soyez, mayor; Thomas W. Ewart, recorder; Robert Crawford, treasurer; Joseph Skinner, marshal; William R. Putnam, surveyor; John O. Cram, Lewis Mixer, Thomas J. Westgate, Joseph Jones, Theodore Scott and Anselm T. Nye, council.

1849.—Anselm T. Nye, mayor; Selden S. Cooke, recorder; Robert Crawford, treasurer; Samuel H. Fuller, marshal; William R. Putnam, surveyor, Israel W. Andrews; street commissioner; John O. Cram, Lewis Mixer, Joseph E. Hall, Theodore Scott, David C. Skinner and Ira Ellis, council.

1850.—Louis Soyez, mayor; Selden S. Cooke, recorder; Abner L. Guitteau, treasurer, James W. Clogston, marshal; Israel W. Andrews, surveyor; Israel W. Andrews, street commissioner; John O. Cram, Joseph E. Hall, Ethan H. Allen, David C. Skinner, Thomas W. Ewart and Jacob D. Leonard, council.

1851.—James Dunn, mayor; Selden S. Cooke resigned, and William S. Ward, recorder; Abner L. Guitteau, treasurer; John Wilson, marshal; Israel W. Andrews, surveyor; John O. Cram, street commissioner; Joseph E. Hall, William F. Curtis, George H. Richards, Beman Gates, James Dutton and Thomas W. Ewart, council.

1852.—James Dunn, mayor; Davis Green, recorder; Abner L. Guitteau, treasurer, John Snyder, marshal; Rufus E. Harte, surveyor; John Slocomb, Bernard Maloy; William F Curtis, Marcellus J. Morse, Joseph E. Hall, William P. Skinner, George M. Woodbridge and Davis Green, council.

1853.—James Dunn, mayor; George Wyllys Dodge, recorder; Abner L. Guitteau, treasurer; William Babcock, marshal; Joseph B. Ward, surveyor; Joseph B. Ward, street commissioner, Joseph E. Hall, Thomas J. Westgate, Joseph Holden, jr., George M. Woodbridge, William N. Stewart and James Dunn, council.

1854.—Daniel Protsman, mayor; Melvin Clark, solicitor; George Wyllys Dodge, clerk; Abner L. Guitteau, treasurer; Joseph Deeble, marshal; A. Devine, civil engineer; John Preston, street commissioner; William F. Curtis, Nelson S. Alcock, Thomas F. Jones, Henry Van Bergen, James B. Hovey and J. Dexter Cotton, council.

1855.—Daniel Protsman, mayor, Melvin Clark, solicitor; John Test, clerk; Abner L. Guitteau, treasurer; Joseph Deeble, marshal; Alexander L. Haskin, civil engineer; Joseph Deeble, street commissioner; William F. Curtis, Nelson S. Alcock, Henry Van Bergen, Thomas F. Jones, James B. Hovey and J. Dexter Cotton, council.

1856.—William A. Whittlesey, mayor; Melvin Clark, solicitor; Anselm T. Nye, clerk; Abner L. Guitteau, treasurer; James I. Goldsmith, marshal; Edward P. Walker, civil engineer; Bernard Maloy, street commissioner; Nelson S. Alcock, William F. Curtis, Thomas F. Jones, Anselm T. Nye, J. Dexter Cotton and James B. Hovey, council.

1857.—William A. Whittlesey, mayor; Melvin Clark, solicitor; Anselm T. Nye, clerk; Abner L. Guitteau, treasurer; James I. Goldsmith, marshal; Edward P. Walker, civil engineer; Bernard Maloy, street commissioner; William F. Curtis, Marcellus J. Morse, Anselm T. Nye, Thomas F. Jones, James B. Hovey and J. Dexter Cotton, council.

1858.—Ethan H. Allen, mayor; Melvin Clark, solicitor; Anselm T. Nye, clerk; John O. Cram, treasurer; James I. Goldsmith, marshal; Alexander L. Haskin, civil engineer; Edward W. T. Clark, street commissioner; Marcellus J. Morse, Michael H. Needham, Thomas F. Jones, Anselm T. Nye, J. Dexter Cotton and James B. Hovey, council.

1859.—Ethan H. Allen, mayor; Melvin Clark, solicitor; Anselm T. Nye, clerk; Abner L. Guitteau, treasurer; James I. Goldsmith, marshal; Alexander L. Haskin, civil engineer; John M. Hook, street commissioner; Michael H. Needham, Charles F. Buell, Anselm T. Nye, Thomas F. Jones, James B. Hovey and J. Dexter Cotton, council.

1860.— William A. Whittlesey, mayor; Franklin Buell, solicitor; John Test, clerk; John O. Cram, treasurer; Henry Kelley, marshal; Alexander L. Haskin, civil engineer; John M. Hook, street commissioner; Charles F. Buell, Nathaniel F. Bishop, Thomas F. Jones, Anselm T. Nye, J. Dexter Cotton and Charles Jones, council.

1861.—William A. Whittlesey, mayor; Franklin Buell, solicitor; John Test, clerk; Charles B. Hall, treasurer; Henry Kelley, marshal; Alexander L. Haskin, civil engineer; John M. Hook, street commissioner; Nathaniel F. Bishop, Charles F. Buell, Anselm T. Nye, George S. Jones, Charles Jones and J. Dexter Cotton, council.

1862.—William A. Whittlesey, mayor; William B. Loomis, solicitor; John Test, clerk; Charles B. Hall, treasurer; Henry Kelley, marshal; Rufus E. Harte, civil engineer; John M. Hook, street commissioner; Charles F. Buell, William Pitt Racer, George S. Jones, William I. Rolston, J. Dexter Cotton, George H. Eells (resigned), and Frederick A. Wheeler, council.

1863.—William A. Whittlesey, mayor; William B. Loomis, solicitor; Anselm T. Nye, clerk; Henry Kelley, marshal; Rufus E. Harte, civil engineer; John M. Hook, street commissioner; William Pitt Racer, John Snyder, William L. Rolston, Thomas F. Jones, Daniel R. Sniffen and James B. Hovey, council.

1864.—Samuel S. Knowles, mayor; William B. Loomis, solicitor; Anselm T. Nye, clerk; Henry Kelley, marshal; Rufus E. Harte, civil engineer, John M. Hook, street commissioner; John Snyder, Michael H. Needham, Thomas F. Jones, Jasper S. Sprague, James B. Hovey and James Dunn, council.

1865.—Samuel S. Knowles, mayor, William B. Loomis, solicitor; Anselm T. Nye, clerk; Darius Towsley, marshal; Rufus E. Harte, civil engineer; John M. Hook, street commissioner; Michael H. Needham, Nathan Fawcett, Jasper S. Sprague, Thomas F. Jones, Allen R. Darrow and Theodore G. Field, council.

1866.—Samuel S. Knowles, mayor; Hiram L. Sibley, solicitor; Anselm T. Nye, clerk; Darius Towsley, marshal; John McGee, civil engineer; John M. Hook, street commissioner; Nathan Fawcett, Michael H. Needham, Thomas F. Jones, Anselm T. Nye, jr., Theodore G. Field and Allen R. Darrow, council.

1867.—Samuel S. Knowles, mayor; Hiram L. Sibley, solicitor;

Anselm T. Nye, clerk; Darius Trowsley, marshal; John McGee, civil engineer, John B. Hook, street commissioner; Michael H. Needham, James H. Dye, Anselm T. Nye, jr., John Hall, George H. Eells and Martin Schmidt, council.

1868.—Frederick A. Wheeler, mayor; Hiram L. Sibley, solicitor; Anselm T. Nye, clerk; Darius Towsley, marshal; John McGee, civil engineer; John M. Hook, street commissioner; James H. Dye, Michael H. Needham, John Hall, Anselm T. Nye, jr., Martin Schmidt and John Newton, council.

1869.—Frederick A. Wheeler, mayor; Hiram L. Sibley, solicitor; Daniel B. Torpy, clerk; Leander K. Dutton, marshal; Rufus E. Harte, civil engineer, John M. Hook, street commissioner; Michael H. Needham, James H. Dye, Anselm T. Nye, jr., John Hall, John Newton and Martin Schmidt, council.

1870.—Frederick A. Wheeler, mayor, Reuben L. Nye, solicitor; Daniel B. Torpy, clerk; Leander K. Dutton, marshal; John McGee, civil engineer; Lewis Anderson, treasurer (ex officio city treasurer); John M. Hook, city commissioner; James H. Dye, Michael H. Needham, John Hall, George S. Jones, Martin Schmidt and Dudley S. Nye, council.

1871.—Frederick A. Wheeler, mayor; Reuben L. Nye, solicitor; Daniel B. Torpy, clerk; Darius Towsley, marshal; Theodore F. Davis, civil engineer; Ernst Lindner, treasurer (ex officio city treasurer); John M. Hook, city commissioner; Michael H. Needham, Samuel A. Cooper, George S. Jones, John Hall, Dudley S. Nye and Martin Schmidt, council.

1872.—John V. Ramsey, mayor; Reuben L. Nye, solicitor; Daniel B. Torpy, clerk; Darius Towsley, marshal; Theodore F. Davis, civil engineer; Ernst Lindner, treasurer (ex officio city treasurer); John M. Hook, city commissioner; Michael H. Needham, Samuel A. Cooper, George S. Jones, John Holst, Dudley S. Nye and Daniel G. Mathews, council.

1873.—John V. Ramsey, mayor; Reuben L. Nye, solicitor; Willis H. Johnson, clerk; Darius Towsley, marshal; Theodore F. Davis, civil engineer; Ernst Lindner, treasurer (ex officio city treasurer); John M. Hook, city commissioner; Michael H. Needham, Samuel A. Cooper, George S. Jones, John Holst, Dudley S. Nye and Daniel G. Mathews, council.

1874.—Jewett Palmer, mayor; Seymour J. Hathaway, solicitor; Willis H. Johnson, clerk; Darius Towsley, marshal; Theodore F. Davis, civil engineer; Ernst Lindner, treasurer (ex officio city treasurer); John M. Hook, city commissioner, Samuel A. Cooper, Thomas K. Wells (resigned February, 1875), John Holst, George S. Jones, Daniel G. Mathews and William Styer, council.

1875.—Jewett Palmer, mayor; Seymour J. Hathaway, solicitor; Willis H. Johnson, clerk; Darius Towsley, marshal; John A. Plumer, civil engineer; John M. Hook, city commissioner; George S. Jones, Josiah Coulter, G. Christian Best, William Styer, George T. Elston and William R. Armstrong, council.

1876.—Jewett Palmer, mayor; William G. Way, solicitor; G. C. Best, jr., clerk; Darius Towsley, marshal; John A. Plumer, civil engineer; John M. Hook, city commissioner; Josiah Coulter, J. D. Strauss and William Styer (newly elected members), council.

1877.—Jewett Palmer, mayor (November 5th, by special election, William Glines was chosen mayor to fill vacancy caused by Mr. Palmer's resignation; William G. Way, solicitor; G. C. Best, jr., clerk; Jacob H. Dye, marshal; James A. Plumer, civil engineer; John M. Hook, city commissioner; G. C. Best, G. T. Elston and John Mills, jr., (newly elected members), council.

1878.—William Glines, mayor; William G. Way, solicitor; G. C. Best, jr., clerk; Jacob H. Dye, marshal; Joseph A. Plumer, civil engineer; John M. Hook, city commissioner; Josiah Coulter, J. D. Strauss and Andrew Wagner (newly elected members), council.

1879.—William Glines, mayor; William G. Way, solicitor; G. C. Best, jr., clerk; Jacob H. Dye, marshal; Joseph A. Plumer, civil engineer; John M. Hook, city commissioner; G. C. Best, G. T. Elston and John Mills, jr. (newly elected members), council.

1880.—R. E. Harte, mayor; William G. Way, solicitor; Charles H. Newton, clerk; Jacob H. Dye, marshal; John A. Plumer, civil engineer; John M. Hook, city commissioner; J. S. Sinclair, T. K. Wells, John Hall (newly elected members), council.

1881.—R. E. Harte, mayor; William G. Way, solicitor; Charles H. Newton, clerk; Jacob H. Dye, marshal; John A. Plumer, civil engineer; John M. Hook, city commissioner; G. C. Best, G. T. Elston, John Mills, jr. (newly elected members), council.

HARMAR MAYORS.

We have already mentioned the fact that Harmar was incorporated as a separate municipality March 23, 1837. Unfortunately, the records containing the names of corporation officers for nearly all of the years intervening between 1837 and 1870 have been destroyed, so that it is impossible to present in these pages the civil list of Harmar. The first mayor was James Whitney, a well known steamboat captain, and boat builder and owner. The first recorder or clerk was J. P. Whiteman. The second mayor was John C. McCoy. Since his time the following men have filled the office, in the order in which their names are mentioned: William Smith, Harlow Chapin, Courtland Shepherd, Harlow Chapin, Amos Layman, A. S. Curtis, Harlow Chapin, William Smith, George Stephens.

CHAPTER XXXVI.

MARIETTA—THE ANCIENT REMAINS—BURIAL PLACES.

Description of the Mound Builders' Fortifications and Monuments—Extent of the System of Works—Quadranaou, Capitolium and Sacra Via—The Great Mound—Its Partial Excavation in 1788—Measures for the Preservation of the Works—Marietta Burial Places—Location of Early Graves—Mound Cemetery—Harmar Burying Ground—Old Grave at Harmar—Oak Grove Cemetery.

DESCRIPTION OF THE PRE-HISTORIC REMAINS AT MARIETTA.*

The antiquities of the Ohio and Mississippi valleys afford a rich field for plodding science, and one of mysterious and romantic interest for poetical imagination.

The vastness of the questions suggested by the simple but enduring earth monuments which dot the valleys and crown the hills throughout the west and south—the very fact that absolute knowledge concerning the people who reared them is so meagre, and the domain of speculation so vast, renders the whole subject fascinating in the extreme.

The student who endeavors to solve any of the mightier problems to which examination of ancient remains leads, will find himself almost at the outset confronted by the great black curtain of oblivion through which no gaze can penetrate. He can only discern what the great mound, the *Quadranaou*, the *Capitolium*, the far extending walls of fortified towns, and the thousands of tumuli occupying coignes of vantage along the Ohio and its tributaries, silently and solemnly attest that a vast race once dwelt in the land and has passed away. Concerning the origin, career and final fate of the people he will gain no positive information. There is, to be sure, a general trend of evidence that the race, who have been given the name of Mound Builders, came from Asia, by way of Behring straits, passed southward to the central region of North America, occupied for a considerable period the great basin of the Mississippi, and then by a slow, long continued migration along the shores of the Father of Waters, reached the gulf, and ultimately Mexico, where they obtained their highest civilization. The wide geographical distribution of the earthworks received by this people (they extend from the Alleghanies to the Missouri and Platte rivers), and the great size of many of the remains, indicate that the population must have been very large and was long resident in the country. Caleb Atwater estimated that in 1819 the population of Ohio was no greater than that which the same territory sustained in the age unknown. It is highly probable that the ancient people were even more numerous than the present population along the tributaries. The spontaneous yieldings of the earth, and the products of the chase could not have sustained so numerous a people as the Mound Builders. They undoubtedly followed agriculture. A study of the graves gives many hints as to the character of the race. There are many indications that the people were semi-civilized. They had a rude knowledge of the arts. Spinning and weaving were among the industries they practiced. They constructed pottery, some of which exhibits fine workmanship. That they had a knowledge of some science or art similar to modern surveying is indisputable. Most of the larger earthworks remaining give proof of this, in the absolute regularity and exactness of the circles, squares and octagons of which they are constituted. It has been the almost universal opinion of those who have given the subject much study, that the ancient people were strongly governed, that they were the devotees of a superstitious religion observed with elaborate rites, and that some form of vassalage prevailed among them.

That the race was either divided against itself or had an aggressive enemy is indisputably indicated by the great number of that class of works designed solely for

---

* The pre-historic remains at Marietta have engaged many pens. Probably no others in the Ohio valley or in the vast basin of the Mississippi have been so often described. This fact is accreditable to two causes: First, the peculiar character of the ancient works, as compared with others in the Northern Central States; and second, the marked attention drawn to them by the planting of the colony of the Ohio company upon the site of the old town. General Samuel Holden Parsons wrote of the fortifications in private letters in 1785. Joseph Buell mentions them in his journal for the year 1786. Captain Jonathan Heart, of Fort Harmar, wrote a letter upon them in January, 1791, which was published in the transactions of the American Philosophical Society, volume III. Dr. Manasseh Cutler spent considerable time in examining the works when he visited the settlement in 1788, and assisted Rufus Putnam in making measurements of them. He afterwards incorporated much information concerning them in his notes to the charge at the ordination of the Rev. Daniel Story, and constituted a valuable paper to one of the French scientific or literary societies upon the subject. Caleb Atwater devoted a large space to the Marietta remains in his general description of antiquities in the west, published in the Archæologia Americana in 1819. Thaddeus Mason Harris wrote of them in his Tour, printed in 1805. Ashe, the wholly unreliable English traveller, had much to say of them in his works, and so had the erudite but eccentric Josiah Priest, whose American Antiquities was published in 1833. It remained for Charles Whittlesey, esq., of Cleveland, to make the first survey and accurate map of these wonderful creations of a lost race, in 1837. Among other writers who have given them consideration we may mention William Henry Harrison, Professor Rofinesque, Dr. S. P. Hildreth, and Squier and Davis, whose valuable work, published in 1848, formed the first of the Smithsonian Institute Contributions to Knowledge. In this volume, among a wealth of accurate plates and fine illustrations, is the map prepared by Mr. Whittlesey, and two views—one of the Great Mound, and one of the whole system of works—from paintings by Charles Sullivan, now in the possession of A. T. Nye, esq., of Marietta.

defence. It is commonly believed by archæologists that the exodus of this people was enforced by their antagonists, who, it is supposed, swept down upon them from the north, and very likely waged war upon them for a long period.

The ancient remains in this State, consisting of the various varieties of mounds, graded ways, enclosures, etc., are chiefly confined to the valleys of the Ohio and its tributary streams, and are most numerous along the Scioto, though they abound also upon the Great and Little Miami, upon the Muskingum and the lesser streams. The number of tumuli in the State may be safely estimated at ten thousand, and the number of enclosures at one thousand or fifteen hundred.* One circumstance in the location of the greater works is very noticeable. They occupied in numerous instances the sites destined for the present cities and village. The centres of the ancient and present population were the same in southern Ohio. Like Marietta, the towns of Cincinnati, Chillicothe, Portsmouth, Circleville, and many others that might be mentioned, are built over the embankments and mounds indicating an ancient occupation of the country.

The ancient works at Marietta occupied the "plain," and were included within the territory north of Putnam street and east of Third (with the exception of the graded way, extending down to the lower river terrace, at a point between Second and Front streets).

These works consisted originally of two enclosures (irregular squares, one of which contained about forty and the other twenty acres), together with several truncated pyramids or elevated platforms of earth, the graded way, the great mound now enclosed in the cemetery, several embankments flanking it, and numerous lesser tumuli. The portions of this interesting group of works remaining are the two truncated pyramids known as *Quadranaou* and *Capitolium*, and the mere bed or bottom of the graded way, *Sacra Via*.

When the settlement was made at Marietta these works were covered with a heavy forest. "When I arrived," says Dr. Cutler, "the ground was in part cleared, but many large trees remained on the walls and mounds. The only possible data for forming any probable conjecture respecting the antiquity of these works, I conceived must be derived from the growth upon them. By the concentric circles, each of which denotes the annual growth, the age of the trees might be ascertained. For this purpose a number of trees were felled; and in the presence of Governor St. Clair and many other gentlemen the number of circles was carefully counted. The trees of the greatest size were hollow. In the largest of those which were found there were from three to four hundred circles. One tree, somewhat decayed at the centre, was found to contain at least four hundred and sixty-three circles. Its age was undoubtedly more than four hundred and sixty-three years. Other trees in a growing state were, from their appearance, much older. There were likewise the strongest marks of a previous growth, as large as the present. Decayed stumps could be traced at the surface of the ground, on different parts

* Squier and Davis' Ancient Monuments of the Mississippi Valley.

of the works, which measured from six to eight feet in diameter. In one of the angles of a square a decayed stump measured eight feet in diameter at the surface of the ground; and though the body of the tree was so moldered as scarcely to be perceived above the surface of the earth, we were able to trace the decayed wood under the leaves and rubbish for nearly a hundred feet. A thrifty beech, containing one hundred and thirty-six circles, appeared to have first vegetated within the space that had been occupied by an ancient predecessor of a different kind of wood."

Upon the hypothesis that the growth which he saw had occupied four hundred and sixty-three years, and that it had been preceded by one of equal size and age, Dr. Cutler estimated that at least nine hundred years had elapsed since the works had been deserted by the people who constructed them.

We may remark in this connection that Clavigero, in his History of Mexico, says that the emigration of the Toltecs commenced from their native country about the middle of the sixth century.

The larger of the two square (or nearly square), fortifications, of which we have spoken, was commonly called by the early inhabitants of Marietta, "the town." The walls were, at the time when first observed and measured, from six to ten feet in height, and from twenty-five to thirty-five feet broad at the base. Through these walls there were, upon three sides, three openings or gateways, of which the central ones were the largest. The central one in the front facing the Muskingum, was one hundred and fifty feet wide. Immediately in front of this great gateway, and leading from it toward the river, its walls running at right angles to those of "the town," was the immense graded way, sometimes called the covert or covered way, and named by some pioneer, of classical education, *Sacra Via*. This was a broad avenue, excavated so as to descend by a perfect grade to the lower or latest formed terrace of the Muskingum, at the foot of which it is supposed the stream flowed when the work was constructed. The grade remains, but the walls thrown up at either side have long since been demolished. They began at a distance of sixty feet from the gateway, were exactly parallel, and six hundred and eighty feet long. They were one hundred and fifty feet apart at their bases and two hundred and thirty at their summits, and the broad "way" between them was rounded and raised like a modern city street. At the base of the grade the walls were twenty-one feet in perpendicular height, measuring from the inside, while at the same point upon the outside they were from eight to ten feet high, and much less at the upper end of the avenue. This portion of the Marietta works alone would be a stupendous piece of construction even in this age; and in the era when it was executed must have been a marvel of engineering and have required the patient, long continued toil of a vast number of men. Not less remarkable were the four squares or truncated pyramids (of which the two principal ones have been preserved), enclosed within the walls of the ancient town. The largest of these, the *Quadranaou*, the location of which is now best

Jno. D. Phillips

So soon as the early comers to Marietta had secured covering for their heads, they planned to secure the services of proper persons to impart education to their children. Ever since that period this feeling has prevailed, and in the history of the county can be read with clearness this resolve. Many have taught and left their impressions for good. As early as the year 1849 a system called the Akron system of schools was adopted for the city, and in the year 1861, Mr. John D. Phillips, a graduate of Marietta college in 1854, was chosen principal of the Green Street grammar school. This was an experiment, as he had never been a regular instructor, although he had taught winter schools for a few years previous to that date. The board of education, charmed with his success from year to year, secured his services, increasing his salary as he became more and more valuable, for sixteen years, when, much to the regret of all who knew his value, he resigned his position and accepted work elsewhere.

During this period Mr. Phillips was twice elected by the board of education as principal of the high school and superintendent of all the schools, which position,

after due consideration for reasons that were satisfactory to himself, he declined.

The name is legion of those who, in all those years, were under his instruction, were prepared for life's business and duties. They are to be found in all of the departments of business and trade, in law, medical, editorial and mechanical offices, doing their work with credit to themselves and honoring their early instructor.

His school for years was the "model school" of the State, and so fully impressed were our citizens with this fact, that with pride they took the scholar, the teacher, the man of culture, and in fact all interested in education and the advancement of our youth, who came to our city, to visit this far-famed school. His kind disposition, unassuming manners and sterling integrity, have won for him scores of friends, but few enemies, and a reputation of which he may justly feel proud.

For the last fourteen years Mr. Phillips has held, with the approval of our best citizens, the position of school examiner and clerk of the board for this county.

Long may he live to witness the fruits of his labor and secure the plaudits of his fellow citizens.

described by saying that it is upon the west side of Fourth street, north of Warren, was in the northwest corner of the great enclosure. It was described by Squier and Davis in 1847 as being one hundred and eighty-eight feet long, by one hundred and thirty-two wide and ten feet high. Its apparent height is now a little less than this figure. It contains more than a quarter of a million cubic feet of earth. At the centre of each of the four sides the earth projects, forming gradual and easy ascents to the top. The elevated square, next in importance, is the *Capitolium*, which is situated upon the northwest corner of of Washington and Fifth streets. The southern wall of "the town" originally extended along Washington street very near the *Capitolium*. This elevated square is one hundred and fifty feet long by one hundred and twenty wide, and is about eight feet high. Upon three sides are projections or inclined ways leading to the level platform, but upon the south side the graded ascent is a recess, the measurements of which are equal to those of the projections, or about twenty feet in width by forty in length. East of this square there was originally another and a smaller one, which was known in earlier days as *St. Cecelia*. It was a truncated pyramid, similar in general characteristics to the *Quadranaou* and *Capitolium*, one hundred and twenty feet long by fifty wide and five or six feet high. It had graded ascents only at the ends. In the northern angle of the enclosure was another rectangular elevation which was never of as great a height as the others, and unlike them, had no ascents.

The purpose for which these elevated squares and the great graded way leading down to the Muskingum can of course, only be conjectured. The former, it has been generally thought by students of archæology, were designed as the sites of temples, and were originally so occupied, but with edifices which, having been constructed of perishable material, long since crumbled into dust. The surface of the elevated squares which we have described is perfectly level, except where it has been upheaved by the roots of falling trees, or burrowing animals. The squares bear a close resemblance to the *Teocalli* of Mexico, upon which temples still stand. In Ohio there are but few of these peculiar formations in connection with the great groups of works, and, in fact, besides the Marietta squares there are none, except at Portsmouth, Newark and in the vicinity of Chillicothe. At no one of these localities are the squares as large as those we have here described. Works of this kind occur more frequently in the South, and investigators who have travelled down the valley of the Mississippi and thence into Mexico, report that there is exhibited quite a uniform and constant increase in the size of the squares until they lead up to the mighty temple crowned *Teocalli*, in the land of Montezuma. Upon the other hand, as we journey southward we find a decrease in the size and in the number of enclosures of similar nature to those which abound in Ohio.

We have so far said but little of the smaller of the two enclosures which existed at Marietta. As we have said its area was about twenty acres. This area is now about equally divided north and south by Wooster street, and lies above Fourth street. This enclosure, which formed the connection in the great system of the Marietta works between the larger enclosure and the great mound, was many years ago obliterated. Its walls were never as high as those of the larger enclosure called "the town." There were openings or gateways at the centre of each side and at the corners, which were defended by mounds. It is conjectured that these two enclosures were not designed for defence although they may of course have served that purpose. The ditch or fosse which often occurs in connection with the walls of similar enclosures was wanting here, but it is not improbable that palisades were planted upon the top of the embankments.

The most reasonable hypothesis to be adopted in accounting for the construction of the so-called "forts" is that they were simply enclosures designed to protect the temples and the sacred altars of the ancient people from the profane gaze or touch of an alien race, or to guard them from desecration by animals. They may also have served as the place for great civic or religious assemblages, or the practice of something analogous to the Olympian games. Very likely they contained the residences of the priests or rulers of the people.

Most of the earth of which the so-called "forts" were constructed must have been taken evenly from the surface of the ground within and around them, although excavations commmonly designated as "dug holes" were at an early day observable in several places not far from the works. Several of these have been supposed to be wells, funnel-shaped like those in eastern countries, so that the water-carriers could go down into them.

The large mound now inclosed in the cemetery, the most interesting feature of the Marietta group of works, remains to be described. It is not larger than some others in Ohio, but is probably higher in proportion to its base measurement, and is uniqe in its accessories of embankment and fosse. It is thirty feet in height and its base is one hundred and fifteen feet in diameter. It is surrounded by a ditch about fifteen feet wide and four feet deep, outside of which is a wall about four feet high, and twenty feet or more in breadth. There is an opening in this wall upon the north side and a filling in the fosse, each about twenty feet in width. The surrounding wall and ditch do not form a perfect circle but an elipse, the longer diameter of which is two hundred and thirty feet, and the shorter two hundred and fifteen feet. Originally there were a number of fragmentary walls of slight elevation west and south of the great mound, forming an imperfect reenclosure. There was also a wall extending from a point near the filling of the fosse toward the south embankment of the smaller enclosure.

The mound was described by Squier and Davis in 1847 as being truncated. It so appears at present and the memory of the oldest inhabitant cannot recall a time when it was otherwise. The writer, however, has reason to believe that the mound as originally constructed was a perfect mammalian. The Marietta mound is, doubtless, a sepulchral mound, and it is probable that it contains (or did once contain) two chambers like the great mound at the mouth of Grave creek, in West Virginia—one chamber being situated upon a level with the surrounding plain, and the other midway between the base and the apex of the mound. The flattening of the top may have been caused by the crushing in of one or both of these chambers (the chambers are, in most cases, constructed of timber), or by the uprooting of the great oak which Dr. Cutler's journal tells us stood upon the top in 1788. It is not generally known that the mound has been partially excavated, but such is the fact. Dr. Cutler, as quoted by Mr. Harris,* says that "an opening being made at the summit of the great conic mound" (and it is worthy of note that he uses the word conic) "there were found the bones of an adult in a horizontal position, covered with a flat stone. Beneath this skeleton were three stones placed vertically at small and different distances, but no bones were discovered. That this venerable monument might not be defaced, the opening was closed without further search." The skeleton found was doubtless not lower down than the middle of the mound, that is to say, fifteen feet from the apex. In everyone of the few large mounds excavated, which have a chamber near the top, there has been found another at the base, and hence there is presumptive evidence that the bones of some mighty personage of the ancient race lie as they were originally deposited in an unknow age, amidst the pomp and splendor of strange and superstitious rites. While this mound is undoubtedly monumental in its character, its unique accessory formations—the fosse and wall—would suggest that the Builders had in view some other purpose than the rearing of a massive sepulchre. It may have been utilized as a place for the observance of religious ceremonies.

Small mounds are usually to be found upon the hills overlooking the larger works in the valleys. These are not wanting at Marietta. Harmar hill and the other eminences in the vicinity of the great group we have described, are crowned with them, and they occur at intervals along the whole length of the Muskingum valley, and also those of the Tuscarawas and the Ohio. It is conjectured that these mounds served the purpose of coignes of vantage from which the approach of an enemy could be descried, and also that they were signal stations from which beacon lights have flashed forth at night and columns of smoke arisen in the day time as warnings of impending danger, or the means of conveying quickly other information. It will be found that from one of these mounds upon the valley wall, another similar mound can nearly always be seen, and that the second commands a third, and so on. It is probable that these mounds formed systems extending along the valleys and across the country.

There are in Washington county many small works and mounds, the most interesting of which are mentioned in the histories of the localities in which they occur. It is scarcely necessary to say that there are none which approach in magnitude the ancient remains at Marietta.

PRESERVATION OF THE ANCIENT WORKS.

The pioneers at Marietta exhibited a laudable disposi-

tion to preserve the strange monuments left by a prehistoric people, and although much has necessarily been swept from existence, the most interesting portions of the great system have been preserved, and nearly in the condition in which they were found. While the Goths and Vandals at Circleville were razing to the ground the wonderful works which gave their town its name, the citizens of Marietta were taking steps not only to guard against the immediate obliteration of the remains within the town plat, but to secure their protection for all time. The names which have been used in this chapter, *Quadranaou Capitolium*, and *Sacra Via*, were bestowed upon the several works during the year 1788. A little later the Ohio company passed the following resolution, which was the first measure adopted looking toward the preservation of the ancient works:

Resolved, That Colonel Battelle, Colonel Crary, and Major Sergeant be a committee to lease the public squares (to Samuel H. Parsons, Rufus Putnam and Griffin Greene, esqs.), the ones on which the great mound stands, the *Quadranaou* and *Capitolium*, for so long a time as they are not wanted for the uses for which they were reserved. The committee are to point out the mode of improvement for ornament, and in what manner the ancient works shall be preserved, and also to ascertain the amount of what is to be given.

In March, 1791, the company decided to lease public square No. 1 (Marie Antoinette), containing the great mound, to Rufus Putnam for twelve years, on condition that he should set out trees and make other improvements. On similar terms it was proposed to lease square No. 2 (*Capitolium*), to Dudley Woodbridge for eight years, and square No. 3 (*Quadranaou*), to Benjamin Tupper for ten years. It was resolved at the same time that *Sacra Via* be not leased but that General Putnam should retain control of it, seed it down, plant trees upon it, etc. It was specified that the trees to be set out on the ancient works were to be of native growth. Subsequently Rufus Putnam, Paul Fearing, and Dr. Jabez True were appointed trustees to take charge of the public squares until the town should become incorporated, and lease them to proper persons, the avails of the rent to be applied to the education of indigent orphans.

The large trees growing upon the *Quadranaou* are all of second growth and were set out in accordance with the requirements of the Ohio company. This work, or rather the question of its preservation and the right of the lessee to obliterate or deface it, was the subject of a very warm controversy in 1820. The square containing the *Quadranaou* had been leased to D. Hartshorn and he had transferred the right of possession to the Rev. Joseph Willard. He began plowing down the truncated pyramid and the citizens protested. Caleb Emerson, who was a member of the council, was active in opposing Willard's action. The council removed the square from Willard's possession and leased to C. D. G. Bonny, and a number of citizens turned out and repaired the damage done by plowing. A discussion of the merits of the case was carried on for some months in the newspapers between a writer who signed himself "Fair Play," and Mr. Willard, and the case was carried into the court, where it was decided in favor of the town. The council claimed the square as a reservation granted to the town

---

*Harris' Tour, page 152.

for public works, or public buildings, and for the benefit of indigent orphan children.

The public squares had not been fenced, up to 1837, and some damage had been caused to the ancient works, but in the year mentioned the citizens raised a sufficient sum of money to repair the injuries effected and to build fences around the squares. Ichabod Nye and Thomas Vinton were appointed by the council as a committee to make the needed improvements and restorations. The large mound has, perhaps, been injured more than either of the other remains, the water having washed the sides where the earth was loosened by the feet of climbers. The uneven places were filled, the defective trees cut down, and the entire surface of the mound sown with grass. In order that the symmetry of the mound should not again be impaired by the displacement of earth consequent upon many persons climbing its steep sides, a flight of stone steps was constructed by which the summit could be easily gained. The mound has since been kept, by occasional slight labor bestowed upon it, in the best possible condition, as have also the other remains. The Capitolium is, however, at present unprotected by a fence, and is in danger of being defaced.

MARIETTA BURIAL PLACES.

In Mound cemetery rest the dead of two races of men.* The largest and probably the most enduring monument here, the great mound, covers the crumbling skeleton of a might personage, a great ruler, a king perchance of that vast race which once dwelt in the land. Reared by the patient toil of many hands in posthumous honor of a personage of power, in perpetuation of the renown of warriors, heroism, or ruler's virtue, the huge pile of earth remains not as a monument to mortal greatness, but the exact reverse—a reminder of the mutations of time and the vain glory of human ambition. Such is the irony of fate. Not alone is the fame of the personage lost in oblivion, but the whole of a mighty race swept away, and there remains in the entire world absolutely no knowledge of its history.

Thickly crowding the plain around the ancient monument are the stones which mark the graves of the dead of our century, and even from these memorial shafts, of comparatively recent years, the hand of time is effacing names and epitaphs. In the shadow of the great mound, by the grassy graves and the crumbling sandstone slabs, the aphorism of Marcus Aurelius—"Near is thy forgetfulness of all things, and near the forgetfulness of thee by all"—recurs to the mind with impressive force. One realizes that the time must inevitably come when memory of the dead who lie here must pass from the minds of the living, and tombstone inscriptions no longer proclaim to the passer-by the names, and the deeds, and the virtues of those who rest beneath the little hillocks of earth. In Mound cemetery rest the ashes of "the fathers of the hamlet," the pioneers of civilization in the great west;

* At Eaton, Preble county, Ohio, there is also a "Mound cemetery." In the ancient sepulchral tumulus, which gives that burial place its name, repose the remains of fourteen brave soldiers of St. Clair's army, who fell near the spot in 1791.

the founders of the State; men of lofty character, noble purpose, heroic achievements. One by one their careers of danger and vicissitude, of patient toil and strenuous manly endeavor for the accomplishment of good were closed, and all that remained of these struggling, hopeful, aspiring men, who were among the natural nobles of the earth, was buried here. So passes the glory of earth. But the thought will arise with irresistible might in him who walks among the closely crowded graves of the old cemetery (whether it takes the form of Christian faith or philosophers' belief) that death is merely the closing of life's earth chapter, which is an introduction to and preparation for existence beyond. It is strangely true that faith in immortal life is ever stronger in the presence of death, and so in this burial place, amidst the closely crowded tombstones which mark the graves of Marietta's dead, alike by the sepulchers of those whom death took from all the joys of the brightest life, and by the sepulchres of those who have only found surcease from sorrows and woe, generations of the living, enduring the pangs of their greatest bereavement, have also been cheered by the sweetest consolation, and the grandest hope, which is vouchsafed to humanity.

The earliest burials at Marietta were not made in Mound cemetery, as is quite commonly believed, but in a lot upon the ridge south of the present Oak Grove cemetery, laid off when the settlement was first made, by the Ohio company, and consisting of about ten acres of land. It was at this place that the first person who died in Marietta—the little child of Major Nathaniel Cushing—was buried, and also General Varnum, the second person who died in the settlement. Several other persons were buried in this locality prior to 1791, but during the Indian war this ground, being in an exposed situation, was forsaken, and burials were made on the brow of the sand hill now dug off, just above Wooster street, on the line of Third street.

Captain Joseph Rodgers, one of the rangers at Campus Martius during the early part of the Indian war, and who was killed March 13, 1791, was buried in Third street, then unimproved. A daughter of Governor St. Clair, named Margaret, a son of Major Ezra Putnam, Matthew Kerr, killed by the Indians, June 17, 1791, James Wells, wife, and daughter, and others who died of the small-pox in 1793, also William Moulton, were buried there. In 1839 the remains of most of these persons were exhumed, and reinterred in Mound cemetery. There were still some graves remaining, however, back of Third street, as late as 1849.

General Benjamin Tupper, who died in 1792, was buried under an apple tree between Third and Fourth streets, opposite the *Quadranaou* on Warren street, this locality being commanded by one of the cannons of Campus Martius. At the same place was buried a child of Colonel Ichabod Nye, and, at a later date, Major Anselm Tupper.

After the close of the Indian war there were other burials on the ridge in the original cemetery. Among them were the following: A little daughter of Colonel Nathaniel Cushing, aged thirteen years, who died August 25, 1788—the first death in Marietta; General James Mitchell Varnum, director of the Ohio company, who died January 10, 1789; a Mr. Welch, from Kentucky, who landed at Marietta sick with smallpox; eight other persons, adults, who died from the same disease, and several children; Mrs. Rowena (Tupper) Sargent, who died in 1790; Mrs. Shepherd, first wife of Colonel Enoch Shepherd; Mrs. Clark, first wife of Major John Clark; a son of the latter; Captain Josiah Munroe, one of the party of forty-seven pioneers, and second postmaster at Marietta.

The remains of Captain Munroe were removed to Mound cemetery in the winter of 1869-70. The remains of twenty-six persons were exhumed in 1871, and removed to Oak Grove cemetery. The grave of General Varnum was identified without a doubt, but all of the others, with one exception (that of a Mr. Boutelle, who was buried as late as 1835), were entirely lacking in distinguishing marks.

Mound cemetery, originally designated as Marie Antoinette square, was made a burial place in the year 1800, and placed in the control of the corporation as such. The first person buried here was Colonel Robert Taylor, who died September 30, 1801, at the age of sixty-five years.

The cemetery in Harmar is older than Mound cemetery. It was laid out by the Ohio company in 1796, and the first entry in the journal of the company's proceedings which refers to it is dated January 11th of that year. After specifying the appropriation of city square No 33, upon the east side of the Muskingum, as a place of burial, the resolution continues that "that there be also laid out three acres on the west side of the Muskingum river, adjoining the two acre lot appropriated to make up the deficiencies of city lots, and in the rear of a tier of city lots, which is appropriated forever for the like purpose." It is not known who was the first person buried here.

One of the earliest deaths which occurred at the Muskingum settlements was that of a non-commissioned officer named Hopper, who belonged to the garrison at Fort Harmar. The grave remained a relic of the pioneer times until the winter of 1880-81, when the few crumbling bones which it contained were removed, under the direction of Colonel William R. Putnam, to Oak Grove cemetery. The location of the grave was upon the line dividing the lots of Colonel Barber and the widow Pugh. A simple slab of sandstone marked the soldier's resting place, which was transferred to Oak Grove cemetery at the same time that the remains were exhumed. The inscription, partly obliterated but still legible, reads: "Here lieth the body of Englehard Hopper, who departed this life November 21, 1788, aged twenty-four years."

The beautiful Oak Grove cemetery consists of thirty-three acres of land bought by the city of Judge Arius Nye in 1861, at an expence of about three thousand seven hundred dollars. The site was selected by Dr. J. D. Cotton and Mr. C. F. Buell, who were appointed by the city council for that purpose. The first adult buried

in Oak Grove was Timothy Cone, who died April 24, 1864, and was born, as the inscription on the stone states, May 20. 1777. Two children were interred here prior to this burial.

CHAPTER XXXVII.

MARIETTA—MORAL AND MATERIAL ADVANCEMENT.

History of Temperance Reform—The Beginning at Newport in 1828—Subsequent Movements Down to 1881—Institutions for the Advancement of Knowledge—Marietta Library—Lyceums—Appearance of the Town—Modern Public Improvements and Ornamentation—The Park Tree Association—Boat House—Business Spirit—Centennial Celebration.

COULD all the causes that combine to advance the moral and material well being of a community be discovered and grouped together the result would be a perfect history of the bright side of that community's life and growth. It is not our purpose in this chapter to sum up or review those topics which have already been dwelt upon, but to introduce a number of important subjects which have not heretofore been considered. The development of mercantile business, manufacturing and navigation has already been set forth, and the history of the three great institutions of civilization—the church, the school, and the press—which have been in part the cause and in part the effect of the religious, moral and intellectual advancement of the people, has been given at length. A considerable space has also been given to a description of the state of society in Marietta in pioneer times, and the reader is supposed to be already familiar with the virtues and vices of those days. We have (in the first chapter of the history of Marietta) stated that in the infant settlement, notwithstanding the generally high standard of morals and the intellectual culture of a majority of the pioneers, intemperance was a very serious evil. It was an evil not confined to the settlements of the frontier, nor in such a degree, as at present, to the baser elements of society, but existed among all classes, and probably had more victims in the upper than in the lower. The use of liquor was a universal custom, and drunkenness was proportionally more common then than now, as the number of drunkards in every hundred or thousand persons was larger. As no moral sentiment had been created against the use of liquor, there was but little odium attached to inordinate indulgence. A gradual change has been worked in the public mind upon the subject of temperance, which we propose to follow from its beginning down to to the present, as it has been the greatest moral improvement that the people have known.

Temperance reform may be said to have had its origin in Washington county early in 1828. A number of good Methodists were assembled some time during thay tear at a quarterly meeting held at Ebenezer Battelle's, in Newport, which was one of the best settlements in this part of the country. Any host or hostess who did not offer his or her guests liquor, in those days, was regarded

JAMES H. DYE

MRS. JAMES H. DYE

The father of James H. Dye, Samuel Dye, familiarly known among the early settlers as "Esquire Dye," was born in Prince William county, Virginia, in 1779. At the age of twenty-six years he came to Lawrence township, this county. His wife, Susan Hoff, was the second daughter and sixth child of Rev. Daniel Hoff, a farmer near Alexandria, Virginia, where she was born in 1776. She died in Lawrence township at the age of seventy-one years. She was an excellent housewife. Esquire Dye was a very large, corpulent man, and quite sympathetic in his nature. He served as magistrate in Lawrence township for thirty-one years. He died at his residence on the Woodsfield road, nine miles from Marietta, in 1860, in his eightieth year.

James Hoff Dye, third son of Samuel Dye, was born on the Little Muskingum in Lawrence township, in 1815. The family residence was on the farm just below the present residence of A. J. Dye, esq. At the age of fourteen he engaged in the tanning business at Marietta. In 1837 he married Clarissa Jackson. In 1862 he disposed of his tanning interests, and became sutler for the Seventh Ohio cavalry. In 1864 he purchased a livery stable in Marietta, which he continued to manage until his death in 1880. Mr. Dye was very social in his habits, and sympathetic in his disposition. He was a sharp trader withal.

Mr. Dye's family consisted of nine children, one of whom, Catharine, is dead. Harriet lives with Mrs. Dye, who still survives, in Marietta; George married Sarah Snider, and lives on Cow Run, Lawrence township; Mary is married to Madison Holmes, and lives in Marshfield, Athens county. William and Marcillus manage the livery business at Marietta; Louisa, wife of Wallace Scott, lives in Warren township; Henry is a practicing physician at Logan, Hocking county, and Fannie at home in Marietta.

as inhospitable, mean and niggardly. On this occasion the liquor happened to be a most excellent and powerful article of home-made peach brandy. The little company, among whom were several church dignitaries, drank their brandy to the health of Deacon Battelle, and followed with a health to some minister who was present. They drank copious draughts from large glasses, refilled from a great decanter, which was passed around with such rapidly increasing frequency that it had in turn soon to be refilled from the cask. The party became more merry, and with the recklessness born of incipient intoxication, drank oftener than before. All this was while Mrs. Battelle was making ready a substantial dinner for the assembled brethren. When dinner was announced they took one drink more, and at the table another. And now the effects of the potations began to appear. Several of the pious brothers who sat down to partake of the steaming dinner that Mrs. Battelle's skill in cooking had produced, were unable to eat, and left the table. Nearly all were visibly affected by the liquor, and several were decidedly drunk. Only a few being able to attend the meeting which had been arranged for in the afternoon, it was postponed. All were ashamed of their over-indulgence, but Mrs. Battelle was sorrowful and indignant. She was a woman of fine sensibilities, great strength of character, and deep convictions. Seeing clearly the great evil to which the use of liquor led, and that it was a reproach to the cause of religion, she resolved that nevermore should the temptation be placed before her guests. Her husband agreed with her, and the next day, in meeting, speaking sorrowfully of what had occurred, expressed his conviction that the custom of drinking was unbecoming to a Christian people, and made known the decision that had been arrived at regarding the banishment of liquor from his board. The sentiment was endorsed by nearly or perhaps quite all of the people present, many of whom were smarting under their recent humiliation. Most of the brethren pledged themselves to discontinue the use of liquor, and to use their influence with others to do the same. There was much earnest talk upon the subject, and the feeling of which it was the expression did not die away when the meeting adjourned, but each man, going to his home, carried with him the determination to do all in his power to promote the principle of total abstinence among the people in his neighborhood.

The movement was taken up at Marietta, and in the month of March, 1828, there was drawn up and subscribed to the first temperance pledge which had an existence in the town. Previous to this whiskey had been kept upon the counters of all the stores, for the free use of customers, but now a number of the leading merchants resolved to discontinue the time-honored custom, and bound themselves so to do in the following compact, which was drawn up in the handwriting of John Mills, and is still in existence:

"MARIETTA, March 17, 1828.

"The undersigned do hereby agree that they will not retail any kind of spirituous liquors, nor give any away in the stores, from and after the first day of May next. It is understood that we may retail French brandy and wines. This agreement remains in force as long as the majority shall direct.

                    JOHN MILLS & CO.
                    AUGUSTUS STONE.
                    MORGAN & CO."

The "Co." with John Mills consisted of John and Luther Edgarton, and the unnamed partner of Mr. David Morgan was Dudley Woodbridge.

In 1829 the Skinners—David and William—and several other prominent merchants followed the example of Messrs. Mills, Morgan, Stone, Edgarton and Woodbridge. In the same year the shipbuilders announced that they would no longer furnish their employes with liquor as they had done for years, and the result was a general strike. They remained firm, however, and after a few days the men went to work without their whiskey.

The temperance movement was vigorously carried on in Marietta for several years after the beginning, in 1828. Caleb Emerson was a leader in the reform. He made public speeches, and did perhaps more than any other one man to procure signers to the total abstinence pledge. Ephraim Cutler was another prominent worker in the cause. In the year 1830 the first Temperance society was organized, with Ephraim Cutler as president; Rev. Jacob Young and Robert Crawford as vice-presidents; Rev. L. G. Bingham, secretary; Wyllys Hall, treasurer; and Caleb Emerson, Junia Jennings, Douglass Putnam and Samuel Shipman composing the executive committee.

The next important action in temperance reform occurred in 1840, and was called the "Washingtonian Movement." It differed from the movement of 1828 in that it was originated and carried on by reformed inebriates.

The movement of 1840 was one of great excitement, as might be judged from the character of its leaders. It began in Marietta, but soon spread over the whole of the surrounding country. Large meetings were held and addresses made by reformed drunkards. Although it was a movement of intense excitment, yet it was regularly organized. But its results are not generally considered to have been so beneficial as those of the calmer and more deliberate work of 1828. Its duration was very short. Among the most prominent men connected with this work were Warren Wilcox, John Greiner and James Clogstone.

The next important movement in temperance reform was made in 1844. It took the form of the organization of total abstinence societies. The first society was formed in Marietta, and others were soon started all over the county. This movement was originated and carried on entirely by men who had always been temperate.

In 1852 there was another period of temperance work. Lodges of the order of "Sons and Daughters of Temperance" were organized throughout the county. In these, many of the most prominent citizens were interested, and worked faithfully.

In 1869—May 24th—was organized the Marietta Lodge No. 289, of the Independent Order of Good Templars, with the following charter members, viz: Richard Richardson, Mary J. Morse, Rufus B. Battelle,

Lewis C. Haddox, Susie Vinton, M. H. Booth, A. W. Williams, Sarah Dutton, A. E. Warnet, James L. Adams, Anna Booth, Sarah E. Hudson, Maggie Vinton, J. L. Guiton, Henrietta Geisen, James Gesien, Lizzie Dutton, Eliza Calvert, J. Radenbaugh, Sarah Johnson, Dudley Gesien, George Pixley, Joseph Fenn, A. M. Lenhart, and Thomas Morse. Starting with twenty six members the lodge grew in six months to a membership of one hundred and twenty-eight. It remained in active existence until the time of the women's crusade.

The women's crusade reached Marietta in February, 1874. On the sixteenth of that month a general meeting of the ladies of Harmar and Marietta was held in the Centenary Methodist church, and a woman's league organized. Mrs. J. M. Woodbridge was the first president of this league. Meetings for prayer and consultation were held as often as every three days until March 3d, when the first band started out to visit the saloons. But before this committees had been appointed who visited all the physicians and druggists and obtained promises from them all that they would not sell, give, or prescribe liquors, except for strictly medicinal or mechanical purposes.

On March 3, 1874, the first band of ladies visited the saloons; it consisted of seven ladies, as follows: Mrs. George M. Woodbridge, Mrs. S. S. Knowles, Mrs. William A. Whittlesey, Mrs. J. W. Stanley, Miss Lillie W. Stone, Mrs. Thomas W. Ewart, and Mrs. Z. D. Walter. The band visited six saloons on Front street, and were received in a very polite manner; and as a rule, were so treated throughout the whole movement. After this date large bands went out every day until about the tenth of May, when this phase of the work was discontinued.

In connection with the regular work of the crusade, meetings of children were held and addresses were made before them.

The visible results of this crusade in Marietta were not great, only three out of the forty saloons having been closed by its agency.

The Womans' Christian Temperance Union, of Marietta, Ohio, was a direct offspring of this crusade movement. It was organized June 14, 1877. This union has a membership of about a hundred. Its work consists in distributing temperance literature, keeping up a reading-room, juvenile meetings, and raising money for temperance lectures. The present officers are as follows: Mrs. S. S. Knowles, president; Mrs. E. A. Tenney, vice-president; Mrs. W. B. Thomas, corresponding secretary; Mrs. W. P. Bennet, recording secretary; Miss H. Hobby, treasurer.

The people of Marietta have ever exhibited a regard for mental improvement, which is very appropriate to the first settlement made under an ordinance which declared that as knowledge in common with religion and morality were necessary to good government, "schools and the means of education should ever be encouraged." Such institutions arose naturally upon the soil settled by a colony of cultured men from Massachusetts. We have seen that a literary society was in existence as early as 1790. From time to time various other institutions have come into being and exerted an influence for good. The Marietta Library was founded as early as 1829, and its free use has ever since been enjoyed by the people of the town. The corporators were John Mills, A. T. Nye, John Cotton, Samuel P. Hildreth and Daniel H. Buell. In 1832 John Mills, Arius Nye and William Slocomb were appointed as a building committee, and erected the brick edifice on Front street, near the corner of Putnam, in which the library is now, and most of the time has been kept. At the time this institution was chartered by the State, there were many precautions taken in granting acts of incorporation for any purpose, lest the charters should be made to cover a banking business. Hence this corporation was restricted in clear annual income to two thousand dollars per year, and it was stipulated that none of the funds should "ever be applied to the purpose of banking." The library contains over three thousand books judiciously selected, and representing all of the principal departments of literature.

In 1831, a lyceum was formed which remained in existence for a term of ten years, and was productive of an unusually large benefit. John Cotton was the first president of this literary organization; Caleb Emerson, vice-president; Arius Nye, corresponding secretary; James M. Booth, recording secretary; John Mills, treasurer; Arius Nye and S. P. Hildreth, curators. Several valuable series of lectures were delivered under the auspices of this body, by Dr. John Cotton, Dr. S. P. Hildreth, John Delafield, jr., William A. Whittlesey, John Brough and others. When this lyceum passed out of active existence, about the year 1841, another was immediately organized which was conducted on similar principles. Lectures were delivered before this organization by various members of the college faculty, and by Dr. Cotton and Judge Arius Nye.

There has probably been no period in the last forty years when there has not been in existence in Marietta, a flourishing society for the discussion of public questions and literary topics. The present literary society has a large membership, and is an institution of great value to the community.

The influence of the college has doubtless been a powerful factor in the creation of a literary spirit in Marietta. The library alone is of great value to the community. It contains upwards of fifteen thousand volumes, is the largest college library west of the Alleghanies, and with the exception of the Cleveland, Columbus, and Cincinnati libraries, is probably the largest in the State. The beneficial effect of educational institutions upon the towns in which they are located is well known and needs no comment. It is proper, however, to remark that in Marietta the effect has probably been more positive than in most communities. Town and college have ever been in close sympathy. The people have supported the institution of learning with remarkable generosity, and the benefit of their gifts has been felt in a large measure by the citizens.

In the line of material improvements Marietta is fully abreast with other towns of similar size in the west. The town is dual in its character as regards appearance.

Henry and Bernard Rodick came to Marietta with [the]ir parents in the fall of 1850, from Oldenburg, North [Ge]rmany. At the time of emigrating, the former was [...]teen, the latter twelve years old. They had pursued [... r]egular German course of schooling, and after com[in]g to America acquired the English language. At an [earl]y age both entered business, Henry with the firm of [... W]osworth, Wells & Company, and afterwards with A. T. [...]ye, in whose store he served for a period of several [ye]ars until the firm of Smith & Rodick began business, [in] 1867. Bernard Rodick acquired most of his busi[ness] experience in the store of John M. Woolbridge, [whe]re he clerked until 1869. He then engaged in [...] boat-ing on the Ohio and Muskingum rivers, as

Henry Rodick

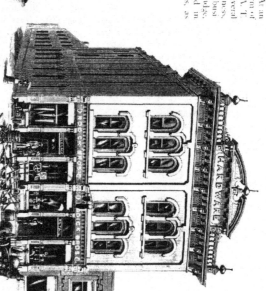

Bernard Rodick

clerk and master. He was one of the owners of the Muskingum river packet "Progress and Soerhic." In 1867 he became one of the partners in the firm of Smith & Rodick.

The hardware store which, in 1867, was opened by John Smith, of Lowell, and Henry and Bernard Rodick, was transferred in 1871, by the death of Mr. Smith, to Rodick Brothers. Under their management the business has been one of the most successful mercantile enter-prises in Marietta. The entire capital in 1867, was five thousand five hundred dollars, at the end of five years an inventory after the death of Mr. Smith showed a net profit of thirty two thousand dollars.

Viewed from the bosom of the Ohio it presents the somewhat unfavorable aspect common to the river villages. That portion of the town, however, which is made up of residences will compare favorably with that of any town in the State, and in some particulars it has no rivals, as for instance in the thoroughly home-like appearance of a majority of the houses. There is but little of modern architecture exhibited, but there are many substantial old-time houses, which have as peculiar and distinctive an expression as have human faces. Few towns have the natural picturesqueness of Marietta. The location of many of the best residences upon the gently rising hillside which terminates in the "plain" was a circumstance of great value æsthetically. Many beautiful situations were afforded house builders, and the frequent introduction of terraces and stone walls has created a pleasing and refreshing variety which could never have been attained in building upon a level site. The broad, cleanly, and well shaded streets of the town are very generally commented upon by visitors, and are a source of pride to the citizens. Because of the nature of the soil, and also owing to the hilly or uneven character of the surface, considerable difficulty has been experienced in constructing and maintaining good paved sidewalks, but all of the principal streets are now provided with well laid brick or stone flagged walks. Most of this work in the residence portion of the town has been accomplished within the last twenty years. A very effective and valuable public improvement was made in 1875. Until that time the now beautiful Riverside park was an unfenced, weed-grown common or cow pasture. The project of improving the common and making it an ornament to the town was entertained by a few citizens and favored by the city government, at the head of which, at that time, was Major Jewett Palmer. The city council made a levy, the first year of five hundred dollars, and the succeeding year one of two hundred and fifty dollars. For this sum the long neglected and unsightly common was made the attractive pleasure ground which it now is. The money was expended by, and the work done under the supervision of, a committee consisting of M. P. Wells, the late Mr. Oldham and J. L. Mills.

Mr. Wells, the leading spirit in making this improvement, during his forty years residence in Marietta, has done very much to advance the condition of the place, and has been instrumental in securing many public improvements. In 1878, principally through his exertions, the Marietta Shade Tree association was organized. The object of the association was to supply the town plentifully with shade trees, and for this purpose thirty persons subscribed five dollars per year for five years, seven persons three dollars per year, and thirty persons one dollar per year. With the modest sum thus realized annually the association has, in the past three years, set out over eleven hundred small elm trees, one hundred and fifty of which are in the park. The improvement is one in which time must make perfect, but when those who are now children shall have reached mature life they will have occasion to thank Mr. Wells and his companions of the Tree association for making Marietta one of the most beautiful embowered villages in Ohio.

The boat-house built in 1880 is a great ornament to the park and an establishment of decided value to the town. It was built for the joint benefit of the citizens and the college, at an expense of about two thousand seven hundred dollars. A large proportion of this amount came from heavy mercantile houses in the large cities of Ohio and the east; but the citizens made liberal contributions to the fund.

In 1878 an organization was effected which is worthy of note, because illustrating one phase of Marietta's public-spirit and growth. We refer to the military company known as the Putnam light artillery, one of the best of its kind in the State. The battery comprises seventy-seven members, and its equipment consists of four first-class twelve-pound Napoleon brass guns. The artillery company built, the same year it was organized, at a cost of more than one thousand dollars, the armory on Putnam street. The battery is kept in all respects fully up to the standard required in the regular army, and as an example of its military spirit is very creditable to the town.

Very recently there have appeared several evidences of the progressive spirit and enterprise of Marietta business men. We mention, as an example, the organization and incorporation in February, 1881, of the Marietta Electric Light company, with a capital of twenty-five thousand dollars. It is composed of the following gentlemen: Edward R. Dale, Murray McMillen, Robert B. Hoover, Theodore D. Dale, James W. Nye, and Reuben L. Nye.

It is not improbable that in the near future the town reaping some advantage from the construction of the ice harbor, from the restoration of those railroad privileges of which it has been unjustly deprived, and from the slowly but surely increasing importance of its manufactures, may show considerable improvement as a matter of trade, but the brightest hope of its future seems to an impartial observer to lie in the development of its educational resources, the building up of intellectual life, and the extension of a noble influence. Upon the Centennial anniversary of American independence, when historical orations were delivered in all the principal towns and villages of the country, we doubt if any one was shown to have a fairer record in all that pertains to the highest well being of the people, than had Marietta.* There is certainly no community of equal size in the State of Ohio in which a greater number of people are living above mere sordid gain, than in Marietta.

*The Centennial was celebrated in Marietta with interesting and appropriate ceremonies. The town was full of visitors who, together with the citizens, made a concourse, numbering not less than ten thousand people. A grand procession promenaded the streets for several hours after which the exercises of the day were opened at the city park. Honorable P. B. Buell was the presiding officer. The Declaration of Independence was read by W. H. Gurley, esq., and president Israel Ward Andrews, of Marietta college, the orator of the day, began the delivery of his historical address, but was compelled to stop on account of a hard rainfall. The meeting was then adjourned to the city hall, at half-past 2 o'clock P. M. There was a fine display of fireworks in the park in the evening, and an open air concert was given by Regnier's band. No accidents marred the pleasures of the day.

BIOGRAPHICAL SKETCHES.

GENERAL RUFUS PUTNAM.

The New England Putnams have their descent from a common ancestor, John Putnam, who came from Buckinghamshire, England, in 1634, and settled in Salem, Massachusetts. He had three sons—Thomas, Nathaniel, and John. Rufus Putnam was descended from Thomas, his father, Elisha, being the son of Edward, the son of Thomas. The celebrated Israel Putnam was also a grandson of Thomas, and, therefore, cousin to Elisha, the father of Rufus.

The Putnams seem to have belonged to that respectable middle class that has furnished to the world so many of its best workers and most useful citizens. In his old age, Edward, the grandfather of Rufus, said "he could say with the Psalmist, 'I have been young, and now I am old, yet have I not seen the righteous forsaken nor his seed begging bread,' except from God, who provides for all; for he hath given the generation of my father Agur's petition, neither poverty nor riches, but hath fed us with food convenient for us, and their children have been able to help others in their need."

Elisha Putnam, the father of Rufus, was born in Salem, Massachusetts, November 3, 1685. He married Susanna Fuller, of Danvers. In 1725 he, with his wife and three children, moved to Sutton. After he removed to Sutton three sons were born to him, of whom Rufus, born April 9, 1738, was the youngest. The Rev. Dr. Hall said of him, "Deacon Elisha Putnam was a very useful man in the civil and ecclesiastical concerns of the place. He was for several years deacon of the church, town clerk, town treasurer, and representative in the general court or colonial assembly of Massachusetts. He died in June, 1745, in the joyful hope of the glory of God."

Misfortune set its mark upon Rufus before he had half started on the journey of life. His father died when he was but little more than seven years old. To the little boy the loss of such a father was a calamity that could not be measured, and the consequences were as lasting as his life. The first two years of his orphanage were passed in the home of his maternal grandfather, Mr. Fuller, in Danvers. During this time he went to school and learned to read, and thus secured the clue to the labyrinth of knowledge. But evil days were in store for him. In 1747 his mother married Captain John Sadler, and Rufus went back to his home. But it was a home without a father, for Captain Sadler but illy supplied the place of the good man that death had taken away. He was illiterate himself, and, what was worse and more to be deplored, he despised learning. He neither sent Rufus to school, nor allowed him opportunities to learn at home. No books were furnished him, and if by chance he succeeded in getting them, he had but little opportunity to use them. His aspirations were scoffed at, and his efforts to quench his thirst for knowledge at living fountains were ridiculed and derided.

Captain Sadler kept a house of entertainment, and by diligent waiting upon guests, Rufus sometimes became the happy possessor of a few pence. These he invested in ammunition, and with the help of an old shot-gun, killed partridges, which he sold. With the proceeds of the sale he bought a spelling book and an arithmetic. From these, without help or guidance, he learned what he could. There were discouragements thrown in the way of his doing this. He was not allowed even the faint light of a tallow candle to enable him to use, in his own behalf, the long winter evenings. But worse than this, and harder to bear, was the ridicule with which he was visited for his endeavors, from the man who stood to him in the place of a father. Yet all of this did not make him give up his determination *to know*. There is something very pathetic in the way this little fatherless boy struggled to obtain knowledge in the face of discouragements that might well have appalled the stout heart of one who was older than he.

In his latter days he wrote out some of the main facts in his life for the benefit of his children and their descendents. The paper is yellow with age, the orthography is often incorrect. But there is a pathos in his simple, direct statements in regard to his early aspirations that no fine writing could equal. He says: "After I was nine years old I went to school in all only three weeks." Yet, not deterred by either abuse or ridicule, he went as far as the "Rule of Three" in arithmetic, and learned to write so as to be intelligible.

In March, 1754, when in his sixteenth year, he was apprenticed to Daniel Mathews, of Brookfield, to learn the trade of millwright. He says: "By him my education was as much neglected as by Captain Sadler, except that he did not deny me the use of a light for study in the winter evenings. I turned my attention chiefly to arithmetic, geography and history; had I been as much engaged in learning to write well, with spelling and grammar, I might have been much better qualified to fulfil the duties of the succeeding scenes of life, which in Providence I have been called to pass through. I was zealous to obtain knowledge, but having no guide I knew not where to begin nor what course to pursue. Having neglected spelling and grammar when young, I have suffered much through life on that account." From sixteen to nineteen he was engaged in learning the trade of a millwright, interspersed with more or less farming. How much soever his mental faculties may have suffered from neglect, the physical powers were surely in a most prosperous condition. He had at eighteen the stature and strength of a mature man. He was nearly six feet in height, with brawny limbs and great muscular power. He was as good as the best in every part that required strength of muscle or power of endurance. A brave heart beat in his bosom, in which abode the high resolve to act manfully and well the part that should be allotted to him in the drama of life. Always faithful, always on the side of the right, as he construed it, from the beginning to the end of his varied career, he was never known to prove recreant to a trust or fail to meet dutifully and well any just requirement. He was in every way well fitted for the life of peril and adventure that a common soldier in a frontier army was compelled to encounter. The time drew near when he was to lay aside the implements of trade and husbandry and take up the weapons of war.

Hostilities began between England and France in 1754. Accounts of military adventure formed the staple of conversation in the long winter evenings during his apprenticeship. The prowess of his father's cousin, Captain Israel Putnam, especially took hold of his imagination and made him emulous of the glory that seemed to rest upon the heads of heroes. As soon as the time for which he was indentured expired, when only nineteen, he enlisted as a private in a company, the term of service in which was less than a year.

A journal of this campaign was kept by the young soldier, in which the events of each day are worded, often without note or comment. The ravages of time have spared this journal, and the exact and methodical manner in which it is kept, are prophetic of the careful and thorough work that would distinguish the life, that as yet in great part, lay before the writer. Captain Larned's company marched to Stillwater in June, and from thence to Fort Edward. There seems to have been but little actual service performed during the campaign, which ended in October, and Mr. Putnam returned home in February. He spent the remainder of the winter there and in the spring enlisted again in a company commanded by Captain Joseph Whitcomb and belonging to Colonel Ruggles' regiment, which rendezvoused at Northampton, Massachusetts. They started for Albany June 3rd, and reached Greenbush June 8th. Mr. Putnam says in his journal, "from Northampton street to this place was through a wilderness, with but one house in the whole distance, except the little fort above mentioned." What a change since then! The young soldier was not destined to see much of the honor or horror of war during this campaign. The regiment was discharged in October. Mr. Putnam went home and spent the winter and in the spring enlisted for the third campaign. During this time of service he was promoted to the post of orderly sergeant. He was in Colonel Ruggles' regiment, and went to Ticonderoga. He was, however, during the whole campaign compelled to work on mills or block-houses instead of doing military duty, which was that for which he had enlisted. He did not think it just right, and he determined to leave the service. He passed the winter of 1759 in New Braintree working on a farm of fifty acres which he had bought with the avails of his savings while in the army. He gave his time to farming and building mills for a time, but meanwhile he was diligently studying practical surveying, in which he was assisted by Colonel Timothy Dwight. He soon became sufficiently master of the business to leave other things and devote himself to it. His thoroughness and exactness made it easy for him to find employment.

In 1761 Mr. Putnam was married to Elizabeth Ayres, daughter of William Ayres of Brookfield. She died within a year, and after a few months their infant son was laid beside his mother.

In January, 1765, he was married again to Persis Rice, daughter of Zebulon Rice, of Westborough, Massachusetts. He lived on the small farm he had previously bought until 1780, when he purchased a large farm in Rutland, Massachusetts. There was upon it a spacious house, which is still standing and in good repair. This property belonged to a Tory, and was confiscated, which enabled Mr. Putnam to purchase it on favorable terms.

During a considerable part of the years 1772 and 1773 Mr. Putnam devoted his time and effort to an enterprise that at the time excited much interest in New England. Soon after the close of the French and Indian war, General Lyman was sent to England by Colonial officers and soldiers, for the purpose of securing, if possible, from the British government a grant of land as a reward for military service performed during the war. He was detained there several years, making vain endeavors to obtain that for which he went. He returned in 1772. A meeting of "The Military Adventurers" was called in Hartford, and General Lyman assured those concerned that an order had been passed by the king in council, authorizing the governor of West Florida to grant lands in that province, to Colonial officers and soldiers in the same proportion and manner as had been given elsewhere to his Majesty's regular troops. As they had been liberally provided for in the provinces assigned during the war, the prospect seemed good that the Colonial officers and soldiers would also reap a reward for duties well done.

General Lyman brought no written vouchers to make the grant sure, but it was thought that the word of a king was a sufficient word. The company, therefore, appointed a committee to explore the country, and lay out the tracts to be divided among the adventurers. The associates of the military company chartered a sloop, in which the exploring committee sailed from New York January 10, 1773. Rufus Putnam and his father's cousin, Colonel Israel Putnam, were two of the committee. They entered the bay of Pensacola March 1st. Governor Chester and his council received them kindly, but no order for a grant of land to the Provincials had yet arrived. This was discouraging, but they took comfort in the hope the order had been delayed, and would yet come. The committee, therefore, set about their explorations.

Among the papers left by General Putnam, which are now in the safe-keeping of the Marietta College library, there is a carefully prepared plan of the Mississippi river, with all its windings and eccentricities, to the mouth of the Yazoo, which was as far as their explorations extended in that direction. Nearly four months were occupied in the thorough examination of the country, which was also extended to a considerable distance up the Yazoo. When the committee returned to Pensacola early in July, they were chagrined and disappointed to find that the expected order had not yet been received. Governor Chester, however, took the responsibility of making an offer of lands upon terms that it was thought upon the whole best to accept, and preparations were made to begin a settlement. Accordingly, when the committee returned, they made so favorable a report in regard to the soil, climate, and conditions of the country that several hundred families from Massachusetts, Connecticut, and other parts of New England, embarked for West Florida to find there new homes for themselves and their children. Unfortunately for them Governor Chester, in October, received orders from the Crown to neither sell nor grant lands upon any conditions until the King's further pleasure should be signified. Thus, when they reached the place, the land office was closed to the poor immigrants. Some of them spent all they had in getting there, and it was late in the season to return, even if they had the means to do so. In this emergency the governor kindly allowed the immigrants to take possession of any unoccupied lands they could find. Many of them, on account of change of climate and exposure, sickened and died, and to the greater part the venture was an unprofitable one. Mr. Putnam was occupied more than eight months in these explorations, and for his time and services received the munificent sum of eighty dollars, which was also to cover his expenses.

The cloud, big with portentous events, that had been hanging over the colonists burst in 1775. Rufus Putnam had too brave a heart and was too zealous a lover of his country to sit tamely by and see other men struggle for liberty and all that was dear to them. He girded on his sword at the first onset and it was not laid aside until peace again smiled upon the land. He entered the army as lieutenant colonel of a regiment commanded by Colonel David Brewer. The regiment was stationed at Roxbury, and was attached to the corps of General Thomas.

Colonel Putnam had not long to wait for a chance to give efficient aid to the cause he had so zealously espoused. After the battle of Charlestown, June 17th, the patriot army was in a most exposed situation. There were no fortifications to protect the town and nothing but a board fence as a shelter for the army in case of an attack, which they had reason to expect at any moment. It was decided in a council of officers, that some kind of defence should at once be commenced. But where was the engineer who would plan the works and superintend their erection. It was one of the misfortunes connected with the situation of the colonies, that they were destitute of men skilled in the arts of war. There were no schools for training them, and in previous wars the colonists had, to a great extent, been subordinate. They had obeyed; those with whom they were now at war had commanded. Colonel Gridley was sent for, but he was needed at Cambridge, where he was, and could not be spared. No other engineer was known. Officers who knew the ability of Colonel Putnam, and knew also that he had been employed to some extent upon fortifications under British engineers during the French and Indian war, spoke of him as a man capable of doing what was needed. He protested—said that he had never read a work on fortifications, and was altogether unqualified to undertake to do what it was needful to have done. But no excuses availed, and he was too good and too patriotic a man to refuse to do the best he could when the need was so

urgent. He then went to work and traced lines in front of Roxbury toward Boston and various other places on the Roxbury side, particularly toward Sewall's Point. While he was occupied in doing this, Generals Washington and Lee came and examined the works and expressed their satisfaction and entire approval, which greatly encouraged Colonel Putnam. General Lee thought the works at Sewall's Point much better constructed than those on the Cambridge side. Colonel Putnam laid out works at Dorchester, Roxbury, Brookline, and late in the fall the Norton Cobble hill, near Charlestown mill-pond. He says in his Memoir, "in the course of this campaign I surveyed and delineated the courses, distances and relative situation of the enemy's works in Boston and Charlestown with our own in Cambridge and Roxbury. In December he went with General Lee to Newport, where he laid out some works, particularly a battery from whence to command the harbor, and some works near Howland's ferry, to secure the communication of Rhode Island with the mainland.

During the months of January and February, 1776 General Washington was anxiously considering the situation with a view to finding some solution to the problem as to what would be done to change the aspect of things. Lord Howe occupied Boston with an army of eight thousand well organized and well appointed troops. These would be supplemented at any time by others from the ships of war that rode gaily in the harbor. Large reinforcements were expected in the spring. This fact emphasized the necessity of speedy action. Meanwhile the winter was passing pleasantly to the officers and soldiers of the British army, who were not only well housed and fed, but the officers especially were finding their pleasure in occupations and amusements suitable to their tastes, without being over scrupulous as to ways and means. The old South church was turned into a riding school, and Fanueil hall converted into a theatre for amateur acting. With war chests well supplied, a national treasury upon which to draw, there was every reason why hope should be exultant. The circumstances were greatly different in the Patriot army. The troops had been paid to December, but had received nothing since, nor did there seem to be anything as the basis for the hope that they would be paid in the future. There was no national treasury—there was not even a national government. There was no money, and what was worse there was no credit. The soldiers were poorly clad, badly sheltered, and the army was deficient in all the munitions of war. One hundred barrels of powder was all there was in store, and there was no artillery except what had been captured from the enemy. It seemed impossible either to drive the enemy from the city or to attack him therein; and it was very galling as well as inconvenient to have him retain possession of the most renowned city in the whole country. The necessity for doing something seemed urgent, and the anxious question was, what? What was possible; what was wisest and best? After much anxious thought and careful examination it was decided, if possible, to take possession of Dorchester heights and erect fortifications which would command both city and harbor. Howe would then be compelled to either evacuate or come out and fight. There were great difficulties in the way of doing this, but as being the only thing possible, it was decided that it was best to undertake it. Preparations were carefully and promptly made. The night of the third of March was selected for the attempt. Everything was reduced to system. Each man knew his place and exactly what was expected of him. The ground was frozen to the depth of eighteen inches, but hay was spread over the surface so that the three hundred carts that went to and fro with material could go noiselessly. The men worked with a will and in silence. In the morning the result was manifest. Strong redoubts looked down on the city and harbor from the tops of two hills. "Perhaps there never was so much work done in so short a space of time." When Lord Howe saw what had been accomplished in a single night, he declared that it must have taken twelve thousand men to do it. He saw at once that his position was untenable. At first he was inclined to risk an engagement, but obstacles intervened and he chose to evacuate. He sent a messenger to Washington to say that he would withdraw if he would be allowed to do so without molestation. General Washington was only too glad to get rid of the enemy upon such terms This was the first substantial gain made by the Patriot army, and then and there, by the aid of an unskilled and untaught engineer, the corner-stone of American Independence was laid. General Putnam's account of the part he acted in this grand drama is very interesting. While the commander in chief was anxiously revolving the question as to what should be done, he called a council of the officers and laid the matter before them. The decision was, fortify Dorchester heights. But there was no engineer capable of laying out and superintending so important a work. Colonel Putnam was mentioned, and what he had already successfully done spoken of. He was invited to dine with General Washington, and after dinner the matter was talked over. Colonel Putnam expressed his reluctance to undertake the work because of his ignorance. He had read nothing on the subject, and was altogether unacquainted with scientific rules. But such was General Washington's confidence in his ability and good judgment that he would accept of no excuse, and Colonel Putnam was compelled to consent to do the best he could. On his way back to his quarters he called on General Heath, and while there he chanced to see lying on the table a book entitled Muller's Field Engineer. He asked General Heath to lend him the the book, and the request was rather uncourteously answered in the negative. But Colonel Putnam persisted, and finally General Heath consented to his taking it. The next morning, upon examining the book, Colonel Putnam found a description of chandeliers, and at once decided that that was what he wanted, and immediately drew a plan for fortifying Dorchester heights. The plan was approved and executed, and the result was the evacuation of Boston by the British army.

In March, 1776, General Washington ordered Colonel Putnam to go to New York by way of Newport, where he assisted Governor Cook in constructing works for the defence of the town. He reached New York April 2nd, and was appointed chief engineer, with orders to lay out works for the protection of New York, Long Island, Fort Washington, etc. He gave himself wholly to the business, working not only during the day, but oftentimes a considerable part of the night. Already General Washington seems to have had more confidence in his skill and ability than he had in any other man. During the summer he received the following letter:

August 11, 1776.

Sir. I have the pleasure to inform you that Congress have appointed you an engineer, with the rank of colonel, and pay sixty dollars per month.

I am, Sir,
Your assured friend and servant,
G. WASHINGTON.

In regard to this appointment, Colonel Putnam, with characteristic modesty, remarks: "My being appointed engineer by Congress was wholly unexpected. I had begun to act in that capacity through pure necessity, and had continued to conduct the business more from necessity and respect for the General than from any opinion of my own abilities. True it is that after my arrival in New York I had read some books on fortification, and I knew much more than when I began at Roxbury, but I had not the vanity to suppose that my knowledge was such as to give me the first rank in a corps of engineers. Yet my experience convinced me that such a corps was necessary to be established. Therefore, near the last of September, I drew up a plan for such an establishment, and presented it to General Washington, and which he transmitted to Congress with a recommendation concluded in these words: 'I commend it as a matter worthy of their consideration, being convinced from experience and from the reasons suggested by Colonel Putnam, who has acted with great diligence and reputation in the business, that some establishment of the sort is highly necessary, and will be productive of the most beneficial consequences.'"

The need of well-taught as well as skilful engineers, was greatly felt. Those that came from France seemed not to have learned from their books the knowledge necessary to make new and unexpected applications. In Colonel Putnam, therefore, General Washington found what he sorely needed and could not find elsewhere—a man with will in plentiful measure, with good, sound, common sense, great industry, unbending integrity, and an intuitive knowledge of the way to adopt means to ends, so as always to accomplish the thing he sought to do. We shall see that he was always in demand. He had no chance to be idle. When the army was in winter quarters he was laying out roads, superintending fortifications, or in some way advancing the cause he had so zealously espoused.

In October of the year 1776, Colonel Putnam, by his shrewdness and energy, was enabled to do a very important service for the army and the country. A large quantity of valuable stores had been placed at White Plains, by order of the commander-in-chief, under the impression that they would there be secure. They were guarded only by three hundred militia. Colonel Putnam was sent out upon a reconnoitring expedition, with a force of some fifty men as a guard. He soon satisfied himself that what he wished to do could be better done without soldiers to attract attention. He therefore dismissed his guard and sent them back, and set out alone. The country was strange to him, for he had never been there before, and he knew that the inhabitants were generally tories, so that it was not safe for him to stop and make inquiries. The enemy had a considerable force at New Rochelle, only nine miles from White Plains, and there were good roads between the two places. On the other side was the Hudson river, upon which were five or six armed vessels belonging to the enemy. With careful scrutiny, and skilful avoidance of danger, he saw and took in the situation. The principal depot of supplies for the American army was at the mercy of the enemy, who had but to reach out his hand and grasp the tempting prize. It was only the entire certainty that he could take it when he wished that made him delay. After a full survey of the situation, Colonel Putnam set out on his return to headquarters, near Kingsbridge. He had ten miles to ride, and reached there about 9 o'clock in the evening, and reported to General Washington, who, he says, "complained very feelingly" of the difficulty of getting correct information in regard to the country and the situation of affairs. Colonel Putnam had made a sketch of the country, and showed the danger there was of losing the stores, upon which so much depended. He was sent with orders for immediate action to Lord Sterling's headquarters, which he reached at 2 o'clock in the morning, and before daylight a detachment was on its way to White Plains, where they arrived about 9 o'clock. "Thus was the American army saved by an interposition of Providence," but that "interposition," the *machinery*, was the fidelity, and courage and shrewdness of Colonel Putnam.

In December he left the engineer corps, and took the command of a Massachusetts regiment, much to the regret of General Washington, who said in a letter to Congress, "I know of no other man even tolerably well qualified for the conducting of that business. None of the French gentlemen whom I have seen with appointments in that way appear to know anything of the matter."

After recruiting his regiment in Massachusetts in the summer of 1777 Colonel Putnam joined the brigade to which he belonged, near Fort Edward.

There was a dark cloud hanging over the north at this time. Burgoyne, at the head of seven thousand troops and a large number of Canadians and Indians, had invaded western New York, coming over the old war path through Vermont. Another large force, under Sir Henry Clinton, was expected to come from the southward, by way of the Hudson river, to meet them. Ticonderoga, the Gibraltar of the north, had fallen into the hands of the enemy. The fall of this fort sent an electric shock through New England. Consternation and alarm spread over the land. Troops were hurried forward to prevent, if possible, a worse disaster that might be impending. Affairs culminated in the battle of Saratoga, which Burgoyne was forced to fight before Clinton could join him.

This battle turned the tide in the concerns of the new nation, and success seemed ere long to be assured.

Colonel Putnam acted well his part in the battle. He was posted in front of the German reserves, and showed great bravery and military skill in the management of his troops. Kosciusko was at this time at the head of the engineering department in General Gates' army, and showed his appreciation of the skill and good judgment of Colonel Putnam by often consulting him in regard to matters pertaining to his business. After the surrender of Burgoyne, Nixon's brigade, to which Colonel Putnam belonged, went into winter quarters at Albany.

Early in the following year, 1778, Colonel Putnam was ordered to West Point to superintend the erection of fortifications at that important point. A French engineer had been employed, but his work was so unsatisfactory that it was thought best that another should take his place. He went at the head of his regiment and went to work with his usual energy both to undo and to do. The French engineer had laid out the main fort on an extreme point next the river. Colonel Putnam abandoned it and simply placed a battery there to annoy the enemy's shipping. The principal fort was built by his own regiment under his superintendence, and named by General McDougal, Fort Putnam. It is on a rocky eminence and commands both the plain and the river. It is said that even now engineers and those learned in the art of fortification from European countries wonder and admire when they see the plans that were made and the work that was done by this self-taught millwright. Colonel Putnam was occupied in laying out and constructing the defences at West Point until June. In July he marched to White Plains and united his regiment with the main army under the commander-in-chief. There was but little more active service performed during the campaign, and in September the army was broken into divisions and that of General Gates, to which Colonel Putnam belonged, was sent to Danbury, Connecticut.

But Colonel Putnam was the possessor of abilities that very effectually kept him from being laid on the shelf with idlers. When there was no fighting to be done, there were surveys to be made and plans for defence. He was employed for some time in laying out roads in the vicinity of Danbury, and later in the season with General Greene, he made reconnoisance along the Hudson river. When this was done he obtained a furlough to visit his home, where he had not been since December, 1777, more than a year.

Mr. Putnam with his family of small children, the oldest not more than twelve, lived on a farm of fifty acres and those acres not of the richest and best. Colonel Putnam's salary was meagre and not promptly paid. When it was paid the currency in which it was done was so greatly depreciated that it was inadequate to meet the wants of the family. Mrs. Putnam eked out their scanty income by the diligent use of the distaff and the needle. Rigid economy prevailed in the household and industry that would seem a marvel to some of their descendents. If the fathers of the Revolution deserve credit for patriotism the mothers should also share in the renown;

much they did and more they endured; and inasmuch as patient waiting is more difficult and harder to endure than active serving, they are worthy to be held in grateful remembrance as having had a large share in securing for us the inheritance of a free country, blessed with civil and religious liberty.

In July, 1779, Colonel Putnam was sent to do special service in the examination of Stony and Verplank's Points, previous and preparatory to the attack upon the former so successfully and brilliantly made by General Wayne. He encountered many difficulties in performing this duty, but as usual accomplished what he had set out to do with great skill and carefulness. Soon after this, he was appointed to the command of a regiment of light infantry in the brigade of General Wayne, made up of the very *elite* of the army.

The greater part of the winter of 1780 he spent in Boston in endeavors to obtain from the legislature redress of grievances for the officers and soldiers in the army. Their sufferings, for want of pay and necessary supplies, were extreme, and had reached the point when endurance seemed no longer possible. The officer of General Nixon's brigade had, by an unanimous vote, chosen Colonel Putnam to represent their interests and intercede for them, both with Congress and the legislature of Massachusetts. He was partially successful in securing relief, and received a note of thanks for the help he obtained.

General Washington seems fully to have appreciated the trustworthiness as well as the ability of Colonel Putnam, and he lost no opportunity of manifesting his interest in him, and his desire to do for him whatever lay in his power. In the Memoir written by General Putnam, he speaks modestly, but with just pride, of the sincere and unwavering regard shown him, by the commander-in-chief. During this year he consulted him in regard to the best plan for arranging a military peace establishment. Colonel Putnam drew up a plan in which he went very much into detail. In 1782 he had become dissatisfied with the service, and was about to retire, but he was made a brigadier-general, and his promotion left him without an excuse for leaving the service. But the war was over, and peace was again come to shed gladness over the land. Early in 1783 General Putnam resigned his commission, and went back to his farm and to surveying. But it was not easy for him to be content with the interests of so narrow a life, after being accustomed to act in stirring events that took hold upon public interests. In June, 1783, a petition signed by two hundred and eighty-three officers was presented to Congress, asking for a grant of land in the west. General Putnam addressed a letter to General Washington, enforcing the terms of the petition, and begging him to use his influence with Congress to induce them to act promptly. In this letter he very forcibly and clearly presents arguments in favor of immediate action. The arguments were drawn from both the needs of the officers and the best interests of the country. He says the probability is that the country between Lake Erie and the Ohio will be filled with inhabitants. He goes on to say that he

thinks there are thousands that would emigrate thither and settle if Congress would grant favorable terms, and urges the necessities of officers and soldiers as a reason for immediate action. General Washington seconded him with all the influence he could bring to bear on the subject, but all was not sufficient to overcome the inertia of Congress. Nothing was done at that time. The history of General Putnam's connection with the Ohio company and the great work that he accomplished in superintending the establishment of the first permanent settlement in the Northwest Territory is given elsewhere, and will be omitted here, except the brief statement of a few facts to fill out the outline of his life.

While in this waiting posture, General Putnam was employed by the State of Massachusetts to survey a tract of land bordering upon Passamaquoddy bay and so entire was the satisfaction felt with the manner in which the work was done that in 1785 he was again employed by the legislature to survey their eastern lands. While he was thus engaged, Congress waked up enough to take action in regard to the proposed settlement in the west, and appointed General Putnam to superintend the work of surveying and laying out the land. But he felt himself in honor bound to keep his engagement with the State of Massachusetts, and at his request General Tupper was appointed in his place. April 7, 1788, forty-eight colonists with General Putnam in command landed at the confluence of the Muskingum and Ohio rivers, and began the settlement of Marietta. General Putnam administered the affairs of the colony with good judgement and wise forethought. There were educated men among the colonists, graduates of Havard and Yale—men who had filled honorably and well high positions, and it is proof, if proof were wanted, of the rare endowments of General Putnam, that he, without the training of school or college, among these men was *facile princeps*. Always cool and clear-headed, he was one to be depended on in emergencies. Inflexible in his integrity, just and upright in all his dealings, it was safe to commit to him any interest no matter how important. It is not strange, then, that he was so often employed to conduct difficult negotiations and manage business, when sound judgment and unimpeachable honesty were necessary to success. It is especially noticeable that in everything he tried to do he always succeeded. There is no failure on record in any enterprise he ever undertook, when the plans and execution were in his own hands.

He went to work at once, as soon as the colony arrived, to arrange securities for them in case of hostilities on the part of the Indians. The wise forethought shown in this, probably saved the colonists in the Indian war that broke out in 1791 and continued for five years.

General Putnam presided over the first court held in the territory and gave the charge to the grand jury in an appropriate and impressive manner. In 1790 he received a commission as judge in the United States court, and in the same year moved his family, consisting of his wife, six daughters, two sons, and two grand-children, to Marietta. In May, 1792, General Putnam was made a brigadier general in the United States army.

He accepted the duty under protest. The first duty assigned him under his new office was to "attempt to be present at the general council of the hostile Indians, about to be held on the Miami river, of Lake Erie, in order to convince them of the humane disposition of the United States, and thereby to make a truce, or peace, with them." Accompanied by the Rev. John Heckewelder, he went to Post Vincent. He succeeded in making a treaty of peace and amity, which was signed by thirty-one kings, chiefs, and warriors, who represented eight of the Wabash tribes. This treaty was of great importance, as it detached a large body of warriors from the war party, though the Shawnees and Miamis were still too much elated by their recent victory over General St. Clair to be induced to sign the treaty.

Soon after this General Putnam resigned his commission as brigadier general, but he was not allowed to retire from public service. Colonel Pickering, the postmaster general, wanted to establish a line of boats to carry the mail from Pittsburgh to Cincinnati. The arrangements were placed under the superintendence of General Putnam, and so wisely and so well was the business managed, that the boats continued to make their regular trips during the Indian war, with the loss of but one life. And again, when a road was wanted to connect Wheeling with Limestone, now Maysville, General Putnam was appointed to superintend the laying out of the same. And finally, through the influence of General Washington, he was made surveyor general of the United States, an office of great responsibility, requiring much wisdom and good judgment to properly meet its requirements. Large tracts of land were to be surveyed and put into the market, grants to be laid out, and many delicate and difficult duties to be done. But he was sufficient for all these things, and discharged the duties of the office with honor to himself, and to the satisfaction of all concerned, until 1803, when he was removed by President Jefferson. He says, in regard to his removal: "I am happy in having my name enrolled with many, who have suffered the like political death, for adherence to those correct principles and measures, in the pursuance of which our country rose from a state of weakness, disgrace, and poverty, to strength, honor, and credit."

In 1802, General Putnam was elected by the citizens of Washington county as one of their representatives in the convention called to form a constitution for the new State. He did good service therein in fighting against the introduction of slavery, which, notwithstanding the prohibition in the ordinance of 1787, was kept out by a majority of only one vote.

In 1807 he drafted a plan for a church which was large and imposing for the time. He gave his services in superintending its erection, and also very liberal contributions in the way of money. The church is still used by the Congregationalists for their regular place of worship. He took great interest in establishing a Bible society in the county, and also in establishing a Sabbath-school, which was a new thing in the young west. He felt the want of educational advantages in his own early life so keenly that he was always ready to lend a helping hand to any effort to provide ways and means to save others from the evils that he suffered. While yet in Massachusetts, he was one of the corporators and trustees of Leicester academy one of the best and earliest started in the State, and to it he gave liberally of his means. In his new western home the cause still lay near his heart. But a brief period was allowed to pass after the Indian war was over before he was at work to get the "Muskingum academy" started and in working condition. This school was organized in 1798, and was the first in which anything higher than the common English branches was taught in all the great northwest, now so dotted with high schools, academies and colleges. He was elected in 1801 by the territorial legislature, one of the trustees of the Ohio university, the first college established in Ohio. He felt a warm interest in securing endowments and getting the college upon a solid foundation; and then, when all these things were accomplished, his public work was done. Surrounded by his children and their children, with a thriving community to bear witness to his wisdom and far-seeing philanthropy, honored with the respect of all who knew him, and cheered by the gratitude of those he had benefitted, he waited in serene old age for the summons to again start for a new and better country. The companion with whom he travelled the journey of life for more than half a century was called before him. Mrs. Putnam died in 1820, but his maiden daughter, Elizabeth, devoted herself to his comfort and did all that love and care could do to make his last years happy. At length his summons came. He died in 1824, in the eighty-seventh year of his age. He was borne to his rest and his remains laid down in the "Mound cemetery" in Marietta, under the shadow of a monument erected by a forgotten race to chieftains of their own, who had, perhaps, in their day, done deeds worthy of commemoration. He left numerous descendents, who are God fearing men and women, useful citizens and many of them active workers in the cause of Christ.

It is scarcely necessary to sum up the character of the man whose life has been so inadequately sketched. His work is his best epitaph. He was not brilliant, he was not quick, but he had good common sense in abundant measure, united with sound judgement and clear discrimination. When he saw what was needed to be done, he was wise in the seelction of the means to secure the desired end. His integrity was never called in question, he was always found on the side of the right, and no good cause was ever brought before him from which he willingly turned away. His personal appearance was imposing. He was courtly in his manners, after the old style of gentlemen, though oftentimes a little abrupt, as is the way of the Putnams. Being a much experienced man, he was very interesting as well as instructive in conversation. He had a large fund from which to draw, for he had seen much of distinguished men and of many remarkable events. He could say, if he would—*quorum magna pars fui*. A granite monument recently erected by his grandson, Colonel W. R. Putnam, marks the place of his rest. It has this inscription:

GEN. RUFUS PUTNAM,

A Revolutionary officer, and the leader of the colony which made the first settlement in the Territory of the Northwest at Marietta, April 7, 1788.

Born April 9, 1738.
Died May 4, 1824.
Persis Rice, wife of
Rufus Putnam,
Born November 19, 1737,
Died September 6, 1820.

The memory of the just is Blessed.

The children of General Rufus Putnam were: Ayres, born 1761, died 1762; Elizabeth, born 1765, died 1830; Persis, born 1767, died ———; Susanna, born 1768, died 1840; Abigail, born 1770, died 1805; William Rufus, born 1771, died 1855; Franklin, born 1774, died 1776; Edwin, born 1776, died 1843; Patty, born 1777, died 1842, and Catharine, born 1780, died 1808. William Rufus married in 1803, Jerusha Guitteau. Their son William Rufus Putnam, jr., was born June 13, 1812. Edwin Putnam married a Miss Safford and had a family of five children, three sons and two daughters. Susanna married Christopher Burlingame. Abigail married William Browning, of Belpre. Persis married Perly Howe, of Belpre. Martha married Benjamin Tupper, of Putnam (now Zanesville). Catharine married Ebenezer Buckingham.

REV. MANASSEH CUTLER, LL., D.

The interest which a majority of those who consult this volume, have in Dr. Manasseh Cutler centres in his splendid services for the New England Ohio company and his immeasurable influence for good, as exerted through the ordinance of 1787, of which much has been already said within these pages, but it is desirable that in a work devoted to the history of a settlement, of which he was one of the founders, a personal sketch of the man should be given to convey, however inadequately, some idea of his life, his talents, and his worth.

Rev. Manasseh Cutler, son of Hezekiah and Susanna (Clark) Cutler, was born in Killingly, Connecticut, May 28 (old style), 1742. His father was a respectable farmer and the son spent his earlier years in the usual manner of a New England farmer's boy. He early displayed promising tokens of genius and made rapid progress in study. He prepared for college under the Rev. Aaron Brown—a Killingly preacher—and entered Yale in 1761. He graduated with high honor in 1765. In the following year he married Mary Balch, daughter of the Rev. Thomas and Mary (Sumner) Balch. He studied law, was admitted to the bar in 1767, and pleaded a few cases in the Norfolk county, Massachusetts, courts, but having entertained, for some years, serious thoughts of entering the ministry, he began in earnest his theological studies in 1769, under the directions of his father-in-law, who was the first pastor of the South church, of Dedham, Massachusetts. In his diary under date of November, of the preceding year, appears an entry showing that he had even then given much consideration to the subject. He says: "Prosecuted my studies—began to make ser-

mons. May God grant me his blessing in so important an undertaking, and make me servicable to the cause of religion and the souls of my fellow-men." After completing the course of study usual at that day he was ordained at Ipswich Hamlet (afterward Hamilton), Massachusetts, September 11, 1771. His pastorate here continued fifty-two years, until his death, in 1823. Dr. Cutler regarded himself as consecrated to the ministry and repeatedly refused opportunities to enter other, and very tempting, avenues of life. His labors in the church were very successful. The Rev. Dr. Benjamin Wadsworth thus spoke of him: "Christ crucified was the great theme of his preaching. His public discourses were prepared in Gospel style, but with studied accuracy, argumentative energy, and persuasive pathos. They were serious and practical, rather than speculative and metaphysical; he could be a son of thunder, and a son of consolation; his object was to win souls to Christ, and to establish them intelligent, judicious, and exemplary Christians." Another writer has said of him: "As a preacher, he was grave, dignified, and impressive in manner, and select in the matter of his discourses. In doctrine, a moderate Calvinist, he steadily maintained the religious opinions with which he commenced his ministry, to the end of his life." Felt, in his history of Ipswich, Massachusetts, says: His voice in preaching was not loud, but distinct and audible to his congregation. . . . His style of writing was clear, perspicuous and strong." His published sermons are: "Charge at the Ordination of Rev. Daniel Story, 1798" (the first ordained minister in the northern territory). "A National Fast Sermon, 1799," "A Sermon before the Bible Society of Salem and vicinity, 1813," and "A Century Discourse of Hamilton Church, 1814."

Dr. Cutler became, while a young man, very fond of scientific study, and, later in life, it is not too much to say, was more distinguished as a scientist than any man in America, except Benjamin Franklin. In the early part of the Revolutionary war an American privateer captured and brought into port a British prize, containing among other valuables a fine library, consisting chiefly of medical and botanical works. These books became the neucleus of what is now the Salem athaneum. The botanical department—a field till then but little cultivated in this country—being very congenial to Dr. Cutler's taste, engaged his eager attention. He prepared a paper on botany which the American Society of Arts and Sciences published in their memoirs, and which Dr. Franklin (as he himself afterward assured Dr. Cutler) caused to be republished in the Columbian Magazine, printed at Philadelphia. In the year 1785 Dr. Cutler published four papers in the Memoirs of the American Academy, in three departments of science—astronomy, meteorology, and botany.

Dr. Cutler, who had already taken degrees in law and divinity, soon after the breaking out of the war of the Revolution, became a student and practitioner of medicine. The regular physician of the hamlet had been called to active military service, and the people were obliged to send to neighboring towns for medical aid.

58

In this exigency Dr. Cutler qualified himself to fill the place made vacant. In due time he acquired a high reputation as a physician, and in the treatment of some difficult cases his success became quite proverbial. Many valuable medical papers are preserved among his manuscripts. His knowledge of botany was blended advantageously with that of medicine. It may be remarked that one of his papers upon a topic of the former science was instrumental in bringing into use lobelia and other indigenous plants.

The public honors conferred upon him give some idea of the estimation in which Dr. Cutler was held as a man of literature and science—such an accumulation as is rarely annexed to the ministerial character. They rank in the following order: He graduated from Yale in 1765; received the degree of Master of Arts from Harvard in 1770; was elected a member of the Academy of Arts and Sciences, 1781; of the Philosophical society, Philadelphia, 1784; and an honorary member of the Massachusetts Medical society, 1785; received the degree of Doctor of Laws from Yale college, 1789; was elected member of the Agricultural society, 1792; of the Historical society, 1792; a representative to Congress from 1800 to 1804; an honorary member of the Linnæan society, Philadelphia, 1809; president of the Bible society of Salem and vicinity, 1811; a member of the American Antiquarian society, 1813; and of the New England Linnæan society, 1815. Dr. Cutler was better and more widely known during his life as a scientist than as a preacher. And now the popularity of the preacher and the renown of the scientist are both eclipsed by the fame of the author of the ordinance of 1787. As the agent who introduced and who secured the adoption of the clause in that immortal instrument which gave it the name of the Ordinance of Freedom, he organized the force which, swelling steadily and irresistibly as the years rolled on, changed the destiny of the Nation and of millions of human beings by barring its progress and so making possible the final overthrow of American slavery. Only in recent years has Dr. Cutler's name been covered with the glory of this great deed. But his agency in the formation of the ordinance—in the insertion and passage of the clause prohibiting slavery in the Northwest Territory—has been established beyond a doubt.

The events which led to Dr. Cutler's great opportunity, if not forming as long a train as that of the steps by which he was fitted to take advantage of the opportunity, were nevertheless numerous. It is not necessary that they should here be recounted. He took a deep interest in the success of the American patriots. He served during two campaigns as chaplain in the Revolutionary army. He was thus personally acquainted with many of the officers and soldiers in that noble body beside those who dwelt in Hamilton and its vicinity. When the great struggle was ended and independence secured, he deeply sympathized with the survivors who had sacrificed all but life itself in the battle. When a number of those men organized the New England Ohio company for the purpose of planting a colony in the west, and there retrieving their spent fortunes, he was elected a director.

Subsequently he was appointed the agent of the company to negotiate for a purchase of lands from Congress. In June, 1787, he journeyed to New York upon his important mission. How perfectly he fulfilled and how mightily he exceeded the object of that mission has already been told in a lengthy chapter of this volume. He not only made the purchase on advantageous terms, but he succeeded, by the exercise of his splendid abilities, in planting upon that land to which the colony was to journey, and upon the soil of the whole Northwest Territory, the law of Massachusetts. He succeeded in securing the eternal prohibition of slavery, and the enactment of wise measures for the support of schools, and the ministry, and the founding of a university.

Dr. Cutler kept a journal during his visit to Congress. That journal (from which ample extracts are given in chapter VI of this work) contains much of the evidence of Dr. Cutler's agency in the formation of the Ordinance of Freedom, and is an invaluable historical document. It was not meant for the public eye, but to give his daughters a glimpse of the world beyond their quiet New England home. The diary was kept at the request of his daughter, Mary, who, as her father was about to depart, ran to him with a book in which she enjoined him, girl-like, to write not only of his negotiations, but to give descriptions of the people whom he met—of ladies as well as gentlemen—of costumes, entertainments, etc. The journal was many years afterwards in Marietta in the hands of Judge Ephraim Cutler. Portions of it were copied by Miss Julia Cutler, and this manuscript is now in the hands of Mrs. Sarah Cutler Dawes, of Marietta. The original was returned to New England and passed into the possession of Daniel Webster. After his death it was found among his papers by the Rev. Edwin Stone, of Massachusetts, who has been for many years engaged in writing a biography of Dr. Cutler, and who still retains the document. Such in brief is the history of this journal. It will, doubtless, some day be deposited in the library of Marietta college.

While his negotiations with Congress were pending Dr. Cutler journeyed to Philadelphia to visit Benjamin Franklin (a man, by the way, whom he resembled in tastes, talents and achievements, as will be seen, when the story of his life is fully told). James Parton, in his life of Franklin, introduces Dr. Cutler's description of this visit as one of the best contemporary accounts of the distinguished American. The following extracts from this description we reproduce as showing something of the character of the writer and the esteem in which he was held by Franklin.

The Journal reads:

Dr. Franklin's house stands up a court at some distance from the street. We found him in the garden, sitting upon a grass plot, under a very large mulberry tree, with several other gentlemen and two or three ladies. . . . He rose from his chair, took me by the hand, expressed his joy at seeing me, welcomed me to the city and begged me to seat myself close to him. His voice was low; his countenance open frank and pleasing. I delivered him my letters. After he had read them, he took me again by the hand and with the usual compliments introduced me to the other gentlemen. . . . Here we entered into a free conversation and spent our time most agreeably, until it was quite dark . . . After it was dark we went into the house, and he invited me into the library, which is likewise his study.

Here Franklin exhibited to his scientific friend many interesting objects,—a glass machine for representing the flow of the blood in the arteries and veins of the human body, a copying press, a long artificial arm and hand (his own invention) for taking books down from high shelves, and other devices and curiosities. Dr. Cutler continues:

But what the doctor wished principally to show me was a huge volume on botany, which, indeed, afforded me the greatest pleasure of any one thing in his library. It was a single volume, but so large, that it was with great difficulty that he was able to raise it from a low shelf and lift it on the table. But with that senile ambition, which is common to old people, he insisted on doing it himself, and would permit no person to assist him, merely to show us how much strength he had remaining. It contained the whole of Linnaeus *Sytema Vegetabilium* with large cuts of every plant colored from nature. It was a feast to me, and the doctor seemed to enjoy it as well as myself. We spent a couple of hours in examining this volume, while the other gentlemen amused themselves with other matters. The doctor is not a botanist, but lamented he had not in early life attended to the science. He delights in natural history and expressed an earnest wish that I should pursue the plan that I had begun and hoped this science so much neglected in America would be pursued with as much ardor here as it is now in every part of Europe. I wanted for three months at least to have devoted myself to this one volume, but fearing that I should be tedious to him, I shut up the volume, though he urged me to examine it longer.

He seemed extremely fond, through the course of the visit of dwelling on philosophical subjects, and particularly that of natural history, while the other gentlemen were swallowed up with politics This was a favorable circumstance for me, for almost the whole of his conversation was addressed to me, and I was highly delighted with the extensive knowledge he appeared to have of every subject, the brightness of his memory and clearness and vivacity of all his mental faculties, notwithstanding his age. His manners are perfectly easy, and everything about him seems to diffuse an unrestrained freedom and happiness. He has an incessant vein of humor accompanied by an uncommon vivacity, which seems as natural and involuntary as his breathing He urged me to call on him again, but my short stay would not admit.

Dr. Cutler, in the summer of 1788, visited the infant settlement which he had been instrumental in founding, for the purpose of attending a meeting of the directors of the Ohio company. He left Hamilton, in his sulky, July 21st, and arrived at Marietta August 19th. On the twenty-seventh of the month he performed the burial service for a child of Major Nathaniel Cushing, the first funeral among the settlers here. He preached on the Sabbath in the hall at Campus Martius; and was present in the same hall September 2, 1788, at the opening of the first court held northwest of the river Ohio, under the forms of civil jurisprudence, officiating as chaplain on that occasion. He was greatly interested in examining the ancient mounds, squares, and other earthworks at Marietta, which he thought were a thousand years old, and were made by some nation more civilized and powerful than any Indians known to exist in America. After his arrival in Massachusetts he wrote to General Rufus Putnam: "On my return home I found several letters from different parts of Europe. The most of them request me to send a particular account of the ancient works found in North America. These works seem to have engaged the attention of the literati in Europe, and I wish to gratify those with whom I have the honor to correspond, as far as possible. I must beg you to forward to me the surveys of the works at Marietta. Accurate measurements I find to be of consequence in their

minds. Pray attend to the width of the openings, and the distances and relative situations of all the works to one another." Dr. Cutler gives an account of these remarkable earthworks in a note to his charge at the ordination of Rev. Daniel Story.

Dr. Cutler at one time contemplated removing his family to the new purchase, but after this visit he writes that he could not do so without making great sacrifices, and, although the country equalled, and in some respects much exceeded his expectations, especially as a grazing country, and he felt the warmest interest in the success and prosperity of the settlement, he finally abandoned the plan.

Soon after the peace made by General Wayne with the western Indians, in 1795, President Washington tendered to Dr. Cutler a commission as judge of the supreme court in the Ohio Territory, which he declined.

Although Dr. Cutler was not of the pioneers at Marietta, two of his sons, Ephraim and Jervis, were, and a third, Charles, was also an early resident of Ohio. Another son died in infancy. Temple, the youngest of the four who lived to maturity, never removed to the west, and died in New England in 1857. Dr. Cutler had three daughters: Mary, who became the wife of Dr. Joseph Torry, of Hamilton; Elizabeth, who married Fitch Poole and lived in Danvers; and Lavinia, who married Captain Jacob Berry.

In the autumn of 1800 Dr. Cutler was elected a member of Congress, and again in 1802, when, having served two terms, he declined a reelection. His people entertained a high estimate of his talents and patriotism, and he accepted the honors conferred with the modest diffidence which true dignity inspires. Whether at home or abroad, his mind was intent on projecting great and good plans, consulting the benefit of generations to come; and his persevering genius rarely failed of carrying them into effect. In politics Dr. Cutler was a Federalist.

Felt's History of Ipswich (Massachusetts), says: "In person Dr. Cutler was of light complexion, above the common stature, erect and dignified in his appearance. His manners were gentlemanly; his conversation easy and intelligent. As an advisor he was discerning and discreet. . . . His mental endowments were high."

This great and good man having nobly fulfilled his life duty passed away July 28, 1823 at the ripe age of eighty-one years.

In a discourse delivered July 30, 1823, in Hamilton, at the interment of the Rev. Manasseh Cutler, by Benjamin Wadswords, D. D., he said: "All who enjoyed the privilege of an acquaintance with the Rev. Dr. Cutler knew that nature had been liberal of her gifts; enriching an elegant form with a penetrating and enterprising mind, capacitated for literary and scientific attainments, and with talents formed to shine on the public stage of life," and he adds, "his name will stand enrolled on the list of the early literati."

Dr. Cutler's old home in Hamilton remains, little changed since he dwelt in it, except that the beautiful gardens which he had in connection with the house have long since disappeared. In the village burying-ground

is a monument to his memory bearing the following inscription:

REV. MANASSEH CUTLER, LL., D.

He died July 28, 1823, in the 81st year of his age.

He was beloved for his domestic and social virtues.

His talents were of a high order. He was eminent for his Botanical,
Medical, Political and Theological knowledge. He was a member of
literary and scientific societies in both Europe and America. After a
useful ministry of fifty-two years in this place, he expired, with a firm
and peaceful reliance on his Redeemer.

"They that trust in the Lord shall be as Mount Zion,
which cannot be removed but abideth forever."

This stone is erected to his memory by his church.

On the reverse is the following:

Sacred to the memory of
MRS. MARY CUTLER,
Consort of Rev. Dr. Cutler, who deceased
Nov. 3, 1815, in the 73d year of her age.

"Blessed are the dead who die in the Lord."

GENERAL BENJAMIN TUPPER.*

The important part taken by General Benjamin Tupper in the measures leading to settlement at Marietta,
makes his personal career a subject of general interest.
He was born at Staughton, Massachusetts, in 1738.
While yet quite young his father died, and he was apprenticed to a tanner named Whitherton, in Dorchester.
He left Dorchester at the age of sixteen, and lived on a
farm at Easton.

He served as a private soldier in the French war most
of the time for about three years. About this time he
also taught school at Easton two or three winters.

He was married November 18, 1762, to Huldah
White, of Easton. She was a woman of much strength
and beauty of character, and was well fitted to be the
companion of a public man during a trying epoch of
history. A short time after their marriage they removed
from Easton to Chesterfield, which continued to be the
family residence until they came to Marietta.

Mr. Tupper, at the opening of the Revolution, was
lieutenant in a militia company at Chesterfield, and
under command of Major Halley, of Northampton,
participated in preventing the supreme court from sitting
under authority of the British Crown. He thus early
joined the illustrious line of revolutionists. When the
war had actually begun, he entered the service with the
rank of major, and was an actor in the events which took
place at Boston harbor.

Mr. Tupper was promoted to the colonelcy in 1776.
He participated in the battle of Long Island. During
the campaign of 1777, he served under General Gates.
In 1778, he was under General Washington, and had a
horse killed under him at the battle of Monmouth. In
1780, he served in the army of the Hudson. About the
close of the war he was promoted to the rank of brigadier general by brevet. When the war had closed, he
returned to his family at Chesterfield.

The circumstances which brought him to the valley of
the Ohio, the survey under the ordinance of 1785, his

*From a sketch written by his grandson, A. T. Nye.

visit to Fort Harmar, his conference with General Putnam and its result, are already known to the reader.

General Tupper's last military services were in the
suppression of Shay's rebellion in Massachusetts, in
which he performed an important part.

General Tupper came to Marietta with the first company of families, August 19, 1788. He served as judge
of the court of quarter sessions until his death in June,
1792. His wife died at Putnam, Ohio, February 21,
1812.

Their family consisted of three sons and four daughters. Major Anselm Tupper died at Marietta, December 25, 1808; Colonel Benjamin Tupper died at Putnam in February, 1815; General Edward W. Tupper
died at Gallipolis in 1823; Rowena, the oldest daughter
of General Tupper, and wife of Secretary Winthrop
Sargeant, died at Marietta in 1790; Sophia, wife of
Nathaniel Wilys, esq., of Connecticut, died in October,
1789; Minerva, wife of Colonel Ichabod Nye, died at
Marietta in April, 1836; the other daughter died young,
before the family emigrated to Ohio.

SAMUEL HOLDEN PARSONS.

Samuel Holden Parsons was an honorable soldier and
able diplomat during the early period of our country's
existence. He was born in New London county, Connecticut, May 14, 1837. His father was Jonathan Parsons, a distinguished clergyman, and his mother was a
descendant of Henry Wolcot, of Connecticut. He
graduated from Harvard college, and studied law. His
first appointment was to the position of colonial auditor
with power to collect and adjust accounts. He became
a member of the committee on western land claims in
1773. His diplomatic services in this connecton were
found of great service to his colony.

In 1783 he was made a member of the intercolonial
standing committee of correspondence and inquiry. As
a member of this committee he suggested to Samuel
Adams the propriety of holding annual meetings of commissioners of the colonies to consult on their general
welfare. Historians have attributed to Samuel Adams
the honor of originating the American Congress, but a
letter on file among the papers of Samuel Adams from
Colonel Parsons proves him to have been the originator
of the idea.

His strong and caustic pen was employed during the
whole of the preliminary struggle with Great Britain in
inspiring his countrymen with a spirit of resistance
against oppression. The fact that a National Congress
was first suggested by Colonel Parsons, has been referred
to. It was through his diplomacy that the legislature of
Connecticut was led to pass a resolution in 1774, recommending a meeting of representatives of the colonies.
Massachusetts, with Samuel Adams in the lead, seconded
this resolution. Colonel Parsons joined the lines at the
opening of the war, and served with distinction till its
close, when he was retired with the rank of major-general.
He had succeeded General Putnam in command of the

Hudson River division, and was one of the committee which tried Major Andre.

In 1786 his ability as a diplomat was called into use when he was appointed to a place on the commission, to treat with the Shawnee Indians for extinguishing the aboriginal title to certain lands within the Northwestern Territory. The other members of the commission were Generals Richard Butler, of Pittsburgh, and George Rogers Clark, of Kentucky. The treaty was held January 31, 1786, near the mouth of the Great Miami, and resulted in the cession to the United States of a large tract of land, on which Cincinnati now stands.

General Parsons was appointed one of the supreme judges under the ordinance of 1787, and came to Marietta in May, 1788. In 1789 he was commissioned chief judge of the territory. In the fall of 1789 he went to the northern part of the State in the service of Connecticut, to treat with the Wyandots relative to their claim on the Reserve lands. While returning to Marietta, he was drowned in the rapids of the Big Beaver November 17, 1789.

JAMES MITCHELL VARNUM.

Americans patriotically cherish the memory of the Revolutionary heroes. But in the character of James Mitchell Varnum we have a man whose services extend beyond the establishment of independence into the period of the establishment of government and the formation of constitutions, a man who devoted to the service of his country the talents of a ready commander, able lawyer and pure statesman.

James Mitchell Varnum was born in Middlesex county, Massachusetts in 1749, on the ancestral estate, which was purchased from the Indians and settled by Samuel Varnum in 1664. His life is briefly summed up in the published memoirs of the Bar of Rhode Island: "The career of General Varnum was active but brief. He graduated at Brown university at twenty; was admitted to the bar at twenty-two; entered the army at twenty-seven; resigned his commission at thirty-one; was member of Congress the same year; resumed practice at thirty-three and continued four years; was elected to Congress again at thirty-seven; emigrated to Ohio at thirty-nine, and died at the early age of forty." Varnum soon after admission to the bar acquired an extensive practice. He had a natural taste for military life, and his keen mind doubtless foresaw the dark future of his country, for he joined the Kentish guards and was in 1774 appointed commander. This was one of the most celebrated companies of the colonial militia. Thirty-two of its members entered the Revolution as commissioned officers. Besides the commander among the number were General Green, Colonel Crary and Colonel Whitemarsh. The prominent part Varnum had taken in the colonial controversies and his position in the militia service caused him to be chosen to the command of one of the first regiments of infantry raised by authority of the colonial legislature. He afterwards received a commis-

sion from Washington. He served as colonel in Washington's division at Trenton and Princeton. In February, 1777, Colonel Varnum was promoted to the rank of brigadier general and served with distinction until 1779, when he retired to his own State which sent him to Congress in 1780. But we cannot detail his important public services. His power as a lawyer was shown in an important case which involved the destiny of the State. The idea took possession of the impoverished people, inexperienced in affairs of government, that money could be manufactured by State authority (an idea since several times revived). Laws had actually been enacted making it an offense finable by law to refuse to accept at par the worthless fiat money of an impoverished State. Interest had become as high as four per cent. per month, and all business was on the verge of ruin. This paper money system gave rise to a case which gave General Varnum a national reputation as a lawyer. The case in itself was simple. John Trevett bought meat of John Weeden and tendered him in payment State bills, which Weeden refused. The whole State was interested in this case. "If the complaint should be sustained by the judgment of the court all the commerce and business of the State would be destroyed and all previous obligations cancelled by this irredeemable trash," General Varnum's plea on this occasion was a masterpiece. He succeeded not only in having the laws adjudged unconstitutional, but the effect of his logic was so powerful that the dominant party was forced to a change of policy.

General Varnum became a member of the Ohio company in 1787, and was elected one of its directors. He was also appointed one of the supreme judges of the territory. He left Rhode Island in the spring of 1788 and arrived in Marietta in June. He delivered the oration at the first Fourth of July celebration in Marietta. After coming to Ohio his health gave way. In the fall of 1788 he determined to go South in the hope of recuperating, but rapid decline saved him a death among strangers. He died of consumption January 10, 1789. His burial was attended with the ceremony due his high character and distinguished public services.

COMMODORE ABRAHAM WHIPPLE.

In the Mound cemetery at Marietta is a tombstone bearing the following inscription:

Sacred
to the memory of
COMMODORE ABRAHAM WHIPPLE,
whose name, skill, and courage,
will ever remain the pride and
boast of his country.
In the late Revolution he was the
first on the seas to hurl defiance at proud Britain,
gallantly leading the way to wrest from
the mistress of the ocean her scepter,
and there to wave the star-spangled banner.
He also conducted to the sea
the first square-rigged vessel ever built on the Ohio,
opening to commerce
resources beyond calculation.*

*This inscription was written by Judge Ephraim Cutler, his warm friend and admirer.

While Ohio is pointing with pride to her many great sons, she should not neglect to know the life, and honor the memory of the brave men who planted ripe civilization on her savage soil. The high position of so many of these among the celebrated men of the Revolution is a source of pride and congratulation.

Abraham Whipple, a descendant of John Whipple, one of the original proprietors of the Providence plantations, was born in Providence, Rhode Island, in the year 1733. In early life he was drawn into ocean commerce, and attained to the command of a vessel engaged in the West India and St. Croix trade. He followed the sea for many years before the Revolution, during which he acquired a practical knowledge of navigation and an intimate acquaintance with the ocean and its harbors. Near the close of the French war he was given command of a privateer. During this period he exhibited qualifications which brought him into notice. He was brave and confident and his ready mind was never at a loss for an expedient. The reputation acquired during the French war drew him into the incipient acts of the Revolution. In 1772 he headed a company of his townsmen who burned an odious British schooner, stationed at Narragansett bay, for the purpose of enforcing oppressive maritime laws. One thousand pounds was offered for the detection of the leader, and five hundred pounds for any member of the company. But England was at that time so universally hated that although more than fifty knew the secret none were found willing to inform. Historians generally consider the burning of the Gaspe, June 17, 1772, by Captain Whipple and the Providence company, the overt act of the Revolution.

Little Rhode Island was first to renounce allegiance to the British crown, and the first to send to sea under legislative authority a vessel of war. Two days before the battle of Bunker Hill, two sloops were purchased and armed, one with twelve the other with eight guns. The larger was placed under command of Captain Whipple, with orders to clear the bay of British tenders, to the frigate Rose under command of Sir James Wallace, who blockaded the harbors and rivers, preventing a large number of homeward bound vessels from entering the port. Captain Whipple sailed on the fifteenth of June, down the Narragansett bay and attacked two of the enemy's traders. He forced one to retire and took the other a prize. This bold stroke cleared the bay and entitles Whipple to the honor of having fired the first gun at the British on the sea, in the opening of the Revolutionary war.

But to narrate the life of Commodore Whipple during the next seven years would be telling an important part of the naval history of the Revolution, and belongs to a book of wider scope. Our purpose here is to give the citizens of Washington county an idea of the National importance of one of the founders of society in their own State and community.

In 1782 he was excused from the service, and returned to his farm at Cranston. He was given command, in 1784, of one of the first merchant vessels sent to Great Britain after the peace. "To Commodore Whipple was given the honor of first unfurling the American flag on the Thames." After his return he again retired to his farm, and was a member of his State legislature during the first rage of the paper money lunacy.

In a pitiful petition to Congress, in 1786, he sets forth his financial condition. His grievances are similar to those of many others who took part in the battles for freedom, and in this age of pensions the prayer of the petition may not be uninteresting. After setting forth his military services, he says:

Thus having exhausted the means of supporting myself and family, I was reduced to the sad necessity of mortgaging my little farm, the remnant I had left, to obtain money for a temporary support. The farm is now gone, and, having been sued out of possession, I am turned into the world at an advanced age, feeble and valetudinary, with my wife and children, destitute of a house or a home that I can call my own, or have the means of hiring. This calamity has arisen from two causes, viz.: First, from my disbursing large sums in France and Charleston. In the former I expended in the service of the United States to the amount of three hundred and sixty French guineas—a large part of that sum was appropriated to the pay of marine, the other part for sea stores to accommodate a number of gentlemen passengers sent on board by the commissioners to take passage for America, and for which I have never been recompensed; and, secondly, my having served the United States from the fifteenth of June, 1775, to December, 1782, without receiving a farthing of wages or subsistance from them since December, 1776. My advances in France and Charleston amount in the whole to nearly seven thousand dollars in specie, exclusive of interest. The repayment of this, or a part of it, might be the happy means of regaining the farm I have been obliged to give up, and snatch my family from misery and ruin."

The whole amount due from the United States was about sixteen thousand dollars. He received in final settlement securities the nominal amount expended in France. He was forced to sell these securities at a discount of eighty per cent. This amount, however, enabled him to regain his Cranston farm, which he sold in 1788 and came to Ohio. During the Indian war he lived in comparative quiet in the house of his son-in-law, Colonel Sproat. He, indeed, considered the whites aggressors in the Indian country, and was inclined to deal with the red men as peaceably as possible.

In 1796, in his sixty-third year, he removed with his wife to a farm of twelve acres, located on the Muskingum, two miles from Marietta, and depended upon its productions and his own labor for a livelihood. The fact of his having gone to Havana with a cargo of produce, in 1801, will be found in the chapter on commerce and navigation.

In 1811, when failing health and reduced circumstances were oppressing him, he followed the advice of friends and applied to Congress for a pension. In answer to his petition he was allowed half the pay of a captain, which was at that time sixty dollars a month. The remaining years of his life were free from anxiety.

His sympathetic life companion was Sarah Hopkins, sister of Governor Hopkins, of Rhode Island. Their family consisted of two daughters and one son. The oldest daughter married Colonel Ebenezer Sproat, and the younger, Dr. Comstock, of Rhode Island. She never came to Ohio. John, the only son, left Marietta at an early period and followed a seafaring life. He never married, and with him the family name became extinct.

Mrs. Sarah Whipple died in October, 1818, in her

eightieth year. Commodore Whipple died May 29, 1819, on his farm. He was a leading actor from beginning to end of that trying struggle which resulted in the establishment of our Nation. Impoverished, he struggled in later life in the midst of the events incident to the first settlement of the northwest. It is pleasant to reflect that his last years were spent in ease and contentment.

COLONEL ROBERT OLIVER.

It is a fortunate circumstance that so many of the colony of first settlers were men of superior character and ability. One of the most useful members of the Ohio company was Colonel Robert Oliver. He was born in 1738 in the north of Ireland. His parents moved to America while Robert was young, and settled on a farm in Worcester county, Massachusetts. His education was as good as the schools of that period afforded.

He entered the Revolution as a lieutenant, but at the close of the war had advanced to the position of colonel. He served under General Rufus Putnam in the campaign against Burgoyne, and was highly complimented as a disciplinarian. After the close of the war he again settled on a farm, where he lived quietly until 1786, when he volunteered to assist in putting down Shay's rebellion.

Upon the formation of the Ohio company he invested in two shares of their land and came to Marietta in the summer of 1788. The formation of the Millsburgh colony and the erection of Wolf Creek mills is fully noticed in the chapter on Watertown.

In 1790 Colonel Oliver was elected to fill the vacancy on the board of directors of the Ohio company caused by the death of General Parsons. His services in that capacity were of great value, especially during the trying period of the Indian war.

Colonel Oliver was the colleague of Colonel Meigs in the first territorial legislature, and was selected as one of the council, which was composed of five representatives, nominated by the governor and commissioned by the President of the United States. In 1800 he was chosen president of the council. He served as colonel of militia, and judge of the court of common pleas. He served his township as magistrate until his death, which occurred in May, 1810.

The few persons yet living who knew him bear testimony of the high regard in which he was held, especially in Waterford, where his private life was known and appreciated.

MAJOR HAFFIELD WHITE.

The few old settlers of the community of Waterford whom time has spared to tell reminiscences of past events frequently mention the name of Major White. He was born in Danvers, Massachusetts, where, at the opening of the Revolution, he was an officer in a company of minute men. His company hastened to the scene of action as soon as the news of the actual opening of hostilities reached them, and arrived in time to pour a round of rifle-balls into the retreating British lines. He served as an officer in line and as commissary until the close of the war.

He became a member of the Ohio company in 1787 and acted as commissary for the first detachment to Marietta. His son, Peletiah, was one of the forty-eight who arrived April 7, 1788. In 1789, Major White, in company with Captain Dodge and Major Oliver, built the first mill in Ohio—Wolf creek mill in Watertown township. This property eventually passed under control of the White family. After the death of the major his son, Peletiah, managed the mill.

Major White was held in high regard by his customers, who were prejudiced by his affable manner and sterling qualities.

COLONEL EBENEZER SPROAT.

A distinguished character in the early history of Ohio is the tall sheriff who headed the procession at the opening of the first court in the territory, and whose imposing figure so impressed the Indians that they gave him the name of Hetuck (Big Buckeye). There is a tradition that from this circumstance the term Buckeye came to be applied to all Ohioians.

Colonel Sproat was born in Middleborough, Massachusetts, in 1752. He had the advantage of early education and became familiar with the principles and practice of surveying. He assisted his father on the farm and was remarked for his strong vigorous frame. He stood erect six feet four inches tall. At the opening of the Revolution Mr. Sproat was given command of a company but soon rose to the position of major in the Tenth Massachusetts regiment, under Colonel Sheppard. In 1778 he became lieutenant colonel in Glover's brigade. It has been said that he was not only the tallest man in the brigade, but also the most complete disciplinarian. At the close of the war he retired to Providence and employed himself at surveying. While here he became attached to Catharine Whipple, whom he married. Colonel Sproat now turned his attention to mercantile pursuits, for which he was singularly unfitted. He was fond of company and freehanded, and as a natural result failed after a short period, losing his own fortune and his wife's patrimony. In 1786, Colonel Sproat was given an appointment on the survey of the seven ranges, and the following year was made one of the surveyors of the Ohio company's purchase. In the fall of that year he led a detachment to Simrell's ferry, where he superintended the building of the Mayflower. Colonel Sproat continued as surveyor for the company until 1791, when the Indian war prevented further operations. He held the position of high sheriff, under commission of Governor St. Clair, for fourteen years. He invested the office with all the dignity of ancient ceremony, which his commanding presence gave a peculiar effect. He always carried a sword as the badge of office. During the Indian war he served as paymaster of the troops. The family of Colonel Sproat consisted of his wife and one daughter, who came to Marietta with Commodore Whipple. His daughter married Solomon Sibley, esq. Colonel Sproat was a friend of General Washington and an acquaintance of Lafayette. He was a staunch Federalist and saw the fall of his party with regret. He took a live interest in agriculture, particularly gardening. His garden covered nearly an acre of ground and was tastefully laid out in squares and walks. He died suddenly in February, 1805.

COLONEL RETURN JONATHAN MEIGS.

Another of the celebrated spirits of the Revolution, and one, too, who figures prominently in the early history of Ohio, was Colonel Return Jonathan Meigs. He was apprenticed a hatter in early life and afterwards had a shop in his native State of Connecticut.

Mr. Meigs was a member of the Colonial military company, of Middletown, and when the war became iminent was chosen captain. After the news of the first bloodshed at Lexington, Captain Meigs volunteered and was received into the service with the rank of major.

After his release he again signified his willingness to enter the service, and was commissioned colonel by Congress. He raised a regiment of volunteers, known in history as the "Red Cap regiment." The expedition of this regiment against Sagg Harbor, Long Island, is celebrated, and its conduct at Stony Point highly honorable. After the war Clonel Meigs returned to Middletown, where he remained until the formation of the Ohio company. His services were engaged by the company as a surveyor, and in the spring of 1788 he entered on the duties of his office. Before the territorial officers had arrived Colonel Meigs had drawn up a code of rules, which served for the government of the territory. After the organization of the government, under the ordinance of Congress he was made one of the associate justices and justice of the peace. He was also commissioned clerk of the court of quarter sessions and prothonotary of the court of common pleas.

Colonel Meigs was commissary of the clothing department during the treaty of 1795, at Greenville. It was through his exertions that Joseph Kelly, the boy captive, was restored to his mother.

Washington county was ably represented in the first territorial legislature by Colonels Meigs and Oliver. This was an important session, and Colonel Meigs' intimate knowledge of affairs made him a superior member.

In 1801 he was appointed by President Jefferson Indian agent in the Cherokee nation, where he removed and resided until his death, which occured in 1823.

His family consisted of three sons—Return Jonathan, John, and Timothy. Colonel Meigs was held in the highest esteem in the army, in Marietta, and among the Indians, where he spent the evening of his busy life.

ARTHUR ST. CLAIR.

Arthur St. Clair, first and, practically, the only governor of the Northwest Territory, was born in Scotland in 1734.

He became a subaltern in the British army, and was detailed to America for duty during the French war. He was present at the storming of Quebec. In 1763 he was given command of Fort Ligonier, in Pennsylvania, where he settled and received one thousand acres of land. He sympathized with the colonies in their difficulties with Great Britain, and at the opening of the Revolution was given command of a regiment of continentals. He was afterwards promoted to the rank of brigadier general, and before the close of the war was made major general. He had command of Ticonderoga when it was captured by Burgoyne, and was charged with everything reflecting on his honor as a military man, but a court-martial sustained his conduct and fully exonerated him. His military career although not brilliant was creditable.

In 1785 he was elected a representative of Legonier, where he settled after the war, to the Continental Congress, and was afterwards chosen president of that body.

The Northwest Territory was formed in 1787, and General St. Clair received the appointment of governor. His home in Legonier, Westmoreland county, was known as "Pott's Grove." He had made some improvements when his duties called him to Ohio. In the winter of 1790 he removed to Marietta with all his family, excepting his wife, who remained to superintend the homestead. His household at Marietta consisted of a son, Arthur St. Clair, jr., and three daughters—Louisa, Jane, and Margaret, and an aged colored woman who acted as cook. Arthur studied law, and engaged in practice in Cincinnatti; Louisa was a young lady of eighteen; Jane was two years younger, "a girl of retiring manners and feeble constitution;" Margaret, the youngest child, died that year with fever. Louisa has been the subject of much comment. She was quick and vigorous both in mind and body. She seemed in her element amid the wild and dangerous surroundings of the period. She was often to be seen riding on a wild and spirited horse at full speed through the thick woods and over logs and streams. She was one of the best pedestrians at the garrison, and frequently came out victorious in walking or running races. She could shoot a rifle with the accuracy of a skilled woodsman, and was exceedingly fond of the chase. Although she had a passion for athletic sports, intellectual pursuits were by no means neglected. She had been educated with much care in Philadelphia.

Governor St. Clair was removed by President Jefferson a few months before the formation of the State Government in 1803. He had suffered great financial loss, and the last years of his life were spent in poverty. He returned to his Pennsylvania farm and in vain appealed to Congress for a bounty. The legislature of his State recognized his services by voting him an annuity of three hundred dollars, which was afterwards increased to six hundred. He died on his farm in the Legonier valley, August 31, 1818.

ICHABOD NYE.

Ichabod Nye was from Tolland, Connecticut. His ancestors, both on his mother's side and his father's were

English, and came from England to America in 1639. They were of those who came here to escape religious persecution. They first settled in Scituate, and then Barnstable, Massachusetts, the church to which they belonged coming over almost in a body. A part of the family after some years moved westward to Tolland, Connecticut. The father of Ichabod Nye was George Nye. His mother was Thankful Hinckley. George Nye owned a farm at Tolland on which he resided. December 21, 1763, Ichabod Nye was born. At the age of fifteen he was apprenticed to a tanner in Hadley, for the purpose of learning the trade. In this it was considered he had an advantage not shared by his brothers who were reared on the farm. It is probable that he finished his apprenticeship, though he entered the Revolutionary army at the early age of sixteen. Among the names of Revolutionary soldiers found at the State house in Boston is the following: "Ichabod Nye, age sixteen, five feet, eleven inches high, black hair; Colonel Porter's regiment, 1779." He afterwards served in Colonel Sear's regiment, which belonged to the northern army under Gates. He was with this branch of the army during the campaign which terminated with the surrender of Burgoyne at Saratoga.

In 1785 Ichabod Nye married Minerva, daughter of General Benjamin Tupper. At the close of the war they were residing with General Tupper, at Chesterfield, Massachusetts.

General Tupper, immediately on his return from the army in 1783, made known to his friends and neighbors his intention to go to the western territory. They regarded it as mere talk on his part. He, however, immediately set about the formation of the Ohio company. Mr. Nye has written: "I had engaged to come west to settle with him, and we began to prepare for the undertaking. Soon after the defeat of Shay I began to collect timber to build wagons, and went with a sleigh to Williamsburgh for timber of oak as there was none to be obtained in Chesterfield, nor was there a wagon fit for such a journey to be obtained in the State of Massachusetts, and but one man in our part of the State who could make one. I engaged him, however, and he built us two wagons, one for the family, or rather both families, and one for the goods and utensils belonging to them. With these we made our destination on the Ohio bank at Wellsburgh, Virginia, in company with Colonel Cushing and family, Major Goodale and family, and were joined there by Major Coburn and family, and his son-in-law, Andrew Webster and family. I left this company at Wellsburgh and came overland on the Virginia side with the horses and two hired men, reaching Marietta ten days before them." They descended the river in the Mayflower, which had been sent up for that purpose, and arrived at Marietta August 19, 1788. Their journey had occupied ten weeks, having been detained at Wellsburgh waiting for Major Coburn.

When these families arrived in Marietta, Campus Martius was in process of building, but not finished. They occupied such houses as they could obtain near Campus Martius, generally small log houses. General Tupper soon put up a dwelling in the Campus Martius, on the southwest side, on the ground afterwards

occupied by the residence of Ichabod Nye. In September, 1788, Mrs. Nye wrote as follows to some friends in New England: "We now live in the city of Marietta, where we expect to end our days. We find the country much more delightsome than we had any idea of." And in November Miss Rowena Tupper writes: "The country has been so often spoken of that it is needless for me to say more than that it answers every expectation." In 1790 Mr. Nye began to sink vats for a tanyard in the extreme northern portion of the town on Seventh street. These vats were built from the timbers of the boat in which his brother, Ebenezer Nye, had descended the river, and were the first tan vats in the Northwestern Territory. This situation was during the Indian war, which soon followed, a hazardous one, but no attack was made upon him there. He afterwards sunk some vats near the upper end of Third street, but the ground was unfavorable, and he finally erected buildings near the corner of Seventh and Putnam streets, where the main building of the chair company now stands. At that time Putnam street was not opened beyond Fifth. It was at this place that the heaviest part of his business was carried on. His customers were from all parts of the surrounding country, and the reputation of the leather made there was of the highest character.

During the Indian war Mr. Nye lived in General Tupper's house in Campus Martius. His brother, Ebenezer Nye, with his family and Mrs. Kelley (a widow) with her children, lived in the southeast block-house. After the close of the war Ichabod Nye purchased the southwest block-house, which had been the residence of Governor St. Clair, and resided there until 1814. He owned four lots on the south end of the square, north of Scammel street, and he left the stockade and lived for a time in a house standing on the lot corner of front and Scammel. In 1820 he built his dwelling house on the stockade, where he resided during the remainder of his life, and where two of his sons have always lived until 1880. In 1809 he erected the brick store on Putnam street, now (1881) occupied by Jacob Pfaff as a bakery. The upper story was used for the Masonic lodge hall; the lower story for a store. In the spring of 1810 he opened a store in this building, in which he kept dry goods, groceries, shoes—in fact such goods as were in demand. In August, 1813, he entered into a partnership with Mr. Charles Shipman, and they removed the goods to Athens and opened a store there under charge of Mr. Shipman, then a young man. In 1816 this partnership was dissolved and Mr. Nye reopened his store on Putnam street, Marietta. He had also formed, in 1805, a partnership with Colonel Benjamin Tupper, his brother-in-law, and they had opened a store in Springfield, now the Ninth ward of Zanesville, Ohio. He afterwards withdrew from this partnership, and established two of his sons in the mercantile business with himself, one under the firm name of I. & A. Nye, and the other A. Nye & Co. These were also in Springfield. He finally transferred the goods from the Marietta store and the store of I. & A. Nye, in Putnam, to Waterford, Ohio. In March, 1819,

A. T. Nye took charge of the business there, and in 1824 he purchased the stock and continued the business under his own name. After 1824, Mr. Ichabod Nye had no further interest in mercantile business.

Colonel Nye, as he was always called, having been commissioned in militia about 1804, was very little engaged in public business. He was a subscriber to Muskingum academy, and was always interested in educational matters. He was a member of the Masonic lodge in Marietta. In his youth his opportunities for obtaining an education were limited, but he was a man who read a great deal, and of the very best, and he also kept himself well informed on all public affairs. He had a strong and vigorous mind, and generally formed his own opinions. He was strongly attached to the administration of General Washington, and belonged to the Federal party as long as that party existed, and afterwards to the Whig party. He died November 27, 1840. His first wife, Minerva Tupper, died April 20, 1836. Their children who survived infancy were: Horace, Panthea, who married Rothius Hayward, of Waterford, Ohio; Arius, Anselm Tupper, Sophia, who married Rev. Cyrus Byington, of the Choctaw Mission; Rowena, who married William Pitt Putnam, of Belpre; Huldah, died June 22, 1838, not married; Ichabod Hinckley, Edward White. The only children who now survive (1881) are Anselm T. Nye, born in Campus Martius, November 9, 1797, and Edward White Nye, born April 13, 1812. Ichabod Hinckly Nye, so well known and highly esteemed in Marietta, died at the homestead, on the stockade, in June, 1880. Colonel Nye married, in 1840, Mrs. Rebecca Howe Beebe, who survived him some years.

Ebenezer Nye, brother of Ichabod Nye, settled in Rainbow. His descendants live in Athens, Meigs and Muskingum counties. From these two brothers are descended all of the name in southeastern Ohio, who are of English descent.

REBECCA GILMAN.

The centre of a circle of cultured intellects during the period of early settlement was Rebecca Ives Gilman, wife of Joseph Gilman. She was the daughter of Benjamin Ives and granddaughter of Hon. Robert Hall, under whose direction a fine mind was store with useful information, and a taste cultivated for polite literature. Her early associties were people of culture and education.

Mrs. Gilman was bright and fascinating in conversation. Her friendship was much sought and highly valued. But she never permitted her polite studies to interfere with domestic duty. She is described as a model housekeeper and mother. After the death of her husband in 1806, she lived in her own house at Harmar until 1812, when she removed with her son, Benjamin Ives Gilman, to Philadelphia, where she died in 1820.

MRS. MARY LAKE.

The name of Mary Lake was for many years a household word in the pioneer families of Marietta. Her example both in the Revolution and here demonstrated the capability of a kind hearted, strong minded woman in seasons of distress. Mary Bird was born in Bristol, England, in 1742. At the age of twenty she married Archibald Lake, a seaman, and moved to St. John, New Foundland. Here he followed fishing until the place came into possession of the French, when he removed to New York and engaged in ship building. New York at an early period of the war was occupied by the British, and Mrs. Luke determined to be of use to her adopted countrymen, for she enlisted heartily in the American cause, deserted the city and went into the hospitals at Fishkill and then at New Windsor, where she was the comforting angel of many suffering soldiers. The war over her husband was at a loss for profitable employment, and welcomed the news of the opening of the new territory west of the Ohio, where he could find a home.

The family came to Marietta in 1789. Mrs. Lake's kindness of heart and skill in the sick room were soon found out. Her superior intelligence and purity of character, placed her in high esteem in the new settlement. In the spring of 1790 small-pox broke out in Campus Martius. Most of the physicians were young, and knew little of the disease. Her experienced services during this trying period were found of the highest value.

Mrs. Lake was a lady af intense purity, and wore all the graces of pure religion. She taught the first Sunday-school in the territory, and it has been said the second in America, but there is good ground for disputing this statement. After the regular preaching service, Mrs. Lake gathered the children about her and instructed them from the Westminister catechism and the Bible.

After the peace in 1795, she moved to the Rainbow settlement on the Muskingum, where she died in 1802, leaving an estimable family.

ISAAC AND REBECCA WILLIAMS.

During the toilsome period of early settlement two inhabitants of Virginia by kind offices so endeared themselves to the residents of this side, that a sketch of their lives belongs in this volume. The village facing the mouth of the Muskingum bears their name.

Isaac Williams was born in Pennsylvania in 1737. In early life his parents removed to Winchester, Virginia, then a frontier town. He was fond of hunting, and soon became acquainted with the out of the way places of the wild country in which he lived. When he was eighteen years old the Colonial Government employed him as a spy to watch the movements of the Indians. He served in the army of General Braddock, and was connected with the military movements in the west during the French and Indian war. He was one of the first settlers of Brooks county, West Virginia. He removed west about 1769. He had previously visited the Ohio on hunting and trapping expeditions, which he made annually. He accumulated large tracts of land by making entries under the Virginia laws. Clearing and planting one acre in corn entitled the holder to four hundred dollars.

While residing in Brooks county he became acquainted with and married Rebecca Martin, a widow. Her first husband had been killed by the Indians.

Mr. Williams accompanied Lord Dunmore in his campaign against the Indians in 1774, and was present when the treaty was made near Chillicothe. Mrs. Williams had come to Virginia in 1771, and was living with her brothers near the mouth of Grave creek. While living here an incident occurred which proves that she was a very remarkable woman. She made an expedition to her sister's, fifty miles down the river, in a canoe. On her return, night overtook her, and she determined to go ashore and wait for the rising of the moon. On returning she found it necessary to wade a few steps to reach the canoe. When just in the act of stepping on board her foot rested on the cold, dead body of an Indian who had been murdered a few days before. Without screaming, she stepped into the canoe and rowed on her way homeward.

In the spring of 1773 Joseph and Samuel Tomlinson, her brothers, entered four hundred acres of land in the bottom opposite the mouth of the Muskingum, which they presented to their sister Rebecca, in consideration for previous services. In 1786, Fort Harmer having been built and garrisoned, Mr. and Mrs. Williams desired to occupy their land. Saplings had grown on the clearing made fifteen years before, but the land was easily reduced to a state of cultivation.

This early settlement on the Virginia side was a fortunate circumstance for the early settlers of Marietta. Mr. Williams, by the time the New England colony arrived, had his farm under a good state of cultivation, and during the distressing famine of 1790 supplied the hungry pioneers on the other side of the river with corn, of which he had a large crop. Speculators, always ready to take advantage of people's misfortunes, urged him to take a dollar and a quarter a bushel for his whole crop. "Dod rot 'em," said the old man, "I would not let 'em have a bushel." When a purchaser came he proportioned the number of bushels to the number of members in the family, in order that he might be able to serve all alike. He charged no one more than fifty cents per bushel, the current price in plentiful years. In the fullest sense he improved his opportunity for doing good.

Rebecca was skilled in the healing art, and often relieved distressed pioneers and hunters by the application of simple remedies. Mr. and Mrs. Williams were always social, clever, and kind. They liberated their slaves in later years, and left them substantial tokens of friendship. Mr. Williams never missed an opportunity to indulge his passion for hunting, even in his old age. The citizens of Marietta mourned his death in September, 1820, as one of their own number.

COLONEL WILLIAM STACEY.

Colonel William Stacey, a man highly esteemed for his many excellent qualities, and honored for his services and sufferings in the cause of freedom, has many descendants yet living in the county. He was a native of Massachusetts, and when the outbreak at Lexington aroused American patriotism, he was the first member of the New Salem militia company to renounce his allegiance to the king. The company was reorganized, and entered the American service with Mr. Stacey as captain.

In 1778 Captain Stacey was promoted to the rank of lieutenant colonel of Colonel Ichabod Alden's regiment of the Massachusetts line. He was with his regiment on the perilous campaign, in 1778, against the Indians and tories in the Cherry valley, New York, and was a witness of the slaughter of November 11th in Oneida county. Colonel Stacey was here taken prisoner, and was taken a distance of about two hundred miles to an Indian village near the present site of Geneva. After a council of the chiefs he was sentenced to be burned. The Indians were under the command of Joseph Brant whom Colonel Stacey saw in the surrounding crowd, while the fires were being kindled under him. It is said that he gave Brant the sign of Free Masonry, and that that chief, whose word was law, directed his release.

Colonel Stacey was held as a prisoner by the Indians for four years. After his release he returned to his farm at New Salem until 1789, when he removed with his five sons and one son-in-law with their family to Marietta. Two of the sons, John and Philemon, were victims of the attack on Big Bottom, January 2, 1791. John was killed, and Philemon was taken prisoner, and died in captivity. Gideon, the youngest son, settled in New Orleans, and established a ferry across Lake Pontchatrain. The remaining member of the family settled in this county.

After the death of his first wife Colonel Stacey married Mrs. Sheffield, a lady of high rank. He died at Marietta in 1804.

MAJOR ANSELM TUPPER.

Anselm Tupper, eldest son of General Benjamin Tupper, came to Marietta as one of the surveyors of the Ohio company, April 7, 1788. Previous to that time he had been in the western country with his father, engaged in the survey of one of the seven ranges.

General Tupper entered the service of his country immediately after the battle of Bunker Hill. At that time his son Anselm was very young, only thirteen, but he was with his father in an engagement on North river, in August, 1776. In 1779 when sixteen years of age, he received the appointment of adjutant in the regiment of Colonel Sproat, of the Massachusetts line, in which position he served until the close of the war. This regiment was engaged at Trenton, Princeton, Monmouth and other battles. Major Tupper enjoyed the confidence and personal friendship of his commanding officer.

Immediately upon their arrival at the Muskingum,

in 1788, the surveyors began their work, and continued it until driven into the forts by the hostility of the Indians. During the Indian war Major Tupper lived in Campus Martius. He taught the first school opened there, in the northwest block-house. He was a man of intellectual ability, and especially in mathematics had the reputation of being a good scholar. He is said to have possessed a refined and polished address, and was of fine personal appearance and military bearing. An oil portrait exists, representing him when very young, in the uniform of the Massachusetts regimental officers. He was appointed post major of Campus Martius, and continued in this position during the war. He was the favorite of the officers in the garrison, especially of Colonel Sproat, and his wit sometimes in verse, seemed to give them great satisfaction, though at their expense. On one occasion, when Colonel Sproat was left behind in a foot race with Dr. Story, the minister, Major Tupper wrote some lines, in which the following gave a momentary offence to Colonel Sproat:

It was a point, they all gave in,
Divinity could outstrip sin.

Some poetic pieces were written by him in connection with Masonic celebrations, he being a member of the Masonic lodge. His verses generally had for their subject some local event, among others "The Indian Feast," to commemorate the dinner given to the Indian chiefs at Campus Martius. Another piece was a parody on the "Battle of the Kegs," and was called the "Battle of the Muskingum," a humorous account of the affairs which occurred at Marietta in connection with the capture of Blennerhassett's boats, usually called Burr's flotilla. This was published in a Lancaster paper, and afterwards in Safford's Life of Blennerhassett.

About 1801 Edward W. Tupper engaged in ship building in Marietta. One of his vessels, the Indiana, was built five miles up the Muskingum. Another, called the Orlando, was built at the foot of Putnam street, Marietta. The Orlando went out under the command of Captain Matthew Miner, and Major Tupper went out as second officer. The vessel arrived at New Orleans the fourth of July, 1804, and found the city in great commotion, celebrating the first fourth of July since the cession of Louisiana to the United States Government. They then crossed the Atlantic to the Mediterranean sea, up to Trieste, at the head of the Adriatic. She was sold, and Major Tupper returned home by way of England. After his return to America he went to Gallipolis, to be with his brother Edward. His health failing, he returned home to Marietta, where he died, December, 1808, at the house of his sister, Mrs. Ichabod Nye. He is buried in Mound cemetery, by the side of his father, and near his old friend and commander, Colonel Sproat.

COLONEL BENJAMIN TUPPER.

Benjamin Tupper, youngest son of General Tupper, was born in Chesterfield, Massachusetts. He came to Marietta with his father in 1788. In 1802 he married Martha, daughter of General Rufus Putnam. For several years he was receiver of the United States land office at Marietta. In 1806 he removed to Springfield, afterwards Putnam, Ohio, and entered into a mercantile business with his brother-in-law, Ichabod Nye. He afterwards formed another partnership, which continued until his death, in 1814. Of his children but one is now (1881) living, Mrs. Catharine Munam, of Zanesville, Ohio. His only son, Benjamin, died some years since. His youngest grandson, Theodore Tupper, died on the battlefield at Shiloh, at the age of nineteen. His body was not recovered. In his death the name of Tupper became extinct in the family line of General Benjamin Tupper.

GENERAL JOSEPH BUELL.

General Buell was not a member of the Ohio company, but he was a soldier who spent two years in the western country before the pioneers arrived. The greater part of those two years he spent at Fort Harmar. He kept a diary, in which he describes the country west of the Ohio and the people who were then in it, and mentions many occurrences which, though apparently of small moment then, are now eagerly sought for as matters of history. In trying to reproduce some of the events of his life, we shall not dwell upon his ancestry or early youth. He was from Killingworth, Connecticut, where he was born February 16, 1760. His parents were David and Mary (Hurd) Buell, and he was the second of their twelve children. His first ancestor in America was William (1630), whose eldest son, Samuel, settled in Killingworth, now Clinton, Connecticut, in 1664.

At the age of twenty-two, in September, 1785, Joseph Buell conducted a company of ninety-four recruits for the army from Hartford, Connecticut, to West Point, in the capacity of orderly sergeant. At West Point the men were assigned to Captain Strong's company of Colonel Harmar's regiment. November 20th the company was ordered to the western frontier. They marched across the mountains and arrived at Fort McIntosh, at the mouth of Beaver river, on the Ohio, December 26, 1785, where they remained in barracks during the remainder of the winter. May 4, 1786, Captain Strong's company and that of Captain Zeigler embarked for the mouth of the Muskingum, where, on the west point, Fort Harmar had been built, though not completely finished, in the fall of 1785. They reached the fort on the eighth, but encamped outside at the edge of some woods until the tenth, when Captain Zeigler's company proceeded down the Ohio to the Miami, and Captain Strong's company moved into Fort Harmar.

On the twenty-seventh of May, 1787, Captain Strong's company was ordered to report at Post St. Vincent, now Vincennes. They descended the river in two keel-boats to Fort Finney, opposite Louisville, which they reached on the thirty-first. There they remained until July 8th, when they started for Post St. Vincent, arriving there on the nineteenth. After a very sickly summer, in which nearly half the men were unfit for duty, they were ordered to return to Fort Harmar, at which place they arrived November 21st.

The succeeding summer was spent at Fort Harmar. Early in November Sergeant Buell obtained his discharge and returned to Connecticut.

In August, 1788, Sergeant Buell purchased four hundred acres of land of Judge Symmes, at half a dollar an acre, paying one-half in cash, the other half to be paid in one year. It was his intention when he bought this to settle in the Miami country, of which he writes, "I think it exceeds any part of the western world." Whatever may have been Mr. Buell's plans for ultimate settlement, he set his face toward home as soon as he had received his discharge from the army, and reached Killingworth November 27, 1788. After visiting his friends he taught school for three months, at the same time trying to perfect his plans for returning to the western country for settlement. February 15, 1789, he was married to Siba Hand. He seems to have felt much doubt about taking her into the new country, but finally decided to do so. He visited Mr. Joshua Shipman, of Saybrook, and bargained with him to furnish half the wagon and half the team which was to carry the two families to Ohio. By the first of May, however, Mr. Shipman had given up the plan, and this, with other difficulties, led Mr. Buell to leave his wife in New England for two years. In May, 1789, he set out for Marietta with his brother, Timothy, afterwards sheriff of Washington county. Arriving safely at Marietta, Mr. Buell was joined by his friend, Mr. Levi Munsell, with whom he had been associated in the army, and they went to North Bend to join Judge Symmes' colony. Probably from fear of the Indians they soon returned to Marietta, many others leaving North Bend for the same reason.

In 1790 Messrs. Buell and Munsell opened a tavern at the Point, Marietta. This was a large frame building, and it was erected in 1789 on the lots at the corner of Front and Green streets. The frame of the building was made at the headwaters of the Ohio and floated down to Marietta. During the Indian war it was within the enclosure which formed the "Point" garrison. At this time Messrs. Buell and Munsell both lived there—Mrs. Buell having joined her husband in 1790, and Mr. Munsell having married a daughter of Colonel Alexander Oliver, of Belpre.

In 1795, peace having been declared, life was once more infused into the plans of the colonists; men left the garrisons and went to their farms; others engaged in occupations in town. Mr. Buell remained in Marietta, and built for his own residence, in 1801, a brick house, on the corner of Green and Second streets. This house is still standing, and is said to be the oldest brick house in the State of Ohio. He also built, a year or two later, the brick house on "Boiler corner." The tavern business was continued under the charge of Mr. Munsell, and became about 1801 very remunerative to the proprietors. Owing to the activity in the business of ship-building, many carpenters, calkers, and other artisans connected

with the business came into Marietta, and they largely patronized this tavern. In August, 1807, there were five ships on the stocks at Marietta. Soon after, in consequence of the embargo, the business was suddenly discontinued, and several prominent business men failed and left Marietta, and laborers connected with them were obliged to seek employment elsewhere. The tavern business suffered in consequence. Mr. Munsell left Marietta in a few years, and General Buell died in 1812; but the tavern was kept as a public house by other parties until about 1830. In 1832 Mr. Joseph Holden, who had bought the property, pulled down the old frame and erected brick buildings on the lots, in which he engaged in a mercantile business. About thirty years after, these buildings were remodelled (having escaped the great fire of 1859), and finally became the property of the First National bank.

From the time that Mr. Buell decided to make Marietta his home he took an active interest in all that concerned the welfare of the town, especially in civil, political, and military affairs. In the early days of Marietta all were adherents of General Washington, and of his administration. A few years later party strife arose and Marietta people became divided in political sentiment. Mr. Buell became an adherent of Jefferson's administration. He was elected a member of the senate of the State of Ohio and served in the first, second, third and fourth assemblies—1803 to 1805. His military service had fitted him to take part in military affairs and he was appointed major general of militia, a position at that time a very responsible one. While he was major general the so called "Burr conspiracy" arose, and Marietta became the scene of considerable military activity. In December, 1806, General Buell received an order from the governor for the arrest of Blennerhassett and the prevention of certain "acts hostile to the tranquility and peace of the United States,"—i. e. the departure of the boats intended for the Burr expedition from the Muskingum. Acting under this authority, General Buell, with characteristic energy and method, took measures to arrest the batteaux, which had been building at Judge Joseph Barker's, on the Muskingum river. "These boats," writes one who saw them, "were very frail, built like a skiff, sharp at both ends, and sided up with thin weatherboarding and covered. There were ten of them, of two or three tons each, and they were built under contract of Mr. Blennerhassett with Colonel Barker. They were called in derision 'Burr's flotilla.'"

One evening in December, 1806, the company of militia from the Point (there were two companies in Marietta), passed up Front street to the Washington street landing. They entered a building there and prepared to remain for the night. Their purpose was not understood by those who saw them, and it was thought singular that the militia should be out at that hour. In the morning it became known that they had arrested nine of Burr's flotilla while attempting to pass down the river—one boat having gone on in the darkness.

A Marietta man, blind in one eye, named Clark Green, had sole charge of two of these boats to bring them down the river; two sons of Green, about eleven and twelve years old, managed another, and had one man each to work the balance—except one—and guide them. The boat which passed by had on it three young men from Belpre. The boats were taken by the militia down into the mouth of the run below Putnam street. They laid in the run until they began to decay, and in time men and boys broke them up and carried them off in pieces. A lot of parched corn taken from them was stored in General Buell's barn, and the academy boys used to go there and help themselves to it, filling their pockets. Mr. Blennerhassett made no effort to recover his property but was obliged to flee from his home.

After the arrest of the boats General Buell proclaimed martial law, and the militia was ordered to be in readiness to appear, "armed and equipped as the law directs," immediately on the firing of the cannon. There was but one cannon in town. In the guard-house, a building which stood on Ohio street just above the "Boiler corner," a constant guard was kept. A gun was placed on the river bank, and all boats passing down the Ohio river were hailed and stopped; and as a further precaution all boats passing down the Muskingum were brought over to Marietta. These measures were taken in order to be prepared for any attempt to rescue the captured batteaux from the direction of Blennerhassett's island, and to stop any men or supplies which might attempt to pass down to aid Burr's expedition. The whole country from Pittsburgh to New Orleans was in a state of great excitement, and Burr made no attempt to resist but endeavored to conceal himself.

General Buell had no sympathy with Aaron Burr. When Burr was in Marietta, General Buell was living in a brick house* which he had erected on "Boiler corner." In this house he entertained Burr at dinner. Mrs. Buell in after years told her children that she "somewhat anxiously watched her husband on that occasion to see whether Burr's insinuating talk had any influence on her husband, and that he failed to enlist sympathy." In carrying out the orders of the governor, General Buell obeyed as a soldier, having no other idea than to do his duty. The position of major general he held until his death. Form 1803 to 1810 General Buell was associate judge in the court of common pleas. The appointment to this office under the State Constitution of 1802 was made by the legislature.

During his life, and at the time of his death, he owned a large number of city lots in Marietta. At one time he owned nearly all of square No. 57, below the alley which connects Front street and Canal street, and the greater part of the square on which his dwelling stood, with parts of "Flat-iron square." These lots lying on Front, Green, Second and Ohio streets, are now many of them occupied by business houses. Other lots lay further out on Green street, beyond Fourth, and some on the plain. At the time of his death he also owned

over two thousand five hundred acres of land in the counties of Washington, Athens, and Meigs.

General Buell died in Marietta, June 13, 1812. He is buried in Mound cemetery. Mrs. Buell died in 1831. Of their eight children, those best known in Marietta were: Daniel Hand, Hiram Augustas, Joseph and Siba (Mrs. William Slocomb).

Daniel Hand Buell, the eldest child of General Joseph Buell, was born October 1, 1790. His early childhood was spent in the garrison at the Point. When of a suitable age he was sent to New England to be educated, returning to Marietta when about twenty-one years of age, he spent the remainder of his life in that place. While he was still a young man his father died, and the management of the estate and the care of the family interests devolved chiefly upon him. In 1814 he was engaged in editing the newspaper called the *American Friend,* of which he was one of the owners. He was one of the founders of Marietta library in 1829, which was for many years an institution highly prized by the reading public. As a public man he stood high in the estimation of his fellow citizens, and held several important offices. He was for many years justice of the peace, and was mayor of the city. June, 1817, to October, 1834, he was county recorder. From 1825 to 1829 he was postmaster. In 1839 he was county commissioner. He was in the latter part of his life an earnest worker for the Episcopal church in Marietta, of which he was a member, doing much to aid it financially, and performing the office of lay reader when the church was destitute of a pastor. After a long and painful illness he died, October 12, 1843. His second wife, Theodosia Hall Buell, survived him and died in 1875. His sons became citizens of Marietta. Charles Ferdinand, the eldest, died June, 1881. He was a member of the Marietta bar. Edward W. and William H. Buell entered the drug business as partners when they were very young. They were also largely engaged as partners in the oil business for several years previous to 1869. Edward W. Buell died in May, 1875.

Hiram A. Buell, fourth son of General Joseph Buell, was born in Marietta, May 29, 1801, and was well known in that place when a young man. He was for some years in the recorder's office as an assistant, and was also engaged in other business in connection with his brother, Daniel H. Buell. In 1833 he left Marietta and went to Holly, in western New York, where he established himself in business as a merchant, with his brother, Joseph. This partnership, cemented by brotherly affection, was dissolved by the death of Hiram A. Buell, February 24, 1875.

Joseph Hand Buell, born February 22, 1809, the youngest child of General Joseph Buell, left Marietta and engaged in business with his brother Hiram, in Holly, New York, where he still resides.

REV. DANIEL STORY.

Dr. Cutler was happy in his selection of a chaplian for the Ohio company. Dr. Story was well qualified for the

---

* This house covered the same ground as the house which now stands on that corner. The present house was built by Mr. Woodbridge.

place which he filled for about fifteen years, first in the employ of the Ohio company and then of the Congregational church, or of the First Religious society as it was known.

He was born in Boston in 1755. Judge Story, the emminent lawyer, was his uncle. He graduated at Dartmouth college. Dr. Story's connection with the religious history of the early settlement has been sufficiently sketched elsewhere. His services in the ministry before coming to Marietta gave promise of usefulness and the choice of Dr. Cutler was received with great satisfaction. His sermons were logical and scholarly, his conversation interesting and his manners agreeable. The last two circumstances were particularly fortunate, for his salary was extremely meagre and generous friends had to be depended upon for relief. He was compelled to mortgage his property in New England to support his contingent expenses, and after death his estate was found insolvent. He severed his connection with the church as pastor March 15, 1804, on account of poor health. His death occurred on the 15th of the following December.

FREDERICK J. CUTTER.

Frederick J. Cutter, son of Lewis J. Cutter, sr., and Eve E. (Wagner) Cutter, was born in Watertown township, Washington county, Ohio, October 5, 1839. In the spring of 1842 his father moved to Union township, where he had bought a farm in the fall of 1841. Frederick remained on the farm with his father until the spring of 1854, when he engaged to drive team on the Marietta & Cincinnati railroad, then building, about two miles below Harmar. He continued to work there until the August following, when he returned home.

In September, 1855, he began work for the Hon. W. P. Cutler on his farm about six miles below Marietta; continuing there until November, 1859. The last three winters he was with Mr. Cutler he attended school, doing chores mornings and evenings to pay for his board. In December, 1859, young Cutter went to Cincinnati and that winter attended Gundry's Commercial college. The next spring he was employed in a furniture store, where he continued until about December, 1860. Not being satisfied with the education received up to that time, he determined if possible, to find a situation where he could earn enough to pay expenses and go to school at the same time. About January, 1861, he secured a route of the Cincinnati *Daily Gazette*, which he kept until June, 1865.

In the fall of 1861 he entered Herron's seminary in Cincinnati, which school he attended until June, 1864, when it was closed in consequence of the death of Prof. Herron, the principal. He then attended Professor Clive's private school in the same city, one year.

By the preparation thus obtained Mr. Cutter was enabled in 1865 to enter the Sophomore class of Marietta college, graduating in 1868 with Rev. W. H. Pearce, now deceased, Professor W. G. Ballantine, and Theodore D. Dale, esq. Rev. D. W. Rhodes, Professor H.

P. Smith of Lane seminary, Rev. H. M. Walker, Charles H. Turner and J. M. Fuller were also members of his class, but none of them, except Mr. Fuller, graduated at Marietta. Two of the winters while at college he taught school to earn means to defray expenses. Mr. Cutter entered college largely upon the advice of Mr. Cutler, who, while the former was working for him, had kindly promised any necessary aid in getting through the college course.

For two years after graduating his time was divided between teaching school and working at home on the farm. In June, 1870, Mr. Cutter took entire charge of the home farm, his father, on account of age, being no longer able to attend to it.

In the fall of 1872 he began reading law with Hon. T. W. Ewart, in connection with his farm labor; and was admitted to the bar in April, 1875. After his admission he remained in the law office of Ewart & Sibley until December, 1876, when he engaged in the practice on his own account, so continuing until the present time, building up quite a good practice. He has also managed the affairs of the farm in connection with his law practice.

In the fall of 1873 Mr. Cutter was elected one of the managers of the Washington County Agricultural and Mechanical association, and continued to serve in that capacity, with the exception of one year, until March, 1880, when he was elected president of the association. In the fall of the same year he was reelected to serve for the year 1881.

In politics Mr. Cutter has always been a Republican, beginning first to take an interest in politics during the memorable campaign of 1860. Since his graduation in 1868 he has been each year connected with campaign work in his county, either as a member of the central or of the county executive committees, having served as secretary of the former for 1876 and 1877, and of the latter from 1878 to 1881. In 1878 he was the Republican candidate for probate judge, but his party being in the minority in the county at that time was defeated with the rest of the ticket. During 1877 and 1878 he served as deputy United States marshal for Washington county, which is the only office of a political nature he ever held. He drew up the application for, and was mainly instrumental in, securing the establishment of the Churchtown postoffice and the tri-weekly mail between Watertown and Marietta.

He also drew the petition for the division of Union township among the four adjoining townships, and the success of that project was due, in a great measure, to his efforts.

Mr. Cutter, in 1879, took quite an active and prominent part in the movement to build free bridges across the Muskingum river. He served as secretary of the free bridge campaign committee, with Dr. P. H. Kelley, of Waterford, as chairman.

In religion, Mr. Cutter was brought up in the Lutheran faith. He was at first a member of the German Lutheran church, of Watertown; afterwards, of the English Lutheran church, of Cincinnati; and, in the spring of 1874, he transferred his membership to the Presbyterian church, of Watertown. While in Cincinnati, he was connected with the Union Bethel Sunday-school as a teacher, from February, 1860, to June, 1865.

His parents were both born in Durkeim, Bavaria, Germany, and came to this country in 1838. His father was born March 7, 1799, and died February 15, 1874. His mother, born January 23, 1807, is still living. There were five sons and seven daughters in the family, all of whom are living, except his brother William, who was a member of company B, seventy-seventh Ohio volunteers, and was killed in the battle of Jenkin's Ferry, on the Saline river, Arkansas, April 30, 1864. His brother Lewis was also a member of the same company, and was a prisoner for ten months in Camp Ford, near Tyler, Texas, having been captured at Marks Mills, Arkansas, April 25, 1864.

GOVERNOR RETURN JONATHAN MEIGS.

The oldest son of Colonel R. J. Meigs was Ohio's first governor, R. J. Meigs, jr., who was born in Middle-town, Connecticut, in the year 1675. He graduated at Yale college in his twentieth year, and was admitted to the bar of his native State. In his younger years he was much given to writing poetry, but never had an ambition to come before the public as a poet. His compositions were generally of a light character, written for amusement and recreation. In 1788 he married Miss Sophia Wright and the same year came to Marietta, where he engaged in professional pursuits and farming.

After the organization of the State government, Mr. Meigs was elected chief justice of the Supreme court, which consisted of three judges. This situation was at that time difficult, as he was required to hold court in every county in the State once a year. He discharged the duties of this distinguished position until October, 1804, when he received the appointment of colonel and commandant of the upper part of the district of Louisiana which included the greater part of the Mississippi valley. In 1805, he was appointed one of the judges of the territory, a position more congenial to his tastes.

The seat of justice in Upper Louisiana, was at St. Louis. It once became the duty of Judge Meigs to pronounce sentence of death upon an Indian convicted of murder. After the execution on the same day a large athletic Indian whom he endeavored to prevent injuring some women and children on the street, assailed him with a tomahawk and struck him several times on the head, cutting through his hat at every stroke. At last seizing the Indian by the arm, he wrested the tomahawk from him and threw it away. Furious at this occurrence, the Indian sprang upon him like a tiger, Mr. Meigs being unable to retain a grip on his naked adversary. The Indian had a belt around him from which in the scuffle he attempted to draw a large knife. A young gentleman, Mr. Hammond, seeing the knife, half removed from its scabbard, and not doubting the purpose for which it was being removed, approached with a pistol and shot the Indian in the back. He let go the knife, started back and fell dead. This is one of a number of Governor Meigs' perilous situations. Once during the Indian war he narrowly escaped from an encounter with a party of Indians on the bank of the Muskingum. While at Detroit acting as diplomat for Governor St. Clair, he was one day leisurely standing on a boat. An Indian on the shore was aiming his rifle. At that instant a white man standing near, snatched the gun from the Indian's hands and shook out the priming. Upon one occasion while reviewing some troops at St. Louis, a salute was fired. A musket was fired, loaded with buck-shot, many of which passed through his vest, cravat and ruffles of his shirt, and one of his epaulets was cut away. This occurrence was altogether accidental.

While serving as judge in Louisiana his health gave way, and he returned to Marietta in 1806 much enfeebled. In April, 1807, he was commissioned judge of the territory of Michigan. He resigned his commission in October and accepted the candidacy for governor of Ohio. This was one of the most exciting campaigns in the early politics of the State. His competitor was General Nathaniel Massie, one of the earliest settlers of the Scioto valley. Meigs received a majority of the votes but his election was contested on the ground that he had not been a resident of the State four years as required by the constitution. The contest resulted in favor of Massie. The contest did not seem to impair his popularity, for at the same session of the legislature he was elected supreme judge, and in September following was chosen to fill the unexpired term of John Smith in the United States senate. He was subsequently reelected senator for the full term.

The campaign of 1810 was one of the most bitter in Ohio political history. An act of the legislature increasing the jurisdiction of justices of the peace had been decided unconstitutional by the supreme court. Politicians endeavored to gain favor with the people by making the discussion appear to have been rendered in favor of a class and in opposition to popular rights. The majority in the legislature pandered to prejudice and passed the "sweeping resolution," a measure intended to remove a number of judges that their places might be filled by members of what was known as the "popular" party. Tammany societies were organized in different parts of the State for the purpose of making nominations and controlling the election. These societies were secret, and in order to insure fidelity an oath was imposed upon the members. General Worthington was their candidate for governor. The opposition was sensible of the necessity of making the strongest possible nominations. Senator Meigs was finally selected to make the race and was elected by two thousand majority. His inaugural address was remarkably strong. In it he enunciated a principle of his private life and public policy. "Public excellence ascends from domestic purity and just principles, extending from families to communities, enlarges the sphere of utility and give to patriotism its proudest devotion."

Governor Meigs' administration extended over a trying and difficult period. His management of affairs during the opening period of the War of 1812 was by no means free from criticism, but the honesty of his intentions and the wisdom of his general policy were recognized by the people, who a third time elected him to the chief magistracy of the State by an increased majority.

During his second term of office he was called, in 1814, by President Madison, to the position of postmaster general. He discharged the duties of this important position until June, 1823, when he tendered his resignation. It is not surprising that he was accused of mismanagement of public affairs. The criticism of political opponents is not necessarily an imputation against the character of an official. Governor Meigs had the confidence of Madison and Monroe. Mr. Monroe observed at the time of his resignation: "I have never had but one opinion towards you since the commencement of the war, when you were governor, and that was friendship. I believe you to be an honest man and a friend of your country. I wish you to retain your office as long as I remain President. If you resign it must be from considerations purely your own."

After his resignation, which closed a long term of public service, Governor Meigs retired to his home in Marietta, where he died March 29, 1825.

Governor Meigs was held in high personal regard among the citizens of Marietta. He was the first post master, and is said to have been quite social among the friends of his youth without regard to their condition in life. He at one time owned a square of land on which he erected in 1806 the finest house in town. The house was not completed for several years afterwards. It is now owned by M. D. Follett. His land extended from Scammel to below the Congregational church lot on Front street. An old citizen relates an incident which proves him to have been large hearted. In 1816 the corn crop was generally a failure, and those possessing this necessary article for food could command almost any price. It happened that Governor Meigs that year had an exceptionally good crop, for which speculators offered tempting prices. He directed that the corn should be sold at the low price of former years, and in small quantities, thus giving poor people an opportunity of supplying their families with this staple food.

On the stone erected to his memory is inscribed the following epitaph, written by Dr. John Cotton:

Here lies the body of
RETURN JONATHAN MEIGS,
Who was born at Middletown, Connecticut, 1765,
And died at Marietta, March 29, 1825.
For many years his time and talents were devoted
To the service of his country.
He successively filled the distinguished places of
Judge of the Territory Northwest of the Ohio,
Judge of the Supreme Court of the State of Ohio,
Senator in the Congress of the United States,
Governor of the State of Ohio, and
Postmaster General of the United States.
To the honored and revered memory of
An ardent Patriot,
A practical Statesman,
An enlightened Scholar,
A dutiful Son,

An indulgent Father,
An affectionate Husband,
This monument is erected by his mourning widow,
SOPHIA MEIGS.

EPHRAIM CUTLER.

Ephraim Cutler, the eldest son of Rev. Dr. Manasseh Cutler, was born in Martha's Vineyard, Massachusetts, April 13, 1767. At the age of three years he was placed with his grandfather, Hezekiah Cutler, in Killingly, Connecticut, and remained with his grandparents until their death, when, having lands in the Ohio company's purchase, he determined to remove to the Northwest Territory. He began this journey with his wife and four children on the fifteenth of June, 1795, and reached Marietta September 18th, having been three months on the way, and buried two of his children in the wilderness between Simrell's Ferry and Marietta.

The first location was at Waterford, where he engaged for a short time in mercantile business, but in 1799 he moved with his family to lands he owned in Ames township, now Athens county. In 1806 he located in Warren, and built the stone house which continued to be his residence until his death in 1853.

His life was one of great activity and usefulness. He contributed his full share to the work of laying the foundations of civil society and material prosperity in the section of country which he had chosen for a home.

He received, in 1796, the appointments from Governor St. Clair of captain of militia, justice of the peace and quarter sessions, and judge of the court of common pleas. In 1801 he was elected a member of the territorial legislature, and subsequently, in 1802, a member of the convention that formed the first constitution of Ohio. In the convention he took a prominent part in securing the adoption of the clauses that excluded slavery from the State, and made the encouragement of schools and education obligatory upon future legislatures.

In these matters of most vital importance to a new commonwealth he followed up, in practical application upon the soil of Ohio, the same principles of organic law that had been placed in the ordinance of 1787 by the efforts of his father, Dr. Manasseh Cutler, when he negotiated with Congress for the purchase of lands for the Ohio company.

He also exerted himself successfully in introducing into the constitution a judiciary system, which, in opposition to a proposed Virginia plan, brought the courts of justice within convenient reach of all the people, instead of compelling them to resort with their suits to the political centre of the State.

He was appointed by the territorial legislature one of the commissioners to take charge of the school and ministerial lands in this part of the State, and to provide for their lease and improvement.

In 1819 he was elected to the legislature, where he devoted himself unceasingly to the accomplishment of two of the most important objects that ever engaged the attention of that body. One was an *ad valorem* system of

60

taxation—the other a system of common schools. Although the constitution had imposed a positive obligation upon the law making power to encourage schools, nothing had been done or attempted until he introduced the first bill in 1819, providing for a school system. He was a member of either the lower house or the senate until 1825, and had the satisfaction of seeing both of his favorite measures so far matured that it could be said that Ohio had systems of taxation and schools. These systems have both progressed in their application to growing wants, and have been perfected by subsequent legislation; but at no period of their progress was more ability, industry, and energy required than was given to them in their incipient stage by Ephraim Cutler.

In presenting the unjust burden imposed upon this section of Ohio by the prevailing system of taxation, under which lands in Hamilton county worth fifty dollars per acre paid no more tax than our land worth fifty cents per acre, Dr. Andrews in his History of Washington County thus alludes to Mr. Cutler's success:

In the winter of 1819-20 Judge Ephraim Cutler, a representative from this county, introduced into the legislature a joint resolution that property should be taxed according to its true value, which passed the house of representatives. In the fall of 1823 he was elected to the senate and again renewed his efforts to secure a reform in the revenue system. He was appointed the chairman of the committee on the revenue. The project of a canal between Lake Erie and the Ohio river had come up, and Judge Cutler had succeeded in convincing the friend of that measure that it must inevitably fail unless based upon a broad, judicious, and equitable system of taxation. To him more than any other are we indebted for the law then enacted. The language of his cotemporaries clearly shows that he was regarded as the author.

Hon. Samuel F. Vinton writes from Washington, December 21, 1824: "We ought to offer up our most unceasing prayers that your plan for the equalization of taxes may at the same time be adopted. Without it, inevitable ruin would await the sparse peopled and sterile parts of the State. In fact, those parts of the State will be virtually ruined under the present system of taxation in defraying the ordinary expense of the Government.

Ingenuity, in my opinion, could not devise a system more unequal, unjust, and offensive. I am decidedly in favor of improving the inland navigation of the State by canals, if possible, but I hope you will perseveringly press upon the legislature your plan of taxation in conjunction with it."

The Hon. Eleutheros Cooke, in a letter dated Sandusky, October 13, 1828, thus speaks of Mr. Cutler's services: "As the author and founder of our new and excellent system of revenue and taxation, I shall ever consider you as richly entitled to the gratitude of the State. In this part of the country you are known as the author."

Caleb Atwater, in a letter to Judge Cutler, dated Circleville, January 22, 1825, says: "You are doing nobly, Press forward with your equal taxation, the school system, and the canals, and immortalize this legislature. What must be your sensations on the prospect you now have of carrying into effect the greatest objects ever presented to our legislature. Press forward I say in your career of doing good. Posterity will call you blessed."

Henry Dana Ward writes: Shrewsburg, Masachusetts, August 14, 1825. "I have heard from you and of you through my brother (Nahum Ward, esq., of Marietta), and have felt with you and for you in wishing your revenue and school bills into legislative being, and now rejoice with you in the commencement of the grand Ohio and Lake Erie canal; and pray that the school bill may go

into as effectual operation as the revenue law. These are great works, long and ardently desired, and perseveringly labored for. You have borne a distinguished part in giving them life, and I hope they may long continue a source of satisfaction to you."

Nahum Ward, esq., writes, Marietta, Ohio, January 12, 1825: "We are greatly indebted to you for you services in the senate and all acknowledge it."

He was positive and earnest in his political views, and never swerved from his convictions upon questions of National policy. In his youth he adopted the principles that governed Washington, Adams, and their compeers, and thus incurred the stigma of Federalist. This, of course, was enough to shut his way to political promotion or success, but it is true that no man in Ohio, in 1825, stood higher as a statesman of integrity, ability, and comprehensive views of State policy than himself.

He was ever the active promoter of every useful public enterprise and accepted an appointment from the citizens of Marietta in 1837, and again in 1839, to visit Baltimore for the purpose of securing the examination of a railroad route to the Ohio river, with a view to making Marietta its crossing point.

In 1839, he represented the Whigs of this district at the National convention that nominated General Harrison for president.

In 1836 he was a member of the General Assembly of the Presbyterian church which met in Pittsburgh, and also in 1837 at their meeting in Philadelphia, at which time the separation of the church into Old school and New school took place.

He was early appointed a member of the board of trustees of the Ohio university at Athens, and gave the interests of that institution his constant and devoted attention for many years.

In all the private relations of life he was faithful and true to his personal obligations; as husband, father, neighbor, and friend. In 1828, he united with the Presbyterian church in Warren, then in its infancy, and continued as a member, ruling elder, and Sabbath-school teacher, to be during his life, one of its main supports and ornaments. On the eighth of July, 1853, he was gathered to his fathers—a shock of corn fully ripe.

He was one of the busy workers, who at the right time, and in their appointed sphere, "dug deep and laid broad the foundations of many generations." Such labors may not be heeded, may even be desecrated and destroyed—but history must make their record "well done."

HARMAN BLENNERHASSETT.

The story of Blennerhassett has been often told, and volumes have been written upon his romantic and melancholy career; but as he was, in a measure, identified with the early history of the locality of which this work treats (though never a resident of Washington county), we propose giving a brief sketch of his life.

He was a descendant of one of the families most prominent among the gentry of Ireland, and was born in the year 1767, in Hampshire, England, while his parents were there upon a visit. Shortly after his birth, the family returned to their residence, Castle Conway, in the county Kerry. When Harman became of proper age, he is known to have been sent to the famous Westminster school, and he completed his education at Trinity college, Dublin, as a classmate of the celebrated Thomas Addis Emmitt. They read law together at the King's court, Dublin, and were admitted upon the same day, in 1790, to practice in the courts. Blennerhassett, however, being the heir expectant of a large fortune, paid but little attention to the law; but travelled considerably, and cultivated his tastes for literature, science, and music. His father died in 1796, leaving Harman his splendid estate. About this time he became involved in political troubles in Ireland, and resolved to cast his fortune in the new world, with the republican principles of which he was in close sympathy. Accordingly, he sold his estate to his cousin, Lord Ventry, and went to England, preparatory to removing to America. Here he married the beautiful and accomplished Miss Margaret Agnew, (daughter of the lieutenant governor of the Isle of Man), who was to share his beautiful island home upon the Ohio and his sad misfortunes. They arrived in New York in 1797, and in the fall of the same year, drawn by the fame of the western country, he came to Marietta, in which place he passed the winter. His time was spent in social pleasure and in seeking a location for a home in the vicinity. It is said that at one time he had a thought of building a castle upon Mount Dudley, being influenced toward that end by Dudley Woodbridge, esq. He finally, however, selected the island in the Ohio near Belpre, and fourteen miles below Marietta, with which his name has ever since been connected. The island was the property of Elijah Backus, and had been originally located in 1770 by George Washington, who owned an extensive tract of land upon the Virginia shore, just below, which was known as Washington bottom. The upper portion of this island, containing about one hundred and seventy acres, was purchased by Mr. Blennerhassett for the sum of four thousand five hundred dollars, in March, 1798. Soon after he moved to it with his wife and one child, and took up his residence in one of the block-houses that remained as a relic of the Indian war. In this block-house he lived for two years, while his mansion was in process of construction. The family residence near the upper end of the island was completed in the year 1800, and was the wonder of the western country. "It was built," says Hildreth, "with great taste and beauty, no expense being spared in its construction that could add to its usefulness or splendor." The main building was fifty-two feet long and thirty feet wide. Porticos extending in front half encircled a beautiful lawn, and connected with the central structure two large offices. The entire front measured over one hundred feet. Colonel Joseph Barker, of Belpre, was one of the architects and builders. The beautiful house was fittingly surrounded. The forest trees in the immediate vicinity were cleared away, the unevenesses of the ground were smoothed, and a lawn containing several acres was secured in front of the mansion, while gardens were laid off at either side and made rich with the bloom of every flower which was native to, or could be grown in, the climate. From the house to the head of the island a broad avenue was opened through the thick wood, affording a view of the river for several miles above. Carriage-ways and nicely gravelled walks led in and out among the forest trees, the planted shrubs and the well kept gardens. Bowers and grottos lent their beauty to the scene. Nature and art were combined to produce all that could be desired in a luxurious and tasteful home. Nor was the useful neglected. Beyond the ornamental gardens were planted fine orchards, and beyond these—occupying the central portion of the island—was a farm of an hundred acres of rich land, upon which grew bountiful crops. The farm was kept under the most perfect cultivation, and the gardens and grounds carefully tended by men who were skilled in their callings, and who had at their command a large number of slaves, which Mr. Blennerhassett, being within the jurisdiction of Virginia, was permitted to own. Within the residence of the Blennerhassetts all things were in keeping with the surroundings. The house was finished in a high style of art, and in perfect taste. The lofty ceilings were bordered with beautiful plaster cornices, or gold mouldings; the floors were covered with carpets of richest color, the walls with pictures and elegant mirrors. The furniture was massive and grand—the most beautiful that the foreign markets afforded. Mr. Blennerhassett had a large library, embracing all departments of literature, which he had bought in London, and an ample apparatus for making those experiments in natural philosophy and chemistry, of which he was fond. He spent much of his time in literary and scientific investigation, but devoted all of the attention that was needful to the beautifying of his wonderful home. Mrs. Blennerhassett, like her husband, was cultured and elegant. She possessed rare accomplishments, was very charming in conversation, and immediately became an admired favorite in the refined society of Marietta and Belpre. The Blennerhassetts often visited these places, and, by both their substantial qualities of mind and many graces, shone brightly in the social circles of the pioneers. When at home they were seldom without visitors, and they entertained their guests with all of the ease, dignity and elegance that good taste and culture, with wealth at their command, can exhibit. Domestic felicity was not wanting in their beautiful home. Husband and wife, according to all accounts, were exceedingly fond. Whether entertaining a gay throng of visitors, or secluded in their forest-embowered and water-begirt villa, their days passed joyously, and in an almost ideal happiness. But into this Eden the tempter came.

Aaron Burr made his first appearance in the west in the spring of 1805. He visited Mr. Blennerhassett and filled his mind with the prospect of a splendid land speculation in the far southwest—an innocent plan which concealed a scheme of foulest treason and revolution. The next summer he returned to the west again, visited the island home and remained for some time in Marietta, a number of the leading citizens receiving him with marked attention, while others did not attempt to conceal their abhorrence of him as the murderer of Alexander Hamilton. Burr was now busy in developing his plans for dissevering the west from the east and founding a vast empire in the Mississippi valley and the Mexican provinces, but his design was carefully concealed under the pretense that what was designed was the colonization of a rich country. Dark suspicions, however, were whispered about, that the wily and subtle schemer meant much more than he openly avowed. Interest in the proposed mysterious adventure ran high, and there was much of conversation upon the subject, and the newspapers were filled with communications approving and disapproving of Burr's plans. A series of articles of the former nature, written by "Querist" were severely censured by another series signed "Regulus," the authorship of which was unknown at the time, and for many years later, but which were undoubtedly from the pen of Jared Mansfield, who had located in Marietta in 1803, having been appointed surveyor general of the United States by Jefferson.[*] But notwithstanding the very general opposition to Burr's schemes, the leader rallied around him, by his fascinating ways and persuasive tongue, many young men of the vicinity. His brilliancy blinded many people to the monstrosity of his character, and he made himself during his stay in Marietta an almost universal favorite. The lady who would not dance at the "Burr ball" in Marietta was regarded as a person who carried her prejudice altogether too far.[†] It was not strange that Blennerhassett should have been beguiled by the artful plotter, nor that having once consented to enter into the project represented to him he should have become deeply interested in it, and devoted his time and money freely to its advancement.

Early in September, 1806, the contract was made for the building of the boats which were to convey the adventurers to their settlement. Mr. Blennerhassett became responsible for the payment and furnished money also for the purchase of provisions. By the last of October the public mind had become filled with vague apprehensions of danger. In the vicinity of Marietta many people began to look upon the preparations of Burr and Blennerhassett with curiosity not unmixed with disfavor. The attention of the general Government had been called to the fact that they were at work organizing an expedition thought by some to be inimical to the interests of the United States, and Jefferson had sent spies to watch the conspirators. The fact that Blennerhassett was entirely innocent of a design to do aught against the United States, was shown at this time. He called upon the Government agent, and talked frankly about the proposed settlement. The surmises of

*Personal Memoirs, by E. D. Mansfield.

†This lady, as we learn from an obituary of her sister, Mrs. Margaret Patterson, published in a Terre Haute newspaper, was the late Mrs. William Skinner. "She withheld her presence from the ball room and gave as a reason that Colonel Burr was plotting treason against the Government.

President Jefferson being communicated to the legislature, that body passed an act authorizing the governor, Edward Tiffin, who was at the State capital, Chillicothe, to call out the militia to capture and detain any boats descending the Muskingum or Ohio under suspicious circumstances. Blennerhassett, hearing of the action of the legislature, it is said, intended to abandon the cause in which he had engaged, but urged by his wife and a party of men who had, under Comfort Tyler, arrived at the island, with the purpose of joining the expedition, he unfortunately adhered to his original design. Under the legislative act, a company of militia was called out, placed under the command of Captain Timothy Buell, and stationed on the bank of the Muskingum, near the site of the stockade. A cannon was planted on the bank, regular sentries set day and night for several weeks, and every passing boat examined. Many amusing jokes were played upon the military during this campaign and the final capture of the half dozen small boats was made the subject of some ludicrous verses in imitation of the "Battle of the Kegs," by General Edward W. Tupper.

In the meantime the people had become much excited about the organization of the expedition, and there was a growing feeling in favor of seizing upon the persons and property of those engaged in it. Upon the ninth of December Blennerhassett learned that the militia of Wood county, Virginia, purposed arresting him, and upon the tenth he left surreptitiously, to join Burr. Colonel Phelps, in command of the Virginia militia, took possession of the island. Mrs. Blennerhassett was in Marietta at this time, and she returned to find her elegant house full of soldiers, who were making themselves at home in a very rough manner, appropriating to their own use whatever stores and liquors they needed, and destroying much valuable property. In a few days she left the once happy home, being assisted in her departure by A. W. Putnam, of Belpre. With her two little sons, Harman and Dominic, she pursued her way down the river to join her husband, and reached him late in January. The history of the expedition is well known. When it broke up Blennerhassett went to Natchez, Mississippi, and was shortly after arrested there. He stood trial and was acquitted. Starting north to visit his home, he was, however, again arrested and sent to Richmond. After ten weeks' imprisonment he was discharged, as no evidence of a sinister design toward the Government could be proven against him. One year from the time he had left it, he returned to the island where he had passed eight happy years of his life. The place was desolate. Property had been seized for debts. Many articles had been stolen. The slaves had escaped. The house had been gutted of its contents. Narrowly escaping a rearrest, Blennerhassett journeyed southward and rejoined his family at Natchez. Purchasing a plantation near Gibson Port, Mississippi, he engaged in the growing of cotton, but the War of 1812 put an end to that business. The plantation was sold for twenty-seven thousand dollars, which sum scarcely more than satisfied Mr. Blennerhassett's creditors. His island home was destroyed in 1811 by fire. Consequently the family removed to

New York, where its head engaged in the practice of law. His efforts, however, were not attended with success. He was a ruined man. Subsequently he had fair prospects in Canada, and removed there in 1819, but ill fate attended him. Mr. Blennerhassett went to Ireland, thinking to avail himself of the benefits of a reversionary claim which he had never deemed worthy of prosecution during the period of his prosperity, but the claim was barred by the statute of limitation. Mrs. Blennerhassett found a home for a time in New York, where she was assisted by the Emmitts; she went afterward to Pennsylvania, and again to Montreal. Here she was joined by her husband. After a short stay the family went to England, and from there to St. Aubin, on the island of Jersey. Their next abiding place was the island of Guernsey, and there upon the first of February, 1831, the gifted, but impracticable, unfortunate Harman Blennerhassett passed away.

In 1842 Mrs. Blennerhassett revisited the United States with the hope of obtaining some redress from the Government which had impoverished, through undeserved prosecution, her husband, and by whose soldiers his home had been despoiled. Mrs. Blenerhassett brought her claim before the proper tribunal, and set forth the amount of damage caused by the Virginia militia, made out by Dudley Woodbridge, esq., of Marietta. This claim would doubtless have been paid, but just as the object she was striving to gain was about to be accomplished, Mrs. Blennerhassett died. Worn out with sorrow and toil and privation, she who had once been the mistress of the splendid house upon the "fairy island" passed away in a dreary tenement house in New York, attended only by her son, Harman, and a black servant, a former slave, who had accompanied her in all her wanderings, served without money, and been faithful through all. Mrs. Blenerhassett's later years were rendered sorrowful by more misfortunes than the loss of property, station, home, and husband. One of her sons proved almost an imbecile, and the other became a confirmed sot—a pitiful wreck, whose life ended in the Blackwell's Island alms-house in 1854.[*]

DAVID PUTNAM.

David Putnam, third son of Colonel Israel Putnam (of whom an account is given in the Belpre history), and grandson of General Israel Putnam, was born in Pomfret, Connecticut, February 24, 1769. He graduated at Yale college in the class of 1793. After his graduation, with the view of entering upon a mercantile life, he accepted a place on a vessel in a voyage to London in the winter of 1794. A journal kept at the time describes the seasickness and discomfort of the voyage, the abuse of an arbitrary and domineering captain, the disgusting association of an ignorant and wicked crew, and the utter distaste for the life on which he had entered. After a

rough and dangerous passage, the vessel was wrecked on the coast of France, the officers and crew making a narrow escape to land. Here they were detained some months, mostly at the city of Nantes, with short rations and general distress, in the period of the French revolution, and the attempt to improve the morals and prosperity of the country, by the substitution of a tenth, instead of a seventh portion of time for rest and relaxation. The journal is a graphic description of the prevailing wretchedness. It says, March 4, 1795:

Since we have been in Nantes, we have lived twenty of us in one chamber, have had two very scanty meals of victuals, one about 12 o'clock, the other at 8 in the evening, consisting of tripe, lights, a little veal, etc., all cooked after the French fashion, and a half pound bread per day, which we draw from the commissary store—for such fare the American consul pays one hundred and ten livres per day.

He availed himself of the first opportunity to return to the United States, and landed in New York July 2, 1795. On meeting an acquaintance, he was informed of the removal of his father's family (during his absence) from the home in Pomfret to the then distant Ohio, and says: "It was unexpected, it surprised, and in some respect agitated my mind—my plans were disconcerted. I returned on board, walked the deck, was pleased, disappointed and pleased again, was miserable, was alone, was happy."

Mr. Putnam's brief experience abroad, proved an effectual cure for a desire of mercantile life or foreign travel.

He taught school in Brooklyn, Connecticut, during the winter of 1795, and during the following year, made a brief visit to Ohio. He then, for about two years, pursued the study of law with Hon. Calvin Goddard, of Plainfield, Connecticut. On the sixteenth of September, 1798, he was married to Betsey Perkins, daughter of Dr. Elisha Perkins, of Plainfield. They came immediately after, on horseback, to Marietta, where he commenced the practice of law. He became the teacher of the Muskingum academy in Marietta, established about this time, the first institution of the kind in the Northwest Territory. He was postmaster in Marietta from 1800 to 1802. In 1805 he built the stone residence on Front street in Harmar (now occupied by a grandson), where he continued until his death in 1856. He became cashier of the Bank of Marietta at its organization in or about 1807 (General Rufus Putnam, Benjamin Ives Gilman, Paul Fearing, William Skinner and others, directors or stockholders), the business being done at his residence in Harmar until about the year 1815, when the bank was transferred to Marietta, and a new cashier appointed.

He continued in the practice of law nearly thirty years, and then retired from it, to an extensive agency which had devolved on him in connection with lands in the Ohio Company's Purchase. This he continued until the year 1845, when at the age of seventy-five, he relinquished it to his son.

He was a faithful adherent, during his active life, of the First Religious Society of Marietta. He donated the lots now occupied by the Congregational church and parsonage in Harmar, and was a liberal contributor to the erection of their meeting-house.

---

[*]A pathetic account of the sorrows of Mrs. Blennerhassett, and the melancholy fate of the family, is given by Miss Maria P. Woodbridge, in Lippincott's Magazine for February, 1879. From it many of the foregoing facts are taken.

Mr. Putnam had no aspiration for public life or political distinction, but in his sphere of a private citizen, was known, recognized and honored as a firm, reliable and intelligent friend of order, morals, education and religion.

He was the father of twelve children, only two of whom survive—his sons, Douglas Putnam and David Putnam, of Harmar.

He died at his homestead in Harmar, March 31, 1856, aged eighty-seven.

NAHUM WARD.

Nahum Ward came to the West so early that had he located almost anywhere else than in the primal settlement, he would have been in the strictest sense of the term a pioneer. Although not of the vanguard of the great army of peace he was one of the conspicuous figures in the ranks which closely followed. He was the pioneer of an era of advancement rather than a movement of population—an era of enlarged scope and great achievement. The inception of Mr. Ward's enterprises in the country round about Marietta, and the inauguration of the period of great improvements and material prosperity were nearly simultaneous. The subject of this sketch was the first man in southeastern Ohio who entered deliberately and determindly upon a thorough system for the development of its landed interests. He conducted a colossal business, was identified with almost every progressive movement of his time, and he made a deep impression upon the community in which he dwelt. It has been said of him by one who is shrewd in his estimates of men, that although he took no active part in politics and did not enter public life, he was probably the most prominent man in Marietta. Certainly he was one of its strongest and most notable characters.

Nahum Ward was born October 23, 1785, in Shrewsbury, Massachusetts. He was a son of Thomas W. Ward and grandson of Artemas Ward, the first major general of the Revolutionary army—the officer to whom legitimately belonged the place accorded to Washington, and to whom it would undoubtedly have been given had not public policy suggested the appointment of a Virginian as commander in chief of the army. The subject of our sketch upon attaining suitable age attended Leicester academy and studied there several years, under the preceptorship of Timothy Fuller (father of that strange literary genius, Margaret Fuller, Countess D'Ossoli, who was the original of Zenobia in Hawthorn's Blithdale romance). After obtaining an education young Ward entered, as a clerk, the store of his uncle, a Mr. Brigman. Four years service in the village store gave him the rudiments of that splendid business knowledge which made him successful in later years. His experience as clerk was supplemented by two years of independent mercantile business, his father giving him in 1807 the sum of five hundred dollars with which to open a store of his own. He seems to have become dissatisfied with the small scope which the management of the

store afforded his abilities, and two years after he had opened it—in June, 1809—he set out for the then far distant west to seek his fortune. His objective point was Marietta, and he had in his possession a letter of introduction to General Rufus Putnam. One may easily imagine the reception given to a young man of Mr. Ward's character, coming to a comparatively new settlement well introduced and recommended. Very naturally he was encouraged to examine the country and given some facilities for so doing. He remained about six weeks; visited various portions of the Ohio company's purchase; acquired considerable information in regard to the lands for sale, and then returned to Shrewsbury, as he had come out—upon horseback. Shortly after his arrival in Massachusetts he received an appointment as deputy sheriff, and took up his residence at Worcester. He had doubtless formed, when in Ohio, a determination to return to the west at an early date, and it is not probable that he swerved for an instant from that purpose. At any rate he had not been long in Worcester before he began purchasing lands from Ohio company shareholders in that place and its vicinity. He had only a very small capital—the five hundred dollars which his father had given him, and the profits from two years' business in his store—but it was sufficient to secure a total of about five thousand acres of lands at the low prices then prevailing. Two years from the time of his first visit—in the fall of 1811—he again journeyed to Ohio; this time to become a citizen. He located in Marietta, which place was henceforth his home, until his death in the year 1860. Mr. Ward examined most of the lands already purchased within a few months from the time of his arrival, and after familiarizing himself with the country, made a trip to his old home in the winter of 1812-13, and bought several more tracts. During the first ten years of his residence in the country Mr. Ward's whole attention was given to buying lands, and he made no attempts to sell. He made annual visits to the east in the winter seasons until 1817, and every year added to his possessions, until he had secured more than thirty-seven thousand acres of land, lying principally within the counties of Washington, Athens, Morgan, Gallia, Lawrence, and Meigs. He was more largely identified with the landed interests of southeastern Ohio than any other one man. His career in his chosen line of business was a successful one, and it could hardly have been otherwise with the possession of such qualities as were combined in Mr. Ward's nature. He was a man of sanguine temperament, and yet so well balanced with a kind of business conservatism that even with the great temptations that arose before him he steadily avoided all forms of wild speculation. His aim was to attain success by slow, sure, safe methods rather than sudden, daring venture based upon the turn of fortune. Yet no man could be more bold in following a line of action after it had once been decided upon; no man could more persistently push forward in a chosen pathway. He had an indomitable will, great energy, self reliance, and patience, and an uncommon development of common sense. Misfortune may come to a man who possesses these characteristics, but it will come only occasionally as the diversifying incident in a career which, as an entirety, is successful. Mr. Ward, while generally fortunate in his undertakings, met some reverses which no human foresight, however far reaching, could discover or forefend. One of the first of his measures for the settlement and improvement of his great tracts of land fell short of its full effect through circumstances entirely beyond his knowledge. Conceiving the idea that the Scotch would make an industrious, frugal, and intelligent element in the agricultural districts, he went to Scotland in the fall of 1822 for the purpose of bringing over a colony of the "canny people." He published in Edinburg a small pamphlet giving descriptions of the country, derived principally from the pamphlet of Dr. Manasseh Cutler, printed at Salem, Massachusetts, in 1787; from the works of Thomas Hutchins, United States geographer, and from the Ohio press. A letter from Return Jonathan Meigs, postmaster general of the United States and ex-governor of Ohio, and a note from the United States consul in Edinburgh were published on the inner leaf of the cover and served as Mr. Ward's credentials. Mr. Ward was so far successful in his measure that he induced about one hundred and seventy-five persons to emigrate to the United States and to the lands which he owned. But the season when they arrived—the summer of 1823—was one during which a terrible epidemic prevailed in Marietta and all the Ohio river region. Nearly all of the Scotch emigrants were stricken down with fever, and thus afflicted, and some of their number dying, these people began their life in a strange land. To the credit of Mr. Ward, be it said, that he was unremitting in his attentions to the unfortunate foreigners. He hired large public rooms for their comfortable lodging, and supplied them with medical attendance and nurses. Many of the descendants of these Scotch emigrants who settled on Mr. Ward's lands now live in Barlow and Wesley townships, and form one of the best elements of the population of Washington county.

Prior to his departure for Scotland, Mr. Ward had disposed of some small pieces of land, but he still retained the greater part of his original purchases, and after his return he constantly added to his possessions. But he did not retain lands and simply leave them unimproved awaiting an increase in value. Had he done so his influence for the good of the country would have been much smaller than it was. His policy was to improve. It had been said of him that "he was not a mere pioneer farmer clearing a few acres for a home, but a pioneer prince, with large estates, improving them all, and at once benefitting himself, his tenants, and the entire community." Some idea of the magnitude of his business operations may be suggested by the statement of the fact that at one time he had one hundred and thirty-one tenants clearing and cultivating lands within the Ohio company's purchase, under his proprietorship. The title to over one hundred thousand acres of land in southeastern Ohio was vested in Mr. Ward during the period he dwelt in Marietta, which was about forty-eight years.

Personal interest, a laudable pride and public spirit combined, led this great land owner to make the most thorough and systematic improvements. His farms throughout the southeastern part of the State—forty or fifty in Washington county—could be easily distinguished by their fine buildings, neat fences, well cultivated acres, and general appearance of thrift. Along many of the country roads Mr. Ward set out shade trees. Taste and utility were alike thought of. He lent aid to the building of many country school-houses, and contributed liberally to every turnpike, bridge, or other improvement of value to the public.

The fact that nearly all of Mr. Ward's farms were improved before they were sold redounded to the advantage of the purchasers and the tenants by whose labor those improvements were made, having easy terms of rental, also prospered. In many cases the renters became owners. It was the theory of Mr. Ward that the best condition of the country was attained when the greatest number of people possible secured homes, and so becoming fixed, had a permanent interest in the welfare of the community. Most of his lands were sold in small parcels, and to men of small means. Many of the purchasers were people who had absolutely no capital but their industry. In selling to hundreds, or perhaps thousands, of this class, it was only natural that many cases should occur in which the buyer was unable to fulfill his contract. And it is a notable fact that in no one of these cases did the proprietor foreclose the property. In every instance he made a settlement with the occupant of the farm forfeited by non-fulfilment of the contract, either refunding any payments already made, or making suitable compensation for improvements put upon it. Hundreds of well-to-do farmers in southeastern Ohio, who bought their lands of Mr. Ward by paying annual instalments, can attest the perfect equity of his business method and the liberality of his terms. And yet he did not escape entirely the obloquy which usually bears upon the large land-owner and dealer. While he never brought suit for foreclosure against those who were unable to pay for lands, Mr. Ward left no legal means unused in his dealings with other real estate owners, and would contest a title, when he believed justice was upon his side, as long as a vestige of hope remained. Becoming the owner of nearly all the shares of the Ohio company, he obtained an amount of Georgia Revolutionary certificates, which, owing to an irregularity in their issue, had not been included in the partition of the company's property, and remained as its only undivided assets.

The value of the certificates was, of course, contingent upon their being recognized by the United States Treasurer. Mr. Ward had a firm faith in the equity of his claim, employed able lawyers, who amassed evidence in support of it, and spent a long term in litigation with the United States and upon his death enjoined in his will the continuance of the great suit. This determination to succeed in whatever he once undertook was a marked characteristic of Mr. Ward, and numerous instances illustrating it might be cited.

Mr. Ward's justness in his business dealings with those who took up his lands or who were his tenants, has been already touched upon. It may be added that in his constant intercourse with even the poorest and humblest he exhibited a simple, natural affability which put them at perfect ease. He was a true friend of the laboring people and deeply interested in them. It was a favorite idea with him that the working man's holidays should be multiplied, within a proper limit, and that such a measure with the introduction of healthful entertainments in which they might participate would elevate their tastes and ambitions. Mr. Ward was by birth and education the equal of the highest class, and found pleasure in refined and cultured society; but it was with his equals that he exhibited something of those qualities which made him appear to many persons as unduly cold and reserved. His manner was dignified and courtly, and he was not a man with whom his associates would be familiar, but if his demeanor was one in which there was much of austerity it covered none but the kindliest feelings toward humanity in general. He was doubtless an aristocrat of the old school at heart, but he possessed also the thoughts of the true Democrat, and his acts indicated one class of feelings as much as the other. Mr. Ward's personal appearance was an expression (if we may use the term) of his nature. It indicated strength, will, energy, and dignity. He was a sturdy man physically as well as mentally; about six feet high, erect in carriage, and well proportioned. His features were strong, clearly cut and expressive. Citizens who remember him speak of Mr. Ward's appearance as always being that of the gentleman. He was almost invariably attired in the sober but elegant broadcloth which one is accustomed by an association of ideas to regard as the appropriate dress of that generation of substantial, sterling men who have nearly all passed away in the last quarter century, and which one imagines so in keeping with their character.

We have said in the beginning of this sketch that Mr. Ward, while not properly a public character, was probably the most prominent man who lived in Marietta. His prominence was naturally obtained through the magnitude of his business operations and the simple strength and solidity of his character. He held no important public offices. He was a Federalist in politics (like most of the leading men of Marietta), and this fact prevented him from accepting in 1812 the position of Aid to Governor Meigs. While the office was in many respects attractive to him he could not consistently with his principles accept it. Had he done so he would doubtless have led a bright and useful career in the service of the State, as civil advancement would have been the legitimate consequence of military success—and success he could scarcely have failed to achieve, with his abilities and strength of purpose.

Mr. Ward's home was the house on the north side of Putnam street, between Front and Second, built by General Edward W. Tupper. When he purchased it, in 1817, it was the largest and most elegant residence in Marietta, and an appropriate dwelling for a man of Mr. Ward's tastes and hospitality. Among other distinguished visitors whom he entertained here was General Lafayette (See chapter XXXIV), whom he had visited in Paris, and whose visit to this country, by the way, was largely the result of Mr. Ward's solicitation and his representations of the deep interest that the people of the United States felt in him.

In 1845 his fellow citizens elected Mr. Ward to the office of mayor, a position which he retained for a long term of years. It was soon after his election that the first extensive improvements in Marietta were made. prior to this time there were no paved sidewalks in the village. It was through Mr. Ward that these were introduced and shade trees set out along the streets. He was unable, however, to carry out all of the plans which he deemed for the interest of the public.

The kindness of his nature was exhibited in the constant exercise of benevolence. Through various channels, religious and secular, private and public, he contributed aid to individuals and to causes. The greatest of his benevolent acts, however, was that which supplied the Unitarians of Marietta with a house of worship. He had been an adherent of the Unitarian faith from his early manhood, and in middle life began to labor zealously to establish a society of that denomination in Marietta. "At length," says a biographer, "as advancing years admonished him, that whatever was to be done, must be done quickly, he determined to build a church and organize a society, and leave the rest to this silent influence of the testimony of truth, and to the gradual softening of prejudice and increase of freedom." The church (upon the corner of Putnam and Third streets) was completed and dedicated with appropriate services, June 4, 1857, at a cost to Mr. Ward of not less than twenty-five thousand dollars. The edifice was donated to the First Unitarian society, and Mr. Ward, not resting, satisfied with what he had done, continued to promote, by every means in his power, the well-being of the society. Ever since his arrival in Marietta he had endeavored to further the growth of Unitarian sentiment by personal persuasion and by the distribution of tracts. Whenever he prepared for a journey through the country he was accustomed to fill one of his saddle-bags with tracts of the American Unitarian association, which he gave to those with whom he came in contact. He always kept a supply of these tracts in his office, which he placed in the hands of his tenants and the men who purchased homesteads from him. His pastor, Rev. E. C. Guild, said: "A very large number were distributed in this way, making the more impression from the fact that a kind word and encouraging tone went with them. It is impossible to estimate the amount of influence exerted in this way, so widespread and deep-seated." Mr. Ward's religious convictions were of the most positive kind, and his devotion to the principles of Christianity, constant and unremitting. He passed away "with a faith as clear, and a confidence in the mercy of God as strong in death as it had been through life." His death occurred upon the sixth of April, 1860, and the funeral services were conducted upon the Sunday following, at the

Isaac Spaulding

The subject of this sketch was born in Townsend, Massachusetts, December 4, 1807. His father, Captain Isaac Spaulding, was a son of Lieutenant Benjamin Spaulding, a lineal descendant of Edward Spaulding, who came to America from England in 1630. His mother was Lucy Emery, a daughter of Lieutenant Emery of Revolutionary fame.

The early education of Mr. Spaulding was somewhat limited, owing to the fact that the large family and the limited means of the father prevented his being sent to college, while the schools of his native village furnished but from six to eight weeks tuition per year. His father, Captain Isaac, in addition to being a good farmer, was also a cooper, and this trade he taught Isaac. At the age of twenty, his father gave him his option of taking his freedom, or of remaining on the farm until twenty-one, when he should receive one hundred dollars. He chose the former, and went to work in a cooper-shop for Captain Davis, of Townsend. At the expiration of a year, he went to Vermont and engaged in the manufacture of barrels and cheese-stones for a dairyman. Finishing this contract, and being unable to get his pay from the dairyman, he accepted a yoke of oxen as part pay, and set out for Massachusetts, driving his oxen before him over the Green mountains, a distance of over one hundred miles. In 1830 he married Elmina Kibling, of Chester, Vermont, whose parents had been drowned in the Connecticut river some years before. In 1832, Mr. Spaulding was elected a captain in the second regiment of Massachusetts militia, receiving his commission from Governor Levi Lincoln. In the same year he went to Lake Champlain, Vermont, and in company with two friends engaged in the cooper business. The company had the contract for furnishing nail kegs for a nail factory in Troy, New York. He continued to manufacture kegs for the Troy firm until December, 1834, when the death of his father recalled him to Townsend to take charge of his father's estate.

Buying the interest of the remaining heirs to his father's estate, he remained at the old homestead until the death of his wife in 1836. Mr. Spaulding then rented the homestead and went to Pittsburgh, Pennsylvania, where he engaged in the manufacture of pumps, associating with him in this business, Silas T. Jewell, under the firm name of Spaulding & Jewell. While here he married Cynthia A. Matthews, of Pittsburgh, the wedding ceremony being performed October 24, 1839, by Rev. C. D. Battelle, one of the pioneer Methodist preachers of the west. In the spring of 1840, he removed to Harmar, Washington county, Ohio, and engaged in the manufacture of pumps with his old partner, Silas T. Jewell. He conducted the business in company with Mr. Jewell for about two years, when he sold out his interest to Richard Pattin, Esq. and returned to Massachusetts to look after his property.

Purchasing a team of horses and a spring wagon, he set out from the Ohio river in company with his wife and infant daughter, Almira, in the early part of June, and reached the banks of the Connecticut about the first of July. The entire journey of about one thousand miles was completed in six weeks. The dusty and travel-worn appearance of the company frequently caused them to be mistaken for homeless wanderers by the villagers along the route, and their kindly offers of help and sympathy had to be declined with thanks a number of times.

In 1846, Mr. Spaulding sold his farm to his brother, and determined to return to Harmar, Ohio. Being fully acquainted with his experience in common road wagons, he made the return trip with his wife and daughter by steamboat and cars to Philadelphia, and thence to Pittsburgh by canal. Arriving at Harmar he resumed the pump business with his old partner, Silas T. Jewell. This partnership, however, was dissolved within a year, Mr. Jewell retiring, and Mr. Spaulding continuing the business. Mr. Spaulding continued the manufacture of pumps down to the time of the Rebellion, supplying the larger amount of pumps sold to eastern and southeastern Ohio, and likewise supplying several dealers in Pittsburgh and Indiana.

Mr. Spaulding is a man of careful business habits, and by practicing the strictest economy, has succeeded in accumulating considerable property. He has not, however, always been fortunate in his investments outside of his regular business, having lost more than ten thousand dollars in various ventures. He was one of the victims of the ill-fated Harry Dean that burst her boilers in the river, and himself, to the water's edge in 1861. He was also a stockholder in the Harmar Bucket factory, which stock proved a total loss. His property at present consists of real estate in Harmar, farming lands in Washington county, Ohio, and western lands, and has likewise a partner in the queensware establishment of Richards & Co., Zanesville, Ohio.

Mr. Spaulding had no issue by his first wife, but ten children were the result of his second marriage. Of these four died in their infancy. Of those living, Almira P., the eldest, is the wife of Captain John A. Livesay, of the Pomeroy and Big Sandy line of steamers; Abbie H. is the wife of Mr. A. D. Hale; Mary S. was married in 1871 to Professor John T. Duff; Ella married Charles W. Jenkins, who is engaged in the dry goods business with Bosworth, Wells & Co., Marietta; and Sarah is the wife of Lyman B. Fuller, who is engaged in the bank business in Marietta with C. E. Glines, Esq. Mr. Spaulding has but one son, Isaac, and he is yet unmarried.

Mr. Spaulding has never held a civil office further than to represent his village in the town council, and in other like capacities, where his sound judgment and his conservative views have always been held in high esteem.

church he had built and which is the noblest monument to his memory. The master workmen who had been employed by him in the erection of this edifice, in accordance with Mr. Ward,s expressed desire, bore his remains to the grave, in Mound cemetery.

We have omitted mention of Mr. Ward's domestic relations. His home was one of happiness, and his family ever received his closest attention and most loving ministry. His first wife, whom he married in the autumn of 1817, was Miss S. C. Skinner, daughter of William Skinner, a prominent pioneer merchant of Marietta. Mr. Ward had seven children, five of whom survived him. One daughter, Ann Maria, who had reached maturity, died in 1839, and a son, Lafayette, died in infancy. William S. Ward, the remaining son, who, after his father's death, carried on his business, died in 1871. He left a son and a daughter, Agnes (the wife of A. B. White, of Lafayette, Indiana). The family name became extinct with the death of the son referred to, William Nahum Ward, in March, 1874. The four daughters of Nahum Ward are Sarah C. (Mrs. W. L. Rolston), Mary E. (Mrs. Charles R. Rhodes), Harriet C. (wife of Goodrich H. Barbour, of Cincinnati), and Henrietta D. (widow of E. G. Leonard, of the same city).

Nahum Ward's first wife died in 1844, and in 1848 he married Harriet Denny, of Worcester, Massachusetts, who survived her husband about twelve years, dying July 16, 1872, and leaving, by will, a large bequest to the church which Mr. Ward had founded.

JOSEPH HOLDEN.

Joseph Holden, for thirty years a prominent figure in the mercantile business, and for sixty years a universally respected and valuable citizen of Marietta, was born in Shirley, Massachusetts, December, 1769. He learned the carpenter trade and in 1803 came to Marietta. until 1807 he engaged in house-building exclusively, and after that time worked at the trade in connection with his mercantile business. He took a deep interest in building as long as he lived. In his old age he was frequently found where improvements were going on, offering friendly criticism. He opened a store in 1807, and continued in trade until 1837. He did business on an honest, straightforward liberal basis, and a large patronage enabled him to acquire a competence which was in after years, generously shared with the needy poor. Mr. Holden always had a place in the local political councils of his party, but never had aspirations for office. He was a Jeffersonian and in 1814 the majority party nominated him for county commissioner which he declined. He was afterwards appointed county treasurer, and discharged the duties of the office seven years. He became a Whig in Whig days, and his store was the place of meeting for the county politicians, when in town. Esquire Booth, Robert Johnson, Judge Rosing of Belpre, Judge Barker of Newport, and others were so often found there in consultation that the Brophy house, which was Democratic headquarters, named the store "Uncle

Joe Holden's senate." He was a Republican after the organization of that party. Mr. Holden was for years a director of the bank, and was held as a careful and sagacious business man. He was always kind to tenants and lenient to borrowers. He was modest and often secret in doing good works. It was his habit to quietly assist worthy young business men particularly, when selfish opposition placed them in need of a friend. He manifested his public spirit in another way. So far as he was able to prevent it, no one was permitted to leave town on account of inability to secure property on favorable terms. He was always ready to sell, when by so doing he could encourage worthy enterprises. Mr. Holden died November 14, 1863 in the ninety-fourth year of his age. "As 'a fine old gentleman,' Mr. Holden was a model."

WILLIAM SLOCOMB.

William Slocomb was born in Franklin, Massachusetts, February 5, 1783. He came to Marietta, Ohio, as a resident in 1816. "At this place he became a teacher, and for many years was regarded as the leading instructor of youth, and as a prime authority on school matters in the Upper Ohio valley. The scene of his labors was partly in Wheeling, West Virginia. A whole generation in these regions felt the beneficent power of his influence in this relation."

In 1817 he became superintendent of a Sunday-school, established in what was known as the Buell school-house, near the corner of Greene and Second streets, Marietta. He was probably the founder of this school, which was the third established in Marietta—that of Mary Lake, in Campus Martius, being the first, and that established in Muskingum academy, under the influence of David Putnam, esq., in May, 1817, being the second. Mr. Slocomb's Sunday-school was opened about two weeks later than that in Muskingum academy.

William Slocomb was reared on his father's farm, and in his early manhood was a practical farmer. The hopes and expectations of his youth—to obtain an education in some college—were disappointed, but his zeal in the pursuit of learning was not wholly repressed by untoward circumstances. He diligently used the means within his reach, and soon devoted himself wholly to teaching.

The difficulties under which he labored turned his mind to the consideration and devising some organization by which young men similarly situated in pecuniary matters might receive aid in the prosecution of studies, especially those desiring to labor in the Christian ministry. (He had made a profession of his faith in Christ at the age of seventeen.) With this object in view he was the leading instrument in the formation, in 1812, of the "Religious Charitable Society for the County of Worcester, Massachusetts," the principal design of which was the education of young men for the work of the ministry. This was one of the earliest movements in this direction in the country, and its influence, with that of some similar organizations, culminated in the formation of the American Education Society, in Boston, in 1816.

As before stated, Mr. Slocomb engaged in teaching when he came to Marietta. Failing health induced him to relinquish teaching. He then went into active business, at first engaged in the lumber business, afterwards in boots and shoes, in partnership with F. Buck. Books were soon added, as the call for them by the students of the college made such a business necessary in the town. Slocomb & Bigelow succeeded this firm.

William and S. Slocomb were, for a number of years, prominent merchants in Marietta. In 1844 William and S. Slocomb, with others, became members of the Marietta Ship company.

William Slocomb was intimately connected with the college during all his life here. He was a Presbyterian, but was for many years connected with the Congregational church, Marietta. He retired from business and removed to Rochester, New York, in 1855. "For seventeen years he officiated as elder in St. Peter's (Presbyterian) church, Rochester, and kept the records of the church until he was eighty years of age. On his ninetieth birthday he received the sacrament of the Lord's Supper. Three months later 'he fell asleep in Him who hath brought life and immortality to light', in the full exercise of his mental powers." He died in Rochester, New York, May 9, 1873.

NATHANIEL DODGE—JONATHAN CRAM.

Nathaniel Dodge was an older brother of Oliver Dodge, one of the first pioneers. He was from Hampton Falls, New Hampsheir, and came to Ohio in 1804. With him came his wife and four sons and two daughters. He purchased the brick house on Putnam street, of late years occupied by A. T. Nye, and which had been built by a Mr. Pool in 1802. Two of his sons—Oliver and Nathaniel—engaged in general mercantile business in Marietta. Oliver was in partnership with Augustus Stone, and afterwards belonged to the company which erected the Stone steam mill in Harmar. Nathaniel formed a partnership with Jonathan Cram, and opened a store on Ohio street. He afterwards removed to Parkersburgh and engaged in business there.

Mr. Cram moved his store to the Muskingum, just above where the Phœnix mills stand.

William Dodge, son of Nathaniel, was educated at Athens, Ohio, and died while studying for the ministry in 1825.

Dudley Dodge, another of his sons, died at the age of eighteen.

Nathaniel Dodge, jr., married Betsey Burlingame, granddaughter of General Rufus Putnam. They had no children.

Oliver Dodge married Eudocia Wing, of Lowell, Ohio, and the children of their only son live in St. Louis. There are none bearing the name of Dodge, who belong to the family of Nathaniel Dodge, living in Ohio now. The daughters of Nathaniel Dodge, who came to Ohio

with him, were Rebona and Hannah. Rebona married Colonel Augustus Stone, of Harmar; Hannah married Daniel Bosworth, of Marietta. In 1816 Jonathan Cram, who had married his daughter Sally in New Hampshire, came to Ohio with his family—wife and three children— for permanent residence. He had previously visited his father-in-law here in 1807 or 1808, having with him at that time his wife and one child. Mr. Cram's household goods were sent out by way of Philadelphia and Pittsburgh and Ohio river to Marietta. He, with his family, came by way of Clarksburgh, Virginia. Mrs. Cram and the children rode in a covered carriage, or gig. Mr. Cram and others in his employ had a large spring wagon. These were far more comfortable carriages than those in which the first pioneers came. Mr. Cram engaged in a successful mercantile business, and bought considerable real estate in Marietta, but he died at the early age of forty-one in 1821. His widow and children remained in Marietta. His sons became prominent citizens. John Oliver Cram, his oldest son, was a man of great energy, and became a leader in affairs relating to the improvement of the town. He established the mills now known as the Phœnix mills. He died at the age of forty-eight, November 7, 1860. Rebona, oldest daughter of Jonathan Cram, married A. T. Nye, of Marietta.

Nathaniel Dodge was a soldier of the Revolution on the sea, and was taken prisoner by the British and confined in the terrible Jersey ship. He belonged to a family who never seemed to know what fear was. He was a good citizen; firm in his support of law and order. At one time when certain parties threatened to turn the court out of doors if some of their guilty friends were punished for their crimes, Captain Dodge quietly attended the sittings of the court for several days, carrying a very heavy cane and sitting near the judges. His presence intimidated the disaffected parties, and no disturbance occurred. In common with all the Revolutionary soldiers who came to Ohio in early days, he was a firm supporter of General Washington and his administration, and belonged to the Federal party. In the Jackson campaign some of the Jacksonians in derision of his political views, and probably of his New England birth, stuffed a cannon with cod-fish and fired it off toward his residence on the other side of the Muskingum. (He was then living near Harmar). Probably the captain had his revenge on them for he was a man of wit and of resources. At one time his family, being married and settled in Marietta, formed a very pleasant family circle, but their lives were short, and he and his wife and children have long rested side by side in Mound cemetery. He died May 1, 1838.

COLONEL JOHN MILLS.

John Mills was born in Marietta, in what was then the Northwest Territory, December 2, 1795. His father, William Mills, left Massachusets and came to this then four-year-old town in 1792. He was a captain in the regular army and was made commandant of the town, the war with the Indians having begun the previous year.

The mother of John Mills was a notable woman, of earnest religious convictions, of strong intellect and large heart. She was clear headed to see and warm hearted to do whatever good work came to her hand. Her gracious manners and her cordial hospitality made her house a pleasant place of refuge to the wayfarer in the new country, and the door of her "Prophet's chamber" always opened easily to give entrance to any servant of the Master. When she went to her grave, in a good old age, she left the legacy of a good and pure repute to be handed down from mothers to daughters in the town in which the greater part of her long life was spent.

John Mills was thus blessed with beneficent home influences. He also enjoyed such means of education as the young town afforded, but had nothing beyond. Judging from results, he must have made good use of his opportunities. When he was eighteen years of age he entered the mercantile establishment of Dudley Woodbridge, who was at the time a leading merchant, and for many years after a prominent citizen of Marietta. The ability and integrity shown by the young clerk gained the confidence and approbation of his employer to such an extent that in three years, at the early age of twenty-one, he was taken into partnership by Mr. Woodbridge and placed in charge of a new store.

In this new position, his unwearied attention to business, his good judgment, and above all his incorruptible integrity, gained for him the respect and confidence of those with whom he dealt, and in consequence a large and profitable business was built up, the profits of which soon enabled him to buy out his senior partner and become sole owner and manager. Colonel Mills continued in the mercantile business for forty years, associating with himself now and then a young man who as a clerk had gained his confidence, and whom in this way he could help to make a better start in life.

Colonel Mills never confined his energies and his interests to the building up of a fortune, in order to add to the comforts and amenities of his private life. He was made on too large a scale for that. It is safe to say that for more than half a century no enterprise has been started in the community where he has lived that promised to result favorably to the mental, moral, or pecuniary interests of the people, to which he has not given his thoughts, his interest, and his money. He has always been ready to put his shoulder to the wheel and give what impulse he could to every good cause, bearing in all things his full share of the burden, and generally making a liberal estimate as to what that share was. He has been a trustee in Marietta college from its establishment in 1835, and was the treasurer, without compensation, for fifteen years. His duty, as he construed it, in this position, was quite beyond the common. He paid out money, sometimes to the extent of thousands of dollars, when the treasury of the college presented the sight of that abhorred thing—a vacuum. Besides these temporary loans he has given outright to the village about twenty-five thousand dollars. But his counsel and his influence have been worth more to the institution than

his money, acceptable as that has been. With an intellect acute and logical, it is one of his peculiarities to always provide for whatever difficulties there are in the present, or are likely to be in the future; and to know where breakers are to be approached often secures their avoidance. With judgment as cool and careful as it was clear, with an interest altogether untiring and never changing, except to increase in proportion to difficulties, he has always been ready to help steer the bark, no matter how rough the waters through which the craft was forced to go.

For more than forty years Colonel Mills has been an efficient member of the Congregational church, through which his contributions have gone out to bless the world in all the channels through which the church has made its influence felt. Among the members of the church, he is, and always has been, one of the most liberal givers, both for the support of the church and the various objects it has sought to promote.

During fifteen years he was president of the Bible society in Washington county, and to this, as to every other good cause, he gave his earnest effort and efficient help.

The record of Colonel Mills in connection with banks and banking interests is one of which he might well be proud if he were ever proud of anything. The bank of Marietta, the first National in the State, was incorporated in 1808. Of this bank Colonel Mills was chosen director in 1824. David Putnam, William R. Putnam, James Whitney, William Skinner, Colonel A. Stone, and Joseph Holden, all prominent men, made up the board of directors. It was something of an honor for John Mills, the youngest man in the board, to be chosen president of the bank in 1825. This position he retained until, by limitation, the charter of the bank expired in 1843. Colonel Mills was a director and a part of the time president of the Marietta branch of the State bank, established in 1845 and continued till 1863, at which date the Marietta National bank was organized. He was a director in this bank during its continuance. He is now (January, 1881) a director in the First National bank of Marietta. There have been diverse and terrible commercial crises during this long period, in which banks have gone down like ships in a raging sea, yet no bank with which Colonel Mills was connected has ever struck its colors, or declared itself insolvent.

Colonel Mills is the largest stockholder in the Marietta Chair company, and president of the same. This is the largest manufacturing establishment in the place, and gives employment to some two hundred and fifty laborers. This manufactory has been an invaluable benefit to many in the town who depend upon labor for their support. During the recent years of hard times and scant employment, now happily over and gone, the work furnished by the chair factory kept the wolf from entering the door of many a home. In the days when ship-building was one of the industries of the place, Colonel Mills took an interest in it and gave it his influence and his aid.

He has been for years, and still is, president of the Marietta gas company.

The town of Marietta, having two rivers, ready made, for travel and commerce, was thought by the average inhabitant to be sufficiently blessed for either and both purposes. But these rivers were nearly dry one part of the year, and frozen up another part, so that as modes of transit they were not so convenient as might be. To the far-seeing eye of Colonel Mills it seemed certain that there must be a surer and swifter way of coming and going, if this mother of the great State of Ohio were not to be left behind and looked down upon by her more enterprising and thriving daughters. Conviction led to effort, and to him as much as to anyone else was due the inception of the Marietta & Cincinnati railroad, the first to connect the place by iron bars with the outside world. The obstacles to the completion of the work were numerous, and the difficulties great, but the work was finally accomplished, though, as is often true, the pecuniary profits went into the pockets of those who came into the field at the eleventh hour and had no share in bearing the heat and burden of the day. The originators and chief executors of the enterprise lost every dollar they invested therein. As a reward for their labors and losses they have the comfort of feeling that they have been the means of bestowing a benefaction upon the community. Only this, and nothing more.

One of the leading characteristics of the subject of this sketch has always been a spirit of helpfulness. Quick to see a want, he has also a nice discrimination that shows him how and when to relieve it. There are many men scattered over the country who are ready to rise up and call him blessed for the helping hand he has extended to them in a critical time, when they would not have breasted the waves that were gaping to overwhelm them without the aid he gave them. And here, where his home has been for so many long years, there are many men who have comfortable homes, with the title deed in their own names, who are indebted to him for the timely aid which enabled them to secure the desired possession. A loan of a few hundred dollars, with easy terms of payment, has helped them to obtain the boon which otherwise would have been beyond their reach. And when a poor woman wanted a cow to assist her in the support of her children, she knew that he was the one to whom to go to get the help she needed, for had not her neighbor done the same and been successful? The fine humanity of the man is better shown in these private and unostentatious charities, of which no one knows but the recipient, than in those larger works of which the world cannot help taking cognizance. They also show that with a mind capacious enough to comprehend the largest interests and work out great problems to satisfactory results, there is also room for the small things of life, and those that affect the happiness of the lowly.

Colonel Mills has been twice married. First in 1824 to Deborah Selden Wilson, who belonged to a family noted for ability, and she possessed a full share of the family inheritance. She had the tact and energy and large mindedness that enabled her to fill well the position in which her marriage placed her. Well fitted to be a leader any where, if she chose, she curbed her ambi-

tion and made it subservient to ruling well her household, and making her guests, who were many, feel the charm of her cordial hospitality and ready appreciation of their wants and feelings. Her death, in 1842, was a sad calamity to her family, and a loss to the church of which she was a member, and the society which she had graced by her presence. She left three daughters, Martha Spencer Mills, who married the Rev. George M. Maxwell, D. D., and now lives in Wyoming, Ohio, and Sarah Mills, the wife of Colonel I. C. Elston, a banker in Crawfordsville, Indiana. In 1845 Colonel Mills was married to Dorotha Webster, of Newburyport, Massachusetts. They have two sons—John, who is in business in Marietta, and William Webster, who is connected with a bank in Crawfordsville, Indiana. Fortunately for him and for the world, the mother of the sons is still living; and now at the age of four score and five years, Colonel Mills presents almost an ideal picture of a serene and beautiful old age. His mind is as far-seeing and shrewd as ever, a spice of humor, which has always given piquancy to his conversation, still shows itself; even the merry twinkle in his eye has not forsaken its place. He takes catholic views of all subjects, is never narrow, never confined in his sympathies by creeds or partial interests. His sympathies are as broad as the needs of humanity, and he takes an eager interest in all that concerns the world's progress. Of fine personal appearance, his graciousness is only equalled by his modesty, which has always encompassed him as a garment. He possesses the reverent respect of all with whom he has had to do, and the love of those who have had the privilege of drawing near to him. His pleasant home is surrounded by tasteful grounds, in which beautiful flowers, cultivated to a considerable extent by his own hands, love to give out their fragrance and show their beauty. But to him the crowning blessing is the companionship of her who is keeping step with him in the way that takes hold on eternal life—one for whom heaven is waiting, and who seems to have been lent to earth for a season, in order to show what manner of spirit they are of, who walk by the River of Life.

And so Colonel John Mills, full of years, of charity, of patience, of hope and of faith, is waiting for the summons to join the innumerable company of those who have fought a good fight, and have been received into the Home prepared for them, to go no more out forever.

ANSELM TUPPER NYE.

Anselm Tupper Nye, son of Ichabod Nye, pioneer of 1788, was born in the southwest block-house at Campus Martius, Marietta, November 9, 1797. This block-house had been the residence of Governor St. Clair, and was purchased by Ichabod Nye after the close of the Indian war. The mother of Anselm T. Nye was Minerva, daughter of General Benjamin Tupper. The first school he attended was kept by Miss Henrietta Morris in the stockade. All the public instruction which he received after leaving Miss Morris was obtained at the

Muskingum academy. His first teacher there was David Putnam; other teachers were David Gilmore, Benjamin F. Stone, Morris B. Belknap, Timothy E. Davidson. In 1816 he was a pupil in the academy six months under Elisha Huntington, a graduate of Dartmouth college. At that time he studied Murray's grammar, higher arithmetic and rhetoric. This ended his school days, but in 1817 he united with Mr. Huntington, Benjamin Putnam and Alexander Lawson in a reading club. The meetings of this club were held in the bank, usually called the old bank, which stood near the Meigs house, on Front street. Each member had selections to make and to read from good authors. A record was kept of books read. The benefit derived from this club was marked, historical, political and scientific works being chiefly read and discussed.

The business career of Mr. Nye began when he was very young. In 1812 he was placed by his father in his store on Putnam street, during the absence of his brother, Horace Nye, the manager of the business in the northwest frontier, where he had gone as brigade major and inspector. While in this store, however, his spare time was occupied in the study of arithmetic, geography and history, without a teacher. Here he continued six months, and in 1813 was sent by his father to assist his brothers, who were engaged in the mercantile business in Putnam, Ohio. In 1816 he returned to school for a time. In 1817, 1818 and a part of 1819, he was again in the store at Marietta. In 1819 he was placed by his father in charge of a stock of goods at Waterford, Ohio. In 1824 he purchased the stock of goods at Waterford of his father, and engaged in business under his own name. For several years after this, business was in a state of great depression. The sales of farm products were very limited. The only outlet for the products of this vicinity was down the river, and there was some trade with the Kanawha salt works, but money was extremely scarce. Nothing could be sent across the mountains at that time with profit, except wool, the expense of transportation being so great. The construction of the New York canal and the Ohio canal helped the country very much, opening a trade with the east which had not been enjoyed before. The Ohio canal was commenced in 1825, and the connection thus made with the Erie and New York canal gave a permanent market for western produce. From that time, wheat, flour and pork have been staple commodities of Ohio.

In May, 1826, Mr. Nye put his business at Waterford into the care of a young man, and came to Marietta to assist his brother, Arius, who had been appointed cashier of the bank of Marietta, supposing he could give a portion of his time to the business at Waterford. But his duties at the bank absorbed his whole time, and in the fall of 1828 he entered into a partnership with Dr. George N. Gilbert, of Belpre, and removed his goods from Waterford to that place, where a new store was opened under the name of George N. Gilbert & Co. At the end of four years, in consequence of a change in the proportion of capital engaged, the firm was changed to Nye & Gilbert; in 1836 the firm was again changed to Gilbert,

Tyler & Co. In 1840 Mr. Nye ceased to be connected with the business. In January, 1830, he entered into the foundry business, which is still continued under the name of A. T. Nye & Son, and of which an account is given elsewhere. In this business his brother, Ichabod H. Nye, was associated with him, and at a later date his nephew, Rothius Hayward. As all the business connections of Mr. Nye are elsewhere mentioned in this book, it is not necessary to enter into any detailed account of them here. From 1826 to 1838 he was assistant cashier of the bank of Marietta; from 1838 to 1842, cashier, and from 1842 to 1847, clerk of the trustees of the bank.

He was a member of the Marietta Ship company, 1844 to 1848, and of the Marietta Bucket factory, 1847 to 1869, and in 1848 began under his own supervision the hardware business now known as the Nye Hardware company.

The public offices he has held are as follows: 1818 and 1824 to 1827, captain in the militia; for several years, beginning 1824, justice of the peace in Waterford; mayor of Marietta several years after 1836, and again in 1849, one year; 1856 to 1862, member of the city council of Marietta; 1863 to 1868, city clerk; 1827 to 1833, county commissioner; and was also township trustee. He was one of the original corporators of Marietta library, founded in 1829. He is one of the trustees of Marietta college, having held that position from its foundation, and in his connection with the college has been trustee of the permanent charitable fund, and was for about thirty years financier of the college.

In February, 1833, he united with the Congregational church in Marietta, and in 1834 was elected deacon. He continued to hold that office until 1878, when he was elected by the church deacon *emeritus*. In connection with his duties as church member, he served as clerk from 1839 until 1873, and was for a number of years superintendent of the Sunday-school, having been a teacher in it from its first organization, in 1817.

About 1869, his eyesight having become very much impaired, Mr. Nye was compelled to retire from active business, his sons taking the management for him.

Mr. Nye has seen almost the whole growth of the State of Ohio. He was born before the old pioneers had passed away, and knew them. In everything that has been for the good of the town in which he has spent his life he has been a ready helper, advancing every moral and civil interest, and often the leader in important reforms. The cause of temperance has always had his support. He was among the first to aid in forming a temperance society in Marietta, and was perhaps the very first among the merchants to discontinue the sale of liquor in his business, having stopped in 1828.

Since retiring from active business he has contributed much to our local history in the preparation of historical articles published in the Marietta *Register*.

DOUGLAS PUTNAM.

Douglas Putnam, of Harmar, is the fourth son of David Putnam, and was born at the old homestead (the stone house still standing near the west bank of the Muskingum), April 7, 1806. He had five brothers and two sisters who lived to maturity, viz: Benjamin, Charles Marsh, Peter Radcliffe, David, George, and Catharine H., and Elizabeth. Mr. Putnam's christian name, it may be remarked, was derived from his grandmother, the wife of Dr. Elisha Perkins, who was originally a Douglas, and a descendant of the Scotch family of that name, famous in history.

Mr. Putnam's boyhood was passed at his home, but in 1820, at the age of fourteen, he was sent away to school. He attended academy in Plainfield and Norwich, Connecticut, and entered Yale college in 1822. He would have graduated from this institution with the class of 1826, but in the fall of 1825, his brother Benjamin having died, and his father's health being poor, it was deemed advisable that he should return to Marietta and assist him in his business. His father, in addition to landed interests of his own, had become agent for a large number of the non-resident shareholders of the Ohio company. The son, entering the office in 1825, remained for twenty years his father's assistant. He developed early those correct and exact business methods which, later in life, led to a very pronounced success. In 1845 his father transferred to him his entire business. During all the years since that time Mr. Putnam has carried on the real estate business, devoting the larger part of his time and attention to it, although many other interests have claimed a share. He was director for fifteen years of the old Cincinnati & Belpre railroad company, and with others labored zealously to secure such a location of the great east and west road as would give Marietta the fullest advantages of rail communication. He was a director of the old bank of Marietta, before its charter expired in 1842, and of the Marietta branch of the State bank; also a director in the Marietta National bank, and for a few years its president. The wooden ware factory, now operated by Putnam, Sons & Co., was established by Mr. Putnam, and during the past thirty years has been most of the time in active operation, benefitting the community by giving employment to a large number of men. The subject of our sketch was also interested for some years in the operation of an iron furnace in Vinton county.

The real estate business, however, conducted by him continuously and constantly for the past thirty-five years, has been, as we have already said, the principal field of Mr. Putnam's business activity and the chief source of the liberal fortune which he has amassed. Mr. Putnam has dealt almost entirely in the Ohio company's lands and has sold generally in small parcels to people who have made themselves homes. His business has thus been one of more solidity of character than it would have possessed had it been conducted on a purely speculative basis, and its profits if more slowly accruing have perhaps been surer than those which could have been obtained from a more rapid handling of property and heavier transactions. Doubtless the manner in which Mr. Putnam's wealth has been obtained has in some measure influenced him in the method of its disposition

He is conservative and careful; has always maintained an exactness of method in all of his dealings; and giving his personal attention to the details as well as to general features, has had a knowledge of his affairs far more definite than is usually possessed by men controlling equally extensive business. He has dealt directly with the men who have bought and settled upon his lands, and while usually enforcing with proper and necessary firmness the conditions of agreements, he has never been in the least degree oppressive in his measures nor taken undue advantages of a purchaser. Not an acre of the many thousands which have passed through Mr. Putnam's hands has been conveyed except upon terms which were intended to be just. Few men in a business so beset with difficulties, by its very nature so frequently looked upon with a prejudice, could escape reasonable or unreasonable censure as Mr. Putnam has done.

But it is not alone as the substantial and successful man of business that we have to speak of Douglas Putnam. He has been a man of sterling worth to the community in which he has dwelt and filled a sphere of noble usefulness. The acts of his benevolence have been many, large, varied in their nature, practical and judicious. His use of money has demonstrated his worthiness of the possession of wealth. He was one of the founders of Marietta college and has ever been its steadfast friend, giving the institution the constant benefit of his influence, services and benevolence. His first gift to the college was two hundred dollars, his largest twenty-five thousand dollars and the total amount of his contributions has been upwards of fifty thousand dollars. The successive donations seem to have been increased in amount with the increase of ability to give. The maintainance and constant development of this line of benevolence has indicated a remarkable continuance of interest and a devoted friendship. While Mr. Putnam has been the largest donor to the college he has aided its advancement by other means. The trustees and the faculty have ever felt the influence of his sanguine hope for the future of the institution and his encouragement during the less promising period of its history. He has often in the time of need assisted the college by securing for it credit, and his practical business knowledge has been of large value in the management of its finances. Mr. Putnam was one of the first trustees of the college and has continuously served in that capacity during the period of its existence—over forty-five years. During most of these years he has been also a member of the executive committee. He has been secretary of the college from the first and has signed in that capacity every diploma that has been issued from 1838 to 1881 inclusive. Mr. Putnam's length of service to this substantial institution of learning, the varied forms of his assistance and the unswerving constancy of his devotion to its interests have rendered the relation one of peculiar and almost unique value and pleasantness. President Andrews has said that, without two such friends as Mr. Putnam and Colonel John Mills, Marietta college could scarcely have maintained an existence.

Many private acts of charity have been performed by

Mr. Putnam, of which only the recipients and himself have had knowledge, and the church has also been a channel through which his benevolence has had a constant outlet. In this connection we may remark that he became a member of the Congregational church of Marietta soon after his return from college, in 1825, and remained one of its communicants until the organization of a society of the same denomination in Harmar, in 1840. He was for ten years a deacon in the Marietta church, and for the past forty-one years has held that office in the Congregational church of Harmar. He is well known in Congregational circles throughout the State. It is worthy of note that, while Mr. Putnam has been prominently identified with local charities, his philanthropy has also been directed to the broader field of the betterment of humanity in general. His reputation for benevolence has not been confined to his home. We find his name enrolled among those of the leading spirits of the great philanthropic societies of the east. Since 1851 he has been a vice-president of the American Home Missionary society, and is the third oldest upon the roster. Since 1853 he has been a corporate member of the American board of commissioners for foreign missions, and he is one of the vice-presidents of the American Missionary association.

Mr. Putnam has not been a public man in a political capacity. The people of Washington county elected him early in life as one of their commissioners, and he held that office by successive reelections for fifteen years. He has been affiliated with the Whig and Republican parties, but has taken only a citizen's interest in politics. While he has not sought elective office, and has had a distaste for political preferment, he has occupied by appointment (or by election entirely unsought) several positions of honor and prominence for which he was peculiarly fitted. Thus, in 1846, his knowledge of the lands in southeastern Ohio led to his choice as a member of the first State board of equalization ever constituted in Ohio, and he served by appointment of Governor Hayes, upon the board of 1870. Very appropriately, considering his extensive practical knowledge of the subject in general, he was appointed by Governor Hayes, in 1866, a member of the first board of State charities, in which capacity he served two terms, or until the efficiency of the board was annulled by the unwise refusal of the legislature to make appropriations for it.

Mr. Putnam has been married three times. His first wife, to whom he was joined February 16, 1831, was Mary Ann, daughter of Dr. Samuel P. Hildreth. She died in 1842, and upon May 16, 1844, Mr. Putnam married Mrs. Eliza Tucker, a daughter of Levi Whipple, of Putnam (now the ninth ward of Zanesville), Ohio. Her death occurred September 9, 1862. In 1867 Mr. Putnam was united, at Springfield, Massachusetts, with his present wife, who was Mrs. Sarah C. Dimond.

Mr. Putnam has been the father of seven children— five by his first wife and two by his second. Two died in infancy, and a third, Benjamin Perkins Putnam, in maturity, in the year 1870. Those now living are: Samuel Hildreth, who occupies the old homestead in Har-

mar; Douglas, jr., located at Ashland, Kentucky, in charge of a large furnace; Mary Hildreth (the wife of Dr. Frank H. Bosworth, of New York) and Lizzie, living at home.

The residence of Mr. Putnam was built in the year 1859.

WILLIAM PARKER CUTLER.

The Hon. William Parker Cutler, of Marietta, belongs to a family which in three generations has performed distinguished service for the State. He is the grandson of Manasseh Cutler, LL. D., and the son of Judge Ephraim Cutler.

Mr. Cutler was born in Warren township, Washington county, Ohio, July 12, 1812. He became a member of the class which graduated from the Ohio university at Athens in 1833, but was prevented by ill health from advancing farther than the junior year in his studies.

He was elected by the Whigs a member of the Ohio legislature in 1844, and twice re elected, He was speaker of the house in the session of 1846-47.

In 1850 he was a member of the convention that formed the present constitution of the State of Ohio.

In 1860 he was elected by the Republicans a member of the Thirty-seventh Congress. Mr. Cutler's public services have been of a high and noble kind. The measures which he has labored to promote have been great and good ones. It has been his splendid privilege to labor for and witness the final complete triumph of the principle of freedom which Manasseh Cutler made possible in the ordinance of 1787, and which Judge Ephraim Cutler assisted fifteen years later. It is pleasant to note that in Congress Mr. Cutler made ringing speeches in denunciation of slavery, and in favor of its abolishment before it was commonly considered that the overthrow of that evil would follow as a result of the war, and that in earlier years his influence was exerted in advancing public opinion upon the "peculiar institution." He has ever held the radical views upon the slavery question which might be expected from his parentage, if from no other source. In May, 1857, he was a member of the United States Presbyterian general assembly which met in Cleveland, and offered a resolution to that body designed to make the advocacy and support of slavery a subject of church discipline as contrary to its standards.

But not in political life alone has Mr. Cutler been useful to the community, in which he has lived, and to the State. He has been a zealous laborer in almost every line of moral and material improvement. The cause of education has always received his hearty support, both in the exercise of influence and in financial aid. He has been for a long term of years a trustee of Marietta college. The church with which he is connected and others have had in him a warm friend, as has also every good institution of the community, every substantial reform and progressive movement. From 1847 to 1868 he was much engaged in promoting the construction of the Marietta & Cincinnati railroad, and during that period he was either president or vice-president and general superintendent of the road. To no man have the people of Marietta and southeastern Ohio been more indebted for their railroad advantages than to Mr. Cutler. He was the prime mover in the establishment of the Hocking Valley railroad in 1867, and in the inauguration of the Marietta, Pittsburgh & Cleveland railroad enterprise, in 1868. Since then he has, as contractor, built over four hundred miles of railroad in Indiana and Illinois. His career of activity is not closed. What may be its achievements time will develop. That his remaining years will not be spent in idleness the character of the man and the nature of his past works are sufficient guarantee. Whatever the future may add, however much or little, it will be said of Mr. Cutler's life that it has been one of success—one of broad benefit to his fellow men, flowing from a conscientious devotion to the highest human duties.

Mr. Cutler married, November 1, 1849, Elizabeth Williamson Voris, daughter of Dr. William and Elizabeth W. (Means) Voris, of Adams county, Ohio, and granddaughter of Colonel John Means, who, "believing slavery to be a moral and political evil," removed from South Carolina in 1819, to Ohio, bringing his slaves with him, setting them free, and providing liberally for their support. Mr. and Mrs. Cutler have had six children, of whom but one is living. William Ephraim was born October 20, 1851, and died August 21, 1852, aged ten months. Annie Elizabeth, born July 24, 1853, died January 11, 1864. Sarah Julia, born January 10, 1856, is living with her parents. Ephraim Sumner, born April 9, 1858, died August 5, 1860. Margaret Jane, born January 9, 1861, died April 18, 1861. William Means, born January 29, 1867, died October 8, 1870.

ISRAEL WARD ANDREWS, LL. D.

"Israel Ward Andrews, son of William and Sarah (Parkhill) Andrews, was born at Danbury, Connecticut, January 3, 1815. After his graduation from Williams college in 1837, he taught an academy at Lee, Massachusetts, and was appointed tutor at Marietta college in the fall of 1838. In April, 1839, he was elected professor of mathematics, and in January, 1855, president."

Such is the autobiography furnished by the third oldest college president in the United States.

The following notice of Dr. Andrews understood to be from the pen of Professor George R. Rosseter, appeared in the *College Olio* of June 29, 1880, which date was the twenty-fifth anniversary of his accession to the presidency of the college:

For many reasons we are expecting that the coming commencement will be of unusual interest. On each return of this fete day of our Alma Mater all her children and all her friends have their hearts warm with kindly feeling. Many an alumnus and many an old friend of the college will find a special reason for emotions both tender and joyful in the fact that at this commencement, Dr. Andrews will have filled out the term of twenty-five years in the service of the college as its president.

Graduated at Williams in 1837, in 1838 Dr. Andrews came here as tutor. In 1839 he was elected professor of mathematics and natural philosophy. For sixteen years he occupied this chair. During all this time his natural aptness for affairs, and his willingness to do all he could for the college, resulted in the assignment to him of many of the incidental duties of the faculty, which belong to no one professor's work, and yet whose prompt and accurate performance is essential to the welfare of the college. For five years, from 1850 to 1855, he was the college treasurer. Upon the resignation of the presidency by Dr. Smith in 1855, the trustees, without for a moment looking elsewhere, elected Professor Andrews, president of the college.

Twenty-five years have passed since he was inducted into this office. Forty-two years of service he has given to Marietta college. Of the four hundred and ninety-eight alumni of our college, President Andrews has known each one personally. It is doubtful if a similar record can be found in the annals of any of our American colleges.

There are few offices which bring with them heavier burdens and responsibilities than that of president of a college. The duty of instruction—the duty of government, the duty of general oversight and of financial management, all rest heavily upon the president.

The old students of Marietta never tire of telling of the excellence of Dr. Andrews, as an instructor—of his masterly grasp of the subject, his clearness in unfolding it—his power of interesting the student, and of inspiring enthusiasm, and above all of the influence of his example of thorough scholarship, in stimulating them to thoroughness in all their work. Undoubtedly it is in the recitation room that a college officer must show himself strong. The unanimous voice of his students for forty-two years has pronounced Dr. Andrews, STRONG.

In the discipline and general government of the college, President Andrews has been remarkably happy. Unyielding in essentials, he has yet been flexible in minor matters, and good order and thoroughly faithful study have been the rule. There have been but few serious cases of discipline, and none which have not readily yielded to his skill. The quiet assumption that the students have gathered here for study, and for gentlemanly conduct toward officers and fellow-students, has been largely successful in securing what was desired. The kindly greetings which Dr. Andrews finds awaiting him all over the land, when he meets one of the alumni, is a sufficient proof that the memory of college days recalls him with only agreeable associations.

The growth of Marietta college in all the essentials of a sound institution of learning—sure and enduring, even if it has been slower than her friends would wish—establishes clearly the wisdom of the management of its affairs by Dr Andrews.

It was indeed a fortunate day for Marietta college when President Mark Hopkins recommended I. W. Andrews to the trustees of Marietta as one from whom they might expect faithful and efficient service.

We trust that for many years his strength may endure and his labors be continued in the interests of our Alma Mater.

DYER BURGESS.

Rev. Dyer Burgess was born in Springfield, Vermont, December 27, 1784. At the age of sixteen years, soon after his conversion, he began to preach as a Methodist minister, but finding his views more in accordance with Congregationalism, he joined that church and studied theology with the Rev. Dr. Wines. He was ordained at Colebrook, Vermont, but came to Ohio in 1816 and was received into Miami Presbytery from the Northern association of Vermont September 2, 1817. About this time he established the Presbyterian church in Piqua, Ohio. His early ministerial labors were in the southeastern part of Ohio. In 1840, he was employed to preach in Warren, Washington county. His first marriage was with Miss Isabella Ellison, with whom he lived in West Union, Adams county, until her death in 1829. In 1842 he married Mrs. Elizabeth W. Voris, but had no children by either wife.

For many years prior to his removal to Warren he was a member of the Chillicothe presbytery, the associate and peer of Dr. R. G. Wilson, president of the Ohio university, Drs. Williamson, Gililand, Carothers, Dickey,

Rankin and others, leading and influential ministers of the Gospel in that region. These gentlemen were born and educated in South Carolina amidst the influences of slavery, and left their native clime in obedience to the dictates of an enlightened conscience, aroused to the evils resulting from that system. They were all strong men, and Mr. Burgess entered most heartily into their views upon the subject of slavery, and became the leading and prominent abolitionist of that day. He was a member of the Presbyterian general assembly of 1818, and presented a paper upon the subject of slavery, which led to the adoption of the celebrated declaration of that body condemning the whole system. His personal appearance and address were such as well qualified him to lead in the discussion of a subject that absorbed the attention of all, and at that time excited the positive hostility of a large majority of his hearers. At one time, while travelling on an Ohio river steamboat, a rope was prepared for his neck, from which he was saved only by the prompt and efficient interference of friends.

He was strongly enlisted in opposition to Masonry, and at one time published a newspaper in Cincinnati upon that subject. His views upon temperance and the use of tobacco were as positive as upon other subjects; and boldness as well as the personal power that he exhibited in the discussion of all such topics gave him the marked characteristics of a radical reformer. Notwithstanding the energy and decisive persistency with which he supported his own views, often giving the impression of rancor and ill-will, yet he was one of the most enjoyable of companions. Having an extensive personal acquaintance, and a memory fully stored with early reminiscences, he possessed also a most happy faculty of communicating his thoughts, while all acrimony disappeared by close contact in social intercourse.

He not only maintained his early literary acquisitions, but kept his knowledge of the classics bright by daily use of the Greek Testament, making it a constant and special study. His labors as minister of the Gospel were in the Presbyterian churches of Belpre, Warren and Watertown, although not confined to any as pastor. He died August 31, 1872.

His second wife was the daughter of Colonel John Means, who moved from South Carolina at the same time and for the same reasons that induced Drs. Wilson, Gilliland, Williamson and others to seek in Ohio a refuge from the evils of slavery. Colonel Means brought all his slaves with him to Adams county, gave them their freedom there, and supplied their wants until they could support themselves. Mrs. Burgess still lives with her daughter, Mrs. W. P. Cutler, a most intelligent lady, the liberal friend of the poor, whose Christian virtues and deeds reach back through more than half a century, and brighten the evening sky of a devoted and most useful life.

HARLOW CHAPIN.

It is a pleasure to outline the life of a prominent and wealthy man, whose success is the reward of earnest, honest and intelligent effort. Such a man is Harlow Chapin, of Harmar. The Chapin family in the United States is descended from Deacon Samuel Chapin, who emigrated from England and settled at Springfield, Massachusetts, and perhaps, more remotely, from a French Huguenot family of that name. The descendants of Deacon Samuel Chapin number more than fifteen hundred individuals. Seymour Chapin his great-grandson, was related to the Seymours of Connecticut. He married Achsa Hulet, of Massachusetts, in 1802, and settled in New Marlborough, Berkshire county, Massachusetts, where Harlow, the subject of our sketch, was born, November 29, 1804. The family consisted of five children, Harlow being the oldest. Levi L. lives in Medina village; Joshua died in Harmar, where he was engaged in business enterprises; Caroline L., wife of William C. Hall, lives in Medina; Electa, first wife of William C. Hall, died at Medina; and Oscar D., died at Saginaw, Michigan, where he had been engaged in the lumber trade.

In 1816 Seymour Chapin with his family emigrated from Massachusetts and settled in Medina county, Ohio, then a thick and almost unbroken forest. But little favored with opportunities for acquiring an education, Harlow yet advanced rapidly, especially in mathematics, for which he had a special aptitude. Hunting the game and fur-bearing animals of the forest was his favorite sport, and solving the abstract propositions of mathematics his favorite study. After completing a partial course at the school at Canton he began life for himself, first as a school teacher. Whatever he undertook was carried through with that spirit of determination and self-reliance which is an important element in the character of the man.

Mr. Chapin taught school at Massillon, Ohio, then a small village, for two winters. In 1829 he was given a place on the corps of engineers then at work on the Ohio canal. A field of labor for which he was peculiarly qualified was now open. Although received under a temporary engagement, his services were found too valuable to be dispensed with. Upon the completion of the canal he was given a section to superintend. This employment occupied his time until 1834, when he was called to Dresden, Ohio, to supervise the erection of a lock near that place. It was found expedient by the board of public works to enlarge the reservoir at Licking Summit, Licking county, and the supervision of this important work was intrusted to the man who seven years before, without any experience, was received to fill a temporary vacancy.

In 1837 an act was passed by Congress authorizing the improvement of the Muskingum by the construction of dams and locks. The most difficult and extensive of these works is at the mouth of the river, the contract for the construction of which was awarded to Mr. Chapin, for the sum, in round numbers, of one hundred and thirty thousand dollars. After this contract had been fulfilled, he took two small contracts, on Ohio river improvements, with which he ended his labors in that direction.

While engaged on the Ohio canal at Massillon, Mr. Chapin formed an attachment for Hannah Earl, daughter of Gilbertharp Earl, a highly respected farmer in the vicinity. She was born July 26, 1807. They were married October 23, 1833. Her brother, William Earl, will be remembered as an early merchant at Beverly where he managed a store owned by Chapin, Fearing & Earl. He is also well known among Odd Fellows, having for many years been secretary of the Grand Lodge of the State.

Mr. and Mrs. Chapin have had six children. Cornelia Maria, was born September 25, 1834. She was married, November 19, 1856, to William H. Crawford, and is now living in Bay City, Michigan. Sarah Earl was born July 20, 1836; she was married to Charles B. Collier, September 22, 1857, and resides in Philadelphia. Henry E. Chapin, born July 16, 1838, married Anna Chappelle, and resides in Bay City, Michigan. Arthur B., was born December 28, 1840; married Electa W. Barber, November 29, 1866, and lives in Saginaw City, Michigan. Charles Seymour was born October 25, 1844; died February 16, 1848. Leander R. was born May 19, 1848; married Anna Young, and lives in Harmar.

Mr. and Mrs. Chapin resided at Zanesville from 1834 till 1835, and at Hebron till 1837, since which time Harmar has been their home. Mr. Chapin in charge of a company of twenty-one men, crossed the continent in 1849, and engaged in mining and dealing in stock in California, for a period of two years. Since his return he has been living in comparative retirement.

The citizens of Harmar have testified their appreciation of his character by electing him mayor of their village twenty-one years. Out of deference to his wishes they occasionally gave him a rest, during the period of one term, but at the end of that term he was again pressed into the service. Mr. Chapin was a member of the Electoral college of Ohio in 1844, and is proud of having cast a vote for the distinguished patriot and statesman, Henry Clay, who was at the time the most able representative of his political ideas. He was a member of the Constitutional convention of 1873. To represent Washington county in a body of this character is no ordinary honor. His practical knowledge of public works and a long experience in business affairs, gave him a peculiar fitness for the place, which his fellow citizens recognize by voting for him regardless of party lines.

Mr. Chapin is a man of affairs and a close student of current events as presented and discussed in the public press. Dogmas and theories have little attraction for him. His intellect is deep enough and broad enough to solve the problems, which daily intrude themselves upon every active man, in a simple and practical way.

Grace and hospitality characterize the Chapin home. Mr. Chapin is strong in body, keen in mind and interesting in conversation. Mrs. Chapin, while physically not so fortunate, is a woman of rare beauty of character.

The California company, referred to above, is worthy of more extended notice. The discovery of gold, in 1848, caused an excitement in which the whole civilized world participated. This excitement in Washington county resulted in the formation of a company to carry on mining operations. Two boards of directors were chosen—one to watch over the interests of the company at home, the other to carry on operations in California. The Harmar board consisted of Darwin E. Gardner, agent; Henry Fearing, E. W. T. Clark, L. Chamberlain, and Asa Soule, advisors. The California board consisted of Harlow Chapin, agent; Abijah Hulet and A. G. Hovey, advisors.

The object of the company was to send a party of men to labor in California for the company. The primary stock was to be at least three thousand dollars. The third article of the rules declared "At least twenty able-bodied men shall be selected by the company, who shall bind themselves to go to California and faithfully labor under the direction of the agents duly appointed, from the time of their departure from Harmar, in April A. D., 1849, until first of April, A. D., 1851." The party which accepted the pledge and left Harmar on the steamer Hamburgh, April 23, 1849, consisted of the following gentlemen: Harlow Chapin, agent; Abijah Hulet and Albert G. Hovey, advisors; Henry Clark, clerk; Charles Cutler, Gage H. Drown, Moses A. Williams, T. Johnson, Allen M. Crabaum, William Bisbee, William Irwin, Edward Hulett, Almer P. Soule, Henry Erehom, John Mills (of Virginia), E. C. Carter, Samuel R. Hammet, Jeremiah Evans, William Flick, George Roe and Paul Fearing.

The trip was made overland. Four of the party—Messrs. Hulet, Drown, Clark and Cutler—died of cholera on the way. On reaching California, representatives from almost every nation were found. They lived without law, in perfect peace and security for a time, but gamblers, roughs and robbers eventually came in, and a dangerous state of affairs followed.

CAPTAIN CAIUS MARCUS COLE.

The earliest account we have of the Cole family of which the subject of this sketch is a representative, shows that in the past century three brothers, Englishmen, settled on Long Island. They were attacked by Indians and fled to save their lives, one of them being killed by the pursuing savages. The two who were spared did not return to the dangerous locality they had originally chosen for a home, but settled in New York State upon the Hudson river. John Cole was the son of one of these brothers. His son Asa was the father of Sardis, who was the father of Captain Cole of Harmar. Sardis Cole was born upon the Hoosac river, January 26, 1795. In 1799 his parents emigrated to the western frontier and locating at Wheeling, Virginia, were for two years or thereabouts residents of the historical old block-house at that place. The father, Asa, was during this period engaged in packing salt from the Atlantic seaboard over the mountains to Wheeling for Zane, the founder of the settlement. In the spring of 1801 the family became settlers on Indian Wheeling creek within the present limits of Belmont county, Ohio, and in 1806 they removed to Warren township, Washington county, where the father pursued the avocations of farming and keel-boating for a number of years. He finally returned to Belmont county, where he died. John Cole, the father of Asa, also settled in Warren township in 1806, and kept the tavern at the roadside on the river bank known as "the Half Way house," because about equidistant from Marietta and Belpre. Here he entertained the wayfarer and the stranger, and as was the universal custom in his time set forth the "gigger" of whiskey to his guests, until he passed away at the ripe age of ninety-five years, about 1817. His grandson, the young Sardis Cole, who was eleven years of age when the family came into Washington county, upon coming of sufficient age to care for himself, entered the then very common, popular and then lucrative occupation of keel-boating. He made trips up the Ohio to Pittsburgh and as far down generally as Cincinnati, and also engaged in the navigation of the Big Kanawha, plying between the salt works on that stream and the best markets on the Ohio. He finally located on the Kanawha, engaged in salt manufacture, and remained there until 1827 having a full experience of that peculiar phase of pioneer life. On leaving the Kanawha salt works Mr. Cole located at Briscoe run in Wood county, Virginia, five miles below Marietta, a locality settled principally by Germans and a place of considerable note on the river, though seemingly without cause. Briscoe Run post office was established in 1838 and Mr. Cole was commissioned as the first postmaster, and held the office as long as he lived. By occupation he was a cooper, but he combined with his trade several other kinds of employment such as there was need for in the little community where he dwelt. He is described as a very clever, social man, and one who, despite the rough surroundings amid which his early life was passed as a keel-boatman and a resident of the isolated salt-making colony on the Kanawha, he was not only noted for his strict integrity but for a correctness of deportment and a freedom from the small vices and careless habits of life which it might naturally be supposed he would possess. He died in the spring of 1871, having passed through the alloted three score years and ten, loved and respected by all who knew him. Sardis Cole married, in 1817, Mary Uhl, of Briscoe Run, who died at the age of sixty-one years, in 1858.

They resided for a few years after their marriage in Warren township, Washington county, in the immediate neighborhood of Judge Ephraim Cutler's homestead, and it was there that their second child, the subject of this sketch, was born, January 6, 1821. A sister, older, Jane Ann (Webb) and a brother younger, Arius Nye, are now living at Briscoe Run. Caius Marcus Cole was in his seventh year when his parents removed to the little village which was to be their permanent home. When he was about eleven years old his father began the business of keeping a wood yard for the steamers plying up and down the river. He made some money at this business and invested most of it in land, the sterile, rough, rocky bank along the Ohio, valuable for little else than its stone and the timber it bore. The business of wooding steamers increased, and Briscoe Run became a favorite station among the river men. Before the subject of our sketch was twenty-one his father had practically turned over his business to him, and its prosperity was not abated under his management. He had become well acquainted with nearly all of the captains or pilots on the river, and was much liked by them. He slipped off occasionally upon boating trips "learned the river" easily, and at thirty years of age was a skilful pilot, (though he was never licensed to act regularly in that capacity until 1862.) It was natural that he should have a fondness for the water, and that he should take to it to gain a livelihood, for many of the Cole family before him had been watermen. Nevertheless, his whole attention was not given to river navigation. He became a jobber, and for years did a large business in furnishing, from his own land at Briscoe Run, building stone, to be used in Parkersburgh and Marietta. Among other extensive works, he built the fine landing at Marietta. Stone quarrying and boating were alternately or jointly his occupations. Since 1866 he has been a government contractor, and during a period of fourteen years has completed twenty-five contracts, of from five to twenty-five thousand dollars each, and he has now on hand two contracts on the Ohio, which amount to one hundred thousand dollars. The scene of the work is eighteen miles above the mouth of the river. Large dykes are there being constructed for the improvement of what is known to river men as the "grand chain," by turning the current from some very dangerous rocks to the smooth side of the bed. These dykes are to be each three thousand feet in length, and eight feet above low water. Mr. Cole's contracts have been both for construction and improvement of navigation through the removal of obstructions, such as snags, wrecks and rocks. This work, whether of one kind or the other, has always been done thoroughly, conscientiously, and to the complete satisfaction of the Government, and has made him an enviable reputation as a contractor. While the promptness and reliability which characterize the captain in his business affairs, have won for him the confidence of the government officials on the one hand, and the sub-contractors, furnishers of material and employes, upon the other, his strict probity of character has made him universally respected by those who know him simply as the man. He has been uncompromising in his devotion to principle, even when, by violating the rigid dictates of conscience, he might very largely have advanced his own monetary interests. As an example of his strictness in this respect, we may state that he does not believe it right to do any work upon Sunday, and when that day comes his boats and men must lie still. Even should he be journeying down the river to engage in the prosecution of some large and important work, the boat must be tied up at the shore before the last hours of Saturday night are gone, and the line not loosed until Monday morning. As it would be impossible to carry out so literal and rigid a Sunday law in the passenger traffic, the captain has always refused to enter into that branch of business, and for the same reason would not become the owner of the Marietta and Williamstown ferry. Something of the same inflexibility of principle is shown in his attitude upon temperance. He is himself a total abstinence man, and he will not employ men who are addicted to the drink habit, even though their indulgence might be only what would ordinarily be termed moderate drinking. It is probable that the influence of his example and counsel has done much good upon the river in this matter. Captain Cole became in early years a member of the Methodist Episcopal church. For the past eight years he has resided in Harmar, and during the greater portion of that term has been connected with the First Congregational church, of which he is now a deacon.

Captain Cole had the misfortune of losing his life companion and helpmeet upon the twelfth of November, 1880. She was a lady of most rare and estimable qualities, and her death was a sad loss to her husband and children. Her maiden name was Nancy Scott, and she was the daughter of John and Nancy Scott, who came from the vicinity of Wheeling, West Virginia, to Warren township, Washington county, in 1839. She was born on the eleventh of December, 1815, and was consequently nearly sixty-five years of age when she died. Her marriage to Captain Cole took place in 1842. Eight children blessed their union. Nancy, the eldest, born November 20, 1842, married Leonard H. Robbins, and is now living in Lincoln, Nebraska; John Sardis, born December 31, 1843, was one of the many thousands of his generation who fell as victims to the civil war. He enlisted in the eleventh regiment, Virginia infantry, and was killed March 30, 1865, at Fort Baldwin on Hatchers run, re-named by the Federals Fort Harris, and his remains lie in the soldier's burying-ground at Petersburgh; the third child and second son, C. Mark, born January 2, 1846, lives in Warren township; Mary Ann, born November 6, 1847, married Thomas Tyrrell, and now resides in Nebraska; James Franklin, born June 16, 1849, and Amanda Jane, born December 27, 1850, are in Harmar; Horace Dryden, born May 4, 1853, is a resident of Lincoln, Nebraska; and Charles Arthur, born December 20, 1857, is a citizen of Harmar.

SETH HART, M. D.

About the middle of the seventeenth century Stephen Hart emigrated with his family from Scotland, and settled on the Connecticut river. At the place of their settlement there was a ford in the river, which became known as Hart's ford. The land which Mr. Hart owned and on which he settled, is now occupied by the flourishing capital city of Connecticut—Hartford.

Joel Hart, a descendant of Stephen Hart, lived in Hartford county. He married Lydia North, of Berlin, Connecticut, by whom he had four children.

Stephen settled in Illinois where he practiced law for a short time, and then engaged in fruit raising in Illinois and Florida; Lidia married Carlyle Olmstead; Mary married Salmon Baldwin; both settled in Oswego county, New York; Lidia is dead.

Seth, the second son, was born in Berlin, Hartford county, Connecticut, November 13, 1804. When he was two years old his father moved with the family to Delaware county, New York, at that time a new county, so that his youth was spent amid the experiences of pioneer life. Joel Hart died October 17, 1811, and Seth spent the next four years of his life at the home of his grandfather, Jedidiah North, in Connecticut, where he enjoyed school privileges. At the age of twelve he returned to Delaware county, New York, where he was placed under the instruction of a tutor and received a liberal education. He remained in New York, teaching school, studying medicine, and clerking in a drug store, until 1824, when he came to New Philadelphia, Ohio, and taught school during the winter of 1824-5.

Mr. Hart, in 1824, received a diploma certifying that he had read medicine three years and qualifying him to enter the practice, and in 1858 he received an honorary degree from an Eclectic college in New York. He came to Washington county in the spring of 1825, and on the ninth of April of that year opened an office in Watertown. He remained in practice until September 27th, when he returned to New York and attended a course of lectures at Fairfield.

He married, February 19, 1826, Vestie Curtis, daughter of Dr. Bildad Curtis, of Delaware county, in whose office Mr. Hart had read medicine. Dr. Curtis was one of the leading physicians in Delaware county, and after coming to Watertown in 1827, he had a full practice until his death. He was born in Braintree, Massachusetts, October 31, 1775.

Mrs. Hart died in Watertown, March 22, 1827, leaving one child, Vestie Curtis, born December 1, 1826. She was married to F. H. Kemper, and lived in Cincinnati, where she died September 29, 1879, leaving one son and four daughters.

Dr. Hart married for his second wife, June 7, 1729, Mary Wilson, daughter of Deacon David Wilson, of Round Bottom, Waterford township. She was born in Waterford, July 18, 1798. She left eight children to mourn her death, which occurred June 14, 1863. Samuel, the oldest, was born June 7, 1830. He graduated at Cincinnati Medical college, and has since been in active practice. During the war he was surgeon for the Seventy-seventh regiment, and afterwards, army physician.

Mary Wilson was born November 26, 1831. She was married to James Nixon November 20, 1878, and resides at Ironton, Ohio.

Romeyn Beck was born November 30, 1833. November 11, 1856, he married Martha E. Metcalf, who was born September 22, 1834. He lives in Harmar. Henry L. and Samuel Munson were born October 11, 1835. Henry married Lucy Wolcott Deming, and resides in Warren township. Samuel Munson married October 16, 1878, Mary Roan. He is a practicing dentist in Marietta.

David Wilson was born November 26, 1838. He married Mariam Cox December 23, 1865, and resides in Denver, Colorado. Lydia North, the youngest child, was born August 30, 1840. She has for many years been a successful teacher in the public schools of Harmar.

Dr. Hart married for his third wife Ella Lula Hiett October 22, 1863. She was the daughter of James Hiett, of West Virginia, and was born December 28, 1842. She died February 16, 1865.

Dr. Hart married November 16, 1870, Elizabeth D. Marshall, daughter of Gideon Marshall of Morgan county. She was born September 30, 1830. They have one child, Minnie HaHa Grace, born November 8, 1872.

Dr. Hart practiced in Watertown from the spring of 1825 until 1836, excepting the time he was absent, attending lectures in New York. Since 1836 his office has been located in Harmar, with but two breaks. In 1865 he was called to Tennessee to assist his son at the army hospital at Telahoma. After the close of the war he remained two years. In 1869 he took charge of a mining enterprise in the Rocky Mountains and remained one year.

Dr. Hart, ever since entering the practice in 1825, has made a habit of keeping and preparing his own medicines. His first experience in compounding medicines was at a drug store at Palmyra, New York. Since then a long and busy life of practice has given him an intimate acquaintance with drugs and their use.

During the period of his practice in this county—more than fifty years—Dr. Hart has always maintained the highest reputation for efficiency as a doctor and integrity as a man. He is a man of vigorous physique and well preserved faculties. His life has been useful not only to himself and family but also to the community which he has served for half a century. His visits have been an inspiration to thousands of families in the hour of pain and distress, and his life has been an example of industry and uprightness. He joined the Presbyterian church at the age of sixteen. When he came to Harmar, he united with the Congregational church, where he still holds his membership.

CAPTAIN HIRAM BURCH.

Hiram Burch, of Marietta, one of the best known of Ohio river men, was born October 13, 1796, near Newtown, Connecticut, and is a son of William and Grace (Northrup) Burch. His father was in early life a seafaring man. In the year 1804 the family moved to Pittsburgh, and the father engaged in keel-boating. As soon as he was old enough young Hiram also adopted this avocation, and served as a keel-boat pilot before he had fairly entered his teens. In 1809 or 1810, his sister having married and located at Belpre, the lad removed to that place and it became his home, so far as one following the river for a living can be said to have a home. He served six months in the War of 1812, entering the ranks as a substitute. Although only sixteen years of age he was well grown, and his active life had made him muscu-

lar and hardy. As early as the year 1814 the young man engaged in the business of making brick, which he followed for many years in Belpre, when not engaged upon the river. He was successively pilot, captain, and owner, and for many years combined the two latter functions. As a pilot he "learned the river" easily, and was regarded as one of the very best upon the western waters. In his later years, when he owned, either alone or in company with others, several steamboats, he made a great deal of money, but met with some reverses. In one case he lost a fine steamer outright, by the carelessness of employes during his absence. But the most remarkable of Captain Burch's misfortunes were those which occurred to him in person—accidents with which he met upon the river. He was four times blown up, yet, strange to say, except in the latest instance, his most serious inconvenience was the mere loss of situations by the destruction or disablement of the boats on which he was employed. The first experience that Captain Burch had in steamboat explosions was in June, 1816, when the Washington exploded her boiler at Marietta. Although this was a serious accident, and one in which several persons lost their lives, while others were injured, Captain Burch escaped unhurt. In 1817, however, he was slightly injured by the explosion of the Lawrence at Sugar Creek bend, below Cincinnati. The third miraculous escape was in 1819. Captain Burch was coming from St. Louis on the Kanawha, as pilot. Henry Fearing, of Harmar, was a passenger. When the boat was near the Guyandotte riffles her boiler exploded, and Captain Burch, who was upon the deck, immediately over it, was thrown a distance of nearly a hundred feet. He fell in the water and sustained no injury. In fact, he was able to assist a wounded man to the shore, and so save his life. In 1857, when the Harry Dean was blown up at Gallipolis, Captain Burch did not escape so luckily as he had in these former instances. He was frightfully injured, but his tough constitution, good medical attendance, and a very favorable condition of the weather, combined to restore him. The captain is a man of unusual strength and hardiness, and now, at the age of eighty-five years, retains his mental faculties and physical health in a very remarkable degree. He has led a retired life since 1857, making his home with his daughter, Mrs. Iams.

Captain Burch was married February 18, 1821, to Nancy Whitney (daughter of Josiah Whitney), who was born in one of the old block-houses at Belpre, in 1798. She died December 7, 1855. Four children were the offspring of this marriage, viz: Lucy Amanda; Mary Whitney (Mrs. R. P. Iams, of Marietta); Ellen Elosha, who married Henry Deming, of Watertown; and Sarah Frances, who married Robert A. Garrison, and lived at Ashland, Kentucky. Mrs. Iams is the only one now living.

MARTIN DEWEY FOLLETT.

Martin Dewey Follett, esq., of Marietta, born in Franklin county, Vermont, is the son of John Fassett Follett, and grandson of Martin Dewey Follett. The family is an old New England one, some of its members having been prominent actors in the colonial movements and in the war of the Revolution. Captain John F. Follett removed from Vermont and settled in Licking county, Ohio, with his entire family, consisting of his wife and nine children. Of the six sons three are now engaged in the practice of law in Ohio; one of them, Judge Charles Follett, of Newark; another, Hon. John F. Follett, of Cincinnati; and the third, the subject of this sketch. Another son is Dr. Alfred Follett, of Granville, Ohio; and the others, George and Austin W. Follett, wool merchants in New York city.

Martin was but nine years of age when the family settled on an uncleared farm in a log cabin, where they lived until, by the labor of father and sons, a hundred acres had been cleared, a barn built, and a frame house, into which they removed. During this time he attended school or taught during the winters until he was twenty-one years of age. After this, having determined to secure a liberal education, he prepared for college, supporting himself meanwhile by his own labor, and in 1853 graduated at Marietta college, with the highest honors of his class. To defray expenses incurred in his course he engaged in teaching and taught in the public schools of Marietta, in Newark high school, and as tutor in Marietta college for one year, and was superintendent of the public schools of Marietta for two years, at the same time reading law.

He married in 1856 Miss Harriet L. Shipman, an old resident of Washington county. In 1875 he again married Abbie M. Bailey, of Lowell, Massachusetts. He has but two children living—both boys.

Mr. Follett was admitted to practice law at Marietta in the fall of 1858, and afterwards to the United States courts at Cincinnati. During his residence in Marietta, since 1851 (with the exception of one year in Newark), he has taken a deep interest in education in the city and county, holding for many years the position of president of the Washington County Teachers' association, and being for twelve years a member of the board of education of Marietta city.

Mr. Follett has been a member either of the Presbyterian or Congregational church since he was seventeen years of age, and is at present a member of the First Religious society (Congregational church) of Marietta, and a deacon of that body. He has served as Sabbath-school superintendent for the past three years, and occupied the same position in 1857, 1858, and 1859.

In 1879 Mr. Follett was sent by Governor Bishop as delegate from Ohio to the National conference of charities, which met in Chicago, and in 1880 was sent by Governor Foster as delegate to the same body, which met at Cleveland; and at present he is counselor for Ohio of the National association for the protection of the insane and the prevention of insanity.

Mr. Follett represented this congressional district in the National Democratic convention of 1864, at Chicago, that nominated General George B. McClellan, for president. He was a candidate for Congress in 1866 and again in 1868. Both years he ran ahead of his party ticket in nearly every county in the district. In 1880 he was nominated by his party as a candidate for judge of the supreme court of Ohio.

He continues in the practice of his profession in Marietta, with his elder son, A. Dewey Follett, as partner, and occupies the residence built by Governor Return Jonathan Meigs, which is pleasantly situated on the banks of the Muskingum river.

REV. DR. JOHN BOYD,

rector of the First Episcopal church of Marietta, is the son of John and Sarah (Pierce) Boyd, who emigrated from Uniontown, Pennsylvania, to Ohio in 1797. He located at first in Franklinton on the Scioto, opposite the site of the city of Columbus, but removed from there to Hillsborough, Highland county, two or three years later, and was the first physician in that place. The subject of our sketch was born in Hillsborough, December 6, 1823.

His youth was spent in his native town and in Gambier, Ohio. He finished his literary course at Kenyon college in 1844, and his health being poor, gave up for a time, intellectual work. As soon, however, as his condition had so improved as to make study possible, he went back and took a theological course, graduating from the seminary in 1850. On the fourth of August of that year, he was ordained at Mount Vernon, Ohio, by the Right Reverend Bishop McIlvaine, and in the same summer he came to Marietta and began his labors with the church which still commands his services. His pastorate, which has extended through a period of thirty-one years, has been rich in rewards, and the church has prospered greatly under his charge. It was a young organization at the time Dr. Boyd became its rector, and small in membership. Now it is one of the most vigorous societies in the State. The length of Dr. Boyd's pastorate and the devotion of his energies to the church are remarkable. About 1870 he had a call to Trinity church of Columbus, which in all probability, had he been governed by personal ambition alone, he would have accepted. He refused the offer because, after careful deliberation, he felt satisfied that the field of his best influence was in Marietta, and with the church which at that time he had been ministering to for twenty years.

Dr. Boyd has been four times sent to the general conventions as representative of his diocese.

In the year 1845, Dr. Boyd was married to Eliza Sharpe, of Highland county, who is still living. They have had six children, four of whom are living.

REV. DR. WILLIAM ADDY,

the pastor of the Fourth Street Presbyterian church, of Marietta, was born in Montreal, Canada, August 11, 1836. He was a graduate from Union college, Schenectady, New York, in 1857, and from Union theological seminary, New York city, in 1861. He served his first pastorate at Windham, New York; removed to Franklin, in the same State, in 1866, and to Marietta in 1869. Most of the growth of the Fourth Street Presbyterian church has been made during the twelve years of Mr. Addy's labors, and it has been a growth of very considerable proportions. Mr. Addy has been, since 1879, a trustee of Marietta college. He was married December 25, 1866, to Mrs. Frances A. Barnes, of Franklin, New York.

REV. DR. T. H. HAWKS.

Dr. Hawks, pastor of the First Religious society (Congregational church) of Marietta, is a native of Charlemont, Massachusetts. He graduated from Williams' college in 1844, and from the Union theological seminary, in New York city, in 1851. His first pastoral charge was the Congregational church of West Springfield, Massachusetts, where he went immediately after graduating from the seminary. He was afterward located in Cleveland, Ohio, and since 1869 has been in Marietta, serving effectively his present society.

MAJOR JEWETT PALMER.

Jewett Palmer, third child of John Pemberton and Abigail Jewett Palmer, and father of the subject of our sketch, was born at Oxford, New Hampshire, May 18, 1797. He enlisted at the age of sixteen, and served two years in the War of 1812. In 1818 he came to Ohio with his father's family, and with it settled in Fearing township, Washington county. Here, on the thirteenth day of March, 1822, he married Rachel Campbell, by whom he had eight children, each of whom lived to rear a family.

Jewett Palmer, youngest child of Jewett and Rachel (Campbell) Palmer, was born May 7, 1840, in Fearing township, Washington county. He is descended on the paternal side, from staunch old New England stock. The Palmers were among the early emigrants to New England, the head of this branch of the family being found at Rowley, Massachusetts, soon after the settlement of that place, in 1639. His ancestry on the maternal side is Scotch. William Campbell, his great grandfather, was born in Scotland, married there, emigrated to this country in 1766, and settled in Mifflin county, Pennsylvania. His third child, William, was the father of Rachel Campbell, mother of our subject.

Jewett remained on the farm with his parents until his twentieth year, when he went to Chicot Pass, Louisiana, at which place he spent the winter of 1860–61, engaged in the lumbering business with a brother-in-law. During the winter political affairs grew more and more threatening, until, believing war to be inevitable, and desiring to be where he could cast in his lot with the defenders of the Union, he left, early in the spring of 1861, for Ohio. He arrived at his home in Salem, on the eleventh day of April. On the seventeenth, at Marietta, he enrolled himself as a recruit in Captain Frank Buell's company,

afterwards company B, Eighteenth Ohio infantry, three months troops—this course seeming to afford the best opportunity of speedily getting into active service. At the expiration of its term of service, the regiment returned from the field the latter part of July, and disbanded at Marietta. On reaching home, he began recruiting a company for the Thirty-sixth Ohio infantry, then forming at Camp Putnam, Marietta, in which he was assisted by James Stanley, of Salem, a comrade in the three months service. On the twelfth of August they went into camp with a company of ninety-eight men, recruited in eleven days. At an election of officers held on the nineteenth, he was unanimously chosen captain of the company. The regiment left for the field, *via* Parkersburgh, on the twenty-ninth, to join Rosecrans' forces on the Gauley river, in West Virginia. From this time his history and that of his company were substantially that of the officers and men of the gallant regiment, whose subsequent reputation for efficiency and valor was second to none in the armies of the Union.

He was promoted to major, to date from May 9, 1864; was severely wounded in the left thigh at Kernstown, Virginia, July 24th. On his return to the field, he lost a horse, shot under him while in temporary command of the regiment, moving to the front to repulse a reconnoissance, made in force by the enemy, at Cedar Creek. He participated in the famous battle of Cedar Creek on the nineteenth of October,—the last action in which the regiment took part. On the twenty-ninth of November he resigned his commission, and returned home.

In 1865 he was elected on the Republican ticket, clerk of the courts of Washington county, and was reelected in 1868. Declining a third nomination, he retired from the office at the close of his second term.

On the nineteenth of September, 1866, he married Miss Saida M. Scott, only child of Theodore Scott, of Marietta.

During his second term as clerk, he entered upon the study of the law with Messrs. Ewart, Gear & Ewart, and in April, 1872, was admitted to the bar, and at once entered upon the practice of the law at Marietta. In April, 1874, he was elected mayor of the city, and was reelected in 1876. He was chairman of the Republican central committee of Washington county during the years 1875–6, was one of the delegates from the fifteenth district of Ohio, to the National Republican convention, held in Cincinnati in May, 1876, and was one of Ohio's "Forty-four for Hayes," who stood by the governor, until he received the nomination. In November, 1877, he resigned the office of mayor, to accept the position of collector of internal revenue for the fifteenth district of Ohio, tendered him by President Hayes, which position he still holds.

GENERAL B. D. FEARING.

Benjamin Dana Fearing, the youngest son of Henry Fearing, esq., and Eliza Dana Fearing, was born at Harmar, Ohio, October 10, 1837. He is the grandson of Hon. Paul Fearing and Benjamin Dana, who was the son of John Winchester Dana and Hannah Pope Dana, the daughter of General Israel Putnam, and through his mother a lineal descendant of the fourth generation from General Israel Putnam. His early life was spent in his native place. He graduated at Marietta college in 1856, at the age of nineteen. During the five years following his graduation he was in business, first at Cincinnati and afterwards at Philadelphia. While on a visit to Cincinnati in the spring of 1861, news came of the firing upon Fort Sumter—then the call of the President for troops. There was a meeting of the citizens at the old stone church on Walnut Hills, to organize. He was at the meeting, and among the first to offer himself in response to the call of the President. The next day he selected from the companies being formed the one which he thought would soonest be ready, and telegraphed his father, "Have joined the Zouave guards. Leave for Columbus on eighteenth, at 6 A. M." The next day, the nineteenth of April, found him speeding away as fast as the iron horse could carry him to the fore-front of the battle. It seems a singular coincidence that 'twas on the same day of the same month, eighty-seven years before, that his ancestor, General Putnam, "left his plow in the furrow" and hurried off on flying hoof to Concord to repel the British and enter upon the war of the Revolution. Upon the organization of regiments at Harrisburgh, Pennsylvania, the Zouave guards became company D of the Second Ohio volunteer infantry. With this regiment they went to Washington, and thence into Virginia, under General Schenck. Here they remained, doing service until their term of enlistment had expired. They were then entitled to their discharge, but as a battle seemed impending they, by a unanimous vote, resolved to remain and share in it. On the day of the battle of Manasses they were detailed as skirmishers. At 4 o'clock A. M. they had brisk work with the enemy's cavalry, driving them over Cut run, and to the banks of Bull run where the line of battle was developed. In the subsequent events of the day, its wild and terrific experiences of battle, carnage, panic, rout and disaster they bore their full share.

During his three months service Fearing received his first promotion, being made forth corporal of his company. After the battle of Manasses the adjutancy of the Thirty-sixth Ohio was offered him by Hon. William P. Cutler, then member of Congress from his district. The offer was again pressed upon him at Columbus when being mustered out at Camp Chase, but was declined as he then expected to join the National guard regiment at Philadelphia.

He accompanied them into West Virginia, and there served in the double capacity of acting adjutant general to General Slemmer and as adjutant to Major Andrews, then in command of the Thirty-sixth. Here he remained for three months, devoting himself assiduously to the drill of officers and men, often spending eighteen hours a day in this service. The high standing this regiment subsequently attained was no doubt largely due to the drill and discipline learned in this their early campaign in West Virginia.

General Slemmer appreciating the value of his services, and recognizing his zeal and ability, recommended to the governor of Ohio, the appointment of Fearing to the colonelcy of the Thirty-sixth regiment. Major Andrews started for Columbus with the recommendation, but at the headquarters of General Rosecrans he was met by Captain George Cook of the Fourth regulars, who had already been appointed to the command of the regiment. Fearing continued acting as adjutant at Somerville with Colonel Cook until he received the appointment of major of the Seventy-seventh regiment Ohio volunteer infantry. He reported at once to Colonel Heildbud at Camp Putnam, and entered upon the duties of his command.

Immediately after the organization of this regiment, although as yet without equipments of any kind, it was transferred to Camp Dennison. The regiment had been in this camp but a short time when orders came from General Grant at Fort Donelson to "move at once and report to General Sherman at Paducah, Kentucky," and at the same time the inquiry "How soon?" The superior officers being absent Major Fearing replied, *"In an hour;"* and so prompt were his movements that his regiment was the first of all the nine ordered from Ohio to arrive at Paducah. He went thence with the main army up the Tennessee river.

While General Sherman was conducting an expedition for the destruction of railroad bridges near Iuka, Mississippi, a heavy shower flooded Yellow creek so as to render his return impossible. Fearing reported the danger and asked permission to build a bridge of boats. This was done with so much expedition and skill as to secure the highest commendation of his commander, and General Sherman ever afterwards "entrusted him with a large share of the bridging operations over railroads, over streams and in the construction of corduroy-roads through the great swamp lands."

At the battle of Pittsburgh Landing Colonel Hildebrand being in command of a brigade and the lieutenant colonel absent, the command of the regiment devolved upon the major. The regiment was stationed at Shiloh church, its line being across the main Corinth road. This Sherman regarded as the most important point of his position. Of this Fearing was aware and realizing the necessity of maintaining his post he held it with unyielding tenacity. The repeated charges of the enemy in their desperate efforts to capture Taylor's battery A, of Chicago, he repulsed with great gallantry, and thus held the battery till orders came for its withdrawal. The general commanding commended the regiment for its brave and determined maintenance of the position at the church, and for its gallantry in defence of the battery.

The official report of the brigade commander says: "Major Benjamin D. Fearing, who commanded the Seventy-seventh Ohio volunteer infantry, was cool and brave, and acquitted himself with as much skill as an old officer of larger experience, and was not excelled by any other field officer who came within my observation."

Major E. C. Dawes, of the Fifty-third Ohio volunteer infantry, himself a participant in the fight, a gallant officer of cool and accurate judgment, writes: "I think the conduct of Major Fearing at Shiloh the most creditable to him and valuable to the cause of anything in his long service. The *Seventy-seventh regiment held the key point* in Sherman's first line of battle, and maintained this position long enough to enable McClernand's and Hulburt's divisions to get into action, and Major Fearing by his reckless personal courage *held the Seventy-seventh* regiment. The conduct of the major and of the Seventy-seventh regiment in that hell of fire has never been appreciated."

The casualties of the regiment, amounting in total to one hundred and sixty-eight officers and men killed and wounded, tells the story of its fighting. In the disasters which befell the regiment on the next day, the major was in a subordinate position, Lieutenant Colonel DeHass being then in command.

While at Fort Pickering after the capture of Corinth and return of the regiment to Memphis, Major Fearing received the appointment of lieutenant colonel of the Ninety-second regiment then being organized at Camp Putnam, Ohio. The first service of this regiment was in the Kanawha valley, where it had a "stirring period of marching and fighting."

In January, 1863, he joined the Army of the Cumberland at Nashville. In March he was made colonel of the regiment, Colonel Van Vorhes being compelled by sickness to resign. At Murfreesborough he was assigned to the Fourteenth army corps under General George H. Thomas. On the twenty-fourth of June he went to the relief of Wilder at Hoover's Gap. On the night of the eighteenth of September he made the march to Chickamauga. His regiment formed a part of the famous "Turchin's brigade" and with it passed through the terrible fighting on the nineteenth and twentieth. In this battle he was severely wounded, a minnie ball passing through the front part of his right and thick part of his left thigh. On the following day the enemy captured the hospital to which the wounded had been removed, but Colonel Fearing and four of his officers were saved by the coolness of his colored servant who carried them to an ambulance and drew them through a continuous fire to a point within the protection of our lines.

As soon as the condition of his wounds would admit of partial duty he was detailed upon courts-martial at Cincinnati and Louisville. During his absence his regiment, under command of Lieutenant Colonel Douglas Putnam, a soldier and officer of spirit kindred to his own, made its memorable record in the storming of Mission Ridge. He returned to his regiment at Ringgold, Georgia, in March 1864. In May he went south, and with Turchin's brigade "fought through that wondrous campaign, a hundred days continuous fighting." He was in the "march to the sea." At Savannah, upon the recommendation of his corps commander, General J. C. Davis, he received a commission from President Lincoln as brigadier general by brevet, bearing date December 2, 1864, "for gallant and meritorious services during the campaign from Chattanooga to Atlanta, and from Atlanta to Savannah." He was assigned to the command

of Colonel Daniel McCook's "fighting brigade," Second division Fourteenth army corps. At the battle of Bentonville when the enemy had broken the union left and centre, General Davis ordered General Fearing to move to the left and "check the enemy's advance," if it "cost him his whole brigade." The charge was glorious. The check was made. The action was terrible. Fearing's horse was shot under him, and a minnie ball tore away the thumb, the fore-finger, and part of his right hand. Van Horne, in summing up the history of the battle, says: "That the battle turned upon the action of the brigades of Mitchell, Vanderveer and Fearing, there can be no doubt. The two former did not give an inch of ground to the enemy, though thrown into single lines and compelled to fight in front and rear. The action of Fearing's brigade was not less important, as it disturbed and defeated General Johnston's combination to utilize for complete success his first advantage. General Fearing was brought in complete isolation for some time, without defences, and when his right flank was struck by the enemy with such force as to shatter it, he charged his front upon his left, rallied his shattered troops and held the ground essential to the stability of the new line. The latter dispositions and resistance by the whole command gave a symmetry and brilliancy to the conflict which have seldom found expression in such urgent improvision."

At the close of the war General Fearing was mustered out of the service at the age of twenty-seven years, having as a private taken part in the first, and as a commander of a brigade in the last, great battle of the war. He was offered the rank of major in the regular army, but declined. The battles in which he participated are memorable in the history of the war:—Manasses, the battles of West Virginia, Shiloh, Catlin Mountain, Iuka, Corinth, Carthage, Hoover's Gap, Tullahoma, Catlit's Gap, Lane's Church, Chickamauga, Chattanooga, Buzzard's Roost, Rocky Face Ridge, Resaca, Etowah, Altoona Pass, Pine Knob, Kenesaw, Nicojack, Peach Tree Creek, Chattahoochee, Utoy Creek, Rough and Ready, Jonesborough, Atlanta, Savannah, through the Carolinas, Averysborough and Bentonville.

The biographical encyclopædia of Ohio says of the General: "As a field officer he was ever ready night or day for active service; was quick to seize upon all the salient points of a position for defence, attack or picket; was admirably careful in the selection of good camping ground; attended personally to the instruction and comfort of his troops; knew the men of his regiment by name, and also their qualities; possessed the ability which organizes rapidly and effectually in the camp or during action; was strict in discipline and under all circumstances was extremely wary in his measures to avoid surprises, while incessantly devising new measures to ensure the safety of his command; once engaged he never hesitated to expose it or himself, when extremities demanded a sacrifice."

For some years after the war, General Fearing was engaged in business in Cincinnati, but being compelled to withdraw from active labor, he returned to his old home in Harmar, where he now resides, devoting himself to literary pursuits, to his friends, and to caring for his health, still rendered precarious by the wounds of Chickamauga and Bentonville.

HIRAM LUTHER SIBLEY*

was born on a farm in Gustavus township, Trumbull county, Ohio, May 4, 1836. His immediate ancestry on both sides were of New England birth. The mother, born at Colebrook, Connecticut, June 13, 1815, was the only daughter of Luther and Chene (Waters) Simons— the former born January 26, 1794, also at Colebrook, and the latter at Granville, in that State, July 22, 1795.

In early and middle life Mr. Simons was a farmer and school-teacher. After his daughter's birth he came to the Western Reserve, in Ohio. Joshua R. Giddings married a sister to his wife, and the families were long in intimate acquaintance.

For more than twenty years before his death, in consequence of an injury to the spine, Mr. Simons was unable to walk. Such, however, was his intellectual force and activity that, while prostrate in bed and suffering from incurable disease, he so mastered the science of medicine as to rank high in knowledge and skill with educated physicians of his time and place.

On the father's side the line is traceable to John Sibley, who came from England in the Fleet A. D. 1629, settling in Salem, Massachusetts. He was a selectman of that town, and went to the general court at Boston. His son Joseph, born in 1655, settled at Sutton, Massachusetts. Joseph's son Benjamin, born September 19, 1703, went to Connecticut, dying at Ashford, November 2, 1789. His last will contains these words: "I recommend my soul to God who gave it, my body to the dust, to be buried with decent Christian burial, nothing doubting but soul and body will be united at the last day, by the Almighty power of God."

Benjamin's son, Ezekiel, married May 3, 1753. From this union came a son, Ezekiel, born October 2, 1766. He went to the more fertile soil near Westfield, Massachusetts, where he reared a large family, the eldest of which, also named Ezekiel, was born August 27, 1789. Among the children of the latter was a son, Ezekiel, born at Westfield, Massachusetts, October 22, 1814. Not long after his birth the family removed to Genesee county, New York, and thence, about 1830, to Trumbull county, Ohio. There on the twenty-ninth of October, 1834, the younger Ezekiel married Phebe, the daughter, as stated above, of Luther and Chene Simons. The subject of this sketch was their first child.

In 1841, Ezekiel, jr., with his family, removed to Gallia county, Ohio, and in 1847 to Middleport, Meigs county. In 1855 he became a member of the Ohio conference, Methodist Episcopal church, with which body he is still connected, in active work.

Except home training, the early educational advantages of Hiram L. were limited to the common schools of the

* By O. B. Chapman, Pomeroy, Ohio.

time. At the age of thirteen, he went to the trade of shoemaker. When sixteen, he got six months in a select school, earning enough in the shop, however, nights and mornings to pay for his tuition, board, and clothes. In 1856, another six months of school were added to those previously enjoyed. The winter following he taught his only term of school.

April 22, 1858, Mr. Sibley was married to Miss Esther Ann Ellis, eldest daughter of John R. and Elizabeth O. Ellis, of Racine, Meigs county, Ohio. From this union have come six children, three of whom are living—the oldest, William Giddings, graduating from Marietta college this year, 1881.

In the fall of 1858, Mr. Sibley, still working at his trade, began to spend his spare hours in the study of law. This continued until October, 1860, when he was elected clerk of the courts, for Meigs county, Ohio. During the canvas he was called upon to address a political club at Pomeroy. He spent the time in showing the position of the founders of the Government with respect to slavery, and especially as regards the doctrine that all men, regardless of race or color, are by nature equally entitled to life, liberty, and the pursuit of happiness. This principle, he claimed, affords the only justification for the Revolution, and of necessity, therefore, was declared by the "fathers," upon a clear apprehension of that fact. In this view, after referring to the almost absolute powers of the British parliament, and its assertion of the right to "bind the colonies in all cases whatsoever," the address said:

From this determination of the highest power to which they could resort, there was no appeal by any established forms of law. They might question its justice, and vehemently denounce the wrongs of its enforcement, as did Pitt, they might reason and philosophise upon its obvious impolicy, as did Burke; and in the eloquent, indignant sarcasm of Barre, they might hold up the British government to the scorn and detestation of mankind, yet, as a question of mere legal and constitutional authority, with Lord Mansfield, they were compelled to admit its binding force upon them. Would it have answered the great end in view to assert—as Chief Justice Taney and Senator Douglas say they intended only to assert—the equal rights of white British subjects in America, with white British subjects in England? This, certainly, could avail them nothing, for the power which by existing law was the final arbiter, had declared against them. Their only hope therefore lay in resting their action upon some great principle, the assertion of which would justify them in rising above and resisting the long-established, lawful authority of the mother country. Our fathers saw and felt their peculiar situation. They appreciated the critical position in which they stood. Clearly comprehending the vast responsibilities resting upon them, conscious that every other resource had been tried only to meet with disheartening failure, were they not compelled to declare the natural right of every human being to life, liberty, and the pursuit of happiness, as the only doctrine upon which they could appeal to God for support, in resistance to tyranny, and with which they could justify their action before the judgement-bar of human opinion.

Mr. Sibley entered upon the duties of his office as clerk February 12, 1861, continuing, however, the study of law. The opening events of the Rebellion came quickly on. He was often called upon to speak at Union meetings, and in gatherings to call for volunteers. In August, 1862, feeling unwilling longer to ask others to go without entering the service himself, he accepted a second lieutenant's commission, dated the twelfth of that month, and helped enlist a body of men, who became

Hiram L. Sibley

company B, One Hundred and Sixteenth Ohio volunteer infantry, going to camp at Marietta, Ohio. Mr. Sibley soon after resigned the office of clerk, and went with his regiment into West Virginia, as part of Major General R. H. Milroy's command. From November to April, 1863, Lieutenant Sibley, in the absence of the regimental adjutant, was detailed to act in his place. In the latter month, also, he was recommended by the officers of his regiment for provost marshal of the Fifteenth congressional district of Ohio. The matter coming to General Milroy's attention, he wrote a letter to the provost marshal general saying:

I have known Lieutenant Sibley for the last six months, while with his regiment in my command, and have observed that he is an able, energetic, and efficient officer—always prompt and attentive to duty—a true gentleman of high moral character, and excellent business talents and habits. He is just the man for provost marshal—who will deal promptly with deserters and other delinquents—and I should be pleased to see him get the position.

Mr. Sibley, with the regiment, was first under fire, at Moorfield, West Virginia, early in January, 1863. Most of the winter was spent at Romney, he doing the work of judge advocate in a court martial. In March the regiment moved to Winchester, Virginia. Here Mr. Sibley was appointed recorder of a military commission. While thus engaged he was prostrated with fever. Getting out for the first time, he was asking to be relieved from the commission, because of ill health, when the post was attacked by the advance of Lee's army, then on its way north. Too feeble to walk, he rode from the hospital to camp and joined his company. The regiment was not engaged until Monday, June 15th, when in retreat, three miles north of Winchester. In battle there, with part of his regiment, and about half of the command, he was made a prisoner of war. June 23rd, suffering still from sickness, Lieutenant Sibley entered the noted Libby prison, in Richmond, Virginia, where he remained until May 7, 1864, when he was taken to Danville, Virginia, and thence to Macon, Georgia, which place he reached May 17th. The last of July he went to Savannah, and on the thirteenth of September to Charleston, South Carolina, where, with other prisoners, he was placed under fire; that is, in the "shelled district" of the city, within range of the Union guns bombarding it. In this situation they remained until October 5th, when they were carried to Columbia, South Carolina, and located near the city in what became known as Camp Sorghum. December 10, 1864, in Charleston harbor, Lieutenant Sibley was exchanged. But his health was so broken by the semi-starvation and other hardships of his long imprisonment, that, in consequence of disability, he was honorably discharged, January 11, 1865. While a prisoner, Governor Brough had commissioned him first lieutenant.

April 14, 1865, Mr. Sibley was admitted to the bar at Pomeroy, Ohio. The next summer he did a few weeks' work as assistant assessor of internal revenue. This led to a position in the office of the district assessor at Marietta, Ohio, to which place Mr. Sibley removed in August, 1865. At the end of a year there, he began the practice of law, as one of the firm of Ewart, Shaw &

Sibley. In 1867 he was nominated by the Republicans of Washington county as their candidate for prosecuting attorney. The question of negro suffrage was in issue. While a prisoner in Libby, Mr. Sibley had led a protracted and exciting debate in favor of giving the ballot to the colored man, and he heartily entered this canvas for the same proposition. But on a close vote the county was lost, and he was defeated. During the fall he delivered a speech which, on request, was written out for publication. We extract a few passages. After referring to the riot and bloodshed in the south, since the war, he said:

During such a deplorable condition of things, Congress assembled in December, 1866. The great problem of the session was still that of reconstruction. After much deliberation they framed the present plan. It has two features, the first is temporary, the other permanent. For the time being the Nation protects its loyal sons from rebel outrage, by the strong arm of military power. But in the nature of things this cannot be permanent. Military government, except as a necessity limited by the occasion, is incompatible with the genius of our Constitution, and the spirit of our free institutions. Some other mode must therefore be devised, by which, in accordance with the fundamental principle of self-government, the spirit of rebellion might be broken, the duty of loyalty cherished, and patriots everywhere protected in all the rights of American citizens. By what means could these ends be accomplished? Only, I answer, by the great protective power of free institutions everywhere—the ballot. By rebel proscription, under Johnson's policy, the large majority of Union men in the rebellious States, were denied the elective franchise. And by this alone, traitors ruled in those States. Hence, the permanent feature of the present plan, by which the southern patriot, black as well as white, is armed with the mighty power of the ballot. Thus military power was rendered but temporarily necessary in the south, and thus negro suffrage wisely became the mode of reconstructing the rebellious States upon a loyal basis, in the strictest accordance with the American idea of self-government.

Coming to the suffrage question in Ohio, he further said:

I do not hesitate to declare warmly in favor of striking the word white from our State constitution. It is demanded alike by the principles of free government, and by sound policy in the public administrations of the State. Political injustice is ever the ground of discord, and a perennial source of trouble. Hence to remove all difficulty—to put the "nigger question" forever at rest in our borders—as well as to conform our fundamental law to the idea of self-government, I approve and shall vote for the change . . We tax negroes as other people. They fight for the country like white folks. They were everywhere brave soldiers, noble and true, who never faltered on any of the bloody fields where their lives were given, and their bones lie moldering with those of white comrades who fell with them, to "save us a nation." After calling for the help and accepting the aid of the colored citizens of Ohio, after putting upon them all the burdens of taxation that white men endure; can we draw a line of right between them and ourselves, and claim the ballot for our protection as men, while we refuse it to them? I think not.

Touching the subject of taxing United States bonds, this was said:

The fact is the Union party has upon this point followed in the footsteps of every administration that ever sold a National bond, and its action is sanctioned by precedents old and uniform, from nearly every Democratic administration in our history. Hence, if wrong here, it became so in following in the well-beaten tracks of all the old Democratic parties of the country. In pursuing this uniform policy of the Government, at the time these bonds were issued, I think the Union party acted wisely. Union statesmen, however, were sagacious enough to issue these bonds upon as short periods as would be at all compatible with National credit, so that when our day of triumph came—when National unity was established—when the Nation should be able thoroughly to organize and to handle its debt—the maturing bonds might be called in and replaced by a different issue, made subject to local or National taxation, or at a reduced rate of interest which would be equivalent to taxation.

Late in 1867 Mr. Sibley and Hon. R. L. Nye formed a law firm which continued till 1869, when ill health compelled the former to retire. But health returning he resumed practice at Pomeroy, Ohio, in the fall of 1870, as one of the partnership of Paine & Sibley. Shortly prior to this, in response to an invitation of the Teachers' institute in Meigs county, he delivered an address upon the "Nature and True End of Education," which, by request of his hearers, was published. On the first branch of the subject, in summary view, this was said:

Bearing in mind now the distinctions made, separating from education the knowledge which is ever its genial companion, the system of motherly discipline under which it is obtained, the exhilerating mental activity without which it could not be born, and tracing it as an idea to its metaphysical root, we affirm it to be, in its essential nature, simply the volume of disciplined mental power, the aggregate of trained intellectual ability, called forth by the various agencies of the educational course. In this view the activities, learning, and dicipline of the curriculum are only so many instruments used for the attainment of the great result. The enlarged, cultivated capacity evolved through these instrumentalities is the end to which they stand in the relation of means, and to reaching which it is their purpose to contribute. Education itself soars far higher than the learning of the books, its gaze reaches beyond the intellectual gymnastics of the schools. These are but favorable conditions for it, the shell in which its life begins, but out of which it breaks in fully entering upon its own career.

As to the true end of education we have this:

In virtue of a law penetrating to the centre of his being, for a man habitually to exert his powers for self alone, is moral debasement, spiritual defilement, and death. Selfishness is a malignant cancer in the best impulses and tenderest affections of the heart, a fatal blight upon the noblest desires and holiest aspirations of the soul. Like a darkness that can be felt, unless dispelled by the light and power of love, it settles down upon the spirit, enshrouding it from the healthful, life-giving influences of goodness, and shutting up the soul to die from moral and spiritual inanition. Under this general law of his constitution, therefore, man is forbidden the use of the power of education for self alone. Hence, considered with exclusive reference to its subject, the true end of culture reaches beyond himself, and shrivelling moral and spiritual death confront him as the divinely ordained penalty for clipping the wings of education until its powers and ends are cooped in the narrow limits of his own soul. . . . Wherever Christian thought has penetrated, and the best results of philosophical inquiry are known, the oneness of our race in nature and general capability is recognized and believed. Out of the notion of common endowment, and the idea of unity in origin, arises the conception of the brotherhood and social nature of man, with all their sequences of mutual obligations and duties, in virtue of which, if we live in obedience to the law of our being, we necessarily become reciprocating co-workers for the common good. Alike, therefore, upon the principles of philosophy and Christianity, every one stands in correlated obligation with all his fellows to use his various abilities and powers for others as well as himself, so long as he remains a subject of social relations. . . . The educated man, as a member of society, by virtue of his moral constitution, is imperatively bound to use his culture for the elevation of his kind. He is to raise up those bowed down in ignorance, to establish the weak in knowledge, to open the eyes of the blind to truth, to aid in breaking the power and dominion of passion, and keep in the work of dispelling the thick clouds of prejudice that everywhere overshadow the uneducated mind. In brief, he is to consecrate his culture to the doing of good, and exalt it thereby into an instrumentality of human progress. Here the true social and individual ends of education meet as brethren to dwell "together in unity."

About this time, also, Mr. Sibley published some essays upon the constitutional law of Ohio respecting religious liberty. Looking back of the conceded rights of conscience to the principle upon which they depend, its true statement was considered to be this:

That before the State, or in the eye of the law, one man's convic-

tions, beliefs, or faith, in regard to any and all matters of religion, are equally sacred with every other man's, no matter what their nature or character may be, and, therefore, with all other convictions, beliefs, or faiths, equally entitled to the protection of the law, and to the respect of the State authorities. This imports absolute equality before the law in all matters of religion, and utter independence of State authority as to religious convictions, beliefs, or faiths.

Passing then to a discussion on the rights of conscience, he said:

I.—What is a "Right of conscience," in the sense of our Constitution? We answer—

1. The right to entertain any opinion, conviction or faith, whatever, in regard to morality or religion, without question or molestation.

2. The right, also, to act in accordance with the opinion, conviction or faith entertained, so long as the conduct is consistent with an equal right in all others, and is not palpably destructive of social order.

II.—As to the condition of the citizen with reference to these rights, we affirm—

1. That in matters of conscience all persons are equal before the law.

2. And are entitled to full and adequate protection therein.

III.—The power and duty of the State in the premises, is—

1. To extend to every citizen the protection to which he is entitled, in the exercise of his rights of conscience.

2. Beyond that, to refrain from any interference whatever, in matters of conscience.

These propositions seem to us so nearly self-evident that we support them only by a reference to section seven, article I, of our Constitution. That section, in its first clause, embodies the principle of our definition of the rights of conscience, and of the equality of all therein, by declaring the natural, indefeasible right of all men to worship God according to the dictates of their own consciences. This idea is fundamental in the controversy—is, indeed, the very tap-root of religious liberty. Logically following it, also, are certain restrictions upon the power of the State, which, if observed, renders its intervention in any matter of conscience; except to protect the citizen where his rights are assailed, morally impossible. No person can be compelled to support any form or place of worship, against his consent, "nor shall any interference with the rights of conscience be permitted." Finally, the General Assembly is directed to pass suitable laws for the protection of all religious denominations, in their chosen forms of worship. Hence, in view of these considerations, we feel justified in regarding the following as a correct although summary statement of the doctrines of our Constitution upon this question, viz.:

"That in rights of conscience all persons are equal, whether they be Christians, Jews, or Pagans; the State can interfere in no matter of conscience, except for the sole purpose of affording protection when its rights are assailed; and that all matters of religious belief, and of conduct in accord therewith, not inconsistent with equal rights in others, nor manifestly dangerous to society, are included in rights of conscience, and are legally open to every person in virtue of his religious freedom."

Finally in answer to a critic, was the following :

Your fallacy is, in confounding every *conviction* of conscience with a *right* of conscience. These are not always convertible. Either may exist in the absence of the other. A right of conscience, in legal and constitutional sense, is the right to entertain any opinion whatever, in regard to religion or morality, without question, and to act in accordance therewith, so long as the conduct is consistent with an equal right in all others, and not palpably destructive of social order. These rights the State obligates itself in the constitution to protect. Hence, when the conviction of conscience coincides with the rights of conscience, the ægis of the constitution is thrown around it, but not otherwise. This distinction will dissipate a thousand sophistries, grounded upon a tacit assumption of the necessary and unvarying identity of a conviction with a right of conscience.

In April, 1874, Mr. Sibley returned to Marietta, and became one of the law firm of Ewart & Sibley. The summer following he discussed the "license question," as connected with the adoption of the proposed new constitution. We quote:

To license an act is (1) to consent to and authorize it; (2) to consent to and authorize the probable consequences of the act. Hence, a license to sell intoxicating liquors, for common drinking as a beverage, is a consent to, and authorization of, such sales, together with their usual and probable consequences. . . Another usual and probable consequence of selling liquor for common drinking, even to adults who are not habitual drunkards, is vice and crime. These cancerous sores upon the body politic radiate from the liquor traffic as their focal centre. They are so interwoven with the abominable business as practically to be inseparable, if they do not, indeed, co-exist in the relation of effect to cause. Hence, so long as the liquor traffic continues vice and crime will remain—its natural, necessary con-comitants. Therefore, to license it, is to consent to and authorize festering nurseries of vice and crime all over the State. . . . But, as clinching the pro-license argument, it is stated that free trade in liquors, within certain limits, now in fact exists. But how? We say by sufferance, merely; for lack of a public sentiment sufficiently powerful to destroy it. But what does license propose but to sur-round this practical free trade with the affirmative sanction of law? Any bond that license might exact from the liquor seller can be had now, by simply enacting the law requiring it, before he can begin selling at all. Every mill of tax that a license would bring may be levied by an excise, if the legislature so direct. Hence, all the fancied "responsi-bility" of the liquor seller, under the license system, about which its advocates prate so much, is equally attainable under the no-license plan. The failure to burden the liquor traffic with special taxation, and bonds against illegal sales, is not from lack of power in the legis-lature, for that already exists, but because of unwillingness to exercise the power.

Mr. Sibley published an article on the questions con-nected with counting the electoral vote of 1876. After discussing what a counting imports, and the election of a president by the *electors*, he comes to the question of his election by the house of representatives. We extract this:

The exact point in issue is whether it rests with the State, or the house of representatives finally to determine the validity of an ap-pointment of certain persons as electors No express restriction upon the broad power to appoint electors, in any manner the legislature of a State may direct, is found in the constitution. Nor is it qualified by necessary implication, unless in the right of the house to elect, in the one contingency, which will be noticed hereafter. Nevertheless, it is urged, that while the State appoints, the house is the final arbiter of the legal validity of the appointment of electors, under the laws of the State by which it is made. The grant is of the exclusive power, to the State, or rather, it is a declaration of power in the States which had never been conferred upon any department of the National govern-ment, a specification of power not delegated, and therefore reserved to the States respectively. Does it include the authority not only to make the appointments in question, but also the right conclusively to determine their validity for all purposes ulterior to that fact? Argu-ment seems inadequate to make the proposition clearer than the fair import of the words of the constitution itself. The whole matter is referred to the State authorities. All regulations respecting the ap-pointment of electors, except as to the day when made, and the dis-qualification of members of Congress, and others, for the position, are left to them. Had it been intended to vest in Congress the power to say whether or not the act of a State in appointing electors, con-forms to its own laws—thus, in effect, making the assent of that body necessary to a legal appointment—some hint, at least, of so important an authority should be found in the constitution. · · · · · But it is said that the house elects the President, in a certain contin-gency, and therefore it must determine when its right arises. But how? The answer to this requires one to follow the plain provisions of the constitution.

The appointment of electors by a State, is conclusive of their right to represent the State in the electoral college. The duties of their of-fice are to vote for a president and vice-president, and to make, certify, and transmit, to certain officers, including the president of the United States senate, lists of these votes. The votes thus certified, the presi-dent of the senate is to open in the presence of the senate and house, when they "shall be counted." If upon the counting of these votes no person has the majority required to an election in that mode then—and not till then—"from the persons having the highest numbers, not ex-ceeding three on the list of those voted for as President, the house of representatives shall choose · immediately the President." Hence, if it obeys the constitution, the house decides upon its right to elect, sole-

ly by the result of a count—the simple enumeration—of the votes of elec-tors certified to the president of the senate, and opened by him in the presence of both houses. And this is all there is in the decision the house is to make. Certainly, by no necessary implication does it in-volve the power to question the act of the State in appointing its electors —to declare the action of those officers void because of defects in their appointment, when the vice, if it existed, would be incurable—thus disfranchising the State, and drawing to the house alone the power it otherwise could not have—to elect the President.

So far, for the sake of clearness, and in order to show in strong light what are conceived to be the principles which should guide in this mat-ter, the discussion has been confined to the assumed case of one set of electors, in each State, who, in formal compliance with the law of le-gitimate local government are accredited as such. Upon the state of facts thus presupposed, the case is plain, on the theory of action set out Furthermore, with these doctrines distinctly in mind, one is in position to consider other possible cases, which, in entire harmony therewith, may open to Congress, within certain limits, defined by the nature of each particular case, the right to inquire respecting the ap-pointment of electors, and their action in voting for a President. For example, suppose what purports to be the votes of two sets of electors from one State are certified and transmitted to the President of the senate, in due form of law, and that the election of a President by the electors, turns upon the votes of that State. · · This condi-tion of affairs is probable only when there is the formal existence of two state governments, as during the Dorr rebellion in Rhode Island, or the possible case, in view of the late war, of a legal and insurrec-tionary government in the same State. · · For the purpose of ascertaining whether or not a lawful State government in fact had ac-credited certain persons as electors, where that is in doubt, and the genuineness of the votes certified as theirs, on the states of fact sug-gested, Congress would, we think, be authorized to look behind the certificates transmitted to the president of the senate. Evidently, however, the power arises *ex-necessitate*, and therefore upon principles perfectly settled. The extent of the inquiry it authorizes will be limited strictly by circumstances which gave it birth, and the end it is to sub-serve. Hence, in all cases, when the vote of a set of electors in fact appointed by the recognized lawful State government, is ascertained the utmost limit of this extraordinary inquiry is reached, and the power that authorized it is exhausted. Confusion has worked into the dis-cussion of this question, and the true principle of action has been clouded, in consequence of not distinguishing, upon the basis of their essentially different states of fact, the cases where Congress may look beyond the certificates of votes returned, and the ordinary one in which it cannot. · · · · · ·

Upon the occasion of decorating the graves of Union soldiers at Marietta, Ohio, in May, 1877, Mr. Sibley wrote an address which was published, and from which we extract the following:

But with emotions aroused by the memories with which the associa-tions of the hour come trooping upon us, may we not examine for a few moments the grounds of the honors we are paying our fallen brothers? Not everyone who dies deserves even to be remembered. There is a deep philosophy implied by the assertion that the "way of the wicked shall perish." · · · Truly estimated, the wars and quarrels of kings and potentates, entitled to a place in history rank but little above the petty contentions of school-boy strife, except as they involve a question of public right or affect the interests and welfare of communities and States.

We must not forget that rectitude is an inseparable element of true greatness. Doing right in the hour of supreme trial, at the great-est possible cost, has gradually come to embody our noblest concep-tion of real heroism—the most exalted ideal of moral perfection in character—which, as in themselves a permanent power for good, through their influence upon mankind, justly entitle one thus worthy to high historic honors. The act performed may not seem to be intrinsically great; no more, perhaps, than that some poor widow gives the last pittance she possesses, and which appears as her only earthly support, for the good of others. Or it is the noble deed of a com-mon soldier, who with heroic purpose in itself sublime, and which shall be an inspiration to patriots for all time—

"Made way for Liberty, and died."

Yet history will preserve remembrance of names like these, and poetry embalm their acts in song, when the Alexanders, with all the army of tyrants who scrupled not to "wade through slaughter to a throne," shall be forgotten!

Who noble ends by noble means obtains,

Like good Aurelius let him reign, or bleed
Like Socrates, that man is great indeed.

Our proposition is that the great act is of necessity a right act. Putting the other side of the truth here, wrong action, however able or brilliant in daring and genius, tested by the highest criterion, lacks an indispensable element of true greatness and one link in a title to the first honors of history. For a time, we agree, transcendant powers devoted to bad ends may excite admiration and secure a measure of renown. There is almost a fascination in the great poet's picture of the angel fallen, "who durst defy the Omnipotent to arms." The frightful audacity of the act inspires a degree of respect for the dauntless courage which dared to undertake it. And thus it is, we presume, as to the homage paid certain characters in history, many of whose most famous deeds are in fact great crimes, but as the years roll on the meteoric splendor of wicked actions pales and fades. Later generations, aided by better and more elevated ideas of the end of life, estimate the fame of those whose names and acts come down to them, nearer their real value. By the operation of the laws of our moral being, we come to assign the honors of history not merely to great abilities or wondrous success in what men undertake, but more to the royal qualities found in intrepid uprightness of character—the genius for being *right* as well as able and successful in the affairs of life. The fond remembrances and spontaneous honors of generations to come will be more and more largely reserved for the real benefactors of the race, and for him who, when thrust into the furnace of some fiery trial or facing some mighty temptation, shall be found—

Among the faithless, faithful * ;
Among innumerable false, unmoved,
Unshaken, unseduced, unterrified;

. . . . .

Nor number, nor example with him wrought
To swerve from the truth.

. . . . .

We linger not to argue the righteousness of the cause in maintaining which these soldiers fell. The result of the dread ordeal of battle, to whose final arbitrament the south in frenzy appealed, and the nearly unanimous judgment of civilization, concur at this point, and we have no reason to think that posterity will not confirm their verdict.

It is right here, however, in the application of the principle we have endeavored to present and illustrate, that we touch upon the real grounds of distinction in the honors which history will confer upon the brave men who fell on opposing sides in this terrible struggle. They were all Americans. Speaking in general terms, both armies were equally heroic in the field. Upon the whole, perhaps their leaders will not be found to differ largely in military genius and skill. Yet the proud record of those who fought for the American Union, and human liberty, will shine in ever increasing brightness and glory when compared with that of our equally gallant countrymen behind whose line of battle were the flag of disunion and the clanking chains of slavery. Those who followed the nation's "banner of beauty and glory" were allied by their cause to the most exalted aspirations and hopes of the future, and consequently were fighting a battle for the elevation and progress of the race. Government by the people, for the people, was inwrapped with their success. On the other side was the principle of civil disintegration, the fact of human bondage—iron links which bound our brave but erring fellow-citizens to the dead body of a barbaric past. In truth, the Lost Cause was lost before its fight with arms began. The thing itself—disruption and slavery—was an anachronism. Judged by the moral sense of mankind, as well as the law of the land, the attempt to sustain it by war was a crime. The spirit of the age, the conclusions of the best political thought, and the high demands of the immediate future were all in league against this cause. It received no sympathy, and was entitled to none, from the toiling millions of civilization, but only the deceptive, baleful, friendship of tottering despots, or aristocracies whose very foundations were crumbling under pressure of the great ideas of popular government. Hence, though we saw it not, if faithful to our duty, the success of this cause was from the beginning impossible. No human genius or bravery could save it. And for the same reasons the heroism of those who fell, its devoted victims in the carnage of battle, cannot lift them to the position in history forever to be occupied by the soldiers of "Liberty and Union," who in the mighty conflict "perished for the Right."

In the summer of 1877, by a decisive majority of the Republican convention of Washington county, Mr. Sibley was declared its candidate for common pleas judge. His competitor, however, not abiding by the action of the convention, as it was supposed and implied by the circumstances that he would do, when the matter was submitted to its decision, in a triangular contest going to the fifty-eighth ballot, Mr. Sibley was defeated in the nomination, by a close vote, in the District convention.

At its annual commencement for 1878, Marietta college conferred upon Mr. Sibley the honorary degree of Master of Arts.

Excepting the period of his army service, and a season of bad health, Mr. Sibley on the stump has advocated the principles of the Republican party in every year from 1856 to 1880, inclusive. During the late Presidential canvas he delivered a speech at Pomeroy, Ohio, which was published on request of gentlemen hearing it, and from which we extract a few passages:

The doctrines of State rights, or, more properly, State supremacy, as against the power and authority of the National Government, under the Constitution, have been in contest ever since that instrument was before our people for ratification. They constituted, indeed, the chief ground of opposition to its adoption; and when that could not be prevented became the basis first of personal effort and then of party organization, designed by narrow and false constructions of the Constitution to emasculate the National Government of its legitimate powers and authority. The country was fortunate, however, from the first, in having able statesmen of National views, to combat the notions of State supremacy, declared by some, and point out the consequences of their general acceptance. . . . .

But it is to the administrations of Washington that the country is most deeply indebted for the assertion and practical establishment of the powers and authority of the General Government upon the National principles embodied in the constitution. The laws enacted by Congress during that period provided for a National judiciary invested with the power of final, authoritative decision, in all cases at law or in equity, arising under the constitution itself, the laws of Congress, and treaties made by the Nation. They also armed the President with the authority and means of performing his sworn duty to "preserve, protect, and defend the constitution," and of taking "care that the laws be faithfully executed." Moreover, as a matter of wise policy, Washington, against the bitter opposition of the State Rights school of his time, made the National constitution and laws supreme in fact, as they were in legal theory, by crushing, with military force, in 1794, armed resistance to them in what is familiarly known as the Whiskey Insurrection of Western Pennsylvania. It was during this contest, felt at the time to be a crucial one between the friends of the constitution and the partizans of State Rights, that in answer to the suggestion in some way to "influence" the insurgents to submission, instead of compelling obedience to the laws, Washington expressed a truth of profound and vital import, upon which he also acted, by declaring that "influence is not government." Before his retirement from the Presidency, therefore, the true theory of the constitution and of National power had become essentially settled, not only in the letter of law, but in the vastly higher efficiency of its actual enforcement by the combined civil and military power of the people acting in National capacity. The result was a second and most signal defeat of the advocates of State rights, or State supremacy, the first having been in the adoption of the constitution by the people. At a later period the same principles respecting the National authority and laws were emphatically asserted and acted upon by the Supreme Court of the United States, through the great Chief Justices Jay and Marshall; were sanctioned and carried into execution with patriotic vigor by the prompt, decisive action of Jackson in his conflict with State rights, as nullification; and were made clear and intelligible, and thus immensely strengthened in the popular mind, through the masterly expositions of Webster. Thus vitalized, they from time to time overcame the "political heresy" of State supremacy, even when supported by the name and fame of Jefferson, the acute and subtle argument of Calhoun, the influence of a great party organization, and, finally, by an armed rebellion of unprecedented magnitude and power. Whether these principles, so potent for good in the past, can be made efficient to protect the citizen and preserve a pure and free ballot in National elections, as against open fraud, intimidation and murderous violence, under cover of State rights, is the great question now dividing the Republican and Democratic parties, and yet to be settled by the political action of the people.

John C. Calhoun may justly be characterized as eminently the metaphysician of our politics. Beginning public life as a politician rather of National than narrow State rights views, the circumstances of his political career finally carried him over to the full acceptance, and elaborate exposition and advocacy of the Jeffersonian dogmas of State supremacy. To comprehend the public life of this distinguished leader of political thought, one must understand that in the latter part of his public career he was wholly devoted to two objects—the perpetuation of slavery in the south, and the maintenance of southern control in the government of the nation. This, of course, made him what his public action in later life shows him to have been—an extreme sectionalist and bitter enemy to the idea of universal human freedom In 1816 he had been favorable to and had voted for a protective tariff, but in 1832 the scheme of tariff protection to American industry had become in his opinion not only unwise and impolitic, but clearly unconstitutional. The secret of the change is easy to penetrate Calhoun had the sagacity to see that the south, with its system of slave labor, could never successfully engage in manufactures, and that, aided by the protective system, the north would inevitably outstrip her in the closely contested race between the two sections for population, wealth, and political ascendancy. Regardless of personal consistency or party relations, therefore, he attacked the idea of protection, and as a means of securing its defeat by the power of a single State, planted himself firmly upon the principles of State supremacy untruly termed State rights On the tariff question, as we all know, he failed Old Hickory even drove him into a corner, where he was compelled to vote for a tariff to save being arrested and tried for treason. But with the sagacity of one born to lead, and a courage which snatches victory from the very jaws of defeat, Calhoun suddenly changed his line of battle and organized a "Solid South" for negro slavery and southern sectional control of the Nation; or, in the alternative of failure in the latter point, secession and a confederacy of slave-holding States.

No man more thoroughly understood the power of political ideas in the government of this country than Calhoun. At once, therefore, he set about the work of indoctrinating the people with the notion that negro slavery was right, and the Democratic party with the principles of State supremacy. The labors of this great but misguided man in which his life was literally worn away, are not more astonishing in the magnitude of what, for the benefit of southern sectionalism and slavery, he undertook, than in the extraordinary measure of his success. He ultimately broke down the scheme of protection which Henry Clay had fondly called the American system; he compelled the great parties of his day to bow in abject submission at the feet of the slave power, and pledge resistence to northern discussion of the sin and crime of slavery, and barely missed seeing his most signal triumph in the adoption by the "Jackson Democracy" of those very principles of State supremacy which the old hero had put his foot upon, with such crushing effect, in 1830-32.

With the exception of one year Mr. Sibley has been in full practice as a lawyer since 1866. He has gained a high position at the bar in the counties where he has practiced, and, we believe, commands the respect of his legal brethren for ability, learning, and personal and professional integrity and honor. He has written arguments in a number of important cases in the supreme court of Ohio, and has appeared in oral and written arguments before the United States courts of the State. In a letter now before us, his powers are thus estimated by a distinguished member of the legal profession, who has known Mr. Sibley well ever since he began practice:

As a lawyer he is possessed of an unusual degree of aptitude for the analysis of complicated facts, and a very happy faculty of lucidly stating them. He readily masters legal principles, and is logical and accurate in their application. His style of composition is terse, chaste, and accurate. He is master of good English, in the true sense; that is, he uses good words, and no more of them than is necessary.

We merely add that Mr. Sibley is a forcible public

speaker, but one who aims at clearness of statement and logical method rather than rhetorical display.

Since 1856 Mr. Sibley has been a member of the Methodist Episcopal church, and for ten years past has held the local relation therein. In 1867 he was the delegate from Marietta to the international convention of Young Men's Christian associations at Detroit, Michigan. By the Ohio conference of 1879 he was elected alternate lay delegate to the general conference of the Methodist Episcopal church for 1880. He is now the head of the law firm of Sibley & Ewart, Marietta, Ohio.

HON. THOMAS WATSON MOORE.

The subject of this sketch was born in Allegheny county, Pennsylvania, March 22, 1825. His father, Joseph, was a well-to-do farmer of the region, and his mother, whose maiden name was Rebecca Watson, sprang from a race of quiet but thrifty farmers of the same region. At the age of seventeen, young Thomas resolved to quit the life of farmer, and accordingly went to Pittsburgh, Pennsylvania, where he engaged himself to the firm of J. B. Warden & Co., machine builders, and began to learn the trade of an engine forger. He served as an apprentice in the shops of this firm for four years, and then, his task being completed, he was employed by Messrs. Warden & Co. as a journeyman. In this capacity he served for the next two years, at the expiration of which he engaged as engineer on the steamer Northern Light, then plying between St. Louis and New Orleans. Remaining as an engineer on the Northern Light for a year, he next engaged in a like capacity on the Pennsylvania, a fine passenger steamer plying from Pittsburgh to Cincinnati. In this position he remained only about a year, when he abandoned this kind of life and determined to engage in business on the land.

Within a year after completing his trade as an engine forger and while yet employed by Messrs. J. B. Warden & Co., Mr. Moore married, taking as his wife Margaret McClelland, of Pittsburgh. In January, 1850, this lady died, leaving two children: Mary, aged two years, and Margaret, but a few weeks old. These children lived but a few years, Mary being three, and Margaret six years old when they died.

In the fall of 1849, a short time previous to the death of his first wife, Mr. Moore, by industry and frugality, having saved some twelve hundred dollars out of his earnings, came to Warren township, Washington county, Ohio, and invested the entire amount of his savings in a farm near what is now known as Tunnel Station, on the Old Line railroad. In April, 1850, Mr. Moore removed with his two children from Allegheny to his new purchase, and for the next four years engaged in farming and in buying and selling stock.

In April, 1853, Mr. Moore married a second time, taking as his wife Mary Green, daughter of Caleb Green, esq., of Washington county. As a result of this marriage, three children were born. The eldest,

Julia Fremont, was born in August, 1856; she is now the wife of F. M. Reed, esq., the business partner of Colonel Moore, and is the mother of one child, Gertie May. Rowena Green was born in November, 1858, and Flora Rebecca in March, 1864. The last two are yet unmarried.

In 1854, when the construction of the Marietta & Cincinnati railroad was in progress, Mr. Moore removed from his farm to the line of the road, and built what is now known as Tunnel station and a dwelling house adjoining. Here he opened out a line of general merchandise, and at the same time took a contract from the railroad company. He remained here selling goods and filling out contracts for the railroad company until 1858. During these years Mr. Moore held a number of local offices, serving as justice of the peace for seven years in succession.

In 1858, he took a contract for constructing a tunnel near White Sulphur Springs, Virginia, on what is now known as the Chesapeake & Ohio railroad. At the breaking out of the Rebellion in 1861, this work was still uncompleted, but Mr. Moore, foreseeing the difficulties likely to be met by an uncompromising Union man in that section, immediately sold out his interest in the contract and returned home.

About this time, the Marietta & Cincinnati railroad company determined to tunnel the hill near the station already spoken of, and the contract for this work was let to the Hon. W. P. Cutler and Mr. Moore. In July, 1861, the railroad company, for want of funds, suspended work on this tunnel, and Mr. Moore at once raised a company of one hundred volunteers in Warren and Barlow townships, and offered the services of himself and the company to the United States. They were accepted, and Captain Moore's company became a part of the famous Thirty-sixth Ohio volunteer infantry. He remained at the head of his company until the next February, when the Marietta & Cincinnati railroad company, having secured funds for the completion of the tunnel above mentioned, demanded that the contractors proceed to finish their contract, and Captain Moore was compelled to resign his position in the army. This work was finished in 1863. Shortly after its completion, Mr. Moore purchased his beautiful home on the banks of the Ohio, three miles distant from Marietta, where he has since resided. This home consists of about six hundred acres of land, upland and bottom, with forest and orchard interspersed here and there, the whole being kept in condition by a number of tenants, whose houses are built on the premises.

In the spring of 1864 Mr. Moore raised a company

of National guards in Warren township, and held himself and company in readiness to enter the service whenever a call should be made. During the same spring he took a contract to build a portion of the Baltimore Short Line railroad, and had just entered on this work, when his military company was ordered into active service. His and a number of other companies rendezvoused at Marietta, May 2nd, where Mr. Moore was at once elected colonel of the regiment, and placed in command. The regiment was ordered to Harper's Ferry, and from there to Point of Rocks, via Washington City; from thence to Bermuda Hundred, where the regiment performed garrison service until their muster out of the service.

Colonel Moore was made commandant of the post at Bermuda Hundred, and to these important duties were afterwards added those of assistant inspector general.

Upon his return from the service, Colonel Moore renewed the work on the Baltimore Short Line, which he completed in 1865. Finishing this work, he went to Missouri, buying a farm of one thousand acres in sight of Sedalia, and embarked in the stock business, at the same time assisting in the organization and establishment of the First National bank at Sedalia. In 1868 he abandoned the stock business, and went to Saginaw, Michigan, and engaged for the next two years in the lumber trade.

In 1870 Colonel Moore engaged in the business of merchandising in Harmar, which, together with his operations in farming, he has continued down to the present.

He has frequently been urged to accept office, which he persistently refused to do until 1879, when the exigencies of the party to which he is attached seemed to point him out as the proper standard bearer. Accordingly, he was nominated by the Republicans of the county for the legislature, to which he was elected by a handsome majority. During his service in the legislature, his conduct has been marked by conservative wisdom and practical common sense, and, to quote the editorial language of the Marietta *Register*, under date of April 28, 1881, "Washington county has not had a more efficient and influential member of the lower house for a long time."

In business affairs, the Hon. T. W. Moore has been singularly successful.

Beginning life without a dollar, he has amassed a considerable fortune. Every dollar of his wealth has been secured by means the most upright and honorable. Energy and fair dealing seem to have been his mottoes through life, and these have secured him, not only wealth and influence, but the confidence and esteem of a wide circle of friends.

CHAPTER XXXVIII.

BELPRE TOWNSHIP.

As BELPRE township stood prior to the year 1856 so was it established December 20, 1790, by act of the court of quarter sessions, expressed as follows:

Resolved, That townships numbered one and two in the tenth range, and township numbered one in the ninth range, be and they are hereby incorporated and included in one township by the name of Belpre.

In 1797 the court declared that all the territory south of the townships of Waterford and Marietta and north of Gallipolis, be known as Belpre township, embracing parts of the present counties of Athens, Vinton, and Ross, together with fractions of Hocking, Meigs, Jackson, and Pike as they stand to-day.

The lines marked out in 1790 were bounded north by territory now embraced in Warren, Barlow and Fairfield, east and south by the Ohio river and west by what became Athens county, Decatur and a section of Fairfield township.

In 1856, by an act of the county commissioners, town one, range nine, and town two, range ten were bisected from east to west and the northern division incorporated into a new township, known as Dunham.

The general form of Belpre is similar to that of Washington county, of which it is the most southern township. Resembling a triangle, it has about eight miles of northern line and nearly seven miles on the west, while the Ohio river as an irregular hypothenuse meanders in a southwesterly direction. North and west, with a general tendency toward the south, are ranges of hills which alternately approach toward and recede from the valley of the Ohio. These hills have no special geological features. They are in many respects similar to their sister hills in the eastern part of the county, save that there are

no large deposits of coal or petroleum. Towards the southern portion of the township there are slight indications of oil, and their seams of coal have occasionally been worked, but the labor is unremunerative. All along the line of the ridge which determines the course of the streams and extends from northeast to southwest, may be found in the out-croppings of the rocky sides an excellent quality of sandstone, especially adapted for building purposes, and in many places affording an excellent grind-stone grit. The principal quarry is a short distance above Little Hocking, and stone is taken from the vicinity of Belpre village.

The streams naturally seek the Ohio river, whose principal tributary in Belpre township is the Little Hocking, whose eastern and western forks, with their numerous branches, converge in the western part of the township, directing the enlarged stream towards the Ohio. Congress and Crooked creeks, in the eastern part of the township, Davis run in the centre, and Sawyer's and Big runs toward the southern extremity, are the only considerable streams independent of the Little Hocking. The hillsides rising from the glens and valleys bordering on these streams are covered with an abundant growth of forest trees, principally oak. Of late years the hill country has, in a measure, been cleared and cultivated. As in the other hilly portions of the county the hill-tops are especially adapted to the growth of apple trees, and numerous orchards are found back of the valleys.

Descending the hills by winding and almost circuitous routes the traveller soon reaches the valleys which nature with bountiful hand has distributed throughout the length and breadth of the township. The valley of the Little Hocking is limited, although it has its fertile tracts. The land along the Ohio is a vast stretch or fertility. By a natural division there are three principal areas where the valley broadens into a plain, and with adjoining second bottoms affords a farming country unsurpassed by any in Washington county. Beginning at the northern boundary of the township the Ohio river flows directly south three miles until it reaches the mouth of the Little Kanawha and the opposing hills of West Virginia, when by an abrupt turn it takes a westerly course thus embracing the first of the areas of rich land. About a mile below this bend the river, as if hesitating which way to turn, has impartially divided, leaving in the centre a rich alluvion, afterwards made an object of national attention by the misfortune of the Blennerhassetts. A little below the head of the island the river is confronted by a precipitous bluff which crowds the valley into the river and continues westward about half a mile. This bluff, which is over thirty feet high, is an extension of the plain land and acting as a spur from the ridge to the north separates the valley. This plateau or peninsula of the hill country is still made beautiful by evergreens, principally cedar, thus giving to the vicinity the name of Cedarville. As will be seen hereafter, this was an attractive spot to the early settlers. Leaving the bluff as the eastern boundary, the Ohio, by a graceful inward curve, has marked out the second and central alluvion from a quarter to a third of a mile wide and about

63

three miles long, being contracted in the narrows just above the mouth of the Little Hocking. The bottom lands gradually lose themselves in adjoining plain land which is thirty or forty feet higher than the alluvial land, and varies in width from a third of a mile to a mile. This upland soil is of a rich and very productive sandy loam. Higher up on the hills the soil is of red clay for the most part, and is not of great value for farming purposes.

The opposing hills and plains on the Virginia shore complete the beauty of the scene. Especially broad and fertile is the plain below Blennerhassett island, and it is not much wonder that General Washington, during his trip down the Ohio, was induced to purchase its broad expanse, and there is but little doubt but that he would have added to his purchase the bottom land opposite, concerning which he speaks in his journal, had this land not been on the "Indian side" of the river.

Along the river bottoms there was a heavy growth of beech, maple, and sycamore trees, while the higher land was shaded by native poplar and oak. In the spring time there was a multitude and endless variety of flowers, and the scene was well nigh enchanting. This garden spot was appropriately named, for there is a beauty and poetry in the name—"Belle Prairie on the Belle Rivier."

Before the advent of the white man this fair land was the dwelling place of wild beasts. The invasions of strong and warlike Indian tribes kept sister tribes from locating villages along this part of the Ohio. It was a common hunting ground, and long ago the buffalo fed in the meadows. As late as the time of the coming of the first white men, the clumsy bear might have been seen galloping into the hills or scaling some neighboring tree; the timid deer ran startled from the water courses, and at night the harmony of the place was interrupted by the howling of the wolves, or the screaming of the panthers. But the Indians while waiting at Harmar to make the treaty of 1788 had pretty effectually driven out the game in the vicinity of Belpre. Deer became scarce, and a bear was not a common sight. Wild turkeys continued to be abundant, and wolves made sheep raising hazardous.

BEFORE THE INDIAN.

In Belpre township there are several mounds which are the work of the pre-historic race. They are all in view of the Ohio.

There is now but one mound of considerable size remaining in Belpre. This is located near the river, just east of Cedarville, on the land now owned by Stephen Druse. The mound was undoubtedly of conical shape, but has gradually been worn and flattened until now it is not more than four or five feet high with a circumference at the base of twenty-five or thirty feet. It is surrounded by a circular ditch which appears to have been several feet deep. This ditch is surmounted by a parapet three or four feet high extending all the way around, and having a diameter of nearly one hundred feet. The whole is laid out with mathematical exactness. This mound has not been opened.

There are several smaller mounds in the same neighborhood that are plainly artificial, but are without the circular ditch and the parapet. There is a small mound of this kind on the property of Charles Ames, and another in the garden of Cyrus Ames, west of Cedarville. Mounds are also found on the land of E. W. Petty and J. Ollum a short distance north of the Druse mound.

Until a few years ago, there stood on the land of J. M. Farson, just below Cedarville, a mound of large proportions. Like its smaller neighbors it was without surrounding ditch or parapet. It stood on the left of, and partially in the road opposite the residence of Mr. Farson. It was shaped like a sugar-loaf, save that at some early day there had been made an excavation in the top which gave it the appearance of an extinct volcano. At the time of its removal it was fourteen feet high and had a circumference of one hundred feet at the base. There was no attempt to ascertain its contents until 1874. During this and the subsequent year Mr. Farson decided to remove it, and while engaged in the work made some very interesting discoveries. As had been surmised, the mound proved to be one of the tumuli with which the surface of the whole country is dotted. The excavation at the top was renewed. After digging downward a short distance the first skeleton was discovered. It was in a fair state of preservation, in fact so sound that the doubt at once arose as to its antiquity. A closer examination of the skull indicated that it was that of an Indian, and a bullet hole in the forhead just above the eye at once suggested the probability that the death and burial took place less than an hundred years ago, although there is no history or even tradition concerning such death and burial.

Toward the centre of the mound a skeleton was found which upon being exposed to the air at once proved its great age by crumbling to dust. As the work proceeded there were found, at different depths, eight more skeletons, irregularly arranged. Exposure soon reduced these bones to their original element. With each skeleton was found a stone pipe, beads, buttons, and balls of muscle-shells, and an occasional collection of arrow-heads. A remarkable harpoon with a bone-bearded point was among the relics found. With one skeleton there was found a pair of horns. This suggests that the builders of the mounds believed in a *post mortem* combat with an evil one, and that weapons were selected with reference to the homeopathic principle "*similia similibus curantur.*" One of these horns is artificial and was carved from the bone of some animal, the outside only being finished; the mate to this rough and hastily made counterpart was a real horn over six inches in length.

In the centre and a little below the base of the mound there were found the remains of a skeleton mingled with burned charcoal and calcined bones. It was evident that the body had been cremated. The lower extremities evidently had not been subjected to the intensity of a flame, and there is evidence that the body prior to cremation had been placed in a sitting posture, so that the head and trunk speedily consumed, leaving unburned the rest of the body.

In various parts of the mound there were found in all

twenty-two arrow-heads from three to five inches in length; numerous stone axes, pipes, and harpoons; nine hollow cylindrical tubes, eight of which were found together away from the skeletons, and the ninth was with the remains of the burned skeleton and was much smaller than the others. These tubes were made of soapstone and the first mentioned are about a foot in length. The maker of these tubes was thoroughly acquainted with the art of glazing, as their polished surfaces attest. As many of these relics as would bear exposure to the air were preserved. The mound was entirely taken away and furnished nearly two thousand cubic yards of earth.

There are several small mounds farther down the river. On the more elevated plains and hilltops have been found heaps of stone which bear evidence of orderly arrangement. There was until a few years ago such a structure on the hillside on the farm of Edwin Guthrie. One was also erected on the adjoining farm of C. W. Oakes. They were constructed of large flat stones, piled up loosely until ten or twelve feet high. Ashes and other indications of fire were discovered.

THE SETTLEMENT.

Belle Prairie was naturally adapted to the wants of the pioneers in the Ohio company, and was quickly selected by the committee sent out to explore, and which reported to the company as the most suitable place for the establishment of the first community separate from the one at the mouth of the Muskingum. The natural beauty of the fair land, combined with the knowledge of the great fertility of the soil, made the place desirable for farmers; and, above all, the good land was close joined by the river, thus enabling the settlers to form a continuous chain of farms and farm-houses, thereby making communication easier. The settlement was composed of more than twenty-five of the original proprietors of the land, and a number of others who had either purchased land of the original proprietors, or else secured it soon after the first settlement. For the most part this was a settlement of Revolutionary officers, brave men and wise, who had struggled for independence with their leader, Washington.

As will be seen, the settlements were made at Belpre in the years 1789 and 1790, principally. Few came during the Indian troubles. After the war a number of additional settlements were made. The fact, however, is that Belpre township was settled, prior to the year 1800, almost as thickly as it is to day. Now and then, during the intervening years, there is a record of a settlement. The country back of the river was principally owned by those living on the bottom land, and hence the back settlement is of recent date, and even to-day is very sparse. The first houses were built near the river, and of necessity very close together, as the lots were very narrow, some of them being less than forty rods wide. The first business of the settler was to build a log house and make a clearing for the first crop. A rapid method of freeing the land to be cultivated from the overhanging shade was to girdle the trees, letting them stand until a more convenient season for felling them. Many of the first houses

were hastily constructed of unhewn logs, and in later years gave way to the more substantial hewed log or frame houses which were usually built farther back from the river. The cattle grazed in the woods back of the clearings, which were generally surrounded by "stake and rider" fences. There was a continuous path from field to field, whereby the settlers kept up the strong feeling of friendliness and sociability which has ever characterized these families, many of the descendants being residents of Belpre township to-day. It will be noticed that the first settlements were made in the upper part of the township, and quickly extended toward the southwestern corner. In the survey of lands they were platted in three divisions, known as the upper, the middle, and the lower settlements. The upper settlement extended down the river to the land drawn by A. W. Putnam; the middle, thence to the mouth of the Little Hocking; and the lower included the remaining portion of river land, afterwards known as the Newbury settlement. The farms of the pioneers will be noted as parts of one of these three divisions.

THE UPPER SETTLEMENT.

From time to time, during the days of early settlement, transient people "squatted" on the Congress section, north of the site of Belpre village, but these soon gave way to permanent settlers, and went further down the river.

Captain William Dana settled on the land now occupied by his grandson, George Dana, a short distance below the present village of Belpre. He was born at Little Cambridge, now Brighton, Massachusetts, in 1745. His ancestors were French Huguenots. In 1770 he married Mary Bancroft, who was born in 1752, and died in 1823, surviving her husband fourteen years. After Captain Dana's marriage he resided in Charleston, but just before the battle of Lexington removed to Worcester. He became a captain in the army, and did good service, but having sold his property for worthless continental currency, he was obliged to quit the army, and for a time worked on a farm near Amherst, New Hampshire, working during the winter at the carpenter trade that he might supply his family with the necessities of life. Leaving his family at Amherst, he came to the Ohio country with his two oldest sons in 1788. He made some money in Marietta by burning brick, the first known to have been made in the territory. In the spring of 1788 he built a log cabin on land in Belpre, a short distance below the present village. In the autumn of 1789 he arrived with his family at Marietta, and there being no accommodations there, proceeded down the river with the intention of living in the log house which he had built in the previous spring, but unfortunately it had burned in the interim, and it was necessary to hastily erect what is known among the pioneers as "salt box." So small was this abode that two of the boys had to sleep in the covered wagon during the winter. Notwithstanding this first misfortune Captain Dana was elated at the thought of having reached such a goodly land, and immediately set about to clear the surrounding forest. In the following year he built a more comfortable hewed log house. There were nine children—Luther, William and Stephen settled in New-port township; Edmond, Augustus, Elizabeth, Mary and George (married), and settled in Washington county. Edmond built the present Dana residence. Mary and Fanny were born in the garrison. George Dana, sr., was born in 1790. By his wife, Deborah A. Fisher, he had five children, three of whom are living, viz: Mrs. E. W. Dodge, of Avondale, Cincinnati; Mary W. Linn, of Zanesville; and George Dana living on the old place in Belpre township. He was born in 1821. He married Licia Byington, by whom he has had eleven children, nine of whom are living.

John and Rebecca Rouse, with their family, arrived at Belpre in 1789, having came from Massachusetts in 1788, accompanied by Major Jonathan Haskell and Captain Jonathan Devol. An interesting circumstance is related concerning their departure from their Massachusetts home. A neighboring farmer boy was in love with Bath-sheba, the oldest daughter of Mr. Rouse, and just before the family left for the west, the boy's father urgently begged Bathsheba to remain, offering as an inducement to marry his son, the deed for a fine farm. But the faithful daughter would not desert her father and mother. She became very useful in the community at Belpre, and for a number of years taught school, she being the first female teacher in the Northwest Territory. The other children were: Cynthia, who married Hon. Paul Fearing; Betsy, wife of Colonel Levi Barber; Michael, Ruth, Stephen, Robert and Barker, the two latter being twins. Robert died of scarlet fever, and the others married and settled in the county, some of the descendants being on the old place in Belpre township.

Colonel Ebenezer Battelle, of Massachusetts, joined the Belpre associates, and early in the spring of 1789 went to Belpre and proceeded to clear his farm, which was located partially on and just east of the site of the Castle. He cleared quite a patch of land, and proceeded to erect a stout block-house for the reception of his family. On the day after Captain King had been killed by the Indians, Colonel Battelle, with his two sons, and Esquire Greene, set forth from Marietta in a large canoe loaded with provisions and farming tools. Before they reached Belpre they were informed of the death of their friend, and for a time they consulted with each other on the river bank, as to the advisability of proceeding, but concluding that they should run the risk they proceeded, and that night, with the assembled settlers, kept guard at their block-houses, which being near together supplied the lack of a fort.

Early in April, before any families had moved on to the grounds, a party of officers and ladies from Marietta visited Belpre. Colonel Battelle accompanied their barge on the return trip up the Ohio. A bear was seen swimming in the river, and the escort that was proceeding by land banged away at him without touching him. The canoe containing Colonel Battelle approached, and he forthwith got a "tail hold" of bruin, whom he immersed every time he tried to bite the hand of his captor. The bear was finally killed with an axe. He weighed over three hundred pounds.

Colonel Battelle soon afterwards removed his family to Belpre. He had three sons and one daughter. Cornelius and Thomas became wealthy merchants in the West Indies; Thomas married the daughter of Governor Livingston, of New York, and Cornelius the daughter of a wealthy planter; Louisa married Rev. Joseph I. Foot, and lived in West Brookfield, Massachusetts, where he was pastor of the Presbyterian church from 1827 to 1829.

Between the years 1802 and 1804 Colonel Battelle and his son Ebenezer moved to Newport township. The former died in 1815.

Colonel Battelle was the first religious instructor appointed for Belpre. During the Indian war his block-house, which formed the northeast corner of Farmer's castle, was used as a place for public worship. Further particulars of the early life of this good man are narrated in the history of Newport township.

Major Jonathan Haskell was one of the first settlers in Belpre, and built his cabin on land a short distance east of the site of the castle. He commenced clearing his farm, and was getting his home in order when the Indian war broke out, and he left Belpre to accept an appointment in the regular service. He went to Rochester, Massachusetts, and returned in December, 1791, to Marietta, where he was stationed for the defence of the settlement. He received his commission as major in 1795. After the war he returned to his home at Belpre, where he remained until his death in 1814. He was born in Massachusetts in 1775. After coming to Belpre he married Phœbe Greene. Some of the descendants are living in Washington county, the daughter of Major Haskell, Mrs. Lawton, being a resident of Barlow township.

Colonel Nathaniel Cushing, the original proprietor of lot twenty-seven on the site of Farmer's castle, moved to his land in 1789. He was born in Massachusetts in 1753, and in 1775 married Elizabeth Heath, by whom he had twelve children, six sons and six daughters. The family has representatives in this county, in the Goodnos, who are grandchildren of Colonel Cushing.

Colonel Cushing achieved military renown in the war of the Revolution. After the close of the war he lived in Boston, whence, in 1788, he removed to Marietta. In August after his arrival he was, by Governor St. Clair, appointed captain in the First regiment of territorial militia, and in 1797 was made colonel of the regiment. After the capture of Major Goodale by the Indians, Colonel Cushing was chosen to command the garrison at Farmer's castle. He was one of the most active men in the affairs of the garrison. He was highly esteemed by Blennerhassett, and both Colonel and Mrs. Cushing were treated with marked attention, and were put in charge of the island when Blennerhassett left.

Colonel Israel Putnam, the eldest son of General Putnam, was born in Salem, Massachusetts, in 1739. In 1764 he married Sarah Waldo. When his father heard of the battle of Lexington, and hurried from the plow to the army, Israel immediately followed with a company of volunteers which he had raised. Though naturally brave and strong, he was unsuited to the army, and after doing good service for three years, retired to the farm. When the Ohio company was formed he became an associate, and started for the west with two of his sons, crossing the mountain with a wagon loaded with farming utensils. While crossing North river the raft on which his son Waldo and the yoke of oxen were crossing began to sink. But Waldo was equal to the emergency, unyoked the oxen, and being unable to swim, seized one of the oxen by the tail and launched him into the river. The astonished ox, after considerable effort, landed his passenger, and the journey proceeded without further incident. The Putnams passed the winter at Marietta, in the Campus Martius, and in the spring of 1789, they proceeded to their lands at Belpre, Colonel Putnam being opposite the mouth of the Little Kanawha, and Waldo's in the middle settlement. Colonel Putnam put up a log house, and remained clearing and fencing his land until the fall of 1790, when he returned to Pomfret, Connecticut, for his family, and owing to the Indian war did not return until after the peace of 1795. Soon after bringing his family to Belpre he erected a large frame house, which, in those early days was considered to be quite a mansion. This house is now known as the Benedict house. Colonel Putnam was a practical agriculturist, and gave an impetus to the growth of the farming interests of Belpre, and was an influential man in the settlement. He frequently led the religious meetings during the absence of the preacher. He had five sons and three daughters. Israel settled in Muskingum township; William Pitt was a physician and located in Marietta in 1792; David also settled in Marietta, in 1798; the fifth son was George W.; Aaron W. located in the middle settlement. Sarah married Samuel Thorniley; Mary, Daniel Mayo; and Elizabeth Joel Craig. The two latter settled in Newport, Kentucky.

Captain Jonathan Stone, one of the Belpre pioneers of 1789, was a settler at Marietta the year before. A full biography appears at the close of this chapter.

Colonel Alexander Oliver, of Massachusetts, and a valiant soldier during the Revolutionary war came to Belpre in 1789 and settled on lot No. 19, just below what is now known as Cedarville. There were eleven children, all of whom settled in Ohio. Two of Alexander's sons became ministers; David became a physician in western Ohio; Launcelot and John were the other sons. The daughters were: Lucreta, wife of Levi Munsel, who lived several years in Marietta; Betsy, married Hon. Daniel Symmes, of Cincinnati; Sally, married Major Austin, United States army, and settled in Cincinnati; Lucreta, wife of George Putnam, son of Colonel Israel Putnam; Mehala, married Calvin Shepherd, of Marietta; Electa, wife of O. M. Spencer, of Cincinnati; and Mary, married Oliver Wing, who settled in Washington county. During the Indian war the family took shelter in Farmer's castle.

William Browning came to Marietta from Massachusetts in 1789, and married Abigail, the daughter of General Rufus Putnam. He settled in Belpre on the land now a part of the village. Here he continued to live until his death which occurred in 1823. There were four children, three of whom lived to maturity, viz: William R., George, and Samuel M. William R., was born in 1792, and in 1819 married Sophia Barker, who was born in 1797 and is still living. Mr. Rufus Browning was at one time county surveyor, and was one of the early justices in the township. In the early days he kept a ferry and his wife kept a tavern. The seven children were: Joseph, Abigail, William, Cynthia, A. H., R. P., and E. P. Browning, and Sophia. A. H. Browning was the original proprietor of the town plat of the village of Belpre. The second son, William, was born in 1824; he married Mary Parker. Their five children survive. Mr. George Browning, son of William Browning, sr., went to Mt. Vernon, Ohio, where he lived and died. His brother, Samuel, was a lawyer and died at Burlington, in Lawrence county, Ohio. He married Miss Lucy Dana, of Newport, Washington county, Ohio.

Nathaniel Little, a native of Massachusetts, was among the first to make settlement in Belpre. During the Indian troubles he and his wife and son, Charles, took refuge in the castle. Afterwards he lived in the Middle settlement, and in a few years removed to Newport where he died. He had five sons and one daughter. His wife was Pamelia Bradford, whose ancestors came from England in the May Flower.

Griffin Greene, esq., located in Belpre in 1790, building his house near the Ohio a little over a mile below the present village of Cedarville, and just below the site of the castle. He was born in Warwick, Rhode Island, in 1749, and was bred in the smith and anchor business. He married Sarah Greene, of a family not connected by blood with his own. She was a sister of Colonel Christopher Greene, who, during the Revolution, commanded the noted black regiment. There were four children by this marriage—Richard, Philip, Griffin, and Susan, all of whom lived to years of maturity, and came to Belpre with their parents. Phœbe Greene, a niece, lived with them and married Major Jonathan Haskell, who settled at Belpre. Richard, Philip, and Susan Greene married and settled in Ohio. Griffin died in Marietta. Esquire Greene early became an important personage in Belpre. He was perhaps the first squire in the neighborhood, and by him were some of the earliest marriages solemnized, and some of the first disputes settled. But he was particularly noted for his inventive genius. He assisted Captain Devol in the invention of the floating mill, and he ingeniously contrived a machine for perpetual motion, which, though it would stop, would run for several hours in a wonderful manner. In 1795 he turned his attention to the feasibility of applying steam to the moving of boats on the western streams, and invented an engine, and in company with Elijah Backus went to Philadelphia, and after an expenditure of about a thousand dollars in a vain effort to construct the engine the project was dropped. In 1794 Squire Greene was active in the formation of the company which discovered the Scioto salines. In 1801 he removed with his family to Marietta. He was faithful to his country during the Revolution, and because he took part in the war was, with his illustrious cousin, General Nathaniel Greene, excommunicated from the Friend's society. He lived in Marietta, after leaving Belpre, until his death which occurred in 1804.

Among those who came to Belpre about 1790 was the family of Colonel Daniel Bent, of Massachusetts. He was accompanied on the journey from Rutland to the Ohio by his family and Silas, in whose name the share of land was drawn. Colonel Bent was the father of several children. Nahum settled after the war near Centre Belpre, eventually becoming the first postmaster at Bent's Post Office, as the Centre Belpre office was once called. Silas Bent, with his wife and several children, located in the upper settlement. He became one of the most prominent men in the township. He was one of the judges of the court of common pleas appointed by Governor St. Clair. After the purchase of Louisiana he removed to St. Louis, and was there engaged in the survey of United States lands. His son, Silas, lived for a time just above Foster's tavern, where Belpre village now stands, and he afterwards removed to the far west, becoming the head of a fur company, and establishing a fort and trading post up the Arkansas river. Of the other children of Colonel Bent, Dorcas married William Dana, of Newport township; Susan married Joel Oakes, of Newbury; and there was another son, Daniel by name, who lived on the old home place and died there.

Captain Isaac Barker removed from New Bedford, Massachusetts, in 1788, and journeyed westward with the family of Captain William Dana. On the way across the mountains an amusing incident occurred. The oxen that Captain Barker was driving, becoming footsore, were exchanged for a fresh yoke at a Dutch tavern at which they stopped. They had scarcely got out of sight of the tavern when the new team balked on a rough place in the road, and all efforts to coax them to go on were futile. The boys sagely concluded that the oxen could not understand English, and quickly sent for the Dutch tavern-keeper, who scared the oxen over the rough place by a rapid flow of Dutch swearing. On arriving at Marietta the family spent several months with the family of Paul Fearing. Early in 1790 they moved to their farm in the upper settlement at Belpre, just below that of Captain Devol. There were eight children—Michael, Isaac, Joseph, William, Timothy, Anna, Rhoda, and Nancy. During the war they lived in Farmer's castle and at Stone's stockade. The Barkers continued on their farm until 1798, when they removed to Athens county, where the sons became prominent.

Captain Jonathan Devol, of Rhode Island, was one of the passengers on the May Flower, which he constructed for the use of the first company of emigrants to Ohio. He erected a house in the Campus Martius in 1788, and was joined by his wife and children in December of that year. Being a skilful builder, and in fact ingenious in any work, he was detained from taking possession of the lot which he had drawn in Belpre. He was one of the committee of three appointed to explore the country in search of suitable places for the location of mills and farming settlements. His lot in Belpre upper settlement was numbered seven, and thither in February, 1791, he repaired with his family. He succeeded in clearing a patch of land, and built a log cabin not far below the house of Captain William Dana, his next neighbor. The news of the Big Bottom massacre reached him while attending court at Marietta, and he hurried home, fearing that his family would be murdered. Mrs. Devol, upon hearing that the Indians were on the war path, ordered the children to lie down with their clothes on, ready to run at a moment's notice. But, fortunately, Captain Devol found his family safe. He at once prepared the plans and directed the building of Farmer's castle, where he and his family remained during the dangerous period. He became famous by building the wonderful "floating mill." For the gratification of Squire Greene, he constructed the perpetual motion machine. He also constructed a cane mill for the use of the inhabitants of the garrison. In 1792 he built a twelve-oared barge, of about twenty-five tons burthen, for General Putnam. The red cedar, of which it was built, was procured at the hazard of Captain Devol's life, on the Little Kanawha, a few miles above its mouth. The barge was a model of beauty, and was said to have excelled any boat ever seen on the Ohio. After the war Captain Devol moved to Marietta, and in 1797 to Wiseman's bottom, in Muskingum. Belpre was a great loser by his removal.

Noah Sparhawk was born in New Hampshire in 1730. He married Miriam Greene, who was born in 1752, and died in 1847, surviving her husband forty years. They settled in Belpre shortly after the Indian war, and secured land of Captain George Ingersoll, who had made some improvement on the lot below Cedarville, of which he was the orignal proprietor, and after the war returned to his home at Boston. Nathan, son of Noah Sparhawk, was born in 1803. In 1834 he married Susan Stone, who was born in Belpre in 1802, and died in 1873. Two children resulted from this union: George W. resides in St. Louis, and Caroline resides with her father in Belpre village. In his younger days he took an active part in all good enterprises.

Edward Henderson, who acted as a ranger at Marietta during the war, at its close settled in Belpre. He was the first man that received pay from the Government for military duty performed at Marietta. He was born in Connecticut in 1761. He married Sarah Lufkin, who was born in 1770 and died in 1832. Mr. Henderson died at Philadelphia in 1800. That same year his son Josiah was born, on the same day that Mr. Blennerhasset moved to his island home. Josiah lived with his mother until he arrived at the years of maturity, and in 1827 married Catharine Hutchison, who was born in 1806. There are three children surviving, viz: George W., in Oakland, California; Lucy Spencer; and Fanny Cay-Wood, in Belpre. Captain Henderson has been on the river during the most of his life, and is now living in honored retirement in the village of Belpre.

Peregrine Foster and Mary his wife settled in the township about 1796, coming immediately from Morgan county, Virginia, whither they had gone for refuge during the war. Mr. Foster was born in New England in 1749, and was one of the forty-eight who came to the Ohio country in 1788. As narrated above, he soon went to Virginia. After his arrival in Belpre he started a ferry, the first concerning which anything is known, and erected a frame house, in which he kept tavern until his death, in 1804, when the business was conducted by his wife, who in after years became the wife of William Browning, and died in 1823. Mr. Foster served as one of the judges of the territorial court of common pleas prior to 1802. He was also one of the surveyors for the Ohio company, and went back to New England for his family. On his way back to Ohio, he and his family stopped in Morgantown, Virginia, on account of the Indian war. His early decease was a great loss to the community in which he dwelt.

Zadoc Foster, a native of Maccachusetts, moved with his family to the Northwest Territory in 1796. He came with an ox team as far as Olean point, on the Allegheny river, and thence by raft to Marietta, where he remained until the spring of 1797, when he settled in Belpre, and remained there until he went to Athens county in 1809, where his descendants are living.

Among the earliest settlers was William Smith, of New England. He married the daughter of Captain Gates. A son is living in Belpre.

Josiah Whiting, a soldier from Boston, was present at St. Clair's defeat. After the Indian war he came to Belpre and settled just above the Putnam place in the upper settlement, afterwards removing back from the river. He was a shoemaker by trade.

Daniel Ellenwood, of Massachusetts, came to Belpre in 1795 and settled just below the Howe farm in the upper settlement. He had three sons and three daughters, none of whom are living in the township.

Cyrus Ames, sr., emigrated from Massachusetts in 1798, and after the usual journey by wagon and boat arrived at Belpre and made settlement a short distance below the present village of Cedarville. He married Polly Rice by whom he had the following children, viz: Cyrus, residing in Belpre, as does also Abigail, widow of Charles H. Brough; Susan C. (McKibben), who settled in Kansas; William, in Illinois; and Azuba, of Belpre. Cyrus, the eldest son, was born in Belpre township in 1812. He married Sarah Porter in 1844. They have had five children, four of whom are still living, viz: Emma, Charles B., living near his father; Frank P., and Mary E. Their oldest son, Edward L., born in 1847, died in 1863. Mr. Ames is a large land owner, he having three hundred and twenty acres of land, mostly of second bottom. He makes a specialty of sheep raising. The father of Cyrus Ames, sr., was an Episcopal clergyman, a graduate of Harvard, and a chaplain in the Revolutionary war. He died at Valley Forge in the hard winter of 1777-8.

Daniel Fisher landed on Blennerhassett Island on New Year's day, 1800. He lived on the Island a few years and then bought land of Colonel Battelle. He had in all a family of ten children, two sons and two daughters remaining at the old home in Dedham, Massachusetts. The other children were William, who became

quite prominent; Seth; Andrew, a hatter by trade, died in Athens county, Elizabeth, married Bartholomew Gilman; Hannah, married Seth Fuller, and Deborah, the wife of George Dana.

Joseph Newbury, a native of New York State, settled at Cedarville at an early day. He had a large family and was a strict Methodist. Believing in the strict adherence to biblical admonition, he refused to be called anything but "dad," because the Bible says "call no man father." His son Joe was a scriptural prodigy and could recite chapter after chapter and understand not a word.

Sherabiah Fletcher was one of the first settlers in Belpre township. He was a Revolutionary soldier and was present at the taking of West Point, Afterwards coming to Belpre he settled on the back part of the lot upon which Cyrus Ames settled. His second wife was a Bellows and is still living near the mouth of the Little Hocking. As an instance of the integrity of Mr. Fletcher it is related that his father, who lived at Lowell, Massachusetts, died and left property to his children, a part of this property being the land on which Lowell was built. Sherabiah told his brothers that he would forego his share of the property if they would assume the responsibility of caring for their aged mother. This they did. In the course of time Mr. Fletcher was informed that according to law he had a right to the land on which Lowell is. This was technically true, but Mr. Fletcher honorably refused to make any effort to reclaim what others had paid for. The citizens of Belpre made the old gentleman a present of three hundred dollars as a token.

John Breck settled just below Major Haskells' place about the year 1800. He married a daughter of Judge Foster, of Belpre, and afterwards removed to the Duck creek settlement. His father was a prominent member of the Ohio company. He preached the first sermon in the settlement.

Joseph O'Neal, sr., emigrated from old Virginia in 1812, and settled a short distance north of the present village of Belpre. He was born in 1770, and died in Belpre in 1807. His two sons, Joseph and Colbert, continued to live on the home place. The latter, who is still living, was born in Virginia in 1805. He married Sarah Dana, born in 1808. These two have had three children, viz: Foster, Amanda, and Russel.

Joseph O'Neal, jr. was born in Virginia in 1800, and died in Belpre in 1840. He married Eunice Cole, who died February 27, 1881. The children are J. L. O'Neal, of Belpre; Ezra H., of Colorado; and J. C. O'Neal, of Belpre. The former, born in 1829, married Jennie Rardin, by whom he has had five children. For the last five years Mr. O'Neal has been justice of the peace, with his office in Belpre village, where he resides.

Joseph Cook was born in Virginia in 1785, and in 1813 with his family emigrated to Ohio, and settled in Belpre township, locating near where the village now stands. His house was a very popular resort for travellers, and was known far and wide as the Cook house. Mr. Cook's wife, Clarissa Devol, was born in 1791, and died in 1859.

They were the parents of three children, viz: Charles D., Maria D., and Elizabeth. Charles D. was born in 1813, in what is now West Virginia, and in that same year was brought by his parents to Belpre. He married Mary Curtis, who was born in Belpre township in 1825. Four of the five children born by this marriage are living, viz: Ada, wife of E. P. Cook; Clara L., wife of Alfred Williams; Mary V., and Ella B.

In 1816 Ebenezer Benedict, a native of Connecticut, removed to Belpre from Trumbull county, Ohio. He lived in a frame house about one hundred yards above the ferry landing, near the present village of Belpre. This house was carried away in the flood of 1832, and was wrecked on the head of Blennerhasset island. Mr. Benedict remained in Belpre until 1866, the time of his death. His widow, Irenea (Barnum) survived him seven years. They had three children: Polly, deceased; George, residing in Marietta; and Irenea (Allen), living in Hamilton county, Ohio.

Levi Benedict, a brother of Ebenezer, came to Belpre in 1816, and died of fever in the sickly season of 1824.

Dr. G. N. Gilbert emigrated from Vermont to Ohio in 1817, and settled in Waterford, and in 1821 located in Belpre middle settlement, where he lived until his death, in 1870. His professional career is noted elsewhere in this work. When he first came to Belpre he boarded at Dr. Beebe's house, and afterwards became a member of the family of A. W. Putnam, whose daughter, Lucy E., he married in 1825. They lived together just forty-five years, the doctor dying on the anniversary of their marriage. They had ten children, of whom eight are living. In 1835 Dr. Gilbert was appointed to take charge of the post office at Cedarville, which he kept at his house a short distance below the old Congregational church. In 1864 he met with a severe runaway accident which deprived him almost entirely of his eyesight. After this time his wife acted as deputy postmaster, and after his death was appointed postmistress, which office she held until in 1873, when the office was discontinued. Mrs. Gilbert, who was born in 1804, is still living, and is one of the few survivors of the early days of Belpre settlement.

THE MIDDLE SETTLEMENT.

In April, 1789, Major Nathan Goodale and family arrived at Belpre, he being a leading associate in the colony. His land was that now occupied by the hamlet of Center Belpre. He was conceded to be one of the most honest, industrious, and intelligent farmers in the settlement, and he went at the heavy task of clearing and making ready for cultivation his land, in such a way as to prove his capabilities for sermounting every difficulty. He was born in Brookfield, Massachusetts, in 1743. He learned the trade of a bricklayer, and received a fair education. He married Elizabeth Phelps, and lived for a time in Rutland, where his three oldest children, Betsy, Cynthia, and Sally, were born. These daughters married and settled in Ohio. The sons were Lincoln, who studied medicine in Belpre, with Dr. Jewett, but afterwards became a merchant in Columbus, where Goodale park keeps his memory green. Timothy was

a grown man during the Indian war and done did as a ranger. He located on the lot just below that on which his father settled, and died a short time after the return of peace. Major Goodale was a soldier in every respect. He was a minute-man, and then a gallant officer in the Revolution. After coming to Marietta in 1789 he was appointed captain of a company of militia which he drilled in view of the approaching war. He was one of the most active in the planning and erection of Farmer's castle. When the building was ready for occupancy what better man than Major Goodale could they get to command the garrison? He was in command in the winter of 1793, when, for convenience, the branch forts were built. Stone's stockade above and Goodale's stockade below. Major Goodale had been in the new garrison scarcely a week when he was ruthlessly seized by savages and carried away to die a captive, a fuller account of his seizure being given elsewhere in this work. He left a vacancy hard to fill. His family, overwhelmed with grief, remained in the neighborhood several years and finally scattered. None of the descendants are living in the county at present.

Daniel Loring, of Massachusetts, with his family took refuge in Farmer's castle during the Indian war. His farm was just below what is now Centre Belpre. His first wife was Miss Howe, of Sudbury, Massachusetts. The children by this marriage were Israel, Charlotte, wife of A. W. Putnam, and Ezekial. His second wife was the widow of a brother of Oliver Rice. The children by the second marriage were Bathsheba, married Mr. Washburne, of Marietta; Daniel, removed to Chillicothe; Polly, wife of Dr. William Beebe; Oliver Rice, who held the office of associate justice of the court of common pleas; and Jesse, who was sheriff of Washington county for a number of years. The two latter remained on the homeplace in Belpre. Rice married Fannie Warren, by whom he had three children, viz: Warren, Lucy, and Jesse. By his second wife Orinda Howe, he had five children: Francis H., and Corwin, who died in the army; a daughter married a Mr. Ford; Delia, married Rev. Mr. Morris; and one child died in infancy.

Jesse Loring married first Deborah Gray, and afterwards Maria Fisher, who lives now in Belpre village. Five children died in early childhood.

Major Oliver Rice, of Massachusetts lived for many years in the middle settlement. He was a widower and generally had a family in his house with whom he boarded. He was an ex-Revolutionary soldier and a man of sterling worth.

Cornelius Delano came to Belpre with Major Goodale, whose daughter he married. He came from Massachusetts and acted as a spy two or three years. He finally settled on lot number ten hundred and twenty, in the northern part of the township, on land now owned by S. McPherson. There he and his wife lived and died. Their only surviving child is living at Columbus, Ohio, where most of the family settled. A grandson is living in Ross county.

Among the old army officers who were original propritors of the Belpre land, was Major Robert Bradford, who drew lot numbered thirty-seven in the middle settlement, a little over a mile below Farmer's castle. He came to Belpre in 1789, and almost immediately erected on the upland, a short distance back of the river, a two-story hewed log house, which is still standing in a good state of preservation, and is undoubtedly the oldest house in Belpre township. In later years it was weather-boarded, and to-day it presents quite a modern appearance, although there are evidences of age in the tumbled down stoop and general deserted appearance. Major Bradford came to Belpre *via* Marietta from Plymouth, Massachnsetts, where he was born in 1750. He was a lineal descendent of Governor Bradford. He married Keziah, the daughter of Captain Nathaniel Little. He was actively engaged in nearly all the battles of the Revolution. A sword which he received from the Marquis Lafayette, is still in possession of the Bradford family. Lafayette, while on a visit to Marietta in 1826, upon learning that his old friend, Major Bradford was dead, was deeply moved. The most prominent enterprise in which Major Bradford engaged during his residence at Belpre, was his association with Esquire Griffin Green on the discovery of the Scioto salines. During the prevalence of the putrid sore throat in Belpre in 1792, the Bradford family was the most sorely afflicted in the settlement, all of the children, who were then born, dying but one. The children born afterwards were, Sarah, in 1794 in the stockade; Robert, 1796; Samuel A. and Otis L. The latter was born in 1799, and is the only survivor, and is living at a ripe old age at Parkersburgh, West Virginia. Major Bradford was struck down by the fearful fever of 1822, and died in his seventy-second year.

Aaron Waldo Putnam, whose journey to Belpre is noted with that of his father, Colonel Israel Putnam, located in the middle settlement on the land now occupied by his grandson, I. W. Putnam. He immediately commenced a clearing, and the erection of a small log cabin, after some years putting up a frame house back from the river, which is the oldest frame in the township, having been built in 1800. His land lay about half a mile below the garrison. While in the garrison, he went down daily to feed his cattle and milk the cows. While at this work on two different occasions he had exciting experiences with the indians. The first incident is related in connection with the opening of Indian hostilities. Not long afterwards, when Mr. Putnam was on a stack in his fodder yard throwing down hay for his cattle, he heard the click of a gun-lock, and turning, saw an Indian behind the fence in the act of recocking his gun, which had failed to go off the first time. Mr. Putnam jumped and ran for life. The Indian fired and missed, and being joined by two others, pursued their supposed victim, who, fortunately crossing the log bridge over the ravine before the Indians reached it, was saved. Mr. Putnam alarmed the garrison but the Indians were not caught. On the return of the Indians from the pursuit of Mr. Putnam, they spitefully shot a yoke of oxen belonging to Captain Benjamin Miles.

In the spring of 1793 great anxiety was caused by

the continued absence of Mr. Putnam, who had gone into the hills in search of stray cattle. On his safe return it was learned that he had traced the cattle to Fort Harmar, fifteen miles distant, and had found the lost animals at Waterford. He returned by the rangers path leading from Waterford to the mouth of the Little Hocking. All this journey was made alone and on foot at a time when Indians were hostile and numerous. During his sojourn in the castle, he was married to Charlotte Loring, who was born in 1773. Both died in 1822, during the fever epidemic. Mr. Putnam, at the time of his death, was fifty-five years old. He was the father of nine children: William P., Charlotte L., Julia H., Albigience W., Israel, Lucy E., Catharine, Bathsheba and Elizabeth. Of these, Lucy E. and Catharine are living. William Pitt was born in Farmer's castle in 1792, and died in 1871.* He married Lorena Nye, who is still living. Of their ten children, five are living. Of these, the oldest, Israel W., was born in 1825. He married Harriet Ripley, by whom he has had six children, five of whom survive. He resides on the old homestead. He, like his father, has been prominent as a township officer and leading citizen.

Captain Benjamin Miles, who early became one of Belpre's most prominent citizens, came to Ohio from Rutland, Massachusetts. He came to Belpre in 1789, and located on the farm which he had drawn in the middle settlement. His land is now occupied by S. R. W. McFarland. Captain Miles built a log house near the river, and soon after the war erected a brick two-story house, the first in the township. Here he kept tavern, and here the first town election was held. He was the proprietor of the first mill on the Little Hocking. During the war the family took refuge in the garrisons. At the beginning of hostilities the Indians, mad because they couldn't catch Waldo Putnam and Nathaniel Little, forthwith killed Captain Miles' five yoke of oxen, the pride of the settlement. The old records, religious and civil, show that Captain Miles, during his residence at Belpre, was eminently a public man. He died in 1817, aged sixty-three, and his wife, Hannah, died in 1825, aged sixty-nine years. The children were: Benjamin Buckminster and Hubbard (twins), William, Tappan and Polly. Benjamin B. became a merchant in Athens county; Solomon S. became a minister of the gospel; Hubbard settled in Illinois; and William and Polly remained in Belpre township, and their descendants are still living.

Among the first families in the middle settlement was that of Isaac Pierce. His farm was the next above Major Bradford's, and it was on the line between their farms that the pioneer school-house was built. The family of Mr. Pierce consisted of his wife and three children—Samuel, Joseph and Phœbe. They took refuge first in Farmer's castle, and afterwards in the Goodale stockade, during the war. After coming to years of maturity, the children scattered. Joseph became a prominent citizen of Dayton; Samuel followed the sea; and Phœbe married Judge Steele, and settled in Dayton.

Joseph Tilton settled on the back lots owned by

Oliver Rice, on the west branch of the Little Hocking. He came to Belpre in the early days of settlement. He afterwards, in 1817, sold his land to Benjamin Robbins, who came with his family from Massachusetts. Mr. Tilton removed a short distance farther up the Little Hocking. His wife was Azubah, daughter of Daniel Durham, who died in 1791.

Daniel Goodno came to Belpre after the Indian war. He was born in Massachusetts in 1770, and lived in Belpre township at the time of his death in 1832. In 1802 he married Sallie, daughter of Nathaniel Cushing. She was born in Massachusetts in 1784, and died in Belpre township in 1864. Three of the children born of this union are still living, viz: Adaline, born in 1803, living in Belpre township; Daniel H., born in 1805, residing in West Virginia; and James, born in 1817, residing in the old home place. The latter married Elizabeth Mathers, who was born in West Virginia in 1824. Their only child, Daniel, is dead. Mr. Goodno is a general farmer. He served three years as township treasurer, and is a prominent citizen of his community.

Bial Stedman, of Vermont, was among the first to locate in the middle settlement. He married Mary Miles. His second wife was Betsy Beebe. He had a large family, many of whom removed to Athens county. He, for a number of years, operated the mill north of Centre Belpre. His father, Alexander, lived on the Goodale farm until 1802, when he removed to Athens county.

Reuben Robbins settled on the Stedman place in 1814. The family remained in the township a few years and then returned to their friends in New York State.

Prior to 1815 Daniel Goss, a native of New England, settled near Miles' mill. He had a tan-yard. He was a leader in the Methodist church, and helped organize its first society.

John Bartlet, a native of England, emigrated to Ohio from Maryland, and about 1820 came to Belpre township and settled above Little Hocking. His wife was Eleanor Felcon. Of the surviving members of the family William, Polly (Miller), and Caroline (S'Keen), live in Belpre, and Elizabeth (Johnson) is in Marion county. William, who was born in 1812, married Elizabeth Allen, who was born in Virginia in 1803. Eight of their eleven children are living: John in Parkersburgh, Reuben in Missouri, Caroline (Walker) in West Virginia, Elizabeth (Dunfee), Adalaide (Collins), and Ann (Dalzell) in Belpre, and Francis (Davis), and William in Virginia.

NEWBURY SETTLEMENT.

Truman Guthrie made the first permanent settlement in Newbury, coming to Belpre in 1790. He proceeded to clear and erect a cabin on the land which his father, Joseph Guthrie, had drawn, he being one of the original proprietors in the Ohio company. Truman, who was born in Connecticut in 1765, came on in advance of his father, as above narrated. He arrived at Marietta on the third of July, 1788, and remained in the vicinity of Fort Harmar for nearly two years. He it was who planted the first wheat in Ohio, near Harmar, with seed that he had obtained on his way west while harvesting in

Pennsylvania. He is also supposed to have put out the first wheat crop in Newbury. During the war he took shelter in Farmer's castle, and for a time in the Newbury stockade. After the war he married Elizabeth, daughter of Israel Stone, who settled in Rainbow. He had returned to Connecticut in 1789 and had brought to Belpre his farming tools, together with chains, shovels, crowbars, etc. This load was brought to Brownsville, Pennsylvania, in an ox-cart, and thence by flatboat down the river. He became the father of eight children. The eldest child, who died in infancy is thought to have been the first born in the lower settlement. The other children were named as follows: Truman, Augustus, James H., Charles L., Benjamin F., Edwin, and David Q. All these children eventually settled in Gallia county, except Edwin, who remained on the home place, where he still resides. He was born in 1810, and has been twice married; first to Amelia Knowles, by whom he had two children, and after her death he was married to Charlotte Bent, by whom he had two children.

Nathaniel Sawyer was the original proprietor of the land on which the post office at Little Hocking now stands. He was a native of Newburyport, Massachusetts, and it is he who gave the lower settlement the name of Newbury. He built his house near the mouth of the Little Hocking, about the time of the first settlements in the township. He was reckless of danger, and frequently exposed himself to the attacks of the Indians. At one time while plowing in a field not far from the house the Indians shot one of his oxen, thus, as he expressed it, spoiling his day's work. He built the first "corn cracker" mill in Newbury settlement, locating it on what was afterwards known as Sawyer's run, about a mile from the Ohio. In 1801 his son Nathaniel was drowned in the Ohio river, and he was buried in what is now the Little Hocking cemetery. Mr. Sawyer married Lydia Porter in Massachusetts.

Joel Oakes, who acted as a scout for the settlements at Belpre and Waterford during the Indian war, after the peace made his permanent residence in Newbury, not far from the old stockade. His exploits as a ranger are elsewhere related. He was born in Massachusetts in 1766, and in 1790 came to Washington county. He married Susan, the daughter of Colonel Silas Bent. She died in 1865, aged ninety-three years. There were seven children in the Oakes family, viz: Susan, Elizabeth, William, Daniel, Sumner, Charlotte, and Lucy. All except Charlotte, who removed to Gallia county, lived in the neighborhood of Newbury, and there died. Daniel Oakes, who is represented in this township by his son, S. B. Oakes, was born in 1801. He married Julia Clough, who was born in 1807. Their three children are living, viz.: Cynthia C., Wiliam, and Silas B. The latter, who lives on the old homestead, was born in 1848. He married Elizabeth Wells, of Bellville, West Virginia. They have two children—Julia and Lizzie. Mr. Oakes is a farmer and stock raiser.

In 1791 Captain Eleazer Curtis and family settled in lower Newbury. Captain Curtis, who died in 1801, was born in Connecticut in 1759. His wife, Eunice Hoyt, died in 1814, aged forty-nine years. There were eight children—Eleazer, Walter, Benajah, Jason, Horace, Polly, Clara, and Lucy. Eleazer moved to Gallipolis. Jason, who was a pilot on the Ohio, died in Marietta in 1833, the first victim of cholera in that city. The daughters married and removed to Athens county; and Walter and Horace always lived in Newbury. Walter, afterwards Judge Curtis, was born in Litchfield county, Connecticut, in 1787, and died in Belpre township in 1876. He married Almira, daughter of Stephen Guthrie. She was born in 1800, and died in 1880. There were four children—Caroline, Austin L, Augustus S., of Harmar, and Marion (deceased). Caroline and Austin L live in Newbury settlement. Their father served as associate judge from 1824 to 1837. During the years 1834 and 1835 he represented the county in the legislature. His son, Austin L., was in the legislature of 1866. Horace Curtis, brother of the judge, was born in 1793, and died in 1871. In 1819 he married Lydia Cole, born in 1796, and died in 1863. Ten children were born by this marriage. Eight of these children are living, viz.: Daniel W., of Pomeroy; Harvey G. and Mary J. (Cook), of Belpre township; Eunice S. (Reed), of Pomeroy; Henry C. Columbus B., and Leroy R., of Little Hocking; Roland L., of Marietta. Harvey G., who was born in Belpre township in 1823, married Augusta Fuller, who was born in Athens county in 1834. Seven of their eight children survive. Mr. Curtis was for twelve years postmaster at Little Hocking. His brother, the present postmaster, Leroy R., was born in 1838. He married Amanda Minor, by whom he has had four children, all of whom are living. He has been in the general store business for twenty-two years.

Daniel Coggeshall and family settled on the lot just below Nathaniel Sawyer. He emigrated from the eastern States and came to Belpre about the time of the outbreak of the Indian troubles, and remained during the subsequent war in the castle, settling in Newbury directly after the peace. His first house was built near the river, but a house was subsequently erected farther back. He was an eccentric genius, and a great lover of fun. He was the father of five children, viz.: Job, Daniel, David, John, and Abigail. John and Daniel moved to Meigs county. Abigail married Peter Stephens, and died near Newbury. Job remained on the home place until his death, where his widow and surviving children are now living.

The ministerial section number twenty-nine is located in Newbury settlement. As early as 1795 there were two families who had squatted on this land, although they had no legal right to remain thereon. One of these early pioneers of section twenty-nine was a man named Littleton, who afterwards removed to Gallia county with his son James. His daughter married Benjamin Bellows, and remained in Newbury.

Anthony Spacht built a cabin on ministerial land in 1789. It was located just north of Truman Guthrie's place. During the war with the Indians, he with his wife Catharine, took refuge in the Newbury stockade, and in the castle up the river. They both died at a very early day, and are buried in the pioneer graveyard on the Guthrie place. Their descendants went farther west, and some of them are well-to-do citizens of Preble county.

Soon after the war Aaron Clough settled on the Ohio, opposite Newbury island, on the farm now in possession of his son Seymour. He was born in Connecticut in 1765, and died in Belpre township in 1823. He married Sarah Delano, who was born in 1781, and died in 1844. Five of the nine children survive, viz: Sarah A. (Greene), Julia (Oaks), Seymour and Mary E., all in Belpre township, and Cynthia A. (Knowles), residing in California. Seymour B., born in 1815, married Mary A. Hitchcock who was born in 1830, and died in 1860. There were no children.

Joseph Guthrie, the father of Truman and Stephen, came to Belpre from Connecticut in 1796, accompanied by his wife and son Stephen. The old gentleman made his home with his son Truman, and while in Newbury, his wife, Hannah Guthrie, died, and was buried in the pioneer cemetery. In 1801 or 1802 he removed to Athens county, where he became a prominent citizen.

Stephen Guthrie who came from Connecticut with his father, married Sallie Chappell, and settled on the land just above the Curtis residence in the southwest corner of the township. He was the father of nine children, viz: Laura, who married Amos Dunham; Almira, wife of Walter Curtis; Julius, Erastus, Austin, and Sheldon living in New Orleans; Stephen and George in Zanesville; and Columbus.

Ebenezer Porter, wife, and children settled on the next lot below Coggeshall's in 1796. Mr. Porter was born in 1732, and on account of his age was familiarly called Grandsir Porter. He lived to the ripe old age of over ninety-four years. He emigrated to Ohio from Massachusetts. None of the children now survive: Cummings lived on the old place at Little Hocking until his death; John moved to Athens county; Samuel lived, and died in Newbury; and Polly married Amos Knowles, of Newbury. The descendants of the Porters are some of them in the neighborhood.

About the year 1801 James Bellows, with his wife and children, settled below Little Hocking at the mouth of Sawyer's run. They emigrated from New Jersey to Ohio, coming down the Ohio in a flat-boat. There were five children, none of whom are now living. Benjamin and James remained on the home place for many years. The other children were: William, Simon and Elias. These died in Meigs county. The land on which the elder Mr. Bellows settled, was drawn by Asa Coburn who lived on it a short time, and then sold it to Mr. Bellows.

Reuben and Magdalene Allen came to the lower settlement in 1807, having emigrated from their native State of Virginia. They settled at the mouth of the Little Hocking, buying the Sawyer farm, where they remained until their death. Mr. Allen died in 1821, and his wife ten years later, both aged sixty-four at the time of their death. The old stock is represented by Davis Allen, their son, who lives on the old homestead. He was born in Virginia in 1801. His wife, Parmelia Barrows, was born in Athens county in 1812. They have had eight children, of whom seven are living, viz: Harvey G.,

Parker L., Corwin D., Viola (McPherson), and Waldo E. in Belpre, and Eunice S. (King) in Morgan county, Ohio, and Mary L. (Boswell) in Kentucky. Mr. Allen is the founder of the hamlet of Little Hocking.

John Cole came from New York State to Ohio in 1808 and settled on the upper part of section twenty-nine. His wife was a Miss Townsend, and by her he had children as follows, viz: Sally, Dolly, Polly, Cynthia, Lydia, John, Henry, and Samuel. Of these John is living on the homeplace and Henry is in the neighborhood. The rest of the family are scattered.

John Cole, sr., came here before 1808 at a very advanced age.

James and Martha Knowles emigrated to Ohio from New Jersey in 1810 and located in Belpre township in the lower settlement, on the ridge, on the land now occupied by Samuel B. Knowles. The old people were originally from Connecticut. They had eight children, as follows, viz: Reuben, James removed to Meigs county, Jesse, Samuel, who removed to Athens county; Amos, William, Esther, who married Eleazar Curtis, jr., and removed to Gallipolis; and an older daughter who remained in the east.

Jeremiah Van Gilder came to Belpre township about 1810, and settled in the back part of Newbury, on the farm now occupied by his son Jesse H. He married Asenath Hubbard, by whom he had six children, viz: Hubbard, Amasa, Jesse H., Asenath, Clarissa, and Louisa. Most of the family removed to Gallia county. The only survivors of the old stock are Amasa, in Gallia county, and Jesse H., who resides on the old homestead farm.

About 1815 Caleb and Alice Barstow settled in Newbury neighborhood, coming to Belpre from Rhode Island. They had eight children, viz: Russel, Richmond, Israel, Lydia, Salvina, Maria, Cornelia, and Abbie. Part of these children lived and died in this township, and the remainder scattered into Gallia and Meigs counties.

William Dumfee settled in the vicinity of Newbury in 1818, and in later years removed to Athens county where he died. He was born in New Jersey in 1772. He married Elizabeth Johnson, who was born in 1775 and died in 1845. They had eleven children, seven of whom are still living, viz: William, Thomas, David, George B., Ludlow, Maria, and John. None of these children are in Washington county save George B., who has a hotel at Little Hocking. He was born in 1816, and was two years old when his father came to Belpre township. In 1837 he married Nancy Tipton, by whom he has had eight children, seven of whom survive, viz: Jonathan and William, in Decatur township; Mary (Brown), in Athens county; Caroline (Self), in Athens county; Francis, in Athens county; Nancy V. (Curtis), in Belpre township, and George W., in Decatur township.

Amos Fisher came from New Hampshire in 1819 or 1820. He settled below Little Hocking, on the Ohio, on what is now the Coalhause farm. He had three sons —Gustavus, Daniel, and Theodoric. In 1833 the whole family emigrated to Kentucky.

The settlement of the lots below the Curtis farm was made by transient persons who remained but a short time, and it was not until a comparatively recent date that permanent settlements have been made thereon.

THE FIRST DEATH

that occurred in the new settlement was that of Captain Zebulon King, who was assassinated by the Indians May 1, 1789. While busily engaged in clearing his lot in the middle settlement, he was shot and scalped, it is supposed by two Indians who had escaped from Fort Harmar, where they were confined by reason of their treacherous conduct towards the whites during the previous summer at Duncan's Falls. The news of the murder cast the first shadow of the troublous events to follow, and already was the hope of the pioneer mingled with fear. Captain King was universally esteemed. He was from Rhode Island, and at the time of his death was preparing a home in Belpre for the family.

THE FAMINE.

An unlooked for and painful experience awaited the colonists. In the land of plenty there was great want. This anomaly was the result of a combination of unavoidable circumstances. Although settlements were begun in the early spring of 1789, so great was the task of clearing the farms that it was late in June before the ground was ready for corn planting. Even then the land was trimmed rather than cleared, and the thick branches of the girdled trees robbed the fields of solar nourishment, thus greatly retarding the growth of the young corn. However, the crop would have matured had not an early October frost blasted the hopes of harvest. Nearly three hundred acres of corn was destroyed in a night. Having lost their bread the anxious pioneers turned to the surrounding forests for meat, but the hunters found little game in the whole region around. The envious Indians, powerless to prevent the coming of the white man had determined to make his subsistence precarious by killing the wild animals. While on their way to witness the treaty at Harmar in 1788, they had almost literally carried out their malicious design.

There were few hogs and cattle in the country, and consequently but little meat had been salted down for winter use. However, they vigorously strove to make the best of discouraging circumstances.

The moldy corn was carefully preserved and ground in the hand-mills. The meal thus obtained, as poor as it was, readily sold for nine shillings, or a dollar and fifty cents a bushel. Those having money succeeded in "keeping the wolf from the door" a little longer than did their less fortunate neighbors, but there was no display of selfishness. Hunters were lured to scour the woods in search of game, the principal supply being obtained from the settlement at Belleville, on the Virginia side of the Ohio.

At a time during the fore part of the winter when the people were well nigh perishing for lack of bread, Isaac Williams came to them as a benefactor. Three years before this good man had settled opposite the mouth of the Muskingum, and during the first summer of his residence there, had put out a large crop of corn, several hundred bushels of which he still possessed when the land was visited by famine. He made an equitable distribution of the corn to the people of Belpre at a moderate price, and those absolutely unable to pay received subsistence gratuitously, with the understanding that the corn might be paid for when plenty made it convenient.

Thus the inhabitants of the colony managed to live for a time, but by spring they were reduced to extremities of want. The corn of Isaac Williams' was gone, and so scarce had the moldy remains of the blighted crop become that it was necessary to dole out the supply, grain by grain. Strong men were appalled and mothers wept at the cries of their children for bread. So great was the suffering that in one family the children were allowed but one potato a day, and afterwards had to subsist on half of one.

In the latter part of winter sugar water began to run, and had there been kettles enough an abundance of nutritious sugar could have been made. As it was, however, it was only possible to collect small quantities of the saccharine juice of the maple, and by mixing it with musty meal make a sap porridge which was not unpalatable, and was very nutritious.

In the spring the scant supply of animal food was eked out by the liberal use of esculent plants that made their appearance in abundance, springing up in the patches of ground cleared the year before. Of these the nettle furnished the earliest supply. The tender plants of the celandine were very palatable, and the luxuriant purslane springing up in the newly broken patches of cleared ground was used as a salad and gave relish to the scanty allowance of meat.

By the middle of July the signs of returning plenty were abundant. The new crop of corn was in the milk and fit for boiling or roasting. Before the grains of corn fully formed they were boiled with salt, forming a very nourishing soup. The very dogs devoured the young crop in the night time, and had to be tied up until the corn became too hard for them. The scarcity of animal food was still great. But the following fall brought corn and meat in abundance, and the famine was over. Wild turkeys came into the settlement by the hundred and the men and boys easily killed them with clubs.

THE PERIOD OF THE INDIAN WAR.[*]

As has been previously noticed, the inhabitants of Belpre were scattered along the banks of the Ohio, so that while communication was easy, defence was difficult. Scarcely had the famine been driven out before the ominous cloud of war obscured the horizon of peace.

The murder of two boys at Neil's station, a point up the Kanawha about a mile above the present village of Belpre, indicated the hostile spirit of the Indians, but for the time no serious apprehensions of danger were felt. But the storm was approaching, and on the memorable second of January, 1791, it burst in a shower of innocent blood upon the settlement at Big Bottom, and

[*]For a more detailed account of many of the incidents of the Indian war, the reader is referred to chapters IX and X.

had it not been for timely warning the settlement at Belpre would have shared the same fate. An examination of the old record of the court of quarter sessions reveals the fact that nearly all the men of Belpre able to bear arms were in Marietta attending court on the Monday that the news was carried to their homes. The consternation of the defenceless women and children can with difficulty be imagined. Their fears were in a measure allayed by the speedy return of their absent loved ones, and all turned their attention to the immediate provision of a place of safety. Monday night the women and children were gathered into the small block-house dwelling which Captain Jonathan Stone had erected in the upper settlement.

Tuesday morning there was held a council of war, and it was decided that the families of the colony, more than thirty in number, be temporarily assembled in the two large log houses which had been erected by Colonels Battelle and Cushing. These block-houses formed the nuclei for the building of the famous stronghold appropriately called

FARMER'S CASTLE.

The site was naturally adapted to purposes of defence. It was situated on the river about half a mile below the bluff, and nearly opposite the centre of Backus', now Blennerhasset island. With the river in front and a swamp a few rods to the rear, the place could only be approached by the natural roadways on either side along the river bank.

The work of erecting this stronghold was commenced immediately, and was vigorously pushed, inasmuch as the lives of the people depended upon their expedition. The block-houses were occupied as fast as they could be erected. Dr. Hildreth thus describes the buildings:

These were thirteen in number, arranged in two rows, with a wide street between them. The basement story was in general twenty feet square, and the upper about twenty-two feet, thus projecting over the lower one, and forming a defence from which to protect the doors and windows below in an attack. They were built of round logs a foot in diameter, and the interstices nicely chinked and pointed with mortar. The doors and window shutters were made of thick oak planks, or puncheons, and secured with stout bars of wood on the inside. The corner block-houses on the back side of the enclosure were provided with watch towers running up eight feet above the roof, where a sentry was constantly kept. The spaces between the houses were filled up with pickets, and occupied three or four times the width of the houses, thus forming a continuous wall or enclosure, about eighty rods long and six rods wide. The pickets were made of quartered oak timber, growing on the plain back of the garrison, and formed from trees about a foot in diameter. They were fourteen feet in length, and set four feet in the ground, leaving a wall ten feet high, over which no enemy could climb without a ladder. The smooth side was set outwards, and the palisades strengthened and kept in place by stout ribbons or wall pieces, pinned to them with inch tree nails on the inside. The palisades on the river side filled the whole space, and projected over the edge of the bank, leaning on rails and posts set to support them. Gates of stout timber were placed in the east and west ends of the garrison, opening in the middle, ten feet wide, for the ingress and egress of teams and stock. A still wider gate opened at the centre of the back wall, through which wood was hauled.

The military regulations were of the most perfect order. Major Nathan Goodale was put in charge of the garrison, and maintained the position until 1793, when he removed to his own garrison further down the river, and his place was taken by Colonel Cushing. There were seventy able-bodied men mustered for military duty. Absence at roll-call at sunrise was punished by compelling the offender to cut out one of the many stumps within the stockade. It is said that the stumps rapidly disappeared.

A point a few yards west of the back gate, and not far from the block-house of Colonel Cushing, was well named the "*place d' armies*" of the castle. Over this place floated the stars and stripes, and here was planted the howitzer whose loud reports caused the Indians to keep their distance.

More than two hundred people found homes within the walls of the castle during the first year of its history. There were twenty-eight heads of families, with numerous small children, besides many young men and women. The following is a list of the occupants of the several houses which, as has been stated before, were arranged on either side of the passage way, six on the north side, and seven on the south: In No. 1, the northeastern, were Colonel Ebenezer Battelle, wife, and four children; in No. 2, going westward, Captain William James, wife, and ten children, also, Isaac Barker, wife, and eight children, and Daniel Coggeshall, wife, and five children; in No. 3, Captain Jonathan Stone, wife, and three children; in No. 4, Colonel Nathaniel Cushing, wife, and six children, also Captain Jonathan Devol, wife, and six children; in No. 5, Isaac Pierce, wife, and three children, Nathaniel Little, wife, and one child, and Joseph Barker, wife, and one child; in No. 6, Major Goodale, wife, and seven children; in No. 7, in the southwest corner of the garrison, A. W. Putnam, wife, and one child, Daniel Loring, wife, and seven children, also Major Rice, and Captain Benjamin Miles, wife, and five children; in No. 8, Squire Griffin Green, wife, and four children; in No. 9, John Rouse, wife, and eight children, and Major Robert Bradford, wife, and four children; in No. 10, Captain John Levins, wife, and six children, and Captain William Dana, wife, and eight children. Between No. 10 and No. 11, in a building called the barracks, the soldiers were quartered; in No. 11, were Mrs. Dunham, widow of Daniel Dunham, with one son and two daughters, also, Captain Israel Stone, wife, and ten children, afterwards removed to Rainbow settlement; in No. 12, the families of Benjamin Patterson and Benoni Hulburt, the rangers; in No. 13, Colonel Alexander Oliver, wife, and eleven children, afterwards removed to Waterford, also Colonel Daniel Bent, wife, and four children. Joshua Fleehart, the hunter, with his family, lived in a small cabin east of house No. 3.

Of the single men in the castle may be mentioned Jonathan Waldo, of Pomfret, Connecticut; Daniel Mayo, of Boston; Jonathan Baldwin, Cornelius Delano, spy from Massachusetts; Joel Oaks, spy from Connecticut; James Caldwell, from Wheeling, also a spy; Wanton Casey, married Betsy Goodale and returned, after the war, to Rhode Island; Stephen and Truman Guthrie; Captain Ingersoll, returned to Boston; Ezra Philips, Stephen Smith and Howell Bull; Samuel Cushing, moved to Natchez, Mississippi; William and John Smith, of Rhode Island; Jonas Davis; Dr. Samuel Barnes, from

Massachusetts; and last but not least "Kitt" Putnam, the colored boy who had been the body servant of General Israel Putnam during the latter years of his life, and was brought to Marietta in the fall of 1798 by Colonel Israel Putnam. "Kitt" was a universal favorite. After the war he lived on the Muskingum with Captain Devol. He was probably the first black voter in the country, inasmuch as he helped elect the delegates, under the territory who met to form a constitution for Ohio.

The rangers who served from time to time were Cornelius Delano, Joel Oaks, Benjamin Patterson, Benoni Hulburt, Joshua Fleehart, George Kerr, John Shepherd, and James Caldwell. These spies served the country every day, making a circuit of twenty-five to thirty miles, with a radius of eight or ten miles. Their circuit in Belpre was over the hills on to the waters of the Little Hocking river, and up the easterly branches across to the Ohio, striking this stream a few miles above the entrance of the Little Kanawha, and thence down the Ohio to the garrison. These men received five shillings or eighty-four cents a day, as appears from the old pay rolls. Prowling Indians were sure to be caught by these wary rangers, and hence to a great extent the woods were kept clear of the foe, and the inhabitants were permitted to cultivate their farms in comparative safety. However, as subsequent events proved, this mode of defence, though measurably effective, was not sufficient. It was on the morning of the twelfth of March, 1791, that Aaron W. Putnam, accompanied by Nathaniel Little, visiting his farm, a half mile below the garrison, for the purpose of milking and feeding his cows, was attacked by Indians and had a very narrow escape from death.

The second attack by the Indians resulted in the death of one of the spies, Benoni Hulburt, on the twenty-eighth of the following September. Hulburt, in company with Joshua Fleehart, went with a canoe to the mouth of the Little Hockhocking to examine some traps they had set. On the way down the Ohio they were tempted to land by what they had supposed were the "gobbling" of wild turkeys, a sound probably made by the Indians to lure them on. The two scouts on reaching the Little Hocking steered their canoe up the stream, and Hulburt, on landing, was immediately shot down by the Indians who were in ambush. His body was recovered the next day and buried near "the Castle."

It was not infrequently that the cattle and hogs of the settlers were stolen by the Indians or lost in the woods, and it was owing to this fact that a Mutual Assurance company was organized in the first part of the war. Each one was accountable for his losses in proportion to his property. This equalization of losses subsequently proved its wisdom, as is shown by the following incident. Late in the fall of 1791 the fat hogs were slaughtered and hung up in a house near the garrison during the night. Before morning the building caught fire and the whole winter supply of meat for the inhabitants of the garrison was destroyed. The few remaining hogs were driven into the woods by the Indians, and there was, consequently, a great scarcity of meat during the winter. Two men were sent to the headwaters at Redstone to buy provisions, but they were delayed by inclement weather and did not succeed in getting back with supplies until the following March.

On the twenty-fourth of April, 1794, a band of marauding Wyandots, while proceeding up the river on the Virginia shore, came to the cabin of John Armstrong, who had but recently moved to a point nearly opposite to the castle that he might be nearer a little floating mill which he and a man named Peter Misner had built. The Indians at once prepared for an assault upon the defenceless inhabitants of the cabin. Mrs. Armstrong and her two youngest children were killed and three others taken prisoners. They were subsequently restored to freedom. A broken monument in the old cemetery at Cedarville, erected by Mr. George Dana, marks the last resting place of Mrs. Armstrong and her two children. The captive children all lived to be restored to the whites.

INDIANS AT NEWBURY.

As is more fully stated elsewhere in this work, one of the points of settlement was at Newbury, on the Ohio, six miles below Farmer's castle. At the first Indian alarm the inhabitants of this lower settlement sought protection in the castle. But early in the following spring, finding it very inconvenient to go so far to cultivate their fields, the brave men of Newbury built a stockade opposite the point in the river known as Newbury bar, and for a time lived with their families in this place in safety. There were three or four families in this little community, and the seeming safety from attack made the people careless. Among the settlers there was a man by the name of Brown, who had recently come from Pennsylvania with his family, which consisted of his wife and four children. On Sunday, March 15th, his wife went with him to see him set out some fruit trees, and the place being near the stockade, she took with her the children, one of whom was but an infant in arms. A young girl named Persis Dunham, a sister of Mrs. Tilton, accompanied them, taking care of the two older children. Just as they approached the spot where Mr. Brown was, two Indians sprang from an ambush near by, and ere flight could be thought of, one of the savages had brained Mrs. Brown with his tomahawk, while the other Indian killed the young girl. The child Mrs. Brown was leading was also killed, and a cruel blow at the baby in its mother's arms it was supposed at first had killed it. The baby, however, after careful nursing by the matrons of Farmer's castle, finally recovered, and the bereaved husband and father soon afterwards took the remnant of his family back to their old home in the east. The spot in which the victims of this massacre are buried afterwards became the burial place of the neighborhood, and near the bank of the river may be seen the plain marble shaft which preserves their names and memory. The people of the Dunham neighborhood, after this occurence, went up to Goodale's stockade and Farmer's castle for protection.

THE EXTENSION OF THE DEFENCES

became necessary in the early spring of 1793, by reason of the crowded condition of Farmer's castle, and the many inconveniences incident to confinement in such close quarters. For the accommodation of those whose land was further up the river, Stone's garrison was built on the land of Jonathan Stone, a short distance below the present site of Belpre village; and, for the same reason, a similar stockade was erected a half a mile down the river, on Major Goodale's land, and named Goodale's garrison. The upper stockade enclosed four blockhouses, a school-house, and a number of log cabins, accommodating in all ten families; the lower garrison consisted of two block-houses, and was the rendezvous of safety for six families. Scarcely had Major Goodale moved to his new abode when, on the first day of March, 1793, he was kidnapped by Indians while he was working not more than sixty rods back of the garrison. The details of this occurrence have already been given in chapter X. The community at Stone's garrison was also visited by the crafty savages, and thereby lost one of the most promising young men, Jonas Davis, who was killed the last of February, 1795.

BELPREANS DISCOVER THE SCIOTO SALINES.

Only those who have suffered the privation know how important it is to be well supplied with salt. Not only the inhabitants of Belpre but in fact all who resided in the territory of the Northwest, had great difficulty in maintaining the supply of marine salt which of necessity was brought in small quantities across the mountains on pack-horses and thence conveyed down the river. In various parts of the country it was noticed that the deer were wont to congregate in particular localities where they would gnaw and lick the clay banks which investigation proved to be impregnated with saline particles and were hence called "salt licks." Inasmuch as eastern salt retailed in the west at between eight and ten dollars a bushel, the value of the salt licks became of great general interest. A white man who had escaped from captivity by the Indians had reported that while he was with his captors he had seen them make salt from the waters of a spring on a tributary of the Scioto at a point presumably not far from the present town of Jackson. 'Squire Griffin Greene, of Farmer's castle, learned of this report and immediately organized a company to proceed with the search. He associated with him in the enterprise Major Robert Bradford and Joel Oakes; he taking half the risk and his partners guaranteeing the remainder. A large pirogue was provided with provisions for ten to twelve men for ten days, and with a number of men from the neighboring settlement at Bellville, Virginia, the company started from Farmers' Castle in the fall of 1794. Proceeding down the Ohio until they reached the mouth of Leading creek, where they landed, and after hiding their boat continued their journey on foot. After several days' travel they came to a stream which led in the direction in which the salt springs were supposed to be. This conjecture proved to be correct. Paths or trails leading to the springs were soon discovered, and the remains of fires were seen along the banks of the creek. After a toilesome search a hole was found scooped out in the sand rock, and filled with blackish water, which proved the presence of the long sought for and much coveted salt. A small quantity was made, but fearing the approach of Indians from the neighboring village of Chillicothe they only remained a day and a half, and then started home with the good news. Just as the party had launched their boat at the mouth of Leading creek, and had got it out into the middle of the Ohio, a large party of pursuing Indians appeared on the bank but the whites were fortunately out of range. A party of Indians while hunting had discovered the men while at work boiling the salt water, and being too weak in numbers to make an attack had hurried to Chillicothe for assistance. The party with 'Squire Green soon reached the garrison, much to the relief of those who awaited their coming. The right of the discovery of the salines was sold by the exploring company to a Philadelphia merchant named John Nicholson, for fifteen hundred dollars. So valuable was the land of salt springs, however, that the State of Ohio long continued to own them, and during the earlier years of Ohio's history these springs furnished almost the entire supply of the southern and middle portions of the State.

THE THEORY OF PERPETUAL MOTION.

'Squire Griffin Greene had an ingenious and inventive mind. Having suggested the idea of the floating mill, and seeing its success, his ever busy mind turned toward something new. He thought of a plan to propel boats up and down the streams. His theory as finally developed was given to his brother mechanic, Captain Devol, to materialize. The latter with his more practical mind at once saw the fallacy in 'Squire Green's reasoning, and thinking to prove its absurdity set about the construction of the machine, whose mechanism was as follows: It consisted of a large wheel with numerous projecting arms; along the side of each of these arms there was a groove containing a leaden ball of one or two pounds weight. As the wheel rotated on its axis the balls rolled out to the extremity of the descending arms, while on the opposite side, as the arms rose, the balls descended to the foot of the arms, thus lessening the weight on the ascending, and increasing it on the descending. The machine worked for some time and then stopped—for lack of force to overcome the resistance offered.

THE GRINDING OF THE GRIST

early occupied the attention of the settlers. During the period of the famine the hand-mill could easily furnish the miserable dole which barely sufficed to sustain life. But with returning plenty the hand-mills were unable to supply the necessary breadstuff, and the erection of a regular grist-mill became a necessity. The Little Hocking was naturally selected as a suitable stream on which to locate this first mill, and the eastern branch being near the central point of Belpre it was decided to build thereon. The spot chosen was on the extreme southwestern corner of section nine, on the land now occupied by A. Fish, a mile and a half north of Centre Belpre. A broad, low gap in the line of hills promised an easy access. A number of the enterprising men of the settlement undertook the erection of the building, necessary

machinery was purchased, and two millwrights employed —Baldwin and Applegate—who had recently assisted in the construction of the Wolf Creek mill at Waterford settlement. The Ohio company, ever anxious to increase the prosperity of the colonies, donated one hundred and sixty acres of land adjoining the site. The dam was built, and the timbers for the building were being made ready, and by the first of January, 1791, were ready for raising. But the dangers of the Indian war forbade further work, and the people, bitterly disappointed, once more labored at the hand-mill. The mill on the Little Hocking thus commenced was never finished,[*] not because the builders had neglected to count the cost, but because they had not counted the Indians.

THE FLOATING MILL.

Early in the summer of 1791, says Dr. Hildreth, the settlers being disappointed in completing the mill commenced on the Little Hock-hocking, by the Indian war, concluded to build what might be called a "floating mill." This could be anchored out in the river and be safe from destruction by the Indians. The labor of grinding corn with a hand-mill, for a community of more than one hundred and fifty persons, was a task only known to those who have tried it. Esquire Griffin Green had travelled in France and Holland three or four years before, and in the latter country had seen a mill erected on boats and the machinery moved by the current. He mentioned the fact to Captain Devol, an ingenious mechanic of ardent temperament and resolute to accomplish anything that would benefit his fellow men; and although Squire Green had not inspected the foreign mill so as to give any definite description, yet the bare suggestion of such a fact was sufficient for Captain Devol, whose mechanical turn of mind immediately devised the machinery required to put it in operation. A company was formed and the stock divided into twelve shares, of which Captain Devol took one-third; the remaining stock being divided among five other persons. When finished it cost fifty-one pounds eight shillings, Massachusetts currency, according to the old bill of expenditures now in the Devol family. The mill was erected on two boats; one of them being five, the other ten feet wide and forty-five feet long. The smaller one was a pirogue made of the trunk of a large hollow sycamore tree, and the larger of timber and plank like a flat-boat. The boats were placed eight feet apart and fastened firmly together by heavy cross beams covered with oak planks. The smaller boat on the outside supported one end of the waterwheel, and the larger boat the other, in which was placed the millstones and running gear covered with a light frame building or mill-house for the protection of machinery, meal, and miller. The space between the boats was covered with planks, forming a deck fore and aft of the waterwheel. This wheel was turned by the natural current of the water and was put in motion or stopped by pulling up or pushing down a set of boards, similar to a gate in front of the wheel. It

---

[*] Dr. Hildreth in his Pioneer says that this mill was completed after the war, but investigation has shown that this is a mistake.

COLONEL JOHN STONE

STONE FAMILY.*

Among the worthy and honorable men who formed the Belpre colony was Captain Jonathan Stone. Captain Stone first came to Marietta in the fall of 1788, and made preparations for the reception of his family. He located his farm in Upper Belpre in the first bottom, a short distance below the mouth of the Little Kanawha. He returned to Massachusetts, and in the summer of 1789 left Brookfield, his former home, with his family, and finally located in Belpre, in December of that year. Two two-ox teams with a large wagon, cows for family use, and a horse for each of the ladies, composed the outfit. After crossing the mountains he procured a flat-boat, in which they came down the river. The boards of this boat were used for the doors and floors of the first house which Captain Stone built at Belpre.

Captain Stone was born at Braintree, Massachusetts, in the year 1751. His father, who had been a soldier in the king's service, died in 1859, leaving him with limited opportunities for obtaining an education, but he acquired a knowledge of surveying, which became useful to him. He served as an apprentice in his father's tannery, and afterwards went on a whaling expedition. On his return he enlisted in the Revolutionary army with the rank of orderly sergeant. He served with credit in the northern army under General Rufus Putnam and General Gates, and was commissioned captain in 1781, in which capacity he served till the end of the war. He was afterwards employed by General Putnam in the survey of lands on the coast of Maine and assisted to put down Shay's rebellion in 1786. On the formation of the Ohio company Captain Stone purchased two shares.

When the Indian war broke out Captain Stone removed his family to Farmer's castle, but after the garrison known as Stone's fort was constructed, they removed into it and remained there until the close of the war. Captain Stone was second to none in courage and ability, and he was one of the most useful defenders of the Belpre garrisons. He was appointed treasurer of Washington county in 1792. After the war he was engaged with Jeffrey Mathewson to complete the survey of the Ohio company's lands, and in 1799 was appointed with General Rufus Putnam and B. I. Gilman to lay out the university lands at Athens. He died before this work was completed, March 24, 1804. Captain Stone was a man highly esteemed, and his early death much regretted. In politics he was a Federalist, as were all the efficient men at Belpre.

Mrs. Stone, (Susannah Mathews), was a niece of General Rufus Putnam. She survived her husband many years, her death occurring November 5, 1833. Their children were: Grace, wife of Luther Dana, of Newport; Benjamin F., of Belpre; Rufus Putnam, removed to Morgan county; John, Belpre; and Melissa W., wife of Joseph Barker, Newport.

Colonel John Stone, of Belpre, is the only member of the family yet living. He was born June 23, 1795. He married, in 1819, Charlotte P. Loring, daughter of Ezekiel Loring. The marriage occurred at the residence of Daniel Loring, in Belpre. He has always lived on the homestead. The house in which he resides originally stood near the river, but was removed to its present position with thirty-eight yoke of oxen in four hours. This was one of the memorable frolics in early times.

In 1826 Mr. Stone was made colonel of militia and has always since been known by that title. He is a man of strong character and convictions based on intelligent ideas. During the days of slavery he was an Abolitionist from principle, and took an active part in some of the stormy incidents along the Belpre shore of the Ohio. He took an active interest in negroes who sought homes in Ohio. He watched with impatient interest the trial at Parkersburgh which involved the boundary line controversy, and once ironically told Caleb Emerson as the ferry was pushing for Virginia, to ask General Jackson what objection there would be to him watering his horse in Virginia's river.

Colonel Stone's family consisted of eight children, six of whom are living, viz: Samuel, Melissa Barker, Simeon Boliver, Lydia Loring, John Loring, Augustus Dana, Jonathan Franklin and Bradley Burgess. Four of the sons were in the late war: Bradley B. was a volunteer in the Ninety-second Ohio volunteer infantry, and when discharged, wearing a captain's commission; Simon Boliver, Augustus D., and Jonathan F. were out over one hundred days at City Point and Bermuda Hundred when Boliver died with malarial fever.

* Taken mainly from published sketches.

could grind, according to the strength of the current, from twenty-five to fifty bushels of grain in twenty-four hours. The larger boat was fastened by a chain cable to an anchor made of timbers and filled with stones, and the smaller one was fastened by a grapevine to the same anchor, and thus independent of the shore could the mill operate. It was placed in a rapid portion of the Ohio about the middle of Backus', now Blennerhassett Island, a few rods from the shore and in sight of the castle. The current here was strong and the position safe from the Indians. With the aid of a bolting-cloth in the garrison very good flour was made. This floating mill was a great relief to the settlers and was visited by all the settlers on both sides of the Ohio for the distance of twenty miles, in their canoes, the only mode of transportation at a period when there were neither roads nor bridges in the country.

THE FIRST STATIONARY MILLS.

During the enforced stay in the castle the floating mill sufficed, but as soon as the settlers returned to their farms, the necessity for a centrally located stationary mill became even more urgent than it was before the war. Captain Miles erected his saw- and grist-mill on the Little Hocking, at a point about a quarter of a mile below the dam that had been erected in 1790 for the mill that was never built. The mill put up by Captain Miles commenced operations shortly prior to the year 1800, and there has been a mill on the same site ever since.

Before its erection the people of Belpre had most of their grinding done at Captain Devol's mill, on the Muskingum; but the long journey of twelve miles up the Ohio and five miles up the Muskingum, was wearisome, and right glad did they avail themselves of the privileges of Captain Miles' mill. It passed into the hands of Bial Stedman, and for many years was known as Stedman's mill. Afterwards the mill was owned by A. Fish, and is now operated by Counsel & Flowers.

Nathaniel Sawyer put up a "corn cracker" in the Newbury settlement, prior to the year 1800. He located it on what is now known as Sawyer's run, about a mile above the entrance into the Ohio. One of the mill stones used in this mill is still preserved as a relic in the neighboring town of Hockingport, Athens county. The people of Newbury patronized the Steadman mill, and the mill on the west branch of the Little Hocking, in what is now Decatur township, until 1877, when a steam flouring mill was erected at Little Hocking by J. T. Seyler.

EPIDEMICS.

In the summer of 1792, the inhabitants of Farmer's castle were visited with a malignant form of scarlet fever, and putrid sore throat. It was especially fatal among children, and the light of many a household was put out in a day. Major Robert Bradford lost his four children, their deaths occurring within a short time of each other. The disease, which was confined to the settlement at Belpre, continued for several weeks, and then gradually subsided. Bilious and intermittent fevers were also prevalent.

65

In September, 1793, that dread disease, the small-pox, was brought into the garrison by Benjamin Patterson, one of the spies. He had become alarmed while at Marietta, lest he should be attacked by the disease, and, as the surest way of escaping danger, had himself and family inoculated by Dr. Barnes, who at that time was in Marietta. Patterson rashly came to Belpre, thus spreading the disease. Few except the old soldiers and officers of the colony had undergone the terrors of the loathsome plague. A meeting was immediately called, and it was decided that, inasmuch as it would be impossible to prevent the spread of the contagion, the people be innocculated by Dr. True, of Marietta. Thus the castle was turned into a hospital, but out of over one hundred patients, not one died. The disease also prevailed in the Goodale garrison, where Dr. Barnes was located. Several cases occurred in Stone's garrison. Dr. Barnes lost several patients, because of partial and tardy innocculation.

During the sickly seasons of 1821-3, many died of fever. The fever was of a low, lingering type, and numbered among its victims many prominent citizens of the township.

FIRST ROADS AND BRIDGES.

The pioneers came to Belpre down the Ohio river, and for a time after their settlement were too busy in the clearing of their land and erection of their houses to be concerned about their ways of inland communication.

However roads soon became a necessity, and they were constructed at a very early day. The first important road was from the mouth of the Little Hocking along the Ohio river to the line of Marietta township, whence there was a continuation to the mouth of the Muskingum. The construction of this road was ordered by the court of quarter sessions convened in 1792. There were two separate petitions, each signed by twelve citizens of Belpre township, the first petition praying that a road be constructed from the Congress lot, so-called, to the settlement on the bluff; and the second petition asking that a road be built from the bluff to the mouth of the Little Hocking. The court ordered Jonathan Stone as surveyor and Nathan Goodale and Oliver Rice as his assistants to construct the upper road; and Richard Greene as surveyor and Jonathan Stone and Wanton Casey as assistants to lay off the lower road. This road was constructed close by the river bank, and to-day there is little of it that has escaped being washed away by the steadily approaching river. This first road was not macadamized, and at times became very muddy, but in general it was a delightful and most useful thoroughfare, by means of which a journey to Marietta could be readily accomplished. The emigrants from Virginia on their way south were in the habit of crossing the river at Parkersburgh that they might travel over this road. Although sixty feet wide, there was room for it to pass between the river and the old burying-ground. So rapidly has the river been wearing away the Ohio shore that not only the road but a part of the burying-ground has been destroyed, and the only vestige of the road in the upper settlement is a piece extending about fifty rods, which still remains near the little hamlet of Blennerhassett.

This road from Marietta was continued across the mouth of the Little Hocking to Chillicothe, and the whole was known as the old Chillicothe road. At first it was customary to ford the Little Hocking near its mouth, but this was both inconvenient and dangerous. In 1804 the citizens of Belpre appointed Dr. Leonard Jewett, Truman Guthrie, and Benjaman Miles, a committee to petition the county commissioners for a grant of three hundred dollars, to assist them in building a bridge. The money was given and the bridge built, but unfortunately the timbers used in its construction were far too heavy, and its strength was impaired to such an extent that it became dangerous to cross on it. There is a common story that the last crossing was made by a drove of cattle on the run. However this was, a new bridge afterwards took the place of the first bridge in the township.

At the time of the construction of the first road there was a bridge built over Davis run, in the vicinity of Waldo Putnam's place. Some of the timbers used in the construction may still be seen at the mouth of the run.

FRUIT GROWING IN BELPRE.

Both apples and peaches have been plenty in the township since the earliest days. The fresh, rich soil along the Ohio was especially adapted to the rapid growth of fruit trees. The early settlers brought with them apple seeds and planted them at the first opportunity, and it was not long before each man had a little nursery of seedlings.

In May, 1794, Israel Putnam, son of Colonel Israel Putnam, arrived at Belpre, bringing with him many scions of the choicest apple trees, which scions were afterwards grafted on the seedlings. This was the first grafting done in the Territory of the Northwest, and the fact is generally admitted among fruit growers. The following is the list of the first scions introduced into Ohio: Putnam Russel, Early Chandler, Gilly Flower, Naturalings, Yellow Greenings, Long Island Pippin, Honey Greening, Kent Pippin, Striped Gilly Flower, Juneings, Green Pippin, Seek-no-Further, Late Chandler, Pound Royal, Rhode Island Greening, Golden Pippin, Tollman Sweeting, Streaked Sweeting, Cooper Apple, Beauty, English Pearmain, Blue Pearmain and Spitzenberg, in all twenty-two varieties. These scions were carefully distributed, and fruit raising was for the time a leading industry.

The first orchard of any pretentions to size was planted by A. W. Putnam in 1798, although a number of the trees had been previously set out. Several of the old trees are still standing west of the old homestead. There may be seen of these first trees three or four of the Putnam Russets, two Rhode Island Greenings, and one Prolific Beauty. These trees are all still bearing, although one would think that the time of their fruitfulness had passed.

George Dana, sr., was among those fortunate to be possessed of some of the early scions, and there is a tree still standing on the farm which was planted in 1792, and engrafted about 1796, when it was about five feet high. In six or eight years time the young apple trees were loaded with apples. The peach trees often bore the second year after being set out, producing fruit of a size and quality not now seen in Ohio. The depredations of the peach insect were not known for more than twenty years, and the climate was much less changeable than it is to-day. On this account peach raising was a very important industry. This fruit was usually taken to market in a liquid form, for along the lower Mississippi, and even in foreign ports, the peach brandy and apple jack of Belpre were in demand, and no small quantity was consumed at home. Every well to-do farmer had a still of his own before the days of temperance reform, and then one by one did these manufactories close, and to-day there is little strong drink sold and none made in the township.

The fruit growers found a ready market down the river for their apples and peaches, and it was customary to take them down in flat-boats. The peach crop has become very uncertain, and nearly the whole attention is given to apples.

The township has become well known as a fruit township, and of late years George Dana has been drying fruit very successfully, doing the work by evaporators since 1880. The principal market for the apples raised in the neighborhood is at the

VINEGAR WORKS.

The vinegar works of Mr. Dana, were started by his father, in 1834, they being located where they now are on the Dana farm, below Belpre village. They were continued by George Dana, jr, after the death of his father. The present building was erected in 1872. Thousands of gallons of pure cider vinegar are made here annually.

THE FIRST LIBRARY ASSOCIATION IN THE NORTHWEST.

Until a few years ago it was supposed that the old "Coonskin Library," of Ames township, Athens county, was the first library established in the Northwest Territory. Examining the history of this library, as prepared by the most thoroughly informed men in Athens county, it is found that there is no claim to a priority earlier than 1804, when a valuable collection of books was purchased in Boston for the use of the literati of the townships of Ames and Dover in Athens, then Washington, county. Other libraries formed shortly afterwards were the Dayton Library society incorporated February 21, 1805; a library at "Granville in the county of Fairfield," January 26, 1807; one at Newton, Hamilton county, February 10, 1808. The "Coonskin library" was incorporated under the name of the "Western Library Association," February 19, 1810, and hence the claim of the Ames people is not to priority of incorporation but to priority of existence and it is this claim that the people of Belpre are enabled by positive proof to overthrow.

The library in Belpre was a part of the family library of General Israel Putnam, who, during his life, collected a large library of useful books, embracing history, travels, belles-lettres, and the like for the benefit of himself and children, and called it the Putnam Family library. At General Putnam's death in 1790, this library was divided among the heirs, and quite a number found their way to Ohio, being brought out by his son, Colonel Israel Putnam. It is supposed that the books were brought to Belpre upon Colonel Putnam's second arrival, in 1795, at the close of the Indian war, when the Colonel returned from Pomfret, Connecticut, with his family.

There is abundant evidence that stock in this library was sold at a very early day. The worth of the books and the intellectual cravings of the highly cultured and educated settlers of Belpre would not permit that this library be exclusive, and the generous nature and sound sense of Colonel Putnam would not deprive the community of its wanted mental nourishment. There was formed a regular organized company of shareholders in this, the first public library northwest of the Ohio river, and for aught that is known the first west of the Alleghanies. The shares were ten dollars, as is shown by the following receipt now in possession of Colonel John Stone:

MARIETTA, twenty-sixth October, 1796.

Received of Jonathan Stone, by the hand of Benjamin Mills, ten dollars, for his share in the Putnam family library.

W. P. PUTNAM, Clerk

In the records of the probate office of Washington county, among the items in an inventory of the estate of Jonathan Stone, dated September 2, 1801, there is found "One share in the Putnam family library, ten dollars."

This library, managed by the stockholders, was a source of great benefit, not only to the people of Belpre, but to settlers for miles around. In the Ohio Historical Collections, under Meigs county, there is an account of this library, by Amos Dunham, who settled in Belpre township, in what was then Washington county, in 1802. He says, "in order to make the long winter evenings pass more smoothly, by great exertion I purchased a share in the Belpre library, six miles distant. Many a night have I passed (using pine knots instead of candles) reading to my wife while she sat hatcheling, carding or spinning."

Soon after its establishment, the library was known as the Belpre Farmers' library, and later as the Belpre library. For a number of years the books were kept at the house of Isaac Pierce, the librarian. Colonel John Stone remembers attending meetings at Pierce's, near Centre Belpre, for the drawing of books, and distinctly recollects that in 1815 or 1816 the association was dissolved by mutual consent. The books were distributed among the shareholders, and many of these old volumes are still preserved.

Colonel Stone selected The Travels of Jonathan Carver. Captain George Dana has in his possession six volumes as follows: John Locke's Essays Concerning the Haman Understanding, London, 1793, and has on the fly leaf "Putnam Family library, No. 5," which is erased, and "Belpre library, No. 29," substituted; the Practical Farmer, dedicated to Thomas Jefferson in 1792, and marked "Putnam Family library, No. 5," changed to

"Belpre library, No. 6;" he has also Robertson's History of Scotland, in two volumes, inscribed "Belpre Farmers' library, No. 24;" and Johnson's Lives of the English Poets, in three volumes, inscribed "Belpre Farmers' library, No. 10." These last two books were published in 1811. Mr. I. W. Putnam has in his library several relics of the old library, viz: The History of Vermont, 1794, one volume; Bassett's History of England, four volumes; Hume's History of England, six volumes; and Goldsmith's Animated Nature. In the family of Mrs. O. H. Loring there are four volumes of Gibbons' Decline and Fall of the Roman Empire, published in England in 1783. There are then in these three families twenty-three volumes belonging to the original Belpre library. One of the books is numbered eighty, which would indicate that at least that many volumes were in the library. The books remaining are solid and well preserved and will be handed down as valuable relics of the olden time as proofs of the literary tastes and enterprises of the early pioneers of one of the oldest settlements in Ohio.

THE ORGANIZATION OF THE TOWNSHIP.

When the geographical limits of Belpre were determined in 1790, the court of quarter sessions named the following township officers: Town clerk, Colonel Ebenezer Battelle; overseer of the poor, Wanton Casey; constable, Colonel Nathaniel Cushing. The court made annual appointments of officers for Belpre and exercised a general supervision over it as late as 1802.

In the records of the first town book of Belpre there may be found an account of the first election. The first town meeting was held on Monday, May 2, 1802. Colonel Cushing was chairman and Daniel Loring, clerk. After due deliberation the qualified electors chose the following officers for the ensuing year, viz: Colonel Israel Putnam, Colonel Cushing, Isaac Pierce, Benajah Hoyt, and Asahel Cooley, trustees; Major Jonathan Haskell and Dr. Leonard Jewett, overseers of the poor; Captain Benjamin Miles and Aaron Clough, fence viewers; Captain William Dana and Isaac Pierce, appraisers of houses; Colonel Nathaniel Cushing, lister of taxable property; Colonel Cushing, Stephen Guthrie, and Pearley Howe, constables; Aaron W. Putnam, Dr. L. Jewett, Benjamin B. Stone, Truman Guthrie, Asahel Cooley, and Joseph Tilton, supervisors of highways.

This the first town meeting adjourned to meet again on the first Monday of the following April, at the house of Captain Benjamin Miles. It is probable that the first election was held at Captain Miles' residence. His house continued to be the voting place for many years. Elections were sometimes held in the old treadmill at A. W. Putnam's, and sometimes at the meeting house on the bluff, at the pine meeting house two miles north of Centre Belpre, at the house of Bial Stedman, and afterwards at the brick school-house at Centre Belpre. Here the elections continued to be held for many years. The present town house was afterwards built on the hillside, less than a mile north of Centre Belpre. This was the only voting place in the township prior to 1870, at which time a second precinct was established in Belpre village.

The officers of the township elected for the year 1880-81, are as follows, viz: John Dana Browning, John G. Waterman, and John A. Brown, trustees; I. W. Putnam, clerk; S. R. W. McFarland, treasurer; I. E. Stone and J. L. O'Neal, justices of the peace; L. R. Curtis, C. W. Oakes, H. M. Yates, I. W. Putnam, C. E. Ames, S. P. Kesterson, George G. Johnson, L. M. Batten, and A. P. Sherman, board of education.

The first justices of the peace in the township were Daniel Loring and Isaac Pierce. The old marriage records show that these 'squires tied many a hymenial knot.

EARLY SCHOOLS.

From the very first the people of Belpre have been devoted to education, and the results of this long continued interest are seen in the flourishing schools of the present time. While the parents were busily engaged in establishing homes they did not forget the intellectual needs of their children. Money was scarce and teaching at first was little more than a labor of love. Bathsheba Rouse, the daughter of John Rouse, one of the emigrants from New Bedford, Massachusetts, was employed in the summer of 1789 to teach the small children, and for several subsequent summers she taught a school in Farmer's castle. She is believed to have been the first female who ever kept a school within the present bounds of Ohio. During the winter months a male teacher was employed for the larger boys and young women. Daniel Mayo was the first teacher in Farmer's castle. He came from Boston, a young man, in the family of Colonel Battelle, in the fall of the year 1788, and was a graduate of Cambridge university. The school was kept in a large room in Colonel Battelle's block-house. Jonathan Baldwin, another educated man, also taught school during a part of the confinement in the garrison.

At the time of the erection of Stone's stockade in 1793, a school-house was among the log cabins enclosed in the stockade. Of the twelve families within this place of refuge there were no less than forty children.

Joseph Barker taught the school during the first winter. He had been educated in Exeter academy in New Hampshire, and made an excellent teacher. Shortly afterwards another school-house was built a short distance west of the stockade. Peregrine Foster was the first teacher of this school. Among subsequent instructors may be mentioned Pearley Howe and Caleb Emerson.

In 1811 another log school-house was built in the same neighborhood, a short distance from the river, not very far from where the Belpre hotel now stands. Deacon Howe set the first copy and wielded the first rod in this school.

The first school-house located in the middle settlement was not far from what is now known as Centre Belpre, and was located on the line between the farms of Esquire Isaac Pierce and Major Robert Bradford. A few years afterwards the brick school-house at Centre Belpre, near by, was built. It was used for school purposes for many years, elections and church meetings being frequently held therein. It is now used as a dwelling house. Among the prominent teachers of this

school were James B. Gardner and Weston Thomas.

The pioneer school at Newbury was just above and in sight of the stockade. It was built about the year 1800. A man by the name of Mahes was the first teacher.

The first teachers of these schools were thoroughly educated, many of them being college graduates of classical institutions. They consented to teach at very reasonable rates, as there was at that early time no other convenient field in which to employ their talents. In July 1790, the Ohio company appropriated one hundred and fifty dollars for the support of schools in the three settlements in the territory, and in December of the same year Belpre received a share of the money distributed. But the burden of these pay schools fell principally upon the people, many of whom being in moderate circumstances, were obliged to stint themselves that they might keep their children in school.

RELIGIOUS HISTORY.

The first sermon in Belpre was preached in the early summer of 1789, by Rev. Daniel Story, the chaplain of the Ohio company. In February, 1790, the agents and proprietors of the company decided that Mr. Story "preach three Sundays at Marietta, and two Sundays at Belpre and Waterford, in rotation." This gave Belpre preaching every four weeks. During the other three Sundays meetings were held. By common consent, Colonel Battelle, a man of fine education, usually presided. It was customary to have a sermon read from the writings of some eminent divine, and prayers read or extemporaneously offered by leaders who were regularly appointed. In March, 1791, it is recorded that twenty dollars were voted to Colonel Battelle for religious instruction at Belpre. In the following April, at a meeting of the agents of the Ohio company, out of one hundred and sixty dollars appropriated for religious instruction in the settlements, it was resolved that Belpre receive fifty dollars, provided that a suitable teacher be supported for seven months. Rev. Daniel Story's visits to Belpre were made in a canoe down the Ohio. During the war, the blood-thirsty savages made a trip from Marietta to Belpre very dangerous, but, nevertheless, Mr. Story came whenever he could, always accompanied by an armed guard of soldiers. Religious services were regularly kept up at Farmer's castle in the residence of Colonel Battelle, who still continued to be the religious instructor. When the time for service arrived, Ebenezer Battelle, jr., then a youth of about sixteen, was accustomed to beat the drum, the church bell of war, and thus call the people together.

THE CONGREGATIONAL CHURCH THE FIRST SOCIETY.

The record of the organization of this, the first religious society in Belpre, has not been preserved. It is probable, however, that the organization was not effected until shortly after the evacuation of Farmer's castle in 1796. The same people, who, during the war had been wont to listen to the reading of the Word in the blockhouse of Colonel Battelle, now united in hearty thanksgiving for the long prayed for peace. The members of the society were by no means all Congregationalists, neither were many of them professing Christians, but a glance at the earliest record, dated 1802, reveals the fact that many of the more prominent members, and the succession of early ministers were of the Congregational church.

After the establishment of peace, Rev. Daniel Story preached once a month at Belpre. On the occasions when the minister was not present, the people did not "forsake the assembling of themselves together," but regularly held "meeting" on the three Sundays on which there was no preaching. Prominent among the first members were, Colonel Ebenezer Battelle, Colonel Nathaniel Cushing, Perley Howe, Benjamin Miles, Judge Peregrine Foster, Judge Loring, Israel Putnam, and William Browning. It was customary to select some leading member to direct the religious services during the absence of the minister. At a business meeting of the society, held March 1, 1802, it was resolved "that the society meet every Sabbath at 10 o'clock, and that the preacher perform fore- and afternoon service, with one hour's intermission, and that persons be appointed to read the sermons and prayers, also that the singers be earnestly invited to atttend; also, that a contribution be taken on the first Sabbath of every month, to enable us to pay for regular preaching." The above resolution is the first of importance which was passed in the then new meeting-house on the Bluff. A glance at the earliest record, shows that at a meeting held February 24, 1802, Perley Howe, Judge Foster and William Browning were appointed a committee to collect subscriptions, and to appropriate the amount towards the building of a school or meeting-house on the Bluff, and to adjust all accounts relative thereto. A sufficient amount must have been raised, for it is recorded, that at the next meeting held in the "meeting-house on the Bluff," as it was ever afterward known, the building committee reported an excess over the amount expended of twelve shillings, nine pence, which sum was laid aside for current expenses. Perley Howe was appointed the first sexton, and continued in that office for a number of years. There is now no vestige of the old house which stood just east of the old burying-ground. The early settlers of Belpre came, some of them, from homes several miles away, and in this, the first sanctuary, worshipped the God of Sabbaoth.

Rev. Samuel P. Robbins was preaching at Belpre in 1805 coming from Marietta. At a meeting held April 4th, of the above named year, it was voted that Rev. Samuel P. Robbins be paid four dollars by Benjamin Miles, who is supposed to have been the treasurer. It is not known how many sermons this money paid for, but at the time the preacher's salary was nominal, and his work was purely a labor of love. At this same spring meeting Colonel Cushing was appointed a committee to manage the prudentials of the society during the next year, and measures were taken to have the meeting-house repaired and the burial-ground cleared. In 1806, Mr. Robbins was hired to act as the regular preacher of the congregation. It was voted, October 27th of the same year, that Isaac Pierce, Daniel Loring, and Nathaniel Cushing, be requested to read sermons,

alternating, during the three Sundays of the month when Mr. Robbins would be absent. It was further voted, that Deacon Miles and Colonel Putnam be appointed to pray at these meetings. In 1809, Decon Miles, Perley Howe and Benjamin F. Stone were appointed to read and pray, and in 1810, this duty devolved on Isaac Pierce, B. F. Stone and Colonel Cushing. At a meeting July 29th, Rev. Mr. Langdon was hired for one year.

As early as 1808 there was a motion made to see if the people were willing either to build a new meeting-house or to repair the old building. It was decided to repair the old house; and it was not until 1819 that there was made another strong effort to build a new church. A committee was appointed to draft plans for the new meeting-house, but owing to some inexplicable reason the report of the committe was not accepted. However, in 1822 a brick church was built and a lot secured for a burying ground at a point a little over half a mile from Cedarville. The building was made perfectly square with a pyramidal roof, and in this modern day presents a quaint appearance, as it stands solitary and deserted, a faithful sentinel over the graves of the members who built it. For some time after the building had been enclosed and roofed it was not finished. In 1831 the house was complete, and the fact was recognized by appropriate services.

THE ORGANIZATION OF THE CHURCH.

During all these years of the history of the society the Congregationalists at Belpre were nominal members of the church at Marietta. Gradually, however, had the society been assuming the prerogatives of a regularly organized church. As early as 1818 there is found the record of the dismission of a member as from a regular Congregational church. On Friday, November 25, 1826, it was stated at a meeting in the brick church that twenty-four members would request dismission from the Marietta church, deciding that each receive an individual letter of dismission. Deacon Perley Howe, Benjamin Miles, and Stephen Guthrie were appointed to present the petitions for dismission and request that the pastor and two delegates from the Marietta church assist in forming a church at Belpre on the first of January, 1827. The following resolution passed by the Marietta church was sent to Belpre: "That the prayer of the petitioners be granted, and that they be formed into a distinct church, enjoying all the privileges and immunities of the same." Accordingly, on New Year's day, 1827, the organization was effected through the instrumentality of Rev. L. G. Bingham, of Marietta. The covenant and articles of faith were adopted and subscribed to by the following named persons: Irene Benedict, Sophia Browning, Hannah Stone, Susan Stone, Deborah Dana, Abijah Wedge, Deacon Perley Howe, Lucy E. Gilbert, Josiah and Sarah Whiting, Elihu and Deborah Clark, Rowena Putnam, Charlotte L. Putnam, Sally Goodno, Benjamin H. Miles, P. Maria Miles, Elizabeth Bell, Priscilla and Hannah Miles, Amos and Huldah Fisher, and Stephen Guthrie. Of these twenty-four original members only three are living, viz.: Mrs. Browning, Mrs. Gilbert, and Mrs. Putnam. In March, 1827, William R. Browning was received into the church—the first member after the organization. Rev. Jacob Little, the first minister, remained about one year, and was succeeded by Rev. Augustus Pomeroy. In 1829, in connection with the Presbyterian church at Warren, a call was made out for, and accepted by, Rev. Addison Kingsbury. He was installed pastor October 3, 1829, by a delegation sent from the presbytery. In a brief minute of the services it is noted "that Rev. Calvin Ransom charged the people. Rev. John Spaulding preached the sermon from the words "What is truth?'' found in John, xviii, 38; that Rev. R. G. Wilson charged the pastor elect, and Rev. L. G. Bingham delivered the charge to the people." Dr. Kingsbury preached his farewell sermon November 10, 1839, having been in the pastorate just ten years. Professor D. H. Allen, of Marietta college, preached at Belpre during 1840; Rev. Tenney served in 1841; Rev. Dyar Burgess, during 1842 and 1843; and Rev. Joseph Edwards until the first of January, 1845. There were temporary supplies until in 1847 Rev. W. A. Smith came. In 1849 he was installed pastor. February 17, 1853, on account of the continued ill health of Mr. Smith, his resignation was accepted. There was no regular preaching until 1854, when Rev. John Williams became the supply. May 27, 1857, Rev. Francis Bartlett, the third and last pastor of the two churches, was installed and remained until the close of 1861. Rev. C. D. Curtis, who came in the spring of 1862, acted as pastor until the fall of 1866, when by mutual consent, the union previously existing between Belpre and Warren churches was dissolved; and here begins the history of the church entirely independent of any other organization.

In February, 1867, Rev. J. A. Bates became the first pastor, whose whole time was devoted to the Belpre church. He continued until May, 1872. From the fall of 1872 to the fall of 1874 the minister was Rev. D. I. Jones. Rev. E. Janes was called in February, 1875, and continued for two years. In the spring of 1877, the church secured the services of Rev. M. K. Pascal, and since 1879 has been without a regular minister. During the union with the Warren church preaching was held at Belpre every two weeks, and on each alternate Sabbath there was a reading service as of old. Weekly prayer meetings have always been kept up, and thanksgiving day has always been faithfully observed.

Perley Howe was deacon at the time of the organization of the church, and at an election held May 3, 1827, Benjamin H. Miles became deacon. At this same time William R. Browning became the first clerk. The present officers of the church are: A. W. Glazier, William Armstrong, George Dana, George A. Howe, and Milton Pelton, trustees; A. W. Glazier and George Dana, deacons; Edward B. Dana, clerk; and John M. Stone, treasurer.

The brick church was located centrally to accommodate a wide circle of members living in the surrounding country, but the springing up of the village of Belpre made it necessary that meetings be held there. About 1862 services for prayer and occasional preaching were held in available rooms in the village, and a Sunday-school organized. Finally there was permanent preaching every Sunday in the academy building, and the old brick church was gradually abandoned, the congregation down the river holding services in the school building near the town-house.

The erection of a church in Belpre village had become a necessity, and without delay the work proceeded. The site chosen is on Main street, just north of the railroad bridge. A. Walker was the architect of the building, which is of brick, forty feet wide by sixty long, with basement story, the whole surmounted by a spire one hundred and twenty-seven feet high, in which swings a good bell. The building was commenced in the fall of 1868 and was not completely finished until the fall of 1869, although the basement was occupied late in the summer.

In 1867 a neat two-story frame parsonage was erected in Belpre, so that at the completion of the church both pastor and people had a home.

From the earliest days the Sunday-school has been maintained, both at the old brick church and in adjoining neighborhoods. Deacon Benjamin Miles was the first superintendent. The system of catechetical instruction, which was in vogue before the days of Sunday-schools, has, in a measure, been adopted by the several schools. The first library was secured in 1827, at the organization of the church. This library was well selected, and formed the nucleus for the present full library. During the year 1880 there was an average attendance of about one hundred scholars. A prominent feature of the church is its active sympathy with all the great religious movements of the world, especially is this the case in the work of missions. The church is now repaying with interest the aid which, when she was weak, was granted to her by the board of home missions. Throughout the whole history of the church one meeting in each month has been set apart for prayer for missions. The people not only pray that the gospel may fly to the corners of the earth, but very sensibly furnish the wings by liberal contributions. There has always been an active interest in all objects of benevolence; a bitter warfare against slavery was waged, and the battle is still fierce against intemperance. The old brick church was sold in 1878.

THE CENTRE BELPRE CHURCH

was formed in October, 1880, by thirty-one members, who were dismissed from the church from the village, which was too far away for this portion of the congregation to attend regularly. The new congregation has not as yet been able to build a house of worship, but assembled regularly in the school building, near the town-house, at Centre Belpre. They are supplied by the minister who may be preaching for the Belpre church.

METHODIST EPISCOPAL.

In 1799 Rev. Robert Marley, of the Baltimore circuit, preached in the Belpre settlement, which at first was under the supervision of the Kanawha, and in 1800 became a part of the circuit known as the Muskingum and Little Hocking. But there was no regular Methodis preaching in Belpre until 1820. At this time Rev. Jacob Young was the presiding elder, and Rev. John McMahon was preacher of the Little Hocking circuit. During the fall and winter of 1820–21 a society was organized, there being in the first class books thirteen names, as follows: Daniel Goss and his wife Lydia, Samuel Hooper, Clarissa Ackley, William P. Howe, A. Gridley, Elizabeth Howe, Leroy Gridley, Susan Oaks, Susan O'Brien, Chester and Caroline Gridley, and Louis Bradford. Daniel Goss, who was one of the most energetic of the early Methodists, whs appointed class leader. Among his papers there was found the old subscription paper for the building of the church:

We, the undersigned subscribers, believing that it would be of importance to the Methodist society in Belpre to build a house of worship, not only for their own convenience but for all those who may be willing to attend; that it is desired by all those who are acquainted with the form of Methodist meeting-houses that the seats are free for those who do not belong to the society, in time of worship—we, the undersigned, do hereby agree to pay the amount to our respective names to the trustees of the Methodist church in said township, who may be appointed to superintend the building of said meeting-house, to be applied as they may think proper:

Daniel Goss	$40 00	Joseph Newbury	$40 00
James Moore	20 00	Joseph O'Neal	10 00
W. P. Leabody	5 00	W. Burroughs	10 00
Samuel Barkley	3 00	S. Cockshott	5 00
A. H. Duffer	5 00	S. W. Grady	1 00
John Kurney	1 00	H. Robinson	2 00
M. Rouse	2 00	Cyrus Ames	3 00
Francis Stone	1 00	N. Sparkhawk	1 00
Isaac Cogshall	1 00	John Bickford	1 00
Barker Rouse	3 00	G. N. Gilbert	3 00
James Whitney	10 00	John Crawford	5 00
—— Protsman	2 00	J. Jennings	2 00
Joseph Kelly	2 00	Solomon Goss	2 00
L. Record	3 00	James Dunn	1 00
Stephen Devol	1 00	Alusha Cole	50
J. M. Calder	1 00	B Bridges	50
S. Ellenwood	1 00	B. Ellenwood	50
J. Knowles	5 00	T. Guthrie	6 00
Andrew Ballard	5 00	Clarissa Cook	5 00
Andrew Fisher	4 50		

A log church was built near the forks of the Little Hocking north of Centre Belpre, of which church there is now no vestige. The quarterage paid in 1821 and '22 was twelve dollars and thirteen and one-fourth cents, and was subscribed in the following sums:

Daniel Goss, cash	$2 50
A. Cote, six bushels of corn	2.25
William Howe, 16¾ quarts cherries	1.97¾
Joseph Place	1.25
C. Ackley	75
Ellen Dilley	1.50
Joseph Dilley, two bushels meal	66¾
Samuel Hooper	1 25

In 1823 Joseph O'Neal was appointed class leader, and there were in all twenty members. The following year a second class was formed and given to the care of Samuel Hooper. During the winter of 1826, a two days meeting resulted in the conversion of a number of people. Seventeen members were added during the next winter, and Methodism in Belpre began to be strong. The ministers up to this time had been as follows: 1823, Cornelius Springer and W. J. Kent; 1824, Philip Greene; 1825, Daniel Limerick and John Steward; 1826, John W. Kinney and Curtis Goddard; 1827, Leroy Swormstedt; 1828, Leroy Swormstedt and James Callahan;

1829, Samuel Hamilton and William Herr; 1830, Jacob Young and Samuel Hamilton; 1831, John W. Gilbert and Gilbert Blue. These latter received twenty-seven dollars and eighteen and three-fourths cents quarterage for their services.

THE CEDARVILLE CHURCH.

By the year 1832 the Methodists in Belpre decided to build a house of worship at Cedarville, on the Ohio. Daniel Goss and Daniel Ellenwood were among the first trustees and members of the building committee. The house is frame, much of the lumber having been floated from Little Hocking in the back water caused by the flood of 1832. The church prospered, and became the local centre of Methodism. During the first year of its history the pastor's salary amounted to one hundred and twenty dollars and seventy-five cents. In 1836 there were fifty-five members. In the following year the church was incorporated into a new circuit known as Belpre circuit. At this time there were in the circuit six Sunday-schools. Mission stations were established at Barlow and other points. In 1838 there was a committee appointed to build a parsonage for the circuit. There were seventy-five members in 1842, and the name of the circuit was changed to Barlow. Nine years later there were one hundred members and four classes. Thus the Cedarville church prospered until 1867, when Belpre was set off as an independent station with three appointments, viz: Cedarville, Belpre village church known as Lewis chapel, and the Centenary church, both of the last named churches having been organized in 1866. The ministers at the Cedarville church, since its building in 1832, have been as follows, viz:

1832, Absalom Fox and Joseph Carper; 1833, Nathan Emery and William Young; 1834, Adam Poe and E Roe; 1835, E. Roe and William H Lawder; 1836, David Lewis and M. P. Kellog; 1837, Dudley Woodbridge and M. P. Strickland; 1838, James D. Webb and Joseph Gosner; 1839, Matthew Scoville and Sheldon Parker; 1840, Joseph Morris and Martin Wolf; 1841, James B. Austin and Samuel Maddox; 1842, James B. Austin and John W. Devilbiss; 1843, John W. Dillon and J. Barringer; 1844, A. Murphy and Richard Arthur; 1845, A. Murphy and Charles Warren; 1846, A. Brown and J. W. Fowble; 1847, D. D. Mather and L. Cunningham; 1848, D. D. Mather and J. McCutchen; 1849, J McCutchen and J F. Given; 1850, J. Barringer and S. C. Frampton; 1851, A. Carthck and J. R. Prose; 1852, A Carthck and C Benjamin; 1853, Isaac Reynolds and David Mann; 1854, Isaac Reynolds and Michael Sheets; 1855, W. W. Cherrington and W. C. Filler; 1856, W. W. Cherrington and A. C. Kelly; 1857, Levi Munsell and J. W. Lewis; 1858, Levi Munsell and E Frost; 1859, Pardon Cook and E. Nichols; 1860, Pardon Cook and E. Nichols; 1861, Stephen Ryland and J. P. Calvert; 1863, F. S. Thurston and George Murray; 1864; F. S. Thurston and F. S. Davis; 1865, W. S. Benner and F. S. Davis; 1866, W. S Benner and J. S. Davis; 1867; T S. Stevens and J. D. Fry.

Since Belpre was made an independent station, the ministers at the three churches above named have been: Revs. J. E. Sowers, Jesse Van Law, Isaac Mackey, T. H. Braderick, M. V. B. Evans, J. F. Williams and James Mitchell. The church officers are: J. Farson, C. Le Seur and S. R. W. McFarland, stewards; G. W. Hensell, J. H. Horton, E. Rysley, E. W. Petty, J. Farson, J. Simpson and J. Waterman, trustees.

LEWIS CHAPEL

in Belpre village was named in honor of Frederick and Mary Lewis, who gave one thousand dollars for the building of the church. The house, a neat frame structure, was erected in the year 1866-7, at an expense of about six thousand and five hundred dollars. Six persons gave five hundred dollars each, and the remainder was raised by subscription. Captain Josiah Henderson presented the bell which cost four hundred and forty dollars. The house was dedicated February 24, 1867, the dedicatory sermon being preached by Rev. J. M. Reed, D.D., the editor of the *Western Christian Advocate.* At this service the debt of the church was cleared. The membership of the church has gradually increased until 1881, and there are two hundred and fifty members.

The organization of the Sunday-school was effected at the time of the dedication of the church. E. E. Cunningham continued to be superintendent until 1871, since which time N. B. Adams has held the office.

The church officers are as follows, viz: S. Druse, J. Alderman and N. B. Adams, stewards; J. Alderman, S. Druse, A. D. Sherman, O. L. Davis, John Brown and J. C. O'Neal, trustees.

CENTENARY CHURCH.

This church branched from the Cedarville church in 1866. Robert Bess's daughter was a prime mover in the work of organization. The first and present stewards are: James Dunlevy, R. C. Menzie, John Berry and Thomas McFarland, sr. The building of the frame meeting-house was commenced in 1866, and the church was dedicated in 1867. There were twenty members at first, and there are now over thirty. About the year 1876 the Centenary church was transferred from the Belpre to the Newbury station. The minister for 1880-1801 is Rev. W. H. Gibbons.

THE NEWBURY CHURCH

was formed about 1811 or 1812, in the Newbury settlement. The first meeting was held at a school-house just west of the cemetery. There were less than a dozen members at first, among them being Mrs. Joel Oakes, Truman, and Elizabeth Guthrie, John Wetherby, and others. The organization was effected by Rev. Marcus Linsey, of Kentucky. Services were held at the school-house until 1829, when a frame church was erected, which was occupied for fifty years. Since 1879 the meetings have been held in the school-house at Little Hocking, where a church building is to be built. There were at one time about thirty-five members, but changes in population have reduced the number to nineteen. The pastor of the church is Rev. W. H. Gibbons. The stewards are A. S. Tidd, Sheppard Humphrey, James Palmer, and N. Coggeshall. The trustees are Edwin Guthrie, Nicholas Baker, C. W. Oakes, and L. R. Curtis.

THE UNIVERSALIST CHURCH.

The first Universalist society of Belpre was organized May 23, 1823, in the old brick school house at Centre Belpre. Many of the first members had previously been members of the society at the meeting-house on the bluff. William Pitt Putnam, chairman, and Daniel Loring, clerk of the first meeting, were appointed to draft articles of association, which were adopted at the second meeting, held, January 17, 1834. There were seventeen

members at first, as follows: Daniel Loring, Hobson Beebe, Oliver Rice, Perley Eastman, O. R. Loring, Beal Stedman, Robert and Otis L. Bradford, William Pitt Putnam, Jesse Loring, R. Gridley; John Birkenshay, sr., John Birkenshay, jr., Julius Chappell, Jasper Needham, Sylvester Haynes, and Joseph C. King.

The history of the society is brief. When there was no preaching, reading meetings were held. The society had occasional preaching from the Rev. Asa Stearns, of Athens county, and Elder Croy, of Galia county. In 1826 the Rev. Eliphath Case preached the thanksgiving sermon, and continued for some time as supply. A number of the members in the society deeming it advisable to form church relations,

THE FIRST UNIVERSALIST CHURCH

was organized in the brick school-house March 1, 1827. There were, besides the membership of the society, twelve additional members at the time of the church organization. The names of these new members are: Luke Reynolds, Jacob Springer, Jonathan Root, Mary Blizzard, Fanny Loring, Anthony Robinson, John Brown, Renssalaer Johnson, Stephen Needham, Susanna Gilbert, and Philip Cole. Sylvester Haynes and William Pitt Putnam were chosen deacons, and the bond of union and profession of faith adopted.

Soon after the organization of the church, Rev. Case left for New Hampshire. In 1829, Rev. Alpheus Sweet became the pastor. Since that time there has been a numerous succession of ministers, viz: Revs. Waldo, W. H. Jolly, Francis H. Johnson, D. S. Morey, Timothy Crow, L. L. Saddler, M. L. Edwards, H. P. Sage, George Rodgers, T. C. Eaton, George Flanders, G. S. Weaver, —— Bartlett, Paul Kendall, Thompson Barrow, Benard Peters, —— Hicks, J. W. McMaster, T. C. Druley, and Rev. Earl, who came in 1880. Rev. J. W. McMaster was pastor for nineteen years.

For several years after the organization of the church the meetings were held in the school-house. The first meeting of the Universalist association was held in the old treadmill on Putnam farm. The church, a frame building, was built in 1835, on a lot presented by Jesse Loring. It stands on the river road, midway between Cedarville and Centre Belpre. It was dedicated August 30, 1835. Elder W. H. Jolly preached the dedicatory sermon, and was assisted in the service by Father Truman Strong.

The Sunday-school, which is in a very properous condition, was organized in 1835, and William P. Putnam and O. R. Loring among the first superintendents. S. H. Stone is the superintendent for 1880, and James Howser, librarian. The library consists of four hundred volumes, and is very valuable.

In 1876 a missionary school was organized in Belpre village. The first meetings were held in Odd Fellows' hall, and are now held in the school hall. Preaching services are held in Belpre once a month. The church has been very appropriately called "the old hive," from the fact that no less than five churches have been formed of members of the first church, viz: Newbury, Dunham, Barlow, and Fairfield in this county, and one church in Illinois. In all, there have been two hundred and nine members of the old church, there being at the beginning of 1881, fifty-seven active members. The officers of the church are as follows: Moderator, J. B. Mawhinney; clerk, J. W. Putnam; treasurer, Mrs. A. W. Brough; trustees, B. B. Stone, Emma Ames, and J. B. Mawhinney; stewards, S. H. Stone, and James Houser; deacons, Nathan Sparhawk, and William P. Cole. The church is ever active in missionary effort, and contributions are made to every good cause.

THE NEWBURY CHURCH,

as has been already remarked, is a branch of the First Universalist church. It was established in 1852. The building is located in the southwestern part of Belpre township, about three miles below Little Hocking. In the year above mentioned nine members applied for a dismission from the mother church in order that they might organize a church in their immediate neighborhood. The nine original members are—Mrs. Elvira Curtis, John Cole and wife, Seymore Clough, Cynthia Clough, Caroline Curtis, J. H. and M. G. Van Gilder, and Marion Curtis. The pulpit is supplied regularly by the pastor of the upper church, this arrangement for preaching having been made at the time of the new organization.

ST. MARY'S CATHOLIC CHURCH.

This church is located at Little Hocking. It was organized in 1878 by the first pastor, Rev. M. M. A. Hartnedy. The house is a neat frame structure, and was built in the same year that the church was organized. The dedicatory services were held June 9, 1878. The membership of the church is quite large, it being comprised of people that come from miles around, and it is probable that about two hundred and fifty people worship at St. Mary's. The priests from Athens have been supplying the church since its organization. After Rev. Father Hartnedy the congregation enjoyed the ministrations of Father T. I. Lane. The present pastor is Father I. C. Madden.

AFRICAN METHODIST EPISCOPAL CHURCH.

This is the oldest colored church in Belpre. It commenced in a humble way and has since become quite strong. In 1868 a little band of ten met in the room of Henry Baker and organized the church through the instrumentality of Rev. James McTerry, of Marietta. He left the class in charge of Henry Baker, who is a local preacher, and came to visit the flock every alternate Sunday. About two years after the organization the people were able to build a little board house, which, though far from being comfortable, served as a place for worship for some time. Afterwards the school board permitted the people to meet in a wing of the colored school-house. In 1876 they put up a neat and commodious building on Florence street, in North Belpre, at a total cost of nearly seven hundred dollars, which sum is about all paid. In the second year of Rev. McTerry's service to this people he was called away by death. His place was supplied by Rev. John Lee. Since then the ministers have been Revs. Isaac Bell, Jacob Cole, Jacob Whitman,

Arthust, and the present pastor, Elder Davis. The officers of the church are: Trustees, John Turner, Robert Sawyer, Henry Baker, and Dow Robinson; stewards, John Roody and James Williams.

JACKSON CHAPEL.

In 1870 there were twenty-five members of a little church that was organized in Belpre by John Jackson, sr., then a local preacher of the Methodist faith. He effected the organization of the church, and after considerable effort a little frame house of worship was erected on North Walnut street, and was dedicated as Jackson chapel. The first regular pastor was Rev. A. Posey, who served the people for two years, and was succeeded by Rev. E. Henderson, who also remained two years. Jacob Skinner and A. A. Price were the pastors during the next two years, being succeeded by Rev. D. Tucker, and by the present pastor, Rev. S. R. Cattrell, who is serving out his two years. This church has lived one decade, and during that time has more than doubled its membership, there being now on the roll over fifty names of active members. In 1870 the officers of the church were: Trustees, H. C. Miller, Henry Baker, and Stroter Thomas; stewards, Douglas Taylor and Charles Burns. In 1880 the trustees were Aaron Williams, John Jackson, jr., Harrison Williams, Esquire Thomas, and James E. Atkins. The stewards are John C. Austin, Adams Patterson, and Samuel M. Taylor. The leaders are H. Williams, John Jackson and Nannie Simms.

ITEMS OF INTEREST.

The first white child born in Belpre township was Joseph Barker. He was born February 28, 1790, at the house of his grandfather, Captain William Dana, where Mrs. Barker had been residing since the breaking out of the small-pox at Marietta, early in January. The little boy became a great man, and held high office in the State. He died in Newport township in 1859, and was the first buried in the new cemetery at Lower Newport.

The first brick house erected in the township was the tavern of Deacon Benjamin Miles, in the middle settlement. This was also the place at which the first town election was held. For years it was a popular hostelrie.

The first frame house was built by Colonel Israel Putnam, and is still standing on the old site at Belpre village, and is now known as the "Benedict House." It was a house of two stories, and in the early days was considered to be quite a mansion.

The first sheep were introduced in the year 1797, the first lot coming from Pennsylvania. During earlier years much of the clothing worn was home-spun. However, the raising of sheep has never been a specialty. During the first years wolves were too numerous, and now the mongrel dogs make the business hazardous.

The shrewd Yankees of the settlement tried to raise everything at first. For the first few years cotton was raised in small quantities, and the genius of Captain Devol quickly invented a "gin," or machine with rollers, which separated the cotton from the pods in a very satisfactory manner.

As early as the year 1800 silk worms were raised,

66

being fed on the leaves of the white mulberry, raised from seed brought from Connecticut. The cocoons were spun into sewing thread.

Judge Barker, in his MSS., says that, in the spring of 1790, Captain William Dana sowed a piece of flax, pulled it early in June, while it was yet in blossom, water-rotted it in a swamp near the river, had it dressed out and spun, and woven into substantial cloth by his son William. It was made into shirts and trousers for the boys, and worn at the celebration of the Fourth of July in Belpre that year.

THE FARMERS' LODGE OF BELPRE

was organized by the Free Masons of the settlement. The records have been lost, but there is every reason to believe that the organization was effected prior to the year 1800. The following are known to have been members, viz.: Daniel Loring, Nathaniel Cushing, Oliver Rice, W. P. Putnam, Major Bradford, Cyrus Ames, sr., Dr. Gilbert, Major Haskell, Deacon Howe, Dr. Pier, Dr. Webb, George Dana, Edmond Dana, Judge Joseph Barker, Rufus B. Stone, William Leabody, Hezekiah Lewis, Andrew Fisher, and Elias Gates, a resident of Virginia. The lodge meetings were held at the house of Major Haskell. Gradually, by the death of the old members, the lodge decreased in numbers and finally expired.

BELPRE LODGE INDEPENDENT ORDER OF ODD FELLOWS, NO. 619.

This lodge was instituted August 10, 1875, by Joseph Dowell, grand master. There were seven charter members, viz: John Brown, David Oliver, J. R. King, B. W. Compton, John B. Badger, A. F. Downer and A. T. Shahan. At the first meeting John F. King and I. H. Henderson were admitted by card, and George Dunberger, L. M. Cunningham, Joseph Richards, and I. B. Kinkead were initiated. The following is a list of the first officers elected; John Brown, N. G.; David Oliver, V. G.; J. R. King, secretary; B. W. Compton, permanent secretary; A. F. Downer, treasurer; I. H. Henderson, warden; James King, conductor; John F. King, inside guardian; I. B. Kinkead, right supporter to noble grand; C. E. Ames, left supporter to N. G.; Joseph Richards, R. S. V. G.; John G. Waterman, L. S. V. G.; A. T. Shahan, R. S. S.; L. M. Cunningham, L. S. S.; John B. Badger, J. R. King, and A. T. Shahan.

The first meetings were held in Browning's building, on Main street, just north of the railroad. In August, 1880, the lodge removed to the present commodious hall on South Main street. Since the first meeting up to 1881 there have been forty initiations, ten admissions by card, five withdrawals by card, and one death. So that the present number of members is fifty-eight. The lodge has been only once visited by death, when in August, 1880, James Williams was called away. Obstacles thrown in the way have only increased the prosperity of the lodge. At times public entertainments are given and are always followed by an accession of new members. The hall is tastefully furnished and handsomely equipped with regalia. The

present officers are: W. P. McKinney, N. G.; M. Mulligan, V. G.; A. Conley, secretary; C. B. Ames, permanent secretary; J. L. O'Neal, treasurer; A. F. Downer, chaplain; B. W. Compton, warden; D. R. Rood, conductor; F. M. Page, inside guardian; K. McCuaig, outside guardian; O. D. Davis, R. S. N. G.; M. C. Nichols, L. S. N. G.; David Oliver, R. S. V. G.; George Dunberger, L. S. V. G.; Austin Templer, R. S. S.; P. S. Cole, L. S. S.; J. L. O'Neal, N. B. Adams, and A. F. Downer, trustees.

STAR OF BELPRE LODGE, NO. 1910, GRAND UNITED ORDER OF ODD FELLOWS,

is the rather high sounding title which the lodge of colored Odd Fellows in Belpre has inscribed upon its banners. The lodge was organized in 187–, by the Naomi Lodge of Pargersburgh, West Virginia. There were thirty-one charter members. There are now eighteen members, and it is hoped the decrease of quantity has improved the quality of the membership. The first officers were as follows, viz: H. C. Miller, N. G.; R. G. Whiteman, permanent secretary; David Tucker, noble father; George Williams, elective secretary; J. W. Scott, treasurer; Robert Williams, chaplain; Harrison Boggs, P. N. G. The meetings are held every Wednesday in the hall over the colored school-room. The present officers are as follows: S. T. Jackson, N. G.; Thomas Blake, P. N. G.; H. C. Miller, permanent secretary; John Turner, V. G.; C. W. Posey, elective secretary; Adams Patterson, N. F.; Ezekial Fry, P. N. F.; John Washington, treasurer; John Jackson, chaplain.

THE BELPRE FARMERS' CLUB.

Ever since the first plow entered the virgin soil and the first grain took root, farming in Blepre township has been a science. True, in the earlier days this knowledge was not formulated and issued as law, but it is evident that an intelligent appreciation of a thorough agricultural education was the basis of the practical knowledge of the early farmers. However, it has been reserved to the modern day to effect the organization of the farmers. July 19, 1879, the people of Belpre township received a visit from the Muskingum Farmers' club, which had been flourishing for five years and more. The accounts which were given of the objects and work of this organization awakened an earnest desire that a similar society be formed in Belpre. On motion of Hon. A. L. Curtis it was decided that a meeting be held in the yard of Mr. Cyrus Ames to effect the organization of a Belpre Farmers' club. This meeting was held July 26th, and, after discussion, it was resolved that a club be organized. Accordingly the constitution was adopted and signed by twenty-four members, which number has since increased to sixty-three. The first officers elected were: Hon. A. L. Curtis, president; J. M. Farson, vice-president; Miss Emma Ames, recording secretary; E. B. Dana, corresponding secretary; S. H. Stone, treasurer. The present officers are the same as at first, save that S. R. W. McFarland is the president. The object of the club is the promotion of farming, gardening, and agriculture, together with the social and intellectual enjoyment of its members. The membership of the club is not confined to Belpre township, and persons in all townships are invited to attend with their families. The meetings are held once a month at the houses of members of the club. The annual meeting is held on the first Saturday of January of each succeeding year. The exercises consist of readings, recitations, music, and an essay and discussion, the discussion being generally concerning some farm topic. There is always time left for sociability, and a dinner is a part of the programme.

PHYSICIANS.

Dr. Samuel Barnes was the first physician who practiced in Belpre township. The humane policy of the directors of the Ohio company suggested the appointment of men to act as physicians and surgeons of the respective garrisons. The committee selected for Belpre Dr. Barnes, who had but recently come to the neighborhood from Massachusetts. He received his instruments and medicines, his board, and a small sum of money from the company. He remained with the family of Major Goodale, whose daughter he married. After the division at Farmer's castle he made his headquarters at the Goodale stockade, and during the plague of the smallpox in 1793 he devoted himself more especially to the people in this garrison. Soon after the close of the war he removed with his family to Athens county, locating not far from the town of Athens.

In 1802, shortly after Dr. Barnes' departure, Dr. Leonard Jewett became the physician of Belpre. He lived in the middle settlement, near the Ohio, and about half a mile below what is now Centre Belpre post office. His practice extended for many miles up and down the river, and in the adjoining country. He was a gentleman of fine intelligence and professional ability. He was born in Massachusetts in 1770. In 1792 he graduated from the Boston Medical college. In 1796 he married Mary Porter. He afterwards served four years as assistant surgeon in a New York hospital. About the year 1805, after remaining at Belpre nearly three years, he removed to the town of Athens, where he died in 1816, from the effects of blood poisoning.

Dr. S. P. Hildreth located in Belpre December 10, 1806, on the very day that Blennerhasset left his fairy island. Dr. Hildreth's professional career is more particularly noticed in the history of the early physicians of Marietta. When twenty-three years old he started on horseback from New Hampshire, September 29, 1806, arriving at Marietta October 4th, whence, on the invitation of leading citizens, he removed to Belpre, where he remained until March, 1808, when he returned to Marietta. In 1807 he married Rhoda Cook, whose mother kept the hotel opposite the mouth of the Little Kanawha. At this place the doctor made his headquarters, practicing up and down and on both sides of the river.

Dr. Ira W. Pier was among the early physicians of the township. He came at a very early day, when he was quite a young man. He married a daughter of Major Bradford. From Belpre he went to Circleville, thence to Indiana, and thence to Cleveland, where he died a few years ago.

Dr. Erastus Webb located in Belpre township prior to 1810. He studied medicine in New York State, whence he came to Ohio. He married a Miss Cook, and after practicing in Belpre several years removed about 1815 to Circleville, Ohio, where he died in 1848.

Dr. William Beebe was the successor of Dr. Webb and Dr. Pier, and came to Belpre about 1816. He located in the Middle settlement, his house being the first west of Davis' run, at its entrance into the Ohio; buying the property of Squire Pierce. He served during the War of 1812 as the assistant of Dr. Jewett, who was the surgeon in General Tupper's command at the time of the expedition to the Maumee river. After the war Dr. Beebe spent some time in the vicinity of the Kanawha salt works, and then came to Belpre as above stated. He married Polly Lorin. His son, Dr. William Beebe, is living in Barlow township, and his daughter, Mrs. Booth, is in Marietta. Dr. Beebe's life as a physician was very vigorous, he being almost constantly in the saddle. There are those living who still cherish the memory of their old family physician. He died in 1821 aged fifty-one. He is buried in the old burying-ground by the river. Dr. Beebe was a pupil of Dr. Jewett.

After Dr. Beebe's death for a time the people of Belpre were without a physician, and were very much perplexed that a suitable man did not offer his services. Acting on the principle that they should help themselves in the emergency, they immediately got up a petition, which was signed by the representative citizens of the community, and forthwith expressed it to the young physician who had settled at Waterford in 1817, Dr. Gilbert. After due deliberation he decided to locate at Belpre, although there was a strong effort made to keep him at Waterford. His first office was that of Dr. Beebe. He afterwards had his headquarters at Major A. W. Putnam's, whose daughter he married. After his marriage in 1825 he located half a mile below Cedarville, where he resided during the remainder of his life. He was always hard worked, he being the only physician in the neighborhood for many years. Hardly had he located in Belpre when the sickly season of 1823 kept him unceasingly busy. His practice, large from the first, gradually widened until his circuit of professional duty was widespread. He continued to practice until 1864, when an accident at once put an end to his professional career. His horse threw him to the ground and dragged him some distance, severely injuring his head and causing an almost entire loss of eyesight. Dr. Gilbert died in 1870.

Dr. Norval Pinnell located in Belpre village in 1863, he being the first physician who settled in the town. He was a graduate of the Cleveland Medical college. After remaining in Belpre one year he removed to Barlow township, and returned in 1865, remaining in practice at Belpre until the time of his death, which occurred in the year 1870.

The physicians at present in the township are as follows: in Belpre village, Drs. C. J. Guthrie, C. W. Goodno, G. W. Reed, and G. N. Pinnell; at Little Hocking, Drs. J. W. Quarles, and B. F. Price.

BELPRE VILLAGE.

For more than sixty years after the first settlement there was no village of considerable size in Belpre township. The stores up and down the river sufficed to answer the demands of trade, and Parkersburgh and Marietta were easily accessible. The multiplicity of farm houses along the river front of the township made, as it were, a village long drawn out.

As early as 1796, Peregrine Foster had established a ferry and tavern opposite the mouth of the Little Kanawha, and the first post office was also at this point. As early as 1800, Cook's tavern, in what is known as the old Benedict house was the rendezvous for emigrants who had crossed from Virginia and were enroute down the Ohio river roads. Close by the river, in what is now the southern part of the village, was the house of William Browning, on whose land the first town plat was surveyed. Thus we see at a very early day there were several houses on the present village site, but there would have been no village to this day had it not been for outside influences. Until the building of the Baltimore & Ohio railroad, the point opposite Parkersburgh was simply a farming community. The building of the railroad suggested the laying out of the village, and accordingly the plat of Belpre was surveyed by L. W. Chamberlain, December 29, 1852, on lots ten, eleven and twelve, for A. H. Browning, the proprietor. The plat was acknowledged before esquire B. F. Stone, March 8, 1853. It contained eighteen town lots, and was bounded on the north by Second street, on the east by the Ohio river, on the south by Cunningham, and on the west by Main street. There have been no less than fifteen additions since 1853, by Messrs. A. H. Browning, Stephen Druse, Colbert O'Neal, L. E. Stone, C. Cole, C. D. Cook, and L. Johnson. The village did not grow rapidly at first. The post office was then in the Benedict house. About this time B. F. Stone, jr., erected a building for a store, near the corner of Main and Cunningham streets. About 1860 E. E. Cunningham built the store now kept by J. D. Browning, and thither was the post office removed. At this time there was less than a dozen houses in the village proper, and it was little more than a hamlet until 1865. Then was ushered in a decade of prosperity. The oil discoveries in the adjoining territory in West Virginia, gave the impetus to the rapid growth of Belpre. Property increased in value so that lots eighty by one hundred and sixty feet, sold for five hundred dollars. The owners of the oil region sold their land at an enormous price, and many of them desiring to locate in a good village, purchased lots and built residences in Belpre. The line of growth extended along the whole extent of Main street. Stores multiplied, and manufactories promised to succeed. It was at this time that the academy was built. A flouring mill was erected and operated by Leseur, Hadley & Co. This mill, located near the ferry, is now operated by L. E. Stone, who has added a planing mill and lumber yard. In 1866, C. H. Johnson opened a drug store in the building on south Main street now occupied by A. S. Combs. In 1868 or 1869, Barkley & Downer opened a tannery in the northern part of the village, on the premises now owned by Kuhn Brothers & Co. A pump factory was owned by Messrs. Porter, Rathbone, and Hale. Alderman & Scott established a pottery, which is not now in operation. Boat-building has been engaged in to some extent. In 1874, the Building asociation that had been formed erected many new houses. In the same year the Baltimore & Ohio railroad company began building the "Short line" from Athens to Parkersburgh. In the summer of 1874, the Baltimore & Ohio company purchased of Mr. George Dana twelve acres of land lying just northwest of the village, and immediately proceeded to construct the stockyards. For the accommodation of passengers and stockmen, a commodious three-story frame hotel was built near by* and Belpre station established thereon. For a time there was a prospect that the railroad car-shops would be located on the Belpre side of the river, but the hope was not realized.

There were about one thousand inhabitants in 1874, and accordingly one hundred and ten citizens presented a petition to the county commissioners urging the immediate incorporation of the village. A remonstrance from seventy leading citizens induced the commissioners to suspend judgment until the December meeting, at which meeting it was decided not to grant the petition for the reason that the boundaries of said proposed incorporation embraced farm lands, which, in justice ought not to be incorporated within said village.

No less than three newspaper enterprises have struggled to gain a foothold in Belpre, but they were short-lived. In 1875, J. B. Kinkead became the editor of the *Courant*. The next paper was the *News*, by Mrs. Mary J. Adams, in 1878. David Goshorn published the *Herald* during the years 1879 and 1880.

Although lack of capital has greatly crippled enterprise, the business interests of the place are well represented, as follows: Groceries, J. M. Stone, C. A. Brown, J. D. Browning, G. N. Pinnell. Dry Goods, J. Alderman. Hardware, O. L. Davis. Drugs, N. B. Adams, Guthrie Brothers, and A. S. Combs. Egg packers, S. B. Kirby & Co. Books, C. A. Brown. Flouring and planing mill with lumber yard, L. E. Stone. Tannery, Kuhn Brothers & Co. Bakery, Henry Gettel. Undertaking, John Brown. Insurance agencies, J. M. Stone, D. R. Rood, and J. L. O'Neal. Physicians, C. J. Guthrie, C. W. Goodno, C. W. Reed, and G. N. Pinnell. Hotels, Belper hotel, S. J. Stribbling; Belpre House, Mrs. S. Williams; attorney D. R. Rood.

The churches of the village are mentioned elsewhere.

THE GRADED SCHOOLS.

Too much cannot be said of the good influence of the schools of Belpre village upon the character of the citizens. The good name of the high school attracted intelligent people, many of whom removed to the village that they might educate their children.

On the twenty-third of March, 1872, a special school district was established in the village. W. W. Northrup was the prime mover in the work of securing and form-

---

*The land for this was bought of Colonel John Stone.

OLIVER RICE LORING.

Daniel Loring, the father of the Loring family of this county, emigrated from Massachusetts to Ohio during the early period of settlement. He had married at Sudbury, Massachusetts, in "Wayside inn," a Miss Howe, one of the family which for generations had presided at that historic place, now celebrated in American poetry. She died before the settlement at Marietta, leaving three children, who accompanied their father to the west, viz: Israel, Charlotte (wife of A. W. Putnam) and Ezekiel. He married for his second wife Mrs. Rice, of Belpre township, and by her had four children, the youngest of whom was Oliver Rice, whose portrait appears above. Daniel Loring was the head of the church at Sudbury, and after coming to Belpre was commonly known as "Priest Loring." He was one of the founders of Universalism in Belpre, and was also prominent among the early Masons. He held the office of justice of the peace for nearly two decades. This was at a period when the best and most intelligent men were elected to the magistracy. The death of Daniel Loring occurred during the sickly seasons of 1822-3.

Oliver Rice Loring was born June 17, 1790. During his youth he received the best instruction the neighborhood afforded, which at the present day would not be considered more than a secondary school. He was sent to Athens a short time to "complete his course" in grammar, arithmetic, geography, and other common branches. He married for his first wife Fanny Warner, and settled on the homestead. She died in 1827, and the following year he married Orinda Howe, who was born in 1799 and still survives.

Mr. Loring held the office of associate judge of the court of common pleas, and was highly complimented by older members of the bar as an officer. He once held the office of ensign of militia, and, at various times, local township offices. He was for many years a Whig leader in that end of the county, and was one of the council which frequently met in Joseph Holden's store in Marietta, and was sardonically designated by John Brophy and his Democratic friends as "Joe Holden's sinate."

Judge Loring was a man of strong sense, and always had a certain influence in the community. He was reserved in his manners, and never sought notoriety.

He died November 21, 1873.

ing the district. The formation was completed by the election of the first board of education, which was composed of the following gentlemen, viz.: N. B. Adams, W. W. Northrup and C. A. Brown. Mr. Northrup was the first president of the board. The officers in 1880-81 are: President, John C. O'Neal; clerk, R. T. Moore; and treasurer, C. A. Brown.

The two-story frame school-house on Main street became the educational home of the united districts. The building was enlarged by the addition of a one-story wing on either side, thus making four rooms, which accommodated as many departments or grades. J. P. Hulburt was the first principal of the high school department, with Mary E. Barkley, Edna Hibbard and Park S. Browning, assistants in the grammar, intermediate and primary grades.

In 1873, E. S. Cox became the superintendent. He systematized the course and thoroughly organized the several departments. L. D. Brown was elected in 1874, and was followed in 1875 by Rev. W. U. Spencer, who, in turn, was succeeded in 1876 by C. K. Wells. J. G. Schofield was superintendent during the year 1878-9, and was succeeded by the present incumbent, C. E. Keyes.

Shortly after the organization of the school, the rapid increase of scholars and the consequent need of more commodious quarters, caused the subject of a new school building to be agitated. The question was decided by a large majority when put to vote, in the spring of 1875, and immediate preparations were made for the construction of the new house. The vote authorized an appropriation of ten thousand dollars for the building, and eight hundred for the purchase of a lot in the northern part of the village, at the corner of Main and Fifth streets. The contract was awarded to M. J. O'Connor, who, for nine thousand two hundred and fifty dollars, agreed to furnish a complete house, with the exception of the seats. The building was constructed from plans designed by A. C. Nash, and is a brick structure that would do credit to larger towns than Belpre. Both the first and second floors are divided from east to west by a hall twelve feet wide. On the first floor there are two rooms on either side of the hall. The south side of the second floor has two rooms, and the other side is left in one large room, which is used as a public hall, which, on suitable occasions, is rented for the benefit of the school fund. There are two stairways, one in the front and the other in the rear of the building. Through the central part of the house there is a large stack, to be used for heating by means of a furnace in the cellar, but so far the rooms have been heated by stoves. In due time the hall was handsomely furnished with a stage, chandeliers and comfortable seats. In 1880 a piano was bought far the school, and placed in the hall where the morning exercises are held. The school grounds are well supplied with shade trees, set out through the instrumentality of Mr. Northrup.

The first commencement took place in June, 1877, at which time there were four graduates, viz.: Anna B. Paden (deceased), Anna Guthrie, David P. Guthrie and Anna Lockwood. In 1878 there were three graduates, two in 1879 and two in 1880.

Through the special efforts of Superintendent L. D. Brown there was formed a library association, the interest in which is still kept up.

THE COLORED SCHOOL.

At the time of the organization of the special district there were about fifteen colored children of school age, and a separate school was established for them. The school now numbers about thirty-five members, and is held in the frame building made vacant by the removal of the white school. Mrs. Martha T. Wattaker taught until 1873, and was succeeded by J. H. Cole and C. W. H. Bell in 1874; W. W. Kinkead, the first white teacher, taught until 1875, when H. C. Day was appointed. From 1877 to 1879 Daniel Tucker taught, and the teacher for 1880 and 1881 is Anna Stephens.

During the summer of 1880 the building was thoroughly overhauled and refitted, and the wings taken off, so that it now presents a very neat appearance.

THE POST OFFICE.

Mail was received and distributed at the tavern of Peregrine Foster as early as 1798. William Browning became the first postmaster, and in 1812 Colonel John Stone became his deputy. Squire Browning held the office until 1821, the time of his death, at which time Pardon Cook was appointed. He was successively followed by Colonel Stone, Ebenezer Benedict, Josiah Henderson, E. E. Cunningham, John Fisher, and in 1865 by John M. Stone who is still in office.

SMALLER VILLAGES.

There are groups of houses below the village of Belpre, which are named respectively, Blennerhassett, Cedarville, Center Belpre and Little Hocking.

Blennerhassett is just opposite the head of the famous island whence the name is derived. It was laid out June 28, 1876, by William and Mary C. Mullen, the proprietors.

Cedarville was laid out by John Ball, John B. Day, Prashel Bailey, Peter Voshel, Cyrus R. Ames and William Clark. The plat was surveyed April 22, 1837. The village is located about two miles below Belpre, on the Ohio river. There are two groceries, a Methodist Episcopal church, and about a dozen houses. The post office, known as Rockland, was established in 1873. The first postmaster, Mr. Mawhinney, is still in office.

The Centre Belpre post office was also established in 1873, and the present incumbent, Parker Lewis, was appointed postmaster. At a very early day what was known as the Bent post office was established with Nahum Bent as postmaster. The office was removed in 1836 or 1837, to the house of Dr. Gilbert, and was known as Centre Belpre post office until discontinued in 1873, at which time the new offices of Rockland and Centre Belpre were established. In connection with the latter office Mr. Lewis keeps a general store.

Little Hocking is situated on the Baltimore & Ohio railroad at the mouth of the Little Hocking, whence the village took its name. The plat was surveyed March 8,

1875, for the proprietors, Davis and Permelia Allen. However, the village was begun years before this survey. About 1824 a post office and store were established by Horace Curtis, first at his residence, and soon afterwards in the store-room now occupied by Leroy R. Curtis, the present postmaster. Until October, 1879, the name of the office was Little Hockhocking, and for convenience the reduplication was dropped. The second postmaster was Jacob King, who held the office from 1854 to 1856. Eli Davidson, his successor, remained in office until 1858, at which time H. G. Curtis was appointed, holding the position until 1866, when he was succeeded by Leroy R. Curtis, who is still in charge of the office, and is the proprietor of the store. In 1848 S. M. Skeen opened a general store, which, since 1878, has been exclusively a drug store. There is also a hotel in the village. The only church is St. Mary's Catholic. The physicians are: Drs. J. W. Quarles and B. F. Price. In 1876 Selden McGirr erected a planing mill and sash factory, and in 1877 J. T. Seyler built a steam grist- and saw-mill now owned by Frank McGirr.

CEMETERIES.

There are no less than six places for burial in the township. Death and the narrow house were contemporaneous with the settler and his cabin. War and insidious disease soon made the "first house" a necessity, and too rapidly have the silent cities been established.

The oldest burying-ground in the township is located on the bluff at Cedarville, and was set apart for this purpose by the Ohio company. The pioneers were buried almost within the shadow of the old meeting-house. When the lot was laid off, it was a short distance from the river high up on a site, upon which nature smiled. In the river beneath with its accompanying stretches of scenery, and in the many evergreens on every side there were suggestions of peace and immortality.

Still surrounded by these emblems we found the last abodes of the fathers of the settlements east of the Little Hocking. The Ohio has gradually been encroaching upon this graveyard until it is feared that the whole will eventually be swallowed up by the rapacious stream. On account of this insecurity of the land there have been few interments since the earlier days, and there have been a number of removals. The cemetery is kept in good order, as in the days when Deacon Perley Howe was its sexton. Most of the graves are marked by head stones taken from the neighboring hills. The inscriptions are rudely chiselled, and on many monuments are illegible. It is impossible to give the name of the first person buried in this cemetery, inasmuch as both name and date have faded from public memory, and may never have been recorded on a headstone, for there are many unmarked graves. The earliest inscription is found on the monument of Israel Stone, jr., who was drowned in the Ohio April 25, 1791, aged thirteen. He who strolls among the graves and deciphers the moss-grown inscriptions, will find among the more prominent names and early dates the following, viz:

Jonathan Stone, died in 1801, Peregrine Foster, in 1804; Noah Sparhawk, 1807; Jonathan Haskell, 1816; Captain William Dana, 1809,

and his son Charles, in 1817, Deacon Benjamin Miles, 1817; Major Robert Bradford, 1822; Benjamin F. Stone, 1824; Theodore Foster, 1825; Amos Sternes, 1813; William Browning, 1823; Reuben Robbins, 1821; Colonel Silas Bent, 1848; Daniel Loring, 1825; Dr. William Beebe, 1821; Benoni Lewis, 1821; Joseph O'Neal, 1810; Levi Benedict, 1824, and others.

On one stone is found an interesting inscription in substance as follows:

In this vicinity Mrs. Armstrong* and her children were killed by the Indians on the Virginia shore in 1795. This stone is erected to rescue their names and fate from oblivion. Eerected by G. Dana, 1836.

In the vicinity of Newbury the traveller on the Ohio is attracted by the sight of a plain marble stone standing on the brink of the river. This monument is on the land cleared by Stephen Guthrie, and marks the graves of a number who died during the first years of settlement. The following is the inscription :

PIONEERS OF OHIO.

Anthony Spacht and his wife Catharine; Hannah, wife of Joseph Guthrie; Stratton, Levins, Bliss, †Denham; one woman and two children killed by the Indians. These and some other names, not remembered, died and were buried near this spot, between 1790 and 1810. Erected by some of their descendants as a token to their memory.

The mounds have sunk out of sight, and the old headstones which were once over the graves are now piled in a heap near the monument which was erected in 1871. Captain Eleazar Curtis, his daughter Eunice, and Noah and William Oakes, who were buried here were, in 1825, removed to the second graveyard, which was laid out back of the river, a little over a half mile directly west of the first burying-ground.

This second place of sepulture, though only one of "God's acres," is rich with the dust of those who were the pioneers of the neighborhood. The mounds are thickly strewn about as the autumn leaves. Whole families are here sleeping side by side, and almost every grave is marked by some memorial tablet or monument. With a praiseworthy regard for the beauty of the cemetery, it is kept green with numerous evergreens, and those who control it see that the graves are neatly kept. The first burial was that of Mrs. Eunice (Hoyt) Curtis, wife of Captain Eleazar Curtis, who died May 6, 1814, aged forty-nine years. An examination of the monuments shows that some are here buried who died prior to this date, but these were brought from other cemeteries. There are found the graves of the following of the most prominent pioneers: Joel Oakes, died in 1822; Captain Eleazar Curtis, 1801; Judge Walter Curtis, 1876; Truman Guthrie, 1841; Stephen Guthrie, 1827; Captain Charles Devol, 1845; Benajah Hoyt, 1807; James Knowles, 1830; Joseph Levins, 1814; Aaron Clough, 1824; Daniel Oakes, 1801; and many others. This cemetery is known as the Newbury burying-ground.

A little further west of the last named ground there is a family burying-ground belonging to R. C. Knowles. The first person buried there was Rebecca White. Those buried in this lot are members of the Knowles family.

The Little Hocking cemetery is one of the oldest in

---

* An account of this tragedy is given elsewhere in this chapter.

† This refers to Persis Dunham, killed by the Indians. The mistake in spelling occurred on the old stone, and was transferred to the new.

the township. The first one buried here was Nathaniel Sawyer, jr., who was drowned in the Ohio, June 14, 1801. Here among others are buried John Bartlett and Eleanor his wife; Mary Ann, wife of Elias Bellows; Ebenezer Porter and his wife Lydia, and Reuben Allen with Magdelene his wife. Here, too, are many forgotten graves. There is a neighborhood burying-ground about two miles due north of Centre Belpre post office. In this place are buried the families of the Delanos, the Coles, the Eastmans, and others who formally lived in the vicinity.

The principal burying-ground in the township adjoins the old brick Congregational church. The cemetery was laid out about the same time that the church was built. It was ready just in time for the reception of the remains of those who died during the sickly seasons of 1821-3. The first burial was that of Mrs. Mary Fisher. Other burials quickly followed, among them being Colonel Daniel Fisher, Charles Medburry, and Major Putnam and wife. Several additions have been made to the grounds, which now comprise several acres. It is not possible to note the names of even a small portion of the numerous burials that have taken place in this quiet country churchyard. Suffice it to say that since its beginning it has been the burying-ground of the neighborhood for miles around, and in this place sleep the departed friends and relatives of the majority of the people of Belpre township. The grounds have always been in charge of Cyrus Ames, who keeps them in good order. By a special act of the legislature in 1851 this cemetery was handed over to the management of the township trustees. All the other public cemeteries of the township are under the same control.

PERSONAL MENTION.

Stephen Druse, sr., settled in Warren township in 1817, having emigrated to Ohio from New York State, where he was born. He died in 1818 and his wife Nannie Denslow died in 1844. Of their children Riley and Stephen settled in Belpre township; Lucy (Cooper) lives in Iowa; Harrison is in Illinois, and Warren and Joseph are in Missouri. Riley who settled in Belpre was born in New York in 1806. He married in 1839 Mary Cockshott, a native of England. Six of their eight children survive, viz: Sarah, Mary A., Maria, Melissa, Olivia, and Lucy.

Hon. Charles H. Brough, brother of the famous "war governor" of Ohio, was born in Marietta in 1813. He lived in Marietta until about twenty years of age, during which he learned the painter's trade and assisted his brother in the publication of the *Register*. He afterwards removed to Fairfield county, Ohio, where he published a paper called the *Ohio Eagle*. He also represented that county in the legislature. In 1844 he removed to Cincinnati and purchased the Cincinnati *Advocate*, the name of which he subsequently changed to the Cincinnati *Enquirer*, the same paper now published by Faran & McLean. Mr. Brough was Colonel of the Fourth regiment in the Mexican war. In 1839 he was married to Abigail Ames of Belpre. He died in 1849, and his widow is still living in this township.

Mr. C. A. Brown was born in Marietta in 1835. His father was sheriff of the county. He afterwards removed to Athens county, but soon came back. Mr. C. A. Brown served through three years of the late war, and on his return in 1865 settled at Brown's Mills, Washington county, Ohio. Thence he removed to Belpre, in 1869, where he engaged in the grocery, book, and stationery business. He is still engaged in this business. He was married in 1856 to Miss Martha J. Breckenridge. He has two sons.

Mr. Andrew Breckenridge was born in Argyleshire, Scotland, in 1814 In 1836 he married Miss Jean Mackay, and the young couple immediately came to this country. They came to Washington county and settled in Belpre village. In 1869 Mr. Breckenridge moved to his present residence in Centre Belpre. In 1877 his wife died. Seven of the nine children of this marriage are still living, three sons and four daughters. His eldest son is a Congregational minister in Iowa. Mr. Breckenridge was married a second time, in February, 1881, to Mrs. Naomi Higly. Mr. Breckenridge started out as a poor boy, and has steadily risen by his industry and perseverance until he now owns a fine farm of two hundred acres.

Mr. George B Dunfee was born in 1816, in New Jersey. When he was two years old he removed with his parents to Washington county, Ohio, and from thence to Athens county, and thence to Little Hocking. In 1837 he was married to Miss Nancy Tipton, who is still living. They have had eight children, of whom seven are living. Mr. Dunfee is proprietor of the Dunfee house in Little Hocking. He has in his possession a passport given to his father in 1796, signed by Timothy Pickering, Secretary of State; also a description of his father, sworn to when he embarked on his journey to Jamaica in this same year. These papers are of great interest.

Parker Lewis was born in Harrison county in 1827, and in 1846 came to Belpre middle settlement. He married Elizabeth Pickering, born in Harrison county in 1828. They have had ten children, of whom nine survive. Mr. Lewis is engaged in the general store business. From 1846 to 1861 he was in the pork business, and has been engaged in the manufacture of grape wine. At one time he owned seventy acres of orchard land. He has been postmaster at Centre Belpre since the establishment of the office in 1873. He was township treasurer from 1866 to 1880. The names of his children are as follows: Morgan E., born February 22, 1847; Leonora, August 30, 1849; Levi L., June 10, 1851; Sylvanus P., September 14, 1853 (died January, 1860); Lizzie P., July 28, 1855; Isaac T., June 29, 1859; Lillie M., March 19, 1862; William P., December 2, 1863; Lincoln G., September 26, 1860; Seth E., January 12, 1868.

J. W. Davis came to Belpre in 1855 from Bellaire, where he was born in 1825. His wife, Anna Krebs, was born in 1831, and died in 1879. Their son, O. L. Davis, who is a hardware dealer in Belpre, married Julia Campbell, by whom he has one child living.

S. J. Spencer came to Belpre in 1858. He has been a river pilot during the last twenty-four years. He was born in Maysville, Kentucky, in 1829, and came to Ohio from West Virginia. In 1832 he married Lucy A. Henderson, by whom he has had six children: Josiah, William, Robert, Caywood, Emma Jane and Fanny. The two last named are now dead.

Dr. C. C. J. Guthrie located in Belpre in 1863, and is now in a large practice in the neighborhood. He was married in 1854, to Miss M. F. Collier. In 1871 they lost a child, Frank, who was killed by falling off the railroad bridge. There are three surviving children, viz: Anna, D. P., and George W. The sons own a drug store in Belpre village.

J. B. Mawhinney came to Ohio from Parkersburgh in 1866, whither he had come from Pennsylvania in 1858, and started a store in Cedarville. He has five children by his wife, Amy Wiley. He has been postmaster of the Rockland office, at Cedarville, since 1873, when it was established.

George M. Pinnell, born in West Virginia in 1850, came to Belpre in 1871. In that year he married Rosa E. Paden, by whom he has three children. Dr. Pinnell is a practicing physician in Belpre village and neighborhood.

J. M. Farson became a resident of Belpre upper settlement in 1866, having emigrated from West Virginia, where he was born in 1824. He married Catharine Stag, by whom he had nine children, five of whom survive. His first wife died in 1861, and he was married to Anna E. MacTaggart, a native of Wood county, West Virginia. It was on Mr. Farson's land that the old relic of the Mound Builders stood until he removed it several years ago.

H. W. Gettel, a resident of Belpre village, was born in Marietta in 1845, he being the son of Michael and Margaret (Molder) Gettel. He is one of the nine surviving children of a family of ten. He married Emeline Collins, who was born in Athens county in 1843. They have four children. Mr. Gettel has been in the bakery business during the last twenty years. He served on a gunboat during the late war.

In 1847 Thomas Hibbard located in the middle settlement, where he has since resided. He came from New York State to Ohio in 1822, stopping first in Meigs and then in Athens county. In 1848 he married Sarah M. Porter, born in this township in 1824. They have had two children—Sarah A., and Edna Amelia (deceased). The latter married David P. Guthrie, and left two children—Frank H., and Hattie A. Mr. Hibbard pays special attention to the raising of Spanish merino sheep.

Jonathan S. Plumly settled north of Little Hocking in 1839. He emigrated from Pennsylvania, where he was born in 1806. In 1828 he was married to Rebecca Nicholson, who was born in 1808. By this marriage nine children were born, five of whom are living, most of them being in Decatur township. J. N. Plumly was born in Belmont county in 1829, and came to Belpre with his father when ten years old. In 1857 he married

Susan Shotwell, of Belpre township. Six of their seven children are living.

James Gandee, born in Parkersburgh in 1825, went to Missouri, whence, in 1851, he emigrated to Ohio, locating in Belpre. In 1853 he married Maria Smith, by whom he has had two children—George W., and Mary A.—both living. Mr. Gandee is a farmer and stock-raiser, and has practiced medicine for over thirty years.

Robert Bess did not come into this township until 1851. He was born in Pennsylvania in 1817. In 1841 he married Ann Coates, who was born in England in 1823. Twelve of their fourteen children are living. He resides a short distance above Little Hocking, on the Ohio river.

Mr. William Mullen was born in October, 1822, in Newport, Washington county, and lived there until he was fifty-two years old. He was married in 1853 to Miss Mary C. Cook. Mr. and Mrs. Mullen have had four children, of whom three are living. All of the children were daughters, and the three surviving ones live in the county, the two youngest with their parents. Mr. Mullen has a fine farm near Belpre village. His parents were old settlers of the county, having moved to Newport in 1815. His mother is still living with him at the advanced age of ninety years. In spite of her great age she is still very active and vigorous.

Mr. Robert Brewster was born in 1820 in Watertown township. He removed with his parents when two years old to Chenango county, New York. At the age of thirteen he moved into what was then Roxbury township. He moved into Belpre township in 1864, where he now lives. He was married in 1859 to Miss Annie Bachelor, who died in 1853. By her he had one son who is now living. Mr. Brewster was married again in 1864 to Miss Sarah E. Knowles, who is still living. By this marriage Mr. Brewster has had three children, who are still living.

Dr. G. W. Reed was graduated in March, 1873 from Miami Medical college, Cincinnati, Ohio. At that time he resided in Harmar, Washington county. In June of the same year he removed to Lowell, where he practiced until September, 1880. He then removed to Belpre where he now has his office.

James Gandee was born in Parkersburgh, West Virginia, in 1823. He attended the schools in his native town until he moved with his parents to the State of Missouri. He stayed there about six years, making frequent visits to his old home for the sake of his health. He then came back and settled in Belpre township where he still resides. Mr. Gandee was married to Miss Maria Smith in 1858. They have two children, a daughter and son.

William H. Barkley has been a resident of Belpre all his life—fifty-nine years. The farm he now occupies his father purchased in 1822, but he came to the township as early, probably, as 1810. The tannery of William H. Barkley was established in 1867, and sold by him in October, 1880, to Kuhn & Brothers. Mr. Barkley was married in 1842, and has had three children, one having died.

JUDGE WALTER CURTIS.

PIC NIC GROUNDS.

RES. OF G. A. HOWE.

1798—Res. PERLEY HOWE.   1846—Res. R. W. HOWE.

BIOGRAPHICAL SKETCHES.

WALTER CURTIS.

In September, 1791, Eleazer Curtis, with his wife and six children, in company with Stephen Guthrie and a number of other young men, left their home in Warren, Litchfield county, Connecticut, destined for Marietta. The outfit consisted of one wagon drawn by two horses, and one drawn by four oxen. After a tedious journey of several weeks, the party reached McKeesport, and there sold one wagon and team, and bought a small flatboat, in which the whole company, with their goods and cattle were crowded. "All went along without any particular incident, until one cold, blustering day in November, the boat was permitted to drift too close to the Virginia shore at the head of Wheeling Island. One of the studding caught in an overhanging tree, causing it to spring off a plank." Mr. Curtis, "seeing the imminent danger of the flat sinking from taking in water, seized a feather bed and pressed it into the opening; the women and children were put into a canoe, the boat landed, and the stock driven ashore, and the boat was kept from sinking. Having repaired the boat, the next object was to hunt the stock that had strayed off into the woods, which caused a delay of nearly two weeks."

The Curtis family remained at Marietta about two years, and then joined the Lower Belpre settlement at Newbury.

Walter Curtis, the subject of this sketch, was born at Warren, Litchfield county, Connecticut, September 20, 1787, and was consequently four years old when the family came to the county. "About the year 1798," he says in a reminiscence of early events, my father was clearing land back of the hill; I was sent to the spring near by for drinking water, and while dipping up water, heard an animal walking in the woods, looking up, I saw a beautiful bay mare going toward the east. I ran and told my father, who went across the hill and caught her; this was the first horse owned at Newbury. The mare had undoubtedly been stolen from Virginia by the Indians, taken to the Scioto and was endeavoring to reach her old home.

Mr. Curtis' early education was quite limited, and in 1809 he spent about six months in college at Athens. Soon after becoming of age he commenced building keelboats, the lumber for which was prepared by the slow process of whipsawing, there being no saw-mills in the vicinity. The boats were loaded with produce and pushed up the Big Kanawha to Charlestown, where the produce was traded for salt, which was taken to Pittsburgh and sold.

Mr. Curtis, although deficient in early intellectual culture, had a thirst for knowledge, and by diligent study became a man of more than ordinary intelligence. An accurate memory and reliable judgment made him one of the leaders of society, as the several official positions to which he was chosen testify. Few men had a more intelligent acquaintance with history, and his reading

covered a wide range of literature. In conversation he was particularly interesting, always having at command a refreshing fund of anecdotes and quotations for illustration. He always interested himself in politics, was a Whig until the decline of that party, and then, until his death, acted with the Republicans. In religion he held decided views, but never subscribed to any creed.

Mr. Curtis represented his county in the legislature in 1827-8, was associate judge from 1824 till 1827, and served as county commissioner from 1852 till 1855. In the township and district offices he performed his share of duty.

Walter Curtis died, after a profitable life of nearly ninety years, June 27, 1876, having lived in the same community nearly eighty-five years, and at the same place eighty-three years.

For the benefit of relatives and friends the following family record is appended:

Eleazer Curtis was born in Warren, Connecticut, October 20, 1759. Eunice Starr, of Bridgefield, Connecticut, was born August 1, 1766, and was married to Eleazar Curtis, November 7, 1782. Their children were: E. S. Curtis, born in 1783; Jason R. Curtis, 1785; Walter Curtis, 1787; Mary Curtis, 1789; Benjamin Curtis, 1791; Horace Curtis, born at Belpre, 1793; Clarissa Curtis, 1796, and Lucy Curtis, 1800.

Walter Curtis was married to Almira Guthrie, February 3, 1819. They had four children, viz: A. S., born April 7, 1822; C. C., born April 11, 1824; Marian, born August 8, 1826; and A. L., born December 19, 1828. Mrs. Almira Curtis died May 13, 1880, aged seventy-nine years.

HOWE FAMILY.

Among the early settlers at Marietta, the name of Perley Howe appears. He was born at Killingly, Connecticut, May 14, 1768. He came to Ohio at the early period of settlement and was one of the first male teachers at the stockade. While there he formed the acquaintance of Persis Putnam, daughter of General Rufus Putnam, whom he married May, 2, 1798. He soon after came to Belpre and settled on a farm given him by General Putnam, on which his grandson, George A. Howe now lives. Mr. Howe was familiarly known among the old settlers, as "Master Howe." He, for a long time taught school in Upper Belpre, and the few old men yet living, remember him as their first teacher. He was one of the best teachers of the community, a good writer, and "good in figures." He lived to see the farm on which he settled, well improved, and the border country to which he came, developed into a well organized community. He died May 17, 1855. His first wife, Persis Putnam, died September 16, 1822. He married for his second wife, Sarah Emerson, September 2, 1827; she died February 19, 1863. By his first wife he had five children, viz: Joseph, born July 4, 1800; Perley, born May 28, 1802; Abigail Putnam, wife of William R. Walker of Athens county, born December 31, 1804;

67

Rufus William, born June 17, 1807, and Persis, born September 7, 1810, only two of whom married—William and Abigail.

Mr. Howe was commissioned Captain of the first brigade, third division of the Washington county militia, in 1804, by Governor Tiffin. At the time of Aaron Burr's conspiracy, this company stood guard, and Captain Howe was a witness at the trial.

Mr. Howe was one of the organizers of the Presbyterian church in Belpre, and was a deacon until his death, in his eigthy-eighth year.

Rufus William Howe was a farmer all his life. In his youth, after passing through the country schools, he attended the academy at Marietta, and boarded with General Rufus Putnam, his grandfather. He married for his first wife, Lucy Eastman, May 23, 1833, of the Lower Belpre settlement. She died September 22, 1834, leaving no children. He married for his second wife, Polly Proctor, of Watertown township, June 24, 1835; the family consisted of four children, viz: Joseph Perley, born April 6, 1836; George Augustus, born October 1, 1838; Rufus Putnam, born May 16, 1841; and Persis Putnam born January 1, 1844; two of whom are living—George Augustus and Persis Putnam. George, the second son, is the only member of the family who married. He married Charlotte Ann Wyatt, of Amestown, Athens county, October 26, 1865. They had five children, viz: Charlotte Wyatt, Mary Emily, Persis Putnam, Blanche and Jessie, the three oldest of whom are living. He married for his second wife, Mary S. Chapman, of College Hill, Ohio, February 12, 1880.

William Howe lived in a house facing Blennerhasset Island first, afterwards removed to the plain. A pictorial sketch of the residence of George A., which stands on the plain overlooking the valley and river, will be found on an adjoining page.

CHAPTER XXXIX.

WATERFORD TOWNSHIP.

Second Association Formed –Colony Lands at Tuttle's Run—Small Lots Drawn—Spring Crop—Military Company Organized—Game Plenty—General Prosperity—Inhabitants of the Garrison—Agriculture During the Indian War—Growth of the Colony after the Indian War—General Description of the Township—Plainfield, its Settlement—Beverly—Incorporation—Business Development—Stores — Mills and Factories—Machine Shop—Banks—Post Office—Olive Green Colony—Names of Families—Sherman Families—A Tradition — Round Bottom—Coal Run — Business—Coal Mines — Economic Geology—Coal Run Churches—Grange—Coal Run Post Office —Physicians—The Dana Farm and Family—Settlement of Federal Bottom—The Peninsula—Ownership — Business — Waterford Post Office—Tick Ridge—Ludlow—McIntosh — "Luke Chute"—White Cemetery—Religious Societies — A Benevolent Society — Masonic Lodge—Odd Fellows—The Encampment — Waterford Grange— Physicians — Township Organization—Early Justices of the Peace —The Beverly Press — Educational History — Early Schools — Beverly Academy —River Incidents—Union Fair—Salt Making— Discovery of Salt Springs—Salt Spring Company Formed—Success of the Industry—Pioneers and Prominent Families of the Township.

THE second association was formed in April, 1789, at Marietta. It was composed of thirty-nine members, most of whom had families. On the twentieth of April nineteen left the garrison at Marietta in a pirogue, and that evening arrived at the mouth of Tuttle's run, a small stream about one mile below Beverly. Here they pitched their tents, and began life in the woods.

The scene which on the following morning was presented to these adventurous pioneers furnishes food for the imagination. The alluvial bottom, both up and down the river, was heavily timbered with sugar, oak, and beech, and with a thick undergrowth of sapplings. About eighty rods back lay an extensive plain, which had at one time probably been an Indian clearing. Annual fires had prevented the growth of timber, and the whole area, about one mile long and half a mile wide, was covered with a matting of briers and underbrush. The forest on the fertile bottom on the opposite side of the river was unbroken. The bold cliff farthur up, beyond the bend, towered above the tall trees intervening. The settlers industriously plied their axes, and in a few days each family was living in a comfortable log cabin, and within a month each had cleared and fenced a small lot for a garden. Early in May another party came up from Marietta, and the settlement then consisted of the following families and single men: Those with families were Gilbert Devol, William Gray, William Sprague, Jonathan Sprague, Major John White, Noah Fearing, Major Coburn, Joshua Sprague, Henry Maxon, Andrew Story, Benjamin Beadle, Allen Devol, David Wilson, William Wilson, Wanton Devol, and Nathan Kinny. The single men were Asa Coburn, Nicholas Coburn, Phineas Coburn, Andrew Webster, Jonathan Devol, Samuel Cushing, Wilbur Sprague, Daniel Convers, Joseph Kitchen, and Andrew McClure.

The whole area of Waterford township lies within the tract donated by the Ohio company to encourage settlement, as has previously been explained in the general history of the county. But the presence of Indians of uncertain disposition, made it necessary that the settlement should be compact, so that the inhabitants might be able to give each other assistance in case of danger. A tract beginning where the town of Beverly now stands and extending about two miles down the river, was laid out in ten and fifteen acre lots. These lots were drawn by holders of titles to full lots lying further back.

On the west side of the river, Wolf creek bends around a gentle elevation which flattens out towards the west, leaving an irregular tract so nearly surrounded by watter, as to be called "the peninsula." This tract was laid off in five acre lots on the plan of the New England villages; one street running through the centre, another at right angles, and a third around the outside.

After providing plans of residence, the first work which engaged the attention of the associates, was preparing for the spring crop. It was a fortunate circumstance, not only for the Waterford settlers, but also for those of Marietta and Belpre, that the plain was already cleared. On a dry day in May, while a strong wind was blowing, fire was applied to the accumulated covering of leaves and decaying logs, and in a few hours the surface was ready for the planters' hoe. About eighty acres were planted in corn which grew rapidly in the mellow mold, and, aided by a favorable season, ripened early, thus escaping the destructive frost early in October, which threatened famine in Marietta and Belpre. Those settlements received considerable assistance during the following year from Waterford, where about three thousand bushels of sound corn was produced. The Waterford associates were saved at least one month's labor by the happy circumstance of this plain being already cleared. The soil having long been exposed to the sun, was warm and ready to receive the crop, and there were no trunks of deadened trees to retard its growth. The first block-house was built early in the summer of 1789 on the east side of the river. This was done in obedience to an order from General Putnam, notifying them of the murder of Captain King, of Belpre. A military company was organized, with William Gray captain, David Wilson sergeant and Andrew Webster corporal. Although the associates took these precautions and prepared themselves for an emergency, they had little fear of danger. Indians frequently visited them and traded with them, and Allen Devol says in his written statement, all worked at clearing, sowing and planting, without much fear, until the news of the massacre of Big Bottom.

The "Peninsula" was mostly cleared during the first season. Dean Tyler, Jarvis Cutter, and John Gardner owned lots on that fertile point. A block-house was built on the river bank just east of the road now leading to Watertown. It was occupied by Dean Tyler, and known by his name. In the latter part of September of this year, John Gardner was taken prisoner by the Indians while working on his lot on the "Peninsula.."

The winter was passed quietly by the settlers in their clearings and improving their homes. They had no fears of an attack on their settlement by the Indians, many of whom spent the winter in the neighborhood and traded at the settlement. Game was plenty. Allen Devol, in 1841 wrote: "We, in general, had plenty of provisions, wild meat in abundance,—turkeys, deer, and some bear. Deer were as plenty as sheep are now. We fattened some pork. Salt was hard to get in sufficient quantities. The inhabitants were healthy and in but little need of a doctor, or his medicines." There were yet no mills, Wolf Creek mill not being in operation until the spring of 1790.

The spring of 1790 brought to Waterford a number of families from the east, and a few from the other settlements. The abundant crop of corn of the previous summer gave some idea of the agricultural resources of the Muskingum bottoms, and donation lots were eagerly sought.

The clearings on both sides the river were being rapidly extended. Eighty acres had been sown in wheat, and preparations were going on for a large corn crop. Domestic animals and ground meal from the mill on Wolf creek greatly improved the table fare. Everything seemed propitious for a prosperous and happy year. In the fall a good crop of corn was harvested; wheat looked promising. At the opening of the winter of 1790–91 the two settlements of Plainfield—as the east side of the

river was called—and Millburgh, numbered about forty able-bodied men.

The principal events of the next four years have already been detailed in the history of the Indian war. To narrate them here would be simply a repetition of what has been said. Millburgh was evacuated, the neat little cabins by the riverside were left empty, and all were compelled to live together in the garrison, which stood opposite the high cliff east of Waterford village. The following are the names of the occupants of Fort Frye, as the garrison was called, during the war. Captain William Gray, wife and two children; Major Phinehas Coburn, wife and three sons, young men, Phineas, Nicholas and Asa; Judge Gilbert Devol, wife and two sons, Gideon and Jonathan, also one daughter; Wanton Devol wife and one child; Allen Devol, wife and three or four children; Andrew Story, wife and five children; widow of B. Convers, and eight children, James, a young man, and Daniel, a lad of fifteen years old; George Wilson, wife and two children; Jeremiah Wilson, two sons and two daughters; Benjamin Shaw, wife and two sons and two daughters; Nathan Kinny and wife; Joshua Sprague, wife and two children; Major John White and wife; William Sprague, wife and two children; Noah Fearing, wife and several children; Andrew Webster and son; Harry Maxon and wife; David Davis, wife and two sons, William and Daniel; David Wilson, wife and one child; Benjamin Beadle and wife. Single men, William McCullock, Neal McGuffy, Andrew McClure, William Newell, who served as rangers for the garrison; Samuel Cushing, William Lunt, Jabez Barlow, Nathaniel Hinkley; Dr. Thomas Farley (physician); Dr. Nathan McIntosh was surgeon's mate, appointed by the Ohio company for the soldiers. The spring after the war began eight or ten soldiers were sent up from Fort Harmar to assist in defence of the settlement.

During the Indian war the settlers always went out to work in parties. Two or more men were detailed to walk around the field and report signs of danger. This duty was considered the most perilous. The guns were stacked near the centre of the field under charge of a sentinel. When work had been done on one lot the party went to the next, and so on until all had been planted. The settlers were annoyed most by the Indians driving away their cows. This was the common device for decoying the men away from the garrisons.

The donation act of 1794, spoken of in the general history, brought many emigrants from the east, and the garrison at Waterford became too small to accommodate all. During the spring the Indians gave the settlement but little trouble, their attention being attracted by Wayne's army, then assembling on the frontier. The crowded condition of the garrison at Waterford, and the anxiety on the part of emigrants and settlers to improve and cultivate their lands, led to the formation of the Olive Green Creek colony in the spring of 1794.

The seventh of April was regularly celebrated by the associates with games of ball, foot races and other favorite masculine sports. We are told that "old and young zealously engaged." But there were also amusements in which the ladies could participate. Dancing was a diversion much encouraged by the elders and eagerly participated in by the younger members of the colony.

The establishment of peace in 1795 found the settlement in a very flourishing condition. They had become expert in dealing with their savage foes, and knew when danger was at hand and how to meet it. Their clearings and cultivated fields had been enlarged, the soil brought under a good state of cultivation, and abundant crops produced. In the fall of 1794 two hundred bushels of corn were marketed at the army posts at Fort Washington and Cincinnati. They received for this forty cents per bushel. This handsome income from the fall crop was a great relief, for home-spun linen and deer skin was their only materal for making clothing. Deer skin was much worn for pantaloons and jackets for a long time after the first settlement of the country. Sheep were not yet introduced, but hogs were fattened on the great crops of acorns and beechnuts, but little corn being required. Their table fare was all that could be desired, but the most important article for seasoning was wanting—salt. It could very seldom be obtained, and then only at an immense price.

The news of the permanent establishment of peace with the Indians was glad tiding of great joy to the inhabitants of the garrison. Clearings were opened and cabins erected on every bottom. Garrisons were abandoned, and the settlement, which had hitherto been compact, now scattered. The fertility of the soil had already become celebrated. Every week added new arrivals, and but a few years elapsed before every lot, with few exceptions, embraced within the present limits of the township, had been improved.

The donation of one hundred acre lots to actual settlers performed no unimportant part in the rapid progress of the settlement and development of the superior agricultural resources of the township. The township, as at present constituted, embraces a territory four miles wide and eight miles long, in the northwest corner of the county. The Muskingum river divides it into two approximately equal parts. The river flowing northward constitutes the western boundary. Thence, with many a curve, it flows in a southeast direction through the centre of the township. Along most of its course on one side or both fertile alluvions extend back to considerable distance. There is, therefore, in this township an unusual area of river bottom land. No part of Ohio can show richer soil or finer farms. No township in the county disputes the supremacy of Waterford in agricultural resources. Her tax per capita is higher than that of any other township. Two large tributaries empty into the Muskingum within its boundary. Wolf creek, the two branches of which unite just outside the township line, empties from the west opposite Beverly. Olive Green creek flows from Morgan county, and empties into the Muskingum two miles above Beverly. Along the courses of these streams are narrow and fertile bottoms. The extensive level tract on the west side of the river, east of the village of Beverly, is known as "Federal Bottom;" many things of interest are connected with its history,

and are narrated further on. In the lower part of the township, on the east side of the river, is the extensive level tract known as "Round Bottom." It receives its name from its shape, the bow of the river being opposite to the bow of the range of hills. Further up is the "Dana Farm." From near the mouth of Olive Green creek a ridge extends in an easterly direction, familiarly called, by the early settlers, "Tick Ridge," because of the unusual number of pestiferous wood-ticks. On the west side of the river the ridge, in the western part of the township, is commonly known as "Righteous Ridge," but contrary to what might be expected, it is said to have been so named because of the wickedness of a former class of settlers.

THE PLAIN.

From Tuttle's run, above the "Dana Farm," the narrow alluvion rises gradually to an extensive plain, already spoken of as the place of the first settlement. As has been explained, this tract was divided into small lots of ten or fifteen acres each. When the war closed, these lots had been cleared, and commanded the highest price. Many lot holders of "Plainfield" traded for lands in the other districts of settlement, and gradually these small portions were grouped together into large farms.

Joshua and William Sprague lived at the lower part of this tract for a short time. George Wilson had a cabin near the garrison which he afterwards sold to Ephraim Cutler, esq. Gilbert Devol owned the farm further down now owned by some of his descendents. Wanton Devol owned an adjoining farm. The Convers family, Captain William Gray, Captain Daniel Davis, George Wilson, William Wilson, and Nathan Kinney lived in this neighborhood. William Gray originally owned the sixty-eight acre lot, on which most of the town of Beverly now stands. It was transferred by him to Exphraim Cutter and by him, in turn to John Dodge in exchange for about six hundred acres on Federal creek, Athens county. Two stores were kept on the east side of the river at an early day. The first was opened by Ephraim Cutter, esq., who continued to do a general mercantile business till the Amestown colony was organized in 1799. This was probably the first store in the township. He was succeeded by a Mr. Allen. A Mr. Hart was in mercantile business in 1806, but on which side of the river is not remembered.

BEVERLY.

Work on the Muskingum river improvements, from 1837 to 1841, brought to the community a great many laborers, for whom houses and stores had to be provided. The want of a village had long been felt by a populous and wealthy community. But something out of the ordinary current of affairs was needed to draw capital into a business channel. The impetus was furnished by the Muskingum river improvements in two ways; first by attracting laborers; second, by furnishing means of transportation, and water power for mills and factories. John Dodge saw his opportunity and laid out a portion of his land in town lots. Aside from the advantages of water-power, the site for a town is very favorable. The river flows on three sides and affords excellent drainage.

George Bowen

The subject of this sketch was born at Hartford, Connecticut, August 25, 1796. While yet in youth, his father, Consider Bowen, removed to Pittsford, Vermont, and here George received the benefit of the earlier district school education and training. In 1818 he came to Ohio and stopped at Waterford, to visit his brothers, and was advised by Dr. Ebenezer Bowen, at that time in full practice, to study medicine. He was without money, but the services of efficient men were in demand to supply the schools. Too many of the schools of that period were taught by shabby pedagogues, of which class of individuals there was an overplus; but a young man of good training and strong character had no difficulty in getting a situation, although the wages were not a great temptation. Mr. Bowen taught a school and studied medicine for a period and then attended medical lectures. He began practice in partnership with his brother, Ebenezer Bowen, during the sickly season of 1822-3. His success in treating fever during that distressing period gave him a deservedly high reputation for tact and skill as a physician, which he maintained during the whole of his long and useful life. He continued in partnership with his brother until the latter removed to Rochester, New York, in 1838. As long as he was able to attend to professional calls—until a few years before his death—Dr. Bowen was the favorite family physician and was counseled in all difficult or serious cases in the community. He was a man of unusual tact, being peculiarly happy in his ability to cheer the patient and encourage the family. In this particular his large soul and happy disposition were a positive professional benefit. His wife was Mary J. Wheeler, of Bridgeport, and his family consisted of three sons and two daughters, whose names and addresses are given in the body of this chapter.

Dr. Bowen's political affiliations were with the Whig party in Whig days, but he became a Republican when that party was organized. His love of country and respect for the constitution moulded every act of his life. During the Rebellion he supported actively the cause of the Union, giving the weight of his influence to the raising of troops, and generously handing out his money for their support in the hour of suffering. He showed his faith in the cause of our armies and his confidence in their final triumph, by freely buying Government securities when half the north assisted the Confederacy, by hesitation and doubt.

Dr. Bowen was a man of strong religious convictions, although a member of no religious organization. He sought an intelligent knowledge of the Bible and Christian doctrine. Distinguished for his upright and honorable disposition, few have ever to-day received more fully the confidence and respect of his fellow citizens, and few have discharged the duties imposed upon them with greater fidelity. He was a business man of rare sagacity, but used his accumulated capital for the benefit of the community. In later life he was an extensive lender of money, but his leniency in dealing with honest and industrious young men is remembered with gratitude by many who have been the recipients of such favors. He was one of the founders of the First National bank of Beverly, and was for many years its president.

Dr. Bowen's personal appearance was commanding and dignified. He was thoroughly democratic in feeling, associating freely with the masses, attending all who desired his professional services, whether rich or poor, and whenever money was wanted for a needy charity he responded with a free hand. He never failed to meet a professional engagement, was methodical in his habits, and diligent in the performance of every duty. Dr. Bowen was widely known as a practitioner. Had he devoted himself less assiduously to practice and given more attention to writing, his fame might be wider. He devoted his life to the service of a community which recognized in him a personal friend. He died in Waterford, May 24, 1874.

C. Bowen

The late Charles Bowen, of Waterford, was born in or near Hartford, Connecticut, September 25, 1798. His parents were Consider and Sabra (Hosmer) Bowen. When the subject of our sketch was very young, the family removed to Pittsford, Vermont, and it was from that place that Charles Bowen emigrated to Ohio. He came out as a young man some time prior to 1820, with his brother, Ebenezer. The journey, as far as Rochester, New York, was made in a sleigh, from thence to the Allegheny by wagon, and from thence to Marietta by a flat-boat or raft. The location at Waterford was influenced by the fact that an older brother, James, had already settled there. No sooner had Charles Bowen reached his destination than he began the exercise of that remarkable industry which made his career one of marked success. His employment was carding and fulling. He was first engaged with his brother James, at the old Creek mill, known as the Dodge mill. The brothers afterward built a mill at Federal bottom, but while that was being fitted up, Charles Bowen went to Sistersville and worked for a year or so for a Mr. Greer. The Federal bottom mill did not long occupy the attention of the brothers, but they returned to the mill at Waterford, on Wolf creek, which they conducted until 1831. They added saw-mill machinery, and carried on the business of making lumber in connection with the carding and cloth fulling. On coming to Waterford, Charles Bowen knew nothing of the trade upon which he entered, and relied at first upon the experience and skill of his brother James, who had learned the trade in Vermont. Charles, however, soon became familiar with the work, and, in addition, developed considerable general business ability.

In 1831 the Bowen brothers bought the store at Waterford, owned by Abigal Brooks, and some years previous by A. T. Nye, of Marietta. Charles Bowen gave his attention to this store until 1866, when he sold out to General H. F. Devol. The last fifteen years he conducted the business alone, having bought out his brothers in 1851. He increased the business to proportions, which, considering the small size of the place, were immense. The business consisted largely in the handling of produce and Mr. Bowen became so popular as a buyer, that he received the grain and pork from many farmers to whom Marietta, Zanesville, or other points would have been more convenient markets. His repu-

tation he always paid cash, gave him a great advantage, both in buying from the farmers throughout the country, and in purchasing goods from the New York merchants whom he went on to see regularly twice a year, as was the common custom. Mr. Bowen seemed to have a feeling against going into debt which was so strong that it amounted to an abhorrence. He refused to avail himself of his credit which was as good as that of any man in Washington county, and invariably refused to make purchases unless able to pay cash for them. Beginning with absolutely nothing except his energy and industry, he accumulated a large fortune. Nearly the whole of it was made in his mercantile business. Mr. Bowen had few business interests outside of his store. He was, however, as long as he lived after its establishment, a director of the First National bank of Beverly. He had no taste for speculation, and upon the other hand evinced no disposition to hoard money. His interest in money and gain was only that of the conservative business man. He was liberal of his means toward worthy causes, and did much to advance the interests of the community in which he dwelt, and of the country around about. In early times when most of the improvements upon roads were made by personal donations, he probably did as much as any man in the county to keep them in good condition, and was a frequent and generous subscriber to funds for building bridges, etc. Although not a member of any church, he was a supporter of religious organizations all of his life, after he became able, and when he died he left bequests to the Methodist Episcopal church of Waterford, and the Presbyterian church of Beverly. He was a man of exemplary morals, and of blameless life. His integrity was of the strictest kind. With what may be called his business and moral characteristics were combined fine social qualities. He was very pleasant in intercourse with his fellow men; treated every one with kindly consideration, and was a warm friend. He was very widely known and everywhere liked for his sterling qualities and genial, cheery ways. Politically he was affiliated with the Whig and Republican parties. Mr. Bowen never married. He made his home with his brother, Dr. George Bowen, in the brick house in Waterford built in 1824, and latterly the home of General H. F. Devol and family. Mr. Bowen died suddenly, either from heart disease or apoplexy, April 7, 1874.

The lots and streets are rolling and dry, and the surrounding scenery is beautiful.

There are in the village four churches,—Presbyterian, Methodist, Universalist, and Baptist; an academy, which has always enjoyed a good reputation; a variety of stores for all kinds of trade, and a variety of manufacturing establishments.

The village was named Beverly by John Dodge in honor of his native town in Massachusetts.

INCORPORATION AND OFFICERS.

Section nineteen of the act of the legislature, passed February 18, 1845, reads:

That so much of the township of Waterford in the county of Washington as is comprised within the following boundaries, to wit. Beginning at the Beverly dam in the middle of the Muskingum river, thence down the river to the southwest corner of the parsonage residence of the Cumberland Presbyterian church (lot now owned by V. Adams), thence north to the northeast corner of the college lot on which the college building stands, thence northwest to the place of beginning; is hereby created a town corporate to be designated and known by the name of Beverly, and by that name shall be a body corporate and politic, with perpetual succession, but all lands, town and out-lots within said boundary not numbered as town lots shall be exempt from taxation for incorporation purposes until the same be laid out and numbered as town lots.

An election was held for corporation officers March 7, 1845, which resulted in the choice of Samuel Anderson, mayor; Thomas Hodge, recorder; and John McCane, William McIntosh, Ellis Slater, Leroy B. Harwood, and Joseph Nickerson, council.

At a subsequent meeting of the council, ordinances of a general character were passed. A marshal was appointed and a tax of two mills on the dollar for corporation expenses levied. The town government was now fully organized.

BUSINESS DEVELOPMENT.

The first store of any considerable size was opened in 1837 by Colonel E. S. McIntosh, in the brick building on Canal street, now known as the "Danley hotel." Mr. McIntosh had built this house for the purpose the previous year. Mr. McIntosh disposed of his business to S. F. Seely, who held a large patronage till 1871, when he died.

Oliver Tucker began the hardware business in the large frame building on the corner of Fourth and Canal streets in 1855. The house had been built about five years before by Samuel McConnel and John Buck. In 1866 Lycurgus Tucker started a dry goods store in the other room of the building. The two stores were consolidated in 1869 and have since been owned and managed by Oliver Tucker. Both stores are stocked with goods varying in both price and quality. General produce is purchased. Mr. Tucker has for a number of years held the leading trade in the village.

In 1864 Richards & Brother opened a store on the corner of Fifth and Canal streets. In 1868 it was purchased by J. A. Wood, who, in 1861, sold to C. M. Devol.

The drug trade was commenced in Beverly by Dr. A. S. Clark in 1856. He has been engaged in the business since that time.

Dr. Joseph Parker opened a drug store in 1865 and has been engaged in the business since, on Canal street.

J. B. Bane opened the first shoe store in Beverly, about 1850, on the south corner of Fifth and Canal streets. D. C. Staley began business with him in 1865. Mr. Staley established a business of his own in 1872. He now has a neat and extensive store and a flattering trade. He also owns a store in Athens, and an interest in one in Boston.

The Grange supply house, a corporation, was established in May, 1877.

C. R. Stull opened a large double store on Fourth street, in 1873. He deals in books, stationery and notions, also fire-clay, piping and casing.

MILLS AND FACTORIES.

The first mill in Waterford township (as the lines now run) was built at the first rapids on Wolf creek, on the neck of the peninsula, by Jonathan Devol. This mill had a good run of custom in seasons of high water, but in dry weather the water power was insufficient to run the machinery. At such times the whole neighborhood, for miles around, were dependent upon the Featherston mill, on the Muskingum, which is mentioned under the head of "Federal Bottom." Jonathan Devol sold his mill to John Dodge, about 1814, and, in 1816, connected with it a carding machine, which he placed in charge of James Bowen. Bowen afterwards moved the machinery to the Featherston mill, down the river, where the business was carried on for several years.

The manufacture of cloth was a slow and tedious process. Machinery was used for carding alone. The spinning and weaving belonged to the women's list of duties.

Charles Bowen, after a few years, associated with his brother James in the business of wool manufacturing. Fulling the cloth, after it had been spun at home, became a part of the work of the factory.

The Muskingum improvements changed the location of the milling industry. The Lowell dam destroyed the water-power at Dana's Island, but made it applicable at Beverly.

E. S. McIntosh built the first grist-mill on the east side, below the Beverly dam, in 1843. This mill is now owned by Whissen & Worstell. Its capacity is about seventy barrels a day.

In 1849 S. G. Hodge and Thomas Irwin leased from the State water-power, and built a woollen factory, known as the Beverly woollen mills. William McIntosh purchased this establishment in 1859. It was transferred by him to D. T. Brown, in 1863, and has been conducted by him since that time. Two improved sets of machinery were put in by Mr. Brown, who has engaged extensively in the manufacture of cassimeres, jeans, blankets and yarns. He also does a jobbing and retail trade, and custom work. In 1880 Mr. Brown connected with his factory a saw-mill. He manufactures wagon and carriage supplies, and does a general custom business.

In 1856 Dodge, Bane & Co. built a grist-mill on the island, between the canal and river, known as the Island mills. They are the largest in the township, having a capacity of about eighty barrels a day. The property was purchased by Higens, Whissen & Co., in 1860. In 1862 Whissen, Green & Co. became the name of the firm. In 1867 they connected with it a woollen factory, known as the Island factory, which cost twenty-two thousand dollars. The firm of E. Lindner & Co. purchased the entire establishment in 1876, and failed in 1878. Clark & Stull purchased the grist mill in 1880, from the receiver, C. R. Stull, for three thousand and fifty dollars. It originally cost sixteen thousand dollars. In May, 1880, W. H. Bush purchased the woollen factory for two thousand six hundred and sixty-six dollars. The machinery in the woollen mill is of the best quality, enabling the proprietor to manufacture all kinds of woollen goods. The capacity of this establishment is about one hundred and forty yards per day.

The next mill was operated by H. C. Baldwin, and was called the Novelty mill. The machinery was afterwards sold, and the building is now used by Denny & Spooner as a saw-mill and grain cradle factory. The manufacture of grain cradles is made a specialty by this firm.

The old machine shop at the foot of Canal street was converted into a grist-mill, and is now operated by H. C. Baldwin.

The saw-mill on Canal street, owned by A. Pomeroy, has been operated since 1856. Mr. Pomeroy has had connected with it a lumber yard, and during Beverly's years of prosperity, had a large trade.

It is to these mills and factories that Beverly has owed her prosperity in past years. Excellent water power, superior shipping faculties, and a productive farming territory attracted capital and trade. But the completion of an immense system of railroads has left Beverly behind with regard to shipping faculties, and not until an ample connecting link with the outside world is furnished will there begin a new era of prosperity.

FOUNDRY AND MACHINE SHOP.

The first foundry in Beverly was built by John Dodge in 1852, at the foot of Second street. It was operated and owned by Sidney and Patterson Dodge until 1857, when it was purchased by Mathew Patterson and W. F. Robertson. The manufacture of stoves and plows and general repairing was the class of work done by the Dodge brothers. In 1859 W. F. Robertson sold his interest to Dr. James Little. The firm name was Patterson & Little until 1863, when Dr. Little purchased his partner's interest and conducted the business until May, 1864, when the firm of W. F. Robertson & Co. was organized and rented the shops from Dr. Little for a period of five years. The members of this firm were W. F. Robertson, W. Preston, Benjamin McAtee, and Robert Clark—all trained mechanics except Mr. Robertson, who took charge of the business office. In 1868 the firm built the shop on Fourth street, and in January of the following year the new building was occupied. J. D. Lashley was made a member of the firm in 1872. In January, 1881, the firm purchased the property of the Marietta Lock works, at Harmar. They manufacture plows, cook and heating stoves, hollow ware, etc., and do general machine work.

BANKING.

By 1863 Beverly had become a flourishing village, and her business men felt the want of a banking institution. The matter was discussed, but no definite action was taken until the National banking act opened up the prospect of a profitable investment.

FIRST NATIONAL BANK.

A meeting of citizens was called in Union hall, September 19, 1863, at which it was decided to establish a National bank, and books were opened for subscription of stock. At the same meeting the following named gentlemen were elected directors: George Bowen, P. O. Dodge, E. S. McIntosh, H. C. Fish, J. B. Bane, Charles Bowen, and C. M. Devol. At a subsequent meeting of the directors Dr. George Bowen was elected president, and William McIntosh, cashier. The capital stock was at first seventy-five thousand dollars, which was increased to one hundred thousand dollars, and afterwards to one hundred and fifty thousand dollars. George Bowen subsequently resigned the presidency, and William McIntosh was elected to fill the vacancy. S. R. McIntosh became cashier. In 1871 E. S. McIntosh was elected president in place of William McIntosh, deceased, and C. W. Reynolds became cashier. In 1874 the bank went into liquidation.

CITIZENS' BANK.

In March, 1875, the Citizens' bank was organized. E. S. McIntosh was elected president, and C. W. Reynolds, cashier. This organization continues to the present time. Business has been conducted since the organization of the first bank in the same room, on the corner of Fifth and Ferry streets.

POST OFFICE.

Beverly post office was established in 1838, John Keyhoe, postmaster. It was kept in Reil Darfris' tavern, near the foot of Second street. It was afterwards moved to Fifth street. Mr. Keyhoe died in 1857, and was succeeded by his wife, and after her death by his son, Ephraim. J. C. Preston was in charge of the office from 1861 till 1877, when A. J. Spooner succeeded and remained in charge till December, 1880. S. G. Hough has been postmaster since that time.

OLIVE GREEN COLONY.

Olive Green creek, one of the principal streams of Morgan county, empties into the Muskingum about two miles above Beverly. For about one mile up from the Waterford curve, a bold hill of unusual height rises from the eastern bank, presenting to the river a fine cliff of sandstone, shale and limestone. From the summit of this hill a view of unusual beauty is obtained. Above this ridge the river flows through a rich bottom about two miles in length. The alluvial belt on the east side is from a quarter to a half mile wide, and is divided into two almost equal parts by Olive Green creek. In this fertile bottom, which is all included in Olive Green allotment, Ezra Shermrn drew lot No. 1, Aaron DeLong, 2; Abel Sherman, 3; Nicholas Hoyt, 4; George Ewing, 5; Josiah Sherman, 6; Mathew Gallant, 7; John Coulter, 8.

These men were all heads of families. Abel Sherman built a block-house on DeLong's lot, and the other families built around it and the whole collection of houses was picketed in, thus forming a garrison. The inhabitants of this garrison numbered thirty souls, one of whom—Thomas Ewing—Ohio remembers as one of her greatest men.

The Sherman family is particularly interesting on account of the melancholy fate of the head of the family. An account of the murder of Abel Sherman will be found in the General Indian History, in this volume. About 1789 the Sherman family, consisting of Abel Sherman and wife, two sons—Ezra and Josiah—and one small daughter, Amy (since Mrs. Samuel Beach), removed from Connecticut to Short Creek, Virginia. At a later period, probably about 1793, they came to Waterford and remained in Fort Frye until the next spring, when the Olive Green colony was organized and Sherman station established. The murder of Mr. Sherman occurred August 14, 1794, near a small stream one mile above Beverly, which to this day bears the name of "Dead Man's Run." The body was first buried on his own land, then on his son's—the lot now owned by John Nulton. In 1877, Joseph and Jackson Beach, grandsons, removed the remains to the cemetery at Waterford. The lower jaw-bone was found in a perfect state of preservation. The teeth are all sound and clear. A peculiarity of the skull, too, seems to confirm a tradition of the death of "Silver Heels," a noted Indian warrior, who after the peace lived near a ripple in the Muskingum called "Silver Heels' ripple." About four years after peace with the Indians Silver Heels chanced to visit one of the salt furnaces in Muskingum county, and while there imbibed freely of the whiskey offered him. He soon lost his discretion and began to boast of the great things he had done during the war. He had taken seventeen scalps. One was of a man, he said, who had two crowns on his head. He had shot him in the evening below the mouth of Olive Green creek. He made two scalps by carefully dividing it, and received fifty dollars for each. He further related that the man was gathering May apples and had the bosom of his shirt full of them at the time. He described the gun which had been set against a tree while engaged in picking fruit, as a musket with iron bands around it. He said he had placed it in a hollow log a few rods up the creek.

The story corresponded so well with the known facts of the tragedy that a son of Mr. Sherman, who happened to be present, was induced to make search for the gun, which he found near the spot where he had four years before found the dead body of his father. Silver Heels was found a few days after this night's revel lying in a by-path in the woods, pierced by a rifle bullet.

Most of the families of Sherman station, after the country was cleared and became quiet, sought homes elsewhere. The fertile bottom which they cleared has always been preferred land, and is now in a well improved condition.

The cemetery on the Nulton farm, in which the bodies of a number of pioneers were interred after Sherman's murder, has been abandoned and the remains moved to Waterford.

ROUND BOTTOM.

The settlement of "Round Bottom" began early in 1795. Some of the heavy timber had been cut before that time, but property owners were not willing to risk the dangers of a residence so far away from the garrison before permanent peace with the enemy was established. Some of the most worthy of the settlers improved farms on this extensive alluvian—Samuel Cushing, Allen Devol, David Wilson, Benjamin Shaw, Andrew Story, and at a later period Samuel Beach. Boylston Shaw next came into possession of the Shaw farm. It is now owned by William Shaw.

A cemetery was laid out at an early period on the Cushing farm, which has since borne the name of "Round Bottom cemetery." A school-house was also built at an early period of the settlement. The bottom proper is an exclusively agricultural district, and in fertility of soil is equal to any part of the township or county. The farm residences are nearly all large and in good repair, showing a healthy condition of worldly prosperity.

COAL RUN.

At the lower end of Round Bottom is situated the thriving little village of Coal Run. It sprang into existence upon the completion of the Muskingum improvements, and until the building of the Duck Creek railroad was one of the best shipping points on the river. The produce of the eastern part of Morgan and southern part of Noble was marketed here. This trade made a village which coal mines continue to support.

The first store was opened in 1837 by Elijah Stephens, in a log building which stood on the Marietta & Beverly road. Successive merchants after him were Andrew Oliphant, W. R. Sprague, and Wilson & Brown. At present there are two general stores and one drug store. The Rose Brothers began business in 1878, and have since been favored with a large patronage.

George Hughes was the pioneer wheat merchant at this point. Silas Thurlow followed him in the business, and in 1857 Alonzo Hall engaged in the trade and continued twenty years. He has probably handled more grain than any one man between Marietta and McConnellsville. J. C. Farnsworth and Rose Brothers are now engaged in the trade.

Samuel Beach built a distillery in the neighborhood, and operated it by horse power for a number of years. In 1831 he purchased steam fixtures and connected with it a mill. This was the first mill on Round Bottom, and the first steam mill in the township. He sold both distillery and mill in 1837.

COAL MINES.

The most valuable feature in the economic geology of Waterford township is in the heavy seam of coal, cropping out at the foot of the hill just back of the village. This seam is about four feet thick. The coal is of fine quality and easily mined.

The Sycamore bank was opened by Henry Laughery

& Co. in 1857, on the farm of William McAtee. This bank is now operated by Keever & Hardin, who employ about fifteen men.

The seminary bank, now operated by the same company, is situated in Adams township on land owned by Beverly college. It was opened by J. N. Henry and I. R. Rose in 1876. This bank gives regular employment to fifteen or twenty men.

In 1874 an unsuccessful attempt was made to open a coal mine on the Dana farm. Good coal was found, but the expense of operating was too great to justify the continuance of the mine.

The geology of the region around Coal Run may be worthy of attention. The upper rock stratum is heavy white sand, selected portions of which would be fine enough for glass making. Other portions might be profitably used for hearthstones for furnaces. There is a seam of coal lying under this sandrock, but it is too thin for profitable mining. There is also a stratum of limestone which is of proper quality for making excellent cement.

The manufacture of fire brick was once engaged in to a limited extent. It could, perhaps, be made a paying industry.

CHURCHES.

In 1852 the growing village felt the need of a church; money was raised by subscription among all classes of citizens, and a neat frame house, called the Union church, was built. It was intended for the use of all denominations, but the church-going people were nearly all Disciples and Methodists, so that its use was confined to those two denominations. The old adage "that two families cannot live in the same house" is, perhaps, also true of churches. In 1858 the Methodist congregation, which, through the labors of Rev. George Willis, had perfected its organization the year previous, decided to build a house for its own use. The Methodist congregation has had the services of a regular pastor since the date of organization. A list of ministers will be found in connection with the Beverly church, with which Coal Run has been connected since 1858. The most prominent of the first members were Silas Thurlow and wife, John Flag, Martha Thurlow, Elijah Sprague, Lewis Pyle, Thomas Hilton and wife, Ann P. Wilson, Mrs. Henry, Erastus Eddy and wife, and John Sprague and wife.

The Disciple church was organized in 1852, and was for many years a flourishing congregation. Of late years, however, its strength has declined. Its ecclesiastical connections have always been with Adams township, where the reader is referred for a list of ministers. Services are now held only occasionally.

GRANGE.

Adams Grange No. 260 was instituted at Coal Run December 23, 1873. The charter members were W. A. Devol, Joseph S. Sprague, W. W. Mason, Miles Humiston, H. O. W. Ross, Sylvester Mason, J. W. Frye, Philip Trapp, Mrs. Ross, Mrs. Devol, and Mrs. Sprague. This society is yet in a healthy condition. Meetings are held in the room over Rose Brothers' store.

POST OFFICE.

Coal Run post office was established in 1839, with Hiram Beach in charge. Successive postmasters since have been J. D. Beach, Benjamin Wilson, Jeremiah Wilson, Alonzo Hall, James Morrison, F. M. Hilton, Josiah Johnston, and Manning Rose.

PHYSICIANS.

The first physician established at Coal Run was William Henry, who opened an office in 1879, and remained in the community one year. He is now located at Lowell.

Manly H. Sprague, a graduate of Columbus Medical college, opened an office in 1880.

The community is said to be unusually healthy, and the services of those useful members of society are fortunately not often needed.

THE DANA FARM.

The large estate, lying within the bow of the river, below Tuttle's run, containing more than fourteen hundred acres of excellent bottom and plain land, was accumulated by a single individual—Benjamin Dana. The Dana family are descended from a French Huguenot family, which left France in 1629 and settled in England. Richard Dana was born in England in about 1640. He emigrated to America and settled at Cambridge, Massachusetts, where he married Ann Bullard. From them all the Danas in this county are descended. Benjamin, third son of Richard Dana, was born in Cambridge in 1660; he married Jane Buckminster. Isaac, third son of Benjamin, was born in 1698, and lived in Pomfret, Connecticut, where he married Sarah Winchester. His son, John Winchester Dana, married Hannah Pope Putnam, daughter of General Israel Putnam. We now come to the generations in whom we have a local interest. Benjamin Dana, third son of John Winchester, was born in Pomfret, Vermont in 1770, where he received a farmer's training. He came to Ohio in 1794 and engaged to clear four acres of heavy timber in Wiseman's bottom for his cousin, Israel Putnam, for which he received a yoke of oxen. In 1796 he purchased two lots (one hundred acres each) from Charles Mills, opposite the island now known as Dana's island. The whole reach of fertile bottom was then a dense forest of heavy timber, mostly sugar. Mr. Dana built a cabin near the centre of his farm, and continued to add lot after lot on all sides, until he owned thirteen hundred acres of land, equal in quality to any land in the county. In 1818 he erected the farm house which is still standing.

Mr. Dana was at that time perhaps the most energetic and progressive farmer along the Muskingum. He made the most of all the resources of his land. Sugar making was an industry in which he engaged very extensively. Improved methods of refining were adopted and the productions of his camp found a ready market.

Mr. Dana was the pioneer shepherd of the Muskingum valley. He stocked his farm with sheep at an early period, and was largely instrumental in securing to the early settlers of the county a market for their wool. One other fact bearing on his farming economy is worthy of imitation. He provided substantial and comfortable outbuildings in which to shelter his stock and preserve their food. Many farmers of the present period would find it to their financial advantage to imitate this example of one of the most successful of the pioneers.

A community is always interested in the personal history of its leading men. Mr. Dana was cool in temperament and decided in his opinions, which were the product of mature deliberation. In religion he held strongly to the school of Free Thinkers, and it was not until after he had spent several months in New England visiting the pious Deacon Fitch Pool, at Danvers, Massachusetts, that he was convinced of the truth of Christian doctrine. During the latter years of his life he was an orthodox believer.

In 1801 Mr. Dana was married to Sallie Shaw, daughter of Benjamin Shaw, one of the forty-eight who came to Marietta in April, 1788. A family of six daughters and one son was the result of this union, viz: Mary, wife of Benjamin Putnam; Eliza, wife of Henry Fearing; Eunice, died single; Charlotte, wife of Dr. Joseph Allen; Hannah, wife of Joseph Chambers; Caroline, wife of D. Edward Dawes; and John Winchester Dana, into whose possession the farm came after the death of his father, July 22, 1838. Mrs. Dana died August 22, 1842. All the members of this old family are now dead. John Winchester, the only son, married Catharine Devol, by whom he had two children: Marietta, wife of J. H. Hubbell, and Caroline, both living in Boston. They own the estate, which is probably the finest in Washington county.

FEDERAL BOTTOM.*

There were squatters on the bottom at a very early day, but among the first land-holding settlers was James Convers, in whose name lot number six was drawn. He had a little grocery near the run at the upper end of the bottom, probably for the accommodation of the settlers going over to the floating mill. He afterward went down on the Mississippi. The distillery mentioned further along probably had the same line of customers. The seasons being a week or two earlier, and the bottoms more ample on the left bank, determined the earliest settlers to that side of the river.

Early in his career Benjamin Dana was undecided on which side to settle. He had a small clearing made and an orchard of grafted trees (probably obtained from General Putnam's nursery at Marietta) planted on the right bank of the river, a short distance above the bend. A two-story log house was built about one fifth of a mile above the bend, and sometime between 1800 and 1802 it was occupied by Stephen Devol and his mother. In 1802 Theophilus H. Powers, of New Canaan, Fairfield county, Connecticut, came out and settled at a point somewhat further up the river. But he soon came down to the bottom, married a sister of Stephen Devol, and built a log house, with a cellar under it, close to the river, about one hundred and fifty yards below Still brook. He and his wife soon separated, and she eloped with a man named McAtee.

----

* By Stephen Powers.

Still brook (now known as Hanford's run) derived its name from the circumstance that a distillery was built on its banks at a very early day by some person unknown. It did not remain long; it was destroyed by a cloudburst which was so heavy that cattle were swept by it down into the river; not a timber of the structure was left on the foundations.

Another incident of very early times was the death of Gideon Devol, November 21, 1795. He had been out gunning, and wandered about until he became hungry and exhausted, when, on his return home, he sat down at the foot of an immense sycamore in the sugar-camp, about a half mile above the mouth of Congress run, and froze to death.

In 1805 Andres Powers followed his brother to Ohio. The two seemed to have bought together the upper third of the bottom; and November 20, 1805, Andres bought of Benjamin Dana the lower portion, two hundred and thirty-five acres, for one thousand three hundred and eighty dollars. The brothers now owned the entire bottom. Their neighbor on the east was Cushing Shaw, on the south, "lands unknown."

Andres settled first in a log house at the mouth of Still brook. He lived here a year or so, then moved down into the house occupied by Stephen Devol and his mother, who moved down the river about Lowell, I believe. In this house William H. Powers was born in 1807. After this time Stephen Devol returned, married Betsy Gray, a daughter of Captain William Gray, and took up his abode in the house at the mouth of Still brook. A few months after her second child was born she was crossing the river with the babe in her arms in a canoe propelled by her brother, William Gray. He being unskilful drove the canoe on a snag within three rods of the shore, and Mrs. Devol and the babe were thrown out and drowned. Gray sank to the bottom and crawled ashore. The body was not recovered for some days, when Theophilus Powers, standing in the mill, chanced to see it go over the dam. This was April 11, 1811.

For his second wife he married, in 1815, a daughter of Deacon David Wilson. In 1812 he bought of Theophilus Powers, for four hundred dollars, twenty acres of land, on which stood the two-story house. After several removes Andres Powers finally built a plank house on the brow of the second plateau, a little below the bend, with a cellar under it, and provided with the first well on the bottom.

The orchard mentioned above was just coming into bearing in 1805. It yielded a large amount of fruit. A good deal was shipped to Zanesville in canoes and pirogues, where it frequently sold as high as fifty cents for a dozen apples. One early Chandler tree finally attained the remarkable height of sixty feet and upward, and some of the yellow russets had a diameter of over two feet. Having grown with great rapidity in the rich virgin soil, it decayed with corresponding rapidity, and the remaining trees, being nearly useless, were cut down about 1860.

Benjamin Knott took a small lot to clear and fence with a log fence just below the orchard, for which he was to have two crops from it. He built a log house a little above the bend. About 1812 Andrew McClure took, on similar terms, another lot, two hundred yards above the mouth of Congress run, on which he also built a log house. Andrew had been a scout in the Indian war, and was somewhat unsteady and inclined to drink too much. He married Polly Devol, sister of Gideon. She was a notable housekeeper and an exemplary woman. She was a member of the Presbyterian church, a useful member of society, and reared seven children, most of whom turned out well.

Phineas Palmer is mentioned in Andres Powers's account-book as early as 1811. He built a log house on the plain about 1814. He made shoes for the settlers, of buckskin and rawhide, and took his pay in corn, potatoes, and whiskey.

The pioneers had little variety in their bill of fare except what they procured with the gun. The deer frequently came in and ate their pumpkins all hollow for the sake of the seeds. Theophilus Powers used to shoot them from his door. Wild turkey abounded; when scared from the corn-field they would run out of it in a long string, single file. Taking advantage of this habit, Theophilus once killed seven at one shot. For weeks together there would be no bread on the table but "Johnny Constant," as the Virginians called it. It was baked in a thin cake on a board set slanting on a block before the fire. The blackened board and block were a staple article of household furniture, being generally seen lying in the corner of the huge fireplace. One Pliny Danielson, who came to learn the cooper's trade of Andres Powers, after being on a straight Johnny-cake regimen for several weeks, on coming in one day and seeing the corn-cake going to the table, stopped short and pulled a doleful face as he exclaimed: "I wish the man who invented Johnny-cake had died in his infancy!"

There was a floating mill on the other side of the river, opposite the upper end of the bottom, which was run in connection with the post, and owned by Truman Peet and Asa Davis. They afterwards sold it to James Mann. It had a wide run of custom, even from this side of the river. But the inconvenience in crossing was considerable, and the back country on this side was now filling up with settlers as early as 1810.

Andres Powers threw a dam diagonally nearly across the river at the head of Dana's island, and built a grist- and saw-mill at the mouth of Congress run. The people came to this mill from places twenty-five or thirty miles distant, long lines of pack-horses wending their way through the forest. The grinding went so slowly, that the men sometimes had to wait for their grists several days, subsisting the while on raw wheat, pawpaws, apples and nuts. Methodists coming to the mill, were frequently entertained while waiting by Stephen Devol.

My father remembers that the children from the other side crossed the river to school a whole three months' term on the ice. Another winter, when the ice broke up, partly demolished Benjamin Knott's house, and bent numbers of the young apple trees down stream—a position which some of them still retained when two feet in

diameter. The first school on the bottom was probably taught by Reuben Culver, in the little log house at the mouth of Still brook. An old school-bill for 1818 shows the following number of scholars: A. Powers, eight; T. H. Powers, three; S. Devol, three; T. Featherston, two; P. Palmer, two; William Crawford, one. The teacher got ten dollars a month. All the sons of Andres were like him in character,—quiet, hard-working, God-fearing —except Stephen. He loved his gun, and loved the girls—a jolly soul, and when a boy, he was sometimes set to plowing corn with an old man named Lyons, who kept him at it early and late. In passing a stump, he would slip down off the horse on the stump, and take to his heels, the old man in hot pursuit.

Among the early inhabitants of the bottom was the widow Bolls. During the Indian war she was in the fort on the other side of the river. Going out for some green corn one day, in company with her father and younger sister—both girls then—they fell into an Indian ambuscade, the father was killed, and the girls captured. After a march of some days the Indians halted and went out foraging, leaving the girls in charge of an old Indian. The Indian fell asleep, whereupon the elder of the girls dispatched him with an axe, and they escaped, and after a fatiguing and perilous journey of several days they arrived at the fort.

Theophilus Powers, was a noted politician, a keen observer, a great reader of the Bible, and a heated controversialist, always defending Calvin in religion (notwithstanding his loose practice), and the Federalists, in politics. During the War of 1812 political discussion waxed hot. There were some noted Democrats at Waterford —Captain James Leget, Robert Leget and John Patterson among them—and Theophilus would frequently stay up there until long after midnight, waging a wordy battle with them and others. His delight knew no bounds when he could worst them, which he generally did, for he was a man of large information. His prominence and the number of other Federalists on the bottom procured for it its present name. Congress run was named by the surveyors.

Keel-boating was much followed in these early days. About 1815 two men named Pedingale and Dutton, built and launched one a little below the bend, named her the Dutton, freighted her with hoop-poles, and ran them down to the Kanawha salt-works. The keel-boats were constructed much after the fashion of a canal-boat nowadays, handsomely trimmed and painted, and having a "race-board" on each side for the crew to walk on in pushing. These race-boards were supported by rows of "knees," which were pieces of timber sawn or hewn from a stump, forming right angles. They were firmly pinned to the sides of the craft, and afforded a strong basis not only for the crew, but also for barrels and other heavy freight to be tumbled about on. The regular crew was six men and a captain. On the ponds all the crew set their poles at once; but in ascending ripples, they had to "break hands," as it was termed. The captain (always at the helm) would cry out "Up at the head!" when the two nearest the bow would go forward and set. Then he would cry out again "Seconds, two!" when the two next would go up. Then "Up behind!" when the two nearest the stern would go up and set. In this way there would always be at least two poles set, so that the boat could not get the advantage of them. They were sometimes half a day in foraging up in this laborious way by Dana's island. Sometimes they would come up on this side, when they would probably fall foul of Andres Powers' dam, and then would ensue much cursing, and they would get out and rip up the dam. This caused considerable trouble, but still the dam was maintained.

Andres was not a miller (he was a cooper by trade), so he did not make head with his mills. He left his farm to be carried on by his boys, and they did, as boys will, and he became involved in debt. May 15, 1817, he sold the two mills and thirty acres of land adjoining to Thomas Featherston for four hundred and fifty dollars. John Featherston, a son of Thomas, and subsequently Abner Fish, a son-in-law, were the principal millers. From about 1816 Andrew McClure attended the saw-mill, what little work it did.

Thomas Featherston, commonly known as "Daddy," was a small man but mighty in exortation, an ignorant but sincere zealot, and the first Methodist speaker on the bottom. He held meetings in his little house by the mill, and many hearers were gathered, some of whom were greatly moved. He sang, shouted, and prayed; some of them were seized with "the power;" women laid off their bonnets and shawls that they might not injure them when pirouetting about over the benches. Bill Cooey, a notorious counterfeiter and thorough-paced rascal, shouted loudest of all; but the sound of his shouting was not orthodox, he "could not get the hang of it," and the brethren received him not. The meetings were subsequently adjourned to the little log school-house which was built a few rods up the river. It was here the writer first went to school, and sat on backless slab benches through which the wooden legs protruded in an inconvenient fashion.

A very different character was Isaac Childs—"Old Daddy Childs"—a Revolutionary soldier, who strayed on to the bottom about 1819. He was a queer old cock; would eat only two meals a day; fond of his grog; fond of a good horse; delighted to boast of the soldier days when he lived on quarter rations. Still he contrived to do a good deal of work for Andres Powers. He cleared a patch at the first fork of Congress run, still known as Childs' place, where he built a log hut and "took up" with a strolling woman. To make him a suit of clothing she would lay him down on the floor, on the cloth, and cut it out by his figure. They had two children, but their paternity was involved in obscurity. Finally the neighbors interfered and had them married in due form.

As early as June 27, 1814, Andres Powers had a carding machine in the garret of his mill, and it was managed by one Samuel Andrews, who carded wool at ten cents a pound. It did not continue many years in operation.

About 1822 or 1823 James Bowen bought the saw-mill, in company with his brother Charles, and they enlarged it and put up a carding- and fulling-mill. The saw-mill stood close to the shore, the fulling-mill next beyond, and the grist-mill quite out over the water. The three were propelled by two long undershot wheels. James subsequently erected much the best dwelling which had yet appeared on the bottom. Mrs. Bowen was an excellent woman; and the genial, liberal hospitality of herself and husband, together with the hearty manner in which they entered into the celebration of the holidays, etc., rendered their house the delight of children.

In 1825, worn out with his many and arduous labors, Andres Powers went to his premature death. He was a simple, sincere Christian; one of those plain, strong men who are builders of the States. Deborah, his wife, was a worthy helpmate to him, a genuine type of the Puritan wife and mother. She ruled her house in the strictest fashion; she never would allow but one cooked meal to be eaten on the Sabbath, that was breakfast; the remaining meals must be bread and milk lunch. When she came to live with us my mother never ventured to transgress this tradition of the house; and even when my wife ascended the throne, long after grandmother had gone to her grave, although she gradually introduced a cooked dinner, she never dared wholly to break over this family usage; and to this day the pitcher of milk standing on the table at our Sunday dinner bears silent but eloquent testimony to the strong will and the rigorous creed of this revered mother in Israel.

A little hamlet grew up about the mills. Benjamin Knott had built a log house at the mouth of the run about 1807. Featherston's house was close to the mill. William Wilson, a chair-maker (about 1829), David McNeal, a blacksmith (about 1833), John Ormiston, a wagon-maker (about 1839), established their trades here. As yet Beverly had not even a beginning. Featherston had sold a part or the whole of the grist-mill to Abner Fish and Robert Leget (two sons-in-law), and in 1833 Daniel Gage bought it of them for eight hundred dollars, and thirty acres of land from Featherston for two hundred dollars.

In 1828 Stephen Devol sold to the trustees of the Methodist church, for one dollar, a lot near the river, on which, largely through his efforts, a church was erected. During quarterly meetings forty guests would sometimes be quartered on his hospitality. His excellent wife labored unceasingly to provide for them. The church was built close to the land of Theophilus Powers, who chose to consider it an affront; and he assailed it in eccentric ways, with profane and bitter hostility, boasting to his dying day that he never had entered it.

Daniel Gage and his large family of daughters were of the more genial New England type—genuine money-loving Yankees, but fond of gaiety, and several of them artistically and poetically gifted. The arrival of so many blooming girls in a new country was very refreshing to the young men, and they straightway laid siege to them. They furnished an even half-dozen of the best wives and housekeepers in the whole country-side.

One H. Windsor burned a brick-kiln and built a distillery at the extreme lower end of the bottom at an early day. In keeping an account with him Andres Powers makes this quaint entry in his book: August 3d. Commenced pasturing oxen at one-half gallon of whiskey per week." Jacob Proctor, a pioneer schoolmaster, is charged with a barrel of whiskey at eight dollars. Andres and an ex-clergyman named Shattuck, or Chadwick, laid the foundation for a distillery on the plain, but abandoned the enterprise. Notes of hand in those days often read, "to be paid in wheat, rye, corn, beef, pork, whiskey, or neat stock."

The dead were at first buried at the upper end of the bottom, but a cemetery was afterward established on the high ground back of the mound, and the dead were removed to it.

The completion of slack-water navigation rendered the dam and the mills useless, and the hamlet gradually went down. Daniel Gage received from the State nine hundred and fifty dollars as compensation, and James Bowen, one thousand dollars.

THE PENINSULA.

The only building on the "Peninsula" during the Indian war was the block-house occupied by Major Dean Tyler. At the close of the war these lots, like those on the "plain," were grouped together in small farms. One lot had been set aside for a cemetery, and is still used for that purpose.

John Patterson, after the War of 1812, opened a tavern at the ferry. For a long time his was the only house of entertainment in the neighborhood.

Jonathan Devol built a mill on the rapids of Wolf creek, which he afterwards sold to John Dodge, who connected with it a carding machine and fulling apparatus, under the management of James Brown.

It appears from deeds and transfers that the greater part of the peninsula farms was at one time owned by Dr. Seth Baker. Jonathan Sprague, Thomas Featherston, and Dr. Pardee, owned individual lots. Rotheus Hayward afterwards purchased the lower part and Joseph Chambers the upper part.

MERCHANDISING.

Waterford has always been a good trading station. Joseph Chambers was probably the pioneer in business at this point. He opened a general store on the Watertown road before 1814, and continued in trade until the year 1839.

Ichabod Nye established a store on the opposite side of the street in 1817. A. T. Nye took charge of this establishment in 1819, and continued in business till 1828, when Abijah Brooks bought him out. About 1833, Charles Bowen began merchandising on this corner, and may be said to have built up the large concern now owned and managed by H. F. Devol. General Devol purchased this establishment from Mr. Bowen in 1866, since which time he has been engaged in general produce and mercantile trade.

Mr. Vaughan has a store on the site of the old tavern stand of John Patterson.

John Patterson was the first postmaster. Hiram Beebe is the present incumbent.

OTHER SETTLEMENTS.

The bottom opposite and west of Beverly was originally settled by William Gray, Andrew McClure and Major John White.

Captain William Burnham was one of the first to make an improvement on the ridge on the west side of the river. Reuben Culver was the pioneer on the ridge south of Waterford village.

Thomas Seely made the first improvement on the ridge on the east side of the river. During the Indian troubles he lived in the garrison at Marietta. In 1795 he removed to "Tick Ridge," where he lived until his death, in 1829. He was a native of Stanford, Connecticut, and was one of a family of twenty children. His wife, whose maiden name was Holcraft, also had nineteen brothers and sisters. Other early settlers of this ridge were Benjamin McAtee, Oliver Shoot, Peter Keath, Mr. Gibbs, Peter Sachel, Jesse Davis, Abram Stevens, and Elias Boudinot. E. S. McIntosh carried on merchandising near the county line from 1823 to 1835. He also had at his store a post office called "Ludlow," from 1827 to 1835. He then moved down the river below the mouth of Olive Green, where he had a post office called "McIntosh," for about eighteen months.

"Luke Chute" is the name of a post office, and also of a trading-post, on the Muskingum river, on the western border of the township. A. Nickerson has for a number of years had a store at that point, and was in 1880 commissioned postmaster. The tradition for the origin of this name is that during the early settlement a father and his young hopeful son, whose name was Luke, were out hunting. The boy, of course, had the gun. In a deep thicket both were startled to see a bear walking upright towards them. Luke took steady aim but hesitated to fire. The father trembled for a moment and then screamed in impatient fright: "Luke shoot or give up the gun." Luke shot and the bear dropped dead.

The cemetery on the hill west of the site of the old Wolf Creek mills is one of the oldest in the township. It is known as the "White burying-ground." It was laid out and first used by the Haffield White family.

The soil on the ridges of this township produces fair crops but is inferior to the river alluvions. The population is rather sparse and the farms are large.

LEAF FROM AN ACCOUNT BOOK.

The index of E. Cutter's ledger, which was opened at Waterford in 1795, and closed in 1800, gives an approximately accurate list of persons who traded at this point during that period. Then as now all the neighboring settlements made this a centre of trade, it is therefore probable that many whose names are given lived without the present limits of the township; we know some of them did. Attention is called to the peculiar arrangement of names. The fact that they stand in alphabetical order with reference to the first name, seems to indicate that people were known more by their Christian than their family name. The index is as follows: Andrew Webster, Abraham Stevens, Abigail Dye, Andrew Story, Andrew McClure, Asa Coburn, Amos Harvey, Aaron Delong,

STEPHEN DEVOL, Jr.   MRS. STEPHEN DEVOL.

An outline of the Devol family is given at another place in this history, but our subject was so widely and favorably known and characterized by so many interesting eccentricities, that a fuller sketch is demanded.

Stephen Devol, jr., was born at Tiverton, Rhode Island, March 2, 1786. He came to Ohio with the family and was seventeen years old at time of the death of his father. His educational facilities were necessarily very limited, but he became inured to hard, patient labor, and until the beginning of the sickness which terminated his life, Mr. Devol rarely sought rest. He married for his first wife Betsy Gray, December 5, 1808. She was a daughter of Captain William Gray, of the Waterford garrison. Two children were the fruit of this marriage—Tillinghast, the oldest, born 1809, followed flat-boating and steam-boating and acquired considerable money. He died at St. Louis. While Hiram, the second child, was yet a babe, Mr. Devol was bereaved of both wife and child. April 10, 1811 was muster-day, and Mrs. Devol desired to cross the river to witness the drill of the militia company of which her husband was a member. While crossing, the skiff which was in charge of her little brother Willie Gray, became unmanageable and upset near the shore. Mrs. Devol and her child were drowned; her brother escaped by crawling to the shore on the bottom of the river.

Mr. Devol married for his second wife, Rebecca Wilson in March, 1815; one year later he followed her remains to the grave.

He married, October 27, 1818, Silence Buell, widow of Mathew Buell. Her maiden name was Silence Hatch and she was born in Connecticut, June 23, 1795. By her first husband, Mathew Buell, she had three children —William, Louisa and Helen, the last of whom married James Sheldon, and resides in Zanesville. By this marriage Mr. Devol had five children, viz: Theodore, born February 28, 1820; Hiram, born February 7, 1824, died September 6, 1829; Emily (Hayward), born September 1827; Hiram F., born August 6, 1841; Betsy (McCaddon), born January 12, 1835, and Louisa (Shaw), December 29, 1836.

Mr. Devol's industry has already been spoken of. He owned about fifty acres of land on Federal bottom, which was in an excellent state of cultivation and produced remarkable crops. He was methodical in his agriculture as in other things, doing all his work with regularity and according to system.

One of his most interesting characteristics was his hospitality. Early in life he joined the Methodist church, and from that time on his house was made the stopping place of preachers and members. During the early days of Methodism in this county, churches were supplied entirely by circuit preachers, "who had no home but the back of a horse." They visited each preaching place periodically, and the membership being widely scattered people came great distances to church. The quarterly meeting services were particularly well attended. The meeting-house stood on one corner of Mr. Devol's farm, and his doors were always open to all who came. Circuit preachers, local preachers, and laymen with their families, made themselves at home at his house, but not always at the farm, for the even temper of the boys was not unfrequently disturbed by having a sufficient number of horses to take care of to supply a cavalry company. As many as forty guests sometimes dined at the Devol residence. But Methodists were not the only class who were benefitted by his hospitality. Farmers who came to the Featherston mill and waited for their grists also found comfortable entertainment here. The Masonic lodge, of which Mr. Devol was a member, were sometimes given a banquet.

Mr. Devol was a pillar of the church. Through his influence the first Methodist meeting-house in the community was built and service mainly supported by him. He was unable to pray or speak in public, but performed his part of the service by leading the singing. His usual seat was at the side of the pulpit, and no service could proceed until he had concluded two or three songs. Mr. Devol's inability to speak or pray was probably owing to his naturally retiring disposition, although he sometimes made feeble efforts.

With all his peculiarities Mr. Devol was a good neighbor, a good Christian, and a good man. He was crippled by disease late in life and compelled to resign his labors, which had been performed as regularly as clock-work all his life.

Mrs. Devol was a woman well fitted for the trying duties of her position. Always cheerful, always kind, a murmur or complaint rarely escaped her lips. She was in every regard an excellent housewife, mother and Christian. During the last years of her life she suffered physical distress, but was resigned until death called her home.

Mr. and Mrs. Devol spent the last years of their life at the house of their daughter, Mrs. Hayward. They lived to see their children all comfortably situated in life, and the burdens of invalid old age were lightened by the sympathetic care of an affectionate daughter.

Mr. Devol died at Waterford, January 21, 1875, having almost completed his ninetieth year.

Allen Devol, Aden Waterman, Benjamin Beadle, Benjamin Carter, Benjamin Shaw, Benjamin Dana, Benjamin Rogers, Charles H. Martin, Charles Williams, Charles Coleman, Conrad Sherman, Captain Daniel Davis, Dean Tyler, Daniel Convers, David Wilson, Daniel Walsworth, David Stephens, Daniel McCulloch, David Randal, Daniel Davis, jr., Eben Cony, Eben Sproat (lived at Marietta); Francis Pearce, George Wilson, Gilbert Devol, esq., George Ewing, Hezekiah Davis, Major Haffield White, Ensign John White, Jesse Gibbs, Joseph Pierce, Joseph Parker, Josiah Sherman, Captain James Brown, James Convers, Joseph Frye, Jonas Ward, Jonathan Devol, Joshua Sprague, James Mann, Colonel Joseph Thompson, John Brown, James Vaughn, John Green, John Leget, Jesse Brown, Levi Allen, Matthew Gallant, Moses Davis, Nathan Hinkley, Nehemiah Sprague, Nicholas Hoyt, Nathan Kinny, Nathan Abbot, Nicholas Coburn, Phinehas Coburn, Peter Shaw, Peter Van Cliep, Peter Noblaise, Richard Woith, Robert Oliver, Simon Nott, Sylvanus Olney, Samuel Cushing, Simon Convers, Samuel Sprague, Samuel Baker, Samuel Baker, jr., Timothy Boothby, Titan Kimble, Thomas Seely, William Davis, William Whitten, William Gray, Wilbur Sprague, William Smith, Captain William Burnhans, Wanton Devol, William Wilson, William Sprague.

The following suggestive coincidence appears from these books:

May 15, 1795, yesterday William Wilson, William Kinny, and Mr. Whipple were drowned.

May 16, 1795, Nathan Kinny (father of William Kinny) to one Bible, eight shillings.

RELIGIOUS SOCIETIES.

The Waterford settlers had a deep regard for religion and the Sabbath. The Ohio company had provided for regular preaching, but the state of the country prevented the perfect working of the system. Dr. Story, during the whole period of the war, occasionally came up from Marietta, by water, and attended by guards and scouts. These visits were highly appreciated by the settlers, who nearly all attended the services. Major Dean Tyler, who was a deeply religious man and fine scholar, regularly held service in his block-house, except on the Sabbaths when Dr. Story was present. The settlers united in the songs, and the venerable major read a sermon from the works of one of the old standard divines. In this way, while the settlement was for the most part without a preacher, they had the benefits of preaching and the privilege of participating in religious worship.

FIRST PRESBYTERIAN CHURCH OF BEVERLY.

In 1795 the country rapidly filled up, churches being organized and society rapidly improving. Between this time and 1804 the Presbyterian church of Waterford was organized, and in September of that year Rev. Jacob Lindley was installed pastor. The services, which were very impressive, were held in a meadow. Many people came fifteen or twenty miles. A few years later a church was built on the east bank of the Muskingum, at the lower edge of the town of Beverly. It was built on the general plan of country churches of that day, being two

stories high, with spacious galleries. The pews were rented, and several wealthy members rented several of them, which they generously gave up to those who had none. Many years afterward it was remodelled after a modern fashion. It was finally abandoned, and the present commodious brick edifice, in the centre of the town, was occupied.

The church remained Presbyterian, as organized, until 1833. Rev. Jacob Lindley had become president of the Ohio university, at Athens, and had changed his church relation and united with the Cumberland Presbyterian church. The pastors, up to this time, were Revs. Jacob Lindley, Chadwick, Boise, and John Pitkin. In December, 1832, Mr. Lindley, in company with Revs. Sparks, Donald, and John Morgan, came to Beverly and held a protracted meeting, resulting in a great revival and many conversions and additions to the church. As another result of this memorable occasion, on the first Sabbath of January, 1833, by a unanimous vote of the congregation they became the First Cumberland Presbyterian church of Beverly, and continued as such until April, 1878, when they were received into the Presbytery of Athens, and are now known as the First Presbyterian church of Beverly. During their connection with the Cumberland Presbyterian body the pastors were Revs. Lindley, McCollum, Barclay, Martin, Thomas, Moore, Brice, and Tenny. In June, 1878, the Rev. W. M. Grimes was chosen pastor, and entered upon his labors the first Sabbath of August, and is faithfully laboring to build up and increase the influence of the church.

In the earlier years of this church the observance of the Sabbath was a peculiar feature. At sundown on Saturday all labor was suspended, and until sundown of the Sabbath the time was strictly kept sacred, no secular duty being performed, and all light reading and conversation strictly forbidden. After sundown on Sabbath evening all who chose might engage in their ordinary avocations.

It is recollected that some fifty years ago, during the pastorate of Rev. Mr. Moore he preached many sermons four hours long, commencing at nine o'clock A. M., and closing at one o'clock P. M. Then came an hour of intermission followed by another sermon of *three hours* in delivery. Many families came from five to twenty miles and attended these services with remarkable regularity. Not only so, but the matter of each sermon was carefully digested and fully studied and discussed the week following by those zealous Christians and their households. The house is said to have been greatly crowded, and the attentive audience could not all be seated. The character of the preaching was doctrinal, homilitical in great part, though occasional exhortatory sermons were preached. The singing was remarkably good. In the church were several persons who had received a careful training in vocal music during their youth in New England. The choir was composed only of those who were regarded as proficient in the art of singing. The chorister, Colonel Simeon Deming, used an old-fashioned wooden pitch-pipe with which to find the key note. The old church-goers assure us that, assisted by his chosen choir he performed Bridgewater, Easter Anthem, Mortality, St. Marlins, etc., with a style and grandeur quite unapproachable by modern singers. Instrumental music was early introduced, and with little interruption has always continued.

God has signally blessed this church. The pastors have been superior men, both as students of the Bible and as teachers, and consecrated their time and talents to the service of God and the church with that cheerful zeal which God has promised to bless.

In addition to the great meeting in 1832, during the winter of 1836-7, under the preaching of Revs. Thomas Squier and Baird, occurred a wondrous revival. The meetings continued several weeks and about one hundred professed religion, many of whom united with the church. During the pastorate of Rev. S. McCollum, more than forty persons made profession of religion and united with the church in a single season, and in the winter of 1866, under the ministry of Rev. Dr. Brice, there were nearly forty accessions. Since that time accessions have been made which more than balance the losses by deaths and removals.

The following are the present officers and societies: Rev. W. M. Grimes, M. A., pastor; Stephen Powers, D. C. Aikin, H. F. Devol, Oliver Tucker, L. Skipton, ruling elders; Oliver Tucker, H. S. Clark, J. R. Sheldon, trustees; Mrs. C. W. Reynolds, organist; Miss Hattie Devol, assistant; Mrs. A. P. Clark, chorister.

Sabbath-school—H. F. Devol, superintendent; D. C. Aikin, assistant; Miss Alice Tucker, secretary and treasurer; H. C. Baldwin, librarian.

Saving Fund society—Mrs. L. Seeley, president; Mrs. J. B. Devol, vice-president; Miss Alice Tucker, secretary; Mrs. Jane Tucker, treasurer.

Woman's Foreign Missionary society—Mrs. C. F. Hayward, president; Mrs. L. Seely, vice-president; Mrs. C. W. Reynolds, secretary; Miss Georgie Shaw, treasurer. Board of Cheerful Givers—Miss Georgie Shaw, leader.

METHODIST CHURCHES.

Methodist meeting was held in the vicinity of Waterford soon after the establishment of the church in this county in 1800. Methodism at Waterford, as at Marietta, was at first unpopular, but vigorous preaching and untiring missionary work soon prepared the people for the organization of a class. The first meeting-house in this part of the county was on the west branch of Wolf creek, in Watertown township. Waterford was a preaching station in 1815, and may have been earlier. The first church stood in Federal bottom. Stephen Devol was the leading member. The present building is the third house of worship. Waterford was connected with the Barlow circuit until September, 1879, when the Waterford circuit was instituted.

At the time of the organization of the Waterford class it belonged to Marietta circuit. Leroy Swomstedt's preaching greatly strengthened the cause, but two years later Jacob Young says he found the church very weak. This was about 1829. "Methodism, in the earlier history of Waterford, had to stem a current of popular opinion, and when the ship was badly managed she floated down stream."

When Barlow circuit was instituted Waterford was made one of the preaching stations.

The ministers of Waterford circuit have been Homer C. Bright, A. B. Cochran, and E. W. Ellis.

The first Methodist Episcopal class in Beverly was formed with three members in 1837, by Revs. E. L. Miller and Chester Morrison. William H. Preston, of Ludlow, was appointed class leader. The society met and held its services in a small school-house on the corner of what is now Seventh and Center streets. It was made one of the preaching places of the McConnelsville circuit, Barnsville district. The society grew rapidly, and in 1844 began the erection of a house of worship on the corner of Sixth and Centre streets. This house was built of brick, but was defective in its masonry, and was never finished. It was, however, used for the services of the church until 1858, when the present commodious edifice was built on the same site, and near the close of the year was dedicated by Rev. Dr. D. W. Clark (afterwards bishop). Rev. G. G. Walters was pastor at this time. The congregation has enjoyed a steady growth in membership from the date of its organization, and is now strong and prosperous. It belongs to Cambridge district, East Ohio conference. The Sunday-school is well attended, and the Woman's Foreign Missionary society has been highly praised for the efficiency of its work. The following is a list of ministers who have served the society since its organization: Chester Morrison, William Athey, Abner Jackson, Pardon Cook, John Mercer, A. D. McCormick, James Means, George G. Walters, A. Ward, John Grant, Edward Ellison, J. Crisman, A. Huston, J. Keagle, David Cross, H. B. Edwards, F. W. Veitican, J. E. Hollister, D. C. Knowls, E. B. Edywell, A. R. Chapman, Theodore Finley, W. H. Piggot, F. D. Fast, J. C. Feitt, and T. F. Phillips.

UNIVERSALIST SOCIETY.

In the summer of 1841, G. T. Flanders, who was at that time editing a Universalist paper at Zanesville, stopped at Waterford on his return from a trip to Marietta and preached in the school-house at Beverly. The families in the neighborhood who at that time held to the faith of the church were: The McIntosh family, Beach family, Ezekiel Emerson's family, and G. L. Chamberlain and sister Mrs. Lucy Hough. The orthodox churches refused admission to Universalist preachers, but services were occasionally held in the school-house until January 1, 1843, when the church in the upper part of the town was completed and dedicated. The society was organized the following year. In 1845 Mr. Flanders was engaged as regular preacher. He was followed by Mr. Eaton. After his resignation the pastorate was vacant for several years till the services of J. W. McMaster were secured. He preached regularly at two different periods, and occasionally the remainder of the time till 1878, when T. C. Dooley became regular preacher, and services were held once a month for one year. The society is at present without a settled pastor.

The congregation has never been numerically strong

BAPTIST CHURCH.

The Baptist society at Beverly was formed through the influence and labor of Job T. Cook, who moved from Newport to Beverly, and naturally desired a religious home of his own faith. Other citizens had been members of the Baptist church at other places, and welcomed Rev. J. H. Barker when he came, in 1856, as a missionary of the Meigs Creek association. Mr. Barker, from this time, preached regularly, and on January 15, 1857, the church, with fifteen members, was reorganized by the association. The members were: Job T. Cook, Sarah A. Cook, J. H. Barker, Juliet Barker, Joseph and Lavina Wood, William and Isabella Glass, Rachel Devol, Elvira Harwood, Robert Vaughan, Nancy Whissen and three others. Mr. Barker served the church until 1859. Succeeding pastors were: William Mears, a short time; G. W. Churchill, two years; J. D. Leonard, till August, 1854; S. Seigfried, one year; vacancy till January 1, 1868; E. Stillwell served for a time, but the membership was small and the field of labor was considered difficult. J. H. Barker and J. W. Riddle have since acted as supplies, but the congregation has been without a pastor since Mr. Stillwell left. In 1860 the church seemed on a fair way toward getting a foothold in this territory. During that winter twenty-seven were received by baptism, and the members were greatly encouraged.

BENEVOLENT SOCIETY.

It appears from the books of Captain Rotheus Hayward that a society known as the Washington benevolent society, was organized in November, 1815. Captain Hayward was treasurer, and his accounts are the only data at our command. It was a branch of the county society, but seems to have been operated on an independent basis. Members were assessed and the money spent for clothing, caring for the sick, meals, etc. The organization was carrying on its work in 1821.

SECRET SOCIETIES.

Mount Moriah Lodge No. 37, Free and Accepted Masons, was established at Waterford, in accordance with a dispensation issued by Henry Brush, grand master, to Ebenezer Bowen, master; Eli Cogswell, S. W.; and Obediah Scott, J. W., to hold a lodge of Ancient York Masons. This dispensation was issued September 28, 1816, and on the fourth of the following November a meeting was held at the residence of John Dodge, at which officers were elected as follows: Ebenezer Bowen, master; Eli Cogswell, S. W.; Obediah Scott, J. W.; William Ripley, secretary; William Rand, treasurer; William White, S. D.; Elias Woodruff, J. D.; John Dodge and Andrew Story, stewards; and Samuel Andrews, tyler. R. Culver was also present at this meeting.

Lodge meetings were held thereafter at 3 o'clock on the Thursday preceding every full moon, at the residence of John Dodge. The first initiations were Jeremiah Wilson and Samuel Beach, November 28, 1816. Stephen Devol was received at the next meeting.

It will be seen that age is not this society's only claim

for respect. Its first members were the leading men in the community.

At a meeting held May 1, 1817, the following resolution was passed:

Resolved, That the thanks of this lodge be returned to Brother Eli Cogswell for his assistance and strict attention in forming this lodge.

Samuel Cushing, afterwards a prominent Mason, was initiated at this meeting.

At the celebration of St. John's Day, 1817, the following members were present: E. Bowen, William Ripley, Jesse Davis, J. K. Cooledge, James Bowen, William Rand, R. Culver, Samuel Andrews, Stephen Devol, J. Wilson, E. Martin, Cook Devol, Samuel Cushing, M. Story, Samuel Beach, J. Greenman, Conrad Thurman, John Dodge, R. Hayward, and three visitors—Nathaniel Hinkley, Dr. Spooner and Thomas Rawson. The members paraded to the church with music. This was the common practice of the time. James Bowen acted as marshal of the ladies. The rites of the order were at that time observed with the greatest precision. The periodical performance of ceremonies threw around the order an air of mystery, which affected both those within and those without the mystic circle.

In 1819 Dr. George Brown became a Mason. J. D. Chamberlain was received the previous year. Both were prominent members until their death.

When we consider the customs of the times nothing remarkable is found in the following resolution:

Resolved That the stewards be empowered to purchase half a barrel of liquor and other refreshments for the use of the lodge.

Stephen Devol's hospitality was not confined to the Methodist church. The records show that he frequently entertained the lodge.

The first death was that of Samuel Cushing, October 9, 1823. The members, as a token of regard, wore a blue ribbon about the left arm from the time of his death to the next regular communication.

In the winter of 1825 the lodge changed its place of meeting to the residence of Ebenezer Bowen, on the west side of the river. In 1827 a charter was issued by the Grand lodge ranking Mt. Moriah lodge in precedence from February 4, 1819. During the year 1828 the lodge met at the house of Bazillia Coburn; in 1829 in a room in the building in Waterford which stood where the store of General Devol now is. During the year 1831 but three meetings were held, this being the year of the anti-Masonic movement which swept over the country in consequence of the reported murder of John Morgan. In June, 1831, eight members met at the hall and decided to defy popular feeling by celebrating St. John's Day with a public procession. The members who participated in this demonstration were: Benjamin Soule, James Bowen, Adelpha Webster, Charles Bowen, Stephen Devol, George Bowen, Jeremiah Wilson, and Barzillia Coburn. The procession organized at the hall and marched with music to the church, where they organized a meeting and pledged each other to stand by the order, regardless of popular clamor.

A lodge of Master Masons was organized March 15, 1832. Benjamin Soule, J. D. Chamberlain, William

Wilson, George Bowen, Charles S. Cory, and James Bowen constituted the membership.

It became necessary during this year for the lodge to give up their room, and no suitable place of meeting could be found. Work was suspended and no meetings were held until October, 1843. On that date John Keyhoe, William Wilson, Ambrose Elliott, William Kearns, Jeremiah Wilson, Charles S. Cory, John Dodge, Charles Bowen, Charles Story, Atkinson Hill, and George Bowen met and memorialized the Grand lodge. That body instructed Mt. Moriah lodge to resume its labors. The first regular meeting was held January 4, 1844. Officers were duly elected, and from that time regular meetings have been held.

The lodge, after reorganization, met in the building on the corner of Fifth and Canal streets until July, 1845. Owing to a sale of the property another room had to be sought, and no suitable place for meetings could be found in Waterford or Beverly. Samuel Beach, of Coal Run, opened his house for the use of the lodge, and meetings were held there until the close of the year. The lodge then removed to Beverly and held its meetings in the building then used by Samuel Hammontree as a cabinet shop. A resolution had long before been passed discarding whiskey from the list of refreshments.

Meetings were held in the Hammontree building till 1846 (this building is now known as the Central house). The lodge then rented and furnished in a very attractive style a room in the building on the corner of Canal and Fifth streets, now occupied by J. M. Truesdell. Meetings were held in the college building, in a room in the third-story, which they rented in connection with the Odd Fellows until 1857. A room in the third-story of the Tucker building was occupied from 1857 until the completion of Masonic block in 1879.

In 1878 the lodge began, what had long been contemplated, the erection of a building dedicated to its own use. The corner-stone was laid according to Masonic regulations, June 24, 1878, by Special Deputy Grand Master W. M. Shinnick. On that occasion an address was delivered by Rev. A. B. Brise of the Presbyterian church. The first lodge meeting was held in the building June 18, 1879.

The structure is a credit to the lodge, being the largest and finest building in the village. The walls are brick with stone columns and arched doors and windows. In size it is forty by seventy-two feet. On the ground floor are two store rooms, the second story is a commodious hall, and the third floor is arranged for the use of the lodge, with reception and private rooms, and a hall for the use of the lodge and chapter. The whole cost was six thousand and twenty-one dollars.

The membership of the lodge January, 1881, was seventy.

ODD FELLOWS.

On the evening of March 4, 1847, Samuel Thompson, Robert Ramsey, Charles L. Bowen, W. V. Z. Wheeler, and W. F. Leget, met in the second story of the frame building on the northwest corner of Fifth and Canal streets and were duly instituted a lodge of the Independent Order of Odd Fellows, known as Beverly Lodge No. 84. The ceremonies of the occasion were conducted by Deputy Grand Master William Chidsey, of Cincinnati. The first officers were: Samuel Thompson, noble grand; Robert Ramsey, vice grand; C. L. Bowen, secretary; W. V. Z. Wheeler, treasurer. The lodge occupied the room in which it was instituted until the spring of 1848, when a room in the college building was secured and used until 1858, a room in Tucker's building was then fitted up and occupied until July, 1868. Since that time the hall on Fifth street has been used.

At the legislative session of 1861 the lodge was incorporated under the laws of Ohio. In 1858 this district was represented at the meeting of the Grand lodge by J. M. Truesdell, of Beverly, A. J. Morrison, who was initiated into the fraternity at this place, was elected to the position of grand master, in Iowa in 1878.

Beverly lodge has initiated about two hundred members. The present membership is seventy-nine. The membership of Lowell, Keaths and Stockport lodges was largely drawn from Beverly. For reference we give the names of the past noble grands: 1847, Samuel Thompson; 1848, C. L. Bowen, J. T. Wilson; 1849, J. W. Fox, E. B. Leget; 1850, W. V. Z. Wheeler, James Brown; 1851, T. Devol, J. M. Truesdell; 1852, S. B. Robinson, Rufus Leget; 1853, Joseph Parker, Isaac Johnson; 1854, Thomas Sweesey, James Mullen; 1855, A. J. Morrison, J. W. Fouts; 1856, W. Preston, L. C. Coburn; 1857, R. B. Cheatham, J. C. Preston; 1858, S. H. Brooks, H. C. Fish; 1859, Frank Hammontree, J. L. W. Newton; 1860, William C. Glines, H. A. Staley; 1861, Alexander Clark, C. L. Bowen, 1862, H. S. Clark, Henry Jordan; 1863, S. H. Jewett, S. Legett; 1864, Parley Chapman, J. G. Hutchinson; 1865, Joseph Parker, J. D. Hand; 1866, Andrew Denney, T. B. Townsend; 1867, J. H. Jordan, Henry S. Clark; 1868, John Henderson, J. J. Barr; 1869, J. H. Jordan, T. E. Clark; 1870, M. B. Johnston, B. F. Jackson; 1871, Linsey Leget, L. L. Grubb; 1872, James Cooney, W. A. Howell; 1873, S. R. Nichel, A. M. Jordan; 1874, Alexander Jackson, W. S. Jordan; 1875, D. C. Blondin; 1876, L. L. Grubb, A. Webster; 1877, C. R. Stull, A. Pomeroy; 1878, P. S. Whissen, A. L. Crooks; 1879, George S. Worstel, W. S. Jordan; 1880, R. S. Rowlands, Joseph T. Palmer; 1881, T. M. Chapman.

THE ENCAMPMENT.

Beverly Encampment, No. 158, was instiuted July 23, 1872, with J. W. Fouts, A. M. Jordan, S. H. Jewett, E. B. Leget, J. H. Jordan, and Isaac Johnson as charter members. The first officers were: S. H. Jewett, chief patriarch; J. H. Jordan, high priest; E. B. Leget, scribe. Past chief patriarchs, in their order, are: S. H. Jewett, J. H. Jordan, L. L. Grubb, A. M. Jordan, D. M. Walker, W. A. Howell, W. S. Jordan, J. M. Shoemaker, W. Preston, A. Pomeroy, P. S. Whissen, J. M. Truesdell, George S. Worstell, B. F. Jackson and H. A. Staley. J. M Truesdell and W. A. Howell have each served two terms.

WATERFORD GRANGE.

Waterford township is the seat of the grange movement in Washington county. Waterford grange was the first

COLONEL E. S. McINTOSH.

The portrait and biography of no man is more deserving of a place in a volume of local history than the subject of this outline. The life of a man who, by persevering labor and force of character, accumulates a fortune and then uses it for the benefit of society, furnishes an example worthy of imitation.

. E. S. McIntosh, eldest son of Dr. Nathan McIntosh, was born in Marietta in what was known as the "old red house," May 23, 1793. When quite young, his parents removed to Clarksburgh, Virginia, and remained there until 1795, when they returned to Marietta.

The school privileges for boys and young men at that period were very limited. The country being new, money was scarce and work plenty. Luther Shepard, a brother of Mrs. Dr. McIntosh, operated a brickyard in which the doctor owned an interest. Enoch S. was placed in this yard as a laborer at the age of nine years, and during the first summer was one of two boys who carried from the moulds three hundred thousand bricks. He thus early began a life of severe and unremitting toil, which occupied all his time until fortune rewarded his labors. At the age of twelve Mr. McIntosh began to lay bricks, and many of the old houses in Marietta were erected under his supervision. The two first cotton factories were built by him.

In 1814, he was engaged by Thomas Seely, of Waterford township, to make bricks for his house. From that time Waterford has been his residence. In 1815 he built Mr. Seely's house, doing all the masonry from the foundation to the roof. Although cutting stone was not his trade, Mr. McIntosh was never afraid to undertake a piece of work placed in his way, and being naturally an expert mechanic, cut and laid stone in a manner entirely satisfactory.

While working for Mr. Seely he won the affections of his daughter Elizabeth, whom he married November 26, 1816. His reputation as a mason was now established, and his services were employed for the best work in the community. It is a fact to his credit as a mechanic that his work commanded higher wages than other brick masons. In 1817, Mr. Benjamin Dana began the erection of the house on the Dana farm, which is still standing. He engaged a workman at one dollar and a half a day, but soon became dissatisfied with the slow progress of the work. He came to Mr. McIntosh and tried to engage his services at the usual wages, but two dollars a day were demanded and finally given. The walls from that time grew rapidly, and the dollar-and-a-half man became thoroughly tired of his partner. Mr. McIntosh was engaged to plaster the house, and after that he did all of Mr. Dana's work, and no questions were asked about wages.

Mr. McIntosh's capacity for work at this time was phenomenal. In 1818 he was engaged to build a brick

MRS. E. S. McINTOSH.

house for Captain Rotheus Hayward, and by October of that year had made and laid one hundred thousand bricks. He worked at the trade until 1823. The Regnier house on Duck creek and large houses for Benjamin Putnam and Colonel Mills, in Marietta, were built by him.

In the spring of 1823 Mr. McIntosh determined to start a store near the Ludlow line, near the northern limit of Waterford township, where he had previously purchased land. He handed to Colonel John Mills, who was then in business, in Marietta, five hundred dollars, and requested him to buy with it such goods as would sell in the country. Colonel Mills doubted the expediency of the enterprise, but conformed to the request. A small store was opened and conducted on the general plan of buying and selling everything. The enterprise, which looked doubtful to a man of Mr. Mills' experience and sagacity, was made a success largely through the tact and force of the proprietor.

Whiskey was one of the staple articles of trade in all the stores at that time. About 1830 a feeling began to develop against the use of intoxicating liquors, and Mr. McIntosh was the first merchant in this part of the county who abandoned its sale. He was strongly importuned by his friends not to take this step and some even went so far as to warn him that his trade would be ruined. But he showed a moral courage equal only to his business energy. Once convinced that vending liquors was wrong, he could not be persuaded to continue the trade.

In 1835 Mr. McIntosh placed his store in charge of John Seely and removed to a farm down the river. He soon after opened a store in Beverly, where he was the first merchant. He also built the first mill in Beverly. Mr. McIntosh continued merchandising until 1850. He has since been dealing in real estate and banking. Through him the First National bank of Beverly was instituted. He has been a director of the bank since its establishment and its president since 1870.

Mr. McIntosh has in all his business affairs been prosperous. When he came to Waterford township in 1814, he had one dollar and twenty-five cents. He has accumulated his property since then by sheer industry and hard work. Speculation has never had any attraction for him. He believes the only way to make money is to earn it, and he has earned his. Once, soon after he was married, a merchant at Waterford refused to trust him to the amount of three dollars for a plow. Although he had never failed to pay a debt in his life, Mr. McIntosh was determined to have the plow, and walked to his farm a distance of three miles and a half and got the money— seven miles for a plow worth less than a half dollar. He had previously walked eighteen miles, on the same day. He resolved that Joseph Chambers should see the day when he would regret the trouble he had caused him.

Mr. McIntosh has been a lender of money for half a century, but it can be said to his credit he has never sued a man. Many testify to the assistance they have received at his hand. He never withholds his assistance from a worthy young man just starting in life. The part taken by him in the war of the Rebellion cannot be omitted from any sketch of his life. The firing in Sumter aroused his patriotism, and his energies from then till the close of the war were devoted to the cause of the Union.

When the first company was organized he expended about seventy-five dollars for supplies for the men and gave to Captain Henderson on the boat, one hundred dollars to be expended for the benefit of the men. Afterwards, when demands were made for money, Colonel McIntosh stepped forward with a subscription of three hundred dollars. He then passed his subscription paper to Dr. and Charles Bowen, who each equalled the sum. Mrs. McIntosh knit one hundred and thirty-seven pairs of woollen socks and sent to the soldiers in the field. Colonel McIntosh was too old to join the army, but his services at home were nevertheless effective in raising troops and supplies.

Mr. McIntosh's first wife, Elizabeth Seely, died April 3, 1868. Both her father and her mother were members of families of twenty children each. She gave birth to three children, viz.: Ann Elizabeth, born June 18, 1821, died August 14, 1824; Satina, born June 6, 1826, died June 22, 1828; and William, the oldest child, born November 15, 1817, died December 28, 1870. Mr. McIntosh married for his second wife Mrs. C. J. Russel, daughter of Major John Clark and Laura Shepard. Major Clark came to Marietta from Quincy, Massachu-

setts, in 1794. While at Quincy he was a playmate of John Quincy Adams. He married Rosanna McCallister, by whom he had four children, viz.; Sally, born in Maine; John and Polly, in Pennsylvania; and Isaac, in Marietta. She died in 1796. In 1798, he married Laura Shepard, daughter of Colonel Enoch Shepard, of Marietta. By her he had nine children, only two of whom are living— Laura and Clarinda Jane. Polly was married to Jason Curtis, and resides in Marietta. Laura was married to Lawrence Chamberlain, and lives in Harmar. Clarinda was born February 17, 1811. She was married to Charles Russel, in 1838, who died in 1841. She was married to Colonel McIntosh December 22, 1868. The remaining children of Major Clark were: Melissa, Timothy Y., Edward T., Tupper, Esther Ann, Nancy C., Samuel D., and Hannah.

In politics, Colonel McIntosh was a Whig, and has been a Republican since the organization of that party. He never asked for an office, although he has been occasionally pressed into the service. His interest in political affairs was stimulated by the Rebellion. He received his title of Colonel in the militia service.

Colonel McIntosh is a man of strong vital and moral force. His health has been uniformly good, and a strong, robust body supports him at the advanced age of eighty-eight years. He began life in a period which tried men's souls, but in all his years has never tasted intoxicating liquor or tobacco in any form.

instituted and naturally attracted considerable attention. The meeting for organization was held November 26, 1873, at the residence of James Hastings. The society was instituted by J. W. Workman, deputy master for Morgan county, with twenty members, twelve men and eight women, as follows: James Hastings, M. A. Malster, G. B. Bartlett, G. B. Palmer, D. S. Ward, Jacob Jones, John Tucker, Charles Beebe, Samuel Tucker, Owen Henry, D. B. Shaw, D. P. Leonard, Mrs. James Hastings, Mrs. Emily Ward, Mrs. Sarah Tucker, Mrs. E. A. Shaw, Mrs. Owen Henry, Miss Lucinda Chadwick, Miss Ellen Henry, and Miss P. G. Shaw. The society rented the third story of the blacksmith shop in Waterford for a period of twelve years. The first meeting was held in this hall January 11, 1874. The secretary's report for the year 1876 showed a membership of one hundred. At the close of the year 1880 there were forty paying members, one hundred dollars in the treasury, and fifty dollars stock in the grange store.

Literary exercises receive a share of attention at meetings. One difficulty has been settled by arbitration.

Masters have served as follows: 1873-4-5, M. A. Malster; 1876, Thomas Lamsdon; 1877, M. A. Malster; 1878, Alexander Hill; 1879, G. B. Bartlett; 1880-1, L. W. Shipton.

The secretaries have been: D. P. Leonard, three years; D. B. Shaw, two years; G. B. Bartlett, two years; A. Danielson, two years; Hiram Beebe, the present incumbent.

PHYSICIANS.

We know but little more of the early physicians of Waterford township than their names. Dr. Nathan McIntosh was not in the proper sense a resident physician. He served during the Indian war in the garrison as surgeon's mate, first under the employ of the Ohio company, then of the United States. Dr. Farley was the practicing physician of the colony at that time. Drs. Baker and Pardee lived on the Peninsula in 1812, how much longer is not known.

Dr. Ebenezer Bowen began the practice of medicine at Waterford in 1816. He was a thoroughly educated man, and trained practitioner. He was successful in practice, and his success was founded upon genuine merit. He continued in practice about sixteen years, and then removed to Rochester, New York, where he died.

Dr. George Bowen was for forty years a leading physician, and for thirty years the leading physician in this part of the State. He came to Waterford in 1818 and studied medicine and taught school for a few years. He began practice with his brother, under whom he read, during the sickly seasons of 1822-3. From that time till his health gave way he was in full and active practice. He was a man of agreeable presence, quick perception, and iron constitution.

Dr. Gilbert practiced at Waterford at an early period. He removed to Belpre, where he settled in practice.

Dr. Campbell and Dr. Berkley each practiced at Waterford a short time.

Dr. L. Reynolds entered the practice on the Beverly side in 1839. He enjoyed the confidence of a large class of people to the time of his death, which occurred in 1865.

Dr. Ramsey came to Beverly about 1849, and practiced in partnership with Dr. Reynolds two years, when his career was ended by death.

Dr. James Little met with commendatory success in this community. He was here from about 1846 to 1857. He then moved away, but afterwards returned, and followed the profession for a number of years. He was also engaged in business enterprises.

Dr. P. Kelley is a native of Morgan county. He came to Waterford in 1846, and entered a course of study under Dr. George Bowen. He attended lectures at Ohio Medical college, at Cincinnati, where he graduated in 1850. For two years from that date he practiced in partnership with Dr. Bowen. He has from the first enjoyed a full and profitable practice.

Dr. Joseph Parker read medicine in Belmont county, Ohio, and graduated at Starling Medical college in 1850. He opened an office in Beverly in 1851, and continues in the practice.

Dr. Kennon practiced in Beverly from 1855 till 1863. He was for a time in partnership with Dr. Thomas Ross, who came from Watertown to Beverly in 1857, and remained till 1862. Dr. Ross represented the county in the legislature, and, after leaving Beverly, enlisted in the army.

Dr. William Hedges began practice in Beverly in 1875. After an encouraging career of about four years he removed to Delaware.

Dr. John Reynolds entered the profession soon after the death of his father in 1865.

Dr. Culver, a man of very respectable ability, practiced in Beverly from about 1865 to 1867.

Dr. C. M. Humiston removed from Kentucky to Beverly, where he is now engaged in the practice.

Dr. Adair has been practicing in Beverly for the past few years and is meeting with complimentary success.

Dr. Arthur Bowen graduated at Cincinnati in 1877. He had an office in Waterford for about three years from that time.

Dr. E. Kelly graduated at Ohio Medical college in 1878. He was associated with his father during the following year.

Henry S. Clark began the study of dentistry in 1868. The carpenter trade had engaged his attention for eighteen years previous to that time. He was admitted to practice in June, 1871, and has since enjoyed a full practice.

Dr. Clark takes a deep interest in educational affairs, having served six years as member of the school board, and has been a member of the board of directors of Beverly academy since 1872.

ESTABLISHMENT OF TOWNSHIP.

At the December session of the court of quarter sessions in 1790, it was ordered that the territory included in the Seventh and Eighth townships of the Eleventh range, and the Fourth and Fifth townships of the Tenth range and the mile square lot, No. 33, in the Fourth township of the ninth range, be incorporated in one township to be known and denominated "Waterford."

The settlement on the Muskingum had previously been known as "Plainfield." The establishment of Adams, Union, Wooster, and Palmer townships, and Morgan and Noble counties, reduced the original territory to the present limits.

The early township records have been lost. We are therefore unable to give the first township officers. The magistracy at that early day was esteemed an important office, and the best men in the community were chosen to serve in that capacity. The present generation would do well to imitate the example of their forefathers in this respect. Colonel Robert Oliver, whose qualifications would have fitted him to preside over a higher court, served his community in the capacity of justice of the peace until his death. Major Dean Tyler and Judge Cutler gave the office a dignity which, unfortunately, in this latter day has been lost.

THE PRESS.

The Beverly *Gazette* was the first paper published in this township. It was owned and edited by Louis C., and Jonathan Baker. The first issue made its appearance in the spring of 1852. It was at first a sprightly little sheet devoted to local and general news, but in 1853 rushed body and soul into the Know Nothing movement and died with its party. Louis C. Baker is now editor of the Wheeling *Register*, and has been clerk of the West Virginia house of representatives.

The *College Minor* was a weekly paper, which made its appearance in January, 1854. It was edited mainly in the interest of Beverly college but gave the local news of the community. It was edited by the students, and by creating an interest in the art of practical composition was of considerable consequence from an educational point of view. It was published one year.

The Beverly *Advertiser* was a small monthly started by J. C. Preston, esq., in January, 1862. In the summer of 1865 Mr. Preston sold the paper to W. F., and Howard Atherton, who changed the name to Beverly *Times* and issued a semi-monthly edition. After about four months its publication was suspended.

W. F. Atherton & Brother began in the winter of 1866 the publication of the Good Templars' Magazine, devoted to temperance news and literature. Only four numbers were issued.

In the spring of 1865 the first number of the Beverly *Citizen and Washington County Advertiser* made its appearance. It was a seven-column paper of respectable size but devoid of local interest. William Porter was editor and his sons, P. P., and William, publishers. At the close of the first year business men withdrew their support and the paper perished.

In the spring of 1879, C. E. F. Miller came from Dresden to Beverly, with a view to starting a paper. He was encouraged to go on with the enterprise, and in December of that year the first issue of the *Dispatch* was placed before the public, with C. E. F. Miller and William C. Walter, as editors. Mr. Walter, the senior edi-

tor, sold his interest in the spring of 1880, to C. N. Mc-Cormick, of Bellefontaine. The *Dispatch* is a five column, eight page weekly, devoted to local interests. The office is equipped for general job work.

SCHOOLS.

From the first settlement the youth of this township have enjoyed the privilege of superior instruction. A school was opened by Major Tyler in the lower story of his block-house. He was assisted during the war and after by Joseph Frye. Both were college-educated men and highly cultured. The impress of their character was left upon the pupils who sat under their instruction. But the community could not always have the services of such men. There came a time when at Waterford, as at other settlements, every new-comer who knew of the elements of arithmetic, wanted to teach a school. Captain Hayward says in his diary: "The country is full of people who want to make money with their education." It is an unpleasant reflection that the professional school teachers of a pioneer community are, as a rule, an inferior class of people. It was particularly fortunate for Waterford that the first teachers were competent men. Only for a short time after the services of the cultured major had been lost, was the community dependent upon strangers. His pupils became able to take charge of educational affairs, and the township has since had superior educational facilities. Waterford was one of the first townships in the state to organize schools under the act of 1825. The township was divided into eight districts at a meeting of the trustees held April 30, 1825, and a school-house was ordered built in each.

The Beverly independent school district is worthy of special attention. It was formerly known as district No. 2, Waterford township. July 25, 1838, the township clerk made the following entry on the journals of the township: "In this district the school house is so poor as to be wholly unfit for a school; but during the summer a female teacher was engaged in it, who appeared to understand the business of teaching and governing the children under her care. She had no certificate of examination. Her daybook was correctly kept, with the exception of distinguishing males and females, and setting the ages of children."

The same clerk, Mr. E. Marsh, made the following entry in 1839: "District No. 2.—Visited the school in this district and found a large number of children collected together in an unfinished school house. The lower floor was loose and consequently the house was cold and uncomfortable; the day being cold the children were crowded around the stove and many of them were in great disorder. The teacher had but little command over them and did not appear to understand the government of a school. I noticed no great improvement in any branch of learning except writing. I believe the teacher was a man of science; his school continued three months, commencing in the winter." The directors were John Dodge, S. B. Robinson, and Samuel Hammontree. During the year two male teachers were employed. The number of pupils enumerated, eighty-three.

From a condensed report by J. Heston we learn that the number of pupils enumerated in 1844 was one hundred and twenty-five, in 1849, one hundred and ninety-two. In 1849 there was drawn from the treasury for school purposes in this district eighty six dollars and thirty-nine cents.

Teachers were supported prior to the act of 1853, mainly by subscription. The salary was usually small, and they were expected to board around. This practice of a former generation exists yet in some rural districts, although it has entirely passed away in Waterford. The teacher, like the preacher, was looked upon as a necessary charity by many of the hewers of the forest and tillers of the soil. The result was a few families had the teacher to board.

The boundaries of the districts under the subscription system were somewhat arbitrary, so that the central and naturally best schools drew many pupils, to the detriment of the more sparsely populated districts. The pay of ordinary teachers had been one dollar to one dollar and a-half per week.

The act providing for the reorganization, supervision and maintenance of public schools, was passed by the legislature in March, 1853. Beverly school district was instituted under the section of the law relating to villages in 1854. The first directors were Thomas Skillington, Thomas Thomas and James Little. A. S. Clark was clerk; and J. M. Hart, treasurer. The board this year built a school-house which cost three thousand dollars. The names of the teachers were: John Tarbell, who received one hundred and eighteen dollars; Miss E. Brown, forty-five dollars; John Shivington, eighty-seven dollars; Sarah Thomas, thirty dollars, making a total of three hundred and eighty-three dollars.

During the year 1855 sixty-six volumes were received for a school library. This was the first, and is yet the only public library in the township. Some school apparatus was also received during this year. In 1858 the school is spoken of in the records as Beverly independent school district. Z. G. Bundy was the superintendent, and to him is due the credit of establishing the graded system. He had been connected with the schools six years, and served as principal four years. The schools under his supervision are said to have been well managed. He received forty dollars per month.

In 1865 Mr. Smith was principal, and from 1866 to 1878 Jefferson Heston served in that capacity. To him is due the credit of establishing a course of study.

In the fall of 1878 school opened with the following corps of teachers in charge: T. C. Ryan, superintendent and teacher in high school; H. B. Caldwell, grammar; Miss Mary Devol, secondary; Miss Maria Clymer, primary. The salary of the superintendent was fixed at seventy-five dollars per month.

School opened in January, 1881, with two hundred and five pupils enrolled. The following was the corps of teachers: T. C. Ryan, superintendent; Mina Burrows, assistant in high school; Maria Clymer, grammar; Mary Devol, secondary, and Retta Israel, primary. The first class to complete the course and graduate, consists

(1881) of Yola M. Williams, Ettie H. Worstell, Frank B. Adams, and Charles R. Applegate.

Professor Heston says in his report in 1876:

Honorable mention should be made of those connected with the school board during the past ten years. Of the directors, Dr. James Little and Dr. William Glines visited the schools most frequently.

Be it said to their credit that their remarks were generally suggestive and encouraging. Dr. John Reynolds was always ready to sustain the teacher. The credit of placing the school in a healthy, financial condition and of making the most improvement in and about the school-building, such as putting on shutters, repainting, reseating and beautifying the building and grounds, is due to E. B. Teget and Dr. H. S. Clark. They, with J. D. Lashley, have shown a fair degree of liberality to pay teachers liberal wages.

A good philosophical apparatus has been supplied by the present board.

BEVERLY ACADEMY.

Benjamin Dana is properly the founder of this institution of learning. Feeling the need of such a school in the community, he left as a legacy for its support a coal mine in Adams township and two lots (Nos. 32 and 33) in Olive Green allotment. Various persons contributed toward the erection of a building, the largest donors being John Dodge, who gave the land, and Mr. Dana. The building was completed in 1842, and was formally opened on the first of November of that year, under the charge of the Pennsylvania synod of the Cumberland Presbyterian church. A charter was afterwards granted by the State. The institution opened with a full corps of teachers: J. P. Whitten, president; Rev. Charles B. Barclay, professor of rhetoric; Rev. Milton Bird, professor of moral science; J. Laughron, professor of languages.

The two lots donated by Mr. Dana were sold for two thousand two hundred dollars. This money was placed on interest as an endowment, and, together with the coal bank is held in trust by a board of directors. For a number of years the buildings have been rented to such individuals as were willing to risk the possibility of financial deficiencies. Under Professor E. S. Cox the institution was quite prosperous. But the too frequent changes in the principalship during the period which followed, until April, 1875, was not conducive to an increase in the number of students, or the promotion of public confidence. The academy has been of considerable benefit by educating teachers and creating among the youth higher aspirations in regard to mental training. Since Mr. Smith came in charge, in April, 1875, a steady policy has been pursued. During the year just ended ninety-eight students have been enrolled.

RIVER INCIDENTS.

The history of navigation on the Muskingum river has been fully treated in a general chapter on that subject. But a few facts of local interest belong in this connection. Navigation by keel-boats and pirogues was at best difficult, but the building of dams at Dana's island and other places greatly obstructed traffic. Boatmen often suffered aggravating experiences at Dana's island. Their boats would lodge on the dam, and hard lifting and prying was required to push them over. This dam was often the occasion of shocking profanity.

The explosion of the boilers of the Buckeye Belle created a great sensation. It was one of the fastest packets on the river. On the day of the explosion, in 1852, the cabin was full of passengers, and the distance from Lowell to Beverly was travelled with unusual rapidity. Just as she was entering the guard lock at Beverly a loud explosion aroused the citizens, and a scene of disaster and suffering was before them. Twenty-one men were killed and eight fatally wounded. A strange fact is the entire escape of the occupants of the ladies' cabin. The safe was not found till recently.

The explosion of the L. C. McCormick, in February, 1879, was not disastrous, except to property. It occurred about two miles below Beverly, while the boat was coming up.

The Muskingum, before the erection of dams, was well stocked with choice fish. Angling was a favorite sport of the early settlers, and many are the "fish stories" which live in tradition. Time never prunes a fishing or hunting exploit.

UNION FAIR.

At a meeting of citizens of Washington, Morgan, and Noble counties held in Beverly July 6, 1878, an organization was formed known as the Union Fair association. E. S. McIntosh was elected president; William Buchanan, vice-president and D. C. Staley, secretary. Twenty directors were elected at this meeting.

The use of the lot on the Marietta road, below Beverly was offered to the association by Colonel McIntosh under certain conditions. The association accepted the proposition and began to prepare the grounds for the first annual exhibition. An adjoining lot was leased, and the grounds are now the finest with regard to situation in the county.

Three very creditable exhibitions have been held, although in a financial point of view they have not been a success. The fair-grounds have annually required the expenditure of considerable money. It is expected that the enterprise will be self-sustaining now since the grounds are improved.

SALT MAKING.

During the period of the early settlement, culinary salt was not only expensive, but scarce and hard to be obtained. The homely tablefare was frequently entirely without that article of seasoning which has become a necessity in civilized life. Means for realizing money were very limited, and the price of seven or eight dollars a bushel placed this staple article beyond the reach of many. It had been rumored that salt springs lay within the bounds of the Ohio Company's purchase, and during the war an exploring party was sent from Marietta up the Muskingum to search for the springs, but the trip was hazardous, and the explorers in their haste did not find them. Some of the Waterford prisoners while in custody of the Indians were taken to these springs, which were located about forty miles from Waterford on a small stream now known as Salt creek, in the territory of Muskingum county. Judge Culter says in his notes:

Mr. George Ewing, who lived near the mouth of Olive Green creek,

informed me, soon after I settled at Waterford (1795) that he had discovered salt springs, which had furnished salt for the Indians. The Wyandots and Shawnees often visited us for the purpose of trading. One of these had given Mr. Ewing such information, that he succeeded in finding the place.

When the springs were discovered, a public meeting was held, and a salt spring company formed from the settlements at Waterford, Wolf Creek Mills, Olive Green, and Cat's Creek, for the purpose of making salt. They were divided into four classes, bearing the names of these places, who, at stated times, relieved each other in the work. Judge Cutler says:

We took possession of the spring, cleared it out, set the large iron kettles we had for making sugar, into the arches, and began boiling the water for salt. It was a slow, tedious business. By a week of hard work four men could make six bushels. We succeeded so far as to make a full supply for the several settlements represented in the company, and had some to spare. Afterwards, when our conveniences were improved, we could by our best efforts make five bushels per day, and it was a great relief to the whole country.

From an old account book we learn that this company sold salt at two dollars for fifty pounds. The improved conveniences spoken of by Judge Cutler were introduced in 1796, when the capital of the company was increased to fifty shares, at one dollar and a half each. Twenty-four kettles were purchased at Pittsburgh and transported to Duncan's Falls by water, and from there they were carried to the springs on pack-horses. A furnace was erected and a well dug near the edge of the creek, fifteen feet deep, from which the salt water was raised through a casing made of the trunk of a hollow sycamore tree, three feet in diameter. A tent was erected over the furnace, and a cabin for the workmen.

The works were run night and day, the men taking turns as watchers. An ox team and one man was employed to draw wood, an enormous quantity of which was required. Eight hundred gallons of water had to be reduced to produce fifty pounds of salt. The workmen were dependent upon the settlements in Waterford for provisions, which were brought on pack-horses and the salt returned in the same way. One who was employed at the salt works was Thomas Ewing, since United States Senator. The company disbanded in 1799, and the springs fell into other hands.

FIRST SETTLERS.

The military leader of the Waterford settlement was Captain William Gray, many of whose descendants are yet residents of the township. He was born in Lynn, Massachusetts, March 26, 1761. He caught the spirit of the Revolution in very early life and at the age of seventeen gave all his energies to the service of his country. He was one of the first who scaled the walls of Stony Point, and for valiant service was promoted to the rank of lieutenant.

After the close of the war he married Mary Diamond of Salem, Massachusetts, and began business at Danvers. His uncle William Gray, of Boston, treated his nephew with great kindness, giving him much needed financial assistance, even after he came to Ohio.

Captain Gray joined the Ohio company in 1788, and was given charge of one of the wagons that transported the first band of pioneers to Ohio. On this wagon was

WILLIAM McINTOSH.

William McIntosh was born on his father's farm near the southern limit of Morgan county, November 15, 1810. He was the only son of Enoch and Elizabeth Seely McIntosh, and was associated with his father in business during his whole life. He inherited the characteristic energy of the family, and during boyhood had a thirst for work unequalled only by his power of accomplishment. He assisted his father in the store when his services were needed there, but took advantage of every opportunity to earn money for himself by working for the neighbors on their farms. An incident occurred when he was thirteen years old which is worthy of repetition as showing that unyielding energy which characterized his whole life. In the spring he started to Marietta with four horses to buy goods. Big run was high and had to be crossed on a flat-boat. Night came on and his parents became anxious, and the colonel started to meet him. At eleven o'clock they met. The boy had just crossed Big run and was coming bravely on, regardless of the lateness of the hour and the dangers of the road.

William McIntosh began business in Beverly in 1837, and was closely identified with its interest until failing health compelled him to retire. He built the first woollen factory in the town, and was engaged in the bank in the capacity of cashier and president. His business interests were so intimately associated with those of his father that to enumerate would be only repetition. In all his affairs

he was progressive. No real improvement escaped his attention. Generosity was another characteristic. An appeal for money in a worthy cause was never made in vain or had to be repeated. "He was at all times the same straightforward, honest, liberal business man.

His ability was versatile. He succeeded alike as mechanic and tradesman. When a boy he made a left-hand grain cradle with which he earned one dollar and a quarter a day. In mature life he was master of a steamboat in the Zanesville and Pittsburgh trade, and was also engaged in the southern produce market. He succeeded in all his undertakings whether as a farmer, manufacturer, steamboatman, merchant or banker.

He married, April 13, 1841, Eliza M. Fearing, daughter of Randolph Fearing, of Beverly. She was born March 23, 1823. Their family consisted of three children, viz.: Shepard R., born January 10, 1842, died September 6, 1872; Florence Elizabeth, born October 4, 1849, died in infancy; and Jessie Fearing, born August 14, 1856, was married to Dr. Charles M. Humiston, of Kentucky, May 30, 1876. They have one child—Shepard McIntosh Humiston, born Jun 28, 1879.

Shepard McIntosh succeeded his father to the cashiership of the bank.

William McIntosh died December 28, 1870, after a protracted sickness.

written in large letters "For Ohio." He joined the second association in the spring of 1789, and at the opening of the Indian war was chosen commander of the garrison. When peace had been established he purchased a farm near the mouth of Wolf creek, and lived there until his death in 1812. His family consisted of ten children, four boys and six girls. The four boys were: William, who lived on the Peninsula; Austin, settled in Massachusetts; Chauncy, in Brown county, and Hanford in Beverly, where he engaged in tanning. Betsy, the eldest of the girls, married Stephen Devol, 2d (an account of her death is given in the sketch of "Federal Bottom;") Polly was married to William Fisher; Debra, to Jesse Loring, of Belpre; Rebecca, to Rotheus Hayward; and Clarissa, to Josiah Hart, a tanner in Waterford.

In a small community versatility is one of the most useful traits of character. Complete division of labor is impossible, and the man who can turn his hand to whatever the eye sees to do, is held in the highest esteem. The man in the early settlement of Waterford more than any other blessed with this kind of genius was Major Dean Tyler. He possessed a brilliant mind, liberal college education, an agreeable person and refined manners. He was brave and active in time of danger, cool and thoughtful in time of peace. Judge Cutler in his diary tersely sums up the regard in which he was held. He says: "When I came here (in 1795) I found Major Dean Tyler, a graduate of Harvard college, a scholar and a gentleman." He was a native of Haverhill, Massachusetts. In early life he formed an attachment to a young lady, which cast a dark shadow over his whole life. The path of these lovers was full of rough places, and young Tyler sought to free himself of haunting dreams by going to Europe. On his journey he had many perilous experiences and narrow escapes. Jealousy subsided, and he determined to return to the woman of his choice. But it was too late. Her death had taken place in the meantime, and he was conscious of being the cause. The shock threw him into a delirium, and he narrowly escaped death. After a slow and tedious recovery he left the scenes of his boyhood and joined the colony at the mouth of the Muskingum. In April, 1789, he drew a donation lot and came to Waterford. The block-house on the west side of the river, opposite the site of the present town of Beverly, was named in his honor and used by him as a residence until his death. Here he instructed the youth and held services on Sunday. He never married, but sought to drown his melancholy in books, and in his later life in the inebriating bowl.

The Dodge family is conspicuous in the history of the Waterford settlement. The family is descended from Lord John Dodge, of Rotham, Kent county, England, to whose ancestors were granted estates in Chestine county, by Anne for service done in the reign of Edward First, and for valiant conduct at the sieges of Berwick and Dunbar. The grandson of Lord John Dodge was Captain John Dodge, who came to Ohio in 1788, and the following year, in partnership with Colonel Robert

Oliver and Major Haffield White, built the first mill in Ohio, near the forks of Wolf creek. He entered six lots in the "donation tract." Part of his land was in the present territory of Watertown township, where he lived. Captain Dodge brought with him from Beverly, Massachusetts, his wife, who was Susanna Morgan, a relative of General Daniel Morgan, and a woman of much strength and beauty of character. Their children were John and William M., born in Massachusetts; Susannah, Sidney, Ethel, Solomon, Mary, and Andrew, born in this county. Captain Dodge died October 8, 1805.

John Dodge, the eldest son, inherited that part of the estate which his father had received from Judge Cutler in exchange for a tract of six hundred acres on Federal creek, in Athens county. The lot originally embraced sixty-eight acres. The first business house in the township was on this lot, and it seemed to possess peculiar advantages as a village site. Mr. Dodge laid out his land in town lots, setting apart lots for churches and other purposes. He named the town Beverly in honor of his native home in Massachusetts. He assisted to found a college for general educational purposes, and used his influence and capital for the encouragement of business enterprise. He married, in 1806, Mary B. Stone. Their children were: Israel S., who was for forty years a prominent physician in Cincinnati; Christopher, William M., Mary M., Sidney, Elvina, and John. Mary Stone Dodge, his wife, died in 1822. He married for his second wife Nancy N. Patterson, of Virginia, by whom there were two children—Patterson Oliphant Dodge and Colina N., wife of S. B. Robinson, esq. Mr. Dodge died January 11, 1854. His wife had preceded him twelve years.

During the Indian war the most active and brave of the young men were deputized to act as rangers. It was their duty to make daily circuits of four or five miles and report the condition of affairs at the garrison. One who served in this dangerous office and remained to clear and cultivate the land he had helped to defend, was Andrew McClure. He was born in Maine in 1771. In his eighteenth year the settlement of the Northwestern Territory attracted his attention, and possessing a brave heart, he resolved to link his fortunes with the pioneers of the border. Not being a member of the Ohio company he drew a lot in the donation tract, and in April, 1789, joined the second association and came to Waterford with the nineteen first settlers. He was regarded a valuable man in the settlement, and during the Indian troubles his skill and courage became celebrated. In 1794 he married Polly Devol, and the following year built a cabin and began cultivating the farm just above the mouth of Wolf creek. His family consisted of nine children, one of whom was Henry McClure, mentioned under the head of Dunham township. In 1806, McClure having met with financial misfortune, removed to Federal Bottom, where he took charge of the saw-mill. He died in Lancaster, Ohio, in 1830. His wife survived him twenty-five years.

The little State of Rhode Island was the birth place of the most numerous family of the Muskingum valley settlers,—the Devol* family. Their paternal ancestor was a Frenchman, who settled in Tiverton, Rhode Island, and engaged in the West India trade. His wife was a Quaker of the mild, peace-loving school. The family consisted of seven sons, three of whom became residents of this county, and the sons of the fourth also joined the pioneer band. Two of the brothers and one of the nephews were settlers of Waterford township.

Gilbert Devol was born in Tiverton, Rhode Island, in 1736. In 1788 he emigrated with his wife and family to Ohio, and stopped in Marietta until April, 1788, when he joined the second association and came to Waterford with the first nineteen. At the opening of the Indian war, he lived in the block-house on the Waterford side of the river, but afterwards removed his family to the garrison. At the close of the war, he settled on the bottom below Beverly, where he died in 1821. He was a man of more than ordinary prominence in the early community. He had served as judge in Rhode Island, and was always known by that title here. He had a large family. Gideon owned a donation lot on the plain adjoining the present site of the Beverly fair grounds. He had improved fourteen acres on his farm when he met an untimely death. He went out hunting on a cold day and was found at the trunk of a tree frozen to death. He was buried on his own farm, in a small lot which has since become a family burying-ground. An incident is told in this connection of the fidelity of a favorite dog. He was found guarding the body of his master, and was unwilling to permit anyone to touch it. When the body was removed the animal seemed grief-stricken, refused food, and finally starved to death.

Wanton, second son of Judge Devol, was one of the forty-eight who first arrived at Marietta. He married Sally Lake, of Rhode Island before emigrating, and by her had a large family. He came to Waterford in the spring of 1789, but it appears, from family records, did not move his family here at that time. He died in 1812, at the age of fifty years. His sons were Alpha, who was born in the Campus Martius, in 1789. He was soon after brought with his mother to Waterford, where the family lived till the close of the war. He married Nancy Champlain, of Connecticut, and settled, first, on Federal Bottom and then on the opposite side of the river, where he died in 1871.

Phillip, second son of Wanton Devol, was born in the garrison in 1791. He married Hannah Hatch, of Connecticut, and settled near the mouth of Tuttles run. He died in 1852.

William, the third son, was born in 1793. He married Sally Silva, and lived where Beverly now stands. He died in 1823.

The daughters of Wanton Devol, were Ruth, died in 1873, aged seven years; Nancy, wife of William Brown, died in Kansas in 1878; Hannah, wife of Charles Story, of Round Bottom, this township; Sally, born 1805, lives on the homestead.

Silas, the youngest son of Wanton Devol, was born in 1802, died on the homestead in 1865.

* Sometimes spelled Duval.

Jonathan, third son of Gilbert Devol, came with his parents from Rhode Island, and was in the garrison at Waterford during the Indian war. He married Clara Sherman, and after the close of hostilities, improved his farm on Wolf creek, where he built a mill. His family consisted of three daughters and two sons, viz: Lecta, wife of John Burris; Betsy, wife of Elmer Drury, of the "Tick Ridge" settlement; and Cyntha; Gideon moved out of the county, and Wanton was drowned in the Muskingum while engaged in keel boating.

Gilbert, forth son of Judge Gilbert Devol, studied medicine and engaged in the practice of his profession in Belpre township.

Isaac, fifth son, was drowned when a boy.

The daughters of Judge Devol were, Sally Hinkley, of Athens county; Betsy Cushing, of Round Bottom settlement; Basha White, of Athens county, and Polly, wife of Andrew McClure.

Stephen Devol, sr., emigrated to Ohio after peace with the Indians. He had learned the ship-building trade in Rhode Island, and was the builder of the first ocean ship—brig St. Clair, which entered the gulf from the Mississippi. This vessel is spoken of at some length in another chapter. In 1802 Mr. Devol removed his family to Waterford, and the following year, October 23, 1803, died. His wife, Rosannah Cook, was born April 14, 1751 (O. S). She died November 10, 1835. Their family consisted of ten children. Presberry was born in 1770. He settled in Morgan county, where he died at the age of ninety-two years. Joseph was born in 1772; he settled in Morgan county, and lived to be more than ninety years old. Philip was born in 1774, and was lost at sea. Wing was born in 1775; he settled, and died in Muskingum township. These four had all been sailors before coming to Ohio, and after the settlement of the family here made ocean voyages. In older years they entertained their friends with stories of seafaring life. Philip was at one time in the bottom of a wrecked vessel three days, living on cracker diet, and water caught by spreading clothes in the rain. Sarah, the fifth child, died in early life. Cook, the fifth son, was very young when he came to Ohio, having preceded the other members of the family. From tradition we learn that he did good service as a scout during the Indian war. After the establishment of peace he married Hannah Convers, and settled in "Quigley Hollow." He is buried in Waterford cemetery, where a stone bearing the following, marks his grave:

In memory of
COOK DEVOL,
Who died August 9, 1831, in the fifty-fifth year of his age. He emigrated from Rhode Island at the early period of 1791, and suffered many privations and hardships during the Indian war, in the early settlement of Marietta.
"Therefore be ye all ready, for ye know not the hour the Son of Man cometh."

Alfaxid, the sixth of the sons of Stephen Devol, was killed by his team running away. Charlotte died at New Albany, Indiana. Stephen, jr., was born at Tiverton in 1786, and died at Waterford in 1875. Rosannah, the youngest daughter, was born in 1792. She was married to Benjamin F. Stone, of Rainbow.

Theodore, oldest son of Stephen Devol, jr., was born in 1820. In 1842 he married Jane F. Clark, who was born in 1825, at Waterford. He settled in Muskingum township, where he now owns a fine farm. His family consists of five children, viz: Frances H. (Barker), Muskingum township; Stephen C., Noble county; Augusta J., Milton H. and Louis A., Muskingum township. Stephen C. was in the Thirty-sixth regiment during the war.

Three brothers, Allen, Isaac and Daniel Devol, came to the county in its first settlement. They were nephews of Gilbert, sr., Stephen, sr., and Captain Jonathan, sr., and grandsons of the original settler at Tiverton, Rhode Island. Allen came with the first company to Marietta in the spring of 1788. In the winter of the following year he drew a donation lot, and joined the second association in April, 1789. He lived at the garrison until the close of Indian hostilities, and then began improving his land on Round bottom, just below the cemetery. Previous to his coming to Waterford, he was married to Ruth Jennings, by whom he had seven children: Simeon, settled opposite Coal run; Lucinda, wife of Wayne; Sprague lived on Big run, Adams township; Daniel on the plain below Beverly; Bennett in Zanesville; Betsey (Mason), opposite Lowell; Allen, jr., in Round bottom; Charlotte, opposite Lowell.

Daniel Devol went south, married a Spanish woman, and located at Mobile, Alabama, where he died in 1824.

Isaac Devol settled in Adams township, where an account of him is given.

Simeon M., son of Allen Devol, was born January 14, 1800. He was married January 10, 1822, to Rubia Sprague, who was born in Waterford township January 16, 1795. The fruit of this union was ten children, five of whom are still living—Emeline M., Ruth B., William A., Betsy, and Adelia. Mrs. Devol died November 24, 1864. William A., the seventh child, was born in Adams township, February 23, 1824. September 25, 1859, he married Catharine, daughter of Peter Angle, of Watertown township, who was born June 3, 1840. Their family consists of three children—Eva E., Roscoe G., and Howell S. Eva E. is married to Russell A. Humiston, of Adams township.

Captain Daniel Davis, one of the Waterford associates, came to Marietta from Killingly, Connecticut. His family were William, afterwards captain of militia and magistrate; Jesse, afterwards colonel of militia and magistrate; Asa, Daniel, jr., and Hezekiah; Betsy married first to Mr. Perrin, and then to Mr. Wilson; and another daughter who married Colonel James Mann. They were all very respectable people and acquired property.

Benjamin Convers, esq., emigrated with his family from Killingly to Marietta, and thence to Waterford the following spring. He died of small-pox at Waterford the first year of the settlement. His family were James, who died about 1804; Daniel was taken prisoner by the Indians and afterwards became a successful merchant at Zanesville; Wright settled at Baton Rouge, Louisiana; Simon and Grosvenor, both respectable and prosperous men; one of the daughters married Jasper Stone, esq.; another Benjamin Beadle.

George Wilson, David Wilson, and William Wilson, came from Killingly, Connecticut, to Marietta in 1788. They joined the second association in the spring of 1789, and were valuable members of the colony during the Indian war. William was drowned in 1797. Jeremiah Wilson, at Coal Run, is a descendant of this Wilson family.

LATER SETTLERS.

Robert Leget, son of John Leget, was born in Pennsylvania in 1795. He lived in Waterford from 1799 until his death in 1876. He was a soldier in the War of 1812, and justice of the peace for twenty-five years. The office of magistrate was once no trifling honor. Judge Cutler and Colonel Robert Oliver had served in that capacity and given the office a dignity which was not lost until later years. Robert Leget married Susanna Featherston, who was born in 1798 and died in 1872. Their daughter Jane was born in 1817 at Beverly. She was married in 1853 to Augustus Cram, who was born in 1813.

Jesse Brown was born in Connecticut in 1776. He immigrated to Ohio in 1800, and settled in Waterford township. His wife, Relief Story, was born in 1781. Both died in Morgan county in 1816. Mrs. Harriet Culver, of Waterford; S. S. Brown, of Waterford, and Parley Brown, of Iowa, are the only children.

S. S. Brown was born in 1807. In 1835 he married Harriet Lagrange, who was born in New York in 1811. They have seven children living, one of whom was in the army from 1862 to 1865. Mr. Brown served as school director for fifteen years.

John Bacon, whose settlement is mentioned in the history of Watertown township, was born in England in 1764. He first emigrated to New York, and then to Ohio soon after the Indian war. His death occurred in Waterford township in 1854. Sarah Comer, his wife, was born in 1774, and died in 1848. Their children were: William, born 1795, died 1880; Sarah, born 1797; John, born 1798, died 1861; Martha, born 1800; Mary Taylor, lives in Noble county; Martin, born 1803; Ellen, born 1805, deceased; Isaac, born 1807, died 1878; Martha, lives in Marietta; Maria, lives in Iowa; Eliza, born 1815, died 1830; Melissa Beach, lives in Waterford township; Bentrand, lives in Iowa, and Martin, who was born in 1804. In 1829 Martin married Mary M. Hurlbut, who died in 1866. In 1868 he married Sarah Mason, who was born in Adams township in 1830. Mr. Bacon is father of five children, viz.: Rachel J. Lawrence, of Waterford township; Mary E. Hill, of Watertown; Betsy Baldwin, of this township; Andrew J. and John E. He has buried three children—Emily, Merandah and Sarah. Mr. Bacon is one of the wealthiest farmers in the township, owning nine hundred and ninety-five acres of land.

Captain Rotheus Hayward was a lineal descendent of Thomas Hayward, who emigrated from England in 1635 and was one of the founders of Bridgewater, Massachusetts. Rotheus, the oldest son of Joseph Hayward, of Eaton, Massachusetts, came to Marietta in 1805. He there became acquainted with Panthia Nye, whom he married January 19, 1807. He had the previous year purchased the McClure farm just above the mouth of Wolf creek, where he spent the active years of his life. This farm, consisting of one hundred and five acres, was sold at sheriff's sale to General Tupper for six hundred and fourteen dollars. It was purchased the same day by Captain Hayward for six hundred and forty-five dollars. Under date of January 29, 1807, the following quaint entry is made in the captain's diary:

I spent this day in town; took breakfast at Colonel Nye's, dinner at General Tupper's, and supper at Colonel Nye's. This night I was married for which I paid three dollars and a half.

Mrs. Panthia Hayward died January 24, 1821, in her thirty-third year. Her family consisted of seven children of whom but two survive—Joseph, of this township, and Rotheus, of Marietta. In 1822 Captain Hayward married Rebecca Gray, daughter of William Gray. She was born in Fort Fry October 4, 1791. The children by this marriage are: Charlotte Gray, born December 25, 1822; Daniel W., born November 15, 1827, residing in Oregon; Columbus F., born April 13, 1831; Cyrus B., born January 21, 1837.

Rotheus Hayward died May 22, 1842; his wife died September 28, 1876.

Joseph Hayward was born in 1808. In 1833 he married Mary Ann Hart, who was born in Watertown in 1813. Five children survive: Charles A., living at Lima, Ohio; Mary S. (Leonard), Josephine A., Arthur W., and Emma A. Oliphant, living at Salem, Oregon.

C. F. Hayward was born in 1831. In 1869 he married Emily Wilson, who was born in 1829. They have one child, born in 1871, Edwin Theodore.

Edward Hayward, a brother of Rotheus, came to the township and settled about three miles up the river from Waterford.

Laban Vincent was born in Rhode Island in 1750. He emigrated to Ohio in 1806 and settled in Marietta. By his wife, Anna Waterman, he had eleven children. John Vincent, their son, was born in Providence, Rhode Island. He came to Ohio with his parents and settled in Union township, now Muskingum. In 1808 he moved to Waterford township, where he died in 1852. He was one of the first settlers on the east side of the river in the upper part of the township. He married Rachel, daughter of Asa Olney, who was one of the earliest settlers of the township. They had ten children, two of whom live in this township—Clarinda Beckett and John Vincent, jr. The latter was born in this township in 1818. In 1839 he married Mary A. Bacon, who was born in 1820. He served as supervisor fourteen years. He has had seven children, four of whom are living, viz: Mary A., at home· John B., in Dakota; Eli B., in Dakota; and Prussia, at home. Prudence, Eliza J., and Thirza died young.

William Henry Cooley was born in New York in 1790. He came to Ohio in 1810 and settled in Marietta. In 1812 he married Mary Vincent, who was born in Rhode Island in 1793. They had four children, two of whom survive—Mrs. Caroline Wood, of Watertown township, and George V. Cooley, who was born in 1820. In 1850

he married Laura E. Sherman, who was born in Waterford township in 1830. They had eight children, viz: Charlotte, Amos E., Emeline C. (Jackson), Sibyl D. (Vincent), Mary M. (West), George W., Martha J., deceased, and Laura R. George W. Vincent served as school director twelve years.

Frederick Chapman, son of Parley and Mary Ogle Chapman, was born in 1811. In 1840 he married Rebecca Chapman, who was born in 1817. They have one child, Frances M.

Nathaniel Chapman and wife emigrated from Massachusetts to Ohio in 1797.

Parley Chapman was one of the first settlers of Aurelius township. He afterwards moved to Morgan county, where he died in 1851.

Rev. Jacob Young, the noted Methodist itinerant, says in his autobiography: "There lived in Waterford at this time (1828) a very conspicuous family by the name of Bowen—men of great energy and decision of character —two of them were physicians, the other two business men. They had an amiable sister, who was the ornament and bond of the family. We brought them all to the threshold of the church, but could not bring them in. When money was called for to support preachers, to send missionaries to foreign lands, to circulate Bibles, or to build churches, they were always ready to give liberally, and there they remain to the present day." A brief personal sketch of a family so intimately connected with the affairs of this part of the county, with the business and life of the community, for sixty years, demands a place in a work of this character.

Consider Bowen, the father of the Ohio members of the Bowen family, was born in Rhode Island in 1756, of Welsh parentage. He was married to Sabra Hosmer, by whom he had nine children, five of whom belong to Washington county, viz: Ebenezer, born 1789; James, born 1794; George, born 1796; Charles, born 1798; and Rebecca, wife of James Whitney, of Harmar, born 1787.

James and Ebenezer came to Waterford in 1816. James had served an apprenticeship in one of the manufacturing establishments on the Connecticut river and understood the art of carding and fulling. Ebenezer had studied medicine, and after settling at Waterford began the practice of his profession. His professional life is mentioned under the proper head. He died in Rochester, New York, May 22, 1865.

James Bowen, for the first several years of his residence at Waterford, engaged in the carding and fulling business, on the peninsula and at the mills on the Muskingum. He afterwards engaged in merchandising at Waterford. In 1818 he married Betsy Cushing, who was born at Waterford in 1796; she died June 28, 1820, leaving one child—Charles L. In 1834 he married Catharine Wheeler, by whom he had two children: Hosmer W. and Julia R. Charles L. was born January 14, 1819. On April 18, 1842, he married Mary W. Deming, daughter of David Deming, of Watertown township; she was born August 18, 1818. They had three children, one of whom is dead: Arthur C., born January 15, 1847, died December 6, 1849; Ella A., born April 7,

WILLIAM H. POWERS

William H. Powers was born within gunshot of his present residence; and with the exception of a few visits he has never been off the farm above two weeks at a time. In him was strongly developed that earth-hunger which is one of the best characteristics of the Anglo-Saxon race—not only the laudable ambition to add field to field, which is common to the American pioneer, but also that better ambition, so seldom seen in this class, to preserve the rich patrimony of the soil intact. To him the soil was ever sacred, and not only was it his constant study to conserve its virgin fertility, but he wished to retain its original physical outlines and with careful, tireless industry he sought to heal the wounds and rents with which the elements, assisted by the necessary operations of agriculture, are always prone to gash the earth. What maledictions does he not deserve from posterity who wastefully and infamously strips the ground of its natural covering of forest, and then allows the rains with slow, cruel, trickling persistence to scar it with villainous gullies, washing down into the rivers, which bear onward to the ocean, the priceless silt that should have been retained upon the hilltops.

Hon. W. I. Chamberlain, in an address to the farmers of Ohio, said: "We should know enough of geology to appreciate the countless years it has cost to clothe our globe with its present fertility and verdure." Then, speaking of the man who burned the great temple of Diana in Ephesus, he added: "Of almost equal infamy shall not we deem him worthy who, in a few short years of wretched, spendthrift farming, exhausts all of the available fertility stored in his farm by nature through all the patient lapse of centuries?" Such, though unspoken, was the one great life-thought of William Powers. Com-

ing to manhood at a time when the settlers were unavoidably plunged in the deepest poverty, and without the guidance or assistance of a father, he made his own little share of the inheritance purchase seven others in succession. A deep and abiding fear of God, an inexorable sense of duty, rigid economy, an iron constitution, an industry which absolutely knew no rest throughout the year, save the rest of sleep and of the Sabbath—these were the secrets of his success.

Too confiding in the honesty of others, and too busy in earning money to concern himself greatly about the fate of it after it was earned, he made many mistakes in business. But all his mistakes he at once set himself uncomplainingly and with a bovine patience to correct. All the eddies in his life-current he turned into the steadily widening channels of success.

After reaching manhood he was never known, even under the bitterest provocation, to speak an angry word to a human being. Strictly just and impartial to his children, he regarded them with an affection which was sincere but so entirely undemonstrative that they knew nothing of its depth until they grew up and the hour of parting arrived. The most harmless and innocent of men, he is regarded by the gay and frivolous with a sentiment approaching to awe. He has the proverbial taciturnity of the farmer.

Shunning a lawsuit as he would poison, a very pillar in the councils and finances of the church (Presbyterian), minding his own business, wronging no soul—a plain, self-contained, simple man—he has borne well his part amid that remarkable race of pioneers, now almost passed away, and of which this region will behold the like no more.

STEPHEN POWERS.

Stephen Powers, farmer, was born in Waterford, July 21, 1840. He obtained his early education in the district school, and when sufficiently able-bodied to plow corn, committed to memory while doing so, two books of Paradise Lost, the book lying in the fence corner for reference every alternate row. He graduated from Michigan university in 1863, and was selected by the faculty from a class of forty to be offered the assistant professorship of Latin, but an older graduate applied for and secured the position. He then went to Cincinnati and engaged in the service of the *Commercial* as army correspondent. In this occupation he wrote letters from West Virginia and East Tennessee, followed Sherman to Atlanta, witnessed and described the battles of Kennesaw and Atlanta, and later the battle of Nashville; reported the funeral of President Lincoln, and subsequently the first reconstruction conventions of Mississippi, Alabama, Georgia, and Texas. He went to Washington and was summoned to testify before the reconstruction committee on Florida and Texas. Went to Europe and remained fifteen months, writing for the *New York Times* and *Nation*, and while thus engaged made pedestrian tours along the Rhine and in Switzerland and in Italy, and at Nuremburgh, in Saxony, was arrested as an Austrian spy, but soon released after a searching examination. In January, 1868, he started from Raleigh, North Carolina, to Savannah, thence from the Atlantic to the Pacific, arriving at San Buenaventura, and going from there to San Francisco, in all a foot journey of three thousand seven hundred miles, and occupying ten months in its performance. He then published at Hartford, Connecticut, a book entitled Afoot and Alone, A Walk from Sea to Sea, a graphic, but in his own estimation, a valueless

work. He then published Muskingum Legends, a collection of tales in imitation of Irving's Sketch Book.

Afterwards he roved about California and Oregon nearly seven years; herded sheep part of the time, part of the time wrote articles for Atlantic, Overland, and other magazines. He bought one hundred and sixty acres of land in the Sierra Nevada, on which he herded goats and studied Indians two years. They tattooed him, and their old men called him "Oan-koi-tu-peh," prophet or deliver. Getting tired of this kind of life he sold out, with "miner's luck," a little too soon as a valuable quartz vein was soon after, by the purchaser, discovered on his ranch.

Returning to New York in 1874 he visited the old farm, and in August, 1875, was, by the Secretary of the Interior, appointed special commissioner to make a collection of Indian art specimens and curiosities in California and western Nevada for the Centennial—a work that occupied five months.

During his residence in California, engaged as mentioned on his farm there, he had prepared an elaborate and original account of the habits, customs, legends, geographical boundaries, religious ideas, etc., of the California Indians, of which the principal portion was published generally in the Overland Monthly, running through the greater part of two years. In its completed form the Government published this work in 1878 at an expense of six thousand five hundred dollars, as a part of the reports of the United States geological and geographical survey of the Rocky Mountain region, under the supervision of J. W. Powell, the explorer. It constitutes volume third of "Contributions to American Ethnology," a work that is intended to embrace about ten volumes from the pens of a number of writers. The third volume is a book of six hundred and thirty-five pages, and includes forty or fifty vocabularies of different Indian tribes. It was distributed gratutiously among the prominent libraries and scientific men of both continents, and its author has been elected a member of the American Association for the Advancement of Science, and a corresponding member of the California Academy of Sciences.

For several years he has been married and settled down quietly on the old farm. From this sketch of him, rapidly drawn, comes the moral that all biography to profit anything, should teach. We have written Stephen Powers a farmer, and to-day he is. He has been also that which taught him the valuable lesson he improved by returning to his farm after exhausting years of wild adventure of all that could be obtained from them. Like many others, in his early manhood he mistook a keen appreciation of profitable literature for ability to produce it, and succeeded in all but the profit. Heir to a noble farm, he sought literary fame, and was made to feel his infinitely small importance, while dancing attendance at a publisher's ante-room, with a roll of poor sophomorical manuscript under his arm, and deference

to insolence of position in his manners; and this continued for weeks before the folly of his literary conceit was pestled out of him. With subsequent ability to earn thirty-five dollars a day, he has been in a position where a scrap of mal-oderous meat begged from an Indian and toasted on a greasewood twig, has given him keen gustatory pleasure.

To-day, under the growing sense of ownership, looking over broad acres of tasselled and silken eared corn, and through granaries filled with old wheat, hay and wool, he looks back on those prodigal, vagabondizing days, sometimes with unspoken contempt, and sometimes with infinite commiseration. The profits of newspaper literature are the keen zest of the journalist in his work, and little else even for him An impecunious old age, if not the poor-house as our subject tells us, stared him in the face, and he had the common sense to see his mistake, and the courage to correct it and take hold of the farm in his younger manhood, where, if he has found little glory, there is much safety. His adventurous life offers a sage lesson, but a lesson, nevertheless, that few possessing his youthful promptings and courage, will profit by.

[The foregoing is from the Biographical Cyclopedia of Ohio.]

1843, is married to Rev. I. F. King, of Columbus; Dr. Arthur H., was born December 7, 1852.

Charles Bowen came to Waterford in 1817, and was for a time associated with his brother James in the wool manufacture He, however, made his reputation and his money in mercantile pursuits, at Waterford. His extensive business is spoken of in another connection. He died unmarried, April 8, 1874.

George Bowen came to the township in 1818. He taught school and pursued his medical studies for a short time after his arrival, and then engaged in the practice of the profession, which he honored until a few years before his death, which occurred May 24, 1874. Dr. Bowen was married to Mary Wheeler, of Connecticut, in 1837, by whom he had five children, viz: Charles W., at Centerville, Iowa; Harriet E., wife of General H. F. Devol; Henry C., deceased; Mary J. Case, of Kansas City; and Edgar G., of Zanesville. Dr. Bowen was as successful in business affairs as in his profession. He was clear headed and far sighted.

Philander and Anna Andress Andrews emigrated from New York and settled in Morgan county, near Beverly, in 1810. They had a family of ten children. Their daughter Amy, who was born in 1811, was married in 1832 to Charles Swift, jr. He was born in this county in 1807. They had six children, of whom Samuel is the fifth. He was born in 1848, in Waterford township. In 1875 he married Alice J. Bartlett, who was born in this township in 1857. They had one child, Charles Swift, jr., who died in 1873.

Seneca Clark emigrated from New York and settled in Waterford township in 1818, near the mouth of Olive Green creek. He married, in this township, Catharine Stull, daughter of Peres Stull, who was a native of New Jersey and settled in Waterford township in 1806. The Clark family consisted of four children, three of whom are living—Augustine S., Jane, wife of Theodore Devol, and Henry S. Augustine S. married Catharine Ross, and is a practicing physician in Beverly; Henry married Martha Cooksey and is practicing dentistry in Beverly.

Adelphia Webster and wife emigrated from New England and settled in Morgan county, Ohio, about 1814. They had a family of five children — Sibyl married Lyman Swift in 1839. He was born in 1815 and died in 1864, leaving five children, viz: Rosamond (Danley), Mary (Owens), Lucinda (Vincent), Adaline (Murray), and Louisa. Francis died at the age of three years.

Samuel Beach was a son of John Beach of New Jersey, who served at the opening of the Revolution as a minute-man, and served at Valley Forge. Samuel Beach purchased a lot near the mouth of Olive Green in 1797, but probably lived at Putnam (Zanesville) some time after that. In 1814 he purchased the old Beach homestead at Coal Run, where he lived until his death in 1855. He operated a mill and distillery, and was a prominent man in the community. He purchased his farm of Joseph Forest, whose history belongs to the record of crime. By profession he was a counterfeiter, and the discovery of his crime made it necessary for him to leave the country. Mr. Beach met him at Lan-

caster, and there purchased the property at a very low figure.

Mr. Beach, at the age of seventeen, married Amy Sherman, who was in her fifteenth year. She was a daughter of Abel Sherman, who was killed during the Indian war. She possessed an accurate memory and a keen appreciation of the romance of life. Her death occurred August 3, 1875. The family of Mr. and Mrs. Beach consists of five children, viz: Hiram and Joseph, Waterford township; Mrs. Jane Newton, Noble county; Mrs. Eliza Sprague, Missouri; and Jackson, Coal Run.

Joseph Beach was born in 1814. His wife, Elizabeth Finney, was born in 1818. Their family consists of four children—Lucy L. Stephens, of Zanesville; Charlotte D. Hilton, Dexter, Iowa; John S., Zanesville; and Amy, at home. John, during the war, was in the regular army.

Mrs. Mary Ross, one of the family of eleven children of John and Margaret Patterson, was born in Pennsylvania in 1809. In 1831 she married William Ross, who was born in Waterford township in 1809. Richard, their only child, was born in 1838. In 1871 he married Viola F. Rardin, who was born in 1852. They have three children—Jessie B., Mary M., and Carl W. William Ross came from McConnelsville in 1857 and located where his son Richard now lives.

Joseph Nickerson was born in Massachusetts in 1816. He emigrated to Ohio with his parents, who settled on Duck creek in 1818. In 1836 he married Mary Taylor, who was born in 1813, and died in 1852. They had a family of six children, viz: Anna (Clogston), who resides in Iowa; Eliza (Murray), who died in Iowa in 1880; Amanda (Wilson), who resides in Morgan county; Cyrus and Hugh, who are both dead; Allen, who was born in Noble county in 1840, and in 1861 married Dorinda C. Swift, who was born in Waterford township in 1840. In 1853 Joseph Nickerson married Cynthia A. Beach, who was born in Guernsey county in 1827. He had by his second wife two children—Harry W. and Charles S. Allen Nickerson had a shoe shop at Luke Chute from 1861 to 1873 excepting the three years he was absent in the army. He has also been engaged in merchandizing at Luke Chute since 1866.

Perez Stull was born in New Jersey in 1767. He emigrated from New York to Belpre township in 1806, and died in Waterford township in 1826. He engaged in distilling in Waterford township for a number of years. Frances Wickham, his wife, was born in 1778, in New York, and died in 1859. The surviving members of their family are Mrs. Catharine Clark, of Beverly; Frances Roberts, of Waterford township; Henry Stull, of California; Electa A. Fouts, of Washington territory; and Mrs. Anna Davis, who was born in 1798 in New York. In 1816 she was married to Marvil Davis, who was born in Belpre township in 1794, and died in Waterford township in 1855. They had seven children, five of whom are still living, viz: Hester A. lives in Waterford township, Juliet in Nebraska, Mindwell (Mason) in Zanesville, Marvil W. on the homestead, Electa A. (Keyhoe) in Waterford township. Patience is dead.

In 1860 Marvel Davis, jr., married Nancy Patent, who

70

was born in Belmont county in 1842. They have nine children—Ralph H., Dema P., Stella B., Trevelyn E., Mabelle, Beryl, Dan, Ada M., and Cecil. Mr. Davis makes fruit culture a specialty.

Cyrus Morey, son of Nathaniel and Elizabeth Morey, who settled in Barlow township in 1808, was born in Waterford township in 1810. He was the fourth and youngest child. Benson, the oldest, resides in Delaware county; Julia died in 1872 and Maria in 1874. Cyrus Morey was married in 1829 to Rebecca Hagerman. Their family consisted of ten children, seven of whom are living: Arilie (Abbey) resides in Wisconsin, Rebecca (Coffman) and Seneca C. in Waterford township, Maria (Boggs) in Wisconsin, Mary (Dolan) in Morgan county, Retta Padgett in Waterford township, and C. L. at home. Betsy, Harris, and Nathaniel are dead. Mr. Morey followed keel and steamboating from 1823 to 1834.

John Jackson was born in Maryland in 1802. He engaged during the greater part of his life in dealing in horses. He was married in 1827 to Nancy Craig, who was born in 1805, and died at Beverly in 1850. He died at the same place in 1856. The surviving members of his family are Alexander, who resides at Beverly; Temperance W. (Morrison), in Iowa; James C., in Rock Island, Illinois; Charlotte O. (Henderson), in Iowa; and B. F., who was born in Beverly in 1840, and in 1863 married Sarah E. Wood, who was born in Virginia in 1840. They have two children—Harry and Carrie. By trade Mr. Jackson is a painter. A. J. Morrison, husband of Temperance W. Jackson, was a member of the Odd Fellows lodge at Beverly, and has, since removing to Iowa, served as grand master of the order in that State.

Daniel Roberts was born in Pennsylvania in 1792. In 1817 he married Hannah Bedagrew, who was born in Pennsylvania in 1800. They had twelve children, six of whom—Alexander, Daniel, John, James, Richard and Nancy C. (Davis)—reside in Missouri. William resides in Illinois. Margaret (Keath), Jeremiah and Isaiah are dead. Amos was born in Perry county in 1818. In 1838 he married Charlotte Taylor, who was born in 1818. She died in 1843, leaving two children—Margaret (Beckett), who lives in Oregon, and Elisha, who was killed at New Madrid in 1862, while in his country's service. Palmer, the first child, died in infancy. Mr. Roberts married, in 1844, Mrs. Frances White, widow of Harris White, by whom he had three children. Henry S., the oldest, lives on the homestead. He is married to Rosanna A. Webster, and has a family of three children. Harris White, first husband of Mrs. Amos Roberts, was born in 1808 and died in 1842. He was father of five children, only one of whom is living. Hiram W. resides in Washington Territory.

William Beckett was born in Jefferson county in 1807. In 1829 he married Anna Watson. She died in 1835, leaving three children—Mary A. (Alton), who lives in Virginia, John P., in Waterford township, and Erasmus W., at McConnelsville. William Beckett was married the second time in 1838, to Clarissa Vincent, who was born in Waterford township in 1810. He had by his second wife five children, viz.: Sarah E. (Kean), lives in

Morgan county; Lucina, at home. Roena and Martha are dead. Marion, third child served in the army for a short time. He is now engaged in farming.

Enos W. Slater removed from Belmont county, where he was born in 1815, to this county and settled in Waterford township in 1837. He was mayor of Beverly in 1860, and took a deep interest in the public schools, having served on the board two terms. In 1844 he married Margaret Turner, who was born in 1818. They have had seven children, two of whom, Calvin and Fletcher (twins), are dead. The five living are Hester A. (Wilson), of Coal Run; Mary (Sprague), of Marietta; Sarah Ruttie, of Cincinnati; Susan L. L. Dyar, of Marietta, and David, who lives at home. David Slater, sr., and his wife Martha West, emigrated from Maryland and settled in Belmont county in 1802. They afterwards moved to Guernsey county, where they lived till 1835, when Morgan county became their home. Mr. Slater died in 1850, Mrs. Slater in 1864.

John and Charlotte Cheffey emigrated from Maryland to Virginia and thence to Ohio in 1822, and settled in Jefferson county. They had a family of fourteen children. John T., one of the sons, was born in Virginia in 1822. In 1846 he married Salina Skivington, who was born in 1823 in Morgan county. They have had three children, but one of whom—John H.—is living. Robert and Amanda are dead.

Oliver Tucker was born in Washington county, Pennsylvania, in 1833; came to Washington county in 1839, and has for many years been engaged in mercantile business in Beverly. His wife, Mary J., daughter of John Buck, was also born in Washington county, Pennsylvania. Their family consists of two children—Alice Rowie, and Mary Jane.

Adelphia Webster and wife, Mary, emigrated from New England and settled in Morgan county in 1814. They had a family of five children. Sibyl was born in 1817, and in 1839 married Lyman Swift, who was born in 1815. They had six children—Rosamond (Danley), resides in Kansas; Mary (Owens), in Waterford; Lucinda (Vincent), at home; Adelia Murry, on the homestead; Francis, died in 1851; Louisa is at home.

David and Elizabeth Creighton emigrated from Ireland in 1829, and settled in Columbiana county. William, one of their five children, was born in Ireland in 1827. In 1877 he married Ruby A. Gifford. She was born in 1840. They have one child. Mr. Creighton was trustee of Waterford township three years, and is one of the most prosperous farmers in his community.

John W. and Henrietta Hernsworth Becket were natives of Maryland. They emigrated to Ohio and settled opposite Wheeling in 1817. About 1847 they moved to Morgan county. They had nine children, three of whom are still living, viz: Julia A. (Bone), resides at McConnelsville; Sarah Harvey, at Coshocton; Mary Beckett, who was born in Maryland in 1808, and was married to John Beckett in 1826. He was born in Virginia in 1805. They had eleven children, eight of whom are still living. Samuel and John live in Oregon; William died there; Humphrey lives on the homestead;

J. COONEY

James Cooney was born in County Donegal, Ireland, in 1818. His father, Mark Cooney, was a freeholder, and until he was eighteen years old James assisted at farming and attended school. He studied mathematics at the neighboring coast town of Ballyshannon, with the intention of becoming a surveyor. During this period he was offered a position in the service of his father's landlord, Colonel Conley, M. P., but his older brother, John, induced him to emigrate to America. In 1837 he joined his brother in Canada, and remained with him until 1840, when he accepted a position on the Muskingum river public works and came to Beverly. He worked here four years, and then returned to Canada, where he taught school three years.

In 1847 he returned, and was employed on public works till 1859. He clerked in stores and in the woollen factory, and owned a small clothing store, until 1873, when a company, consisting of Thomas Clark, George Preston, George Worsted and himself, built a boat for the trade between Marietta and Beverly and intermediate points. Mr. J. H. Hubble at that time owned a saw-mill on his farm below Beverly, and was particularly accommodating with regard to getting out lumber for the mill. The company named the boat in his honor—a compliment which Mr. Hubble acknowledged by presenting her a twenty dollar flag.

Mr. Cooney acted as clerk on the Hubble until 1878, when he became entire owner, and has since been master.

The Hubble does the people along the Munkingum an important service. Her regular daily trips at convenient hours afford them an opportunity of marketing and trading in Marietta, and choosing between intermediate points. Captain Cooney is always found prompt, accommodating and trusty in the performance of duty, and courteous in his treatment of passengers, always solicitous for their comfort and entertainment.

Captain Cooney is a member of the Presbyterian church of Beverly and a conscientious Christian. He has a natural capacity for mathematics, has a clear recollection of the scenes of his boyhood, and is an interesting and pleasant companion.

Jesse lives in Virginia, served through the war in the Second Virginia cavalry; Elizabeth Ross lives on the homestead; Louisa Milner lives in Morgan county; George lives in Plymouth; Jacob is dead; and Erasmus lives in Waterford.

Luther P. Allen was born in Waterford township in 1808. He married Ellen Edgar, who was born in 1812. She was the daughter of Daniel Edgar, who was born in 1788 and died in 1858. Mr. Allen was a preacher for about forty years, also a farmer. They had twelve children, of whom Levi is the third. He was born in 1847, and lives on the homestead with his mother. His father died in 1877.

Asahel Pomeroy was born in Massachusetts in 1812, emigrated to Morgan county in 1848, and removed to Beverly in 1850, where he engaged in the lumber trade in 1856, and still continues at that business. He married Rosamond Webster, who was born in Morgan county in 1815. They had nine children: Susan Brown, Lyman, Adelphia, and Lydia Clark, living at Beverly; Mary, Moses, George, Francis, and Sibyl are dead.

H. A. Staley was born in Virginia in 1814. In 1842 he married Elizabeth Matthews, who was born in Pennsylvania in 1817. Mr. Staley began the manufacture of woollen goods in Harrison county in 1832. In 1850 he removed to Beverly, where he engaged in the same business until 1876, when he retired from business. He served the village of Beverly as councilman nine years. His son David is engaged in the shoe business in Beverly. William lives in Athens, and Ella in Beverly. Sarah E., Mary A., Albert, and Elizabeth, are dead.

Joseph Parker, M. D., was born in Belmont county on November 5, 1821. He graduated from Starling Medical college, Columbus, in 1850, and begun practice in Beverly in 1851. In 1852 he married Adeline Bliss, who was born in Marietta January 28, 1832. They have had one child: Florence Bliss Parker. Dr. Parker's father was a native of North Carolina.

Samuel B. Robinson, esq., was born in Pennsylvania in 1815. He came to Waterford township in 1834, and died at Beverly January 2, 1877. In May, 1846, he married Colina N. Dodge, who died December 3, 1871. The surviving members of the family are W. P. Robinson, Beverly; Alice C. Robinson, Cromwell, Iowa, and Louis C. Robinson, of Marietta.

Joseph Wood emigrated with his family from Virginia and settled in Waterford township in 1855. He was born in Virginia in 1808, and married Lovina Cook, who was born in New York in 1812. The surviving members of the family are: James M., who lives in Illinois; Elizabeth (Jackson); Joseph N., Watertown; Frank M., in Illinois; Amanda, residing with her father on Wolf creek, this township; Mary W. (Ethell), in Illinois; Hervey D. and Charles J., at Waterford. Charles J. married, in 1858, Isabel Devol, who was born at Waterford in 1838.

David T. Brown, son of Isaac M. Brown and Christina Kyle, was born in Loudoun county, Virginia, in 1825. In 1832 his parents, with their family, removed to Ohio and settled at Zanesville. David, at the age of nineteen, began life on the river in the capacity of engineer on a steamboat, and served in that position twelve years. He then became captain of a boat, and during seven years' service in that responsible position won by his skill and courtesy an enviable reputation. In 1863 he purchased the Beverly woollen mills, which he continues to own and operate. In 1852 he was married to Miriam Lowe, daughter of John Lowe, of Aurelius township. The fruit of this marriage was five children, viz: George W., born April 5, 1854, died August 3, 1855; Alice C., born November 12, 1856; Willard M., born February 14, 1860; Lewis K., born December 30, 1865; and Eva Louise, born February 5, 1872. Alice C., the second child, was married November 12, 1874, to Rev. Theodore Finley, who was pastor of the Methodist Episcopal church at Beverly in 1872. Her husband died March 28, 1876, leaving one child, Theodore G., born September 17, 1875.

Isaac D., fifth son of Cyrus Spooner, M. D., was born in Lowell in 1838. He married, in 1866, Sarah Denney, who was born in Noble county in 1843. They have two children—Edward H., and Grace G. He served in the army from 1862 to 1865, in the Ninety-second Ohio volunteer infantry. The hardware business at Lowell and Beverly engaged his attention from 1866 to 1876. He is now manufacturing grain cradles at Beverly.

Joseph Bush emigrated with his wife from Connecticut and settled in Noble county, Ohio, in 1852. W. H. Bush, his son, was born in Noble county, Ohio. In 1873 he married Ella J. Carl, who was born in Perry county in 1853. Media W. and Lester are their children. Mr. Bush carried on the manufacture of woollen goods at McConnelsville from 1875 to 1880, when he came to Beverly and engaged in the same business.

David C. Aikin came to Beverly in 1868 from Harrison county, where he was born in 1822. His wife, whose maiden name was Violet Anderson, was born in 1824. They were married in 1845, and have a family of seven children, viz: Mary M. Seaman, Beverly, Ohio; Harriet Jenks, Illinois; James, Philadelphia; John, Beverly; Jennie, at home; Isaac, Tennessee; and Samuel, at home. Mr. Aikin was in the Twenty-second Ohio battery during the war. He has been engaged at wagon-making in Beverly since 1868.

In 1870 Professor E. S. Cox came from West Virginia to Waterford, where he married Frances McCullum, who was born at Beverly in 1845. Their family consists of three children—Edward L., Frank, and Annie L. Professor Cox organized and graded the public schools of Belpre in 1874.

CHAPTER XL.

ADAMS TOWNSHIP.

Geography, Soil and Scenery—Mineral Wealth—The Adams Garrison—Names of First Settlers—Other Early Settlers—German Emigration—Negro Colony—Societies—Masonic Lodge—Odd Fellows Lodge—Grange—Churches—Eearly Religious Meetings—Physicians—Early Events—Township Organization—Lowell Business Enterprises.

ADAMS, a large township lying east of Waterford, and bordering on Noble county, possesses a variety of soil and scenery. The Muskingum river flows through a fertile alluvial valley of variable width in the southern half. High terraces rise abruptly on both sides and extend to the borders. These terraces on the north are drained by Coal run, Big run, Cat's creek and Bear run. There are no streams worthy of a name emptying into the Muskingum from the south. The bluff which faces the river on this side is higher than the terraces lying further back, and throws the water from them into Rainbow and its branches.

The hills along Coal run, Big run, and Cat's creek, contain heavy seams of coal of a fair quality, which would be an unlimited source of wealth were it not for the unfortunate circumstance that the market in this region is very meagre. Great repositories of coal can only be of value in the presence of manufacturing establishments, and at this age of the world railroads are as necessary to manufacturing operations as steam pipes to an engine. As has been noted in the chapter on Waterford, mines about the mouth of Coal run have been opened and supply the local needs of the community, but the economic resources of the township can be fully developed only by railroad facilities.

The soil of this township, considering its physical features, is upon the whole superior. The river alluvians are as productive though not as extensive as those of Waterford. The soil on the terraces has been made fertile by disintegrated limestone, and produces satisfactory crops of wheat and other cereals.

THE SETTLEMENT.

The improvement of the territory of Adams township was retarded about four years by the Indian war. Donation lots were drawn in 1789, and many of the owners joined the Waterford colony, or more properly the Second association, and were confined within the garrison at that place. A few others remained at Marietta—the owners of Bear Creek allotment nearly all resided in Campus Martius.

The settlement of Adams was cotemporary with the settlement of the block-house colony on the south branch of Wolf creek, but fortunately suffered no such disaster as the murder of Sherman Waterman, although that event caused great anxiety in the frail garrison located nearly opposite the site of the present town of Buell's Lowell. The inhabitants of this garrison were four families and four single men, all of whom owned land in the vicinity and employed the time during the first summer at clearing and building cabins. The garrisoned cabins which stood near each other on the river bank belonged

to, and were occupied by, Nicholas Coburn, with whom Asa, his brother, then a single man, boarded; Robert Allison, with whom Oliver Dodge boarded; Nathan Kinny and family, admitted to their cabin Joseph Simons, and William Davis, whose cabin was the home, during the first summer, of Daniel Davis.

By the close of the summer of 1795, a clearing had been made on each man's farm, and a cabin had been erected by those with families. Permanent peace with the Indians broke the pickets from the garrison fence, and the little band which necessity had made neighbors scattered to their possessions. The improvement of other lots now commenced, and in a few years much of the thick and heavy forest of the Muskingum alluvians gave place to fields of stout corn. Of the eight first settlers three—Robert Allison, Oliver Dodge and Joseph Simons, were at Marietta during the war, the other five were at Waterford.

The Coburns and their descendants are prominent in the history of the township. Major Coburn, who came to Marietta in the latter part of 1788, was one of three brothers who entered the Colonial army at the opening of the Revolution. Andrew, the eldest, was killed at Bunker Hill. Abraham also lost his life in battle. Asa served as captain, and after the recognition of the Government was retired with the rank of major. All three belonged to the Massachusetts line. Phineas, eldest son of Asa, joined the first company of Ohio emigrants. Major Asa, with his sons Nicholas and Asa, came half a year later. The father and three sons joined the second association. The burial place of Major Coburn is unknown. He died at Waterford during the Indian war. Nicholas and Asa settled on the bottom, opposite the mouth of Cat's creek, on adjoining lots. Asa died in 1827, leaving seven children, three of whom, Sibyl, Asa and Minerva, live on the homestead; Sarah, Samuel and Parsis are dead; Lucy is married to Joseph Frye, who lives on the Coburn farm. Mrs. Coburn, whose maiden name was Rhoda Baker, daughter of Dr. Baker, died in 1816.

Joseph Frye, father of Joseph Frye, jr., came from Maine to Waterford, where he was one of the early school teachers. He married Sally Becker, by whom he had three children: Sophrania, died young; Rhoda, married John Wilkins, of Adams township, and Joseph, in 1840, married Lucy Coburn, who was born in the year 1809. Joseph was born in the year 1810. Their family consists of two children—Sarah, wife of Oliver Keil, of Darke county, and John W., of this township, who was born January 14, 1841. He married, August 19, 1863, Melinda Mason, who was born October 10, 1840. They have four children—Henry C., Harley E., Joe W., and Nellie M. The permanent settlement of Phineas Coburn, eldest son of Major Coburn, was in Morgan county. Nicholas Coburn, after making considerable progress in improving his land, traded with James Owens and removed to Morgan county. Three daughters of Major Asa Coburn married Ohio pioneers. Sibyl, first wife of Andrew Webster, died in Massachusetts. Her husband and two sons—Adelpha and Asa

C., belonged to the second association. Mary, second daughter of Major Coburn, was married to Gilbert Devol. Susanna was married to William Mason.

Of the little group of pioneer families of 1795, Robert Allison's was the largest. Mr. Allison came to the county from Pennsylvania in the fall of 1788, and lived in the stockade until the spring of 1795, when he joined the Adams colony. He had drawn lot fourteen, in Cat's Creek allotment, and in the fall he removed his family into a cabin erected during the summer. The family consisted of eleven children, the second of whom, Nancy, was born in Fayette county, Pennsylvania, October 22, 1784. She was married to Stephen Frost, son of Samuel Frost, December 18, 1800. They had seven children—Robert, Clarissa, Louisiana, Rosetha, Nancy, Stephen, and Eliza. Louisiana, the third child, was born September 16, 1807. She was married to John Stacy, son of Joseph Stacy, of Muskingum township. Five children was the fruit of this marriage—Miles, Austin, Luceba, Sophia, and Mary. Austin, the second child, was born in Adams township, September 25, 1830. He married, April 22, 1858, Lydia Pixley, daughter of of Fremont Pixley, of Marion county, Ohio. She was born October 9, 1837. Eight children have blessed this union—Albert F., Jessie M., George P., Osmer O., William, Harry, Mary, and Littie; all of whom are living. Mrs. Frost, now in her ninety-seventh year, is a remarkably well preserved woman. Her memory of events at Marietta, during the Indian war is clear, and to her the writer of this chapter is indebted for his information concerning the first settlement. Longevity was a characteristic of some of her ancestors. The father of Robert Allison lived to the extreme old age of one hundred and four.

Oliver Dodge was one of the forty-eight who came to Ohio in April, 1788. He had seven brothers, but one of whom, Nathaniel, one of Marietta's early merchants, came to Ohio. Oliver was born at Hampton Falls, New Hampshire, in 1776. He was in Campus Martius during the Indian war, and joined the Adams colony in the spring of 1795. He frequently walked to Marietta to purchase provisions, and carried them home on his back. In January, 1800, he married Mrs. Nancy Manchester. Her maiden name was Devol. Her first husband died before she came to Ohio. Mr. Dodge, after the first summer, had lived alone in the lonely neighborhood, one year in a hollow sycamore tree. He lived on the farm until his health failed, when he came to Marietta for medical treatment, and died at the residence of his brother on Putnam street. He was buried on his farm in Adams township, with Masonic honors, the lodge conducting his body for burial in a barge up the river. He had two children: Richard Hubbard, born in 1801, and Mary Manchester, born in 1807. Richard married, October 4, 1825, Betsy H. McCoy, who was born in this county in 1801. Richard was familiarly termed an odd genius, and many anecdotes are told of him. He never permitted anything to change his plans. Upon one occasion his wife was intending to go on horseback with him to church. "Dick" brought out a favorite horse

saddled for two, and rode to the block, where he waited a short time for his companion, whose coming was not as prompt as he desired, and without a word he hastened alone to the church. He had a mania for horses, and once, while riding to church with his wife, the horse struck a gait so satisfactory to the head rider that he was not permitted to stop until the meeting-house had been left five miles behind. Richard had no children, and with him the family in this line became extinct. They lived for many years at the homestead, until his health failed, and then removed to McConnelsville, where he died November 2, 1866. Mary Manchester, only daughter of Oliver Dodge, was married to Perley B. Johnson, of Marietta. Oliver and his son Richard were tall, thin men. "The Dodges always lived as they pleased and died as they pleased."

Nathan Kinny, who has been mentioned as one of the eight, and whose name appears in the early history of Waterford, was a native of Nova Scotia, and a descendant of an aristocratic English family. Mr. Kinny married Massa Wilson, a member of the Wilson family of Waterford township. He owned the farm on which the garrison stood during the first summer. The friendship formed between these pioneer families seems to have been of a permanent character, for two of the sons of Robert Allison, William and Stephen, married two of the daughters of Nathan Kinny, Elizabeth and Abigail, respectively. Sarah, the second daughter of Mr. Kinny, married Wyram Bartlett, of Waterford.

William and Daniel Davis, sons of Captain Daniel Davis, one of the forty-eight first emigrants, owned lots in Bear Run allotment. After Wayne's treaty they left the garrison on the Kinny farm, and moved to their own land, a part of which was cleared and planted the first summer. Williard, one of the sons of William Davis, was born March 5, 1806. He married, in 1827, Caroline Shepard, who was born in New York, November 27, 1811. Their family consisted of five children, viz: Elizabeth, Walter, Susan, Willard H., and Mary C., three of whom are living, Elizabeth, Walter, and Willard. Walter was born August 8, 1832. He married, May 17, 1863, Elizabeth Trapp, daughter of Philip Trapp. They have had five children, four of whom are living: Willard F., Katie, Rosa, and Walter. Mr. Davis has been in mercantile business in Lowell for about seventeen years.

James Owen, who came into possession of the Nicholas Coburn lot, emigrated to Ohio with his family in the spring of 1788, from Rhode Island. His first wife was Mary Gardner. After her death he married Ruby Brown. Daniel Owen, one of the sons, afterwards became a resident of this township. He was born in Rhode Island, November 25, 1782. He married, April 10, 1804, Hannah Allison. He married, for his second wife, February 20, 1820, Betsy Green, and for his third, February 29, 1828, Deborah Sprague Swift. By his first wife he had seven children: Sally, Polly, Azabah, Vincent, Leander, and Allison; by his second, Oliver G., and by his third, Hannah, Daniel, and Henry. Daniel, the only survivor of the last named three, was born November 28, 1831. He was married May 9, 1852, to Mercy Chapman, who was born November 23, 1830. They have three children: Florence, Alice, and Linnie.

William Mason, a native of Massachusetts, joined the Forty-eight Ohio emigrants in April, 1788, and it is said was the second man to leave the boat at Marietta. He married, March 14, 1790, Susanna Coburn. He had received the title of colonel in the Revolution and was a man of prominence in the early community. He settled in Adams in 1796 or 1797, on the bottom and plain nearly opposite the site of Upper Lowell, where he died September 26, 1813. Of a family of twelve children but one is yet living, Jonas, the third child. There is a tradition that he was the first child born in the township, but this is disputed by others. Adams was at that time a new community and medical services could be obtained only at Marietta or Waterford. This circumstance made it prudent for the wives of the youthful Adams settlement to spend the period of expectancy in one of the older communities. It is said that for more than two years after its first settlement, no child was born on Adams territory. We are unable to say positively whether or not Mr. Mason was born in this township. He was born May 23, 1797. He married Beulah Stacey, who was born in Rainbow, October 8, 1804. They were married January 24, 1822. The other members of the family of Colonel Mason will be remembered by the old people of this township. Pamela married John Roach, of Adams; Joseph finally settled in Missouri; William lived and died in Upper Lowell; Susan married in Marion county, where she died; Elijah lived back of Upper Lowell; Simeon settled in Missouri; Sophronia married Solomon Parke, of Watertown; Clarinda married Abner Devol, of Adams; and Adelpha Coburn Mason, who was born April 12, 1814. He married, in 1836, Patience Simons and settled on lots 8 and 9 of Cat's Creek survey. He had six children who settled as follows: Reuben S., on the Nicholas Coburn farm; Oscar F., in Kansas; William W., killed in the war; Vestie S., (Foster), in Waterford township; Elijah J., in Marietta; and Electa K. (Owen), in Illinois. Reuben S., the oldest son, married Miss L. L. Stacy, by whom he had four children.

Isaac, youngest son of William and Sarah Mason, was born August 7, 1826. He married, March 25, 1847, Delia Allison, who was born April 10, 1821, and died December 21, 1876. He married for his second wife Anthia Simons, March 22, 1877. She was born October 17, 1838. By his first wife he had six children: Amy, Chester, Delia A., Melissa A., Stephen, and Rachel C. By his second wife, two: Cloyd R., and Mertie.

William B., second son of Colonel Mason, was born in 1800, and in 1821 married Henrietta McDonald, who was born in the District of Columbia, in 1804. Two children by this marriage are living: Elizabeth, wife of Warner Green, of Harmar, and William B., jr. The latter, born in 1823, was married in 1852, to Lucetta B. Mason, by whom he has two children: Mary E., and William B. Mrs. Mason's family were not related to the

family by her husband, although her father's name, curiously enough, was William B. Mason. Colonel W. B. Mason was county recorder from 1855 to 1861, when he left for the war, entering the army as a private and coming out in 1865 as colonel of the Sixty-third regiment. In 1866 he was elected county treasurer, holding the office during one term. From 1870 to 1878, he was postmaster at Marietta. In 1880 he engaged in the hat business in Marietta.

Mr. Isaac Devol, of Tiveston, Rhode Island, was born in August, 1774; married Elizabeth Brownell, of Portsmouth, in 1798, and came to Ohio the same year in company with two brothers, Allen and Daniel, two sisters and a widowed mother. He bought a farm on the Muskingum, not far from Big run. He built on his farm a large stone house, which is still standing. He followed the sea for several years previous to his marriage and visited both the East and West Indies. He died November 4, 1851, and his wife eleven years afterward. They were the parents of eleven children—George W., Clarissa, Rebecca, Abner, Richmond, David, Patience, Isaac, Nathan B., Charles M., and Cynthia—of whom are living: Richmond, in Missouri, Patience, wife of Edmund Morse, in Athens county, and Charles M., in Muskingum township, this county. The latter married Celina M. Olney, and has five children—Russell S., who is professor of mathematics in the Ohio university, Athens; Mary E., (Mrs. Cook) in Morris, Illinois; Alice D., in Kansas; Silian, in Muskingum, and Charles M., jr., at home.

William Mason, a native of Pennsylvania, emigrated to Ohio and settled in Adams township in 1797. He married Rebecca Sharp, by whom he had eight children, three boys and five girls. William, the fifth child, was born in Pennsylvania, September 9, 1796. He married twice; first Luna Sprague, April 18, 1818. She died in 1839. He married for his second wife Nancy Sprague. His family consisted of ten children: Lydnay, Rachel, Eliza, Adeline, Lucy, Sarah, and Sylvester, by his first wife; and Melinda, Melissa, and William W., by his second. Sylvester married, July 22, 1856, Harriet Barnes. She died March 16, 1880, leaving two children, Vestie L. and George D. He married for his second wife, November 18, 1880, Caroline Reaney.

It was once said by a census enumerator, that he only asked the first names of the inhabitants of the Muskingum valley, between rainbow and the mouth of Wolf creek. He could tell by family resemblance whether they were Devols, Masons, or Spragues. An effort has already been made to briefly trace the other two families.

The Sprague family, in Washington county, is descended from an old English family of that name. Joshua Sprague, second, was born in Providence, Rhode Island, in 1729. He married twice, first to Amy Darling, second to Abigail Wilber, from whom the Spragues of Adams township are descended. The family were living in Nova Scotia at the opening of the Revolution, but at that time removed to Massachusetts. Joshua served during the war as major. He lost all his property during the war. In 1788, accompanied by his two sons, Jonathan and William, he came to Simrell's ferry with a horse and two wheeled vehicle. They came by water to Marietta, arriving in June. Mr. Sprague and his sons took the contract of building one of the block-houses, for which they recived one hundred dollars. They joined the second association in the spring of 1789, and were at Waterford during the Indian war. In the spring of 1784 the remaining members of the family were removed to Waterford. Joshua lived in Waterford until 1812, when he removed to Adams township, where he died October, 1816. Abigail, his wife died at the same place, December 10, 1825, in her ninety-fifth year. Joshua's descendants at the time of his death numbered one hundred and sixty-three. The sons of Joshua numbered nine and the daughters four. Of these, William settled and died in Adams township; James in Muskingum county; Samuel on Meigs creek; Wilber in Jackson county; Frederick, in Columbus; Nehemiah, in Adams township; and Jonathan, the head of the Spragues, now living in Adams, settled on the bottom opposite Coal Run, in 1803, and built the stone house now occupied by his son, Elijah. He also built a mill which is still standing; it was known as the Island mill. He also had a distillery. His sons were Wayne, who lived on the old Lord farm, and died in 1848; Jonathan is still living in the valley, near the homestead; Joshua died in 1828, on a farm near the mill; Elijah occupies the old house; Seaman lives in the west; and Benjamin lived in Waterford. The family has always been highly respectable as well as numerous.

Stephen Frost improved the farm now owned by A. O. Stacey, nearly opposite Buell's Lowell. Michael Cyphers, a Pennsylvanian, came to this township about 1803, and made an improvement on the Flick farm. John Green and a Mr. Brown were temporary settlers on the upper end of the Coburn bottom. Esquire Lord lived at Marietta during the Indian war. He afterwards purchased a lot on the west side of the river, above the dam.

Benjamin Beadle and Andrew McClure, two of the Waterford associates, drew lots in the Cats Creek allotment. Andrew McClure made some improvement on his farm, but soon sold and removed to Waterford. Benjamin Beadle removed at an early date to Athens county.

The first farm below the mouth of Cats creek was improved by Esquire Joseph Wells. David Wells lived near the mouth of the creek. They were sons of Major Wells, and lived in the stockade during the Indian war.

The brick house now occupied by Walter Davis was built by Alexander Oliver, who purchased three lots at an early period of the settlement, and removed from Belpre, where he had been during the war.

Enoch Wing improved the farm and built the house now owned by Hanson Dutton.

Gilbert Seamans and his three sons, Benijah, Gilbert and Preserved, owned lots in Bear Creek allotment. They were at Harmar during the Indian war.

Joseph Simons owned and improved lot ten in Cats Creek allotment.

Amos Wilson, a native of Maine, came to Washington county about the year 1804. He died in 1837. His wife was Betsy Newhall, who bore him nine children as follows: Caroline, Charles, Charlotte, David, Eliza, Newhall, Polly, Nelson, and one that died in infancy. Newhall was born in this township in 1817, and has resided here since. He has been twice married—to Susan Lewis, in 1845, and after her death (in March 1877,) was married in May, 1878, to Margaret A. Stacy.

George N. Cox, a native of Pennsylvania, was born in 1787, and removed to Virginia about the year 1816, and resided there until 1838, when he came to this county and settled in Aurelius township. He afterwards moved to Salem township, and still later to Adams, and continued to live here until his death, which took place April 5, 1879. He was the father of eleven children, named as follows: Jane A., James F., Samuel N., William F., Benjamin M., Joseph, George W., John F., Charles, Margaret, Edwin R. All the children are living except Jane, George and Charles. Joseph, a well-known resident of this township, was born in what is now Marshal county, Virginia, in 1820. He came to Adams in 1844. He was formerly a tinner by trade, and followed his trade some ten years, when he engaged in merchandising in Lowell, in which he continued some twenty-three years. In 1877 he sold out to Sprague & Wolfram. In 1849 he was married to Harriet Porter, of Salem, born in 1826. They have one child, Flora M., wife of A. W. Tompkins, of Harmar.

The aged mother of Mr. Cox is still living, at the advanced age of eighty-nine. She and her husband had lived together as man and wife for sixty-seven years.

Alfred Hall was born in West Virginia in 1802. In 1822 he moved to Ohio and settled in Adams township. He died at Coal Run in 1878. His wife, whose name was Narcissa Ross, was born in 1803. The surviving members of their family are: Matilda Mackay, who resides in Missouri; Malissa Yates, Beverly; Alfred J., Coal Run; Eliza Blackmer, Iowa; Sarah Keever, Coal Run; and Alonzo, who was born in 1828. He married Mary Wilson in 1852. She was born in 1831. They have two children—Clara A. Rose and Charley. Mr. Hall was engaged in merchandising at Coal Run from from 1857 to 1877. He is now retired from business.

John J. Wood, son of Morgan Wood, was born in Adams township, October 24, 1824, and was a resident of the township until his death, which occurred December 21, 1880. January 1, 1868, he married Martha J. Campbell, of Noble county, who was born July 14, 1835. Her father, Patriarch Campbell, was once a resident of this county. Mrs. Wood has a family of five children. She continues to farm the homestead, one-half mile north of Upper Lowell.

John C. Farnsworth was born in Monroe county in 1826. In 1841 he removed to Washington county and settled in this township. In 1845 he married Emeline Devol, who was born in 1822. Mr. Farnsworth is a veteran school director, having served his district in that capacity from 1854 till 1878. Three of the seven children of his family are still living. Simeon and Frank live at Coal Run, and William at home with his father. Mr.

Farnsworth engaged in farming and flat-boating from 1845 to 1859. He has since been engaged as a dealer in general produce. Mr. Farnsworth now lives in Waterford township.

David M. Reed, a native of Ireland, came from New York State to Ohio, and settled first in Morgan county, coming to this county in 1849, and settling in Adams township. By his wife, Lucinda Buchanan, he had three children, viz.: George W., of Belpre, Lucy D. (Echalbury) of Missouri, and Frances M., of Harmar, this county. George W. who is a practicing physician in Belpre, was born in Morgan county in 1846. He married Mary J. Chandler, of Adams township. After the doctor's graduation he practiced for a time at Lowell.

James H. Rose was born in Virginia in 1810. He emigrated to Ohio and settled in this township in 1844. He married Mary Shafer, who was born in 1812 and died in 1871. Mr. Rose died at Coal Run in 1880. He was a substantial member of the Methodist church and a worthy man. His surviving children are: Anna (Hickman), Coal Run; Isaiah and Lemuel, Coal Run; Silas, Bellaire; Edward, Coal Run; James, born 1849, in 1871 married Clara J. Hall, born in 1853; Manning, born in 1856, married Louisa M. Bish in 1877. James and Manning have been in business at Coal Run since 1878.

Richard Fouraker was born in Stafford county, Virginia, in 1809. In the fall of 1852 he settled in that part of Union township now embraced in Adams township. His farm of two hundred acres was, when he came to it, a vast wilderness, which hard work has converted into a pleasant home. By his wife, Caroline, he has had seven children. Of this family Joseph N., Elizabeth, Levi J., Douglas W., and Martha E. are deceased, Lewis K. and Eliza J. being the survivors.

Mr. Fouraker was captain of company H of the Seventy-seventh Ohio volunteer infantry, in which company his sons, Douglas W. and Lewis K. enlisted in 1861. Douglas died from wounds received at the battle of Shiloh. Lewis was wounded there but finally recovered. Mr. Fouraker has served as justice of the peace, trustee, constable, and the like.

Albert Chandler removed to Adams in the winter of 1844, coming from Muskingum county, where he was born in 1823. Mr. Chandler enlisted in the Mexican war, but on arriving at Camp Washington, Cincinnati, found that his services were not needed, as the quota required had been filled. He was therefore sent back home. In the war of the Rebellion he again offered his services to the Government with better success. He was captain of company K, Ohio volunteer infantry, and served three years and three months. Previous to the war he had been engaged in the lumber and mercantile business, and subsequently in merchandise and commission, and also ran a flouring mill. At the present time he is farming. In the spring of 1848 he was married to a daughter (Ethella) of Alfred Regnier, esq., born in 1827. They have one daughter, Mrs. Dr. G. W. Reed, of Belpre.

James F. Putnam became a resident of Adams in 1870, having removed from Pickaway county, Ohio, where he was born in 1839. In the fall of 1873 he was married to Harriet Brown, a native of this township, born in 1841. They have four children—Wade W., James B., Hattie, and Anna. Mr. Putnam is now serving his second term as justice of the peace, and has also held the office of township assessor for the last six years. He has been engaged for the past eleven months in the drug business in Lowell. Mr. Putnam was captain of the Eighth battery in the war of the Rebellion.

The value of the terraces of Adams township, was not appreciated until about 1840, when the German emigration begun. On Cats creek, above the river bottom, there was no improvement before 1833, when Alvey Hoyt purchased a lot and built a house. The population of the hill districts is, at the present time, more than eighty per cent. German. Fearing and Adams are the German townships of the county. The village of Lowell is more than sixty per cent. German, and it is to the people of this nationality, that the township owes a large proportion of its wealth.

Philip Mattern, county commissioner and postmaster at Lowell, was born in Germany, in July 1836, and emigrated to this country with his father, Henry Mattern, who settled and afterwards lived in Salem township. Henry Mattern was born in 1790, and died in 1860. He was the father of four children, of whom Philip was the youngest. Philip remained in Salem township until the fall of 1855, when he moved to Adams, and has since resided here. He has been twice married, first in 1855 to Mary, daughter of John Chandler, who died April 19, 1872, leaving two children—John and Philip. His present wife was Christina Minich, whom he married in June, 1873, and by whom he has one child—Clarence. As previously mentioned, Mr. Mattern is serving as county commissioner, and postmaster at Lowell, having held the latter office for sixteen years. He has also served as township clerk for two years.

Jacob Snyder emigrated with his family from Germany, where he was born in 1795, and settled in Belpre township, this county, in 1847. Three years afterward he moved to Warren, and in 1852 came to Adams, and died in this township in June, 1853. His wife was Margaret Baker, by whom he had seven children. Of these, five are living, viz: Jacob, Charles, Elizabeth, George and Daniel. George, a resident of this township, was born in Germany in 1831, and in 1864 married Elizabeth, daughter of Willard Davis, also born in 1831. They had two children—Caroline D., and Jessie D. Mr. Snyder has served as trustee of his township three terms, and was appraiser of real estate in 1870.

Thomas Spratt, who was born in Northumberland county, England, in 1829, became a resident of this county in 1856. Since his settlement, he has earned, by unceasing energy, his present farm of two hundred and twenty acres of land. He took part in the war of the Rebellion before becoming a citizen of the United States, and served faithfully in the hundred day service. Both in his native land and in this country he has been an extensive dealer in fine sheep. By his wife, Jane Heslop, he has had five children: Lizzie A., Alice J., Matthew, George and Mary.

MANLY W. MASON.

Mr. Mason is a representative of one of the oldest families of Washington county, being a grandson of William Mason, whose settlement is noted elsewhere. His father, John Mason, was born in Adams township, in 1803. In 1831 he was married to Rosannah Scribner, who was born in the year 1815. They raised a family of eight children, of whom the subject of this notice was the second son. He was born in Adams township, Washington county, Ohio, August 13, 1835, and resided there until 1857, since which time he has lived at Coal Run village, in Waterford township. His occupation had been that of a farmer, until October, 1871, when he was admitted by the supreme court of Ohio to practice law in the several courts of the State, and since then he has followed the practice of his profession. He was commissioned a notary public for Washington county, Ohio, in May, 1877, and is still holding that office. At the September term of the circuit court of Wood county, West Virginia, in 1880, he was admitted to practice in that State.

Mr. Mason was married March 15, 1855, to Sophia A. Hall, who died February 23, 1862, leaving four small children. July 23, 1862, he married Lucy A. Dyer.

Jacob Becker, son of Theobold Becker, was born in Germany in 1836. He came to America with his father in 1847, and settled in Fearing township. He married in 1860, Mary E. Wilking, who was born in Union township in 1839. In 1867 he came to Lowell, and has since been engaged as a carpenter and contractor. His family consists of eight children—John, Philip, Caroline, Harman, Lavina, Flora, Ellen and Anna.

Jacob Rietz was born in Bavaria in 1815. February 8, 1840, he married Margaret Gloss, who was born in Germany, August 20, 1820. They came to America in 1840, and settled in Salem township. In 1857 he removed to Lowell and operated the lowell saw-mill. He sold the mill in 1872, and is now engaged in business. The family consists of six children—Jacob, Caroline, (Weis), Margaret Blankenbühler, Katie (deceased), Phœbe and Henry.

In 1875, a colored colony obtained a foothold near the line of Adams and Muskingum townships. The colony at present consists of eight families, who deserted the plantations of Rockingham county, Virginia, about 1855, and settled in Belmont county, Ohio, whence they came about six years ago. They organized a religious society in 1880, and are regularly ministered to by Rev. J. Andrews, the Wesleyan Methodist preacher at Parkersburgh.

SOCIETIES.

Lowell Lodge, No. 436 F. and A. M., was chartered October 21, 1867. The charter members were John Farbell, Albert Chandler, John Williamson, Philip Mattern, Joseph Cox, John W. Frye, Sylvester Mason, Cyrenus Buchanan, S. N. Meriam, William Mason, William Engler, and A. O. Stacey. The first officers were John Farbell, W. M.; Albert Chandley, S. W.; John Williamson, J. W.; Philip Mattern, treasurer; Joseph Cox, secretary; J. W. Frye, S. D.; Sylvester Mason, J. D; Cyrenus Buchanan, tyler.

The following is a list of masters with the date of the expiration of their term of service: John Farbell, December, 1870; A. Chandler, 1871; J. W. Frye, 1872; A. Chandler, 1873: John Williamson, 1874; Jacob Landsettle, 1875; Sylvester Mason, 1876; George Snyder, 1877; J. Landsettle, 1878; P. Mattern, 1880; J. Landsettle, since December, 1880. The lodge was constituted December 25, 1869, by David Aikin, P. M., in Philip Mattern's building, where meetings were held until September, 1870, when the lodge removed its quarters to the Snyder building.

Lowell Lodge, No. 438, I. O. O. F., was chartered August 23, 1869, with the following members: Henry Wolf, Jacob Hopp, Jacob Becker, Jacob Landsettle, Franz Wilking, jr., Franz Wilking, sr., Jacob Rietz, William Wendell, John Wilking, Aberus Judd, sr., E. W. Sprague, Parley Rummer, J. S. Donalson, S. M. Devol. The first officers were: A. Judd, sr., noble grand; Franz Wilking, jr., secretary; E. W. Sprague, treasurer. The lodge was constituted by Grand Marshal H. G. Hollister and Grand Marshal Snider. The noble grands have been: A. Judd, jr., Franz Wilking, sr., I. D. Spooner, J. L. Delong, E. C. Farquhar, O. A. Stacey, H. Porter,

Albert Chandler, Jacob Landsettle, William Bosner, Franz Wilking, 2d, Jacob Becker, J. A. Fleck, Henry Spies, R. S. Mason, John Williamson, William Wendell, David Wilking, 2d, C. E. Judd, Christian Doeberiner, J. A. Fleck, David Wilking, Henry Spies, and Theobald Becker. This lodge has always had a large membership.

Lowell Grange, No. 1035, was organized September 30, 1874, with nineteen members. The first officers were: George Snyder, master; O. A. Stacey, overseer; R. S. Mason, lecturer; A. Chandler, chaplain; S. C. Kile, steward; T. M. Alexander, assistant steward; Walter Davis treasurer; Mrs. Emily Mason, ceres; Mrs. Lydia Stacey, pomona; Mrs. Elizabeth Davis, flora; Mrs. Jane Alexander, lady assistant steward. George Snyder was master till 1877; J. W. Frye, till 1880; A. O. Stacey, till 1881; R. S. Mason is present master.

In the spring of 1878, the Union Grange Fair association was formed by delegates from Lowell, Liberty Hill and Adams granges. The first fair which was held at Lowell, in September, 1878, proved a success. Since then four other granges—Jackson, Ridge, Valley and Waterford—have been admitted to the association. The fair of 1879 was satisfactory, but bad weather greatly impaired the exhibition of 1880. Lowell grange at present has a membership of twenty.

RELIGIOUS SOCIETIES.

The first religious services in the township were held soon after the first settlement, by Dr. Story, of Marietta. The residence of Robert Allison was for some time used for religious meetings by all denominations—Baptists, Congregationalists, and Methodists—after the formation of Marietta circuit. Mrs. Stacey has given us a picture of one of these meetings. She writes:

Previous to the building of the Baptist church at Upper Lowell, they had meetings in private houses and school-houses, in cold weather; in warm weather in barns and groves. I attended meeting in a private log house with two rooms, about twelve feet square. During the meeting a woman proceeded to examine a small sack hanging up. Being unable to determine its contents by feeling, she opened it and exclaimed, "There, it is candles, and I have spoiled them!" On another occasion the speaker being somewhat animated, raised a chair and brought it down so violently on the foot of a man that it took the nail off the great toe. I saw him limp out of the house. I have seen a large proportion of the congregation in their bare feet. The ladies were in the habit of carrying their shoes near the church. They then put them on but soon removed them after leaving the meeting."

The Methodist church, usually strong in country districts, never made progress in Adams. A house of worship was once erected at Lowell, but owing to the weakness of the congregation was finally abandoned. The Baptist church absorbed religious interests in the early history of the township.

BAPTIST CHURCH.

The first Baptist church in the county and second religious society of any denomination, was organized in Adams township in 1797. The history of this early organization, its successes and dissensions, has been given in connection with the history of the church at Marietta. The present society is a reorganization of the old Rainbow church, which was effected in 1832, with fifty-seven members. It had been a branch of the Marietta church from 1827 until that date. During the year of its establishment (1832) a house of worship was built near the site of Upper Lowell. The location was unfortunate, as the centre of population in a few years moved further down the river. The present house in Buell's Lowell was built in 1868. The church has always incurred strong opposition from the outside and suffered dissension within its own membership. Good Hope and Watertown churches originated in an interest at Lowell. The successive pastors have been: A. Dana, A. Darrow, H. Gear, M. White, A. J. Sedwick, William Pearce, J. M. Winn, M. Madox, S. W. Churchill, H. Lyon, S. Seigfried, W. A. Blake, H. Lyon, F. Stanley, J. C. Richardson, H. M. Prince. Mr. Stanley is the present pastor. The pastorate was vacant from 1870 to 1874.

DISCIPLE CHURCH.

Through the efforts of John Reed and others a society of Disciples in Christ was organized in 1831, with a large and influential membership. A house of worship was built below the present site of Lowell. The pulpit has been supplied by John Reed, Reuben Davis, Nathan J. Mitchell, George Lucy, John Sargeant, and others. There was an awakening revival in 1858 which resulted in sixty accessions to the church. The new house was built in 1872. The congregation has been for some time without a settled minister, and is not as strong as formerly.

EVANGELICAL PROTESTANT CHURCH.

A German congregation of the Protestant Evangelical church was organized in Lowell about 1857. In the absence of early records we are unable to give exact dates. A society was organized and constitution adopted in 1860. In 1863 the present brick church was built. May 6, 1879, the roof was burned and the building otherwise injured, necessitating extensive repairs. F. Juergeus was pastor till 1867, and Alfred Kretschmar succeeded. F. Eschenfld became pastor in 1871, and remained about one year. C. G. Freidrich succeeded and remained till July, 1880. Since September, 1880, E. A. Frienfstick has been pastor. The present membership is about sixty.

CONGREGATIONAL CHURCH.

The Congregational society of Lowell was organized by Charles Weatherby. In 1860 the most commodious church building in the township was erected. Since Mr. Weatherby resigned the pastorate, the society has never been strong in numbers, but the field is large and there yet remains hope of final success. Mr. Weatherby's successors have been: Messrs. Noble, Frye, Fay, Moore, Ransom, Mills, Louis, Reed, and Irwin.

PHYSICIANS.

The first of these useful members of society who settled in Adams was Thomas Hearsay. He opened an office about the beginning of the century and held a full practice for a number of years. Drs. Baker and Dergy, of Waterford, and Regnier, of Duck Creek, were relied upon in serious cases. A fair share of the practice passed to Dr. Cyrus Spooner after he began practice. Dr. Spooner had a strong love of natural science, and spent his leisure time experimenting in mechanics.

Dr. James Sales was for a number of years in partnership with Dr. Spooner.

Dr. Sirenus Buchanan will be remembered as a physician who enjoyed the confidence of a large class of people during a full practice extending over a period of many years. It is a fact worthy of mention in this connection, that with these exceptions, and a few others, Adams township during past years has suffered inefficient or inexperienced medical service. There are at present four physicians located at Lowell.

MISCELLANEOUS NOTES.

The first school in the township was kept by Enoch Wing, esq., in his cabin, about 1797. This school was attended by the youth of the whole settlement for a distance of four miles along the river. The first summer school was taught in a cabin on the farm of Esquire Wells, by Nancy Hanson. Schools were regularly supported after that by subscription until the public school law went into effect. The first school-house was built by a gathering of the neighbors, about the beginning of the century.

The public burying ground of Adams township was set apart for cemetery purposes by the Ohio company. It is located on a beautiful plain and were proper care given to its ornamentation would be a resting place worthy of the memory of past generations, whose legacy the children of the present are enjoying. The first man buried in this cemetery was Benijah Seamans; the first woman, Lottie, wife of Alexander Oliver.

Mention must be made of some old mills on the Muskingum. Esquire Wells built a small horse-mill near the mouth of Cats creek at an early period of the settlement. It was afterwards purchased by Esquire Wing, who attached water-power. This mill next came into possession of Dr. Spooner, who made considerable improvement in the method of grinding and then sold to Mr. Fleck. The dam took away the power and the mill went down.

The second mill on the river was built by Jonathan Sprague.

Adams was constituted a corporate town by the court of quarter sessions in 1797. Its boundaries have undergone numerous changes since that time as has been detailed in the chapters on the neighboring townships. No records remain of the early official acts of the town. We are therefore unable to give anything concerning elections.

There is an extensive group of well defined ancient works on the plain above Lowell. For theories concerning their origin the reader is referred to the special chapter on that topic.

LOWELL.

The first goods were sold in Adams township in 1816 by S. N. Meriam. The first store was opened by E. Short in 1822 where Upper Lowell now stands. The improvement of the Muskingum made Buell's Lowell. A great many men were employed and thousands of dollars expended on the dam, lock, and canal. The place became a natural centre of trade during these four years, and the opening of navigation perpetuated the favorable conditions.

Truckson, Lyon & Buck, in 1842, built the Lowell mills, which are now owned by Dirks & Baldwin.

Buell's Lowell was laid out by P. B. Buell. who encouraged business enterprises and succeeded in starting a village which has become a seat of trade.

The principal stores at present are owned by P. Mattern, D. W. Sprague & Co., Davis & Trapp, P. Rummer, S. N. Meriam, and James F. Putnam.

Oak mill, built in 1859 by A. Judd, is now owned by Mr. King. The Lowell planing-mill, a manufacturing establishment of considerable importance, was burned May 6, 1879.

There are in Lowell two steam tanneries; one built by Wilking, Wendell & Co. in 1866, was purchased in 1875 by Rice & Wendell. It has a capacity of twenty-five hundred heavy sides per year. The other tannery was built by Franz Wilking in 1877 and is about equal in capacity. The Lowell woollen factory was built by C. T. Weatherby.

E. Short was the first postmaster at Lowell, or Adams as it was originally. He held the office nearly twenty years—until about 1840, when Henry Wolf succeeded. Philip Mattern has held the office since December, 1863, with the exception of one year, during which John Spooner was in charge.

Buell's Lowell was incorporated May 10, 1851, with town privileges. The following persons were elected to conduct the affairs of the town: Theodore Schreiner, mayor; S. N. Meriam, recorder; John Scott, Solomon Sharpe, John B. Regnier, Joseph Cox, and George Fleck, trustees. William Bartlett was elected first marshal by the board of trustees.

CHAPTER XLI.

NEWPORT TOWNSHIP.[*]

Scenery—Blennerhassett's Visit to Mt. Dudley—Fruit-raising—Newell's Run Uplift—Coal Banks—Deserted Derricks—Action of the Court of Quarter Sessions in 1798—A Large Township—Gradual Partition—Population, Past and Present—Three Points of Settlement: Upper, Lower, Hills—The Belpre Colony—Later Settlements—Trade on the Ohio—Record of the Floods—Description of Pioneer Schools—Whiskey in the Early Settlements—The Newport Graveyard—Other Burying Places—First Worship in Private Houses—Growth of Churches—Luther Barker, the First Postmaster—A "Corn Cracker" on Little Muskingum in 1800—William Dana's Philanthrophy Builds a Mill—The Only Town—First Houses—Squire Greene's Tavern—Plat of Newport Village Surveyed in 1839—Its Fortunate Location.

PHYSICAL FEATURES.

As Newport township has stood since 1840, it is separated from West Virginia on the east and south by the broad belt of the Ohio river; Marietta township is on the

[*] The writers of the chapters on Newport and Lawrence townships are especially indebted to Dr. J. M. McElhinney, of Newport for valuable information. They have been given free access to his imposing manuscript volumes.

west, and Lawrence and Independence townships are north.

The general contour of the township is that of the right angle triangle. Mathematically consistent with the well known problem, the Ohio valley as the hypothenuse is by far the most valuable of the three bounding tracts.

The general aspect of the surface is hilly, and back of the Ohio strips of level land are rarely found. In general, the slopes are drained by the Ohio and Little Muskingum rivers, the tendency of the watercourses being to the south and southwest, the Ohio ultimately receiving the whole supply.

The watershed temporarily separating the Little Muskingum from the Ohio, crosses the northern boundary of the township in section eighteen, sends out an eastern and a western spur in section seventeen, and continues southwest, leaving the township in section thirty-two. The slopes above the spurs supply on the east the eastern branches of Newell's run, and on the west the stream known as Eight Mile run, while the territory, south of the spurs, is drained on the southeast by numerous branchlets of the Ohio, and on the southwest by Long run, a tributary of the Little Muskingum. The main ridge extends into Lawrence and Independence townships, and the southern drainage of these townships is towards the Ohio. At a point between sections six and thirty-six a southern branch of the main ridge enters the township, and passes through it almost due south to the Ohio. The eastern slope of this secondary ridge is towards Dana's run, and the western slope supplies Newell's run.

The dividing ridge between the Little Muskingum and Ohio is made up of an exceedingly elevated line of vertebrated hills frequently penetrated by the deep and narrow valleys of small streams which are gradually eroding their limiting hills, thus giving these rugged barriers a weird and romantic beauty which cannot fail to be appreciated by the passing traveller. A birds-eye view of the township as thus shaped, gives a grand view of an intricate labyrinth of natural beauty which no art of man could enhance. The whole surface is but a constant continuity of mountainous hills. One of the more prominent of these overlooks the Ohio between the village of Newport and Newell's run. This precipitous height is called Mt. Dudley after Dudley Woodbridge. On a clear day, it is said that the distant city of Marietta is visible from the top of this elevation. When Herman Blennerhassett sought for a suitable site for the proposed palace, he visited this hill in company with Dudley Woodbridge, who was desirous that Mr. Blennerhassett locate on its slope. It is related that while the party was about half way up the ascent, Mr. Blennerhassett becoming fatigued, sent his servant to the top to see if he could see Marietta. The servant reported that the city was not to be seen. Mr. Blennerhassett never ascended Mt. Dudley, and his subsequent purchase of Backus' island ended the prospect of a palace on this the most prominent elevation in Newport township.

Even the careless observer cannot fail to note that the hills a mile back of the Ohio and the village of Newport are bordered by a remarkable depression, which would at once suggest the action of flowing water. Geological researches prove that during the era of high water of the Drift period, the river or a portion of it, flowed through this depression and deposited drift, sand and gravel. It is generally conceded that the land to the south of this depression was once an island. The Ohio now sweeps around this strip of land, making an opposing curve on the south. During the flood of 1832, when the waters of the Ohio were highest, it was noticed that the water line was within three and a half feet of the line of this ancient river bed. The land adjoining this depression on the south is rich with alluvial deposits and is an excellent territory for farming.

The valleys of the Ohio and Little Muskingum mark the course of the most extended areas of level ground. In general these valleys are quite narrow, and they soon lose themselves in surrounding hills, which like walls, hem them in on either side. Especially is this the case in the Narrows just below Newport village, where the course of the Ohio is straightened and narrowly confined by opposing hills in Ohio and West Virginia.

The more level territory in the township is utilized in the cultivation of corn and considerable tobacco, while the hill land with its drier atmosphere and vigorous clay upland soil is most valuable in the production of wheat and other small grain. The hill tops and slopes are in many places still crowned with their native forests of oak, hickory, and some poplar, while the first and second bottoms were covered principally with a growth of black oak.

Fruit raising is a characteristic feature of the farmer in this township, and the cleared hill tops are planted with large orchards of apple and other fruit trees. The proximity of the Ohio affords ample opportunity to get the fruit to a good market.

In general the eastern slopes of the hill ranges are the most productive areas in the uplands. While there are some tracts that are of little value, there is scarcely any land in the township that the patient industry of practical farmers has not caused to produce at least one mite towards the general prosperity. For many years after the first settlements roads were not numerous and considerable difficulty was experienced in traversing the hilly regions. But for many years the system of roads has been good, and ingress and egress is now comparatively an easy matter.

RESEARCHES AMONG THE ROCKS.*

The western part of the township shows little of interest in its geological structure. The hills are composed largely of shales and sandstones. The most remarkable feature in the geology of the township is what is termed the Newell's run uplift, a continuation of the great West Virginia uplift. The line of this uplift was found to be a line of gas springs, oil springs, and of the few wells at that time obtained. The centre of this uplift on the Newport side is at or very near the mouth of Conley's

*The above is from Professor E. B. Andrews' Report in the Ohio Geological Survey.

run, a little above the mouth of Newell's run. In the immediate bank of the Ohio we find by far the lowest rocks, geologically considered, in the county, for the bottom of this uplift is, geologically, about one hundred and sixty-five feet lower than the bottom of the Cow run uplift. The sand rock in which the old Newton well on Cow run found its oil, is here seen in the Ohio river bank. This uplift, toward the north, becomes a broad and flattened arch, and gradually dies away.

At the feet of the rocky hills in the courses of the small streams there are many opportunities for quarrying a fair quality of building stone. But the only quarry that has been extensively worked is located on the Ohio river, a short distance above Newport village. Much of the stone used in the construction of the ice harbor at Marietta in 1880 and 1881, was taken from this quarry.

OIL AND COAL.

Says Professor Andrews: "At some points in West Virginia, by a careful study of the 'break,' as it is called, I was enabled to predict, upon the position of the rocks on the surface, where the large oil fissures must almost necessarily be found, and these predictions were abundantly verified. But in Newport the same 'break' or uplift so flattens and fades away that it has been found impossible to make similar predictions, and yet there is but little doubt that there are beneath the surface large quantities of oil."

Wells have been bored in the centre and on either slope, and, although some of them were sunk very deep, no large reservoirs of oil have been discovered, and the oil business in Newport township has consequently never been very profitable. At the time of the outbreak of the oil excitement numerous wells were sunk in the vicinity of Newell's run, and with them was sunk considerable sums of money. To-day in a number of places only the deserted derrick stands as a monument of a dead enterprise. However, there is some oil still produced in Newport township. There are six wells on Northup's run, a tributary of Newell's, which yield the Wideawake oil company about sixty barrels per month. These are the only wells in operation in this township.

On the Ohio, at a point called Petrolia, a little over a mile below the mouth of Newell's run, is an iron oil tank of ten thousand barrels' capacity, which was erected in the winter of 1869–70 by the Cow Run Iron Tank company. The oil from Cow run, in Lawrence township, is carried a distance of five and a half miles by means of a two-inch iron pipe which discharges fifty barrels per hour. This tank is not now used.

The West Virginia Transportation company has wooden tanks at Petrolia, and is handling the Cow run oil.

Coal has been discovered and mined to some extent in this township, but the seams are thin generally, and mining soon becomes unprofitable. The conditions favorable to the growth and accumulation of the vegetable materials for seams of coal appear not to have existed, although this territory is very near the centre of our great coal basin. At present in the township of Newport there is but one coal mine in operation. This mine is

DR. JOSEPH M. McELHINNEY.   MRS. DR. J. M. McELHINNEY

Joseph M. McElhinney, the subject of this sketch of a somewhat eccentric life and character, was born in Artasooman, in the parish of Faghanvale, about two miles east of the city of Londonderry, in the north of Ireland, on Good Friday, April 16th. He was the oldest son of Joseph McElhinney. His paternal ancestors, being dissenters, went over to Ireland for refuge during the persecution in Scotland. His mother, Mary Miller, whom he describes as a woman of rare merit, was of a family which trace their lineage back several centuries in Scotland and England. His father, wishing to give him a liberal education, had him at a very early age placed under the care of Mr. William Wright, a celebrated teacher, of Greenan, in the county of Londonderry, where he received the rudiments of his education. From his infancy he was fond of books, and was soon distinguished for his love of learning. He made such early improvement in literature that in his seventh year he was in advance of most children of his age, and attracted the attention of his tutors. In his boyhood he evinced a partiality for the exact sciences, in which he excelled, and which engrossed almost his whole time and attention. So great was his passion for the mathematics that to them for some years he applied all the powers of his mind, and his attention was so given to these branches that he was often abstracted from surrounding objects and circumstances. In the solution of mathematical problems he seldom followed the rules of arithmetic, or the ordinary methods of demonstrating geometrical propositions.

In the summer of 1831 he emigrated to the United States, and settled on the Little Muskingum, in the northeast part of Lawrence township, where he lived until 1848. In 1840 his father's death left on him a great part of the care of the family, the youngest of which was but six weeks old. The same year he commenced his diary or daily account of his transactions, and of events worthy of note, which came within the range of his observation; also the weather, extremes of temperature, barometric pressure, etc. No day passed without something noted.

In 1842 he left off farming and commenced teaching, which was his main calling for twelve years. About this time, although he had been reared in a pious family and was particularly careful as to his moral conduct, so that he never in his life so much as used one profane word, yet he began to see his moral depravity, and to realize the deep sinfulness of his heart. And being influenced by an ardent desire to become a Christian, he was brought through the good providence of God to repentance and evidence of regeneration in February, 1843, and united with the Presbyterian church, under the ministry of Rev. J. M. Woodbridge.

On the second of February, 1850, he helped to revive the Newport Lyceum, which had in its possession a fine library. On the seventeenth of June, 1851, he organized the Newport Literary Institute, which he

conducted with some degree of success for about three years. In this society he gave a series of lectures on Astronomy in 1851, on Natural Philosophy in 1852, and on Mental Philosophy in 1853.

In June, 1844, he invented his "Self-acting Calculator," or machinery applied to calculation. This he constructed in two parts; the first part applied to all the different arithmetical calculations, and the second to the problems in trigonometry, including logarithms, sines, tangents, secants, etc.

In December, 1846, he invented a new method of proving numerical calculations, which he did in two minutes, right from which he published at St. Louis, etc., in 1847.

His most elaborate performance was that of compiling his "Medical and Surgical Notes," which he did in two volumes, rising from 1860 till 1880, and in which he has made more than twenty-two thousand references to diseases and morbid symptoms.

In his twentieth year he married Miss Arabella R. Hannold, a daughter of Major J. M. Hannold, who was then superintendent of the Washington county infirmary. Their marriage was solemnized by Rev. Levi L. Fay, to whom Dr. McElhinney always felt indebted for the assistance which he rendered him through the use of his library, to which the latter had free access.

Miss Arabella Ross Hannold was born June 6, 1827, near Strattonville, about a mile from the Clarion river, in what was then Armstrong county, Pennsylvania. She received her education in Marietta, under the care of Professor Lionel Terry. She taught in Lawrence and Fearing townships, and in Newport from 1847 till 1849. She was industrious, economical, persevering, and neat as a housewife; but her chief delight was in floriculture, in which she excelled. During the spring and summer her flower garden bloomed with the greatest variety of flowers, and through the winter months, her east and south bay windows might be seen crowded with rare and choice flowers and foliage. She was a member of the Presbyterian church, and warmly advocated the total abstinence reform and opposed the liquor traffic in toto. And she also took an active part in the Woman's Christian Temperance Union.

In the year 1850, through the medium of the "Journal of Man," Joseph M. McElhinney became acquainted with the editor, Dr. J. R. Buchanan, of Covington, Kentucky, one of nature's noblemen, and through his influence he was induced to undertake the study of medicine systematically. He had the advantage of being already acquainted with the Latin language, and of being a teacher of the elementary branches of medical science, botany, chemistry, anatomy, physiology and neurology. He attended the lectures at the Eclectic Medical college in Cincinnati, and commenced the practice of medicine and surgery in Newport, where he had been teaching. In practice he endeavored to shun the *"via mediorum,"* and take the course suggested by a sound philosophy and the best authorities, as being the safest. This success in practice was indicated by his case-book, which, while it shows over six hundred cases annually for the first ten years, shows at the same time an average mortality of but one and one-fourth per cent.

In May, 1850, he was initiated a Son of Temperance in Newport division, No. 402, in which he presided as worthy patriarch in 1852. From that time he became an advocate of the temperance reform. He organized the Newport temperance alliance May 17, 1853. The same year he was made secretary of the Washingtonian society, of Newport, a place which he continued to fill for several years. In March, 1869, he joined the Independent Order of Good Templars, and was afterwards made State deputy grand worthy chief templar for Ohio, and became well known as an advocate of total abstinence in opposition to the liquor traffic. In May, 1873, he helped to organize the Newport temperance league. He co-operated with the Prohibition party from its commencement, and was the unsuccessful candidate for the Ohio State senate in 1877, and for congress in the Thirteenth district in 1878.

His sentiment in opposition to the use of tobacco was alike marked, but, as he said: "The time has not yet arrived for us to deal with the tobacco evil, let us first put down the liquor traffic."

When the rebellion broke out, owing to the distracted state of the nation, his medical practice was to a degree interrupted. In May, 1861, he was elected first lieutenant of the Newport company of volunteer militia, under Captain Christopher Greene. This was the first volunteer company ever raised in Newport township. In September, 1862, he was elected captain of the Newport home guards, a company of one hundred volunteers, organized for home protection. In August, 1863, he was elected captain of company H, of the forty-sixth battalion of Ohio volunteer militia, a company raised in Newport for State service. May 2, 1864, his company was called into the United States service, and took its place as company G, of the One Hundred and Forty-eighth regiment, Ohio infantry volunteers. The regiment was discharged on the fourteenth of September of the same year. During this short term of four and one-half months, Captain McElhinney served in the double character of captain and assistant surgeon of the regiment.

In 1866 he was made a Mason in American Union lodge No. 1, A. F. and A. M., and in 1867 was exalted to the degree of Royal Arch Mason in American Union chapter No. 1, at Marietta, Ohio.

The subject of this sketch, like every man of positive character, had some peculiarities or ways of his own. In his childhood he was habitually silent, and when he spoke his language was laconic. In his boyhood and youth his hours of study were from seven o'clock P. M. until one o'clock A. M., but at the age of thirty years he was threatened with paralysis of the eyelids as a result of these late hours, and was compelled to give up this habit. His most prominent trait of character, morally, was that of firmness, which he sometimes carried to the extent of stubbornness. He was scrupulously exact in his dealings, and acted up to his obligations, whether expressed or implied. He was seldom or never known to shed tears under any circumstances, and was habitually cheerful. His favorite amusements were those of sailing and hunting. As a teacher he avoided all appearance of partiality and labored hard to be successful, and knowing as he did that no teacher could please everyone, he determined to have his own method of teaching and so be sure that one was pleased. During the war his motto was "The United States against the World." In the church his motto was: "Do right and be happy." In medicinal practice it was: "One nurse is worth two doctors." But in respect to the doubtful occurrences of every day life he was sure to remark: "We can tell better afterwards."

A prominent element in his character was the love of children, which he cultivated on all occasions. While a teacher the younger scholars would each try to be nearest to the teacher, and when in his office the smaller children of the town would often visit him. This led him into Sabbath-school work, for which he had a preference. In his boyhood he used often to walk down to the old Cavwood church to attend Sabbath-school, a distance of nine miles. He had no devotion or adherence to any sect, but had an aversion to sectarianism either in religion or medicine; and so little interest had he in the politics of the country that he never voted until over forty years old, and the safety of the Republic seemed to demand it. His aversion to litigation and strife was no less marked, and the only suit he ever had in court was the notorious case of Amos Dye vs. Joseph M. McElhinney. He was charged with having slanderously circulated an old report that the former had

murdered a pedler. Against this claim both conscience and justice required his efforts to defend himself; and after a contest of over two years—1867 to 1869—the court decided that his defence was true, and that he was justified in what he had said.

Unlike as he was to almost everybody else, he often claimed to be decidedly an average man, being, as he said, "neither very big nor very little, neither very old nor very young, neither very rich nor very poor, and neither very good nor yet desperately bad."

The following is a genealogical account of the McElhinney family—as prepared by Dr. McElhinney himself.

McELHINNEY FAMILY.

FIRST GENERATION.

(1) William McElhinney resided in the county of Londonderry in the north of Ireland, where he died about the year 1762. His first wife was a—
(2) Miss Marshall. His second wife was—
(3) Miss Agnes Mclevery. He had two brothers—
(4) Samuel McElhinney, a resident of the same county, and—
(5) John McElhinney, " " "

SECOND GENERATION.

Children of William McElhinney by his first wife (Nos. 1 and 2).
(10) Joseph McElhinney, farmer, near Londonderry. After the death of his father he supported the widow and the younger children.
(12) Mary McElhinney married a—
(13) Mr. Purling near the city of Londonderry.
Children of William McElhinney by his second wife (1 and 3)—
(15) Jane McElhinney married—
(16) George O'Dare, who resided near Londonderry.
(17) William McElhinney, jr., emigrated to England while a young man.
(20) John McElhinney, farmer, was born about the year 1754. He lived near the Point of Colmore below the city of Londonderry until after the birth of his youngest child. He removed to Artnagunnig, a village about two miles east of Londonderry, where he resided until 1832, when he emigrated to the United States, and settled on the Little Muskingum near the upper corner of Lawrence township, where he died in January, 1834. He was a member of the Covenanter church. He married
(21) Nancy Hettrick, of the county of Londonderry, Ireland. She was a member of the same church with her husband. She was remarkable for neatness of person and propriety of speech. She died in Artnagunnig about the year 1825 of pulmonary consumption.
(22) Samuel McElhinney, the youngest of the family, emigrated to India, where he married and had a large family.

THIRD GENERATION.

Children of Mary McElhinney and Mr. Purling (12 and 13)—
(30) William Purling, born in Londonderry.
Children of John McElhinney and wife (20 and 21)—
(76) John McElhinney, jr., a linen weaver; born at the Point of Colmore about the year 1775. He was a young man of amiable character, and had a habit of giving good precepts to those about him. He died at Artnagunnig at the age of twenty-three years.
(77) Anne McElhinney was born at Colmore Point about 1778; came with her father to the United States in 1832. After the death of her father she made her home with the family of her brother Joseph. She died of paralysis October 19, 1870, at the residence of her niece, Mrs. M. M. Chambers, in Marietta, where she had made her home for several years. She was a member of the Presbyterian church, and remarkably gentle in her disposition. Dr. McElhinney remarks of her that he felt greatly indebted to her for her affection and kindness to him in his childhood.
(78) Joseph McElhinney, farmer, was born at the Point of Colmore, near the city of Londonderry, about the year 1780. He was educated at Cloghhole, where he continued at school until about thirty years of age; and, in the old, slow methods of teaching and learning, he became what was considered a good scholar, especially in mathematical and philosophical science. He married at the age of forty years. In the spring of 1831 he emigrated to the United States, had a long, rough voyage of about fifty days on the ocean, came over the Alleghany mountains by wagon, and settled on the Little Muskingum, in the upper corner of Lawrence township, in this county, at what was called the "Long Narrows," where he purchased two hundred acres of land. He died September 5, 1840. When in Ireland he was a member of the Covenanter church, but when he came to Ohio he joined the Presbyterian church for convenience of attendance. His wife—
(80) Mary Miller, daughter of John Miller, was born in Middle

Edenreagh, in Muff Glen, near Londonderry, May 12, 1798. She was the youngest of nine children. Her mother was Gressy Withro, a daughter of Alexander Withro, of the "Back hill" near Londonderry. Mary Miller was a member of the Presbyterian church until her sixtieth year, when she united with the New Jerusalem church. Her children describe her as a woman of rare merit, and with a keen, penetrating mind. Mrs. McElHinney was passionately fond of reading and a fine Bible scholar. She, with her husband, taught the first Sabbath-school ever organized on the Little Muskingum. She died October 8, 1874, at the residence of her oldest daughter, Mrs. M. M. Chambers, in Marietta.

FOURTH GENERATION.

Children of Joseph McElHinney and wife (78 and 79)—

(98) Matilda McElHinney was born near Londonderry, Ireland, in July, 1821, and in her tenth year came with her parents to Lawrence township, in this county. At the age of sixteen years she married—

(99) Joseph Chambers, a farmer and carpenter of Lower Lawrence, in this county. In 1850 she induced her husband to remove to Harmar, and afterward to Marietta, for the purpose of educating their children.

(100) Joseph M. McElHinney, M. D., physician and surgeon, Newport, Washington county, Ohio, was born near Londonderry, in the north of Ireland, on Good Friday, April 16th; emigrated to the United States in 1831; received his education first in Londonderry, and afterwards in Pittsburgh, Marietta, St. Clairsville, and Cincinnati; taught in this county for twelve years, and then went into the practice of medicine and surgery. In 1849 he married—

(101) Arabella R. Hannold, a daughter of Major I. W. Hannold, who was the superintendent of the Washington county infirmary. Miss Arabella R. Hannold was born near Strattonsville, Clarion county, Pennsylvania, June 6, 1821; received her education in Allegheny City, Newport, Ohio, and Marietta, Ohio; taught school from 1847 to 1849. She was noted for her success in floriculture.

(102) John A. McElHinney was born near Londonderry, Ireland, in June, 1827; died of croup in 1829, and was buried at Enoch Kirk, a very ancient ruin, near Londonderry.

(103) Nancy J. McElHinney, teacher, was born near Londonderry, December 31, 1829; came with her parents to the United States; received her education in Marietta, under the care of Professor L. Tenny; married in 1849 to (104) Rev. George V. Fry, a Congregational minister. In 1863 they removed from this county to Richmond county. In 1867 she became insane and was placed in the Central Ohio lunatic asylum, at Columbus.

(105) Catharine A. McElHinney, was born February 27, 1832, and died in October, the same year.

(106) David W. McElHinney, teacher, merchant, brickmaker, and builder, was born in Lawrence township, Washington county, Ohio, January 9, 1834; was educated in Allegheny City college; removed to Nebraska City in 1869, and afterwards to Hastings, Nebraska In 1873 and 1874 he was grand master of the order of Odd Fellows, of the State of Nebraska. He married (107) Miss Harriet Barnes of Allegheny City.

(108) Alexander M. McElHinney, teacher, photographer, merchant, land-dealer, and miner, postmaster in Silver Cliff, Colorado, was born in Lawrence township, February 23, 1838; removed to Pittsburgh, Pennsylvania, about 1858, and to Lincoln City, Nebraska, in 1868. Afterwards he removed to Silver Cliff, Colorado; married (109) Miss Lizzie Ellis, only daughter of Dr. Ellis, of Greenupsburgh, Kentucky.

(110) Catharine G. McElHinney, teacher, was born in Lawrence township, July 25, 1840. She was educated in Allegheny City college, where in 1860 she graduated with the highest honors of her class. She taught in the grammer school, in Columbus, until 1869, when she married (111) Samuel Adalbert Squier, a merchant, of Chicago. About the year 1879 he removed to Silver Cliff, Colorado, and was made mayor of the city in 1880.

FIFTH GENERATION.

Children of Matilda McElHinney and Joseph Chambers (No. 98 and 99)—

(132) Lucy A. Chambers, teacher, born in Lawrence township, July 19, 1838, educated in Marietta and Harmar Union schools in which latter she became a teacher in 1856. She died of typhoid remittent fever, February 23, 1858.

(133) Mary E. Chambers, teacher, born in Lawrence township, May 13, 1840. In 1867 she married (134) Walter Brown, a farmer, of Wade, Ohio.

(135) Nancy M. Chambers, teacher, born in Lawrence township, September 28, 1842, educated in Harmar and Marietta. At the age of sixteen years she married (136) James Steele, miller and farmer, Smithton, West Virginia, who had been divorced from his first wife (137) who was a daughter of Henry Harper, of Tigert's valley, West Virginia.

(138) Dr. Joseph M. Chambers, dentist, Marietta, Ohio, born in Lawrence township, July 15, 1847, received his education in Marietta and Cincinnati.

Children of Dr. Joseph M. McElHinney and wife (100 and 101)—

(140) Joseph McElHinney, M. D., physician and surgeon, Hills, Ohio, bor in Newport, Ohio, October 13, 1850; educated in Newport, Marietta and Cincinnati; married September 18, 1877, to (141) Mary Elizabeth Greene, a daughter of Christopher Greene, of Newport, Ohio.

(142) Adella A. McElHinney, artist, born in Newport, Ohio, May 16, 1852, received her education in Newport, Marietta and Delaware, Ohio, and in Steubenville, Ohio; graduated in the Ohio Wesleyan female college in 1873.

(144) Francois B. McElHinney, M. D., physician and surgeon, Columbus, Ohio, born in Newport, September 18, 1853; educated in Newport, Delaware and Cincinnatti, Ohio. On the first of October, 1878, he married Sophie F. Jones, daughter of Edward A. Jones, a merchant, of Newport, Ohio.

Children of Nancy J McElHinney and Rev. G. V. Fry (103 and 104)

(150) George Vincent Fry, jr., merchant, Allegheny City, Pennsylvania, born October 17, 1850; educated in Marietta. In 1872 he married (151) Josephine Wintrode, of Lexington, Ohio.

(152) James Melanchthon Fry, died in infancy.

(153) Eva H. Fry, born in Salem, in this county, February 22, 1854; educated in Lexington, Ohio; married in April, 1875, to (154) William A. Sackett, farmer, Ruggles, Ohio.

(155) Clara C. Fry, born in Salem, in this county, April 20, 1856; educated in Lexington, Ohio; married in January, 1876, to (156) William W. Beach, teacher, Ruggles, Ohio.

Children of David McElHinney and wife (106 and 107)—

(160) Bessie B. McElHinney, born in Uniontown, Pennsylvania, March 9, 1863.

(162) Frank Alex. McElHinney, born in Wellsburgh, West Virginia, November 25, 1866.

Children of Alex. M. McElHinney and wife (108 and 109)—

(170) Lucy E. McElHinney, born August 27, 1871.

(172) Samuel A McElHinney, born December, 1873.

Children of Kate McElHinney and S. A. Squier (110 and 111)—

(180) Edward A. Squier, born in Chicago, May 26, 1870.

(182) James M. Squier, born in Chicago, January 17, 1872.

(184) Marshall M. Squier, born in Chicago, February 23, 1874.

(186) Esther Squier, born in Silver Cliff, Colorado, December 31, 1879; died of hydrocephalus, September 8, 1880.

located in section five on the land of George W. Smith. It produces a fair supply of good coal.

ESTABLISHMENT.

At the regular meeting of the court of quarter sessions in December, 1798, it was deemed expedient to organize a distinct township in the eastern part of the county. Acccordingly, all that portion of Washington county lying east of the western boundary of the Seventh range was set apart and named Newport township. The portion of the county included within this new township was bounded on the north by what are now portions of Noble and Monroe counties, on the east and south by the Ohio river, and on the west by Marietta and Salem townships.

A special study of the several townships of which Newport is the common parent will show that this eastern third of the county is no mean territory.

Increased population and growing prosperity called for the gradual partition of this huge township, which, in time, would have become unwieldy. Communities springing up here and there justified independent organizations for each. By successive acts of the county commissioners, from year to year, this work was effected. Six townships were erected in this eastern territory, leaving Newport as their corner-stone. The records show that in 1802 the extreme eastern part of Newport township was made separate and named Grand View. By subsequent partition, in 1815, the township of Lawrence reduced the northern boundary of Newport. Ludlow, in 1819, was located diagonally northeast of Lawrence, and in 1832 Liberty was made the western boundary of Ludlow. In 1840 the new township of Independence bounded Lawrence on the east, and Jolly crowned the head of Grand View. Five of the six townships thus established have survived, and still exist as separate organizations. In 1840, however, it was ordered by the county commissioners that sections seventeen, eighteen, twenty-two, twenty-three, twenty-eight, twenty-nine, and thirty-four, in town two, range seven, Lawrence township, be attached to Newport township. Jolly township was short-lived, a part being annexed to Monroe county in 1851, and the remainder becoming a part of Grand View in 1859.

Thus, little by little, has the territory of Newport township been encroached upon, not by the slow advance of decay, but by the quick and vigorous step of progressive enterprise. The cutting off of the several branches has but quickened the life of the parent vine whence they sprang.

ORGANIZATION.

The exact time and locality of the first election of officers for the township of Newport cannot be ascertained. Settlement had scarcely begun when, in 1798, Newport was established. It is believed, however, that the first election was held in the immediate vicinity of the present village of Newport. John Greene, sr., was the first justice of the peace, and there is a record that in 1805 he made Benjamin and Sarah Raser happy by tying the matrimonial knot. Luther Dana was a justice as early as 1806. William Nixon served in the same ca-

pacity in 1810, and was followed by Jeremiah Dare. William Dana and Ebenezer Battelle, sr., were soon afterwards elected justices, the former in 1813, and the latter in 1816. William Knowlton was clerk in 1810, and was soon followed by Ebenezer Battelle, sr.

For several years prior to 1820 the Newport elections were regularly held at a point just below the present residence of J. B. Greene, a short distance below Newport village. It is to be regretted that the records of all official proceedings prior to 1834 have not been preserved. About 1830 Joseph Barker and Thomas Ferguson served as justices. For years the elections have been held at Newell's Run. The town hall is located in section nine, on the Newport pike, a short distance west of Newell's Run post office.

The following is a list of officers elected at successive spring elections from 1834 to 1880, as taken from the earliest records extant:

TRUSTEES.

1834, Oliver Woodson, jr., John Rowland, Thomas Ferguson; 1835, Clark Middleswart, Ezra O'Neal, Thomas Ferguson; 1836, Ira Hill, John Rowland, Thomas Ferguson; 1837, Joseph Barker, jr., Robert Rowland, Peregrine Dana, 1838, John Chambers, Jacob Middleswart, S. Harvey; 1839, Richard Greene, William A. Bosworth, Clark Middleswart, 1840, James Ferguson, John Chambers, Jacob Middleswart; 1841, James Ferguson, Joseph Barker, John Hill, 1842, Clark Middleswart, Charles Dana, John Hill, 1843, Peter Snyder, Charles Dana, Ira Hill; 1844, George Greenwood, Reuben McVay, Ira Hill; 1845, Robert Rowland, Reuben McVay, Richard Greene; 1846, George Greenwood, Benjamin Rightmire, Richard Greene; 1847, George Greenwood, Benjamin Rightmire, Jacob Middleswart; 1848, Henry Obleness, Benjamin Rightmire, William Lyons, 1849, A. B. Battelle, C. Greene, E. O'Neal; 1850, A. B. Battelle, Peter Snyder, E. O'Neal; 1851, James Ferguson, John Hill, E. O'Neal, 1852, Joseph Barker, P. F. Dana, Reuben McVay, 1853, Benjamin Rightmire, R. Rowland, Reuben McVay; 1854, James Mackey, R. Rowland, James Ferguson; 1855, James Mackey, Joseph Bell, James Ferguson; 1856, R. Rowland, Charles McVay, James Ferguson; 1857, R. Rowland, John Hill, ———, 1858, R. Rowland, John Hill, Evan Scott; 1859, E. O'Neal, John Hill, Evan Scott; 1860, Henry Sheets, John Hill, Evan Scott, 1861, Benjamin Rightmire, John Hill, Aaron Edgell, 1862, Benjamin Rightmire, John Hill, Evan Scott; 1863, B. Rightmire, Isaac Adkins, James Sankey; 1864, B. Rightmire, Isaac Adkins, James Sankey; 1865, B. Rightmire, Jesse Whiston, T. Ferguson; 1866, William Hill, Jesse Whiston, T. Ferguson, 1867, William Hill, Jesse Whiston, T. Ferguson; 1868, William Hill, J. W. Collett, Henry Sheets, 1869, William Hill, Jesse Whiston, ———; 1870, John Reynolds, Jesse Whiston, C. McVay, 1871, James Hanna, Jacob Cooper, C. McVay; 1872, Wesley Brown, William Hill, C. McVay, 1873, Lewis Phillips, William Hill, John Reynolds, jr.; 1874, Lewis Phillips, William Hill, B. Ferguson; 1875, Lewis Phillips, S. A. Whiston, B Ferguson; 1876, Lewis Phillips, S. A. Whiston, B. Ferguson; 1877, Lewis Phillips, S. A. Whiston, A. B. Little, 1878, Lewis Phillips, P. G. Hays, A. B. Little; 1879, Lewis Phillips, William Hill, A. B. Little; 1880, Lewis Phillips, William Hill, A. B. Little.

CLERKS.

1834-5, Edwin West; 1836, Charles Dana; 1837, J. G. Brown; 1838-9, Joseph Barker, jr.; 1840-5, E. Battelle, jr.; 1845-6, Christopher Greene; 1847, E. Battelle, jr; 1848, Isaac Adkins; 1849, George Greenwood; 1850, J. B. Brown, 1851, Anthony Reed; 1852, G. Greenwood; 1853, S. Amlen; 1854, J. G. Brown, 1855, C. Greene; 1856, A. Leonard, 1857, Thomas O'Neal; 1858-70, Samuel Amlin; 1871, J. W. Ker, 1872, Dr. C. T. Gale; 1873, J. M. Willis, 1874-79, G. W. Haight; 1880, Fred Koerner.

TREASURERS.

1834-49, John Greene; 1850, A. B. Battelle; 1851, E. O'Neal; 1852-4, L. Edgerton; 1855-6, Charles Dana; 1857, Robert Rowland; 1858-61, E. Battelle, jr.; 1862-4, James Ferguson; 1865, John Reynolds, jr.; 1866, James Ferguson; 1867-72, J. K. Burge; 1873, George Cassady; 1874-8, P. G. Hays; 1879-80, J. W. Ker.

The present justices of the peace are: Monroe Greenwood, Alvin Adkins, and J. T. Hill, the two former residing at Newport, and the latter near Hills post office.

Out of a population of two thousand five hundred and thirty-five, there were, at the Presidential election in 1880, five hundred and twenty-four electors in the township.

EARLY SETTLERS.

The population of Newport township has from the earliest times increased very rapidly. Taking a brief review of the last forty years it is discovered that in 1880 the population was 2,535; in 1870, it was 2,002; in 1860, 1,804 were enumerated; and in 1840, after Independence and Jolly had been made separate townships, the township of Newport counted one thousand six hundred and seventy-eight citizens. The ratio of growth prior to 1840 is much larger, and constantly increases towards the beginning of the century, at which early time even, a community was established in the township. A community to grow so rapidly must have a healthy animus, and it is surprising to learn by actual research that the pioneers were men who possessed great strength of character as well as strength of body. With few exceptions the early settlers came to stay, and their children are now moving in the places which only their death made vacant. In giving the history of the settlement of Newport township, let it be understood that it is a history of the settlement of the territory of the township as it now stands.

No permanent settlement was made prior to 1798, although the actual settlers found several squatters ahead of them.

William Tison, Neal Cortner, John Cotton, and David Stokely, once lived in what was afterwards known as the Upper settlement, in the vicinity of the present village of Newport. Here, too, had Joseph Luckey erected a little cabin. All of these men soon disappeared from the neighborhood, and gave way to the permanent settlers, the real pioneers of the township.

It will appear that there were three principal points or centres of settlement, around which as many early communities clustered, viz: the Upper settlement, near Newport; the Lower settlement, around Lower Newport; and the Hill settlement in the northwest corner of the township. Gradually the intermediate spaces have been filled with inhabitants.

The Danas and the Greenes share the honor of having made the first permanent settlement in Newport township. Both came in the same year, 1798, and about the same time in the year. They owned most of the bottom land north of the river from Newport, and much of it is still in the possession of the two families.

William and Luther Dana secured a large tract of land, and erected thereon log houses. The brothers fell vigorously to work in an effort to make for themselves and families a comfortable and pleasant home. The work was arduous, and required patience. The trees had to be felled, and the brush cleared away before a crop could be raised. They were far from neighbors, and in the midst of dense forests full of dangers. But they did not grow faint-hearted, and they succeeded in the accomplishment of their work. The brothers were sons of Captain William Dana, a Revolutionary soldier, who, in 1789, settled at Belpre, where he died in 1809. At the edict of Nantes the family fled to England, whence Richard Dana emigrated to the United States, and settled in the vicinity of Boston. Captain Dana, his great grandson, married Mary Bancroft, by whom he had eight sons and three daughters. William Dana who built his cabin near the present site of Milltown on Dana's run, was a man of sterling worth and uncommon enterprise. He built several manufactories, prominent among which was his flouring mill at Milltown. He was a man of public enterprise, and one of the strongest supporters of the church. He was twice married, first to Polly Foster, and after her death, to Maria Taylor, the widow of Benjamin Guitteau. By his first wife he had five children; Betsey married Charles Haskell, who was drowned near Newport, and afterwards she married Dr. John McCracken, of Pittsburgh; Fannie married Rev. Israel Archibald, of the Methodist Episcopal church; Pamelia was never married; Samuel married Elizabeth Thornily; Rev. Charles, a Methodist Episcopal preacher, who afterwards became insane, married Eunice Churchill. By his second wife William Dana had three children: Polly is the wife of Rev. M. Dustin, of the Methodist Episcopal church; Grace married Thomas Ewart, of Marietta, and Dorcas was the wife of Melvina Clark, of Marietta. None of the children are now living in the township. The two sons of Charles Dana reside at Milltown. William Dana died in 1851, aged seventy-six years.

Luther Dana entered land in section twenty-eight, and built his house on that part of the farm now known as the Adkins place, just north of Newport village. He was born in Massachusetts in 1773, and had all of the good qualities of the New Englander. He made one of the first clearings in the settlement. He came to Newport township from Belpre, where he had married Grace Stone. They had five children, four of whom arrived at years of maturity. It is noticeable that the only son became a minister of the Gospel while the daughters became the wives of ministers. Lucy married Rev. Samuel Browning; Alfred married Ann Pratt, and was an earnest and effective Baptist minister; Susan became the wife of Rev. Joseph A. Waterman, a preacher and a doctor; Maria married Rev. Peter McGowan, a Methodist Episcopal preacher. Luther Dana did not live many years to enjoy the home that he had worked so hard to establish. He died in 1813, aged forty years. His family is not now represented in this township.

John Greene, sr., and members of his family came to Newport township in 1798, the year of the first settlements. He built his log house on the farm now occupied by William C. Greenwood near the present village of Newport. He, from the first, was a leading and influential citizen as were also his sons who settled near him. He early became Squire Greene, and in this capacity was the arbiter of many a dispute.

John and Mary Greene had a family of ten children, all of whom were born in Rhode Island, and all of whom came to this county. The first John Greene came from

Salisbury, England, to Massachusetts, in 1635, and went with Roger Williams to Rhode Island, becoming the ancestor of a numerous progeny. His son Thomas and his descendants continued to reside in "Stone Castle" from 1660 to 1795, when John Greene made preparations to remove to the far famed territory of the Northwest. In 1796 the family arrived at Belpre, and in 1798, as above narrated, came to this township. The children all lived to years of maturity, and the family is by nature of long life. They are all deceased. Phœbe Greene married Major Jonathan Haskell, of Marietta. Daniel, the sea captain, built the first brick house in Newport township, and resided in Marietta. Eliza became Mrs. Pilcher, of Athens county. Mary married Ebenezer Battelle, jr., who settled in Newport. Ruth, the seventh child, married James Whitney, of Harmar. The next daughter was Sarah. Caleb, Philip, John and Richard settled in the township.

Caleb Greene married Catharine McMasters, and Philip married Martha Brooks. Both lived for a while in the southwestern part of the township, on the farm now owned by Henry Sheets. Caleb removed to Union county, and Philip, who became a Methodist Episcopal preacher, worked in eastern Ohio and West Virginia, in which latter State he died.

John Greene, jr., married Mary Hill and settled above the present village of Newport, on the place now occupied by their son, Rufus H. Greene. He was very active in every early enterprise, and took a very prominent place in the community. He became the father of ten children—nine sons and one daughter—viz.: Christopher, William H., John, Daniel, Sarah, Charles, Rufus H., Richard, and Luther. One child died in infancy. Of these, Christopher, Charles, Rufus, and Sarah settled in this township, and are still living, with the exception of Sarah, who became the wife of P. F. Dana and died in 1857. Christopher resids in Newport village. Rufus H. married Eleanor Echols, by whom he has four children.

Richard Greene, a brother of John Greene, jr., settled about a mile below Newport village soon after the settlement of his brother. The home place is now occupied by his son, Hon. James B. Greene. His first wife, Rebecca Lawton, died in 1831. In that same year he married Harriet Brown, who was born in Waterford township in 1798, and died in 1877, surviving her husband four years, the latter dying in 1873, at the advanced age of ninety years. His son, James B. Greene, married Melissa Wood, who died in 1860. He afterwards married Mary Adkins. He has eight children. In the winter of 1866-7 he was a member of the general assembly of Ohio.

Prior to the year 1800 George, the eldest son of William Templeton, of "Burnt Cabins," Pennsylvania, emigrated to Ohio and settled at the mouth of Eight-mile run, in the northwest part of Newport township. From thence he removed to the mouth of Newell's run, or on to the island opposite, and in 1825 moved to Lawrence township where he died in 1850. He is described as a tall, sedate man, who was never known to laugh, and yet no man was more sociable. He was a prominent man in Lawrence township in which his children all settled.

Probably the next family that settled in Newport township was that of Joseph and Grace Holden, who came from Pennsylvania in 1800, and located on the present site of Newport. Their house, which was of logs, was erected on the lot in the present village upon which Frank Greenwood's residence now stands. Mr. Holden's daughter, Grace, married Thomas Ferguson of Newport township.

David McKibben came from Pennsylvania to Ohio in 1800, and settled in Newport township, near the mouth of Eight-mile run. He lived on this place until his death. He married for his first wife Elizabeth, daughter of Judge Sharp, of Lawrence township, and after her death he was married to Hulda Johnson. He was the father of eleven children, none of whom reside in Newport township.

The father of James Nichols settled near Newport in 1800.

The next settlement was made in the northwestern corner of the township on the Little Muskingum, when, in 1801, William Hill, sr., emigrated from Pennsylvania to this county and township, and entered land in section thirty-six, on the east bank of the Muskingum. He built the first house in the neighborhood which is now known by his name. He was the son of John Hill, a native of Ireland. He married first Rhoda Stephenson, and after her death married Sarah Twiggs, who died in 1833. By his first wife he had eight children, viz.: John, who married Martha Richey and lived in Newport; Mary, wife of John Greene, sr., Elizabeth, married Jasher Taylor, of Marietta; James, died aged eighteen; Margaret married Reuben McVay, who lived near by; Sarah, died aged twenty-two; William Hill, jr., married Sarah Amlen. He was born near Pittsburgh in 1800, while his parents were detained on their journey to Ohio. He was a prominent man in Newport township, where he resided until his death, which occurred in 1853. He had twelve children. John T., a justice of the peace at Hills post office, married Cynthia Carver. Jonathan A. married Lucinda Reckard. William married Mary Ann Caywood, and resides near the old homestead. Sarah married William Caywood, living just beyond the line in Lawrence township. Charles became a Presbyterian minister; and Maria married B. F. Twiggs, living on the homestead farm, where Mrs. Hill, sr., still resides.

Thomas Ferguson was born in Loudoun county, Virginia, and in 1801 emigrated from Washington county, Pennsylvania. He settled in Newport township, about a mile and a half above the village, on the Ohio river just below what is known as Ferguson's landing. By his wife, Grace Holden, he had thirteen children, ten of whom became men and women, and seven of whom are still living, four being in this township, and three in Independence township. Lucy married Jeremiah and Mary married Ira Bosworth. Bazil and James live near Ferguson's landing.

Colonel Ebenezer Battelle, and his son, Captain Ebenezer Battelle came to the upper settlement in 1802, locating on the land on which Captain Battelle afterwards laid out the village of Newport. The ground was soon cleared for the erection of the family residence, which is still standing—the oldest if not the first house in the village. It was built two stories high, of hewed logs, and at that early day was considered quite a palatial residence. Colonel Battelle died here in 1815, and his son continued to hold the old house, which was afterwards the property of his son, also named Ebenezer. It is now owned by Captain Jack Harrison. The Battelles were very important factors in the early growth of the settlement.

Colonel Batelle, only son of Ebenezer Battelle, of Dedham, Massachusetts. graduated at Harvard college, at Cambridge, Massachusetts, engaged in business in Boston, and was there married to Miss Anna Durrant.

April 6, 1788, he set out on the journey to Marietta, arriving there after six weeks toilsome journeying. In 1789 he removed to Belpre, and afterwards, as above narrated, came to Newport, where he ended his days. His son, Captain Battelle, married Mary, the daughter of John Greene. They reared a family of six children. The eldest son, Cornelius, became a Methodist minister. He married Elizabeth Greene, and now resides at Zanesville. Phœbe married Mr. Browning. Thomas has attained distinction in California. Gordon became a Methodist minister, and died in the army as chaplain of a West Virginia regiment. He was very active in the work of securing a State constitution for West Virginia. Ebenezer, the fourth son, married Julia, the daughter of Judge Joseph Barker, of Lower Newport. At present he resides at Newark, Ohio. He was the founder of Newport village. Andrew married Elizabeth Barker and resides at Bellaire.

Samuel Bell, born in Ireland about 1780, emigrated to Brownsville, Pennsylvania, and from there to Marietta in 1800. He settled in Newport township in the southwestern part, and at the time of his death in 1848 he was the owner of eleven hundred acres of land. He was a soldier in the War of 1812. His wife, Mary Lyons, was born in 1790 and died in 1842. They had twelve children, of whom five survive, viz: Samuel, Joseph, Nathan, Hiram, and William.

Nathan Bell was born in 1811. His first wife, Adaline Reckard, lived about eight years after her marriage. Three children were born of the first union. By his second wife, Maria Broome, born in 1827, he had seven children.

William Plumer settled in this county in 1804, having emigrated from Pennsylvania, where, in 1799, his son, John M., was born. The latter, in his early manhood, constructed a flat-boat of his own, and for five years followed the river, making trips to New Orleans, and various other points. He married Jane H. Fulton, who was born in 1804 and died in 1871. Five of their six children are living, viz: William F., in Iowa; John A., in Marietta; Happy F., at home; Eliza, and Charles S., at home. Mr. Plumer has a beautiful farm of two hundred acres, which was a dense forest when he came to it; but by hard work and honest toil it has been converted into one of the finest homes in Washington county.

Among the earliest settlers in the township were the children of Thomas and Mary Ann Reynolds, who emigrated from Maryland and settled opposite Newport township, in West Virginia. All of their children but one settled in Newport. John and Samuel settled near Ferguson's landing in 1805. The former died in 1877, leaving a widow and three children who reside in the neighborhood. John had eight children, three of whom live in the neighborhood. He enjoys the proud distinction of being the sole survivor of the soldiers of the War of 1812 who went from this township. Margaret married Jacob Seevers, of Newport. The other children were James E., Nancy, George, Rebecca, Daniel and Thomas. The latter settled at Lower Newport.

Daniel S. Reynolds, son of Thomas Reynolds, was born in 1819, in section twenty-four of this township. By his wife, Elizabeth Gill, he has had nine children, four of whom survive. He is a cooper by trade and has a farm of seventy-eight acres. He served four years—from 1861 to 1864—in the Thirty-ninth Ohio volunteer infantry.

As early as 1805, William Nixon came from Fayette county, Pennsylvania, and settled in the northwest corner of the township, on the Marietta line, a short distance below the mouth of Eight Mile run. He was a tanner by trade, and did some work in that line. He had eight children by his first wife, Mary Petit, and three by his second wife, Elizabeth Stephenson. Of these, Sarah became the wife of John Chambers, formerly of Newells Run, and Harriet married Samuel Rightmire, of this township. Other representatives of the family are living on Cow run.

John Rowland emigrated from Pennsylvania in 1805. and located in this township below Newells Run, and nearly opposite the Lower Brother Island. He was a prominent officer of the township during the earlier years of its civil history. Representatives of his family are still in the neighborhood in which he first settled.

Nathaniel Little was among the early settlers who came from Belpre township. He made a permanent settlement about the year 1805, locating about three-fourths of a mile above Newport village. His wife's maiden name was Pamelia Bradford, daughter of Major Robert Bradford, of Belpre. There were five sons and one daughter in the Little family, viz: Wealthy married Ira Hill, a farmer of Lower Newport; Charles died on the homestead in 1876; his wife's name was Mary A. Frazier; Harry went to Cuba and from thence to California, afterwards returning to Newport, where he died in 1873; Lewis settled near McConnelsville, Ohio, where he died; Nathaniel, an itinerate preacher, is the only survivor. George resided in Cincinnati. Charles Little had a large family, five of whom are living. His son, Arthur B. Little, lives on the old homestead near Newport village.

Although Stephen Dana entered a large tract of land in section twenty-nine, where he afterwards erected his house, it was not until the year 1807, that he became a resident of the township. He was born in Massachusetts in 1779. He married Elizabeth Foster, who was born in 1788, and died in 1870, surviving her husband thirty-six years. Mr. Dana was not one whit behind his brothers in his active zeal for the promotion of the welfare of the community. His family is represented in this township by his son S. A. Dana, who resides on the home place, which now consists of four hundred and thirty-three acres. The younger Mr. Dana was born in 1819, in this township, and married Jane Little, born in 1822, by whom he has two children, viz: Permelia L. and Frederick F.

Reuben McVay, born in Pennsylvania in 1791, came to Ohio about 1810. His first settlement in this township was near Ferguson's Landing, in the upper settlement. He afterwards removed in the neighborhood of the Hill settlement. He married Margaret, the daughter of William Hill, sr. He had twelve children, of whom Luther and his wife Martha J. Hill, are in Newport township. Reuben McVay died in 1866.

Peter Snyder came from Pennsylvania in 1810, and settled in section thirty-five of this township. The old man, while yet living east of the mountains, was made prisoner by the Indians, who barbarously mutilated his ears before releasing him. His son Peter lives in Marietta township.

Ira Hill married Wealthy Little. He came from Salem township in 1810, and settled on the Ohio, about five miles below Newport village, his daughter living near where he settled.

Pressly Petty was born near Harper's Ferry in 1791, and in 1810 came to Ohio, locating on section twelve of Newport township, where he died in 1862. His widow, Margaret Jennings, born 1794, is living with her son, Henry W. The family consisted of nine children, of whom six survive, viz: Mariah (Dye), in Lawrence township, Betsy (Harris), in West Virginia, Rosannah (Smith), in Watertown township, Margaret (Lee), in Iowa, Stephen, in Illinois, and Henry W. in Newport township. The latter was born in 1838, married Nancy McAllister, by whom he has had ten children, nine of whom are living. Mr. Petty was in the hundred day service, company B., One Hundred and Forty-eighth Regiment, Ohio National Guards.

William Burch, the father of Captain Hiram Burch, of Marietta, was an early settler in Newport. He came from Newtown, Connecticut, about the year 1806. He brought with him a stock of goods and established a store on the opposite side of the river, at the mouth of Bull creek. In 1808 he brought out his family. Mr. Burch traded his store for a tract of land in that vicinity, which he afterwards lost through defect in title, and then removed to this township and settled on the Adkins place. He was subsequently engaged in brickmaking, and he erected some of the earliest brick houses in the township and elsewhere in the county. He removed to Mason county, Virginia, in 1823, where he afterwards lived. He had a family of five sons and five daughters, only two of whom are now living—Captain Burch, in Marietta, and William, in Virginia.

About 1813 Benjamin Hartwell settled two miles above Marietta, on the Ohio. He was soon afterwards drowned in the river between Newport and St. Marys.

Jacob Kinsor settled on Dana's run in 1814 or 1815,

locating three miles from the Ohio. His wife was Ellen O'Hanlin. He died in Missouri. His daughter, Elizabeth, became the wife of Jonathan Ker, and Margaret married Samuel Ker.

Luther and Joseph Barker settled in the southwestern part of the township, about the year 1815. They were the sons of Colonel Joseph Barker, whose early settlement in Wiseman's bottom is fully noticed in the history of Muskingum township.

Luther, after remaining two years in Newport township, removed to McConnelsville, where he died in 1845. By his wife, Maria Devol, he had ten children.

Joseph Barker, jr., better known as Judge Barker, remained in Newport township until his death, which occurred at the old Newport farm, in 1859. He was born in 1791. His first wife was Melissa Stone, of Belpre. His second wife was Mrs. Mary Ann Shipman. He was elected to the legislature in the three years 1829, 1830 and 1834. He succeeded his father as associate judge of the common pleas court. He was elected in 1844, and served until 1852, when the adoption of the new constitution abolished the office. He was seventy-one years of age when he died. He was the father of nine children.

A Mr. Kinder settled about a mile above Milltown in 1816, in section thirty, in the neighborhood now known by the name of Kinderhook.

In 1817 Samuel Smith and family came from near Lancaster, Pennsylvania, and settled first on Dana's run, three miles from the Ohio, and afterwards removed to the farm of Reynolds' run, now occupied by James Smith.

William Mullen settled in Newport township, section nine, in 1818. He was born in Pennsylvania in 1797, and died six years after coming to Ohio. His wife, Sarah Poland, whom he married in 1820, was born in 1792. Of their three children two survive, and are living in Belpre township, viz.: Mary Campbell and William. The latter, born in 1822, married Mary C. Cook in 1853, and became a resident of Belpre. Three of their four children are living.

In 1818 Isaac Davis came into the township and settled on the small stream that bears his name. He emigrated from Virginia. He settled in the woods and among the hills. The logs with which he built his cabin were poled down the steep hill slope. By his first wife he had six children. His wife's maiden name was Betsy Miller. By his second wife, Elizabeth Williamson, he had five children.

Charles Ker, a farmer, carpenter, and hunter, lived for several years in Allegheny, Pennsylvania. He married Jane McNulty. In 1821 he and family removed to this township and settled just behind Mount Dudley. He died on the east fork of Newell's run, which took the name of Ker's hollow. He had ten children; of these, Jonathan married Elizabeth Kinsor, and, prior to 1871, lived in this township; Margaret married George Reece, of Newell's run; Samuel, a farmer, cooper, and cattle dealer, settled in section twenty-one, on the east branch of Newell's run, and died in 1872, was twice married

72

and had six children; Barbara married Joshua Britton, and Hannah married David McKibben, both of Newell's run. Five of the six children of Samuel Ker are living. Of these, the second son, James W., born in 1845, married Hattie Jewell, born in 1848. They have five children. Mr. Ker is a large stock dealer, and has a farm of two hundred and twenty acres of land in section five. He has held the offices of township treasurer and clerk.

George Greenwood was born in West Virginia, as was also his wife, Isabella Clarke, who died in 1811. Their son, William C. Greenwood, was born in 1804 in West Virginia, emigrating from that State to Ohio in 1821. He settled in Washington county, Newport township, where he owns a beautiful home, surrounded by two hundred and fifteen acres of land. He is one of the two children remaining* of the original family of three sons and four daughters. He married Parmelia Little, who was born in 1818. Five children have been born to them, four of whom survive, viz: George C., Frank A., Monroe, and Junius.

Dr. George W. Gale was born in New Hampshire in 1798. He emigrated to West Virginia, practicing medicine in Pleasant and Wood counties until 1825, when he came to Newport township. His wife, Catharine A. Mills, was born in 1815. Ten of the twelve children survive, viz: Alcinda, Rachel, Ellen, Nicholas, Constantine, Mrs. V. Stephenson, Hammit, Ada, and Bernard. Of the sons, Constantine, George T., and Bernard are physicians, and Hammit is a dentist. Dr. Gale died in the village of Newport in 1878. His son, Dr. George T. Gale, is practicing in Newport.

Edward Francis was born in Maryland in 1786, removed to Virginia about 1812, and to Ohio about 1826. He settled on Eight Mile run, in Newport township, where he lived several years, and then removed to Dana's run, two and a half miles north of the village of Newport, were he died about 1848. His widow, Ann Francis, a daughter of George and Elizabeth Pritchett, died in 1880. They had six sons and seven daughters. Of those who remained in the township, Edward remained until 1865; Allen lived on Dana's run; Susan, the wife of W. H. Ballentine, lived first in Newport village and then on Long run; Ann married John Baldwin, of Long run; Amanda married Sanford Davis, of Dana's run; Jackson died in the army, and Sophia married Lester Francis, of Dana's run.

Ezra O'Neal was born in Virginia in 1802, and in 1826 came to this county, and settled in Newport township, near the mouth of Newell's run. He married Matilda Ferguson, who was born in 1805, and died in 1872. Seven of the ten children survive, viz: George, Thomas, Joseph, Judah, Jane, Huldah, and Gilbert. The latter, born in section three, Newport township, in 1837, married Sarah Broome, born in 1844. They have four children. Mr. O'Neal is postmaster at Newell's Run, where he has a general store.

In 1832 Hugh Brown settled on Newell's run, where he died in 1852. His wife, Mary Griffin, daughter of Benoni Griffin, was a vocalist of much power. After the death of her husband she lived with her youngest son,

Wesley, until her death in 1856. Mr. and Mrs. Brown had nine children—Joseph G. married M. E. Crawford, and in 1832 settled at the mouth of Newell's run; Sarah married James Little, of Eight Mile run, this township; Leonard married Jane Carr, and settled in this township; Hannah married Samuel Ker; Wesley, a boat builder, pilot, and farmer, married Elizabeth Reece.

Jacob Ritchey, the son of Abraham and Jane (Willoughby) Ritchey, was born in Pennsylvania; and settled on Newell's run, Newport township, in 1833. In that same year he married Nancy Edmendson. His daughter, Maria, married Stephen Noland, of Newell's Run, and Mary married Joseph L. Conner, of Newport township. Mr. Ritchey was drowned in 1861, in the Ohio, near the mouth of Newell's run.

Among those living in the township at an early day was Samuel Rightmire, who married Harriet, daughter of William Nixon, whose settlement has been noticed. Mr. Rightmire was born in 1810, and died in 1868. His wife was born in 1817. They have had six children born to them, all of whom survive, viz: Susan E. (Miller); Lucy A. (Davis); Sarah R. (Lackey); Mary H. (Dye); Martha H. (Doan); and Eliza J. (Lucans). Mrs. Rightmire has a farm of one hundred and four acres of well improved land.

William Warren settled in Marietta in 1814. He was born in Massachusetts in 1772, and died in Noble county, Ohio, in 1854. By his wife Hannah Dickinson, born in 1780 and died in 1853, he had fourteen children, viz: Priscilla Berry, William, Nancy Hutchison, Sophia Daniels, James S. of Noble county, Sarah Rayley, Delia, deceased; Ai, Caroline Weber of Noble county, Marilla Hussey, Elmira Hussey, dead; Andrew, deceased; Western of Noble county, and Elbridge G. The latter born in Morgan county in 1826, married Sarah Mitchell, by whom he has had five children, four of whom survive. He has a farm of one hundred acres of land in Newport township, in section twenty-one.

LATER SETTLEMENT.

After 1835 settlements in Newport township became very numerous, and it would be well nigh impossible to mention each and every one of these later settlers. However an effort has been made to note as many as limited space will permit.

'Squire Samuel Amlin, as he was familiarly called, was the son of John and Sarah Amlin. He became a resident of this township about 1840, having emigrated from New Jersey to Marietta township as early as 1809. He lived for many years in the village of Newport and died in 1872 at a ripe old age. The records show that for many years he was active in the affairs of the township.

James Cree and his wife Nancy Gadd emigrated to Ohio from Pennsylvania in 1840, and located in this township. Both died in 1876. Three of the five children survive. Alfred is in Grand View township, and John and David H. are in Newport. The latter, born in 1847, married Louisa Heintzelman, born in 1846. They have

---

* Deceased since this was written.

one child. Mr. Cree has been connected with the hotel business since 1877. His wife is a milliner.

Jacob Day, native of Pennsylvania, settled in Washington county, Newport township, in 1843. He died in 1876, aged eighty-two years, and his wife Catharine died two years later than her husband aged seventy-five years. Their son John Day was born in Pittsburgh, Pennsylvania, in 1818, and emigrated to this county with his father. He flat-boated from Marietta to New Orleans for ten years and finally settled in section thirty-five of this township, where he cleared and improved his farm of about one hundred and twenty-five acres of land, which is now adorned by the handsome buildings which Mr. Day has erected. He married Mariah Cisler, who was born in 1827. Six of their nine children are living, all in this township except one—Cecelia—in Lawrence township; Edward, Augustus, Lucinda, Daniel, and Frank.

Thomas Noland, born in Virginia in 1794, married Sarah Frazee, who was born in 1810. Mr. Noland came to Ohio in 1844, and settled in section eleven of this township, where he died in 1859. Six of his twelve children are living, viz: Stephen, Edmund, Johnston, Lewis, William, and Augustus. The latter, born in 1837, married Nancy Haynes, who was born in 1852. They have three children. Mr. Noland has a farm of eighty-three acres. Mr. Noland was in the hundred day service, as were his brothers Stephen and Johnston. His brothers Justice and Philip were in the Ohio volunteer cavalry. In 1844 Stephen and Anna (Ballard) Bull settled on the north branch of Eight Mile run in Newport township. He was a millstone maker and farmer. He was born in Pennsylvania and emigrated to this county from Guernsey county, Ohio, in 1844. He died in Kansas in 1861.

Nicholas Cisler, born in Pennsylvania in 1788, whence, in 1819, he emigrated to Marietta, subsequently settled in Newport township, where he died in 1853. He was a carpenter and farmer. His wife, Sarah Newton, was born in 1790, and died in 1864. They had nine children—Elizabeth, Margaret, Mary, J. N., Eliza, William, Harriet, Maria, and Lucinda. Four of these survive. J. N. Cisler was born in Marietta in 1822, and married Elizabeth McVay, born in 1824. Two of their five children survive. Mr. Cisler has a farm which consists of one hundred and three acres, situated on the Little Muskingum.

Noah Smith settled in Newport township in 1848. He was born in New Jersey in 1783, and died in 1865. His wife, Christianne, was born in 1785, and died in 1864. Of their children, Rebecca (Rasher), resides in Steubenville; James is in Watertown; George W. in Newport township, as is Samuel T. The latter was born in Steubenville in 1829. He married Mary Kidd in 1862, who was born in 1837 in Belmont county. He enlisted in the regular service in 1864 in company G, One Hundred and Forty-eighth Ohio volunteer infantry. In 1863 he became a member of the Ohio national guard.

Robert Edwards settled in section six of Newport township in 1849. He was born in Virginia in 1810.

His wife, Mary Workman, was born in 1803, and died in 1874. Four of their five children survive. John is dead. Jane lives in Middleport, Ohio; the fourth is Dennis, and the youngest, Mary, is living in Virginia. Benjamin F., the second son, was born in 1832, and married Nancy E. Need, by whom he has four children, the oldest, Alice, being a natural artist. Mr. Edwards has a farm of eighty-six acres of land.

John Metheny is the son of Noah and a grandson of Nathan Metheny, both of whom resided in Lawrence township. He was born in 1830. He married Mary Seevers, born in 1832, and settled in Newport township, where he owns a farm. Their four children are married. Mr. Metheny served three years in the Seventh Ohio volunteer cavalry during the late war.

In 1850 James Conner, who was born in 1805 in Pennsylvania emigrated from that state to Ohio and located in Newport township. By his wife, Sarah Macon, he had seven children, of whom Joseph L., Eliza (Johnson), and Thomas J., reside in this township. The latter, born in Guernsey county in 1841, married Isabel Dye, of Lawrence township. From 1871 he served three years as township trustee, and is at present the president of the township board of education. He served three years during the late war in company B, Thirty-ninth regiment. He is now filling the position of postmaster at Cow Run.

William Seevers came to Newport township in 1852 from Noble county. He was born in Fearing township in 1799; married Elizabeth Devol. He settled in section thirty, and built the first house in the little settlement called Kinderhook. His house was a pioneer preaching place. He died in 1867. Of the children Daniel came to this township in 1840; Richard in 1842; Abraham and his wife, Polly Morrison, in 1855; and others have become residents of the township. Abraham and Polly Seevers had fourteen children, five of whom are deceased. Those living are Andrew, Martha, Amariah, John, Levi, Harvey, Polly, Mary, and Abraham. Mr. Seevers was in the hundred day service.

James Mackey was born in Columbiana county, Ohio, in 1814, and in 1857 settled in section thirty-five, Newport township. By his wife, Susan B. Corner, he has five children—Louella, Susannah, J. Noble, Frank, and Anna. Mr. Mackey has a beautiful home, consisting of two hundred and twenty-five acres of land well improved. He and his family are staunch members of the Congregational church.

D. A. Conger was born in Monroe county, Ohio, in 1818, and removed to Washington county in 1857, settling in Newport township on a farm in sections twenty-one and twenty-seven. For ten years he was in the oil business. His wife, Catharine Lippincott, was born in 1820. They have had ten children, eight of whom are living.

George Stephens, born in France in 1827, married Mary Rabel, born in 1838. In 1859 they settled in Newport township, section twelve, where Mr. Stephens owns two hundred and eighty acres of land. Thirteen of the fourteen children are living, twelve in the township. Mr. Stephens, in addition to his farming, deals extensively in stock.

Moses Hanna settled in Newport township, section six, in 1860, and died in 1879. He was born in Pennsylvania in 1800. By his wife, Mary Watson, he had ten children, four of whom survive. Of these, James, the second son, was born in Pennsylvania in 1825, coming to this township in 1868. He married Harriet Case, by whom he has had five children, four of whom are living. Mr. Hanna has been trustee and supervisor.

Jonathan Burge was born in Pennsylvania in 1834, afterwards removed to Virginia, and in 1865 came to Ohio and Washington county, settling upon thirty five acres of land in sections three and four in Newport township. He is a blacksmith by trade. He has been township treasurer, supervisor, etc. He married Ellen B. Raby, who was born in 1832. They have nine children. In 1862 Mr. Burge enlisted and served two years and three months in the Fifteenth Pennsylvania, company B.

Frederick Koerner was born in Allegheny county, Pennsylvania, in 1843, and in 1866 settled in Salem township, this county. He enlisted and served in the Pennsylvania Reserve, battery B. Since the war he has been engaged in boring for oil, in which business he has been actively engaged for ten years. He is at present engaged in the mercantile business at Newell's Run post office. He is the township clerk. By his wife, Mary, he has had three children, one of whom is deceased.

Henry Bate, born in England in 1833, became a resident of this county in 1875, and settled in section twelve, of Newport township, where he died in 1880. He married Martha Etitt, who was born in 1833. By her he had four children, three of whom, Sarah, Joseph, and George H., are living. George H. was born in 1854, in Noble county. He cultivates a farm of two hundred and forty acres of land.

John Butler, born in New Jersey in 1830, settled in Independence township, this county, in 1861, and afterwards removed to Newport township, section eighteen, where he owns one hundred and thirty-five acres of land. He has been trustee and supervisor. By his wife, Amelia Boyd, who was born in 1833, he has had ten children, nine of whom survive.

John Braun, who was born in Germany in 1830, became a resident of Washington county in 1853, and settled in Salem township. He married Eva D. Wohlrab, who was born in 1834. Ten children are living. Mr. Braun is a general farmer, and has about one hundred acres of land, and now resides in Newport township.

THE OHIO RIVER

is an invaluable means of transportation. Ever since the first settlers brought their flat-boats down by means of its current, it has been a grand highway for trade. During the greater portion of the year a railroad in Newport township along the Ohio valley would be almost superfluous.

Newport township furnishes no small portion of the trade of the river boats. Lower Newport, Newell's Run, Newport, together with Little's and Ferguson's Landings are the principal stopping points.

An island of ninety-five acres opposite Newell's Run, and Middle island, opposite sections twenty-two and twenty-three are the only considerable islands along the Newport line.

A more general account of the floods in the Ohio will be found in another part of this work. The record of these floods in the vicinity of Newport has been preserved by Dr. J. M. McElhinney. The store room now occupied by E. A. Jones has been used as the standard of measurement in determining the various heights to which the water has risen.

February 12, 1832, during the greatest flood, in the evening at Newport, the water was four feet and two inches above the store counter, and was out of its banks for nine days, destroying an immense amount of property. In December, 1847, the water reached the level of the store floor. April 21, 1852, at 8 A. M., the water was five inches above the counter, and was three feet and eight inches lower than during the flood of 1832. April 13, 1860, although higher at Marietta than in 1852, the water was two inches below the counter's top, and seven inches below the mark of 1852. Late in the night of the twenty-first of January, 1862, the river reached the level of the store floor, and was one foot higher than the subsequent flood of 1873. March 19, 1865, the river was over its banks and came within one foot and six inches of Jones' cellar door, and within six inches of 1873's high water. December 15, 1873, the water line was six inches higher than in 1865. This is commonly called the "corn fodder" flood. In 1874, January 9th, at 5 P. M., the water was even with the bank at the foot of Greene street in the village of Newport. During these floods it often becomes necessary for people living near the river to remove their families and goods to drier quarters, and the unwonted spectacle of boats sailing in the streets, and even within the houses, is occasionally seen. Although the destruction of property by the rampant river has at times been great, there have been few accidents to human life during the floods. Persons have been drowned during the ordinary stages of water.

THE DROWNING OF CHARLES HASKELL.

The drowning of Charles Haskell is perhaps the most remarkable and the saddest case of this kind on record. Charles Haskell was, at the time of his tragic death, a respected citizen and a prominent member of the Baptist church. He resided near the river where he had his store. Saturday, July 23, 1831, he observed that some boats that he had secured to the Ohio shore were being blown by the wind towards the Virginia side. Without a second thought he plunged into the river, and his wife happening to come to the door for a moment, saw him swimming towards the boats. Having confidence in her husband's strength, she went into the house, but upon looking towards the river shortly afterwards she was horrified by the non-appearance of her husband, and the terrible thought was at once suggested that he had sank under the cruel water. This proved too true. It is supposed that he was seized with cramps while trying to get into the boat, and thus met a watery grave. A long search in the vicinity failed to discover any trace of the drowned man, and it was not until the third day that the body was found in the river at a point opposite Marietta. At the time of his death Mr. Haskell was clerk of the Baptist church, and it is recorded that Charles Little was elected to fill the vacancy caused by the death of their beloved brother.

THE ONLY "RAILROAD."

The township records show that August 28, 1872, a petition signed by one hundred citizens of Newport township was presented by virtue of an act of the general assembly, April 23, 1872, "to authorize counties, cities, incorporated villages and townships to build railroads and to lease and operate the same."

The termini in the township were an eligible point in the north line of the township in the valley of the Ohio, and an eligible point in the west line of the township in the valley of the Ohio.

An appropriation of thirty thousand dollars was to be raised by the issue of bonds executed by the township clerk and trustees, payable semi-annually at the office of the county treasurer, with interest at eight per cent. Three thousand dollars to be paid in eleven years, and the remainder in nine annual payments of three thousand dollars each.

There was some prospect of a road, which, however, never became more than an imaginary line. At an election held February 27, 1873, the people of Newport township decided that the construction of the road would be expedient.

THE MEDICAL PROFESSION.

The pioneer physician of Newport township was Dr. George W. Gale. In 1822 he settled on the Ohio in West Virginia, opposite Rea's Run, and about six miles above Newport. He practiced throughout the neighboring country for miles around, and ere he had actually become a resident of Newport township he was practising in every part of it. About the year 1837 he removed to the Barker settlement, near Lower Newport, and there made his headquarters until in 1840, he removed to the village of Newport, and remained there until his death, which occurred in 1877. He was a successful physician and an esteemed citizen.

The second physician who located in the township was Dr. George S. Smith. He was a native of Belmont county, Ohio, and in 1844 came to Newport township and settled about two miles north of the village. He practiced his profession in connection with horticulture until the time that St. Mary's was made the county seat of Pleasanton, in West Virginia (about 1850), when he removed to St. Mary's. In 1854 he returned to his old location, and in 1858 removed to Missouri, and is now practising in Illinois.

Dr. Joseph M. McElhinney has been identified with the interests of this township since 1848. He was born in Ireland, and in 1831 came, with his father, to Ludlow township. After teaching in Newport township for five or six years, he went through a course of study in medi-

cine at Cincinnati, and in 1855 commenced the practice of medicine and surgery in the village of Newport, where he has continued in practice up to the present date, only being interrupted by the late war in which he served. He became captain of company H, Forty-sixth Ohio volunteer infantry. During the hundred day service he was assistant surgeon of the regiment. His two sons, Joseph H. and Francois B., chose the medical profession, and practiced with their father in Newport, the elder from 1872 to 1875, when he removed to Marietta township, near Hills, and the younger practising from 1875 to 1877, when he removed to Hocking county, and afterwards to Columbus.

The mantle of Dr. Gale, sr., very appropriately fell upon his son, George T. Gale. He commenced the study of medicine under the tutelage of his father, and after his graduation commenced practicing in Newport, where he continued for two years, and then removed to Matamoras, Grand View township. In 1877 he returned to Newport village, and took the place vacated by his father.

PIONEER SCHOOLS.

The first school in the township was held in the upper settlement. At first the children were instructed by Caleb Greene at the family residence. This was as early as 1801, or 1802. Subsequently, the first school-house in the township was erected, about fifty yards north of where Little's tannery stands, the only mark of the deserted site being a growth of locust trees thereon. This first school-house was rude in its architectural design, being built wholly of rough round logs, and having a puncheon floor and seats. It was heated by an old-fashioned fireplace, and lighted by means of greased paper windows. Among the first teachers were John Watterman, Wealthy Little, Rebecca Ellis, Mary Fraizer, and Luther Barker.

In the course of time, with the advancing growth and prosperity of the settlement, it was thought best to build a more enduring structure, and hence the primitive log school-house was replaced by a more modern brick building. This latter building was destroyed by fire, and another building, erected in its place, has since been torn down by the hand of progress.

The first school in the hill neighborhood, in the extreme northwestern part of the township, was contemporary with the school settlement at Newport. It was a round log cabin, and stood on Hill's run, about half way between the residence of William Hill and the mouth of the run at the Little Muskingum. The first teacher was Annie Plumer, the sister of Dr. William Plumer.

Another round log school-house was soon erected near by, on the east bank of the Little Muskingum on the land now owned by Joseph Gracey, less than half a mile west of the Beech Grove church.

The flood of 1832 caused the Little Muskingum to overflow its banks, and the little school-house was swept away. Then a hewed log house was built on the spot, which house is now occupied by Mr. Gracey.

In 1816, in section twenty-six, at Lower Newport, a hewed log school-house was erected on the land then owned by Philip Greene. George Greenwood was the first teacher in this building, which stood near by the Ohio river.

These pioneer schools were kept up by subscription, and although in the early days of Newport township it required a strong effort to find time and money for schooling purposes, the thought of this very fact, combined with a natural intelligence and a due appreciation of knowledge, served to stimulate the energies of the youth, who very properly disregarding the maxim that "a little learning is a dangerous thing," struggled on over multitudinous obstacles, wisely striving to gain as many invigorating drops from the Pierian fount as possible. Thus has the whole community gradually risen in intellectuality. The development and progress of the common school system has given tone to

THE PRESENT SCHOOLS,

with which the township is well supplied. Always prospering and never retrograding, they are eminently successful in the accomplishment of popular practical education. In 1881 there are eight school districts, besides the special district at Newport village. The board of education consists of the following named gentlemen: Henry M. Hill, Charles Dana, E. T. Miller, Joseph Conner, James W. Ker, John Butler, Michael Lawrence, and Martin Hall.

OLD DISTILLERIES

were very numerous in the early days when it was a breach of hospitality not to pass the bottle when guests were present. The purity of the liquor made by the honest pioneer distillers was unquestioned, and everybody used it, until they noticed that they were beginning to yield to whiskey the mastery, and then they quit the use and the manufacture, and to-day there is but little spirituous liquor sold, and none made, in this township. During the first years of the settlement, "whiskey mills" were even more numerous than grist-mills.

John Greene, jr., Ebenezer Battelle, sr., and Richard Greene had a small distillery in the northwest corner of section twenty-eight, in 1805. They had three copper stills in operation, and devoted most of their time to the manufacture of apple jack and peach brandy. They continued at the business for about ten years, and now there is no sign of their place of business.

William Dana started a still about 1815, and continued until 1832 or 1833, when, being convinced that he was not doing right, he ceased operations in this line.

There was once a log distillery on the Little Muskingum, nearly opposite the old Sharp mill, owned by Reuben Northup. This was burned about 1826. A remnant of the old fixtures was recently found deeply buried in the river bank.

From 1820 to 1832 Thomas Ferguson had a still-house on his place above Newport, in section twenty-two.

Reference to the old account book of John Greene, which is in the possession of his son, Christopher, proves that in the early days whiskey was legal tender for all debts, for in those days it was supposed that whiskey was even better than water. From the same old book it is also learned that the consumers of the fiery liquid wanted it like water in two respects—pure and free, for they always bought on credit.

CEMETERIES.

There are at least five burying-grounds in Newport township that have been used for many years. The cemetery adjoining the Beech Grove Presbyterian church serves as a neighborhood burying-ground. The first person buried therein was Mrs. Rhoda Hill, the first wife of William Hill, sr. She died in 1807, aged forty-eight years.

The cemetery at Newport is the largest in the township. It is in the northern part of the village, next to the Methodist church. The first person buried here was Nathaniel Little, who died November 20, 1808, aged forty-nine. There had been others buried in private grounds in the vicinity before the death of Mr. Little. In this cemetery lie buried nearly all of the early settlers of the territory around Newport. They have one by one passed over to the "silent majority," and are too numerous to mention.

The old cemetery at Lower Newport is located in section thirty-three. The first burial, which took place in 1818, was that of a young man who was killed by the falling of a tree. His name is unknown.

The new graveyard was laid out in 1860, the first burial taking place therein being that of Judge Joseph Barker, jr. The cemetery is located in section twenty-five, not far from the Ohio river. The trustees who control it are Jacob Middleswart, H. D. Hill, and Joseph Bell.

The cemetery adjoining the Beech Grove United Brethren church, at Newell's run, is also very old. The first person buried there was an unknown man who was found floating in the Ohio. The graveyard, though small, contains the remains of a great many people.

CHURCHES.

Before the erection of any church building the people were wont to assemble in private houses and school-houses that they might enjoy the benefits of the gospel. In the earliest days they seldom were able to have preaching services, inasmuch as the ministers were nearly all travelling evangelists, whose circuit of preaching places was almost boundless. When practicable, the people would go to Marietta to church, but there was scarcely any road and the distance was too great. In such a community as was formed by the early settlers of Newport township churches and schools must spring up, and it is not strange that among the cabins erected we find the pioneer school-house and church. The results of their early support of intellectual and religious institutions have been manifest in the proportion of young men and women of intelligence and high moral worth, many of them having entered the profession as ministers, physicians, lawyers, or journalists. The number of ministers' wives which Newport has furnished is truly remarkable.

As time advanced, the several denominations in the settlement that had representative members were organized into distinct societies, and each one has become the centre of a wide circle of good influence.

THE METHODIST CHURCH.

In the summer of 1799 Robert Manley, the first Methodist preacher in Washington county, visited the Newport settlement, it being one of his stopping places in his evangelistic tour. The ministers who followed him to Marietta did not neglect the way station, and consequently it was not long before the first Methodist church was erected. As early as 1815, at Lower Newport settlement, in section sixteen, on the bank of the Ohio, there was a Methodist church. The building was of hewed logs, and stood on the land of Philip Greene, now owned by Henry Sheets. Philip Greene early became a Methodist minister, and it is probable that he was the means of having the church built, and that he was its first preacher. The house has long since disappeared.

An old Methodist church once stood on the spot now occupied by the Beech Grove United Brethren church, on Newell's run. It was organized by Rev. Jones, now at Williamstown, West Virginia. The church, which was of log, was erected prior to 1840. It was afterwards deserted, and at the time that it was torn down was used as a tobacco house.

A Methodist church known as the German church was organized at an early day, and a little log church erected on the west bank of Newell's run, in the northwestern part of the township. It was occupied until about 1873, when the society transferred its membership to the Pine Ridge Methodist Episcopal church, in Lawrence township.

THE NEWPORT CHURCH.

The upper settlement was one of the earliest preaching points. Rev. Jacob Young, who came to the Marietta circuit in 1804, occasionally preached in the vicinity of the present village of Newport. In 1821 the appointment at Newport was attached to the Duck Creek circuit. In 1825 it was deemed advisable to organize a regular church at Newport, and accordingly less than twenty members formed a society.

However, it was not until 1829, that a house of worship was ready for occupancy. Rev. David Young was the first preacher after the house was occupied and dedicated. Many ministers have followed him, among whom were Revs. Philip Greene, John Smothers, John Waterman, William Lippet, Peter McGowan, William Waterman, Cornelius Battelle, Wesley Browning, Pardon Cook, and Richard Armstrong. After 1860 the ministers have been, Revs. Andrew Huston, John Z. Moore, Joseph H. White, John W. Hamilton, D. C. Knowles, John H. Doar, Henry M. Rader, Frank D. Fast, W. H. Piggott, C. J. Feitt, George W. Dennis, and the pastor in 1880-1 J. H. Doan, who was pastor in 1871-2.

Of the earlier ministers of this church: Philip Greene died a superanuated minister of the West Virginia conference, after a long life spent in preaching in eastern Ohio and western Virginia. Rev. Waterman, once of the Ohio conference, later of the church South, sleeps with his fathers; Cornelius D. Battelle, now among the older members of the Ohio conference, has given half a century to the work of the ministry.

From a mere handful the membership of the church has increased to almost sixty members. Revivals were experienced from time to time, and many memories are clustered around the old but never to be forgotton Methodist *mourners' bench*.

In 1866 and 1867, it having been determined that a new house of worship was to be erected, large centenary subscriptions were raised, and the work of building a good-sized brick church proceeded. However, it was not until May, 1870, that the Centenary church was finished and dedicated. The work was begun under the pastorate of Rev. J. H. Hamilton, and dedicated while Rev. D. C. Knowles was the minister. The building cost seven thousand dollars, which is now about paid for.

The church owes much of the prosperity to the energy of the ladies who by their efforts have paid much of the debt. The Ladies' Foreign Mission society and the Mite society are vigorous organizations, and are doing a noble work.

The "wheel within a wheel," the Sabbath-school within the church, has wrought a glorious work. The school was started in Newport by Mr. Everett and Miss Louisa Battelle, now Mrs. Foote. Those two were on a visit from Massachusetts, and siezing the opportunity organized the school and succeeded in awakening an interest that continues to the present day. Each additional revival in the church met its response in the Sabbath-school, and the result has been that the school is as the nursery to the church. The present superintendent is D. J. States.

THE NEWPORT PRESBYTERIAN CHURCH

was organized in the village of Newport June 9, 1838, by Rev. Bennett Roberts, an Evangelist. The nine constituent members were, David and Mary Murdock, John and Mary Greene, Jane Moreland, Eleanor K. Cook, Mariah H. Bailey, Sarah E. Dana, and Ira H. Bosworth. They held their meetings in the pioneer school-house just north of Newport, and after it was burned meetings were held at the other school-house and at the Methodist and Baptist churches. The congregation was never strong. They had occasional supplies from Marietta, but not until Rev. Henry Smith, D. D., president of Marietta college, came did they have a stated supply. For fifteen years he preached to this people twice a month. He was accustomed to remark that his visits to the little flock at Newport were green spots in his life. Certain it is that no little church for miles around was favored with the services of so talented a minister as was Dr. Smith. Rev. John Noble also supplied the church.

In 1869 the presbytery of Athens formally dissolved Newport church, and the following were at their own request transferred to the Fourth Street Presbyterian church in Marietta: Eleanor Cook, Dr. J. H. McElhinney and wife, Ira H. Bosworth and wife, Eleanor C. Bosworth, Augustus Leonard and wife. Luther Edgarton, the only surviving elder, afterwards became a member of the Forth Street church.

BEECH GROVE PRESBYTERIAN CHURCH.

This church is located in the northwest corner of the township on the Little Muskingum, not far from Hill's post office. The history is closely identified with that of the First Presbyterian church of Marietta, of which this church is the successor, and, in fact, the remnant. When the Marietta church was formed in 1841, those Presbyterians living in the Hill neighborhood attended services in town ocsasionally. But most of them attended more regularly a church that had been formed just over the line in Lawrence township, near William Caywood's.

In 1844 or '45 a Congregational sentiment having arisen in the church near Caywoods, the members of the Presbyterian church withdrew and with members who had hitherto belonged to the Marietta church established a branch society on the Little Muskingum, and in 1848 erected the present house of worship, which was at first a mere shell of a frame building but has since been remodelled and is now a very neat structure.

The ministers have been Revs. J. M. Farris, James Stewart, William Reed, T. S. Leason, Benjamin I. Lowe, M. R. Miller, Samuel Forbes, W. M. Galbreath, and the present supply, J. Strauss. Of these ministers only Revs. Leason and Lowe were installed as pastors of the church.

When the church was first organized William Hill was the first elder. Joseph Caywood was soon afterwards elected. Others have served since then. William Caywood and William Hill, jr., are the present elders.

February 23, 1861, the church at Marietta having died, it was decided that the church be afterwards known as the Beech Grove First Presbyterian church, which name it still retains. At present there are about sixty members.

The church has furnished one minister, viz: Rev. Charles Hill, who is now preaching in Tennessee.

The Sunday-school of about fifty scholars is under the charge of William Hill.

THE BAPTIST CHURCH.

The earliest history of the Baptist church of Newport is a part of the history of the church in Marietta township near the mouth of the Little Muskingum, which church the Newport people attended. The first meetings in the Upper settlement were at the house of Jacob Churchill, at Newport. Elder James McAboy was the first minister. The first recorded meeting was held September 21, 1822, and at that time, "after prayer by Elder McAboy, Sarah Howard, David Canfield, and Ira Hill, jr., after relating their experience were received into the church, and baptized the following Sunday, together with Abigail Churchill, Melissa Barker, and Susan S. Dana, who had united with the church at its last meeting on Little Muskingum." The next month Joseph Barker, and L. D. Barker and wife were received, and at the close of the year 1822 William and Lucy Bosworth, Grace Ferguson, and Mary Little became members. Thus, little by little, was the nucleus of the Newport church formed.

In 1823 regular meetings were not held on account of prevailing sickness in the neighborhood, and by reason of the death of the clerk, Jacob Churchill, the record was neglected. Joseph Barker was the next clerk. After

the death of Mr. Churchill the meetings at Newport were held in the old brick school-house, where they were continued until the church was built. Gradually as the years advanced did the meetings at this school-house church multiply, and it was evident that a church would be located in the neighborhood. November 19, 1825, Elder McAboy requested to be released from the pastoral charge, and on the next day Elder Jeremiah Dale was ordained and installed, receiving a solemn charge from the retiring pastor.

September 19, 1830, Alfred Dana was ordained assistant pastor, Elder Dale going to Massachusetts to visit relations. Elder Dale was in poor health and died at Danvers, Massachusetts, September 4, 1831, in the forty-fourth year of his age.

At a meeting held October 15th "the solemn and affecting letter concerning the death of the beloved pastor Elder Dale was read, and then the congregation asked Rev. Alfred Dana to become its pastor. Mr. Dana continued in the pasrorate until 1834, when Elder A. Darrow was called, Elder Dana for a time remaining the assistant pastor.

The time had now come for the establishment of an entirely separate church, and on the third of January, 1838, a meeting of the members of the regular Baptist church was held at Newport for the purpose of effecting an organization. William Dana, Ira Hill, Joseph Barker, Charles Little and Jacob Middleswart were the members of the committee who drafted the constitution. It was resolved to invite delegates from Marietta, Adams, Vienna, Mt. Vernon, and Mill Creek churches to join the council, together with Revs. H. Geer, C. Rector, A. Dana, and the pastor, A. Darrow, and also Revs. Gabriel and J. Whitney, with their churches. The council met January 20, 1838, and adopted articles of faith. The members of the council were: Elders H. Geer, A. Dana, A. Darrow, with Brothers Thornily, P. Snyder, F. Wood, and others. Rev. A. Darrow became pastor of the new church, and William Dana and Ira Hill were elected deacons.

In the latter part of the year 1839 there was some talk of a meeting-house, and in the early part of 1841 it was decided to erect a house of worship. Joseph Barker, jr., William Dana, A. Darrow, Ira Hill and William Leonard were appointed members of the building committee. A commodious brick church was erected where the present building stands, in the northern part of the village of Newport. The house was dedicated on New-Year's day, 1842, Elder Geer preaching the sermon. There had been paid on the church nine hundred and fifty-one dollars and twenty-four cents, leaving a debt of three hundred and thirty-six dollars and forty-four cents. William Dana paid this, and took the note of the trustee for the amount. At the death of Mr. Dana search for the note was made, but it could not be found. In this quiet way did Mr. Dana pay the debt, having destroyed the note as soon as received. The following trustees were elected: William Dana, Joseph Barker, Ira Hill, Jacob Middleswart, Charles Little, Jacob Leonard, Ezekiel Slagle, William A. Bosworth, Carlton Palmer, P. F. Dana

^and Amos Adkins. Elder Darrow resigned in 1843, and in July, 1844, Elder H. S. Dale received a call to the pastorate, in which he continued until 1851. He was followed by Rev. John D. Riley. Rev. Z. C. Rush was called May 18, 1868, and remained until 1871. Then came Elder Hiram Geer, who remained until 1874. In 1875 Elder William Dunn was called, and stayed until the first of July, 1876. Since that time the church has been without a pastor, and the pulpit has received occasional supplies. The services of a regular pastor will be secured as soon as practicable.

Meanwhile, the people have not been idle. In 1877 there was talk of fixing up the old church, but in 1878 it was decided that the house be thoroughly remodelled. This was done at an expense of two thousand dollars, most of which is paid. The building, as it now stands, is neat and commodious, and an ornament to the village. A clear-sounding bell swings in the steeple. The building is fully insured, and there is the most complete order in the business affairs. The new house was dedicated on the twenty-first of March, 1880, the dedicatory sermon being preached by Rev. W. P. Walker.

The present officers of the church are: James Ferguson, Stephen A. Dana and Arthur Little, trustees; James Ferguson, clerk.

The Sabbath-school was established in 1841, and has been prospering ever since. The attendance is good, and the teachers have a mind to the work. Bazel Ferguson is the superintendent.

UNITED BRETHREN IN CHRIST.

In the early history of the work of this denomination in Ohio, there was occasional preaching at or near Marietta, and the adherents of the church living in the eastern portion of the county were at first under the care of the Wills Creek circuit. The churches at Newport are now under the jurisdiction of the Beech Grove circuit, which embraces six churches, four in this county and two in Newport township, viz.: Kinderhook and Beech Grove churches. The former is located in section thirty, about three miles north of Newport village. This church owes its origin to the church in Noble county, of which William Seevers was a leading member. About the year 1854 or 1855, when Mr. Seevers came to this township, a United Brethren church was organized by Rev. Hazel Cecil, from near Woodsville, Ohio. The land upon which the church building was subsequently erected was obtained from Mr. Seevers. The building is of frame, and the congregation being small, has been unable to fit up the house as it would have done had it been possible. The inside of the house has not yet been finished, the room being unplastered and the seats being of the roughest pattern.

In 1856 Rev. H. Rice, having been appointed to take charge of what is now Beech Grove circuit, became the pastor of the Kinderhook church. Since then, among the ministers who have served this people may be mentioned: Revs. George Athey, A. L. Moore, Joseph Miller, M. S. Riddle, George Moore and the present pastor, Rev. John Coleman.

The Beech Grove church was organized in the schoolhouse at Newell's Run, in 1868. The congregation was not large, but, with the firm conviction that they would prosper did they but do their duty, the people went forward and made arrangements for the erection of a church. The site of the old Methodist church, near the mouth of Newell's Run, was thought the most eligible, and it was accordingly purchased. The old church which had years before been deserted by the Methodists, and had been since used as a tobacco shed, was torn down and a very neat little frame building put in its place. This was in 1870, and in the following year the house was dedicated to the honor and glory of God. The first minister of this little church was Rev. George Athey, who effected its organization. The succeeding ministers have been Revs. A. L. Moore, Riddle, Miller, George Moore and the present pastor, Rev. John Coleman. Mr. Athey has been returned to the church once since he first had charge of it.

The trustees of the church are Isaiah Bogard, L. Phillips, William Guiten, Jacob Gans and Peter Hasley.

POSTAL MATTERS.

Four years prior to the settlement of Newport township a line of mail boats was established on the Ohio between Wheeling and Cincinnati, but of course no stops were made within the territory of Newport.

In the year of the first settlements (1798) this system of carrying the mails was discontinued, and the better plan of the overland route was adopted.

There was an early call at Newport for the establishment of a post office, and very soon after the formation of the community Luther Barker received his commission as postmaster. The office was kept in the brick residence now owned by Isaac K. Adkins. In 1825 the late Ebenezer Battelle was appointed to take charge of the office, which he removed to his residence at Newport. He remained in the office until 1843, when he was succeeded by Dr. George W. Gale. Since then the office has been held successively by Joseph W. Crandall, Thomas O'Neal, Samuel Amlin, Alfred Cree, George Davenport, John M. Gano, and the present incumbent, E. A. Jones, who took the office in 1876.

The post office at Lower Newport was established in 1841, with Jacob Middleswart as postmaster. He was succeeded in 1849 by Ira Hill. John Plumer served from 1850 to 1857, and was followed by Henry Sheets, who held the office until 1879, when the present incumbent, H. F. Middleswart, was appointed.

The Newell's Run post office, situated on the Ohio river, was established in 1865. Thomas J. Conner was the first postmaster. The present incumbent is F. Koerner.

Hills post office was established in 1869, with Amos Crum as the first postmaster, and Philip Becker assistant. Hills is located in the extreme northwest corner of the township, and is the successor of Lower Lawrence post office, in the adjoining township. The present postmaster, Philip Becker, took the office three years after its establishment.

73

The mails at Newport and other river stations are received by way of the United States mail steamers, which run regularly on the Ohio.

GRIST- AND SAW-MILLS.

As early as 1800 there was a log-mill in section thirty-six, on the banks of the Little Muskingum, where the present mill now is. At first it was nothing more than a "corn cracker," but soon afterwards became a flouring-mill, with a sawing apparatus attached. Prior to 1820 this mill was burned, and a frame mill, erected by Elisha Rose, stood until a better one was built in its place by Thomas Dye. This building was burned, and the site purchased by James Lafaber, who erected and is still running a grist- and saw-mill which, as were the previous mills, is operated by horse-power. At one time there was a fulling-mill near the grist-mill, which was kept by Jasher Taylor.

In 1816 there was a mill run by horse-power, owned by William Dana and located midway between Dana's store and the larger water-mill that was built by Mr. Dana in 1820. This latter mill is still standing in Milltown, on Dana's run, and is used as a tobacco warehouse. The mill was built under peculiar circumstances. A number of Irish families en route for some point down the river were hindered from proceeding further than Newport by the ice, and were obliged to remain in Newport until the river opened. They were destitute, and appealed for work to Mr. Dana, who being a man of kind sympathies, sought to devise some means by which he could give them employment. Remembering that Irishmen could dig, he set them to digging a long mill-race, which work occupied most of the winter. Afterwards the mill was constructed. Mr. Dana spent in all about seven thousand dollars in this humane enterprise. The mill ceased operations about twenty-two years ago.

A small horse-power mill commenced to operate on the Ohio at the village of Newport in 1855. The owner, John S. Moore, at first only ground feed for his own horses, but gradually the operations became enlarged, and in 1859 he erected a frame steam flouring mill, which was afterwards enlarged. In 1879 the Newport Mill company bought the old mill, tore it down, and disposed of the machinery. The company was incorporated July, 1879, with a capital stock of twelve thousand dollars, in shares of one hundred dollars each. Victor Torner is president, James Johnson, secretary and treasurer, and John Hadley, director. The company contracted with the Cooper Manufacturing company of Mt. Vernon for a complete new process mill of four run of buhrs. The company erected the mill building, which is of frame. The mill was completed and in operation September 1, 1879, the total cost being ten thousand dollars.

There is a steam saw-mill in section sixteen belonging to Benjamin Goddard; another one near Lower Newport, by J. W. Gitchell; and still another at Hills post office, which has been mentioned.

NEWPORT VILLAGE.

This village is located on the Ohio river, six miles above Marietta. It is the centre of the semi-circular territory in which the first settlement in the township was made.

It must have been evident to the keen observer who watched the progress of the upper settlement, that the interests of the community would eventually centre around this spot in the Ohio valley. The idea of a village was suggested by the natural advantages surrounding on every side.

In front and beyond the Ohio river and the abrupt hills of West Virginia, behind and on either side the wide spread and fertile valley jointly contributed to make the locality attractive, so that even at first there was a hamlet where the village now stands.

The present site of Newport was conveyed by Messrs. Cotton and Caldwell to the late Ebenezer Battelle, sr., about the year 1801. As has been previously remarked, there were two or three little cabins in the vicinity as early as 1798. John Cotton had his house near by and it is known that Joseph Luckey's cabin stood on the present site of the village. This house probably stood near the river. The first house built on the second bottom in what is now the upper part of Newport, was built by Joseph Holdren on the lot now owned by George Greenwood and occupied by Frank Greenwood. The first house in Newport of any considerable size was the substantial log residence erected by Ebenezer Battelle, sr., the subsequent founder of the town. The house, which has since been weather-boarded and otherwise modernized, is still standing, and is now the property of Captain Jack Harrison.

The first brick house in Newport town and township was erected by Captain Daniel Greene about 1809, and is now owned and occupied by William C. Greenwood. There was a tavern opened at a very early day near the river. Esquire John Greene, sr., was its first proprietor from 1798 to 1810.

Thus was formed the nucleus of the future village. Gradually, as the river facilities for river transportation increased, and the prosperity of the community created a trade, the number of houses increased, and ere the official act the village of Newport was established. On the pages of the records of Washington county is found "a plat of the village of Newport, comprising forty lots in section twenty-seven, in the original surveyed township, numbered one, in range numbered six of the old seven ranges; surveyed January 30 and 31, 1839, for Ebenezer Battelle, the proprietor, the streets to be ninety-one links and the alleys sixteen links in width." This is witnessed by the county surveyor, Benjamin F. Stone, and by the proprietors of the village, Ebenezer and Mary Battelle. The ground was surveyed anew May 27, 1839.

The following is the record of the vacation of the town plat by the original proprietor:

In the court of common pleas, September term, 1839, on application of Ebenezer Battelle, he having produced to the court satisfactory evidence that notice of his intention to vacate the town plat of Newport had been given according to law, and a statement in writing filed from the persons, to whom by verbal contract said Battelle had given an equitable claim on lots in said town, of their consent to said vacation. It is ordered by the court that said proprietor be permitted to vacate said town plat of Newport.

As the village now stands the main group of buildings is near the river, while along the county road, known as Green street, extending as far north as the Methodist church, the village is elongated by a continuous line of houses, mostly on the right hand side. The village contains about fifty houses and three hundred inhabitants. Its growth has been gradual, and has probably attained its maximum. Besides the steam flouring-mill there are no considerable manufacturing establishments. There are two blacksmith shops, one wagon shop, a cigar manufactory, a harness and a shoe shop, besides seven stores and three hotels. The number of general stores is as remarkable as is their general prosperity. The first regular store in the village was on the river bank opposite the store now owned by E. A. Jones, which was probably the second in the village. Mention has been made of the first hotel. The Cree house and the City hotel are the leading hotels at present, and are doing a good business. The resident physicians are Drs. McElhinney and Gale. The history of the Methodist and Baptist churches appear in another part of this work.

Fortunately there is no place in the village where liquor is sold. The people of Newport and vicinity have for many years been bitter enemies of intemperance. A few years ago there was an attempt to start a saloon at the southeast corner of Greene and Merchant streets. For a time the establishment flourished, and the proprietor began to hope that he would succeed. But one night a crowd, with perhaps more impatient enthusiasm on their side than law, unceremoniously stoned the saloon, breaking windows and creating havoc among the bottles within. One adventurous stone liquidated the saloonists' debts to the community by striking and turning the spigot of the "fire box," and thus deluging the floor with the stock in trade. In this way was the liquor business broken up in Newport, and the law-abiding citizens, while not in favor of violent measures, will see to it that there be no necessity for them in the future.

The post office is kept at the store of E. A. Jones, it having been previously kept at the Battelle residence.

The schools of Newport are exceptionally good, and are embraced in what is known as the Newport special school district, which was established in 1866. There are three buildings in this district, the two primary schools being at either extremity, and the graded school midway between them. The primary school in Newport is taught by Susan F. Moore, the primary school in the back settlement being taught by Julia Rea. Professor D. J. States has charge of the high school where the more advanced branches are taught. The building now occupied by this school was formerly the Methodist church. The schools are in a flourishing condition, and the good work of higher education is advancing in this intelligent community.

CHAPTER XLII.

SALEM TOWNSHIP.

The Four Watersheds—Mt. Pisgah—Anthony's Rock—A Township Rich in Soil and Coal—Singular Natural Water Works—Why Called Salem—Establishment—First Officers—How Salem was Settled—The First Family—From Youghiogheny to Marietta—A Crude Shelter—Improvements—The First Birth—The First Bereavement and Burial—Neighbors Arrive—The First "Hired Man"—A Poorly Furnished House—The Namesake of Noble County—A Colony leaves Salem—The First Colored Man—Beginning of Settlement Near Bonn—Other Settlers—Schools—Old Log School-houses—Wages of Old Time Teachers—Orthodox Text Books—Frame Buildings Erected—The First Cellar—Mills—Prehistoric Stone Cutters—Tanneries—Stores—A Temperance Society in 1822—Salem Obtains a Post Office—Physicians—The Oldest Church—A Temperance Plank in its Platform—Religious History—Odd Fellowship—Cemeteries—The Oldest—The Good Hope Cemetery—Other Graveyards—The Villages of Salem, Warner, and Bonn—An Attempt to Introduce the Manufacture of Silk.

THIS is the fourth township in the eighth range. It is in the shape of a parallelogram, six miles from east to west, and nearly five and a half miles from north to south, with the exception that a tract four miles east and west by a mile and a third from north to south is missing from the northwest corner. This space is occupied by the southern part of Aurelius township. The rest of the north boundary is Noble county, which also bounds the township for a half a mile on the east. For the rest, Liberty township lies to the east, Fearing and over half of Muskingum on the south, and Adams on the west.

The hills, though numerous here, are not so abrupt as those farther north. About a half mile east of Bear creek, the ridge or watershed between that stream and Duck creek enters and extends through the township nearly due north.

Passing through the southeast corner of Aurelius another ridge enters, separating the east and west forks of Duck creek.

In the northeast part, to the east of the East fork of Duck creek another watershed enters, extending approximately in a southwesterly direction and ending not far east of Salem village. A fourth dividing ridge controls the drainage of the southeastern part of the township in respect to the claims of Pawpaw and Duck creek.

It will be seen from this that with the single exception of Pawpaw valley, the drainage of the township is toward the south. All Salem belongs to the Duck creek basin, except a narrow north and south strip in the western part.

The rains that fall in this tract are carried to the Muskingum by Bear creek, which rises about a mile west of what is known as the Good Hope church, and flows south in an unusually, for this region, straightforward course, until it leaves the township, when it immediately turns west and finds the Muskingum.

Not so easily described is the course of Duck creek, for it waddles through the township in a most incomprehensible manner. The west branch crosses the Ludlow line about half way between the east and west boundaries of the township. It leaves the township, after being joined by the west fork, at a point due south. Its first large bend is a mile south of where it enters—thence it flows a little south of east, or as far as the "forks," a mile east of Salem village. The east fork enters in the north boundary, bisects the northern extension of the township, then flows southwesterly to the junction of the streams. The combined waters immediately proceed to form the first, or upper ox-bow, almost enclosing a triangle of land extending to the south a mile, and there having a breadth of over half a mile, while the northern neck is not wider than thirty rods. To advance this short distance, the stream goes about two miles. Turning, it flows south, parallel to the last mile of its former course, and when two miles away, it forms the second ox-bow, which is a narrow peninsula extending half a mile northwest. In three more marked bends, this meanderer leaves the township. From the right, the west fork receives the contents of Buell's run, whose waters are mostly from Aurelius township. The east branch is recruited by three runs, draining the northern extension, and the crooked Pawpaw creek, which enters the township a mile and a half north of the southeast corner, and flows west, then nearly north to Salem village.

At the first ox-bow are the sharply defined bluffs known as Mount Pisgah—a favorite resort for picnicers, and easily accessible by railroads. A couple of depressions in the rock resembling footprints are pointed out, doubtless to the great edification of the children at the Sunday-school picnics, as the place "where Moses stood, to view the landscape o'er."

The only other topographical feature that has received a name is "Anthony's Rock," on Pawpaw creek—a favorite resort for the pioneer, Anthony Perkins, in his hunting days. The soil is much richer than would appear to one used to the broad stretches of bottom land in some other parts of Ohio. It is largely made up of limestone of great fertilizing power, and on the ridges can produce many bushels of wheat per acre. Elsewhere, the land is very good corn land. Here, as in other places in the county, are many orchards, especially of apple and peach trees.

The native forests are of oak, chestnut, and kindred trees, sugar maple, walnut, beech, buckeye and the like. So far as known, Salem township is the richest in the county in coal. One seam is generally found roofed with a heavy sandstone, from which it derives its name. This deposit is undoubtedly the most extensive formation of coal in the county. On Bear creek it is thickest toward the north, having been mined when it was as thick as five feet. The coal in the Bowen mine, farther south, is three and a half feet thick. It was sent, as fast as mined, to the Muskingum, by means of a road up the creek, built for that purpose. But the best development of this seam is on Duck creek, especially in the hills bordering the East fork, and in different places between the two forks.

The limestone seam, or lower Salem coal, corresponds with the Pittsburgh seam. It appears in the lower course of Bear creek; on Duck creek, directly across the ridge and up that stream and the East fork; for miles along Pawpaw creek; in places along Coal run, a branch of the latter stream; near the village of Salem; and near the

south line of the township on Moses Blake's farm, where it appears as cannel.* This seam thins to the north and disappears.

Oil has not been found in remunerative quantities at its present price. Several wells have been dug, however, along the East fork of Duck creek and along Pawpaw. In the upper end of Salem village, on the right bank of Duck creek, Mr. John Kiggens was sinking a well in October, 1880, and struck at the depth of six hundred and eighty-four feet, a vein of mineral water, which gives rise to some striking phenomena. Under the impulses of gas, it boils over the top about once every hour, and at irregular intervals, averaging forty-eight hours, perhaps, the impulsive force of the gas throws a vertical stream a hundred and fifty feet above the mouth of the well. This display excites considerable interest in the neighborhood and regularly attracts its quota of spectators at times when the "blast" is expected. This great supply of gas indicates the presence of petroleum somewhere in the neighborhood. The water has a strong odor, and tastes much like brine, although it is reported that no salt can be obtained from it by boiling. Many believe it to be of great medicinal virtue.

ESTABLISHMENT.

Salem was originally a part of Adams. But the following petition was handed in to the court of quarter sessions, part of whose business it was to establish townships:

To the Honorable Court of General Quarter Sessions of the Peace for the County of Washington:

GENTLEMEN: Your petitioners, the inhabitants of Duck Creek, beg your honors to take into consideration the local situation they are in from other settlements, and whereas, your honors at your last session in March did at that time form the different settlements into towns, and at the same time put us, the inhabitants of Duck Creek, into an association with the inhabitants of Virgin Bottom, Rainbow, Cattle Creek, and Bear Creek (into one town called by the name of Adams), whose situation is inconvenient for us to associate with as respects a town by reason of the inconvenience of passing the hills and ridges where it is not practicable to make roads to pass from Duck Creek to Muskingum at the same time, our numbers are almost if not quite equal to some of the other towns already laid out by your Honors being in number on Duck Creeek thirty-four families and upwards of sixty men capable of bearing arms.

For this and other good motives, your petitioners request your Honors would take the matter into consideration, and make a division in the town of Adams west by a division line between the waters of Duck Creek and Muskingum, and as far south as Shephard's old mills, so called, as far as your Honors in their wisdom shall judge best.

We also would inform that the people on Duck creek did on the second day of May last, make choice of us, the subscribers, to prefer a petition to your Honors for the above mentioned purposes.

DUCK CREEK, June 3, 1797.
                [Signed],

Levi Chapman,	James Amlin,
John Amlin,	Jonathan Amlin,
John Amlin, sr.,	Conrad Rightner,
Joel Tuttle,	Joseph Chapman,
John Campbell,	Daniel Bradstreet,
Jonathan Delong,	Patrick Campbell,
Samuel Fulton,	Robert Campbell,
Samuel Nash,	Daniel Campbell,
Robert Colewell,	Ebenezer Tolman,
Seth Tolman,	Uriah Wheeler,
Benjamin Tolman,	Amos Porter,
Samuel Amlin,	Amos Porter, jr.

* Compiled from E. B. Andrews in Ohio geological report.

Petition from the inhabitants of Duck Creek relative to a division of the township, received June, 1797.

By the Court ordered on file.

Salem bounded north on the northern boundary line of the county, east on the west boundary line of the seventh range, south on Marietta township, and west on a line which shall be parallel to, and one mile east of the western boundary of the eighth range.

CAPTAIN NASH, assessor.
LEVI CHAPMAN, constable.

These last two names are the appointment of the court, and hence were the first officers of the township.

The word Salem in this document is probably a memorandum of the christening. Many of the first settlers were from near Salem, Massachusetts, which sufficiently accounts for the name.

In the journal of the above court appears this entry, dated the first Tuesday of December, 1797:

The court proceeded to establish a new township by the name of Salem. Samuel Nash appointed assessor for said township of Salem.

The first changes in the boundary of this township were made March 8, 1808, when Fearing was established, thus cutting away over three miles from the south end of the township, in compensation the commissioners on the same day:

Ordered that the west range of sections in township four in eighth range formerly belonging to Adams, be attached to the town of Salem.

In December, 1818, when Aurelius township was established, sections Nos. 25, 26 and 27, and fractional sections Nos. 34, 35 and 36 were excepted from that township, they being reserved for Salem.

In the June session, 1842, the commissioners:

Resolved, That section twenty-seven and fractional section thirty-four in township five, range eight, heretofore belonging to township Salem, is hereby annexed to Aurelius.

It will be seen that these changes leave Salem its present size and shape.

The township officers in the territorial days, before 1802, were appointed by the court of quarter sessions. The two officers first appointed we have noticed. In March, 1798, they were: Ephraim True, Amos Porter, jr., overseers of the Poor; Levi Chapman, constable; Richard Maxon, Ebenezer Tollman, supervisors of highways; Andrew Gaylor, Dudley Davies, fence viewers. On the second Tuesday of May, 1800, the officers were: Allen Putam, constable, *vice* Henry Maxon, resigned; Samuel Nash, Joel Tuttle, and John Amlin, supervisors of the highway; Dudley Davis, Andrew Galor, Seth Tolman, fence viewers; Ephraim True, Amos Porter, jr., Joseph Chapman, committee of freeholders; Ephraim True, Amos Porter, overseers of the poor. The present township officers are: Joseph Elliott, John Thomas, Charles Schrumm, trustees; Walter Thomas, clerk; Theobald Young, treasurer; C. J. Pfaff, assessor; William J. Sprout, Pemberton Palmer, justices of the peace. Township elections were formerly held in an old log church, hereafter to be mentioned.

The first elections for representative to general assembly were: first—William R. Putnam, thirty-two; Griffin Greene, two; Elijah Backus, thirty; second—in October, 1802—William Rufus Putnam, thirty-eight; Ephraim Cutler, thirty-eight; Griffin Greene, one; William Wells,

one. In 1880 Garfield electors received one hundred and eighty-nine votes; Hancock electors, one hundred and ninety-nine.

The population of the township in 1840 was eight hundred and eighty-one; in 1860, one thousand five hundred and twenty-seven; in 1870, one thousand six hundred and ten, which, added to one hundred and eighty-seven in Salem village, makes one thousand seven hundred and ninety seven; in 1880 it was one thousand six hundred and thirty-eight.

SETTLEMENT.

The first family that settled in what is now Salem township is supposed to have been that of Amos Porter. As a biographical sketch of the family is given elsewhere in this work, it will not be necessary to make further mention of them in this place.

Soon after the arrival of the Porters came Samuel Nash and Jonathan Delong. Captain Nash established himself on lot No. 18, just above Salem village on Duck creek. His farm included the site of Salem village. He was, as has been seen, the first assessor of the township. His children were David, Chester, one daughter, who afterwards became Mrs Fuller, and two or three other girls. A number of years before 1816, he sold his farm and moved away.

Jonathan Delong first settled on Pawpaw about a mile and a half from its mouth. He sold this farm to Samuel Fulton and moved on Duck creek, on the north side of the lower "ox bow." He was a very shrewd man, and one of the foremost in the neighborhood. His children were: Isaac, who died at Macksburg, Jonathan, David, James, Chauncey, Mary, and Lydia. He died in Salem, and was buried on his own farm.

Ebenezer, Seth, and Benjamin Tolman came at this period, and entered the adjoining lots, nine, six, and twelve, above Samuel Nash. They were also from Massachusetts. Ebenezer and Benjamin, soon after, moved down to the forks of the creek, and afterwards up the West fork. Benjamin Tolman and his wife, Elizabeth, had the following children: Jerusha, who married John True, an early school teacher, Eben, Chester, Joel, Nancy, and Urania. Seth Tolman's wife was a Miss Reed. His children were: George, Silas, James, Ora, and several daughters. Just before Benjamin settled on the West fork of Duck creek, he and his brother Seth went to Urbana, whence Seth went to Iowa, and remained there until his death.

The father of Benjamin and Seth Tolman started with them from the east, but while on the road he, from some cause, fell before a moving wagon, which crushed the life from him.

Then came to the settlement Mr. McCune, and made his home at the mouth of Pawpaw creek. His children were Mary, Hannah, and one other. Mr. McCune was a day laborer, and found employment among the neighboring farmers. He left the settlement about 1809.

Samuel Fulton bought the place of Mr. DeLong when a man of, perhaps, forty-five years. About the same time he married Louisa Jackson. He had a family of five or six children.

Dudley Davis was a soldier of the Revolution who came with a comrade, Levi Dains. He built his house on the right bank of Duck creek, in the first bend below the lower ox-bow, and entered lot number sixty-two. He afterwards removed to Noble county. Mention of him may be found in the history of Aurelius township, in connection with Indian run. He was a justice of the peace, and had the honor of performing the marriage ceremony for each one of his seven or eight children.

John Noble was another of this community, living on the south side of the lower ox-bow. He soon moved up to a settlement in the county that now bears his name.

In these times, too, there was living in the neighborhood one named Ogle. He lived two miles south of the forks, in a hollow, named, at that time, after him, and remarkable for its low temperature. Ogle's children were George, William, and James. The father died in the settlement, and the children moved northward to the Caldwell settlement, where James acquired quite a fortune. In this connection it may be remarked that very many from Salem settlement, about the year 1810, went to the Caldwell settlement, forming a nucleus about which has clustered the present people and improvements of Noble county.

Other settlers who were present when the township was established were Robert Campbell and Robert Colewell, or Caldwell.

Campbell took up his abode near where Salem village is, on the other side of the creek. One of his children was Patrick Campbell, whose name occurs elsewhere in the county history.

Caldwell, as the name has since become, soon made a part of the north settlement just referred to, and from his family the city in Noble county gets its name.

Richard Fisher, a mulatto, was in the settlement before October, 1801. He lived on the West fork of Duck creek. The course of true love between himself and his wife did not run smooth. Separations frequently occurred, and after each one they considered it necessary to be re-united by a justice, thus keeping 'Squire Porter in steady and light employment.

By the beginning of 1798 Anthony Perkins had moved into lot No. 116, just south of the present village of Bonn. Three years later, William Perkins moved into the adjoining farm where his son Ezra now lives. He died in 1816, aged about fifty-five. His wife, Elizabeth Oatly, died in 1816, being in the neighborhood of fifty-three years of age.

The children of Ezra Perkins are Percival, Asa, Augustus, Ezra, Osborne, Mrs. Doane, Mrs. Thomas, at Salem village, and Mrs. Bennett, of Louisville, Kentucky.

In 1808 Ephraim True moved from what is now Fearing township to the farm in Salem township which is now occupied by his son Moses. Ephraim True was born in Salisbury, Massachusetts, in 1756. He came west first in 1789 and again in 1796. In 1807 or 1808 he married Betsy Amlin, whose father settled about the same time as Mr. True did. Both men were in the Revolutionary war.

Moses True, Ephraim's son, was born in 1810 in the township, and has spent his seventy years in the old place. He was married in 1836 to Mehitabel Alden. Of their seven children, five are living: Melvin C., Wilbur L., Hiram. Abbie L., and Julia. All but one live in the county and that one lives in Monroe county. Moses True has held various offices in the township.

Melvin C. True married Mixenda Hovey in 1867. Three children have been born to them—Eugenie Mabel, Annie G., and Clarke E. Mr. M. C. True served as sergeant in the army in the Thirty-sixth Ohio volunteer infantry during the civil war, and was lieutenant colonel of the militia regiment organized in Salem since the war.

By this time the settlers were so numerous that it would occupy beyond the limits allotted to mention them in detail. A few, only, of the many representative ones will be noticed.

The first one to settle in Salem, on Bear creek, was David Jackson, who married Sarah Morris and, about 1807, located near the stream opposite where is now the Good Hope church. The children of this pioneer couple were Hugh, David, Robert, Mary, Rebecca, Margaret (now at Harrietville), Ruhama, Jane, Nancy, Sally, Betsy (now at Newport), and Phœbe. All are dead but three. Jane married Joseph Reed in 1817, and moved to Caldwell, Noble county, but returned in 1836 to near Schrumm's mill, West fork of Duck creek. She is now living in Salem village, an aged lady of eighty-four years, and the mother of six sons and five daughters.

Daniel Ward came to Ohio in 1808, and lived the greater part of his life in Salem township, arriving about 1810.

Benjamin Gould came to the settlement from Massachusetts, where he was born in 1767, October 3rd. He came to Washington county, Marietta township, in 1808. Thence he removed to Salem township in 1813. He died in 1849. His son, Ephraim Gould, was born in 1805, in Massachusetts, and still lives at the well known Gould place with his daughter, Miss Annie Gould. His connection with the old temperance society and the Methodist church on his place is given elsewhere.

Isaiah Hallett was a settler in 1813, coming with his family from Kennebec county, Maine, where he was born. He is said to have made the first pegged shoe made in Washington county. He had seven children— Ruthey, Orrellane, Solomon, Isaiah, Isaac, Hannah, and Zenas. Solomon, Hannah, Isaac, and Zenas are living.

Orrellane Hallett was born in Maine in 1807, and came to Washington county with his father in 1813. In 1831 he married Lucy L. Blake. They had seven children—Mary A., Lynda, Angenora, Corwin, Cynthia, Howard, and Anna. All but Corwin are living, Lynda in Kansas, Cynthia in Noble county, and the rest in Washington county. Captain Howard Hallett served three years in the Twenty-fifth Ohio volunteer infantry, and is now captain of the Salem guards.

In 1770 the pioneer, Simeon Blake, was born. He came to Adams township first, and died in Noble county in 1833. By 1801 he had moved into what is now Fearing township, on the farm now occupied by John Flanders. He served as captain of the militia. His wife, Lavina Peck, was born in Connecticut, and died in 1843. Of the children, two are living—Simeon, in Illinois, and Matilda. Simeon Blake, jr., grandson of the pioneer, and son of Benjamin Blake, was born January 18, 1822. He married Mary J. Cunningham in 1840, and has had eight children, three of whom are living—Susan, Jane, and Edward. His second wife, Diana Morgan, he married in 1875. He is a general farmer in Salem township.

John McGee was an early settler who came with his wife, Mary Higgins, in 1814, and built his house on the east bank of Duck creek, west of Amos Porter's. He was born in 1790 and died in 1861. His wife, though born in 1795, is still living in the place and is the mother of Joseph, Ann Eliza, Rebecca, Henry H., Diantha, Sarah, Sophia, Julia, Martha, John, Clark, Barker, Mary, and Francis. Her father and mother were Joseph and Mary Higgins, who settled on the Ohio river.

A man by the name of Babson settled in Aurelius at first, and afterwards removed to Salem. He was born in 1795, in Gloucester, Massachusetts, whence he emigrated. His marriage to Nancy Marr occurred in 1818. He has three sons and six daughters: John and Oliver, who live in Athens county; Albert, yet in Salem; and Sarah Ann, Mary, Betsy, Lydia, and Francis. Mary died in Iowa, the rest are living.

Lot Hull came to Salem township about the year 1819. Of his children, John and Darius are in Illinois, L. R. and Charlotte Kelly are in Salem township.

Henry Schofield has been in the township since 1824. He was born in Pennsylvania in 1809, his father being William Schofield.

Richard Doane came to the county in 1807. He was born about 1765 and died in 1823. His wife was Anna Post, who died in her seventieth year in 1846. They were married about 1798. They came first to Noble county from Cincinnati, where both were born. Richard Doane enlisted in the Revolutionary war when only sixteen years old. His children were Curtis, Lyman, Ashael, Anna, Philo, Joshua, Linda, Diana, Richard, William, and Lydia.

Curtis Doane married Esther Chapman, in 1825. The children are Richard, David C., E. P., J. M., A. S., E. T., H. P., and L. C., all in Washington county. Curtis died in 1880.

E. P. Doane was born in 1832, and married Mary A. Babson, in 1859. His children are Curtis and Preston. He is a carpenter and undertaker by trade.

S. C. Doane was born in 1846 and married Pauline Fuller, of Marietta, in 1876. They have one child, Guy Frederick. Mr. Doane is a farmer and lives on the old homestead.

H. C. Hovey, another one who has passed the limit of three score and ten, is living in Salem township, having been born in New York in 1797. He married Clarissa Stanley, and his children, Benjamin, Simon and Lucy, are now in Illinois; Mary and Lucinda are in Kansas, and G. S. and Mixenda C. are in Salem. G. S. Hovey married Mary A. Hallett. Their three children are Judso H., Grace R., and Alice E., who married Jacob

Matz of Salem township. Although he did not come into what is now Salem until 1830, Mr. H. C. Hovey is really a much older resident, as he moved first into Fearing in 1818, at the age of twenty-one. His mother was born in 1761, and died in 1858. He married Clarissa Stanley in November, 1822. His wife was born in 1803, in Fearing. His father, Thomas Stanley, died there in 1816.

John R. Hardy came to the State about 1830, and settled first on the Western Reserve. He was born in Maine in 1812, commenced the practice of medicine in 1846. In 1831 he married Julia M. Goodrich. Three children were born to them—M. V., Susan C., and Andrew J. Susan is Mrs. P. Palmer; M. V. has chosen the profession of his father, and has been engaged in it since 1853. In 1854 he married Adaline Collins and now has three children: John C., who is a practicing physician, Ella F., and Edward. John R. was married the second time, in 1840, and has had two children—James M. and Josephine. The latter is dead. James M. was born in 1844, was three years in the Seventh Ohio cavalry, in which he was corporal, and was married to Miss Mary E. Miller in 1872, by whom he had three children —Eva May, Maurice Luther, and Arthur Garfield, the latter born in 1880.

Joseph Palmer came to Washington, Ohio, as early as 1818. He was born in 1815 in New Hampshire. In 1837 he married Matilda Ward, and by her had three children, the youngest being dead. His daughter married Jacob Flanders and now lives in Kansas; Milo L. lives at Whipple, married to Mary J. Flanders since 1861. Both his children, Edward W. and Dudley R., are living. Mr. Joseph Palmer was justice of the peace twenty four years. Miles L. served two years and ten months in the Seventh Ohio cavalry. Mrs. Joseph Palmer died in 1861, aged forty-five years.

Thomas Bay was born in Germany in 1797; emigrated to Philadelphia in 1835, moved to Pittsburgh in 1836, and to this county in 1837, settling in Salem township on a farm. He now lives in Marietta. He married Miss S. Gruishalber, born in Germany in 1804, and by her has had six children, of whom four survive, viz: Thomas, in Salem township; Jacob, in Lowell; Samuel, on the old Salem homestead, and William Lewis.

George Stanley, another settler of the township, has now a representative descendant by the name of W. W. Stanley, who married Ida Babson in 1876. He served in the army in the Twelfth Ohio volunteer infantry, and was wounded at South Mountain in the arm.

Willard Twiggs was born in 1836 in Salem township. In 1865 he was married to Jane Blake. Soon after his marriage he removed to Salem village, where he now resides. Mr. and Mrs. Twiggs have two children. Mr. Twiggs is an artist by profession. He has been constable for the last fifteen or twenty years.

David W. Schofield was born in the township in 1832. In 1856 he married Miss Drucilla Marshall, a native of Virginia. There have been born to them three children, two of whom are now living; the oldest, Lilly M., married G. W. Stanley; the name of the other is Mary E.

Since 1865 Mr. Schofield has been a merchant at Warren. Previously he was engineer on Ohio, Mississippi and Red river steamboats. During the war he was in the service of the Government.

In 1806 Asa Doane came to the county and took up his residence in Fearing. He was born in 1802 in Saybrook, Connecticut, whence he came to this county. In 1825 he married Sarah Stanley. He had five children, four of whom are now living: Emily, William A., Harriet A., and Armarilla G. Asa Doane first settled at Stanleyville and afterwards returned to Salem, where he now lives. By patient and honest toil he has become owner of a farm of one hundred and twenty-seven acres near Salem village.

William A. Doane was born in 1832 on the farm where he now lives. In 1855 he married Annie Palmer, by whom he has had thirteen children, ten of whom are now living.

In 1836 Jacob Lauer came to the county from Germany. His wife's name was Barbara, and she was the mother of seven children, viz: Jacob, now living in Salem township; Theobald, Daniel, Phœbe Hahn, in Tuscarawas county; and Catharine, Margaret, and John, who are dead.

Daniel Lauer and his wife, Catharine, had five children—all living. His second wife was Mary Kilthary.

George P. Lauer, born in 1796, died in 1869, came from Bavaria to Ohio and made his home in Salem township in 1840. His wife, Margaret, lived from 1791 to 1875. His children were as follows: Jacob, Margeret, who is the wife of John Gearhart, of Muskingum township; and Elizabeth, who married Lewis Plaff, and moved to Missouri, where both died. Jacob lives in Salem township. George Lauer was a member of the council, and acted as clerk for a village in Rhinephalz, Bavaria. Jacob Lauer's children are as follows: George, Jacob, Daniel, William (now in Nebraska), Lewis (now in Nebraska), Christopher, Magdalene, and Mary. Jacob Lauer married Catharine Close in January, 1847, has been elected to different township offices, and still lives on the old homestead. His son George keeps a dry goods and grocery store in Salem village. His father founded this business under the name of J. Lauer & Son in 1868.

L. Haas, born in Bavaria in 1789, came to Salem township in 1840 from Pennsylvania, where he had been four years. He was one of Napoleon's soldiers for four years, and engaged in the battles at Moscow and Waterloo. In 1809 he married Sophia Lorentz, in Bavaria. His children are Mrs. Elizabeth Trapp, of Lowell; Matthias Haas, of Warner; Christina, who is unmarried, and Valentine, of Salem township. The latter married Joanna M. Boger in 1841, and has these children, all living: Charles, Wallace, Jacob, William, Elizabeth, and Rosa.

William Kelly came to the county in 1824 from Pennsylvania, and settled first in Fearing township. He was born in 1788, and died in 1870. His wife's name was Elizabeth Scott, and their children were called John, William, and Margaret. William Kelly, jr., is the representative of the family in Salem. He married Charlotte

Hall in 1842, and has had eleven children. Eight are living: Lucy, Calvin, William R., Mary J., Elizabeth, Clara, John, and Charles.

Franz Reiss, born in Germany in 1793, emigrated to this county in 1835, and two years later, in the spring of 1837, came to Salem township, this county, where he resided until his death in October, 1840. He was married in 1815 to Susan Wendell, and had a family of five boys and six girls. Peter, the second child, was born in Bavaria, Germany, in 1817; came to Salem township with his father in 1837, and in 1849 settled in Adams, where he has since resided. In September, 1843, he was married to Christena, daughter of Henry Mattern. She is also a native of Germany, born in 1822. Mr. Reiss was formerly in the mercantile business in Lowell, but is now proprietor of a tannery in that place.

Henry Mattern emigrated to this country from Germany, where he was born in 1790, and settled in this township, where he resided until his death in 1860. He was the father of four children—George, Christina, Madaline, and Philip, all living but Madaline.

David Hunter, born in Pennsylvania in 1801, settled in Salem township, this county, in 1841, and died in Marietta in 1856. By his wife, Elizabeth Mellan, he had seven children, of whom five survive, viz.: John in Illinois; Samuel, and David, Lavina and Amanda are in West Virginia. Samuel Hunter was born in Pennsylvania in 1833; married Ellen Ritchie, who was born in 1832. Their three children are dead. They have an adopted son, Emerson Burnett Hunter. Mr. Hunter has a farm of sixty-seven acres in Newport township, where he resides.

William Best, born in Bavaria in 1801, emigrated to Washington county, Ohio, in 1840, and located in Salem township. In 1824 he married Catharine Burkey, who died in 1832. Two of the four children are living—William and George C. The latter, born in 1825, married Hannah Snyder, by whom he has had seven children, all living. In 1865 he engaged in the grocery business in Marietta, in which business he is still engaged.

One of the natives of the township is Mr. Samuel Bay, who was born in 1844, and married Henrietta M. Conrad, by whom he has three children—Mary C., Henry, and Louis William. He has a farm in Salem township, and makes a specialty of stock-raising and stock-dealing. He has been supervisor two or three terms, and is a member of the order of Odd Fellows.

Paul Smith came to the county in 1845 with his son J. L., who was born in Bavaria, Germany, in 1835. Paul had four other children—Eva B., in Noble county; J. J., in Quincy, Illinois; Katy and Michael, in Salem township.

William Thomas came from Wales originally, and emigrated from Pennsylvania to Ohio in 1848. He was born in 1810, and is therefore now seventy-one years of age. Besides serving the township in various official capacities, he has been county commissioner several terms. The children of himself and his wife, who was Eliza Ruse, are Walter, Margaret, Ruse, David, John,

Jane, Mary and William. Ruse married Angenora Babson in 1866, and has two children, Freddie K. and William W. He has been township clerk, and is now postmaster at Lower Salem. He was in the Third Ohio volunteer infantry over three years, and is a merchant.

In 1849 Pemberton Palmer moved into Salem township from Fearing, where he had been living since he was three years old. He was born in Liberty township in 1827. In 1852 he married Susan C. Hardy. Three boys and three girls were the remainder of the family. One died. Moses and John married respectively Matilda and Catherine Beck. Julia is Mrs. William Wolfert. Clarence and Maud are still at home. Pemberton Palmer has served the county as commissioner, has taken great interest in agricultural societies, attending fairs in many places, and is prominently connected with the county board of agriculture.

John A. Palmer was born October 12, 1829, and died March 26, 1863. In 1856 he married Margaret A. McAfee. Two children were the result of this union—Eva, who died in 1863; and Ida, who was born in 1861.

Frederick Boye came to Salem at the close of the year 1849. He was born in the kingdom of Hanover, June 11, 1796, and his death occurred March 27, 1878. The maiden name of his wife was Christina Belmann, and their children are F. W. and Theodore, at Cincinnati; Philip and Almer, in Salem township; Ernest, in Salem township; August, farming in Colorado; and Bertha, married to David Thomas.

Joseph Elliot was another accession to the township in 1850. He was born in 1835, in Morgan county, Ohio. He is a stock dealer and farmer, and has held several local offices. The name of his wife was Susan Blake, whom he married in 1858. His children are Mary E., who is now at home, and Charles E., who died in infancy. His parents, John and Mary, came from the State of Pennsylvania.

John Haskins was born in 1809. He married Mehitabel Littlefield, by whom he had six children, Joanna, Roswell, David, Lydia, John, and Sarah. Joanna is in Liberty township, Roswell in Salem, Lydia in Noble county, David in Salem, John in Salem, and Sarah is dead.

David Haskins married Mary Sutton. They have three children, who live at home—Victoria, Oscar, and Eunice.

Jacob Matz, sr., a native of Germany, came to Salem from Pennsylvania in 1855. He married Catharine Kilzer, and their children are Carrie, who married O. J. Pfaff, of Salem; Catharine, who is unmarried; George, the husband of Elizabeth Stom, of Salem; Jacob, jr., who married, in 1878, Alice Hovey; Henry, who died young; Emma, wife of Frederick Feldner; and Elizabeth, widow of Matthew Haas.

Thomas Mathews came to Noble county from Maryland about 1828. He was married to Maria Magruder about 1822. They had six children, five of whom are living. Mrs. Mathews died in 1875. Mr. Mathews is now in Louisiana. Their son, William P., born in 1823, moved into Salem township, Washington county, in 1839.

He married Jerusha True in 1845. They have one child living, Allen, a young man of twenty-two years. Mr. Mathews has a farmer and is engaged principally in shipping stock.

German Hall was born in 1805. His wife, Edith Chandler, was born in 1812. They were married in 1830. Their children are: Phœbe, in Indiana; W. D., in Salem; Nancy, in Salem; Elizabeth, in Warner; Norman, dead; Mary, in Iowa; Eunice, in Salem; James A., in Salem township; Rebecca, in Iowa; and Lydia J., in Macksburgh. German Hall died in Salem township in 1863. He was a farmer and was several times called upon to serve the township in an official capacity. His son, James Hall, was married to Jane Longfellow in 1869, and their offspring are Minnie, Edith, Blanche, and Ara.

George Kilzer is a native of Germany, born in 1820, who arrived in Salem in 1858, in which township he has been engaged in running a steam-mill. His wife's name was Catharine Burkhard. His sister, Mrs. Matz, is also in the township. A brother is in Columbus, and a brother and sister are in Noble county.

David Feldner was born July 5, 1837. His parents came from Germany. In 1862 he married Rebecca Elliott, who was born in Morgan county, Ohio, July 26, 1842. Their only child, Charles H., is now eighteen years old. Mr. Feldner has a farm in Salem township and pays especial attention to stock-raising and shipping.

Daniel G. Stanley came to Marietta from Massachusetts when a small boy. He was born May 4, 1785, and his wife, Rosella Putnam, was born two years later. They were married December 27, 1807. They had the following children: Anna, Lot Putnam, James, Thomas, Lydia Porter, Rosella, Daniel G., Mary Augusta, and Augustus Little, who died in the shipwreck of the General Warren, at the mouth of the Columbia. Lot P. was killed in the Confederate army in the seven days' fight about Richmond. All but James are dead.

James Stanley was born in 1813, in Washington county. He was married in 1837 to Grace Racer. They have had six children: Susannah, Benjamin, Thomas J., Charles W., Joseph L., and James H. Thomas J. was killed at Cloyd's Mountain, May 9, 1864, aged twenty-two; C. W. and J. H. are living. The former is a merchant in Salem village, and the latter a farmer in the township. Mr. Stanley served through the civil war, coming out as captain.

Moses Blake was born October 30, 1820, in Fearing township, whither his parents had come from Maine. He lived in Fearing township until about 1849, when he moved to the farm in Salem township now occupied by his son Benjamin. Mr. Blake married Martha J. Chapman in 1845. They had five children: Hannah D., born July 22, 1847; Benjamin, born January 14, 1851; George, born December 1, 1852; John, born June 1, 1856; and Charles, born December 27, 1860. George is a merchant in Salem village; John has a farm in the township, and makes a specialty of thoroughbred Devon cattle; Charles owns a farm adjoining the old homestead; Benjamin owns the old home farm, where he lives, paying most of his attention to sheep-raising, making a specialty of thoroughbred sheep; Hannah D. is dead.

EARLY EVENTS.

The earliest residents of the township being mostly from New England, and especially from Massachusetts, schools were no doubt established at a very early date, in fact, the oldest ones now living remember log school-houses in different localities, but do not know who first taught in them, or when they were built. It is known that John True kept a school in Salem about the year 1807. His salary would hardly be satisfactory to the school teacher of to-day. It was ten hard (and hard-earned) dollars every month. With this he was expected to feed and clothe himself and lay by the rest for the proverbial rainy day.

About 1813, in the summer, Rebecca Perkins, a young lady of twenty or twenty-one, taught a school in the house of Amos Porter, jr.; she was a daughter of Hannah Perkins and a niece of Anthony Perkins.

A log school-house stood on the Magee place at a very early date. Probably the first teacher in it was Barton Wells, who taught there one summer. The second school-house was built on the opposite side of the little run that traverses the farm. This was one of the houses in which John True taught. These schools were attended by the neighborhood children that have been mentioned in the preceeding pages. The text books were Testament and the spelling book. The "Bible in the schools" was a question not mooted at that time.

It is not known just when or by whom the custom of building their dwellings from logs was broken in upon, but it is known that the frame house of Seth Tolman was standing at a very early date, and that Squire Ira Hill built a frame house very early. The house of Amos Porter, jr., in which Rebecca Perkins held her school, was also a frame. It was situated over a cellar dug in a hill—this being probably the first cellar in the township.

At the beginning of the War of 1812, the Porter brothers determined to introduce frame barns instead of the old log structures. At the barn raising at Amos Porter's, a recruting officer appeared upon the scene from Marietta. The men in those days were brave and quick in their decisions, so in an amazingly short time, six men who had gone to the place with the expectation of merely aiding a neighbor in the peaceful construction of a shelter, enrolled their names and devoted themselves to the aid of the Nation, the destruction of her foes, the strengthening of the great shelter of government. These men were Amri Sutton, Thomas Taylor, Hugh Jackson, James Walker, "Doc" DeLong, and one whose name was forgotten. The latter alone was killed. The term of enlistment was three years.

In those early and unartificial times, every one was direct in his dealings with others, free in his opinions, rough and practical in his jokes. Yet neighbors were bound strong in friendship, and, as one who lived there recently remarked, "It seemed as if neighbors thought more of each other then, than kinsefolk do now." This is not to be wondered at, for though human nature

changes as little, perhaps, as anything else, yet the lone-someness of the surroundings, the scarcity of help, a common lot of hardships and danger, bound stronger than ties of blood alone. As an illustration of the broad, rough ways, though occurring later than the earlier days of the settlement, old residents will remember the trick played on John Mead, about 1825. At one of these "mutual aid societies," a barn raising or similar assembly. They were gathering the briars away from some patch of ground, and quite a heap had been collected at the foot of a hill. John with many others was proceeding toward the heap, arms full of the prickly things and grasping them with gingerly embrace. John himself had ducked somebody in the creek sometime before and somebody was going to get even. Suddenly Mr. Mead was tripped up and forward upon his burden that felt anything but a bed of roses. As he rolled permiscuously down the hill, others paved the way with their thorny bundles, and so, betimes, he plunged into the great brush heap below. Some thoughtless one set fire to it. In an instant the mass was ablaze, and John was draged out by one leg as a brand from the burning, his clothes hanging in strips. The only complete covering he had was the scratches of briars. But he took it goodnaturedly after all, so it is said, which is the most marvelous part of the story.

Considering that the whole business of these early communities was to produce grain, a comparatively useless article until taken to mill and ground, it is not strange that the few mills then in existence were so crowded with work.

At first the inhabitants of Salem went down Duck creek to mills near Marietta, or over to the Muskingum by horse-paths, or, later, to Dr. Regnier's mills in Aurelius; and many a trip did the farmer make after his pulverized grist only to find it lying where he left it with many unground grists ahead of him yet. As one who knew by experience remarked, "It seemed as if I went a hundred miles after one grist." In such cases the ingenuity of the housewife would be sorely taxed to get up a meal without meal, and contrive to appease the appetites of the young and growing "flower of the family" when the bottom of the flour barrel had been reached long ago. It was not until near 1820 that Elisha Allen erected a mill in the township, on Duck creek, below the lower ox-bow. This was the first. He had built a saw-mill at the same place a short time before.

Shortly after Thomas Porter constructed a horse-mill that helped to meet the wants of the community.

The first steam saw-mill was built by S. N. Merriam on upper ox-bow in 1831, followed by his steam grist-mill in 1832. He hired John Magee to get out the mill-stones. Mr. Magee went south of the upper ox-bow and worked out a stone that lay under a layer a foot thick. It is said that above the quarry grew an oak tree perhaps eighteen inches in diameter. Altogether it is quite reasonable to suppose that no human hand had touched the stone for centuries upon centuries. Yet he found that a line had been chiseled across it and wedges inserted, but failed to split the rock since they were working across the grain. The unknown workmen, or workman, had knocked out all the wedges but one, which the rock had held too tightly, and there was the wedge, just such a short iron instrument as quarrymen use to-day. Mr. Magee cut out the stone, leaving the wedge in it, and there it staid in the upper mill-stone of Merriam's mill, a sight for the curious. The stones were afterward removed and placed in a mill near the mouth of Bear creek, and the mill being disused and dismantled they probably lie there to-day. Now who made that iron wedge? Does it prove that the "stone age" is more ancient than has been supposed, or that rock can be deposited much faster than geology has allowed?

Another mill was built by William Mackintosh in 1836 or 1837. This was on the site occupied by Boye's mill to-day.

The first tannery in the township was the enterprise of Thomas Gilkerson, and was carried on as early, probably, as 1813; certainly before 1816. The enterprise was brought to a conclusion by the removal of himself and wife, who was Sarah DeLong, to the Caldwell settlement.

In 1820 Thomas Porter built a tannery about a hundred yards below the residence of Almer Porter. In the fall of 1832 he set in operation another on the hill south of Salem village.

Before Mr. Merriam built his mill, he kept a store, probably about the year 1829. At about the same time, part of Elisha Allen's mill was utilized for mercantile purposes, but whether Meriam's or the store in Allen's mill was the first in the township, is unsettled. The probability is in favor of the latter.

In 1832 or 1833 Daniel Hill kept a store about a mile and a half from Salem, on the Aurelius road. He resorted to the store of William Mackintosh, at Macksburgh for his stock.

The first Sunday-schools in the place were held by Daniel J. Stanley, in a school-house, and by William Porter, John Magee, and the Goulds, about 1825.

Very near the year 1822 arose what was a very remarkable organization for the times when everybody drank "good whiskey," and considered it a necessity at the social and industrial merrymaking and assemblies. It is claimed that this organization in question was the first temperance society in the west. The honor of its establishment belongs to Ephriam Gould, then a youth of seventeen years, and his brother Dennis, nineteen years old. While working in the field the idea occurred to Ephraim that whiskey was doing more harm than good, and that a society that would induce people to do without it would be a benefit. Together with Dennis, then fresh from Lane seminary, and full of the ardor of reform, he arranged a pledge that they called "teetotal"—thus divorcing it completely from the old Washingtonian movement. The first members were the immediate members of the family, and by means similar to those now in use, such as home-made speeches, persuasion, and the like, others were induced to sign, until the list comprised the great part of the community. Mr. Ephraim Gould, for one, has kept his vow in all its strictures, ever since.

In a few years after this, the first post office was granted to the township. Daniel J. Stanley was the first postmaster, and held his office about 1827. Before that, the people in the northern part of the township went to Macksburgh for their mail.

For many years after the settlement, the people of Salem were obliged to send to Marietta for their medical attendance. In this way Drs. Hildreth and Regnier were well known to all. It was not till about 1837 or 1838 that a physician established an office among the Salem people. This was Dr. William Hield. Since then, there have been at various times, Dr. Owens, Dr. Stone, Dr. Rose, Dr. Bishop, Dr. Samuel McGeary, Dr. Blackledge, and Dr. J. R. Hardy, who began his practice in 1848. At present there are Drs. J. M. Hardy, M. V. Hardy, and G. W. Blake.

CHURCHES.

Salem township is remarkable for the number of its churches. The first one organized was the old Presbyterian church. It started in Fearing township. Members were the Stanleys, Chapmans, William Perkins (who was a deacon), Messrs. Fulton, Davis, Linn, Swan, and others. From a sketch, drawn from the records by Mrs. George Hovey, it appears that the first meeting recorded was on April 25, 1810. James Amlin and Jesse Baldwin were declared elders. May 6, 1810, the first session convened at the house of Rev. James Cunningham. The first death in the church was that of Mrs. McMillen, in Fearing, May 22, 1812. The first meeting of the session in Salem was October 12, 1812, when the following joined: Amos Porter, Eleanor Waterman, and Mrs. Lydia Gould. In about 1830 the building now standing at Salem village was erected, the second one in the township. The ministers who served the church and presided at sessions at various times are Revs. James Cunningham, Ebenezer Everett, John Hunt, John Pitkin, Jacob Little, Tyler Thatcher, Luke De Witt, L. G. Bingham, N. H. Allen, M. J. Hickok, Samuel Dunham, Thomas Wicks, Bennett Roberts, N. C. Coffin, R. Tenney, and G. V. Fry, who was a Congregationalist minister and remained until 1861. The early elders were James Amlin, Jesse Baldwin, Amos Porter, William Perkins, Daniel G. Stanley, and Elisha Allen. In 1834 the records bear a resolution that no one shall be admitted to the church who will not abstain from the use of ardent spirits as a beverage. In 1845 the church had seventy-two members. Two new places of worship were organized, one in Harrietsville, and one in Bonn. Since 1861 no record has been kept and no pastor has been in charge. "Only a few members remain, like sheep without a shepherd, and the old house of worship, the second one built in Salem, yet stands a monument of what once was but now is not."

About 1810 a series of meetings were held in a school-house at the forks of Duck creek, and at other places, under the auspices of the Freewill Baptist denomination. The services were by David Wells, who would come over from the Muskingum, where he lived. These meetings ceased in two or three years, without any organization being effected.

Methodist meetings were held in the neighborhood from

time immemorial to the oldest inhabitants. The earliest remembered preacher was a local exhorter known as Father Goss, who lived in the Chapman settlement, in Fearing township, and came to the Salem settlement to preach every two weeks. These meetings were held in the house of some settler, oftenest at the residence of Amos and Simon Porter.

Some time before 1815 a Methodist church was organized in the school-house at Salem. One of the earliest preachers of this church was Elder Young. The original membership comprised Simon Porter and wife, John True and wife, Ebenezer Tolman and his mother, the two Amos Porters, and Margaret Hale. Their first building was on the site occupied by the present one in Salem village. Moses True constructed it in 1836. The new building was dedicated in 1873 by Rev. McCormick, the present preacher.

Of late years a disagreement occurred in the congregation, and the Protestant Methodist church was established. In the summer of 1878 their place of worship was completed, not far from the other church building. The land on which it stands was given by H. Magee. Messrs. Simeon Blake, Joseph Elliott, David Feldner, M. D. Morse, and H. Magee, were some of the members and had the church building constructed.

The Mount Ephraim Methodist church, whose building is some two miles above Salem, dates from the earliest times when meetings were held from house to house in the neighborhood; and in the absence of any regular preacher, the farmers took turns at reading discourses from a book of Erskine's sermons, which one of the neighbors possessed. In 1846 the little association felt able to afford a building which was erected on land given by Ephraim Gould. In 1873 the present building was finished, and the old one is now used as a stable near by.

A Baptist church, of long standing in the township, is the Good Hope church, situated on the ridge west of Duck creek. On the eleventh day of October, 1835, various persons in the community met at the house of Deacon Hugh Wilson and organized this church. The chairman of the meeting was Elder Jacob Drake, and Enoch Rector was clerk. The members that joined the church were James Bell, Calvin Crawford, Hugh Wilson, Eli Vaughn, William Wharff, Lucy Driskill, Elizabeth Driskill, Eleanor Bell, Maria Bell, F. Congleton, Nancy Culver, sr., Nancy Culver, jr., Mary Crawford, Harriet Retcher, Mary Wilson, Margaret Jackson, Electa Vaughn, Sarah Babson, Deborah Wharff, Esther Still, Eleanor Stewart, Nancy Wharff, and Mary Spears—twenty-three in all.

The first pastor was Elder Levi Culver, who was chosen for that place in October, 1835, the same month in which the church was organized, and who held it until his death, December 17, 1835. The next pastor was Enoch Rector. Since these two, Benjamin Blake, D. G. Hanley (supply), Henry Billings, J. C. Skinner, W. E. Mathuss (supply), Henry Lyon, John Ables, J. H. Barker, E. W. Daniels, E. Adkins, W. A. Blake (missionary), J. S. Covert, William McPeak, J. C.

Richardson, and H. M. Prince, have acted at various times as pastors. In 1874 we find that the church had been disbanded and reorganized. In 1871 the total membership was one hundred and thirteen. In 1874 twenty-seven members were enrolled. The present number of members is fifty-two.

The first house of worship was built in 1836 of logs. In 1851 it was superseded by a frame church building, which is the one now in use.

The Bonn German Methodist church was organized in 1840 by Rev. Koaneke. The first regular minister was Rev. J. Miller. The first members were Henry Otton, Mr. Barand, Jacob Schlohn, P. Bahrenburg, I. Mier, and I. Bakehaus. Two years after the organization, a house of worship was erected. This was replaced in 1871 by a new building. About 1852 a parsonage was built, and the first one to make use of this was a man by the name of Jahraus. This, too, was, in turn, thought too old for use, and in 1874 a new parsonage was built. Before the meeting-house was built meetings were held in private houses—principally at the residence of I. Bakehaus.

The Disciple church at Bonn was organized about 1852 at a meeting in the school-house. The first preacher was J. J. M. Dickey; then followed Elders Hughes, Solomon Devoir, and J. M. Harvey. Services were discontinued about 1858. The first members were William Sprout and wife, Hill and wife Julinda Kidd, A. Zollars and wife, J. Zollars and wife, Thomas Farley and wife, and Captain Collins. They had no church building, but met from house to house.

The next Disciple church started at Warner in 1872, under the charge of J. M. Harvey, though services had been held for some time just before. The original members were William J. Sprout, William Sherfick, Isaac Hill, and their wives, Julinda Kidd and Malin Martin. The Elders, from Mr. Harvey to the present, have been John Moody, Nathan Moody, Joseph M. Thomas; irregular supply, O. W. Kyle and Mr. Cox. At present the church has no regular elder. In 1876 the present edifice at Warner station was constructed.

At a meeting in the public school-house in Salem village, December 13, 1859, the Universalist church of the township was organized. The pastor was J. W. McMaster, who has remained in charge ever since. The first members were William Thomas, Eliza Thomas, Jewett Palmer, sr., Jewett Palmer, jr., John A. Palmer, Thomas Williams, Mrs. Mary Williams, Henry Schofield, Mrs. Sarah Schofield, Dr. Ernest Lintner, Mrs. Caroline Lintner, Mrs. Sarah Williams, Mrs. Anna Doane, Mrs. Mary Chapman, Miss Jane Thomas, Miss Ellen Crawford, Miss Julia Wiley, and Robert Fulton. The first officers were Jewett Palmer, sr., moderator; Jewett Palmer, jr., clerk; Thomas Williams, Dr. Lintner, Robert Fulton, trustees; William Thomas, John A. Palmer, stewards. J. W. McMaster preached monthly a year before the church was organized in the Salem school-house. The church building now in use a mile north of Salem was dedicated in 1861.

In the western part of the township is a German Lutheran church, which was organized about 1859. The first minister was named Juergen. The first members were Theobald Jung, Theobald Schramm, Theobald Boesshar, Jacob Boesshar, Adam Baltz, Jacob Baltz, Jacob Motz, Jacob Pfaff, Peter Pfaff, Wilhelm Wagner, their wives, John Schramm, and Michael Feldner. The preachers since have been Daniel Hirsch, Revs. Boedenshatz, Esschenfeld, Trapp, and Engelhardt. The church building has been in existence since the organization.

The Corinth church is in the southeast part of the township near Bonn. Its membership formerly belonged to and attended a church which met further up Pawpaw, in Liberty township. In 1860, however, they began to hold meetings in their own neighborhood, there listening to the preaching of Henry Lyon and W. A. Blake. In 1863 this part of the old church was organized separately and held meetings in a school-house on the farm of John Fulton. In 1876 a building that had till then been standing near Pawpaw creek in Liberty township was moved to the neighborhood, in which the meetings of this church have since been held. The original members of the church are George Twiggs and wife, Almund Cluss, John Fulton, Jane Haskins, and Joanna Fulton. At the first regular meeting as the Corinth church, Andrew Twiggs, Mrs. Fulton, Margaret Fulton, and Cornelia Twiggs became members. In 1870 and 1872 the church had fifty members, which number diminished to fifteen in 1880. Since the pastors mentioned there have been placed over the flock from time to time the following ministers: John Ables, William McPeak, J. D. Riley, G. F. Dix, and H. M. Prince.

The Baptist church of Lower Salem was organized under the leadership of Rev. J. D. Riley, August 26, 1877, with seventeen members. At first they worshipped in the old Presbyterian church building. A new frame building was put up in Salem village in the winter of 1880–81 and dedicated in the latter year. The church has now twenty-eight members.

The only secret society of any permanence in the township is the Odd Fellow lodge at Salem. Its origin was in this wise: In April, 1859, William Thomas, John A. Palmer, Pemberton Palmer, William A. Doan and Walter Thomas met at the house of John A. Palmer, to organize, if possible, a lodge. Their endeavor was successful, for in May the charter was made out, in July the meeting was held at the "Valley House," and thus began the Palmer Lodge, No. 351. The first officers of the Lodge were William Thomas, noble grand; John A. Palmer, vice-grand; P. Palmer, recording secretary; William A. Doan, treasurer. The present officers are August Decker, noble grand; Jonas Neun, vice-grand; Evan Williams, recording secretary; W. W. Stanley, permanent secretary; Daniel Lauer, treasurer. The meetings are held once a week in Blake's store, in Salem.

Some time ago Margaret Palmer, Anna Doan, and Mrs. William Thomas organized as Daughters of Rebecca.

Mention has been made of the Amos Porter cemetery as the first in the township. It stands on a high hill back of the Salem school-house and contains the graves of many fathers and mothers of the community. Here we find represented the Stanleys, the Trues, the Tolmans, the Porters, the Pettys, Armstrongs, and others.

Another comparatively old burying-ground is the cemetery on Bear Creek ridge near the Good Hope church. Here lies Elder Levi Culver, the first one buried in it, whose stone bears the record, "Died December 17, 1835 in his sixtieth year." Here also are the remains of members of the first families in the neighborhood—Hugh Wilson, who settled in 1819, some of the Hutchesons, Felix Mayer, who died aged one hundred and seven years. Representatives are here of the Bells, Simons, Montgomerys, Carlins, Hayts, Dixons, Halls, and others.

A visitor at Orgilleas Doan's by the name of William McBane, died in 1823 and Mr. Doan came to Mr. Gould to arrange a place of burial. A spot was selected near where a barn of Mr. Kilmer's stands. In a few days Mr. Doan was seized with the same disease and died. The burying place was afterwards changed to where it now is, near the church. Here lie buried the dead of the Goulds, Hoveys, Halletts, Hills, Doans, Aldens, Trues, and also Rev. Denton Watkins.

About 1839, Henry Whittock gave a half acre to the township for a burying-ground. It is located near the Universalist church. On one stone is the inscription, "Henry B., son of S. and M. Whittock, died June 20, 1839, aged twelve years, one month and four days," being the first person interred in this yard.

The last cemetery in the township is on a hill west of Warner station. The first one buried there was Frederick Feldner, who was killed by a boiler explosion about four years ago.

The graveyard at the Bonn German Methodist church dates from 1842, when a child of Henry Bahrenburg was buried in it, the first.

Salem is the largest village in the township. It was laid out by James Stanley in 1850. The occasion was the building of a plank road from Marietta to the place, and it was thought that this advantage would make the place quite a fair sized town. The resident stockholders in this enterprise were William Thomas, Madison R. Morse, H. McGee, and Moses True. A toll-house was built at the terminus, and was the first building in the village. But the road did not pay, the boards were allowed to rot, while the village that it started kept on to its present size. The first house, except the toll-house, was built by Benjamin Hovey and is now occupied by a saloon.

Though a small place at present, of less than three hundred population, it can boast of quite a number of business houses. It contains a hotel, livery stable, gristmill, saw- and planing-mill, a tannery, six grocery and dry goods stores, a tobacco packing house, two carriage shops, three blacksmith shops, two shoe stores, one harness shop, a cigar factory, and four churches. A two-story brick school building was erected eight years ago, at a cost of over three thousand dollars. The first teachers were W. R. and Talma Goddard. The present are Mr. C. E. Bailey, principal, and Miss Mary Ames.

Warner village, a station on the Cleveland & Marietta railroad, and named in honor of General A. J. Warner, was laid out by P. and E. Boye in about 1873. It now has a store, harness shop, blacksmith shop, cooper shop, shoe shop, a church and two hotels. The store was begun in August, 1871, and is therefore the first enterprise in the village. It was kept formerly in the railroad depot.

Bonn is the oldest of the three towns and is in the southeastern part of the township. Mr. Nahum Ward owned land at the place and by his characteristic and energetic endeavors induced a considerable emigration to the locality, principally of Germans, in whose honor the town was called Bonn, from the town of that name on the Rhine.

Bonn was laid out near 1835. It will be remembered that Mr. Ward expected to introduce the manufacture of silk to the place and for that purpose planted a grove of white mulberry trees, bought spinning machinery and introduced workmen. But the enterprise failed and Bonn was left to the fate of an inland agricultural village. The first store in the place was by Rufus Payne who began to carry on the business about the time the town was platted. The place now contains a store, carpenter shop, blacksmith shop and shoe shop.

BIOGRAPHICAL SKETCHES.

PORTER FAMILY.

The Porter family, of Salem township, came from Danvers, Massachusetts. Amos Porter, the head of the family, was born in Danvers, November 24, 1742, and married in 1764, Anne Bradstreet, of Topsfield. This couple, Amos Porter and Anna Bradstreet, were descended respectively from John Porter and Governor Simon Bradstreet.

John Porter was born in England, in 1596. It is not known just when he arrived in the Massachusetts colony, but he was there as early as 1635. Settled first at Hingham, but soon removed to Salem. At the time of his death, in 1676, he was the largest landholder in Salem. He was a man of energy and influence, well known in the colony, and held many official positions. His wife's name was Mary ———, and they had eight children. The record of descent to Amos Porter is as follows: John Porter and Mary ———, Joseph Porter and Ann Hathorne, Joseph Porter and Mary ———, Joseph Porter and Mary ———, Amos Porter and Anne Bradstreet.

Governor Simon Bradstreet, son of a nonconforming minister, was born at Horbling, England, in March, 1603; spent one year at Emanuel college, Cambridge; came to Massachusetts with Winthrop, Dudley, and other distinguished persons in the Arbella, in 1630. Was chosen an assistant in the government of the colony before leaving England, and annually reelected for fifty years; was afterwards deputy governor and governor. He married Anne Dudley, daughter of Thomas Dudley, first deputy governor of the colony, who was never out of the magistracy, and most of the time deputy governor or governor

until his death, in 1653. The record of descent to Anne Bradstreet runs thus: Simon Bradstreet and Anne Dudley, John Bradstreet and Sarah Perkins, Simon Bradstreet and Elizabeth Capen, Simon Bradstreet and Anne Flint, Amos Porter and Anne Bradstreet.

The children of Amos Porter and Anne Bradstreet, all born in Massachusetts, were: Lydia, born March 20, 1765; Anna, born December 6, 1766; Amos, born February 20, 1769; Jonathan, born June 6, 1771; Simon, born November 18, 1779. Lydia died in Danvers at the age of ten; Anna married Allen Putnam.

The parents, with their son-in-law and three sons, came to Ohio in the spring of 1795. Mr. Putnam settled on a farm in Fearing township, not far from Stanleyville. Mr. Porter and his sons settled in Salem township, just below the present village of Salem, pushing much farther into the wilderness in that direction than any previous settlers.

Amos Porter, jr., purchased a farm on the same side of the creek that the village is, and extending from the village to near the West fork of the stream. Amos Porter, sr., and his sons Jonathan and Simon took a farm directly across the creek from that of Amos Porter, jr.

Amos Porter, sr., died in 1807; Jonathan shortly afterward, leaving the farm to Simon, who also had the care of his mother until her death, several years later.

On these farms these two brothers lived the remainder of their days, Simon dying March 10, 1843, aged sixty-three, and Amos dying November 28, 1861, aged ninety-two.

Men of integrity, industry, and sobriety and of simple habits, they became well-to-do farmers, lived quiet but useful lives, were prominent in church and township affairs, and rendered valuable assistance to later settlers and to the poor generally. It is believed that among their descendants not one has become a drunkard or even a tippler.

Amos was for some years an elder in the Presbyterian church of Fearing and Salem, of which his mother and brother Jonathan were members. But the church being without a pastor for several years, and possibly for other reasons, he changed his church relations, uniting with the Methodists, with whom he continued to the time of his death.

Simon was the chosen leader of the Methodist society in Salem nearly all the time from its organization to the time of his death. His home was the chief stopping place for the Methodist ministers. The door-string always out, was especially so when ministers were about, and on occasions of quarterly meetings. Methodist preachers in those days were fond of, and needed good horses, and, to this end, they wanted them well cared for; and they soon learned that "Father Porter" or "Uncle Simon" (as more commonly called) would not only look well to their own comfort, but equally well to the condition of their horses.

The term "Uncle Simon" was so common, so well nigh universal, that the younger children scarcely knew their father had any other name, as the following incident will show. "Uncle Simon," busy at work, and wanting more nails. than he had, called upon his little boy to make his first trip to a neighboring store about a mile off to get a few pounds. The little fellow having received his instructions, set out for the store. Arrived there, he announced that "Father wants some nails." Looking at the lad, the storekeeper asked "Who is your father?" "Uncle Simon," was the ready response.

Amos was one of the number that landed at Marietta April 7, 1788, and the last survivor of that famous band. The return trip to Boston, at the end of two years, was made all the way on foot. He married for his first wife, Sabra Tolman. She was the mother of all his children. For his second wife he married Mrs. Sally (Perkins) Sutton. His children were: Amos, William, Samuel, Thomas, Rufus, Hiram, Lydia, Jerusha and Almer. Amos died in early manhood, unmarried. Rufus and Hiram died in childhood. William married three times: First, Mary Sutton; second, Polly Stanley; and third, Mrs. Betsey (Fowler) Tolman. He had ten children. He and six of his children removed to southern Illinois, where he died. Samuel married Mary Palmer; he had three children, and died in Salem. Thomas married: first, Rhoda Sutton, and second, Polly Stille, and had six children. The children are all dead, except Mrs. Joseph Cox, of Lowell. He is living at Belpre, and has been a man of remarkable physical strength and activity, and was a noted conductor on the "Underground Railway" in years gone by. Lydia married Mr. S. N. Merriam, of Lowell, this county, where they now reside, a well preserved, aged couple, who have passed their "Golden Wedding" by several years, but are remarkably youthful for persons of their ages, and are still actively engaged in their usual pursuits,—he, at the age of eighty-two, conducting a general merchandise store, and she, at the age of seventy-five, doing all their household duties with that punctilious care which has ever characterized her.

Jerusha married Mr. Davis, and had three children. She has long been a widow. It is supposed she is still living in the west.

Almer, an invalid for some years, lives on a part of the old homestead in Salem. He married Mary Babson. They have six children.

Simon, son of Amos, sr., married Elizabeth Stille. Their children were: Hiram, Lois, Anne Bradstreet, Mary Vincent, Irum, Ruth, Simon Swormstead and Cyrus Fox. No death occurred in this family for thirty-six years, viz: From January 9, 1807, to January 29, 1843. Hiram died in infancy. Cyrus died in early manhood unmarried. Anne never married. Lois married Ephraim Gould, had ten children, and died October 23, 1859. One son, Jasper Porter, graduated at Alleghany college, Pennsylvania, and was for a time principal of Marietta high school. He married Mary Taylor, of Lee, Massachusetts. One daughter, Mary Melissa, married Rev. Mr. Brady, who left the ministry to help put down the Rebellion. Mary married Madison R. Morse, had nine children, and died September 29, 1863. At one time her husband and five of her sons were in the Union army. Her oldest son Wallace was killed before

Lynchburgh. Irum married Elizabeth True. Their two children died in infancy. He died in Minnesota June 1, 1872.

Ruth married Dr. William Heald, had one son, and died November 26, 1843.

Simon S., the only member of the family now living, married Euretta S. Hill. They have three children: Ida Precia, Mary Waldena and Edwin Horace.

Beside several years' teaching in district and select schools in this county and Crawford county, Pennsylvania, Mr. Porter has been principal of the Washington Street grammar school, Marietta, eighteen years, and entered upon the duties of that position in January, 1854. In March, 1864, he resigned on account of ill health. In the spring of 1865 he was chosen a member of the board of education, in which capacity he served until 1873, when he was reelected to his former position in the schools, which place he still holds. It will thus be seen that he has been connected with the public schools of Marietta as teacher or member of the board of education for the past twenty-seven years, with but one year's exception.

FAMILY OF IRA HILL.

Among the early families of Salem township was that of Ira Hill, esq. Mr. Hill came to Ohio from Vermont, but was born in Goshen, Litchfield county, Connecticut. He was the son of Zenas and Kezia Hill (probably cousins.) His grand parents were Ebenezer Hill and Martha Dibble, the former born at Guilford, Connecticut, November 23, 1687, and the latter at Hartford, November 13, 1697.

Ira Hill married Esther Post, of Norwich, Connecticut, February 2, 1786. Their children were: Ira, Harry, Sally, Urania, Speedy, Guy and Dan. These were all born in New England except Dan, who was born in Salem, January 31, 1803.

The family arrived in Marietta in the year 1800, and after remaining a while in Marietta, settled on a farm in Salem, about one mile north of Salem village.

Mr. Hill came west, thinking a change of climate might improve his health; and he seems to have realized the object of his search, for he lived to the ripe old age of four-score and six, dying October 13, 1841. Mild and amiable in disposition, frank, honest and upright in his intercourse with others, he was not only respected, but trusted and honored by the community.

His wife was a woman of rare social qualities, and of great courage, energy and endurance. She lived to the age of ninety-two, dying August 15, 1851.

The parents and most of the children were members of the Presbyterian church of Fearing and Salem. The boys were fond of military displays, and figured somewhat prominently in the musters and drills of those early times. Harry became a colonel, Ira a major, and Guy and Dan were musicians.

Ira Hill, jr., married Wealthy Little, of Newport, in 1816, and, in 1819, settled on a farm in Newport, next above the late Joseph Barker's. Here he lived until his death in 1866. He was a deacon in the Baptist church, a prominent member of that denomination, and widely known in other denominations as a zealous Christian worker. He was a genial companion, a most liberal giver for religious purposes, and a man of the highest integrity. His children were: Luther, Ira, Emily, Cynthia, Mary, Charles, Hervey and Judson.

Luther, a graduate of Marietta college, class of 1842, and of Newton theological seminary, Massachusetts, is a Baptist minister in Maine. Ira is a farmer in Iowa. Emily (Mrs. Charles Fuller) removed to Iowa some years since, and died there. Cynthia, an intelligent and deeply religious maiden lady, resides near her father's farm, in Newport. Mary is the worthy wife of Mr. Adams, an Iowa farmer. Charles and Judson died in early manhood at their father's. (Charles was preparing for the ministry at the time of his death) Hervey, who lived on the homestead, died soon after his father, leaving the farm to his widow and children, who still occupy it.

Colonel Harry Hill married Mrs. Jerusha (Chapman) Doan, of Salem. They lived for a time in Salem, then removed to Lancaster, Ohio, where he died. Their children were: Jerusha, Louisa, Harry and Abigail. Jerusha married Mr. Prindle, a farmer. They live in Wisconsin. Louisa died in infancy. Harry is a farmer near Lancaster. Abbie is Mrs. Major Carey, Aberdeen, Ohio. Sally and Guy never married, living and dying at the old home in Salem. Speedy died in infancy in Vermont. Urania married James Stanley, of Fearing. They had nine children: Urania, Laura, Lucy, Cynthia, James, Caroline, Diantha, Clement and Paul. Urania, James and Clement went to Wisconsin, married and settled at Necedah, Juneau county. (Urania is Mrs. Harry Smith.) Laura married James Ewing, of Salem. Lucy is Mrs. James Calland, of Noble county. She resides near Summerfield. Cynthia married Isaac T. Lund, a successful farmer of Aurelius, active in township affairs, and a noted abolitionist in times when it required backbone to avow such sentiments. Caroline is Mrs. Daniel Morgan, of Salem. Diantha died in early womanhood, and Paul while yet a youth.

Dan, the youngest of the family, married Mary Merriam, daughter of Reuben Merriam and Mary Noyes, who came from Troy, New York, to Lowell, in 1816. He remained on the farm in Salem, and, beside carrying on the farm, engaged in merchandizing, first with William McIntosh, afterward alone, and for many years conducted an extensive and profitable business. He was a keen observer of men and nature, and a man of excellent judgment. His counsel and sympathy were extensively sought in times of trouble and distress, and his kind, sympathetic nature extended to all a helping hand. He was active in the formation of the first temperance society west of the Alleghanies, and drafted its pledge. Deprived by death of his beloved wife, on whom he greatly relied, not only for the management of the household but also in business matters, he nevertheless succeeded in rearing his family of six children, watching over them with a father's care and a mother's tenderness. His children were: Edwin, Euretta, Archibald, Oladine, Deming,

Esther and Erwin. Edwin died in infancy. Euretta is Mrs. S. S. Porter, Marietta. Archibald is a merchant in Columbus, Ohio. Oladine is the wife of S. B. Hildreth, a well-off farmer near Marietta. Deming is a farmer in California. Esther is the wife of J. A. Woods, superintendent of schools and farmer, Clarinda, Iowa. Erwin is a farmer near Marietta.

CHAPTER XLIII.
GRAND VIEW TOWNSHIP.

A Picturesque Locality—Location, Soil, Timber, Etc.—Organization of Township—Early Settlement and Personal Sketches—Lease Run Settlement—Churches—Schools—Cemeteries—Railroad—Vineyard—Matamoras and Grand View—Odd Fellows and Masonic Lodges—Grange Societies—Mills—Casualties and Tragedies—Newspapers—"Petticoat Ford."

ASCENDING the highest hill immediately southwest of Matamoras, and turning our gaze toward the east, a scene of rare beauty is revealed. At first the eye will naturally seek the view of the great, majestic sweep of the Ohio, whose waters can be traced for full twenty miles away. Then beyond are the Virginia hills rolling away into mere perspective of blue sky and vapory clouds. On either hand the Buckeye hills, with rugged brows of abutting sandstone, stand revealed in strongest outline, amidst gnarled trunks of trees, variagated oaks and evergreen pine.

Below is the town of Matamoras toward the north, and the village of Grand View at the south with pointed church-spires and the scarce-heard echoes of their school bells mingle with the hum of manufacture, the bustle of farm life, and the piercing whistle of the river steamers. The squares of fenced fields, dotted with farm houses; the winding roads and noisy teamsters, the orchards, field and woodland, in one unbroken vista—how natural the exclamation: "What a grand view!"

So general was this expression by visitors to this place that it naturally and appropriately became the name of the locality and township.

It is the extreme northeast township of the county, and lies in the shape of the letter V pointed at the south; is joined on the north by Monroe county, and the southwest course of the Ohio river shapes the inclination of the eastern boundary, while Independence and Ludlow townships join Grand View on the west. Along the banks of the Ohio level stretches of fertile bottom lands of the variable breadth of a mile and less extend the entire length of the township, and the soil of sand and clay is highly productive of wheat, corn, potatoes and tobacco, the latter being extensively cultivated.

The highlands rise abruptly from the river bottoms, and extend in high ridges throughout the western part of the township, some of the elevations reaching a height of over eight hundred feet. The soil is generally what is known as "white oak," and of variable degrees of productiveness.

The timber lands are mostly of the different varieties of oak, while some hickory, walnut and poplar may be found. The whole length of the township, between the extreme north and south points, is ten miles and the greatest width five and one half miles, embracing an area of near thirty thousand acres of land. The settlements were made along the banks of the Ohio, and Matamoras is the only incorporated town. Grand View village, Ward Station, and Yellow House are points of trade and post offices. The population, according to the last census, is two thousand six hundred and sixty-four. The drainage is generally by small branches into the Ohio river; the principal branch is Sheet's run, which takes its rise in the northwestern part, and flowing directly south, empties into the Ohio at the extreme southwest corner of the township. Mill Creek run carries the waters of the northern part into the Ohio above Matamoras.

The chief productions belong mostly to the agricultural department, though there is considerable cooperage, tanning and other minor branches of manufacture in operation in this township.

ORGANIZATION.

"Grand View was struck off from Newport in 1803," and the first election for township officials was held the first Monday of the April following, and resulted as follows: Samuel Williamson, Philip Witten, and David Jackson, trustees; Arthur Scott, clerk; Nathan Parr, William Ramsey, and John McBride, supervisors; Alexander Mayers, constable. In the following year the list was increased: Philander B. Stewart and William Cline, constables; Arthur Scott, lister of property; James Riggs and John Collins, overseers of poor; Nathan Parr and Henry Dickerson, appraisers of houses.

EARLY SETTLEMENTS.

The old Dickerson farm was the first land cleared in Grand View township, and on it was built the first log cabin by David Shepherd, in very early times. This cabin stood east of the present residence of Aurelius Ellis, near the river. David Shepherd is supposed to have been but temporarily settled here as nothing concerning him can now be found, and, after selling his property, in all probability he removed further down the Ohio. The cabin which he built was occupied by the Dickerson family when they first came to this locality. Kinsey Dickerson first purchased the farm of David Shepherd "for a consideration of eighty-five pounds, current money of Virginia," and it was described as fractional section twenty-seven, township one, range five, in the territory northwest of the Ohio river then belonging to Virginia, and containing one hundred and seventy acres of land. The deed conveying the land in this transaction was recorded in 1796.

Mr. Dickerson, the purchaser, was a well known hunter in the early days, and with rifle, tomahawk, and a knife in his belt, delighted in the chase after the wild animals among the hills and along the banks of the Ohio, and any adventure promising any extraordinary demand for skill, prowess, or heroism, was hailed with delight by Kinsey Dickerson. He was also many times in active pursuit of thieving or hostile Indians that frequently visited the early settlements.

Thomas Dickerson, brother of Kinsey, settled on this farm in 1795. He was born October 15, 1757, and had a family of nine children—Joseph, Frederick, Rebecca, Vachel, Isabella, Eleanor, Elizabeth, Thomas, and Sarah. He lived on this farm, an industrious and respected citizen, until his death, when the estate was divided among his children. Among his papers were found several ancient documents, some of which are here given:

Feb. 20th, 1786.

Received of Thomas Dickerson one discharge for three years' service in the 8th Penn. Regulars. Given at Ft. Pitt Oct. 9th, 1779, by Col. Bayard, com. of 8th Penn. Regulars.

(Signed) JOHN MUNN.

WASHINGTON, D. C., Dec. 18th, 1818.

This is to certify that Thomas Dickerson, private in the army of the Revolution, is entitled to a pension of $8.00 per month.

(Signed) J. C. CALHOUN,
Sec. of War.

The neighbors of Thomas Dickerson in early times were David Shepherd, John Mitchell, Philip Whitton, and others, of whom no further record can now be found. They are remembered as the men of pioneer times in this locality, whose personal efforts, privations, and industry began the work now blooming in fruition, as exhibited by the present prosperity of Grand View township, and measured by the position she holds in the rank of progress and civilization of Washington county.

James Riggs came from Maryland and made the first settlement in what is now Matamoras, about 1799, and built his log cabin on what is now First street, where the residence of Mr. Thornbury now stands. This house was made of hewn logs, after the style of early times. He first encamped on the opposite side of the river, where he kept his family until the cabin in Ohio was completed, when he moved over. He was born in what is now Washington, District of Columbia, in 1742, and died February 27, 1815. He was accompanied by his wife, Mary Johnson, and children—Basil, Hezekiah, John, Samuel, Edmund, Maxey, Polly, and Prissa; also his son-in-law, Martin Sheets. He, with the latter, entered two hundred acres of land along the Ohio river, he taking the northern, and the son-in-law the southern part, all of which subsequently was transferred to Martin Sheets. On the northern part of this land the town of Matamoras was founded. Basil Riggs was born in Maryland in 1775, and died in 1850. Mary Robey, his wife, was born in 1777, and died in 1836. Their children were—James, Susan, Harriet, Isaac, Edmund, William, Hezekiah, Hazil, Asbury, and Squire Dilly. Hezekiah was born in 1810, and was married to Elizabeth Moorland, who was born in 1812. They had a family of eight children—James W., Mary, Susan, Daniel, Hezekiah, Nancy E., Angeline, and Harriet.

Anthony Sheets and wife emigrated from Maryland to Ohio and settled in Grand View township sometime during the latter part of the eighteenth century. He died in 1834, aged seventy-five, and his wife died in 1840, aged eighty years. Their son, Henry Sheets, who was born in Grand View township in 1807, married Rebecca Parr, who was born in 1811. To them have been born thirteen children, of whom there survive, viz: Minerva, in Iowa; Jesse P., in Kansas; Leander and William H., in West Virginia; Rebecca M., and Ruth B., in Kansas; and Hamilton and Malinda. Henry Sheets laid out the first lots in the town of Matamoras, of which he was the originator. During the years 1836–52 he was engaged in the mercantile business on the site of Matamoras. In 1855 he removed to his present farm in Newport township. During the years 1826–79, inclusive, he was postmaster at Lower Newport.

Rufus Ellis came from New York and landed at Newell's Run in 1808, having floated down the Ohio on a lumber raft. His wife was Ruth Ingalls, and they had children, viz: Martin, Benjamin, Silas, Rufus, Henry, Rebecca, Sibyl, Sabra, and Diana. Silas Ellis settled on the old Dickerson farm in 1806. He was married to Eleanor Dickerson, who died in 1859, his decease occurring the same year. To them were born seven children —Charles D., William M., Ruth, Minerva, Solon, Aurelius and Aurelia (twins), and Henry. William McGee Ellis was born on the Dickerson farm in 1819, and was married to Clarissa Ankrom. He moved to Matamoras in the spring of 1847, and erected for John Scott, on First street, the first brick house in the town, now the residence of Dr. Richardson. The grandmother of Silas Ellis, father of William M. Ellis, was a Ballou, sister to the mother of James A. Garfield, President of the United States.

Aurelius Ellis was born in 1823, and was married in 1845 to Eveline Morgan, who was born in 1824. To them were born ten children, nine of whom are now living: Leander, Lafayette, Evan, Aurelius, Elizabeth, Sarah, Mary, Paulina, and Bertha.

Mr. Ellis was pilot on the Ohio river, running from Wheeling to St. Louis for twenty-six years. At present he is a farmer, and owns a farm of one hundred acres in Grand View township.

John Burris settled just above Leath's run, about 1800. His wife was Betsey McMahon, and their children were: Benjamin, Van, Stinson, Swangum, Martin, John, Lavina, and David. He was quite a remarkable man physically, and stood six feet six in his stockings. His wit and sociability made him very popular in the settlement, and he was also given to poetry, confining his genius, however, to local events, and the satire of local characters. These compositions he would sing to very appreciative audiences. On one occasion he had a lawsuit with William Rea, and after the trial he placed his back against the door, thus confining his victim in the room, and then entertained the crowd and the 'squire with a song against his late opponent. On account of his well known physical endurance he was appointed to carry dispatches from Cincinnati to Fort Duquesne during the Indian war.

Henry Jolly settled about half a mile below Grand View village in 1799. His wife, when a child, had a very narrow escape from death by the Indians as she was on her way with her parents from Virginia to Ohio. The family were attacked at night, and all the rest of them murdered. She was also felled by a blow from a tomahawk, and scalped

as she lay helpless on the ground, where she was left for dead. A party of whites the following day found the bodies of the murdered family, and upon proceeding to bury them they found that one was yet alive, and after some difficulty she was resuscitated and lived to become the wife of Judge Jolly. To them were born four children: Albert, William, Kinsey, and Sidney.

John Collins was the oldest member of the family that came to this county in 1803. He was born in 1754 and died in 1842. His wife was Sarah (Henthorn), who died in 1814. They had a family of three sons and four daughters. He was afterward married to Deborah (Dickerson) Dyson, who died in 1847.

Henry Collins came with his father, John Collins, and settled in Grand View township in 1803. He was born in Pennsylvania in 1778, and was married in 1810 to Frances Ewart, widow of William Peyton (now Mrs. Cordery), who was born in 1781. They had a family of six children, of whom five are now living: Elliott H., Sardine Y., Francis E., John H., and Jeremiah.

Francis E. Collins was born in 1818, and was married in 1851 to Margaret M. Bill, who was born 1829. To them were born four children, three now living—John H., Mary E., Francis B. Mr. Collins has been, and is, one of the successful farmers of this township. He owns a farm of two hundred and thirty acres, most of which he cleared himself; is one of the leading men of this locality, and has furnished for himself and family one of the most elegant and comfortable homes of this township.

Joseph Holdren was born in New Jersey and came to this township about 1803, and was married in 1805 to Ruth Coleman. They had three children, two now living—Thomas and George. His son Thomas was born in 1808 and in 1839 was married to Mary A. Riggs, who was born in 1812. They have a family of eight living children—James, Joseph, Edmund, George, Allen, Josiah, Mary, Eliza. When Mr. Holdren first came here he was possessed of little or no property, but by his own industry he accumulated twelve hundred and fifty acres of land, which he has deeded to his sons, only a part of which is located in this township, on which is a very fine orchard.

Richard Talbott was a native of Wales, and emigrated to Washington county, Pennsylvania, and afterwards to Grand View township, in 1812, and settled on the farm now owned by Robert Amos in the extreme northeast corner of the township on the Ohio. The site of the cabin in which he lived was located at the mouth of Talbott's run, but has long since been washed down the river.

Charles W. Talbott, sr., was born in Washington county, Pennsylvania, in 1791, and came to this township after a service in the War of 1812. He was married to Eliza McMunn who was born in 1798. They had a family of twelve children, namely: Temperance, Absalom O., John Marshall, Martha, Charles W., Elizabeth, Basil, Ephriam, Nancy B., Cornelia, Elvisia, and Mary. He was a farmer and well known local preacher in the Methodist Episcopal church. He died October 22, 1874, in Lawrence county, Ohio.

Charles W. Talbott, jr., was born in Matamoras on First street, south of the public well, in an old house that stood where the street now runs, in 1826. He was married in 1849 to Nancy Talbott. To them were born five children—Emma, Dorinda, Alma, Eliza and Luna Lee. He has served as captain on the Ohio and Mississippi. He now resides in Matamoras.

William Williamson was born about 1790, and died in Texas about 1855. He was married about 1809 to Sarah McMahn, who was born about 1788, and died 1838. They had three children—Narcissa, Hannah and Hannibal. Hannibal Williamson was born in Grand View in 1813, and was married in 1831 to Temperance Hubbard, born in 1824. They had a family of eleven children, of whom are now living—Belmont, Jerome, Narcissa, Hannibal, Eva, and Althea Temperance. He has held the office of treasurer eleven years, trustee several years, and now owns a farm of nine hundred acres, part of which he cultivates himself, and is a prominent citizen of the township.

Bemont Hubbard was born in Connecticut about 1780, and was married to Miss A. Talbott, who was born about 1791. To them were born eight children, five now living: John, Richard, William, Temperance, and Jemima. His decease occurred at Matamoras in 1866, the death of Mrs. Hubbard having occurred in 1845. He was trustee several years, and served as teamster in the transport service during the War of 1812, and by his industry had accumulated considerable property.

Isaac Rinard, father of John Rinard, came from Pennsylvania and first settled on Leath run in 1814, and removed to this township in 1824, on Mill creek about one mile north of Matamoras. His wife was Mary Young. They had a family of two children—Sarah and John; and by his second wife—Isaac, James, Peggy, Polly, Nancy, and Cynthia. John went to Muskingum in 1826, and returned to Mill creek in 1829, where he lived until 1870, when he removed to his present residence near the public school building in Matamoras.

Nicholas Lisk was born in Virginia in 1803, and was married to Susan Hill, who was born in 1805 and died in 1846. Six of their thirteen children are now living—Edmund, Jonas, Jasper, Nicholas, Pauline, and Harriet. He was again married, in 1848, to Mary A. Lippincott, and died in Monroe county in 1874. Edmund Lisk was born in 1829 and was married in 1855 to Maria Salsbury, who died in 1868. They had a family of five children, three now living: Alexander, Mary E., and Jasper. He was married again in 1870 to Sarah Fox, who was born in 1851, and they have five children: James, Nicholas, Thomas, Anna, and John. He has been constable three times, and has given much attention to the study of law, and is a prominent farmer and citizen.

Samuel Pool, a native of Virginia, came to this county about 1835, where he resided until his death, which occurred August 29, 1846. He was married to Mary E. Kidwell, December 23, 1813, who died June 6, 1875. They had a family of ten children: Samuel, John, Ellen, Catharine, and Richard, are now living. John, the fifth son, was born in Virginia, October 18, 1824, and

came to this county with his father; was married August 12, 1856, to Hannah Rinard, who was born December 12, 1833. He has served as county commissioner one term; assessor of township three years; and like his father and mother before him, is an active and efficient member of the Baptist church, which he has served as deacon for thirty years, and is one of the leading citizens of the township.

John Hinds was born in Washington county in 1835, and was married in 1855 to Margaret Frey, who was born in 1831. They now have a family of ten children: John F., Sarah, Eliza A., Mary S., William C., David H., Charlotta, James, Hannah and Rosie. He is one of the leading farmers and citizens of this township. By the death of his father he was early called upon to support his mother and younger brothers and sisters. He came with the family to Ohio in his seventeenth year, in order to give his brothers and sisters educational advantages. He was entirely without assistance, but by industry, has accumulated considerable property. He was a member of company C, Seventy-seventh Ohio volunteer infantry, serving from 1862 to the close of the war; was detailed as orderly to Colonel Hildebrand, and was in the battles of Shiloh, Corinth, Little Rock, Spanish Fort, Mark's Mills, Siege of Mobile, and was at the surrender of Kirby Smith at Mobile.

William L. West, M. D., was born in Moundsville, West Virginia, 1850; began the study of medicine under Dr. G. W. Brue; graduated in 1875 at Jefferson Medical college of Philadelphia, and moved to Matamoras in 1877, where he has since practiced. He is now mayor of Matamoras, and one of the leading physicians.

Francis P. Martin, M. D., was born in Monroe county, in 1836, and was married in 1860 to Adaline A. Davis, who was born in 1842. They had a family of eight children, six now living—John H., Thaddeus, Luther, Lilian, Nimrod, and Matilda. He came to Matamoras in 1862, where he has since been engaged in the practice of medicine; is a graduate of the Cincinnati College of Medicine and Surgery; belongs to the Allopathic school of medicine, and is known as a successful practitioner.

John Webber came to this township in 1837, was born about 1798 in New England, and died in Minnessota in 1863. He was married to Mary Gilson, who was born about 1796, and died in 1864. Six of their children are now living—Hadessa, John P., Sarah, Richard Gilson, Mary and Jerry. He held several township offices, and remained in the township, one of the leading citizens, until 1854, when he removed to Minnesota.

Richard Gilson Webber was born in 1826, and was married in 1856 to Mary Farraborn, who was born in 1834. They have a family of five children—William Emmett, James Madison, Samuel G., Richard C., and Marion. He came to this township with his father in 1837; has held the office of school director, and is entirely a self-made man, receiving no assistance from his father. He has, as the fruit of his own industry, a farm of one hundred and sixty acres of land in Missouri, and two hundred and eighty in this township. He is a prominent member of the Presbyterian church.

Samuel Hensell was born in West Virginia in 1810, and was married to Miss R. A. Keck, who was born in Pennsylvania in 1816, and died in 1877. They have three children now living: Catherine, John F., and Anna. He first settled in what was then Jolly township, where he resided until 1871, when he came to Matamoras, where he now lives. He has been a class leader in the Methodist Episcopal church for twenty years, and is a leading citizen of the town in which he lives.

John Hensell was born in Jolly township in 1834, and was married in 1858 to Martha C. States, who was born in 1837, and died in 1873. He was afterward married to Mary J. Cambell, who was born in 1850, and they have three children—Samuel T., Cora Jane, and Z. David. He has held the office of corporation treasurer, and is now undertaker and cabinet-maker in Matamoras on First street. He also owns a small farm of fifteen acres of bottom land, with a good orchard. In 1860 he had the misfortune to lose his left lower limb in the horse power of a threshing machine. He is a member of the Methodist Episcopal church, in which he has held the office of leader and trustee.

Conrad Emery came to this township in 1846. Was born in Germany about 1810, and married to Catharine Kraft, who was born in the same country in 1820. He died in 1877. They had a family of seven children, five surviving: Catharine, John, Mary, Margaret, and Laura. John Emery was born in Pennsylvania in 1834, and was married in 1860, to Mary Hays, who was born in 1828. They have five children: Ira, Allen, Mary, Elizabeth, and Alice. He held the office of school director, and owns a farm of one hundred and twenty acres.

John Hays was born in 1780, came to this township in 1838. His wife was Elizabeth Waters, born in 1790. They have six children living: Ann, Sarah, Allen, Mary, John, and David. He died in 1872, one year after the decease of his wife.

Samuel S. Dorff was born about 1776, and died in 1870. He was married to Violet Evans, who was born in 1782, and died in 1845. Five of their children are now living: Joshua, Charles, William, Violet, and Russell. They came to this township in 1844.

Russell Dorff was born in 1817, and was married in 1843 to Elizabeth Barnett, who was born in 1819. Six of their ten children are now living: William, Sarah, Eveline, Margaret, Stillman, and Mary. He was previously (1831) married to Jane Evans, who was born in 1816, died in 1841. He has held the office of justice of the peace for twenty-three years, and also many other offices. His son William was a member of the First battery, Ohio volunteer artillery, from 1861 to 1865, and was at Gettysburgh, Bull Run, Petersborough, and many other battles.

Edward Shapley came to this township with his stepfather, John Edmonds, where he has since resided. Was born in 1820, and married in 1841, to Mary Cameron, who was born in Virginia in 1824, and died in 1864. Their family consisted of five children, four now living: Jerome, George, Marshall, and Sarah. He was again married in 1869, to Martha Edmonds, born in 1850, and

died in 1873. They had one child, William. He has been school director; is a cooper by trade, and has succeeded in accumulating considerable property, and is a well known citizen of Grand View.

George A. Shapley, son of Edward Shapley, was born in Grand View in 1845, and was married in 1870, to Josephine McCracken, who was born in 1849. They have a family of four children: Fanny B., Maud, Charles P., and Frederick. He is now engaged in coopering, and manufactures one hundred barrels per week, sending them to the markets of Pittsburgh and Wheeling.

James Ward came from Pennsylvania and settled in Grand View township, in section five, in 1845. He was born in 1813, and was married in 1834. His wife, Margaret, was born in 1815. They now have seven children living: David, Mary, Richard, Eliza Jane, Albert, Joseph, and Margaret. He has by his own industry accumulated a large property, part of which he has distributed among his children, and is a leading citizen of the county.

Joseph P. was born in 1846, and in 1877 was married to Nancy M. Covert, who was born in 1858. They have one child—Asa Evart. He has studied law for a number of years, and is now notary public and holds half interest in the general store under the name of Ward Brothers. He is the present postmaster, located about eight miles west of Matamoras. The general store of Ward Brothers is the only business house at what is known as Ward station. The merchandizing of quite a large and thickly settled community is done here. The business firm is composed of Albert and Joseph P. Ward, and was established in in 1862 under the name of Richard Ward. It consists of dry goods, general merchandising, produce, and buying tobacco. The Ward family now owns about three hundred and fifty acres of land in this township.

Silas F. Cochran, son of Zachariah Cochran, was born in this township in 1839, and was married in 1872 to Emma Dorsey, who was born in 1848. They have a family of three children—Lulu, Eddie, and Harry. He commenced life as a farmer, but started for himself in the dry goods and groceries at Longreach, West Virginia, after which he came to his present business situation in Grand View. He is postmaster of Grand View, which position he has held for the past five years.

Theodore Perry Biddle came to this township about 1840 and settled between Matamoras and Grand View. He was born in September, 1820, and was married to Maria Willis in 1840. They had a family of seven children—Alonzo, Lloyd, John, Margaret, Josephine, Ella, and Grace. He enlisted in 1861 in company I, Seventy-seventh Ohio volunteer infantry, and was in the battle of Pittsburg Landing. He died in 1864 at Little Rock, Arkansas.

Lloyd Biddle was born in this township in 1844, and was married in 1867 to Sarah Mitchell, born in Monroe county in 1844. To them were born six children—Eva, Abbie, and Jessie now living. He enlisted in 1861 in company C, Seventy-seventh regiment, Ohio volunteer infantry, and was mustered out in 1866—after having served during the entire war. He was in the battles of

Pittsburgh Landing, Little Rock, and Mark's Mills, where he was captured with about fifteen thousand others, and was confined in the rebel prisons at Tyler, Texas, for ten months. When captured they were stripped of their clothing, except shirt and drawers, confined in an open stockade without shelter except what they themselves provided by digging caves in the earth, and were compelled to subsist on one pint of meal and three-fourths of a pound of beef, per day, and that issued irregularly. Many died from the severe treatment, and naturally every means was sought to escape from the prison. At one time a New York prisoner was detailed to haul dirt from the prison with a dump-cart and mule, and as many as three hundred of the prisoners escaped, one by one concealing themselves in the load of dirt and were dumped into the garbage holes outside the prison, but just before Mr. Biddle's time came the guards discovered the trick, and, as a precautionary measure, would prod the loads of dirt with their bayonets as they passed out. One very extensive tunnel was worked entirely beyond the guards, requiring from June to October to complete it, but the anxiety of the prisoners to escape overcame their precaution, and the tunnel was opened at the wrong time and discovered by the guards in time to prevent any escapes. Punishment for such offences was ten days standing on a stump.

The year 1847 brought a settler to Grand View by the name of Walter Brown, a native of Tyler county, Pennsylvania. He lived in the township the rest of his life, which ended in 1874. Of his eleven children, his namesake, Walter Brown, jr., was the second child, and was born in Ohio county, West Virginia, in 1834. He went to Independence township from Grand View in 1867, where he now lives. His wife, Mary E., is a daughter of Joseph Chambers, and was born in Lawrence township in 1840. Their marriage, in 1867, has resulted in seven children—Walter E., Mary A., Richard C., Edward T., Joseph H., Walter M., and Carl—all living but Walter and Mary. Mr. Brown is a farmer, township trustee, and ex-boatman. John and Mary, his brother and sister, live with him at present.

Samuel Hutchison was born in Belmont county, Ohio, in 1818, and was married in 1843 to Jane Morton, who was born in 1824, in Washington county, Pennsylvania. To them were born ten children, seven of whom are now living: Arthur, Morton, William, Elizabeth, Edward, John, and Mary. He came to Grand View township in 1851, and settled in Matamoras, where he established his present business of general merchandising. In 1857 he established the tannery, which he carried on until 1863, when he sold to Machetanz & Son. He was prominent in getting the post office established in the town in 1851, and was the first postmaster, and has held several other offices. He was elected justice of the peace in 1851, and served six years. He was mayor two terms, and was elected representative in the Ohio legislature on the Republican ticket in 1855. He was an ardent supporter of the Union cause during the late war, and raised a company of militia, of which he was made the captain. He has been identified with all the public movements of

this locality. At present he is a member of the United Presbyterian church. He owns a farm of three hundred and twenty-three acres, located in the north part of the township.

Under the name of Samuel Hutchison & Sons, he is assisted in the largest merchandizing establishment in the township by his two sons, Morton and William, located on the east side of First street, in the north part of Matamoras.

Samuel Shannon, son of John and Hannah (Rabe) Shannon, was born in 1813, and was married in 1844 to Susan Dennison. They have a family of the following children: John, Thomas, Samuel, and Mary. He first came to Matamoras and purchased the general store of Henry Sheets (the first store in the town), and began business in 1852, where he remained until about 1870, when he purchased the present steam flouring-mill of Clement Waters, where at present he is engaged in milling with his son John.

Mr. Shannon is one of the substantial and highly respected citizens of Matamoras, but careful and industrious attention to his business affairs has prevented him from accepting any public office.

Thomas A. Masters settled in Grand View village in 1856. He was born in 1838, and married in 1868 to Phœbe Titus, who was born in Rhode Island in 1841. They have four children, viz: Flora, Netta, Etta, and Fairy. He enlisted in 1861 in company B, Twenty-fifth Ohio volunteer infantry, and was mustered out in 1864. He was the color sergeant of his company, and received a serious wound in his side at Chancellorsville. He was also in the second battle at Manassas, at Gettysburgh, and several other engagements, serving under Generals McLean, Hooker, and Meade. He has held the office of justice of the peace since 1877, and was elected assessor the following year, which offices he now holds.

George West was born in England in 1821, and was married there to Susan Knowles, who was born in 1819 and died in 1857. They had a family of five children, four now living—Michael, Samuel, George, and Anna. He was again married to Rebecca Chambers, born in 1823. To them were born five children, three now living—Susan E., David O., and Mahala.

He settled in Matamoras in 1856, and in 1865 moved to his present location and commenced business as dry goods and general business merchant in what is known as the Yellow House west of Matamoras. He now owns a farm of two hundred and ten acres and is one of the leading citizens of his neighborhood.

Andrew Vauple (Fawble) was born in Germany in 1830 and came to the United States in 1857, and settled in Matamoras. He was married in 1860 to Elizabeth Bendal, and to them were born three children—Louisa, William, and Mary. Mr. Vauple first engaged in butchering in Matamoras and by hard work and economy succeeded in purchasing a farm of one hundred and seven acres, which lies west of the town. In 1868 he built his present brick residence in Matamoras, and was elected as member of the council in 1876.

Robert E. Wilson settled in Grand View township in

1856. He was born in 1815 and died in 1877; was married in 1833 to Mary Van Eman, who was born in 1820. Five of the ten children are now living, namely: Alexander D., Andrew, Sarah, Anna, and Lily. His son Andrew V., was born in 1842; married in 1869 to Jennie S. Hutchinson, born in 1852 and died in 1880, leaving three children—Clifford Guy, Emmett C., and Stella A. He was a member of company C, Seventy-seventh Ohio volunteer infantry, from 1861 to 1864, as corporal, color sergeant, and orderly; was in Sherman's brigade Sixteenth army corps and in the engagements of Shiloh, Little Rock, and at the battle of Fallen Timber, Tennessee, was captured by the enemy but was recaptured by the Union cavalry; is now farmer by occupation.

Robert Lovett was born in Pennsylvania in 1823, and was married in 1845 to Susan Nelson, who was born in 1823. They had a family of eight children, six of whom are now living—George, Jay, Ella, Madison, Brady, and Frank. He came to this township in 1858; is a carpenter by trade, having previously been a tanner, and has served his township as road master for eleven years. He now owns a farm of one hundred and twenty-eight acres of land and considerable other property as the result of a busy and industrious life.

Theodore Barnes, sr., son of Charles T. Barnes, settled in this township in 1860; was born in 1813, and died in 1880. He was married in 1842 to Euphemia Benninghaus, who was born in 1820, and died in 1852. Four of their six children are now living—Francis A., Charles W., Theodore B., and Lizette. He was again married in 1856 to Jane Grimes, who was born in 1830. To them were born three children—Anna, Laura and William. His son Theodore was born in 1849; married in 1873 to Margaret Bell, who was born in 1847, and they now have a family of two children—Louisa Belle and Jennie Leslie. He is now conducting a livery stable at Matamoras, owns a farm of twenty-one acres of bottom land, and is a well known citizen of Matamoras.

John Swan, son of John Swan, sr., settled in this township in 1856; was born in Jefferson county, Ohio, in 1820. He was married in 1846 to Mary Ann Aten, born in 1828, and died in 1877. Five of their seven children are now living—George, John C., William, Jane, and Silas Darwin. He commenced life with but the clothes on his back, and they unpaid for; but by industry has made himself possessor of a farm of eighty acres, and has been enabled to start some of his children in life. He is a respected citizen of the township.

John Brooks was born in 1829, and was married in 1857 to Miss N. J. Davis, who was born in 1838. They now have five living children—William, Charles, Frank, Anna, and Effie. He came to Matamoras in 1862, and began the practice of medicine, having studied at Antioch, Ohio. In the year 1814 he was called to the pastorate of the Brownsville Baptist church, which position he now holds, and during this pastorate he has baptized one hundred and one converts. He was a member of company D, Fifty-first Ohio volunteer infantry, being drafted in September, 1864, and mustered out in 1865.

Matilda Efan, widow of Wesley Cline, was born in West Virginia in 1829. Her family now consists of nine children by her first husband—Alpheus, who now resides in Newport; Rosetta, wife of James Merride, in West Virginia; Nancy A., wife of George W. Coss; Martha Jane, wife of James W. Bruce; Solomon, and Jacob M., the four latter now living in Monroe county; Sarah E., Susanna, and James Monroe, all now living at home.

Thomas Mitchell was the first member of his family who came to Grand View township; he arrived in Matamoras in 1861. He was born in Pennsylvania, in 1804, and was united in marriage to Elizabeth Clarke, who was born in 1803. To them were born ten children; five now living: Thomas, Elizabeth, John C., Joseph M., and Sarah A. He was a prominent citizen of Monroe county, being elected sheriff two terms in this county. He gave his attention to farming and accumulated considerable property, but reverses in later life reduced his effects considerably. He died in 1870, and the decease of his wife followed the next year. Thomas Mitchell, his son, was first lieutenant and afterwards captain of company H, Seventy-seventh Ohio volunteer infantry; enlisted December, 1861, and discharged in 1864. He was wounded at the battle of Fallen Timber, in Tennessee. John was second lieutenant of company I, One Hundred and Ninety-fourth Ohio volunteer infantry, and served one year. Joseph M. Mitchell was born in 1841, and was married in 1867, to Mary E. Swarts, who was born in 1850. They have five children now living: James T., Tolo, George C., Mabel, Delia. He enlisted in 1861, in company C, Seventy-seventh Ohio volunteer infantry, and was promoted to first lieutenant of company A, which position he held until the close of the war. He was engaged at Shiloh, Fallen Timber, Corinth, Mobile, and Marks Mills, Arkansas, in which battle he was taken prisoner and was confined ten months in Tyler prison, Texas, during which time he suffered from exposure and insufficient food, and general ill-treatment, the effects of which he yet feels. (For further particulars of life in this prison see sketch of Lloyd Riddle). He is now one of the leading business men of Matamoras, engaged under the firm name of Mitchell & Rice, as general merchandise and provision merchants, in which they were established in 1879. The shipments are made by boat to Pittsburgh, consisting mostly of butter, eggs, beans, dried fruits, etc. The business is increasing and every indication points to a deserved success.

George Davenport was born in 1832, and was married in 1858, to Mary E. Reckard, who was born in 1839. To them were born eleven children, nine of whom are now living: William C., Frank E., Ella L., Olivia R., John A., George A., Mary E., Martha, and Carl B. He came to this county in 1855, and first settled in Marietta, where he resided until 1866, and was engaged in the clothing business, when he removed to Newport and engaged in the dry goods business, until 1873, when he was elected sheriff of the county. He commenced business in Matamoras in 1877. He enlisted, in 1862, in the First Ohio light artillery, battery H, as first lieutenant, where he served until discharged on account of physical disability, in 1863. He was at the first battle at Winchester, Port Republic; Second Bull Run, and Fredericksburgh.

Nathan Kirkbride first came to this county in 1840, and settled in Ludlow township; was born in Maryland in 1795, and died in 1865. He was married to Sarah Farley, who was born in 1805. She still resides on the old homestead in Independence township. Andrew Kirkbride was born in 1827, and was married in 1855 to Mary Decker, who was born in 1839. They had a family of ten children, eight now living: Sarah, Ellen, Charles, Mary, Elizabeth, Frank, Frederick, and Andrew. He has followed the occupation of butchering for the past twenty years, and is also dealer in cattle, and has accumulated considerable property, and now resides in Matamoras.

Henderson Rice was born in 1819, and was married to Elizabeth Miller, who was born in 1818. They have five children: Frances, Edmund, Alice, William, and Oscar. He came to this county about 1842, and first settled in Harmar, but since removed to Monroe county, where he now resides. He was a minister in the United Brethren church. Edmund M. Rice was born in 1847, and was married in 1868 to Caroline Grove, who was born in 1849. They had a family of four children, three living: Ettie, Effie, and Kate. He engaged in the dry goods business in 1878 with George Davenport in Matamoras, and sold to Mr. Davenport in 1879, and in the fall of the same year began the same class of business with Joseph Mitchell, under the name of Mitchell & Rice, where he is now engaged.

Gottfried Machetanz was born in Germany in 1808, and was married to Maria Jacob, who was born in 1814. To them were born ten children, eight now living: Sophia, Jacob, Martha, Elizabeth, Maria, Louisa, Amelia, and Edward. He emigrated from Germany in 1858, and came to Matamoras in 1863, purchased the tannery and residence of Samuel Hutchinson, which business he has since conducted—first under the firm name of Machetanz & Son, but now Machetanz & Brother. His son Jacob was born in 1837, and came to America with his father. He was married in 1868 to Elizabeth Lentz, who was born in 1836. He is now engaged in the business with his brother Edward as successors to their father. He has held several town offices, and is at present treasurer of the township.

The tannery of Machetanz and Brother was established by Samuel Hutchison, and passed into the hands of the Machetanz family in 1863. They tan all kinds of shoe and harness leather, and are doing a business of fifteen thousand to twenty thousand dollars, employing a capital of seven thousand to ten thousand dollars. They have a large and extended market demand which taxes their fullest capacity and energy. They employ six hands on full time, and the business is fast increasing. They are located in the northwest part of Matamoras.

James K. Libbey settled in Grand View township in 1850, and died in 1860. He was born in Maine in 1784. He was a soldier in the War of 1812. His wife, Phœbe Benson, died in 1859. Of the four children, two reside

in this county, viz: Eliza, a wife of Henry Myers, of Ludlow township; and Elisha B., who was born in Maine in 1812, married, in 1854, Nancy Campbell, born in Pennsylvania in 1813. Five children survive. His sons, Virgil and Jason, were in the late war. Virgil was wounded at Fredericksburgh, and never fully recovered. He died in 1864. Mr. Libbey is a general farmer, and owns one hundred and six acres of land.

Jacob Fox, a native of Germany, was born in 1846, and settled in Grand View in 1868. In 1870 he was married to Rosa Roth, who was born in 1851. They have now a family of six children—Mary, Charles, George, Cora, Arthur, and an unnamed babe. Mr. Fox is clerk of the township, which office he has held two years. He is one of the leading merchants of Grand View, where he commenced business in 1878, in dry goods, etc., and also owns a farm of two hundred acres located in this township.

William Patterson was born in Pennsylvania in 1827, and was married in 1849 to Barbara Ambler, who was born in Ohio in 1828. They had a family of five children, three of whom are now living—Lucinda, Sarah M., and James Winfield. They came to the township in 1869. He was formerly engaged in mining, but on coming to this township he began operations on the farm which he now owns as the result of his own industry. It contains one hundred and nine acres. He is a member of the Methodist Protestant church, and a prominent citizen.

John Marshall Wells was born in 1852, and was married in 1873 to Mary L. Barnes, who was born in 1850. They have two children—Chauncy T., and Harry H. He came to this township with his mother in 1855, and was originally a farmer, but in 1873 he began as a ship-carpenter, which occupation he now follows. In 1872 became a member of the Masonic order in Matamoras, and has taken four degrees in that order; also, has held the offices of senior and junior wardens. He is now a prominent member of the Methodist Episcopal church.

LEASE RUN SETTLEMENT.

Benjamin Pinney came from New York and made the first opening in this settlement in 1834. He built the first cabin on the bank above what is known as White Oak spring. Soon after, Thomas Flowers moved into this settlement, after him John Hecathorn, James McCullough, and others. This has grown to be a thickly settled neighborhood, located about three-fourths of a mile southeast of Ward station.

CHURCHES.

THE PRESBYTERIAN CHURCH.

This church was organized by an appointment made by the Presbytery of St. Clairsville, and the committee met in the village of Grand View June 7, 1850. Rev. John Moffat acted as moderator. James McWilliams and Joseph A. Barton, elders from Brownsville church, were invited to assist in the organization. The following persons were received on certificate at this meeting: Anthony and Caroline Sheets, Dr. Moses and Nancy Curry, John M. and Margaret Conkey, Mrs. Joseph Harvey Curry, Tirzah F. Curry, and Rebecca McWilliams.

At the first election of elders, Anthony Sheets, John M. Conkey, and Joseph H. Curry were chosen, and the ordination of these elders, which took place on Sabbath evening, June 9, 1850, completed the organization of the first Presbyterian church in this township. Among the first ministers who were sent as supplies to the new church were Revs. Williams, Hall, Alexander, Grimes, and Dool. Rev. R. Armstrong was the first ordained minister of this congregation, which ceremony took place June 25, 1851.

The work of building a house of worship began immediately and was soon ready for dedication, which occurred October 2, 1852. The dedication sermon was preached by Rev. W. S. Dool, using for his text the following words: "I will glorify the house of my glory."

The society of Grand View prospered for a time, but eventually, for unknown reasons, the membership decreased and the organization was abandoned. The friends of this denomination living in and about Matamoras called a meeting, to be held in the Baptist church of that place, for the purpose of organizing a society and building a church at Matamoras. The necessary arrangements having been made the building was begun in 1877 and was completed in July, 1878.

The church building is located on First street, in the northern part of the town, on a beautiful situation fronting the river. It is a frame building of modern finish and has an eighty-five feet spire. The ceremony of laying the corner stone was performed by the present pastor, Rev. C. D. Curtis, in 1879. The base stone was hollowed by a square mortise in which are deposited a copy of the Bible, records of the church, names of members, and several different pieces of coin. The trustees of the church at the present time are R. G. Webber, Israel Early, and M. M. Hutchison. Present elders, R. G. Webber, John Emery, and M. M. Hutchison.

METHODIST EPISCOPAL CHURCH.

The first meetings were held by this denomination in very early times in Grand View, at the houses of the pioneers, by the itinerent ministers as they passed to and from the annual conferences. Among the early ministers were Revs. Abel Robinson, Denison, David Smithers, and others. The first permanent organization was made some time prior to 1852, in which year the present church building was erected in Grand View village. The dedication sermon was preached by Pardon Cook. Among the leading members were James Williamson, Anthony Sheets, Polly Talbott, Warren Wells, Martin Sheets, William Peaden and wife.

In 1865 the appointments at Grand View and Matamoras were added to Brownsville circuit, from whose present secretary, C. Sander (Jolly post office), we are indebted for the following history, which then belonged to McConnellsville district, of Pittsburgh annual conference:

The first quarterly meeting was held at Grand View June 3, 1865. The trustees of this church at that time were: J. Martin, C. T. Barnes, F. Collins, C. Masters,

and J. H. Stewart, who was also a local preacher. The preachers in charge on this circuit were, viz: From 1864 to 1867, Rev. C. P. Hamilton; from this time to 1871 were Revs. F. C. Hatfield and H. McCall.

At the fourth quarterly conference, held at Matamoras, February 26, 1870, the following committee was appointed to estimate the cost of a proposed church edifice in Matamoras, viz: C. T. Barnes, C. Deiters, H. R. Riggs, G. W. Cline, and J. H. Stewart, and at the conference held at Brownsville in September 24, 1870, the following trustees of this church were appointed: G. W. Cline, W. Wells, H. Hensell, S. Pope, H. R. Riggs, C. Deiters, A. Nuger, J. Hensell, and J. H. Stewart. The present Methodist Episcopal church building was completed in 1871, at a cost of over three thousand dollars, and the following ministers have served this congregation and the circuit from 1871 to the present time, viz: Revs. P. K. McCue, William Smith, John Wright, J. J. Exell, and William Piggott, the present pastor.

THE METHODIST EPISCOPAL CHURCH (BELL'S CHAPEL).

The lot on which the first log meeting-house of this society was built in 1855, was donated by Alexander Bell, who was a local preacher, and it was located in the southwest corner of the roads, three quarters of a mile west of Ward's station, in the extreme western part of the township.

The society then belonged to Brownsville circuit, and among the early ministers were: E. Ellison, Pardon Cook, James A. White, and many others. The present building, a frame, twenty-eight by forty feet, was erected in 1879, and stands on the land donated by John Drake, immediately west of the site of the old log church. John Stewart, John Twinem, Joseph Dodds, Thomas Flowers, and Andrew McMasters, trustees. Present membership sixty-four, services every three weeks, and Sabbath-school every Sunday — under the superintendence of Rev. Doan, Newport circuit.

THE METHODIST EPISCOPAL CHURCH (GERMAN)

is located in the western part of the township, and is a frame building, about twenty-six by thirty, and was erected about 1860.

Among the early ministers of this church were Henry Henkey, Frederick Schimmelfenig, Carl Melitzer, John Kupp and the present one, J. G. Reiber. The first trustees were John Neun, Peter Englehart and Tunis Neun, and the present trustees are Peter Englehart, Conrad Miller and John Kellneer. The membership numbers about fifty; services every three weeks, and Sunday-school every Sunday.

UNITED BRETHREN CHURCH.

The first church building of this denomination was built on west corner of farm owned by Francis Collins, south of Grand View village. The house was a rude log built about 1869. Henry Jones, Dwight Berentz and Levi Clark were leading men and officials in this first organization. Among the early ministers were Rev. George Athy, Reasacker, Hendrickson and others. Rev. Reasacker was a minister of remarkable powers, and many very extraordinary revivals occurred in this church under his ministry. It is related that at one time a lame man was made to walk about the church as though he were not lame. A young lady—Laura Emory—passed over the tops of the benches and the heads of the people in a manner clearly impossible to mere human power, and as many as ten persons lay helpless on the floor at one time, and many other remarkable manifestations are related as having occured in these revival meetings.

Some few years after this society moved to the present location where, under the ministry of Rev. Anson Roach, they now hold regular services near Ward's station.

THE FAIRVIEW (CHRISTIAN) CHURCH

is located in the western part of the township; is a substantial frame, twenty-four by thirty-four, and was erected in 1880. This congregation was built up from a general revival in 1819, under the preaching of Revs. Barker and Singer, when about forty members were taken into the church. Trustees: James Knowlton, Anderson Hall, Daniel Little, and Revs. Bonner and Nugent were among the former ministers of this denomination. Services are now held once every month; Sabbath-school every Sabbath superintended by Daniel Little.

The present membership is about fifty, and is the only congregation of this denomination in the township.

BAPTIST CHURCH (MATAMORAS).

The Baptist denomination had the earliest representation in the religious element of this locality. They first held services in the old log school-house near the mouth of Mill creek in very early times, but no organization was made until 1859.

The council called for the purpose of organizing a church at Matamoras was held May 28, 1859. T. W. Ewart acting as moderator and Okey Johnson, clerk, and the delegates in attendance from the various points, who were previously solicited to attend, were as follows: Rev. Henry Lyons, John Pool, Stacy and John P. Stephens, and John Davis, Brownsville; Morris Covert, Samuel Morgan, Basil Stewart, Michael Stine, and Richard Stacy, Unity; Rev. J. D. Riley and James Furguson, Newport; Andrew Dare, George Stewart, William and E. D. Johnson, Long Reach, Va.; L. G. Leonard, D. D., T. W. Ewart, Isaac Adkins, Isaac Talbott, Charles Pearce, Marietta; Elder J. D. Riley, Little Muskingum; Sterling Jones, Woodfield; S. B. Sickman, Pleasants, Virginia.

The following persons were admitted by letter at the first meeting: Lucy Cochran, Levi and Mary Hoffman, Charlotta Eastham, Robert McCormick, Joseph Bonar, Emma Brown, Thomas R. and Maria Smith, Jonas and Nancy Unger, J. D. Nancy, Mary, Virginia, Albert, and Cynthia Leonard, Diana Furguson, Temperance Scott, Mary Young, and Thomas Reynolds.

The organization having been thus successfully effected, Rev. J. D. Leonard received the first call to the regular pastorate of this church and among those who have since served this society as ministers were T. L. Rinehart, J. P. Stephens, Watson Dana, L. Hamlin, M. J. Dunn, and the present pastor, Rev. Mungo Taylor.

76

The first officials were—Andrew Snider, Zachariah Cochran, H. G. Hubbard, trustees; Thomas Reynolds, treasurer; Jasper Bonar, clerk.

The lot on which the church was erected was donated by the "Womens' Sewing society," which was organized for the purpose of making up articles of wearing apparel, the proceeds of the sale of such articles to be devoted to religious purposes. The above lot was purchased by this society in this way at the cost of one hundred dollars, and was first intended as a donation for a Union church, but finally came into the possession of the Baptists, as they were greatly in the majority over other denominations. The present building is located on the southwest corner of Third and Main streets, is a frame, about forty by fifty, and has a cupola and bell.

The present membership numbers about one hundred and twelve. The present pastor holds services here every alternate Sunday and the Sabbath-school meets every Sunday; and in connection with this society the same pastor serves Lawrence and Unity, and the pastoral charge is now in a good, flourishing condition.

SCHOOLS.

The first school-house of which an account can now be found was built at the mouth of Mill creek on the banks of the river. The teacher of this school was a Mr. Edgington, of whom little is now remembered.

Another school was afterward established in a deserted cabin, near what is now Cochransville, and was taught by Mr. Oakey. These were known as subscription schools, the teacher receiving so much from the parents or guardian of each scholar. About 1852 the present school building in Matamoras was erected, originally containing two rooms, under the control of Abram Loman. Among those who have taught in this school building are, Messrs. Tuttle, Alexander, Charles D. Young and others. The fourth separate district in which the building is located includes the town of Matamoras and a considerable extent of territory beyond the corporation limits. The building has been improved to accommodate the increasing number of pupils, until there are now four departments, and four rooms of equal size and the whole building eighty-five by thirty feet. The number now enrolled is two hundred and twenty-five; average daily attendance, one hundred and seventy-five, under the present corps of teachers—Professor S. W. Barber, principal; John Martin, intermediate A; Miss Emma Greene, intermediate B; and Miss Lida Hinds, primary.

GRAND VIEW VILLAGE SCHOOL.

The first school-house in this locality stood where the Methodist Episcopal church now stands, and was the old log building elsewhere mentioned as the place where the early meetings of the pious settlers were held. Mr. Flack was the first teacher who presided over the school here. In a few years the school was removed to the old tannery belonging to Hannibal Williamson, where it was continued until 1863, when the present house was built and was improved in 1874, now having two rooms. The present teachers are Professor E. B. Hutchinson and Mrs. S. E. Altsman. Number of pupils enrolled, eighty; daily average attendance, fifty-five. In good, prosperous condition.

CEMETERIES.

The first cemetery in this township was the old burying-ground immediately south of Matamoras, and was the first half-acre of cleared land in this locality, and the first person buried there was Prissa (Riggs) Sheets, about 1800. The next burial place was the lot in the rear of Andrew Vauple's residence in Matamoras.

These old grounds have long since been abandoned, and many of the bodies removed to other places. In 1840 Amos Ridgway donated three acres of land to the public for a cemetery, which is located on the hill northwest of the town, which is now the principal cemetery, though there are other places of interment in other localities.

RAILROAD.

A line of railroad was projected through this township following the course of the Ohio river leading from Marietta to Bellaire, and extending the entire length of the township from south to north. Many very extensive bridges and culverts were completed and grading done, but for some reason the enterprise failed and the unfinished work abandoned. This rather extensive and very costly failure was begun by the Baltimore & Ohio railroad, in 1854, and but little hopes are now entertained of the final completion of the road.

VINEYARD.

The Machetanz Brothers also have a vineyard located on the hill back of Matamoras, containing two acres of land and about twelve hundred plants, and having a southeast front. It was first planted in 1875, and the first crop taken in 1877. The plants are of many kinds, embracing some of the finest grapes in the United States, including the Concord, Ives, Seedling, Norton, Virginia, White Wine, Taylor, Cynthiana, Martha, and others. They have a press of four hundred gallon capacity, and they propose soon to establish a shipping business.

MATAMORAS—NEW MATAMORAS POST OFFICE.

The proprietor of the town was Henry Sheets, who made the survey of the first plat on his land lying along the Ohio river. Beginning with the big road, which extended along the banks of the river, the original plat extend west three blocks to Third street, and north three blocks from Merchants street, to the first alley above the flour mill now belonging to Samuel Shannon. The only houses within the boundry of the original plat were the stove and dwelling house, also the flour mill of the proprietor. The streets were, beginning at the river, Water street, which has now almost disappeared beneath the encroachments of the river; the next was First, then Second and Third streets, all running north and south; then those extending east and west were Merchants and Ferry. The first addition was made by Stinson Burris, and extended from Merchants down to Vine, including two lots beyond; and from Water back to third, thus extending Water, First, Second, and Third streets, and adding two new streets—Main and Vine. The second addition was made on the north extending Water, First and

Second streets three blocks, and adding another street—Togler—and eighteen new blocks, which in 1849 included the full dimensions of the town. Afterwards many other large additions were made on the southwest.

The town began slowly to improve, and houses, one by one, began to appear along First street of the old plat, then on Main and Second, until 1861 the incorporation was made, and at the election James McWilliams was elected mayor.

The present town officials are: Dr. W. L. West, mayor; Jasper Lisk, clerk; Philip Hanshumaker, treasurer; Hezekiah Riggs, marshal; J. N. Simmons, street commissioner; John Shannon, H. B. May, Edward Machetanz, George Davenport, John Hays, and I. Walters, councilmen. The commercial importance of Matamoras is represented by the following business firms: First street, Samuel Shannon & Son, flour mill; Samuel Hutchison & Sons, general store and post office; August Andrea, druggist; Adam Brown, saloon; Hosea B. May, hardware and tinner; John Richard, Richards House; Philip Reinherr, confectionary and bakery; Dr. S. M. Richardson, druggist and physician; John Hensell, furniture and undertaker; Charles Miller, general store; M. Burbaker, merchant tailor; Jacob Gautchi, cigarmaker and barber; A. Unger, boot and shoemaker; Frederick Glaso, merchant tailor; Jacob Grohs, saddler and harness; Mitchell & Rice, general store and fowarding; Charles Nelly, Nelly House; Philip Hanshumaker, dry goods; Dr. F. P. Martin, physician and surgeon; W. F. Powell, New Matamoras *Herald*; T. B. Barnes, livery. Main street: Dr. W. L. West, physician and surgeon; I. Walters, boots and shoes; A. Kirkbride, butcher; Elliott Brothers, general store; Lloyd Biddle, saloon; James McMunn, boots and shoes; A. P. Cree, grocery and commission; Mrs. Young, book store; T. H. Huffman, Huffman House; Isaac Young; blacksmith; Alexander Minder, saloon; Jonas Lisk, wagonmaker. Second street: John Graham, carpenter; Charles Keddy, butcher; Levi Huffman, drayman. Third street: William Gist, carpenter; H. C. Cunningham, carpenter; John Hays, cooper; Dr. A. R. Anderson, physician and surgeon; Machetanz & Brother, tannery. Merchant street: John Craig, livery.

The location of the town on the Ohio river makes it a convenient shipping point for a large territory.

GRAND VIEW VILLAGE

is a small place located immediately south of Matamoras, and was first surveyed in very early times, but the old plat was annuled by Hannibal Williamson in 1848-9, who immediately proceeded to make a new plat on the same grounds, by running two rows of lots from the river, six rods deep, with an alley between, ten feet wide. The buildings are mostly located on the one main street and facing the river. There are at present one grange store, two general stores, three cooper shops, one church, one graded school, one drug store, and one saloon.

LODGES.

The Matamoras Lodge, Independent Order of Odd Fellows, No. 524, was organized by Right Worthy of Ohio

Grand Lodge at its May session 1872, when the charter was granted. The charter members were—Philip Hanshumaker, O. F. Flint, William S. Potter, George Schmidt, Charles Hill, Charles Miller, and Philip Reinherr, and the lodge was instituted July 9, 1812, by Special Deputy Grand Master, H. R. Williams. Officials elected were—Philip Hanshumaker, N. G.; Charles Hill, vice N. G.; O. F. Flint secretary; Philip Reinherr, treasurer; William S. Potter, chaplain. Members of fifth degree are, viz: Jasper Lisk, Philip Reinherr, Philip Hanshumaker, W. S. Potter, George A. Shapley, Samuel Snodgrass, Esau Knowlton, Mathias Merckle, W. W. Glesencamp, William Pool, Charles Hill, George Schmidt, W. T. Steadman, Harvey Holland, jr., Barnet Adamson, Israel Early, Lloyd Biddle, Jacob Machetanz, David Thomas, Richard Edwards, A. W. Minder, A. Cutler, A. R. Newman, Jacob Gautchi, George Davenport, George Emery, J. McBaker, R. A. Shaw, Jacob Grohs. The benefits paid by this lodge are, in case of sickness, four dollars per week after first week, and funeral expenses of fifty dollars. Meetings are held over store room of Miller & Hanshumaker.

New Matamoras Lodge of Free and Accepted Masons, No. 374, was organized by charter, granted October 16, 1867. Charter members, viz: Dr. F. P. Martin, J. R. Algeo, George S. Algeo, Frederick Beegle, William S. Potter, Dr. S. M. Richardson, Vachel Barnes, Cameron Bishop, Charles McMunn, C. W. True, Clement Watters, William Hubbard, C. W. Ridgeway, Charles Algeo, Rolla Meredith, G. C. Renetts. First official, John W. Jackson, master; F. P. Martin, senior warden; Joseph Algeo, junior warden. The hall in which the lodge held its meetings was destroyed by fire August 17, 1874, and all the property of the lodge totally destroyed.

It was, however, reorganized, and another charter granted with full power of the original. The hall in which the lodge now meets, on the corner of Main and Second streets, in Matamoras, is fully refurnished with the equipments necessary to Masonry. The present officials are: John Wells, master; George Algeo, senior warden; Samuel F. Koontz, junior warden; Charles McMunn, treasurer: J. M. Mitchell, secretary; Jasper Lisk, senior deacon; James L. Amos, junior deacon; David A. Cochran, tyler.

THE GRANGES.

The organization of farmers known as the Grange is in active operation in this township, and several lodges have been organized in various localities. These granges —Greene Mountain, Salem Hall—together with Archer's Fork, Mt. Vernon, Bethel, Low Gap and Jericho, have organized an incorporated joint-stock company for the purpose of operating what is known as a cooperative store. This store is now located at Grand View, under the control of Jacob Fox, and is now in successful operation on what is known as the Rockdale plan.

Greene Mountain Grange, No. 1,040, is located on Lease Run, about four miles west of Grand View village, and was organized about 1872. The following were the original officials: William H. Fullmer, master; Jacob Fox, secretary; William Heddleston, lecturer; and John Delong, treasurer. The charter members, including the above officials, were: John M. Walker, August Suck and Conrad Felton. The present membership is about thirty, and the society is in active, prosperous condition.

Salem Hall Grange is located in the western part of the township, and was organized in February, 1875. The first officials were, viz.: William Fry, master; C. Fox, lecturer; William Smith, secretary; Henry Roudebaugh, treasurer; Burgess Hall, chaplain; Joseph Bashor, gatekeeper. The hall building is a frame structure about eighteen by thirty-seven, and was erected in 1877, at a cost of about three hundred dollars. The membership, originally about fifty, has decreased almost one-half.

MILLS.

The first mill in this township was known as "Bucks Mill," and was operated on Mill creek in very early times, about one mile north of Matamoras. This mill was rebuilt in 1829 by Isaac Rinard. It is remarkable that this only flour-mill within twelve miles of this locality used No. 4 bolting cloth, and every kind of grinding was done on one run of stone. After this some time, Henry Sheets erected the steam mill on the site of the present steam mill of Samuel Shannon, in Matamoras.

Mr. Shannon has made some very material improvements on the mill, and it is now a frame structure about thirty-three feet square, four stories high, and has three run of stone of usual capacity, propelled by steam.

GRAND VIEW MILL.

This mill is located immediately north of Grand View village, and was erected by Hannibal Williamson in 1864, and is a flour- and saw-mill combined. It is a frame structure (thirty-six by twenty-four) having two run of stone of usual capacity. Gilbert Hubbard now has the mill rented, and is doing only the general custom work of the locality.

CASUALITIES AND TRAGEDIES.

On the Fourth of July, 1856, every preparation was being made by the people of Matamoras and the vicinity for a grand celebration of the national holiday. William Ellis, Isaac Cline, Amos Ridgway, and Sylvester Martin had charge of a small swivel gun, and were on the hill back of the town very early in the morning, firing salutes. While Martin was loading a premature discharge carried away both of his arms, and, singularly as it may appear, one of his thumbs was blown off with such force as to enter the arm of Joseph Cline above the elbow, and, following the muscle almost to the shoulder, remained imbedded in the flesh until extracted by the physician. Martin exhibited great power of endurance under the suffering the accident necessarily must have cost him, and when under the physician's hands, enduring the necessary amputation, he was even humorous, and inquired flippantly of the physicians what they intended to make out of him, and expressed the very plain fact that they could never "fix him up for a fiddler." He recovered, and is now living, though having left this locality after many years here, where he supported himself in several lucrative lines of trade.

On the evening of the third of July a crowd was collected at the wharf at Grand View, for the purpose of firing salutes preparatory to the celebration on the following day. They had a singular machine for making a loud noise—a fifty-six pound weight with a hole drilled in it, in which the powder was confined by driving a plug. The fuse at one time failed to ignite with the powder, and Dr. Drake, a young physician, proposed to ignite it with a lighted cigar, which he did, and the explosion which followed tore his head from his shoulders, producing instant death.

In 1860 David Burnet was instantly killed by a falling tree, about one and a quarter miles west of Frank Collins', near Grand View. Near this same place a few years after, John Burnet was killed by a falling tree while coon-hunting at night. He was a son of the former victim. Following this a few years, in the same locality, Albert Hutchison, while fox-hunting at night, ran against a stump, receiving injuries from which he soon died. All these accidents happened within one-half mile of each other.

In 1863 William Little and Reason Kendall quarrelled about some domestic troubles, and one day as Little was riding along the road about three miles northwest of Matamoras, Kendall, who was secreted behind an old chimney that stood near the road, fired upon Little with a rifle. The ball took effect in the back of the head and passing through lodged near the right eye, producing instant death. Kendall was convicted, and served a time in the State prison, but was pardoned.

In 1866 John Hupp was knocked down and beaten to death in a drunken quarrel at Grand View, but the murderers were never apprehended, and the particulars were not fully known.

On the river about one-half mile below Grand View, a man by the name of Fuller, from Virginia, was engaged to row William Brian, and a woman known as Kate King, from the Virginia side to Grand View, some time in 1860-1. The boat did not proceed to suit the parties, and a quarrel ensued in which Fuller received a blow on the head by an oar, and his body was found drifting in his boat the following day.

NEWSPAPERS.

The first newspaper published in this township was issued by L. L. Harvey, editor and proprietor, on Friday, November 15, 1861, and was called the Matamoras *Herald*. The editorial prospectus lays claim to the usual unselfish object of "filling a long felt want" by publishing the only paper on the Ohio river between Marietta and Belaire, a distance of seventy-eight miles. An article is clipped from the New York *Observer* in which the impatience of the people in that stage of the late war was sought to be silenced by explanations of the crippled condition of the Government at the beginning of the war, and that the real designs of pretended leaders in the Union cause were fast being discovered, and confidence restored by the elevation of men of undoubted loyalty to places of command, and promising an immediate advanced movement when these difficulties were satisfactorily adjusted. Also an article from the Richmond (Virginia) *Whig*, complaining of the failure of the Confederate army to advance, deprecating a defensive policy, and earnestly entreating the leaders of the rebel hosts to carry the war into the enemy's country. The removal of General Fremont was interpreted by the editor of the *Herald* as propitiatory to the pro-slavery element of the north.

Among the professional and business men that patronized the advertising columns of the paper were: Dr. W. W. Plummer, office First street; D. R. Marks, physician and surgeon, Second street; wagons repaired by H. Bebout; Blue Bird mills give notice that without ten bushels of custom work to begin with on Wednesdays and Fridays, no grinding would be done—Knapp & Calhoun; blacksmithing, for cash or produce, by Isaac Young; W. M. Harvey, and J. N. Hills, dealers in dry goods; I. C. Land, tailor, First street; Em. Andrea, drug store. W. T. Robinson, second lieutenant, Ohio volunteer infantry, opens a recruiting office for the Seventy-seventh Ohio volunteer infantry, offering thirteen dollars per month. The paper existed for some time, but finally ceased.

The New Matamoras *Herald* was first issued by W. T. Powell, editor and proprietor, August 5, 1880, and though in operation but a short time there are many encouraging indications of future success. It is now a sprightly journal of twenty-four columns, soon to be increased, and, maintaining an independence in all things, can be supported as it ought by the citizens throughout this locality.

"PETTICOAT FORD"

is the name given a former shallow place in the Ohio river, below Grand View village. A man living on the Virginia side of the river had a large family of girls who frequently visited their neighbors on the Ohio side, and in order to do so they were compelled to wade the river, and this operation necessitated the exposure of the well known article of female apparel called the petticoat, and the usually gay colors of which this garment is made did not escape the prying eyes of the boatmen as they passed up and down the river, and the jesting remarks occasioned thereby gave the name to this ford.

BIOGRAPHICAL SKETCH.

H. A. WILLIAMSON.

On an accompanying page will be found a view of Grand View farm. The township derives its name from the magnificent view within the range of an observer standing on a point on this farm. Between the Virginia hills in the distance and the plain on which is situated the village of Grand View, lies the winding course of the Ohio, with willow-dressed shores and bearing on its bosom noisy tugs and gracefully floating packets. This farm, possessing greater scenic interest than any other in the county, is owned by H. A. Williamson.

The Williamsons were among the first settlers of the

RESIDENCE OF H. A. WILLIAMSON GRAND VIEW WASHINGTON Co. O.

H. A. WILLIAMSON

OLD HOMESTEAD

MRS H. A. WILLIAMSON

township, and it is proper that the portrait of a well-known representative of the family, and a pictorial sketch of his finely situated farm, should have a place in this volume. Mr. Williamson was born in Grand View township, November 13, 1813. He married, January 14, 1841, Temperance Hubbard, who was born May 16, 1824. Since he began life for himself, Mr. Williamson has accumulated a great deal of property. His farm includes nine hundred acres of choice land and is well improved. Before the war he was engaged in the southern trade, and about 1850 was a partner in a store at Grand View. He has been identified with the educational interests of his community all his life, having served term after term, in the capacity of school director. He is not a member of any church, but his means contributed largely toward building the Methodist and Presbyterian meeting-houses. Mr. Williamson is known in the community and will be remembered as an industrious, liberal man, whose life has been honorable and useful.

CHAPTER XLIII.

MUSKINGUM TOWNSHIP.

The Township in Embryo—Boundaries Defined in 1861 by Legislative Act—Part of Union Annexed—The Muskingum's Influence on Physical features—Wolves Troublesome—Piscatorial Amusements—The Last Beaver—Donation Lots Drawn—The River a Refuge—A Block-house built—Pioneers of Rainbow—First Settlement in Wiseman's Bottom—The Virginia Squatter—First Orchard Planted Under Difficulties—Growth of the Community—First Schools and Teachers—A Singing School—An Old Subscription Paper—The Only Church—Pioneer Burying-Grounds—The Putnam Monument—Jonathan Devol's Floating Mills—Stationary Mills—Ships on the Muskingum—Children's Home Established—Mrs. Ewing's Home—An Organization of Farmers.

THE territory now comprised in this township was originally a part of Adams township as established by the court of quarter sessions convened at Marietta in March, 1797. From time to time since that early day the several northern townships have come into existence by the crumbling away of old Adams, and prior to the year 1861, Muskingum township was in an embryonic state within the confines of Marietta, Fearing and Union townships.

ESTABLISHMENT.

April 18, 1861, the Ohio legislature passed the following bill:

AN ACT

To erect the township of Muskingum in Washington county.

SECTION 1. *Be it enacted by the General Assembly of the State of Ohio,* That the territory now constituting parts of the townships of Marietta, Union, and Fearing, in the county of Washington, and bounded as follows, to wit: Beginning at a point on the Muskingum river, where the same is intersected by the west line of a seventy-eight acre lot, numbered sixteen, in Bear Creek allotment of donation lands, running thence south on said line to the southwest corner of said lot numbered sixteen, thence west to the northwest corner of an eighty-five acre lot, numbered twenty-two, in Rainbow Creek allotment of donation lands, thence south on the west line of said lot numbered twenty-two, to the north line of Wiseman's bottom allotment of the donation lands, thence east on said line to the Muskingum river, thence down said river

on the west bank thereof the same is intersected by the west line of one hundred and sixty acre lot, numbered four hundred, thence south on said line and its continuation to the south line of township numbered three, in range numbered eight, thence east on said line to the east bank of the Muskingum river, thence down said river to the south line of commons lot numbered twenty-eight, thence northeasterly along the corporation line of the city of Marietta to the southwest corner of commons lot numbered seventeen, thence easterly along the south line of commons lot numbered seventeen, to the southwest corner of commons lot numbered twelve, thence easterly along the south line of commons lot numbered twelve, to the southwest corner of commons lot numbered fourteen, thence north on line of original survey to the south line of Fearing township, thence east on said line to the east line of three acre lot numbered three hundred and two, thence north on the east line of a range of three acre lots numbered three hundred and eighty-nine, thence west to the east line of section numbered twenty-five in township numbered three, of range eight, thence north on the section line to the south line of Salem township, thence west on said township line to Bear creek, thence down said creek to the Muskingum river, thence up said river to a point due north of the place of beginning, thence south across the river to the place of beginning, be and the same is hereby erected and constituted into a new township to be designated as Muskingum township, and that the eastern boundary of Union township, the western boundary of Fearing, and the northern boundary of Marietta township be so changed as to conform to the lines of said Muskingum township.

SECTION II. This act shall take effect and be in force from and after the date of its passage.

Thus were the boundaries of the new township defined, and then as now Muskingum was bounded on the north by Adams and Salem, on the east by Fearing and Marietta, on the south by Marietta city and township, and Warren, and on the west by Watertown.

ORGANIZATION.

The records show that the first election for officers in the new town of Muskingum was held at the school-house in sub-district number two of said township, December 28, 1861, the judges of the election being Augustine Dyar, William Devol, and C. F. Stacy. After balloting the following named persons were declared elected: Abraham Zellers, Augustine Dyer, and C. F. Stacy, trustees; Wesley Combs, clerk; James Ward, treasurer; A. D. C. Stacy, and John Gerhart, constables; J. P. Devol, and Smith Bartlett, justices of the peace; A. R. Stacy, R. Fearing, A. Dyar, Daniel Wilking, and Jacob Wagner, board of education.

At succeeding annual elections the following officers were chosen:

TRUSTEES.

1862, A. Zellers. Jacob Schramm, J. Stacy; 1863, A. Zellers, Jacob Schramm, A. Dyar; 1864, Anthony Smith, A. R. Stacy, George Matthews; 1865, John Gerhart, A. Smith, William Devol, 1866, John Gerhart, A. S. Marshal, W. Devol; 1867, J. B Dyar, Theodore Devol, Levi Bartlett; 1868, R. G. Alden, George Wagner, Levi Bartlett; 1869, R. G. Alden, Jacob Oesterle, Levi Bartlett; 1870, O. J. Wood, Jacob Oesterle, Levi Bartlett; 1871, Joseph Dyar, Jacob Oesterle, L. Bartlett; 1872, A. Dyar, A. R. Stacy, S. S. Olney; 1873, G. A. Wood, Jacob Spies, S. S. Olney; 1874, John Gerhart, J. Strecker, S. S. Olney; 1875, George Oesterle, J. Strecker, S. S. Olney; 1876, A. Dyar, A. Smith, Charles Weinheimer; 1877, S. S. Stowe, A. Smith, C. Weinheimer; 1878, M. A. Stacy, A. Smith, C. Weinheimer; 1879, G. P. Smith, A. Smith, C. Weinheimer; 1880, G. P Smith, Jacob Neu, A. Dyar.

CLERKS.

1862-7, W. D. Devol, 1866-75, James Weeks; 1875-80, James Weeks; 1880-1, James Weeks

TREASURERS.

1862-7, James Ward; 1867-75, James Ward;* 1875-80, W. D. Devol; 1880-1, M. A. Stacy.

* Mr. Ward dying during his term of office, John Strecker was appointed.

The elections are now held at Grimm's wagon shop at Union landing, on the Muskingum river.

AN ADDITION.

At the June session of the board of county commissioners in 1877, a petition was presented by Matthew Jurden and others, praying for the dissolution of Union Township, and at the regular session of the commissioners in December, 1877, the following was ordered:

The petitioners having made application at the June session of 1877 for the partition of Union township among the townships of Adams, Muskingum, Warren and Watertown, and the board being of opinion that it is necessary and expedient that the prayer of said petitioners be granted, hereby order that said Union township be divided, and annexed to the adjoining townships as follows: . . . . . to Muskingum—the territory beginning at the northeast corner of one hundred and sixty acre lot No. 392, west to the northwest corner of said lot No. 392, thence north to Wiseman's bottom, thence west to the southwest corner of Wiseman's bottom, thence east to the Muskingum river, thence following the course of the Muskingum to the northeast corner of one hundred and sixty acre lot No. 413, thence south to the place of beginning, containing section eight, one hundred and sixty acre lot No. 413, part of Donation line (lot No. 418), and all of Wiseman's bottom allotment that lies in Union township.

. . . .

It was further ordered that the above go into effect April 1, 1878, and that the boundary of the township of Muskingum be so changed as to conform to that given above.

THE NAME OF THE TOWNSHIP

is very naturally and very appropriately derived from the beautiful Muskingum river, which meanders through its whole longitudinal extent, and keeps fertile the garden spots along its banks.

PHYSICAL FEATURES.

The surface of the township is greatly diversified. The course of the Muskingum river has greatly influenced the contour of the land on either side. The eastern and western boundaries of the township embrace rugged hills which gradually slope towards their common central valley, which has been marked out in sinuous course among the surrounding uplands and hill country. The ascent from the river to the terminal hills is by four distinct steps, which are generally apparent. Including the river from Marietta on the south to Bear creek on the north, the township contains a large area of the immediate valley of the Muskingum. In places this valley or bottom land is scarcely perceptible. However, there are considerable areas of broad low lands extending first on one side and then on the other. The three abrupt bends in the course of the river indicate the boundaries of as many areas of plain land, and especially is it true of the two northerly intervals, that they are the garden spots of the township and hence the centres of thriving agricultural communities.

The first and most northerly curve of the river bears so strong a resemblance to the bow in the clouds that the included district was early called the Rainbow territory. Immediately south of this land and only separated from it by the waters of the Muskingum, is a stretch of bottom land which took the name Wiseman's bottom from its first settler. Still further south is a smaller stretch of lowland. The first two areas are from one-half to nearly a mile wide. Opposite these respective bottoms the hills approach very nearly to the water's edge as if jealous of their sister lowland. One step back from the first bottoms will be found a slightly more elevated region known as the second bottom, which swells into the higher plain land beyond, which in turn borders the outstretching slopes of the hill land. The hill country is very much broken and consists of alternate swells and falls. The hills vary in height and are separated by deep hollows through which run small streams of water, many of which are fed by springs, especially abundant in the northeastern part of the township. Many of these hills are symetrically moulded by nature's hand, and there are numerous mounds very suggestive of the artificial. Towards the western boundary the hills are not as prominent as on what is known as the ridge, which extends north and south along the western line.

The general tendency of the various branching watercourses is in a southerly direction toward the Muskingum river.

SOIL.

The bottoms consist of rich alluvions deposited by the river. The soil is of the richest quality. Adjacent to these are the second bottoms, of a thinner soil, and of a more loamy or sandy character. The plain land immediately adjacent to the hills has a gravelly soil. It is not expedient to attempt to determine which of the two bottoms, Rainbow or Wiseman's, is the more productive, inasmuch as they vie with each other for the palm. Both are very fertile and are consequently very productive, and are clear of timber. The uplands afford a fertile, clayey soil well adapted to the culture of wheat and all the small grains. The hill-tops which in the early days of settlement were regarded as little more than sterile obstructions have, by reason of the industry of the farmer, been crowned with golden harvests and dotted with grazing cattle. The bottom land averages in value fifty dollars per acre; and the lowest valuation is set on the hill land, which is worth from twenty-five down to ten dollars an acre.

Wheat is the staple production, corn being raised principally for home consumption. In the territory among the hills, and distant from the markets the raising of stock is made a specialty, and especial attention is paid to sheep raising where the soil is adapted to pasturage.

Throughout the whole territory of the township great pains are taken to raise fruit. The stipulation in the early allotment of land that fruit trees be set out has left a lasting impression on the settlers, and consequently fruit is now abundant.

The uplands and hill slopes are covered with a growth of beech and sugar trees, which the higher elevations and tops of the hills are heavily clothed with forests, principally of white oak. At the time of the first settlement when there was such a scarcity of salt for culinary operations, it was thought that there were saline indications near the entrance of March run from the east, into the Muskingum. The deer, by congregating in that vicinity, suggested the presence of a "salt-lick." A man named Miller, from McConnelsville, was employed to bore a well, and for a number of years the remnants of the machinery then used might have been seen along the shores of the creek.

Along the eastern ridge of the township there are indications of the presence of coal, although not in quantities sufficient to warrant mining. Coal has been found on the land of John Spies, in the northern extremity of the township; also not far from the residence of B. F. Dyar in section seven. A thin seam of coal has been discovered on the land of Jacob Sutter on Second creek.

In the bed of this last named stream abundant modules of rich iron ore are found, which have been used in the puddling furnaces in the Marietta rolling mill.

NATIVE ANIMALS.

Originally, the forests bordering the Muskingum teemed with almost every variety of wild animals which are native of this western country. Before the advent of the white man, the Indians, in passing up and down the river, would turn aside to indulge in their favorite sport. These native nimrods rapidly scaring the abundant game from their native haunts, when the settlers arrived the buffalo had disappeared, and bears and panthers were scarce; but wolves, deer, and wild turkey, besides smaller game, were yet plenty.

The early settlers of Muskingum were frequently disturbed by the inroads of wolves among their cattle, but seldom had cause to fear for their personal safety, although at times lonely travellers had to run for their lives. It is related, that at one time a fiddler was en route down the Muskingum for Marietta, where he was to preside at some jollification, and when several miles above town, was attacked by a pack of wolves and forced to take to a tree and there fiddle for his life until the first gray streaks of early dawn.

Deer and wild turkeys kept the larder well supplied with fresh meat, while the waters of the Muskingum were overstocked with hundreds of the finny tribe, which furnished no small part of the animal food of the early settlers. The black cat and pike were the largest of these natives of the water. Fishing at the time of the settlements at Rainbow and Wiseman's bottoms was a comparatively easy task, as there were generally about two bites for every hook.

The last beaver were seen at the time of the settlement of Judge Joseph Barker in Wiseman's bottom in the winter of 1795. These sagacious animals had a lodge behind an island about a mile below the Barker place, and another a short distance above, at the mouth of Rainbow creek. They were the last of the race seen in this country, and were ere long caught by the old trapper, Isaac Williams.

SETTLEMENT.

Prior to the Indian war there had been no permanent settlement made in that part of the Muskingum valley within the limits of this township. While Virginia claimed the right to the Northwest Territory, a backwoodsman named Wiseman entered about four hundred acres of the bottom land lying east of the Muskingum. He strove to hold his land by asserting what was known as the claim right, and forthwith made a clearing near

river. He remained only long enough to give his name to the territory he occupied, and soon afterwards disappeared from this part of the country.

During the Indian war many families were compelled to dwell within the refuge afforded them at Marietta, where they remained until after the peace of Greenville. By virtue of an act of congress, April 21, 1792, donating to the agents of the Ohio company a tract of a hundred thousand acres of land lying north of Marietta, they were enabled to offer settlers tracts of land which were to be conveyed in fee simple upon the fulfillment of certain stipulated conditions. Naturally, the first settlements were made on the donation land, whose southern boundary line passes through Muskingum township about four miles above Marietta.

At the close of the war the brave men who had been for so long a time harassed by the bloodthirsty savages were eager to settle on their land, and at the first opportunity made preparations for emigration from their prison houses. Accordingly, in the spring of 1795, those who drew land located on the Muskingum river, made preparations for an early migration, so that they could get a good start with their spring work. In those days the winding river was the only avenue of ingress and egress and along the shores of the Muskingum there was no road on which to journey; then, too, the settlers, for fear of the Indians, kept no horses; so it became a necessity that the company journey by boat up the river, which they accordingly did.

Few of these pioneers of Muskingum township had much more property than their household goods, but they all possessed determined spirits and unusual intelligence. Compelled to undergo every hardship incident to pioneer life, these hardy settlers went energetically into the laborious task of subduing the forest and preparing the virgin soil for the first crop. Their success has been attested by their subsequent history. Naturally the areas of such bottom land were chosen as centres of settlement, and hence it is that we find that the earliest settlements in the township were made in Rainbow and Wiseman's bottoms.

THE RAINBOW SETTLEMENT.

The Rainbow settlement was commenced April 29, 1795, when a company of several families arrived from Marietta and landed on the western shore of the Muskingum river, and then and there proceeded to make for themselves homes. At that time the whole surrounding country was a labyrinth of forest, and a mile was an almost interminable distance, when its course lay through dangers innumerable. On this account and for purposes of mutual protection and comfort, it was thought best to establish a community along the river bank. Hence they desired and received a portion of their allotted land adjoining the river, and built their cabins close to the stream, which was their only effective means of egress and ingress. In the midst of the settlement, on the land now owned by Aurelius Stacy, was erected a blockhouse which served as a shelter and protection until the neighboring cabins could be built.

In the first company of settlers in the Rainbow district

was Israel Stone and family. He settled on the farm now occupied by Sardine S. Stowe. Mr. Stone was of Welsh ancestry, and the ninth child of the fifth generation in America. He was born at Rutland, Massachusetts, in 1749, and in 1768 was married to Lydia Barrett, by whom he had twelve children. His first wife died in 1792, at Belpre, and he married Mary Broadhurst Carner, by whom he had one child. He settled first at Belpre prior to 1790, and in 1795 removed to this township, in which he finally settled. His children were: Elizabeth, wife of Truman Guthrie; Matilda, wife of Stephen Smith, whose settlement in this township is noted; Jasper, married Mary L. Converse; Lydia, married Ezra Hoyt; Mary, married John Dodge, of Beverly; Augustus, married Miss Rebecca Dodge; Benjamin F., married Miss Rosanna Devol, sister of Stephen Devol; Christopher Columbus, married Cyrinthia Graham; Harriet, married James Knowles; and John B. married for his first wife Celina Bosworth, and for his second, Sarah Taylor. Israel Stone, jr., was drowned at Belpre in 1791, when but thirteen years of age. Israel Stone, sr., died in 1808, at his home. Mrs. Harriet Knowles is the sole survivor of the family, being eighty-eight years old.

Stephen Smith came from Massachusetts among the earliest western emigrants. He married Matilda, daughter of Israel Stone, in Farmer's castle, at the time of the siege in the block-house. At the declaration of the peace he, with his family, started up the Muskingum for the Rainbow district, and settled on the farm now owned by his son, Columbus C. Smith. Mr. and Mrs. Smith had a family of eleven children: Percival, Harriet, Matilda, Lydia, Augustus and Franklin are dead; Dudley settled and now lives in West Virginia; Melissa married Jonathan Sprague, and lives in Adams township, this county; Columbus married Orrilla Davis; Mary married a Mr. Davis, of West Virginia; and Cyrinthia was married to a Mr. Morris, whose first wife died when they were coming to this country from England. Mrs. Morris is now a widow, living in Salem. The family of Columbus C. Smith, who resides on the home place, consisted of seven children, who became men and women. George P. married Adaline Wolcott; Cyrinthia married S. S. Stowe, of this township; Caroline is the wife of F. W. Rayley; C. C. Smith, jr., married Jane Moore; Sarah E. married A. McNeal; and Eva became the wife of Sardine S. Stowe. George and C. C. Smith, jr., were both in the late war, the former remaining in the army until mustered out in 1865, and the latter being discharged on account of physical disability, in 1864.

After the treaty with the Indians, Ebenezer Nye and his two elder sons went to Rainbow and made ready a home for the family. He had, in the spring of 1790, at the suggestion of his brother in Ohio, exchanged his farm in Connecticut for a share in the Ohio company's purchase. He started for his western home, crossing the Hudson at Newburgh, reaching Robstown, on the Youghiogeny, about harvest time in 1790. Here he bought, in connection with Joshua Shipman, a flat-boat, in which the two families came to Marietta. Mr. Nye and family at first lived in a house in which it was almost impossible

to stand erect. During the Indian war they lived in the northeast block-house of the garrison. The farm in Rainbow is opposite the mouth of March run, and is now occupied by Thomas Ridgway. Reviewing Mr. Nye's family history, it is found that he was born in Tolland, Connecticut, in 1750, and that he removed when twenty-three or twenty-four years of age to Litchfield county, where he married Desire Sawyer, who died in 1800, aged forty-two years. He afterwards married the widow Gardiner, and continued in Rainbow until his death in 1823. He had six sons and one daughter. Lewis died near Zanesville; Neal lived and died at Kerr's run, above Pomeroy; Melzer died in Meigs county and George in Athens; Nathan moved west, and Sarah, wife of Azariah Pratt, after living for many years in Marietta, removed to Sunday Creek, in Athens county.

Simon Wright was also one of the original settlers of Rainbow. He was a native of Massachusetts. He married Mrs. Maria Witham. About the time of the first emigration to Ohio, he with others, came to the Marietta settlement, and remained at the garrison until after the cessation of Indian hostilities. Then he took charge of his portion of land on the Muskingum, settling with his family on the farm, upon which the Wood family now reside. Mr. Wright was a soldier in the War of 1812. His family consisted of four children—three sons and one daughter. Henry, Simeon and Horace have since died. The only daughter, Lorana, married and removed to Wolf creek. After remaining a few years on his farm in Rainbow, Mr. Wright sold his place to Joseph Wood, who emigrated from the State of New Jersey prior to the Indian war. His wife was a Miss Pewther. He was the father of the following named children: Emelius married Adaline Fuller, the daughter of the man, who at one time owned the land, on which the city of New York now stands. Caius Martius, the second son, married Sophia Hall, who is still living with her son and daughter, Gustavus and Cornelia, both of whom are unmarried. Joseph lives in the neighborhood, having married first Anna Wilber, and after her death, Susan Wood. His children are Imogene J. and John A. He owns ninety acres of land, and is a small fruit grower. The other children of Joseph Wood, sr., are James and Nancy, the latter being a resident of Marietta. Some years after Mr. Wood's settlement, he was called to Marietta to take charge of the land office. He died about thirty years ago, being universally respected.

Among the first settlers of Rainbow were Archibald and Mary Lake, who located on the place now owned by Israel Devol. Archibald Lake married Mary Bird, of London, and being a seafaring man, removed to New Foundland, where he was employed in the fisheries, which at that time were very profitable, as the strict observance of Lent in Catholic Europe caused a great demand for fish. When that place came into the possession of the French he moved his family to New York and worked in the ship-yards. During the Revolution, when General Washington evacuated the city of New York, the Lake family followed the army up North river, where Mrs. Lake served as matron, first at Fishkill, and then at New Windsor hospital. Mr. Lake was appointed a deputy commissary to the hospital, and ranged the adjacent country in search of provisions for the sick. More than once did Mrs. Lake receive the personal thanks of General Washington in recognition of her valuable services. After the army was disbanded Mr. and Mrs. Lake returned to New York. After the war, ship-building being a poor business, and Mr. Lake accidentally hearing of the Marietta colony, decided to emigrate to the west. Accordingly, in 1789, he removed to Marietta. His family consisted of eight children, of whom three sons, James, Thomas and Andrew, were young men. The spring after their arrival the small-pox broke out, and during the terrible pestilence Mrs. Lake heroically served as nurse, and her superior knowledge of the art of nursing, in all probability, saved many a valuable life. Probably one of the first Sunday-schools in America was taught by her, in 1791, at the Campus Martius. Being early converted she felt it to be her duty to care for the souls, as well as the bodies, of those with whom she was wont to be associated. She collected in her little room on Sabbath afternoons the children who were wont to indulge in all sorts of amusements upon the holy day. After the conclusion of the service by Rev. Mr. Story she held Sunday-school, giving the youth instruction from the Bible and the Westminster catechism. She was peculiarly adapted to impart religious instruction to the children, and hence her work was crowned with merited success. April 27, 1795, the Lake family became residents of Rainbow. Mrs. Lake died the next year after her settlement, and her husband did not long survive. Their son Andrew was a carpenter by trade, at which business he worked whenever an opportunity was afforded, and during the remainder of the time he was an honest tiller of the soil. In 1797 he married Miss Elizabeth Goss, whose parents resided on Duck creek. The marriage ceremony was performed at the bride's house by 'Squire Monroe, and the young couple at once came to Rainbow, where the young people treated them to a genuine, old-fashioned house warming. They had nine children, of whom William, Tirzah, Jane, Mary and Dauphin are dead; Hannah is the wife of Courtland Sheppard, of Harmar; Sarah is the widow of Isaac Monett, and resides with her son in Marietta; Preston and Daniel are in Iowa, and Solomon is living in Kansas.

Captain Abel Matthers was among those who, with his wife and children, resided at the Point prior to the peace with the Indians. He was a native of Hartford, Connecticut, whence he emigrated during the first days of the Ohio colony. His wife was a widow named Elizabeth Woodard. John, the eldest son, served as drummer to the garrison, and eventually married Penelope Morris. Philo married Penelope Woodard. Hannah and Charlotte never married. Captain Matthers became a resident of Rainbow settlement about three years after the first cabin had been erected. By that time the people had discovered that it was not safe to build so close to the bank of the river, because of occasional overflows which flooded their houses, and hence it was that Captain Matthers erected his cabin a short distance back of

the river, making his settlement in the northeastern part of the township.

William Stacy settled on the farm now owned by his grandson, Cyrenius F. Stacy. His father was a native of Massachusetts, and a proprietor in the Ohio company. He came early to the Northwestern Territory. In the early part of his life he engaged in the seafaring business, probably at Salem, and afterwards became a farmer near New Salem. At the outbreak of the Revolution he took the initiatory step in reorganizing his company of home militia, becoming their captain by unanimous choice, he having gallantly torn up his royal commission, saying: "Fellow-soldiers, I don't know exactly how it is with the rest of you, but for one I will not serve a king that murders my own countrymen." In 1778 he had become lieutenant colonel in Colonel Ichabod Allen's regiment of the Massachusetts line. In the summer of 1778 his regiment was ordered up to Cherry valley to protect the inhabitants from the threatened attack of the Torries and Indians. The commander of the soldiers at the fort being unacquainted with Indian warfare, was surprised and defeated by a combined force of Indians and Tories, and among the rest Colonel Stacy was taken prisoner by the Indians, and was only released from the stake by giving to an Indian the sign of Free Masonry, which act saved his life. After four years captivity he was released and returned to his family at New Salem, whence, in 1789, he emigrated to Marietta, remaining there until his death, which occurred in 1804. His sons, John and Philemon, were massacred at the Big Bottom settlement. William and Joseph became the pioneers of Muskingum township. To William and Mehitabel Stacy were born five children, who grew to maturity. Sophia married Moses Varnum, of West Virginia. The oldest daughter became the wife of James McClure, of the Rainbow settlement, who finally settled in Millersport, Ohio. William married Vilata Howe, and is deceased; Joel was the husband of Lorilla Howe, and Samuel married Elizabeth Price, and is also deceased. A. R. and C. F. Stacy are the sons of Joel Stacy, and reside in this township. C. F. Stacy was born in 1817, and married Lucy Withom, by whom he has had eight children. He was township clerk for fifteen years, and has held other offices. A. R. Stacy, his brother, is also a native of Washington county. His first wife was Sarah Ross, and his second Diana Malster. He is the father of four children. He is a general farmer and stock-raiser.

Joseph Stacy, also a son of Colonel William Stacy, settled on a farm now occupied by Aurelius Stacy. He married a Miss Perry, by whom he had several children. Joseph married Fanny Williams, whose ancestors came from England. Their children are in Iowa, and the parents are both dead. John, the second son, was married three times and raised quite a family of children. His first wife, Lucebe Rice, had one child that died in infancy. By his second wife, Lousiana Frost, he had four children, two sons and two daughters. Miles A., living in Wiseman's bottom, married Harriet Dyar, by whom he has had five children—Adalaide, Amelia, Ella,

Grace, and Joseph. In 1861, at the call of his country, he enlisted in the Thirty-sixth Ohio volunteer infantry, company A, and soon rose to the position of captain. He was discharged after three years and a half of service on account of physical disability. The third wife of John Stacy was Claryna Frost, by whom he had five children. The two little girls when about nine or ten years of age were attacked by a severe bleeding at the nose which caused their death. James, a son by the last marriage, married a Miss Ann Von, and John married Miss McNeal, and resides near Lowell. Joseph Stacy, sr., had a daughter, Mary, who married, first, Elijah Boyce, and after his death, Luke Emerson.

Preserved Seamon, with his family, emigrated very soon after the arrival of the first company at Marietta. They came from Nova Scotia. The family of children consisted of four sons—Samuel, Gilbert, Preserved, and Benajah. Samuel had a wife and two or three children and occupied the guard-house of Fort Harmar, where the whole family remained during the Indian war. At the Peace they drew donation lots and settled on the Muskingum.

Cogswell Olney was born in Nova Scotia September 28, 1791, and was brought to Ohio by his parents when only six weeks old. His father, Elaezer Olney, was one of the twenty-seven proprietors who settled the most of the donation lands in the tract known as "Rainbow Creek allotment of donation lands." He lived on his farm there until his death. Cogswell Olney married, November 3, 1816, Matilda P. Smith, who was born in Farmer's castle, Belpre, December 12, 1794. She lived until eighty-four years of age, dying at Harmar, December 18, 1878. Their daughter, Celina, is the wife of Charles M. Devol, of Muskingum township.

John Dyar, sr., was born in Boston, Massachusetts. Thence he removed to Nova Scotia, where he lived for a number of years and was married. Here he engaged in navigation. He emigrated thence to Ohio in 1816 and settled in what is now Muskingum township, in Rainbow settlement. He was an eye-witness of the battle of Bunker Hill. After an eventful life in Muskingum he died in 1832. His wife, Sarah Potter, born in 1778, survived him forty-two years. They had ten children, only two of whom survive: J. B. and B. F. Dyar, of Muskingum.

J. B. Dyar has been a resident of his present neighborhood since he was sixteen years old. He has been twice married, first to Amanda Hall, by whom he had seven children, viz: Augustine, who married Elizabeth Pollard; James (deceased), Joseph, who married Fanny Kendrick; Alary, Adelaide (deceased), Edwin, and Charles. By his second wife, Abigail Proctor, Mr. Dyar has had two daughters, viz: Harriet, wife of M. A. Stacy, and Amelia, wife of Reece Cole. Joseph, who was in the Thirty-sixth Ohio volunteer infantry, was wounded at the battle of Lewisburgh, and on that account discharged in 1863.

B. F. Dyar was born in 1817 in Washington county, the year after his father arrived in the county. When he was about a year old his parents removed to the farm where he still resides. Mr. Dyar was married in 1843 to Miss Polly P. Hensy, who still lives. Mr. and Mrs. Dyar have had eight children, four sons and four daughters, all of whom are living. Camillus is married and engaged in the mercantile business in western Iowa. His brother, Frank B., is in business with him. Louisa married Mr. Chapman and resides in Fearing township, of this county. The remaining children reside at home. Mr. Dyar has a farm of one hundred acres in Muskingum township.

SETTLEMENT IN WISEMAN'S BOTTOM.

As has already been mentioned, the first who made a clearing in the above named territory was the man whose memory is perpetuated in the name of the locality in which for a time he dwelt. It is probable that not holding a clear title to his land, he was forced to yield to the claims of the rightful owners in the Ohio company. Geographically considered, Wiseman's bottom is but the southern extension of Rainbow, and hence the two settlements being contiguous, and having a community of interests, were almost blended into one.

The pioneers of Wiseman's bottom were well satisfied that their lot had fallen in such a pleasant place, and joyfully did they make ready to establish their right to their allotted land.

Colonel Joseph Barker was the advance guard of the little colony. In April, 1795, having drawn his donation lot of one hundred acres, he left the garrison in a canoe, with two of his wife's brothers, William and Edmond Bancroft Dana, together with his faithful dog Pedro, and ere long reached his destination—the land now owned by James S. Stowe. Colonel Barker brought with him—in addition to his cooking utensils, farming tools and provisions—fifty young apple, and a dozen cherry trees; it being a condition of a clear title to their land that the recipients of donation land set out fruit trees immediately upon settlement.

At the time of Colonel Barker's settlement the Indians had not been wholly pacified, and soon after his arrival he heard of the death of a man on Wolf creek at the hands of the treacherous savages. Each night the little party was wont to seek shelter in the block-house, which had been erected on the opposite side of the river by General Putnam. Each morning they returned to their work, and although harassed and embarrassed by dangers and difficulties, they never faltered in their arduous undertaking. While at work felling the trees, one of the party was constantly on the watch, for it was a pioneer's first principle to ever be on the alert and ready for any emergency. The faithful dog Pedro, who had been the family guard ever since leaving New Hampshire, was quick to scent danger from afar.

They were thus occupied for about three weeks, and made the first permanent improvement in Wiseman's bottom. During this time they cleared about two acres of the thick forest near the river, and with infinite labor succeeded in getting the ground ready for cultivation. Their first work was to set out the orchard. While they were setting out the apple trees the dog showed signs of alarm, and they therefore remained only long enough to finish the planting of the apple trees, and thinking that they had almost transgressed the limit of safety, hurriedly got ready and were soon rapidly paddling down the Muskingum. In May Colonel Barker returned to his farm and cleared an additional acre of wood-land, making in all about two acres of cleared land, which he planted in corn. This new land, rich with vegetable mold, needed no plowing, but became productive by having the soil stirred up just deep enough to shelter the grain. Colonel Barker's corn-field was carefully watched from the ravages of the squirrels and other animals destructive to the growing corn, and at the harvest the field yielded one hundred and twenty-five bushels. He succeeded in erecting a log cabin sixteen feet square, to one side of which he attached a corn crib four or five feet in width, made of poles, and in this crib he stored his first crop.

In the following December Colonel Barker, with his wife and three children, left the garrison, and on the eighteenth of that month arrived at their new and rather dreary home. The nearest neighbors were distant. During the winter the clearing was considerably enlarged and two hundred peach trees were set out in the orchard in the spring. The hand-mill across the river, at the block-house, was their only dependence for meal, but with a good crib of corn and this resource they thought themselves fortunate. During the year he erected a hewed log house, which was distinguished by the unwonted luxury of a brick chimney, something that humbler houses could not boast of for several years. He had erected his new house just in time, for soon after leaving his first cabin it was destroyed by fire. This was a very heavy loss to Colonel Barker, inasmuch as in this cabin, which was used as a general storehouse, was kept his stock of carpenter tools, and in the loft was stored away the well rotted crop of flax, ready for dressing, and on which depended the family's supply of material for making cloth. His provisions, as well as his fine stock of tools, were lost. But in no wise disconcerted by this misfortune, he sought employment at his old trade of carpentering. In Marietta he erected the Muskingum academy, and the dwellings of Hon. Paul Fearing, William Skinner, Rev. Daniel Story, and others. In 1799 and 1800 he built the mansion of Herman Blennerhassett, on the island called by his name. He was one of the first justices of the peace in Washington county. In 1818 he was elected representative for Washington county in the Ohio legislature. He served for a number of years as county commissioner, and in 1822 drew the plan for the new court house, which was built in that year. During the years 1830-42 he was an associate judge of the common pleas court. He died in 1843, aged seventy-eight years, he having been born at New Market, New Hampshire, in 1765. While working at the carpenter trade in New Boston he became acquainted with Elizabeth, the daughter of Captain William Dana, and in 1789 he was married. In September of the same year the young couple emigrated in an ox wagon to Ohio, suffering every hardship on the way, stopping at Belpre and Marietta, before making a final settlement in Wiseman's bottom. Mrs. Barker died in 1835. They had ten children, four sons and six daughters: Joseph; Elizabeth, wife of Rufus

Stone, of Belpre; Luther married Maria Devol; Sophia married Rufus Browning; George; Mary, still living; Catharine resides in Tennessee; Fanny lives in New Jersey; and Charlotte is also a survivor. Most of the children married and moved away. Joseph and Luther settled in Newport township. George W., better known as Major Barker, was the only member of the family who remained many years on the old homestead farm. He was born in 1801 in Wiseman's bottom. He married Emeline, daughter of Captain Wing Devol. He became the owner of the old homestead. He was twice elected sheriff of Washington county, and filled the office from 1842 to 1846. In the latter year he was elected representative to the legislature, and in 1847 was elected senator, and served two years, he being the last State senator under the old constitution of Ohio. In 1873 he sold his farm, and with four of his sons removed to Missouri, where he died in 1875, aged seventy-four years. His widow, now seventy-one years old, is living in Muskingum township with her son, J. G. Barker.

Israel Putnam settled on the Muskingum on the farm now occupied by S. S. Stowe, and he soon became one of the leading men of his enterprising neighborhood. He was a grandson of General Putnam and a son of Colonel Israel Putnam, of Revolutionary fame. He was born in Pomfret, Connecticut, in 1776. He had four brothers and three sisters. Of this family none survive. In 1789, his father settled at Belpre where, in May, 1794, he arrived, and stopped for a time with his brother Aaron Waldo Putnam. He was a young man of rare powers of observation and had, while travelling from place to place, become imbued with that spirit of enterprise which marks the practical and successful man. He had learned in the east to engraft fruit trees, and almost his first act after landing in Ohio was to graft some fruit trees for his brother with scions which he had brought with him. This is thought to have been the first grafting this side of the Alleghanies. In 1796, he, with his family, settled in Wiseman's bottom, locating on the farm now owned by S. S. Stowe. The first wife of Mr. Putnam was Clarina Chandler, by whom he had two daughters, Fanny and Clarina, both of whom are deceased. His second wife, Elizabeth Wiser, was born in 1769, and died in 1842. Seven children were born by this marriage. Pascal is dead; Helen P. (Mrs. Devol); Lewis J. is living in Marietta, Laura is dead; Fanny, deceased; Catharine, wife of John Newton, is deceased; and the youngest, Elizabeth, is also dead. Mr. Putnam, being a man of great intelligence, encouraged education in the new settlement and did all that he could to assist in the establishment of the first school-house. In the early days of the settlement he erected a substantial brick house, a thing that was rarely done in those days. In 1818, he was the first to undertake the rather difficult task of raising merino sheep. He purchased at Steubenville a flock of over one hundred of these sheep, and succeeded very well in the business of sheep raising. Mr. Putnam died in 1824, aged fifty-nine years.

In 1796, the families of Captain J. Devol and John Russel moved into Wiseman's bottom and soon there was a decreased sense of loneliness in the surrounding forest which rang at the stroke of the woodman's ax.

Captain Jonathan Devol built his house upon the land now owned by Robert Ward, at the place on the Muskingum where he afterwards built a mill. Rapidly reviewing his history, it is found that Jonathan Devol was born at Tiverton, Rhode Island, in 1756, and there in 1776 he married Miss Nancy Barker, daughter of Captain Isaac Barker, a noted ship master, who was lost at sea several years before his daughter's marriage. At the time of the formation of the Ohio company, Captain Devol, who was an ingenious mechanic, built the "May Flower," in which the first company came down the Ohio. The further exploits of this remarkable man will be particularly noticed elsewhere in this work. He settled first at Belpre, where he became famous by reason of his construction of the first floating-mill. After the peace, which ended the Indian war, he removed to Marietta, and cultivated the land of Paul Fearing, and in 1797, made a settlement on the Muskingum, as above narrated. His family consisted of six children, most of whom are deceased. Sarah married James McFarland; Charles, Barker, Tillinghast, and Frank were the sons; Mariah married Luther Barker who removed to McConnelsville.

Wing Devol was among the first settlers in Wiseman's bottom, coming from Marietta soon after the Indian war. He married Clarissa Hart, by whom he had eight children. William, B. F., James, Harris, Josiah, Cynthia, and Emeline (Barker). William Devol, whose family still live in Muskingum, was born in 1803. He married Helen P. daughter of Israel Putnam, and died in August, 1873. Mrs. Devol is still living. She is the mother of three children, John P., William Dudley and Israel P. Dudley Devol married Bitha Marshall, and has had three children, two living. He resides on what is known as the Walnut Hill Farm. Israel P. married Diantha Stowe and has six children. He owns the old farm purchased by his father in 1829.

Benjamin Franklin Devol, a son of Wing Devol, married Ruth B. Cross, by whom he had fourteen children, twelve of whom are living. He died in 1876 and his widow is still living in this township. Her sons, Charles William, and Benjamin were soldiers in the late war.

Joseph, a brother of Wing Devol, at the time of the first settlement, entered land in Wiseman's bottom. Joseph Devol and family lived but a comparatively short time in this township, and then moved to Morgan county, Ohio, where they both died. The family has been scattered, and is not now directly represented in Washington county. The land upon which Joseph Devol settled is now owned by W. D. Devol.

John Russell and family were among the earliest settlers in Wiseman's bottom. They located on the farm which is at present in the possession of Allen Marshall. Mr. Russell was born in Connecticut, in 1764. He married Elizabeth Smith, a native of Massachusetts. To them were born nine children, of whom three are living. Jonathan, Elizabeth, Lucy, Charles, Jane and Caroline are dead. Mary, the widow of Pardon Cook, lives in Marietta; Hiram resides at Centre Point, Iowa, and

William resides beyond Williamstown, West Virginia. Mr. Russell emigrated to the Northwestern Territory about the time that the Ohio company's first colony arrived. During the Indian troubles, he remained at Marietta, and soon after the cessation of hostilities drew his land, and proceeded up the Muskingum to make a settlement. He died in 1829, and his family is not now represented in this township.

Squier Prouty and his wife, Diantha Howe, emigrated to Ohio shortly after the first settlement was made at Marietta. They were natives of Vermont. Mr. Prouty being a blacksmith, located about a quarter of a mile south of Devol's dam, and after building a shop, worked at his trade whenever there was opportunity. Mr. and Mrs. Prouty had two daughters—Rachel and Louisa, both of whom are deceased. Squier Prouty moved away years ago, and the name is without a representative in the township.

Peter Howe and his wife, Orinda Fuller, were from Vermont, and were among the first settlers on the Muskingum. They reared a large family, the only representative of which is Orinda, the wife of Rice Loring, of Belpre. There were fourteen children in all. The Howes lived about a mile south of John Russell's place. Mr. Howe afterwards removed to the vicinity of New England, this State.

John Dyar, a son of John Dyar, sr., and brother of J. B. Dyar, elsewhere mentioned, was born in 1804, in Nova Scotia, and in 1816, emigrated to Ohio from Massachusetts. He settled in section nine of Union township, in that part now embraced in Muskingum. Here he remained until his death in 1835. His wife was Rosanna Stone. His son, John W. Dyar, married Charlotte Beebe, by whom he has had two children—Helen and Harry.

Levi Bartlett was born in 1805, in Rhode Island, from which State he emigrated to Ohio. He settled in Warren, since called Muskingum township, and remained there until his death which occurred in 1879. He married first, Maria Dickey in 1837, by whom he had five children, four of whom are living; she died in 1846. For his second wife he married Mrs. Phœbe Green in 1851, by whom he had nine children, all living. The farm consists of two hundred acres. Mr. Bartlett was justice of the peace and county surveyor, and in 1852–4 represented Washington county in the State legislature. His widow still resides on the farm.

Thomas Ridgway was born in Nova Scotia in 1796, and afterwards removed to Louisiana. In 1822 he came to Ohio, and settled on the west bank of the Muskingum, where Ridgway ferry is located. By his first wife, Esther Ann Dyar, he had four children: James, John, George, William, and Francis. By his second wife, Sarah Abagail Doane, five children were born: Caroline, Thomas, Mary, Isaac, and Sidney. The farm consists of thirty acres of bottom land, and eighty acres of hill land. Stock and fruit are raised to a considerable extent.

James S. Stowe, sr., was born in Meigs county in 1806, and when nineteen years old came to Washington county and became a resident of the Muskingum valley. In

THOMAS RIDGWAY, Muskingum Tp.

Thomas Ridgway was born January, 22, 1796, of English ancestors. At the time of his birth, Thomas' parents were living at Shelbourne, Nova Scotia, at which place they continued to reside until he was thirteen years of age, when they removed to Halifax, at which place Thomas obtained the rudiments of an education by perseveringly applying himself at night school, kept for those whose daily task forbade their attendance in daylight.

Trained to the trade of a cooper from boyhood, Thomas was called (in that fishing town) to the fisheries, and at an early age was engaged in superintending the cooperage department of one of the great mackerel fisheries on Cape Breton island.

At other times during the fishing seasons he was employed in the cod fisheries of the coast of Newfoundland. During the War of 1812-15 he was, as a British subject, aboard many of the American prizes, among which was the ill-fated Chesepeake, and at an advanced age of eighty-five years his recollection of that terrible wreck is clear and vivid. In 1821 Thomas Ridgway started to seek his fortunes in the southwestern States, and early in that year landed at New Orleans. There he worked at his trade in the great sugar establishments until, losing his health, he returned to Halifax late in the same year. In the spring of 1822 he returned to New Orleans and pursued his trade until autumn, when he came north to see the country and visit the Dyar family, living then on the old homestead, on the Muskingum river, in this county, to whom he was distantly related. In the following spring of 1823, in company with Joseph B. Dyar, he loaded a boat with produce of various kinds and floated it up the great Kanawha to the salt wells, near the site of the present town of Malden, West Virginia. There they disposed of the cargo to advantage, and entered into a contract with one of the salt firms to furnish salt barrels in exchange for salt, at the rate of one bushel and a peck of salt for a barrel. In the succeeding fall they brought a cargo of salt up the Ohio river, and sold it at various points from Marietta up as far as Wheeling.

In February of 1824 they returned to the salt wells, and recommenced the making of barrels and shipping of salt with renewed vigor, Joseph Dyar doing the shipping. During that season Mr. Ridgway, with his own hands, unaided, made three thousand barrels in nine months, about twelve and a half per day. They lived in true bachelor style, and did a thriving business, selling their salt down the Ohio at thirty-five cents per bushel. In the autumn of 1825, after they had closed their contract at the wells, they were wind-bound with their last load of salt, at a point near Ironton, and were offered a piece of land, at three dollars per acre, upon which the city now stands.

After they had disposed of the cargo, Mr. Ridgway returned to Washington county and with Mr. Dyar purchased the property in Muskingum township upon which he now lives. They also purchased what is known as the Davis farm one mile further up river. At the termination of their partnership Mr. Ridgway took the farm upon which he now lives at a valuation of nine hundred dollars. February 16, 1826 he was married to Esther Ann Dyar, the sister of his late partner, by whom he had five children: James, John, George, William, and Francis. His wife dying in 1836, he was married to Mrs. Sarah A. Doane December 6, 1838, by whom he had five children: Caroline, Thomas, Mary, Isaac, and Sidney. Mrs. Sarah A. Ridgway dying May, 1862, he married Mrs. Caroline Johnson on the fourteenth of November, 1866. Mrs. Caroline Ridgway lived but five years. and Mr. Ridgway was again left a widower on the thirtieth of November, 1871. Shortly after his first marriage Mr. Ridgway entered the Methodist church, and has since continued to live the life of a consistent Christian.

The church of his first adoption becoming enfeebled by removals, he entered the Congregational church of Lowell, that he might do more effectual work, and the frequent donation made to that society after he had secured a home for his family testifies his devotion to the cause.

In politics, as in religion, nothing was done by halves. With his earnest acquaintance with our form and principles of government he espoused the cause of the Whig party, and from his sense of justice and humanity became an avowed enemy to slavery. He continued with the Whig party until its faltering, wavering course upon the question of slavery gave rise to the Free Soil party, where he found a better expression of his sentiments. Mr. Ridgway voted the anti-slavery ticket almost alone in his precinct. No taunts or opposition could cause him to hesitate or waver in the support he gave the choice of his conscience. Before and during the fugitive law Mr. Ridgway's house was ever the asylum for the pursued; and from first to last of those bitter slavery days over fifty fugitives have found food and shelter at his hand from their pursuers. From the rise of the Republican party Mr. Ridgway has been found in its ranks. During the war he was a firm Unionist, losing two sons in the support of the cause he upheld, and in his old age has the sweet pleasure of seeing the fulfillment of the most sanguine expectations of his younger days.

1831 he commenced boating, which he followed until prevented by the outbreak of the late war. About 1830 he married Anna Merriam, by whom he had four children. She died in 1842. About 1844 he married Eliza Davis, by whom he had six children, all of whom survive. His eldest son, Sardine S., married for his third wife, Eva Smith, and has seven children: Nancy, married to A. S. Marshal; Diantha, married to Israel Devol; Seldon S., married to Ellen Smith, and has had three children, two of whom survive. He served during the Rebellion in the Thirty-sixth Ohio volunteer infantry. Lucy Stowe married J. C. Drake; Dudley D. became a resident of the township in 1850, married Sybil Wood, and has one son, David H. Stowe. He lives on the homestead farm, where he owns three hundred and twenty-nine acres. James Smith Stowe, jr., born in 1856, married in 1880 Lucy W. Franks, whose parents were early settlers in Marietta. In the summer of 1880 he commenced the grocery business at Marietta. Pittman L. Stowe resides at home.

Randolph Fearing was born in 1825, and died in 1873. His wife, Julia Hill, born in 1830, is the daughter of William Hill, an old settler. Mr. and Mrs. Fearing became the parents of ten children, of whom three are deceased. The farm in Muskingum township consists of twenty-four acres.

Charles Weinheimer came from Prussia in 1853, and settled in this township. He was born in 1831, and married Elizabeth Shoemaker, born in 1829. They have five children. Mr. Weinheimer farms one hundred acres of land. He has been a member of the board of education and trustee of the township.

A. S. Marshall owns one hundred acres of land in Wiseman's bottom. His father, John Marshall, emigrated from West Virginia in 1832, and became a resident of Marietta township, dying in 1874. A. S. Marshall married Nancy Stowe, by whom he had five children, four of whom survive.

Thomas Drake bought land in Wiseman's bottom in 1866, coming from Chester, Pennsylvania, where he was born in 1825. His wife, Sarah J. Oliver, born in 1830, is still living. They have had four children—John, Margaret, James and Mary. John, who was born in 1848, married Lucy J. Stowe, who was born in 1847. They have two sons. Mr. Drake has two hundred and sixty acres of land, is a general farmer and a cattle and sheep raiser, making a specialty of Jersey cattle and fine Merino sheep.

Dr. Simeon D. Hart became a resident of Muskingum township in 1869, when he became the superintendent of the Children's Home. He is one of the seven children of Benjamin and Honor (Deming) Hart. His father was born in Connecticut in 1781 and died in Newport township in 1867. His mother, born in 1789, died in 1825. Dr. Hart married Lydia M. Lawrence, who was born in 1822. He has been superintendent of the Home during the past eleven years. During the years 1864–66 he was county coroner.

Peter Armstrong settled on the Muskingum in Wiseman's bottom allotment in 1870. He was born at Har-

risonburgh, Virginia, in 1839. He married Catharine Burke, by whom he has had seven children, six of whom survive. He has a farm of thirty-seven acres of land.

THE SETTLEMENT OF THE RIDGE.

The territory forming the eastern boundary of the township, and known as the ridge because it divides the waters of Duck creek from the Muskingum, was not generally settled until a comparatively recent date. This is on account of the hilly, and consequently somewhat sterile nature of the soil whose unproductiveness was early a proverb among the more fortunate settlers of the lower and richer valley lands. But it has been demonstrated that a living can be obtained on these high places by honest and persevering toil, combined with practical intelligence.

Although the neighborhood is now almost entirely peopled with Germans, who in fact made the first permanent settlements, yet is it discovered that settlers of American birth first had little farms among the hills. The representatives of these first settlers of that part of the ridge lying in the present township of Muskingum are scattered, and it is impossible to give them more than a passing mention.

In all probability a number of these settlers were in this section prior to 1825. A Mr. Page resided for a short time on the present Garver place.

A settler named Steit, residing just north of where the Wagners settled, removed to the west about the year 1840, declaring his inability to make a livelihood by tilling his farm.

Mr. Johnson, with his wife and children, resided on the place upon which Ulrich Ulmer now lives. He also moved to the west.

Stephen Otis and wife, with five or six children, lived first on the Decker place, on the river, and afterwards moved on the hill, upon what is now known as the Frank Rayley place. Mr. Otis was one of the prominent men in his community forty years ago, and it was he who presented the ground upon which the German church was erected.

There were settlers on the Wilking and Gerhart places prior to the German settlement.

In 1833 quite a company of Bavarians left their native Germany and, after the long and tedious voyage necessary to travel in a slow sailing vessel, they arrived in New York, and most of them came immediately to Ohio and secured land on the ridge. In this company were the families of Abraham Arend, Daniel Cemmer, and Jacob Peters. They were also accompanied by Theodore Schreiner, who afterwards became the pastor of their church.

Daniel Cemmer, born in 1781, was one of the first German settlers on the ridge. In 1833 he, with his wife, Barbara, and nine or ten children, settled on what was originally the Steit place. Both of the old folks are dead, and the children are scattered through the county.

Jacob and Catharine Peters settled in 1833 on the Page farm. They had two sons and one daughter—Charles, Philip, and Margaret. In 1836 they removed to Watertown. Both parents are now deceased.

In 1834, in the forepart of the year, Abraham Arend and his wife, M. Sarah Arend, settled in the neighborhood. They left their native land in August, 1833, and stopped for a while after landing at Wheeling, West Virginia. After remaining there for seven months they got a farm in Washington county, and settled on the farm upon which Mrs. Arend still resides with her daughter, Mrs. Jacob Wagner. Seven of their eight children are living, two of them residing on the home-place. The eldest daughter, Mary Elizabeth, became the wife of Jacob Wagner.

In 1834 Jacob and Mary Gerhart came to the vicinity, being emigrants from Germany, and settled on the farm now occupied by their son, John Gerhart, with whom the mother still resides. John Gerhart is quite prominent as a township officer.

John and Elizabeth Wagner emigrated also from Germany and settled on the farm near the church on the place now occupied by John Wagner. There had been a clearing made in the forest which surrounded them by B. Briggs, who was a hunter in that region some time before the advent of the Wagners. Mr. and Mrs. Wagner had ten children in all, three of whom were born in this county. Six of the children are living, and five are in this township.

In 1836 Adam and Margaret Seiler settled on the farm which had been previously owned by Jacob Peters. Mrs. Seiler had five daughters, of whom three are living.

In 1836 Theobald, a brother of Jacob Gerhart, settled on Second creek, on the place now owned by Jacob Millbach. His wife died soon afterwards, and his children are scattered. He moved to Marietta and there died some years ago.

In 1839, or thereabouts, Jacob Grimm and his wife Caharine, settled on the ridge between Second creek and the Muskingum, on the place now occupied by their daughters, Elizabeth and Catharine.

In 1837 Daniel and Catharine Long, with their three children, settled on what is now known as the Youngblood farm. Mr. and Mrs. Long had three children born to them in America.

Theobald Wagner settled about the same time on the same place with the Longs. He married Margaret Cemmer, by whom he had eight children. Jacob Wagner is still living on the place.

F. W. Rayley was born in Aurelius township in 1839, and afterwards became a resident of Muskingum. He married Caroline Smith, who was born in 1840. They have three children—Raymond W., Maynard, and an infant. Mr. Rayley farms eighty acres of land.

John Phillips emigrated to this county from Massachusetts in 1815, and settled in Muskingum township. He married Mary Dean, who was born in Massachusetts in 1795. He died in 1840, aged sixty-six years. Two of their seven children are living: Mary, the widow of Captain Hathaway, living in Massachusetts; and Joseph, residing east of Marietta. The latter was born in 1805. He married Anna Terny, by whom he had seven children, six of whom survive. For thirty years Mr. Phillips was in the employ of Dr. Moore, and then purchased his present farm, where he has a nice, comfortable home.

Mr. J. N. Bishop was born in 1800, in Hoosac Falls, New York. When he was a small boy, his parents removed to the vicinity of Parkersburgh, West Virginia. Thence after several years, they removed to Morgan county, Ohio, where they died. Before the death of his parents, Mr. Bishop had settled in Marietta. In 1830 he married Miss Lucetta A. M. Seely, of Washington county. Miss Seely's parents were among the oldest settlers in Marietta. Mr. and Mrs. Bishop had four children. Their three daughters are still living. Their only son died in 1863, in Virginia, from wounds received in battle. His father died a few weeks after from a disease contracted while nursing his son in the camp. Mrs. Bishop still lives in the old place in Muskingum township.

Mr. W. W. Rathbone was born in Columbus, Ohio, in 1829. He removed with his parents to Louisville, Kentucky, when he was about six years old. Here the family lived five or six years. Thence they removed to Belpre village, Washington county, Ohio, which was the old home of Mr. Rathbone's mother, she being a member of the Putnam family. Here Mr. Rathbone lived until his twenty-second year, when he removed to his present residence, about a mile north of Marietta, in Muskingum township. He was married in 1852 to Miss Julia Furguson. Mr. and Mrs. Rathbone have three daughters. Mr. Rathbone makes a specialty of raising sweet potatoes, and probably does the largest business in that line in the west.

EARLY SCHOOLS.

It is not strange that in such highly intellectual communities as are found in this township that the first school-house was built about the time the first cabin was erected in the several settlements. The earlier settlements in Wiseman's bottom and Rainbow were made by people who had enjoyed the privileges of a New England education, and were unwilling with the loss of numerous comforts and privileges to give up the school-house. They very sensibly foresaw that their children needed intelligence to assist them in the arduous task of overcoming the numerous obstacles which blocked up the road to success in the west. Hence it is that from the earliest beginnings the foundations of present prosperity were laid in the ground of a broad intelligence. The first schools were of course subscription schools, and continued as such until the formation of our present excellent system of free schools.

The first school in Wiseman's bottom was located on the Muskingum river, on the land then owned by Israel Putnam. It was a round log structure of the true pioneer type, with puncheon floor and seats, windows covered with greased paper, and huge fireplace across one end of the room. The logs of which the house was constructed were of beech and sugar principally, and ere very long they became rotten and hollow in places, which were frequently occupied by snakes, chipmunks, etc. On one occasion an unusually large black-snake was discovered in the recess of the fireplace trying to get at a nest of swallows in the chimney above. It was recess in that school until the big boys and teacher killed the snake.

The earliest teacher whose name can be ascertained was Miss Esther Levings. Abigail Poole was in all probability the next. She was followed by Theophilus Cotton. Not long after the erection of the school-house on the river it was found that the building was too near the water and was liable to be surrounded during a heavy rise in the river. On this account it was deemed advisable to remove the school-house farther back on higher ground. Accordingly this was done, the building being located on Israel Putnam's farm, where, in 1816, through Mr. Putnam's instrumentality, a commodious brick school-house was erected, which served the double purpose of school-house and church. In this building the people of the neighborhood continued to worship for a number of years. The people were of various denominations, but in those early days they worshipped in common. Rev. Joseph Willard, an Episcopal clergyman of talent, is remembered to have been the first minister who preached in the school-church. When the school-house was first moved back from the river, the teachers were Colonel Stone, Mr. Brown, of New England, a Mr. Allen, and perhaps others. Whipple Spooner was the first teacher in the brick house.

In early times Rainbow had two neighborhood schoolhouses, which, in this modern day have been consolidated into one. There was what was known as the upper and lower school-house, the former being located on the Muskingum, not far from Stephen Smith's place, and the latter being on the site of the present school-house of the neighborhood, immediately in the bow of the river. Both structures were built of logs and were primitive in the style of their architecture. In these two buildings did the children of the first settlers of Rainbow receive the rudiments of education. School was kept three months in each year, and the children were allowed and encouraged to attend whenever the work at home permitted. Nathaniel Dodge is believed to have been the first teacher in what was known as the lower school. Benjamin F. Stone succeeded him, and he in turn was succeeded by Sidney McClung. A. Pixley was the next teacher. To his pedagogical duties he added those of the singing master, and was accustomed to teach the young folks how to sing, and there were consequently many good singers in the neighborhood. They did not learn the common *tra la la* of modern days, but were trained in such music as Judgment and Easter anthems. Among succeeding teachers are found the names of Elijah Boyce, Nancy Plummer, Harriet Williams, Orinda Howe, Amanda Hall, Melissa Smith, and Sarah Thornily, and later came Mordecai Sanders, William Otis, Jonathan Gibbs, Dudley Smith, Whiting Hollaster, and others. The log school-house gave place to a frame and then the present brick structure. From the earliest date in the settlement of Rainbow the people in addition to their love for education, were firm in maintaining religious principles, and the school-houses and neighboring private houses were used as places of worship.

The first teacher at the upper Rainbow school was a Mr. Walbridge. B. F. Stone and Lydia Smith were among the succeeding early instructors. The original log building was the first and last school-house on this site, and years ago the two schools were consolidated, and the children of the upper school became attendants of the one farther down the river.

It was customary for the two schools to hold joint spelling matches, which drew to the front all the orthographical talent of which the settlement could boast, and many a night's sport did the fun-loving young folks of that day have in these contests.

The first school-house in the settlement of Germans on the ridge was located on the land which was then owned by Adam Seiler, and is now on the Arend place. It was a hewed log building, and during the first years of its history was a German school, in which no English was taught. The first German teacher was Carl Young. He was followed by John Paff, Adam Wilking, Jacob Morningstar and Jacob Miegle. Gradually the children of the neighborhood learned the English language, and there was consequently a demand for English teaching. The first one who taught an English school was Mrs. Mary A. Grant. This was in the year of 1843, and since then English has become predominant, alternating at first with the German, and gradually taking precedence. The log school-house has given place to a comfortable frame.

At the passage of the law establishing schools throughout the county which were to be supported by taxation, the pay schools were discontinued and the district schools took their places. There are at present nine school districts in the township. The first township board of education consisted of the following named gentlemen: A. R. Stacy, R. Fearing, Augustine Dyar, Daniel Wilking, and Jacob Wagner. The present board consists of the following persons, one for each district, viz: Anthony Smith, M. A. Stacy, John Wellspring, Joseph Dyar, J. G. Barker, Jacob H. Wagner, Joseph Jurden, Henry Cline, and J. W. Dyar. The schools are under good management and the high standing of education which has ever been maintained, has made this township a most intellectual community.

About thirty years ago Samuel Maxwell, a retired professor of Marietta college, erected a large brick residence which is now used as a part of the Children's Home. In an upper room in the rear part of the house, over what is now the kitchen of the Home, Professor Maxwell established an academy for boys, and there instructed them. At times he had as high as twenty scholars, and for a while the school was successful, but it eventually failed.

AN OLD SUBSCRIPTION PAPER.

Although because of the proximity of neighboring churches a house of worship was not erected in the territory now comprised in this township, the people have always been enthusiastic in religious work, and from the earliest time strove to care for their souls as well as for their intellects. An interesting bit of paper remains to testify to their Christian fidelity. This witness is an old subscription paper drawn up in 1810, which appears to be in the handwriting of Colonel Joseph Barker. The object of the subscription was to establish divine worship in Rainbow and Wiseman's bottom. None of those whose names appear below are now living. It reads thus:

Please pay in money or produce to Mr. Thomas Lake, on or before the fifteenth day of December next, for the purpose of introducing the regular preaching of the Gospel of Jesus Christ, and for inculcating and introducing habits of good order, morality, and piety, by holding up to public view examples worthy the imitation and practice of the rising generation.

The subscription paper provided for a cash subscription, but there was none made of that kind.

Then comes a list of the subscribers:

ADAMS, April 2, 1810.

Subscribers' names.	Produce.
Joseph Barker	$5 00
Jasper Stone	3 00
Joseph Stacy	4 00
Sylvanus Newton	6 00
Sardine Stone	2 00
Joseph Stacy, jr	1 00
Stephen Smith	1 00
Thomas Lake	6 00
John Russell	3 00
Simeon Wright	2 00
Isaac Walbridge	1 00
Benjamin F. Stone	3 00
William Stacy, jr	1 00
John Deem	1 00
William Stacy	3 00
Ephraim Matthews, thirty cents for each day's preaching.	
Squier Prouty	2 00
Joseph Wood	4 00
Resolved Fuller	1 00

Preaching services were regularly held in the several school-houses from time to time when a minister could be found.

THE EVANGELICAL PROTESTANT CHURCH.

This, the only church within the confines of Muskingum township, is formed exclusively of the German settlers on the ridge and vicinity. The first company of emigrants had with them him who was to establish in their midst a church, in which, as was their wont in the Fatherland, they could worship the God of their fathers. Sometimes they would attend English preaching services at the Cedar Narrows, on Duck creek, in Fearing township. But this was, of course, unsatisfactory to people who could not as yet speak the English language, and they were all very anxious to establish a church of their own, where they might hear the gospel in their native tongue. The material for the organization was at hand and the people had a mind to work, but as yet they knew of no one who would serve them as pastor. But Providence had been kind to them, and they soon discovered that they had the right man in their midst. Theodore Schreiner, who emigrated from Germany in 1833, was the son of a clergyman, and had been carefully reared and educated. While in the midst of his studies, his father died, and he was consequently deprived of further educational advantages. Feeling that his future success depended entirely upon his own efforts, he decided to come to the new world. At the time of the organization of the church he was living in Fearing township, near by. Being a man of education, a minister's son, and withal a godly man, what more proper than that he be called to become the shepherd of this little flock among the hills. Having decided to pick up the ministerial duties which

his father had been compelled to lay down at his death, he went heartily into the work, and soon effected the organization of a society of not less than twenty members.

The first building was a hewed log structure, erected upon the site of the present building. The lot for the building and adjoining burying-ground was donated by Stephen Otis. In this house the congregation continued to worship for a number of years, and in 1849 the hewed log gave place to the present frame church, which was built by Theobald Baker.

Rev. Theodore Schreiner continued in the pastorate for nineteen years, and was followed by Rev. F. Ciolina. He, in turn, was followed by Rev. Ferdinand Jurgens, who remained eight years. Revs. F. Wald and August Walther stayed about one year each. The next pastor, Rev. G. F. Englehardt, remained seven or eight years, being followed by Rev. Trapp, who remained about one year. Then the people called the present pastor, Rev. S. Beach, who has faithfully ministered unto them for seven years.

The church at present is in a prosperous condition, and is well sustained. There are ninety-seven members on the church roll. The trustees are: Anthony Smith, John Wilking and Wallace Smith. John Gerhart is the clerk. About twelve years ago another acre of ground was added to the church lot.

GRAVEYARDS.

Each neighborhood had its pioneer burying-ground, for death was common to them all. There are now three such enclosures in Muskingum township, which are sacred to the memory of the past and the resting place of hopes to be realized only in that future day that is yet to come. In each one of these God's acres sleep the forefathers of the township's early settlers.

The pioneer graveyard of Wiseman's bottom was located on the farm of Israel Putnam. Here were buried the Putnams, Barkers, Russells, Devols, and in fact nearly all of the earliest settlers. In later years the place was not used, and it became neglected. About the year 1820 a new cemetery was laid out about half a mile northeast of Devol's dam, and in this ground was buried most of those who had lain in the old cemetery. Since 1820 burials have been frequent, and the cemetery is well filled. The grounds are neatly kept, and are adorned with numerous evergreens that form a pleasing background to the many handsome monuments. Conspicuous among these monuments is a Scotch granite which Colonel Putnam erected to the memory of his fathers. The inscription reads:

To the memory of General Israel Putnam, born at Salem, Massachusetts, in 1718, a confidential friend of Washington, died May 19, 1790. Israel Putnam, his grandson, died March 9, 1824, aged fifty-nine. This monument was erected by Major L. J. P. Putnam.

The monument of Colonel Barker is also conspicuous.

There is another pioneer graveyard on the Walnut Hills farm, now owned by Dudley Devol. Therein were buried a number of the first settlers. It is not now used, and has been sadly neglected.

The pioneer graveyard of the Rainbow settlement is located on the Joseph Wood farm. The first person

J. B. DYAR.

MRS. J. B. DYAR.

buried in this ground was Mrs. Mary Lake, wife of Archibald Lake, who died the next year after his settlement on the Muskingum. The grounds have from time to time been greatly improved, and at present the cemetery presents a very attractive appearance. Within its boundaries reposes the dust of the early settlers of Rainbow, sleeping in the midst of the land which they redeemed from the wilderness and made prosperous by their early efforts.

There is a cemetery adjoining the Evangelical Protestant church in the northeastern part of the township. It originally consisted of about an acre of ground, but a few years ago received an additional acre. It is under the control of the church. The first person buried in this cemetery was the mother of Henry Spies, and since then most of the original settlers have been buried there.

FLOATING MILL ON THE MUSKINGUM.

In another place there is a history of the floating mill which Captain Jonathan Devol so ingeniously built for the use of the settlers along the Ohio at Belpre. When, in 1796, he moved up the Muskingum and joined the community located in the present township, he found that the settlers were in great need of a mill in which to grind their grain. The clumsy hand mills, then in common use, were inefficient, and it was difficult to keep a sufficient supply of meal. Captain Devol with becoming and characteristic enterprise, at once proceeded to alleviate the difficulty by constructing a floating mill similar to the one he had built at Belpre in 1791. It was built on two boats, the one supporting the machinery for grinding, and the other the shaft for the water wheel. The boats were joined at the bow and stern by stout planks, which served the double purpose of floor and girder, binding the boats to a parallel course. The mill machinery was enclosed by a little frame structure which sheltered the miller, and protected the machinery and grain from the wet weather. People came by water from all parts of the country for fifty miles around, and the mill supplied them with plenty. In 1803, he built a larger mill which produced an excellent quality of flour. This floating mill was constructed at the instance of Griffin Green, esq., after the pattern of similar mills in Holland. During its operation on the Muskingum it was moved at a point in the river where Captain Devol afterwards built the dam for his large stationary mill.

OTHER MILLS

of various kinds have been erected from time to time. In 1807, Captain Devol erected a very large frame flouring mill near where the present mill now stands. Its large under shot wheel is said to have been more than forty feet in diameter, it being the largest mill wheel ever seen in the west. The mill did a fair business, but with the lapse of years was allowed to fall into decay. It stood for a number of years a deserted monument to early enterprise, and full fifty years ago it tottered to its fall, and with a crash was scattered prone upon the earth. Like an aged man, having finished its appointed tasks, it mingled with its original dust, and gave way in later years to a modern structure which is still standing.

78

Some time after the desertion of the old mill, Captain Devol's grandson, J. L. Devol, put up a building near by to be used as a saw-mill and chair factory. He also kept, in connection with it a small general store. The buildings, which are now owned by Colonel L. J. P. Putnam, are still standing in a very dilapidated state. There was a corn cracker in connection with the saw-mill that did some grinding for the neighborhood. This saw-mill and chair factory, prior to its purchase by Major Putnam, was owned by Dana & Wendleken. After the close of the late war it was for a time operated by Putnam, Bragg & Straw.

In 1866, Major Putnam erected at Devol's dam, a large mill with three run of buhrs, which was considered to be the best mill on the river. After operating this mill for a year, Major Putnam put it in charge of I. P. and H. C. Putnam, and is now operated by I. P. Putnam, under the name of Union mills.

Sheep raising had become such an important industry among the farmers in the year 1809, that it was highly important that the work of the hand cards be made easier by the use of machinery. Accordingly, with his usual enterprising energy, Captain Devol purchased and put in operation, necessary machinery for wool carding.

During the previous year he erected works for cloth dressing and fulling, both of which operations being carried on by Captain Devol prior to any other operations of like kind west of the mountains. The machinery for cloth dressing could not be found in Ohio, and was purchased at McConnelsville, on the Youghiogeny river.

The saw-mill at Union Landing or "Pinchville," was built at a comparatively early day by George T. Elston.

John Strecker, jr's. glue factory just north of Marietta, began operations in 1863, and now has an invested capital of four or five thousand dollars. Thirty-five thousand pounds of glue, valued at thirty-five thousand dollars, are made annually.

SHIP-BUILDING ON THE MUSKINGUM.

The community in Wiseman's bottom was fortunate in having among its numbers two men of such marked mechanical skill as Colonel Joseph Barker and Captain Jonathan Devol. Both of them were skilled architects, Captain Devol being a shipwright by trade, and Colonel Barker a house-builder. About the year 1800, shipbuilding having become an important industry at Marietta and on the Muskingum, these men readily took part in the work for which they were so well adapted by previous education and natural skill. The dense forests on either side of the river furnished excellent material for the work. Giant oaks were felled, and under the skilful hands of these men were joined together and moulded into symmetrical shape. Noting first the work of Colonel Barker, we find that his shipyard was on his farm on the east bank of the Muskingum. In 1802, he constructed two ocean vessels. One was a brig, built for Messrs. Blennerhassett and Woodbridge, and named the Dominic, after the name of Mr. Blennerhassett's oldest son. The other was a schooner, called the Indiana. This last named vessel, together with the Louisa, built in 1803, were for E. W. Tupper, of Marietta. During the fall of 1806 he was employed by Herman Blennerhassett to construct fifteen large bateaux for the use of the expedition of Aaron Burr to Mexico. The fate of these boats and this intended expedition is more fully described elsewhere in this work.

Captain Devol's ship-building was quite extensive. He also worked along the Muskingum upon his farm. In 1801 he built a sloop of four hundred tons for B. J. Gilman, a merchant of Marietta. The vessel was wholly constructed of black walnut, and was named after the river by whose side it was built. In 1802 he built two brigs, of two hundred tons each, the Eliza Green, and the Ohio. In 1804, the schooner Nonpareil was built. The passage of the embargo act, in 1807, suspended all further operations in this line.

THE CHILDREN'S HOME.

This institution is beautifully situated on an eastern bluff of the Muskingum river about one mile from the city of Marietta. The idea of the institution was a gradual growth, founded on the increased necessity for some refuge besides the infirmary for the numerous little ones left without parental care. The act establishing children's homes in the several counties of the State was passed March 20, 1866, and then with the means in their hands the county commissioners proceeded to establish a Home in this county, appointing, in accordance with law, five trustees, to serve one year each. The act of 1867 reduced this number to three, whose term of service extended to three years.

The first board of trustees was composed of the following members, viz: Douglas Putnam, William R. Putnam, Frederick A. Wheeler, William S. Ward, and Augustine Dyar. Of this number, Frederick A. Wheeler is still in office. Colonel W. R. Putnam, the chairman of the board from its commencement, resigned after a faithful service of ten years; and William S. Ward died during his term of office. Wylie H. Oldham, who was appointed in 1871, also died while in office. In 1875 W. Dudley Devol was appointed, and in 1877 George Benedict became a member of the board which now consists of Messrs. Wheeler, Devol, and Benedict.

There was no lack of children anxious to enter the Home. As early as 1858 Miss Catharine Fay, now Mrs. Ewing, began caring for the little waifs which were left without parental care. They were provided for at the Home in Lawrence township under an arrangement made with the directors of the county infirmary. At the time of the establishment of the Home on the Muskingum there were thirty children under Miss Fay's charge, who were brought to their new abode April 1, 1867. Mrs. A. G. Brown, who had been appointed matron on the first of March, continued to serve until April 1, 1868, when she was succeeded by Rev. Ira M. Preston and wife as superintendent and matron, who served one year, being succeeded by the present incumbents, Dr. Simeon D. Hart and wife.

Since the advent of Dr. Hart numerous improvements have been made. A frame addition in the shape of an L. has been put up on the north side of the back part of the original brick building. This part is used principally as a nursery for the younger children.

In 1874 the increased numbers justified the erection of a second brick building just behind the first house. It was occupied January 1, 1875. It is three stories high, seventy-five feet long, and thirty feet wide. As soon as there is need of additional room it is proposed that a similar structure be added to the north side, and that the two wings thus formed be wrought into one building. The first floor of the wing that has been built is occupied by the Home school. The second floor is the boys' dormitory, and the third is for the girls. Everything is kept neat and clean, as perfect order is maintained in every department. The attendance at the school in 1880 averaged over sixty pupils, none being exempt from school duty except those very small and those of the larger ones detailed to assist in the work. The school is under the management of Miss Augusta Nixon, who has had charge of it for over ten years. Inasmuch as the scholars are all quite young, only the common branches are taught. Music is taught to such as evince a taste for it. On Sundays, and at other times, religious instruction is given and many of the children have a thorough knowledge of Bible history. The progress of their education is very satisfactory and the results of thorough system in training are seen in the bright eyes and quick looks of intelligence which greet the visitor. That the bodily powers may not flag the children regularly go through exercises in calisthenics. They are well fed, well dressed, and kindly cared for, and are therefore happy.

The farm land is much better adapted to grazing and pasturing than to the raising of grain and other crops. Except the lawn and garden, and about twelve acres of woodland, the farm is in pasture and fruit land. Milk being considered an almost indispensable article of diet, especially for children, a sufficient quantity is provided to give them a generous supply each day. To do this, from ten to twelve cows are required, and pains are taken to secure the best breeds for the purpose. The orchard provides an abundance of healthful fruit.

The object of the Home is not simply to feed and clothe these children, but to nurture them by inculcating those principles which shall enable them to go out into the world and make homes for themselves. They are not allowed by the law to remain at the home after reaching the age of sixteen years. Long before that time most of the children are either restored to their parents or adopted into responsible families. The average number of inmates during the year 1880 was about seventy-five, there being twice as many boys as girls. The number of children has been less during the past year than it has been in any of the last ten years previous.

This institution was the first in the State organized under the law authorizing county homes for children. Those charged with its management accepted their positions fully sensible of the difficulties to be encountered, and with the knowledge that they were without the advantages to be derived from the experience of similar institutions. Its history shows that the Home has succeeded in fulfilling the full measure of expectation. The general management of its affairs by the superintendent and matron have been eminently satisfactory, and their annual reappointment since 1868 attests the estimation with which their services are regarded by those most familiar with the history, success, and progress of the Home.

THE MUSKINGUM FARMERS' CLUB

was organized January 1, 1874, for the double purpose of promoting the agricultural and social interests of the community. Most trades and professions have their associations for the advancement of their interests, and it is equally fitting that farmers assemble to talk over their business and social affairs, and to make more interesting and profitable the great industry which is the foundation of all prosperity. Moreover society in the country is usually more nominal than real, and it is invigorated by the frequent assembling together of farmers and their families. The Muskingum Farmers' club has succeeded admirably in the accomplishment of these very important ends. During the six years of its existence the meetings have been well attended, the average attendance being about forty. Formerly bi-monthly, the meetings are now held on the first Saturday of every month, at the house of some member or friend of the club. In winter it is customary to assemble at 11 A. M., dine at 12 and transact business from 1 to 4 P. M. During the summer season the meetings are in the afternoon with supper at the close. The ladies of the club share with the hostess the duties of entertainment, and the culinary department is fully equipped in true picnic style, and thus happily is business combined with social enjoyment, and it is no wonder that there are always a number of ever welcome friends who enjoy the club's hospitality.

The usual order of exercises is as follows: Reading of the minutes of the previous meeting; vocal and instrumental music; a recitation by one of the younger members; the reading of a selected article and of an original essay; general remarks; miscellaneous business, and the discussion of a question previously assigned. The subjects for reading, writing and discussion are left entirely to the discretion of the appointees who gratify their own convenience and tastes, though party questions are carefully avoided. The regular question for discussion is generally of practical importance to the farmer, and much practical good is derived.

Premiums have from time to time been offered for the best articles and yields of farm produce. The most noticeable of these premiums is a handsome silver medal presented to the club by M. P. Wells, of Marietta, to be given each year to the member raising the best acre of corn.

It is the intention of the club hereafter to give more attention and encouragement to careful experiment in regard to the comparative values of different farm products and methods of culture.

The present officers of the club are: J. G. Barker, president; W. D. Devol, vice-president; Kate Rathbone, secretary; C. P. Dyar, corresponding secretary, and M. A. Stacy, treasurer.

Taking all things into consideration, the Muskingum club has been a success, and has realized the anticipations of its founders. It has done much to make enjoyable a life usually of much toil and little healthful intellectual and social enjoyment. No means which can improve the welfare and increase the happiness of the great farming class of the country should be neglected, and the Muskingum Farmers' club has, in great measure, met this great want.

BIOGRAPHICAL SKETCHES.

THE DYAR FAMILY.

John Dyar, the first representative of this family in Washington county, was a native of Boston. After the Revolution he removed to Nova Scotia and became engaged in navigation, and accumulated some money, but during the Napoleonic wars his vessel was captured and his fortune ruined. He married, in Nova Scotia, Sally Potter, whose father was also a native of Boston. Mr. Dyar returned to Massachusetts with his family, and in 1816 emigrated to Ohio. The journey from Boston to Marietta was made with teams, and occupied thirty days. At this time his family consisted of eight children; two more were born after coming to this county. Joseph, the oldest, was born October 1, 1800, in Arcadia (Annapolis Royal), Nova Scotia. His facilities for obtaining an education were very limited, owing to his father's occupation and circumstances. He remained at home six years after coming to Ohio, and assisted his father to acquire a small estate in Muskingum township.

Joseph Dyar made his first business venture at the age of twenty-two. He built a flat-boat and loaded it with a cargo of hoop-poles, staves, and produce, for the Kanawha trade. He pushed his boat to the salt regions, and traded and sold his freight for a cargo of salt, which he floated down to Cincinnati and sold with the boat for two hundred dollars. This was the first money of his own which came into his possession. An episode on the way home shows his energy. The steamer Rufus Putnam, on which he took passage, was wrecked near Maysville, Kentucky, and Mr. Dyar set out on foot, reaching home in good spirits. The same year Mr. Dyar and Thomas Ridgway purchased a keel-boat, and engaged in the Kanawha trade. The second year of their partnership they purchased the Nye farm, in the Muskingum valley. This was the first settled farm in the township. They paid for it one thousand dollars in cash. The Kanawha trade was continued for one year longer, and then Mr. Dyar began flat-boating and trading along the river as far south as New Orleans. He was the first trader in this section who paid cash for goods. This gave him great advantage in buying. For ten years he continued buying produce, and flat-boating. The productions of his own farm by this time amounted to considerable, and added materially to his yearly dividends. One peculiarity of

Mr. Dyar's business operations is deserving of special notice. He never insured either his boats or goods. He always kept a personal supervision over all operations, and depended upon no one but himself to guard against loss. Although he experienced many narrow escapes, and sometimes approached the brink of destruction, he never suffered any material loss.

Since he quit flat-boating Mr. Dyar has been engaged in farming, dealing in real estate, and managing his accumulations. Care and industry are his predominant characteristics. He owes much of his success to his ability to read a line ahead in the chapter of current events.

Mr. Dyar married in February, 1827, Amanda Hall, of Muskingum township. She died June 25, 1837, leaving six children. Augustine, the oldest, was born December 10, 1827; he is married and lives in Muskingum township. Edwin was born February 1, 1829; he died in the south January 29, 1852. Charles C. was born October 22, 1830, died January 24, 1857. Mary was born October 2, 1830; she lives on the homestead. James H. died in youth. Joseph was born February 24, 1836; he lives in Muskingum township. Adelaide was married to General H. F. Devol in 1856, and died at Waterford in 1860.

Mr. Dyar married for his second wife Abigail Proctor, daughter of Nathan Proctor, of Muskingum township, January 24, 1839. Her father emigrated to Ohio, from Massachusetts, at an early period of the setttlement, and after the Indian war, returned and brought to the county his family. They stopped with his brother, Jacob Proctor, in Watertown township, and then removed to Barlow as soon as a cabin could be erected. Mr. Proctor made the first improvement in the township, and Abigail (Mrs. Dyar) was the second child born in the township. She was one of seven children. By his second wife Mr. Dyar had three children, two of whom are living, viz: Amelia E., wife of E. N. Cole, of Harmar, born December 28, 1841; and Harriet A., wife of Miles A. Stacey, born December 26, 1844.

Mr. Dyar can look over his possessions with the comforting consciousness that they are the product of his own labor, care, and business sagacity. He has made it a rule in life to attend strictly and closely to his own business and operated on a cash basis. He earned his start, and has never since ventured beyond his ready capital.

In politics he acted with the Democrats until 1856, since when he has been a Republican. He has never connected himself with any organized society.

JAMES S. STOWE.

Erastus Stowe, father of the subject of this sketch, was born at Cooverstown, New York. While yet a child, one of the celebrated Indian massacres of the Revolution occurred in that valley, and both his parents were murdered by the savage woodsmen. The child was carried away and left in a corn field and there found by Abijah Hubble who adopted him into his family. About 1800, Mr. Stowe, then more than twenty years old, came with the Hubble family to Ohio, and settled in Meigs county. He married in Meigs county, Jane Smith, a daughter of James Smith, who, like many others, sold his property in New England, in the hope of bettering his condition by joining the Ohio emigrants, but also like many others, he received for his property continental money and was in consequence reduced to penury. The family lived at the Marietta garrison during the Indian war and afterwards settled in Meigs county. Mr. Stowe, after he was married, engaged in farming. He died in Meigs county at the age of sixty-five years; his wife died at the age of ninety-three years.

James S. Stowe, whose portrait appears above, was the oldest son of Erastus Stowe, and was born in Meigs county, in 1806. He was a spirited youth and never afraid to undertake anything assigned for him to do. His services were always in demand on the farms in the neighborhood. When a small boy, he made a lonely trip on horseback through the cow-paths in the woods to Athens to mill; at the age of seventeen he was apprenticed to a cabinet-maker, in Gallipolis. He was sadly afflicted with homesickness, which the religious practices of his boss were not calculated to alleviate, and, as he expressed it, "the man fortunately died soon," being stricken with the prevailing epidemic. He returned home and was variously employed in Meigs county until the age of twenty, when he began work for his uncle, Sardine Stone, in Muskingum township. At the end of five years he became impatient and affected an arrangement by which the Stone farm came into his possession.

In 1829, Mr. Stowe began flat-boating—a business which he pursued with great profit for more than thirty years. The first load was fitted out at an expense of five hundred dollars, which was borrowed for the purpose. The load was disposed of at a profit of three hundred dollars. This was the beginning of a long and successful business career. Every planter along the river knew Smith Stowe. He had the reputation of being a sharp but honest dealer. In all his experience he never lost money on a season's trade. But the winter of 1861 was full of danger for flat-boatmen. The opening of rebellion is characterized by a certain enthusiasm which is worn off by the fatigue of military movements. Mr. Stowe, although well acquainted, did not escape the general threat against Ohio men and abolitionists. At Lake Providence an incident occurred which shows the spirit of the times in the south and also Mr. Stowe's sagacity. The boat was tied up at the shore and he had been doing considerable trading when the news came of the secession of South Carolina. The community was thrown into a whirlwind of excitement, and flat-boatmen notified that it was unsafe for them to remain. Mr. Stowe fastened a line to the bottom of his boat, where it could not be seen. That night the main line was cut, and when he appeared on the roof a shot was fired. The next morning a deputation waited on him and warned him against remaining, declaring that "no Lincoln abolitionists could land at their shores." He was given till four o'clock to leave. This is one of many similar incidents which shows the feeling at the south during the formation of

MRS. JAMES S. STOWE.

JAMES S. STOWE.

the confederacy. One fact is worthy of mention in connection with the subject of this sketch in regard to the use of fire-arms. He has been down the Mississippi and up Red river and in the most dangerous parts of the south at the most dangerous times, and yet has never owned a revolver or carried a firearm. Mr. Stowe, in connection with the produce trade, carried on farming and milling. He always kept things moving, employed hands and paid them and in that way has been a useful man in his community. His first possession was the Stone farm, but since then he has invested as much as ninety thousand dollars in land lying in the fine bottom within the bow of the Muskingum, just above Devol's dam, and forty thousand dollars in farms in the Rainbow bottom. He has made his money by industrious, hard work and sharp dealing. He attributes a large measure of his success to punctuality, whether working by the day in his boyhood, or in business transactions throughout life.

Mr. Stowe was married in 1830, to Anne Meriam of Lowell, by whom he had six children; four of whom are now living: Sardine, Nancy (Marshall), Diantha (Devol), and Seldon. Mrs. Stowe died in 1842. In 1843 he married for his second wife, Mrs. Eliza Ferrin, daughter of Freeman Davis, and widow of Davis Ferrin. She had by her first husband one son, Liman Ferrin, who was killed in the war. By Mr. Stowe she had five children, viz.: Charles, died in 1866; Lucy (Drake), Dudley, J. Smith, and Pitt. All the children live on farms within the sound of the dinner-bell at their parents' house, except J. Smith, who is in business at Marietta.

CHAPTER XLV.

WATERTOWN TOWNSHIP.

Geography and Survey—Donation Lands—Surface Features—Establishment and Change of Boundaries—Change of Name—The First Settlement—Wolf Creek Mills—The Pioneers—Millsburgh—First Sermon—Millsburgh Evacuated—New Mill Built—The Watertown Settlement—Sherman Waterman Killed by Indians—West Branch Settlers—Other Settlers—Review of Settlement—Educational History—Character of Early Traders—Wolf Creek Mills Rebuilt—South Branch Mills—Watertown Mill—An Indian Incident—A Church Scene—The Nine Cemeteries—Watertown Village—Church-town Post Office—Manufacturing—Physicians—Watertown Grange—Churches—Methodist, Presbyterian, Universalist, Lutheran, Catholic, United Brethren.

WATERTOWN in extent of territory is the largest township in Washington county. From the southeastern corner to the northwestern is a distance of twelve miles, and forty-two and one-half miles of area lie within its boundaries. About one-third of this area was originally Ohio company land, and was laid out in one hundred and sixty acre lots; the remaining two-thirds was a part of the donation tracts set apart by the Ohio company for the encouragement of settlement. Rainbow allotment, South Branch allotment, North Branch allotment, are included in this township. A part of Between Rainbow and Waterford allotment, and Wolf Creek and Waterford allotments are also included.

DRAINAGE.

Watertown is chiefly drained by Wolf creek, the two branches of which unite in the northern part. The east branch, which rises in Warren township, takes almost a direct northward course in Watertown. The hills along its valley are not as abrupt as those in most other parts of the county. Back from the creek valley the surface is comparatively level except along the tributaries, where the hills reaching to the plain are steep, but not abrupt. The west branch flows into Watertown from Morgan county, and joins the east branch near the Waterford line. This stream flows alternately between regular and picturesque hills and through beautiful valleys, which spread out into fertile bottoms. The part of the township drained by the west branch is the most hilly and broken. Rainbow creek carries off the waters of the northeastern part of the township.

THE SOIL.

This township is generally finely situated for agricultural purposes, but the soil is not as fertile as that in some other portions of the county. The rock strata, by the disintegration of which soil is mostly formed, is shale and sandstone with very little limestone. The heavy stratum of limestone in the bed of the west branch of Wolf creek does not crop out anywhere on the hills, and can only be made available by artificial methods. A seam of slaty coal appears near the village of Watertown.

GEOGRAPHY.

At the date of its establishment, June 4, 1806, Watertown, then Wooster, included only the fourth township of the tenth range. The commissioners at a subsequent meeting set off of Waterford and attached to Wooster, that part of the town of Waterford lying in the third township of the tenth range, and the seventh township of the eleventh range, and so much of the eighth township of the eleventh range as lies south of the west branch of Wolf creek.

At the September session of the commissioners, 1813, six sections, thirty-one to thirty-six, of Union, were set off and annexed to Wooster. The name of the township was changed from Wooster to Watertown, December 6, 1824, the object being to avoid the annoyance of having two Woosters in the same State, there being a town and township bearing that name in Wayne county. The name "Watertown" was selected in honor of the Waterman family, one of whose members lost his life in the early settlement.

Watertown received an important addition of territory in 1877 when Union township was partitioned. Union township when originally established in 1812 included the whole of township three, range nine, and sections thirty-one, thirty-two, thirty-three, thirty-four, thirty-five and thirty-six, of township three, range nine. This tract had previously been a part of Marietta and Adams. Watertown as it existed before 1813 had originally been a part of Waterford.

The territory of Union had grown smaller by annexations to Watertown, Adams, and Muskingum, and finally the town, December, 1877, lost its identity entirely. The part bounded by a line beginning at the southwest corner of section twenty-six, and running due east to the southwest corner of section eight, then north to the south line of "Wiseman's bottom allotment," then west to the southwest corner of Wiseman's bottom, then north to the southeast corner of lot number five, in Rainbow Creek allotment, then west to the southwest corner of lot number ten, in same allotment, then north to the northeast corner of lot number sixteen, then west to the line of Watertown township, then south to the place of beginning, was annexed to Watertown township. The territory constituting Watertown was originally embraced in Marietta and Waterford. Legal divisions generally became smaller as the population grows more dense, out every change of boundaries but one (when Palmer was established) has resulted in the enlargement of this territory.

THE SETTLEMENT.

On the bottom bordering the north bank of the west branch of Wolf creek, near the forks, was made the first settlement in the township. Here is also the site of the first mill in Ohio, known as Wolf Creek mills. In the spring of 1789 a company, composed of Colonel Robert Oliver, Captain John Dodge, and Major Haffield White, made a small clearing, erected three log cabins, and began operations for the erection of a mill, which was of great utility to the early settlers.

The place is interesting, both to the historian and the artist. The stream goes over a rapids of several feet fall, and spreads itself out to the width of one hundred feet, over a bed of solid limestone, from which protrudes irregular masses of rock. From the southern bank there rises a high hill clothed with cedars, pines, and heavy trees. On the other side, a beautiful plain extends from the rocky shore to the base of a picturesque range of hills in the distance. This plain became the residence of three of Washington county's most worthy pioneers: Major White, Colonel Oliver, and Captain Dodge. The construction of a dam and mill required much labor, and workmen were industriously occupied until the following March before the mills were put in operation. The building was made of round logs, and stood on the bank of the stream, just at the foot of the rapids. The crank for the saw-mill was made at New Haven, Connecticut, and is said to have been brought to Symrill's ferry on a pack-horse. The millstones were made of a conglommerate rock, procured at Laurell hill, near Brownsville. One of these stones is preserved as a relic by Mrs. Patterson Dodge, of Beverly. This enterprise proved of great benefit to the whole settlement. The stones were not of proper texture for grinding wheat, but corn, which was the staple product for the first few years, could be ground when the water was high, at the rate of a bushel in four minutes. A large portion of the meal, both for the Marietta and Waterford settlements, was ground at this mill. It was accessible by water during freshets, and flatboats of considerable size brought grain

from Waterford and carried meal back to the settlements at Marietta and Belpre.

It was ordered by the Ohio company that a block-house should be built at this settlement, known as Millsburgh, before July 20, 1789, but no danger was apprehended, and the workmen, being busily engaged in the construction of the mill, no provision was made for a place of safety in time of danger.

The mill company seemed devoted to but one object. The clearing was very limited, and no attempt was made at cultivating the extensive bottom which spreads its fertile acres toward the north and west. The names of the laborers employed at Millsburgh are not known. The first religious service held in the Muskingum settlements was at this station, in July, 1789, by the Rev. Daniel Story, who was then in the employ of the Ohio company. There was no house large enough for the meeting, which was attended by many of the Plainfield residents. The congregation assembled in the open air, under a beech tree.

Operations at Millsburgh were undisturbed until January, 1791, when the massacre at Big Bottom made the settlers conscious of their danger. A council was held with the Waterford settlers, and the erection of a garrison decided upon. At this time the colony at the mills numbered about thirty souls, all of whom gathered in the cabin of Colonel Oliver when the fate of the Big Bottom colony, and the danger of the other settlements was made known. This and other events relating to the Indian war are fully treated in a general chapter on that subject, and to narrate them here would be mere repetition of what has already been given.

The leading families went into the garrison at Marietta, the other members of the colony moved to the garrison at Waterford, and from there with the greatest caution operated the mills, which were cunningly left unmolested by the Indians during the whole period of the war.

It required fifteen or twenty men to grind a load of corn during this period. It was necessary for sentries to guard the boat, and then when the grist was grinding guards were posted on all sides to protect the millers from a sudden attack, which might be expected any moment, as the mill was probably left standing for the purpose of decoying the whites.

At the close of the war, in 1795, the proprietors reoccupied their cabins and repaired the mill, which, in a short time, was found to be too small for the accommodation of the rapidly growing settlement, and a new frame mill was built just about the former site.

The settlement, reenforced from the east, now began in earnest the work of clearing and cultivating the land.

In the spring of 1795 the second colony, composed of five young men—William Ford, William Hart, Jacob Proctor, John Waterman and Sherman Waterman—was formed for the purpose of clearing their lands in company. A block-house was built about three miles from the township line, on the south branch of Wolf creek. Although little danger was apprehended at this time, it was thought prudent to remain together, and day by day they alternately worked on each other's farms. The spring passed away quietly and peacefully until the twentieth of May, when one of this brave and hardy band fell a victim of the red man's cunning. During the fore part of the day frequent showers had driven them from their accustomed work in the clearing to the garden near the house. Sherman Waterman went across the creek, a few yards distant, to procure some bark to repair the bottom of his bed, and while he was engaged at this work the men in the garden heard the report of a gun, and stepped to a port-hole in the enclosure. Waterman was running towards the house calling for help, while the enemy continued to fire at him from an ambush a short distance away. Waterman fell exhausted in the creek. William Hart rushed out and brought him to the house. Hart carried the news of the disaster to Waterford, whence a party of men came and took the body of the wounded man to the residence of Dean Tyler, where he died the following day. He had been shot in the region of the liver. On examination, it was found that the Indians had encamped near a log on which the settlers had been in the habit of crossing a narrow ravine as they went to and came from their work. Near the end of this log was found a blanket and some silver brooches, left as a decoy. It had doubtless been the plan of the Indians to charge upon the settlers while examining these articles, and had it not been for the fact that the day was rainy and disagreeable, the scheme might have succeeded, a result which would have materially affected the character of the settlement of the township.

A few years after this tragedy an unknown Indian, while in a state of intoxication, told a man named McFarlan, who lived in the eastern part of the township, the story of the murder of Waterman, and said they knew they had killed him, for they saw blood in the water down the creek. Waterman is buried in the Waterford cemetery. A stone bearing the following inscription marks his grave:

Memento Mori—1795.
SHERMAN WATERMAN,
Who was wounded by the savages, being shot through the body twenty-first, and died the twenty-second of May, 1795, aged twenty-five years.

As soon as permanent peace had been established with the Indians, the donation lands in the north part of the township were rapidly cleared and reduced to a state of cultivation. The south and southeast part of the territory remained a wilderness when the stumps of the northern sections were fast disappearing.

The valley of the west branch of Wolf creek above the mills was occupied about 1797 by an English settlement. The pioneer of this colony was Samuel Mellor, who settled on the farm in the bend of the creek now owned by his son, John Mellor. A few years later brought to the bottom, on the opposite side of the creek, Matthew Corner and John Bacon, and the elliptical bottom further down was occupied by James Quigley, whose name it still retains.

Peter Taylor, who was brought from England by Blennerhassett and employed by him as gardener, after the ruin of his patron's estate became a resident of this valley; also 'Cajoe Phillips, a colored servant of Blennerhassett.

William Ford, shortly after the close of Indian hostilities, was joined by his brother Giles, accompanied by his wife and son, Giles Harry. Giles died soon after their settlement, and William became the husband of his widow, by whom he had a large family. Joseph, Ansel and Ammon settled in this township, and had families; Lucien, Romanta B. and Isaiah N. studied for the Presbyterian ministry. Romanta died before he had completed his studies. Lucien died in early manhood in Cincinnati; Isaiah at Jackson, Ohio.

Ansel B. Ford was born in Licking county in 1805. In 1833 he married Lucy Deming, who was born in this township in 1809. He served for a number of years as justice of the peace, and after a useful life died in 1879, leaving four children—Sarah L., Mira M., Eliza J., and Charlotte G.

Ammon Ford was born September 9, 1807, in this township. November 27, 1827, he was married to Hannah Parke, who was born in New York, September 15, 1809. They had seven children—John, Seth, Sarah, Lucy and Laura (twins), Judah, and William—of whom three—John, Sarah and Judah—are dead. Seth, the second child, was born in Barlow township, September 12, 1830. In 1852 he went to California, where he remained until 1863, since which time he has been a resident of Watertown. December 20, 1863, he married Margaret Ross, who was born in Perry county, May 1, 1840. They have three children living—Frank, Hattie and Fred—and one dead, Mary.

Juda Ford emigrated with his father from Connecticut in 1795, and was a resident of the township to the time of his death, which occurred September 24, 1851. He married Betsy Deming, who was born in Massachusetts, June 17, 1791, by whom he had seven children. Daniel, the sixth child, was born on the farm, where he now lies October 30, 1820. February 23, 1854, he married Louisa Morris, who was born March 15, 1829. Their family consists of three children—Charles, Myron and Edward.

John Waterman, a brother of Sherman, and one of the associates of the block-house company, settled on Wolf creek, in the neighborhood of the old block-house. He came to an untimely death at the hand of his son, who was insane.

Ferrand Waterman came to the township in 1796. He emigrated from Connecticut with his brothers, John and Sherman, but remained in Marietta one year before making a permanent settlement.

Dougle Walker was probably the first Scotch emigrant to this township. He left his native Highlands and settled in the northwestern part of the township before 1800. He died in 1821, leaving a large family.

Jacob Proctor, who has already been mentioned, married Betsy Wells, and lived in the centre of the township. His brother, Nathan, came from Danvers, Massachusetts, with the Deming family in 1797. He afterwards removed to Barlow township.

Benjamin Hart came from Berlin, Connecticut, during the early settlement of the township. He married Honor Deming, by whom he had seven children—Austin died in Michigan; Columbus lives in Indiana; Dr. Simeon is superintendent of the Children's Home; Dr. Franklin, a practicing physician in Marietta; Mary Ann (Hayward), and Lucy Payne. After the death of his wife in 1825 he married Mrs. Ester Minor. Henry C., who lives near Marrietta, is one of the children by this wife. He was married a third time to Mrs. Lawrence, widow of Rufus Lawrence.

Sila Hart lived with a large family on an adjoining farm. He left the township at an early date.

Pelig Springer cleared a farm on the south branch of Wolf creek, near the forks. He had four sons. Joseph, the oldest, was a school teacher; Clark, the second son, married a daughter of Elijah Wilson, who came to the township in 1797, and was employed in Wolf Creek mills.

Among the early pioneers of Washington county was John McNeal, sr. He was of Scotch parentage, born about the year 1743. When fourteen years of age he was taken prisoner by the Indians in Pennsylvania and remained in captivity for seven years. During his captivity he and another white boy accompanied three Indian chiefs as servants from Pennsylvania to the headwaters of the Missouri, as he called the country which is now Dakota or Montana. They visited on their journey the principal Indian tribes and consulted their chiefs. He did not know positively the object of the visit, but supposed it was to unite the various tribes in a general war against the whites. If such was the case it did not succeed. The journey both ways consumed three years. When the treaty of November, 1764, was concluded, he was set at liberty. He made his way back to Pennsylvania, where he found one sister still living. He subsequently married Anna Howell who was a native of New Jersey, born in 1760, and some time prior to the summer of 1791 removed to Morgantown, Virginia. In the spring of 1796 he decided to remove to the Northwest Territory and floated down the Monongahela and Ohio rivers to Marietta, arriving in the latter part of April. He drew his donation lot (No. 28) between Rainbow and Waterford. He first settled on Duck creek, near what is now Stanleyville, where he lived until the spring of 1799 when he moved to his claim where he resided until his death, which occurred probably in the fall of 1819. His wife survived him many years, dying in 1846. Their children, who grew to mature years, were James, Elizabeth, John, Susan and Margaret (twins), William, Andrew, Levi and David. Of these Anna is still living and is the only survivor of the family. William, whose whole life was spent in Washington county was born March 25, 1799, during the residence of his parents near Stanleyville. He possessed much energy of character, and bore the name of an honest, upright man. He was trustee of his township for many years and was school director for upwards of forty years. He died April 9, 1879. His wife, Matilda Bellows, daughter of the late Elias Bellows, sr., of Little Hocking, Belpre township, was born November 21, 1809, died July 13, 1875. They were married in March, 1828, and had a large family. Those who grew to adult age

were the following: Andrew, Ira, Cromwell, Diana, Elias, Franklin, Thomas, Ason and Margaret. Andrew is a surveyor and resides in Cedar county, Nebraska; Ira died in Illinois in 1852; Cromwell was a physician, entered the army in the fall of 1861 from Illinois, and died at Paducah, Kentucky, while in charge of a floating hospital, June, 1862; Diana (Mrs. Wilson) resides in California; Elias lives in Missouri; Franklin resides in Watertown, on the old homestead and owns half of the old donation lot before mentioned. He was deputy surveyor of Christian county, Illinois, in 1867, and of Clay county, Kansas, in 1871. He has served one term as justice of the peace of this township. He was born April 8, 1839, married Mary Alexander and had two children. Thomas resides in Kansas, Ason is a resident of this county, as is also Margaret (Stacy).

John Mellor, son of Samuel Mellor, was born in England, August 17, 1793. The family emigrated to America in 1795, and were among the first settlers of this township. Abigail Briggs was married to John Mellor in 1818. She died in 1874, leaving eleven children—six boys and five girls.

William Woodford made the first improvement on the Ohio company lands in 1796. He came from Connecticut, a single man, and became possessor of a large tract, on which the village of Watertown now stands. Some time after his arrival in Ohio, he returned to his old home in Connecticut on foot, and came back to Ohio by the same laborious method of travel. He married Dianna Ford, daughter of William Ford, by whom he had four children, viz: Seth, who married Mecy Deming; Miles, who became a trader on the river; Laura, wife of A. Brooks, the first storekeeper at Watertown, and William G., who was born February 2, 1811. He married September 27, 1832, Sophia Shields, who was born in Virginia June 2, 1811. They had nine children: Laura, Caroline, Hial, William L., Sarah A., James, Giles, Dianna and Miles, only four of whom are still living, viz: Laura, wife of George Buchannan; James, Dianna, wife of Michael Ryan, of Belpre township, and Miles, who resides in Palmer township. William G. Woodford was in merchantile business in Watertown for several years. He was also engaged in milling.

Simon Starlin, with his wife and three sons, emigrated from Connecticut about the close of the Indian war, and moved upon donation lots they had drawn in Rainbow allotment, but after a short period the family constantly haunted by the presence of the Indians, determined to wait for more congenial times for commencing pioneer life. They all removed to Vienna, Virginia, except Marvel, the oldest son, who went to Marietta. In 1798 Marvel made an improvement on his lot in the northeast part of the township, and about two years later the other members of the family returned from Virginia, and settled in the same neighborhood.

The fall of 1796 brought to Ohio the first representative of the most numerous and prominent families in the township. A party consisting of Colonel Simeon Deming and family, Horace Wolcot, Ezekiel Deming and Dr. Hart, left Sandusfield, Massachusetts, in November, and

JOHN MALSTER.

One of the first and perhaps the first improvement in the present territory of Palmer township was made by Christopher Malster, who came to Ohio in the summer of 1795, from Lycoming county, Pennsylvania. He was a native of Delaware, and had lived in Pennsylvania about two years. He drew a donation lot and purchased one, and during the first year of his residence in this county cleared and planted a part of his land. He also built a cabin with puncheon floors and doors. While living in Pennsylvania he married Margaret Mahaffy, who remained there until 1797, when taking her son William, then about two years old, on a horse, she joined a party of emigrants and came to her husband's home. They at that time had no neighbors nearer than three or four miles.

John Malster, a son of Christopher Malster, was born in Palmer township September 2, 1800. During his boyhood he labored on his father's farm part of the time and part of the time worked out by the day or month. He made his first trip south on a flat-boat in 1822. During his younger years he suffered the misfortune of losing his health in a manner not highly commendable to a German physician of that period. He had been troubled with rheumatism and laid his case before the quack doctor who prescribed "a dose heavy enough," as Mr. Malster expresses it, "to kill a calf." The prescription was: "Dissolve in a quart of whiskey one ounce of saltpetre and one ounce of gumgnac; take a gill every

morning before breakfast on an empty stomach." Mr. Malster followed the prescription, but has been a sufferer ever since in consequence.

Mr. Malster is one of the few men yet living who in his youth wore buckskin pantaloons. He tells some comical experiences in connection with this article of clothing of a by-gone generation. They were particularly hard to remove after being wet, and the boys at retiring time were compelled to give each other assistance. It was a happy way of keeping a bond of union in the family, for an unbrotherly brother could be easily punished for his offences by help being withheld, leaving him to remain in his trousers all night. It is easy to imagine the effects of putting on buckskin in a cold morning; many of the young men wore nothing else. A pair would last two winters. The common mode of cleaning was to rub them on the grindstone or with a piece of sandstone.

His poor health prevented him from engaging in the severe labor of the farm, and in 1828 he was given the contract for carrying the mail between Marietta and Lancaster for four years, for the sum of three hundred and ten dollars a year. He performed the contract for a year and a half, but his health being poor he sold out and sought relief at the mineral springs at Bedford, Pennsylvania. In 1831 he received treatment at Saratoga springs, New York. In 1834 he opened a store in Palmer township for Colonel Augustus Stone, of Harmar, for whom he did business four years. He afterwards clerked for Colonel Stone, Abijah Brooks, at Harmar, and Chapin & Fearing at Beverly.

In 1841 Mr. Malster purchased a farm in Palmer township and began raising and dealing in cattle. He says, "I could make more money by raising cattle than by cultivating grain, and do it easier." He kept on his farm facilities for weighing, and in consequence was able to make purchases and sales to the best advantage. In 1853 he took one hundred and ten head of cattle over the mountains and sold them in Pennsylvania. He showed his speculative turn on one occasion in Athens county. He purchased, of a man named Dew, eighty fat cattle, and in less than three hours sold them on the premises to a drover from Circleville at a handsome advance. In 1855 he took a trip south for his health, and visited Galveston, Texas, New Orleans, and Memphis, returning in 1856.

Mr. Malster possessed the ability to make money and the habits of life to save it. From the time of first starting out in life for himself, when, as he has entered in a memorandum, he "bought and raised wheat and made twenty-five barrels of flour, which I sold to Colonel A. Stone, in Harmar, for two dollars and fifty cents a barrel, and trusted him six months without interest. I have bought and sold wheat for twenty-eight cents a bushel, and oats for twelve and a half cents and hauled them to Harmar." He has made the following quaint memorandum of his real estate transactions: "I sold the first farm I bought in 1854 for thirteen hundred dollars more than I paid for it. The winter of 1859 I bought a farm of John Palmer; paid four thousand dollars; swapped farms with my brother, Thomas, and got eight hundred dollars 'to boot,' and then sold this farm for six thousand one hundred dollars to John Hague, who got with the farm about fifteen hundred dollars worth of stock, grain, and farming tools." He has dealt largely in real estate and in old age is a heavy tax-payer. He is interesting in conversation and cordial in manner. He never married, and for more than four years he has been living with his nephew, M. A. Malster.

after a few weeks hard travelling reached Symrill's ferry, where the party separated. Ezekiel Deming and Dr. Hart came on to Waterford, where they spent the winter. In February Colonel Deming started the other members of the party and the goods down the river on a flatboat. He then started overland with the stock. They reached their destination near the latter part of the mouth, and sought out the lands they had drawn in the Rainbow allotment of the donation tract. A cabin was erected, where they all lived until the opening of spring, when the work of clearing and planting was commenced. During the following season an epidemic of smallpox spread across the county, and the young men of the neighborhood made the Deming cabin a pest house. Ezekiel Deming, Joseph Wolcott, Asa Beach, William Woodford, Forest Meeker and probably some others, Horace Wolcott and his family, and Colonel Deming's family were all confined within this one cabin, where they were waited upon by a physician from Virginia.

The Demings and Wolcotts formed what was known as the Sandusfield settlement, so named from the place from which they emigrated. Ezekial Deming cleared his land, and planted an orchard. He then returned to Massachusetts, where in September, 1799, he married Hannah Parke. He came back to the settlement the same fall. A family of the children blessed this union, viz: Lucinda (Bingham), Mercy (Woodford), Hiram, J. Harvey, Harley, Mary Ann, John T., R. J. Meigs, David V. and Hannah. Mr. Deming was a Jeffersonian in politics, and served three terms as associate judge.

Colonel Simon Deming's family, at the time of his emigration to Ohio, consisted of his wife, whose maiden name was Lucy Wolcott, and four children—one son and three daughters. Honor, the oldest daughter, was married to Benjamin Hart, Betsy to Juda Ford, and Sally to L. J. Convers. David, the third child was born in Sandusfield, Massachusetts, April 25, 1793. He married, August 27, 1816, Anna Henry, who was born in Washington county, Pennsylvania. They had seven children—Mary W., William H., Horace W., Lucy A., Amanda E., Edwin A., and Martin L.—all dead except Mary W. and William H. William H. was born July 15, 1819. April 6, 1848 he married Matilda J. Hutchinson, who died May 10, 1849. May 29, 1854, he married Ellen E. Burch. She died September 10, 1859. Mr. Deming married Mary B. Parke, daughter of Robert B. Parke, November 6, 1851. She was born June 11, 1826. Mr. Deming's family consists of four children. After coming to Ohio six children were added to the family, of whom Joel of Warren township is the only surviving son, and Mrs. Lucy Ford, of Centre Belpre the only surviving daughter. Colonel Deming was a man of positive character and strong convictions. In politics he was a Federalist, in religion a Presbyterian.

The settlement was increased in 1798 by the arrival of the Wolcotts, the Woodruffs, and other families which have been prominent in the township ever since. Elias Wolcott was a single man when he came to the State, but soon after married Delinda Howe, who bore him a family of eight children—six boys and two girls. Horace, an

older brother, came to Ohio with Colonel Deming the year previous. They both settled in the Sandusfield or eastern settlement. Horace, after a residence in the county of about fourteen years, moved with his family to Granville. Elias H., oldest son of Elias Wolcott, was born June 17, 1803. May 30, 1826, he married Loraina Starlin, a daughter of Marvel Starlin. She was born June 10, 1807. The fruit of this union was thirteen children, viz.: Lucien M., Vesta, Delinda, Orlow, Walter B., Peter H., Adeline H., Roscoe, Rosaltha, Fremont, Orinda, Lydia A., and one died in infancy, seven of whom are still living. Mrs. Wolcott died March 25, 1868. Mr. Wolcott lost his eyesight October 1, 1873. He lives with his son Roscoe, who was born June 17, 1842. He was married June 17, 1868, to Emma Bridge, of Waterford township, who was born November 19, 1846. Their family consists of two children—Anna L. and Brooks. Mr. Wolcott, when a young man, was a teacher of vocal music.

Abner Woodruff emigrated from New Jersey with his family and first settled in the "Sundusfield" neighborhood, but soon moved to the south part of the township, in the valley of Wolf creek, where he made the first improvement about 1800. He was born in 1766, in New Jersey, where he married Catharine Roll. He died in Barlow township in 1836. His wife survived him two years. They had six children: Abner, Isaac, Polly, Elias, Nancy, and Hannah. Abner was born in Watertown in 1801. He married Miss Pilcher in 1838, by whom he had two children—Emily and Amanda, the latter of whom survives. Mr. Woodruff resides in Belpre. Elias, the fourth child of Abner Woodruff, settled in the south part of the township. He married Hannah McGuire, by whom he had eight children, viz: Jacob R., Sarah A., Oren J., Emeline, Henry C., Betsy J., Hannah C., and Eunice, four of whom are still living. Sarah was married first to Ragita Kalvini, and after his death to Weir Browning, who was born in England. The fruit of this marriage, which occurred in November, 1853, was two children—Francis M., and Victor. She had by her first husband two children—Thea and Adelpha. Emeline, the fourth child of Elias Woodruff, was born January 27, 1826. She was married first to Columbus D. Barkley; after his death to William Brown, January 4, 1878. By her first husband she had eight children: Cecil, Eugene H., Earnest, Minerva M., Eva V., Mary C., Arthur D., and one who died in infancy.

Jason Humiston settled in this township about 1798. He was born in 1768, at Wellington, Connecticut, from which State he emigrated to Ohio in 1796, and remained for a period at Marietta, and then, with his wife and family, moved to Watertown. Mr. Humiston's first wife, whose maiden name was Anna Peck, died in 1809, in her thirty-eighth year. There were six children, four of whom are living: Lyndes, in Adams township; Sally (Chandler), in Minnesota; Julania (Chandler), in Brooklyn, New York; Lavinia McClure, in Dunham township. By his second wife, Margaret McNeal, Mr. Humiston had six children. Lines lived for a time in the north part of the township, then moved to Illinois; Henry lives in Chicago. Lyedes, son of Jason Humiston, was born

79

in this county in 1797, and was eighteen months old when his father removed to Watertown. April 6, 1820, he married Betsy Starlin, and two years later he removed to Adams township. Their family consisted of seven children, four of whom survive, viz: Hiram, Eliza, Sally, and Miles. The youngest son, Miles, was born November 28, 1840. He married September 6, 1866, Emeline Beebe, daughter of George W. Beebe, of Watertown township, born October 24, 1847. They have one child—David M.

John Laflin, a native of Vermont, emigrated to Ohio in 1800, and after remaining in Adams township one year settled in this township, where he remained until the time of his death, in December, 1852. He married Abigail Richards, by whom he had four children: Kyman, Harley, Huldah, and Tuman R. Harley and Tuman are the only members of the family yet living. Tuman, the youngest child, was born November 11, 1818. He married Susan E. Leely, who was born in West Chester county, New York, August 10, 1826. Her father, William G. Leely came to Waterford in 1839, and remained there two years, when he settted in Watertown. Susan E. was born August 10, 1826, and married August 12, 1849. She gave birth to four children, viz: Flora E., Albretta M., James H., and Lorin, who died May 30, 1862. Mrs. Laflin is a member of the Universalist church. Mr. Laflin has served his township as trustee four terms.

Abijah Beebe permanently settled in Watertown in 1810. He emigrated with his family from Connecticut and remained in Marietta township about ten years before coming to this township. He died in 1853, after having had a family of twelve children. Thomas, the third child, was born June 19, 1804. He married, March 10, 1840, Kate Skipton, who was born in Cumberland county, Pennsylvania, April 27, 1809. Eleven children blessed this union: Mary A., wife of Conrad Bohl; George W., died December 14, 1852; Harriet, wife of William Myers; Jeremiah, married Martha Myers; Richard, married Christina Brabham; Franklin, married Ella Coaler; Sarah, married Joseph Newton; Joliana, married Jacob Stuber; Maria D., died October 4, 1852; Saddie, married James R. Powers; Prentiss, married Margaret Baker, died October 15, 1878. All the children living reside in Watertown.

John Johnson emigrated from Pennsylvania and settled in this township in the summer of 1817. In 1814 he married Mary Wilson; she died December 15, 1872, leaving one son, Isaac, who was born in Chemung county, New York, November 5, 1816 December 5, 1838, he married Laura A. Stanton, who was born in Connecticut, June 16, 1815. They have had six children, viz: Willis H., Winchester B., Josephine, Wealthy V., Mary I., Sarah L., and Emma J.; all living except Winchester B. Mrs. Johnson died February 14, 1862. Mr. Johnson has been assessor of Watertown township since 1862.

Seth Humphrey emigrated from Connecticut to Ohio and settled on Wolf creek, near the centre of the township, in 1817, where he died in 1837. He was the father of five children, four boys and one girl. Joseph L., the oldest child, was born in Litchfield, Connecticut, September 12, 1805, He came to this township with his father's family, and October 17, 1842, married Elmira Muchler. Their family consisted of three children: Laura A., Elisha O., and Edward M. Elisha O. married Elmira Jennings, Edward M. married Jelpha Skipton, both reside in Watertown township.

Joseph Arnold, a native of Rhode Island, emigrated to Ohio with his father, and settled in Watertown township in 1817. He was married in Rhode Island about 1803 to Mary Steer, by whom he had seven children, five boys and two girls. Mr. Arnold died August 21, 1868. Benjamin W., the sixth child, was born December 4, 1814, being three years old when his father came to Ohio. He was married October 7, 1846 to Sarah Parke, the fruit of this marriage was six children—Joseph P., Alice C., William C., Eunice, Myra, and Mary; Eunice and Myra are dead. Mrs. Arnold died June 8, 1862. December 2, 1862, Mr. Arnold married Mrs. Rosanna Jennings, widow of Daniel Jennings, and daughter of Peter Stotlar. She was born in Washington county, October 23, 1828. Mrs. Arnold had three children by her first husband—Mary J., Almira and Henry, all living. Mr. Arnold is a member of the Presbyterian church, Mrs. Arnold of the Methodist church.

Levi Brewster settled in Watertown township in 1818. He was born in Norwich, Connecticut, in 1789, and came to Ohio from New York state. In 1820 he married Lydia Waterman, who was born in New York in 1792, and died in 1864. They had two children, Richard and Sherman. Mr. Brewster died in Union county, Ohio, in 1873. Richard, born in 1820, married Annie Bachelor, by whom he had three children. His first wife died in 1859, and in 1861 he married Sarah E. Knowles, by whom he has had three children, He is a large land owner and resides in Belpre township.

Deacon Dennis Adams was born in Whitehall, New York, in 1792. In 1809 he removed with his father's family to Pennsylvania, and in 1813 to this county. He remained here about a year, then returned to Pennsylvania and married Miss Jane Patterson. In 1818 he returned to this county with his family, and settled in Watertown township, where he lived until 1837, when he sold his property and moved to Marietta. Here he spent the remainder of his life, his death occurring in April, 1873, in his eighty-first year. His wife died in 1851, in her forty-second year. They had a family of two sons and three daughters, all of whom are deceased, except one son, D. P. Adams, a machinist of Marietta.

William Quinby, third child of Daniel and Martha Quinby was born in New York, November 20, 1822. He emigrated to Ohio with his father, and remained in Marietta township one year, after which he settled in Watertown, April 16, 1846; he married Finatta Parke, by whom he had six children, viz: William W., Lewis C., Martha E., Lucy E., Harley P. William W., Martha E., and Lucy E. are still living. Mrs. Quinby died November 18, 1870. Mr. Quinby was married subsequently to Mrs. Martha Jones, widow of George Jones and daughter of John Meloney, who was born July 17, 1834.

They were married August 20, 1879. Mrs. Quinby had by her first husband six children, but one of whom is living—Samuel, William W. Quinby married Philipena Steeber; Martha married Frank Clinger. Both are residents of Watertown.

John Morris settled in this township in 1829. He was born in Loudoun county, Virginia, January 17, 1797. He first emigrated to Belmont county, Ohio, where he remained until he permanently settled in Watertown. He was married November 22, 1827, to Delilah Biggins, daughter of John Biggins of this township. She was born January 22, 1805. The fruit of this union was eight children, viz: William, Minerva, John, Nancy, Temer, Elwood, Eliza and Harvey, four of whom are still living—John, Nancy, Temer, and Harvey.

Prominent among the Scotch emigrants to this county, is Edward Breckenridge, who was born in Argylshire, June 25, 1803. He emigrated to America and settled in Watertown township in the fall of 1830. He married in February, 1832, Jane Fleming, who was born in Argylshire April 23, 1806. They have have had nine children, viz: Andrew, John, William, Edward, James F., Agnes, Jane C., Mary, and Elizabeth, of whom six are living—Andrew, William, Edward, Agnes, Jane C., and Mary. Mrs. Breckenridge died December 16, 1865. Edward, jr., is married to Nancy Greenlees. William, the third child of Edward Breckenridge, sr., was born March 24, 1835. He was married April 20, 1866, to Ermina L. Deming, daughter of Daniel and Lois Deming, born March 30, 1840. Their family consists of three children—Daniel D., James E., and William K. Mr. Breckenridge will be remembered as one of the old schoolteachers of the township, having taught fifteen winters. Mrs. Breckenridge was also an experienced teacher, having taught from the time she was fourteen until she was married, in 1866.

Conrad Bohl was one of the earliest of the German emigrants to this township. He came to America in July, 1834, and settled in the eastern part of the township, and lived there until his death, which occurred June 6, 1873. He was married to Margaret Smith in 1813, by whom he had six children, viz: Elizabeth, Nicholas, Barbara, Philip, Conrad, and John. The last named was born in Bavaria, October 21, 1828. He married April 15, 1851, Mrs. Elizabeth Manche, widow of Michael Manche, and daughter of Nicholas Willis. The fruit of this marriage was four children—Mary, Elizabeth, Jacob, and John. Mary, wife of Dr. Lintner, resides in Kansas; Elizabeth, wife of Dr. J. A. Reynolds, resides in Minnesota. Conrad, jr., fifth son of Conrad Bohl, was born in Bavaria March 4, 1826. He came to America with his father in 1834, and has been in mercantile business in Watertown village since 1861. He was married August 27, 1847, to Mary A. Beebe, daughter of Thomas Beebe. She was born January 30, 1830, in Watertown. They have had seven children, viz: William H., George B., Lewis W., Emily, Edward B., Benjamin W., and Ernest L., all living except Emily, who died in November, 1873. Mr. Bohl was postmaster from 1861 till 1873.

Levi A. Newbanks, third child of Archibald Newbanks, is one of the substantial farmers of this township. He was born April 27, 1834, and has been a resident of the township all his life, except about five years which were spent in Grant county, Wisconsin. He was married February 6, 1854, to Caroline Walbridge, daughter of Ira and Cynthia Walbridge, who was born in Palmer township, February 18, 1835. The fruit of this union was three children—Joseph J., George A., and Elza. Mr. and Mrs. Newbanks are both members of the Presbyterian church.

Otis Nixon, a native of Massachusetts, emigrated to Ohio and settled in Gallia county in 1818. In 1825 he removed to New York, where he lived till 1832, when he came to Washington county and settled in Waterford township. In 1834 he removed to Watertown, where he died March 11, 1877. His family consisted of five boys and four girls. George H. Nixon was born in Herkimer county, New York, April 7, 1828. He came to Watertown township with his father, Otis Nixon, and married October 28, 1851, Adaline Smith, who was born in Fairfield township, August 22, 1831. They have seven children—Charles T., Mary E., Emma C., George D., William W., and two that died in infancy. Mary E., Emma C., and George D. are also dead. William W. is still at home. Charles T. married Miss Dena Benning, and resides in this township. Albert Nixon, fifth child of Otis Nixon was born in New York February 9, 1830. He came with his father's family to Ohio, and February 12, 1856, married Eleanor Morris, who was born in Tuscarawas county, Ohio, May 28, 1833. Three children blessed this union—Frederick L., Francis M., and Mary L. Frederick L. is dead. Mr. Nixon is a carpenter, and works at that trade; he is also engaged in farming.

Philip Schilling settled in Washington county in 1837. His son, John, was born in 1838, and married Elizabeth Snyder, who was born in 1844. In 1865 John Schilling settled in the territory in Union township now included in Watertown. Mr. and Mrs. Schilling have one child—William. Mr. Schilling enlisted in 1861 in company F, Ohio volunteer infantry, and was a faithful soldier. He has a fine farm of one hundred acres of land. At one time he was township treasurer, holding that office seven years.

James McDermott, one of the earlier settlers of Washington county, became a resident of Union township in 1840, in that part of the township now embraced in Waterertown township. He is still living. He married Margaret Dyar, by whom he has four children, viz: Philip, Ella, Jane, and Thomas; the latter was born in 1845. He owns a farm of eighty acres which he has reclaimed from the native forest. He and his family are faithful members of the Roman Catholic church.

About 1847 Jeffrey Buchannan became a resident of this township. He emigrated from New York to Ohio in 1813 and settled in Marietta, where he remained about eight years. He removed to Athens county where he lived five years and then moved to Morgan county and remained there twenty-one years. He died in this township July 12, 1876. His wife, whose maiden name was Rachel Prouty, survived him three years. Their descendants are nine children, forty-six grandchildren, and seventeen great-grandchildren. Mr. Buchannan's private life was highly commendable. Walter, the second child, was born in Muskingum township December 15, 1821. He married Mary A. Malster, who was born in Palmer township August 29, 1832. They were married November 5, 1850. Their family consists of five children, viz: Sarah A., Vesta A., Delia A., Emma D., and John M. Sarah A is married to Clarence C. Smith, who resides in Wesley township. Vesta A. is the wife of James Wells and resides in West Virginia.

David Henry, fourth child of David Henry, sr., was born in Watertown township April 30, 1849. He has been a resident of the township all his life, except about one year during which he lived in Palmer township. He was married December 23, 1869, to Susan, daughter of Thomas G. Graham. The fruit of this marriage was one child—Susan. Mr. Henry was married the second time April 3, 1873, to Mrs. Emily Woodford, widow of William L. Woodford and daughter of Harley L. Deming. She was born October 14, 1838. They have had three children—David, Emily, and Florence, who is dead. Mrs. Henry is a member of the Universalist church.

Bilgad Curtis, with his wife and family, emigrated from Massachusetts to Athens county, Ohio, in 1826, and remained there until 1850 when they became residents of this township. Mr. Curtis died July 11, 1866, at the age of ninety years and eight months. He had eight children, six boys and two girls. Lois, the fifth child, was born October 26, 1813. She was married to Daniel Deming April 20, 1834, by whom she had six children. She was again married in 1874 to William Powers, of Waterford township.

Edward H. Corner, son of George Corner, one of the oldest settlers of Morgan county, was born April 14, 1814. He settled in Watertown township with his family in 1852, and has since been one of the prominent occupants of the valley of the west branch of Wolf creek. He married, December 6, 1843, Hannah Thornton, daughter of Henry Thornton. She was born in Wood county, West Virginia, in 1820. This union was blessed with fourteen children, seven boys and seven girls, only seven of whom are living, viz: Isabella, William, Willard, John, Jane, Matthew, and Nancy.

Joseph Wynn was born in Dauphin county, Pennsylvania. In 1814 he married Sarah Yocum, of Lebanon county, Pennsylvania. He emigrated to Ohio with his family in 1853, and settled in Watertown township, where he lived till the time of his death which occurred in 1874. His family consisted of eleven children, seven boys and four girls. Joseph D., the seventh child, December 8, 1864, married Mary A. Anderson, who was born in Pennsylvania, May 2, 1840. They had ten children, eight boys and two girls, all of whom are living except one girl. By trade Mr. Wynn is a blacksmith. He also cultivates a good farm.

Henry Jorres was born in Prussia, Germany, July 31, 1818; emigrated to America and settled in Pittsburgh in 1848. He remained there about eighteen months, when he came to this county and settled in Watertown township. He was married, in the month of September, 1845, to Anna T. Struif, a native of Germany. He is by trade a moulder, and has worked at the trade some thirty years.

John Layner, a native of Ireland, emigrated from New Jersey in 1854, and settled on lot three hundred and ninety—then in that part of Watertown township formerly in Union. In 1873 he removed to Kansas. He had five children by his first wife, and seven by his second wife, Margaret Lightfritz. Austen, of the second family, was born in 1851, and married Sarah Hagerman, born in 1855. They have one child. Mr. Layner has a farm of forty acres.

Burr W. Power, fourth child of Robert and Amanda Burr was born in Loudoun county, Virginia, December 26, 1836. He came to Ohio and remained for a short time in the territory formerly included in Union township. In the spring of 1863 he became a resident of Watertown. He married, March 27, 1862, Mary T. Sullivan, who was born in Virginia, April 29, 1841. Ten children blessed this union, viz: Estella G., Hattie P., Joseph and Mary (twins), Edith B., Charles G., Lillie F., Elliander M., John L., and Anna B., all living except Joseph and Mary. Mr. and Mrs. Power both are members of the Baptist church. Mr. Power is a minister of that denomination.

Frank Henker, one of the most prominent of the German settlers of this township, was born in Germany, March 24, 1838. He emigrated to America and settled in Watertown in 1867. He married, February 25, 1868, Christina Rowe. She died March 19, 1871. He was married again August 3, 1871, to Cila Straller, who was born in Germany March 19, 1852. The fruit of this union was five children: Frank, Henry, Katie, Jessie, and Mary, all at home. Mr. and Mrs. Henker are both members of the Catholic church.

Matthew Jurden was born in Aix-la-Chapelle, Prussia. He afterwards emigrated to Pennsylvania, whence in 1865 he came to Ohio, and settled in this county, in that part of Union township now embraced in Watertown. He was elected township clerk in 1869, served for six years as justice of the peace, and since 1875 has been postmaster at Churchtown. His wife, Catharine De Temple, was born in France in 1832. To them have been born eleven children, all of whom are living. Mr. Jurden has a beautiful upland farm of two hundred acres of land, most of which he cleared by his own labor. He is also proprietor of an extensive vineyard.

In 1869 William Sharp, born in Belmont county, Ohio, March 10, 1815, moved with his family to Washington county, and settled in Watertown township, April 1, 1846. Mr. Sharp married Martha McPherson, daughter of Eleander McPherson, of Morgan county. She was born January 7, 1822, in Lancaster county, Pennsylvania. Mr. and Mrs. Sharp lived in Barlow township from about 1849 till 1869. Mr. Sharp died May 3, 1876, leaving a family of ten children—Joseph, Nancy J., Sarah R., Lettia C., Catharine, Reese, Mary R., Martha E., Jefferson D. and George Q., all living in this county except Cath-

WILLIAM G. WOODFORD.

WILLIAM G. WOODFORD AND WIFE.

The subject of this sketch was born in Watertown township, February 2, 1811. His father, William Woodford, was a native of Connecticut, from which State he emigrated in 1797, in company with the family of William Ford, whose daughter, Dianna, he subsequently married. Mr. Woodford first settled in the northern part of the township, but finally made permanent settlement near the site of the present village. His family consisted of four children: Seth, Miles, Laura, and William G. Seth was a business man in Watertown, and also a farmer. He served in the legislature two terms, and died in his native township. Miles engaged in the southern produce trade. He died in Cincinnati. Laura was married to Abijah Brooks, a merchant at Watertown, afterwards at Waterford, Harmar, and in the south, where he died. She is living in Cincinnati. William G., the youngest son, remained with his father until he was twenty-one years old. He attended the district school, which stood on the present site of Dunbar's store. This was at a period when school-houses were made of logs, with undressed puncheons for seats and desks. When he was eighteen years old he made two trips to Baltimore for his brother Miles, with cattle, on foot. This was not an easy task, as the course lay through large tracts of woodland, and over the mountains, which were covered with greenbriers. The following year he made a similar trip for his brother Seth. At the age of twenty-one he began life for himself. He bought a small farm adjoining the vil-

lage and engaged in trade in the stand formerly occupied by his father. He had been trained to severe toil and now had a double incentive to activity. He continued trade for about two years and during the same time started the first carding machine in the township. At the end of that time he took advantage of a favorable opportunity and made a trade of his farm and carding machine for the Burchet farm, west of the village, with a financial result which encouraged him to continue in the real estate business. His next move was to sell this farm and buy the Patton farm, situated just across the creek from the village, which then belonged to John Paine. While living here he again engaged in the grocery and produce trade and at a later period, in partnership with Dennis Ryan, went into merchandising, where Dunbar is now located. About a year and a-half later, Mr. Woodford bought the Watertown mills, consisting of a gristmill, saw-mill, and an oil mill. He pushed business here with characteristic energy for about three years, when he traded for a farm in Palmer township. This is said to have been the best farm in the township. He now devoted himself to accumulating land and trading farms. He at different periods owned several farms in Watertown, Belpre, and Warren townships, also six hundred and forty acres in Indiana, half of which he retains, and one-third interest in a ten thousand acre tract in Illinois. During this period he has dealt largely in stock, produce, and wool. No man in the township has handled more money or property of different kinds than Grove Wood-

MRS. WILLIAM G. WOODFORD.

ford. He knows everybody and is known by everybody in the community. During his whole life his fortune grew steadily, until in 1875 he met a serious reverse. He then suffered a loss of twenty-five thousand dollars by having gone security for another, a loss which he met out of his hard-earned savings.

Mr. Woodford, in the spring of 1881, in partnership with his son, opened a store in Watertown for general trade. His friends were pleased to again greet him in a place, where they had so long and favorably known him—behind the counter.

In the Watertown cemetery is a large and handsomely built stone vault which bears the inscription over the front entrance: "William Woodford's family vault, 1853." It was built by the combined contributions of the father and sons, and on the lids to its occupied cells are found the following inscriptions: "William Woodford died August 3, 1858, aged 83 years, 11 months and 14 days." "Seth Woodford died April 4, 1860, aged 59 years, 6 months and 1 day." "Mercy, wife of Seth Woodford, died March 19, 1871, aged 69 years, 5 months and 8 days." "Miles Woodford died January 26, 1855, in the 51st year of his age." "Mary, wife of Miles Woodford, died August 22, 1854, in the 28th year of her age."

William G. Woodford married September 27, 1832, Sophia Shields, who was born in Virginia June 2, 1811. She was the daughter of David and Sarah Loyd Shields, who emigrated from Virginia, and settled in Watertown township about 1818. Their family consisted of twelve children, of whom Sophia was the sixth.

Mr. and Mrs. Woodford have had nine children: Laura was born June 23, 1833, is married to George Buchannan, and lives in Watertown township; Caroline was born June 6, 1835, and died at the age of seven years and ten days; Hial was born January 5, 1837, and died November 7, 1842; William S. was born August 4, 1839, married Emily Deming, died April 16, 1872, leaving five children—William G., James H., Minnie, Mary and Annie; Sarah Ann was born December 5, 1841, and was married to Juda Ford, who owned a large tannery at Watertown, and then moved to Kansas, where they died in 1878 within a period of three days, leaving two children: Adaline and Douglas Ammon; James K. P. was born September 23, 1844, and is in business in Watertown; Giles his twin brother, died October 3, 1844; Dianna Amanda was born August 8, 1846, married first Thomas Ryan, who died in Watertown, married for her second husband, Michael Ryan, lives in Belpre, and has two children—James Dennis and Delia May; Miles was born August 29, 1849, married Amelia Martin, lives in Palmer township, and has two children—Carrie Belle and Ottie Sophia.

Mr. Woodford, although he has met reverses, still has a large competence, and old age does not seem to have affected his business sagacity. His standing has always been honorable. In politics he stands alone in his family, always having been a warm Democrat. He has never sought office, but has frequently been honored with local trusts.

arine, who resides in Illinois; Reese, in Missouri; and Mary in West Virginia.

Father E. L. Fladung, who was born in Prussia, in 1847, emigrated to this country, and is now the pastor of St John's Catholic church, which is located in that part of Union township which is now included in Watertown township. He has been the pastor of the church for the last eight years.

James K. is the seventh of a family of eleven children of Noah Smith, of Newport township. He was born in Jefferson county, September 15, 1821. He came to Washington county with his father, and settled in Newport in 1848, where he remained until 1874, when he came to this township. He was married April 7, 1850, to Rosannah Petty, who was born in Newport township, September 22, 1829. Twelve children blessed this union, viz.: Jeanette A., Mary L., Maria V., Presly H., Edward M., John W., Oliver R., Edith M., Joseph L., James W., William M. and Adda C., all living. Jeanette is married to William H. McCowan, of Watertown. The other members of the family are still at home.

Jacob Hall, oldest child of James Hall, was born in the part of Noble county formerly belonging to Washington, September 1, 1837. He lived in Marietta from 1861 to 1863. He removed to Wheeling, but in less than a year returned to Marietta township, where he remained till 1874, when he settled in Watertown. August 1, 1858, he married Elizabeth Birchall, who was born in Noble county, September 6, 1838. They had five children: Anna E., Alice M., Mary J., Ele B. and one deceased. Alice is also dead. Mr. Hall, although one of the more recent settlers of the township, is regarded as a leading citizen.

James R. Sheldon was born in Noble county, Ohio, August 13, 1840. He removed with his family to Watertown township in 1874. He married, April 18, 1861, Mary Haynes, by whom he had three children, two of whom are living. Mrs. Haynes died October 17, 1869. April 24, 1872, he married Elizabeth Yarnall, who was born December 9, 1845. This union was blessed with three children. Mrs. Sheldon, whose maiden name was Elizabeth Way, was bereaved of her first husband January 13, 1870. Mr. Sheldon served in company A, One Hundred and Sixty-first Ohio volunteer infantry during the Rebellion. Both Mr. and Mrs. Sheldon are members of the Presbyterian church.

Mrs. Mary E. Blakeley, daughter of William Sheldon, was born in Noble county, Ohio, December 5, 1835. She was married to Edward Blakeley, July 28, 1859. He was born in England, August 3, 1836, and emigrated with his father, John Blakeley, to America, in 1843. Mr. Blakely died in Noble county, leaving two children— John A. and Mary A., who were born October 18, 1867. Mrs. Blakeley settled with her family in Watertown township, in 1878. She is a member of the United Brethren church.

It will be seen from this general synopsis of the settlement of the township that the first improvements were made at the forks of Wolf creek. The bottoms along the South branch as far as the donation line were next occupied. The English emigrants chose the valley of the West branch. The first settlement at the headwaters of Rainbow was made by the Sandusfield, Massachusetts, party in 1797. The Starlins and a few others were the only early settlers north of this neighborhood.

The German emigration began in 1835, Conrad Bohl being one of the first. The population of the northern part of the territory formerly included in Union, is largely German. It remained unimproved till as late as 1840. The southern part of this portion of the township is inhabited by people of Irish nativity, who settled in 1842-4. They were mostly engaged as laborers on the Muskingum river improvements, and then invested their earnings in the adjacent lands which at that time could be purchased at low rates. They are an industrious, hard-working class of people, and have done much towards improving the county.

EARLY SCHOOLS.

Watertown enjoyed school privileges very early in her history. A school was taught during the winter of 1799, in the Sandusfield neighborhood, by Nathaniel Gates. He was a popular teacher and pupils attended from the creek settlements. The closing exercises of Mr. Gates' school were attended by the parents, who manifested a live interest in the education of their children. Good teachers were, however, at that period very scarce. Teachers, as a rule, had no training, and it seems little sense. The unsparing use of the rod made the schoolroom a place of persecution, and the murder of the king's English was lamentable. The girls were taught reading and writing, while arithmetic was added to the course of study for the boys. Webster's spelling book and the Bible were the only text books used at first; in later years the American Preceptor and Columbian Orator came into use. Miss Peck, Colonel Augustus Stone, Judge Deming, Jason Humiston, and Horace Wolcott, were among the early teachers in the Sandusfield district. Another early school-house was in the West Branch neighborhood. Some old citizens retain vivid recollections of whippings received in this building. Smith Green is one of the best remembered teachers. Another early school-house was located in the Starlin neighborhood. Mr. McGehan was one of the first teachers. The building was also used as a meeting-house, by the settlers of all denominations in that neighborhood, but chiefly by the Methodists.

MILLS.

Wolf creek furnishes good water power except during dry seasons. At many places along its course a rapid current and high banks provide excellent mill sites, but periodical low water is a discouraging circumstance.

We have already mentioned the old Wolf creek mill owned by Captain Dodge, Colonel Oliver and Major White. After Indian hostilities had subsided this mill was found too small to meet the demands of the flourishing settlement, and a frame mill was constructed just above the old building, which, after the death of Major White, was in charge of his son, Peletiah White. This structure was swept away by high water, and a third and larger one built near the same site which was in after years owned and run by Haffield White, jr., grandson of the major. The foundations of these buildings are yet to be seen, and many interested persons have procured pieces of the decaying timbers and are preserving them as relics.

Solomon Lewis, a son-in-law of Mr. White, built the second mill in the township. It was located on the south branch near the forks. This was also a combination of saw-mill and grist-mill. It next came into possession of a Mr. Bartlett, and was owned by him when destroyed by fire.

The mill now known as the Ryan mill, on the south branch, about two miles below the village, was built about 1830 by William and Samuel Beswick.

The Watertown mill was built by John Paine, about 1825. He came with a party from Rhode Island on their way to one of the western States, but was delayed in this township by high water, there being at that time no bridges. While stopping with the hospitable people of the neighborhood the party were strongly impressed with the country, and after sending one of the party to examine the locality to which it had been their intention to go, they purchased lands and settled in this township. Samuel Paine, who was a miller, commenced operations for the construction of this mill. It was afterwards owned by Dennis Ryan.

EARLY INCIDENTS AND CUSTOMS.

A meagre light is thrown upon the character of the brave and prudent women of the early settlement by an incident which occurred at Wolf Creek mills shortly after peace with the Indians, but while straggling natives were yet frequent visitors at the cabins of the settlers. An Indian in a state of intoxication came to the mills and was roughly treated by a miller named Fry. He showed signs of anger, and indicated a purpose to have revenge. Mrs. Oliver, who understood Indian character, gained his attention at this point and induced him to engage in a game of quoits with herself and two other women. He finally left the settlement in the best of humor, and no occasion for anxiety remained behind.

A meeting in Wolf Creek chapel is humorously described by an old resident. Rev. Mr. Mitchell, the ardent evangelist, had just concluded a stirring sermon to a packed audience. One of the good, old-fashioned choruses was started, and everybody joined in. The singing grew louder and more enthusiastic until the more emotional of the members broke forth in a general shout of joy, which provoked a shout of fun among the wicked boys in the back corners. A general confusion, which lasted till all were exhausted, ensued. Children cried, boys sang, women shouted, and men prayed.

It was in this same chapel upon another occasion, while the meeting was in progress, a wind and hail storm set in, which struck terror in the congregation. Heavy trees were falling, lightning was striking in every direction, and large hail stones thundered on the roof. The preacher was unmoved by all these demonstrations of nature, but in a happy manner turned them to his own advantage by exclaiming "Oh, Lord, you strike outside while I strike inside." One old lady thought it was safer out, and was detained only by main force.

CEMETERIES.

There are in this township nine cemeteries. Three of them are owned by churches; the remaining six are controlled by the township and private individuals.

The oldest one in the township is located on the Waterman farm, near the place of the second settlement. This is the burial lot of the oldest families in the township—the Watermans, Fords, Harts, Curtises, Humphries, Beaches, Rodgers, and others.

At the death of Simon Starlin a burying lot was fenced off on his farm. Here are interred representatives of the Starlin, Ezekial Deming, Parke, and Beebe families.

Horace Wolcott, at the death of his child, set apart a lot on his farm for burial purposes. The Wolcott family, Simeon Deming family, the Humiston family, the Green family, and the Henry family have used this cemetery.

The cemetery near the west branch was formerly the churchyard of Wolf Creek chapel, long since torn down. The land was given by George Corner. Most of the members of the English colony, mentioned in the settlement, are buried here.

The Woodruff cemetery in the south part of the township is the burial place of the family whose name it bears.

The cemetery at Watertown village was set apart by Seth Woodford at the death of Miss Caroline Woodford. The location is exceptionally fine. It is now used more than any other cemetery in the township.

The Catholic cemetery near the brick church in the eastern part of the township, set apart from the McDermott farm at the death of James McDermott, in March, 1846. It now belongs to St. John's church.

Eva Merae churchyard was laid out at the building of that church in 1866.

St. John's Lutheran churchyard was laid out in 1855.

POST OFFICES AND WATERTOWN.

The village of Watertown is at the intersection of the two oldest roads running through the township—the Marietta and Lancaster, and county road leading from Waterford. The first store was opened in 1828 by Abijah Brooks, who was also the first postmaster. The succeeding postmasters have been: William Woodford, Miles Woodford, Michael Ryan, Conrad Bohl, Prudie Woodruff, and Nicholas Wiles.

The first tavern was kept by a Mr. Carlton, who lived on the Lancaster road a short distance from the present town. Burris Cruson opened the first house of entertainment in the village of Watertown. John Keil and Lewis Thornbery will be remembered by travellers of a later period. Watertown is now a town of about thirty families, having three churches, Universalist, Methodist, and Presbyterian; a mill, a school, two stores, one opened by Conrad Bohl in 1861, the other by James T. Duncan in 1867, and both doing a large business; and other village conveniences.

Churchtown post office, at the Catholic church in the eastern part of the township, was established in February, 1875, with M. Jurden, the present incumbent, in charge.

Carding and fulling was at one time carried on in this village by Miles Woodford. Wolf creek does not furnish sufficient water power for carrying on this industry extensively, and consequently, after the building up of large establishments at other places, these smaller concerns were abandoned.

W. G. Woodford engaged in the manufacture of flaxseed oil. For a few years his business was quite profitable.

The tanning business, begun by Jude Ford, was the most extensive industry ever carried on in the township. At one time fifteen men were regularly employed.

PHYSICIANS.

Watertown for a long time was dependent entirely upon her neighbors for medical service in cases of sickness. Dr. Baker, Dr. Dergy, and Dr. Pardee, were called from Waterford during the early years of the settlement, and later Dr. Seymour, of Waterford, and Dr. Hildreth, of Marietta, were the medical counselors. Dr. Regnier, the Duck Creek physician, also had a good practice in this township, and at a later period the Bowens, of Waterford. Dr. Seth Hart opened the first office in the township, and had a complimentary practice. Dr. Curtis had an office in the township, and enjoyed a full practice until his death. Dr. Cottle, Dr. Ross, and Dr. Howell, were among the more recent practitioners. Several have opened offices, but their residence was too short to merit notice in this connection.

Dr. Bohl, the only physician in the township at this writing, has had a large practice since 1852, when he first placed himself before the public. Of late years he has had more calls than he has been able to give attention to.

THE GRANGE.

Watertown grange was organized in 1874 with sixty members. The first officers were: Wallace Wolcott, master; H. McGrew, overseer; Roscoe Wolcott, secretary. The society had a hall in Watertown, and during the first four years created considerable interest. Meetings were discontinued in April, 1879, owing to a general indifference on part of the members, which began as soon as the enthusiasm, naturally inspired by novelty, had died out.

RELIGIOUS WORSHIP—METHODISTS.

In the early period of the settlement of Washington county, the Methodists made it a special object to establish their form of worship in the rural districts. Peter Cartwright said: "The towns were given to Deism, Spiritualism and Calvanism." Methodist circuit riders were the only preachers who visited the sparse settlements. They did an effectual and good work.

A meeting-house, forty feet square, was built about 1802, on the west branch, known as Wolf Creek chapel. A frame church was afterwards built near the site of the first church. Services have long since been abandoned here, and the house removed.

The "First Methodist Society of Wooster" was incorporated in June, 1819. The trustees were Samuel Mellor, Samuel Mellor, jr., Seth Green, and Duty Green.

A Methodist church was built on the North Marietta road, in the part of the township formerly included in Union in 1830. The house was rented to the Lutherans at the organization of that body.

Salem church was built in 1871. The class had been organized long previously.

Watertown church was organized in 1860. The following were the members of the class: B. N. Sparks, S. Ryland, J. P. Culver, Ezra Michner, Sarah Michner, Martha Flower, Joseph Yarnell and Roena Ford. Meetings were held in a school-house for a time. Satisfactory arrangements were then made with the Presbyterians, by which the use of their house at Watertown was secured.

The churches of Watertown have been connected with Barlow circuit since its establishment, previous to that time Marietta preachers supplied these churches.

PRESBYTERIAN CHURCH.

Many of the prominent early families of Watertown township were Presbyterians, and when the society at Waterford was formed, connected themselves with that body. The charge was very early divided into two preaching stations, the services for the southern part of the district being held in the open air and in residences and barns. William Ford's barn on Wolf creek was very frequently used for this purpose. Measures were taken in 1821 for the building of a house of worship. Due notice having been given, a meeting of a sufficient number of inhabitants of the township was held at the house of Benjamin Hart, November 17, 1821, for the purpose of forming a religious society. As a result of this meeting the First Presbyterian society of Wooster was incorporated November 20, 1821. Simeon Deming, William Woodford, and Benjamin Hart, are named in the record of incorporation, as trustees. A church organization separate from the church at Waterford was not formed till ten years afterward. This society was merely a business auxilliary; the conditions of membership were monetary. A meeting-house was built opposite the bend of the creek, two miles below Watertown. This house was built on the New England plan, being a combination of sanctuary and township house for election and other purposes. A school was also accommodated in one of the rooms.

Here, as at Waterford, vocal music was made a special feature of the church service. The choir was led by Colonel Simeon Deming, and assisted by the music of two violins and a violoncello. This choir became quite celebrated and aided greatly in filling the house on occasions of public worship.

On the eighth of May, 1831, Rev. Luther G. Bingham, commissioned by the presbytery of Athens, formed a church in Watertown, consisting of persons who had till then belonged to the church of Waterford, and persons living in Watertown and Barlow townships, the number of members being eighty-four. Dennis Adams and Benjamin Hart were chosen ruling elders.

August 31, 1831, Rev. P. Kimball was ordained pastor.

He also taught school in the church building, which was repaired and changed in its construction during his pastorate. Rev. S. N. Manning was ordained in 1834; Rev. Bennett Roberts in 1836; Rev. E. Garland in 1840; Rev. James Holmes in 1842; Rev. A. Thompson in 1847. About this time a division arose relative to the place of meeting. Those living in the vicinity of Watertown village furnished for meeting purposes the room in the upper story of the brick school-house. The other portion of the congregation desired to continue services in the old church. The matter was laid before the Presbytery, which resulted in the appointment of Rev. L. C. Ford and Roswell Tenny, as a committee to organize a second Presbyterian church at Watertown. August 11, 1848, a meeting was held at Watertown, at which a society, styling itself the Village Presbyterian church, was organized with twenty-seven members, all from the first church. G. H. Ford, Seth Woodford, and B. W. Arnold were elected ruling elders. Rev. A. Thompson was pastor till the summer of 1850. James S. Walton was ordained pastor in 1851.

The first church continued to hold service at the old meeting-house. Supplies from Marietta college filled the pulpit for some time. Rev. Dyer Burgess, the great abolition advocate, also ministered to this church.

The presbytery of Athens at its meeting in Barlow, April 13, 1853, resolved "That the First Presbyterian church of Watertown and the Village Presbyterian church of Watertown, be united under the name of the First Presbyterian church of Watertown, and that the records of the two churches be put into the hands of the session of the united church." The pastors since the union have been: James McNeal, G. R. Rossetter, D. C. Perry, Thomas McLeon, J. M. Howard, William H. Galbreath, J. Strauss, John Noble, and William H. Bay. During the greater part of the time since 1871, Watertown and Barlow have been served by one pastor, preaching being on alternate Sabbaths at each place. A comfortable frame church was built on the hill just above the village, in 1869, which was dedicated January 16, 1870. The use of this house is shared with the Methodists.

UNIVERSALIST CHURCH.

The First Universalist church of this township was built in 1835 in the vicinity of the old block-house, below Watertown village, in the Wolf Creek valley. Rev. Mr. Sage was the only regular minister this church ever had. Services were held at irregular intervals by itinerant preachers. The house was burned in 1857, and the congregation disorganized. In 1870, through the efforts of Rev. J. M. McMaster of Marietta, the congregation was reorganized and a church built in the village. Mr. McMaster continued as pastor till 1878, when he was succeeded by Rev. E. M. Earl, who remained one year. The pastorate has since been vacant.

ST. JOHN—LUTHERAN.

Conrad Bohl, who settled in this township in 1834, was the father of this church. Preachers from Marietta occasionally held service in the neighborhood until 1845, when a congregation was organized, and the frame build-ing erected by the Methodists some years previous, was purchased. The present house was built in 1855. In 1878 it was repaired, and is now a neat and comfortable house of worship. The congregation was connected with the Marietta church until 1865, since then with Lowell. The present membership is thirty families.

ST. JOHN THE BAPTIST—CATHOLIC.

A Catholic congregation was organized in Union township, now Watertown, about 1850, which was supplied by the pastor of the Marietta parish until 1865. In 1853 Michael McDermott donated to the church a lot on which they built a frame house. In 1865 the members in this locality were constituted a parish, and Magnus Eppank sent by the diocese as priest. The congregation had, the year previous, built a comfortable parsonage which has been the residence of succeeding pastors since that time. In 1866 it was thought desirable to divide the congregation, and two meeting-houses were built that year, one was located on Rainbow, on land donated by Andrew Schemdernan, which was christened Ave Maria. The membership of this congregation is German. The other was built on land donated by M. Jurdon. The membership of this congregation is both Irish and German. The old building was sold for a school-house. The new building is the handsomest church edifice in the township, and the largest Catholic church in the county. It cost about twelve thousand dollars. The following have been the priests: Magnus Eppank from 1865 to 1869; Gebhardt Schneader and Lawrence Schneader in 1869; Leonard McKeinen in 1870; Lewis Grammer in 1871; E. L. Fladung to the present time (1881). The membership of "St. John" church is seventy-five families, of "Ave Maria," fifty-five families.

UNITED BRETHREN CHURCHES.

Watertown church was organized by Rev. Mr. Lease, an early minister on Plymouth circuit. The first members were Peter Stollar, Susan Stollar, William Sampson, Elizabeth Sampson, Daniel Jennings, Rosanna Jennings, Andrew Stollar, Elizabeth Stollar, Eleazer Smith, and Eunice Smith. The ministers of the Plymouth circuit supplied this church until 1878, when Pleasant Grove circuit was formed, J. W. Shell was given charge of the new circuit, and remained in charge two years. The present pastor, J. W. Willis, has served since 1880. In the fall of 1880 the name of the circuit was changed from "Pleasant Grove" to "Watertown." The class worshipped in private houses for some time, and then in the East Watertown school-house until 1871, when Pleasant Grove chapel was built. The present membership of this church is thirty-five. Four of the original members are yet living.

A class consisting mostly of persons living in old Union township, was organized by Rev. J. Watts in 1870. The names of the first members were, James Willis, Candace Willis, John Skipton, sr., Sally Skipton, J. W. Willis (present pastor), Bartha J. Willis, and Harriet Power. The ecclesiastical connections of this church have been with Pleasant Grove. The present membership is twenty-seven; services are held in a school-house.

BIOGRAPHICAL SKETCH.

JOHN DRESSER CHAMBERLAIN

was born at Goshen, Hampshire county, Massachusetts, September 10, 1789, and died at Fairfield, Washington county, Ohio, February 10, 1880. His parents, Asa and Prudence (Dresser) Chamberlain, were of the hardy New England stock known as Yankees, but in their later life forsook their eastern home to make a new one in Ohio, their son having preceded them a few years.

John D. Chamberlain crossed the mountains on foot in the early part of the year 1811, arriving at Marietta in March, and immediately wended his way up the Muskingum river to Waterford. Remaining there a short time, he finally settled in Wooster, now Watertown, where he purchased land and resided more than sixty years.

He enlisted in the War of 1812, and served until its close, in 1814, when he received an honorable discharge with the rank of captain.

He was for many years a teacher, having taught school upon Cat's creek, where Lowell now stands, and at Waterford, in Washington county, and at the old settlement of Amesville, in Athens county. He served in many civil offices, and was a county commissioner for fifteen years. He was a man of remarkable physical strength and of strong intellect, alike well qualified to endure the hardships and privations of pioneer life, and to enjoy the amenities of that period in which his old age was passed.

For many years he was engaged with others in the manufacture and sale of clocks at Cincinnati, the firm at first being Reed, Watson & Chamberlain, and afterwards Watson & Chamberlain. (This Mr. Watson's first name was Luman. It was after him that John D. Chamberlain's son, Luman W. was named). Many of the clocks manufactured by these two firms, more than sixty years ago, are still keeping time, although the hands that wrought them and the minds that planned them have ceased from labor.

Mr. Chamberlain married as his first wife Thirza A. Grow, of Chester, Meigs county. Nine children were the offspring of this union, viz: Diana M., Ason G., Amanda E., Anna M., Melissa E., Luman W., Prudence N., Alma A., and Thirza R. After the death of his first wife, Mr. Chamberlain married Mrs. Sarah Williams, of Morgan county, Ohio, whose death occurred prior to that of her husband. Two children were the fruits of this marriage—Sarah J., and John D.

CHAPTER XLVI.
WARREN TOWNSHIP.

Topography—Quality of Sandstone—Boundaries—Incorporation and Survey—Settlement Retarded—Appearance of Squatters—First Permanent Settlers—Back Settlements—Settlers of a Later Period—Hunters—Post Office—Cemeteries—A Thanksgiving Incident—Epidemics—Population—Roads—Educational Matters—Warren Graduates at Marietta College—Presbyterian, Methodist, Disciple, and United Brethren Churches—Early Sunday-Schools—The Use of Spirituous Liquors—Temperance Reformation.

WARREN may properly be styled the "grindstone township" of Washington county. Along the whole course of the Ohio river hills, three strata of heavy sandstone rock present transverse sections, and an almost inexhaustible supply of stone of the very finest quality might be quarried. A high range of precipitous hills borders the river from Harmar, to a point nearly opposite Muskingum island, where it recedes and the intervening tract of bottom, about six miles long and from one half to one mile wide, includes the most fertile farming land in the township.

Back of this bluff the whole area of the township may be described by the familiar phrase "up hill and down hill." The drainage in the interior seems to be without system. Streams flow in every direction, and following their course is the only means of determining their destination. The altitude of the township makes it a headwater territory. The streams which flow into the Ohio —Mile run, Scott's run, Bailey's run, and a few others— are all short and small, the sources of none of them being more than three miles from the river. The east branch of the Little Hocking rises on the ridge near the centre of the township, and takes a southerly course. The waters of the northwestern part of the territory unite to form Wolf creek. The principal branch from the north is Horse run. Branches from the south are Turkey Hen creek and Brown's run, the mouth of which is in Barlow township. From this general outline of the water courses some idea can be gleaned of the irregularity of the surface slopes. Wolf creek, a stream sixty miles long, which empties into the Muskingum at Beverly, has its source in the ridge fronting the Ohio and Muskingum at their junction. The annoying oddity of the names of two of these streams, excite a spirit of inquiry into their origin. It is said that in early times, peavine grew in abundance along the north branch of Wolf creek. This is a species of grass greatly relished by many kinds of stock, and collections of horses, cows, etc., were frequently seen along the valley. Cow run, in Lawrence township, had for a similar reason received its name, and the pioneers of Warren took advantage of the alternative and called this stream Horse run. Turkey Hen creek was named by a party of Virginia hunters who, upon one occasion, left their own hills and came to the wilds of Ohio in search of game. The deep valley of the first southern branch of Wolf creek was made the camping ground. But game was not to be found, and the disgusted Virginians returned with a solitary turkey hen. This valley, aesthetically the most interesting in the township, by its homely name perpetuates the memory of an incident in itself unimportant.

In quality of soil the township may be divided into three distinct sections. The river bottom consists mostly of a rich loam, and produces abundant crops. The dividing ridge which borders this bottom is covered with a shaly soil rich in concretions of lime, and is fairly productive. The third belt, extending from Turkey Hen creek in a southwesterly direction, is composed of disintegrated sandstone and shale, and is not adapted to the culture of most crops without a liberal use of fertilizers.

The most valuable feature of the economic geology is the heavy ledges of sandsone of superior quality for grindstones and building purposes, lying along the Ohio river. The first layer, a coarse building stone, is thirty feet thick. This is followed by ten feet of blue shale, which rests upon a twenty-five foot stratum of sand rock of the finest quality. The texture and grit varies greatly with the locality. Everything conspires to the successful manufacture of grindstones. The quarries are easily accessible, and are inexhaustible, and the proximity of the railroad and river affords ample shipping facilities. Grindstones have been manufactured along this outcrop for more than seventy years. At the present time the principal quarries are owned by Calvin Finch, J. H. Deming, H. H. Cole, P. L. Cole, Mr. O'Connor, and Dean Briggs. The "constitution stone" of the Ohio River Stone company became quite celebrated, being admirably adapted to ornamental architectural work. It was introduced into Chicago and other cities. Capability of resisting great pressure without fracture, and resistance to the influence of heat, make it superior for building purposes to limestone or marble. For grindstones, Warren sand-rock will compare with any stone in the world. On comparison of a specimen from J. H. Deming's quarry with the best Nova Scotia grit, they were found almost identical in texture, and equal in quality for grinding.

The stretch of alluvial bottom along the river was heavily timbered with walnut, maple, beech, sycamore, hickory, and other trees, which a network of thrifty grapevines tied together so firmly that in the progress of clearing it was sometimes necessary to cut half a dozen before the first could be brought to the ground. On the uplands the trees were much smaller. At present the bottom lands and more fertile terraces are entirely cleared. Native forest continues to cover the steep hills and tracts not adapted to agricultural uses. The scenery of Warren has many attractions for the lover of nature. The streams are clear, the valleys narrow and the hills steep and at some places precipitous. The dividing ridge, extending through the township almost parallel with the river, overlooks the surrounding territory, and its highest peak—Owl hill—near the Lancaster road, affords a splendid view of the Virginia hills and the basin of Wolf creek and Turkey Hen.

LEGAL BOUNDARIES AND ORGANIZATION.

The boundaries of Warren have frequently been changed since its incorporation by the county commissioners on the tenth of September, 1810. The original town consisted of all the territory included by a line beginning at the Ohio river where the line between the eighth and ninth ranges strikes it, thence north on said range line to the northeast corner of section twenty-five, in town two, range nine; thence west to northwest corner of section seventeen, in same township; thence north to the north line of same township; thence west to the northwest corner of the township; thence south to the southwest corner of the same; thence west to the northwest corner of section twelve, in town two, range ten; thence south to the southwest corner of section ten, in said township; thence east to the Ohio river; thence up the river to the place of beginning.

In 1813 it was ordered that all that part of Marietta township lying between the eighth and ninth ranges be annexed to Warren.

The boundaries were afterwards changed several times. A personal enmity between two prominent citizens resulted in a tract one-half mile wide and two miles long being set off and annexed to Barlow. When the town of Dunham was established, June 5, 1855, considerable territory was cut off from Warren, and the partitionment of Union added four sections on the north in 1877.

The territory now included in Warren was laid out in the original survey in eight acre lots excepting three sections—ministerial section number twenty-nine, school section number sixteen, and Congress reservation section number eight.

THE SETTLEMENT.

The plan adopted by the Ohio company for allotting lands to its members retarded for several years the settlement of Warren township. Many of the eight-acre lots were owned by non-residents, who held them for speculative purposes. This made it difficult for any one desiring to make an improvement to procure a sufficiently large and connected tract of land for a suitable farm. Settlers naturally preferred to go further back, where large tracts could be purchased from a single individual.

Soon after the close of the Indian war, squatters began to make improvements on Congress section number eight. These people, with a few exceptions, were afflicted with a roving disposition and an aversion to the labor necessary to the making of more than a temporary improvement. On section eight a community of these people had gathered previous to the permanent settlement of the township. A few of them were industrious and frugal, and afterwards became good citizens, but by far the greater number sought dwelling places elsewhere, when driven from the land they occupied by actual owners. The first of this class of improvements were made in Warren township by Isaac Nogle, George Nogle, Thomas Dickey and Isaac Hardin. These were soon followed by Thomas Patton, William Patton, Dr. Morse, Samuel Friend, John Rardin, John Chevington and others. This collection of uninviting cabins was called Nogletown. These transient inhabitants did not bear an enviable reputation among the more solid settlers who followed them, and their departure was not regretted.

The rich lands along the river were naturally chosen by the first settlers. The first permanent improvements were made by Seth Bailey, Elias Newton and the Cole family, in 1804 and 1805. About one year later Isaac Humphreys, Ezekial Finch and Judge Ephraim Cutler purchased land and made improvements. These old families were not only the pioneers of the township, but the leading characters in its history for more than thirty years. They were men of culture and energy, who were ambitious to build up the community as well as their private fortunes.

Thomas Dickey was one of the earliest residents of the township. He came from Pennsylvania to Washington county in 1798. About 1810 he was employed by Timothy Cone to carry the mail. After working two years for Mr. Cone, he took the mail contract for himself, and remained in the employ of the Government till 1816. In 1818 he was married to Betsy G. Brown, and in 1820 moved to Athens county, afterwards removing to Morgan county, where he died in 1863. He had four boys and three girls. His eldest son, Charles, was born in Athens county, in 1823. He is now a resident of this township. He has had three sons, two of whom are living.

Philip Cole was the first representative of his family who settled in Warren township. John Cole, his father, was a native of Rhode Island, where he was married twice. By his first wife he had three children—Asa, Nathan, and Noah. By his second wife, Sasannah Salisbury, he had five children—Elizabeth, Candace, Philip, Ichabod, and John. He emigrated from Rhode Island to West Virginia, and then settled in Belpre where he remained two years. Philip, during the stay of the family in Wood county, West Virginia, married Eunice Gates, a Vermont lady, and in 1803, or early in 1804, sought a home up the river. He settled on the farm now owned by J. H. Deming. His nearest neighbor down the river was Wilbur Harris, one of the earliest settlers of the township. The nearest improvement up the river was Nogletown. In 1804, John Cole with his family removed from Belpre and settled below Vienna Island, on the farm now owned by Henry Cole. He opened the first house of entertainment in the neighborhood and kept the first ferry between Belpre and Marietta. His son, Asa, retained the homestead; Nathan settled on the territory now included in Dunham, where he afterwards opened a tavern. Elizabeth, the oldest daughter, married William Green; Candace married Willard Harris and settled, in 1806, on Little Hocking. Philip Cole's family consisted of eight children—Eunice (O'Neil), Lucinda (Whiteman), Diantha (Deming), Caroline (Lewis), William, Louisa (Shields), Henry H., and Mary Ann (Ballard). Philip Cole was an enterprising citizen and a useful member of his pioneer community. He was one of the first magistrates of his township. He died January 25, 1831; his wife died December 11, 1857.

Captain Willard Green lived on the farm now owned by Dean Briggs. He married Lizzie Cole, a daughter of John Cole. Before coming to Warren they lived for a time at Hughes River, Virginia, where the forest was dense and full of wild animals. The captain was necessarily absent most of the time, and Mrs. Green was herself compelled to hunt the cow in the woods. One evening,

taking her baby, she set out, and guided by the sound of the bell, came to a small ravine, and through the shadow of the trees and underbrush she thought she saw a man approching. She caught occasional glimpses of him as she went down into the ravine, but on coming nearer was startled to find herself in the presence of a large black bear. It suddenly occurred to her that animals could be controlled by the human eye. She hastily wrapped the baby in her stout apron, and looking the monster steadily in the eye, clapped her hands vigorously. The bear, to her great relief, turned and walked away. Mrs. Green lived to be ninety-six years old, and died in Warren township May 4, 1869.

Henry H. Cole, the sixth child of Philip and Eunice Cole, was born in Warren in 1816. He married Sarah, the daughter of David Varner, born in Pennsylvania in 1815. The result of this union was two children—Philip L. and Sarah J., both residing in this township. Mr. Cole has been engaged extensively in the manufacture of grindstones for the past forty years. Mr. Cole has for many years served as trustee of his township.

J. H. Deming married Diantha Cole, by whom he had seven children, six of whom survive, viz.: Diantha, Elizabeth, Lucinda, Mary, Wallace, and Hiram. Mr. Deming, besides being a large farmer, is also engaged in the manufacture of grindstones. He has been township trustee for fifteen years, and has been postmaster at Constitution for a like period.

Elias Newton settled on the bottom in 1805, and was followed by his son Oren, several years later. Oren engaged in the manufacture of grindstone at an early period. His sons, Stephen and John, now living at Marietta, received their early training in the quarries.

Seth Bailey, a native of Massachusetts, emigrated to Virginia in 1793. While in Virginia he married Polly, the daughter of Captain William James, who, at that time, owned Vienna island, Neil's island, and a large tract in Virginia. Polly received as a marriage portion, Vienna island. Mr. Bailey built a cabin on the island and began the work of clearing in 1802. He, at this time, owned one horse, two oxen, and one cow. The island was densely covered with immense trees and clearing progressed slowly and involved the hardest kind of labor. Winter set in before a shelter could be provided for the stock, but nature had supplied that. A sycamore tree seventeen feet in its greatest diameter, and fifteen in its shortest, was discovered to be hollow. A door was cut in one side and the interior found large enough to afford a comfortable stable for all the stock. In after years this tree caught fire and burned to the ground. Mr. Bailey, one year, planted corn inside the remaining snags and harvested from it one bushel. Early in 1805, a frame house was built opposite the head of the island, a short distance below the present site of Mr. Scott's brick residence. This house became the Bailey homestead. The family consisted of eleven children: Maria (Shipman), who died in Marietta; Elizabeth, Seth, jr., living in Athens county; Charles, died in Virginia; John, settled in Warren township; Bennet, settled in Warren but afterwards moved to Kansas; William, living in Marietta;

George, in Warren; Augustus, in Kansas; and Thomas, in Dunham township.

William Bailey was born May 24, 1816. He lived at home until he reached the age of twenty, when he entered Marietta college. After graduating, in 1843, he read medicine, but the practice was not congenial to his disposition. A short time was spent in mercantile business in the west, after which he opened a store in Warren township, on the Cutler homestead. From 1855 to 1871, he engaged in the grindstone trade. He has since engaged in fruit culture and gardening in Marietta. In 1848, Mr. Bailey was married to Mary A. Ward, who died the following year. The fruit of this union was one daughter, Mary Annett, wife of James Walton. She died in Nebraska, in 1875. October 1, 1850, Mr. Bailey was married to Elizabeth Smith Emerson, daughter of Caleb Emerson, esq. They have three children: Ella F., Lucy D., and Charles Emerson.

Seth Bailey, after settling in Warren, erected a forge, and "picked up" the blacksmithing trade. Besides accommodating his neighbors, he occupied rainy days at making nails. His example was imitated by many of the young men in the neighborhood, and pounding nails became a common occupation.

William Johnson, a native of Ireland, settled in Washington county in 1815, where he remained until his death in 1826. He was the father of three children: Jane, William and Ellen. Of these Jane and Ellen are living. Jane was born in New Jersey in 1813. She married George Bailey, of Warren township. They became the parents of one child, M. L. George Bailey died in 1852. His widow and son reside on the home place.

Congress section eight was purchased by Isaac Humphreys in 1805. It made the largest and best farm in the township. Mr. Humphreys was a native of Ireland, and is remembered by the early settlers as a sharp business man. He moved to Harmar in 1839. He was one of the early magistrates of the township, and represented Washington county in the legislature a few years. He had six children: Mary, wife of Joel Deming, Charles, Emeline died in Harmar; Harriet, wife of Stephen Newton; Charity deceased, and Henry, who was drowned in the Ohio.

William Smith, one of the settlers on the river bank in 1805, had rather an eventful life. He came to Ohio with General Varnum in 1788, as an attendant. He was then young, but brave and ambitious. When the Big Bottom colony was formed, he became a member, and afterwards seemingly by chance escaped the horrible massacre of that unfortunate settlement. He had been sent to Marietta on the day previous to the tragedy, and on his way back was detained at Waterford, just long enough to be absent from the sack of his settlement. In 1805 he settled in Warren, on the bottom below Philip Cole's, where he made a clearing, built a cabin, and planted an orchard. His fruit and flower gardens were the joy of the youth of the neighborhood. The family consisted of six children: John and William left the county; Elijah settled in Harmar; Sally, wife of John

Newton, moved to Ironton; Mary married Richard Patton, and Huldah, John Test, ex-county sheriff.

Ezekiel Finch was one of the earliest pioneers of Warren township. He was born in New York State in 1769, and emigrated to Ohio in the fall of 1806, settling in the southern part of the territory now known as Warren township, where he resided until his death, which occurred in 1848. His children were: Morris, Lewis, Harris, Reuben, Samantha, Calvin, Darius, Sarah, Charles, and Alfred W. Calvin is the only survivor of this large family. He was born in Pennsylvania in 1806, and in that same year was brought to this county by his father and mother. He married Mrs. Sarah Cunningham in 1837. Seven children resulted from this marriage, all living but one. William W. married Eliza Jones; Lewis J. married Lucy Skipton; Henry C. married Sabra C. Thompson, and resides in Dakota; the other three children are living at home. Mr. Finch has been engaged in the grindstone business since 1850.

Morris Finch was a soldier in the War of 1812. He first went into the service as a substitute for Seth Bailey, but when his time had expired he volunteered and was present at the perilous battle of Bladensburgh.

Ephraim Cutler, eldest son of Rev. Manasseh Cutler, LL. D., was born at Edgarton, Martha's Vineyard, Massachusetts, April 13, 1767. He first married Polly Leah Atwood, April 8, 1787, at Killingly, Connecticut, where he settled. She was born Auguet 14, 1765, and died November 4, 1807. He married, for his second wife, Polly Parker, April 13, 1808. She was born at Newburyport, Massachusetts, June 6, 1777, and died June 30, 1846. He died July 8, 1853. Mr. Cutler settled in Warren in 1806, having previously lived at Waterford and at Ames, Athens county. The old stone house, which is still standing was completed in 1809. A biographical sketch of Judge Cutler will be found in this volume.

John Henry, a native of Ireland, came to Warren township in 1807, where he engaged in the manufacture of wheels for spinning flax. He owned a tract of land now included in the farm of Charles Cone, esq., which he sold to Mr. Brewster, and removed to Ames, Athens county, in 1817. He afterwards became a successful farmer and influential citizen. He had eighteen children. The patriarch of a large and respectable family, he died in 1854.

William Hutchinson was a resident of the township in 1807. He owned an eight acre lot north of Congress section eight.

Gideon Rathbun was the eccentric character among the settlers of 1807. He first settled on an eight acre lot which was afterwards included in Judge Cutter's farm. When he sold this he moved down on Little Hocking. His only source of revenue was the fur bearing animals he was enabled to capture. For a time he owned a pony on which he was accustomed to go to Marietta with a small grist of corn and skins to barter for other necessities of life. As he grew older his luck at hunting turned, and then to add misfortune to misery the old pack horse died, and Gideon was compelled to

SAMUEL DYE, Sr.

Among the early settlers of the eastern part of Washington county who endured all the privations of pioneer life, in order to subdue the wilderness and plant the seed of civilization and improvement, none perhaps deserve more credit than John Dye. He was a native of New Jersey, and emigrated to Virginia when young, locating near where the first battle of Bull Run was fought, where he married Miss Hannah Hoff. After remaining there for several years, and having become disgusted with slavery, they decided to emigrate to Ohio, which they did in the year 1806. Stopping about a year on Duck creek, thence moving in the spring of 1807 to what is now Lawrence township, on the farm now owned by A. J. Dye, esq. Of a large family (there were fifteen children, the majority of whom attained the age of maturity), only three are now living. The two years known as the epidemical years (1822 and 1823) were very destructive in that vicinity, and several of this family fell victims to the fell destroyer, including the father, who died in 1823. The three now living are Samuel, the subject of this sketch; J. W., and A. J.

Samuel Dye, esq., was born September 24, 1806, in Fearing township, whence he removed with his father to Lawrence township in 1807, where he resided over sixty years. The early part of his life was spent in helping fell the forest and aiding in the support of a large family, for his father was of a delicate constitution and unable to withstand the more arduous duties of pioneer life. As means for acquiring an education at that time were very meagre, his attainments in that direction were of course limited, but his ambition and natural propensities were too great to allow misfortune and adverse circumstances to prevent him from acquiring a good education. He married Miss Lucinda Dye, December 16, 1830. Her parents were pioneers of what is now Noble county. She was a woman of most generous impulses, and a most affectionate wife and mother. Like Lucretia of old, her hands were never idle, and such was her devotion to her husband and children that however arduous her domestic duties her words of cheer and comfort and her helping hand were always unreserved. She was a most exemplary Christian wife and mother, and when, on February 1, 1870, after a short illness of a few days the Lord called her away, the husband mourned the loss of a most worthy and faithful wife; the children a mother in every sense of the word, and the neighbors and friends one whose heart was imbued with generosity and kindness. The names of their children are as follows: Morgan L., married Miss Lucretia Bell and resides on the old homestead in Lawrence township; John J., married Miss Emily Brown who died in 1862, and resides in Macon county, Missouri; Amos Newton, died December 25, 1870; D. H., died in infancy; Charlotte M., married Rev. Leander Rhinehart, died November 6, 1858; Daniel U., married Miss L. A. Wakefield, and resides in Kankakee, Illinois; Furman J., residing in Warren township; Sarah E., married

Austin Middleswart, and resides in Warren township; Thomas M., died July 20, 1876; Joseph R., married Miss Elvira Torner, and resides on Cow run; Hattie R. and Samuel live with their father; W. Wirt, died May 25, 1867; William Chase, died January 24, 1863; Franklin U., died December 13, 1880.

Mr. Dye held the office of justice of the peace twelve years, and was noted for his just and impartial disposition of all questions which he was called upon to decide. He has been a prominent member of the Baptist church for forty years, serving as deacon about thirty years, and aiding with great liberality in the dissemination of the Gospel. In politics he is a Republican and has labored hard for the success of that party from its infancy. His loyalty is evinced by the fact that he cheerfully gave up three of his sons to battle for the preservation of the Union in the late war. Daniel U., Morgan L., and Thomas M. served creditably in different regiments until they were honorably discharged. He always took a great interest in the cause of education, sparing neither pains nor money in providing for his children in that respect. John J. graduated at Marietta high school. Amos Newton graduated at Marietta college in 1864, and at Rochester Theological seminary in 1868. He was excelled in eloquence by few, if any, in his conference, and was stricken down just as he was entering the temple of fame and distinction. Daniel U. and Furman J. graduated at Marietta college in 1871. Daniel U. afterwards graduated at the Theological seminary of West Chester, Pennsylvania, and has had charge of the Baptist church at Kankakee, Illinois, six years. Furman J. has been engaged in teaching the greater part of the time since his graduation. Although none of his other children were graduates, still they received more than an ordinary education.

The first petroleum found in paying quantities in the vicinity of Cow run was obtained in 1860 on the farm of Mr. D. Nye, and his income from that resource increased his already large accumulations until he was by far the wealthiest man in Lawrence township. Having disposed of the eighty acres of oil territory to an eastern company he purchased a large farm on the Ohio river about four miles below Marietta, and removed thereto in 1867, where he still resides. Though trouble seems to have marked him for its victim, yet he his still to be seen attending to the duties of the farm, patiently submitting to the decrees of an all wise Providence. One by one has death snatched from that home-circle until the father has seen the flowers of spring bloom over the graves of just one half of those upon whom he had founded hopes of long life and influence. His success in business and his popularity have brought him in contact with the best business men of the county, by whom he is esteemed for his strict adherence to rectitude and honesty. He is indeed one of the kindest and most affectionate of men, generous to a fault and holding firmly the regard and friendship of all who know him

carry corn to mill on his own back. One day as he was sweltering under his burden, a neighbor made friendly inquiry concerning his circumstances. Gideon despondingly replied, "Oh, I haint got nothin' to git nothin' with, nor I haint got nothin' to bring nothin' home on." The latter part of his life was not free from want.

John Shipton, a native of Pennsylvania and one of the oldest men now living in the township, settled on the farm just above the present site of Scott's station before 1810. In 1837 he moved to the farm on which he now lives, on the ridge fronting the river bottom.

In the early part of the century after permanent and substantial improvements had been made along the river, the settlement of the interior of the township was very sparce.

Robert Bulby was probably the first settler on Horse run. He and an Irishman named McGarry, who made an improvement on Wolf creek, came into the township about 1806. Shortly after William Coleby erected a cabin between Turkey Hen and Brown's run. Richard Poland made the first improvement on the ridge between Brown's run and east branch of Little Hocking. The two prominent early families in this part of the township were the Cunningham and the Bridges families.

John Cunningham was a native of Virginia. He settled in Warren township about 1807, on land lying south of Turkey Hen. He had six children, of whom Levi, a well known preacher of the Methodist church, is the youngest. Levi is described to have been a remarkable young man. He was pious and able but without education. He exhorted the small Methodist classes so effectively that he was chosen to serve the church as a local preacher, and was afterwards given a circuit. During the first year of his ministry he devoted himself assiduously to the study of English grammar and composition. Mr. Cunningham has reached a high place in the church, and is truly a self-made man. He lives near Columbus.

Jacob Bridges, esq., came from Northern Ohio about 1812 and settled near the site of Tunnel Station. Mr. Bridges was a leading man of the community. He was a magistrate several years and was the business counselor of his neighborhood. 'Squire Bridges and Mr. Cunningham were the organizers of Methodism in the township and the influence of their labor has not yet died out. About 1850 Mr. Bridges sold out and moved to Iowa. His two sons Silas and Benjamin accompanied him. His daughter, Sarah, was married to Charles Tidd and settled in Iowa. She died soon afterwards.

William White was the first settler on the Pinkerton farm on the Lancaster road.

The settlement was most rapid between 1835 and 1845. The earliest settlers improved the inviting river bottoms. The next class of settlers pushed further on into the State, and it was not until the Scioto and Miami valleys had been occupied that the hills of Washington county were in demand.

William Perdew was one of the earliest settlers of the interior of the township. He was born in Pennsylvania in 1789. At the age of seventeen he emigrated to Wood county, Virginia, where he lived about six months. About 1806 he became a resident of Washington county, and was one of the prominent citizens of Warren township until his death, which occurred January 5, 1869. In 1815 Mr. Perdew was married to Susanna Harris, who was born in New York in 1795. She died February 12, 1880. The family consisted of twelve children, six boys and six girls. Both were earnest members of the Methodist church, and labored faithfully and successfully for the upbuilding of the church in the community.

Charles, the second son, was born October 3, 1818, in Warren township, where he has resided ever since. May 26, 1842, he married Polly Lamma, daughter of Andrew and Rachel Lamma, of Virginia. The fruit of this union is seven boys and five girls. William W. Perdew, jr., was born August 9, 1827, and in 1853 married Sarah Seffens, born December 20, 1827. They have had nine children, as follows: Anne L., born November 2, 1854; Abbie A., October 17, 1856; John E., March 28, 1858; Mary J., December 28, 1859; Lizzie L., April 26, 1862; Hannah L., February 8, 1864; Joseph W., March 4, 1866; Benjamin W., May 17, 1871, and Clara L., May 8, 1874.

William M. Stage, eighth child of James Stage, was born in Washington county June 4, 1827, and resided in the county till the time of his death, which occurred September 9, 1871. He was married to Miss Drucilla Lightfrits, a daughter of John Lightfrits, who settled in Warren township in 1820. His death occurred March 31, 1841. His family consisted of ten children, five boys and five girls. Drucilla was born October 5, 1836. She married Mr. Stage October 14, 1849. They had seven children: William J., Samuel G., Jerry, Adda, Sarah R., Samantha B., and Perry, all living. With the assistance of her son Perry she continues to farm the old homeplace.

Philip, son of Thomas and Margaret Roe, was born in Delaware in 1811. In 1830 he removed from Muskingum county, Ohio, to Washington county, and located in Warren township. In 1839 he married Rebecca Lammery, by whom he had thirteen children, eight boys and five girls. Of this family nine children survive, three still living at home. Two of Mr. Roe's sons served in the late war, George for three years and Philip during the hundred days service.

Henry McAffee was born in Columbiana county, Ohio, and when quite young came to this county with his father, Daniel McAffee, and has since been living in that part of Warren which was formerly a part of Union township. He has a farm of forty acres. He is a carpenter by trade.

Thomas Drain, third child of Daniel and Jeanette Drain, was born in Argylshire, Scotland, in 1808, and came to Cincinnati in 1832, and after remaining there two years became a resident of Washington county. He married Jeanette Fullerton, by whom he had two children, viz: James, who married Romayne Bay; and Daniel, who is still at home. Mr. Drain has by economy accumulated much land.

Philip Schilling, born in Germany in 1810, settled in

this township in 1835, in that part formerly included in Union. He emigrated to Ohio from Florida. By his wife, Elizabeth Hopp, he had eleven children, eight of whom survive. George, the fifth son, born in 1849, married Louisa Walter, born in 1852. They have four children. Mr. Schilling, who is a general farmer, possesses ninety-six acres of land.

Duncan Drain settled in this county in 1838, having emigrated from Argylshire, Scotland, where he was born in 1817. He commenced the harness-maker's trade when but twelve years of age, and continued at the work for fifteen years. In 1845 he married Catharine Greenlees, by whom he has had nine children, all of whom are living, viz: Hugh, Jeanette (Curtis), Anna (Trotter), Nancy, Daniel, Mary, Eliza, Margaret, and Rosetta.

Robert Hanna, a native of Westmoreland county, Pennsylvania, emigrated to Monroe county, Ohio, in 1828. He lived there about twelve years, and then moved to Virginia, where he remained about ten months. He resided in Warren township from 1841 to the time of his death, July 13, 1878, aged eighty-three. He was the father of eight children. Andrew, Robert C., Hugh, Thomas, James, and Mary A. are residents of Warren township. Jane C. resides in Harmar. Mr. and Mrs. Hanna were members of the Universalist church. Andrew, the oldest child, was born in Westmoreland county, Pennsylvania, October, 1825. He came to Washington county with his father, August 24, 1848. He married Lydia Inman, who was born in Maine, May 22, 1826. They had three children: James C.; Joseph, married to Lucy Tilton, and living in Warren township; and Henrietta, married to Samuel G. Sage, of Wood county, Virginia. It is very seldom that we mention election to small offices, but a long term of service in any office indicates efficiency and popularity. Mr. Hanna has been elected supervisor six successive terms. Joseph is living with his father on the homestead, and is the father of one child, Myrtha B. James C., the oldest son of Andrew and Lydia Hanna, was born in 1850. He married Sarah Reed in 1871. This union has been blessed with two children. Robert E. Hanna, the second child of Robert Hanna, was born in Westmoreland county, Pennsylvania, September 23, 1827. He came to Warren township with his father, in 1841, and August 20, 1857, married Deborah Inman, who was born September 16, 1832. They have two children—Emma, and George. Hugh, the third child of Robert Hanna, was born in Monroe county, Ohio, in 1830, and came to Washington county, Ohio, with his father, in 1841. He married Jane Seffers, by whom he has been blessed with eight children, seven girls and one boy.

In 1842 William Scott located in this county, and has since lived here with the exception of a brief residence in Iowa. Born in western Virginia in 1810, he married Mary Holiday in 1833. Five of their eight children survive. Three are home. Nancy (O'Neal) lives at Belpre, and David W. who married Louisa Dye, resides in Warren township. Mr. Scott is one of the substantial farmers of his neighborhood.

One of the many who sought homes in Warren township, between 1840 and 1850, was Jacob Cooster, oldest son of Joseph Cooster. He was born in Lancaster county, Pennsylvania, March 15, 1810, and settled in Warren township in 1843. Priscilla Atwood who was born in Connecticut August 27, 1811, became his wife February 18, 1830. Their only child died April 6, 1832. Mr. Cooster's popularity in the township is shown by the frequency with which he is chosen to fill local offices.

The Coffmans are well known and influential citizens of this township. Jacob Coffman was a native of Germany. He came to America when quite young, and remained for a period at Lancaster, Pennsylvania. He came to Washington county in 1795, and settled in Marietta township. He afterwards became a resident of this township, where he remained until 1834, when he removed to Hardin county, where he died. He was the father of five children, viz: Jacob, Polly, Fannie, Deborah and Thomas.

Thomas was born November 8, 1805. He married Rebecca Callahan June 18, 1829. She was born in Waterford township October 18, 1807. The fruit of this union was nine children: Mary J., Harvey, George W., Charles, John Q., Thomas A., Sarah, Lucy and Martha, five of whom are living. Mr. and Mrs. Coffman are well known Methodists. Mr. Coffman was honored with the office of township trustee fifteen successive terms.

George W. Coffman, third son of Thomas Coffman, was born September 23, 1834. March 27, 1856, he married Sarah Patton who was born March 7, 1838. They have five children: Mary E., Sarah E., George F., Fremont D., and Murray E., all living.

Charles, fourth son of Thomas Coffman, was born January 13, 1838. He moved to Warren township in 1847, with his father. He married December 13, 1860, Harriet Roush, who was born in Washington county April 10, 1842. They have had seven children: Lizzie, Vesta H., Lucy M., Charles L., Emma M., William D., and Ida B.; all are living, except Lizzie.

John Coffman, fifth child of Thomas and Rebecca Coffman, was born in Watertown township February 28, 1840. He was married to Jane Miller June 1, 1862, and is now the father of four children: Lizzie, Austin, Franklin and Carrie, all living at home.

Stephen Druse was born in France in 1772. In 1800 he married Annie DeSasle. He emigrated first to New York and then to Ohio, and settled in Warren township in 1816. He died in Warren in 1820. Mrs. Druse died in 1845. The surviving members of the family are: Lucy Cooper, who resides in Iowa; Riley, in Belpre; Harrison in Illinois; Warren and Joseph in Missouri; and Stephen, jr., in Belpre. The last named was born in New York in 1816. In 1837 he married Sarah Barkley, who was born in Belpre in 1818. They have had seven children, five of whom are living, viz.: Lucy, Uriah, Stephen, Jane, and Cora. Amanda Williams, the oldest child, is dead.

Lucas Casady emigrated from Pennsylvania to Ohio in 1819, and settled in Washington county, in Warren township. His son, George Casady, was born in Pennsylvania in 1815, and came to Ohio when but four years of age. His first wife was Hannah S. Dye, born in 1818, and died in 1845. Three children were born of the first marriage. Amaziah volunteered in 1862, aged twenty-three, became a member of the Ninety-second Ohio volunteer infantry, company F, and died at Chattanooga in 1864. Emma B. resides in Lawrence township. In 1850 Mr. Casady was married to Sophia Hoff, who was born in 1825. They have had four children, viz.: Mary L., deceased; Judson; Oran; and Ida, deceased. Mr. Casady has a beautiful farm of two hundred and six acres of well improved land. When he first came to the county there was not a wagon in the township, and game, large and small, was abundant.

George Miller was born in England in 1771. He emigrated to America in 1804 and was employed by Blennerhassett on his farm for ten years. He then moved to Morgan county, where he died January 20, 1829. In 1806 he was married to Louise Taylor, who was born in England in 1782. Their family consisted of seven boys and four girls. William, the second child, was born December 6, 1808. He was taken with his parents when young to Morgan county, where he remained till 1840, when he settled in Warren township. He was married, December 28, 1852, to Mary McVey, who was born in Athens county December 7, 1828. They have had six children—Albert H., Hannah M., George W., Elizabeth J., and Susannah B.—three of whom are living at home. Albert resides in Kansas, Susannah B. in Morgan county, and Elizabeth, wife of J. P. Miller, in Warren township.

Barnet S. Christopher, second son of Decamp and Harriet Christopher, was born in Fayette county, Pennsylvania in 1824, and in 1846 settled in Warren township, Washington county, Ohio. In 1852 he married Emily, daughter of John Lacey, of Jefferson county, Ohio. Ten of their eleven children survive. By hard work and enterprise Mr. Christopher has secured a fine farm and a comfortable home.

James Pinkerton settled in that part of Warren formally included in Union, in the year 1846. He was born in Pennsylvania in 1804. His wife, Mary Wilson, born in 1805, died in 1878; nine of their thirteen children are living—William, Andrew, James, Thomas John, Wilson, Calvert, Robert, and Sarah. The fourth son, Thomas, born in Allegheny county, Pennsylvania, in 1837, came to this county with his father. He married Sarah R. Coffman, born in 1847. Their children are, George, Charles and Emma. Mr. Pinkerton's farm consists of one hundred and thirty-two acres of land.

Robert Smith, sixth son of Thomas Smith, was born in George county, Maryland, April 24, 1805. He came to Warren township in 1848; February 14, 1827, he was married to Eliza Arnold, of Jefferson county, Ohio. Six children have blessed this unison, viz: Oliver E., residing in Warren township; John C., and Thomas, in Illinois; Martha J., in Warren township; James A., in Kansas; and Elizabeth in Illinois. Mr. Smith is a blacksmith by trade, and both he and his wife are members of the Christian church.

March 27, 1855, Martha J. was married to Benjamin Parlin, who was born in Maine, October 9, 1825. They

have had seven children, Ethalinda, John, Verandale, James, George, Lizzie and Mary, of whom two are dead—Ethalinda and John. Mr. Parlin died February 16, 1876, at the age of fifty-one years. He was several times honored with township offices, and much respected in the community.

Adam Freed, fifth son of Benjamin Freed, was born in Columbiana county, Ohio, November 5, 1824. He lived in Jefferson county, Ohio, Mason county, Virginia, and Meigs county, Ohio, until 1851, when he came to Warren township. He was married to Margaret E. Bradshaw, widow of George Bradshaw and daughter of Samuel Oliver. She was born April 14, 1827, and married to Mr. Freed July 10, 1851. They have had eleven children, Martha J., Mary A., Rebecca, Susan A., Margaret M., Dennis F., Lizzie C., Adam A., Sarah E., and two who died in infancy.

In 1851 James Foster became a resident of this township, and remained therein until his death in 1879. His widow, whose maiden name was Eliza Coyle is still living, as are also nine of her ten children. Their second son, John, was born in Belmont county, in 1835, and came with his father to Washington county. He married Eliza J. Price, daughter of Abram Price of this county. The result of their marriage was one boy and one girl. Before settling on his present farm he was section foreman on the Marietta & Cincinnati railroad.

Arthur McMahon, oldest child of Philip McMahon, was born in Ireland, May 14, 1816. He emigrated to America and settled in Chester county, Pennsylvania, in 1843. In 1844 he moved to Reading, Pennsylvania, where he was married in 1847 to Catherine Clark, a native of Ireland. In 1852 he came to Washington county, Ohio. Twelve children, eleven of whom survive, have blessed this union. Mr. McMahon is one of the kind of men who are able to turn their hand to anything. He labored successfully in a machine shop at Reading, Pennsylvania; served the Government during the war in the telegraph department, and is now a successful farmer. Both Mr. and Mrs. McMahon are members of the Catholic church.

John Christie was born in Prussia in 1823, emigrated to New Jersey, and, in 1853, came to this county and settled in that part of Union now Warren township, upon an upland farm of one hundred acres, which are well improved. For three years Mr. Christie served as township trustee. He married Elizabeth Tresth, who was born in 1828. Four of their five children survive. Mr. Christie has just erected a fine frame house.

John Holden, oldest child of Andrew and Margaret Holden, was born in King's county, Ireland, in 1810, and emigrated to New York State about 1850, remaining there two years, thence coming to Warren township, this county. In 1836 he married Julia Dooley, daughter of John Dooley, of Ireland. Twelve children, nine boys and three girls, have blessed their union. Mr. and Mrs. Holden are earnest supporters of the Roman Catholic church. Their oldest son, Andrew, born in 1839, emigrated to New York in 1853, and in that same year came to this township. By his wife, Catharine Highlands, he has had six children, four of whom are still living. Mr. Holden has been township treasurer, and is the present clerk. He served four years during the late war, in company F, Seventy-third Ohio volunteer infantry.

William C. Wright, fourth child of Jesse Wright, was born in Berkeley county, Virginia, in 1805, and in 1853 came to Washington county. In 1833 he married Maria, daughter of David Pattin. Of their ten children but four are living, viz.: John, Friend, Stephen and Elizabeth. Mrs. Wright died in 1876. Mr. Wright, being by trade a miller, has worked many years at the mill in Harmar. He is now on his farm in Warren township.

George Harris, sr., emigrated from Rhode Island to Ohio in 1805, and settled in Marietta. He remained in the county until his death, which occurred June 2, 1856. During this time he lived about three years in Monroe county. He married Mary Harrison, who was born in England, June 21, 1784. The fruit of this union was seven children. George, the youngest child, was born in Fearing township, July 26, 1829. He lived with his father till January 1, 1851, when he was married to Elizabeth Sprague, who was born in Monroe county, June 16, 1826. In 1856 Mr. Harris moved to Warren township. He is the father of nine children: Eldora, Phœbe. Isabella, Abner, Fayette, William R., Orilla, George F. and Della. Mr. Harris was township trustee four years.

John Davis settled in Warren township in 1856. He was born in Ireland in 1815, and emigrated to America with his father when quite young. He remained there until he came to this township. In November, 1838, he married Eleanor Pinkerton, a daughter of Andrew D. Pinkerton. She was born January 1, 1816. The children are: Andrew G., Malinda, Elizabeth, William W., James and Thomas P. All are living except Andrew G.

Frederick Hart, a native of Pennsylvania, emigrated to Ohio in 1854 and settled in Warren township, where he died April 12, 1857. He was the father of nine children: Samuel M., Mary A., Andrew J., Margaret, Miller H., Alexander, William, Elizabeth, and George, all living. Samuel M., the oldest child, was born in Allegheny county, Pennsylvania, September 21, 1827. He came to Warren township with his father in 1854. He was married April 26, 1856, to Mary McKee, who was born in Ireland March 6, 1831. Their family consists of four children—William, Ellenworth, George, and Frank, all living except Frank. Mr. Hart served during the war in company K, One Hundred and Forty-eighth National guard.

James A. Mercer, second child of Caleb Mercer, was born in Frederick county, Virginia, June 7, 1819. In 1841 he moved to Monroe county and remained there four years. He lived in Lawrence and Newport townships until 1857, when he settled in Warren township. September 3, 1841, he was married to Tabitha Cecil, who was born February 28, 1826, in Harrison county, Ohio. The fruit of this marriage was ten children, nine boys and one girl. Eight are still living—four married and four single. Mr. Mercer worked at backsmithing for thirty years before coming to Warren township.

James Cooper, fifth son of James Cooper, sr., was

born in Butler county, Pennsylvania, June 28, 1820. He emigrated to Ohio in 1859, and settled in Warren township. January 12, 1858, he married Sarah McCue, of Ireland. The fruit of this union was four children—Mary C., Nancy J., Sarah M., and James, all living at home. Mr. Cooper is a member of the Presbyterian church and a useful man in the community. He is a stonemason by trade, but since coming to Ohio has devoted all his attention to farming.

Uriah Cooper, youngest son of James Cooper, sr., was born in Butler county, Pennsylvania, February 22, 1836. He was married May 14, 1863, to Miss Werner, daughter of Aaron Werner, a native of Germany. She was born in Germany February 6, 1843. The family of Mr. and Mrs. Cooper consists of five children—Amos L., Sophia W., Minerva I., Marion M., and Wilmina M., three of whom are living. Both Mr. and Mrs. Cooper are faithful members and liberal supporters of the church.

Ernest Roeper, the ninth son of John H. Roeper, was born in Prussia March 6, 1818. He emigrated to America and settled in Cincinnati in 1852, and remained there until 1855, when he came to Harmar. After residing in Harmar ten years he moved to Locust Forks, in Warren township, and is now engaged in business at that place. He married Fredericka Grasle May 26, 1857, and is now the father of five children—George H., Katie E., Louisa F., William L., and Herman P., and one died in infancy. Mr. and Mrs. Roeper are both members of the Lutheran Church.

John J. Kaylor, sixth son of Altonis Kaylor, was born in Butler county, Pennsylvania, November 26, 1826. He married, May 6, 1852, Johannah Burger, who was born in Germany September 28, 1830. They had ten children—George, Mary A., Martha, Lizzie, Josephine, John, Henrietta, Joseph, William H., and Matilda, all living except John. Mr. Kaylor came to Washington county and settled in Warren township in 1868. The whole family are members of the Catholic church. Mr. Kaylor has worked at blacksmithing since 1845, and was employed one year during the war in one of the Government shops. He is also an enterprising farmer.

Harriet Price, daughter of John Gosset, was born in Watertown township October 10, 1813. Mrs. Price has twice been bereaved of her husband. She was first married to John Wilson, by whom she had seven children. Abram Price, to whom she was married July 10, 1863, was born April 8, 1800. Mrs. Price is a member of the Brethren church. With the assistance of her grandsons she cultivates the old farm in Warren township.

George Seibert was born in Baden, Germany, January 3, 1822. He emigrated to America and settled in Pennsylvania, where he remained until 1874, when he settled in Warren township, Washington county, Ohio. He was married in 1845 to Elizabeth Kaylor. This union was blessed with five children, all boys. In October, 1867, he was married a second time, and has since had seven children, three boys and four girls. Both Mr. and Mrs. Seibert are members of the Catholic church. Mr. Seibert worked at the machinest trade thirty-five years previous to 1874. Since that time he has been farming.

CONSTITUTION FARM.

RESIDENCE OF H. LYMAN HART, WARREN TP., WASHINGTON CO., O.

HUNTERS.

Warren township, in the early years of the settlement, was a favorite hunting ground. Game was abundant along the small streams in the interior of the township. Excellent shelter was afforded by the density of the forest and size of the trees. Wild-cats and wolves were numerous and troublesome, and occasionally a panther was shot. The most noted hunters were Amos Delano, Ichabod Cole, Willard Harris, and the Ferrils.

POST OFFICES.

There have never been but two post offices in the township. The first one was established January 21, 1832, and was named Constitution, in honor of the first postmaster, Judge Ephraim Cutler, who was one of the most prominent members and latest survivors of the convention which framed the first constitution of Ohio. Judge Cutler was postmaster about twenty years. His successors have been, William D. Bailey, J. H. Deming, Lizzy M. Bailey, and Lucinda Reid. "Tunnel" was established in 1855. T. W. Moore was appointed first postmaster, and held the office two years. Succeeding postmasters have been I. J. Vandewalker, James Tuttle, William Heald, and Charles Tretsel.

VILLAGES.

There is not within this township any collection of houses large enough to be called a village. Tunnel, while the old line of the Marietta & Cincinnati railroad was being built, was a temporary collection of small huts, which were deserted when the work which called their occupants there was ended. Charles Tretsel, at Tunnel, and Earnest Roeper, at Locust Forks, conduct good country stores.

CEMETERIES.

Before any cemetery had been laid out a small lot along the river, near the present location of the Presbyterian church, was used for a burying ground by the early settlers. A man named Ruter, two of the Green children, and a few others, were buried here; but river floods made the place unsuitable for a cemetery. Seth Bailey, at the death of his sister Mary, set apart a lot on his farm to be used as a public burying-ground. The lot was afterwards enlarged and deeded to the first religious society, by which it is controlled at present. In 1856, at the death of Lucy D. Brabham, Walter Brabham fenced off for cemetery purposes a finely located lot on the Lancaster road. It was owned by Mr. Brabham, but given to the use of the public until 1877, when the Warren township cemetery association was founded and the lot transferred to that association by Mr. Brabham. The trustees are Samuel M. Hart, Joseph A. Mercer, and Earnest Roeper.

A THANKSGIVING.

An incident is remembered by an old settler of a thanksgiving service which was held in the early history of the settlement, in the first school-house. The services were conducted by the Rev. Mr. Robbins, of Marietta, and at their conclusion the men got on their horses and rode down to Cole's tavern, where the usual refreshments were served. But before partaking, Mr. Robbins, while yet remaining on his horse, asked an impressive blessing, on the stimulating beverage contained in the glasses.

THE EPIDEMICS.

The epidemics of 1807 and 1821-3 were particularly severe in Warren township. The intensely cold winter of 1806-7 was followed by high water in the spring, which completely flooded the alluvial bottom. Distressing sickness prevailed during the summer, and the work of clearing and improving farms was greatly retarded. The epidemic of 1821-3 was devastating. Fever visited almost every house, and in many cases proved fatal within a week after the first attack. One familiar with the history of this terrible period writes: "No family and few individuals escaped. In the family of William Smith, consisting of eleven persons, all were sick at the same time, and in other instances none were able to nurse the sick. This season and the next was very dry. In 1822 the Ohio was lower than ever before known; the water was nearly stagnant, and green with scum and vegetable matter, while grass and aquatic plants covered the sandbars and extended into the water several rods from the shore. The sickness began early in June, was very severe in August and September, and did not abate until the heavy frosts in November. This year the disease prevailed especially along the river valley, and, as during the previous season, many deaths occurred. The next year much rain fell, and the river kept well up during the summer. But in June the fever again made its appearance, not only along the water courses, but also on the uplands, and was in many cases fatal. So general was the sickness that the corn grew unattended among the weeds, and remained unharvested until late, and the orchards were laden with fruits which perished. These sickly seasons will long be remembered in the traditions of the afflicted and bereaved families. Many valuable citizens were numbered with the dead. A remarkable fatality attended the families of Mr. Tiffany Adams and his nephew, James Adams, who occupied the Gilman farm in the upper part of the township. They were attacked by the fever and fourteen graves in the Adams' row, in the old cemetery in Warren, tell the result. Of six remarkably fine healthy sons of Tiffany Adams two survived, and returned to Connecticut, from where the family emigrated in 1817.

POPULATION.

In 1820 Warren had a population of four hundred and sixty. During the next decade the sickly season occurred, and the population was only six hundred and forty-two. From 1830 to 1840 the population increased to nine hundred and thirty-one, and in 1850 reached one thousand four hundred and sixty-one. In 1860 it enumerated one thousand seven hundred and fifteen, but density of settlement increased more rapidly than the figures seem to indicate, for the area of the township was considerably reduced during this decade. During the next ten years the war deprived the township of many of its best citizens, and the number of inhabitants decreased to one thousand six hundred and four. In 1880 it enumerated one thousand nine hundred and six.

81

ROADS.

The first road through the township was laid out in 1793 from Marietta to Belpre. This road, through the present territory of Warren, was located at the foot of the river hills. It was afterwards changed to run along the river bank, crossing many streams that required bridges. These, together with frequent sinking of the river bank, caused by freshets, made the road expensive and burdensome on the sparce population.

The second road through the township was a State road from Marietta to Lancaster, built in 1797. The location of this road has never been materially changed.

The Marietta and Athens road, commonly known in Warren township as the State road, was constructed about 1800, although the survey was made before that time. Along this road the first improvements were made after the river bottom had been taken up.

A road connecting the Lancaster and Belpre roads was laid out in 1804, but remained for a long time nothing but a cow-path through the woods. The construction of roads among the hills required much labor before they could be made serviceable. At present the roads in Warren are in good condition, considering the roughness of the surface.

The stranger riding along the Belpre road can see in the large farm houses the agricultural thrift of the community. These houses, many of them, are old, and were built by the first settlers to replace the original cabins. The bricks with which they were built were made by Oren Newton on the Newton farm.

The first frame houses in the township were built by Messrs. Bailey, Newton, and Cole. The frames were made at the headwaters of the Ohio and floated down on rafts. The oldest house in the township at present is the old stone Cutler residence, which was built in 1807. Its massive masonry is emblematic of the mind and character of its builder and occupant, for nearly half a century.

In the interior of the township the farm buildings average fairly with those of other upland portions of the county. Warren, in respect to improvements and productiveness of soil, is somewhat typical of the whole county. It has its alluvial bottom, its limestone terraces, and its shale and sand hills, and the quality of improvements varies with the productiveness of these different kinds of soil. As would naturally be expected, the character of the population is, in a measure, affected in the same way.

SCHOOLS.

Happily we have in the memoranda of Judge Ephraim Cutler a complete and accurate account of the early schools of the township. We give entire the first contract:

Memoranda of an agreement entered into this third day of February, 1807, by and between Isaac Humphreys, John Henry, and Ephraim Cutler and John D. W. Kip, on the other part witnesseth: That for the consideration of the sum of twenty-five dollars for every three months, to be paid him at the expiration of said term by Humphreys, Henry and Cutler, he, the said Kip, doth engage to keep a school at such place as they shall direct and to teach reading, writing and arithmetic, and to govern himself and school by the following rules and regu-

lations, to-wit: He shall keep school from nine o'clock in the morning till twelve at noon, and from one in the afternoon until four; provided that during the months of June, July, August and September school may commence at half-past one and close at half-past four. He shall be excused from keeping school on Saturdays in the afternoon, on the Fourth of July, when he shall be called to attend trainings, and on election days.

The whole school shall be arranged into two or more classes at the direction of the master, the senior class to be admitted to the exercise of writing and arithmetic, the lower classes shall be employed in reading and spelling, and that no time may be lost they shall have portions assigned them for study, from which at proper hours the master shall ask them to spell, and in order to promote emulation, the priority in standing shall be determined by their accuracy in spelling.

Particular attention shall be paid in the upper class in teaching them punctuation; and that in reading they be taught to observe the stops and points, notes of affection and interrogation, also accenting and emphasizing.

The master shall consider himself as in the place of parent to the children under his care, and endeavor to convince them by mild treatment that he feels a parental affection for them. He shall be sparing as to promises or threatenings, but punctual in the performance of one and execution of the other, and that he inculcate upon the scholars the propriety of good behavior during their absence from school.

He will endeavor on all suitable occasions to impress upon the minds of his scholars a sense of the being and providence of God, and the obligations they are under to love and serve Him; of their duty to their parents; the beauty and excellency of truth, the duty which they owe to their country, and the necessity of a strict observance to its laws.

He shall caution, and as far as he can, restrain them from the prevailing vices, such as lying, profaneness, gaming, and idleness.

From these general rules he may form particular rules, and if they are broken, he must be particular to punish the offender, but mildness in punishment is recommended.

This contract shows that the early settlers had high ideas of the influence of a school and the power of a school-master. The lack of confidence in Mr. Kip, shown by the minuteness of the rules laid down in the contract, proved to be well founded, for the memoranda goes on to state that Mr. Kip found himself unequal to the task, and in less than a week resigned the charge. "He could not reduce to order the stalwart lads and buxom lasses committed to his care."

In the winter of 1809–10 the first successful school was accommodated in the south room of Judge Culler's stone house. The teacher was General John Brown, late treasurer of Ohio university, at Athens. He was an intelligent young man, of kind and genial disposition and strong common sense. He is remembered and spoken of with the highest respect by those who enjoyed his instructions.

In 1810 the first school-house was built. It was a log building, and stood where Dole's blacksmith shop now (1881) is.

In 1813 the winter school was in charge of John McMillan. John Adams, a well educated young man from Connecticut, taught in 1819.

In 1814 a summer school, designed particularly for girls, was opened by Miss Sallie Rice; she received as compensation one dollar and twenty-five cents per week. Her contract prescribed that she should teach reading and instruct the young misses in sewing. Miss Rice was a very successful teacher, and held the position until 1818. Mary Ann Cutler was a succeeding female teacher. In addition to the usual "reading, writing and arithmetic" grammar and geography were taught by her.

The common school law, which was passed in 1825

went into effect in Warren township about 1827. The township was divided into four districts, but there were probably five school-houses within the limits of the township at that time.*

April 18, 1853, the school board of the township met and reorganized the schools under the act of March 11, of that year. The township was divided into twelve school districts. The establishment of Dunham in 1855 reduced the number to ten, which number was afterwards reduced to nine. In 1867 the two river districts were separated from the rest of the township, and established into a special district. This action created a bitter feeling throughout the township. The township had the year previous appropriated six hundred dollars to build a school-house in each one of these districts, and the people of the township at large considered it unfair to permit the two wealthier districts to withdraw, especially while new houses were needed all over the township. The object of the movers for a special district was, to establish a graded school. An attempt was made to carry this object into execution, but failed. The tax duplicate shows that the special district is benefitted financially to the detriment of the township districts. In 1869 the Warren township board appropriated one hundred dollars toward the building of a house for a colored school, a similar appropriation having been made by Barlow township. There were at that time fifteen colored children in the township.

The annexation of four sections from Union added two schools to Warren, making the whole number of township schools, in 1877, nine. Most of the buildings are in good condition, and the schools are conducted as liberally as common schools generally are.

After the adoption of the common school system, higher branches than formerly were taught in the river districts, by well qualified teachers, in both summer and winter. Since 1835 the winter schools have generally been taught by students from Marietta college. Since 1820 it has been the custom to send the youth of either sex to Marietta or more distant places to complete their education. A number of young men who did not take a college course, availed themselves for a time of the instructions afforded at Marietta, and perhaps a still larger proportion of the young ladies have pursued their studies at the female seminaries in the State—thus forming an intelligent community. We append a list of natives of Warren who have graduated at Marietta college: William Dennison Bailey, class of 1843; George Washington Bailey, class of 1845; Oren Henry Newton, class of 1845; Ephraim Cutler Dawes, class of 1861; Seth Packard Bailey, 1874; Charles Lindley Dickey, class of 1877; Amos Austin Dickey, class of 1877; Charles Emerson Bailey, class of 1880. The following graduates were residents but not natives of Warren: Joseph Cone Blackington, class of 1875; Daniel Wayland Dye, class of 1871; Freeman J. Dye, class of 1871; Salathiel Smith De Garmo, class of 1876.

*In the absence of complete records we are compelled to rely upon the recollection of the oldest and best informed citizens of the township.

POLITICS.

The majority at State and National elections has always been given in favor of the Democratic candidate, with but one exception—the Presidential election of 1840, when Harrison carried the township. But at the preceding Presidential election the vote stood: Whig, 28; Democratic, 68. During the slavery agitation the leading Democrats stood by the traditions of their party. The Whigs were of the conservative order, while but two or three straight-out abolitionists resided in the township. Samuel Brown, then of Warren, and Mr. Burges were the only aggressive opponents of the system of slavery.

PRESBYTERIAN CHURCH.

In the winter of 1825-6, while navigation was suspended on the Ohio, two missionaries, Messrs. Chamberlyn and West, on their way to the southwest, were ice-bound at Marietta, and did missionary work in adjacent communities. Through their influence the Domestic missionary society of Connecticut sent Rev. Jacob Little to labor as an evangelist in Washington county. He preached in Belpre, and occasionally in Warren and other places. Services were held in the old tavern stand of Nathan Cole, in the present territory of Dunham township. Here Mr. Little, who was well fitted for a pioneer preacher, organized a Bible-class of twenty-four, mostly young ladies, and a Sunday-school.

April 18, 1827, an agreement was entered into between Mr. Little and Samuel S. Spencer, Ephraim Cutler, Seth Bailey, Timothy Cone, Oren Newton, and Isaac Humphreys, by which they were to pay him two hundred dollars for half his time and labors. About this time, however, Mr. Little received and accepted a call to Granville, Ohio.

Rev. Augustus Pomeroy came in the summer of 1827, and held meetings in the brick school-house, which had just been built, on the upper part of Seth Bailey's farm. In this house the "Presbyterian church of Warren" was formed February 23, 1828. We quote the first entry in the record:

In compliance with the indications of Providence and the ardent wishes of Christians in Warren, agreeably to previous notice, the people of Warren and vicinity assembled, and after sermon by L. G. Bingham, of Marietta, James Harvey and Catharine, his wife, James Harvey, jr., William Fleming, William Frazer and Christina, his wife, Mrs. Elizabeth Fulcher, Mrs. Sarah Johnston, Samuel S. Spencer, Charles Humphreys, Mrs. Seth Bailey, and Mrs. Hezekiah Lewis presented letters of recommendation, and were duly constituted into a church of Christ, in Warren, by the Rev. A. Pomeroy, missionary.

Samuel S. Spencer and William Fleming were unanimously elected elders. On Sabbath, the day following, eight were admitted to membership on examination, viz: Ephraim Cutler, James Frazer, Mrs. Samuel S. Spencer, Mrs. Harvey Lewis, Mrs. Lucy Cooper, Sarah Smith, Sarah Cutler, and Calvina Waterman. The sermon was preached in the morning by Rev. T. Thacher, and in the afternoon by Rev. A. Pomeroy. It is recorded: "This day was one of great apparent solemnity and interest, and it is believed will be remembered forever."

The Warren church was first represented in the Athens presbytery April 17, 1828. About that time Rev. A. Kingsbury took charge. During the first two years of his pastorate two interesting revivals occurred, and sixty-six members were added to the church. Dr. Kingsbury served the church until 1839, when he accepted a call to Putnam, Ohio, to the deepest regret of the Warren church, then numbering over one hundred members.

In 1837 the present meeting-house, on the river road, was built at an expense of about one thousand four hundred dollars, which was borne mainly by Oren Newton, Ephraim Cutler, William P. Cutler, and Seth Bailey. An act incorporating the "First Presbyterian Society of Warren" was passed February 13, 1838. After Dr. Kingsbury left, the church was supplied for short seasons by Dr. Linsley, Professor Allen, and Rev. John Woodbridge. In 1841 Rev. Roswell Tenny accepted a call and remained one year. He was succeeded by Rev. Dyar Burgess, "an eccentric but strong man," who filled the pulpit two years. During this time a few additions were made to the church. During the two years' pastorate of Rev. Joseph S. Edwards, which began in 1841, twenty-seven were added to the church. Rev. Windsor A. Smith came in 1846 and was installed pastor. He was an acceptable minister, but on account of ill health resigned and retired in September, 1852. Up to this time Warren and Belpre united in sustaining a minister. It was now agreed that each church should support its own pastor.

Rev. Prof. E. B. Andrews, of Marietta college, supplied the pulpit during 1853. January 1, 1854, Rev. James S. Walton became pastor. Under his persuasive preaching a revival took place in 1856, which resulted in thirty-two accessions to the church. Mr. Walton removed to Illinois in 1858, and from that time till 1862, no record was kept. Rev. Charles D. Curtis had charge of Warren and Belpre churches from November, 1862, till June, 1866, when he was elected president of Farmers' college, Cincinnati. Rev. John L. Mills, of Marietta, supplied the pulpit until December, 1868, when John Noble was installed pastor. Mr. Noble was succeeded by Mr. Strauss in 1876. Mr. Strauss remained pastor till 1880.

The fifty-two years this church has existed, more than three hundred members have been connected with it. It has always sustained temperance and Sabbath-schools, and according to its means and numbers supported liberally, missionary and other benevolent institutions.

This church, considering its age, has had but few ruling elders. Samuel S. Spencer was a good worker particularly in the Sabbath-school. He died, much lamented, July 27, 1832. William Fleming faithfully served the church as ruling elder for a period of forty years—from its foundation till his death in 1868. He was born in 1781. April 7, 1833, Ephraim Cutler and Harry McClure were set apart as ruling elders. Mr. Cutler served the church and Sabbath-school ably and faithfully until his death July 8, 1853. He was twice a member of the Presbyterian general assembly. Mr. McClure was a delegate to the general assembly which met in St. Louis in 1855. Returning, he died of cholera on an Ohio river boat, in sight of his home, May 18, 1845. William P. Cutler and Joel Deming were made ruling elders.

Both are still living. Mr. Cutler left the place in 1872, and about that time George W. Bailey was added to the eldership.

METHODISM.

The late Bishop Morris, when a young man, preached occasionally in Warren, and was probably the pioneer preacher of the township. He formed a class in the part of the township which has since been set off to Dunham and one in the interior. A union meeting-house was built on the site of the present town-house, which was mainly used by itinerant Methodists, who carried their missionary work into the country. Had it not been for these zealous itinerants, the sparsely populated portions of the county would have been deprived of the elevating and moralizing influences of Christian preaching. A large share of the credit for the systematic organization of the church is due to Rev. Levi Cunningham, who served first as a local preacher in the community, and was finally given charge of a circuit. When the settlement began to increase more rapidly, two classes were organized, one on Brown's run called "Zoar," the other on the Lancaster road, denominated "Bethel," and churches were built and cemeteries laid out for the accommodation of both classes. "Zoar" disbanded its organization at the beginning of the Rebellion. "Bethel" continues to maintain its organization, although preaching has been temporarily suspended. Warren chapel is at present (1881) the only preaching station in the township. Its membership is partially drawn from Zoar and Bethel. Warren churches are included in Barlow circuit.

MT. MORIAH UNITED BRETHREN CHURCH.

This church was organized about 1850, at which time a log meeting-house was built near the site of the present church on the Lancaster road near Wolf creek. The congregation was connected with Plymouth circuit until 1879, when the circuit was divided and Mt. Moriah was attached to Pleasant Grove, now Watertown circuit. The ministers connected with the Plymouth circuit, a list of whom will be found elsewhere, supplied this church. Rev. Mr. Willis is the present pastor.

DISCIPLE CHURCH.

In 1862 Jesse Thomas, Samuel Sprague, Robert Smith, and a few others holding the doctrines of Alexander Campbell, met and organized a society known as the Warren Disciple church. The society has never had the services of a regular pastor, but have been irregularly supplied by various ministers, Rev. Mr. Newgen preaching most frequently. A church building was erected near the residence of Nathan Thomas in 1880. The church, although not large, is in a healthy condition.

EARLY SUNDAY-SCHOOL.

The first Sunday-school was established in Warren township by Miss Mariam Cutler, a niece of Judge Cutler, in the spring of 1819. There were at that time in the whole community but five professors of religion, and three of those were considered recent settlers. Judge Cutler writes: "At the commencement the scholars had very little previous knowledge of the design of the insti-

MRS. JESSE MELLOR

JESSE MELLOR

THE OLD HOME

RESIDENCE OF J. MELLOR, WARREN TP., WASHINGTON CO., O.

tution; many of them had been in the habit of considering the Sabbath a holiday. But five were able to recite anything at the first meeting. There was, however, improvement." The following is the roll of scholars probably at the first meeting: boys—M. Cutler, William Cutler, J. Ranger, E. Smith, Seth Bailey, C. Baily, John Bailey, B. Bailey, A. Wood, William Cole, M. Wood, E. Ridgly, and W. Bailey; girls—M. Cutler, J. Cutler, C. Simpson, Sally Smith, Linda Cole, S. Jenks, D. Cole, C. Cole, C. Ridgly, M. Bailey, E. Bailey, S. Bailey, S. Harris, H. Smith, P. Smith, J. Cutler, C. Cutler, E. Cutler, and J. Ridgly. In 1836 there were three schools in the township, designated Nos. 1, 2 and 3. School No. 1 was superintended for some time by ladies. At the formation of the Presbyterian church eight scholars were received on profession and some of them were afterwards the most useful members. Four of this number had been teachers. After the establishment of the church the school was intimately connected with it. In 1836 there were sixty-one scholars, one superintendent and eight teachers, and a library of three hundred and sixty-four volumes.

School No. 2 was organized in 1833, and received through the agent of the Sunday-school union, J. M. McAboy, five dollars. Its library contained, in 1836, seventy-five volumes. There were at that time twenty-five scholars and four teachers.

School No. 3 was organized in 1833. In 1836 it had one hundred volumes in its library, three teachers and twenty scholars.

The several churches in the township maintain Sabbath-schools during the summer and others have been organized in school-houses. The three mentioned were the only early schools.

TEMPERANCE SOCIETY.

The free use of intoxicating and stimulating liquors have frequently been remarked. The much relished beverage was used to stimulate the brain and muscle while at work and to quiet the nerves during the hours of rest. A well filled bottle was the emblem of hospitality, and all grades of society united in drinking each other's health. The subscription papers of one of the oldest churches in the county show that the minister received several gallons of whiskey on account of salary and another minister of the same period owned an interest in a distillery.

That there has been a revolution of opinion on the subject of temperance is proved by the change of customs, and it is interesting to know when and in what way this revolution was effected. We shall confine ourselves to the territory which forms the subject of this chapter. Mr. Cutler says in his notes:

The first check to intemperance which had so generally prevailed as to almost forbid the hope that it could be arrested, was matured under the blessing of God through the labors of Rev. Mr. Kingsbury and a few others, it was suggested as likely to have a favorable effect to invite the Rev. John Spaulding, then living at Athens, to deliver an address on this important subject. He accepted the invitation. A committee of five was appointed and a constitution was prepared, ready for the purpose of forming a society, to be presented for signatures immediately after the address.

The meeting was held April 22, 1832. Mr. Spaulding and Mr. Kingsbury each made thrilling addresses, and we were surprised to find forty-nine pledging themselves, by signing the constitution, to abandon the use of ardent spirits, except as medicine, and we hope the entire number with nearly one hundred others whose names are added to this constitution, have remained faithful to their promise.

This temperance movement resulted in a genuine reformation. It was approved and promoted by the most influential inhabitants. Intoxicating liquors were no longer provided at huskings and raisings, and were banished from the harvest field. At first additional wages were offered, but soon all acquiesced in the innovation. Nearly half a century has passed and the good effects remain.

BIOGRAPHICAL SKETCHES.

JESSE MELLOR.

About the year 1795, Samuel Mellor and his brother-in-law, Matthew Corner, emigrated with their families from England, and settled on donation lands along the west branch of Wolf creek, in Watertown township. The Mellor family consisted of five sons and four daughters. One of the sons was Samuel Mellor, jr., who married Nancy Jadon, of this county, and improved a farm in the Wolf Creek bottom. Their family consisted of seven children: Susan (Dunsmore), Jesse, Mary (Adams), Prudence (Adams), Nancy (Godfrey), Joannah (Rodgers), and Walter. All of these are dead except Joannah, and Jesse, the subject of this sketch.

Jesse Mellor was born September 14, 1810. The nearest school-house being three miles distant, his early training was very limited, and the severe labor of a new farm deprived him of educational advantages later in life. He was married March 22, 1831, to Mary Ann Kidwell. He rented a farm in Wesley township, and served as a tenant four years. During that period, by industry and economical habits, he accumulated money enough to purchase a small tract of land, which he cleared, and afterwards traded for property in Marietta. In turn, the town property was exchanged for a farm on Wolf creek, above the homestead, but before removing to this place he cultivated his father's farm for a period of three years. Thirty-three years ago Mr. Mellor came into possession of his present property in Warren township.

Mary Ann Mellor, first wife of Jesse Mellor, died in February, 1844, in her thirty-fourth year, leaving seven children, all of whom are living. The children are: Mary Ann (Higgins), Harmar, born February 11, 1832; Columbus Mellor, Marietta, born November 16, 1833; Jefferson Mellor, Barlow, born March 29, 1836; Charles Mellor, Muskingum township, born April 31, 1838; Edward Mellor, Warren township, born February 10, 1840; Samuel Austin Mellor, Muskingum township, born November 23, 1841; Jane (Coffman), Warren township, born November 9, 1843.

Mr. Mellor married for his second wife, Matilda Elliott, July 12, 1845, by whom he had five children, viz: George Mellor, Warren township, born June 25, 1846; David Higgins Mellor, born May 28, 1848; Joannah (Mercer), Warren township, born March 12, 1851; Susannah Mellor, Harmar, born June 3, 1854; Thomas, born July 30, 1856, died in infancy; Mrs. Mellor died in 1865.

Mr. Mellor married for his third wife, January 1, 1866, Mrs. Ann Eliza Farrish, daughter of Joseph and Susannah Leach. Her father emigrated from Pennsylvania to Belmont county, Ohio, where she was born March 12, 1828. The family afterwards removed to this county. Her first husband was Thomas L. Farrish, who died in September, 1859, leaving three children: Virginia Ann, deceased, Tute M., and Joseph Leach. Mr. Mellor has by his third wife one son, Jesse L., born July 24, 1867.

Mr. Mellor has been during all his life a hard worker. He has cleared and improved four farms. In his clearing he departed from the general custom of the period, of making log-rolling frolics, finding it more profitable to do his own work with oxen and chains. Although never having learned the trade, Mr. Mellor is a skilled worker in wood. He has built three houses, made wagons, carts, plows, and other farming utensils for his own use and for his neighbors. In the kitchen, at the present time, stands an old-fashioned cupboard, made by him fifty years ago, with a drawing knife. He never indulged in any games, preferring to use his time more profitably making churns, buckets, etc., etc. His self-made tools and implements have frequently taken premiums at agricultural fairs.

Mr. Mellor has given special attention to fruit culture, having large plumb, peach, and apple orchards. One year he placed on exhibition, at the county fair, more than one hundred varieties of apples. Some of the specimens in the Ohio collection at the Centennial exposition were taken from his orchard. He has for many years sold fruits and vegetables to a large patronage in Marietta. He engaged in butchering and selling meat from his wagon for eight years. In addition to regular farming he has dealt largely in stock. Every agricultural fair in this county has received his support, and he always comes away with a fair share of premiums, the number at the county fair one year aggregating to forty-seven.

Mr. Mellor's habits have been unusually regular. He has never tasted strong drink or tobacco, or indulged in needless luxuries. He has never bought for his children candies, preferring to give them books for presents. He is a well preserved man, being, at the age of three-score and ten, able to fell three-foot trees, leaving "a right and left cut stump."

His first vote was for Andrew Jackson; but the next four years made him a Whig, with which party he co-operated until 1856, when he became a Republican. During the half-century he has been a voter his name has been enrolled at every election until the spring of 1881, when sickness detained him.

TIMOTHY AND SARAH H. CONE.

Timothy Cone was born in East Haddam, Connecticut, May 20, 1777. He would look back to an honorable ancestry. He was the son of Joseph Cone and Martha Spencer, the daughter of Joseph Spencer, a major general in the war of the Revolution. Her mother was Martha Brainard, the sister of David and John Brainard.

Joseph Cone, the father of Timothy, was a naval officer, and laid down his life for his country during the struggle for independence, so that Timothy never knew what it was to enjoy a father's care and protection, but his mother made good the loss as far as lay in her power. Her memory was sacred to him through all his long life. His opportunities for education were scant, and entailed a lack that he never ceased to deplore.

Soon after he attained his majority he went to Belfast, Maine, and engaged in business in which he was having good success, when he was attacked by disease and compelled to leave all and devote himself to the recovery of his health. He went to Saratoga springs and remained there eighteen months, at the end of which time the savings of the previous years were consumed, but he had received in exchange the inestimable boon—recovered health.

In the spring of 1802 he started from Saratoga, on horseback, for the Ohio. His uncle, Dr. Joseph Spencer had bought a tract of land in Virginia, six miles below Marietta and removed his family thither. Mr. Cone went to his uncle's, and his home was there until in 1806 he married Sarah H. Bailey, the daughter of Seth Bailey, who emigrated from Easton, Massachusetts, in 1804, and settled in Virginia, a few miles below Marietta.

Sarah H. Bailey was born in Easton, March 9, 1790, and was but sixteen and a half years old at the time of her marriage. They began housekeeping in a very humble way in Ohio on the bank of the river, six miles below Marietta. After a year or two Mr. Cone bought land back of the river, on what was known as the "State road," to which he removed, and there he remained four or five years, when he moved to Harmar. He lived there until 1826, when he bought a farm in Warren, four miles below Marietta, which from thenceforth became his home. The two youngest of his ten children were born there, and all grew to manhood and womanhood. Two of his children still live on the home place.

Mr. Cone felt so keenly his own want of education that he was determined to save his children, if possible, from like suffering. He was unwearied in his efforts to give them educational advantages, and counted no self denial too great if he would advance their interests in this respect. The low prices obtained for farm products at that time made it difficult to satisfy the wants and provide for the necessities of so large a family. Mr. Cone died in 1864 when nearly eighty-seven years old. His last years were clouded by the great affliction of blindness. For the greater part of twelve years he saw but dimly, and during the last two or three he saw not at all. His resignation and cheerfulness under this great affliction were something wonderful. Notwithstanding his great age his mental faculties were but little impaired at the time of his death; his memory, especially, was remarkably tenacious.

Mrs. Cone survived till 1870. She was a woman of great strength of character, of untiring industry and the most careful economy, whose home was her world. Her children "arise up and call her blessed." Mr. and Mrs. Cone were both members of the Presbyterian church, and died in the blessed hope of a glorious immortality. They are buried in Oak Hill cemetery, in Marietta.

Of their ten children seven are living. The youngest was the first to go to the "better land." Ellen married Hiram A. Peck, of Salem, Indiana, and died, leaving two children, in 1862. Deborah Packard, the eldest, married Mr. Silas Slocomb, and died in Marietta in 1863. Martha Spencer married Mr. J. B. Blackinton, who died in 1871. She and her three children live on a part of the home place. Mary is unmarried and lives in Marietta. Alice Sparrow married Edmund Brush, esq., of Zanesville, and was left a widow in 1861. She lives in Marietta. Of the four sons two are in California. George lives at Sacramento and Joseph Spencer at Red Bluff. The latter has been greatly successful in business and has accumulated a large property. Charles lives in the house his father built, and has been extending the area of his farm by adding acre to acre. Timothy is unmarried and lives in Marietta.

CHAPTER XLVII.

DUNHAM TOWNSHIP.

Establishment — Boundaries Changed — Drainage — Coal — Sandstone—The Survey—The First Improvement—Elihu Clark—The Dunhams—Description of the Forest in 1804—Inconveniences—Other Settlers—Early Events—First Tavern—Dancing—First Presbyterian Meeting—Veto, Dunham and Briggs' Post Offices—Cemeteries—Agricultural Fair—Churches—First School—Public Schools—Politics—Industries.

ON THE fifth of June, 1855, the tract of territory three miles wide and eight miles long, bounded on the north by Warren and Barlow, on the east by the Ohio, on the south by Belpre, and on the west by Decatur and Fairfield, was established by the county commissioners an independent township, with corporate powers. On the petition of William P. Cutler, Dean Briggs and others, the boundary line between Warren and Dunham was changed and established as it now exists, October 19, 1855.

Along the river the hills are high and abrupt, presenting heavy sandstone ledges. The wide and fertile valley of the Little Hocking runs in a southwesterly direction through the centre of the township. The western end of the territory is drained by the Little East branch of the Hocking. The northern branches of Congress creek carry off the waters of the southwest part. The streams which empty into the Ohio are short and small. The same seam of coal found in Belpre, Fairfield and Warren, is found in Dunham. Its black stain can be seen in many places in the township. There are in places well defined strata of limestone, and some of the shales contain limestone in small concretions. Wherever these limestone concretions occur, the soil produces abundant crops. Sandstone is the characteristic rock of the hills. Large quarries have been opened along the river and in the northern part of the township, on both sides of the Little Hocking valley. The body of this rock is of excellent quality for building purposes, and the selected stone makes superior grindstones. Many of these hills were once covered with yellow pines, a tree that thrives only on highly silicious soil. The Creek valley was a dense forest of chestnut, oak and hickory—the productions of shale and limestone land. This township possessed two important natural sources of wealth, exhaustless ledges of the finest sandstone, and an abundant and valuable growth of timber. The development of the stone industry has only commenced. The forest has almost entirely passed away, the best of it in the form of barrels and casks.

The soil of the valley is well adapted to all sorts of agricultural products. Wool growing is the principal industry of the upland districts.

THE SURVEY.

This township is located in that portion of the Ohio company's purchase, which was laid out in one hundred and sixty acre lots. The ministerial section of township one, range nine, and township two, range ten, and also school section sixteen, of township two, range ten, and Congress reservation, section eleven, of township two, range ten, are included within the limits of the legal township of Dunham. Little Hocking creek flows through Congress section eleven, and school section sixteen. The ministerial sections are at the opposite ends of the township.

THE SETTLEMENT.

The first improvement on the territory of Dunham township was probably made by Elihu Clark, on school section number sixteen. He was followed by Benjamin Bickford, Hezekiah Bickford, and in 1803 Lemuel Cooper also had a cabin on the same section. At that time the forest in the direction of Marietta was unbroken as far as the squatter settlement known as Nozletown, on the Warren township bottom.

Elihu Clark was a native of Pennsylvania. He first came to Belpre township, where he worked at the carpenter trade. After he moved to the present territory of Dunham, he devoted his labor to the clearing of land and farming. He died in 1830. His wife, Helen McCune Clark, died the same year. Miller, son of Elihu Clark, was born February 24, 1799. He died November 4, 1874. Miller Clark and wife left a family of two children, Jehiel, who resides in Allen county, and Ethlinda R., wife of Samuel G. Gorham, who was killed August 9, 1864, by the explosion of an ordnance steamer, near City Point, Virginia. They had three children: Charles E., Stacy B., and Lewis C., all living in Dunham township.

Lemuel Cooper was the typical squatter of the period. He lived mostly on game and dwelt in log huts constructed with the least possible labor. He was generally found in the settlements amusing the boys with thrilling adventures and hair-breadth escapes. He was master of the boxer's art and considered himself a great fighter.

In the summer of 1803, Jonathan Dunham undertook to follow the range line from Turkey Hen creek to Belpre. He followed the line until he came to a point near the farm now owned by Sylvester Ellenwood, where he lost his bearings and had no other means of finding his way out than to follow the creek down. The land now owned by Mr. George Goddard struck his fancy, and he sought out the owner from whom he purchased the lot on long time, at two dollars an acre. This lot was divided into three parts, Jonathan Dunham taking half, Amos Dunham sixty acres, and Amos Delano twenty acres. Amos Dunham says in his address at a meeting for the celebration of the establishment of Dunham township:

In the spring of 1804, I commenced working on my lot and lived in quite a retired manner. I slept in my little camp a short distance back of where Mr. Goddard now lives; cooked my own pork and potatoes; kept a good fire in front of my camp at night; laid myself down on my bed of leaves and was soon hushed to sleep by the united melody of wolves and owls; and from Monday morning till Saturday night was not disturbed by the sight of a single human being. Every night the wolves would commence howling on one hill and be answered by another hill, and another, until it seemed the woods were full of them. Sheep had to be enclosed in yards near the house or they would be caught. I had fourteen killed in one night, one of them was not more than twelve feet from where I was sleeping.

For several years after I commenced farming, the wild turkeys would come to my fields in such numbers, after the wheat was sown, that the ground was black with them, and in the winter and spring the deer would come in droves and take what the turkeys had left.

Jonathan Dunham, in honor of whose family the township was named, was a lineal descendant of Rev. Jonathan Dunham, the first preacher at Martha's Vineyard. Each succeeding generation had left but one son to inherit the family name. Amos, after the death of his father, was the sole representative of the family. At his death the name became extinct. Betsey Dunham, only sister of Amos Dunham, was married to Asahel Hollister.

Asahel Hollister came to Washington county with his family in 1816 from Litchfield county, Connecticut, and settled in Warren, now Dunham, township. He was born in 1772, and died in 1850. His wife, Betsey (Dunham), survived him twelve years, dying in 1862. They raised a family of eight children, three dying in infancy. The only survivors are three brothers: Albert G., Jonathan J., and Whiting B. The former two reside in Dunham; Jonathan, on the old homestead where his father settled in 1816; W. B. lives in Harmar, where for nearly forty years he has been in the marble business. He began in 1844, bringing the first marble to southern Ohio. At that time there were but three pieces of marble in the cemetery and those only two inch slabs. He married in the spring of 1844 Amanda B. Burroughs, who died in 1852, and in 1853 he was married to Aurelia R. Stone, daughter of Benjamin F. Stone, who is still living.

The early settlement of the township was greatly retarded by the inconvenience of having no roads. Mills and markets were at great distances, and packing farm products on the back of a horse was slow work. Milling was particularly inconvenient, especially in dry weather, when Devol's mill on the Muskingum had to be de-

pended upon. It not only took several days for the Dunham pioneers to go to and come from this mill, but they not unfrequently had to wait a week before their turn came for grinding.

Stephen Taylor lived where the Dunham cemetery now is, and the small stream emptying into Little Hocking, near by, was named in his honor. In a short time his house was consumed by fire. He enlisted in the War of 1812 and never returned.

Gideon Rathbun made a squatter's improvement on section eleven, near the present residence of J. J. Hollister. A man named Munn also made an improvement on the same farm. In 1816 Rathbun moved to another quarter of the same section. He was one of those eccentric wanderers so frequently met with in pioneer history, who are content as long as they have anything to eat and a place to sleep.

Benedict Rathbun, a native of Rhode Island, settled in Dunham in 1816. He was the first victim of the epidemic of 1822-3.

Thomas and Amos Delano emigrated from Connecticut to Ohio in 1804. They stopped for a short time on their way in New York. They remained in Lower Belpre until 1808, and then improved their land in Dunham. Amos owned land adjoining the farm of his stepfather, Jonathan Dunham. After his death Thomas married his widow and lived on the same farm. By her first husband, Mrs. Delano (Cynthia Cole), had two children, Julia and Lucy A., by her second husband she had five children—Lewis T.; Phœbe E.; Clark, who lives in Iowa; Amos P., and Sarah J., deceased. Lewis T., who yet resides in the township, married Mary E. Vincent. She died February 26, 1860, leaving one child, Elmer L.

Captain James Moore was in Dunham as early as 1810. His cabin stood where the house of the late Harry McClure now stands, below the narrows. He had one son and seven or eight daughters, one of whom, Melissa, was drowned in the Ohio river, near the house. Captain Moore belonged to that rough and ready, now extinct class, once so important in the commerce on our western rivers—the keel boatmen. He sometimes pushed his boat up the Big Kanawha to the salines, and returned with a cargo of salt, or made longer trips in the freighting business. He did not as others did, spend a hatful of dollars in a single spree, and come home empty handed; but he often returned from the long and tedious journey with loss rather than profit. The law at that time allowed imprisonment for debt, and Captain Moore, for this cause, was sometimes cast behind the bars. On his way to Marietta he would call at the door of Judge Cutler and say frankly: "Well, judge, I am on my way to jail and you must go bail for me," or, failing to find the judge at home, the message was left: "Tell the judge I have gone to jail and he must come up to-morrow and bail me out," which was generally done. Captain Moore was an adept in breaking and swingling flax. His labor was in great demand, and was readily promised, but the patience of the good women was often sorely tried, waiting for their flax. The late Bishop Morris, the pioneer of Methodism in this community, occasionally preached here. A class was formed and Captain Moore was appointed leader. They met at his house and were instructed to the best of their leader's ability, he being a man of good intentions. He removed with his family from the county about 1830.

Benjamin Ellenwood, a native of Maine, emigrated with his three sons—Benjamin, Daniel and Samuel—from Pennsylvania to Ohio in 1811, and settled on school section sixteen. Samuel Ellenwood was a pushing farmer and highly esteemed man in the settlement. He purchased the first wagon used on the east branch of the Little Hocking. He died June 25, 1857, in his seventy-second year. His wife died in 1862 in her seventy-sixth year. Their children were: Sylvester D., Samuel S., Milton, Harvey B., Benjamin, and Cynthia, who still reside in Dunham township, and Augustus and Corinda (Chevalier), who reside in Iowa.

Sylvester Ellenwood married Lucy A., daughter of Amos Dunham. She died December 3, 1862. The maiden name of his second and present wife was Mary Chevelier. These two marriages were blessed with eight sons and one daughter, four of whom are living—Horace D., Orville O., Lowell W., and Cynthia A.—the two oldest and two youngest. Sylvester Ellenwood owns a fine farm in the north part of the township on Little Hocking. The first improvement was made on this farm by Francis Dilly.

Milton Ellenwood, a son of Benjamin Ellenwood, jr., was born January 7, 1817. September 23, 1840, he married Sophronia Needham, a daughter of Jasper Needham, who, with his brother Stephen, settled in the township in 1816. The family of Milton Ellenwood and wife consists of two sons and five daughters, three of whom reside in Dunham township—Rowena R., Oscar N., and Ida E.; Flora B. (Gard) resides in Barlow township; Milton E., in Clay county, Kansas; Parmelia S. (Starkweather), in Hamilton, Illinois; Delia L. Lewis, in Iowa.

Harvey B. Ellenwood, a son of Samuel Ellenwood, was born August 7, 1822. He married, May 1, 1856, Elizabeth A. Paulley, who was born September 11, 1823. The fruit of this marriage was three children, two of whom—Kemper D. and Ella L.—reside in Dunham township. Samuel E. is dead.

Amos Paulley, father of Mrs. Ellenwood, came to Belpre in 1818, and died there in 1825.

Frederick Lewis is one of the principal real estate owners of the township. His farm of three hundred and twenty acres lies along the Ohio river. Benoni Lewis, his father, was born in Rhode Island in 1752. In 1802 he emigrated with his family to Virginia, and in 1807 settled on the Ohio side. He had been captain of an ocean ship and was employed during the Revolution in the commissary department. He died in 1821. Mary Walton Lewis, his wife, was born in Connecticut in 1753, and died in 1845. Frederick is the only one of eleven children yet living. He was born in Rhode Island in 1793. At the breaking out of the War of 1812 he enlisted, but was rejected on account of physical infirmity.

Loring W. Lewis, a son of Henry, and grandson of Benoni Lewis, was born in Massachusetts in 1805. He came to Ohio with his father in 1813, and in 1835 married Caroline Cole, who was born in 1811. Henry Lewis was born in 1779 in Connecticut. After living in Ohio for a period he moved to Illinois, where he died in 1847.

Hapgood Goddard, a native of New Hampshire, settled in Washington county in 1814. He was married to Rebecca Wood. His death occurred in Fairfield township in 1866. The surviving members of his family are Eliza, Wesley township; William P. P., Wesley township; Abram W., Fairfield township; Julia P., Jackson county, Ohio; Sarah S., Missouri; Charles H., Fairfield township; George R., Dunham; and Lucy, Fairfield. George R. married Ester J. Smith April 7, 1867. She is a daughter of Carmi Smith, of Fairfield township. The fruit of this marriage was four children, three of whom are living, viz: Loring H., Selvan C., and Harford H.

The first settler of the territory west of the Little Hocking valley was Joseph Tilton, who moved from Belpre township and made an improvement in that part of the township in 1817.

In 1820 James Harvey and family, Daniel Shaw, and William Fleming came from Scotland, and sought homes in Washington county. Mr. Harvey settled on the farm now owned by Neil McTaggart. Mr. Shaw purchased land in the back part of the township where he resided until his death in 1871. His widow, Catharine McKay Shaw, still resides on the farm. He had ten children, eight sons and two daughters, of whom six are living.

Thomas and Samuel Drain, sons of Daniel and Jeanette Templeton Drain, emigrated from Argyleshire, Scotland, and settled in Washington county; Thomas in Waren township, and Samuel in Dunham. October 28, 1841, Samuel married Isabella Dunlap, who was born in Argyleshire, Scotland, in July, 1818. Six sons and two daughters blessed this union, viz: John D., Daniel (deceased), Roland S., Daniel R., Jeanette, Mary, Thomas, and James N., all of whom reside in this township except three—Jeanette, McFarlan, Barlow township; Robert in Illinois, and Daniel R. in Adams county, Iowa.

Almond Henderson, a grandson of Edward Henderson, is the principal proprietor of school section sixteen. Edward Henderson was a native of Glasgow, Scotland, whence he emigrated to Massachusetts and then to Washington county, where he was employed as a spy. Josiah Henderson, of Belpre, and James, who was born in 1791 and died in 1835, were his sons. James married Jane Lucas, daughter of Nathaniel Lucas, who was born in 1805. They had three sons—Israel, Almond, and Edward. Israel lives in Minnesota, and Edward in Vinton county, Ohio. On March 10, 1859, Almond married Jane Dunlap, who was born March 17, 1818. The fruit of this marriage was one daughter—Elizabeth.

John Mitchel, the son of Hugh Mitchel was born September 8, 1835. Hugh Mitchel emigrated from Scotland in 1841 and first settled in Barlow township. He afterward located in Dunham, where he died October 5, 1856, in his forty-ninth year. He married Margaret Dunlap, who was born in 1815, and is still living.

82

The surviving members of the family are: John, living in Dunham township; Jeanette Drain, in Belpre; Robert, in Boone county, Illinois; Jane, in Winnebago county, Illinois; Mary, in Wood county, West Virginia; Hugh, in Belpre township, and Archibald B. in Boone county, Illinois. John was married to Hannah E. Burnett, February 26, 1863. They have a family of seven children, three sons and four daughters, viz: Charles H., Mary A., Maggie E., Sarah E., Nettie M., John E., and Daniel T. All are living in Dunham township.

Charles O. Pond is descended from one of the earliest settlers of Barlow township. His great-grandfather, Samuel B. Pond, came to that township from Vermont. Leonidas P., a son of Samuel B. Pond, was born May 23, 1826, and died January 25, 1874. November 23, 1854 he married Mary M. Gard, daughter of Hiram Gard, who was born March 31, 1834. They had four children: Hiram O., Charles V., Beman L., and Sylvester P. Hiram O. lives in Columbus, the other three live in Dunham township.

In 1815 Alexander Calder settled near the present line between Warren and Dunham townships. He was born in 1789 in New York, where he married Phœbe Mabey, about 1810. She was born in New York in 1780 and died in 1820, having had six children, of whom but one survives—Margaret (Swan) of Meigs county. He was married in 1825 to Cecy Casey, who was born at Fairfax, Virginia, in 1800. The fruit of this union was six children, five of whom survive, viz: William, David B., Philip C., and Wallace, who reside in Dunham township, and Van Buren who lives in Belpre township. Alexander died in 1848. During the War of 1812, Mr. Calder was living in Canada. He was imprisoned as a citizen of the United States, but soon received his pardon. After coming to Washington county, he opened a large stone quary on his farm and engaged in the manufacture of grindstones.

David B., son of Alexander Calder, was born in 1829. In 1855 he married Mary E. McClure, who was born in 1832. Their family consists of five children: Ida L., Flora M., Witmer A., Stella E., and David R. Mr. Calder's connection with the stone producing and manufacturing industry, is fully noted further along.

William Calder, oldest son of Alexander Calder, was born in 1827. In 1857 he married Jane H. King, who was born in Pittsburgh in 1838. They have seven children, viz: Mary R., Clara Estella, Geneverive M., Lizzie Gertrude, Louis W., Mable L., and Myrtle L. Both William and D. B. Calder have worked in the quarries along the river ledges all their lives. Their quarries produce stone of superior quality.

Harry McClure, son of Andrew McClure, of Waterford township, was born in Waterford township in 1803. In 1827 he married Lavinia Humiston, daughter of Jasen Humiston, of Watertown. She was born about 1805. They had nine children, seven of whom are living. The military record of the sons deserves special mention in this connection: Emeline lives at home; William lives in Sioux city, Iowa; Mary, wife of D. B. Calder, in Dunham; Andrew J., in Lincoln, Nebraska;

Henry O., in Missouri; Theodore died from sickness contracted in the army. He was wounded at Shiloh, and was color bearer at Mission Ridge; Dyar B. died in 1862, from the effects of a wound received at Lewisburgh, West Virginia; William was train master for the Thirty-sixth Ohio volunteer infantry, and Andrew in the First Iowa infantry and First Iowa battery. Alonzo went out in the hundred days' service. Harry McClure died in Dunham township in 1855.

William P. Cole, a son of Philip Cole, was born in Warren township in 1814. In 1840 he married Louisa Shield, who was born in Wood county, West Virginia, in 1810. They have had eight children, five of whom are living: Sarah S., David, Philip S., Effie and Arthur W.

Freman Hopkins emigrated from Connecticut, and settled in Warren township in 1816. He soon removed however, to the part of Dunham which was formerly included in Belpre, where he died in 1857, aged seventy-two years. In 1808 he married Sarah Leech, who was born in Sharon, Connecticut, in 1790. She died in 1856. When Mr. Hopkins came to Ohio, he was a poor man. He worked at the shoemaker trade in winter, and farmed during the summer. By that means he acquired financial independence. He had eleven children, eight of whom are living: Joline P., Mrs. Harrington, Louisa, Frances (Burrows), Sarah and Morgan live in Dunham; Mrs. Annie Patton lives in Watertown, and Mrs. Henriette Crosen lives in Barlow.

Joline P. Hopkins was born in 1809, in Connecticut. In 1835 he married Electa French, who was born in the part of Dunham formerly included in Warren in 1817. They had six children: Le Roy lives at home; Isaac, in Barlow township; Mrs. Melissa Martin, in Pittsburgh, Pennsylvania, and Mrs. Nettie Meddlesweart, in Warren. Mr. Hopkins owns and lives on the farm formerly owned by his father-in-law, Isaac French.

William Seffens, a native of Lancashire, England, emigrated to America in 1841, and settled in Pennsylvania, where he remained until 1850, when he came to Dunham township. Both Mr. Seffens and his wife, Ann Shackleton, were born in 1801. She died in 1849; he in 1858. They had fourteen children, six of whom are living: Mary Ann (Taylor), of Highland county; Sarah (Perdew), Warren township; Hannah (Welshaus), Alleghany, Pennsylvania; Elizabeth (Eaton), Allegheny, Pennsylvania; Jane Hanna, of Warren township; and John, Dunham township. John, youngest son of William Seffens, was born in 1838. In 1869 he married Harriet Taylor, who was born in England in 1837. They have had ten children, of whom the following are living, viz: James, John, Ann, Edward, Joseph, Hugh, and Flora. Mr. Seffens gives particular attention to sheep-raising.

William Mankin emigrated from Maryland to Ohio in 1824, and settled in the part of Dunham township formerly included in Warren. He died in 1870, in his ninetieth year. His wife, Elizabeth Carey, was born in 1783, and died in 1875. They had four children. William F., Francis F., and John live in Dunham township; Joseph W. lives in Henry county, Illinois. William F.

Mankin was born in 1816. In 1839 he married Harriet Dodge, who was born in Delaware in 1820. They have four children. Charity, Ezra, and Rhoda (Bingham) live in Dunham; Martha (Beech), in Barlow.

Alexander McTaggart was born in Argylshire, Scotland, in 1817. He emigrated to America in 1838, his older brother, Neil, having preceded him about five years. Neil had made a permanent settlement in the part of Dunham formerly included in Belpre, and Alexander on arriving joined him. In 1843 he married Jeanette Fleming, who was born in 1823. They have one child, Alexander, who lives at home. When Mr. McTaggart came to Ohio he was in debt. He is now one of the wealthiest men in the township.

EARLY EVENTS.

The first frame house in the township was built for Amos Dunham, by a carpenter named Graves.

A tavern was opened near the head of Neil's island, in 1805, by Nathan Cole. One large room was suitable for dancing, and parties frequently gathered there to practice the art, which was much cultivated at that time. Willard Green was the usual fiddler. The ideal of grace in dancing was to keep the body erect and steady and move with a noiseless step. Some attained such proficiency that they could perform any of the fashionable dances of the day with a butter bowl on their heads.

Mr. Cole sold his tavern stand to James Harvey, and it was in the ball-room of this building that the first Presbyterian meeting was held between Belpre and Marietta. In this room the first steps were taken toward the organization of the Presbyterian church of Warren.

POST OFFICES.

There are in this township no villages, but the citizens have nothing to complain of in the way of postal facilities, there being an office at each end and one near the centre of the territory.

Veto was the first post office established within the present limits of the township. William Chevalier was commissioned postmaster in 1850. He was succeeded by Mr. Deshler. Malcolm Shaw has held the office a number of years.

Dunham post office was established in 1857. Postmasters—Jasper Needham, J. J. Hollister, and Justine Hollister.

In 1875 the citizens along the river asked for an office in their neighborhood. Their petition was granted and Briggs post office established in March of that year. William Calder, the present incumbent, was appointed to take charge of the office.

CEMETERIES.

The first cemetery within the present limits of Dunham township is located on Hocking, near the mouth of Taylor's run. Upon the death of Lucinda, a daughter of Amos Dunham, a small lot was set apart by Jonathan Dunham as a public burying-ground. This lot next passed into possession of Betsey Hollister and from her to her son, R. D. Hollister. It was transferred by him to George and Charles Goddard, who made it a public cemetery and placed it under the charge of the township trustees.

The cemetery on the Shaw farm, near Veto post office, was set apart for the use of the public upon the death of Joseph Tilton, one of the first settlers of that section of the township. It has been entensively used by the citizens of Scotch descent.

The burying-ground on the farm now owned by L. D. Hopkins was fenced off for burial purposes at the death of Isaac French, who was at the time of his death owner of the farm.

AGRICULTURAL ASSOCIATION.

About 1850 the farmers of Dunham fell into the habit of holding plowing exhibitions, which excited a great deal of interest throughout the community. These tests of skill soon became more general, and finally grew into a general agricultural fair. An association, of which J. J. Hollister was chosen president, was formed, grounds near Veto post office were leased and improved, and interesting annual exhibitions were held until the second year of the war, when for various reasons the enterprise was abandoned.

CHURCHES AND SOCIETIES.

It was said of Dunham township at the time of its establishment in 1855, that neither a church nor a saloon was located within its boundaries. There had been churches, and a church has since been built, but no one has ever engaged in the sale of intoxicating liquors.

A temperance society, which was organized in 1837, exercised an important influence. Its membership was composed of the leading citizens, who felt the necessity of a revolution of opinion relative to the free use of distilled liquors. This society was under charge of men of sense and experience, and avoided those extremes into which similar associations too frequently fall. Meetings were held at private houses and at school-houses; meetings were addressed by members and others, and conversation relative to the subject freely indulged in by all. In that way a healthy public sentiment was created, without which reform of any kind is impossible. After a number of years, meetings ceased to be held and the organization broke up, its purposes having to a considerable degree been accomplished.

As in most other rural communities, the Methodist was the pioneer church. A class was formed soon after the first settlement, which was supplied by the preachers of Marietta circuit and later by those of Barlow circuit. A frame building was erected about 1830 on the Little Hocking, in which services were held occasionally until 1855. The building was removed before the war.

A Universalist society was organized by members from the Belpre church in 1845. This society was ministered to by Thompson Barron and J. M. McMaster. Meetings were held in school-houses. The society was never strong in numbers, and soon dissolved and reunited with the Belpre church.

The opening up of extensive quarries along the Little Hocking brought to the township many laborers, most of whom were members of the United Brethren church.

They naturally desired a house of worship, but felt themselves unable to bear the expense of building. William P. Cutler, who at that time was operating the principal quarries, donated a lot, and In 1871 erected a neat frame church, which bears the name "Cutler chapel." He deeded this property to the "United Brethren church," specifying, however, that the house should always be open for the use of all denominations. When Mr. Cutler's quarries in that community ceased to be operated, many of the members were thrown out of employment and the congregation became small. Preaching service is yet maintained. It was connected with Plymouth circuit until 1879; since that time with Watertown circuit.

SCHOOLS.

The earliest settlers along the Little Hocking sent their children to school at Belpreville, where Amos Dunham was the teacher. About 1814, a school-house was built by subscription on the Goddard farm. In this house the first, and for a long time the best, school within the present territory of the town was maintained. Ethlinda Clark taught there in the summer of 1816 and the following winter Samuel Clark from Massachusetts was the teacher. In 1818, Dr. Robertson, a superannuated physician from New Jersey, taught a family school at the house of Asahel Hollister where he lived. During the next winter he taught in the school-house. In 1820, a log school-house was built near the forks of the Little Hocking. During the following winter this school was taught by Amos Dunham and attended by seventy scholars. An anecdote is told in this connection of the eccentric Gideon Rathbun. Scholars under a certain age were received at half price, and the subscription paper in consequence showed many halves the subscriptions running, "scholars, three and a half, two and a half, etc. Gideon determined to be accurate, wrote his subscription "scholars, 20 halves" (Two scholars, no halves) succeeding teachers in this school were: R. D. Hollister, Jonah Robbins, Sally Smith, Mr. Tenny, W. B. Hollister, J. J. Hollister, Mr. Proctor, and others. Mr. Proctor has since become one of the leading journalists of Iowa. The second school-house in the township was built near the river, but this in early times was regarded an inferior school, the more advanced pupils of the northern part of the neighborhood going to Warren and those in the southern, to Belpre. The third was west of the Little Hocking. The house was built by a portion of those who had formerly belonged to the Hocking district. Mr. Hand and A. G. Hollister were the first teachers. The township, after its establishment in 1855, was divided into five full and two fractional districts. The compliments of the fractional districts are in Belpre, in which township one of the school-houses is located. The houses in this township are generally comfortable, and good talent is employed.

ELECTIONS.

The first election was held June 30, 1855, at the school-house near the forks of the Little Hocking. Succeeding elections were held for a few years at the same place, afterwards at Glendale school-house in the Hollister settlement. In 1871 a town-house was built, where elections have since been held.

In politics Dunham has always been Democratic, the lowest majority for that party having been nineteen in 1861.

STONE QUARRIES AND GRINDSTONE MANUFACTURE.

The first stone quarries in Dunham were opened up by Averal Harris, Mr. Schwan and Oren Newton about 1820. At this time there was no demand for building stone, but the manufacture of grindstones was found a profitable industry. Flat-boats were used exclusively for transporting the handcut stones down the river to the Cincinnati market, and walking back was part of the business. A. Calder opened a fine quarry in the river ledges, and as navigation improved, the industry grew in extent and importance. Along the Little Hocking the industry was carried on most extensively in 1870–71, by the Ohio River Stone company, William P. Cutter, Malcolm Blue and O'Connor & Blue. O'Connor & Blue at present operate the largest quarries in this section of the stone district.

A. B. and W. Calder have been operating extensive quarries along the river since 1870. The piers for the railroad bridge at Parkersburgh, and the stone for the ornamental work of the Episcopial church at Parkersburgh came from their quarry. An establishment was erected near the river, by Mr. O'Connor for sawing out building stone, but did not prove as successful as was anticipated.

Well informed operators estimate that the sandstone ledges in Dunham and Warren township have already been the source of more than three hundred thousand dollars revenue. These stone in quality, are unexcelled anywhere on the continent, are convenient both to river and railroad and will for years be the source of great wealth.

COOPERING.

The number of fine chestnut-oaks in the forest determined the industry of the pioneer community. Many farmers became coopers, and trained tradesmen engaged in the business of making barrels, for which there was a constant demand. The home consumption of farm products was at that time very small, and slack barrels were required for shipping apples, potatoes, etc., to Cincinnati, New Orleans, and other markets. Meat tubs and other casks were also extensively manufactured in this portion of the county.

NOTE.—Whenever the term Dunham township is used in the preceding narrative, the territory within the boundaries of the legal township, as established in 1855, is meant.

BIOGRAPHICAL SKETCH.

GEORGE R. GODDARD.

One of the most prosperous and well-known farmers in Washington county is Mr. G. R. Goddard, of Dunham

RESIDENCE OF G. R. GODDARD, DUNHAM TP., WASHINGTON CO., O.

township. His father, Hapgood Goddard, was one of the early settlers of the county.

Hapgood Goddard was born in Swansey, New Hampshire, April 12, 1783. His father was the minister of the Congregational church in Swansey, for over twenty years. He was rather too liberal in his theological views for large popularity in those strict, old Puritan days. Hapgood Goddard married, on May 7, 1807, Miss Rebecca Wood, who was born in Chesterfield, New Hampshire, August 29, 1787. Her father was minister of the Congregational church in Chesterfield for fifty-one years. He was of the most rigid, orthodox views.

Mr. Goddard, at the time of his marriage, was engaged in the mercantile business, but his business was broken up by Jefferson's embargo, he having at the time a large amount of produce on hand. He settled up his business as far as he was able, leaving only two hundred dollars unpaid. The creditor of this debt bade him go and prosper, and pay the debt when he was able. Mr. Goddard then started for Ohio on horseback. This was in 1812. He came to Washington county, and, while in Belpre, heard the Goverment strongly denounced for the war in a Fourth of July oration. He was satisfied with what he saw of the country, and returned for his family. The family, consisting of Mr. and Mrs. Goddard and three children, commenced their journey in September 1814, in a wagon drawn by a team consisting of one blind mare, and another one twenty-one years old. With this team they started for Belpre, Washington county, Ohio, eight hundred miles distant, and that, too, over the mountains across which there were no roads.

At one time in the journey he was within hearing of the battle of Plattsburgh, but so tardy was communication in those early days that he reached the Ohio river before he heard the result of the battle. At another time, while in the mountains, they were belated, and the night came upon them before they could find a lodging place. While they were travelling in almost total darkness, the wagon upset. Mr. Goddard spread a blanket on the ground, and here his wife seated herself, took one child in her lap and one under each arm, and waited while her husband went, she knew not how far, for help to right the wagon. At that time the woods were full of bears and other wild animals. No doubt her heart leaped with joy when, after an anxious suspense, lights appeared, and her husband came with three men to help them on.

Mr. Goddard arrived in Marietta in October, 1814, with a two-dollar and a three-dollar bill in his pocket. The ferryman over the Muskingum refused to take either of these, saying that they were counterfeit. On their arrival at Major Putnam's, in Belpre, the bills were found to be genuine. Mr. Goddard immediately returned to pay the ferryman. He found his bill charged to "Mr. Yankee," the ferryman never expecting to see him again.

The family lived for one year on Blennerhassett's island, and one year in what is known as the "Old Beebe house," in Belpre. During the winter of 1816–17 Mr. Goddard taught school, and in March, 1817, moved his family to what was then known as "White Oak settlement," in Wooster township. Here they underwent such hardships,

frequent in that early day, as the present generation would consider unendurable. There was scarcely any money. But the greatest cause of distress was the lack of salt; Mr. Goddard paid four dollars for a hundred pounds, and carried it from the river on his horse. At this time wheat would not bring twenty-five cents a bushel.

It was during his residence in Wooster township that Wesley and Fairfield townships were made. He was clerk of these townships for many years. He was a candidate for commissioner at one time. Although his party were largely in the minority, yet he lacked but five votes of an election, his personal popularity outweighing much party prejudice.

In 1837 he returned to his native State and paid his last debt of two hundred dollars. After visiting his friends he returned to Ohio, about the fourth of July, 1837. His return trip was the fourth one he had made over those eight hundred miles on horseback. Each time he made the trip in sixteen days. He made the trip once in a wagon, when he brought his family out, in twenty-eight days. As late as 1837 there was no better means of travelling than by horses.

In 1847 Mr. Goddard retired from active life, and his two sons, C. H. and G. R., took charge of the farm of one hundred and seventy acres which he had acquired, and also his stock. After this date he lived with his son, C. H. Goddard, of Fairfield township, until his death, which occurred January 21, 1865, he being eighty-two years old. His wife survived him ten years, dying at the same place February 27, 1875, at the age of eighty-eight years.

Mr. and Mrs. Goddard had ten children, five sons and five daughters; of these, eight are now living; their names and births are as follows: Frances Amanda, born February 17, 1810, died August 19, 1844; Edward Hapgood, born May 20, 1811, died November 27, 1853; Eliza Alvisa, born January 23, 1813; William Pitt Putnam, born December 24, 1814; Abraham Wood, born March 11, 1817; Julia Putnam, born September 30, 1819; Sarah Loring, born February 19, 1822; Charles Howe, born December 24, 1824; George Rodney, born April 7, 1827; Lucy Eaton, born September 1, 1829.

Mr. Goddard was a man of intense energy and indomitable will. Such characteristics were necessary to conquer the difficulties of those early days. He was devoted to his family, and, being a man of good education himself, determined that all his children should have as good an education as could be gotten at that day. He was very poor and scarcely able to pay their school bills. The following incident will serves to illustrate the straits to which he was put to meet these demands.

At one time a Mr. Dexter taught a six-months' school. Mr. Goddard sent his children but was not able to pay the tuition in money, and so an agreement was made with the teacher, who consented to take his pay in tow-and-linen cloth. Mrs. Goddard spun and wove thirty-two yards to pay his bill.

By such determination and such sacrifices this worthy couple succeeded in giving all their children the best education that could be gotten in those days. By such energy, also, Mr. Goddard acquired a comfortable fortune, having started out with almost nothing. He was a man of most scrupulous honesty, as instances of his carefulness in paying his last debt in New Hampshire, even when he had to wait twenty-three years to do it. Both he and his wife were earnest Christians, being members of the Universalist church. His wife was for many years a member of the Methodist church, but in the latter part of her life joined her husband in the Universalist church.

George R. Goddard was born April 7, 1827, in Wesley township, Washington county, Ohio. He was the youngest of Hapgood Goddard's five son's, and the next to the youngest child in the family. He lived on the old place until he was thirty-two years old, and received his education in the school near his father's house. When he was twenty years old, he and his brother, C. H., as has been already stated, took charge of his father's farm. In 1859 he removed to his present farm in Dunham township. On the seventh of April, 1867, he married Miss Esther J. Smith, daughter of Carmi Smith, of Fairfield township, who was born May 2, 1843, in Homer township, Morgan county, Ohio. When she was four years old her parents moved back to Fairfield township, Washington county, where they reside. Mr. and Mrs. Goddard have had four children, whose names are as follows: Loring Hapgood, born December 21, 1869; an infant, who died twelve days after its birth, born October 6, 1873; Selvin Carmi, born October 1, 1876; Harford Bishop, born March 28, 1878. Mr. Goddard has a farm of six hundred acres and a fine residence in Dunham township. He makes a specialty of stock-raising, and is particularly interested in the raising of short-horned cattle. He is one of the most wealthy and influential citizens of the township.

CHAPTER XLVIII.

LAWRENCE TOWNSHIP.

General Physical Features and Geological Formation—First Settlement—Old Families—Eccentric Characters—German Emigration—Scotch Emigration—Organization of Government—List of First Voters—Schools—Religious Societies—Cemeteries—Early Sunday-schools—First Children's Home—Post Offices—Societies—Physicians—Oil Production—Population.

LAWRENCE is the only square township in the county. Its territory bounded on the north by Liberty, on the east by Independence, on the south by Newport, and on the west by Fearing, is coextensive with township No. 3, range seven, in the original survey. In its physical features this township is peculiarly interesting, for by the relief-forms is shown the geological formation which makes possible the existence of the chief source of wealth. The Little Muskingum enters at the northeast corner and flows diagonally across this township, dividing it into two almost equal parts. Along its entire

course narrow alluvial bottoms lie between the shallow channel and the steep ascent to the hight plateaus on either side. The territory is divided into three surface slopes, one toward the northwest and emptying its waters into the Little Muskingum, one toward the southeast and emptying its waters into the same stream, and the third in the northwest corner, sloping toward the west and emptying its waters into Duck creek. The principal streams of the southwestward slope are Cow run, Bear run, and Archer's fork. The streams of the southeastward slope are Morse run and Fifteen creek. Whippel's fork, a tributary of Duck creek, rises in the northward slope. These streams, which on account of the rapid descent of the general slope are very swift, flow through narrow channels from which rise steep and sometimes precipitous hills to the elevated plateaus above. The surface on these elevations between these streams is comparatively level, and the soil is productive. The smaller streams are numerous and their valleys are narrow and deep, thus cutting the elevated table lands into small and irregular tracts, giving the country a rough and broken appearance.

Cow run, which we shall frequently have occasion to mention in this history, rises on the ridge in the southeastern part of the township, flows westerly and empties into the Little Muskingum about one mile from the Newport township line. The name of this stream, though not euphonious, is suggestive. There are saline springs along the entire valley, which before the land was fenced attracted cattle from the territory for miles around. This was the creek on which the milkmaid was accustomed to find her cows, and it is not strange that Cow run soon became the common designation.

Bear run, which rises in the highlands in the southeastern part of the township and takes a northwesterly direction, derives its name from an event in the life of Archer, the hunter. It is said that on the banks of this stream Archer met a bear in a hand to paw combat in which the veteran hunter triumphed, not, however, without receiving severe injuries. His thigh was horribly minced and his life barely saved.[*]

Archer's fork properly belongs to Independence, only about one mile of its course being in Lawrence. The sources of Fifteen creek are in Liberty township and along the water-shed between the basins of Duck creek and the Little Muskingum. It flows almost due south and empties into Little Muskingum near the centre of the township. Morse run has its source in the water-shed, and empties into the Little Muskingum about two miles above the mouth of Cow run. The hill, along this stream are the hghest in the township. These hills were once thickly covered with fine chestnut trees, and the first industry in the township was the manufacture of chestnut shingles. One of the principal operators was a man named Morse, who had a cabin in the wilderness and after whom the stream was named. Little Morse run is a stream flowing into Morse run from the north-

---

*Another and more commonly accepted origin for the name of this stream is that a bear was killed in the valley through which it flows in comparatively recent times.

west. Cow run flows through a ravine known as Dark Valley, which requires special mention. Here the channel of the stream is verry narrow, and its course is due north and south. A range of hills on each side rises almost perpendicularly to the altitude of four hundred feet above the level of the stream. A series of conical peaks castelate these ranges and present a strikingly picturesque scene. From the bottom of the valley the sun can never be seen more than four hours during the day, hence the name Dark Valley.

THE SOIL AND CROPS.

The body of the soil on the terraces is red sand, sufficiently mixed with disentegrated limestone to make it fertile. Where the limestone is wanting satisfactory production can only be secured by the liberal application of fertilizers. In most portions of the township the land is naturally productive and easily cultivated. Wheat yields fairly, and of late years tobacco culture has been extensively and successfully pursued. The rich loam of the Little Muskingum valley yields large crops of Indian corn. That Lawrence is adapted to stock-raising is proved by the experience of the Scotch settlement in the north part of the township, a notice of which will be found further on. The German settlement in the northwest corner of the township occupies, probably, the most sterile portion, but under industrious and careful cultivation the hills in that section, once considered valueless, are enriching their owners.

But it is not fertility of soil that gives the lands of Lawrence their chief value. Nature has deposited her richest treasures in the underlying strata. Before, however, we proceed to the history of the discovery and production of petroleum, it will be necessary to study briefly

THE GEOLOGICAL FORMATION.

Oil is found only where there are fissures or breaks in the rock strata, caused by subterranean disturbance. At the time these fissures were formed they extended to great depths, and through them vapors from the distillation of bitumuous materials came up, condensed to a liquid state and filled the pores and crevices.

There is in Lawrence township a well marked uplift, the centre of which is on the hill on the south side of Cow run, near the line of the Exchange company's territory. From this point the axis of the break slopes gradually toward the north until at Burning Spring, on Fifteen, the anticlinal feature is scarcely perceptible. The eastern and western dips on Cow run are very rapid, and oil men are guided by surface indications where to locate wells. Further north on Morse run and Fifteen, the surface indications of subterranean fissures are so slight that it is impossible to locate them. The break also declines from Cow run toward the south, and is no longer perceptible at Eight Mile run.

The best coal mines in the township are on Morse run, where the seam on the Myers and Martin farms is three and one-half to four feet thick. The Exchange company obtains the coal with which to operate their oil wells on their own territory on Cow run.

On the summit of the uplift the first sandrock which contains oil lies one hundred and thirty-five feet below the bed of the stream, and the second sandrock containing oil is four hundred feet deeper. Oil is found on Fifteen creek in blue shale at the depth of four hundred feet, and on Morse run in first sandrock.

There are a few salt springs in the township, and water, ladened with saline materials, has been struck during the sinking of oil wells.

THE FOREST.

The terrace woodlands originally consisted of tall, straight poplars, heavy chestnuts and majestic oaks, with smaller timber intervening. Small pines, buckeye, ash, sugar, beech and hickory also abounded, making the forest almost impenetrable; wide-spreading sycamores skirted the streams, and but few spots of surface were exposed to the sun. This dense forest was inhabited by wolves, bears, deer, wild-cats, panthers, raccoons, foxes, and the other smaller and more common animals. Altogether this tract of territory presented few attractions for the emigrant in search of a home, and the comparative tardiness of settlement is not to be wondered at. Bears greatly annoyed the earliest settlers by carrying off their hogs and other domestic animals, but they retreated when the work of clearing began to be pushed. Wolves remained until a later date. Deer have many years since ceased to run the hills, but foxes are yet numerous.

Thus nature has left Lawrence township with a surface broken and hilly, with a soil variable in fertility, but on the whole inferior, with productive seams of good coal and underlying rocks filled with petroleum. The civil history of a community depends so much upon the geography of the territory occupied that a previous knowledge of natural environments is necessary to a correct understanding of its social and industrial development.

THE SETTLEMENT.

It is not definitely known who the first settler of Lawrence was. The Dye family, the Hoff family, and the Chambers family all made permanent improvements in the Little Muskingum valley before 1810. As would be expected, the first settlers chose the rich bottom land along the river, the more distant terraces not being entered till comparatively recent times.

John Dye and Samuel Dye emigrated from Virginia and settled in the valley of the Little Muskingum, a short distance above the mouth of Cow run, in 1805. A few years later their father, John Dye, sr., with the remainder of the family, settled in the same neighborhood. John Dye, second, was born in New Jersey, in 1774. He emigrated with his family to Virginia, and then to Ohio, and settled in Lawrence township. He was married to Hannah Hoff, who was born in 1774, and died in 1857. He died during the epidemic of 1823. They had eleven children: Enoch, who died at the age of twenty; Thomas, Mophet, Susan, wife of Robert Pierce, of Newport township; Eliza, wife of Nathan Davis; Samuel, second, esq., a resident of Warren township; Emma, wife of William

Chambers; Daniel, deceased; John W.; A. Jackson, and Hannah, wife of George Casady, of Newport township.

A. Jackson Dye, son of John Dye, jr., was born in 1816, in Lawrence township. In 1838 he married Maria Petty, who was born in 1818. He owns one hundred acres of the old homestead. His family consists of nine children: D. H., who resides in Lawrence township; L. P., in Marietta; P. C., in Nebraska; G. P., in Marietta; William A., in Nebraska; H. M., wife of Gideon Campbell, on Cow run; S. A., in Lawrence township; Lottie and Emma at home.

Samuel Dye, brother of John Dye, jr., is well remembered by the older citizens of the township. He emigrated from Virginia and began life among the wooded hills of Lawrence, in 1805. He died in 1860, at the age of eighty-one years. Susan Hoff, his wife, was born in Virginia, in 1776 and died in 1849. The family consisted of ten children: John H., the oldest, was born in Virginia, in 1799. In 1822 he married Eliza O'Bleness, who was born in New York in 1803. The remaining children of Samuel Dye were: Hannah, first wife of Joseph Caywood; Sophia, wife of Amos Dye, second; Betsy, wife of Ezekial Dye, second; Mary, wife of Ezekial Reed; Annie, wife of William Templeton, and afterwards of William McGee; Jonathan and James H., of Marietta; Nancy, wife of John R. Hill, of Newport township; and George, deceased. Hannah and Sophia married cousins of their father; Betsy and Mary their second cousins.

When Samuel and John Dye settled in Lawrence township, the nearest post office was Marietta, and the tract of country toward the north was an unbroken wilderness. The native animals of the forest nightly visited the improvement in search of prey. Domestic animals were in constant danger, and even children were unsafe beyond sight of the cabin. In dry weather the nearest mill was at Devol's dam, twelve miles away, which could only be reached by traversing a cow path through the woods. Samuel Dye was a man of eccentric appearance. In cold weather a long cloak, covered with shorter capes, the number depending on the temperature, protected his tall and corpulent body. He was always in a good humor and called everybody "bub," which gave him the nickname "bub Sam." The electors of his township made him justice of the peace for thirty-one successive years. The brothers and sisters of John and Samuel Dye were: Jane, wife of Henry Chamberlain; Polly, wife of James Hoff; Ezekiel and Jonathan, farmers of Lawrence township; Bettie, Sallie, wife first of Thomas Worthington, then of James Britton; Patience, wife of John Cadwell, of Marietta township; and Amos, a farmer and one of the early millers of Lawrence.

Two sons of Jonathan Dye, sr., were the victims of fatal accidents. Amos died from the effect of a falling limb striking him on the head. The accident which resulted in the death of Alexander was horrible. In 1873, during the oil excitement at Cow Run, Alexander's son, a small boy, found a can of fluid which his parents supposed to be refined coal oil. The lamp, which was more than half full of crude oil, was filled with what was supposed to be the superior article, and the evening was spent as usual around the open hearth. The lamp was noticed to flicker now and then, but no apprehension was excited. Before retiring it was turned down and left burning on the table. Soon after retiring the flickering became more frequent and excited the fears of Mrs. Dye, who asked her husband to blow out the light. He hurried to obey the request, but when he picked up the lamp the flickering became frequent and more intense. Just as he was in the act of pitching the dangerous bowl from the cabin, the explosion of the half pint of nitro-glycerine which it contained, filled the air with small particles of the body of its victim, left the cabin in ruins and wounded every member of the family except the baby.

Mrs. Abigal Dye, wife of Jonathan T. Dye, who was born in 1835 and died in 1878, is the daughter of James Jamison, who was born in Pennsylvania in 1795, and settled in Liberty township, Washington county. Mr. Jamison was married to Elizabeth Gordon, who was born in 1803 and died in 1866. The surviving members of the family are: Elizabeth, wife of William Mosburgh, of Kansas; John H., James M., and Mark B., who reside in Virginia; Susan, wife of John Phunister; Rebecca, wife of Earstus Magee; and Abigal, who was born in 1841, in Liberty township.

Diarca A. Dye, son of John H. Dye, was born in 1840. In 1860 he married Mary E. Clogston, who was born in Marietta in 1840. They have a family of six children. Mr. Dye went into the oil business in 1862, and continued to operate wells until 1875, when he engaged in the lumber business.

Dr. William L. McCowan was born in Philadelphia in 1815, and came to Ohio in 1846, stopping for a time at Harmar, and eventually locating in this township at Morse run, where he has been postmaster since 1862. By his first wife, Marinda J. Matthews, who died in 1870, he had ten children, of whom eight survive, viz: Elizabeth, Harriet (Bab) of Cow Run, Marinda (Dye) of West Virginia, Asa, Nancy H. (Dye) of Dexter City, William H., and Edward. By his second wife, Dr. McCowan has two children, Emma and Viola.

One of the early, and possibly the first, settlers of Lawrence township, was John Chambers, who was born in County Down, Ireland. He emigrated to America in 1798 and settled in Lawrence township about 1799. He settled at the mouth of Chambers' run a short distance below and opposite the mouth of Cow run. From the time of his arrival in Ohio, until he settled in Lawrence, he lived at the mouth of Wingett's run, in Ludlow township. He built the first saw-mill in the township, on the Little Muskingum at the mouth of Chambers' run. His wife, Annie Greer, was a Scotch lady. It was chiefly through Mr. Chambers' benevolence and influence that the Little Muskingum church was built. He died in 1823.

William Chambers, an older brother, settled in Lawrence on the farm opposite the mouth of Chambers' run, about 1810. A younger sister who emigrated from Ireland at the same time, was the wife of Hugh Wilson, of Aurelius township.

James P., a son of William Chambers, was a natural

land surveyor. Without the aid of an instrument he could run lines and measure land with remarkable accuracy.

James G., the oldest son of John Chambers, was distinguished for two traits of character, fine social qualities and an uncontrolable temper. When in a fit of passion his swearing was shocking. William, a younger brother was killed by lightening at the age of seventeen. Joseph Chambers was a farmer and carpenter who lived on the east side of the Little Muskingum until 1850, when he moved to Marietta. He married Matilda McElHinney.

Joseph Caywood settled about one mile below and opposite the mouth of Cow run in 1806. He died without children in 1820. His nephew, Joseph, a son of William Caywood, settled in Lawrence, on what is yet known as the Joseph Caywood farm. He was a leading member of the Presbyterian church.

About 1805 the Hoff family, consisting of Susan Hoff, the widow of Daniel Hoff, and seven children, four sons and three daughters, came from Alexandria, Virginia, and settled in Lawrence township, above the mouth of Cow run. Enoch Hoff, the oldest, had been a slave master and trader. He settled near the mouth of Morse run. He was married five times. The children by his third wife were: James P., Angeline and Mary. Both James P. and his father were known in the community as "nigger catchers." Refugee slaves on several occasions were induced into the Hoff residence, and there captured and carried back to bondage.

Hannah Hoff married John Dye. Jonathan married Betsy Duncan and settled on Duck creek.

William Hoff was born in old Virginia in 1780, and settled in Lawrence township, where he died in 1844. His wife, Elizabeth Dutton, born in 1785, died in 1839. Of their children, Daniel died in Iowa; James died in Muskingum township; Lida died in Lawrence township; John died in Iowa; Margaret resides in Lawrence; Alfred, in Muskingum township; George is in Illinois, and Amos is in Iowa. Alfred Hoff is the father of eight children, of whom seven survive. He was captain of the transfer boat that carried the first regiment out of the State at the outbreak of the late war. He established a woollen mill at Marietta. Susan was the wife of Samuel Dye. Polly married Isaac Hill, and moved to Hocking river. James, the youngest of the family, married three times, and had five sons and eleven daughters.

John Sharp, well known all over the county as associate judge of common pleas, was born in Pennsylvania in 1771, and came to Ohio about 1800. He made an improvement on the east side of the Little Muskingum near the Newport township line. The first orchard on the Little Muskingum was planted by him. He was a very large, corpulent man, and was looked upon as the Solon of the community. He served as judge of common pleas several years, and a few days before his death in 1823, was commissioned judge of the superior court. His wife, whose maiden name was Mary Mitchell, and ten children survived him.

About the year 1812 Nathan Matheney (originally spelled Metheny), a native of Virginia, came from Athens county, Ohio, and settled above and opposite the mouth of Fifteen creek, and improved the farm now owned by Polly Martin. He had, by his first wife, Elizabeth Everly, eight children; by his second, Barbara Fultz, two; by his third, Katie Farley, six. Of these, sixteen children but one settled in Lawrence township. Noah, the oldest, made the first improvement on Bear run. Nathan Matheny, sr., returned to Athens county in 1835. Noah moved to Tunnel, Ohio, in 1858. His son John resides in Newport township.

George Templeton, esq., came to Lawrence township from Newport, and made an improvement on the Little Muskingum about two miles above the mouth of Fifteen, in 1819. He served as justice of the peace in Lawrence for thirty-three years. In partnership with Beniah Snodgrass and Benjamin Burres, he built a saw-mill in 1834, about one mile further up the river. He died about 1850. He was the father of twelve children. His son William was killed by accident. Joseph settled on Bear run, where he is still living. James is living on Fifteen creek. Lettie who is unmarried, has always been the main support of the Lawrence Baptist church.

Zeptha Treadway was one of the earliest settlers of the upper part of the township. About 1820 he came from New Jersey, and entered land below and opposite the mouth of Archer's fork. Two of his sons are living: Jonathan, near the same place, and the other, Jerre who was a self-constituted preacher, is in the county infirmary.

Every royal household has its jester, every circus a clown, and no community is complete without a professional story teller. Lawrence, in the person of Jacob Bartmess, possessed a Munchausen in whom was combined the cunning of a wit and the oddity of a genius. "Jake" lived in a cabin on the east side of the Little Muskingum, nearly opposite the Baptist church, as early as 1825. He cared nothing about domestic affairs, and was happy only when tramping the woods with his gun on his shoulder, or entertaining his neighbors with the story of the mighty deeds of "my brother George." George was always the hero of his blood chilling stories. A few pecularities of the house are worthy of mention. The black-eyed children had a terror of strangers. A rustle of bare feet followed a rap on the door, and the entering visitor could see nothing of children save several pairs of sparkling black eyes peering from under the bed. When the boys grew older, they were given an outfit of buckskin pantaloons. Although the boys were growing longer, the pantaloons from time to time became shorter, they being Jake's only recourse for thongs. He died on a hunting expedition down the river near Cairo, in 1876, aged seventy-seven years.

Hiram Snodgrass emigrated from Bull Creek, West Virginia, and settled on Bear run in Lawrence township, in 1812. He died on the same place in 1879. His wife's maiden name was Drucilla Olliver. Eli Snodgrass, a brother of Hiram, and husband of Polly Templeton, was one of the early settlers of Lawrence. Beniah Snodgrass is well remembered by all the old settlers of Lawrence. He was married twice, first to Anna McKibban and then to Julia Anne Clark. He settled in section ten, and in partnership with Burris & Templeton, built the Templeton mill in 1834.

Lucas Casady settled in Lawrence township, about one mile below the mouth of Fifteen, in 1821. He continued to reside in Lawrence township until 1850, when he was killed by accident in Maysville, Kentucky. His family consisted of three sons and one daughter. Morton settled opposite Painter run; George at the head of Morse run, and William J. on Morse run. Diadamia was married to Samuel Dye, third, from whom she was afterwards divorced, and married to Carlton Palmer, of Newport township.

The McAllister improvement is the oldest in the upper part of the township. About five acres were cleared as early as 1820, but no house was built. It is not probable that anyone lived there until the later settlement of the township.

Joe Harris, who settled near the mouth of Morse run in 1825, was the hero of the woods. In manners he was somewhat rough, but possessed a kind heart and accommodating disposition. He was a useful man in the clearing, and could always be relied upon at a raising.

The mill at the mouth of Fifteen was owned by George W. Reynolds in 1832. It came into possession of Charles Akinson in 1836. Charles was a grandson of Cornelius Akinson, who was wounded seven times in one battle in the Revolution. Charles was born on the Juniata in 1796, and in early life learned milling and boatbuilding. His death occurred in Marietta in 1880. William, his oldest son, made an improvement on Bear run in 1838, where he is still living. His first wife was Jane Templeton, daughter of 'Squire Templeton. He married for his second wife Theda Patterson, sister of Dr. Patterson. He is a prominent man in the community.

In the autumn of 1832, Joseph McElHinney with his aged father, John McElHinney, and his only sister Anne, come from the north of Ireland and settled on the Little Muskingum, a short distance above and opposite the mouth of Elk run. He found there a clearing of six acres and a small orchard and cabin which had been made by Jacob Newlin some twelve years previous. This was at that time the uppermost improvement in the township, and there was no improvement above on the county road nearer than that of Jacob Wingett, at the mouth of Wingett's run. Zephtha Treadway was the nearest neighbor on the same road below. John McElHinney died in 1874, in his eightieth year. His daughter Anne made her home with her brother Joseph, until his death in September, 1840; Mary, wife of Joseph McElHinney, died at the home of her daughter, Mrs. Chambers, in Marietta, in 1874. They had a family of six children: Matilda, wife of Joseph Chambers, Marietta; Joseph M. McElHinney, M. D., Newport; Nancy Jane, wife of Rev. George D. Fry, Morgan county; David M. McElHinney is mayor of Hastings, Nebraska, and was, in 1873-4, grand master of Nebraska State lodge, I. O. O. F.; Alexander M., Silver Cliff, Colorado; and Kate, wife of S. A. Squier, mayor of Silver Cliff, Colorado.

John Rake made the first improvement on section six.

He sold to A. Campbell and Samuel Bush, and purchased the McAllister improvement in 1835. He died opposite the mouth of Bear run in 1875.

Solomon Tice, an early settler of Ludlow township, pushed into Lawrence township in the pursuit of his ambition to suddenly make a great fortune. At the mouth of a small stream emptying into the Little Muskingum, the "Governor," as he was nicknamed, discovered a composite rock which he supposed to contain silver. This circumstance gave the stream its present name, Silver Mine run. As early as 1825 he bored a well on Fifteen creek, opposite the mouth of Mill fork, to the depth of three hundred feet, in search of salt. His tools were inadequate to the further progress of the work, and the attempt was abandoned. It is said that his confidence of obtaining a productive salt well was broken by the appearance, at the depth of two hundred feet, of a black, greasy liquid, which later investigations prove to have been oil.

Archibald Campbell settled in the northeast corner of Lawrence township in 1833. He was born in Pennsylvania in 1806, and married Hannah Sample, who was born in 1820. Mr. Campbell was the first postmaster of Lawrence post office. The surviving members of the family are: John M., who lives in Marietta; Rebecca J., wife of Thomas Hall, of Ludlow township; Sarah A., wife of Ross N. Dye, of Marietta township; Joseph L., who lives in Marietta; Gideon, Samuel M., and Luna, who live at Cow Run. Samuel M., the druggist at Cow Run, was born in 1844. He married Mary E. Maxon in 1866. In 1863 he enlisted in company H, Seventh Ohio cavalry, and served till 1865, when he was discharged at Nashville. He was appointed census enumerator in 1880.

The first store in Lawrence township was opened by William Powell in 1838, in the upper part of the township, near the corner of Independence. He removed from Lawrence to Grand View township, where he engaged in the practice of medicine.

John Barnhart was one of the early settlers of the upper corner of the township. He was a nervous and superstitious character, who was in constant dread of ghosts. One night, while passing through a clearing, a man without a head appeared, and in a few days it was announced that Barnhart had died of nervous prostration.

Rev. Levi I. Fay was born in the State of Massachusetts in 1814. He married Caroline Hill, who was born in 1816, and died in 1854. In 1855 he married Minerva Bachelor. He settled in Marietta township in 1835, and removed to Lawrence township in 1844. He is a Congregational minister, and is now in charge of the churches at Morse Run, Cow Run, Stanleyville, and Cedar Narrows. His surviving children do not live in this county.

Major Isaac M. Hannold was the seventh son of Isaac Hannold, jr., a blacksmith and wagon-maker of Camden, New Jersey, whose father, Isaac Hannold, came from Germany and settled in Haddonfield, New Jersey. Isaac M. Hannold was born in Barnsborough, New Jersey, June 29, 1791, and was brought up in Camden. He was a brick-layer, stone-cutter, shoemaker, carpenter, and farmer. In 1814 he was elected first lieutenant of the Camden Blues, and was in the service till the close of the war. In 1815 he married Patience F. Ross, of Philadelphia, who was of an English family. In 1817 he removed to Pennsylvania, and in 1819 he was elected captain of militia, and in 1824 was commissioned major of the Fifteenth regiment. He was elected colonel in 1836, but before receiving his commission he removed to Natchez, Mississippi, where a railroad contract occupied his time until 1838, when he returned to Pennsylvania and was employed two years in the construction of the Hann Street bridge between Allegheny City and Pittsburgh. In 1840 he removed to this county and purchased a farm eight miles from Marietta, in Lawrence township, on the ridge between Duck creek and Little Muskingum. He was for four years superintendent of the infirmary, and was one of the partners in the Old Elm well, the second producing oil well on Cow run. In 1865 he removed to Monitor, Indiana, where he died in 1867, two years after the death of his wife.

We have now given a sketch of the best known of the early settlers along the Muskingum valley. The large tract of territory at the head of Fifteen creek was settled mostly by Scotch families who came to this county between 1840 and 1850. They are an intelligent and industrious class of people, and have contributed largely toward the wealth of the county. Wool growing is the predominant industry of the Scotch communities.

George Heslop was born in England in 1790. He emigrated to America and settled in Lawrence township in 1844. His death occurred in 1878. Agnes Dixon, his wife, was born in 1794, and died in 1840. The surviving members of the family are: Elizabeth, wife of Thomas Lumsdon, who resides in Pennsylvania; Agnes, wife of Andrew Johnson, Fearing township; Jane, wife of Thomas Spratt, Adams township; William, Lawrence township; Isabel, wife of Alexander Ormiston, Barlow township; and John, who was born in 1828. In 1865 he married Anna Thompson, who was born in 1845. They have six children. John Heslop came from England in 1844, and settled on one hundred and forty acres of land in the north part of Lawrence township.

Ralph Cuthbert emigrated from England, where he was a master shepherd, in 1842. He settled in Lawrence township, on Fifteen creek, and engagedn in general farming and wool growing. His wife, Isabel Thompson, was born in 1819, she died in 1876. The family consisted of eight children, six of whom are living. Ralph W., third child, died in 1865, from a wound which he received at Nashville, Tennessee. Mr. Cuthbert owns two hundred and forty acres of good land.

John Slobaum was the first German settler on the highlands in the northwest part of the township, known as German ridge. He entered land and made an improvement previous to 1840. This ridge is now settled by people of German descent, who are becoming wealthy on the products of once rejected terraces.

John D. Pape, sr., born in Hanover, Germany, in 1794, emigrated to this country in 1838, came to Wash-

ington county, and settled in Lawrence township, where he died. His wife, Hedwick Mehrtens, was born in 1797, and is still living. Six of the eight children are living. In 1812 John D. Pape served in Bonaparte's army.

John D. Pape, jr., married Christiana Fitchen, who came from Germany in 1845. Six of the seven children are living. Mr. Pape owns a farm of two hundred and fifty acres of land, on the Ohio river, in Marietta township. In 1877 he started a grocery in Marietta, where he resides.

John W. Gitchell settled in Lawrence township in 1852, he having emigrated from Steubenville, Ohio, where he was born in 1836. For the past sixteen years he has been connected with the saw-mill business in the township of Newport. He has a farm of one hundred and eighty acres of land. Was in the hundred days service, and in 1864 was drafted into the Sixty-second Ohio volunteer infantry, serving until the close of the war. By his wife, Samantha T. Tidd, he has had eight children.

John Q. Pepper settled in Lawrence township in 1853, having emigrated from Virginia. He married Olive Maxon, who was born in 1822. They had eight children. Sarah E. was born in Noble county in 1851. In 1872 she was married to Augustus T. Dye, who was born in 1850. He died in 1876, leaving two children.

The most rapid growth of population was between 1863 and 1870, caused by the extensive production of oil within that period.

Eldridge G. Gilbert was born in Massachusetts in 1828, emigrated to Aurelius township, Washington county, in 1858, and to Cow Run, Lawrence township, in 1864, where he built a machine shop. His wife, Mary A. Davis, was born in 1840, in Adams township. They have a family of three children: Juna B., born in 1870; Laura M., in 1874; and Ethel S., in 1879.

Victor Torner was born in Europe in 1815 and emigrated to Virginia, and in 1861 settled in Belpre township, afterwards coming to Lawrence, where he is superintendent of the Exchange company's oil wells. He built the flouring mill at Newport. In 1848 he married Charlotta G. Weiss, who was born in 1819. They have three children, viz: Elvira, wife of J. R. Dye, of Cow Run; Hugo T., living at Cow Run, and William V., at Newport.

Alfred Hoff was born in Lawrence township, Washington county, June 24, 1817. He was married in 1839 to Miss Mary N. Atkinson, who died in the same year. In 1840 he was a second time married, to Miss Elizabeth Fuller, who still lives. Eight children have been born of this marriage, of whom seven are living. Mr. Hoff was for twenty-five years chief engineer on boats on the Ohio, its tributaries, and on southern rivers. When the civil war broke out he was in the south, and immediately after the fall of Sumter transported two confederate regiments from Arkansas to New Orleans. Not relishing such work, he immediately set out for home. On his arrival, he with two others chartered a boat and took out the first troops that left Ohio. He served through the whole war. After the war he was interested in manufacturing, building the Marietta woollen mills. In 1861 he purchased a farm in Muskingum township, on which he now lives in retirement.

In 1868 George E. Lehmer emigrated to Lawrence from Pennsylvania, in which State he was born in 1837. He married Annie E. Stickle, who was born in 1840. To Mr. and Mrs. Lehmer has been born one son, Willie H., living in this township. In 1873 Mr. Lehmer was elected to the office of school director. He has charge of six oil wells, which produce about five barrels per day. While serving in Company F of the Pennsylvania reserves he was wounded at Antietam and also at Fredericksburgh.

W. Strachan was born in England in 1831. He came to America in 1843, and remained in Allegheny county, Pennsylvania, until 1869, when he came to Cow Run and engaged in the oil business. He has been justice of the peace for nine years. He married Sarah Johnson, of this township, a granddaughter of Alderman Johnson, an early settler of this township, and daughter of Edward Johnson. He has five children, viz: David, Mary, Margaret, Sarah and Edward.

ESTABLISHMENT AND ORGANIZATION.

A petition was laid before the commissioners at their June session, 1815, signed by Nathaniel Mitchell, John Mitchell, Elisha Rose, John Sharp and others, "praying that a new township may be laid out and set off from the township of Newport." It was resolved by the board "that the whole of the original surveyed township number three, range seven, together with sections 17, 18, 22, 23, 24, 28, 29, 30, 32, 34, 35 and 36 in the second township, range seven, be and hereby is established into an incorporated town, to be called and denominated Lawrence, and the inhabitants within said district are entitled to all the immunities and privileges of incorporated towns within the State. The elections in said town will meet at the house of John Mitchell on the second Saturday of July, at 10 o'clock A. M., for the purpose of electing township officers." The court of quarter sessions directed that an election for two justices of the peace should be held at the same time and place. The election which was held agreeably to this order resulted in the choice of the following officers: Trustees, William Hoff, John Newton and Elisha Rose; clerk, John Sharp; constables, James Hoff and Elijah Wilson; fence viewers, Jonathan Dye and James Mitchell; treasurer, John Dye; supervisors, George Nixon and Nathaniel Mitchell; justices of the peace, Samuel Dye and John Mitchell. The township officers were sworn in by Samuel Dye, justice of the peace.

On the first of April, 1816, the electors met at the house of Nathaniel Mitchell to elect township officers. John Dye was chosen chairman, and Elisha Rose and John Newton judges of the election. John Sharp was clerk. At this second election eighteen votes were cast. The following is the list of voters: John Sharp, William Hoff, James Hoff, David McKibbon, Isaac Wilson, Nathan Davis, Nathanial Mitchell, Jonathan Dye, John

Newton, Elisha Rose, John Dye, Samuel Dye, Henry Chamberlain, John Mitchell, Isaac Hill, Ezekiel Dye, James Mitchell and Alderman Johnson.

Nearly half of this list of voters resided in that part of the township which has since been set back to Newport. James Hoff was elected first "lister of taxable property," and John Mitchell appraiser of houses. The first grand jurors from the township were Nathaniel Amlin and Nathaniel Mitchell. John Dye was the first petit juror.

The election of 1820 and subsequent elections for many years were held in a school-house on John Dye's farm near the mouth of Cow run. In 1827, section thirty-two of township two was reannexed to Newport, and at the June session, 1840, Lawrence was reduced to its present limits. William Hill and others made an effort in 1816 to have this change made, but the commissioners deemed it inexpedient. A township house has since been built near the center of the township, where elections are now held by the citizens of the northern precinct. The second voting precinct was established, for the convenience of the residents of the southern end, in 1872.

Before the war Lawrence gave large Democratic majorities. From the opening of the war till 1872, the township was carried by the Republicans; from 1872 it was carried by the Democrats till 1880, when the Republicans had a small majority.

SCHOOLS.

The first school in the township was opened about 1810, by a young man from Virginia, named Dunkin, in a log building which stood on the Joseph Haywood farm, a short distance below the mouth of Cow run. A school-house was afterwards built on the farm owned by John Templeton, in which school was maintained until the common school system went into operation in 1838. A school was opened about 1835 on the J. H. Dye farm, by Peggy Hill. This school was quite popular among the settlers, and was well patronized. The only other private school in the township was on Fifteen creek.

In 1838, when the public school system went into effect, the township was divided into eight districts, and a log house built in each. The number of districts was increased to ten, and in 1880 to fourteen.

Lawrence township has been peculiarly fortunate with regard to her school fund. In 1869, when profitable oil wells were being obtained almost everywhere in the Cow run region, a company known as the School-house company leased from the school board the lot on which the Cow Run school-house then stood. The company, under the conditions of the lease were to receive two-thirds of all the oil yielded by the territory. The school-house was moved and operations began which resulted, on the twenty-second of October, in procuring, probably, the best well in the township. At first it produced one hundred and twenty barrels a day. This well has since been the source of a steady income to the township school fund, its production at the present time being about sixteen barrels per week. The school fund has derived

J. T. Dye

Amos Dye, father of Jonathan T., was one of the old settlers of Lawrence township, where he lived from the time of his settlement until his death. He came from Noble county, Ohio. He died in 1877, leaving six sons, viz: Thomas, Devol, John Wesley, Jonathan T., Joseph and Fay. All of these are living except Jonathan T. John W. and Fay live in Washington county; Thomas lives in Virginia, Devol and Joseph live in Ross county, Ohio.

Jonathan Titus Dye was born January 26, 1838, in Lawrence township, and received his education in the schools of the township. He was always noted as a particularly bright scholar, and acquired a very good common school education. At the age of seventeen, he began to teach, and followed this profession until his twenty-sixth year. His schools were all in Lawrence township.

On the thirteenth of March, 1862, Mr. Dye was married to Miss Abigail E. Jameson, who survives him. Miss Jameson was born in Liberty township, March 13, 1843. Her father was one of the oldest settlers of the county. He first settled in Liberty township, whence he removed with his family to Kansas in 1853. Here he died in the fall of the same year, his wife having preceded him to the grave a few months before. The four children moved back to Lawrence township, this county, in the following spring.

After his marriage, Mr. Dye taught school for two years, then moved to Marietta, where he engaged in the oil business. After being thus employed for two or three years, he engaged in the dry goods and grocery business on Greene street, in the firm of Westgate & Dye. But, as his health was always very delicate, Mr. Dye felt that life in the country was better for him than an active business life in town. Hence, after about six months, he purchased a part of his father's homestead in Lawrence township, and moved his family thither. Here he lived until his death, which occurred February 28, 1879, of consumption.

Mr. and Mrs. Dye had seven children, as follows: Martin L. P., born April 13, 1863, died August 23, 1864; Clara M., born September 13, 1865; Ida Sophia, born February 21, 1868; Sherman Edwin, born August 14, 1870; Abbie C., born November 8, 1872; Furman Victor, born September 7, 1875, died March 10, 1877; and Carl M., born February 6, 1878.

Mr. Dye's home farm consisted of one hundred and twelve acres. He also owned other lands in various parts of the county, and some in Ross county, amounting altogether to about three hundred acres. This land is still owned by his widow, who lives on and manages the home farm.

Mr. Dye made a specialty of stock-raising, paying especial attention to the raising of sheep.

Mr. Dye was township clerk, and also a trustee of the township for several years. At one time he was appointed land appraiser.

He was a man of great energy, although that energy was constantly hampered by ill health. He was very widely known and always very highly respected. He was an earnest and sincere Christian, being a member of the Congregational church, which body he joined at the early age of seven.

from it about forty thousand dollars, out of which the schools of the township have been maintained and a number of new houses built. There is now a balance bearing interest, of twenty-four thousand seven hundred and seventy-nine dollars and fifty-seven cents. To what use this fund shall be appropriated is an issue in the township. Some favor permanently endowing the common schools, and others advocate the establishment of a school for higher instruction.

CHURCHES.

The first church built in Lawrence township was located in the neighborhood of the first settlement, on the Little Muskingum, near the Newport line, principally through the influence of John Chambers. It was a small log building covered with clapboards, and used by all the settlers in the neighborhood, regardless of denominational differences. The church, after 1835, was regularly supplied by Revs. L. D. Bingham and Addison Kingsbury, of Marietta, until October, 1844, when Rev. Levi L. Fay became regular pastor. During this time the congregation was under the care of the presbytery and was Presbyterian in form of government. The ruling elders were J. H. Dye and Joseph Caywood. On the eleventh of July, 1846, a Congregational meeting was held, at which it was decided to reorganize the church and unite it with the Congregational conference. During the summer of 1846 the old building was abandoned and a new one built on Morse run. Rev. Mr. Fay was ordained pastor of this society, known as as the Little Muskingum Congregational church in 1849. The present house of worship was built in 1866, and dedicated May 28, 1867. Twelve hundred dollars toward the expense of this building was donated by the pastor, and a bell which cost one hundred dollars has since been purchased by him and dedicated to the use of the congregation. Mr. Fay labored successfully until 1877, when ill health compelled him to retire. The pulpit was supplied two years by Rev. Mr. Riddle. The congregation since 1879 has been without a pastor. The present membership of the society is about fifty.

BAPTIST CHURCHES.

The Lawrence Baptist church was constituted in 1840. A log meeting-house was built and the few communicants met every Sunday, although no regular preacher visited the congregation until 1844. During these four years, while the existence of the organization was hanging between doubt and fear, the courageous labor of Lettie Templeton carried the helpless infant beyond the period of danger. She is entitled to the proud distinction of god-mother of the church. J. D. Riley became pastor in 1844; Henry Lyon, in 1853; John Ables, in 1854; B. M. Stout, in 1863; D. Sechman, in 1866. Mr. Sechman was succeeded by Mungo Taylor.

At Cow Run a meeting-house was built for the use of all denominations, but passed under the control of the Baptist society which was constituted in 1870. Mungo Taylor was the pastor for a time, but regular service has been discontinued.

GERMAN METHODIST.

The first German society in the township was organized about 1845, as the German Methodist church. A log building was put up, and a burying-ground laid out on the ridge in the northwest corner. This house is still standing, and services are held at irregular intervals.

LUTHERANS.

There are in the township two German Evangelical churches—one on the Little Muskingum, a short distance above the mouth of Cow run, established in 1853, and the other on the ridge, established in 1868. Neither of these societies enjoys the privilege of regular preaching. Cemeteries adjoin both church buildings.

UNITED BRETHREN.

The United Brethren have a strong hold in the southern part of the township. The largest society of this denomination worship at the Mount Zion meeting-house, about one mile south of Cow Run post office. This society was organized about 1860, and now has a membership of sixty. Sunday-school is held every week during the whole year. G. W. Athey, A. L. Moor and M. S. Riddle have been the most prominent preachers. The Union Chapel congregation is not as large, though about five years older than the Mount Zion. Union chapel, a log structure, about twenty-five years old, is situated at the head of Eight Mile run. Both these congregations are connected with Beach Grove circuit.

METHODIST CHURCH.

Pine Ridge Methodist Episcopal church, located in the southeast part of the township, at the head of Bear run, was organized in 1866 by Rev. J. W. Hamilton. In 1868, when D. C. Knowles became pastor, the membership numbered seventeen. A log meeting-house was built in 1870. In 1873 the remnant of a German Methodist church, which had existed in the neighborhood, united with Pine Ridge. The number of members has been steadily increasing from year to year, until there are more than seventy communicants. The congregation belongs to Newport circuit, the preachers of which have been, since 1871: John H. Doan, to 1873; H. M. Rader, to 1874; T. D. Fast, to 1876; W. H. Piggot, to 1877; C. J. Feitt, to 1878; G. W. Dennis, to 1880. J. H. Doan is the present pastor.

Methodist meeting is occasionally held in the Good Templars' hall at Cow Run.

DISCIPLE CHURCH.

A society of Disciples of Christ, popularly known as Campbellites, was organized in 1869, and built a meeting-house known as Mount Pisgah church, at the head of Cow run. The society is small, and does not enjoy the privilege of regular preaching.

PRESBYTERIAN CHURCH.

The Scotch settlers in the north part of Lawrence organized a church September 3, 1847. The society was organized by T. M. Galloway under the authority of the presbytery of Steubenville. Rev. D. M. Sleth is the present pastor.

METHODIST CHURCH.

Gross chapel, Methodist Episcopal church was built about 1872. The structure is comfortable, but the congregation is small.

CEMETERIES.

Besides the churchyards, there are in the township two family cemeteries. After the log meeting-house on the Little Muskingum was abandoned, the cemetery, in which the graves of many old settlers, are marked by mossy slabs of marble, reverted to the Chambers family and has since been used by them as a private burying-place.

The Dye cemetery, on the farm of A. J. Dye, was laid out by John Dye, at the death of his oldest son, Enoch, in 1812. The bodies of more than fifty members and relatives of the Dye family have been laid away in this historic lot. The tombs faithfully record the resistless march of time and keep fresh in the minds of surviving members, the memory of days gone by. The use of the cemetery has never been denied the public, and many are buried there who were in no way connected with the family. But it is not probable that a lot so sad and precious, in which are consigned the relatives of five generations, will ever become the property of the public.

There is a cemetery on the line, between the old Snodgrass farm and the Esquire Templeton farm opposite the mouth of Beaver run. It has been used as a public burying-ground since the settlement of that portion of the township.

FIRST CHILDREN'S HOME.

The first Children's Home in the State, established by Miss Catharine A. Fay, was located in Lawrence township, at the mouth of Morse run. This was properly a county institution, and has already been treated of in the general history. But the plan of its management had a local bearing upon the affairs of the township, which makes a brief sketch necessary in this connection. The Home was opened on the first of April, 1858, with eight boys and one girl, in a temporary, one story building. On the first of May when school opened, Miss Fay led those of proper age to the public school-house, but the teacher sent them home. Miss Fay then took the proper legal steps toward having her wards admitted. Great indignation prevailed throughout the neighborhood, and it was determined if possible to prevent these "pauper children" from being received into the public school of the district. When the matron, a second time, took her children to the school, she was confronted by two directors and eleven men, but she was armed with letters of guardianship, and there was no legal way of preventing the execution of her plans. This conflict inspired throughout the whole township, a deep prejudice against Miss Fay and her institution. There were some people who supported her enterprise and gave her assistance, but the prevailing sentiment was adverse.

This conflict has been the subject of much comment, and the people of Lawrence township, to some extent at least, have suffered unjust criticism. Miss Fay's work of benevolence was in behalf of the whole county, but the citizens of the township were not disposed to be in any way coerced into the support of that work. The school was maintained by the taxpayers of Lawrence township for the benefit of the people of Lawrence township, and it is but natural that a majority should be averse to educating the poor of all the townships. We are not disposed to espouse the cause of either party. Miss Fay did not receive the support and sympathy from her neighbors which the benevolent character of her work entitled her to. But there was a cause for the unpopularity of her institution, and it is but justice that that cause should be known. All occasion for complaint was removed, the second year, by the establishment of a private school. The scales of prejudice, however, which gather about the eyes of the public, can only be removed by time.

POST OFFICES.

The official name of the first post office was Lawrence Township, John W. Dye, postmaster. Mr. Dye's farm was central in location, and one office met the wants of the settlers until 1843, when Archibald Campbell, who resided in the northeast corner was commissioned postmaster of Lawrence, and Joseph Caywood, who resided in the southwest corner, became postmaster of Lower Lawrence. This office was discontinued when Hill's was established. Moss Run was established in 1858; Dr. McCowan has been postmaster since 1863. The post office known as Fifteen was established in 1867, and placed in charge of Leonard Button. In 1879 it was deemed advisable to discontinue Fifteen and establish an office at Heslop's, in Liberty township. The rapid growth of Cow Run in 1869, made the establishment of an office at that place a necessity. The department granted the request of the citizens in December of that year, and commissioned William P. Guitteau postmaster. T. J. Connor is the present incumbent. Lunville, located at the headwaters of Bear run, was established in 1879. Moss Run, Cow Run, and Lunville are the three offices now in existence in the township.

SUNDAY-SCHOOLS.

The first Sunday-school in the Little Muskingum valley, so far as is known, was taught by Mr. and Mrs. McElHinney, who resided above and opposite the mouth of Elk run. This school was attended by the parents and children of the settlement within a radius of four miles. It was an itinerant school, and was held at the houses in the neighborhood, most frequently at the houses of Joseph McElHinney, in Lawrence, and Robert McKenzie and Jesse Fleming, of Independence. This school was organized in 1833.

The next school of which we have any knowledge was opened in 1835, in the Presbyterian church, in the opposite corner of the township, by Thomas Hughes, then a student at Marietta college. Mr. Hughes was in the habit of delivering an exhortation at the conclusion of the lesson, and by his stirring addresses, created a lively interest throughout the lower settlement. He soon afterwards (about 1836) opened a school in the school-house above the mouth of Fifteen. Messrs. Bingham,

Bosworth, Dye, and Reynolds were also among the pioneers in Sunday-school work in the township.

SOCIETIES.

Among the young men of the early settlement of the upper part of the township, J. M. McElHinney took the lead in matters looking to mental improvement. In February, 1842, Mr. McElHinney, Evan Nomans, and William Powell, organized the Little Muskingum Lyceum, the first organization for literary improvement in the Little Muskingum valley. This society did good work for about three years in the development of literary taste and talent among its members. A considerable number of young persons in the neighborhood could not be induced to join this society, for they claimed it was too aristocratic, and their clothing was not suitable to appear at the meetings. On their account the old lyceum was allowed to go down, and in 1845 Mr. McElHinney organized a new society, consisting at first of sixteen members, called the Singed Cat society, declaring to them that they, like singed cats, were better than they appeared. The idea was popular and the society prospered for nearly three years. But there was another element among the settlers of the community—the poor and illiterate—who claimed that the Singed Cats thought themselves better than they. In order to help this class and if possible to help the poor fellows along, Mr. McElHinney organized a reading club in the spring of 1848 giving it the significant name of Tarnal Critters. This was a decidedly democratic institution, anyone being eligible to membership provided he could half behave himself. But after reading through the Western Adventures, and a few other Indian stories, they ceased to be interested, and the plan proved a failure. Soon after Mr. McElHinney removed to Newport and left the Tarnal Critters.

One organization comes under this head which deserves special prominence, and that is the Good Templars lodge of Cow Run. The village of Cow Run, even at its most prosperous period, was a sober and orderly community, being widely different in that regard from most camps of similar character. The lodge of Good Templars exercised no small influence in the maintenance of this healthy state of morality. This society was formed in December, 1870. Meetings were held in the Baptist church for about six months, and then the only saloon in the settlement was purchased and converted into a hall for meetings. The hall was thrown open on Sundays for preaching, ministers of all denominations being invited to come and hold service. The society ceased to hold meetings in 1879, the membership having become very small on account of the removal from the village of most of the members.

PHYSICIANS.

William Powell read medicine while he was keeping store in the upper part of the township. Although not a professional practitioner he attended his neighbors when the services of a medical man were needed.

Dr. Tyler was the first professional practitioner who located in the township. He opened an office about one mile above the mouth of Fifteen in 1839, and maintained a successful practice for about two years.

Dr. Joshua Rogers settled a short distance above the mouth of Fifteen and began the practice of his profession in 1842. Death deprived the community of his services in 1847.

Dr. William T. Patterson comes next on the list of Lawrence township physicians. William Patterson, his father, came from Jefferson county to Ludlow township in 1844, and soon afterwards settled on section five, where William T. opened an office.

Dr. William McCowan, a native of Philadelphia, removed from Harmar and located on Morse run in 1860. He has from the first enjoyed a large practice and the confidence of the community.

Dr. George W. Flemming, a nephew of Dr. Patterson, located at the mouth of Archers fork and began the practice of medicine in 1864. In 1876 he moved to Bear Run where he now resides.

Dr. Ullman practiced a short time in this township. His office was near the mouth of Morse run.

OIL PRODUCTION.

The development of Lawrence township's richest resource began in 1860. William Guyton had for twenty years made use of the gas emitting from a fissure on Cow run, to light his shop, and a "burning spring" on Mill creek had been known since the earliest settlement. But it had never occurred to any one that these phenomena indicated the presence of oil. Besides it was not known that the geological conditions were favorable to the procurement of profitable wells.

John Newton was the first to anticipate the possibilities, and in partnership with Mophet Dye, began to sink the first shaft, near the summit of the break, on Cow run. Oil was found at the depth of one hundred and forty feet. They drilled but a short distance further through the "first sand" rock when a stream began to flow from the top through the sucker rods, and continued to flow at the rate of twenty barrels per day. The great success of this first attempt raised the neighborhood on tiptoe. The early operators and pioneers in the business were Newton Dye, Perkins, Jonathan Hoff, Logan, List, Hervey Ablinas, Green, Brown and Nailor. The third well belonging to Ablinas, Green and Brown, produced at first about fifteen barrels per day, but was soon pumped dry. This fact was an indication that the fissures leading to the prime sources of oil, were closed, and that these wells were an outlet to that only which was imprisoned in the crevices and pores of the rocks. The first engine was brought to Cow Run by Jonathan Hoff. The first wells were all drilled by spring pole. The first machinery for drilling was used by George McFarlan in 1864, when the first attempt was made to strike oil in a lower strata. The success of McFarlan's enterprise gave the business a new impetus. Many of the first sand wells had failed, and the production of others was declining. The discovery of the second sand deposit seemed to insure permanent production. When McFarlan struck oil in the second sand, there was great rejoicing among the holders of the leases, who carried him in triumph on their shoulders. Property became food for speculation, and capital was lavishly and wrecklessly invested. The excitement was confined to Cow run. Sufficient oil was obtained on Fifteen to enhance the value of property four hundred per cent., and even on Morse run, where there were no productive wells, land commanded extravagant prices. One hundred and twenty acres in the Cow run region cost the Bergen Oil company one hundred thousand dollars.

The principal operators during 1864–5 were McFarlan, Camden & Co., Colonel Weare, Rathbone, Perkins and Hervey. McFarlan, Rathbone, Camden, Weare and others came from Virginia in 1863, and purchased three hundred and twenty acres on the western slope of the break, and divided by Cow Run valley. They also purchased a tract on Fifteen. The whole tract passed into the hands of Colonel Weare and Tillotson & Bro., and finally in 1865 came into full possession of Weare, who struck twelve profitable wells in succession, which produced ten to seventy barrels per day. In 1867 Weare sold half his territory to the Exchange Oil company of Cincinnati, and in 1873 disposed of the remaining half interest to the same company.

Cow run became the centre of interest in the fall of 1866, when Perkins and Hervey struck in second sand rock at the depth of five hundred and ninety-four feet, on a five acre tract leased from the Bergen company, a crevice from which the oil was forced at intervals to the height of seventy-five feet above the ground. This well caught fire on the following night, and produced one of the most threatening conflagrations ever seen in these regions. This was the first flowing well in second sand, and its production of one hundred barrels per day proved that the supply was not yet exhausted.

Cow Run now began to assume the appearance of a large camp. Plank houses dotted the hills and at meal time the valley was a swarm of busy humanity.

In 1869 and 1870 about five hundred wells were being operated, and shafts were being sunk wherever a show of success presented itself. The production decreased rapidly from 1872 to 1876, since which time it has been very uniform. In 1870 the daily production was four hundred and fifty barrels. At present about sixty wells are operated, which produce sixty-five barrels daily; of these sixty, the Exchange company own thirty-five; H. G. Thomas, six, and most of those remaining are on the Bergen territory. The Exchange company owns its own coal mine and its own machine shop. There is a marked difference in the character of the wells on the eastern and western slopes. Those on the Bergen territory on the western slope, terminate in crevices, and generally blow faster, but fail sooner than those on the eastern slope, which terminate in sand rock known as honey comb. A shaft was once sunk on the Exchange territory to the depth of nearly twenty-two hundred feet, but the result was unsatisfactory.

In 1868, a transportation company was organized with a capital of twenty-five thousand dollars, which constructed pipes and the necessary tanks and machinery for the transportation of oil from the tanks to the river. The main pipe passes over a hill four hundred feet above the level of Cow run.

The first productive well of Fifteen, was struck in 1870 (an attempt in 1863 having failed), at the depth of four hundred feet, in shale. In that region there is now but one producing well. The only producing well on Morse run is on the land of John Myers. This well terminates in first sand rock.

INCIDENTS.

It appears from an entry in the township book bearing date May, 1819, that the township was troubled with pauper preachers. An order directed to Reuben McVey, constable, reads: "Whereas, a certain person calling himself a preacher, is likely to become a township charge, you are hereby directed to order said preacher out of the township."

In 1839, Elisha Rose, a well known citizen of Newport township, engaged in a horse race with a man named Hinkel, on the banks of the Little Muskingum near the mouth of Archer's fork, which proved fatal to his life. A purse of three dollars was put up and the contestants started on the race. When Rose had reached the terminus, he arose in his saddle and looked for his opponent. The horse at that moment stumbled and pitched the rider against a rock. Rose died in a few days from the wound, and his estate received the purse.

In 1859, Porter Flint and one of the Mitchell boys were drowned in the Little Muskingum at Proute's mill. A raft which they were floating became unmanageable at the mill dam, and both were precipitated into the stream.

The most abhorrent of the many cases of drowning in the township, occurred at Cow run. A daughter of one of the workmen one day went to a tank to get some oil with which to start a fire. While she was stooping over the top of the tank, her foothold gave way, and she was taken from the reservoir in a lifeless condition.

Thomas Flemming was drowned at Chamber's mill below the mouth of Cow run, while running lumber over the dam.

POPULATION.

The population of the township increased very rapidly during the decade ending 1870, at which time there were two thousand six hundred and fifty-five native, and one hundred and ninety-five foreign inhabitants. The population on the first of June 1880, was two thousand three hundred and thirty-six. Cow run in 1870, was a camp of one thousand five hundred people, at present there are less than five hundred.

CHAPTER XLIX.

PALMER TOWNSHIP.

A Progressive Township—The Pioneer of the Settlement—Census in 1796—The Pioneer Babies—The Palmers—To the Legislature—The Pioneer Marriage—The First Brick House—Sudden Death—The Old Veteran—The First Death—Fire—The First Frame House—A New Settlement on the Creek—Brown's Mill—Horse-Mill—An Exhibition—A Portable Post Office—A Historic Log House—Civil History—Record of Officers from 1851 to 1880—Early and Late Justices of the Peace—Educational—The First School—Ashcroft—Other Teachers—A New Building—A School for Teachers—The Freewill Baptist Meetings—Early Methodist Gatherings—The First Preachers—First Circus Rider—Organization—The Corner Chapel—The Different Circuits—Temperance in Palmer—A Blow at Prevailing Customs—Palmer Anti-License—A Fine Company of Riflemen—Gard Graveyard—Death at a Barn-Raising—The Murdock Cemetery—A Giant Skeleton—Roads—The Old Indian Trail—The First Road Made by White Men—Doctors—Industries—Stores—The First Blacksmith—Tanneries—Agriculture—Sheep Raising—Palmer Pastures—A Bit of Geology—Native Trees—The Old Pine Grove—A Well-Farmed Land—Census.

IT HAS been said, "Happy is the native whose annals are tiresome." To those who love the tales of war, danger, and sacrifice, of startling change, or scenes of destruction, rather than wholesome growth and quiet advance, this is indeed true. But there are some who delight in watching the tranquil and steady progress of a community, from its doubtful and unsteady first steps to a prosperous present, a course as undisturbed as the glide of a boat down a widening river. To these is addressed this record of the pleasant and balmy progress of the township of Palmer.

In the upper part of their courses the West fork and the left branch of the South fork of Wolf creek approach within less than half a mile of each other. Thence diverging far before they meet, these streams enclose a large and compactly shaped tract of land, in the upper part of which is included the most of the fourteen thousand or more acres that, since 1851, have been known as Palmer township. Wolf creek's west fork courses diagonally through the northwest corner. The smaller stream just mentioned traverses from end to end the southern half of the township. The dividing ridge between these creeks extends from the west end of the donation tract belonging to Palmer through the centre of the township, and bends sharply to the northwest--shaped much like a great J and standing a perpetual judge of the claims of the two streams to the drainage of the township. In remarkable exception to the general rule that first settlements proceed along streams, the first settlers of Palmer choose homes along this ridge. This is partly due to the fact that the region between the creeks, the scene of this sketch, is beautifully rolling, the billowy land nowhere breaking into ruggedness. Thus it was that Christopher Malster, as he was choosing a place for a future home, in the year 1796, found it convenient to penetrate the then roadless wilderness without confining himself to the pathways worn by the waters. Christopher Malster was a native of Delaware, where he was born December 27, 1755. He had married Margaret Mehaffy, who was born in 1776, in Lycoming county, Pennsylvania, and settled in her native shire.

Here their first child, William, was born December 11,

1795. The following year the father, then in the prime of life, determined to wrest a home from the wilds of the west. Going first to the mouth of Wolf creek, he finally chose lot No. 15, now in Palmer, and bought of a man named Burnham lot sixty-three. On this latter place he erected his cabin home, and the population of what is now Palmer numbered one. The next year the problem presented itself of transportation. Far to the east was his wife and babe of two years. Woman's pluck solved it. All the toilsome way from Williamsport, Pennsylvania, the mother rode horseback, carrying her child in her arms. As Virgil says: "*Tantae molis erat Romanam condere gentem*," it was that much trouble to start the settlement.

After arrival the family was increased by the birth of six more children. John kept his brother William company after September 2, 1800, and was the first born of the township. After him at intervals of two years, Thomas, Benjamin, and Moses were born. The daughters Elizabeth and Mary were born in 1810 and 1814 respectively.

In 1832, January 11, the father finished his work, and was laid to rest in the Gard cemetery. His wife survived him thirty years, and now lies by his side. William, the infant pioneer married in 1822, Sarah Baker, who was born in the county in 1800. Five of their six children are living: Roxana, John L., Moses A., Rowena, and Mary. Roxana is in Palmer. Moses A. was born in 1826, married Martha White in 1835, lives in Watertown, and is the father of four children, all living. His uncle, John, also lives in the place—the only surviving child of Christopher Malster. Rowena is Mrs. George B. Quinn; Mary E. married Walter Buchanan, of Watertown township. William Malster died February 12, 1876.

In March, 1802, the Palmers moved to the tract of land now under consideration. They settled on the land now occupied by Brown's Mill post office. The head of the family was Joseph Palmer, born in Windom, Connecticut, January 13, 1761, with his wife Hannah Fox, who was born in Windom August 2, 1763. His removal was from Rutland county, Vermont, where he had been a resident. The family came to King's settlement, at the head of the Allegheny river. Accompanied by Messrs. Howe, Prouty, Thaddeus, Pond, and Elijah Pond, they made their way down the rivers to Marietta in Keel-boats in the fall of 1801. On the way an accident occurred in the rapids, upsetting the boat containing the Palmers, spilling out their effects and giving the occupants a cool, but not dangerous bath. Jerusha Palmer, then a little girl, was rescued by Mr. Howe. The Palmers then consisting of the two parents and their children Joseph, Jabez, Jerusha, Isaac, and perhaps Ephraim, went immediately to the settlement at Wolf Creek mills. Winter was at hand and some place to spend it had to be found immediately. Mr. Palmer finally decided upon a building that had been used as a shelter for sheep. As might be expected, it was not in condition to suit the notions of a housekeeper who had any regard for cleanliness, but it was soon put in condition for occupation. Arriving at Palmer next spring, they found in the well known pine grove that then occupied the place, a man before them. He was one of that profession that in those days found employment in gathering knots from the pine trees and burning them for the tar they afforded. This man's name was Mallery—a singular character in some respects—well known in the Waterford settlement. He was a bachelor and had constructed a very neat lodge in the vast pine wilderness, and as he was through with his work there Mr. Palmer ushered in his family and began in earnest the life of a settler. The first care was to provide a more commodious and permanent shelter for a large family than that afforded by a bachelor's shanty, which was done. In the spring of the following year, 1803, the last child of the family, Elizabeth, was born. In 1805 or 1806 another log cabin was built by Mr. Palmer, into which they soon moved. By the year 1810 Mr. Palmer had constructed a third house, of hewed pine logs, two stories in height, and in this the family lived until the death of its builder, in 1831, in his seventy-first year. Then Isaac Palmer built and lived in a two-story frame building, now remodelled and occupied by A. F. Breckenridge. Joseph Palmer, sr., was quite a prominent character in the settlement that he had helped to found. He was the first justice of the peace. In 1807 he was sent to the legislature as a representative of Washington county. Towards the close of his life his brain became affected, the general opinion being that this misfortune originated from too assiduous duties performed while at Columbus. His wife survived him five years and died at the age of seventy-three years.

Joseph Palmer, jr., the eldest son, married, in 1808, Sarah Martin. This, the first marriage ceremony of the settlement, was to have been performed by a preacher at Wolf Creek mills, by the name of Lindley. Everything was made ready—

"The bridegroom's doors are opened wide
    To all the kith and kin:
The guests are met, the feast is set:
    Mayst hear the merry din—"

but the minister comes not. The impatient couple wait long, for they cannot know that Mr. Lindley has received and accepted an offer of a position at Athens, Ohio, and is busily engaged in removing thence. The position is becoming embarrassing. Brilliant thought! The old gentleman suddenly remembers he is a justice of the peace. He performs the ceremony himself, thus doing his son the last favor possible while yet a member of his family, pronouncing the closing words, we may well imagine, amid many smiles, much merriment, and good-natured comment of the assembled guests—"the twain are made one"—and the wedding fee remains in the family. The happy couple immediately entered upon their wedding tour, which was the nearest route to their new home, about a quarter of a mile distant. In 1852 Joseph and his wife both died, aged respectively sixty-six and sixty-four years. They were buried side by side in the old Gard graveyard. Of their children, the first-born, Harris, made his home in the township and married Annie Hougling, of Barlow township. They have four children: Sarah, who married George Camp, of Palmer;

Edward R., husband of Mary J. Thornbury; Ruth, now Mrs. Ezra Chapman, of Palmer; and Ephraim. Joseph and John E. are dead. Edward R. was born in 1837, and married in 1858. His wife was born in 1841. His children are Jesse A., Emma N., and Mary. James Martin, another child of Joseph, jr., was born in 1813. He married Sophia Gard in 1835. Six children blessed this union, one of whom, James D., died in the army in the late war. Jabez, the second son of Joseph, sr., married Lydia Brown and settled in Palmer. He built the first brick house in the township, in 1828. It was thirty by forty feet. In the fall of 1844, while cutting corn, he fell dead in the field. He was aged fifty-five. Ten years after, his wife died, at the age of sixty-four. Benjamin F. Palmer, the third son of the original family, married Margaret Hougland, and lives in Barlow township. Jerusha married Caleb Green, of Barlow, who accidentally killed himself. Isaac was born in 1797, and married Persis Tilton. He moved to Waterford township, and had seven boys and four girls. Ephraim, the next younger, married Mary Densmore, went on a western trip and died there about 1835. Elizabeth, the first girl baby of the township, died in 1867. She was never married. The last thirteen years of her life were spent in darkness, for the checking of a running sore in the back of her head produced blindness. Of the original family, all were noted for their great size. Jabez was the largest.

The third family in the settlement was that of Jason Rice and his wife, who was a Miss Hibbard. Their children were Reuben, Joseph, Ambrose, Mary, Deborah, Jonas, Sabinas, and Jason. They moved to the neighborhood in the spring of 1802, a very little later than the Palmers. In about two years they sold out to Cornelius Gard, and went to Federal creek. Mr. Rice was from New England, and lived a short distance north of where the town-house now stands. For several years after his removal he paid visits to the neighborhood.

In 1803 John Danley brought his family to the settlement, and in a few years, together with David Gard, bought lot No. 1,065, and settled on the eastern half. He was a Virginian from near Winchester, and a farmer, though before moving west he was engaged in teaming over the mountains. He was noted as a hunter, and was very fond of the society of his neighbors, especially of children. He had never seen his father, and superstition used to bring people from miles around with children who had sore mouths. Though he had none of the superstition himself, yet he would gratify them by breathing into the mouths of his patients, their parents trusting that they would be cured in that way. His first removal west was to Marietta, in 1797. There he stayed for two years, working for Paul Fearing. Thence he moved to Round bottom, whence he finally came to the Palmer settlement. His wife was Amy Pugh. His children were: Benjamin, who died on attaining his majority; Mary, who married John Cornes; John; Eliza, who became Mrs. William Groves; Elizabeth, wife of J. Leonard; Amy, who married Thomas Malster; Robert, who became the husband of a daughter of Edmund Perry, and has three children; Joel, and, finally, Joseph. John Danley, sr., died in 1858, in his eighty-fourth year—nine years after the death of his wife, in her seventy-first year. Robert and his wife are still living, but by themselves, where the old man of sixty-seven still works at his last. He is widely known as the "old veteran," is entrusted with the care of the old Gard cemetery, and takes great pride in his charge. His quaint communications on the subject of bygone days often appear in print, and indicate how prone he is to think of the "days that are no more."

Cornelius Gard, Mary Hancher, his wife, and their two children, David and Timothy, the former of whom married Mary Hiett two years before, were the next accession to the township. They came from West Virginia, near the Ohio river. Cornelius settled in 1804 on lot No. 1,068. All the family were shoemakers. Cornelius paid more attention to that trade than his sons, however, the latter turning farmers. The father is remembered as a large man, with a deep, heavy voice, and a pleasant though bluff manner. A negro servant accompanied the Gards, Chloe, by name, whose little daughter died the summer of their arrival, and was buried without funeral services on the Breckenridge place. This was the first death and burial in the settlement. In a year or two the Gards sold out to Henry Cornes. Timothy moved on Jonathan's creek, near Zanesville. His wife was Nancy Davis, an orphan girl raised by Isaac Williams, the pioneer who named the West Virginia town opposite Marietta. David, in 1805, moved back to West Virginia, returning in the spring of 1809. He, with John Danley, bought one hundred and sixty acres, lot No. 1,065, and for his part settled with his father on the west half.

Cornelius was born in East Jersey, October 30, 1749, (O. S.) and died November 2, 1842, in his ninety-fourth year. Mary, his wife, was born in 1757, and died in 1840.

David's wife, Mary Hiett, was a daughter of Timothy Hiett, one of the earliest settlers of West Virginia, near Marietta. The children of David were: Hiram, Maria, Rowena, Sophia, Jane and James, the latter two not now living. Hiram is the oldest, was born in 1806, and is in Barlow township; Maria married Mason Brown; Rowena, Edward Camp, Sophia; Martin Palmer.

On his second settlement in the Palmer neighborhood, David Gard built a two-story house of hewed logs, which in 1816 was destroyed by fire. In all probability this was the first conflagration in the settlement. It left the family in a rather uncomfortable plight, none having any clothes but the single suits they were wearing that day.

At one time a servant was working for David Gard, by the name of Isaac Cherry. A poplar tree was standing by the road side, much deflected from the perpendicular by a large limb, that, for some reason, it was considered advisable to remove. This could only be done by standing on a limb below, holding on with one hand and using an axe with the other. The man volunteered to undertake the task; but, as soon as the limb was freed the tree, relieved of its weight, straightened and began a series of vibrations that loosened Mr. Cherry's

foothold, and, while he hung by one hand, swung him violently against the trunk again and again. However, he held on, and when the tree ceased vibrating, came down with no worse injuries than a few bruises.

Benjamin M. Brown, who was born in New York State in 1797, emigrated to Ohio in 1806, and lived in Palmer township, this county, until his death, which occurred in 1849. In 1826 he married Maria Gard, who was born in 1806 and died in, 1880. The surviving children are as follows, viz: C. A. Brown, who married Martha J. Breckenridge and does business in Belpre village, and John A. Brown, who resides in Union county. The elder Mr. Brown was a prominent man in Palmer township, having served nine years as magistrate and four years as county sheriff.

The sixth family to enter the neighborhood was the first German family. Henry Cornes and his wife Catharine came probably from Pennsylvania and remained in the settlement until 1832. His settlement has been described before, as the purchase, near the year 1806, of the farm of Cornelius Gard and his moving thereon. He was noted for his fondness for horses. In 1809 or 1810 he built the first frame house in the settlement. Part of it is standing yet, on what is known as the Stacey farm. The Cornes children were William, Elizabeth, John, James, Rachel and Henry. William was married before his arrival. His second wife was Mary Perry, whom he married about 1820. Upwards of seven of his children are yet living. He himself died in 1831, at the age of sixty years. Elizabeth married Asa Beach, of Watertown; John, Mary Dauley; James, Mary Miller, of England; Rachel, Miller Clark, on Little Hocking; Henry, Mary Pugh, of Virginia. The second and third deaths in the settlement were those of two children of William Cornes.

For a period of seven years, more or less, no additional families came to the settlement. Finally, in 1813, Joseph Atkinson with his wife, a niece of Paul Fearing, moved in from Waterford. His children were John, Luan, Frank, Deborah, and a little girl whose name is not known. Atkinson was a disorderly character. Returning intoxicated from Wolf Creek mills one evening in 1818, he fell by the roadside and died from exposure. There he was found by one of his sons.

During all this period, the settlement was confined to the upland country. The course of the West fork of Wolf creek now included in Palmer, was, it is remarkable, not settled at all. But in 1815, Timothy Hiett, who, up to that time, was living in West Virginia, a few miles below Marietta, began the erection of a saw-mill with one run of buhrs on this stream. This was the second mill on Wolf creek. Samuel Brown, a millwright of Athens, was employed to build the mill for six hundred dollars. When finished it was bought by its builder, while Mr. Hiett, with his wife, who was Elizabeth Pewthers before marriage, bought a farm near where Robert Breckenridge now lives. In 1834 he sold to John Breckenridge and returned to the mill, which he operated until his death, in 1839, at which time he was fifty years of age. His wife survived him until 1861, dying in her seventieth year.

Samuel Brown was a brother of General Brown, of Athens, and learned his trade of Sharp & Hunt, for whom he worked in the construction of Wolf Creek mills. Hiett had a cabin put up, in which he intended to live when his mill should be finished. Brown and his family occupied it during the building of the mill, and continued to remain there upon his purchase of the mill. Mr. Brown did not make such a financial success of his business as a less sympathetic man would have done. Never a needy person, however, unable to pay, came to his mill and went away empty handed. After the sale of his mill, he lived with his son-in-law, a Frenchman, named Eugene Pierrot. Brown's first wife was Mary Poole, who died in Athens county. Her children were Sophia, Lucinda, Affa, and Alvina. By his second wife, Sarah Jenkins, his children were: Mary and Amy. Samuel Brown died in 1872, aged ninety-one years. His last wife died in 1856, aged sixty-four.

Before the construction of these mills, the neighborhood went principally to those on Wolf creek. A hand-mill in Watertown township also did them some service. In this connection it may be mentioned that Brown's was the only grist-mill ever run by water in the territory of Palmer. Between 1820 and 1825, John Hurlbut came to the settlement, bought the farm now owned by widow Stoller, erected a horse-power tread-mill, and with his brother-in-law, John Miller, did grinding for the neighborhood. This mill will be remembered by old settlers in connection with an exhibition, consisting of literary exercises by home talent, and held in the building shortly after its erection. This performance was perhaps the first of the kind in the neighborhood. The frame of the mill is now used in a barn on the same place. Hurlbut went to Waterford about 1842, and lived there until his death. Two miles above Brown's mill, about 1835, Hiram Gard put up a saw-mill.

The only post office that is now, or ever has been, in the neighborhood now called Palmer, is called Brown's Mill's post office. Its name indicates its origin. Samuel Brown was the first postmaster, beginning in that capacity about 1821, and locating the office in his dwelling-house, near the mill. At that time there was no post office between it and Harmar. The mail was carried by Colonel Ullmore, of Massachusetts, on the route between Marietta and Lancaster, which was opened at that time. The next postmaster was Hiram Gard, who held it for about a score of years, beginning with 1826 or 1827. The succeeding one was Thomas Breckenridge. The present postmaster is Andrew Breckenridge. The office was changed successively to the residences of the different postmasters.

George Quinn was born in Columbiana county, Ohio, and afterwards came to Palmer township in 1820-30. His wife, Jane Bruce, was born in Beaver county. Pennsylvania. Six children were born to them, of whom five are living: Charles lives in McClellan county, Texas; David J. is in Harrison county; George B. is in Palmer township; and Elizabeth is at home. They had a daughter, Annie, who is dead. George B. was born in Washington county in 1845, and married, in 1867, Roena Malster, who was born in 1830. Mr. Quinn has a large farm of some three hundred and seventy-seven acres, on which he is extensively engaged in the important interest of Palmer township—that of sheep-raising.

Thomas Perry, born in Pennsylvania in 1746, emigrated to Ohio in 1824, and died in what is now Palmer township. By his wife, Catharine Fisher, he had three sons and seven girls. Of these, John settled in Washington county in 1829. He married Abigail, the daughter of Samuel Patterson, who was born in 1801. Five of their eleven children survive. James, the fourth child, was born in 1823, and has been in this township since he was five years of age.

Isaac Perry was a Pennsylvanian, who came to the southern end of the settlement in 1829. He lived from 1775 to 1868. In 1819 he married Mary Armstrong, who was born in 1801. Six children were born—James B.; Isabelle, who is married and lives in Fairfield; Margaret, now Mrs. Smith, of Palmer; Mary Ann, a resident with her parents; Sarah, wife of Dock V. Smith, and an inhabitant of Washington Court House; and Armstrong H., who lives in Palmer.

James B. Perry was born in 1819 in Pennsylvania. He came to this county with his parents. In 1844 he married Esther, daughter of William Huston, and is the father of the following seven children: Euphemia, Orange C., Charles B., Chauncey, Mahala, Caroline, and Lewis. His first wife lived from 1827 to 1878. He married, in 1880, Mrs. Phœbe Smith, who was born in 1846. Her children by her first husband are Minnie, Leslie, and Clara B. Mr. Perry's name appears frequently in the table of the township officers, and he was also in the one hundred days' service during the war.

Dock V. Smith, mentioned above, was a son of Vincent Smith. He was born in 1832 in this county, and in 1855 was married. He removed from the county in 1877. Of his five children Ralph W., is living in Palmer township with his grandparents. He was born in 1856, and in 1880 married Ruth Rardin, who was born in 1862. He is a general farmer and stock-raiser. Ada, the second child of Dock Smith, is at home; Ella married Dr. Bansier, a native of England; Frank and Fred are at home. Vincent Smith had another son by the name of S. S., who was born in this county in 1825, and married, in 1862, Deborah Graham, who was born in 1830 and died in 1856. Three children resulted from this marriage—two survive—Anna N., and Eva J., who married George Chamberlain; both live in Columbiana county. In 1861 S. S. Smith married Margaret Perry, who was born in 1823. Their two children are Sidner E., and Idella M. S. S. Smith is a farmer on a ninety acre farm.

In April, 1828, Elias Murdock came to the settlement from Harmar, to which place he had moved from Wood county, Virginia, in 1826. His parents, John Murdock and Mary Dilse, had moved to the latter place from Pennsylvania in 1804. In 1825, Elias married Malinda, a daughter of James Pewthers, who had come from Scotland prior to 1790, and settled on the Vienna bottom, on the Ohio river. The Pewthers family was of the Bellville garrison during the Indian war.

Elias Murdock, born 1807 and died 1880. His wife in 1870. The children were: Elizabeth A., James M., Mary P., George W., Virginia A., Jesse G., Sarah C., and Charles J. James M. was born March 4, 1828, and married in 1849, Nancy Breckenridge, who was born in the county in 1828. Their five children are named respectively: Hugh B., George D., Henry G. (died in 1865), Robert H., and Ellie A.

William Hickman, the third son of William and Mary (Tumblinson) Hickman, natives of Virginia, was born in Columbiana county, Ohio, in 1819, and settled in Palmer township in 1838. He married Susan, the daughter of Thomas and Catharine Perry. They have three children, viz: Charlotte (Varner), of this township; Selena, at home, and Mary (Lake), in Decatur township. Mr. Hickman owns one hundred and sixty acres of land. He has held important township offices.

Owen Pattent, the son of Richard Pattent, was born in Washington county, in 1812, and married Anna, daughter of Freeman Hopkins. She was born in 1814, Seven children were born: Andrew, Freeman, Sarah, Thomas, John, Owens, and Robert. Thomas was born in 1840, in the county, and in 1866 married Mary, daughter of William Cornes. She was born in 1847. The fruit of this union is two children: Ida and Earl, both of whom are with their parents. Mr. Pattent is actively engaged in stock raising on a hundred and twenty acre farm. Mr. Pattent enlisted in 1861 in company L, First Ohio cavalry.

An example of what industry will do, is that afforded by Robert and Margaret Graham, the parents of Thomas Graham. When they arrived in America, their capital consisted of twenty-five cents, and hope. By hard work they in time attained a competence. Thomas, who was born in Pennsylvania, in 1800, was a miller and farmer, and lived with his parents until he was forty-five years of age. Then, having already married Susan Gilchrist in 1841, he began life for himself in Palmer township. Their children were: Robert, Maria, and Susan; the latter is dead. Thomas Graham's second wife was Miss Dennis, and his third a daughter of Peleg Lincoln, who was born in 1812 and still lives in Palmer.

She is the daughter of Peleg and Bettie Lincoln, and a native of Franklin county, Massachusetts. She came to Morgan county in 1817, and was married in 1849. Her only child, Amanda, still lives with her on a two hundred acre farm.

Mariah, daughter of Thomas Graham and his first wife, still lives in Palmer on a farm of two hundred and twelve acres, which she is managing herself.

The Scotch settlement, which owed its existence to the energy of Nahum Ward, and which began in Barlow about 1817—began in Palmer in 1820, with the advent of John and Hugh Breckenridge. Following his settlement, in order, were the arrivals of Hugh Greenlees in 1834, David Ferguson, and Duncan Drain. This is the extent of that settlement in Palmer.

Robert Breckenridge settled in the territory, now a part of Palmer township, in 1818. He was one of a numerous family that emigrated from Scotland and settled in the county of Washington. His father was Andrew Breckenridge, who married Nancy Brown, by whom he had the following children: Robert, Isabel, John, Hugh, Edward, William, Elizabeth and Nancy, all of whom were born in Argylshire. Robert, the first settler, married Catharine Harvey and left Scotland in June, 1818, coming from New York to Philadelphia, whence he walked nearly all the way to Pittsburgh, coming thence in a keel-boat down the Ohio and landing at Marietta. His wife still survives. They had six children. John and Hugh, who were twins, settled in Palmer township in 1820. John married Agnes Fleming, by whom he had three sons and three daughters—Andrew, John, Robert, Jane, Nancy, and Martha, who married C. A. Brown of Belpre. Mr. Breckenridge was elected county commissioner in 1849 and served three years. His first wife dying, he was again married in 1852, his second wife dying in 1871. The eldest son, Andrew, in 1848, married Elizabeth, only daughter of Joseph and Sarah Palmer. Four children were born of this union. Mr. Breckenridge has been postmaster at Brown's Mills since 1861. He has been the treasurer of Palmer township. Robert Breckinridge married Mary P. Murdock. They have had seven children, five of whom are living. The Breckenridge family is of the old Scotch Presbyterian faith.

On the Breckenridge place stands a log house that has something of a history. It is two stories in height, and built by Mr. Hutchinson when he owned the farm. Timothy Hiett bought the place, and in 1834 sold it to John Breckenridge, who already had a home on an adjoining farm. The house, accordingly, not being used by himself, he devoted it to the shelter of the Scotch families who were frequently coming in search of places in which to live, and they thus used the house temporarily until more permanently settled. Nor was this the only use made of the house. As the Breckenridge daughters would be married at different times, they would begin housekeeping in this *quasi* hotel until their husbands could construct dwellings of their own. Thus this structure has seen many families within its hospitable walls.

Nathan, the third child of Samuel and Rebecca (Shipley) Browning was born in Maryland in 1816, and when young came to Morgan county, Ohio, with his parents. He married Jane, daughter of Levin and Nancy Shipley. Six of their ten children are living, viz: Edward, George, Charles and Annis, at home; Francis, in Michigan; John in Marietta. Mr. Browning is one of Washington county's most worthy farmers and respected citizens.

One of the later accessions to the township is William R. Stacy, who was born in Muskingum township in 1850; married Eliza J. Breckenridge in 1872 and settled in Palmer township in 1873. His wife was born in 1858. They have four children, three of whom, Len. E., Clide C., and Ned E., are living. John R. is dead.

Orlando Trotter, son of Richard and Caroline Trotter, was born in 1850, and married Anna, daughter of Duncan and Catharine Drain. One child is the result of their marriage. Mr. Trotter has been a township officer, and owns a farm of one hundred and fifteen acres of land.

POLITICAL HISTORY.

The territory that is the subject of these pages, has undergone many changes in regard to township lines. One man, long a resident of the Palmer neighborhood, recollects having been, without moving, successively in Waterford, Wooster (afterwards called Watertown) Roxbury, Wesley and Palmer. Prior to the formation of Noble county in 1851, a man standing on the northeast corner of section six, now in Palmer, could have placed himself by a single step, either northeast, in Watertown, southeast in Barlow, southwest, in Wesley, or northwest, in Roxbury. From this point, the dividing lines ran toward the four points of the compass in two straight lines through the present township. But, by the formation of Noble, Morgan county lost large areas, and was partially recompensed by the addition of the larger part of Roxbury, taken from Washington county. At a special session of the commissioners, May 19, 1851, the remaining portions of Roxbury, with parts of the other townships just mentioned were consolidated into a new township, named after the family so much concerned in the settlement and growth of its territory and interests. The entry on the journal reads as follows:

A petition was received from citizens of Roxbury and parts of Wesley, Watertown and Barlow for the erection of a new township composed of territory embraced within the following boundaries, viz : Commencing at at the northwest corner of one hundred and sixty acre lot No. 1,079, range eleven, town eight; thence south to the southwest corner of said lot; thence to the northwest corner of one hundred and sixty acre lot No. 1,080; thence south to the southwest corner of section thirteen, range eleven, town eight; thence south to the southwest corner of section No. 17, range eleven, town seven; thence to the southeast corner of section No. 5, range eleven, town seven; thence east to the southeast corner of section No. 35, range ten, town three; thence north to the southwest corner of one hundred and sixty acre lot No. 780; thence east to the southeast corner of one hundred and sixty acre lot No. 780; thence north to the northeast corner of section No. 30, range ten, town three; thence north to the northeast corner of fractional lot No. 838, range ten, town four; thence north to the southeast corner of one hundred acre lot No. 47, range ten, town four, south branch allotment; thence to the northeast corner of one hundred acre lot No. 47 aforesaid; thence west to the northwest corner of one hundred acre lot No. 14, range ten, town four, west branch allotment; thence south to the southwest corner of one hundred acre lot No. 15, range ten, town four, west branch allotment; thence westwardly to follow the line which divides the late township of Roxbury, setting off the said township to Morgan county, to the place of beginning.

An order was issued for the first election of township officers, and bore the date, May 18, 1851. The place appointed for the election was the "school-house in district No. 1, formerly of Roxbury township." Here, May 30, 1851, the election was held. The officers elected were: Hiram Gard, John Danley, jr., and George Quin, trustees; Hiram M. Brown, clerk; Joseph Leonard, treasurer; O. M. Cook, assessor; John Palmer, Thomas Breckenridge, constables; John Breckenridge, jr., B. S. Malster, James H. Gard, Albert Thomas, Hugh Greenlees, and William Leget, supervisors. Supervisors appointed the same day—Albert Ward, Andrew Brown, Nathan Witham, William Ormiston, William Creighton, Thomas Drain, Richard Trotter, George Hildebrand, David Hildebrand, and Isaac Aigin. The judges of this election were George Quin, John Danley, jr., and J. L. Palmer. Hiram Gard and Joseph Leonard were the clerks of the election.

Since that time the township trustees elected at each spring election are: 1852, William Malster, John Danley, jr., Horace Dunsmore; 1853, Richard Trotter, William Malster, Isaac Perry; 1854, O. M. Cook, David Ferguson, Joseph W. Danley; 1855, William Hickman, jr., Joseph W. Danley, Gabriel Payne; 1856 and 1857, William Hickman, jr., J. M. Mordough, R. I. Danley; 1858, R. I. Danley, J. B. Perry, Thomas Drain; 1859 and 1860, William Malster, William Hickman, Thomas Drain; 1861, J. M. Murdock, William Hickman, J. H. Gard; 1862–67, J. M. Murdock, James M. Palmer, William Hickman; 1868, J. M. Murdock, David Ferguson, John M. Danley; 1869, J. M. Murdock, David Ferguson, Henry L. Pugh; 1870-2, R. Breckenridge, David Ferguson, I. W. Danley; 1873 and 1874, R. Breckenridge, David Ferguson, O. M. Cook; 1875, R. Breckenridge, David Ferguson, G. B. Quinn; 1876–8, R. Breckenridge, A. G. Pugh, D. W. Shinn; 1879–80, R. Breckenridge, S. J. Henry, D. W. Shinn.

The clerks of the township for the same time are: 1852-3, H. M. Brown; 1854-5, James H. Gard, 1856-7, John Palmer; 1858-60, Joseph Leonard; 1861-2, Thomas Breckenridge; 1863-5, H. M. Brown; 1866-8, D. P. Leonard; 1869-72, J. J. Montgomery; 1873, C. J. Gibson; 1874-7, J. P. Daugherty; 1878, H. M. Palmer; 1879-80, T. E. Ferguson.

Treasurers: 1852, Joseph Leonard; 1853, James M. Mordough; 1854, Joseph Leonard; 1855, John W. Danley; 1856-7, Joseph W. Danley; 1858, D. L. Brown; 1860-66, John Breckenridge; 1867, C. A. Brown; 1868, James Breckenridge; 1869-71, John L. Pugh; 1872-78, J. G. Murdock; 1879-80, L. Daugherty.

Assessors: 1852-3, Hiram Gard; 1854-7, Isaac Perry; 1858, Richard Trotter; 1859, John Breckenridge; 1860, Isaac Perry; 1861-2, Richard Trotter; 1863, Robert Breckenridge; 1864, Richard Trotter; 1865-6, Robert Breckenridge; 1867, Richard Trotter; 1868-9, Robert Breckenridge; 1870, Richard Trotter; 1871, S. S. Smith; 1872-3, William Campbell; 1874-5, Robert Breckenridge; 1876, Richard Trotter; 1877, J. M. Murdock; 1878, Ell. Miller; 1879, Richard Trotter; 1880, Samuel Caskey.

The early justices in the neighborhood are not all known. Joseph Palmer has already been mentioned as the first one in the settlement. Others were: Silas Cook, the father of O. M. Cook, about 1815-20; Hiram Gard, in the neighborhood of 1834; Evan Jenkins, about 1840-7; and Squires Trotter and Pewthers. In the June term, 1851, the court of common pleas ordered the first election of Palmer township justices to be held the third Saturday of the following July. July 19th the election was held, resulting in the choice of Hiram Gard and Edwin West. In 1854 Richard Trotter and Thomas Breckenridge were elected; 1857, Richard Trotter, A. F. Breckenridge; June 13, 1857, Joseph W. Danley was elected; April, 1860, Richard Trotter; June, 1863, Joseph W. Danley; 1865, Edward Camp; 1867, Henry L. Pugh.

May 31, 1851, an election was held on the Marietta & Cincinnati railroad question. Those who favored a county subscription of two hundred thousand dollars for the railroad, numbered seventy-six; those against, thirty-three.

Palmer township has always been Republican. A few elections indicative of its political drift are: 1851, Samuel F. Vinton, Republican, sixty-three; Reuben Wood, Democrat, thirty-eight. In 1852 General Scott received twenty-one majority. October 10, 1854, Joseph R. Swan, for supreme judge, sixty; Shep. Norris, twenty-five. In 1855 the Republican majority was forty. In 1862 the Republican majority was twenty-six; in 1866, fifty-six. In October, 1880, for secretary of State, there were eighty-eight Republican, fifty-one Democratic, and one Greenback votes cast. For the last fifteen years the average vote has been one hundred and fourteen, and the average Republican majority, forty-three.

Palmer township began with thirteen road districts; in 1878 it had fifteen. In 1880, in accordance with the Moore law, which affects only Washington county, the township was divided into two road districts, "all north of and including lots Nos. 1085, 1075, 1070, 805, and 1804," being one district, and the remainder of the township the other.

The first election after Palmer township was established has already been referred to as in a school-house. From then up to 1856 elections were usually held in an old dwelling-house near A. F. Breckenridge's residence. In 1856, when the present school-house was built, the former one was appropriated as a town-house, in which all elections have since been held.

SCHOOLS.

These began almost with the settlement. It will be remembered that Joseph Palmer built three houses. In the winter, probably, of 1805-6, Russell Darrow, a young man from New England, who married a daughter of Frederick Evelyn, engaged by Mr. Palmer, taught school a month. This was the first school in the settlement, and was held in the second house built by Mr. Palmer, a log cabin into which Palmer had not yet moved. The pupils were the seven Palmer children and Benjamin Danley—then a lad of some seven or eight summers. The wages the young teacher received were twelve dollars for his month's work.

Probably the next school was that taught by James Ashcroft in 1809 or 1810. By this time the Palmers had moved out of the house that Darrows had used, leaving it free to be occupied by Mr. Ashcroft for his work, and hence his school was held in the same building in which was Mr. Darrow's. The pupils were the Palmer children, except Joseph, the Malsters, named William, John, Thomas, and Benjamin; seven or eight of the Cornes children, three Danley children, and last, perhaps least at that time, Hiram Gard. Ashcroft was an Englishman whose folks lived at the mouth of Wolf creek. He was a peevish, spiteful man, and on account of a difficulty with David Gard, carried on a series of petty persecutions against little Hiram, keeping him most of the time on the dunce block, which, it is said, was a large bible. Almost every day he would deputize some larger pupil to "take Hiram Gard by the ear and lead

him to the dunce block;" but at one time the laugh was turned on him by the wit of one of his scholars. This one, being appointed as Hiram's guide, led him up to the teacher's seat, which at that time was unoccupied.

In one respect Ashcroft was an extreme hypochondriac. He was mortally afraid of getting damp. Many a housewife would often recall to memory the half opened door, the head thrush in, and the inquiry from the owner thereof: "Have you been scrubbing your floor? If you have, I can't come in." How near this dread approached insanity may be seen by the fact that at one time, at an apple-paring, he declared that the "damp from the apple-peelings affected his system." It may easily be imagined what amusement, and even scorn, this would excite among a community schooled to all manner of hardship, with whom strength and manliness was virtue, and weakness and effeminacy crime; whose women were men in fortitude, and whose men were hardy beyond their race—a people that admired virility in men, and would hardly tolerate womanly weakness in women.

Ashcroft, however, was a good scholar, and received maximum wages—twelve dollars per month.

After Ashcroft, three more teachers taught in the same building. Their probable order was Jabez Palmer, John T. Dumont, and William Brown. The little flock which all these led through educational pastures was composed of substantially the same lambs as heretofore mentioned.

By 1814 a building, for educational and religious uses, was constructed of hewed pine logs and on the small plat of ground where now stands the schools and town-house. The first teacher in this building was Solomon N. Cook, who taught two winters. Other teachers were Peter B. Lake, William Cowee, Rufus Humphrey, B. M. Brown, and Hiram Gard, who, let us hope, remembered Ashcroft and was merciful. Two lady teachers—Eliza Danley and Elizabeth Palmer—taught a summer school in this same building.

Not far from the year 1825 the log building was superceded by a frame school-house, which was so used until 1856, when it was appropriated for a town-house, and may yet be seen. In the spring of this year, however, a select school was begun and held in it. It was conducted by Z. G. Bundy, and principally designed for the instruction of teachers whose winters were occupied at their profession. In the summers of 1857, 1858 and 1859 it was continued under the instruction of Jefferson Yarnell, in the school-house yet standing, which was built in 1856. The higher branches were taught both in language and mathematics, so that it was possible for a student in the school to prepare himself for college. Its patronage was from quite a large territory, members being from Noble and Morgan counties. The number of pupils ranged from fifty to seventy-five. Among them was E. R. Alderman, the present editor of the Marietta Register, who attended in 1857, 1858 and 1859, in the latter year hearing some classes. After 1859 the enterprise was discontinued.

CHURCHES.

In the early days of the settlement, a man named Straight held Freewill Baptist meetings. Meetings of this denomination were frequently held through the different settlements at that time, and rarely resulted in an organization of a church. That was the case here. Straight became involved in social difficulties and left the neighborhood. No more meetings of this class were held after.

The first Methodist meetings were held in the neighborhood of 1807, under the management of Philip or John Green, a local preacher. Succeeding him was one named Mitchell. The place of these meetings was the house of Henry Cornes. These exercises were discontinued, after a short time, until 1813, when the circuit rider, Isaac Quinn, at that time of the Marietta circuit, revived the cause of Methodism and held meetings in the former dwelling house of Joseph Palmer, sr., the house referred to as taught in by Ashcroft. Meetings were held in this for only a year or less, when they were transferred to the hewed pine log house that had just been made as a school and meeting-house. At this time, or very soon after, the church was organized. The first class-leader was Joseph Palmer, jr. The members, as far as can be recalled by old residents, were no more than Joseph Palmer and wife, and William Cornes and his mother. Not long after Christopher Malster joined the little band. Some time before the organization of the church, many from the neighborhood attended in what was known as Corner chapel, in the Miller neighborhood. An early preacher there was named Stone. In 1827, after the building that now stands as a town-house was put up, meetings were held in that until the fall of 1837, when the present church building was constructed. The land for this latter building was given by Isaac Palmer. The present minister of the church is D. M. Smith, of the Plymouth circuit. In 1799, this settlement was included in the Little Kanawha circuit. In 1805 it became part of the Little Muskingum circuit. In 1807, it was Muskingum and Little Kanawha. After 1808, it was the Marietta circuit. This order of things continued until 1836, when it was transferred to the Belpre circuit. In 1843, it became part of the Barlow circuit. In 1856, it was part of Plymouth circuit, where it has remained ever since.

TEMPERANCE.

Palmer township, situated at a distance from large towns with their excitements and other influences which make cities always allurements to intemperance, settled by men of steady habits, devoted to the tranquil pursuits of agriculture and sheep-raising—this township, it may be readily inferred, is the home of a strong, decided, and active temperance sentiment. As early as December 24, 1840, this sentiment had crystallized into a temperance society, and the aggressive character of this sentiment was well expressed by the title, "the Roxbury Society for the Promotion of Temperance." John Hurlbert was the president, Jesse Leasure was vice-president, and Edward Camp was secretary at the organization of this society. Four times a year they met, keeping time with the seasons, thus literally fulfilling the injunction to be "instant in season and out of season." Business meetings were held on the first Saturday of April.

The first meeting saw the subscription of twenty-eight names—which roll was, by the year 1851, increased to nearly a hundred and fifty—to the following pledge which was a part of their constitution:

We the undersigned do agree that we will abstain from intoxicating liquors as a beverage except in cases of sickness or bodily hurt; that we will not traffic in them; that we will not provide them as an article of entertainment for persons in our employment, and in all suitable ways we will discontinue their use throughout the community.

It will be noticed that one clause of this agreement is aimed at the then prevailing practice of rewarding neighborly aid at log-rollings, barn-raisings, and similar gatherings, also furnishing harvest hands with whiskey.

This society was succeeded by the Sons of Temperance in 1851—which body existed in Palmer until 1854. This was the period, it will be remembered, of the contest concerning the Maine Liquor law. June 17, 1851, soon after its establishment, Palmer township voted as follows on the license question: For license, thirty; against the same, fifty-two; majority against license, twenty-two.

April 9, 1852, a branch society of the Washington County Temperance Union was organized in Palmer with J. M. Palmer as president, John Breckenridge, jr., as vice-president and J. M. Murdock as secretary. This was also organized principally with the object of aiding the temperance interests in the approaching political contest.

Early meetings of the first society, as well as those of the Sons of Temperance, were held in the old Palmer house—the one mentioned as built of hewed pine logs and lived in by Joseph Palmer, jr., all the latter part of his life. When the death of the old man ended its use as a dwelling house, this building was put to many public uses. It was a general resort for the neighborhood. Isaac Palmer fitted it up, at one time as a dancing hall, and its old walls, many a time, rang to the strains evoked from his violin by the indispensable well known, country fiddler. Fourth of July and other celebrations were held in this building. It was also used many years, as a store, but more of this hereafter.

Among all these organizations in Palmer, must not be forgotten that of the Independent Rifle company. This owed its existence to a similar organization in Barlow township, about the year 1822, to which some of the residents of what is now Palmer belonged. These afterwards organized a separate company in their own neighborhood, thus bringing it in the range of this sketch. There were from a hundred to a hundred and thirty members in it. The early captains were Michael Gard, Ephraim Palmer, and Henry Abbott. Both officers and men were very finely uniformed, and their parades were very much admired by the neighborhood.

CEMETERIES.

March 15, 1817, Jane, a six months old daughter of David Gard, was accidentally and fatally scalded. This was the fourth death in the settlement. She was buried on a high plat of ground a short distance north of the residence of R. I. Danley. This was the origin of the Gard cemetery. It is in a beautiful situation, and is well kept by R. I. Danley, in whose charge it now remains.

It is rare that one sees a graveyard so filled with the patriarchs and pioneers of a community. It contains, on a close estimate, two hundred and seventy-five graves. Of the old residents of the land enclosed in Palmer township, there lie here Joseph Pierrot, a native of France, died in 1856, aged sixty-five; Henrietta, his wife, of Berne, Switzerland, died in 1875, aged seventy-four; F. L. Liengme, also of Berne, died in 1848, aged forty-four; Thomas G. Graham; Sybil Piper, died in 1853, aged seventy; Esther Michener, of Pennsylvania, died in 1867, born in 1778; Benjamin G. Brockway, died in 1856, aged seventy-four; Ruth, his wife; Dr. John Hemphill; Nathan Gard, died in 1821, aged fifty-two, the third buried in the yard; Eleanora Gard, died in 1824, aged fifty; Benjamin Pugh, died in 1870, aged eighty-four; Mary, his wife; James Henderson, died in 1835, aged forty-three; William Groves, died in 1841, aged forty-two; Eliza, his wife; Benjamin Danley, died in 1820, aged twenty-two, the second buried in the cemetery; Henry Cornes, died in 1826, aged seventy-two; Elias Pewthers, died in 1840, aged thirty-seven; Benjamin M. Brown, born in Washington county, New York, in 1797, was sheriff of the county from 1834 to 1838, died in 1849; Phœbe Groves, died in 1856, aged seventy-six; John Hurlbut, died in 1855, aged seventy-six; John Multon, died in 1850, aged sixty-five; Lucy, his wife, died in 1848, aged seventy-two. Here, also, lie many whose deaths and ages have already been given—of the Palmers, the Malsters, the Gards, the Cornes, the Danleys, the Breckenridges, and many others. Many well-known names of Barlow, Watertown, and Windsor townships also appear on the marble stones.

In the year 1838, shortly after the arrival of John and Hugh Breckenridge in the settlement, they were at a barn raising. While they were at work, one of the rafters fell, killing Hugh and injuring John. In accordance with a wish expressed by Hugh a short time before, he was buried on that part of his land now embraced by the cemetery, near the house of J. M. Murdock. This was the beginning of that graveyard. The next burial in it was that of the wife of John Breckenridge. In this yard are buried persons of the names of Breckenridge, Murdock, Palmer, Mitchell, Ferguson, Greenlees, Bryan, Reed, and others. It now contains about forty graves. Both these graveyards are in the care of the township, the Murdock cemetery having been entrusted to it some four years ago.

These are not the only burying-grounds in the township. There existed another, containing one grave, but the date of its origin, and facts about the life of its occupant, are destined, probably, forever to remain mysteries. The grave was situated west of Brown's mills, on a ridge, and was what is ordinarily known as an Indian mound. It was on the farm of G. W. Murdock. In 1838, Ludley Gard, D. W. Shinn, and others, opened it, and discovered in it a vault eight feet long, four feet deep, and walled with stone. This contained a skeleton seven feet long, a tomahawk, arrow-heads, and stones ground into divers shapes. This mound was situated near what might be styled the first road in the township.

This was no more or less than an old Indian trail, which crossed the stream below Brown's mills, and ran in the direction of the Hocking river from the Ohio. Its situation indicates that it was a line of communication from the western villages of the Indians to the frontier. In addition to the mound above mentioned, many Indian relics were found along its course.

The first white man's road in Palmer, however, was built from Waterford to within three miles of Plymouth; that is, to the State road between Marietta and Athens. The course of this road through Palmer was along the high ground to the east of the West fork of Wolf creek, and lay directly through the site of the earliest settlement. In those days of few roads, and no steamboats or railroads, articles imported into the settlement were, of course, very high priced. Salt at that time was carried over the mountains on horseback. Residents of the neighborhood were obliged to go to Marietta for this article, and pay five dollars per bushel for it.

PHYSICIANS.

The first physician in Palmer was Dr. John Hemphill, a native of New Hampshire, who was a young man of thirty-five when he arrived. His arrival was, in all probability, in 1836. He married Mary Ann Gage, of Waterford, and settled near Brown's mill. He had two children, Orson and Joseph. He was a quiet, unassuming man and a good practitioner. He practiced until within a few years of his death, which occurred in 1869, of softening of the brain. He was sixty-seven years old at the time of his death.

In 1850 Dr. West came to the settlement. He was of the eclectic school of physicians, and was very successful, especially in fevers. He did not remain but about four years. While in the settlement he lived at different places, but most of the time his residence was near the neighborhood store.

The third and last doctor in Palmer was H. Bryan, who came in 1856. He was a botanical doctor, and practiced about a dozen years.

INDUSTRIES.

The first store in the territory included in Palmer was kept by Hiram Gard, between 1825 and 1830. It was situated on the West fork.

Upon the death of Joseph Palmer, sr., in 1831, his two-story hewed pine log dwelling house, so often mentioned in this article, was used as a store. Colonel Stone, of Harmar, filled it with goods. Beginning with 1834 and continuing for four years, John Malster kept it. The building itself after being used for the various purposes referred to, was torn down. The upper story was fitted up as a dwelling house, and so used by David Richards, and after him many other store-keepers. This part of the historic building is still standing and in good preservation, but would hardly be recognized now as the last of the three houses of old Joseph Palmer.

The first blacksmith in the neighborhood, as near as can be recollected, was William Chute, who began pounding iron there about 1825. He located his shop just east of Brown's mill. At first he had no anvil, and was

85

obliged to use instead an old cast-off saw-mill crank. When business got better he doubtless indulged in an anvil of a more approved pattern.

The first tannery was put up near Brown's mill on the Hemphill farm, by James Jenkins. This was probably a few years after the mill was built. The enterprise lasted but a few years. About 1833 Edward Camp bought a few acres of the Gards and started the second tannery. In 1847 Robert I. Danley bought this of its founder and managed it two or three years, when the enterprise was discontinued. This tannery was situated in the depression between Mr. Robert Danley's present dwelling house and the residence of Mr. Brown.

In the summer of 1879, Ezra Michner, at Brown's mills, began what promised to be an important work to the neighborhood—the manufacture, by grinding, of limestone flour—thus furnishing a good fertilizer for farms. But the main industries, and what must always be the main industries of Palmer, are the cultivation of farms and the raising of sheep. The land, as before remarked, is rolling, nowhere so steep as to make cultivation impossible or even difficult. The soil, though in many places of a whitish color, still yields fairly on the whole, and good cultivation is supplementing other deficiencies.

Within a comparatively few years the attention of Palmer township people has largely been turned to the raising of sheep, many of the farmers dealing in the finest varieties. So far has this interest progressed, that as the traveller traverses the country and notices the grassy surfaces, apparently swelling and falling in great waves of land on every side, he is struck with the idea that Palmer is certainly the township of meadows.

Limestone is situated in most places through this county too low to be of much value as a fertilizer. Sandstone is a remarkable factor in the rocks that underlie these farms, and where this sandstone rests on a more solvent shale, exposed to the action of water, the very beautiful waterfalls are formed that appear to one passing along the often romantic valleys of the streams.

Coal is not present in paying quantities. The only seam that appears, according to Professor E. B. Andrews, is the Hobson seam. This is not of remarkable thickness, but it gives the coal miner of Palmer a Hobson's choice—that or nothing. Mr. Andrews avers that about a hundred and twenty feet above the coal appears iron ore of two or three feet in thickness. This is said to cover a considerable area in the neighborhood. It yields a very small per cent.—only nine and seventy-two hundredths of iron.

The native trees of the county are, among others, the white oak, and hickory on the flat lands. The pine grove referred to as settled in by Mr. Palmer, and furnishing tar under the skill of a Mallery, was a remarkable growth confined to that immediate neighborhood, and well remembered by those who lived within sight of it, or spent their noons, while attending the select school, beneath its shade. Within the present year, under the destroying influence of the portable saw-mill, it has entirely disappeared from the landscape.

The numerous white oak trees have christened this, in common with settlements in adjoining townships, the White Oak settlement, which has always been famous for its thrift and intelligence. The results of this, as well as of the steady progress which the preceding pages attempt to convey, are well attested by the eye that views the neat and often beautiful houses, the well kept fences and farm improvements, and the general air of order that everywhere exists in this pleasant section.

In 1860 the population of Palmer township was six hundred and eighteen; in 1870, six hundred and seventy-one; in 1880, five hundred and ninety-three. The decrease in the last decade is partly due to the fact that increase in individual wealth resulted in larger farms and consequently fewer farmers.

CHAPTER L.

AURELIUS TOWNSHIP.

Position and Dimensions — Establishment — Name — Organization— Table of Township Officers — Changes in Boundary—Population and Vote—Physical Features—Origin of the Name Indian Run—Soil— Coal—Salt—Oil—The Dutton Well—Present State of the Oil Industry—Settlement—How Ben Beat the Boat—Early Days—Trouble with a Panther—First Marriage, Birth and Death—Dr. Regnier's Brick House—First Orchard, Road, Post Office, Sunday-school and Store—Mills—Churches—Schools—Aurelius Lodge of Masons— Cemeteries—Macksburgh—Elba—Physicians.

THIS township is the extreme northern one of the county. It is technically known as township five, range eight, and at present contains only sections seven, sixteen, seventeen, eighteen, nineteen, twenty, twenty-one, twenty-two, twenty-seven, twenty eight, twenty-nine, thirty and the fractional sections between the southern boundary of these last four sections, and what is called the "Ludlow line," viz., sections thirty-one, thirty-two, thirty-three and thirty-four. On the north, west, and all of the east side, except the eastern boundary of sections twenty-seven and thirty-four, is Noble county. These sections are bounded on the east by Salem township, which also bounds Aurelius on the south. Originally the present territory of Aurelius was a part of Monroe county. Shortly before 1819 Dr. John Regnier, then a commissioner of Washington county, succeeded in getting this territory taken from Monroe county and added to Washington county. In 1818 John S. Corp and Judah M. Chamberlain headed a petition to the commissioners of Washington, praying the establishment of this addition as a township.

ESTABLISHMENT.

On the commissioners' journal, dated December 15, 1818, appears this record:

On petition of John S. Corp, Judah M. Chamberlain, and others, praying for the establishment of a new town in the county of Washington, therefore

Resolved, by the board of commissioners, That that township, numbered five in the eighth range, excepting sections No. 25, 26 and 27, and fractional sections No. 34, 35 and 36 be and the same is hereby declared and established into an incorporated town, to be hereafter known and distinguished by the name and denomination of *Aurelius*, and the inhabitants residing in said district are hereby declared entitled to all the privileges and immunities of incorporated towns in the State. The electors in said town will meet at the house of Mr. Judah M. Chamberlain on the second Monday of January, 1819, at 10 o'clock, A. M., to elect their township officers agreeably to law.

The godfather of this singularly named township was Dr. Regnier. Having been so prominent in all matters pertaining to the public welfare of this district, and being universally beloved and respected by the citizens, by common consent Dr. Regnier was to name the township. He accordingly christened it with the same name he gave one of his sons. Whether he derived the name from the old Roman, Marcus Aurelius, or from a friend or relation, is not now known.

ORGANIZATION.

At the date mentioned in the above extract, the citizens of the infant township met at Mr. Chamberlain's house. The result of the election is not known. The old citizens cannot remember the event, and the township records prior to 1847 have been lost.

It is known, however, that Gileas Doane and Judah M. Chamberlain were elected justices of the peace.

The officers of the township from 1847 to 1880 are given in the following list, the regular township elections being held in April of each year:

TRUSTEES.

John Smithson, John Hutchins, John Corp, 1848; John Low, 1849; John Smithson, James Weeks, Joseph Wallace, 1850; John Smithson, A. G. Grubb, Ely Vaughn, 1851; John Smithson, A. G. Grubb, Ely Vaughn, May 30, 1851; James W. Smith, I. T. Lund, William Rayley, 1852; James W. Smith, John Hutchins, Joseph Gatwood, 1853; Hanson Dutton, I. T. Lund, J. Ward, 1854; I. T. Lund, Hanson Dutton, Calvin Burt, 1855; G. W. St. John, Hanson Dutton, Calvin Burt, 1856; G. W. St. John, I. T. Lund, George Wickens, 1857; J. Hutchins, J. Zollers, George Wickens, 1858; Hanson Dutton, J. Zollers, George Wickens, 1859; A. T. Warren, John Ward, I. Atkinson, 1860; George Wickens, I. I. Dutton, T. J. Berkely, 1861; George Wickens, I. I. Dutton, R. Dilly, 1862; Joseph Dixon, I. T. Lund, R. Dilly, 1863; Joseph Dixon, Abram Dilly, R. Dilly, 1864; Joseph Dixon, T. J. Delong, R. Dilly, 1865; J. V. Davis, Owen Barnes, R. Dilly, 1866; Hanson Dutton, J. Hutchins, Joseph Dixon, 1867; Theo. Gevrez, I. T. Lund, (died) Simeon Blake, J. W. Smith, 1868; Theo. Gevrez, Joseph Dixon, James Briggs, 1869; Theo. Gevrez, Joseph Dixon, James W. Smith, 1870; Theo. Gevrez, William R. Dutton, James W. Smith, 1871; Theo. Gevrez, William R. Dutton, James W. Smith, 1872; Theo. Gevrez, Joseph Dixon, H. G. Jackson, 1873; A. Dutton, Joseph Dixon, H. G. Jackson, 1874; A. Dutton, Joseph Dixon, John Smith, 1875; Henry Mickens, Daniel J. Ward, J. S. Snyder, 1876; Charles Schimmel, J. Dixon, H. M. Cox, 1877; John Smith, J. F. Briggs, H. M. Cox, 1878; John Smith, J. F. Briggs, Charles Schimmel, 1879; John Smith, J. F. Briggs, J. F. Ayres, 1880.

CLERKS.

Theodore Gevrez, April, 1847; Theodore Gevrez, 1848; John Smithson, jr., 1850; John Smithson, jr., 1851; John Smithson, jr., May 30, 1851; I. H. Delong, 1852; A. G. Grubb, 1853; Thomas Ellison, 1854; Thomas Ellison, 1855; Thomas Ellison 1856; T. J. Berkely, 1857; J. Smithson, jr., 1858; J. Smithson, jr., 1859; R. W. St. John. 1860; R. W. St. John, 1861; Thomas Ellison, 1862; E. L. St. John, 1863; Thomas Ellison, 1864; Thomas Ellison, 1865; Theodore Gevrez, jr., 1866; R. C. Smithson, 1867; R. W. St. John, 1868; B. F. Atkinson, 1869; B. F. Atkinson, 1870; R. W. St. John, 1871; R. W. St. John, 1872; R. W. St. John, 1873; R. C. Smithson, 1874; R. W. St. John, 1875; W. E. Rayley, 1876; R. W. St. John, 1877; J. O. Dutton, 1878; J. O. Dutton 1879; J. O. Dutton, 1880.

TREASURERS.

Thomas Scott, 1848; W. L. Rayley, 1849; I. T. Lund, 1850; Thomas Delong, 1851; Thomas Delong, May 30, 1851; T. J. Delong, 1852; John Smithson, 1853; James W. Smith, 1854; James W. Smith, 1855; James W. Smith, 1856; R. W. St. John, 1857; S. J. Berkely, 1858; James W. Smith, 1859; S. L. Berkely, 1860; S. L. Berkely, 1861; S. L. Berkely, 1862; S. L. Berkely, 1863; J. W. Smith, 1864; S. L. Berkely, 1865; William H. Markey, 1866; S. W. Clark, 1867; W. H. Markey, 1868; R. C. Smithson, 1869; J. H. Delong, 1870; J. H. Delong, 1871; J. H. Delong, 1872; J. H. Delong, 1873; J. H. Delong, 1874; J. A. Morrison, 1875; J. H. Delong, 1876; R. C. Smithson, 1877; R. C. Smithson, 1878; W. T. Morris, 1879; W. T. Morris, 1880.

ASSESSORS.

James Lancaster, 1849; Theodore Gevrez, 1850; Theodore Gevrez, 1851; Theodore Gevrez, May 30, 1851; J. Smithson, jr., 1852; Daniel Bates, 1854; Simeon Blake, 1855; Simeon Blake, 1856; Matthew Brown, 1857; Simeon Blake, 1858; W. L. Rayley, 1859; W. L. Rayley, 1860; Thomas Ellison, 1861; Alexander Simmons, 1862; John Hilton, 1863; Webster Gray, 1864; A. T. Warren, 1865; Theodore Gevrez, sr., 1866; James L. Dilly, 1867; James L. Dilly, 1868; R. W. St. John, 1869; James F. Briggs, 1870; I. T. Briggs, 1871; J. F. Briggs, 1872; J. F. Briggs, 1873; J. F. Briggs, 1874; J. F. Briggs, 1875; J. F. Briggs, 1876; J. F. Briggs, 1877; W. H. Wolfe, 1878; W. H. Wolfe, 1879; W. H. Wolfe and C. W. Atkinson, 1880.

It will be noticed that the establishing act did not give Aurelius sections twenty-seven and thirty-four. The date of this accession, as ascertained from the commissioners' journal was that of their June session, 1842. For they

Resolved, that section twenty-seven and fractional section thirty-four, in township five, range eight, heretofore belonging to township Salem, is hereby annexed to Aurelius.

Aurelius was reduced to its present small dimensions by the act of the legislature forming Noble county. It was passed March 11, 1851. That part of the boundary line of Noble county which affects Aurelius is described as follows:

Thence south to the southeast corner of section eighteen, township four, range seven, thence west to the east line of township five, range eight, thence north to the northeast corner of section twenty-five, in township five, thence west to the southwest corner of section twenty-three, thence north to the northwest corner of section twenty-three, thence west to the southwest corner of number fifteen, thence north to the southwest corner of section ten, thence west to the southwest corner of section eight, thence north to the northwest corner of section eight, thence west to the west line of township five, thence south to the southeast corner of Morgan county.

The citizens in the despoiled township immediately petitioned that Aurelius be recognized as still a township, and accordingly, the commissioners, on May 19, 1851, constituted the fractional township left them an entire township, under the same old name, Aurelius, and ordered a special election of officers to be held May 30, 1851. Then as per township record,

Agreeable to a notice from the commissioners of Washington county, authorizing the electors in the fractional part of the township of Aurelius, now set off into a separate township, to hold an election for township officers on Friday, the thirtieth day of May, 1851, met and elected *viva voce*, John Perkins, Russell St. John, and Eli Vaughn, judges of said election, and John Smithson, jr., and William L. Rayley, clerks. They, after having taken the oath of office, proceeded to the election of township officers.

This resulted, as a reference to the table will show, in a reelection of the whole administration, and so John Smithson, A. G. Grubb, Eli Vaughn, John Smithson, jr., I. T. Lund, and Theodore Gevrez, may be considered the first officers of the present Aurelius township. No further change has been made in the political structure of Aurelius, save that in the winter of 1876-7, two voting precincts were formed; one at Macksburgh and one at Elba.

In the census of 1840, Aurelius had eight hundred and eighty-six inhabitants; in 1860, eight hundred and thirty-two; in 1870, seven hundred and ninety-nine; in 1880, one thousand and four.

The vote in 1880 was as follows: Elba precinct—Long (Democrat), forty-six; Townsend (Republican), seventy-six; Lloyd (Greenback), six; total one hundred and twenty-eight. Macksburgh precinct—Long, fourteen; Townsend, forty-eight; Lloyd, ten; total, seventy-two. Total vote of Aurelius, two hundred.

PHYSICAL FEATURES.

While it has always been considered an impossibility to have two hills without a valley between them, yet this township comes very near solving the problem. The hills here are rather high knobs with rounded tops, and separated by narrow ravines with almost precipitous sides. The west fork of Duck creek, the principal stream of the township affords comparatively little bottom land, the valley being, perhaps, not more than a half a mile broad in the widest part, which is about half way between Macksburgh and Elba. The east fork of Duck creek is entirely outside the township.

The drainage is altogether by means of Duck creek and the small tributary streams. The principal ridge or water-shed is in the western part, entering at the extreme southwest on the farm of J. Dixon, esq., and with devious course passing north through the farms of Messrs. Ward, Davidson and Wickens. Here it widens, and finally divides, one branch of the ridge ending at Indian

run in the middle of the north part of section nineteen, the other turning west, and leaving the township in the southern part of the west boundary of the same section.

A second ridge east of Duck creek skirts the eastern boundary of the township, finally crossing the line in section twenty-two.

The course of these ridges may be graphically and approximately ascertained by reference to the so called "ridge roads" as they appear in the atlas. The other roads in the county are the valley roads. These two kinds are all they have, for the rough nature of the country permits the people of Aurelius to build them not always where they are needed, but only where they can be built.

The drainage of the township is, as implied by this description of the water-sheds, simple and complete. Duck creek is the main stream. It is supposed to derive its name from the numberless flocks of wild ducks that the pioneers of its valley noticed. It enters the township in the extreme northwest corner, flows southeast to Elba, there turns and flows southward, leaving Aurelius in the eastern part of section thirty-three. Though quite a small stream, it often gets high enough to be navigable by small boats as Elder Daniel Hilton and others proved long ago. Its descent is rapid enough for all purposes as a water power.

One of the principal tributaries is Indian run which enters the west boundary at section nineteen, and flows a little east of north to Duck creek at a point southeast of Macksburgh.

By this name, Indian run, "hangs a tale." At the beginning of the century when there was a peace between the Indians and whites, hunting parties of Indians were frequent in Duck Creek valley. A party of three Indians on such an expedition, went down to Marietta, and became slightly intoxicated. It is said one of the three insulted a white boy of the place by relating to him how he had killed the boy's father—that afterwards he asked the boy to ferry him across the Muskingum. The fate of the Indian is only surmised. The other two companions waited about Marietta in vain for their missing one, finally gave up, and returned to their camp on the stream in question. Here they packed their utensils, left those of their comrade, and returned whence they had come, blazing the trees, as they went, for the benefit of the lost Indian, should he ever return. Squire Davis and Levi Dean, then of Salem and Fearing townships, respectively, found the cooking utensils, blanket, and the like of the ill-fated Indian, and preserved them in their families, where they have been seen by many now living. But the stream where they were found, has been called Indian run ever since.

At the village of Macksburgh is the mouth of Big run, often called Goose run since the oil discoveries, which flows south from Noble county. Elba is likewise possessed of a stream running through the place called Long run. The largest tributary does not all lie in the township. It is Buell's run and has three sources on the farms of Messrs. Ward and Pierce and the heirs of Mary Ward, in sections nineteen, twenty, and twenty nine. It leaves the township by flowing south through the eastern part of section thirty-two.

A streamlet, called Jackson's run, rises near the "Smith church," about a mile and a half west of Elba, and runs southeast to Duck creek at Kingsbury station. It is important in that it affords a route for a road connecting the western ridge road with that up Duck Creek valley.

The soil in Aurelius is, for the most part, of two kinds: that formed by the action of water on sandstone and that resulting from the disintegration of limestone. The former kind of soil is not at all fertile, but in many localities fine farms are afforded by the latter. This is noticable among the hills and on the ridges in the western half of the township. From the nature of the surface and soil, the Aurelian farmers deal largely in stock, especially sheep, and plant extensive orchards. One farmer mentioned that he had twenty-three kinds of apple trees on his farm.

Enough has been told of the winding, narrow course of Duck creek, the steep yet finely-rounded hills, which are yet, in many places, covered with their original forests of oak, walnut, poplar, and the like, and the romatic and intricate system of ravines tell the stranger that a ride up the tortuous Marietta & Cincinnatti railroad, commonly called the "Duck Creek road," is an admission to a moving diorama of picturesque scenery, at the low price of three cents per mile of canvas.

Coal exists in abundance everywhere over this district. It is of fine quality but not extensively mined on account of the cost of getting it to market. It is plenty and cheap enough, however, to render the old time country fireplace and "Christmas back-log" a thing unknown to the farmers of Aurelius. In its place is the more city-reminding grate and the coal-scuttle, for almost every farmer has his own private coal bank, and when he wants his fire replenished he digs rather than chops.

The lower or "limestone" seam of coal is not well developed, but the seam above it is thick and exists everywhere. The coal has been mined on Hugh Jackson's land and also in other places. In many places toward the north it is found six feet thick, and is easily obtained from the sides of the hills skirting Duck creek. In the northeast the thickness of the coal increases, in the west diminishes. A branch railroad from Macksburgh runs to the Ohio Coal company's mines in Noble county, where the coal seam is six feet thick.

Salt is found, in solution, of course, at depths of from ninety to three hundred feet in the valley near Macksburgh, but salt-boiling is not a business in Aurelius, as the drills that find the brine are after deeper things, for Aurelius township is one of the best in the county for petroleum.

About 1858-9 John McKee, near Caldwell, Ohio, while drilling for salt, found a vein of oil. It came bubbling up and overflowing in great quantity, and the discoverer celebrated the event by a bonfire of the oil. Afterwards a Mr. Duff came from Pittsburgh and put a pump in the well. But this incident set Mr. James Dutton to thinking. Many a time as he was swimming in the holes in Duck creek when a youth, he had noticed that "jumping up and down" in the water caused oil to rise and float away on the surface. Finally he, with William Dutton, John Smithson, and Alden Warren formed a copartnership and began on the since famous Dutton well, on the right bank of Duck creek about a mile below Macksburgh. At twenty-eight feet they came to a rock with oil in the crevices. They drilled a foot-square hole for the "conductor" and worked by hand through eight feet of rock, striking oil. When four feet further a second vein was touched, and when twenty-eight feet in the rock, or fifty-six feet below the surface, they struck, in October, 1859, the "big vein." Hand pumping furnished a stream "as thick as my arm," says Mr. Dutton, and he pumped an eighty-barrel tank full in half a day. For a whole year the oil was sold at twenty-eight dollars a barrel. The well itself sold for one hundred thousand dollars. This was the first paying well in the county, and the first large well in the State.

After this came a furor of speculation and drilling. Companies bought lands, farmers turned oil men, and derricks arose as quickly as the palaces of a dream. But first the war, and now the low price of oil have conspired to moderate the fever, and the oil business in this, one of the best oil townships in the county, is now conducted on every day practical principles. Yet the visitor in the valley can still count a derrick for every house, and the wells about Macksburgh present a lively appearance. One of the best is Mr. George Rice's "deep well," bored one thousand five hundred and seventy-six feet, which has been flowing a year, and now yields seven or eight barrels per diem of light oil. Another of Mr. Rice's wells has been yielding oil for sixteen years. Within a fortnight of the present writing Mr. Z. O. Patton struck oil at a depth of five hundred feet, and is now obtaining a hundred barrels a day from it. The date of this find is December 28, 1880.

SETTLEMENT.

The first settler of Aurelius—Levi Dains—was a soldier in the Revolution, and moved to Ohio in company with Squire Davis, a comrade. His wife was Chloe, and their children's names were: Levi, Eben, Parley, Benjamin, Luther, Simeon, Lucy, Julia, and Lavina. The family moved from Fearing township, and remained in Aurelius from 1806 or 1807 until a colony left on a boat for Illinois. This event will be mentioned hereafter.

A little episode, however, might be mentioned here. When the family made arrangements to leave, Benjamin was not included in their plans, as he was not considered possessed of the requisite brightness and activity for an emigrant. They remembered how on one occasion it took him three days to go with an ox team from home to Marietta. So Benjamin was to be left behind to live and die in Aurelius, while the rest of the family went rejoicing to their new home. But Benjamin had quietly made other arrangements, and when the boat with the family approached the Illinois shore, where they expected to land, the first object described was the aforesaid Benjamin, with a broad grin upon his face, apparently at the pleasure it would give them to see him. Slow and dull as he was, he had walked the entire distance, and beat them at that. Shortly after their arrival in Illinois the dread cholera carried away all the children except Benjamin and Lucy. The father had died shortly before this, and the mother had remarried and moved away.

Joseph Dutton was the second pioneer of the township. The stone that marks his resting place in the private burying-ground on the Dutton place gives his death as September 1, 1844, in his sixty-sixth year; hence he was born in 1778 or 1779. His wife, Amy Job, was born on the twentieth of October, 1767, and died March 27, 1860, at the advanced age of over ninety-two years. Their children were: Sallie, Mary, James, Jane, Susan, and Betsey. On Christmas, 1805, the family moved to Fearing township from Virginia, and in 1806 or 1807 they moved to Aurelius and settled on twenty-five acres bought from Levi Dean. He afterwards entered the southwest quarter of section seventeen.

Joseph Dutton's birthplace was in Pennsylvania. He married in Loudoun county, Virginia, about 1795. His wife was an orphan at the time, and came from New Jersey. Of the children, Mary lives at Cat's creek, near Lowell, married to Samuel Davis; Sallie was the first bride of the township; Levi and Mrs. Dains, jr., died with the cholera in Illinois; Jane is the widow of William True, and lives at Salem; Susan is the wife of William Penwill and is in Bradford, Pennsylvania; Betsey married William Garrett, and moved to near the Ozark mountains, Missouri. They are both dead.

James Dutton was born July 23, 1801, in Virginia. After the death of his father he lived in Aurelius until April, 1864, when he moved to Marietta, where he still lives. His first wife was Barbara Ann Rayley, whom he married in 1823. In 1870, he married Esther A. Suthers, a widow whose maiden name was Miss Blower. When a boy, in the wilds of the township he was known as a fearless hunter. When fourteen he killed a full grown bear with a small tomahawk. To prevent the escape of a wolf with one of his traps, he bestrode the animal and held it by the ears until help came. His boyish soubriquet was "Wolf" Dutton, and this christian name changed to "Oil" after his discoveries in that article mentioned elsewhere.

In 1809-10, Jacob Bouser, in company with his son John, their wives, and John's four children, entered land in sections seventeen and eighteen. They were Dunkers and lived there until Dr. Regnier bought them out, which was in six or eight years. They removed to beyond Zanesville.

John Hutchins, sr., the fourth or fifth to make a home in the settlement, was born in 1770. He married Joanna Weeks and came in a company of about thirty-two or three, among whom were, David and another brother. His children were: Hollis, John, Rosanna, and Shubel. Hollis died in August, 1880, Morgan county. Rosanna died fourteen or fifteen years ago. Shubel died about 1840. The father himself died in 1852, in his eighty-second year.

John Hutchins, jr., was born in the eastern part of Maine, August 31, 1797, and has been living in Aurelius

since 1811. His wife was Jane Rowland, born in the Isle of Wight in 1804, who came straight to Aurelius in 1820. The marriage was in 1824, and the children are: Julia Ann, born in 1825; George, born in 1827; John, Caroline, born in 1831; and Jane Joanna, born in 1837. All of this family are yet living; the parents in the identical frame house built for them in 1823, by Hollis Hutchins, which is probably the first frame house in the township.

Elder Daniel Hilton came from Maine in 1810-12, and left on the Illinois bound boat about 1817. His wife is spoken of by all who knew her as a remarkably fine woman and very popular.

Dr. Hodge was the first doctor in the settlement. He had been persuaded to go to Aurelius by Dr. Regnier, who owned land there, but had not yet moved upon it and wanted it tenanted. He left upon the arrival of Dr. Regnier soon after. He came from New York.

I. H. Delong, sr., was born in the last century, in 1790. While in Aurelius he was justice of the peace twenty-one years, and was a volunteer in the War of 1812, being prevented from serving by the sudden close of the war. He married a Miss Hill, and she dying, his second wife was Nelsie Lancaster, who also died in 1864. His children were: Matilda, dead; Eliza, in Indiana; Jonathan, in West Virginia; William in Aurelius; and Margaret. These were children of his first wife. By his second wife were: David, dead; Thomas J., in Nebraska· I. H., in Macksburgh; Nancy, in Iowa; Martha in Kansas; Mary Jane, in Illinois; Juliette, and Hannah, also in Illinois; James in Pennsylvania; and David, who died unmarried.

Theodore Gevrez came to Aurelius from Marietta in 1817-18 with his widowed mother. He was born in 1812, in Washington county. He has been married three times—to Jane Smithson, Eliza Week, and his present wife, Elizabeth Lupardis. His children by his first wife were Didier, Jane, Theodore, and Lafayette; by his second wife, Lafayette, Frances, Charles, and Evaline; by his present wife, Willie Francis. Mr. Gevrez has held, as a reference to the table of officers will show, various township offices, and has taught school three years.

Eli Vaughn, one of the early settlers, emigrated from New York, where he was born in 1792, to Aurelius as early as 1817. His death occurred in 1864, in the township. He was honored at different times with many township offices, and was justice of the peace for several years. His wife's name was Electa Burch, and the children are, Polly, A. R., Hannah, married to Joseph Hutchins; Lydia, in Adams township; Caroline, wife of Abram Zollars, in Salem; Adeline, married to William Hoyt, of Iowa; George, husband of Patty Simms, and in Wisconsin; Electa, wife of John Dixon, of Aurelius. The dead are, John, who married Rowena Perkins and died in the army; Celestia, who married and died in Iowa; Betsey Davis, and P. B. A. R. Vaughn married Sallie Wharf in 1842, by whom he has had twelve children, ten of whom are now living.

William Raylay was born in Yorkshire, England, in 1781 and came to New York in 1799. In 1801, while still in New York, he married Martha Duncan. She died soon, and in 1804 he married Sarah Chamberlin, who was born August 7, 1781, being just one day older than her husband. In 1815, with his wife and children he moved to a point on the Ohio opposite Marietta, and in 1817 he came to Aurelius township and settled in the northwest quarter of section seventeen. He bought this of Dr. Regnier, who had bought it of Jacob Rouser. The children accompanying him to the township were. Barbara Ann, who afterwards became the wife of James Dutton, and who was the only child of his first wife, born in 1802; also William L.; Content Adeline, born in 1807; and Gurdon, born in 1810. Ralph Woodell, born in 1808, died in New York. William Rayley came to Aurelius to work for Dr. Regnier who was getting a grist- and saw-mill built. It will be seen afterward that he was the prime mover in the establishment of the Methodist society, which is the parent of so many yet existing in the neighborhood. William L. Rayley, at present living in Macksburgh, was born July 4, 1805, and married Sarah Warren in 1828, and has a large family. William Rayley has been township clerk, postmaster twenty-three years, United States marshal, and held various other offices. Content Adeline married Dr. Benjamin Brown.

In 1818 another addition was made to the settlement in the person of Mr. James Bill, a Scotchman by birth, which occurred in East London in 1777. This farmer from which he last came was New York. This farmer married Margaret Sinclair, born in 1778, died in 1855, he himself dying two years before his wife. Of their large family, Margaret became Mrs. Jackson, and is in Salem. Ellen married Thomas Carlin. Marion married Edmund Simmons, of Wisconsin. Elizabeth's husband was Norman Hall, and is in Illinois. James is the husband of Mary Carlin. Another child was Catharine. John died in youth. Isabella married John Moffett, and Jane, Samuel Patton. James Bill married in 1843, and is the father of five children.

Another of the old settlers of Aurelius was Justus Hall, who located in 1818 in section thirty. Though born in Canada, he was by 1812 so far Americanized as to fight for Uncle Sam. He came to Ohio from New York. Leaving Aurelius, he finally went to Illinois, where he died. His wife, whose name before her marriage was Diantha Burch, died in the year 1860. The names and places of residence of the surviving members of the family are: Leonard, in Illinois; J. B. Hall, in Aurelius township; Justus, in Missouri; Nelson, in Illinois; Diantha, married Simon Selix; and Samantha, married Lyman Hunt. Other members of the family were Electa Omstead, who died in 1855; Ephraim, who was drowned by the upsetting of a boat; German, who died in Salem township in 1863; Hely, who was killed when only eight years old; and Norman, who died a natural death at the age of fifty years.

Joseph B. Hall was married June 6, 1833, to Mary J. Bartlett. Their children are: John R., W. H., Margaret A., James, George W., R. B., W. A., Levi., and W. W., who are living; Diantha, Charlotte, Justus W., Mary E., Joseph H., and an infant, who are dead. Justus W. died

in the army. B. B. and W. A. are physicians at Chillicothe. W. W. is assistant surgeon in the army at Fort Reno, Indian Territory. W. H. is in Osceola, Iowa, where he has a store.

Dr. John B. Regnier, the greater portion of whose participation in the settlement of Aurelius will be found recorded elsewhere throughout this history, seems to have been of a remarkably rare nature, always working for the public good, and of great enterprise and energy. His birth-time, birth-place, and death will be found elsewhere, in his epitaph. He married Content Chamberlain in New York State, came to Marietta about 1806, from Stanleyville, and went to Aurelius about 1819 or 1820. His arrival at Stanleyville was before 1800. Before moving to Aurelius he bought land there, and built the mill referred to at another place. He had seven children: Alfred, Hannah, Felix, Julius, Francis, John, and Aurelius, the township name. All are dead but Felix.

Dr. Regnier's death occurred at Marietta, of epidemic fever. He may really be regarded as the father of the township. He got it into the county, obtained many improvements for it, for he was county commissioner from 1815 till his death, got the post office, the first road, and many other benefits elsewhere mentioned. His intention was to plat Macksburgh, and open a drugstore in the place, but death intervened. His son Alfred was married to Mary A. Rowland, who settled in Aurelius in 1820, and who is still living. She resides with her daughter, Mrs. Albert Chandler, in Adams township.

Russell St. John was born in 1792, in Connecticut and came to Aurelius in 1821, from New York, and settled upon a farm in section twenty-two. He died in 1874. He was a blacksmith and farmer, and was frequently called upon to fill various offices in the township. His wife was Isabella Chamberlin. R. W., his son, is a farmer in Aurelius; George W. is in Kansas; Erastus L. is in Monroe county; Ruth E., Caroline C., Morris S. and Lorine are dead. R. W. St. John has seven children: Emma, C. R., William H., Arthur L., Leora H., Clara L., and Austin H. C. R. St. John studied law in Noble county under Dalzell & McGinnis, and was admitted to the bar in May, 1880. This was after four years spent as a teacher.

George Wickens settled in Aurelius in 1832, in section twenty-nine. He was a native of England, born in the Isle of Wight in 1780. He married Charlotte Rowlands, who was born in the Isle of Wight in 1792. He died in 1870, and his wife in 1868, in Aurelius. Their children are George, Elizabeth, William R., John and Henry. George moved to Illinois, John to Kansas, and the rest live in Aurelius. William R. in 1849 married Sarah L. Cadwell, and Henry married Elizabeth Roff in 1855.

John Dixon, sr., was a native of England, and came to Aurelius township in the year 1834. His son, John Dixon, jr., is living in the township, is married and has three children. He married, in 1853, Electa Vaughan, and has three children—Hannah, wife of W. Mincks, Abraham Lincoln and Fred.

Dr. Benjamin Brown was a graduate at Glasgow, Scotland, and his talents are mentioned as of a high order by all who have spoken about him. He came to the place about the time he married, which was in 1835, and to Content Adeline Rayley, the daughter of William Rayley, the pioneer. He had a very successful practice. The family, which consisted of the parents and three children, was divided by the separation of Dr. Brown and his wife.

William Davidson settled in section thirty, this township, in the spring of 1836. He was born in Northumberland, England, November 11, 1797, and emigrated to this country in 1829. He first settled in Virginia, and moved to Ohio, where he resided until his death, in 1869. His wife, Jane Richardson, died in 1840, aged forty years. Their children, five in number, were: Catharine, born in 1824; Elizabeth, born in 1826; George, born in 1828; Thomas, born in 1831; Margaret A., born in 1828, died in 1846. Two years after the death of his first wife, Mr. Davidson married Harriet Coles, who died in 1876. By this marriage there were seven children, six now living. George Davidson, one of the sons, married, November 30, 1854, M. M. Nesselrode, jr., and has had eight children, as follows: Emily A., born in 1856, married William Wilson in 1876; William C., born in 1858; Charles S., born in 1860, died in 1879; George M., born in 1862; Jennie, born in 1864; Maggie, born in 1866; Harry W., born in 1870; Kate, born in 1873.

About this time settlers began to come into the ridge country in the western part of the township. Among them was William Smith, who, with his wife, Elizabeth, was a native of Pennsylvania, and moved to this State in 1830. The settlement of this couple in Aurelius was seven years later. Their son, James W. Smith, is still living in the place.

The little settlement having got fairly upon its feet by the time two or three families were there, improvement began, and the various events growing out of the social life of man began to take place. Thus it is that man always gives an impetus to history.

Levi Dains had already distinguished himself as the builder of the first house in the township. It was, of course, a log cabin, and the tenderer portion of the family found it all ready for their entrance, the thoughtful care of the good man having prepared it before the family moved. A sheep pen had been made in the angle formed by the great chimney and the end of the house, and about the first one outside the family to discover this fact was a huge panther which made an incursion on the sheep the first night. The male portion of the family turned out *en masse* and drove the invader off.

Soon after Mr. Dutton moved there, while as yet there were but two families in the settlement, the society of the place was set all on the *qui vive* by a marriage between the two "first families" of the neighborhood. The woods that had before echoed to the howl of the wolf, and more lately to the blow of the axe and the crack of the rifle, now rang with the music of marriage bells—if they had any. Levi Dains, jr., and Sallie Dutton were the contracting parties. Their wedding tour was limited by the bounds of their fathers' lands, for they settled on a portion of the paternal acres.

In 1809 an addition was made to the settlement, but not by way of immigration. In the first family that settled was born the first child in the township. In a few short months, however, the little flower of the wilderness faded, and the first funeral saw little Simeon Dains burie at the edge of a field, and no stone marks the place where they laid him. Thus the little baby's short life was marked only by its birth and death. The funeral was preached at the house of Levi Dains by a Mr. Goss, who was the first Methodist preacher ever in the county. Only the Dains and Duttons attended the funeral; there were as yet no other settlers in the township.

It is not known certainly whether John Hutchins, jr., built the first frame house or Mr. John Jewell. Certain it is that the Hutchins house is the first frame house whose date we can obtain. It is about a mile above Macksburgh, and was built by Hollis Hutchins in 1823 for John Hutchins, jr., and his intended wife. They were married the next year and moved into it. It is a substantial building, containing plenty of hewn logs, which can be seen supporting the ceiling in a way that looks very substantial.

The first frame barns were built by the heirs of Dr. Regnier and by Joseph Dutton in 1822-3.

The first brick building was built by Dr. Regnier. It is described as a very large, fine house, employing many hands in its construction. On one of the walls the figures 1820 were built in with black brick, thus fixing the date very accurately. When the mansion was about ready to be occupied Dr. Regnier died. It has since been, for the most part, torn down, and the part of the walls remaining is concealed by the boards of the building of George Rice, esq.

As an orchard is considered one of the first requisites of a Washington county farm, it may be readily inferred that the first orchard in the township was on the first farm and planted by the first farmer. Levi Dean planted it in 1810.

The first road through the township was the ridge road, from Marietta to Cambridge. The first road for the benefit of the township was from Cat's creek mouth, at the upper end of Lowell, to Middleburgh, through Macksburgh. This road may be credited to the efforts of Dr. Regnier. It was built about 1815.

The first post office was obtained, the reader is ready to surmise by this time, by the influence of the public-spirited Dr. Regnier. He obtained it about the year 1819, and was himself the first postmaster—the office being in his own house. His son, Felix, succeeded him in the office. Next was another son, Julius; following him was William Rayley, who held it for twenty-three and a half years; next was I. H. Long.

The first Sunday-school was instituted by Benjamin Corp shortly before he built and presented the Methodist church, probably in 1823.

Dr. Regnier's son-in-law, William W. Mackintosh, kept the first dry goods store about 1827. This was the first store of any kind in the township. The first blacksmith shop was built about the year 1820, and the vulcan was William Way.

MILLS.

Dr. Regnier built the first grist- and also the first saw-mill in about the year 1818. The grist-mill is still standing, the saw-mill is now torn down, but was about four or five rods distant from the grist-mill. The building of these mills was, indirectly, the cause of the first Methodist church, as will appear hereafter.

The mill that the traveller on the railroad notices just below Elba was built by Thomas Girby forty or fifty years ago. It was a grist- and saw-mill combined, but is now only a saw-mill.

CHURCHES.

THE FREEWILL BAPTIST CHURCH.

This was undoubtedly the first church organized in the township. About 1810–12 Elder Daniel Hilton came from Maine. He found several people in the settlement and proceeded to establish a church of the above denomination. They met at no set place but held meetings from house to house, most frequently at Dean's and Hilton's. Some of the original members of this church were the families of Hilton, Dean, Bartlett, Judah Chamberlin, Jehu Chamberlin, Benjamin Blake, from what is now Noble county; also Nancy and Mary Dutton, and some of the Davises. This church flourished until 1817, when Elder Hilton, the Deans, Bartletts, and others went away in a boat to Illinois, below St. Louis. The colony left in two boats; one was built on the Muskingum, and the other, on which the Duck creek families left, in the woods below Macksburgh. The boat was launched by means of trees felled, trimmed, and used for "skids," over which the boat was pushed by the united efforts of some of their neighbors.

Such a depletion of their numbers destroyed the little church, and the few members remaining either ceased to attend church or joined the

REGULAR, OR HARD-SHELL BAPTIST CHURCH,

which had been formed a short while before. The most of the members of this church were from what is now Noble county, and most of the meetings were held there. For this church, too, like the other one, was not possessed of a set place in which to worship, nor, like the children of Israel, did it have even a tabernacle, but depended on the hospitality of its different members. We may be sure that these pioneers welcomed it to their houses not less cordially than a mortal stranger, and that they were none the losers.

The originator of this church was Elder Joseph Clark. It comprised in its membership John Hutchins, sr., and wife, Simeon Morgareidge, Joseph Davis, Robinson Sandford, Walter Stevens, Joseph Dutton, and their wives. John Hutchins, jr., and his consort joined in 1830 or 1831. Their pulpit was often supplied from Zanesville. The second preacher was Levi Jewell. Another minister was Mr. Sedgewick.

In time, however, the church died, and the only denomination now represented in Aurelius is the

METHODIST CHURCH.

This was organized about the year 1818, principally by the efforts of William Rayley, who came to Aurelius at that time to board the hands and help build the mills for Dr. Regnier. This worker procured the services of Methodist ministers, notably Bishop Morris. Then came Nathan Walker and organized the church, the accompanying preacher sent by the Pittsburgh conference being Thomas McLeary. The original members included William Rayley and his wife, Sarah; John S. Corp and his wife, Elizabeth; and a young man working at the mills—only these five. Benjamin Corp, John's father, joined next. About 1824 he built, and presented to the church, a frame building twenty-five feet square, situated about half a mile above Macksburgh. Being rallied about its small size, he affirmed that when the congregation got large enough to fill it he would enlarge it. The first meeting the house was jammed, and so Mr. Corp had it cut in the middle, the parts separated fifteen feet and the space built in, making a building twenty-five by forty feet.

In the meantime, however, some of this society had been meeting about at the houses, notably at Dutton's, as the church building was not so convenient. This, again, as it increased divided into two parts, and those living nearest Macksburgh finally, in 1855, built the church now at that place. The land on which this building stands was donated by Mr. John Hilton. The building itself was constructed by Mr. John Eagler. Elder James Henderson was in charge at that time. Since then, because of the characteristic itinerent system of the Methodist church, there have been many pastors. For the past fifteen years they have been as follows: Revs. Thomas Winstanly and White; Revs. Gordon and Doane; Revs. Phillips and Strahl; Revs. L. Timberlick and Ruckman; Revs. A. D. McCormick, N. C. Worthington, George Wilson, and W. F. Smith; the last named being the pastor now. The church now belongs to the Dexter circuit. It was made from the Sharon circuit in 1875. This itself was not an original circuit, but formed from another.

The Corp meeting-house having been found unsuitable in position by this time, ceased to be used, some of the attendants coming to the Macksburgh church and others going to the "Crooked Tree" in Noble county.

The other part of the society before referred to as meeting at Dutton's, and other places, when the division occurred, held meetings in a log school-house near where the present school-house now stands, on James W. Smith's place, about a mile and a half west of Elba. This school-house, by the way, was built in 1846, and the first teacher who used it was Hannah Ellison. In time, a meeting-house was constructed, and in 1854 dedicated by Rev. Thomas Winstanley, of the Pittsburgh conference. The land on which it stands was the gift of James W. Smith. In about 1875 preaching was discontinued, and the congregation, for the most part, attend at Elba.

The Methodist society at Elba is not an offshoot of the foregoing, but was organized independently in about 1842. In the summer of 1874, James Morrison, a merchant of Elba, donated land as a church site, and the present church at that place was built. The preachers who first used the church were Revs. Webster and Mc-Cormick.

Thus we find that all these numerous societies of this denomination have finally graviated to the two towns of Macksburgh and Elba.

SCHOOLS.

It is a fact creditable to the pioneers of Aurelius that the date of settlement and the date of the first school differ by a very small figure. The first formal attempt at the instruction of youth was made by Nancy Dutton, who started and successfully completed a three months school in the winter of 1808-9 or of 1809-10. Her pupils were, of course, drawn principally from the Dean and Dutton families. After this, Polly Stanley taught, and when the year 1819 had arrived, a Mrs. Free took charge of a school for the whole winter. Before that, Elder Davis had taught in 1812.

In the neighborhood of 1815, a log school-house was built near Dexter, two miles above Macksburgh. At the close of the War of 1812, Mr. John Jewell taught in the second school-house in the township, situate about a mile below Macksburgh.

The largest building and school in the township is at Macksburgh, and is the best public building in the place. It is a two-story white frame, surmounted by a steeple, and would be easily mistaken for a church. There are two departments taught, the upper room being presided over by Charles W. Atherton, and the lower by Charles St. John. There is a full attendance at both rooms.

SECRET SOCIETIES.

The only one now in existence in the township is the Aurelius lodge of Free Masons, with headquarters at Macksburgh. The date of this charter is October 20, 1859, to take effect December 24, 1850. The society, however, ran a couple or so of years before, under a dispensation. The charter members were: Thomas Morris, F. M. Mason, E. S. Tingley, G. L. Chamberlin, S. L. Berkely, Mark Weeks, R. E. Smithson and Jacob Wharton. The first officers were: Master, S. L. Berkely; senior warden, G. L. Chamberlin; junior warden, J. D. James. The lodge is now in a flourishing condition, if membership be the criterion, as it has about sixty members. The present master is R. C. Smithson.

The only other secret organization known to have existed here is the Good Templars, a lodge of which sprang up in the fall of 1873 and lasted about a year.

BURIAL PLACES.

The one below Macksburgh a short distance was established by Dr. Regnier, who gave the ground, nearly an acre, little thinking that he was providing a home for his own body in the near future. The first person buried in it was Mrs. Phineas Beardsley, and the second one was Dr. Regnier himself. This was the first burial place in the township. It contains the graves of many old settlers and the tombstone of Dr. Regnier. The stone may be seen leaning against the tree in the southwest corner of the lot. It is fitting that this memorial of the foremost man of the township be preserved, and, as far

as possible, it shall be done right here. The inscription is:

In memory of
DR. JOHN B. REGNIER,
Who died August 16, 1821,
In the fifty-third year of his age.
A native of Paris, in France.

"Behold and see, as you pass by,
As you are now, so once was I;
As I am now, so you must be,
Prepare for death and follow me."

The cemetery near the "Smith church" dates from 1856, when Lucinda F. Taylor, an infant, was buried in it. This place of interment contains the graves of many other older inhabitants—the Smiths, the Walfords, the Wards, Elliotts and Gilmores, the Harveys and Blakes, and many others. The ground was given by James W. Smith, and has since been incorporated.

VILLAGES.

The two towns of the township are Macksburgh and Elba. Macksburgh is a place of about three hundred inhabitants, and is situated a few rods from the left bank of Duck creek, in the southeast quarter of section seven. It is a station on the Marietta & Cleveland railroad, and lies between this road and a coal road, which branches off to the north to a coal mine in Noble county. Its site is neither valley nor hill, but on the rise between, and the surface is much diversified, giving the place a rather irregular appearance. This is partly owing to the fact that the town was never regularly surveyed into lots until largely built. Dr. Regnier had planned to lay out the town but died before accomplishing his end. Old citizens unite in regarding this untoward death as a great misfortune to the prosperity of the village. It is now essentially an oil place, the numerous wells in its vicinity supplying employment for many of its residents. At present it contains the school-house and Methodist church, elsewhere described, a post office, three general stores, a shoe store, a blacksmith shop, a hotel by the name of the Ohio House, and two saloons. Directly south of the town, across the creek, is a gathering of dwellings along the road, which in many districts would be called a town. It might be considered a suburb of Macksburgh. This collection of houses is really as old as Macksburgh itself. The name Macksburgh is owing to the fact that William W. Mackintosh lived there, and probably because he kept the first dry goods store. It was never formally named at all; the name gradually grew to the place.

ELBA.

This town lies on a beautiful situation on the line between sections twenty-one and twenty-two, and on the left bank of Duck creek. Its site is a pretty nook, surrounded on three sides by hills. The railroad on which it is a station and the valley road passes along the west side of the place. A small stream runs through the village to join Duck creek, finding its way to the town by a romantic ravine. This village was laid out by James Morrison, then proprietor of the land. The survey was made in the fall of 1873, by Ralph St. John. It has a post office, two general stores, a shoe store, blacksmith shop, and a tobacco warehouse.

THE PHYSICIANS.

The physicians who have been in the township are Dr. John B. Regnier, Dr. Hodge, and Dr. Benjamin Brown. More particular mention of them will be found in the "settlement" elsewhere. The present physicians are Dr. Hopkin and Dr. Neiswonger at Macksburgh, and Dr. Brock at Elba.

CHAPTER LI.

FEARING TOWNSHIP.

Establishment of the Township— First Election—Statistics—Commodore Whipple for Once Gets Too Much of the Water—A Stream Named from a Dinner—Cannel Coal—The Duck Creek Settlement in General—Thomas Stanley—The Mill Question—Levi Chapman—A Block-house Built—Names of Settlers Before 1800—Allen Putnam's Death—Later Settlers—The Doctors of Fearing—The Mills Destroyed by Flood and Indian—Forgotten Schools—Charles Shipman the Earliest Teacher Remembered—Discipline in the Olden Time—Pioneer School-ma'ams—School in a Barn—An Early Library Association—The Fearing Religious Society—The Congregational Church—Methodism in Fearing—An Old-time Camp-Meeting—The Zion Methodist Episcopal Church—The Church at Cedar Narrows—The Two German Churches—The Stanley Cemetery—An Old Man —The Chapman Cemetery.

TOWNSHIP number three, in range number eight, was, on petition of John Porter and others, established March 8, 1808. As formed, it was six miles square. On the eighth of February of the following year the western tier of sections, were detached and annexed to other townships. The further diminution of territory, which made the township as it now stands, occurred in 1861, when the township of Muskingum was formed.

The township was named for Hon. Paul Fearing, who was, at the time of its establishment, serving as county commissioner.

On the fourth day of April, 1808, the electors met at the house of Henry Maxon and elected the following officers: Henry Maxon, clerk; Thomas Stanley, John Porter and Resolved Fuller, trustees; Simeon Wright and Joel Tuttle, overseers of the poor; Solomon Goss and John W. White, fence viewers; William Stacy, jr., and John Miller, appraisers; Didier Gerez, Isaac Hill, Daniel Dunchew, Henry Maxon, John Porter and Ebenezer Nye, supervisors; Daniel G. Stanley and George Nye, constables; Solomon Goss, treasurer.

The present officers are: Henry Knock, Jacob Schramm, Daniel Ludwig, trustees; Charles Schimmel, clerk; Christian Gerber, assessor; J. J. D. McVaig, treasurer, and Daniel Marsch, justice of the peace.

The population of Fearing in 1840 was ten hundred and nineteen; in 1860, one thousand five hundred and eighty-nine; in 1870, one thousand three hundred and fifty-eight; in 1880, one thousand two hundred and seventy-five. In the Presidential election of 1880,

Fearing township voted as follows: Hancock, Democrat, one hundred and ninety-six; Garfield, Republican, one hundred and four.

The township as it now exists, is six miles of a transverse section of the lower basin of Duck creek, extending almost across the basin, from the Little Muskingum ridge to that of its larger namesake, being four miles in breadth, and thus containing twenty-four square miles. Salem, Lawrence, Marietta and Muskingum townships bound it from the north around to the west. The boundary ridges of the basin of Duck creek lie partly within and partly without its eastern and western borders, and aside from these, Fearing has no important water-sheds. It therefore gives all its water to Duck creek, which stream enters the township three-quarters of a mile east of the northwest corner, and leaves it on the southern boundary three-fourths of a mile further east, making one huge bend to the east in the lower half of this course. The tributaries flow, for the most part, east or west, with a southerly tendency. The principal one is Whipple's run. It rises in Liberty township, a mile and a half from the southwest corner, near which it enters Fearing and flows west, with a large southerly bend, to Duck creek. In early days, it is said, Abraham Whipple and a party of surveyors, finding the stream too high to be crossed, felled a tree across it, and while using that for a foot log, the old sea captain fell in and nearly met his death. The unnamed stream was afterward described as the "run Whipple fell in," and this soon became condensed into "Whipple's run."

Passing down the left bank of Duck creek, and crossing several small and mostly unnamed streams, a creek is reached a mile below Stanleyville, called Sugar run. Farther down, an inconsiderable stream flows north into Duck creek, named Brush run.

In the winter of 1794-5, as the Chapman family were pushing their way up the wilderness by the natural pathway of Duck creek, to their future home near Whipple's run, they passed near what is now the Cedar Narrows, at the mouth of an unknown stream that flowed from the west. It was New Year's day, and they celebrated the holiday by the only practical, and, no doubt, acceptable way they could—by eating their dinner. Naturally enough, they afterwards would refer to that stream as New Year's creek, and the name still distinguishes the run. So the story goes.

The only other considerable run that drains the western part of the township enters Duck creek just above Stanleyville.

The country is not so rough as further north in Aurelius township and in Noble county. Still the hills are numerous and upright. To escape from among these barriers the larger streams are obliged to pursue very devious courses, and, as it were, to exercise all their ingenuity to find the Ohio.

As is characteristic of Duck Creek valley, bottom lands are not extensive when compared with those of most streams; still, in some places, as just above Stanleyville, the spectator can overlook from some bordering hill quite a stretch of rich, level farms. This is, of course, very desirable farming lands, except where too liable to sudden visits from Duck creek after heavy rains. In the higher lands the soil is not uniformly rich, the red being the most esteemed, and the light-colored or white soil being very poor. Limestone, the foundation of fertility, is not as abundant here as in other parts of the basin. Perhaps the largest formation of this rock appears in the neighborhood of Stanleyville.

SETTLEMENT.

From Marietta as a centre there issued three secondary colonies—to Belpre, Waterford and Duck creek. The latter was the smallest, and is least mentioned in previous histories. It is generally referred to as situated on the forks of Duck creek, but settlers made homes at different points farther down the stream. The necessity for a mill was perhaps the strongest influence that opened up this creek to the settlers. At the close of the Indian war, which began in 1791 and lasted some four years, the settlement lost most of the element of danger, and it is then we find the oldest permanent settlers of Fearing and Salem moving up the Duck Creek valley. Levi Chapman and Thomas Stanley, sr., were the first two to settle within the twenty-four square miles now called Fearing. Stanley was one of the prominent men in the Marietta settlement, to which he and his family had already come in 1790. In 1792 he was appointed constable of Marietta. He remained in this town till the close of the Indian war, when the family came to what is now section eight in Fearing township. His connection with the mills at that early date will more properly be treated further on. He was born in 1752. Mixenda, his wife, was born July, 1766. Anna S., his first wife, was born in 1760. She was the mother of Daniel G., who was born in 1785, in Connecticut, and of Thomas F., who was born in 1787. Francis R., born 1738 and dying in Illinois, was the son of his second wife, as was James, born 1789; Nancy, born 1791; Lucy, born 1793; Cynteia, born 1795; Mary, born 1798; Elizabeth, born 1801; Clarissa, in 1803; Sarah, in 1804; Mixenda, in 1806; and George, in 1812. Thomas, sr., died in 1816 and his wife in 1851. In 1816 Thomas, jr., married Angelina Goldsmith, who was born in Virginia in 1798. Of their children, Joseph Ford is the eldest, and is living at Stanleyville, married Harriet Doan and is the father of Frederick A., Helen A., Edna L., Abbey G., Percival J., Harriet E., and Adelina E. The other children of Thomas are Timothy T., John W., Eliza, Lucy, and Charles A., who is a missionary in China.

The nucleus of another settlement near the present site of Whipple station was formed by the settlement of Levi Chapman, sr., who landed at Marietta in 1794, with a family of eight boys and four girls, having emigrated from Saybrook, Connecticut. He remained in the fort a short time, and then moved to the above mentioned place, attended by a guard of soldiers, who aided him in the construction of a block-house. With this place, the commander of the fort kept communication until peace was made with the Indians.

Shortly afterward Joel Tuttle settled about a mile and a half above Stanleyville. He first came to Waterford township in 1789, having been born in Connecticut in 1740. He died in Fearing in 1823. He served as justice of the peace, and held various other township offices. His wife, Lucy Calkings, died in New England.

Simeon Tuttle came from Connecticut to Ohio in 1791, aged fourteen years, and settled in Fearing township. His death occurred in 1817. He was an 1812 soldier, justice of the peace several years, and husband of Phœbe Everett, of Pennsylvania, whom he married in 1801, and of whose ten children are living: Lucy M., married to Robert Ward, of Fearing, and Simeon E., in San Francisco. Five died young. Three died at maturer years: August, Sarah C. Maxon and Phœbe E. Bevins.

Jonathan Chapman came about this time with his wife, Mary Smith. The rest of the family was David, Levi, Simeon, Jonathan, Ruth and Clara. David married Martha Wheeler, and the children of this couple were Asahal, Selden, Enos, Wheeler, Jonathan, Esther, Antha and Mary Ann. Wheeler was born in Cape May county, New Jersey, about 1809, and married Louisa True in 1837. His children are Leander, Hiram and Sylvester. Enos was born about 1801, and came to the township in 1811. Selden, who was born in 1799, and died in 1839, married Elizabeth Stanley in 1820. The children were Oren S., Nancy S., William, Wheeler, Elizabeth A., Louisa M., Julia F., and Esther A. Oren S. was born in 1821, and in 1877 married Ellen S. Palmer. Their young child, Don Selden Thomas, was born in 1880. The common parents of all these sleep in the Chapman burying-ground. Jonathan died in 1820 at the age of seventy-two years, and Mary died in 1837 in her eighty-fourth year.

Simeon Blake came to Adams township from Rhode Island, where he was born in 1770. He died in 1833. He was a militia captain, and owned the old cabin, which stood on the banks of the Muskingum in the mill-yard. He moved into Fearing about 1800, on the farm occupied at present by John Flanders. His wife's name was Lavina Peck, who was born in Connecticut, and died in 1843. Of the children, Susan married Joseph Elliott; Jane, Willard Twiggs; Edward S. is unmarried; George married Cynthia Smith, while Louisa, Martha, and Charles F. died young. Mr. Simeon Blake married Mary Jane Cunningham in 1840. There were eight children. Mrs. Blake died January 30, 1874.

The following is a list compiled from signatures to old petitions of the settlers in Fearing before 1800. Of the Amlins, John, sr., John, jr., Jonathan, James, and Samuel. According to the records of the Ohio company, these occupied five lots just east of the present German church on Whipple's run. John Amlin, sr., was born in Germany, and came to New Jersey, whence he emigrated to Fearing township, where he died in 1816, at which time he was an old man. Sarah, his wife, lived until after 1825. John Amlin, jr., was one of his sons and a farmer. He married Jane Campbell. Elizabeth, a daughter of John, sr., married Ephraim True, another old settler of Fearing. James Amlin married Nancy Campbell. Jona-

CHARLES F. BISZANTZ

One of the early German emigrants to this county was Conrad Biszantz, who came to America with his family, consisting of a wife and nine children, and settled on a tract of land a short distance above Stanleyville, in Fearing township. This tract is still known as the Biszantz farm, and contains about three hundred acres.

Charles F., one of the best known of the children on account of his active business career, was born in Germany August 7, 1830. He worked on his father's farm until he was eighteen years old, when he began clerking in a steamboat. He afterwards engaged in the grocery and dry goods business in St. Louis. In 1854 he returned to Marietta, and opened a dry goods store on Front street.

He married May 27, 1855, Phœbe Zimmer, who was born in Germany April 21, 1832. Her father, Daniel Zimmer, came to America with his family early in 1833, and settled on March Run hill in Fearing township. He was one of the earliest settlers of that locality. His family consisted of eleven children, who came to maturity. Daniel Zimmer died June 10, 1875. Mrs. Zimmer died July 13, 1878, on the homestead. Conrad Biszantz, father of Charles F., died February 2, 1877. His wife had preceded him, having died August, 1875.

Charles F. Biszantz, the subject of this sketch, continued his dry goods business until June, 1861, when his store was consumed by fire. He again began mercantile business on Front street, in partnership with his brothers, but this partnership did not continue long. In 1863 Mr. and Mrs. Biszantz opened a restaurant on Front street, known as the Sigle House. Mr. Biszantz's next business was to buy the Lowell mill which he continued to own but a short time. In 1864 he purchased the historic old house on Butler street, which was built by Colonel Lord, and converted it into a hotel. He presided over the Biszantz house as landlord for fourteen years, when failing health made it necessary for him to retire. During the same period he was engaged in the oil business. He also had an interest in the Harmar mill, and in a ferryboat across the river. He removed to the farm at the extremity of Green street in 1878, and died there January 13, 1880.

Through all his life he had a faculty for acquiring money and property. But while we are paying him the respect his busy life demands, we must not fail to give due credit to his energetic, economical helpmeet who still survives. To her as well as him is due the credit of acquiring a competence which will soften the path of old age, and give the children a start in the course of life.

The family consists of three children: Ella Louisa was born June 14, 1856. She was married November 16, 1880, to Peter Kuntz, of Marietta. Charles was born January 10, 1858, and died when ten months old. Frank Boell was born November 25, 1859. He lives on the farm with Mrs. Biszantz.

than Amlin was a stone mason in Fearing township who moved afterwards to Marietta and died in Newport, Washington county, in 1846, at the age of seventy years. He married Elizabeth Twiggs. Samuel Amlin was also a farmer, who died in 1872, at the age of ninety-four years. He was married successively to Elizabeth Mitchell, Miss Hill, and Hannah La Rue. Samuel lived at Newport for many years.

Isaac Chapman was below Whipple station. Patrick and Daniel Campbell settled a mile and a half northeast of Stanleyville. Levi Dains mentioned more fully in the history of Aurelius township, of which he was the first settler, occupied the lot just above the Chapman burying-ground. Charles Daugherty owned lot one hundred and twelve, a mile east of Whipple station. John Forthner owned a lot two miles west of the Whipple Run church. Andrew and Daniel Galer held lots opposite Stanleyville, near the west line of the township. Seth Jones owned the northwest corner lot of the township. Henry and Rickard Maxon were on Duck creek just above Stanleyville. The Maxons were a part of the original Marietta boat-load. Allen Putnam held lot one hundred and thirty, a mile northeast of Stanleyville. Conrad Rightner adjoined the Amlins. Mr. Seevers was just north of Mr. Rightner. The Tuttles were on Duck creek, south of the Chapman cemetery. Allen Putnam, who also belonged to the generous boat-load of 1788, the friend of Amos Porter, jr., of Salem township, was another of these early settlers of Fearing. He married Anna Porter, and settled about a mile north of Stanleyville very soon after the spring of 1797. He was a ship-carpenter by trade, and met his death by falling through a hatchway, while he was at work at Marietta.

Charles H. Morton was at the mouth of Sugar run. Ephraim True, who afterwards moved to Salem township, was on lot one hundred and thirty-eight, northeast of Stanleyville. John Widger was on lot seventy-nine, near Whipple's station.

It will be seen from this that there was no inconsiderable settlement here by the beginning of the century. The great majority of these names occur on petitions dated 1797, showing that their owners came up the creek immediately on the complete return of security from the Indians.

In the southern part of Fearing a family settled early, by the name of Caywood, whence the name of the station on the Marietta, Pittsburgh & Cincinnati railroad at that place. William Caywood settled on the farm now occupied by Henry Pape. His wife before marriage was named Phœbe Moore. Of his family, Thomas married Harriet Maxon, and settled in Fearing; Jonathan married Eliza Huston, and also remained in the township; Phœbe married William Gill, and went to Marietta; Joseph Caywood settled in Lower Lawrence. He was a leading member of the Presbyterian church, and was born in Prince William county, Virginia, in 1799. He joined the family in this county in 1820. Eliza Caywood married Joshua Reed, of Marietta township. A. Jackson lives in Fearing, at Caywood station. He married Eliza Stanley and Elizabeth Hill.

Other early settlers of Fearing were the McKees, Robert, William, John, and Alexander. These moved to the settlement where Caldwell now stands, and their descendants are prominent members of that community to-day.

In the year 1806 another addition was made to the neighborhood. Nathaniel Kidd came from Pennsylvania, where he was born in 1800, and lived until 1880. His wife, Mary Hill, born in 1796, died in 1866, and was the mother of Isaac, C. J., N. E., and Jesse M. The first two live respectively in Lawrence township and Marietta; the latter two live in Fearing township.

Walter Athey came from east Virginia, and settled in Fearing in 1810. There he died in 1855, after holding various local offices, marrying Clarissa Goldsmith, and raising the following children: Walter, now in Bonn; John, in Nebraska; Elizabeth, in Indiana; Solomon, in Kansas; Hezekiah, in Fearing; William, in Fearing; Sarah, in Elba; and Samuel, in Illinois.

Hezekiah married Phœbe M. Huggins in 1855, and has these four children: Frances, Elizabeth, Rufus, and Etta. By his first wife, Mary Ann Tidd, the children were: C. W., James L., and Annie.

In 1811 one who is yet a resident of the township, Mr. William S. Price, came, then an infant of a year. He is a native of Virginia, and is possessed with a very distinct recollection of early times, in all that made them so different from the present. His home is about a mile from Caywood station.

Philo Doan was a settler in the northern edge of the township in 1812. His antecedents were settlers in Noble county, and are mentioned more particularly in the history of Salem township. Philo married Sibyl Chapman in 1839, when he was thirty-one years old. About 1856 he moved to Stanleyville. His children are Anna Kemp, William Henry, William P., Joshua P., and Ansel.

Reuben McVay was another one of the early settlers. The date of his settlement is 1813, when he came from Pennsylvania, where he was born in 1792, and died in 1860, in Newport township. During his life he was justice of the peace, and held other township offices. Margaret Hill was the name of his wife before her marriage, and she was the mother of Charles, Joseph, Elizabeth, Rosanna, and Luther, of Newport township, and J. J. D., of Fearing. Two died in childhood. Martha Cable, Mary Ann, Marie, and William are also dead. J. J. D. McVay married Miss Ann E. Kidd in 1855, and has had ten children: Dudley died when small; George F., Mary R., Ellsworth, Elizabeth J., Francis A., J. J. D., jr., Dewey F. and Juliette D. (twins), Augustus, and Otto are living with their parents. Mr. J. J. McVay has been a teacher for eighteen years, and several times honored with offices by the citizens of the township.

James Dowling came to the township in 1814, from Ireland. The immediate place from which he removed, however, was New York. He taught one of the first schools in Fearing township, and was a teacher for twelve years. He married Sallie Harris, and died in 1841. His son, John, still lives in Fearing; James is in Illinois; and

Margaret Post is at McConnelsville; Lewis, Elisha, and Harriet are dead. John married Phœbe Perkins in 1836, and has four children living—Sarah J., Wilson S., Belle, and Henry A. Mr. Dowling has been justice of the peace and infirmary director nine years each, and has held many other local offices. Thomas B. Dowling married Hattie Smithson, and has one child.

Robert Ward emigrated to this county in 1818, with his father, Thomas Ward. He married Lucy M. Tuttle in 1827, and had ten children, six of whom are living: Julia Ann Douthett, of Salem; Simeon T., of Kansas; Matilda E. Hill, of Fearing; and John C., Everett R., and Alice M., also of Fearing. Phœbe Augustus, Augustus T., and two infants are dead. Robert Ward was never naturalized.

James Lowe was another settler, who hailed from Virginia, married Rosanna Haback, and died in 1818 in Morgan county.

In 1818 H. C. Hovey also came to Fearing, and in 1822 married Clarissa Stanley. The two removed in 1830 to Salem township.

John P. Palmer, another settler, is now represented in the township by his son, Thomas, who married his wife, Ellen, in 1847, and has the following children: William, Albert (dead), Ellen S., Jewett, A., Thomas F. (dead) Margaret J., John P., Emiline S., Almerta, Alzora, Gifford, and Sivellus. Thomas P. has held offices in the township, and is much interested in politics, taking an active part in that line.

About 1820, Dr. Hicks entered the township, but practised very little. Heretofore, all the medical service in Fearing was done by Marietta physicians. In about 1830 Dr. Quimby settled just above Mr. Guetteau's place.

Dr. J. F. Ullman, the only doctor now in Fearing, has been practicing here for two years, ever since his settlement. He came from Monroe, but was born in Noble county in 1853. His wife, Mary E. Lane, was born in this county in 1858. Mary Leona, their child, was born in 1877.

Amos Dye was an emigrant to Lawrence township in 1804 from east Virginia, where he was born in 1796. He died at Marietta. His wife was Marie Taylor, and children were Sophronia Chamberlain, Perlina Spencer, Edith Webster, Eliza Brooks, Charlotte Groff, Dudley Dye and Amos Dye, jr., John R., Annie, Henry, George W. and Mary, infants, are dead.

John Whittock, a native of England, was a resident of the township until 1879, when his death occurred. He was born in 1794, and married Miss Julia R. Chapman, who was born in 1816.

John Young, sr., was an emigrant from Virginia, who came to the township in 1833. His birth and death were in 1764 and 1854. He was a native of Scotland, and his father fought on the side of the British in the Revolutionary war, from the battle of Lexington to the surrender of Cornwallis. Mary Darling, born in 1770, died in 1855, was his wife and the mother of John and Betsey, of Fearing.

William Brown first settled in Belmont county in 1806.

He came to Washington county in 1834. His birth place was near Harper's Ferry, Virginia, and he died March 4, 1878. His wife, Margaret Nicol, was born in 1810 and died 1858. The children were Marie Yeomans, James P., and Frank S., of Fearing; Kate Broadhurst, of Barlow; John B., of California; Daniel N., of Dexter City; and William H., of Marietta. Annie M., Mary E., and Hattie A. are dead. James Brown still lives on the old homestead.

About this time was the beginning of that German emigration to Fearing that has since made it essentially a German township. In 1832 the Donaker family came from Germany and settled in Fearing. This was probably the first beginning of the German movement to this township. Shortly after, the Sayler family arrived, also from Germany.

Conrad Biszantz and wife, Eva Huffman, settled in Fearing township in 1834. He was born in Germany in 1801, and his wife was also born in Germany. Six of their ten children are living, three in Washington county. Mr. Biszantz died in Marietta in 1876, surviving his wife four years.

Jacob Zimmer came to Fearing in 1836 from Bavaria, where he was born in 1789. He married Elizabeth Schramm, and the children were: David, Charles, and Daniel, of Fearing; Elizabeth Lehnard, Catharine Buck, and Caroline Strauss, of Marietta; John, of Ironton; and Jacob, who died in 1878. Daniel Zimmer married Elizabeth Young in 1855. Eleven children are living—Catharine, Daniel J., Elizabeth M., Amelia Matilda, Lewis, Jacob, Caroline, Clara, Edward, Ella Lena, and Helen Frances.

Theobald Zimmer came to Fearing in 1836. He was a native of Bavaria, Germany, and was born there in 1817. His wife, Catharine Hoffman, was born in 1824. Their children now in Fearing are Charles and Daniel; Elizabeth Lehnard, Catharine Buck and Caroline Strauss are in Marietta. Jacob died in 1880.

C. W. Zimmer married Carrie E. Lehnard in 1876, and has two children—Nettie and an infant. He is president of the township board of education, and takes great interest in politics.

John D. Pape settled in Lawrence township in 1839, whence he came from Germany, where he was born in 1798. He died in Lawrence in 1842. The children of Mr. Pape reside as follows: John D., Marietta; Adeline Dinkleman, Cincinnati; Detrick and Henry, Fearing; Martha Wischmire, Cincinnati; Annie Geiger, Cincinnati. Two died in infancy.

Detrick Pape married Mary F. Eifler in 1849, and has six children—Adeline Brown, Marietta; Francis Stevenson, Marietta; George H., Fearing; Charles, Marietta; Clinton A., unmarried; Nora A., unmarried, and William, who died when young.

Theobald Boesshar was the son of Jacob and Louisa Boesshar, and came to Fearing in 1852. He was born in 1833, and in 1856 married Elizabeth Schramm, who was born in 1838. She died in 1878. The children are Caroline, Maria, Elizabeth, Jacob, Catharine, Maria Magdalena, John Jacob, Louisa, Edward Theobald, Bertha,

WILLIAM BROWN.

William Brown was a native of Virginia, and was born near Harper's Ferry, in 1804. When he was four years old his parents removed to Belmont county, Ohio, and during his younger years our subject operated a distillery. He married in Belmont county, in January, 1830. Margaret Nicol, a daughter of Daniel Nicol, of Fearing township, this county. Her parents were Scotch people of high respectability. They were rigid members of the Methodist church, and exacting in their honesty and morality.

Soon after he was married, Mr. Brown purchased a farm near the present homestead, at Caywood station, in Fearing township. He afterwards purchased the farm on which he died, and which is now owned by his heirs. The family consisted of ten children: Cathraine was born in November, 1830. She married Whittington Broadhurst. Maria was born in 1832. She married Richard Yeomans, and died in 1869. John was born in 1834, and lives in California; Daniel was born in 1836, and lives in Dexter city, Noble county, Ohio; William H. was born in 1838, and lives in Marietta; Ann H. was born in 1840, and died in 1876; James P. and Mary E. (twins) were born in 1844. James P. lives on the homestead, Mary E. died in 1860; Frank S. was born in 1847, and lives on the homestead. Hattie, the youngest, was born in 1850, and died in 1868. Mrs. Brown passed away in 1858.

Mr. Brown was a man of modest and retiring habits. He was a farmer, and his only ambition was to earn a comfortable competence and lead an honest, upright life. Aside from the routine of farming, he dealt in cattle, and in that way formed a large acquaintance among the agricultural classes.

Both Mr. and Mrs. Brown were members of the Methodist church, and to the last were contented by a simple and religious doctrine, undisturbed by that skepticism so common to more pretentious people.

Mr. Brown died in 1878, having lived an honorable and profitable life.

Emma, and twins named Wilhelmina Philipina and Philipina Wilhelmina.

Lewis Motter emigrated from Germany to this county in 1850, and located in Fearing township with his parents, John and Elizabeth (Huffman) Motter, who had fourteen children, eight of whom are living. In 1860 he married Elizabeth Biszantz, daughter of Conrad and Eva Biszantz. By this marriage there are two children. Mr. Motter has been in the bakery and confectionary business in Marietta since 1865.

John Bules settled in Stanleyville in August, 1872, in which month he married Kate Trautner. He has been engaged in blacksmithing ever since his arrival. His children are Lizzie, Phœbe, Kate, and John.

F. C. Trapp, a German preacher of Fearing township, first came to this part of the county embraced in Muskingum township in 1872. The following year he removed to Fearing, where he is now engaged in ministerial work. He was born in Germany in 1831. In 1860 he married Catharine Kaiser, whose birth occurred in 1825. His children are Charles, Mary, Anna, and Henry.

The virtual beginning of the settlement, as has been implied before, was the attempted and finally successful erection of mills on Duck creek. In 1790 Colonel Ebenezer Sproat and Enoch Shephard commenced building mills in the southern part of the township, under an agreement that they were to receive one thousand acres of land if the mills were finished by September 1, 1790. But a freshet destroyed their dam and did such other damage that the terms of the agreement could not be met.

In the same year, farther down the creek, Mr. Robert Potts began a mill, but lost his labor and expense by the breaking out of the Indian war. The Indians swept through this valley and destroyed everything that could be found, these works not being excepted.

Also Thomas Stanley attempted to build mills and a still-house further up the creek, five miles from Marietta, but failed with the rest. But although the mills and other enterprises were not put in successful operation, yet reference is made to them in fixing locations as if they existed. Thus we find mention in the road records of "Stanley's still-house" as early as January, 1794. But we find that the mills were rebuilt.

But we find that the mills were rebuilt. In a petition for a road, dated January 5, 1797, is mention of "White's mill." As the petition was accepted March, 1798, the first date is probably an error for 1798, caused by the not uncommon *lapsus pennæ* at the beginning of a year. In a subsequent petition, dated 1799, White's, and Sproat's mills are referred to; also, "Esquire Stanley's old mill on congress lot," and in the plat of the road, the position of the former mill is fixed at the crossing of the road, which goes past the Methodist church near Wesley station. In fact, the petition was for this very road.

Thomas Stanley made his second and successful attempt at a mill in about a year after the close of the Indian war. He also built with it a saw-mill, which was the first in the township. In connection with it was a powder-mill, a fulling-mill, and a distillery, all three alike

being a necessity in those days. At the same time he erected the first frame dwelling in the township.

The first brick building was not constructed until about 1831, when Isaac Chapman built one. In about 1811, Mr. Stanley built the mill at Stanleyville, on the site now occupied, after being rebuilt two or three times, by the mill of Theobald Bœschar. Shortly after, and before 1812, Carlisle's mills were constructed, near the north boundary of the township.

In the neighborhood of 1836, William I. Gray built a saw-mill and machine shops, and did, for a short time, some manufacturing of furniture. The turned pieces were mostly forwarded to Marietta, and there made into furniture. Mr. Gray called his works the Stanleyville mills, and in this way the town took its name, and very properly, too, from the old settler who had done so much for it.

The town is at present the only one in the township, and contains two stores, two blacksmith shops, a Congregational church, a grist-mill, carpenter shop, and a post office.

In a collection of manuscripts, made by Dr. Hildreth, is the following petition for one of the early roads through Fearing township. With the aid of what has been stated regarding the position of the farms referred to in the petition, the road can be easily traced and identified with existing ones:

To the Honorable Court of General Quarter Sessions of the Peace of the County of Washington:

Your petitioners request that a road may be laid out from Marietta to the forks of Duck creek and on to Mr Tolman's in the most eligible situation to be taken past Pott's mills, so called, or any other place that should be found more convenient hereafter, from thence on to a ridge, keeping the same ridge to the Cedar Narrows, so called, thence following the creek by Mr. Widger's, then past Mr. Levi Chapman's, and crossing the creek and on to the forks of Duck creek, from thence to the mouth of Pawpaw and on to Mr. Tolmon's.

Which your petitioners, as in duty bound, request a committee may be appointed for that purpose.   Signed,

SAMUEL NASH,	JOSEPH CHAPMAN,
LEVI CHAPMAN,	AMOS PORTER,
DUDLEY DAVIS,	SETH JONES,
LEVI DAINS,	JOEL TUTTLE,
LEVI CHAPMAN, JR.,	EZRA CHAPMAN,
LINUS TUTTLE,	SIMEON TUTTLE,
JOHN WIDGER,	ISAAC CHAPMAN,
JOHN CAMPBELL,	

Thomas Stanley, Surveyor, June, 1797.

The settlement having been formed so early, and yet being the object of no little attention by earlier historians, it becomes difficult, and sometimes impossible, to find the first events and enterprises. The first school is probably not retained in the mind of any one now living. It is remembered that Charles Shipman taught a school in 1804 or near then—that in the northeastern part of the township, Hannah Perkins, near 1807, and afterward Clarissa Plummer, taught.

In about 1812, a Mr. Coleman taught below Stanleyville. The pupils, raised in the open air, trained to hardy pursuits, and free from most of the restraints now everywhere existing, were very little inclined to obey the pedagogue. He accordingly submitted to superior physical force and abandoned the job of teaching before his term was out. A Mr. Gallant was employed in his place with the agreement that he was to teach his term out or he would receive no pay. One day the larger pupils brought their skates to school and disobeyed a rule by skating, that "nooning." Gallant excused all the smaller ones, locked in himself and the disobedient ones, produced a heavy ball bat, which he had charge of when not used in their play, and engaged in a lively knockdown melee with the young giants, in which he came out completely victorious. It is said that he had no trouble thereafter. This illustrates the spirit of those pioneer times—the preeminence accorded to physical courage and force and the rough and ready way of settling difficulties. Gallant was followed by Corner, who, in turn, was succeeded by James Dowling, who taught for twelve years at different schools. One of the early lady teachers was Miss Betsey Maxon, who taught at the mouth of Sugar run.

About 1814, Mary Gross taught a small school of young scholars in an old log barn. It was one of those double barns consisting of two "pens" separated by a third division which alone had a floor. In one of these pens was held her school, consisting of Philo and Anna Doan; Betsey, Rebecca, and John Carlisle; Betsey and Julinda Kidd; Hiram Chapman, and others. The school was held in summer time. Before that, school was kept in a school-house on Whipple's run. The principal text books then in use, were the Testament and Webster's spelling-book. Not much improvement has since been made on either. It is known that Walter Stevens taught school at Cedar Narrows, at a very early date. In 1851, the last select school in the township was taught by John Douglas.

While on the subject of education, it should be noticed that Fearing township was the seat of one of the very early libraries of the west. About 1810-13, the books were purchased by inhabitants of the township. It was a private affair, and in 1816 was incorporated The articles of incorporation limit the property besides books, maps, charts, and the like, to three thousand dollars. As officers until an election could be held: Thomas Stanley, Robert Baird, and Elisha Allen were made directors; John Miller treasurer, and Daniel G. Stanley librarian. In time the association dissolved, the books were distributed among the shareholders and many remain yet in private libraries of their descendants. Many books are of a religious nature, and all are of the weightier class of reading. The latest date noticed on the title page as date of publication, is 1813. In the back fly leaves of many books, are the notes of damages and fines written by the librarian on the return of the book. The principal disasters to the works are from grease spots—suggesting the light of other days.

CHURCHES.

A record of the earliest church in the township (the old Presbyterian church of 1810) appears in the history of Salem township, although it belongs alike to both townships. The old church-building was constructed in 1814, in Stanleyville, on land given by Thomas Stanley. Regular religious services continued until about 1848. An organization styled the Fearing religious society,

was incorporated January 29, 1813, by John H. White, Simeon Tuttle, William Caywood, Daniel G. Stanley, Robert Baird, Isaac Hill, and associates. It was under the auspices of no particular denomination. It was reorganized in 1837, and going down again, was reorganized again in 1853, for business purposes—a dispute having arisen about the ownership of the church property hitherto owned by the Presbyterian church.

On the demise of the Presbyterian church in Stanleyville, three years elapsed and a Congregational church was organized in 1851. A building was erected in 1856, which is still standing. The pastor at that time was Rev. G. L. Fryes. L. L. Fay followed him, and his successor was Rev. Riddle. The present pastor is Rev. C. S. Erwin.

About 1820, a Methodist church was organized in the southern part of the township. One of the most energetic, and perhaps the principal of the organization, was Elder Swormstead, who is well remembered as possessed of a powerful voice, his sermons being audible to a great distance. The meetings then were held in an old school-house, not far from the site of the present Methodist church building, near Wesley station. Among the old members of this church were Underhill Lynch, Abraham Daniels, John Price, Daniel Nicholls, James Brown, William Brown, Lewis Dowling, and their wives, also Mr. Quimby and Deborah Craff.

Quarterly meetings were held sometimes at the house of Mr. Underhill Lynch. In 1847 the church-building was completed, on land given by Mr. Lynch. About 1863 the parsonage was built.

The first camp-meeting in the township was held in 1822, in a sugar grove, on Mr. Lynch's place, near what is called the "overhead bridge" on the railroad. At the second camp-meeting, in about 1840, the pulpit was built between two large sugar trees. Now there was a singular character in the neighborhood at that time—an old worn-out slave, nobody knew how old. He was one of those whose appearance would indicate almost any age—the older, the better the guess. Complexion as black as coal, long, skinny, claw-like fingers, known to everyone as "Frank" (his real name was Francis Lee). He lived the existence of a local nomad, sleeping oftentimes in a hollow log in the woods. This character, some of the wilder sort, who attended this camp meeting, armed with a horn of loud and blatant tone. While the preachers were at supper, Frank and horn ascended one of the sugar trees that guarded the pulpit. The foliage screened him from immediate observation by the large audience which assembled at the evening meeting, and so he remained until the fervor of the meeting was at its height. Then, at a signal from one of the crowd, the impersonator of Gabriel awoke the echoes with a terrific blast. The audience, however, was not so superstitious as that of Lorenzo Dow in the old story, for both they and the minister preaching saw and recognized the trumpeter. In an instant the preacher was transformed into an axeman, and to save himself from being cut down, Frank, who had made his debut as Gabriel, assumed the role of Crocket's coon, and came down, or rather slid down, with more velocity than dignity.

JOHN C. WARD

was born in Fearing township, Washington county, Ohio, May 6, 1843. His father, Robert Ward, was a native of Cheshire, England, and emigrated to this country when a single man. He eventually found his way to this county, where he married Lucy M. Tuttle, and settled in Fearing township. He died July 28, 1879. His widow still survives and is living with her son.

Our subject spent his youth upon the farm, and enjoyed such educational advantages only as the common schools furnished, but of them he made diligent use. When he was nineteen he commenced teaching school, and subsequently taught seventeen terms, generally during the winter months, and working on the farm in the summer. Two winters he taught the Wagner school

in Muskingum township, and walked from his home to his school and back again every day, a distance of three miles. He was elected township clerk of Fearing in the spring of 1866, and reelected in 1867. He served for four years as member of the school board of his township, and has always shown a lively interest in the cause of education. He was an orderly sergeant in the militia, and served in the Morgan raid.

Mr. Ward is in politics a Democrat, and in 1872 was a delegate to the State convention held at Cleveland, and again in 1875 was a delegate at Columbus, when Hon. William Allen was renominated for governor. He is a member of Palmer Lodge, No. 351, Independent Order of Odd Fellows, and past grand of said lodge.

A second Methodist church was organized perhaps half a century ago, and held meetings at first in a schoolhouse, just above Stanleyville. The preachers at the time were Messrs. Kellogg and Lewis. Members were Walter Athey, who was class-leader; John Collins, John Whittock, Joseph Cass, and their wives, also Jesse Hill, Maria Whittock, and Jennie Britton. About 1839, the congregation built a log structure in which they worshipped for eighteen or twenty years. Then the present frame church, east of Stanleyville, was erected by Mr. H. Athey.

Mr. Lewis, of Lowell, has now charge of the church which is known as the Zion Methodist Episcopal church, and belongs to the Lynch circuit.

A branch of the Congregational church of Stanleyville, finding it inconvenient to attend from a distance, built a church for themselves near the Cedar Narrows. The building was erected in 1873, by Thomas Flanders. The church flourished under the pastorship of Rev. Levi L. Fay and has now about thirty members.

The advent of the Germans, among other things, has resulted in the establishment of two churches in Fearing —the First Protestant Evangelist church, and the St. Jacob's church. The former was founded at almost the beginning of this phase of the settlement. As is characteristic of the German churches, the building was erected cotemporaneously with the organization of the church. It was located near Whipple run, and may yet be seen. In 1872 a new building was erected, and the old, having finished its work, was forsaken. The land on which it stands was purchased from Daniel Biehl. The ministers have been as follows: From the organization until 1852, Rev. Schreiner; from 1852 to 1873, Daniel Hirsch; thence to the present, F. C. Trapps. The church has now fifty-two members.

The St. Jacobs church originated in 1858, as follows: In the summer of that year a number of Germans of the southern part of the township met for the purpose of establishing a church. Several concluded to withdraw from the enterprise, leaving only eight heads of families to continue the work. Nothing daunted, they undertook their great task. Their first step was to obtain a church site. This they did of Mr. Chapman, who owned land a mile west of Stanleyville, and who gave a part of it for this purpose on very liberal conditions. The church was erected, a plat set apart for a graveyard, and when the building was complete it was dedicated by Rev. David Hirsch. The eight builders organized and framed a constitution for a congregation.

This was in the early part of January, 1859. The names of these eight founders are: Jacob Biehl, Theobald Mueller, Friedrich Bules, Mr. Trautner, Franz J. Spindler, Michael Mueller, George Adam Trautner and Jacob Schumann.

Since then nineteen families have joined the organization, making in all twenty-seven. Eight of these have withdrawn—three on account of removal from the township, and five from a wish to be unconnected with the church.

The nineteen families composing the church in March,

1881, include five of the original eight families. An admission fee of three dollars is charged for the privilege of membership.

Six ministers, besides Mr. Hirsch, have attended the spiritual wants of the congregation. Mr. Hirsch, with a trifling exception, has been pastor twelve years—the first six years of the existence of the church, and also since April, 1873.

The oldest burying-ground in the township is that at Stanleyville. Perhaps the oldest grave is the one containing the remains of Major Thomas Stanley, who died March 14, 1816. Besides other members of the Stanley family, we find that many old families of the township have availed themselves of this spot as a resting place for their dead. The tombstones bear such names as Collins, Leedham, Whittock, Hodge, Blake, Caywood, Lankford, Cousins, Amlin, Athey, Hill, Kidd, Miller and Morris. The oldest person buried in the yard is Robert Collins, who was born in England in 1762, and died May 6, 1871, in the one hundred and ninth year of his age.

A half mile to the south of the Cedar narrows is the old Chapman cemetery. Originally a private burying-place of that family—begun in about 1816—others availed themselves of their courtesy until, besides the Chapmans, some of the Johnsons, Carlisles, Flanders, Tuttles, Warrens, Guitteaus, Beardsleys, Morgans, Sinclairs and Hazens rest in the little plot.

At the church near Whipple's run, east of the Cedar narrows, there are two graveyards. The later one was begun in 1875, the old ground being filled with graves. This old one has been in existence since 1846, when Peter Biehl died and was buried there.

Near the Cedar narrows is a burial place on the Flanders farm. Members from the families of Flanders, Stewards, Penns and Seevers are here laid to rest.

CHAPTER LII.

INDEPENDENCE TOWNSHIP.

Position and Division—The Ohio River Settlement—Prehistoric Inhabitants—The Valley of Dry Bones—Permanent Settlement—The Leath family—Other Pioneers—The First Orchard—An Early Tavern—The Settlement in 1808—Isaac Rinard and His Mills—The Captivity of Thomas Simons—A Girl Kills a Bear—The Vocalist of the Community—John Rea, the Irish Miller—The Rea Graveyard—Early Schools—A Temperance Movement—The First Store—A Union Church Building—The First Public School—A Useful Settler —First Frame Dwelling—The First Post Office—A Victim of the Freshet of 1832—"One Niggah Enough"—Other Mills—Beginning of German Immigration—Anecdote of Washington—The First Four Wheeled Wagon—The Western End of the Settlements—A Heroine Kills a Ruffian—A Few Doctors—An Incipient Town—It's Store—Early Preaching—Three Churches and the Tripartite Agreement— The First Sunday-school—The Little Muskingum Settlement—The Archer's Fork Settlement—Archer's Home in a Tree—The First Marriage—The First Schools—Private Burial Places—The Decker Mill—The Settlement of the Germans—Other Settlers—The Scotch Neighborhood—The Waernicke Mansion—Churches—Independence Declared a Township—The First Election—A Novel Ballot Box.

INDEPENDENCE township, as now constituted, is that political division of the county bounded on the north by

Ludlow, on the east by Grand View, on the south by Newport and the Ohio river, and on the west by Lawrence. In its physical features it is divided into three parts, one of which directly slopes to the Ohio river, another contributes its waters to form Archer's fork, while the third part embraces the Little Muskingum valley.

The latter division barely lies within the township limits, the bounding ridge cutting, in a diagonal direction, sections thirty, thirty-six and thirty-five. The Ohio river division is a southeasterly slope of some two or three miles, beginning at a ridge entering near the encroaching corner of Grand View and reaching southwesterly to the further corner of section thirty-two. This portion of the township, a territory approximating thirteen square miles, was settled before the other two. The tide of emigration always seeks the valleys of the large streams first. The rivers were the only highways of the settlers, the banks of the rivulets their first foot-paths.

It does not belong here to treat at length of the first human beings who are known to have existed here, nor of that later race that made the country that our forefathers found, so much worse than uninhabited. This has been done at the beginning of the book. The most lasting reminders of their existence that were left here by these races were the graves and skeletons of their dead. One of the most remarkable of these traces existed until as late as, it may be, 1840. About a hundred yards from the Ohio, on the land now owned by John Butler, first owned by John Burris, is a rocky ledge, eight or nine feet high, under which was a collection of about a cart load of human bones, some of them of remarkable size. This circumstance gave name to the little stream—Bone run—in this vicinity.

SETTLEMENT.

The first white family that is known to have chosen what is now Independence for their home, was the Leath family. They settled at the mouth of the run bearing their name. This stream, rising far in Grand View, near its western boundary, as far north as Matamoras, takes a southerly course through one of the romantic valleys in which the country abounds, almost parallel to the Ohio, and empties into the latter river a few hundred yards on the Independence side of the Grand View line.

Little is known about this man or his family. He probably cleared the first land in the township, presumably above the mouth of the run. His settlement was either in the latter part of 1700 or first of 1800. His stay was short, for he moved away soon after burying his wife, Sarah, who died in 1804. She was buried in Grand View township near the line and the river. This, the first death in the township, was the origin of the first graveyard in the settlement.

In it now rest all that is earthly of the loved ones of the first families in the settlement: The Littles, Morelands, Riggs, Browns, Haldrens, as well as those of the settlement in Grand View—Burris, Dye, McMahon, Parr and others.

A few years ago the land composing the graveyard, was deeded by Mr. Haldren to the township, the matter having been neglected until then.

The second family was that of William Little. He and his household, which at that time consisted of himself, wife and three children, came from the Emerald Isle in 1805, in company with the family of William Rea. In 1806 he settled at the mouth of Leath's run, on land purchased and presented to him by his oldest son James, the son of his first wife, Mary Thompson. James had preceded his father and stepmother, Mary McKee, to America, settling in the Shenandoah valley, and rapidly amassing a fortune. William Little was a physician, having graduated at a medical college in Ireland. But his surroundings in that country were such that he could not succeed. He died in 1807, in his seventieth year. He was born in County Down, Ireland.

Of his two children by his second wife, Jane and Mary, Jane married Rhesa Moreland, and Mary married David Murdock.

As Mr. Little came down the Ohio on his way to his new western home, he stopped at Steubenville, and purchased young apple trees which he planted on his arrival, thus starting the first orchard in the township. The last tree was cut down in the winter of 1880–1—a truly patriarchal tree, the trunk measuring eleven feet in girth. The Ridgeway orchard in the same settlement was older than this, but was situated in Grand View.

The William Rea mentioned as the companion of Mr. Little in his emigration from Ireland, also settled as a neighbor, belonging to Independence. His land was that now belonging to Walter Brown. When he left Ireland, his family consisted, besides himself, of his wife, who was Nancy Martin, and two children. The latter number was subsequently increased to seven: William, Samuel, Martin, Margaret, Mary, Eliza, and Nancy. All are now dead, but Nancy, who lives in Mason county, West Virginia. Her first husband was H. A. Riggs; her second, J. P. Harvey.

The travel along shore and stream of the Ohio—the great thoroughfare between the east and her western children—increasing with the growth of the new settlements, it became necessary to provide more suitable accommodations than could be afforded to the belated travellers by the incommodious cabin of the pioneer. William Rea attempted to fill this demand by keeping a tavern at his home. In a short time, about the year 1808, he removed it to the mouth of the stream since named for him, Rea's run—a pretty stream, flowing two miles southeast to a point on the Ohio shore, a mile and a quarter below the mouth of Leath's run. Its waters are swelled by but one stream south, Farnsworth's branch, which enters it from the left, in the lower third of its course. The name that Mr. Rea thought appropriate for his hotel, was "The Travellers' Rest." Mr. Rea abandoned the enterprise, probably soon after the death of his wife in 1821. Mr. Rea was born in Ireland in 1777, and died in this township about 1848, being buried in the graveyard at the mouth of the run.

At this period of the settlement, a family arrived, whose domestic troubles alone cause it to be remembered.

John (or George) Cline was the name of the head of the family, and his wife's maiden name was Clarissa Mc-Cardle, of Middle Island. Cline was constantly inflicting corporal chastisement upon his spouse, and his excuse or pretext for this was that she was too much a friend to alcoholic stimulus. The troubles of this interesting pair furnished a theme for a song that is yet spoken of among the oldest inhabitants. Some time after 1808, Cline with his wife moved away, leaving his first name and his destination to be a subject of differing opinion by his quondam neighbors.

Joseph Holdren and his wife, whose name before marriage was Ruth Ferguson, settled on the place left by Cline. Their children were Thomas, George and Grace. The first two live in Grand View; the daughter is not living. Coleman Holdren, Joseph's brother, settled on the river. He afterwards moved to the middle part of the Newport township shore. He had several children, two were named Joseph and James; the latter lives in Marietta.

By the year 1808 the settlers had become numerous enough to give the settlement a definite form. It lined the bank of the river, beginning with Oliver Aplin's home, over two miles in Grand View, extending down the river embracing the fields of Dickinson, Nathan Parr, David Smothers, Joseph Holdren, Benjamin Ridgeway, and Joseph Burris—all in what is to-day Grand View territory. Those of the settlement in what is at present Independence township have been mentioned. Above Alpin's there was no settler for a considerable distance; the next settlement below was that of Newport. It will thus be seen that the history of the Ohio settlement of Independence merges into that of Grand View and Newport.

The next addition to this settlement was the widow of Samuel French and her children. She came from Tyler county, West Virginia, in which State her husband had died. She was poor and compelled to obtain a living as best she could, nowhere certain of a long stay, and working in different places. She died about 1845. The children of Mr. French and herself were three—two boys and a girl. Only one of these is now living, namely, Charles, who was born in Tyler county in 1803. Since his arrival he has always lived in the township. He was in those early days a youth who worked at odd jobs, helping Mr. Walker to construct Ridgeway's brick house for one thing, spending his leisure, which was probably ample, about the tavern with playmates, or learning to hunt with his stepfather, Thomas Simms. As Mr. French grew older he engaged in the nursery business—was connected with the boating interests of the river, was something of a farmer and has never been married. He lives now with his nephew, Martin O. Hanlon.

The next was the Rizhar family, which settled up Leath's run. This stream has considerable fall, and at one point the valley is very narrow, affording a good place for a dam.

Up to this time the settlement had been without a mill, and in their extremity the pioneers were obliged to resort for their flour and meal to Mills so distant as

Devol's, on the greater Muskingum. Accordingly, a very important accession to the settlement was the skilful and enterprising Isaac Rinard, a German who came about 1809 or 1810 down the river, bearing on his raft millstones that were obtained at Laurel Hill, West Virginia. At the site before mentioned he built a dam and put up a mill. He built a cabin at the same place, which is still standing, though the old mill has long since been at rest. Not content with one enterprise, he built another mill at Mill creek, in Green View township, about 1822, also one on the Little Muskingum, in Monroe county, about four miles above Bloomfield. The children of Mr. Rinard and his first wife were John and Sarah; of the second wife Hester Elder, Isaac, James, Mary, Rebecca, Cynthia, Margaret, and Nancy.

Cotemporary with the settlement of Mr. Rinard was that of Rhesa Moreland, who came from Maryland in company with a friend. He was born about the beginning of the Revolution. He married Jane Little and was the father of three girls and one boy. The latter, John, was killed by the kick of a horse in the summer of 1875.

THOMAS SIMMS AND HIS CAPTIVITY.

About 1810 a man arrived, of adventurous and eventful history. When Thomas Simms was a boy of some eight years of age, living with his kindred near Wheeling, Virginia, the Indians attacked and massacred his grandfather, and several of the family to which he belonged, but spared his life. They took Thomas to what was called Sandusky plains, where they raised him in the ways of their tribe. He seems to have met with great favor in their eyes, for they made him their companion rather than their slave. They trained him carefully and well in the preeminent Indian accomplishment of hunting, teaching him all the subtleties of Indian woodcraft. In his youth he played with Indian playmates, whose almost constant sport was with the bow and arrow. He accompanied the tribe in their warlike expeditions, and was with them in their retreat from near Marietta, when the whites had almost starved them, when they buried their kettle and other utensils, only to have them dug up again by the whites. He learned their language. He was always well treated, except when they had their drunken carousals. During one of these orgies he was chased and wounded in the calf of the leg by a large knife, the blade passing completely through the fleshy part. He luckily managed to secrete himself in a hollow log where he lay all night, listening fearfully to the steps of his temporary enemies as they passed to and fro over his very hiding place, but luckily never thinking to peer in the end of it.

When Simms had reached the years of manhood, the longing came strong upon him to visit the homes of his own race and learn of his friends and kindred. It is said that the Indians allowed him to go "on his own recognizance," having such confidence in his honor as to trust his promise to return. At any rate he did make a visit to his old neighborhood, returning to his foster tribe in a very short time. In a little while he went again to Virginia, and thus severed his connection with the Indians forever. The story is that he escaped from them by frightening an old squaw who was with him at some distance from the camp with the exclamation that the whites were coming. She hurried back to the main body of the Indians, while Simms went in the opposite direction.

Once more with the white people, Simms found himself a child in the knowledge of his race. He took up his abode with James McMahon, in West Virginia, and set earnestly to work under the tuition of the Misses McMahon to retrieve as far as possible the lost years of his captivity. Under his fair preceptresses his progress was, no doubt, rapid, and he soon left the family to enter our settlement, marry Mrs. French, and devote himself to the arts of peace and civilization. He entered the farm where Mr. Charles French now resides, near the Ohio river, a few hundred yards west of Leath's run. Three daughters were born to him, but he took the most interest, apparently, and was oftenest in company with his stepson, Charles, then a youth of seven or eight years. Him he taught in the Indian ways, tutored in their language, told stories of their adventures, of their ways and customs, took with him when hunting—of which occupation the man was very fond, and in which Indian skill had made him an adept—taught to fire the rifle, to carry a deer as the Indians do—with a strip of bark against the forehead. Many other things he taught and told his young companion, most of which have been, unfortunately, forgotten. He identified himself with the tribe which had adopted him, to that extent that to insult or ridicule the tribe was a personal affront to him. A fellow-harvester, by the name of Benjamin Hartwell, once derided the defeat, before mentioned, of his tribe by the whites. Simms started for him with up-raised sickle and flashing eyes, and had not Hartwell run from the field it is probable that a tragedy would have been enacted. Now about that time a delegation of Indians came up the river in three keel-boats, bound for the capital. They stopped at this settlement two or three days, and the Indians frequently came to the house of Simms after learning that he could speak in the Indian tongue. It was on this account that they would eat at his house, refusing food at other places for fear of poison. Simms could converse with only one Indian, who had once belonged to the same tribe that Simms lived with, but had killed one of their number, and taken refuge with the nation he was then representing.

Simms was drafted in the War of 1812, but was excused from service on account of a running sore in his leg. He is described as a small, but heavy-set man, of medium weight, with black hair and quick, dark eyes, but fair complexion. He was the swiftest runner in the whole region about him, and was in every way quick and active. He died about 1816, when a man of apparently forty-five years of age. His death was due to a cold caught from exposure while chasing a bear.

These bears seem to have been more numerous at that time in the neighborhood than in many other parts of the county. In 1815 a young woman of perhaps twenty years, named Susan Riggs, while crossing the Ohio, opposite the settlement, in a canoe, saw a bear about a year old, swimming in the river, and, it is said, killed it with the canoe paddle.

Isaac Wilson and his wife, Margaret, settled a little below the mouth of Rea's run. He came, probably, during the War of 1812. He had but one child, a son named Abijah. He came from near Wheeling, and moved away in a short time to Marion county, as nearly as can be ascertained. He was a relative of Nathan Parr, who was a resident of the Grand View part of the settlement.

Near 1814 George Lewis arrived, from Virginia, it is thought, where he married a lady by the name of Cooper. Two of his children were Nathan and Polly. He was celebrated for his great talent as a singer. He moved down the river to Indiana, where his son, "Nace," has since achieved some political distinction.

In 1820 John Rea, a brother of William Rea, came to the settlement and bought the Rinard property. He had two sons and one daughter. The daughter built the wall about their private graveyard, which is still in existence, and contains but four graves.

John Rea was, of course, an Irishman. He immediately began running the old Rinard mill, which was then in a rather dilapidated condition. The creek got rather high one day when the mill was running, for in hilly countries, such as Independence township, rivulets rise and fall with great rapidity. The rumbling wheel gathered speed; the buhrs began to hum; the old mill tottered as if there were an earthquake, and the Irish miller, too much frightened to shut the water off, cried out to his oldest son: "Sam! Sam! let's go out on the bank an' let her run a weal of hours by hersilf until the wather ebbs."

In about eight or nine years Rea abandoned the old affair, and the site has been without a mill until three or four years ago, when John Yost constructed one at that place.

Samuel Rea, the Sam of the preceding narrative, was quite enterprising. With the exception of William Rea, who made, perhaps, one trading trip, he was the first one of the settlement to carry produce, by boat, to New Orleans. He began this business about the year 1824. His method was to build a flat-boat in the summer, and in the meanwhile scour the country for its produce of dried fruit, such as peaches and apples, buying flour and meal of the millers, and also investing to some extent in other products. At that time vast quantities of peaches were raised in this region, the bottoms being almost covered with peach trees.

At this period an important industry of the district was the manufacture of tar. The forests abounded in fine, yellow pine trees, especially in the territory now included in Independence, Liberty, and Ludlow townships. The pine knots from these trees were gathered and burnt in kilns, furnishing the tar, which was sold to traders in the article. Bazil Riggs, living across the river, was a principal dealer in the tar, finding a market for it at Mr. Berry's rope works at Wheeling.

Returning to the year 1821, the death and burial of Nancy Rea, sr., at that date, was the beginning of the first graveyard within the township—that at the mouth of Rea's run. Since then his yard has received all that is mortal of many other of the oldest families—bearing such names as Farnsworth, Ellifrits, Kiddar, Price, Barkwill, and among them, four soldiers named Thompson Rea, Kemper Rea, Isaac Booth, and a Mr. Wolf. The land was given for the yard by William Rea, and is now filled with graves, so that burials in it have ceased.

At an uncertain date, but one not much later than this, a settler came to the neighborhood by the name of Martin O. Hanlon. He was the oldest child of Richard Hanlon and was born in 1818 in what is Pleasant county, West Virginia. He was quite young, when he settled here. He has lived in the neighborhood ever since. His first wife was named Louisa Hearn and his marriage to her was in 1843. She dying in 1878, in 1879 he married Mary A. Heinselman, a daughter of Christian Heinselman, born in 1834. The children are named Charles L. and Mathias F. Charles married Lydia A. Sloan of West Virginia.

Not far from 1823, William Cathers taught a subscription school in a little dwelling house near the Grand View line.

Soon after, Alcinda Bridget, a sister of Dr. Gale, of Newport, opened a like school in a little house on the farm of Rhesa Moreland. These were the first schools in the settlement, as far as ascertained.

In 1830, David Murdock came to the township. His marriage to Mary Little has already been chronicled in the sketch of that family. Though a comparatively late settler, he took a prominent part in making the history of the township. He was born in 1768 in Pennsylvania; married in 1815; settled in the Shenandoah valley—then went to Newport village in 1827, where he kept store three years. He died in 1853; his wife in 1850.

The first temperance movement in the township began through his agency. He kept a temperance pledge in a store which he was managing. Many of the settlement were induced to sign it by his efforts. The store referred to was the first one in the township. By his endeavors, a movement originated, and was carried through successfully, to construct a building of hewed logs, twenty-four feet square, for the use of all religious denominations for worship, and for a public school as well. Thus this structure was at the same time the first church building and the first public school-house in the township.

The first teacher in this building, and consequently, of the first public school in Independence, was Matilda Foster. She began her work in the summer of 1835, and received for it six dollars per month, existing in the meanwhile by "boarding around." She had about twenty pupils. That winter, Ebenezer Battelle taught in the same building for ten or twelve dollars per month. The district school teacher of to-day, who justly, perhaps, feels that his thirty to fifty dollars per month is not a sufficient return for the preparation that a competent teacher must undergo, can still see considerable advance in his monthly salary over his scantily paid pioneer predecessor.

Another settler was Stillman Harvey, of Maine, who came to the settlement in the neighborhood of 1831. His wife was Lona Prescott, and his children were Stillman, John, Asa, Albion, Lona, Ann, James B., Edson Jackson, Barizillar Washington, William Morgareidge, Mary Louisa, Lucien Levant, and Franklin Clariville. He settled on the farm before occupied by Isaac Wilson, owned, however, by John Burris. Mr. Harvey lost all his property by the great freshet of 1832. With characteristic generosity John Burris gave Mr. Harvey his own time to pay for the land.

Mr. Harvey was a farmer and blacksmith, and built the first blacksmith shop in what is now the township. This was upon his first arrival, before which, the neighborhood was obliged to go to Newport village for blacksmithing. He also built, in 1836 or 1837, the first frame dwelling in the township. His views were decided. He was a very strong temperance man, and so strongly inclined to Democracy that he would not patronize, it is said, a store kept by a Republican, although at one time he had to do without his coffee on this account.

In 1845 or 1846, he traded his farm for a store-boat, went to Harmar, and kept store there for a while. He changed his residence often, at one time returning to Independence township and finally passing to his rest in Matamoras. His wife returned to Maine.

By the efforts of Mr. Harvey, David Murdock, Hezekiah Riggs, William Rea, jr., and perhaps one or two others, a post office was established at the settlement, with Mr. Harvey as the first postmaster, and the first, as well, in the township. This was called Ostend. Mr. Harvey was succeeded in this position by Mr. William Rea; the third postmaster was S. C. Riggs, who held the position throughout the administrations of Grant and Lincoln. He had the name changed from Ostend to Wade, in honor of Ohio's bluff senator. The present postmaster is John Bliss. The mail was originally carried to and from this office by a hack that ran between Marietta and Wheeling. Before the establishment of Ostend, post office, the neighborhood went to the town of Newport for their mail.

The freshet just now referred to, that occured in 1832, did great damage to others in the settlement as well as to Mr. Harvey. All along the river, dwellings were swept away, and lives, too, were lost. In the summer of 1880, the erosion of the bank uncovered a large human skeleton that was but eighteen inches below the surface. This was about a quarter of a mile below the mouth of Leath's run, in a place built up by previous river deposits. All the circumstances indicate that this great 1832 freshet had drowned the victim.

By this time the wild animals that were so numerous in the inception of the settlement were comparatively scarce. The first game to disappear is uniformly the bear. In the year 1834 the said bear was killed in the Ohio river division of the township, George Berridge wounded it while he was hunting squirrels at the foot of the hills on Leath's run. The bear took to the river just above the mouth of the run. Bazel Riggs, who lived on the opposite shore, saw the animal and notified the boys at the house, who embarked in two boats. Two or three shots were fired; the bear attempted to board one boat, at the same time a negro occupant of the vessel, with that delicate consideration and sense of the fitness of things often displayed by the darkey race, began to climb out over the opposite gunwale. The bear was dispatched with an oar. The darkey explained his course of procedure by asserting that he considered "one niggah in de boat enough at one time."

In this year the Rinard mill having been abandoned for five or six years, the settlement was without a mill, and Isaac and Hezekiah Riggs supplied the want by the construction of one further up the run. It was a grist and saw-mill combined. The next mill in the settlement was built in about 1840 on the same stream by John Edwards, a native of England, who was born in 1794. He came to the township in 1735, from Pennsylvania. The children of himself and wife, Ann Jeffre, were John, who yet lives in Independence; Susan, who married a Mc-Mahon, a resident of Grand View; Jane, now Mrs. E. Pinning, of Grand View; Richard, of Independence; Mary Ann, now wife of P. Hutchison, of Grand View, and James, now dead. John, the eldest, was born in England in 1820. When twenty-seven years old he married Maria, a daughter of Charles and Phœbe Weber, also a native of England, where she was born in 1828. Their children were ten, seven of whom are now living. The fourth child, Richard, was born in England in 1827. He came to the township with his father, is still living in it, married Ann Weber, sister of Phœbe, in 1853, and is the father of eight children, all living. Both Richard and John are farmers. The next mill in the neighborhood was built by Henry Goodman, on Rea's run.

The old settlement of Independence has been largely replaced by a German element. It may be interesting to note that this phrase of immigration dates from about 1836, when Hans Huffman and John Kinsel came to the township together. Huffman paid Kinsel's passage over the Atlantic, and Kinsel paid the debt after his arrival by work. Huffman and wife, Catharine, had two children, Conrad and Catharine. He was a farmer and died lately. John Kinsel and wife, Catharine, were childless. He was a stonecutter and blacksmith. He died in the county infirmary in 1880, where his wife still lives. The third German family was that of Charles Berlett, a wagonmaker, who, however, removed in a few years to Sunfish, West Virginia.

In 1842 Squire D. Riggs crossed the river from Pleasant county, Virginia, where he was born in 1816. He was the ninth son and eleventh child of Bazel Riggs, whose father was an old settler in Grand View. Bazel was born in Bedford county, Pennsylvania, in 1774. When but three years old he called forth a manifestation by George Washington. Bazel and his oldest sister, Mary, were witnessing, near their Pennsylvania home, the movement of troops during the Revolution. The little child, Bazel, was bewildered and frightened by the unwonted sights and sounds, and began to cry. This attracted the attention of Washington, and he came to the little fellow, and in the kindest manner soothed and reassured the boy.

Mr. Squire D. Riggs married Nancy R. Moreland, a daughter of Rhesa and Jane Moreland, and born in 1818 in the township. The marriage, which was in 1838, resulted in twelve children: Luther P., David M., Asberry A., Mary E., William N., Theodore J., Henry M., Luther M., Benjamin F., Adaline M., Walter L., and Hattie G. Luther P., Mary, and Luther M. are dead. David M. married Loretta Flint, and is a resident of Monroe county; Asberry A. married Mary Morrell, and lives in the township; William married Mary Howell, and lives in Meigs county; Theodore married Rebecca Davis, and is a resident of Independence; Adaline M. married A. Farnsworth, and lives in Richland county; three children are still at home, and Henry lives with his brother Theodore.

The vehicles of the earlier times were crude beyond comprehension by one used to nothing but the stylish and finished affairs that glide along the modern highway. It was not until near 1843 that a four-wheeled wagon was introduced in the township. This was owned by Mr. Riggs. He also bought the first combined reaper and mower a few years ago.

The Chapman graveyard was formed about this time (1843-5) by the burial of George Chapman. By permission of this family, several other families have availed themselves of this ground as a resting place for their dead.

By this time settlement was proceeding in the western part of that division of Independence which is now under consideration. One of the representative settlers in this neighborhood was Richard Bayles, youngest child of Richard, sr., born in New York in 1816. He came to Independence in 1849, and has resided there ever since, his home being on Dana's run, a stream flowing almost due south to the Ohio river, near Newport town. He married Nancy, a daughter of Charles Haynes, and born in Noble county in 1819. This union, which was in 1837, resulted in three children: Mary M., Richard, and Westley.

The next incident, in point of time worthy of record, is a tragedy. The settlement had long stood in fear of a desperate character by the name of George McCammick, who seemed to threaten and commit violence without motive. His wife was in constant dread of him. One evening in January, 1852, he left her and her children with a threat of murder when he should return. About dusk he arrived at the home of John Cisk, an inoffensive citizen, and after threatening to kill the family, aimed a pistol at Cisk, who would doubtless have been murdered had he not possessed a courageous wife. She seized a chair and demolished it over McCammick's head. Then with another chair gave him a second blow, leaving him prostrate outside the house. Leaving her husband in care of the household, she made her way through the snow in her stocking feet to the house of a neighbor, a considerable distance away and brought back assistance. McCammick was found dead, his skull having been fractured. The homicide was considered perfectly justifiable and no account was taken of the matter by the courts.

From the time of Dr. Little, down to the war of the

Rebellion, there was no physician in the township. During the war Dr. Wilson located here; next to him was Dr. Sloan, who came at the close of the war, and left a short time ago. The present practicing physician is James Taylor, who began his practice in 1881.

The landing and post office at the mouth of Rea's run, has caused the erection of a few houses at the place. One of these is a store kept by Robert W. Bedilion, who came to the place in 1864. He is the seventh child of Abraham Bedilion, and was born in Pennsylvania in 1837. In 1864 he married Mary L., daughter of Samuel Mansbarger, whose birth was in West Virginia in 1840. His eight children are: William D. J., Nancy M. R., Robert H. B., Mamie, Abbie L., Clem E., Julia L., and Sarah E. Mamie is dead. Mr. Bedilion has been justice of the peace and township treasurer.

It is remarkable, that not until this stage of the narrative the writer is able to chronicle the digging of the first well on the Ohio river bottom in the township. This was by James Louderback in 1874.

Two years after, in 1876, the exigencies of travel on the river, justified the establishment of a light station on the Independence shore. This is some three-fourths of a mile below the mouth of Rea's run.

It must not be supposed that during all these years the people of the settlement neglected their religious interests. It is almost certain that the first preaching in the community was done by Mr. Davis Smothers in the first decade of the century. He had a charge in West Virginia opposite his home, which was in Grand View. He also preached on the Ohio side from house to house. But from that time until the erection of the public church building before referred to, the dwellers in the settlement under consideration repaired to Newport for religious exercises. The building of this hewed-log church in 1835 obviated the necessity of this. It was begun in January and finished in May. Immediately three separate organizations of respectively Presbyterian, Methodist, and Baptist belief, began to use it. By an amicable arrangement they used it in rotation. This continued without difficulty or disagreement until 1855, when the Presbyterians consolidated with their brethren at Newport and ceased to use the building. In 1858 the Methodists built a meeting-house on the upper side of Rea's run. The Baptists continued in their old place of meeting until 1867, when they began to use a school-house built about that time near the church. The old public meeting-house thus deserted is now used as a barn.

The first members of the above organization of Presbyterians were John Green, David Murdock—who were also the first elders—Mary Murdock, Jane Moreland, Maria Bailey, John Green's wife, daughter and two sons; Ira Bosworth; Luther Edgerton, his wife and daughters, Ellen Cook, and William Rea. The church was organized under the leadership of Rev. Bennett Roberts. The first regular preacher was Rev. Luke Dewitt, who was employed by the Home Missionary society.

The Methodist church was organized with the following membership: Samuel Rea, class leader; Elizabeth Moreland, John Moreland, Eliza Rea, John Berridge,

his wife and two daughters, Daniel Dye and wife, and others. The second class leader was Martin Rea, a brother of Samuel. The three earliest preachers were Charles Talbott, Pardon Cook, and Philip Green. At this time the church belonged to the Woodsfield circuit. They now worship in their building mentioned above, the dedication sermon of which was preached by Alexander Bell. Their present preacher is J. H. Doan. The church belongs to the Newport circuit, and the class leader is Henry Whetstone.

The Baptists started with a very small membership— the Holdrens, Prices, and McMahons, with one or two others. The first preacher in the township was the father of Jeremiah Dale—the next was Jeremiah Dale himself. He began about 1825 to preach from house to house. In 1831 he died. The minister who held the first Baptist meetings in the union church building was Allen Darrow. The church is now without a pastor, the last one being Rev. Hanlon.

The first Sabbath-school in this division of Independence was held in a little house on Rigg's landing. This building was constructed by William Rea, jr., who used it as an office whence he watched for the arrival of steamers and employed his time in shoemaking and the like work. About 1834 Elizabeth Moreland organized and conducted a Sabbath-school in this building, whence it was removed to the union church. The next superintendent was Samuel Rea.

THE LITTLE MUSKINGUM SETTLEMENT.

Next to the Ohio settlement, in point of time, is that of the northwest corner of the township, which, by virtue of its location on the Little Muskingum river, is cotemporary with the old settlement along that valley, in Ludlow and Lawrence townships. Its history more properly belongs to either of those townships, but as township lines were not run for the convenience of the historian, a sketch of the little district will be inserted here.

It is something less than four square miles in area, and contains about a mile of the course of the Little Muskingum. This stream, passing diagonally through the corner section, cuts off about a quarter of it in its northwest part. The winding creek pays a second and very short visit to the township in section thirty-five, to receive the waters of Elk run, which stream rises in the centre of section thirty.

The first families to settle here were those of Jesse Flemming and Vachel Dickerson. It is not known who made the first settlement, but the distinction probably belongs to the Flemmings.

Jesse was the son of Peter Flemming, whose wife, Nancy, was the widow of James Burris, and daughter of James Wilson. Peter Flemming was one of the earliest settlers of Ludlow township, and died in 1833. Jesse was born at the mouth of Fishing creek, in 1791. He is said to have been the first white male child born between Wheeling and Marietta. His settlement was very early, and on section thirty-six. Paralysis ended his life at Matamoras, in 1872. His wife's name was Nellie Collins, who said she was born on "the eastern shore." The children were Thomas, Joseph, Wealthy and four or five others.

Vachel Dickerson was raised in this part of the county, and was the son of Thomas Dickerson. He settled before 1818.

The early settlers of this section of so limited extent were necessarily few. The later settlers, however, cannot be treated in detail, but one or two representative families deserve mention.

In 1846 Joseph A. Duval, the third child of Marion and Mary (Chambers) Duval, came from Jefferson county, where he was born in 1823. He married, in 1845, Nancy C., daughter of Joseph Carle. Their eleven children are named respectively: Margaret E., Ephraim F., a resident of Kansas, Eva A., William B., Rebecca J., Joseph C., Maria A., Washington M., Jackson B., George E. and Mary C. Mr. Duval is a farmer, and still lives in Indiana.

The year of 1859 brought Henry Mead to the settlement. His father was named Uriah. Henry was born in Maryland in 1816. He changed his residence several times, finally coming to the township from Monroe county. In 1833 he married Orpha Dodd, of Belmont county. Eight children were born to them: Elizabeth C., Anna D., David G., Nancy A., Mary E., Joseph H., Rachel C. and Samuel H., one of whom, Elizabeth, is now dead.

In *ante bellum* times a post office was established here, on the Little Muskingum, and appears under the title of Lawrence. The postmaster is William Flemming.

ARCHER'S FORK SETTLEMENT.

The third and last division of the township is that drained by Archer's fork, an area of between twelve and thirteen square miles. The region lies between the two ridges, elsewhere described, and furnishes to Archer several runs, named usually from some owner of the land through which they run. One stream, a short run, entering from the right near the centre of this district, is named Coal run, from the attempts formerly made to mine that article from the hills that line its valley. It may be remarked here, that the coal of Independence township is not in thick enough seams to warrant profitable mining.

Archer's fork is named from an early settler or squatter, about whose settlement there is a difference of opinion. One story places Mr. Archer at the mouth of this stream, another relates that he was the first settler, or rather the first squatter in the division of the township now under consideration. According to tradition Archer eloped with another man's wife, came to this secluded region, chose his home about three hundred yards below the mouth of Cady's run, on the banks of the main stream, and there lived romantically with his companion in a hollow sycamore tree, with no gossiping neighbors to molest or make them afraid. Whether the pair tired of their solitude or wished to find some spot more likely to remain unpeopled by others is not known, but before the first permanent settler came into this valley, the couple had taken their departure.

The upper course of Archer's fork was settled first. The first permanent settler was James Cady, who came

from the Ohio river January 8, 1818, to this valley, and settled on Archer, about a quarter of a mile below the mouth of Cady's run. He moved into a house built by Alexander Walker, a settler of Grand View, who had been on Archer the year previous, and lived in it from spring to fall. Mr. Cady was in this house until spring, then he moved into a building of his own erection.

James Cady was born in Vermont, near the year 1779, and died about 1865, aged eighty-six years. He was a soldier in the War of 1812, his business being that of a teamster. His wife was Elizabeth Chandler, who was born about 1783, and died about 1860. The children were: Charles C., Ira, Abijah, James, and Eliza. Only Ira and James survive. The latter moved to Indiana in 1861. Ira, who was born in 1810, married Veronica Sipple in 1849, and settled on Cady's run, a stream flowing west to the centre of the region under discussion. The children are: Norman S., George, Ira H., and Margaret Ellen, all living in the neighborhood.

The second family in the settlement was that of Benjamin Burris, who came from Grand View in the spring of 1818. His wife was Susan Riggs, and they had no children when they came, but during their residence on Archer's fork, eleven children were born to them, viz: Mary, Johnson, Basil, Jackson, Lemuel, Benson, Elizabeth, Harriet and Lavina (twins), Volney, and Adaline. Two other children were born in Texas, whither the family moved in 1839. About the year 1828 Mr. Burris built the first mill in the settlement, a saw-mill, situated just below the mouth of Coal run. After the freshet of 1832 he added to it the machinery of a grist-mill. Burris was a lumberman, running his lumber down the Little Muskingum, also from his own mill down Archer. The usual destination of the lumber was Cincinnati. He was also a stock raiser and trader. He made a trip or two to New Orleans in the latter business. He was one of the three that built the Templeton mill below the mouth of Archer's fork. He was a Free Mason. His oldest child, Mary, was born in 1818, and was the first person born in the settlement.

A considerable time having elapsed, the next arrival was that of Mr. Burris' paternal grandmother and her daughter, Nancy. They settled in a cabin probably built by the resident grandson, across the stream from the historic Archer sycamore. At that time the elder of the two was the widow of Peter Flemming, mentioned before as the parent of Jesse Flemming, the pioneer on the Little Muskingum. After two or three years the pair moved over to the Little Muskingum, where Mr. Flemming died. Nancy lived a while in Ludlow, and is now an inmate of the infirmary.

Following these was Jeremiah Treadway, who settled down Archer, near where the township line is, in 1824. His wife's maiden name was Hopp. They moved away in five or six years.

The next settlement was probably that of Samuel Parr, who came from Virginia to the Little Muskingum, in Ludlow township, and then arrived at Archer in 1828. His mother, then a widow of Obseliah Peyton, accompanied him, also two half brothers and a half sister. He made his home about a half mile above the mouth of Cady's run. While in Ludlow, having become acquainted with Eliza, the daughter of James Cady, he married her, and thus she became the first bride in the settlement. Their marriage took place in 1825, Squire Felix Hanlon officiating.

About this time Solomon Tice moved into the neighborhood, and located at the mouth of Road run, a stream entering Archer's fork in section eleven, on the farm now owned by R. O. Hanlon. Solomon and his wife had eleven children: David, Catharine, Susan, John, Mary, Solomon, Lavina, Louis, Amaziah, George, and Cynthia. In this decade the first school on Archer's fork was opened. It was a summer school, maintained by subscription, and taught in 1829. The teacher was Miss Anna Aplin, and the school-room was an up-stairs room in the hewed log house of Benjamin Burris. There were nine pupils: Diana Cady, James Cady, Mary Burris, Johnson Burris, Bazel Burris, Lemuel Burris, Jackson Burris, Adaline Riggs, and Nancy Burns. The latter lived with John Burris in Grand View, on the Ohio river, but, there being no school in that neighborhood, she was sent to this settlement.

In 1834 or 1835 another subscription school was taught in the neighborhood by Elizabeth Moreland.

Near the year 1830, began the oldest cemetery in this district—the private one of the Cady family, although others also now use the ground. The occasion of its formation was the death of an infant child of Mr. Cady. The burial of the baby was the first in the cemetery. It is situated on land owned by Messrs. Hill and Schrader, and contains the graves of Zebulon Chandler, who came to the neighborhood about 1825, from Pennsylvania; James Cady and his venerable wife, David Cline and Sarah Cline.

The next oldest burying-ground is on the farm of Moses Decker. The first burial was that of a little daughter of Levi Decker, in 1830. Buried here are members of the Decker family, Joseph Luddington, who was killed by the fall of a tree, James Monroe Smith, and others. This, too, is a private yard. The settlement contains no public cemetery.

The next mill after the Burris mill, was built about 1833, by the Deckers—Abraham, Moses, and Levi. This was a saw-mill, and the furniture that the Decker brothers manufactured is described as very fine work. Specimens of their handiwork—tables, cupboards, and the like—generally made from wild cherry, still exist in the houses of some of the old residents.

The wave of German immigration that has so largely covered the township, reached Archer's fork about 1835. The first families were those of Goodballet, Sipple, and Yost. By this time settlers came in too rapidly to fully mention. About 1845 one of those moving in was Daniel Stewart, a native of Pennsylvania, who came to Monroe county, Ohio, in the first place, and removed thence to Independence. In 1857, or near that time, he returned to Monroe county and there died. He was the father of nine children—two boys and seven girls: John II., the oldest son, was born in Monroe county June

25, 1822; came to the township in 1853; has lived here since. He married Mahala, daughter of James Elson, who was born in 1827. This marriage was in 1843, and resulted in thirteen children: James P., Hiram, Whitten, Stanton E., Landora, Harriet I., William W., Louisa, Mary L., Bishop M., Eliza J., John E., and T. L. All are living but James P. and Louisa.

Andrew McMaster became a member of the community in 1848. He came from Belmont county, where he was born in 1818. In 1841 he married Lavina, daughter of Zebulon Day, and born April 28, 1823. Mr. McMaster has been justice of the peace and notary public for several years.

Those acquainted with the township have noticed on the boundary ridge, between the Ohio slope and the valley, a small Scotch settlement. This originated with the advent of David Deuchers, a son of James Deuchers. David was born in Perthshire, Scotland, in 1820. He came from West Virginia to Independence and settled where he now lives, in 1852. He married Isabel, a daughter of Daniel Murray, and a native of Scotland, where she first saw the light in 1827. The wedding was in 1846, and the children born to them number eleven: James, Isabel, Virginia, David, Daniel, George, Catharine, Sarah, Alexander, Elizabeth and Maggie. All are living but Catharine and David. James married Martha Griffin. Isabel became Mrs. Timothy Bliss. Daniel wedded Eliza Bliss, and George became the husband of Margaret A. Sprague, all residents of Independence. David Deuchers is a blacksmith, and has been honored with the position of township trustee. James, the first born, keeps a store opposite his father's house that does a flourishing trade. The year of his marriage is 1873, and his children are David, Burton E., and Mary E.

Another and later settler in the settlement is James Taylor, the fourth child of Mungo Taylor, and born in Perth county, Scotland, June, 1814. His settlement in Independence dates from the year 1856. In 1839 he married Margaret Deuchers. His children number eight, as follows: Mungo, Isabel, Catharine, John, James, William, David, and a child deceased. Mr. Taylor has been township trustee, and is a farmer.

In the following year (1857), William O. Riley came to the settlement. He was the fifth child of Dennis O. and Mary. His birth was in Belmont county, in 1826, whence he moved to Independence. His wife, Elizabeth, is the daughter of Abraham Ramsey, was born 1839; married in 1856, and is the mother of fourteen children; eight boys and six girls.

Near the residence of Mr. Deuchers is a church and cemetery. The latter began in April, 1864, when a child of Mr. Beaver died. This was the first burial in the yard.

About this time the first brick house in the township was erected—the building of Ernest Waernicke, a wealthy and enterprising citizen of the community.

The next enterprise in the vicinity that is worthy of remark was that of Nicholas Schar, who, about the year 1868, came from Monroe county with his family, settled in section eleven, and started a cheese factory. The enterprise lasted some three or four years, when, the business failing to prove remunerative, he abandoned it.

Until within three or four years the dwellers on Archer's fork were without a post office in their midst. At that time, however, one was established, close to the town-house, with Augustus Hill as postmaster. The mail is carried overland, there being no other way at present to get there.

The history of the churches in this neighborhood begins with that of the Methodist organization. Sometime before 1843 the Methodist meetings, held as circumstances permitted, resulted in an organization of that denomination, comprising as members Abraham Decker and his wife, Jacob Shockey and wife, William Chapman and wife, and others. The meetings from house to house continued until 1847, when a log meeting-house was built on a half-acre deeded for the purpose by David Cline. Then in a few years the organization went down.

But a United Brethren minister by the name of Cecil came shortly before 1851, and organized a church of that denomination in the building. The membership embraced several of the old members of the Methodist organization. The new church lasted but two or three years.

For nearly a score of years the old structure was without regular services. Occasionally meetings would be held in it, oftenest by Alexander Bell. In 1869 the Christian Union church began to use it, and continued to do so until the building of their own meeting-house in 1874. The old log building is now used by the Methodists again, they having taken possession in March, 1879. The church belongs to the Newport circuit, and the minister at present is Rev. J. H. Doan.

By the year 1847 or 1848, the German element in the vicinity had become strong enough to establish the German Lutheran church. The first members of this were Adam Yost, Martin Sippel, Henry Goodballet, Christian Hanselman, John Kinsel, John Wagner, William Saelick, and their wives, also Mrs. Huffman, then a widow, and others. A church building was erected on land given by Messrs. Yost and Holstein. The first preacher was the Rev. Bairnes. The present minister (1880) is Rev. Wintrin.

A series of meetings under the auspices of the Christian, or Disciple, denomination began to be held in the neighborhood about the year 1853. The leader of these meetings was John Henderson, of West Virginia, who may be called the founder of the church that resulted. About the year 1870, at a meeting in the Eddy school-house, not far from the head of Coal run, an organization was effected, embracing in its membership Henry and Alfred Eddy, Simeon Bennett, Levi Thomas, Timothy and Stephen Ward, Savannas More, and their wives. For a period of about three years the church met in the school-house and other places. Then, near the year 1873, during the ministry of John Henderson, a meeting-house was erected on the ridge at the head of Coal run. Alfred Eddy bought and presented the ground on which it stands. Since that time the ministers who have served the congregation are John Moody, Joseph Thom-

as, Ezra Barker, and John Henderson, who is now pastor. The church has thirty-seven members, and is known by the name of Mount Hope.

Among many institutions that refer their origin to the great Rebellion is the Christian Union church. During the latter part of this war, Rev. C. F. Given, a graduate of Marietta college, a Methodist preacher, and a Democrat, claiming that his Methodist brethren treated him unfairly on account of his politics, issued a call for the organization of a new church with the avowed object of excluding politics from its doctrine, discussions, and practice. Several churches were organized in obedience to this call, under the name of the Christian Union church. A minister by the name of Daniel Keller, from the interior of the State, came to the neighborhood and held meetings under the auspices of this new denomination at "Duval's Knoll, called Point Pleasant." Afterwards, William Weddele came and organized the church in Independence. Within the first year, about sixty members joined. This church held meetings on Archer's fork, some distance below Point Pleasant, but residents of that place were among the organizers of the church. Afterwards they organized a separate branch in their own neighborhood.

The building of this first church has already been referred to as erected in 1874. The land on which it stands is owned by Thomas Cline, who has given a lease to the church, permitting it to use the land as long as it chooses for church purposes. At present this branch has no pastor.

The Point Pleasant church, just mentioned, was organized about two years after the above body. The first minister was Mr. Weddele; the second, John Camden; and the third and present one, Thomas Cline. The meetings were held in a school-house until within three years of the present. Then a church building was erected and dedicated a year or two afterward.

The Little Valley church, another one of this denomination, was organized in the spring of 1872. Then the meetings were held in the so called "Hanlon school-house." Before organization meetings were held in Grand View, in the Delong school-house. In 1873 a meeting-house was built on land furnished by George Tice. The church now worships in this.

In the midst of the little Scotch settlement before referred to, is a small Baptist church building. The society organized in 1864, under the auspices of L. K. Adkins, of Newport. It was originally named Davis Run chapel—the meetings being at first held near the upper course of that stream. The building used for that purpose was a log school-house. Afterwards the present church building was erected, and is now familiarly known as "Deuchers chapel." This structure dates from 1871. Although at first called the Davis Run church, it was reorganized in 1870 by the efforts of David Deuchers, Isaac Atkins, A. C. Yonally, and the Rev. Rush. But it was not disconnected from the Newport church, of which it was a part from the first, until March 15, 1879. At that time, a request was presented and granted for the separation and independent existence of the Regular Baptist church, of Independence. The following persons signed the petition and may hence be considered the charter members of the church: Margaret A. Sloan, Loretta Yonally, D. Deuchers, Sarah M. Deuchers, Isabel Deuchers, George Deuchers, Virginia A. Deuchers, Isabel Bliss, Asa Yonally, Mary L. Yonally, Samantha Sloan, William Todd, Julia A. Todd, Sarah E. Yonally F. C. Richardson, and S. T. Echols. The ministers were Revs. Messrs. Rush, Hiram Gear, Dunn, and Luther Hanlon.

The territory which was the scene of all that precedes was originally a part of Newport township. In March, 1840, the two eastern tiers of sections in the township were attached to Grand View. When Independence was established the sections numbered five, six, eleven and twelve were still allowed to remain with Grand View. In the commissioner's journal, under the date June 3, 1840, appears the establishing act, which may not be inaptly styled the declaration of Independence. It reads as follows:

On the petition of sundry inhabitants of the township of Newport, praying to be set off into a new township separately and apart from said Newport, on consideration of said petition, the commissioners do hereby agree to constitute a new township in the county of Washington, to be known and designated as the township of Independence, and to be constituted of the following territory, to-wit: Sections No. 2, 3, 4, 8, 9, 10, 14, 15, 16, 17, 18, 19, 20, 21, 22, 23, 24, 25, 26, 27, 28, 29, 30, 31, 32, 33, 34, 35, 36, and fractional sections Nos. 1, 7, and 13.

The early records of Independence township are missing from the clerk's office. Fortunately, however, something is remembered of the first election, which was for township officers. It was held in the cabin built by Benjamin Burris, after he came to Archer's fork. At that time it was occupied by John Goodman. It is thought that William Rea, jr., was the clerk of the election. The ballot "box" was a teakettle. The first justice of the peace was Stillman Harvey. Before his term expired, another justice was created by the election of James S. Cady. The latter was the first treasurer of the township, and remained in that office for many years.

For the past decade, the officers have been as follows: Trustees, 1870, Ruben Cline, Samuel Farnsworth, John Hoppel; 1871, George Brown, James Braden, John Hoppel; 1872, George Brown, William Sipple, Ira Cady; 1873, George Brown, John Hoppel, David G. Mead; 1874, David Mead, John Hoppel, James Braden; 1875-6, John Hoppel, Ira Cady, David G. Mead; 1877, John Hoppel, David G. Mead, George Brown; 1878-9, George Brown, John Hollstein, Samuel Miller; 1880, Walter Brown, John Hollstein, J. H. Bohlen. Clerks: 1870, J. W. Richardson; 1871, 2, 3, 4, and 5, Abner Powell; 1876, 7, 8, and 9, J. W. Richardson; 1880, J. M. Twinem. Treasurers: 1871-2, Ernest Waernicke; 1873 and 4, R. W. Bedillion; 1875, Charles Schrader; 1876, George Brown; 1877, 8, 9, and 1880, Charles Schrader. Assessor: 1871-80, Malachi Scott.

In 1880 the minority judge of elections was Henry Whetstone, and the constables were, L. H. Wells and W. B. Duval. The township has now eight ward districts and eight school districts. One of the latter is an independent district, and out of the control of the township board of education.

After the organization of the township, a log building was constructed as a town house. This has since been torn down, and about 1864 the present one was built

The population of Independence in 1840, was three hundred and thirty-five; in 1860, one thousand five hundred and seven; in 1870, one thousand three hundred and ninety-five; in 1880, one thousand eight hundred and twenty-eight.

CHAPTER LIII.

LUDLOW TOWNSHIP.

Birth of the Township—Changes in Territory—Records—Early Elections—A Poor Place for Whigs—Population—The Little Muskingum and Its Tributaries—Scenery—The Earliest Settlement—The "Oldest Inhabitant"—A Governor Without a Subject—Silver Mining—Salt Boring—A Long-lived Family—A Grave Perplexity—First Birth—Early Agricultural Wants and Contrivances—Bark Harness—First Blacksmith Shop—First Road—A House Founded Under a Rock—David Cline and His Town—Abner Martin, the Pioneer Preacher—The Methodists—The Disciples—The Catholics—Solomon's Temple and the Baptists—Schools—Physicians—Mills—Bloomfield—Scotttown

THIS township derives its name indirectly from a surveyor of that name, who ran the north boundary of the donation land called the Ludlow line. On July 17, 1819, the county fathers established the township and named it after the line that now bounds it on the north. At that time, however, the township extended two miles north of this line. The establishing act, as found in the commissioners' journal, is as follows:

July 17, 1819.

On the petition of Joseph Dickerson, John Davis, and Kinzer D. Jolly and others, inhabitants of the third township in the sixth range.

The board of commissioners of Washington county establish the third township in the sixth range, together with section No. 36 of township two, in said sixth range, into a new and independent township and election district, to be hereafter known and distinguished by the name and denomination of Ludlow. And order that the qualified electors of said district meet at the house of Daniel Hearn, in said town, on the fourth Monday of August next, at 10 o'clock A. M., to elect their township officers agreeably to law.

In 1851 all above the Ludlow line became a part of Monroe county. In 1840 the establishment of Independence declared the "section No. 36 in township two" a part of that township. These are the only two changes that Ludlow has suffered territorially since its establishment. It now contains twenty-two and a half square miles, and is bounded north by Monroe county, east by Grand View, south by Grand View and Independence, and west by Liberty.

As is, unfortunately, often the case, the township records for the earlier political history of Ludlow are wanting. They were destroyed by fire. Consequently, dependence must be placed in the uncertain memory of man for what few early township officers he may chance to recall. The earlier elections were held principally at the house of Christopher Dickson, sr. This continued for a great many years. Afterwards a school-house was used for the purpose, then a log town house was built about 1840, at Bloomfield. This was replaced two or three years ago by a frame township house, in which elections are now held.

The early justices of the peace that are remembered are Joseph Dickerson, who was probably the first; Charles McIntyre, David McIntyre, and, later, Daniel Flint.

By the year 1840 there were about sixty voters in the township, but this number was of small benefit to the Whig party. A list of those who through these years stuck to the Whigs would begin and end with the names Samuel Kean, Solomon Hearn, Porter Flint, and George Adams, who says he was at one time the only Whig in the township.

The township officers for the year 1880–81 are: Elijah Haught, James Drum and Jonathan Cline, trustees; E. G. Smith, clerk; A. J. Watson, treasurer; Christopher Dickson, assessor; William Hendershot and Samuel Boston, constables; Isaac Tucker and John Hall, justices of the peace.

The population of Ludlow in 1840 was five hundred and thirty-nine; in 1860, one thousand and forty-three; in 1870, one thousand and eighty-two; and in 1880, one thousand three hundred and seventy-four.

TOPOGRAPHY.

The principal stream of the township is the Little Muskingum river, which, with very crooked course, bisects the township from northeast to southwest, so that the two halves dovetail together in much the same way as the different pieces of a child's puzzle block. The runs that enter the river from the left flow from a water-shed in the southeast part of township, and take, in general, a direction north of west. The principal of these creeks are, beginning up the river, Edwards' run, Wilson's run, Cedar run, Pice run and Hendershot run. Wilson's run is named from an old hunter by the name of Israel Wilson, who made its valley his favorite hunting ground. The derivation of the name of Cedar run is evident. The others are named from the owners of farms near their mouths.

The tributaries entering the Little Muskingum from the right flow almost due south from a water-shed in Monroe county. Those named are, proceeding down the river, Long eddy, Sackett's run and Winget's run. The first was named from the eddy formed at its mouth by its current and the conformation of the banks of the Little Muskingum at that point. Sackett's run was the resort of a hunter by that name, and Jacob Winget was the first settler on the stream by that name.

The township, like the others in its vicinity, is quite hilly. Many of these hills, however, are covered with the red soil that yields so well, and, if carefully tilled, affords good crops. The seams of coal are the same as in Liberty and Salem townships, but not so thick or extensive.

The Little Muskingum valley is famed for its beauty. Almost any of the hills that overlook this stream afford fine prospects. This may be particularly remarked of the ridge at one of the southern bends of the river, about a mile above the mouth of Pice's run. Through the trees on this ridge, whose limbs form a rustic frame for the scene, near two miles of the course of the river can be descried as it swings far to the south, laps the foot of the ridge under the spectator's feet, and bears off to the west. In the elbow thus formed lies the "made land of many an acre of the proverbial breadth"—the child of the river and the northern hills. By almost insensible gradations, the level merges to the rolling, and finally to the hill land back of it. Far back the dividing ridge, and to the right and left the ridge that turns the stream from sight bound the view. When the leaf and grain have painted this prospect in green and gold, it must be a sight for an artist. Unfortunately for the description, however, the writer was forced to be content with a winter view, when the snow was gone. A rain was falling, alike dampening to soil, clothes and appreciation of the beautiful, and in this case the bleak prospect proved the untruth of the adage that "beauty unadorned 's adorned the most."

SETTLEMENT.

As is everywhere the case, the first settlements were along the streams, usually in the order of the size of these streams. All the early settlements in Ludlow were along the Little Muskingum, and generally, at the mouths of its tributaries. The oldest in Ludlow is the Tice run. The first ones to make a home here, and, consequently, the pioneers of the township, was the family of Solomon Tice.

Solomon Tice, sr., was known as "Governor" Tice. He was a blacksmith, farmer, and hunter, and came from New York city. He settled in Ludlow in 1797, on the east side of the Little Muskingum, about two miles below Bloomfield, where he died about 1838, at the age of ninety-three.

At one time he was in Virginia, and while there, received one vote for governor of that State. This gave him the cognomen of governor which stuck to him until the day of his death. He was a man of remarkable energy, which did not desert him even in his old age. One of his ruling passions was the desire to amass wealth suddenly. In 1833 he dug for silver on "Silver Mine run" known afterwards as Campbell's run, in the upper part of the township. He found shining metal which he took to be silver, probably thinking that the saying "All that glitters is not gold," did not apply to silver. He took a half bushel of it to Wheeling as a test, and there learned his mistake. This was not his only attempt. The hills of Independence and other places were the scene of his prospecting expeditions. In 1825 he bored for salt on Fifteen Mile creek opposite the mouth of Mill fork, penetrating the earth three hundred feet. Petroleum, of whose value he was then ignorant, calling it the "Devil's grease," stopped his enterprise. Throughout his long life, he boasted he had never attended church. His family was remarkable for longevity. He had seventy grandchildren, eighteen great-grandchildren, and a few great-great-grandchildren before he died. He was noted for his wit and sociability. He related as his own experience the well known story of the capture of seven Indians by knocking the wedge from a partially split log, which they had been induced to try to pull apart.

His parents were Martin and Mary; his wife was Mary Collier. He had six sons and two daughters. Martin died young. James was born in 1775, and owned six hundred acres of land. His mania was the acquisition of land. He owned a saw-mill on the Little Muskingum above the mouth of Hendershot's run. He died on the way to Oregon in 1851. His wife was Sarah Strimback.

The first death in his family was that of a daughter. The longevity of the Tices has been remarked. James and family had not been in the habit of attending funerals. They therefore were at a loss to know the customary way in which funerals were conducted, and had to seek their neighbors to learn how. John, another son of Solomon, was born in 1780, and settled near his father in Ludlow. His two wives were sisters: Catharine and Christina Cline. Another son, Solomon, jr., was born in 1782, and settled on Archer's fork in Independence. He married another of the Cline sisters, Rosanna. The next son, Jacob, shot himself at a sugar camp in trying to kindle a fire with a loaded gun. Mary died in infancy. David settled in Virginia, from whence he went to Missouri in 1850. Sarah was born in 1798, and is the only one still living. She is the wife of Jacob Newlin, who was a soldier of the War of 1812. Sarah was probably the first white child born in Ludlow township.

The next to settle was the family of Abraham Devees. They came in about the decade of this century, probably near the year 1808. Mr. Devees had five children named William, Sarah, Archibald, Abraham, and Nellie. They settled near the mouth of Tice's run.

Following the family of Mr. Devees, was Daniel Hearn, a native of England. His migration to this county, however, was from Sussex county, Delaware. About the year 1807 he came with his family down the Ohio river, the freezing of which compelled him to stop where is now Matamoras. He leased a farm of, perhaps, eighty acres near that place, and remained there about four years. Then he changed his quarters to Ludlow, moving over by the aid of Solomon Tice, jr., who brought over the household goods on a sled. At that time Mr. Hearn's family consisted of his wife, who was Betsy Wilson before marriage, and five children named Hiram, Josiah, Solomon, Mary, and Daniel, jr. This number was subsequently increased to thirteen by the birth of Henry, Elizabeth, Nancy, Narcissa, Louisa, Perry, Luther, and Nehemiah.

Mr. Hearn settled in the same section of land with his neighbors Devees and Tice, section twenty. He, also, chose his home on the banks of the creek. Solomon Hearn was celebrated for his fondness for litigation. He practiced law himself to a limited extent. He also did something in the way of loaning money. Nehemiah married Elizabeth, daughter of John Medley. Nancy married James Bowie. Daniel, jr., was born in 1810 and was therefore a year old when he came to the township. He married Margaret Elder in 1840. Mrs. Daniel Hearn was born in 1818. Their surviving children are three boys and one girl.

The next two families to arrive were those of John Elder and Christopher Dickson. Elder probably came first. His arrival was in the neighborhood of 1812. He was accompanied by his two sons, James and John, from Ireland, although his son, John, never came to Ludlow. James married Sarah Rinard and was blessed with twelve children, one of whom, Margaret, has been referred to as the wife of Daniel Hearn. James Elder was a farmer, miller, distiller, and, in fact, worked at almost anything. John and James Elder settled on opposite sides of the creek on the farm now owned by Luther Rinard.

Christopher Dickson, sr., came in 1813 or 1814, and settled on the hill above Bloomfield, with his wife, who was Fanny Lewis, and children: Christopher, Jane, Elizabeth, Susan, and Mary. Afterwards Sarah, Jemima, Lavina, Nancy, Cythia, Alexander, and Jacob were born. All are now dead but Jacob, Christopher, jr., Susan and Cynthia. Jacob lives on the right side of the Little Muskingum, a short distance above Bloomfield. Cynthia is the widow of John Thomas, and lives farther down the stream. Susan is the widow of Truman Payne and lives near by. Christopher, who was born in 1808, lives just above Bloomfield. In 1834 he married Ann Elizabeth Snyder, who was born in 1815 and died in 1878. The children are Amanda, Albert, Lavina, Cynthia, Lewis, Margaret E., Abner, Clarissa, and Selena. Lewis, Cynthia, Albert, and Lavina are dead. Amanda became Mrs. John Woods and lives in Pennsylvania. Margaret married R. L. White and lives in Indiana. Abner married Mary E. Kirkpatrick. Christopher Dickson, jr., has been honored with many offices in the gift of his township. His father died about thirty years ago aged not far from eighty years; he lies in the Bloomfield cemetery.

The makeshifts and contrivances resorted to by these early settlers in the absence of harness-makers, blacksmiths, and the like, are difficult of comprehension by one who did not live at that time. Thus, in the toilsome task of loosening the soil on the hill-sides, the farmers would harness their horses to their rude plows with bark stripped from bushes and saplings. The settlers were obliged to get their blacksmithing done outside the township until the arrival of Stephen Parr, who opened the first blacksmith shop a little below where Scot Town now is.

The difficulties of travel were greatly ameliorated by the building of the first road in the township. It was the Woodsfield and Marietta road, and ran along the Little Muskingum. A branch was afterwards built up Winget's run. The distances were marked by means of mile-trees.

Mention must also be made of the old settler, Jacob Winget, who named the stream just referred to and settled at a very early date at its mouth.

David Edwards settled in Ludlow in 1819, and resided there until his death in 1848. He was born in Maryland in 1792, and in 1817 was married to Rachel Riggs, a native of West Virginia, born in 1795. She died in 1863. Mr. Edwards was a soldier in the War of 1812. He was the father of eight children, seven of whom survive and reside as follows: Mrs. Mary Scott, in Washington Territory; Mrs. Priscilla Griffiths, in

Brooklyn, New York; James, in Belpre, this county; Charles, in West Virginia; William A. W., in Missouri; B. W. in Ludlow, and Mrs. Elizabeth Hooper, in West Virginia; Harriet is deceased; Baswell W., born in 1833, married in 1856 to Arminta Hooper, born in 1838, and has ten children: Nancy J., wife of S. Cline; Rachel E., wife of L. Moore; Benson B., Priscilla I., Mary B., Minerva J., Margaret A., Rebecca, Amanda E., and Sarah L.

Another very early settler was Patrick O'Hanlon. He was born in Ireland, whence he came with his parents. His children were: Margaret Ellen, John, Phelix (sic) James, Mary, and Richard. Ellen married Jacob Kinser, a laborer, who was the first settler on Dana's run. At first their dwelling was under a rock. He removed down the river where he died. Phelix became the husband of Mary Musser, who lived in Ludlow township; James married Sarah Tice and lived in Ludlow; Mary became Mrs. George Musser, of Ludlow.

John Rinard, born in Pennsylvania in 1801, came to Washington county with his parents, Isaac and Mary Rinard. In 1824 he married Nancy Ray, who was born in 1802. They reared a family of twelve children, ten of whom survive, as follows: Isaac, John W., and Luther, who reside in Ludlow; Samuel, Mrs. A. Smith, David, Nelson, and Theodore, who reside in Iowa; Mrs. J. Pool, in Grand View township, and Mrs. H. Monteith, in West Virginia. Luther, one of the leading farmers of this township, was born in 1834 in Grand View township. In 1865 he married Charlotte Martin, who died in 1879, at the age of forty years. He has had seven children, six of whom are living, namely: Matilda and Delilah A. (twins), Delilah (deceased), David A., John, Hannah, Charlotte B., and Ida Dell.

David Cline came to Ludlow about 1840, and lived a few years at the mouth of Sackett's run. Then he moved about a mile below, back on the high ground. He laid out a village, which he called Clinesville, on the corner of a road just surveyed, hoping that this road would build the town. He left in a few years for Archer's fork, in Independence township.

Porter Flint was a millwright and farmer. He built Flint's mills before 1832 on the Little Muskingum, at what is now Bloomfield. His wife was a Miss Bell, of Newport township. He was drowned in 1859 while running a raft.

Daniel Flint, his brother, kept the first store in the township. It was opposite Flint's mills, and subsequently kept by Holland. He afterwards moved out of the State.

Joseph Reese, a native of Loudoun county, Virginia, born in 1798, removed to Washington county in 1840, and settled in Ludlow township. He remained here until 1862, when he moved to Germantown, Liberty township, and died the following year. His wife, Maria, born in 1796, survived him some ten years. He had twelve children, three of whom are living. David, merchant and postmaster at Dalzell, was born in Jefferson county, Ohio, in 1835, and removed to this county with his parents in 1840. He was married, in 1859, to Malinda Scott, who was born in Ludlow in 1840. They

have seven children—Howard B., Jewett A., Laura L., James R., Albert O., John C., Melvin F., living, and Charles S., deceased. Mr. Reese served in the war of the Rebellion, from September 14, 1861, to July 27, 1865, being a member of company G, Thirty-sixth Ohio volunteer infantry. He had also four brothers in the service, viz: Joseph, Oliver, Jonathan, and Thomas. He was appointed postmaster at Dalzell in 1874, and continues in that position.

William Fox, born in County Tyrone, Ireland, emigrated to this country with his family in 1841 and settled in this township. He settled in a sugar-camp and entered the first land in section one and seven. In the winter of 1842 a catamount was killed in the springhouse. At that time the milling was all done by horsepower at E. Reed's. Mr. Fox and wife, and son James, were the first Catholic citizens of the county outside of Marietta. The locality in which they settled was called the Fox settlement. Mr. Fox died in 1857. His wife, whose maiden name was Jane Maginnis, died in 1876, aged eighty-four. They had five children. Patrick, James, and Mrs. Sarah McCormick reside in Ludlow; Mrs. Mary McKinney in Grand View, and the family of William, who is deceased, live in Iowa. James was born in Ireland in 1819. He married, in 1847, Margaret McKinney, who was born in 1824. They have had ten children living, as follows: Thomas, John, Sarah, William, Jane, Mary, Maggie, James, Anna, John, Catharine, and Bell. The first two are dead. Mr. Fox served about nine months in company D, Fifty-first Ohio volunteer infantry in the war of 1861-5.

Samuel L. Day came to Washington county and settled in Ludlow in 1849. He was born in 1820, and died in 1854. He married, in 1844, Drazilla Johnston, who was born in 1825. There were to them nine children, of whom three only are now living, viz: William A., Rachel E. (Mrs. Scott), and Lavinia (Mrs. Ridgway). The last two reside in Kansas. William A. was born in 1845; married, in 1867, Joanah Hendershot, and has four children—Samuel L., Clara B., and George and Minnie, twins. He was a member of company G, Seventy-seventh Ohio volunteer infantry, and served from the fall of 1861 to the spring of 1865. He was postmaster of Winget Run office for two years.

In 1853 Robert Giffin came to Ludlow, from Belmont county, Ohio, in company with his mother. Though born in 1798, the aged lady is still living with him. Robert Giffin was born in 1829. In 1858, he married one of the same surname—Miss Mary Giffin, who was born in 1833. Their children are: Emeline Asa, Anna M., Eunice M., Huldah J., and Reginald R. Huldah is dead.

One of the later settlers to the township is A. J. Watson, who came in 1878 and began keeping a store at Bloomfield. He was born October 30, 1855; his parents are James and Maria Watson, the former a native of Scotland. In 1880 he married Anna K. Poole. Although so short a time in the neighborhood, he has been already selected to fill township offices, that of clerk and treasurer.

CHURCHES.

The "advance guard of civilization," which came on foot armed with axe and rifle, would, in the early settlement of the country, be followed in no long time by the pioneers of mind and soul—the itinerant preacher on horseback, equipped with Bible and calling the hunters and farmers together as he passed, to worship God. By 1824, one of these preachers, Abner Martin by name, addressed meetings at different houses in the neighborhood often, for one, at the house of Christopher Dickson. These meetings soon bore fruit in the organization of the first church in the township. This was of the Methodist denomination. Before 1848, it became strong enough to build a meeting-house at Bloomfield. This lasted about twenty-five years, and was finally torn down. The organization has long since ceased to exist.

The next church was of the Christian denomination, otherwise and more properly called the Disciple church. This was near 1850. The original members, so far as learned, were: Ezra McMullins, Joseph Rees, Richard Scott, Samuel Thomas, Isaac Thomas, Levi McMullin, and their wives. The first minister was Richard Atherton. Following him were Isaac Thomas, Rev. Ashley, and David Hendershot. In about ten years after their organization, the members built a place of worship on Winget's run in section thirty-four, where they now hold meetings.

In the southeastern part of the township are many Irish, mostly of Catholic proclivities, making the field a favorable one for the planting of a Catholic church. This was accordingly done by Father Brumer, not far from 1860. At the same time a log church building was erected, principally through the agency of Messrs. Fox, Patrick Cawley, Charles Cawley, and James McCormick. The land on which it stands was donated for the purpose by Charles Cawley. The present officiating priest is Father Newmonger.

On April 29, 1866, Rev, John S. Covert preached in a school-house called "Solomon's temple." About twenty people only, attended the morning service, but in the afternoon the house would not hold the people. In May, 1866, a Sabbath-school was organized with Thomas Reynolds as superintendent. This school furnished itself a library and all the necessary accessories to its successful work.

The religious work thus inaugurated was continued by Elder Covert, who preached in May, July and August of that year. He was granted an involuntary vacation in June by the prevalence of floods, preventing his access to the place. Thus at different intervals, the work was kept alive until February, 1867. At that time the great flood of religious interest in Lawrence township to the south, arose and lapped the sides of the southern hills of Ludlow. Large meetings were held in the little school-house and five persons were baptized by Elder Seckman.

On the last day of March, 1837, a council was called of delegates from the churches at Brownsville, Graysville, Matamoras, Unity, Woodsfield, Liberty, Rood Fork, and Lawrence. The elders were present and the organization of the Baptist church of Ludlow was effected. The first members were: Mary Thomas, Isaac R. Rinard, Luther Rinard, Alfred Graham, Eunice Graham, Martha Thomas, and Eliza Swallow, all of whom yet live in the neighborhood. G. W. Harvey and Mary E. Harvey, who are now dead; and Ellen Hendershot,—Reynolds, Sarah Powell, Sarah Baker, James Pratt, Mary J. Pratt, Burgess Hall, Hannah Hall, Jonah Walters, and Mary J. Walters, who have moved away.

In a few years the little band determined to have a special place of worship, but it was not until May, 1870, that this was dedicated. The exercises lasted from the twenty-seventh to the twenty-ninth of that month, under the guidance of Elders Covert and Dana, and pastor D. Seckman, who was the regular preacher at that time. The building is a neat frame structure, situated on a bluff on Pice's run.

In November, 1870, at a meeting held in the church building, it was decided to incorporate the church. The trustees were elected for three years, consisting of Luther Rinard, Luther M. Hearn, Isaac Graham, and G. W. Harvey.

SCHOOLS.

Usually, when a settlement has so far progressed as to include four or five families, some maiden lady undertakes the task of keeping the little ones out of the way of the harvesters or other summer laborers, by instructing them in the mysteries of A, B, C, and the like branches of knowledge. About the year 1816 two such schools were taught. No trace of earlier ones in the neighborhood have been found. Nothing definite is learned that will determine which of these two schools were the first. The probability is, however, that the first one was by Miss Daly. It was a summer school of three months duration. Quite a number of pupils attended for the time of year, probably fifteen. This was held in a log school-house, about a mile and a half below Bloomfield. The attendants were the little ones of the families of Dickson, Tice, Hearn, French, Martin and others. The wages paid were a dollar and a half per pupil. The next school was taught by a man by the name of Gale.

At a school-house on the land of Daniel Hearn, the first teacher was Elizabeth McIntyre, about the year 1816. She was succeeded by Washington Williams. She had over a dozen pupils.

The settlers of Ludlow were without the benefits of a physician within easy access until 1838. Before that they were obliged to summon assistance, when sickness of such gravity as justified it attacked any of them, from Newport, Woodsfield, or even more distant points. But in the year referred to Dr. Philip D. Cocks settled in the vicinity. About the same time Dr. Jesse Ward, one of those physicians peculiar to the times called "steam doctors," made his home in what was then Ludlow but since has become Monroe county. Since then Drs. Russell and William Mitchell have settled in the township.

The first mill in the township not turned "by hand" was the horse-mill of James Tice. Soon after James Elder built one. These mills partially relieved the necessities of the people in that direction, until about the year 1818 or 1820 when Richard Taylor built the first water mill in the settlement. It was constructed on the Little Muskingum at the site of Bloomfield. It was both a grist- and a saw-mill. The first dam was a brush dam; this being swept away, it was replaced by a log dam. So anxious were the farmers to have this great convenience that when it was proposed to build the mill they subscribed aid enough, principally in lumber, work, etc., to insure its probable completion. This mill was afterwards rebuilt by Porter Flint, and still afterwards by Mr. Edwards and Solomon Tice.

About 1850 J. C. Ashley built a saw-mill farther down, in the neighborhood of Scott Town, but it has not been running since about 1870. Near this town, also, the firm of Best & Bates moved in and in the spring of 1869 started a woollen mill on Winget's run.

The oldest of the graveyards in Ludlow is what is known as the Tice cemetery. This dates from the year 1815, at which time Cynthia, a daughter of Jacob Wright, was buried—the first one in the yard. This cemetery has received the bodies of many old citizens and many of their families. Here Solomon Tice was buried; here William Snively and his wife; here are gravestones bearing the names of Dickson, Hearn, and others.

The next oldest is the Hall graveyard. This is in the southwest part of the township, and is nearly as old as the Tice burying-ground.

About forty years ago the graves of four children from the families respectively, of Daniel Flint, Jacob Flint, Elijah Reed, and George Snyder, situated near the site of Bloomfield, were found to be too close to the Little Muskingum. The bodies were accordingly removed to what is now the Bloomfield cemetery, which thus originated. Here are buried Daniel Hearn, sr., and his wife, Porter Flint, his wife and his mother, Christopher Dickson, sr., and his wife, David McIntyre, and others.

The Catholic cemetery is about twenty-five years old. It is situated in the southwestern part of the township, in section seven.

After the erection of the Baptist church building, near the school-house, that bears the singular name of Solomon's Temple, a cemetery was started. Necessarily, it is a burying-place for only the comparatively modern settlers.

At present there are two villages in the township, Bloomfield and Scott Town. The attempted enterprise of Clinesville has been referred to in the treatment of the settlement.

About forty years ago Porter Flint laid out the town of Bloomfield. The flouring and saw-mill there, as well as a furniture shop, distillery, and store carried on by Harvey and Horace Holland, seemed to warrant the expectation that a town could be successfully started. About that time, also, a post office was started which is yet in operation. At present Bloomfield is a small place on the left bank of the Little Muskingum, and situated principally in section twenty-one. The post office is on the other side of the stream.

In 1865 Isaac Scott opened a store at the mouth of Wingate's run. This was the origin of and the first building in Scott Town. In 1873 the place was granted

a post office, with A. C. Alexander as postmaster. W. A. Day succeeded him and he was followed by the present postmaster, Isaac Scott.

Biographical Sketch.

ROBERT GIFFIN.

The subject of this sketch was born in Belmont, county, Ohio, August 5, 1829. His father, Archibald Giffin, was a native of Scotland, and was born September 24, 1771. He emigrated to America and settled in Belmont county, Ohio. He owned a farm and lived in Richland township until his death, July 26, 1833. In November, 1814, he married Agnes Belville, who was born in Newcastle county, Delaware, July 14, 1798. She is of French parentage.

The Giffin family consisted of six children. Cornelius lives in Belmont county; John died in Belmont county; Archibald lives at St. Clairsville, Belmont county; William lives in Newport township, this county; Agnes died at the age of four years; and Robert, a pictorial sketch of whose residence in Ludlow township is presented on an adjoining page.

Robert Giffin purchased the farm on which he now lives while that portion of the county was comparatively new. Ninety acres was the extent of his property at that time. This was a part of the old Solomon Tice farm, an eccentric character who came from Virginia at an early period. The clearing and cabin of the "Governor," as he was known among the early settlers, stood near the site of Mr. Giffin's residence. But a small portion of the land was cleared, and to our subject is due the credit not only of accumulating acres, but also of improving them. John Giffin lived on the farm during the first year of Robert's proprietorship. The following year, his father having died, Mr. Giffin removed to the farm on which he has resided ever since. His mother accompanied him, and still makes his residence her home.

Mr. Giffin married Miss Mary Giffin, of Belmont county, York township, who was born June 10, 1833. The fruit of this union was six children, viz: Emeline, born August 29, 1861; Asa, born October 29, 1863; Anna Martha, born November 6, 1865; Eunice, born April 26, 1868; Huldah J., born December 12, 1872; Reginald R., born November 15, 1874. Huldah J. died October 25, 1873.

Mr. Giffin has been adding to his possessions from time to time until he now has in the farm on which he lives two hundred and twenty-seven acres. He also owns a farm on Tice run, embracing one hundred and twenty acres.

Mr. Giffin served during the war in the Thirty-sixth Ohio volunteer infantry. He enlisted February 24, 1865, and was discharged from the service July 27, 1865.

Mr. Giffin is one of the most progressive farmers of

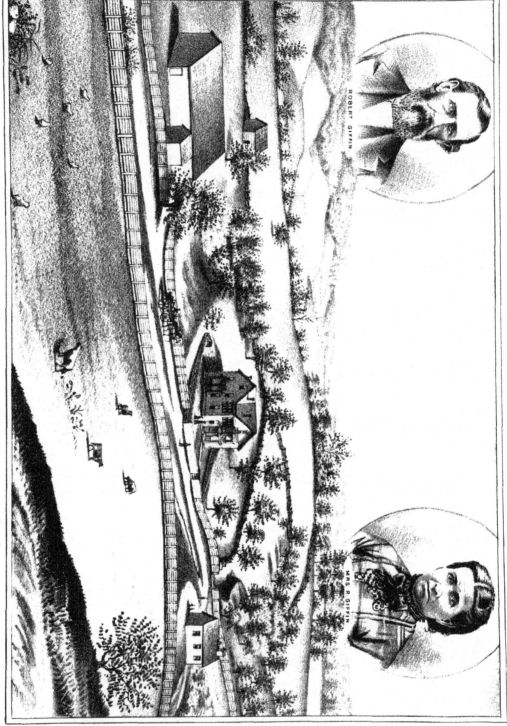

Residence of ROBERT GIFFIN, Esqre., Tp. Waterloo, Co. ...

ROBERT GIFFIN

MRS R GIFFIN

the township. In addition to the routine of farming he deals largely in sheep, and in that way has added materially to his competence. In the community he is looked upon as a leading citizen, and in consequence is frequently called upon to act in the capacity of guardian or administrator of estates.

His farm is probably the best improved in the township. The large, square house, presented in the view, is surrounded by picturesque hills. Few more picturesque or more desirable places, so far as scenic effect goes to give interest to a locality, could be found in the county.

CHAPTER LIV.

LIBERTY TOWNSHIP.

The Territory Described—Ancient Smelting Works—Coal Mines and Oil Wells—The Birth of Liberty—Early Elections—Settlement—The First Child Born—The Germantown Settlement—A Departed Generation—Unfavorable Opinion of the Country Dispelled—New Life Given to the Settlement—The First Doctor—Oakwood and His Herbs—Other Physicians—The Last of the Deer—A Mill in a Stump—Mill of the Miller Miller—The Cluss Mill—The Germantown Mill—Early Schools—Pioneers in Religious Matters—The Christian Church—The Scott Ridge Church—German Churches—Pleasant Ridge Church—The Baptists—The Free Methodists in Liberty—Cemeteries—Germantown—Industries—Statistics.

THIS is the name that the county fathers, in 1832, applied to that part of the county now bounded on the north, for four miles, by Noble county; for the remaining northern two miles of boundary, by Monroe county; on the east by Ludlow township, on the south by Lawrence township, and on the west by Salem township. The name, which probably originated in the tact of some one of the commissioners, is appropriately bestowed, for if it be true that mountainous countries have always been the fastnesses of freedom, it is in keeping with it that a hilly region should be the abode of liberty. These hills, in general, arrange themselves into one principal and many subsiding ridges. The main ridge extends from the north projection of the township (section twelve), in almost a straight southwestern course, leaving the western boundary a mile from the southern line. From this back-bone extend many ribs, a few reaching westward toward Pawpaw creek, but the most and the longest, stretching southward and southeastward, as arbitrators of the claims of the various tributaries of Fifteen Mile creek. The longest of these ridges extends directly south from the north end of the main ridge for the six miles that it is in the township. The eastern slope of this is drained by the smaller streams, such as the west branch of Winget's run, which reaches the Little Muskingum directly. Along the foot of the western slope, the East fork of Fifteen Mile creek flows. This is divided from the West fork of the same stream by another remarkably straight ridge, which extends south from the upper end of the main ridge, four miles. These forks, after flowing almost directly south, unite in the northern part of section seven, and leave the

township two miles west of its southeast corner. The three main tributaries of this stream from the west are, beginning with the most northerly, which rises in the centre of the township, Sycamore, Goss fork, and Dean's fork. The eastern slope of this main ridge, belongs, of course, to the Little Muskingum basin. The western slope furnishes three main streams, flowing nearly west to Pawpaw. Beginning at the north, they are Saltpetre, Koon run, and Campbell run. The first owes its name to the fact that some time in the thirties, a Mr. Davis was wont to come from the north to a cave in its bank, a short distance from where Germantown now is, and containing crude nitre. He would use it in the manufacture of gun-powder, in which he was engaged. The derivation of Koon run is obvious. It is so called from the residents of that name who first settled, and whose descendants still exist, along its valley. Campbell run is so called from the pioneer, Patrick Campbell, who settled on the stream very early. At that time it was called Horse run.

The two western tributaries of Pawpaw are known respectively as Long run and Laurel run. The latter is the southerly one, and takes its name from the laurel thickets that grew in its valley, and used to poison the cattle that found them in the course of their daily browsings.

Pawpaw itself enters the township about two miles and a half east of the northwest township corner, and flows southwest to a point two miles directly north of the southwest corner. Its waters eventually find the Ohio by means of Duck creek. Along its banks the traces of the wonderful Mound Builders appeared in the shape of remains of ancient furnaces of stone with hearths of clay. These were probably used for smelting, for they contained, when found, cinder and pieces of stone coal. These furnaces evidently existed in great numbers along the creek.

Although the hills would present rather a discouraging appearance to a farmer unused to them, yet the limestone under the farms, wherever it was crumbled into soil, has fertilized them to that extent that farming them is quite remunerative.

The coal, though not mined to the extent that it is in Salem, is everywhere prevalent, and up almost every run the traveller can see the pile of "slack" perhaps smouldering where it has been fired to keep the laborer warm, the terminus of the short railway, and the little car, perhaps emptying its black freight into the wagon below, or entering the grimy corridor to the heart of the hill. The seam mined is the Salem or sandstone seam. In one or two places the "Hobson" seam has been found in its usual place above the Salem coal, and borings made for oil have discovered the limestone seam far below, at its usual depth.

Although oil wells have been pushed downward at various places, the oil business as such does not exist in the township. Hitherto no oil has been found in paying quantities.

ESTABLISHMENT AND ORGANIZATION.

It appears that Liberty township was established without the preliminary petition from the citizens that is usually presented. We find in the commissioners journal, under the date of March 5, 1832, the establishing act beginning with the rather abrupt

Resolved, That the tract of country contained in range number seven, in town number four, in the county of Washington, be, and the same is hereby established into an incorporated town, to be called and designated Liberty; and the inhabitants residing within said surveyed township are declared to be entitled to all the privileges and immunities of incorporated towns within this State; and said inhabitants will meet at the house of Matthew Gray, in said township, on the first day of April next, at 10 o'clock, A. M., to elect township officers agreeably to law.

It will thus be seen that, at first, the surveyed township and the established township were identical, and thus, accordingly, Liberty began life with her full thirty-six square miles of territory. No record of township elections appears until 1838, although the book which contains this record was in possession of the township for four years previous.

The memories of the oldest residents of the township, however, retain the facts that Matthew Gray was in all probability the first justice of the peace, that at anyrate, he was a "squire" in 1834, at which time William Gray was a constable. It is said that at one time there were not available men enough to fill the offices, and that Salem township was asked in a neighborly way to lend them a man for constable, but who was the man thus obligingly furnished, tradition has provokingly forgotten. It appears also that these early elections were held in a log school-house about where Germantown stands.

The first township officers on record in the township were chosen April 2, 1838, at an election held at the residence of Joseph Barnhart. William Koon, Matthew Gray, and Gideon Keeder, presided over the election, and James Schofield and Richard Albery were clerks. The election resulted in the choice of Newman Meridith, Marcellus Marsh, and Richard Albery, for trustees; David Hendershot, clerk; Elijah Gray, constable; Isaac Cline and John Miller, overseers of the poor; Eben Speers, Amlin True, and William Walters, fence viewers; James Martin, Daniel Michael, and William Harsheys, road supervisors.

The omission to elect a treasurer was corrected by the appointment in May, 1838, of Matthew Gray to fill that office. This appointment was made by the trustees of the township.

On the twenty-sixth of May, in the same year, a division was made of the township into two school districts. This number has kept step with the increase of the population and growth of educational sentiment, until now Liberty township has eight school districts. At present the road districts number nineteen.

The present township officers were elected in 1880, and are: Isaiah Neff, T. C. Congleton, and J. W. Bowers, trustees; David Rees, treasurer; Joseph Congleton, assessor; J. J. Schenkel, clerk; Daniel Stephens and Michael Doyle, constables; S. D. Spear and Andrew C. Johnston, justices of the peace.

It is remembered that as far back as 1837, there were but five voters in the township as now bounded. On a full vote the Democrats could obtain a majority of one over the Whigs, provided some popular Whig did not run ahead of his ticket. These five were Philip Cline,

William Walters, Levi Woods, David Hendershot, and Matthew Gray. Of these, Cline and Gray joined the Whig element. This voting population has grown until in November, 1880, it polled one hundred and eighty-six Republican, one hundred and fifty-one Democratic, and four Greenback votes; total, three hundred and forty-one.

In 1851, when Noble county was formed, part of Liberty township was sacrificed, among other of the northern territory of Washington. Thus the township lacks sections 5, 6, 18, 24, 30, and 36. Sections 5 and 6 belong to Monroe county, and the rest to Noble county.

SETTLEMENT.

The oldest settlement in the surveyed township is in the Harrietville neighborhood, in the part of Liberty since assigned to Noble county.

The first person known to have penetrated the wilderness of the present territory of Liberty was Jewett Palmer, who moved in from Lawrence township, where, about 1823, he had first settled. This removal was in 1825, and was to the farm now owned by C. Abicht, on the upper corner of Whipple run. Mr. Palmer remained in the place but five years, then went to Fearing, and finally, in the neighborhood of 1845, to Salem township. During his stay in Liberty occurred what was probably the first birth in the township, that of Pemberton Palmer, in December, 1827. Jewett Palmer was remarkable for his bold and pronounced partizanship in regard to all the questions of the day, and several which at that time were questions of the future. He was bitterly opposed to the universal presence of whiskey and the like at old-time merry-makings, and industrial gatherings; was connected with the "Underground railroad," and was one of the very few early Free Soilers.

Shortly after the pioneer, Patrick Campbell, ventured into the wilderness as far as Horse run. About 1835 Richard Albery moved in on the head of Whipple run. But this settlement, thus begun in the southern part of the township, was of short life. It was destined that the northern part, that about the site of Germantown, was to be the scene of the final permanent settlement. The first one to make his home here was Matthew Gray, who came from the Harrietville settlement. As usual with the first settlers, he made his way along the natural pathway, worn for him by the rapid flowing of a stream. In this case he came to the banks of Pawpaw, about half a mile above the mouth of Saltpetre. Those who shared his danger and his home with him were his wife, whose name before marriage was Amy Enochs, and his 'children. There were nine of these in all, named William, David, Elijah, Jesse, George, James, Elizabeth, Rhoda, and one whose name has been forgotten.

Matthew Gray seems to have been a man of great intelligence and force of character, as is evident by the character of the offices to which he was chosen, and the manner in which he is mentioned by those who knew him. The date of his settlement cannot be long before 1832.

By the year 1834 five other families had moved into

the township. Two of these—Levi Woods and Isaac Koon—settled in the part since cut off. The other families were those of William Koon, Michael Koon, and Joseph Barnhart.

William Koon lived on Pawpaw, opposite the mouth of Koon run, with his wife, whose former name was Margaret Brown, and seven children.

Michael Koon's wife was Barbara Stackhouse, and he was the father of eight children.

Joseph Barnhart, who settled a little below Saltpetre, married Betsey Geer. Their children were William, George, Asa, Rosanna, and others.

Although the settlement was begun so late, it is a singular fact that none of these first settlers now live in the township. Facts about the settlement are consequently difficult to obtain, and to that extent less reliably learned. The next one to come to the township is now the oldest living settler. In 1834 Stephen Harris moved into that singularly isolated valley now called Koon run, where he has lived ever since. His wife's name was Rhoda Koon. Their children are Mary, Amy, Barbara, George, Stephen, who died in the army, and Esau.

George Kesselring, a native of Maryland, settled in what is now Liberty township in 1828, where he died in 1844. By his wife, Elizabeth Haltsman, born in 1806, he had eight children, six of whom survive, viz.: Elizabeth, Robinson, of Virginia; Mary Redfox, Rebecca Hendershot, Ezra, John, and Samuel. John, who was born in 1828, married Anna Eliza Gray, by whom he has nine children. He has a farm of ninety-four acres, and is a tobacco-packer. He resides in Newport township.

Soon after, the settlers came in more rapidly. At first there seemed to prevail an opinion that it was not possible to live in Liberty township, the land being considered too rough and barren. Many came from Salem township and elsewhere for a short time and returned discouraged. At last, however, it was found that these settlers, mentioned before, survived and even enjoyed it. Then settlement received new encouragement and more rapid progress was made toward its present population. Early and late, the most of the settlers have found their way over the ridges from more northern counties, especially Guernsey and Monroe. Shortly after 1834 came the families of William Walters, who settled near Germantown, Joshua Cunningham, a man named Stackhaus, who settled in section thirty-three, but left as early as 1848, and many others. In 1839 Cephas Hendershot arrived —a young man of twenty-two. He chose his home immediately below Germantown, where he has lived until now. His wife was Delilah Sloan, and his children living are Elias, George W., Sarah Ann, Caroline, Charles, Margaret, and Jane. Five others are dead.

About 1840 the little settlement was increased by the advent of a new neighbor—Philip Cline, from Monroe county. He settled on section thirty-three, on the farm at present occupied by Lewis Stickrath. His wife was Elizabeth Newman before marriage. The children were eight in number; four are dead. Philip, jr., and Samuel are in Iowa; Sarah lives in Liberty township; Andrew married Nancy McDonald and has four children living,

one of whom, William, still lives in this township, and, with his wife, Rebecca, has five children.

The first doctor in the township arrived at this period. His name was Dr. Ekholtz, and he would sometimes be called by its English equivalent—Oakwood. His remedies were simple and confined entirely to the vegetable kingdom in its crude form. Such physicians were common in early times, and in the colloquial style of the people were termed "Yarb" doctors.

Between 1845 and 1850 a Dr. Patterson arrived, followed by Dr. J. M. Warren in 1851, Dr. Sparling in 1860, and the present Drs. Warren, jr., E. S. Divine, and Ridley Sparling.

Another comparatively late settler in Liberty township is Lewis Young, who is the son of Philip Young. He and his wife, Julia, are the parents of Jacob, now married and living in Fearing township; Lizzie, Charlotte, Caroline, Henry, and Otto.

John Bowers was born in Guernsey county, Ohio, in 1808, and settled in this township in 1845. He married Sarah McPeek in 1828. She died in 1878 at the age of seventy-one. They were the parents of twelve children, eight of whom are living, as follows: John W. and Valentine, in Liberty; Josiah A., in Noble county; Jacob A., Marietta township; Sarah Vanowey, in West Virginia, Mrs. Mrs. Rebecca A. Glove, in Bellaire, Ohio; Mrs. Elizabeth Congleton, in Liberty; and Mrs. Margaret E. Willison, in Marietta. Hester J., William T., Mary A., and James are deceased. Four of the sons served in the war of the Rebellion, to wit: John W., company D, seventy-seventh Ohio volunteer infantry; Valentine, company H, One Hundred and Seventy-fifth Ohio volunteer infantry; Josiah A, company K, Ohio volunteer infantry.

Thomas Hamilton, a native of North Carolina, born in 1784, emigrated to Ohio in 1804, and settled in Tuscarawas county. In 1849 he removed with his family to this county, and settled in Liberty township. He died February, 1872. His first wife was Mary A. Taylor, who was born in North Carolina in 1784. She died in 1828. The children by this marriage were six in number, three living, viz: Archibiald A. in Indiana; William in Tuscarawas county; Thomas F. in Pike county, Ohio. He married for his second wife, Sarah Manlow, born in 1817; died in 1840. The fruits of this union were four children as follows: Mrs. J. Smith in Illinois; Mrs. J. Swiggert in Coshocton county, Ohio; Lewis in Liberty and Leonard in Kansas. The latter was born in Tuscarawas county, Ohio, in 1834; married in 1855, Asaminta Parish, who was born in 1840, and has a family of nine children, viz: Ruanna, Anna, Mary, Thomas and Lillie deceased; and Emma J., Susannah, William, and Fredonia, living.

Hiram Dearth was among the more recent settlers of the county, having removed here in 1869. He was born in 1828 in Monroe county, Ohio. He married Hester J. Kasey, born in 1830, and has the following children: James, Ephraim, Lewis, John, Robert, Martha A., Arizona, Russell, and George S., all living, and Nancy J., Kasey and Frank, deceased.

The wild animals in the township, when it was settled,

were of the same kinds that the pioneers found elsewhere in the county, except that the settlement having been made so late, the bear disappeared. Many of the settlers were hunters rather than farmers, and were rarely seen without their guns. But in time the wolves and the deer left. The last deer killed was by Joshua Powell, about 1840, at the mouth of Saltpetre.

"In early days" as the old pioneers like to say, one of the greatest difficulties of the farmers was to prepare their grain for consumption. Other wants, though quite as pressing, were supplied by much simpler means, but the machinery of a mill was a matter of great moment, when everything had to be obtained from the raw material, water-mills being so "few and far between" various expedients were resorted to by the farmers, who could not at times take the long journey to the nearest mill or spare the time waiting until the grists ahead of them were ground or perhaps, on account of low or high water, be unable to find a mill that could run at all. Many owned hand-mills. A few farmers made rough horse-mills such as would make the miller of to-day smile. One way of making a hand-mill was to saw off a section of a hollow sycamore, making what is known as a "gum." In this was firmly planted the nether millstone at the proper height, a hole was bored in the stump to allow the meal to escape. The upper stone contained two apertures at a distance from the centre, one extending through the stone, and through this, the feeding was done. The other, extended deep enough to hold firmly a wooden rod, the upper end of which turned in a socket several feet above the centre of the stone. From one to three or four persons would seize this rod and turn the upper stone with it, while one dextrously dropped handfuls of grain in the hole for that purpose, as the revolution brought it past. Such were the primitive hand-mills, at least in Liberty township. Perhaps the first one of this kind was on the farm now occupied by Nathan Miller, then by Matthew Gray.

The first water-mill was built about 1844, by John Miller, on Saltpetre creek, about a half mile from its mouth. He was mechanic enough to build his mill himself. It was his custom to put the grist in the hopper, turn on the water, and retire calmly to rest, telling the customer that the "grist would be ready to-morrow morning." Shortly after this time a man by the name of Cluss built a mill on Pawpaw. He also had one in Salem township. John Miller afterwards built the mill now at Germantown.

The first road in the new settlement, and consequently in the township, went, as might be surmised from the position of the settlers' homes, up Pawpaw creek to the site of the town of Lebanon, north of the township.

The first orchard in the settlement was planted by Stephen Harris, probably who bought the trees of Joseph Barker, at a nursery on the Ohio river.

Perhaps the first frame house in the township was built by Frederick Gruver. It now belongs to Caleb Hendershot.

The first school-house was a log one, and stood a quarter of a mile north of Germantown, in about 1838. At that time ten or fifteen pupils attended. Very early,

perhaps before any other school had been inaugurated, a daughter of John Doffatt, of Salem township, came to the settlement and taught in an old log cabin that was considered the common property, where all sorts of meetings were held, principally church meetings of the denominations of Methodists, United Brethren, etc. This school was a private enterprise, and the teacher received a dollar and a half for each pupil that she taught three months. She had about a half dozen pupils, thus reaping the very moderate harvest of perhaps nine dollars for her work of a quarter of a year.

The first religious denomination that began work in the township was the Methodist. A hewed log church was built in 1839 or 1840, just above Germantown, and there they held their meetings. These meetings have long been transferred to a point further down stream. In 1848 Mr. Abraham Alban set apart some ground for the purpose, and a church building was erected on it. This was during the ministry of Rev. Thomas McCormick. The members of the church at that time were: Andrew Cline, Jeremiah Burton, William Myers, Amos Lacey, Elijah Gray, Abraham Alban, New Meredith, William Harmiger, and their wives, John Koon, Betty Koon, Margaret Koon, John Meredith, Catharine Amos, and George Casselring. This church still continues its meetings, which are at present conducted by Rev. Paugh. The building may still be seen standing on a high bank to the right of Pawpaw, a little above the road from Salem to Dalzell. The church belongs to the Lebanon circuit.

The next church that originated in the township was the one whose building now stands above Germantown, just over the border of the township. It being so closely connected with the settlers of the township, a sketch of it will be given. It dates from the vicinity of 1840, and was organized by the following members: Nathan Miller, David Hendershot, Levi Woods, Daniel Michael, Daniel McPeek, John Miller, Hammond Miller, John Walters, and their wives. About 1850 Daniel Michael gave land for the purpose, and a building was constructed by John Walters and John Powell. Before this meetings were held in the building used by the township for election purposes. The church building is still standing, but the members now meet at the church at Dalzell.

By the spring of 1855 the southern part of the township had become settled thickly enough to warrant the establishment of a church in that region. Accordingly John and William Love, Robert, John, and James Scott, with their wives, and Robert Love, banded themselves together as a separate congregation of Methodists. It was about the time of the ministry of Cook, of Marietta, that they met at the house of Robert Scott.

Thus matters went on for two or three years, when the advantage of a special house of worship became so obvious that they constructed one of logs for the purpose. This was replaced about 1873 by a frame structure, made by John Scott. In this they still meet and are known as the Scott Ridge church. Rev. Paugh supplies the pulpit, and the church is now a part of the Lebanon circuit.

Some fifteen or twenty years ago a German church was organized, and met in a building on Fifteen Mile creek. In a short time the building was destroyed by fire, and the church ceased to exist.

A German Lutheran church is in existence, and meets in their church edifice in section thirty-two. The organizers of this church were Jacob Schramm, Samuel Bruny, Christian Best, Peter Gruver, Charles Brown, their wives, and Catharine Hartwig, Frederick and William Epler. The meetings were at first held from house to house. This state of affairs continued for only two or three years, when the present building was put up. The preacher now is the Rev. F. C. Trapp.

The little village of Dalzell contains a neat-looking little edifice, in which the Pleasant Ridge Christian church of that place worships. The organization was effected in May, 1867, by Robert Miller, John Gregory, James T. Rogers, Joel C. Gregory, S. D. Spear, George Beardsmore, William Beardsmore, William Jarvis, D. N. Rogers, Francis Rogers, Wilford Howell, J. H. Gray, Elizabeth Farnsworth, Agnes Howell, Ellen Gregory, Eliza J. Howell, Abigail Rogers, Arminda Gregory, Milicent Beardsmore, Mary Taylor and Sarah Martin.

The officers elected first were: William Jarvis, John Gregory and D. N. Rogers, elders; Francis Rogers and Wilford Howell, deacons; John Gregory, J. H. Gray and S. D. Spear, trustees.

The officers now (1881) are: Elders, David Rees, William Roberts, S. D. Spear; deacons, John B. Booth, E. C. French, Thomas Forshey and Enoch Griffin.

The church numbers eighty-two members. It first held meetings in a log church, built at the time of organization. In 1880 the present frame structure was reared.

Where the two forks of Fifteen Mile creek unite is a church building which was built in 1874, and in which worships the Liberty Baptist church. The land was donated by John Congleton. Before the building of the church, the organization met in Noble county for worship. This church was constituted in 1842. The ministers have been: Revs. William Stone, John D. Young, J. C. Skinner, John Ables, H. Lyons, D. Ross, William McPeek and J. D. Riley. The church has now twenty-nine members.

On Fifteen Mile creek there is a Free Methodist church organization, which began about three years ago to hold meetings in what is known as "Jordan's hall." In the fall of 1879 they purchased a school-house, and dedicated it in the summer of 1880 as a church. The present preacher is Rev. Bennett.

The only graveyard in Liberty before 1834 was a private burying-ground of the Koon families. In that year it contained but one grave—that of a little daughter of William Koon. About the same time John Barnhart died, but was buried north of the present county line. These two deaths, so far as can be ascertained, were the first in the township.

The next oldest cemeteries are those at the Methodist and Christian churches in Pawpaw valley. Although the latter yard is partially outside the county, yet many old residents of the township lie there. The ground was set apart for the purpose by William and John Walters, about 1848 or 1849. The first one to be buried in it was a little child of David McPeek. In this yard rest the remains of some from the families of Hendershot, Miller, Walters, Beardmore, Roberts and other families. The yard now contains about a hundred graves.

The other yard, the one near the Methodist church, begun with the burial of Mrs. Thomas Robinson, in 1849. Here lie buried some of the Laceys, Clines, Kidds, Myers, Merediths and Burtons. Dr. Warren's grave is here. These three cemeteries are the oldest in the township.

Turning from the cities of the dead to the towns of the living, the oldest village in the township is Germantown, which was laid out, in 1852, by David Hendershot. Before this there was no building in the place but a sawmill. The first building put up after the sale of lots was by John Holtz, and intended for a storehouse. The post office was obtained in 1873, and Charles Coleman was the postmaster. The village now contains, besides the dwelling houses, a store, a mill, a blacksmith shop, a shoe shop and a saloon.

The other hamlet in the township is named in honor of Private Dalzell, of Noble county. It was laid out March 13, 1871, by R. W. St. John, surveyor for Francis Rogers, who owned the land. The first settler on the site of the town was S. D. Spear. The first house was a log house, on lot No. 16, and belongs now to George Kelzer. In January, 1872, Dalzell became a post office, with S. D. Spear as postmaster. The second and present postmaster is David Rees, who began his labors in that department in 1877. At present, Dalzell contains a store, blacksmith shop, wagon shop and shoe shop.

Before leaving the history of the township, it would be well to take a brief view of the population and its occupation. The people mainly represent the English, German and Irish races. A few are of Scotch extraction. About one-third can speak German, and about one in six are of German blood and English speech. Guernsey and Monroe counties, and Pennsylvania, furnished most of the settlers. Agriculture is, of course, the principal employment. Besides grain, much tobacco is raised, and, perhaps, this plant has brought more money to the people than any other. Cattle and sheep do well here, as much of the ground is better fitted for pasture than for raising grain.

In 1840 the population of Liberty was five hundred and fifteen; in 1860, one thousand three hundred and twenty-seven; in 1870, one thousand six hundred and thirty-two; in 1880, one thousand six hundred and twenty.

CHAPTER LV.

BARLOW TOWNSHIP.

A Progressive Township—Description—Establishment and Organization—Early Provision Made for Schools and Churches—Settlement—
Religious Organizations—Educational Interests—Temperance Society—Agricultural Association—Wool Growers' Association—Patrons
of Husbandry—Mills—Barlow Village.

THIS township, for the public spirit of its citizens, the
industry, enterprise, and general thrift of its farmers, is
known as one of the leading townships of the county.
The many farms showing thorough culture, the successful operation of the agricultural fair, the Wool Growers'
association, the church and school interests, and many
other prominent indications of industry and intelligence,
entitle her to that position. It is situated in the western
part of the county, and is bounded on the north by Watertown, on the east by Warren, south by Dunham, and
west by Fairfield and Palmer. The southern part is
drained by branches of Little Hocking, and the north
by branches of Wolf creek. In the central and northern
parts the land is rather smooth, and the hill-slopes gradual, while the southern part is more inclined to abrupt
declivities and higher elevations.

The soil is of red and yellow clay, and in many localities are found beds of shale of considerable thickness,
containing small concretionary lumps of limestone in
large quantities, thus giving the shales (or "marls," as
they are popularly called) great value in fertilization.
The chief productions are fruits, wheat, corn, and the
ordinary farm products of this section. The chief branch
of industry is wool growing, which is carried on quite
extensively. The Merino sheep is the favorite breed in
this locality, producing fleeces of fine wool, commanding
good prices. The market for this production is local
and ample, thus rendering the operations of trade both
easy and profitable to the producers.

The township—barring a protrusion of two half-sec-
tions on the east, and a half-section taken from the northwest corner—is five sections wide and six long, making
in all thirty and one-half sections, or nineteen thousand
five hundred and twenty acres of land. It is almost entirely rural in its settlements, having no incorporated
towns within its limits, and but three important points of
trade—Barlow village, Vincent station, and Fleming post
office—and has, according to the last census (1880), a
population of one thousand two hundred. The main
thoroughfare is the State road, leading from Marietta to
Athens, and passing almost directly through the centre
from east to west, receiving the Belpre and Watertown
road at Barlow. The abandoned line of the Marietta &
Cincinnati railroad passes through the southern part of
the township.

Several seams of coal are found in this township,
known as the Hobson seam, and generally found along
the course of Wolf creek, but none of the seams are
thick enough for practical mining—so far as the discoveries yet made are concerned. The probabilities are that
future need of fuel will stimulate research that will be rewarded by the discovery of deeper seams of more superior coal.

Jesse Lawton some years ago discovered on his farm
near the village of Barlow, which is situated in the midst
of the marl regions, a locality of fossil fresh water shells
of the genus *Unio*. These shells were imbedded in coarse
sand or gravel, cemented by ferruginous matter, and the
specimens are casts replaced by argillacious oxide of iron.
This locality bears evidence of once having been the bed
of a lake or pond, but is now a valley surrounded by low
hills, extending some four miles in length and a mile in
width. The waters of this valley are drained by a small
branch of the Little Hocking.

ORGANIZATION.

On petition of Nathan Proctor, Benjamin Baker, and
others, the inhabitants of township three, of range ten,
were declared entitled to the privileges and immunities
of incorporated towns, and said territory to be known as
Barlow township. The inhabitants were notified to meet
at the residence of James Lawton for the purpose of
electing township officers, on the third Monday of July,
1818. The only records of any election that can now be
found is that of the election of trustees and other officials for managing the school and ministerial lands, which
was held on the third day of January, 1818, at the Old
Hickory school-house. At this meeting Benajah Howe
was made both chairman and clerk pro tem. Judges of
election were Cornelius Houghland and Isaac Hutchinson. The election resulted as follows: Cornelius Houghland, S. N. Cooke, and Caleb Greene, trustees; Duty
Greene, treasurer; and, in the following April, Benjamin
F. Palmer was appointed to fill the vacancy occasioned
by the death of Cornelius Houghland.

In all probability, Cornelius Houghland was the first
justice of the peace who exercised the functions of that
office in Barlow township, as he held commissions as
justice of the peace here long before the township was
stricken from Wesley. The oldest of these commissions
bears date of October 9, 1810, aud is signed by Governor Samuel Huntington. Another is dated October 30,
1813, and bears the celebrated signature of Return Jonathan Meigs, governor and commander in chief of the
State of Ohio.

SCHOOL AND MINISTERIAL FUND.

Section sixteen was granted by Congress for school
and section twenty-nine for church purposes. These
sections were surveyed and laid out in lots April 12,
1812, by Joseph Palmer, Cornelius Houghland, and Nathan Proctor, and they were viewed and appraised by
Duty Greene. Five lots, Nos. 1, 2, 3, 4, and 5, of
eighty acres each, were first laid out in section twenty-
nine and valued at one dollar and seventy-five cents, to
two dollars per acre. This land was rented to settlers,
the rents collected by the trustees and applied to payment of teachers and preachers. In 1823 it was resolved
by the trustees that any kind of goods in merchantable
trade would be received for rents at following prices, viz:
wheat, seventy-five cents per bushel, corn fifty cents,
rye fifty cents, oats thirty-three cents, pork four dollars
and fifty cents, and tow-linen cloth fifty cents per yard.
Duty Greene as agent for the Methodist Episcopal

church made the first demand for the ministerial funds, and on June 19, 1824, he received all the *property* in the treasury.

The first lease of land was made to William Dunbar, dated April 12, 1812, for No. 5 of section twenty-nine, valued at two dollars per acre—"six per cent. of this valuation to be paid every year as rent for said lands." This lease was witnessed by David Ewell, Samuel Clark, and Thomas Dunbar, and the trustees were Joseph Palmer, John Curtis and Edmund Neal.

EARLY SETTLEMENTS.

In the spring of 1800, James Lawton (to whom we are indebted for many of the facts contained in the history of Barlow), and Nathan Proctor made the first opening in what was then known as "White Oak settlement." The first cleared fields were on the small elevation just west of the present residence of Mrs. James Lawton, jr., southeast of Barlow village, and were made along the dividing lines between the only settlers in the wilderness. Nathan Proctor and his brother Jacob, erected a tent about forty rods south of the present Methodist Episcopal church.

Soon after, James Lawton began the erection of the first cabin, which was built immediately east of the present brick farm residence above mentioned—a relic of this first cabin in Barlow township is preserved, in the shape of a cane made from one of the walnut logs, and is now in possession of the Lawton family.

During the erection of this cabin the men engaged, who were hired from Marietta, passed the nights in Nathan Proctor's tent, where they were often entertained by the singing of Watts' hymns and the psalms, by the Proctor boys, who were then considered remarkably good singers.

In the summer of 1800, William Vincent and family, Cornelius Houghland, his brother-in-law, Thomas McGuire, and their families arrived in this vicinity. Duty Greene came the following year, and was probably the first Methodist in this locality. He was one of the leading men in the religious work of those early days, especially as a leader in the singing, and was very partial to a familiar methodist hymn called the "Good Old Way," which he sang on very frequent occasions.

Nathan Proctor came from Danvers, Massachusetts, and after he cleared the land and erected his cabin, his aged father and mother and his sister came to the new settlement. He died in Barlow in his seventieth year—of whose death the Marietta *Register* thus speaks: "Shortly after the first settlement at Marietta, he emigrated to what is now Barlow township, and selected his dwelling place where his residence now stands, and felled the first tree in the new settlement. In the death of this gentleman society has lost a valuable member; the family, a kind husband and affectionate parent. He was a Christian and a Republican."

Cornelius Houghland, an early settler of what is now Barlow township, was a native of Hampshire county, Virginia, where he was born in 1773. In the spring of 1796 he married Anna Stalcut, and the fall of the same year left for Kentucky. He soon found his way to the

vicinity of Williamstown opposite Marietta, where he made a settlement on a branch of Big run since known as Houghland's run. In April, 1801, with his brother-in-law Thomas McGuire, he removed to what was then known as "White Oak settlement," and located on the farm now owned by Neal Loynachan's heirs, one mile west of Barlow village. In his log cabin he kept the first licensed tavern in the township. The license was issued January 5, 1806, for the township of Wooster, and was signed by E. W. Tupper. Mr. Houghland was killed March 10, 1818, while cutting timber, a tree falling upon him. His wife died April 29, 1824, in her forty-eighth year. Their children were Polly, Margaret, Ruth, John, Eleanor, Elza, Lewis, David, and Anna. All are now dead except Anna (widow of Harris Palmer), who lives in Palmer township, aged sixty-four. Polly was the wife of Rev. Edmund McGinnis. Margaret married Benjamin F. Palmer, of Barlow. She died May 19, 1875, in her seventy-seventh year. She had four children: Joah F., Joseph, Cornelius (who died young), and Elza H. Ruth Houghland died in childhood. Eleanor became the wife of Vincent Smith, of Plymouth, this county.

Thomas McGuire who came to Barlow (then Wooster) with his brother-in-law, Cornelius Houghland, in the spring of 1801, settled on Wolf creek, northeast of where Barlow village now is. His cabin stood a short distance below the old hickory school-house.

The settlements made by these families formed the centre of what has now grown to be Barlow township.

The roads were then known only as "tracks" through the unbroken wilderness. One leading from Marietta to Athens, from east to west now known as the State road, passed a few rods north of the Lawton cabin, and the other from Belpre to Watertown was a short distance west. These routes sustained all the travel to and from these points, and the travellers, on account of the difficulties of the unbroken road, were often compelled to remain over night with some of the settlers, and among these early visitors are remembered—Dr. Perkins, of Athens, Griffin Greene, sr., of Marietta, Colonel Israel Putnam, and Colonel Fisher, of Belpre, Colonel Oliver, and Major White, of Waterford.

James Lawton, sr., was born in Rhode Island in 1760, and settled in Marietta in 1796, and died in Barlow in 1843. He was the first settler of Barlow township, and a man of superior intelligence and public spirit. He was married to Susannah Gould, who was born in 1764, and died in 1852. They had four children: one now living—Mrs. Sarah Branson, who lives in Illinois. His son Jesse was born in 1789, and came to Ohio with his parents in 1796, and was married to Maria Haskell in 1821, and settled in Barlow township in 1800. They had a family of six children—five now living: Arthur, Isaac and Phœbe (twins), Isaiah B., and Richard, who was born in 1824, and was married in 1862, to Persis Walker, who was born in 1828. He was in the United States army during the late war, in the hundred day service, and is one of the leading and respected farmers of Barlow.

William Vincent settled in Barlow in 1800. He was born in 1770, in Rhode Island, and died in this township in 1825. His wife, Elizabeth Earl, was born in 1767, and died in 1852. Of this family two yet survive—Mariah, widow of the late Obediah Gardner, of near Columbus, and John, who now resides in the township. He was trustee for eight years, also overseer of the poor for a number of years. John Vincent was born in 1809, and was married to Elizabeth Dustin in 1832, who was born in 1808. They have thee children living. His son John C. was an orderly sergeant in the hundred day service. He is the inventor of the "Vincent rifle," and is engaged in the manufacture of these guns, and in other mechanical pursuits at his shop, just east of Vincent station. The popularity of this gun is increasing, and orders for them are received from various and distant places. Mr. Vincent is known as a workman of rare skill and proficiency in many departments of mechanical art.

Henry Earl Vincent was born in 1802, in Barlow township, where he died in 1873. He held the office of justice of the peace for many years, and was also clerk, treasurer, and trustee, and a leading pioneer citizen of the township. He was married in 1830 to Rhoda Clark, who was born in 1806. Her father, Elisha Clark, was born in New Jersey, in 1765, and settled in Belpre in 1798, and was married to Helen Brown, who was born in 1765. She has six living children, and is now living on the farm of eighty acres at Vincent station, engaged in farming and fruit growing. Osmer B. was in the hundred day service, and Henry C. was employed as telegraph operator, by the Government, under General Thomas, in Tennessee.

Daniel N. Dunsmore was born in 1817, and was married in 1843 to Isabel Fleming, who was born in Scotland, in 1817. They have two children. He is a farmer and stock-raiser and engaged particularly in raising thoroughbred Merino sheep. Hiel Dunsmore was in the hundred day service.

Duty Greene settled in Barlow, in 1800, and was born in New York, in 1760, and died in 1842. He had a family of six children, one of whom is now living—Pamelia, widow of S. H. Reynolds, now living in Missouri. Smith Greene, his son, was born in New York, in 1792, and came to Barlow with his father; was married to Sarah Mellor in 1813, who was born in England, in 1789. To them were born six children—two now living—Edna and Cynthia; the latter was born in 1814, and was married to Simeon Evans in 1842. He served in the Union army as member of company F, Thirty-sixth Ohio volunteer infantry. They had a family of four children—two now living—Harriet F. and Charles E., who was in the hundred day service; David E., enlisted in 1861, in company F, Thirty-sixth Ohio volunteer infantry, and died from injuries received in the army in 1863.

Isaac Woodruff was born in New Jersey in 1787; emigrated to this country and settled in Barlow township, in 1801. He was justice of the peace four years, and served in various township offices. He was married to Margaret Greene, who was born in 1790, and died in 1853. The following children of this family are now living: Silas, Chester, Caroline, Jeanette, and Duty. Mrs. Pamelia Bell was born in 1819, in Barlow township, and was married in 1838, to William Bell, who was born in 1811, and died in 1868. He was trustee of the township for a number of years, and was a member of the Methodist Episcopal church from 1837 until his death. Mrs. Bell is a cripple for life, having been injured by a fall in 1879. She has seven children living and owns two hundred and twenty-five acres of land.

Silas Woodruff, son of Isaac Woodruff, was born in 1811, and was married to Mary Stump, in 1833, who was born in 1812, and died in 1859. To them were born seven children; the following are now living: Hiram, David, and Anson, all living in Kansas; Maria, wife of J. L. Palmer, of California; and Mary, wife of H. M. Morter, this township. He was again married in 1859, to Elizabeth Stollar, who was born in Pennsylvania, in 1830. They had four children: Alpharetta, Calvin E., Marian G., and Clarence L. At present he has a farm of three hundred and fifty acres and is a general farmer.

In 1801, John Laflin settled in Watertown township. He was born in Vermont in 1773, and died in 1851. His wife, Abigail Richards, was born in 1777, and died in 1847. The surviving members of this family are Luman and Harley, the latter was the second son and was born in Wooster township, in 1807, and was married to Anna Shields, in 1831, who was born in 1809. They had a family of four children—three now living: Diantha, now Mrs. John Seeley, of Watertown; Mary A., wife of James Morrison; and Charles S., who now lives on the homestead, and was born in 1839, and married to Caroline Cooksey, in 1868. They have three children: Charles E., Morrison, and Lizzie.

Harley Laflin has held the office of justice of the peace for twelve years, and was elected to the legislature in 1854, and now resides on his estate of one hundred and sixty acres of land, a respected citizen and farmer of Barlow.

Benjamin F. Palmer came to Barlow in 1816 and built his log cabin bachelor's hall about twenty feet east of his present residence north of Barlow. While clearing his farm he gave two days' work of each week for his board, and passed the nights in his cabin, sleeping on the floor. He was married in 1817 to Margaret Houghland, who was born in 1798, and three of their children are now living in Barlow—Sarah, Joseph, and Elza H. He was a soldier in the War of 1812, serving under Captain Timothy Buell, and was one of the pioneers of the township. He now owns a farm of two hundred and sixty acres as the result of his own industry. E. H. Palmer, his youngest son, occupies the old homestead, and is largely engaged in the raising of fine stock.

Robert Breckenridge first settled in Wesley township in 1811; was born in Scotland in 1794, and died in Barlow 1871. He was one of the first elders of the Presbyterian church, which office he held until his death. Was married to Catharine Harvey, who was born in 1794. The surviving members of their family are Nancy, Elizabeth, Mary, and James H. The latter was born in 1832 in Barlow, and was married to Catharine Reed in 1860, who was born in West Virginia in 1835. He now owns a farm of eighty acres, and is one of the substantial farmers of the township.

Cyrus W. Morey was born in New York in 1807 and came to this township with his parents in 1808. The family consisted of four children—Benson, who now resides in Delaware county, Ohio; Julia, who died in 1872; Maria, who died in 1874; and Cyrus.

Heman Chapman was born in Connecticut in 1764 and first settled in Marietta in 1806, and died in Barlow in 1851. He was married in 1785 to Marcy Potter, who was born in 1767 and died in 1834. His son, Samuel Chapman, was born in New York in 1793 and came to Ohio in 1816, in which year he was married to Catharine Clark, who was born in 1797, and they settled in Watertown township in 1816. To them was born one son—Hiel Chapman—who was born in 1829, and in 1857 was married to Abigail Hutchins, who was born in 1831, and are now living in Barlow. He has held the office of constable and justice of the peace. Was a member of company F, One Hundred and Forty-eighth Ohio national guards, and is now a general farmer, owning a farm of eighty acres, on which he resides.

Jesse Pugh settled in Barlow township in 1814. He was born in Virginia, and married Sarah McDonald. They reared a family of five boys and three girls, viz.: Benjamin, Jesse, John, James, and Robert. Of these children, James, who was born in 1804, married Margaret Gard, the daughter of John Gard. Of their five children, two are living—James A. and John L. The latter lives in Noble county. James A., born in 1845, married Dora E. Cook, born in 1856. One child has blessed this union. They live in Palmer township, where Mr. Pugh owns one hundred and fifty acres of land.

Asa Beach was born in Connecticut in 1780 and first settled in Watertown in 1799, where he died in 1847. His wife, Betsey Corns, was born in 1782 and died in 1859. The following members of this family yet survive: David, Pardee, Bernard, Sarah, Elizabeth, and Rufus. The latter was born in 1814, and in 1840 was married to Emily Thompkins, who was born in 1820. To them were born the following children: Josephine, Alfred, Cydnor T., Leander, Roena, Alice, Ruth, and Ada May. Alfred was a member of company F, Thirty-sixth Ohio volunteer infantry; was wounded at Winchester in 1863 and discharged in 1865. Cydnor enlisted in same company in 1863, and was discharged in 1865. Mr. Beach has held the office of trustee for five years, and resides on his farm of one hundred and sixty acres of land in Barlow.

One of the well known citizens of this township is John McCuiag, who came from Scotland and first settled in Warren township in 1821. He was born in Scotland in 1797, and was married to Catharine Harvey, who was born in 1801, and died in 1860. He has two children now living—Margaret, widow of Alexander Gordon, and Mary C., wife of David Scott. He served his appenticeship as a blacksmith in Scotland, and after

coming to this country he worked at his trade for a number of years at Barlow, where he now resides an honored and respected citizen, having retired from business, on his farm, adjoining the village.

Margaret Gordon was born in 1828 and was married in 1851 to Alexander Gordon, who was born in Scotland in 1818, and died in 1873. She has two children living with her on the old homestead—Kate G., now Mrs. Frank Palmer, and John, who was married to Carrie Hart in 1879.

James W. Merrill was born in 1832 and was married in 1854 to Rebecca Greene, who was born in 1832. He came to the township in 1842 and located where he now resides, in Barlow village. He entered the army as first lieutenant of company B, Ninety-second Ohio volunteer infantry, and was wounded in the right knee at the battle of Chickamauga and, being disabled, was honorably discharged in 1864. He immediately entered the dry goods business at the present location, where he has since been engaged, and has accumulated considerable wealth, owning a farm of one hundred acres, a dwelling in the village, and one-half interest in the present store.

David H. Merrill was born in 1835 and came to Barlow in 1850. He first began work on a farm; afterwards taught school until in 1857 he commenced merchandising at his present location in Barlow. In 1864 he was joined by his brother in partnership, under the name of Merrill Brothers, and they are now successfully operating the largest business in this section, consisting of general merchandising in all its departments, milling and buying wool—amounting to a business of forty thousand dollars per year.

Thomas G. Graham was born in Pennsylvania in 1800, and came to Barlow in 1842, having previously served as captain of militia in Pennsylvania. He was married to Susan Gillchreast, who was born in 1822 and died in 1848. The surviving children are: Maria, who lives in Palmer township; and Amanda, also living in Palmer.

Robert Graham was born in 1842, and was married to Mary L. Lamb, in 1868, who was born in 1846. They have four children living, and he is a farmer and stock raiser, owning a farm of one hundred and sixty acres of land. He enlisted in the Union army in 1862, company G, Nineteenth Ohio volunteer infantry, and was discharged in 1865.

Christiana Lamb, whose father, William Fraser, was born in Scotland, in 1783, and settled in Warren township in 1823, where he died in 1837, and whose mother, Christiana McKinsey, was born in 1772, and died in 1848, was born in Scotland in 1809, and was married to William Lamb, in 1827, who was born in 1803 and died in 1878. She has four children—Agnes, Christiana, Mary L. and Sarah, and now lives in Barlow.

Amos Benedict was born in New York in 1806, and settled in Warren township in 1844, where he died in 1879. He was married to Hannah Hobby, who was born in 1806, and died in 1853. They left three children, now living, Henry N., George E., and A. H. He was again married in 1854, to Anna Moffit, who was born in England in 1816.

A. H. Benedict was born in 1843, and was married in 1867 to Lucy E. Gould, who was born in 1847 in Barlow township, and they have a family of three children. He was admitted to the bar in 1867, has served as correspondent of the Marietta *Register*, has taught school in Barlow for the past twenty years, and at present possesses seventy-five acres of land, where he resides in Barlow township.

Josiah Scott, son of John and Nancy, was born in 1820, and was married to Louisa Finch, in 1855, who was born in 1822. They have one child living—Frank L., who resides at home. He now lives on his farm in Barlow, containing one hundred acres of land.

His father, John Scott, first settled in Warren township in 1839, was born in Pennsylvania in 1773, and died in Harmar in 1874. He was married to Nancy Patterson, who was born in 1778, and died in 1861. They have six children now living—William, now residing in Warren township; Mary A., wife of Seth Baily, of Coolville; James, now in Kentucky; Lydia, widow of John Scott, of Harmar; Moses, of Pomeroy, Ohio, and Josiah, who lives in Barlow.

David Breckenridge settled in Barlow in 1832, was born in Scotland in 1773, and died in 1843. His wife, Charlotta McMillen, was born in 1785, and died in 1875. The names of the living members of this family are, viz: Elizabeth, now Mrs. William Andrew; Charlotte, wife of John Dunlap; David, now living in Barlow; Margaret, wife of James McKay; Duncan and John, both living in Iowa; Charles, now in Indiana, and Thomas. The latter was born in Scotland, in 1811, and was married to Margaret Harvey, in 1836, who was born in Scotland, in 1812. He has served as trustee, supervisor and school director for several years, and now owns a farm of one hundred and thirty-five acres of land, on which he resides.

James Ormiston, third, was born in Scotland, in 1822, and in 1845 was married to Polly Conchrite, who was born in 1826. They have seven children now living, and he is general farmer and mechanic, and has made himself possessor of three hundred and fifty acres in Barlow, and served as constable for six years. His father, David Ormiston, first settled in Warren township, in 1828, was born in Scotland in 1800, and died in Illinois in 1880. The living members of this family are: John, living in Barlow; William, in Missouri; A. S., in Kansas; David and Jane in Illinois; Mary, widow of David Taylor, of Indiana, and Benjamin F., now living in Illinois.

James Ormiston, sr., was born in Scotland, in 1769, and settled in Barlow township in 1831, where he died in 1852. His wife, Christiana Lamb, was born in 1771, and died in 1834. Their children were Agnes and James. The latter was born in 1806 in Scotland, and was married in 1834 to Lucinda Willworth, born in 1813. The living members of this family are, viz: Alexander, Isaac, Christiana, James, Merat, Rufus, Anna J., Ruth L., and Thomas L. Alexander enlisted in 1861, in company G, Sixty-third Ohio volunteer infantry, and was with Sherman on his march to the sea. Isaac and James served in the hundred days service.

Mr. Ormiston was a carpenter in his early days, but now resides on his farm of two hundred and thirty acres in Barlow township, and is a general farmer and stock-raiser.

Thomas Fisher, sr., first settled in Aurelius township, in 1837, afterwards in Barlow in 1840. He was born in England in 1811. His wife, Mary Cousins, to whom he was married in 1835, was born in 1814. They have a family of six children, five now living—Richard, John, Sarah, Thomas, Hezekiah and Joseph.

Thomas Fisher, jr., is a general farmer of the township, and is also engaged in raising sheep, and has a farm of one hundred and fifty acres of land.

Marcus Anderson, sr., a native of Ireland, born in 1809, and came to Ohio in 1841. His wife, Rebecca Rodgers, was born in 1812. The members of this family now living are: Elizabeth, Edward, Mary, William, James, Susan, Agnes, Jane, Thomas, Marcus, and Rebecca. Edward was in the hundred day service. William was a member of company F, Thirty-sixth Ohio volunteer infantry, and James of the "Pierpont battery." Mr. Fisher now owns three hundred acres of land and is engaged in sheep raising.

D. H. Tompkins settled in Barlow in 1845; was born in Belmont county in 1818, and died in 1880. He was married in 1843 to Betsey Windsor, who was born in 1823 and died in 1879. Two of the children are now living—A. W., who lives in Harmar, and W. E., citizen of this township. The latter was born in 1851, and now resides on the homestead containing over two hundred acres.

William Beebe, M. D., the leading physician of Barlow township, began the practice of medicine here in 1845. He was born in Belpre in 1822, and was married to Elizabeth Rathbone in 1846, who was born in 1827. To them were born five children now living—W. L., practicing physician in Minnesota; Brooks F., physician in Cincinnati; William P. physician in Texas. Lucy L. and Lizzie H. are both living at home. The doctor has a large practice, and is regarded in the community as an able practitioner in his profession.

In 1834, Robert Haddow came from Scotland and settled in Barlow township. He was born in 1799, and was married to Jeanette Ormiston, who was born in 1795 and died in 1866. The members of this family are—John, Nancy, Mary, Jane, and James.

James Haddow was born in 1827, and was married to Lucy Dustin in 1853, who was born in 1834. He was a member of company F, Thirty-sixth Ohio volunteer infantry from 1861 to 1865, and was wounded at the battle of Winchester, Virginia, and discharged in 1865. He has a family of eight children, and owns one hundred and twenty acres of land, where he resides as a farmer and citizen.

John Haddow was born in 1821, and married in 1843 to Jane C. Fleming, born in 1824, and has seven children now living. He is present postmaster at Barlow, which office he has held since 1861; has held the office of justice of the peace for nineteen years, and township clerk eighteen years. In 1860 he was elected to the legislature, and through his influence Muskingum township was organized.

Ezekiel Deming was born in Massachusetts in 1772, and died at Marietta in 1858. He was judge of the supreme court twenty-one years; was also school teacher, and was married to Hannah Parke, who was born in 1777, and died in 1818. To them were born the following children: Hiram R., James H., Lucinda, Mary, and J. T. Deming, who was born in 1810, and was married in 1841 to Mary A. Richards, who was born in 1824. They have nine children living. Henry R. was sergeant in the hundred day service. Mr. Deming has over one hundred acres of land, and is engaged in farming and raising fine wool sheep.

William H. Cunningham, son of B. F. Cunningham, who was born in 1818, and married to Sabra Harvey, born in 1824, was born in 1842, and was married to Caroline Childers in 1867, who was born in 1848, and died in 1875, leaving two children. He is undertaker and cabinetmaker at Barlow. Of his father's family the following are now living, viz: John W., Melissa J., Orlando, Loring, Mary E., Ister C., Sarah R., and Robert.

John Fleming settled in Barlow in 1820. He was born in Scotland in 1778 and died in 1854. He was married to Jane Colvell, who was born in 1782 and died in 1852. His family consists of David, Isabella, and Mrs. Mary Harvey, who was born in Scotland in 1804, and was married to James Harvey in 1825, born in 1802 and died in 1856. She has six children now living. Her son, David, enlisted in 1861 in company F, Seventy-seventh Ohio volunteer infantry, and died in 1863 from injuries received in the army. Also her son Robert enlisted in 1861 in company A, Thirty-sixth Ohio volunteer infantry, and gave his life to his country at the battle of Cloyd Mountain, Virginia, in 1864. Mrs. Kate W. Harvey was born in 1855, and was married in 1875 to Andrew Harvey, who was born in 1846 and died in 1880. She has three children living, and is also possessor of a farm of two hundred acres of land located in Barlow.

James Fleming was born in Scotland in 1792, and settled in Barlow township in 1820, and died in 1851. His wife was Margaret Breckenridge, and to them were born the following children: J. C., Sarah, Robert, Jane, Margaret, and Thomas. The latter was born in 1836, and was married to Margaret Breckenridge, who was born in 1840. They have seven children now living. He is extensively engaged in raising fine sheep, and has a farm of three hundred acres of land.

Enoch Preston first settled in Harmar in 1838. He was born in Maryland in 1806, and was united in marriage to Miss Margery Lytton, who was born in 1812. The surviving members of this family are Margaret A., wife of John W. Tuttle; Daniel L., Maria E., William L., and Mary J.

Miss Mary J. Preston was born in 1840 in Dunham township, and is now engaged in keeping a general supply store at Vincent station, where she began about one year ago, and at present carries a stock valued at two thousand dollars.

John Jones was born in Pennsylvania in 1803, and married Sarah Lavan, who was born the same year. In 1850 they became residents of Barlow township, remaining there until 1877; thence removing first to Fairfield and finally to Palmer township. His first wife dying in 1875, he married Mrs. Sarah E. Winner, daughter of Ansel and Lida Forbes. Mr. Jones has eight children living, and Mrs. Jones has nine children by her first husband. Mr. Jones has held township office.

CHURCHES.

METHODIST EPISCOPAL CHURCH—BARLOW VILLAGE.

The first meetings of this society were held in the old Hickory school-house, and was then on Marietta circuit. David Young was one of the early ministers, and is remembered as having at one time selected for his text the twenty-third verse of the fifth chapter of Judges—"Curse ye, Meroz, curse ye bitterly the inhabitants thereof, because they came not to the help of the Lord." In the exposition of this text the minister, as was the custom in those days, repeated the text frequently, and each time with greater emphasis. An elderly lady from West Virginia happened to be present, and being afterward asked how she liked the sermon, replied: "The sermon was very good, but I am afraid the old man swore most too much."

The Methodists, after holding services in the Hickory school-house for a number of years, built a log meeting-house in 1808, north of Barlow village, where they held services until the present church building was erected in the village, which was completed in 1836, though it has been much improved since then, having at present a cupola and bell; and is a good substantial frame, thirty-five by forty. Among the early preachers of this society was Jacob Young, a brother of David Young, who is remembered as a very efficient minister in building up this part of the circuit. The present parsonage, located near the church building, was completed in 1839, and was first occupied by Rev. James B. Austin. Among the ministers who preached on this circuit after the church was built, were: John Furree, presiding elder, William Strickland, Samuel Hamilton, presiding elder, (1838) James D. Webb and Joseph Gasner, Matthew Scoville, Sheldon Parker, Joseph Morris, Martin Wolf. In 1844 the circuit was changed to Barlow, after having been Marietta, then Belpre circuit for a number of years. The society at Barlow village is now in a flourishing condition under the present ministry of Rev. S. B. Ricketts, and has a membership of one hundred and fifteen. The Sabbath-school, under the superintendence of Daniel Canfield, meets every Sunday. In connection with the church is the Woman's Missionary society, organized and carried on by the ladies of the society, and succeeds in adding about thirty dollars yearly to the missionary fund of the general church.

PRESBYTERIAN (OLD SCHOOL) CHURCH—BARLOW VILLAGE.

The Proctor family were the pioneer Presbyterians of this locality, and the house of Nathan Proctor was the stopping place of the ministers of this denomination, and he would make an appointment for them to preach at night, or probably secure their services for Sabbath.

Revs. S. P. Robbins, Jacob and Stephen Lindley, were among the early ministers of this denomination. The present church building was erected in 1833, and the first organization was effected three years after (1836) by Revs. Addison Kingsbury and Luther Bingham, "the petition to presbytery having been signed by John Henry, John and Hugh Breckenridge, and others." The sermon, from First Samuel, seventh chapter and second verse, was delivered by Rev. Kingsbury, and at the first meeting the following persons were received into communion by letter: Nill and Agnes McGeachy, Jeanette Johnson, and Elizabeth Bowman; afterwards, Joshua, Elizabeth, James and Hannah Rodgers, Thomas Breckenridge, John and Mary Martin, John Breckenridge, Charlotta Dunlap, David F. and Sophia Fleming, Michael Ormiston, and Duty Greene.

Revs. Manning and Roberts served this congregation as supplies until the first regular pastor, Rev. Samuel P. Dunham, was installed. In 1839 the "New School" society withdrew from this church, and erected a small frame building just east of Barlow village. Among the prominent members of this society were Robert Haddow, William Lamb, and Nelson Ford. They held services in this building until 1870, when the two Presbyterian societies again united, and the building was abandoned, the reunited society choosing the present house of worship. The present pastor, Rev. William Bay, has served this congregation about four years, and they have a present membership of about seventy-five, and are enjoying a good degree of prosperity. Services are held regularly every Sabbath, after which the Sabbath-school is convened, and an hour spent in the study of the Scripture and imparting the knowledge thereof to the children.

UNITED PRESBYTERIAN CHURCH—BARLOW VILLAGE.

This congregation was organized October 8, 1849, by Samuel Findly, D. D. It was formed mainly of those who had withdrawn from the "Old School" congregation worshipping in the same village. Since its organization the following have been ministers in charge: Revs. S. M. Hutchinson, James McNeal, Julian Straus, and W. S. Harper. The pastoral work of Rev. J. D. Palmer, the present minister, began in May, 1876. Ruling elders: Daniel Drain, Almond Henderson, W. B. McGill, and Anderson Ferguson. Trustees: F. P. Deming, Andrew McFarland, and James Drain. The membership now numbers about one hundred, holding services in the brick building located in Barlow village. Services and Sabbath-school every Sabbath.

THE UNION CHURCH—VINCENT STATION.

This building is located in the northeast part of the village; is a frame twenty-five by forty feet, and was erected in 1867 by general subscription as a union church for the use of all denominations. The Universalists, Methodists, and Presbyterians hold services here, but the former has regular services under the ministerial charge of Rev. J. W. McMasters. The original trustees were John Ormiston, Isaac Hopkins, and Isaac Dunlap. In 1866 Mrs. Sarah Hill first inaugurated the movement which resulted in the organization of the present union Sabbath-school, which now meets regularly at the church. The leading men in this congregation were Henry M. Amlin, John Ormiston, Osmer B. Vincent, and Hiram Gard. The object of the organization was to promote a general study of the bible without sectarian bias. The first officials were H. M. Amlin, superintendent; John Ormiston, assistant superintendent; O. B. Vincent, secretary; J. Caleb Vincent, treasurer. At present there are eight teachers, one hundred and seventeen scholars, with a library of about one hundred and fifty volumes. The present officials are: John Ormiston, superintendent; J. C. Vincent, assistant superintendent; Emmett Agin, secretary; Florence M. Hayes, treasurer. The school is now in very prosperous condition, and is regarded as an institution productive of much good, morally, socially and intellectually, and great interest is felt among the moral people of this community for the continued success of the union Sabbath-school.

The Christian church was organized in 1846 under the administration of Rev. William Kelso. The first meeting was held at the house of Amos Pryor, who was the first elder of the church. In 1859 the present church building was erected. The ministers of the society have been, in the order of their services, Zephaniah Zollers, Isaac Newton, John Beard, Nathan Moody, H. Bingman, Adam Cardner, John Moody, J. Neugent, Joseph Thomas, Ezra Barker, A. B. Wade, J. A. Walters, R. A. Pickens, Joseph Dunn, Joseph Dutton, and A. Calvert, the present clergyman. The society now numbers about thirty members, and has a prosperous Sabbath-school, of which A. Pryor is superintendent.

SCHOOLS.

In the fall of 1808-9 the first school-house was built on the northwest part of section sixteen, and was known as the old Hickory school-house. The first teacher was a young man—John Treat Deming—from Sandersfield, now Watertown. The next teacher was a venerable Irishman—Samuel Clark—who was well educated in mathematics and penmanship. He went from here to the vicinity of Fishtown in Fairfield, and afterwards removed to Columbus. For the following abstract of a description of this pioneer school-house we are indebted to the papers left by Henry Earle Vincent:

The house in which the pioneer children of Barlow township first learned their A, B, C, and to repeat "In Adam's fall we sinned all," was built entirely of rough hickory logs, with chimney of "cat and clay," and a broad fireplace wide enough to receive logs the length of a common fence-rail, which not only furnished fuel for fire but seats for the young urchins while warming themselves. The floor, benches and writing table were all made of rough-hewn puncheons—that is, logs split into slabs and some of the roughness "scutched" off with a broad-axe. Small cavities were left in the back wall in which the ink-stands, containing the *maple* ink, were kept to protect it from the frost. The windows were made by cutting out a piece of a log six or eight feet in length and placing small sticks perpendicularly across the space at intervals, thus making a sash over which paper was pasted. The paper used was generally the well-scribbled leaves of old copy-books, as there were no newspapers in those days and blank paper was too scarce and too valuable to be used for such purposes. This paper was made transparent by being first generally coated with coon's grease, possum fat, and a fire-brand held to it until well melted.

The old schoolmaster was so deaf that the scholars would "talk right-out-loud," and often he would go to sleep and then the way the

Hiram Gard

Ataline G Gard

Cornelius Gard, grandfather of the subject of this sketch, was born near Morristown, New Jersey, on the thirtieth of October, 1744, (Old Style), was of English extraction, and married near Pughtown, in Frederick county, Virginia, on the first of October, 1774, Mary Harsher, whose parents were from Wales, and who was born June 22, 1757. Cornelius Gard came to Ohio from Frederick county, Virginia, in 1802, was a shoemaker by trade, lived in Washington and Licking counties, was a genial and companionable man, and died in Palmer township, Washington county, November 2, 1841, aged ninety-seven years, his wife having preceded him in death about one year, dying August 17, 1840, aged eighty-three years. Both of them were members of the Methodist church. They left two sons—Timothy, the oldest, born February 21, 1785, and David, born April 15, 1792. Timothy married Nancy Davis, a relative of Isaac Williams, a pioneer who lived in Virginia, opposite the mouth of the Muskingum and Ohio rivers. Timothy died July 14, 1858, at Granville, Licking county, Ohio, leaving four sons—Isaac, Jeremiah, Timothy, Samuel, and one daughter, Polly.

David Gard, the father of Hiram Gard, was born in Hampshire county, Virginia, and married Mary Hiett, March 11, 1800, of same place. Came to Vienna, Virginia, six miles above Parkersburgh the same spring, lived there one year, and in 1803 moved to the White Oak settlement, in what is now Palmer township, Washington county, Ohio, at which place Hiram was born. In 1805 David returned to Vienna, Virginia, and remained there until the spring of 1812 when he returned to the White Oak settlement, then Wesley township, near where Brown's Mills were afterwards built, on Wolf creek, where he lived until his death February 15, 1859. His wife, Mary Hiett Gard, followed him in death from the same place May 15, 1861. David Gard was a man of sterling integrity, and honest in the fullest sense of the term, a man of very limited education but of good judgment, and much respected in society. He and his wife were both devoted and worthy members of the Methodist church for the last twenty years of their lives; were quiet in demeanor, much beloved and respected.

David Gard left two sons—Hiram, born May 11, 1804, and James Hiett, born January 2, 1828, and four daughters—Maria, born August 20, 1801, Rowena, born December 20, 1805, Sophia, born January 6, 1813, and Jane, born March 15, 1817 (died in infancy by accidental scalding).

Of the daughters, Maria married Benjamin Mason Brown, of Athens county, on the eleventh of May, 1826, and died at Belpre, July 17, 1885, at the home of her son-in-law, Justice Alderman, where she had lived many years in widowhood, receiving the kindest attention and best care that could be bestowed during a long illness. She left sons—Hiram McNeal, who died some years before his mother, leaving a wife, Mrs. Jane Brown, and one son, John Mason Brown; Charles Alonzo and John Arza both enlisted in the service of the United States against the Rebellion, and were honorably discharged at the close of the war, Charles Alonzo having received a wound at the battle of Chickamauga, from which he finally recovered; Charles Alonzo, who married Martha Breckenridge; John Arza, who married Henrietta Stacy; and Sophronia Josephine, who married the aforesaid Justice Alderman and lives in Belpre village.

Rowena married Edward Camp October 3, 1833, and reared two sons, George L., and David H., both of whom served honorably in the war against the Rebellion (George L., during an engagement with the enemy, at the battle of Mission Ridge, stopped one of the enemy's balls, which passed through many thick-

nesses of blanket and his trousers, and stopped in the midst of his silver lever watch, after entirely destroying it), and three daughters—Josephine, who married William Vincent; Augusta, who married twice—Dr. William Bates and J. K. Hornaday, and Emma, unmarried.

Sophia Gard married James M. Palmer November 4, 1835, and had three sons—David E., who married Miss Shradley Dudley, who died in the Union army in Tennessee; and Hiram, who married Augusta Evans; and three daughters—Mary, who married Jesse Murdock, and Lydia and Laura, who are unmarried. Jane Gard died in infancy by a scald.

James H. married Ruth G. Palmer December 2, 1851. He also enlisted in the Union army and served a term of some three months. He left two daughters—Clara and Laura, their oldest daughter, Ella, having died young. James H. died August 5, 1859. His widow and the two little daughters moved to Oregon where they still reside.

Hiram Gard, the oldest son of David Gard, married Ataline Gage Dunsmoor February 23, 1831. They have reared four sons—Edward Dunsmoor, Charles Edgar, Daniel Hosmer, and Huel Abner, and three daughters, Mary Melissa, Martha Jane, and Helen Josephine.

Edward, first son, married Jane Breckenridge April 26, 1853, and died November 20, 1858. His daughter, Martha Atema, was born after his death, on May 15, 1859, and died April 15, 1861. Edward D. was a very industrious and persevering young man, and had already founded a comfortable home at the time of his premature death.

Charles Edgar, second son, was born March 31, 1832, and married Rachel Breadwell September 1, 1859, who was born April 10, 1841, at Mt. Carmel, Ohio. They have two sons—Ord Lark, born November 6, 1861, Otto Brent, born February 12, 1867, and one daughter—Grace Adena, born May 16, 1869. Charles was a surveyor and engineer before being reared on a farm, where he studied and worked hard for an education, but finally settled down to merchandising, to which business he applied himself closely and shrewdly. He has served as justice of the peace one term and also as county surveyor.

Daniel Hosmer, third son, was born at Palmer February 24, 1844, and married Ella E. Rider November 5, 1868. They have one son, born May 3, 1876, named Wentworth. He is a telegraph operator; has always made that his business, and is now superintendent of two lines of railway telegraph, viz. Hocking Valley and Columbus & Toledo railroads. He lives at Columbus, Ohio, where he has built a fine residence on Long street, near the crossing of Lexington avenue. He is a man of close application and good business habits, and stands high with his associates and the railroad companies.

Huel Abner, third and youngest son, born August 19, 1853, married Flora Bell Ellenwood, November 13, 1870, is a young farmer, a man of good judgment, and prides himself on raising good stock and having everything near around him, and carries on the home farm at Vincent. Three sons, together with the daughters, whose names will follow, were all born at Palmer, Washington county, Ohio.

Mary Melissa, the oldest daughter, was born March 31, 1834, and married Francisca Pitt Pond November 27, 1854, who died January 24, 1875. Mr. Pond was hauling wood at a distance from his house, the ground was sloping and frozen but slightly thawed on top, the wagon slipped and upset, horses and all, into a broad gulley, the wood under the wagon and Mr. Pond under one of the horses, which was also down He was dead when found by his wife several hours afterward. He left four sons. Hiram Otis, the oldest, born November 15, 1855, was a telegraph operator in the principal office of the Columbus & Toledo railroad at Columbus, Ohio; is now chief train dispatcher on the same road. He was born minus one hand, the arm terminating a few inches below the elbow, an apparent evil perhaps working for his good. Charles Orland, second son, born November 26, 1858, a promising young man of six feet three inches; Beman Lew, third son, born June 9, 1867, and Sylvester Pitt, fourth and last son, born February 22, 1870.

Martha Jane, second daughter of H. Gard, was born January 29, 1836, and married Joel Mason Danley June 19, 1859, who enlisted in the Union army in the spring of 1862 for three years, and before he had seen many months services took the measles, followed by pneumonia, which caused his death at Carthage Ferry while in the service of his country He reared one son, Robert Joel Mason, born September 26, 1861 (this son is also a telegraph operator in the principal office of the Hocking Valley railroad at Columbus), and one daughter, Ida Leona, born June 21, 1858, married to Stewart E. Crewson.

Helen Josephine, third daughter, was born August 22, 1839, and was married to Henry C. Vincent January 20, 1864. They have one son, Fred Wilber, born July 1, 1864 Mr. Vincent lives at Vincent, Ohio; he is also a telegraph operator, one of the first who learned to operate on the old Marietta and Cincinnati railroad; he has followed the business most of his life.

Hiram Gard, the subject of the portrait, was born in Washington county, in what was then called the White Oak settlement, which is now included in Palmer township. From 1805 to 1810 he was absent in Virginia, after which he returned and remained until 1854, when he removed to Vincent, in Barlow township. He was absent from that place some five years, living at New England, Athens county; at the expiration of which he returned to Vincent, where he now resides. In early life he was engaged to some extent in driving and dealing in stock, also in merchandising and milling Subsequently at Vincent he graded about one and a half miles of the old Marietta & Cincinnati railroad track. At the age of nineteen he was elected a captain of militia and a year or two later, lieutenant colonel of the same. In 1840 he was elected county commissioner for Washington county He was frequently called to serve as viewer of State and county roads, and as justice of the peace in different townships in Washington and Athens counties. He once received a tie vote for nomination as representative of Washington county. He married, February 25, 1830, Ataline Gage Dunsmoor, the daughter of Phineas and Polly Dunsmoor, of Goshen, Sullivan county, New Hampshire. On February 25, 1880, they celebrated the fiftieth anniversary of their happy wedded life, surrounded by all their children, most of their grandchildren, and many of their friends.

Hiram Gard, to a character of sterling worth unites a genial, hearty temperament, which rejoices in the society of friends, and finds the chief pleasure of life in their companionship. A good talker, he possesses a fund of anecdote and reminiscence which makes him excellent company. He has that self-depreciation and that lack of self-consciousness which render him always more thoughtful for the happiness of others than of himself. His incorruptible honesty as well as his strong hold on the affections of his acquaintances and friends are illustrated by an incident in his business career. At one time he became deeply involved in debt, and his friends urged him to avail himself of the advantage of the bankrupt law He refused to do so, saying in substance that it was a law for sneaks. "There is my property," said he, "take it and divide it up among you as far as it will go, and if I ever make any more I will pay the whole debt; but I will not take advantage of the bankrupt law." Several judgments were secured against him, and articles of his property were, in pursuance thereof, offered at sheriff's sale, but in no instance, save one, was there one of his neighbors who was willing to bid, and, consequently, the property remained unsold. He redeemed himself and paid all in full.

Phineas Dunsmoor was born in Townsend, Massachusetts, December 29, 1771. Polly Gage, his wife, was born in Pelham, New Hampshire, July 16, 1782, and was the daughter of Abner Gage, a soldier in the Revolutionary war, and at the battle of Bunker Hill had a portion of his foot taken off by a cannon ball. They were married April 10, 1798. He owned a large farm at Charleston, New Hampshire, where they resided until Ataline was about five years old, when he sold his farm and purchased a hotel stand and farm adjoining, at Goshen, Sullivan county, New Hampshire, where they resided until Ataline was ten years old; he then sold his property in New Hampshire, and bought of J. Buck a farm of nine hundred and five acres, situated in the Ohio company's purchase, Wesley township, Washington county, Ohio. They left New Hampshire the same spring and arrived in Wesley, July 25, 1822. He died May 6, 1823, at the same place, leaving his widow with seven children. These were: Horace, born October 11, 1799; Abner G., born March 17, 1804; Mary K., born August 13, 1805; Hiel, born October 20, 1807; Lucius P., born January 25, 1810, Ataline G., born September 18, 1812 (all the above born at Charleston, New Hampshire); Daniel N., born in Goshen November 26, 1817. Their mother died at Barlow March 20, 1857. Their ancestors came to this country in 1719, and settled in Londonderry, New Hampshire. They descended from Lord John Dinsmore, of Achimeed, Scotland, who possessed a large tract of land in the north of Ireland, Londonderry county.

Londonderry, New Hampshire, derived its name from Londonderry, Ireland—name given by first settlers there. From the above are descended all the Densmores, Dunsmoors, and Dinsmores of this county.

young rogues in "home-spun and linsey" would "cut-up" was nobody's business but the teacher's and he did not know it. When dismissed for noon, the first one on the ice was the best fellow—but the best *fellow* in this case happened to be a tall, portly *girl*, who generally led the van in all the sports. The old school-house has long since, with the youthful actors in the scenes about its portals, passed away forever.

The early schools received some support from the rents of the lands granted by Congress for that purpose. The other expenses were paid by subscription from the parents who had children to send to school. As an illustration of how teachers were engaged the following contract is appended:

The article of agreement between James Lawton, jr. and his employers:

Witnesseth, that he on his part agrees to teach the school during the term of three months in which he is to teach the different parts of learning that may be required according to his best ability.

For the above service (when performed) the undersigned agree to give the said James Lawton the sum of $36.00, half in cash or store orders the other in the following articles of produce, viz: Merino wool (not less than one-fourth blooded) at 50 c. per lb., flax at 12½ whiskey at 31 c. per gal., linen cloth 30 c., and that which is called four and thirty linen.

This township has now eight school districts, all provided with school buildings and teachers supported under the present public school system at public expense. At the present time there are three hundred and forty-three pupils enrolled, with an average daily attendance of two hundred and twenty-seven. And the average number of weeks these schools were in session during the last year (1880) was twenty-six. The present educational advantages as compared with the past is not better exemplified in any other locality than in Barlow when we recall old Hickory school-house, with its unhewn logs, its copy-book windows, clapboard seats, and few, if any books, with the present comfortable houses and many appliances and facilities in educational pursuits.

THE BARLOW AGRICULTURAL ASSOCIATION.

In response to a call for a meeting to organize an agricultural society, about fifteen persons assembled at the town house in Barlow August 24, 1872. Daniel Canfield was called to the chair, and I. B. Lawton was appointed secretary. The election of officers resulted as follows: William Thompson, president; Thomas Fleming, vice-president; directors—for two years, John Ormiston, Daniel Canfield, C. S. Prugh, James H. Breckenridge; for one year, D. N. Dunsmore, Robert Dunlap, Rufus Beach, and C. H. Goddard; I. F. Palmer, secretary.

The grove of C. D. Ford, about a mile west of Barlow village, was immediately fitted up for the first exhibition, which was held September 24 and 25, 1872. The first exhibition was very much larger than was anticipated, there being over three hundred entries, and general interest was awakened and deepened by the discussion of various questions of farm interest.

The total receipts for the first year were seventy-five dollars and thirty-five cents; expenses, fifty-six dollars and ninety-four cents; leaving a balance of eighteen dollars and forty-one cents in the treasury, to begin the improvements and make arrangements for the next exhibition. The grounds are now amply fitted for a very creditable display; having a domestic and art hall twenty by sixty feet, farm products hall twenty by sixty feet, an ornamental flower pavilion with a fountain, a sheep shed of fifty-six pens, arranged in a circle, enclosing an open space in the centre for exhibition; cattle and horse sheds containing over over one hundred and fifty stalls; and the enclosure of the grounds embraces an area of about fifteen acres, well supplied with water. The gross receipts of last year were six hundred and forty-six dollars and ninety-six cents, and expenditures five hundred and ninety-four dollars and ninety-nine cents. The present officers are: William Thompson, president; Robert Breckenridge, vice-president; directors, Thomas Fleming, C. S Prugh, Roscoe Walcott, John Ormiston, C. S. Laflin, D. R. Shaw, J. H. Breckenridge; I. F. Palmer, treasurer; F. P. Deming, secretary.

BARLOW TEMPERANCE UNION.

The object of this society is to increase the interest in the cause of temperance. The Murphy pledge is used and the meetings are public, which are enlivened and made attractive by literary exercises. The first meeting was held February 26, 1880, at the Methodist Episcopal church. Rev. J. D. Palmer was called to the chair, and prayer offered by Rev. S. B. Ricketts. Sixty-five persons signed the pledge at the first meeting, and the membership has increased to two hundred and twenty-five. The election of officers resulted as follows: D. H. Merrill, president; J. H. Breckenridge, vice-president; Miss Nettie Loynacan, secretary; Miss Anna R. Ford, treasurer. The Union is now in active and successful operation, and is considered as an effectual agent in promoting moral reform in this locality.

WOOL GROWERS' ASSOCIATION.

The sheep breeders and wool growers of Washington county met at the residence of William Thompson, in Fairfield township, March 24, 1876, for the purpose of organizing an association. Thomas Fleming was called to the chair, and G. B. Quinn, secretary; R. Breckenridge, treasurer. The committee appointed to draft a constitution and by-laws reported as the object of the association, the promotion of harmony and more intelligent action among sheep breeders by the interchange of ideas and information, and the careful and unprejudiced comparison of stock and productions. On motion it was decided that a "shearing" be held the following spring at the residence of William Thompson, and a committee was appointed to arrange for the meeting. James Hiett, Andrew Harvey, William R. Putnam, James Trotter, George Coffman, and Pemberton Palmer were appointed judges of sheep. At this shearing, which was held May 1, 1876, the examinations were made as to the breed, age, age of fleece, weight of carcasses and of fleece, quality of wool and condition, length of staple, density of fleece, yolkiness, covering of belly, head, and legs, wrinkliness, form and constitution. The sheep were first examined by the committee, then sent to the shearer; the shearer turns the fleeces over to the committee on fleeces, and, after examination, they are bundled and labelled, and recorded by the secretary. Over one hundred and fifty head of sheep were presented for examination at the first meeting.

The meetings of the association are held regularly once a month from October to May. The present officials are: Joseph H. Gage, president; John Ormiston, vice-president; F. P. Deming, secretary; R. Breckenridge, treasurer.

BARLOW GRANGE NO. 712 PATRONS OF HUSBANDRY.

The organization of this grange was effected in April, 1874, and the original officials were: D. N. Dunsmore, master; J. B. Lawton, overseer; C. C. Lawton, lecturer; J. W. Bradhurst, chaplain; D. Hartson, steward; Andrew Harvey, assistant steward; S. W. Harvey, secretary; D. H. Fleming, treasurer; Mrs. S. W. Harvey, Ceres; Mrs. P. Dunsmore, Pomona; Mrs. D. H. Fleming, Flora; Miss Hannah Fleming, stewardess. The charter members, including the above, were: E. F. Greene, P. Dunsmore, D. A. Dunsmore, William Fleming, J. W. Morris, Josiah Scott, Tremont Malster, Misses Emma Fleming, Nettie and Sarah Henry.

The building in which the meetings are held is located in East Barlow, and is a frame twenty by forty feet, erected by the grange in 1874. The meetings have been harmonious, though in debate on various questions affecting general interests, opinions are freely expressed, no serious discussions have occurred, and at present, though somewhat embarrassed by financial difficulties, in which this and other granges became involved by departing from grange principles and attempting to conduct business on plans not contemplated by the organization. This embarrassment has seriously injured the grange movement, although, so far as this society is concerned, every effort is being made to push the finances to final and satisfactory settlement, and to continue the organization, and make it an organization of substantial benefit to all classes as well as the farmer. The present membership is about twenty, though but about half of the original membership, it embraces among its numbers many of the substantial and reliable farmers of this locality.

CEMETERIES.—BARLOW CENTRAL CEMETARY ASSOCIATION.

This association was formed February 14, 1859, at a meeting called for that purpose, held at the town house in Barlow village. The officers of the association were elected, viz: D. C. Perry, John Vincent, James W. Merrill, James Haddow, and J. H. Breckenridge, trustees; James W. Merrill, treasurer; John Lawton, sexton. An addition was made to the old burying-grounds immediately east of Barlow village, on the Proctor farm. The lots were surveyed twelve by twenty feet, with an alley four feet wide between. These grounds are kept in repair by the association, and are now the principal burying-grounds of the township.

MILLS.

In early times "going to mill" was a pilgrimage requiring long absence from home, and at best, an uncertain return, and accompanied by many difficulties unknown to the present generation. Henry E. Vincent leaves on record a very full description of a journey of this kind from this locality to the mill on Big Hocking, some fifteen or twenty miles distant. The roads were but paths through the woods, and often led dangerously near the deep gorges and precipices of the rough country through which he passed. In the route he passed along the Big West branch, and here met with an accident. By a sudden slide of the wagon his load was precipitated over a precipice; down went sack after sack bounding over the rocks and tumbling over each other in their rapid descent, and to crown all, his bucket of biscuits burst from their confinement and went skipping down over the rocks after the sacks of grain, causing the hapless victim to smile in the midst of the disaster. He finally arrived at the mill, though it was fast growing dark, on Friday, and was informed that he could not have the grist before the following Sunday. But there were several others there patiently waiting for their supply of meal, and they camped around the miller's fire, where they passed the time in telling jokes, and the fun and mirth that went gaily around the miller's fire during those long nights must be imagined. The trip home was performed on the following Sunday, and by the assistance of a neighbor who rode with him from the mill, he was finally enabled to reach home in safety.

Barlow mill, located in the village of Barlow, was erected in 1859, by Haynes & Basim, and now belongs to Merrill & Ford, operated by D. E. Basim. It is a substantial frame building, two stories high, and has two run of stone, with capacity of two hundred bushels per day.

Since the abandonment of the railroad no shipping has been done, the trade being generally confined to custom work. This is the only flour mill within the bounds of the township, and now furnishes a large and growing community with all the usual commodities of the trade.

BARLOW VILLAGE.

The plat of this village was originally made in 1840, with John McCuig, Horatio Ford and Lyman Laflin, proprietors, and consisted of eleven lots of fifty-four acres each, and located near the Marietta and Belpre roads. The first house within the plat was a small frame located on the southeast corner (now used as a kitchen to J. W. Merritt's residence), and was built by Elias Woodruff and John Pratt for a grocery. The first store was where the present store of Merrill Bros. now stands, and Lyman Laflin kept the first post office south of the present store. At present the village has one general store, one blacksmith shop, one tin shop, one shoe shop, one wagon shop, one cabinet-maker and undertaker and one flour mill, two physicians and three churches.

Fleming station is a small collection of houses with one store and post office kept by Lyman Tullis in east part of township on the old Marietta & Cincinnati railroad.

VINCENT STATION.

This small village, located in the southwestern part of the township on the old line of the Marietta & Cincinnati railroad, was first laid out in lots, August 3, 1853, by Henry Earle Vincent, proprietor. The first house built within the original plat was erected by Enoch Preston on lot eight, where he kept the first house of entertainment and where he yet lives as proprietor of the Preston house. The first post office was kept by Henry E. Vincent in the present station house (1857), and the first store was kept by Church B. Tuttle on the lot, where the present store house of H. Gard & Son now stands. The village now contains two general stores, one saloon, one church, and one cooper-shop. The abandonment of the Marietta & Cincinnati railroad was a serious blow to the rather flattering prospects of the village from which there are small hopes of recovery.

CHAPTER LVI.

WESLEY TOWNSHIP.

The Township Established—Physical Features—First Election of Township Officers—Roads Established—Banishment of a Destitute Family—Wheat Received for Taxes—Census in 1826—Settlement— Societies—Schools—Churches—Cemeteries—Villages—Mills—Tannery—Incidents—Underground Railroad.

WESLEY township was established on petition of Joseph Palmer and others, in 1810, and originally embraced the territory of township three, range ten, and township seven, range eleven, then belonging to Wooster, also the south half of township eight, range eleven, belonging to Roxbury. Afterwards sections one, two, three, four, five, six of township seven, and sections one, two, three of township eight were added. At present it is nine miles long from north to south, and four miles wide, containing in all thirty sections, embracing an area of almost twenty thousand acres, It is bounded on the north by Morgan county, east by Palmer and Fairfield, south by Decatur, on the east by Athens county, and has a population of fourteen hundred and seventy-seven. The surface maintains the general aspect common to this section of country—high rolling lands, and in various localities broken in high hills and deep ravines. The soil is of yellow and red clay, productive chiefly of fruits of all kinds, wheat, corn and other ordinary cereals. The industries belong mostly to the agricultural, though there are several flouring-mills, saw-mills, tannery, and other minor manufactures. The timber consists mostly of white and red oak, with some walnut and poplar. The west branch of Wolf creek enters the township in the extreme northwest corner, and following a zigzag course southwest, enters Fairfield from section twenty-six. This stream usually furnishes sufficient force for flour-mills during most of the year.

Coal run, a small stream, enters the township at the northwest, and, flowing in a southeast course, empties into Wolf creek, north of Coady & Gage's mill. Several other unimportant branches are found in the west and south.

The State road leading from Harmar, on the Ohio river, to Athens was first laid out by the county commissioners, January 27, 1848. It extends across the central part of the township, from east to west, through the villages of Pleasanton and Plymouth, where it receives the main north and south thoroughfares.

ORGANIZATION.

The first officials of the township were appointed August 12, 1810, viz.: Trustees, Joseph Palmer, Cornelius Houghland and John Rardin; township clerk, Samuel Clark; overseer of poor, Abner Woodruff and Duty Greene; fence-viewers, John Danley and Henry Coons; lister of taxes, James Lawton; appraiser, William Vincent; supervisors, Robert Miller, David Gard, Isaac Woodruff, William Rardin and Edmund Neal; constables, David Ewell and Isaac Woodruff; treasurer, John Curtis. In the following October, Joseph Palmer and Cornelius Houghland were elected justices of the peace.

The first general election was held April 1, 1811, resulting as follows: Trustees, John Rardin, Duty Greene and John Danley; clerk, Samuel Clark; overseers of poor, Edmund Neal and Nathan Proctor; fence-viewers, Joshua Shuttleworth and James Corns; lister of taxes, Isaac Woodruff; appraiser, William Vincent; constables, David Ewell and Jabez Palmer; treasurer, John Curtis. Members of grand jury were first selected in 1815— David Ewell and David Gard; petit jury, Samuel Pond and John Danley. The first settlement by the treasurer, of which any record is found, was made by Samuel Pond, treasurer, March 16, 1815, showing the receipt from all sources of thirty-four dollars and twenty-three and one-half cents, and leaving in the treasury after settlement, four dollars and ninety-three and one-half cents.

On the thirteenth of April, 1816, the road districts were first laid out by Cornelius Houghland, John Danley and William Rardin, under Benajah Horse, township clerk. The first notice against the poor was issued by Joseph Palmer and William Coons, overseers, March 4, 1818, warning "James Lockwood and Phœbe, his wife, and all their children, to depart out of this township, as it is found they have no visible means of support and are in danger of coming onto the township." This notice was served by Michael Gard, constable, and it is supposed that its purpose was effected and that the poor family was compelled to "move on" out of the township.

At a meeting of trustees, April 2, 1821, a resolution was passed enabling those indebted to the township for taxes to pay the same in wheat, to be delivered at the mill of Samuel Brown, now in Palmer township, on Wolf creek, at fifty cents per bushel.

In 1826 the first recorded census of the householders of Wesley township shows a list of ninety-four names. This then included what is now Fairfield township with Wesley. This great expanse of territory had less than one hundred families as late as 1826, shows something of the progress this township has made in the past fifty years.

EARLY SETTLEMENTS.

Among the earliest pioneers of Wesley, we find the name of Honorable Thomas Ewing, who settled on the farm now owned by James W. Smith, just west of Plymouth. He built his log-cabin about seventy-five rods southwest of the present farm residence of Mr. Smith. A few fruit trees still stand as the only mark of the spot where the venerable statesman lived.

Moses Woodruff, who came from Pennsylvania, built his log-cabin two miles north of Plymouth, near the present residence of John Morrow, in section thirty.

John Rardin's cabin stood just where the present residence of Dr. Munroe now stands in Pleasanton.

Henry Rardin erected his cabin on the farm now owned by John Morrow, in section thirty. These settlements were all made prior to 1810, in which year James Ward Smith settled on the farm now owned by his son, James, immediately west of Plymouth, and occupied the cabin built by Thomas Ewing.

Robert Brackenridge lived about one mile southeast of Pleasanton, in the cabin which stood on the opposite side of the road from the present residence of Charles Haines, in section thirty-four.

Jacob Mullen erected his cabin on the west branch of Little Hocking river, about fifty rods southeast of the present farm-house of James A. McGrew, in section twenty-seven.

William Coaley lived on the farm now owned by Cyrus Wilson in section twenty-eight.

Soloman Gable erected his cabin on the site of the present residence of James King, in section twenty-seven.

Joseph Ames settled on the farm now owned by E. Hollingsworth, north of the State road, in section twenty-two.

Levi Arnold, two miles east of Plymouth, where Dixon Graham now lives, in section twenty-two.

James W. Smith was born in 1809, and came with his father's family to this township in 1810, and has lived on the homestead farm ever since. He was married in 1830, to Eliza Goddard, who was born in New Hampshire in 1813. To them were born eight children—six of whom are now living, viz.: Pherona T., wife of James W. Barnes, now resides in Cincinnati; Elonzo H., now living in Dunham township; Edward F., resides in Dakota Territory; Waldo, living in this township; Lucy, at home; and Clarence C., now living in Wesley township. Mr. Smith has filled several township offices, and has been a citizen of this township longer than any one now living within its boundaries—a period of three score years and ten.

James Waldo Smith, jr., was born in this township in 1838, and was married to Mary A. Gage in 1864, who was born in 1847. They have a family of four children, viz.: Oscar B., Myron A., Lucy S., Ethel F. Mr. Smith's farm is located about one mile north of Plymouth. He is quite extensively engaged in raising stock.

Soloman N. Cook settled in Wesley township in 1814, coming from New Hampshire in 1814, where he was born in 1785. He married Mary Cook, whose parents were early settlers of Palmer township. She was born in 1786, and died in 1868. Mr. and Mrs. Cook have five children, three of whom are still living, all in this county.

Philip Schrader, sr., was born in Maryland, and was married to a daughter of Michael Montgomery in 1805. He first settled in Wesley township in September, 1816, having purchased three hundred and twenty acres of land from William Skinner, sr., for which he paid eight hundred dollars. He located about one mile north of the present village of Plymouth. He had a family of eleven children, eight boys and three girls, all of whom have grown to maturity in Washington county. He died in Licking county, Ohio, in 1865, his wife having died in Athens county in 1862.

Levi Arnold came from Wood county, Virginia, and first settled on the farm now owned by Dixon Graham on the State road, two miles east of Plymouth, section twenty-two. He was born in Virginia in 1801, and was married to Sarah Ingram, who was born in 1803, and died in 1867. He died in Missouri in 1867. While he resided in Wesley he was one of the leading citizens, and held the office of clerk and trustee, and was justice of the peace sixteen years.

Benjamin F. Arnold, son of Levi, was born in Wesley township in 1825, and was married to Maria Palmer, who was born in 1827. To them were born twelve children, seven of whom are now living, viz.: Laura Orinda, wife of Oliver Miller, now living in Wesley township; Dena Johnson resides in Helena, Montana; Lucy Jane, wife of Charles Barnes, living in Morgan county, Ohio. Levi Sibley, Anzonetta, Alpha Diena, and Frank Benjamin are all at home. Mr. Arnold has been justice of the peace for twelve years. He entered the army in May, 1864, as second lieutenant, under Captain W. F. Dawson, One Hundred and Forty-eighth Ohio National guard. After serving four months he returned to his business of tanning at the present place, where he has operated since 1859.

George Martin, a native of Scotland, was born in 1780, and died in 1832. He was married to Rebecca Mc-Kollister, born in 1780, and died in 1862. They had a family of twelve children; nine are yet living.

Alexander, fifth child of George and Rebecca Martin, was born in Wesley township in 1816, and was married in 1848 to Phœbe Coaler, who was born in 1823. The names of their children are as follows: John, who now resides in Palmer township; Lucy, Ordelia, Douglas, and William, all now at home. He resides on his farm, which is located in the northwest part of the township, section twenty-six.

Stephen Randolph, son of James and Margery, was born in 1831. His wife, Sarah Kester, to whom he was married in 1852, died in 1853. Marian, their only child, now resides in Hocking county, Ohio. He was again married, in 1856, to Narcissa Chamberlain, who was born in 1831. To them were born six children, as follows: Cameron W., Laura J., Clarence M., Everett L., Lowell W., and Lucy E., all residing at home. He has served as trustee and constable, and was in the three months service during the late war. He resides on his farm in section thirty-three.

Milton D. Fowler, the present postmaster of Bartlett post office (Plymouth), was born in 1822, and was mar-

JAS. W. SMITH.

MRS. J. W. SMITH.

RESIDENCE OF J. W. SMITH, WESLEY TP., WASHINGTON CO., O.

ried in 1863 to Susan James, who was born in 1832. He came to Wesley in 1838, and was raised on the farm which he cleared for his father, and afterwards moved to his present location in 1872, and engaged in the grocery business; was appointed postmaster in 1873, which position he yet holds. He is a member of the Friends society; also a member of the Masonic order, and is known as a straightforward and respected citizen of Wesley township.

James King was born in Pennsylvania in 1818. He removed to Morgan county, Ohio, in 1824. In 1841 he was married to Deborah Stephen, born in Berks county, Pennsylvania, in 1819. In 1843 he came to this county and settled in Wesley, where he now resides. He has had a family of eleven children, eight of whom are living, viz: Rebecca, wife of A. W. Naylor, banker, Des Moines, Iowa; Nora, wife of Professor D. R. Moore, of Mahaska, Iowa; Anna M., Ida A., wife of J. C. Picket; James S., a Methodist minister; Mary, wife of Professor J. Wolf; Helen A. and Charles. Mr. King has served nine years as township trustee; was elected three times as land appraiser of the township; was one of the two who first advocated the establishing of Bartlett academy, of which he has since been a trustee. He became a member of the Masonic order in 1852, and was one of the charter members of Bartlett Lodge, No. 293. He has always been an active temperance man.

John L. Brill, son of John and Mary, was born in Bradford county, Pennsylvania, in 1801. His wife, Eleanor Shively, to whom he was married in 1828, was born in 1808 in Loudoun county, Virginia. He settled in Wesley, where he now resides, in 1836. To them were born ten children, nine now living, viz: Ezra, resides in Morgan county, Ohio; Isaiah, in Athens county, Ohio; Hamilton, in Kansas; Commillia J., wife of Aaron Kester; William, in Washington county; Benjamin, at Ironton, Ohio; Margery, at home; John R., at Oscaloosa, Iowa, and Sarah J., wife of William Jewell. Mr. and Mrs. Brill are prominent members of the Methodist Episcopal church, and as the result of industry now possess a farm of one hundred acres of land.

James Bowman, son of Isaac and Ann, was born in Stark county, Ohio, December 15, 1818, deceased 1880. He was married in 1842 (May 25th), to Elizabeth Baily, who was born December 1, 1820.

Henry Bowman, third child, was born in Wesley township, in 1847, and was married in 1868 to Rachel B. Crew, who was born in 1845. They have a family of four children, namely: Joseph T., Elizabeth J., Edith A., and Mattie C. His father settled in Wesley in 1837, where he resided until his death. Henry now owns a farm of sixty acres, eight acres where he now resides engaged in raising stock—section thirty-seven.

John Morris, son of Benjamin and Lydia, was born in North Carolina in 1790, and was married in 1814 to Rachel Coppark, who was born in Pennsylvania in 1790, deceased in 1843. He settled in this county in 1838. They had a family of twelve children, only one of whom survives.

Joshua Morris, jr., the only living member of this

family, was born in Belmont county, Ohio, September 3, 1824, and was married in 1847 to Eliza Ann Tullis, who was born in 1822. To them were born nine children, seven now living, viz: Hannah, Emeline, Rachel, Linley, Ruthana, Benjamin F., and Richard E. Mr. Morris now owns two hundred and seventy-five acres of land, where he resides—section thirty-one.

Gideon Mills, a native of North Carolina, settled in Washington county in 1839. His children now living are Isaac, Reuben, Esther, Ezra and Lewis. Lewis Mills was born in 1814, and deceased in 1880. He was married in 1844, to Ann Smith, who was born in Virginia in 1821. They had six children, namely: Job S. who resides in Franklin county, Ohio; Simon G. and John A., both at home; W. J., in Franklin county, Ohio; Sarah L., wife of M. Tuttle; Rebecca, now at home; Emma is dead. He held the office of justice of the peace for nine years; T. W. Mills enlisted in company D, Seventy-seventh Ohio volunteer infantry in 1861, and now lies in an unknown southern grave; J. S. Mills is a member of the United Brethren church.

Robert Williams, son of John and Mary, was born in 1813, and was united in marriage in 1838, to Phœbe Boker, who was born in 1810. They have a family of five children now living: Eli H., Jason B., Sarah M., now Mrs. William H. Beazell; John T., and Robert H., both at home. He emigrated to this county in 1858, and settled in Wesley township, where he has since resided on his present farm, and located in the eastern part of the township, section six.

John Speais was born in Pennsylvania in 1813. He was married to Margaret Zumbro, who was born in 1816, and settled in Wesley township in 1852. He has a family of four children, namely: Jane, who resides at home; Henry, who lives in Athens county, Ohio; William and Malinda, both at home.

Mr. and Mrs. Spears are members of the United Brethren church and among its most liberal and earnest supporters. He located in the northern part of the township, where he now lives in section thirty.

Job Addis, son of John and Mary, was born in Fayette county, Pennsylvania, in 1816. His wife, Hester A. Hartman, to whom he was married in 1847, was born in 1822. They emigrated from Pennsylvania in 1858, and settled in Wesley township, where they have since resided. He now resides on his farm located in the northern part of the township in section twenty-four. They hold affiliation with the Disciples church, are strong advocates of social order and morality in the community, in which they live as respected members.

Elisha J. Holloway, son of James and Phœbe Holloway, was born in Belmont county, Ohio, in 1819, and was married in 1840, to Lydia Vanlaw, daughter of John and Sarah Vanlaw, who was born in 1820, in Belmont county. To them were born five children: Phœbe L., Mary, Lucinda, Edwin, and Samuel. Lucinda, the only one now living, was married to William Steele, and lives in Plymouth, and has a family of three children: Horatio, Samuel R., and Rufus. Phœbe L. was married to Samuel Kirby, and resided in Plymouth, where she died,

91

leaving one child, Walter. Mr. and Mrs. Holloway are members of the Friends church, and were zealous friends of the slave during the agitation of the slavery question. He is now in the produce business in Plymouth.

James Morrow, son of James and Rebecca, was born in Pennsylvania in 1796, and was married to Sarah More, who was born in 1798, and died in 1866. They emigrated to Ohio and settled in this township in 1850, on the farm where he now lives, section thirty. He had a family of five children: John, who now lives on the farm; Rebecca, deceased; Polly, wife of Thomas Williamson, now deceased; Charles and Jesse C., both living in Plymouth. Captain Jesse C. Morrow was born in Beaver county, Pennsylvania, and was married in 1856 to Mary A. Pewthers, who was born in Washington county, Ohio, in 1836, and deceased in 1860. To them were born two children: Lucia A., now living at home; and Charles L., living in St. Paul, Minnesota. He was remarried in 1867 to Mrs. Lucia A. Vanlaw, daughter of Thomas Swaim, born in 1842. They have two children—Emma L. and Myron M.—both living at home. He enlisted in the Union army during the late war in company B, Thirty-sixth Ohio volunteer infantry, and was first made orderly sergeant, and was promoted successively in the several offices until he was made captain of company D. He was honorably discharged after having served from 1861 to 1865, from the beginning to the close of the war. He has held the offices of trustee and treasurer of the township, is a blacksmith by profession, and is at present engaged in this vocation where he resides, at Plymouth.

E. Hollingsworth, son of Elisha and Sarah Hollingsworth, was born in Columbiana county, Ohio, in 1827, and was married in 1848 to Mary J., daughter of William and Eleanor Harris, who was born in 1832 and died in 1866. They had a family of six children: Jemima L., wife of A. W. Graham; E. T. J. resides in this county; William D. and George R., both at home; Sarah F. and Phœbe E., deceased. He was again married in 1866, to Sarah J., daughter of Jonah and Nancy Tabenner, who was born in 1836. They have one child, Mary J. They are both efficient and prominent members of the Methodist Episcopal church. They reside on their farm, section twenty-two.

John Zumbro, sr., came from Pennsylvania in 1848, and settled about one mile north of the present store of his son, John, section twenty-six. He was born April 26, 1806, and married February 5, 1829, to Catharine Price, who was born July 20, 1809. They had a family of seven children—Abraham, Joseph, Henry, John, Jacob, Mary E., and Benjamin. John Zumbro, jr., was born in Pennsylvania February 28, 1842, and was married to Louisa Jane Haas. They have three children—Emma A., Minnie C., and Alpha Adelia. He came to this township when he was six years old, and was reared on the farm where he remained until 1863, when he began teaching school, in which he continued until 1866. He bought his uncle's farm in 1867. In 1871 he sold the farm and began keeping store at his present location, about three miles north of Plymouth (Patten's Mills post office).

Ranson S. Gage was born September 25, 1862, in Fairfield township. His father, Horace D. Gage, was born in 1842, and was married to Margaret Josephine Coady. They have a family of seven children—Ranson S., Alice, Alva, May, Jay, Lucy, and Lena. Ranson began to assist his father in the flour-mill in 1876, and took charge of the present mills, known as Patten's mills, under the name of Coady & Gage, December 1, 1880, where he at present operates. He is a young man of energy and perseverance, and, though having undertaken the mill under some embarrassments, present indications are favorable for his future success.

Henry S. Barnes was born in Greene county, Pennsylvania, in 1810, son of Otho and Anna Barnes. He was married to Maria Price, daughter of John and Sarah, born in Maryland in 1809, and deceased in 1833. They had one child, Otho, who now resides in Belmont county, Ohio. He was again married in 1838 to Eliza A. Whittington, who was born in Maryland in 1817, and died in 1877. To them were born eight children, five now living —Anna, Amanda, Euphemia, and Caleb, all at home. Charles resides in Morgan county, Ohio. Lewis was in the Union army, and was one of the martyrs who gave their lives for their country in the prison pen at Andersonville. Mr. Barnes settled in this township in 1847, on his present farm, section six.

Richard J. Barton was born in Guernsey county, Ohio, in 1824—son of Alexander and Frances—and was married in 1847 to Sarah J. Keigley, daughter of William and Mary Keigley, who was born in 1827. They had a family of seven children, five of whom are now living —William A., resides at Portsmouth; Sarah C., wife of George W. Hance, Newark, Ohio; Virginia, now Mrs. E. Stanton, Athens county, Ohio; Susan, and Mary, both at home. He has a farm located in the northwest part of the township, section six. He has been a resident of this township since 1869.

Jason Williams, son of Robert and Phœbe, was born in Pennsylvania in 1845. His wife, Jane Hance, daughter of Kinsey and Charlotta, to whom he was married in 1877, was born in Belmont county, Ohio, in 1848. They have a family of two children—Archie, and an infant daughter. Mrs. Williams is a member of the Methodist Episcopal church; but he, though a strong advocate of law and order, does not belong to any religious organization. He now owns eighty acres of land, on which he resides, section five.

LODGES.

The Bartlett lodge of Free and Accepted Masons, No. 293, was organized October 24, 1856. The charter members were: S. C. Vanlaw, R. Hodgin, S. Heald, C. C. Cheadle, James King, H. S. Barnes, John Hass, D. Shinn, Elias Bundy, Benjamin Pickering, S. W. Phillips, and Jacob Perkins. Officials: C. C. Cheadle, master; S. C. Vanlaw, senior warden; James King, junior warden.

This organization has held its meetings regularly since the charter was granted, and has a very neat and tasty lodge room over the hardware store in Plymouth.

The Sons of Temperance and Good Templars have both had organizations here; but while these special meetings have now ceased and the organizations abandoned, their influence has made its mark on the moral history of this township. United with the religious societies the battle against intemperance was earnest, bold and decisive; and the fact that at one time there were three saloons here, while now there is not a place within the township where intoxicating liquors are sold, is justly claimed as a great victory in a great moral contest.

SCHOOLS.

The first school-house in this township was built about one mile north of Plymouth, about 1819. It was constructed of round, unhewn logs after the style common in these early days. The first teacher was Miss Hewitt, after her were Neil Rowell and Isaac Runnels.

School-houses after this same style were soon erected in various localities throughout the township, and for many years they were supported by private subscription, and the sessions were necessarily short and irregular, and affording the children of the early settlers very meagre opportunities for intellectual improvement. Under the present public school system there are twelve school districts, all supplied with teachers and good school-buildings. The number of scholars now enrolled is four hundred and fifty-seven; average daily attendance, two hundred and fifty-four; average weeks in session during the year, twenty-seven; average monthly wages, forty-four dollars.

These early teachers experienced difficulties incident to those early days, when it was of ordinary occurrence to "bar the teacher out" and compel him to treat the school, before he was allowed to enter. The Rardin boys and John Mullin are remembered as leaders in these sports. One time, on a Christmas, they barred Neal Rowell out, and after a long trial to gain access, he promised to sign a paper obligating himself to furnish the cider and apples for the school, but he signed "Neal Rowell, not bound" and it is safe to say that the cider and apples were never produced under that contract.

BARTLETT'S ACADEMY.

This institution was organized in 1856. The first board of trustees were: Joseph Penrose, president, Joseph K. Bucy, Isaac Emmons and James King, and Jefferson M. Heston was first principal with one assistant. The first building was purchased of the Presbyterian church for seven hundred dollars, and has been remodelled and improved, is now two stories high, with cupola and bell; and is a substantial frame structure, forty by thirty-five. The recitation rooms are on the first floor, and it has seating capacity for more than seventy-five on the second floor. The boarding hall for students joins the academy on the east, and is operated by a joint-stock company. The institution has continued for now almost a quarter of a century with variable degrees of success. The location is considered healthy, the community radically temperate and eminently moral. Present number of students, seventy-four. The object of the present administration is to impart good academic instruction, prepare students for college, and to train teachers by thorough normal drill. Faculty, Professor

Z. G. Bundy, president; Professor William Eldridge, languages and mathematics; Professor D. R. Emmons, penmanship.

CHURCHES.

The first religious meetings in this township were held in the log cabins of the pioneers, until the school-houses were built in which the public services were then held. The first church building in the township was erected by the Methodist Episcopal society about one and a half miles north of Plymouth, 1825. Among the first ministers were: David Young (Protestant Episcopal), Jacob Young and Samuel Hamilton; first trustees were James W. Smith, sr., John Rardin, and Frederick Cradlebaugh. Services were held in this rude log-cabin until 1855, when the present house at Pleasanton was built. The building is a plain frame, forty by fifty, and is located in the northwest part of the village. This denomination has a parsonage in the village, and occupies the site of the former one destroyed by fire in 1871. Present pastor, Rev. D. M. Smith. Services every alternate Sabbath, Sabbath-school every Sunday.

FRIENDS' CHURCH (PLYMOUTH).

The first organization of this society was made in 1837. The meeting for this purpose was held at the residence of Edward McConnell one quarter of a mile east of Plymouth, on north side of State road. The first minister was Lydia McConnell, who preached here for a number of years; then Sarah Mott took charge, holding services at private houses until 1842, when they built a log meeting-house one quarter of a mile east of Plymouth, where regular services were held until 1856, when the present frame house located one quarter of a mile north of Plymouth was erected. Services are now held every first and fourth days, under the ministry of Daniel Mott. Membership, eighteen families.

FRIENDS' CHURCH (SOUTHLAND).

This society is the outgrowth of the Plymouth organization, and is under the same ministry. The present meeting-house (frame, eighteen by thirty) was erected in 1850, and is located four miles southwest of Plymouth. It has a membership of ten or twelve families. Regular services are held here every first and fifth days. Daniel Mott is the present minister.

UNITED BRETHREN CHURCH.

In early times this denomination held meetings in a log cabin church, located about one-half mile west of Patten's mills, and was the first building erected by this society in the township. In 1870 the present house, located about three-fourths of a mile south of Patten's mills, was erected. It is a substantial frame, about twenty-eight to thirty feet.

Among the early ministers of this denomination were Revs. Lease and Hood, who preached here for a number of years.

Rev. John Phillips is the present minister, holding services every Sunday. Present membership about thirty.

This denomination has another society and church building, located in the northwest part of the township.

The church building was erected about 1870, and is a frame structure of about twenty-eight to thirty feet. This society has a membership of about thirty, and is under the same ministerial charge with the other society. Services every Sunday.

CEMETERIES.

The burial grounds of this township, like all rural cemeteries, are located near the several churches. Some of them in this township are controled by township trustees.

The first interments were made in the now abandoned grounds near the Methodist Episcopal church in Pleasanton, but no record can now be found to determine who were the first victims of the common destroyer.

VILLAGES.

Plymouth is a small village on the State road in the central part of the township, and was founded by Harvey Smith in 1835. The first business in the town was carried on by the founder, Harvey Smith, who manufactured hats in a log cabin in the rear of the present residence of Mrs. Crow, opposite the Faires House. James W. Smith kept the first licensed house of entertainment near the present residence of his son, just west of the town. Harvey Smith soon started a grocery in connection with his hat factory. He would string a few hats across his horse's back and ride to Marietta and exchange them for groceries and small articles, and carried his whole stock home with him in his saddle-bags.

The town has now grown to contain one general store, two shoe stores, one hotel, one fancy goods store, one hardware, and one millinery store.

Pleasanton was laid out by Milton Smith about three years after Plymouth, during the time when there was a movement made to organize a new county, of which this should be the county seat, and was called Pleasanton from the fact that it would be a pleasant place for the new court house. It joins Plymouth on the east, and so closely that it is difficult to determine where Plymouth leaves off and Pleasanton begins. The village now has one drug store, one general store, three blacksmith shops, one harness, and one wagon shop, one church, and one academy.

The post office is now in Pleasanton, and was established some time before Plymouth was laid out, and was called Bartlett post office, in honor of Amos Bartlett, who was instrumental in having an office established at this point, and who was the first postmaster.

The two villages are now really considered as one, and together have, by the late census, a population of two hundred and forty, and never having had the required population were never incorporated.

MILLS.

In early times the settlers of this township were compelled to go to what was known as the Barris mill, then located on Federal creek, eight miles north of Plymouth. The first flour-mill was built on Wolf creek in 1816, by George and John Martin. It was located on the opposite side of the creek from the present mill of Coady & Gage, known as Patten's mills, and was a frame building

having two run of stone. From this mill the settlers received all their grists until the present mill, now operated by Ranson S. Gage for Coady & Gage, was erected. The present building is a frame of forty by sixty feet, has four run of stone with a capacity of four hundred bushels per day. The reaction wheels are propelled by water power.

The farmers' mill was built by Ferguason Brothers in 1877. It is a substantial frame, thirty-six by forty feet; has two run of stone, with a daily capacity of two hundred bushels. The power is received from a fifty horse-power engine. Its trade is a general local custom, yielding an income of about fifteen hundred dollars. It is located one-fourth of a mile north of Plymouth, and is now operated and owned by Messrs. Clark & Glen.

TANNERY.

As early as 1840 Hiram Rhodes operated a tannery on the site of the present tannery of B. F. Arnold. After him was Robert Hodgins for two or three years, and with some other changes of proprietorship it came into the hands of the present owner, B. F. Arnold. He has made very many improvements, adding a new structure. The present building is of three stories with basement, and is seventy by twenty feet. A stone wall eight feet high extends the whole length of one side and the ends, and two partition stone walls divide the basement into three rooms, in which the wet shaving, scouring, etc., are done; in the second room, beam-work, unhairing hides, and working vats; third room for bark. On the second floor is located the sale room, finishing department and bark mill. The third floor is used for drying. The capacity of the yard is as follows: Eighteen lay away vats, two vats for liming and two for vatsing, in the beam room, and three leeches, capable of tanning one thousand hides yearly. The local demand is all that is now sought to be supplied. Considerable shipments have been made from this tannery to Cincinnati, Philadelphia and New York.

INCIDENTS.

Levi Arnold was a hunter of some skill, and at one time he killed a deer in the forest, and bent down a sapling and swung the carcass up out of the reach of wild animals that infested the neighborhood. "Bill Wason," a common vagabond of the settlement, stole the carcass and carried it to his log hut, which stood on a by-path near the present residence of James King. Unfortunately for Wason, he failed to cover his tracks and Mr. Arnold with several of his neighbors followed the track to Wason's cabin door. The evidence of Wason's guilt was sufficient, and without the formalities of law the thief was taken and tied to a tree near his cabin and was severely lashed with hickory wyths. This is, no doubt, the first and only administration of justice by corporal punishment in this township.

The great Indian trail leading off Wolf creek extended southwest, passing the present southwest corner of the road in the northwest corner of section six. In this corner, as early as 1837 and for an unknown time before, hanging in a tree was the skull of an Indian horse. It was hung there no doubt by the Indians as a guideboard on the only pathway through the wilderness, but became regarded with some superstitious wonder and dread by the settlers, and the place was known as the "Horse Skull fork."

UNDERGROUND RAILROAD.

This name was given to the secret operations of the friends of freedom, known as abolitionists, in assisting the slaves of the neighboring slave States, to escape from bondage, to freedom in the north, or in Canada. The line extended from the Ohio river through Decatur and on through this township, along which the fleeing refugee was guided through the dark ravines and deep recesses by day, and hidden in the caves and caverns of these hills by night. They were passed along from station to station, where stood the secret friend to guide them on, to feed, and clothe, and cheer the panting fugitive, fleeing from the shackles and the lash in a land of boasted freedom. It is estimated that over one hundred slaves escaped to freedom through this township during that time.

Mr. James Ward Smith, grandfather of James Waldo, was one of the early settlers of the county. He was born in Genesee county, New York, and came thence to Wesley township, Washington county, Ohio, in 1810. He married, in New York State, a Miss Alderman. By her he had nine children, as follows: Vincent, Milton, Lawson, Harvey, James, Carmi, Talma, Eli, and Lucy. Of these, Milton, Carmi, and James are living; Carmi and James live in Washington county, Milton in the northern part of the State.

Mr. James Smith was born in 1809. He married Eliza Goddard, who is still living. Mr. and Mrs. Smith have had eight children, who, in the order of age, are as follows: Ferona T., Alonzo H., Edward F., James Waldo, Alphonso W., Sarah A., Lucy R., and Clarence C. Alphonso W. and Sarah A. are dead. Ferona T. married J. W. Barnes, and is living in Cincinnati, Ohio. Alonzo H., James Waldo, and Clarence C., are all farmers in Washington county. Lucy R. keeps a store in Plymouth, this county. Edward F. lives on his farm in Lincoln county, Dakota.

James Waldo Smith was born on the first day of June, 1838. He was educated in the common schools near his father's home. On coming to man's estate he bought a farm in Fairfield township, this county, which he, in 1862, traded to his brother, Edward F., for a part of his present farm. By additional purchase from time to time this property has grown to its present size. It is situated in Wesley township. Mr. Smith was married in 1864 to Miss Mary A. Gage, of Fairfield township. Four children are the fruit of this union: Roscoe B., born in 1865; Myron A., born in 1866; Lucy G., born in 1868; and Ethyl F., born in 1877. All of these are still living. Mr. Smith makes a specialty of stock-raising, paying especial attention to sheep-raising.

CHAPTER LVIII.

FAIRFIELD TOWNSHIP.

Situation—Principal Products—Timber and Streams—Organization and First Election—Settlement—Schools—Churches—Cemeteries—Societies and Associations—First Mill—Towns and Villages—Epidemic—Mineral Spring.

FAIRFIELD township is situated in the western part of the county, and is bounded on the north by Palmer, east by Barlow, south by Decatur, and west by Wesley. The original boundary lines were as follows: From northwest corner, section sixteen, township seven, range eleven, to northeast corner Fr. eighteen; thence to northwest corner, Fr. eighteen; thence east to southwest corner, section twenty-four, township six, range eleven; thence east to southeast corner of section thirty-six, township two, range ten, and thence to the beginning. At present, with the exceptions of part of a section taken from the northwest, and also part of a section taken from the southwest, the township presents a map of symmetrical boundary, and contains an area of more than fifteen thousand acres, and has a population of seven hundred and thirty-one.

The soil is generally of yellow and red clay, with the common sandstone base, which extends, generally, through this part of the State. This soil is abundantly productive of all kinds of fruits, apples of all kinds, pears, etc., and an ample profusion of the smaller fruits, are found in all parts of the township. Peaches are also produced in some seasons, but are not certain of fruition, owing to climatic influences. Wheat, oats, and corn are the chief agricultural productions. Wool growing is carried on quite extensively throughout the township, and fine-wool sheep are now being generally introduced, among which are found the Shermanoes, Merinoes, and some Leicesters. The fleeces from this locality command the highest market price.

The timber lands abound mostly in white and red oak, with some hickory, walnut, and poplar. The sandstone, outcroppings of which are found in various localities in the township, is used generally for building purposes, but is quarried only for local use at the present time.

Little Hocking river takes its rise in the western part of the township, and, receiving several unimportant tributaries, flows in a southeastern direction until it reaches a point southeast of Dunbar post office, where it turns westward for a short distance, and thence directly south, leaving the township west of the central part of the southern boundary. Other small branches drain the various parts of the township, flowing both north and south from the great highland divide extending across the township.

The Marietta & Cincinnati railroad extends across the south part of the township, but is not now in operation, having been abandoned some two years ago.

ORGANIZATION.

The organization of this township was effected by the county commissioners at the December session of 1851. It was formed from parts of Wesley, on the northwest,

Barlow on the northeast, Belpre on the southeast, and Decatur on the southwest.

The first election was held December 20, 1851, which resulted as follows: Trustees, Peter B. Lake, John Burfield and James Smith; township clerk, Charles H. Goddard; treasurer, Peter B. Lake; assessor, Torren Gilmore; constable, Augustine Stephens.

The first election for justice of the peace occurred August 17th, 1852, resulting in the election of Torrens

EARLY SETTLEMENTS.

Gilmore and Augustine Stephens.

The early settlers of this township came up over the Ohio river hills from Marietta, following the only broken route through the wilderness, since known as the State road. This route extended along its present course, following the ridge of highlands now known as the "divide," which extends across the northern part of the township from east to west. Near this road the settlers naturally fixed the site of their pioneer homes, erected their log cabins, and began the work of development and civilization of what is now known as Fairfield township.

Among the earliest settlers, of whom any account can now be obtained, were David Ewell, who came from Virginia some time prior to 1814, first settled about one-half mile south of the present village of Fishtown, where he erected his log-cabin home—section three, and Joshua Shuttleworth (also from Virginia) at this same time lived immediately south of Ewell.

Of these earliest pioneers very little is known concerning their personal history, for with them have passed away forever the records of their lives and deeds, save what they have impressed upon the unwritten history of the rise and progress of this locality from the wilds of wilderness and forest to its present position in the ranks of civilization.

William Dunbar settled in this township in the early part of 1814, and erected his cabin on the site of the present residence of his son Daniel, just east of Fishtown—section four. In this same year Walter Kidwell, from Fairfax county, Virginia, came and settled about one-quarter mile north of the present residence of his son John, where he built his cabin. He was accompanied by his wife and two sons, John and William.

William Dunbar was born in the year 1740, and was married to Polly Shelton some time previous to his settlement in Ohio. They had six children—Catharine, Sarah, Nancy, Thomas, William and Daniel. He was a private soldier in the Revolutionary war, and was discharged after honorable service to his country.

Daniel Dunbar, the only surviving child of William Dunbar, was born in Fairfax county, Virginia, in 1800, and came to this township with his father. He was married to Mary C. Lake in 1827, who was born in 1804, and died in 1840. They have five children, three of whom are now living, viz: Jane Ann, now the widow of Jacob Hueston, living in Athens county, Ohio; India, in Athens county, and James. James, the fifth child of Daniel Dunbar, was born in this township July 6, 1840. In the spring of 1866 he became a resident of Watertown, where he has since lived. He was married to Flora F.

Gage, who was born in this township, December 5, 1850. The fruit of this union was one child, Dayton G. He has been treasurer of Watertown since 1871, and store-keeper since 1867.

Thomas Dunbar, son of William, was born in Virginia in 1790, and died in 1874. He came with his father to this locality, where he spent his life. He was married to Esther Owens, who was born about 1794 in Virginia. They had six children, three of whom are now living, viz.: Shelton, David and Louisa, widow of Samuel Hull, now living in Marietta. He served as private in the War of 1812, and also held several township offices.

Shelton Dunbar was born in this township in 1820, and was married to Sarah A. Varner (born in 1827) in 1844. They had four children—Emily J., wife of Knotley McCain, now living in this township; Mary Ann, Eliza and Angeline, the latter now teaching school. He has served several years as school director, and supervisor and has been postmaster at Dunbar station for over twenty-six years, and has also been connected with the mercantile business at Dunbar, Belpre and Parkersburgh.

Hapgood Goddard was born in Swansey, New Hampshire, in 1783, and was married to Rebecca Wood (born 1787,) in 1809. In the year 1817 he settled on section fifteen this township. His decease occurred in 1865, his wife surviving him ten years. He was one of the leading men in the township, and served as township clerk for fifteen years. Previous to his coming to the west he was engaged in the mercantile business in New Hampshire, but the financial policy of President Jefferson, known as Jefferson's embargo, ruined him, and he came to this township with but five dollars. He lived to own a farm of one hundred and twenty acres of land, and left an honorable name as citizen and farmer. He had a family of ten children, eight of whom are now living, viz: Eliza, wife of James Smith, in Plymouth; William, P. P., in Wesley; Abraham W., in Fairfield; Julia, widow of Lanson Smith, now living in Jackson county, Ohio; Charles H., in Fairfield; George R., in Dunham; Lucy E., wife of Joseph C. Coulter, in Fairfield; and Sarah, wife of John V. Farris, now residing in Missouri.

Abraham W. Goddard was born in 1816, in Belpre, and was married in 1843 to Mary Jane Coulter, who was born in 1825, in Coshocton county, Ohio. They had nine children, eight of whom are now living: Emeline, wife of William Quinn, Palmer township; William R. now resides in Athens county, Ohio; Edna, wife of James Randolph, Wesley; Talma, wife of William Rowlands, now living at Racine, Wisconsin; Edgar W., Fairfield; Harmar H., Fairfield; Zaidie E., Columbus, Ohio, and Minnie, who is now at home. Mr. Goddard has been a prominent man in this township, treasurer for fifteen years, and justice of the peace twenty-five years, and now owns a farm of three hundred and twenty-four acres, on which he resides, located in the southwestern part of township—section 19.

Charles H. Goddard was born in this township in 1824, and was married in 1847 to Melissa E. Chamberlain, who was born in 1826 (Watertown). They have a family of ten children, eight of whom are now living viz: Rowena, who now lives at home; Rodney Watson (Welston, Ohio), Harley C., S. A. Douglas, Ason A., Frank E., Bertha, and Webster B. He has held the offices of clerk and trustee of township for thirty-one years, having been clerk of four townships—Wesley, Fairfield, Warren and Dunham. He now owns about four hundred acres of land and has distributed three hundred and fifty acres among his children. He has been one of the most active citizens in all the public movements in the township.

Carmi Smith was born August 6, 1812, and was married October 20, 1831, to Sarah Bishop, who was born December 21, 1813, in the State of New York. To them were born seven children, three of whom are now living, viz: Gilbert, who now resides in this township; Talma, wife of Sylvester Williams, who now lives in Belpre, Ohio; Esther Jane, married to George R. Goddard (Dunham); Sarah Clorinda, wife of Dixon Graham (Wesley). He has been among the leading men of his locality; has held the office of justice of the peace for sixteen years; was merchant and general tradesman at Fishtown for many years, and has been prominently identified with the Methodist Episcopal church.

Gilbert Smith, only son of Carmi Smith, was born in Wesley township in 1832, and was married to Rowena G. Williams, born in 1833, in the year 1857. He has had the honorable distinction of representing his district in the Ohio legislature two successive terms—from 1875 to 1879. He was also assessor three years, and has held many other township offices. At present he owns three hundred acres of land located in the northwest part of the township. He had no family but took a girl named Ida, whom he reared as his own. She was married to Oscar Thompson.

Phinehas Dunsmore came to this county in 1822 with his family, and settled about one mile north of Fishtown, then in Wesley but now in Fairfield township, where he had previously purchased a tract of land of nine hundred acres. He was a native of Townsend, Massachusetts, born December 29, 1771. In 1798 he married Polly Gage, who was born in Pelham, New Hampshire, July 16, 1782. Their children were Horace, Hiram, Abner G., Mary K., Hiel, Lucius P., Adaline G., and Daniel N. Phinehas Dunsmore was a captain of a cavalry company in the War of 1812, but did not perform any active service, being only ordered to hold his company in readiness to march to Portsmouth at one day's notice. He died in less than a year after he came west—May 6, 1823. His wife lived until March 20, 1857.

Jordon Swesey, father of James Swesey, was born in Pennsylvania in 1788, and settled in Wesley township in 1828, on section five. He died in Palmer township in 1862. He was a man of versatile abilities, and skilful in various ways, such as splitting shingles, and roofing houses and barns. He was also a shoemaker, and in these pursuits obtained money to purchase seventy acres of land. He was united in marriage to Elizabeth Barr, who was born in Pennsylvania in 1790, and died in Palmer township in 1865. They had six children, three of whom are now living, viz: James, the oldest, is married,

and at present resides in Iowa; Jordon lives in Fairfield, and Jane, wife of Robert Miller, lives in Palmer. Jordon Swesey was born in Pennsylvania in 1822, and was married in 1848 to Nancy Campbell, who was born in 1827 in Guernsey county, Ohio. Mr. Swesey farms sixty acres of land, part of which is located in the northeastern part of Fairfield township, on which he now lives. He is one of the trustees of the Methodist Episcopal church and also a member of the Sons of Temperance.

William Moore came from Pennsylvania with his father, John Moore, and first settled in the central part of the county about 1845. He was born in 1828, and was married to Mrs. Louisa Chute in 1860. They had a family of seven children, viz: Fremont A., James G., William L., Lucy I., Clara O., Brooks B., Theora Belle, all of them are living at home. Mrs. Moore is a daughter of James Kidwell, and was first married to Samuel S. Chute, who died in 1859, leaving three children, viz: Sarah M., who now lives in Iowa; Sophronia, wife of Joseph Moore, living in Iowa; and Samuel S., now living at home.

Moses Campbell settled in this township about 1830; was born in Ireland, in 1800, and died in 1874. He was married in 1810 to Margaret Stranahan, who died in 1835. They had five children, four now living—Nancy, wife of Jordon Swesey; James and William, both married and living in this township. Martha, the only daughter, is also living in this township. He was afterward married to Eleanor Roberts in 1844, whose decease occurred in 1876. They had six children, all now living, viz: Caroline, widow of Martin Corns (Decatur township), Amos (Palmer township), Thomas (Columbiana county), Charles (Pittsburgh, Pennsylvania), David (Fairfield township), and Jane, wife of C. H. Bracken (Kansas). Thomas and Charles (orderly sergeants), served three years in the late war, both were members of the Seventy-seventh Ohio volunteer infantry.

James Campbell was born in 1829, and was married in 1845 to Nancy Laughlin, who was born in 1830 and died in 1858. They had two children, one now living: Esther Ann, wife of Isaac Jones, living in Michigan. He was again married, in 1860, to Rebecca J. Kenny, who was born in Columbiana county, Ohio, in 1833. To them were born four children, three of whom are living: Emma, Ella, and William W.—all at home. He has held several township offices—constable and supervisor, and was called out in the militia during the Morgan raid. He is a farmer and owns one hundred and sixty acres of land, located in section sixteen, in the northwestern part of the township.

David N. Campbell was born in this township in 1844, and was married to Jennie Irvine in 1876, who was born in Ireland in 1846. They have two children—Forest Wade and Willis Scott, both now living at home. He was trustee of the township, and owns the homestead farm of one hundred and fifty acres, where he now lives, and where his father settled and died.

Alexander A. Campbell (Cutler station) came to this township in April, 1856; he was born in Butler county, Pennsylvania, in 1821. His wife, Mary Myers, to whom he was married in 1844, was born in Guernsey county, Ohio, in 1825. Their family consists of eight children, five of whom are now living, namely: Samantha A., wife of E. G. Bundy (Kansas); Mary, wife of Jesse Bentley (Clinton county, Ohio); William is married and lives at Cutler Station; Charles and Ulysses Grant both live at home. He was in the late war serving in the Seventy-third Ohio volunteer infantry, company F, from October, 1861, to January, 1865, during which time he was in thirty-two engagements, which includes the second battle of Manasses, Gettysburgh and Mission Ridge, in General Hooker's brigade. At present he keeps the hotel at Cutler station, and is on the construction corps of the Marietta & Cincinnati railroad.

Joseph H. Gage settled in this township on section sixteen, in 1837. He was born in New Hampshire in 1815, and was married, in 1838, to Mary A. Cook, who was born in Vermont, in 1814. Of their nine children, six are now living, viz: Horace D. (Wesley township); John A., now living at home; Mary Ann, wife of J. Waldo Smith (Wesley township); Flora, wife of J. T. Dunbar (Watertown township). George is married, and lives in this township. Myron lives at home. He is a stone-cutter by trade, but is now farming, owning at present over four hundred acres of land, as the result of his own industry.

William Thompson was born in Guernsey county, Ohio, in 1828, and settled in this township on section hree, in 1851. He was elected county commissioner in 1880, and has held most of the offices of his township; was married in 1853 to Angeline Smith, who was born in 1834 and died in 1856, leaving two children—Carmi Orville, deceased, and Oscar, who is married and lives in Barlow township. He was married in 1858 to Laura A. Ford, who was born in Barlow township in 1834. They have three children, namely: John Ford, William Elmer, and Phœbe Putnam, all of whom are living at home. He was a member of company F, One Hundred and Forty-eighth Ohio national guards, and served from May to September, 1864; was stationed at Bermuda, on the James river, near Richmond, Virginia. He was first president of the Barlow agricultural board, elected in 1872, and has held the office until the present time. He was also a member of the county board for nine years; is at present a farmer, owning four hundred and five acres of land on which he resides, located in the northeastern part of the township. Mr. Thompson has borne a leading part in public affairs, and has been efficient in most of the organizations of his own and adjoining townships, also of the county.

Owen Clark settled in Fairfield township in 1855. He was born in Ireland in 1813. He married Catharine O'Malia, who died in 1870. They have had seven children, viz: John H., Annie, Bridget, Edward, Thomas, Mary and Catharine; of these, Bridget is dead. John H., born in 1849, married in 1875, Miss Bridget Clark, by whom he has had three children, all born in Belpre township, where the younger Mr. Clark resides, he having charge of the depot of the Marietta & Cincinnati railroad.

SCHOOLS.

The first school-house was built on the north side of the present State road, about one-half mile west of Fishtown, about 1819. It was known as Lake's school-house, after Thomas Lake, who lived near it. Oliver Miller, father of Jonathan Miller, now living at Cutler station, was the first teacher who "wielded the birchen" and directed the intellectual development of the sturdy pioneer sons and daughters in this primitive log-cabin schoolhouse. A few crumbling stones now remain to mark the spot of this first school-house, and Daniel Dunbar and John Kidwell are the only surviving members of the school.

The next school-house was built near the present residence of Daniel Dunbar, on the extreme west corner of his land, near the State road, in 1840. These early schools were taught by teachers engaged by the parents of the scholars, and were supported by general subscription. In this way the schools were supported in the various localities until the increase in population necessitated the organization of school districts. At present there are seven separate school districts, all supplied with teachers and good, substantial school buildings, where the means for the ordinary common school education are amply supplied under the present public school system.

CHURCHES.

The first religious services were held at the cabins of the pious settlers by the itinerant preachers who might happen in the settlement, until the school-houses were built, when the religious services were held in them. Probably the first general service was held in the old Lake school-house, in which many of the different religious organizations of the township were effected. The first church building was erected by the Methodist Episcopal society about 1824, on the site of the present Methodist Episcopal church at Fishtown, and was called "Kidwell meeting-house," in honor of Walter Kidwell, who was then a prominent member of the church. The house was built of hewn logs. This house stood until 1863, when it was pulled down, and another house erected on the same site by general subscription, as a union church, for the common use of all denominations. This new house was accidentally burned down on the twelfth of the following February. The workmen, after finishing the house, gathered the shavings and other inflammable material and stowed it under the house through an aperture left under the front door, which was to be closed by the stone steps; but before the steps were put up, on an occasion of public worship, a young lady took a fire-brand from a neighboring house to the church for the purpose of building a fire, and on entering the door the fire-brand fell from her hands and ignited the debris under the house, and before help could be obtained the building was destroyed.

The present frame building — forty-five by twenty-eight feet — was erected on the same site, by the Methodist Episcopal society, and was completed the following year, 1864. The dedication sermon was preached by Rev. John Frazier, presiding elder, and

LUCIUS P. DUNSMORE.

Phineas Dunsmore with his wife, Polly, and seven children, among whom was Lucius P., came to what is now Fairfield township, then Wesley, Washington county, Ohio, in 1822. The family came from Goshen, New Hampshire. Lucius was then twelve years old, having been born on the twenty-fifth of January, 1810. Mr. Dunsmore brought his family through New York State and travelled along the beach of Lake Erie until they reached Ashtabula county, Ohio. Here the rest of the family tarried with friends until Mr. Dunsmore, with his brother and eldest son, Horace, came down to Washington county to "view the land." The result of this inspection was that Mr. Dunsmore traded his property in New Hampshire for a section and a fraction in Wesley township, comprising nine hundred and five acres. This purchase was made of James Brick, who was one of the Ohio company. Mr Dunsmore then went for his family, and they came down in the same wagons in which they had come from New Hampshire, arriving at their new home on the fourth of July, 1822. A log house was immediately put up. It was of very primitive construction. They had no nails, and so were compelled to secure their roof with weight poles. This house stood about a mile northwest of where Layman post office now is.

In the early part of 1823 Phineas Dunsmore died and was buried on his own land, whence his body was removed to the Union cemetery a few years ago. Mrs. Dunsmore survived her husband about eighteen years, dying in 1841.

The children of Phineas and Polly Dunsmore, in order of age were as follows: Horace, born in 1799; Abner, born in 1802; Mary, born in 1804; Hiel, born in 1806; Lucius P., born in 1810; Adaline, born in 1812; and Daniel, born in 1816. Horace died in March, 1878, and Abner in 1853. The rest of the children are still living.

In 1836 Lucius P. Dunsmore married Mahala Williams, of Wood county, Virginia, who was born in 1813. He built a frame house about half a mile from the old homestead, and thither he took his bride. Their new home was in the midst of a dense forest, and they went to work to clear a farm for cultivation. The work proceeded very slowly, and only four or five acres were cleared a year.

In 1838 their first child was born—Elbina. She married, in 1856, Jesse Hildebrand, and now lives just above her father's home. She has three children. In 1840 their second daughter, Polly C., was born. She married Isaac P. Hanes in 1860. They reside on the old Dunsmore homestead and have two children. Rachel J. was born in 1842. She married John T. Hanes in 1862. They live in Palmer township near Mr. Dunsmore's and have one child. Mahala J. was born in 1843 and died in 1870. Lucius Jasper was born in 1845 and died in 1868. Laura Anne was born in 1848. She married Dr. Elisha Tinker. They lived in Plymouth, of this county. Mrs. Tinker died in 1872. Lorina A. was born in 1852. She married R. F. Runels in 1874. They live with Mr. Dunsmore in Fairfield township and have two children. Mr. Dunsmore's wife died on the twenty-first of May 1876.

When Mr. Dunsmore came to the county the comforts and luxuries of civilization had not yet reached this part of the country. Everything was in a rude state. When the family needed meal one of them was obliged to go to a mill six miles distant, of which the motive power was an old horse. Here he would sometimes be obliged to wait three days before getting the meal. They were obliged to go to Marietta to do their trading and also to haul their wheat there over rough roads, and then get only thirty-seven and one half cents a bushel for it. At that day the forests were filled with wolves, which did great damage to the flocks. The farmers were obliged to build large sheepfolds to protect their flocks. Mr. Dunsmore has a farm of two hundred and sixty-two acres, being a part of the original purchase of his father. This land is farmed by a son in law, Mr. Runels, who makes a specialty of sheep raising.

Mr. Dunsmore was township treasurer for seven years. He is a member of the Universalist church. He now lives on his farm and is highly respected throughout the township.

the first trustees were Carmi Smith, Peter Lake, John Kidwell, Philip Moore, Theodore Hull, Reuben Ellis, and John V. Farris. Among the early local ministers of this denomination were Osborn, Thompson, Lippett, and others, and the first regular ministers were Revs. David and Jacob Young, Daniel Limerick, James Furee, James and William McMahon. Regular services are held every alternate Sabbath.

The Centenary Methodist Episcopal church is located in the southwest part of the township, three-fourths of a mile north of Cutler station, and was erected in 1867—a substantial frame building, about forty by forty-five. This congregation formerly worshipped in a log meeting-house, situated about two miles east of the present church building, and was known as "Zion" church.

The first minister of this charge was Rev. Hathaway, and among the prominent ministers on this (Bartlett) circuit were Revs. Sayers, Morgan, Callahan, O'Neal, and others. The first trustees were Theodore Hull, John V. Farris, W. D. Jones, R. D. Carothers, and B. H. Dawson. The membership numbers about sixty, holding services every alternate Sabbath.

The Universalist church located near the present residence of Charles H. Goddard, on the State road, west of Fishtown, was the first erected in the township by this denomination. It was first built in 1867, as a union church, but at present is controlled by the Universalists. It is a frame building, thirty by forty, and the first trustees were Daniel Dunbar, A. W. Goddard, and J. F. Haines. Services are held every month by the present pastor, Rev. Earl.

This denomination has another church building, located at Fishtown, which was erected as a union church in 1868. It is a frame building (thirty by thirty-six) and was dedicated by Rev. Cantwell, and is now under the control of the same trustees as the other church, with the same minister who officiates alternately with the other congregation.

The first meetings of this denomination were conducted by Father Sweet and Rev. Jolly, and the original organization was effected by Hapgood Goddard, Isaac Perry, Hiel Dunsmore, Jacob Minton, and George Hildebrand. Naturally there were many conflicts among the different religious societies of this locality, differing, as they did, so widely on the doctrines of the Bible.

CEMETERIES.

The burial places in this township are mostly connected with the churches near which they are located. Some are now under the control of the township trustees.

The first burying-ground was just south of Fishtown, where Mrs. Dunbar was buried in very early times. Then the Methodist Episcopal church graveyard at Fishtown was opened, where many of the early pioneers were buried. The cemetery at the forks of the road, near the Universalist church, west of Fishtown, is now under the control of the township trustees, and is one of the principal ones. A cemetery has also been opened near the Centenary Methodist Episcopal church, north of Cutler station.

ASSOCIATIONS AND SOCIETIES.

The Wool Growers' association was first organized at the residence of William Thompson, in 1876. The membership extends throughout this whole section of country, embracing Fairfield, Barlow, Wesley, Palmer, Watertown, and Warren townships. Meetings are held regularly in April and November, at the residence of some one of the members. The object of the organization is to have a general interchange of ideas on the subject of sheep raising, the best breeds to raise, what to feed, etc. At the meetings each member brings specimens of his breed of sheep and a general shearing is made and the fleeces compared. The general expenses are paid by a tax of twenty-five cents per capita, and the society is now in good condition in every way.

Sons of Temperance, Lyman division, No. 52, was organized in the Methodist Episcopal church, at Fishtown, in 1857, with the following officers: William Thompson, W. P.; Mrs. William Thompson, W. A.; G. W. Morris, R. S.; Orlando Trotter, F. S.; Jordan Swesey, treasurer; G. Y. Palmer, chaplain. This society has done much effectual work in the suppression of intemperance in this township and the fact that there is no place within the bounds of the township where intoxicating liquors are sold, attest the good results of labor in this cause. The society now holds its meetings at the private houses of the members—having no lodge room of its own—and has enrolled among its members some of the best and most influential citizens of the community.

Grange No. 872 was organized in 1874, by M. A. Malster. The original officials were as follows: Charles A. Goddard, master; J. H. F. Browning, secretary; David Dunbar, overseer; Reuben Hull, lecturer; William Thompson, treasurer; George Varner, steward; Caroline Varner, pomona; E. A. Varner, flora; Elma Addis, lady steward; and Josephus Harrington, gate-keeper. At present this organization has a membership of about twenty, and is highly regarded for the social benefits arising from the regular meetings, as many of the leading families of the township are members of the organization.

THE FIRST MILL.

The first and only grist-mill in this township was constructed on a very rude plan. Two stones were placed in a hollow log. The upper one had a shaft inserted through the top of the log, and had a handle attached, and with this power the mill was operated by hand. This structure was the common property of the settlers, and stood near the present residence of W. W. Morris at Fishtown. To this mill the early settlers brought their grists of corn, and each one in his turn ground out his supply of meal, from which the well known article of diet familiarly known as "mush" was made. This "mush" with bear meat and venison formed the common food of the first settlers.

TOWNS AND VILLAGES.

Cutler station is a small village located in the extreme southwestern part of the township, on the Marietta & Cincinnati railroad. It was first laid out in 1857, and received the name of Harshaville after John M. Harsha, M. D., who owned the land on which the original plat was made. Dr. Harsha afterward voluntarily relinquished the honor thus conferred upon him, in favor of William P. Cutler, and the town was rechristened Cutler station. The log cabin in which Dr. Harsha lived was the only house within the bounds of the plat, and it stood about four rods west of the present residence of Dr. Trickle, on the north side of the railroad, west of Main street. The first store was kept by Harvey Smith & Son on the southwest corner of Main and Front streets. At the same time Gilbert & Smith kept a store on the southeast corner of the same streets.

The postoffice was first established in the house of Dr. Harsha, who was appointed postmaster.

In the fall of 1857, A. A. Campbell built the first hotel on the southwest corner of Broadway and Front streets. In 1862 William Coulter kept a house of entertainment on the northeast corner of Main and Putnam. The Cutler house was built on the southwest corner of Clinton and Front streets, in 1865, but was destroyed by fire June 11, 1868, and the present house was erected on the same site in the following year. At present the village contains two general stores, one drugstore, one hotel, two shoe shops and one doctor's office.

The town has not fulfilled the hopes entertained by its founders, never having reached the dimensions necessary for incorporation.

Dunbar post office is located on the now abandoned branch of the Marietta & Cincinnati railroad, in the southern part of the township. Shelton Dunbar is postmaster.

Wesley post office, one of the old post offices of this section, is now, as for many years, kept at the private residence of Joseph H. Gage, postmaster, located east of Fishtown, on the State road, in the northeastern part of the township. These with the offices at Fishtown (W. W. Morris, postmaster) and Cutler station, constitute very ample mail facilities for this township.

Fishtown (Layman post office) is a small village of a few houses on the State road, in the northeastern part of the township. James Lake kept the first store here in 1837, which stood immediately west of the present store. He was succeeded in the business by Daniel Fish, after whom the town was named.

The post office was first established about 1857, and was kept in the store of Carmi Smith, who was the postmaster, and was removed to its present location, in the store-room of W. W. Morris, in 1861. Fishtown now contains six dwellings houses, one general store and post office, one blacksmith shop, one cabinet shop, one Methodist Episcopal and one Universalist church.

EPIDEMIC.

In 1820 this locality was visited by some kind of fever called by the settlers the "cold plague," and such were the ravages of the disease that it required all the energies of the able-bodied citizens to care for the afflicted ones. It is stated that over fifty persons were carried off by this awful scourge. What may have been the cause of this disease was never known; but its ravages were unchecked until a whole neighborhood was almost depopulated and the messenger of death had darkened almost every household.

On the farm of William Thompson, about ten rods north of his present residence, is a mineral spring, whose waters are found to be very beneficial in malarial diseases. No complete analysis has been made, but salts and iron with some eight other constituents are found contained in the water. No efforts, however, have been made to make the spring available to the general public, though many very notable cures of long-protracted and hopeless cases of ague have been effected by the use of this mineral water.

CHAPTER LVII.

DECATUR TOWNSHIP.

Establishment of the Township—Boundaries—Physical Features—Soil—Products—Streams and Roads—Settlement—Educational—Religious Organizations—Mills—Incidents—An Unsuccessful Enterprise—A Night in a Cave.

THE establishment of this township was effected in 1820, on the petition of sundry persons not named, residents in sixth township, range eleven. Said locality was declared an incorporated town and an election district to be thereafter known as Decatur, and it was ordered that the inhabitants residing in said district were thereby entitled to the privileges and immunities of incorporated towns within the State. The electors were notified to meet at the residence of William Johnson, on Thursday, November 30, 1820, to elect town officers, but the records of this first election cannot now be found, and the names of the first officials, therefore, cannot be definitely ascertained.

At present the township is bounded on the north by Wesley and Fairfield, east by Dunham and Belpre, and on the south and west by Athens county. The boundary lines, barring eight and a half sections on the northwest, enclose a perfect square of five sections on each side, making altogether thirty-three and a half sections, or an area of over twenty-one thousand acres. The population in 1870 was fourteen hundred and thirty-seven, and the last census (1880) gives the township a population of fifteen hundred and five, an increase of sixty-eight in ten years.

The surface consists generally of very high rolling lands, broken in rugged and precipitous hills, especially in the southwest. The soil is of red and yellow clay, though in localities some sand is found. The chief productions are wheat, corn, etc., and all kinds of fruits are produced in abundance, never failing orchards being found in various localities throughout the township. In early times considerable tar was manufactured near Fillmore, and was floated down the Little Hocking in canoes to the Ohio, but now only the small local demand is supplied from the old kilns. Shallow veins of an inferior quality of coal are found in various places.

The west branch of Little Hocking river, a considerable stream, enters the township from Fairfield at the northwest, and, flowing in a southeast course, leaves the township at the extreme southeast corner. Many other minor and unimportant branches, mostly tributary to the river, drain the lands of this locality.

The abandoned branch of the Marietta & Cincinnati railroad extends across the extreme northwest corner. The principal thoroughfare is the State road, leading from Hill's Landing to McConnelsville, extending from southeast toward north through the principal settlements —Fillmore and Decaturville. All sections of the township are also provided with road communications.

Along the water courses, and in various localities throughout the township, are found numerous outcroppings of sandstone, which is generally used for building purposes. This stone is found to make very desirable and certainly very beautiful residences, and promises to become utilized more in this way than heretofore. Specimens of these buildings are found here. Caves and deep caverns among towering hills, ribbed with the abutting sandstone and skirted with evergreen pine, are constantly in sight of the traveller, presenting a view grand and picturesque.

EARLY SETTLEMENT.

The first settler in this township was Joseph Lovdell, who came here in the spring of 1816. He was the first to accept an offer of forty acres of land made by David Putnam, agent of the Ohio company, to any one who would locate in this township, build a cabin, and plant an orchard of one hundred trees. He located forty acres on the northeast part of the farm now owned by Joshua McGirr, at Fillmore, and built his cabin in the extreme southwest corner of what is now section three.

Another forty acres adjoining this tract, on the northeast, was first bargained for by a Mr. Frost, who never came to the township; but William Johnson, having purchased this claim, arrived here about three weeks after Joseph Lobdell, and built his cabin just northeast of his only neighbor in the then western wilderness, about fifteen rods northeast of the present forks of the road.

Among the settlers who came after these earliest ones were Able Dufer, Hiram Fairchilds, Ebenezer Bachelor, John and James Dunn, John Giddings, Andrew Ballard, and others, all of whom settled in this locality, forming what was then known as the "Lower Settlement," now called Fillmore post office. It is located in the southeastern part of the township, on the State road, and is the centre of trade for the surrounding country. A general store, that of Mr. Russell, is kept here.

The settlement made around what is now known as Decaturville post office was then known as the "Upper Settlement," and was made soon after the original settlement.

George Ball built his cabin about fifty rods southwest of the present residence of his son, Henry L., immediately south of Decaturville, section seventeen.

Daniel Morey's cabin stood about one hundred rods west of Ball's, near the cave on the north side of the run.

Peter Brewer built his cabin on the farm now owned by C. F. Frazyer, about ten rods from the northeast corner of section sixteen.

Isaac Place erected his cabin near the present residence of C. Booker, section sixteen.

Barnabas Nolan lived in a log cabin in the southwest part of section eleven.

John Storts entered two hundred acres of land, on which he built his cabin, near the present residence of P. Storts, section seventeen.

Nathaniel Place settled on section ten, near the present farm house of Austin place.

Joseph Place lived west of Decaturville, section sixteen, and Eli Gilbert built his log cabin house in central part of section sixteen.

Canada settlement is located west of Fillmore, beyond Little Hocking river, and was made soon after the "Upper Settlement." Jonathan Root and Alexander Johnson were among the early settlers. This locality, though having a general name, is but a thickly settled community, having no trading place or post office, and how it received the name of Canada is not certainly known.

Abel Dufer was a native of New York, and was born in 1802; deceased 1870. He emigrated to Washington county in 1814, and was married in 1823 to Polly Fairchild, who was born in 1809 and died in 1842. To them were born six children—Lucy M., Eva, Abel, Edmund P., John and Abigail. He was married the second time to Eunice Bachelder, daughter of Ebon and Eunice Bachelder, who was born 1817. They had a family of two children—Eunice A. and Daniel F. Daniel F. was born in 1851 and resides in the township. He has held the office of school director and is now county surveyor. He owns a farm on section two.

Philip Schrader, jr., was born in Pittsburgh, Pennsylvania, November 12, 1808, and was married in 1828 to Clarissa Cheedle, who was born in 1810. To them were born twelve children—nine boys and three girls. Five of the boys and the three girls are now living. He came to this township with his father (whose history appears in Wesley) in 1837, and settled on the farm that he now owns. His father built the house in which he resides. He has lived in this township continuously for forty-four years; has held several important offices; is at present justice of the peace and postmaster.

James Smith, a native of Ireland, son of James and Jane Smith, was born in 1792, and died in 1859. He was married in 1823 to Margaret Morrison, daughter of John and Catherine (McCausland) Morrison, who was born in Ireland in 1802. They settled in this township in 1832, section twenty-four, and to them were born twelve children—Anna Jane; William, resides in Decatur; Percilla, wife of B. H. Dawson (Fairfield township); Alexander F. (Kansas); John M. (Kansas); Eliza, wife of Henry Hibbard (Kansas); James H., enlisted during the late war in the One Hundred and Forty-eighth Ohio and was killed by the explosion of an ordnance boat; Margaret, at home; Joseph A. (Decatur); Matilda, wife of

W. H. Burk (Michigan); Lucinda, wife of P. Roe (Chillicothe); Frances, wife of C. Payne (Missouri).

Joseph A. Smith was born in this township 1840, and was married in 1871 to Susan Dela Grange, born in 1849. They have one child—Arthur H. He enlisted in 1864 in company K, Thirty-ninth Ohio volunteer infantry, and was discharged in 1865; has held the office of district assessor and all the other township offices, except constable and clerk, and at present is engaged in farming, owning a farm of one hundred and eighty acres, on which he now resides as one of the respected farmers and citizens of the township, section twenty-four.

Richard W. Fields was born in Virginia in 1831, and settled in this township in 1847. He was married in 1851 to Mary J. Richards, born in Pennsylvania in 1831, died in 1878. Mr. Fields has a family of sixteen children, all living—Abdallah, Thornton, Mary, Joseph W., Amanda, Maria, George W., Sarah L., Martha; Frances E., Lydia, Ruth, Joshua R. G., Benoni, Arthur, and Jesse. Mr. Fields is a prominent member of the Baptist (colored) church, and one of its most liberal and earnest supporters, and has by his own industry made himself possessor of a farm of eighty acres, where he now resides a highly respected representative of his race—section twenty-three.

Richard Irwin was born in Ireland in 1810, and died in 1858. He was married in Ireland to Jane Wilkinson and settled in Decatur township in 1850. They had a family of five children, four now living—Richard J., Robert M., Sarah J., William G., living in the township. William G. Irvine was born in this county 1853, and was united in marriage in 1879 to Sarah A. Lyde, who was born in 1855. He is now elder in the Presbyterian church and has a farm on which he resides—section eleven.

William Gamble was born in Washington county, Pennsylvania, and was married to Elizabeth Corns. They had a family of nine children, eight now living—Amos L., William, Walter, Joseph, Harley E., Randolph E., Camby and Reese. William Gamble, jr., was born April 15, 1851; and was married to Sarah E. Nist (daughter of George Nist) who was born 1858. They have one child, Cornelia E. Mr. Gamble has been trustee for three years, and has a farm on which he now lives—section seven.

Henry Welch was born in 1804, and was married to Barbara Smith, who was born in 1806. They came to Washington county in 1841, and first settled in Wesley township. To them were born ten children, five now living—Peter, Susan, John, James, and George H. Peter Welch was born in Columbiana county, Ohio, in 1830, and was married in 1852 to Hannah Gilmore—daughter of Torrens and Polly Gilmore—born 1834. Mr. and Mrs. Welch had a family of thirteen children—John, Noah, Emily, wife of Isaac Bradenberry, Martin, Barbara (now Mrs. Charles Weaver), McClellan, Warren, Estella, Lucy, Ella, Dow, George and Marion. He has served as trustee, and now owns three hundred and twenty-five acres of land on which he resides—section twenty-two.

Elijah Sawyer, born in North Carolina in 1800, became a resident of Decatur township in 1854. He married Maria Kendall, who is still living. Three of their children survive, viz: R. F. in Belpre township, and William H. and James K. in Decatur township. Of these R. F. Sawyer married Elizabeth Tate, by whom he has one child. Mr. Sawyer is running on the river, and has his residence in Belpre.

Conrad Miller was born in Stark county, Ohio, in 1806, and was married to Elizabeth Burk, who was born in 1802. They had ten children, eight now living—Daniel, now living in Iowa; Emanuel, Decatur township; Conrad, Decatur; Nancy, wife of Samuel Lee, Wesley; Elizabeth, wife of R. Weir, Athens county, Ohio; Magdaline, Decatur; Jadida, wife of Robert Martin, Pennsylvania; Emeline, wife of David Martin. Emanuel Miller was born in Columbiana county, Ohio, in 1827, and came to this township with his parents in 1840, and was married in 1850 to Eliza Sharp—daughter of Isaac and Lydia Sharp—who was born in 1832. To them were born fourteen children, twelve now living—Elizabeth M., wife of J. Fish, lives in Decatur township; Lydia, wife of T. D. Meek, Fairfield; Isaac A., at home; Mary B., wife of D. B. Brooks, Belpre township; Henry B., at home; Enoch, Thomas, Samuel, Addie, Joel, Wyatt and Lucy, all at home. Mr. Miller served nine months in the late war, and is now possessor of one hundred and sixty acres of land on which he resides as a general farmer and respected citizen—section thirty-six.

Charles Russell was born in Coshocton county, Ohio, in 1808 and died in 1880. He was married in 1837 to Elizabeth, daughter of Jacob Reigel, who was born 1809. To them were born eight children. All but one (Sarah) are now living—Emanuel, Mary M., Washington, Solomon, Elizabeth, Charles, Lucretia.

Emanuel Russell was born in 1838, in Coshocton county, and was married in 1867 to Frances E. Gearhart, daughter of Jacob and Mary, who was born in Carroll county in 1847. Mr. and Mrs. Russell have a family of three children—Eva, Ella, and Alfred. Mr. Russell has held the office of treasurer for twelve years, justice of the peace nine years, and is now postmaster at Fillmore. He enlisted in the Union army during the war of the Rebellion, August, 1862, in the One Hundred and Sixteenth Ohio volunteer infantry, company I, and was a prisoner in the well known rebel prison pen of Andersonville for six months where, with thousands of his fellow comrades, he endured the horrors of hunger, thirst, and inhuman treatment, the details of which are too atrocious to be repeated, but, like the sufferings of the martyrs, will live in the annals of our country's heroic history forever. He is now engaged in the mercantile business at Fillmore, a highly respected and deserving citizen.

Dr. Edward Hamilton Trickle was born in Belmont county, Ohio, July 1, 1836; removed to Coolville, Ohio, in 1854 where, in 1857, he was married to Jane Hamilton, who was born in 1838. His family consists of five children—William Arthur, Mattie Jane, Frank Hamilton, Bessie Evelyn, and Phœbe Luella. He began the study of medicine in 1859, which was interrupted by the late civil war, in which he was engaged as member of company E, Fourth West Virginia volunteer infantry, and during the siege of Vicksburgh, Mississippi, was promoted to lieutenant. He was engaged in the battles of Charleston, West Virginia, the capture of Jackson, Mississippi, Mission Ridge, Lynchburgh, and the ensuing campaign under General Sheridan, and was discharged after a service of three years and three months, much impaired in health. He immediately resumed his medical studies, and in 1867 attended the Ohio Medical college at Cincinnati, and after practising his profession two years at Parkersburgh, West Virginia, he returned to Cincinnati and received a diploma from the Miami Medical college. He then returned to Racine, Ohio, where, with the exception of one winter in the hospital in New York, he practiced his profession until 1879, when he came to his present location at Cutler station. On his removal to this place he resigned the position of examining surgeon of the United States bureau, and also the presidency of the Meigs County Medical society.

SCHOOLS.

The first school-house was a log building erected about ten rods north of the old Methodist church. This school was first taught by Oliver Root, and after him was Abel Stanton. The early schools of this township, like all the early schools, were supported by special subscription, and the history connected therewith is identical with the schools generally of this period. Section sixteen of this township was reserved for school land, and the rents of this land were devoted to the support of the schools, thus rendering very material assistance to the needy settlers in furnishing educational facilities to their children. Time has brought many changes to the educational advantages in this township, and there are now ten school districts all supplied with teachers and school buildings at the expense of the general public, where the means for the common school education are amply provided for the rich and the poor alike. If the rising generation do not surpass their forefathers it will not be because the means for their advancement have not been provided.

CHURCHES.

Methodism planted the first Christian standard in this township leading the way as the pioneer church. Preaching was held in the woods, in the log cabins or in the school-houses. Whenever the pioneers found a lodgement in the wilderness, Methodism followed with a church. The first church building in this township was the old log meeting-house located in the eastern part of the township, built about 1840-5. Andrew Ballard was the leading member of this early church, and he often officiated as local preacher. This old house was the general place of meeting for the neighborhood, and all the religious organizations of the locality were effected within its walls. The early members have all passed away, and for some reason have left no one upon whom the mantles of succession in the religious work have fallen—and the society has been allowed to go down—and the churches of the township are now abandoned or occupied by other denominations. The Canada M. E. church was built some time

after the settlement was made, but is now occupied by the United Brethren.

The Friends society in early times had an organization here and built a church at Fillmore, but it has been long abandoned.

UNITED BRETHREN CHURCH.

The first services of this denomination were held in the house of Mrs. Philip Schrader's father, now where George Dunsmore lives, northeast part of section seventeen. About 1850 Jonathan Root was the leading member of this church, and Joshua Montgomery is remembered as the first minister. They now occupy the house built by the Methodist Episcopal society, near Decaturville, of which Henry Bennett and Lucius Root are the present trustees. This denomination also has another class which meets in the Methodist Episcopal church west of Fillmore. Both congregations are small and are supplied as missions. The present minister is Rev. George Geiger.

PRESBYTERIAN OLD SCHOOL CHURCH,

located one mile east of Decaturville, was organized in 1847 in the old log Methodist church, under the ministry of Rev. Moses Hoag. The first elders were William Bennett and William Campbell, and the first regular preacher was Rev. William Farris. The church building was first erected in 1849 and was rebuilt in 1856. The present building is a frame twenty-four by thirty. The congregation now numbers about seventy-five, under the ministry of Rev. Robert C. Stewart, and eldership of Philip Bennett, John P. Knox, Robert Cray, William Campbell, William Scott and William G. Irvine. Services and Sabbath-school every Sunday.

BAPTIST CHURCH (COLORED)

is located in the northern part of the township, northwest corner of section twenty-three. The first minister was Nathan B. Henry, and first trustees John Williams, James A. Harris and R. W. Field. The first house in which this society met was built in 1856, and was used for the colored select school was situated about twenty rods south of R. W. Fields—section twenty-three. The present board house was built in 1860, and the society was reorganized by Revs. Atkins and Pierce. During the agitation of the slavery question this society withdrew from the regular Baptist and became what was known as Anti-Slavery Baptist. Present membership twenty-six; services once every month; Sabbath-school every Sunday, Rev. William Norman, present pastor.

MILLS.

The first flour mill in this township was the one erected by Hiram Fairchild about 1822, and was located in the northwest part of section one, south of Fillmore. About the same time another mill was built northwest of the first one, but it has long since been abandoned. On the site of the original mill Dion Neal now operates a flour mill, having two run of stone with the usual capacity. The building is a frame of two stories and hip roof; the local demand only is supplied. The flour mill now known as Root's Mill, is located on west branch of Little Hocking river and is now operated by Rufus Root. This mill was first erected in 1860, but Mr. Root has made many improvements; it is now a substantial frame building about thirty-six by forty feet, having two run of stone, with a capacity of one hundred and seventy-five bushels per day. The power is derived from a forty-horse power engine. The trade is mostly local custom, which requires the full capacity of the mill to supply.

INCIDENTS.

The general route of the well-known underground railroad led through this township, and many of the prominent men of this locality were engaged in this work. Many incidents in this memorable struggle for freedom occurred here, but among them the following is perhaps the most noted, and will better illustrate the spirit of the contest:

On the night of July 9, 1845, a party of Ohioans from this locality went to Hall's Landing, on the Ohio river, for the purpose of assisting a party of six slaves, belonging to John W. Harwood, who lived just below Blennerhassett island, to escape. They were unarmed, and just as the boat on which the slaves were concealed reached the landing, a posse of armed officials, having had information of this movement and concealed themselves in the bushes, rushed out and captured five of the slaves and three of their intended liberators. The three Ohioans were Peter M. Garner, Crayton Loraine and Mordecai Thomas, and they were taken by force of arms and lodged in the Parkersburgh jail. The Virginia officials claimed that the Ohio citizens were "felons," amenable to Virginia law for an alleged offence not known in Ohio law. Bail was refused the prisoners, and all intercourse with their friends in Ohio denied, and lawyers employed in Marietta to defend them were rejected.

August 16, 1845, a public meeting was called, to meet in the court house at Marietta, "to take into consideration means for liberation of Ohio citizens confined in the Parkersburgh (Virginia) prison, and the vindication of the rights of Ohio citizens." This call brought forth quite a concourse of citizens, and the indignation of the friends of freedom was freely expressed, while the interest in the all-absorbing question deepened. September 2nd the prisoners were taken from the jail to the court house in Parkersburgh, and they pleaded "not guilty." Bail was again refused, and they were again remanded to prison.

On the seventeenth of the following November their trial was held, and they received a verdict of guilty. The case was taken to a higher court on the question of jurisdiction. The case was argued before the court of appeals, December 10th and 13th, and the court divided equally on the question whether the State line was the low or high water mark, the prisoners having been captured at the low water mark. At the following special term, at Parkersburgh, the men were admitted to bail on their own recognizance, and were set at liberty. January 10, 1846. Thus ended a very exciting local episode in the history of African slavery.

Garner lived in this township, at the Cross-roads, on the northwest corner, where the store now stands. He was born June 14, 1808, and died at Columbus, Ohio, at the age of sixty-one years. Loraine lived one-fourth of a mile west of Fillmore, but has since removed to Illinois, where he is now living. Thomas resided west of Loraine, but is now living in Belmont county, Ohio.

In 1826 the old school-house north of Lobdell's was mysteriously destroyed by fire, and at the time no cause could be assigned for the origin of the fire until some time after, in removing the debris, the charred remains of a man were found, which afterwards proved to be the body of a stranger who had come into the neighborhood the day before the fire, and was noticed as being very peculiar in his actions. An open razor was found with the body, and it is supposed that he fired the house and then cut his throat with the razor.

In early times a "refined" young man from New York purchased what he supposed was a desirable mill site, on one of the chasms of Little Hocking, and brought several first-class workmen with him to construct a dam. But no human genius could construct a framework that would withstand the sudden rush of water down any of these hill branches, and the grand enterprize became the laughing-stock of the practical settlers of the neighborhood, and the young man from New York was compelled to return whence he came, a wiser but somewhat poorer man.

It is related that one Christmas, J. D. Chamberlain, William Chute, Isaac Palmer and James Lawton were surveying a road through this township and that night overtook them in the wilds of hill and forest, and, as the cabins of the settlers were very few, and separated by long distances, and the roads were little better marked than the blazes on the trees indicated, they were compelled to seek shelter in one of the caves. They finally found one suitable for the purpose, and it was located on the steep brow of a hill nearly one hundred feet from the bottom of the ravine below. To this cave they made their way, pulling themselves over the rocks by branches of scrub oaks and pine. They lowered the wood for a fire from above to the shelf of a rock protruding from the cave. A hunter of the party easily procured a deer. The venison was soon on the fire, and the party, in true hunter style, passed a Christmas night in the cave, retiring at last with their saddles for pillows, and overcoats for blankets, while the glare of fire reflected from the rocks, illuminated the ravine below, where the horses of the party were quietly feeding.

ADDITIONAL PERSONAL NOTES.

Colonel Levi Barber was born in Connecticut in 1777 and emigrated from Vermont to Marietta, Ohio, in 1799. He settled in Harmar, where he remained until his death, which occurred in 1833. His wife was Eliza Rouse, whom he married about 1802. She was born in Rhode Island in the same year as was her husband, and died in 1830. To them were born five children, viz: David, living in Carthage, Illinois; Elizabeth, deceased; Austin, residing at Pittsfield, Illinois; Levi, who died in infancy, and a second son Levi, living in Harmar.

David Barber, nephew of Colonel Levi Barber, came to Harmar in 1819 from the State of New York, where he was born in 1799. In 1827 he married Miss Lydia N. Stanley, who was born in 1807, in Connecticut, and whose parents emigrated from that State in 1813, settling at Marietta. To Mr. and Mrs. David Barber have been born nine children, of whom four survive: Eliza, widow of Oscar D. Chapin, lives in Saginaw, Michigan; Levi A. resides in Bay City, Michigan; Julia is at home; and Electa W. is the wife of A. B. Chapin, of Saginaw, Michigan. In 1823, Mr. David Barber entered into mercantile business in Meigs county, Ohio, and, after remaining there nearly twenty-three years, returned to Marietta and continued in business, first with Levi Barber and then with his son Levi A. Since 1875, he has been a retired merchant, quietly enjoying the reward of his toil.

Hugh and Celia Brenan, natives of Ireland, emigrated to this country from the West Indies in 1840, and settled in Marietta. He was engaged here in general merchandise until his death, in 1869. They had twelve children, of whom Joseph, William, Francis R., and Celia (Mrs. Van Buskirk), are living. The three brothers are engaged in the grocery business in Marietta, each having a store of his own. Joseph was born in the West Indies in 1829, and was eleven years old when he came to Marietta. Since 1852 he has been engaged in the grocery business.

William Corner, who came in 1795, was from Macclesfield, England, where he was born February 3, 1789. He died August 17, 1878. He worked two years for General Israel Putnam. His wife's name was Sally Maxon, born in 1782, died in 1854. Of the children, Henry W. married Lucinda Robb, and is in Kansas; Lucy married James Anderson, who is now dead; Celinda married J. P. Sandford, and Mary E. was the wife of Benjamin Posey. Two children died in youth. The first land cleared on the Little Muskingum was by William Corner. Mrs. Sandford says that Henry Maxon cut the first tree in Ohio.

Another of the very early settlers was George Corner, who came to the township in 1795. He was born in England in 1783, lived with General Putnam when a boy, was a surveyor, and married Susanna Burlingame, who was born in 1790. She was a granddaughter of General Putnam. The places of residence of the living members of the family are: Persis R., Barstow, Iowa; George S., Marietta township; John B., Virginia; Mary S. Leggett, Iowa; Edwin L., Oregon; Susan B. Mackey, Newport township; Elizabeth P. Rood, Marietta. Henry H., Rebecca, Maria Racer, Sarah F., and Melville R., are dead.

Joseph C. Cole was another old resident, who came in 1802. He was born in 1769, in England, and engaged in farming and especially in raising small trees and nurseries. His wife, Polly Case, lived from 1781 to 1847, while he survived her until 1866. Children: Mary E., still lives on the old homestead; Candis is dead, as is Joseph C.; F. C. married Mary S. Dye, and Richard C. was unmarried; both are now dead.

Jacob Ebinger was born in Sweigern, Germany, in 1825, came to New York in 1847, lived for two years at Pottsville, Pennsylvania, and then came to Marietta, since which time he has been in the harness business. In 1849 he married Catharine Abendschan, who died in 1876. Eight of their nine children are living.

From Massachusetts emigrated William Fay, in 1832, who died at home in 1866. For many years he was deacon in the Congregational church. In 1812 he married Elizabeth Lankton, who was born July 23, 1790. Their children were: Levi L., who married Caroline Hill first, then Minerva Batchelor; Elizabeth, wife of Dr. Gillman, and now dead; Bula S., now Mrs. Dr. James Tenney, of Toledo; William A., married, and in Springfield, Ohio; Solomon P., in Boston, married to Marie Brigham; Catharine A., in Marietta, and wife of Archibald Ewing; Eunice S., wedded to Dr. Johnson.

In 1863, section nine furnished a home for Jacob Hendershot, who was a native of this State and born in 1825, although he came to Marietta from Virginia. He had a farm there on which several oil-wells were drilled, but sold out and came here. His wife was Mary S. Joy, born in 1835 and married in 1855. One child died young; another, Ella Adaline, is now at home.

Stephen Hildreth, father of Calvin, came to Washington county in January, 1814, having left Shirley, Massachusetts, the November previous. He was a son of John Hildreth, and a descendant of Richard Hildreth, who came to this country from England in 1650, and settled in Massachusetts. John Hildreth was a native of Westford, Massachusetts. He was twice married. His second wife was Elizabeth Gates, by whom he had six children, viz: Simeon, Sallie, Stephen, Lemuel, Betsey and Polly.

Stephen Hildreth was born July 15, 1777, and married Miss Cynthia Brown, who was born October 9, 1783, in Shirley, Massachusetts. On coming to this county, he bought the farm now occupied by his son and grandson. He died here in 1858, his wife having preceded him, dying in 1823. They had four children—Caloin, born April 1, 1804, in Shirley, Massachusetts; Mary, born February 10, 1806, in Bath, Maine; Rebecca Ann, born August 29, 1808, in Charlestown, Massachusetts; Louisa, born August 4, 1811, in Shirley, Massachusetts.

Calvin married in 1830 Miss Susan E. Maxon, who was born in Fearing township, this county, in 1807. There have been born to them two children, Stephen B. and Cynthia, the latter dying in infancy. Stephen B. was born on the old farm October 19, 1831; married in 1856 Miss Oladine S. Hill, who was born February 26, 1834. The issue of this marriage is one child, Zenas Brownhill, born August 21, 1878.

Thomas Hutchinson was born in the block-house at Marietta, in 1794. He married Nancy Warren, who was born in Massachusetts in 1802, and is still living, having been a widow since 1841. Four of the seven children born to Mr. and Mrs. Hutchinson are living: William resides in Harmar; Susan, wife of Rev. Irwin, lives in Kansas; Dudley is in Iowa; and Julia resides in Kansas. The eldest son, William W. Hutchinson, born in Harmar in 1822, married Phœbe Sutton, born in New York in 1821. Two of their six children are living, both in Harmar. Mr. Hutchinson has been a farmer during the most of his life, but is now in the grocery business in Harmar.

Lewis Lehnhard came to Marietta in 1838, having emigrated from Germany, where he was born in 1818. He has always followed the carpenter business for a livelihood. He married Elizabeth Cimmer, born in Germany in 1821. Four of the five children of this marriage are living—Lewis C., Lucinda, wife of Harman Angart; John H., who married Carrie L. Miller; Mary E., wife of Lewis Blohm. Mr. Lehnhard and his brother, John, are the only surviving members who organized the Evangelical church.

John Lehnhard was born in Germany in 1809, and married Christina Bescardor, a native of Prussia. In 1836 he landed in Baltimore, where he was married to Catharine Philipina Bock, by whom he has had twelve children, seven of whom survive. In 1838 Mr. Lehnhard came to Marietta. He has been a carpenter during his whole life.

Jacob Lorenz, a native of Germany, born in 1817 came to this country in 1846. Soon after his arrival at New Orleans he went to Louisville, Kentucky. In 1847 he married Catharine Reiter, and after a residence of two or three years in Louisville he moved to Marietta and settled in Union township. Mrs. Lorenz came to the county with her mother, Magdaline, who died here in 1859, aged eighty-nine years. Her father died in

Germany. Henry and Mary Lorenz, the parents of Jacob, died, he in 1855 and she in 1861. To Jacob Lorenz have been born ten children, six of whom are living: Henry, Charles, Catharine (Shafer), Jacob, David, and Wilhelmina. Mr. Lorenz now lives in Marietta.

William W. Lucas was born in New Jersey in 1844, and came to Marietta in 1860, and after remaining but a short time went to Athens, where he was employed by the Marietta & Cincinnati railroad company for two years, when he left for Philadelphia, and in 1864 was again employed at Marietta, where he has since been ticket and freight, and, since 1877, express agent of the Marietta & Cincinnati road. In 1875 he married Marion Curtis. They have three children.

Emery Luthringer, sr., was born in Alsace, France, in 1809. He emigrated to America, and lived in Pittsburgh, Pennsylvania, until 1857, when he removed to Marietta where he resided until his death, which occurred in 1871. His wife, Agatha Dryer, is living with her son Joseph. She was born in Alsace in 1805. Their two sons are Emery and Joseph. Emery is in the tin business in Harmar. He was born in 1839 and married Mary M. Shilshott, who was born in Columbiana county, Ohio, in 1842. Joseph, born in Germany in 1842, came to Marietta with his parents. He married Margaret Henn, born in New York city in 1846. Five of their seven children are living. Since 1867, Mr. Luthringer has been in the tin and hardware business in Marietta.

In the year 1815 came William McAllister from New Hampshire, and settled on section sixteen. He was born in 1768 and died in 1819. A son of this farmer, John, was born in 1807, and married Olive F. Owen in 1834. Mrs. McAllister was born in 1815, and is still living. Mr. McAllister died in 1880. Their daughter, Mary, became Mrs. William Cecil in 1867. Mr. McAllister was much interested in meteorology, and kept a record of semi-daily observations for twenty years. Another son, Madison, married Sallie Whitehouse in 1842, and his second wife, Harriet Posey, in 1867. Two children—Kennett and Mahala. William's wife died in 1865, at the extreme age of ninety-three. Other children are Rebecca and Irene, now Mrs. Ebenezer Buell.

In 1829 John C. McCoy came to Harmar from Richland county, and engaged in the tailoring business. He moved to Athens county in 1856, where he died in 1875. He was one of the first Abolitionists in the county of Washington. He was born in Virginia in 1792, married Mary Comley born in 1799, and died in 1829. Two of their six children are living, viz: W. W. in Harmar, and Asa S. in Bloomington, Illinois. William W., born in 1822, came with his parents to Harmar. He was married in 1850 to Elizabeth Davis in St. Louis, Missouri. Six of their ten children are living. Mr. McCoy is a contractor and does a large business. His father was the mayor of Harmar about 1843. His brother Asa graduated from Marietta college in 1849, and is now a Methodist minister.

Gottlob Meister, born in Germany in 1821, arrived in New York in 1847, lived over a year in Philadelphia, and in Cincinnati until 1855, where he was engaged in the tanning business. Coming to Marietta he went into partnership with Ebinger and Killinger. He afterwards became a partner of A. Roemer. He now has a business aggregating about thirty thousand dollars per annum. In 1844 he married Elizabeth R. Stuhr, born in Germany in 1824. Eight of their twelve children are living, all in this county.

John Miller, father of Robert T. Miller, was born in Westchester county, New York, in 1777 and came to Washington county in 1806. He died in 1840. His wife was Jane Taylor, born in Providence, Rhode Island, in 1769. They had three children, one of whom only survives: Robert T. He was born in 1809 and in 1838 married Marietta Fuller, who was born in Rhode Island, in 1812. Her parents, Charles and Nancy Fuller, were early residents of this county and died here. Mr. Miller was county infirmary director from 1854 to 1860. His farm east of Marietta was entered by Colonel Robert Taylor, who came to the county from Rhode Island in 1799.

Jacob Miller came to Marietta in 1858, and started a bakery and confectionery and a mineral water establishment. Born in Germany in 1830, he emigrated in 1847, stopping first at Erie, Pennsylvania, and then removing to Cincinnati, where he lived ten years prior to coming to Marietta. From 1874 to 1880 he was a member of the board of education. In 1859 he married Mary Keller, born in Germany in 1842. By her he has had seven children, six of whom survive, and all at home.

Of the later additions to the population of the township, was John W. Miller, who married Margaret J. Scott, and had a family of five young children, namely: Fannie, Abbie, Bertha, John and Sarah. The father, however, died some time ago.

Another citizen of the township, Mr. C. A. Miller, married Margaret Bell in 1869. He served two years and ten months in the Seventh Ohio volunteer corps.

Marcellus J. Morse was born in the town of Marietta, in 1812, and died in 1880. He married Louisa Shankland, who was born in Virginia in 1813. They had five children, but two of whom are living: Kent, residing in Indianapolis, and William M., of Harmar. The latter was born in 1843 and married Charlotte Palmer, born in 1843. To them have been born three children: Jennie, Laura and Frank. Mr. Morse has been an engineer on the Marietta & Cincinnati railroad since 1861. He is at present a member of the city council of Harmar, and is also a member of the school board. The elder Mr. Morse was sheriff for two terms, also a member of the council and board of health at Harmar. During Grant's administration, he was inspector for this district.

John Otterbein emigrated from Germany to this country in May, 1860. Soon after his arrival in Marietta the war of the Rebellion commenced, and Mr. Otterbein enlisted as private in company F, Thirty-ninth regiment, and was mustered out of service as a commissioned officer in August, 1865. Soon after his return to Marietta he opened a meat market, which he carried on for a short time, and then engaged in the sale of liquors until 1875.

Richard Pattin, sr., was born in 1806, married Miss Mary Smith, who was born in 1807, and was the father of six children, three of whom are living: Sabra, widow of Luther Burlingham, living in Harmar; William S. residing in Portsmouth, Ohio; and Richard, jr., of Harmar. He was born in 1839, married Amanda Wells, born in 1844, and has three children living and one dead. Mr. Pattin is the superintendent of the Lubricating Oil Company.

Among the colonists of 1788 was Azariah Pratt, who married Sarah Nye, by whom he had ten children, three of whom survive. Their son Elisha was born in 1798, in the block-house standing on the corner of Second and Washington streets. In 1826 he married Lydia Smith, who was born in 1800, and died in 1851, six years before the death of her husband. Their only child, Sarah M., was married in 1852, to Alexander McGirr, born in 1825. They have four children, all living at home. Mr. McGirr entered the One Hundred and Forty-eighth Ohio national guard, company A, as sergeant, and was honorably discharged in September, 1864.

Benjamin Racer was one of the very first settlers, for he came to Marietta in 1789, and settled in Newport township. He was born in Pennsylvania in 1785, and died in the township in 1872. His business was farming and hunting. For many years he lived in the garrison at Marietta, and has mentioned that he heard the gun that killed Robert Warth. His wife, Susannah Holdren, was born March, 1784, and died in 1833. Their son David married Maria Corner, and afterward Susan Flagg; Francis D. is single; William P. married Hattie Fulton, and is in Marietta; Charles' wife is Margaret Day; E. O. married Jane Posey; Susan is the wife of S. B. Smith; all these live in Marietta. Grace's husband is James Stanley, of Salem; Cynthia is Mrs. John A. West; and Annie is the widow of Thomas Alcock; Dennis, Benjamin, Dudley, Mary, Sophia, Rachel, and Elizabeth are dead. E. O. is a farmer on the old homestead, living in a house built in 1831.

In 1811, Joseph Leonard Reckard emigrated to Marietta township from Massachusetts, where he was born in 1795. He engaged in the blacksmith trade and the manufacture of axes. In 1816, he married Delilah Jennings, born in Pennsylvania in 1798. Six of their eleven children are living. Mr. Reckard opened the first livery stable in Marietta, in which business he continued until his death, which occurred in 1870. His son, Joseph L. Reckard, who continued the business, was born in 1839; he married Mary E. Morse, who was born in 1839. They have two children.

Alfred J. Richards commenced the dry goods business in Marietta in 1875, having for six years prior to that time been in the employ of W. H. Buell. He was born in 1849, and married Sarah Eggleston, born in Philadelphia in 1853. They have one daughter.

William Rowland came to Newport township in 1816, originally from Maryland, where his birth occurred in 1790, but immediately from Pennsylvania. He died in

1854. He was a farmer and trader, and held the office of justice of the peace several times. His wife, Ann E. Clark, born in 1799, died in 1876. Several children were born them: Eliza J. is now Mrs. William Thornley; Thomas married Amanda Neal, and with Charles, whose wife was Jane D. White, and Lewis C., who married Barbara McKibben, is in Newport. Virginia A. married J. B. Hovey, of Marietta; George W. married Paulina Ann Corner and lives in Marietta township. Rufus H. is the husband of Charlotte Rood, and resides in Kansas. William (dead), was wedded to Catharine P. Cline and went to Illinois. The rest died young.

In the year 1820 Thomas J. H. Sandford arrived from England and made his home on section four of Marietta township. He was born October 15, 1776, and died in 1823. He had served in the British navy, was paymaster on board a British man of war in the East Indies. His wife was Mary Broadhurst, who was born in 1790, and died in 1867. His son, J. P. Sandford, married Celinda Corner, and has had nine children. Eliza C. is unmarried; S. H. married Caroline Haas. Seven children died young.

John Schneider was born in Germany in 1827, and came to this country in 1846, and has since been engaged in the brewery business in Buffalo, Cincinnati and Harrison. In 1879 he opened a brewery in Marietta. In 1853 he was married to Elizabeth Zapf,* by whom he has five children. Mr. Schneider's aged father is still living in Germany.

Henry Schwitzer, born in Prussia in 1821, came to Baltimore in 1848, then to Wheeling, and shortly afterward to Harrison county, where he worked at his trade for two years. In 1851, coming to Marietta, he engaged in the wagon-making trade. He was married to Elizabeth Lehnhard, born in Germany. They have three girls and three boys, of whom two are at home.

Edward Shaldon was born in New Jersey in 1789, and died in 1847, in Marietta township, where he settled in 1818. Of the six surviving children, Elizabeth, wife of Caleb Thornly, lives in Marietta township, as does Eliza. Sarah was born in Gallia county in 1836. She married Henry Reckard in 1857. He died in 1872.

Mr. George P. Stevens came to this county from Portage county, in 1867. He engaged in the mercantile business in 1870, in which he continued for six years. In 1879 he was elected a member of the board of education of Harmar, and in the spring of 1880 was elected mayor of Harmar, which office he still holds. Mayor Stevens and his father, Dr. Stevens, who is still living in Harmar, established and mainly built up the rolling-mill, which was successfully conducted while it had their attention. In 1863 Mr. Stevens was married to Harriet Harmond, and has one child.

John D. Strauss, born in Germany in 1819, emigrated to Virginia in 1848, coming to this county on foot in 1850. He lived, until 1851, on land purchased in West Virginia, and has since lived in Marietta. Until 1861 he worked at the cabinet-making business, and then bought the mill in partnership with F. Coleman, and in 1873 he retired from the firm. In 1878 he again bought the flouring-mill, which is now operated under the name of the Buckeye Flouring Mill, by Strauss, Elston & Co. In 1853 he married Caroline Zimmer, who came to this county with her parents, who died several years ago. Seven of the eleven children of Mr. Strauss are living, six being at home. Mr. Strauss has been in the city council for two terms.

John Strecker, born in Germany in 1804, came to the United States in 1846, and settled in Pittsburgh, and after one year had passed he came to Marietta. His wife was born and died in Germany prior to Mr. Strecker's emigration. Their son, George, came to this country with his father. In 1856 he married Johannah Abenchoen. Eight of the nine children are living. George Strecker, in 1868, started the Harmar boiler works, which are still in operation.

Ernst Styer was born in the Kingdom of Hanover, Germany, in 1798; emigrated to this country in 1837, and afterwards came to Marietta. Here he has resided since, except two years when he lived at Vicksburgh, Mississippi, working at his trade, that of carpentering. William, a brother of Ernst, came over from Germany in 1838, and to this county in the spring of 1839. He was born in 1806. His trade has also been that of carpentering, and he also spent some months in Vicksburgh. His oldest son William has been a druggist in Cincinnati, and now resides in Marietta.

William Thornily was born in England in 1774, and in 1795 emigrated to New York city, where he was soon afterwards married to Elizabeth Markham, born in London in 1775. Soon after their marriage they emigrated to Ohio, and settled on a farm in Marietta township. Mr. Thornily was at one time in the merchandise business, both at Marietta and Pittsburgh. Of a family of seven children, but one survives, viz., Augusta Beswick, living in Iowa.

Philip Van Thornily was born in New York city, in 1799, and came with his parents to Marietta township. In 1830 he married Nancy C. Martin, who was born in Virginia, in 1811. Eleven children have been born to them, seven of whom are living. Farming and boat-building have principally engaged Mr. Thornily's attention, but for some time previous to his death he led a retired life upon the garden spot of his large farm, which from year to year he distributed among his children. He died April 26, 1881, after an illness of a few weeks, in his eighty-second year.

William Thornily, another son of William Thornily, sr., was born in the township, section two, in 1808, and died in 1853. His business was that of shipping produce. He married Esther A. Smith, who was born in 1813. There were born to them: Samuel, who married Frances Middleswart; Thomas J., who died young; Elizabeth M., who is now Mrs. Samuel King; Augusta B., who is Mrs. George Harness; Eliza D., who is the wife of Daniel Reynolds, of Warren; and Laura J., who married Timothy Buell, of Marietta township.

Major John Thornily came to Marietta township in 1795, from Cheshire, England. Born July 17, 1780, he died in Marietta township, August, 1844. He was in the War of 1812, captain under General Harrison, major in Washington county militia, and one of the seven members who formed the first Baptist church in Ohio. His wife, Mary Compton, was born in 1788, and survived her husband till 1875. Their children married as follows: William, to Eliza J. Rowland; Mary Ann, to Aaron Howe, of Illinois; Thomas E., to Mary C. Ralston; John, to Jane Temple, Harmar; Elizabeth, to Lemuel Wells, in Missouri; C. S. to Betsy Sheldon, in Marietta; Adaline, to James C. West, in Marietta township; James is unmarried, and lives in Marietta; John, Thomas, and George are dead. William T. is now seventy years old, has never lain on a sick bed, and all his teeth are as sound as ever. His marriage was in 1834, and the living children are Minerva A., wife of M. B. Gates, of Ironton; Rinaldo R., married to Mary Snyder, in Newport township; Alice, now Mrs. H. Scott, of Marietta; Newton I., married to Clara S. Kidd, also in Marietta; John R. died young.

Colonel William West settled in Marietta township, section eight, in 1829. He was born in 1796 at Bull Run, Virginia, and served six months in the War of 1812. He married Elizabeth Compton, born in 1794 in Virginia, near Winchester. Four of their nine children are living, viz: John A., James C., William W. and Thomas J. The elder Mr. West served two terms as county commissioner, was infirmary director, and held other important offices. During the war he was a strong Abolitionist, and made the first speech of that character in the county. He owned three hundred and ninety-five acres of land. Of his children, the eldest son, John A., was born in 1821 in Virginia; and married Cynthia Racer, who was born in 1819 in this county. Two of their three children are living: Henry C. and Leslie C. Their daughter Lelia (Hoffman) died in 1880, leaving one son. Mr. West owns a farm at the mouth of the Little Muskingum. He has been trustee of his township nineteen years. His son Henry C. married Phebe McKibben, and has two children. Leslie C., the second son, married Arvilla Middleswart and lives in Kansas. James C., the second son of William and Elizabeth West, was born in 1824, married Adaline Thornily, who was born in Marietta township in 1832. Their sons, George F. and James W. are living. Mr. West has been an important officer in his township. He owns a farm of nearly two hundred acres of land.

Robert Williams was a native of Carnarvonshire, North Wales, where he was born October 31, 1762. He emigrated to this country with his wife and three oldest children, in 1794, and after living some ten years in New Jersey and Pennsylvania, removed to Washington coun-

ty in 1804. The following year he located on a farm four or five miles east of Marietta, in what afterwards became known as the "Fuller settlement,"—several members of a family of the name of Fuller settling there, whose farms adjoined one another. Robert Williams built himself a substantial log house, the best for many miles around. He was naturalized a citizen of the United States in 1808, and the naturalization papers are now in possession of his daughter, Mrs. Greene. Mr. Williams first married Jane Roberts, who died in 1816. He afterwards married Mrs. Mary H. Needham, widow of Noah Needham. He had six children by his first wife. David, the oldest, was a Methodist minister. Thomas was a farmer of this county. Of the four daughters, Mrs. Dickinson and Mrs. Baker removed to the west several years ago; Mrs. Winters, at her death, resided in Cincinnati, and the other died in childhood. By his second marriage there were five children, three daughters and two sons, twins. The two oldest daughters, Mrs. Susan W. Greene and Mrs. Mary A. Rood, reside in Marietta. The other daughter (Margaret) died quite early. One of the sons, Rev. John Williams, lives in Ottumwa, Iowa; the other, William, died in 1860. Robert Williams died April, 1843, aged eighty-one, and his wife, Mary, in 1857. Of the children of Mrs. Williams, by her first husband, only one lived to years of maturity, the late M. H. Needham, of Marietta, a well known architect, who died in 1878.

John Willis was born in Washington county, in 1839. In the year 1859 he married Rosa E. Grimes, who was born January 13, 1835. To this couple were born six children, four of whom are still living, viz: Osmer M., who is attending medical college at Columbus; Arthur C., Lemuel C., and Freddie N. Mr. Willis was elected superintendent of the county infirmary in 1877. This infirmary was erected in 1841, on land (one hundred and sixty acres) purchased for that purpose in 1839. Mr. Willis has been for nine years a pastor in the Methodist Episcopal church, but for the greater part of his life has been a farmer.

Stephen Wood was born in Tyler county, West Virginia, in 1809. He came to Marietta in 1829, and worked in the Phœnix mills, and was also connected with a ferry boat across the Ohio. He married Elizabeth Kennedy, who was born in 1811. Eight children still survive, viz: D. H., A. S., W. W., B. F., Mrs. Mahala Oliver, Mrs. Sarah J. Akerson, Mrs. Mary O. Bunch, and Mrs. Martha S. Pflug. Mr. Wood died in 1876. He was a temperance man from 1846 until his death. He joined the United Brethren church in 1856.

CPSIA information can be obtained
at www.ICGtesting.com
Printed in the USA
BVOW04s1120051217
501449BV00029B/126/P